The National Hockey League

Official Guide & Record Book

1997-98

Published by the National Hockey League.
Compiled by the NHL Public Relations Department
and the 26 NHL Club Public Relations Directors.
Copyright © 1997 by the National Hockey League

THE NATIONAL HOCKEY LEAGUE
Official Guide & Record Book/1997-98

Staff

For the NHL: David McConnachie; Supervising Editor: Greg Inglis; Statistician: Benny Ercolani; Editorial Staff: David Keon, Sherry McKeown, Jackie Rinaldi, Kelley Rosset, Chris Tredree

Managing Editors: Ralph Dinger, James Duplacey

Contributing Editor: Igor Kuperman

Production Editors: John Pasternak, Alex Dubiel

Assistant Editor: Mark Paddock

Contributors: Jeremiah Bartz, Mike Berger, Ray Boetto, Bob Borgen, Bob Duff, Gene Dupras, Peter Fillman, Ernie Fitzsimmons, Andy Foster, Mel Foster, Scott Fowler, Dan Gognavic, Lloyd Hamshaw (WHL), Martin C. Harris, James Karkoski, Gunter Klein, Marina Klein, Steve Luse (AHL), Al Mason, Terry Matheson, Philip A. Mendel, Dave Mishkin, Herb Morrell (OHL), John Moritsugu, NHL Broadcasters' Association, NHL Central Registry, NHL Players' Association, Robert Newton, Terry Owens, Jim Price (CHL), Valentina Riazanova, Jim Thies, Jeff Weiss (CCHA).

Consulting Publisher: Dan Diamond

Photo Credits

Historical and special event photos: Bruce Bennett, David Bier, Michael Burns, Graphic Artists Collection, NHL Images/Allsport, New York Rangers, Rice Studio, Robert Shaver, Imperial Oil Turofsky Collection, Hockey Hall of Fame.

Current photos: Graig Abel, Toronto; Action Image, Detroit; Joe Angeles, St. Louis; Steve Babineau, Boston; Al Bello, NHL Images; Bruce Bennett Studios, NY Islanders and Philadelphia; Bob Binder, Anaheim; Denis Brodeur, Montreal; Mark Buckner, St. Louis; Cassidy, Philadelphia; Denny Cavanaugh, Pittsburgh; Steve Crandall, New Jersey; Edmonton Northlands; Bob Fisher, Montreal; Art Foxall, Los Angeles; Ray Grabowski, Chicago; John Hartman, Detroit; Jonathan Hayt, Tampa Bay; J. Henson Photographics, Washington; Mark Hicks, Detroit; Glenn James, Dallas; George Kalinsky, NY Rangers; Deborah King, Washington; David Klutho, St. Louis; Robert Laberge, Montreal; V.J. Lovero, Anaheim; Jim Mackey, Detroit; Doug MacLellan; McElligott-Teckles Sports Focus Imaging, Ottawa; Al Messerschmidt, Florida; Jack Murray, Vancouver; Tim Parker, St. Louis; Andre Pichette, Montreal; Richard Pilling, New Jersey; Harry Scull, Jr., Buffalo; Don Smith, San Jose; Diane Sobolewski, Hartford; John Soohoo; Gerry Thomas, Edmonton; Jim Turner, New Jersey; Brad Watson, Calgary; Rocky Widner, San Jose; Bill Wippert, Buffalo.

Distribution

Canadian representatives:
North 49 Books, 35 Prince Andrew Drive, Toronto, Ontario M3C 2H2
416/449-4000; FAX 416/449-9924

NHL Publishing, 194 Dovercourt Road, Toronto, Ontario M6J 3C8
416/531-6535; FAX 416/531-3939

U.S. representatives: Triumph Books,
644 South Clark Street, Chicago, Illinois 60605   312/939-3330; FAX 312/663-3557

International representatives: Barkers Worldwide Publications,
155 Maybury Road, Woking, Surrey, England GU21 5JR
Tel. and FAX: 011/44/483/776-141

Data Management and Typesetting: Caledon Data Management, Hillsburgh, Ontario
Film Output and Scanning: Stafford Graphics, Toronto, Ontario
Printing: Moore Data Management Services, Scarborough, Ontario
Production Management: Dan Diamond and Associates, Inc., Toronto, Ontario

The National Hockey League
1251 Avenue of the Americas, 47th Floor, New York, New York 10020-1198
1800 McGill College Ave., Suite 2600, Montreal, Quebec H3A 3J6
75 International Boulevard, Suite 300, Toronto, Ontario M9W 6L9

COOLEST GAME on earth™

Table of Contents

Table of Contents *continued*

Introduction

WELCOME TO *THE NHL OFFICIAL GUIDE & RECORD BOOK FOR 1997-98.* This 66th edition of the *Guide* incorporates three new features, each of which reflects significant changes in hockey.

The National Hockey League's best will play at the 1998 Winter Olympic Games in Nagano, Japan in February of 1998. The NHL regular-season schedule has been designed to accommodate Olympic competition as no NHL games will take place from February 8 to February 24. A comprehensive Olympic Preview begins on page 12 of this edition of the *NHL Guide & Record Book.* It includes a 1998 Olympic schedule, complete results and standings from all previous Olympic competitions, an all-time medal winners table, a comparison of NHL and International Ice Hockey Federation rules and the Olympic scoring and goaltending statistics for all active NHL players.

International hockey was also center stage in September of 1996 when the NHL and the NHL Players' Association staged the first World Cup of Hockey tournament in cooperation with the IIHF. This eight-nation event saw games take place in four European cities—Helsinki, Garmisch, Prague and Stockholm—and in five NHL venues—Montreal, New York, Ottawa, Philadelphia and Vancouver. In the three-game final, Team USA defeated Team Canada two games to one. Canada won game one in overtime before Team USA captured games two and three by identical 5-2 scores. World Cup game scores, standings and leading scorers are found on page 129.

Mario Lemieux, one of hockey's greatest players, announced his retirement at the end of the 1996-97 season. Pittsburgh's big number 66 ended his superb 12-season career with his sixth NHL scoring championship and eighth All-Star selection. From his 100-point rookie season in 1984-85 through three MVP selections and two Stanley Cup championships, Mario's scoring feats lifted fans out of their seats throughout the hockey world. A salute to Lemieux begins on page 164. In addition to his regular-season, playoff and All-Star Game records, Lemieux's milestones and a top ten ranking of players assisting on his 613 career goals are also featured. Special thanks to Steve Bovino and Brian Coe of the Pittsburgh Penguins media relations department for compiling this information.

The Player Register begins on page 257. This edition's comprehensive listing of career data for NHL players and prospects includes more players than ever before. A key to abbreviations and symbols used in the individual player and goaltender data panels that make up the Registers as well as a list of NHL clubs' minor-league affiliates are found on page 255. The Retired Player Index, beginning on page 407, contains much new statistical research. *Guide & Record Book* editors have resolved many discrepancies in games played, points and penalty minutes for forwards and defensemen as well as minutes, decisions and shared shutouts for goaltenders. The result is that this edition of the Retired Player Index contains many small changes that enhance its accuracy. The Retired Goaltender Index begins on page 459. It also benefits from this research and employs a new symbol (**§**) to indicate the goaltending statistics of forwards, defensemen and coaches playing in goal. Before teams carried two goaltenders, injuries or penalties to the regular goalkeeper would occasionally force a skater to "climb into the barrel," to use an expression of the era.

For 1997-98, the NHL welcomes the Carolina Hurricanes who will play in the Northeast Division of the Eastern Conference. Roster, coaching information and franchise records can be found beginning on page 33. In 1997-98, the Hurricanes will play their home games in the Greensboro Coliseum in Greensboro, North Carolina (20,800 capacity). As well, the Washington Capitals will begin play in the new MCI Center (20,000 capacity) on December 5 vs. the Florida Panthers.

THE **1997-98 NHL S**CHEDULE will see each of the League's 26 member clubs play 82 games, 41 at home and 41 on the road. Each club will play either five or six games against its divisional opponents, four games against teams in the other division of its own conference and two games against each of the 13 teams in the League's other conference. The Mighty Ducks of Anaheim and the Vancouver Canucks will open their seasons with two games in Tokyo on October 3 and 4. The first contest will count as Vancouver's home game; the second, Anaheim's.

As always, our thanks to readers, correspondents and members of the media who take the time to comment on the *Guide & Record Book.* Thanks as well to the people working in the communications departments of the NHL's member clubs and to their counterparts in the AHL, IHL, ECHL, Central, Colonial/United and junior leagues as well as in college athletic conferences and European hockey federations.

Best wishes for an enjoyable 1997-98 NHL season and Winter Olympics.

ACCURACY REMAINS THE *GUIDE & RECORD BOOK'*S TOP PRIORITY.

We appreciate comments and clarification from our readers. Please direct these to:

Greg Inglis   47th floor, 1251 Avenue of the Americas, New York, New York 10020-1198 . . . or . . .

David Keon   75 International Blvd., Suite 300, Rexdale, Ontario M9W 6L9.

Your involvement makes a better book.

NATIONAL HOCKEY LEAGUE

New York – 1251 Avenue of the Americas, 47th Floor, New York, NY 10020-1198, (212)789-2000, Fax: (212)789-2020
Montreal – 1800 McGill College Avenue, Suite 2600, Montreal, Quebec H3A 3J6, (514)288-9220, Fax: (514)284-0300
Toronto – 75 International Blvd., Suite 300, Rexdale, Ontario M9W 6L9, (416)798-0809, Fax: (416)798-0819
NHL Enterprises, L.P. – 1251 Avenue of the Americas, 47th Floor, New York, NY 10020-1198, (212)789-2000, Fax: (212)789-2020
NHL Enterprises Canada, L.P. – 75 International Blvd., Suite 301, Rexdale, Ontario M9W 6L9, (416)798-9388, Fax: (416)798-9395
NHL Productions – 183 Oak Tree Road, Tappan, NY 10983-2809, (914)365-6701, Fax: (914)365-6010
NHL Europe – Signaustrasse 1, 8008 Zurich – Switzerland, 41(0)1 389-8080, Fax 41(0)1 389-8090

Executive

Commissioner.. Gary B. Bettman
Senior Vice President and Chief Operating Officer.................... Stephen J. Solomon
Senior Vice President Legal Affairs.. William L. Daly
Senior Vice President and Director of Hockey Operations........................Brian P. Burke
Executive Assistant to the Commissioner..Debbie Jordan

Administration

Director.. Debbie Jordan
Director, Human Resources.. Janet A. Meyers

Broadcasting / NHL Productions

Vice President.. Glenn Adamo
Coordinating Producer..Ken Rosen
Senior Producer...Darryl Lepik
Director, Broadcasting... Adam Acone
Director, Broadcast Operations / NHLP...Patti Fallick
Director, Scheduling and Operations..Steve Hatzepetros
Assistant Director, Broadcast Business Affairs............................ Samuel Esposito, Jr.
Manager, Broadcasting.. Todd Goodman

Corporate Communications

Vice President.. Bernadette Mansur
Director, Corporate Communications..Mary Pat Clarke
Manager, Corporate Communications.......................................Tracey Cohen
Publicist, Corporate Communications / USA Hockey........................ Amy Early
Director, Creative Services.. David F. Haney

Finance

Group Vice President and Chief Financial Officer.........................Craig Harnett
Vice President, Finance...Joseph DeSousa
Controller, Broadcasting..Megan O'Donnell
Controller and Office Manager (Montreal).................................Olivia Pietrantonio
Director, Accounting Operations...Belinda Haeberlein

Hockey Operations

Vice President (Toronto)..Jim Gregory
Director, Central Registry (Montreal)..Garry Lovegrove
Assistant Director, Central Registry (Montreal)............................Madeleine Supino
Director of Central Scouting (Toronto).......................................Frank Bonello
Director of Officiating (Toronto)..Bryan Lewis
Officiating Coordinator (Toronto)...Robert Bouchard
Hockey Operations Manager..David Nonis
Consultant (Montreal)..Brian F. O'Neill
Video Director, Hockey Operations...Rob Schoenbach
Office Manager (Toronto).. Kelly Rossett

Information Systems

Director.. Peter DelGiacco
Assistant Director (Montreal).. Luc Coulombe
Manager, Network Communication...Patrick Powers

Legal

Vice President and General Counsel.. David Zimmerman
Assistant General Counsel.. Katherine Jones

Pension

Director (Montreal)..Yvon Chamberland
Controller, Pension (Montreal).. Mary Skiadopoulos
Manager, Pension (Montreal).. Lise DeJocas

Public Relations

Vice President Public Relations... Arthur Pincus
Managing Director, Public Relations (Toronto)............................. Gary Meagher
Chief Statistician (Toronto)..Benny Ercolani
Director, Public Relations..Andrew McGowan
Manager, Media Services... Susan Aglietti
Manager, News Services.. Greg Inglis
Public Relations Coordinator (Toronto)...................................... David Keon
Public Relations Coordinator.. Magdale L. Labbe

Security

Vice President and Director..Dennis Cunningham
Assistant Director...Joseph Caporicci

Special Events / Event Marketing

Vice President Special Events..Frank Supovitz
Director, Special Events.. Karen Ayoub
Director, Special Events.. Lori Boesch
Director, Special Events..Anne I. Grotefeld
Manager, Special Events... Ken Chin
Manager, Special Events... Patricia L. Conrad
Manager, Special Events... Debbie Hodkinson
Manager, Special Events... Bill Miller
Manager, Special Events... Sally Printz

Television and Business Affairs

VP Television and Business Affairs..Ellis T. "Skip" Prince III
Director, New Business Development...Bryant S. McBride
Manager, Television and Business Affairs, International....... Susanna Mandel-Mantello
Manager, Team Television..John A. Tortora

NHL Enterprises, L.P.

President..Rick Dudley

Consumer Products / Retail Sales Marketing

Vice President...Brian Jennings
Group Director, Special Projects and Promotional Services..................... Glenn Horine
Director, Consumer Products Marketing, Canada................................... Karen Hanson
Director, Apparel.. Jim Haskins
Director, Non-Apparel..Judith Salsberg
Sales Manager, Eastern Region...Brian Way
Sales Manager, Midwest Region...Cathy Groves
Manager, Center Ice Program.. Lloyd Haymes
Manager of Retail Sales and Marketing, Canada.............................Barry Monaghan

Marketing

Group Vice President, Marketing.. Ed Horne

CORPORATE MARKETING
   Director, Corporate Marketing..Todd Parker
   Director, Corporate Marketing..Tim Conway
   Director, Corporate Marketing, Canada...................................Paul MacLaren
   Director, Corporate Sales and Marketing.................................Mark Donovan
   Manager, Corporate Marketing, Canada..................................Laurie Kepron

YOUTH MARKETING
   Vice President, Youth Marketing..Dina Gilbertie
   Director, Youth Marketing...Ilene Kent
   Manager, Youth Marketing.. Ann Kiely

CLUB MARKETING
   Director, Club Marketing.. Scott Carmichael

PRINTED PRODUCTS MARKETING
   Director, Printed Products Marketing.......................................David McConnachie

FAN DEVELOPMENT
   Vice President, Fan Development... Ken Yaffe
   Director, Off-Ice Programs.. Brian Mullen
   Director, Fan Development Programs...................................... Alysse Soll
   Manager, Fan Development Programs...................................... Kamini Sharma

INTERNATIONAL CONSUMER PRODUCTS MARKETING
   Managing Director, NHL Enterprises B.V...................................Brad Kwong
   Director, International Marketing, Asia / Pacific...........................Frank Nakano
   Manager, International Marketing..................................Francesca Giordano Ferrara

Finance

Controller, Consumer Products Marketing..................................Mary McCarthy
Controller, Marketing & NHL ICE... Pam Wakoff
Finance Manager, Events..Scott Weinfeld

Legal

Senior Vice President and General Counsel.................................Richard Zahnd
Associate General Counsel – Intellectual Property......................... Mary Sotis
Associate Counsel..Leslie Gittess
Associate Counsel..Douglas Perlman
Assistant General Counsel.. Thomas Gowan
Director, Consumer Products Marketing and Trademark Compliance....... Ruth Gruhin
Director, Contract Administration..Heather Bell
Senior Intellectual Property Administrator..................................Maria Liuzzo

NHL Interactive CyberEnterprises (NHL ICE)

General Manager and Executive Producer...................................Charlie Schmitt
Senior Producer..Refet Kaplan
Director of Advertising...Susan Conig

BOARD OF GOVERNORS

Chairman of the Board : Harley N. Hotchkiss

MIGHTY DUCKS OF ANAHEIM
Disney Sports Enterprises, Inc.

Tony Tavares..Governor
Michael D. Eisner.........................Alternate Governor
Jack Ferreira..................................Alternate Governor

BOSTON BRUINS
Boston Professional Hockey Association, Inc.

Jeremy M. Jacobs...Governor
Louis Jacobs................................Alternate Governor
Harry J. Sinden.............................Alternate Governor

BUFFALO SABRES
Niagara Frontier Hockey, L.P.

Northrup R. Knox...Governor
Michael J. Rigas..........................Alternate Governor
Robert O. Swados.........................Alternate Governor
Lawrence Quinn...........................Alternate Governor
John J. Rigas...............................Alternate Governor
Seymour H. Knox, IV...................Alternate Governor

CALGARY FLAMES
Calgary Flames Limited Partnership

Harley N. Hotchkiss......................................Governor
Al Coates.....................................Alternate Governor
Ron Joyce....................................Alternate Governor
Byron J. Seaman..........................Alternate Governor
Ron Bremner................................Alternate Governor

CAROLINA HURRICANES
KTR Hockey Limited Partnership

Peter Karmanos, Jr. ....Governor
Jim Rutherford.............................Alternate Governor

CHICAGO BLACKHAWKS
Chicago Blackhawks Hockey Team, Inc.

William W. Wirtz..Governor
Gene Gozdecki.............................Alternate Governor
Thomas N. Ivan............................Alternate Governor
Robert J. Pulford..........................Alternate Governor
W. Rockwell Wirtz........................Alternate Governor

COLORADO AVALANCHE
Colorado Avalanche, LLC

Charlie Lyons...Governor
Pierre Lacroix..............................Alternate Governor

DALLAS STARS
Dallas Stars, L.P.

Tom Hicks..Governor
James R. Lites.............................Alternate Governor

DETROIT RED WINGS
Detroit Red Wings, Inc.

Michael Ilitch...Governor
Jay A. Bielfield............................Alternate Governor
Jim Devellano..............................Alternate Governor
Atanas Ilitch...............................Alternate Governor
Christopher Ilitch.........................Alternate Governor

EDMONTON OILERS
Oilers Hockey Inc.

Peter Pocklington...Governor
Glen Sather..................................Alternate Governor

FLORIDA PANTHERS
Florida Panthers Hockey Club, Ltd.

William A. Torrey...Governor
Richard H. Evans..........................Alternate Governor
H. Wayne Huizenga......................Alternate Governor
Dean Jordan.................................Alternate Governor

LOS ANGELES KINGS
Los Angeles Kings Hockey Club, L.P.

Robert Sanderman...Governor
Philip F. Anschutz........................Alternate Governor
Timothy J. Leiweke........................Alternate Governor
Edward Roski, Jr...........................Alternate Governor
Dave Taylor..................................Alternate Governor

MONTRÉAL CANADIENS
Le Club de Hockey Canadien, Inc.

Ronald L. Corey..Governor
Rejean Houle...............................Alternate Governor
Fred Steer....................................Alternate Governor

NEW JERSEY DEVILS
Meadowlanders, Inc.

Dr. John J. McMullen....................................Governor
Lou A. Lamoriello.........................Alternate Governor
Peter McMullen............................Alternate Governor

NEW YORK ISLANDERS
New York Islanders Hockey Club, L.P.

William M. Skehan, Esq. ....Governor
John H. Krumpe............................Alternate Governor
Arthur J. McCarthy........................Alternate Governor
Barrett Pickett, Esq. ....Alternate Governor

NEW YORK RANGERS
Madison Square Garden, L.P.

David W. Checketts......................................Governor
Marc Lustgarten...........................Alternate Governor
Kenneth W. Munoz........................Alternate Governor
Neil Smith....................................Alternate Governor

OTTAWA SENATORS
Ottawa Senators Hockey Club Limited Partnership

Roderick M. Bryden.......................................Governor
Roy Mlakar...................................Alternate Governor
David Ferguson.............................Alternate Governor
Pierre Gauthier.............................Alternate Governor

PHILADELPHIA FLYERS
Philadelphia Flyers Limited Partnership

Edward M. Snider...Governor
Bob Clarke..................................Alternate Governor
Richard Ruben..............................Alternate Governor
Ronald K. Ryan.............................Alternate Governor
Philip I. Weinberg.........................Alternate Governor

PHOENIX COYOTES
BG Hockey Ventures

Richard Burke...Governor
Steven Gluckstern........................Alternate Governor
Robert D. Smith............................Alternate Governor

PITTSBURGH PENGUINS
Pittsburgh Hockey Associates

Howard L. Baldwin..Governor
Craig Patrick................................Alternate Governor
Roger M. Marino...........................Alternate Governor
Don Patton...................................Alternate Governor

ST. LOUIS BLUES
St. Louis Blues Hockey Club, L.P.

Jerry E. Ritter..Governor
Ron Caron....................................Alternate Governor
Mark Sauer...................................Alternate Governor

SAN JOSE SHARKS
San Jose Sharks, L.P.

George Gund III..Governor
Gordon Gund................................Alternate Governor
Greg Jamison...............................Alternate Governor
Irvin A. Leonard...........................Alternate Governor
Dean Lombardi.............................Alternate Governor

TAMPA BAY LIGHTNING
Lightning Partners, Ltd.

David E. LeFevre...Governor
Phil Esposito................................Alternate Governor
Steve Oto.....................................Alternate Governor
Chris Phillips...............................Alternate Governor

TORONTO MAPLE LEAFS
Maple Leaf Gardens Limited

Steve A. Stavro..Governor
Brian P. Bellmore.........................Alternate Governor
Ken Dryden..................................Alternate Governor

VANCOUVER CANUCKS
Vancouver Hockey Club Ltd.

John E. McCaw, Jr...Governor
Arthur Griffiths............................Alternate Governor
John H. Chapple...........................Alternate Governor
Stanley McCammon........................Alternate Governor
J.B. Patrick Quinn.........................Alternate Governor

WASHINGTON CAPITALS
Washington Capitals, L.P.

Abe Pollin..Governor
Richard M. Patrick........................Alternate Governor
Peter O'Malley.............................Alternate Governor
David Osnos.................................Alternate Governor

Commissioner and League Presidents

Gary B. Bettman

Gary B. Bettman took office as the NHL's first Commissioner on February 1, 1993. Since the League was formed in 1917, there have been five League Presidents.

NHL President	Years in Office
Frank Calder	1917-1943
Mervyn "Red" Dutton	1943-1946
Clarence Campbell	1946-1977
John A. Ziegler, Jr.	1977-1992
Gil Stein	1992-1993

NHL Europe, B.V.

Signaustrasse 1
8008 Zurich – Switzerland
Phone: 41(0)1 389-8080
Fax: 41(0)1 389-8090

Brad Kwong – Managing Director
Cyril Speijer – Authorized Agent

Hockey Hall of Fame

BCE Place
30 Yonge Street
Toronto, Ontario M5E 1X8
Phone: 416/360-7735
Executive Fax: 416/360-1501
Resource Center/Retail Fax: 416/360-1316
www.hhof.com

Ian "Scotty" Morrison – Chairman
Bryan Black – Vice-President, Marketing
Jeff Denomme – Vice-President, Operations and Treasurer
Kelly Massé – Executive Assistant
Craig Baines – Manager, Business Development
Jan Barrina – Manager, Special Events and Facility Sales
Craig Beckim – Associate Manager, Merchandising
Sandra Buffone – Manager, Accounting and Office Services
Barry Eversley – Manager, Building Services
Anthony Fusco – Manager, Information Systems
Jeff Graham – Manager, Guest Services
Tim McWilliams – Associate Manager, Retail Operations
Ray Paquet – Manager, Exhibit Development and Technology
Phil Pritchard – Manager, Resource Centre and Acquisitions

National Hockey League Players' Association

777 Bay Street, Suite 2400
Toronto, Ontario M5G 2C8
Phone: 416/408-4040
Fax: 416/408-3685
E-mail: media@nhlpa.com   Internet: http://www.nhlpa.com

Robert W. Goodenow – Executive Director and
  General Counsel
JP Barry – Associate Counsel
Jeffrey Citron – Associate Counsel
Ian Pulver – Associate Counsel
Ted Saskin – Senior Director, Business Affairs and Licensing
Mike Ouellet – Associate Counsel, Licensing
Ken Kim – Marketing Manager, "Be A Player" and
  Promotional Licensing
Michael Merhab – Director, Trading Cards and Collectibles
Alison McDonald – Television and Media Projects Director
Chris Allard – Communications Co-ordinator
Barbara Larcina – Director of Business Administration
Ian Sanderson – Manager, Information Technology
Kim Murdoch – Manager, Pensions and Benefits

NHL On-Ice Officials

Total NHL Games and 96-97 Games columns count regular-season games only.

Referees

#	Name	Birthplace	Birthdate	First NHL Game	Total NHL Games	96-97 Games
9	Blaine Angus	Shawville, Que	9/25/61	10/17/92	54	21
30	Bernard DeGrace	Lameque, N.B.	5/1/67	10/15/91	*157	0
10	Paul Devorski	Guelph, Ont.	8/18/58	10/14/89	390	70
11	Mark Faucette	Springfield, MA	6/9/58	12/23/87	507	72
2	Kerry Fraser	Sarnia, Ont.	5/30/52	4/6/75	1043	66
4	Terry Gregson	Erin, Ont.	11/7/53	12/19/81	934	70
95	Conrad Haché	Sudbury, Ont.	5/15/72	2/27/95	*24	*4
8	Dave Jackson	Montreal, Que.	11/28/64	12/23/90	191	68
18	Greg Kimmerly	Toronto, Ont.	12/8/64	11/30/96	1	1
12	Don Koharski	Halifax, N.S.	12/2/55	10/14/77	**1066	70
14	Dennis LaRue	Savannah, GA	7/14/59	3/26/91	83	27
28	Mike Leggo	North Bay, Ont.	10/7/64		0	0
27	Kevin Maguire	Toronto, Ont.	5/1/63		0	0
6	Dan Marouelli	Edmonton, Alta.	7/16/55	11/2/84	706	60
26	Rob Martell	Winnipeg, Man.	10/21/63	3/14/84	**3	1
7	Bill McCreary	Guelph, Ont.	11/17/55	11/3/84	796	66
19	Mick McGeough	Regina, Sask.	6/20/57	1/19/89	386	68
15	Dan O'Halloran	Leamington, Ont.	3/25/64	10/14/95	26	16
20	Lance Roberts	Edmonton, Alta.	5/28/57	11/3/89	272	65
31	Lyle Seitz	Brooks, Alta.	1/22/69	10/6/92	*102	0
16	Rob Shick	Port Alberni, B.C.	12/4/57	4/6/86	591	64
22	Paul Stewart	Boston, MA	3/21/55	3/27/87	624	64
17	Richard Trottier	Laval, Que.	2/28/57	12/13/89	288	66
21	Don Van Massenhoven	London, Ont.	7/17/60	11/11/93	182	67
24	Stephen Walkom	North Bay, Ont.	8/8/63	10/18/92	183	63
23	Brad Watson	Regina, Sask.	10/4/61	2/5/94	3	1
29	Scott Zelkin	Wilmette, IL	9/12/68	4/13/97	1	1

* All games worked as a linesman.   ** Includes some games worked as a linesman.

Linesmen

#	Name	Birthplace	Birthdate	First NHL Game	Total NHL Games	96-97 Games
75	Derek Amell	Port Colborne, Ont.	9/16/68		0	0
94	Wayne Bonney	Ottawa, Ont.	5/27/53	10/10/79	1235	66
55	Gord Broseker	Baltimore, MD	7/8/50	1/14/75	1596	75
74	Lonnie Cameron	Victoria, B.C.	7/15/64	10/5/96	65	65
35	Pierre Champoux	Ville St-Pierre, Que.	4/18/63	10/8/88	566	75
50	Kevin Collins	Springfield, MA	12/15/50	10/13/77	1547	81
88	Mike Cvik	Calgary, Alta.	7/6/62	10/8/87	644	67
33	Pat Dapuzzo	Hoboken, NJ	12/29/58	12/5/84	931	1
44	Greg Devorski	Guelph, Ont.	8/3/69	10/9/93	241	74
68	Scott Driscoll	Seaforth, Ont.	5/2/68	10/10/92	297	75
36	Gerard Gauthier	Montreal, Que.	9/5/48	10/16/71	1944	77
66	Darren Gibbs	Edmonton, Alta.	9/30/66		0	0
91	Don Henderson	Calgary, Alta.	9/23/68	3/10/95	56	37
64	Shane Heyer	Summerland, B.C.	2/7/64	10/5/88	633	77
48	Swede Knox	Edmonton, Alta.	3/2/48	10/14/72	1846	72
71	Brad Kovachik	Woodstock, Ont.	3/7/71	10/10/96	27	27
86	Brad Lazarowich	Vancouver, B.C.	8/4/62	10/9/86	751	70
46	Dan McCourt	Falconbridge, Ont.	8/14/54	12/27/80	1142	72
90	Andy McElman	Chicago Heights, IL	8/4/61	10/7/93	233	68
39	Randy Mitton	Fredericton, N.B.	9/22/50	2/2/74	1643	31
41	Jean Morin	Sorel, Que.	8/10/63	10/5/91	348	71
93	Brian Murphy	Dover, NH	12/13/64	10/7/88	582	79
40	Thor Nelson	Westminister, CA	1/6/68	2/16/95	39	20
43	Tim Nowak	Buffalo, NY	9/6/67	10/8/93	233	70
79	Mark Paré	Windsor, Ont.	7/26/57	10/11/79	1327	72
51	Baron Parker	Vancouver, B.C.	3/5/67	1/25/95	174	68
72	Stephane Provost	Montreal, Que.	5/5/67	1/25/95	184	70
34	Pierre Racicot	Verdun, Que.	2/15/67	10/12/93	237	74
32	Ray Scapinello	Guelph, Ont.	11/5/46	10/17/71	2019	72
47	Dan Schachte	Madison, WI	7/13/58	10/6/82	1053	70
57	Jay Sharrers	Jamaica, West Indies	7/3/67	10/6/90	432	73
56	Mark Wheler	North Battleford, Sask.	9/20/65	10/10/92	316	72

NHL History

1917 — National Hockey League organized November 22 in Montreal following suspension of operations by the National Hockey Association of Canada Limited (NHA). Montreal Canadiens, Montreal Wanderers, Ottawa Senators and Quebec Bulldogs attended founding meeting. Delegates decided to use NHA rules.

Toronto Arenas were later admitted as fifth team; Quebec decided not to operate during the first season. Quebec players allocated to remaining four teams.

Frank Calder elected president and secretary-treasurer.

First NHL games played December 19, with Toronto only arena with artificial ice. Clubs played 22-game split schedule.

1918 — Emergency meeting held January 3 due to destruction by fire of Montreal Arena which was home ice for both Canadiens and Wanderers.

Wanderers withdrew, reducing the NHL to three teams; Canadiens played remaining home games at 3,250-seat Jubilee rink.

Quebec franchise sold to P.J. Quinn of Toronto on October 18 on the condition that the team operate in Quebec City for 1918-19 season. Quinn did not attend the November League meeting and Quebec did not play in 1918-19.

1919-20 — NHL reactivated Quebec Bulldogs franchise. Former Quebec players returned to the club. New Mount Royal Arena became home of Canadiens. Toronto Arenas changed name to St. Patricks. Clubs played 24-game split schedule.

1920-21 — H.P. Thompson of Hamilton, Ontario made application for the purchase of an NHL franchise. Quebec franchise shifted to Hamilton with other NHL teams providing players to strengthen the club.

1921-22 — Split schedule abandoned. First and second place teams at the end of full schedule to play for championship.

1922-23 — Clubs agreed that players could not be sold or traded to clubs in any other league without first being offered to all other clubs in the NHL. In March, Foster Hewitt broadcasts radio's first hockey game.

1923-24 — Ottawa's new 10,000-seat arena opened. First U.S. franchise granted to Boston for following season.

Dr. Cecil Hart Trophy donated to NHL to be awarded to the player judged most useful to his team.

1924-25 — Canadian Arena Company of Montreal granted a franchise to operate Montreal Maroons. NHL now six team league with two clubs in Montreal. Inaugural game in new Montreal Forum played November 29, 1924 as Canadiens defeated Toronto 7-1. Forum was home rink for the Maroons, but no ice was available in the Canadiens arena November 29, resulting in shift to Forum.

Hamilton finished first in the standings, receiving a bye into the finals. But Hamilton players, demanding $200 each for additional games in the playoffs, went on strike. The NHL suspended all players, fining them $200 each. Stanley Cup finalist to be the winner of NHL semi-final between Toronto and Canadiens.

Prince of Wales and Lady Byng trophies donated to NHL.

Clubs played 30-game schedule.

1925-26 — Hamilton club dropped from NHL. Players signed by new New York Americans franchise. Franchise granted to Pittsburgh.

Clubs played 36-game schedule.

1926-27 — New York Rangers granted franchise May 15, 1926. Chicago Black Hawks and Detroit Cougars granted franchises September 25, 1926. NHL now ten-team league with an American and a Canadian Division.

Stanley Cup came under the control of NHL. In previous seasons, winners of the now-defunct Western or Pacific Coast leagues would play NHL champion in Cup finals.

Toronto franchise sold to a new company controlled by Hugh Aird and Conn Smythe. Name changed from St. Patricks to Maple Leafs.

Clubs played 44-game schedule.

The Montreal Canadiens donated the Vezina Trophy to be awarded to the team allowing the fewest goals-against in regular season play. The winning team would, in turn, present the trophy to the goaltender playing in the greatest number of games during the season.

1930-31 — Detroit franchise changed name from Cougars to Falcons. Pittsburgh transferred to Philadelphia for one season. Pirates changed name to Philadelphia Quakers. Trading deadline for teams set at February 15 of each year. NHL approved operation of farm teams by Rangers, Americans, Falcons and Bruins. Four-sided electric arena clock first demonstrated.

1931-32 — Philadelphia dropped out. Ottawa withdrew for one season. New Maple Leaf Gardens completed.

Clubs played 48-game schedule

1932-33 — Detroit franchise changed name from Falcons to Red Wings. Franchise application received from St. Louis but refused because of additional travel costs. Ottawa team resumed play.

1933-34 — First All-Star Game played as a benefit for injured player Ace Bailey. Leafs defeated All-Stars 7-3 in Toronto.

1934-35 — Ottawa franchise transferred to St. Louis. Team called St. Louis Eagles and consisted largely of Ottawa's players.

1935-36 — Ottawa-St. Louis franchise terminated. Montreal Canadiens finished season with very poor record. To strengthen the club, NHL gave Canadiens first call on the services of all French-Canadian players for three seasons.

1937-38 — Second benefit all-star game staged November 2 in Montreal in aid of the family of the late Canadiens star Howie Morenz.

Montreal Maroons withdrew from the NHL on June 22, 1938, leaving seven clubs in the League.

1938-39 — Expenses for each club regulated at $5 per man per day for meals and $2.50 per man per day for accommodation.

1939-40 — Benefit All-Star Game played October 29, 1939 in Montreal for the children of the late Albert (Babe) Siebert.

1940-41 — Ross-Tyer puck adopted as the official puck of the NHL. Early in the season it was apparent that this puck was too soft. The Spalding puck was adopted in its place.

After the playoffs, Arthur Ross, NHL governor from Boston, donated a perpetual trophy to be awarded annually to the player voted outstanding in the league.

1941-42 — New York Americans changed name to Brooklyn Americans.

1942-43 — Brooklyn Americans withdrew from NHL, leaving six teams: Boston, Chicago, Detroit, Montreal, New York and Toronto. Playoff format saw first-place team play third-place team and second play fourth.

Clubs played 50-game schedule.

Frank Calder, president of the NHL since its inception, died in Montreal. Meryn ''Red'' Dutton, former manager of the New York Americans, became president. The NHL commissioned the Calder Memorial Trophy to be awarded to the League's outstanding rookie each year.

1945-46 — Philadelphia, Los Angeles and San Francisco applied for NHL franchises.

The Philadelphia Arena Company of the American Hockey League applied for an injunction to prevent the possible operation of an NHL franchise in that city.

1946-47 — Mervyn Dutton retired as president of the NHL prior to the start of the season. He was succeeded by Clarence S. Campbell.

Individual trophy winners and all-star team members to receive $1,000 awards.

Playoff guarantees for players introduced.

Clubs played 60-game schedule.

1947-48 — The first annual All-Star Game for the benefit of the players' pension fund was played when the All-Stars defeated the Stanley Cup Champion Toronto Maple Leafs 4-3 in Toronto on October 13, 1947.

Ross Trophy, awarded to the NHL's outstanding player since 1941, to be awarded annually to the League's scoring leader.

Philadelphia and Los Angeles franchise applications refused.

National Hockey League Pension Society formed.

1949-50 — Clubs played 70-game schedule.

First intra-league draft held April 30, 1950. Clubs allowed to protect 30 players. Remaining players available for $25,000 each.

1951-52 — Referees included in the League's pension plan.

1952-53 — In May of 1952, City of Cleveland applied for NHL franchise. Application denied. In March of 1953, the Cleveland Barons of the AHL challenged the NHL champions for the Stanley Cup. The NHL governors did not accept this challenge.

1953-54 — The James Norris Memorial Trophy presented to the NHL for annual presentation to the League's best defenseman.

Intra-league draft rules amended to allow teams to protect 18 skaters and two goaltenders, claiming price reduced to $15,000.

1954-55 — Each arena to operate an ''out-of-town'' scoreboard. Referees and linesmen to wear shirts of black and white vertical stripes.

1956-57 — Standardized signals for referees and linesmen introduced.

1960-61 — Canadian National Exhibition, City of Toronto and NHL reach agreement for the construction of a Hockey Hall of Fame on the CNE grounds. Hall opens on August 26, 1961.

1963-64 — Player development league established with clubs operated by NHL franchises located in Minneapolis, St. Paul, Indianapolis, Omaha and, beginning in 1964-65, Tulsa. First universal amateur draft took place. All players of qualifying age (17) unaffected by sponsorship of junior teams available to be drafted.

1964-65 — Conn Smythe Trophy presented to the NHL to be awarded annually to the outstanding player in the Stanley Cup playoffs.

Minimum age of players subject to amateur draft changed to 18.

1965-66 — NHL announced expansion plans for a second six-team division to begin play in 1967-68.

1966-67 — Fourteen applications for NHL franchises received.

Lester Patrick Trophy presented to the NHL to be awarded annually for outstanding service to hockey in the United States.

NHL sponsorship of junior teams ceased, making all players of qualifying age not already on NHL-sponsored lists eligible for the amateur draft.

1967-68 — Six new teams added: California Seals, Los Angeles Kings, Minnesota North Stars, Philadelphia Flyers, Pittsburgh Penguins, St. Louis Blues. New teams to play in West Division. Remaining six teams to play in East Division.

Minimum age of players subject to amateur draft changed to 20.

Clubs played 74-game schedule.

Clarence S. Campbell Trophy awarded to team finishing the regular season in first place in West Division.

California Seals changed name to Oakland Seals on December 8, 1967.

1968-69 — Clubs played 76-game schedule.

Amateur draft expanded to cover any amateur player of qualifying age throughout the world.

1970-71 — Two new teams added: Buffalo Sabres and Vancouver Canucks. These teams joined East Division: Chicago switched to West Division.

Clubs played 78-game schedule.

1971-72 — Playoff format amended. In each division, first to play fourth; second to play third.

1972-73 — Soviet Nationals and Canadian NHL stars play eight-game pre-season series. Canadians win 4-3-1.

Two new teams added. Atlanta Flames join West Division; New York Islanders join East Division.

1974-75 — Two new teams added: Kansas City Scouts and Washington Capitals. Teams realigned into two nine-team conferences, the Prince of Wales made up of the Norris and Adams Divisions, and the Clarence Campbell made up of the Smythe and Patrick Divisions.

Clubs played 80-game schedule.

NHL History — *continued*

1976-77 — California franchise transferred to Cleveland. Team named Cleveland Barons. Kansas City franchise transferred to Denver. Team named Colorado Rockies.

1977-78 — Clarence S. Campbell retires as NHL president. Succeeded by John A. Ziegler, Jr.

1978-79 — Cleveland and Minnesota franchises merge, leaving NHL with 17 teams. Merged team placed in Adams Division, playing home games in Minnesota.
   Minimum age of players subject to amateur draft changed to 19.

1979-80 — Four new teams added: Edmonton Oilers, Hartford Whalers, Quebec Nordiques and Winnipeg Jets.
   Minimum age of players subject to entry draft changed to 18.

1980-81 — Atlanta franchise shifted to Calgary, retaining ''Flames'' name.

1981-82 — Teams realigned within existing divisions. New groupings based on geographical areas. Unbalanced schedule adopted.

1982-83 — Colorado Rockies franchise shifted to East Rutherford, New Jersey. Team named New Jersey Devils. Franchise moved to Patrick Division from Smythe; Winnipeg moved to Smythe Division from Norris.

1991-92 — San Jose Sharks added, making the NHL a 22-team league. NHL celebrates 75th Anniversary Season. The 1991-92 regular season suspended due to a strike by members of the NHL Players' Association on April 1, 1992. Play resumed April 12, 1992.

1992-93 — Gil Stein named NHL president (October, 1992). Gary Bettman named first NHL Commissioner (February, 1993). Ottawa Senators and Tampa Bay Lightning added, making the NHL a 24-team league. NHL celebrates Stanley Cup Centennial. Clubs played 84-game schedule.

1993-94 — Mighty Ducks of Anaheim and Florida Panthers added, making the NHL a 26-team league. Minnesota franchise shifted to Dallas, team named Dallas Stars. Prince of Wales and Clarence Campbell Conferences renamed Eastern and Western. Adams, Patrick, Norris and Smythe Divisions renamed Northeast, Atlantic, Central and Pacific. Winnipeg moved to Central Division from Pacific; Tampa Bay moved to Atlantic Division from Central; Pittsburgh moved to Northeast Division from Atlantic.

1994-95 — A labor disruption forced the cancellation of 468 games from October 1, 1994 to January 19, 1995. Clubs played a 48-game schedule that began January 20, 1995 and ended May 3, 1995. No inter-conference games were played.

1995-96 — Quebec franchise transferred to Denver. Team named Colorado Avalanche and placed in Pacific Division of Western Conference. Clubs to play 82-game schedule.

1996-97 — Winnipeg franchise transferred to Phoenix. Team named Phoenix Coyotes and placed in Central Division of Western Conference.

1997-98 — Hartford franchise transferred to Raleigh. Team named Carolina Hurricanes and remains in Northeast Division of Eastern Conference.

Major Rule Changes

1910-11 — Game changed from two 30-minute periods to three 20-minute periods.

1911-12 — National Hockey Association (forerunner of the NHL) originated six-man hockey, replacing seven-man game.

1917-18 — Goalies permitted to fall to the ice to make saves. Previously a goaltender was penalized for dropping to the ice.

1918-19 — Penalty rules amended. For minor fouls, substitutes not allowed until penalized player had served three minutes. For major fouls, no substitutes for five minutes. For match fouls, no substitutes allowed for the remainder of the game.
   With the addition of two lines painted on the ice twenty feet from center, three playing zones were created, producing a forty-foot neutral center ice area in which forward passing was permitted. Kicking the puck was permitted in this neutral zone.
   Tabulation of assists began.

1921-22 — Goaltenders allowed to pass the puck forward up to their own blue line.
   Overtime limited to twenty minutes.
   Minor penalties changed from three minutes to two minutes.

1923-24 — Match foul defined as actions deliberately injuring or disabling an opponent. For such actions, a player was fined not less than $50 and ruled off the ice for the balance of the game. A player assessed a match penalty may be replaced by a substitute at the end of 20 minutes. Match penalty recipients must meet with the League president who can assess additional punishment.

1925-26 — Delayed penalty rules introduced. Each team must have a minimum of four players on the ice at all times.
   Two rules were amended to encourage offense: No more than two defensemen permitted to remain inside a team's own blue line when the puck has left the defensive zone. A faceoff to be called for ragging the puck unless short-handed.
   Team captains only players allowed to talk to referees.
   Goaltender's leg pads limited to 12-inch width.
   Timekeeper's gong to mark end of periods rather than referee's whistle. Teams to dress a maximum of 12 players for each game from a roster of no more than 14 players.

1926-27 — Blue lines repositioned to sixty feet from each goal-line, thereby enlarging the neutral zone and standardizing distance from blueline to goal.
   Uniform goal nets adopted throughout NHL with goal posts securely fastened to the ice.

1927-28 — To further encourage offense, forward passes allowed in defending and neutral zones and goaltender's pads reduced in width from 12 to 10 inches.
   Game standardized at three twenty-minute periods of stop-time separated by ten-minute intermissions. Teams to change ends after each period.
   Ten minutes of sudden-death overtime to be played if the score is tied after regulation time.
   Minor penalty to be assessed to any player other than a goaltender for deliberately picking up the puck while it is in play. Minor penalty to be assessed for deliberately shooting the puck out of play.
   The Art Ross goal net adopted as the official net of the NHL.
   Maximum length of hockey sticks limited to 53 inches measured from heel of blade to end of handle. No minimum length stipulated.
   Home teams given choice of goals to defend at start of game.

1928-29 — Forward passing permitted in defensive and neutral zones and into attacking zone if pass receiver is in neutral zone when pass is made. No forward passing allowed inside attacking zone.
   Minor penalty to be assessed to any player who delays the game by passing the puck back into his defensive zone.
   Ten-minute overtime without sudden-death provision to be played in games tied after regulation time. Games tied after this overtime period declared a draw.
   Exclusive of goaltenders, team to dress at least 8 and no more than 12 skaters.

NHL Attendance

Season	Regular Season Games	Regular Season Attendance	Playoffs Games	Playoffs Attendance	Total Attendance
1960-61	210	2,317,142	17	242,000	2,559,142
1961-62	210	2,435,424	18	277,000	2,712,424
1962-63	210	2,590,574	16	220,906	2,811,480
1963-64	210	2,732,642	21	309,149	3,041,791
1964-65	210	2,822,635	20	303,859	3,126,494
1965-66	210	2,941,164	16	249,000	3,190,184
1966-67	210	3,084,759	16	248,336	3,333,095
1967-68[1]	444	4,938,043	40	495,089	5,433,132
1968-69	456	5,550,613	33	431,739	5,982,352
1969-70[2]	456	5,992,065	34	461,694	6,453,759
1970-71	546	7,257,677	43	707,633	7,965,310
1971-72	546	7,609,368	36	582,666	8,192,034
1972-73[3]	624	8,575,651	38	624,637	9,200,288
1973-74	624	8,640,978	38	600,442	9,241,420
1974-75[4]	720	9,521,536	51	784,181	10,305,717
1975-76	720	9,103,761	48	726,279	9,830,040
1976-77	720	8,563,890	44	646,279	9,210,169
1977-78	720	8,526,564	45	686,634	9,213,198
1978-79	680	7,758,053	45	694,521	8,452,574
1979-80[5]	840	10,533,623	63	976,699	11,510,322
1980-81	840	10,726,198	68	966,390	11,692,588
1981-82	840	10,710,894	71	1,058,948	11,769,842
1982-83	840	11,020,610	66	1,088,222	12,028,832
1983-84	840	11,359,386	70	1,107,400	12,466,786
1984-85	840	11,633,730	70	1,107,500	12,741,230
1985-86	840	11,621,000	72	1,152,503	12,773,503
1986-87	840	11,855,880	87	1,383,967	13,239,847
1987-88	840	12,117,512	83	1,336,901	13,454,413
1988-89	840	12,417,969	83	1,327,214	13,745,183
1989-90	840	12,579,651	85	1,355,593	13,935,244
1990-91	840	12,343,897	92	1,442,203	13,786,100
1991-92[6]	880	12,769,676	86	1,327,920	14,097,596
1992-93[7]	1,008	14,158,177[8]	83	1,346,034	15,504,211
1993-94[9]	1,092	16,105,604[10]	90	1,440,095	17,545,699
1994-95	624	9,233,884	81	1,329,130	10,563,014
1995-96	1,066	17,041,614	86	1,540,140	18,581,754
1996-97	1,066	17,640,529	82	1,494,878	19,135,407

[1] First expansion: Los Angeles, Pittsburgh, California (Cleveland), Philadelphia, St. Louis and Minnesota (Dallas)
[2] Second expansion: Buffalo and Vancouver
[3] Third expansion: Atlanta (Calgary) and New York Islanders
[4] Fourth expansion: Kansas City (Colorado, New Jersey) and Washington
[5] Fifth expansion: Edmonton, Hartford, Quebec (Colorado) and Winnipeg
[6] Sixth expansion: San Jose
[7] Seventh expansion: Ottawa and Tampa Bay
[8] Includes 24 neutral site games
[9] Eighth expansion: Anaheim and Florida
[10] Includes 26 neutral site games

Major Rule Changes — *continued*

1929-30 — Forward passing permitted inside all three zones but not permitted across either blue line.

Kicking the puck allowed, but a goal cannot be scored by kicking the puck in.

No more than three players including the goaltender may remain in their defensive zone when the puck has gone up ice. Minor penalties to be assessed for the first two violations of this rule in a game; major penalties thereafter.

Goaltenders forbidden to hold the puck. Pucks caught must be cleared immediately. For infringement of this rule, a faceoff to be taken ten feet in front of the goal with no player except the goaltender standing between the faceoff spot and the goal-line.

Highsticking penalties introduced.

Maximum number of players in uniform increased from 12 to 15.

December 21, 1929 — Forward passing rules instituted at the beginning of the 1929-30 season more than doubled number of goals scored. Partway through the season, these rules were further amended to read, ''No attacking player allowed to precede the play when entering the opposing defensive zone.'' This is similar to modern offside rule.

1930-31 — A player without a complete stick ruled out of play and forbidden from taking part in further action until a new stick is obtained. A player who has broken his stick must obtain a replacement at his bench.

A further refinement of the offside rule stated that the puck must first be propelled into the attacking zone before any player of the attacking side can enter that zone; for infringement of this rule a faceoff to take place at the spot where the infraction took place.

1931-32 — Though there is no record of a team attempting to play with two goaltenders on the ice, a rule was instituted which stated that each team was allowed only one goaltender on the ice at one time.

Attacking players forbidden to impede the movement or obstruct the vision of opposing goaltenders.

Defending players with the exception of the goaltender forbidden from falling on the puck within 10 feet of the net.

1932-33 — Each team to have captain on the ice at all times.

If the goaltender is removed from the ice to serve a penalty, the manager of the club to appoint a substitute.

Match penalty with substitution after five minutes instituted for kicking another player.

1933-34 — Number of players permitted to stand in defensive zone restricted to three including goaltender.

Visible time clocks required in each rink.

Two referees replace one referee and one linesman.

1934-35 — Penalty shot awarded when a player is tripped and thus prevented from having a clear shot on goal, having no player to pass to other than the offending player. Shot taken from inside a 10-foot circle located 38 feet from the goal. The goaltender must not advance more than one foot from his goal-line when the shot is taken.

1937-38 — Rules introduced governing icing the puck.

Penalty shot awarded when a player other than a goaltender falls on the puck within 10 feet of the goal.

1938-39 — Penalty shot modified to allow puck carrier to skate in before shooting.

One referee and one linesman replace two referee system.

Blue line widened to 12 inches.

Maximum number of players in uniform increased from 14 to 15.

1939-40 — A substitute replacing a goaltender removed from ice to serve a penalty may use a goaltender's stick and gloves but no other goaltending equipment.

1940-41 — Flooding ice surface between periods made obligatory.

1941-42 — Penalty shots classified as minor and major. Minor shot to be taken from a line 28 feet from the goal. Major shot, awarded when a player is tripped with only the goaltender to beat, permits the player taking the penalty shot to skate right into the goalkeeper and shoot from point-blank range.

One referee and two linesmen employed to officiate games.

For playoffs, standby minor league goaltenders employed by NHL as emergency substitutes.

1942-43 — Because of wartime restrictions on train scheduling, regular-season overtime was discontinued on November 21, 1942.

Player limit reduced from 15 to 14. Minimum of 12 men in uniform abolished.

1943-44 — Red line at center ice introduced to speed up the game and reduce offside calls. This rule is considered to mark the beginning of the modern era in the NHL.

Delayed penalty rules introduced.

1945-46 — Goal indicator lights synchronized with official time clock required at all rinks.

1946-47 — System of signals by officials to indicate infractions introduced.

Linesmen from neutral cities employed for all games.

1947-48 — Goal awarded when a player with the puck has an open net to shoot at and a thrown stick prevents the shot on goal. Major penalty to any player who throws his stick in any zone other than defending zone. If a stick is thrown by a player in his defending zone but the thrown stick is not considered to have prevented a goal, a penalty shot is awarded.

All playoff games played until a winner determined, with 20-minute sudden-death overtime periods separated by 10-minute intermissions.

1949-50 — Ice surface painted white.

Clubs allowed to dress 17 players exclusive of goaltenders.

Major penalties incurred by goaltenders served by a member of the goaltender's team instead of resulting in a penalty shot.

1950-51 — Each team required to provide an emergency goaltender in attendance with full equipment at each game for use by either team in the event of illness or injury to a regular goaltender.

1951-52 — Home teams to wear basic white uniforms; visiting teams basic colored uniforms.

Goal crease enlarged from 3 x 7 feet to 4 x 8 feet.

Number of players in uniform reduced to 15 plus goaltenders.

Faceoff circles enlarged from 10-foot to 15-foot radius.

1952-53 — Teams permitted to dress 15 skaters on the road and 16 at home.

1953-54 — Number of players in uniform set at 16 plus goaltenders.

1954-55 — Number of players in uniform set at 18 plus goaltenders up to December 1 and 16 plus goaltenders thereafter. Teams agree to wear colored uniforms at home and white uniforms on the road.

1956-57 — Player serving a minor penalty allowed to return to ice when a goal is scored by opposing team.

1959-60 — Players prevented from leaving their benches to enter into an altercation. Substitutions permitted providing substitutes do not enter into altercation.

1960-61 — Number of players in uniform set at 16 plus goaltenders.

1961-62 — Penalty shots to be taken by the player against whom the foul was committed. In the event of a penalty shot called in a situation where a particular player hasn't been fouled, the penalty shot to be taken by any player on the ice when the foul was committed.

1964-65 — No bodily contact on faceoffs.

In playoff games, each team to have its substitute goaltender dressed in his regular uniform except for leg pads and body protector. All previous rules governing standby goaltenders terminated.

1965-66 — Teams required to dress two goaltenders for each regular-season game. Maximum stick length increased to 55 inches.

1966-67 — Substitution allowed on coincidental major penalties.

Between-periods intermissions fixed at 15 minutes.

1967-68 — If a penalty incurred by a goaltender is a co-incident major, the penalty to be served by a player of the goaltender's team on the ice at the time the penalty was called. Limit of curvature of hockey stick blade set at 1-$\frac{1}{2}$ inches.

1969-70 — Limit of curvature of hockey stick blade set at 1 inch.

1970-71 — Home teams to wear basic white uniforms; visiting teams basic colored uniforms.

Limit of curvature of hockey stick blade set at $\frac{1}{2}$ inch.

Minor penalty for deliberately shooting the puck out of the playing area.

1971-72 — Number of players in uniform set at 17 plus 2 goaltenders.

Third man to enter an altercation assessed an automatic game misconduct penalty.

1972-73 — Minimum width of stick blade reduced to 2 inches from 2-$\frac{1}{2}$ inches.

1974-75 — Bench minor penalty imposed if a penalized player does not proceed directly and immediately to the penalty box.

1976-77 — Rule dealing with fighting amended to provide a major and game misconduct penalty for any player who is clearly the instigator of a fight.

1977-78 — Teams requesting a stick measurement to be assessed a minor penalty in the event that the measured stick does not violate the rules.

1979-80 — Wearing of helmets made mandatory for players entering the NHL.

1980-81 — Maximum stick length increased to 58 inches.

1981-82 — If both of a team's listed goaltenders are incapacitated, the team can dress and play any eligible goaltender who is available.

1982-83 — Number of players in uniform set at 18 plus 2 goaltenders.

1983-84 — Five-minute sudden-death overtime to be played in regular-season games that are tied at the end of regulation time.

1985-86 — Substitutions allowed in the event of co-incidental minor penalties. Maximum stick length increased to 60 inches.

1986-87 — Delayed off-side is no longer in effect once the players of the offending team have cleared the opponents' defensive zone.

1991-92 — Video replays employed to assist referees in goal/no goal situations. Size of goal crease increased. Crease changed to semi-circular configuration. Time clock to record tenths of a second in last minute of each period and overtime. Major and game misconduct penalty for checking from behind into boards. Penalties added for crease infringement and unnecessary contact with goaltender. Goal disallowed if puck enters net while a player of the attacking team is standing on the goal crease line, is in the goal crease or places his stick in the goal crease.

1992-93 — No substitutions allowed in the event of coincidental minor penalties called when both teams are at full strength. Wearing of helmets made optional for forwards and defensemen. Minor penalty for attempting to draw a penalty ("diving"). Major and game misconduct penalty for checking from behind into goal frame. Game misconduct penalty for instigating a fight. Highsticking redefined to include any use of the stick above waist-height. Previous rule stipulated shoulder-height.

1993-94 — High sticking redefined to allow goals scored with a high stick below the height of the crossbar of the goal frame.

1996-97 — Maximum stick length increased to 63 inches.

Roy "Shrimp" Worters drops to the ice and deftly "stacks the pads" to keep an enemy puck from crossing the goal line. Until 1917-18, it was illegal for netminders to leave their feet, and any goaltender caught "praying" on his knees in an effort to make a save, was sent to the penalty box for three minutes to reflect on his sins.

NHL PLAYERS AT THE 1998 WINTER OLYMPICS

NATIONAL HOCKEY LEAGUE PLAYERS will participate for the first time in the 1998 Winter Olympic Games in Nagano, Japan. As the result of an agreement reached by the NHL, the National Hockey League Players' Association and the International Ice Hockey Federation, players from the NHL will join national teams of Canada, the United States of America, Russia, Sweden, Finland and the Czech Republic. These teams will begin play in the final round of the tournament.

For the first time in League history, the regular-season schedule will be interrupted to allow the game's top players to play in the Olympics.

The Olympic hockey tournament will be played in two phases: a preliminary round and a final round. From Feb. 7 to Feb. 10, eight teams will each play three games. Austria, Italy, Kazakhstan and Slovakia will compete in Group A, while Group B will consist of Belarus, France, Germany and Japan. The winners of Group A and B will advance to the final round.

Beginning February 13, the eight teams in the final round will each play three games to determine seedings for the quarterfinals.

Single-game playoffs will determine the winners of the quarterfinals, semifinals and gold medal match.

1998 Men's Olympic Hockey Schedule

Preliminary Round

Feb. 7	Italy	vs.	Kazakhstan
Feb. 7	Austria	vs.	Slovakia
Feb. 7	Germany	vs.	Japan
Feb. 7	France	vs.	Belarus
Feb. 8	Austria	vs.	Kazakhstan
Feb. 8	Slovakia	vs.	Italy
Feb. 9	Germany	vs.	Belarus
Feb. 9	Japan	vs.	France
Feb. 10	Belarus	vs.	Japan
Feb. 10	Kazakhstan	vs.	Slovakia
Feb. 10	Italy	vs.	Austria
Feb. 10	France	vs.	Germany
Feb. 12	13th place game		
Feb. 12	11th place game		
Feb. 12	9th place game		

Final Round

Feb. 13	USA	vs.	Sweden
Feb. 13	Finland	vs.	Czech Republic
Feb. 13	Canada	vs.	Qualifier 1
Feb. 13	Qualifier 2	vs.	Russia
Feb. 14	Qualifier 1	vs.	USA
Feb. 14	Sweden	vs.	Canada
Feb. 15	Russia	vs.	Finland
Feb. 15	Czech Republic	vs.	Qualifier 2
Feb. 16	Canada	vs.	USA
Feb. 16	Czech Republic	vs.	Russia
Feb. 16	Finland	vs.	Qualifier 2
Feb. 16	Sweden	vs.	Qualifier 1

Quarterfinals	**Semifinals**
Feb. 18	Feb. 20

Bronze Medal Game	**Gold Medal Game**
Feb. 21	Feb. 22

1998 Women's Olympic Hockey Schedule

Feb. 8	Sweden	vs.	Finland
Feb. 8	Canada	vs.	Japan
Feb. 8	China	vs.	USA
Feb. 9	Finland	vs.	Japan
Feb. 9	USA	vs.	Sweden
Feb. 9	Canada	vs.	China
Feb. 11	Sweden	vs.	Canada
Feb. 11	Japan	vs.	China
Feb. 11	USA	vs.	Finland
Feb. 12	China	vs.	Sweden
Feb. 12	USA	vs.	Japan
Feb. 12	Finland	vs.	Canada
Feb. 14	Japan	vs.	Sweden
Feb. 14	Finland	vs.	China
Feb. 14	Canada	vs.	USA

Bronze Medal Game	**Gold Medal Game**
Feb. 17	Feb. 17

Olympic Hockey Results

Lillehammer, Norway • 1994

Group A

Team	GP	W	L	T	GF	GA	PTS
Finland	5	5	0	0	25	4	10
Germany	5	3	2	0	11	14	6
Czech Republic	5	3	2	0	16	11	6
Russia	5	3	2	0	20	14	6
Austria	5	1	4	0	13	28	2
Norway	5	0	5	0	5	19	0

Group B

Team	GP	W	L	T	GF	GA	PTS
Slovakia	5	3	0	2	26	14	8
Canada	5	3	1	1	17	11	7
Sweden	5	3	1	1	23	13	7
USA	5	1	1	3	21	17	5
Italy	5	1	4	0	15	31	2
France	5	0	4	1	11	27	1

Quarterfinals

Canada	3	Czech Republic	2
Finland	6	USA	1
Sweden	3	Germany	0
Russia	3	Slovakia	2

Semifinals

Canada	5	Finland	3
Sweden	4	Russia	3

Bronze Medal Game

Finland	4	Russia	0

Gold Medal Game

Sweden	3	Canada	2 (shootout)

1994 Final Standings

1. Sweden GOLD
2. Canada SILVER
3. Finland BRONZE
4. Russia
5. Czech Republic
6. Slovakia
7. Germany
8. USA
9. Italy
10. France
11. Norway
12. Austria

1994 Scoring Leaders

Player	Team	GP	G	A	PTS	PIM
Zigmund Palffy	Slovakia	8	3	7	10	8
Miroslav Satan	Slovakia	8	9	0	9	0
Peter Stastny	Slovakia	8	5	4	9	9
Hakan Loob	Sweden	8	4	5	9	2
Gates Orlando	Italy	7	3	6	9	41
Patrik Juhlin	Sweden	8	7	1	8	16
Jiri Kucera	Czech Republic	8	6	2	8	4
Marty Dallman	Austria	7	4	4	8	8
Mika Nieminen	Finland	8	3	5	8	0
David Sacco	USA	8	3	5	8	12
Peter Forsberg	Sweden	8	2	6	8	6

Albertville, France • 1992

Group A

Team	GP	W	L	T	GF	GA	PTS
USA	5	4	0	1	18	7	9
Sweden	5	3	0	2	22	11	8
Finland	5	3	0	1	22	11	7
Germany	5	2	3	0	11	12	4
Italy	5	1	4	0	18	24	2
Poland	5	0	5	0	4	30	0

Group B

Team	GP	W	L	T	GF	GA	PTS
Canada	5	4	1	0	28	9	8
Unified Team*	5	4	1	0	32	10	8
Czechoslovakia	5	4	1	0	25	15	8
France	5	2	3	0	14	22	4
Switzerland	5	1	4	0	13	25	2
Norway	5	0	5	0	7	38	0

* Soviet Union/Russia played as Unified Team in 1992.

Medal Round

Canada	4	Germany	3
Czechoslovakia	3	Sweden	1
USA	4	France	1
Unified Team	6	Finland	1

Semifinals

Canada	4	Czechoslovakia	2
Unified Team	5	USA	2

Bronze Medal Game

Czechoslovakia	6	USA	1

Gold Medal Game

Unified Team	3	Canada	1

1992 Final Standings

1. Unified Team GOLD
2. Canada SILVER
3. Czechoslovakia BRONZE
4. USA
5. Sweden
6. Germany
7. Finland
8. France
9. Norway
10. Switzerland
11. Poland
12. Italy

1992 Scoring Leaders

Player	Team	GP	G	A	PTS
Joe Juneau	Canada	8	6	9	15
Andrei Khomutov	Unified Team	8	7	7	14
Robert Lang	Czechoslovakia	8	5	8	13
Teemu Selanne	Finland	8	7	4	11
Eric Lindros	Canada	8	5	6	11
Hannu Jarvenpaa	Finland	8	5	6	11
Viacheslav Bykov	Unified Team	8	4	7	11
Yuri Khmylev	Unified Team	8	4	6	10
Mika Nieminen	Finland	8	4	6	10
Nikolai Borschevsky	Unified Team	8	7	2	9

Calgary, Alberta, Canada • 1988

Group A

Team	GP	W	L	T	GF	GA	PTS
Finland	5	3	1	1	22	8	7
Sweden	5	2	0	3	23	10	7
Canada	5	3	1	1	17	12	7
Switzerland	5	3	2	0	19	10	6
Poland	5	0	4	1	3	13	1
France	5	1	4	0	10	41	0

Group B

Team	GP	W	L	T	GF	GA	PTS
Soviet Union	5	5	0	0	32	10	10
W. Germany	5	4	1	0	19	12	8
Czechoslovakia	5	3	2	0	23	14	6
USA	5	2	3	0	27	27	4
Austria	5	0	4	1	12	29	1
Norway	5	0	4	1	11	32	1

Final Round

Team	GP	W	L	T	GF	GA	PTS
Soviet Union	5	4	1	0	25	7	8
Finland	5	3	1	1	18	10	7
Sweden	5	2	1	2	15	16	6
Canada	5	2	2	1	17	14	5
W. Germany	5	1	4	0	8	26	2
Czechoslovakia	5	1	4	0	12	22	2

1988 Final Standings

1. Soviet Union GOLD
2. Finland SILVER
3. Sweden BRONZE
4. Canada
5. W. Germany
6. Czechoslovakia
7. USA
8. Switzerland
9. Austria
10. Poland
11. France
12. Norway

1988 Scoring Leaders

Player	Team	GP	G	A	PTS	PIM
Vladimir Krutov	Soviet Union	8	6	9	15	0
Igor Larionov	Soviet Union	8	4	9	13	4
Viacheslav Fetisov	Soviet Union	8	4	9	13	6
Corey Millen	USA	6	6	5	11	4
Dusan Pasek	Czechoslovakia	8	6	5	11	8
Sergei Makarov	Soviet Union	8	3	8	11	10
Erkki Lehtonen	Finland	8	4	6	10	2
Anders Eldebrink	Sweden	8	4	6	10	4
Igor Liba	Czechoslovakia	8	4	6	10	8
Gerd Truntschka	W. Germany	8	3	7	10	10
Raimo Helminen	Finland	7	2	8	10	4

Sarajevo, Yugoslavia • 1984

Group A

Team	GP	W	L	T	GF	GA	PTS
Soviet Union	5	5	0	0	42	5	10
Sweden	5	3	1	1	34	15	7
W. Germany	5	3	1	1	27	17	7
Poland	5	1	4	0	16	37	2
Italy	5	1	4	0	15	31	2
Yugoslavia	5	1	4	0	8	37	2

Group B

Team	GP	W	L	T	GF	GA	PTS
Czechoslovakia	5	5	0	0	38	7	10
Canada	5	4	1	0	24	10	8
Finland	5	2	2	1	27	19	5
USA	5	1	2	2	16	17	4
Austria	5	1	4	0	13	37	2
Norway	5	0	4	1	15	43	1

Final Round

Team	GP	W	L	T	GF	GA	PTS
Soviet Union	3	3	0	0	16	1	6
Czechoslovakia	3	2	1	0	6	2	4
Sweden	3	1	2	0	3	12	2
Canada	3	0	3	0	0	10	0

Consolation Round

Team	GP	W	L	T	GF	GA	PTS
W. Germany	1	1	0	0	7	4	2
USA	1	1	0	0	7	4	2
Finland	1	0	1	0	4	7	0
Poland	1	0	1	0	4	7	0

1984 Final Standings

1. Soviet Union **GOLD**
2. Czechoslovakia **SILVER**
3. Sweden **BRONZE**
4. Canada
5. W. Germany
6. Finland
7. USA
8. Poland

1984 Scoring Leaders

Player	Team	GP	G	A	PTS	PIM
Erich Kuhnhackl	W. Germany	6	8	6	14	12
Peter Gradin	Sweden	7	9	4	13	6
Nikolai Drozdetski	Soviet Union	7	10	2	12	2
Viacheslav Fetisov	Soviet Union	7	3	8	11	8
Petri Skriko	Finland	6	6	4	10	8
Vladimir Ruzicka	Czechoslovakia	7	4	6	10	6
Raimo Summanen	Finland	6	4	6	10	4
Darius Rusnak	Czechoslovakia	7	4	6	10	6
Jiri Hrdina	Czechoslovakia	7	4	6	10	10
Vincent Lukac	Czechoslovakia	7	4	5	9	2
Viktor Tjumenev	Soviet Union	6	0	9	9	2

Lake Placid, New York • 1980

Red Division

Team	GP	W	L	T	GF	GA	PTS
Soviet Union	5	5	0	0	51	11	10
Finland	5	3	2	0	26	18	6
Canada	5	3	2	0	28	12	6
Poland	5	2	3	0	15	23	4
Holland	5	1	3	1	16	43	3
Japan	5	0	4	1	7	36	1

Blue Division

Team	GP	W	L	T	GF	GA	PTS
Sweden	5	4	0	1	26	7	9
USA	5	4	0	1	25	10	9
Czechoslovakia	5	3	2	0	34	16	6
Romania	5	1	3	1	13	29	3
W. Germany	5	1	4	0	21	30	2
Norway	5	0	4	1	9	36	1

Final Round

Team	GP	W	L	T	GF	GA	PTS
USA	3	2	0	1	10	7	5
Soviet Union	3	2	1	0	16	8	4
Sweden	3	0	1	2	7	14	2
Finland	3	0	2	1	7	11	1

1980 Final Standings

1. USA **GOLD**
2. Soviet Union **SILVER**
3. Sweden **BRONZE**
4. Finland
5. Czechoslovakia
6. Canada
7. Poland
8. Holland
9. Romania
10. W. Germany
11. Norway
12. Japan

1980 Scoring Leaders

Player	Team	GP	G	A	PTS	PIM
Milan Novy	Czechoslovakia	6	7	8	15	0
Peter Stastny	Czechoslovakia	6	7	7	14	6
Jaroslav Pouzar	Czechoslovakia	6	8	5	13	6
Alexander Golikov	Soviet Union	7	7	6	13	6
Jukka Porvari	Finland	7	7	4	11	4
Boris Mikhailov	Soviet Union	7	6	5	11	2
Vladimir Krutov	Soviet Union	7	6	5	11	4
Sergei Makarov	Soviet Union	7	5	6	11	2
Marian Stastny	Czechoslovakia	6	5	6	11	4
Mark Johnson	USA	7	5	6	11	6

Innsbruck, Austria • 1976

Group A

Team	GP	W	L	T	GF	GA	PTS
Soviet Union	5	5	0	0	40	11	10
Czechoslovakia	5	3	2	0	17	10	6
W. Germany	5	2	3	0	21	24	4
Finland	5	2	3	0	19	18	4
USA	5	2	3	0	15	21	4
Poland	5	0	5	0	9	37	0

Group B

Team	GP	W	L	T	GF	GA	PTS
Romania	5	4	1	0	23	15	8
Austria	5	3	2	0	18	14	6
Japan	5	3	2	0	20	18	6
Yugoslavia	5	3	2	0	22	19	6
Switzerland	5	2	3	0	24	22	4
Bulgaria	5	0	5	0	19	38	0

1976 Final Standings

1. Soviet Union **GOLD**
2. Czechoslovakia **SILVER**
3. W. Germany **BRONZE**
4. Finland
5. USA
6. Poland
7. Romania
8. Austria
9. Japan
10. Yugoslavia
11. Switzerland
12. Bulgaria

1976 Scoring Leaders

Player	Team	GP	G	A	PTS	PIM
Vladimir Shadrin	Soviet Union	5	6	4	10	0
Alexander Maltsev	Soviet Union	5	5	5	10	0
Victor Shalimov	Soviet Union	5	5	5	10	2
Erich Kuhnhackl	W. Germany	5	5	5	10	10
Valeri Kharlamov	Soviet Union	5	3	6	9	6
Ernst Kopf	W. Germany	5	3	5	8	2
Vladimir Petrov	Soviet Union	5	4	3	7	8
Alexander Yakushev	Soviet Union	5	3	4	7	2
Bob Dobek	USA	5	3	4	7	4
Lorenz Funk	W. Germany	5	2	5	7	4
Victor Zhluktov	Soviet Union	5	1	6	7	2

Sapporo, Japan • 1972

Group A

Team	GP	W	L	T	GF	GA	PTS
Soviet Union	5	4	0	1	33	13	9
USA	5	3	2	0	18	15	6
Czechoslovakia	5	3	2	0	26	13	6
Sweden	5	2	2	1	17	13	5
Finland	5	2	3	0	14	24	4
Poland	5	0	5	0	9	39	0

Group B

Team	GP	W	L	T	GF	GA	PTS
W. Germany	4	3	1	0	22	10	6
Norway	4	3	1	0	16	14	6
Japan	4	2	1	1	17	16	5
Switzerland	4	0	2	2	9	16	2
Yugoslavia	4	0	3	1	9	17	1

1972 Final Standings

1. Soviet Union **GOLD**
2. USA **SILVER**
3. Czechoslovakia **BRONZE**
4. Sweden
5. Finland
6. Poland
7. W. Germany
8. Norway
9. Japan
10. Switzerland
11. Yugoslavia

1972 Scoring Leaders

Player	Team	GP	G	A	PTS	PIM
Valeri Kharlamov	Soviet Union	5	9	6	15	2
Vaclav Nedomansky	Czechoslovakia	5	6	3	9	0
Vladimir Vikulov	Soviet Union	5	5	4	9	0
Craig Sarner	USA	5	4	5	9	0
Kevin Ahearn	USA	5	4	3	7	0
Alexander Maltsev	Soviet Union	5	4	3	7	0
Anatoli Firsov	Soviet Union	5	2	5	7	0
Yuri Blinov	Soviet Union	5	3	3	6	0
Jiri Kochta	Czechoslovakia	5	3	3	6	0
Richard Farda	Czechoslovakia	5	1	5	6	0

Grenoble, France • 1968

Group A

Team	GP	W	L	T	GF	GA	PTS
Soviet Union	7	6	1	0	48	10	12
Czechoslovakia	7	5	1	1	33	17	11
Canada	7	5	2	0	28	15	10
Sweden	7	4	2	1	23	18	9
Finland	7	3	3	1	17	23	7
USA	7	2	4	1	23	28	5
W. Germany	7	1	6	0	13	39	2
E. Germany	7	0	7	0	13	48	0

Group B

Team	GP	W	L	T	GF	GA	PTS
Yugoslavia	5	5	0	0	33	9	10
Japan	5	4	1	0	27	12	8
Norway	5	3	2	0	15	16	6
Romania	5	2	3	0	22	23	4
Austria	5	1	4	0	12	27	2
France	5	0	5	0	9	32	0

1968 Final Standings

1. Soviet Union **GOLD**
2. Czechoslovakia **SILVER**
3. Canada **BRONZE**
4. Sweden
5. Finland
6. USA
7. W. Germany
8. E. Germany
9. Yugoslavia
10. Japan
11. Norway
12. Romania
13. Austria
14. France

1968 Scoring Leaders

Player	Team	GP	G	A	PTS	PIM
Anatoli Firsov	Soviet Union	7	12	4	16	4
Vladimir Vikulov	Soviet Union	7	2	10	12	2
Vyatch. Starshinov	Soviet Union	7	6	6	12	2
Victor Populanov	Soviet Union	7	6	6	12	10
Josef Golonka	Czechoslovakia	7	4	6	10	8
Jan Hrbaty	Czechoslovakia	7	2	7	9	2
Fran Huck	Canada	7	4	5	9	10
Marshall Johnston	Canada	7	2	6	8	4
Jack Morrison	USA	7	2	6	8	10
Vaclav Nedomansky	Czechoslovakia	7	5	2	7	4

Innsbruck, Austria • 1964

Group A

Team	GP	W	L	T	GF	GA	PTS
Soviet Union	7	7	0	0	54	10	14
Sweden	7	5	2	0	47	16	10
Czechoslovakia	7	5	2	0	38	19	10
Canada	7	5	2	0	32	17	10
USA	7	2	5	0	29	33	4
Finland	7	2	5	0	10	31	4
W. Germany	7	2	5	0	13	49	4
Switzerland	7	0	7	0	9	57	0

Group B

Team	GP	W	L	T	GF	GA	PTS
Poland	7	6	1	0	40	13	12
Norway	7	5	2	0	40	19	10
Japan	7	4	2	1	35	31	9
Romania	7	3	3	1	31	28	7
Austria	7	3	3	1	24	28	7
Yugoslavia	7	3	3	1	29	37	7
Italy	7	2	5	0	24	42	4
Hungary	7	0	7	0	14	39	0

1964 Final Standings

1. Soviet Union GOLD
2. Sweden SILVER
3. Czechoslovakia BRONZE
4. Canada
5. USA
6. Finland
7. W. Germany
8. Switzerland
9. Poland
10. Norway
11. Japan
12. Romania
13. Austria
14. Yugoslavia
15. Italy
16. Hungary

1964 Scoring Leaders

Player	Team	GP	G	A	PTS	PIM
Sven Tumba	Sweden	7	8	3	11	0
Ulf Sterner	Sweden	7	6	5	11	0
Victor Yakushev	Soviet Union	7	7	3	10	0
Boris Mayorov	Soviet Union	7	7	3	10	0
Jiri Dolana	Czechoslovakia	7	7	3	10	0
Vyatch. Starshinov	Soviet Union	7	7	3	10	6
Josef Cerny	Czechoslovakia	7	5	5	10	2
Anders Andersson	Sweden	7	7	2	9	8
Konstantin Loktev	Soviet Union	7	4	5	9	8
Gary Dineen	Canada	7	3	6	9	10

Squaw Valley, California, USA • 1960

Group A

Team	GP	W	L	T	GF	GA	PTS
Canada	2	2	0	0	24	3	4
Sweden	2	1	1	0	21	5	2
Japan	2	0	2	0	1	38	0

Group B

Team	GP	W	L	T	GF	GA	PTS
Soviet Union	2	2	0	0	16	4	4
W. Germany	2	1	1	0	4	9	2
Finland	2	0	2	0	5	12	0

Group C

Team	GP	W	L	T	GF	GA	PTS
USA	2	2	0	0	19	6	4
Czechoslovakia	2	1	1	0	23	6	2
Austria	2	0	2	0	2	30	0

Final Round

Team	GP	W	L	T	GF	GA	PTS
USA	5	5	0	0	29	11	10
Canada	5	4	1	0	31	12	8
Soviet Union	5	2	2	1	24	19	5
Czechoslovakia	5	2	3	0	21	23	4
Sweden	5	1	3	1	19	19	3
W. Germany	5	0	5	0	5	45	0

Consolation Round

Team	GP	W	L	T	GF	GA	PTS
Finland	4	3	0	1	50	11	7
Japan	4	2	1	1	32	22	5
Austria	4	0	4	0	8	57	0

1960 Final Standings

1. USA GOLD
2. Canada SILVER
3. Soviet Union BRONZE
4. Czechoslovakia
5. Sweden
6. W. Germany
7. Finland
8. Japan
9. Austria

1960 Scoring Leaders

Player	Team	GP	G	A	PTS	PIM
Fred Etcher	Canada	7	9	12	21	0
Bobby Attersley	Canada	7	6	12	18	4
Bill Cleary	USA	7	7	7	14	2
Bill Christian	USA	7	2	11	13	2
George Samolenko	Canada	7	8	4	12	0
Lars Erik Lundvall	Sweden	7	8	4	12	0
Vaclav Panucek	Czechoslovakia	7	7	5	12	0
John Mayasich	USA	7	7	5	12	2
Nisse Nilsson	Sweden	7	7	5	12	4
Venjamin Alexandrov	Soviet Union	7	7	5	12	8
Butch Martin	Canada	7	6	6	12	14
Ronald Petersson	Sweden	7	4	8	12	2

Cortina d'Ampezzo, Italy• 1956

Group A

Team	GP	W	L	T	GF	GA	PTS
Canada	3	3	0	0	30	1	6
W. Germany	3	1	1	1	9	6	3
Italy	3	0	1	2	5	7	2
Austria	3	0	2	1	2	32	1

Group B

Team	GP	W	L	T	GF	GA	PTS
Czechoslovakia	2	2	0	0	12	6	4
USA	2	1	1	0	7	4	2
Poland	2	0	2	0	3	12	0

Group C

Team	GP	W	L	T	GF	GA	PTS
Soviet Union	2	2	0	0	15	4	4
Sweden	2	1	1	0	7	10	2
Switzerland	2	0	2	0	8	16	0

Final Round

Team	GP	W	L	T	GF	GA	PTS
Soviet Union	5	5	0	0	25	5	10
USA	5	4	1	0	26	12	8
Canada	5	3	2	0	23	11	6
Sweden	5	1	3	1	10	17	3
Czechoslovakia	5	1	4	0	20	30	2
W. Germany	5	0	4	1	6	35	1

Consolation Round

Team	GP	W	L	T	GF	GA	PTS
Italy	3	3	0	0	21	7	6
Poland	3	2	1	0	12	10	4
Switzerland	3	1	2	0	12	8	2
Austria	3	0	3	0	9	19	0

1956 Final Standings

1. Soviet Union GOLD
2. USA SILVER
3. Canada BRONZE
4. Sweden
5. Czechoslovakia
6. W. Germany
7. Italy
8. Poland
9. Switzerland
10. Austria

1956 Scoring Leaders

Player	Team	GP	G	A	PTS	PIM
Jim Logan	Canada	8	7	5	12	2
Paul Knox	Canada	8	7	5	12	2
Vsevolod Bobrov	Soviet Union	7	9	2	11	4
Gerry Theberge	Canada	8	9	2	11	8
Jack McKenzie	Canada	8	7	4	11	4
John Mayasich	USA	7	7	3	10	2
Alexei Guryshev	Soviet Union	7	7	2	9	0
Vlastimil Bubnik	Czechoslovakia	7	5	4	9	14
George Scholes	Canada	8	5	3	8	2

Oslo, Norway • 1952

Team	GP	W	L	T	GF	GA	PTS
Canada	8	7	0	1	71	1	15
USA	8	6	1	1	43	21	13
Sweden	8	6	2	0	48	19	12
Czechoslovakia	8	6	2	0	47	18	12
Switzerland	8	4	4	0	40	40	8
Poland	8	2	5	1	21	56	5
Finland	8	2	6	0	21	60	4
W. Germany	8	1	6	1	21	53	3
Norway	8	0	8	0	15	46	0

1952 Final Standings

1. Canada GOLD
2. USA SILVER
3. Sweden BRONZE
4. Czechoslovakia
5. Switzerland
6. Poland
7. Finland
8. W. Germany
9. Norway

Cumulative Medal Standings, 1924-1994					
	Gold	Silver	Bronze	Total	Last Medal
1. Canada	5	4	2	11	Silver 94
2. Russia/USSR	8	1	1	10	Gold 92
3. USA	2	5	1	8	Gold 80
4. Sweden	1	2	4	7	Gold 94
5. Czechoslovakia	0	4	3	7	Bronze 92
6. Great Britain	1	0	1	2	Gold 36
7. Finland	0	1	1	2	Bronze 94
8. W. Germany	0	0	2	2	Bronze 76
9. Switzerland	0	0	2	2	Bronze 48

St. Moritz, Switzerland • 1948

Team	GP	W	L	T	GF	GA	PTS
Canada	7	6	0	1	57	2	13
Czechoslovakia	7	6	0	1	76	15	13
Switzerland	7	5	2	0	62	17	10
Sweden	7	4	3	0	53	23	8
Great Britain	7	3	4	0	36	43	6
Poland	7	2	5	0	25	74	4
Austria	7	1	6	0	31	64	2
Italy	7	0	7	0	23	125	0

1948 Final Standings

1. Canada GOLD
2. Czechoslovakia SILVER
3. Switzerland BRONZE
4. Sweden
5. Great Britain
6. Poland
7. Austria
8. Italy

Garmisch-Partenkirchen, Germany • 1936

Group A

Team	GP	W	L	T	GF	GA	PTS
Canada	3	3	0	0	24	3	6
Austria	3	2	1	0	11	7	4
Poland	3	1	2	0	11	12	2
Latvia	3	0	0	3	3	27	0

Group B

Team	GP	W	L	T	GF	GA	PTS
Germany	3	2	1	0	5	1	4
USA	3	2	1	0	5	2	4
Italy	3	1	2	0	2	5	2
Switzerland	3	1	2	0	1	5	2

Group C

Team	GP	W	L	T	GF	GA	PTS
Czechoslovakia	3	3	0	0	10	0	6
Hungary	3	2	1	0	14	5	4
France	3	1	2	0	4	7	2
Belgium	3	0	3	0	4	20	6

Group D

Team	GP	W	L	T	GF	GA	PTS
Great Britain	2	2	0	0	4	0	4
Sweden	2	1	1	0	2	1	2
Japan	2	0	2	0	0	5	0

Group A Semifinal Round

Team	GP	W	L	T	GF	GA	PTS
Great Britain	3	2	0	1	8	3	5
Canada	3	2	1	0	22	4	4
Germany	3	1	1	1	5	8	3
Hungary	3	0	3	2	22	0	0

Group B Semifinal Round

Team	GP	W	L	T	GF	GA	PTS
USA	3	3	0	0	5	1	6
Czechoslovakia	3	2	1	0	6	4	4
Sweden	3	1	2	0	3	6	2
Austria	3	0	3	0	1	4	0

Final Round

Team	GP	W	L	T	GF	GA	PTS
Great Britain	3	2	0	1	7	1	5
Canada	3	2	1	0	9	2	4
USA	3	1	1	1	2	1	3
Czechoslovakia	3	0	3	0	0	14	0

1936 Final Standings

1. Great Britain GOLD
2. Canada SILVER
3. USA BRONZE
4. Czechoslovakia
5. Germany
5. Sweden
7. Hungary
7. Austria

Lake Placid, New York, USA • 1932

Team	GP	W	L	T	GF	GA	PTS
Canada	6	5	0	1	32	4	11
USA	6	4	1	1	27	5	9
Germany	6	2	4	0	7	26	4
Poland	6	0	6	0	3	34	0

1932 Final Standings

1. Canada GOLD
2. USA SILVER
3. Germany BRONZE
4. Poland

St. Moritz, Switzerland • 1928

Group A

Team	GP	W	L	T	GF	GA	PTS
Great Britain	3	2	1	0	10	6	4
France	3	2	1	0	6	5	4
Belgium	3	2	1	0	9	10	4
Hungary	3	0	3	0	2	6	0

Group B

Team	GP	W	L	T	GF	GA	PTS
Sweden	2	1	0	1	5	2	3
Czechoslovakia	2	1	1	0	3	5	2
Poland	2	0	0	1	4	5	1

Group C

Team	GP	W	L	T	GF	GA	PTS
Switzerland	2	1	0	1	5	4	3
Austria	2	0	0	2	4	4	2
Germany	2	0	0	1	0	1	1

Final Round

Team	GP	W	L	T	GF	GA	PTS
Canada	3	3	0	0	38	0	6
Sweden	3	2	1	0	7	12	4
Switzerland	3	1	2	0	4	17	2
Great Britain	3	0	3	0	1	21	0

1928 Final Standings

1. Canada — GOLD
2. Sweden — SILVER
3. Switzerland — BRONZE
4. Great Britain
5. France
5. Czechoslovakia
5. Austria
8. Belgium
8. Poland
8. Germany
11. Hungary

Chamonix, France • 1924

Group A

Team	GP	W	L	T	GF	GA	PTS
Canada	3	3	0	0	85	0	6
Sweden	3	2	1	0	18	25	4
Czechoslovakia	3	1	2	0	14	41	2
Switzerland	3	0	3	0	2	53	0

Group B

Team	GP	W	L	T	GF	GA	PTS
USA	3	3	0	0	52	0	6
Great Britain	3	2	1	0	34	16	4
France	3	1	2	0	9	42	2
Belgium	3	0	3	0	8	35	0

Final Round

Team	GP	W	L	T	GF	GA	PTS
Canada	3	3	0	0	47	3	6
USA	3	2	1	0	32	6	4
Great Britain	3	1	2	0	6	33	2
Sweden	3	0	3	0	3	46	0

1924 Final Standings

1. Canada — GOLD
2. USA — SILVER
3. Great Britain — BRONZE
4. Sweden
5. Czechoslovakia
5. France
7. Switzerland
7. Belgium

Earlier Results

Hockey was also played at the 1920 Summer Olympics in Antwerp, Belgium. This tournament usually is not counted in cumulative Winter Olympic Hockey statistics.

Results

Elimination Round

Sweden	8	Belgium	0
USA	29	Switzerland	0
Canada	15	Czechoslovakia	0
Sweden	4	France	0
Canada	2	USA	0

Final Round

USA	7	Sweden	0
USA	16	Czechoslovakia	0
Canada	12	Sweden	1
Sweden	4	Switzerland	0
Czechoslovakia	1	Sweden	0
Russia	3	Slovakia	2

1920 Final Standings

1. Canada — GOLD
2. USA — SILVER
3. Czechoslovakia — BRONZE
4. Sweden
5. Switzerland

NHL and IIHF Rules Compared

Abuse of Officials
NHL: If a player deliberately strikes an official, causes an injury or attempts to injure the minimum suspension will be 20 games. **IIHF:** Any action taken against an official will, at the referee's discretion, result in a misconduct, a game misconduct or a gross misconduct.

Board Checking
NHL: When a major penalty is assessed for boarding (with injury to head and face), a game misconduct follows. **IIHF:** When a major penalty is assessed for roughing, elbowing or kneeing, a game misconduct follows.

Butt-ending
NHL: An attempt to butt-end without making contact will result in a double minor; when contact is made, the penalty will be a major plus a game misconduct. **IIHF:** An attempt to butt-end without making contact will result in a double minor plus a misconduct; when contact is made, a major plus a game misconduct will be assessed, or a match penalty if injury is caused.

Charging the goalkeeper
NHL: For charging a goalkeeper in his crease, a minor or major will be assessed. **IIHF:** Any foul against a goalkeeper in his crease incurs a double minor or major penalty.

Checking from Behind
NHL: There is no minor for checking from behind. A crosscheck, push or charge from behind against a player who is unable to defend himself will incur a major and a game misconduct. **IIHF:** For checking from behind, a minor plus a misconduct, or a major plus a game misconduct, will be assessed.

Crosschecking
NHL: Crosschecking will be penalized with a minor or a major plus a game misconduct. **IIHF:** Crosschecking will be penalized with a minor, or major plus a game misconduct.

Calling of Penalties
NHL: If a delayed minor is signalled against a shorthanded team and a goal is scored, the first minor is terminated and the delayed penalty assessed. **IIHF:** In the same case, the delayed minor is terminated instead.

Elbowing
NHL: Elbowing will be penalized with a minor or major and a game misconduct if an injury to the face or head occurs. **IIHF:** Elbowing will be penalized with a minor or major plus game misconduct if injury occurs.

Faceoffs
NHL: In a faceoff, the visiting center must place his stick down first. **IIHF:** In a faceoff, the attacking center must place his stick down first.

Fisticuffs
NHL: Any player deemed to be the instigator of an altercation will receive a minor, a major and a game misconduct. **IIHF:** Any player starting a fight will receive a match penalty.

Goalkeeper's Penalties
NHL: A goalkeeper may freeze the puck anywhere in the defensive zone provided he is being checked at the time. **IIHF:** A goalkeeper incurs a minor penalty if he falls on the puck beyond the hash marks or behind the goal line.

Goalkeeper's Stick
NHL: A goalkeeper's stick must have a knob of white tape at the top of the shaft. **IIHF:** No rule applies here.

NHL: No limit to the curvature of the blade of a goalkeeper's stick. **IIHF:** The blade of a goalkeeper's stick cannot be curved any more than that of a regular player.

Icing
NHL: Defending team must touch the puck to complete icing after it crosses the goal line. **IIHF:** Icing is called automatically when the puck crosses the goal line.

Illegal Stick and Penalty Shot
NHL: A stick measurement may be requested during any stoppage. If a player scores on a penalty shot and then is found to have an illegal stick, the goal will be nullified. If no goal is scored, the player will receive a minor penalty. A minor penalty plus a 10-minute misconduct will be assessed to a player who refuses to surrender his stick for a measurement. **IIHF:** A stick measurement may be requested before a penalty shot. If the stick is found to be illegal, the player may take the shot with a legal stick and then serve a penalty.

NHL: If a player scores on a penalty shot, and his stick is then found to be illegally curved, the goal is disallowed but no penalty is given. If he does not score and his stick is then found illegal, he receives a minor penalty. **IIHF:** No stick measurement is allowed during a play stoppage after any goal. If a penalty shot is missed, a measurement is allowed.

Kneeing
NHL: Kneeing will be penalized with a match penalty for deliberate or attempted kneeing during an altercation. **IIHF:** Kneeing will be penalized with a minor or a major plus a game misconduct if injury occurs.

Leaving the Bench
NHL: The first and second player on either team to leave the players bench or penalty bench to start or enter an altercation will receive game misconducts in addition to any penalties incurred by participating in the altercation. **IIHF:** The first player on either team to leave the players bench or penalty bench to start or enter an altercation will receive a double minor plus a game misconduct.

Linesmen
NHL: The Linesman may stop play to call double minors for butt-ending, head-butting, high-sticking or spearing. The Linesman may also stop play and impose any major penalty when a serious incident occurs. The Linesman may also report goalkeeper interference. **IIHF:** Linesmen have no authority in these areas.

Major Penalties, Misconducts and Suspensions
NHL: When an injured player receives a major penalty, his team must place a substitute in the penalty box before the penalty expires. **IIHF:** The substitute player must enter penalty box immediately.

NHL: For statistical purposes, a game or gross misconduct penalty is 10 minutes long. **IIHF:** For statistical purposes, a game or gross misconduct penalty is 20 minutes long.

NHL: Automatic suspension for multiple game misconducts but not for gross misconducts. **IIHF:** Automatic minimum-game suspension for gross misconducts but not for multiple game misconducts.

NHL: When a team official is assessed a misconduct, the team does not automatically receive a bench minor. **IIHF:** When a team official is assessed a misconduct, the team automatically receives a bench minor.

NHL: For statistical purposes, a match penalty is 5 minutes long and there is no minimum suspension. In the event of deliberate injury, the offending player is suspended until the circumstances surrounding the infraction are reviewed by the League. **IIHF:** For statistical purposes, a match penalty is 25 minutes long and carries a minimum one-game suspension. The player concerned is immediately suspended until judgement is passed.

Penalty Shots
NHL: The fouled player must take the penalty shot; if he cannot, a player who was on the ice at the time of the foul must take it. **IIHF:** Any player may take a penalty shot.

Protection of Goalkeeper
NHL: Play will not be stopped if an attacking player deliberately stands in the goal crease unless goaltender interference is called. **IIHF:** When an attacking player deliberately stands in the goal crease, play will be stopped and a faceoff held in the neutral zone.

Rink Dimensions
NHL: Dimensions of rink: width 85 feet (26 meters); length 200 feet (61 meters). Goal lines are 11 feet (3.3 meters) from each end of the rink. **IIHF:** Maximum dimensions of rink: width 30 meters (98.5 feet); length 61 meters (200 feet). Minimum dimensions of rink: width 26 meters (85 feet); length 56 meters (184 feet). Goal lines are 4 meters (13 feet) from each end of the rink.

Spearing
NHL: An attempt to spear without making contact will result in a double minor; when contact is made, the penalty will be a major plus a game misconduct. **IIHF:** An attempt to spear without making contact will result in a double minor plus a misconduct; when contact is made, a major plus a game misconduct will be assessed, or a match penalty if injury is caused.

Termination of Minor Penalties
NHL: When a goal is scored against a team that is shorthanded by reason of one or more minor penalties, the minor penalty that caused the team to be shorthanded is nullified. **IIHF:** When a goal is scored against a team that is shorthanded the first minor penalty on the clock is nullified.

NHL: If a shorthanded team is scored upon when a delayed minor penalty is called, the player already in the penalty box (with the least amount of time remaining) returns to the ice if the penalty he was serving was a minor. The player being assessed the delayed penalty goes to the penalty box. **IIHF:** If a shorthanded team is scored upon when a delayed minor penalty is called, the delayed penalty is nullified.

Throwing the Stick
NHL: For throwing a stick or any object at the puck in the defending zone, the Referee will award a penalty shot if a goal does not follow the infraction. If the offense occurs in any zone, a minor penalty will be assessed, unless a goal follows. If a stick or object is thrown when the defending team's goalkeeper has been removed for an extra skater, a goal shall be awarded unless the play results in a goal. **IIHF:** In the same situation, a major penalty is assessed.

Time-Outs
NHL: Only one team is permitted a time-out during a stoppage. **IIHF:** Both teams are permitted a time-out during a stoppage, but the second team calling a time-out must notify the referee before the first time-out has expired.

Active NHL Players in the Olympics 1980-1994

• – Gold medal win. Note that teams from the Russia and the former Soviet Union are listed as USSR until 1988 and as RUS thereafter.

Date	Name	Country	GP	G	A	Pts	PIM	97-98 Club
1994	Alinc, Jan	CZE	6	2	0	2	4	Europe
1988	Andersson, Mikael	SWE	8	3	3	6	4	T.B.
1992	Archibald, David	CAN	8	7	1	8	18	IHL
1994	Astley, Mark	CAN	8	0	1	1	4	IHL
1994	Aucoin, Adrian	CAN	4	0	0	0	2	VAN
1992	Augusta, Patrick	CZE	8	3	2	5	0	IHL
1992	Bautin, Sergei	RUS	8	0	0	0	6	IHL •
1994	Beaufait, Mark	USA	8	1	4	5	2	IHL
1994	Berezin, Sergei	RUS	8	3	2	5	2	TOR
1992	Borschevsky, Nikolai	RUS	8	7	2	9	0	Europe •
1988	Bradley, Brian	CAN	7	0	4	4	0	T.B.
1980	Broten, Neal	USA	7	2	1	3	2	•
1988	Brown, Greg	USA	6	0	4	4	2	Europe
1992	Brown, Greg	USA	7	0	0	0	2	Europe
1992	Butsayev, Viacheslav	RUS	8	1	1	2	4	AHL •
1994	Campbell, Jim	USA	8	0	0	0	6	STL
1984	Chelios, Chris	USA	6	0	3	3	8	CHI
1994	Ciavaglia, Peter	USA	8	2	4	6	0	IHL
1984	Courtnall, Russ	CAN	7	1	3	4	2	
1994	Crowley, Ted	USA	8	0	2	2	8	PHO
1994	Dackell, Andreas	SWE	4	0	0	0	0	OTT •
1992	Dahl, Kevin	CAN	8	2	0	2	6	PHO
1984	Daigneault, J.J.	CAN	7	1	1	2	0	ANA
1984	Dineen, Kevin	CAN	7	0	0	0	4	CAR
1992	Donato, Ted	USA	8	4	3	7	8	BOS
1984	Driver, Bruce	CAN	7	0	4	4	10	NYR
1992	Drury, Ted	USA	7	1	1	2	0	ANA
1994	Drury, Ted	USA	7	1	2	3	2	ANA
1992	Emma, David	USA	6	0	1	1	6	
1994	Ferraro, Peter	USA	8	6	0	6	6	NYR
1980	Fetisov, Vyacheslav	USSR	7	5	4	9	10	DET
1984	Fetisov, Vyacheslav	USSR	7	3	8	11	8	DET •
1988	Fetisov, Vyacheslav	USSR	8	4	9	13	6	DET •
1984	Flatley, Pat	CAN	7	3	3	6	70	
1994	Forsberg, Peter	SWE	8	2	6	8	6	COL •
1984	Gagner, Dave	CAN	7	5	2	7	6	FLA
1988	Granato, Tony	USA	6	1	7	8	4	S.J
1988	Gusarov, Alexei	USSR	8	1	3	4	6	COL •
1994	Gusmanov, Ravil	RUS	8	3	1	4	0	IHL
1992	Hannan, Dave	CAN	8	3	5	8	8	
1994	Harlock, David	CAN	8	0	0	0	8	AHL
1994	Hauer, Brett	USA	8	0	0	0	10	AHL
1992	Hedican, Brett	USA	8	0	0	0	4	VAN
1992	Heinze, Steve	USA	8	1	3	4	8	BOS
1994	Hendrickson, Darby	USA	8	0	0	0	6	TOR
1994	Hlushko, Todd	CAN	8	5	0	5	6	CGY
1984	Iafrate, Al	USA	6	0	0	0	2	S.J
1988	Janney, Craig	USA	5	3	1	4	2	PHO
1994	Johnson, Craig	USA	8	0	4	4	4	L.A.
1994	Johnson, Greg	CAN	8	0	3	3	0	PIT
1994	Jonssen, Jorgen	SWE	6	0	0	0	0	Europe •
1994	Jonsson, Kenny	SWE	3	1	0	1	0	NYI •
1994	Juhlin, Patrik	SWE	8	7	1	8	10	AHL •
1992	Juneau, Joe	CAN	8	6	9	15	4	WSH
1988	Kamensky, Valeri	USSR	8	4	2	6	4	COL •
1994	Kapanen, Sami	FIN	8	1	0	1	2	CAR
1994	Kariya, Paul	CAN	8	3	4	7	2	ANA
1994	Karpov, Valeri	RUS	8	3	1	4	2	ANA
1992	Kasparaitis, Darius	RUS	8	0	2	2	2	PIT •
1992	Khmylev, Yuri	RUS	8	4	6	10	4	•
1994	Kiprusoff, Marko	FIN	8	3	3	6	4	Europe
1994	Koivu, Saku	FIN	8	4	3	7	12	MTL
1994	Kontos, Chris	CAN	8	3	1	4	2	IHL
1992	Kovalenko, Andrei	RUS	8	1	1	2	2	EDM •
1992	Kovalev, Alexei	RUS	8	1	2	3	14	NYR •
1988	Kravchuk, Igor	USSR	6	1	0	1	0	OTT •
1992	Kravchuk, Igor	RUS	8	3	2	5	6	OTT •
1994	Kudashov, Alexei	RUS	8	1	2	3	4	Europe
1980	Kurri, Jari	FIN	7	2	1	3	6	COL
1992	Lachance, Scott	USA	8	0	1	1	6	NYI
1984	LaFontaine, Pat	USA	6	5	3	8	0	BUF
1992	Lang, Robert	CZE	8	5	8	13	8	Europe
1984	Larionov, Igor	USSR	7	1	4	5	6	DET •
1988	Larionov, Igor	USSR	8	4	9	13	8	DET •
1992	Laukkanen, Janne	FIN	8	0	1	1	6	OTT
1994	Laukkanen, Janne	FIN	8	0	2	2	12	OTT
1988	Leach, Stephen	USA	6	1	2	3	0	CAR
1988	Leetch, Brian	USA	6	1	5	6	4	NYR
1994	Lehtera, Tero	FIN	4	0	1	1	0	Europe
1994	Lehtinen, Jere	FIN	8	3	0	3	0	DAL
1984	Lidster, Doug	CAN	7	0	2	2	2	NYR
1994	Lilley, John	USA	8	3	1	4	16	IHL
1992	Lindros, Eric	CAN	8	5	6	11	6	PHI
1988	Lumme, Jyrki	FIN	6	0	1	1	2	VAN
1992	Malakhov, Vladimir	RUS	8	3	0	3	4	MTL •
1992	Manderville, Kent	CAN	8	1	2	3	0	CAR
1994	Marchant, Todd	USA	8	1	1	2	6	EDM

Date	Name	Country	GP	G	A	Pts	PIM	97-98 Club
1994	Martin, Matt	USA	8	0	2	2	8	TOR
1992	McEachern, Shawn	USA	8	1	0	1	10	OTT
1992	McInnis, Marty	USA	8	5	2	7	4	CGY
1984	Millen, Corey	USA	6	0	0	0	2	CGY
1988	Millen, Corey	USA	6	6	5	11	4	
1988	Miller, Kevin	USA	5	1	3	4	4	CHI
1992	Mironov, Dmitri	RUS	8	3	1	4	6	ANA
1988	Mogilny, Alexander	USSR	6	3	2	5	2	VAN •
1984	Muller, Kirk	CAN	6	2	1	3	0	FLA
1994	Nedved, Petr	CAN	8	5	1	6	6	PIT
1994	Nikolishin, Andrei	RUS	8	2	5	7	6	WSH
1994	Norris, Dwayne	CAN	8	2	2	4	4	Europe
1988	Norton, Jeff	USA	6	0	4	4	4	T.B.
1988	Numminen, Teppo	FIN	6	1	4	5	0	PHO
1984	Olczyk, Ed	USA	6	2	6	8	0	PIT
1994	Palffy, Zigmund	SLO	8	3	7	10	8	NYI
1984	Patrick, James	CAN	7	0	3	3	4	CGY
1994	Peltonen, Ville	FIN	8	4	3	7	0	S.J
1994	Petrovicky, Robert	SLO	8	1	6	7	18	STL
1992	Plavsic, Adrien	CAN	8	0	2	2	0	IHL
1994	Richter, Barry	USA	8	0	3	3	4	BOS
1994	Roberts, David	USA	8	1	5	6	4	VAN
1994	Rohlin, Leif	SWE	8	0	1	1	10	VAN •
1994	Rolston, Brian	USA	8	7	0	7	8	N.J.
1994	Roy, Jean-Yves	CAN	8	1	0	1	0	
1994	Sacco, David	USA	8	3	5	8	12	AHL
1992	Sacco, Joe	USA	8	2	0	2	0	ANA
1984	Sandstrom, Tomas	SWE	7	2	1	3	6	ANA
1994	Satan, Miroslav	SLO	8	9	0	9	0	BUF
1994	Savage, Brian	CAN	8	2	2	4	6	MTL
1992	Selanne, Teemu	FIN	8	7	4	11	6	ANA
1988	Semenov, Anatoli	USSR	8	2	4	6	6	•
1992	Slegr, Jiri	CZE	8	1	1	2	14	PIT
1992	Smehlik, Richard	CZE	8	0	1	1	2	BUF
1988	Stevens, Kevin	USA	5	1	3	4	2	NYR
1992	Svehla, Robert	CZE	8	2	1	3	8	FLA
1994	Svehla, Robert	SLO	8	2	4	6	26	FLA
1992	Sweeney, Tim	USA	8	3	4	7	6	
1994	Therien, Chris	CAN	4	0	0	0	4	PHI
1992	Tkachuk, Keith	USA	8	1	1	2	12	PHO
1994	Varis, Petri	FIN	5	1	1	2	2	CHI
1994	Vopat, Jan	CZE	8	0	1	1	8	L.A.
1994	Warriner, Todd	CAN	4	1	1	2	0	TOR
1988	Weinrich, Eric	USA	3	0	0	0	0	CHI
1994	Werenka, Brad	CAN	8	2	2	4	8	PIT
1992	Woolley, Jason	CAN	8	0	5	5	4	PIT
1988	Yawney, Trent	CAN	8	1	1	2	6	
1988	Young, Scott	USA	6	2	6	8	4	COL
1992	Young, Scott	USA	8	2	1	3	2	COL
1992	Yushkevich, Dmitri	RUS	8	1	2	3	4	TOR •
1988	Zalapski, Zarley	CAN	8	1	3	4	2	CGY
1992	Zhamnov, Alexei	RUS	8	0	3	3	8	CHI •
1992	Zhitnik, Alexei	RUS	8	1	0	1	0	BUF •
1992	Zubov, Sergei	RUS	8	0	1	1	0	DAL •

NHL Goaltenders in the Olympics 1980-1994

Date	Name	Country	GPI	Mins	GAA	%	97-98 Club
1988	Burke, Sean	CAN	4	238	3.02	.893	CAR
1992	Burke, Sean	CAN	8	429	2.37	.928	CAR
1994	Dunham, Mike	USA	3	180	5.02	.826	N.J.
1988	Hasek, Dominik	CZE	5	217	4.97	.833	BUF
1994	Hirsch, Corey	CAN	8	495	2.05	.930	VAN
1992	Kidd, Trevor	CAN	0				CAR
1992	LeBlanc, Ray	USA	8	462	2.20	.943	IHL
1994	Legace, Manny	CAN	0				CAR
1988	Moog, Andy	CAN	4	240	2.25	.900	MTL
1988	Richter, Mike	USA	4	230	3.91	.842	NYR
1994	Salo, Tommy	SWE	6	370	2.11	.895	NYI •
1992	Shtalenkov, Mikhail	RUS	8	440	1.63	.919	ANA •
1994	Snow, Garth	USA	5	299	3.41	.881	PHI
1992	Soderstrom, Tommy	SWE	8	298	2.61	.838	
1988	Terreri, Chris	USA	3	128	6.58	.774	CHI
1992	Trefilov, Andrei	RUS	0				BUF •
1994	Turek, Roman	CZE	2	120	1.50	.931	DAL

Mighty Ducks of Anaheim

1996-97 Results: 36W-33L-13T 85PTS. Second, Pacific Division

Year-by-Year Record

Season	GP	Home W	Home L	Home T	Road W	Road L	Road T	Overall W	Overall L	Overall T	GF	GA	Pts.	Finished		Playoff Result
1996-97	82	23	12	6	13	21	7	36	33	13	245	233	85	2nd,	Pacific Div.	Lost Conf. Semi-Final
1995-96	82	22	15	4	13	24	4	35	39	8	234	247	78	4th,	Pacific Div.	Out of Playoffs
1994-95	48	11	9	4	5	18	1	16	27	5	125	164	37	6th,	Pacific Div.	Out of Playoffs
1993-94	84	14	26	2	19	20	3	33	46	5	229	251	71	4th,	Pacific Div.	Out of Playoffs

1997-98 Schedule

Oct.	Fri.	3	at Vancouver†
	Sat.	4	Vancouver†
	Fri.	10	Ottawa
	Mon.	13	Boston
	Wed.	15	Philadelphia
	Fri.	17	Edmonton
	Sun.	19	NY Islanders
	Tue.	21	at Phoenix
	Wed.	22	Detroit
	Sat.	25	at NY Islanders*
	Sun.	26	at NY Rangers
	Tue.	28	at Toronto
	Thu.	30	at Boston
Nov.	Sun.	2	at Detroit*
	Wed.	5	Tampa Bay
	Fri.	7	at Calgary
	Sat.	8	at Vancouver
	Mon.	10	San Jose
	Wed.	12	Montreal
	Fri.	14	Vancouver
	Sun.	16	Dallas
	Tue.	18	at San Jose
	Wed.	19	Chicago
	Sat.	22	at St. Louis
	Mon.	24	at Dallas
	Wed.	26	New Jersey
	Fri.	28	at Edmonton
	Sat.	29	at Calgary
Dec.	Tue.	2	at Toronto
	Wed.	3	at Buffalo
	Sat.	6	at Pittsburgh
	Wed.	10	Pittsburgh
	Fri.	12	Washington
	Wed.	17	Toronto
	Fri.	19	Phoenix
	Sun.	21	San Jose
	Mon.	22	Calgary
	Sat.	27	at St. Louis
	Sun.	28	at Chicago
	Tue.	30	at Carolina
Jan.	Thu.	1	at Washington*

	Sat.	3	at Tampa Bay
	Sun.	4	at Florida
	Wed.	7	Buffalo
	Fri.	9	Edmonton
	Sun.	11	Dallas
	Mon.	12	at Los Angeles
	Wed.	14	Colorado
	Wed.	21	Florida
	Thu.	22	at Colorado
	Sat.	24	Los Angeles*
	Tue.	27	at San Jose
	Wed.	28	Calgary
Feb.	Sun.	1	Chicago
	Wed.	4	NY Rangers
	Sat.	7	Los Angeles*
	Wed.	25	at Vancouver
	Fri.	27	at Edmonton
Mar.	Sun.	1	St. Louis
	Wed.	4	Detroit
	Fri.	6	San Jose
	Sun.	8	Carolina
	Mon.	9	at Los Angeles
	Wed.	11	Toronto
	Fri.	13	at Dallas
	Sun.	15	Colorado
	Wed.	18	at New Jersey
	Thu.	19	at Philadelphia
	Sat.	21	at Montreal
	Sun.	22	at Ottawa
	Wed.	25	at Chicago
	Thu.	26	at Detroit
	Sat.	28	at Colorado*
Apr.	Wed.	1	Phoenix
	Fri.	3	at Phoenix
	Sun.	5	Calgary
	Wed.	8	Edmonton
	Thu.	9	at San Jose
	Mon.	13	Colorado
	Wed.	15	at Edmonton
	Sat.	18	at Los Angeles*
	Sun.	19	St. Louis

* Denotes afternoon game.   † in Tokyo.

Franchise date: June 15, 1993

WESTERN
NHL
CONFERENCE

**PACIFIC
DIVISION**

**5th
NHL
Season**

Above: Despite missing 13 games at the start of the 1996-97 season, Paul Kariya recovered to score 44 goals, win the Lady Byng Trophy and lead the League in game-winning goals (10) and shots-on-goal (340). Left: One of the few players to graduate to the NHL from the Canadian university program, Steve Rucchin centered Anaheim's top line and recorded a plus/minus of +26, the third-best rating on the club.

1997-98 Player Personnel

FORWARDS	HT	WT	S	Place of Birth	Date	1996-97 Club
AALTO, Antti	6-2	190	L	Lappeenranta, Finland	3/4/75	TPS
ANTOSKI, Shawn	6-4	235	L	Brantford, Ont.	3/25/70	Pittsburgh-Anaheim
BANHAM, Frank	6-0	190	R	Calahoo, Alta.	4/14/75	Anaheim-Baltimore
CHOUINARD, Marc	6-5	187	R	Charlesbourg, Ont.	5/5/77	Halifax
CULLEN, Matt	6-1	195	L	Virginia, MN	11/2/76	St. Cloud-Baltimore
DRURY, Ted	6-0	185	L	Boston, MA	9/13/71	Anaheim
JANSSENS, Mark	6-3	212	L	Surrey, B.C.	5/19/68	Hartford-Anaheim
JOMPHE, Jean-Francois	6-1	195	L	Harve' St. Pierre, Que.	12/28/72	Anaheim
KARIYA, Paul	5-11	175	L	Vancouver, B.C.	10/16/74	Anaheim
KNUTSEN, Espen	5-11	180	L	Oslo, Norway	1/12/72	Djurgarden
LeBOUTILLIER, Peter	6-1	205	R	Minnedosa, Man.	1/11/75	Anaheim-Baltimore
LECLERC, Mike	6-1	205	L	Winnipeg, Man.	11/10/76	Anaheim-Baltimore
NIECKAR, Barry	6-3	205	L	Rama, Sask.	12/16/67	Anaheim-Long Beach
NIELSEN, Jeff	6-0	200	R	Grand Rapids, MN	9/20/71	NY Rangers-Binghamton
NIKULIN, Igor	6-1	200	L	Cherepovets, USSR	8/26/72	Baltimore-Fort Wayne-Anaheim
PARK, Richard	5-11	190	R	Seoul, S. Korea	5/27/76	Pittsburgh-Cleveland-Anaheim
PRONGER, Sean	6-2	205	L	Dryden, Ont.	11/30/72	Anaheim-Baltimore
REICHERT, Craig	6-1	200	R	Winnipeg, Man.	5/11/74	Anaheim-Baltimore
RUCCHIN, Steve	6-3	215	L	London, Ont.	7/4/71	Anaheim
RYCHEL, Warren	6-0	205	L	Tecumseh, Ont.	5/12/67	Anaheim
SACCO, Joe	6-1	195	L	Medford, MA	2/4/69	Anaheim
SANDSTROM, Tomas	6-2	205	L	Jakobstad, Finland	9/4/64	Pittsburgh-Detroit
SELANNE, Teemu	6-0	200	R	Helsinki, Finland	7/3/70	Anaheim
STEVENSON, Jeremy	6-2	220	L	San Bernadino, CA	7/28/74	Anaheim-Baltimore
TODD, Kevin	5-10	180	L	Winnipeg, Man.	5/4/68	Anaheim
WREN, Bob	5-10	185	L	Preston, Ont.	9/16/74	Baltimore
DEFENSEMEN						
BRISKE, Byron	6-3	195	R	Humboldt, Sask.	1/23/76	Baltimore
DAIGNEAULT, Jean-Jacques	5-10	186	L	Montreal, Que.	10/12/65	Pittsburgh-Anaheim
DOLLAS, Bobby	6-2	212	L	Montreal, Que.	1/31/65	Anaheim
KARPA, Dave	6-1	210	R	Regina, Sask.	5/7/71	Anaheim
MARSHALL, Jason	6-2	200	R	Cranbrook, B.C.	2/22/71	Anaheim
MIRONOV, Dmitri	6-3	215	R	Moscow, USSR	12/25/65	Pittsburgh-Anaheim
MORO, Marc	6-1	220	L	Toronto, Ont.	7/17/77	Kingston-S.S. Marie
SALEI, Ruslan	6-2	205	L	Minsk, USSR	11/2/74	Anaheim-Baltimore-Las Vegas
SHAW, Lloyd	6-3	220	R	Regina, Sask.	9/26/76	Red Deer
TREBIL, Daniel	6-3	210	R	Edina, MN	4/10/74	Anaheim-Baltimore
TRNKA, Pavel	6-3	200	L	Plzen, Czech.	7/27/76	Baltimore
TSULYGIN, Nikolai	6-3	210	R	Ufa, USSR	5/29/75	Anaheim-Baltimore-Fort Wayne
VAN IMPE, Darren	6-1	195	L	Saskatoon, Sask.	5/18/73	Anaheim

GOALTENDERS	HT	WT	C	Place of Birth	Date	1996-97 Club
ASKEY, Tom	6-2	185	L	Kenmore, NY	10/4/74	Baltimore
HEBERT, Guy	5-11	185	L	Troy, NY	1/7/67	Anaheim
MASON, Chris	6-0	200	L	Red Deer, Alta.	4/20/76	Prince George
RUSSELL, Blaine	5-11	180	L	Wetaskawin, Sask.	1/11/77	Lethbridge-Prince Albert
SHTALENKOV, Mikhail	6-2	185	L	Moscow, USSR	10/20/65	Anaheim

General Manager

FERREIRA, JACK
Vice-President/General Manager, The Mighty Ducks of Anaheim.
Born in Providence, RI, June 9, 1944.

Jack Ferreira was named as the first vice president/general manager of the Mighty Ducks on March 23, 1993. A veteran of over 23 years in professional hockey, Ferreira's expertise lies in evaluating talent. He is responsible for the overall hockey operations of the club.

Experienced in building an NHL team from the ground up, Ferreira assembled a nucleus in Anaheim that tied a record for most wins by an NHL first-year club (33), as the Mighty Ducks stayed in contention for a Western Conference playoff berth for most of the season in 1993-94. Anaheim's solid foundation that included Bobby Dollas, Guy Hebert, Joe Sacco and Mikhail Shtalenkov was strengthened over the next few seasons with his additions of players like Paul Kariya, David Karpa, Steve Rucchin and Teemu Selanne. During the 1996-97 season, Ferreira made trades that added veteran talent and experienced players including J.J. Daigneault, Ted Drury, Mark Janssens and Dmitri Mironov. Those additions were a big reason the Mighty Ducks finished with the West's fourth seed and home-ice advantage in the first round of the 1997 Stanley Cup Playoffs. After a tough October, Anaheim had the third-best record in the West after November 1, 1996 (35-24-10) and had the top record in the West from February 22, 1997 (13-3-7). The Ducks finished the 1996-97 season with a franchise-record 85 points, including 36 wins and a first round playoff series victory over Phoenix.

A Providence, RI, native, Ferreira's professional career began in 1972 with the New England Whalers of the World Hockey Association, where he served in many capacities, including head scout, assistant coach and assistant general manager through 1977.

From 1977-80, Ferreira served as a New England scout for the NHL's Central Scouting Service before moving to the Calgary Flames as a U.S. and college scout from 1980-86.

Ferreira took a post as director of player development for the New York Rangers in 1986, serving in that capacity until 1988. He then joined the Minnesota North Stars, where he served as vice president and general manager from 1988-90.

Ferreira helped start up the San Jose Sharks franchise, serving as the team's executive vice president and general manager from 1990-92. Ferreira made acquisitions during the Sharks' first season that would be part of the foundation in San Jose's success over the 1993-94 and 1994-95 campaigns.

A former All-American goaltender at Boston University, Ferreira owns the NCAA record for most shutouts in one season (nine in 1964-65) and a career (13 from 1963-66). He served as an assistant coach on the collegiate level at Princeton in 1969. He also was an assistant coach with Brown University from 1970-72.

In addition, Ferreira served as assistant general manager for Team USA at the 1996 World Cup of Hockey which defeated Canada in the finals.

1996-97 Scoring

* – rookie

Regular Season

Pos	#	Player	Team	GP	G	A	Pts	+/–	PIM	PP	SH	GW	GT	S	%
R	8	Teemu Selanne	ANA	78	51	58	109	28	34	11	1	8	2	273	18.7
L	9	Paul Kariya	ANA	69	44	55	99	36	6	15	3	10	0	340	12.9
C	20	Steve Rucchin	ANA	79	19	48	67	26	24	6	1	2	1	153	12.4
D	15	Dmitri Mironov	PIT	15	1	5	6	-4	24	0	0	1	0	19	5.3
			ANA	62	12	34	46	20	77	3	1	1	0	158	7.6
			TOTAL	77	13	39	52	16	101	3	1	2	0	177	7.3
C	17	Jari Kurri	ANA	82	13	22	35	-13	12	3	0	3	0	109	11.9
L	23	Brian Bellows	T.B.	7	1	2	3	-4	0	0	0	0	0	17	5.9
			ANA	62	15	13	28	-11	22	8	0	1	0	151	9.9
			TOTAL	69	16	15	31	-15	22	8	0	1	0	168	9.5
C	12	Kevin Todd	ANA	65	9	21	30	-7	44	0	0	1	0	95	9.5
R	14	Joe Sacco	ANA	77	12	17	29	1	35	1	1	2	0	131	9.2
D	36	J.J. Daigneault	PIT	53	3	14	17	-5	36	0	0	1	0	49	6.1
			ANA	13	2	9	11	5	22	0	0	0	0	13	15.4
			TOTAL	66	5	23	28	0	58	0	0	1	0	62	8.1
D	29	* Darren Van Impe	ANA	74	4	19	23	3	90	2	0	0	0	107	3.7
R	46	Jean-Francois Jomphe	ANA	64	7	14	21	-9	53	0	1	0	0	81	8.6
C	13	Ted Drury	ANA	73	9	9	18	-9	54	1	0	2	1	114	7.9
D	2	Bobby Dollas	ANA	79	4	14	18	17	55	1	0	1	1	96	4.2
L	16	Warren Rychel	ANA	70	10	7	17	6	218	1	1	1	0	59	16.9
C	54	* Sean Pronger	ANA	39	7	7	14	6	20	1	0	1	1	43	16.3
D	33	Dave Karpa	ANA	69	2	11	13	11	210	0	0	1	0	90	2.2
L	22	Ken Baumgartner	ANA	67	0	11	11	0	182	0	0	0	0	20	0.0
D	28	Jason Marshall	ANA	73	1	9	10	6	140	0	0	0	0	34	2.9
C	24	Mark Janssens	HFD	54	2	4	6	-10	90	0	0	0	0	30	6.7
			ANA	12	0	2	2	-3	47	0	0	0	0	9	0.0
			TOTAL	66	2	6	8	-13	137	0	0	0	0	39	5.1
D	34	* Daniel Trebil	ANA	29	3	3	6	5	23	0	0	0	0	30	10.0
L	27	* Mike Leclerc	ANA	5	1	1	2	2	0	0	0	1	0	3	33.3
C	32	Richard Park	PIT	1	0	0	0	-1	0	0	0	0	0	1	0.0
			ANA	11	1	1	2	0	10	0	0	0	0	9	11.1
			TOTAL	12	1	1	2	-1	10	0	0	0	0	10	10.0
R	11	Valeri Karpov	ANA	9	1	0	1	-2	16	0	0	0	0	4	25.0
R	52	* Peter LeBoutillier	ANA	23	1	0	1	0	121	0	0	0	0	5	20.0
D	26	* Nikolai Tsulygin	ANA	22	0	1	1	-5	8	0	0	0	0	10	0.0
D	5	* Ruslan Salei	ANA	30	0	1	1	-8	37	0	0	0	0	14	0.0
G	31	Guy Hebert	ANA	67	0	1	1	0	4	0	0	0	0	0	0.0
G	1	Michael O'Neill	ANA	1	0	0	0	0	0	0	0	0	0	0	0.0
L	42	Barry Nieckar	ANA	2	0	0	0	0	5	0	0	0	0	0	0.0
R	39	* Frank Banham	ANA	3	0	0	0	-2	0	0	0	0	0	1	0.0
R	51	* Craig Reichert	ANA	3	0	0	0	-2	0	0	0	0	0	3	0.0
L	40	* Jeremy Stevenson	ANA	5	0	0	0	-1	14	0	0	0	0	1	0.0
D	25	Adrian Plavsic	ANA	6	0	0	0	-5	2	0	0	0	0	3	0.0
L	19	Shawn Antoski	PIT	13	0	0	0	0	49	0	0	0	0	3	0.0
			ANA	2	0	0	0	1	2	0	0	0	0	0	0.0
			TOTAL	15	0	0	0	1	51	0	0	0	0	3	0.0
G	35	M. Shtalenkov	ANA	24	0	0	0	0	4	0	0	0	0	0	0.0

Goaltending

No.	Goaltender	GPI	Mins	Avg	W	L	T	EN	SO	GA	SA	S%
31	Guy Hebert	67	3863	2.67	29	25	12	2	4	172	2133	.919
35	M. Shtalenkov	24	1079	2.89	7	8	1	4	2	52	539	.904
1	Michael O'Neill	1	31	5.81	0	0	0	0	0	3	10	.700
	Totals	**82**	**4994**	**2.80**	**36**	**33**	**13**	**6**	**6**	**233**	**2688**	**.913**

Playoffs

Pos	#	Player	Team	GP	G	A	Pts	+/–	PIM	PP	SH	GW	OT	S	%
L	9	Paul Kariya	ANA	11	7	6	13	-2	4	4	0	1	1	61	11.5
D	15	Dmitri Mironov	ANA	11	1	10	11	0	10	1	0	0	0	36	2.8
R	8	Teemu Selanne	ANA	11	7	3	10	-3	4	3	0	1	0	38	18.4
D	36	J.J. Daigneault	ANA	11	2	7	9	-6	16	1	0	1	0	24	8.3
L	23	Brian Bellows	ANA	11	2	4	6	-7	2	1	0	0	0	36	5.6
C	20	Steve Rucchin	ANA	8	1	2	3	-2	10	0	0	0	0	8	12.5
C	17	Jari Kurri	ANA	11	1	2	3	2	4	0	0	0	0	18	5.6
R	14	Joe Sacco	ANA	11	2	0	2	-4	2	0	0	0	0	20	10.0
D	33	Dave Karpa	ANA	8	1	1	2	-2	20	0	0	1	0	13	7.7
C	54	* Sean Pronger	ANA	9	0	2	2	0	4	0	0	0	0	7	0.0
D	29	* Darren Van Impe	ANA	9	0	2	2	-3	16	0	0	0	0	11	0.0
L	16	Warren Rychel	ANA	11	0	2	2	-2	19	0	0	0	0	16	0.0
C	13	Ted Drury	ANA	10	1	0	1	-2	4	0	0	0	0	17	5.9
D	28	Jason Marshall	ANA	7	0	1	1	1	4	0	0	0	0	3	0.0
D	34	* Daniel Trebil	ANA	9	0	1	1	-6	6	0	0	0	0	10	0.0
L	22	Ken Baumgartner	ANA	11	0	1	1	0	11	0	0	0	0	0	0.0
C	32	Richard Park	ANA	11	0	1	1	-2	2	0	0	0	0	10	0.0
L	27	* Mike Leclerc	ANA	1	0	0	0	0	0	0	0	0	0	0	0.0
R	21	* Igor Nikulin	ANA	1	0	0	0	0	0	0	0	0	0	1	0.0
C	12	Kevin Todd	ANA	4	0	0	0	-3	2	0	0	0	0	3	0.0
G	35	M. Shtalenkov	ANA	4	0	0	0	0	2	0	0	0	0	0	0.0
G	31	Guy Hebert	ANA	9	0	0	0	0	0	0	0	0	0	0	0.0
D	2	Bobby Dollas	ANA	11	0	0	0	-2	4	0	0	0	0	10	0.0
C	24	Mark Janssens	ANA	11	0	0	0	-3	15	0	0	0	0	13	0.0

Goaltending

No.	Goaltender	GPI	Mins	Avg	W	L	EN	SO	GA	SA	S%
31	Guy Hebert	9	534	2.02	4	4	1	1	18	255	.929
35	M. Shtalenkov	4	211	2.84	0	3	1	0	10	162	.938
	Totals	**11**	**747**	**2.41**	**4**	**7**	**2**	**1**	**30**	**419**	**.928**

Club Records

Team

(Figures in brackets for season records are games played; records for fewest points, wins, ties, losses, goals, goals against are for 70 or more games)

Most Points	85	1996-97 (82)	
Most Wins	36	1996-97 (82)	
Most Ties	13	1996-97 (82)	
Most Losses	46	1993-94 (84)	
Most Goals	245	1996-97 (82)	
Most Goals Against	251	1993-94 (84)	
Fewest Points	71	1993-94 (84)	
Fewest Wins	33	1993-94 (84)	
Fewest Ties	5	1993-94 (84)	
Fewest Losses	33	1996-97 (82)	
Fewest Goals	229	1993-94 (84)	
Fewest Goals Against	233	1996-97 (82)	

Longest Winning Streak
Overall .... 6 Mar. 8-22/96
Home .... 5 Twice
Away .... 4 Nov. 19-24/93

Longest Undefeated Streak
Overall .... 12 Feb. 22-Mar. 19/97
  (7 wins, 5 ties)
Home .... 14 Feb. 12-Apr. 9/97
  (10 wins, 4 ties)
Away .... 5 Jan. 2-19/94
  (3 wins, 2 ties)

Longest Losing Streak
Overall .... 8 Oct. 12-30/96
Home .... 5 Oct. 16-30/96
Away .... 6 Three times

Longest Winless Streak
Overall .... 9 Twice
Home .... 5 Oct. 16-30/96
Away .... 10 Mar. 26-Oct. 11/95
  (9 losses, 1 tie)

Most Shutouts, Season 6 1996-97 (82)
Most PIM, Season 1,710 1996-97 (82)
Most Goals, Game .... 7 Six times

Individual

Most Seasons	4	Four
Most Games	278	Joe Sacco
Most Goals, Career	112	Paul Kariya
Most Assists, Career	134	Paul Kariya
Most Points, Career	246	Paul Kariya
Most PIM, Career	650	Todd Ewen
Most Shutouts, Career	12	Guy Hebert

Longest Consecutive
Games Streak .... 159 Bobby Dollas
Most Goals, Season .... 51 Teemu Selanne
  (1996-97)
Most Assists, Season .... 58 Paul Kariya
  (1995-96)
Most Points, Season .... 109 Teemu Selanne
  (1996-97; 51G, 58A)
Most PIM, Season .... 285 Todd Ewen
  (1995-96)

Most Points, Defenseman,
Season .... 46 Dmitri Mironov
  (1996-97; 12G, 34A)

Most Points, Center,
Season .... 67 Steve Rucchin
  (1996-97; 19G, 48A)

Most Points, Right Wing,
Season .... 109 Teemu Selanne
  (1996-97; 51G, 58A)

Most Points, Left Wing,
Season .... 108 Paul Kariya
  (1995-96; 50G, 58A)

Most Points, Rookie,
Season .... 39 Paul Kariya
  (1994-95; 18G, 21A)

Most Shutouts, Season .... 4 Guy Hebert
  (1995-96, 1996-97)
Most Goals, Game .... 3 Seven times
Most Assists, Game .... 4 Shaun Van Allen
  (Mar. 9/95)
Most Points, Game........... 5 Twice

* NHL Record.

General Managers' History

Jack Ferreira, 1993-94 to date.

Coaching History

Ron Wilson, 1993-94 to 1996-97; Pierre Page, 1997-98.

Captains' History

Troy Loney, 1993-94; Randy Ladouceur, 1994-95 to 1995-96;
Paul Kariya, 1996-97 to date.

All-time Record vs. Other Clubs

Regular Season

	At Home							On Road							Total						
	GP	W	L	T	GF	GA	PTS	GP	W	L	T	GF	GA	PTS	GP	W	L	T	GF	GA	PTS
Boston	3	1	1	1	6	9	3	3	1	2	0	10	14	2	6	2	3	1	16	23	5
Buffalo	3	2	1	0	8	7	4	3	1	1	1	7	6	3	6	3	2	1	15	13	7
Calgary	11	4	5	2	31	29	10	11	4	7	0	26	32	8	22	8	12	2	57	61	18
Chicago	8	2	5	1	17	22	5	9	3	5	1	16	23	7	17	5	10	2	33	45	12
Colorado	6	3	2	1	16	11	7	4	1	1	2	23	28	4	10	4	3	3	39	39	11
Dallas	9	4	5	0	23	26	8	7	0	5	2	15	34	2	16	4	10	2	38	60	10
Detroit	8	2	4	2	20	32	6	7	2	5	2	20	32	4	15	4	9	4	40	64	10
Edmonton	10	7	2	1	33	23	15	5	5	0	0	23	20	10	15	12	7	1	56	43	25
Florida	3	1	1	1	8	9	3	3	1	2	0	7	7	2	6	2	3	1	16	16	5
Hartford	3	2	1	0	15	10	4	3	1	2	0	6	9	2	6	3	3	0	21	19	6
Los Angeles	11	6	3	2	42	29	14	11	3	6	2	24	34	8	22	9	9	4	66	63	22
Montreal	3	1	2	0	12	13	2	3	1	1	1	10	12	3	6	2	3	1	22	25	5
New Jersey	3	2	1	0	12	8	4	3	1	2	0	7	11	2	6	3	3	0	19	19	6
NY Islanders	3	1	1	1	7	7	3	3	1	2	0	9	8	2	6	2	3	1	16	15	5
NY Rangers	3	3	0	0	15	8	6	3	1	2	0	7	10	2	6	4	2	0	22	18	8
Ottawa	3	3	0	0	13	6	6	3	2	1	0	8	9	4	6	5	1	0	21	13	10
Philadelphia	3	1	2	0	11	11	2	3	1	1	1	5	7	3	6	2	3	1	16	18	5
Phoenix	8	7	1	0	30	14	14	8	4	4	0	29	31	8	16	11	5	0	59	45	22
Pittsburgh	3	1	2	0	13	15	2	3	0	2	1	7	12	1	6	1	4	1	20	27	3
St. Louis	8	3	4	1	23	21	7	8	3	5	0	25	30	6	16	6	9	1	48	51	13
San Jose	11	5	6	0	33	39	10	10	6	3	1	36	30	13	21	11	9	1	69	69	23
Tampa Bay	3	1	1	1	7	7	3	3	1	2	0	7	6	2	6	2	3	1	14	13	5
Toronto	8	4	3	1	26	18	9	8	1	5	2	17	27	4	16	5	8	3	43	45	13
Vancouver	11	3	7	1	24	35	7	11	4	7	0	28	40	8	22	7	14	1	52	75	15
Washington	3	1	1	1	9	11	3	3	2	1	0	6	5	4	6	3	2	1	15	16	7
Totals	**148**	**70**	**62**	**16**	**454**	**418**	**156**	**148**	**50**	**83**	**15**	**379**	**477**	**115**	**296**	**120**	**145**	**31**	**833**	**895**	**271**

Playoffs

	Series	W	L	GP	W	L	T	GF	GA	Last Mtg.	Round	Result
Detroit	1	0	1	4	0	4	0	8	13	1997	CSF	L 0-4
Phoenix	1	1	0	7	4	3	0	17	17	1997	CQF	W 4-3
Totals	**2**	**1**	**1**	**11**	**4**	**7**	**0**	**25**	**30**			

Playoff Results 1997-94

Year	Round	Opponent	Result	GF	GA
1997	CSF	Detroit	L 0-4	8	13
	CQF	Phoenix	W 4-3	17	17

Abbreviations: Round: F – Final;
CF – conference final; CQF – conference quarter-final;
CSF – conference semi-final; DF – division final;
DSF – division semi-final; SF – semi-final;
QF – quarter-final; PR – preliminary round.

Colorado totals include Quebec, 1993-94 to 1994-95.   Phoenix totals include Winnipeg, 1993-94 to 1995-96.

1996-97 Results

Oct.	5	at Toronto	1-4	10		Buffalo	5-2
	7	at Montreal	6-6	12	at	Vancouver	3-2
	9	at Chicago	2-0	15	at	Calgary	1-2
	10	at Colorado	6-6	22		New Jersey	3-1
	12	at Phoenix	2-4	23	at	Phoenix	3-6
	16	Philadelphia	3-4	25	at	Los Angeles	2-2
	18	San Jose	1-4	27	at	St. Louis	4-1
	20	Boston	1-5	29	at	Dallas	1-3
	22	at Philadelphia	0-3	31		Hartford	6-3
	24	at Hartford	1-4	Feb. 2		Colorado	2-5
	27	Calgary	1-4	4	at	NY Islanders	3-4
	30	Vancouver	3-6	5	at	Toronto	2-4
Nov.	1	San Jose	4-3	8	at	Edmonton	2-1
	3	Colorado	1-1	9	at	Calgary	1-6
	6	Montreal	5-6	12		Toronto	5-2
	8	Los Angeles	7-4	15	at	Vancouver	2-4
	11	Dallas	2-3	17		Edmonton	5-1
	13	Toronto	3-2	20	at	Los Angeles	1-3
	15	at Dallas	3-4	22		Phoenix	4-2
	17	at St. Louis	2-4	23		Vancouver	5-2
	20	NY Islanders	2-2	26		Edmonton	3-3
	23	at San Jose	3-0	28	at	Washington	4-1
	24	Detroit	3-1	Mar. 2	at	Detroit	1-1
	27	St. Louis	2-3	5		Ottawa	2-4
	29	Chicago	2-0	7		NY Rangers	5-2
Dec.	1	Edmonton	4-2	9	at	Colorado	2-2
	4	Tampa Bay	3-1	12		Detroit	2-3
	6	at Buffalo	1-1	14		St. Louis	4-4
	7	at Pittsburgh	3-5	16		Calgary	2-2
	9	at Boston	5-2	19		Los Angeles	6-2
	11	Pittsburgh	3-7	21	at	Colorado	3-4
	13	Washington	5-4	23	at	Edmonton	4-1
	20	Calgary	7-0	25	at	Calgary	2-3
	23	Phoenix	1-2	26	at	Vancouver	3-5
	27	at NY Rangers	2-3	28	at	Chicago	4-3
	28	at New Jersey	3-5	30	at	Detroit	1-0
	30	at Ottawa	4-3	Apr. 1		Chicago	3-3
Jan.	1	at Florida	3-0	2	at	San Jose	5-5
	3	at Tampa Bay	2-3	4		Dallas	3-2
	6	Vancouver	1-5	9		Los Angeles	4-1
	8	Florida	3-2	11	at	San Jose	4-3

Entry Draft
Selections 1997-93

1997
Pick
18	Mikael Holmqvist
45	Maxim Balmochnykh
72	Jay Legault
125	Luc Vaillancourt
178	Tony Mohagen
181	Mat Snesrud
209	Rene Stussi
235	Tommi Degerman

1996
Pick
9	Ruslan Salei
35	Matt Cullen
117	Brendan Buckley
149	Blaine Russell
172	Timo Ahmaoja
198	Kevin Kellett
224	Tobias Johansson

1995
Pick
4	Chad Kilger
29	Brian Wesenberg
55	Mike Leclerc
107	Igor Nikulin
133	Peter Leboutillier
159	Mike Laplante
185	Igor Karpenko

1994
Pick
2	Oleg Tverdovsky
28	Johan Davidsson
67	Craig Reichert
80	Byron Briske
106	Pavel Trnka
132	Jon Battaglia
158	Mark (Rocky) Welsing
184	John Brad Englehart
236	Tommi Miettinen
262	Jeremy Stevenson

1993
Pick
4	Paul Kariya
30	Nikolai Tsulygin
56	Valeri Karpov
82	Joel Gagnon
108	Mikhail Shtalenkov
134	Antti Aalto
160	Matt Peterson
186	Tom Askey
212	Vitaly Kozel
238	Anatoli Fedotov
264	David Penney

Coach

PAGE, PIERRE
Head Coach, The Mighty Ducks of Anaheim.
Born in St. Hermas, Que., April 30, 1948.

Pierre Page was named as the second coach in Mighty Ducks history on August 9, 1997. A veteran of 13 seasons as a coach in the National Hockey League, Page is respected as one of the top hockey minds in the game today. He is entering his eighth campaign as a head coach in the NHL.

Page comes to the Mighty Ducks from the Calgary Flames, where he spent the last two seasons as head coach. In 1996-97, he took a team that included 13 new players and nine rookies under the age of 24 and kept the club in contention for a playoff spot until the final week of the season. In his first season as Flames head coach in 1995-96, Page led the team to a second place finish in the Pacific Division despite a slow start of only five wins in the first 25 games.

Before his latest stint with Calgary, Page spent the 1994-95 season working as a pro scout for the Toronto Maple Leafs and assisting Canada's National Team.

Perhaps Page's most valuable experience and success came during his tenure with the Quebec Nordiques. He joined Quebec as general manager in May, 1990, and one season later added the responsibilities of head coach. Upon joining the Nordiques, Page inherited a team that was coming off a 31-point season and failed to qualify for post-season play for the third consecutive year. In 1992-93, Quebec finished fourth overall in the League with 104 points and qualified for the playoffs for the first time in six seasons.

Page spent four seasons (1990-93) in Quebec, and in that time was responsible for acquiring several players who made significant contributions in helping the Colorado Avalanche win the 1996 Stanley Cup.

The 1988-89 season was Page's first as a head coach in the NHL, when he joined the Minnesota North Stars under general manager Jack Ferreira.

His first NHL experience came in the Calgary Flames' organization where he spent eight seasons (1980-88), serving in several capacities. He joined the Flames in 1980-81 as an assistant coach under Al MacNeil, serving in that post through the 1981-82 season. The Flames went to the NHL semifinals in 1980-81, the club's first season in Calgary. Page's responsibilities increased in 1982-83 when he took on the role of general manager and head coach of the Flames' primary development affiliate in Denver, and later, Moncton (1984-85). He returned to Calgary as an assistant coach to Bob Johnson in 1985-86, helping guide the Flames to their first Stanley Cup Finals appearance. Page remained with Calgary, also serving under Terry Crisp in 1987-88 before joining Minnesota. During his tenure with Calgary, he also served as a guest coach with the 1980 Canadian Olympic Team and an assistant coach to Scotty Bowman with Team Canada in the 1981 Canada Cup.

Prior to coming to the NHL in 1980, Page served as head coach of Dalhousie University in Halifax, Nova Scotia, during the late 1970s. He led the university team to the number two ranking in Canadian college hockey in 1978-79, capturing the Maritime title for the first time in 60 years.

Page and his wife Donna have one daughter, Lauren (1/31/86). The family resides in Tustin, CA.

Coaching Record

Season	Team	Games	Regular Season W	L	T	%	Playoffs Games	W	L	%
1978-79	Dalhousie (CIAU)	....	....	....	....	....	....	....	....	....
1982-83	Denver (CHL)	80	41	36	3	.531	6	2	4	.333
1983-84	Denver (CHL)	76	48	25	3	.651	6	2	4	.333
1984-85	Moncton (AHL)	80	32	40	8	.450	....	....	....	....
1988-89	**Minnesota (NHL)**	80	27	37	16	.438	5	1	4	.200
1989-90	**Minnesota (NHL)**	80	36	40	4	.475	7	3	4	.429
1991-92	**Quebec (NHL)**	62	17	34	11	.362	....	....	....	....
1992-93	**Quebec (NHL)**	84	47	27	10	.619	6	2	4	.333
1993-94	**Quebec (NHL)**	84	34	42	8	.452	....	....	....	....
1995-96	**Calgary (NHL)**	82	34	37	11	.482	4	0	4	.000
1996-97	**Calgary (NHL)**	82	32	41	9	.445	....	....	....	....
	NHL Totals	554	227	258	69	.472	22	6	16	.273

Club Directory

Anaheim Sports, Inc.
Arrowhead Pond of Anaheim
2695 Katella Ave.
Anaheim, CA 92806
Phone **714/940-2900**
FAX 714/940-2953
Ticket Information 714/704-2701
Capacity: 17,174

Executive Management
President and Governor	Tony Tavares
Vice President/General Manager (Alternate Governor)	Jack Ferreira
Vice President of Finance/Administration	Andy Roundtree
Assistant General Manager	David McNab
Vice President, Business Affairs	Kevin Gilmore
Vice President, Sales and Marketing	Ken Wachter
Administrative Assistant, President	Jennifer Mitchell
Administrative Assistant, General Manager	Mary Leer
Administrative Assistant, Business Affairs	Tia Wood
Administrative Assistant, Sales and Marketing	Roberta Maslanka

Coaching Staff
Head Coach	Pierre Page
Associate Coach	Walt Kyle
Assistant Coach	Don Hay
Goaltending Consultant	Francois Allaire

Hockey Club Operations
Chief Amateur Scout	Alain Chainey
Chief Pro Scout	Paul Fenton
Assistant to the General Manager	Angela Gorgone
Scouts	Thommie Bergman, Richard Green, Mark Odnokon
Scouting Staff	Donald Marier, Mike McGraw, David McNamara, Ed Wright, Pavel Beranek, Konstantin Krylov, Matti Pettonen
Head Athletic Trainer	Greg Smith
Equipment Manager	Mark O'Neill
Assistant Equipment Manager	John Allaway
Cincinnati Mighty Ducks (AHL) Head Coach	Moe Mantha
Team Physicians	Dr. Ronald Glousman, Dr. Craig Milhouse
Oral Surgeon	Dr. Jeff Pulver
Visiting Team Equipment Attendant	Chris Kincaid

Communications Department
Director, Communications	Bill Robertson
Manager, Media Services	Rob Scichili
Manager, Publications	Doug Ward
Administrative Assistant, Communications	Cynthia Jacobs
Community Relations Representatives	Paul Desaulniers, Jennifer Guran
Web Site Editor	Paul Nowosad
Team Photographer	V.J. Lovero (Lovero Group)

Finance and Administration Department
Director, Finance	Martin Greenspun
Manager, Business Development	Lawrence Cohen
Controller	Jon Sullivan
Manager, Human Resources	Jenny Price
Manager, Information Services	Andy Roe
Assistant Controllers	Cristina Fisher, Melody Martin
Accountants	Jean Ouyang, Roseanna Sitzman, Lorlei Largey
Accounting Assistants	Roberta Billings, Karen Wilson
Office Manager	Barbara Potts
Administrative Assistant, Human Resources	Cindy Williams
Human Resources Assistant	Lisa Giancanelli
General Manager, Disney ICE	Art Trottier
Office Assistant	Paul Zessau

Sales & Marketing Department
Director, Marketing	Bill Holford
Director, Advertising Sales/Sponsorship Services	Bob Wagner
Manager, Marketing	Lisa Manning
Manager, Advertising and Broadcasting Sales	John Covarrubias
Manager, Sponsorship Services	Sue O'Shea
Manager, Group Sales	Andy Silverman
Manager, Ticket Sales	Don Engle
Manager, Hispanic Sales & Marketing	Marie Moreno
Advertising Sales Managers	John Davis, Hap Deneen, Richard McClemmy, Dave Severson
Sponsorship Services Representative	Chris Sinta
Sponsorship Services Coordinator	Brian Strohecker
Account Executives	June Clayton, Mark LaFerr, Keith Rowe
Group Ticket Sales Executives	Ken Bamberg, Joe Furmanski, Laury Wedin
Premium Account Executives	Kristen Atkinson, Jennifer Flaa, Mike Gullo, David Mann
Administrative Assistants	Natalie Caldera, Patty Leemhuis, Christi Le Narz, Pat Lissy

Television and Radio Broadcasting Department
Director, Broadcasting	Mark Vittorio
Producer	Tim Davis
Associate Producer	Aaron Teats
Television	KCAL (Ch. 9) & Fox Sports West 2 (Cable) Chris Madsen, Brian Hayward
Radio	KRLA (1110 AM) & Mighty Ducks Radio Network Brian Hamilton, Darren Eliot

Ticketing Department
Manager, Ticket Operations	Don Boudreau
Ticketing Supervisors	Rick Capstraw, Kevin Gidden, Heather Holter
Manager, Premium Ticket Services	Anne McNiff

Entertainment Department
Director, Entertainment	Marty Berg
Staging Supervisor	Marianne Herman
Administrative Assistant, Entertainment	Susan Jackson
Receptionist	Sue Felix

Boston Bruins

1996-97 Results: 26W-47L-9T 61PTS. Sixth, Northeast Division

Despite missing 20 games to injury, Ray Bourque still led the Bruins in shots (230) and game-winning goals (3). He also became only the second defenseman and fifth player to reach the 1,000-assist plateau in the NHL.

1997-98 Schedule

Oct.	Thu.	2	Los Angeles
	Sat.	4	Montreal
	Tue.	7	at Colorado
	Wed.	8	at Phoenix
	Sat.	11	at San Jose
	Mon.	13	at Anaheim
	Wed.	15	at Los Angeles
	Fri.	17	at Vancouver
	Sat.	18	at Calgary
	Tue.	21	at Edmonton
	Thu.	23	Tampa Bay
	Sat.	25	Florida
	Thu.	30	Anaheim
Nov.	Sat.	1	Edmonton
	Sun.	2	at Ottawa
	Thu.	6	Washington
	Sat.	8	at New Jersey
	Wed.	12	at Dallas
	Thu.	13	at St. Louis
	Sat.	15	Ottawa
	Mon.	17	at Ottawa
	Wed.	19	at Pittsburgh
	Thu.	20	Buffalo
	Sat.	22	Dallas
	Wed.	26	at Florida
	Fri.	28	Vancouver*
	Sat.	29	Washington
Dec.	Mon.	1	at Carolina
	Wed.	3	at Philadelphia
	Sat.	6	Carolina
	Thu.	11	Buffalo
	Sat.	13	Montreal
	Mon.	15	at Florida
	Wed.	17	at Tampa Bay
	Thu.	18	at Philadelphia
	Sat.	20	NY Islanders
	Mon.	22	Detroit
	Sat.	27	at Tampa Bay*
	Sun.	28	at NY Rangers
	Wed.	31	at Toronto
Jan.	Thu.	1	Ottawa

	Sat.	3	San Jose
	Wed.	7	at Montreal
	Thu.	8	Phoenix
	Mon.	12	New Jersey
	Wed.	14	Pittsburgh
	Wed.	21	at Montreal
	Sat.	24	at Pittsburgh*
	Sun.	25	at Washington*
	Tue.	27	Ottawa
	Thu.	29	Pittsburgh
	Sat.	31	NY Rangers*
Feb.	Sun.	1	at NY Islanders*
	Wed.	4	at Buffalo
	Thu.	5	St. Louis
	Sat.	7	Carolina*
	Thu.	26	Buffalo
	Sat.	28	Pittsburgh*
Mar.	Sun.	1	at NY Islanders*
	Tue.	3	at Washington
	Thu.	5	at New Jersey
	Sat.	7	Chicago*
	Tue.	10	at Detroit
	Thu.	12	Calgary
	Sat.	14	NY Rangers*
	Mon.	16	Tampa Bay
	Thu.	19	Toronto
	Sat.	21	at Buffalo*
	Sun.	22	at Chicago*
	Thu.	26	Philadelphia
	Sat.	28	Florida*
	Mon.	30	Colorado
Apr.	Wed.	1	at NY Rangers
	Fri.	3	at Buffalo
	Mon.	6	Carolina
	Tue.	7	at Ottawa
	Thu.	9	NY Islanders
	Sat.	11	New Jersey
	Mon.	13	at Carolina
	Wed.	15	at Montreal
	Sat.	18	at Pittsburgh*
	Sun.	19	Philadelphia*

* Denotes afternoon game.

Franchise date: November 1, 1924

NORTHEAST DIVISION

74th NHL Season

Year-by-Year Record

		Home			Road			Overall						
Season	GP	W	L	T	W	L	T	W	L	T	GF	GA	Pts.	Finished	Playoff Result
1996-97	82	14	20	7	12	27	2	26	47	9	234	300	61	6th, Northeast Div.	Out of Playoffs
1995-96	82	22	14	5	18	17	6	40	31	11	282	269	91	2nd, Northeast Div.	Lost Conf. Quarter-Final
1994-95	48	15	7	2	12	11	1	27	18	3	150	127	57	3rd, Northeast Div.	Lost Conf. Quarter-Final
1993-94	84	20	14	8	22	15	5	42	29	13	289	252	97	2nd, Northeast Div.	Lost Conf. Semi-Final
1992-93	84	29	10	3	22	16	4	51	26	7	332	268	109	1st, Adams Div.	Lost Div. Semi-Final
1991-92	80	23	11	6	13	21	6	36	32	12	270	275	84	2nd, Adams Div.	Lost Conf. Championship
1990-91	80	26	9	5	18	15	7	44	24	12	299	264	100	1st, Adams Div.	Lost Conf. Championship
1989-90	80	23	13	4	23	12	5	46	25	9	289	232	101	1st, Adams Div.	Lost Final
1988-89	80	17	15	8	20	14	6	37	29	14	289	256	88	2nd, Adams Div.	Lost Div. Final
1987-88	80	24	13	3	20	17	3	44	30	6	300	251	94	2nd, Adams Div.	Lost Final
1986-87	80	25	11	4	14	23	3	39	34	7	301	276	85	3rd, Adams Div.	Lost Div. Semi-Final
1985-86	80	24	9	7	13	22	5	37	31	12	311	288	86	3rd, Adams Div.	Lost Div. Semi-Final
1984-85	80	21	15	4	15	19	6	36	34	10	303	287	82	4th, Adams Div.	Lost Div. Semi-Final
1983-84	80	25	12	3	24	13	3	49	25	6	336	261	104	1st, Adams Div.	Lost Div. Semi-Final
1982-83	80	28	6	6	22	14	4	50	20	10	327	228	110	1st, Adams Div.	Lost Conf. Championship
1981-82	80	24	12	4	19	15	6	43	27	10	323	285	96	2nd, Adams Div.	Lost Div. Final
1980-81	80	26	10	4	11	20	9	37	30	13	316	272	87	2nd, Adams Div.	Lost Prelim. Round
1979-80	80	27	9	4	19	12	9	46	21	13	310	234	105	2nd, Adams Div.	Lost Quarter-Final
1978-79	80	25	10	5	18	13	9	43	23	14	316	270	100	1st, Adams Div.	Lost Semi-Final
1977-78	80	29	6	5	22	12	6	51	18	11	333	218	113	1st, Adams Div.	Lost Final
1976-77	80	27	7	6	22	16	2	49	23	8	312	240	106	1st, Adams Div.	Lost Final
1975-76	80	27	5	8	21	10	9	48	15	17	313	237	113	1st, Adams Div.	Lost Semi-Final
1974-75	80	29	5	6	11	21	8	40	26	14	345	245	94	2nd, Adams Div.	Lost Prelim. Round
1973-74	78	33	4	2	19	13	7	52	17	9	349	221	113	1st, East Div.	Lost Final
1972-73	78	27	10	2	24	12	3	51	22	5	330	235	107	2nd, East Div.	Lost Quarter-Final
1971-72	**78**	**28**	**4**	**7**	**26**	**9**	**4**	**54**	**13**	**11**	**330**	**204**	**119**	**1st, East Div.**	**Won Stanley Cup**
1970-71	78	33	4	2	24	10	5	57	14	7	399	207	121	1st, East Div.	Lost Quarter-Final
1969-70	**76**	**27**	**3**	**8**	**13**	**14**	**11**	**40**	**17**	**19**	**277**	**216**	**99**	**2nd, East Div.**	**Won Stanley Cup**
1968-69	76	29	3	6	13	15	10	42	18	16	303	221	100	2nd, East Div.	Lost Semi-Final
1967-68	74	22	9	6	15	18	4	37	27	10	259	216	84	3rd, East Div.	Lost Quarter-Final
1966-67	70	10	21	4	7	22	6	17	43	10	182	253	44	6th,	Out of Playoffs
1965-66	70	15	17	3	6	26	3	21	43	6	174	275	48	5th,	Out of Playoffs
1964-65	70	12	17	6	9	26	0	21	43	6	166	253	48	6th,	Out of Playoffs
1963-64	70	13	15	7	5	25	5	18	40	12	170	212	48	6th,	Out of Playoffs
1962-63	70	7	18	10	7	21	7	14	39	17	198	281	45	6th,	Out of Playoffs
1961-62	70	9	22	4	6	25	4	15	47	8	177	306	38	6th,	Out of Playoffs
1960-61	70	13	17	5	2	25	8	15	42	13	176	254	43	6th,	Out of Playoffs
1959-60	70	21	11	3	7	23	5	28	34	8	220	241	64	5th,	Out of Playoffs
1958-59	70	21	11	3	11	18	6	32	29	9	205	215	73	2nd,	Lost Semi-Final
1957-58	70	15	14	6	12	14	9	27	28	15	199	194	69	4th,	Lost Final
1956-57	70	20	9	6	14	15	6	34	24	12	195	174	80	3rd,	Lost Final
1955-56	70	14	14	7	9	20	6	23	34	13	147	185	59	5th,	Out of Playoffs
1954-55	70	16	10	9	7	16	12	23	26	21	169	188	67	4th,	Lost Semi-Final
1953-54	70	22	8	5	10	20	5	32	28	10	177	181	74	4th,	Lost Semi-Final
1952-53	70	19	10	6	9	19	7	28	29	13	152	172	69	3rd,	Lost Final
1951-52	70	15	12	8	10	17	8	25	29	16	162	176	66	4th,	Lost Semi-Final
1950-51	70	13	12	10	9	18	8	22	30	18	178	197	62	4th,	Lost Semi-Final
1949-50	70	15	12	8	7	20	8	22	32	16	198	228	60	5th,	Out of Playoffs
1948-49	60	18	10	2	11	13	6	29	23	8	178	163	66	2nd,	Lost Semi-Final
1947-48	60	12	8	10	11	16	3	23	24	13	167	168	59	3rd,	Lost Semi-Final
1946-47	60	18	7	5	8	16	6	26	23	11	190	175	63	3rd,	Lost Semi-Final
1945-46	50	11	5	4	13	13	4	24	18	8	167	156	56	2nd,	Lost Final
1944-45	50	11	12	2	5	18	2	16	30	4	179	219	36	4th,	Lost Semi-Final
1943-44	50	15	8	2	4	18	3	19	26	5	223	268	43	5th,	Out of Playoffs
1942-43	50	17	3	5	7	14	4	24	17	9	195	176	57	2nd,	Lost Final
1941-42	48	17	4	3	8	13	3	25	17	6	160	118	56	3rd,	Lost Semi-Final
1940-41	**48**	**15**	**4**	**5**	**12**	**4**	**8**	**27**	**8**	**13**	**168**	**102**	**67**	**1st,**	**Won Stanley Cup**
1939-40	48	20	3	1	11	9	4	31	12	5	170	98	67	1st,	Lost Semi-Final
1938-39	**48**	**20**	**2**	**2**	**16**	**8**	**0**	**36**	**10**	**2**	**156**	**76**	**74**	**1st,**	**Won Stanley Cup**
1937-38	48	18	3	3	12	8	4	30	11	7	142	89	67	1st, Amn. Div.	Lost Semi-Final
1936-37	48	14	9	1	9	14	1	23	18	7	120	110	53	2nd, Amn. Div.	Lost Quarter-Final
1935-36	48	15	8	1	7	12	5	22	20	6	92	83	50	2nd, Amn. Div.	Lost Quarter-Final
1934-35	48	17	7	0	9	9	6	26	16	6	129	112	58	1st, Amn. Div.	Lost Semi-Final
1933-34	48	11	11	2	7	14	3	18	25	5	111	130	41	4th, Amn. Div.	Out of Playoffs
1932-33	48	20	2	3	5	13	5	25	15	8	124	88	58	1st, Amn. Div.	Lost Semi-Final
1931-32	48	11	10	3	4	11	9	15	21	12	122	117	42	4th, Amn. Div.	Out of Playoffs
1930-31	44	17	1	5	11	9	1	28	10	6	143	90	62	1st, Amn. Div.	Lost Semi-Final
1929-30	44	21	1	0	17	4	1	38	5	1	179	98	77	1st, Amn. Div.	Lost Final
1928-29	**44**	**16**	**6**	**1**	**10**	**7**	**4**	**26**	**13**	**5**	**89**	**52**	**57**	**1st, Amn. Div.**	**Won Stanley Cup**
1927-28	44	13	4	5	7	9	6	20	13	11	77	70	51	1st, Amn. Div.	Lost Semi-Final
1926-27	44	15	7	0	6	13	3	21	20	3	97	89	45	2nd, Amn. Div.	Lost Final
1925-26	36	10	7	1	7	8	3	17	15	4	92	85	38	4th,	Out of Playoffs
1924-25	30	3	12	0	3	12	0	6	24	0	49	119	12	6th,	Out of Playoffs

1997-98 Player Personnel

FORWARDS	HT	WT	S	Place of Birth	Date	1996-97 Club
ALLISON, Jason	6-3	205	R	North York, Ont.	5/29/75	Washington-Boston
AXELSSON, Per-Johan	6-1	174	L	Kungalv, Sweden	2/26/75	V. Frolunda
BARTANUS, Karol	6-2	185	L	Liptovsky Mikulas, Slovakia	6/9/78	Drummondville
BATES, Shawn	5-11	205	R	Melrose, MA	4/3/75	Boston U.
BAUMGARTNER, Ken	6-1	205	L	Flin Flon, Man.	3/11/66	Anaheim
CARTER, Anson	6-1	175	R	Toronto, Ont.	6/6/74	Wsh-Portland (AHL)-Bos
DiMAIO, Rob	5-10	190	R	Calgary, Alta.	2/19/68	Boston
DONATO, Ted	5-10	183	L	Boston, MA	4/28/69	Boston
DOYLE, Jason	6-1	200	R	Toronto, Ont.	5/15/78	S.S. Marie-Owen Sound
DROUIN, P.C.	6-2	208	L	St. Lambert, Que.	4/22/74	Boston-Providence (AHL)
HEINZE, Stephen	5-11	202	R	Lawrence, MA	1/30/70	Boston
KHRISTICH, Dimitri	6-2	195	R	Kiev, USSR	7/23/69	Los Angeles
KUSTER, Henry	6-0	195	R	Edmonton, Alta.	11/11/77	Medicine Hat
MANN, Cameron	6-0	194	R	Thompson, Man.	4/20/77	Peterborough
McCAULEY, Bill	6-1	195	L	Detroit, MI	4/20/75	Providence (AHL)-Charlotte
McCLEARY, Trent	6-0	180	R	Swift Current, Sask.	9/8/72	Boston
NAUD, Eric	6-1	187	L	Lasarre, Que.	10/2/77	Rouyn-Noranda-Hull
NIELSEN, Kirk	6-1	205	R	Grand Rapids, MN	10/19/73	Providence (AHL)
ODGERS, Jeff	6-0	200	R	Spy Hill, Sask.	5/31/69	Boston
ROBITAILLE, Randy	5-11	195	L	Ottawa, Ont.	10/12/75	Miami-Ohio-Boston
ROY, Andre	6-3	202	L	Port Chester, NY	2/8/75	Boston-Providence (AHL)
SAMSONOV, Sergei	5-8	184	R	Moscow, USSR	10/27/78	Detroit (IHL)
SULLIVAN, Mike	6-2	190	L	Marshfield, MA	2/27/68	Calgary-Adirondack
THORNTON, Joe	6-4	198	L	London, Ont.	7/2/79	S.S. Marie
WHITFIELD, Trent	5-11	176	L	Estevan, Sask.	6/17/77	Spokane
WILSON, Landon	6-2	216	R	St. Louis, MO	3/13/75	Col-Bos-Providence (AHL)
DEFENSEMEN						
ABRAHAMSSON, Elias	6-3	227	L	Uppsala, Sweden	6/15/77	Halifax
AITKEN, Johnathan	6-4	205	L	Edmonton, Alta.	5/24/78	Brandon
BOURQUE, Ray	5-11	219	L	Montreal, Que.	12/28/60	Boston
BROWN, Thomas	6-4	200	R	Hamilton, Ont.	11/11/77	Sarnia-Sudbury
CHYNOWETH, Dean	6-1	191	R	Calgary, Alta.	10/30/68	Boston-Providence (AHL)
CORNFORTH, Mark	6-1	193	L	Montreal, Que.	11/13/72	Providence (AHL)-Cleveland
ELLETT, Dave	6-2	205	L	Cleveland, OH	3/30/64	Toronto-New Jersey
GILL, Hal	6-6	200	L	Concord, MA	4/6/75	Providence
LANE, Chris	6-1	192	R	Edmonton, Alta.	2/16/78	Spokane
MALKOC, Dean	6-3	215	L	Vancouver, B.C.	1/26/70	Boston-Providence (AHL)
MASTAD, Milt	6-4	233	L	Regina, Sask.	3/5/75	Providence (AHL)-Charlotte
McLAREN, Kyle	6-4	219	L	Humbolt, Sask.	6/18/77	Boston
MYRVOLD, Anders	6-2	200	L	Lorenskog, Norway	8/12/75	Hershey-Boston-Providence (AHL)
PAQUETTE, Charles	6-1	220	L	Lachute, Que.	6/17/75	Providence (AHL)
RICHTER, Barry	6-2	200	L	Madison, WI	9/11/70	Boston-Providence (AHL)
ROHLOFF, Jon	6-0	221	R	Mankato, MN	10/3/69	Boston-Providence (AHL)
SHALDYBIN, Yevgeny	6-2	198	L	Novosibirsk, USSR	7/29/75	Boston-Providence (AHL)
SWEENEY, Don	5-10	184	L	St. Stephen, N.B.	8/17/66	Boston
TIMANDER, Mattias	6-3	210	L	Solleftea, Sweden	4/16/74	Boston-Providence (AHL)
YAKHANOV, Andrei	5-11	190	R	Ufa, USSR	7/23/73	Ufa Salavat

GOALTENDERS	HT	WT	C	Place of Birth	Date	1996-97 Club
CAREY, Jim	6-2	205	L	Dorchester, MA	5/31/74	Washington-Boston
DAFOE, Byron	5-11	175	L	Sussex, England	2/25/71	Los Angeles
GRAHAME, John	6-2	210	L	Denver, CO	8/31/75	Lake Superior
SCHAFER, Paxton	5-9	164	L	Medicine Hat, Alta.	2/26/76	Bos-Providence (AHL)-Charlotte
TALLAS, Robbie	6-0	163	L	Edmonton, Alta.	3/20/73	Boston-Providence (AHL)

Captains' History

No Captain, 1924-25 to 1926-27; Lionel Hitchman, 1927-28 to 1930-31; George Owen, 1931-32; "Dit" Clapper, 1932-33 to 1937-38; "Cooney" Weiland, 1938-39; "Dit" Clapper, 1939-40 to 1945-46; "Dit" Clapper and John Crawford, 1946-47; John Crawford 1947-48 to 1949-50; Milt Schmidt, 1950-51 to 1953-54; Milt Schmidt, Ed Sanford, 1954-55; Fern Flaman, 1955-56 to 1960-61; Don McKenney, 1961-62, 1962-63; Leo Boivin, 1963-64 to 1965-66; John Bucyk, 1966-67; no captain, 1967-68 to 1972-73; John Bucyk, 1973-74 to 1976-77; Wayne Cashman, 1977-78 to 1982-83; Terry O'Reilly, 1983-84, 1984-85; Ray Bourque, Rick Middleton (co-captains) 1985-86 to 1987-88; Ray Bourque, 1988-89 to date.

Coach

BURNS, PAT

Coach, Boston Bruins. Born in St-Henri, Que., April 4, 1952.

Pat Burns enters his first season as the Bruins head coach with a lifetime NHL record of 307-211-83 in 601 regular season games (a .580 winning percentage) and a playoff coaching record of 53-49 in 102 games (a .520 winning percentage). He is one of four coaches to have twice won the Jack Adams Trophy as the NHL's top coach. His teams have finished with either the first or second best defensive records in five of his seven full regular seasons behind an NHL bench and have won two division titles.

Burns began his coaching career with the Hull Olympiques of the QMJHL. During his four seasons behind the Hull bench, he compiled a 138-136-6 record and a berth in the 1986 Memorial Cup finals. In 1987-88, he moved to the professional ranks, assuming the head coaching position with Montreal's AHL affiliate in Sherbrooke. After leading that team to a 42-34-4 record, he was named as the head coach in Montreal.

He was the NHL's winningest coach over his four-year tenure in Montreal, with a 174-104-42 record and .609 winning percentage from 1988-89 through 1991-92.

On May 29, 1992, Burns was named as the head coach for the Toronto Maple Leafs. In his first season with Toronto, he led the team to the highest single-season turnaround in club history with club records in regular season wins, points and home wins and playoff games and victories. Their 44-29-11 record in 1992-93 was a 32-point improvement from their 1991-92 campaign. His second season behind the Toronto bench earned the team consecutive 40-win seasons for the first time in club history.

1996-97 Scoring

* – rookie

Regular Season

Pos	#	Player	Team	GP	G	A	Pts	+/–	PIM	PP	SH	GW	GT	S	%
C	16	Jozef Stumpel	BOS	78	21	55	76	-22	14	6	0	1	0	168	12.5
L	21	Ted Donato	BOS	67	25	26	51	-9	37	6	2	2	0	172	14.5
D	77	Ray Bourque	BOS	62	19	31	50	-11	18	8	1	3	1	230	8.3
R	41	Jason Allison	WSH	53	5	17	22	-3	25	1	0	1	0	71	7.0
			BOS	19	3	9	12	-3	9	1	0	0	0	28	10.7
			TOTAL	72	8	26	34	-6	34	2	0	1	0	99	8.1
R	19	Rob Dimaio	BOS	72	13	15	28	-21	82	0	3	2	0	152	8.6
D	32	Don Sweeney	BOS	82	3	23	26	-5	39	0	0	0	0	113	2.7
R	23	Steve Heinze	BOS	30	17	8	25	-8	27	4	2	2	0	96	17.7
R	43	Jean-Yves Roy	BOS	52	10	15	25	-8	22	2	0	1	1	100	10.0
L	42	Tim Sweeney	BOS	36	10	11	21	0	14	2	0	2	0	65	15.4
R	27	* Landon Wilson	COL	9	1	2	3	1	23	0	0	0	0	7	14.3
			BOS	40	7	10	17	-6	49	0	0	0	0	76	9.2
			TOTAL	49	8	12	20	-5	72	0	0	0	0	83	9.6
C	11	* Anson Carter	WSH	19	3	2	5	0	7	1	0	1	0	28	10.7
			BOS	19	8	5	13	-7	2	1	1	1	0	51	15.7
			TOTAL	38	11	7	18	-7	9	2	1	2	0	79	13.9
R	33	Sheldon Kennedy	BOS	56	8	10	18	-17	30	0	4	0	0	65	12.3
D	46	Barry Richter	BOS	50	5	13	18	-7	32	1	0	0	0	79	6.3
L	65	Brett Harkins	BOS	44	4	14	18	-3	8	3	0	2	0	52	7.7
L	20	Todd Elik	BOS	31	4	12	16	-12	16	1	0	0	0	72	5.6
R	36	Jeff Odgers	BOS	80	7	8	15	-15	197	1	0	1	0	84	8.3
L	29	Troy Mallette	BOS	68	6	8	14	-8	155	0	0	2	1	61	9.8
D	18	Kyle McLaren	BOS	58	5	9	14	-9	54	0	0	1	0	68	7.4
R	45	Sandy Moger	BOS	34	10	3	13	-12	45	3	0	0	0	54	18.5
D	47	* Mattias Timander	BOS	41	1	8	9	-9	14	0	0	0	1	62	1.6
D	38	Jon Rohloff	BOS	37	3	5	8	-14	31	1	0	0	0	69	4.3
C	25	Trent McCleary	BOS	59	3	5	8	-16	33	0	0	1	0	41	7.3
D	34	Bob Beers	BOS	27	3	4	7	0	8	1	0	0	0	49	6.1
C	37	Clayton Beddoes	BOS	21	1	2	3	-1	13	0	0	0	0	11	9.1
D	28	Dean Chynoweth	BOS	57	0	3	3	-12	171	0	0	0	0	30	0.0
D	14	* Anders Myrvold	BOS	9	0	2	2	-1	4	0	0	0	0	8	0.0
L	49	* Andre Roy	BOS	10	0	2	2	-5	12	0	0	0	0	12	0.0
D	62	* Yevgeny Shaldybin	BOS	3	1	0	1	-2	0	0	0	0	0	5	20.0
L	17	* Davis Payne	BOS	15	0	1	1	-4	7	0	0	0	0	8	0.0
L	26	Cameron Stewart	BOS	15	0	1	1	-2	4	0	0	0	0	21	0.0
C	48	* Randy Robitaille	BOS	1	0	0	0	0	0	0	0	0	0	0	0.0
G	31	Tim Cheveldae	BOS	2	0	0	0	0	0	0	0	0	0	0	0.0
L	14	* Kevin Sawyer	BOS	2	0	0	0	0	0	0	0	0	0	0	0.0
G	1	* Paxton Schafer	BOS	3	0	0	0	0	0	0	0	0	0	0	0.0
L	40	* P.C. Drouin	BOS	3	0	0	0	1	0	0	0	0	0	1	0.0
C	52	David Emma	BOS	5	0	0	0	-1	0	0	0	0	0	3	0.0
G	39	* Scott Bailey	BOS	8	0	0	0	0	0	0	0	0	0	0	0.0
G	35	* Robbie Tallas	BOS	28	0	0	0	0	0	0	0	0	0	0	0.0
D	44	Dean Malkoc	BOS	33	0	0	0	-14	70	0	0	0	0	7	0.0
G	30	Jim Carey	WSH	40	0	0	0	0	2	0	0	0	0	0	0.0
			BOS	19	0	0	0	0	0	0	0	0	0	0	0.0
			TOTAL	59	0	0	0	0	2	0	0	0	0	0	0.0

Goaltending

No.	Goaltender	GPI	Mins	Avg	W	L	T	EN	SO	GA	SA	S%
31	Tim Cheveldae	2	93	3.23	0	1	0	1	0	5	33	.848
35	* Robbie Tallas	28	1244	3.33	8	12	1	1	1	69	587	.882
30	Bill Ranford	37	2147	3.49	12	16	8	0	2	125	1102	.887
39	* Scott Bailey	8	394	3.65	1	5	0	2	0	24	181	.867
30	Jim Carey	19	1004	3.82	5	13	0	2	0	64	496	.871
1	* Paxton Schafer	3	77	4.68	0	0	0	1	0	6	25	.760
	Totals	**82**	**4982**	**3.61**	**26**	**47**	**9**	**7**	**3**	**300**	**2431**	**.877**

Coaching History

Arthur Ross, 1924-25 to 1927-28; Cy Denneny, 1928-29; Arthur Ross, 1929-30 to 1933-34; Frank Patrick, 1934-35 to 1935-36; Arthur Ross, 1936-37 to 1938-39; "Cooney" Weiland, 1939-40 to 1940-41; Arthur Ross, 1941-42 to 1944-45; "Dit" Clapper, 1945-46 to 1948-49; George Boucher, 1949-50; Lynn Patrick, 1950-51 to 1953-54; Lynn Patrick and Milt Schmidt, 1954-55; Milt Schmidt, 1955-56 to 1960-61; Phil Watson, 1961-62; Phil Watson and Milt Schmidt, 1962-63; Milt Schmidt, 1963-64 to 1965-66; Harry Sinden, 1966-67 to 1969-70; Tom Johnson, 1970-71 to 1971-72; Tom Johnson and "Bep" Guidolin, 1972-73; "Bep" Guidolin, 1973-74; Don Cherry, 1974-75 to 1978-79; Fred Creighton and Harry Sinden, 1979-80; Gerry Cheevers, 1980-81 to 1983-84; Gerry Cheevers and Harry Sinden, 1984-85; "Butch" Goring, 1985-86; "Butch" Goring and Terry O'Reilly, 1986-87; Terry O'Reilly, 1987-88 to 1988-89; Mike Milbury, 1989-90 to 1990-91; Rick Bowness, 1991-92; Brian Sutter, 1992-93 to 1994-95; Steve Kasper, 1995-96 to 1996-97; Pat Burns, 1997-98.

Coaching Record

		Regular Season					Playoffs			
Season	**Team**	**Games**	**W**	**L**	**T**	**%**	**Games**	**W**	**L**	**%**
1983-84	Hull (QMJHL)	70	25	45	0	.357	....	....	....	....
1984-85	Hull (QMJHL)	68	33	34	1	.493	5	1	4	.200
1985-86	Hull (QMJHL)	72	54	18	0	.750	15	15	0	1.000
1986-87	Hull (QMJHL)	70	26	39	5	.407	8	4	4	.500
1987-88	Sherbrooke (AHL)	80	42	34	4	.550	6	2	4	.333
1988-89	**Montreal (NHL)**	**80**	**53**	**18**	**9**	**.719**	**21**	**14**	**7**	**.667**
1989-90	**Montreal (NHL)**	**80**	**41**	**28**	**11**	**.581**	**11**	**5**	**6**	**.455**
1990-91	**Montreal (NHL)**	**80**	**39**	**30**	**11**	**.556**	**13**	**7**	**6**	**.538**
1991-92	**Montreal (NHL)**	**80**	**41**	**28**	**11**	**.581**	**11**	**4**	**7**	**.364**
1992-93	**Toronto (NHL)**	**84**	**44**	**29**	**11**	**.589**	**21**	**11**	**10**	**.524**
1993-94	**Toronto (NHL)**	**84**	**43**	**29**	**12**	**.583**	**18**	**9**	**9**	**.500**
1994-95	**Toronto (NHL)**	**48**	**21**	**19**	**8**	**.521**	**7**	**3**	**4**	**.429**
1995-96	**Toronto (NHL)**	**65**	**25**	**30**	**10**	**.462**	....	....	....	....
	NHL Totals	**601**	**307**	**211**	**83**	**.580**	**102**	**53**	**49**	**.520**

Club Records

Team

(Figures in brackets for season records are games played; records for fewest points, wins, ties, losses, goals, goals against are for 70 or more games)

Most Points	121	1970-71 (78)
Most Wins	57	1970-71 (78)
Most Ties	21	1954-55 (70)
Most Losses	47	1961-62 (70), 1996-97 (82)
Most Goals	399	1970-71 (78)
Most Goals Against	306	1961-62 (70)
Fewest Points	38	1961-62 (70)
Fewest Wins	14	1962-63 (70)
Fewest Ties	5	1972-73 (78)
Fewest Losses	13	1971-72 (78)
Fewest Goals	147	1955-56 (70)
Fewest Goals Against	172	1952-53 (70)

Longest Winning Streak

Overall	14	Dec. 3/29-Jan. 9/30
Home	*20	Dec. 3/29-Mar. 18/30
Away	8	Feb. 17-Mar. 8/72, Mar. 15-Apr. 14/93

Longest Undefeated Streak

Overall	23	Dec. 22/40-Feb. 23/41 (15 wins, 8 ties)
Home	27	Nov. 22/70-Mar. 20/71 (26 wins, 1 tie)
Away	15	Dec. 22/40-Mar. 16/41 (9 wins, 6 ties)

Longest Losing Streak

Overall	11	Dec. 3/24-Jan. 5/25
Home	*11	Dec. 8/24-Feb. 17/25
Away	14	Dec. 27/64-Feb. 21/65

Longest Winless Streak

Overall	20	Jan. 28-Mar. 11/62 (16 losses, 4 ties)
Home	11	Dec. 8/24-Feb. 17/25 (11 losses)
Away	14	Three times
Most Shutouts, Season	15	1927-28 (44)
Most PIM, Season	2,443	1987-88 (80)
Most Goals, Game	14	Jan. 21/45 (NYR 3 at Bos. 14)

Individual

Most Seasons	21	John Bucyk
Most Games	1,436	John Bucyk
Most Goals, Career	545	John Bucyk
Most Assists, Career	1,001	Ray Bourque
Most Points, Career	1,363	Ray Bourque (362G, 1,001A)
Most PIM, Career	2,095	Terry O'Reilly
Most Shutouts, Career	74	Tiny Thompson
Longest Consecutive Games Streak	418	John Bucyk (Jan. 23/69-Mar. 2/75)
Most Goals, Season	76	Phil Esposito (1970-71)
Most Assists, Season	102	Bobby Orr (1970-71)
Most Points, Season	152	Phil Esposito (1970-71; 76G, 76A)
Most PIM, Season	304	Jay Miller (1987-88)
Most Points, Defenseman, Season	*139	Bobby Orr (1970-71; 37G, 102A)
Most Points, Center, Season	152	Phil Esposito (1970-71; 76G, 76A)
Most Points, Right Wing, Season	105	Ken Hodge (1970-71; 43G, 62A), Ken Hodge (1973-74; 50G, 55A), Rick Middleton (1983-84; 47G, 58A)
Most Points, Left Wing, Season	116	John Bucyk (1970-71; 51G, 65A)
Most Points, Rookie, Season	102	Joe Juneau (1992-93; 32G, 70A)
Most Shutouts, Season	15	Hal Winkler (1927-28)
Most Goals, Game	4	Several players
Most Assists, Game	6	Ken Hodge (Feb. 9/71), Bobby Orr (Jan. 1/73)
Most Points, Game	7	Bobby Orr (Nov. 15/73; 3G, 4A), Phil Esposito (Dec. 19/74; 3G, 4A), Barry Pederson (Apr. 4/82; 3G, 4A), Cam Neely (Oct. 16/88; 3G, 4A)

* NHL Record.

Retired Numbers

2	Eddie Shore	1926-1940
3	Lionel Hitchman	1925-1934
4	Bobby Orr	1966-1976
5	Dit Clapper	1927-1947
7	Phil Esposito	1967-1975
9	John Bucyk	1957-1978
15	Milt Schmidt	1936-1955

All-time Record vs. Other Clubs

Regular Season

		At Home							On Road							Total					
	GP	W	L	T	GF	GA	PTS	GP	W	L	T	GF	GA	PTS	GP	W	L	T	GF	GA	PTS
Anaheim	3	2	1	0	14	10	4	3	1	1	1	9	6	3	6	3	2	1	23	16	7
Buffalo	89	51	27	11	359	274	113	89	31	44	14	275	335	76	178	82	71	25	634	609	189
Calgary	41	25	10	6	145	111	56	40	21	16	3	143	150	45	81	46	26	9	288	261	101
Chicago	278	159	86	33	1008	786	351	280	93	143	44	748	904	230	558	252	229	77	1756	1690	581
Colorado	57	30	19	8	227	178	68	59	33	20	6	255	214	72	116	63	39	14	482	392	140
Dallas	55	40	6	9	248	131	89	55	29	15	11	207	157	69	110	69	21	20	455	288	158
Detroit	281	151	87	43	992	747	345	280	76	152	52	702	938	204	561	227	239	95	1694	1685	549
Edmonton	25	17	6	2	110	73	36	24	12	9	3	86	84	27	49	29	15	5	196	157	63
Florida	8	3	3	2	19	20	8	7	4	3	0	16	16	8	15	7	6	2	35	36	16
Hartford	63	43	14	6	252	167	92	61	27	27	7	217	215	61	124	70	41	13	469	382	153
Los Angeles	56	42	10	4	267	154	88	55	30	19	6	208	192	66	111	72	29	10	475	346	154
Montreal	317	145	118	54	938	863	344	316	88	183	45	737	1078	221	633	233	301	99	1675	1941	565
New Jersey	42	27	11	4	184	133	58	39	22	9	8	138	105	52	81	49	20	12	322	238	110
NY Islanders	45	25	10	10	177	130	60	47	23	19	5	158	157	51	92	48	29	15	335	287	111
NY Rangers	284	151	92	41	1029	800	343	288	109	125	54	809	875	272	572	260	217	95	1838	1675	615
Ottawa	14	11	3	0	65	42	22	13	10	1	2	49	25	22	27	21	4	2	114	67	44
Philadelphia	62	40	14	8	254	180	88	59	26	27	6	175	204	58	121	66	41	14	429	384	146
Phoenix	24	17	4	3	112	79	37	25	13	10	2	95	91	28	49	30	14	5	207	170	65
Pittsburgh	63	45	12	6	292	187	96	65	27	27	11	246	233	65	128	72	39	17	538	420	161
St. Louis	53	34	11	8	233	143	76	54	23	22	9	190	171	55	107	57	33	17	423	314	131
San Jose	5	4	0	1	21	15	9	5	3	0	2	24	13	8	10	7	0	3	45	28	17
Tampa Bay	8	6	1	1	31	18	13	9	4	3	2	28	26	10	17	10	4	3	59	44	23
Toronto	282	151	84	47	926	754	349	282	86	148	48	734	961	220	564	237	232	95	1660	1715	569
Vancouver	45	36	5	4	201	105	76	46	24	14	8	196	154	56	91	60	19	12	397	259	132
Washington	42	24	13	5	166	119	53	43	41	11	10	155	122	52	83	45	23	15	321	241	105
Defunct Clubs	164	112	39	13	525	306	237	164	79	67	18	496	440	176	328	191	106	31	1021	746	413
Totals	**2406**	**1391**	**686**	**329**	**8795**	**6525**	**3111**	**2406**	**915**	**1114**	**377**	**7096**	**7866**	**2207**	**4812**	**2306**	**1800**	**706**	**15891**	**14391**	**5318**

Playoffs

	Series	W	L	GP	W	L	T	GF	GA	Last Mtg.	Round	Result
Buffalo	6	5	1	33	19	14	0	132	113	1993	DSF	L 0-4
Chicago	6	5	1	22	16	5	1	97	63	1978	QF	W 4-0
Colorado	2	1	1	11	6	5	0	37	36	1983	DSF	W 3-1
Dallas	1	0	1	3	0	3	0	13	20	1981	PR	L 0-3
Detroit	7	4	3	33	19	14	0	96	98	1957	SF	W 4-1
Edmonton	2	0	2	9	1	8	0	20	41	1990	F	L 1-4
Florida	1	0	1	5	1	4	0	16	22	1996	CQF	L 1-4
Hartford	2	2	0	13	8	5	0	24	17	1991	DSF	W 4-2
Los Angeles	2	2	0	13	8	5	0	56	38	1977	QF	W 4-2
Montreal	28	7	21	139	52	87	0	339	430	1994	CQF	W 4-3
New Jersey	3	1	2	18	7	11	0	52	55	1995	CQF	L 1-4
NY Islanders	2	0	2	11	3	8	0	35	49	1983	CF	L 2-4
NY Rangers	9	6	3	42	22	18	2	114	104	1973	QF	L 1-4
Philadelphia	4	2	2	20	11	9	0	60	57	1978	SF	W 4-1
Pittsburgh	4	2	2	19	9	10	0	62	67	1992	CF	L 0-4
St. Louis	2	2	0	8	8	0	0	48	15	1972	SF	W 4-0
Toronto	13	5	8	62	30	31	1	153	150	1974	QF	W 4-0
Washington	1	1	0	4	4	0	0	15	6	1990	CF	W 4-0
Defunct Clubs	3	1	2	11	4	5	2	20	20			
Totals	**98**	**46**	**52**	**476**	**228**	**242**	**6**	**1405**	**1422**			

Calgary totals include Atlanta, 1972-73 to 1979-80. Colorado totals include Quebec, 1979-80 to 1994-95. Dallas totals include Minnesota, 1967-68 to 1992-93. New Jersey totals include Kansas City, 1974-75 to 1975-76, and Colorado Rockies, 1976-77 to 1981-82. Phoenix totals include Winnipeg, 1979-80 to 1995-96.

Playoff Results 1997-93

Year	Round	Opponent	Result	GF	GA
1996	CQF	Florida	L 1-4	16	22
1995	CQF	New Jersey	L 1-4	5	14
1994	CSF	New Jersey	L 2-4	17	22
	CQF	Montreal	W 4-3	22	20
1993	DSF	Buffalo	L 0-4	12	19

Abbreviations: Round: F – Final; **CF** – conference final; **CQF** – conference quarter-final; **CSF** – conference semi-final; **DF** – division final; **DSF** – division semi-final; **SF** – semi-final; **QF** – quarter-final; **PR** – preliminary round.

1996-97 Results

Oct.	5		NY Rangers	4-4	11 at Montreal	3-6
	7		Phoenix	2-5	13 Ottawa	3-4
	12	at	San Jose	5-3	14 at New Jersey	2-4
	14	at	Vancouver	5-4	20 Washington	2-3
	17	at	Los Angeles	2-4	22 at Ottawa	4-1
	20	at	Anaheim	5-1	23 Florida	1-4
	24		Toronto	1-2	25 Colorado	4-1
	26		Detroit	1-2	30 at Florida	1-3
	29		New Jersey	5-2	Feb. 1 at Tampa Bay	3-0
	31		Hartford	4-4	2 at NY Rangers	3-3
Nov.	2		NY Rangers	2-5	4 Ottawa	3-4
	4		Los Angeles	4-4	6 Hartford	3-5
	6	at	Hartford	1-5	8 St. Louis	1-3
	7		Edmonton	0-6	11 at Calgary	1-5
	9	at	Ottawa	4-3	12 at Edmonton	3-4
	14		Pittsburgh	2-1	15 at Phoenix	4-5
	18		San Jose	4-2	18 at Colorado	3-5
	19	at	Washington	2-2	20 at Chicago	3-5
	21		Montreal	2-6	23 at Buffalo	1-5
	23		Buffalo	2-5	24 at Washington	1-5
	26		Philadelphia	2-0	27 Tampa Bay	6-2
	29		Vancouver	7-3	Mar. 1 Philadelphia	5-5
	30	at	Pittsburgh	2-6	3 at Toronto	2-4
Dec.	4	at	Montreal	4-3	6 at NY Islanders	2-5
	5		Hartford	2-4	8 at Tampa Bay	6-4
	7		Calgary	1-1	9 at Florida	3-1
	9		Anaheim	2-5	12 at Hartford	3-6
	12		New Jersey	4-7	13 Montreal	4-3
	14		Buffalo	0-4	15 NY Islanders	5-2
	15	at	Philadelphia	0-6	17 at Buffalo	1-5
	17	at	Pittsburgh	6-4	19 at Detroit	1-4
	19		Tampa Bay	3-0	22 Ottawa	4-5
	21		Washington	4-3	24 at Montreal	1-3
	23		Chicago	3-3	27 NY Islanders	3-6
	27	at	Dallas	4-6	29 at NY Islanders	2-8
	29	at	St. Louis	2-4	Apr. 3 at NY Rangers	4-5
Jan.	1	at	Ottawa	2-3	5 Florida	4-2
	2	at	Hartford	5-4	8 at Pittsburgh	1-3
	4		Dallas	3-2	10 at Buffalo	1-2
	7	at	Philadelphia	3-7	11 at New Jersey	0-2
	9		Montreal	5-4	13 at Pittsburgh	7-3

Entry Draft
Selections 1997-83

1997
Pick
1	Joe Thornton
8	Sergei Samsonov
27	Ben Clymer
54	Mattias Karlin
63	Lee Goren
81	Karol Bartanus
135	Denis Timofeev
162	Joel Trottier
180	Jim Baxter
191	Antti Laaksonen
218	Eric Van Acker
246	Jay Henderson

1996
Pick
8	Johnathan Aitken
45	Henry Kuster
53	Eric Naud
80	Jason Doyle
100	Trent Whitfield
132	Elias Abrahamsson
155	Chris Lane
182	Thomas Brown
208	Bob Prier
234	Anders Soderberg

1995
Pick
9	Kyle McLaren
21	Sean Brown
47	Paxton Schafer
73	Bill McCauley
99	Cameron Mann
151	Yevgeny Shaldybin
177	Per Johan Axelsson
203	Sergei Zhukov
229	Jonathan Murphy

1994
Pick
21	Evgeni Ryabchikov
47	Daniel Goneau
99	Eric Nickulas
125	Darren Wright
151	Andre Roy
177	Jeremy Schaefer
229	John Grahame
255	Neil Savary
281	Andrei Yakhanov

1993
Pick
25	Kevyn Adams
51	Matt Alvey
88	Charles Paquette
103	Shawn Bates
129	Andrei Sapozhnikov
155	Milt Mastad
181	Ryan Golden
207	Hal Gill
233	Joel Prpic
259	Joakim Persson

1992
Pick
16	Dmitri Kvartalnov
55	Sergei Zholtok
112	Scott Bailey
133	Jiri Dopita
136	Grigori Panteleev
184	Kurt Seher
208	Mattias Timander
232	Chris Crombie
256	Denis Chervyakov
257	Evgeny Pavlov

1991
Pick
18	Glen Murray
40	Jozef Stumpel
62	Marcel Cousineau
84	Brad Tiley
106	Mariusz Czerkawski
150	Gary Golczewski
172	John Moser
194	Daniel Hodge
216	Steve Norton
238	Stephen Lombardi
260	Torsten Kienass

1990
Pick
21	Bryan Smolinski
63	Cameron Stewart
84	Jerome Buckley
105	Mike Bales
126	Mark Woolf
147	Jim Mackey
168	John Gruden
189	Darren Wetherill
210	Dean Capuano
231	Andy Bezeau
252	Ted Miskolczi

1989
Pick
17	Shayne Stevenson
38	Mike Parson
57	Wes Walz
80	Jackson Penney
101	Mark Montanari
122	Stephen Foster
143	Otto Hascak
164	Rick Allain
185	James Lavish
206	Geoff Simpson
227	David Franzosa

1988
Pick
18	Robert Cimetta
60	Stephen Heinze
81	Joe Juneau
102	Daniel Murphy
123	Derek Geary
165	Mark Krys
186	Jon Rohloff
228	Eric Reisman
249	Doug Jones

1987
Pick
3	Glen Wesley
14	Stephane Quintal
56	Todd Lalonde
67	Darwin McPherson
77	Matt Delguidice
98	Ted Donato
119	Matt Glennon
140	Rob Cheevers
161	Chris Winnes
182	Paul Ohman
203	Casey Jones
224	Eric Lemarque
245	Sean Gorman

1986
Pick
13	Craig Janney
34	Pekka Tirkkonen
76	Dean Hall
97	Matt Pesklewis
118	Garth Premak
139	Paul Beraldo
160	Brian Ferreira
181	Jeff Flaherty
202	Greg Hawgood
223	Staffan Malmqvist
244	Joel Gardner

1985
Pick
31	Alain Cote
52	Bill Ranford
73	Jaime Kelly
94	Steve Moore
115	Gord Hynes
136	Per Martinelle
157	Randy Burridge
178	Gord Cruickshank
199	Dave Buda
210	Bob Beers
220	John Byce
241	Marc West

1984
Pick
19	Dave Pasin
40	Ray Podloski
61	Jeff Cornelius
82	Robert Joyce
103	Mike Bishop
124	Randy Oswald
145	Mark Thietke
166	Don Sweeney
186	Kevin Heffernan
207	J.D. Urbanic
227	Bill Kopecky
248	Jim Newhouse

1983
Pick
21	Nevin Markwart
42	Greg Johnston
62	Greg Puhalski
82	Alain Larochelle
102	Allen Pederson
122	Terry Taillefer
142	Ian Armstrong
162	Francois Olivier
182	Harri Laurilla
202	Paul Fitzsimmons
222	Norm Foster
242	Greg Murphy

Club Directory

FleetCenter
One FleetCenter, Suite 250
Boston, Massachusetts
02114-1303
Phone **617/624-1900**
FAX 617/523-7184
Capacity: 17,565

Executive
Owner and Governor	Jeremy M. Jacobs
Alternative Governor	Louis Jacobs
President, General Manager and Alternative Governor	Harry Sinden
Vice President	Tom Johnson
Assistant General Manager	Mike O'Connell
Sr. Assistant to the President	Nate Greenberg
General Counsel	Michael Wall
Director of Administration	Dale Hamilton
Assistant to the President	Joe Curnane
Administrative Assistant/Team Travel Coord.	Carol Gould
Receptionist	Karen Ondo

Coaching Staff
Head Coach	Pat Burns
Assistant Coaches	Jacques Laperriere, Bob Francis
Coach, Providence Bruins	Tom McVie
Assistant Coach, Providence Bruins	Rod Langway
Coach, Charlotte Checkers	John Marks

Scouting Staff
Director of Scouting	Scott Bradley
Director of Player Evaluation	Bart Bradley
Director of Development	Bob Tindall
Director of Scouting Information	Jeff Gorton
Scouting Staff	Daniel Dore (Quebec/Ontario); Scott McLellan (Ontario); Jean Ratelle (New England); Don Saatzer (Minnesota/USHL); Don Matheson (Quebec); Ernie Gare (WHL); Svenake Svensson (Europe); Yuri Karmanov (CIS); Gerry Cheevers, Jim Morrison and Tim O'Connell (Pro Leagues)

Communications Staff
Director of Media Relations	Heidi Holland
Media Relations Assistant	Greg Post
Director of Community Relations, & Marketing Services	Sue Byrne
Community Relations & Marketing Services Assistant	Brian Oates
Director of Alumni Services	John Bucyk
Administrative Assistant, Alumni Office	Mal Viola

Ticketing and Finance Staff
Director of Ticket Operations	Matt Brennan
Assistant Director of Ticket Operations	Jim Foley
Ticket Office Assistants	Linda Bartlett, Justin Brennan
Accounting Manager	Rick McGlinchey
Accounts Payable	Barbara Johnson

Medical and Training Staff
Athletic Trainer	Don Del Negro
Physical Therapist	Tim Trahant
Rehabilitation Consultant	Jim Kausek, AdvantageHEALTH Corp.
Equipment Manager	Ken Fleger
Assistant Equipment Manager	Keith Robinson
Team Physicians	Dr. Bertram Zarins, Dr. Ashby Moncure, Dr. John J. Boyle
Team Dentists	Dr. Edwin Riley, DMD; Dr. Bruce Donoff, DMD, MD; Dr. Kenneth Kahn, DDS
Team Opthalmic Consultant	Dr. Bradford Shingleton
Team Psychologist	Dr. Fred Neff

Television and Radio
TV Outlets	New England Sports Network (NESN) and UPN38-WSBK
Radio Station	WBZ (1030 AM)
Broadcasters, UPN38-WSBK	Dave Shea and Andy Brickley
NESN	Dale Arnold and Gord Kluzak
Radio	Bob Neumeier and Bob Beers

Miscellaneous
Club Colors	Gold, Black and White
Ice Surface	200 feet by 85 feet
Website	www.bostonbruins.com

General Managers' History

Arthur Ross, 1924-25 to 1953-54; Lynn Patrick, 1954-55 to 1964-65; Leighton "Hap" Emms, 1965-66 to 1966-67; Milt Schmidt, 1967-68 to 1971-72; Harry Sinden, 1972-73 to date.

President and General Manager

SINDEN, HARRY
President and General Manager, Boston Bruins.
Born in Collins Bay, Ont., September 14, 1932.

Harry Sinden enters his ninth season as the Bruins' president and his 26th season as the club's general manager.

Sinden's name is synonymous with the Bruins organization for over 35 years. He has been instrumental in bringing a Stanley Cup, six Conference titles and ten Division championships to Boston. On October 17, 1995 with a 7-4 Boston win at St. Louis, he became the first general manager in the history of the NHL to record 1,000 victories as a GM.

His many accomplishments, in addition to his knowledge and experience, led to his 1983 induction into the Hockey Hall of Fame in the esteemed Builder's category as he became the 23rd Bruin enshrined.

Sinden was a top amateur player in Canada as a defenseman who captained his Whitby Dunlops team to both the 1957 Allan Cup as Canada's Senior Amateur Champions and the 1958 World Championship title. He also competed in the 1960 Olympics in Squaw Valley, bringing a silver medal home to Canada.

He came to the Bruins organization in 1961 as he assumed the position of player-coach in Kingston, Ontario. After coaching Boston's minor league affiliate in Minneapolis, he became a player-coach in Oklahoma City and led that team to the 1966 CHL championship with eight consecutive victories. He moved to Boston to assume the Bruins head coaching reins in 1966-67.

In 1972 he served as coach of Team Canada in the classic series between NHL players and the Soviet Union.

Sinden and his wife, Eleanor, reside in Winchester, MA. They have four daughters.

NHL Coaching Record

Season	Team	Games	Regular Season W	L	T	%	Playoffs Games	W	L	%
1966-67	Boston	70	17	43	10	.314				
1967-68	Boston	74	37	27	10	.568	4	0	4	.000
1968-69	Boston	76	42	18	16	.658	10	6	4	.600
1969-70	Boston	76	40	17	19	.651	14	12	2	.857*
1979-80	Boston	10	4	6	0	.400	9	4	5	.444
1984-85	Boston	24	11	10	3	.521	5	2	3	.400
	NHL Totals	330	151	121	58	.545	42	24	18	.571

* Stanley Cup win.

Buffalo Sabres

1996-97 Results: 40w-30l-12t 92pts. First, Northeast Division

Derek Plante's dramatic overtime goal in game seven of the Eastern Conference Quarter-finals against Ottawa propelled Buffalo to its first playoff round win since 1993.

1997-98 Schedule

Oct.	Wed.	1	at St. Louis		Thu.	8	at Los Angeles
	Fri.	3	at Washington		Sat.	10	at San Jose
	Sun.	5	at Tampa Bay		Wed.	14	at Toronto
	Tue.	7	Dallas		Thu.	15	Vancouver
	Thu.	9	Washington		Tue.	20	at Philadelphia
	Sat.	11	at New Jersey		Wed.	21	Carolina
	Wed.	15	at Carolina		Fri.	23	Tampa Bay
	Fri.	17	Montreal		Tue.	27	St. Louis
	Sun.	19	at Chicago*		Fri.	30	Phoenix
	Wed.	22	Calgary	Feb.	Sun.	1	at Florida
	Sun.	26	at Phoenix		Mon.	2	at Tampa Bay
	Tue.	28	at Colorado		Wed.	4	Boston
	Fri.	31	at Carolina		Fri.	6	Pittsburgh
Nov.	Sat.	1	at Florida		Sat.	7	at Montreal
	Thu.	6	Florida		Wed.	25	Toronto
	Sat.	8	at Pittsburgh		Thu.	26	at Boston
	Mon.	10	Edmonton	Mar.	Sun.	1	at Washington*
	Thu.	13	Washington		Mon.	2	at NY Rangers
	Sat.	15	New Jersey		Fri.	6	NY Islanders
	Thu.	20	at Boston		Sat.	7	at Montreal
	Sat.	22	NY Islanders*		Tue.	10	at NY Islanders
	Mon.	24	at Pittsburgh		Thu.	12	San Jose
	Wed.	26	Philadelphia		Sat.	14	at Pittsburgh*
	Fri.	28	NY Rangers		Sun.	15	Pittsburgh*
Dec.	Mon.	1	at Philadelphia		Tue.	17	Chicago
	Wed.	3	Anaheim		Thu.	19	Florida
	Fri.	5	Tampa Bay		Sat.	21	Boston*
	Sat.	6	at Ottawa		Tue.	24	at Calgary
	Thu.	11	at Boston		Thu.	26	at Vancouver
	Fri.	12	Carolina		Fri.	27	at Edmonton
	Mon.	15	at Dallas		Sun.	29	at Detroit
	Wed.	17	at NY Islanders	Apr.	Wed.	1	Los Angeles
	Fri.	19	Montreal		Fri.	3	Boston
	Sun.	21	at NY Rangers		Sun.	5	Ottawa*
	Tue.	23	Detroit		Wed.	8	Carolina
	Fri.	26	NY Rangers		Fri.	10	Montreal
	Sat.	27	at Carolina		Sat.	11	at Ottawa
	Mon.	29	New Jersey		Mon.	13	Philadelphia
	Wed.	31	Ottawa		Wed.	15	at New Jersey
Jan.	Fri.	2	Colorado		Sat.	18	at Montreal
	Wed.	7	at Anaheim		Sun.	19	Ottawa

* Denotes afternoon game.

Franchise date: May 22, 1970

EASTERN NHL **CONFERENCE**

NORTHEAST DIVISION

28th NHL Season

Year-by-Year Record

		Home			Road			Overall							
Season	GP	W	L	T	W	L	T	W	L	T	GF	GA	Pts.	Finished	Playoff Result
1996-97	82	24	11	6	16	19	6	40	30	12	237	208	92	1st, Northeast Div.	Lost Conf. Semi-Final
1995-96	82	19	17	5	14	25	2	33	42	7	247	262	73	5th, Northeast Div.	Out of Playoffs
1994-95	48	15	8	1	7	11	6	22	19	7	130	119	51	4th, Northeast Div.	Lost Conf. Quarter-Final
1993-94	84	22	17	3	21	15	6	43	32	9	282	218	95	4th, Northeast Div.	Lost Conf. Quarter-Final
1992-93	84	25	15	2	13	21	8	38	36	10	335	297	86	4th, Adams Div.	Lost Div. Final
1991-92	80	22	13	5	9	24	7	31	37	12	289	299	74	3rd, Adams Div.	Lost Div. Semi-Final
1990-91	80	15	13	12	16	17	7	31	30	19	292	278	81	3rd, Adams Div.	Lost Div. Semi-Final
1989-90	80	27	11	2	18	16	6	45	27	8	286	248	98	2nd, Adams Div.	Lost Div. Semi-Final
1988-89	80	25	12	3	13	23	4	38	35	7	291	299	83	3rd, Adams Div.	Lost Div. Semi-Final
1987-88	80	19	14	7	18	18	4	37	32	11	283	305	85	3rd, Adams Div.	Lost Div. Semi-Final
1986-87	80	18	14	8	10	26	4	28	44	8	280	308	64	5th, Adams Div.	Out of Playoffs
1985-86	80	23	16	1	14	21	5	37	37	6	296	291	80	5th, Adams Div.	Out of Playoffs
1984-85	80	23	10	7	15	18	7	38	28	14	290	237	90	3rd, Adams Div.	Lost Div. Semi-Final
1983-84	80	25	9	6	23	16	1	48	25	7	315	257	103	2nd, Adams Div.	Lost Div. Semi-Final
1982-83	80	25	7	8	13	22	5	38	29	13	318	285	89	3rd, Adams Div.	Lost Div. Final
1981-82	80	23	8	9	16	18	6	39	26	15	307	273	93	3rd, Adams Div.	Lost Div. Semi-Final
1980-81	80	21	7	12	18	13	9	39	20	21	327	250	99	1st, Adams Div.	Lost Quarter-Final
1979-80	80	27	5	8	20	12	8	47	17	16	318	201	110	1st, Adams Div.	Lost Semi-Final
1978-79	80	19	13	8	17	15	8	36	28	16	280	263	88	2nd, Adams Div.	Lost Prelim. Round
1977-78	80	25	7	8	19	12	9	44	19	17	288	215	105	2nd, Adams Div.	Lost Quarter-Final
1976-77	80	27	8	5	21	16	3	48	24	8	301	220	104	2nd, Adams Div.	Lost Quarter-Final
1975-76	80	28	7	5	18	14	8	46	21	13	339	240	105	2nd, Adams Div.	Lost Quarter-Final
1974-75	80	28	6	6	21	10	9	49	16	15	354	240	113	1st, Adams Div.	Lost Final
1973-74	78	23	10	6	9	24	6	32	34	12	242	250	76	5th, East Div.	Out of Playoffs
1972-73	78	30	6	3	7	21	11	37	27	14	257	219	88	4th, East Div.	Lost Quarter-Final
1971-72	78	11	19	9	5	24	10	16	43	19	203	289	51	6th, East Div.	Out of Playoffs
1970-71	78	16	13	10	8	26	5	24	39	15	217	291	63	5th, East Div.	Out of Playoffs

1997-98 Player Personnel

FORWARDS	HT	WT	S	Place of Birth	Date	1996-97 Club
AUDETTE, Donald	5-8	184	R	Laval, Que.	9/23/69	Buffalo
BARNABY, Matthew	6-0	188	L	Ottawa, Ont.	5/4/73	Buffalo
BIENVENUE, Daniel	6-0	196	L	Val d'Or, Que.	6/10/77	Val d'Or
BROWN, Curtis	6-0	190	L	Unity, Sask.	2/12/76	Buffalo-Rochester
BURRIDGE, Randy	5-9	188	L	Fort Erie, Ont.	1/7/66	Buffalo
DAVIDSON, Matt	6-2	190	R	Flin Flon, Man.	8/9/77	Portland (WHL)
DAVIS, Ryan	6-2	185	R	Hamilton, Ont.	2/16/78	Owen Sound
DAWE, Jason	5-10	189	L	North York, Ont.	5/29/73	Buffalo
DUTIAUME, Mark	6-0	200	L	Winnipeg, Man.	1/31/77	Brandon-Rochester
GROSEK, Michal	6-2	207	R	Vyskov, Czech.	6/1/75	Buffalo
HAMEL, Denis	6-2	200	L	Lachute, Que.	5/10/77	Chicoutimi
HOLZINGER, Brian	5-11	190	R	Parma, OH	10/10/72	Buffalo
LaFONTAINE, Pat	5-10	182	L	St. Louis, MO	2/22/65	Buffalo
MAY, Brad	6-1	206	L	Toronto, Ont.	11/29/71	Buffalo
NICHOL, Scott	5-8	160	R	Edmonton, Alta.	12/31/74	Rochester
PECA, Michael	5-11	181	R	Toronto, Ont.	3/26/74	Buffalo
PLANTE, Derek	5-11	181	L	Cloquet, MN	1/17/71	Buffalo
PRIMEAU, Wayne	6-3	193	L	Scarborough, Ont.	6/4/76	Buffalo-Rochester
RASMUSSEN, Erik	6-2	205	L	Minneapolis, MN	3/28/77	U. Minnesota
RAY, Rob	6-0	203	L	Belleville, Ont.	6/8/68	Buffalo
SATAN, Miroslav	6-1	195	L	Topolcany, Czech.	10/22/74	Edmonton-Buffalo
TARDIF, Patrice	6-2	202	L	Thetford Mines, Que.	10/30/70	Phoenix (IHL)-Detroit (IHL)
VARADA, Vaclav	6-0	200	L	Vsetin, Czech.	4/26/76	Buffalo-Rochester
WALSH, Kurt	6-2	205	R	St. John's, Nfld.	9/26/77	Owen Sound
WARD, Dixon	6-0	200	R	Leduc, Alta.	9/23/68	Buffalo
ZANUTTO, Mike	6-0	190	L	Burlington, Ont.	1/1/77	Oshawa

DEFENSEMEN	HT	WT	S	Place of Birth	Date	1996-97 Club
BOUGHNER, Bob	6-0	206	R	Windsor, Ont.	3/8/71	Buffalo
GRAND PIERRE, Jean-Luc	6-3	207	L	Montreal, Que.	2/2/77	Val d'Or
HURLBUT, Mike	6-2	200	L	Massena, NY	10/7/66	Houston
KLIMENTJEV, Sergei	5-11	200	L	Kiev, USSR	4/5/75	Rochester
MARTONE, Mike	6-2	200	R	Sault Ste. Marie, Ont.	9/26/77	Peterborough
McKEE, Jay	6-3	195	L	Kingston, Ont.	9/8/77	Buffalo-Rochester
NDUR, Rumun	6-2	200	L	Zaria, Nigeria	7/7/75	Buffalo-Rochester
SHANNON, Darryl	6-2	208	L	Barrie, Ont.	6/21/68	Buffalo
SMEHLIK, Richard	6-3	222	L	Ostrava, Czech.	1/23/70	Buffalo
WILSON, Mike	6-6	212	L	Brampton, Ont.	2/26/75	Buffalo
WRIGHT, Shayne	6-0	189	L	Welland, Ont.	6/30/75	Rochester
ZHITNIK, Alexei	5-11	204	L	Kiev, USSR	10/10/72	Buffalo

GOALTENDERS	HT	WT	C	Place of Birth	Date	1996-97 Club
BALES, Michael	6-1	180	L	Prince Albert, Sask.	8/6/71	Ottawa-Baltimore
BIRON, Martin	6-1	154	L	Lac St. Charles, Que.	8/15/77	Beauport-Hull
HASEK, Dominik	5-11	168	L	Pardubice, Czech.	1/29/65	Buffalo
SHIELDS, Steve	6-3	210	L	Toronto, Ont.	7/19/72	Buffalo-Rochester
TREFILOV, Andrei	6-0	190	L	Kirovo-Chepetsk, USSR	8/31/69	Buffalo

General Manager

REGIER, DARCY
General Manager, Buffalo Sabres. Born in Swift Current, Sask., Nov. 27, 1957.

Darcy Regier, 39, became the sixth general manager of the Buffalo Sabres on June 11, 1997 after a lengthy management apprenticeship in the New York Islanders organization. As a player, Regier played eight pro seasons, including parts of the 1982-83 and 1983-84 campaigns with the New York Islanders.

He began his career as an administrator with the Islanders in 1984-85 and went on to serve in a variety of capacities including director of administration, assistant director of hockey operations, assistant coach and assistant general manager. He also served as an assistant coach with Hartford in 1991-92.

While with the Islanders, Regier benefitted from working with talented managers and coaches including Bill Torrey and Al Arbour. As a minor pro player with Indianapolis of the CHL he became associated with another important influence on his hockey career, current Detroit Red Wing executive Jim Devellano.

Regier and his wife Katherine have three sons: Jonathan, 16; Justin, 12; and Jarrett, 4.

Head Coach

RUFF, LINDY
Head Coach, Buffalo Sabres. Born in Warburg, Alta., February, 17, 1960.

A former captain of the Sabres, Lindy Ruff was appointed as the club's 15th head coach on July 21, 1997. As a player, Ruff was drafted 32nd overall by the Sabres in the 1979 Entry Draft. He played both defense and left wing in an NHL career that spanned 12 seasons including 608 regular-season games with Buffalo. He became a playing assistant coach with Rochester of the AHL in 1991-92 and San Diego of the IHL in 1992-93. Ruff's San Diego club set a pro hockey record with 62 wins. In 1993-94 he became an NHL assistant coach for the Florida Panthers, handling the defense and penalty killing units for coach Roger Neilson.

Ruff and his wife Gaye have four children: Brett, 7; Eryn, 6; and twins Brian and Madeleine, 2.

1996-97 Scoring
* – rookie

Regular Season

Pos	#	Player	Team	GP	G	A	Pts	+/-	PIM	PP	SH	GW	GT	S	%
C	26	Derek Plante	BUF	82	27	26	53	14	24	5	0	6	1	191	14.1
C	19	Brian Holzinger	BUF	81	22	29	51	9	54	2	2	6	0	142	15.5
R	28	Donald Audette	BUF	73	28	22	50	-6	48	8	0	5	1	182	15.4
C	27	Michael Peca	BUF	79	20	29	49	26	80	5	6	4	0	137	14.6
R	17	Jason Dawe	BUF	81	22	26	48	14	32	4	1	3	0	136	16.2
R	15	Dixon Ward	BUF	79	13	32	45	17	36	1	2	4	0	93	14.0
R	36	Matthew Barnaby	BUF	68	19	24	43	16	249	2	0	1	0	121	15.7
L	81	Miroslav Satan	EDM	64	17	11	28	-4	22	5	0	2	0	90	18.9
			BUF	12	8	2	10	1	4	2	0	1	0	29	27.6
			TOTAL	76	25	13	38	-3	26	7	0	3	0	119	21.0
D	3	Garry Galley	BUF	71	4	34	38	10	102	1	1	1	0	84	4.8
D	18	Michal Grosek	BUF	82	15	21	36	25	71	1	0	2	1	117	12.8
D	44	Alexei Zhitnik	BUF	80	7	28	35	10	95	3	1	0	1	170	4.1
L	12	Randy Burridge	BUF	55	10	21	31	17	20	1	3	0	0	85	11.8
D	42	Richard Smehlik	BUF	62	11	19	30	19	43	2	0	1	0	100	11.0
D	8	Darryl Shannon	BUF	82	4	19	23	23	112	1	0	1	0	94	4.3
D	4	Mike Wilson	BUF	77	2	9	11	13	51	0	0	1	0	57	3.5
R	32	Rob Ray	BUF	82	7	3	10	3	286	0	0	1	0	45	15.6
D	74	* Jay McKee	BUF	43	1	9	10	3	35	0	0	0	0	29	3.4
C	16	Pat LaFontaine	BUF	13	2	6	8	-8	4	1	0	0	0	38	5.3
D	6	Bob Boughner	BUF	77	1	7	8	12	225	0	0	0	0	34	2.9
C	37	* Curtis Brown	BUF	28	4	3	7	4	18	0	0	1	0	31	12.9
L	10	Brad May	BUF	42	3	4	7	-8	106	1	0	1	0	75	4.0
C	93	Anatoli Semenov	BUF	25	2	4	6	-3	2	1	0	1	0	21	9.5
C	76	* Wayne Primeau	BUF	45	2	4	6	-2	64	0	0	0	0	25	8.0
R	5	Ed Ronan	BUF	18	1	4	5	4	11	0	0	0	0	10	10.0
G	39	Dominik Hasek	BUF	67	0	3	3	0	30	0	0	0	0	0	0.0
D	22	Charlie Huddy	BUF	1	0	0	0	-1	0	0	0	0	0	0	0.0
D	40	* Rumun Ndur	BUF	2	0	0	0	1	0	0	0	0	0	0	0.0
G	30	Andrei Trefilov	BUF	3	0	0	0	0	0	0	0	0	0	0	0.0
L	25	* Vaclav Varada	BUF	5	0	0	0	2	0	0	0	0	0	2	0.0
G	31	* Steve Shields	BUF	13	0	0	0	4	0	0	0	0	0	0	0.0

Goaltending

No.	Goaltender	GPI	Mins	Avg	W	L	T	EN	SO	GA	SA	S%
39	Dominik Hasek	67	4037	2.27	37	20	10	3	5	153	2177	.930
31	* Steve Shields	13	789	2.97	3	8	2	2	0	39	447	.913
30	Andrei Trefilov	3	159	3.77	0	2	0	1	0	10	98	.898
	Totals	82	5003	2.49	40	30	12	6	5	208	2728	.924

Playoffs

Pos	#	Player	Team	GP	G	A	Pts	+/-	PIM	PP	SH	GW	OT	S	%
C	26	Derek Plante	BUF	12	4	6	10	4	4	1	0	2	1	26	15.4
R	28	Donald Audette	BUF	11	4	5	9	-3	6	3	0	0	0	33	12.1
C	19	Brian Holzinger	BUF	12	2	5	7	-3	8	0	1	1	0	20	10.0
L	12	Randy Burridge	BUF	12	5	1	6	-5	2	3	0	0	0	26	19.2
L	18	Michal Grosek	BUF	12	3	3	6	3	8	0	0	0	0	18	16.7
D	3	Garry Galley	BUF	12	0	6	6	2	14	0	0	0	0	22	0.0
D	8	Darryl Shannon	BUF	12	2	3	5	-1	8	1	0	0	0	8	25.0
D	15	Dixon Ward	BUF	12	2	3	5	2	6	0	1	1	0	23	8.7
R	36	Matthew Barnaby	BUF	8	0	4	4	4	36	0	0	0	0	12	0.0
R	17	Jason Dawe	BUF	11	2	1	3	-2	6	0	0	0	0	19	10.5
L	10	Brad May	BUF	12	1	2	3	4	32	0	0	1	0	7	14.3
C	27	Michael Peca	BUF	10	0	2	2	-3	8	0	0	0	0	20	0.0
D	42	Richard Smehlik	BUF	12	0	2	2	4	4	0	0	0	0	17	0.0
R	5	Ed Ronan	BUF	6	1	0	1	-1	6	0	0	1	1	6	16.7
D	44	Alexei Zhitnik	BUF	12	0	1	1	-9	16	0	0	0	0	16	6.3
D	4	Mike Wilson	BUF	10	0	1	1	3	2	0	0	0	0	15	0.0
D	6	Bob Boughner	BUF	11	0	1	1	0	9	0	0	0	0	1	0.0
R	32	Rob Ray	BUF	12	0	1	1	-3	28	0	0	0	0	4	0.0
G	30	Andrei Trefilov	BUF	1	0	0	0	0	0	0	0	0	0	0	0.0
G	39	Dominik Hasek	BUF	3	0	0	0	0	0	0	0	0	0	0	0.0
D	74	* Jay McKee	BUF	3	0	0	0	0	0	0	0	0	0	1	0.0
L	81	Miroslav Satan	BUF	7	0	0	0	-1	0	0	0	0	0	4	0.0
C	76	* Wayne Primeau	BUF	9	0	0	0	-2	6	0	0	0	0	4	0.0
G	31	* Steve Shields	BUF	10	0	0	0	0	9	0	0	0	0	0	0.0

Goaltending

No.	Goaltender	GPI	Mins	Avg	W	L	EN	SO	GA	SA	S%
30	Andrei Trefilov	1	5	.00	0	0	0	0	0	4	1.000
39	Dominik Hasek	3	153	1.96	1	1	0	0	5	68	.926
31	* Steve Shields	10	570	2.74	4	6	3	1	26	334	.922
	Totals	12	734	2.78	5	7	3	1	34	409	.917

General Managers' History

George "Punch" Imlach, 1970-71 to 1977-78; John Anderson (acting), 1978-79; Scotty Bowman, 1979-80 to 1985-86; Scotty Bowman and Gerry Meehan, 1986-87; Gerry Meehan, 1987-88 to 1992-93; John Muckler, 1993-94 to 1996-97; Darcy Regier, 1997-98.

Coaching History

"Punch" Imlach, 1970-71; "Punch" Imlach, Floyd Smith and Joe Crozier, 1971-72; Joe Crozier, 1972-73 to 1973-74; Floyd Smith, 1974-75 to 1976-77; Marcel Pronovost, 1977-78; Marcel Pronovost and Billy Inglis, 1978-79; Scotty Bowman, 1979-80; Roger Neilson, 1980-81; Jim Roberts and Scotty Bowman, 1981-82; Scotty Bowman, 1982-83 to 1984-85; Jim Schoenfeld and Scotty Bowman, 1985-86; Scotty Bowman, Craig Ramsay and Ted Sator, 1986-87; Ted Sator, 1987-88 to 1988-89; Rick Dudley, 1989-90 to 1990-91; Rick Dudley and John Muckler, 1991-92; John Muckler, 1992-93 to 1994-95; Ted Nolan, 1995-96 to 1996-97; Lindy Ruff, 1997-98.

Club Records

Team

(Figures in brackets for season records are games played; records for fewest points, wins, ties, losses, goals, goals against are for 70 or more games)

Most Points	**113**	1974-75 (80)
Most Wins	**49**	1974-75 (80)
Most Ties	**21**	1980-81 (80)
Most Losses	**44**	1986-87 (80)
Most Goals	**354**	1974-75 (80)
Most Goals Against	**308**	1986-87 (80)
Fewest Points	**51**	1971-72 (78)
Fewest Wins	**16**	1971-72 (78)
Fewest Ties	**6**	1985-86 (80)
Fewest Losses	**16**	1974-75 (80)
Fewest Goals	**203**	1971-72 (78)
Fewest Goals Against	**201**	1979-80 (80)
Longest Winning Streak		
Overall	**10**	Jan. 4-23/84
Home	**12**	Nov. 12/72-Jan. 7/73, Oct. 13-Dec. 10/89
Away	***10**	Dec. 10/83-Jan. 23/84
Longest Undefeated Streak		
Overall	**14**	Mar. 6-Apr. 6/80 (8 wins, 6 ties)
Home	**21**	Oct. 8/72-Jan. 7/73 (18 wins, 3 ties)
Away	***10**	Dec. 10/83-Jan. 23/84 (10 wins)
Longest Losing Streak		
Overall	**7**	Oct. 25-Nov. 8/70, Apr. 3-15/93, Oct. 9-22/93
Home	**6**	Oct. 10-Nov. 10/93, Mar. 3-Apr. 3/96
Away	**7**	Oct. 14-Nov. 7/70, Feb. 6-27/71, Jan. 10-Feb. 3/96
Longest Winless Streak		
Overall	**12**	Nov. 23-Dec. 20/91 (8 losses, 4 ties)
Home	**12**	Jan. 27-Mar. 10/91 (7 losses, 5 ties)
Away	**23**	Oct. 30/71-Feb. 19/72 (15 losses, 8 ties)
Most Shutouts, Season	**9**	1993-94 (84)
Most PIM, Season	**2,712**	1991-92 (80)
Most Goals, Game	**14**	Jan. 21/75 (Wsh. 2 at Buf. 14), Mar. 19/81 (Tor. 4 at Buf. 14)

Individual

Most Seasons	**17**	Gilbert Perreault
Most Games	**1,191**	Gilbert Perreault
Most Goals, Career	**512**	Gilbert Perreault
Most Assists, Career	**814**	Gilbert Perreault
Most Points, Career	**1,326**	Gilbert Perreault
Most PIM, Career	**2,032**	Rob Ray
Most Shutouts, Career	**19**	Dominik Hasek
Longest Consecutive Games Streak	**776**	Craig Ramsay (Mar. 27/73-Feb. 10/83)
Most Goals, Season	**76**	Alexander Mogilny (1992-93)
Most Assists, Season	**95**	Pat LaFontaine (1992-93)
Most Points, Season	**148**	Pat LaFontaine (1992-93; 53G, 95A)
Most PIM, Season	**354**	Rob Ray (1991-92)
Most Points, Defenseman, Season	**81**	Phil Housley (1989-90; 21G, 60A)
Most Points, Center, Season	**148**	Pat LaFontaine (1992-93; 53G, 95A)
Most Points, Right Wing, Season	**127**	Alexander Mogilny (1992-93; 76G, 51A)
Most Points, Left Wing, Season	**95**	Richard Martin (1974-75; 52G, 43A)
Most Points, Rookie, Season	**74**	Richard Martin (1971-72; 44G, 30A)
Most Shutouts, Season	**7**	Dominik Hasek (1993-94)
Most Goals, Game	**5**	Dave Andreychuk (Feb. 6/86)
Most Assists, Game	**5**	Gilbert Perreault (Feb. 1/76, Mar. 9/80, Jan. 4/84), Dale Hawerchuk (Jan. 15/92), Pat LaFontaine (Dec. 31/92, Feb. 10/93)
Most Points, Game	**7**	Gilbert Perreault (Feb. 1/76; 2G, 5A)

* NHL Record.

Retired Numbers

2	Tim Horton	1972-1974
7	Rick Martin	1971-1981
11	Gilbert Perreault	1970-1987
14	Rene Robert	1971-1979

Captains' History

Floyd Smith, 1970-71; Gerry Meehan, 1971-72 to 1973-74; Gerry Meehan and Jim Schoenfeld, 1974-75; Jim Schoenfeld, 1975-76 to 1976-77; Danny Gare, 1977-78 to 1980-81; Danny Gare and Gil Perreault, 1981-82; Gil Perreault, 1982-83 to 1985-86; Gil Perreault and Lindy Ruff, 1986-87; Lindy Ruff, 1987-88; Lindy Ruff and Mike Foligno, 1988-89; Mike Foligno, 1989-90; Mike Foligno and Mike Ramsey, 1990-91; Mike Ramsey, 1991-92; Mike Ramsey and Pat LaFontaine, 1992-93; Pat LaFontaine and Alexander Mogilny, 1993-94; Pat LaFontaine, 1994-95 to date.

All-time Record vs. Other Clubs

Regular Season

	At Home							On Road							Total						
	GP	W	L	T	GF	GA	PTS	GP	W	L	T	GF	GA	PTS	GP	W	L	T	GF	GA	PTS
Anaheim	3	1	1	1	6	7	3	3	1	2	0	7	8	2	6	2	3	1	13	15	5
Boston	89	44	31	14	335	275	102	89	27	51	11	274	359	65	178	71	82	25	609	634	167
Calgary	40	22	13	5	166	123	49	40	15	15	10	134	143	40	80	37	28	15	300	266	89
Chicago	47	29	12	6	178	122	64	45	15	24	6	125	147	36	92	44	36	12	303	269	100
Colorado	58	34	16	8	235	189	76	58	18	29	11	182	218	47	116	52	45	19	417	407	123
Dallas	47	25	12	10	173	126	60	48	20	22	6	144	149	46	95	45	34	16	317	275	106
Detroit	47	32	8	7	212	131	71	49	18	26	5	148	182	41	96	50	34	12	360	313	112
Edmonton	25	10	10	5	100	94	25	24	4	18	2	66	106	10	49	14	28	7	166	200	35
Florida	8	6	1	1	30	9	13	7	2	5	0	19	22	4	15	8	6	1	49	31	17
Hartford	62	35	20	7	258	195	77	63	29	25	9	195	191	67	125	64	45	16	453	386	144
Los Angeles	47	23	15	9	191	145	55	48	22	18	8	171	166	52	95	45	33	17	362	311	107
Montreal	84	41	24	19	267	233	101	84	24	49	11	255	346	59	168	65	73	30	522	579	160
New Jersey	40	27	8	5	178	125	59	40	22	10	8	148	122	52	80	49	18	13	326	247	111
NY Islanders	47	25	15	7	166	136	57	47	20	20	7	134	136	47	94	45	35	14	300	272	104
NY Rangers	54	32	16	6	237	177	70	52	15	24	13	143	183	43	106	47	40	19	380	360	113
Ottawa	13	11	2	0	58	19	22	15	10	3	2	52	30	22	28	21	5	2	110	49	44
Philadelphia	49	24	19	6	176	153	54	53	13	31	9	144	196	35	102	37	50	15	320	349	89
Phoenix	24	20	2	2	112	58	42	24	12	10	2	86	77	26	48	32	12	4	198	135	68
Pittsburgh	57	29	13	15	242	157	73	56	16	27	13	190	220	45	113	45	40	28	432	377	118
St. Louis	46	29	12	5	190	142	63	45	13	26	6	117	167	32	91	42	38	11	307	309	95
San Jose	6	6	0	0	34	20	12	5	1	2	2	21	19	4	11	7	2	2	55	39	16
Tampa Bay	9	3	5	1	21	35	7	9	8	1	0	30	16	16	18	11	6	1	51	51	23
Toronto	52	33	16	3	221	149	69	51	23	19	9	188	158	55	103	56	35	12	409	307	124
Vancouver	47	23	16	8	170	140	54	46	14	22	10	150	174	38	93	37	38	18	320	314	92
Washington	42	28	8	6	175	116	62	42	25	10	7	159	112	57	84	53	18	13	334	228	119
Defunct Clubs	23	13	5	5	94	63	31	23	12	8	3	97	76	27	46	25	13	8	191	139	58
Totals	**1066**	**605**	**300**	**161**	**4225**	**3139**	**1371**	**1066**	**399**	**497**	**170**	**3379**	**3723**	**968**	**2132**	**1004**	**797**	**331**	**7604**	**6862**	**2339**

Playoffs

	Series	W	L	GP	W	L	T	GF	GA	Last Mtg.	Round	Result
Boston	6	1	5	33	14	19	0	113	132	1993	DSF	W 4-0
Chicago	2	2	0	9	8	1	0	36	17	1980	QF	W 4-0
Colorado	2	0	2	8	2	6	0	27	35	1985	DSF	L 2-3
Dallas	2	1	1	7	3	4	0	28	26	1981	QF	L 1-4
Montreal	6	2	4	31	13	18	0	94	114	1993	DF	L 0-4
New Jersey	1	0	1	7	3	4	0	14	14	1994	CQF	L 3-4
NY Islanders	3	0	3	16	4	12	0	45	59	1980	SF	L 2-4
NY Rangers	1	1	0	3	2	1	0	11	6	1978	PR	W 2-1
Ottawa	1	1	0	7	4	3	0	14	13	1997	CQF	W 4-3
Philadelphia	4	0	4	21	5	16	0	49	74	1997	CSF	L 1-4
Pittsburgh	1	0	1	3	1	2	0	9	9	1979	PR	L 1-2
St. Louis	1	1	0	3	2	1	0	7	8	1976	PR	W 2-1
Vancouver	2	2	0	7	6	1	0	28	14	1981	PR	W 3-0
Totals	**32**	**11**	**21**	**155**	**67**	**88**	**0**	**475**	**514**			

Calgary totals include Atlanta, 1972-73 to 1979-80. Colorado totals include Quebec, 1979-80 to 1994-95. Dallas totals include Minnesota, 1970-71 to 1992-93. New Jersey totals include Kansas City, 1974-75 to 1975-76, and Colorado Rockies, 1976-77 to 1981-82. Phoenix totals include Winnipeg, 1979-80 to 1995-96.

Playoff Results 1997-93

Year	Round	Opponent	Result	GF	GA
1997	CSF	Philadelphia	L 1-4	13	21
	CQF	Ottawa	W 4-3	14	13
1995	CQF	Philadelphia	L 1-4	13	18
1994	CQF	New Jersey	L 3-4	14	14
1993	DF	Montreal	L 0-4	12	16
	DSF	Boston	W 4-0	19	12

Abbreviations: Round: F – Final;
CF – conference final; **CQF** – conference quarter-final;
CSF – conference semi-final; **DF** – division final;
DSF – division semi-final; **SF** – semi-final;
QF – quarter-final; **PR** – preliminary round.

1996-97 Results

Oct.	4	at	Edmonton	3-4		9	at	Los Angeles	3-6
	6	at	Calgary	0-3		10	at	Anaheim	2-5
	9	at	Vancouver	2-1		12	at	Phoenix	3-2
	12		Detroit	1-6		15	at	NY Islanders	2-1
	15		Tampa Bay	0-4		20		Chicago	2-1
	17		Pittsburgh	4-1		22		Montreal	6-1
	18	at	Washington	4-1		24		Edmonton	1-3
	24		Montreal	6-3		25		Hartford	1-5
	26		Hartford	6-3		29		Pittsburgh	3-1
	27	at	NY Rangers	4-6		31		Dallas	3-1
	30	at	Dallas	0-2	**Feb.**	2		Washington	2-2
Nov.	1	at	St. Louis	4-2		4	at	Philadelphia	1-1
	2	at	Colorado	0-0		6		Florida	1-1
	7		Philadelphia	2-5		8	at	Tampa Bay	3-1
	9	at	Hartford	3-4		9		Ottawa	2-1
	11		Florida	3-2		12		Montreal	2-2
	12	at	Pittsburgh	0-3		16		San Jose	6-2
	14		Colorado	5-4		18		Calgary	5-5
	19	at	Toronto	3-4		21		NY Islanders	5-2
	21		Toronto	6-3		23		Boston	5-1
	23	at	Boston	3-2		27	at	New Jersey	1-4
	26	at	Florida	3-4	**Mar.**	1	at	Ottawa	3-1
	27	at	Tampa Bay	3-0		5		Pittsburgh	4-2
	29		Ottawa	3-0		8	at	Montreal	3-3
	30	at	NY Islanders	3-2		9		New Jersey	1-4
Dec.	4		Vancouver	6-7		11		Philadelphia	3-2
	6		Anaheim	1-1		15	at	Philadelphia	7-5
	7	at	Hartford	4-6		17		Boston	5-1
	11	at	Montreal	3-2		18	at	Pittsburgh	3-5
	13		NY Rangers	0-3		21	at	Washington	4-1
	14	at	Boston	4-0		22	at	Florida	2-3
	18		Tampa Bay	5-3		26		NY Islanders	2-3
	20		Los Angeles	6-2		28	at	Detroit	1-2
	21	at	Ottawa	3-2		30	at	Chicago	2-3
	23	at	New Jersey	0-0	**Apr.**	1	at	NY Rangers	1-1
	26		Hartford	5-1		2		Ottawa	0-2
	28	at	Pittsburgh	0-2		4		NY Rangers	5-1
	31		New Jersey	6-5		7	at	Hartford	2-4
Jan.	3		St. Louis	2-2		10	at	Boston	5-1
	5		Phoenix	5-1		12	at	Ottawa	0-1
	7	at	San Jose	1-1		13		Washington	3-8

Entry Draft Selections 1997-83

1997
Pick
21 Mika Noronen
48 Henrik Tallinder
69 Maxim Afinogenov
75 Jeff Martin
101 Luc Theoret
128 Torrey Diroberto
156 Brian Campbell
184 Jeremy Adduono
212 Kamil Piros
238 Dylan Kemp

1996
Pick
7 Erik Rasmussen
27 Cory Sarich
33 Darren Van Oene
54 Francois Methot
87 Kurt Walsh
106 Mike Martone
115 Alexei Tezikov
142 Ryan Davis
161 Darren Mortier
222 Scott Buhler

1995
Pick
14 Jay McKee
16 Martin Biron
42 Mark Dutiaume
68 Mathieu Sunderland
94 Matt Davidson
111 Marian Menhart
119 Kevin Popp
123 Daniel Bienvenue
172 Brian Scott
198 Mike Zanutto
224 Rob Skrlac

1994
Pick
17 Wayne Primeau
43 Curtis Brown
69 Rumun Ndur
121 Sergei Klimentjev
147 Cal Benazic
168 Steve Plouffe
173 Shane Hnidy
176 Steve Webb
199 Bob Westerby
225 Craig Millar
251 Mark Polak
277 Shayne Wright

1993
Pick
38 Denis Tsygurov
64 Ethan Philpott
116 Richard Safarik
142 Kevin Pozzo
168 Sergei Petrenko
194 Mike Barrie
220 Barrie Moore
246 Chris Davis
272 Scott Nichol

1992
Pick
11 David Cooper
35 Jozef Cierny
59 Ondrej Steiner
80 Dean Melanson
83 Matthew Barnaby
107 Markus Ketterer
108 Yuri Khmylev
131 Paul Rushforth
179 Dean Tiltgen
203 Todd Simon
227 Rick Kowalsky
251 Chris Clancy

1991
Pick
13 Philippe Boucher
35 Jason Dawe
57 Jason Young
72 Peter Ambroziak
101 Steve Shields
123 Sean O'Donnell
124 Brian Holzinger
145 Chris Snell
162 Jiri Kuntos
189 Tony Iob
211 Spencer Meany
233 Mikhail Volkov
255 Michael Smith

1990
Pick
14 Brad May
82 Brian McCarthy
97 Richard Smehlik
100 Todd Bojcun
103 Brad Pascall
142 Viktor Gordiyuk
166 Milan Nedoma
187 Jason Winch
208 Sylvain Naud
229 Kenneth Martin
250 Brad Rubachuk

1989
Pick
14 Kevin Haller
56 John (Scott) Thomas
77 Doug MacDonald
98 Ken Sutton
107 Bill Pye
119 Mike Barkley
161 Derek Plante
183 Donald Audette
194 Mark Astley
203 John Nelson
224 Todd Henderson
245 Michael Bavis

1988
Pick
13 Joel Savage
55 Darcy Loewen
76 Keith E. Carney
89 Alexander Mogilny
97 Robert Ray
106 David Di Vita
118 Mike McLaughlin
139 Mike Griffith
160 Daniel Ruoho
181 Wade Flaherty
223 Thomas Nieman
244 Robert Wallwork

1987
Pick
1 Pierre Turgeon
22 Brad Miller
53 Andrew MacVicar
84 John Bradley
85 David Pergola
106 Chris Marshall
127 Paul Flanagan
148 Sean Dooley
153 Tim Roberts
169 Grant Tkachuk
190 Ian Herbers
211 David Littman
232 Allan MacIsaac

1986
Pick
5 Shawn Anderson
26 Greg Brown
47 Bob Corkum
56 Kevin Kerr
68 David Baseggio
89 Larry Rooney
110 Miguel Baldris
131 Mike Hartman
152 Francois Guay
173 Shawn Whitham
194 Kenton Rein
215 Troy Arndt

1985
Pick
14 Calle Johansson
35 Benoit Hogue
56 Keith Gretzky
77 Dave Moylan
98 Ken Priestlay
119 Joe Reekie
140 Petri Matikainen
161 Trent Kaese
182 Jiri Sejba
203 Boyd Sutton
224 Guy Larose
245 Ken Baumgartner

1984
Pick
18 Mikael Andersson
39 Doug Trapp
60 Ray Sheppard
81 Bob Halkidis
102 Joey Rampton
123 James Gasseau
144 Darcy Wakaluk
165 Orvar Stambert
206 Brian McKinnon
226 Grant Delcourt
247 Sean Baker

1983
Pick
5 Tom Barrasso
10 Normand Lacombe
11 Adam Creighton
31 John Tucker
34 Richard Hajdu
74 Daren Puppa
94 Jayson Meyer
114 Jim Hofford
134 Christian Ruutlu
154 Don McSween
174 Tim Hoover
194 Mark Ferner
214 Uwe Krupp
234 Marc Hamelin
235 Kermit Salfi

Club Directory

Marine Midland Arena
One Seymour H. Knox III Plaza
Buffalo, NY 14203
Phone **716/855-4100**
Fax 716/855-4110
Ticket Office: 716/888-4000
Capacity: 18,595

Board of Directors

Chairman of the Board	Northrop R. Knox
Vice-Chairman of the Board and Counsel	Robert O. Swados
Vice-Chairman of the Board	Robert E. Rich, Jr.
Chairman of the Executive Committee	John J. Rigas
Treasurer	Joseph T.J. Stewart
Board of Directors **Niagara Frontier Hockey, L.P.** (includes above listed officers)	Edwin C. Andrews, Peter C. Andrews, William C. Cox, III, John B. Fisher, George T. Gregory, John E. Houghton, Seymour H. Knox, IV, Michael J. Rigas, Timothy J. Rigas, Richard W. Rupp, Howard T. Saperston, Jr., Paul A. Schoellkopf, George Strawbridge, Jr., William H. Weeks

Executive Department

President/Chief Executive Officer	Lawrence Quinn
Executive Vice-President/Sports & Arena Operations	Dan DiPofi
Senior Vice-President/Legal and Business Affairs	Kevin Billet
Vice-President/Finance	John Cudmore
Vice-President/Corporate Relations	Seymour H. Knox, IV
Vice-President/Marketing	Christye Peterson
Vice-President/Ticket Sales and Operations	John Sinclair
Assistant to the President	Chris Schoepflin
Special Consultant to the President	Joe Crozier
Executive Assistants	Elaine Burzynski, Debbie Driscoll, Toni Addeo, Eleanore MacKenzie

Hockey Department

General Manager	Darcy Regier
Assistant to the General Manager	Larry Carriere
Director of Player Personnel	Don Luce
Director of Team Operations	Jeff Holbrook
Director of Scouting	Jack Bowman
Professional Scout	Terry Martin
Scouting Staff	Don Barrie, Jim Benning, Paul Merritt, Mike Racicot, Rudy Migay, David Volek
Head Coach	Lindy Ruff
Associate Coach	Don Lever
Assistant Coach	Mike Ramsey
Strength & Conditioning Coach	Doug McKenney
Goaltender Consultant	Mitch Korn
Administrative Assistant Coach	Jon Christiano
Head Trainer/Massage Therapist	Jim Pizzutelli
Physical Therapist	Joe Acquino
Equipment Manager	Rip Simonick
Assistant Equipment Manager	George Babcock
Administrative Assistant	Cindy Blais
Team Travel Coordinator	Verna Wojcik

Medical

Club Doctor	John L. Butsch, M.D.
Orthopedic Consultant	John Marzo, M.D.
Club Dentist	Daniel Yustin, D.D.S., M.S.
Oral Surgeon	Steven Jensen, D.D.S.
Team Psychologists	Max Offenberger, Ph.D. & Dan Smith, Ph.D.

Administration

Human Resources Coordinator	Vanessa Barrons
Management Information Systems Manager	Ken Bass
Distribution Manager	Gerry Magill
Receptionists	Olive Anticola, Evelyn Battleson

Broadcast Production

Director of Broadcasting	Joe Guarnieri
Broadcast Coordinator	Lisa Tzetzo
Editor/Technical Director	Eric Grossman
Producer	Lowell MacDonald
Feature Producer/Avid Editor	Martin McCreary
Director	Phil Mollica
Senior Commercial Producer/Editor	Joe Pinter
Broadcast Team	Rick Jeanneret (play-by-play), Jim Lorentz (color commentary), Danny Gare (reporter), Dave Miller (radio host/producer)

Communications

Director of Communications	Mike Gilbert
Media Relations Director	Gil Chorbajian
Director of Community Relations	Ken Martin, Jr.
Community Relations Coordinator	Deidre Daniels
Director of Alumni Relations	Larry Playfair
Corporate and Community Relations Liaison	Gilbert Perreault
Team Photographer	Bill Wippert

Empire Sports Sales

Director of Corporate Sales	Dan Rozanski
National Sales Manager	Nick DiVico
Senior Account Managers	Steve Cuccia, Jim DiMino
Vendor Programs Manager	Jim Harrington
Account Managers	Kathleen Kane, Matt Schobert
Sales Support Account Executive	Len Synor
Traffic Coordinators	Corinne Moyer, Terese Schmidle
Administrative Assistant	Stephanie LeMaitre

Finance

Controller	Chuck LaMattina
Financial Analyst	Elizabeth McPartland
Administrative Assistant to Finance	Toni Addeo
Accounting Manager – Buffalo Sabres	Chris Ivansitz
Accounting Manager – Marine Midland Arena	Scott Haima
Payroll Manager	Birgid Haensel
Finance Assistants	Mary Jones, Sally Lippert
Staff Accountant	Dave Eisenreid

Legal

Associate Counsel	Richard Mugel

Marketing

Director of Promotions & Advertising	Tanya Isherwood
Director of Game Presentation & Special Events	Kathy Manley
Promotions & Advertising Coordinator	Tara Doster
Game Presentation Coordinator	Mark Mashiotta
Game Presentation/Matrix Coordinator	Dawn Reed

Ticket Sales & Operations

Director of Ticket Sales	Gary Rabinowitz
Assistant Director of Group & Retail Promotions	Nick Turano
Season & Group Account Representatives	Dan Carroll, Dave Forman, Jr., Mike Jones, Grant Weber
Canadian Sales & Marketing Manager	Steve Katzman
Sales Associate	Todd Langdon
Account Services Manager	Rose Thompson
Account Service Representatives	Roxanne Anderson, Damion Chatmon, Gretchen Huzinec
Box Office Manager	Mike Tout
Assistant Box Office Manager	Christopher Makowski
Group Sales Coordinator	Paul Barker
Ticket Administrators	Lisa Jacobs, Marty Maloney, Cindi Reuther, Elaine Fredo, Andrea Giambra
Cash & Settlement Administrator	Jennifer Glowny

Merchandise

Director of Merchandise	Julie Regan
Merchandise Manager	Mike Kaminska
Store Manager	Tammy Preteroti
Inventory Control Manager	Glenn Barker
Administrative Assistant	Brenda Hawkins

Marine Midland Arena

Director of Facilities Management	Stan Makowski
Director of Operations	Sam Aceti
Event Bookings & Promotion Manager	Jennifer Stich
Event Managers	Matt Rabinowitz, John Faso
Assistant Event Manager	Scott Lasker
Telecommunications Director	Al Wiessman
Communications Technician	Mike Queeno
Chief Engineer	Barry Becker
Assistant Chief Engineer	Brian Drabek
Engineers	John Blake, Patrick Needham
Maintenance Supervisor	Bill Graf
Utility Crew Manager	Bud Redding
Cleaning Supervisor	Brian Hall
Administrative Assistants	Pat Chimera, Tracey Gilbert
Director of Suite Sales & Services	Mark Stone
Suite Services Manager	Sue Smith
Coordinator of Suite Services	Emily Eberhardt
Director of Lacrosse and Amateur Athletics	Kurt Silcott
Assistant Managers of Lacrosse & Amateur Sports	Joe Baldini, Chris Colleary
Administrative Assistant	Donna Webb

Calgary Flames

1996-97 Results: 32W-41L-9T 73PTS. Fifth, Pacific Division

1997-98 Schedule

Oct.	Wed.	1	Detroit		Wed.	31	Montreal
	Fri.	3	Colorado	Jan.	Sat.	3	at St. Louis
	Tue.	7	Toronto		Mon.	5	at Chicago
	Thu.	9	NY Rangers		Tue.	6	at Colorado
	Sun.	12	at Detroit		Fri.	9	Florida
	Tue.	14	at Dallas		Sat.	10	St. Louis
	Fri.	17	Colorado		Wed.	14	at Edmonton
	Sat.	18	Boston		Tue.	20	at Los Angeles
	Wed.	22	at Buffalo		Wed.	21	at San Jose
	Thu.	23	at Philadelphia		Sat.	24	Vancouver
	Sat.	25	at Toronto		Wed.	28	at Anaheim
	Tue.	28	Pittsburgh		Thu.	29	at Los Angeles
	Thu.	30	Phoenix		Sat.	31	New Jersey
Nov.	Sat.	1	at Colorado	Feb.	Tue.	3	Los Angeles
	Sun.	2	at Phoenix		Thu.	5	San Jose
	Wed.	5	Toronto		Sat.	7	Edmonton
	Fri.	7	Anaheim		Fri.	27	Vancouver
	Sun.	9	at Detroit	Mar.	Sun.	1	Ottawa
	Mon.	10	at Chicago		Tue.	3	Tampa Bay
	Thu.	13	Carolina		Thu.	5	at Vancouver
	Sat.	15	at Edmonton		Sat.	7	at Ottawa
	Tue.	18	at New Jersey		Mon.	9	at Washington
	Thu.	20	at Florida		Wed.	11	at Pittsburgh
	Sat.	22	at Tampa Bay		Thu.	12	at Boston
	Sun.	23	at Carolina		Sat.	14	at Toronto
	Thu.	27	Chicago		Mon.	16	at Montreal
	Sat.	29	Anaheim		Fri.	20	NY Islanders
Dec.	Mon.	1	San Jose		Sun.	22	St. Louis
	Wed.	3	Detroit		Tue.	24	Buffalo
	Fri.	5	at Dallas		Thu.	26	Washington
	Sat.	6	at St. Louis		Sat.	28	Los Angeles*
	Tue.	9	at NY Islanders		Mon.	30	at Edmonton
	Wed.	10	at NY Rangers	Apr.	Wed.	1	Dallas
	Fri.	12	Colorado		Sun.	5	at Anaheim
	Tue.	16	Chicago		Tue.	7	at San Jose
	Thu.	18	Dallas		Thu.	9	Vancouver
	Sat.	20	Los Angeles*		Sat.	11	Edmonton
	Mon.	22	at Anaheim		Mon.	13	at Los Angeles
	Tue.	23	at Phoenix		Wed.	15	San Jose
	Sat.	27	Philadelphia		Fri.	17	at Vancouver
	Mon.	29	Phoenix		Sat.	18	at San Jose

* Denotes afternoon game.

Franchise date: June 24, 1980
Transferred from Atlanta to Calgary.

**26th
NHL
Season**

**PACIFIC
DIVISION**

Jarome Iginla finished third among rookie scorers in 1996-97 with 21 goals and established himself as a hard-working forechecker on the ice and a potential team leader in the dressing room.

Year-by-Year Record

		Home			Road			Overall							
Season	GP	W	L	T	W	L	T	W	L	T	GF	GA	Pts.	Finished	Playoff Result
1996-97	82	21	18	2	11	23	7	32	41	9	214	239	73	5th, Pacific Div.	Out of Playoffs
1995-96	82	18	18	5	16	19	6	34	37	11	241	240	79	2nd, Pacific Div.	Lost Conf. Quarter-Final
1994-95	48	15	7	2	9	10	5	24	17	7	163	135	55	1st, Pacific Div.	Lost Conf. Quarter-Final
1993-94	84	25	12	5	17	17	8	42	29	13	302	256	97	1st, Pacific Div.	Lost Conf. Quarter-Final
1992-93	84	23	14	5	20	16	6	43	30	11	322	282	97	2nd, Smythe Div.	Lost Div. Semi-Final
1991-92	80	19	14	7	12	23	5	31	37	12	296	305	74	5th, Smythe Div.	Out of Playoffs
1990-91	80	29	8	3	17	18	5	46	26	8	344	263	100	2nd, Smythe Div.	Lost Div. Semi-Final
1989-90	80	28	7	5	14	16	10	42	23	15	348	265	99	1st, Smythe Div.	Lost Div. Semi-Final
1988-89	**80**	**32**	**4**	**4**	**22**	**13**	**5**	**54**	**17**	**9**	**354**	**226**	**117**	**1st, Smythe Div.**	**Won Stanley Cup**
1987-88	80	26	11	3	22	12	6	48	23	9	397	305	105	1st, Smythe Div.	Lost Div. Final
1986-87	80	25	13	2	21	18	1	46	31	3	318	289	95	2nd, Smythe Div.	Lost Div. Semi-Final
1985-86	80	23	11	6	17	20	3	40	31	9	354	315	89	2nd, Smythe Div.	Lost Final
1984-85	80	23	11	6	18	16	6	41	27	12	363	302	94	3rd, Smythe Div.	Lost Div. Semi-Final
1983-84	80	22	11	7	12	21	7	34	32	14	311	314	82	2nd, Smythe Div.	Lost Div. Final
1982-83	80	21	12	7	11	22	7	32	34	14	321	317	78	2nd, Smythe Div.	Lost Div. Final
1981-82	80	20	11	9	9	23	8	29	34	17	334	345	75	3rd, Smythe Div.	Lost Div. Semi-Final
1980-81	80	25	5	10	14	22	4	39	27	14	329	298	92	3rd, Patrick Div.	Lost Semi-Final
1979-80*	80	18	15	7	17	17	6	35	32	13	282	269	83	4th, Patrick Div.	Lost Prelim. Round
1978-79*	80	25	11	4	16	20	4	41	31	8	327	280	90	4th, Patrick Div.	Lost Prelim. Round
1977-78*	80	20	13	7	14	14	12	34	27	19	274	252	87	3rd, Patrick Div.	Lost Prelim. Round
1976-77*	80	22	11	7	12	23	5	34	34	12	264	265	80	3rd, Patrick Div.	Lost Prelim. Round
1975-76*	80	19	14	7	16	19	5	35	33	12	262	237	82	3rd, Patrick Div.	Lost Prelim. Round
1974-75*	80	24	9	7	10	22	8	34	31	15	243	233	83	4th, Patrick Div.	Out of Playoffs
1973-74*	78	17	15	7	13	19	7	30	34	14	214	238	74	4th, West Div.	Lost Quarter-Final
1972-73*	78	16	16	7	9	22	8	25	38	15	191	239	65	7th, West Div.	Out of Playoffs

* Atlanta Flames

1997-98 Player Personnel

FORWARDS	HT	WT	S	Place of Birth	Date	1996-97 Club
ANDERSSON, Erik	6-3	210	L	Stockholm, Sweden	8/19/71	U. of Denver
BEGIN, Steve	5-11	180	L	Trois-Rivieres, Que.	6/14/78	Val d'Or-Saint John
BRIGLEY, Travis	6-1	190	L	Coronation, Alta.	6/16/77	Lethbridge
BROWN, Bobby	6-0	200	R	Winnipeg, Man.	9/26/75	Roanoke-Baton Rouge
CASSELS, Andrew	5-11	177	L	Bramalea, Ont.	7/23/69	Hartford
COWAN, Jeff	6-2	185	L	Scarborough, Ont.	9/27/76	Saint John-Roanoke
DINGMAN, Chris	6-4	225	L	Edmonton, Alta.	7/6/76	Saint John
DOMENICHELLI, Hnat	6-0	175	L	Edmonton, Alta.	2/17/76	Hartford-Sprfld-Cgy-Saint Jn
DOWD, Jim	6-1	190	R	Brick, NJ	12/25/68	NY Islanders-Utah-Saint John
FLEURY, Theoren	5-6	160	R	Oxbow, Sask.	6/29/68	Calgary
GAVEY, Aaron	6-1	194	L	Sudbury, Ont.	2/22/74	Tampa Bay-Calgary
GUSMANOV, Ravil	6-3	185	L	Naberezhnye Chelny, USSR	7/25/72	Indianapolis-Saint John
HLUSHKO, Todd	5-11	185	L	Toronto, Ont.	2/7/70	Calgary
HOGLUND, Jonas	6-3	200	R	Hammaro, Swe.	8/29/72	Calgary
IGINLA, Jarome	6-1	193	R	Edmonton, Alta.	7/1/77	Calgary
KARPOV, Valeri	5-10	176	L	Chelyabinsk, USSR	8/5/71	Anaheim-Baltimore-Long Beach
KOHN, Ladislav	5-10	180	L	Uherske Hradiste, Czech.	3/4/75	Saint John
LANDRY, Eric	5-11	185	L	Gatineau, Que.	1/20/75	Hamilton
MATTSSON, Jesper	6-0	185	L	Malmo, Sweden	5/13/75	Saint John
McCARTHY, Sandy	6-3	225	R	Toronto, Ont.	6/15/72	Calgary
McINNIS, Marty	5-11	183	R	Hingham, MA.	6/2/70	NY Islanders-Calgary
MOISE, Martin	6-0	197	L	Valleyfield, Que.	1/18/79	Beauport
MURPHY, Burke	6-0	180	L	Gloucester, Ont.	6/5/73	Saint John
MURRAY, Marty	5-9	175	L	Deloraine, Man.	2/16/75	Calgary-Saint John
NYLANDER, Michael	5-11	190	L	Stockholm, Sweden	10/3/72	Lugano
PETROVICKY, Ronald	5-11	185	R	Zilina, Czech.	2/15/77	Prince George
READY, Ryan	6-2	185	L	Peterborough, Ont.	11/7/78	Belleville
SCHULTE, Paxton	6-2	217	L	Onaway, Alta.	7/16/72	Calgary-Saint John
SCHUTZ, Derek	6-2	185	R	Yorkton, Sask.	3/5/79	Spokane
STERN, Ron	6-0	195	R	Ste. Agathe, Que.	1/11/67	Calgary
STILLMAN, Cory	6-0	180	L	Peterborough, Ont.	12/20/73	Calgary
TITOV, German	6-1	190	L	Moscow, USSR	10/16/65	Calgary
TKACZUK, Daniel	6-0	190	L	Toronto, Ont.	6/10/79	Barrie
TRIPP, John	6-2	207	R	Kingston, Ont.	5/4/77	Oshawa
WARD, Ed	6-3	205	R	Edmonton, Alta.	11/10/69	Cgy-Saint John-Detroit (IHL)
WILM, Clarke	6-0	202	L	Central Butte, Sask.	10/24/76	Saint John

DEFENSEMEN						
ALBELIN, Tommy	6-1	190	L	Stockholm, Sweden	5/21/64	Calgary
ALLISON, Jamie	6-1	190	L	Lindsay, Ont.	5/13/75	Calgary-Saint John
BOUCHARD, Joel	6-0	190	L	Montreal, Que.	1/23/74	Calgary
GAUTHIER, Denis	6-2	195	L	Montreal, Que.	10/1/76	Saint John
HELENIUS, Sami	6-5	225	L	Helsinki, Finland	1/22/74	Calgary-Saint John
HULSE, Cale	6-3	210	R	Edmonton, Alta.	11/10/73	Calgary
LEFEBVRE, Christian	6-5	212	L	Montreal, Que.	3/3/78	
McCAMBRIDGE, Keith	6-2	205	L	Thompson, Man.	2/1/74	Saint John
MORRIS, Derek	5-11	180	R	Edmonton, Alta.	8/24/78	Regina-Saint John
O'SULLIVAN, Chris	6-2	185	L	Dorchester, MA	5/15/74	Calgary-Saint John
PATRICK, James	6-2	198	R	Winnipeg, Man.	6/14/63	Calgary
ST. CROIX, Chris	6-1	186	R	Voorhees, NJ	5/2/79	Kamloops
SIMPSON, Todd	6-3	215	L	North Vancouver, B.C.	5/28/73	Calgary
THOMPSON, Rocky	6-2	192	R	Calgary, Alta.	8/8/77	Medicine Hat-Swift Current
ZALAPSKI, Zarley	6-1	215	L	Edmonton, Alta.	4/22/68	Calgary

GOALTENDERS	HT	WT	C	Place of Birth	Date	1996-97 Club
GARNER, Tyrone	6-1	164	L	Stoney Creek, Ont.	7/27/78	Oshawa
GIGUERE, Jean-Sebastien	6-0	175	L	Montreal, Que.	5/16/77	Hartford-Halifax
GORDON, Ian	5-10	160	L	Yorkton, Sask.	5/15/75	Saint John-Grand Rapids
LINDSAY, Evan	6-1	180	L	Calgary, Alta.	5/15/79	Prince Albert
MOSS, Tyler	6-0	184	R	Ottawa, Ont.	6/29/75	Adi-Grand Rap-Musk-Saint Jn
ROLOSON, Dwayne	6-1	180	L	Simcoe, Ont.	10/12/69	Calgary-Saint John
TABARACCI, Rick	6-1	180	L	Toronto, Ont.	1/2/69	Calgary-Tampa Bay

1996-97 Scoring

* – rookie

Regular Season

Pos	#	Player	Team	GP	G	A	Pts	+/-	PIM	PP	SH	GW	GT	S	%
R	14	Theoren Fleury	CGY	81	29	38	67	-12	104	9	2	3	3	336	8.6
C	51	Dave Gagner	CGY	82	27	33	60	2	48	9	0	4	1	228	11.8
L	13	German Titov	CGY	79	22	30	52	-12	36	12	0	4	0	192	11.5
R	12	* Jarome Iginla	CGY	82	21	29	50	-4	37	8	1	3	0	169	12.4
R	18	Marty McInnis	NYI	70	20	22	42	-7	20	4	1	4	1	163	12.3
			CGY	10	3	4	7	-1	2	1	0	0	0	19	15.8
			TOTAL	80	23	26	49	-8	22	5	1	4	1	182	12.6
L	44	* Jonas Hoglund	CGY	68	19	16	35	-4	12	3	0	6	1	189	10.1
C	34	Corey Millen	CGY	61	11	15	26	-19	32	1	0	0	0	82	13.4
C	16	Cory Stillman	CGY	58	6	20	26	-6	14	2	0	0	0	112	5.4
C	23	Aaron Gavey	T.B.	16	1	2	3	-1	12	0	0	0	0	8	12.5
			CGY	41	7	9	16	-11	34	3	0	1	1	54	13.0
			TOTAL	57	8	11	19	-12	46	3	0	1	1	62	12.9
L	20	Todd Hlushko	CGY	58	7	11	18	-2	49	0	0	0	0	76	9.2
R	22	Ronnie Stern	CGY	79	7	10	17	-4	157	0	1	1	0	98	7.1
D	36	Yves Racine	CGY	46	1	15	16	4	24	1	0	0	0	82	1.2
D	5	Tommy Albelin	CGY	72	4	11	15	-8	14	2	0	0	0	103	3.9
D	27	* Todd Simpson	CGY	82	1	13	14	-14	208	0	0	1	0	85	1.2
L	42	Ed Ward	CGY	40	5	8	13	-3	49	0	0	0	0	33	15.2
L	32	Mike Sullivan	CGY	67	5	6	11	-11	10	0	3	2	0	64	7.8
D	4	Glen Featherstone	HFD	41	2	5	7	0	87	0	0	0	0	40	5.0
			CGY	13	1	3	4	-1	19	0	0	0	0	27	3.7
			TOTAL	54	3	8	11	-1	106	0	0	0	0	67	4.5
D	19	* Chris O'Sullivan	CGY	27	2	8	10	0	2	1	0	1	0	41	4.9
D	6	* Joel Bouchard	CGY	76	4	5	9	-23	49	1	0	0	0	61	6.6
R	15	Sandy McCarthy	CGY	33	3	5	8	-8	113	1	0	1	0	38	7.9
D	29	* Cale Hulse	CGY	63	1	6	7	-2	91	0	0	0	0	58	1.7
L	17	* Hnat Domenichelli	HFD	13	2	1	3	-4	7	1	0	0	0	14	14.3
			CGY	10	1	2	3	1	2	0	0	0	0	16	6.3
			TOTAL	23	3	3	6	-3	9	1	0	0	0	30	10.0
D	3	James Patrick	CGY	19	3	1	4	2	6	1	0	0	0	22	13.6
C	41	* Dale McTavish	CGY	9	1	2	3	-4	2	0	0	0	0	14	7.1
G	37	Trevor Kidd	CGY	55	0	2	2	0	16	0	0	0	0	0	0.0
D	8	Sami Helenius	CGY	19	0	1	1	1	0	0	0	0	0	1	0.0
L	38	Sasha Lakovic	CGY	19	0	1	1	-1	54	0	0	0	0	10	0.0
L	35	* Paxton Schulte	CGY	1	0	0	0	1	2	0	0	0	0	1	0.0
D	33	Zarley Zalapski	CGY	2	0	0	0	0	2	0	0	0	0	7	0.0
C	28	* Marty Murray	CGY	2	0	0	0	0	4	0	0	0	0	2	0.0
C	45	* Marko Jantunen	CGY	3	0	0	0	-1	0	0	0	0	0	7	0.0
D	2	* Jamie Allison	CGY	20	0	0	0	-4	35	0	0	0	0	8	0.0
G	30	Dwayne Roloson	CGY	31	0	0	0	0	2	0	0	0	0	0	0.0

Goaltending

No.	Goaltender	GPI	Mins	Avg	W	L	T	EN	SO	GA	SA	S%
31	Rick Tabaracci	7	361	2.33	2	4	0	0	1	14	155	.910
37	Trevor Kidd	55	2979	2.84	21	23	6	4	4	141	1416	.900
30	Dwayne Roloson	31	1618	2.89	9	14	3	2	1	78	760	.897
	Totals	**82**	**4990**	**2.87**	**32**	**41**	**9**	**6**	**6**	**239**	**2337**	**.898**

General Manager

COATES, AL
Executive Vice President/General Manager, Calgary Flames.
Born in Listowel, Ont., December 3, 1945.

Al Coates was named executive vice president of the Calgary Flames on June 22, 1995. On November 3, he was designated the interim general manager, replacing Doug Risebrough. Coates' appointment as general manager became official on May 31, 1996. In this role, he is responsible for all aspects of hockey operations for the club.

Coates had been a member of the Flames senior management team since the club's arrival in Calgary in 1980. He has over 26 years of professional hockey experience, including 17 years of service with the Calgary Flames.

Following a playing career in Europe, Coates joined the Detroit Red Wings organization in 1971. He spent nine seasons with the Red Wings, working in various capacities. In the summer of 1980, he joined the Flames as the team's director of public relations. In August, 1982, Coates was named as the assistant to the president, working directly with then president and general manager Cliff Fletcher in a number of hockey administrative capacities. Later, on August 1, 1989, he was promoted to director of hockey administration. He continued his progression through the organization when, on September 8, 1991, he was named the team's assistant general manager, a position he held until his promotion to executive vice president and general manager.

Coates' work has involved player contracts, coordinating professional scouting, and working with the Flames development team in Saint John (AHL). Coates also now serves as the chairman of the executive committee of the American Hockey League. His progressive management and leadership style has helped shape the Flames franchise into a successful, respected organization both on and off the ice.

General Managers' History

Cliff Fletcher, 1972-73 to 1990-91; Doug Risebrough, 1991-92 to 1994-95; Doug Risebrough and Al Coates, 1995-96; Al Coates, 1996-97 to date.

Coaching History

Bernie Geoffrion, 1972-73 to 1973-74; Bernie Geoffrion and Fred Creighton, 1974-75; Fred Creighton, 1975-76 to 1978-79; Al MacNeil, 1979-80 (Atlanta); 1980-81 to 1981-82 (Calgary); Bob Johnson, 1982-83 to 1986-87; Terry Crisp, 1987-88 to 1989-90; Doug Risebrough, 1990-91; Doug Risebrough and Guy Charron, 1991-92; Dave King, 1992-93 to 1994-95; Pierre Page, 1995-96 to 1996-97; Brian Sutter, 1997-98.

Club Records

Team

(Figures in brackets for season records are games played; records for fewest points, wins, ties, losses, goals, goals against are for 70 or more games)

Most Points	117	1988-89 (80)
Most Wins	54	1988-89 (80)
Most Ties	19	1977-78 (80)
Most Losses	41	1996-97 (82)
Most Goals	397	1987-88 (80)
Most Goals Against	345	1981-82 (80)
Fewest Points	65	1972-73 (78)
Fewest Wins	25	1972-73 (78)
Fewest Ties	3	1986-87 (80)
Fewest Losses	17	1988-89 (80)
Fewest Goals	191	1972-73 (78)
Fewest Goals Against	226	1988-89 (80)

Longest Winning Streak

Overall	10	Oct. 14-Nov. 3/78
Home	9	Oct. 17-Nov. 15/78, Jan. 3-Feb. 5/89, Mar. 3-Apr. 1/90, Feb. 21-Mar. 14/91
Away	7	Nov. 10-Dec. 4/88

Longest Undefeated Streak

Overall	13	Nov. 10-Dec. 8/88 (12 wins, 1 tie)
Home	18	Dec. 29/90-Mar. 14/91 (17 wins, 1 tie)
Away	9	Feb. 20-Mar. 21/88 (6 wins, 3 ties), Nov. 11-Dec. 16/90 (6 wins, 3 ties)

Longest Losing Streak

Overall	11	Dec. 14/85-Jan. 7/86
Home	4	Eight times
Away	9	Dec. 1/85-Jan. 12/86

Longest Winless Streak

Overall	11	Dec. 14/85-Jan. 7/86 (11 losses), Jan. 5-26/93 (9 losses, 2 ties)
Home	6	Nov. 25-Dec. 18/82 (5 losses, 1 tie), Nov. 18-Dec. 9/95 (4 losses, 2 ties)
Away	13	Feb. 3-Mar. 29/73 (10 losses, 3 ties)
Most Shutouts, Season	8	1974-75 (80)
Most PIM, Season	2,655	1991-92 (80)
Most Goals, Game	13	Feb. 10/93 (S.J. 1 at Cgy. 13)

Individual

Most Seasons	13	Al MacInnis
Most Games	803	Al MacInnis
Most Goals, Career	314	Joe Nieuwendyk
Most Assists, Career	609	Al MacInnis
Most Points, Career	822	Al MacInnis (213G, 609A)
Most PIM, Career	2,405	Tim Hunter
Most Shutouts, Career	20	Dan Bouchard

Longest Consecutive

Games Streak	257	Brad Marsh (Oct. 11/78-Nov. 10/81)
Most Goals, Season	66	Lanny McDonald (1982-83)
Most Assists, Season	82	Kent Nilsson (1980-81)
Most Points, Season	131	Kent Nilsson (1980-81) (49G, 82A)
Most PIM, Season	375	Tim Hunter (1988-89)

Most Points, Defenseman, Season	103	Al MacInnis (1990-91; 28G, 75A)
Most Points, Center, Season	131	Kent Nilsson (1980-81; 49G, 82A)
Most Points, Right Wing, Season	110	Joe Mullen (1988-89; 51G, 59A)
Most Points, Left Wing, Season	90	Gary Roberts (1991-92; 53G, 37A)
Most Points, Rookie, Season	92	Joe Nieuwendyk (1987-88; 51G, 41A)
Most Shutouts, Season	5	Dan Bouchard (1973-74), Phil Myre (1974-75)
Most Goals, Game	5	Joe Nieuwendyk (Jan. 11/89)
Most Assists, Game	6	Guy Chouinard (Feb. 25/81), Gary Suter (Apr. 4/86)
Most Points, Game	7	Sergei Makarov (Feb. 25/90; 2G, 5A)

Records include Calgary Flames, 1972-73 through 1979-80.

Retired Numbers

9	Lanny McDonald	1981-1989

Captains' History

Keith McCreary, 1972-73 to 1974-75; Pat Quinn, 1975-76, 1976-77; Tom Lysiak, 1977-78, 1978-79; Jean Pronovost, 1979-80; Brad Marsh, 1980-81; Phil Russell, 1981-82, 1982-83; Lanny McDonald, Doug Risebrough (co-captains), 1983-84; Lanny McDonald, Doug Risebrough, Jim Peplinski (tri-captains), 1984-85 to 1986-87; Lanny McDonald, Jim Peplinski (co-captains), 1987-88; Lanny McDonald, Jim Peplinski, Tim Hunter (tri-captains), 1988-89; Brad McCrimmon, 1989-90; alternating captains, 1990-91; Joe Nieuwendyk, 1991-92 to 1994-95; Theoren Fleury, 1995-96 to 1996-97.

All-time Record vs. Other Clubs

Regular Season

		At Home							On Road							Total					
	GP	W	L	T	GF	GA	PTS	GP	W	L	T	GF	GA	PTS	GP	W	L	T	GF	GA	PTS
Anaheim	11	7	4	0	32	26	14	11	5	4	2	29	31	12	22	12	8	2	61	57	26
Boston	40	16	21	3	150	143	35	41	10	25	6	111	145	26	81	26	46	9	261	288	61
Buffalo	40	15	15	10	143	134	40	40	13	22	5	123	166	31	80	28	37	15	266	300	71
Chicago	49	22	19	8	154	148	52	47	15	21	11	141	165	41	96	37	40	19	295	313	93
Colorado	28	15	7	6	118	87	36	28	10	11	7	105	117	27	56	25	18	13	223	204	63
Dallas	48	28	9	11	187	128	67	48	18	23	7	163	180	43	96	46	32	18	350	308	110
Detroit	46	26	14	6	189	146	58	45	14	23	8	140	171	36	91	40	37	14	329	317	94
Edmonton	62	35	21	6	283	227	76	62	22	32	8	226	256	52	124	57	53	14	509	483	128
Florida	3	2	1	0	7	6	4	3	1	2	0	7	7	2	6	3	3	0	14	13	6
Hartford	24	19	4	1	124	79	39	24	13	8	3	93	79	29	48	32	12	4	217	158	68
Los Angeles	79	49	21	9	371	260	107	76	30	37	9	282	296	69	155	79	58	18	653	556	176
Montreal	39	12	22	5	123	141	29	40	11	23	6	97	144	28	79	23	45	11	220	285	57
New Jersey	38	27	5	6	173	99	60	39	24	12	3	147	112	51	77	51	17	9	320	211	111
NY Islanders	45	21	13	11	162	138	53	45	11	25	9	121	184	31	90	32	38	20	283	322	84
NY Rangers	45	26	10	9	204	138	61	46	20	21	5	166	165	45	91	46	31	14	370	303	106
Ottawa	4	3	0	1	26	10	7	4	1	1	2	11	8	4	8	4	1	3	37	18	11
Philadelphia	47	23	15	9	192	155	55	46	13	31	2	122	183	28	93	36	46	11	314	338	83
Phoenix	57	35	15	7	266	186	77	56	21	26	9	203	227	51	113	56	41	16	469	413	128
Pittsburgh	40	24	9	7	177	122	55	40	10	20	10	128	150	30	80	34	29	17	305	272	85
St. Louis	48	24	20	4	169	141	52	49	20	21	8	153	171	48	97	44	41	12	322	312	100
San Jose	17	11	6	0	80	48	22	19	15	3	1	72	44	31	36	26	9	1	152	92	53
Tampa Bay	4	2	2	0	16	10	4	5	2	2	1	20	18	5	9	4	4	1	36	28	9
Toronto	48	30	13	5	208	150	65	46	17	22	7	173	179	41	94	47	35	12	381	329	106
Vancouver	79	53	15	11	346	223	117	80	33	30	17	268	284	83	159	86	45	28	614	507	200
Washington	34	23	6	5	149	83	51	35	13	17	5	124	132	31	69	36	23	10	273	215	82
Defunct Clubs	13	8	4	1	51	34	17	13	7	3	3	43	33	17	26	15	7	4	94	67	34
Totals	**988**	**556**	**291**	**141**	**4100**	**3062**	**1253**	**988**	**369**	**465**	**154**	**3268**	**3647**	**892**	**1976**	**925**	**756**	**295**	**7368**	**6709**	**2145**

Playoffs

	Series	W	L	GP	W	L	T	GF	GA	Last Mtg.	Round	Result
Chicago	3	2	1	12	7	5	0	37	33	1996	CQF	L 0-4
Dallas	1	0	1	6	2	4	0	18	25	1981	SF	L 2-4
Detroit	1	0	1	2	0	2	0	5	8	1978	PR	L 0-2
Edmonton	5	1	4	30	11	19	0	96	132	1991	DSF	L 3-4
Los Angeles	6	2	4	26	13	13	0	102	105	1993	DSF	L 2-4
Montreal	2	1	1	11	5	6	0	32	31	1989	F	W 4-2
NY Rangers	1	0	1	4	1	3	0	8	14	1980	PR	L 1-3
Philadelphia	2	1	1	11	4	7	0	28	43	1981	QF	W 4-3
St. Louis	1	1	0	7	4	3	0	28	22	1986	CF	W 4-3
San Jose	1	0	1	7	3	4	0	35	26	1995	CQF	L 3-4
Toronto	1	0	1	2	0	2	0	5	9	1979	PR	L 0-2
Vancouver	5	3	2	25	13	12	0	82	80	1994	CQF	L 3-4
Winnipeg	3	1	2	13	6	7	0	43	45	1987	DSF	L 2-4
Totals	**32**	**12**	**20**	**156**	**69**	**87**	**0**	**529**	**590**			

Calgary totals include Atlanta, 1972-73 to 1979-80.   Colorado totals include Quebec, 1979-80 to 1994-95.
Dallas totals include Minnesota, 1972-73 to 1992-93.   New Jersey totals include Kansas City, 1974-75 to 1975-76, and
Colorado Rockies, 1976-77 to 1981-82.   Phoenix totals include Winnipeg, 1979-80 to 1995-96.

Playoff Results 1997-93

Year	Round	Opponent	Result	GF	GA
1996	CQF	Chicago	L 0-4	7	16
1995	CQF	San Jose	L 3-4	35	26
1994	CQF	Vancouver	L 3-4	20	23
1993	DSF	Los Angeles	L 2-4	28	33

Abbreviations: Round: F – Final;
CF – conference final; **CQF** – conference quarter-final;
CSF – conference semi-final; **DF** – division final;
DSF – division semi-final; **SF** – semi-final;
QF – quarter-final; **PR** – preliminary round.

1996-97 Results

Oct.	5	at	Vancouver	1-3		7	Toronto	4-3
	6		Buffalo	3-0		9	Hartford	2-2
	9		St. Louis	1-3		11	Florida	1-4
	11	at	Detroit	2-1		15	Anaheim	2-1
	13	at	Philadelphia	1-0		21	at	Pittsburgh	2-4
	14	at	NY Rangers	4-5		22	at	Toronto	3-5
	16	at	Montreal	2-4		24	at	Ottawa	2-2
	20		Edmonton	6-3		28		NY Islanders	4-3
	22		Colorado	5-1		30		San Jose	3-6
	24		Pittsburgh	7-5	Feb.	1		Vancouver	3-0
	26	at	Los Angeles	0-0		3		Los Angeles	2-3
	27	at	Anaheim	4-1		5	at	Edmonton	2-5
	30	at	San Jose	1-3		7		Washington	2-5
Nov.	1		Phoenix	2-3		9		Anaheim	6-1
	2	at	Vancouver	3-4		11		Boston	5-1
	9		St. Louis	2-3		13		Edmonton	3-2
	13	at	Dallas	3-3		15		Toronto	3-0
	14	at	Chicago	2-1		18	at	Buffalo	5-5
	16	at	St. Louis	0-2		19	at	Detroit	0-4
	18		NY Rangers	5-3		21	at	Dallas	2-4
	20		Dallas	1-3		23	at	St. Louis	5-3
	22		Chicago	2-5		26		Phoenix	2-5
	23	at	Edmonton	2-3		28		Montreal	3-2
	26		Edmonton	1-10	Mar.	2		Dallas	4-1
	28		Los Angeles	2-0		4	at	Washington	1-2
	30	at	Phoenix	1-3		5	at	Hartford	0-2
Dec.	3	at	NY Islanders	1-3		7	at	Florida	3-1
	5	at	New Jersey	1-2		9	at	Tampa Bay	1-2
	7	at	Boston	1-1		12	at	Colorado	3-2
	10		Ottawa	5-5		15	at	Los Angeles	5-2
	12	at	Los Angeles	5-1		16	at	Anaheim	2-2
	14		Colorado	4-1		19		San Jose	4-2
	16		New Jersey	0-5		21		Tampa Bay	3-4
	18		Detroit	3-3		25		Anaheim	3-2
	20	at	Anaheim	0-7		29		Vancouver	2-5
	22	at	Phoenix	7-2	Apr.	2		Colorado	1-5
	23	at	Colorado	3-4		4	at	Vancouver	3-3
	29		Philadelphia	2-4		6		Chicago	1-2
	31		San Jose	1-5		8		Detroit	2-3
Jan.	2	at	Colorado	2-3		11	at	Chicago	3-7
	4	at	San Jose	4-3		12	at	Toronto	1-4

Entry Draft Selections 1997-83

1997

Pick	
6	Daniel Tkaczuk
32	Evan Lindsay
42	John Tripp
51	Dimitri Kokorev
60	Derek Schutz
70	Erik Andersson
92	Chris St. Croix
100	Ryan Ready
113	Martin Moise
140	Ilja Demidov
167	Jeremy Rondeau
223	Dustin Paul

1996

Pick	
13	Derek Morris
39	Travis Brigley
40	Steve Begin
73	Dmitri Vlasenkov
89	Toni Lydman
94	Christian Lefebvre
122	Josef Straka
202	Ryan Wade
228	Ronald Petrovicky

1995

Pick	
20	Denis Gauthier Jr.
46	Pavel Smirnov
72	Rocky Thompson
98	Jan Labraaten
150	Clarke Wilm
176	Ryan Gillis
233	Steve Shirreffs

1994

Pick	
19	Chris Dingman
45	Dmitri Ryabykin
77	Chris Clark
91	Ryan Duthie
97	Johan Finnstrom
107	Nils Ekman
123	Frank Appel
149	Patrick Haltia
175	Ladislav Kohn
201	Keith McCambridge
227	Jorgen Jonsson
253	Mike Peluso
279	Pavel Torgayev

1993

Pick	
18	Jesper Mattsson
44	Jamie Allison
70	Dan Tompkins
95	Jason Smith
96	Marty Murray
121	Darryl Lafrance
122	John Emmons
148	Andreas Karlsson
200	Derek Sylvester
252	German Titov
278	Burke Murphy

1992

Pick	
6	Cory Stillman
30	Chris O'Sullivan
54	Mathias Johansson
78	Robert Svehla
102	Sami Helenius
126	Ravil Yakubov
129	Joel Bouchard
150	Pavel Rajnoha
174	Ryan Mulhern
198	Brandon Carper
222	Jonas Hoglund
246	Andrei Potaichuk

1991

Pick	
19	Niklas Sundblad
41	Francois Groleau
52	Sandy McCarthy
63	Brian Caruso
85	Steven Magnusson
107	Jerome Butler
129	Bobby Marshall
140	Matt Hoffman
151	Kelly Harper
173	David St. Pierre
195	David Struch
217	Sergei Zolotov
239	Marko Jantunen
261	Andrei Trefilov

1990

Pick	
11	Trevor Kidd
26	Nicolas P. Perreault
32	Vesa Viitakoski
41	Etienne Belzile
62	Glen Mears
83	Paul Kruse
125	Chris Tschupp
146	Dmitri Frolov
167	Shawn Murray
188	Mike Murray
209	Rob Sumner
230	invalid claim
251	Leo Gudas

1989

Pick	
24	Kent Manderville
42	Ted Drury
50	Veli-Pekka Kautonen
63	Corey Lyons
70	Robert Reichel
84	Ryan O'Leary
105	F. (Toby) Kearney
147	Alex Nikolic
168	Kevin Wortman
189	Sergei Gomolyako
210	Dan Sawyer
231	Alexander Yudin
252	Kenneth Kennholt

1988

Pick	
21	Jason Muzzatti
42	Todd Harkins
84	Gary Socha
85	Thomas Forslund
90	Scott Matusovich
126	Jonas Bergqvist
147	Stefan Nilsson
168	Troy Kennedy
189	Brett Peterson
210	Guy Darveau
231	Dave Tretowicz
252	Sergei Priakhan

1987

Pick	
19	Bryan Deasley
25	Stephane Matteau
40	Kevin Grant
61	Scott Mahoney
70	Tim Harris
103	Tim Corkery
124	Joe Aloi
145	Peter Ciavaglia
166	Theoren Fleury
187	Mark Osiecki
208	William Sedergren
229	Peter Hasselblad
250	Magnus Svensson

1986

Pick	
16	George Pelawa
37	Brian Glynn
79	Tom Quinlan
100	Scott Bloom
121	John Parker
142	Rick Lessard
163	Mark Olsen
184	Warren Sharples
205	Doug Pickell
226	Anders Lindstrom
247	Antonin Stavjana

1985

Pick	
17	Chris Biotti
27	Joe Nieuwendyk
38	Jeff Wenaas
59	Lane MacDonald
80	Roger Johansson
101	Esa Keskinen
122	Tim Sweeney
143	Stu Grimson
164	Nate Smith
185	Darryl Olsen
206	Peter Romberg
227	Alexander Kozhevnikov
248	Bill Gregoire

1984

Pick	
12	Gary Roberts
33	Ken Sabourin
38	Paul Ranheim
75	Petr Rosol
96	Joel Paunio
117	Brett Hull
138	Kevan Melrose
159	Jiri Hrdina
180	Gary Suter
200	Petr Rucka
221	Stefan Jonsson
241	Rudolf Suchanek

1983

Pick	
13	Dan Quinn
51	Brian Bradley
55	Perry Berezan
66	John Bekkers
71	Kevan Guy
77	Bill Claviter
91	Igor Liba
111	Grant Blair
131	Jeff Hogg
151	Chris MacDonald
171	Rob Kivell
191	Tom Pratt
211	Jaroslav Benak
231	Sergei Makarov

Coach

SUTTER, BRIAN
Coach, Calgary Flames.
Born in Viking, Alta., October 7, 1956.

Brian Sutter was named the tenth coach in Flames franchise history on July 3, 1997. The appointment serves as a homecoming to the Alberta-born Sutter. Of the six Sutter brothers involved in hockey, none has ever before played or coached at the NHL level in Alberta.

The Sutter family has combined for 87 years of cumulative experience in the NHL. The Sutter name is synonymous with intensity, honesty, hard work and tenacity. These are trademark qualities which Brian lives by and instills in the players he coaches.

Following a 12 season playing career (1976-1988) with St. Louis, Sutter immediately joined the NHL coaching ranks as head coach of the team he captained for nine of his twelve seasons. He coached the Blues for four years (1988-92), before moving on to coach the Boston Bruins between 1992-95. In each of his seven seasons as an NHL head coach, Sutter has led the teams under his direction to the playoffs.

During his three seasons as head coach of the Boston Bruins, Sutter led the Bruins to the third best record in the NHL (120-73-23). During the 1992-93 season, Sutter coached his team to the second best overall record in the league (51-26-7, 109 points). The 1992-93 season marked the first time in ten years the Bruins posted a 50-win season and earned Sutter runner-up honors in the balloting for the Jack Adams Trophy as the league's top coach. In his second season behind the Bruins bench, Sutter coached one of the league's youngest rosters, including Bryan Smolinski and Joe Juneau, to 42 wins. Sutter's win percentage during his tenure with the Bruins was an impressive .609.

Sutter spent four seasons (1988-92) behind the bench of the St. Louis Blues where he exceeded Scotty Bowman's record to become the winningest coach in Blues history, posting a Blues' career record of 153-124-43 and .545 winning percentage. Sutter won coach-of-the-year honors in 1990-91 after leading his charges to a 47-22-11 record, second overall in the league.

Following his junior career with Lethbridge (WHL), Sutter was drafted by the St. Louis Blues as their second pick, 20th overall, in the 1976 Amateur Draft. Sutter played his entire twelve year NHL career with the Blues. His number 11 was retired by the Blues on December 30, 1988. Sutter ranks second all-time among Blues players in games played and assists and third all-time in goals and points.

Sutter and his wife, Judy, return to "Sutter Country" Alberta in the Sylvan Lake area during the off-season. They have one son, Shaun and one daughter, Abigail.

Coaching Record

		Regular Season					Playoffs			
Season	Team	Games	W	L	T	%	Games	W	L	%
1988-89	St. Louis (NHL)	80	33	35	12	.488	10	5	5	.500
1989-90	St. Louis (NHL)	80	37	34	9	.519	12	7	5	.583
1990-91	St. Louis (NHL)	80	47	22	11	.656	13	6	7	.462
1991-92	St. Louis (NHL)	80	36	33	11	.519	6	2	4	.333
1992-93	Boston (NHL)	84	51	26	7	.649	4	0	4	.000
1993-94	Boston (NHL)	84	42	29	13	.577	13	6	7	.462
1994-95	Boston (NHL)	48	27	18	3	.594	5	1	4	.200
	NHL Totals	536	273	197	66	.571	63	27	36	.429

Club Directory

Canadian Airlines Saddledome
P.O. Box 1540 Station M
Calgary, Alberta T2P 3B9
Phone **403/777-2177**
FAX 403/777-2195
Capacity: 18,882

Owners Grant A. Bartlett, N. Murray Edwards, Harley N. Hotchkiss, Ronald V. Joyce, Alvin G. Libin, Allan P. Markin, J.R. (Bud) McCaig, Byron J. Seaman, Daryl K. Seaman

Management
President & Cheif Executive Officer . . . . Ron Bremner
Executive Vice-President & General Manager . . . . . Al Coates
Vice-President, Finance & Administration . . . . Michael Holditch
Vice-President, Corporate Development . . . . Lanny McDonald
Vice-President, Marketing . . . . Garry McKenzie

Hockey Club Personnel
Director, Player Personnel . . . . Nick Polano
Director, Hockey Operations . . . . Al MacNeil
Head Coach . . . . Brian Sutter
Assistant Coaches . . . . Rich Preston, Steve Smith
Development Coordinator . . . . Jamie Hislop
Director, Hockey Administration . . . . Mike Burke
Pro Scout . . . . Tod Button
St. John Flames Head Coach . . . . Bill Stewart
St. John Assistant Coach . . . . Jeff Perry
Amateur Scouting Coordinator . . . . Mike Kelly
Scouts . . . . Jiri Hrdina, Ian McKenzie, Kelly Kisio, Guy Lapointe
Scouting Staff . . . . Glen Giovanucci, Larry Popein, Larry Johnston, Mike Polano, Raimo Summanen, Normand Poisson
Secretary to President/CEO & VP, Finance . . . . Yvette Mutcheson
Secretary to GM and Hockey Operations. . . . . Brenda Koyich
Secretary to VP, Finance & Corporate Development Nancy Nelson

Administration
Controller . . . . Jackie Manwaring
Assistant Controller . . . . Dorothy Stuart

Public Relations
Director, Communications . . . . Peter Hanlon
Assistant Director, Public Relations . . . . Kathy Gieck
Public Relations Assistant . . . . Sean O'Brien
Secretary, Public Relations . . . . Bernie Doenz

Marketing
Manager, Marketing and Special Events . . . . Roger Lemire
Director, Executive Suites/Club Sales . . . . Bob White
Director, Advertising and Publishing . . . . Pat Halls
Account Executive . . . . John Vidalin
Director, Retail Operations . . . . Mark Mason
Director, Game Presentation . . . . Karla Piper

Sales/Customer Services
Director, Sales & Ticket Operations . . . . Jack Maloney
Manager, Ticket Office . . . . Brad Andrews
Manager, Customer Service . . . . Wendy Kennelly
Manager, Ticket Sales . . . . Judy McCord

Medical/Training Staff
Physiotherapist & Fitness Coordinator . . . . Terry Kane
Head Trainer/Equipment Manager . . . . Bobby Stewart
Trainer . . . . Brian Patafie
Strength & Conditioning . . . . Rich Hesketh
Head Physician – Sport Medicine . . . . Dr. William Meeuwisse
Orthopedic Surgeon . . . . Dr. Nicholas Mohtadi
Internal Medicine . . . . Dr. Terry Groves
Team Dentist . . . . Dr. Bill Blair
Dressing Room Attendant . . . . Les Jarvis

Canadian Airlines Saddledome
GM, Building Operations . . . . Libby Raines
Operations Manager . . . . George Greenwood
Director of Marketing/Facilities . . . . Dale Ryan
Food Services Asst. Manager . . . . Art Hernandez
Concessions Manager . . . . Sheila Parisien
Maintenance Superintendant . . . . Ron Leopold

Facility
Location of Media Boxes . . . . Print – north side
TV & Radio – south side
Dimensions of Rink . . . . 200 feet by 85 feet

Broadcast Stations
Radio . . . . 66 CFR Radio (660 AM)
Television . . . . Channels 2 & 7

Carolina Hurricanes
1996-97 Results: 32W-39L-11T 75PTS. Fifth, Northeast Division

Year-by-Year Record

Season	GP	Home W	L	T	Road W	L	T	Overall W	L	T	GF	GA	Pts.	Finished		Playoff Result
1996-97*	82	23	15	3	9	24	8	32	39	11	226	256	75	5th,	Northeast Div.	Out of Playoffs
1995-96*	82	22	15	4	12	24	5	34	39	9	237	259	77	4th,	Northeast Div.	Out of Playoffs
1994-95*	48	12	10	2	7	14	3	19	24	5	127	141	43	5th,	Northeast Div.	Out of Playoffs
1993-94*	84	14	22	6	13	26	3	27	48	9	227	288	63	6th,	Northeast Div.	Out of Playoffs
1992-93*	84	12	25	5	14	27	1	26	52	6	284	369	58	5th,	Adams Div.	Out of Playoffs
1991-92*	80	13	17	10	13	24	3	26	41	13	247	283	65	4th,	Adams Div.	Lost Div. Semi-Final
1990-91*	80	18	16	6	13	22	5	31	38	11	238	276	73	4th,	Adams Div.	Lost Div. Semi-Final
1989-90*	80	17	18	5	21	15	4	38	33	9	275	268	85	4th,	Adams Div.	Lost Div. Semi-Final
1988-89*	80	21	17	2	16	21	3	37	38	5	299	290	79	4th,	Adams Div.	Lost Div. Semi-Final
1987-88*	80	21	14	5	14	24	2	35	38	7	249	267	77	4th,	Adams Div.	Lost Div. Semi-Final
1986-87*	80	26	9	5	17	21	2	43	30	7	287	270	93	1st,	Adams Div.	Lost Div. Final
1985-86*	80	21	17	2	19	19	2	40	36	4	332	302	84	4th,	Adams Div.	Lost Div. Semi-Final
1984-85*	80	17	18	5	13	23	4	30	41	9	268	318	69	5th,	Adams Div.	Out of Playoffs
1983-84*	80	19	16	5	9	26	5	28	42	10	288	320	66	5th,	Adams Div.	Out of Playoffs
1982-83*	80	13	22	5	6	32	2	19	54	7	261	403	45	5th,	Adams Div.	Out of Playoffs
1981-82*	80	13	17	10	8	24	8	21	41	18	264	351	60	5th,	Adams Div.	Out of Playoffs
1980-81*	80	14	17	9	7	24	9	21	41	18	292	372	60	4th,	Norris Div.	Out of Playoffs
1979-80*	80	22	12	6	5	22	13	27	34	19	303	312	73	4th,	Norris Div.	Lost Prelim. Round

* Hartford Whalers

1997-98 Schedule

Oct.	Wed.	1	at Tampa Bay
	Fri.	3	Pittsburgh
	Sat.	4	at Ottawa
	Tue.	7	Los Angeles
	Fri.	10	New Jersey
	Sat.	11	at Pittsburgh
	Mon.	13	at St. Louis
	Wed.	15	Buffalo
	Sat.	18	at Detroit*
	Mon.	20	at NY Rangers
	Wed.	22	St. Louis
	Fri.	24	at Colorado
	Sun.	26	at Chicago
	Fri.	31	Buffalo
Nov.	Mon.	3	Vancouver
	Wed.	5	Detroit
	Fri.	7	NY Islanders
	Sun.	9	Ottawa
	Wed.	12	at Edmonton
	Thu.	13	at Calgary
	Sun.	16	at Vancouver*
	Wed.	19	Montreal
	Fri.	21	NY Rangers
	Sun.	23	Calgary
	Wed.	26	at Pittsburgh
	Fri.	28	Tampa Bay
	Sat.	29	Colorado
Dec.	Mon.	1	Boston
	Wed.	3	NY Islanders
	Fri.	5	Phoenix
	Sat.	6	at Boston
	Wed.	10	Florida
	Fri.	12	at Buffalo
	Tue.	16	Ottawa
	Thu.	18	at Ottawa
	Sat.	20	Washington
	Tue.	23	at Philadelphia
	Fri.	26	Florida
	Sat.	27	Buffalo
	Tue.	30	Anaheim
	Wed.	31	at Pittsburgh

Jan.	Sat.	3	Dallas
	Mon.	5	Ottawa
	Tue.	6	at NY Rangers
	Thu.	8	Philadelphia
	Sat.	10	at NY Islanders*
	Mon.	12	Pittsburgh
	Wed.	14	Chicago
	Wed.	21	at Buffalo
	Thu.	22	at Ottawa
	Sat.	24	at Montreal*
	Tue.	27	at Florida
	Wed.	28	at Tampa Bay
	Fri.	30	at NY Islanders
Feb.	Sun.	1	Montreal
	Wed.	4	Tampa Bay
	Sat.	7	at Boston*
	Sat.	28	at New Jersey
Mar.	Mon.	2	at San Jose
	Thu.	5	at Los Angeles
	Fri.	6	at Phoenix
	Sun.	8	at Anaheim
	Thu.	12	New Jersey
	Sat.	14	San Jose
	Sun.	15	Edmonton
	Wed.	18	at Washington
	Fri.	20	at Dallas
	Mon.	23	at Florida
	Thu.	26	NY Rangers
	Sat.	28	at Philadelphia*
	Sun.	29	Philadelphia
	Tue.	31	Montreal
Apr.	Wed.	1	at New Jersey
	Sat.	4	at Montreal
	Mon.	6	at Boston
	Wed.	8	at Buffalo
	Thu.	9	Toronto
	Sat.	11	at Toronto
	Mon.	13	Boston
	Thu.	16	Pittsburgh
	Sat.	18	Washington*
	Sun.	19	at Washington*

* Denotes afternoon game.

Franchise date: June 22, 1979
Transferred from Hartford to Carolina,
June 25, 1997.

NORTHEAST DIVISION

19th NHL Season

The only NHL player from Canada's icy Northwest Territories, Geoff Sanderson chilled opposing goalies last season with a team-leading 36 goals. He's shown here in the uniform of the NHL's Eastern Conference All-Stars at the 1997 All-Star Game in San Jose.

1997-98 Player Personnel

FORWARDS	HT	WT	S	Place of Birth	Date	1996-97 Club
BROWN, Kevin	6-1	212	R	Birmingham, England	5/11/74	Hartford-Springfield
BUCKLEY, Tom	6-1	204	L	Buffalo, NY	5/26/76	Springfield-Richmond
DANIELS, Jeff	6-1	200	L	Oshawa, Ont.	6/24/68	Hartford-Springfield
DINEEN, Kevin	5-11	190	R	Quebec City, Que.	10/28/63	Hartford
EMERSON, Nelson	5-11	175	R	Hamilton, Ont.	8/17/67	Hartford
GRIMSON, Stu	6-5	227	L	Kamloops, B.C.	5/20/65	Detroit-Hartford
KAPANEN, Sami	5-10	170	L	Vantaa, Finland	6/14/73	Hartford
KRON, Robert	5-11	185	L	Brno, Czech.	2/27/67	Hartford
LEACH, Stephen	5-11	197	R	Cambridge, MA	1/16/66	St. Louis
MacDONALD, Craig	6-2	180	L	Antigonish, N.S.	4/7/77	Harvard
MacNEIL, Ian	6-2	171	L	Halifax, N.S.	4/27/77	Oshawa
MANDERVILLE, Kent	6-3	210	L	Edmonton, Alta.	4/12/71	Hartford-Springfield
MARTINS, Steve	5-9	175	L	Gatineau, Que.	4/13/72	Hartford-Springfield
MURRAY, Chris	6-2	209	R	Port Hardy, B.C.	10/25/74	Montreal-Hartford
O'NEILL, Jeff	6-1	190	R	Richmond Hill, Ont.	2/23/76	Hartford-Springfield
PETRUNIN, Andrei	5-9	169	L	Moscow, USSR	2/2/78	CSKA
PRIMEAU, Keith	6-4	210	L	Toronto, Ont.	11/24/71	Hartford
RANHEIM, Paul	6-1	210	R	St. Louis, MO	1/25/66	Hartford
RICE, Steven	6-0	217	R	Kitchener, Ont.	5/26/71	Hartford
RITCHIE, Byron	5-10	180	L	Burnaby, B.C.	4/24/77	Lethbridge
ROBERTS, Gary	6-1	190	L	North York, Ont.	5/23/66	
SANDERSON, Geoff	6-0	185	L	Hay River, N.W.T.	2/1/72	Hartford
WASYLKO, Steve	6-1	173	L	Ottawa, Ont.	7/11/78	Detroit (OHL)
WASYLUK, Trevor	6-1	187	L	Saskatoon, Sask.	5/4/78	Medicine Hat-Springfield
WILLIS, Shane	6-0	176	R	Edmonton, Alta.	6/13/77	Prince Albert-Lethbridge

DEFENSEMEN						
BROWN, Jeff	6-1	204	R	Ottawa, Ont.	4/30/66	Hartford
BURT, Adam	6-2	207	L	Detroit, MI	1/15/69	Hartford
CHIASSON, Steve	6-1	205	L	Barrie, Ont.	4/14/67	Calgary-Hartford
CICCONE, Enrico	6-5	220	L	Montreal, Que.	4/10/70	Chicago
FEDOTOV, Sergei	6-1	185	L	Moscow, USSR	1/24/77	Saratov-Detroit (OHL)
HALKO, Steven	6-1	195	R	Etobicoke, Ont.	3/8/74	Springfield
HALLER, Kevin	6-2	195	L	Trochu, Alta.	12/5/70	Philadelphia-Hartford
LESCHYSHYN, Curtis	6-1	205	L	Thompson, Man.	9/21/69	Colorado-Washington-Hartford
McBAIN, Jason	6-2	180	L	Ilion, NY	4/12/74	Hartford-Springfield
McMAHON, Mark	6-1	179	L	Geralton, Ont.	2/10/78	Kitchener
PRATT, Nolan	6-2	195	L	Fort McMurray, Alta.	8/14/75	Hartford-Springfield
RUCINSKI, Mike	5-11	179	L	Trenton, MI	3/30/75	Richmond-Springfield
WESLEY, Glen	6-1	197	L	Red Deer, Alta.	10/2/68	Hartford

GOALTENDERS	HT	WT	C	Place of Birth	Date	1996-97 Club
BAKER, Aaron	6-1	174	R	Eckville, Alta.	2/17/78	Tri-City
BURKE, Sean	6-4	208	L	Windsor, Ont.	1/29/67	Hartford
FOUNTAIN, Mike	6-1	176	L	North York, Ont.	1/26/72	Vancouver-Syracuse
JABLONSKI, Pat	6-0	180	R	Toledo, OH	6/20/67	Montreal-Phoenix
KIDD, Trevor	6-2	190	L	Dugald, Man.	3/29/72	Calgary

General Managers' History

Jack Kelly, 1979-80 to 1980-81; Larry Pleau, 1981-82 to 1982-83; Emile Francis, 1983-84 to 1988-89; Ed Johnston, 1989-90 to 1991-92; Brian Burke, 1992-93; Paul Holmgren, 1993-94; Jim Rutherford, 1994-95 to date.

Coaching History

Don Blackburn, 1979-80; Don Blackburn and Larry Pleau, 1980-81; Larry Pleau, 1981-82; Larry Kish, Larry Pleau and John Cuniff, 1982- 83; Jack "Tex" Evans, 1983-84 to 1986-87; Jack "Tex" Evans and Larry Pleau, 1987-88; Larry Pleau, 1988-89; Rick Ley, 1989-90 to 1990-91; Jim Roberts, 1991-92; Paul Holmgren, 1992-93; Paul Holmgren and Pierre Maguire, 1993-94; Paul Holmgren, 1994-95; Paul Holmgren and Paul Maurice, 1995-96; Paul Maurice, 1996-97 to date.

Captains' History

Rick Ley, 1979-80; Rick Ley and Mike Rogers, 1980-81; Dave Keon, 1981-82; Russ Anderson, 1982-83; Mark Johnson, 1983-84; Mark Johnson and Ron Francis, 1984-85; Ron Francis, 1985-86 to 1990-91; Randy Ladouceur, 1991-92; Pat Verbeek, 1992-93 to 1994-95; Brendan Shanahan, 1995-96; Kevin Dineen, 1996-97.

1996-97 Scoring

* – rookie

Regular Season

Pos	#	Player	Team	GP	G	A	Pts	+/−	PIM	PP	SH	GW	GT	S	%
L	8	Geoff Sanderson	HFD	82	36	31	67	-9	29	12	1	4	1	297	12.1
C	21	Andrew Cassels	HFD	81	22	44	66	-16	46	8	0	2	0	142	15.5
L	27	Derek King	NYI	70	23	30	53	-6	20	5	0	3	0	153	15.0
			HFD	12	3	3	6	0	2	1	0	0	0	28	10.7
			TOTAL	82	26	33	59	-6	22	6	0	3	0	181	14.4
C	55	Keith Primeau	HFD	75	26	25	51	-3	161	6	3	2	2	169	15.4
R	11	Kevin Dineen	HFD	78	19	29	48	-6	141	8	0	5	2	185	10.3
R	16	Nelson Emerson	HFD	66	9	29	38	-21	34	2	1	2	0	194	4.6
R	12	Steven Rice	HFD	78	21	14	35	-11	59	5	0	2	0	159	13.2
D	20	Glen Wesley	HFD	68	6	26	32	0	40	3	1	0	0	126	4.8
C	92	Jeff O'Neill	HFD	72	14	16	30	-24	40	2	1	0	0	101	13.9
D	3	Steve Chiasson	CGY	47	5	11	16	-11	32	1	2	1	0	112	4.5
			HFD	18	3	11	14	-10	7	3	0	0	0	56	5.4
			TOTAL	65	8	22	30	-21	39	4	2	1	0	168	4.8
R	24	Sami Kapanen	HFD	45	13	12	25	6	2	3	0	2	0	82	15.9
R	18	Robert Kron	HFD	68	10	12	22	-18	10	2	0	4	1	182	5.5
D	7	Curtis Leschyshyn	COL	11	0	5	5	1	6	0	0	0	0	8	0.0
			WSH	2	0	0	0	0	2	0	0	0	0	0	0.0
			HFD	64	4	13	17	-19	30	1	1	1	0	94	4.3
			TOTAL	77	4	18	22	-18	38	1	1	1	0	102	3.9
L	28	Paul Ranheim	HFD	67	10	11	21	-13	18	0	3	1	0	96	10.4
D	14	Kevin Haller	PHI	27	0	5	5	-1	37	0	0	0	0	34	0.0
			HFD	35	2	6	8	-11	48	0	0	0	0	43	4.7
			TOTAL	62	2	11	13	-12	85	0	0	0	0	77	2.6
D	6	Adam Burt	HFD	71	2	11	13	-13	79	0	0	0	0	85	2.4
C	44	Kent Manderville	HFD	44	6	5	11	3	18	0	0	1	0	51	11.8
R	17	Chris Murray	MTL	56	4	2	6	-8	114	0	0	0	0	32	12.5
			HFD	8	1	1	2	1	10	0	0	0	0	9	11.1
			TOTAL	64	5	3	8	-7	124	0	0	0	0	41	12.2
D	5	Alexander Godynyuk	HFD	55	1	6	7	-10	41	0	0	1	0	34	2.9
D	23	* Marek Malik	HFD	47	1	5	6	5	50	0	0	1	0	33	3.0
L	32	Stu Grimson	DET	1	0	0	0	-1	0	0	0	0	0	0	0.0
			HFD	75	2	2	4	-7	218	0	0	0	0	17	11.8
			TOTAL	76	2	2	4	-8	218	0	0	0	0	17	11.8
R	46	Kevin Brown	HFD	11	0	4	4	-6	6	0	0	0	0	12	0.0
D	41	* Nolan Pratt	HFD	9	0	2	2	0	6	0	0	0	0	4	0.0
L	37	Jeff Daniels	HFD	10	0	2	2	2	0	0	0	0	0	6	0.0
G	1	Sean Burke	HFD	51	0	2	2	0	14	0	0	0	0	0	0.0
D	7	Brian Glynn	HFD	1	1	0	1	2	2	0	0	0	0	2	50.0
C	26	* Steve Martins	HFD	2	0	1	1	0	0	0	0	0	0	2	0.0
G	29	Jason Muzzatti	HFD	31	0	1	1	0	18	0	0	0	0	0	0.0
D	27	Jeff Brown	HFD	1	0	0	0	0	0	0	0	0	0	0	0.0
D	25	* Jason McBain	HFD	6	0	0	0	-4	0	0	0	0	0	1	0.0
G	47	* J Sebastien Giguere	HFD	8	0	0	0	0	0	0	0	0	0	0	0.0

Goaltending

No.	Goaltender	GPI	Mins	Avg	W	L	T	EN	SO	GA	SA	S%
1	Sean Burke	51	2985	2.69	22	22	6	6	4	134	1560	.914
29	Jason Muzzatti	31	1591	3.43	9	13	5	1	0	91	815	.888
47	* J Sebastien Giguere	8	394	3.65	1	4	0	0	0	24	201	.881
	Totals	**82**	**4996**	**3.07**	**32**	**39**	**11**	**7**	**4**	**256**	**2583**	**.901**

Coach

MAURICE, PAUL
Coach, Carolina Hurricanes. Born January 30, 1967.

Paul Maurice is entering his third year as the franchise's head coach and is the first head coach of the Carolina Hurricanes. Under his direction, the Whalers were 61-72-19 and have narrowly missed the playoffs in each of the past two seasons. Last season, Maurice's club finished just two points out of the playoff hunt. Maurice became the Whalers' tenth coach in the 17-year history of the franchise on November 6, 1995, just 12 games into the 1995-96 season. Maurice, who was born on January 30, 1967, stepped in as the youngest coach in the National Hockey League.

Maurice, who has been a member of the Compuware hockey organization for the past 12 years, joined the Whalers in June of 1995 as an assistant coach after serving as the head coach of the Detroit Junior Red Wings for two seasons. The Junior Wings won the OHL Western Division regular season title and played for the 1995 Memorial Cup by winning the OHL playoffs. The Wings lost in the Cup finals to Kamloops. For his efforts, Maurice was the runner-up for OHL coach of the year honors in 1995. In the 1993-94 season, Maurice's squad won the OHL Hap Emms Division title and advanced to the finals of the OHL playoffs before losing in seven games to North Bay.

Maurice began his coaching career in 1986 as an assistant coach for the Detroit Junior Red Wings after an eye injury ended his junior playing career. He served six seasons in that capacity before taking over the head coaching responsibilities in the 1993-94 season.

Maurice resides in West Hartford, Connecticut, with his wife, Michelle.

Coaching Record

Season	Team	Regular Season					Playoffs			
		Games	W	L	T	%	Games	W	L	%
1993-94	Detroit (OHL)	66	42	20	4	.697	17	11	6	.647
1994-95	Detroit (OHL)	66	44	18	4	.727	21	16	5	.762
1995-96	Hartford (NHL)	70	29	33	8	.471	....	....	....	....
1996-97	Hartford (NHL)	82	32	39	11	.457	....	....	....	....
	NHL Totals	152	61	72	19	.464	....	....	....	....

Club Records

Team

(Figures in brackets for season records are games played; records for fewest points, wins, ties, losses, goals, goals against are for 70 or more games)

Most Points	93	1986-87 (80)
Most Wins	43	1986-87 (80)
Most Ties	19	1979-80 (80)
Most Losses	54	1982-83 (80)
Most Goals	332	1985-86 (80)
Most Goals Against	403	1982-83 (80)
Fewest Points	45	1982-83 (80)
Fewest Wins	19	1982-83 (80)
Fewest Ties	4	1985-86 (80)
Fewest Losses	30	1986-87 (80)
Fewest Goals	226	1996-97 (82)
Fewest Goals Against	256	1996-97 (82)

Longest Winning Streak

Overall	7	Mar. 16-29/85
Home	5	Mar. 17-29/85
Away	6	Nov. 10-Dec. 7/90

Longest Undefeated Streak

Overall	10	Jan. 20-Feb. 10/82 (6 wins, 4 ties)
Home	7	Mar. 15-Apr. 5/86 (5 wins, 2 ties)
Away	8	Nov. 11-Dec. 5/96 (4 wins, 4 ties)

Longest Losing Streak

Overall	9	Feb. 19/83-Mar. 8/83
Home	6	Feb. 19/83-Mar. 12/83, Feb. 10-Mar. 3/85
Away	13	Dec. 18/82-Feb. 5/83

Longest Winless Streak

Overall	14	Jan. 4/92-Feb. 9/92 (8 losses, 6 ties)
Home	13	Jan. 15-Mar. 10/85 (11 losses, 2 ties)
Away	15	Nov. 11/79-Jan. 9/80 (11 losses, 4 ties)

Most Shutouts, Season	6	1995-96 (82)
Most PIM, Season	2,354	1992-93 (84)
Most Goals, Game	11	Feb. 12/84 (Edm. 0 at Hfd. 11), Oct. 19/85 (Mtl. 6 at Hfd. 11), Jan. 17/86 (Que. 6 at Hfd. 11), Mar. 15/86 (Chi. 4 at Hfd. 11)

Individual

Most Seasons	10	Ron Francis
Most Games	714	Ron Francis
Most Goals, Career	264	Ron Francis
Most Assists, Career	557	Ron Francis
Most Points, Career	821	Ron Francis (264G, 557A)
Most PIM, Career	1,368	Torrie Robertson
Most Shutouts, Career	13	Mike Liut
Longest Consecutive Games Streak	419	Dave Tippett (Mar. 3/84-Oct. 7/89)
Most Goals, Season	56	Blaine Stoughton (1979-80)
Most Assists, Season	69	Ron Francis (1989-90)
Most Points, Season	105	Mike Rogers (1979-80; 44G, 61A), (1980-81; 40G, 65A)
Most PIM, Season	358	Torrie Robertson (1985-86)

Most Points, Defenseman, Season	69	Dave Babych (1985-86; 14G, 55A)
Most Points, Center, Season	105	Mike Rogers (1979-80; 44G, 61A), Mike Rogers (1980-81; 40G, 65A)
Most Points, Right Wing, Season	100	Blaine Stoughton (1979-80; 56G, 44A)
Most Points, Left Wing, Season	89	Geoff Sanderson (1992-93; 46G, 43A)
Most Points, Rookie, Season	72	Sylvain Turgeon (1983-84; 40G, 32A)
Most Shutouts, Season	4	Mike Liut (1986-87), Peter Sidorkiewicz (1988-89), Sean Burke (1995-96, 1996-97)
Most Goals, Game	4	Jordy Douglas (Feb. 3/80), Ron Francis (Feb. 12/84)
Most Assists, Game	6	Ron Francis (Mar. 5/87)
Most Points, Game	6	Paul Lawless (Jan. 4/87; 2G, 4A), Ron Francis (Mar. 5/87; 6A, Oct. 8/89; 3G, 3A)

Records include Hartford Whalers, 1979-80 through 1996-97.

Hartford Whalers Retired Numbers

2	Rick Ley	1972-1981
9	Gordie Howe	1977-1980
19	John McKenzie	1976-1979

All-time Record vs. Other Clubs

Regular Season

	At Home							On Road							Total					
	GP	W	L	T	GF	GA	PTS	GP	W	L	T	GF	GA	PTS	GP	W	L	T	GF	GA	PTS
Anaheim	3	2	1	0	9	6	4	3	1	2	0	10	15	2	6	3	3	0	19	21	6
Boston	61	27	27	7	215	217	61	63	14	43	6	167	252	34	124	41	70	13	382	469	95
Buffalo	63	25	29	9	191	195	59	62	20	35	7	195	258	47	125	45	64	16	386	453	106
Calgary	24	8	13	3	79	93	19	24	4	19	1	79	124	9	48	12	32	4	158	217	28
Chicago	25	11	11	3	85	84	25	24	6	15	3	68	107	15	49	17	26	6	153	191	40
Colorado	57	24	22	11	193	199	59	59	17	34	8	180	252	42	116	41	56	19	373	451	101
Dallas	25	9	13	3	87	97	21	24	10	13	1	77	98	21	49	19	26	4	164	195	42
Detroit	24	14	9	1	88	68	29	25	7	12	6	71	96	20	49	21	21	7	159	164	49
Edmonton	24	9	10	5	100	91	23	25	4	18	3	73	105	11	49	13	28	8	173	196	34
Florida	8	4	4	0	26	20	8	8	2	4	2	14	23	6	16	6	8	2	40	43	14
Los Angeles	25	13	9	3	100	99	29	24	7	14	3	96	109	17	49	20	23	6	196	208	46
Montreal	63	24	31	8	192	228	56	61	12	42	7	181	272	31	124	36	73	15	373	500	87
New Jersey	29	13	9	7	107	92	33	31	11	17	3	101	114	25	60	24	26	10	208	206	58
NY Islanders	31	14	12	5	115	114	33	29	9	16	4	80	109	22	60	23	28	9	195	223	55
NY Rangers	29	16	10	3	108	98	35	30	9	18	3	89	131	21	59	25	28	6	197	229	56
Ottawa	12	11	1	0	44	26	22	14	8	3	3	47	34	19	26	19	4	3	91	60	41
Philadelphia	30	10	15	5	112	126	25	29	7	20	2	78	118	16	59	17	35	7	190	244	41
Phoenix	24	12	7	5	95	76	29	26	13	12	1	93	89	27	50	25	19	6	188	165	56
Pittsburgh	33	17	14	2	137	128	36	31	10	16	5	127	151	25	64	27	30	7	264	279	61
St. Louis	26	10	14	2	81	83	22	25	8	15	2	81	101	18	51	18	29	4	162	184	40
San Jose	6	3	3	0	22	16	6	5	2	3	0	20	30	4	11	5	6	0	42	46	10
Tampa Bay	9	7	2	0	32	23	14	9	3	5	1	25	28	7	18	10	7	1	57	51	21
Toronto	24	14	6	4	112	79	32	24	13	8	3	95	83	29	48	27	14	7	207	162	61
Vancouver	24	10	10	4	78	85	24	25	9	10	6	74	90	24	49	19	20	10	152	175	48
Washington	31	11	15	5	88	107	27	30	10	18	2	87	106	22	61	21	33	7	175	213	49
Totals	**710**	**318**	**297**	**95**	**2496**	**2450**	**731**	**710**	**216**	**412**	**82**	**2208**	**2895**	**514**	**1420**	**534**	**709**	**177**	**4704**	**5345**	**1245**

Playoffs

	Series	W	L	GP	W	L	T	GF	GA	Last Mtg.	Round	Result
Boston	2	0	2	13	5	8	0	38	47	1991	DSF	L 2-4
Colorado	2	1	1	9	5	4	0	35	34	1987	DSF	L 2-4
Montreal	5	0	5	27	8	19	0	70	96	1992	DSF	L 3-4
Totals	**9**	**1**	**8**	**49**	**18**	**31**	**0**	**143**	**177**			

Playoff Results 1997-93

(Last playoff appearance: 1992)

Year	Round	Opponent	Result	GF	GA

Abbreviations: Round: F – Final;
CF – conference final; **CQF** – conference quarter-final;
CSF – conference semi-final; **DF** – division final;
DSF – division semi-final; **SF** – semi-final;
QF – quarter-final; **PR** – preliminary round.

Calgary totals include Atlanta, 1979-80. Colorado totals include Quebec, 1979-80 to 1994-95.
Dallas totals include Minnesota, 1979-80 to 1992-93. New Jersey totals include Colorado Rockies, 1979-80 to 1981-82.
Phoenix totals include Winnipeg, 1979-80 to 1995-96.

1996-97 Results

Oct.	5		Phoenix	1-0		10	at	Vancouver	3-5
	8		Pittsburgh	7-3		12	at	Edmonton	1-2
	12	at	Florida	0-6		15		Pittsburgh	0-3
	17	at	NY Islanders	3-1		20		Toronto	3-1
	19		New Jersey	6-2		22		Florida	2-1
	24		Anaheim	4-1		24		NY Islanders	2-5
	26	at	Buffalo	3-6		25	at	Buffalo	5-1
	30		NY Islanders	2-2		30	at	Los Angeles	3-5
	31	at	Boston	4-4		31	at	Anaheim	3-6
Nov.	2		Los Angeles	2-3	Feb.	5	at	NY Rangers	2-5
	4	at	Detroit	1-5		6	at	Boston	5-3
	6		Boston	5-1		8	at	Montreal	2-3
	8		Detroit	1-4		12		New Jersey	2-3
	9		Buffalo	4-3		13	at	New Jersey	0-4
	12	at	San Jose	4-3		15		Ottawa	2-1
	14	at	Phoenix	2-1		16	at	Ottawa	2-4
	16	at	Colorado	2-2		19	at	Philadelphia	2-2
	20		Montreal	3-1		21		NY Rangers	7-2
	22		Pittsburgh	1-7		22		Washington	2-0
	23	at	Ottawa	3-3		26		Chicago	2-2
	27		Vancouver	2-6		28		San Jose	2-3
	29	at	Florida	1-1	Mar.	2		Philadelphia	2-5
	30	at	Tampa Bay	6-3		5		Calgary	2-0
Dec.	3	at	Pittsburgh	4-4		7		Montreal	2-0
	5	at	Boston	4-2		8	at	Toronto	1-1
	7		Buffalo	6-4		12		Boston	6-3
	11		Florida	5-2		13	at	New Jersey	0-6
	12	at	Philadelphia	2-3		15		Edmonton	2-4
	14		Philadelphia	0-4		16	at	Washington	3-5
	16	at	NY Rangers	2-5		20	at	St. Louis	1-4
	17		St. Louis	5-3		21	at	Dallas	0-2
	20		Dallas	1-5		25		Colorado	0-4
	21		Tampa Bay	6-5		27	at	Tampa Bay	5-2
	26	at	Buffalo	1-5		29		NY Rangers	2-1
	28		Ottawa	3-2	Apr.	2		Montreal	1-4
	29	at	Chicago	3-4		3	at	Pittsburgh	2-3
Jan.	1	at	Washington	2-3		5	at	Montreal	4-1
	2		Boston	4-5		7		Buffalo	4-2
	4		Washington	1-1		9	at	Ottawa	4-5
	6	at	Montreal	4-5		11	at	NY Islanders	4-6
	9	at	Calgary	2-3		13		Tampa Bay	2-1

Entry Draft
Selections 1997-83

1997		1993		1989		1986	
Pick		**Pick**		**Pick**		**Pick**	
22	Nikos Tselios	2	Chris Pronger	10	Robert Holik	11	Scott Young
28	Brad Defauw	72	Marek Malik	52	Blair Atcheynum	32	Marc Laforge
80	Francis Lessard	84	Trevor Roenick	73	Jim McKenzie	74	Brian Chapman
88	Shane Willis	115	Nolan Pratt	94	James Black	95	Bill Horn
142	Kyle Dafoe	188	Emmanuel Legace	115	Jerome Bechard	116	Joe Quinn
169	Andrew Merrick	214	Dmitri Gorenko	136	Scott Daniels	137	Steve Torrel
195	Niklas Nordgren	240	Wes Swinson	157	Raymond Saumier	158	Ron Hoover
199	Randy Fitzgerald	266	Igor Chibirev	178	Michel Picard	179	Robert Glasgow
225	Kent McDonell			199	Trevor Buchanan	200	Sean Evoy
		1992		220	John Battice	221	Cal Brown
1996		**Pick**		241	Peter Kasowski	242	Brian Verbeek
Pick		9	Robert Petrovicky				
34	Trevor Wasyluk	47	Andrei Nikolishin	**1988**		**1985**	
61	Andrei Petrunin	57	Jan Vopat	**Pick**		**Pick**	
88	Craig MacDonald	79	Kevin Smyth	11	Chris Govedaris	5	Dana Murzyn
104	Steve Wasylko	81	Jason McBain	32	Barry Richter	26	Kay Whitmore
116	Mark McMahon	143	Jarret Reid	74	Dean Dyer	68	Gary Callaghan
143	Aaron Baker	153	Ken Belanger	95	Scott Morrow	110	Shane Churla
171	Greg Kuznik	177	Konstantin Korotkov	116	Corey Beaulieu	131	Chris Brant
197	Kevin Marsh	201	Greg Zwakman	137	Kerry Russell	152	Brian Puhalsky
223	Craig Adams	225	Steven Halko	158	Jim Burke	173	Greg Dornbach
231	Askhat Rakhmatullin	249	Joacim Esbjors	179	Mark Hirth	194	Paul Tory
				200	Wayde Bucsis	215	Jerry Pawlowski
1995		**1991**		221	Rob White	236	Bruce Hill
Pick		**Pick**		242	Dan Slatalla		
13	J-Sebastien Giguere	9	Patrick Poulin			**1984**	
35	Sergei Fedotov	31	Martin Hamrlik	**1987**		**Pick**	
85	Ian MacNeil	53	Todd Hall	**Pick**		11	Sylvain Cote
87	Sami Kapanen	59	Mikael Nylander	18	Jody Hull	110	Mike Millar
113	Hugh Hamilton	75	Jim Storm	39	Adam Burt	131	Mike Vellucci
165	Byron Ritchie	119	Mike Harding	81	Terry Yake	173	John Devereaux
191	Milan Kostolny	141	Brian Mueller	102	Marc Rousseau	193	Brent Regan
217	Mike Rucinski	163	Steve Yule	123	Jeff St. Cyr	214	Jim Culhane
		185	Chris Belanger	144	Greg Wolf	234	Pete Abric
1994		207	Jason Currie	165	John Moore		
Pick		229	Mike Santonelli	186	Joe Day	**1983**	
5	Jeff O'Neill	251	Rob Peters	228	Kevin Sullivan	**Pick**	
83	Hnat Domenichelli			249	Steve Laurin	2	Sylvain Turgeon
109	Ryan Risidore	**1990**				20	David Jensen
187	Tom Buckley	**Pick**				23	Ville Siren
213	Ashlin Halfnight	15	Mark Greig			61	Leif Carlsson
230	Matt Ball	36	Geoff Sanderson			64	Dave MacLean
239	Brian Regan	57	Mike Lenarduzzi			72	Ron Chyzowski
265	Steve Nimigon	78	Chris Bright			104	Brian Johnson
		120	Cory Keenan			124	Joe Reekie
		141	Jergus Baca			143	Chris Duperron
		162	Martin D'Orsonnens			144	James Falle
		183	Corey Osmak			164	Bill Fordy
		204	Espen Knutsen			193	Reine Karlsson
		225	Tommie Eriksen			204	Allan Acton
		246	Denis Chalifoux			224	Darcy Kaminski

Club Directory

Greenboro Coliseum

Carolina Hurricanes
5000 Aerial Center Parkway
Suite 1000
Morrisville, NC 27560
Phone **919/467-7825**
FAX 919/462-7030
Capacity: 20,800

Ownership
Chief Executive Officer/Governor. . . . . Peter Karmanos, Jr.
General Partner . . . . Thomas Thewes
Chief Operating Officer/General Manager . . . . Jim Rutherford

Coaching Staff
Head Coach. . . . . Paul Maurice
Assistant Coaches . . . . Randy Ladouceur, Tom Webster
Goaltender Coach/Pro Scout . . . . Steve Weeks

Hockey Operations
Vice President of Hockey Operations . . . . Terry McDonnell
Director of Amateur Scouting/Player Personnel . . . . Sheldon Ferguson
Scouting Staff . . . . Laurence Ferguson, Claude Larose, Willy Langer,
Willy Lindstrom, Bert Marshall, Ken Schinkel,
Tony MacDonald

Head Athletic Therapist/Strength and
   Conditioning Coach . . . . Peter Friesen
Equipment Managers . . . . Skip Cunningham, Wally Tatomir
Assistant Equipment Managers . . . . Bob Gorman, Rick Szuber
Massage Therapist . . . . TBA
Executive Assistant, Hockey Operations. . . . . Kristina Owens

Finance and Administration
Vice President of Finance and Administration . . . . . Mike Amendola
Consultant on Business Affairs . . . . Lou Beer
Accounting Staff . . . . Melissa Anderson, Sharon Battle, Patty Hilliard
Receptionist. . . . . Regina Bennett

Merchandise
Director of Merchandise . . . . Kevin Murphy
Merchandising Assistant . . . . Casey Fellenz

Marketing
Vice President of Marketing and Sales. . . . . Rick Francis
Account Executives . . . . Robert Douglas, Robert Hawkins, Susan Schmidt,
Bruce Weber
Greensboro Account Executive . . . . Jed McMillan
Marketing Coordinator . . . . Sheila Carter

Public Relations
Director of Public Relations . . . . Jim Loria
Director of Media Relations/Team Services . . . . Chris Brown
Public and Media Relations Manager. . . . . Jerry Peters
Motivational Consultant & Community
   Relations Development. . . . . Doris E. Barksdale
Community Relations Manager . . . . Peggy Sue Hawkins
Game Night Operations & Promotions Assistant . . . Jason Neiberg

Ticket Sales
Director of Ticket Operations. . . . . Jim Baldwin
Ticket Sales Manager/RDU Account Executive . . . . . Scott Tippins
Ticket Office Managers . . . . Mike Gilsenan, Ryan Meyer
Ticket Sales Representatives . . . . Derrill Smith, Kevin Patton, Kyle Prairie
Raleigh Durham Account Executive . . . . John Miller
Greensboro Account Executives . . . . Durand Arnold, Joe Barbetta

Arena Operations
Vice President of Arena Management . . . . Sims Hinds
Director of Arena Operations. . . . . David Olsen

General Manager

RUTHERFORD, JIM
General Manager, Carolina Hurricanes. Born in Beeton, Ont., Feb. 17, 1949.

Jim Rutherford, a former NHL goaltender, was named the president and general manager of the Hartford Whalers when KTR Partnership purchased the club on June 28, 1994. He is the franchise's seventh general manager and the first general manager of the Carolina Hurricanes. Entering his fourth season, Rutherford has taken an aggressive approach towards turning the fortunes of the franchise through trades and the NHL draft.

A veteran of 13 NHL seasons, Rutherford began his professional goaltending career in 1969 as a first-round selection of the Detroit Red Wings. While playing for Pittsburgh, Toronto, Los Angeles, and Detroit, Rutherford collected 14 career shutouts. For five seasons he also served as the Red Wings' player representative. Rutherford also played for Team Canada in the IIHF World Championships in Vienna in 1977 and Moscow in 1979.

After his playing days with the Red Wings, Rutherford joined Compuware to serve as the director of hockey operations for Compuware Sports Corporation. Rutherford gained a wealth of experience in youth hockey and junior programs. As a former player, coach, and general manager, his ability to develop players and produce winning programs is widely respected throughout the hockey community.

He started his management career by guiding Compuware Sports Corporation's purchase of the Windsor Spitfires of the Ontario Hockey League in April of 1984. During the next four years, Rutherford acted as general manager of the Spitfires. After the Spitfires advanced to the 1988 Memorial Cup finals, Rutherford led Compuware's efforts to bring the first American-based OHL franchise to Detroit on December 11, 1989. In the following five years, the Detroit Junior Whalers became one of the premier teams in the OHL. The 1993-94 Detroit team won the Emms Division championship and Rutherford was voted the 1993 executive of the year award in both the OHL and the Canadian Hockey League. He won the OHL executive of the year award again in 1994.

Chicago Blackhawks

1996-97 Results: 34W-35L-13T 81PTS. Fifth, Central Division

Jeff Hackett played superbly in 1996-97, finishing third in GAA (2.16) among NHL netminders. He also tied for second in save percentage (.927)

1997-98 Schedule

Oct.	Wed.	1	at Phoenix	Mon.	5	Calgary
	Sat.	4	at San Jose	Fri.	9	Phoenix
	Thu.	9	Tampa Bay	Sat.	10	at Toronto
	Fri.	10	at Dallas	Mon.	12	Vancouver
	Mon.	13	at Phoenix	Wed.	14	at Carolina
	Wed.	15	Washington	Thu.	15	at Washington
	Fri.	17	St. Louis	Tue.	20	NY Islanders
	Sun.	19	Buffalo*	Thu.	22	Toronto
	Wed.	22	at NY Rangers	Sat.	24	St. Louis*
	Fri.	24	Dallas	Thu.	29	at San Jose
	Sun.	26	Carolina	Sat.	31	at Los Angeles*
	Mon.	27	at Montreal	Feb. Sun.	1	at Anaheim
	Wed.	29	Vancouver	Tue.	3	at Phoenix
	Fri.	31	San Jose	Thu.	5	at Colorado
Nov.	Sun.	2	Pittsburgh	Sat.	7	at Dallas*
	Thu.	6	St. Louis	Thu.	26	Los Angeles
	Sat.	8	at NY Islanders	Sat.	28	at Colorado*
	Mon.	10	Calgary	Mar. Sun.	1	Dallas*
	Tue.	11	at Toronto	Tue.	3	at St. Louis
	Thu.	13	Toronto	Thu.	5	at Pittsburgh
	Sun.	16	Detroit	Sat.	7	at Boston*
	Wed.	19	at Anaheim	Mon.	9	Edmonton
	Thu.	20	at Los Angeles	Thu.	12	at Detroit
	Sat.	22	at Vancouver	Sat.	14	at Tampa Bay*
	Tue.	25	at Edmonton	Sun.	15	at Florida
	Thu.	27	at Calgary	Tue.	17	at Buffalo
	Sat.	29	at Ottawa	Thu.	19	Montreal
Dec.	Thu.	4	Colorado	Sun.	22	Boston*
	Sun.	7	Edmonton	Mon.	23	at Detroit
	Wed.	10	Phoenix	Wed.	25	Anaheim
	Fri.	12	Philadelphia	Fri.	27	Ottawa
	Sun.	14	San Jose*	Sun.	29	Florida*
	Tue.	16	at Calgary	Tue.	31	at Philadelphia
	Wed.	17	at Edmonton	Apr. Thu.	2	Colorado
	Sat.	20	at Vancouver	Sat.	4	Detroit*
	Mon.	22	Los Angeles	Sun.	5	NY Rangers*
	Fri.	26	at St. Louis	Thu.	9	at St. Louis
	Sun.	28	Anaheim	Sun.	12	Phoenix
	Tue.	30	at New Jersey	Wed.	15	at Toronto
Jan.	Thu.	1	Toronto	Thu.	16	New Jersey
	Sun.	4	Detroit	Sat.	18	at Dallas*

* Denotes afternoon game.

Franchise date: September 25, 1926

WESTERN CONFERENCE

CENTRAL DIVISION

72nd NHL Season

Year-by-Year Record

		Home			Road			Overall						
Season	GP	W	L	T	W	L	T	W	L	T	GF	GA	Pts.	Finished	Playoff Result
1996-97	82	16	21	4	18	14	9	34	35	13	223	210	81	5th, Central Div.	Lost Conf. Quarter-Final
1995-96	82	22	13	6	18	15	8	40	28	14	273	220	94	2nd, Central Div.	Lost Conf. Semi-Final
1994-95	48	11	10	3	13	9	2	24	19	5	156	115	53	3rd, Central Div.	Lost Conf. Championship
1993-94	84	21	16	5	18	20	4	39	36	9	254	240	87	5th, Central Div.	Lost Conf. Quarter-Final
1992-93	84	25	11	6	22	14	6	47	25	12	279	230	106	1st, Norris Div.	Lost Div. Semi-Final
1991-92	80	23	9	8	13	20	7	36	29	15	257	236	87	2nd, Norris Div.	Lost Final
1990-91	80	28	8	4	21	15	4	49	23	8	284	211	106	1st, Norris Div.	Lost Div. Semi-Final
1989-90	80	25	13	2	16	20	4	41	33	6	316	294	88	1st, Norris Div.	Lost Conf. Championship
1988-89	80	16	14	10	11	27	2	27	41	12	297	335	66	4th, Norris Div.	Lost Conf. Championship
1987-88	80	21	17	2	9	24	7	30	41	9	284	328	69	3rd, Norris Div.	Lost Div. Semi-Final
1986-87	80	18	13	9	11	24	5	29	37	14	290	310	72	3rd, Norris Div.	Lost Div. Semi-Final
1985-86	80	23	12	5	16	21	3	39	33	8	351	349	86	1st, Norris Div.	Lost Div. Semi-Final
1984-85	80	22	16	2	16	19	5	38	35	7	309	299	83	2nd, Norris Div.	Lost Conf. Championship
1983-84	80	25	13	2	5	29	6	30	42	8	277	311	68	4th, Norris Div.	Lost Div. Semi-Final
1982-83	80	29	8	3	18	15	7	47	23	10	338	268	104	1st, Norris Div.	Lost Conf. Championship
1981-82	80	20	13	7	10	25	5	30	38	12	332	363	72	4th, Norris Div.	Lost Conf. Championship
1980-81	80	21	11	8	10	22	8	31	33	16	304	315	78	2nd, Smythe Div.	Lost Prelim. Round
1979-80	80	21	12	7	13	15	12	34	27	19	241	250	87	1st, Smythe Div.	Lost Quarter-Final
1978-79	80	18	12	10	11	24	5	29	36	15	244	277	73	1st, Smythe Div.	Lost Quarter-Final
1977-78	80	20	9	11	12	20	8	32	29	19	230	220	83	1st, Smythe Div.	Lost Quarter-Final
1976-77	80	19	16	5	7	27	6	26	43	11	240	298	63	3rd, Smythe Div.	Lost Prelim. Round
1975-76	80	17	15	8	15	15	10	32	30	18	254	261	82	1st, Smythe Div.	Lost Quarter-Final
1974-75	80	24	12	4	13	23	4	37	35	8	268	241	82	3rd, Smythe Div.	Lost Quarter-Final
1973-74	78	20	6	13	21	8	10	41	14	23	272	164	105	2nd, West Div.	Lost Semi-Final
1972-73	78	26	9	4	16	18	5	42	27	9	284	225	93	1st, West Div.	Lost Final
1971-72	78	28	3	8	18	14	7	46	17	15	256	166	107	1st, West Div.	Lost Semi-Final
1970-71	78	30	6	3	19	14	6	49	20	9	277	184	107	1st, West Div.	Lost Final
1969-70	76	26	7	5	19	15	4	45	22	9	250	170	99	1st, East Div.	Lost Semi-Final
1968-69	76	20	14	4	14	19	5	34	33	9	280	246	77	6th, East Div.	Out of Playoffs
1967-68	74	20	13	4	12	13	12	32	26	16	212	222	80	4th, East Div.	Lost Semi-Final
1966-67	70	24	5	6	17	12	6	41	17	12	264	170	94	1st,	Lost Semi-Final
1965-66	70	21	8	6	16	17	2	37	25	8	240	187	82	2nd,	Lost Semi-Final
1964-65	70	20	13	2	14	15	6	34	28	8	224	176	76	3rd,	Lost Final
1963-64	70	26	4	5	10	18	7	36	22	12	218	169	84	2nd,	Lost Semi-Final
1962-63	70	17	9	9	15	12	8	32	21	17	194	178	81	2nd,	Lost Semi-Final
1961-62	70	20	10	5	11	16	8	31	26	13	217	186	75	3rd,	Lost Final
1960-61	70	20	6	9	9	18	8	29	24	17	198	180	75	3rd,	**Won Stanley Cup**
1959-60	70	18	11	6	10	18	7	28	29	13	191	180	69	3rd,	Lost Semi-Final
1958-59	70	14	12	9	14	17	4	28	29	13	197	208	69	3rd,	Lost Semi-Final
1957-58	70	15	17	3	9	22	4	24	39	7	163	202	55	5th,	Out of Playoffs
1956-57	70	12	15	8	4	24	7	16	39	15	169	225	47	6th,	Out of Playoffs
1955-56	70	9	14	12	10	20	5	19	39	12	155	216	50	6th,	Out of Playoffs
1954-55	70	6	21	8	7	19	9	13	40	17	161	235	43	6th,	Out of Playoffs
1953-54	70	8	21	6	4	30	1	12	51	7	133	242	31	6th,	Out of Playoffs
1952-53	70	14	11	10	13	17	5	27	28	15	169	175	69	4th,	Lost Semi-Final
1951-52	70	9	19	7	8	25	2	17	44	9	158	241	43	6th,	Out of Playoffs
1950-51	70	8	22	5	5	25	5	13	47	10	171	280	36	6th,	Out of Playoffs
1949-50	70	13	18	4	9	20	6	22	38	10	203	244	54	6th,	Out of Playoffs
1948-49	60	13	12	5	8	19	3	21	31	8	173	211	50	5th,	Out of Playoffs
1947-48	60	10	17	3	10	17	3	20	34	6	195	225	46	6th,	Out of Playoffs
1946-47	60	10	17	3	9	20	1	19	37	4	193	274	42	6th,	Out of Playoffs
1945-46	50	15	5	5	8	15	2	23	20	7	200	178	53	3rd,	Lost Semi-Final
1944-45	50	9	14	2	4	16	5	13	30	7	141	194	33	5th,	Out of Playoffs
1943-44	50	15	6	4	7	17	1	22	23	5	178	187	49	4th,	Lost Final
1942-43	50	14	3	8	3	15	7	17	18	15	179	180	49	5th,	Out of Playoffs
1941-42	48	15	8	1	7	15	2	22	23	3	145	155	47	4th,	Lost Quarter-Final
1940-41	48	11	10	3	5	15	4	16	25	7	112	139	39	5th,	Lost Semi-Final
1939-40	48	15	7	2	8	12	4	23	19	6	112	120	52	4th,	Lost Quarter-Final
1938-39	48	5	13	6	7	15	2	12	28	8	91	132	32	7th,	Out of Playoffs
1937-38	48	10	10	4	4	15	5	14	25	9	97	139	37	3rd, Amn. Div.	**Won Stanley Cup**
1936-37	48	8	13	3	6	14	4	14	27	7	99	131	35	4th, Amn. Div.	Out of Playoffs
1935-36	48	15	7	2	6	12	6	21	19	8	93	92	50	3rd, Amn. Div.	Lost Quarter-Final
1934-35	48	12	9	3	14	8	2	26	17	5	118	88	57	2nd, Amn. Div.	Lost Quarter-Final
1933-34	48	13	4	7	7	13	4	20	17	11	88	83	51	2nd, Amn. Div.	**Won Stanley Cup**
1932-33	48	12	7	5	4	13	7	16	20	12	88	101	44	4th, Amn. Div.	Out of Playoffs
1931-32	48	13	5	6	5	14	5	18	19	11	86	101	47	2nd, Amn. Div.	Lost Quarter-Final
1930-31	44	13	8	1	11	9	2	24	17	3	108	78	51	2nd, Amn. Div.	Lost Final
1929-30	44	12	9	1	9	9	4	21	18	5	117	111	47	2nd, Amn. Div.	Lost Quarter-Final
1928-29	44	3	13	6	4	16	2	7	29	8	33	85	22	5th, Amn. Div.	Out of Playoffs
1927-28	44	2	18	2	5	16	1	7	34	3	68	134	17	5th, Amn. Div.	Out of Playoffs
1926-27	44	12	8	2	7	14	1	19	22	3	115	116	41	3rd, Amn. Div.	Lost Quarter-Final

1997-98 Player Personnel

FORWARDS	HT	WT	S	Place of Birth	Date	1996-97 Club
AMONTE, Tony	6-0	195	L	Hingham, MA	8/2/70	Chicago
BLACK, James	6-0	202	L	Regina, Sask.	8/15/69	Chicago
CALDER, Kyle	5-11	180	L	Mannville, Alta.	1/5/79	Regina
CLEARY, Daniel	6-0	203	L	Carbonear, Nfld.	12/18/78	Belleville
CUMMINS, Jim	6-2	219	R	Dearborn, MI	5/17/70	Chicago
DAHLEN, Ulf	6-2	195	L	Ostersund, Sweden	1/12/67	San Jose-Chicago
DAZE, Eric	6-6	222	L	Montreal, Que.	7/2/75	Chicago
DUBINSKY, Steve	6-0	190	L	Montreal, Que.	7/9/70	Chicago-Indianapolis
HUSKA, Ryan	6-2	194	L	Cranbrook, B.C.	7/2/75	Indianapolis
JONES, Ty	6-3	210	R	Richland, WA	2/22/79	Spokane
KLIMOVICH, Sergei	6-3	189	R	Novosibirsk, USSR	3/8/74	Chicago-Indianapolis
KRIVOKRASOV, Sergei	5-11	185	L	Angarsk, USSR	4/15/74	Chicago
LeCOMPTE, Eric	6-4	190	L	Montreal, Que.	4/4/75	Wor-Ind-FtWayne
LEROUX, Jean-Yves	6-2	211	L	Montreal, Que.	6/24/76	Chicago-Indianapolis
MANLOW, Eric	6-0	190	L	Belleville, Ont.	4/7/75	Baltimore-Columbus
MILLER, Kevin	5-11	190	R	Lansing, MI	9/2/65	Chicago
MILLS, Craig	6-0	190	R	Toronto, Ont.	8/27/76	Indianapolis
MOREAU, Ethan	6-2	205	L	Huntsville, Ont.	9/22/75	Chicago
NABOKOV, Dmitri	6-2	209	R	Novosibirsk, USSR	1/4/77	Soviet Wings-Regn-Ind
PETERS, Geoff	6-0	180	L	Hamilton, Ont.	4/30/78	Erie (OHL)
PROBERT, Bob	6-3	225	L	Windsor, Ont.	6/5/65	Chicago
REICH, Jeremy	6-1	185	L	Craik, Sask.	2/11/79	Seattle
SHANTZ, Jeff	6-0	185	R	Duchess, Alta.	10/10/73	Chicago
SUTTER, Brent	6-0	188	R	Viking, Alta.	6/10/62	Chicago
TARDIF, Steve	6-1	180	L	St-Agnes, Que.	3/29/77	Drummondville
VARIS, Petri	6-1	200	L	Varkaus, Finland	5/13/69	Jokerit
WHITE, Todd	5-10	180	L	Kanata, Ont.	5/21/75	Clarkson
ZHAMNOV, Alexei	6-1	195	L	Moscow, USSR	10/1/70	Chicago
DEFENSEMEN						
CARNEY, Keith	6-2	205	L	Providence, RI	2/3/70	Chicago
CHELIOS, Chris	6-1	190	R	Chicago, IL	1/25/62	Chicago
GRONMAN, Tuomas	6-3	219	R	Viitasaari, Finland	3/22/74	Chicago-Indianapolis
HUSSEY, Marc	6-4	210	R	Chatham, N.B.	1/22/74	Saint John-Utah-Indianapolis
JOHNSON, Andy	6-3	188	L	Fredericton, N.B.	3/6/78	Peterborough
KOZYREV, Andrei	6-1	200	L	Tomsk, USSR	6/17/73	Cherepovets
LAFLAMME, Christian	6-1	202	R	St. Charles, Que.	11/24/76	Chicago-Indianapolis
McLAREN, Steve	6-0	194	L	Owen Sound, Ont.	2/3/75	Indianapolis
NASREDDINE, Alain	6-1	201	L	Montreal, Que.	7/10/75	Carolina-Indianapolis
PAUL, Jeff	6-3	203	R	London, Ont.	3/1/78	Erie (OHL)
RISIDORE, Ryan	6-4	195	L	Hamilton, Ont.	4/4/76	Springfield
ROYER, Remi	6-2	185	R	Donnacona, Que.	2/12/78	Rouyn-Noranda-Indianapolis
RUSSELL, Cam	6-4	200	L	Halifax, N.S.	1/12/69	Chicago
SUTER, Gary	6-0	205	L	Madison, WI	6/24/64	Chicago
SYKORA, Michal	6-5	225	L	Pardubice, Czech.	7/5/73	San Jose-Chicago
TWERDUN, Chris	6-0	200	R	Saskatoon, Sask.	2/11/78	Moose Jaw
VELLINGA, Mike	6-1	218	R	Chatham, Ont.	8/19/78	Guelph
WEINRICH, Eric	6-1	210	L	Roanoke, VA	12/19/66	Chicago
WILFORD, Marty	6-0	216	L	Cobourg, Ont.	4/17/77	Oshawa

GOALTENDERS	HT	WT	C	Place of Birth	Date	1996-97 Club
HACKETT, Jeff	6-1	195	L	London, Ont.	6/1/68	Chicago
LAMOTHE, Marc	6-1	204	L	New Liskeard, Ont.	2/27/74	Indianapolis
TERRERI, Chris	5-8	160	L	Providence, RI	11/15/64	San Jose-Chicago
WAITE, Jimmy	6-1	180	L	Sherbrooke, Que.	4/15/69	Chicago-Indianapolis
WEIBEL, Lars	6-0	178	L	Rapperswil, Switz.	5/20/74	Lugano

Coach

HARTSBURG, CRAIG

Coach, Chicago Blackhawks. Born in Stratford, Ont., June 29, 1959.

Craig Hartsburg, 38, enters his third season as coach of the Chicago Blackhawks.

Hartsburg was introduced as the 30th head coach in the history of the Chicago Blackhawks at a press conference on June 29, 1995. Hartsburg comes to the Blackhawks from the Guelph Storm (OHL), where he was named OHL coach of the year after leading the Storm to a 47-14-5 record.

Hartsburg received his first head coaching position at Guelph in 1994-95 after spending four seasons as an assistant coach with the Philadelphia Flyers (1990-94) and one season as an assistant coach with the Minnesota North Stars (1989-90).

Hartsburg played his entire 10-year NHL career with Minnesota. Known as an offensive-defenseman, Hartsburg was the North Stars' captain for six seasons, until injuries forced him to retire from active play on January 13, 1988.

Hartsburg lists winning the Canada Cup championship in 1987 as his most memorable hockey moment. He participated in three NHL All-Star Games (1980, 1982 and 1983) and also competed in three World Championship tournaments for Team Canada — and was chosen best defenseman of the 1987 World Championships. In February of 1992, Hartsburg was voted to the North Stars' 25th Anniversary Dream Team by Minnesota fans.

Hartsburg and his wife Peggy have two children, Christopher and Katie.

Coaching Record

		Regular Season					Playoffs			
Season	Team	Games	W	L	T	%	Games	W	L	%
1994-95	Guelph (OHL)	66	47	14	5	.750	14	10	4	.714
1995-96	**Chicago (NHL)**	**82**	**40**	**28**	**14**	**.573**	**10**	**6**	**4**	**.600**
1996-97	**Chicago (NHL)**	**82**	**34**	**35**	**13**	**.494**	**6**	**2**	**4**	**.333**
	NHL Totals	**164**	**74**	**63**	**27**	**.534**	**16**	**8**	**8**	**.500**

1996-97 Scoring

* – rookie

Regular Season

Pos	#	Player	Team	GP	G	A	Pts	+/–	PIM	PP	SH	GW	GT	S	%
R	10	Tony Amonte	CHI	81	41	36	77	35	64	9	2	4	2	266	15.4
C	26	Alexei Zhamnov	CHI	74	20	42	62	18	56	6	1	2	0	208	9.6
D	7	Chris Chelios	CHI	72	10	38	48	16	112	2	0	2	0	194	5.2
L	55	Eric Daze	CHI	71	22	19	41	-4	16	11	0	4	0	176	12.5
C	32	Murray Craven	CHI	75	8	27	35	0	12	2	0	1	0	122	6.6
R	22	Ulf Dahlen	S.J.	43	8	11	19	-11	8	3	0	1	0	78	10.3
			CHI	30	6	8	14	9	10	1	0	3	0	53	11.3
			TOTAL	73	14	19	33	-2	18	4	0	4	0	131	10.7
D	2	Eric Weinrich	CHI	81	7	25	32	19	62	1	0	0	1	115	6.1
L	19 *	Ethan Moreau	CHI	82	15	16	31	13	123	0	0	1	1	114	13.2
R	16	Kevin Miller	CHI	69	14	17	31	-10	41	5	1	2	0	139	10.1
C	11	Jeff Shantz	CHI	69	9	21	30	11	28	0	1	1	0	86	10.5
D	20	Gary Suter	CHI	82	7	21	28	-4	70	3	0	0	1	225	3.1
C	18	Denis Savard	CHI	64	9	18	27	-10	60	2	0	2	0	82	11.0
R	25	Sergei Krivokrasov	CHI	67	13	11	24	-1	42	2	0	3	0	104	12.5
L	38	James Black	CHI	64	12	11	23	6	20	0	0	3	0	122	9.8
L	24	Bob Probert	CHI	82	9	14	23	-3	326	1	0	3	0	111	8.1
D	4	Keith Carney	CHI	81	3	15	18	26	62	0	0	1	0	77	3.9
D	6	Michal Sykora	S.J.	35	2	5	7	0	59	1	0	0	0	39	5.1
			CHI	28	1	9	10	4	10	0	0	0	0	38	2.6
			TOTAL	63	3	14	17	4	69	1	0	0	0	77	3.9
C	12	Brent Sutter	CHI	39	7	7	14	10	18	0	0	1	0	62	11.3
R	15	Jim Cummins	CHI	65	6	6	12	4	199	0	0	0	1	61	9.8
D	39	Enrico Ciccone	CHI	67	2	2	4	-1	233	0	0	1	0	65	3.1
C	22	Adam Creighton	CHI	19	1	2	3	-2	13	0	0	0	0	20	5.0
D	8	Cam Russell	CHI	44	1	1	2	-8	65	0	0	0	0	19	5.3
L	37 *	Jean-Yves Leroux	CHI	1	0	1	1	1	5	0	0	0	0	0	0.0
D	44 *	Christian Laflamme	CHI	4	0	1	1	3	2	0	0	0	0	3	0.0
D	46 *	Tuomas Gronman	CHI	16	0	1	1	-4	13	0	0	0	0	9	0.0
G	31	Jeff Hackett	CHI	41	0	1	1	0	6	0	0	0	0	0	0.0
C	17 *	Sergei Klimovich	CHI	1	0	0	0	0	2	0	0	0	0	0	0.0
G	29	Jim Waite	CHI	2	0	0	0	0	0	0	0	0	0	0	0.0
C	14	Steve Dubinsky	CHI	5	0	0	0	2	0	0	0	0	0	4	0.0
R	23 *	Mike Prokopec	CHI	6	0	0	0	-1	6	0	0	0	0	2	0.0
L	54	Dave Chyzowski	CHI	8	0	0	0	1	6	0	0	0	0	6	0.0
L	17	Basil McRae	CHI	8	0	0	0	-2	12	0	0	0	0	1	0.0
D	5	Steve Smith	CHI	21	0	0	0	4	29	0	0	0	0	7	0.0
G	40	Chris Terreri	S.J.	22	0	0	0	0	0	0	0	0	0	0	0.0
			CHI	7	0	0	0	0	0	0	0	0	0	0	0.0
			TOTAL	29	0	0	0	0	0	0	0	0	0	0	0.0

Goaltending

No.	Goaltender	GPI	Mins	Avg	W	L	T	EN	SO	GA	SA	S%
31	Jeff Hackett	41	2473	2.16	19	18	4	2	2	89	1212	.927
40	Chris Terreri	7	429	2.66	4	1	2	1	0	19	192	.901
20	Ed Belfour	33	1966	2.69	11	15	6	4	1	88	946	.907
29	Jim Waite	2	105	4.00	0	1	1	0	0	7	58	.879
	Totals	**82**	**5000**	**2.52**	**34**	**35**	**13**	**7**	**3**	**210**	**2415**	**.913**

Playoffs

Pos	#	Player	Team	GP	G	A	Pts	+/–	PIM	PP	SH	GW	OT	S	%
R	10	Tony Amonte	CHI	6	4	2	6	2	8	0	2	0	0	24	16.7
D	20	Gary Suter	CHI	6	1	4	5	1	8	0	0	0	0	12	8.3
C	11	Jeff Shantz	CHI	6	0	4	4	4	6	0	0	0	0	7	0.0
L	24	Bob Probert	CHI	6	2	1	3	-4	41	1	0	1	0	10	20.0
L	55	Eric Daze	CHI	6	2	1	3	-1	2	0	0	0	0	15	13.3
L	38	James Black	CHI	5	1	1	2	1	2	0	0	0	0	8	12.5
D	4	Keith Carney	CHI	6	1	1	2	-2	2	0	0	0	0	7	14.3
C	18	Denis Savard	CHI	6	0	2	2	-3	2	0	0	0	0	14	0.0
C	14	Steve Dubinsky	CHI	4	1	0	1	0	4	0	0	0	0	6	16.7
R	25	Sergei Krivokrasov	CHI	6	1	0	1	-2	4	0	0	1	1	11	9.1
L	19 *	Ethan Moreau	CHI	6	1	0	1	3	9	0	0	0	0	10	10.0
R	22	Ulf Dahlen	CHI	5	0	1	1	0	0	0	0	0	0	2	0.0
D	7	Chris Chelios	CHI	6	0	1	1	-2	8	0	0	0	0	18	0.0
R	16	Kevin Miller	CHI	6	0	1	1	0	0	0	0	0	0	10	0.0
D	2	Eric Weinrich	CHI	6	0	1	1	-1	4	0	0	0	0	8	0.0
D	6	Michal Sykora	CHI	1	0	0	0	-2	0	0	0	0	0	1	0.0
C	32	Murray Craven	CHI	2	0	0	0	-4	2	0	0	0	0	5	0.0
C	12	Brent Sutter	CHI	2	0	0	0	-2	6	0	0	0	0	3	0.0
G	40	Chris Terreri	CHI	2	0	0	0	0	2	0	0	0	0	0	0.0
D	5	Steve Smith	CHI	3	0	0	0	0	4	0	0	0	0	3	0.0
D	8	Cam Russell	CHI	4	0	0	0	0	4	0	0	0	0	1	0.0
D	39	Enrico Ciccone	CHI	4	0	0	0	0	18	0	0	0	0	6	0.0
G	31	Jeff Hackett	CHI	6	0	0	0	0	0	0	0	0	0	0	0.0
R	15	Jim Cummins	CHI	6	0	0	0	-5	24	0	0	0	0	3	0.0

Goaltending

No.	Goaltender	GPI	Mins	Avg	W	L	EN	SO	GA	SA	S%
40	Chris Terreri	2	44	4.09	0	0	0	0	3	28	.893
31	Jeff Hackett	6	345	4.35	2	4	0	0	25	190	.868
	Totals	**6**	**391**	**4.30**	**2**	**4**	**0**	**0**	**28**	**218**	**.872**

Club Records

Team

(Figures in brackets for season records are games played; records for fewest points, wins, ties, losses, goals, goals against are for 70 or more games)

Most Points	107	1970-71 (78), 1971-72 (78)
Most Wins	49	1970-71 (78), 1990-91 (80)
Most Ties	23	1973-74 (78)
Most Losses	51	1953-54 (70)
Most Goals	351	1985-86 (80)
Most Goals Against	363	1981-82 (80)
Fewest Points	31	1953-54 (70)
Fewest Wins	12	1953-54 (70)
Fewest Ties	6	1989-90 (80)
Fewest Losses	14	1973-74 (78)
Fewest Goals	*133	1953-54 (70)
Fewest Goals Against	164	1973-74 (78)
Longest Winning Streak		
Overall	8	Dec. 9-26/71, Jan. 4-21/81
Home	13	Nov. 11-Dec. 20/70
Away	7	Dec. 9-29/64
Longest Undefeated Streak		
Overall	15	Jan. 14-Feb. 16/67 (12 wins, 3 ties)
Home	18	Oct. 11-Dec. 20/70 (16 wins, 2 ties)
Away	12	Nov. 2-Dec. 16/67 (6 wins, 6 ties)
Longest Losing Streak		
Overall	13	Feb. 25-Oct. 11/51
Home	11	Feb. 8-Nov. 22/28
Away	17	Jan. 2-Oct. 7/54
Longest Winless Streak		
Overall	21	Dec. 17/50-Jan. 28/51 (18 losses, 3 ties)
Home	15	Dec. 16/28-Feb. 28/29 (11 losses, 4 ties)
Away	23	Dec. 19/50-Oct. 11/51 (15 losses, 8 ties)
Most Shutouts, Season	15	1969-70 (76)
Most PIM, Season	2,663	1991-92 (80)
Most Goals, Game	12	Jan. 30/69 (Chi. 12 at Phi. 0)

Individual

Most Seasons	22	Stan Mikita
Most Games	1,394	Stan Mikita
Most Goals, Career	604	Bobby Hull
Most Assists, Career	926	Stan Mikita
Most Points, Career	1,467	Stan Mikita (541G, 926A)
Most PIM, Career	1,442	Keith Magnuson
Most Shutouts, Career	74	Tony Esposito
Longest Consecutive Games Streak	884	Steve Larmer (1982-83 to 1992-93)
Most Goals, Season	58	Bobby Hull (1968-69)
Most Assists, Season	87	Denis Savard (1981-82, 1987-88)
Most Points, Season	131	Denis Savard (1987-88; 44G, 87A)
Most PIM, Season	408	Mike Peluso (1991-92)
Most Points, Defenseman, Season	85	Doug Wilson (1981-82; 39G, 46A)
Most Points, Center, Season	131	Denis Savard (1987-88; 44G, 87A)
Most Points, Right Wing, Season	101	Steve Larmer (1990-91; 44G, 57A)
Most Points, Left Wing, Season	107	Bobby Hull (1968-69; 58G, 49A)
Most Points, Rookie, Season	90	Steve Larmer (1982-83; 43G, 47A)
Most Shutouts, Season	15	Tony Esposito (1969-70)
Most Goals, Game	5	Grant Mulvey (Feb. 3/82)
Most Assists, Game	6	Pat Stapleton (Mar. 30/69)
Most Points, Game	7	Max Bentley (Jan. 28/43; 4G, 3A), Grant Mulvey (Feb. 3/82; 5G, 2A)

* NHL Record.

Retired Numbers

1	Glenn Hall	1957-1967
9	Bobby Hull	1957-1972
21	Stan Mikita	1958-1980
35	Tony Esposito	1969-1984

Captains' History

Dick Irvin, 1926-27 to 1928-29; "Duke" Dutkowski, 1929-30; Ty Arbour, 1930-31; Cy Wentworth, 1931-32; Helge Bostrom, 1932-33; Chuck Gardiner, 1933-34; no captain, 1934-35; Johnny Gottselig, 1935-36 to 1939-40; Earl Seibert, 1940-41, 1941-42; Doug Bentley, 1942-43, 1943-44; Clint Smith 1944-45; John Mariucci, 1945-46; "Red" Hamill, 1946-47; John Mariucci, 1947-48; Gaye Stewart, 1948-49; Doug Bentley, 1949-50; Jack Stewart, 1950-51, 1951-52; Bill Gadsby, 1952-53, 1953-54; Gus Mortson, 1954-55 to 1956-57; no captain, 1957-58; Eddie Litzenberger, 1958-59 to 1960-61; Pierre Pilote, 1961-62 to 1967-68, no captain, 1968-69; Pat Stapleton, 1969-70; no captain, 1970-71 to 1974-75; Stan Mikita and "Pit" Martin, 1975-76; Stan Mikita, "Pit" Martin and Keith Magnuson, 1976-77; Keith Magnuson, 1977-78, 1978-79; Keith Magnuson, Terry Ruskowski, 1979-80; Terry Ruskowski, 1980-81, 1981-82; Darryl Sutter, 1982-83 to 1984-85; Darryl Sutter and Bob Murray, 1985-86; Darryl Sutter, 1986-87; no captain, 1987-88; Denis Savard and Dirk Graham, 1988-89; Dirk Graham, 1989-90 to 1994-95; Chris Chelios, 1995-96 to date.

All-time Record vs. Other Clubs

Regular Season

	At Home							On Road							Total						
	GP	W	L	T	GF	GA	PTS	GP	W	L	T	GF	GA	PTS	GP	W	L	T	GF	GA	PTS
Anaheim	9	5	3	1	23	16	11	8	5	2	1	22	17	11	17	10	5	2	45	33	22
Boston	280	143	93	44	904	748	330	278	86	159	33	786	1008	205	558	229	252	77	1690	1756	535
Buffalo	45	24	15	6	147	125	54	47	12	29	6	122	178	30	92	36	44	12	269	303	84
Calgary	47	21	15	11	165	141	53	49	19	22	8	148	154	46	96	40	37	19	313	295	99
Colorado	27	15	10	2	102	90	32	26	10	12	4	99	109	24	53	25	22	6	201	199	56
Dallas	95	61	24	10	388	248	132	97	42	40	15	314	321	99	192	103	64	25	702	569	231
Detroit	318	146	122	50	960	888	342	317	93	195	29	777	1085	215	635	239	317	79	1737	1973	557
Edmonton	30	17	9	4	126	111	38	31	14	15	2	120	125	30	61	31	24	6	246	236	68
Florida	3	1	1	1	13	11	3	3	2	1	0	11	8	4	6	3	2	1	24	19	7
Hartford	24	15	6	3	107	68	33	25	11	11	3	84	85	25	49	26	17	6	191	153	58
Los Angeles	61	31	22	8	233	184	70	60	29	25	6	215	205	64	121	60	47	14	448	389	134
Montreal	269	91	123	55	724	754	237	269	51	170	48	634	1045	150	538	142	293	103	1358	1799	387
New Jersey	41	23	10	8	170	116	54	40	15	15	10	122	119	40	81	38	25	18	292	235	94
NY Islanders	43	22	16	5	145	148	49	41	11	17	13	123	148	35	84	33	33	18	268	296	84
NY Rangers	280	126	112	42	853	778	294	281	110	116	55	797	833	275	561	236	228	97	1650	1611	569
Ottawa	4	2	1	1	11	10	5	4	3	1	0	15	9	6	8	5	2	1	26	19	11
Philadelphia	55	25	11	19	198	156	69	56	16	29	11	151	182	43	111	41	40	30	349	338	112
Phoenix	34	23	8	3	153	98	49	35	12	19	4	118	130	28	69	35	27	7	271	228	77
Pittsburgh	54	37	8	9	228	146	83	53	23	25	5	178	189	51	107	60	33	14	406	335	134
St. Louis	99	56	29	14	389	303	126	95	33	45	17	298	317	83	194	89	74	31	687	620	209
San Jose	11	7	3	1	41	30	15	12	6	6	0	36	31	12	23	13	9	1	77	61	27
Tampa Bay	7	3	2	2	17	15	8	6	2	3	1	17	18	5	13	5	5	3	34	33	13
Toronto	307	154	112	41	946	798	349	307	93	161	53	794	1048	239	614	247	273	94	1740	1846	588
Vancouver	57	37	14	6	220	135	80	58	17	27	14	166	177	48	115	54	41	20	386	312	128
Washington	34	21	8	5	141	103	47	35	12	19	4	111	130	28	69	33	27	9	252	233	75
Defunct Clubs	139	79	40	20	408	268	178	140	52	67	21	316	346	125	279	131	107	41	724	614	303
Totals	**2373**	**1185**	**817**	**371**	**7812**	**6488**	**2741**	**2373**	**779**	**1231**	**363**	**6574**	**8017**	**1921**	**4746**	**1964**	**2048**	**734**	**14386**	**14505**	**4662**

Playoffs

	Series	W	L	GP	W	L	T	GF	GA	Last Mtg.	Round	Result
Boston	6	1	5	22	5	16	1	63	97	1978	QF	L 0-4
Buffalo	2	0	2	9	1	8	0	17	36	1980	QF	L 0-4
Calgary	3	1	2	12	5	7	0	33	37	1996	CQF	W 4-0
Colorado	2	0	2	12	4	8	0	28	49	1997	CQF	L 2-4
Dallas	6	4	2	33	19	14	0	119	119	1991	DSF	L 2-4
Detroit	14	8	6	69	38	31	0	210	190	1995	CF	L 1-4
Edmonton	4	1	3	20	8	12	0	77	102	1992	CF	W 4-0
Los Angeles	1	1	0	5	4	1	0	10	7	1974	QF	W 4-1
Montreal	17	5	12	81	29	50	2	185	261	1976	QF	L 0-4
NY Islanders	2	0	2	6	0	6	0	6	21	1979	QF	L 0-4
NY Rangers	5	4	1	24	14	10	0	66	54	1973	SF	W 4-1
Philadelphia	1	1	0	4	4	0	0	20	8	1971	QF	W 4-0
Pittsburgh	2	1	1	8	4	4	0	24	23	1992	F	L 0-4
St. Louis	9	7	2	45	27	18	0	166	129	1993	DSF	L 0-4
Toronto	9	3	6	38	15	22	1	89	111	1995	CQF	W 4-3
Vancouver	2	1	1	9	5	4	0	24	24	1995	CSF	W 4-0
Defunct Clubs	4	2	2	9	5	3	1	16	15			
Totals	**89**	**40**	**49**	**406**	**187**	**214**	**5**	**1153**	**1283**			

Calgary totals include Atlanta, 1972-73 to 1979-80. Colorado totals include Quebec, 1979-80 to 1994-95. Dallas totals include Minnesota, 1967-68 to 1992-93. New Jersey totals include Kansas City, 1974-75 to 1975-76, and Colorado Rockies, 1976-77 to 1981-82. Phoenix totals include Winnipeg, 1979-80 to 1995-96.

Playoff Results 1997-93

Year	Round	Opponent	Result	GF	GA
1997	CQF	Colorado	L 2-4	14	28
1996	CSF	Colorado	L 2-4	14	21
	CQF	Calgary	W 4-0	16	7
1995	CF	Detroit	L 1-4	12	13
	CSF	Vancouver	W 4-0	11	6
	CQF	Toronto	W 4-3	22	20
1994	CQF	Toronto	L 2-4	10	15
1993	DSF	St. Louis	L 0-4	6	13

Abbreviations: Round: F – Final; **CF** – conference final; **CQF** – conference quarter-final; **CSF** – conference semi-final; **DF** – division final; **DSF** – division semi-final; **SF** – semi-final; **QF** – quarter-final; **PR** – preliminary round.

1996-97 Results

Oct.	5	at	Washington	5-2	**Jan.**	2		Phoenix	2-4
	6	at	St. Louis	4-1		5		Detroit	5-5
	9		Anaheim	0-2		8		Edmonton	4-1
	11		Colorado	0-2		10	at	New Jersey	3-3
	13		Dallas	3-5		11	at	Detroit	3-1
	15	at	Toronto	3-1		13		Tampa Bay	0-2
	17		Detroit	2-1		20	at	Buffalo	1-2
	20		Los Angeles	2-1		22		Vancouver	3-4
	24		St. Louis	6-4		24		Toronto	1-2
	25	at	Detroit	2-2		25	at	NY Islanders	2-3
	27		San Jose	2-6		27	at	NY Rangers	2-1
	29	at	Tampa Bay	2-2	**Feb.**	1	at	Los Angeles	3-2
	30	at	Florida	2-3		3	at	San Jose	4-2
Nov.	1	at	Dallas	3-2		6	at	Phoenix	2-3
	3		Edmonton	4-2		8	at	Colorado	4-2
	7		New Jersey	2-4		13		San Jose	7-3
	9	at	Philadelphia	4-1		15		NY Rangers	2-0
	10		Ottawa	2-0		17	at	St. Louis	2-4
	14		Calgary	1-2		20		Boston	5-3
	15	at	Ottawa	3-4		22	at	Pittsburgh	5-2
	17		Los Angeles	2-4		25		Dallas	0-1
	19	at	Edmonton	4-4		26	at	Hartford	2-2
	21	at	Vancouver	1-2	**Mar.**	1	at	Colorado	1-2
	22	at	Calgary	5-2		2	at	Phoenix	4-0
	27	at	San Jose	2-3		5	at	Vancouver	1-1
	29	at	Anaheim	0-2		8		Phoenix	0-2
	30	at	Los Angeles	5-3		10		Vancouver	2-2
Dec.	6		Montreal	1-3		12	at	Toronto	3-2
	7	at	Montreal	2-3		14	at	Dallas	4-4
	9		Toronto	1-3		16		NY Islanders	5-4
	12	at	Detroit	2-6		20		Phoenix	2-4
	13	at	St. Louis	4-1		23		Detroit	5-3
	15		Pittsburgh	2-1		26		Washington	5-3
	18		Dallas	2-3		28		Anaheim	3-4
	20		Florida	1-3		30		Buffalo	3-2
	22		Philadelphia	2-2	**Apr.**	1	at	Anaheim	3-3
	23	at	Boston	3-3		3	at	Edmonton	2-4
	26		St. Louis	4-4		6	at	Calgary	2-1
	28	at	Toronto	4-5		9		St. Louis	0-1
	29		Hartford	4-3		11		Calgary	7-3
	31		Colorado	1-4		13	at	Dallas	5-2

Entry Draft
Selections 1997-83

1997 Pick		**1993** Pick		**1989** Pick		**1985** Pick	
13	Daniel Cleary	24	Eric Lecompte	6	Adam Bennett	11	Dave Manson
16	Ty Jones	50	Eric Manlow	27	Michael Speer	53	Andy Helmuth
39	Jeremy Reich	54	Bogdan Savenko	48	Bob Kellogg	74	Dan Vincellette
67	Mike Souza	76	Ryan Huska	111	Tommi Pullola	87	Rick Herbert
110	Benjamin Simon	90	Eric Daze	132	Tracy Egeland	95	Brad Belland
120	Peter Gardiner	102	Patrik Pysz	153	Milan Tichy	116	Jonas Heed
130	Kyle Calder	128	Jonni Vauhkonen	174	Jason Greyerbiehl	137	Victor Posa
147	Heath Gordon	180	Tom White	195	Matt Saunders	158	John Reid
174	Jerad Smith	206	Sergei Petrov	216	Mike Kozak	179	Richard LaPlante
204	Sergei Shikhanov	232	Mike Rusk	237	Michael Doneghey	200	Brad Hamilton
230	Chris Feil	258	Mike McGhan			221	Ian Pound
		284	Tom Noble	**1988** Pick		242	Rick Braccia
1996 Pick				8	Jeremy Roenick		
31	Remi Royer	**1992** Pick		50	Trevor Dam	**1984** Pick	
42	Jeff Paul	12	Sergei Krivokrasov	71	Stefan Elvenas	3	Ed Olczyk
46	Geoff Peters	36	Jeff Shantz	92	Joe Cleary	45	Trent Yawney
130	Andy Johnson	41	Sergei Klimovich	113	Justin Lafayette	66	Tommy Eriksson
184	Mike Vellinga	89	Andy MacIntyre	134	Craig Woodcroft	90	Timo Lehkonen
210	Chris Twerdun	113	Tim Hogan	155	Jon Pojar	101	Darin Sceviour
236	Alexei Kozyrev	137	Gerry Skrypec	176	Mathew Hentges	111	Chris Clifford
		161	Mike Prokopec	197	Daniel Maurice	132	Mike Stapleton
1995 Pick		185	Layne Roland	218	Dirk Tenzer	153	Glen Greenough
19	Dimitri Nabokov	209	David Hymovitz	239	Andreas Lupzig	174	Ralph DiFiorie
45	Christian Laflamme	233	Richard Raymond			194	Joakim Persson
71	Kevin McKay			**1987** Pick		215	Bill Brown
82	Chris Van Dyk	**1991** Pick		8	Jimmy Waite	224	David Mackey
97	Pavel Kriz	22	Dean McAmmond	29	Ryan McGill	235	Dan Williams
146	Marc Magliarditi	39	Michael Pomichter	50	Cam Russell		
149	Marty Wilford	44	Jamie Matthews	60	Mike Dagenais	**1983** Pick	
175	Steve Tardif	66	Bobby House	92	Ulf Sandstrom	18	Bruce Cassidy
201	Casey Hankinson	71	Igor Kravchuk	113	Mike McCormick	39	Wayne Presley
227	Mike Pittman	88	Zac Boyer	134	Stephen Tepper	59	Marc Bergevin
		110	Maco Balkovec	155	John Reilly	79	Tarek Howard
1994 Pick		112	Kevin St. Jacques	176	Lance Werness	99	Kevin Robinson
14	Ethan Moreau	132	Jacques Auger	197	Dale Marquette	115	Jari Torkki
40	Jean-Yves Leroux	154	Scott Kirton	218	Bill Lacouture	119	Mark Lavarre
85	Steve McLaren	176	Roch Belley	239	Mike Lappin	139	Scot Birnie
118	Marc Dupuis	198	Scott MacDonald			159	Kevin Paynter
144	Jim Enson	220	A. Andriyevsky	**1986** Pick		179	Brian Noonan
170	Tyler Prosofsky	242	Mike Larkin	14	Everett Sanipass	199	Dominik Hasek
196	Mike Josephson	264	Scott Dean	35	Mark Kurzawski	219	Steve Pepin
222	Lubomir Jandera			77	Frantisek Kucera		
248	Lars Weibel	**1990** Pick		98	Lonnie Loach		
263	Rob Mara	16	Karl Dykhuis	119	Mario Doyon		
		37	Ivan Droppa	140	Mike Hudson		
		79	Chris Tucker	161	Marty Nanne		
		121	Brett Stickney	182	Geoff Benic		
		124	Derek Edgerly	203	Glen Lowes		
		163	Hugo Belanger	224	Chris Thayer		
		184	Owen Lessard	245	Sean Williams		
		205	Erik Peterson				
		226	Steve Dubinsky				
		247	Dino Grossi				

General Manager

MURRAY, BOB
General Manager, Chicago Blackhawks.
Born in Kingston, Ont., November 26, 1954.

Bob Murray was named as the sixth general manager in the history of the Chicago Blackhawks on July 3, 1997. Murray has been with the Blackhawk organization for more than 23 years, dating back to 1974 when he was drafted by the Blackhawks.

Murray spent his entire NHL playing career in Chicago, playing 1,008 games in a Blackhawk uniform. He became only the fourth player in team history to reach the 1,000-game plateau and during the 1990 Stanley Cup Playoffs, he became the first defenseman in team history to play over 100 playoff games.

He ranks first among All-Time Blackhawk defensemen in games played and ranks second among All-Time Blackhawk defensemen in career points with 514. During his 15-year Blackhawk career, Murray scored 132 goals (26th overall) and 382 assists (8th overall) totalling 514 points (12th overall). He played in two NHL All-Star Games (1981 and 1983) and recorded an assist.

Murray's playing career was marked by tremendous skill, endurance and determination. His great effort and preparation were well noted by the organization, along with his organization and management skills. All these traits convinced the Blackhawks to sign Murray as a pro scout in 1990. Within a year he was appointed director of player personnel, mastering the computerized system which keeps tabs on all players observed by the scouting staff.

Murray has directed the Blackhawks in the NHL Entry Draft since 1992, and his selections over the last six Drafts have provided a solid foundation for the future of the organization. Murray's keen eye for talent has brought young NHL players like Eric Daze, Ethan Moreau and Jeff Shantz into the Blackhawks' organization. Murray has spent considerable time over the last six seasons scouting individual amateur players while coordinating Blackhawk scouting efforts in North America and Europe.

Prior to the 1995-96 season Murray was named as the club's assistant general manager. In that role, he has spent the last two seasons learning about the business side of management working closely with general manager Bob Pulford.

Club Directory

United Center

Chicago Blackhawk Hockey Team, Inc.
1901 W. Madison Street
Chicago, IL 60612
Phone **312/455-7000**
FAX 312/455-7041
Internet Address
www.chicagoblackhawks.com
Capacity: 20,500

President	William W. Wirtz
Vice President & Assistant to the President	Thomas N. Ivan
Senior Vice President	Robert J. Pulford
Vice President	Jack Davison
General Manager	Bob Murray
Head Coach	Craig Hartsburg
Assistant Coach	Lorne Henning
Assistant Coach	Newell Brown
Goaltending Consultant	Vladislav Tretiak
Development Coach/Comm. Relations Ambassador	Denis Savard
Pro Scout	Dirk Graham
Pro Scout	Phil Russell
Chief Amateur Scout	Michel Dumas
Amateur Scout	Bruce Franklin
Amateur Scout	Tim Higgins
Amateur Scout	Dave Lucas
Amateur Scout	Steve Lyons
Amateur Scout	Steve Richmond
European Scout	Jan Blomgren
European Scout	Lars Norrman
Assistant to the General Manager	Tom Finks

Medical Staff

Club Doctors	Mark Bowen, Gordon Nuber
Team Dentist	Dr. Daniel Mackey, Dr. Dean Sana
Oral Surgeon	Dr. Eric Pulver
Eye Doctor	Dr. Robert Stein
Head Trainer	Michael Gapski
Equipment Manager	Troy Parchman
Asst. Equipment Mgr.	Lou Varga
Massage Therapist	Pawel Prylinski
Strength & Conditioning Trainer	Mark Kling

Finance

Controller	Robert Rinkus
Assistant to the Controller	Penny Swenson
Staff Accountant	Dave Jorns
Accounting Secretary	Pat Dema

Ticketing

Director of Ticket Operations	James K. Bare
Sales Manager	Doug Ryan
Sr. Season & Group Sales Rep	Danny Lucier
Season & Group Sales Rep.	Steve Rigney
Sr. Ticket Operations Rep.	Kathie Ralmondi
Ticket Operations Rep.	Martha Webster

Public Relations/Marketing

Vice President of Marketing	Peter R. Wirtz
Executive Director of Public Relations	Jim DeMaria
Director of Community Relations/PR Assistant	Barbara Davidson
Director of Publications/PR Assistant	Brad Freeman
Executive Director of Marketing/Merchandising	Jim Sofranko
Dir. of Corporate Partnerships	Elliot Bell
Manager, Client Services	Kelly Bodnarchuk
Dir. of Projects & Development	Carol Kolbus
Manager, Special Events	Matt Colleran
Marketing Associate	Alison Tragesser

Miscellaneous Information

Team Photographers	Ray Grabowski, Rob Grabowski
Organist	Frank Pellico
Public Address Announcer	Harvey Wittenberg
Executive Offices/Home Ice	United Center
Location of Press Box	North Side of United Center
Dimensions of Rink	200 feet by 85 feet
Ends of Rink	Plexi-glass extends above boards all around rink
Club Colors	Red, White & Black
Radio Station	WMAQ (AM 670)
Television Station	Fox Sports Chicago
Broadcasters	Pat Foley, Dale Tallon, Dave Pasch

Coaching History

Pete Muldoon, 1926-27; Barney Stanley and Hugh Lehman, 1927-28; Herb Gardiner, 1928-29; Tom Shaughnessy and Bill Tobin, 1929-30; Dick Irvin, 1930-31; Dick Irvin and Bill Tobin, 1931-32; Emil Iverson, Godfrey Matheson and Tommy Gorman, 1932-33; Tommy Gorman, 1933-34; Clem Loughlin, 1934-35 to 1936-37; Bill Stewart, 1937-38; Bill Stewart and Paul Thompson, 1938-39; Paul Thompson, 1939-40 to 1943-44; Paul Thompson and Johnny Gottselig, 1944-45; Johnny Gottselig, 1945-46 to 1946-47; Johnny Gottselig and Charlie Conacher, 1947-48; Charlie Conacher, 1948-49, 1949-50; Ebbie Goodfellow, 1950-51 to 1951-52; Sid Abel, 1952-53 to 1953-54; Frank Eddolls, 1954-55; Dick Irvin, 1955-56; Tommy Ivan, 1956-57; Tommy Ivan and Rudy Pilous, 1957-58; Rudy Pilous, 1958-59 to 1962-63; Billy Reay, 1963-64 to 1975-76; Billy Reay and Bill White, 1976-77; Bob Pulford, 1977-78, 1978-79; Eddie Johnston, 1979-80; Keith Magnuson, 1980-81; Keith Magnuson and Bob Pulford, 1981-82; Orval Tessier, 1982-83 to 1983-84; Orval Tessier and Bob Pulford, 1984-85; Bob Pulford, 1985-86 to 1986-87; Bob Murdoch, 1987-88; Mike Keenan, 1988-89 to 1991-92; Darryl Sutter, 1992-93 to 1994-95; Craig Hartsburg, 1995-96 to date.

General Managers' History

Major Frederic McLaughlin, 1926-27 to 1941-42; Bill Tobin, 1942-43 to 1953-54; Tommy Ivan, 1954-55 to 1976-77; Bob Pulford, 1977-78 to 1989-90; Mike Keenan, 1990-91 to 1991-92; Mike Keenan and Bob Pulford, 1992-93; Bob Pulford, 1993-94 to 1996-97; Bob Murray, 1997-98.

Colorado Avalanche

1996-97 Results: 49W-24L-9T 107PTS. First, Pacific Division

1997-98 Schedule

Oct.				Jan.			
	Wed.	1	Dallas	Fri.	2	at Buffalo
	Fri.	3	at Calgary	Sat.	3	at Pittsburgh
	Sun.	5	at Edmonton	Tue.	6	Calgary
	Tue.	7	Boston	Thu.	8	Vancouver
	Thu.	9	San Jose	Sat.	10	Ottawa
	Sat.	11	Phoenix	Mon.	12	Florida
	Wed.	15	at Edmonton	Wed.	14	at Anaheim
	Fri.	17	at Calgary	Thu.	15	San Jose
	Sun.	19	at Vancouver*	Wed.	21	at Dallas
	Wed.	22	Washington	Thu.	22	Anaheim
	Fri.	24	Carolina	Sat.	24	Dallas*
	Sat.	25	at Dallas	Mon.	26	Edmonton
	Tue.	28	Buffalo	Wed.	28	Vancouver
	Thu.	30	at St. Louis	Sat.	31	at San Jose*
Nov.	Sat.	1	Calgary	Feb. Mon.	2	at Vancouver
	Wed.	5	NY Rangers	Thu.	5	Chicago
	Sat.	8	St. Louis*	Sat.	7	Philadelphia*
	Tue.	11	at Detroit	Wed.	25	at Phoenix
	Thu.	13	at Philadelphia	Thu.	26	Phoenix
	Fri.	14	at New Jersey	Sat.	28	Chicago*
	Sun.	16	at NY Rangers*	Mar. Mon.	2	Edmonton
	Tue.	18	at Washington	Wed.	4	at Toronto
	Fri.	21	Toronto	Thu.	5	at Ottawa
	Sun.	23	Los Angeles	Sat.	7	at NY Islanders
	Wed.	26	at Tampa Bay	Mon.	9	Tampa Bay
	Fri.	28	at Florida*	Wed.	11	St. Louis
	Sat.	29	at Carolina	Sat.	14	at Los Angeles*
Dec.	Tue.	2	Edmonton	Sun.	15	at Anaheim
	Thu.	4	at Chicago	Thu.	19	at Phoenix
	Sat.	6	Vancouver	Sat.	21	at San Jose*
	Mon.	8	at Montreal	Thu.	26	New Jersey
	Wed.	10	at Toronto	Sat.	28	Anaheim*
	Fri.	12	at Calgary	Mon.	30	at Boston
	Sat.	13	at Vancouver	Apr. Wed.	1	at Detroit
	Mon.	15	Toronto	Thu.	2	at Chicago
	Wed.	17	Detroit	Sat.	4	at St. Louis*
	Fri.	19	Pittsburgh	Mon.	6	Los Angeles
	Tue.	23	Los Angeles	Sat.	11	at Los Angeles*
	Sat.	27	at Edmonton	Mon.	13	at Anaheim
	Mon.	29	Montreal	Thu.	16	San Jose
	Wed.	31	NY Islanders	Sat.	18	Detroit*

* Denotes afternoon game.

Franchise date: June 22, 1979
Transferred from Quebec to Denver,
June 21, 1995

**PACIFIC
DIVISION**

**19th
NHL
Season**

Despite missing 17 games with a knee injury, Peter Forsberg still led the Avalanche in points (86), short-handed goals (4) and plus/minus (+31).

Year-by-Year Record

		Home			Road			Overall							
Season	GP	W	L	T	W	L	T	W	L	T	GF	GA	Pts.	Finished	Playoff Result
1996-97	82	26	10	5	23	14	4	49	24	9	277	205	107	1st, Pacific Div.	Lost Conf. Championship
1995-96	**82**	**24**	**10**	**7**	**23**	**15**	**3**	**47**	**25**	**10**	**326**	**240**	**104**	**1st, Pacific Div.**	**Won Stanley Cup**
1994-95*	48	19	1	4	11	12	1	30	13	5	185	134	65	1st, Northeast Div.	Lost Conf. Quarter-Final
1993-94*	84	19	17	6	15	25	2	34	42	8	277	292	76	5th, Northeast Div.	Out of Playoffs
1992-93*	84	23	17	2	24	10	8	47	27	10	351	300	104	2nd, Adams Div.	Lost Div. Semi-Final
1991-92*	80	18	19	3	2	29	9	20	48	12	255	318	52	5th, Adams Div.	Out of Playoffs
1990-91*	80	9	23	8	7	27	6	16	50	14	236	354	46	5th, Adams Div.	Out of Playoffs
1989-90*	80	8	26	6	4	35	1	12	61	7	240	407	31	5th, Adams Div.	Out of Playoffs
1988-89*	80	16	20	4	11	26	3	27	46	7	269	342	61	5th, Adams Div.	Out of Playoffs
1987-88*	80	15	23	2	17	20	3	32	43	5	271	306	69	5th, Adams Div.	Out of Playoffs
1986-87*	80	20	13	7	11	26	3	31	39	10	267	276	72	4th, Adams Div.	Lost Div. Final
1985-86*	80	23	13	4	20	18	2	43	31	6	330	289	92	1st, Adams Div.	Lost Div. Semi-Final
1984-85*	80	24	12	4	17	18	5	41	30	9	323	275	91	2nd, Adams Div.	Lost Conf. Championship
1983-84*	80	24	11	5	18	17	5	42	28	10	360	278	94	3rd, Adams Div.	Lost Div. Final
1982-83*	80	23	10	7	11	24	5	34	34	12	343	336	80	4th, Adams Div.	Lost Div. Semi-Final
1981-82*	80	24	13	3	9	18	13	33	31	16	356	345	82	4th, Adams Div.	Lost Conf. Championship
1980-81*	80	18	11	11	12	21	7	30	32	18	314	318	78	4th, Adams Div.	Lost Prelim. Round
1979-80*	80	17	16	7	8	28	4	25	44	11	248	313	61	5th, Adams Div.	Out of Playoffs

* Quebec Nordiques

1997-98 Player Personnel

FORWARDS	HT	WT	S	Place of Birth	Date	1996-97 Club
BEAUDOIN, Nic	6-3	205	L	Ottawa, Ont.	12/25/76	Hershey
CORBET, Rene	6-0	187	L	Victoriaville, Que.	6/25/73	Colorado
DEADMARSH, Adam	6-0	195	R	Trail, B.C.	5/10/75	Colorado
DRURY, Chris	5-10	180	R	Trumbull, CT	8/20/76	Boston U.
FORSBERG, Peter	6-0	190	L	Ornskoldsvik, Sweden	7/20/73	Colorado
JONES, Keith	6-2	200	L	Brantford, Ont.	11/8/68	Washington-Colorado
KAMENSKY, Valeri	6-2	198	R	Voskresensk, USSR	4/18/66	Colorado
KURRI, Jari	6-1	195	R	Helsinki, Finland	5/18/60	Anaheim
LACROIX, Eric	6-1	205	L	Montreal, Que.	7/15/71	Colorado
LARSEN, Brad	5-11	212	L	Nakusp, B.C.	1/28/77	Swift Current
LEMIEUX, Claude	6-1	215	R	Buckingham, Que.	7/16/65	Colorado
MARHA, Josef	6-0	176	L	Havlickuv Brod, Czech.	6/2/76	Colorado-Hershey
MATTE, Christian	5-11	166	R	Hull, Que.	1/20/75	Colorado-Hershey
NIEMINEN, Ville	5-11	205	L	Tampere, Finland	4/6/77	Tappara
RICCI, Mike	6-0	190	L	Scarborough, Ont.	10/27/71	Colorado
SAKIC, Joe	5-11	185	L	Burnaby, B.C.	7/7/69	Colorado
SARAULT, Yves	6-1	170	L	Valleyfield, Que.	12/23/72	Colorado-Hershey
SEVERYN, Brent	6-2	211	L	Vegreville, Alta.	2/22/66	Colorado
SHEARER, Rob	5-10	190	R	Kitchener, Ont.	10/19/76	Hershey
SIMON, Jason	6-1	210	L	Sarnia, Ont.	3/21/69	Phoenix-Las Vegas
YELLE, Stephane	6-1	162	L	Ottawa, Ont.	5/9/74	Colorado
YOUNG, Scott	6-0	190	R	Clinton, MA	10/1/67	Colorado
DEFENSEMEN						
BELAK, Wade	6-4	213	R	Saskatoon, Sask.	7/3/76	Colorado-Hershey
FOOTE, Adam	6-1	202	R	Toronto, Ont.	7/10/71	Colorado
GUSAROV, Alexei	6-3	185	L	Leningrad, USSR	7/8/64	Colorado
KLEMM, Jon	6-3	200	R	Cranbrook, B.C.	1/8/70	Colorado
KRUPP, Uwe	6-6	235	R	Cologne, West Germany	6/24/65	Colorado
LEFEBVRE, Sylvain	6-2	205	L	Richmond, Que.	10/14/67	Colorado
MESSIER, Eric	6-2	200	L	Drummondville, Que.	10/29/73	Colorado-Hershey
MILLER, Aaron	6-3	197	R	Buffalo, NY	8/11/71	Colorado
OZOLINSH, Sandis	6-1	195	L	Riga, Latvia	8/3/72	Colorado
RATCHUK, Peter	6-0	175	L	Buffalo, NY	9/10/77	Bowling Green
SMITH, Dan	6-2	195	L	Fernie, B.C.	10/19/76	Tri-City-Hershey
TREPANIER, Pascal	6-0	205	R	Gaspe, Que.	4/9/73	Hershey

GOALTENDERS	HT	WT	C	Place of Birth	Date	1996-97 Club
BILLINGTON, Craig	5-10	170	L	London, Ont.	9/11/66	Colorado
DENIS, Marc	6-0	188	L	Montreal, Que.	8/1/77	Colorado-Chicoutimi-Hershey
FISCHER, Kai	5-11	176	L	Forst, Germany	3/25/77	Dusseldorf
PETRUK, Randy	5-9	178	R	Cranbrook, B.C.	4/23/78	Kamloops
ROY, Patrick	6-0	192	L	Quebec City, Que.	10/5/65	Colorado
THOMAS, Tim	5-11	180	L	Flint, MI	4/15/74	U. of Vermont

General Manager

LACROIX, PIERRE
President and General Manager, Colorado Avalanche.
Born in Montreal, Que., August 3, 1948.

Pierre Lacroix was appointed to the general manager's post on May 24, 1994 after 21 years as a respected player agent. In his first season (1994-95) as general manager, his leadership was instrumental in moving the team from 11th to second place in the NHL. Lacroix's second season began with the club's move to Denver. He set out to improve the team and did so through acquisitions that brought Claude Lemieux, Sandis Ozolinsh, Patrick Roy and Mike Keane to Colorado. The revamped Avs finished atop the Pacific Division and went on to win the Stanley Cup. He was named NHL executive of the year by *The Hockey News* and became president of the club's hockey operations in August, 1995.

Lacroix and his wife Colombe have two children. Martin (27) is a player agent. Eric (26) plays left wing for the Avalanche.

Coach

CRAWFORD, MARC
Coach, Colorado Avalanche. Born in Belleville, Ont., February 13, 1961.

Marc Crawford became the tenth head coach in franchise history on July 6th, 1994. In 1994-95, he led the franchise (Quebec) to second place overall in the NHL and became the first rookie coach to win the Jack Adams Award.

In June 1996, he led the Avalanche to the Stanley Cup, becoming the first coach to lead a team to the championship in its first year in a new city.

Crawford played seven seasons with the Vancouver Canucks beginning in 1981. He became general manager and coach of the Cornwall Royals in the Ontario Hockey League in 1989 and joined the Maple Leafs organization as coach of Toronto's AHL farm club two years later. He reached the Calder Cup finals in his first AHL season and was named top coach in the league in 1992.

One of nine children, his father and two of his brothers also played pro hockey. Crawford and his wife Helene have two children, Dylan and Kaitlin.

Coaching Record

		Regular Season					Playoffs			
Season	Team	Games	W	L	T	%	Games	W	L	%
1989-90	Cornwall (OHL)	66	24	38	4	.394	6	2	4	.333
1990-91	Cornwall (OHL)	66	23	42	1	.356	....	....	....	....
1991-92	St. John's (AHL)	80	39	29	12	.562	16	11	5	.688
1992-93	St. John's (AHL)	80	41	26	13	.594	9	4	5	.444
1993-94	St. John's (AHL)	80	45	23	12	.638	11	6	5	.545
1994-95	**Quebec (NHL)**	**48**	**30**	**13**	**5**	**.677**	**6**	**2**	**4**	**.333**
1995-96	**Colorado (NHL)**	**82**	**47**	**25**	**10**	**.634**	**22**	**16**	**6**	**.727***
1996-97	**Colorado (NHL)**	**82**	**49**	**24**	**9**	**.652**	**17**	**10**	**7**	**.588**
	NHL Totals	**212**	**126**	**62**	**24**	**.651**	**45**	**28**	**17**	**.622**

* Stanley Cup win.

1996-97 Scoring

* – rookie

Regular Season

Pos	#	Player	Team	GP	G	A	Pts	+/–	PIM	PP	SH	GW	GT	S	%
C	21	Peter Forsberg	COL	65	28	58	86	31	73	5	4	4	0	188	14.9
C	19	Joe Sakic	COL	65	22	52	74	-10	34	10	2	5	0	261	8.4
D	8	Sandis Ozolinsh	COL	80	23	45	68	4	88	13	0	4	1	232	9.9
L	13	Valeri Kamensky	COL	68	28	38	66	5	38	8	0	4	1	165	17.0
R	18	Adam Deadmarsh	COL	78	33	27	60	8	136	10	3	4	0	198	16.7
R	11	Keith Jones	WSH	11	2	3	5	-2	13	1	0	0	0	12	16.7
			COL	67	23	20	43	5	105	13	1	7	0	158	14.6
			TOTAL	78	25	23	48	3	118	14	1	7	0	170	14.7
R	48	Scott Young	COL	72	18	19	37	-5	14	7	0	0	0	164	11.0
L	28	Eric Lacroix	COL	81	18	18	36	16	26	2	0	4	0	141	12.8
C	9	Mike Ricci	COL	63	13	19	32	-3	59	5	0	3	0	74	17.6
R	22	Claude Lemieux	COL	45	11	17	28	-4	43	5	0	4	0	168	6.5
L	20	Rene Corbet	COL	76	12	15	27	14	67	1	0	3	1	128	9.4
R	25	Mike Keane	COL	81	10	17	27	2	63	0	1	1	0	91	11.0
C	26	Stephane Yelle	COL	79	9	17	26	1	38	0	1	1	0	89	10.1
D	24	Jon Klemm	COL	80	9	15	24	12	37	1	2	1	0	103	8.7
D	4	Uwe Krupp	COL	60	4	17	21	12	48	2	0	1	0	107	3.7
D	52	Adam Foote	COL	78	2	19	21	16	135	0	0	0	0	60	3.3
D	3	* Aaron Miller	COL	56	5	12	17	15	15	0	0	3	0	47	10.6
D	5	Alexei Gusarov	COL	58	2	12	14	4	28	0	0	0	0	33	6.1
D	2	Sylvain Lefebvre	COL	71	2	11	13	12	30	1	0	0	0	77	2.6
D	23	Brent Severyn	COL	66	1	4	5	-6	193	0	0	0	0	55	1.8
L	15	Yves Sarault	COL	28	2	1	3	0	6	0	0	0	0	41	4.9
R	27	* Christian Matte	COL	5	1	1	2	1	0	0	0	0	0	6	16.7
G	1	Craig Billington	COL	23	0	2	2	0	2	0	0	0	0	0	0.0
C	10	* Josef Marha	COL	6	0	1	1	0	0	0	0	0	0	6	0.0
G	33	Patrick Roy	COL	62	0	1	1	0	15	0	0	0	0	1	0.0
G	30	* Marc Denis	COL	1	0	0	0	0	0	0	0	0	0	0	0.0
D	32	* Richard Brennan	COL	2	0	0	0	0	0	0	0	0	0	0	0.0
D	6	* Wade Belak	COL	5	0	0	0	-1	11	0	0	0	0	1	0.0
D	29	* Eric Messier	COL	21	0	0	0	7	4	0	0	0	0	11	0.0

Goaltending

No.	Goaltender	GPI	Mins	Avg	W	L	T	EN	SO	GA	SA	S%
33	Patrick Roy	62	3698	2.32	38	15	7	3	7	143	1861	.923
1	Craig Billington	23	1200	2.65	11	8	2	2	1	53	584	.909
30	* Marc Denis	1	60	3.00	0	1	0	1	0	3	26	.885
	Totals	**82**	**4980**	**2.47**	**49**	**24**	**9**	**6**	**8**	**205**	**2477**	**.917**

Playoffs

Pos	#	Player	Team	GP	G	A	Pts	+/–	PIM	PP	SH	GW	OT	S	%
C	19	Joe Sakic	COL	17	8	17	25	5	14	3	0	0	0	50	16.0
R	22	Claude Lemieux	COL	17	13	10	23	7	32	4	0	4	1	73	17.8
L	13	Valeri Kamensky	COL	17	8	14	22	-1	16	5	0	2	0	49	16.3
C	21	Peter Forsberg	COL	14	5	12	17	-6	10	3	0	0	0	35	14.3
D	8	Sandis Ozolinsh	COL	17	4	13	17	-1	24	2	0	1	0	39	10.3
R	18	Adam Deadmarsh	COL	17	3	6	9	-6	24	1	0	1	0	39	7.7
C	26	Stephane Yelle	COL	12	1	6	7	5	2	0	0	0	0	19	5.3
R	48	Scott Young	COL	17	4	2	6	-1	14	2	0	0	0	21	19.0
R	11	Keith Jones	COL	6	3	3	6	2	4	1	0	0	0	16	18.8
C	9	Mike Ricci	COL	17	2	4	6	1	17	0	0	1	0	21	9.5
L	28	Eric Lacroix	COL	17	1	4	5	2	19	0	0	0	0	15	6.7
R	25	Mike Keane	COL	17	3	1	4	2	24	0	0	1	0	17	17.6
L	20	Rene Corbet	COL	17	2	2	4	0	27	0	0	0	0	31	6.5
D	52	Adam Foote	COL	17	0	4	4	3	62	0	0	0	0	17	0.0
D	3	* Aaron Miller	COL	17	1	2	3	3	10	0	0	0	0	8	12.5
D	5	Alexei Gusarov	COL	17	0	3	3	3	14	0	0	0	0	9	0.0
D	24	Jon Klemm	COL	17	1	1	2	-1	6	0	0	0	0	20	5.0
G	1	Craig Billington	COL	1	0	0	0	0	0	0	0	0	0	0	0.0
L	15	Yves Sarault	COL	5	0	0	0	0	2	0	0	0	0	2	0.0
D	29	* Eric Messier	COL	6	0	0	0	0	4	0	0	0	0	1	0.0
D	23	Brent Severyn	COL	8	0	0	0	1	12	0	0	0	0	3	0.0
D	2	Sylvain Lefebvre	COL	17	0	0	0	-1	25	0	0	0	0	15	0.0
G	33	Patrick Roy	COL	17	0	0	0	0	12	0	0	0	0	0	0.0

Goaltending

No.	Goaltender	GPI	Mins	Avg	W	L	EN	SO	GA	SA	S%
33	Patrick Roy	17	1034	2.21	10	7	2	3	38	559	.932
1	Craig Billington	1	20	3.00	0	0	0	0	1	13	.923
	Totals	**17**	**1060**	**2.32**	**10**	**7**	**2**	**3**	**41**	**574**	**.929**

General Managers' History

Maurice Filion, 1979-80 to 1987-88; Martin Madden 1988-89; Martin Madden and Maurice Filion, 1989-90; Pierre Page, 1990-91 to 1993-94; Pierre Lacroix, 1994-95 to date.

Coaching History

Jacques Demers, 1979-80; Maurice Filion and Michel Bergeron, 1980-81; Michel Bergeron, 1981-82 to 1986-87; André Savard and Ron Lapointe, 1987-88; Ron Lapointe and Jean Perron, 1988-89; Michel Bergeron, 1989-90; Dave Chambers, 1990-91; Dave Chambers and Pierre Page, 1991-92; Pierre Page, 1992-93 to 1993-94; Marc Crawford, 1994-95 to date.

Club Records

Team

(Figures in brackets for season records are games played; records for fewest points, wins, ties, losses, goals, goals against are for 70 or more games)

Most Points	107	1996-97 (82)
Most Wins	49	1996-97 (82)
Most Ties	18	1980-81 (80)
Most Losses	61	1989-90 (80)
Most Goals	360	1983-84 (80)
Most Goals Against	407	1989-90 (80)
Fewest Points	31	1989-90 (80)
Fewest Wins	12	1989-90 (80)
Fewest Ties	5	1987-88 (80)
Fewest Losses	24	1996-97 (82)
Fewest Goals	236	1990-91 (80)
Fewest Goals Against	205	1996-97 (82)

Longest Winning Streak

Overall	7	Four times
Home	10	Nov. 26/83-Jan. 10/84, Mar. 6-Apr. 16/95
Away	5	Feb. 28-Mar. 24/86

Longest Undefeated Streak

Overall	12	Dec. 23/96-Jan. 20/97 (9 wins, 3 ties)
Home	14	Nov. 19/83-Jan. 21/84 (11 wins, 3 ties)
Away	8	Feb. 17/81-Mar. 22/81 (6 wins, 2 ties), Dec. 23/96-Jan. 20/97 (5 wins, 3 ties)

Longest Losing Streak

Overall	14	Oct. 21-Nov. 19/90
Home	8	Oct. 21-Nov. 24/90
Away	18	Jan. 18-Apr. 1/90

Longest Winless Streak

Overall	17	Oct. 21-Nov. 25/90 (15 losses, 2 ties)
Home	11	Nov. 14-Dec. 26/89 (7 losses, 4 ties)
Away	33	Oct. 8/91-Feb. 27/92 (25 losses, 8 ties)

Most Shutouts, Season	8	1996-97 (82)
Most PIM, Season	2,104	1989-90 (80)
Most Goals, Game	12	Three times

Individual

Most Seasons	11	Michel Goulet
Most Games	813	Michel Goulet
Most Goals, Career	456	Michel Goulet
Most Assists, Career	668	Peter Stastny
Most Points, Career	1,048	Peter Stastny (380G, 668A)
Most PIM, Career	1,545	Dale Hunter
Most Shutouts, Career	8	Patrick Roy

Longest Consecutive Games Streak	312	Dale Hunter (Oct. 9/80-Mar. 13/84)
Most Goals, Season	57	Michel Goulet (1982-83)
Most Assists, Season	93	Peter Stastny (1981-82)
Most Points, Season	139	Peter Stastny (1981-82; 46G, 93A)
Most PIM, Season	301	Gord Donnelly (1987-88)
Most Points, Defenseman, Season	82	Steve Duchesne (1992-93; 20G, 62A)
Most Points, Center, Season	139	Peter Stastny (1981-82; 46G, 93A)

Most Points, Right Wing, Season	103	Jacques Richard (1980-81; 52G, 51A)
Most Points, Left Wing, Season	121	Michel Goulet (1983-84; 56G, 65A)
Most Points, Rookie, Season	109	Peter Stastny (1980-81; 39G, 70A)
Most Shutouts, Season	7	Patrick Roy (1996-97)
Most Goals, Game	5	Mats Sundin (Mar. 5/92), Mike Ricci (Feb. 17/94)
Most Assists, Game	5	Six times
Most Points, Game	8	Peter Stastny (Feb. 22/81; 4G, 4A), Anton Stastny (Feb. 22/81; 3G, 5A)

Records include Quebec Nordiques, 1979-80 through 1994-95.

Quebec Nordiques Retired Numbers

3	J.C. Tremblay	1972-1979
8	Marc Tardif	1979-1983
16	Michel Goulet	1979-1990

Captains' History

Marc Tardif, 1979-80, 1980-81; Robbie Ftorek and Andre Dupont, 1981-82; Mario Marois, 1982-83 to 1984-85; Mario Marois and Peter Stastny, 1985-86; Peter Stastny, 1986-87 to 1989-90; Joe Sakic and Steven Finn, 1990-91; Mike Hough, 1991-92; Joe Sakic, 1992-93 to date.

All-time Record vs. Other Clubs

Regular Season

	At Home							On Road							Total						
	GP	W	L	T	GF	GA	PTS	GP	W	L	T	GF	GA	PTS	GP	W	L	T	GF	GA	PTS
Anaheim	7	4	1	2	28	23	10	6	2	3	1	11	16	5	13	6	4	3	39	39	15
Boston	59	33	20	6	214	255	46	57	19	30	8	178	227	46	116	39	63	14	392	482	92
Buffalo	58	29	18	11	218	182	69	58	16	34	8	189	235	40	116	45	52	19	407	417	109
Calgary	28	11	10	7	117	105	29	28	7	15	6	87	118	20	56	18	25	13	204	223	49
Chicago	26	12	10	4	109	99	28	27	10	15	2	90	102	22	53	22	25	6	199	201	50
Dallas	27	17	7	3	119	78	37	26	10	14	2	85	95	22	53	27	21	5	204	173	59
Detroit	27	15	9	3	109	96	33	26	10	15	1	88	105	21	53	25	24	4	197	201	54
Edmonton	27	11	14	2	115	120	24	27	8	17	2	85	138	18	54	19	31	4	200	258	42
Florida	5	1	2	2	14	16	4	6	5	1	0	25	15	10	11	6	3	2	39	31	14
Hartford	59	34	17	8	252	180	76	57	22	24	11	199	193	55	116	56	41	19	451	373	131
Los Angeles	27	13	11	3	115	106	29	28	10	16	2	94	119	22	55	23	27	5	209	225	51
Montreal	59	29	26	4	200	211	62	58	13	36	9	185	247	35	117	42	62	13	385	458	97
New Jersey	28	15	10	3	108	85	33	30	12	15	3	106	123	27	58	27	25	6	214	208	60
NY Islanders	28	16	10	2	107	89	34	27	11	15	1	96	113	23	55	27	25	3	203	202	57
NY Rangers	29	15	11	3	123	113	33	27	6	17	4	76	114	16	56	21	28	7	199	227	49
Ottawa	10	10	0	0	55	26	20	12	7	3	2	58	36	16	22	17	3	2	113	62	36
Philadelphia	28	9	9	10	105	103	28	29	6	21	2	76	111	14	57	15	30	12	181	214	42
Phoenix	27	13	11	3	108	103	29	26	11	10	5	104	101	27	53	24	21	8	212	204	56
Pittsburgh	27	14	12	1	126	110	29	30	11	15	4	123	130	26	57	25	27	5	249	240	55
St. Louis	26	12	11	3	96	88	27	26	6	18	2	85	117	14	52	18	29	5	181	205	41
San Jose	8	6	2	0	44	21	12	10	6	4	0	49	37	12	18	12	6	0	93	58	24
Tampa Bay	7	5	1	1	33	18	11	7	1	6	0	18	26	2	14	6	7	1	51	44	13
Toronto	27	15	7	5	105	84	35	27	13	12	2	114	94	28	54	28	19	7	219	178	63
Vancouver	28	12	11	5	89	79	29	27	12	11	4	117	107	28	55	24	22	9	206	186	57
Washington	28	12	12	4	91	103	28	28	9	16	3	90	116	21	56	21	28	7	181	219	49
Totals	**710**	**350**	**265**	**95**	**2800**	**2493**	**795**	**710**	**243**	**383**	**84**	**2428**	**2835**	**570**	**1420**	**593**	**648**	**179**	**5228**	**5328**	**1365**

Playoffs

	Series	W	L	GP	W	L	T	GF	GA	Last Mtg.	Round	Result
Boston	2	1	1	11	5	6	0	36	37	1983	DSF	L 1-3
Buffalo	2	2	0	8	6	2	0	35	27	1985	DSF	W 3-2
Chicago	2	2	0	12	8	4	0	49	28	1997	CQF	W 4-2
Detroit	2	1	1	12	6	6	0	32	32	1997	CF	L 2-4
Edmonton	1	1	0	5	4	1	0	19	11	1997	CSF	W 4-1
Florida	1	1	0	4	4	0	0	15	4	1996	F	W 4-0
Hartford	2	1	1	9	4	5	0	34	35	1987	DSF	W 4-2
Montreal	5	2	3	31	14	17	0	85	105	1993	DSF	L 2-4
NY Islanders	1	0	1	4	0	4	0	9	18	1982	CF	L 0-4
NY Rangers	1	0	1	6	2	4	0	19	25	1995	CQF	L 2-4
Philadelphia	2	0	2	11	4	7	0	29	39	1985	CF	L 2-4
Vancouver	1	1	0	6	4	2	0	24	17	1996	CQF	W 4-2
Totals	**22**	**12**	**10**	**119**	**61**	**58**	**0**	**386**	**378**			

Playoff Results 1997-93

Year	Round	Opponent	Result	GF	GA
1997	CF	Detroit	L 2-4	12	16
	CSF	Edmonton	W 4-1	19	11
	CQF	Chicago	W 4-2	28	14
1996	**F**	**Florida**	**W 4-0**	**15**	**4**
	CF	Detroit	W 4-2	20	16
	CSF	Chicago	W 4-2	21	14
	CQF	Vancouver	W 4-2	24	17
1995	CQF	NY Rangers	L 2-4	19	25
1993	DSF	Montreal	L 2-4	16	19

Abbreviations: Round: F – Final; **CF** – conference final; **CQF** – conference quarter-final; **CSF** – conference semi-final; **DF** – division final; **DSF** – division semi-final; **SF** – semi-final; **QF** – quarter-final; **PR** – preliminary round.

Calgary totals include Atlanta, 1979-80. Colorado totals include Quebec, 1979-80 to 1994-95.
Dallas totals include Minnesota, 1979-80 to 1992-93. New Jersey totals include Colorado Rockies, 1979-80 to 1981-82.
Phoenix totals include Winnipeg, 1979-80 to 1995-96.

1996-97 Results

Oct.	4	at	St. Louis	2-4	8	at New Jersey	1-1
	5	at	Dallas	1-4	9	at Ottawa	2-0
	8		San Jose	6-0	11	at Toronto	3-2
	10		Anaheim	6-6	15	Tampa Bay	4-2
	11	at	Chicago	2-0	20	at Florida	4-2
	15		Edmonton	7-2	21	at Tampa Bay	2-3
	17		Florida	1-2	23	at Pittsburgh	4-3
	19		Vancouver	9-2	25	at Boston	1-4
	22	at	Calgary	1-5	27	at Toronto	5-2
	23	at	Vancouver	4-1	29	Los Angeles	6-3
	26	at	Edmonton	4-2	Feb. 1	at San Jose	1-2
	28		Washington	1-0	2	at Anaheim	5-2
	30		St. Louis	6-3	8	Chicago	2-4
Nov.	2		Buffalo	0-0	11	Los Angeles	3-1
	3	at	Anaheim	1-1	13	at Phoenix	3-2
	6	at	San Jose	4-1	15	at St. Louis	5-2
	8	at	Phoenix	4-1	18	Boston	3-3
	9		Montreal	5-2	21	at Edmonton	4-3
	11	at	NY Islanders	6-2	23	Ottawa	4-3
	13	at	Detroit	4-1	25	at Los Angeles	1-3
	14	at	Buffalo	4-5	27	Dallas	2-6
	16		Hartford	4-4	Mar. 1	Chicago	2-1
	20		Phoenix	6-0	3	Vancouver	5-1
	22		NY Islanders	3-2	5	at Montreal	7-3
	27		NY Rangers	2-5	8	at Washington	3-6
	30		New Jersey	2-1	9	Anaheim	3-2
Dec.	4		Edmonton	2-0	12	Calgary	2-3
	6		St. Louis	3-4	15	Pittsburgh	6-3
	7	at	Los Angeles	2-4	16	Detroit	4-2
	11	at	Vancouver	6-1	18	Vancouver	4-2
	14	at	Calgary	1-4	21	Anaheim	4-3
	17		Detroit	4-3	23	at Philadelphia	0-2
	18	at	Edmonton	4-4	25	at Hartford	4-0
	21		Toronto	2-6	26	at Detroit	5-6
	23		Calgary	4-3	29	Toronto	2-3
	28	at	Los Angeles	5-2	Apr. 2	at Calgary	5-1
	29		Dallas	3-2	5	at San Jose	6-7
	31	at	Chicago	4-1	6	Phoenix	2-1
Jan.	2		Calgary	3-2	9	San Jose	1-4
	4		Philadelphia	4-4	11	at Dallas	2-1
	6	at	NY Rangers	2-2	13	Los Angeles	2-4

Entry Draft
Selections 1997-83

1997
Pick
26	Kevin Grimes
53	Graham Belak
55	Rick Berry
78	Ville Nieminen
87	Brad Larsen
133	Aaron Miskovich
161	David Aebischer
217	Doug Schmidt
243	Kyle Kidney
245	Stephen Lafleur

1996
Pick
25	Peter Ratchuk
51	Yuri Babenko
79	Mark Parrish
98	Ben Storey
107	Randy Petruk
134	Luke Curtin
146	Brian Willsie
160	Kai Fischer
167	Dan Hinote
176	Samuel Pahlsson
188	Roman Pylner
214	Matthew Scorsune
240	Justin Clark

1995
Pick
25	Marc Denis
51	Nic Beaudoin
77	John Tripp
81	Tomi Kallio
159	Brent Johnson
155	John Cirjak
181	Dan Smith
207	Tomi Hirvonen
228	Chris George

1994
Pick
12	Wade Belak
22	Jeffrey Kealty
35	Josef Marha
61	Sebastien Bety
72	Chris Drury
87	Milan Hejduk
113	Tony Tuzzolino
139	Nicholas Windsor
165	Calvin Elfring
191	Jay Bertsch
217	Tim Thomas
243	Chris Pittman
285	Steven Low

1993
Pick
10	Jocelyn Thibault
14	Adam Deadmarsh
49	Ashley Buckberger
75	Bill Pierce
101	Ryan Tocher
127	Anders Myrvold
137	Nicholas Checco
153	Christian Matte
179	David Ling
205	Petr Franek
231	Vincent Auger
257	Mark Pivetz
283	John Hillman

1992
Pick
4	Todd Warriner
28	Paul Brousseau
29	Tuomas Gronman
52	Emmanuel Fernandez
76	Ian McIntyre
100	Charlie Wasley
124	Paxton Schulte
148	Martin LePage
172	Mike Jickling
196	Steve Passmore
220	Anson Carter
244	Aaron Ellis

1991
Pick
1	Eric Lindros
24	Rene Corbet
46	Richard Brennan
68	Dave Karpa
90	Patrick Labrecque
103	Bill Lindsay
134	Mikael Johansson
156	Janne Laukkanen
157	Aaron Asp
178	Adam Bartell
188	Brent Brekke
200	Paul Koch
222	Doug Friedman
244	Eric Meloche

1990
Pick
1	Owen Nolan
22	Ryan Hughes
43	Bradley Zavisha
106	Jeff Parrott
127	Dwayne Norris
148	Andrei Kovalenko
158	Alexander Karpovtsev
169	Pat Mazzoli
190	Scott Davis
211	Mika Stromberg
232	Wade Klippenstein

1989
Pick
1	Mats Sundin
22	Adam Foote
43	Stephane Morin
54	John Tanner
68	Niklas Andersson
76	Eric Dubois
85	Kevin Kaiser
106	Dan Lambert
127	Sergei Mylnikov
148	Paul Krake
169	Viacheslav Bykov
190	Andrei Khomutov
211	Byron Witkowski
232	Noel Rahn

1988
Pick
3	Curtis Leschyshyn
5	Daniel Dore
24	Stephane Fiset
45	Petri Aaltonen
66	Darin Kimble
87	Stephane Venne
108	Ed Ward
129	Valeri Kamensky
150	Sakari Lindfors
171	Dan Wiebe
213	Alexei Gusarov
234	Claude Lapointe

1987
Pick
9	Bryan Fogarty
15	Joe Sakic
51	Jim Sprott
72	Kip Miller
93	Rob Mendel
114	Garth Snow
135	Tim Hanus
156	Jake Enebak
177	Jaroslav Sevcik
183	Ladislav Tresl
198	Darren Nauss
219	Mike Williams

1986
Pick
18	Ken McRae
39	Jean-Marc Routhier
41	Stephane Guerard
81	Ron Tugnutt
102	Gerald Bzdel
117	Scott White
123	Morgan Samuelsson
134	Mark Vermette
144	Jean-Francois Nault
165	Keith Miller
186	Pierre Millier
207	Chris Lappin
228	Martin Latreille
249	Sean Boudreault

1985
Pick
15	David Latta
36	Jason Lafreniere
57	Max Middendorf
65	Peter Massey
78	David Espe
99	Bruce Major
120	Andy Akervik
141	Mike Oliverio
162	Mario Brunetta
183	Brit Peer
204	Tom Sasso
225	Gary Murphy
246	Jean Bois

1984
Pick
15	Trevor Stienburg
36	Jeff Brown
57	Steve Finn
78	Terry Perkins
120	Darren Cota
141	Henrik Cedergren
162	Jyrki Maki
183	Guy Ouellette
203	Ken Quinney
244	Peter Loob

1983
Pick
32	Yves Heroux
52	Bruce Bell
54	Iiro Jarvi
92	Luc Guenette
112	Brad Walcott
132	Craig Mack
152	Tommy Albelin
172	Wayne Groulx
192	Scott Shaunessy
232	Bo Berglund
239	Jindrich Kokrment

Club Directory

McNichols Arena
1635 Clay Street
Denver, CO 80204
Phone **303/893-6700**
FAX 303/893-0614
Capacity: 16,061

Owner	Ascent Entertainment Group, Inc.
Governor and Chairman	Charlie Lyons

Hockey Operations
President, General Manager and Alternate Governor	Pierre Lacroix
Executive Assistant	Charlotte Grahame
Assistant General Manager	Francois Giguere
Administrative Assistant	Heidi Beitz
Head Coach	Marc Crawford
Assistant Coach	Mike Foligno
Assistant Coach	Jacques Cloutier
Video Coach	Paul Fixter
Director of Media Relations and Team Services	Jean Martineau
Assistant Director of Media Relations	Sally Christgau
Media Relations Assistant	Jennifer Hofmeister
Strength and Conditioning Coach	Skip Allen
Director of Player Personnel	Michel Goulet
Chief Scout	Dave Draper
Scouts	Yvon Gendron, Jan Janda, John Gill, Brian MacDonald, Don McKenney, Orval Tessier, Don Paarup
Pro Scouts	Brad Smith, Shawn Dineen
Athletic Trainer	Pat Karns
Kinesiologist	Matthew Sokolowski
Massage Therapist	Leo Vyssokov
Equipment Manager	Rob McLean
Assistant Equipment Manager	Mike Kramer
Equipment Assistant	Wayne Fleming
Team Physician/Orthopedist	Andrew Parker
Team Physician/Cardiologist	Steve Freidrich
Team Dentist	Steve Barker

Business Operations
President – Ascent Sports	Ellen Robinson
Executive Assistant	Mary Draper
Senior Vice President/Business Affairs	Steve Story
Executive Assistant	Jo Ann Kratz
ExecutiveVice President/Sales and Marketing	Mimi Brown
Vice President/Community Relations	Kathleen MacDonald
Senior Vice President and General Counsel	Ron Sally
Special Assistant to General Counsel	Sharon Chinn
Vice President of Operations	Kirk Dyer
Vice President/Broadcasting	Lou Personett
Vice President/Corporate Sales	Mike Arthur
Advertising Manager	Ed O'Brien

Finance
Vice President/Finance	Mark Waggoner

Director of Accounting	Jerry Girkin
Assistant Controller	Greg Sherman
Accounting Assistant	Karen Becker
Accounting Assistant	Loretta Harmon
Accounting Assistant	Lori McLaren
Accounting Assistant	Devin Brown

Ticket Sales
Director of Ticket Operations	Rob Winston
Ticket Operations Managers	Lori Blanche, Glenn Hives
Manager Ticket Bus	Carlos Jimenez
Ticket Operations Assistants	Ann Harmon, Flo Kunze, Bryan Horan

Sales
Director of Ticket Sales	Paul Andrews
Sales Consultants	Dan Sweeney, Allison Levy, Robert Kinnard, Aimee Ahlers, Amy Cashel, Jack Breedon, Heather Kolon, Jason Linscott

Service
Manager of Season Ticket Service	Amy Seltenreich
Season Ticket Representatives	Scot Billups, Sabrina Slater, Kelly Fallin, Che Vialpando, Derek Matthews, John Ellis

Marketing and Corporate Partnership
Vice President Corporate Sales	Michael Arthur
Executive Assistant	Kathleen Snead
Senior Corporate Account Executives	Brian Jones, Mike Kurowski Molly Mueller, Deanna Poyfair
Corporate Account Executives	Cindy Gerrity, Jon Moore, Jeff Plush

Game Operations
Director of Game Operations	Rene Doubleday
Marketing	Kenn Solomon
Game Operations and Promotions Coordinators	Kim Erwin, Christy Baird
Director of Special Events	Cydni Bickerstaff
Special Events Manager	Cydni Bickerstaff
Senior Events Coordinator	Becky Grupe
Operations, Sales and Special Events Assistant	Kirsten Nissler

Broadcasting
Vice-President/Broadcasting	Lou Personett
Executive Producer	Robb Moody
Producer	Mike Schanno
Associate Producer	Kyle Keefe
TV Play-by-Play Announcer	John Kelly
TV Color Commentator	Peter McNab
Radio Play-by-Play Announcer	Michael Haynes
Radio Color Commentator	Norm Jones

Retail
Arena Retail Manager	Johnny Duke
Buyer/Arena Coordinator	Kevin Walsh
Mail Order/Central Distribution Manager	Bill McAdoo
Administrative Assistant/Merchandising	TBA
Assistant Warehouse Manager/Arena Coordinator	Bill Howell

Creative Services
Senior Art Director	Kelly Kocher
Art Director	Chris Austin
Graphic Artist	Krysia Taylor
Team Photographer	Tim DeFrisco

Community Relations
Community Fund President	Chopper Travaglini
Community Relations Program Coordinator	Jason Johanning
Community Relations Program Coordinator	Meredith Kaplan
Community Relations Assistant	Tamara Walker
Community Relations Program Coordinator	Derek Williams

Administration
Director of Administration	Cheryl Miller
Administrative Services Coordinator	Lou Carroll
Administrative Assistant	Jennifer Walters
Receptionists	Heather Ellsworth, Gina Silletto
Courier	Paul Bartch

Dallas Stars

1996-97 Results: 48w-26l-8t 104pts. First, Central Division

In his sophomore season, right-winger Jere Lehtinen matured into one of the League's top defensive forwards, finishing third in the Selke Trophy race while compiling a plus/minus rating of +26.

1997-98 Schedule

Oct.	Wed.	1	at Colorado
	Sat.	4	St. Louis
	Tue.	7	at Buffalo
	Wed.	8	at Detroit
	Fri.	10	Chicago
	Tue.	14	Calgary
	Thu.	16	Florida
	Sat.	18	at Toronto
	Sun.	19	at Ottawa
	Tue.	21	Vancouver
	Fri.	24	at Chicago
	Sat.	25	Colorado
	Tue.	28	at NY Rangers
	Wed.	29	at Washington
Nov.	Sun.	2	at Philadelphia*
	Mon.	3	at Montreal
	Wed.	5	at Pittsburgh
	Fri.	7	NY Rangers
	Mon.	10	St. Louis
	Wed.	12	Boston
	Sat.	15	at Los Angeles
	Sun.	16	at Anaheim
	Wed.	19	Edmonton
	Fri.	21	at Detroit
	Sat.	22	at Boston
	Mon.	24	Anaheim
	Wed.	26	Los Angeles
	Thu.	27	at Phoenix
	Sat.	29	Phoenix
Dec.	Wed.	3	Edmonton
	Fri.	5	Calgary
	Mon.	8	at Toronto
	Wed.	10	Tampa Bay
	Fri.	12	San Jose
	Mon.	15	Buffalo
	Thu.	18	at Calgary
	Sat.	20	at Edmonton
	Tue.	23	at Vancouver
	Sat.	27	Vancouver
	Mon.	29	at Detroit
	Wed.	31	Los Angeles

Jan.	Fri.	2	NY Islanders
	Sat.	3	at Carolina
	Mon.	5	at New Jersey
	Wed.	7	Ottawa
	Fri.	9	Detroit
	Sun.	11	at Anaheim
	Mon.	12	at San Jose
	Wed.	14	at St. Louis
	Wed.	21	Colorado
	Sat.	24	at Colorado*
	Mon.	26	Toronto
	Thu.	29	at Florida
	Sat.	31	at St. Louis*
Feb.	Mon.	2	at Toronto
	Wed.	4	Philadelphia
	Sat.	7	Chicago*
	Wed.	25	at NY Islanders
	Sat.	28	Phoenix*
Mar.	Sun.	1	at Chicago*
	Wed.	4	Montreal
	Sat.	7	at St. Louis*
	Sun.	8	Phoenix
	Thu.	12	at Phoenix
	Fri.	13	Anaheim
	Tue.	17	at Los Angeles
	Wed.	18	at San Jose
	Fri.	20	Carolina
	Sun.	22	Pittsburgh*
	Thu.	26	Toronto
	Sat.	28	San Jose*
	Sun.	29	New Jersey
Apr.	Wed.	1	at Calgary
	Fri.	3	at Edmonton
	Sat.	4	at Vancouver
	Mon.	6	Toronto
	Wed.	8	Washington
	Sat.	11	at Tampa Bay*
	Sun.	12	St. Louis
	Wed.	15	Detroit
	Thu.	16	at Phoenix
	Sat.	18	Chicago*

* Denotes afternoon game.

Franchise date: June 5, 1967
Transferred from Minnesota to Dallas beginning with 1993-94 season.

CENTRAL DIVISION

31st NHL Season

Year-by-Year Record

		Home			Road			Overall							
Season	GP	W	L	T	W	L	T	W	L	T	GF	GA	Pts.	Finished	Playoff Result
1996-97	82	25	13	3	23	13	5	48	26	8	252	198	104	1st, Central Div.	Lost Conf. Quarter-Final
1995-96	82	14	18	9	12	24	5	26	42	14	227	280	66	6th, Central Div.	Out of Playoffs
1994-95	48	9	10	5	8	13	3	17	23	8	136	135	42	5th, Central Div.	Lost Conf. Quarter-Final
1993-94	84	23	12	7	19	17	6	42	29	13	286	265	97	3rd, Central Div.	Lost Conf. Semi-Final
1992-93*	84	18	17	7	18	21	3	36	38	10	272	293	82	5th, Norris Div.	Out of Playoffs
1991-92*	80	20	16	4	12	26	2	32	42	6	246	278	70	4th, Norris Div.	Lost Div. Semi-Final
1990-91*	80	19	15	6	8	24	8	27	39	14	256	266	68	4th, Norris Div.	Lost Final
1989-90*	80	26	12	2	10	28	2	36	40	4	284	291	76	4th, Norris Div.	Lost Div. Semi-Final
1988-89*	80	17	15	8	10	22	8	27	37	16	258	278	70	3rd, Norris Div.	Lost Div. Semi-Final
1987-88*	80	10	24	6	9	24	7	19	48	13	242	349	51	5th, Norris Div.	Out of Playoffs
1986-87*	80	17	20	3	13	20	7	30	40	10	296	314	70	5th, Norris Div.	Out of Playoffs
1985-86*	80	21	15	4	17	18	5	38	33	9	327	305	85	2nd, Norris Div.	Lost Div. Semi-Final
1984-85*	80	14	19	7	11	24	5	25	43	12	268	321	62	4th, Norris Div.	Lost Div. Final
1983-84*	80	22	14	4	17	17	6	39	31	10	345	344	88	1st, Norris Div.	Lost Conf. Championship
1982-83*	80	23	6	11	17	18	5	40	24	16	321	290	96	2nd, Norris Div.	Lost Div. Final
1981-82*	80	21	7	12	16	16	8	37	23	20	346	288	94	1st, Norris Div.	Lost Div. Semi-Final
1980-81*	80	23	10	7	12	18	10	35	28	17	291	263	87	3rd, Adams Div.	Lost Final
1979-80*	80	25	8	7	11	20	9	36	28	16	311	253	88	3rd, Adams Div.	Lost Semi-Final
1978-79*	80	19	15	6	9	25	6	28	40	12	257	289	68	4th, Adams Div.	Out Of Playoffs
1977-78*	80	12	24	4	6	29	5	18	53	9	218	325	45	5th, Smythe Div.	Out of Playoffs
1976-77*	80	17	14	9	6	25	9	23	39	18	240	310	64	2nd, Smythe Div.	Lost Prelim. Round
1975-76*	80	15	22	3	5	31	4	20	53	7	195	303	47	4th, Smythe Div.	Out of Playoffs
1974-75*	80	17	20	3	6	30	4	23	50	7	221	341	53	4th, Smythe Div.	Out of Playoffs
1973-74*	78	18	15	6	5	23	11	23	38	17	235	275	63	7th, West Div.	Out of Playoffs
1972-73*	78	26	8	5	11	22	6	37	30	11	254	230	85	3rd, West Div.	Lost Quarter-Final
1971-72*	78	22	11	6	15	18	6	37	29	12	212	191	86	2nd, West Div.	Lost Quarter-Final
1970-71*	78	16	15	8	12	19	8	28	34	16	191	223	72	4th, West Div.	Lost Semi-Final
1969-70*	76	11	16	11	8	19	11	19	35	22	224	257	60	3rd, West Div.	Lost Quarter-Final
1968-69*	76	11	21	6	7	22	9	18	43	15	189	270	51	6th, West Div.	Out of Playoffs
1967-68*	74	17	12	8	10	20	7	27	32	15	191	226	69	4th, West Div.	Lost Semi-Final

* Minnesota North Stars

1997-98 Player Personnel

FORWARDS	HT	WT	S	Place of Birth	Date	1996-97 Club
ADAMS, Greg	6-3	195	L	Nelson, B.C.	8/1/63	Dallas
BASSEN, Bob	5-10	185	L	Calgary, Alta.	5/6/65	Dallas
BOTTERILL, Jason	6-3	205	L	Edmonton, Alta.	5/19/76	U. of Michigan
CARBONNEAU, Guy	5-11	186	R	Sept-Iles, Que.	3/18/60	Dallas
COTE, Patrick	6-3	199	L	Lasalle, Que.	1/24/75	Dallas-Michigan
DOURIS, Peter	6-1	195	R	Toronto, Ont.	2/19/66	Milwaukee
ERREY, Bob	5-10	185	L	Montreal, Que.	9/21/64	Detroit-San Jose
HARVEY, Todd	6-0	195	R	Hamilton, Ont.	2/17/75	Dallas
HOGUE, Benoit	5-10	194	L	Repentigny, Que.	10/28/66	Dallas
HRKAC, Tony	5-11	170	L	Thunder Bay, Ont.	7/7/66	Milwaukee
JINMAN, Lee	5-10	160	R	Toronto, Ont.	1/10/76	Michigan
LANGENBRUNNER, Jamie	5-11	185	R	Duluth, MN	7/24/75	Dallas
LEHTINEN, Jere	6-0	192	R	Espoo, Finland	6/24/73	Dallas
LIND, Juha	5-11	178	L	Helsinki, Finland	1/2/74	Jokerit
MARSHALL, Grant	6-1	193	R	Mississauga, Ont.	6/9/73	Dallas
MODANO, Mike	6-3	200	L	Livonia, MI	6/7/70	Dallas
NIEUWENDYK, Joe	6-1	195	L	Oshawa, Ont.	9/10/66	Dallas
REID, David	6-1	217	L	Toronto, Ont.	5/15/64	Dallas
SAWYER, Kevin	6-2	205	L	Christina Lake, B.C.	2/21/74	Boston-Providence (AHL)
TANCILL, Chris	5-10	185	L	Livonia, MI	2/7/68	San Jose-Kentucky
VERBEEK, Pat	5-9	192	R	Sarnia, Ont.	5/24/64	Dallas
DEFENSEMEN						
BUZEK, Petr	6-0	205	L	Jihlava, Czech.	4/26/77	Michigan
CHAMBERS, Shawn	6-2	200	L	Sterling Hts., MI	10/11/66	New Jersey
GUSEV, Sergey	6-1	195	L	Nizhny Tagil, USSR	7/31/75	Michigan
HATCHER, Derian	6-5	225	L	Sterling Heights, MI	6/4/72	Dallas
JACKMAN, Richard	6-2	180	R	Toronto, Ont.	6/28/78	S.S. Marie
KECZMER, Dan	6-1	190	L	Mt. Clemens, MI	5/25/68	Dallas-Michigan
LUDWIG, Craig	6-3	220	L	Rhinelander, WI	3/15/61	Dallas
LUKOWICH, Brad	6-1	170	L	Cranbrook, B.C.	8/12/76	Michigan
MATVICHUK, Richard	6-2	200	L	Edmonton, Alta.	2/5/73	Dallas
SYDOR, Darryl	6-0	195	L	Edmonton, Alta.	5/13/72	Dallas
ZUBOV, Sergei	6-1	200	R	Moscow, USSR	7/22/70	Dallas

GOALTENDERS	HT	WT	C	Place of Birth	Date	1996-97 Club
BELFOUR, Ed	5-11	182	L	Carman, Man.	4/21/65	Chicago-San Jose
FERNANDEZ, Emmanuel	6-0	185	L	Etobicoke, Ont.	8/27/74	Michigan
TUREK, Roman	6-3	190	R	Pisek, Czech.	5/21/70	Dallas-Michigan

Coach

HITCHCOCK, KEN
Coach, Dallas Stars. Born in Edmonton, Alberta, December 17, 1951.

In his first full season as head coach of the Dallas Stars, Ken Hitchcock added to his very impressive list of credentials by guiding the Stars to a first place in the Central Division. The 1996-97 Stars were only the ninth team in NHL history to go from last to first in their division in one season. The head coach for the Western Conference at the 1997 NHL All-Star Game, he led the Stars to team records in wins and points during the 1996-97 season, posting a 48-26-8 record (104 points).

Selected as *The Hockey News* and *The Sporting News* 1996-97 coach of the year, Hitchcock also finished as runner-up for the NHL's Jack Adams Trophy. Having coached in his 100th career NHL game on February 12 vs. Phoenix, he now has the highest career winning percentage in Stars history for coaches with over 100 games behind the bench (.556).

Named to his position on January 8, 1996, the 44-year old native of Edmonton has posted a winning record in every season as a head coach prior to joining the Stars, including record-breaking numbers in the Western Hockey League in the late 1980's.

Getting his start behind the bench as a head coach in the Canadian Triple A Midget ranks with Sherwood Park, a suburb of Edmonton, Hitchcock posted an incredible 575-69 mark during his ten-year reign there.

Named head coach of the Kamloops Blazers of the WHL in 1984, he began a dominating run at the junior level which saw his team finish first in the Western Division in five of his six seasons at the helm. The WHL coach of the year in 1986-87 and 1989-90, Hitchcock was named the top coach in all of Canadian Major Jr. Hockey in 1989-90 after the Blazers won the WHL title and finished third at the Memorial Cup. His .693 winning percentage (291-125-15) at Kamloops is the highest in the history of the Western Hockey League while his .695 playoff winning percentage (66-29) with the Blazers is fourth best in league annals. Adding to his amateur success, he served as an assistant coach for the gold medal-winning 1987 Team Canada squad at the World Juniors in Russia.

After a three-year stint (1990-93) as an assistant coach for the Philadelphia Flyers, Hitchcock returned to head coaching duties for the 1993-94 season, manning the bench for the Kalamazoo Wings, the Stars minor league affiliate in the International Hockey League. Hitchcock also coached in both the 1993-94 and 1994-95 IHL All-Star Games.

Coaching Record

		Regular Season					Playoffs			
Season	Team	Games	W	L	T	%	Games	W	L	%
1984-85	Kamloops (WHL)	71	52	17	2	.746	15	10	5	.667
1985-86	Kamloops (WHL)	72	49	19	4	.708	16	14	2	.875
1986-87	Kamloops (WHL)	72	55	14	3	.785	13	8	5	.615
1987-88	Kamloops (WHL)	72	45	26	1	.632	18	12	6	.667
1988-89	Kamloops (WHL)	72	34	33	5	.507	16	8	8	.500
1989-90	Kamloops (WHL)	72	56	16	0	.778	17	14	3	.824
1993-94	Kalamazoo (IHL)	81	48	26	7	.636	5	1	4	.200
1994-95	Kalamazoo (IHL)	81	43	24	14	.617	16	10	6	.625
1995-96	Michigan (IHL)	40	19	10	11	.613	....	....	....	....
	Dallas (NHL)	**43**	**15**	**23**	**5**	**.407**	....	....	....	....
1996-97	**Dallas (NHL)**	**82**	**48**	**26**	**8**	**.634**	**7**	**3**	**4**	**.429**
	NHL Totals	**125**	**63**	**49**	**13**	**.556**	**7**	**3**	**4**	**.429**

1996-97 Scoring

* – rookie

Regular Season

Pos	#	Player	Team	GP	G	A	Pts	+/–	PIM	PP	SH	GW	GT	S	%
C	9	Mike Modano	DAL	80	35	48	83	43	42	9	5	9	2	291	12.0
R	16	Pat Verbeek	DAL	81	17	36	53	3	128	5	0	4	0	172	9.9
C	25	Joe Nieuwendyk	DAL	66	30	21	51	-5	32	8	0	2	2	173	17.3
D	5	Darryl Sydor	DAL	82	8	40	48	37	51	2	0	2	0	142	5.6
L	33	Benoit Hogue	DAL	73	19	24	43	8	54	5	0	5	0	131	14.5
R	26	Jere Lehtinen	DAL	63	16	27	43	26	2	3	1	2	0	134	11.9
D	56	Sergei Zubov	DAL	78	13	30	43	19	24	1	0	3	0	133	9.8
L	14	Dave Reid	DAL	82	19	20	39	12	10	1	1	4	0	135	14.1
C	15	* Jamie Langenbrunner	DAL	76	13	26	39	-2	51	3	0	3	0	112	11.6
L	23	Greg Adams	DAL	50	21	15	36	27	2	5	0	4	1	113	18.6
C	10	Todd Harvey	DAL	71	9	22	31	19	142	1	0	2	0	99	9.1
C	41	Brent Gilchrist	DAL	67	10	20	30	6	24	2	0	2	0	116	8.6
D	2	Derian Hatcher	DAL	63	3	19	22	8	97	0	0	0	0	96	3.1
C	21	Guy Carbonneau	DAL	73	5	16	21	9	36	0	1	0	0	99	5.1
C	7	Neal Broten	N.J.	3	0	1	1	-1	0	0	0	0	0	3	0.0
			L.A.	19	0	4	4	-9	0	0	0	0	0	17	0.0
			DAL	20	8	7	15	6	12	1	1	2	0	35	22.9
			TOTAL	42	8	12	20	-4	12	1	1	2	0	55	14.5
D	12	Grant Ledyard	DAL	67	1	15	16	31	61	0	0	0	0	99	1.0
D	3	Craig Ludwig	DAL	77	2	11	13	17	62	0	0	1	0	59	3.4
C	28	Bob Bassen	DAL	46	5	7	12	5	41	0	0	2	0	50	10.0
D	24	Richard Matvichuk	DAL	57	5	7	12	1	87	0	2	0	0	83	6.0
L	17	Bill Huard	DAL	40	5	6	11	5	105	0	0	0	0	34	14.7
R	29	Grant Marshall	DAL	56	6	4	10	5	98	0	0	0	0	62	9.7
R	39	Mike Kennedy	DAL	24	1	6	7	3	13	0	0	1	0	26	3.8
D	18	Mike Lalor	DAL	55	1	1	2	3	42	0	0	0	0	32	3.1
G	32	Arturs Irbe	DAL	35	0	2	2	0	8	0	0	0	0	0	0.0
D	22	Dan Keczmer	DAL	13	0	1	1	3	6	0	0	0	0	10	0.0
G	35	Andy Moog	DAL	48	0	1	1	0	12	0	0	0	0	0	0.0
L	44	* Patrick Cote	DAL	3	0	0	0	0	27	0	0	0	0	1	0.0
R	42	Sergei Makarov	DAL	4	0	0	0	-2	0	0	0	0	0	0	0.0
G	1	Roman Turek	DAL	6	0	0	0	0	0	0	0	0	0	0	0.0
L	27	Marc Labelle	DAL	9	0	0	0	-4	46	0	0	0	0	2	0.0

Goaltending

No.	Goaltender	GPI	Mins	Avg	W	L	T	EN	SO	GA	SA	S%
1	Roman Turek	6	263	2.05	3	1	0	0	0	9	129	.930
35	Andy Moog	48	2738	2.15	28	13	5	0	3	98	1121	.913
32	Arturs Irbe	35	1965	2.69	17	12	3	3	3	88	825	.893
	Totals	**82**	**4979**	**2.39**	**48**	**26**	**8**	**3**	**6**	**198**	**2078**	**.905**

Playoffs

Pos	#	Player	Team	GP	G	A	Pts	+/–	PIM	PP	SH	GW	OT	S	%
C	9	Mike Modano	DAL	7	4	1	5	2	0	1	1	2	0	27	14.8
C	28	Bob Bassen	DAL	7	3	1	4	3	4	0	0	0	0	12	25.0
C	41	Brent Gilchrist	DAL	6	2	2	4	0	2	0	0	0	0	20	10.0
L	33	Benoit Hogue	DAL	7	2	2	4	-1	6	1	0	0	0	16	12.5
C	25	Joe Nieuwendyk	DAL	7	2	2	4	-1	6	0	0	0	0	21	9.5
R	26	Jere Lehtinen	DAL	7	2	2	4	1	0	0	0	0	0	15	13.3
R	16	Pat Verbeek	DAL	7	1	3	4	-2	16	1	0	0	0	19	5.3
D	56	Sergei Zubov	DAL	7	0	3	3	4	2	0	0	0	0	9	0.0
C	15	* Jamie Langenbrunner	DAL	5	1	1	2	1	14	0	0	1	0	15	6.7
R	29	Grant Marshall	DAL	5	0	2	2	2	8	0	0	0	0	4	0.0
D	12	Grant Ledyard	DAL	7	0	2	2	-3	0	0	0	0	0	8	0.0
D	3	Craig Ludwig	DAL	7	0	2	2	1	18	0	0	0	0	5	0.0
D	2	Derian Hatcher	DAL	7	0	2	2	1	20	0	0	0	0	7	0.0
D	5	Darryl Sydor	DAL	7	0	2	2	-2	0	0	0	0	0	24	0.0
L	14	Dave Reid	DAL	7	1	0	1	-2	4	0	0	0	0	10	10.0
C	7	Neal Broten	DAL	2	0	1	1	0	0	0	0	0	0	3	0.0
L	23	Greg Adams	DAL	3	0	1	1	2	0	0	0	0	0	4	0.0
C	21	Guy Carbonneau	DAL	7	0	1	1	-3	6	0	0	0	0	9	0.0
G	35	Andy Moog	DAL	7	0	1	1	0	0	0	0	0	0	0	0.0
D	24	Richard Matvichuk	DAL	7	0	1	1	-1	20	0	0	0	0	8	0.0
C	10	Todd Harvey	DAL	7	0	1	1	-2	10	0	0	0	0	15	0.0
G	32	Arturs Irbe	DAL	1	0	0	0	0	0	0	0	0	0	0	0.0

Goaltending

No.	Goaltender	GPI	Mins	Avg	W	L	EN	SO	GA	SA	S%
32	Arturs Irbe	1	13	.00	0	0	0	0	0	4	1.000
35	Andy Moog	7	449	2.81	3	4	0	0	21	214	.902
	Totals	**7**	**462**	**2.73**	**3**	**4**	**0**	**0**	**21**	**218**	**.904**

Coaching History

Wren Blair, 1967-68; Wren Blair and John Muckler, 1968-69; Wren Blair and Charlie Burns, 1969-70; Jackie Gordon, 1970-71 to 1972-73; Jackie Gordon and Parker MacDonald, 1973-74; Jackie Gordon and Charlie Burns, 1974-75; Ted Harris, 1975-76, 1976-77; Ted Harris, André Beaulieu and Lou Nanne, 1977-78; Harry Howell and Glen Sonmor, 1978-79; Glen Sonmor, 1979-80 to 1981-82; Glen Sonmor and Murray Oliver, 1982-83; Bill Mahoney, 1983-84 to 1984-85; Lorne Henning, 1985-86; Lorne Henning and Glen Sonmor, 1986-87; Herb Brooks, 1987-88; Pierre Page, 1988-89 to 1989-90; Bob Gainey, 1990-91 to 1994-95; Bob Gainey and Ken Hitchcock, 1995-96; Ken Hitchcock, 1996-97 to date.

Captains' History

Bob Woytowich, 1967-68; "Moose" Vasko, 1968-69; Claude Larose, 1969-70; Ted Harris, 1970-71 to 1973-74; Bill Goldsworthy, 1974-75, 1975-76; Bill Hogaboam, 1976-77; Nick Beverley, 1977-78; J.P. Parise, 1978-79; Paul Shmyr, 1979-80, 1980-81; Tim Young, 1981-82; Craig Hartsburg, 1982-83; Craig Hartsburg, Brian Bellows, 1983-84; Craig Hartsburg, 1984-85 to 1987-88; Curt Fraser, Bob Rouse and Curt Giles, 1988-89; Curt Giles, 1989-90 to 1990-91; Mark Tinordi, 1991-92 to 1993-94; Neal Broten and Derian Hatcher, 1994-95; Derian Hatcher, 1995-96 to date.

Club Records

Team

(Figures in brackets for season records are games played; records for fewest points, wins, ties, losses, goals, goals against are for 70 or more games)

Most Points	104	1996-97 (82)
Most Wins	48	1996-97 (82)
Most Ties	22	1969-70 (76)
Most Losses	53	1975-76, 1977-78 (80)
Most Goals	346	1981-82 (80)
Most Goals Against	349	1987-88 (80)
Fewest Points	45	1977-78 (80)
Fewest Wins	18	1968-69 (76), 1977-78 (80)
Fewest Ties	4	1989-90 (80)
Fewest Losses	23	1981-82 (80)
Fewest Goals	189	1968-69 (76)
Fewest Goals Against	191	1971-72 (78)

Longest Winning Streak

Overall	7	Mar. 16-28/80, Mar. 16-Apr. 2/97
Home	11	Nov. 4-Dec. 27/72
Away	7	Nov. 18-Dec. 5/92, Jan. 26-Feb. 21/94

Longest Undefeated Streak

Overall	12	Feb. 18-Mar. 15/82 (9 wins, 3 ties)
Home	13	Oct. 28-Dec. 27/72 (12 wins, 1 tie), Nov. 21-Jan. 9/80 (10 wins, 3 ties), Jan. 17-Mar. 17/91 (11 wins, 2 ties)
Away	8	Jan. 26-Feb. 21/94 (7 wins, 1 tie)

Longest Losing Streak

Overall	10	Feb. 1-20/76
Home	6	Jan. 17-Feb. 4/70
Away	8	Oct. 19-Nov. 13/75, Jan. 28-Mar. 3/88

Longest Winless Streak

Overall	20	Jan. 15-Feb. 28/70 (15 losses, 5 ties)
Home	12	Jan. 17-Feb. 25/70 (8 losses, 4 ties)
Away	23	Oct. 25/74-Jan. 28/75 (19 losses, 4 ties)

Most Shutouts, Season	7	1972-73 (78)
Most PIM, Season	2,313	1987-88 (80)
Most Goals, Game	15	Nov. 11/81 (Wpg. 2 at Min. 15)

Individual

Most Seasons	16	Neal Broten
Most Games	992	Neal Broten
Most Goals, Career	342	Brian Bellows
Most Assists, Career	593	Neal Broten
Most Points, Career	867	Neal Broten (274G, 593A)
Most PIM, Career	1,883	Shane Churla
Most Shutouts, Career	26	Cesare Maniago
Longest Consecutive Games Streak	442	Danny Grant (Dec. 4/68-Apr. 7/74)
Most Goals, Season	55	Dino Ciccarelli (1981-82), Brian Bellows (1989-90)
Most Assists, Season	76	Neal Broten (1985-86)
Most Points, Season	114	Bobby Smith (1981-82; 43G, 71A)

Most PIM, Season	382	Basil McRae (1987-88)
Most Points, Defenseman, Season	77	Craig Hartsburg (1981-82; 17G, 60A)
Most Points, Center, Season	114	Bobby Smith (1981-82; 43G, 71A)
Most Points, Right Wing, Season	107	Dino Ciccarelli (1981-82; 55G, 52A)
Most Point, Left Wing, Season	99	Brian Bellows (1989-90; 55G, 44A)
Most Points, Rookie, Season	98	Neal Broten (1981-82; 38G, 60A)
Most Shutouts, Season	6	Cesare Maniago (1967-68)
Most Goals, Game	5	Tim Young (Jan. 15/79)
Most Assists, Game	5	Murray Oliver (Oct. 24/71), Larry Murphy (Oct. 17/89)
Most Points, Game	7	Bobby Smith (Nov. 11/81; 4G, 3A)

Records include Minnesota North Stars, 1967-68 through 1992-93.

General Managers' History

Wren A. Blair, 1967-68 to 1973-74; Jack Gordon, 1974-75 to 1976-77; Lou Nanne, 1977-78 to 1987-88; Jack Ferreira, 1988-89 to 1989-90; Bob Clarke 1990-91 to 1991-92; Bob Gainey, 1992-93 to date.

Minnesota North Stars Retired Numbers

8	Bill Goldsworthy	1967-1976
19	Bill Masterton	1967-1968

All-time Record vs. Other Clubs

Regular Season

	At Home							On Road							Total						
	GP	W	L	T	GF	GA	PTS	GP	W	L	T	GF	GA	PTS	GP	W	L	T	GF	GA	PTS
Anaheim	8	7	1	0	34	15	14	9	5	4	0	26	23	10	17	12	5	0	60	38	24
Boston	55	15	29	11	157	207	41	55	6	40	9	131	248	21	110	21	69	20	288	455	62
Buffalo	48	22	20	6	149	144	50	47	12	25	10	126	173	34	95	34	45	16	275	317	84
Calgary	48	23	18	7	180	163	53	48	9	28	11	128	187	29	96	32	46	18	308	350	82
Chicago	97	40	42	15	321	314	95	95	24	61	10	248	388	58	192	64	103	25	569	702	153
Colorado	26	14	10	2	95	85	30	27	7	17	3	78	119	17	53	21	27	5	173	204	47
Detroit	92	48	30	14	338	277	110	91	31	47	13	301	368	75	183	79	77	27	639	645	185
Edmonton	31	12	13	6	114	103	30	30	8	16	6	104	136	22	61	20	29	12	218	239	52
Florida	3	0	1	2	11	12	2	3	1	1	1	10	11	3	6	1	2	3	21	23	5
Hartford	24	13	10	1	98	77	27	25	13	9	3	97	87	29	49	26	19	4	195	164	56
Los Angeles	65	38	16	11	268	183	87	64	19	27	18	191	226	56	129	57	43	29	459	409	143
Montreal	54	14	29	11	141	196	39	53	10	36	7	128	235	27	107	24	65	18	269	431	66
New Jersey	39	23	10	6	154	103	52	39	17	19	3	121	132	37	78	40	29	9	275	235	89
NY Islanders	41	15	19	7	122	155	37	41	10	23	8	117	161	28	82	25	42	15	239	316	65
NY Rangers	55	16	30	9	165	209	41	56	12	34	10	152	198	34	111	28	64	19	317	407	75
Ottawa	5	4	1	0	25	11	8	4	3	1	0	14	10	6	9	7	2	0	39	21	14
Philadelphia	61	24	23	14	204	206	62	62	9	41	11	140	244	29	122	33	64	25	344	450	91
Phoenix	36	19	13	4	150	121	42	34	16	16	2	121	121	34	70	35	29	6	271	242	76
Pittsburgh	59	33	21	5	225	199	71	58	17	36	5	161	223	39	117	50	57	10	386	422	110
St. Louis	100	45	36	19	343	299	109	103	28	56	19	294	379	75	203	73	92	38	637	678	184
San Jose	11	6	4	1	40	30	13	11	6	5	0	37	30	12	22	12	9	1	77	60	25
Tampa Bay	6	4	1	1	22	15	9	7	4	1	2	17	12	10	13	8	2	3	39	27	19
Toronto	91	44	33	14	349	292	105	94	31	47	16	296	337	78	185	78	80	27	645	629	183
Vancouver	57	32	15	10	223	168	74	57	21	26	10	177	217	52	114	53	41	20	400	385	126
Washington	34	15	11	8	130	101	38	35	14	14	7	111	110	35	69	29	25	15	241	211	73
Defunct Clubs	33	19	8	6	123	86	44	32	10	16	6	84	105	26	65	29	24	12	207	191	70
Totals	**1179**	**548**	**444**	**187**	**4181**	**3771**	**1283**	**1179**	**343**	**646**	**190**	**3410**	**4480**	**876**	**2358**	**891**	**1090**	**377**	**7591**	**8251**	**2159**

Playoffs

	Series	W	L	GP	W	L	T	GF	GA	Last Mtg.	Round	Result
Boston	1	1	0	3	3	0	0	20	13	1981	PR	W 3-0
Buffalo	2	1	1	7	4	3	0	26	28	1981	QF	W 4-1
Calgary	1	1	0	6	4	2	0	25	18	1981	SF	W 4-2
Chicago	6	2	4	33	14	19	0	119	119	1991	DSF	W 4-2
Detroit	2	0	2	12	4	8	0	29	40	1995	CQF	L 1-4
Edmonton	3	1	2	16	7	9	0	48	57	1997	CQF	L 3-4
Los Angeles	1	1	0	7	4	3	0	26	21	1968	QF	W 4-3
Montreal	2	1	1	13	6	7	0	37	48	1980	QF	W 4-3
NY Islanders	1	0	1	5	1	4	0	16	26	1981	F	L 1-4
Philadelphia	2	0	2	11	3	8	0	26	41	1980	SF	L 1-4
Pittsburgh	1	0	1	6	2	4	0	16	28	1991	F	L 2-4
St. Louis	10	5	5	56	30	26	0	174	162	1994	CQF	W 4-0
Toronto	2	2	0	7	6	1	0	35	26	1983	DSF	W 3-1
Vancouver	1	0	1	5	1	4	0	11	18	1994	CSF	L 1-4
Totals	**35**	**15**	**20**	**187**	**89**	**98**	**0**	**608**	**645**			

Calgary totals include Atlanta, 1972-73 to 1979-80. Colorado totals include Quebec, 1979-80 to 1994-95. Dallas totals include Minnesota, 1967-68 to 1992-93. New Jersey totals include Kansas City, 1974-75 to 1975-76, and Colorado Rockies, 1976-77 to 1981-82. Phoenix totals include Winnipeg, 1979-80 to 1995-96.

Playoff Results 1997-93

Year	Round	Opponent	Result	GF	GA
1997	CQF	Edmonton	L 3-4	18	21
1995	CQF	Detroit	L 1-4	10	17
1994	CSF	Vancouver	L 1-4	11	18
	CQF	St. Louis	W 4-0	16	10

Abbreviations: Round: F – Final; **CF** – conference final; **CQF** – conference quarter-final; **CSF** – conference semi-final; **DF** – division final; **DSF** – division semi-final; **SF** – semi-final; **QF** – quarter-final; **PR** – preliminary round.

1996-97 Results

Oct.	5	Colorado	4-1		8		Detroit	6-3
	8	Washington	5-3		10		Phoenix	3-4
	10	at NY Rangers	2-1		13	at	Montreal	2-1
	12	at New Jersey	4-2		14	at	Pittsburgh	1-3
	13	at Chicago	5-3		21	at	Philadelphia	3-3
	15	Detroit	3-1		24	at	Washington	5-2
	17	Vancouver	1-6		25	at	Toronto	5-1
	19	Toronto	2-0		27		Los Angeles	7-2
	23	at Detroit	1-4		29		Anaheim	3-1
	26	Ottawa	5-1		31	at	Buffalo	1-3
	30	Buffalo	2-0	Feb.	2	at	Detroit	3-4
Nov.	1	Chicago	2-3		5		Tampa Bay	4-0
	3	at St. Louis	3-6		6	at	St. Louis	4-6
	6	at Phoenix	3-2		8	at	Phoenix	5-4
	8	at San Jose	1-3		9		Los Angeles	2-1
	11	at Anaheim	3-2		12		Phoenix	0-5
	13	Calgary	3-3		14		Detroit	4-3
	15	Anaheim	4-3		17	at	Los Angeles	2-1
	17	at Edmonton	7-3		18	at	San Jose	1-3
	19	at Vancouver	0-2		21		Calgary	4-2
	20	at Calgary	3-1		23		Edmonton	6-1
	22	Florida	1-2		25	at	Chicago	1-0
	27	New Jersey	2-3		27	at	Colorado	6-2
	29	at Tampa Bay	1-2	Mar.	1	at	Calgary	1-4
	30	Toronto	5-2		5		St. Louis	3-2
Dec.	4	San Jose	1-2		7		Edmonton	2-1
	6	Philadelphia	3-6		10	at	Toronto	3-3
	8	at Florida	1-1		14		Chicago	4-4
	11	St. Louis	5-5		16		Pittsburgh	6-2
	13	Vancouver	2-1		19		Phoenix	7-2
	15	at Ottawa	4-0		21		Hartford	2-0
	18	at Chicago	3-2		23	at	St. Louis	4-1
	20	at Hartford	4-1		30	at	Vancouver	3-2
	21	at NY Islanders	3-2		31	at	Edmonton	3-1
	23	San Jose	1-2	Apr.	2		NY Islanders	5-4
	27	Boston	6-4		4	at	Anaheim	2-3
	29	at Colorado	2-3		5	at	Los Angeles	3-3
	30	NY Rangers	2-3		7	at	Phoenix	2-2
Jan.	1	Montreal	4-6		9		Toronto	3-2
	3	at Detroit	1-2		11		Colorado	1-2
	4	at Boston	2-3		13		Chicago	2-5

Entry Draft
Selections 1997-83

1997
Pick
25	Brenden Morrow
52	Roman Lyashenko
77	Steve Gainey
105	Marc Kristoffersson
132	Teemu Elomo
160	Alexei Timkin
189	Jeff McKercher
216	Alexei Komarov
242	Brett McLean

1996
Pick
5	Richard Jackman
70	Jonathan Sim
90	Mike Hurley
112	Ryan Christie
113	Evgeny Tysbuk
166	Eoin McInerney
194	Joel Kwiatkowski
220	Nick Bootland

1995
Pick
11	Jarome Iginla
37	Patrick Cote
63	Petr Buzek
69	Sergei Gusev
115	Wade Strand
141	Dominic Marleau
173	Jeff Dewar
193	Anatoli Kovesnikov
202	Sergei Luchinkin
219	Stephen Lowe

1994
Pick
20	Jason Botterill
46	Lee Jinman
98	Jamie Wright
124	Marty Turco
150	Yevgeny Petrochinin
228	Marty Flichel
254	Jimmy Roy
280	Chris Szysky

1993
Pick
9	Todd Harvey
35	Jamie Langenbrunner
87	Chad Lang
136	Rick Mrozik
139	Per Svartvadet
165	Jeremy Stasiuk
191	Rob Lurtsema
243	Jordan Willis
249	Bill Lang
269	Cory Peterson

1992
Pick
34	Jarkko Varvio
58	Jeff Bes
88	Jere Lehtinen
130	Michael Johnson
154	Kyle Peterson
178	Juha Lind
202	Lars Edstrom
226	Jeff Romfo
250	Jeffrey Moen

1991
Pick
8	Richard Matvichuk
74	Mike Torchia
97	Mike Kennedy
118	Mark Lawrence
137	Geoff Finch
174	Michael Burkett
184	Derek Herlofsky
206	Tom Nemeth
228	Shayne Green
250	Jukka Suomalainen

1990
Pick
8	Derian Hatcher
50	Laurie Billeck
70	Cal McGowan
71	Frank Kovacs
92	Enrico Ciccone
113	Roman Turek
134	Jeff Levy
155	Doug Barrault
176	Joe Biondi
197	Troy Binnie
218	Ole-Eskild Dahlstrom
239	John McKersie

1989
Pick
7	Doug Zmolek
28	Mike Craig
60	Murray Garbutt
75	Jean-François Quintin
87	Pat MacLeod
91	Bryan Schoen
97	Rhys Hollyman
112	Scott Cashman
154	Jonathan Pratt
175	Kenneth Blum
196	Arturs Irbe
217	Tom Pederson
238	Helmut Balderis

1988
Pick
1	Mike Modano
40	Link Gaetz
43	Shaun Kane
64	Jeffrey Stop
148	Ken MacArthur
169	Travis Richards
190	Ari Matilainen
211	Grant Bischoff
232	Trent Andison

1987
Pick
6	David Archibald
35	Scott McCrady
48	Kevin Kaminski
73	John Weisbrod
88	Teppo Kivela
109	Darcy Norton
130	Timo Kulonen
151	Don Schmidt
172	Jarmo Myllys
193	Larry Olimb
214	Mark Felicio
235	Dave hields

1986
Pick
12	Warren Babe
30	Neil Wilkinson
33	Dean Kolstad
54	Eric Bennett
55	Rob Zettler
58	Brad Turner
75	Kirk Tomlinson
96	Jari Gronstrand
159	Scott Mathias
180	Lance Pitlick
201	Dan Keczmer
222	Garth Joy
243	Kurt Stahura

1985
Pick
51	Stephane Roy
69	Mike Berger
90	Dwight Mullins
111	MikeMullowney
132	Mike Kelfer
153	Ross Johnson
174	Tim Helmer
195	Gordon Ernst
216	Ladislav Lubina
237	Tommy Sjodin

1984
Pick
13	David Quinn
46	Ken Hodge
76	Miroslav Maly
89	Jiri Poner
97	Kari Takko
118	Gary McColgan
139	Vladimir Kyhos
160	Darin MacInnis
181	Duane Wahlin
201	Mike Orn
222	Tom Terwilliger
242	Mike Nightenale

1983
Pick
1	Brian Lawton
36	Malcolm Parks
38	Frantisek Musil
56	Mitch Messier
76	Brian Durand
96	Rich Geist
116	Tom McComb
136	Sean Toomey
156	Don Biggs
176	Paul Pulis
196	Milos Riha
212	Oldrich Valek
236	Paul Roff

General Manager

GAINEY, BOB
Vice President of Hockey Operations/General Manager, Dallas Stars.
Born in Peterborough, Ont., December 13, 1953.

Bob Gainey enters his second season as the full-time general manager for the Dallas Stars after relinquishing his head coaching duties on January 8, 1996. Named general manager of the team on June 8, 1992, he held the dual role of coach and g.m. for over four seasons. Having been appointed head coach for the Stars on June 19, 1990, his five-plus consecutive seasons behind the bench was the longest tenure of any head coach in franchise history. He is the Stars' sixth general manager and was the team's 16th head coach.

Under Gainey's tutelage, the Stars improved their regular-season record in each of Gainey's first four seasons as coach, going from 27 wins and 68 points in his first year to 42 wins and 97 points in 1993-94. In his first season, 1990-91, Gainey led the Stars through to the Stanley Cup finals, surprising Chicago and St. Louis and eliminating defending champion Edmonton before bowing in six games to Pittsburgh. He finished his reign behind the Stars bench with a 165-190-60 regular season record.

Elected to the Hockey Hall of Fame in 1992, Gainey was Montreal's first choice (eighth overall) in the 1973 Amateur Draft. During his 16-year career with the Canadiens, Gainey was a member of five Stanley Cup-winning teams and was named the Conn Smythe Trophy winner in 1979. He was a four-time recipient of the Frank Selke Trophy (1978-81), awarded to the League's top defensive forward, and participated in four NHL All-Star Games (1977, 1978, 1980 and 1981). He served as team captain for eight seasons (1981-89). During his career, he played in 1,160 regular-season games, registering 239 goals and 262 assists for 501 points. In addition, he tallied 73 points (25-48-73) in 182 post-season games.

NHL Coaching Record

Season	Team	Regular Season					Playoffs			
		Games	W	L	T	%	Games	W	L	%
1990-91	Minnesota	80	27	39	14	.425	23	14	9	.643
1991-92	Minnesota	80	32	42	6	.438	7	3	4	.429
1992-93	Minnesota	84	36	38	10	.488	....	....	....	....
1993-94	Dallas	84	42	29	13	.577	9	5	4	.556
1994-95	Dallas	48	17	23	8	.438	5	1	4	.200
1995-96	Dallas	39	11	19	9	.397	....	....	....	....
	NHL Totals	**415**	**165**	**190**	**60**	**.470**	**44**	**23**	**21**	**.523**

Club Directory

Reunion Arena

Dallas Stars Hockey Club, Inc.
Dr Pepper StarCenter
211 Cowboys Parkway
Irving, TX 75063
Phone **214/868-2890**
FAX 972/868-2860
P.R. Office 214/GO STARS
Capacity: 16,924

Executive
Chairman of the Board and Owner	Thomas O. Hicks
President and Alternate Governor	James R. Lites
Vice President of Hockey Operations	Bob Gainey
Vice President of Marketing and Broadcasting	Bill Strong
Vice President of Marketing and Promotion	Jeff Cogen
Vice President and Chief Financial Officer	Rick McLaughlin
Office Manager	Rene Marshall
Assistant to the President	Kim Smith

Hockey
General Manager	Bob Gainey
Assistant General Manager	Les Jackson
Head Coach	Ken Hitchcock
Assistant Coaches	Doug Jarvis, Rick Wilson
Assistant to the General Manager	Doug Armstrong
Director of Scouting	Craig Button
Chief Scout	Bob Gernander
Scout	Tim Bernhardt
Pro Scout	Doug Overton
Regional Scouts	E.J. Hradek, Jimmy Johnston, Brad Robson, Jeff Twohey, Ray Robson, Serge Savard Jr., Kevin Pottle, Bob Richardson, Jim Pederson, Evgeny Larionov, Hans Edlund
Director of Team Services	Dan Stuchal
Head Athletic Trainer	Dave Surprenant
Equipment Managers	Dave Smith, Rich Matthews
Strength and Conditioning Coach	J.J. McQueen
Equipment Assistant	Matt Benolkin
Video Coordinator	Paul McGrath
Administrative Assistant	Lesa Moake

Public Relations
Director of Public Relations	Larry Kelly
Public Relations Manager	Kurt Daniels
Art Director	Rainer Uhlir
Community Relations Manager	Kristin Reaugh
Community Relations Coordinator	Julie Berkhouse

Ticket Sales
Director of Ticket Sales	Brian Byrnes
Senior Account Executives	Tom Fireoved, Frank Hubach
Account Executives	Brad Alberts, Paige Jackson, Kimberly Marriott, Misha Pfaff, Patricia Schmidt, Jason Sivils, Jeff Tummonds
Sales Coordinator	Leah Deniger
Sales/Marketing Assistant	Becky Thielen

Corporate Services
Director of Corporate Services	Jill Cogen
Corporate Service Assistants	Annemarie Baker, Christi Langas

Marketing and Promotion
Director of Marketing and Promotion	Christy Martinez
Manager of Events & Sponsor Services	Lee Smith
Marketing Manager	Rebecca Miller

Merchandising
Director of Merchandising	Steve Shilts
Retail Manager	Tiffani McCallon
Merchandise Operations Manager	Mike Groom
Arena & Warehouse Manager	Oscar Garza

Corporate Sales
Assistant V.P. of Advertising Sales	David Peart
Director of Corporate Sales	Jamie Norman

Broadcasting
Director of Broadcasting	Kevin Spivey
Announcers, TV/Radio	Ralph Strangis, Daryl Reaugh
Announcer, Arena	Bill Oellerman
Manager, Broadcast and Sales Services	Hilary Roberts

Finance, Legal & Business Development
Assistant V.P. of Finance	Therese Baird
Director of Legal Affairs & Business Development	Lance Lankford
Controller	Sharon Arellono
Tax Manager	Denise Gilbert
Accounting Supervisor	Tracy Goldsack
Payroll Accountant	Dina Ferreira
Staff Accountant	Jeff Cook
Accounting Assistant	Cliff Johnson

Box Office Operations
Director of Box Office Operations	Augie Manfredo
Box Office Manager	Stacey Marthaler
Phone Room Supervisor	Ben Marthaler
Box Office Assistant	Chris Oliver

Dr. Pepper StarCenter Operations
Director of Business Operations	Ed Reusch
Director of Building Operations	Geoff Moore
Skating Programs Manager	Alexandra LaFave
Hockey Programs Manager	Jouni Lehtola
Building Manager	Dan Ryan
Operations Manager	Robert Santana
Assistant Skating Programs Manager	Aerin Williams
Assistant Hockey Programs Manager	Mark Spain
Front Desk Manager	Brent Swarbrick
Head Skating Professional	Lorraine Borman
Office Assistants	Rachel Brezina, Sheree Smith

Detroit Red Wings

1996-97 Results: 38W-26L-18T 94PTS. Second, Central Division

1997-98 Schedule

Oct.	Wed.	1	at Calgary	**Jan.**	Wed.	31	St. Louis
	Fri.	3	at Edmonton		Fri.	2	San Jose
	Wed.	8	Dallas		Sun.	4	at Chicago
	Fri.	10	Tampa Bay		Tue.	6	Phoenix
	Sun.	12	Calgary		Fri.	9	at Dallas
	Tue.	14	at Toronto		Sun.	11	Washington*
	Wed.	15	Toronto		Mon.	12	at NY Islanders
	Sat.	18	Carolina*		Wed.	14	Vancouver
	Mon.	20	St. Louis		Tue.	20	at New Jersey
	Wed.	22	at Anaheim		Wed.	21	Toronto
	Thu.	23	at Los Angeles		Sat.	24	Philadelphia*
	Sun.	26	at Vancouver		Wed.	28	Phoenix
	Wed.	29	San Jose		Sat.	31	at Pittsburgh*
	Fri.	31	Los Angeles	**Feb.**	Sun.	1	at Washington*
Nov.	Sun.	2	Anaheim*		Tue.	3	at Florida
	Wed.	5	at Carolina		Thu.	5	at Tampa Bay
	Fri.	7	Pittsburgh		Sat.	7	at St. Louis*
	Sun.	9	Calgary		Wed.	25	Los Angeles
	Tue.	11	Colorado		Fri.	27	Florida
	Thu.	13	at Ottawa	**Mar.**	Mon.	2	at Phoenix
	Sat.	15	at St. Louis		Wed.	4	at Anaheim
	Sun.	16	at Chicago		Thu.	5	at San Jose
	Wed.	19	NY Islanders		Sat.	7	at Los Angeles*
	Fri.	21	Dallas		Tue.	10	Boston
	Sat.	22	at Montreal		Thu.	12	Chicago
	Wed.	26	Ottawa		Sat.	14	at Philadelphia*
	Fri.	28	Montreal		Tue.	17	Edmonton
Dec.	Mon.	1	at Vancouver		Wed.	18	at Toronto
	Wed.	3	at Calgary		Sat.	21	at NY Rangers*
	Fri.	5	at Edmonton		Mon.	23	Chicago
	Tue.	9	Vancouver		Thu.	26	Anaheim
	Fri.	12	Edmonton		Sat.	28	at St. Louis*
	Sun.	14	at Phoenix		Sun.	29	Buffalo
	Tue.	16	at San Jose	**Apr.**	Wed.	1	Colorado
	Wed.	17	at Colorado		Sat.	4	at Chicago*
	Fri.	19	New Jersey		Tue.	7	St. Louis
	Mon.	22	at Boston		Thu.	9	Phoenix
	Tue.	23	at Buffalo		Sat.	11	NY Rangers*
	Fri.	26	Toronto		Tue.	14	at Phoenix
	Sat.	27	at Toronto		Wed.	15	at Dallas
	Mon.	29	Dallas		Sat.	18	at Colorado*

* Denotes afternoon game.

Franchise date: September 25, 1926

WESTERN NHL CONFERENCE
CENTRAL DIVISION

72nd NHL Season

Darren McCarty's inspirational play was a key to the Red Wings' success in 1996-97. The tough winger capped the team's playoff run by scoring the Stanley Cup-winning goal against Philadelphia.

Year-by-Year Record

Season	GP	Home W	L	T	Road W	L	T	Overall W	L	T	GF	GA	Pts	Finished	Playoff Result
1996-97	82	20	12	9	18	14	9	38	26	18	253	197	94	2nd, Central Div.	**Won Stanley Cup**
1995-96	82	36	3	2	26	10	5	62	13	7	325	181	131	1st, Central Div.	Lost Conf. Championship
1994-95	48	17	4	3	16	7	1	33	11	4	180	117	70	1st, Central Div.	Lost Final
1993-94	84	23	13	6	23	17	2	46	30	8	356	275	100	1st, Central Div.	Lost Conf. Quarter-Final
1992-93	84	25	14	3	22	14	6	47	28	9	369	280	103	2nd, Norris Div.	Lost Div. Semi-Final
1991-92	80	24	12	4	19	13	8	43	25	12	320	256	98	1st, Norris Div.	Lost Div. Final
1990-91	80	26	14	0	8	24	8	34	38	8	273	298	76	3rd, Norris Div.	Lost Div. Semi-Final
1989-90	80	20	14	6	8	24	8	28	38	14	288	323	70	5th, Norris Div.	Out of Playoffs
1988-89	80	20	14	6	14	20	6	34	34	12	313	316	80	1st, Norris Div.	Lost Div. Semi-Final
1987-88	80	24	10	6	17	18	5	41	28	11	322	269	93	1st, Norris Div.	Lost Conf. Championship
1986-87	80	20	14	6	14	22	4	34	36	10	260	274	78	2nd, Norris Div.	Lost Conf. Championship
1985-86	80	10	26	4	7	31	2	17	57	6	266	415	40	5th, Norris Div.	Out of Playoffs
1984-85	80	19	14	7	8	27	5	27	41	12	313	357	66	3rd, Norris Div.	Lost Div. Semi-Final
1983-84	80	18	20	2	13	22	5	31	42	7	298	323	69	3rd, Norris Div.	Lost Div. Semi-Final
1982-83	80	14	19	7	7	25	8	21	44	15	263	344	57	5th, Norris Div.	Out of Playoffs
1981-82	80	15	19	6	6	28	6	21	47	12	270	351	54	6th, Norris Div.	Out of Playoffs
1980-81	80	16	15	9	3	28	9	19	43	18	252	339	56	5th, Norris Div.	Out of Playoffs
1979-80	80	14	21	5	12	22	6	26	43	11	268	306	63	5th, Norris Div.	Out of Playoffs
1978-79	80	15	17	8	8	24	8	23	41	16	252	295	62	5th, Norris Div.	Out of Playoffs
1977-78	80	22	11	7	10	23	7	32	34	14	252	266	78	2nd, Norris Div.	Lost Quarter-Final
1976-77	80	12	22	6	4	33	3	16	55	9	183	309	41	5th, Norris Div.	Out of Playoffs
1975-76	80	17	15	8	9	29	2	26	44	10	226	300	62	4th, Norris Div.	Out of Playoffs
1974-75	80	17	17	6	6	28	6	23	45	12	259	335	58	4th, Norris Div.	Out of Playoffs
1973-74	78	21	12	6	8	27	4	29	39	10	255	319	68	6th, East Div.	Out of Playoffs
1972-73	78	22	12	5	15	17	7	37	29	12	265	243	86	5th, East Div.	Out of Playoffs
1971-72	78	25	11	3	8	24	7	33	35	10	261	262	76	5th, East Div.	Out of Playoffs
1970-71	78	17	15	7	5	30	4	22	45	11	209	308	55	7th, East Div.	Out of Playoffs
1969-70	76	20	11	7	20	10	8	40	21	15	246	199	95	3rd, East Div.	Lost Quarter-Final
1968-69	76	23	8	7	10	23	5	33	31	12	239	221	78	5th, East Div.	Out of Playoffs
1967-68	74	18	15	4	9	20	8	27	35	12	245	257	66	6th, East Div.	Out of Playoffs
1966-67	70	21	11	3	6	28	1	27	39	4	212	241	58	5th,	Out of Playoffs
1965-66	70	20	8	7	11	19	5	31	27	12	221	194	74	4th,	Lost Final
1964-65	70	25	7	3	15	16	4	40	23	7	224	175	87	1st,	Lost Semi-Final
1963-64	70	23	9	3	7	20	8	30	29	11	191	204	71	4th,	Lost Final
1962-63	70	19	10	6	13	15	7	32	25	13	200	194	77	4th,	Lost Final
1961-62	70	17	11	7	6	22	7	23	33	14	184	219	60	5th,	Out of Playoffs
1960-61	70	15	13	7	10	16	9	25	29	16	195	215	66	4th,	Lost Final
1959-60	70	18	14	3	8	15	12	26	29	15	186	197	67	4th,	Lost Semi-Final
1958-59	70	13	17	5	12	20	3	25	37	8	167	218	58	6th,	Out of Playoffs
1957-58	70	16	11	8	13	18	4	29	29	12	176	207	70	3rd,	Lost Semi-Final
1956-57	70	23	7	5	15	13	7	38	20	12	198	157	88	1st,	Lost Semi-Final
1955-56	70	21	6	8	9	18	8	30	24	16	183	148	76	2nd,	Lost Final
1954-55	70	25	5	5	17	12	6	42	17	11	204	134	95	1st,	**Won Stanley Cup**
1953-54	70	24	4	7	13	15	7	37	19	14	191	132	88	1st,	**Won Stanley Cup**
1952-53	70	20	5	10	16	11	8	36	16	18	222	133	90	1st,	Lost Semi-Final
1951-52	70	24	7	4	20	7	8	44	14	12	215	133	100	1st,	**Won Stanley Cup**
1950-51	70	25	3	7	19	10	6	44	13	13	236	139	101	1st,	Lost Semi-Final
1949-50	70	19	9	7	18	10	7	37	19	14	229	164	88	1st,	**Won Stanley Cup**
1948-49	60	21	6	3	13	13	4	34	19	7	195	145	75	1st,	Lost Final
1947-48	60	16	9	5	14	9	7	30	18	12	187	148	72	2nd,	Lost Final
1946-47	60	14	10	6	8	17	5	22	27	11	190	193	55	4th,	Lost Semi-Final
1945-46	50	16	5	4	4	15	6	20	20	10	146	159	50	4th,	Lost Semi-Final
1944-45	50	19	5	1	12	9	4	31	14	5	218	161	67	2nd,	Lost Final
1943-44	50	18	5	2	8	13	4	26	18	6	214	177	58	2nd,	Lost Semi-Final
1942-43	50	16	4	5	9	10	6	25	14	11	169	124	61	1st,	**Won Stanley Cup**
1941-42	48	14	7	3	5	18	1	19	25	4	140	147	42	5th,	Lost Final
1940-41	48	14	5	5	7	11	6	21	16	11	112	102	53	3rd,	Lost Final
1939-40	48	11	10	3	5	16	3	16	26	6	90	126	38	5th,	Lost Semi-Final
1938-39	48	14	8	2	4	16	4	18	24	6	107	128	42	5th,	Lost Semi-Final
1937-38	48	8	10	6	4	15	5	12	25	11	99	133	35	4th, Amn. Div.	Out of Playoffs
1936-37	48	14	5	5	11	9	4	25	14	9	128	102	59	1st, Amn. Div.	**Won Stanley Cup**
1935-36	48	14	5	5	10	11	3	24	16	8	124	103	56	1st, Amn. Div.	**Won Stanley Cup**
1934-35	48	11	8	5	8	14	2	19	22	7	127	114	45	4th, Amn. Div.	Out of Playoffs
1933-34	48	15	5	4	9	9	6	24	14	10	113	98	58	1st, Amn. Div.	Lost Final
1932-33*	48	17	3	4	8	12	4	25	15	8	111	93	58	2nd, Amn. Div.	Lost Semi-Final
1931-32	48	15	3	6	3	17	4	18	20	10	95	108	46	3rd, Amn. Div.	Lost Quarter-Final
1930-31**	44	10	7	5	6	14	2	16	21	7	102	105	39	4th, Amn. Div.	Out of Playoffs
1929-30	44	9	10	3	5	14	3	14	24	6	117	133	34	4th, Amn. Div.	Out of Playoffs
1928-29	44	11	6	5	8	10	4	19	16	9	72	63	47	3rd, Amn. Div.	Lost Quarter-Final
1927-28	44	9	10	3	10	9	3	19	19	6	88	79	44	4th, Amn. Div.	Out of Playoffs
1926-27***	44	5	16	0	7	12	4	12	28	4	76	105	28	5th, Amn. Div.	Out of Playoffs

* Team name changed to Red Wings. ** Team name changed to Falcons. *** Team named Cougars.

1997-98 Player Personnel

FORWARDS	HT	WT	S	Place of Birth	Date	1996-97 Club
AUDET, Philippe	6-2	175	L	Ottawa, Ont.	6/4/77	Granby-Adirondack
BROWN, Doug	5-10	185	R	Southborough, MA	6/12/64	Detroit
CLOUTIER, Sylvain	6-0	195	L	Mont-Laurier, Que.	2/13/74	Adirondack
DANDENAULT, Mathieu	6-0	174	R	Sherbrooke, Que.	2/3/76	Detroit
DRAPER, Kris	5-11	185	L	Toronto, Ont.	5/24/71	Detroit
FEDOROV, Sergei	6-1	200	L	Pskov, USSR	12/13/69	Detroit
GILCHRIST, Brent	5-11	180	L	Moose Jaw, Sask.	4/3/67	Dallas
HOLMSTROM, Tomas	6-0	200	L	Pitea, Sweden	1/23/73	Detroit-Adirondack
KNUBLE, Michael	6-3	208	R	Toronto, Ont.	7/4/72	Detroit-Adirondack
KOCUR, Joe	6-0	205	R	Calgary, Alta.	12/21/64	San Antonio-Detroit
KOZLOV, Vyacheslav	5-10	180	L	Voskresensk, USSR	5/3/72	Detroit
LAPLANTE, Darryl	6-1	185	L	Calgary, Alta.	3/28/77	Moose Jaw
LAPOINTE, Martin	5-11	200	R	Ville Ste. Pierre, Que.	9/12/73	Detroit
LARIONOV, Igor	5-9	170	L	Voskresensk, USSR	12/3/60	Detroit
MALTBY, Kirk	6-0	180	R	Guelph, Ont.	12/22/72	Detroit
McCARTY, Darren	6-1	210	R	Burnaby, B.C.	4/1/72	Detroit
ROEST, Stacy	5-9	192	R	Lethbridge, Alta.	3/15/74	Adirondack
SHANAHAN, Brendan	6-3	218	R	Mimico, Ont.	1/23/69	Hartford-Detroit
TAYLOR, Tim	6-1	185	L	Stratford, Ont.	2/6/69	Detroit
YZERMAN, Steve	5-11	185	R	Cranbrook, B.C.	5/9/65	Detroit
DEFENSEMEN						
ERIKSSON, Anders	6-3	218	L	Bollnas, Sweden	1/9/75	Detroit-Adirondack
FETISOV, Viacheslav	6-1	220	L	Moscow, USSR	4/20/58	Detroit
GILLAM, Sean	6-2	187	R	Lethbridge, Alta.	5/7/76	Adirondack
GOLUBOVSKY, Yan	6-3	183	R	Novosibirsk, USSR	3/9/76	Adirondack
KUZNETSOV, Maxim	6-5	198	L	Pavlodar, USSR	3/24/77	Moscow D'amo-Adirondack
LIDSTROM, Nicklas	6-2	185	L	Vasteras, Sweden	4/28/70	Detroit
MURPHY, Larry	6-2	210	R	Scarborough, Ont.	3/8/61	Toronto-Detroit
PUSHOR, Jamie	6-3	192	R	Lethbridge, Alta.	2/11/73	Detroit
ROUSE, Bob	6-1	210	R	Surrey, B.C.	6/18/64	Detroit
WARD, Aaron	6-2	200	R	Windsor, Ont.	1/17/73	Detroit
GOALTENDERS	**HT**	**WT**	**C**	**Place of Birth**	**Date**	**1996-97 Club**
BACH, Ryan	6-1	180	L	Sherwood Park, Alta.	10/21/73	Utica-Adirondack-Toledo
HODSON, Kevin	6-0	182	L	Winnipeg, Man.	3/27/72	Detroit-Quebec
MARACLE, Norm	5-9	175	L	Belleville, Ont.	10/2/74	Adirondack
OSGOOD, Chris	5-10	160	L	Peace River, Alta.	11/26/72	Detroit

Director of Player Personnel/Coach

BOWMAN, WILLIAM SCOTT (SCOTTY)
Director of Player Personnel/Coach, Detroit Red Wings.
Born in Montreal, Que. September 18, 1933.

Last season, Scotty Bowman led the Detroit Red Wings to their eighth Stanley Cup championship in the franchise's 71-year history, ending the team's 42-year drought since the 1955 title. Individually, Bowman now has won eight Cups (seven as coach, one as director of player development) over the course of his 26 seasons (25 seasons as a head coach) in the NHL and becomes the first to win the Cup with three different teams. Entering his fifth season as Detroit's head coach, Scotty Bowman aims to match one of the few remaining NHL records he does not already own — the most Stanley Cup titles as coach (8), held by the legendary Toe Blake. After guiding the St. Louis Blues into the championship round in three consecutive seasons from 1968-70, Bowman was appointed head coach of the Montreal Canadiens, who captured five Stanley Cup titles under Bowman's supervision.

Following an eight season term as the general manager of the Buffalo Sabres, and a brief stint as a commentator for CBC Television, Bowman joined the Pittsburgh Penguins as director of player development, but returned to coaching when head coach Bob Johnson became ill in September, 1991. Bowman was elected to the Hockey Hall of Fame as a builder in 1991.

NHL Coaching Record

		Regular Season					Playoffs			
Season	Team	Games	W	L	T	%	Games	W	L	%
1967-68	St. Louis	58	23	21	14	.517	18	8	10	.444
1968-69	St. Louis	76	37	25	14	.579	12	8	4	.667
1969-70	St. Louis	76	37	27	12	.566	16	8	8	.500
1970-71	St. Louis	28	13	10	5	.554	6	2	4	.333
1971-72	Montreal	78	46	16	16	.692	6	2	4	.333
1972-73	Montreal	78	52	10	16	.769	17	12	5	.706*
1973-74	Montreal	78	45	24	9	.635	6	2	4	.333
1974-75	Montreal	80	47	14	19	.706	11	6	5	.545
1975-76	Montreal	80	58	11	11	.794	13	12	1	.923*
1976-77	Montreal	80	60	8	12	.825	14	12	2	.857*
1977-78	Montreal	80	59	10	11	.806	15	12	3	.800*
1978-79	Montreal	80	52	17	11	.719	16	12	4	.750*
1979-80	Buffalo	80	47•	17	16	.688	14	9	5	.643
1981-82	Buffalo	35	18	10	7	.614	4	1	3	.250
1982-83	Buffalo	80	38	29	13	.556	10	6	4	.600
1983-84	Buffalo	80	48	25	7	.644	3	0	3	.000
1984-85	Buffalo	80	38	28	14	.563	5	2	3	.400
1985-86	Buffalo	37	18	18	1	.500	....	....	....	....
1986-87	Buffalo	12	3	7	2	.333	....	....	....	....
1991-92	Pittsburgh	80	39	32	9	.544	21	16	5	.762*
1992-93	Pittsburgh	84	56	21	7	.708	12	7	5	.583
1993-94	Detroit	84	46	30	8	.595	7	3	4	.429
1994-95	Detroit	48	33	11	4	.729	18	12	6	.667
1995-96	Detroit	82	62	13	7	.799	19	10	9	.526
1996-97	Detroit	82	38	26	18	.573	20	16	4	.800*
	NHL Totals	**1736**	**1013**	**460**	**263**	**.659**	**283**	**178**	**105**	**.629**

* Stanley Cup win.

1996-97 Scoring

* – rookie

Regular Season

Pos	#	Player	Team	GP	G	A	Pts	+/–	PIM	PP	SH	GW	GT	S	%
L	14	Brendan Shanahan	HFD	2	1	0	1	1	0	0	1	0	0	13	7.7
			DET	79	46	41	87	31	131	20	2	7	2	323	14.2
			TOTAL	81	47	41	88	32	131	20	3	7	2	336	14.0
C	19	Steve Yzerman	DET	81	22	63	85	22	78	8	0	3	0	232	9.5
C	91	Sergei Fedorov	DET	74	30	33	63	29	30	9	2	4	0	273	11.0
D	5	Nicklas Lidstrom	DET	79	15	42	57	11	30	8	0	1	0	214	7.0
C	8	Igor Larionov	DET	64	12	42	54	31	26	2	1	4	0	95	12.6
R	25	Darren McCarty	DET	68	19	30	49	14	126	5	0	6	1	171	11.1
L	13	Vyacheslav Kozlov	DET	75	23	22	45	21	46	3	0	6	0	211	10.9
D	55	Larry Murphy	TOR	69	7	32	39	1	20	4	0	0	1	137	5.1
			DET	12	2	4	6	2	0	1	0	1	0	21	9.5
			TOTAL	81	9	36	45	3	20	5	0	1	1	158	5.7
R	28	Tomas Sandstrom	PIT	40	9	15	24	4	33	1	1	0	0	73	12.3
			DET	34	9	9	18	2	36	0	1	2	1	66	13.6
			TOTAL	74	18	24	42	6	69	1	2	2	1	139	12.9
D	16	Vlad. Konstantinov	DET	77	5	33	38	38	151	0	0	0	0	141	3.5
R	20	Martin Lapointe	DET	78	16	17	33	-14	167	5	1	1	0	149	10.7
D	2	Viacheslav Fetisov	DET	64	5	23	28	26	76	0	0	1	0	95	5.3
C	33	Kris Draper	DET	76	8	5	13	-11	73	1	0	1	0	85	9.4
R	17	Doug Brown	DET	49	6	7	13	-3	8	1	0	0	0	69	8.7
D	3	Bob Rouse	DET	70	4	9	13	8	58	0	2	0	0	70	5.7
R	11	Mathieu Dandenault	DET	65	3	9	12	-10	28	0	0	0	0	81	3.7
D	4 *	Jamie Pushor	DET	75	4	7	11	1	129	0	0	0	0	63	6.3
L	15 *	Tomas Holmstrom	DET	47	6	3	9	-10	33	3	0	0	0	53	11.3
L	18	Kirk Maltby	DET	66	3	5	8	3	75	0	0	0	0	62	4.8
C	37	Tim Taylor	DET	44	3	4	7	-6	52	0	1	0	2	44	6.8
D	27 *	Aaron Ward	DET	49	2	5	7	-9	52	0	0	0	0	40	5.0
D	34 *	Anders Eriksson	DET	23	0	6	6	5	10	0	0	0	0	27	0.0
R	26	Joey Kocur	DET	34	2	1	3	-7	70	0	0	1	0	38	5.3
G	30	Chris Osgood	DET	47	0	2	2	0	6	0	0	0	0	0	0.0
R	22 *	Michael Knuble	DET	9	1	0	1	-1	0	0	0	0	0	10	10.0
G	31 *	Kevin Hodson	DET	6	0	1	1	0	0	0	0	0	0	0	0.0
D	23	Mike Ramsey	DET	2	0	0	0	0	0	0	0	0	0	3	0.0
L	40	Mark Major	DET	2	0	0	0	0	5	0	0	0	0	0	0.0
G	29	Mike Vernon	DET	33	0	0	0	0	35	0	0	0	0	0	0.0

Goaltending

No.	Goaltender	GPI	Mins	Avg	W	L	T	EN	SO	GA	SA	S%
31	* Kevin Hodson	6	294	1.63	2	2	1	0	1	8	114	.930
30	Chris Osgood	47	2769	2.30	23	13	9	3	6	106	1175	.910
29	Mike Vernon	33	1952	2.43	13	11	8	1	0	79	782	.899
	Totals	**82**	**5031**	**2.35**	**38**	**26**	**18**	**4**	**7**	**197**	**2075**	**.905**

Playoffs

Pos	#	Player	Team	GP	G	A	Pts	+/–	PIM	PP	SH	GW	OT	S	%
C	91	Sergei Fedorov	DET	20	8	12	20	5	12	3	0	4	0	79	10.1
L	14	Brendan Shanahan	DET	20	9	8	17	8	43	2	0	2	1	82	11.0
L	13	Vyacheslav Kozlov	DET	20	8	5	13	3	14	4	0	2	1	58	13.8
C	19	Steve Yzerman	DET	20	7	6	13	3	4	3	0	2	0	65	10.8
C	8	Igor Larionov	DET	20	4	8	12	8	8	3	0	1	0	29	13.8
R	20	Martin Lapointe	DET	20	4	8	12	8	60	1	0	1	1	37	10.8
D	55	Larry Murphy	DET	20	2	9	11	16	8	1	0	1	0	51	3.9
D	5	Nicklas Lidstrom	DET	20	2	6	8	12	2	0	0	0	0	79	2.5
L	18	Kirk Maltby	DET	20	5	2	7	6	24	0	1	1	0	35	14.3
R	25	Darren McCarty	DET	20	3	4	7	1	34	0	0	2	0	34	8.8
R	17	Doug Brown	DET	14	3	3	6	4	2	0	0	0	0	23	13.0
C	33	Kris Draper	DET	20	2	4	6	5	12	0	1	0	0	30	6.7
R	26	Joey Kocur	DET	19	1	3	4	5	22	0	0	0	0	16	6.3
D	2	Viacheslav Fetisov	DET	20	0	4	4	2	42	0	0	0	0	27	0.0
R	28	Tomas Sandstrom	DET	20	0	4	4	-3	24	0	0	0	0	36	0.0
D	16	Vlad. Konstantinov	DET	20	0	4	4	-1	29	0	0	0	0	29	0.0
D	4 *	Jamie Pushor	DET	5	0	1	1	-1	5	0	0	0	0	3	0.0
G	29	Mike Vernon	DET	20	0	1	1	0	12	0	0	0	0	0	0.0
L	15 *	Tomas Holmstrom	DET	1	0	0	0	-1	0	0	0	0	0	0	0.0
C	37	Tim Taylor	DET	2	0	0	0	-1	0	0	0	0	0	0	0.0
G	30	Chris Osgood	DET	2	0	0	0	0	2	0	0	0	0	0	0.0
D	27 *	Aaron Ward	DET	19	0	0	0	1	17	0	0	0	0	9	0.0
D	3	Bob Rouse	DET	20	0	0	0	8	55	0	0	0	0	14	0.0

Goaltending

No.	Goaltender	GPI	Mins	Avg	W	L	EN	SO	GA	SA	S%
29	Mike Vernon	20	1229	1.76	16	4	0	1	36	494	.927
30	Chris Osgood	2	47	2.55	0	0	0	0	2	21	.905
	Totals	**20**	**1280**	**1.78**	**16**	**4**	**0**	**1**	**38**	**515**	**.926**

Club Records

Team

(Figures in brackets for season records are games played; records for fewest points, wins, ties, losses, goals, goals against are for 70 or more games)

Most Points	**131**	1995-96 (82)
Most Wins	***62**	1995-96 (82)
Most Ties	**18**	1952-53 (70), 1980-81 (80), 1996-97 (82)
Most Losses	**57**	1985-86 (80)
Most Goals	**369**	1992-93 (84)
Most Goals Against	**415**	1985-86 (80)
Fewest Points	**40**	1985-86 (80)
Fewest Wins	**16**	1976-77 (80)
Fewest Ties	**4**	1966-67 (70)
Fewest Losses	**13**	1950-51 (70), 1995-96 (82)
Fewest Goals	**167**	1958-59 (70)
Fewest Goals Against	**132**	1953-54 (70)
Longest Winning Streak		
Overall	**9**	Mar. 3-21/51, Feb. 27-Mar. 20/55
Home	**14**	Jan. 21-Mar. 25/65
Away	**7**	Mar. 25-Apr. 14/95
Longest Undefeated Streak		
Overall	**15**	Nov. 27-Dec. 28/52 (8 wins, 7 ties)
Home	**18**	Dec. 26/54-Mar. 20/55 (13 wins, 5 ties)
Away	**15**	Oct. 18-Dec. 20/51 (10 wins, 5 ties)
Longest Losing Streak		
Overall	**14**	Feb. 24-Mar. 25/82
Home	**7**	Feb. 20-Mar. 25/82
Away	**14**	Oct. 19-Dec. 21/66
Longest Winless Streak		
Overall	**19**	Feb. 26-Apr. 3/77 (18 losses, 1 tie)
Home	**10**	Dec. 11/85-Jan. 18/86 (9 losses, 1 tie)
Away	**26**	Dec. 15/76-Apr. 3/77 (23 losses, 3 ties)
Most Shutouts, Season	**13**	1953-54 (70)
Most. PIM, Season	**2,393**	1985-86 (80)
Most Goals, Game	**15**	Jan. 23/44 (NYR 0 at Det. 15)

Individual

Most Seasons	**25**	Gordie Howe
Most Games	**1,687**	Gordie Howe
Most Goals, Career	**786**	Gordie Howe
Most Assists, Career	**1,023**	Gordie Howe
Most Points, Career	**1,809**	Gordie Howe (786G, 1,023A)
Most PIM, Career	**2,090**	Bob Probert
Most Shutouts, Career	**85**	Terry Sawchuk
Longest Consecutive Games Streak	**548**	Alex Delvecchio (Dec. 13/56-Nov. 11/64)
Most Goals, Season	**65**	Steve Yzerman (1988-89)
Most Assists, Season	**90**	Steve Yzerman (1988-89)
Most Points, Season	**155**	Steve Yzerman (1988-89; 65G, 90A)
Most PIM, Season	**398**	Bob Probert (1987-88)
Most Points, Defenseman, Season	**77**	Paul Coffey (1993-94; 14G, 63A)
Most Points, Center, Season	**155**	Steve Yzerman (1988-89; 65G, 90A)
Most Points, Right Wing, Season	**103**	Gordie Howe (1968-69; 44G, 59A)
Most Points, Left Wing, Season	**105**	John Ogrodnick (1984-85; 55G, 50A)
Most Points, Rookie, Season	**87**	Steve Yzerman (1983-84; 39G, 48A)
Most Shutouts, Season	**12**	Terry Sawchuk (1951-52, 1953-54, 1954-55), Glenn Hall (1955-56)
Most Goals, Game	**6**	Syd Howe (Feb. 3/44)
Most Assists, Game	***7**	Billy Taylor (Mar. 16/47)
Most Points, Game	**7**	Carl Liscombe (Nov. 5/42; 3G, 4A), Don Grosso (Feb. 3/44; 1G, 6A), Billy Taylor (Mar. 16/47; 7A)

* NHL Record.

Retired Numbers

1	Terry Sawchuk	1949-55, 57-64, 68-69
6	Larry Aurie	1927-1939
7	Ted Lindsay	1944-57, 64-65
9	Gordie Howe	1946-1971
10	Alex Delvecchio	1951-1973
12	Sid Abel	1938-43, 45-52

All-time Record vs. Other Clubs

Regular Season

	At Home							On Road							Total						
	GP	W	L	T	GF	GA	PTS	GP	W	L	T	GF	GA	PTS	GP	W	L	T	GF	GA	PTS
Anaheim	8	5	1	2	32	20	12	8	4	2	2	32	20	10	16	9	3	4	64	40	22
Boston	280	152	76	52	938	702	356	281	87	151	43	747	992	217	561	239	227	95	1685	1694	573
Buffalo	49	26	18	5	182	148	57	47	8	32	7	131	212	23	96	34	50	12	313	360	80
Calgary	45	23	14	8	171	140	54	46	14	26	6	146	189	34	91	37	40	14	317	329	88
Chicago	317	195	93	29	1085	777	419	318	122	146	50	888	960	294	635	317	239	79	1973	1737	713
Colorado	26	15	10	1	105	88	31	27	9	15	3	96	109	21	53	24	25	4	201	197	52
Dallas	91	47	31	13	368	301	107	92	30	48	14	277	338	74	183	77	79	27	645	639	181
Edmonton	30	14	13	3	116	113	31	30	11	14	5	121	136	27	60	25	27	8	237	249	58
Florida	3	2	1	0	13	9	4	3	2	1	0	9	8	4	6	4	2	0	22	17	8
Hartford	25	12	7	6	96	71	30	24	9	14	1	68	88	19	49	21	21	7	164	159	49
Los Angeles	65	28	27	10	265	240	66	66	18	35	13	208	279	49	131	46	62	23	473	519	115
Montreal	276	127	96	53	790	708	307	276	63	170	43	620	983	169	552	190	266	96	1410	1691	476
New Jersey	34	19	13	2	141	117	40	35	10	17	8	100	125	28	69	29	30	10	241	242	68
NY Islanders	39	21	16	2	140	126	44	40	16	22	2	122	151	34	79	37	38	4	262	277	78
NY Rangers	280	160	75	45	983	689	365	278	87	133	58	712	857	232	558	247	208	103	1695	1546	597
Ottawa	4	2	2	0	16	10	4	4	2	1	1	13	11	5	8	4	3	1	29	21	9
Philadelphia	53	25	18	10	191	173	60	54	13	30	11	161	215	37	107	38	48	21	352	388	97
Phoenix	36	19	13	4	152	128	42	34	11	13	10	110	114	32	70	30	26	14	262	242	74
Pittsburgh	60	38	11	11	239	165	87	59	15	40	4	177	264	34	119	53	51	15	416	429	121
St. Louis	90	37	38	15	323	288	89	91	27	49	15	257	328	69	181	64	87	30	580	616	158
San Jose	11	11	0	0	58	16	22	12	9	2	1	63	37	19	23	20	2	1	121	53	41
Tampa Bay	6	5	1	0	26	15	10	8	6	1	1	45	26	13	14	11	2	1	71	41	23
Toronto	310	163	101	46	930	756	372	308	101	162	45	821	1028	247	618	264	263	91	1751	1784	619
Vancouver	52	30	15	7	216	156	67	51	19	25	7	165	198	45	103	49	40	14	381	354	112
Washington	42	18	13	11	151	125	47	40	16	20	4	126	154	36	82	34	33	15	277	279	83
Defunct Clubs	141	76	40	25	430	307	177	141	49	63	29	364	375	127	282	125	103	54	794	682	304
Totals	**2373**	**1270**	**743**	**360**	**8157**	**6388**	**2900**	**2373**	**758**	**1232**	**383**	**6579**	**8197**	**1899**	**4746**	**2028**	**1975**	**743**	**14736**	**14585**	**4799**

Playoffs

	Series	W	L	GP	W	L	T	GF	GA	Last Mtg.	Round	Result
Anaheim	1	1	0	4	4	0	0	13	8	1997	CSF	W 4-0
Boston	7	3	4	33	14	19	0	98	96	1957	SF	L 1-4
Calgary	1	1	0	2	2	0	0	8	5	1978	PR	W 2-0
Chicago	14	6	8	69	31	38	0	190	210	1995	CF	W 4-1
Colorado	2	1	1	12	6	6	0	32	32	1997	CF	W 4-2
Dallas	2	2	0	12	8	4	0	40	29	1995	CQF	W 4-1
Edmonton	2	0	2	10	2	8	0	26	39	1988	CF	L 1-4
Montreal	12	7	5	62	29	33	0	149	161	1978	QF	L 1-4
New Jersey	1	0	1	4	0	4	0	7	16	1995	F	L 0-4
NY Rangers	5	4	1	23	13	10	0	57	49	1950	F	W 4-3
Philadelphia	1	1	0	4	4	0	0	16	6	1997	F	W 4-0
St. Louis	5	2	3	29	16	13	0	88	79	1997	CQF	W 4-2
San Jose	2	1	1	11	7	4	0	51	27	1995	CSF	W 4-0
Toronto	23	11	12	117	59	58	0	321	311	1993	DSF	L 3-4
Winnipeg	1	1	0	6	4	2	0	20	10	1996	CQF	W 4-2
Defunct Clubs	4	3	1	10	7	2	1	21	13			
Totals	**83**	**45**	**38**	**408**	**206**	**201**	**1**	**1137**	**1091**			

Playoff Results 1997-93

Year	Round	Opponent	Result	GF	GA
1997	**F**	**Philadelphia**	**W 4-0**	**16**	**6**
	CF	Colorado	W 4-2	16	12
	CSF	Anaheim	W 4-0	13	8
	CQF	St. Louis	W 4-2	13	12
1996	CF	Colorado	L 2-4	16	20
	CSF	St. Louis	W 4-3	22	16
	CQF	Winnipeg	W 4-2	20	10
1995	F	New Jersey	L 0-4	7	16
	CF	Chicago	W 4-1	13	12
	CSF	San Jose	W 4-0	24	6
	CQF	Dallas	W 4-1	17	10
1994	CQF	San Jose	L 3-4	27	21
1993	DSF	Toronto	L 3-4	30	24

Abbreviations: Round: F – Final; **CF** – conference final; **CQF** – conference quarter-final; **CSF** – conference semi-final; **DF** – division final; **DSF** – division semi-final; **SF** – semi-final; **QF** – quarter-final; **PR** – preliminary round.

Calgary totals include Atlanta, 1972-73 to 1979-80. Colorado totals include Quebec, 1979-80 to 1994-95. Dallas totals include Minnesota, 1967-68 to 1992-93. New Jersey totals include Kansas City, 1974-75 to 1975-76, and Colorado Rockies, 1976-77 to 1981-82. Phoenix totals include Winnipeg, 1979-80 to 1995-96.

1996-97 Results

Oct.	5	at	New Jersey	1-3		9	at	Phoenix	5-4
	9		Edmonton	2-0		11		Chicago	1-3
	11		Calgary	1-2		14		Los Angeles	3-3
	12	at	Buffalo	6-1		20	at	Montreal	1-4
	15	at	Dallas	1-3		22		Philadelphia	2-2
	17	at	Chicago	1-2		25	at	Philadelphia	4-1
	19		NY Islanders	4-2		29		Phoenix	0-3
	21		Los Angeles	3-0	**Feb.**	1	at	St. Louis	4-1
	23		Dallas	4-1		2		Dallas	4-3
	25		Chicago	2-2		4		St. Louis	1-1
	26	at	Boston	2-1		6		Vancouver	4-7
	30		Montreal	5-3		8	at	Pittsburgh	6-5
Nov.	1	at	Ottawa	2-2		12		San Jose	7-1
	2	at	Toronto	2-6		14	at	Dallas	3-4
	4		Hartford	5-1		16	at	Florida	4-2
	6		New Jersey	0-2		17	at	Tampa Bay	3-3
	8	at	Hartford	4-1		19		Calgary	4-0
	10		Tampa Bay	4-2		22	at	St. Louis	2-2
	13		Colorado	1-4		24	at	Phoenix	5-3
	15		San Jose	5-1		27		Pittsburgh	4-1
	18	at	Phoenix	2-2	**Mar.**	1		NY Rangers	3-0
	21	at	San Jose	6-1		2		Anaheim	1-1
	23	at	Los Angeles	6-0		5	at	Toronto	4-4
	24	at	Anaheim	1-3		8	at	Vancouver	5-3
	27		Toronto	5-2		10	at	Los Angeles	3-3
Dec.	1		Florida	2-4		12	at	Anaheim	1-2
	3		Vancouver	2-2		15	at	San Jose	7-4
	4	at	Washington	2-0		16	at	Colorado	2-4
	10		Edmonton	0-0		19		Boston	4-1
	12		Chicago	6-2		21	at	NY Rangers	1-3
	15		Toronto	3-1		23	at	Chicago	3-5
	17	at	Colorado	3-4		26		Colorado	6-5
	18	at	Calgary	3-3		28		Buffalo	2-1
	20	at	Vancouver	2-3		30		Anaheim	0-1
	22	at	Edmonton	6-2	**Apr.**	1		St. Louis	1-1
	26		Washington	5-4		3		Toronto	2-2
	28	at	NY Islanders	7-1		5	at	Toronto	4-2
	30		Phoenix	3-5		8	at	Calgary	3-2
Jan.	3		Dallas	1-2		9	at	Edmonton	3-3
	5	at	Chicago	5-5		11		Ottawa	2-3
	8	at	Dallas	3-6		13		St. Louis	1-3

Entry Draft
Selections 1997-83

1997 Pick		1993 Pick		1989 Pick		1986 Pick	
49	Yuri Butsayev	22	Anders Eriksson	11	Mike Sillinger	1	Joe Murphy
76	Petr Sykora	48	Jonathan Coleman	32	Bob Boughner	22	Adam Graves
102	Quintin Laing	74	Kevin Hilton	53	Nicklas Lidstrom	43	Derek Mayer
129	John Wikstrom	97	John Jakopin	74	Sergei Fedorov	64	Tim Cheveldae
157	B.J. Young	100	Benoit Larose	95	Shawn McCosh	85	Johan Garpenlov
186	Mike Laceby	126	Norm Maracle	116	Dallas Drake	106	Jay Stark
213	Steve Wilejto	152	Tim Spitzig	137	Scott Zygulski	127	Per Djoos
239	Greg Willers	178	Yuri Yeresko	158	Andy Suhy	148	Dean Morton
		204	Vitezslav Skuta	179	Bob Jones	169	Marc Potvin
1996 Pick		230	Ryan Shanahan	200	Greg Bignell	190	Scott King
26	Jesse Wallin	256	James Kosecki	204	Rick Judson	211	Tom Bissett
52	Aren Miller	282	Gordon Hunt	221	Vladimir Konstantinov	232	Peter Ekroth
108	Johan Forsander			242	Joseph Frederick		
135	Michal Podolka	**1992** Pick		246	Jason Glickman	**1985** Pick	
144	Magnus Nilsson	22	Curtis Bowen			8	Brent Fedyk
162	Alexandre Jacques	46	Darren McCarty	**1988** Pick		29	Jeff Sharples
189	Colin Beardsmore	70	Sylvain Cloutier	17	Kory Kocur	50	Steve Chiasson
215	Craig Stahl	118	Mike Sullivan	38	Serge Anglehart	71	Mark Gowans
241	Evgeniy Afanasiev	142	Jason MacDonald	47	Guy Dupuis	92	Chris Luongo
		166	Greg Scott	59	Petr Hrbek	113	Randy McKay
1995 Pick		183	Justin Krall	80	Sheldon Kennedy	134	Thomas Bjur
26	Maxim Kuznetsov	189	C.J. Denomme	143	Kelly Hurd	155	Mike Luckraft
52	Philippe Audet	214	Jeff Walker	164	Brian McCormack	176	Rob Schenna
58	Darryl Laplante	238	Daniel McGillis	185	Jody Praznik	197	Erik Hamalainen
104	Anatoly Ustugov	262	Ryan Bach	206	Glen Goodall	218	Bo Svanberg
125	Chad Wilchynski			227	Darren Colbourne	239	Mikael Lindman
126	David Arsenault	**1991** Pick		248	Donald Stone		
156	Tyler Perry	10	Martin Lapointe			**1984** Pick	
182	Per Eklund	32	Jamie Pushor	**1987** Pick		7	Shawn Burr
208	Andrei Samokvalov	54	Chris Osgood	11	Yves Racine	28	Doug Houda
234	David Engblom	76	Michael Knuble	32	Gordon Kruppke	49	Milan Chalupa
		98	Dmitri Motkov	41	Bob Wilkie	91	Mats Lundstrom
1994 Pick		142	Igor Malykhin	52	Dennis Holland	112	Randy Hansch
23	Yan Golubovsky	186	Jim Bermingham	74	Mark Reimer	133	Stefan Larsson
49	Mathieu Dandenault	208	Jason Firth	95	Radomir Brazda	152	Lars Karlsson
75	Sean Gillam	230	Bart Turner	116	Sean Clifford	154	Urban Nordin
114	Frederic Deschenes	252	Andrew Miller	137	Mike Gober	175	Bill Shibicky
127	Doug Battaglia			158	Kevin Scott	195	Jay Rose
153	Pavel Agarkov	**1990** Pick		179	Mikko Haapakoski	216	Tim Kaiser
205	Jason Elliot	3	Keith Primeau	200	Darin Bannister	236	Tom Nickolau
231	Jeff Mikesch	45	Vyacheslav Kozlov	221	Craig Quinlan		
257	Tomas Holmstrom	66	Stewart Malgunas	242	Tomas Jansson	**1983** Pick	
283	Toivo Suursoo	87	Tony Burns			4	Steve Yzerman
		108	Claude Barthe			25	Lane Lambert
		129	Jason York			46	Bob Probert
		150	Wes McCauley			68	David Korol
		171	Anthony Gruba			86	Petr Klima
		192	Travis Tucker			88	Joey Kocur
		213	Brett Larson			106	Chris Pusey
		234	John Hendry			126	Bob Pierson
						146	Craig Butz
						166	Dave Sikorski
						186	Stu Grimson
						206	Jeff Frank
						226	Charles Chiatto

Club Directory

Joe Louis Arena
600 Civic Center Drive
Detroit, Michigan 48226
Phone **(313) 396-7544**
FAX PR: (313) 567-0296
Capacity: 19,983

Owner	Mike Ilitch
Owner/Secretary-Treasurer	Marian Ilitch
Vice-Presidents	Atanas Ilitch, Christopher Ilitch
Senior Vice-President	Jim Devellano
General Manager	Ken Holland
Assistant General Manager	Don Waddell
Head Coach	Scotty Bowman
Associate Coaches	Barry Smith, Dave Lewis
Director of Amateur Scouting and Player Development	Jim Nill
NHL Scout	Dan Belisle
Pro Scout/Minor League Player Development	Mark Howe
Eastern Scout	Joe McDonnell
Western Scout	Bruce Haralson
USA, High School and College Scout	Mark Leach
Director of European Scouting	Hakan Andersson
Czech and Slovak Republic Scout	Vladimir Havluj
Russian Scout	Ruslan Shabanov
Scout	Paul Crowley
Scout	Marty Stein
Director of Finance	Paul MacDonald
General Manager – Joe Louis Arena/ V.P. of Operations	John Pettit
General Sales Manager	Bill Ley
Marketing Director	Ted Speers
Box Office Manager	Bob Kerlin
Season Ticket Sales Director	Brad Ebben
Executive Assistant	Nancy Beard
Senior Account Executives	Jeffrey Ajluni, Michael Mazurek, Dan Frank, Scott Miller
Broadcast Coordinator	Jason O'Connell
Advertising Sales Coordinator	Andy Loughnane
Marketing Coordinator	Kevin Vaughn
Marketing Assistant	Lori Shiels
Public Relations Coordinators	Karen Davis, Michael Kuta
Season Ticket Coordinator	Chuck Smith
Hockey Group Sales Coordinator	Mary Greener
Accounting Assistant	Cathy Witzke
Administrative Assistant	Kristin Armstrong
Athletic Therapist	John Wharton
Equipment Manager	Paul Boyer
Assistant Equipment Manager	Tim Abbott
Team Physicians	John Finley, D.O., David Collon, M.D.
Team Dentist	C.J. Regula, D.M.D.

General Managers' History

Art Duncan, 1926-27; Jack Adams, 1927-28 to 1961-62; Sid Abel, 1962-63 to 1969-70; Sid Abel and Ned Harkness, 1970-71; Ned Harkness, 1971-72 to 1973-74; Alex Delvecchio, 1974-75 to 1975-76; Alex Delvecchio and Ted Lindsay, 1976-77; Ted Lindsay, 1977-78 to 1979-80; Jimmy Skinner, 1980-81 to 1981-82; Jim Devellano, 1982-83 to 1989-90; Bryan Murray, 1990-91 to 1993-94; Jim Devellano (Senior Vice President), 1994-95 to 1996-97; Ken Holland, 1997-98.

Coaching History

Art Duncan, 1926-27; Jack Adams, 1927-28 to 1946-47; Tommy Ivan, 1947-48 to 1953-54; Jimmy Skinner, 1954-55 to 1956-57; Jimmy Skinner and Sid Abel, 1957-58; Sid Abel, 1958-59 to 1967-68; Bill Gadsby, 1968-69; Bill Gadsby and Sid Abel, 1969-70; Ned Harkness and Doug Barkley, 1970-71; Doug Barkley and John Wilson, 1971-72; John Wilson, 1972-73; Ted Garvin and Alex Delvecchio, 1973-74; Alex Delvecchio, 1974-75; Doug Barkley and Alex Delvecchio, 1975-76; Alex Delvecchio and Larry Wilson, 1976-77; Bobby Kromm, 1977-78 to 1978-79; Bobby Kromm and Ted Lindsay, 1979-80; Ted Lindsay and Wayne Maxner, 1980-81; Wayne Maxner and Billy Dea, 1981-82; Nick Polano, 1982-83 to 1984-85; Harry Neale and Brad Park, 1985-86; Jacques Demers, 1986-87 to 1989-90; Bryan Murray, 1990-91 to 1992-93; Scotty Bowman, 1993-94 to date.

Captains' History

Art Duncan, 1926-27; Reg Noble, 1927-28 to 1929-30; George Hay, 1930-31; Carson Cooper, 1931-32; Larry Aurie, 1932-33; Herbie Lewis, 1933-34; Ebbie Goodfellow, 1934-35; Doug Young, 1935-36 to 1937-38; Ebbie Goodfellow, 1938-39 to 1940-41; Ebbie Goodfellow and Syd Howe, 1941-42; Sid Abel, 1942-43; "Mud" Bruneteau, Bill Hollett (co-captains), 1943-44; Bill Hollett, 1944-45; Bill Hollett and Sid Abel, 1945-46; Sid Abel, 1946-47 to 1951-52; Ted Lindsay, 1952-53 to 1955-56; Red Kelly, 1956-57, 1957-58; Gordie Howe, 1958-59 to 1961-62; Alex Delvecchio, 1962-63 to 1972-73; Alex Delvecchio, Nick Libett, Red Berenson, Gary Bergman, Ted Harris, Mickey Redmond, Larry Johnston, 1973-74; Marcel Dionne, 1974-75; Danny Grant, Terry Harper, 1975-76; Danny Grant, Dennis Polonich, 1976-77; Dan Maloney, Dennis Hextall, 1977-78; Dennis Hextall, Nick Libett, Paul Woods, 1978-79; Dale McCourt, 1979-80; Errol Thompson, Reed Larson, 1980-81; Reed Larson, 1981-82; Danny Gare, 1982-83 to 1985-86; Steve Yzerman, 1986-87 to date.

General Manager

HOLLAND, KEN
General Manager, Detroit Red Wings. Born in Vernon, B.C., Nov. 10, 1955.

Entering his 14th year with the Detroit Red Wings, Ken Holland begins his tenure as the club's general manager after serving as assistant general manager for the previous three seasons. Holland was elevated to his present position July 18, 1997.

In his new and expanded role, he oversees all aspects of hockey operations including all matters relating to player personnel, development, contract negotiations and player movements. Holland also continues to be Detroit's point person at the NHL Entry Draft, as he has for the past seven years. In that capacity, he was instrumental in selecting some of Detroit's best young talent, including Vyacheslav Kozlov, Darren McCarty, Chris Osgood and Martin Lapointe, along with several other top prospects.

Holland, 42, has deftly handled several different front-office duties for the club over the past 13 years. At the conclusion of his playing days as a goaltender, spending most of his pro career at the American Hockey League level, Holland began his off-ice career in 1985 as a western Canada scout followed by five years as amateur scouting director before promotions leading to his current position as general manager.

A native of Vernon, BC, Holland played in the junior ranks for Medicine Hat (WHL) in 1974-75. He was Toronto's 13th pick (188th overall) in the 1975 draft but never saw action with the Maple Leafs. Holland twice signed with NHL teams as a free agent — in 1980 with Hartford and 1983 with Detroit. He spent most of his pro career with AHL clubs in Binghamton and Springfield, along with Adirondack, but did appear in four NHL games, making his debut with Hartford in 1980-81 and playing three contests for Detroit in 1983-84.

Ken and wife Cindy have four children, Brad, Julie, Rachel and Greg, and reside in suburban Detroit.

Edmonton Oilers

1996-97 Results: 36w-37l-9t 81pts. Third, Pacific Division

1997-98 Schedule

Oct.	Wed.	1	at San Jose	Sun.	4	Los Angeles*
	Fri.	3	Detroit	Wed.	7	Florida
	Sun.	5	Colorado	Fri.	9	at Anaheim
	Wed.	8	NY Rangers	Sat.	10	at Los Angeles
	Sat.	11	Toronto	Mon.	12	St. Louis
	Mon.	13	at Vancouver*	Wed.	14	Calgary
	Wed.	15	Colorado	Tue.	20	Phoenix
	Fri.	17	at Anaheim	Fri.	23	at San Jose
	Sun.	19	at Los Angeles	Sat.	24	at Phoenix
	Tue.	21	Boston	Mon.	26	at Colorado
	Fri.	24	Pittsburgh	Wed.	28	New Jersey
	Wed.	29	Phoenix	Sat.	31	Vancouver
Nov.	Sat.	1	at Boston	Feb. Mon.	2	Los Angeles
	Mon.	3	at NY Rangers	Wed.	4	San Jose
	Wed.	5	at NY Islanders	Fri.	6	at Vancouver
	Thu.	6	at Philadelphia	Sat.	7	at Calgary
	Sat.	8	at Washington	Wed.	25	Ottawa
	Mon.	10	at Buffalo	Fri.	27	Anaheim
	Wed.	12	Carolina	Sat.	28	San Jose
	Sat.	15	Calgary	Mar. Mon.	2	at Colorado
	Mon.	17	at Phoenix	Wed.	4	Tampa Bay
	Wed.	19	at Dallas	Sat.	7	at Toronto
	Thu.	20	at St. Louis	Mon.	9	at Chicago
	Sat.	22	at Ottawa	Wed.	11	at Tampa Bay
	Tue.	25	Chicago	Fri.	13	at Florida
	Fri.	28	Anaheim	Sun.	15	at Carolina
	Sun.	30	San Jose	Tue.	17	at Detroit
Dec.	Tue.	2	at Colorado	Wed.	18	at Pittsburgh
	Wed.	3	at Dallas	Sat.	21	St. Louis
	Fri.	5	Detroit	Sun.	22	NY Islanders
	Sun.	7	at Chicago	Wed.	25	Washington
	Wed.	10	at New Jersey	Fri.	27	Buffalo
	Fri.	12	at Detroit	Mon.	30	Calgary
	Sat.	13	at St. Louis	Apr. Wed.	1	at Vancouver
	Wed.	17	Chicago	Fri.	3	Dallas
	Sat.	20	Dallas	Mon.	6	Vancouver
	Mon.	22	at Montreal	Wed.	8	at Anaheim
	Tue.	23	at Toronto	Thu.	9	at Los Angeles
	Sat.	27	Colorado	Sat.	11	at Calgary
	Tue.	30	Philadelphia	Wed.	15	Anaheim
Jan.	Fri.	2	Montreal	Sat.	18	Toronto

* Denotes afternoon game.

Year-by-Year Record

		Home			Road			Overall						
Season	GP	W	L	T	W	L	T	W	L	T	GF	GA	Pts.	Finished	Playoff Result
1996-97	82	21	16	4	15	21	5	36	37	9	252	247	81	3rd, Pacific Div.	Lost Conf. Semi-Final
1995-96	82	15	21	5	15	23	3	30	44	8	240	304	68	5th, Pacific Div.	Out of Playoffs
1994-95	48	11	12	1	6	15	3	17	27	4	136	183	38	5th, Pacific Div.	Out of Playoffs
1993-94	84	17	22	3	8	23	11	25	45	14	261	305	64	6th, Pacific Div.	Out of Playoffs
1992-93	84	16	21	5	10	29	3	26	50	8	242	337	60	5th, Smythe Div.	Out of Playoffs
1991-92	80	22	13	5	14	21	5	36	34	10	295	297	82	3rd, Smythe Div.	Lost Conf. Championship
1990-91	80	22	15	3	15	22	3	37	37	6	272	272	80	3rd, Smythe Div.	Lost Conf. Championship
1989-90	80	23	11	6	15	17	8	38	28	14	315	283	90	**2nd, Smythe Div.**	**Won Stanley Cup**
1988-89	80	21	16	3	17	18	5	38	34	8	325	306	84	3rd, Smythe Div.	Lost Div. Semi-Final
1987-88	80	28	8	4	16	17	7	44	25	11	363	288	99	**2nd, Smythe Div.**	**Won Stanley Cup**
1986-87	80	29	6	5	21	18	1	50	24	6	372	284	106	**1st, Smythe Div.**	**Won Stanley Cup**
1985-86	80	32	6	2	24	11	5	56	17	7	426	310	119	1st, Smythe Div.	Lost Div. Final
1984-85	80	26	7	7	23	13	4	49	20	11	401	298	109	**1st, Smythe Div.**	**Won Stanley Cup**
1983-84	80	31	5	4	26	13	1	57	18	5	446	314	119	**1st, Smythe Div.**	**Won Stanley Cup**
1982-83	80	25	9	6	22	12	6	47	21	12	424	315	106	1st, Smythe Div.	Lost Final
1981-82	80	31	5	4	17	12	11	48	17	15	417	295	111	1st, Smythe Div.	Lost Div. Semi-Final
1980-81	80	17	13	10	12	22	6	29	35	16	328	327	74	4th, Smythe Div.	Lost Quarter-Final
1979-80	80	17	14	9	11	25	4	28	39	13	301	322	69	4th, Smythe Div.	Lost Prelim. Round

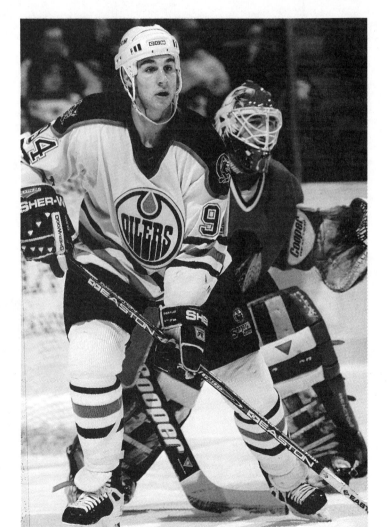

Super-sniper Ryan Smyth blossomed in 1996-97, leading the Oilers in goals (39) and tying for the League lead in power-play markers (20).

Franchise date: June 22, 1979

PACIFIC DIVISION

19th NHL Season

1997-98 Player Personnel

FORWARDS	HT	WT	S	Place of Birth	Date	1996-97 Club
ARNOTT, Jason	6-3	220	R	Collingwood, Ont.	10/11/74	Edmonton
BONSIGNORE, Jason	6-4	220	R	Rochester, NY	4/15/76	Hamilton
BONVIE, Dennis	5-11	205	R	Antigonish, N.S.	7/23/73	Hamilton
BUCHBERGER, Kelly	6-2	200	L	Langenburg, Sask.	12/2/66	Edmonton
DAW, Jeff	6-3	190	R	Carlisle, Ont.	2/28/72	Wheeling-Hamilton
DEVEREAUX, Boyd	6-2	195	L	Seaforth, Ont.	4/16/78	Kitchener-Hamilton
FRIEDMAN, Doug	6-1	195	L	Cape Elizabeth, ME	9/1/71	Hershey
GRIER, Michael	6-1	225	R	Detroit, MI	1/5/75	Edmonton
HUARD, Bill	6-1	215	L	Welland, Ont.	6/24/67	Dallas
HULBIG, Joe	6-3	215	L	Norwood, MA	9/29/73	Edmonton-Hamilton
INTRANUOVO, Ralph	5-8	185	L	East York, Ont.	12/11/73	Toronto-Edmonton-Hamilton
KELLY, Steve	6-1	190	L	Vancouver, B.C.	10/26/76	Edmonton-Hamilton
KOVALENKO, Andrei	5-10	215	L	Balakovo, USSR	6/7/70	Edmonton
LACOUTURE, Dan	6-3	210	L	Hyannis, MA	4/18/77	Boston U.
LARAQUE, Georges	6-3	235	R	Montreal, Que.	12/7/76	Hamilton
LINDGREN, Mats	6-2	200	L	Skelleftea, Sweden	10/1/74	Edmonton-Hamilton
MARCHANT, Todd	5-10	175	L	Buffalo, NY	8/12/73	Edmonton
McAMMOND, Dean	5-11	185	L	Grand Cache, Alta.	6/15/73	Edmonton
MOORE, Barrie	5-11	175	L	London, Ont.	5/22/75	Buf-Rochester-Edm-Hamilton
MURRAY, Rem	6-2	195	L	Stratford, Ont.	10/9/72	Edmonton
MYHRES, Brantt	6-4	222	R	Edmonton, Alta.	3/18/74	Tampa Bay-San Antonio
PADEN, Kevin	6-3	190	L	Woodhaven, MI	2/12/75	Nashville (CHL)-Huntington
PETERSON, Kyle	6-4	220	L	Calgary, Alta.	4/17/74	Michigan Tech
RANDALL, Bryan	6-3	190	L	Winnipeg, Man.	8/8/78	Medicine Hat-Regina
RIESEN, Michel	6-2	185	R	Oberbalm, Switzerland	4/11/79	Biel
SCHMIDT, Colin	5-11	185	L	Regina, Sask.	2/3/74	Hamilton-Wheeling
SMYTH, Ryan	6-1	195	L	Banff, Alta.	2/21/76	Edmonton
TUOMAINEN, Marko	6-3	203	R	Kuopio, Finland	4/25/72	Hamilton
WATT, Mike	6-2	212	L	Seaforth, Ont.	3/31/76	Michigan State
WEIGHT, Doug	5-11	200	L	Warren, MI	1/21/71	Edmonton
DEFENSEMEN						
BANNISTER, Drew	6-2	200	R	Belleville, Ont.	9/4/74	Tampa Bay-Edmonton
BROWN, Sean	6-2	205	L	Oshawa, Ont.	11/5/76	Edmonton-Hamilton
De VRIES, Greg	6-3	218	L	Sundridge, Ont.	1/4/73	Edmonton-Hamilton
DESCOTEAUX, Matthieu	6-3	220	L	Pierreville, Que.	9/23/77	Shawinigan-Hull
FERGUSON, Scott	6-1	195	L	Camrose, Alta.	1/6/73	Hamilton
HAJT, Chris	6-3	206	L	Saskatoon, Sask.	7/5/78	Guelph
LOWE, Kevin	6-2	200	L	Lachute, Que.	4/15/59	Edmonton
MARCHMENT, Bryan	6-1	205	L	Scarborough, Ont.	5/1/69	Edmonton
McGILLIS, Daniel	6-2	225	L	Hawkesbury, Ont.	7/1/72	Edmonton
MILLAR, Craig	6-2	200	L	Winnipeg, Man.	5/10/77	Rochester-Edmonton-Hamilton
MIRONOV, Boris	6-3	220	R	Moscow, USSR	3/21/72	Edmonton
MUIR, Bryan	6-4	220	L	Winnipeg, Man.	6/8/73	Hamilton-Edmonton
POTI, Tom	6-2	185	L	Worcester, MA	3/22/77	Boston U.
SANDWITH, Terran	6-4	210	L	Edmonton, Alta.	4/17/72	Hamilton
SYMES, Brad	6-2	210	L	Edmonton, Alta.	4/26/76	Wheeling-Hamilton
YERKOVICH, Sergei	6-3	210	L	Minsk, USSR	9/3/74	Las Vegas
ZHURIK, Alexander	6-3	195	L	Minsk, USSR	5/29/75	Hamilton

GOALTENDERS	HT	WT	C	Place of Birth	Date	1996-97 Club
DOVIGI, Patrick	6-0	180	L	Sault Ste. Marie, Ont.	7/2/79	Erie (OHL)
HULTBERG, John	5-11	211	L	Skokie, IL	4/25/77	Kingston-Barrie
JOSEPH, Curtis	5-10	185	L	Keswick, Ont.	4/29/67	Edmonton
LABBE, Jean-Francois	5-9	170	L	Sherbrooke, Que.	6/15/72	Hershey
MINARD, Mike	6-3	205	L	Owen Sound, Ont.	11/1/76	Hamilton-Wheeling
PASSMORE, Steve	5-9	165	L	Thunder Bay, Ont.	1/29/73	Hamilton-Raleigh
WICKENHEISER, Chris	6-1	185	L	Lethbridge, Alta.	1/20/76	Red Deer-Portland (WHL)

Coach

LOW, RONALD ALBERT (RON)
Head Coach, Edmonton Oilers. Born in Birtie, Man., June 21, 1950.

The 1997-98 season sees Ron Low enter his fourth season as head coach of the Edmonton Oilers. After serving as an assistant coach with the Edmonton Oilers for six seasons, Ron Low became the team's fifth head coach when he was named to the position on April 6, 1995.

Low has become known around the League as a coach who successfully develops talented, young prospects into solid NHL performers. This was evident during the 1996-97 season as Low guided the Oilers to a third place finish in the Pacific Division with a 26-37-9 record and a return to post-season play.

On August 3, 1989, Low was appointed to the Edmonton Oilers' coaching staff as an assistant coach. He also played parts of four seasons with Edmonton from 1979-80 to 1982-83.

The Oilers were one of six teams, the Birtie, Manitoba native played for in an 11-year NHL career that saw him tend goal for Toronto, Washington, Detroit, Quebec, Edmonton and New Jersey. From 1972-73 to 1984-85, he played 382 NHL games and registered a 4.28 goals-against average with four shutouts and a 102-203-37 record.

In 1985-86 he was named assistant playing coach with the Nova Scotia Oilers, Edmonton's American Hockey League affiliate. Following two years as an assistant coach he was named Nova Scotia's head coach in 1987-88 and kept that position when the team became the Cape Breton Oilers in 1988-89. Low compiled a 62-83-15 record as an AHL head coach before joining the NHL coaching ranks.

Ron and his wife, Linda, have two daughters, Alexandra Juliana, born in June of 1992, and Taylor.

Coaching Record

		Regular Season					Playoffs			
Season	Team	Games	W	L	T	%	Games	W	L	%
1987-88	Nova Scotia (AHL)	80	35	36	9	.506	5	1	4	.200
1988-89	Cape Breton (AHL)	80	27	47	6	.375	....	....	....	....
1994-95	**Edmonton (NHL)**	**13**	**5**	**7**	**1**	**.423**	....	....	....	....
1995-96	**Edmonton (NHL)**	**82**	**30**	**44**	**8**	**.415**	....	....	....	....
1996-97	**Edmonton (NHL)**	**82**	**36**	**37**	**9**	**.494**	**12**	**5**	**7**	**.417**
	NHL Totals	**177**	**71**	**88**	**18**	**.452**	**12**	**5**	**7**	**.417**

1996-97 Scoring

* – rookie

Regular Season

Pos	#	Player	Team	GP	G	A	Pts	+/–	PIM	PP	SH	GW	GT	S	%
C	39	Doug Weight	EDM	80	21	61	82	1	80	4	0	2	0	235	8.9
L	94	Ryan Smyth	EDM	82	39	22	61	-7	76	20	0	4	0	265	14.7
L	51	Andrei Kovalenko	EDM	74	32	27	59	-5	81	14	0	2	0	163	19.6
C	7	Jason Arnott	EDM	67	19	38	57	-21	92	10	1	2	1	248	7.7
R	21	Mariusz Czerkawski	EDM	76	26	21	47	0	16	4	0	3	0	182	14.3
R	16	Kelly Buchberger	EDM	81	8	30	38	4	159	0	0	3	0	78	10.3
C	26	Todd Marchant	EDM	79	14	19	33	11	44	0	4	3	0	202	6.9
R	25	* Mike Grier	EDM	79	15	17	32	7	45	4	0	2	0	89	16.9
D	2	Boris Mironov	EDM	55	6	26	32	2	85	2	0	1	0	147	4.1
L	17	* Rem Murray	EDM	82	11	20	31	9	16	1	0	2	0	85	12.9
L	37	Dean McAmmond	EDM	57	12	17	29	-15	28	4	0	6	0	106	11.3
L	14	* Mats Lindgren	EDM	69	11	14	25	-7	12	2	3	1	0	71	15.5
D	23	* Daniel McGillis	EDM	73	6	16	22	2	52	2	1	2	0	139	4.3
D	55	* Drew Bannister	T.B.	64	4	13	17	-21	44	1	0	0	0	57	7.0
			EDM	1	0	1	1	-2	0	0	0	0	0	2	0.0
			TOTAL	65	4	14	18	-23	44	1	0	0	0	59	6.8
D	24	Bryan Marchment	EDM	71	3	13	16	13	132	1	0	0	0	89	3.4
R	85	Petr Klima	L.A.	8	0	4	4	-7	2	0	0	0	0	12	0.0
			PIT	9	1	3	4	-4	4	0	0	0	0	21	4.8
			EDM	16	1	5	6	-1	6	0	0	0	0	22	4.5
			TOTAL	33	2	12	14	-12	12	0	0	0	0	55	3.6
D	4	Kevin Lowe	EDM	64	1	13	14	-1	50	0	0	0	0	46	2.2
D	22	Luke Richardson	EDM	82	1	11	12	9	91	0	0	0	0	67	1.5
L	18	* Barrie Moore	BUF	31	2	6	8	1	18	1	0	0	0	42	4.8
			EDM	4	0	0	0	0	0	0	0	0	0	1	0.0
			TOTAL	35	2	6	8	1	18	1	0	0	0	43	4.7
D	5	* Greg De Vries	EDM	37	0	4	4	-2	52	0	0	0	0	31	0.0
L	29	Louie Debrusk	EDM	32	2	0	2	-6	94	0	0	0	0	10	20.0
C	9	* Ralph Intranuovo	TOR	3	0	1	1	-1	0	0	0	0	0	4	0.0
			EDM	5	1	0	1	0	0	0	0	0	0	2	50.0
			TOTAL	8	1	1	2	-1	0	0	0	0	0	6	16.7
G	31	Curtis Joseph	EDM	72	0	2	2	0	20	0	0	0	0	0	0.0
C	10	* Steve Kelly	EDM	8	1	0	1	-1	6	0	0	1	0	6	16.7
D	34	Donald Dufresne	EDM	22	0	1	1	-1	15	0	0	0	0	10	0.0
D	35	* Craig Millar	EDM	1	0	0	0	0	2	0	0	0	0	1	0.0
D	8	* Sean Brown	EDM	5	0	0	0	-1	4	0	0	0	0	2	0.0
C	12	Jesse Belanger	EDM	6	0	0	0	-3	0	0	0	0	0	8	0.0
L	15	* Joe Hulbig	EDM	6	0	0	0	-1	0	0	0	0	0	4	0.0
G	30	Bob Essensa	EDM	19	0	0	0	0	4	0	0	0	0	0	0.0

Goaltending

No.	Goaltender	GPI	Mins	Avg	W	L	T	EN	SO	GA	SA	S%
30	Bob Essensa	19	868	2.83	4	8	0	3	1	41	406	.899
31	Curtis Joseph	72	4100	2.93	32	29	9	3	6	200	2144	.907
	Totals	**82**	**4982**	**2.97**	**36**	**37**	**9**	**6**	**7**	**247**	**2556**	**.903**

Playoffs

Pos	#	Player	Team	GP	G	A	Pts	+/–	PIM	PP	SH	GW	OT	S	%
C	39	Doug Weight	EDM	12	3	8	11	0	8	0	0	0	0	54	5.6
L	94	Ryan Smyth	EDM	12	5	5	10	-4	12	1	0	2	1	48	10.4
D	2	Boris Mironov	EDM	12	2	8	10	-6	16	2	0	0	0	31	6.5
C	7	Jason Arnott	EDM	12	3	6	9	-3	18	1	0	0	0	27	11.1
R	16	Kelly Buchberger	EDM	12	5	2	7	-1	16	0	0	1	1	19	26.3
L	51	Andrei Kovalenko	EDM	12	4	3	7	1	6	3	0	0	0	35	11.4
C	26	Todd Marchant	EDM	12	4	2	6	2	12	0	3	1	1	40	10.0
D	23	* Daniel McGillis	EDM	12	0	5	5	8	24	0	0	0	0	20	0.0
R	25	* Mike Grier	EDM	12	3	1	4	-2	4	1	0	1	0	21	14.3
L	14	* Mats Lindgren	EDM	12	0	4	4	-2	0	0	0	0	0	22	0.0
R	21	Mariusz Czerkawski	EDM	12	2	1	3	-2	10	0	0	0	0	19	10.5
L	17	* Rem Murray	EDM	12	1	2	3	-1	4	0	0	0	0	7	14.3
D	22	Luke Richardson	EDM	12	0	2	2	-4	14	0	0	0	0	6	0.0
L	15	* Joe Hulbig	EDM	6	0	1	1	2	2	0	0	0	0	5	0.0
D	5	* Greg De Vries	EDM	12	0	1	1	4	8	0	0	0	0	16	0.0
D	4	Kevin Lowe	EDM	1	0	0	0	-1	0	0	0	0	0	0	0.0
D	34	Donald Dufresne	EDM	3	0	0	0	0	0	0	0	0	0	0	0.0
D	24	Bryan Marchment	EDM	3	0	0	0	-3	4	0	0	0	0	2	0.0
D	35	* Bryan Muir	EDM	5	0	0	0	-2	4	0	0	0	0	7	0.0
R	85	Petr Klima	EDM	6	0	0	0	0	4	0	0	0	0	2	0.0
L	29	Louie Debrusk	EDM	6	0	0	0	0	4	0	0	0	0	1	0.0
C	10	* Steve Kelly	EDM	6	0	0	0	1	2	0	0	0	0	2	0.0
G	31	Curtis Joseph	EDM	12	0	0	0	0	2	0	0	0	0	0	0.0
D	55	* Drew Bannister	EDM	12	0	0	0	-4	30	0	0	0	0	9	0.0

Goaltending

No.	Goaltender	GPI	Mins	Avg	W	L	EN	SO	GA	SA	S%
31	Curtis Joseph	12	767	2.82	5	7	1	2	36	405	.911
	Totals	**12**	**771**	**2.88**	**5**	**7**	**1**	**2**	**37**	**406**	**.909**

Coaching History

Glen Sather, 1979-80; Bryan Watson and Glen Sather, 1980-81; Glen Sather, 1981-82 to 1988-89; John Muckler, 1989-90 to 1990-91; Ted Green, 1991-92 to 1992-93; Ted Green and Glen Sather, 1993-94; George Burnett and Ron Low, 1994-95; Ron Low, 1995-96 to date.

General Managers' History

Larry Gordon, 1979-80; Glen Sather, 1980-81 to date.

Club Records

Team

(Figures in brackets for season records are games played; records for fewest points, wins, ties, losses, goals, goals against are for 70 or more games)

Most Points	119	1983-84 (80), 1985-86 (80)
Most Wins	57	1983-84 (80)
Most Ties	16	1980-81 (80)
Most Losses	50	1992-93 (84)
Most Goals	*446	1983-84 (80)
Most Goals Against	327	1980-81 (80)
Fewest Points	60	1992-93 (84)
Fewest Wins	25	1993-94 (84)
Fewest Ties	5	1983-84 (80)
Fewest Losses	17	1981-82 (80), 1985-86 (80)
Fewest Goals	240	1995-96 (82)
Fewest Goals Against	247	1996-97 (82)

Longest Winning Streak

Overall	8	Five times
Home	8	Jan. 19-Feb. 22/85, Feb. 24-Apr. 2/86
Away	8	Dec. 9/86-Jan. 17/87

Longest Undefeated Streak

Overall	15	Oct. 11-Nov. 9/84 (12 wins, 3 ties)
Home	14	Nov. 15/89-Jan. 6/90 (11 wins, 3 ties)
Away	9	Jan. 17-Mar. 2/82 (6 wins, 3 ties), Nov. 23/82-Jan. 18/83 (7 wins, 2 ties)

Longest Losing Streak

Overall	11	Oct. 16-Nov. 7/93
Home	9	Oct. 16-Nov. 24/93
Away	9	Nov. 25-Dec. 30/80

Longest Winless Streak

Overall	14	Oct. 11-Nov. 7/93 (13 losses, 1 tie)
Home	9	Oct. 16-Nov. 24/93 (9 losses)
Away	9	Three times
Most Shutouts, Season	7	1996-97
Most PIM, Season	2,173	1987-88 (80)
Most Goals, Game	13	Nov. 19/83 (N.J. 4 at Edm. 13), Nov. 8/85 (Van. 0 at Edm. 13)

Individual

Most Seasons	14	Kevin Lowe
Most Games	1,030	Kevin Lowe
Most Goals, Career	583	Wayne Gretzky
Most Assists, Career	1,086	Wayne Gretzky
Most Points, Career	1,669	Wayne Gretzky (583G, 1,086A)
Most PIM, Career	1,557	Kelly Buchberger
Most Shutouts, Career	9	Grant Fuhr
Longest Consecutive Games Streak	521	Craig MacTavish (Oct. 11/86-Jan. 2/93)
Most Goals, Season	*92	Wayne Gretzky (1981-82)
Most Assists, Season	*163	Wayne Gretzky (1985-86)
Most Points, Season	*215	Wayne Gretzky (1985-86; 52G, 163A)
Most PIM, Season	286	Steve Smith (1987-88)

Most Points, Defenseman, Season	138	Paul Coffey (1985-86; 48G, 90A)
Most Points, Center, Season	*215	Wayne Gretzky (1985-86; 52G, 163A)
Most Points, Right Wing, Season	135	Jari Kurri (1984-85; 71G, 64A)
Most Points, Left Wing, Season	106	Mark Messier (1982-83; 48G, 58A)
Most Points, Rookie, Season	75	Jari Kurri (1980-81; 32G, 43A)
Most Shutouts, Season	6	Curtis Joseph (1996-97)
Most Goals, Game	5	Wayne Gretzky (Feb. 18/81, Dec. 30/81, Dec. 15/84, Dec. 6/87), Jari Kurri (Nov. 19/83), Pat Hughes (Feb. 3/84)
Most Assists, Game	*7	Wayne Gretzky (Feb. 15/80, Dec. 11/85, Feb. 14/86)
Most Points, Game	8	Wayne Gretzky (Nov. 19/83; 3G, 5A), Wayne Gretzky (Jan. 4/84; 4G, 4A), Paul Coffey (Mar. 14/86; 2G, 6A)

* NHL Record.

Captains' History

Ron Chipperfield, 1979-80; Blair MacDonald and Lee Fogolin, 1980-81; Lee Fogolin, 1981-82 to 1982-83; Wayne Gretzky, 1983-84 to 1987-88; Mark Messier, 1988-89 to 1990-91; Kevin Lowe, 1991-92; Craig MacTavish, 1992-93 to 1993-94; Shayne Corson, 1994-95; Kelly Buchberger, 1995-96 to date.

Retired Numbers

3	Al Hamilton	1972-1980

All-time Record vs. Other Clubs

Regular Season

	GP	W	L	T	GF	GA	PTS	GP	W	L	T	GF	GA	PTS	GP	W	L	T	GF	GA	PTS
			At Home							On Road							Total				
Anaheim	10	5	5	0	20	23	10	10	2	7	1	23	33	5	20	7	12	1	43	56	15
Boston	24	9	12	3	84	86	21	25	6	17	2	73	110	14	49	15	29	5	157	196	35
Buffalo	24	18	4	2	106	66	38	25	10	10	5	94	100	25	49	28	14	7	200	166	63
Calgary	62	32	22	8	256	226	72	62	21	35	6	227	283	48	124	53	57	14	483	509	120
Chicago	31	15	14	2	125	120	32	30	9	17	4	111	126	22	61	24	31	6	236	246	54
Colorado	27	17	8	2	138	85	36	27	14	11	2	120	115	30	54	31	19	4	258	200	66
Dallas	30	16	8	6	136	104	38	31	13	12	6	103	114	32	61	29	20	12	239	218	70
Detroit	30	14	11	5	136	121	33	30	13	14	3	113	116	29	60	27	25	8	249	237	62
Florida	3	1	2	0	9	8	2	3	0	2	1	8	12	1	6	1	4	1	17	20	3
Hartford	25	18	4	3	105	73	39	24	10	9	5	91	100	25	49	28	13	8	196	173	64
Los Angeles	63	33	16	14	309	240	80	62	25	24	13	271	262	63	125	58	40	27	580	502	143
Montreal	25	13	12	0	87	80	26	24	7	14	3	75	87	17	49	20	26	3	162	167	43
New Jersey	27	14	8	5	128	101	33	27	13	12	2	92	95	28	54	27	20	7	220	196	61
NY Islanders	25	16	5	4	98	71	36	25	5	12	8	93	109	18	50	21	17	12	191	180	54
NY Rangers	24	11	12	1	92	87	23	24	13	6	5	98	92	31	48	24	18	6	190	179	54
Ottawa	4	3	1	0	18	12	6	4	2	2	0	12	9	4	8	5	3	0	30	21	10
Philadelphia	24	14	6	4	90	71	32	25	6	18	1	72	114	13	49	20	24	5	162	185	45
Phoenix	58	36	18	4	262	196	76	57	31	22	4	260	235	66	115	67	40	8	522	431	142
Pittsburgh	25	19	5	1	134	87	39	25	12	12	1	116	100	25	50	31	17	2	250	187	64
St. Louis	30	15	12	3	123	117	33	30	13	13	4	122	117	30	60	28	25	7	245	234	63
San Jose	18	13	2	3	73	40	29	18	7	10	1	56	65	15	36	20	12	4	129	105	44
Tampa Bay	5	4	1	0	12	12	8	5	1	2	2	12	18	4	10	5	3	2	24	30	12
Toronto	30	17	7	6	149	105	40	30	14	14	2	136	125	30	60	31	21	8	285	230	70
Vancouver	62	41	15	6	300	194	88	63	31	24	8	268	241	70	125	72	39	14	568	435	158
Washington	24	10	10	4	93	81	24	24	9	13	2	87	103	20	48	19	23	6	180	184	44
Totals	**710**	**404**	**220**	**86**	**3083**	**2406**	**894**	**710**	**287**	**332**	**91**	**2733**	**2881**	**665**	**1420**	**691**	**552**	**177**	**5816**	**5287**	**1559**

Playoffs

	Series	W	L	GP	W	L	T	GF	GA	Last Mtg. Round	Result
Boston	2	2	0	9	8	1	0	41	20	1990 F	W 4-1
Calgary	5	4	1	30	19	11	0	132	96	1991 DSF	W 4-3
Chicago	4	3	1	20	12	8	0	102	77	1992 CF	L 0-4
Colorado	1	0	1	5	1	4	0	11	19	1997 CSF	L 1-4
Dallas	3	2	1	16	9	7	0	57	48	1997 CQF	L 3-4
Detroit	2	2	0	10	8	2	0	39	26	1988 CF	W 4-1
Los Angeles	7	5	2	36	24	12	0	154	127	1992 DSF	W 4-2
Montreal	1	1	0	3	3	0	0	15	6	1981 PR	W 3-0
NY Islanders	3	1	2	15	6	9	0	47	58	1984 F	W 4-1
Philadelphia	3	2	1	15	8	7	0	49	44	1987 F	W 4-3
Vancouver	2	2	0	9	7	2	0	35	20	1992 DF	W 4-2
Winnipeg	6	6	0	26	22	4	0	120	75	1990 DSF	W 4-3
Totals	**39**	**30**	**9**	**194**	**127**	**67**	**0**	**802**	**616**		

Calgary totals include Atlanta, 1979-80. Colorado totals include Quebec, 1979-80 to 1994-95.
Dallas totals include Minnesota, 1979-80 to 1992-93. New Jersey totals include Colorado Rockies, 1979-80 to 1981-82.
Phoenix totals include Winnipeg, 1979-80 to 1995-96.

Playoff Results 1997-93

Year	Round	Opponent	Result	GF	GA
1997	CSF	Colorado	L 1-4	11	19
	CQF	Dallas	W 4-3	21	18

Abbreviations: Round: F – Final;
CF – conference final; **CQF** – conference quarter-final;
CSF – conference semi-final; **DF** – division final;
DSF – division semi-final; **SF** – semi-final;
QF – quarter-final; **PR** – preliminary round.

1996-97 Results

Oct.	4		Buffalo	4-3		7	at St. Louis	5-2
	6		Vancouver	2-0		8	at Chicago	1-4
	8	at	Toronto	0-2		11	San Jose	1-4
	9	at	Detroit	0-2		12	Hartford	2-1
	11		St. Louis	1-3		15	Florida	4-0
	14	at	Phoenix	6-3		21	at NY Rangers	4-4
	15	at	Colorado	2-7		22	at NY Islanders	1-8
	20	at	Calgary	3-6		24	at Buffalo	3-1
	22		Pittsburgh	5-2		26	at Washington	3-1
	24	at	Los Angeles	8-2		29	San Jose	2-1
	26		Colorado	2-4		31	NY Islanders	1-0
	30		Phoenix	4-1	Feb.	5	Calgary	5-2
Nov.	1		Vancouver	4-5		8	Anaheim	1-2
	3	at	Chicago	2-4		9	Washington	4-1
	6	at	Pittsburgh	2-5		12	Boston	4-3
	7	at	Boston	6-0		13	at Calgary	2-3
	9	at	Toronto	3-7		15	at Los Angeles	2-2
	11	at	Montreal	2-3		17	Anaheim	1-5
	13	at	Ottawa	4-0		19	Toronto	6-5
	17		Dallas	3-7		21	Colorado	3-4
	19		Chicago	4-4		23	at Dallas	1-6
	21		NY Rangers	3-2		26	at Anaheim	3-3
	23		Calgary	3-2		27	at Los Angeles	3-6
	26	at	Calgary	10-1	Mar.	1	Montreal	4-5
	27		Los Angeles	1-5		4	Los Angeles	4-1
	29	at	San Jose	4-2		7	at Dallas	1-2
Dec.	1	at	Anaheim	2-4		9	at St. Louis	4-1
	4	at	Colorado	0-2		11	at New Jersey	1-6
	6		Ottawa	5-2		13	at Philadelphia	4-5
	8		St. Louis	2-3		15	at Hartford	4-2
	10	at	Detroit	0-0		19	Tampa Bay	3-1
	12	at	Tampa Bay	2-2		23	Anaheim	1-4
	15	at	Florida	3-6		24	at San Jose	5-1
	18		Colorado	4-4		28	at San Jose	3-4
	20		New Jersey	2-3		29	at Phoenix	3-1
	22		Detroit	2-6		31	Dallas	1-3
	23	at	Vancouver	7-0	Apr.	3	Chicago	4-2
	27		Philadelphia	4-6		5	Vancouver	2-2
	28		San Jose	5-3		9	at Detroit	3-3
	30		Los Angeles	2-1		11	at Phoenix	2-6
Jan.	3		Toronto	4-3		12	at Vancouver	4-5

Entry Draft
Selections 1997-83

1997
Pick
14 Michel Riesen
41 Patrick Dovigi
68 Sergei Yerkovich
94 Jonas Elofsson
121 Jason Chimera
141 Peter Sarno
176 Kevin Bolibruck
187 Chad Hinz
205 Chris Kerr
231 Alexandre Fomitchev

1996
Pick
6 Boyd Devereaux
19 Matthieu Descoteaux
32 Chris Hajt
59 Tom Poti
114 Brian Urick
141 Bryan Randall
168 David Bernier
170 Brandon Lafrance
195 Fernando Pisani
221 John Hultberg

1995
Pick
6 Steve Kelly
31 Georges Laraque
57 Lukas Zib
83 Mike Minard
109 Jan Snopek
161 Martin Cerven
187 Stephen Douglas
213 Jiri Antonin

1994
Pick
4 Jason Bonsignore
6 Ryan Smyth
32 Mike Watt
53 Corey Neilson
60 Brad Symes
79 Adam Copeland
95 Jussi Tarvainen
110 Jon Gaskins
136 Terry Marchant
160 Curtis Sheptak
162 Dmitri Shulga
179 Chris Wickenheiser
185 Rob Guinn
188 Jason Reid
214 Jeremy Jablonski
266 Ladislav Benysek

1993
Pick
7 Jason Arnott
16 Nick Stajduhar
33 David Vyborny
59 Kevin Paden
60 Alexander Kerch
111 Miroslav Satan
163 Alexander Zhurik
189 Martin Bakula
215 Brad Norton
241 Oleg Maltsev
267 Ilja Byakin

1992
Pick
13 Joe Hulbig
37 Martin Reichel
61 Simon Roy
65 Kirk Maltby
96 Ralph Intranuovo
109 Joaquin Gage
157 Steve Gibson
181 Kyuin Shim
190 Colin Schmidt
205 Marko Tuomainen
253 Bryan Rasmussen

1991
Pick
12 Tyler Wright
20 Martin Rucinsky
34 Andrew Verner
56 George Breen
78 Mario Nobili
93 Ryan Haggerty
144 David Oliver
166 Gary Kitching
210 Vegar Barlie
232 Evgeny Belosheikin
254 Juha Riihijarvi

1990
Pick
17 Scott Allison
38 Alexandre Legault
59 Joe Crowley
67 Joel Blain
101 Greg Louder
122 Keijo Sailynoja
143 Mike Power
164 Roman Mejzlik
185 Richard Zemlicka
206 Petr Korinek
227 invalid claim
248 Sami Nuutinen

1989
Pick
15 Jason Soules
36 Richard Borgo
78 Josef Beranek
92 Peter White
120 Anatoli Semenov
140 Davis Payne
141 Sergei Yashin
162 Darcy Martini
225 Roman Bozek

1988
Pick
19 Francois Leroux
39 Petro Koivunen
53 Trevor Sim
61 Collin Bauer
82 Cam Brauer
103 Don Martin
124 Len Barrie
145 Mike Glover
166 Shjon Podein
187 Tom Cole
208 Vladimir Zubkov
229 Darin MacDonald
250 Tim Tisdale

1987
Pick
21 Peter Soberlak
42 Brad Werenka
63 Geoff Smith
64 Peter Eriksson
105 Shaun Van Allen
126 Radek Toupal
147 Tomas Srsen
168 Age Ellingsen
189 Gavin Armstrong
210 Mike Tinkham
231 Jeff Pauletti
241 Jesper Duus
252 Igor Vyazmikin

1986
Pick
21 Kim Issel
42 Jamie Nichols
63 Ron Shudra
84 Dan Currie
105 David Haas
126 Jim Ennis
147 Ivan Matulik
168 Nicolas Beaulieu
189 Mike Greenlay
210 Matt Lanza
231 Mojmir Bozik
252 Tony Hand

1985
Pick
20 Scott Metcalfe
41 Todd Carnelley
62 Mike Ware
104 Tomas Kapusta
125 Brian Tessier
146 Shawn Tyers
167 Tony Fairfield
188 Kelly Buchberger
209 Mario Barbe
230 Peter Headon
251 John Haley

1984
Pick
21 Selmar Odelein
42 Daryl Reaugh
63 Todd Norman
84 Rich Novak
105 Richard Lambert
106 Emanuel Viveiros
126 Ivan Dornic
147 Heikki Riihijarvi
168 Todd Ewen
209 Joel Curtis
229 Simon Wheeldon
250 Darren Gani

1983
Pick
19 Jeff Beukeboom
40 Mike Golden
60 Mike Flanagan
80 Esa Tikkanen
120 Don Barber
140 Dale Derkatch
160 Ralph Vos
180 Dave Roach
200 Warren Yadlowski
220 John Miner
240 Steve Woodburn

General Manager

SATHER, GLEN CAMERON
President and General Manager, Edmonton Oilers.
Born in High River, Alta., Sept. 2, 1943.

The architect of the Edmonton Oilers' five Stanley Cup championships, Glen Sather is one of the most respected administrators in the NHL. The 1997-98 season is his 17th as general manager of the NHL Oilers and his 22nd with Edmonton since joining the organization in August of 1976.

Named coach and vice president of hockey operation for the Oilers when the franchise joined the NHL on June 15, 1979, Sather became coach, general manager and club president in May of 1980. He coached through the 1988-89 season and also returned for 60 games behind the bench in 1993-94. His .616 winning percentage in 842 regular-season games ranked seventh on the NHL's all-time coaching list. His playoff winning percentage of .706 ranks first.

Sather-coached teams won the Stanley Cup four times in the 1980s. As general manager, Sather was instrumental in the Oilers' fifth Cup triumph in 1990.

He has extensive international hockey experience, most recently as g.m. and coach of Team Canada at the 1996 World Cup of Hockey. He has also coached or managed tournament-winning teams at the Canada Cup and the IIHF World Championships.

Sather played for six different teams during a nine-year NHL career. He scored 80 goals in 660 games.

NHL Coaching Record

Season	Team	Games	Regular Season W	L	T	%	Playoffs Games	W	L	%
1979-80	Edmonton	80	28	39	13	.431	3	0	3	.000
1980-81	Edmonton	62	25	26	11	.492	9	5	4	.555
1981-82	Edmonton	80	48	17	15	.694	5	2	3	.400
1982-83	Edmonton	80	47	21	12	.663	16	11	5	.687
1983-84	Edmonton	80	57	18	5	.744	19	15	4	.789*
1984-85	Edmonton	80	49	20	11	.681	18	15	3	.833*
1985-86	Edmonton	80	56	17	7	.744	10	6	4	.600
1986-87	Edmonton	80	50	24	6	.663	21	16	5	.762*
1987-88	Edmonton	80	44	25	11	.619	18	16	2	.889*
1988-89	Edmonton	80	38	34	8	.538	7	3	4	.429
1993-94	Edmonton	60	22	27	11	.458	....	....	....	....
	NHL Totals	842	464	268	110	.616	126	89	37	.706

* Stanley Cup win.

Club Directory

Edmonton Oilers
11230 – 110 Street
Edmonton, Alberta T5G 3G8
Phone **403/414-4000**
Ticketing 403/414-4400
FAX 403/414-4659
Capacity: 17,099

Owner/Governor . . . . Peter Pocklington
Alternate Governor . . . . Glen Sather
President/General Manager . . . . Glen Sather
Exec. Vice President/Assistant G.M. . . . . Bruce MacGregor
Vice President, Hockey Operations . . . . Doug Risebrough
Coach . . . . Ron Low
Assistant Coaches . . . . Ted Green, Bob McCammon
Chief Scout . . . . Barry Fraser
Director of Player Personnel/Hockey Operations . . . Kevin Prendergast
Director of Hockey Administration . . . . Steve Pellegrini
Video Coordinator . . . . Brian Ross
Scouting Staff . . . . Ed Chadwick, Lorne Davis, Harry Howell, Gilles Leger, Chris McCarthy, Kent Nilsson, Dave Semenko

Executive Secretary to the President . . . . Betsy Freedman
Executive Secretary to the Vice Presidents . . . . Yvonne Ewaskow
Receptionist/Secretary . . . . Melahna Matan

Medical and Training Staff
Athletic Trainer/Therapist. . . . . Ken Lowe
Equipment Manager . . . . Barrie Stafford
Assistant Equipment Manager. . . . . Lyle Kulchisky
Massage Therapist. . . . . Stewart Poirier
Team Medical Chief of Staff/Director of Glen
   Sather Sports Medicine Clinic. . . . . Dr. David C. Reid
Team Physicians. . . . . Dr. Don Groot, Dr. Boris Boyko
Team Dentists . . . . Dr. Tony Sneazwell, Dr. Brian Nord
Fitness Consultant . . . . Dr. Art Quinney
Physical Therapy Consultant . . . . Dr. Dave Magee
Team Acupuncturist . . . . Dr. Steven Aung
Fitness Consultant . . . . Daryl Duke

Finance
Vice President, Finance . . . . Richard Hughes
Business Manager . . . . Darryl Boessenkool
Manager of Human Resources . . . . Pat Stanic
Financial Analysis . . . . Janice Mah
Systems Administrator . . . . Terry Rhoades
Finance Staff . . . . Connie Muller, Lynn Schmidl, Colleen Stewart

Public Relations
Vice President, Public Relations . . . . Bill Tuele
Information Coordinator . . . . Steve Knowles
Public Relations Manager . . . . Bryn Griffiths
Public Relations & Communications Coordinator. . . Fiona Liew
Community Relations & Special Events Assistant . . . Dan Taylor

Business Operation
Executive VP of Business Operations . . . . Doug Piper
Vice President, Sponsorships, Sales & Services . . . . Allan Watt
Vice President, Corporate Communications . . . . . . Trish Kerr
Manager, Corporate Sponsorships . . . . Brad MacGregor
Manager, Corporate Sponsorships . . . . Greg McDannold
Coordinator, Sponsorships, Sales & Services . . . . . Nicole Wiens
Corporate Sponsorship Representative . . . . Sean Price
Marketing Coordinator . . . . Dave Myers
Director of Broadcast. . . . . Don Metz
Game Night Operations. . . . . Glenn Wiun
Coordinator of Publications and New Media . . . . . Amanda Rose

Properties
Director of Properties. . . . . Darrell Holowaychuk
Properties Coordinator . . . . Brent Gibbs
Administrative Coordinator . . . . Linda Malito
Merchandising Manager . . . . Kerri Hill
Administrative Assistant. . . . . Heather Allen

Ticketing Operations
Director of Ticketing Operations . . . . John Yeomans
Ticket Client Services. . . . . Sheila McCaskill, Marcella Kinsman, Sandy Langley, Sherry Smith, Sheri Fitzgerald

Ticketing Sales
Director of Ticket Sales . . . . Kyle Draper
Sales and Marketing Assistant . . . . Melanie Dudek
Client Services Representative . . . . Lisa Johnson
Manager, Group Sales . . . . Michael Lake
Group Sales Representatives . . . . Brian Furman, Greg Hope
Corporate Sales Representatives . . . . D'Arcy Evans, David Grout, Darren Simmons, Robbin Tylor, Mark Wollen

Miscellaneous
Location of Press Box. . . . . East Side at top (Radio/TV)
   West Side at top (Media)
Dimensions of Rink . . . . 200 feet by 85 feet
Ends of Rink . . . . Herculite extends above boards around rink

Team Information
Team Founded . . . . 1972 (WHA), 1979-80 (NHL)
Club Colours . . . . Midnight Blue, Metallic Copper, Red & White
Team Uniforms . . . . Home: Base colour White, trimmed with midnight blue, copper and red
   Away: Base colour midnight Blue, trimmed with white, copper and red
Training Camp Site . . . . Edmonton Coliseum, Edmonton, Alberta
Television Outlets . . . . A-Channel
   CBXT TV (Channel 5, Cable 4)
Radio Flagship Station . . . . 630 CHED (AM)
   Rod Phillips, Morley Scott

Florida Panthers

1996-97 Results: 35w-28l-19t 89pts. Third, Atlantic Division

Year-by-Year Record

Season	GP	Home W	L	T	Road W	L	T	Overall W	L	T	GF	GA	Pts.	Finished		Playoff Result
1996-97	82	21	12	8	14	16	11	35	28	19	221	201	89	3rd,	Atlantic Div.	Lost Conf. Quarter-Final
1995-96	82	25	12	4	16	19	6	41	31	10	254	234	92	3rd,	Atlantic Div.	Lost Final
1994-95	48	9	12	3	11	10	3	20	22	6	115	127	46	5th,	Atlantic Div.	Out of Playoffs
1993-94	84	15	18	9	18	16	8	33	34	17	233	233	83	5th,	Atlantic Div.	Out of Playoffs

1997-98 Schedule

Oct.	Wed.	1	at Philadelphia
	Sat.	4	at Pittsburgh
	Sat.	11	at St. Louis
	Mon.	13	NY Islanders
	Wed.	15	Tampa Bay
	Thu.	16	at Dallas
	Sun.	19	Pittsburgh
	Wed.	22	at Montreal
	Thu.	23	at Ottawa
	Sat.	25	at Boston
	Tue.	28	Los Angeles
	Thu.	30	Ottawa
Nov.	Sat.	1	Buffalo
	Wed.	5	New Jersey
	Thu.	6	at Buffalo
	Sun.	9	Washington
	Wed.	12	NY Islanders
	Fri.	14	Philadelphia
	Sat.	15	at NY Islanders
	Tue.	18	NY Rangers
	Thu.	20	Calgary
	Sat.	22	at New Jersey*
	Sun.	23	Washington
	Wed.	26	Boston
	Fri.	28	Colorado*
	Sun.	30	at NY Rangers*
Dec.	Mon.	1	Phoenix
	Fri.	5	at Washington
	Sun.	7	Washington*
	Wed.	10	at Carolina
	Fri.	12	at NY Rangers
	Sat.	13	at NY Islanders
	Mon.	15	Boston
	Wed.	17	NY Rangers
	Thu.	18	at Washington
	Sat.	20	at Philadelphia*
	Tue.	23	St. Louis
	Fri.	26	at Carolina
	Sat.	27	at NY Islanders
	Tue.	30	San Jose
Jan.	Thu.	1	New Jersey*

	Fri.	2	at Tampa Bay
	Sun.	4	Anaheim
	Wed.	7	at Edmonton
	Fri.	9	at Calgary
	Sat.	10	at Vancouver
	Mon.	12	at Colorado
	Wed.	14	at Phoenix
	Wed.	21	at Anaheim
	Thu.	22	at Los Angeles
	Sat.	24	at San Jose
	Tue.	27	Carolina
	Thu.	29	Dallas
	Sat.	31	Tampa Bay*
Feb.	Sun.	1	Buffalo
	Tue.	3	Detroit
	Sat.	7	at Toronto*
	Wed.	25	New Jersey
	Fri.	27	at Detroit
Mar.	Wed.	4	NY Rangers
	Sat.	7	at Washington*
	Mon.	9	at Montreal
	Wed.	11	at Ottawa
	Fri.	13	Edmonton
	Sun.	15	Chicago
	Tue.	17	Vancouver
	Thu.	19	at Buffalo
	Sat.	21	at Tampa Bay*
	Mon.	23	Carolina
	Thu.	26	Montreal
	Sat.	28	at Boston*
	Sun.	29	at Chicago*
Apr.	Wed.	1	Montreal
	Sat.	4	at Philadelphia*
	Sun.	5	Pittsburgh
	Tue.	7	Toronto
	Thu.	9	Philadelphia
	Sat.	11	at Pittsburgh*
	Sun.	12	at New Jersey
	Tue.	14	Ottawa
	Thu.	16	Philadelphia
	Sat.	18	at Tampa Bay*

* Denotes afternoon game.

John Vanbiesbrouck's rapier-like glove enabled him to post a .919 save percentage, the fifth-best mark in the League.

Franchise date: June 14, 1993

ATLANTIC DIVISION

5th NHL Season

1997-98 Player Personnel

FORWARDS	HT	WT	S	Place of Birth	Date	1996-97 Club
BROWN, Mike	6-5	185	L	Surrey, B.C.	4/27/79	Red Deer
BUCKBERGER, Ashley	6-2	206	R	Esterhazy, Sask.	2/19/75	Carolina
DUERDEN, Dave	6-2	201	L	Oshawa, Ont.	4/11/77	Peterborough
DVORAK, Radek	6-2	187	R	Tabor, Czech.	3/9/77	Florida
FERGUSON, Craig	5-11	190	L	Castro Valley, CA	4/8/70	Florida-Carolina
GAGNER, Dave	5-10	180	L	Chatham, Ont.	12/11/64	Calgary
GARPENLOV, Johan	5-11	184	L	Stockholm, Sweden	3/21/68	Florida
HULL, Jody	6-2	195	R	Cambridge, Ont.	2/2/69	Florida
JOHNSON, Ryan	6-2	185	L	Thunder Bay, Ont.	6/14/76	Carolina
KVASHA, Oleg	6-5	205	R	Moscow, USSR	7/26/78	CSKA
LINDSAY, Bill	5-11	190	L	Big Fork, MT	5/17/71	Florida
LOWRY, Dave	6-1	200	L	Sudbury, Ont.	2/14/65	Florida
MELLANBY, Scott	6-1	199	R	Montreal, Que.	6/11/66	Florida
MULLER, Kirk	6-0	205	L	Kingston, Ont.	2/8/66	Toronto-Florida
NEMIROVSKY, David	6-1	192	R	Toronto, Ont.	8/1/76	Florida-Carolina
NIEDERMAYER, Rob	6-2	201	L	Cassiar, B.C.	12/28/74	Florida
NILSON, Marcus	6-1	183	R	Stockholm, Sweden	3/1/78	Djurgarden
POIRIER, Gaetan	6-2	200	L	Moncton, N.B.	12/28/76	Carolina
SHEPPARD, Ray	6-1	195	R	Pembroke, Ont.	5/27/66	Florida
SMITH, Nick	6-1	165	L	Hamilton, Ont.	3/23/79	Barrie
VASILJEVS, Herbert	5-11	170	R	Riga, USSR	5/27/76	Carolina-Port Huron
WASHBURN, Steve	6-2	191	L	Ottawa, Ont.	4/10/75	Florida-Carolina
WELLS, Chris	6-6	223	L	Calgary, Alta.	11/12/75	Cleveland-Florida
WORRELL, Peter	6-6	249	L	Pierre Fonds, Que.	8/18/77	Hull
DEFENSEMEN						
ARMSTRONG, Chris	6-0	198	L	Regina, Sask.	6/26/75	Carolina
CARKNER, Terry	6-3	210	L	Smiths Falls, Ont.	3/7/66	Florida
COUTURE, Alexandre	6-4	197	R	Hamnord, Que.	12/18/77	Victoriaville
DOYLE, Trevor	6-3	212	R	Ottawa, Ont.	1/1/74	Carolina
EAKINS, Dallas	6-2	195	L	Dade City, FL	2/27/67	Pho-Springfield-NYR-Binghamton
JAKOPIN, John	6-5	220	R	Toronto, Ont.	5/16/75	Merrimack-Adirondack
JOVANOVSKI, Ed	6-2	205	L	Windsor, Ont.	6/26/76	Florida
KUBA, Filip	6-3	202	L	Ostrava, Czech.	12/29/76	Carolina
LANKSHEAR, Mike	6-2	185	L	Calgary, Alta.	9/8/78	Guelph
LAUS, Paul	6-1	216	R	Beamsville, Ont.	9/26/70	Florida
MURPHY, Gord	6-2	191	R	Willowdale, Ont.	3/23/67	Florida
SVEHLA, Robert	6-1	190	R	Martin, Czech.	1/2/69	Florida
SWINSON, Wes	6-2	183	L	Peterborough, Ont.	5/26/75	Tallahasee-Carolina
WARRENER, Rhett	6-1	209	L	Shaunavon, Sask.	1/27/76	Florida

GOALTENDERS	HT	WT	C	Place of Birth	Date	1996-97 Club
FITZPATRICK, Mark	6-2	198	L	Toronto, Ont.	11/13/68	Florida
KHLOPTONOV, Denis	6-4	198	L	Moscow, USSR	1/27/78	CSKA
LEMANOWICZ, David	6-2	190	L	Edmonton, Alta.	3/8/76	Carolina-Port Huron
MacDONALD, Todd	6-0	167	L	Charlottetown, P.E.I.	7/5/75	Carolina-Cincinnati
VANBIESBROUCK, John	5-8	176	L	Detroit, MI	9/4/63	Florida
WEEKES, Kevin	6-0	158	L	Toronto, Ont.	4/4/75	Carolina

General Manager

MURRAY, BRYAN CLARENCE
Vice President and General Manager, Florida Panthers.
Born in Shawville, Que., December 5, 1942.

Bryan, 54, is entering his fourth season as vice president and general manager of the Panthers. Since being named to the position on August 1, 1994, he has helped construct a team that's become a perennial Stanley Cup contender. Under Bryan's watch, the Panthers have gone 96-81-35, good for a winning percentage of .535.

Bryan has acquired several players who've become cornerstones of the franchise. Ray Sheppard, Johan Garpenlov, Kirk Muller, Dave Gagner, Robert Svehla, Terry Carkner, Chris Wells and Radek Dvorak have all joined the team in the last three years, while Radek Dvorak was Bryan's first draft choice as GM of the Panthers. Marcus Nilson (1996) and Mike Brown (1997) are other first-round picks who are expected to contribute in the future. Bryan's efforts were recognized in 1996 when *The Sporting News* selected him as its NHL executive of the year.

This is Bryan's eighth season as a general manager. Before joining the Panthers, he served as coach and general manager of the Detroit Red Wings from 1990-93 and as general manager during the 1993-94 campaign. In 328 games under Murray's control, the Wings won a total of 170 games, while losing 121 and tying 37, an average of 43 wins and 94 points a season. Bryan left his mark in the NHL record book as a coach with a career record of 467-337-112,(.571 winning pct.) in 916 regular-season games, placing him seventh on the all-time victory list.

Murray broke into the NHL coaching ranks with the Washington Capitals on November 11, 1981. He spent the next 8½ seasons with the Caps and earned the Jack Adams Award as the NHL's coach of the year in 1983-84. In 1988-89, he led the Capitals to the Patrick Division title, the only first-place finish in team history. On January 15, 1990, Bryan was replaced by his brother, Terry.

Born in Shawville, Quebec on Dec. 5, 1942, Bryan is a graduate of McGill University in Montreal. He spent four years as athletic director and hockey coach at the school before leaving to coach the Regina Pats to a WHL title in 1979-80. Bryan moved up to the Hershey Bears (AHL) the following season and was named *The Hockey News'* minor league coach of the year after guiding that team to its best record in 40 years.

Bryan and his wife, Geri, have two daughters, Heide, 26 and Brittany 12.

1996-97 Scoring

* – rookie

Regular Season

Pos	#	Player	Team	GP	G	A	Pts	+/–	PIM	PP	SH	GW	GT	S	%
R	26	Ray Sheppard	FLA	68	29	31	60	4	4	13	0	7	0	226	12.8
R	27	Scott Mellanby	FLA	82	27	29	56	7	170	9	1	4	0	221	12.2
D	24	Robert Svehla	FLA	82	13	32	45	2	86	5	0	3	0	159	8.2
C	9	Kirk Muller	TOR	66	20	17	37	-23	85	9	1	3	0	153	13.1
			FLA	10	1	2	3	-2	4	1	0	1	0	21	4.8
			TOTAL	76	21	19	40	-25	89	10	1	4	0	174	12.1
R	19	Radek Dvorak	FLA	78	18	21	39	-2	30	2	0	1	0	139	12.9
C	44	Rob Niedermayer	FLA	60	14	24	38	4	54	3	0	2	0	136	10.3
L	29	Johan Garpenlov	FLA	53	11	25	36	10	47	1	0	1	2	83	13.3
L	11	Bill Lindsay	FLA	81	11	23	34	1	120	0	1	3	0	168	6.5
L	10	Dave Lowry	FLA	77	15	14	29	2	51	2	0	2	1	96	15.6
C	28	Martin Straka	FLA	55	7	22	29	9	12	2	0	1	0	94	7.4
D	4	Per Gustafsson	FLA	58	7	22	29	11	22	2	0	1	0	105	6.7
R	21	Tom Fitzgerald	FLA	71	10	14	24	7	64	0	2	1	1	135	7.4
D	5	Gord Murphy	FLA	80	8	15	23	3	51	2	0	0	0	137	5.8
D	55	Ed Jovanovski	FLA	61	7	16	23	-1	172	3	0	1	0	80	8.8
C	20	Brian Skrudland	FLA	51	5	13	18	4	48	0	0	2	0	57	8.8
R	12	Jody Hull	FLA	67	10	6	16	1	4	0	1	2	1	92	10.9
L	18	Mike Hough	FLA	69	8	6	14	12	48	0	0	2	0	85	9.4
R	15 *	David Nemirovsky	FLA	39	7	7	14	1	32	1	0	0	1	53	13.2
D	2	Terry Carkner	FLA	70	0	14	14	-4	96	0	0	0	0	38	0.0
D	7	Rhett Warrener	FLA	62	4	9	13	20	88	1	0	1	0	58	6.9
D	3	Paul Laus	FLA	77	0	12	12	13	313	0	0	0	0	63	0.0
C	22 *	Steve Washburn	FLA	18	3	6	9	2	4	1	0	0	0	21	14.3
C	23	Chris Wells	FLA	47	2	6	8	5	42	0	0	0	0	29	6.9
G	34	J. Vanbiesbrouck	FLA	57	0	2	2	0	8	0	0	0	0	0	0.0
G	30	Mark Fitzpatrick	FLA	30	0	1	1	0	13	0	0	0	0	0	0.0
R	8 *	Craig Martin	FLA	1	0	0	0	0	5	0	0	0	0	1	0.0
D	25	Geoff Smith	FLA	3	0	0	0	1	2	0	0	0	0	2	0.0
C	16	Craig Ferguson	FLA	3	0	0	0	-1	0	0	0	0	0	5	0.0
C	16	Craig Fisher	FLA	4	0	0	0	-2	0	0	0	0	0	2	0.0

Goaltending

No.	Goaltender	GPI	Mins	Avg	W	L	T	EN	SO	GA	SA	S%
34	J. Vanbiesbrouck	57	3347	2.29	27	19	10	3	2	128	1582	.919
30	Mark Fitzpatrick	30	1680	2.36	8	9	9	4	0	66	771	.914
	Totals	**82**	**5041**	**2.39**	**35**	**28**	**19**	**7**	**2**	**201**	**2360**	**.915**

Playoffs

Pos	#	Player	Team	GP	G	A	Pts	+/–	PIM	PP	SH	GW	OT	S	%
D	24	Robert Svehla	FLA	5	1	4	5	-4	4	1	0	0	0	13	7.7
D	5	Gord Murphy	FLA	5	0	5	5	0	4	0	0	0	0	18	0.0
C	44	Rob Niedermayer	FLA	5	2	1	3	-1	6	1	0	0	0	5	40.0
C	9	Kirk Muller	FLA	5	1	2	3	-3	4	1	0	0	0	20	5.0
L	29	Johan Garpenlov	FLA	4	2	0	2	0	4	2	0	1	0	6	33.3
R	26	Ray Sheppard	FLA	5	2	0	2	-4	0	1	0	0	0	12	16.7
R	27	Scott Mellanby	FLA	5	0	2	2	-1	4	0	0	0	0	6	0.0
R	15 *	David Nemirovsky	FLA	3	1	0	1	-2	0	0	0	0	0	4	25.0
L	18	Mike Hough	FLA	5	1	0	1	-2	2	0	0	0	0	10	10.0
L	11	Bill Lindsay	FLA	3	0	1	1	0	8	0	0	0	0	4	0.0
R	21	Tom Fitzgerald	FLA	5	0	1	1	-1	0	0	0	0	0	14	0.0
D	3	Paul Laus	FLA	5	0	1	1	-3	4	0	0	0	0	6	0.0
C	23	Chris Wells	FLA	3	0	0	0	-1	0	0	0	0	0	1	0.0
R	19	Radek Dvorak	FLA	3	0	0	0	0	0	0	0	0	0	1	0.0
C	28	Martin Straka	FLA	4	0	0	0	-2	0	0	0	0	0	2	0.0
D	2	Terry Carkner	FLA	5	0	0	0	-3	6	0	0	0	0	7	0.0
R	12	Jody Hull	FLA	5	0	0	0	-1	0	0	0	0	0	12	0.0
L	10	Dave Lowry	FLA	5	0	0	0	-3	0	0	0	0	0	8	0.0
G	34	J. Vanbiesbrouck	FLA	5	0	0	0	0	0	0	0	0	0	0	0.0
D	55	Ed Jovanovski	FLA	5	0	0	0	-4	4	0	0	0	0	7	0.0
D	7	Rhett Warrener	FLA	5	0	0	0	0	0	0	0	0	0	5	0.0

Goaltending

No.	Goaltender	GPI	Mins	Avg	W	L	EN	SO	GA	SA	S%
34	J. Vanbiesbrouck	5	328	2.38	1	4	0	1	13	184	.929
	Totals	**5**	**329**	**2.37**	**1**	**4**	**0**	**1**	**13**	**184**	**.929**

Captains' History

Brian Skrudland, 1993-94 to 1996-97.

General Managers' History

Bob Clarke, 1993-94; Bryan Murray, 1994-95 to date.

NHL Coaching Record

		Regular Season					Playoffs			
Season	Team	Games	W	L	T	%	Games	W	L	%
1981-82	Washington	76	25	28	13	.477	....	....	....	....
1982-83	Washington	80	39	25	16	.588	4	1	3	.250
1983-84	Washington	80	48	27	5	.631	8	4	4	.500
1984-85	Washington	80	46	25	9	.631	5	2	3	.400
1985-86	Washington	80	50	23	7	.669	9	5	4	.556
1986-87	Washington	80	38	32	10	.538	7	3	4	.429
1987-88	Washington	80	38	33	9	.531	14	7	7	.500
1988-89	Washington	80	41	29	10	.575	6	2	4	.333
1989-90	Washington	46	18	24	4	.435	....	....	....	....
1990-91	Detroit	80	34	38	8	.475	7	3	4	.429
1991-92	Detroit	80	43	25	12	.613	11	4	7	.364
1992-93	Detroit	84	47	28	9	.613	7	3	4	.429
	NHL Totals	**916**	**467**	**337**	**112**	**.571**	**78**	**34**	**44**	**.436**

Club Records

Team

(Figures in brackets for season records are games played; records for fewest points, wins, ties, losses, goals, goals against are for 70 or more games)

Most Points	92	1995-96 (82)
Most Wins	41	1995-96 (82)
Most Ties	19	1996-97 (82)
Most Losses	34	1993-94 (84)
Most Goals	254	1995-96 (82)
Most Goals Against	234	1995-96 (82)
Fewest Points	83	1993-94 (84)
Fewest Wins	33	1993-94 (84)
Fewest Ties	10	1995-96 (82)
Fewest Losses	28	1996-97 (82)
Fewest Goals	221	1996-97 (82)
Fewest Goals Against	201	1996-97 (82)

Longest Winning Streak

Overall	7	Nov. 2-14/95
Home	5	Nov. 5-14/95
Away	4	Dec. 2-12/95, Nov. 13-Dec 1/96

Longest Undefeated Streak

Overall	12	Oct. 5-30/96 (8 wins, 4 ties)
Home	8	Nov. 5-26/96 (7 wins, 1 tie)
Away	7	Twice

Longest Losing Streak

Overall	5	Twice
Home	5	Feb. 20-Mar. 4/94
Away	5	Feb. 25-Mar. 11/96

Longest Winless Streak

Overall	9	Feb. 24-Mar. 13/96 (7 losses, 2 ties)
Home	6	Mar. 21-Apr. 12/94 (3 losses, 3 ties)
Away	10	Feb. 25-Apr. 6/96 (9 losses, 1 tie)

Most Shutouts, Season	6	1994-95 (48)
Most PIM, Season	1,628	1996-97 (82)
Most Goals, Game	8	Jan. 24/94 (Mtl. 3 at Fla. 8)

Individual

Most Seasons	4	Several Players
Most Games	289	Scott Mellanby
Most Goals, Career	102	Scott Mellanby
Most Assists, Career	109	Scott Mellanby
Most Points, Career	211	Scott Mellanby (102G, 109A)
Most PIM, Career	796	Paul Laus
Most Shutouts, Career	9	John Vanbiesbrouck
Longest Consecutive Games Streak	191	Bill Lindsay
Most Goals, Season	32	Scott Mellanby (1995-96)
Most Assists, Season	49	Robert Svehla (1995-96)
Most Points, Season	70	Scott Mellanby (1995-96; 32G, 38A)
Most PIM, Season	313	Paul Laus (1996-97)
Most Shutouts, Season	4	John Vanbiesbrouck (1994-95)

Most Points, Defenseman, Season	57	Robert Svehla (1995-96; 8G, 49A)
Most Points, Center, Season	61	Rob Niedermayer (1995-96; 26G, 35A)
Most Points, Right Wing, Season	70	Scott Mellanby (1995-96; 32G, 38A)
Most Points, Left Wing, Season	51	Johan Garpenlov (1995-96; 23G, 28A)
Most Points, Rookie, Season	50	Jesse Belanger (1993-94; 17G, 33A)
Most Goals, Game	3	Five times
Most Assists, Game	3	Seven players
Most Points, Game	4	Jesse Belanger (Jan. 19/94; 2G, 2A); Scott Mellanby (Jan. 4/97; 1G, 3A)

* NHL Record.

All-time Record vs. Other Clubs

Regular Season

	At Home							On Road							Total					
	GP	W	L	T	GF	GA	PTS	GP	W	L	T	GF	GA	PTS	GP	W	L	T	GF	GA	PTS
Anaheim	3	1	1	1	7	8	3	3	1	0	2	9	8	4	6	3	1	2	16	16	7
Boston	7	3	4	0	16	16	6	8	3	3	2	20	19	8	15	6	7	2	36	35	14
Buffalo	7	5	2	0	22	19	10	8	6	1	1	9	30	3	15	6	8	1	31	49	13
Calgary	3	2	1	0	7	7	4	3	1	2	0	6	7	2	6	3	3	0	13	14	6
Chicago	3	1	2	0	8	11	2	3	1	1	1	11	13	3	6	2	3	1	19	24	5
Colorado	6	1	5	0	15	25	2	5	2	1	2	16	14	6	11	3	6	2	31	39	8
Dallas	3	1	1	1	11	10	3	3	1	0	2	12	11	4	6	2	1	3	23	21	7
Detroit	3	1	2	0	8	9	2	3	1	2	0	9	13	2	6	2	4	0	17	22	4
Edmonton	3	2	0	1	12	8	5	3	2	1	0	8	9	4	6	4	1	1	20	17	9
Hartford	8	4	2	2	23	14	10	8	4	0	4	20	26	8	16	8	2	6	43	40	18
Los Angeles	3	2	0	1	11	4	5	3	2	1	0	13	8	4	6	4	1	1	24	12	9
Montreal	8	3	3	2	28	22	8	7	2	1	4	21	19	9	15	5	4	6	49	41	17
New Jersey	10	5	2	3	25	20	13	10	3	6	1	16	26	7	20	8	8	4	41	46	20
NY Islanders	10	6	3	1	33	28	13	10	5	3	2	24	22	12	20	11	6	3	57	50	25
NY Rangers	10	5	4	1	26	30	11	10	3	4	3	25	28	9	20	8	8	4	51	58	20
Ottawa	8	6	1	1	30	17	13	8	5	2	1	28	18	11	16	11	3	2	58	35	24
Philadelphia	9	2	7	0	24	29	4	10	4	3	3	27	23	11	19	6	10	3	51	52	15
Phoenix	3	1	2	0	8	9	2	4	2	1	1	12	10	5	7	3	3	1	20	19	7
Pittsburgh	8	4	4	0	23	20	8	8	1	6	1	21	30	3	16	5	10	1	44	50	11
St. Louis	3	1	1	1	6	7	3	3	1	2	0	6	8	2	6	2	3	1	12	15	5
San Jose	3	1	0	2	9	6	4	3	1	1	1	9	7	3	6	2	1	3	18	13	7
Tampa Bay	10	6	2	2	28	17	14	10	5	3	2	29	20	12	20	11	5	4	57	37	26
Toronto	4	1	1	2	12	10	4	3	2	0	1	10	10	2	7	3	2	3	22	20	6
Vancouver	3	2	0	1	9	7	5	3	1	1	1	8	12	3	6	3	1	2	17	19	8
Washington	10	4	4	2	30	25	10	9	3	3	3	23	26	9	19	7	7	5	53	51	19
Totals	**148**	**70**	**54**	**24**	**431**	**378**	**164**	**148**	**59**	**61**	**28**	**392**	**417**	**146**	**296**	**129**	**115**	**52**	**823**	**795**	**310**

Playoffs

	Series	W	L	GP	W	L	T	GF	GA	Last Mtg.	Round	Result
Boston	1	1	0	5	4	1	0	22	16	1996	CQF	W 4-1
Colorado	1	0	1	4	0	4	0	4	15	1996	F	L 0-4
NY Rangers	1	0	1	5	1	4	0	10	13	1997	CQF	L 1-4
Philadelphia	1	1	0	6	4	2	0	15	11	1996	CSF	W 4-2
Pittsburgh	1	1	0	7	4	3	0	20	15	1996	CF	W 4-3
Totals	**5**	**3**	**2**	**27**	**13**	**14**	**0**	**71**	**70**			

Playoff Results 1997-94

Year	Round	Opponent	Result	GF	GA
1997	CQF	NY Rangers	L 1-4	10	13
1996	F	Colorado	L 0-4	4	15
	CF	Pittsburgh	W 4-3	20	15
	CSF	Philadelphia	W 4-2	15	11
	CQF	Boston	W 4-1	22	16

Abbreviations: Round: F – Final;
CF – conference final; **CQF** – conference quarter-final;
CSF – conference semi-final; **DF** – division final;
DSF – division semi-final; **SF** – semi-final;
QF – quarter-final; **PR** – preliminary round.

Colorado totals include Quebec, 1993-94 to 1994-95.   Phoenix totals include Winnipeg, 1993-94 to 1995-96.

1996-97 Results

Oct.	5	at	Philadelphia	3-1		11	at	Calgary	4-1
	6	at	NY Rangers	5-2		14	at	Vancouver	4-4
	8		NY Rangers	1-1		15	at	Edmonton	0-4
	12		Hartford	6-0		20		Colorado	2-4
	16	at	San Jose	3-3		22	at	Hartford	1-2
	17	at	Colorado	2-1		23	at	Boston	4-1
	20	at	Phoenix	1-1		25		Tampa Bay	3-2
	23		Ottawa	5-2		28		Montreal	5-1
	25		NY Rangers	6-4		30		Boston	3-1
	27	at	Philadelphia	3-2	**Feb.**	1		Washington	1-3
	29	at	NY Rangers	1-1		3	at	Montreal	2-2
	30		Chicago	3-2		6	at	Buffalo	1-1
Nov.	2		Philadelphia	2-3		7	at	New Jersey	2-2
	7		Washington	4-2		9		NY Rangers	4-3
	9		Pittsburgh	4-2		12		Tampa Bay	5-2
	11	at	Buffalo	2-3		15	at	NY Islanders	0-1
	13	at	Montreal	5-3		16		Detroit	2-4
	15		NY Islanders	3-3		18	at	Pittsburgh	2-4
	18		Washington	2-4		20		New Jersey	2-2
	20		Los Angeles	4-1		22		Philadelphia	3-4
	22	at	Dallas	1-3		25		San Jose	2-2
	23	at	St. Louis	3-1		27		St. Louis	3-2
	26		Buffalo	4-3	**Mar.**	1	at	Tampa Bay	0-2
	29		Hartford	1-1		2	at	Phoenix	0-3
Dec.	1	at	Detroit	4-2		4	at	Calgary	1-3
	3	at	New Jersey	0-2		7		Boston	1-3
	5		NY Islanders	4-2		11		NY Islanders	3-2
	8		Dallas	1-3		13		Vancouver	5-4
	10	at	Philadelphia	4-5		15		Toronto	3-3
	11	at	Hartford	2-5		17	at	New Jersey	4-1
	15		Edmonton	6-3		19	at	NY Islanders	4-7
	19	at	Ottawa	3-1		20	at	Ottawa	2-2
	20	at	Chicago	3-1		22		Buffalo	3-2
	22	at	NY Rangers	3-7		27		Ottawa	2-3
	23	at	NY Islanders	4-3		29		Tampa Bay	1-1
	26	at	Tampa Bay	3-3		31	at	Pittsburgh	3-4
	28	at	Washington	1-1	**Apr.**	2	at	Toronto	1-3
	29		Montreal	1-2		5	at	Boston	2-4
Jan.	1		Anaheim	0-3		6	at	Washington	3-3
	4	at	Los Angeles	5-0		9		New Jersey	4-2
	8	at	Anaheim	2-3		11		Pittsburgh	4-2

Entry Draft
Selections 1997-93

1997 Pick		1995 Pick		1993 Pick	
20	Mike Brown	10	Radek Dvorak	5	Rob Niedermayer
47	Kristian Huselius	36	Aaron MacDonald	41	Kevin Weekes
56	Vratislav Cech	62	Mike O'Grady	57	Chris Armstrong
74	Nick Smith	80	Dave Duerden	67	Mikael Tjallden
95	Ivan Novoseltsev	88	Daniel Tjarnqvist	78	Steve Washburn
127	Pat Parthenais	114	Francois Cloutier	83	Bill McCauley
155	Keith Delaney	166	Peter Worrell	109	Todd MacDonald
183	Tyler Palmer	192	Filip Kuba	135	Alain Nasreddine
211	Doug Schueller	218	David Lemanowicz	161	Trevor Doyle
237	Benoit Cote			187	Briane Thompson
				213	Chad Cabana
1996 Pick		**1994 Pick**		239	John Demarco
20	Marcus Nilson	1	Ed Jovanovski	265	Eric Montreuil
60	Chris Allen	27	Rhett Warrener		
65	Oleg Kvasha	31	Jason Podollan		
82	Joey Tetarenko	36	Ryan Johnson		
129	Andrew Long	84	David Nemirovsky		
156	Gaetan Poirier	105	Dave Geris		
183	Alexandre Couture	157	Matt O'Dette		
209	Denis Khloptonov	183	Jasson Boudrias		
235	Russell Smith	235	Tero Lehtera		
		261	Per Gustafsson		

Coaching History

Roger Neilson, 1993-94 to 1994-95; Doug MacLean, 1995-96 to date.

Coach

MacLEAN, DOUG
Coach, Florida Panthers. Born in Summerside, P.E.I., April 12, 1954.

Doug, 43, compiled a record of 76-59-29 (.552 winning pct.) in his first two seasons behind the Panthers' bench. Only six teams — Detroit (100), Colorado (96), Philadelphia (90), Pittsburgh (87), New Jersey (82) and the New York Rangers (79) — posted more wins than Florida over that span. In 1996-97, Doug guided the Panthers to one of the fastest starts in NHL history (8-0-4) and earned the right to coach in the All-Star Game for the second year in a row. He recorded his second straight win in the event as the East defeated the West, 11-7, in San Jose, California.

In his first season as an NHL head coach (1995-96), Doug led the Panthers to the Eastern Conference Championship and a berth in the Stanley Cup Finals against the Colorado Avalanche. Known for his wit and the ability to get the most out of his players, he was also named a finalist for the Jack Adams Award as the NHL's Coach of the Year and was selected as *The Hockey News'* coach of the year.

Born in Summerside, Prince Edward Island on April 12, 1954. Doug's NHL career began in 1986-87 when he was hired by the St. Louis Blues as an assistant to head coach Jacques Martin. Doug spent two seasons in St. Louis, helping guide the Blues to first and second place finishes in the Norris Division, before becoming Bryan Murray's assistant coach in Washington at the start of the 1988-89 campaign.

Doug spent two seasons in the Capitals' organization. He spent all of 1988-89 as Murray's assistant and began the 1989-90 campaign in that capacity until he was named head coach of the Capitals' American Hockey League affiliate in Baltimore midway through the season. Doug was Baltimore's head coach for the final 35 games of 1989-90 and he compiled a record of 17-13-5, as the Skipjacks finished third in the AHL's South Division with an overall record of 43-30-7.

The following season, 1990-91, Doug left the Capitals' organization to become Murray's assistant coach in Detroit. MacLean spent two seasons behind the Red Wings' bench, the second season as associate coach, and helped guide Detroit to third and first place finishes, respectively. In 1992-93, he left the coaching ranks to concentrate on the Red Wings' player development. Doug spent the entire 1992-93 and 1993-94 seasons as Detroit's assistant general manager, as well as general manager of the Adirondack Red Wings, Detroit's AHL affiliate. He left the Wings' organization before the start of 1994-95 and once again was reunited with Bryan Murray. Doug became the Panthers' director of player development and pro scout in October 1994 and was named the team's head coach on July 24, 1995.

Doug played collegiate hockey at the University of P.E.I., where he graduated with a bachelor's degree in education. He also played for the Montreal Junior Canadiens, and in 1974, was invited to attend the St. Louis Blues' training camp. After his playing career, Doug enrolled at the University of Western Ontario, where he received his master's degree in educational psychology. While attending Western Ontario, Doug began his coaching career as an assistant with the London Knights of the Ontario Hockey League. After graduating from Western Ontario, he returned home where he taught high school and became head coach of Summerside's junior A hockey team. In 1985-86, Doug became head coach at the University of New Brunswick, and after only one season there, was tabbed by Jacques Martin to join his coaching staff in St. Louis.

Doug and his wife, Jill, have two children, a son, Clark, 9 and a daughter, MacKenzie, 6. The family lives in Coral Springs, FL.

Coaching Record

Season	Team	Regular Season					Playoffs			
		Games	W	L	T	%	Games	W	L	%
1985-86	U. of New Brunswick (CIAU)	22	8	14	0	.364	....	....	....	....
1989-90	Baltimore (AHL)	35	17	13	5	.557	12	6	6	.500
1995-96	**Florida (NHL)**	**82**	**41**	**31**	**10**	**.561**	**22**	**12**	**10**	**.545**
1996-97	**Florida (NHL)**	**82**	**35**	**28**	**19**	**.543**	**5**	**1**	**4**	**.200**
	NHL Totals	**164**	**76**	**59**	**29**	**.552**	**27**	**13**	**14**	**.481**

Club Directory

Miami Arena
100 Northeast Third Avenue
2nd Floor
Fort Lauderdale, FL 33301
Phone **954/768-1900**
FAX 954/768-1920
Capacity: 14,703

Chairman and CEO	H. Wayne Huizenga
President & Governor	William A. Torrey
Executive Vice President & Alternate Governor	Dean J. Jordan
Special Consultant	Richard C. Rochon
Executive Assistants to Presidents	Deanna Cocozzelli, Cathy Stevenson
Executive Assistant to Executive Vice President	Janine Shea

Finance & Administration

Vice President of Finance and Administration/CFO	Steve Dauria
Director of Finance/Controller	Evelyn Lopez
Assistant Controller	Cheryl Balaban
Manager of Information Services	Kelly Connor
Office Manager/Accounts Payable Supervisor	Laura Barrera
Staff Accountants	Ana Carrasquilla, Karen Walker
Payroll Coordinator	Kathy Graham
Information Systems Staff	Kerri Gustin, Jon Paul Hernandez
Executive Assistant to Vice President, Finance & Administration	Judy O'Donovan
Office Services	Anthony Vandaley
Manager of Payroll/Human Resources	Mary Santimaw
Head Receptionist	Marilyn Klees
Backup Receptionist/Office Services	Lee Bancroft

Hockey Operations

Vice President and General Manager	Bryan Murray
Assistant General Manager	Chuck Fletcher
Head Coach	Doug MacLean
Assistant Coaches	Duane Sutter, Joe Cirella
Goaltending Coach	Bill Smith
Director of Player Development	Paul Henry
Amateur Scouts	Ron Harris, Matti Vaisanen, Tim Murray, Wayne Meier, Billy Dea
Pro Scouts	Micheal Abbamont, Jim Clark
Assistant to the General Manager	Kevin Dessart
Executive Assistant to Vice President and General Manager	Vanessa Rey
Head Medical Trainer	David Smith
Equipment Manager	Mark Brennan
Training Staff	Tim LeRoy, Scott Tinkler
Team Services Coordinator	Marni Share
Training Staff Assistant	Andre Szucko
Internist	Charles Posternack, M.D.
Orthopedic Surgeon	David E. Attarian, M.D.
Assistant Physicians	Stephen R. Southworth, M.D., James Guerra, M.D.
Plastic Surgeon	Harry K. Moon
Team Dentist	Marty Robins, D.D.S.
Minor League Affiliates	New Haven (AHL), Fort Wayne (IHL), Tallahassee (ECHL) & Port Huron (UHL)

Communications Department

Director of Communications	Mike Hanson
Communications Associate	Jon Kramer
Communications Assistant	Tom Ziermann
Community Programs Manager	Liz Ridley
Assistant to the Director of Communications	Stephanie Cuzzacrea
Manager of Archives	Jonas Kalkstein

Marketing Department

Vice President of Marketing	Declan J. Bolger
Director of Corporate Sales & Sponsorship	Kimberly Terranova
Manager of Corporate Sales & Sponsorship	Scott Baynes
Senior Manager of Promotions	Ed Krajewski
Corporate Account Manager	Brette Sadler
Promotions Coordinator	Tim Dieter
Publications Sales Coordinator	Chris Gallagher
Mascot Coordinator	Phil Crowhurst
Director of Season & Group Sales	Chris Trinceri
Account Executives	Craig Petrus, Brent Flahr, Leo Sarmiento
Executive Assistant to Vice President of Marketing	Andria Cunningham
Administrative Assistant to Director of Corporate Sales & Sponsorship	Susan Ferro
Admin. Assistant, Promotions and Sales	Kali Blosch

Ticket Operations

Vice President of Operations	Steve Dangerfield
Director of Ticket Operations	Scott Wampold
Director of Merchandising	Ron Dennis
Manager of Ticket Operations	Matt Coyne
Ticket Operations Representative	Lauri Carr
Executive Assistant to Vice President of Operations	Mary Lou Poag
Admin. Assistant to Director of Merchandising	Alex Fernandez

General Information

Arena Phone Number	(305) 530-4444
Location of Press Box	Mezzanine, Sec. 211
Press Box Phone	(305) 372-3540
Dimensions of Rink	200 feet by 85 feet
Practice Arena	Gold Coast Ice Arena (954) 784-5500
Team Colors	Red, Navy Blue, Yellow, Gold
Television Announcers	Jeff Rimer, Denis Potvin
Panthers Radio Network	WQAM, 560 AM
Radio Announcers	Chris Moore, Randy Moller

Los Angeles Kings

1996-97 Results: 28W-43L-11T 67PTS. Sixth, Pacific Division

1997-98 Schedule

Oct.	Wed.	1	at Pittsburgh		Mon.	5	at Vancouver
	Thu.	2	at Boston		Thu.	8	Buffalo
	Sun.	5	at NY Rangers		Sat.	10	Edmonton
	Tue.	7	at Carolina		Mon.	12	Anaheim
	Thu.	9	at St. Louis		Wed.	14	at San Jose
	Sun.	12	Ottawa		Tue.	20	Calgary
	Wed.	15	Boston		Thu.	22	Florida
	Fri.	17	Philadelphia		Sat.	24	at Anaheim*
	Sun.	19	Edmonton		Thu.	29	Calgary
	Tue.	21	NY Islanders		Sat.	31	Chicago*
	Thu.	23	Detroit	**Feb.**	Mon.	2	at Edmonton
	Sun.	26	at Tampa Bay		Tue.	3	at Calgary
	Tue.	28	at Florida		Thu.	5	NY Rangers
	Fri.	31	at Detroit		Sat.	7	at Anaheim*
Nov.	Sat.	1	at NY Islanders		Wed.	25	at Detroit
	Tue.	4	at New Jersey		Thu.	26	at Chicago
	Thu.	6	Tampa Bay		Sat.	28	St. Louis*
	Sat.	8	Montreal	**Mar.**	Mon.	2	Vancouver
	Tue.	11	Vancouver		Thu.	5	Carolina
	Thu.	13	San Jose		Sat.	7	Detroit*
	Sat.	15	Dallas		Mon.	9	Anaheim
	Thu.	20	Chicago		Tue.	10	at Phoenix
	Sun.	23	at Colorado		Thu.	12	Toronto
	Wed.	26	at Dallas		Sat.	14	Colorado*
	Thu.	27	at St. Louis		Mon.	16	at San Jose
	Sat.	29	New Jersey		Tue.	17	Dallas
Dec.	Wed.	3	at Montreal		Sat.	21	Phoenix*
	Thu.	4	at Ottawa		Tue.	24	at San Jose
	Sat.	6	at Toronto		Thu.	26	San Jose
	Tue.	9	Pittsburgh		Sat.	28	at Calgary*
	Sat.	13	Washington		Mon.	30	at Toronto
	Mon.	15	at Vancouver	**Apr.**	Wed.	1	at Buffalo
	Thu.	18	Toronto		Thu.	2	at Philadelphia
	Sat.	20	at Calgary*		Sat.	4	at Washington*
	Mon.	22	at Chicago		Mon.	6	at Colorado
	Tue.	23	at Colorado		Thu.	9	Edmonton
	Sat.	27	Phoenix		Sat.	11	Colorado*
	Mon.	29	Vancouver		Mon.	13	Calgary
	Wed.	31	at Dallas		Wed.	15	at Vancouver
Jan.	Thu.	1	at Phoenix		Thu.	16	St. Louis
	Sun.	4	at Edmonton*		Sat.	18	Anaheim*

Denotes afternoon game.

Franchise date: June 5, 1967

**PACIFIC
DIVISION**

**31st
NHL
Season**

Stephane Fiset's .906 save percentage and career-high four shutouts
in 44 games played provided the Kings with solid netminding in 1996-97.

Year-by-Year Record

		Home			Road			Overall						
Season	**GP**	**W**	**L**	**T**	**W**	**L**	**T**	**W**	**L**	**T**	**GF**	**GA**	**Pts.**	**Finished**	**Playoff Result**
1996-97	82	18	16	7	10	27	4	28	43	11	214	268	67	6th, Pacific Div.	Out of Playoffs
1995-96	82	16	16	9	8	24	9	24	40	18	256	302	66	6th, Pacific Div.	Out of Playoffs
1994-95	48	7	11	6	9	12	3	16	23	9	142	174	41	4th, Pacific Div.	Out of Playoffs
1993-94	84	18	19	5	9	26	7	27	45	12	294	322	66	5th, Pacific Div.	Out of Playoffs
1992-93	84	22	15	5	17	20	5	39	35	10	338	340	88	3rd, Smythe Div.	Lost Final
1991-92	80	20	11	9	15	20	5	35	31	14	287	296	84	2nd, Smythe Div.	Lost Div. Semi-Final
1990-91	80	26	9	5	20	15	5	46	24	10	340	254	102	1st, Smythe Div.	Lost Div. Final
1989-90	80	21	16	3	13	23	4	34	39	7	338	337	75	4th, Smythe Div.	Lost Div. Final
1988-89	80	25	12	3	17	19	4	42	31	7	376	335	91	2nd, Smythe Div.	Lost Div. Final
1987-88	80	19	18	3	11	24	5	30	42	8	318	359	68	4th, Smythe Div.	Lost Div. Semi-Final
1986-87	80	20	17	3	11	24	5	31	41	8	318	341	70	4th, Smythe Div.	Lost Div. Semi-Final
1985-86	80	9	27	4	14	22	4	23	49	8	284	389	54	5th, Smythe Div.	Out of Playoffs
1984-85	80	20	14	6	14	18	8	34	32	14	339	326	82	4th, Smythe Div.	Lost Div. Semi-Final
1983-84	80	13	19	8	10	25	5	23	44	13	309	376	59	5th, Smythe Div.	Out of Playoffs
1982-83	80	20	13	7	7	28	5	27	41	12	308	365	66	5th, Smythe Div.	Out of Playoffs
1981-82	80	19	15	6	5	26	9	24	41	15	314	369	63	4th, Smythe Div.	Lost Div. Final
1980-81	80	22	11	7	21	13	6	43	24	13	337	290	99	2nd, Norris Div.	Lost Prelim. Round
1979-80	80	18	13	9	12	23	5	30	36	14	290	313	74	2nd, Norris Div.	Lost Prelim. Round
1978-79	80	20	13	7	14	21	5	34	34	12	292	286	80	3rd, Norris Div.	Lost Prelim. Round
1977-78	80	18	16	6	13	18	9	31	34	15	243	245	77	3rd, Norris Div.	Lost Prelim. Round
1976-77	80	20	13	7	14	18	8	34	31	15	271	241	83	2nd, Norris Div.	Lost Quarter-Final
1975-76	80	22	13	5	16	20	4	38	33	9	263	265	85	2nd, Norris Div.	Lost Quarter-Final
1974-75	80	22	7	11	20	10	10	42	17	21	269	185	105	2nd, Norris Div.	Lost Prelim. Round
1973-74	78	22	13	4	11	20	8	33	33	12	233	231	78	3rd, West Div.	Lost Quarter-Final
1972-73	78	21	11	7	10	25	4	31	36	11	232	245	73	6th, West Div.	Out of Playoffs
1971-72	78	14	23	2	6	26	7	20	49	9	206	305	49	7th, West Div.	Out of Playoffs
1970-71	78	17	14	8	8	26	5	25	40	13	239	303	63	5th, West Div.	Out of Playoffs
1969-70	76	12	22	4	2	30	6	14	52	10	168	290	38	6th, West Div.	Out of Playoffs
1968-69	76	19	14	5	5	28	5	24	42	10	185	260	58	4th, West Div.	Lost Semi-Final
1967-68	74	20	13	4	11	20	6	31	33	10	200	224	72	2nd, West Div.	Lost Quarter-Final

1997-98 Player Personnel

FORWARDS	HT	WT	S	Place of Birth	Date	1996-97 Club
BARNEY, Scott	6-4	198	R	Oshawa, Ont.	3/27/79	Peterborough
BELANGER, Eric	5-11	170	L	Sherbrooke, Que.	12/16/77	Beauport-Rimouski
BYLSMA, Dan	6-2	215	L	Grand Haven, MI	9/19/70	Los Angeles
DALE, Andrew	6-1	196	L	Sudbury, Ont.	2/16/76	Mississippi-Phoenix (IHL)
FERRARO, Ray	5-10	185	L	Trail, B.C.	8/23/64	Los Angeles
GREEN, Josh	6-3	197	L	Camrose, Alta.	11/16/77	Medicine Hat-Swift Current
JOHNSON, Craig	6-2	197	L	St. Paul, MN	3/8/72	Los Angeles
JOHNSON, Matt	6-5	230	L	Welland, Ont.	11/23/75	Los Angeles
JOKINEN, Olli	6-2	198	L	Kuopio, Finland	12/5/78	HIFK
LaFAYETTE, Nathan	6-1	200	R	New Westminster, B.C.	2/17/73	L.A.-Phoenix (IHL)-Syracuse
LAPERRIERE, Ian	6-1	195	R	Montreal, Que.	1/19/74	Los Angeles
MacLEAN, Donald	6-2	174	L	Sydney, N.S.	1/14/77	Hull
McKENNA, Steve	6-8	247	L	Toronto, Ont.	8/21/73	Los Angeles-Phoenix (IHL)
MOGER, Sandy	6-3	214	R	100 Mile House, B.C.	3/21/69	Boston-Providence (AHL)
MORGAN, Jason	6-1	185	L	St. John's, Nfld.	10/9/76	L.A.-Phoenix (IHL)-Mississippi
MURRAY, Glen	6-2	220	R	Halifax, N.S.	11/1/72	Pittsburgh-Los Angeles
O'BRIEN, Sean	6-1	200	L	Belmont, MA	2/9/72	Tallahassee-Utah-Phoenix (IHL)
PERREAULT, Yanic	5-11	182	L	Sherbrooke, Que.	4/4/71	Los Angeles
ROBITAILLE, Luc	6-1	195	L	Montreal, Que.	2/17/66	NY Rangers
ROSA, Pavel	5-11	180	L	Most, Czech.	6/7/77	Hull
SCHMIDT, Chris	6-3	200	L	Beaverlodge, Alta.	3/1/76	Mississippi-Phoenix (IHL)
SHEVALIER, Jeff	5-11	180	L	Mississauga, Ont.	3/14/74	Los Angeles-Phoenix (IHL)
SMYTH, Brad	6-0	200	L	Ottawa, Ont.	3/13/73	Fla-L.A.-Phoenix (IHL)
STUMPEL, Jozef	6-3	210	R	Nitra, Czech.	7/20/72	Boston
TAYLOR, Chris	6-0	189	L	Stratford, Ont.	3/6/72	NY Islanders-Utah
TSYPLAKOV, Vladimir	6-0	185	L	Moscow, USSR	4/18/69	Los Angeles
VOPAT, Roman	6-3	216	L	Litvinov, Czech.	4/21/76	Los Angeles-Phoenix (IHL)
YACHMENEV, Vitali	5-9	180	L	Chelyabinsk, USSR	1/8/75	Los Angeles
ZULTEK, Matt	6-4	218	L	Windsor, Ont.	3/12/79	Ottawa (OHL)

DEFENSEMEN						
BATYRSHIN, Ruslan	6-1	185	L	Moscow, USSR	2/19/75	Phoenix (IHL)
BERG, Aki-Petteri	6-3	198	L	Turku, Finland	2/28/77	Los Angeles-Phoenix (IHL)
BLAKE, Rob	6-3	215	R	Simcoe, Ont.	12/10/69	Los Angeles
BLANCHARD, Sean	6-0	201	L	Sudbury, Ont.	3/29/78	Ottawa (OHL)
BOUCHER, Philippe	6-3	190	R	St. Apollinaire, Que.	3/24/73	Los Angeles
FINN, Steven	6-0	191	L	Laval, Que.	8/20/66	Los Angeles
GALLEY, Garry	6-0	204	L	Montreal, Que.	4/16/63	Buffalo
MODRY, Jaroslav	6-2	195	L	Ceske-Budejovice, Czech.	2/27/71	Los Angeles-Phoenix (IHL)-Utah
NORSTROM, Mattias	6-1	205	L	Stockholm, Sweden	1/2/72	Los Angeles
O'DONNELL, Sean	6-3	225	L	Ottawa, Ont.	10/13/71	Los Angeles
VOPAT, Jan	6-0	205	L	Most, Czech.	3/22/73	Los Angeles-Phoenix (IHL)
ZMOLEK, Doug	6-2	220	L	Rochester, MN	11/3/70	Los Angeles

GOALTENDERS	HT	WT	C	Place of Birth	Date	1996-97 Club
FISET, Stephane	6-1	195	L	Montreal, Que.	6/17/70	Los Angeles
GUZDA, Brad	6-3	180	L	Banff, Alta.	4/28/73	Knoxville-Phoenix (IHL)
STORR, Jamie	6-0	170	L	Brampton, Ont.	12/28/75	Los Angeles-Phoenix (IHL)
VALIQUETTE, Stephen	6-5	205	L	Etobicoke, Ont.	8/20/77	Sudbury

General Managers' History

Larry Regan, 1967-68 to 1972-73; Larry Regan and Jake Milford, 1973-74; Jake Milford, 1974-75 to 1976-77; George Maguire, 1977-78 to 1982-83; George Maguire and Rogatien Vachon, 1983-84; Rogatien Vachon, 1984-85 to 1991-92; Nick Beverley, 1992-93 to 1993-94; Sam McMaster, 1994-95 to 1996-97; Dave Taylor, 1997-98.

Coaching History

"Red" Kelly, 1967-68 to 1968-69; Hal Laycoe and John Wilson, 1969-70; Larry Regan, 1970-71; Larry Regan and Fred Glover, 1971-72; Bob Pulford, 1972-73 to 1976-77; Ron Stewart, 1977-78; Bob Berry, 1978-79 to 1980-81; Parker MacDonald and Don Perry, 1981-82; Don Perry, 1982-83; Don Perry, Rogie Vachon and Roger Neilson, 1983-84; Pat Quinn, 1984-85 to 1985-86; Pat Quinn and Mike Murphy 1986-87; Mike Murphy, Rogie Vachon and Robbie Ftorek, 1987-88; Robbie Ftorek, 1988-89; Tom Webster, 1989-90 to 1991-92; Barry Melrose, 1992-93 to 1993-94; Barry Melrose and Rogie Vachon, 1994-95; Larry Robinson, 1995-96 to date.

Captains' History

Bob Wall, 1967-68, 1968-69; Larry Cahan, 1969-70, 1970-71; Bob Pulford, 1971-72, 1972-73; Terry Harper, 1973-74, 1974-75; Mike Murphy, 1975-76 to 1980-81; Dave Lewis, 1981-82, 1982-83; Terry Ruskowski, 1983-84, 1984-85; Dave Taylor, 1985-86 to 1988-89; Wayne Gretzky, 1989-90 to 1991-92; Wayne Gretzky and Luc Robitaille, 1992-93; Wayne Gretzky, 1993-94 to 1994-95; Wayne Gretzky and Rob Blake, 1995-96; Rob Blake, 1996-97 to date.

1996-97 Scoring

* – rookie

Regular Season

Pos	#	Player	Team	GP	G	A	Pts	+/–	PIM	PP	SH	GW	GT	S	%
L	8	Dimitri Khristich	L.A.	75	19	37	56	8	38	3	0	2	0	135	14.1
C	20	Ray Ferraro	L.A.	81	25	21	46	-22	112	11	0	2	1	152	16.4
L	9	Vladimir Tsyplakov	L.A.	67	16	23	39	8	12	1	0	2	0	118	13.6
L	25	Kevin Stevens	L.A.	69	14	20	34	-27	96	4	0	1	1	175	8.0
R	43	Vitali Yachmenev	L.A.	65	10	22	32	-9	10	2	0	2	1	97	10.3
D	4	Rob Blake	L.A.	62	8	23	31	-28	82	4	0	1	0	169	4.7
R	27	Glen Murray	PIT	66	11	11	22	-19	24	3	0	1	0	127	8.7
			L.A.	11	5	3	8	-2	8	0	0	0	0	26	19.2
			TOTAL	77	16	14	30	-21	32	3	0	1	0	153	10.5
L	21	Kai Nurminen	L.A.	67	16	11	27	-3	22	4	0	1	1	112	14.3
C	44	Yanic Perreault	L.A.	41	11	14	25	0	20	1	1	0	0	98	11.2
D	28	Philippe Boucher	L.A.	60	7	18	25	0	25	2	0	1	0	159	4.4
C	22	Ian Laperriere	L.A.	62	8	15	23	-25	102	0	1	2	0	84	9.5
D	14	Mattias Norstrom	L.A.	80	1	21	22	-4	84	0	0	0	0	106	.9
R	11	* Brad Smyth	FLA	8	1	0	1	-3	2	0	0	0	0	10	10.0
			L.A.	44	8	8	16	-7	74	0	0	1	1	74	10.8
			TOTAL	52	9	8	17	-10	76	0	0	1	1	84	10.7
D	6	Sean O'Donnell	L.A.	55	5	12	17	-13	144	2	0	0	0	68	7.4
D	27	John Slaney	L.A.	32	3	11	14	-10	4	1	0	1	0	60	5.0
L	19	* Jeff Shevalier	L.A.	26	4	9	13	-6	6	1	0	0	0	42	9.5
C	12	* Roman Vopat	L.A.	29	4	5	9	-7	60	1	0	2	0	54	7.4
D	33	* Jan Vopat	L.A.	33	4	5	9	3	22	0	0	1	1	44	9.1
L	42	* Dan Bylsma	L.A.	79	3	6	9	-15	32	0	0	0	0	86	3.5
D	5	Aki Berg	L.A.	41	2	6	8	-9	24	2	0	0	0	65	3.1
C	23	Craig Johnson	L.A.	31	4	3	7	-7	26	1	0	0	0	30	13.3
L	41	Brent Grieve	L.A.	18	4	2	6	-2	15	0	0	1	0	50	8.0
D	15	Jaroslav Modry	L.A.	30	3	3	6	-13	25	1	1	0	0	32	9.4
L	40	Barry Potomski	L.A.	26	3	2	5	-8	93	0	0	1	0	18	16.7
D	29	Steven Finn	L.A.	54	2	3	5	-8	84	0	0	1	0	35	5.7
C	24	Nathan Lafayette	L.A.	15	1	3	4	-8	8	0	0	0	0	26	3.8
L	17	* Matt Johnson	L.A.	52	1	3	4	-4	194	0	0	0	0	20	5.0
C	37	Paul Dipietro	L.A.	6	1	0	1	-2	6	0	0	0	0	10	10.0
D	2	Doug Zmolek	L.A.	57	1	0	1	-22	116	0	0	0	0	28	3.6
G	32	J.C. Bergeron	L.A.	1	0	0	0	0	0	0	0	0	0	0	0.0
C	26	* Chris Marinucci	L.A.	1	0	0	0	-2	0	0	0	0	0	1	0.0
C	52	* Jason Morgan	L.A.	3	0	0	0	-3	0	0	0	0	0	4	0.0
G	1	* Jamie Storr	L.A.	5	0	0	0	0	0	0	0	0	0	0	0.0
D	7	* Steve McKenna	L.A.	9	0	0	0	1	37	0	0	0	0	0	0.0
G	34	Byron Dafoe	L.A.	40	0	0	0	0	0	0	0	0	0	0	0.0
G	35	Stephane Fiset	L.A.	44	0	0	2	0	0	0	0	0	0	0	0.0

Goaltending

No.	Goaltender	GPI	Mins	Avg	W	L	T	EN	SO	GA	SA	S%
1	* Jamie Storr	5	265	2.49	2	1	1	1	0	11	147	.925
34	Byron Dafoe	40	2162	3.11	13	17	5	4	0	112	1178	.905
35	Stephane Fiset	44	2482	3.19	13	24	5	4	4	132	1410	.906
32	J.C. Bergeron	1	56	4.29	0	1	0	0	0	4	35	.886
	Totals	82	4985	3.23	28	43	11	9	4	268	2779	.904

General Manager

TAYLOR, DAVE
General Manager, Los Angeles Kings. Born in Levack, Ont., December 4, 1955.

No player in the history of the Kings ever wore the uniform with more distinction and class than Dave Taylor. For 17 seasons, Taylor gave his all, both on and off the ice, receiving All-Star status for his outstanding play.

Fittingly, after finishing his illustrious career during the 1993-94 season, Taylor remains a key part of the Kings organization, now serving as vice president and general manager for the NHL club. Taylor, 41, assumed his current responsibilities on April 22, 1997, becoming the seventh GM in team history. He joined the Kings front office three years ago as an assistant to his predecessor, Sam McMaster.

An All-American hockey player while at Clarkson University, Taylor was relatively unknown when the Kings' picked him in the 15th round of the 1975 draft. His grit and work ethic kept him around long enough to hook up with a center named Marcel Dionne, who virtually ignited Taylor's career. As a member of the renowned "Triple Crown" line with Dionne and left winger Charlie Simmer, Taylor became a prolific scorer who also packed a fearsome check. Taylor's NHL career stats include a Kings-record 1,111 games, 431 goals, 638 assists and 1,069 points.

A five-time NHL All-Star Game selection, Taylor served as the Kings captain for four seasons (1985-89). After posting career highs in goals (47) and points (112) during the 1980-81 season, Taylor earned a spot on the NHL Second All-Star Team. On April 3, 1995, Taylor's jersey No. 18 was retired, joining Rogie Vachon (No. 30) and Marcel Dionne (No. 16) on the wall of the Great Western Forum. For all his individual accomplishments in hockey, his crowing glory was reaching the Stanley Cup Finals with the 1992-93 Kings.

Away from the ice, Taylor has worked tirelessly for numerous charities throughout the years. Each year he hosts the Dave Taylor Golf Classic benefiting the Cystic Fibrosis Foundation, which annually raises more than $125,000. In 1991, the NHL honored Taylor's contributions to hockey and the community by awarding him both the Masterton and King Clancy trophies.

Dave and his wife, Beth, live in Tarzana, CA with their daughters Jamie, 13, and Katie, 10.

Club Records

Team

(Figures in brackets for season records are games played; records for fewest points, wins, ties, losses, goals, goals against are for 70 or more games)

Most Points	105	1974-75 (80)	
Most Wins	46	1990-91 (80)	
Most Ties	21	1974-75 (80)	
Most Losses	52	1969-70 (76)	
Most Goals	376	1988-89 (80)	
Most Goals Against	389	1985-86 (80)	
Fewest Points	38	1969-70 (76)	
Fewest Wins	14	1969-70 (76)	
Fewest Ties	7	1988-89 (80), 1989-90 (80)	
Fewest Losses	17	1974-75 (80)	
Fewest Goals	168	1969-70 (76)	
Fewest Goals Against	185	1974-75 (80)	

Longest Winning Streak
Overall .... 8 Oct. 21-Nov. 7/72
Home .... 12 Oct. 10-Dec. 5/92
Away .... 8 Dec. 18/74-Jan. 16/75

Longest Undefeated Streak
Overall .... 11 Feb. 28-Mar. 24/74
(9 wins, 2 ties)
Home .... 13 Oct. 10-Dec. 8/92
(12 wins, 1 tie)
Away .... 11 Oct. 10-Dec. 11/74
(6 wins, 5 ties)

Longest Losing Streak
Overall .... 10 Feb. 22-Mar. 9/84
Home .... 9 Feb. 8-Mar. 12/86
Away .... 12 Jan. 11-Feb. 15/70

Longest Winless Streak
Overall .... 17 Jan. 29-Mar. 5/70
(13 losses, 4 ties)
Home .... 9 Jan. 29-Mar. 5/70
(8 losses, 1 tie),
Feb. 8-Mar. 12/86
(9 losses)
Away .... 21 Jan. 11-Apr. 3/70
(17 losses, 4 ties)
Most Shutouts, Season 9 1974-75 (80)
Most PIM, Season 2,228 1990-91 (80)
Most Goals, Game .... 12 Nov. 28/84
(Van. 1 at L.A. 12)

Individual

Most Seasons	17	Dave Taylor
Most Games	1,111	Dave Taylor
Most Goals, Career	550	Marcel Dionne
Most Assists, Career	757	Marcel Dionne
Most Points Career	1,307	Marcel Dionne
Most PIM, Career	1,846	Marty McSorley
Most Shutouts, Career	32	Rogie Vachon

Longest Consecutive
Games Streak .... 324 Marcel Dionne
(Jan. 7/78-Jan. 9/82)
Most Goals, Season .... 70 Bernie Nicholls
(1988-89)
Most Assists, Season .... 122 Wayne Gretzky
(1990-91)
Most Points, Season .... 168 Wayne Gretzky
(1988-89; 54G, 114A)
Most PIM, Season .... 399 Marty McSorley
(1992-93)

Most Points, Defenseman,
Season .... 76 Larry Murphy
(1980-81; 16G, 60A)
Most Points, Center,
Season .... 168 Wayne Gretzky
(1988-89; 54G, 114A)
Most Points, Right Wing,
Season .... 112 Dave Taylor
(1980-81; 47G, 65A)
Most Points, Left Wing,
Season .... *125 Luc Robitaille
(1992-93; 63G, 62A)
Most Points, Rookie,
Season .... 84 Luc Robitaille
(1986-87; 45G, 39A)
Most Shutouts, Season .... 8 Rogie Vachon
(1976-77)
Most Goals, Game .... 4 Several players
Most Assists, Game .... 6 Bernie Nicholls
(Dec. 1/88),
Tomas Sandstrom
(Oct. 9/93)
Most Points, Game .... 8 Bernie Nicholls
(Dec. 1/88; 2G, 6A)

* NHL Record.

Retired Numbers

16	Marcel Dionne	1975-1987
18	Dave Taylor	1977-1994
30	Rogatien Vachon	1971-1978

All-time Record vs. Other Clubs

Regular Season

	At Home						On Road							Total					
	GP	W	L	T	GF	GA	PTS	GP	W	L	T	GF	GA	PTS	GP	W	L	T	GF	GA	PTS
Anaheim	11	6	3	2	34	24	14	11	3	6	2	29	42	8	22	9	9	4	63	66	22
Boston	55	19	30	6	192	208	44	56	10	42	4	154	267	24	111	29	72	10	346	475	68
Buffalo	48	18	22	8	166	171	44	47	15	23	9	145	191	39	95	33	45	17	311	362	83
Calgary	76	37	30	9	296	282	83	79	21	49	9	260	371	51	155	58	79	18	556	653	134
Chicago	60	25	29	6	205	215	56	61	22	31	8	184	233	52	121	47	60	14	389	448	108
Colorado	28	16	10	2	119	94	34	27	11	13	3	106	115	25	55	27	23	5	225	209	59
Dallas	64	27	19	18	226	191	72	65	16	38	11	183	268	43	129	43	57	29	409	459	115
Detroit	66	35	18	13	279	208	83	65	27	28	10	240	265	64	131	62	46	23	519	473	147
Edmonton	62	24	25	13	262	271	61	63	16	33	14	240	309	46	125	40	58	27	502	580	107
Florida	3	1	2	0	8	13	2	3	0	2	1	4	11	1	6	1	4	1	12	24	3
Hartford	24	14	7	3	109	96	31	25	9	13	3	99	100	21	49	23	20	6	208	196	52
Montreal	60	17	34	9	187	239	43	59	7	41	11	153	277	25	119	24	75	20	340	516	68
New Jersey	37	26	5	6	192	115	58	37	15	17	5	133	129	35	74	41	22	11	325	244	93
NY Islanders	39	18	14	7	142	127	43	39	13	22	4	113	149	30	78	31	36	11	255	276	73
NY Rangers	54	21	24	9	181	196	51	53	15	33	5	151	214	35	107	36	57	14	332	410	86
Ottawa	4	4	0	0	24	9	8	4	1	2	1	11	14	3	8	5	2	1	35	23	11
Philadelphia	60	18	34	8	175	207	44	58	15	36	7	151	227	37	118	33	70	15	326	434	81
Phoenix	55	21	24	10	237	230	52	58	21	28	9	210	246	51	113	42	52	19	447	476	103
Pittsburgh	64	41	15	8	251	168	90	66	20	38	8	207	249	48	130	61	53	16	458	417	138
St. Louis	64	33	22	9	231	182	75	64	15	41	8	167	244	38	128	48	63	17	398	426	113
San Jose	18	12	5	1	68	50	25	18	6	9	3	61	70	15	36	18	14	4	129	120	40
Tampa Bay	5	0	5	0	11	21	0	4	2	2	0	9	10	4	9	2	7	0	20	31	4
Toronto	62	33	20	9	224	183	75	61	19	31	11	207	245	49	123	52	51	20	431	428	124
Vancouver	84	43	29	12	348	279	98	82	26	42	14	270	324	66	166	69	71	26	618	603	164
Washington	41	24	12	5	166	129	53	40	17	17	6	151	173	40	81	41	29	11	317	302	93
Defunct Clubs	35	27	6	2	141	76	56	34	11	14	9	91	109	31	69	38	20	11	232	185	87
Totals	**1179**	**560**	**444**	**175**	**4474**	**3984**	**1295**	**1179**	**353**	**651**	**175**	**3729**	**4852**	**881**	**2358**	**913**	**1095**	**350**	**8203**	**8836**	**2176**

Playoffs

	Series	W	L	GP	W	L	T	GF	GA	Last Mtg.	Round	Result
Boston	2	0	2	13	5	8	0	38	56	1977	QF	L 2-4
Calgary	6	4	2	26	13	13	0	105	112	1993	DSF	W 4-2
Chicago	1	0	1	5	1	4	0	7	10	1974	QF	L 1-4
Dallas	1	0	1	7	3	4	0	21	26	1968	QF	L 3-4
Edmonton	7	2	5	36	12	24	0	124	150	1992	DSF	L 2-4
Montreal	1	0	1	5	1	4	0	12	15	1993	F	L 1-4
NY Islanders	1	0	1	4	1	3	0	10	21	1980	PR	L 1-3
NY Rangers	2	0	2	6	1	5	0	14	32	1981	PR	L 1-3
St. Louis	1	0	1	4	0	4	0	5	16	1969	SF	L 0-4
Toronto	3	1	2	12	5	7	0	31	41	1993	CF	W 4-3
Vancouver	3	2	1	17	9	8	0	66	60	1993	DF	W 4-2
Defunct Clubs	1	1	0	7	4	3	0	23	25			
Totals	**29**	**10**	**19**	**142**	**55**	**87**	**0**	**459**	**568**			

Calgary totals include Atlanta, 1972-73 to 1979-80. Colorado totals include Quebec, 1979-80 to 1994-95.
Dallas totals include Minnesota, 1967-68 to 1992-93. New Jersey totals include Kansas City, 1974-75 to 1975-76, and
Colorado Rockies, 1976-77 to 1981-82. Phoenix totals include Winnipeg, 1979-80 to 1995-96.

Playoff Results 1997-93

Year	Round	Opponent	Result	GF	GA
1993	F	Montreal	L 1-4	12	15
	CF	Toronto	W 4-3	22	23
	DF	Vancouver	W 4-2	26	25
	DSF	Calgary	W 4-2	33	28

Abbreviations: Round: F – Final;
CF – conference final; **CQF** – conference quarter-final;
CSF – conference semi-final; **DF** – division final;
DSF – division semi-final; **SF** – semi-final;
QF – quarter-final; **PR** – preliminary round.

1996-97 Results

Oct.	4		NY Islanders	1-0		9	Buffalo	6-3
	6		San Jose	6-7		11	St. Louis	2-1
	9	at	Montreal	3-6		14	at Detroit	3-3
	10	at	Philadelphia	4-5		15	at Toronto	3-2
	12	at	Washington	4-3		21	New Jersey	1-4
	15		Philadelphia	3-2		22	at San Jose	2-7
	17		Boston	4-2		25	Anaheim	2-2
	20	at	Chicago	1-2		27	at Dallas	2-7
	21	at	Detroit	0-3		29	at Colorado	3-6
	24		Edmonton	2-8		30	Hartford	5-3
	26		Calgary	0-0	Feb.	1	Chicago	2-3
	29	at	Toronto	5-2		3	at Calgary	3-2
	31	at	Ottawa	2-2		5	at San Jose	2-3
Nov.	2	at	Hartford	3-2		9	at Dallas	1-2
	4	at	Boston	4-4		11	at Colorado	1-3
	7		Montreal	4-1		13	Toronto	4-4
	8	at	Anaheim	4-7		15	Edmonton	2-2
	14		Toronto	4-1		17	Dallas	1-2
	17	at	Chicago	4-2		18	at Phoenix	1-6
	19	at	Tampa Bay	0-3		20	Anaheim	2-2
	20	at	Florida	1-4		22	Vancouver	4-0
	23		Detroit	0-6		25	Colorado	3-1
	27	at	Edmonton	5-1		27	Edmonton	6-3
	28	at	Calgary	0-2	Mar.	1	at Vancouver	3-0
	30		Chicago	3-5		4	at Edmonton	1-4
Dec.	3	at	Phoenix	4-1		6	NY Rangers	2-6
	5		Tampa Bay	1-2		8	Ottawa	3-1
	7		Colorado	4-2		10	Detroit	3-3
	10		Pittsburgh	3-5		13	St. Louis	2-4
	12		Calgary	1-5		15	Calgary	2-5
	14		Washington	4-4		19	at Anaheim	2-6
	17	at	NY Islanders	3-4		22	San Jose	2-1
	18	at	NY Rangers	0-4		24	at Vancouver	2-2
	20	at	Buffalo	2-6		27	at St. Louis	1-2
	22	at	St. Louis	4-7		29	at Pittsburgh	1-4
	26		Phoenix	2-5		30	at New Jersey	3-5
	28		Colorado	2-5	Apr.	3	Phoenix	4-5
	30	at	Edmonton	1-2		5	Dallas	3-3
Jan.	2	at	Vancouver	3-4		9	at Anaheim	1-4
	4		Florida	0-5		12	San Jose	4-1
	7		Vancouver	6-2		13	at Colorado	4-2

Entry Draft
Selections 1997-83

1997
Pick
3	Olli Jokinen
15	Matt Zultek
29	Scott Barney
83	Joseph Corvo
99	Sean Blanchard
137	Richard Seeley
150	Jeff Katcher
193	Jay Kopischke
220	Konrad Brand

1996
Pick
30	Josh Green
37	Marian Cisar
57	Greg Phillips
84	Mikael Simons
96	Eric Belanger
120	Jesse Black
123	Peter Hogan
190	Stephen Valiquette
193	Kai Nurminen
219	Sebastien Simard

1995
Pick
3	Aki-Petteri Berg
33	Donald MacLean
50	Pavel Rosa
59	Vladimir Tsyplakov
118	Jason Morgan
137	Igor Melyakov
157	Benoit Larose
163	Juha Vuorivirta
215	Brian Stewart

1994
Pick
7	Jamie Storr
33	Matt Johnson
59	Vitali Yachmenev
111	Chris Schmidt
163	Luc Gagne
189	Andrew Dale
215	Jan Nemecek
241	Sergei Shalomai

1993
Pick
42	Shayne Toporowski
68	Jeffrey Mitchell
94	Bob Wren
105	Frederick Beaubien
117	Jason Saal
120	Tomas Vlasak
146	Jere Karalahti
172	Justin Martin
198	John-Tra Dillabough
224	Martin Strbak
250	Kimmo Timonen
276	Patrick Howald

1992
Pick
39	Justin Hocking
63	Sandy Allan
87	Kevin Brown
111	Jeff Shevalier
135	Raymond Murray
207	Magnus Wernblom
231	Ryan Pisiak
255	Jukka Tiilikainen

1991
Pick
42	Guy Leveque
79	Keith Redmond
81	Alexei Zhitnik
108	Pauli Jaks
130	Brett Seguin
152	Kelly Fairchild
196	Craig Brown
218	Mattias Olsson
240	Andre Bouliane
262	Michael Gaul

1990
Pick
7	Darryl Sydor
28	Brandy Semchuk
49	Bob Berg
91	David Goverde
112	Erik Andersson
133	Robert Lang
154	Dean Hulett
175	Denis LeBlanc
196	Patrik Ross
217	K.J. (Kevin) White
238	Troy Mohns

1989
Pick
39	Brent Thompson
81	Jim Maher
102	Eric Ricard
103	Thomas Newman
123	Daniel Rydmark
144	Ted Kramer
165	Sean Whyte
182	Jim Giacin
186	Martin Maskarinec
207	Jim Hiller
228	Steve Jaques
249	Kevin Sneddon

1988
Pick
7	Martin Gelinas
28	Paul Holden
49	John Van Kessel
70	Rob Blake
91	Jeff Robison
109	Micah Aivazoff
112	Robert Larsson
133	Jeff Kruesel
154	Timo Peltomaa
175	Jim Larkin
196	Brad Hyatt
217	Doug Laprade
238	Joe Flanagan

1987
Pick
4	Wayne McBean
27	Mark Fitzpatrick
43	Ross Wilson
90	Mike Vukonich
111	Greg Batters
132	Kyosti Karjalainen
174	Jeff Gawlicki
195	John Preston
216	Rostislav Vlach
237	Mikael Lindholm

1986
Pick
2	Jimmy Carson
44	Denis Larocque
65	Sylvain Couturier
86	Dave Guden
107	Robb Stauber
128	Sean Krakiwsky
149	Rene Chapdelaine
170	Trevor Pochipinski
191	Paul Kelly
212	Russ Mann
233	Brian Hayton

1985
Pick
9	Craig Duncanson
10	Dan Gratton
30	Par Edlund
72	Perry Florio
93	Petr Prajsler
135	Tim Flannigan
156	John Hyduke
177	Steve Horner
219	Trent Ciprick
240	Marian Horwath

1984
Pick
6	Craig Redmond
24	Brian Wilks
48	John English
69	Tom Glavine
87	Dave Grannis
108	Greg Strome
129	Tim Hanley
150	Shannon Deegan
171	Luc Robitaille
191	Jeff Crossman
212	Paul Kenny
232	Brian Martin

1983
Pick
47	Bruce Shoebottom
67	Guy Benoit
87	Bob LaForest
100	Garry Galley
107	Dave Lundmark
108	Kevin Stevens
127	Tim Burgess
147	Ken Hammond
167	Bruce Fishback
187	Thomas Ahlen
207	Miroslav Blaha
227	Chad Johnson

Coach

ROBINSON, LARRY
Coach, Los Angeles Kings. Born in Winchester, Ont., June 2, 1951.

Larry Robinson enters his third season as head coach in 1997-98. Robinson became the 18th head coach of the Los Angeles Kings on July 26, 1995, replacing Barry Melrose (Rogie Vachon served as interim coach for the final seven games of the 1994-95 season). He served as an assistant coach with the New Jersey Devils the previous two seasons, helping them win the Stanley Cup in 1995. One of the great defensemen in NHL history, Robinson enjoyed a stellar 20-year playing career with the Montreal Canadiens and the Kings (1972-73–1991-92). In his 17 seasons with Montreal, the Habs won five Stanley Cups, including four straight (1975-76–1978-79). Robinson played in 1,384 career games (9th all-time), scoring 208 goals, 750 assists (3rd all-time) and 958 points (4th all-time defenseman). In playoff action, he holds NHL records for most career games played (227) and most consecutive years in playoffs (20). Robinson's individual honors include two Norris Trophies as the NHL's top defenseman, a Conn Smythe Trophy as playoff MVP, three seasons each as a First Team All-Star and Second Team All-Star, and 10 appearances in the NHL All-Star Game.

Coaching Record

			Regular Season				Playoffs			
Season	Team	Games	W	L	T	%	Games	W	L	%
1995-96	Los Angeles (NHL)	82	24	40	18	.402	....	....	....	....
1996-97	Los Angeles (NHL)	82	28	43	11	.409	....	....	....	....
	NHL Totals	164	52	83	29	.405	....	....	....	....

Club Directory

The Great Western Forum
P.O. Box 17013
3900 West Manchester Blvd.
Inglewood, CA 90308
Phone 310/419-3160
GM FAX 310/672-1490
PR FAX 310/673-8927
Capacity: 16,005

Executive
Owner	Philip F. Anschutz
Owner	Edward P. Roski
Governor	Robert Sanderman
President	Tim Leiweke
Vice President, New Business Development	Mitch Huberman
Vice President and Chief Financial Officer	Dan Beckerman
Vice President, Marketing	John Cimperman
Vice President, General Counsel	Ted Fikre
Vice President, Special Projects	Rogie Vachon
Executive Assistant to the President	Celeste Grant
Executive Assistant to V.P., New Business Development	TBA
Executive Assistant to V.P., Business Operations	TBA
Executive Assistant to V.P., Marketing	Jackie Howard
Executive Assistant to V.P., General Counsel	TBA

Hockey Operations
Vice President/General Manager	Dave Taylor
Director of Player Personnel	Bill O'Flaherty
Assistant to General Manager	John Wolf
Executive Assistant to General Manager	Marcia Galloway
Head Coach	Larry Robinson
Assistant Coaches	Rick Green, Jay Leach
Goaltending Coach	Don Edwards
Director of Amateur Scouting	Al Murray
Director of Pro Scouting	Ace Bailey
Scouting Staff	Serge Aubry, Greg Dreschel, Rob Laird, Vaclav Nedomansky, John Stanton, Ari Vuori
Video Coordinator	Bill Gurney

Medical Staff
Trainer	Pete Demers
Equipment Manager	Peter Millar
Assistant Equipment Manager	Rick Garcia
Equipment Assistant	Greg Brohamer
Rehabilitation Trainer/Strength and Conditioning Coordinator	Robert Zolg
Fitness Consultant	Guy LeMasurier
Massage Therapist	Dan Garcia
Team Physicians	Dr. Ronald Kvitne, Kerlan/Jobe Orthopaedic Clinic
Internist	Dr. Michael Mellman
Dentist	Dr. Jeffrey Hoy
Opthamologist	Dr. Howard Lazerson

Communications
Director, Media Relations	Mike Altieri
Director, Community Relations	Kelly Malcomb Davis
Manager, Fan Development	Steve Bogoyevac
Community Relations Coordinator	Jill Berke
Media Relations/Team Services Coordinator	Jeff Moeller
Media Relations Assistant	Michael Jund
Team Photographer	Andrew Bernstein
Receptionist	TBA

Personnel/Accounting
Director, Human Resources	Barbara Mendez
Director, Finance	Peter Mazur
Manager, Accounting	Lisa Ashworth
Accounts Payable	Emma Harris
Accounts Receivable	Heather O'Conner
Assistant, Human Resources	Elizabeth Tutt

Marketing/Corporate Sales
Director, Corporate Sales	Sergio del Prado
Director, Marketing and Promotions	Kurt Schwartzkopf
Manager, Corporate Sales	Susan Long
Corporate Account Executives	Karen Marumoto, Tracy Hartman, Scott Litner
Client Service Coordinators	Tami Cole, Annie Goshert, David Newman

Ticket Sales/Operations
Director, Sales	Steve DeLay
Director, Ticket Operations	Bill Chapin
Manager, Premium Seating	Anthony Jones
Manager, Group Sales	Lynn Wittenburg
Manager, Ticket Operations	Chris Cockrell
Manager, Information Services	Scott Andrews
Season Seats, Group	Matthew Cohen, Marne Orsillo
Sales Coordinator	Myrna Powell
Ticket Coordinators	Robert Anderson, Nell Nicolas
Account Executives	Garrett Kakita, Chris Maier, Christopher McGowan, Jeff Olsen

Entertainment and Events
Director, Entertainment and Events	TBA
Public Address Announcer	David Courtney
Supervisor, Off-Ice Officials	Bill Meuris

Broadcasting
Play-by-Play Announcer, Television	Bob Miller
Color Commentator, Television	Jim Fox
Play-by-Play Announcer, Radio	Nick Nickson
Color Commentator, Radio	Mike Allison
Television Station	Fox Sports West
Radio Station	XTRA Sports (690 AM)
Spanish Radio Station	KWIZ (1480 AM)

General Information
Dimensions of Rink	200 feet by 85 feet
Colors	Black, White and Silver
Training Camp	Iceoplex, North Hills, CA
Location of Press Box	West Colonnade, Sec. 28, Rows 1-12
Web Site address	www.lakings.com

Montreal Canadiens

1996-97 Results: 31W-36L-15T 77PTS. Fourth, Northeast Division

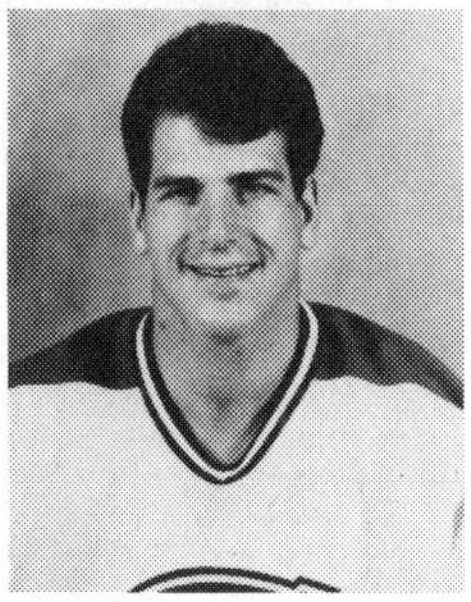

Mark Recchi's hard work, determination and soft hands resulted in a team-leading 34 goals in 1996-97.

1997-98 Schedule

Month	Day	Date	Opponent	Month	Day	Date	Opponent
Oct.	Wed.	1	Ottawa		Wed.	31	at Calgary
	Sat.	4	at Boston	Jan.	Fri.	2	at Edmonton
	Wed.	8	at Pittsburgh		Sat.	3	at Vancouver
	Sat.	11	Philadelphia		Wed.	7	Boston
	Wed.	15	Pittsburgh		Thu.	8	at NY Islanders
	Fri.	17	at Buffalo		Sat.	10	NY Rangers
	Sat.	18	Washington		Mon.	12	at Tampa Bay
	Wed.	22	Florida		Wed.	14	at Philadelphia
	Thu.	23	at New Jersey		Wed.	21	Boston
	Sat.	25	at Ottawa		Sat.	24	Carolina*
	Mon.	27	Chicago		Sun.	25	New Jersey*
	Wed.	29	NY Islanders		Thu.	29	at Philadelphia
Nov.	Sat.	1	Toronto		Sat.	31	Ottawa
	Mon.	3	Dallas	Feb.	Sun.	1	at Carolina
	Wed.	5	Phoenix		Wed.	4	at NY Islanders
	Fri.	7	at San Jose		Sat.	7	Buffalo
	Sat.	8	at Los Angeles		Wed.	25	Pittsburgh
	Wed.	12	at Anaheim		Sat.	28	at Toronto
	Thu.	13	at Phoenix	Mar.	Wed.	4	at Dallas
	Sat.	15	Washington		Thu.	5	at St. Louis
	Mon.	17	Tampa Bay		Sat.	7	Buffalo
	Wed.	19	at Carolina		Mon.	9	Florida
	Sat.	22	Detroit		Wed.	11	Vancouver
	Mon.	24	San Jose		Sat.	14	New Jersey
	Wed.	26	at Washington		Mon.	16	Calgary
	Fri.	28	at Detroit		Wed.	18	at NY Rangers
	Sat.	29	at Pittsburgh		Thu.	19	at Chicago
Dec.	Mon.	1	Pittsburgh		Sat.	21	Anaheim
	Wed.	3	Los Angeles		Wed.	25	at Tampa Bay
	Sat.	6	NY Rangers		Thu.	26	at Florida
	Mon.	8	Colorado		Sat.	28	Tampa Bay
	Wed.	10	St. Louis		Tue.	31	at Carolina
	Fri.	12	at New Jersey	Apr.	Wed.	1	at Florida
	Sat.	13	at Boston		Sat.	4	Carolina
	Mon.	15	Philadelphia		Mon.	6	at Washington
	Fri.	19	at Buffalo		Tue.	7	at NY Rangers
	Sat.	20	Ottawa		Fri.	10	at Buffalo
	Mon.	22	Edmonton		Sat.	11	NY Islanders
	Tue.	23	at Ottawa		Wed.	15	Boston
	Sat.	27	at Pittsburgh		Thu.	16	at Ottawa
	Mon.	29	at Colorado		Sat.	18	Buffalo

* Denotes afternoon game.

Franchise date: November 22, 1917

EASTERN CONFERENCE

NORTHEAST DIVISION

81st NHL Season

Year-by-Year Record

		Home			Road			Overall							
Season	**GP**	**W**	**L**	**T**	**W**	**L**	**T**	**W**	**L**	**T**	**GF**	**GA**	**Pts.**	**Finished**	**Playoff Result**
1996-97	82	17	17	7	14	19	8	31	36	15	249	276	77	4th, Northeast Div.	Lost Conf. Quarter-Final
1995-96	82	23	12	6	17	20	4	40	32	10	265	248	90	3rd, Northeast Div.	Lost Conf. Quarter-Final
1994-95	48	15	5	4	3	18	3	18	23	7	125	148	43	6th, Northeast Div.	Out of Playoffs
1993-94	84	26	12	4	15	17	10	41	29	14	283	248	96	3rd, Northeast Div.	Lost Conf. Quarter-Final
1992-93	**84**	**27**	**13**	**2**	**21**	**17**	**4**	**48**	**30**	**6**	**326**	**280**	**102**	**3rd, Adams Div.**	**Won Stanley Cup**
1991-92	80	27	8	5	14	20	6	41	28	11	267	207	93	1st, Adams Div.	Lost Div. Final
1990-91	80	23	12	5	16	18	6	39	30	11	273	249	89	2nd, Adams Div.	Lost Div. Final
1989-90	80	26	8	6	15	20	5	41	28	11	288	234	93	3rd, Adams Div.	Lost Div. Final
1988-89	80	30	6	4	23	12	5	53	18	9	315	218	115	1st, Adams Div.	Lost Final
1987-88	80	26	8	6	19	14	7	45	22	13	298	238	103	1st, Adams Div.	Lost Div. Final
1986-87	80	27	9	4	14	20	6	41	29	10	277	241	92	2nd, Adams Div.	Lost Conf. Championship
1985-86	**80**	**25**	**11**	**4**	**15**	**22**	**3**	**40**	**33**	**7**	**330**	**280**	**87**	**2nd, Adams Div.**	**Won Stanley Cup**
1984-85	80	24	10	6	17	17	6	41	27	12	309	262	94	1st, Adams Div.	Lost Div. Final
1983-84	80	19	19	2	16	21	3	35	40	5	286	295	75	4th, Adams Div.	Lost Conf. Championship
1982-83	80	25	6	9	17	18	5	42	24	14	350	286	98	2nd, Adams Div.	Lost Div. Semi-Final
1981-82	80	25	6	9	21	11	8	46	17	17	360	223	109	1st, Adams Div.	Lost Div. Semi-Final
1980-81	80	31	7	2	14	15	11	45	22	13	332	232	103	1st, Norris Div.	Lost Prelim. Round
1979-80	80	30	7	3	17	13	10	47	20	13	328	240	107	1st, Norris Div.	Lost Quarter-Final
1978-79	**80**	**29**	**6**	**5**	**23**	**11**	**6**	**52**	**17**	**11**	**337**	**204**	**115**	**1st, Norris Div.**	**Won Stanley Cup**
1977-78	**80**	**32**	**4**	**4**	**27**	**6**	**7**	**59**	**10**	**11**	**359**	**183**	**129**	**1st, Norris Div.**	**Won Stanley Cup**
1976-77	**80**	**33**	**1**	**6**	**27**	**7**	**6**	**60**	**8**	**12**	**387**	**171**	**132**	**1st, Norris Div.**	**Won Stanley Cup**
1975-76	**80**	**32**	**3**	**5**	**26**	**8**	**6**	**58**	**11**	**11**	**337**	**174**	**127**	**1st, Norris Div.**	**Won Stanley Cup**
1974-75	80	27	8	5	20	6	14	47	14	19	374	225	113	1st, Norris Div.	Lost Semi-Final
1973-74	78	24	12	3	21	12	6	45	24	9	293	240	99	2nd, East Div.	Lost Quarter-inal
1972-73	**78**	**29**	**4**	**6**	**23**	**6**	**10**	**52**	**10**	**16**	**329**	**184**	**120**	**1st, East Div.**	**Won Stanley Cup**
1971-72	78	29	3	7	17	13	9	46	16	16	307	205	108	3rd, East Div.	Lost Quarter-Final
1970-71	**78**	**29**	**7**	**3**	**13**	**16**	**10**	**42**	**23**	**13**	**291**	**216**	**97**	**3rd, East Div.**	**Won Stanley Cup**
1969-70	76	21	9	8	17	13	8	38	22	16	244	201	92	5th, East Div.	Out of Playoffs
1968-69	**76**	**26**	**7**	**5**	**20**	**12**	**6**	**46**	**19**	**11**	**271**	**202**	**103**	**1st, East Div.**	**Won Stanley Cup**
1967-68	**74**	**26**	**5**	**6**	**16**	**17**	**4**	**42**	**22**	**10**	**236**	**167**	**94**	**1st, East Div.**	**Won Stanley Cup**
1966-67	70	19	9	7	13	16	6	32	25	13	202	188	77	2nd,	Lost Final
1965-66	**70**	**23**	**11**	**1**	**18**	**10**	**7**	**41**	**21**	**8**	**239**	**173**	**90**	**1st,**	**Won Stanley Cup**
1964-65	**70**	**20**	**8**	**7**	**16**	**15**	**4**	**36**	**23**	**11**	**211**	**185**	**83**	**2nd,**	**Won Stanley Cup**
1963-64	70	22	7	6	14	14	7	36	21	13	209	167	85	1st,	Lost Semi-Final
1962-63	70	15	10	10	13	9	13	28	19	23	225	183	79	3rd,	Lost Semi-Final
1961-62	70	26	2	7	16	12	7	42	14	14	259	166	98	1st,	Lost Semi-Final
1960-61	70	24	6	5	17	13	5	41	19	10	254	188	92	1st,	Lost Semi-Final
1959-60	**70**	**23**	**4**	**8**	**17**	**14**	**4**	**40**	**18**	**12**	**255**	**178**	**92**	**1st,**	**Won Stanley Cup**
1958-59	**70**	**21**	**8**	**6**	**18**	**10**	**7**	**39**	**18**	**13**	**258**	**158**	**91**	**1st,**	**Won Stanley Cup**
1957-58	**70**	**23**	**8**	**4**	**20**	**9**	**6**	**43**	**17**	**10**	**250**	**158**	**96**	**1st,**	**Won Stanley Cup**
1956-57	**70**	**23**	**6**	**6**	**12**	**17**	**6**	**35**	**23**	**12**	**210**	**155**	**82**	**2nd,**	**Won Stanley Cup**
1955-56	**70**	**29**	**5**	**1**	**16**	**10**	**9**	**45**	**15**	**10**	**222**	**131**	**100**	**1st,**	**Won Stanley Cup**
1954-55	70	26	5	4	15	13	7	41	18	11	228	157	93	2nd,	Lost Final
1953-54	70	27	5	3	8	19	8	35	24	11	195	141	81	2nd,	Lost Final
1952-53	**70**	**18**	**12**	**5**	**10**	**11**	**14**	**28**	**23**	**19**	**155**	**148**	**75**	**2nd,**	**Won Stanley Cup**
1951-52	70	22	8	5	12	18	5	34	26	10	195	164	78	2nd,	Lost Final
1950-51	70	17	10	8	8	20	7	25	30	15	173	184	65	3rd,	Lost Final
1949-50	70	17	8	10	12	14	9	29	22	19	172	150	77	2nd,	Lost Semi-Final
1948-49	60	19	8	3	9	15	6	28	23	9	152	126	65	3rd,	Lost Semi-Final
1947-48	60	13	13	4	7	16	7	20	29	11	147	169	51	5th,	Out of Playoffs
1946-47	60	19	6	5	15	10	5	34	16	10	189	138	78	1st,	Lost Final
1945-46	**50**	**16**	**6**	**3**	**12**	**11**	**2**	**28**	**17**	**5**	**172**	**134**	**61**	**1st,**	**Won Stanley Cup**
1944-45	50	21	2	2	17	6	2	38	8	4	228	121	80	1st,	Lost Semi-Final
1943-44	**50**	**22**	**0**	**3**	**16**	**5**	**4**	**38**	**5**	**7**	**234**	**109**	**83**	**1st,**	**Won Stanley Cup**
1942-43	50	14	4	7	5	15	5	19	19	12	181	191	50	4th,	Lost Semi-Final
1941-42	48	12	10	2	6	17	1	18	27	3	134	173	39	6th,	Lost Quarter-Final
1940-41	48	11	9	4	5	17	2	16	26	6	121	147	38	6th,	Lost Quarter-Final
1939-40	48	5	14	5	5	19	0	10	33	5	90	167	25	7th,	Out of Playoffs
1938-39	48	8	11	5	7	13	4	15	24	9	115	146	39	6th,	Lost Quarter-Final
1937-38	48	13	4	7	5	13	6	18	17	13	123	128	49	3rd, Cdn. Div.	Lost Quarter-Final
1936-37	48	16	8	0	8	10	6	24	18	6	115	111	54	1st, Cdn. Div.	Lost Semi-Final
1935-36	48	5	11	8	6	15	3	11	26	11	82	123	33	4th, Cdn. Div.	Out of Playoffs
1934-35	48	11	11	2	8	12	4	19	23	6	110	145	44	3rd, Cdn. Div.	Lost Quarter-Final
1933-34	48	16	6	2	6	14	4	22	20	6	99	101	50	2nd, Cdn. Div.	Lost Quarter-Final
1932-33	48	15	5	4	3	20	1	18	25	5	92	115	41	3rd, Cdn. Div.	Lost Quarter-Final
1931-32	48	18	3	3	7	13	4	25	16	7	128	111	57	1st, Cdn. Div.	Lost Semi-Final
1930-31	**44**	**15**	**3**	**4**	**11**	**7**	**4**	**26**	**10**	**8**	**129**	**89**	**60**	**1st, Cdn. Div.**	**Won Stanley Cup**
1929-30	**44**	**13**	**5**	**4**	**8**	**9**	**5**	**21**	**14**	**9**	**142**	**114**	**51**	**2nd, Cdn. Div.**	**Won Stanley Cup**
1928-29	44	12	4	6	10	3	9	22	7	15	71	43	59	1st, Cdn. Div.	Lost Semi-Final
1927-28	44	12	7	3	14	4	4	26	11	7	116	48	59	1st, Cdn. Div.	Lost Semi-Final
1926-27	44	15	5	2	13	9	0	28	14	2	99	67	58	2nd, Cdn. Div.	Lost Semi-Final
1925-26	36	5	12	1	6	12	0	11	24	1	79	108	23	7th,	Out of Playoffs
1924-25	30	10	5	0	7	6	2	17	11	2	93	56	36	3rd,	Lost Final
1923-24	**24**	**10**	**2**	**0**	**3**	**9**	**0**	**13**	**11**	**0**	**59**	**48**	**26**	**2nd,**	**Won Stanley Cup**
1922-23	24	10	2	0	3	7	2	13	9	2	73	61	28	2nd,	Lost NHL Final
1921-22	24	8	3	1	4	8	0	12	11	1	88	94	25	3rd,	Out of Playoffs
1920-21	24	9	3	0	4	8	0	13	11	0	112	99	26	3rd and 2nd*	Out of Playoffs
1919-20	24	8	4	0	5	7	0	13	11	0	129	113	26	2nd and 3rd*	Out of Playoffs
1918-19	18	7	2	0	3	6	0	10	8	0	88	78	20	1st and 2nd*	Cup Final but no Decision
1917-18	22	8	3	0	5	6	0	13	9	0	115	84	26	1st and 3rd*	Lost NHL Final

* Season played in two halves with no combined standing at end.
From 1917-18 through 1925-26, NHL champions played against PCHA champions for Stanley Cup.

1997-98 Player Personnel

FORWARDS	HT	WT	S	Place of Birth	Date	1996-97 Club
BORDELEAU, Sebastien	5-11	187	R	Vancouver, B.C.	2/15/75	Montreal-Fredericton
BRUNET, Benoit	5-11	195	L	Pointe-Claire, Que.	8/24/68	Montreal
BURE, Valeri	5-10	168	R	Moscow, USSR	6/13/74	Montreal
BUREAU, Marc	6-1	198	R	Trois-Rivières, Que.	5/19/66	Montreal
CORSON, Shayne	6-1	200	L	Midland, Ont.	8/13/66	St. Louis-Montreal
CRONAN, Earl	6-1	210	L	Warwick, RI	1/2/73	Fredericton
DAMPHOUSSE, Vincent	6-1	195	L	Montreal, Que.	12/17/67	Montreal
DELISLE, Jonathan	5-10	186	R	Ste-Anne-des-Plaines, Que.	6/30/77	Hull
HOUDE, Eric	5-11	185	L	Montreal, Que.	12/19/76	Montreal-Fredericton
HOULE, Jean-Francois	5-9	175	L	Charlesbourg, Que.	1/14/75	Clarkson
KOIVU, Saku	5-9	175	L	Turku, Finland	11/23/74	Montreal
LING, David	5-9	185	R	Halifax, N.S.	1/9/75	Saint John-Montreal-Fredericton
MORIN, Olivier	6-1	176	R	Montreal, Que.	4/2/78	Chicoutimi
OLSON, Boyd	6-1	173	L	Edmonton, Alta.	4/4/76	Fredericton
RECCHI, Mark	5-10	180	L	Kamloops, B.C.	2/1/68	Montreal
RICHER, Stephane	6-2	215	R	Ripon, Que.	6/7/66	Montreal
RUCINSKY, Martin	6-0	198	L	Most, Czech.	3/11/71	Montreal
RYAN, Terry	6-2	198	L	St. John's, Nfld.	1/14/77	Montreal-Red Deer
SAVAGE, Brian	6-1	190	L	Sudbury, Ont.	2/24/71	Montreal
STEVENSON, Turner	6-3	215	R	Prince George, B.C.	5/18/72	Montreal
THORNTON, Scott	6-3	210	L	London, Ont.	1/9/71	Montreal
TUCKER, Darcy	5-10	179	L	Castor, Alta.	3/15/75	Montreal
DEFENSEMEN						
BRISEBOIS, Patrice	6-1	188	R	Montreal, Que.	1/27/71	Montreal
BROWN, Brad	6-3	220	R	Baie Verte, Nfld.	12/27/75	Montreal-Fredericton
CHEREDARYK, Steve	6-2	197	L	Calgary, Alta.	11/20/75	Sprfld-Fred-Mississippi
CULLIMORE, Jassen	6-5	225	L	Simcoe, Ont.	12/4/72	Vancouver-Montreal
DARLING, Dion	6-3	220	L	Edmonton, Alta.	10/22/74	Fredericton
DROLET, Jimmy	6-0	187	L	Vanier, Que.	2/19/76	Fredericton
GROLEAU, Francois	6-0	197	L	Longueuil, Que.	1/23/73	Montreal-Fredericton
GUREN, Miloslav	6-2	215	L	Uherske. Hradiste, Czech.	9/24/76	Fredericton
MALAKHOV, Vladimir	6-3	220	L	Sverdlovsk, USSR	8/30/68	Montreal
MANSON, Dave	6-2	202	L	Prince Albert, Sask.	1/27/67	Phoenix-Montreal
POPOVIC, Peter	6-6	235	L	Koping, Sweden	2/10/68	Montreal
QUINTAL, Stephane	6-3	225	R	Boucherville, Que.	10/22/68	Montreal
RIVET, Craig	6-1	190	R	North Bay, Ont.	9/13/74	Montreal-Fredericton
ROBIDAS, Stephane	5-11	192	R	Sherbrooke, Que.	3/3/77	Shawinigan
WILKIE, David	6-2	210	R	Ellensburgh, WA	5/30/74	Montreal

GOALTENDERS	HT	WT	C	Place of Birth	Date	1996-97 Club
CAVICCHI, Trent	6-3	187	L	Halifax, N.S.	8/11/74	Knoxville-Raleigh
MOOG, Andy	5-8	175	L	Penticton, B.C.	2/18/60	Dallas
THEODORE, Jose	5-11	181	R	Laval, Que.	9/13/76	Montreal-Fredericton
THIBAULT, Jocelyn	5-11	170	L	Montreal, Que.	1/12/75	Montreal
VOKOUN, Tomas	5-11	208	R	Karlovy Vary, Czech.	7/2/76	Montreal-Fredericton

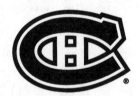

Coach

VIGNEAULT, ALAIN
Coach, Montreal Canadiens. Born in Quebec, Que., May 14, 1961.

Alain Vigneault was named the 24th head coach in the history of the Montreal Canadiens on May 26, 1997. Vigneault coached the QMJHL Beauport Harfangs for the past two seasons, following more than three seasons as an assistant coach with the NHL Ottawa Senators. Before joining the Senators, Vigneault was the head coach of the Hull Olympiques for five years (1987 to 1992), leading his team to the Memorial Cup Tournament in his first season. Alain Vigneault's coaching record at the junior hockey level shows 296 victories, 249 losses and 35 ties. In 580 games, he posted a .541 winning percentage. Vigneault was assistant coach for Canada's National Junior Team in 1989 and 1991, winning the gold medal at the 1991 World Junior Championships. He was honored once as CHL coach of the year (1987-88), and twice as head coach of the QMJHL Second All-Star Team. Alain Vigneault played for two seasons in the NHL after being drafted by the St. Louis Blues in the 1981 NHL Entry Draft. In 46 NHL games (including playoffs), he recorded a total of eight points (2 goals, 6 assists) and 108 penalty minutes.

Coaching Record

		Regular Season					Playoffs			
Season	Team	Games	W	L	T	%	Games	W	L	%
1986-87	Trois-Rivières (QMJHL)	65	26	37	2	.415	....	....	....	....
1987-88	Hull (QMJHL)	70	43	23	4	.643	....	....	....	....
1988-89	Hull (QMJHL)	66	36	25	5	.583	....	....	....	....
1989-90	Hull (QMJHL)	70	36	29	5	.550	....	....	....	....
1990-91	Hull (QMJHL)	65	33	25	7	.562	....	....	....	....
1991-92	Hull (QMJHL)	68	40	23	5	.625	....	....	....	....
1995-96	Beauport (QMJHL)	31	19	7	5	.694	....	....	....	....
1996-97	Beauport (QMJHL)	70	24	44	2	.357	....	....	....	....

1996-97 Scoring

* – rookie

Regular Season

Pos	#	Player	Team	GP	G	A	Pts	+/–	PIM	PP	SH	GW	GT	S	%
C	25	Vincent Damphousse	MTL	82	27	54	81	-6	82	7	2	3	2	244	11.1
R	8	Mark Recchi	MTL	82	34	46	80	-1	58	7	2	3	0	202	16.8
L	49	Brian Savage	MTL	81	23	37	60	-14	39	5	0	2	0	219	10.5
C	11	Saku Koivu	MTL	50	17	39	56	7	38	5	0	3	0	135	12.6
L	26	Martin Rucinsky	MTL	70	28	27	55	1	62	6	3	3	1	172	16.3
R	44	Stephane Richer	MTL	63	22	24	46	0	32	2	0	2	1	126	17.5
R	18	Valeri Bure	MTL	64	14	21	35	4	6	4	0	2	1	131	10.7
D	38	Vladimir Malakhov	MTL	65	10	20	30	3	43	5	0	1	0	177	5.6
L	27	Shayne Corson	STL	11	2	1	3	-4	24	1	0	0	0	19	10.5
			MTL	47	6	15	21	-5	80	2	0	2	0	96	6.3
			TOTAL	58	8	16	24	-9	104	3	0	2	0	115	7.0
L	17	Benoit Brunet	MTL	39	10	13	23	6	14	2	0	2	1	63	15.9
D	5	Stephane Quintal	MTL	71	7	15	22	1	100	1	0	0	0	139	5.0
D	37	Dave Manson	PHO	66	3	17	20	-25	164	2	0	0	0	153	2.0
			MTL	9	1	1	2	-1	23	0	0	0	0	22	4.5
			TOTAL	75	4	18	22	-26	187	2	0	0	0	175	2.3
R	30	Turner Stevenson	MTL	65	8	13	21	-14	97	1	0	0	0	76	10.5
C	24	Scott Thornton	MTL	73	10	10	20	-19	128	1	1	1	0	110	9.1
C	42	* Darcy Tucker	MTL	73	7	13	20	-5	110	1	0	3	1	62	11.3
C	28	Marc Bureau	MTL	43	6	9	15	4	16	1	1	2	0	56	10.7
D	3	* David Wilkie	MTL	61	6	9	15	-9	63	3	0	0	0	65	9.2
D	43	Patrice Brisebois	MTL	49	2	13	15	-7	24	0	0	1	0	72	2.8
D	34	Peter Popovic	MTL	78	1	13	14	9	32	0	0	0	0	82	1.2
C	71	* Sebastien Bordeleau	MTL	28	2	9	11	-3	2	0	0	0	0	27	7.4
D	35	Jassen Cullimore	VAN	3	0	0	0	-2	2	0	0	0	0	2	0.0
			MTL	49	2	6	8	4	42	0	1	1	0	52	3.8
			TOTAL	52	2	6	8	2	44	0	1	1	0	54	3.7
D	52	* Craig Rivet	MTL	35	0	4	4	7	54	0	0	0	0	24	0.0
C	20	* Eric Houde	MTL	13	0	2	2	1	2	0	0	0	0	1	0.0
G	37	* Tomas Vokoun	MTL	1	0	0	0	0	0	0	0	0	0	0	0.0
R	51	* David Ling	MTL	2	0	0	0	0	0	0	0	0	0	0	0.0
L	14	* Terry Ryan	MTL	3	0	0	0	0	0	0	0	0	0	0	0.0
D	48	* Francois Groleau	MTL	5	0	0	0	0	4	0	0	0	0	3	0.0
D	32	* Brad Brown	MTL	8	0	0	0	-1	22	0	0	0	0	0	0.0
L	15	Pierre Sevigny	MTL	13	0	0	0	0	5	0	0	0	0	1	0.0
G	60	* Jose Theodore	MTL	16	0	0	0	0	0	0	0	0	0	0	0.0
G	41	Jocelyn Thibault	MTL	61	0	0	0	0	0	0	0	0	0	0	0.0

Goaltending

No.	Goaltender	GPI	Mins	Avg	W	L	T	EN	SO	GA	SA	S%
41	Jocelyn Thibault	61	3397	2.90	22	24	11	5	1	164	1815	.910
60	* Jose Theodore	16	821	3.87	5	6	2	0	0	53	508	.896
39	Pat Jablonski	17	754	3.98	4	6	2	0	0	50	438	.886
37	* Tomas Vokoun	1	20	12.00	0	0	0	0	0	4	14	.714
	Totals	**82**	**5008**	**3.31**	**31**	**36**	**15**	**5**	**1**	**276**	**2780**	**.901**

Playoffs

Pos	#	Player	Team	GP	G	A	Pts	+/–	PIM	PP	SH	GW	GT	S	%
R	8	Mark Recchi	MTL	5	4	2	6	2	2	0	0	0	0	18	22.2
L	17	Benoit Brunet	MTL	4	1	3	4	4	4	0	1	0	0	8	12.5
C	11	Saku Koivu	MTL	5	1	3	4	1	10	0	0	0	0	10	10.0
D	43	Patrice Brisebois	MTL	3	1	1	2	3	24	0	0	1	1	3	33.3
R	30	Turner Stevenson	MTL	5	1	1	2	1	2	0	0	0	0	5	20.0
L	49	Brian Savage	MTL	5	1	1	2	1	0	0	0	0	0	6	16.7
L	27	Shayne Corson	MTL	5	1	0	1	-5	4	0	1	0	0	8	12.5
C	24	Scott Thornton	MTL	5	1	0	1	1	2	0	0	0	0	11	9.1
D	5	Stephane Quintal	MTL	5	0	1	1	-1	6	0	0	0	0	6	0.0
R	18	Valeri Bure	MTL	5	0	1	1	-4	2	0	0	0	0	7	0.0
D	52	* Craig Rivet	MTL	5	0	1	1	-2	14	0	0	0	0	6	0.0
D	35	Jassen Cullimore	MTL	2	0	0	0	-1	2	0	0	0	0	0	0.0
D	3	* David Wilkie	MTL	2	0	0	0	0	2	0	0	0	0	1	0.0
G	60	* Jose Theodore	MTL	2	0	0	0	0	0	0	0	0	0	0	0.0
D	34	Peter Popovic	MTL	3	0	0	0	-3	2	0	0	0	0	1	0.0
G	41	Jocelyn Thibault	MTL	3	0	0	0	0	0	0	0	0	0	0	0.0
C	42	* Darcy Tucker	MTL	4	0	0	0	0	0	0	0	0	0	4	0.0
C	25	Vincent Damphousse	MTL	5	0	0	0	-5	2	0	0	0	0	7	0.0
D	37	Dave Manson	MTL	5	0	0	0	6	17	0	0	0	0	10	0.0
R	44	Stephane Richer	MTL	5	0	0	0	-3	0	0	0	0	0	9	0.0
D	38	Vladimir Malakhov	MTL	5	0	0	0	-3	6	0	0	0	0	12	0.0
L	26	Martin Rucinsky	MTL	5	0	0	0	-5	4	0	0	0	0	10	0.0

Goaltending

No.	Goaltender	GPI	Mins	Avg	W	L	EN	SO	GA	SA	S%
60	* Jose Theodore	2	168	2.50	1	1	0	0	7	108	.935
41	Jocelyn Thibault	3	179	4.36	0	3	2	0	13	101	.871
	Totals	**5**	**348**	**3.79**	**1**	**4**	**2**	**0**	**22**	**211**	**.896**

Coaching History

"Jack" Laviolette, 1909-10; Adolphe Lecours, 1910-11; Napoleon Dorval, 1911-12 to 1912-13; Jimmy Gardner, 1913-14 to 1914-15; "Newsy" Lalonde, 1915-16 to 1920-21; "Newsy" Lalonde and Léo Dandurand, 1921-22; Léo Dandurand, 1922-23 to 1925-26; Cecil Hart, 1926-27 to 1931-32; "Newsy" Lalonde, 1932-33 to 1933-34; "Newsy" Lalonde and Léo Dandurand, 1934-35; Sylvio Mantha, 1935-36; Cecil Hart, 1936-37 to 1937-38; Cecil Hart and Jules Dugal, 1938-39; "Babe" Siebert, 1939*; "Pit" Lepine, 1939-40; Dick Irvin 1940-41 to 1954-55; "Toe" Blake, 1955-56 to 1967-68; Claude Ruel, 1968-69 to 1969-70; Claude Ruel and Al MacNeil, 1970-71; Scotty Bowman, 1971-72 to 1978-79; Bernie Geoffrion and Claude Ruel, 1979-80; Claude Ruel, 1980-81; Bob Berry, 1981-82 to 1982-83; Bob Berry and Jacques Lemaire, 1983-84; Jacques Lemaire, 1984-85; Jean Perron, 1985-86 to 1987-88; Pat Burns, 1988-89 to 1991-92; Jacques Demers, 1992-93 to 1994-95; Jacques Demers and Mario Tremblay, 1995-96; Mario Tremblay, 1996-97; Alain Vigneault, 1997-98.

* Named coach in summer but died before 1939-40 season began.

Club Records

Team

(Figures in brackets for season records are games played; records for fewest points, wins, ties, losses, goals, goals against are for 70 or more games)

Record		
Most Points	*132	1976-77 (80)
Most Wins	60	1976-77 (80)
Most Ties	23	1962-63 (70)
Most Losses	40	1983-84 (80)
Most Goals	387	1976-77 (80)
Most Goals Against	295	1983-84 (80)
Fewest Points	65	1950-51 (70)
Fewest Wins	25	1950-51 (70)
Fewest Ties	5	1983-84 (80)
Fewest Losses	*8	1976-77 (80)
Fewest Goals	155	1952-53 (70)
Fewest Goals Against	*131	1955-56 (70)
Longest Winning Streak		
Overall	12	Jan. 6-Feb. 3/68
Home	13	Nov. 2/43-Jan. 8/44, Jan. 30-Mar. 26/77
Away	8	Dec. 18/77-Jan. 18/78, Jan. 21-Feb. 21/82
Longest Undefeated Streak		
Overall	28	Dec. 18/77-Feb. 23/78 (23 wins, 5 ties)
Home	*34	Nov. 1/76-Apr. 2/77 (28 wins, 6 ties)
Away	*23	Nov. 27/74-Mar. 12/75 (14 wins, 9 ties)
Longest Losing Streak		
Overall	12	Feb. 13/26-Mar. 13/26
Home	7	Dec. 16/39-Jan. 18/40
Away	10	Jan. 16-Mar. 13/26
Longest Winless Streak		
Overall	12	Feb. 13-Mar. 13/26 (12 losses), Nov. 28-Dec. 29/35 (8 losses, 4 ties)
Home	15	Dec. 16/39-Mar. 7/40 (12 losses, 3 ties)
Away	12	Nov. 26/33-Jan. 28/34 (8 losses, 4 ties), Oct. 20/50-Dec. 13/51 (8 losses, 4 ties)
Most Shutouts, Season	*22	1928-29 (44)
Most PIM, Season	1,847	1995-96 (82)
Most Goals, Game	*16	Mar. 3/20 (Mtl. 16 at Que. 3)

Individual

Record		
Most Seasons	20	Henri Richard, Jean Beliveau
Most Games	1,256	Henri Richard
Most Goals, Career	544	Maurice Richard
Most Assists, Career	728	Guy Lafleur
Most Points, Career	1,246	Guy Lafleur (518G, 728A)
Most PIM, Career	2,248	Chris Nilan
Most Shutouts, Career	75	George Hainsworth
Longest Consecutive Games Streak	560	Doug Jarvis (Oct. 8/75-Apr. 4/82)
Most Goals, Season	60	Steve Shutt (1976-77), Guy Lafleur (1977-78)
Most Assists, Season	82	Peter Mahovlich (1974-75)
Most Points, Season	136	Guy Lafleur (1976-77; 56G, 80A)
Most PIM, Season	358	Chris Nilan (1984-85)
Most Points, Defenseman, Season	85	Larry Robinson (1976-77; 19G, 66A)
Most Points, Center, Season	117	Peter Mahovlich (1974-75; 35G, 82A)
Most Points, Right Wing, Season	136	Guy Lafleur (1976-77; 56G, 80A)
Most Points, Left Wing, Season	110	Mats Naslund (1985-86; 43G, 67A)
Most Points, Rookie, Season	71	Mats Naslund (1982-83; 26G, 45A), Kjell Dahlin (1985-86; 32G, 39A)
Most Shutouts, Season	*22	George Hainsworth (1928-29)
Most Goals, Game	6	Newsy Lalonde (Jan. 10/20)
Most Assists, Game	6	Elmer Lach (Feb. 6/43)
Most Points, Game	8	Maurice Richard (Dec. 28/44; 5G, 3A), Bert Olmstead (Jan. 9/54; 4G, 4A)

* NHL Record.

Retired Numbers

1	Jacques Plante	1952-1963
2	Doug Harvey	1947-1961
4	Jean Béliveau	1950-1971
7	Howie Morenz	1923-1937
9	Maurice Richard	1942-1960
10	Guy Lafleur	1971-1984
16	Henri Richard	1955-1975

All-time Record vs. Other Clubs

Regular Season

	At Home							On Road							Total						
	GP	W	L	T	GF	GA	PTS	GP	W	L	T	GF	GA	PTS	GP	W	L	T	GF	GA	PTS
Anaheim	3	1	1	1	12	10	3	3	2	1	0	13	12	4	6	3	2	1	25	22	7
Boston	316	183	88	45	1078	737	411	317	118	145	54	863	938	290	633	301	233	99	1941	1675	701
Buffalo	84	49	24	11	346	255	109	84	24	41	19	233	267	67	168	73	65	30	579	522	176
Calgary	40	23	11	6	144	97	52	39	22	12	5	141	123	49	79	45	23	11	285	220	101
Chicago	269	170	51	48	1045	634	388	269	123	91	55	754	724	301	538	293	142	103	1799	1358	689
Colorado	58	36	13	9	247	185	81	59	26	29	4	211	200	56	117	62	42	13	458	385	137
Dallas	53	36	10	7	235	128	79	54	29	14	11	196	141	69	107	65	24	18	431	269	148
Detroit	276	170	63	43	983	620	383	276	96	127	53	708	790	245	552	266	190	96	1691	1410	628
Edmonton	24	14	7	3	87	75	31	25	12	13	0	80	87	24	49	26	20	3	167	162	55
Florida	7	2	4	1	19	21	5	8	3	3	2	22	28	8	15	5	7	3	41	49	13
Hartford	61	42	12	7	272	181	91	63	31	24	8	228	192	70	124	73	36	15	500	373	161
Los Angeles	59	41	7	11	277	153	93	60	34	17	9	239	187	77	119	75	24	20	516	340	170
New Jersey	40	27	8	5	158	104	59	40	24	14	2	172	117	50	80	51	22	7	330	221	109
NY Islanders	46	27	11	8	176	138	62	46	21	20	5	137	147	47	92	48	31	13	313	285	109
NY Rangers	276	185	56	35	1087	635	405	276	110	112	54	806	808	274	552	295	168	89	1893	1443	679
Ottawa	15	9	4	2	48	43	20	12	9	3	0	44	33	18	27	18	7	2	92	76	38
Philadelphia	60	30	17	13	223	187	73	59	21	25	13	179	183	55	119	51	42	26	402	370	128
Phoenix	24	21	3	0	127	57	42	24	10	8	6	94	80	26	48	31	11	6	221	137	68
Pittsburgh	67	54	6	7	338	167	115	67	32	23	12	242	205	76	134	86	29	19	580	372	191
St. Louis	54	38	9	7	239	145	83	53	27	11	15	189	136	69	107	65	20	22	428	281	152
San Jose	6	6	0	0	28	9	12	6	2	2	2	15	17	6	12	8	2	2	43	26	18
Tampa Bay	8	4	3	1	19	20	9	9	1	6	2	18	26	4	17	5	9	3	37	46	13
Toronto	316	192	84	40	1124	781	424	317	113	160	44	832	958	270	633	305	244	84	1956	1739	694
Vancouver	47	36	8	3	234	123	75	45	30	7	8	180	111	68	92	66	15	11	414	234	143
Washington	46	30	10	6	194	94	66	45	18	20	7	142	124	43	91	48	30	13	336	218	109
Defunct Clubs	231	148	58	25	779	469	321	230	98	97	35	586	606	231	461	246	155	60	1365	1075	552
Totals	**2486**	**1574**	**568**	**344**	**9519**	**6068**	**3492**	**2486**	**1036**	**1025**	**425**	**7324**	**7240**	**2497**	**4972**	**2610**	**1593**	**769**	**16843**	**13308**	**5989**

Playoffs

	Series	W	L	GP	W	L	T	GF	GA	Last Mtg.	Round	Result
Boston	28	21	7	139	87	52	0	430	339	1994	CQF	L 3-4
Buffalo	6	4	2	31	18	13	0	114	94	1993	DF	W 4-0
Calgary	2	1	1	11	6	5	0	31	32	1989	F	L 2-4
Chicago	17	12	5	81	50	29	2	261	185	1976	QF	W 4-0
Colorado	5	3	2	31	17	14	0	105	85	1993	DSF	W 4-2
Dallas	2	1	1	13	7	6	0	48	37	1980	QF	L 3-4
Detroit	12	5	7	62	33	29	0	161	149	1978	QF	W 4-1
Edmonton	1	0	1	3	0	3	0	6	15	1981	PR	L 0-3
Hartford	5	5	0	27	19	8	0	96	70	1992	DSF	W 4-3
Los Angeles	1	1	0	5	4	1	0	15	12	1993	F	W 4-1
NY Islanders	4	3	1	22	14	8	0	64	55	1993	CF	W 4-1
NY Rangers	14	7	7	61	34	25	2	188	158	1996	CQF	L 2-4
New Jersey	1	0	1	5	1	4	0	11	22	1997	CQF	L 1-4
Philadelphia	4	3	1	21	14	7	0	72	52	1989	CF	W 4-2
St. Louis	3	3	0	12	12	0	0	42	14	1977	QF	W 4-0
Toronto	15	8	7	71	42	29	0	215	160	1979	QF	W 4-0
Vancouver	1	1	0	5	4	1	0	20	9	1975	QF	W 4-1
Defunct Clubs	11*	6	4	28	15	9	4	70	71			
Totals	**132***	**84**	**47**	**628**	**377**	**243**	**8**	**1949**	**1559**			

* 1919 Final incomplete due to influenza epidemic.

Calgary totals include Atlanta, 1972-73 to 1979-80. Colorado totals include Quebec, 1979-80 to 1994-95.
Dallas totals include Minnesota, 1967-68 to 1992-93. New Jersey totals include Kansas City, 1974-75 to 1975-76, and Colorado Rockies, 1976-77 to 1981-82. Phoenix totals include Winnipeg, 1979-80 to 1995-96.

Playoff Results 1997-93

Year	Round	Opponent	Result	GF	GA
1997	CQF	New Jersey	L 1-4	11	22
1996	CQF	NY Rangers	L 2-4	17	19
1994	CQF	Boston	L 3-4	20	22
1993	**F**	**Los Angeles**	**W 4-1**	**15**	**12**
	CF	NY Islanders	W 4-1	16	11
	DF	Buffalo	W 4-0	16	12
	DSF	Quebec	W 4-2	19	16

Abbreviations: Round: F – Final; **CF** – conference final; **CQF** – conference quarter-final; **CSF** – conference semi-final; **DF** – division final; **DSF** – division semi-final; **SF** – semi-final; **QF** – quarter-final; **PR** – preliminary round.

1996-97 Results

Oct.	5		Ottawa	3-3		6		Hartford	5-4
	7		Anaheim	6-6		9	at	Boston	4-5
	9		Los Angeles	6-3		11		Boston	6-3
	12		NY Rangers	5-2		13		Dallas	1-2
	15	at	New Jersey	2-3		14	at	Philadelphia	2-3
	16		Calgary	4-2		20		Detroit	4-1
	19	at	Ottawa	3-6		22	at	Buffalo	1-6
	24	at	Buffalo	3-6		25		St. Louis	1-8
	26		Philadelphia	6-5		26		Pittsburgh	2-5
	28		Phoenix	4-5		28	at	Florida	1-5
	30	at	Detroit	3-5		30	at	Tampa Bay	4-1
Nov.	2	at	San Jose	3-4	**Feb.**	1		New Jersey	4-4
	3	at	Phoenix	4-4		3		Florida	2-2
	6	at	Anaheim	6-5		5		Pittsburgh	3-6
	7	at	Los Angeles	1-4		6	at	Philadelphia	5-9
	9	at	Colorado	2-5		8		Hartford	3-2
	11		Edmonton	3-2		10		San Jose	4-2
	13		Florida	3-5		12	at	Buffalo	2-2
	15	at	Washington	1-3		15		New Jersey	1-4
	16		Vancouver	6-1		17	at	NY Islanders	4-1
	20	at	Hartford	1-3		22		Toronto	1-5
	21	at	Boston	6-2		25	at	Vancouver	4-2
	23	at	Toronto	4-3		28	at	Calgary	2-3
	25		Tampa Bay	4-2	**Mar.**	1	at	Edmonton	5-4
	27	at	Pittsburgh	2-2		5		Colorado	3-7
	30		Washington	0-2		7	at	Hartford	0-2
Dec.	1	at	NY Rangers	2-6		8		Buffalo	3-3
	4		Boston	3-4		10	at	Pittsburgh	2-2
	6	at	Chicago	3-1		13	at	Boston	3-0
	7		Chicago	3-2		15		Ottawa	2-2
	11		Buffalo	2-3		19	at	NY Rangers	5-4
	14	at	New Jersey	3-3		22		Washington	1-3
	16		Tampa Bay	2-4		24		Boston	3-1
	21		NY Rangers	2-3		26		Pittsburgh	8-5
	23		Ottawa	0-6		29	at	Ottawa	2-5
	26	at	Pittsburgh	3-3	**Apr.**	2	at	Hartford	4-1
	28	at	Tampa Bay	4-4		5		Hartford	1-4
	29	at	Florida	2-1		7		NY Islanders	2-1
Jan.	1	at	Dallas	6-4		9	at	NY Islanders	3-1
	2	at	St. Louis	2-2		10	at	Washington	2-3
	4		NY Islanders	3-1		12		Philadelphia	3-3

Entry Draft
Selections 1997-83

1997 Pick		1993 Pick		1989 Pick		1985 Pick	
11	Jason Ward	21	Saku Koivu	13	Lindsay Vallis	12	Jose Charbonneau
37	Gregor Baumgartner	47	Rory Fitzpatrick	30	Patrice Brisebois	16	Tom Chorske
65	Ilkka Mikkola	73	Sebastien Bordeleau	41	Steve Larouche	33	Todd Richards
91	Daniel Tetrault	85	Adam Wiesel	51	Pierre Sevigny	47	Rocky Dundas
118	Konstantin Sidulov	99	Jean-Francois Houle	83	Andre Racicot	75	Martin Desjardins
122	Gennady Razin	113	Jeff Lank	104	Marc Deschamps	79	Brent Gilchrist
145	Jonathan Desroches	125	Dion Darling	146	Craig Ferguson	96	Tom Sagissor
172	Ben Guite	151	Darcy Tucker	167	Patrick Lebeu	117	Donald Dufresne
197	Petr Kubos	177	David Ruhly	188	Roy Mitchell	142	Ed Cristofoli
202	Andrei Sidyakin	203	Alan Letang	209	Ed Henrich	163	Mike Claringbull
228	Jarl-Espen Ygranes	229	Alexandre Duchesne	230	Justin Duberman	184	Roger Beedon
		255	Brian Larochelle	251	Steve Cadieux	198	Maurice Mansi
1996 Pick		281	Russell Guzior			205	Chad Arthur
18	Matt Higgins			1988 Pick		226	Mike Bishop
44	Mathieu Garon	1992 Pick		20	Eric Charron	247	John Ferguson Jr.
71	Arron Asham	20	David Wilkie	34	Martin St. Amour		
92	Kim Staal	33	Valeri Bure	46	Neil Carnes	1984 Pick	
99	Etienne Drapeau	44	Keli Corpse	83	Patrik Kjellberg	5	Petr Svoboda
127	Daniel Archambault	68	Craig Rivet	93	Peter Popovic	8	Shayne Corson
154	Brett Clark	82	Louis Bernard	104	Jean-Claude Bergeron	29	Stephane Richer
181	Timo Vertala	92	Marc Lamothe	125	Patrik Carnback	51	Patrick Roy
207	Mattia Baldi	116	Don Chase	146	Tim Chase	54	Graeme Bonar
233	Michel Tremblay	140	Martin Sychra	167	Sean Hill	65	Lee Brodeur
		164	Christian Proulx	188	Harijs Vitolinsh	95	Gerald Johannson
1995 Pick		188	Michael Burman	209	Yuri Krivokhizha	116	Jim Nesich
8	Terry Ryan	212	Earl Cronan	230	Kevin Dahl	137	Scott MacTavish
60	Miroslav Guren	236	Trent Cavicchi	251	Dave Kunda	158	Brad McCughey
74	Martin Hohenberger	260	Hiroyuki Miura			179	Eric Demers
86	Jonathan Delisle			1987 Pick		199	Ron Annear
112	Niklas Anger	1991 Pick		17	Andrew Cassels	220	Dave Tanner
138	Boyd Olson	17	Brent Bilodeau	33	John LeClair	240	Troy Crosby
164	Stephane Robidas	28	Jim Campbll	38	Eric Desjardins		
190	Greg Hart	43	Craig Darby	44	Mathieu Schneider	1983 Pick	
216	Eric Houde	61	Yves Sarault	58	Francois Gravel	17	Alfie Turcotte
		73	Vladimir Vujtek	80	Kris Miller	26	Claude Lemieux
1994 Pick		83	Sylvain Lapointe	101	Steve McCool	27	Sergio Momesso
18	Brad Brown	100	Brad Layzell	122	Les Kuntar	35	Todd Francis
44	Jose Theodore	105	Tony Prpic	143	Rob Kelley	45	Daniel Letendre
54	Chris Murray	127	Oleg Petrov	164	Will Geist	78	John Kordic
70	Marko Kiprusoff	149	Brady Kramer	185	Eric Tremblay	98	Dan Wurst
74	Martin Belanger	171	Brian Savage	206	Barry McKinlay	118	Arto Javanainen
96	Arto Kuki	193	Scott Fraser	227	Ed Ronan	138	Vladislav Tretiak
122	Jimmy Drolet	215	Greg MacEachern	248	Bryan Herring	158	Rob Bryden
148	Joel Irving	237	Paul Lepler			178	Grant MacKay
174	Jessie Rezansoff	259	Dale Hooper	1986 Pick		198	Thomas Rundqvist
200	Peter Strom			15	Mark Pederson	218	Jeff Perpich
226	Tomas Vokoun	1990 Pick		27	Benoit Brunet	238	Jean-Guy Bergeron
252	Chris Aldous	12	Turner Stevenson	57	Jyrki Lumme		
278	Ross Parsons	39	Ryan Kuwabara	78	Brent Bobyck		
		58	Charles Poulin	94	Eric Aubertin		
		60	Robert Guillet	99	Mario Milani		
		81	Gilbert Dionne	120	Steve Bisson		
		102	Paul DiPietro	141	Lyle Odelein		
		123	Craig Conroy	162	Rick Hayward		
		144	Stephen Rohr	183	Antonin Routa		
		165	Brent Fleetwood	204	Eric Bohemier		
		186	Derek Maguire	225	Charlie Moore		
		207	Mark Kettelhut	246	Karel Svoboda		
		228	John Uniac				
		249	Sergei Martynyuk				

General Manager

HOULE, RÉJEAN
Vice President, Hockey and General Manager, Montreal Canadiens.
Born in Rouyn-Noranda, Que., October 25, 1949.

Réjean Houle was appointed general manager of the Montreal Canadiens on October 21, 1995. Houle played for the Canadiens from 1969 to 1983, with the exception of a three-year stint with the Quebec Nordiques (WHA), and was a recipient of five Stanley Cups with Montreal. Houle played in 635 NHL regular season games, posting totals of 161 goals and 247 assists. Prior to becoming general manager of the Canadiens, and following his playing career, Réjean Houle was an executive with Molson-O'Keefe Breweries.

Captains' History

"Jack" Laviolette, 1909-10; "Newsy" Lalonde, 1910-11; "Jack" Laviolette, 1911-12; "Newsy" Lalonde, 1912-13; Jimmy Gardner, 1913-14 to 1914-15; Howard McNamara, 1915-16; "Newsy" Lalonde, 1916-17 to 1921-22; Sprague Cleghorn, 1922-23 to 1924-25; Bill Coutu, 1925-26; Sylvio Mantha, 1926-27 to 1931-32; George Hainsworth, 1932-33; Sylvio Mantha, 1933-34 to 1935-36; "Babe" Siebert, 1936-37 to 1938-39; Walter Buswell, 1939-40; "Toe" Blake, 1940-41 to 1946-47; "Toe" Blake and Bill Durnan, 1947-48; Emile Bouchard, 1948-49 to 1955-56; Maurice Richard, 1956-57 to 1959-60; Doug Harvey, 1960-61; Jean Beliveau, 1961-62 to 1970-71; Henri Richard, 1971-72 to 1974-75; Yvan Cournoyer, 1975-76 to 1978-79; Serge Savard, 1979-80, 1980-81; Bob Gainey, 1981-82 to 1988-89, Guy Carbonneau and Chris Chelios (co-captains), 1989-90; Guy Carbonneau, 1990-91 to 1993-94; Kirk Muller and Mike Keane, 1994-95; Mike Keane and Pierre Turgeon, 1995-96; Pierre Turgeon and Vincent Damphousse, 1996-97.

Club Directory

Centre Molson
1260 de La Gauchetière St. W.
Montréal, QC H3B 5E8
Phone **514/932-2582**
FAX (Hockey) 514/932-8736
Team Services 514/989-2717
P.R. 514/932-9296
Media 514/932-8285
Capacity: 21,273

Owner: The Molson Companies Limited

Chairman of the Board, President and Governor . . .	Ronald Corey
Vice-President Hockey, General Manager and Alternate Governor	Réjean Houle
Vice-President, Finance and Administration and Alternate Governor	Fred Steer
Vice-President and General Manager, Centre Molson	Aldo Giampaolo
Vice-President, Communications and Marketing Services	Bernard Brisset
Administrative Assistant to the General Manager	Phil Scheuer
Head Coach.	Alain Vigneault
Assistant Coaches	Dave King, Clément Jodoin, Roland Melanson
Director of Scouting	Pierre Mondou
Director of Player Development and Scout	Claude Ruel
Pro Scouts	Jacques Demers, Mario Tremblay
Director of Team Services	Michèle Lapointe
Chief Scout	Doug Robinson
Scouting Staff	Neil Armstrong, Scott Baker, Fred E. Bandel, Elmer Benning, Pierre Dorion, Mats Naslund, Gerry O'Flaherty, Sakari Pietila, Antonin Routa, Richard Scammell

AHL Affiliation

Governor	Fredericton Canadiens
Head Coach.	Phil Scheuer
Assistant Coach	Michel Therrien
Strength, Conditioning Coach.	John Perpich
Director of Operations	Stéphane Dubé
	Wayne Gamble

Medical and Training Staff

Club Physician	Dr. D.G. Kinnear
Athletic Trainer	Gaétan Lefebvre
Assistant to the Athletic Trainer.	Graham Rynbend
Supervisor of Purchasing, Hockey	Eddy Palchak
Equipment Manager	Pierre Gervais
Assistants to the Equipment Manager	Robert Boulanger, Pierre Ouellette

Advertising and Sponsorship

EFFIX Inc.	François-Xavier Seigneur

Communications

Director of Communications	Donald Beauchamp
Assistant to the Director of Communications	Dominick Saillant
Production Supervisor	Frédérique Cardinal
Communications Assistant	Claude Rompré
Supervisor, Production Room.	Paul Sohubin
Show Coordinator	Michel Quidoz

Finance

Director of Finance	Jacques Aubé
Controller	Dennis McKinley
Administrative Supervisor	Dave Poulton
Controller – Financial Reporting	Françoise Brault
Supervisor – Accounting, Centre Molson Operations	Linda Guertin
Accounting Supervisors	Gilles Viens, Paule Jolicoeur
M.I.S. Director	Sylvain Roy

Centre Molson

Director, Building and Operations	Alain Gauthier
Director, Concessions, Food & Beverage	Michel T. Tremblay
Director, Box Office and Customer Service	Richard Primeau
Director, Events	Louise Laliberté
Director, Boutiques Souvenirs	Yves Renaud
Assistant Director, Building and Operations.	Jean-François Garneau
Supervisor, Box Office	Cathy D'Ascoli
Manager, Guest Services and Security	Marc Després

Executive Assistants

President, Lise Beaudry; General Manager, Donna Stuart; V.P. Communications, Normande Herget; V.P. Finance, Susan Cryans; V.P. and General Manager (Centre Molson), Vicki Mercuri; Hockey, Claudine Crépin

Location of Press Box.	Suspended above ice – East side
Location of Radio and TV booths.	Suspended above ice – West side
Dimensions of rink.	200 feet by 85 feet
Club colors	Red, White and Blue
Club trains at.	Centre Molson
Play-by-Play – Radio/TV	Claude Quenneville, Pierre Houde, André Côté, Pierre Rinfret (French) Dino Sisto (English)
TV Channels	CBFT (2), TQS (35) (French), CBMT (6) (English)
Cable TV	RDS (25)
Radio Stations	CKAC (730) (French), CJAD (800) (English)

General Managers' History

Jack Laviolette and Joseph Cattarinich, 1909-1910; George Kennedy, 1910-11 to 1920-21; Leo Dandurand, 1921-22 to 1934-35; Ernest Savard, 1935-36; Cecil Hart, 1936-37 to 1938-39; Jules Dugal, 1939-40; Tom P. Gorman, 1940-41 to 1945-46; Frank J. Selke, 1946-47 to 1963-64; Sam Pollock, 1964-65 to 1977-78; Irving Grundman, 1978-79 to 1982-83; Serge Savard, 1983-84 to 1994-95; Serge Savard and Réjean Houle, 1995-96; Réjean Houle, 1996-97 to date.

New Jersey Devils

1996-97 Results: 45W-23L-14T 104PTS. First, Atlantic Division

1997-98 Schedule

Oct.	Fri.	3	at Tampa Bay
	Sat.	4	at Washington
	Wed.	8	Philadelphia
	Fri.	10	at Carolina
	Sat.	11	Buffalo
	Fri.	17	at Ottawa
	Sat.	18	Tampa Bay
	Thu.	23	Montreal
	Sat.	25	San Jose
	Mon.	27	at Philadelphia
	Thu.	30	Vancouver
Nov.	Sat.	1	Washington
	Tue.	4	Los Angeles
	Wed.	5	at Florida
	Sat.	8	Boston
	Mon.	10	at NY Islanders
	Wed.	12	at NY Rangers
	Fri.	14	Colorado
	Sat.	15	at Buffalo
	Tue.	18	Calgary
	Thu.	20	NY Islanders
	Sat.	22	Florida*
	Wed.	26	at Anaheim
	Fri.	28	at San Jose
	Sat.	29	at Los Angeles
Dec.	Tue.	2	St. Louis
	Thu.	4	at Pittsburgh
	Sat.	6	Tampa Bay
	Wed.	10	Edmonton
	Fri.	12	Montreal
	Sat.	13	at Toronto
	Tue.	16	NY Rangers
	Thu.	18	at St. Louis
	Fri.	19	at Detroit
	Tue.	23	at Washington
	Fri.	26	NY Islanders
	Mon.	29	at Buffalo
	Tue.	30	Chicago
Jan.	Thu.	1	at Florida*
	Sat.	3	Toronto
	Mon.	5	Dallas
	Wed.	7	Pittsburgh
	Fri.	9	Tampa Bay
	Sat.	10	at Pittsburgh
	Mon.	12	at Boston
	Wed.	14	NY Rangers
	Tue.	20	Detroit
	Thu.	22	Pittsburgh
	Sat.	24	at NY Rangers*
	Sun.	25	at Montreal*
	Wed.	28	at Edmonton
	Fri.	30	at Vancouver
	Sat.	31	at Calgary
Feb.	Mon.	2	at Ottawa
	Wed.	4	Ottawa
	Sat.	7	at NY Islanders*
	Wed.	25	at Florida
	Thu.	26	at Tampa Bay
	Sat.	28	Carolina
Mar.	Mon.	2	Philadelphia
	Thu.	5	Boston
	Sat.	7	NY Rangers*
	Mon.	9	at NY Rangers
	Tue.	10	at Philadelphia
	Thu.	12	at Carolina
	Sat.	14	at Montreal
	Wed.	18	Anaheim
	Fri.	20	at Washington
	Sat.	21	Washington
	Tue.	24	Philadelphia
	Thu.	26	at Colorado
	Sat.	28	at Phoenix
	Sun.	29	at Dallas
Apr.	Wed.	1	Carolina
	Fri.	3	Ottawa
	Sun.	5	Phoenix
	Wed.	8	at NY Islanders
	Sat.	11	at Boston
	Sun.	12	Florida
	Wed.	15	Buffalo
	Thu.	16	at Chicago
	Sat.	18	NY Islanders

* Denotes afternoon game.

Franchise date: June 30, 1982
Transferred from Denver to New Jersey, previously transferred from Kansas City to Denver, Colorado.

EASTERN
NHL CONFERENCE

**ATLANTIC
DIVISION**

**24th
NHL
Season**

Year-by-Year Record

| Season | GP | Home | | | Road | | | Overall | | | | | | | |
		W	L	T	W	L	T	W	L	T	GF	GA	Pts.	Finished	Playoff Result
1996-97	82	23	9	9	22	14	5	45	23	14	231	182	104	1st, Atlantic Div.	Lost Conf. Semi-Final
1995-96	82	22	17	2	15	16	10	37	33	12	215	202	86	6th, Atlantic Div.	Out of Playoffs
1994-95	**48**	**14**	**4**	**6**	**8**	**14**	**2**	**22**	**18**	**8**	**136**	**121**	**52**	**2nd, Atlantic Div.**	**Won Stanley Cup**
1993-94	84	29	11	2	18	14	10	47	25	12	306	220	106	2nd, Atlantic Div.	Lost Conf. Championship
1992-93	84	24	14	4	16	23	3	40	37	7	308	299	87	4th, Patrick Div.	Lost Div. Semi-Final
1991-92	80	24	12	4	14	19	3	38	31	11	289	259	87	4th, Patrick Div.	Lost Div. Semi-Final
1990-91	80	23	10	7	9	23	8	32	33	15	272	264	79	4th, Patrick Div.	Lost Div. Semi-Final
1989-90	80	22	15	3	15	19	6	37	34	9	295	288	83	2nd, Patrick Div.	Lost Div. Semi-Final
1988-89	80	17	18	5	10	23	7	27	41	12	281	325	66	5th, Patrick Div.	Out of Playoffs
1987-88	80	23	16	1	15	20	5	38	36	6	295	296	82	4th, Patrick Div.	Lost Conf. Championship
1986-87	80	20	17	3	9	28	3	29	45	6	293	368	64	6th, Patrick Div.	Out of Playoffs
1985-86	80	17	21	2	11	28	1	28	49	3	300	374	59	6th, Patrick Div.	Out of Playoffs
1984-85	80	13	21	6	9	27	4	22	48	10	264	346	54	5th, Patrick Div.	Out of Playoffs
1983-84	80	10	28	2	7	28	5	17	56	7	231	350	41	5th, Patrick Div.	Out of Playoffs
1982-83	80	11	20	9	6	29	5	17	49	14	230	338	48	5th, Patrick Div.	Out of Playoffs
1981-82**	80	14	21	5	4	28	8	18	49	13	241	362	49	5th, Smythe Div.	Out of Playoffs
1980-81**	80	15	16	9	7	29	4	22	45	13	258	344	57	5th, Smythe Div.	Out of Playoffs
1979-80**	80	12	20	8	7	28	5	19	48	13	234	308	51	6th, Smythe Div.	Out of Playoffs
1978-79**	80	8	24	8	7	29	4	15	53	12	210	331	42	4th, Smythe Div.	Out of Playoffs
1977-78**	80	17	14	9	2	26	12	19	40	21	257	305	59	2nd, Smythe Div.	Lost Prelim. Round
1976-77**	80	12	20	8	8	26	6	20	46	14	226	307	54	5th, Smythe Div.	Out of Playoffs
1975-76*	80	8	24	8	4	32	4	12	56	12	190	351	36	5th, Smythe Div.	Out of Playoffs
1974-75*	80	12	20	8	3	34	3	15	54	11	184	328	41	5th, Smythe Div.	Out of Playoffs

* Kansas City Scouts. ** Colorado Rockies.

Martin Brodeur posted a career-high ten shutouts and a miniscule GAA of 1.88, the finest goaltending marks recorded in the NHL in a quarter-century.

1997-98 Player Personnel

FORWARDS	HT	WT	S	Place of Birth	Date	1996-97 Club
ANDREYCHUK, Dave	6-4	220	R	Hamilton, Ont.	9/29/63	New Jersey
BERTRAND, Eric	6-1	205	L	St. Ephrem, Que.	4/16/75	Albany
BICEK, Jiri	5-11	183	L	Kosice, Czech.	12/3/78	Kosice
BRULE, Steve	5-11	185	R	Montreal, Que.	1/15/75	Albany
BRYLIN, Sergei	5-10	190	L	Moscow, USSR	1/13/74	New Jersey-Albany
CARPENTER, Bob	6-0	200	L	Beverly, MA	7/13/63	New Jersey
CRAWFORD, Glenn	5-11	175	L	Orillia, Ont.	2/27/78	Windsor
DAGENAIS, Pierre	6-3	185	L	Blainville, Que.	3/4/78	Moncton-Laval-Rouyn-Noranda
DUCE, Bryan	6-0	190	R	Thunder Bay, Ont.	1/15/78	Kitchener
ELIAS, Patrik	6-0	175	L	Trebic, Czech.	4/13/76	New Jersey-Albany
GILMOUR, Doug	5-11	172	L	Kingston, Ont.	6/25/63	Toronto-New Jersey
GUERIN, Bill	6-2	210	R	Wilbraham, MA	11/9/70	New Jersey
HOLIK, Bobby	6-3	220	R	Jihlava, Czech.	1/1/71	New Jersey
HOUSE, Bobby	6-1	200	R	Whitehorse, Yukon	1/7/73	Albany
LAKOVIC, Sasha	6-0	205	L	Vancouver, B.C.	9/7/71	Calgary-St. John-Las Vegas
LEGG, Mike	5-11	175	R	London, Ont.	5/25/75	U. of Michigan
MacLEAN, John	6-0	210	R	Oshawa, Ont.	11/20/64	New Jersey
MADDEN, John	5-11	185	L	Barrie, Ont.	5/4/75	U. of Michigan
MASON, Wes	6-2	180	L	Windsor, Ont.	12/12/77	Sarnia
McKAY, Randy	6-1	210	R	Montreal, Que.	1/25/67	New Jersey
MORRISON, Brendan	5-11	175	L	N. Vancouver, B.C.	8/12/75	U. of Michigan
OLIWA, Krzysztof	6-5	235	L	Tychy, Poland	4/12/73	New Jersey-Albany
PANDOLFO, Jay	6-1	195	L	Winchester, MA	12/27/74	New Jersey-Albany
PARKER, Scott	6-4	220	R	Hanford, CA	1/29/78	Kelowna
PEDERSON, Denis	6-2	190	R	Prince Albert, Sask.	9/10/75	New Jersey-Albany
RHEAUME, Pascal	6-1	200	L	Quebec, Que.	6/21/73	New Jersey-Albany
ROCHEFORT, Richard	5-9	180	R	North Bay, Ont.	1/7/77	Sudbury-Sarnia
ROLSTON, Brian	6-2	200	L	Flint, MI	2/21/73	New Jersey
SHARIFIJANOV, Vadim	5-11	210	L	Ufa, USSR	12/23/75	New Jersey-Albany
SIMPSON, Reid	6-2	220	L	Flin Flon, Man.	5/21/69	New Jersey-Albany
SKOREPA, Zdenek	6-0	185	L	Duchcov, Czech.	8/10/76	Albany
SKRLAC, Rob	6-4	230	L	Campbell, B.C.	6/10/76	Kamloops
SYKORA, Petr	6-0	190	L	Plzen, Czech.	11/19/76	New Jersey-Albany
THOMAS, Steve	5-11	190	L	Stockport, England	7/15/63	New Jersey
WILLIAMS, Jeff	6-0	175	L	Pointe-Claire, Que.	2/11/76	Raleigh-Albany
ZELEPUKIN, Valeri	6-0	200	L	Voskresensk, USSR	9/17/68	New Jersey
ZEZEL, Peter	5-11	200	L	Toronto, Ont.	4/22/65	St. Louis-New Jersey
DEFENSEMEN						
BOMBARDIR, Brad	6-2	190	L	Powell River, B.C.	5/5/72	Albany
DANEYKO, Ken	6-1	215	L	Windsor, Ont.	4/17/64	New Jersey
DEAN, Kevin	6-3	200	L	Madison, WI	4/1/69	New Jersey-Albany
HELMER, Bryan	6-1	200	R	Sault Ste. Marie, Ont.	7/15/72	Albany
KINNEAR, Geordie	6-1	200	L	Simcoe, Ont.	7/9/73	Albany
KROUPA, Vlastimil	6-3	205	L	Most, Czech.	4/27/75	San Jose-Kentucky
NEHRLING, Lucas	6-4	195	R	Peterborough, Ont.	8/14/79	Sarnia
NIEDERMAYER, Scott	6-0	200	L	Edmonton, Alta.	8/31/73	New Jersey
ODELEIN, Lyle	5-11	210	R	Quill Lake, Sask.	7/21/68	New Jersey
REHNBERG, Henrik	6-2	194	L	Grava, Sweden	7/20/77	Farjestad
SOURAY, Sheldon	6-2	210	L	Elk Point, Alta.	7/13/76	Albany
SRDINKO, Jan	5-11	195	L	Vsetin, Czech.	2/22/74	Vsetin
STEVENS, Scott	6-2	215	L	Kitchener, Ont.	4/1/64	New Jersey
SUTTON, Ken	6-0	200	L	Edmonton, Alta.	11/5/69	Manitoba-Albany
VYSHEDKEVICH, Sergei	6-0	185	L	Dedovsk, USSR	1/3/75	Albany
WARD, Lance	6-3	195	L	Lloydminster, Alta.	6/2/78	Red Deer
WHITE, Colin	6-3	190	L	New Glasgow, N.S.	12/12/77	Hull

GOALTENDERS	HT	WT	C	Place of Birth	Date	1996-97 Club
BRODEUR, Martin	6-1	205	L	Montreal, Que.	5/6/72	New Jersey
DAMPHOUSSE, Jean-Francois	6-0	165	L	St-Alexis-des-Monts, Que.	7/21/79	Moncton
DUNHAM, Michael	6-3	200	L	Johnson City, NY	6/1/72	New Jersey-Albany
HENRY, Frederic	5-11	155	L	Cap-Rouge, Que.	8/9/77	Granby-Albany
LAMBERT, Judd	6-1	175	L	Richmond, B.C.	6/3/74	Colorado
SHULMISTRA, Richard	6-2	185	R	Sudbury, Ont.	4/1/71	Albany
SIDORKIEWICZ, Peter	5-9	180	L	Dabrowa Bialostocka, Pol.	6/29/63	Albany

General Managers' History

(Kansas City) Sid Abel, 1974-75 to 1975-76; (Colorado) Ray Miron, 1976-77 to 1980-81; Billy MacMillan, 1981-82 to 1982-83; Billy MacMillan and Max McNab, 1983-84; Max McNab 1984-85 to 1986-87; Lou Lamoriello, 1987-88 to date.

General Manager

LAMORIELLO, LOU
President and General Manager, New Jersey Devils.
Born in Providence, Rhode Island, October 21, 1942.

Lou Lamoriello's life-long dedication to the game of hockey was rewarded in 1992 when he was named a recipient of the Lester Patrick Trophy for outstanding service to hockey in the United States. Lamoriello is entering his eleventh season as president and general manager of the Devils following more than 20 years with Providence College as a player, coach and administrator. His trades, signings and draft choices helped lead the Devils to their first-ever Stanley Cup championship in 1995. A member of the varsity hockey Friars during his undergraduate days, he became an assistant coach with the college club after graduating in 1963. Lamoriello was later named head coach and in the ensuing 15 years, led his teams to a 248-179-13 record, a .578 winning percentage and appearances in 10 post-season tournaments, including the 1983 NCAA Final Four. Lamoriello also served a five-year term as athletic director at Providence and was a co-founder of Hockey East, one of the strongest collegiate hockey conferences in the U.S. He remained as athletic director until he was hired as president of the Devils on April 30, 1987. He assumed the dual responsibility of general manager on September 10, 1987. He was g.m. of Team USA for the first World Cup of Hockey in 1996 as the U.S. captured the championship. He was also named g.m. for the 1998 U.S. Olympic Team.

1996-97 Scoring

* – rookie

Regular Season

Pos	#	Player	Team	GP	G	A	Pts	+/–	PIM	PP	SH	GW	GT	S	%
C	93	Doug Gilmour	TOR	61	15	45	60	-5	46	2	1	1	0	103	14.6
			N.J.	20	7	15	22	7	22	2	0	0	1	40	17.5
			TOTAL	81	22	60	82	2	68	4	1	1	1	143	15.4
C	16	Bobby Holik	N.J.	82	23	39	62	24	54	5	0	6	0	192	12.0
L	23	Dave Andreychuk	N.J.	82	27	34	61	38	48	4	1	2	1	233	11.6
R	15	John MacLean	N.J.	80	29	25	54	11	49	5	0	6	0	254	11.4
R	12	Bill Guerin	N.J.	82	29	18	47	-2	95	7	0	9	0	177	16.4
L	14	Brian Rolston	N.J.	81	18	27	45	6	20	2	2	3	0	237	7.6
L	25	Valeri Zelepukin	N.J.	71	14	24	38	-10	36	3	0	2	0	111	12.6
D	27	Scott Niedermayer	N.J.	81	5	30	35	-4	64	3	0	3	0	159	3.1
L	32	Steve Thomas	N.J.	57	15	19	34	9	46	1	0	2	0	124	12.1
C	10 *	Denis Pederson	N.J.	70	12	20	32	7	62	3	0	3	0	106	11.3
R	21	Randy McKay	N.J.	77	9	18	27	15	109	0	0	2	0	92	9.8
D	4	Scott Stevens	N.J.	79	5	19	24	26	70	0	0	1	0	166	3.0
D	2	Dave Ellett	TOR	56	4	10	14	-8	34	0	0	1	0	83	4.8
			N.J.	20	2	5	7	2	6	1	0	1	0	22	9.1
			TOTAL	76	6	15	21	-6	40	1	0	2	0	105	5.7
D	29	Shawn Chambers	N.J.	73	4	17	21	17	19	1	0	0	0	114	3.5
C	19	Bob Carpenter	N.J.	62	4	15	19	6	14	0	1	0	0	76	5.3
C	22	Peter Zezel	STL	35	4	9	13	6	12	0	0	1	0	49	8.2
			N.J.	18	0	3	3	4	4	0	0	0	0	13	0.0
			TOTAL	53	4	12	16	10	16	0	0	1	0	62	6.5
D	24	Lyle Odelein	N.J.	79	3	13	16	16	110	1	0	2	0	93	3.2
L	20 *	Jay Pandolfo	N.J.	46	6	8	14	-1	6	0	0	1	2	61	9.8
D	3	Ken Daneyko	N.J.	77	2	7	9	24	70	0	0	0	1	63	3.2
D	28	Kevin Dean	N.J.	28	2	4	6	2	6	0	0	0	0	21	9.5
R	22 *	Patrik Elias	N.J.	17	2	3	5	-4	2	0	0	0	0	23	8.7
C	18	Sergei Brylin	N.J.	29	2	2	4	-13	20	0	0	0	0	34	5.9
L	33	Reid Simpson	N.J.	27	0	4	4	0	60	0	0	0	0	17	0.0
G	30	Martin Brodeur	N.J.	67	0	4	4	0	8	0	0	0	0	0	0.0
C	17	Petr Sykora	N.J.	19	1	2	3	-8	4	0	0	0	0	26	3.8
C	8 *	Pascal Rheaume	N.J.	2	1	0	1	1	0	0	0	0	0	5	20.0
L	26 *	Krzysztof Oliwa	N.J.	1	0	0	0	-1	5	0	0	0	0	0	0.0
R	9 *	Vadim Sharifijanov	N.J.	2	0	0	0	0	0	0	0	0	0	4	0.0
G	35	Jeff Reese	N.J.	3	0	0	0	0	0	0	0	0	0	0	0.0
G	1 *	Mike Dunham	N.J.	26	0	0	0	0	2	0	0	0	0	0	0.0

Goaltending

No.	Goaltender	GPI	Mins	Avg	W	L	T	EN	SO	GA	SA	S%
30	Martin Brodeur	67	3838	1.88	37	14	13	5	10	120	1633	.927
1 *	Mike Dunham	26	1013	2.55	8	7	1	1	2	43	456	.906
35	Jeff Reese	3	139	5.61	0	2	0	0	0	13	65	.800
	Totals	**82**	**4999**	**2.18**	**45**	**23**	**14**	**6**	**13**	**182**	**2160**	**.916**

Playoffs

Pos	#	Player	Team	GP	G	A	Pts	+/–	PIM	PP	SH	GW	OT	S	%
R	15	John MacLean	N.J.	10	4	5	9	1	4	2	1	1	0	32	12.5
D	29	Shawn Chambers	N.J.	10	1	6	7	-2	6	1	0	0	0	17	5.9
D	27	Scott Niedermayer	N.J.	10	2	4	6	0	6	2	0	1	0	34	5.9
L	14	Brian Rolston	N.J.	10	4	1	5	0	6	1	2	0	0	45	8.9
L	25	Valeri Zelepukin	N.J.	8	3	2	5	3	2	1	0	1	0	13	23.1
R	26 *	Patrik Elias	N.J.	8	2	3	5	0	4	1	0	0	0	18	11.1
C	16	Bobby Holik	N.J.	10	2	3	5	1	4	1	0	0	0	29	6.9
D	24	Lyle Odelein	N.J.	10	2	2	4	-3	19	1	0	0	0	27	7.4
C	93	Doug Gilmour	N.J.	10	0	4	4	-2	14	0	0	0	0	21	0.0
D	4	Scott Stevens	N.J.	10	0	4	4	-2	2	0	0	0	0	27	0.0
R	12	Bill Guerin	N.J.	8	2	1	3	-5	18	1	0	1	0	13	15.4
C	19	Bob Carpenter	N.J.	10	1	2	3	2	2	0	0	0	0	15	6.7
D	2	Dave Ellett	N.J.	10	0	3	3	-1	10	0	0	0	0	15	0.0
R	21	Randy McKay	N.J.	10	1	1	2	1	0	0	0	0	0	15	6.7
L	32	Steve Thomas	N.J.	10	1	1	2	-6	18	0	0	0	0	25	4.0
D	28	Kevin Dean	N.J.	1	1	0	1	1	0	0	0	1	0	3	33.3
G	30	Martin Brodeur	N.J.	10	1	0	1	0	0	0	0	0	0	1	100.0
L	20 *	Jay Pandolfo	N.J.	6	0	1	1	-2	0	0	0	0	0	11	0.0
L	23	Dave Andreychuk	N.J.	1	0	0	0	0	0	0	0	0	0	5	0.0
C	22	Peter Zezel	N.J.	2	0	0	0	0	10	0	0	0	0	4	0.0
C	17	Petr Sykora	N.J.	2	0	0	0	1	2	0	0	0	0	10	0.0
L	33	Reid Simpson	N.J.	5	0	0	0	-1	29	0	0	0	0	0	0.0
C	10 *	Denis Pederson	N.J.	9	0	0	0	-2	2	0	0	0	0	6	0.0
D	3	Ken Daneyko	N.J.	10	0	0	0	1	28	0	0	0	0	8	0.0

Goaltending

No.	Goaltender	GPI	Mins	Avg	W	L	EN	SO	GA	SA	S%
30	Martin Brodeur	10	659	1.73	5	5	2	2	19	268	.929
	Totals	**10**	**662**	**1.90**	**5**	**5**	**2**	**2**	**21**	**270**	**.922**

Coaching History

(Kansas City) "Bep" Guidolin, 1974-75; "Bep" Guidolin, Sid Abel, and Eddie Bush, 1975-76; (Colorado) John Wilson, 1976-77; Pat Kelly, 1977-78; Pat Kelly and Aldo Guidolin, 1978-79; Don Cherry, 1979-80; Bill MacMillan, 1980-81; Bert Marshall and Marshall Johnston, 1981-82; (New Jersey) Bill MacMillan, 1982-83; Bill MacMillan and Tom McVie, 1983-84; Doug Carpenter, 1984-85 to 1986-87; Doug Carpenter and Jim Schoenfeld, 1987-88; Jim Schoenfeld, 1988-89; Jim Schoenfeld and John Cunniff, 1989-90; John Cunniff and Tom McVie, 1990-91; Tom McVie, 1991-92; Herb Brooks, 1992-93; Jacques Lemaire, 1993-94 to date.

Captains' History

Simon Nolet, 1974-75 to 1976-77; Wilf Paiement, 1977-78; Gary Croteau, 1978-79; Mike Christie, Rene Robert, Lanny McDonald, 1979-80; Lanny McDonald, 1980-81; Lanny McDonald, Rob Ramage, 1981-82; Don Lever, 1982-83; Don Lever and Mel Bridgman, 1983-84; Mel Bridgman, 1984-85 to 1986-87; Kirk Muller, 1987-88 to 1990-91; Bruce Driver, 1991-92; Scott Stevens, 1992-93 to date.

Club Records

Team

(Figures in brackets for season records are games played; records for fewest points, wins, ties, losses, goals, goals against are for 70 or more games)

Most Points	106	1993-94 (84)
Most Wins	47	1993-94 (84)
Most Ties	21	1977-78 (80)
Most Losses	56	1983-84 (80), 1975-76 (80)
Most Goals	308	1992-93 (84)
Most Goals Against	374	1985-86 (80)
Fewest Points	*36	1975-76 (80)
	41	1983-84 (80)
Fewest Wins	*12	1975-76 (80)
	17	1982-83 (80), 1983-84 (80)
Fewest Ties	3	1985-86 (80)
Fewest Losses	23	1996-97 (82)
Fewest Goals	*184	1974-75 (80)
	230	1982-83 (80)
Fewest Goals Against	182	1996-97 (82)

Longest Winning Streak
Overall	7	Oct. 6-Oct. 23/93
Home	8	Oct. 9-Nov. 7/87
Away	5	Dec. 10-20/96

Longest Undefeated Streak
Overall	13	Jan. 24-Feb. 20/97 (6 wins, 7 ties)
Home	15	Jan. 8-Mar. 15/97 (9 wins, 6 tie)
Away	8	Nov. 5-Dec. 2/93 (5 wins, 3 ties)

Longest Losing Streak
Overall	*14	Dec. 30/75-Jan. 29/76
	10	Oct. 14-Nov. 4/83
Home	9	Dec. 22/85-Feb. 6/86
Away	12	Oct. 19/83-Dec. 1/83

Longest Winless Streak
Overall	*27	Feb. 12-Apr. 4/76 (21 losses, 6 ties)
	18	Oct. 20-Nov. 26/82 (14 losses 4 ties)
Home	*14	Feb. 12-Mar. 30/76 (10 losses, 4 ties), Feb. 4-Mar. 31/79 (12 losses, 2 ties)
	9	Dec. 22/85-Feb. 6/86 (9 losses)
Away	*32	Nov. 12/77-Mar. 15/78 (22 losses, 10 ties)
	14	Dec. 26/82-Mar. 5/83 (13 losses, 1 tie)

Most Shutouts, Season	13	1996-97 (82)
Most PIM, Season	2,494	1988-89 (80)
Most Goals, Game	9	Seven times

Individual

Most Seasons	14	Ken Daneyko
Most Games	908	John MacLean
Most Goals, Career	344	John MacLean
Most Assists, Career	346	John MacLean
Most Points, Career	690	John MacLean (344G, 346A)
Most PIM, Career	2,121	Ken Daneyko
Most Shutouts, Career	22	Martin Brodeur

Longest Consecutive
Games Streak	388	Ken Daneyko (Nov. 4/89-Mar. 29/94)

Most Goals, Season	46	Pat Verbeek (1987-88)
Most Assists, Season	60	Scott Stevens (1993-94)
Most Points, Season	94	Kirk Muller (1987-88; 37G, 57A)
Most PIM, Season	283	Ken Daneyko (1988-89)
Most Points, Defenseman, Season	78	Scott Stevens (1993-94; 18G, 60A)
Most Points, Center, Season	94	Kirk Muller (1987-88; 37G, 57A)
Most Points, Right Wing, Season	*87	Wilf Paiement (1977-78; 31G, 56A)
	87	John MacLean (1988-89; 42G, 45A)
Most Points, Left Wing, Season	86	Kirk Muller (1989-90; 30G, 56A)
Most Points, Rookie, Season	63	Kevin Todd (1991-92; 21G, 42A)
Most Shutouts, Season	10	Martin Brodeur (1996-97)
Most Goals, Game	4	Bob MacMillan (Jan. 8/82), Pat Verbeek (Feb. 28/88)
Most Assists, Game	5	Kirk Muller (Mar. 25/87), Greg Adams (Oct. 10/86), Tom Kurvers (Feb. 13/89)
Most Points, Game	6	Kirk Muller (Nov. 29/86; 3G, 3A)

* Records include Kansas City Scouts and Colorado Rockies, 1974-75 through 1981-82.

All-time Record vs. Other Clubs

Regular Season

	At Home						On Road						Total					
	GP	W	L	T	GF	GA	PTS	GP	W	L	T	GF	GA	PTS	GP	W	L	T	GF	GA	PTS
Anaheim	3	2	1	0	11	7	4	3	1	2	0	8	12	2	6	3	3	0	19	19	6
Boston	39	9	22	8	105	138	26	42	11	27	4	133	184	26	81	20	49	12	238	322	52
Buffalo	40	10	22	8	122	148	28	40	8	27	5	125	178	21	80	18	49	13	247	326	49
Calgary	39	12	24	3	112	147	27	38	5	27	6	99	173	16	77	17	51	9	211	320	43
Chicago	40	15	15	10	119	122	40	41	10	23	8	116	170	28	81	25	38	18	235	292	68
Colorado	30	15	12	3	123	106	33	28	10	15	3	85	108	23	58	25	27	6	208	214	56
Dallas	39	19	17	3	132	121	41	39	10	23	6	103	154	26	78	29	40	9	235	275	67
Detroit	35	17	10	8	125	100	42	34	13	19	2	117	141	28	69	30	29	10	242	241	70
Edmonton	27	12	13	2	95	92	26	27	8	14	5	101	128	21	54	20	27	7	196	220	47
Florida	10	6	3	1	26	16	13	10	2	5	3	20	25	7	20	8	8	4	46	41	20
Hartford	31	17	11	3	114	101	37	29	9	13	7	92	107	25	60	26	24	10	206	208	62
Los Angeles	37	17	15	5	129	133	39	37	5	26	6	115	192	16	74	22	41	11	244	325	55
Montreal	40	14	24	2	117	172	30	40	8	27	5	104	158	21	80	22	51	7	221	330	51
NY Islanders	66	25	31	10	225	253	60	66	8	49	9	183	309	25	132	33	80	19	408	562	85
NY Rangers	67	30	32	5	225	243	65	66	16	39	11	200	282	43	133	46	71	16	425	525	108
Ottawa	9	6	1	2	33	20	14	10	8	1	1	32	15	17	19	14	2	3	65	35	31
Philadelphia	65	32	29	4	237	248	68	67	15	45	7	165	279	37	132	47	74	11	402	527	105
Phoenix	23	7	10	6	73	75	20	25	4	18	3	67	101	11	48	11	28	9	140	176	31
Pittsburgh	63	30	21	12	243	219	72	62	22	36	4	216	255	48	125	52	57	16	459	474	120
St. Louis	41	18	16	7	135	121	43	40	9	25	6	124	176	24	81	27	41	13	259	297	67
San Jose	6	4	2	0	24	10	8	5	3	1	1	16	9	7	11	7	3	1	40	19	15
Tampa Bay	11	9	1	1	41	17	19	11	5	3	3	31	27	13	22	14	4	4	72	44	32
Toronto	34	13	11	10	124	108	36	35	7	24	4	114	155	18	69	20	35	14	238	263	54
Vancouver	43	18	19	6	132	144	42	43	8	24	11	123	163	27	86	26	43	17	255	307	69
Washington	64	29	28	7	203	198	65	64	19	41	4	188	264	42	128	48	69	11	391	462	107
Defunct Clubs	8	4	2	2	25	19	10	8	2	3	3	19	27	7	16	6	5	5	44	46	17
Totals	**910**	**390**	**392**	**128**	**3050**	**3078**	**908**	**910**	**226**	**557**	**127**	**2696**	**3792**	**579**	**1820**	**616**	**949**	**255**	**5746**	**6870**	**1487**

Playoffs

	Series	W	L	GP	W	L	T	GF	GA	Last Mtg.	Round	Result
Boston	3	2	1	18	11	7	0	55	52	1995	CQF	W 4-1
Buffalo	1	1	0	7	4	3	0	14	14	1994	CQF	W 4-3
Detroit	1	1	0	4	4	0	0	16	7	1995	F	W 4-0
Montreal	1	1	0	5	4	1	0	22	11	1997	CQF	W 4-1
NY Islanders	1	1	0	6	4	2	0	23	18	1988	DSF	W 4-2
NY Rangers	3	0	3	19	7	12	0	46	56	1997	CSF	L 1-4
Philadelphia	2	1	1	8	4	4	0	23	20	1995	CF	W 4-2
Pittsburgh	3	1	2	17	8	9	0	47	56	1995	CSF	W 4-1
Washington	2	1	1	13	6	7	0	43	44	1990	DSF	L 2-4
Totals	**17**	**9**	**8**	**97**	**52**	**45**	**0**	**289**	**278**			

Playoff Results 1997-93

Year	Round	Opponent	Result	GF	GA
1997	CSF	NY Rangers	L 1-4	5	10
	CQF	Montreal	W 4-1	22	11
1995	**F**	**Detroit**	**W 4-0**	**16**	**7**
	CSF	Philadelphia	W 4-2	20	14
	CSF	Pittsburgh	W 4-1	17	8
	CQF	Boston	W 4-1	14	5
1994	CF	NY Rangers	L 3-4	16	18
	CSF	Boston	W 4-2	22	17
	CQF	Buffalo	W 4-3	14	14
1993	DSF	Pittsburgh	L 1-4	13	23

Abbreviations: Round: F – Final;
CF – conference final; **CQF** – conference quarter-final;
CSF – conference semi-final; **DF** – division final;
DSF – division semi-final; **SF** – semi-final;
QF – quarter-final; **PR** – preliminary round.

Calgary totals include Atlanta, 1974-75 to 1979-80.   Colorado totals include Quebec, 1979-80 to 1994-95.
Dallas totals include Minnesota, 1974-75 to 1992-93.   New Jersey totals include Kansas City, 1974-75 to 1975-76, and
Colorado Rockies, 1976-77 to 1981-82.   Phoenix totals include Winnipeg, 1979-80 to 1995-96.

1996-97 Results

Oct.	5		Detroit	3-1		12	at	NY Rangers	0-3
	7	at	Philadelphia	1-3		14		Boston	4-2
	12		Dallas	2-4		21	at	Los Angeles	4-1
	15		Montreal	3-2		22	at	Anaheim	1-3
	18		Ottawa	2-2		24	at	San Jose	3-1
	19	at	Hartford	2-6		29		Ottawa	1-1
	24		San Jose	3-1		31		Toronto	3-3
	26	at	Tampa Bay	4-1	Feb.	1	at	Montreal	4-4
	29	at	Boston	2-5		5		NY Islanders	4-1
	30		NY Rangers	1-6		7		Florida	2-2
Nov.	2		Tampa Bay	2-1		8		Philadelphia	4-2
	6	at	Detroit	2-0		12	at	Hartford	3-2
	7	at	Chicago	4-2		13		Hartford	4-0
	9		NY Islanders	4-0		15	at	Montreal	4-1
	12		Washington	3-2		17	at	NY Rangers	2-2
	14		Vancouver	0-3		19	at	NY Rangers	1-1
	16		Tampa Bay	6-3		20	at	Florida	2-2
	19	at	Ottawa	2-1		22	at	Tampa Bay	1-3
	22		Washington	1-5		26	at	NY Islanders	5-3
	23	at	Washington	3-4		27		Buffalo	4-1
	27	at	Dallas	3-2	Mar.	1		Pittsburgh	6-3
	28	at	Phoenix	3-4		4	at	Pittsburgh	3-1
	30	at	Colorado	1-2		5	at	Philadelphia	3-1
Dec.	3		Florida	2-0		8	at	NY Islanders	1-5
	5		Calgary	2-1		9	at	Buffalo	4-1
	7		Phoenix	3-4		11		Edmonton	6-1
	10	at	Toronto	5-2		13		Hartford	6-0
	12	at	Boston	7-4		15		Washington	3-2
	14		Montreal	3-3		17		Florida	1-4
	16	at	Calgary	5-0		19	at	Washington	2-2
	18	at	Vancouver	2-1		22	at	Pittsburgh	3-2
	20	at	Edmonton	3-2		25		Philadelphia	3-3
	23		Buffalo	0-0		27		NY Rangers	4-0
	26	at	NY Islanders	1-4		30		Los Angeles	5-2
	28		Anaheim	5-3	Apr.	1	at	Washington	1-0
	31	at	Buffalo	5-6		4		Tampa Bay	3-0
Jan.	2		Pittsburgh	1-6		6	at	St. Louis	2-0
	3	at	Ottawa	1-0		8	at	Tampa Bay	2-2
	5		St. Louis	3-5		9	at	Florida	2-4
	8		Colorado	1-1		11		Boston	2-0
	10		Chicago	3-3		13	at	Philadelphia	4-5

Entry Draft
Selections 1997-83

1997
Pick
24 J-F Damphousse
38 Stanislav Gron
104 Lucas Nehrling
131 Jiri Bicek
159 Sascha Goc
188 Mathieu Benoit
215 Scott Clemmensen
241 Jan Sorinko

1996
Pick
10 Lance Ward
38 Wesley Mason
41 Joshua Dewolf
47 Pierre Dagenais
49 Colin White
63 Scott Parker
91 Josef Boumedienne
101 Josh MacNevin
118 Glenn Crawford
145 Sean Ritchlin
173 Daryl Andrews
199 Willie Mitchell
205 Jay Bertsch
225 Pasi Petrilainen

1995
Pick
18 Petr Sykora
44 Nathan Perrott
70 Sergei Vyshedkevich
78 David Gosselin
79 Alyn McCauley
96 Henrik Rehnberg
122 Chris Mason
148 Adam Young
174 Richard Rochefort
200 Frederic Henry
226 Colin O'Hara

1994
Pick
25 Vadim Sharifijanov
51 Patrik Elias
71 Sheldon Souray
103 Zdenek Skorepa
129 Christian Gosselin
134 Ryan Smart
155 Luciano Caravaggio
181 Jeff Williams
207 Eric Bertrand
233 Steve Sullivan
259 Scott Swanjord
269 Mike Hanson

1993
Pick
13 Denis Pederson
32 Jay Pandolfo
39 Brendan Morrison
65 Krzysztof Oliwa
110 John Guirestante
143 Steve Brule
169 Nikolai Zavarukhin
195 Thomas Cullen
221 Judd Lambert
247 Jimmy Provencher
273 Michael Legg

1992
Pick
18 Jason Smith
42 Sergei Brylin
66 Cale Hulse
90 Vitali Tomilin
94 Scott McCabe
114 Ryan Black
138 Daniel Trebil
162 Geordie Kinnear
186 Stephane Yelle
210 Jeff Toms
234 Heath Weenk
258 Vladislav Yakovenko

1991
Pick
3 Scott Niedermayer
11 Brian Rolston
33 Donevan Hextall
55 Fredrik Lindqvist
77 Bradley Willner
121 Curt Regnier
143 David Craievich
165 Paul Wolanski
187 Daniel Reimann
231 Kevin Riehl
253 Jason Hehr

1990
Pick
20 Martin Brodeur
24 David Harlock
29 Chris Gotziaman
53 Michael Dunham
56 Brad Bombardir
64 Mike Bodnarchuk
95 Dean Malkoc
104 Petr Kuchyna
116 Lubomir Kolnik
137 Chris McAlpine
179 Jaroslav Modry
200 Corey Schwab
221 Valeri Zelepukin
242 Todd Reirden

1989
Pick
5 Bill Guerin
18 Jason Miller
26 Jarrod Skalde
47 Scott Pellerin
89 Mike Heinke
110 David Emma
152 Sergei Starikov
173 Andre Faust
215 Jason Simon
236 Peter Larsson

1988
Pick
12 Corey Foster
23 Jeff Christian
54 Zdeno Ciger
65 Matt Ruchty
75 Scott Luik
96 Chris Nelson
117 Chad Johnson
138 Chad Erickson
159 Bryan Lafort
180 Sergei Svetlov
201 Bob Woods
207 Alexander Semak
222 Charles Hughes
243 Michael Pohl

1987
Pick
2 Brendan Shanahan
23 Rickard Persson
65 Brian Sullivan
86 Kevin Dean
107 Ben Hankinson
128 Tom Neziol
149 Jim Dowd
170 John Blessman
191 Peter Fry
212 Alain Charland

1986
Pick
3 Neil Brady
24 Todd Copeland
45 Janne Ojanen
62 Marc Laniel
66 Anders Carlsson
108 Troy Crowder
129 Kevin Todd
150 Ryan Pardoski
171 Scott McCormack
192 Frederic Chabot
213 John Andersen
236 Doug Kirton

1985
Pick
3 Craig Wolanin
24 Sean Burke
32 Eric Weinrich
45 Myles O'Connor
66 Gregg Polak
108 Bill McMillan
129 Kevin Schrader
150 Ed Krayer
171 Jamie Huscroft
192 Terry Shold
213 Jamie McKinley
234 David Williams

1984
Pick
2 Kirk Muller
23 Craig Billington
44 Neil Davey
74 Paul Ysebaert
86 Jon Morris
107 Kirk McLean
128 Ian Ferguson
149 Vladimir Kames
170 Mike Roth
190 Mike Peluso
211 Jarkko Piiparinen
231 Chris Kiene

1983
Pick
6 John MacLean
24 Shawn Evans
85 Chris Terreri
105 Gordon Mark
125 Greg Evtushevski
145 Viacheslav Fetisov
165 Jay Octeau
185 Alexander Chernykh
205 Allan Stewart
225 Alexei Kasatonov

Coach

LEMAIRE, JACQUES GERARD
Coach, New Jersey Devils. Born in LaSalle, Quebec, September 7, 1945.

Jacques Lemaire is entering his fifth season as head coach of the New Jersey Devils. With a record of 45-23-14 in 1996-97, the Devils captured their first regular-season division championship. In 1994-95 Lemaire led the Devils to a record of 22-18-8 and their first Stanley Cup championship that included a four-game sweep in the finals. In 1993-94, his first season behind the Devils' bench, he led the team to a franchise-record 106 points and guided the team to the Conference Finals for the first time since 1988. Lemaire was named the winner of the Jack Adams Award as the NHL's outstanding coach following that season and was also honored by *The Sporting News* and *The Hockey News*. Lemaire, who served as the assistant to the managing director of the Montreal Canadiens for seven years, coached the Canadiens from February 24, 1984 to the end of the 1984-85 season. During his successful term as the Habs' coach, he led the team to the Conference Finals in 1984 and to a first place finish in the Adams Division in 1984-85.

A member of the Hockey Hall of Fame as a player, Lemaire coached Sierre of the Swiss League and Longueuil of the Quebec Major Junior Hockey League before joining the Canadiens' organization in 1983.

Coaching Record

Season	Team	Games	W	L	T	%	Games	W	L	%
1979-80	Sierre (Switzerland)					UNAVAILABLE				
1980-81	Sierre (Switzerland)					UNAVAILABLE				
1982-83	Longueuil (QMJHL)	70	37	29	4	.557	15	9	6	.600
1983-84	**Montreal (NHL)**	17	7	10	0	.412	15	9	6	.600
1984-85	**Montreal (NHL)**	80	41	27	12	.588	12	6	6	.500
1993-94	**New Jersey (NHL)**	84	47	25	12	.631	20	11	9	.550
1994-95	**New Jersey (NHL)**	48	22	18	8	.542	20	16	4	.800*
1995-96	**New Jersey (NHL)**	82	37	33	12	.524	....	....	....	....
1996-97	**New Jersey (NHL)**	82	45	23	14	.634	10	5	5	.500
	NHL Totals	393	199	136	58	.580	77	47	30	.610

* Stanley Cup win.

Club Directory

Continental Airlines Arena
50 Route 120 North
P.O. Box 504
East Rutherford, NJ 07073
Phone **201/935-6050**
FAX 201/935-2127
Capacity: 19,040

Chairman	John J. McMullen
President & General Manager	Louis A. Lamoriello
Vice President, General Counsel	Joseph C. Benedetti
Vice President, Finance	Al Duncan
Vice President, Ticket Operations	Terry Farmer
Vice President, Operations & Human Resources	Peter McMullen
Vice President, Communications & Broadcasting	Rick Minch
Executive Assistants to the President/GM	Marie Carnevale, Mary K. Morrison

Hockey Club Personnel

Head Coach	Jacques Lemaire
Assistant Coach	Robbie Ftorek
Goaltending Coach	Jacques Caron
Director of Scouting	David Conte
Scouting Staff	Claude Carrier, Glen Dirk, Milt Fisher, Ferny Flaman, Dan Labraaten, Chris Lamoriello, Joe Mahoney, Larry Perris, Marcel Pronovost, Lou Reycroft, Ed Thomlinson, Les Widdifield
Pro Scouting Staff	Andre Boudrias, Bob Hoffmeyer, Jan Ludvig
Hockey Operations Video Coordinator	Taran Singleton
Scouting Staff Assistant	Callie A. Smith
Strength & Conditioning Coach	Michael Vasalani
Medical Trainer	Bill Murray
Equipment Manager	Dave Nichols
Assistant Equipment Managers	Alex Abasto, Joe Summers
Massage Therapist	Juergen Merz
Team Cardiologist	Dr. Joseph Niznik
Team Dentist	Dr. H. Hugh Gardy
Team Orthopedists	Dr. Barry Fisher, Dr. Len Jaffe
Exercise Physiologist	Dr. Garret Caffrey
Physical Therapist	David M. Feniger
Video Consultant	Mitch Kaufman
Head Coach, Albany	John Cunniff
Assistant Coach, Albany	Dennis Gendron
Athletic Trainer, Albany	Chris Scarlata
Equipment Manager, Albany	Dana McGuane

Finance Department

Senior Director, Finance	Scott Struble
Staff Accountants	Dan Burgers, Gina Durante, Suzanne Folkerts, Michael Merolla
Secretary	Eileen Musikant

Ticket Department

Director, Ticket Operations	Tom Bates
Director, Customer Service/Gold Circle	Gail DeRisi
Director, Group Sales	Neil Desormeaux
Group Account Manager	Dan Sawyer
Customer Service Representative	Andrea Gebhardt

Marketing Department

Senior Director, Corporate Sponsorships	Ken Ferriter
Account Executive	Chris Potenza
Director, Community Development	Mike Kozak
Director, Season Ticket Sales	Kevin Morgan
Account Managers	David Beck, Blaise Bozzelli, Joanne Byrne, Joel De Castro, Mike DeMartino, John Donaldson, Megan Gardner, Nick Toomer, Frank Vella, Mike Yencik
Coordinator, Sponsor Services	Eileen Begg
Coordinator, Marketing Services	Jackie Dooley
Coordinator, Game Presentation	Joe Schilp
Community Development Assistant	Paul Viola
Sales Receptionist	Stephanie Haggan
Merchandising Manager	David Perricone
Merchandising Assistants	Karen Pietz, Stephanie Toskos

Communications Department

Director, Information & Publications	Mike Levine
Coordinator, Communications	Jana Spaulding
Communications Assistant	Jeffrey Altstadter
Staff Assistant	Phil Ratchford
Receptionists	Jelsa Belotta, Pat Maione
Team Photographer	Bruce Bennett Studios

Computer Operations

Dir., Programming & Computer Operations	Jack Skelly
Director, Internet Content	Peter Shankman
Systems Administrator	Mike Tukes

Television/Radio

Television Outlet	SportsChannel
Broadcasters	Mike Emrick, Play-by-Play; Glenn Resch, Color
Radio Outlet	WABC (770 AM)
Broadcasters	Mike Miller, Play-by-Play; Randy Velischek, Color
Dimensions of Rink	200 feet by 85 feet
Club Colors	Red, Black & White

New York Islanders

1996-97 Results: 29W-41L-12T 70PTS. Seventh, Atlantic Division

1997-98 Schedule

Oct.	Fri.	3	at NY Rangers	Sat.	3	at Phoenix
	Sat.	4	Toronto	Tue.	6	Pittsburgh
	Wed.	8	Washington	Thu.	8	Montreal
	Sat.	11	at Washington	Sat.	10	Carolina*
	Mon.	13	at Florida	Mon.	12	Detroit
	Thu.	16	at San Jose	Wed.	14	at Tampa Bay
	Sun.	19	at Anaheim	Tue.	20	at Chicago
	Tue.	21	at Los Angeles	Thu.	22	at St. Louis
	Sat.	25	Anaheim*	Sat.	24	at Ottawa
	Mon.	27	San Jose	Mon.	26	at Philadelphia
	Wed.	29	at Montreal	Wed.	28	Philadelphia
	Thu.	30	NY Rangers	Fri.	30	Carolina
Nov.	Sat.	1	Los Angeles	**Feb.** Sun.	1	Boston*
	Wed.	5	Edmonton	Mon.	2	at Pittsburgh
	Fri.	7	at Carolina	Wed.	4	Montreal
	Sat.	8	Chicago	Sat.	7	New Jersey*
	Mon.	10	New Jersey	Wed.	25	Dallas
	Wed.	12	at Florida	**Mar.** Sun.	1	Boston*
	Fri.	14	at Tampa Bay	Tue.	3	Philadelphia
	Sat.	15	Florida	Fri.	6	at Buffalo
	Wed.	19	at Detroit	Sat.	7	Colorado
	Thu.	20	at New Jersey	Tue.	10	Buffalo
	Sat.	22	at Buffalo*	Thu.	12	Washington
	Wed.	26	NY Rangers	Sat.	14	Vancouver
	Fri.	28	at Philadelphia	Wed.	18	at Ottawa
	Sat.	29	St. Louis	Fri.	20	at Calgary
Dec.	Tue.	2	Ottawa	Sun.	22	at Edmonton
	Wed.	3	at Carolina	Tue.	24	at Vancouver
	Sat.	6	Phoenix	Thu.	26	Pittsburgh
	Tue.	9	Calgary	Sat.	28	at Toronto
	Thu.	11	at Philadelphia	Tue.	31	at Washington
	Sat.	13	Florida	**Apr.** Wed.	1	Tampa Bay
	Tue.	16	at Washington	Sat.	4	NY Rangers*
	Wed.	17	Buffalo	Mon.	6	at Tampa Bay
	Sat.	20	at Boston	Wed.	8	New Jersey
	Mon.	22	Ottawa	Thu.	9	at Boston
	Fri.	26	at New Jersey	Sat.	11	at Montreal
	Sat.	27	Florida	Mon.	13	Washington
	Mon.	29	at Pittsburgh	Wed.	15	at NY Rangers
	Wed.	31	at Colorado	Thu.	16	Tampa Bay
Jan.	Fri.	2	at Dallas	Sat.	18	at New Jersey

* Denotes afternoon game.

Franchise date: June 6, 1972

ATLANTIC DIVISION

26th NHL Season

Zigmund Palffy sparked the Islanders' attack with his elusive moves and rapid release, finishing among the League leaders in goals (48) and points (90).

Year-by-Year Record

		Home			Road			Overall							
Season	GP	W	L	T	W	L	T	W	L	T	GF	GA	Pts.	Finished	Playoff Result
1996-97	82	19	18	4	10	23	8	29	41	12	240	250	70	7th, Atlantic Div.	Out of Playoffs
1995-96	82	14	21	6	8	29	4	22	50	10	229	315	54	7th, Atlantic Div.	Out of Playoffs
1994-95	48	10	11	3	5	17	2	15	28	5	126	158	35	7th, Atlantic Div.	Out of Playoffs
1993-94	84	23	15	4	13	21	8	36	36	12	282	264	84	4th, Atlantic Div.	Lost Conf. Quarter-Final
1992-93	84	20	19	3	20	18	4	40	37	7	335	297	87	3rd, Patrick Div.	Lost Conf. Championship
1991-92	80	20	15	5	14	20	6	34	35	11	291	299	79	5th, Patrick Div.	Out of Playoffs
1990-91	80	15	19	6	10	26	4	25	45	10	223	290	60	6th, Patrick Div.	Out of Playoffs
1989-90	80	15	17	8	16	21	3	31	38	11	281	288	73	4th, Patrick Div.	Lost Div. Semi-Final
1988-89	80	19	18	3	9	29	2	28	47	5	265	325	61	6th, Patrick Div.	Out of Playoffs
1987-88	80	24	10	6	15	21	4	39	31	10	308	267	88	1st, Patrick Div.	Lost Div. Semi-Final
1986-87	80	20	15	5	15	18	7	35	33	12	279	281	82	3rd, Patrick Div.	Lost Div. Final
1985-86	80	22	11	7	17	18	5	39	29	12	327	284	90	3rd, Patrick Div.	Lost Div. Semi-Final
1984-85	80	26	11	3	14	23	3	40	34	6	345	312	86	3rd, Patrick Div.	Lost Div. Final
1983-84	80	28	11	1	22	15	3	50	26	4	357	269	104	1st, Patrick Div.	Lost Final
1982-83	**80**	**26**	**11**	**3**	**16**	**15**	**9**	**42**	**26**	**12**	**302**	**226**	**96**	**2nd, Patrick Div.**	**Won Stanley Cup**
1981-82	**80**	**33**	**3**	**4**	**21**	**13**	**6**	**54**	**16**	**10**	**385**	**250**	**118**	**1st, Patrick Div.**	**Won Stanley Cup**
1980-81	**80**	**23**	**6**	**11**	**25**	**12**	**3**	**48**	**18**	**14**	**355**	**260**	**110**	**1st, Patrick Div.**	**Won Stanley Cup**
1979-80	**80**	**26**	**9**	**5**	**13**	**19**	**8**	**39**	**28**	**13**	**281**	**247**	**91**	**2nd, Patrick Div.**	**Won Stanley Cup**
1978-79	80	31	3	6	20	12	8	51	15	14	358	214	116	1st, Patrick Div.	Lost Semi-Final
1977-78	80	29	3	8	19	14	7	48	17	15	334	210	111	1st, Patrick Div.	Lost Quarter-Final
1976-77	80	24	11	5	23	10	7	47	21	12	288	193	106	2nd, Patrick Div.	Lost Semi-Final
1975-76	80	24	8	8	18	13	9	42	21	17	297	190	101	2nd, Patrick Div.	Lost Semi-Final
1974-75	80	22	6	12	11	19	10	33	25	22	264	221	88	3rd, Patrick Div.	Lost Semi-Final
1973-74	78	13	17	9	6	24	9	19	41	18	182	247	56	8th, East Div.	Out of Playoffs
1972-73	78	10	25	4	2	35	2	12	60	6	170	347	30	8th, East Div.	Out of Playoffs

1997-98 Player Personnel

FORWARDS	HT	WT	S	Place of Birth	Date	1996-97 Club
BELANGER, Ken	6-4	225	L	Sault Ste. Marie, Ont.	5/14/74	NY Islanders-Kentucky
BERTUZZI, Todd	6-3	224	L	Sudbury, Ont.	2/2/75	NY Islanders-Utah
CZERKAWSKI, Mariusz	6-0	195	L	Radomsko, Poland	4/13/72	Edmonton
DUMONT, Jean-Pierre	6-1	187	L	Montreal, Que.	4/1/78	Val d'Or
GREEN, Travis	6-1	193	R	Castlegar, B.C.	12/20/70	NY Islanders
HAGGERTY, Sean	6-1	186	L	Rye, NY	2/11/76	Kentucky
HOUGH, Mike	6-1	197	L	Montreal, Que.	2/6/63	Florida
JACKSON, Dane	6-1	200	R	Castlegar, B.C.	5/17/70	Rochester
KRUSE, Paul	6-0	202	L	Merritt, B.C.	3/15/70	Calgary-NY Islanders
LAPOINTE, Claude	5-9	181	L	Lachine, Que.	10/11/68	NY Islanders-Utah
LAWRENCE, Mark	6-4	215	R	Burlington, Ont.	1/27/72	Michigan
NEMCHINOV, Sergei	6-0	200	L	Moscow, USSR	1/14/64	NY Rangers-Vancouver
ORSZAGH, Vladimir	5-11	173	L	Banska Bystrica, Czech.	5/24/77	Utah
PALFFY, Zigmund	5-10	183	L	Skalica, Czech.	5/5/72	Dukla Trencin-NY Islanders
PLANTE, Dan	5-11	202	R	Hayward, WI	10/5/71	NY Islanders
REICHEL, Robert	5-10	185	L	Litvinov, Czech.	6/25/71	Calgary-NY Islanders
SMOLINSKI, Bryan	6-1	200	R	Toledo, OH	12/27/71	Detroit (IHL)-NY Islanders
STORM, Jim	6-2	200	L	Milford, MI	2/5/71	Michigan
VUKOTA, Mick	6-1	225	R	Saskatoon, Sask.	9/14/66	NY Islanders-Utah
WEBB, Steve	6-0	195	R	Peterborough, Ont.	4/20/75	NY Islanders-Kentucky
DEFENSEMEN						
BERARD, Bryan	6-1	190	L	Woonsocket, RI	3/5/77	NY Islanders
CHARA, Zdeno	6-8	231	L	Trencin, Czech.	3/18/77	Prince George
CHEBATURKIN, Vladimir	6-2	213	L	Tyumen, USSR	4/23/75	Utah
HOLLAND, Jason	6-2	193	R	Morinville, Alta.	4/30/76	NY Islanders-Kentucky
JONSSON, Kenny	6-3	195	L	Angelholm, Sweden	10/6/74	NY Islanders
LACHANCE, Scott	6-1	196	L	Charlottesville, VA	10/22/72	NY Islanders
LIBBY, Jeff	6-3	215	L	Waterville, ME	3/1/74	U. of Maine
McCABE, Bryan	6-1	204	L	St. Catharines, Ont.	6/8/75	NY Islanders
NAMESTNIKOV, Yevgeny	5-11	190	R	Arzamis-Ig, USSR	10/9/71	Vancouver-Syracuse
PILON, Richard	6-0	205	L	Saskatoon, Sask.	4/30/68	NY Islanders
STRUDWICK, Jason	6-3	207	L	Edmonton, Alta.	7/17/75	Kentucky
VASKE, Dennis	6-2	210	L	Rockford, IL	10/11/67	NY Islanders
GOALTENDERS	**HT**	**WT**	**C**	**Place of Birth**	**Date**	**1996-97 Club**
FICHAUD, Eric	5-11	171	L	Anjou, Que.	11/4/75	NY Islanders
FLAHERTY, Wade	6-0	170	L	Terrace, B.C.	1/11/68	San Jose-Kentucky
McARTHUR, Mark	5-10	175	L	East York, Ont.	11/16/75	Utah
SALO, Tommy	5-11	173	L	Surahammar, Sweden	2/1/71	NY Islanders

Captains' History

Ed Westfall, 1972-73 to 1975-76; Ed Westfall, Clark Gillies, 1976-77; Clark Gillies, 1977-78, 1978-79; Denis Potvin, 1979-80 to 1986-87; Brent Sutter, 1987-88 to 1990-91; Brent Sutter and Patrick Flatley, 1991-92; Patrick Flatley, 1992-93 to 1995-96; no captain, 1996-97.

General Managers' History

William A. Torrey, 1972-73 to 1991-92; Don Maloney, 1992-93 to 1994-95; Don Maloney and Mike Milbury, 1995-96; Mike Milbury, 1996-97 to date.

General Manager

MILBURY, MIKE
General Manager, New York Islanders. Born in Walpole, MA, June 17, 1952.

Milbury, 45, came to the Islanders with 20 years of professional hockey experience with the Boston Bruins — as a player, assistant coach, assistant general manager, general manager and coach on both the NHL and AHL levels. Milbury took over as general manager from Don Maloney on December 12, 1995.

The Walpole, MA native joined the Boston organization after graduating from Colgate University with a degree in urban sociology and enjoyed a nine-year playing career with the team. He retired May 6, 1985 and took over as assistant coach. He returned to the ice late in the 1985-86 season when injuries decimated the Bruins' defense.

Milbury's playing career concluded on July 16, 1987 when he took over as coach of the Maine Mariners, Boston's top AHL affiliate. In his first year with the team he guided the Mariners to the AHL's Northern Division title and was named both AHL coach of the year and *The Hockey News* minor league coach of the year.

He was named the assistant general manager and coach of the Boston Bruins May 16, 1989. In two years behind the bench Milbury was the NHL's most successful coach: He guided the Bruins to consecutive 100-point seasons and Adams Division titles, the 1990 Presidents' Trophy and Wales Conference championship, and an appearance in the Stanley Cup finals in 1990. He earned coach of the year honors from both *The Hockey News* and *The Sporting News* for this effort.

Milbury and his wife, Debbie, have two sons, Owen and Luke, and two daughters, Alison and Caitlin.

NHL Coaching Record

		Regular Season					Playoffs			
Season	Team	Games	W	L	T	%	Games	W	L	%
1989-90	Boston	80	46	25	9	.631	21	13	8	.619
1990-91	Boston	80	44	24	12	.606	19	10	9	.526
1995-96	NY Islanders	82	22	50	10	.329	....	....	....	....
1996-97	NY Islanders	45	13	23	9	.389	....	....	....	....
	NHL Totals	**287**	**125**	**122**	**40**	**.505**	**40**	**23**	**17**	**.575**

1996-97 Scoring

* – rookie

Regular Season

Pos	#	Player	Team	GP	G	A	Pts	+/–	PIM	PP	SH	GW	GT	S	%
R	16	Zigmund Palffy	NYI	80	48	42	90	21	43	6	4	6	1	292	16.4
C	39	Travis Green	NYI	79	23	41	64	-5	38	10	0	3	0	177	13.0
C	21	Robert Reichel	CGY	70	16	27	43	-2	22	6	0	3	0	181	8.8
			NYI	12	5	14	19	7	4	0	1	0	0	33	15.2
			TOTAL	82	21	41	62	5	26	6	1	3	0	214	9.8
C	15	Bryan Smolinski	NYI	64	28	28	56	9	25	9	0	1	1	183	15.3
D	34	* Bryan Berard	NYI	82	8	40	48	1	86	3	0	1	0	172	4.7
L	32	Niklas Andersson	NYI	74	12	31	43	4	57	1	1	1	0	122	9.8
D	4	Bryan McCabe	NYI	82	8	20	28	-2	165	2	1	2	0	117	6.8
R	44	Todd Bertuzzi	NYI	64	10	13	23	-3	68	3	0	1	0	79	12.7
D	3	Kenny Jonsson	NYI	81	3	18	21	10	24	1	0	0	0	92	3.3
C	13	Claude Lapointe	NYI	73	13	5	18	-12	49	0	3	3	1	80	16.3
D	7	Scott Lachance	NYI	81	3	11	14	-7	47	1	0	0	0	97	3.1
C	14	* Derek Armstrong	NYI	50	6	7	13	-8	33	0	0	2	0	36	16.7
R	42	Dan Plante	NYI	67	4	9	13	-6	75	0	2	0	0	61	6.6
R	11	Randy Wood	NYI	65	6	5	11	-7	61	0	1	2	0	96	6.3
L	20	Brent Hughes	NYI	51	7	3	10	-4	57	0	0	0	0	47	14.9
D	6	Doug Houda	NYI	70	2	8	10	1	99	0	0	0	0	29	6.9
L	24	Paul Kruse	CGY	14	2	0	2	-4	30	0	0	1	0	10	20.0
			NYI	48	4	2	6	-5	111	0	0	0	0	39	10.3
			TOTAL	62	6	2	8	-9	141	0	0	1	0	49	12.2
R	62	* Steve Webb	NYI	41	1	4	5	-10	144	1	0	0	0	21	4.8
D	2	Richard Pilon	NYI	52	1	4	5	4	179	0	0	0	0	17	5.9
D	28	Dennis Vaske	NYI	17	0	4	4	3	12	0	0	0	0	19	0.0
C	10	Dave McLlwain	NYI	4	1	1	2	-2	0	1	0	0	0	3	33.3
L	33	* Ken Belanger	NYI	18	0	2	2	-1	102	0	0	0	0	5	0.0
D	46	* Jason Holland	NYI	4	1	0	1	1	0	0	0	0	0	3	33.3
R	12	Mick Vukota	NYI	17	1	0	1	-2	71	0	0	0	0	7	14.3
G	35	Tommy Salo	NYI	58	0	1	1	0	4	0	0	0	0	0	0.0
G	30	Tommy Soderstrom	NYI	1	0	0	0	0	0	0	0	0	0	0	0.0
C	25	Chris Taylor	NYI	1	0	0	0	0	0	0	0	0	0	1	0.0
C	21	* Nick Vachon	NYI	1	0	0	0	-1	0	0	0	0	0	0	0.0
L	36	* Jarrett Deuling	NYI	1	0	0	0	0	0	0	0	0	0	0	0.0
L	8	Mike Donnelly	NYI	3	0	0	0	0	2	0	0	0	0	5	0.0
C	28	Jim Dowd	NYI	3	0	0	0	-1	0	0	0	0	0	0	0.0
L	42	* Andrei Vasiliev	NYI	3	0	0	0	-3	2	0	0	0	0	1	0.0
C	24	David Archibald	NYI	7	0	0	0	-4	4	0	0	0	0	4	0.0
D	10	Corey Foster	NYI	7	0	0	0	-2	2	0	0	0	0	1	0.0
G	1	* Eric Fichaud	NYI	34	0	0	0	0	2	0	0	0	0	0	0.0

Goaltending

No.	Goaltender	GPI	Mins	Avg	W	L	T	EN	SO	GA	SA	S%
30	Tommy Soderstrom	1	0	.00	0	0	0	0	0	0	0	.000
35	Tommy Salo	58	3208	2.82	20	27	8	7	5	151	1576	.904
1	* Eric Fichaud	34	1759	3.10	9	14	4	1	0	91	897	.899
	Totals	**82**	**4988**	**3.01**	**29**	**41**	**12**	**8**	**5**	**250**	**2481**	**.899**

Coaching History

Phil Goyette and Earl Ingarfield, 1972-73; Al Arbour, 1973-74 to 1985-86; Terry Simpson, 1986-87 to 1987-88; Terry Simpson and Al Arbour, 1988-89; Al Arbour, 1989-90 to 1993-94; Lorne Henning, 1994-95; Mike Milbury, 1995-96; Mike Milbury and Rick Bowness, 1996-97; Rick Bowness, 1997-98.

Coach

BOWNESS, RICK
Coach, New York Islanders. Born in Moncton, N.B., January 25, 1955.

Rick Bowness is entering his first full season as coach of the New York Islanders. The Moncton, N.B. native took over the coaching duties of the Islanders on January 24, 1997 and led the club to a 16-18-3 mark down the stretch.

After brief stays behind the bench in both Winnipeg and Boston, Bowness was named as the first head coach of the expansion Ottawa Senators on June 15, 1992. He remained behind the Senators' bench until November 20, 1995, becoming only the second coach in NHL history to head an expansion team through its first three seasons.

Prior to joining the Senators, Rick coached the Boston Bruins in 1991-92, guiding the team to a 39-32-12 record and a berth in the conference finals. The Moncton native began his coaching career with the AHL's Sherbrooke Jets as a player/coach in 1981, and returned to his hometown in 1987 as the coach and general manager of the Moncton Hawks, the Jets' AHL development team. In February 1989, Rick took over as interim coach of the Winnipeg Jets (28 games). Bowness then joined the Boston organization, coaching the AHL's Maine Mariners for two seasons before assuming head coaching duties for the Bruins for 1991-92.

Coaching Record

		Regular Season					Playoffs			
Season	Team	Games	W	L	T	%	Games	W	L	%
1987-88	Moncton (AHL)	80	27	45	8	.388	....	....	....	....
1988-89	Moncton (AHL)	53	28	20	5	.576	....	....	....	....
	Winnipeg (NHL)	**28**	**8**	**17**	**3**	**.340**	....	....	....	....
1989-90	Maine (AHL)	80	31	38	11	.457	....	....	....	....
1990-91	Maine (AHL)	80	34	34	12	.500	2	0	2	.000
1991-92	**Boston (NHL)**	**80**	**36**	**32**	**12**	**.525**	**15**	**8**	**7**	**.533**
1992-93	**Ottawa (NHL)**	**84**	**10**	**70**	**4**	**.143**	....	....	....	....
1993-94	**Ottawa (NHL)**	**84**	**14**	**61**	**9**	**.220**	....	....	....	....
1994-95	**Ottawa (NHL)**	**48**	**9**	**34**	**5**	**.240**	....	....	....	....
1995-96	**Ottawa (NHL)**	**19**	**6**	**13**	**0**	**.316**	....	....	....	....
1996-97	**NY Islanders (NHL)**	**37**	**16**	**18**	**3**	**.473**	....	....	....	....
	NHL Totals	**380**	**99**	**245**	**36**	**.308**	**15**	**8**	**7**	**.533**

Club Records

Team

(Figures in brackets for season records are games played; records for fewest points, wins, ties, losses, goals, goals against are for 70 or more games)

Most Points	118	1981-82 (80)
Most Wins	54	1981-82 (80)
Most Ties	22	1974-75 (80)
Most Losses	60	1972-73 (78)
Most Goals	385	1981-82 (80)
Most Goals Against	347	1972-73 (78)
Fewest Points	30	1972-73 (78)
Fewest Wins	12	1972-73 (78)
Fewest Ties	4	1983-84 (80)
Fewest Losses	15	1978-79 (80)
Fewest Goals	170	1972-73 (78)
Fewest Goals Against	190	1975-76 (80)

Longest Winning Streak

Overall	15	Jan. 21/82-Feb. 20/82
Home	14	Jan. 2/82-Feb. 27/82
Away	8	Feb. 27/81-Mar. 31/81

Longest Undefeated Streak

Overall	15	Jan. 21-Feb. 20/82 (15 wins), Nov. 4-Dec. 4/80 (13 wins, 2 ties)
Home	23	Oct. 17/78-Jan. 27/79 (19 wins, 4 ties), Jan. 2/82-Apr. 3/82 (21 wins, 2 ties)
Away	8	Four times

Longest Losing Streak

Overall	12	Dec. 27/72-Jan. 18/73, Nov. 22-Dec. 17/88
Home	5	Jan. 2-23/73, Feb. 28-Mar. 19/74, Nov. 22-Dec. 17/88
Away	15	Jan. 20-Apr. 1/73

Longest Winless Streak

Overall	15	Nov. 22-Dec. 23/72 (12 losses, 3 ties)
Home	7	Oct. 14-Nov. 21/72 (6 losses, 1 tie), Nov. 28-Dec. 23/72 (5 losses, 2 ties), Feb. 13-Mar. 13/90 (4 losses, 3 ties)
Away	20	Nov. 3/72-Jan. 13/73 (19 losses, 1 tie)

Most Shutouts, Season	10	1975-76 (80)
Most PIM, Season	1,857	1986-87 (80)
Most Goals, Game	11	Dec. 20/83 (Pit. 3 at NYI 11), Mar. 3/84 (NYI 11 at Tor. 6)

Individual

Most Seasons	17	Billy Smith
Most Games	1,123	Bryan Trottier
Most Goals, Career	573	Mike Bossy
Most Assists, Career	853	Bryan Trottier
Most Points, Career	1,353	Bryan Trottier (500G, 853A)
Most PIM, Career	1,879	Mick Vukota
Most Shutouts, Career	25	Glenn Resch
Longest Consecutive Games Streak	576	Bill Harris (Oct. 7/72-Nov. 30/79)

Most Goals, Season	69	Mike Bossy (1978-79)
Most Assists, Season	87	Bryan Trottier (1978-79)
Most Points, Season	147	Mike Bossy (1981-82; 64G, 83A)
Most PIM, Season	356	Brian Curran (1986-87)
Most Points, Defenseman, Season	101	Denis Potvin (1978-79; 31G, 70A)
Most Points, Center, Season	134	Bryan Trottier (1978-79; 47G, 87A)
Most Points, Right Wing, Season	147	Mike Bossy (1981-82; 64G, 83A)
Most Points, Left Wing, Season	100	John Tonelli (1984-85; 42G, 58A)
Most Points, Rookie, Season	95	Bryan Trottier (1975-76; 32G, 63A)
Most Shutouts, Season	7	Glenn Resch (1975-76)
Most Goals, Game	5	Bryan Trottier (Dec. 23/78, Feb. 13/82), John Tonelli (Jan. 6/81)
Most Assists, Game	6	Mike Bossy (Jan. 6/81)
Most Points, Game	8	Bryan Trottier (Dec. 23/78; 5G, 3A)

Retired Numbers

5	Denis Potvin	1973-1988
9	Clark Gillies	1974-1986
22	Mike Bossy	1977-1987
23	Bob Nystrom	1972-1986
31	Billy Smith	1972-1989

All-time Record vs. Other Clubs

Regular Season

		At Home							On Road							Total					
	GP	W	L	T	GF	GA	PTS	GP	W	L	T	GF	GA	PTS	GP	W	L	T	GF	GA	PTS
Anaheim	3	2	1	0	8	9	4	3	1	1	1	7	7	3	6	3	2	1	15	16	7
Boston	47	19	23	5	157	158	43	45	10	25	10	130	177	30	92	29	48	15	287	335	73
Buffalo	47	20	20	7	136	134	47	47	15	25	7	136	166	37	94	35	45	14	272	300	84
Calgary	45	25	11	9	184	121	59	45	13	21	11	138	162	37	90	38	32	20	322	283	96
Chicago	41	17	11	13	148	123	47	43	16	22	5	148	145	37	84	33	33	18	296	268	84
Colorado	27	15	11	1	113	96	31	28	10	16	2	89	107	22	55	25	27	3	202	203	53
Dallas	41	23	10	8	161	117	54	41	19	15	7	155	122	45	82	42	25	15	316	239	99
Detroit	40	22	16	2	151	122	46	39	16	21	2	126	140	34	79	38	37	4	277	262	80
Edmonton	25	12	5	8	109	93	32	25	9	11	5	71	98	14	50	17	21	12	180	191	46
Florida	10	3	5	2	22	24	8	10	3	6	1	28	33	7	20	6	11	3	50	57	15
Hartford	29	16	9	4	109	80	36	31	12	14	5	114	115	29	60	28	23	9	223	195	65
Los Angeles	39	22	13	4	149	113	48	39	14	18	7	127	142	35	78	36	31	11	276	255	83
Montreal	46	20	21	5	147	137	45	46	11	27	8	138	176	30	92	31	48	13	285	313	75
New Jersey	66	49	8	9	309	183	107	66	31	25	10	253	225	72	132	80	33	19	562	408	179
NY Rangers	78	49	22	7	321	242	105	78	24	46	8	239	308	56	156	73	68	15	560	550	161
Ottawa	10	3	4	3	38	36	9	9	3	4	2	33	27	8	19	6	8	5	71	63	17
Philadelphia	80	43	24	13	313	235	99	77	23	46	8	233	294	54	157	66	70	21	546	529	153
Phoenix	25	12	7	6	100	80	30	24	14	7	3	94	75	31	49	26	14	9	194	155	61
Pittsburgh	69	36	25	8	285	230	80	70	26	33	11	246	269	63	139	62	58	19	531	499	143
St. Louis	43	23	10	10	166	108	56	42	17	17	8	140	155	42	85	40	27	18	306	263	98
San Jose	6	5	0	1	33	19	11	5	2	2	1	19	13	5	11	7	2	2	52	32	16
Tampa Bay	11	3	8	0	28	41	6	11	4	6	1	33	34	9	22	7	14	1	61	75	15
Toronto	40	23	14	3	173	125	49	42	20	19	3	152	144	43	82	43	33	6	325	269	92
Vancouver	41	23	10	8	157	111	54	43	20	20	3	142	143	43	84	43	30	11	299	254	97
Washington	66	40	25	1	266	205	81	66	29	28	9	220	211	67	132	69	53	10	486	416	148
Defunct Clubs	13	11	0	2	75	33	24	13	4	5	4	35	41	12	26	15	5	6	110	74	36
Totals	**988**	**536**	**313**	**139**	**3858**	**2975**	**1211**	**988**	**362**	**485**	**141**	**3246**	**3529**	**865**	**1976**	**898**	**798**	**280**	**7104**	**6504**	**2076**

Playoffs

									Last			
	Series	W	L	GP	W	L	T	GF	GA	Mtg.	Round	Result
Boston	2	2	0	11	8	3	0	49	35	1983	CF	W 4-2
Buffalo	3	3	0	16	12	4	0	59	45	1980	SF	W 4-2
Chicago	2	2	0	6	6	0	0	21	6	1979	QF	W 4-0
Colorado	1	1	0	4	4	0	0	18	9	1982	F	W 4-0
Dallas	1	1	0	5	4	1	0	26	16	1981	F	W 4-1
Edmonton	3	2	1	15	9	6	0	58	47	1984	F	L 1-4
Los Angeles	1	1	0	4	3	1	0	21	10	1980	PR	W 3-1
Montreal	4	1	3	22	8	14	0	55	64	1993	CF	L 1-4
New Jersey	1	0	1	6	2	4	0	18	23	1988	DSF	L 2-4
NY Rangers	8	5	3	39	20	19	0	129	132	1994	CQF	L 0-4
Philadelphia	4	1	3	25	11	14	0	69	83	1987	DF	L 3-4
Pittsburgh	3	3	0	19	11	8	0	67	58	1993	DF	W 4-3
Toronto	2	1	1	10	6	4	0	33	20	1981	PR	W 3-0
Vancouver	2	2	0	6	6	0	0	26	14	1982	F	W 4-0
Washington	6	5	1	30	18	12	0	99	88	1993	DSF	W 4-2
Totals	**43**	**30**	**13**	**218**	**128**	**90**	**0**	**748**	**650**			

Playoff Results 1997-93

Year	Round	Opponent	Result	GF	GA
1994	CQF	NY Rangers	L 0-4	3	22
1993	CF	Montreal	L 1-4	11	16
	DF	Pittsburgh	W 4-3	24	22
	DSF	Washington	W 4-2	23	22

Abbreviations: Round: F – Final;
CF – conference final; **CQF** – conference quarter-final;
CSF – conference semi-final; **DF** – division final;
DSF – division semi-final; **SF** – semi-final;
QF – quarter-final; **PR** – preliminary round.

Calgary totals include Atlanta, 1972-73 to 1979-80.   Colorado totals include Quebec, 1979-80 to 1994-95.
Dallas totals include Minnesota, 1972-73 to 1992-93.   New Jersey totals include Kansas City, 1974-75 to 1975-76, and
Colorado Rockies, 1976-77 to 1981-82.   Phoenix totals include Winnipeg, 1979-80 to 1995-96.

1996-97 Results

Oct.	4	at	Los Angeles	0-1	11	at Tampa Bay	4-4
	5	at	San Jose	2-2	13	at NY Rangers	4-2
	9	at	Ottawa	3-3	15	Buffalo	1-2
	12		Philadelphia	5-1	20	St. Louis	4-6
	17		Hartford	1-3	22	Edmonton	8-1
	19	at	Detroit	2-4	24	at Hartford	5-1
	22		Tampa Bay	3-6	25	Chicago	3-2
	26		San Jose	2-2	28	at Calgary	3-4
	30	at	Hartford	2-2	30	at Vancouver	1-2
	31		Toronto	3-5	31	at Edmonton	0-1
Nov.	2		Washington	6-1	Feb. 4	Anaheim	4-3
	4	at	Philadelphia	4-3	5	at New Jersey	1-4
	6		NY Rangers	1-8	7	NY Rangers	2-5
	9	at	New Jersey	0-4	11	Ottawa	5-5
	11		Colorado	2-6	12	at Pittsburgh	5-1
	13		Vancouver	5-4	15	Florida	1-0
	15	at	Florida	3-3	17	Montreal	1-4
	16		Ottawa	1-4	21	at Buffalo	2-5
	20	at	Anaheim	2-2	23	Pittsburgh	4-1
	22	at	Colorado	2-3	26	New Jersey	3-5
	23	at	Phoenix	3-3	28	at Ottawa	1-4
	27		Philadelphia	4-1	Mar. 2	at Washington	2-0
	29	at	Washington	2-0	4	Tampa Bay	3-6
	30		Buffalo	2-3	6	Boston	5-2
Dec.	3		Calgary	3-1	8	New Jersey	5-1
	5	at	Florida	2-4	11	at Florida	2-3
	7		Washington	2-0	13	at Tampa Bay	3-0
	10		Phoenix	8-2	15	at Boston	2-5
	11	at	NY Rangers	5-3	16	at Chicago	4-5
	14	at	Tampa Bay	1-4	19	Florida	7-4
	17		Los Angeles	4-3	22	Philadelphia	3-3
	19	at	Philadelphia	0-5	26	at Buffalo	6-3
	21		Dallas	2-3	27	at Boston	6-3
	23		Florida	3-4	29	Boston	8-2
	26		New Jersey	4-1	Apr. 2	at Dallas	4-5
	28		Detroit	1-7	3	at St. Louis	5-5
	30	at	Toronto	0-2	5	Tampa Bay	2-3
Jan.	2	at	NY Rangers	3-4	7	at Montreal	1-2
	7	at	Montreal	1-3	9	Montreal	1-3
	9		Pittsburgh	3-5	11	Hartford	6-4
	10	at	Pittsburgh	2-5	12	at Washington	2-6

Entry Draft
Selections 1997-83

1997
Pick
- 4 Roberto Luongo
- 5 Eric Brewer
- 31 Jeff Zehr
- 59 Jarrett Smith
- 79 Robert Schnabel
- 85 Petr Mika
- 115 Adam Edinger
- 139 Bobby Leavins
- 166 Kris Knoblauch
- 196 Jeremy Symington
- 222 Ryan Clark

1996
Pick
- 3 Jean-Pierre Dumont
- 29 Dan Lacouture
- 56 Zdeno Chara
- 83 Tyrone Garner
- 109 Andy Berenzweig
- 128 Petr Sachl
- 138 Todd Miller
- 165 Joe Prestifilippo
- 192 Evgeny Korolev
- 218 Mike Muzechka

1995
Pick
- 2 Wade Redden
- 28 Jan Hlavac
- 41 Denis Smith
- 106 Vladimir Orszagh
- 158 Andrew Taylor
- 210 David MacDonald
- 211 Mike Broda

1994
Pick
- 9 Brett Lindros
- 38 Jason Holland
- 63 Jason Strudwick
- 90 Brad Lukowich
- 112 Mark McArthur
- 116 Albert O'Connell
- 142 Jason Stewart
- 194 Mike Loach
- 203 Peter Hogardh
- 220 Gord Walsh
- 246 Kirk Dewaele
- 272 Dick Tarnstrom

1993
Pick
- 23 Todd Bertuzzi
- 40 Bryan McCabe
- 66 Vladim Chebaturkin
- 92 Warren Luhning
- 118 Tommy Salo
- 144 Peter Leboutillier
- 170 Darren Van Impe
- 196 Rod Hinks
- 222 Daniel Johansson
- 248 Stephane Larocque
- 274 Carl Charland

1992
Pick
- 5 Darius Kasparaitis
- 56 Jarrett Deuling
- 104 Tomas Klimt
- 105 Ryan Duthie
- 128 Derek Armstrong
- 152 Vladimir Grachev
- 159 Steve O'Rourke
- 176 Jason Widmer
- 200 Daniel Paradis
- 224 David Wainwright
- 248 Andrei Vasiljev

1991
Pick
- 4 Scott Lachance
- 26 Zigmund Palffy
- 48 Jamie McLennan
- 70 Milan Hnilicka
- 92 Steve Junker
- 114 Robert Valicevic
- 136 Andreas Johansson
- 158 Todd Sparks
- 180 John Johnson
- 202 Robert Canavan
- 224 Marcus Thuresson
- 246 Marty Schriner

1990
Pick
- 6 Scott Scissons
- 27 Chris Taylor
- 48 Dan Plante
- 90 Chris Marinucci
- 111 Joni Lehto
- 132 Michael Guilbert
- 153 Sylvain Fleury
- 174 John Joyce
- 195 Richard Enga
- 216 Martin Lacroix
- 237 Andy Shirr

1989
Pick
- 2 Dave Chyzowski
- 23 Travis Green
- 44 Jason Zent
- 65 Brent Grieve
- 86 Jace Reed
- 90 Steve Young
- 99 Kevin O'Sullivan
- 128 Jon Larson
- 133 Brett Harkins
- 149 Phil Huber
- 170 Matthew Robbins
- 191 Vladimir Malakhov
- 212 Kelly Ens
- 233 Iain Fraser

1988
Pick
- 16 Kevin Cheveldayoff
- 29 Wayne Doucet
- 37 Sean LeBrun
- 58 Danny Lorenz
- 79 Andre Brassard
- 100 Paul Rutherford
- 111 Pavel Gross
- 121 Jason Rathbone
- 142 Yves Gaucher
- 163 Marty McInnis
- 184 Jeff Blumer
- 205 Jeff Kampersal
- 226 Phillip Neururer
- 247 Joe Capprini

1987
Pick
- 13 Dean Chynoweth
- 34 Jeff Hackett
- 55 Dean Ewen
- 76 George Maneluk
- 97 Petr Vlk
- 118 Rob DiMaio
- 139 Knut Walbye
- 160 Jeff Saterdalen
- 181 Shawn Howard
- 202 John Herlihy
- 223 Michael Erickson
- 244 Will Averill

1986
Pick
- 17 Tom Fitzgerald
- 38 Dennis Vaske
- 59 Bill Berg
- 80 Shawn Byram
- 101 Dean Sexsmith
- 104 Todd McLellan
- 122 Tony Schmalzbauer
- 138 Will Anderson
- 143 Richard Pilon
- 164 Peter Harris
- 185 Jeff Jablonski
- 206 Kerry Clark
- 227 Dan Beaudette
- 248 Paul Thompson

1985
Pick
- 6 Brad Dalgarno
- 13 Derek King
- 34 Brad Lauer
- 55 Jeff Finley
- 76 Kevin Herom
- 89 Tommy Hedlund
- 97 Jeff Sveen
- 118 Rod Dallman
- 139 Kurt Lackten
- 160 Hank Lammens
- 181 Rich Wiest
- 202 Real Arsenault
- 223 Mike Volpe
- 244 Tony Grenier

1984
Pick
- 20 Duncan MacPherson
- 41 Bruce Melanson
- 62 Jeff Norton
- 70 Doug Wieck
- 83 Ari Haanpaa
- 104 Mike Murray
- 125 Jim Wilharm
- 146 Kelly Murphy
- 167 Franco Desantis
- 187 Tom Warden
- 208 David Volek
- 228 Russ Becker
- 249 Allister Brown

1983
Pick
- 3 Pat LaFontaine
- 16 Gerald Diduck
- 37 Garnet McKechney
- 57 Mike Neill
- 65 Mikko Makila
- 84 Bob Caulfield
- 97 Ron Viglasi
- 117 Darin Illikainen
- 137 Jim Sprenger
- 157 Dale Henry
- 177 Kevin Vescio
- 197 Dave Shellington
- 217 John Bjorkman
- 237 Peter McGeough

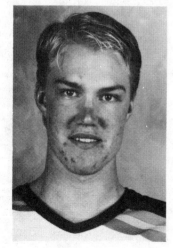

With his steady, stay-at-home style, Kenny Jonsson led all Islander blueliners with a plus/minus rating of +10.

Club Directory

**Nassau Veterans'
Memorial Coliseum**
Uniondale, NY 11553
Phone **516/794-4100**
FAX 516/542-9348
www.xice.com
Capacity: 16,297

Owner	John O. Pickett Jr.
Governor and General Counsel	William Skehan
Senior Vice President, CFO and Alternate Governor	Arthur McCarthy
Alternate Governors	John Krumpe, Barrett N. Pickett

Hockey Operations

General Manager	Mike Milbury
Director of Player Personnel	Gordie Clark
Consultant to the General Manager	Al Arbour
Head Coach	Rick Bowness
Assistant Coaches	Wayne Fleming, Brad McCrimmon
Strength and Conditioning Coach	Steig Theander
Assistants to the General Manager	Joanne Holewa, Mike Santos
Head Amateur Scout	Tony Feltrin
Western Scout	Earl Ingarfield
Director of Pro Scouting	Ken Morrow
Assistant Director of Pro Scouting	Kevin Maxwell
Director of Player Development	Chris Pryor
Scouting Staff	Jim Madigan, Jim McMahon, Mario Saraceno
Video Coordinator	Bob Smith
Administrative Assistant	Pam Genzardi

Medical Staff

Director of Medical Services	Dr. Elliot Pellman
Internist	Dr. Clifford Cooper
Team Orthopedists	Dr. Elliott Hershman, Dr. Stephen Nicholas, Dr. Kenneth Montgomery
Team Dentists	Dr. Bruce Michnik, Dr. Jan Sherman

Training Staff

Head Trainer	Rich Campbell
Assistant Trainer	Sean Donellan

Equipment Staff

Head Equipment Manager	Joe McMahon
Assistant Equipment Manager	Eric Miklich
Lockerroom Attendants	Tom Severance, Charles E. Nass

Communications Staff

Vice President/Communications	Patrick Calabria
Director of Game Events	Tim Beach
Director of Media and Public Relations	Ginger Killian
Director of Publishing/Public Relations Associate	Chris Botta
Director of Game Events	Tim Beach
Director of Special Events	Maureen Brady
Media Relations Assistant	Jason Lagnese
Public Relations Assistant/Manager of Amateur Hockey Development	Tom Bigliani
Administrative Assistant	Giselle Marinello
Office Attendant	Todd Aronovich

Sales and Administration

Vice President/Media Sales	Arthur Adler
Controller	Ralph Sellitti
Assistant Controller	Ginna Cotton
Director of Administration	Joseph Dreyer
Director of Corporate Relations	Bob Nystrom
Director of Corporate Sales	Bill Kain
Director of Executive Suites	Tracy F. Matthews
Director of Marketing and Ticket Sales	Brian Edwards
Director of Merchandising	Gary DiSimone
Director of Suite Operations	Sam Buonogura
Office Manager/Group Administrator	Kathleen Maloney
Accountants	Christine Bowler, Lois Odermatt
Ticket Manager	Vincent DiOrio
Assistant Ticket Managers	Joy Rusciano, Kerry Cornils
Premier Seat Coordinator	Margaret Barrett
Sales Managers	Tom Engel, Brian Rabinowitz, Richard Gaudet, Andrew Smith
Account Executives	Rich Davis, Joseph Graves, Scott Lindquist, Matthew Manfredi, Eric Schiebe, Rob Zampolin
Corporate Sales Representative	Ted Van Zelst
Account Representatives	Larry Fitzpatrick, Brian Reynolds, Frank Gulotta
Marketing Manager	Dierdre Hannett
Team Store Managers	Chris DiPierri, Maryanne Steves
Receptionists	Colleen Touhey-Ramirez, Margaret Petrocelli
Promotional Assistants	Howard Hutton, Brian Huhl, Randy Risorto

Team Information

Colors	Orange, blue, white, silver, Atlantic green
Television Coverage	SportsChannel
Announcers	Howie Rose, Ed Westfall, Stan Fischler
Radio	WLIR – 92.7 & 98.5
Announcers	Jim Cerny, Chris Botta

New York Rangers

1996-97 Results: 38W-34L-10T 86PTS. Fourth, Atlantic Division

Wayne Gretzky reaffirmed his status as the Great One, tying for the League lead with 72 assists and earning his 14th post-season All-Star Team berth.

1997-98 Schedule

Oct.	Fri.	3	NY Islanders		Wed.	31	at Tampa Bay
	Sun.	5	Los Angeles	Jan.	Sat.	3	at Washington
	Wed.	8	at Edmonton		Tue.	6	Carolina
	Thu.	9	at Calgary		Thu.	8	Washington
	Sat.	11	at Vancouver		Sat.	10	at Montreal
	Tue.	14	Pittsburgh		Mon.	12	Toronto
	Wed.	15	at Ottawa		Wed.	14	at New Jersey
	Sat.	18	at St. Louis		Tue.	20	St. Louis
	Mon.	20	Carolina		Thu.	22	Philadelphia
	Wed.	22	Chicago		Sat.	24	New Jersey*
	Fri.	24	Tampa Bay		Mon.	26	Washington
	Sun.	26	Anaheim		Thu.	29	at Ottawa
	Tue.	28	Dallas		Sat.	31	at Boston*
	Thu.	30	at NY Islanders	Feb.	Mon.	2	at San Jose
Nov.	Mon.	3	Edmonton		Wed.	4	at Anaheim
	Wed.	5	at Colorado		Thu.	5	at Los Angeles
	Fri.	7	at Dallas		Sat.	7	at Phoenix
	Wed.	12	New Jersey		Thu.	26	at Toronto
	Fri.	14	Pittsburgh		Sat.	28	Philadelphia*
	Sun.	16	Colorado*	Mar.	Mon.	2	Buffalo
	Tue.	18	at Florida		Wed.	4	at Florida
	Wed.	19	at Tampa Bay		Sat.	7	at New Jersey*
	Fri.	21	at Carolina		Mon.	9	New Jersey
	Sat.	22	at Pittsburgh		Wed.	11	San Jose
	Tue.	25	Vancouver		Sat.	14	at Boston*
	Wed.	26	at NY Islanders		Mon.	16	Ottawa
	Fri.	28	at Buffalo		Wed.	18	Montreal
	Sun.	30	Florida*		Sat.	21	at Detroit*
Dec.	Tue.	2	Washington		Sun.	22	at Philadelphia
	Fri.	5	Philadelphia		Wed.	25	Ottawa
	Sat.	6	at Montreal		Thu.	26	at Carolina
	Mon.	8	Phoenix		Sat.	28	at Pittsburgh*
	Wed.	10	Calgary		Mon.	30	Tampa Bay
	Fri.	12	Florida	Apr.	Wed.	1	Boston
	Tue.	16	at New Jersey		Sat.	4	at NY Islanders*
	Wed.	17	at Florida		Sun.	5	at Chicago*
	Sat.	20	at Tampa Bay*		Tue.	7	Montreal
	Sun.	21	Buffalo		Sat.	11	at Detroit*
	Tue.	23	Tampa Bay		Tue.	14	at Washington
	Fri.	26	at Buffalo		Wed.	15	NY Islanders
	Sun.	28	Boston		Sat.	18	at Philadelphia*

* Denotes afternoon game.

Franchise date: May 15, 1926

EASTERN CONFERENCE

ATLANTIC DIVISION

72nd NHL Season

Year-by-Year Record

		Home			Road			Overall						
Season	GP	W	L	T	W	L	T	W	L	T	GF	GA	Pts.	Finished	Playoff Result
1996-97	82	21	14	6	17	20	4	38	34	10	258	231	86	4th, Atlantic Div.	Lost Conf. Final
1995-96	82	22	10	9	19	17	5	41	27	14	272	237	96	2nd, Atlantic Div.	Lost Conf. Semi-Final
1994-95	48	11	10	3	11	13	0	22	23	3	139	134	47	4th, Atlantic Div.	Lost Conf. Semi-Final
1993-94	**84**	**28**	**8**	**6**	**24**	**16**	**2**	**52**	**24**	**8**	**299**	**231**	**112**	**1st, Atlantic Div.**	**Won Stanley Cup**
1992-93	84	20	17	5	14	22	6	34	39	11	304	308	79	6th, Patrick Div.	Out of Playoffs
1991-92	80	28	8	4	22	17	1	50	25	5	321	246	105	1st, Patrick Div.	Lost Div. Final
1990-91	80	22	11	7	14	20	6	36	31	13	297	265	85	2nd, Patrick Div.	Lost Div. Semi-Final
1989-90	80	20	11	9	16	20	4	36	31	13	279	267	85	1st, Patrick Div.	Lost Div. Final
1988-89	80	21	17	2	16	18	6	37	35	8	310	307	82	3rd, Patrick Div.	Lost Div. Semi-Final
1987-88	80	22	13	5	14	21	5	36	34	10	300	283	82	5th, Patrick Div.	Out of Playoffs
1986-87	80	18	18	4	16	20	4	34	38	8	307	323	76	4th, Patrick Div.	Lost Div. Semi-Final
1985-86	80	20	18	2	16	20	4	36	38	6	280	276	78	4th, Patick Div.	Lost Conf. Championship
1984-85	80	16	18	6	10	26	4	26	44	10	295	345	62	4th, Patrick Div.	Lost Div. Semi-Final
1983-84	80	27	12	1	15	17	8	42	29	9	314	304	93	4th, Patrick Div.	Lost Div. Semi-Final
1982-83	80	24	13	3	11	22	7	35	35	10	306	287	80	4th, Patrick Div.	Lost Div. Final
1981-82	80	19	15	6	20	12	8	39	27	14	316	306	92	2nd, Patrick Div.	Lost Div. Final
1980-81	80	17	13	10	13	23	4	30	36	14	312	317	74	4th, Patrick Div.	Lost Semi-Final
1979-80	80	22	10	8	16	22	2	38	32	10	308	284	86	3rd, Patrick Div.	Lost Quarter-Final
1978-79	80	19	13	8	21	16	3	40	29	11	316	292	91	3rd, Patrick Div.	Lost Final
1977-78	80	18	15	7	12	22	6	30	37	13	279	280	73	4th, Patrick Div.	Lost Prelim. Round
1976-77	80	17	18	5	12	19	9	29	37	14	272	310	72	4th, Patrick Div.	Out of Playoffs
1975-76	80	16	16	8	13	26	1	29	42	9	262	333	67	4th, Patrick Div.	Out of Playoffs
1974-75	80	21	11	8	16	18	6	37	29	14	319	276	88	2nd, Patrick Div.	Lost Prelim. Round
1973-74	78	26	7	6	14	17	8	40	24	14	300	251	94	3rd, East Div.	Lost Semi-Final
1972-73	78	26	8	5	21	15	3	47	23	8	297	208	102	3rd, East Div.	Lost Semi-Final
1971-72	78	26	7	6	22	11	6	48	17	13	317	192	109	2nd, East Div.	Lost Final
1970-71	78	30	2	7	19	16	4	49	18	11	259	177	109	2nd, East Div.	Lost Semi-Final
1969-70	76	22	8	8	16	14	8	38	22	16	246	189	92	4th, East Div.	Lost Quarter-Final
1968-69	76	27	7	4	14	19	5	41	26	9	231	196	91	3rd, East Div.	Lost Quarter-Final
1967-68	74	22	8	7	17	15	5	39	23	12	226	183	90	2nd, East Div.	Lost Quarter-Final
1966-67	70	18	12	5	12	16	7	30	28	12	188	189	72	4th,	Lost Semi-Final
1965-66	70	12	16	7	6	25	4	18	41	11	195	261	47	6th,	Out of Playoffs
1964-65	70	8	19	8	12	19	4	20	38	12	179	246	52	5th,	Out of Playoffs
1963-64	70	14	13	8	8	25	2	22	38	10	186	242	54	5th,	Out of Playoffs
1962-63	70	12	17	6	10	19	6	22	36	12	211	233	56	5th,	Out of Playoffs
1961-62	70	16	11	8	10	21	4	26	32	12	195	207	64	4th,	Lost Semi-Final
1960-61	70	15	15	5	7	23	5	22	38	10	204	248	54	5th,	Out of Playoffs
1959-60	70	10	15	10	7	23	5	17	38	15	187	247	49	6th,	Out of Playoffs
1958-59	70	14	16	5	12	16	7	26	32	12	201	217	64	5th,	Out of Playoffs
1957-58	70	14	15	6	18	10	7	32	25	13	195	188	77	2nd,	Lost Semi-Final
1956-57	70	15	12	8	11	18	6	26	30	14	184	227	66	4th,	Lost Semi-Final
1955-56	70	20	7	8	12	21	2	32	28	10	204	203	74	3rd,	Lost Semi-Final
1954-55	70	10	12	13	7	23	5	17	35	18	150	210	52	5th,	Out of Playoffs
1953-54	70	18	12	5	11	19	5	29	31	10	161	182	68	5th,	Out of Playoffs
1952-53	70	11	14	10	6	23	6	17	37	16	152	211	50	6th,	Out of Playoffs
1951-52	70	16	13	6	7	21	7	23	34	13	192	219	59	5th,	Out of Playoffs
1950-51	70	14	11	10	6	18	11	20	29	21	169	201	61	5th,	Out of Playoffs
1949-50	70	19	12	4	9	19	7	28	31	11	170	189	67	4th,	Lost Final
1948-49	60	13	12	5	5	19	6	18	31	11	133	172	47	6th,	Out of Playoffs
1947-48	60	11	12	7	10	14	6	21	26	13	176	201	55	4th,	Lost Semi-Final
1946-47	60	11	14	5	11	18	1	22	32	6	167	186	50	5th,	Out of Playoffs
1945-46	50	8	12	5	5	16	4	13	28	9	144	191	35	6th,	Out of Playoffs
1944-45	50	7	11	7	4	18	3	11	29	10	154	247	32	6th,	Out of Playoffs
1943-44	50	4	17	4	2	22	1	6	39	5	162	310	17	6th,	Out of Playoffs
1942-43	50	7	13	5	4	18	3	11	31	8	161	253	30	6th,	Out of Playoffs
1941-42	48	15	8	1	14	9	1	29	17	2	177	143	60	1st,	Lost Semi-Final
1940-41	48	13	7	4	8	12	4	21	19	8	143	125	50	4th,	Lost Quarter-Final
1939-40	**48**	**17**	**4**	**3**	**10**	**7**	**7**	**27**	**11**	**10**	**136**	**77**	**64**	**2nd,**	**Won Stanley Cup**
1938-39	48	13	8	3	13	8	3	26	16	6	149	105	58	2nd,	Lost Semi-Final
1937-38	48	15	5	4	12	10	2	27	15	6	149	96	60	2nd, Amn. Div.	Lost Quarter-Final
1936-37	48	9	7	8	10	13	1	19	20	9	117	106	47	3rd, Amn. Div.	Lost Final
1935-36	48	11	6	7	8	11	5	19	17	12	91	96	50	4th, Amn. Div.	Out of Playoffs
1934-35	48	11	8	5	11	12	1	22	20	6	137	139	50	3rd, Amn. Div.	Lost Semi-Final
1933-34	48	11	7	6	10	12	2	21	19	8	120	113	50	3rd, Amn. Div.	Lost Quarter-Final
1932-33	**48**	**12**	**7**	**5**	**11**	**10**	**3**	**23**	**17**	**8**	**135**	**107**	**54**	**3rd, Amn. Div.**	**Won Stanley Cup**
1931-32	48	13	7	4	10	10	4	23	17	8	134	112	54	1st,	Lost Final
1930-31	44	11	5	6	8	9	5	19	16	9	106	87	47	3rd, Amn. Div.	Lost Semi-Final
1929-30	44	11	5	6	6	12	4	17	17	10	136	143	44	3rd, Amn. Div.	Lost Semi-Final
1928-29	44	12	6	4	9	7	6	21	13	10	72	65	52	2nd, Amn. Div.	Lost Final
1927-28	**44**	**10**	**8**	**4**	**9**	**8**	**5**	**19**	**16**	**9**	**94**	**79**	**47**	**2nd, Amn. Div.**	**Won Stanley Cup**
1926-27	44	13	5	4	12	8	2	25	13	6	95	72	56	1st, Amn. Div.	Lost Quarter-Final

1997-98 Player Personnel

FORWARDS	HT	WT	S	Place of Birth	Date	1996-97 Club
BERG, Bill	6-1	205	L	St. Catharines, Ont.	10/21/67	NY Rangers
BLOUIN, Sylvain	6-2	207	L	Montreal, Que.	5/21/74	NY Rangers-Binghamton
BOULTON, Eric	6-0	201	L	Halifax, N.S.	8/17/76	Binghamton-Charlotte
BROSSEAU, David	6-1	190	R	Montreal, Que.	1/16/76	Binghamton-Charlotte
CHERNESKI, Stefan	6-0	195	L	Winnipeg, Man.	9/19/78	Brandon
CHURLA, Shane	6-1	200	R	Fernie, B.C.	6/24/65	NY Rangers
DUBE, Christian	5-11	170	R	Sherbrooke, Que.	4/25/77	NY Rangers-Hull
EASTWOOD, Mike	6-3	205	R	Ottawa, Ont.	7/1/67	Phoenix-NY Rangers
FERRARO, Chris	5-10	185	R	Port Jefferson, NY	1/24/73	NY Rangers-Binghamton
FERRARO, Peter	5-10	185	R	Port Jefferson, NY	1/24/73	NY Rangers-Binghamton
GERNANDER, Ken	5-10	180	L	Coleraine, MN	6/30/69	Binghamton-NY Rangers
GONEAU, Daniel	6-0	194	L	Montreal, Que.	1/16/76	NY Rangers-Binghamton
GRAVES, Adam	6-0	210	L	Toronto, Ont.	4/12/68	NY Rangers
GRETZKY, Wayne	6-0	185	L	Brantford, Ont.	1/26/61	NY Rangers
KEANE, Mike	6-0	185	R	Winnipeg, Man.	5/29/67	Colorado
KOVALEV, Alexei	6-0	210	L	Togliatti, USSR	2/24/73	NY Rangers
LANGDON, Darren	6-1	200	L	Deer Lake, Nfld.	1/8/71	NY Rangers
LINDBOM, Johan	6-2	216	L	Alvesta, Sweden	7/8/71	HV 71
MAUDIE, Bob	5-11	180	L	Cranbrook, B.C.	9/17/76	Binghamton-Charlotte
PELUSO, Mike	6-4	225	L	Pengilly, MN	11/8/65	New Jersey-St. Louis
PEPPERALL, Colin	5-10	160	L	Niagara Falls, Ont.	4/28/78	Erie (OHL)
SAVARD, Marc	5-10	174	L	Ottawa, Ont.	7/17/77	Oshawa
SEVIGNY, Pierre	6-0	195	L	Trois-Rivières, Que.	9/8/71	Montreal-Fredericton
SKRUDLAND, Brian	6-0	195	L	Peace River, Alta.	7/31/63	Florida
SLAMIAR, Peter	5-11	174	R	Zvolen, Czech.	2/26/77	B. Bystrica-Shawinigan
STEVENS, Kevin	6-3	217	L	Brockton, MA	4/15/65	Los Angeles
SUBBOTIN, Dmitri	6-1	183	L	Tomsk, USSR	10/20/77	CSKA-CSKA
SUNDSTROM, Niklas	6-0	185	L	Ornskoldsvik, Sweden	6/6/75	NY Rangers
VANDENBUSSCHE, Ryan	5-11	187	R	Simcoe, Ont.	2/28/73	NY Rangers-Binghamton
VOROBIEV, Vladimir	6-0	185	R	Cherepovets, USSR	10/2/72	NY Rangers-Binghamton
DEFENSEMEN						
BEUKEBOOM, Jeff	6-5	230	R	Ajax, Ont.	3/28/65	NY Rangers
BROWN, Jeff	6-1	215	R	Mississauga, Ont.	4/24/78	Sarnia-London
CAIRNS, Eric	6-5	230	L	Oakville, Ont.	6/27/74	NY Rangers-Binghamton
CAMPBELL, Ed	6-2	212	L	Worcester, MA	11/26/74	Binghamton
DRIVER, Bruce	6-0	185	L	Toronto, Ont.	4/29/62	NY Rangers
FINLEY, Jeff	6-2	205	L	Edmonton, Alta.	4/14/67	Phoenix
FIORENTINO, Peter	6-1	205	R	Niagara Falls, Ont.	12/22/68	Binghamton
GALANOV, Maxim	6-1	195	L	Krasnoyarsk, USSR	3/13/74	Binghamton
HALL, Todd	6-1	212	L	Hamden, CT	1/22/73	Binghamton-Charlotte
HENRY, Burke	6-2	190	L	Ste. Rose, Man.	1/21/79	Brandon
JARVIS, Wes	6-4	203	L	Toronto, Ont.	4/16/79	Kitchener
JOHNSSON, Kim	6-1	175	L	Malmo, Sweden	3/16/76	Malmo
KALLARSSON, Tomi	6-3	194	L	Lempaala, Finland	3/15/79	HPK
KARPOVTSEV, Alexander	6-1	205	R	Moscow, USSR	4/7/70	NY Rangers
KOROBOLIN, Alexander	6-2	189	L	Chelyabinsk, USSR	3/12/76	Chelyabinsk
LEETCH, Brian	5-11	190	L	Corpus Christi, TX	3/3/68	NY Rangers
LIDSTER, Doug	6-1	190	R	Kamloops, B.C.	10/18/60	NY Rangers
MARTIN, Mike	6-2	204	R	Stratford, Ont.	10/27/76	Binghamton
McKIE, Ryan	6-2	198	R	Kenora, Ont.	3/30/78	London-Sudbury
SAMUELSSON, Ulf	6-1	205	L	Fagersta, Sweden	3/26/64	NY Rangers
SMITH, Adam	6-0	190	L	Digby, N.S.	5/24/76	Binghamton
SOROCHAN, Lee	5-11	210	L	Edmonton, Alta.	9/9/75	Binghamton
SUNDIN, Ronnie	6-1	220	L	Ludvika, Sweden	10/3/70	V. Frolunda
THOMPSON, Brent	6-2	200	L	Calgary, Alta.	1/9/71	Pho-Springfield-Phoenix (IHL)
VASILIEV, Alexei	6-1	190	L	Yaroslavl, USSR	9/1/77	Yaroslavl
GOALTENDERS	**HT**	**WT**	**C**	**Place of Birth**	**Date**	**1996-97 Club**
CLOUTIER, Dan	6-1	182	L	Mont-Laurier, Que.	4/22/76	Binghamton
HEIL, Jeff	6-1	190	L	Bloomington, MN	9/17/75	Wisc.-River Falls
MUZZATTI, Jason	6-2	210	L	Toronto, Ont.	2/3/70	Hartford
RICHTER, Mike	5-11	187	L	Abington, PA	9/22/66	NY Rangers
STAUBER, Robb	5-11	180	L	Duluth, MN	11/25/67	Portland (AHL)

General Manager

SMITH, NEIL

General Manager, New York Rangers. Born in Toronto, Ont., January 9, 1954.

Through his first eight years at the helm of the Rangers, Neil Smith has enjoyed great success. The club has posted an overall record of 309-234-77, ranking fifth among NHL teams since 1989-90. New York has captured three divisional titles, two Presidents' Trophies and one Stanley Cup championship.

In 1993-94, the Rangers captured the fourth Stanley Cup in franchise history, defeating Vancouver four games to three. The championship was the culmination of a season in which New York set a club record with 52 wins and 112 points. The Rangers captured their second Presidents' Trophy in three years and became the first team since the Presidents' Trophy was established to win it, along with the Conference Championship and Stanley Cup, in the same year. Following the season, Neil was awarded with *The Hockey News* executive of the year award.

In his first three seasons as general manager after joining the Rangers on July 17, 1989, New York enjoyed the best three consecutive finishes in club history.

On June 19, 1992, he was promoted to the position of president and general manager, becoming the ninth president in Rangers' history and the first president to also hold the title of general manager.

A native of Toronto, Ontario, Smith played junior hockey at Brockville, Ontario, before entering Western Michigan University where he became an All-American defenseman as a freshman and team captain in his second year.

After being selected by the New York Islanders in the NHL Amateur Draft and playing two seasons in the International Hockey League, Neil joined the Islanders scouting department during the 1980-81 season. Following two seasons in that capacity, he joined the Detroit Red Wings in 1982 as director of professional scouting and soon after became director of their farm system.

Smith was then named director of scouting, and general manager/governor of the Adirondack Red Wings of the AHL, where he won two Calder Cup championships.

1996-97 Scoring

* – rookie

Regular Season

Pos	#	Player	Team	GP	G	A	Pts	+/–	PIM	PP	SH	GW	GT	S	%
C	99	Wayne Gretzky	NYR	82	25	72	97	12	28	6	0	2	1	286	8.7
C	11	Mark Messier	NYR	71	36	48	84	12	88	7	5	9	1	227	15.9
D	2	Brian Leetch	NYR	82	20	58	78	31	40	9	0	2	0	256	7.8
L	9	Adam Graves	NYR	82	33	28	61	10	66	10	4	3	5	269	12.3
L	24	Niklas Sundstrom	NYR	82	24	28	52	23	20	5	1	4	0	132	18.2
L	20	Luc Robitaille	NYR	69	24	24	48	16	48	5	0	4	0	200	12.0
D	25	A. Karpovtsev	NYR	77	9	29	38	1	59	6	1	0	0	84	10.7
R	27	Alexei Kovalev	NYR	45	13	22	35	11	42	1	0	0	0	110	11.8
R	21	Russ Courtnall	VAN	47	9	19	28	4	24	1	0	1	0	101	8.9
			NYR	14	2	5	7	-3	2	1	1	1	0	24	8.3
			TOTAL	61	11	24	35	1	26	2	1	2	0	125	8.8
L	10	Esa Tikkanen	VAN	62	12	15	27	-9	66	4	1	2	1	103	11.7
			NYR	14	1	2	3	0	6	0	1	0	1	30	3.3
			TOTAL	76	13	17	30	-9	72	4	2	2	2	133	9.8
D	33	Bruce Driver	NYR	79	5	25	30	8	48	2	0	2	0	154	3.2
R	8	Patrick Flatley	NYR	68	10	12	22	6	26	0	0	2	0	96	10.4
D	5	Ulf Samuelsson	NYR	73	6	11	17	3	138	1	0	1	0	77	7.8
L	18	Bill Berg	NYR	67	8	6	14	2	37	0	2	3	0	84	9.5
L	16 *	Daniel Goneau	NYR	41	10	3	13	-5	10	3	0	2	0	44	22.7
D	23	Jeff Beukeboom	NYR	80	3	9	12	22	167	0	0	0	0	55	5.5
C	32	Mike Eastwood	PHO	33	1	3	4	-3	4	0	0	0	0	22	4.5
			NYR	27	1	7	8	2	10	0	0	0	0	22	4.5
			TOTAL	60	2	10	12	-1	14	0	0	0	0	44	4.5
L	39 *	Vladimir Vorobiev	NYR	16	5	5	10	4	6	2	0	0	0	42	11.9
L	15	Darren Langdon	NYR	60	3	6	9	-1	195	0	0	1	0	24	12.5
D	6	Doug Lidster	NYR	48	3	4	7	10	24	0	0	0	0	42	7.1
R	26	David Oliver	EDM	17	1	2	3	-8	4	0	0	0	0	22	4.5
			NYR	14	2	1	3	3	4	0	0	0	0	13	15.4
			TOTAL	31	3	3	6	-5	8	0	0	0	0	35	8.6
R	14 *	Chris Ferraro	NYR	12	1	1	2	1	6	0	0	0	0	23	4.3
C	19 *	Christian Dube	NYR	27	1	1	2	-4	4	1	0	0	0	14	7.1
R	37 *	Ryan Vandenbussche	NYR	11	1	0	1	-2	30	0	0	0	0	4	25.0
D	29 *	Eric Cairns	NYR	40	0	1	1	-7	147	0	0	0	0	17	0.0
R	22	Shane Churla	NYR	45	0	1	1	-10	106	0	0	0	0	19	0.0
R	36 *	Jeff Nielsen	NYR	2	0	0	0	-1	2	0	0	0	0	1	0.0
C	17 *	Peter Ferraro	NYR	2	0	0	0	0	0	0	0	0	0	3	0.0
D	38 *	Sylvain Blouin	NYR	6	0	0	0	-1	18	0	0	0	0	1	0.0
D	28	Dallas Eakins	PHO	4	0	0	0	-3	10	0	0	0	0	2	0.0
			NYR	3	0	0	0	-1	6	0	0	0	0	2	0.0
			TOTAL	7	0	0	0	-4	16	0	0	0	0	4	0.0
G	30	Glenn Healy	NYR	23	0	0	0	0	4	0	0	0	0	0	0.0
G	35	Mike Richter	NYR	61	0	0	0	0	4	0	0	0	0	0	0.0

Goaltending

No.	Goaltender	GPI	Mins	Avg	W	L	T	EN	SO	GA	SA	S%
30	Glenn Healy	23	1357	2.61	5	12	4	2	1	59	632	.907
35	Mike Richter	61	3598	2.68	33	22	6	9	4	161	1945	.917
	Totals	**82**	**4974**	**2.79**	**38**	**34**	**10**	**11**	**5**	**231**	**2588**	**.911**

Playoffs

Pos	#	Player	Team	GP	G	A	Pts	+/–	PIM	PP	SH	GW	OT	S	%
C	99	Wayne Gretzky	NYR	15	10	10	20	5	2	3	0	2	0	44	22.7
L	10	Esa Tikkanen	NYR	15	9	3	12	2	26	3	1	3	2	45	20.0
C	11	Mark Messier	NYR	15	3	9	12	2	6	0	0	1	0	43	7.0
L	20	Luc Robitaille	NYR	15	4	7	11	7	4	0	0	0	0	43	9.3
D	2	Brian Leetch	NYR	15	2	8	10	5	6	1	0	1	0	56	3.6
R	21	Russ Courtnall	NYR	15	3	4	7	1	0	1	0	0	0	27	11.1
D	6	Doug Lidster	NYR	15	1	5	6	-2	8	0	0	0	0	20	5.0
L	24	Niklas Sundstrom	NYR	9	0	5	5	3	2	0	0	0	0	18	0.0
D	25	A. Karpovtsev	NYR	13	1	3	4	2	20	1	0	0	0	10	10.0
L	9	Adam Graves	NYR	15	2	1	3	1	12	1	0	2	1	39	5.1
C	32	Mike Eastwood	NYR	15	1	2	3	0	22	0	0	0	0	19	5.3
D	5	Ulf Samuelsson	NYR	15	0	2	2	1	30	0	0	0	0	11	0.0
D	23	Jeff Beukeboom	NYR	15	0	1	1	5	34	0	0	0	0	9	0.0
D	33	Bruce Driver	NYR	15	0	1	1	-3	2	0	0	0	0	26	0.0
G	35	Mike Richter	NYR	15	0	1	1	0	0	0	0	0	0	0	0.0
C	17 *	Peter Ferraro	NYR	2	0	0	0	0	0	0	0	0	0	2	0.0
L	18	Bill Berg	NYR	3	0	0	0	-1	2	0	0	0	0	5	0.0
R	26	David Oliver	NYR	3	0	0	0	0	0	0	0	0	0	0	0.0
D	29 *	Eric Cairns	NYR	3	0	0	0	0	0	0	0	0	0	0	0.0
C	19 *	Christian Dube	NYR	3	0	0	0	-2	0	0	0	0	0	0	0.0
D	28	Dallas Eakins	NYR	4	0	0	0	-1	4	0	0	0	0	1	0.0
C	12	Ken Gernander	NYR	9	0	0	0	0	0	0	0	0	0	0	0.0
L	15	Darren Langdon	NYR	10	0	0	0	-1	2	0	0	0	0	1	0.0
R	8	Patrick Flatley	NYR	11	0	0	0	2	14	0	0	0	0	14	0.0
R	22	Shane Churla	NYR	15	0	0	0	-3	20	0	0	0	0	6	0.0

Goaltending

No.	Goaltender	GPI	Mins	Avg	W	L	EN	SO	GA	SA	S%
35	Mike Richter	15	939	2.11	9	6	2	3	33	488	.932
	Totals	**15**	**943**	**2.23**	**9**	**6**	**2**	**3**	**35**	**490**	**.929**

General Managers' History

Lester Patrick, 1927-28 to 1945-46; Frank Boucher, 1946-47 to 1954-55; "Muzz" Patrick, 1955-56 to 1963-64; Emile Francis, 1964-65 to 1974-75; Emile Francis and John Ferguson, 1975-76; John Ferguson, 1976-77 to 1977-78; John Ferguson and Fred Shero, 1978-79; Fred Shero, 1979-80; Fred Shero and Craig Patrick, 1980-81; Craig Patrick, 1981-82 to 1985-86; Phil Esposito, 1986-87 to 1988-89; Neil Smith, 1989-90 to date.

Club Records

Team

(Figures in brackets for season records are games played; records for fewest points, wins, ties, losses, goals, goals against are for 70 or more games)

Most Points .... 112 — 1993-94 (84)
Most Wins .... 52 — 1993-94 (84)
Most Ties .... 21 — 1950-51 (70)
Most Losses .... 44 — 1984-85 (80)
Most Goals .... 371 — 1991-92 (80)
Most Goals Against .... 345 — 1984-85 (80)
Fewest Points .... 47 — 1965-66 (70)
Fewest Wins .... 17 — 1952-53, 1954-55, 1959-60 (70)
Fewest Ties .... 5 — 1991-92 (80)
Fewest Losses .... 17 — 1971-72 (78)
Fewest Goals .... 150 — 1954-55 (70)
Fewest Goals Against .... 177 — 1970-71 (78)
Longest Winning Streak
Overall .... 10 — Dec. 19/39-Jan. 13/40, Jan. 19-Feb. 10/73
Home .... 14 — Dec. 19/39-Feb. 25/40
Away .... 7 — Jan. 12-Feb. 12/35, Oct. 28-Nov. 29/78
Longest Undefeated Streak
Overall .... 19 — Nov. 23/39-Jan. 13/40 (14 wins, 5 ties)
Home .... 26 — Mar. 29/70-Feb. 2/71 (19 wins, 7 ties)
Away .... 11 — Nov. 5/39-Jan. 13/40 (6 wins, 5 ties)
Longest Losing Streak
Overall .... 11 — Oct. 30-Nov. 27/43
Home .... 7 — Oct. 20-Nov. 14/76, Mar. 24-Apr. 14/93
Away .... 10 — Oct. 30-Dec. 23/43
Longest Winless Streak
Overall .... 21 — Jan. 23-Mar. 19/44 (17 losses, 4 ties)
Home .... 10 — Jan. 30-Mar. 19/44 (7 losses, 3 ties)
Away .... 16 — Oct. 9-Dec. 20/52 (12 losses, 4 ties)
Most Shutouts, Season .... 13 — 1928-29 (44)
Most PIM, Season .... 2,018 — 1989-90 (80)
Most Goals, Game .... 12 — Nov. 21/71 (Cal. 1 at NYR 12)

Individual

Most Seasons .... 17 — Harry Howell
Most Games .... 1,160 — Harry Howell
Most Goals, Career .... 406 — Rod Gilbert
Most Assists, Career .... 615 — Rod Gilbert
Most Points, Career .... 1,021 — Rod Gilbert (406G, 615A)
Most PIM, Career .... 1,226 — Ron Greschner
Most Shutouts, Career .... 49 — Ed Giacomin
Longest Consecutive Games Streak .... 560 — Andy Hebenton (Oct. 7/55-Mar. 24/63)
Most Goals, Season .... 52 — Adam Graves (1993-94)
Most Assists, Season .... 80 — Brian Leetch (1991-92)
Most Points, Season .... 109 — Jean Ratelle (1971-72; 46G, 63A)
Most PIM, Season .... 305 — Troy Mallette (1989-90)
Most Points, Defenseman, Season .... 102 — Brian Leetch (1991-92; 22G, 80A)
Most Points, Center, Season .... 109 — Jean Ratelle (1971-72; 46G, 63A)
Most Points, Right Wing, Season .... 97 — Rod Gilbert (1971-72; 43G, 54A), Rod Gilbert (1974-75; 36G, 61A)
Most Points, Left Wing, Season .... 106 — Vic Hadfield (1971-72; 50G, 56A)
Most Points, Rookie, Season .... 76 — Mark Pavelich (1981-82; 33G, 43A)
Most Shutouts, Season .... 13 — John Ross Roach (1928-29)
Most Goals, Game .... 5 — Don Murdoch (Oct. 12/76), Mark Pavelich (Feb. 23/83)
Most Assists, Game .... 5 — Walt Tkaczuk (Feb. 12/72), Rod Gilbert (Mar. 2/75, Mar. 30/75, Oct. 8/76), Don Maloney (Jan. 3/87)
Most Points, Game .... 7 — Steve Vickers (Feb. 18/76; 3G, 4A)

Retired Numbers

1	Eddie Giacomin	1965-1976
7	Rod Gilbert	1960-1978

Captains' History

Bill Cook, 1926-27 to 1936-37; Art Coulter, 1937-38 to 1941-42; Ott Heller, 1942-43 to 1944-45; Neil Colville 1945-46 to 1948-49; Buddy O'Connor, 1949-50; Frank Eddolls, 1950-51; Frank Eddolls and Allan Stanley, 1951-52; Allan Stanley, 1952-53; Allan Stanley and Don Raleigh, 1953-54; Don Raleigh, 1954-55; Harry Howell, 1955-56, 1956-57; George Sullivan, 1957-58 to 1960-61; Andy Bathgate, 1961-62, 1962-63; Andy Bathgate and Camille Henry, 1963-64; Camille Henry and Bob Nevin, 1964-65; Bob Nevin 1965-66 to 1970-71; Vic Hadfield, 1971-72 to 1973-74; Brad Park, 1974-75; Brad Park and Phil Esposito, 1975-76; Phil Esposito, 1976-77, 1977-78; Dave Maloney, 1978-79, 1979-80; Dave Maloney, Walt Tkaczuk and Barry Beck, 1980-81; Barry Beck, 1981-82 to 1985-86; Ron Greschner, 1986-87; Ron Greschner and Kelly Kisio, 1987-88; Kelly Kisio, 1988-89 to 1990-91; Mark Messier, 1991-92 to 1996-97.

All-time Record vs. Other Clubs

Regular Season

	At Home							On Road							Total						
	GP	W	L	T	GF	GA	PTS	GP	W	L	T	GF	GA	PTS	GP	W	L	T	GF	GA	PTS
Anaheim	3	2	1	0	10	7	4	3	0	3	0	8	15	0	6	2	4	0	18	22	4
Boston	288	125	109	54	875	809	304	284	92	151	41	800	1029	225	572	217	260	95	1675	1838	529
Buffalo	52	24	15	13	183	143	61	54	16	32	6	177	237	38	106	40	47	19	360	380	99
Calgary	46	21	20	5	165	166	47	45	10	26	9	138	204	29	91	31	46	14	303	370	76
Chicago	281	116	110	55	833	797	287	280	112	126	42	778	853	266	561	228	236	97	1611	1650	553
Colorado	27	17	6	4	114	76	38	29	11	15	3	113	123	25	56	28	21	7	227	199	63
Dallas	56	34	12	10	198	152	78	55	30	16	9	209	165	69	111	64	28	19	407	317	147
Detroit	278	133	87	58	857	712	324	280	75	160	45	689	983	195	558	208	247	103	1546	1695	519
Edmonton	24	6	13	5	92	98	17	24	12	11	1	87	92	25	48	18	24	6	179	190	42
Florida	10	4	3	3	28	25	11	10	4	5	1	30	26	9	20	8	8	4	58	51	20
Hartford	30	18	9	3	131	89	39	29	10	16	3	98	108	23	59	28	25	6	229	197	62
Los Angeles	53	33	15	5	214	151	71	54	24	21	9	196	181	57	107	57	36	14	410	332	128
Montreal	276	112	110	54	808	806	278	276	56	185	35	635	1087	147	552	168	295	89	1443	1893	425
New Jersey	66	39	16	11	282	200	89	67	32	30	5	243	225	69	133	71	46	16	525	425	158
NY Islanders	78	46	24	8	308	239	100	78	22	49	7	242	321	51	156	68	73	15	550	560	151
Ottawa	9	7	2	0	42	26	14	9	8	1	0	33	22	16	18	15	3	0	75	48	30
Philadelphia	92	42	28	22	305	263	106	91	34	44	13	265	307	81	183	76	72	35	570	570	187
Phoenix	24	14	8	2	115	95	30	25	13	10	2	93	91	28	49	27	18	4	208	186	58
Pittsburgh	83	44	32	7	344	289	95	83	39	33	11	319	302	89	166	83	65	18	663	591	184
St. Louis	55	43	6	6	233	124	92	57	26	22	9	185	168	61	112	69	28	15	418	292	153
San Jose	5	4	0	1	27	15	9	6	6	0	0	29	13	12	11	10	0	1	56	28	21
Tampa Bay	12	5	6	1	44	49	11	10	5	4	1	33	34	11	22	10	10	2	77	83	22
Toronto	270	113	101	56	830	792	282	269	80	151	38	698	920	198	539	193	252	94	1528	1712	480
Vancouver	49	36	8	5	222	122	77	47	32	12	3	193	151	67	96	68	20	8	415	273	144
Washington	67	34	27	6	268	239	74	69	26	34	9	232	261	61	136	60	61	15	500	500	135
Defunct Clubs	139	87	30	22	460	290	196	139	82	34	23	441	291	187	278	169	64	45	901	581	383
Totals	**2373**	**1159**	**798**	**416**	**7988**	**6774**	**2734**	**2373**	**857**	**1191**	**325**	**6964**	**8209**	**2039**	**4746**	**2016**	**1989**	**741**	**14952**	**14983**	**4773**

Playoffs

	Series	W	L	GP	W	L	T	GF	GA	Last Mtg.	Round	Result
Boston	9	3	6	42	18	22	2	104	114	1973	QF	W 4-1
Buffalo	1	0	1	3	1	2	0	6	11	1978	PR	L 1-2
Calgary	1	1	0	4	3	1	0	14	8	1980	PR	W 3-1
Chicago	5	1	4	24	10	14	0	54	66	1973	SF	L 1-4
Colorado	1	1	0	6	4	2	0	25	19	1995	CQF	W 4-2
Detroit	5	1	4	23	10	13	0	49	57	1950	F	L 3-4
Florida	1	1	0	5	4	1	0	13	10	1997	CQF	W 4-1
Los Angeles	2	2	0	6	5	1	0	32	14	1981	PR	W 3-1
Montreal	14	7	7	61	25	34	2	158	188	1996	CQF	W 4-2
New Jersey	3	3	0	19	12	7	0	56	46	1997	CSF	W 4-1
NY Islanders	8	3	5	39	19	20	0	132	129	1994	CQF	W 4-0
Philadelphia	10	4	6	47	20	27	0	153	157	1997	CF	L 1-4
Pittsburgh	3	0	3	15	3	12	0	45	65	1996	CSF	L 1-4
St. Louis	1	1	0	6	4	2	0	29	22	1981	QF	W 4-2
Toronto	8	5	3	35	19	16	0	86	86	1971	QF	W 4-2
Vancouver	1	1	0	7	4	3	0	21	19	1994	F	W 4-3
Washington	4	2	2	22	11	11	0	71	75	1994	CSF	W 4-1
Defunct	9	6	3	22	11	7	4	43	29			
Totals	**86**	**42**	**44**	**386**	**183**	**195**	**8**	**1091**	**1114**			

Calgary totals include Atlanta, 1972-73 to 1979-80. Colorado totals include Quebec, 1979-80 to 1994-95. Dallas totals include Minnesota, 1967-68 to 1992-93. New Jersey totals include Kansas City, 1974-75 to 1975-76, and Colorado Rockies, 1976-77 to 1981-82. Phoenix totals include Winnipeg, 1979-80 to 1995-96.

Playoff Results 1997-93

Year	Round	Opponent	Result	GF	GA
1997	CF	Philadelphia	L 1-4	13	20
	CSF	New Jersey	W 4-1	10	5
	CQF	Florida	W 4-1	13	10
1996	CSF	Pittsburgh	L 1-4	15	21
	CQF	Montreal	W 4-2	19	17
1995	CSF	Philadelphia	L 0-4	10	18
	CQF	Quebec	W 4-2	25	19
1994	F	Vancouver	W 4-3	21	19
	CF	New Jersey	W 4-3	18	16
	CSF	Washington	W 4-1	20	12
	CQF	NY Islanders	W 4-0	22	3

Abbreviations: Round: F – Final; **CF** – conference final; **CQF** – conference quarter-final; **CSF** – conference semi-final; **DF** – division final; **DSF** – division semi-final; **SF** – semi-final; **QF** – quarter-final; **PR** – preliminary round.

1996-97 Results

Oct. 5	at	Boston	4-4		**Jan.** 2		NY Islanders	4-3
6		Florida	2-5		4		Ottawa	6-4
8	at	Florida	1-1		6		Colorado	2-2
10		Dallas	1-2		8		Tampa Bay	3-4
12	at	Montreal	2-5		9	at	Washington	0-2
14		Calgary	5-4		12		New Jersey	3-0
16		Pittsburgh	8-1		13		NY Islanders	2-4
18		St. Louis	2-1		21		Edmonton	4-4
20	at	Tampa Bay	2-5		22	at	Washington	5-3
23		Washington	2-3		25	at	Pittsburgh	7-4
25	at	Florida	4-6		27		Chicago	1-2
27		Buffalo	6-4		**Feb.** 1	at	Philadelphia	4-2
29		Florida	1-1		2		Boston	2-3
30	at	New Jersey	6-1		5		Hartford	5-2
Nov. 2	at	Boston	5-2		8	at	NY Islanders	5-2
4		Tampa Bay	3-5		9	at	Florida	3-4
6	at	NY Islanders	1-1		13	at	St. Louis	1-4
9	at	Washington	2-3		15	at	Chicago	0-2
11		Vancouver	2-3		17		New Jersey	2-2
13		Philadelphia	1-2		19	at	New Jersey	1-1
16	at	Pittsburgh	8-3		21	at	Hartford	2-7
18	at	Calgary	3-5		23	at	Philadelphia	1-2
21	at	Edmonton	2-3		**Mar.** 1	at	Detroit	0-3
23	at	Vancouver	3-5		3		San Jose	5-4
26	at	Phoenix	3-1		6	at	Los Angeles	6-2
27	at	Colorado	5-2		7	at	Anaheim	2-5
Dec. 1		Montreal	6-2		9	at	San Jose	2-1
4		Philadelphia	1-1		12		Washington	3-2
6		Toronto	6-5		14	at	Ottawa	4-3
7	at	Toronto	4-0		17		Ottawa	3-4
9		Phoenix	5-2		19		Montreal	4-5
11		NY Islanders	3-5		21		Detroit	3-1
13	at	Buffalo	3-0		24		Pittsburgh	3-0
16		Hartford	5-2		27	at	New Jersey	0-4
18		Los Angeles	4-0		29	at	Hartford	1-2
21	at	Montreal	3-2		**Apr.** 1		Buffalo	1-1
22		Florida	7-3		3		Boston	5-4
26	at	Ottawa	2-5		4	at	Buffalo	1-5
27		Anaheim	3-2		7		Philadelphia	3-2
30	at	Dallas	3-2		10	at	Philadelphia	6-3
31	at	Tampa Bay	2-4		11		Tampa Bay	2-4

Entry Draft
Selections 1997-83

1997
Pick
19	Stefan Cherneski
46	Wes Jarvis
73	Burke Henry
93	Tomi Kallarsson
126	Jason McLean
134	Johan Lindbom
136	Michael York
154	Shawn Degagne
175	Johan Holmqvist
182	Mike Mottau
210	Andrew Proskurnicki
236	Richard Miller

1996
Pick
22	Jeff Brown
48	Daniel Goneau
76	Dmitri Subbotin
131	Colin Pepperall
158	Ola Sandberg
185	Jeff Dessner
211	Ryan McKie
237	Ronnie Sundin

1995
Pick
39	Christian Dube
65	Mike Martin
91	Marc Savard
110	Alexei Vasiliev
117	Dale Purinton
143	Peter Slamiar
169	Jeff Heil
195	Ilja Gorohov
221	Bob Maudie

1994
Pick
26	Dan Cloutier
52	Rudolf Vercik
78	Adam Smith
100	Alexander Korobolin
104	Sylvain Blouin
130	Martin Ethier
135	Yuri Litvinov
156	David Brosseau
182	Alexei Lazarenko
208	Craig Anderson
209	Vitali Yeremeyev
234	Eric Boulton
260	Radoslav Kropac
267	Jamie Butt
286	Kim Johnsson

1993
Pick
8	Niklas Sundstrom
34	Lee Sorochan
61	Maxim Galanov
86	Sergei Olimpiyev
112	Gary Roach
138	Dave Trofimenkoff
162	Sergei Kondrashkin
164	Todd Marchant
190	Eddy Campbell
216	Ken Shepard
242	Andrei Kudinov
261	Pavel Komarov
268	Maxim Smelnitsky

1992
Pick
24	Peter Ferraro
48	Mattias Norstrom
72	Eric Cairns
85	Chris Ferraro
120	Dmitri Starostenko
144	David Dal Grande
168	Matt Oates
192	Mickey Elick
216	Dan Brierley
240	Vladimir Vorobjev

1991
Pick
15	Alexei Kovalev
37	Darcy Werenka
96	Corey Machanic
125	Fredrik Jax
128	Barry Young
147	John Rushin
169	Corey Hirsch
191	Viacheslav Uvayev
213	Jamie Ram
235	Vitali Chinakhov
257	Brian Wiseman

1990
Pick
13	Michael Stewart
34	Doug Weight
55	John Vary
69	Jeff Nielsen
76	Rick Willis
85	Sergei Zubov
99	Lubos Rob
118	Jason Weinrich
139	Bryan Lonsinger
160	Todd Hedlund
181	Andrew Silverman
202	Jon Hillebrandt
223	Brett Lievers
244	Sergei Nemchinov

1989
Pick
20	Steven Rice
40	Jason Prosofsky
45	Rob Zamuner
49	Louie DeBrusk
67	Jim Cummins
88	Aaron Miller
118	Joby Messier
139	Greg Leahy
160	Greg Spenrath
181	Mark Bavis
202	Roman Oksyuta
223	Steve Locke
244	Ken MacDermid

1988
Pick
22	Troy Mallette
26	Murray Duval
68	Tony Amonte
99	Martin Bergeron
110	Dennis Vial
131	Mike Rosati
152	Eric Couvrette
173	Shorty Forrest
194	Paul Cain
202	Eric Fenton
215	Peter Fiorentino
236	Keith Slifstien

1987
Pick
10	Jayson More
31	Daniel Lacroix
46	Simon Gagne
69	Michael Sullivan
94	Eric O'Borsky
115	Ludek Cajka
136	Clint Thomas
157	Charles Wiegand
178	Eric Burrill
199	David Porter
205	Brett Barnett
220	Lance Marciano

1986
Pick
9	Brian Leetch
51	Bret Walter
53	Shawn Clouston
72	Mark Janssens
93	Jeff Bloemberg
114	Darren Turcotte
135	Robb Graham
156	Barry Chyzowski
177	Pat Scanlon
198	Joe Ranger
219	Russell Parent
240	Soren True

1985
Pick
7	Ulf Dahlen
28	Mike Richter
49	Sam Lindstahl
70	Pat Janostin
91	Brad Stephan
112	Brian McReynolds
133	Neil Pilon
154	Larry Bernard
175	Stephane Brochu
196	Steve Nemeth
217	Robert Burakowsky
238	Rudy Poeschek

1984
Pick
14	Terry Carkner
35	Raimo Helminen
77	Paul Broten
98	Clark Donatelli
119	Kjell Samuelsson
140	Thomas Hussey
161	Brian Nelson
182	Ville Kentala
188	Heinz Ehlers
202	Kevin Miller
223	Tom Lorentz
243	Scott Brower

1983
Pick
12	Dave Gagner
33	Randy Heath
49	Vesa Salo
53	Gordie Walker
73	Peter Andersson
93	Jim Andonoff
113	Bob Alexander
133	Steve Orth
153	Peter Marcov
173	Paul Jerrard
213	Bryan Walker
233	Ulf Nilsson

Club Directory

Madison Square Garden
14th Floor
2 Pennsylvania Plaza
New York, New York 10121
Phone **212/465-6000**
PR FAX 212/465-6494
Capacity: 18,200

Executive Management
CEO and Governor	David W. Checketts
President and General Manager/ Alternate Governor	Neil Smith
Executive Vice President and General Counsel	Kenneth W. Munoz
Vice President and Business Manager	Francis P. Murphy
Vice President, Legal and Business Affairs	Marc Schoenfeld
Controller	Luis R. Perez
Alternate Governors	Marc Lustgarten, Kenneth W. Munoz

Hockey Club Personnel
Assistant General Manager	Don Maloney
Head Coach	Colin Campbell
Assistant Coaches	Craig MacTavish, Bill Moores, Dick Todd
Development Coach	E.J. Maguire
Assistant Development Coach	Mike Busniuk
Goaltending Analyst	Sam St. Laurent
Director of Scouting	Martin Madden
Director of Professional Scouting	John Paddock
Scouting Staff	Darwin Bennett, Ray Clearwater, Herb Hammond, Martin Madden Jr., Kevin McDonald, Christer Rockstrom
Scouting Manager	Bill Short
Video Assistant	Jerry Dineen

Business Operations
Vice President of Operations	Mark Piazza
Director of Business Administration	John Gentile
Coordinator of Team Operations	Darren Blake
Executive Administrative Assistant	Barbara Cahill
Senior Secretary	Yvonne DeLaney

Public Relations Department
Director of Public Relations	John Rosasco
Assistant Director of Public Relations	Rob Koch
Public Relations Assistant	Frank Buonomo
Administrative Assistant	Ann Marie Gilmartin

Marketing Department
Director of Marketing and Community Programs	Jim Pfeifer
Director of Event Presentation	Jeanie Baumgartner
Director of Community Relations	Rod Gilbert
Promotions Manager	Caroline Calabrese
Community and Marketing Programs Assistant	Teri Stewart

Medical/Training Staff
Team Physician and Orthopedic Surgeon	Dr. Barton Nisonson
Assistant Team Physician	Dr. Tony Maddalo
Medical Consultants	Dr. Howard Chester, Dr. Frank Gardner, Dr. Ronald Weissman
Team Dentists	Dr. Irwin Miller, Dr. Don Soloman
Sports Physiologist	Howie Wenger
Medical Trainer	Jim Ramsay
Equipment Manager	Mike Folga
Massage Therapist	Bruce Lifrieri
Assistant Equipment Manager	Acassio Marques
Staff Assistant	Damian Echevarrieta

Home Ice	Madison Square Garden
Press Facilities	33rd Street
Television Facilities	31st Street
Radio Facilities	33rd Street
Rink Dimensions	200 feet by 85 feet
Ends and Sides of Rink	Plexiglass (8 feet)
Club Colors	Blue, Red and White
Practice Facility	Rye, New York

The New York Rangers Hockey Club is part of Madison Square Garden

Coach

CAMPBELL, COLIN
Coach, New York Rangers. Born in London, Ontario, January 28, 1953.

Colin Campbell begins his fourth season as head coach of the Rangers after being named to the post on August 9, 1994. He was promoted to the position after serving in various capacities in the organization over the previous five years, including assistant coach, associate coach and half of the 1992-93 season as head coach of the Rangers American Hockey League affiliate at Binghamton. Colin made his head coaching debut on January 20, 1995 vs. Buffalo and earned his first NHL victory on January 21, 1995 vs. Montreal.

Campbell, 44, began his coaching career in 1985-86 with Detroit, following his retirement as a player after the 1984-85 season. He worked a total of five seasons as a Red Wings assistant coach, one season under coach Harry Neale and four seasons under coach Jacques Demers.

The native of London, Ontario, joined the Rangers organization in August of 1990 as an assistant coach to Roger Neilson. He served in that role until January 4, 1993, when he became head coach of the Binghamton Rangers. He guided Binghamton to a record of 29-8-5, helping the club set AHL records for wins (57) and points (124) in a single season.

On June 21, 1993, Campbell was promoted to associate coach of New York, under head coach Mike Keenan, helping the Rangers capture the Presidents' Trophy, given to the team with the best regular-season record, and the Stanley Cup.

Before joining the coaching ranks, Campbell played 12 seasons of professional hockey as a defensive defenseman. He played in a total of 636 NHL contests, collecting 25 goals and 103 assists for 128 points along with 1,292 penalty minutes.

Coaching Record

Season	Team	Games	Regular Season W	L	T	%	Playoffs Games	W	L	%
1992-93	Binghamton (AHL)	42	29	8	5	.750	14	7	7	.500
1994-95	NY Rangers (NHL)	48	22	23	3	.490	10	4	6	.400
1995-96	NY Rangers (NHL)	82	41	27	14	.585	11	5	6	.455
1996-97	NY Rangers (NHL)	82	38	34	10	.524	15	9	6	.600
	NHL Totals	212	101	84	27	.540	36	18	18	.500

Coaching History

Lester Patrick, 1926-27 to 1938-39; Frank Boucher, 1939-40 to 1947-48; Frank Boucher and Lynn Patrick, 1948-49; Lynn Patrick, 1949-50; Neil Colville, 1950-51; Neil Colville and Bill Cook, 1951-52; Bill Cook, 1952-53; Frank Boucher and "Muzz" Patrick, 1953-54; "Muzz" Patrick, 1954-55; Phil Watson, 1955-56 to 1958-59; Phil Watson and Alf Pike, 1959-60; Alf Pike, 1960-61; Doug Harvey, 1961-62; "Muzz" Patrick and George Sullivan, 1962-63; George Sullivan, 1963-64 to 1964-65; George Sullivan and Emile Francis, 1965-66; Emile Francis, 1966-67 to 1967-68; Bernie Geoffrion and Emile Francis, 1968-69; Emile Francis, 1969-70 to 1972-73; Larry Popein and Emile Francis, 1973-74; Emile Francis, 1974-75; Ron Stewart and John Ferguson, 1975-76; John Ferguson, 1976-77; Jean-Guy Talbot, 1977-78; Fred Shero, 1978-79 to 1979-80; Fred Shero and Craig Patrick, 1980-81; Herb Brooks, 1981-82 to 1983-84; Herb Brooks and Craig Patrick, 1984-85; Ted Sator, 1985-86; Ted Sator, Tom Webster and Phil Esposito, 1986-87; Michel Bergeron, 1987-88; Michel Bergeron and Phil Esposito, 1988-89; Roger Neilson, 1989-90 to 1991-92; Roger Neilson and Ron Smith, 1992-93; Mike Keenan, 1993-94; Colin Campbell, 1994-95 to date.

Ottawa Senators

1996-97 Results: 31w-36L-15T 77PTS. Third, Northeast Division

Year-by-Year Record

		Home			Road			Overall						
Season	GP	W	L	T	W	L	T	W	L	T	GF	GA	Pts.	Finished	Playoff Result
1996-97	82	16	17	8	15	19	7	31	36	15	226	234	77	3rd, Northeast Div.	Lost Conf. Quarter-Final
1995-96	82	8	28	5	10	31	0	18	59	5	191	291	41	6th, Northeast Div.	Out of Playoffs
1994-95	48	5	16	3	4	18	2	9	34	5	117	174	23	7th, Northeast Div.	Out of Playoffs
1993-94	84	8	30	4	6	31	5	14	61	9	201	397	37	7th, Northeast Div.	Out of Playoffs
1992-93	84	9	29	4	1	41	0	10	70	4	202	395	24	6th, Adams Div.	Out of Playoffs

1997-98 Schedule

Oct.	Wed.	1	at Montreal
	Fri.	3	at Philadelphia
	Sat.	4	Carolina
	Tue.	7	at San Jose
	Fri.	10	at Anaheim
	Sun.	12	at Los Angeles
	Wed.	15	NY Rangers
	Fri.	17	New Jersey
	Sun.	19	Dallas
	Wed.	22	at Toronto
	Thu.	23	Florida
	Sat.	25	Montreal
	Wed.	29	at Tampa Bay
	Thu.	30	at Florida
Nov.	Sun.	2	Boston
	Thu.	6	Phoenix
	Sat.	8	Philadelphia
	Sun.	9	at Carolina
	Tue.	11	at Philadelphia
	Thu.	13	Detroit
	Sat.	15	at Boston
	Mon.	17	Boston
	Thu.	20	Pittsburgh
	Sat.	22	Edmonton
	Wed.	26	at Detroit
	Thu.	27	Washington
	Sat.	29	Chicago
Dec.	Tue.	2	at NY Islanders
	Thu.	4	Los Angeles
	Sat.	6	Buffalo
	Thu.	11	St. Louis
	Sat.	13	Tampa Bay
	Mon.	15	at St. Louis
	Tue.	16	at Carolina
	Thu.	18	Carolina
	Sat.	20	at Montreal
	Mon.	22	at NY Islanders
	Tue.	23	Montreal
	Sat.	27	at Washington
	Wed.	31	at Buffalo
Jan.	Thu.	1	at Boston

	Sat.	3	Philadelphia
	Mon.	5	at Carolina
	Wed.	7	at Dallas
	Sat.	10	at Colorado
	Sun.	11	at Phoenix
	Tue.	13	at Washington
	Tue.	20	at Pittsburgh
	Thu.	22	Carolina
	Sat.	24	NY Islanders
	Mon.	26	Tampa Bay
	Tue.	27	at Boston
	Thu.	29	NY Rangers
	Sat.	31	at Montreal
Feb.	Mon.	2	New Jersey
	Wed.	4	at New Jersey
	Thu.	5	Toronto
	Sat.	7	Pittsburgh
	Wed.	25	at Edmonton
	Sat.	28	at Vancouver
Mar.	Sun.	1	at Calgary
	Thu.	5	Colorado
	Sat.	7	Calgary
	Wed.	11	Florida
	Sat.	14	Washington
	Mon.	16	at NY Rangers
	Wed.	18	at NY Islanders
	Fri.	20	Vancouver
	Sun.	22	Anaheim
	Wed.	25	at NY Rangers
	Fri.	27	at Chicago
	Sun.	29	at Pittsburgh*
Apr.	Thu.	2	San Jose
	Fri.	3	at New Jersey
	Sun.	5	at Buffalo*
	Tue.	7	Boston
	Thu.	9	Pittsburgh
	Sat.	11	Buffalo
	Mon.	13	at Tampa Bay
	Tue.	14	at Florida
	Thu.	16	Montreal
	Sun.	19	at Buffalo

* Denotes afternoon game.

Franchise date: December 16, 1991

NORTHEAST DIVISION

6th NHL Season

Rookie blueliner Wade Redden played a poised game at both ends of the ice, playing sound defense while collecting 30 points.

1997-98 Player Personnel

FORWARDS	HT	WT	S	Place of Birth	Date	1996-97 Club
ALFREDSSON, Daniel	5-11	200	R	Goteborg, Sweden	12/11/72	Ottawa
ARMSTRONG, Derek	5-11	188	R	Ottawa, Ont.	4/23/73	NY Islanders-Utah
ARVEDSON, Magnus	6-2	198	L	Karlstad, Swe.	11/25/71	Farjestad
BEDDOES, Clayton	5-11	190	L	Bentley, Alta.	11/10/70	Boston-Providence (AHL)
BONK, Radek	6-3	205	R	Krnov, Czech.	1/9/76	Ottawa
CHORSKE, Tom	6-1	205	R	Minneapolis, MN	9/18/66	Ottawa
CIERNIK, Ivan	6-1	198	L	Levice, Czech.	10/30/77	Nitra
CROWE, Philip	6-2	230	L	Nanton, Alta.	4/14/70	Ottawa-Detroit (IHL)
CUNNEYWORTH, Randy	6-0	198	L	Etobicoke, Ont.	5/10/61	Ottawa
DACKELL, Andreas	5-11	191	R	Gavle, Sweden	12/29/72	Ottawa
DAIGLE, Alexandre	6-0	195	L	Montreal, Que.	2/7/75	Ottawa
GARDINER, Bruce	6-1	193	R	Barrie, Ont.	2/11/71	Ottawa
HOSSA, Marian	6-1	185	L	Stara Lubovna, Czech.	1/12/79	Dukla Trencin
LABELLE, Marc	6-1	215	L	Maniwaki, Que.	12/20/69	Dallas-Milwaukee-Michigan
LAMBERT, Denny	5-11	200	L	Wawa, Ont.	1/7/70	Ottawa
MANELUK, Mike	5-11	188	R	Winnipeg, Man.	10/1/73	Worcester
McEACHERN, Shawn	5-11	195	L	Waltham, MA	2/28/69	Ottawa
PROKOPEC, Mike	6-2	190	R	Toronto, Ont.	5/17/74	Chi-Indianapolis-Detroit (IHL)
VAN ALLEN, Shaun	6-1	200	L	Calgary, Alta.	8/29/67	Ottawa
VIAL, Dennis	6-1	220	L	Sault Ste. Marie, Ont.	4/10/69	Ottawa
YASHIN, Alexei	6-3	215	R	Sverdlovsk, USSR	11/5/73	Ottawa
ZENT, Jason	5-11	204	L	Buffalo, NY	4/15/71	Ottawa-Worcester
ZHOLTOK, Sergei	6-0	190	R	Riga, Latvia	12/2/72	Ottawa-Las Vegas

DEFENSEMEN						
BICANEK, Radim	6-1	195	L	Uherske Hradiste, Czech.	1/18/75	Ottawa-Worcester
GOLDMANN, Erich	6-3	196	L	Dingolfing, West Germany	4/7/76	Kaufbeuren
HARDY, Francois	6-2	185	L	Les Saules, Que.	7/6/78	Val d'Or
HILL, Sean	6-0	203	R	Duluth, MN	2/14/70	Ottawa
HOCKING, Justin	6-4	205	R	Stettler, Alta.	1/9/74	Worcester
KRAVCHUK, Igor	6-1	200	L	Ufa, USSR	9/13/66	St. Louis
LAUKKANEN, Janne	6-0	180	L	Lahti, Finland	3/19/70	Ottawa
MUSIL, Frank	6-3	215	L	Pardubice, Czech.	12/17/64	Ottawa
NECKAR, Stanislav	6-1	212	L	Ceske Budejovice, Czech.	12/22/75	Ottawa
PHILLIPS, Chris	6-2	200	L	Fort McMurray, Alta.	3/9/78	Prince Albert-Lethbridge
PITLICK, Lance	6-0	203	R	Minneapolis, MN	11/5/67	Ottawa
REDDEN, Wade	6-2	193	L	Lloydminster, Sask.	6/12/77	Ottawa
SULLIVAN, Jeff	6-1	185	L	St. John's, Nfld.	9/18/78	Granby-Halifax
VAN DRUNEN, David	6-0	200	R	Sherwood Park, Alta.	1/31/76	Prince Albert
YORK, Jason	6-2	198	R	Nepean, Ont.	5/20/70	Ottawa

GOALTENDERS	HT	WT	C	Place of Birth	Date	1996-97 Club
CASSIVI, Frederic	6-4	205	L	Sorel, Que.	6/12/75	Syracuse
HURME, Jani	6-0	187	L	Turku, Finland	1/7/75	TPS
RHODES, Damian	6-0	180	L	St. Paul, MN	5/28/69	Ottawa
TUGNUTT, Ron	5-11	155	L	Scarborough, Ont.	10/22/67	Ottawa

General Managers' History

Mel Bridgman, 1992-93; Randy Sexton, 1993-94 to 1994-95; Randy Sexton and Pierre Gauthier, 1995-96; Pierre Gauthier, 1996-97 to date.

General Manager

GAUTHIER, PIERRE
General Manager, Ottawa Senators. Born in Montreal, Que., May 28, 1953.

Pierre Gauthier was appointed the third general manager in Senators' history on December 11, 1995. He has, since that time, patiently and quickly built a team that has given the coaching staff a nucleus of players that saw the five-year old franchise post its best regular season record (31-36-15) and compete in its first playoff series in 1996-97 — just 17 months after his appointment.

Prior to joining the Senators, Pierre Gauthier was the assistant general manager with the Mighty Ducks of Anaheim. He was a key part of management in starting up the NHL franchise in 1993.

In the years before the Mighty Ducks of Anaheim, Gauthier had been in the Quebec Nordiques scouting department for 12 years. He had joined the Nordiques in 1983 as a scout, working in that capacity for three years before being named assistant director of scouting in 1986. Gauthier was promoted to chief scout in 1988, serving at that post until he joined Anaheim.

Pierre Gauthier received a master's degree in sports administration from the University of Minnesota in 1983. He is also a graduate of Syracuse University, where he earned a bachelor's of science degree in physical education.

Pierre and his wife Manon have a daughter, Catherine, and a son Vincent.

1996-97 Scoring

* – rookie

Regular Season

Pos	#	Player	Team	GP	G	A	Pts	+/-	PIM	PP	SH	GW	GT	S	%
C	19	Alexei Yashin	OTT	82	35	40	75	-7	44	10	0	5	1	291	12.0
R	11	Daniel Alfredsson	OTT	76	24	47	71	5	30	11	1	1	2	247	9.7
R	91	Alexandre Daigle	OTT	82	26	25	51	-33	33	4	0	5	2	203	12.8
D	28	Steve Duchesne	OTT	78	19	28	47	-9	38	10	2	3	0	208	9.1
L	7	Randy Cunneyworth	OTT	76	12	24	36	-7	99	6	0	3	0	115	10.4
R	10 *	Andreas Dackell	OTT	79	12	19	31	-6	8	2	0	3	0	79	15.2
L	15	Shawn McEachern	OTT	65	11	20	31	-5	18	0	1	2	0	150	7.3
D	6 *	Wade Redden	OTT	82	6	24	30	1	41	2	0	1	0	102	5.9
C	16 *	Sergei Zholtok	OTT	57	12	16	28	2	19	5	0	0	0	96	12.5
L	17	Tom Chorske	OTT	68	18	8	26	-1	16	1	1	1	0	116	15.5
C	22	Shaun Van Allen	OTT	80	11	14	25	-8	35	1	1	2	0	123	8.9
D	25 *	Bruce Gardiner	OTT	67	11	10	21	4	49	0	1	2	0	94	11.7
D	33	Jason York	OTT	75	4	17	21	-8	67	1	0	0	0	121	3.3
D	27	Janne Laukkanen	OTT	76	3	18	21	-14	76	2	0	0	0	109	2.8
L	42	Denny Lambert	OTT	80	4	16	20	-4	217	0	0	1	0	58	6.9
C	76	Radek Bonk	OTT	53	5	13	18	-4	14	0	1	1	0	82	6.1
D	2	Lance Pitlick	OTT	66	5	5	10	2	91	0	0	1	0	54	9.3
L	38 *	Jason Zent	OTT	22	3	3	6	5	9	0	0	0	0	20	15.0
D	23	Christer Olsson	STL	5	0	1	1	1	0	0	0	0	0	2	0.0
			OTT	25	2	3	5	-5	10	1	0	0	0	24	8.3
			TOTAL	30	2	4	6	-4	10	1	0	0	0	26	7.7
R	20	Denis Chasse	OTT	22	1	4	5	0	3	0	0	0	0	12	8.3
D	3	Frank Musil	OTT	57	0	5	5	6	58	0	0	0	0	24	0.0
C	14	Dave Hannan	OTT	34	2	2	4	-1	8	0	1	1	0	16	12.5
G	1	Damian Rhodes	OTT	50	0	2	2	0	2	0	0	0	0	0	0.0
D	29	Phil Vonstefenelli	OTT	6	0	1	1	-3	7	0	0	0	0	2	0.0
L	21	Dennis Vial	OTT	11	0	1	1	0	25	0	0	0	0	4	0.0
D	44 *	Radim Bicanek	OTT	21	0	1	1	-4	8	0	0	0	0	27	0.0
R	26	Philip Crowe	OTT	26	0	1	1	0	30	0	0	0	0	8	0.0
G	31	Ron Tugnutt	OTT	37	0	1	1	0	0	0	0	0	0	0	0.0
G	35 *	Mike Bales	OTT	1	0	0	0	0	0	0	0	0	0	0	0.0
D	4	Sean Hill	OTT	1	0	0	0	1	4	0	0	0	0	9	0.0
D	94	Stanislav Neckar	OTT	5	0	0	0	2	2	0	0	0	0	3	0.0

Goaltending

No.	Goaltender	GPI	Mins	Avg	W	L	T	EN	SO	GA	SA	S%
1	Damian Rhodes	50	2934	2.72	14	20	14	2	1	133	1213	.890
31	Ron Tugnutt	37	1991	2.80	17	15	1	2	3	93	882	.895
35 *	Mike Bales	1	52	4.62	0	1	0	0	0	4	18	.778
	Totals	**82**	**5001**	**2.81**	**31**	**36**	**15**	**4**	**4**	**234**	**2117**	**.889**

Playoffs

Pos	#	Player	Team	GP	G	A	Pts	+/-	PIM	PP	SH	GW	OT	S	%
R	11	Daniel Alfredsson	OTT	7	5	2	7	-1	6	3	0	2	1	23	21.7
C	19	Alexei Yashin	OTT	7	1	5	6	-2	2	1	0	0	0	21	4.8
D	28	Steve Duchesne	OTT	7	1	4	5	-3	0	1	0	1	0	18	5.6
D	6 *	Wade Redden	OTT	7	1	3	4	-4	2	0	0	0	0	11	9.1
L	15	Shawn McEachern	OTT	7	2	0	2	-1	8	1	0	0	0	21	9.5
L	7	Randy Cunneyworth	OTT	7	1	1	2	-3	10	0	0	0	0	18	5.6
C	16 *	Sergei Zholtok	OTT	7	1	1	2	0	0	1	0	0	0	16	6.3
R	10 *	Andreas Dackell	OTT	7	1	0	1	0	0	0	0	0	0	5	20.0
L	17	Tom Chorske	OTT	5	0	1	1	-1	2	0	0	0	0	3	0.0
L	42	Denny Lambert	OTT	6	0	1	1	0	9	0	0	0	0	5	0.0
C	22	Shaun Van Allen	OTT	7	0	1	1	-3	4	0	0	0	0	8	0.0
D	25 *	Bruce Gardiner	OTT	7	0	1	1	0	0	0	0	0	0	3	0.0
D	27	Janne Laukkanen	OTT	7	0	1	1	-1	6	0	0	0	0	7	0.0
C	76	Radek Bonk	OTT	7	0	1	1	-1	4	0	0	0	0	8	0.0
R	26	Philip Crowe	OTT	3	0	0	0	0	16	0	0	0	0	1	0.0
G	31	Ron Tugnutt	OTT	7	0	0	0	0	0	0	0	0	0	0	0.0
D	2	Lance Pitlick	OTT	7	0	0	0	-1	4	0	0	0	0	2	0.0
D	33	Jason York	OTT	7	0	0	0	-3	4	0	0	0	0	18	0.0
R	91	Alexandre Daigle	OTT	7	0	0	0	-5	2	0	0	0	0	16	0.0
D	44 *	Radim Bicanek	OTT	7	0	0	0	0	8	0	0	0	0	4	0.0

Goaltending

No.	Goaltender	GPI	Mins	Avg	W	L	EN	SO	GA	SA	S%
31	Ron Tugnutt	7	425	1.98	3	4	0	1	14	169	.917
	Totals	**7**	**428**	**1.96**	**3**	**4**	**0**	**1**	**14**	**169**	**.917**

Club Records

Team

(Figures in brackets for season records are games played; records for fewest points, wins, ties, losses, goals, goals against are for 70 or more games)

Most Points	77	1996-97 (82)
Most Wins	31	1996-97 (82)
Most Ties	15	1996-97 (82)
Most Losses	70	1992-93 (84)
Most Goals	226	1996-97 (82)
Most Goals Against	397	1993-94 (84)
Fewest Points	24	1992-93 (84)
Fewest Wins	10	1992-93 (84)
Fewest Ties	4	1992-93 (84)
Fewest Losses	36	1996-97 (82)
Fewest Goals	191	1995-96 (82)
Fewest Goals Against	234	1996-97 (82)
Longest Winning Streak		
Overall	4	Mar. 27-Apr. 3/97
Home	4	Mar. 29-Apr. 12/97
Away	3	Oct. 30-Nov. 5/93, Feb. 10-20/96
Longest Undefeated Streak		
Overall	4	Three times
Home	6	Oct. 9-Nov. 7/97 (3 wins, 3 ties)
Away	4	Twice
Longest Losing Streak		
Overall	14	Mar. 2-Apr. 7/93
Home	*11	Oct. 27-Dec. 8/93
Away	*38	Oct. 10/92-Apr. 3/93**
Longest Winless Streak		
Overall	21	Oct. 10-Nov. 23/92 (20 losses, 1 tie)
Home	*17	Oct. 28/95-Jan. 27/96 (15 losses, 2 ties)
Away	*38	Oct. 10/92-Apr. 3/93 (38 losses)
Most Shutouts, Season	4	1996-97 (82)
Most PIM, Season	1,716	1992-93 (84)
Most Goals, Game	7	Four times

** NHL records do not include neutral site games

Individual

Most Seasons	4	Four players
Most Games, Career	263	Alexandre Daigle
Most Goals, Career	101	Alexei Yashin
Most Assists, Career	136	Alexei Yashin
Most Points, Career	237	Alexei Yashin (101G, 136A)
Most PIM, Career	600	Dennis Vial
Most Shutouts, Career	3	Damian Rhodes, Ron Tugnutt
Longest Consecutive Games Streak	135	Stan Neckar (Jan. 22/95-Oct. 18/96)
Most Goals, Season	35	Alexei Yashin (1996-97)
Most Assists, Season	49	Alexei Yashin (1993-94)
Most Points, Season	79	Alexei Yashin (1993-94; 30G, 49A)
Most PIM, Season	318	Mike Peluso (1992-93)
Most Points, Defenseman, Season	63	Norm Maciver (1992-93; 17G, 46A)
Most Points, Center, Season	79	Alexei Yashin (1993-94; 30G, 49A)
Most Points, Right Wing, Season	71	Daniel Alfredsson (1996-97; 24G, 47A)
Most Points, Left Wing, Season	43	Sylvain Turgeon (1992-93; 25G, 18A)
Most Points, Rookie, Season	79	Alexei Yashin (1993-94; 30G, 49A)
Most Shutouts, Season	3	Ron Tugnutt (1996-97)
Most Goals, Game	3	Eleven times
Most Assists, Game	4	Alexei Yashin (Nov. 5/93)
Most Points, Game	6	Dan Quinn (Oct. 15/95; 3G, 3A)

* NHL Record.

Coaching History

Rick Bowness, 1992-93 to 1994-95; Rick Bowness, Dave Allison and Jacques Martin, 1995-96; Jacques Martin, 1996-97 to date.

Captains' History

Laurie Boschman, 1992-93; Brad Shaw, Mark Lamb and Gord Dineen, 1993-94; Randy Cunneyworth, 1994-95 to 1996-97.

Retired Numbers

8	Frank Finnigan	1924-1934

All-time Record vs. Other Clubs

Regular Season

	At Home							On Road							Total						
	GP	W	L	T	GF	GA	PTS	GP	W	L	T	GF	GA	PTS	GP	W	L	T	GF	GA	PTS
Anaheim	3	1	2	0	9	8	2	3	0	3	0	4	13	0	6	1	5	0	13	21	2
Boston	13	1	10	2	25	49	4	14	3	11	0	42	65	6	27	4	21	2	67	114	10
Buffalo	15	3	10	2	30	52	8	13	2	11	0	19	58	4	28	5	21	2	49	110	12
Calgary	4	1	1	2	8	11	4	4	0	3	1	10	26	1	8	1	4	3	18	37	5
Chicago	4	1	3	0	9	15	2	4	1	2	1	10	11	3	8	2	5	1	19	26	5
Colorado	12	3	7	2	36	58	8	10	0	10	0	26	55	0	22	3	17	2	62	113	8
Dallas	4	1	3	0	10	14	2	5	1	4	0	11	25	2	9	2	7	0	21	39	4
Detroit	4	1	2	1	11	13	3	4	2	2	0	10	16	4	8	3	4	1	21	29	7
Edmonton	4	2	2	0	9	12	4	4	1	3	0	12	18	2	8	3	5	0	21	30	6
Florida	8	2	5	1	18	28	5	8	1	6	1	17	30	3	16	3	11	2	35	58	8
Hartford	14	3	8	3	34	47	9	12	1	11	0	26	44	2	26	4	19	3	60	91	11
Los Angeles	4	2	1	1	14	11	5	4	0	4	0	9	24	0	8	2	5	1	23	35	5
Montreal	12	3	9	0	33	44	6	15	4	9	2	43	48	10	27	7	18	2	76	92	16
New Jersey	10	1	8	1	15	32	3	9	1	6	2	20	33	4	19	2	14	3	35	65	7
NY Islanders	9	4	3	2	27	33	10	10	4	3	3	36	38	11	19	8	6	5	63	71	21
NY Rangers	9	1	8	0	22	33	2	9	2	7	0	26	42	4	18	3	15	0	48	75	6
Philadelphia	9	2	6	1	24	32	5	9	1	8	0	19	45	2	18	3	14	1	43	77	7
Phoenix	6	0	5	1	12	28	1	4	2	2	0	16	19	4	10	2	7	1	28	47	5
Pittsburgh	12	2	9	1	26	49	5	13	0	12	1	27	64	1	25	2	21	2	53	113	6
St. Louis	4	1	3	0	8	22	2	4	1	2	1	14	14	3	8	2	5	1	22	36	5
San Jose	4	2	0	2	14	11	6	4	1	3	0	5	8	2	8	3	3	2	19	19	8
Tampa Bay	9	3	6	0	25	26	6	9	4	5	0	23	28	8	18	7	11	0	48	54	14
Toronto	4	1	2	1	10	11	3	5	1	4	0	10	21	2	9	2	6	1	20	32	5
Vancouver	4	2	2	0	10	14	4	4	1	2	1	7	12	3	8	3	4	1	17	26	7
Washington	9	3	5	1	34	35	7	10	2	7	1	22	46	5	19	5	12	2	56	81	12
Totals	**190**	**46**	**120**	**24**	**473**	**688**	**116**	**190**	**36**	**140**	**14**	**464**	**803**	**86**	**380**	**82**	**260**	**38**	**937**	**1491**	**202**

Playoffs

	Series	W	L	GP	W	L	T	GF	GA	Last Mtg.	Round	Result
Buffalo	1	0	1	7	3	4	0	13	14	1997	CQF	L 3-4
Totals	**1**	**0**	**1**	**7**	**3**	**4**	**0**	**13**	**14**			

Playoff Results 1997-93

Year	Round	Opponent	Result	GF	GA
1997	CQF	Buffalo	L 3-4	13	14

Abbreviations: Round: F – Final; **CF** – conference final; **CQF** – conference quarter-final; **CSF** – conference semi-final; **DF** – division final; **DSF** – division semi-final; **SF** – semi-final; **QF** – quarter-final; **PR** – preliminary round.

Colorado totals include Quebec, 1992-93 to 1994-95. Dallas totals include Minnesota, 1992-93. Phoenix totals include Winnipeg, 1992-93 to 1995-96.

1996-97 Results

Oct.	5	at	Montreal	3-3		13	at	Boston	4-3
	9		NY Islanders	3-3		15		Washington	5-1
	11		Pittsburgh	3-2		22		Boston	1-4
	12	at	Pittsburgh	2-3		24		Calgary	2-2
	18	at	New Jersey	2-2		27		Tampa Bay	5-3
	19		Montreal	6-3		29	at	New Jersey	1-1
	23	at	Florida	2-5		30		St. Louis	2-5
	24	at	Tampa Bay	5-2	**Feb.**	1	at	Toronto	2-1
	26	at	Dallas	1-5		3		Vancouver	6-4
	30		Los Angeles	2-2		4	at	Boston	4-3
Nov.	1		Detroit	2-2		8		San Jose	3-3
	2	at	Pittsburgh	3-7		9	at	Buffalo	1-2
	7		Toronto	6-2		11	at	NY Islanders	5-5
	9		Boston	3-4		13	at	Philadelphia	2-4
	10	at	Chicago	0-2		15	at	Hartford	1-2
	13		Edmonton	0-4		16		Hartford	4-2
	15		Chicago	4-3		18	at	Washington	6-1
	16	at	NY Islanders	4-1		20	at	St. Louis	1-1
	19		New Jersey	1-2		23	at	Colorado	3-4
	23		Hartford	3-3		26		Philadelphia	5-8
	27	at	Washington	2-1		28		NY Islanders	4-1
	29	at	Buffalo	0-3	**Mar.**	1		Buffalo	1-3
	30		Philadelphia	3-4		5	at	Anaheim	1-4
Dec.	4		Pittsburgh	2-4		6	at	San Jose	0-2
	6	at	Edmonton	2-5		8	at	Los Angeles	1-3
	7	at	Vancouver	3-2		10	at	Phoenix	4-1
	10	at	Calgary	5-5		14		NY Rangers	3-4
	13		Phoenix	2-4		15	at	Montreal	2-2
	15		Dallas	0-4		17	at	NY Rangers	4-3
	19		Florida	5-2		20		Florida	2-2
	21		Buffalo	2-3		22	at	Boston	5-4
	23	at	Montreal	6-0		25	at	Tampa Bay	0-5
	26		NY Rangers	5-2		27	at	Florida	3-2
	28	at	Hartford	2-3		29		Montreal	5-2
	30		Anaheim	3-4	**Apr.**	2	at	Buffalo	2-0
Jan.	1		Boston	3-2		3		Washington	4-0
	3		New Jersey	0-1		5	at	Pittsburgh	2-5
	4	at	NY Rangers	4-6		6	at	Philadelphia	1-2
	6		Tampa Bay	3-4		9		Hartford	5-4
	9		Colorado	0-2		11	at	Detroit	3-2
	11		Pittsburgh	3-3		12		Buffalo	1-0

Entry Draft
Selections 1997-92

1997
Pick
12	Marian Hossa
58	Jani Hurme
66	Josh Langfeld
119	Magnus Arvedsson
146	Jeff Sullivan
173	Robin Bacul
203	Nick Gillis
229	Karel Rachunek

1996
Pick
1	Chris Phillips
81	Antti-Jussi Niemi
136	Andreas Dackell
163	Francois Hardy
212	Erich Goldmann
216	Ivan Ciernik
239	Sami Salo

1995
Pick
1	Bryan Berard
27	Marc Moro
53	Brad Larsen
89	Kevin Bolibruck
103	Kevin Boyd
131	David Hruska
183	Kaj Linna
184	Ray Schultz
231	Erik Kaminski

1994
Pick
3	Radek Bonk
29	Stanislav Neckar
81	Bryan Masotta
131	Mike Gaffney
133	Daniel Alfredsson
159	Doug Sproule
210	Frederic Cassivi
211	Danny Dupont
237	Stephen MacKinnon
274	Antti Tormanen

1993
Pick
1	Alexandre Daigle
27	Radim Bicanek
53	Patrick Charbonneau
91	Cosmo Dupaul
131	Rick Bodkin
157	Sergei Poleschuk
183	Jason Disher
209	Toby Kvalevog
227	Pavol Demitra
235	Rick Schuwerk

1992
Pick
2	Alexei Yashin
25	Chad Penney
50	Patrick Traverse
73	Radek Hamr
98	Daniel Guerard
121	Al Sinclair
146	Jaroslav Miklenda
169	Jay Kenney
194	Claude Savoie
217	Jake Grimes
242	Tomas Jelinek
264	Petter Ronnqvist

Left: Explosive Alexei Yashin led the Senators to their first-ever playoff berth by scoring 35 goals. Right: Daniel Alfredsson played superbly in Ottawa's playoff against Buffalo, recording five goals in the seven-game series.

Coach

MARTIN, JACQUES
Coach, Ottawa Senators. Born in St. Pascal, Ont., October 1, 1952.

Jacques Martin led the Ottawa Senators to its best season in team history. The club recorded a total of 77 points (31-36-15), a .470 winning percentage, and set club records for wins, ties and points both at home and on the road in a season. Ottawa also posted its best ever conference placing (7th) and played in its first Stanley Cup playoff series, taking the Buffalo Sabres to overtime in the final game of the best-of-seven Eastern Conference quarter-final series.

When appointed the Senators' third head coach on January 24, 1996, Martin brought ten years of NHL coaching experience, including five with the Quebec Nordiques, an organization often compared with the Senators, in that both teams were built around young, talented players requiring patience and teaching.

Martin's coaching career began at the collegiate level in 1976. He was appointed head coach of the Guelph Platers (now Storm) in 1986, winning the OHL title, the Memorial Cup and being named the OHL coach of the year. That summer, Martin became head coach of the St. Louis Blues. In his NHL rookie year, he lead the Blues to the Norris Division Championship and, in two seasons with the Blues, posted a 66-71-23 record. He then spent two seasons as an assistant to Chicago's head coach Mike Keenan, before joining the Nordiques in 1990. With Quebec, he worked four years as assistant coach and one year (1993-94) as both head coach and general manager of the AHL Cornwall Aces.

Coaching Record

Season	Team	Regular Season					Playoffs			
		Games	W	L	T	%	Games	W	L	%
1983-84	Peterborough (OHL)	70	43	23	4	.643	....	....	....	....
1984-85	Peterborough (OHL)	66	42	20	4	.667	....	....	....	....
1985-86	Guelph (OHL)	66	41	23	2	.636	....	....	....	....
1986-87	St. Louis (NHL)	80	32	33	15	.494	6	2	4	.333
1987-88	St. Louis (NHL)	80	34	38	8	.475	10	5	5	.500
1993-94	Cornwall (AHL)	80	33	36	11	.481	13	8	5	.615
1995-96	**Ottawa (NHL)**	**38**	**10**	**24**	**4**	**.316**	**....**	**....**	**....**	**....**
1996-97	**Ottawa (NHL)**	**82**	**31**	**36**	**15**	**.470**	**7**	**3**	**4**	**.429**
	NHL Totals	**280**	**107**	**131**	**42**	**.457**	**23**	**10**	**13**	**.435**

Club Directory

Corel Centre

Corel Centre
1000 Palladium Drive
Kanata, Ontario
K2V 1A5
Phone **613/599-0250**
FAX 613/599-0358
Capacity: 18,500

Executive
Chairman Governor	Rod Bryden
President, CEO & Alternate Governor	Roy Mlakar
General Manager & Alternate Governor	Pierre Gauthier
Executive Vice-President	Steve Violetta
President, Corel Centre & Alternate Governor	Cyril Leeder

Assistants
Secretary to Governor	Sharry Dozois
Executive Assistant and Office Manager	Cheryl Blake
Secretary to the General Manager	Allison Vaughan
Administrative Assistant to the Executive Vice-President	Kelly MacCallum
Secretary to the President, Corel Centre	Gail Martineau

Hockey Operations
Assistant General Manager	Ray Shero
Director of Player Personnel	Marshall Johnston
Head Coach	Jacques Martin
Assistant Coaches	Perry Pearn, Craig Ramsay
Video Coach and Conditioning Coach	Randy Lee
Scouting Coordinator	Trevor Timmins
Head Equipment Manager	Ed Georgica
Head Athletic Trainer	Kevin Wagner
Assistant Equipment Manager	John Gervais
Massage Therapist	Brad Joyal
Team Doctor	Jamie Kissick, M.D.
Chief Scout	Andre Savard
Professional Scout	Phil Myre
European Scouts	Agustin Bubnik, Jarmo Kekalainen
Scouts	Don Boyd, Paul Castron, Dale Engel, George Fargher, John Phelan

Media Relations
Director	Phil Legault
Assistant Director	Morgan Quarry

Administration & MIS
Manager, Computer & Internet Services	Sean Shrubsole
Office Manager	Cheryl Blake
Office Coordinator	Katrina Phelps
Receptionist	Colleen Clark
Computer Services Assistant	Niall Sheehan

Broadcast Services
Vice-President	Jim Steel
Administrative Assistant	Katrina Phelps

Community Development
Director	Brad Marsh
Assistant Director	Sherry Doiron
Coordinator	Marie Olney

Corporate Sales
Vice-President, Sales	Mark Bonneau
Manager of Sponsorship and Corporate Properties	Dan Quinn
Coordinators	Christine Clancy, Deborah Desormeaux
Administrative Assistant	Marie-Danielle Davis
Corporate Account Managers	James Cotie, Bill Courchaine, Gina Hillcoat, Brian Jokat, Marie-Paule McNeill, Steve Powell, Craig Purcell

Finance
Vice-President	Mark Goudie
Controller	Erin Crowe
Administrative Assistant	Sandra Lindsay
Payroll Supervisor	Sandi Horner
Senior Accountant	Lynda Rozon
Accounts Payable	Laurel Neill
Accounts Receivable	Anne Hersey
Staff Accountant	Lisa Saumure

Marketing
Executive Vice-President	Steve Violetta
Managing Editor	Carl Lavigne
Merchandise Manager	Bob Maxwell
Manager, Graphics	Kevin Caradonna
Administrative Assistant	Kelly MacCallum
Director of Game Entertainment and Promotions	Vikki Hultquist
Retail Supervisor	Tracy Ogilby
Graphic Designer	Angie Mulligan
Coordinator, Marketing & Broadcast	Krista Pogue
Promotions Coordinator	Erik Vogel
Coordinator, Sales and Marketing	Erik McDonald

Ticketing
Vice-President	Jeff Kyle
Ticket Sales Manager	Pat Whalen
Customer Service Coordinator	Cindy Kruger
Coordinator, Corporate Ticket Services	Jody Thorson
Administrative Assistant	Laurie Hamilton
Coordinator, Fan Development	Shawn Williams
Program Coordinator, Partners in Caring	Maria Murphy
Customer Service Representatives	Natalie Grandmaison-Farmer, Wendy Duncan, Tracey Bonner
Account Representatives	Jim Armstrong, Gus Ayoub, Gianni Farinon, Joe Lowes, Angela Peppiatt, Serge Rolling, Devon Wingate

Corel Centre
President, Corel Centre & Alternate Governor	Cyril Leeder
Secretary to the President Corel Centre	Gail Martineau

Philadelphia Flyers

1996-97 Results: 45W-24L-13T 103PTS. Second, Atlantic Division

On April 13, 1997, John LeClair scored his 50th goal of the season to become the first Flyer to reach the vaunted mark in back-to-back seasons since Tim Kerr's four consecutive 50-goal seasons in the mid-1980s.

1997-98 Schedule

Oct.	Wed.	1	Florida		Thu.	8	at Carolina
	Fri.	3	Ottawa		Fri.	9	at Washington
	Sun.	5	Phoenix		Sun.	11	at Tampa Bay
	Wed.	8	at New Jersey		Wed.	14	Montreal
	Thu.	9	Pittsburgh		Tue.	20	Buffalo
	Sat.	11	at Montreal		Thu.	22	at NY Rangers
	Mon.	13	at San Jose		Sat.	24	at Detroit*
	Wed.	15	at Anaheim		Mon.	26	NY Islanders
	Fri.	17	at Los Angeles		Wed.	28	at NY Islanders
	Tue.	21	Tampa Bay		Thu.	29	Montreal
	Thu.	23	Calgary		Sat.	31	Washington*
	Mon.	27	New Jersey	Feb.	Wed.	4	at Dallas
	Wed.	29	St. Louis		Thu.	5	at Phoenix
	Fri.	31	at Washington		Sat.	7	at Colorado*
Nov.	Sun.	2	Dallas*		Sat.	28	at NY Rangers*
	Mon.	3	at St. Louis	Mar.	Mon.	2	at New Jersey
	Thu.	6	Edmonton		Tue.	3	at NY Islanders
	Sat.	8	at Ottawa		Thu.	5	Washington
	Tue.	11	Ottawa		Sat.	7	at Pittsburgh*
	Thu.	13	Colorado		Sun.	8	Pittsburgh
	Fri.	14	at Florida		Tue.	10	New Jersey
	Sun.	16	Tampa Bay		Thu.	12	Vancouver
	Wed.	19	at Toronto		Sat.	14	Detroit*
	Thu.	20	San Jose		Mon.	16	Toronto
	Wed.	26	at Buffalo		Thu.	19	Anaheim
	Fri.	28	NY Islanders		Sat.	21	at Pittsburgh*
	Sat.	29	at Tampa Bay		Sun.	22	NY Rangers
Dec.	Mon.	1	Buffalo		Tue.	24	at New Jersey
	Wed.	3	Boston		Thu.	26	at Boston
	Fri.	5	at NY Rangers		Sat.	28	Carolina*
	Thu.	11	NY Islanders		Sun.	29	at Carolina
	Fri.	12	at Chicago		Tue.	31	Chicago
	Sun.	14	Tampa Bay	Apr.	Thu.	2	Los Angeles
	Mon.	15	at Montreal		Sat.	4	Florida*
	Thu.	18	Boston		Wed.	8	at Tampa Bay
	Sat.	20	Florida*		Thu.	9	at Florida
	Tue.	23	Carolina		Sat.	11	Washington*
	Sat.	27	at Calgary		Mon.	13	at Buffalo
	Tue.	30	at Edmonton		Thu.	16	at Florida
	Wed.	31	at Vancouver		Sat.	18	NY Rangers*
Jan.	Sat.	3	at Ottawa		Sun.	19	at Boston*

* Denotes afternoon game.

Franchise date: June 5, 1967

ATLANTIC DIVISION

31st NHL Season

Year-by-Year Record

		Home			Road			Overall						
Season	GP	W	L	T	W	L	T	W	L	T	GF	GA	Pts.	Finished	Playoff Result
1996-97	82	23	12	6	22	12	7	45	24	13	274	217	103	2nd, Atlantic Div.	Lost Final
1995-96	82	27	9	5	18	15	8	45	24	13	282	208	103	1st, Atlantic Div.	Lost Conf. Semi-Final
1994-95	48	16	7	1	12	9	3	28	16	4	150	132	60	1st, Atlantic Div.	Lost Conf. Championship
1993-94	84	19	20	3	16	19	7	35	39	10	294	314	80	6th, Atlantic Div.	Out of Playoffs
1992-93	84	23	14	5	13	23	6	36	37	11	319	319	83	5th, Patrick Div.	Out of Playoffs
1991-92	80	22	11	7	10	26	4	32	37	11	252	273	75	6th, Patrick Div.	Out of Playoffs
1990-91	80	18	16	6	15	21	4	33	37	10	252	267	76	5th, Patrick Div.	Out of Playoffs
1989-90	80	17	19	4	13	20	7	30	39	11	290	297	71	6th, Patrick Div.	Out of Playoffs
1988-89	80	22	15	3	14	21	5	36	36	8	307	285	80	4th, Patrick Div.	Lost Conf. Championship
1987-88	80	20	14	6	18	19	3	38	33	9	292	292	85	3rd, Patrick Div.	Lost Div. Semi-Final
1986-87	80	29	9	2	17	17	6	46	26	8	310	245	100	1st, Patrick Div.	Lost Final
1985-86	80	33	6	1	20	17	3	53	23	4	335	241	110	1st, Patrick Div.	Lost Div. Semi-Final
1984-85	80	32	4	4	21	16	3	53	20	7	348	241	113	1st, Patrick Div.	Lost Final
1983-84	80	25	10	5	19	16	5	44	26	10	350	290	98	3rd, Patrick Div.	Lost Div. Semi-Final
1982-83	80	29	8	3	20	15	5	49	23	8	326	240	106	1st, Patrick Div.	Lost Div. Semi-Final
1981-82	80	25	10	5	13	21	6	38	31	11	325	313	87	3rd, Patrick Div.	Lost Div. Semi-Final
1980-81	80	23	9	8	18	15	7	41	24	15	313	249	97	2nd, Patrick Div.	Lost Quarter-Final
1979-80	80	27	5	8	21	7	12	48	12	20	327	254	116	1st, Patrick Div.	Lost Final
1978-79	80	26	10	4	14	15	11	40	25	15	281	248	95	2nd, Patrick Div.	Lost Quarter-Final
1977-78	80	29	6	5	16	14	10	45	20	15	296	200	105	2nd, Patrick Div.	Lost Semi-Final
1976-77	80	33	6	1	15	10	15	48	16	16	323	213	112	1st, Patrick Div.	Lost Semi-Final
1975-76	80	36	2	2	15	11	14	51	13	16	348	209	118	1st, Patrick Div.	Lost Final
1974-75	**80**	**32**	**6**	**2**	**19**	**12**	**9**	**51**	**18**	**11**	**293**	**181**	**113**	**1st, Patrick Div.**	**Won Stanley Cup**
1973-74	**78**	**28**	**6**	**5**	**22**	**10**	**7**	**50**	**16**	**12**	**273**	**164**	**112**	**1st, West Div.**	**Won Stanley Cup**
1972-73	78	27	8	4	10	22	7	37	30	11	296	256	85	2nd, West Div.	Lost Semi-Final
1971-72	78	19	13	7	7	25	7	26	38	14	200	236	66	5th, West Div.	Out of Playoffs
1970-71	78	20	10	9	8	23	8	28	33	17	207	225	73	3rd, West Div.	Lost Quarter-Final
1969-70	76	11	14	13	6	21	11	17	35	24	197	225	58	5th, West Div.	Out of Playoffs
1968-69	76	14	16	8	6	19	13	20	35	21	174	225	61	3rd, West Div.	Lost Quarter-Final
1967-68	74	17	13	7	14	19	4	31	32	11	173	179	73	1st, West Div.	Lost Quarter-Final

1997-98 Player Personnel

FORWARDS	HT	WT	S	Place of Birth	Date	1996-97 Club
BIALOWAS, Frank	5-11	220	L	Winnipeg, Man.	9/25/70	Philadelphia (AHL)
BOISVENUE, Martin	6-0	192	L	Cornwall, Ont.	4/24/77	Val D'Or
BOWEN, Jason	6-4	215	L	Port Alice, B.C.	11/9/73	Phi-Philadelphia (AHL)
BRIND'AMOUR, Rod	6-1	202	L	Ottawa, Ont.	8/9/70	Philadelphia
BRUININKS, Brett	6-4	235	R	Minneapolis, MN	3/10/72	Philadelphia (AHL)
CERVEN, Martin	6-4	200	L	Trencin, Czech.	3/7/77	Seattle
COLES, Bruce	5-9	183	L	Montreal, Que.	1/12/68	Philadelphia (AHL)
DANIELS, Scott	6-3	214	L	Prince Albert, Sask.	9/19/69	Philadelphia
DARBY, Craig	6-3	200	R	Oneida, NY	9/26/72	Phi-Philadelphia (AHL)
DRUCE, John	6-2	195	R	Peterborough, Ont.	2/23/66	Philadelphia
FALLOON, Pat	5-11	190	R	Foxwarren, Man.	9/22/72	Philadelphia
FORBES, Colin	6-3	205	L	New Westminster, B.C.	2/16/76	Phi-Philadelphia (AHL)
GRATTON, Chris	6-4	218	L	Brantford, Ont.	7/5/75	Tampa Bay
HEALEY, Paul	6-2	196	R	Edmonton, Alta.	3/20/75	Phi-Philadelphia (AHL)
KLATT, Trent	6-1	205	R	Robbinsdale, MN	1/30/71	Philadelphia
KORDIC, Dan	6-5	234	L	Edmonton, Alta.	4/18/71	Philadelphia
LACROIX, Daniel	6-2	205	L	Montreal, Que.	3/11/69	Philadelphia
LeCLAIR, John	6-3	226	L	St. Albans, VT	7/5/69	Philadelphia
LINDROS, Eric	6-4	236	R	London, Ont.	2/28/73	Philadelphia
McCOSH, Shawn	6-0	197	R	Oshawa, Ont.	6/5/69	Philadelphia (AHL)
MONTGOMERY, Jim	5-10	185	R	Montreal, Que.	6/30/69	Koln
OTTO, Joel	6-4	220	R	Elk River, MN	10/29/61	Philadelphia
PAYETTE, Andre	6-2	205	L	Cornwall, Ont.	7/29/76	S.S. Marie-Kingston
PODEIN, Shjon	6-2	200	L	Rochester, MN	3/5/68	Philadelphia
PROSPAL, Vaclav	6-2	185	L	Ceske-Budejovice, Czech.	2/17/75	Phi-Philadelphia (AHL)
WESENBERG, Brian	6-3	187	R	Peterborough, Ont.	5/9/77	Guelph-Philadelphia (AHL)
WHITE, Peter	5-11	200	L	Montreal, Que.	3/15/69	Philadelphia (AHL)
ZUBRUS, Dainius	6-3	215	L	Elektrenai, USSR	6/16/78	Philadelphia
DEFENSEMEN						
BRIMANIS, Aris	6-3	210	R	Cleveland, OH	3/14/72	Phi-Philadelphia (AHL)
COFFEY, Paul	6-0	190	L	Weston, Ont.	6/1/61	Hartford-Philadelphia
DELMORE, Andy	6-1	192	R	LaSalle, Ont.	12/26/76	Sarnia-Fredericton
DESJARDINS, Eric	6-1	200	R	Rouyn, Que.	6/14/69	Philadelphia
HEWARD, Jamie	6-2	207	R	Regina, Sask.	3/30/71	Toronto-St. John's
LANK, Jeff	6-3	205	L	Indian Head, Sask.	3/1/75	Philadelphia (AHL)
MacISAAC, Dave	6-2	225	L	Arlington, MA	4/23/72	Philadelphia (AHL)
NIINIMAA, Janne	6-1	220	L	Raahe, Finland	5/22/75	Philadelphia
RICHARDSON, Luke	6-4	210	L	Ottawa, Ont.	3/26/69	Edmonton
SAMUELSSON, Kjell	6-6	235	R	Tyngsryd, Sweden	10/18/58	Philadelphia
STAPLES, Jeff	6-2	207	L	Kitimat, B.C.	3/4/75	Philadelphia (AHL)
STEVENS, John	6-1	195	L	Completon, N.B.	5/4/66	Philadelphia (AHL)
SVOBODA, Petr	6-1	195	L	Most, Czech.	2/14/66	Philadelphia
THERIEN, Chris	6-5	230	L	Ottawa, Ont.	12/14/71	Philadelphia
VanTIGHEM, Travis	6-1	210	L	Calgary, Alta	3/16/73	Michigan Tech

GOALTENDERS	HT	WT	C	Place of Birth	Date	1996-97 Club
BOUCHER, Brian	6-1	190	L	Woonsocket, RI	1/2/77	Tri-City
HEXTALL, Ron	6-3	192	L	Brandon, Man.	5/3/64	Philadelphia
LITTLE, Neil	6-1	193	L	Medicine Hat, Alta.	12/18/71	Philadelphia (AHL)
ROUSSEL, Dominic	6-1	191	L	Hull, Que.	2/22/70	Philadelphia (AHL)
SNOW, Garth	6-3	200	L	Wrentham, MA	7/28/69	Philadelphia

General Manager

CLARKE, ROBERT EARLE (BOB)
President/General Manager, Philadelphia Flyers.
Born in Flin Flon, Man., August 13, 1949.

Bob Clarke was named president and general manager of the Philadelphia Flyers on June 15, 1994. Clarke's appointment marks the second time he has served as the Flyers' general manager. The Flin Flon native was the Flyers' vice president and general manager from 1984-90. During his nine years as the team's general manager, the Flyers have won five divisional titles, three conference championships, reached the Stanley Cup semifinals five times and the Finals three times.

Prior to re-joining the Flyers' family in 1994, Clarke served as vice president and general manager of the Florida Panthers. In 1993-94, their first season in the NHL, the Panthers established NHL records for wins (33) and points (83) by an expansion franchise. Clarke also served as the vice president and general manager of the Minnesota North Stars from 1990-92, guiding the team to the Stanley Cup Finals in 1991.

As a player, the former Philadelphia captain led his club to Stanley Cup championships in 1974 and 1975 and captured numerous individual awards, including the Hart Trophy as the League's most valuable player in 1973, 1975 and 1976. The four-time All-Star also received the Masterton Memorial Trophy (perseverance and dedication) in 1972 and the Frank J. Selke Trophy (top defensive forward) in 1983. He appeared in nine All-Star Games and was elected to the Hockey Hall of Fame in 1987. He was awarded the Lester Patrick Trophy in 1979-80 in recognition of his contribution to hockey in the United States. Clarke appeared in 1,144 regular season games, recording 358 goals and 852 assists for 1,210 points. He also added 119 points in 136 playoff games.

1996-97 Scoring

* – rookie

Regular Season

Pos	#	Player	Team	GP	G	A	Pts	+/–	PIM	PP	SH	GW	GT	S	%
L	10	John LeClair	PHI	82	50	47	97	44	58	10	0	5	2	324	15.4
C	88	Eric Lindros	PHI	52	32	47	79	31	136	9	0	7	2	198	16.2
L	17	Rod Brind'Amour	PHI	82	27	32	59	2	41	8	2	3	2	205	13.2
R	19	Mikael Renberg	PHI	77	22	37	59	36	65	1	0	4	1	249	8.8
D	37	Eric Desjardins	PHI	82	12	34	46	25	50	5	1	1	0	183	6.6
R	20	Trent Klatt	PHI	76	24	21	45	9	20	5	5	5	0	131	18.3
D	44	* Janne Niinimaa	PHI	77	4	40	44	12	58	1	0	2	0	141	2.8
C	18	Dale Hawerchuk	PHI	51	12	22	34	9	32	6	0	2	0	102	11.8
D	77	Paul Coffey	HFD	20	3	5	8	0	18	1	0	1	0	39	7.7
			PHI	37	6	20	26	11	20	0	1	1	0	71	8.5
			TOTAL	57	9	25	34	11	38	1	1	2	0	110	8.2
L	25	Shjon Podein	PHI	82	14	18	32	7	41	0	0	4	0	153	9.2
C	29	Joel Otto	PHI	78	13	19	32	12	99	0	1	2	1	105	12.4
D	6	Chris Therien	PHI	71	2	22	24	27	64	0	0	0	0	107	1.9
R	15	Pat Falloon	PHI	52	11	12	23	-8	10	2	0	4	0	124	8.9
R	9	* Dainius Zubrus	PHI	68	8	13	21	3	22	1	0	2	0	71	11.3
D	24	Karl Dykhuis	PHI	62	4	15	19	6	35	2	0	1	0	101	4.0
R	26	John Druce	PHI	43	7	8	15	-5	12	1	0	0	0	73	9.6
C	45	* Vaclav Prospal	PHI	18	5	10	15	3	4	0	0	0	0	35	14.3
D	23	Petr Svoboda	PHI	67	2	12	14	10	94	1	0	0	0	36	5.6
D	8	Michel Petit	EDM	18	2	4	6	-13	20	0	0	0	0	30	6.7
			PHI	20	0	3	3	2	51	0	0	0	0	13	0.0
			TOTAL	38	2	7	9	-11	71	0	0	0	0	43	4.7
C	32	Daniel Lacroix	PHI	74	7	1	8	-1	163	1	0	0	0	54	13.0
L	22	Scott Daniels	PHI	56	5	3	8	2	237	0	0	2	0	48	10.4
D	28	Kjell Samuelsson	PHI	34	4	3	7	17	47	0	0	0	0	36	11.1
C	11	Craig Darby	PHI	9	1	4	5	2	2	0	1	0	0	13	7.7
L	21	Dan Kordic	PHI	75	1	4	5	-1	210	0	0	0	0	21	4.8
L	48	* Colin Forbes	PHI	3	1	0	1	0	0	0	0	0	0	3	33.3
D	3	* Aris Brimanis	PHI	3	0	1	1	0	0	0	0	0	0	1	0.0
D	34	Jason Bowen	PHI	4	0	1	1	1	8	0	0	0	0	1	0.0
G	30	Garth Snow	PHI	35	0	1	1	0	30	0	0	0	0	0	0.0
R	38	* Paul Healey	PHI	2	0	0	0	0	0	0	0	0	0	0	0.0
D	2	Frantisek Kucera	VAN	2	0	0	0	0	0	0	0	0	0	3	0.0
			PHI	2	0	0	0	-2	2	0	0	0	0	2	0.0
			TOTAL	4	0	0	0	-2	2	0	0	0	0	5	0.0
D	5	Darren Rumble	PHI	10	0	0	0	-2	0	0	0	0	0	9	0.0
G	27	Ron Hextall	PHI	55	0	0	0	0	43	0	0	0	0	0	0.0

Goaltending

No.	Goaltender	GPI	Mins	Avg	W	L	T	EN	SO	GA	SA	S%
30	Garth Snow	35	1884	2.52	14	8	8	2	2	79	816	.903
27	Ron Hextall	55	3094	2.56	31	16	5	4	5	132	1285	.897
	Totals	**82**	**4995**	**2.61**	**45**	**24**	**13**	**6**	**7**	**217**	**2107**	**.897**

Playoffs

Pos	#	Player	Team	GP	G	A	Pts	+/–	PIM	PP	SH	GW	OT	S	%
C	88	Eric Lindros	PHI	19	12	14	26	7	40	4	0	1	0	71	16.9
L	17	Rod Brind'Amour	PHI	19	13	8	21	9	10	4	2	1	0	65	20.0
L	10	John LeClair	PHI	19	9	12	21	5	10	4	0	3	0	79	11.4
D	44	* Janne Niinimaa	PHI	19	1	12	13	3	16	1	0	1	0	56	1.8
R	19	Mikael Renberg	PHI	18	5	6	11	1	4	2	0	0	0	35	14.3
D	37	Eric Desjardins	PHI	19	2	8	10	9	12	0	0	0	0	49	4.1
R	9	* Dainius Zubrus	PHI	19	5	4	9	3	12	1	0	1	0	28	17.9
D	77	Paul Coffey	PHI	17	1	8	9	-3	6	0	0	0	0	37	2.7
R	20	Trent Klatt	PHI	19	4	3	7	1	12	0	0	2	0	26	15.4
L	25	Shjon Podein	PHI	19	4	3	7	4	16	0	0	1	0	52	7.7
C	18	Dale Hawerchuk	PHI	17	2	5	7	-2	0	1	0	1	0	24	8.3
D	6	Chris Therien	PHI	19	1	6	7	14	6	0	0	1	0	36	2.8
C	29	Joel Otto	PHI	18	1	5	6	3	8	0	0	0	0	23	4.3
R	15	Pat Falloon	PHI	14	3	1	4	-1	2	1	0	0	0	32	9.4
C	45	* Vaclav Prospal	PHI	5	1	3	4	0	4	0	0	0	0	10	10.0
D	23	Petr Svoboda	PHI	16	1	2	3	4	16	0	0	0	0	9	11.1
D	24	Karl Dykhuis	PHI	18	0	3	3	1	2	0	0	0	0	15	0.0
G	30	Garth Snow	PHI	12	0	2	2	0	11	0	0	0	0	0	0.0
L	21	Dan Kordic	PHI	12	1	0	1	1	22	0	0	0	0	3	33.3
R	26	John Druce	PHI	13	1	0	1	2	2	0	1	0	0	10	10.0
C	32	Daniel Lacroix	PHI	12	0	1	1	0	22	0	0	0	0	4	0.0
D	8	Michel Petit	PHI	3	0	0	0	-1	6	0	0	0	0	1	0.0
L	48	* Colin Forbes	PHI	3	0	0	0	0	0	0	0	0	0	3	0.0
D	28	Kjell Samuelsson	PHI	5	0	0	0	-3	2	0	0	0	0	4	0.0
G	27	Ron Hextall	PHI	8	0	0	0	0	0	0	0	0	0	0	0.0

Goaltending

No.	Goaltender	GPI	Mins	Avg	W	L	EN	SO	GA	SA	S%
30	Garth Snow	12	699	2.83	8	4	0	0	33	305	.892
27	Ron Hextall	8	444	2.97	4	3	0	0	22	203	.892
	Totals	**19**	**1146**	**2.88**	**12**	**7**	**0**	**0**	**55**	**508**	**.892**

General Managers' History

"Bud" Poile, 1967-68 to 1968-69; "Bud" Poile and Keith Allen, 1969-70; Keith Allen, 1970-71 to 1982-83; Bob McCammon, 1983-84; Bob Clarke, 1984-85 to 1989-90; Russ Farwell, 1990-91 to 1993-94; Bob Clarke, 1994-95 to date.

Club Records

Team

(Figures in brackets for season records are games played; records for fewest points, wins, ties, losses, goals, goals against are for 70 or more games)

Most Points	**118**	1975-76 (80)
Most Wins	**53**	1984-85 (80), 1985-86 (80)
Most Ties	***24**	1969-70 (76)
Most Losses	**39**	1993-94 (84)
Most Goals	**350**	1983-84 (80)
Most Goals Against	**319**	1992-93 (84)
Fewest Points	**58**	1969-70 (76)
Fewest Wins	**17**	1969-70 (76)
Fewest Ties	**4**	1985-86 (80)
Fewest Losses	**12**	1979-80 (80)
Fewest Goals	**173**	1967-68 (74)
Fewest Goals Against	**164**	1973-74 (78)
Longest Winning Streak		
Overall	**13**	Oct. 19-Nov. 17/85
Home	***20**	Jan. 4-Apr. 3/76
Away	**8**	Dec. 22/82-Jan. 16/83
Longest Undefeated Streak		
Overall	***35**	Oct. 14/79-Jan. 6/80 (25 wins, 10 ties)
Home	**26**	Oct. 11/79-Feb. 3/80 (19 wins, 7 ties)
Away	**16**	Oct. 20/79-Jan. 6/80 (11 wins, 5 ties)
Longest Losing Streak		
Overall	**6**	Mar. 25-Apr. 4/70, Dec. 5-Dec. 17/92, Jan. 25-Feb. 5/94
Home	**5**	Jan. 30-Feb. 15/69
Away	**8**	Oct. 25-Nov. 26/72
Longest Winless Streak		
Overall	**11**	Nov. 21-Dec. 14/69 (9 losses, 2 ties), Dec. 10/70-Jan. 3/71 (9 losses, 2 ties)
Home	**8**	Dec. 19/68-Jan. 18/69 (4 losses, 4 ties)
Away	**19**	Oct. 23/71-Jan. 27/72 (15 losses, 4 ties)
Most Shutouts, Season	**13**	1974-75 (80)
Most PIM, Season	**2,621**	1980-81 (80)
Most Goals, Game	**13**	Mar. 22/84 (Pit. 4 at Phi. 13), Oct. 18/84 (Van. 2 at Phi. 13)

Individual

Most Seasons	**15**	Bobby Clarke
Most Games	**1,144**	Bobby Clarke
Most Goals, Career	**420**	Bill Barber
Most Assists, Career	**852**	Bobby Clarke
Most Points, Career	**1,210**	Bobby Clarke (358G, 852A)
Most PIM, Career	**1,683**	Rick Tocchet
Most Shutouts, Career	**50**	Bernie Parent
Longest Consecutive Game Streak	**320**	Rod Brind'Amour (Feb. 24/93-current)
Most Goals, Season	**61**	Reggie Leach (1975-76)
Most Assists, Season	**89**	Bobby Clarke (1974-75, 1975-76)
Most Points, Season	**123**	Mark Recchi (1992-93; 53G, 70A)
Most PIM, Season	***472**	Dave Schultz (1974-75)
Most Points, Defenseman, Season	**82**	Mark Howe (1985-86; 24G, 58A)
Most Points, Center, Season	**119**	Bobby Clarke (1975-76; 30G, 89A)
Most Points, Right Wing, Season	**123**	Mark Recchi (1992-93; 53G, 70A)
Most Points, Left Wing, Season	**112**	Bill Barber (1975-76; 50G, 62A)
Most Points, Rookie, Season	**82**	Mikael Renberg (1993-94; 38G, 44A)
Most Shutouts, Season	**12**	Bernie Parent (1973-74, 1974-75)
Most Goals, Game	**4**	Thirteen times
Most Assists, Game	**6**	Eric Lindros (Feb. 26/97)
Most Points, Game	**8**	Tom Bladon (Dec. 11/77; 4G, 4A)

* NHL Record.

Retired Numbers

1	Bernie Parent	1967-1971 and 1973-1979
4	Barry Ashbee	1970-1974
7	Bill Barber	1972-1985
16	Bobby Clarke	1969-1984

All-time Record vs. Other Clubs

Regular Season

	At Home							On Road							Total						
	GP	W	L	T	GF	GA	PTS	GP	W	L	T	GF	GA	PTS	GP	W	L	T	GF	GA	PTS
Anaheim	3	1	1	1	7	5	3	3	2	1	0	11	11	4	6	3	2	1	18	16	7
Boston	59	27	26	6	204	175	60	62	14	40	8	180	254	36	121	41	66	14	384	429	96
Buffalo	53	31	13	9	196	144	71	49	19	24	6	153	176	44	102	50	37	15	349	320	115
Calgary	46	31	13	2	183	122	64	47	15	23	9	155	192	39	93	46	36	11	338	314	103
Chicago	56	29	16	11	182	151	69	55	11	25	19	156	198	41	111	40	41	30	338	349	110
Colorado	29	21	6	2	111	76	44	28	9	9	10	103	105	28	57	30	15	12	214	181	72
Dallas	61	41	9	11	244	140	93	61	23	24	14	206	204	60	122	64	33	25	450	344	153
Detroit	54	30	13	11	215	161	71	53	18	25	10	173	191	46	107	48	38	21	388	352	117
Edmonton	25	18	6	1	114	72	37	24	6	14	4	71	90	16	49	24	20	5	185	162	53
Florida	10	3	4	3	23	27	9	9	7	2	0	29	24	14	19	10	6	3	52	51	23
Hartford	29	20	7	2	118	78	42	30	15	10	5	126	112	35	59	35	17	7	244	190	77
Los Angeles	58	36	15	7	227	151	79	60	34	18	8	207	175	76	118	70	33	15	434	326	155
Montreal	59	25	21	13	183	179	63	60	17	30	13	187	223	47	119	42	51	26	370	402	110
New Jersey	67	45	15	7	279	165	97	65	29	32	4	248	237	62	132	74	47	11	527	402	159
NY Islanders	77	46	23	8	294	233	100	80	24	43	13	235	313	61	157	70	66	21	529	546	161
NY Rangers	91	44	34	13	307	265	101	92	28	42	22	263	305	78	183	72	76	35	570	570	179
Ottawa	9	8	1	0	45	19	16	9	6	2	1	32	24	13	18	14	3	1	77	43	29
Phoenix	25	19	6	0	114	70	38	24	12	10	2	82	77	26	49	31	16	2	196	147	64
Pittsburgh	89	67	15	7	392	229	141	88	32	39	17	286	308	81	177	99	54	24	678	537	222
St. Louis	61	41	10	10	245	139	92	61	30	24	7	192	179	67	122	71	34	17	437	318	159
San Jose	5	3	1	1	22	11	7	6	5	1	0	21	11	10	11	8	2	1	43	22	17
Tampa Bay	10	5	1	4	31	20	14	11	7	4	0	32	32	14	21	12	5	4	63	52	28
Toronto	54	35	11	8	217	126	78	54	22	19	13	187	183	57	108	57	30	21	404	309	135
Vancouver	47	32	14	1	209	140	65	47	25	10	12	184	139	62	94	57	24	13	393	279	127
Washington	68	40	23	5	259	194	85	66	29	25	12	228	227	70	134	69	48	17	487	421	155
Defunct Clubs	34	24	4	6	137	67	54	35	13	14	8	102	89	34	69	37	18	14	239	156	88
Totals	**1179**	**722**	**308**	**149**	**4558**	**3159**	**1593**	**1179**	**452**	**510**	**217**	**3849**	**4079**	**1121**	**2358**	**1174**	**818**	**366**	**8407**	**7238**	**2714**

Playoffs

	Series	W	L	GP	W	L	T	GF	GA	Last Mtg.	Round	Result
Boston	4	2	2	20	9	11	0	57	60	1978	QF	L 1-4
Buffalo	4	4	0	21	16	5	0	74	49	1997	CSF	W 4-1
Calgary	2	1	1	11	7	4	0	43	28	1981	QF	L 3-4
Chicago	1	0	1	4	0	4	0	8	20	1971	QF	L 0-4
Colorado	2	2	0	11	7	4	0	39	29	1985	CF	W 4-2
Dallas	2	2	0	11	8	3	0	41	26	1980	SF	W 4-1
Detroit	1	0	1	4	0	4	0	6	16	1997	F	L 0-4
Edmonton	3	1	2	15	7	8	0	44	49	1987	F	L 3-4
Florida	1	0	1	6	2	4	0	11	15	1996	CSF	L 2-4
Montreal	4	1	3	21	6	15	0	52	72	1989	CF	L 2-4
New Jersey	2	1	1	8	4	4	0	20	23	1995	CF	L 2-4
NY Islanders	4	3	1	25	14	11	0	83	69	1987	DF	W 4-3
NY Rangers	10	6	4	47	27	20	0	157	153	1997	CF	W 4-1
Pittsburgh	2	2	0	12	8	4	0	51	37	1997	CQF	W 4-1
St. Louis	2	0	2	11	3	8	0	20	34	1969	QF	L 0-4
Tampa Bay	1	1	0	6	4	2	0	26	13	1996	CQF	W 4-2
Toronto	3	3	0	17	12	5	0	67	47	1977	QF	W 4-2
Vancouver	1	1	0	3	2	1	0	15	9	1979	PR	W 2-1
Washington	3	1	2	16	7	9	0	55	65	1989	DSF	W 4-2
Totals	**52**	**31**	**21**	**269**	**144**	**125**	**0**	**869**	**814**			

Calgary totals include Atlanta, 1972-73 to 1979-80. Colorado totals include Quebec, 1979-80 to 1994-95. Dallas totals include Minnesota, 1967-68 to 1992-93. New Jersey totals include Kansas City, 1974-75 to 1975-76, and Colorado Rockies, 1976-77 to 1981-82. Phoenix totals include Winnipeg, 1979-80 to 1995-96.

Playoff Results 1997-93

Year	Round	Opponent	Result	GF	GA
1997	F	Detroit	L 0-4	6	16
	CF	NY Rangers	W 4-1	20	13
	CSF	Buffalo	W 4-1	21	13
	CQF	Pittsburgh	W 4-1	20	13
1996	CSF	Florida	L 2-4	11	15
	CQF	Tampa Bay	W 4-2	26	13
1995	CF	New Jersey	L 2-4	14	20
	CSF	NY Rangers	W 4-0	18	10
	CQF	Buffalo	W 4-1	18	13

Abbreviations: Round: F – Final; **CF** – conference final; **CQF** – conference quarter-final; **CSF** – conference semi-final; **DF** – division final; **DSF** – division semi-final; **SF** – semi-final; **QF** – quarter-final; **PR** – preliminary round.

1996-97 Results

Oct.	5		Florida	1-3		7		Boston	7-3
	7		New Jersey	3-1		9		Tampa Bay	1-3
	10		Los Angeles	5-4		11		Washington	3-3
	12	at	NY Islanders	1-5		14		Montreal	3-2
	13		Calgary	0-1		21		Dallas	3-3
	15	at	Los Angeles	2-3		22	at	Detroit	2-2
	16	at	Anaheim	4-3		25		Detroit	1-4
	18	at	Phoenix	3-1		28		Phoenix	4-1
	22		Anaheim	3-0		29	at	Washington	2-1
	26	at	Montreal	5-6	**Feb.**	1		NY Rangers	2-4
	27		Florida	2-3		4		Buffalo	1-1
	30	at	Washington	2-4		6		Montreal	9-5
	31	at	Tampa Bay	4-3		8	at	New Jersey	2-4
Nov.	2	at	Florida	3-2		13		Ottawa	4-2
	4		NY Islanders	3-4		15		Pittsburgh	5-1
	7	at	Buffalo	5-2		16	at	Pittsburgh	6-2
	9		Chicago	1-4		19		Hartford	2-2
	10		Toronto	3-1		20	at	Tampa Bay	2-5
	13	at	NY Rangers	2-1		22	at	Florida	4-3
	14		Washington	2-5		23		NY Rangers	2-1
	16		San Jose	2-2		26	at	Ottawa	8-5
	21		Pittsburgh	7-3	**Mar.**	1	at	Boston	5-5
	23	at	Tampa Bay	2-1		2	at	Hartford	5-2
	26	at	Boston	0-2		5		New Jersey	1-3
	27	at	NY Islanders	1-4		8	at	Pittsburgh	2-3
	30	at	Ottawa	4-3		9		Washington	5-0
Dec.	1		Vancouver	4-3		11	at	Buffalo	2-3
	4	at	NY Rangers	1-1		13		Edmonton	5-4
	6	at	Dallas	6-3		15		Buffalo	5-7
	10		Florida	5-4		19	at	Toronto	6-3
	12		Hartford	3-2		22	at	NY Islanders	3-3
	14	at	Hartford	4-0		23		Colorado	2-0
	15		Boston	6-0		25	at	New Jersey	4-3
	19		NY Islanders	5-0		29	at	Washington	5-3
	21		St. Louis	4-0		30	at	St. Louis	2-3
	22	at	Chicago	2-2	**Apr.**	1		Tampa Bay	1-1
	27	at	Edmonton	6-4		6		Ottawa	2-1
	29	at	Calgary	4-2		7	at	NY Rangers	2-3
	31	at	Vancouver	5-3		10		NY Rangers	3-6
Jan.	2	at	San Jose	4-1		12	at	Montreal	3-3
	4	at	Colorado	4-4		13		New Jersey	5-4

Entry Draft
Selections 1997-83

1997 Pick		1992 Pick		1988 Pick		1985 Pick	
30	Jean-Marc Pelletier	7	Ryan Sittler	14	Claude Boivin	21	Glen Seabrooke
50	Pat Kavanagh	15	Jason Bowen	35	Pat Murray	42	Bruce Rendall
62	Kris Mallette	31	Denis Metlyuk	56	Craig Fisher	48	Darryl Gilmour
103	Mihail Chernov	103	Vladislav Buljin	63	Dominic Roussel	63	Shane Whelan
158	Jordon Flodell	127	Roman Zolotov	77	Scott Lagrand	84	Paul Marshall
164	Todd Fedoruk	151	Kirk Daubenspeck	98	Edward O'Brien	105	Daril Holmes
214	Marko Kauppinen	175	Claude Jutras Jr.	119	Gordie Frantti	126	Ken Alexander
240	Par Styf	199	Jonas Hakansson	140	Jamie Cooke	147	Tony Horacek
		223	Chris Herperger	161	Johan Salle	168	Mike Cusack
1996 Pick		247	Patrice Paquin	182	Brian Arthur	189	Gordon Murphy
15	Dainius Zubrus			203	Jeff Dandreta	231	Rod Williams
64	Chester Gallant	**1991 Pick**		224	Scott Billey	252	Paul Maurice
124	Per-Ragna Bergqvist	6	Peter Forsberg	245	Drahomir Kadlec		
133	Jesse Boulerice	50	Yanick Dupre			**1984 Pick**	
187	Roman Malov	86	Aris Brimanis	**1987 Pick**		22	Greg Smyth
213	Jeff Milleker	94	Yanick Degrace	20	Darren Rumble	27	Scott Mellanby
		116	Clayton Norris	30	Jeff Harding	37	Jeff Chychrun
1995 Pick		122	Dmitri Yushkevich	62	Martin Hostak	43	Dave McLay
22	Brian Boucher	138	Andrei Lomakin	83	Tomaz Eriksson	47	John Stevens
48	Shane Kenny	182	James Bode	104	Bill Gall	79	Dave Hanson
100	Radovan Somik	204	Josh Bartell	125	Tony Link	100	Brian Dobbin
132	Dimitri Tertyshny	226	Neil Little	146	Mark Strapon	121	John Dzikowski
135	Jamie Sokolsky	248	John Porco	167	Darryl Ingham	142	Tom Allen
152	Martin Spanhel			188	Bruce McDonald	163	Luke Vitale
178	Martin Streit	**1990 Pick**		209	Steve Morrow	184	Bill Powers
204	Ruslan Shafikov	4	Mike Ricci	230	Darius Rusnak	204	Daryn Fersovitch
230	Jeff Lank	25	Chris Simon	251	Dale Roehl	245	Juraj Bakos
		40	Mikael Renberg				
1994 Pick		42	Terran Sandwith	**1986 Pick**		**1983 Pick**	
62	Artem Anisimov	44	Kimbi Daniels	20	Kerry Huffman	41	Peter Zezel
88	Adam Magarrell	46	Bill Armstrong	23	Jukka Seppo	44	Derrick Smith
101	Sebastien Vallee	47	Chris Therien	28	Kent Hawley	81	Alan Bourbeau
140	Alexander Selivanov	52	Al Kinisky	83	Mark Bar	101	Jerome Carrier
166	Colin Forbes	88	Dan Kordic	125	Steve Scheifele	121	Rick Tocchet
192	Derek Diener	109	Viacheslav Butsayev	146	Sami Wahlsten	141	Bobby Mormina
202	Raymond Giroux	151	Patrik Englund	167	Murray Baron	161	Per-Erik Eklund
218	Johan Hedberg	172	Toni Porkka	188	Blaine Rude	181	Rob Nichols
244	Andre Payette	193	Greg Hanson	209	Shawn Sabol	201	William McCormick
270	Jan Lipiansky	214	Tommy Soderstrom	230	Brett Lawrence	221	Brian Jopling
		235	William Lund	251	Daniel Stephano	241	Harold Duvall
1993 Pick		**1989 Pick**					
36	Janne Niinimaa	33	Greg Johnson				
71	Vaclav Prospal	34	Patrik Juhlin				
77	Milos Holan	72	Reid Simpson				
114	Vladimir Krechin	117	Niklas Eriksson				
140	Mike Crowley	138	John Callahan Jr.				
166	Aaron Israel	159	Sverre Sears				
192	Paul Healey	180	Glen Wisser				
218	Tripp Tracy	201	Al Kummu				
226	E.J. Bradley	222	Matt Brait				
244	Jeffrey Staples	243	James Pollio				
270	Kenneth Hemmenway						

Coaching History

Keith Allen, 1967-68 to 1968-69; Vic Stasiuk, 1969-70 to 1970-71; Fred Shero, 1971-72 to 1977-78; Bob McCammon and Pat Quinn, 1978-79; Pat Quinn, 1979-80 to 1980-81; Pat Quinn and Bob McCammon, 1981-82; Bob McCammon, 1982-83 to 1983-84; Mike Keenan, 1984-85 to 1987-88; Paul Holmgren, 1988-89 to 1990-91; Paul Holmgren and Bill Dineen, 1991-92; Bill Dineen, 1992-93; Terry Simpson, 1993-94; Terry Murray, 1994-95 to 1996-97; Wayne Cashman, 1997-98.

Coach

CASHMAN, WAYNE
Coach, Philadelphia Flyers. Born in Kingston, Ont., June 24, 1945.
Wayne Cashman was named as the 11th head coach of the Philadelphia Flyers on July 7, 1997. Cashman served as an assistant coach for Team Canada in the 1997 World Hockey Championship after working in a similar role with the San Jose Sharks during the 1996-97 season. Prior to joining San Jose, Cashman spent four seasons (1992-93 through 1995-96) working as an assistant coach with the Tampa Bay Lightning. Cashman also served as an assistant coach for the New York Rangers for five seasons (1987-88 through 1991-92). He joined the Rangers organization in August 1986 as a New England scout.

Cashman played 17 seasons in the National Hockey League (1964-65 through 1982-83), all with the Boston Bruins, recording 277 goals and 516 assists for 793 points and 1,041 penalty minutes in 1,027 games. He was a member of the Bruins' 1970 and 1972 Stanley Cup Championship teams and served as captain of the Bruins from the 1977-78 season until his retirement following the 1982-83 season. He was named to the NHL's Second All-Star Team after recording career single-season highs in goals (30), assists (59) and points (89) during the 1973-74 season.

Club Directory

CoreStates Center
1 CoreStates Complex
Philadelphia, PA 19148
Phone **215/465-4500**
PR FAX 215/389-9403
Capacity: 19,511

Executive Management
Chairman	Ed Snider
Limited Partners	Pat Croce, Jay Snider, Sylvan and Fran Tobin
President and General Manager	Bob Clarke
Chairman of the Board, Emeritus	Joe Scott
Chief Operating Officer	Ron Ryan
Executive Vice-President	Keith Allen
Governor	Ed Snider
Alternate Governors	Bob Clarke, Ron Ryan, Phil Weinberg
Executive Assistant	Kathy Nasevich
Receptionist	Suzanne Nast

Hockey Club Personnel
Head Coach	Wayne Cashman
Assistant General Manager	John Blackwell
Associate Coach	Keith Acton
Assistant Coach	Dave Brown
Goaltending Coach	Rejean Lemelin
Director of Player Personnel	Paul Holmgren
Pro Scout	Terry Murray
Chief Scout	Dennis Patterson
Scouting Staff	John Chapman, Inge Hammarstrom, Simon Nolet, Blair Reid, Vaclav Slansky, Evgeny Zimin
Director of Team Services	Barry Hanrahan
Computer Analyst	David Gelberg
Executive Assistant	Dianna Taylor

Medical/Training Staff
Team Physicians	Arthur Bartolozzi, M.D.; Jeff Hartzell, M.D.; Gary Dorshimer, M.D.; Mike Weinik, M.D.; Guy Lanzi, D.M.D.
Athletic Trainer	John Worley
Head Equipment Manager	Jim Evers
Equipment Managers	Rusty Pearl, Anthony Oratorio

Public Relations Department
Director of Media Relations	Joe Klueg
Director of Public Relations	Zack Hill
Director of Community Relations	Linda Panasci
Director of Fan Development	Greg Scott
Director of Fan Services	Joe Kadlec
Assistant Director of Media Relations/ Publications Manager	Linda Held
Assistant Director of Public Relations	Jody Clarke
Public Relations Assistant	Jill Lipson
Youth Hockey Program Coordinator	Melissa Wilson

Sales/Marketing Department
Vice President, Marketing	Bob Schwartz
Vice President, Sales	Jack Betson
Ticket Manager	Ceil Baker
Assistant Director of Season Tickets	Mike Dunphy
Sales/Marketing Assistant	Christina Ruskey
Assistant Ticket Manager	Michelle Hay
Ticket Office Assistants	Pat Piazza, Linda DiTommaso, Lisa Albertson

Finance Department
Vice President, Finance	Dan Clemmens
Director of Finance	Dave Jablonski
Controller	Lisa Cataldo
Payroll Accountant	Susann Schaffer
Accounts Payable Accountant	Renee Drayton

Advertising/Sales Department
Senior Account Executives	Jeff Kirk, Ivan Shlichtman, Joe Watson
Account Executives	Steve Coates, Lisa Fusco, Ron Skotarczak
Sponsorship Coordinator	Alyson Rochvarg
Administrative Assistants	Jennifer Gargiulo, Colleen Molloy

Broadcast Department
TV Play-by-Play, Color Commentary	Jim Jackson, Gary Dornhoefer
Radio Play-by-Play, Color Commentary	Tim Saunders, Steve Coates
Director of Broadcasting	Bryan Cooper
Broadcast Advisor	Gene Hart
Public Address Announcer	Lou Nolan

Flyers Wives Charities
Executive Director	Fran Tobin
Director of Marketing	Rita Johanson
Event Coordinators	Laurie Podall, Diane Smith

Captains' History

Lou Angotti, 1967-68; Ed Van Impe, 1968-69 to 1971-72; Ed Van Impe and Bobby Clarke, 1972-73; Bobby Clarke, 1973-74 to 1978-79; Mel Bridgman, 1979-80, 1980-81; Bill Barber, 1981-82; Bill Barber and Bobby Clarke, 1982-83; Bobby Clarke, 1983-84; Dave Poulin, 1984-85 to 1988-89; Dave Poulin and Ron Sutter, 1989-90; Ron Sutter, 1990-91; Rick Tocchet, 1991-92; no captain, 1992-93; Kevin Dineen, 1993-94; Eric Lindros, 1994-95 to date.

Phoenix Coyotes
1996-97 Results: 38w-37L-7T 83PTS. Third, Central Division

Right: Keith Tkachuk, who used a quick, accurate shot to record a League-leading 52 goals in 1996-97, is the first American-born player to lead the NHL in goals. Below: Jeremy Roenick made his first season in Phoenix a productive one, collecting 29 goals and 40 assists.

1997-98 Schedule

Oct.	Wed.	1	Chicago		Sat.	3	NY Islanders
	Fri.	3	at St. Louis		Tue.	6	at Detroit
	Sun.	5	at Philadelphia		Thu.	8	at Boston
	Wed.	8	Boston		Fri.	9	at Chicago
	Sat.	11	at Colorado		Sun.	11	Ottawa
	Mon.	13	Chicago		Wed.	14	Florida
	Sun.	19	San Jose		Tue.	20	at Edmonton
	Tue.	21	Anaheim		Wed.	21	at Vancouver
	Thu.	23	Washington		Sat.	24	Edmonton
	Sun.	26	Buffalo		Mon.	26	Vancouver
	Wed.	29	at Edmonton		Wed.	28	at Detroit
	Thu.	30	at Calgary		Fri.	30	at Buffalo
Nov.	Sun.	2	Calgary		Sat.	31	at Toronto
	Wed.	5	at Montreal	Feb.	Tue.	3	Chicago
	Thu.	6	at Ottawa		Thu.	5	Philadelphia
	Sat.	8	at Toronto		Sat.	7	NY Rangers
	Tue.	11	Tampa Bay		Wed.	25	Colorado
	Thu.	13	Montreal		Thu.	26	at Colorado
	Sat.	15	at San Jose		Sat.	28	at Dallas*
	Mon.	17	Edmonton	Mar.	Mon.	2	Detroit
	Thu.	20	at Vancouver		Fri.	6	Carolina
	Sat.	22	Toronto		Sun.	8	at Dallas
	Tue.	25	St. Louis		Tue.	10	Los Angeles
	Thu.	27	Dallas		Thu.	12	Dallas
	Sat.	29	at Dallas		Sat.	14	at St. Louis*
Dec.	Mon.	1	at Florida		Mon.	16	at Washington
	Wed.	3	at Tampa Bay		Thu.	19	Colorado
	Fri.	5	at Carolina		Sat.	21	at Los Angeles*
	Sat.	6	at NY Islanders		Sun.	22	San Jose
	Mon.	8	at NY Rangers		Tue.	24	Toronto
	Wed.	10	at Chicago		Sat.	28	New Jersey
	Fri.	12	Pittsburgh	Apr.	Wed.	1	at Anaheim
	Sun.	14	Detroit		Fri.	3	Anaheim
	Wed.	17	Vancouver		Sun.	5	at New Jersey
	Fri.	19	at Anaheim		Tue.	7	at Pittsburgh
	Sat.	20	Toronto		Thu.	9	at Detroit
	Tue.	23	Calgary		Sat.	11	at St. Louis*
	Fri.	26	at San Jose		Sun.	12	at Chicago
	Sat.	27	at Los Angeles		Tue.	14	Detroit
	Mon.	29	at Calgary		Thu.	16	Dallas
Jan.	Thu.	1	Los Angeles		Sat.	18	St. Louis*

* Denotes afternoon game.

Franchise date: June 22, 1979
Transferred from Winnipeg to Phoenix, July 1, 1996

CENTRAL DIVISION

19th NHL Season

Year-by-Year Record

Season	GP	Home W	L	T	Road W	L	T	Overall W	L	T	GF	GA	Pts.	Finished		Playoff Result
1996-97	82	15	19	7	23	18	0	38	37	7	240	243	83	3rd,	Central Div.	Lost Conf. Quarter-Final
1995-96*	82	22	16	3	14	24	3	36	40	6	275	291	78	5th,	Central Div.	Lost Conf. Quarter-Final
1994-95*	48	10	10	4	6	15	3	16	25	7	157	177	39	6th,	Central Div.	Out of Playoffs
1993-94*	84	15	23	4	9	28	5	24	51	9	245	344	57	6th,	Central Div.	Out of Playoffs
1992-93*	84	23	16	3	17	21	4	40	37	7	322	320	87	4th,	Smythe Div.	Lost Div. Semi-Final
1991-92*	80	20	14	6	13	18	9	33	32	15	251	244	81	4th,	Smythe Div.	Lost Div. Semi-Final
1990-91*	80	17	18	5	9	25	6	26	43	11	260	288	63	5th,	Smythe Div.	Out of Playoffs
1989-90*	80	22	13	5	15	19	6	37	32	11	298	290	85	3rd,	Smythe Div.	Lost Div. Semi-Final
1988-89*	80	17	18	5	9	24	7	26	42	12	300	355	64	5th,	Smythe Div.	Out of Playoffs
1987-88*	80	20	14	6	13	22	5	33	36	11	292	310	77	3rd,	Smythe Div.	Lost Div. Final
1986-87*	80	25	12	3	15	20	5	40	32	8	279	271	88	3rd,	Smythe Div.	Lost Div. Final
1985-86*	80	18	19	3	8	28	4	26	47	7	295	372	59	3rd,	Smythe Div.	Lost Div. Semi-Final
1984-85*	80	21	13	6	22	14	4	43	27	10	358	332	96	2nd,	Smythe Div.	Lost Div. Final
1983-84*	80	17	15	8	14	23	3	31	38	11	340	374	73	4th,	Smythe Div.	Lost Div. Semi-Final
1982-83*	80	22	16	2	11	23	6	33	39	8	311	333	74	4th,	Smythe Div.	Lost Div. Semi-Final
1981-82*	80	18	13	9	15	20	5	33	33	14	319	332	80	2nd,	Norris Div.	Lost Div. Semi-Final
1980-81*	80	7	25	8	2	32	6	9	57	14	246	400	32	6th,	Smythe Div.	Out of Playoffs
1979-80*	80	13	19	8	7	30	3	20	49	11	214	314	51	5th,	Smythe Div.	Out of Playoffs

* Winnipeg Jets

1997-98 Player Personnel

FORWARDS	HT	WT	S	Place of Birth	Date	1996-97 Club
BRIERE, Daniel	5-9	160	L	Gatineau, Que.	10/6/77	Drummondville
CHRISTIAN, Jeff	6-2	210	L	Burlington, Ont.	7/30/70	Pittsburgh-Cleveland
CORKUM, Bob	6-2	210	R	Salisbury, MA	12/18/67	Phoenix
DOAN, Shane	6-1	215	R	Halkirk, Alta.	10/10/76	Phoenix
DRAKE, Dallas	6-0	180	L	Trail, B.C.	2/4/69	Phoenix
GARTNER, Mike	6-0	187	R	Ottawa, Ont.	10/29/59	Phoenix
GORDON, Rhett	5-11	175	R	Regina, Sask.	8/26/76	Springfield
HANSEN, Tavis	6-1	180	R	Prince Albert, Sask.	6/17/75	Phoenix-Springfield
ISBISTER, Brad	6-2	198	R	Edmonton, Alta.	5/7/77	Portland (WHL)-Springfield
JANNEY, Craig	6-1	190	L	Hartford, CT	9/26/67	Phoenix
KILGER, Chad	6-3	204	L	Cornwall, Ont.	11/27/76	Phoenix-Springfield
KIMBLE, Darin	6-2	210	R	Lucky Lake, Sask.	11/22/68	Manitoba-Kansas City
LEMIEUX, Jocelyn	5-10	200	L	Mont-Laurier, Que.	11/18/67	Long Beach-Phoenix
LETOWSKI, Trevor	5-10	170	R	Thunder Bay, Ont.	4/5/77	Sarnia
LEVINS, Scott	6-4	210	R	Spokane, WA	1/30/70	Springfield
McKENZIE, Jim	6-3	205	L	Gull Lake, Sask.	11/3/69	Phoenix
MURRAY, Rob	6-1	180	R	Toronto, Ont.	4/4/67	Springfield
ROENICK, Jeremy	6-0	170	R	Boston, MA	1/17/70	Phoenix
RONNING, Cliff	5-8	170	L	Burnaby, B.C.	10/1/65	Phoenix
SHANNON, Darrin	6-2	210	L	Barrie, Ont.	12/8/69	Phoenix
STAPLETON, Mike	5-10	183	R	Sarnia, Ont.	5/5/66	Phoenix
TKACHUK, Keith	6-2	210	L	Melrose, MA	3/28/72	Phoenix
TOCCHET, Rick	6-0	205	R	Scarborough, Ont.	4/9/64	Boston-Washington
YLONEN, Juha	6-0	180	L	Helsinki, Finland	2/13/72	Phoenix-Springfield
DEFENSEMEN						
BARON, Murray	6-3	215	L	Prince George, B.C.	6/1/67	St. Louis-Montreal-Phoenix
CROWLEY, Ted	6-2	188	R	Concord, MA	5/3/70	Cincinnati-Phoenix (IHL)
DIDUCK, Gerald	6-2	217	R	Edmonton, Alta.	4/6/65	Hartford-Phoenix
DOIG, Jason	6-3	216	R	Montreal, Que.	1/29/77	Granby-Springfield-Las Vegas
GAGNON, Sean	6-2	210	L	Sault Ste. Marie, Ont.	9/11/73	Fort Wayne
JOHNSON, Jim	6-1	190	L	New Hope, MN	8/9/62	Phoenix
MACIVER, Norm	5-11	180	L	Thunder Bay, Ont.	9/8/64	Phoenix
MORE, Jayson	6-2	210	R	Souris, Man.	1/12/69	NY Rangers-Phoenix
NUMMINEN, Teppo	6-1	190	R	Tampere, Finland	7/3/68	Phoenix
QUINT, Deron	6-1	182	L	Durham, NH	3/12/76	Phoenix-Springfield
SLANEY, John	6-0	185	L	St. John's, Nfld.	2/7/72	Los Angeles-Phoenix (IHL)
TVERDOVSKY, Oleg	6-0	185	L	Donetsk, USSR	5/18/76	Phoenix
GOALTENDERS	**HT**	**WT**	**C**	**Place of Birth**	**Date**	**1996-97 Club**
KHABIBULIN, Nikolai	6-1	176	L	Sverdlovsk, USSR	1/13/73	Phoenix
LANGKOW, Scott	5-11	190	L	Sherwood Park, Alta.	4/21/75	Springfield
WAKALUK, Darcy	5-11	180	L	Pincher Creek, Alta.	3/14/66	Phoenix

Coach

SCHOENFELD, JAMES GRANT (JIM)
Coach, Phoenix Coyotes. Born in Galt, Ont., September 4, 1952.

The eight-year veteran NHL coach joins the Coyotes after four successful seasons with the Washington Capitals, where he ranked third in team history in games coached (249) and victories (113). In 249 games, Schoenfeld guided the Caps to a 113-102-34 record and a .522 winning percentage. His best season as a head coach came during the 1995-96 season, when Schoenfeld led Washington to a 39-32-11 record with 89 points and a .543 winning percentage. Schoenfeld has a career coaching record of 182-180-54 and a .502 winning percentage.

The 45-year-old native of Galt, Ontario began his coaching career as head coach of the Rochester Americans in the American Hockey League, a position he held for one season before rejoining the Buffalo Sabres as a player. Schoenfeld resumed his career behind the bench during the 1985-86 season, when he compiled a 19-19-5 record with the Sabres until g.m. Scotty Bowman opted to return as head coach. In 1988, Schoenfeld joined the New Jersey Devils, and in his first season led the Devils to within one game of the Stanley Cup Finals. The Devils lost to the Boston Bruins in the Wales Conference Finals.

Schoenfeld's playing career spanned 13 years and three teams (Buffalo, Detroit and Boston). The majority of his career was spent with Buffalo, where Schoenfeld was considered one of the most popular defensemen in Sabres team history. He was best known for his durability and outstanding defensive play.

Schoenfeld was drafted by Buffalo in the first round (fifth overall) in the 1972 NHL Entry Draft. Two years later, he was named the Sabres captain, becoming the youngest team captain in League history at that time. In 1974-75, Schoenfeld played in 20 NHL playoff games, leading the Sabres to the club's first ever berth in the Stanley Cup Finals against Philadelphia. He was named to the NHL's Second All-Star Team in 1979-80 and finished third in Norris Trophy voting that season after setting a current single-season Sabres club record for plus-minus rating with a plus-60. Schoenfeld was also voted the NHL's top rookie defenseman for the 1972 season, and played in the 1977 and 1980 NHL All-Star games, before ending his career in 1985.

Schoenfeld played in 719 career NHL games, scoring 51 goals and adding 204 assists for 255 points. In addition, he racked up 1,132 penalty minutes. His most productive playing season came during the 1979-80 campaign, when he reached career highs in games played (77), goals (9), assists (27) and points (36). Schoenfeld also appeared in 75 NHL playoff games, all with Buffalo, scoring 3 goals and adding 13 assists for 16 points and 151 PIM.

Jim and his wife Theresa have four children; Justin, Katie, Adam and Nathan.

Coaching Record

		Regular Season					Playoffs			
Season	Team	Games	W	L	T	%	Games	W	L	%
1984-85	Rochester (AHL)	25	17	6	2	.720	....	....	....	....
1985-86	**Buffalo (NHL)**	**43**	**19**	**19**	**5**	**.500**	....	....	....	....
1987-88	**New Jersey (NHL)**	**30**	**17**	**12**	**1**	**.583**	**20**	**11**	**9**	**.550**
1988-89	**New Jersey (NHL)**	**80**	**27**	**41**	**12**	**.413**	....	....	....	....
1989-90	**New Jersey (NHL)**	**14**	**6**	**6**	**2**	**.500**	....	....	....	....
1993-94	**Washington (NHL)**	**37**	**19**	**12**	**6**	**.595**	**11**	**5**	**6**	**.455**
1994-95	**Washington (NHL)**	**48**	**22**	**18**	**8**	**.542**	**7**	**3**	**4**	**.429**
1995-96	**Washington (NHL)**	**82**	**39**	**32**	**11**	**.543**	**6**	**2**	**4**	**.333**
1996-97	**Washington (NHL)**	**82**	**33**	**40**	**9**	**.457**	....	....	....	....
	NHL Totals	**416**	**182**	**180**	**54**	**.502**	**44**	**21**	**23**	**.477**

1996-97 Scoring

* – rookie

Regular Season

Pos	#	Player	Team	GP	G	A	Pts	+/–	PIM	PP	SH	GW	GT	S	%
L	7	Keith Tkachuk	PHO	81	52	34	86	-1	228	9	2	7	1	296	17.6
C	97	Jeremy Roenick	PHO	72	29	40	69	-7	115	10	3	7	0	228	12.7
R	22	Mike Gartner	PHO	82	32	31	63	-11	38	13	1	7	1	271	11.8
D	20	Oleg Tverdovsky	PHO	82	10	45	55	-5	30	3	1	2	0	144	6.9
C	15	Craig Janney	PHO	77	15	38	53	-1	26	5	0	1	0	88	17.0
C	77	Cliff Ronning	PHO	69	19	32	51	-9	26	8	0	2	0	171	11.1
R	11	Dallas Drake	PHO	63	17	19	36	-11	52	5	1	1	0	113	15.0
D	27	Teppo Numminen	PHO	82	2	25	27	-3	28	0	0	0	0	135	1.5
L	34	Darrin Shannon	PHO	82	11	13	24	4	41	1	0	2	0	104	10.6
C	21	Bob Corkum	PHO	80	9	11	20	-7	40	0	1	3	0	119	7.6
C	14	Mike Stapleton	PHO	55	4	11	15	-4	36	2	0	1	0	74	5.4
D	5	Deron Quint	PHO	27	3	11	14	-4	4	1	0	0	0	63	4.8
L	17	Kris King	PHO	81	3	11	14	-7	185	0	0	0	0	57	5.3
D	4	Gerald Diduck	HFD	56	1	10	11	-9	40	0	0	1	0	59	1.7
			PHO	11	1	2	3	2	23	1	0	0	0	21	4.8
			TOTAL	67	2	12	14	-7	63	1	0	1	0	80	2.5
D	44	Norm Maciver	PHO	32	4	9	13	-11	24	1	0	1	0	40	10.0
R	19	Shane Doan	PHO	63	4	8	12	-3	49	0	0	0	0	100	4.0
R	23	Igor Korolev	PHO	41	3	7	10	-5	28	2	0	0	0	41	7.3
D	8	Jim Johnson	PHO	55	3	7	10	5	74	0	0	0	0	51	5.9
D	26	Jeff Finley	PHO	65	3	7	10	-8	40	1	0	1	0	38	7.9
L	33	Jim McKenzie	PHO	65	5	3	8	-5	200	0	0	1	0	38	13.2
D	6	Jay More	NYR	14	0	1	1	0	25	0	0	0	0	10	0.0
			PHO	23	1	6	7	10	37	0	0	1	0	18	5.6
			TOTAL	37	1	7	8	10	62	0	0	1	0	28	3.6
D	36	Murray Baron	STL	11	0	2	2	-4	11	0	0	0	0	7	0.0
			MTL	60	1	5	6	-16	107	0	0	0	0	52	1.9
			PHO	8	0	0	0	0	4	0	0	0	0	5	0.0
			TOTAL	79	1	7	8	-20	122	0	0	0	0	64	1.6
C	18	Chad Kilger	PHO	24	4	3	7	-5	13	1	0	0	0	30	13.3
D	10	Brad McCrimmon	PHO	37	1	5	6	2	18	0	0	0	0	28	3.6
G	35	N. Khabibulin	PHO	72	0	3	3	0	16	0	0	0	0	0	0.0
R	32	Jocelyn Lemieux	PHO	2	1	0	1	0	0	0	0	1	0	4	25.0
G	43	Darcy Wakaluk	PHO	16	0	1	1	0	4	0	0	0	0	0	0.0
G	1	Parris Duffus	PHO	1	0	0	0	0	0	0	0	0	0	0	0.0
L	38	Jason Simon	PHO	1	0	0	0	-1	0	0	0	0	0	0	0.0
D	3	Brent Thompson	PHO	1	0	0	0	-1	7	0	0	0	0	0	0.0
C	47	* Tavis Hansen	PHO	1	0	0	0	0	0	0	0	0	0	0	0.0
D	24	Kevin Dahl	PHO	2	0	0	0	0	0	0	0	0	0	2	0.0
C	36	* Juha Ylonen	PHO	2	0	0	0	0	0	0	0	0	0	2	0.0
C	28	Mike Hudson	PHO	7	0	0	0	-4	2	0	0	0	0	9	0.0
G	39	Pat Jablonski	MTL	17	0	0	0	0	0	0	0	0	0	0	0.0
			PHO	2	0	0	0	0	0	0	0	0	0	0	0.0
			TOTAL	19	0	0	0	0	0	0	0	0	0	0	0.0

Goaltending

No.	Goaltender	GPI	Mins	Avg	W	L	T	EN	SO	GA	SA	S%
39	Pat Jablonski	2	59	2.03	0	1	0	1	0	2	24	.917
1	Parris Duffus	1	29	2.07	0	0	0	0	0	1	8	.875
35	N. Khabibulin	72	4091	2.83	30	33	6	7	7	193	2094	.908
43	Darcy Wakaluk	16	782	2.99	8	3	1	0	1	39	386	.899
	Totals	**82**	**4974**	**2.93**	**38**	**37**	**7**	**8**	**8**	**243**	**2520**	**.904**

Playoffs

Pos	#	Player	Team	GP	G	A	Pts	+/–	PIM	PP	SH	GW	OT	S	%
C	77	Cliff Ronning	PHO	7	0	7	7	2	12	0	0	0	0	11	0.0
L	7	Keith Tkachuk	PHO	7	6	0	6	2	7	2	0	0	0	37	16.2
D	27	Teppo Numminen	PHO	7	3	3	6	3	0	1	0	1	0	19	15.8
C	97	Jeremy Roenick	PHO	6	2	4	6	6	4	0	0	0	0	16	12.5
L	34	Darrin Shannon	PHO	7	3	1	4	2	4	0	0	1	0	5	60.0
C	21	Bob Corkum	PHO	7	2	2	4	-1	4	0	0	1	0	9	22.2
R	22	Mike Gartner	PHO	7	1	2	3	-1	4	0	0	0	0	17	5.9
C	15	Craig Janney	PHO	7	0	3	3	1	4	0	0	0	0	6	0.0
D	5	Deron Quint	PHO	7	0	2	2	2	0	0	0	0	0	13	0.0
R	11	Dallas Drake	PHO	7	0	1	1	-2	2	0	0	0	0	12	0.0
D	20	Oleg Tverdovsky	PHO	7	0	1	1	0	0	0	0	0	0	10	0.0
D	36	Murray Baron	PHO	1	0	0	0	0	0	0	0	0	0	0	0.0
D	26	Jeff Finley	PHO	1	0	0	0	-1	2	0	0	0	0	1	0.0
R	23	Igor Korolev	PHO	1	0	0	0	0	0	0	0	0	0	1	0.0
R	32	Jocelyn Lemieux	PHO	2	0	0	0	0	4	0	0	0	0	2	0.0
R	19	Shane Doan	PHO	4	0	0	0	-1	2	0	0	0	0	2	0.0
D	8	Jim Johnson	PHO	6	0	0	0	0	4	0	0	0	0	7	0.0
D	4	Gerald Diduck	PHO	7	0	0	0	2	10	0	0	0	0	8	0.0
L	17	Kris King	PHO	7	0	0	0	-1	17	0	0	0	0	2	0.0
L	33	Jim McKenzie	PHO	7	0	0	0	0	2	0	0	0	0	7	0.0
D	6	Jay More	PHO	7	0	0	0	1	7	0	0	0	0	6	0.0
C	14	Mike Stapleton	PHO	7	0	0	0	-1	14	0	0	0	0	5	0.0
G	35	N. Khabibulin	PHO	7	0	0	0	0	6	0	0	0	0	0	0.0

Goaltending

No.	Goaltender	GPI	Mins	Avg	W	L	EN	SO	GA	SA	S%
35	N. Khabibulin	7	426	2.11	3	4	2	1	15	222	.932
	Totals	**7**	**427**	**2.39**	**3**	**4**	**2**	**1**	**17**	**224**	**.924**

Coaching History

Tom McVie and Bill Sutherland, 1979-80; Tom McVie, Bill Sutherland and Mike Smith, 1980-81; Tom Watt, 1981-82 to 1982-83; Tom Watt and Barry Long, 1983-84; Barry Long, 1984-85; Barry Long and John Ferguson, 1985-86; Dan Maloney, 1986-87 to 1987-88; Dan Maloney and Rick Bowness, 1988-89; Bob Murdoch, 1989-90, 1990-91; John Paddock, 1991-92 to 1993-94; John Paddock and Terry Simpson, 1994-95; Terry Simpson, 1995-96; Don Hay, 1996-97; Jim Schoenfeld, 1997-98.

Club Records

Team

(Figures in brackets for season records are games played; records for fewest points, wins, ties, losses, goals, goals against are for 70 or more games)

Most Points	96	1984-85 (80)
Most Wins	43	1984-85 (80)
Most Ties	15	1991-92 (80)
Most Losses	57	1980-81 (80)
Most Goals	358	1984-85 (80)
Most Goals Against	400	1980-81 (80)
Fewest Points	32	1980-81 (80)
Fewest Wins	9	1980-81 (80)
Fewest Ties	7	1985-86 (80),
		1992-93 (84),
		1996-97 (82)
Fewest Losses	27	1984-85 (80)
Fewest Goals	214	1979-80 (80)
Fewest Goals Against	243	1996-97 (82)

Longest Winning Streak

Overall	9	Mar. 8-27/85
Home	9	Dec. 27/92-Jan. 23/93
Away	8	Feb. 25-Apr. 6/85

Longest Undefeated Streak

Overall	13	Mar. 8-Apr. 7/85
		(10 wins, 3 ties)
Home	11	Dec. 23/83-Feb. 5/84
		(6 wins, 5 ties)
Away	9	Feb. 25-Apr. 7/85
		(8 wins, 1 tie)

Longest Losing Streak

Overall	10	Nov. 30-Dec. 20/80,
		Feb. 6-25/94
Home	5	Oct. 29-Nov. 13/93
Away	13	Jan. 26-Apr. 14/94

Longest Winless Streak

Overall	*30	Oct. 19-Dec. 20/80
		(23 losses, 7 ties)
Home	14	Oct. 19-Dec. 14/80
		(9 losses, 5 ties)
Away	18	Oct. 10-Dec. 20/80
		(16 losses, 2 ties)

Most Shutouts, Season	8	1996-97 (82)
Most PIM, Season	2,278	1987-88 (80)
Most Goals, Game	12	Feb. 25/85
		(Wpg. 12 at NYR 5)

Individual

Most Seasons	14	Thomas Steen
Most Games	950	Thomas Steen
Most Goals, Career	379	Dale Hawerchuk
Most Assists, Career	553	Thomas Steen
Most Points, Career	929	Dale Hawerchuk
		(379G, 550A)
Most PIM, Career	1,338	Laurie Boschman
Most Shutouts, Career	14	Bob Essensa

Longest Consecutive

Games Streak	475	Dale Hawerchuk
		(Dec. 19/82-Dec. 10/88)
Most Goals, Season	76	Teemu Selanne
		(1992-93)
Most Assists, Season	79	Phil Housley
		(1992-93)
Most Points, Season	132	Teemu Selanne
		(1992-93; 76G, 56A)
Most PIM, Season	347	Tie Domi
		(1993-94)

Most Points, Defenseman, Season	97	Phil Housley
		(1992-93; 18G, 79A)
Most Points, Center, Season	130	Dale Hawerchuk
		(1984-85; 53G, 77A)
Most Points, Right Wing, Season	132	Teemu Selanne
		(1992-93; 76G, 56A)
Most Points, Left Wing, Season	98	Keith Tkachuk
		(1995-96; 50G, 48A)
Most Points, Rookie, Season	*132	Teemu Selanne
		(1992-93; 76G, 56A)
Most Shutouts, Season	7	Nikolai Khabibulin
		(1996-97)
Most Goals, Game	5	Willy Lindstrom
		(Mar. 2/82),
		Alexei Zhamnov
		(Apr. 1/95)
Most Assists, Game	5	Dale Hawerchuk
		(Mar. 6/84, Mar. 18/89,
		Mar. 4/90),
		Phil Housley
		(Jan. 18/93)
Most Points, Game	6	Willy Lindstrom
		(Mar. 2/82; 5G, 1A),
		Dale Hawerchuk
		(Dec. 14/83; 3G, 3A,
		Mar. 5/88; 2G, 4A,
		Mar. 18/89; 1G, 5A),
		Thomas Steen
		(Oct. 24/84; 2G, 4A),
		Eddie Olczyk
		(Dec. 21/91; 2G, 4A)

* NHL Record.

Records include Winnipeg Jets, 1979-80 through 1995-96.

General Managers' History

John Ferguson, 1979-80 to 1987-88; John Ferguson and Mike Smith, 1988-89; Mike Smith, 1989-90 to 1992-93; Mike Smith and John Paddock, 1993-94; John Paddock, 1994-95 to 1995-96; John Paddock and Bobby Smith, 1996-97; Bobby Smith, 1997-98.

Captains' History

Lars-Erik Sjoberg, 1979-80; Morris Lukowich, 1980-81; Dave Christian, 1981-82; Dave Christian and Lucien DeBlois, 1982-83; Lucien DeBlois, 1983-84; Dale Hawerchuk, 1984-85 to 1988-89; Randy Carlyle, Dale Hawerchuk and Thomas Steen (tri-captains), 1989-90; Randy Carlyle and Thomas Steen (co-captains), 1990-91; Troy Murray, 1991-92; Troy Murray and Dean Kennedy, 1992-93; Dean Kennedy and Keith Tkachuk, 1993-94; Keith Tkachuk, 1994-95; Kris King, 1995-96; Keith Tkachuk, 1996-97 to date.

Winnipeg Jets Retired Numbers

9	Bobby Hull	1972-1980
25	Thomas Steen	1981-1995

All-time Record vs. Other Clubs

Regular Season

		At Home							On Road							Total					
	GP	W	L	T	GF	GA	PTS	GP	W	L	T	GF	GA	PTS	GP	W	L	T	GF	GA	PTS
Anaheim	8	4	4	0	31	29	8	8	1	7	0	14	30	2	16	5	11	0	45	59	10
Boston	25	10	13	2	91	95	22	24	4	17	3	79	112	11	49	14	30	5	170	207	33
Buffalo	24	10	12	2	77	86	22	24	2	20	2	58	112	6	48	12	32	4	135	198	28
Calgary	56	26	21	9	227	203	61	57	15	35	7	186	266	37	113	41	56	16	413	469	98
Chicago	35	19	12	4	130	118	42	34	8	23	3	98	153	19	69	27	35	7	228	271	61
Colorado	26	10	11	5	101	104	25	27	11	13	3	103	108	25	53	21	24	8	204	212	50
Dallas	34	16	16	2	121	121	34	36	13	19	4	121	150	30	70	29	35	6	242	271	64
Detroit	34	13	11	10	114	110	36	36	13	19	4	128	152	30	70	26	30	14	242	262	66
Edmonton	57	22	31	4	235	260	48	58	18	36	4	196	262	40	115	40	67	8	431	522	88
Florida	4	1	2	1	10	12	3	3	1	0	9	8	4	7	3	3	1	19	20	7	
Hartford	26	12	13	1	89	93	25	24	7	12	5	76	95	19	50	19	25	6	165	188	44
Los Angeles	58	28	21	9	246	210	65	55	24	21	10	230	237	58	113	52	42	19	476	447	123
Montreal	24	8	10	6	80	94	22	24	3	21	0	57	127	6	48	11	31	6	137	221	28
New Jersey	25	18	4	3	101	67	39	23	10	7	6	75	73	26	48	28	11	9	176	140	65
NY Islanders	24	7	14	3	75	94	17	25	7	12	6	80	100	20	49	14	26	9	155	194	37
NY Rangers	25	10	13	2	91	93	22	24	8	14	2	95	115	18	49	18	27	4	186	208	40
Ottawa	4	2	2	0	19	16	4	6	5	0	1	28	12	11	10	7	2	1	47	28	15
Philadelphia	24	10	12	2	77	82	22	25	6	19	0	70	114	12	49	16	31	2	147	196	34
Pittsburgh	24	9	13	2	88	89	20	25	7	18	0	74	109	14	49	16	31	2	162	198	34
St. Louis	37	18	13	6	122	113	42	35	9	17	9	105	132	27	72	27	30	15	227	245	69
San Jose	16	9	4	3	60	47	21	14	5	7	2	57	58	12	30	14	11	5	117	105	33
Tampa Bay	5	2	3	0	13	13	4	5	4	1	0	22	16	8	10	6	4	0	35	29	12
Toronto	35	18	11	6	149	132	42	36	19	15	2	140	131	40	71	37	26	8	289	263	82
Vancouver	55	27	20	8	218	208	62	58	16	34	8	170	229	40	113	43	54	16	388	437	102
Washington	25	13	7	5	95	92	31	24	5	16	3	71	108	13	49	18	23	8	166	200	44
Totals	**710**	**322**	**293**	**95**	**2660**	**2581**	**739**	**710**	**222**	**404**	**84**	**2342**	**3009**	**528**	**1420**	**544**	**697**	**179**	**5002**	**5590**	**1267**

Playoffs

	Series	W	L	GP	W	L	T	GF	GA	Last Mtg.	Round	Result
Anaheim	1	0	1	7	3	4	0	17	17	1997	CQF	L 3-4
Calgary	3	2	1	13	7	6	0	45	43	1987	DSF	W 4-2
Detroit	1	0	1	6	2	4	0	10	20	1996	CQF	L 2-4
Edmonton	6	0	6	26	4	22	0	75	120	1990	DSF	L 3-4
St. Louis	1	0	1	4	1	3	0	13	20	1982	DSF	L 1-3
Vancouver	2	0	2	13	5	8	0	34	50	1993	DSF	L 2-4
Totals	**14**	**2**	**12**	**69**	**22**	**47**	**0**	**194**	**270**			

Playoff Results 1997-93

Year	Round	Opponent	Result	GF	GA
1997	CQF	Anaheim	L 3-4	17	17
1996	CQF	Detroit	L 2-4	10	20
1993	DSF	Vancouver	L 2-4	17	21

Abbreviations: Round: F – Final;
CF – conference final; **CQF** – conference quarter-final;
CSF – conference semi-final; **DF** – division final;
DSF – division semi-final; **SF** – semi-final;
QF – quarter-final; **PR** – preliminary round.

Calgary totals include Atlanta, 1979-80.   Colorado totals include Quebec, 1979-80 to 1994-95.
Dallas totals include Minnesota, 1979-80 to 1992-93.   New Jersey totals include Colorado Rockies, 1979-80 to 1981-82.

1996-97 Results

Oct.	5	at	Hartford	0-1	9		Detroit	4-5

Oct.	5	at	Hartford	0-1			9		Detroit	4-5
	7	at	Boston	5-2			10	at	Dallas	4-3
	10		San Jose	4-1			12		Buffalo	2-3
	12		Anaheim	4-2			13	at	San Jose	4-5
	14		Edmonton	3-6			15		St. Louis	1-4
	18		Philadelphia	1-3			23		Anaheim	6-3
	20		Florida	1-1			25		Vancouver	4-0
	22		St. Louis	1-2			28	at	Philadelphia	1-4
	26	at	Toronto	2-5			29	at	Detroit	3-0
	28	at	Montreal	5-4	**Feb.**	1	at	Pittsburgh	1-4
	30	at	Edmonton	1-4			4		Tampa Bay	0-2
Nov.	1	at	Calgary	3-2			6		Chicago	3-2
	3		Montreal	4-4			8		Dallas	4-5
	6		Dallas	2-3			10	at	St. Louis	4-2
	8		Colorado	1-4			12	at	Dallas	5-0
	14		Hartford	1-2			13		Colorado	2-3
	16		Toronto	3-2			15		Boston	5-4
	18		Detroit	2-2			18		Los Angeles	6-1
	20	at	Colorado	0-6			22	at	Anaheim	2-4
	21	at	St. Louis	3-4			24		Detroit	3-5
	23		NY Islanders	3-3			26	at	Calgary	5-2
	26		NY Rangers	1-3			27	at	Vancouver	2-6
	28		New Jersey	4-3	**Mar.**	2		Chicago	0-4
	30		Calgary	2-3			5	at	Florida	5-0
Dec.	3		Los Angeles	1-4			6	at	Tampa Bay	5-0
	5	at	St. Louis	3-0			8	at	Chicago	2-0
	7	at	New Jersey	4-3			10		Ottawa	1-4
	9	at	NY Rangers	2-5			12		Pittsburgh	5-5
	10	at	NY Islanders	2-8			14	at	San Jose	4-1
	13	at	Ottawa	4-2			17		St. Louis	3-2
	14	at	Toronto	5-3			19	at	Dallas	2-7
	17		Washington	4-3			20	at	Chicago	4-2
	20		Toronto	5-2			22	at	Toronto	3-0
	22		Calgary	2-7			27		Toronto	1-1
	23	at	Anaheim	4-1			29		Edmonton	4-3
	26	at	Los Angeles	2-5	**Apr.**	1		San Jose	7-1
	27		Vancouver	7-4			3	at	Los Angeles	5-4
	30	at	Detroit	5-3			6	at	Colorado	1-2
Jan.	2	at	Chicago	4-2			7		Dallas	2-7
	3	at	Washington	0-3			9	at	Vancouver	4-6
	5	at	Buffalo	1-5			11	at	Edmonton	6-2

Entry Draft
Selections 1997-83

1997
Pick
43	Juha Gustafsson
96	Scott McCallum
123	Curtis Suter
151	Robert Francz
207	Alex Andreyev
233	Wyatt Smith

1996
Pick
11	Dan Focht
24	Daniel Briere
62	Per-Anton Lundstrom
119	Richard Lintner
139	Robert Esche
174	Trevor Letowski
200	Nicholas Lent
226	Marc-Etienne Hubert

1995
Pick
7	Shane Doan
32	Marc Chouinard
34	Jason Doig
67	Brad Isbister
84	Justin Kurtz
121	Brian Elder
136	Sylvain Daigle
162	Paul Traynor
188	Jaroslav Obsut
189	Frederik Loven
214	Rob Deciantis

1994
Pick
30	Deron Quint
56	Dorian Anneck
58	Tavis Hansen
82	Steve Cheredaryk
108	Craig Mills
143	Steve Vezina
146	Chris Kibermanis
186	Ramil Saifullin
212	Henrik Smangs
238	Mike Mader
264	Jason Issel

1993
Pick
15	Mats Lindgren
31	Scott Langkow
43	Alexei Budayev
79	Ruslan Batyrshin
93	Ravil Gusmanov
119	Larry Courville
145	Michal Grosek
171	Martin Woods
197	Adrian Murray
217	Vladimir Potapov
223	Ilja Stashenkov
228	Harijs Vitolinsh
285	Russell Hewson

1992
Pick
17	Sergei Bautin
27	Boris Mironov
60	Jeremy Stevenson
84	Mark Visheau
132	Alexander Alexeyev
155	Artur Oktyabrev
156	Andrei Raisky
204	Nikolai Khaibulin
228	Yevgeny Garanin
229	Teemu Numminen
252	Andrei Karpovtsev
254	Ivan Vologzhaninov

1991
Pick
5	Aaron Ward
49	Dmitri Filimonov
91	Juha Ylonen
99	Yan Kaminsky
115	Jeff Sebastian
159	Jeff Ricciardi
181	Sean Gauthier
203	Igor Ulanov
225	Jason Jennings
247	Sergei Sorokin

1990
Pick
19	Keith Tkachuk
35	Mike Muller
74	Roman Meluzin
75	Scott Levins
77	Alexei Zhamnov
98	Craig Martin
119	Daniel Jardemyr
140	John Lilley
161	Henrik Andersson
182	Rauli Raitanen
203	Mika Alatalo
224	Sergei Selyanin
245	Keith Morris

1989
Pick
4	Stu Barnes
25	Dan Ratushny
46	Jason Cirone
62	Kris Draper
64	Mark Brownschidle
69	Alain Roy
109	Dan Bylsma
130	Pekka Peltola
131	Doug Evans
151	Jim Solly
172	Stephane Gauvin
193	Joe Larson
214	Bradley Podiak
235	Evgeny Davydov
240	Sergei Kharin

1988
Pick
10	Teemu Selanne
31	Russell Romaniuk
52	Stephane Beauregard
73	Brian Hunt
94	Anthony Joseph
101	Benoit Lebeau
115	Ronald Jones
127	Markus Akerblom
136	Jukka Marttila
157	Mark Smith
178	Mike Helber
199	Pavel Kostichkin
220	Kevin Heise
241	Kyle Galloway

1987
Pick
16	Bryan Marchment
37	Patrik Erickson
79	Don McLennan
96	Ken Gernander
100	Darrin Amundson
121	Joe Harwell
142	Tod Hartje
163	Markku Kyllonen
184	Jim Fernholz
226	Roger Rougelot
247	Hans Goran Elo

1986
Pick
8	Pat Elynuik
29	Teppo Numminen
50	Esa Palosaari
71	Hannu Jarvenpaa
92	Craig Endean
113	Robertson Bateman
155	Frank Furlan
176	Mark Green
197	John Blue
218	Matt Cote
239	Arto Blomsten

1985
Pick
18	Ryan Stewart
39	Roger Ohman
60	Daniel Berthiaume
81	Fredrik Olausson
102	John Borrell
123	Danton Cole
144	Brent Mowery
165	Tom Draper
186	Nevin Kardum
207	Dave Quigley
228	Chris Norton
249	Anssi Melametsa

1984
Pick
30	Peter Douris
68	Chris Mills
72	Sean Clement
93	Scott Schneider
99	Brent Severyn
114	Gary Lorden
135	Luciano Borsato
156	Brad Jones
177	Gord Whitaker
197	Rick Forst
218	Mike Warus
238	Jim Edmonds

1983
Pick
8	Andrew McBain
14	Bobby Dollas
29	Brad Berry
43	Peter Taglianetti
69	Bob Essensa
89	Harry Armstrong
109	Joel Baillargeon
129	Iain Duncan
149	Ron Pessetti
169	Todd Flichel
189	Cory Wright
209	Eric Cormier
229	Jamie Husgen

General Manager

SMITH, BOBBY
General Manager, Phoenix Coyotes.
Born in North Sydney, N.S., February 12, 1958.

After 15 outstanding seasons as a National Hockey League player and eight years as the vice president of the NHL Players' Association, Bobby Smith became the Phoenix Coyotes first executive vice president of hockey operations on May 21, 1996.

In 1978, Smith was named the Canadian Major Junior player of the year and was drafted by the Minnesota North Stars first overall in the NHL Entry Draft. A year later, the Ottawa, Ontario native was named the Calder Trophy winner as the NHL's top rookie in 1979 after scoring 30 goals and 74 points in his first season. Smith went on to have a remarkable NHL career with Minnesota and Montreal. Smith played in 1,077 games with the North Stars and Canadiens recording (357-679) 1,036 points. He led the North Stars in scoring four of his first five years with the club. His finest season with Minnesota came during the 1981-82 campaign when Smith achieved career highs in games played (80), goals (43), assists (71) and points (114). He was one of three players who played on both of Minnesota's Stanley Cup Finalist teams in 1981 and 1991. Following a trade to Montreal in 1983, Smith played seven seasons with the Canadiens, recording 70-plus points in five of those years. In 1986, he helped guide the Canadiens to a Stanley Cup victory over the Calgary Flames. Smith scored the Stanley Cup game-winning goal in a 4-3 win over Calgary. After 13 playoff seasons and 184 games with Minnesota and Montreal, Smith retired with 64 goals and 96 assists for 160 points, ranking him 12th on the NHL all-time playoff point leaders list. Smith also played in four NHL All-Star Games (1981, 1982, 1989, 1990) during his career.

After retiring from hockey, Smith focused his energy on education and completed two degrees at the Curt Carlson School of Management at the University of Minnesota; a Bachelor of Science (in business) and a Masters of Business Administration.

Bobby and his wife Elizabeth along with their three children Ryan, Megan and Daniel reside in Scottsdale, AZ.

Club Directory

America West Arena

Phoenix Coyotes Hockey Club
One Renaissance Square
2 North Central, Suite 1930
Phoenix, AZ 85004
Phone **602/379-2800**
FAX 602/379-2828
Website: www.nhlcoyotes.com
Capacity: 16,210

CEO & Governor	Richard Burke
Owner & Alternate Governor	Steven Gluckstern
President & Chief Operating Officer	Shawn Hunter
General Manager & Alternate Governor	Bobby Smith
Chief Financial Officer & Vice President of Administration	Mark Peterson
Administrative Assistant to the President	Lisa Mardeusz
Executive Assistant, Hockey Operations	Lesa Senker

Hockey Operations
Vice President of Hockey Operations/Facilities	Mike O'Hearn
Assistant General Manager	Taylor Burke
Head Coach	Jim Schoenfeld
Assistant Coach	John Tortorella
Assistant Coach/Director of Player Development	Gordie Roberts
Goaltending Coach	Benoit Allaire
Springfield Falcons (AHL) Head Coach	Dave Farrish
Director of Scouting	Bill Lesuk
Director of Player Personnel	Sean Coady
Assistant Director of Scouting	Joe Yannetti
Scouts	Vaughn Karpan, Terry Doran, Connie Broden, Larry Hornung, Blair Mackasey, Evzen Slansky, Claes Wallin, Boris Yemeljanov,
Director of Hockey Administration/Legal Counsel	Laurence Gilman
Director of Hockey Information	Igor Kuperman
Sports Physiologists/Strength and Conditioning Consultants	Dr. Dan Halvorsen, Kevin Ziegler
Video Coordinator	Steve Peters

Broadcasting
Director of Broadcasting	Mark Hulsey
Broadcasting Coordinator	Craig Amazeen
Broadcasting Intern	Scott Eisenstein
TV Play-by-Play	Doug McLeod
TV Color Commentator	Charlie Simmer
Radio Play-by-Play	Curt Keilback
Radio Color Commentator	Tom Kurvers

Corporate Sales and Service
Director of Corporate Sales	Tim Weil
Director of Business Development	Rip Reynolds
Corporate Account Executives	Rob Childs, Kelly Staley, Tara Pisciotta

Ticket Sales and Service
Vice President of Sales & Service	Brenda Tinnen
Director of Ticket Operations	Bruce Bielenberg
Director of Marketing	Tim McBride
Game Operations Coordinator	Staci Grevillius
Customer Service Representative	Marcy Fileccia
Receptionist	TBA
Ticket Sales Manager	Jeff Lane
Account Executives	Nick Roe, Brian Tollefson, Amber Vacha, Jim Willits
Customer Service Representative	Scott Epp
Summer Sales Associates	Adam Link, Amy Sun, Scott Newhouse, Meghan Harrison, Joshua Waggoner

Business Development
Vice President of Business Development	Joe Levy
Director of Suite Sales	Renee Tauer
Suite Sales Intern	Kelly Joyce

Communications
Director of Media & Player Relations	Richard Nairn
Manager of Media Relations	Jeffrey Hecht
Publications Coordinator	Rick Braunstein
Media Relations Intern	John Mellor

Community Relations
Director of Community Relations/Executive Director of Phoenix Coyotes Goals For Kids Foundation	Lori Summers
Admin. Ass't/Event Coordinator - Phoenix Coyotes Goals For Kids Foundation	Aimee Zeff
Coordinator of Fan Development	Justin Maloof

Finance & Administration
Controller	Joe Leibfried
Payroll Administrator	Cheri Sedor
Accounting Assistants	Joanna Savage, June Reynolds

Dressing Room
Athletic Therapist	Gord Hart
Massage Therapist	Jukka Nieminen
Equipment Managers	Stan Wilson, Tony DaCosta
Assistant Equipment Manager	Chris Scoppetto
Team Physicians	Matthew Maddox, D.O., Dana Seltzer, M.D.
Team Dentists	Dr. Rick Lawson, Dr. Lawrence Emmott

Team Information
Team Colors	Black, Brick Red, Hunter Green, Sand, Sienna, and Purple
Home Ice	America West Arena
Dimensions of Rink	200 feet by 85 feet
Training Camp	Phoenix
Press Box Location	East Side of Arena
Cable Station	Fox Sports Arizona
Television Stations	KTVK Channel 3 and WB-61
Radio Stations	KDKB FM (93.3), KUKQ AM (1060)

Pittsburgh Penguins

1996-97 Results: 38W-36L-8T 84PTS. Second, Northeast Division

TM

Year-by-Year Record

Season	GP	Home W	L	T	Road W	L	T	Overall W	L	T	GF	GA	Pts.	Finished		Playoff Result
1996-97	82	25	11	5	13	25	3	38	36	8	285	280	84	2nd,	Northeast Div.	Lost Conf. Quarter-Final
1995-96	82	32	9	0	17	20	4	49	29	4	362	284	102	1st,	Northeast Div.	Lost Conf. Championship
1994-95	48	18	5	1	11	11	2	29	16	3	181	158	61	2nd,	Northeast Div.	Lost Conf. Semi-Final
1993-94	84	25	9	8	19	18	5	44	27	13	299	285	101	1st,	Northeast Div.	Lost Conf. Quarter-Final
1992-93	84	32	6	4	24	15	3	56	21	7	367	268	119	1st,	Patrick Div.	Lost Div. Final
1991-92	**80**	**21**	**13**	**6**	**18**	**19**	**3**	**39**	**32**	**9**	**343**	**308**	**87**	**3rd,**	**Patrick Div.**	**Won Stanley Cup**
1990-91	**80**	**25**	**12**	**3**	**16**	**21**	**3**	**41**	**33**	**6**	**342**	**305**	**88**	**1st,**	**Patrick Div.**	**Won Stanley Cup**
1989-90	80	22	15	3	10	25	5	32	40	8	318	359	72	5th,	Patrick Div.	Out of Playoffs
1988-89	80	24	13	3	16	20	4	40	33	7	347	349	87	2nd,	Patrick Div.	Lost Div. Final
1987-88	80	22	12	6	14	23	3	36	35	9	319	316	81	6th,	Patrick Div.	Out of Playoffs
1986-87	80	19	15	6	11	23	6	30	38	12	297	290	72	5th,	Patrick Div.	Out of Playoffs
1985-86	80	20	15	5	14	23	3	34	38	8	313	305	76	5th,	Patrick Div.	Out of Playoffs
1984-85	80	17	20	3	7	31	2	24	51	5	276	385	53	6th,	Patrick Div.	Out of Playoffs
1983-84	80	7	29	4	9	29	2	16	58	6	254	390	38	6th,	Patrick Div.	Out of Playoffs
1982-83	80	14	22	4	4	31	5	18	53	9	257	394	45	6th,	Patrick Div.	Out of Playoffs
1981-82	80	21	11	8	10	25	5	31	36	13	310	337	75	4th,	Patrick Div.	Lost Div. Semi-Final
1980-81	80	21	16	3	9	21	10	30	37	13	302	345	73	3rd,	Norris Div.	Lost Prelim. Round
1979-80	80	20	13	7	10	24	6	30	37	13	251	303	73	3rd,	Norris Div.	Lost Prelim. Round
1978-79	80	23	12	5	13	19	8	36	31	13	281	279	85	2nd,	Norris Div.	Lost Quarter-Final
1977-78	80	16	15	9	9	22	9	25	37	18	254	321	68	4th,	Norris Div.	Out of Playoffs
1976-77	80	22	12	6	12	21	7	34	33	13	240	252	81	3rd,	Norris Div.	Lost Prelim. Round
1975-76	80	23	11	6	12	22	6	35	33	12	339	303	82	3rd,	Norris Div.	Lost Prelim. Round
1974-75	80	25	5	10	12	23	5	37	28	15	326	289	89	3rd,	Norris Div.	Lost Quarter-Final
1973-74	78	15	18	6	13	23	3	28	41	9	242	273	65	5th,	West Div.	Out of Playoffs
1972-73	78	24	11	4	8	26	5	32	37	9	257	265	73	5th,	West Div.	Out of Playoffs
1971-72	78	18	15	6	8	23	8	26	38	14	220	258	66	4th,	West Div.	Lost Quarter-Final
1970-71	78	18	12	9	3	25	11	21	37	20	221	240	62	6th,	West Div.	Out of Playoffs
1969-70	76	17	13	8	9	25	4	26	38	12	182	238	64	2nd,	West Div.	Lost Semi-Final
1968-69	76	12	20	6	8	25	5	20	45	11	189	252	51	5th,	West Div.	Out of Playoffs
1967-68	74	15	12	10	12	22	3	27	34	13	195	216	67	5th,	West Div.	Out of Playoffs

1997-98 Schedule

Oct.	Wed.	1	Los Angeles	**Jan.**	Sat.	3	Colorado
	Fri.	3	at Carolina		Tue.	6	at NY Islanders
	Sat.	4	Florida		Wed.	7	at New Jersey
	Wed.	8	Montreal		Sat.	10	New Jersey
	Thu.	9	at Philadelphia		Mon.	12	at Carolina
	Sat.	11	Carolina		Wed.	14	at Boston
	Tue.	14	at NY Rangers		Tue.	20	Ottawa
	Wed.	15	at Montreal		Thu.	22	at New Jersey
	Fri.	17	at Tampa Bay		Sat.	24	Boston*
	Sun.	19	at Florida		Mon.	26	St. Louis
	Wed.	22	at San Jose		Wed.	28	at Washington
	Fri.	24	at Edmonton		Thu.	29	at Boston
	Sat.	25	at Vancouver		Sat.	31	Detroit*
	Tue.	28	at Calgary	**Feb.**	Mon.	2	NY Islanders
Nov.	Sat.	1	Vancouver		Wed.	4	Washington
	Sun.	2	at Chicago		Fri.	6	at Buffalo
	Wed.	5	Dallas		Sat.	7	at Ottawa
	Fri.	7	at Detroit		Wed.	25	at Montreal
	Sat.	8	Buffalo		Sat.	28	at Boston*
	Wed.	12	Washington	**Mar.**	Mon.	2	Toronto
	Fri.	14	at NY Rangers		Thu.	5	Chicago
	Sat.	15	at Toronto		Sat.	7	Philadelphia*
	Wed.	19	Boston		Sun.	8	at Philadelphia
	Thu.	20	at Ottawa		Wed.	11	Calgary
	Sat.	22	NY Rangers		Sat.	14	Buffalo*
	Mon.	24	Buffalo		Sun.	15	at Buffalo*
	Wed.	26	Carolina		Wed.	18	Edmonton
	Sat.	29	Montreal		Sat.	21	Philadelphia*
Dec.	Mon.	1	at Montreal		Sun.	22	at Dallas*
	Thu.	4	New Jersey		Thu.	26	at NY Islanders
	Sat.	6	Anaheim		Sat.	28	NY Rangers*
	Tue.	9	at Los Angeles		Sun.	29	Ottawa*
	Wed.	10	at Anaheim	**Apr.**	Wed.	1	San Jose
	Fri.	12	at Phoenix		Sat.	4	at Tampa Bay*
	Tue.	16	Tampa Bay		Sun.	5	at Florida
	Fri.	19	at Colorado		Tue.	7	Phoenix
	Sat.	20	at St. Louis		Thu.	9	at Ottawa
	Fri.	26	at Washington		Sat.	11	Florida*
	Sat.	27	Montreal		Wed.	15	Tampa Bay
	Mon.	29	NY Islanders		Thu.	16	at Carolina
	Wed.	31	Carolina		Sat.	18	Boston*

* Denotes afternoon game.

Franchise date: June 5, 1967

EASTERN CONFERENCE

NORTHEAST DIVISION

31st NHL Season

Despite missing 19 games due to injury, Jaromir Jagr finished seventh in NHL scoring with 47 goals and 48 assists. Jagr is the first European-trained player to win the League's scoring championship, earning the Art Ross Trophy in 1994-95.

1997-98 Player Personnel

FORWARDS	HT	WT	S	Place of Birth	Date	1996-97 Club
AUBIN, Serge	6-1	194	L	Val d'Or, Que.	2/15/75	Cleveland
BARNES, Stu	5-11	174	R	Spruce Grove, Alta.	12/25/70	Florida-Pittsburgh
BERANEK, Josef	6-2	190	L	Litvinov, Czechoslovakia	10/25/69	Vsetin-Pittsburgh
BONIN, Brian	5-10	185	L	St. Paul, MN	11/28/73	Cleveland
CALLAHAN, Brian	6-1	190	L	Melrose, MA	7/13/74	Boston College
DOME, Robert	6-	214	L	Skalica, Czech.	1/29/79	Long Beach-Las Vegas
DZIEDZIC, Joe	6-3	227	L	Minneapolis, MN	12/18/71	Pittsburgh
FITZGERALD, Rusty	6-1	210	L	Minneapolis, MN	10/4/72	
FRANCIS, Ron	6-3	200	L	Sault Ste. Marie, Ont.	3/1/63	Pittsburgh
HICKS, Alex	6-1	195	L	Calgary, Alta.	9/4/69	Anaheim-Pittsburgh
HRDINA, Jan	6-0	190	R	Hradec Kralove, Czech.	2/5/76	Cleveland
JAGR, Jaromir	6-2	216	L	Kladno, Czech.	2/15/72	Pittsburgh
JOHANSSON, Andreas	6-0	205	L	Hofors, Sweden	5/19/73	NYI-Pit-Cleveland
JOHNSON, Greg	5-10	185	L	Thunder Bay, Ont.	3/16/71	Detroit-Pittsburgh
KANE, Boyd	6-1	207	L	Swift Current, Sask.	4/18/78	Regina
NEDVED, Petr	6-3	195	L	Liberec, Czech.	12/9/71	Pittsburgh
OKSIUTA, Roman	6-3	230	L	Murmansk, USSR	8/21/70	Anaheim-Pittsburgh
OLCZYK, Eddie	6-1	205	L	Chicago, IL	8/16/66	Los Angeles-Pittsburgh
PITTIS, Domenic	5-11	190	L	Calgary, Alta.	10/1/74	Pittsburgh-Long Beach
PROTSENKO, Boris	6-0	185	R	Kiev, USSR	8/21/78	Calgary (WHL)
ROCHE, Dave	6-4	227	L	Lindsay, Ont.	6/13/75	Pittsburgh-Cleveland
SAVOIA, Ryan	6-0	195	R	Thorold, Ont.	5/6/73	Johnstown-Cleveland-Fort Wayne
STOJANOV, Alek	6-4	225	L	Windsor, Ont.	4/25/73	Pittsburgh
STRAKA, Martin	5-10	178	L	Plzen, Czech.	9/3/72	Florida
VALK, Garry	6-1	205	L	Edmonton, Alta.	11/27/67	Anaheim-Pittsburgh
WRIGHT, Tyler	5-11	185	R	Canora, Sask.	4/6/73	Pittsburgh-Cleveland

DEFENSEMEN	HT	WT	S	Place of Birth	Date	1996-97 Club
BERGKVIST, Stefan	6-2	224	L	Leksand, Sweden	3/10/75	Pittsburgh-Cleveland
BUTENSCHON, Sven	6-5	201	L	Itzehoe, West Germany	3/22/76	Cleveland
HATCHER, Kevin	6-4	225	R	Detroit, MI	9/9/66	Pittsburgh
KASPARAITIS, Darius	5-10	205	L	Elektrenai, USSR	10/16/72	NY Islanders-Pittsburgh
KRIVCHENKOV, Alexei	6-0	190	L	Novosibirsk, USSR	6/11/74	Jhnstn-Hamp Rds-Long Beach
LEROUX, Francois	6-6	235	L	Ste.-Adele, Que.	4/18/70	Pittsburgh
MATHIEU, Alexandre	6-2	180	L	Repentigny, Que.	2/12/79	Halifax
MELICHAR, Josef	6-3	198	L	Budejovice, Czech.	1/20/79	Budejovice
MORAN, Ian	5-11	195	R	Cleveland, OH	8/24/72	Pittsburgh-Cleveland
OLAUSSON, Fredrik	6-2	195	R	Dadesjo, Sweden	10/5/66	Anaheim-Pittsburgh
PRATT, Harlan	6-1	202	R	Fort McMurray, Alta.	12/10/78	Red Deer-Prince Albert
ROZSIVAL, Michal	6-1	189	R	Vlasim, Czech.	9/3/78	Swift Current
SLEGR, Jiri	6-1	205	L	Jihlava, Czech.	5/30/71	Litvinov-Sodertalje
TAMER, Chris	6-2	212	L	Dearborn, MI	11/17/70	Pittsburgh
VORONOV, Sergei	6-2	200	L	Moscow, USSR	2/5/71	Las Vegas
WERENKA, Brad	6-2	210	L	Two Hills, Alta.	2/12/69	Indianapolis
WILKINSON, Neil	6-3	200	R	Selkirk, Man.	8/15/67	Pittsburgh-Cleveland
WOOLLEY, Jason	6-0	188	L	Toronto, Ont.	7/27/69	Florida-Pittsburgh

GOALTENDERS	HT	WT	C	Place of Birth	Date	1996-97 Club
AUBIN, Jean-Sebastien	5-11	179	R	Montreal, Que.	7/19/77	Laval-Moncton-Sherbrooke
BARRASSO, Tom	6-3	211	R	Boston, MA	3/31/65	Pittsburgh
HILLIER, Craig	6-1	174	L	Cole Harbour, N.S.	2/28/78	Ottawa (OHL)
LALIME, Patrick	6-2	170	L	St. Bonaventure, Que.	7/7/74	Pittsburgh-Cleveland
WREGGET, Ken	6-1	201	L	Brandon, Man.	3/25/64	Pittsburgh

Coach

CONSTANTINE, KEVIN
Head Coach, Pittsburgh Penguins.
Born in International Falls, MN, December 27, 1958.

Recognized as one of the bright young coaches in the game, the 38-year-old Constantine was named head coach of the Penguins on June 12, 1997.

The former college goaltender already has three-plus seasons of NHL coaching experience on his resume, including 157 games as head coach of the San Jose Sharks from 1993-95. Constantine led the young Sharks to two playoff appearances during his tenure, and oversaw a much-publicized playoff upset of Detroit.

Last season, he served as an assistant coach under Pierre Page with the Calgary Flames.

Constantine played three seasons as a goaltender at Rensselaer Polytechnic Institute (RPI) from 1978-80 and was a ninth-round draft choice of the Montreal Canadiens in 1978. He had a brief tryout with the Canadiens in 1980.

He began to attract notice as a young coach when he led Rochester to the USHL title in 1987-88. He landed his first professional head coaching job at age 32 in 1991-92 and rewarded his bosses by leading Kansas City to the International Hockey League championship. In two seasons with the Blades, Constantine compiled a record of 102-48-14, prompting a promotion to the NHL and San Jose in 1993-94. He was 55-78-4 in two-plus seasons with the Sharks.

Coaching Record

		Regular Season					Playoffs			
Season	Team	Games	W	L	T	%	Games	W	L	%
1985-86	North Iowa (USHL)	48	17	31	0	.354	....	....	....	....
1987-88	Rochester (USHL)	48	39	7	2	.833	15	9	4	.692*
1991-92	Kansas City (IHL)	82	56	22	4	.707	15	12	3	.800
1992-93	Kansas City (IHL)	82	46	26	10	.622	12	6	6	.500
1993-94	**San Jose (NHL)**	**84**	**33**	**35**	**16**	**.488**	**14**	**7**	**7**	**.500**
1994-95	**San Jose (NHL)**	**48**	**19**	**25**	**4**	**.438**	**11**	**4**	**7**	**.364**
1995-96	**San Jose (NHL)**	**25**	**3**	**18**	**4**	**.250**	....	....	....	....
	NHL Totals	**157**	**55**	**78**	**24**	**.427**	**25**	**11**	**14**	**.440**

* includes 2 ties.

1996-97 Scoring

* – rookie

Regular Season

Pos	#	Player	Team	GP	G	A	Pts	+/–	PIM	PP	SH	GW	GT	S	%
C	66	Mario Lemieux	PIT	76	50	72	122	27	65	15	3	7	1	327	15.3
R	68	Jaromir Jagr	PIT	63	47	48	95	22	40	11	2	6	1	234	20.1
C	10	Ron Francis	PIT	81	27	63	90	7	20	10	1	2	0	183	14.8
C	93	Petr Nedved	PIT	74	33	38	71	-2	66	12	3	4	0	189	17.5
L	27	Ed Olczyk	L.A.	67	21	23	44	-22	45	5	1	5	0	166	12.7
			PIT	12	4	7	11	8	6	0	0	1	0	29	13.8
			TOTAL	79	25	30	55	-14	51	5	1	6	0	195	12.8
D	4	Kevin Hatcher	PIT	80	15	39	54	11	103	9	0	1	0	199	7.5
C	14	Stu Barnes	FLA	19	2	8	10	-3	10	1	0	0	1	44	4.5
			PIT	62	17	22	39	-20	16	4	0	3	2	132	12.9
			TOTAL	81	19	30	49	-23	26	5	0	3	3	176	10.8
D	23	Fredrik Olausson	ANA	20	2	9	11	-5	8	1	0	0	0	35	5.7
			PIT	51	7	20	27	21	24	2	0	3	0	75	9.3
			TOTAL	71	9	29	38	16	32	3	0	3	0	110	8.2
D	22	Jason Woolley	FLA	3	0	0	0	1	2	0	0	0	0	7	0.0
			PIT	57	6	30	36	3	28	2	0	1	0	79	7.6
			TOTAL	60	6	30	36	4	30	2	0	1	0	86	7.0
C	9	Greg Johnson	DET	43	6	10	16	-5	12	0	0	0	0	56	10.7
			PIT	32	7	9	16	-13	14	1	0	0	0	52	13.5
			TOTAL	75	13	19	32	-18	26	1	0	0	0	108	12.0
C	33	Alex Hicks	ANA	18	2	6	8	1	14	0	0	0	0	21	9.5
			PIT	55	5	15	20	-6	76	0	0	3	0	57	8.8
			TOTAL	73	7	21	28	-5	90	0	0	3	0	78	9.0
D	11	Darius Kasparaitis	NYI	18	0	5	5	-7	16	0	0	0	0	12	0.0
			PIT	57	2	16	18	24	84	0	0	0	0	46	4.3
			TOTAL	75	2	21	23	17	100	0	0	0	0	58	3.4
R	7	Joe Mullen	PIT	54	7	15	22	0	4	1	0	1	0	63	11.1
L	8	Garry Valk	ANA	53	7	7	14	-2	53	0	0	1	0	68	10.3
			PIT	17	3	4	7	-6	25	0	0	0	0	32	9.4
			TOTAL	70	10	11	21	-8	78	0	0	1	0	100	10.0
L	16	Joe Dziedzic	PIT	59	9	9	18	-4	63	0	0	1	0	85	10.6
R	20	Roman Oksiuta	ANA	28	6	7	13	-12	22	2	0	0	1	48	12.5
			PIT	7	0	0	0	-4	4	0	0	0	0	10	0.0
			TOTAL	35	6	7	13	-16	26	2	0	0	1	58	10.3
C	38 *	Andreas Johansson	NYI	15	2	2	4	-6	0	1	0	0	0	21	9.5
			PIT	27	2	7	9	-6	20	0	0	0	0	38	5.3
			TOTAL	42	4	9	13	-12	20	1	0	0	0	59	6.8
L	51	Dave Roche	PIT	61	5	5	10	-13	155	2	0	0	0	53	9.4
D	24	Ian Moran	PIT	36	4	5	9	-11	22	0	0	0	0	50	8.0
D	2	Chris Tamer	PIT	45	2	4	6	-25	131	0	1	0	0	56	3.6
R	25	Alek Stojanov	PIT	35	1	4	5	3	79	0	0	0	0	11	9.1
L	15	Josef Beranek	PIT	8	3	1	4	-1	4	1	0	0	0	15	20.0
L	72	Jeff Christian	PIT	11	2	2	4	-3	13	0	0	0	0	18	11.1
C	29	Tyler Wright	PIT	45	2	2	4	-7	70	0	0	2	0	30	6.7
D	28	Craig Muni	PIT	64	0	4	4	-6	36	0	0	0	0	19	0.0
C	9	Dan Quinn	PIT	16	0	3	3	-6	10	0	0	0	0	16	0.0
D	18	Francois Leroux	PIT	59	0	3	3	-3	81	0	0	0	0	5	0.0
G	31	Ken Wregget	PIT	46	0	1	1	0	6	0	0	0	0	0	0.0
C	23 *	Domenic Pittis	PIT	1	0	0	0	-1	0	0	0	0	0	0	0.0
G	30 *	Philippe De Rouville	PIT	2	0	0	0	0	0	0	0	0	0	0	0.0
G	35	Tom Barrasso	PIT	5	0	0	0	0	0	0	0	0	0	0	0.0
D	3 *	Stefan Bergkvist	PIT	5	0	0	0	-1	7	0	0	0	0	0	0.0
R	44	Ed Patterson	PIT	6	0	0	0	0	8	0	0	0	0	2	0.0
D	6	Neil Wilkinson	PIT	23	0	0	0	-12	36	0	0	0	0	16	0.0
G	40 *	Patrick Lalime	PIT	39	0	0	0	0	0	0	0	0	0	0	0.0

Goaltending

No.	Goaltender	GPI	Mins	Avg	W	L	T	EN	SO	GA	SA	S%
40	* Patrick Lalime	39	2058	2.94	21	12	2	3	3	101	1166	.913
30	* Philippe De Rouville	2	111	3.24	0	2	0	1	0	6	66	.909
31	Ken Wregget	46	2514	3.25	17	17	6	6	2	136	1383	.902
35	Tom Barrasso	5	270	5.78	0	5	0	1	0	26	186	.860
	Totals	**82**	**4969**	**3.38**	**38**	**36**	**8**	**11**	**5**	**280**	**2812**	**.900**

Playoffs

Pos	#	Player	Team	GP	G	A	Pts	+/–	PIM	PP	SH	GW	OT	S	%
R	68	Jaromir Jagr	PIT	5	4	4	8	-4	4	2	0	0	0	18	22.2
C	66	Mario Lemieux	PIT	5	3	3	6	-4	4	0	0	0	0	19	15.8
C	10	Ron Francis	PIT	5	1	2	3	-7	2	1	0	0	0	6	16.7
C	93	Petr Nedved	PIT	5	1	2	3	-2	12	0	1	0	0	10	10.0
D	24	Ian Moran	PIT	5	1	2	3	1	4	0	0	0	0	8	12.5
D	22	Jason Woolley	PIT	5	0	3	3	-1	0	0	0	0	0	9	0.0
D	4	Kevin Hatcher	PIT	5	1	1	2	-5	4	1	0	0	0	12	8.3
L	27	Ed Olczyk	PIT	5	1	0	1	-2	12	0	1	1	0	11	9.1
C	9	Greg Johnson	PIT	5	1	0	1	-1	2	0	0	0	0	2	50.0
D	23	Fredrik Olausson	PIT	4	0	1	1	-1	0	0	0	0	0	5	0.0
C	14	Stu Barnes	PIT	5	0	1	1	0	0	0	0	0	0	4	0.0
L	16	Joe Dziedzic	PIT	5	0	1	1	-1	4	0	0	0	0	5	0.0
C	33	Alex Hicks	PIT	5	0	1	1	-1	2	0	0	0	0	2	0.0
R	7	Joe Mullen	PIT	1	0	0	0	0	0	0	0	0	0	0	0.0
D	18	Francois Leroux	PIT	3	0	0	0	0	0	0	0	0	0	0	0.0
D	28	Craig Muni	PIT	3	0	0	0	0	0	0	0	0	0	0	0.0
D	2	Chris Tamer	PIT	4	0	0	0	-1	4	0	0	0	0	3	0.0
D	6	Neil Wilkinson	PIT	5	0	0	0	-2	4	0	0	0	0	1	0.0
G	31	Ken Wregget	PIT	5	0	0	0	0	2	0	0	0	0	0	0.0
L	15	Josef Beranek	PIT	5	0	0	0	-4	2	0	0	0	0	17	0.0
D	11	Darius Kasparaitis	PIT	5	0	0	0	-4	6	0	0	0	0	7	0.0

Goaltending

No.	Goaltender	GPI	Mins	Avg	W	L	EN	SO	GA	SA	S%
31	Ken Wregget	5	297	3.64	1	4	2	0	18	211	.915
	Totals	**5**	**300**	**4.00**	**1**	**4**	**2**	**0**	**20**	**213**	**.906**

Club Records

Team

(Figures in brackets for season records are games played; records for fewest points, wins, ties, losses, goals, goals against are for 70 or more games)

Most Points	119	1992-93 (84)
Most Wins	56	1992-93 (84)
Most Ties	20	1970-71 (78)
Most Losses	58	1983-84 (80)
Most Goals	367	1992-93 (84)
Most Goals Against	394	1982-83 (80)
Fewest Points	38	1983-84 (80)
Fewest Wins	16	1983-84 (80)
Fewest Ties	4	1995-96 (82)
Fewest Losses	21	1992-93 (84)
Fewest Goals	182	1969-70 (76)
Fewest Goals Against	216	1967-68 (74)
Longest Winning Streak		
Overall	*17	Mar. 9-Apr. 10/93
Home	11	Jan. 5-Mar. 7/91
Away	6	Mar. 14-Apr. 9/93, Nov. 22-Dec. 13/96
Longest Undefeated Streak		
Overall	18	Mar. 9-Apr. 14/93 (17 wins, 1 tie)
Home	20	Nov. 30/74-Feb. 22/75 (12 wins, 8 ties)
Away	7	Three times
Longest Losing Streak		
Overall	11	Jan. 22/83-Feb. 10/83
Home	7	Oct. 8-29/83
Away	18	Dec. 23/82-Mar. 4/83
Longest Winless Streak		
Overall	18	Jan. 2-Feb. 10/83 (17 losses, 1 tie)
Home	11	Oct. 8-Nov. 19/83 (9 losses, 2 ties)
Away	18	Oct. 25/70-Jan. 14/71 (11 losses, 7 ties), Dec. 23/82-Mar. 4/83 (18 losses)
Most Shutouts, Season	6	1967-68 (74), 1976-77 (80)
Most PIM, Season	*2,670	1988-89 (80)
Most Goals, Game	12	Mar. 15/75 (Wsh. 1 at Pit. 12), Dec. 26/91 (Tor. 1 at Pit. 12)

Individual

Most Seasons	12	Mario Lemieux
Most Games	753	Jean Pronovost
Most Goals, Career	613	Mario Lemieux
Most Assists, Career	881	Mario Lemieux
Most Points, Career	1,494	Mario Lemieux (613G, 881A)
Most PIM, Career	980	Troy Loney
Most Shutouts, Career	11	Les Binkley
Longest Consecutive Games Streak	320	Ron Schock (Oct. 24/73-Apr. 3/77)
Most Goals, Season	85	Mario Lemieux (1988-89)
Most Assists, Season	114	Mario Lemieux (1988-89)
Most Points, Season	199	Mario Lemieux (1988-89; 85G, 114A)
Most PIM, Season	409	Paul Baxter (1981-82)
Most Points, Defenseman, Season	113	Paul Coffey (1988-89; 30G, 83A)
Most Points, Center, Season	199	Mario Lemieux (1988-89; 85G, 114A)
Most Points, Right Wing, Season	*149	Jaromir Jagr (1995-96; 62G, 87A)
Most Points, Left Wing, Season	123	Kevin Stevens (1991-92; 54G, 69A)
Most Points, Rookie, Season	100	Mario Lemieux (1984-85; 43G, 57A)
Most Shutouts, Season	6	Les Binkley (1967-68)
Most Goals, Game	5	Mario Lemieux (Three times)
Most Assists, Game	6	Ron Stackhouse (Mar. 8/75), Greg Malone (Nov. 28/79), Mario Lemieux (Three times)
Most Points, Game	8	Mario Lemieux (Oct. 15/88; 3G, 5A, Dec. 31/88; 5G, 3A)

* NHL Record.

Retired Numbers

21	Michel Brière	1969-1970

Coaching History

George Sullivan, 1967-68 to 1968-69; Red Kelly, 1969-70 to 1971-72; Red Kelly and Ken Schinkel, 1972-73; Ken Schinkel and Marc Boileau, 1973-74; Marc Boileau, 1974-75; Marc Boileau and Ken Schinkel, 1975-76; Ken Schinkel, 1976-77; John Wilson, 1977-78 to 1979-80; Eddie Johnston, 1980-81 to 1982-83; Lou Angotti, 1983-84; Bob Berry, 1984-85 to 1986-87; Pierre Creamer, 1987-88; Gene Ubriaco, 1988-89; Gene Ubriaco and Craig Patrick, 1989-90; Bob Johnson, 1990-91 to 1991-92; Scotty Bowman, 1991-92 to 1992-93; Eddie Johnston, 1993-94 to 1995-96; Eddie Johnston and Craig Patrick, 1996-97; Kevin Constantine, 1997-98.

Captains' History

Ab McDonald, 1967-68; no captain, 1968-69 to 1972-73; Ron Schock, 1973-74 to 1976-77; Jean Pronovost, 1977-78; Orest Kindrachuk, 1978-79 to 1980-81; Randy Carlyle, 1981-82 to 1983-84; Mike Bullard, 1984-85, 1985-86; Mike Bullard and Terry Ruskowski, 1986-87; Dan Frawley and Mario Lemieux, 1987-88; Mario Lemieux, 1988-89 to 1993-94; Ron Francis, 1994-95; Mario Lemieux, 1995-96 to 1996-97.

All-time Record vs. Other Clubs

Regular Season

	At Home							On Road							Total						
	GP	W	L	T	GF	GA	PTS	GP	W	L	T	GF	GA	PTS	GP	W	L	T	GF	GA	PTS
Anaheim	3	2	0	1	12	7	5	3	2	1	0	15	13	4	6	4	1	1	27	20	9
Boston	65	27	27	11	233	246	65	63	12	45	6	187	292	30	128	39	72	17	420	538	95
Buffalo	56	27	16	13	220	190	67	57	13	29	15	157	242	41	113	40	45	28	377	432	108
Calgary	40	20	10	10	150	128	50	40	9	24	7	122	177	25	80	29	34	17	272	305	75
Chicago	53	25	23	5	189	178	55	54	8	37	9	146	228	25	107	33	60	14	335	406	80
Colorado	30	15	11	4	130	123	34	27	12	14	1	110	126	25	57	27	25	5	240	249	59
Dallas	58	36	17	5	223	161	77	59	21	33	5	199	225	47	117	57	50	10	422	386	124
Detroit	59	40	15	4	264	177	84	60	11	38	11	165	239	33	119	51	53	15	429	416	117
Edmonton	25	12	12	1	100	116	25	25	5	19	1	87	134	11	50	17	31	2	187	250	36
Florida	8	6	1	1	30	21	13	8	4	4	0	20	23	8	16	10	5	1	50	44	21
Hartford	31	16	10	5	151	127	37	33	14	17	2	128	137	30	64	30	27	7	279	264	67
Los Angeles	66	38	20	8	249	207	84	64	15	41	8	168	251	38	130	53	61	16	417	458	122
Montreal	67	23	32	12	205	242	58	67	6	54	7	167	338	19	134	29	86	19	372	580	77
New Jersey	62	36	22	4	255	216	76	63	21	30	12	219	243	54	125	57	52	16	474	459	130
NY Islanders	70	33	26	11	269	246	77	69	25	36	8	230	285	58	139	58	62	19	499	531	135
NY Rangers	83	33	39	11	302	319	77	83	32	44	7	289	344	71	166	65	83	18	591	663	148
Ottawa	13	12	0	1	64	27	25	12	9	2	1	49	26	19	25	21	2	2	113	53	44
Philadelphia	88	39	32	17	308	286	95	89	15	67	7	229	392	37	177	54	99	24	537	678	132
Phoenix	25	18	7	0	109	74	36	24	13	9	2	89	88	28	49	31	16	2	198	162	64
St. Louis	58	27	19	12	221	178	66	59	14	39	6	160	231	34	117	41	58	18	381	409	100
San Jose	5	3	1	1	30	17	7	6	5	0	1	40	11	11	11	8	1	2	70	28	18
Tampa Bay	9	6	2	1	43	22	13	8	4	3	1	32	30	9	17	10	5	2	75	52	22
Toronto	56	30	20	6	237	182	66	55	18	26	11	185	229	47	111	48	46	17	422	411	113
Vancouver	45	30	8	7	208	153	67	45	21	21	3	173	165	45	90	51	29	10	381	318	112
Washington	69	37	26	6	275	229	80	72	29	37	6	270	312	64	141	66	63	12	545	541	144
Defunct Clubs	35	22	6	7	148	93	51	34	13	10	11	108	101	37	69	35	16	18	256	194	88
Totals	**1179**	**613**	**402**	**164**	**4625**	**3965**	**1390**	**1179**	**351**	**680**	**148**	**3744**	**4882**	**850**	**2358**	**964**	**1082**	**312**	**8369**	**8847**	**2240**

Playoffs

	Series	W	L	GP	W	L	T	GF	GA	Last Mtg.	Round	Result
Boston	4	2	2	19	10	9	0	67	62	1992	CF	W 4-0
Buffalo	1	1	0	3	2	1	0	9	9	1979	PR	W 2-1
Chicago	2	1	1	8	4	4	0	23	24	1992	F	W 4-0
Dallas	1	1	0	6	4	2	0	28	16	1991	F	W 4-2
Florida	1	0	1	7	3	4	0	15	20	1996	CF	L 3-4
New Jersey	3	2	1	17	9	8	0	56	47	1995	CSF	L 1-4
NY Islanders	3	0	3	19	8	11	0	58	67	1993	DF	L 3-4
NY Rangers	3	3	0	15	12	3	0	65	45	1996	CSF	W 4-1
Philadelphia	2	0	2	12	4	8	0	37	51	1997	CQF	L 1-4
St. Louis	3	1	2	13	6	7	0	40	45	1981	PR	L 2-3
Toronto	2	0	2	6	2	4	0	13	21	1977	PR	L 1-2
Washington	5	4	1	31	18	13	0	106	103	1996	CQF	W 4-2
Defunct Clubs	1	1	0	4	4	0	0	13	6			
Totals	**31**	**16**	**15**	**160**	**86**	**74**	**0**	**529**	**516**			

Playoff Results 1997-93

Year	Round	Opponent	Result	GF	GA
1997	CQF	Philadelphia	L 1-4	13	20
1996	CF	Florida	L 3-4	15	20
	CSF	NY Rangers	W 4-1	21	15
	CQF	Washington	W 4-2	21	17
1995	CSF	New Jersey	L 1-4	8	17
	CQF	Washington	W 4-3	29	26
1994	CQF	Washington	L 2-4	12	20
1993	DF	NY Islanders	L 3-4	27	24
	DSF	New Jersey	W 4-1	23	13

Abbreviations: Round: F – Final; **CF** – conference final; **CQF** – conference quarter-final; **CSF** – conference semi-final; **DF** – division final; **DSF** – division semi-final; **SF** – semi-final; **QF** – quarter-final; **PR** – preliminary round.

Calgary totals include Atlanta, 1972-73 to 1979-80. Colorado totals include Quebec, 1979-80 to 1994-95. Dallas totals include Minnesota, 1967-68 to 1992-93. New Jersey totals include Kansas City, 1974-75 to 1975-76, and Colorado Rockies, 1976-77 to 1981-82. Phoenix totals include Winnipeg, 1979-80 to 1995-96.

1996-97 Results

Oct.	5		Tampa Bay	3-4		10		NY Islanders	5-2
	8	at	Hartford	3-7		11	at	Ottawa	3-3
	11	at	Ottawa	2-3		14		Dallas	3-1
	12		Ottawa	3-2		15	at	Hartford	3-0
	16	at	NY Rangers	1-8		21		Calgary	4-2
	17	at	Buffalo	1-4		23		Colorado	3-4
	19		Washington	2-1		25		NY Rangers	4-7
	22	at	Edmonton	2-5		26	at	Montreal	5-2
	24	at	Calgary	5-7		29	at	Buffalo	1-3
	26	at	Vancouver	1-2	**Feb.**	1		Phoenix	4-1
Nov.	1	at	Washington	2-4		4		Vancouver	6-4
	2		Ottawa	7-3		5	at	Montreal	6-3
	6		Edmonton	5-2		8		Detroit	5-6
	8	at	Tampa Bay	5-5		12		NY Islanders	1-5
	9	at	Florida	2-4		15	at	Philadelphia	1-5
	12		Buffalo	3-0		16		Philadelphia	2-6
	14	at	Boston	1-2		18		Florida	4-2
	16		NY Rangers	3-8		22		Chicago	2-5
	19		St. Louis	4-2		23	at	NY Islanders	1-4
	21	at	Philadelphia	3-7		27	at	Detroit	1-4
	22	at	Hartford	7-1	**Mar.**	1	at	New Jersey	3-6
	27		Montreal	2-2		4		New Jersey	1-3
	30		Boston	6-2		5	at	Buffalo	2-4
Dec.	3		Hartford	4-4		8		Philadelphia	3-2
	4	at	Ottawa	4-2		10		Montreal	2-2
	6	at	Washington	5-3		12	at	Phoenix	5-5
	7		Anaheim	5-3		14	at	Colorado	3-6
	10	at	Los Angeles	5-3		16	at	Dallas	2-6
	11	at	Anaheim	7-3		18		Buffalo	5-3
	13	at	San Jose	4-0		20		Toronto	6-3
	15	at	Chicago	1-2		22		New Jersey	2-3
	17		Boston	4-6		24	at	NY Rangers	0-3
	19	at	St. Louis	4-0		26	at	Montreal	5-8
	21		San Jose	3-1		29		Los Angeles	4-1
	23	at	Toronto	6-5		31		Florida	4-3
	26		Montreal	3-3	**Apr.**	3		Hartford	5-5
	28		Buffalo	2-0		5		Ottawa	5-2
	30		Washington	5-3		8		Boston	3-1
Jan.	2	at	New Jersey	6-1		10	at	Tampa Bay	3-4
	4		Tampa Bay	7-3		11	at	Florida	2-4
	7	at	NY Islanders	5-3		13	at	Boston	3-7

Entry Draft
Selections 1997-83

1997
Pick
17	Robert Dome
44	Brian Gaffaney
71	Josef Melichar
97	Alexandre Mathieu
124	Harlan Pratt
152	Petr Havelka
179	Mark Moore
208	Andrew Ference
234	Eric Lind

1996
Pick
23	Craig Hillier
28	Pavel Skrbek
72	Boyd Kane
77	Boris Protsenko
105	Michal Rozsival
150	Peter Bergman
186	Eric Meloche
238	Timo Seikkula

1995
Pick
24	Alexei Morozov
76	J-Sebastien Aubin
102	Oleg Belov
128	Jan Hrdina
154	Alexei Kolkunov
180	Derrick Pyke
206	Sergei Voronov
232	Frank Ivankovic

1994
Pick
24	Chris Wells
50	Richard Park
57	Sven Butenschon
73	Greg Crozier
76	Alexei Krivchenkov
102	Thomas O'Connor
128	Clint Johnson
154	Valentin Morozov
161	Serge Aubin
180	Drew Palmer
206	Boris Zelenko
232	Jason Godbout
258	Mikhail Kazakevich
284	Brian Leitza

1993
Pick
26	Stefan Bergkvist
52	Domenic Pittis
62	Dave Roche
104	Jonas Andersson-Junkka
130	Chris Kelleher
156	Patrick Lalime
182	Sean Selmser
208	Larry McMorran
234	Timothy Harberts
260	Leonid Toropchenko
286	Hans Jonsson

1992
Pick
19	Martin Straka
43	Marc Hussey
67	Travis Thiessen
91	Todd Klassen
115	Philipp De Rouville
139	Artem Kopot
163	Jan Alinc
187	Fran Bussey
211	Brian Bonin
235	Brian Callahan

1991
Pick
16	Markus Naslund
38	Rusty Fitzgerald
60	Shane Peacock
82	Joe Tamminen
104	Robert Melanson
126	Brian Clifford
148	Ed Patterson
170	Peter McLaughlin
192	Jeff Lembke
214	Chris Tok
236	Paul Dyck
258	Pasi Huura

1990
Pick
5	Jaromir Jagr
61	Joe Dziedzic
68	Chris Tamer
89	Brian Farrell
107	Ian Moran
110	Denis Casey
130	Mika Valila
131	Ken Plaquin
145	Pat Neaton
152	Petteri Koskimaki
173	Ladislav Karabin
194	Timothy Fingerhut
215	Michael Thompson
236	Brian Bruininks

1989
Pick
16	Jamie Heward
37	Paul Laus
58	John Brill
79	Todd Nelson
100	Tom Nevers
121	Mike Markovich
126	Mike Needham
142	Patrick Schafhauser
163	Dave Shute
184	Andrew Wolf
205	Greg Hagen
226	Scott Farrell
247	Jason Smart

1988
Pick
4	Darrin Shannon
25	Mark Major
62	Daniel Gauthier
67	Mark Recchi
88	Greg Andrusak
130	Troy Mick
151	Jeff Blaeser
172	Rob Gaudreau
193	Donald Pancoe
214	Cory Laylin
235	Darren Stolk

1987
Pick
5	Chris Joseph
26	Richard Tabaracci
47	Jamie Leach
68	Risto Kurkinen
89	Jeff Waver
110	Shawn McEachern
131	Jim Bodden
152	Jim Kucera
173	Jack MacDougall
194	Daryn McBride
215	Mark Carlson
236	Ake Lilljebjorn

1986
Pick
4	Zarley Zalapski
25	Dave Capuano
46	Brad Aitken
67	Rob Brown
88	Sandy Smith
109	Jeff Daniels
130	Doug Hobson
151	Steve Rohlik
172	Dave McIlwain
193	Kelly Cain
214	Stan Drulia
235	Rob Wilson

1985
Pick
2	Craig Simpson
23	Lee Giffin
58	Bruce Racine
86	Steve Gotaas
107	Kevin Clemens
114	Stuart Marston
128	Steve Titus
149	Paul Stanton
170	Jim Paek
191	Steve Shaunessy
212	Doug Greschuk
233	Gregory Choules

1984
Pick
1	Mario Lemieux
9	Doug Bodger
16	Roger Belanger
64	Mark Teevens
85	Arto Javanainen
127	Tom Ryan
169	John Del Col
189	Steve Hurt
210	Jim Steen
230	Mark Ziliotto

1983
Pick
15	Bob Errey
22	Todd Charlesworth
58	Mike Rowe
63	Frank Pietrangelo
103	Patrick Emond
123	Paul Ames
163	Marty Ketola
183	Alec Haidy
203	Garth Hildebrand
223	Dave Goertz

General Manager

PATRICK, CRAIG
General Manager, Pittsburgh Penguins. Born in Detroit, MI, May 20, 1946.

Known for his calm and patient management style, Patrick has led the Penguins to two Stanley Cups, one Presidents' Trophy and four division championships since taking over as g.m. on Dec. 5, 1989. Under his leadership, Pittsburgh has the League's second-best winning percentage in the 1990s (.594) — trailing only Detroit.

Patrick also has served two stints as interim coach of the Penguins, most recently over the final 20 games of the 1996-97 season.

A member of one of hockey's most famous families — including grandfather Lester, father Lynn and uncle Muzz — Patrick played collegiate hockey at the University of Denver and captained the Pioneers to the NCAA championship in 1969. He played eight NHL seasons with five different teams, registering 72 goals and 163 points in 401 games before retiring in 1979. He made the transition to management and coaching when he landed the dual role of assistant coach and assistant g.m. of the 1980 U.S. Olympic Team that won the gold medal at Lake Placid.

Patrick joined the New York Rangers organization as director of operations in 1980 and became the youngest general manager in club history on June 14, 1981. He served in that capacity through the 1985-86 season, leading his team to the playoffs every year.

Prior to joining the Penguins, Patrick spent two years as director of athletics and recreation at the University of Denver.

NHL Coaching Record

		Regular Season					Playoffs			
Season	Team	Games	W	L	T	%	Games	W	L	%
1980-81	NY Rangers	59	26	23	10	.525	14	7	7	.500
1984-85	NY Rangers	35	11	22	2	.343	3	0	3	.000
1989-90	Pittsburgh	54	22	26	6	.463	....	....	....	....
1996-97	Pittsburgh	20	7	10	3	.425	5	1	4	.200
	NHL Totals	**168**	**66**	**81**	**21**	**.455**	**22**	**8**	**14**	**.364**

Club Directory

Civic Arena
66 Mario Lemieux Place
Pittsburgh, PA 15219
Phone **412/642-1300**
FAX 412/642-1859
Media Relations FAX
412/642-1322
Capacity: 16,958

Ownership	Howard L. Baldwin and Roger M. Marino
Co-Managing Directors	Howard L. Baldwin and Roger M. Marino

Administration
President	Donn Patton
Executive Vice President, Pgh Sports Associates	Jack Kelley
Vice President, General Counsel	Greg Cribbs
Director of Planning and Design	Scott Baldwin
Marketing Consultant	Bill Barnes
Executive Assistants	Elaine Heufelder, Paula Nichols, Amy Hirsh
Receptionist	Pam Douglas
President, Igloo Development Associates	Chuck Greenberg

Hockey Operations
Executive VP/General Manager	Craig Patrick
Assistant General Manager	Ed Johnston
Head Coach	Kevin Constantine
Assistant Coaches	Mike Eaves, Randy Hillier, Don Jackson, Rick Kehoe, Troy Ward
Goaltending Coach & Scout	Gilles Meloche
Head Scout	Greg Malone
Scouts	Les Binkley, Herb Brooks, Charlie Hodge, Mark Kelley, Ralph Cox
Professional Scout	Glenn Patrick
Strength and Conditioning Coach	John Welday
Equipment Manager	Steve Latin
Trainer	Charles "Skip" Thayer
Team Physician	Dr. Charles Burke
Team Dentist	Dr. David Donatelli
Executive Assistant	Tracey Botsford
Assistant Equipment Manager	Paul Flati

Communications
Vice President, Communications	Tom McMillan
Director of Media Relations	Steve Bovino
Assistant Director, Media Relations	Brian Coe
Director of Public Relations	Cindy Himes
Director of Entertainment	Kevin Smith
Manager, Community Relations	Renee Petrichevich

Finance
Vice President, Finance & Administration	Bob Vogel
Controller	Kevin Hart
Accounting Staff	Lisa Kreutzer, Tawni Love, Mark Oresic, Troy Ussack

Ticketing
Vice President, Ticket Sales	Jeff Barrett
Director, Premium Seating	Rich Hixon
Manager, Premium Services	Terry Smith
Assistant Manager, Premium Services	Michelle Follen
Premium Seating Representative	Brian Magness
Managers, Corporate Ticket Sales	Mark Anderson, Bian Slais
Group Sales Director	Fred Traynor
Group Sales Representative	Ward Russell
Box Office Manager	Carol Coulson
Customer Service Manager	Allison Quigley
Telemarketing Manager	James Santilli
Assistant Telemarketing Manager	Chad Slencak
Ticket Sales Representatives	Neil Bossola, Laura Bryer
Ticketing Staff	Heather Abramovitz, Daneen Napolitano

Advertising
Vice President, Advertising	David Soltesz
Managers, Corporate Sponsorships	Jackie Mateosky-Alger, Taylor Baldwin, Kimberly Bogesdorfer, Arden Robbins, Mimi York
Director of Event Marketing	Kevin Saundry
Marketing Manager	Marie Mays
Assistant Marketing Manager	Amy Gillespie, Xander Paumgarten
Marketing and Sales Administrator	Barb Pilarski

Iceoplex at Southpointe
Vice President, General Manager	Howard Baldwin Jr.
Director of Skating	Igor Novodran
Director of Operations	Dan Kaschalk
Assistant Director of Operations	Paul McKean
Director of Hockey Programs	Joanne DeFazio
Administrative Assistant	Nicole Kaschalk
Director of Publicity and Youth Hockey	Harry Sanders
Staff	Robert Dyer, Ryan Mance, Robert Arquillo

General Information
Dimensions of Rink	200 feet by 85 feet
Team Colors	Black, Gold and White
TV Stations	Fox Sports Pittsburgh, WPTT/UPN22 and WPGH/Fox 53
TV Announcers	Mike Lange, Paul Steigerwald
Flagship Radio Station	WDVE (102.5 FM)
Radio Announcers	Matt McConnell, TBA

General Managers' History

Jack Riley, 1967-68 to 1969-70; "Red" Kelly, 1970-71; "Red" Kelly and Jack Riley, 1971-72; Jack Riley, 1972-73; Jack Riley and Jack Button, 1973-74; Jack Button, 1974-75; Wren Blair, 1975-76; Wren A. Blair and Baz Bastien, 1976-77; Baz Bastien, 1977-78 to 1982-83; Ed Johnston, 1983-84 to 1987-88; Tony Esposito, 1988-89; Tony Esposito and Craig Patrick, 1989-90; Craig Patrick, 1990-91 to date.

St. Louis Blues

1996-97 Results: 36w-35L-11T 83PTS. Fourth, Central Division

Year-by-Year Record

		Home			Road			Overall							
Season	GP	W	L	T	W	L	T	W	L	T	GF	GA	Pts.	Finished	Playoff Result
1996-97	82	17	20	4	19	15	7	36	35	11	236	239	83	4th, Central Div.	Lost Conf. Quarter-Final
1995-96	82	15	17	9	17	17	7	32	34	16	219	248	80	4th, Central Div.	Lost Conf. Semi-Final
1994-95	48	16	6	2	12	9	3	28	15	5	178	135	61	2nd, Central Div.	Lost Conf. Quarter-Final
1993-94	84	23	11	8	17	22	3	40	33	11	270	283	91	4th, Central Div.	Lost Conf. Quarter-Final
1992-93	84	22	13	7	15	23	4	37	36	11	282	278	85	4th, Norris Div.	Lost Div. Final
1991-92	80	25	12	3	11	21	8	36	33	11	279	266	83	3rd, Norris Div.	Lost Div. Semi-Final
1990-91	80	24	9	7	23	13	4	47	22	11	310	250	105	2nd, Norris Div.	Lost Div. Final
1989-90	80	20	15	5	17	19	4	37	34	9	295	279	83	2nd, Norris Div.	Lost Div. Final
1988-89	80	22	11	7	11	24	5	33	35	12	275	285	78	2nd, Norris Div.	Lost Div. Final
1987-88	80	18	17	5	16	21	3	34	38	8	278	294	76	2nd, Norris Div.	Lost Div. Final
1986-87	80	21	12	7	11	21	8	32	33	15	281	293	79	1st, Norris Div.	Lost Div. Semi-Final
1985-86	80	23	11	6	14	23	3	37	34	9	302	291	83	3rd, Norris Div.	Lost Conf. Championship
1984-85	80	21	12	7	16	19	5	37	31	12	299	288	86	1st, Norris Div.	Lost Div. Semi-Final
1983-84	80	23	14	3	9	27	4	32	41	7	293	316	71	2nd, Norris Div.	Lost Div. Final
1982-83	80	16	16	8	9	24	7	25	40	15	285	316	65	4th, Norris Div.	Lost Div. Semi-Final
1981-82	80	22	14	4	10	26	4	32	40	8	315	349	72	3rd Norris Div.	Lost Div. Final
1980-81	80	29	7	4	16	11	13	45	18	17	352	281	107	1st, Smythe Div.	Lost Quarter-Final
1979-80	80	20	13	7	14	21	5	34	34	12	266	278	80	2nd, Smythe Div.	Lost Prelim. Round
1978-79	80	14	20	6	4	30	6	18	50	12	249	348	48	3rd, Smythe Div.	Out of Playoffs
1977-78	80	12	20	8	8	27	5	20	47	13	195	304	53	4th, Smythe Div.	Out of Playoffs
1976-77	80	22	13	5	10	26	4	32	39	9	239	276	73	1st, Smythe Div.	Lost Quarter-Final
1975-76	80	20	12	8	9	25	6	29	37	14	249	290	72	3rd, Smythe Div.	Lost Prelim. Round
1974-75	80	23	13	4	12	18	10	35	31	14	269	267	84	2nd, Smythe Div.	Lost Prelim. Round
1973-74	78	16	16	7	10	24	5	26	40	12	206	248	64	6th, West Div.	Out of Playoffs
1972-73	78	21	11	7	11	23	5	32	34	12	233	251	76	4th, West Div.	Lost Quarter-Final
1971-72	78	17	17	5	11	22	6	28	39	11	208	247	67	3rd, West Div.	Lost Semi-Final
1970-71	78	23	7	9	11	18	10	34	25	19	223	208	87	2nd, West Div.	Lost Quarter-Final
1969-70	76	24	9	5	13	18	7	37	27	12	224	179	86	1st, West Div.	Lost Final
1968-69	76	21	8	9	16	17	5	37	25	14	204	157	88	1st, West Div.	Lost Final
1967-68	74	18	12	7	9	19	9	27	31	16	177	191	70	3rd, West Div.	Lost Final

1997-98 Schedule

Oct.	Wed.	1	Buffalo
	Fri.	3	Phoenix
	Sat.	4	at Dallas
	Thu.	9	Los Angeles
	Sat.	11	Florida
	Mon.	13	Carolina
	Fri.	17	at Chicago
	Sat.	18	NY Rangers
	Mon.	20	at Detroit
	Wed.	22	at Carolina
	Thu.	23	Vancouver
	Sat.	25	Washington
	Wed.	29	at Philadelphia
	Thu.	30	Colorado
Nov.	Sat.	1	San Jose
	Mon.	3	Philadelphia
	Thu.	6	at Chicago
	Sat.	8	at Colorado*
	Mon.	10	at Dallas
	Thu.	13	Boston
	Sat.	15	Detroit
	Mon.	17	at Toronto
	Thu.	20	Edmonton
	Sat.	22	Anaheim
	Tue.	25	at Phoenix
	Thu.	27	Los Angeles
	Sat.	29	at NY Islanders
Dec.	Tue.	2	at New Jersey
	Thu.	4	Toronto
	Sat.	6	Calgary
	Mon.	8	Vancouver
	Wed.	10	at Montreal
	Thu.	11	at Ottawa
	Sat.	13	Edmonton
	Mon.	15	Ottawa
	Thu.	18	New Jersey
	Sat.	20	Pittsburgh
	Mon.	22	at Tampa Bay
	Tue.	23	at Florida
	Fri.	26	Chicago
	Sat.	27	Anaheim

	Mon.	29	at Washington
	Wed.	31	at Detroit
Jan.	Sat.	3	Calgary
	Tue.	6	at San Jose
	Wed.	7	at Vancouver
	Sat.	10	at Calgary
	Mon.	12	at Edmonton
	Wed.	14	Dallas
	Tue.	20	at NY Rangers
	Thu.	22	NY Islanders
	Sat.	24	at Chicago*
	Mon.	26	at Pittsburgh
	Tue.	27	at Buffalo
	Thu.	29	Toronto
	Sat.	31	Dallas*
Feb.	Wed.	4	at Toronto
	Thu.	5	at Boston
	Sat.	7	Detroit*
	Thu.	26	at San Jose
	Sat.	28	at Los Angeles*
Mar.	Sun.	1	at Anaheim
	Tue.	3	Chicago
	Thu.	5	Montreal
	Sat.	7	Dallas*
	Mon.	9	at Vancouver
	Wed.	11	at Colorado
	Sat.	14	Phoenix*
	Sat.	21	at Edmonton
	Sun.	22	at Calgary
	Thu.	26	Tampa Bay
	Sat.	28	Detroit*
	Mon.	30	San Jose
Apr.	Wed.	1	at Toronto
	Sat.	4	Colorado*
	Tue.	7	at Detroit
	Thu.	9	Chicago
	Sat.	11	Phoenix*
	Sun.	12	at Dallas
	Thu.	16	at Los Angeles
	Sat.	18	at Phoenix*
	Sun.	19	at Anaheim

* Denotes afternoon game.

Franchise date: June 5, 1967

WESTERN CONFERENCE

CENTRAL DIVISION

31st NHL Season

Acquired from Montreal early in the 1996-97 season, Pierre Turgeon showed his considerable flair in the offensive zone, leading the Blues in assists (49) and game-winning goals (7).

1997-98 Player Personnel

FORWARDS	HT	WT	S	Place of Birth	Date	1996-97 Club
ATCHEYNUM, Blair	6-2	210	R	Estevan, Sask.	4/20/69	Hershey
CAMPBELL, Jim	6-2	185	R	Worcester, MA	4/3/73	St. Louis
CONROY, Craig	6-2	198	R	Potsdam, NY	9/4/71	Fredericton-St. Louis-Worcester
COURTNALL, Geoff	6-1	195	L	Duncan, B.C.	8/18/62	St. Louis
DEMITRA, Pavol	6-0	189	L	Dubnica, Czech.	11/29/74	Dukla Trencin-Vegas-StL-Grand Rapids
HULL, Brett	5-10	201	R	Belleville, Ont.	8/9/64	St. Louis
KENADY, Chris	6-2	195	R	Mound, MN	4/10/73	Worcester
LACHANCE, Bob	5-11	180	R	Northampton, MA	2/1/74	Worcester
LOW, Reed	6-4	220	R	Moose Jaw, Sask.	6/21/76	Moose Jaw
MAYERS, Jamal	6-0	190	R	Toronto, Ont.	10/24/74	St. Louis-Worcester
MURPHY, Joe	6-1	190	L	London, Ont.	10/16/67	St. Louis
PELLERIN, Scott	5-11	180	L	Shediac, N.B.	1/9/70	St. Louis-Worcester
PETROVICKY, Robert	5-11	172	L	Kosice, Czech.	10/26/73	St. Louis-Worcester
POESCHEK, Rudy	6-2	218	R	Kamloops, B.C.	9/29/66	Tampa Bay
RAMSAY, Bruce	6-0	180	L	Dryden, Ont.	5/13/69	Thunder Bay-Grand Rapids
ROY, Stephane	5-10	173	L	Ste-Martine, Que.	1/26/76	Worcester
SHAFRANOV, Konstantin	5-11	176	L	Ust-Kamenogorsk, USSR	9/11/68	St. Louis-Worcester
TOPOROWSKI, Shayne	6-2	210	R	Paddockwood, Sask.	8/6/75	Toronto-St. John's
TURCOTTE, Darren	6-0	178	L	Boston, MA	3/2/68	San Jose
TURGEON, Pierre	6-1	195	L	Rouyn, Que.	8/28/69	Montreal-St. Louis
TWIST, Tony	6-1	220	L	Sherwood Park, Alta.	5/9/68	St. Louis
YAKE, Terry	5-11	190	R	New Westminster, B.C.	10/22/68	Rochester
YORK, Harry	6-2	215	L	Panoka, Alta.	4/16/74	St. Louis
ZUKIWSKY, Jonathan	6-2	185	L	St. Paul, Alta.	10/7/77	Red Deer
DEFENSEMEN						
BERGEVIN, Marc	6-1	197	L	Montreal, Que.	8/11/65	St. Louis
DUCHESNE, Steve	5-11	195	L	Sept-Iles, Que.	6/30/65	Ottawa
FITZPATRICK, Rory	6-1	205	R	Rochester, NY	1/11/75	Montreal-St. Louis-Worcester
GODYNYUK, Alexander	6-0	207	L	Kiev, Ukraine	1/27/70	Hartford
HOLLINGER, Terry	6-1	200	L	Regina, Sask.	2/24/71	Rochester
MacINNIS, Al	6-2	196	R	Inverness, N.S.	7/11/63	St. Louis
McALPINE, Chris	6-0	210	R	Roseville, MN	12/1/71	Albany-St. Louis
PERSSON, Ricard	6-2	205	L	Ostersund, Sweden	8/24/69	New Jersey-Albany-St. Louis
PRONGER, Chris	6-5	220	L	Dryden, Ont.	10/10/74	St. Louis
RIVERS, Jamie	6-0	190	L	Ottawa, Ont.	3/16/75	St. Louis-Worcester
VIRTUE, Terry	6-0	200	R	Scarborough, Ont.	8/12/70	Worcester
ZABRANSKY, Libor	6-3	196	L	Brno, Czech.	11/25/73	St. Louis-Worcester
GOALTENDERS	**HT**	**WT**	**C**	**Place of Birth**	**Date**	**1996-97 Club**
FUHR, Grant	5-9	190	R	Spruce Grove, Alta.	9/28/62	St. Louis
McLENNAN, Jamie	6-0	190	L	Edmonton, Alta.	6/30/71	Worcester
PARENT, Rich	6-3	195	L	Montreal, Que.	1/12/73	Detroit (IHL)
ROCHE, Scott	6-4	220	L	Lindsay, Ont.	3/19/77	North Bay-Windsor
SCOTT, Travis	6-2	185	L	Kanata, Ont.	9/14/75	Baton Rouge-Worcester

Coaching History

Lynn Patrick and Scotty Bowman, 1967-68; Scotty Bowman, 1968-69 to 1969-70; Al Arbour and Scotty Bowman, 1970-71; Sid Abel, Bill McCreary and Al Arbour, 1971-72; Al Arbour and Jean-Guy Talbot, 1972-73; Jean-Guy Talbot and Lou Angotti, 1973-74; Lou Angotti, Lynn Patrick and Garry Young, 1974-75; Garry Young, Lynn Patrick and Leo Boivin, 1975-76; Emile Francis, 1976-77; Leo Boivin and Barclay Plager, 1977-78; Barclay Plager, 1978-79; Barclay Plager and Red Berenson, 1979-80; Red Berenson, 1980-81; Red Berenson and Emile Francis, 1981-82; Emile Francis and Barclay Plager, 1982-83; Jacques Demers, 1983-84 to 1985-86; Jacques Martin, 1986-87 to 1987-88; Brian Sutter, 1988-89 to 1991-92; Bob Plager and Bob Berry, 1992-93; Bob Berry, 1993-94; Mike Keenan, 1994-95 to 1995-96; Mike Keenan, Jim Roberts and Joel Quenneville, 1996-97; Joel Quenneville, 1997-98.

Coach

QUENNEVILLE, JOEL
Head Coach, St. Louis Blues.
Born in Windsor, Ont., September 15, 1958.

Joel Quenneville was named head coach on January 6, 1997, becoming the 19th head coach in Blues history. His first game behind the Blues' bench was on January 7, 1997. Coach "Q" guided the Blues to a 18-15-7 regular season record and a first round playoff match-up with the eventual Stanley Cup champion Detroit Red Wings.

Prior to joining the Blues the former NHL defenseman spent the past three seasons with the Colorado Avalanche organization as an assistant coach. He was instrumental in the Avalanche's drive for their first Stanley Cup during the 1995-96 season.

Prior to joining the Avalanche he was head coach for the Springfield Indians of the American Hockey League during the 1993-94 season. He retired from hockey after the 1991-92 season after serving the St. John's Maple Leafs (AHL) as a player/coach. Quenneville played 13 NHL seasons and finished with 803 career games played, 54 goals, 136 assists and 705 penalty minutes. His best years on the ice were spent with Hartford where he earned most valuable defenseman honors in 1985 and 1986. He played an integral part in helping Hartford win a divisional championship in 1986-87.

Quenneville and his wife Elizabeth have three children: Dylan, Lily and Anna.

Coaching Record

		Regular Season					Playoffs			
Season	Team	Games	W	L	T	%	Games	W	L	%
1996-97	St. Louis (NHL)	40	18	15	7	.538	6	2	4	.333

1996-97 Scoring

* – rookie

Regular Season

Pos	#	Player	Team	GP	G	A	Pts	+/–	PIM	PP	SH	GW	GT	S	%
C	77	Pierre Turgeon	MTL	9	1	10	11	4	2	0	0	0	0	22	4.5
			STL	69	25	49	74	4	12	5	0	7	1	194	12.9
			TOTAL	78	26	59	85	8	14	5	0	7	1	216	12.0
R	16	Brett Hull	STL	77	42	40	82	-9	10	12	2	6	2	302	13.9
L	14	Geoff Courtnall	STL	82	17	40	57	3	86	4	0	2	0	203	8.4
R	17	Joe Murphy	STL	75	20	25	45	-1	69	4	1	2	1	151	13.2
R	10 *	Jim Campbell	STL	68	23	20	43	3	68	5	0	6	1	169	13.6
D	2	Al MacInnis	STL	72	13	30	43	2	65	6	1	1	0	296	4.4
L	32	Stephane Matteau	STL	74	16	20	36	11	50	1	2	2	0	98	16.3
D	44	Chris Pronger	STL	79	11	24	35	15	143	4	0	0	0	147	7.5
C	37 *	Harry York	STL	74	14	18	32	1	24	3	1	3	0	86	16.3
D	5	Igor Kravchuk	STL	82	4	24	28	7	35	1	0	0	0	142	2.8
C	36	Robert Petrovicky	STL	44	7	12	19	2	10	0	0	1	0	54	13.0
R	39	Scott Pellerin	STL	54	8	10	18	12	35	0	2	2	0	76	10.5
C	22	Craig Conroy	STL	61	6	11	17	0	43	0	0	1	0	74	8.1
D	28	Ricard Persson	N.J.	1	0	0	0	0	0	0	0	0	0	2	0.0
			STL	53	4	8	12	-2	45	1	0	0	0	68	5.9
			TOTAL	54	4	8	12	-2	45	1	0	0	0	70	5.7
D	6 *	Jamie Rivers	STL	15	2	5	7	-4	6	1	0	0	0	9	22.2
C	23	Craig MacTavish	STL	50	2	5	7	-12	33	0	0	0	0	26	7.7
L	20	Mike Peluso	N.J.	20	0	2	2	0	68	0	0	0	0	14	0.0
			STL	44	2	3	5	0	158	0	0	0	0	23	8.7
			TOTAL	64	2	5	7	0	226	0	0	0	0	37	5.4
D	43 *	Libor Zabransky	STL	34	1	5	6	-1	44	0	0	1	0	26	3.8
L	26	Sergio Momesso	NYR	9	0	0	0	-2	11	0	0	0	0	11	0.0
			STL	31	1	3	4	-4	37	0	0	0	0	32	3.1
			TOTAL	40	1	3	4	-6	48	0	0	0	0	43	2.3
D	4	Marc Bergevin	STL	82	0	4	4	-9	53	0	0	0	0	30	0.0
R	38	Pavol Demitra	STL	8	3	0	3	0	2	2	0	1	0	15	20.0
R	26	Konstantin Shafranov	STL	5	2	1	3	1	0	0	0	0	0	8	25.0
R	27	Stephen Leach	STL	17	2	1	3	-2	24	0	0	0	0	33	6.1
R	12	Rob Pearson	STL	18	1	2	3	-5	37	0	0	0	0	14	7.1
L	18	Tony Twist	STL	64	1	2	3	-8	121	0	0	0	0	21	4.8
D	33	Trent Yawney	STL	39	0	2	2	2	17	0	0	0	0	8	0.0
G	31	Grant Fuhr	STL	73	0	2	2	0	6	0	0	0	0	0	0.0
L	13	Yuri Khmylev	STL	2	1	0	1	-1	2	0	0	0	0	3	33.3
R	38	Gary Leeman	STL	2	0	1	1	0	0	0	0	0	0	3	0.0
C	21 *	Jamal Mayers	STL	6	0	1	1	-3	2	0	0	0	0	7	0.0
D	42	Rory Fitzpatrick	MTL	6	0	1	1	-2	6	0	0	0	0	5	0.0
			STL	2	0	0	0	-2	2	0	0	0	0	1	0.0
			TOTAL	8	0	1	1	-4	8	0	0	0	0	6	0.0
R	15 *	Alexander Vasilevski	STL	3	0	0	0	-1	2	0	0	0	0	3	0.0
G	30	Jon Casey	STL	15	0	0	0	0	0	0	0	0	0	0	0.0
D	19 *	Chris McAlpine	STL	15	0	0	0	-2	24	0	0	0	0	3	0.0

Goaltending

No.	Goaltender	GPI	Mins	Avg	W	L	T	EN	SO	GA	SA	S%
31	Grant Fuhr	73	4261	2.72	33	27	11	4	3	193	1940	.901
30	Jon Casey	15	707	3.39	3	8	0	2	0	40	299	.866
	Totals	**82**	**4980**	**2.88**	**36**	**35**	**11**	**6**	**3**	**239**	**2245**	**.894**

Playoffs

Pos	#	Player	Team	GP	G	A	Pts	+/–	PIM	PP	SH	GW	OT	S	%
R	16	Brett Hull	STL	6	2	7	9	4	2	0	0	0	0	25	8.0
L	14	Geoff Courtnall	STL	6	3	1	4	0	23	1	0	2	0	11	27.3
R	38	Pavol Demitra	STL	6	1	3	4	3	6	0	0	0	0	8	12.5
D	2	Al MacInnis	STL	6	1	2	3	-1	4	1	0	0	0	22	4.5
C	77	Pierre Turgeon	STL	5	1	1	2	0	2	1	0	0	0	8	12.5
R	17	Joe Murphy	STL	6	1	1	2	-2	10	1	0	0	0	8	12.5
D	44	Chris Pronger	STL	6	1	1	2	0	22	0	0	0	0	19	5.3
R	10 *	Jim Campbell	STL	4	1	0	1	-1	6	1	0	0	0	6	16.7
D	4	Marc Bergevin	STL	6	1	0	1	2	8	0	0	0	0	4	25.0
D	19 *	Chris McAlpine	STL	4	0	1	1	1	0	0	0	0	0	6	0.0
C	23	Craig MacTavish	STL	1	0	0	0	-1	2	0	0	0	0	0	0.0
D	5	Igor Kravchuk	STL	2	0	0	0	-1	2	0	0	0	0	6	0.0
C	36	Robert Petrovicky	STL	2	0	0	0	1	0	0	0	0	0	1	0.0
L	26	Sergio Momesso	STL	3	0	0	0	0	6	0	0	0	0	0	0.0
L	32	Stephane Matteau	STL	5	0	0	0	0	0	0	0	0	0	2	0.0
L	20	Mike Peluso	STL	5	0	0	0	-1	25	0	0	0	0	1	0.0
C	37 *	Harry York	STL	5	0	0	0	-1	2	0	0	0	0	2	0.0
G	31	Grant Fuhr	STL	6	0	0	0	0	4	0	0	0	0	0	0.0
R	27	Stephen Leach	STL	6	0	0	0	-2	33	0	0	0	0	8	0.0
L	18	Tony Twist	STL	6	0	0	0	0	0	0	0	0	0	0	0.0
C	22	Craig Conroy	STL	6	0	0	0	-1	8	0	0	0	0	4	0.0
R	39	Scott Pellerin	STL	6	0	0	0	-1	6	0	0	0	0	7	0.0
D	28	Ricard Persson	STL	6	0	0	0	-1	27	0	0	0	0	1	0.0

Goaltending

No.	Goaltender	GPI	Mins	Avg	W	L	EN	SO	GA	SA	S%
31	Grant Fuhr	6	357	2.18	2	4	0	2	13	183	.929
	Totals	**6**	**360**	**2.17**	**2**	**4**	**0**	**2**	**13**	**183**	**.929**

Captains' History

Al Arbour, 1967-68 to 1969-70; Red Berenson and Barclay Plager, 1970-71; Barclay Plager, 1971-72 to 1975-76; no captain, 1976-77; Red Berenson, 1977-78; Barry Gibbs, 1978-79; Brian Sutter, 1979-80 to 1987-88; Bernie Federko, 1988-89; Rick Meagher, 1989-90; Scott Stevens, 1990-91; Garth Butcher, 1991-92; Brett Hull, 1992-93 to 1994-95; Brett Hull, Shayne Corson and Wayne Gretzky, 1995-96; no captain, 1996-97.

Club Records

Team

(Figures in brackets for season records are games played; records for fewest points, wins, ties, losses, goals, goals against are for 70 or more games)

Most Points	**107**	1980-81 (80)
Most Wins	**47**	1990-91 (80)
Most Ties	**19**	1970-71 (78)
Most Losses	**50**	1978-79 (80)
Most Goals	**352**	1980-81 (80)
Most Goals Against	**349**	1981-82 (80)
Fewest Points	**48**	1978-79 (80)
Fewest Wins	**18**	1978-79 (80)
Fewest Ties	**7**	1983-84 (80)
Fewest Losses	**18**	1980-81 (80)
Fewest Goals	**177**	1967-68 (74)
Fewest Goals Against	**157**	1968-69 (76)
Longest Winning Streak		
Overall	**7**	Jan. 21-Feb. 3/88, Mar. 19-31/91
Home	**9**	Jan. 26-Feb. 26/91
Away	**4**	Four times
Longest Undefeated Streak		
Overall	**12**	Nov. 10-Dec. 8/68 (5 wins, 7 ties)
Home	**11**	Feb. 12-Mar. 19/69 (5 wins, 6 ties), Feb. 7-Mar. 29/75 (9 wins, 2 ties), Oct. 7-Nov. 26/93 (7 wins, 4 ties)
Away	**7**	Dec. 9-26/87 (4 wins, 3 ties)
Longest Losing Streak		
Overall	**7**	Nov. 12-26/67, Feb. 12-25/89
Home	**5**	Nov. 19-Dec. 6/77
Away	**10**	Jan. 20/82-Mar. 8/82
Longest Winless Streak		
Overall	**12**	Jan. 17-Feb. 15/78 (10 losses, 2 ties)
Home	**7**	Dec. 28/82-Jan. 25/83 (5 losses, 2 ties)
Away	**17**	Jan. 23-Apr. 7/74 (14 losses, 3 ties)
Most Shutouts, Season	**13**	1968-69 (76)
Most PIM, Season	**2,041**	1990-91 (80)
Most Goals, Game	**11**	Feb. 26/94 (St.L. 11 at Ott. 1)

Individual

Most Seasons	**13**	Bernie Federko
Most Games	**927**	Bernie Federko
Most Goals, Career	**500**	Brett Hull
Most Assists, Career	**721**	Bernie Federko
Most Points, Career	**1,073**	Bernie Federko
Most PIM, Career	**1,786**	Brian Sutter
Most Shutouts, Career	**16**	Glenn Hall
Longest Consecutive Games Streak	**662**	Garry Unger (Feb. 7/71-Apr. 8/79)
Most Goals, Season	**86**	Brett Hull (1990-91)
Most Assists, Season	**90**	Adam Oates (1990-91)
Most Points, Season	**131**	Brett Hull (1990-91) (86G, 45A)
Most PIM, Season	**306**	Bob Gassoff (1975-76)
Most Points, Defenseman, Season	**78**	Jeff Brown (1992-93; 25G, 53A)
Most Points, Center, Season	**115**	Adam Oates (1990-91; 25G, 90A)
Most Points, Right Wing, Season	**131**	Brett Hull (1990-91; 86G, 45A)
Most Points, Left Wing, Season	**102**	Brendan Shanahan (1993-94; 52G, 50A)
Most Points, Rookie, Season	**73**	Jorgen Pettersson (1980-81; 37G, 36A)
Most Shutouts, Season	**8**	Glenn Hall (1968-69)
Most Goals, Game	**6**	Red Berenson (Nov. 7/68)
Most Assists, Game	**5**	Brian Sutter (Nov. 22/88), Bernie Federko (Feb. 27/88), Adam Oates (Jan. 26/91)
Most Points, Game	**7**	Red Berenson (Nov. 7/68; 6G, 1A), Garry Unger (Mar. 13/71; 3G, 4A)

Retired Numbers

3	Bob Gassoff	1973-1977
8	Barclay Plager	1967-1977
11	Brian Sutter	1976-1988
24	Bernie Federko	1976-1989

All-time Record vs. Other Clubs

Regular Season

	At Home							On Road							Total						
	GP	W	L	T	GF	GA	PTS	GP	W	L	T	GF	GA	PTS	GP	W	L	T	GF	GA	PTS
Anaheim	8	5	3	0	30	25	10	8	4	3	1	21	23	9	16	9	6	1	51	48	19
Boston	54	22	23	9	171	190	53	53	11	34	8	143	233	30	107	33	57	17	314	423	83
Buffalo	45	26	13	6	167	117	58	46	12	29	5	142	190	29	91	38	42	11	309	307	87
Calgary	49	21	20	8	171	153	50	48	20	24	4	141	169	44	97	41	44	12	312	322	94
Chicago	95	45	33	17	317	298	107	99	29	56	14	303	389	72	194	74	89	31	620	687	179
Colorado	26	18	6	2	117	85	38	26	11	12	3	88	96	25	52	29	18	5	205	181	63
Dallas	103	56	28	19	379	294	131	100	36	45	19	299	343	91	203	92	73	38	678	637	222
Detroit	91	49	27	15	328	257	113	90	38	37	15	288	323	91	181	87	64	30	616	580	204
Edmonton	30	13	13	4	117	122	30	30	12	15	3	117	123	27	60	25	28	7	234	245	57
Florida	3	2	1	0	8	6	4	3	1	1	1	7	6	3	6	3	2	1	15	12	7
Hartford	25	15	8	2	101	81	32	26	14	10	2	83	81	30	51	29	18	4	184	162	62
Los Angeles	64	41	15	8	244	167	90	64	22	33	9	182	231	53	128	63	48	17	426	398	143
Montreal	53	11	27	15	136	189	37	54	9	38	7	145	239	25	107	20	65	22	281	428	62
New Jersey	40	25	9	6	176	124	56	41	16	18	7	121	135	39	81	41	27	13	297	259	95
NY Islanders	42	17	17	8	155	140	42	43	10	23	10	108	166	30	85	27	40	18	263	306	72
NY Rangers	57	22	26	9	168	185	53	55	6	43	6	124	233	18	112	28	69	15	292	418	71
Ottawa	4	2	1	1	14	14	5	4	3	1	0	22	8	6	8	5	2	1	36	22	11
Philadelphia	61	24	30	7	179	192	55	61	10	41	10	139	245	30	122	34	71	17	318	437	85
Phoenix	35	17	9	9	132	105	43	37	13	18	6	113	122	32	72	30	27	15	245	227	75
Pittsburgh	59	39	14	6	231	160	84	58	19	27	12	178	221	50	117	58	41	18	409	381	134
San Jose	13	10	3	0	50	29	20	10	9	1	0	38	26	18	23	19	4	0	88	55	38
Tampa Bay	6	5	1	0	25	17	10	7	3	3	1	23	22	7	13	8	4	1	48	39	17
Toronto	92	53	26	13	323	259	119	91	24	57	10	262	347	58	183	77	83	23	585	606	177
Vancouver	57	31	18	8	211	175	70	58	26	25	7	183	180	59	115	57	43	15	394	355	129
Washington	35	14	13	8	144	120	36	34	12	19	3	101	125	27	69	26	32	11	245	245	63
Defunct Clubs	32	25	4	3	131	55	53	33	11	10	12	95	100	34	65	36	14	15	226	155	87
Totals	**1179**	**608**	**388**	**183**	**4225**	**3559**	**1399**	**1179**	**381**	**623**	**175**	**3466**	**4376**	**937**	**2358**	**989**	**1011**	**358**	**7691**	**7935**	**2336**

Playoffs

	Series	W	L	GP	W	L	T	GF	GA	Last Mtg.	Round	Result
Boston	2	0	2	8	0	8	0	15	48	1972	SF	L 0-4
Buffalo	1	0	1	3	1	2	0	8	7	1976	PR	L 1-2
Calgary	1	0	1	7	3	4	0	22	28	1986	CF	L 3-4
Chicago	9	2	7	45	18	27	0	129	166	1993	DSF	W 4-0
Dallas	10	5	5	56	26	30	0	162	174	1994	CQF	L 0-4
Detroit	5	2	3	29	13	16	0	79	88	1997	CQF	L 2-4
Los Angeles	1	1	0	4	4	0	0	16	5	1969	SF	W 4-0
Montreal	3	0	3	12	0	12	0	14	42	1977	QF	L 0-4
NY Rangers	1	0	1	6	2	4	0	22	29	1981	QF	L 2-4
Philadelphia	2	2	0	11	8	3	0	34	20	1969	QF	W 4-0
Pittsburgh	3	2	1	13	7	6	0	45	40	1981	PR	W 3-2
Toronto	5	3	2	31	17	14	0	88	90	1996	CQF	W 4-2
Vancouver	1	0	1	7	3	4	0	27	27	1995	CQF	L 3-4
Winnipeg	1	1	0	4	3	1	0	20	13	1982	DSF	W 3-1
Totals	**45**	**18**	**27**	**236**	**105**	**131**	**0**	**681**	**777**			

Calgary totals include Atlanta, 1972-73 to 1979-80. Colorado totals include Quebec, 1979-80 to 1994-95. Dallas totals include Minnesota, 1967-68 to 1992-93. New Jersey totals include Kansas City, 1974-75 to 1975-76, and Colorado Rockies, 1976-77 to 1981-82. Phoenix totals include Winnipeg, 1979-80 to 1995-96.

Playoff Results 1997-93

Year	Round	Opponent	Result	GF	GA
1997	CQF	Detroit	L 2-4	12	13
1996	CSF	Detroit	L 3-4	16	22
	CQF	Toronto	W 4-2	21	15
1995	CQF	Vancouver	L 3-4	27	27
1994	CQF	Dallas	L 0-4	10	16
1993	DF	Toronto	L 3-4	11	22
	DSF	Chicago	W 4-0	13	6

Abbreviations: Round: F – Final; **CF** – conference final; **CQF** – conference quarter-final; **CSF** – conference semi-final; **DF** – division final; **DSF** – division semi-final; **SF** – semi-final; **QF** – quarter-final; **PR** – preliminary round.

1996-97 Results

Oct.	4		Colorado	4-2		5	at	New Jersey	5-3
	6		Chicago	1-4		7		Edmonton	2-5
	9	at	Calgary	3-1		9	at	San Jose	4-3
	11	at	Edmonton	3-1		11	at	Los Angeles	1-2
	12	at	Vancouver	3-5		15	at	Phoenix	4-1
	17		Toronto	6-1		20	at	NY Islanders	6-4
	18	at	NY Rangers	1-2		23		Vancouver	4-3
	20		San Jose	2-3		25	at	Montreal	8-1
	22	at	Phoenix	2-1		27		Anaheim	1-4
	24	at	Chicago	4-6		29	at	Toronto	4-0
	26		Washington	4-6		30	at	Ottawa	5-2
	30	at	Colorado	3-6	**Feb.**	1		Detroit	1-4
Nov.	1		Buffalo	2-4		4	at	Detroit	1-1
	3		Dallas	6-3		6		Dallas	6-4
	5	at	Toronto	3-6		8	at	Boston	3-3
	8	at	Vancouver	4-2		10		Phoenix	2-4
	9	at	Calgary	3-2		13		NY Rangers	4-1
	14		Tampa Bay	5-3		15		Colorado	2-5
	16		Calgary	2-0		17		Chicago	4-2
	17		Anaheim	4-2		20		Ottawa	1-1
	19	at	Pittsburgh	2-4		22		Detroit	2-2
	21		Phoenix	4-3		23		Calgary	3-5
	23		Florida	1-3		25	at	Tampa Bay	2-3
	27	at	Anaheim	3-2		27	at	Florida	2-3
Dec.	1		San Jose	3-4	**Mar.**	5	at	Dallas	2-3
	3	at	Toronto	0-2		9		Edmonton	1-4
	5		Phoenix	0-3		11	at	San Jose	4-3
	6	at	Colorado	4-3		13	at	Los Angeles	4-2
	8	at	Edmonton	3-2		14	at	Anaheim	4-4
	11	at	Dallas	5-5		17	at	Phoenix	2-3
	13		Chicago	1-4		20		Hartford	4-1
	15		Vancouver	0-8		23		Dallas	1-4
	17	at	Hartford	3-5		25	at	Washington	2-3
	19		Pittsburgh	0-4		27		Los Angeles	2-1
	21	at	Philadelphia	0-4		30		Philadelphia	3-2
	22		Los Angeles	7-4	**Apr.**	1	at	Detroit	1-1
	26	at	Chicago	4-4		3		NY Islanders	5-5
	27		Toronto	2-3		6		New Jersey	0-2
	29		Boston	4-2		9	at	Chicago	1-0
Jan.	2		Montreal	2-2		10		Toronto	5-1
	3	at	Buffalo	2-2		13	at	Detroit	3-1

Entry Draft
Selections 1997-83

1997	**1993**	**1989**	**1986**
Pick	**Pick**	**Pick**	**Pick**
40 Tyler Rennette	37 Maxim Bets	9 Jason Marshall	10 Jocelyn Lemieux
86 Didier Tremblay	63 Jamie Rivers	31 Rick Corriveau	31 Mike Posma
98 Jan Horacek	89 Jamal Mayers	55 Denny Felsner	52 Tony Hejna
106 Jame Pollock	141 Todd Kelman	93 Daniel Laperriere	73 Glen Featherstone
149 Nicholas Bilotto	167 Mike Buzak	114 David Roberts	87 Michael Wolak
177 Ladislav Nagy	193 Eric Boguniecki	124 Derek Frenette	115 Mike O'Toole
206 Bobby Haglund	219 Michael Grier	135 Jeff Batters	136 Andy May
232 Dmitri Plekhanov	245 Libor Prochazka	156 Kevin Plager	157 Randy Skarda
244 Marek Ivan	271 Alexander Vasilevsky	177 John Roderick	178 Martyn Ball
	275 Christer Olsson	198 John Valo	199 Rod Thacker
1996		219 Brian Lukowski	220 Terry MacLean
Pick	**1992**		234 Bill Butler
14 Marty Reasoner	**Pick**	**1988**	241 David O'Brien
67 Gordie Dwyer	38 Igor Korolev	**Pick**	
95 Jonathan Zukiwsky	62 Vitali Karamnov	9 Rod Brind' Amour	**1985**
97 Andrei Petrakov	64 Vitali Prokhorov	30 Adrien Plavsic	**Pick**
159 Stephen Wagner	86 Lee J. Leslie	51 Rob Fournier	37 Herb Raglan
169 Daniel Corso	134 Bob Lachance	72 Jaan Luik	44 Nelson Emerson
177 Reed Low	158 Ian LaPerriere	105 Dave Lacouture	54 Ned Desmond
196 Andrei Podkonicky	160 Lance Burns	114 Dan Fowler	100 Dan Brooks
203 Anthony Hutchins	180 Igor Boldin	135 Matt Hayes	121 Rich Burchill
229 Konstantin Shafranov	182 Nicholas Naumenko	156 John McCoy	138 Pat Jablonski
	206 Todd Harris	177 Tony Twist	159 Scott Brickey
1995	230 Yuri Gunko	198 Bret Hedican	180 Jeff Urban
Pick	259 Wade Salzman	219 Heath DeBoer	201 Vince Guidotti
49 Jochen Hecht		240 Michael Francis	222 Ron Saatzer
75 Scott Roche	**1991**		243 Dave Jecha
101 Michal Handzus	**Pick**	**1987**	
127 Jeff Ambrosio	27 Steve Staios	**Pick**	**1984**
153 Denis Hamel	64 Kyle Reeves	12 Keith Osborne	**Pick**
179 J-Luc Grand-Pierre	65 Nathan Lafayette	54 Kevin Miehm	26 Brian Benning
205 Derek Bekar	87 Grayden Reid	59 Robert Nordmark	32 Tony Hrkac
209 Libor Zabransky	109 Jeff Callinan	75 Darin Smith	50 Toby Ducolon
	131 Bruce Gardiner	82 Andy Rymsha	53 Robert Dirk
1994	153 Terry Hollinger	117 Rob Robinson	56 Alan Perry
Pick	175 Christopher Kenady	138 Todd Crabtree	71 Graham Herring
68 Stephane Roy	197 Jed Fiebelkorn	159 Guy Hebert	92 Scott Paluch
94 Tyler Harlton	219 Chris MacKenzie	180 Robert Dumas	113 Steve Tuttle
120 Edvin Frylen	241 Kevin Rappana	201 David Marvin	134 Cliff Ronning
172 Roman Vopat	263 Mike Veisor	207 Andy Cesarski	148 Don Porter
198 Steve Noble		222 Dan Rolfe	155 Jim Vesey
224 Marc Stephan	**1990**	243 Ray Savard	176 Daniel Jomphe
250 Kevin Harper	**Pick**		196 Tom Tilley
276 Scott Fankhouser	33 Craig Johnson	**1983**	217 Mark Cupolo
	54 Patrice Tardif	DID NOT DRAFT	237 Mark Lanigan
	96 Jason Ruff		
	117 Kurtis Miller		
	138 Wayne Conlan		
	180 Parris Duffus		
	201 Steve Widmeyer		
	222 Joe Hawley		
	243 Joe Fleming		

General Managers' History

Lynn Patrick, 1967-68; Scotty Bowman, 1968-69 to 1970-71; Lynn Patrick, 1971-72; Sid Abel, 1972-73; Charles Catto, 1973-74; Gerry Ehman, 1974-75; Dennis Ball, 1975-76; Emile Francis, 1976-77 to 1982-83; Ron Caron, 1983-84 to 1993-94; Mike Keenan, 1994-95 to 1995-96; Mike Keenan and Ron Caron, 1996-97; Larry Pleau, 1997-98.

General Manager

PLEAU, LARRY
General Manager, St. Louis Blues.
Born in Lynn, MA, June 29, 1947.

Larry Pleau was named general manager on June 9, 1997, becoming the 10th person to hold that position in team history.

Pleau joins the Blues after spending the past eight seasons with the New York Rangers organization, most recently as vice president of player personnel. He joined the Rangers in 1989 as assistant general manager of player development. During Pleau's tenure in New York, the Rangers drafted NHL stars Sergei Zubov, Doug Weight, Alexei Kovalev, Niklas Sundstrom, Todd Marchant and Sergei Nemchinov, along with Corey Hirsch, Daniel Goneau and Mattias Norstrom. Prior to joining the Rangers, Pleau spent 17 seasons with the Hartford Whalers organization as a player, assistant coach, head coach, general manager and minor league general manager and head coach.

He was also instrumental in drafting Ray Ferraro, Ron Francis, Kevin Dineen and Ulf Samuelsson while a member of the Whalers organization.

Pleau played three seasons with the Montreal Canadiens (1969-1972) in the National Hockey League before being the first player signed by the Hartford Whalers of the World Hockey Association. He was a center/left wing for the Whalers from 1972 until his retirement in 1979. He played in 468 regular season games for Hartford, accumulating 157 goals and 215 assists for 372 points. He also played for the 1968 United States Olympic Team, the 1969 U.S. National Team and for Team USA in the 1976 Canada Cup tournament.

Pleau and his wife, Wendy have two children: son, Steve, and daughter, Shannon.

Club Directory

Kiel Center
1401 Clark Avenue
St. Louis, MO 63103-2709
Phone **314/622-2500**
FAX 314/622-2582
Capacity: 19,260

Board of Directors . . . . Jerry Ritter, Robert M. Cox Jr., Juanita Hinshaw, Ted C. Wetterau, Karen Jennings, Lee Liberman, Todd R. Schnuck

Executive
Chairman of the Board . . . . Jerry Ritter
President and CEO. Mark Sauer
Senior Vice President & General Manager . . . . Larry Pleau
Senior Vice President, Marketing
  & Communications. . . . . Jim Woodcock
Senior Advisor . . . . Ronald Caron
Vice President, Sales . . . . Bruce Affleck
Vice President, Finance & Hockey Administration . . Jerry Jasiek
Vice President, Marketing . . . . Jo Ann Miles
Executive Assistant to Chairman . . . . Shirley Langbein
Executive Assistant to President. . . . . Jan Carlock
Executive Assistant to General Manager . . . . Donna Lemke

Hockey Operations
Assistant General Manager . . . . John Ferguson, Jr.
Head Coach. . . . . Joel Quenneville
Assistant Coaches . . . . Roger Nielson, Jim Roberts
Director of Pro Scouting . . . . Bob Plager
Pro Scouts . . . . Rick Meagher, Bill Dineen
Director of Amateur Scouting . . . . Teddy Hampson
Special Assignment . . . . Jack Evans
Amateur Scouts. . . . . Don Boyd, Matt Keator, Anders Steen, Bill Terry
Part-time Scouts . . . . Jim Bzdel, Dick Cherry, Wayne Mundey, Miroslav Termer, Ken Williamson, Georgi Zhuravlev
Director of Team Services . . . . Michael Caruso
Video Coordinator . . . . TBD
Head Coach, Worcester IceCats . . . . Greg Gilbert
Associate Coach, Worcester IceCats . . . . Paul Pickard

Medical Staff
Athletic Trainer . . . . Ray Barile
Massage Therapist. Jeff Cope
Strength & Conditioning Coach . . . . Bob Kersee
Equipment Manager . . . . Burt Godin
Assistant Equipment Manager. . . . . Eric Bechtol
Equipment Assistant . . . . TBD
Orthopedic Surgeon . . . . TBD
Internist . . . . Dr. Aaron Birenbaum
General Surgery. . . . . Dr. Michael Brunt
Dentist. . . . . Dr. Glenn Edwards
Optometrist . . . . Dr. N. Rex Ghormley
Physical Therapist . . . . Randy Craig

Communications/Marketing
Director of Communications . . . . Jeff Trammel
Assistant Director of Communications. . . . . Tony Ommen
Communications Interns . . . . Joe Campbell, Renee St. John
Director of Corporate Sponsorships. . . . . Chris Arger
Manager of Corporate Sales & Promotions . . . . . Rob Rixford
Manager of Community Relations/
  Fan Development . . . . Yvette Horwitz
Manager of Amateur Hockey &
  Community Programs. . . . . Dan Kelly
Marketing/Public Relations Assistant . . . . Donna Quirk
Receptionists . . . . Pam Barrett, Leslie Simon

Finance/Sales
Director of Finance . . . . Jeff Horstmann
Sales Representatives. . . . . John Casson, Wes Edwards, Jill Mann, Kari Palmer, Karen Meyer, Jennifer Gruner
Accounting Staff . . . . Jim Bergman, Craig Bryant, Marsha McBride, Fred Giles, Phil Siddle

San Jose Sharks

1996-97 Results: 27W-47L-8T 62PTS. Seventh, Pacific Division

Year-by-Year Record

		Home			Road			Overall							
Season	GP	W	L	T	W	L	T	W	L	T	GF	GA	Pts.	Finished	Playoff Result
1996-97	82	14	23	4	13	24	4	27	47	8	211	278	62	7th, Pacific Div.	Out of Playoffs
1995-96	82	12	26	3	8	29	4	20	55	7	252	357	47	7th, Pacific Div.	Out of Playoffs
1994-95	48	10	13	1	9	12	3	19	25	4	129	161	42	3rd, Pacific Div.	Lost Conf. Semi-Final
1993-94	84	19	13	10	14	22	6	33	35	16	252	265	82	3rd, Pacific Div.	Lost Conf. Semi-Final
1992-93	84	8	33	1	3	38	1	11	71	2	218	414	24	6th, Smythe Div.	Out of Playoffs
1991-92	80	14	23	3	3	35	2	17	58	5	219	359	39	6th, Smythe Div.	Out of Playoffs

1997-98 Schedule

Oct.	Wed.	1	Edmonton
	Sat.	4	Chicago
	Tue.	7	Ottawa
	Thu.	9	at Colorado
	Sat.	11	Boston
	Mon.	13	Philadelphia
	Thu.	16	NY Islanders
	Sun.	19	at Phoenix
	Wed.	22	Pittsburgh
	Sat.	25	at New Jersey
	Mon.	27	at NY Islanders
	Wed.	29	at Detroit
	Fri.	31	at Chicago
Nov.	Sat.	1	at St. Louis
	Tue.	4	Toronto
	Fri.	7	Montreal
	Sat.	8	Tampa Bay
	Mon.	10	at Anaheim
	Wed.	12	Vancouver
	Thu.	13	at Los Angeles
	Sat.	15	Phoenix
	Tue.	18	Anaheim
	Thu.	20	at Philadelphia
	Sat.	22	at Washington
	Mon.	24	at Montreal
	Tue.	25	at Toronto
	Fri.	28	New Jersey
	Sun.	30	at Edmonton
Dec.	Mon.	1	at Calgary
	Thu.	4	at Vancouver
	Wed.	10	Washington
	Fri.	12	at Dallas
	Sun.	14	at Chicago*
	Tue.	16	Detroit
	Thu.	18	Vancouver
	Sun.	21	at Anaheim
	Fri.	26	Phoenix
	Mon.	29	at Tampa Bay
	Tue.	30	at Florida
Jan.	Fri.	2	at Detroit
	Sat.	3	at Boston
	Tue.	6	St. Louis
	Sat.	10	Buffalo
	Mon.	12	Dallas
	Wed.	14	Los Angeles
	Thu.	15	at Colorado
	Wed.	21	Calgary
	Fri.	23	Edmonton
	Sat.	24	Florida
	Tue.	27	Anaheim
	Thu.	29	Chicago
	Sat.	31	Colorado*
Feb.	Mon.	2	NY Rangers
	Wed.	4	at Edmonton
	Thu.	5	at Calgary
	Sat.	7	at Vancouver
	Thu.	26	St. Louis
	Sat.	28	at Edmonton
Mar.	Mon.	2	Carolina
	Thu.	5	Detroit
	Fri.	6	at Anaheim
	Mon.	9	Toronto
	Wed.	11	at NY Rangers
	Thu.	12	at Buffalo
	Sat.	14	at Carolina
	Mon.	16	Los Angeles
	Wed.	18	Dallas
	Sat.	21	Colorado*
	Sun.	22	at Phoenix
	Tue.	24	Los Angeles
	Thu.	26	at Los Angeles
	Sat.	28	at Dallas*
	Mon.	30	at St. Louis
Apr.	Wed.	1	at Pittsburgh
	Thu.	2	at Ottawa
	Sat.	4	at Toronto
	Tue.	7	Calgary
	Thu.	9	Anaheim
	Sat.	11	Vancouver
	Wed.	15	at Calgary
	Thu.	16	at Colorado
	Sat.	18	Calgary

* Denotes afternoon game.

Franchise date: May 9, 1990

WESTERN CONFERENCE

PACIFIC DIVISION

7th NHL Season

Tony Granato, who returned to the NHL after recovering from brain surgery, was granted a special exemption to play in his home rink at the 1997 All-Star Game in San Jose. At the end of the season, he was awarded the Masterton Trophy for perseverance, sportsmanship and dedication to hockey.

1997-98 Player Personnel

FORWARDS	HT	WT	S	Place of Birth	Date	1996-97 Club
BRADLEY, Matt	6-1	168	R	Stittsville, Ont.	6/13/78	Kingston-Kentucky
BURR, Shawn	6-1	200	L	Sarnia, Ont.	7/1/66	Tampa Bay
COLAGIACOMO, Adam	6-2	206	R	Toronto, Ont.	3/17/79	London-Oshawa
CRAVEN, Murray	6-2	185	L	Medicine Hat, Alta.	7/20/64	Chicago
CYRENNE, Cory	5-9	170	L	Winnipeg, Man.	8/25/77	Brandon
DONOVAN, Shean	6-2	200	R	Timmins, Ont.	1/22/75	San Jose-Kentucky
EWEN, Todd	6-2	230	R	Saskatoon, Sask.	3/22/66	San Jose
FRIESEN, Jeff	6-0	190	L	Meadow Lake, Sask.	8/5/76	San Jose
GRANATO, Tony	5-10	185	R	Downers Grove, IL	6/25/64	San Jose
GUOLLA, Stephen	6-0	180	L	Scarborough, Ont.	3/15/73	San Jose-Kentucky
KOROLYUK, Alexander	5-9	170	L	Moscow, USSR	1/15/76	Soviet Wings-Manitoba
KOZLOV, Viktor	6-5	225	R	Togliatti, USSR	2/14/75	San Jose
MAKINEN, Marko	6-5	200	R	Turku, Finland	3/31/77	Kiekko-Espoo-Kiekko-67
MARLEAU, Patrick	6-2	190	L	Swift Current, Sask.	9/15/79	Seattle
MATTEAU, Stephane	6-3	215	L	Rouyn-Noranda, Que.	9/2/69	St. Louis
NAZAROV, Andrei	6-5	230	R	Chelyabinsk, USSR	5/22/74	San Jose-Kentucky
NICHOLLS, Bernie	6-	185	R	Haliburton, Ont.	6/24/61	San Jose
NITTEL, Adam	6-	215	R	Kitchener, Ont.	7/17/78	Erie (OHL)
NOLAN, Owen	6-1	201	R	Belfast, Ireland	2/12/72	San Jose
POTOMSKI, Barry	6-2	215	L	Windsor, Ont.	11/24/72	Los Angeles-Phoenix (IHL)
ROED, Peter	5-10	210	L	St. Paul, MN	11/15/76	Prince George-Louisville
SKALDE, Jarrod	6-0	175	L	Niagara Falls, Ont.	2/26/71	Saint John
STURM, Marco	5-11	178	L	Dingolfing, Germany	9/8/78	Landshut
SUTTER, Ron	6-0	180	R	Viking, Alta.	12/2/63	San Jose
THIBEAULT, David	6-1	190	L	Trois-Rivieres, Que.	5/12/78	Victoriaville
WOOD, Dody	6-	200	L	Chetwynd, B.C.	3/18/72	San Jose-Kansas City
YEGOROV, Alexei	5-11	195	L	St. Petersburg, USSR	5/21/75	San Jose-Kentucky
DEFENSEMEN						
ALLEN, Peter	6-2	195	R	Calgary, Alta.	3/6/70	Cleveland
BODGER, Doug	6-2	210	L	Chemainus, B.C.	6/18/66	San Jose
BOIKOV, Alexander	6-0	180	L	Chelyabinsk, USSR	2/7/75	Kentucky
BRENNAN, Rich	6-2	200	R	Schenectady, NY	11/26/72	Colorado-Hershey
GILL, Todd	6-0	180	L	Cardinal, Ont.	11/9/65	San Jose
HANNAN, Scott	6-1	210	L	Richmond, B.C.	1/23/79	Kelowna
HOULDER, Bill	6-2	211	L	Thunder Bay, Ont.	3/11/67	Tampa Bay
IAFRATE, Al	6-3	235	L	Dearborn, MI	3/21/66	San Jose
McSORLEY, Marty	6-1	235	R	Hamilton, Ont.	5/18/63	San Jose
ODUYA, Fredrik	6-3	200	L	Stockholm, Sweden	5/31/75	Kentucky
RAGNARSSON, Marcus	6-1	215	L	Ostervala, Sweden	8/13/71	San Jose
RATHJE, Mike	6-6	220	L	Mannville, Alta.	5/11/74	San Jose
WIDMER, Jason	6-0	200	L	Calgary, Alta.	8/1/73	San Jose-Kentucky
ZYUZIN, Andrei	6-1	187	L	Ufa, USSR	1/21/78	Ufa Salavat

GOALTENDERS	HT	WT	C	Place of Birth	Date	1996-97 Club
HRUDEY, Kelly	5-10	189	L	Edmonton, Alta.	1/13/61	San Jose
NABOKOV, Yevgeni	6-0	180	L	Ust-Kamenogorsk, USSR	7/25/75	Moscow D'amo
RAM, Jamie	5-11	175	L	Scarborough, Ont.	1/18/71	Kentucky
VERNON, Mike	5-9	165	L	Calgary, Alta.	2/24/63	Detroit

Captains' History

Doug Wilson, 1991-92 to 1992-93; Bob Errey, 1993-94; Bob Errey and Jeff Odgers, 1994-95; Jeff Odgers, 1995-96; Todd Gill, 1996-97.

General Managers' History

Jack Ferreira, 1991-92; Office of the General Manager: Chuck Grillo (V.P. Director of Player Personnel) and Dean Lombardi (V.P. Director of Hockey Operations), 1992-93 to 1995-96; Dean Lombardi, 1996-97 to date.

General Manager

LOMBARDI, DEAN
Executive Vice President and General Manager, San Jose Sharks.
Born in Holyoke, Massachusetts, March 5, 1958.

Dean Lombardi, 39, is a ten-year veteran of NHL front office duties. A charter member of the Sharks' management team, Lombardi joined the club in 1990 as assistant general manager after having served in a similar capacity with the Minnesota North Stars. He was named San Jose's director of hockey operations on June 26, 1992 and became the club's general manager on March 6, 1996. As the team's top hockey executive, he oversees player personnel decisions, negotiates player contracts and coordinates the efforts of the Sharks' scouting and player evaluation departments.

Lombardi oversaw the acquisition of key veterans for the Sharks: forwards Owen Nolan, Bernie Nicholls, Tony Granato and Darren Turcotte; goaltender Kelly Hrudey and defensemen Doug Bodger, Marty McSorley, Todd Gill and Al Iafrate. He is also firmly committed to building through the Entry Draft. San Jose draft picks making important contributions to the club include forwards Jeff Friesen, Viktor Kozlov, Shean Donovan and Andrei Nazarov along with defensemen Marcus Ragnarsson and Mike Rathje.

After the 1993-94 season that saw the Sharks post an NHL record single-season improvement of 58 points, Lombardi finished third in The Hockey News award voting for executive of the year.

1996-97 Scoring

* – rookie

Regular Season

Pos	#	Player	Team	GP	G	A	Pts	+/–	PIM	PP	SH	GW	GT	S	%
R	11	Owen Nolan	S.J.	72	31	32	63	-19	155	10	0	3	1	225	13.8
C	39	Jeff Friesen	S.J.	82	28	34	62	-8	75	6	2	5	2	200	14.0
C	9	Bernie Nicholls	S.J.	65	12	33	45	-21	63	2	1	0	1	137	8.8
L	25	Viktor Kozlov	S.J.	78	16	25	41	-16	40	4	0	4	0	184	8.7
L	21	Tony Granato	S.J.	76	25	15	40	-7	159	5	1	4	0	231	10.8
C	8	Darren Turcotte	S.J.	65	16	21	37	-8	16	3	1	4	0	126	12.7
R	62	Andrei Nazarov	S.J.	60	12	15	27	-4	222	1	0	1	0	116	10.3
L	17 *	Stephen Guolla	S.J.	43	13	8	21	-10	14	2	0	1	1	81	16.0
D	23	Todd Gill	S.J.	79	0	21	21	-20	101	0	0	0	0	101	0.0
D	4	Greg Hawgood	S.J.	63	6	12	18	-22	69	3	0	0	1	83	7.2
D	10	Marcus Ragnarsson	S.J.	69	3	14	17	-18	63	2	0	0	0	57	5.3
D	33	Marty McSorley	S.J.	57	4	12	16	-6	186	0	1	1	1	74	5.4
D	3	Doug Bodger	S.J.	81	1	15	16	-14	64	0	0	1	0	96	1.0
R	42	Shean Donovan	S.J.	73	9	6	15	-18	42	0	1	0	0	115	7.8
D	43	Al Iafrate	S.J.	38	6	9	15	-10	91	3	0	0	0	91	6.6
C	12	Ron Sutter	S.J.	78	5	7	12	-8	65	1	2	1	0	78	6.4
L	22	Bob Errey	DET	36	1	2	3	-3	27	0	0	0	0	34	2.9
			S.J.	30	3	6	9	-2	20	0	0	0	0	38	7.9
			TOTAL	66	4	8	12	-5	47	0	0	0	0	72	5.6
D	44	Vlastimil Kroupa	S.J.	35	2	6	8	-17	12	2	0	1	0	24	8.3
D	40	Mike Rathje	S.J.	31	0	8	8	-1	21	0	0	0	0	22	0.0
C	16	Dody Wood	S.J.	44	3	2	5	-3	193	0	0	0	0	43	7.0
L	7	Ville Peltonen	S.J.	28	2	3	5	-8	0	1	0	0	0	35	5.7
L	18	Chris Tancill	S.J.	25	4	0	4	-5	8	1	0	0	0	20	20.0
R	19	Tim Hunter	S.J.	46	0	4	4	0	135	0	0	0	0	13	0.0
L	14	Ray Whitney	S.J.	12	0	2	2	-6	4	0	0	0	0	24	0.0
R	36	Todd Ewen	S.J.	51	0	2	2	-5	162	0	0	0	0	22	0.0
D	5 *	Jason Widmer	S.J.	2	0	1	1	1	0	0	0	0	0	0	0.0
R	15 *	Alexei Yegorov	S.J.	2	0	1	1	1	0	0	0	0	0	0	0.0
C	28	Iain Fraser	S.J.	2	0	0	0	-1	2	0	0	0	0	0	0.0
R	91 *	Jan Caloun	S.J.	2	0	0	0	-2	0	0	0	0	0	3	0.0
G	31	Wade Flaherty	S.J.	7	0	0	0	0	0	0	0	0	0	0	0.0
D	26	Chris Lipuma	S.J.	8	0	0	0	-2	22	0	0	0	0	4	0.0
G	20	Ed Belfour	CHI	33	0	0	0	0	26	0	0	0	0	0	0.0
			S.J.	13	0	0	0	0	8	0	0	0	0	0	0.0
			TOTAL	46	0	0	0	0	34	0	0	0	0	0	0.0
G	32	Kelly Hrudey	S.J.	48	0	0	0	0	0	0	0	0	0	0	0.0

Goaltending

No.	Goaltender	GPI	Mins	Avg	W	L	T	EN	SO	GA	SA	S%
40	Chris Terreri	22	1200	2.75	6	10	3	4	0	55	553	.901
32	Kelly Hrudey	48	2631	3.19	16	24	5	4	0	140	1263	.889
20	Ed Belfour	13	757	3.41	3	9	0	1	1	43	371	.884
31	Wade Flaherty	7	359	5.18	2	4	0	0	0	31	202	.847
	Totals	**82**	**4970**	**3.36**	**27**	**47**	**8**	**9**	**1**	**278**	**2398**	**.884**

Coaching History

George Kingston, 1991-92 to 1992-93; Kevin Constantine, 1993-94 to 1994-95; Kevin Constantine and Jim Wiley, 1995-96; Al Sims, 1996-97; Darryl Sutter, 1997-98.

Coach

SUTTER, DARRYL JOHN
Coach, San Jose Sharks. Born in Viking, Alta., August 19, 1958.

Darryl Sutter, 39, became the Sharks' fifth head coach on June 9, 1997. Sutter played eight NHL seasons, all with the Chicago Blackhawks (1979-87). He began his coaching career as an assistant in Chicago in 1987-88 before taking over as head coach of the Blackhawks' IHL affiliate that played in Saginaw (1988-89) and in Indianapolis (1989-90). His club won an IHL Turner Cup championship in 1990 and Sutter was named coach of the year.

He later served as an associate coach under Mike Keenan in Chicago in 1990-91 and 1991-92 and began a three-year tenure as head coach of the Blackhawks in 1992-93. As coach of Chicago, Sutter's teams reached the playoffs in all three seasons. His career winning percentage of .569 ranks second among Chicago coaches. He resigned as head coach following the 1994-95 season to spend more time with his family and worked as a consultant to the Blackhawks for special assignments in 1995-96 and 1996-97.

In 16 years of hockey as a player and coach, Sutter has never failed to qualify for post-season play. During his eight-year playing career, he scored 116 goals and added 118 assists in 406 regular-season games. He added 24 goals and 19 assists in 51 playoff games. Drafted 179th overall by Chicago in the 1978 NHL Entry Draft, he scored a remarkable 40 goals during his rookie season. The left winger served as team captain from 1982-83 until injuries forced his retirement after the 1986-87 season.

He is one of six brothers to play in the NHL. The others are Brian, Brent, Duane, Rich and Ron. All are involved in the Sutter Foundation which raises raises money for non-profit organizations in their home province of Alberta.

Coaching Record

		Regular Season					Playoffs			
Season	Team	Games	W	L	T	%	Games	W	L	%
1988-89	Saginaw (IHL)	82	46	26	10	.560	6	2	4	.333
1989-90	Indianapolis (IHL)	82	53	21	8	.646	14	12	2	.857
1992-93	**Chicago (NHL)**	**84**	**47**	**25**	**12**	**.631**	**4**	**0**	**4**	**.000**
1993-94	**Chicago (NHL)**	**84**	**39**	**36**	**9**	**.518**	**6**	**2**	**4**	**.333**
1994-95	**Chicago (NHL)**	**48**	**24**	**19**	**5**	**.552**	**16**	**9**	**7**	**.563**
	NHL Totals	**216**	**110**	**80**	**26**	**.569**	**26**	**11**	**15**	**.423**

Club Records

Team

(Figures in brackets for season records are games played; records for fewest points, wins, ties, losses, goals, goals against are for 70 or more games)

Most Points	82	1993-94 (84)
Most Wins	33	1993-94 (84)
Most Ties	16	1993-94 (84)
Most Losses	*71	1992-93 (84)
Most Goals	252	1993-94 (84), 1995-96 (82)
Most Goals Against	414	1992-93 (84)
Fewest Points	24	1992-93 (84)
Fewest Wins	11	1992-93 (84)
Fewest Ties	*2	1992-93 (84)
Fewest Losses	35	1993-94 (84)
Fewest Goals	211	1996-97 (82)
Fewest Goals Against	265	1993-94 (84)

Longest Winning Streak
Overall ..... 7 Mar. 24-Apr. 5/94
Home ..... 5 Jan. 21-Feb. 15/95
Away ..... 4 Mar. 24-Apr. 5/94

Longest Undefeated Streak
Overall ..... 9 Mar. 20-Apr. 5/94
(7 wins, 2 ties)
Home ..... 6 Mar. 20-Apr. 13/94
(4 wins, 2 ties)
Away ..... 5 Two times

Longest Losing Streak
Overall ..... *17 Jan. 4/93-Feb. 12/93
Home ..... 9 Nov. 19/92-Dec. 19/92
Away ..... 19 Nov. 27/92-Feb. 12/93

Longest Winless Streak
Overall ..... 20 Dec. 29/92-Feb. 12/93
(19 losses, 1 tie)
Home ..... 9 Nov. 19/92-Dec. 18/92
(9 losses)
Away ..... 19 Nov. 27/92-Feb. 12/93
(19 losses)
Most Shutouts, Season 5 1994-95 (48)
Most PIM, Season 2134 1992-93 (84)
Most Goals, Game ..... 10 Jan. 13/96
(S.J. 10 at Pit. 8)

Individual

Most Seasons ..... 5 Pat Falloon, Jayson More, Jeff Odgers
Most Games, Career ..... 334 Jeff Odgers
Most Goals, Career ..... 76 Pat Falloon
Most Assists, Career ..... 86 Johan Garpenlov, Pat Falloon
Most Points, Career ..... 162 Pat Falloon (76G, 86A)
Most PIM, Career ..... 1,001 Jeff Odgers
Most Shutouts, Career ..... 8 Arturs Irbe
Longest Consecutive
Games Streak ..... 131 Viktor Kozlov
(Dec. 2/95-Mar. 26/97)
Most Goals, Season ..... 31 Owen Nolan (1996-97)
Most Assists, Season ..... 52 Kelly Kisio (1992-93)
Most Points, Season ..... 78 Kelly Kisio (1992-93; 26G, 52A)
Most PIM, Season ..... 326 Link Gaetz (1991-92)

Most Shutouts, Season ..... 4 Arturs Irbe (1994-95)
Most Points, Defenseman, Season ..... 64 Sandis Ozolinsh (1993-94; 26G, 38A)
Most Points, Center, Season ..... 78 Kelly Kisio (1992-93; 26G, 52A)
Most Points, Right Wing, Season ..... 68 Sergei Makarov (1993-94; 30G, 38A)
Most Points, Left Wing, Season ..... 66 Johan Garpenlov (1992-93; 22G, 44A)
Most Points, Rookie, Season ..... 59 Pat Falloon (1991-92; 25G, 34A)
Most Goals, Game ..... 4 Owen Nolan (Dec. 19/95)
Most Assists, Game ..... 4 Three times
Most Points, Game ..... 5 Owen Nolan (Dec. 19/95; 4G, 1A)

* NHL Record.

All-time Record vs. Other Clubs

Regular Season

	At Home						On Road						Total					
	GP	W	L	T	GF	GA	PTS	GP	W	L	T	GF	GA	PTS	GP	W	L	T	GF	GA	PTS
Anaheim	10	3	6	1	30	36	7	11	6	5	0	39	33	12	21	9	11	1	69	69	19
Boston	5	0	3	2	13	24	2	5	0	4	1	15	21	1	10	0	7	3	28	45	3
Buffalo	5	2	1	2	19	21	6	6	0	6	0	20	34	0	11	2	7	2	39	55	6
Calgary	19	3	15	1	44	72	7	17	6	11	0	48	80	12	36	9	26	1	92	152	19
Chicago	12	6	6	0	31	36	12	11	3	7	1	30	41	7	23	9	13	1	61	77	19
Colorado	10	4	6	0	37	49	8	8	3	6	2	21	44	4	18	6	12	2	58	93	12
Dallas	11	5	6	0	30	37	10	11	4	6	1	30	40	9	22	9	12	1	60	77	19
Detroit	12	2	9	1	37	63	5	11	0	11	0	16	58	0	23	2	20	1	53	121	5
Edmonton	18	10	7	1	65	56	21	18	2	13	3	40	73	7	36	12	20	4	105	129	28
Florida	3	1	1	1	7	9	3	3	0	1	2	6	9	2	6	1	2	3	13	18	5
Hartford	5	3	2	0	30	20	6	6	3	3	0	16	22	6	11	6	5	0	46	42	12
Los Angeles	18	9	6	3	70	61	21	18	5	12	1	50	68	11	36	14	18	4	120	129	32
Montreal	6	2	2	2	17	15	6	6	0	6	0	9	28	0	12	2	8	2	26	43	6
New Jersey	5	1	3	1	9	16	3	6	2	4	0	10	24	4	11	3	7	1	19	40	7
NY Islanders	5	2	2	1	13	19	5	6	0	5	1	19	33	1	11	2	7	2	32	52	6
NY Rangers	6	0	6	0	13	29	0	5	0	4	1	15	27	1	11	0	10	1	28	56	1
Ottawa	4	3	1	0	8	5	6	4	0	2	2	11	14	2	8	3	3	2	19	19	8
Philadelphia	6	1	5	0	11	21	2	5	1	3	1	11	22	3	11	2	8	1	22	43	5
Phoenix	14	7	5	2	58	57	16	16	4	9	3	47	60	11	30	11	14	5	105	117	27
Pittsburgh	6	0	5	1	11	40	1	5	1	3	1	17	30	3	11	1	8	2	28	70	4
St. Louis	10	1	9	0	26	38	2	13	3	10	0	29	50	6	23	4	19	0	55	88	8
Tampa Bay	5	0	5	0	15	24	0	5	2	3	0	12	17	4	10	2	8	0	27	41	4
Toronto	12	4	7	1	27	36	9	11	2	8	1	24	45	5	23	6	15	2	51	81	14
Vancouver	18	6	10	2	61	66	14	18	3	14	1	38	76	7	36	9	24	3	99	142	21
Washington	5	2	3	0	15	17	4	5	1	4	0	11	18	2	10	3	7	0	26	35	6
Totals	**230**	**77**	**131**	**22**	**697**	**867**	**176**	**230**	**50**	**160**	**20**	**584**	**967**	**120**	**460**	**127**	**291**	**42**	**1281**	**1834**	**296**

Playoffs

	Series	W	L	GP	W	L	T	GF	GA	Last Mtg.	Round	Result
Calgary	1	1	0	7	4	3	0	26	35	1995	CQF	W 4-3
Detroit	2	1	1	11	4	7	0	27	51	1995	CSF	L 0-4
Toronto	1	0	1	7	3	4	0	21	26	1994	CSF	L 3-4
Totals	**4**	**2**	**2**	**25**	**11**	**14**	**0**	**74**	**112**			

Playoff Results 1997-93

Year	Round	Opponent	Result	GF	GA
1995	CSF	Detroit	L 0-4	6	24
	CQF	Calgary	W 4-3	26	35
1994	CSF	Toronto	L 3-4	21	26
	CQF	Detroit	W 4-3	21	27

Abbreviations: Round: F – Final;
CF – conference final; **CQF** – conference quarter-final;
CSF – conference semi-final; **DF** – division final;
DSF – division semi-final; **SF** – semi-final;
QF – quarter-final; **PR** – preliminary round.

Colorado totals include Quebec, 1991-92 to 1994-95.   Dallas totals include Minnesota, 1991-92 to 1992-93.
Phoenix totals include Winnipeg, 1991-92 to 1995-96.

1996-97 Results

Oct.	5	NY Islanders	2-2	11	at Edmonton	2-1
	6	at Los Angeles	7-6	13	Phoenix	5-4
	8	at Colorado	0-6	20	at Vancouver	1-6
	10	at Phoenix	1-4	22	Los Angeles	7-2
	12	Boston	3-5	24	New Jersey	1-3
	16	Florida	3-3	27	at Vancouver	2-5
	18	at Anaheim	4-1	29	at Edmonton	1-3
	20	at St. Louis	3-2	30	at Calgary	6-3
	22	at Toronto	3-4	Feb. 1	Colorado	2-1
	24	New Jersey	1-3	3	Chicago	2-4
	26	at NY Islanders	2-2	5	Los Angeles	3-2
	27	at Chicago	6-2	8	at Ottawa	3-3
	30	Calgary	3-1	10	at Montreal	2-4
Nov.	1	at Anaheim	3-4	12	at Detroit	1-7
	2	Montreal	4-3	13	at Chicago	3-7
	6	Colorado	1-4	16	at Buffalo	2-6
	8	Dallas	3-1	18	Dallas	3-1
	12	Hartford	3-4	20	Vancouver	1-6
	15	at Detroit	1-5	23	at Tampa Bay	4-3
	16	at Philadelphia	2-2	25	at Florida	2-2
	18	at Boston	2-4	28	at Hartford	3-2
	21	Detroit	1-6	Mar. 1	at Toronto	2-3
	23	Anaheim	0-3	3	at NY Rangers	4-5
	27	Chicago	3-2	6	Ottawa	2-0
	29	Edmonton	2-4	9	NY Rangers	1-2
Dec.	1	at St. Louis	4-3	11	St. Louis	3-4
	4	at Dallas	2-1	14	Phoenix	1-4
	7	Tampa Bay	3-4	15	Detroit	4-7
	11	Washington	3-2	19	at Calgary	2-4
	13	Pittsburgh	0-4	20	at Vancouver	1-2
	17	Toronto	3-6	22	at Los Angeles	1-2
	20	at Washington	2-3	24	Edmonton	1-5
	21	at Pittsburgh	1-3	26	Toronto	1-2
	23	at Dallas	2-1	28	Edmonton	4-3
	26	Vancouver	6-1	Apr. 1	at Phoenix	1-7
	28	at Edmonton	3-5	2	Anaheim	5-5
	31	at Calgary	5-1	4	Colorado	7-6
Jan.	2	Philadelphia	1-4	7	Vancouver	1-4
	4	Calgary	3-4	9	at Colorado	4-1
	7	Buffalo	1-1	11	Anaheim	3-4
	9	St. Louis	3-4	12	at Los Angeles	1-4

Entry Draft
Selections 1997-91

1997
Pick
2	Patrick Marleau
23	Scott Hannan
82	Adam Colagiacomo
107	Adam Nittel
163	Joe Dusbabek
192	Cam Severson
219	Mark Smith

1996
Pick
2	Andrei Zyuzin
21	Marco Sturm
55	Terry Friesen
102	Matt Bradley
137	Michel Larocque
164	Jake Deadmarsh
191	Cory Cyrenne
217	David Thibeault

1995
Pick
12	Teemu Riihijarvi
38	Peter Roed
64	Marko Makinen
90	Vesa Toskala
116	Miikka Kiprusoff
130	Michal Bros
140	Timo Hakanen
142	Jaroslav Kudrna
167	Brad Mehalko
168	Robert Jindrich
194	Ryan Kraft
220	Miiko Markkanen

1994
Pick
11	Jeff Friesen
37	Angel Nikolov
66	Alexei Yegorov
89	Vaclav Varada
115	Brian Swanson
141	Alexander Korolyuk
167	Sergei Gorbachev
193	Eric Landry
219	Yevgeny Nabokov
240	Tomas Pisa
245	Aniket Dhadphale
271	David Beauregard

1993
Pick
6	Viktor Kozlov
28	Shean Donovan
45	Vlastimil Kroupa
58	Ville Peltonen
80	Alexander Osadchy
106	Andrei Buschan
132	Petri Varis
154	Fredrik Oduya
158	Anatoli Filatov
184	Todd Holt
210	Jonas Forsberg
236	Jeff Salajko
262	Jamie Matthews

1992
Pick
3	Mike Rathje
10	Andrei Nazarov
51	Alexander Cherbajev
75	Jan Caloun
99	Marcus Ragnarsson
123	Michal Sykora
147	Eric Bellerose
171	Ryan Smith
195	Chris Burns
219	A. Kholomeyev
243	Victor Ignatjev

1991
Pick
2	Pat Falloon
23	Ray Whitney
30	Sandis Ozolinsh
45	Dody Wood
67	Kerry Toporowski
89	Dan Ryder
111	Fredrik Nilsson
133	Jaroslav Otevrel
155	Dean Grillo
177	Corwin Saurdiff
199	Dale Craigwell
221	Aaron Kriss
243	Mikhail Kravets

Club Directory

San Jose Arena
525 West Santa Clara Street
San Jose, CA 95113
Phone **408/287-7070**
FAX 408/999-5797
Internet hhttp://www.sj-sharks.com
Capacity: 17,442

Executive Staff
Owner & Chairman	George Gund III
Co-Owner	Gordon Gund
President & Chief Executive Officer	Greg Jamison
Senior Executive Vice President & Chief Operating Officer	Frank Jirik
Executive Vice President & General Manager	Dean Lombardi
Vice Chairman	Tom McEnery
Executive Vice President of Development	Matt Levine
Executive Vice President & Chief Financial Officer	Gregg Olson
Executive Vice President of Business Operations	Malcolm Bordelon
Vice President & General Manager (San Jose Arena)	Jim Goddard
Vice President & General Counsel	Don Gralnek
Vice President of Marketing	Elaine Sullivan-Digre
Executive Assistant	Michelle Simmons

Hockey
Assistant General Manager	Wayne Thomas
Head Coach	Darryl Sutter
Assistant Coaches	Paul Baxter, Roy Sommer
Strength & Conditioning Specialist	Steve Millard
Eastern Professional Scout	TBA
Western Professional Scout	John Ferguson
Director of Amateur Scouting	Tim Burke
Chief Scout	Ray Payne
Scouts	Pat Funk, Rob Grillo, George Gund III, Karel Masopust, Bruce Southern
Scouting Coordinator	Joe Will
Video Scouting Coordinator	Bob Friedlander
Team Travel Coordinator	Steve Perry
Executive Assistant	Brenda Will
Head Athletic Trainer	Ray Tufts, ATC
Athletic Trainer	Tom Woodcock
Equipment Manager	Mike Aldrich
Assistant Equipment Manager	Kurt Harvey
Equipment Assistant & Equipment Transportation	Jason Rudee
Equipment Assistant	Tony Silva
Head Coach & Dir. of Hockey Operations, Kentucky Thoroughblades	Jim Wiley
Assistant Coaches, Kentucky Thoroughblades	Mark Kaufman, Vasily Tikhonov
Head Trainer, Kentucky Thoroughblades	Jerry Iannarelli
Team Physician	Arthur J. Ting, M.D.
Team Dentist	Robert Bonahoom, D.D.S.
Team Vision Specialist	Vincent S. Zuccaro, O.D., F.A.A.O.
Medical Staff	Warren King, M.D., Mark Sontag, M.D., Will Straw, M.D.

Business Operations
Director of Broadcasting	Frank Albin
Director of Community Development	Eric Stanion
Director of Media Relations	Ken Arnold
Director of Sponsorship Sales	Greg Elliot
Community Development Manager	Lou Siville
Educational Programs & Arena Tours Manager	Dianna Carthew
Event Services Manager	Kimberly Hargreaves
Mascot Operations Manager	Jason Minsky
Media Relations Manager	Roger Ross
Sponsorship Sales Managers	Kirk Berridge, Mark Foxlon, Andrea Robinson
Youth & Amateur Hockey Program Manager	J.D. Kershaw
Broadcast Traffic & Promotions Coordinator	Patti Sircus
Sponsorship Services Coordinator	Valerie Bigelow
Event Services Assistant	TBA
Media Relations Assistant	Chris Kelleher
Administrative Assistant	Dawn Beres

Marketing
Director of Advertising & Publicity	Beth Brigino

Director of Ticket Sales & Promotions	Kent Russell
Account Sales Managers	Michael Dunnett, Bill Rapp, Gene Wiggins
Account Service Managers	Kris Lyon, Pat Swan, TBA
Marketing Manager	Jim Sparaco
Ticket Operations Manager	Mary Enriquez
Suite Hospitality Manager	Colleen Duncan
Suite Hospitality Assistant Manager	Mike Hollywood
Ticket Operations Coordinator	John Castro
Administrative Assistants	Steward Diner, Kris Lyon

Development
Executive Assistant	Kimberly Brown

Finance
Director of Finance	Ken Caveney
Finance Manager	Steve Calamia
Human Resources Manager	Carol Ross
Management Information Systems Manager	James Struckle
Senior Staff Accountant	Sarah McEnery
Staff Accountant	Tina Park
Accounts Payable Accounting Associate	Tammy Link
Accounts Receivable Accounting Associate	Diane Rubino
Payroll Accounting Associate	Sue Feachen
Management Information Systems Coordinator	TBA
Management Information Systems Assistant	John Huh
Executive Assistant	Tricia Nordquist

Building Operations
Director of Building Operations	Rich Sotelo
Director of Guest Services	Rick Mears
Director of Ticket Operations	Daniel DeBoer
Facilities Technical Director	Greg Carrolan
Booking & Events Managers	Bob Herrfeldt, Steve Kirsner
Building Services Manager	Bruce Tharaldson
Ticket Operations Manager	Judy Jones
Ushering Guest Services Manager	Kellie Elliott
Building Services Coordinators	George Gund IV, Greg Gund
Mailroom Coordinator	Richard Perez
Ticket Office Coordinator	Rossanna Lira
Ushering Guest Services Coordinators	Julie Fuller, Andrea Teed, Darcy Teed
Executive Assistant	Christine de la Cruz
Administrative Assistant	Beth Ganeff

Aramark Leisure Services
General Manager	Dale Haynes
Human Resources Director	Bruce Yamanaka
Concessions Manager	TBA
Financial Controller	Scott McClellan
Executive Chef	Dennis Glafkides
Merchandise Manager	TBA
Restaurant Manager	Tracy Ingram
Suites & Catering Manager	Wendy Riggs
Assistant Concessions Manager	Gretchen La Due

Miscellaneous
Team Colors	Pacific Teal, Gray, Black, White
Dimensions of Rink	200 feet by 85 feet
Television Stations	KICU-TV 36, SportsChannel
Radio Network Flagship	KARA (105.7 FM)
Radio Play-By-Play Broadcaster	Dan Rusanowsky
Radio Color Analyst	Drew Remenda
Television Play-By-Play Broadcaster	Randy Hahn
Television Color Analyst	TBA
Television Studio Host	Ted Rowlands
Team Photographers	Rocky Widner, Don Smith
P.A. Announcer	Joe Ike
Organist	TBA
Mascot	S.J. Sharkie

Tampa Bay Lightning

1996-97 Results: 32w-40L-10T 74pts. Sixth, Atlantic Division

Year-by-Year Record

		Home			Road			Overall							
Season	GP	W	L	T	W	L	T	W	L	T	GF	GA	Pts.	Finished	Playoff Result
1996-97	82	15	18	8	17	22	2	32	40	10	217	247	74	6th, Atlantic Div.	Out of Playoffs
1995-96	82	22	14	5	16	18	7	38	32	12	238	248	88	5th, Atlantic Div.	Lost Conf. Quarter-Final
1994-95	48	10	14	0	7	14	3	17	28	3	120	144	37	6th, Atlantic Div.	Out of Playoffs
1993-94	84	14	22	6	16	21	5	30	43	11	224	251	71	7th, Atlantic Div.	Out of Playoffs
1992-93	84	12	27	3	11	27	4	23	54	7	245	332	53	6th, Norris Div.	Out of Playoffs

1997-98 Schedule

Oct.	Wed.	1	Carolina
	Fri.	3	New Jersey
	Sun.	5	Buffalo
	Thu.	9	at Chicago
	Fri.	10	at Detroit
	Wed.	15	at Florida
	Fri.	17	Pittsburgh
	Sat.	18	at New Jersey
	Tue.	21	at Philadelphia
	Thu.	23	at Boston
	Fri.	24	at NY Rangers
	Sun.	26	Los Angeles
	Wed.	29	Ottawa
Nov.	Wed.	5	at Anaheim
	Thu.	6	at Los Angeles
	Sat.	8	at San Jose
	Tue.	11	at Phoenix
	Fri.	14	NY Islanders
	Sun.	16	at Philadelphia
	Mon.	17	at Montreal
	Wed.	19	NY Rangers
	Sat.	22	Calgary
	Wed.	26	Colorado
	Fri.	28	at Carolina
	Sat.	29	Philadelphia
Dec.	Wed.	3	Phoenix
	Fri.	5	at Buffalo
	Sat.	6	at New Jersey
	Wed.	10	at Dallas
	Sat.	13	at Ottawa
	Sun.	14	at Philadelphia
	Tue.	16	at Pittsburgh
	Wed.	17	Boston
	Sat.	20	NY Rangers*
	Mon.	22	St. Louis
	Tue.	23	at NY Rangers
	Sat.	27	Boston*
	Mon.	29	San Jose
	Wed.	31	NY Rangers
Jan.	Fri.	2	Florida
	Sat.	3	Anaheim

	Wed.	7	Toronto
	Fri.	9	at New Jersey
	Sun.	11	Philadelphia
	Mon.	12	Montreal
	Wed.	14	NY Islanders
	Wed.	21	Washington
	Fri.	23	at Buffalo
	Sat.	24	at Toronto
	Mon.	26	at Ottawa
	Wed.	28	Carolina
	Sat.	31	at Florida*
Feb.	Mon.	2	Buffalo
	Wed.	4	at Carolina
	Thu.	5	Detroit
	Sat.	7	at Washington
	Wed.	25	at Washington
	Thu.	26	New Jersey
	Sat.	28	Washington*
Mar.	Tue.	3	at Calgary
	Wed.	4	at Edmonton
	Sat.	7	at Vancouver
	Mon.	9	at Colorado
	Wed.	11	Edmonton
	Sat.	14	Chicago*
	Mon.	16	at Boston
	Wed.	18	Vancouver
	Sat.	21	Florida*
	Wed.	25	Montreal
	Thu.	26	at St. Louis
	Sat.	28	at Montreal
	Mon.	30	at NY Rangers
Apr.	Wed.	1	at NY Islanders
	Thu.	2	at Washington
	Sat.	4	Pittsburgh*
	Mon.	6	NY Islanders
	Wed.	8	Philadelphia
	Sat.	11	Dallas*
	Mon.	13	Ottawa
	Wed.	15	at Pittsburgh
	Thu.	16	at NY Islanders
	Sat.	18	Florida*

* Denotes afternoon game.

Franchise date: December 16, 1991

ATLANTIC DIVISION

6th NHL Season

Rob Zamuner's dependable defensive play earned him the second-highest plus/minus of any Tampa forward (+3).

1997-98 Player Personnel

FORWARDS

	HT	WT	S	Place of Birth	Date	1996-97 Club
ANDERSSON, Mikael	5-11	181	L	Malmo, Sweden	5/10/66	Tampa Bay
BRADLEY, Brian	5-10	180	R	Kitchener, Ont.	1/21/65	Tampa Bay
CICCARELLI, Dino	5-10	185	R	Sarnia, Ont.	2/8/60	Tampa Bay
CULLEN, John	5-10	182	R	Fort Erie, Ont.	8/2/64	Tampa Bay
DeBRUSK, Louie	6-2	215	L	Cambridge, Ont.	3/19/71	Edmonton
EGELAND, Allan	6-0	175	L	Lethbridge, Alta.	1/31/73	Tampa Bay-Adirondack
EPACHINTSEV, Vadim	5-9	165	L	Orsk, USSR	3/16/76	Spartak
LANGKOW, Daymond	5-11	175	L	Edmonton, Alta	9/27/76	Tampa Bay-Adirondack
PETERSON, Brent	6-3	200	L	Calgary, Alta.	7/20/72	Tampa Bay-Adirondack
POULIN, Patrick	6-1	210	L	Vanier, Que.	4/23/73	Tampa Bay
RENBERG, Mikael	6-2	218	L	Pitea, Sweden	5/5/72	Philadelphia
SELIVANOV, Alexander	6-0	206	L	Moscow, USSR	3/23/71	Tampa Bay
SPRING, Corey	6-4	214	R	Cranbrook, B.C.	5/31/71	Adirondack
TOMS, Jeff	6-5	200	L	Swift Current, Sask.	6/4/74	Tampa Bay-Adirondack
VUJTEK, Vladimir	6-1	190	L	Ostrava, Czech.	2/17/72	Assat
WIEMER, Jason	6-2	219	L	Kimberley, B.C.	4/14/76	Tampa Bay-Adirondack
YSEBAERT, Paul	6-1	194	L	Sarnia, Ont.	5/15/66	Tampa Bay
ZAMUNER, Rob	6-2	206	L	Oakville, Ont.	9/17/69	Tampa Bay

DEFENSEMEN

	HT	WT	S	Place of Birth	Date	1996-97 Club
CROSS, Cory	6-5	219	L	Lloydminster, Alta.	1/3/71	Tampa Bay
DYKHUIS, Karl	6-3	214	L	Sept-Iles, Que.	7/8/72	Philadelphia
HAMRLIK, Roman	6-2	200	L	Gottwaldov, Czech.	4/12/74	Tampa Bay
HUSCROFT, Jamie	6-2	200	R	Creston, B.C.	1/9/67	Calgary-Tampa Bay
LAROCQUE, Mario	6-2	182	L	Montreal, Que.	4/24/78	Hull
McBAIN, Mike	6-2	195	L	Kimberley, B.C.	1/12/77	Red Deer
NORTON, Jeff	6-2	200	L	Acton, MA	11/25/65	Edmonton-Tampa Bay
RABY, Matthieu	6-4	215	L	Hull, Que.	1/19/75	Adirondack-Wheeling
RACINE, Yves	6-0	205	L	Matane, Que.	2/7/69	Kentucky-Quebec-Calgary
SHAW, David	6-2	205	R	St. Thomas, Ont.	5/25/64	Tampa Bay
ULANOV, Igor	6-1	205	L	Krasnokamsk, USSR	10/1/69	Tampa Bay

GOALTENDERS

	HT	WT	C	Place of Birth	Date	1996-97 Club
PUPPA, Daren	6-4	205	R	Kirkland Lake, Ont.	3/23/65	Tampa Bay-Adirondack
SCHWAB, Corey	6-0	180	L	North Battleford, Sask.	11/4/70	Tampa Bay
WILKINSON, Derek	6-0	170	L	Lasalle, Ont.	7/29/74	Tampa Bay-Cleveland

1996-97 Scoring

* – rookie

Regular Season

Pos	#	Player	Team	GP	G	A	Pts	+/–	PIM	PP	SH	GW	GT	S	%
C	77	Chris Gratton	T.B.	82	30	32	62	-28	201	9	0	4	0	230	13.0
R	22	Dino Ciccarelli	T.B.	77	35	25	60	-11	116	12	0	6	0	229	15.3
C	12	John Cullen	T.B.	70	18	37	55	-14	95	5	0	2	1	116	15.5
L	7	Rob Zamuner	T.B.	82	17	33	50	3	56	0	4	3	0	216	7.9
D	44	Roman Hamrlik	T.B.	79	12	28	40	-29	57	6	0	0	1	238	5.0
L	11	Shawn Burr	T.B.	74	14	21	35	5	106	1	0	3	0	128	10.9
R	29	Alexander Selivanov	T.B.	69	15	18	33	-3	61	3	0	4	0	187	8.0
C	18	* Daymond Langkow	T.B.	79	15	13	28	1	35	3	1	1	1	170	8.8
L	28	Patrick Poulin	T.B.	73	12	14	26	-16	56	2	3	1	0	124	9.7
D	2	Bill Houlder	T.B.	79	4	21	25	16	30	0	0	2	0	116	3.4
C	19	Brian Bradley	T.B.	35	7	17	24	2	16	1	2	1	0	93	7.5
L	34	Mikael Andersson	T.B.	70	5	14	19	1	8	0	3	1	0	102	4.9
D	6	Jeff Norton	EDM	62	2	11	13	-7	42	0	0	0	0	68	2.9
			T.B.	13	0	5	5	0	16	0	0	0	0	13	0.0
			TOTAL	75	2	16	18	-7	58	0	0	0	0	81	2.5
L	15	Paul Ysebaert	T.B.	39	5	12	17	1	4	2	0	0	0	91	5.5
L	24	Jason Wiemer	T.B.	63	9	5	14	-13	134	2	0	0	0	103	8.7
D	27	David Shaw	T.B.	57	1	10	11	1	72	0	0	0	0	59	1.7
L	9	* Jeff Toms	T.B.	34	2	8	10	2	10	0	0	1	0	53	3.8
D	4	Cory Cross	T.B.	72	4	5	9	6	95	0	0	2	0	75	5.3
D	5	Igor Ulanov	T.B.	59	1	7	8	2	108	0	0	0	1	56	1.8
R	20	Rudy Poeschek	T.B.	60	0	6	6	-3	120	0	0	0	0	30	0.0
D	8	Jamie Huscroft	CGY	39	0	4	4	2	117	0	0	0	0	33	0.0
			T.B.	13	0	1	1	-4	34	0	0	0	0	7	0.0
			TOTAL	52	0	5	5	-2	151	0	0	0	0	40	0.0
R	74	* Brantt Myhres	T.B.	47	3	1	4	1	136	0	0	1	0	13	23.1
L	17	* Brent Peterson	T.B.	17	2	0	2	-4	4	0	0	0	0	11	18.2
G	32	* Corey Schwab	T.B.	31	0	1	1	0	10	0	0	0	0	0	0.0
G	31	Rick Tabaracci	CGY	7	0	0	0	0	0	0	0	0	0	0	0.0
			T.B.	55	0	1	1	0	12	0	0	0	0	0	0.0
			TOTAL	62	0	1	1	0	12	0	0	0	0	0	0.0
C	25	* Alan Egeland	T.B.	4	0	0	0	-3	5	0	0	0	0	1	0.0
G	35	* Derek Wilkinson	T.B.	6	0	0	0	0	0	0	0	0	0	0	0.0
G	93	Daren Puppa	T.B.	6	0	0	0	0	2	0	0	0	0	0	0.0
R	10	* Paul Brousseau	T.B.	6	0	0	0	-4	0	0	0	0	0	3	0.0
D	26	Jay Wells	T.B.	21	0	0	0	-3	13	0	0	0	0	16	0.0

Goaltending

No.	Goaltender	GPI	Mins	Avg	W	L	T	EN	SO	GA	SA	S%
93	Daren Puppa	6	325	2.58	1	1	2	1	0	14	150	.907
31	Rick Tabaracci	55	3012	2.75	20	25	6	5	4	138	1415	.902
32	* Corey Schwab	31	1462	3.04	11	12	1	2	2	74	719	.897
35	* Derek Wilkinson	5	169	4.26	0	2	1	1	0	12	72	.833
	Totals	**82**	**4984**	**2.97**	**32**	**40**	**10**	**9**	**6**	**247**	**2365**	**.896**

Coaching History

Terry Crisp, 1992-93 to date.

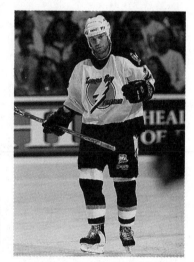

The ageless Dino Ciccarelli celebrated his 17th season with 35 goals, leaving him just 14 shy of the 600-goal plateau.

Coach

CRISP, TERRY
Coach, Tampa Bay Lightning. Born in Parry Sound, Ont., May 28, 1943.

Terry Crisp, 54, enters the 1997-98 season with the longest current tenure among active NHL head coaches, as he has been behind the Lightning bench for all five seasons since his initial appointment in 1992. His 380 games with the Lightning (entering 1997-98) also represent the longest NHL expansion franchise coaching stint ever.

Despite falling three points short of the playoffs in 1996-97, Crisp led the Lightning to the second-best record in franchise history at 32-40-10 (74 points), and kept Tampa Bay in the playoff hunt until the final weekend of the regular season.

In five seasons, Crisp has established the Lightning as a hard-working team ready to compete with every NHL opponent.

Prior to joining the Lightning, Crisp was an assistant coach for the 1992 Canadian Olympic Team, which won the silver medal in Albertville, France, and for Team Canada during the 1992 World Championships.

A native of Parry Sound, Ontario, Crisp is one of only 13 individuals to have coached and played on a Stanley Cup championship team. He coached the Calgary Flames to the 1989 title and played for the 1974 and 1975 Philadelphia Flyers.

Crisp's coaching career began as an assistant to Fred Shero for two seasons in Philadelphia (1977-1979). His first head coaching job was with the Sault Ste. Marie Greyhounds of the Ontario Hockey League beginning in 1979-80. His six-year stint there ended with three consecutive divisional and league championships. He was named Coach of the Year in 1982-83 and again in 1984-85, when his team went 33-0 at home. From Sault Ste. Marie, Crisp moved to Moncton of the American Hockey League where, in two seasons, he posted a combined 77-65-18 mark for Calgary's top minor league affiliate.

He was named Calgary's fifth head coach in 1987 and directed the Flames for three seasons, amassing a combined record of 144-63-33, including a franchise-best 54-17-9 in 1988-89. Crisp was named NHL Coach of the Year by *The Sporting News* after the 1987-88 season and he was the runner-up in NHL balloting that season.

Crisp's 11-year playing career was highlighted by hard work and strong defensive play. Beginning with Boston in 1965, Crisp also played for St. Louis, Philadelphia and the New York Islanders before retiring in 1977. In 536 regular season games, Crisp scored 67 goals, 134 assists and 201 points. He appeared in 110 Stanley Cup Playoff games, netting 15 goals and 28 assists.

Terry and his wife, Sheila, reside in Tampa. They have three children, Tony, Jeff and Caley. Tony serves as manager of international events for Hockey Canada, and Jeff is the director of marketing and public relations for the Peterborough Petes of the OHL.

Coaching Record

Season	Team	Games	Regular Season				Playoffs				
			W	L	T	%	Games	W	L	T	%
1979-80	S.S. Marie (OHL)	68	22	45	1	.331	....				
1980-81	S.S. Marie (OHL)	68	47	19	2	.706	19	8	7	4	.526
1981-82	S.S. Marie (OHL)	68	40	25	3	.610	13	4	6	3	.423
1982-83	S.S. Marie (OHL)	70	48	21	1	.693	16	7	6	3	.531
1983-84	S.S. Marie (OHL)	70	38	28	4	.571	16	8	4	4	.625
1984-85	S.S. Marie (OHL)	66	54	11	1	.826	16	12	2	2	.813
1985-86	Moncton (AHL)	80	34	34	12	.500	10	5	5	0	.500
1986-87	Moncton (AHL)	80	43	31	6	.575	6	2	4	0	.333
1987-88	**Calgary (NHL)**	80	48	23	9	.656	9	4	5	0	.444
1988-89	**Calgary (NHL)**	80	54	17	9	.731	22	16	6	0	.727*
1989-90	**Calgary (NHL)**	80	42	23	15	.619	6	2	4	0	.333
1992-93	**Tampa Bay (NHL)**	84	23	54	7	.315	....				
1993-94	**Tampa Bay (NHL)**	84	30	43	11	.423	....				
1994-95	**Tampa Bay (NHL)**	48	17	28	3	.385	....				
1995-96	**Tampa Bay (NHL)**	82	38	32	12	.537	6	2	4	0	.333
1996-97	**Tampa Bay (NHL)**	82	32	40	10	.451	....				
	NHL Totals	**620**	**284**	**260**	**76**	**.519**	**43**	**24**	**19**	**0**	**.558**

* Stanley Cup win.

Club Records

Team

(Figures in brackets for season records are games played; records for fewest points, wins, ties, losses, goals, goals against are for 70 or more games)

Most Points	88	1995-96 (82)
Most Wins	38	1995-96 (82)
Most Ties	12	1995-96 (82)
Most Losses	54	1992-93 (84)
Most Goals	245	1992-93 (84)
Most Goals Against	332	1992-93 (84)
Fewest Points	53	1992-93 (84)
Fewest Wins	23	1992-93 (84)
Fewest Ties	7	1992-93 (84)
Fewest Losses	32	1995-96 (82)
Fewest Goals	217	1996-97 (82)
Fewest Goals Against	247	1996-97 (82)

Longest Winning Streak
Overall.................. 5 Twice
Home.................... 6 Feb. 15-Mar. 10/96
Away .... 4 Jan. 6-13/97

Longest Undefeated Streak
Overall.................. 7 Feb. 28-Mar. 13/96
(5 wins, 2 ties)
Home.................... 8 Feb. 15-Mar. 13/96
(6 wins, 2 ties)
Away .... 6 Dec. 28/93-Jan. 12/94
(5 wins, 1 tie)

Longest Losing Streak
Overall.................. 8 Mar. 9-23/93
Home.................... 6 Mar. 9-Apr. 11/93
Away.................... 6 Apr. 14-29/95

Longest Winless Streak
Overall.................. 8 Mar. 9-23/93
(8 losses)
Home.................... 9 Mar. 9-Apr. 10/93
(8 losses, 1 tie)
Away .... 10 Oct. 23-Nov. 26/93
(8 losses, 2 ties)

Most Shutouts, Season 6 1996-97 (82)
Most PIM, Season 1,686 1996-97 (82)
Most Goals, Game .... 7 Five times

Individual

Most Seasons	5	Several players
Most Games, Career	340	Rob Zamuner, Roman Hamrlik
Most Goals, Career	109	Brian Bradley
Most Assists, Career	184	Brian Bradley
Most Points, Career	293	Brian Bradley (109G, 184A)
Most PIM, Career	535	Enrico Ciccone
Most Shutouts, Career	10	Daren Puppa

Longest Consecutive
Games Streak .... 174 Chris Gratton
Most Goals, Season .... 42 Brian Bradley (1992-93)
Most Assists, Season .... 56 Brian Bradley (1995-96)

Most Points, Season	86	Brian Bradley (1992-93; 42G, 44A)
Most PIM, Season	258	Enrico Ciccone (1995-96)
Most Shutouts, Season	5	Daren Puppa (1995-96)
Most Points, Defenseman, Season	65	Roman Hamrlik (1995-96; 16G, 49A)
Most Points, Center, Season	86	Brian Bradley (1992-93; 42G, 44A)
Most Points, Right Wing, Season	60	Dino Ciccarelli (1996-97; 35G, 25A)
Most Points, Left Wing, Season	51	Chris Kontos (1992-93; 27G, 24A)
Most Points, Rookie, Season	43	Rob Zamuner (1992-93; 15G, 28A)
Most Goals, Game	4	Chris Kontos (Oct. 7/92)
Most Assists, Game	4	Joe Reekie (Oct. 7/92), Marc Bureau (Dec. 16/92)
Most Points, Game	6	Doug Crossman (Nov. 11/92; 3G, 3A)

Captains' History

No captain, 1992-93 to 1994-95; Paul Ysebaert, 1995-96 to date.

All-time Record vs. Other Clubs

Regular Season

	At Home							On Road							Total						
	GP	W	L	T	GF	GA	PTS	GP	W	L	T	GF	GA	PTS	GP	W	L	T	GF	GA	PTS
Anaheim	3	2	1	0	6	7	4	3	1	1	1	7	7	3	6	3	2	1	13	14	7
Boston	9	3	4	2	26	28	8	8	1	6	1	18	31	3	17	4	10	3	44	59	11
Buffalo	9	1	8	0	16	30	2	9	5	3	1	35	21	11	18	6	11	1	51	51	13
Calgary	5	2	2	1	18	20	5	4	2	2	0	10	16	4	9	4	4	1	28	36	9
Chicago	6	3	2	1	18	17	7	7	2	3	2	15	17	6	13	5	5	3	33	34	13
Colorado	7	6	1	0	26	18	12	7	1	5	1	18	33	3	14	7	6	1	44	51	15
Dallas	7	1	4	2	12	17	4	6	1	4	1	15	22	3	13	2	8	3	27	39	7
Detroit	8	1	6	1	26	45	3	6	1	5	0	15	26	2	14	2	11	1	41	71	5
Edmonton	5	2	1	2	18	12	6	5	4	0	1	12	12	9	10	6	1	3	30	24	15
Florida	10	3	5	2	20	29	8	10	2	6	2	17	28	6	20	5	11	4	37	57	14
Hartford	9	5	3	1	28	25	11	9	2	7	0	23	32	4	18	7	10	1	51	57	15
Los Angeles	4	2	2	0	10	9	4	5	0	0	21	11	10	9	7	2	0	31	20	14
Montreal	9	6	1	2	26	18	14	8	3	4	1	20	19	7	17	9	5	3	46	37	21
New Jersey	11	3	5	3	27	31	9	11	1	9	1	17	41	3	22	4	14	4	44	72	12
NY Islanders	11	6	4	1	34	33	13	11	8	3	0	41	28	16	22	14	7	1	75	61	29
NY Rangers	10	4	5	1	34	33	9	12	6	5	1	49	44	13	22	10	10	2	83	77	22
Ottawa	9	5	4	0	28	23	10	9	6	3	0	26	25	12	18	11	7	0	54	48	22
Philadelphia	11	4	7	0	32	32	8	10	1	5	4	20	31	6	21	5	12	4	52	63	14
Phoenix	5	1	4	0	16	22	2	5	3	2	0	13	13	6	10	4	6	0	29	35	8
Pittsburgh	8	3	4	1	30	32	7	9	2	6	1	22	43	5	17	5	10	2	52	75	12
St. Louis	7	3	3	1	22	23	7	6	1	5	0	17	25	2	13	4	8	1	39	48	9
San Jose	5	3	2	0	17	12	6	5	5	0	0	24	15	10	10	8	2	0	41	27	16
Toronto	7	1	6	0	13	26	2	9	5	4	0	24	30	10	16	6	10	0	37	56	12
Vancouver	4	1	3	0	12	17	2	5	0	5	0	7	26	0	9	1	8	0	19	43	2
Washington	11	2	8	1	18	32	5	11	2	5	4	25	35	8	22	4	13	5	43	67	13
Totals	**190**	**73**	**95**	**22**	**533**	**591**	**168**	**190**	**67**	**102**	**21**	**511**	**631**	**155**	**380**	**140**	**197**	**43**	**1044**	**1222**	**323**

Playoffs

	Series	W	L	GP	W	L	T	GF	GA	Last Mtg.	Round	Result
Philadelphia	1	0	1	6	2	4	0	13	26	1996	CQF	L 2-4
Totals	**1**	**0**	**1**	**6**	**2**	**4**	**0**	**13**	**26**			

Playoff Results 1997-93

Year	Round	Opponent	Result	GF	GA
1996	CQF	Philadelphia	L 2-4	13	26

Abbreviations: Round: F – Final;
CF – conference final; **CQF** – conference quarter-final;
CSF – conference semi-final; **DF** – division final;
DSF – division semi-final; **SF** – semi-final;
QF – quarter-final; **PR** – preliminary round.

Colorado totals include Quebec, 1992-93 to 1994-95.   Dallas totals include Minnesota, 1992-93.
Phoenix totals include Winnipeg, 1992-93 to 1995-96.

1996-97 Results

Oct.	5	at	Pittsburgh	4-3		11	NY Islanders	4-4
	11	at	Washington	2-6		13	at Chicago	2-0
	12	at	Toronto	7-4		15	at Colorado	2-4
	15	at	Buffalo	4-0		21	Colorado	3-2
	20		NY Rangers	5-2		25	at Florida	2-3
	22	at	NY Islanders	6-3		27	at Ottawa	3-5
	24		Ottawa	2-5		30	Montreal	1-4
	26		New Jersey	1-4	Feb.	1	Boston	0-3
	29		Chicago	2-2		4	at Phoenix	2-0
	31		Philadelphia	3-4		5	at Dallas	0-4
Nov.	2	at	New Jersey	1-2		8	Buffalo	1-3
	4	at	NY Rangers	5-3		12	at Florida	2-5
	6		Washington	1-2		14	at Washington	4-5
	8		Pittsburgh	5-5		15	Washington	4-1
	10	at	Detroit	2-4		17	Detroit	3-3
	14	at	St. Louis	3-5		20	Philadelphia	5-2
	16	at	New Jersey	3-6		22	New Jersey	3-1
	19		Los Angeles	3-0		23	San Jose	4-3
	23		Philadelphia	1-2		25	St. Louis	3-2
	25	at	Montreal	2-4		27	at Boston	2-6
	27		Buffalo	0-3	Mar.	1	Florida	2-0
	29		Dallas	1-2		4	at NY Islanders	6-3
	30		Hartford	3-6		6	Phoenix	0-5
Dec.	4	at	Anaheim	1-3		8	Boston	4-6
	5	at	Los Angeles	2-1		9	Calgary	2-1
	7	at	San Jose	4-3		13	NY Islanders	0-3
	12		Edmonton	4-3		15	Vancouver	2-5
	14		NY Islanders	4-1		16	Toronto	1-3
	16	at	Montreal	4-2		19	at Edmonton	1-3
	18	at	Buffalo	3-5		21	at Calgary	4-3
	19	at	Boston	0-3		22	at Vancouver	4-3
	21	at	Hartford	5-6		25	Ottawa	5-0
	23		Washington	1-3		27	Hartford	2-5
	26		Florida	3-3		29	at Florida	1-1
	28		Montreal	2-4	Apr.	1	at Philadelphia	1-1
	31		NY Rangers	4-2		4	at New Jersey	0-3
Jan.	3		Anaheim	3-2		5	at NY Islanders	3-2
	4	at	Pittsburgh	3-7		8	New Jersey	2-2
	6	at	Ottawa	4-3		10	Pittsburgh	4-3
	8	at	NY Rangers	4-3		11	at NY Rangers	4-2
	9	at	Philadelphia	3-1		13	at Hartford	1-2

Entry Draft
Selections 1997-92

1997
Pick
7	Paul Mara
33	Kyle Kos
61	Matt Elich
108	Mark Thompson
109	Jan Sulc
112	Karel Betik
153	Andrei Skopintsev
168	Justin Jack
170	Eero Somervuori
185	Samuel St-Pierre
198	Shawn Skolney
224	Paul Comrie

1996
Pick
16	Mario Larocque
69	Curtis Tipler
125	Jason Robinson
152	Nikolai Ignatov
157	Xavier Delisle
179	Pavel Kubina

1995
Pick
5	Daymond Langkow
30	Mike McBain
56	Shane Willis
108	Konsta Golokhvastov
134	Eduard Pershin
160	Cory Murphy
186	Joe Cardarelli
212	Zac Bierk

1994
Pick
8	Jason Wiemer
34	Colin Cloutier
55	Vadim Epachintsev
86	Dmitri Klevakin
137	Daniel Juden
138	Bryce Salvador
164	Chris Maillet
190	Alexei Baranov
216	Yuri Smirnov
242	Shawn Gervais
268	Brian White

1993
Pick
3	Chris Gratton
29	Tyler Moss
55	Allan Egeland
81	Marian Kacir
107	Ryan Brown
133	Kiley Hill
159	Mathieu Raby
185	Ryan Nauss
211	Alexandre Laporte
237	Brett Duncan
263	Mark Szoke

1992
Pick
1	Roman Hamrlik
26	Drew Bannister
49	Brent Gretzky
74	Aaron Gavey
97	Brantt Myhres
122	Martin Tanguay
145	Derek Wilkinson
170	Dennis Maxwell
193	Andrew Kemper
218	Marc Tardif
241	Tom MacDonald

General Managers' History

Phil Esposito, 1992-93 to date.

General Manager

ESPOSITO, PHIL
General Manager, Tampa Bay Lightning.
Born in Sault Ste. Marie, Ont., February 20, 1942.

No one deserves more credit for the creation of the Tampa Bay Lightning and subsequent rapid development of the fledgling franchise into a playoff team in just its fourth season of competition than General Manager Phil Esposito. While many words can describe Phil — including dynamic, charismatic and creative — perhaps when speaking of the Lightning and Phil's association, none is more appropriate than determined.

It was Phil Esposito's determination and persistence that led to the awarding of an expansion franchise in 1990. Despite predictions that the franchise might not perform well, Phil's determination brought the Lightning a highly competitive — and respected — team in 1992-93 when the Lightning first hit the ice. And it was Phil's determination that has continued the building process to produce a team that is sure to remain in the playoff race for years to come.

One of hockey's greatest performers — he ranks fourth on the NHL all-time goal-scoring list and is a member of the Hockey Hall of Fame — Phil has distinguished himself in his role with the Lightning as the person in charge of all aspects of hockey operations. Phil has utilized every avenue available to improve the Lightning — be it through the expansion draft, entry draft, free agent signings, waiver draft selections and trade.

Esposito's spectacular 18-year playing career was highlighted by two Stanley Cup Championships as a member of the Boston Bruins in 1970 and 1972. Originally a member of the Chicago Blackhawks (1963-67), Esposito was the central figure in one of hockey's biggest trades when he was sent to Boston in 1967. Over the next eight seasons, he virtually rewrote the NHL record books. He became the first player in NHL history to score 100 points in a season (1969-70) and, two seasons later, set single season standards of 76 goals and 152 points, which stood until Wayne Gretzky eclipsed those marks a decade later. Over a five-year period (1970-71 to 1974-75), Phil scored 55 or more goals and totalled 127 points or more in each season with combined totals of 326 goals and 687 points. Once again part of one of hockey's biggest trades in 1975, Esposito was dealt to the New York Rangers where he led the Rangers in scoring for four years and helped them to the Stanley Cup Finals in 1979.

His 717 goals place him fourth on the all-time list behind Gretzky (837), Gordie Howe (801) and Marcel Dionne (731) and his 1,590 points are fourth all-time behind Gretzky, Howe and Dionne.

Phil was also an integral member of several international teams, including Team Canada's memorable come-from-behind effort in the historic first Summit Series in 1972 against Russia. In 1996, Phil journeyed to Japan for a series of Hockey clinics as Japan prepares to host the 1998 Winter Olympics.

Prior to his efforts with the Lightning, Esposito, now 55, was vice-president and general manager of the New York Rangers from 1986-88.

Phil resides in Tampa. He has three daughters, Laurie, Carrie and Cherise and two grandsons, Dylan and Dakota.

NHL Coaching Record

		Regular Season					Playoffs			
Season	Team	Games	W	L	T	%	Games	W	L	%
1986-87	NY Rangers	43	24	19	0	.558	6	2	4	.333
1988-89	NY Rangers	2	0	2	0	.000	4	0	4	.000
	NHL Totals	45	24	21	0	.533	10	2	8	.200

Club Directory

Ice Palace

Ice Palace
401 Channelside Drive
Tampa, FL 33602
Admin. Office **813/229-2658**
FAX 813/229-3350
Ticket Info. 813/229-8800
Capacity: 19,758

Lightning Partners, Ltd.
General Partner . . . . Lightning Partners Inc.

Executive Staff
Majority Owner and Chairman . . . . Takashi Okubo
President, CEO and Alternate Governor . . . . Saburo (Steve) Oto
Governor . . . . David LeFevre
General Manager & Alternate Governor . . . . Phil Esposito
Executive Vice President & Alternate Governor . . . . Chris Phillips
Vice President and CFO . . . . Frank Sato

Administration
Assistant to the President and CEO . . . . Masahiro Yamshita
Executive Assistant . . . . Connie Troy

Hockey Operations
General Manager . . . . Phil Esposito
Director of Hockey Development & Scouting . . . . . Tony Esposito
Counsel . . . . Henry Lee Paul – Lazzara & Paul, P.A.
Head Coach . . . . Terry Crisp
Assistant Coaches . . . . Dave MacQueen, Rick Paterson
Assistant Coach/Strength and
  Conditioning Coach . . . . Chris Reichart
Pro Scout . . . . Peter Mahovlich
Head Scout . . . . Don Murdoch
Scouting Staff . . . . Angelo Bumbacco, Jake Goertzen,
  Doug Macauley, Richard Rose, Luke Williams
Director of Team Services . . . . Phil Thibodeau
Head Trainer . . . . Dennis Brogna
Equipment Manager . . . . Jocko Cayer
Assistant Equipment Manager . . . . James Pickard
Administrative Assistant . . . . Kathy Skelton
Operations Manager . . . . Michael Wall
Video Coordinator . . . . Nigel Kirwan

Finance
Vice President and CFO . . . . Frank Sato
Accounting Manager . . . . Vincent Ascanio
Accounting Supervisor . . . . Kevin Steiger
Executive Administrative Assistant . . . . Evelyn Hicks
Accounts Payable Supervisor/Staff Accountant . . . . Robin Hughes
Accounts Payable Clerk . . . . Alina Simonds
Human Resource Administrator . . . . Katie Lang

Marketing and Sales
Vice President of Corporate Sales . . . . Fred Doremus
Vice President of Marketing . . . . Paul D'Aiuto
Director of Fan Services . . . . Steve Woznick
Corporate Sales Representative . . . . Chris Lahey
Creative Director . . . . Killeen Mullen
Promotions Manager . . . . Debbie Blizzard
Marketing Coordinator . . . . Kim Pryor
Marketing Assistant . . . . Sonya Michael

Ticket Operations
Director of Ticket Sales . . . . Dan Froehlich
Assistant Director of Ticket Sales . . . . Keith Brennan
Director of Group Sales . . . . Cliff Gault
Ticket Office Manager . . . . Marilyn Brace
Ticket Office Assistant . . . . Stephanie Hanchey
Season Ticket Service Manager . . . . Dan Pekarek
Ticket Sales Manager . . . . Brendan Cunningham
Group Sales Manager . . . . Jason Baumgarten
Group Sales Coordinator . . . . Matt Lemay
Sales Representatives . . . . Mike Centanni, Missy Davis

Communications
Vice President/Communications . . . . Gerry Helper
Director of Publications/Corporate PR . . . . Jay Preble
Communications/Community
  Relations Coordinator . . . . Carrie Schuldt
Media Information Manager . . . . John Sternal
Receptionist . . . . Patsy Vold, Mary Sharpe

Medical Staff
Team Physician . . . . Dr. David Leffers
Team Dentist . . . . Dr. Joseph Spoto

Game Night Staff
Team Photographer . . . . Jonathan Hayt
Off-ice Officials . . . . Jim Galluzzi, Ron Brace, Gerry Dollmont,
  Ralph Emery, Chuck Fontana, Mark Losier,
  Tony Mancuso, Jeff Maust, Mike Rees,
  Gary Reilly, John Supak, Rich Wasilewski
NHL Commercial Coordinator . . . . David Rice
Public Address Announcer . . . . Paul Porter
Scoreboard Operation . . . . Bill Heald
Media Services . . . . Jan Porter

Television & Radio
Television Stations . . . . Sunshine Network, &
  Lightning Television Network
Broadcasters . . . . Rick Peckham and Bobby Taylor
Radio Stations . . . . WDAE 1250 AM
  & Lightning Radio Network
Broadcasters . . . . Larry Hirsch and Bobby Taylor

Toronto Maple Leafs

1996-97 Results: 30W-44L-8T 68PTS. Sixth, Central Division

Felix Potvin faced an NHL-record 2438 shots in 74 games in 1996-97, but still managed to record an impressive .908 save percentage.

1997-98 Schedule

Month	Day	Date	Opponent
Oct.	Wed.	1	Washington
	Sat.	4	at NY Islanders
	Tue.	7	at Calgary
	Thu.	9	at Vancouver
	Sat.	11	at Edmonton
	Tue.	14	Detroit
	Wed.	15	at Detroit
	Sat.	18	Dallas
	Wed.	22	Ottawa
	Sat.	25	Calgary
	Tue.	28	Anaheim
Nov.	Sat.	1	at Montreal
	Tue.	4	at San Jose
	Wed.	5	at Calgary
	Sat.	8	Phoenix
	Tue.	11	Chicago
	Thu.	13	at Chicago
	Sat.	15	Pittsburgh
	Mon.	17	St. Louis
	Wed.	19	Philadelphia
	Fri.	21	at Colorado
	Sat.	22	at Phoenix
	Tue.	25	San Jose
	Sat.	29	Vancouver
Dec.	Tue.	2	Anaheim
	Thu.	4	at St. Louis
	Sat.	6	Los Angeles
	Mon.	8	Dallas
	Wed.	10	Colorado
	Sat.	13	New Jersey
	Mon.	15	at Colorado
	Wed.	17	at Anaheim
	Thu.	18	at Los Angeles
	Sat.	20	at Phoenix
	Tue.	23	Edmonton
	Fri.	26	at Detroit
	Sat.	27	Detroit
	Wed.	31	Boston
Jan.	Thu.	1	at Chicago
	Sat.	3	at New Jersey
	Tue.	6	at Washington
	Wed.	7	at Tampa Bay
	Sat.	10	Chicago
	Mon.	12	at NY Rangers
	Wed.	14	Buffalo
	Wed.	21	at Detroit
	Thu.	22	at Chicago
	Sat.	24	Tampa Bay
	Mon.	26	at Dallas
	Thu.	29	at St. Louis
	Sat.	31	Phoenix
Feb.	Mon.	2	Dallas
	Wed.	4	St. Louis
	Thu.	5	at Ottawa
	Sat.	7	Florida*
	Wed.	25	at Buffalo
	Thu.	26	NY Rangers
	Sat.	28	Montreal
Mar.	Mon.	2	at Pittsburgh
	Wed.	4	Colorado
	Sat.	7	Edmonton
	Mon.	9	at San Jose
	Wed.	11	at Anaheim
	Thu.	12	at Los Angeles
	Sat.	14	Calgary
	Mon.	16	at Philadelphia
	Wed.	18	Detroit
	Thu.	19	at Boston
	Sat.	21	Vancouver
	Tue.	24	at Phoenix
	Thu.	26	at Dallas
	Sat.	28	NY Islanders
	Mon.	30	Los Angeles
Apr.	Wed.	1	St. Louis
	Sat.	4	San Jose
	Mon.	6	at Dallas
	Tue.	7	at Florida
	Thu.	9	at Carolina
	Sat.	11	Carolina
	Wed.	15	Chicago
	Sat.	18	at Edmonton
	Sun.	19	at Vancouver

* Denotes afternoon game.

Franchise date: November 22, 1917

CENTRAL DIVISION

81st NHL Season

Year-by-Year Record

		Home			Road			Overall							
Season	GP	W	L	T	W	L	T	W	L	T	GF	GA	Pts.	Finished	Playoff Result
1996-97	82	18	20	3	12	24	5	30	44	8	230	273	68	6th, Central Div.	Out of Playoffs
1995-96	82	19	15	7	15	21	5	34	36	12	247	252	80	3rd, Central Div.	Lost Conf. Quarter-Final
1994-95	48	15	7	2	6	12	6	21	19	8	135	146	50	4th, Central Div.	Lost Conf. Quarter-Final
1993-94	84	23	15	4	20	14	8	43	29	12	280	243	98	2nd, Central Div.	Lost Conf. Championship
1992-93	84	25	11	6	19	18	5	44	29	11	288	241	99	3rd, Norris Div.	Lost Conf. Championship
1991-92	80	21	16	3	9	27	4	30	43	7	234	294	67	5th, Norris Div.	Out of Playoffs
1990-91	80	15	21	4	8	25	7	23	46	11	241	318	57	5th, Norris Div.	Out of Playoffs
1989-90	80	24	14	2	14	24	2	38	38	4	337	358	80	3rd, Norris Div.	Lost Div. Semi-Final
1988-89	80	15	20	5	13	26	1	28	46	6	259	342	62	5th, Norris Div.	Out of Playoffs
1987-88	80	14	20	6	7	29	4	21	49	10	273	345	52	4th, Norris Div.	Lost Div. Semi-Final
1986-87	80	22	14	4	10	28	2	32	42	6	286	319	70	4th, Norris Div.	Lost Div. Final
1985-86	80	16	21	3	9	27	4	25	48	7	311	386	57	4th, Norris Div.	Lost Div. Final
1984-85	80	10	28	2	10	24	6	20	52	8	253	358	48	5th, Norris Div.	Out of Playoffs
1983-84	80	17	16	7	9	29	2	26	45	9	303	387	61	5th, Norris Div.	Out of Playoffs
1982-83	80	20	15	5	8	25	7	28	40	12	293	330	68	3rd, Norris Div.	Lost Div. Semi-Final
1981-82	80	12	20	8	8	24	8	20	44	16	298	380	56	5th, Norris Div.	Out of Playoffs
1980-81	80	14	21	5	14	16	10	28	37	15	322	367	71	5th, Adams Div.	Lost Prelim. Round
1979-80	80	17	19	4	18	21	1	35	40	5	304	327	75	4th, Adams Div.	Lost Prelim. Round
1978-79	80	20	12	8	14	21	5	34	33	13	267	252	81	3rd, Adams Div.	Lost Quarter-Final
1977-78	80	21	13	6	20	16	4	41	29	10	271	237	92	3rd, Adams Div.	Lost Semi-Final
1976-77	80	18	13	9	15	19	6	33	32	15	301	285	81	3rd, Adams Div.	Lost Quarter-Final
1975-76	80	23	12	5	11	19	10	34	31	15	294	276	83	3rd, Adams Div.	Lost Quarter-Final
1974-75	80	19	12	9	12	21	7	31	33	16	280	309	78	3rd, Adams Div.	Lost Quarter-Final
1973-74	78	21	11	7	14	16	9	35	27	16	274	230	86	4th, East Div.	Lost Quarter-Final
1972-73	78	20	12	7	7	29	3	27	41	10	247	279	64	6th, East Div.	Out of Playoffs
1971-72	78	21	11	7	12	20	7	33	31	14	209	208	80	4th, East Div.	Lost Quarter-Final
1970-71	78	24	9	6	13	24	2	37	33	8	248	211	82	4th, East Div.	Lost Quarter-Final
1969-70	76	18	13	7	11	21	6	29	34	13	222	242	71	6th, East Div.	Out of Playoffs
1968-69	76	20	8	10	15	18	5	35	26	15	234	217	85	4th, East Div.	Lost Quarter-Final
1967-68	74	24	9	4	9	22	6	33	31	10	209	176	76	5th, East Div.	Out of Playoffs
1966-67	**70**	**21**	**8**	**6**	**11**	**19**	**5**	**32**	**27**	**11**	**204**	**211**	**75**	**3rd,**	**Won Stanley Cup**
1965-66	70	22	9	4	12	16	7	34	25	11	208	187	79	3rd,	Lost Semi-Final
1964-65	70	17	15	3	13	11	11	30	26	14	204	173	74	4th,	Lost Semi-Final
1963-64	**70**	**22**	**7**	**6**	**11**	**18**	**6**	**33**	**25**	**12**	**192**	**172**	**78**	**3rd,**	**Won Stanley Cup**
1962-63	**70**	**21**	**8**	**6**	**14**	**15**	**6**	**35**	**23**	**12**	**221**	**180**	**82**	**1st,**	**Won Stanley Cup**
1961-62	**70**	**25**	**5**	**5**	**12**	**17**	**6**	**37**	**22**	**11**	**232**	**180**	**85**	**2nd,**	**Won Stanley Cup**
1960-61	70	21	6	8	18	13	4	39	19	12	234	176	90	2nd,	Lost Semi-Final
1959-60	70	20	9	6	15	17	3	35	26	9	199	195	79	2nd,	Lost Final
1958-59	70	17	13	5	10	19	6	27	32	11	189	201	65	4th,	Lost Final
1957-58	70	12	16	7	9	22	4	21	38	11	192	226	53	6th,	Out of Playoffs
1956-57	70	12	16	7	9	18	8	21	34	15	174	192	57	5th,	Out of Playoffs
1955-56	70	19	10	6	5	23	7	24	33	13	153	181	61	4th,	Lost Semi-Final
1954-55	70	14	10	11	10	14	11	24	24	22	147	135	70	3rd,	Lost Semi-Final
1953-54	70	22	6	7	10	18	7	32	24	14	152	131	78	3rd,	Lost Semi-Final
1952-53	70	17	12	6	10	18	7	27	30	13	156	167	67	5th,	Out of Playoffs
1951-52	70	17	10	8	12	15	8	29	25	16	168	157	74	3rd,	Lost Semi-Final
1950-51	**70**	**22**	**8**	**5**	**19**	**8**	**8**	**41**	**16**	**13**	**212**	**138**	**95**	**2nd,**	**Won Stanley Cup**
1949-50	70	18	9	8	13	18	4	31	27	12	176	173	74	3rd,	Lost Semi-Final
1948-49	**60**	**12**	**8**	**10**	**10**	**17**	**3**	**22**	**25**	**13**	**147**	**161**	**57**	**4th,**	**Won Stanley Cup**
1947-48	**60**	**22**	**3**	**5**	**10**	**12**	**8**	**32**	**15**	**13**	**182**	**143**	**77**	**1st,**	**Won Stanley Cup**
1946-47	**60**	**20**	**8**	**2**	**11**	**11**	**8**	**31**	**19**	**10**	**209**	**172**	**72**	**2nd,**	**Won Stanley Cup**
1945-46	50	10	13	2	9	11	5	19	24	7	174	185	45	5th,	Out of Playoffs
1944-45	**50**	**13**	**9**	**3**	**11**	**13**	**1**	**24**	**22**	**4**	**183**	**161**	**52**	**3rd,**	**Won Stanley Cup**
1943-44	50	13	11	1	10	12	3	23	23	4	214	174	50	3rd,	Lost Semi-Final
1942-43	50	17	6	2	5	13	7	22	19	9	198	159	53	3rd,	Lost Semi-Final
1941-42	**48**	**18**	**6**	**0**	**9**	**12**	**3**	**27**	**18**	**3**	**158**	**136**	**57**	**2nd,**	**Won Stanley Cup**
1940-41	48	16	5	3	12	9	3	28	14	6	145	99	62	2nd,	Lost Semi-Final
1939-40	48	15	3	6	10	14	0	25	17	6	134	110	56	3rd,	Lost Final
1938-39	48	13	8	3	6	12	6	19	20	9	114	107	47	3rd,	Lost Final
1937-38	48	13	6	5	11	9	4	24	15	9	151	127	57	1st, Cdn. Div.	Lost Final
1936-37	48	14	9	1	8	12	4	22	21	5	119	115	49	3rd, Cdn. Div.	Lost Quarter-Final
1935-36	48	15	4	5	8	15	1	23	19	6	126	106	52	2nd, Cdn. Div.	Lost Final
1934-35	48	16	6	2	14	8	2	30	14	4	157	111	64	1st, Cdn. Div.	Lost Final
1933-34	48	19	2	3	7	11	6	26	13	9	174	119	61	1st, Cdn. Div.	Lost Semi-Final
1932-33	48	16	4	4	8	14	2	24	18	6	119	111	54	1st, Cdn. Div.	Lost Final
1931-32	**48**	**17**	**4**	**3**	**6**	**14**	**4**	**23**	**18**	**7**	**155**	**127**	**53**	**2nd, Cdn. Div.**	**Won Stanley Cup**
1930-31	44	15	4	3	7	9	6	22	13	9	118	99	53	2nd, Cdn. Div.	Lost Quarter-Final
1929-30	44	10	8	4	7	13	2	17	21	6	116	124	40	4th, Cdn. Div.	Out of Playoffs
1928-29	44	15	5	2	6	13	3	21	18	5	85	69	47	3rd, Cdn. Div.	Lost Semi-Final
1927-28	44	9	8	5	9	10	3	18	18	8	89	88	44	4th, Cdn. Div.	Out of Playoffs
1926-27*	44	10	10	2	5	14	3	15	24	5	79	94	35	5th, Cdn. Div.	Out of Playoffs
1925-26	36	11	5	2	1	16	1	12	21	3	92	114	27	6th,	Out of Playoffs
1924-25	30	10	5	0	9	6	0	19	11	0	90	84	38	2nd,	Lost NHL S-Final
1923-24	24	7	5	0	3	9	0	10	14	0	59	85	20	3rd,	Out of Playoffs
1922-23	24	10	1	1	3	9	0	13	10	1	82	88	27	3rd,	Out of Playoffs
1921-22	**24**	**8**	**4**	**0**	**5**	**6**	**1**	**13**	**10**	**1**	**98**	**97**	**27**	**2nd,**	**Won Stanley Cup**
1920-21	24	9	3	0	6	6	0	15	9	0	105	100	30	2nd and 1st***	Lost NHL Final
1919-20**	24	8	4	0	4	8	0	12	12	0	119	106	24	3rd and 2nd***	Out of Playoffs
1918-19	18	5	4	0	0	9	0	5	13	0	64	92	10	3rd and 3rd***	Out of Playoffs
1917-18	**22**	**10**	**1**	**0**	**3**	**8**	**0**	**13**	**9**	**0**	**108**	**109**	**26**	**2nd and 1st*** **	**Won Stanley Cup**

* Name changed from St. Patricks to Maple Leafs. ** Name changed from Arenas to St. Patricks.
*** Season played in two halves with no combined standing at end.

1997-98 Player Personnel

FORWARDS	HT	WT	S	Place of Birth	Date	1996-97 Club
ADAMS, Kevyn	6-1	182	R	Washington, D.C.	10/8/74	Grand Rapids
BAKER, Jamie	6-0	195	L	Ottawa, Ont.	8/31/66	Toronto
BEREZIN, Sergei	5-10	187	R	Voskresensk, USSR	11/5/71	Toronto
BRAND, Aaron	6-0	190	L	Toronto, Ont.	6/14/75	St. John's
BUTZ, Rob	6-3	191	L	Dewberry, Alta.	2/24/75	St. John's
CARTER, Shawn	6-2	210	L	Eagle River, WI	4/16/73	Orlando-St. John's
CHASE, Kelly	5-11	193	R	Porcupine Plain, Sask.	10/25/67	Hartford-Toronto
CLARK, Wendel	5-11	194	L	Kelvington, Sask.	10/25/66	Toronto
CONVERY, Brandon	6-1	182	R	Kingston, Ont.	2/4/74	Toronto-St. John's
DEMPSEY, Nathan	6-0	170	L	Spruce Grove, Alta.	7/14/74	Toronto-St. John's
DEYELL, Mark	6-0	180	R	Regina, Sask.	3/26/76	St. John's
DOMI, Tie	5-10	200	R	Windsor, Ont.	11/1/69	Toronto
FAIRCHILD, Kelly	5-11	180	L	Hibbing, MN	4/9/73	Toronto-St. John's-Orlando
HAKANSSON, Mikael	6-1	196	L	Stockholm, Sweden	5/31/74	Djurgarden
HENDRICKSON, Darby	6-0	185	L	Richfield, MN	8/28/72	Toronto-St. John's
JOHNSON, Mike	6-2	190	R	Scarborough, Ont.	10/3/74	Bowling Green-Toronto
KALMIKOV, Konstantin	6-4	205	R	Kharkov, USSR	6/14/78	Sudbury-St. John's
KENNEDY, Mike	6-1	195	R	Vancouver, B.C.	4/13/72	Dallas-Michigan
KING, Derek	6-0	212	L	Hamilton, Ont.	2/11/67	NY Islanders-Hartford
KING, Kris	5-11	208	L	Bracebridge, Ont.	2/18/66	Phoenix
KOLESAR, Mark	6-1	188	R	Brampton, Ont.	1/23/73	Toronto-St. John's
KUCHARCIK, Tomas	6-2	200	L	Vlasim, Czech.	5/10/70	Slavia Praha
KYPREOS, Nick	6-0	205	L	Toronto, Ont.	6/4/66	Toronto-St. John's
McCAULEY, Alyn	5-11	185	L	Brockville, Ont.	5/29/77	Ottawa (OHL)-St. John's
MELENOVSKY, Marek	5-9	176	L	Humpolec, Czech.	3/30/77	Dukla Jihlava-St. John's
MODIN, Fredrik	6-3	222	L	Sundsvall, Sweden	10/8/74	Toronto
NEDVED, Zdenek	6-0	180	L	Lany, Czech.	3/3/75	Toronto-St. John's
PEPPERALL, Ryan	6-1	185	R	Niagara Falls, Ont.	1/26/77	Kitchener
PODOLLAN, Jason	6-1	192	R	Vernon, B.C.	2/18/76	Fla-Carolina-Tor-St. John's
PROCHAZKA, Martin	5-11	180	R	Slany, Czech.	3/3/72	AIK
SULLIVAN, Steve	5-9	155	R	Timmins, Ont.	7/6/74	New Jersey-Albany-Toronto
SUNDIN, Mats	6-4	215	R	Bromma, Sweden	2/13/71	Toronto
WARRINER, Todd	6-1	188	L	Blenheim, Ont.	1/3/74	Toronto
DEFENSEMEN						
COOPER, David	6-2	204	L	Ottawa, Ont.	11/2/73	Toronto-St. John's
GUSTAFSSON, Per	6-2	190	L	Osterham, Sweden	6/6/70	Florida
MACOUN, Jamie	6-2	200	L	Newmarket, Ont.	8/17/61	Toronto
MARKOV, Daniil	5-11	176	L	Moscow, USSR	7/11/76	Spartak-St. John's
MARTIN, Matt	6-3	205	L	Hamden, CT	4/30/71	Toronto-St. John's
POSMYK, Marek	6-5	220	R	Jihlava, Czech.	9/15/78	Dukla Jihlava-St. John's
SCHNEIDER, Mathieu	5-11	192	L	New York, NY	6/12/69	Toronto
SMITH, D.J.	6-1	200	L	Windsor, Ont.	5/13/77	Toronto-Windsor-St. John's
SMITH, Jason	6-3	205	R	Calgary, Alta.	11/2/73	New Jersey-Toronto
SMYTH, Greg	6-3	212	R	Oakville, Ont.	4/23/66	Toronto-St. John's
TREMBLAY, Yannick	6-2	185	R	Pointe-aux-Trembles, Que.	11/15/75	Toronto-St. John's
WARE, Jeff	6-4	220	L	Toronto, Ont.	5/19/77	Toronto-Oshawa
WOLANIN, Craig	6-4	215	L	Grosse Pointe, MI	7/27/67	Tampa Bay-Toronto
YUSHKEVICH, Dimitri	5-11	208	R	Cherepovets, USSR	11/19/71	Toronto
ZETTLER, Rob	6-3	200	L	Sept Iles, Que.	3/8/68	Toronto-Utah

GOALTENDERS	HT	WT	C	Place of Birth	Date	1996-97 Club
BONNER, Doug	5-10	175	L	Tacoma, WA	10/15/76	St. John's-Peoria
COUSINEAU, Marcel	5-9	180	L	Delson, Que.	4/30/73	Toronto-St. John's
HEALY, Glenn	5-10	185	L	Pickering, Ont.	8/23/62	NY Rangers
LARIVEE, Francis	6-2	198	L	Montreal, Que.	11/8/77	Granby-Laval-St. John's
POTVIN, Felix	6-0	190	L	Anjou, Que.	6/23/71	Toronto

1996-97 Scoring

* – rookie

Regular Season

Pos	#	Player	Team	GP	G	A	Pts	+/–	PIM	PP	SH	GW	GT	S	%
C	13	Mats Sundin	TOR	82	41	53	94	6	59	7	4	8	1	281	14.6
L	17	Wendel Clark	TOR	65	30	19	49	-2	75	6	0	6	0	212	14.2
R	94	* Sergei Berezin	TOR	73	25	16	41	-3	2	7	0	2	0	177	14.1
C	11	* Steve Sullivan	N.J.	33	8	14	22	9	14	2	0	2	1	63	12.7
			TOR	21	5	11	16	5	23	1	0	1	0	45	11.1
			TOTAL	54	13	25	38	14	37	3	0	3	1	108	12.0
L	8	Todd Warriner	TOR	75	12	21	33	-3	41	2	2	0	1	146	8.2
R	28	Tie Domi	TOR	80	11	17	28	-17	275	2	0	1	0	98	11.2
R	9	Mike Craig	TOR	65	7	13	20	-20	62	1	0	0	0	128	5.5
C	14	Darby Hendrickson	TOR	64	11	6	17	-20	47	0	1	0	2	105	10.5
C	16	Jamie Baker	TOR	58	8	8	16	2	28	1	0	3	0	69	11.6
D	36	Dimitri Yushkevich	TOR	74	4	10	14	-24	56	1	1	1	0	99	4.0
D	2	Rob Zettler	TOR	48	2	12	14	8	51	0	0	0	0	31	6.5
L	19	* Fredrik Modin	TOR	76	6	7	13	-14	24	0	0	0	0	85	7.1
D	72	Mathieu Schneider	TOR	26	5	7	12	3	20	1	0	1	0	63	7.9
D	34	Jamie Macoun	TOR	73	1	10	11	-14	93	0	0	1	0	64	1.6
C	12	* Brandon Convery	TOR	39	2	8	10	-9	20	0	0	0	0	41	4.9
R	10	* Zdenek Nedved	TOR	23	3	5	8	4	6	1	0	0	0	22	13.6
D	25	Jason Smith	N.J.	57	1	2	3	-8	38	0	0	0	0	48	2.1
			TOR	21	0	5	5	-4	16	0	0	0	0	26	0.0
			TOTAL	78	1	7	8	-12	54	0	0	0	0	74	1.4
D	42	* David Cooper	TOR	19	3	3	6	-3	16	2	0	0	0	23	13.0
L	32	Nick Kypreos	TOR	35	3	2	5	1	62	0	0	0	0	18	16.7
R	26	* Jamie Heward	TOR	20	1	4	5	-6	6	0	0	0	0	23	4.3
C	7	* Jason Podollan	FLA	19	1	1	2	-3	4	1	0	0	0	20	5.0
			TOR	10	0	3	3	-2	6	0	0	0	0	10	0.0
			TOTAL	29	1	4	5	-5	10	1	0	0	0	30	3.3
R	20	* Mike Johnson	TOR	13	2	2	4	-2	4	0	1	1	0	27	7.4
D	3	Matt Martin	TOR	36	0	4	4	-12	38	0	0	0	0	30	0.0
D	26	Craig Wolanin	T.B.	15	0	0	0	-9	8	0	0	0	0	12	0.0
			TOR	23	0	4	4	3	13	0	0	0	0	31	0.0
			TOTAL	38	0	4	4	-6	21	0	0	0	0	43	0.0
D	24	Tom Pederson	TOR	15	1	2	3	0	9	1	0	0	0	23	4.3
R	39	Kelly Chase	HFD	28	1	2	3	2	122	0	0	0	0	5	20.0
			TOR	2	0	0	0	0	27	0	0	0	0	1	0.0
			TOTAL	30	1	2	3	2	149	0	0	0	0	6	16.7
G	29	Felix Potvin	TOR	74	0	3	3	0	19	0	0	0	0	0	0.0
L	43	* Nathan Dempsey	TOR	14	1	1	2	-2	2	0	0	0	0	11	9.1
C	7	* Kelly Fairchild	TOR	22	0	2	2	-5	2	0	0	0	0	14	0.0
D	4	* D.J. Smith	TOR	8	0	1	1	-5	7	0	0	0	0	4	0.0
G	31	* Marcel Cousineau	TOR	13	0	1	1	0	0	0	0	0	0	0	0.0
L	22	Scott Pearson	TOR	1	0	0	0	0	2	0	0	0	0	0	0.0
D	25	Greg Smyth	TOR	2	0	0	0	0	0	0	0	0	0	1	0.0
G	33	Don Beaupre	TOR	3	0	0	0	0	0	0	0	0	0	0	0.0
C	15	* Brian Wiseman	TOR	3	0	0	0	0	0	0	0	0	0	1	0.0
R	41	* Shayne Toporowski	TOR	3	0	0	0	0	7	0	0	0	0	3	0.0
D	38	* Yannick Tremblay	TOR	5	0	0	0	-4	0	0	0	0	0	2	0.0
R	44	* John Craighead	TOR	5	0	0	0	0	10	0	0	0	0	0	0.0
R	37	* Mark Kolesar	TOR	7	0	0	0	-3	0	0	0	0	0	3	0.0
D	23	* Jeff Ware	TOR	13	0	0	0	2	6	0	0	0	0	4	0.0

Goaltending

No.	Goaltender	GPI	Mins	Avg	W	L	T	EN	SO	GA	SA	S%
29	Felix Potvin	74	4271	3.15	27	36	7	6	0	224	2438	.908
31	* Marcel Cousineau	13	566	3.29	3	5	1	1	1	31	317	.902
33	Don Beaupre	3	110	5.45	0	3	0	1	0	10	60	.833
	Totals	**82**	**4966**	**3.30**	**30**	**44**	**8**	**8**	**2**	**273**	**2823**	**.903**

General Manager

DRYDEN, KEN
General Manager, Toronto Maple Leafs. Born in Hamilton, Ont., Aug. 8, 1947.

Ken Dryden, 50, was named president of Toronto Maple Leafs on May 30, 1997. He added the duties of the general manager on August 20, 1997.

As a goaltender, Dryden backstopped the Montreal Canadiens to six Stanley Cup championships after joining the team late in 1971. He was instrumental in the Canadiens winning the 1971 Stanley Cup after having been promoted from the minors and playing just six games down the stretch. By playing all 20 games in the playoffs, Dryden won the Conn Smythe Trophy as playoff MVP. He added the Calder Trophy as the NHL's top rookie the following season and went on to win the Vezina Trophy as the League's best goaltender on five occasions. A five-time NHL All-Star, Dryden was inducted into the Hockey Hall of Fame in 1983. He also participated in the historic series between Team Canada and the Soviet National team in 1972.

He played from 1966 to 1969 at Cornell University and was a three-time All-American. While playing for the Canadiens, he successfully completed law school at McGill University. Upon retiring after the 1978-79 season, he wrote two best-selling books about hockey, *The Game* and *Home Game*. He also wrote *The Moved and the Shaken: The Story of One Man's Life* and *In School*. He also authored a report for the University of Moncton pertaining to the attack on a referee and the future of hockey at the university.

Dryden initiated the "Ken Dryden Scholarships" to students from foster homes or group homes for study at a university or college. He also coordinated youth employment programs for the governments of the Yukon and Ontario.

Dryden also possesses a background in hockey broadcasting. He was a color commentator for ABC TV at the 1980, 1984 and 1988 Winter Games.

Ken and his wife Linda live in Toronto with their two children, Sarah and Michael.

General Managers' History

Conn Smythe, 1927-28 to 1956-57; "Hap" Day, 1957-58; "Punch" Imlach, 1958-59 to 1968-69; Jim Gregory, 1969-70 to 1978-79; "Punch" Imlach, 1979-80 to 1980-81; "Punch" Imlach and Gerry McNamara, 1981-82; Gerry McNamara, 1982-83 to 1987-88; Gord Stellick, 1988-89; Floyd Smith, 1989-90 to 1990-91; Cliff Fletcher, 1991-92 to 1996-97; Ken Dryden, 1997-98.

Captains' History

"Hap" Day, 1927-28 to 1936-37; Charlie Conacher, 1937-38; Red Horner, 1938-39, 1939-40; Syl Apps, 1940-41 to 1942-43; Bob Davidson, 1943-44, 1944-45; Syl Apps, 1945-46 to 1947-48; Ted Kennedy, 1948-49 to 1954-55; Sid Smith, 1955-56; Jim Thomson, Ted Kennedy, 1956-57; George Armstrong, 1957-58 to 1968-69; Dave Keon, 1969-70 to 1974-75; Darryl Sittler, 1975-76 to 1980-81; Rick Vaive, 1981-82 to 1985-86; no captain, 1986-87 to 1988-89; Rob Ramage, 1989-90 to 1990-91; Wendel Clark, 1991-92 to 1993-94; Doug Gilmour, 1994-95 to 1996-97.

Club Records

Team

(Figures in brackets for season records are games played; records for fewest points, wins, ties, losses, goals, goals against are for 70 or more games)

Most Points	99	1992-93 (84)
Most Wins	44	1992-93 (84)
Most Ties	22	1954-55 (70)
Most Losses	52	1984-85 (80)
Most Goals	337	1989-90 (80)
Most Goals Against	387	1983-84 (80)
Fewest Points	48	1984-85 (80)
Fewest Wins	20	1981-82, 1984-85 (80)
Fewest Ties	4	1989-90 (80)
Fewest Losses	16	1950-51 (70)
Fewest Goals	147	1954-55 (70)
Fewest Goals Against	*131	1953-54 (70)

Longest Winning Streak

Overall	10	Oct. 7-28/93
Home	9	Nov. 11-Dec. 26/53
Away	7	Nov. 14-Dec. 15/40, Dec. 4/60-Jan. 5/61

Longest Undefeated Streak

Overall	11	Oct. 15-Nov. 8/50 (8 wins, 3 ties), Jan. 6-Feb. 1/94 (7 wins, 4 ties)
Home	18	Nov. 28/33-Mar. 10/34 (15 wins, 3 ties), Oct. 31/53-Jan. 23/54 (16 wins, 2 ties)
Away	9	Nov. 30/47-Jan. 11/48 (4 wins, 5 ties)

Longest Losing Streak

Overall	10	Jan. 15-Feb. 8/67
Home	7	Nov. 10-Dec. 5/84, Jan. 26-Feb. 25/85
Away	11	Feb. 20-Apr. 1/88

Longest Winless Streak

Overall	15	Dec. 26/87-Jan. 25/88 (11 losses, 4 ties)
Home	11	Dec. 19/87-Jan. 25/88 (7 losses, 4 ties)
Away	18	Oct. 6/82-Jan. 5/83 (13 losses, 5 ties)

Most Shutouts, Season	13	1953-54 (70)
Most PIM, Season	2,419	1989-90 (80)
Most Goals, Game	14	Mar. 16/57 (NYR 1 at Tor. 14)

Individual

Most Seasons	21	George Armstrong
Most Games	1,187	George Armstrong
Most Goals, Career	389	Darryl Sittler
Most Assists, Career	620	Borje Salming
Most Points, Career	916	Darryl Sittler (389G, 527A)
Most PIM, Career	1,670	Dave Williams
Most Shutouts, Career	62	Turk Broda
Longest Consecutive Games Streak	486	Tim Horton (Feb. 11/61-Feb. 4/68)
Most Goals, Season	54	Rick Vaive (1981-82)
Most Assists, Season	95	Doug Gilmour (1992-93)
Most Points, Season	127	Doug Gilmour (1992-93; 32G, 95A)
Most PIM, Season	351	Dave Williams (1977-78)

Most Points, Defenseman, Season	79	Ian Turnbull (1976-77; 22G, 57A)
Most Points, Center, Season	127	Doug Gilmour (1992-93; 32G, 95A)
Most Points, Right Wing, Season	97	Wilf Paiement (1980-81; 40G, 57A)
Most Points, Left Wing, Season	99	Dave Andreychuk (1993-94; 53G, 46A)
Most Points, Rookie, Season	66	Peter Ihnacak (1982-83; 28G, 38A)
Most Shutouts, Season	13	Harry Lumley (1953-54)
Most Goals, Game	6	Corb Denneny (Jan. 26/21), Darryl Sittler (Feb. 7/76)
Most Assists, Game	6	Babe Pratt (Jan. 8/44), Doug Gilmour (Feb. 13/93)
Most Points, Game	*10	Darryl Sittler (Feb. 7/76; 6G, 4A)

* NHL Record.

Retired Numbers

5	Bill Barilko	1946-1951
6	Irvine "Ace" Bailey	1927-1934

Honored Numbers

1	Walter "Turk" Broda	1936-43, 45-52
	Johnny Bower	1958-70
7	Francis "King" Clancy	1930-37
	Tim Horton	1949-50, 51-70
9	Ted Kennedy	1942-1955, 56-57
10	Syl Apps	1936-1948

All-time Record vs. Other Clubs

Regular Season

			At Home						On Road						Total			
	GP	W	L	T	GF	GA	PTS	GP	W	L	T	GF	GA	PTS	GP	W	L	T	GF	GA	PTS
Anaheim	8	5	1	2	27	17	12	8	3	4	1	18	26	7	16	8	5	3	45	43	19
Boston	282	148	86	48	961	734	344	282	84	151	47	754	926	215	564	232	237	95	1715	1660	559
Buffalo	51	19	23	9	158	188	47	52	16	33	3	149	221	35	103	35	56	12	307	409	82
Calgary	46	22	17	7	179	173	51	48	13	30	5	150	208	31	94	35	47	12	329	381	82
Chicago	307	161	93	53	1048	794	375	307	112	154	41	798	946	265	614	273	247	94	1846	1740	640
Colorado	27	12	13	2	94	114	26	27	7	15	5	84	105	19	54	19	28	7	178	219	45
Dallas	94	47	31	16	337	296	110	91	33	47	11	292	349	77	185	80	78	27	629	645	187
Detroit	308	162	101	45	1028	821	369	310	101	163	46	756	930	248	618	263	264	91	1784	1751	617
Edmonton	30	14	14	2	125	136	30	30	7	17	6	105	149	20	60	21	31	8	230	285	50
Florida	3	2	1	0	10	10	4	4	1	1	2	10	12	4	7	3	2	2	20	22	8
Hartford	24	8	13	3	83	95	19	24	6	14	4	79	112	16	48	14	27	7	162	207	35
Los Angeles	61	31	19	11	245	207	73	62	20	33	9	183	224	49	123	51	52	20	428	431	122
Montreal	317	160	113	44	958	832	364	316	84	192	40	781	1124	208	633	244	305	84	1739	1956	572
New Jersey	35	24	7	4	155	114	52	34	11	13	10	108	124	32	69	35	20	14	263	238	84
NY Islanders	42	19	20	3	144	152	41	40	14	23	3	125	173	31	82	33	43	6	269	325	72
NY Rangers	269	151	80	38	920	698	340	270	101	113	56	792	830	258	539	252	193	94	1712	1528	598
Ottawa	5	4	1	0	21	10	8	4	2	1	1	11	10	5	9	6	2	1	32	20	13
Philadelphia	54	19	22	13	183	187	51	54	11	35	8	126	217	30	108	30	57	21	309	404	81
Phoenix	36	15	19	2	131	140	32	35	11	18	6	132	149	28	71	26	37	8	263	289	60
Pittsburgh	55	26	18	11	229	185	63	56	20	30	6	182	237	46	111	46	48	17	411	422	109
St. Louis	91	57	24	10	347	262	124	92	26	53	13	259	323	65	183	83	77	23	606	585	189
San Jose	11	8	2	1	45	24	17	12	7	4	1	36	27	15	23	15	6	2	81	51	32
Tampa Bay	9	4	5	0	30	24	8	7	6	1	0	26	13	12	16	10	6	0	56	37	20
Vancouver	53	25	19	9	201	180	59	51	16	26	9	171	179	41	104	41	45	18	372	359	100
Washington	36	20	12	4	151	126	44	37	12	23	2	102	142	26	73	32	35	6	273	268	70
Defunct Clubs	232	158	53	21	860	515	337	233	84	120	29	607	745	197	465	242	173	50	1467	1260	534
Totals	**2486**	**1321**	**807**	**358**	**8690**	**7034**	**3000**	**2486**	**808**	**1314**	**364**	**6836**	**8501**	**1980**	**4972**	**2129**	**2121**	**722**	**15526**	**15535**	**4980**

Playoffs

	Series	W	L	GP	W	L	T	GF	GA	Last Mtg.	Round	Result
Boston	13	8	5	62	31	30	1	150	153	1974	QF	L 0-4
Calgary	1	1	0	2	2	0	0	9	5	1979	PR	W 2-0
Chicago	9	6	3	38	22	15	1	111	89	1995	CQF	L 3-4
Dallas	2	0	2	7	1	6	0	26	35	1983	DSF	L 1-3
Detroit	23	12	11	117	58	59	0	311	321	1993	DSF	W 4-3
Los Angeles	3	2	1	12	7	5	0	41	31	1993	CF	L 3-4
Montreal	15	7	8	71	29	42	0	160	215	1979	QF	L 0-4
NY Islanders	2	1	1	10	4	6	0	20	33	1981	PR	L 0-3
NY Rangers	8	3	5	35	16	19	0	86	86	1971	QF	L 2-4
Philadelphia	3	0	3	17	5	12	0	47	67	1977	QF	L 2-4
Pittsburgh	2	2	0	6	4	2	0	21	13	1977	PR	W 2-1
St. Louis	5	2	3	31	14	17	0	90	88	1996	CQF	L 2-4
San Jose	1	1	0	7	4	3	0	26	21	1994	CSF	W 4-3
Vancouver	1	0	1	5	1	4	0	9	16	1994	CF	L 1-4
Defunct	8	6	2	24	12	10	2	59	57			
Totals	**96**	**51**	**45**	**444**	**210**	**230**	**4**	**1166**	**1246**			

Calgary totals include Atlanta, 1972-73 to 1979-80.   Colorado totals include Quebec, 1979-80 to 1994-95.   Dallas totals include Minnesota, 1967-68 to 1992-93.   New Jersey totals include Kansas City, 1974-75 to 1975-76, and Colorado Rockies, 1976-77 to 1981-82.   Phoenix totals include Winnipeg, 1979-80 to 1995-96.

Playoff Results 1997-93

Year	Round	Opponent	Result	GF	GA
1996	CQF	St. Louis	L 2-4	15	21
1995	CQF	Chicago	L 3-4	20	22
1994	CF	Vancouver	L 1-4	9	16
	CSF	San Jose	W 4-3	26	21
	CQF	Chicago	W 4-2	15	10
1993	CF	Los Angeles	L 3-4	23	22
	DF	St. Louis	W 4-3	22	11
	DSF	Detroit	W 4-3	24	30

Abbreviations: Round: F – Final; CF – conference final; CQF – conference quarter-final; CSF – conference semi-final; DF – division final; DSF – division semi-final; SF – semi-final; QF – quarter-final; PR – preliminary round.

1996-97 Results

Oct.	5	Anaheim	4-1		7	at Calgary	3-4
	8	Edmonton	2-4		11	Colorado	2-3
	12	Tampa Bay	4-7		13	at Washington	3-6
	15	Chicago	1-3		15	Los Angeles	2-3
	17 at	St. Louis	1-6		20	at Hartford	1-3
	19 at	Dallas	0-2		22	Calgary	5-3
	22	San Jose	4-3		24	at Chicago	2-1
	24 at	Boston	2-1		25	Dallas	1-5
	26	Phoenix	5-2		27	Colorado	2-5
	29	Los Angeles	2-5		29	St. Louis	0-4
	31 at	NY Islanders	5-3		31	at New Jersey	3-3
Nov.	2	Detroit	6-2	Feb.	1	Ottawa	1-2
	5	St. Louis	6-3		5	Anaheim	4-2
	7 at	Ottawa	2-6		8	Vancouver	4-2
	9	Edmonton	7-3		12	at Anaheim	2-5
	10 at	Philadelphia	1-3		13	at Los Angeles	4-4
	13 at	Anaheim	2-3		15	at Calgary	1-5
	14 at	Los Angeles	1-4		18	at Vancouver	6-5
	16	Phoenix	2-3		19	at Edmonton	5-6
	19	Buffalo	4-3		22	at Montreal	5-1
	21 at	Buffalo	3-6		25	at Washington	3-5
	23	Montreal	3-4	Mar.	1	San Jose	3-2
	26	Vancouver	3-2		3	Boston	4-2
	27 at	Detroit	2-5		5	Detroit	4-4
	30 at	Dallas	2-5		8	Hartford	1-1
Dec.	3	St. Louis	2-0		10	Dallas	3-3
	6 at	NY Rangers	5-6		12	Chicago	2-3
	7	NY Rangers	0-4		15	at Florida	3-3
	9 at	Chicago	3-1		16	at Tampa Bay	3-1
	10	New Jersey	2-5		19	Philadelphia	3-6
	14	Phoenix	3-5		20	at Pittsburgh	3-6
	15 at	Detroit	1-3		22	Phoenix	0-3
	17 at	San Jose	6-3		26	at San Jose	2-1
	20 at	Phoenix	2-5		27	at Phoenix	1-1
	21 at	Colorado	6-2		29	at Colorado	3-2
	23	Pittsburgh	5-6	Apr.	2	Florida	3-1
	27 at	St. Louis	3-2		3	at Detroit	2-2
	28	Chicago	5-4		5	Detroit	2-4
	30	NY Islanders	2-0		9	at Dallas	2-3
Jan.	3 at	Edmonton	3-4		10	at St. Louis	1-5
	4 at	Vancouver	3-7		12	Calgary	4-1

Entry Draft
Selections 1997-83

1997
Pick
57	Jeff Farkas
84	Adam Mair
111	Frantisek Mrazek
138	Eric Gooldy
165	Hugo Marchand
190	Shawn Thornton
194	Russ Bartlett
221	Jonathan Hedstrom

1996
Pick
36	Marek Posmyk
50	Francis Larivee
66	Mike Lankshear
68	Konstantin Kalmikov
86	Jason Sessa
103	Vladimir Antipov
110	Peter Cava
111	Brandon Sugden
140	Dmitriy Yakushin
148	Chris Bogas
151	Lucio DeMartinis
178	Reggie Berg
204	Tomas Kaberle
230	Jared Hope

1995
Pick
15	Jeff Ware
54	Ryan Pepperall
139	Doug Bonner
145	Yannick Tremblay
171	Marek Melenovsky
197	Mark Murphy
223	Daniil Markov

1994
Pick
16	Eric Fichaud
48	Sean Haggerty
64	Fredrik Modin
126	Mark Deyell
152	Kam White
178	Tommi Rajamaki
204	Rob Butler
256	Sergei Berezin
282	Doug Nolan

1993
Pick
12	Kenny Jonsson
19	Landon Wilson
123	Zdenek Nedved
149	Paul Vincent
175	Jeff Andrews
201	David Brumby
253	Kyle Ferguson
279	Mikhail Lapin

1992
Pick
8	Brandon Convery
23	Grant Marshall
77	Nikolai Borschevsky
95	Mark Raiter
101	Janne Gronvall
106	Chris Deruiter
125	Mikael Hakansson
149	Patrik Augusta
173	Ryan Vandenbussche
197	Wayne Clarke
221	Sergei Simonov
245	Nathan Dempsey

1991
Pick
47	Yanic Perreault
69	Terry Chitaroni
102	Alexei Kudashov
113	Jeff Perry
120	Alexander Kuzminsky
135	Martin Prochazka
160	Dmitri Mironov
164	Robb McIntyre
167	Tomas Kucharcik
179	Guy Lehoux
201	Gary Miller
223	Jonathan Kelley
245	Chris O'Rourke

1990
Pick
10	Drake Berehowsky
31	Felix Potvin
73	Darby Hendrickson
80	Greg Walters
115	Alexander Godynyuk
136	Eric Lacroix
157	Dan Stiver
178	Robert Horyna
199	Rob Chebator
220	Scott Malone
241	Nick Vachon

1989
Pick
3	Scott Thornton
12	Rob Pearson
21	Steve Bancroft
66	Matt Martin
96	Keith Carney
108	David Burke
125	Michael Doers
129	Keith Merkler
150	Derek Langille
171	Jeffrey St. Laurent
192	Justin Tomberlin
213	Mike Jackson
234	Steve Chartrand

1988
Pick
6	Scott Pearson
27	Tie Domi
48	Peter Ing
69	Ted Crowley
88	Leonard Esau
132	Matt Mallgrave
153	Roger Elvenas
174	Mike Delay
195	David Sacco
216	Mike Gregorio
237	Peter DeBoer

1987
Pick
7	Luke Richardson
28	Daniel Marois
49	John McIntyre
71	Joe Sacco
91	Mike Eastwood
112	Damian Rhodes
133	Trevor Jobe
154	Chris Jensen
175	Brian Blad
196	Ron Bernacci
217	Ken Alexander
238	Alex Weinrich

1986
Pick
6	Vincent Damphousse
36	Darryl Shannon
48	Sean Boland
69	Kent Hulst
90	Scott Taylor
111	Stephane Giguere
132	Danny Hie
153	Stephen Brennan
174	Brian Bellefeuille
195	Sean Davidson
216	Mark Holick
237	Brian Hoard

1985
Pick
1	Wendel Clark
22	Ken Spangler
43	Dave Thomlinson
64	Greg Vey
85	Jeff Serowik
106	Jiri Latal
127	Tim Bean
148	Andy Donahue
169	Todd Whittemore
190	Bob Reynolds
211	Tim Armstrong
232	Mitch Murphy

1984
Pick
4	Al Iafrate
25	Todd Gill
67	Jeff Reese
88	Jack Capuano
109	Fabian Joseph
130	Joe McInnis
151	Derek Laxdal
172	Dan Turner
192	David Buckley
213	Mikael Wurst
233	Peter Slanina

1983
Pick
7	Russ Courtnall
28	Jeff Jackson
48	Allan Bester
83	Dan Hodgson
128	Cam Plante
148	Paul Bifano
168	Cliff Albrecht
184	Greg Rolston
188	Brian Ross
208	Mike Tomlak
228	Ron Choules

Coaching History

Conn Smythe, 1927-28 to 1929-30; Conn Smythe and Art Duncan, 1930-31; Art Duncan and Dick Irvin, 1931-32; Dick Irvin, 1932-33 to 1939-40; "Hap" Day, 1940-41 to 1949-50; Joe Primeau, 1950-51 to 1952-53; "King" Clancy, 1953-54 to 1955-56; Howie Meeker, 1956-57; Billy Reay, 1957-58; Billy Reay and "Punch" Imlach, 1958-59; "Punch" Imlach, 1959-60 to 1968-69; John McLellan, 1969-70 to 1970-71; John McLellan and "King" Clancy, 1971-72; John McLellan, 1972-73; "Red" Kelly, 1973-74 to 1976-77; Roger Neilson, 1977-78 to 1978-79; Floyd Smith, Dick Duff and "Punch" Imlach, 1979-80; "Punch" Imlach, Joe Crozier and Mike Nykoluk, 1980-81; Mike Nykoluk, 1981-82 to 1983-84; Dan Maloney, 1984-85 to 1985-86; John Brophy, 1986-87 to 1987-88; John Brophy and George Armstrong, 1988-89; Doug Carpenter, 1989-90; Doug Carpenter and Tom Watt, 1990-91; Tom Watt, 1991-92; Pat Burns, 1992-93 to 1994-95; Pat Burns and Nick Beverley, 1995-96; Mike Murphy, 1996-97 to date.

Coach

MURPHY, MIKE
Coach, Toronto Maple Leafs. Born in Toronto, Ont., September 12, 1950.

Mike Murphy enters his second season as Toronto's head coach in 1997-98.

Named as the Maple Leafs' 24th coach on July 3, 1996, Mike Murphy is familiar with the expectations that accompany coaching in his hometown. Murphy, 47, was an assistant coach with the Leafs from 1991-92 to 1993-94 and served in a similar capacity with the New York Rangers in 1994-95 and 1995-96.

He played 12 NHL seasons at right wing, scoring 328 goals and 318 assists in 821 games. He played for the Rangers and Blues before joining the Los Angeles Kings in 1973. He played 10 seasons with the Kings and served as the club's captain before joining the club's coaching staff in 1984. He worked as an assistant before taking over the head coaching job in January of 1987. He coached 65 games for the Kings before moving to Vancouver as an assistant in 1988. In 1991, he coached Milwaukee, the Canucks' IHL affiliate, before joining the Leafs.

Coaching Record

| Season | Team | | Regular Season | | | | | | Playoffs | | | |
		Games	W	L	T	%		Games	W	L	%
1986-87	Los Angeles (NHL)	38	13	21	4	.395		5	1	4	.200
1987-88	Los Angeles (NHL)	27	7	16	4	.333		....	....	....	....
1990-91	Milwaukee (IHL)	82	36	43	3	.452		6	2	4	.333
1996-97	Toronto (NHL)	82	30	44	8	.415		....	....	....	....
	NHL Totals	147	50	81	16	.395		5	1	4	.200

Club Directory

Maple Leaf Gardens
60 Carlton Street
Toronto, Ontario M5B 1L1
Phone **416/977-1641**
FAX 416/977-5364
Capacity: 15,746 (standing 100)

Board of Directors
Brian P. Bellmore, Robert G. Bertram, John MacIntyre, Dean Metcalf, Steve A. Stavro, Larry Tanenbaum

Advisory Board
J. Donald Crump, Chris Dundas, Terence V. Kelly, Ted Nikolaou, W. Ron Pringle, George E. Whyte

Management
Chairman of the Board and CEO	Steve A. Stavro
President and General Manager, Toronto Maple Leafs	Ken Dryden
Alternate Governor	Brian P. Bellmore
Corporate Secretary	Paul Perantinos
Assistant to the President	Bill Watters
Associate General Manager	Mike Smith
Assistant General Manager and Director of Professional Player Development	Anders Hedberg
Marketing/Community Consultant	Darryl Sittler
Director of Pro Scouting	Nick Beverley
Head Coach	Mike Murphy
Assistant Coach	Mike Kitchen
Assistant Coach	Terry Simpson
Goaltending Coach/Pro Scout	Rick Wamsley
Pro Scout	Tom Watt
Scouting Coordinator	Dan Marr
Scouts	George Armstrong, Mark Hillier, Peter Johnson, Garth Malarchuk, Jack Gardiner, Bob Johnson, Floyd Smith

St. John's Maple Leafs
Head Coach	Al MacAdam
Assistant Coach	Rich Brown
Athletic Therapist	Nick Addey-Jibb
Equipment Manager	Don Alcock

Hockey Administration
Director of Business Operations and Communications	Bob Stellick
Travel Coordinator	Mary Speck
Manager, Media Relations	Pat Park
Manager, Game Operations and Team Services	Casey Vanden Heuvel
Manager, Community Relations	Kristy Fletcher
Manager, Community Development	Angela McManus
Promotions Assistant	Mike Ferriman
Promotions Assistant	Nancy Gilks
Media Relations Assistant	Anthony Alfred
Executive Secretary to the President and G.M.	Ann Clark

Medical and Training Staff
Head Athletic Therapist	Chris Broadhurst
Athletic Therapist	Brent Smith
Equipment Manager	Brian Papineau
Assistant Equipment Manager	Dave Aleo
Team Doctors	Dr. Michael Clarfield, Dr. Darrell Ogilvie-Harris, Dr. Leith Douglas, Dr. Rob Devenyi, Dr. Simon McGrail
Team Dentist	Dr. Ernie Lewis
Team Psychologist	Robert Offenberger, Ph.D.

Sales and Marketing
Director of Marketing	Bill Cluff
Marketing and Promotions Manager	Chris Reed
Manager, Business Development	Duke Dickson
Luxury Suites Coordinator	Nancy Read
Marketing Assistant	Christine McKenna

Retail
| Retail Operations Manager | Jeff Newman |

Ticketing
Box Office Manager	Donna Henderson
Assistant, Box Office Manager	Brenda Roberts
Box Office Coordinator	Bonnie Fox
Box Office Coordinator	Stephen Nichol

Finance and Building Operations
Vice-President of Building Operations	Brian Conacher
Controller	Ian Clarke
Vice-President, Project Director	Tom Anselmi
Executive Assistant to Vice-President, Project Director	Gail Ricci
Assistant Controller	Paul Franck
Assistant Building Manager	Bernie Fournier
Assistant Building Manager, Chief Engineer	Steven Bodolay
Booking Manager	Cindy Ross
Food and Beverage Manager	Garth Essery
Assistant Food and Beverage Manager	James Findlay
Manager, Security and Event Staff	Russ Lauzier
Assistant Manager, Security and Event Staff	Dan Wilkinson

Vancouver Canucks

1996-97 Results: 35W-40L-7T 77PTS. Fourth, Pacific Division

1997-98 Schedule

Oct.	Fri.	3	Anaheim†	Mon.	5	Los Angeles
	Sat.	4	at Anaheim†	Wed.	7	St. Louis
	Thu.	9	Toronto	Thu.	8	at Colorado
	Sat.	11	NY Rangers	Sat.	10	Florida
	Mon.	13	Edmonton*	Mon.	12	at Chicago
	Fri.	17	Boston	Wed.	14	at Detroit
	Sun.	19	Colorado*	Thu.	15	at Buffalo
	Tue.	21	at Dallas	Wed.	21	Phoenix
	Thu.	23	at St. Louis	Sat.	24	at Calgary
	Sat.	25	Pittsburgh	Mon.	26	at Phoenix
	Sun.	26	Detroit	Wed.	28	at Colorado
	Wed.	29	at Chicago	Fri.	30	New Jersey
	Thu.	30	at New Jersey	Sat.	31	at Edmonton
Nov.	Sat.	1	at Pittsburgh	Feb. Mon.	2	Colorado
	Mon.	3	at Carolina	Fri.	6	Edmonton
	Tue.	4	at Washington	Sat.	7	San Jose
	Sat.	8	Anaheim	Wed.	25	Anaheim
	Tue.	11	at Los Angeles	Fri.	27	at Calgary
	Wed.	12	at San Jose	Sat.	28	Ottawa
	Fri.	14	at Anaheim	Mar. Mon.	2	at Los Angeles
	Sun.	16	Carolina*	Thu.	5	Calgary
	Thu.	20	Phoenix	Sat.	7	Tampa Bay
	Sat.	22	Chicago	Mon.	9	St. Louis
	Tue.	25	at NY Rangers	Wed.	11	at Montreal
	Fri.	28	at Boston*	Thu.	12	at Philadelphia
	Sat.	29	at Toronto	Sat.	14	at NY Islanders
Dec.	Mon.	1	Detroit	Tue.	17	at Florida
	Thu.	4	San Jose	Wed.	18	at Tampa Bay
	Sat.	6	at Colorado	Fri.	20	at Ottawa
	Mon.	8	at St. Louis	Sat.	21	at Toronto
	Tue.	9	at Detroit	Tue.	24	NY Islanders
	Sat.	13	Colorado	Thu.	26	Buffalo
	Mon.	15	Los Angeles	Sat.	28	Washington
	Wed.	17	at Phoenix	Apr. Wed.	1	Edmonton
	Thu.	18	at San Jose	Sat.	4	Dallas
	Sat.	20	Chicago	Mon.	6	at Edmonton
	Tue.	23	Dallas	Thu.	9	at Calgary
	Sat.	27	at Dallas	Sat.	11	at San Jose
	Mon.	29	at Los Angeles	Wed.	15	Los Angeles
	Wed.	31	Philadelphia	Fri.	17	Calgary
Jan.	Sat.	3	Montreal	Sun.	19	Toronto

* Denotes afternoon game.   † in Tokyo.

Franchise date: May 22, 1970

PACIFIC DIVISION

28th NHL Season

Year-by-Year Record

		Home			Road			Overall						
Season	GP	W	L	T	W	L	T	W	L	T	GF	GA	Pts.	Finished	Playoff Result
1996-97	82	20	17	4	15	23	3	35	40	7	257	273	77	4th, Pacific Div.	Out of Playoffs
1995-96	82	15	19	7	17	16	8	32	35	15	278	278	79	3rd, Pacific Div.	Lost Conf. Quarter-Final
1994-95	48	10	8	6	8	10	6	18	18	12	153	148	48	2nd, Pacific Div.	Lost Conf. Semi-Final
1993-94	84	20	19	3	21	21	0	41	40	3	279	276	85	2nd, Pacific Div.	Lost Final
1992-93	84	27	11	4	19	18	5	46	29	9	346	278	101	1st, Smythe Div.	Lost Div. Final
1991-92	80	23	10	7	19	16	5	42	26	12	285	250	96	1st, Smythe Div.	Lost Div. Final
1990-91	80	18	17	5	10	26	4	28	43	9	243	315	65	4th, Smythe Div.	Lost Div. Semi-Final
1989-90	80	13	16	11	12	25	3	25	41	14	245	306	64	5th, Smythe Div.	Out of Playoffs
1988-89	80	19	15	6	14	24	2	33	39	8	251	253	74	4th, Smythe Div.	Lost Div. Semi-Final
1987-88	80	15	20	5	10	26	4	25	46	9	272	320	59	5th, Smythe Div.	Out of Playoffs
1986-87	80	17	19	4	12	24	4	29	43	8	282	314	66	5th, Smythe Div.	Out of Playoffs
1985-86	80	17	18	5	6	26	8	23	44	13	282	333	59	4th, Smythe Div.	Lost Div. Semi-Final
1984-85	80	15	21	4	10	25	5	25	46	9	284	401	59	5th, Smythe Div.	Out of Playoffs
1983-84	80	20	16	4	12	23	5	32	39	9	306	328	73	3rd, Smythe Div.	Lost Div. Semi-Final
1982-83	80	20	12	8	10	23	7	30	35	15	303	309	75	3rd, Smythe Div.	Lost Div. Semi-Final
1981-82	80	20	8	12	10	25	5	30	33	17	290	286	77	2nd, Smythe Div.	Lost Final
1980-81	80	17	12	11	11	20	9	28	32	20	289	301	76	3rd, Smythe Div.	Lost Prelim. Round
1979-80	80	14	17	9	13	20	7	27	37	16	256	281	70	3rd, Smythe Div.	Lost Prelim. Round
1978-79	80	15	18	7	10	24	6	25	42	13	217	291	63	2nd, Smythe Div.	Lost Prelim. Round
1977-78	80	13	15	12	7	28	5	20	43	17	239	320	57	3rd, Smythe Div.	Out of Playoffs
1976-77	80	13	21	6	12	21	7	25	42	13	235	294	63	4th, Smythe Div.	Out of Playoffs
1975-76	80	22	11	7	11	21	8	33	32	15	271	272	81	2nd, Smythe Div.	Lost Prelim. Round
1974-75	80	23	12	5	15	20	5	38	32	10	271	254	86	1st, Smythe Div.	Lost Quarter-Final
1973-74	78	14	18	7	10	25	4	24	43	11	224	296	59	7th, East Div.	Out of Playoffs
1972-73	78	17	18	4	5	29	5	22	47	9	233	339	53	7th, East Div.	Out of Playoffs
1971-72	78	14	20	5	6	30	3	20	50	8	203	297	48	7th, East Div.	Out of Playoffs
1970-71	78	17	18	4	7	28	4	24	46	8	229	296	56	6th, East Div.	Out of Playoffs

Martin Gelinas, who reached the 30-goal plateau for the second consecutive year, became a fan favorite in Vancouver with his inspired two-way play.

1997-98 Player Personnel

FORWARDS	HT	WT	S	Place of Birth	Date	1996-97 Club
BOHONOS, Lonny	5-11	190	R	Winnipeg, Man.	5/20/73	Vancouver-Syracuse
BRASHEAR, Donald	6-2	220	L	Bedford, IN	1/7/72	Montreal-Vancouver
BURE, Pavel	5-10	189	L	Moscow, USSR	3/31/71	Vancouver
COURVILLE, Larry	6-1	180	L	Timmins, Ont.	4/2/75	Vancouver-Syracuse
DRUKEN, Harold	5-11	194	L	St. John's, Nfld.	1/26/79	Detroit (OHL)
GELINAS, Martin	5-11	195	L	Shawinigan, Que.	6/5/70	Vancouver
GORDON, Robb	5-11	190	R	Murrayville, B.C.	1/13/76	Syracuse
HOLDEN, Josh	5-11	187	L	Calgary, Alta.	1/18/78	Regina
LINDEN, Trevor	6-4	210	R	Medicine Hat, Alta.	4/11/70	Vancouver
MESSIER, Mark	6-1	205	L	Edmonton, Alta.	1/18/61	NY Rangers
MOGILNY, Alexander	5-11	187	L	Khabarovsk, USSR	2/18/69	Vancouver
NASH, Tyson	6-0	185	L	Edmonton, Alta.	3/11/75	Syracuse
NASLUND, Markus	6-0	186	L	Ornskoldsvik, Sweden	7/30/73	Vancouver
NOONAN, Brian	6-1	200	R	Boston, MA	5/29/65	St. Louis-NY Rangers-Vancouver
ODJICK, Gino	6-3	210	L	Maniwaki, Que.	9/7/70	Vancouver
PROSOFSKY, Tyler	5-11	193	L	Saskatoon, Sask.	2/19/76	Kelowna
ROBERTS, David	6-0	185	L	Alameda, CA	5/28/70	Vancouver
SCATCHARD, Dave	6-2	200	R	Hinton, Alta.	2/20/76	Syracuse
SCHAEFER, Peter	5-11	190	L	Yellow Grass, Sask.	7/12/77	Brandon-Syracuse
SCISSONS, Jeff	6-1	190	L	Saskatoon, Sask.	11/24/76	Minn.-Duluth
SILLINGER, Mike	5-10	190	R	Regina, Sask.	6/29/71	Vancouver
SINCLAIR, Darren	6-0	200	L	Brooks, Alta.	8/24/76	Syracuse
VAIC, Lubomir	5-9	178	L	Spisska Nova Ves, Czech.	3/6/77	Kosice
WALKER, Scott	5-10	189	R	Montreal, Que.	7/19/73	Vancouver
DEFENSEMEN						
ALLAN, Chad	6-1	192	L	Saskatoon, Sask.	7/12/76	Syracuse
AUCOIN, Adrian	6-1	194	R	Ottawa, Ont.	7/3/73	Vancouver
BABYCH, Dave	6-2	215	L	Edmonton, Alta.	5/23/61	Vancouver
BONNI, Ryan	6-4	190	L	Winnipeg, Man.	2/18/79	Saskatoon
CABANA, Clint	6-2	192	R	Bonnyville, Alta.	4/28/78	Medicine Hat-Edmonton (WHL)
FERENCE, Brad	6-3	185	R	Calgary, Alta.	4/2/79	Spokane
HEDICAN, Bret	6-2	195	L	St. Paul, MN	8/10/70	Vancouver
LEDYARD, Grant	6-2	195	L	Winnipeg, Man.	11/19/61	Dallas
LUMME, Jyrki	6-1	205	L	Tampere, Finland	7/16/66	Vancouver
McALLISTER, Chris	6-7	225	L	Saskatoon, Sask.	6/16/75	Syracuse
MURZYN, Dana	6-2	200	L	Calgary, Alta.	12/9/66	Vancouver
OHLUND, Mattias	6-3	209	L	Pitea, Sweden	9/9/76	Lulea
ROBERTSSON, Bert	6-3	205	L	Sodertalje, Sweden	6/30/74	Syracuse
ROHLIN, Leif	6-1	198	L	Vasteras, Sweden	2/26/68	Vancouver
SOPEL, Brent	6-1	190	R	Calgary, Alta.	1/7/77	Swift Current-Syracuse
STAIOS, Steve	6-0	185	R	Hamilton, Ont.	7/28/73	Boston-Vancouver
WOTTON, Mark	5-11	187	L	Foxwarren, Man.	11/16/73	Vancouver-Syracuse
GOALTENDERS	**HT**	**WT**	**C**	**Place of Birth**	**Date**	**1996-97 Club**
CUGNET, Jason	6-1	205	L	North Battleford, Sask.	7/31/76	Colorado
HIRSCH, Corey	5-10	160	L	Medicine Hat, Alta.	7/1/72	Vancouver
HITCHEN, Allan	6-1	195	L	North York, Ont.	3/6/78	Peterborough-London
IRBE, Arturs	5-8	175	L	Riga, Latvia	2/2/67	Dallas
KEYES, Tim	5-11	170	L	Ganonoque, Ont.	5/28/76	Ottawa (OHL)
McLEAN, Kirk	6-0	195	L	Willowdale, Ont.	6/26/66	Vancouver

1996-97 Scoring

* – rookie

Regular Season

Pos	#	Player	Team	GP	G	A	Pts	+/–	PIM	PP	SH	GW	GT	S	%
R	89	Alexander Mogilny	VAN	76	31	42	73	9	18	7	1	4	1	174	17.8
L	23	Martin Gelinas	VAN	74	35	33	68	6	42	6	1	3	1	177	19.8
R	96	Pavel Bure	VAN	63	23	32	55	-14	40	4	1	2	0	265	8.7
C	17	Mike Ridley	VAN	75	20	32	52	0	42	3	0	5	0	79	25.3
L	19	Markus Naslund	VAN	78	21	20	41	-15	30	4	0	4	0	120	17.5
R	16	Trevor Linden	VAN	49	9	31	40	5	27	2	2	2	0	84	10.7
R	26	Mike Sillinger	VAN	78	17	20	37	-3	25	3	3	2	0	112	15.2
D	21	Jyrki Lumme	VAN	66	11	24	35	8	32	5	0	2	0	107	10.3
R	28	Brian Noonan	STL	13	2	5	7	2	0	0	0	0	0	13	15.4
			NYR	44	6	9	15	-7	28	3	0	1	1	62	9.7
			VAN	16	4	8	12	2	6	0	1	0	0	25	16.0
			TOTAL	73	12	22	34	-3	34	3	1	1	1	100	12.0
L	7	David Roberts	VAN	58	10	17	27	11	51	1	1	1	0	74	13.5
D	44	Dave Babych	VAN	78	5	22	27	-2	38	2	0	1	0	105	4.8
C	13	Sergei Nemchinov	NYR	63	6	13	19	5	12	1	0	1	0	90	6.7
			VAN	6	2	3	5	4	4	0	0	1	0	7	28.6
			TOTAL	69	8	16	24	9	16	1	0	2	0	97	8.2
R	14 *	Lonny Bohonos	VAN	36	11	11	22	-3	10	2	0	1	0	67	16.4
D	6	Adrian Aucoin	VAN	70	5	16	21	0	63	1	0	0	0	116	4.3
D	3	Bret Hedican	VAN	67	4	15	19	-3	51	2	0	1	0	93	4.3
C	24	Scott Walker	VAN	64	3	15	18	2	132	0	0	0	0	55	5.5
D	25 *	Steve Staios	BOS	54	3	8	11	-26	71	0	0	0	1	56	5.4
			VAN	9	0	6	6	2	20	0	0	0	0	10	0.0
			TOTAL	63	3	14	17	-24	91	0	0	0	1	66	4.5
D	32	Chris Joseph	VAN	63	3	13	16	-21	62	2	0	1	0	99	3.0
L	8	Donald Brashear	MTL	10	0	0	0	-2	38	0	0	0	0	6	0.0
			VAN	59	8	5	13	-6	207	0	0	2	0	55	14.5
			TOTAL	69	8	5	13	-8	245	0	0	2	0	61	13.1
L	29	Gino Odjick	VAN	70	5	8	13	-5	371	1	0	0	0	85	5.9
D	27	Leif Rohlin	VAN	40	2	8	10	4	8	0	0	0	0	37	5.4
D	4 *	Mark Wotton	VAN	36	3	6	9	8	19	0	1	0	0	41	7.3
D	5	Dana Murzyn	VAN	61	1	7	8	7	118	0	0	0	0	70	1.4
C	20	Alexander Semak	VAN	18	2	1	3	-2	2	1	0	0	0	12	16.7
R	18	Troy Crowder	VAN	30	1	2	3	-6	52	0	0	0	0	11	9.1
L	22 *	Larry Courville	VAN	19	0	2	2	-4	11	0	0	0	0	11	0.0
G	1	Kirk McLean	VAN	44	0	2	2	0	2	0	0	0	0	0	0.0
G	31	Corey Hirsch	VAN	39	0	1	1	0	6	0	0	0	0	0	0.0
D	2	Yevgeny Namestnikov	VAN	2	0	0	0	-1	4	0	0	0	0	1	0.0
G	30 *	Michael Fountain	VAN	6	0	0	0	0	0	0	0	0	0	0	0.0

Goaltending

No.	Goaltender	GPI	Mins	Avg	W	L	T	EN	SO	GA	SA	S%
1	Kirk McLean	44	2581	3.21	21	18	3	3	0	138	1247	.889
31	Corey Hirsch	39	2127	3.27	12	20	4	2	2	116	1090	.894
30 *	Michael Fountain	6	245	3.43	2	2	0	0	1	14	135	.896
	Totals	**82**	**4972**	**3.29**	**35**	**40**	**7**	**5**	**3**	**273**	**2477**	**.890**

General Managers' History

Normand Robert Poile, 1970-71 to 1972-73; Hal Laycoe, 1973-74; Phil Maloney, 1974-75 to 1976-77; Jake Milford, 1977-78 to 1981-82; Harry Neale, 1982-83 to 1984-85; Jack Gordon, 1985-86 to 1986-87; Pat Quinn, 1987-88 to date.

General Manager

QUINN, PAT
President and General Manager, Vancouver Canucks.
Born in Hamilton, Ont., January 29, 1943.

Pat Quinn is entering his eleventh season as president and general manager of the Vancouver Canucks. Before joining the Canucks, he played professional hockey for 14 seasons, coached the Philadelphia Flyers from (1979-82) and Los Angeles Kings (1984-87) and earned his law degree from Widener University, Delaware School of Law.

As a defenceman, Quinn was a member of the Memorial Cup champion Edmonton Oil Kings before his playing career turned pro in 1964 when he joined the Tulsa Oilers of the Central League. Quinn entered the NHL when he joined the Toronto Maple Leafs in 1968, and became an inaugural team member of the Vancouver Canucks on June 10, 1970 when he was selected in the Expansion Draft. In total, Quinn played 133 games as a Canuck before closing out his career with a five-season stint in Atlanta, the last two of which he served as the Flames' captain.

Quinn was named head coach of the Vancouver Canucks in January 1991 and served behind the bench for over three-and-a-half seasons (including six regular season and six playoff games at the end of 1995/96). As head coach, Quinn took the Canucks to post-season play for five seasons, going all the way to a seventh game in the 1994 Stanley Cup Finals. Quinn's accolades include two Jack Adams Awards, signifying top coaching honours in the NHL, with both the Philadelphia Flyers in 1979-80, during which his team set an NHL record of 35 consecutive wins (a record which still stands), and with the Canucks in 1991-92 when he coached the Canucks to their first 40+ win season in franchise history. He has also won *The Hockey News* Coach of the Year in 1979-80 and 1991-92. *The Sporting News* coach of the year in 1979-80 and 1991-92, he coached Team Canada to a bronze medal in the 1986 World Championships. He received the 1994 Jake Milford Award for dedicated service and contribution to hockey in British Columbia and the 1995 Jack Diamond sports personality of the year award.

In his ten years with the Vancouver Canucks, Quinn has earned a reputation as an outstanding administrator, a keen judge of talent and a shrewd negotiator, most recently signing all-star centre Mark Messier to a multi-year deal. These qualities earned him the title of *The Hockey News* executive of the year in 1992 and runner-up in that category in 1994.

Most recently, Quinn served as assistant general manager of the gold medal winning Team Canada at the World Championship tournament in Finland as well as assistant general manager of Team Canada in the 1996 World Cup of Hockey. In the Vancouver community, Quinn is the Co-chair of The Greater Vancouver Open, the first new PGA Tour event in more than ten years. The Vancouver Canucks have taken a leading role in establishing the tournament, and serving as a community partner. The not-for-profit tournament supports many community initiatives throughout British Columbia and this year featured members of both the Vancouver Canucks and Team Canada.

NHL Coaching Record

		Regular Season					Playoffs			
Season	**Team**	**Games**	**W**	**L**	**T**	**%**	**Games**	**W**	**L**	**%**
1978-79	Philadelphia	30	18	8	4	.667	8	3	5	.375
1979-80	Philadelphia	80	48	12	20	.725	19	13	6	.684
1980-81	Philadelphia	80	41	24	15	.606	12	6	6	.500
1981-82	Philadelphia	72	34	29	9	.535	....	....	....	....
1984-85	Los Angeles	80	34	32	14	.513	3	0	3	.000
1985-86	Los Angeles	80	23	49	8	.338	....	....	....	....
1986-87	Los Angeles	42	18	20	4	.476	....	....	....	....
1990-91	Vancouver	26	9	13	4	.423	6	2	4	.333
1991-92	Vancouver	80	42	26	12	.600	13	6	7	.462
1992-93	Vancouver	84	46	29	9	.601	12	6	6	.500
1993-94	Vancouver	84	41	40	3	.506	24	15	9	.625
1995-96	Vancouver	6	3	3	0	.500	6	2	4	.333
	NHL Totals	**744**	**357**	**285**	**102**	**.548**	**103**	**53**	**50**	**.515**

Club Records

Team

(Figures in brackets for season records are games played; records for fewest points, wins, ties, losses, goals, goals against are for 70 or more games)

Most Points	**101**	1992-93 (84)
Most Wins	**46**	1992-93 (84)
Most Ties	**20**	1980-81 (80)
Most Losses	**50**	1971-72 (78)
Most Goals	**346**	1992-93 (84)
Most Goals Against	**401**	1984-85 (80)
Fewest Points	**48**	1971-72 (78)
Fewest Wins	**20**	1971-72 (78), 1977-78 (80)
Fewest Ties	**3**	1993-94 (84)
Fewest Losses	**26**	1991-92 (80)
Fewest Goals	**203**	1971-72 (78)
Fewest Goals Against	**250**	1991-92 (80)
Longest Winning Streak		
Overall	**7**	Feb. 10-23/89
Home	**9**	Nov. 6-Dec. 9/92
Away	**5**	Jan. 14-25/92, Oct. 6-Nov. 2/93
Longest Undefeated Streak		
Overall	**10**	Mar. 5-25/77 (5 wins, 5 ties)
Home	**18**	Oct. 30/92-Jan. 18/93 (16 wins, 2 ties)
Away	**5**	Five times
Longest Losing Streak		
Overall	**9**	Four times
Home	**6**	Dec. 18/70-Jan. 20/71
Away	**12**	Nov. 28/81-Feb. 7/82
Longest Winless Streak		
Overall	**13**	Nov. 9-Dec. 7/73 (10 losses, 3 ties)
Home	**11**	Dec. 18/70-Feb. 6/71 (10 losses, 1 tie)
Away	**20**	Jan. 2-Apr. 2/86 (14 losses, 6 ties)
Most Shutouts, Season	**8**	1974-75 (80)
Most PIM, Season	**2,326**	1992-93 (84)
Most Goals, Game	**11**	Mar. 28/71 (Cal. 5 at Van. 11), Nov. 25/86 (L.A. 5 at Van. 11), Mar. 1/92 (Cgy. 0 at Van. 11)

Individual

Most Seasons	**13**	Stan Smyl
Most Games	**896**	Stan Smyl
Most Goals, Career	**262**	Stan Smyl
Most Assists, Career	**411**	Stan Smyl
Most Points, Career	**673**	Stan Smyl (262G, 411A)
Most PIM, Career	**1,946**	Gino Odjick
Most Shutouts, Career	**19**	Kirk McLean
Longest Consecutive Games Streak	**482**	Trevor Linden (Oct. 4/90-Dec. 3/96)
Most Goals, Season	**60**	Pavel Bure (1992-93, 1993-94)
Most Assists, Season	**62**	André Boudrias (1974-75)
Most Points, Season	**110**	Pavel Bure (1992-93; 60G, 50A)
Most PIM, Season	**371**	Gino Odjick (1996-97)
Most Points, Defenseman, Season	**63**	Doug Lidster (1986-87; 12G, 51A)
Most Points, Center, Season	**91**	Patrik Sundstrom (1983-84; 38G, 53A)
Most Points, Right Wing, Season	**110**	Pavel Bure (1992-93; 60G, 50A)
Most Points, Left Wing, Season	**81**	Darcy Rota (1982-83; 42G, 39A)
Most Points, Rookie, Season	**60**	Ivan Hlinka (1981-82; 23G, 37A), Pavel Bure (1991-92; 34G, 26A)
Most Shutouts, Season	**6**	Gary Smith (1974-75)
Most Goals, Game	**4**	Several players
Most Assists, Game	**6**	Patrik Sundstrom (Feb. 29/84)
Most Points, Game	**7**	Patrik Sundstrom (Feb. 29/84; 1G, 6A)

Retired Numbers

12	Stan Smyl	1978-1991

Captains' History

Orland Kurtenbach, 1970-71 to 1973-74; no captain, 1974-75; Andre Boudrias, 1975-76; Chris Oddleifson, 1976-77; Don Lever, 1977-78; Don Lever and Kevin McCarthy, 1978-79; Kevin McCarthy, 1979-80 to 1981-82; Stan Smyl, 1982-83 to 1989-90; Dan Quinn, Doug Lidster and Trevor Linden, 1990-91; Trevor Linden, 1991-92 to date.

All-time Record vs. Other Clubs

Regular Season

	At Home							On Road							Total						
	GP	W	L	T	GF	GA	PTS	GP	W	L	T	GF	GA	PTS	GP	W	L	T	GF	GA	PTS
Anaheim	11	7	4	0	40	28	14	11	7	3	1	35	24	15	22	14	7	1	75	52	29
Boston	46	14	24	8	154	196	36	45	5	36	4	105	201	14	91	19	60	12	259	397	50
Buffalo	46	22	14	10	174	150	54	47	16	23	8	140	170	40	93	38	37	18	314	320	94
Calgary	80	30	33	17	284	268	77	79	15	53	11	223	346	41	159	45	86	28	507	614	118
Chicago	58	27	17	14	177	166	68	57	14	37	6	135	220	34	115	41	54	20	312	386	102
Colorado	27	11	12	4	107	117	26	28	11	12	5	79	89	27	55	22	24	9	186	206	53
Dallas	57	26	21	10	217	177	62	57	15	32	10	168	223	40	114	41	53	20	385	400	102
Detroit	51	25	19	7	198	165	57	52	15	30	7	156	216	37	103	40	49	14	354	381	94
Edmonton	63	24	31	8	241	268	56	62	15	41	6	194	300	36	125	39	72	14	435	568	92
Florida	3	1	1	1	12	8	3	3	0	2	1	7	9	1	6	1	3	2	19	17	4
Hartford	25	10	9	6	90	74	26	24	10	10	4	85	78	24	49	20	19	10	175	152	50
Los Angeles	82	42	26	14	324	270	98	84	29	43	12	279	348	70	166	71	69	26	603	618	168
Montreal	45	7	30	8	111	180	22	47	8	36	3	123	234	19	92	15	66	11	234	414	41
New Jersey	43	24	8	11	163	123	59	43	19	18	6	144	132	44	86	43	26	17	307	255	103
NY Islanders	43	20	20	3	143	142	43	41	10	23	8	111	157	28	84	30	43	11	254	299	71
NY Rangers	47	12	32	3	151	193	27	49	8	36	5	122	222	21	96	20	68	8	273	415	48
Ottawa	4	2	1	1	12	7	5	4	2	2	0	14	10	4	8	4	3	1	26	17	9
Philadelphia	47	10	25	12	139	184	32	47	14	32	1	140	209	29	94	24	57	13	279	393	61
Phoenix	58	34	16	8	229	170	76	55	20	27	8	208	218	48	113	54	43	16	437	388	124
Pittsburgh	45	21	21	3	165	173	45	45	8	30	7	153	208	23	90	29	51	10	318	381	68
St. Louis	58	25	26	7	180	183	57	57	18	31	8	175	211	44	115	43	57	15	355	394	101
San Jose	18	14	3	1	76	38	29	18	10	6	2	66	61	22	36	24	9	3	142	99	51
Tampa Bay	5	5	0	0	26	7	10	4	3	1	0	17	12	6	9	8	1	0	43	19	16
Toronto	51	26	16	9	179	171	61	53	19	25	9	180	201	47	104	45	41	18	359	372	108
Washington	34	15	14	5	115	112	35	35	11	20	4	104	124	26	69	26	34	9	219	236	61
Defunct Clubs	19	14	3	2	82	48	30	19	10	8	1	71	68	21	38	24	11	3	153	116	51
Totals	**1066**	**468**	**426**	**172**	**3789**	**3618**	**1108**	**1066**	**312**	**617**	**137**	**3234**	**4291**	**761**	**2132**	**780**	**1043**	**309**	**7023**	**7909**	**1869**

Playoffs

	Series	W	L	GP	W	L	T	GF	GA	Last Mtg.	Round	Result
Buffalo	2	0	2	7	1	6	0	14	28	1981	PR	L 0-3
Calgary	5	2	3	25	12	13	0	80	82	1994	CQF	W 4-3
Chicago	2	1	1	9	4	5	0	24	24	1995	CSF	L 0-4
Colorado	1	0	1	6	2	4	0	17	24	1996	CQF	L 2-4
Dallas	1	1	0	5	4	1	0	18	11	1994	CSF	W 4-1
Edmonton	2	0	2	9	2	7	0	20	35	1992	DF	L 2-4
Los Angeles	3	1	2	17	8	9	0	60	66	1993	DF	L 2-4
Montreal	1	0	1	5	1	4	0	9	20	1975	QF	L 1-4
NY Islanders	2	0	2	6	0	6	0	14	26	1982	F	L 0-4
NY Rangers	1	0	1	7	3	4	0	19	21	1994	F	L 3-4
Philadelphia	1	0	1	3	1	2	0	9	15	1979	PR	L 1-2
St. Louis	1	1	0	7	4	3	0	27	27	1995	CQF	W 4-3
Toronto	1	1	0	5	4	1	0	16	9	1994	CF	W 4-1
Winnipeg	2	2	0	13	8	5	0	50	34	1993	DSF	W 4-2
Totals	**25**	**9**	**16**	**124**	**54**	**70**	**0**	**377**	**422**			

Playoff Results 1997-93

Year	Round	Opponent	Result	GF	GA
1996	CQF	Colorado	L 2-4	17	24
1995	CSF	Chicago	L 0-4	6	11
	CQF	St. Louis	W 4-3	27	27
1994	F	NY Rangers	L 3-4	19	21
	CF	Toronto	W 4-1	16	9
	CSF	Dallas	W 4-1	18	11
	CQF	Calgary	W 4-3	23	20
1993	DF	Los Angeles	L 2-4	25	26
	DSF	Winnipeg	W 4-2	21	17

Abbreviations: Round: F – Final; **CF** – conference final; **CQF** – conference quarter-final; **CSF** – conference semi-final; **DF** – division final; **DSF** – division semi-final; **SF** – semi-final; **QF** – quarter-final; **PR** – preliminary round.

Calgary totals include Atlanta, 1972-73 to 1979-80. Colorado totals include Quebec, 1979-80 to 1994-95. Dallas totals include Minnesota, 1970-71 to 1992-93. New Jersey totals include Kansas City, 1974-75 to 1975-76, and Colorado Rockies, 1976-77 to 1981-82. Phoenix totals include Winnipeg, 1979-80 to 1995-96.

1996-97 Results

Oct.	5		Calgary	3-1		12		Anaheim	2-3
	6	at	Edmonton	0-2		14		Florida	4-4
	9		Buffalo	1-2		20		San Jose	6-1
	12		St. Louis	5-3		22	at	Chicago	4-3
	14		Boston	4-5		23	at	St. Louis	3-4
	17	at	Dallas	6-1		25	at	Phoenix	0-4
	19	at	Colorado	2-9		27		San Jose	5-2
	23		Colorado	1-4		30		NY Islanders	2-1
	26		Pittsburgh	2-1	**Feb.**	1	at	Calgary	0-3
	30	at	Anaheim	6-3		3	at	Ottawa	4-6
Nov.	1	at	Edmonton	5-4		4	at	Pittsburgh	4-6
	2		Calgary	4-3		6	at	Detroit	7-4
	8		St. Louis	2-4		8	at	Toronto	2-4
	11	at	NY Rangers	3-2		11		Washington	2-5
	13	at	NY Islanders	4-5		15		Anaheim	4-2
	14	at	New Jersey	3-0		18		Toronto	5-6
	16	at	Montreal	1-6		20	at	San Jose	6-1
	19		Dallas	2-0		22	at	Los Angeles	0-4
	21		Chicago	2-1		23	at	Anaheim	2-5
	23		NY Rangers	5-3		25		Montreal	2-4
	26	at	Toronto	2-3		27		Phoenix	6-2
	27	at	Hartford	6-2	**Mar.**	1		Los Angeles	0-3
	29	at	Boston	3-7		3	at	Colorado	1-5
Dec.	1	at	Philadelphia	3-4		5		Chicago	1-1
	3	at	Detroit	2-2		8		Detroit	3-5
	4	at	Buffalo	7-6		10	at	Chicago	2-2
	7		Ottawa	2-3		11	at	Washington	1-4
	11		Colorado	1-6		13	at	Florida	4-5
	13	at	Dallas	1-2		15	at	Tampa Bay	5-2
	15	at	St. Louis	8-0		18	at	Colorado	2-4
	18		New Jersey	1-2		20		San Jose	1-2
	20		Detroit	3-2		22		Tampa Bay	3-2
	23		Edmonton	0-7		24		Los Angeles	2-2
	26	at	San Jose	1-6		26		Anaheim	5-3
	27	at	Phoenix	4-7		29	at	Calgary	5-2
	31		Philadelphia	3-5		30		Dallas	2-3
Jan.	2		Los Angeles	4-3	**Apr.**	4		Calgary	3-3
	4		Toronto	7-3		5	at	Edmonton	2-2
	6	at	Anaheim	5-1		7	at	San Jose	3-2
	7	at	Los Angeles	2-6		9		Phoenix	6-4
	10		Hartford	5-3		12		Edmonton	5-4

Entry Draft
Selections 1997-83

1997
Pick
10	Brad Ference
34	Ryan Bonni
36	Harold Druken
64	Kyle Freadrich
90	Chris Stanley
114	David Darguzas
117	Matt Cockell
144	Matt Cooke
148	Larry Shapley
171	Rod Leroux
201	Denis Martynyuk
227	Peter Brady

1996
Pick
12	Josh Holden
75	Zenith Komarniski
93	Jonas Soling
121	Tyler Prosofsky
147	Nolan McDonald
175	Clint Cabana
201	Jeff Scissons
227	Lubomir Vaic

1995
Pick
40	Chris McAllister
61	Larry Courville
66	Peter Schaefer
92	Lloyd Shaw
120	Todd Norman
144	Brent Sopel
170	Stewart Bodtker
196	Tyler Willis
222	Jason Cugnet

1994
Pick
13	Mattias Ohlund
39	Robb Gordon
42	Dave Scatchard
65	Chad Allan
92	Mike Dubinsky
117	Yanick Dube
169	Yuri Kuznetsov
195	Rob Trumbley
221	Bill Muckalt
247	Tyson Nash
273	Robert Longpre

1993
Pick
20	Mike Wilson
46	Rick Girard
98	Dieter Kochan
124	Scott Walker
150	Troy Creurer
176	Yevgeny Babariko
202	Sean Tallaire
254	Bert Robertsson
280	Sergei Tkachenko

1992
Pick
21	Libor Polasek
40	Mike Peca
45	Michael Fountain
69	Jeff Connolly
93	Brent Tully
110	Brian Loney
117	Adrian Aucoin
141	Jason Clark
165	Scott Hollis
213	Sonny Mignacca
237	Mark Wotton
261	Aaron Boh

1991
Pick
7	Alex Stojanov
29	Jassen Cullimore
51	Sean Pronger
95	Danny Kesa
117	Evgeny Namestnikov
139	Brent Thurston
161	Eric Johnson
183	David Neilson
205	Brad Barton
227	Jason Fitzsimmons
249	Xavier Majic

1990
Pick
2	Petr Nedved
18	Shawn Antoski
23	Jiri Slegr
65	Darin Bader
86	Gino Odjick
128	Daryl Filipek
149	Paul O'Hagan
170	Mark Cipriano
191	Troy Neumier
212	Tyler Ertel
233	Karri Kivi

1989
Pick
8	Jason Herter
29	Robert Woodward
71	Brett Hauer
113	Pavel Bure
134	James Revenberg
155	Rob Sangster
176	Sandy Moger
197	Gus Morschauser
218	Hayden O'Rear
239	Darcy Cahill
248	Jan Bergman

1988
Pick
2	Trevor Linden
33	Leif Rohlin
44	Dane Jackson
107	Corrie D'Alessio
122	Phil Von Stefenelli
128	Dixon Ward
149	Greg Geldart
170	Roger Akerstrom
191	Paul Constantin
212	Chris Wolanin
233	Stefan Nilsson

1987
Pick
24	Rob Murphy
45	Steve Veilleux
66	Doug Torrel
87	Sean Fabian
108	Garry Valk
129	Todd Fanning
150	Viktor Tumenev
171	Craig Daly
192	John Fletcher
213	Roger Hansson
233	Neil Eisenhut
234	Matt Evo

1986
Pick
7	Dan Woodley
49	Don Gibson
70	Ronnie Stern
91	Eric Murano
112	Steve Herniman
133	Jon Helgeson
154	Jeff Noble
175	Matt Merton
196	Marc Lyons
217	Todd Hawkins
238	Vladimir Krutov

1985
Pick
4	Jim Sandlak
25	Troy Gamble
46	Shane Doyle
67	Randy Siska
88	Robert Kron
109	Martin Hrstka
130	Brian McFarlane
151	Hakan Ahlund
172	Curtis Hunt
193	Carl Valimont
214	Igor Larionov
235	Darren Taylor

1984
Pick
10	J.J. Daigneault
31	Jeff Rohlicek
52	Dave Saunders
55	Landis Chaulk
58	Mike Stevens
73	Brian Bertuzzi
94	Brett MacDonald
115	Jeff Korchinski
136	Blaine Chrest
157	Jim Agnew
178	Rex Grant
198	Ed Lowney
219	Doug Clarke
239	Ed Kister

1983
Pick
9	Cam Neely
30	Dave Bruce
50	Scott Tottle
70	Tim Lorentz
90	Doug Quinn
110	Dave Lowry
130	Terry Maki
150	John Labatt
170	Allan Measures
190	Roger Grillo
210	Steve Kayser
230	Jay Mazur

Coaching History

Hal Laycoe, 1970-71 to 1971-72; Vic Stasiuk, 1972-73; Bill McCreary and Phil Maloney, 1973-74; Phil Maloney, 1974-75 to 1975-76; Phil Maloney and Orland Kurtenbach, 1976-77; Orland Kurtenbach, 1977-78; Harry Neale, 1978-79 to 1980-81; Harry Neale and Roger Neilson, 1981-82; Roger Neilson, 1982-83; Roger Neilson and Harry Neale, 1983-84; Harry Neale and Bill Laforge, 1984-85; Tom Watt, 1985-86, 1986-87; Bob McCammon, 1987-88 to 1989-90; Bob McCammon and Pat Quinn, 1990-91; Pat Quinn, 1991-92 to 1993-94; Rick Ley, 1994-95; Rick Ley and Pat Quinn, 1995-96; Tom Renney, 1996-97 to date.

Coach

RENNEY, TOM
Coach, Vancouver Canucks. Born in Cranbrook, B.C., March 1, 1955.

Tom Renney is entering his second year as the Vancouver Canucks head coach following his hiring on June 4, 1996. Renney, a native of Cranbrook, B.C., joined the National Team program at the beginning of the 1992-93 season and was appointed head coach in August of 1993. Renney coached Canada's National Team to a bronze medal at the 1995 World Championships and won the silver medal at the 1996 World Championships in Vienna, Austria.

Tom Renney coached Canada's Olympic Hockey Team to a silver medal at the 1994 Olympic Winter Games in Lillehammer, Norway and coached the gold medal-winning team at the 1994 World Hockey Championships in Milan, Italy.

Renney, 42, coached the Kamloops Blazers to two WHL regular season pennants during the 1990-91 and the 1991-92 seasons, posting a record of 101 wins, 37 losses and six ties. Under the guidance of Renney, the Kamloops Blazers became the 1991-92 Canadian Hockey League's Memorial Cup champions.

Renney has been honored with the following awards: Sport British Columbia coach of the year in 1991-92, 3M Coaches Canada Award, and WHL coach of the year in 1990-91. He was an assistant coach for the Canadian team at the International Ice Hockey Federation's 1992 World Junior Championship in Fussen, Germany and in the summer of 1992, was the head coach of Canada's National Under-18 Team winning the Phoenix Cup in Japan.

Tom Renney graduated from the University of North Dakota with a degree in physical education. Tom and his wife Glenda have two daughters; Jessica and Jamie.

Club Directory

General Motors Place
800 Griffiths Way
Vancouver, B.C. V6B 6G1
Phone **604/899-4600**
FAX 604/899-4640
Capacity: 18,422

Orca Bay Sports & Entertainment Management
Chairman, Orca Bay Sports & Entertainment; Governor, NHL and NBA.	John E. McCaw, Jr.
Vice-Chairman, Orca Bay Sports & Entertainment; Alternate Governor, NHL and NBA	Arthur R. Griffiths
Deputy Chairman, Orca Bay Sports & Entertainment	Stanley B. McCammon
President & CEO, Orca Bay Sports & Entertainment	Steve Bellringer
Alternate Governor, Orca Bay Sports & Entertainment	John H. Chapple
President, General Manager Vancouver Canucks, Alternate Governor NHL	J.B. Patrick Quinn
President, General Manager, Vancouver Grizzlies, Alternate Governor NBA	Stu Jackson
Executive Vice-President, Business, Orca Bay Sports & Entertainment	Tod Leiweke

Vancouver Canucks Staff
President, General Manager and Alternate Governor	J.B. Patrick Quinn
Executive Assistant to President/GM	Carolyn Marchese-Blanche
Senior Vice President, Hockey Operations	Steve Tambellini
Executive Assistant to Sr. VP, Hockey Operations	Kalli Quinn
Assistant General Manager	Mike Penny
Executive Assistant to Assistant General Manager	Jeanne Mayne
Vice President, Finance, Hockey Operations	Carlos Mascarenhas
Director of Amateur Scouting	Jack Birch
Manager, Media Relations	Devin Smith
Assistant, Media Relations	Chris Brumwell
Manager, Community Relations	Veronica Varhaug
Coordinator, Education and Community Relations	Lisa Ryan
Office Assistant	Brenda Eastcott
Head Coach	Tom Renney
Assistant Coach	Stan Smyl
Assistant Coach	Glen Hanlon
Assistant Coach	Terry Bangen
Strength and Conditioning Coach	Peter Twist
Video Coordinator	Doug Cole
Medical Trainer	Mike Burnstein
Massage Therapist	Dave Schima
Equipment Manager	Pat O'Neill
Assistant Equipment Manager	Darren Granger
Team Doctors	Dr. Ross Davidson, Dr. Doug Clement
Team Dentist	Dr. David Lawson
Team Chiropractor	Dr. Sid Sheard
Head Coach/Syracuse Crunch	Jack McIlhargey
Medical Trainer/Syracuse Crunch	Ralph Krugler
Equipment Manager/Syracuse Crunch	Rodney Blachford
Director of Pro Scouting	Murray Oliver
Scouts	Sergei Chibisov, Ron Delorme, Jim Eagle, Thomas Gradin, Rick Ley, Jack McCartan, Ed McColgan, Ray Miron, Noel Price, Ken Slater

Orca Bay Sports & Entertainment
Vice-President, Finance & Chief Financial Officer	David Cobb
Vice-President, Corporate Communications and Community Investment	Kevin Gass
Vice-President, People Development, Administration & Customer Care	Susanne Haine
Vice-President, Business Development	Leila Bell-Irving
Vice-President, Broadcast	Chris Hebb
Director of Business Development	Ric Thomsen
Manager, Corporate Service	Dave Cannon
Vice-President, Consumer Sales and Service	John Rizzardini
Managing Director, Customer Sales and Service	John Rocha
Director, Customer Sales	Steve Smith
Manager, Customer Communications	Marla Taner
Customer Sales and Service Assistant	Michelle Carriere
Account Managers	Terry Gayton, Bruce Foreman, Mark Roxborough
Manager, Customer Sales	Kelly Smith, Reid Mitchell, Jordan Thorsteinson, Doug Geddes
Assistant Director of Game Presentation	Stephanie Willox
Assistant, Game Presentation	Karen Brydon
Assistant, Game Presentation	Greg Bedard

Coaching Record

Year	Team	Games	Regular Season				Playoffs, Olympics, or World Championships				
			W	L	T	%	Games	W	L	T	%
1990-91	Kamloops (WHL)	72	50	20	2	.708	12	5	7	0	.417
1991-92	Kamloops (WHL)	72	51	17	4	.736	16	11	5	0	.647
1993-94	Canadian National	63	33	26	4	.556	8	5	2	1	.688*
1994-95	Canadian National	57	37	17	3	.675	8	4	2	2	.625**
1995-96	Canadian National	53	33	12	8	.698	8	4	2	2	.625***
1996-97	**Vancouver (NHL)**	**82**	**35**	**40**	**7**	**.470**	....	....	....	....	....
	NHL Totals	**82**	**35**	**40**	**7**	**.470**	....	....	....	....	....

* Olympics (silver medal)
** World Championships (bronze)
*** World Championships (silver)

Washington Capitals

1996-97 Results: 33W-40L-9T 75PTS. Fifth, Atlantic Division

With 46 goals – including 10 power-play and three game-winning markers – Peter Bondra was the foundation of Washington's offense again.

1997-98 Schedule

Oct.	Wed.	1	at Toronto	Sat.	3	NY Rangers
	Fri.	3	Buffalo	Tue.	6	Toronto
	Sat.	4	New Jersey	Thu.	8	at NY Rangers
	Wed.	8	at NY Islanders	Fri.	9	Philadelphia
	Thu.	9	at Buffalo	Sun.	11	at Detroit*
	Sat.	11	NY Islanders	Tue.	13	Ottawa
	Wed.	15	at Chicago	Thu.	15	Chicago
	Sat.	18	at Montreal	Wed.	21	at Tampa Bay
	Wed.	22	at Colorado	Sun.	25	Boston*
	Thu.	23	at Phoenix	Mon.	26	at NY Rangers
	Sat.	25	at St. Louis	Wed.	28	Pittsburgh
	Wed.	29	Dallas	Sat.	31	at Philadelphia*
	Fri.	31	Philadelphia	**Feb.** Sun.	1	Detroit*
Nov.	Sat.	1	at New Jersey	Wed.	4	at Pittsburgh
	Tue.	4	Vancouver	Sat.	7	Tampa Bay
	Thu.	6	at Boston	Wed.	25	Tampa Bay
	Sat.	8	Edmonton	Sat.	28	at Tampa Bay*
	Sun.	9	at Florida	**Mar.** Sun.	1	Buffalo*
	Wed.	12	at Pittsburgh	Tue.	3	Boston
	Thu.	13	at Buffalo	Thu.	5	at Philadelphia
	Sat.	15	at Montreal	Sat.	7	Florida*
	Tue.	18	Colorado	Mon.	9	Calgary
	Sat.	22	San Jose	Thu.	12	at NY Islanders
	Sun.	23	at Florida	Sat.	14	at Ottawa
	Wed.	26	Montreal	Mon.	16	Phoenix
	Thu.	27	at Ottawa	Wed.	18	Carolina
	Sat.	29	at Boston	Fri.	20	New Jersey
Dec.	Tue.	2	at NY Rangers	Sat.	21	at New Jersey
	Fri.	5	Florida	Wed.	25	at Edmonton
	Sun.	7	at Florida*	Thu.	26	at Calgary
	Wed.	10	at San Jose	Sat.	28	at Vancouver
	Fri.	12	at Anaheim	Tue.	31	NY Islanders
	Sat.	13	at Los Angeles	**Apr.** Thu.	2	Tampa Bay
	Tue.	16	NY Islanders	Sat.	4	Los Angeles*
	Thu.	18	Florida	Mon.	6	Montreal
	Sat.	20	at Carolina	Wed.	8	at Dallas
	Tue.	23	New Jersey	Sat.	11	at Philadelphia*
	Fri.	26	Pittsburgh	Mon.	13	at NY Islanders
	Sat.	27	Ottawa	Tue.	14	NY Rangers
	Mon.	29	St. Louis	Sat.	18	at Carolina*
Jan.	Thu.	1	Anaheim*	Sun.	19	Carolina*

* Denotes afternoon game.

Franchise date: June 11, 1974

ATLANTIC DIVISION

24th NHL Season

Year-by-Year Record

		Home			Road			Overall						
Season	GP	W	L	T	W	L	T	W	L	T	GF	GA	Pts.	Finished	Playoff Result
1996-97	82	19	17	5	14	23	4	33	40	9	214	231	75	5th, Atlantic Div.	Out of Playoffs
1995-96	82	21	15	5	18	17	6	39	32	11	234	204	89	4th, Atlantic Div.	Lost Conf. Quarter-Final
1994-95	48	15	6	3	7	12	5	22	18	8	136	120	52	3rd, Atlantic Div.	Lost Conf. Quarter-Final
1993-94	84	17	16	9	22	19	1	39	35	10	277	263	88	3rd, Atlantic Div.	Lost Conf. Semi-Final
1992-93	84	21	15	6	22	19	1	43	34	7	325	286	93	2nd, Patrick Div.	Lost Div. Semi-Final
1991-92	80	25	12	3	20	15	5	45	27	8	330	275	98	2nd, Patrick Div.	Lost Div. Semi-Final
1990-91	80	21	14	5	16	22	2	37	36	7	258	258	81	3rd, Patrick Div.	Lost Div. Final
1989-90	80	19	18	3	17	20	3	36	38	6	284	275	78	3rd, Patrick Div.	Lost Conf. Championship
1988-89	80	25	12	3	16	17	7	41	29	10	305	259	92	1st, Patrick Div.	Lost Div. Semi-Final
1987-88	80	22	14	4	16	19	5	38	33	9	281	249	85	2nd, Patrick Div.	Lost Div. Final
1986-87	80	22	15	3	16	17	7	38	32	10	285	278	86	2nd, Patrick Div.	Lost Div. Semi-Final
1985-86	80	30	8	2	20	15	5	50	23	7	315	272	107	2nd, Patrick Div.	Lost Div. Final
1984-85	80	27	11	2	19	14	7	46	25	9	322	240	101	2nd, Patrick Div.	Lost Div. Semi-Final
1983-84	80	26	11	3	22	16	2	48	27	5	308	226	101	2nd, Patrick Div.	Lost Div. Final
1982-83	80	22	12	6	17	13	10	39	25	16	306	283	94	3rd, Patrick Div.	Lost Div. Semi-Final
1981-82	80	16	16	8	10	25	5	26	41	13	319	338	65	5th, Patrick Div.	Out of Playoffs
1980-81	80	16	17	7	10	19	11	26	36	18	286	317	70	5th, Patrick Div.	Out of Playoffs
1979-80	80	20	14	6	7	26	7	27	40	13	261	293	67	5th, Patrick Div.	Out of Playoffs
1978-79	80	15	19	6	9	22	9	24	41	15	273	338	63	4th, Norris Div.	Out of Playoffs
1977-78	80	10	23	7	7	26	7	17	49	14	195	321	48	5th, Norris Div.	Out of Playoffs
1976-77	80	17	15	8	7	27	6	24	42	14	221	307	62	4th, Norris Div.	Out of Playoffs
1975-76	80	6	26	8	5	33	2	11	59	10	224	394	32	5th, Norris Div.	Out of Playoffs
1974-75	80	7	28	5	1	39	0	8	67	5	181	446	21	5th, Norris Div.	Out of Playoffs

1997-98 Player Personnel

FORWARDS	HT	WT	S	Place of Birth	Date	1996-97 Club
BERUBE, Craig	6-1	205	L	Calahoo, Alta.	12/17/65	Washington
BONDRA, Peter	6-1	200	L	Luck, USSR	2/7/68	Washington
BRUNETTE, Andrew	6-0	212	L	Sudbury, Ont.	8/24/73	Washington-Portland (AHL)
BULIS, Jan	6-0	194	L	Pardubice, Czech.	3/18/78	Barrie
EAGLES, Mike	5-10	190	L	Sussex, N.B.	3/7/63	Washington
GENDRON, Martin	5-9	190	R	Valleyfield, Que.	2/15/74	Las Vegas
HERR, Matt	6-1	180	L	Hackensack, NJ	5/26/76	U. of Michigan
HUNTER, Dale	5-10	198	L	Petrolia, Ont.	7/31/60	Washington
JUNEAU, Joe	6-0	195	L	Pont-Rouge, Que.	1/5/68	Washington
KAMINSKI, Kevin	5-10	190	L	Churchbridge, Sask.	3/13/69	Washington
KLEE, Ken	6-1	205	R	Indianapolis, IN	4/24/71	Washington
KONOWALCHUK, Steve	6-1	195	L	Salt Lake City, UT	11/11/72	Washington
KRYGIER, Todd	6-0	185	L	Chicago Heights, IL	10/12/65	Washington
MILLER, Kelly	5-11	197	L	Lansing, MI	3/3/63	Washington
NELSON, Jeff	6-0	190	L	Prince Albert, Sask.	12/18/72	Grand Rapids
NIKOLISHIN, Andrei	5-11	180	L	Vorkuta, USSR	3/25/73	Hartford-Washington
OATES, Adam	5-11	185	R	Weston, Ont.	8/27/62	Boston-Washington
PEAKE, Pat	6-1	195	R	Rochester, MI	5/28/73	Washington-Portland (AHL)
PIVONKA, Michal	6-2	195	L	Kladno, Czech.	1/28/66	Washington
SIMON, Chris	6-3	219	L	Wawa, Ont.	1/30/72	Washington
SVEJKOVSKY, Jaroslav	5-11	185	R	Plzen, Czech.	10/1/76	Washington-Portland (AHL)
VAN BRUGGEN, Andrew	6-5	220	R	Iowa City, IA	4/24/77	N. Michigan
VOLCHKOV, Alexander	6-1	194	L	Moscow, USSR	9/25/77	Barrie-Portland (AHL)
ZEDNIK, Richard	5-11	172	L	Bystrica, Czech.	1/6/76	Washington-Portland (AHL)

DEFENSEMEN						
BAUMGARTNER, Nolan	6-1	200	R	Calgary, Alta.	3/23/76	Portland (AHL)
BOILEAU, Patrick	6-0	190	R	Montreal, Que.	2/22/75	Washington-Portland (AHL)
CHARRON, Eric	6-3	192	L	Verdun, Que.	1/14/70	Washington-Portland (AHL)
COTE, Sylvain	6-0	190	R	Quebec City, Que.	1/19/66	Washington
GONCHAR, Sergei	6-2	212	L	Chelyabinsk, USSR	4/13/74	Washington
HOUSLEY, Phil	5-10	185	L	St. Paul, MN	3/9/64	Washington
JOHANSSON, Calle	5-11	200	L	Goteborg, Sweden	2/14/67	Washington
MALGUNAS, Stewart	6-0	200	L	Prince George, B.C.	4/21/70	Washington-Portland (AHL)
MROZIK, Rick	6-2	185	L	Duluth, MN	1/2/75	Minn. Duluth
POAPST, Steve	6-0	200	L	Cornwall, Ont.	1/3/69	Portland (AHL)
REEKIE, Joe	6-3	220	L	Victoria, B.C.	2/22/65	Washington
SWANSON, Scott	6-2	190	L	St. Paul, MN	2/15/75	Colorado
TINORDI, Mark	6-4	213	L	Red Deer, Alta.	5/9/66	Washington
TUOHY, John	6-2	190	L	Baldwin, NY	2/2/76	Providence
WITT, Brendan	6-1	205	L	Humbolt, Sask.	2/20/75	Washington-Portland (AHL)
ZIMAKOV, Sergei	6-1	194	L	Moscow, USSR	1/15/78	Soviet Wings

GOALTENDERS	HT	WT	C	Place of Birth	Date	1996-97 Club
BROCHU, Martin	5-10	200	L	Anjou, Que.	3/10/73	Portland (AHL)
KOLZIG, Olaf	6-3	225	L	Johannesburg, South Africa	4/9/70	Washington
RANFORD, Bill	5-11	185	L	Brandon, Man.	12/14/66	Boston-Washington
WENINGER, Dave	6-1	160	L	Calgary, Alta.	2/8/76	Michigan Tech.

1996-97 Scoring
* – rookie

Regular Season

Pos	#	Player	Team	GP	G	A	Pts	+/–	PIM	PP	SH	GW	GT	S	%
C	77	Adam Oates	BOS	63	18	52	70	-3	10	2	2	4	0	138	13.0
			WSH	17	4	8	12	-2	4	1	0	1	0	22	18.2
			TOTAL	80	22	60	82	-5	14	3	2	5	0	160	13.8
R	12	Peter Bondra	WSH	77	46	31	77	7	72	10	4	3	2	314	14.6
C	32	Dale Hunter	WSH	82	14	32	46	-2	125	3	0	5	0	110	12.7
L	22	Steve Konowalchuk	WSH	78	17	25	42	-3	67	2	1	3	1	155	11.0
C	90	Joe Juneau	WSH	58	15	27	42	-11	8	9	1	3	0	124	12.1
R	92	Rick Tocchet	BOS	40	16	14	30	-3	67	3	0	1	1	120	13.3
			WSH	13	5	5	10	0	31	1	0	1	0	37	13.5
			TOTAL	53	21	19	40	-3	98	4	0	2	1	157	13.4
D	96	Phil Housley	WSH	77	11	29	40	-10	24	3	1	2	0	167	6.6
D	55	Sergei Gonchar	WSH	57	13	17	30	-11	36	3	0	3	0	129	10.1
C	13	Andrei Nikolishin	HFD	12	2	5	7	-2	2	0	0	0	0	25	8.0
			WSH	59	7	14	21	5	30	1	0	0	0	73	9.6
			TOTAL	71	9	19	28	3	32	1	0	0	0	98	9.2
L	10	Kelly Miller	WSH	77	10	14	24	4	33	0	1	3	0	95	10.5
D	3	Sylvain Cote	WSH	57	6	18	24	1	28	2	0	0	0	131	4.6
C	20	Michal Pivonka	WSH	54	7	16	23	-15	22	2	0	1	0	83	8.4
L	17	Chris Simon	WSH	42	9	13	22	-1	165	3	0	1	0	89	10.1
D	6	Calle Johansson	WSH	65	6	11	17	-2	16	2	0	0	0	133	4.5
L	21	Todd Krygier	WSH	47	5	11	16	-10	37	1	0	1	0	121	4.1
L	18	* Andrew Brunette	WSH	23	4	7	11	-3	12	2	0	0	0	23	17.4
D	2	Ken Klee	WSH	80	3	8	11	-5	115	0	0	2	0	108	2.8
L	34	* Jaroslav Svejkovsky	WSH	19	7	3	10	-1	4	2	0	1	0	30	23.3
D	29	Joe Reekie	WSH	65	1	8	9	8	107	0	0	0	0	65	1.5
D	24	Mark Tinordi	WSH	56	2	6	8	3	118	0	0	1	0	53	3.8
L	36	Mike Eagles	WSH	70	1	7	8	-4	42	0	0	0	0	38	2.6
L	27	Craig Berube	WSH	80	4	3	7	-11	218	0	0	1	0	55	7.3
D	19	Brendan Witt	WSH	44	3	2	5	-20	88	0	0	0	0	41	7.3
L	44	* Richard Zednik	WSH	11	2	1	3	-5	4	1	0	0	0	21	9.5
C	23	Kevin Kaminski	WSH	38	1	2	3	0	130	0	0	0	0	12	8.3
D	28	Eric Charron	WSH	25	1	1	2	1	20	0	0	0	0	11	9.1
G	30	Bill Ranford	BOS	37	0	0	0	0	0	0	0	0	0	0	0.0
			WSH	18	0	1	1	0	7	0	0	0	0	0	0.0
			TOTAL	55	0	1	1	0	7	0	0	0	0	0	0.0
D	45	* Patrick Boileau	WSH	1	0	0	0	0	0	0	0	0	0	0	0.0
C	14	Pat Peake	WSH	4	0	0	0	1	4	0	0	0	0	4	0.0
D	4	Stewart Malgunas	WSH	6	0	0	0	2	2	0	0	0	0	3	0.0
L	16	Stefan Ustorf	WSH	6	0	0	0	-3	2	0	0	0	0	7	0.0
G	37	Olaf Kolzig	WSH	29	0	0	0	0	4	0	0	0	0	0	0.0

Goaltending,

No.	Goaltender	GPI	Mins	Avg	W	L	T	EN	SO	GA	SA	S%
37	Olaf Kolzig	29	1644	2.59	8	15	4	6	2	71	758	.906
30	Bill Ranford	18	1010	2.73	8	7	2	1	0	46	412	.888
30	Jim Carey	40	2293	2.75	17	18	3	2	1	105	984	.893
	Totals	**82**	**4977**	**2.78**	**33**	**40**	**9**	**9**	**3**	**231**	**2163**	**.893**

Coach

WILSON, RON
Coach, Washington Capitals. Born in Windsor, Ont., May 28, 1955.

Prior to being named the Capitals' 11th head coach on June 9, 1997, Ron Wilson served as head coach of the Mighty Ducks of Anaheim. During his four seasons in Anaheim, the Mighty Ducks posted a 120-145-31 record (.458) and made its first post-season appearance in 1996-97. His NHL coaching experience also includes a three-year stint as an assistant coach to Pat Quinn for the Vancouver Canucks from 1990-93. During Wilson's three seasons in Vancouver, the Canucks posted a 116-98-30 record (.537) and qualified for the Stanley Cup playoffs all three years.

Wilson, 42, also served as the head coach for Team USA at the 1996 World Cup of Hockey. Team USA won the championship series, two games to one, over Canada.

Wilson has significant playing experience in professional, amateur and international hockey. He played four years at Providence College where he was a two-time All-American and four-time All-Hockey East. Wilson was Hockey East player of the year in 1975 when he led the nation in scoring with 26-61-87 points in 26 games. He remains Providence's all-time leading scorer and ranks as the NCAA all-time leading scorer among defensemen with 250 points. Wilson received a Bachelor of Arts degree in economics from Providence College.

Drafted by the Toronto Maple Leafs (132nd overall) in 1975, Wilson began his professional hockey career in 1976-77 with the Dallas Blackhawks in the Central Hockey League. He joined the Toronto Maple Leafs in 1977-78, playing in 64 NHL contests over three seasons. Wilson then moved to Switzerland in 1980 and competed for the Swiss teams Kloten and Davos for six seasons. The former defensemen/winger signed with the Minnesota North Stars as a free agent in 1985 where he played through 1988. Ron enjoyed his finest offensive season in 1986-87 when he recorded 12 goals and 29 assists in 66 games with the North Stars.

Although born in Canada, Wilson was raised in the United States and remains a U.S. citizen. He was a four-time player for U.S. National Teams (1975, 1981, 1983, 1987) and coached the 1994 squad at the World Championships in Italy, leading Team USA to a 4-4-0 record with a fourth-place finish. Wilson also coached the 1996 squad, earning a bronze medal for Team USA.

Wilson and his wife Maureen have two daughters, Kristen (20), and Lauren (17).

Coaching Record

			Regular Season				Playoffs			
Season	Team	Games	W	L	T	%	Games	W	L	%
1993-94	Anaheim (NHL)	84	33	46	5	.423	....	....	....	....
1994-95	Anaheim (NHL)	48	16	27	5	.385	....	....	....	....
1995-96	Anaheim (NHL)	82	35	39	8	.476	....	....	....	....
1996-97	Anaheim (NHL)	82	36	33	13	.518	11	4	7	.364
	NHL Totals	296	120	145	31	.458	11	4	7	.364

Adam Oates joined the Capitals late in the 1996-97 season. Including his 63 games in Boston, he finished the season with 60 assists.

Coaching History

Jim Anderson, "Red" Sullivan and Milt Schmidt, 1974-75; Milt Schmidt and Tom McVie, 1975-76; Tom McVie, 1976-77 to 1977-78; Danny Belisle, 1978-79; Danny Belisle and Gary Green, 1979-80; Gary Green, 1980-81; Gary Green, Roger Crozier and Bryan Murray, 1981-82; Bryan Murray, 1982-83 to 1988-89; Bryan Murray and Terry Murray, 1989-90; Terry Murray, 1990-91 to 1992-93; Terry Murray and Jim Schoenfeld, 1993-94; Jim Schoenfeld, 1994-95 to 1996-97; Ron Wilson, 1997-98.

Club Records

Team

(Figures in brackets for season records are games played; records for fewest points, wins, ties, losses, goals, goals against are for 70 or more games)

Most Points	107	1985-86 (80)
Most Wins	50	1985-86 (80)
Most Ties	18	1980-81 (80)
Most Losses	67	1974-75 (80)
Most Goals	330	1991-92 (80)
Most Goals Against	*446	1974-75 (80)
Fewest Points	*21	1974-75 (80)
Fewest Wins	*8	1974-75 (80)
Fewest Ties	5	1974-75 (80), 1983-84 (80)
Fewest Losses	23	1985-86 (80)
Fewest Goals	181	1974-75 (80)
Fewest Goals Against	204	1995-96 (82)

Longest Winning Streak

Overall	10	Jan. 27-Feb. 18/84
Home	8	Feb. 1-Mar. 11/86, Mar. 3-Apr. 1/89
Away	6	Feb. 26-Apr. 1/84

Longest Undefeated Streak

Overall	14	Nov. 24-Dec. 23/82 (9 wins, 5 ties)
Home	13	Nov. 25/92-Feb. 2/93 (9 wins, 4 ties)
Away	10	Nov. 24/82-Jan. 8/83 (6 wins, 4 ties)

Longest Losing Streak

Overall	*17	Feb. 18-Mar. 26/75
Home	*11	Feb. 18-Mar. 30/75
Away	37	Oct. 9/74-Mar. 26/75

Longest Winless Streak

Overall	25	Nov. 29/75-Jan. 21/76 (22 losses, 3 ties)
Home	14	Dec. 3/75-Jan. 21/76 (11 losses, 3 ties)
Away	37	Oct. 9/74-Mar. 26/75 (37 losses)

Most Shutouts, Season	9	1995-96 (82)
Most PIM, Season	2,204	1989-90 (80)
Most Goals, Game	12	Feb. 6/90 (Que. 2 at Wsh. 12)

Individual

Most Seasons	11	Rod Langway, Michal Pivonka
Most Games	802	Kelly Miller
Most Goals, Career	397	Mike Gartner
Most Assists, Career	406	Michal Pivonka
Most Points, Career	789	Mike Gartner (397G, 392A)
Most PIM, Career	1,798	Dale Hunter
Most Shutouts, Career	14	Jim Carey
Longest Consecutive Games Streak	422	Bob Carpenter
Most Goals, Season	60	Dennis Maruk (1981-82)
Most Assists, Season	76	Dennis Maruk (1981-82)
Most Points, Season	136	Dennis Maruk (1981-82; 60G, 76A)
Most PIM, Season	339	Alan May (1989-90)

Most Points, Defenseman, Season	81	Larry Murphy (1986-87; 23G, 58A)
Most Points, Center, Season	136	Dennis Maruk (1981-82; 60G, 76A)
Most Points, Right Wing, Season	102	Mike Gartner (1984-85; 50G, 52A)
Most Points, Left Wing, Season	87	Ryan Walter (1981-82; 38G, 49A)
Most Points, Rookie, Season	67	Bobby Carpenter (1981-82; 32G, 35A), Chris Valentine (1981-82; 30G, 37A)
Most Shutouts, Season	9	Jim Carey (1995-96)
Most Goals, Game	5	Bengt Gustafsson (Jan. 8/84), Peter Bondra (Feb. 5/94)
Most Assists, Game	6	Mike Ridley (Jan. 7/89)
Most Points, Game	7	Dino Ciccarelli (Mar. 18/89; 4G, 3A)

* NHL Record.

Retired Numbers

7	Yvon Labre	1974-1981

Captains' History

Doug Mohns, 1974-75; Bill Clement and Yvon Labre, 1975-76; Yvon Labre, 1976-77, 1977-78; Guy Charron, 1978-79; Ryan Walter, 1979-80 to 1981-82; Rod Langway, 1982-83 to 1991-92; Rod Langway and Kevin Hatcher, 1992-93; Kevin Hatcher, 1993-94; Dale Hunter, 1994-95 to date.

All-time Record vs. Other Clubs

Regular Season

		At Home							On Road							Total					
	GP	W	L	T	GF	GA	PTS	GP	W	L	T	GF	GA	PTS	GP	W	L	T	GF	GA	PTS
Anaheim	3	1	2	0	5	6	2	3	1	1	1	9	3	6	2	3	1	16	15	5
Boston	41	10	21	10	122	155	30	42	13	24	5	119	166	31	83	23	45	15	241	321	61
Buffalo	42	10	25	7	112	159	27	42	8	28	6	116	175	22	84	18	53	13	228	334	49
Calgary	35	17	13	5	132	124	39	34	6	23	5	83	149	17	69	23	36	10	215	273	56
Chicago	35	19	12	4	130	111	42	34	8	21	5	103	141	21	69	27	33	9	233	252	63
Colorado	28	16	9	3	116	90	35	28	12	12	4	103	91	28	56	28	21	7	219	181	63
Dallas	35	14	14	7	110	111	35	34	11	15	8	101	130	30	69	25	29	15	211	241	65
Detroit	40	20	16	4	154	126	44	42	13	18	11	125	151	37	82	33	34	15	279	277	81
Edmonton	24	13	9	2	103	87	28	24	10	10	4	81	93	24	48	23	19	6	184	180	52
Florida	9	3	3	3	26	23	9	10	4	4	2	25	30	10	19	7	7	5	51	53	19
Hartford	30	18	10	2	106	87	38	31	15	11	5	107	88	35	61	33	21	7	213	175	73
Los Angeles	40	17	17	6	173	151	40	41	12	24	5	129	166	29	81	29	41	11	302	317	69
Montreal	45	20	18	7	124	142	47	46	10	30	6	94	194	26	91	30	48	13	218	336	73
New Jersey	64	41	19	4	264	188	86	64	28	29	7	198	203	63	128	69	48	11	462	391	149
NY Islanders	66	28	29	9	211	220	65	66	25	40	1	205	266	51	132	53	69	10	416	486	116
NY Rangers	69	34	26	9	261	232	77	67	27	34	6	239	268	60	136	61	60	15	500	500	137
Ottawa	10	7	2	1	46	22	15	9	5	3	1	35	34	11	19	12	5	2	81	56	26
Philadelphia	66	25	29	12	227	228	62	68	23	40	5	194	259	51	134	48	69	17	421	487	113
Phoenix	24	16	5	3	108	71	35	25	7	13	5	92	95	19	49	23	18	8	200	166	54
Pittsburgh	72	37	29	6	312	270	80	69	26	37	6	229	275	58	141	63	66	12	541	545	138
St. Louis	34	19	12	3	125	101	41	35	13	14	8	120	144	34	69	32	26	11	245	245	75
San Jose	5	4	1	0	18	11	8	5	3	2	0	17	15	6	10	7	3	0	35	26	14
Tampa Bay	11	5	2	4	35	25	14	11	8	2	1	32	18	17	22	13	4	5	67	43	31
Toronto	37	23	12	2	142	102	48	36	12	20	4	126	171	28	73	35	32	6	268	273	76
Vancouver	35	20	11	4	124	104	44	34	14	15	5	112	115	33	69	34	26	9	236	219	77
Defunct Clubs	10	2	8	0	28	42	4	10	4	5	1	30	39	9	20	6	13	1	58	81	13
Totals	**910**	**439**	**354**	**117**	**3314**	**2988**	**995**	**910**	**318**	**475**	**117**	**2826**	**3485**	**753**	**1820**	**757**	**829**	**234**	**6140**	**6473**	**1748**

Playoffs

	Series	W	L	GP	W	L	T	GF	GA	Last Mtg.	Round	Result
Boston	1	0	1	4	0	4	0	6	15	1990	CF	L 0-4
New Jersey	2	1	1	7	3	6	0	44	43	1990	DSF	W 4-2
NY Islanders	6	1	5	30	12	18	0	88	89	1993	DSF	L 2-4
NY Rangers	4	2	2	22	11	11	0	75	71	1994	CSF	L 1-4
Philadelphia	3	2	1	16	9	7	0	65	55	1989	DSF	L 2-4
Pittsburgh	5	1	4	31	13	18	0	103	106	1996	CQF	L 2-4
Totals	**21**	**7**	**14**	**116**	**52**	**64**	**0**	**381**	**389**			

Playoff Results 1997-93

Year	Round	Opponent	Result	GF	GA
1996	CQF	Pittsburgh	L 2-4	17	21
1995	CQF	Pittsburgh	L 3-4	26	29
1994	CSF	NY Rangers	L 1-4	12	20
	CQF	Pittsburgh	W 4-2	20	12
1993	DSF	NY Islanders	L 2-4	22	23

Abbreviations: Round: F – Final; **CF** – conference final; **CQF** – conference quarter-final; **CSF** – conference semi-final; **DF** – division final; **DSF** – division semi-final; **SF** – semi-final; **QF** – quarter-final; **PR** – preliminary round.

Calgary totals include Atlanta, 1974-75 to 1979-80. Colorado totals include Quebec, 1979-80 to 1994-95. Dallas totals include Minnesota, 1974-75 to 1992-93. New Jersey totals include Kansas City, 1974-75 to 1975-76, and Colorado Rockies, 1976-77 to 1981-82. Phoenix totals include Winnipeg, 1979-80, 1995-96.

1996-97 Results

Oct.	5		Chicago	2-5	9		NY Rangers	2-0
	8	at	Dallas	3-5	11	at	Philadelphia	3-3
	11		Tampa Bay	6-2	13		Toronto	6-3
	12		Los Angeles	3-4	15	at	Ottawa	1-5
	18		Buffalo	1-4	20	at	Boston	3-2
	19	at	Pittsburgh	1-2	22		NY Rangers	3-5
	23	at	NY Rangers	3-2	24		Dallas	2-5
	26	at	St. Louis	6-4	26		Edmonton	1-3
	28	at	Colorado	0-1	29		Philadelphia	1-2
	30		Philadelphia	4-2	Feb. 1	at	Florida	3-1
Nov.	1		Pittsburgh	4-2	2	at	Buffalo	2-2
	2	at	NY Islanders	1-6	7	at	Calgary	2-5
	6	at	Tampa Bay	2-1	9	at	Edmonton	1-4
	7	at	Florida	2-4	11	at	Vancouver	5-2
	9		NY Rangers	3-2	14		Tampa Bay	5-4
	12	at	New Jersey	2-3	15	at	Tampa Bay	1-4
	14	at	Philadelphia	5-2	18		Ottawa	1-6
	15		Montreal	3-1	22	at	Hartford	0-2
	18	at	Florida	4-2	24		Boston	3-3
	19		Boston	2-2	26	at	Toronto	3-1
	22	at	New Jersey	5-1	28		Anaheim	1-4
	23		New Jersey	4-3	Mar. 2		NY Islanders	3-2
	27		Ottawa	1-2	4		Calgary	2-1
	29		NY Islanders	0-2	6		Colorado	6-3
	30	at	Montreal	2-0	9	at	Philadelphia	0-5
Dec.	4		Detroit	0-2	11		Vancouver	4-1
	6		Pittsburgh	3-5	12		NY Rangers	2-3
	7	at	NY Islanders	0-2	15	at	New Jersey	2-3
	11	at	San Jose	2-3	16		Hartford	5-3
	13	at	Anaheim	4-5	19		New Jersey	2-3
	14	at	Los Angeles	4-4	21		Buffalo	1-4
	17	at	Phoenix	3-4	22	at	Montreal	3-1
	20		San Jose	3-2	25		St. Louis	3-2
	21	at	Boston	3-2	26	at	Chicago	3-5
	23		Tampa Bay	3-1	29		Philadelphia	3-5
	26	at	Detroit	4-5	Apr. 1		New Jersey	0-1
	28		Florida	1-1	3	at	Ottawa	0-4
	30	at	Pittsburgh	3-3	6		Florida	3-3
Jan.	1		Hartford	3-2	10		Montreal	3-2
	3		Phoenix	3-0	12		NY Islanders	6-2
	4	at	Hartford	1-1	13	at	Buffalo	8-3

Entry Draft
Selections 1997-83

1997
Pick
9	Nicholas Boynton
35	J-F Fortin
89	Curtis Cruickshank
116	Kevin Caulfield
143	Henrik Petre
200	Pierre-Luc Therrien
226	Matt Oikawa

1996
Pick
4	Alexander Volchkov
17	Jaroslav Svejkovsky
43	Jan Bulis
58	Sergei Zimakov
74	Dave Weninger
78	Shawn McNeil
85	Justin Davis
126	Matthew Lahey
153	Andrew Van Bruggen
180	Michael Anderson
206	Oleg Orekhovsky
232	Chad Cavanagh

1995
Pick
17	Brad Church
23	Miikka Elomo
43	Dwayne Hay
93	Sebasti Charpentier
95	Joel Theriault
105	Benoit Gratton
124	Joel Cort
147	Frederick Jobin
199	Vasili Turkovsky
225	Scott Swanson

1994
Pick
10	Nolan Baumgartner
15	Alexander Kharlamov
41	Scott Cherrey
93	Matthew Herr
119	Yanick Jean
145	Dmitri Mekeshkin
171	Daniel Reja
197	Chris Patrick
223	John Tuohy
249	Richard Zednik
275	Sergei Tertyshny

1993
Pick
11	Brendan Witt
17	Jason Allison
69	Patrick Boileau
147	Frank Banham
173	Daniel Hendrickson
174	Andrew Brunette
199	Joel Poirier
225	Jason Gladney
251	Mark Seliger
277	Dany Bousquet

1992
Pick
14	Sergei Gonchar
32	Jim Carey
53	Stefan Ustorf
71	Martin Gendron
119	John Varga
167	Mark Matier
191	Mike Mathers
215	Brian Stagg
239	Gregory Callahan
263	Billy Jo MacPherson

1991
Pick
14	Pat Peake
21	Trevor Halverson
25	Eric Lavigne
36	Jeff Nelson
58	Steve Konowalchuk
80	Justin Morrison
146	Dave Morissette
168	Rick Corriveau
190	Trevor Duhaime
209	Rob Leask
212	Carl LeBlanc
234	Rob Puchniak
256	Bill Kovacs

1990
Pick
9	John Slaney
30	Rod Pasma
51	Chris Longo
72	Randy Pearce
93	Brian Sakic
94	Mark Ouimet
114	Andrei Kovalev
135	Roman Kontsek
156	Peter Bondra
159	Steve Martell
177	Ken Klee
198	Michael Boback
219	Alan Brown
240	Todd Hlushko

1989
Pick
19	Olaf Kolzig
35	Byron Dafoe
59	Jim Mathieson
61	Jason Woolley
82	Trent Klatt
145	Dave Lorentz
166	Dean Holoien
187	Victor Gervais
208	Jiri Vykoukal
229	Andrei Sidorov
250	Ken House

1988
Pick
15	Reginald Savage
36	Tim Taylor
41	Wade Bartley
57	Duane Derksen
78	Rob Krauss
120	Dmitri Khristich
141	Keith Jones
144	Brad Schlegel
162	Todd Hilditch
183	Petr Pavlas
192	Mark Sorensen
204	Claudio Scremin
225	Chris Venkus
246	Ron Pascucci

1987
Pick
36	Jeff Ballantyne
57	Steve Maltais
78	Tyler Larter
99	Pat Beauchesne
120	Rich Defreitas
141	Devon Oleniuk
162	Thomas Sjogren
204	Chris Clarke
225	Milos Vanik
240	Dan Brettschneider
246	Ryan Kummu

1986
Pick
19	Jeff Greenlaw
40	Steve Seftel
60	Shawn Simpson
61	Jimmy Hrivnak
82	Erin Ginnell
103	John Purves
124	Stefan Nilsson
145	Peter Choma
166	Lee Davidson
187	Tero Toivola
208	Bobby Bobcock
229	John Schratz
250	Scott McCrory

1985
Pick
19	Yvon Corriveau
40	John Druce
61	Rob Murray
82	Bill Houlder
83	Larry Shaw
103	Claude Dumas
124	Doug Stromback
145	Jamie Nadjiwan
166	Mark Haarmann
187	Steve Hollett
208	Dallas Eakins
229	Steve Hrynewich
250	Frank DiMuzio

1984
Pick
17	Kevin Hatcher
34	Steve Leach
59	Michal Pivonka
80	Kris King
122	Vito Cramarossa
143	Timo Iljina
164	Frank Joo
185	Jim Thomson
205	Paul Cavallini
225	Mikhail Tatarinov
246	Per Schedrin

1983
Pick
75	Tim Bergland
95	Martin Bouliane
135	Dwaine Hutton
155	Marty Abrams
175	David Cowan
195	Yves Beaudoin
215	Alain Raymond
216	Anders Huss

General Managers' History

Milt Schmidt, 1974-75; Milt Schmidt and Max McNab, 1975-76; Max McNab, 1976-77 to 1980-81; Max McNab and Roger Crozier, 1981-82; David Poile, 1982-83 to 1996-97; George McPhee, 1997-98.

General Manager

McPHEE, GEORGE
General Manager, Washington Capitals. Born in Guelph, Ont., July 2, 1958.

George McPhee becomes the fifth general manager in Capitals franchise history. McPhee had been with the Vancouver Canucks for the past five seasons, most recently serving as the team's vice president of hockey operations. While with the Canucks, McPhee was responsible for all matters pertaining to contracts and assisted Pat Quinn in all hockey and business related matters. Along with Quinn, he served as an alternate governor for the hockey club.

McPhee enters Washington and his first general manager's position with excellent credentials. He played in the NHL and has earned degrees in both law and business. While attending law school at Rutgers University, he interned at the United States Court of International Trade in 1991 and spent two previous summers working on Wall Street in Manhattan.

A back injury forced McPhee to retire as an active player at the conclusion of the 1988-89 season, after a seven year playing career with the New York Rangers and New Jersey Devils.

McPhee originally signed as a free agent with the Rangers in July, 1982, after graduating from Bowling Green State University with a business degree. McPhee did not waste any time in college, tallying 40 goals and 48 assists in his freshman season and easily winning CCHA rookie of the year honors. His outstanding collegiate hockey career was capped off when he was named the recipient of the Hobey Baker Award as the top U.S. collegiate player in his senior season. McPhee also earned All-America honors as a senior and finished his career at Bowling Green as the CCHA's all-time leading scorer with 114-153-267. He was the first player in CCHA history to make the Conference's all-academic team three straight seasons.

A native of Guelph, Ontario, McPhee brings his wife Leah and one daughter, Grayson to the Washington area.

Club Directory

MCI Center

USAirways Arena
1 Harry S. Truman Drive
Landover, MD 20785
Phone **301/350-3400**
PR FAX 301/386-7012
Capacity: 18,130
After Dec. 15, 1997:
MCI Center
Capacity: Approximately 20,000

Executive Management
Chairman . . . . Abe Pollin
Board of Directors . . . . David P. Bindeman, Stuart L. Bindeman, James A. Cafritz, A. James Clark, Albert Cohen, J. Martin Irving, R. Robert Linowes, Arthur Mason, Dr. Jack Meshel, David M. Osnos, Richard M. Patrick
President and Governor . . . . Richard M. Patrick
Legal Counsel and Alternate Governor . . . . David M. Osnos
VP and Chief Financial Officer . . . . Peter Biche
Vice President of Finance . . . . Ed Stelzer

Washington Sports and Entertainment
President . . . . Susan O'Malley
Executive Vice President . . . . Wes Unseld
Assistant to the President . . . . Pam Medlock

Hockey Operations
General Manager . . . . George McPhee
Head Coach . . . . Ron Wilson
Assistant Coaches . . . . Tim Army, Tim Hunter
Goalie Coach . . . . Dave Prior
Head Trainer . . . . Stan Wong
Assistant Trainer/Equipment Manager . . . . Doug Shearer
Assistant Equipment Managers . . . . Craig Leydig, Rick Harper
Strength and Conditioning Coach . . . . Frank Costello
Massage Therapist . . . . Curt Millar
Director of Hockey Operations . . . . Shawn Simpson
Pro Scout/Special Assignments . . . . Archie Henderson
Chief Amateur Scout . . . . Ross Mahoney
Chief Eastern Scout . . . . Bob Atrill
Chief Western Scout . . . . Ernie Vargas
Scouting Staff . . . . Mike Backman, Alexei Dementiev, Doug Overton, Martin Poulit, Josef Straka, Niklas Wikegard
Administrative Assistant to the General Manager . . Pat Young
Director of Team Services . . . . Todd Warren
Assistant to the Hockey Department . . . . Rick Mulready
Piney Orchard Staff . . . . Alex Walker

Communications Department
Vice President of Communications . . . . Matt Williams
Director of Public Relations . . . . Nancy Yasharoff
Director of Broadcasting and Game Operations . . . Reed Laughlin
Assistant Public Relations Director . . . . Bob Artman
Public Relations Assistant . . . . Jesse Price
Assistant Director of Game Operations . . . . Sara Matelson
Communications Coordinator . . . . Julie Hensley

Phil Housley led all Capitals defenders with 40 points and three power-play goals in 1996-97.

1996-97 Final Statistics

Standings

Abbreviations: GA – goals against; **GF** – goals for; **GP** – games played; **L** – losses;
PTS – points; **T** – ties; **W** – wins; **%** – percentage of games won.

EASTERN CONFERENCE

Northeast Division

	GP	W	L	T	GF	GA	PTS	%
Buffalo	82	40	30	12	237	208	92	.561
Pittsburgh	82	38	36	8	285	280	84	.512
Ottawa	82	31	36	15	226	234	77	.470
Montreal	82	31	36	15	249	276	77	.470
Hartford	82	32	39	11	226	256	75	.457
Boston	82	26	47	9	234	300	61	.372

Atlantic Division

	GP	W	L	T	GF	GA	PTS	%
New Jersey	82	45	23	14	231	182	104	.634
Philadelphia	82	45	24	13	274	217	103	.628
Florida	82	35	28	19	221	201	89	.543
NY Rangers	82	38	34	10	258	231	86	.524
Washington	82	33	40	9	214	231	75	.457
Tampa Bay	82	32	40	10	217	247	74	.451
NY Islanders	82	29	41	12	240	250	70	.427

WESTERN CONFERENCE

Central Division

	GP	W	L	T	GF	GA	PTS	%
Dallas	82	48	26	8	252	198	104	.634
Detroit	82	38	26	18	253	197	94	.573
Phoenix	82	38	37	7	240	243	83	.506
St. Louis	82	36	35	11	236	239	83	.506
Chicago	82	34	35	13	223	210	81	.494
Toronto	82	30	44	8	230	273	68	.415

Pacific Division

	GP	W	L	T	GF	GA	PTS	%
Colorado	82	49	24	9	277	205	107	.652
Anaheim	82	36	33	13	245	233	85	.518
Edmonton	82	36	37	9	252	247	81	.494
Vancouver	82	35	40	7	257	273	77	.470
Calgary	82	32	41	9	214	239	73	.445
Los Angeles	82	28	43	11	214	268	67	.409
San Jose	82	27	47	8	211	278	62	.378

Mats Sundin's ability to elude checkers and thread crisp passes to unprotected teammates lifted him to seventh place in the NHL scoring race with 94 points in 1996-97.

INDIVIDUAL LEADERS

Goal Scoring

Player	Team	GP	G
Keith Tkachuk	Pho.	81	52
Teemu Selanne	Ana.	78	51
Mario Lemieux	Pit.	76	50
John LeClair	Phi.	82	50
Zigmund Palffy	NYI	80	48
Jaromir Jagr	Pit.	63	47
Brendan Shanahan	Hfd.-Det.	81	47
Peter Bondra	Wsh.	77	46
Paul Kariya	Ana.	69	44
Brett Hull	St.L.	77	42

Assists

Player	Team	GP	A
Mario Lemieux	Pit.	76	72
Wayne Gretzky	NYR	82	72
Ron Francis	Pit.	81	63
Steve Yzerman	Det.	81	63
Doug Weight	Edm.	80	61
Adam Oates	Bos.-Wsh.	80	60
Doug Gilmour	Tor.-N.J.	81	60
Pierre Turgeon	Mtl.-St.L.	78	59

Power-play Goals

Player	Team	GP	PP
Brendan Shanahan	Hfd.-Det.	81	20
Ryan Smyth	Edm.	82	20
Paul Kariya	Ana.	69	15
Mario Lemieux	Pit.	76	15
Andrei Kovalenko	Edm.	74	14
Keith Jones	Wsh.-Col.	78	14
Ray Sheppard	Fla.	68	13
Sandis Ozolinsh	Col.	80	13
Mike Gartner	Pho.	82	13
Petr Nedved	Pit.	74	12
Dino Ciccarelli	T.B.	77	12
Brett Hull	St.L.	77	12

Short-handed Goals

Player	Team	GP	SH
Michael Peca	Buf.	79	6
Mark Messier	NYR	71	5
Trent Klatt	Phi.	76	5
Mike Modano	Dal.	80	5

Game-winning Goals

Player	Team	GP	GW
Paul Kariya	Ana.	69	10
Mark Messier	NYR	71	9
Mike Modano	Dal.	80	9
Bill Guerin	N.J.	82	9
Teemu Selanne	Ana.	78	8
Mats Sundin	Tor.	82	8

Game-tying Goals

Player	Team	GP	GT
Adam Graves	NYR	82	5
Theoren Fleury	Cgy.	81	3
Stu Barnes	Fla.-Pit.	81	3
Tim Taylor	Det.	44	2
Jay Pandolfo	N.J.	46	2
Eric Lindros	Phi.	52	2

Shots

Player	Team	GP	S
Paul Kariya	Ana.	69	340
Theoren Fleury	Cgy.	81	336
Brendan Shanahan	Hfd.-Det.	81	336
Mario Lemieux	Pit.	76	327
John LeClair	Phi.	82	324

Shooting Percentage
(minimum 82 shots)

Player	Team	GP	G	S	%
Miroslav Satan	Edm.-Buf.	76	25	119	21.0
Jaromir Jagr	Pit.	63	47	234	20.1
Martin Gelinas	Van.	74	35	177	19.8
Andrei Kovalenko	Edm.	74	32	163	19.6
Teemu Selanne	Ana.	78	51	273	18.7

Penalty Minutes

Player	Team	GP	PIM
Gino Odjick	Van.	70	371
Bob Probert	Chi.	82	326
Paul Laus	Fla.	77	313
Rob Ray	Buf.	82	286
Tie Domi	Tor.	80	275

Plus/Minus

Player	Team	GP	+/-
John LeClair	Phi.	82	44
Mike Modano	Dal.	80	43
Vlad. Konstantinov	Det.	77	38
Dave Andreychuk	N.J.	82	38
Darryl Sydor	Dal.	82	37

Individual Leaders

Abbreviations: * – rookie eligible for Calder Trophy; **A** – assists; **G** – goals; **GP** – games played; **GT** – game-tying goals; **GW** – game-winning goals; **PIM** – penalties in minutes; **PP** – power play goals; **Pts** – points; **S** – shots on goal; **SH** – short-handed goals; **%** – percentage of shots on goal resulting in goals; **+/−** – difference between Goals For (**GF**) scored when a player is on the ice with his team at even strength or short-handed and Goals Against (**GA**) scored when the same player is on the ice with his team at even strength or on a power play.

Individual Scoring Leaders for Art Ross Trophy

Player	Team	GP	G	A	Pts	+/−	PIM	PP	SH	GW	GT	S	%
Mario Lemieux	Pittsburgh	76	50	72	122	27	65	15	3	7	1	327	15.3
Teemu Selanne	Anaheim	78	51	58	109	28	34	11	1	8	2	273	18.7
Paul Kariya	Anaheim	69	44	55	99	36	6	15	3	10	0	340	12.9
John LeClair	Philadelphia	82	50	47	97	44	58	10	0	5	2	324	15.4
Wayne Gretzky	NY Rangers	82	25	72	97	12	28	6	0	2	1	286	8.7
Jaromir Jagr	Pittsburgh	63	47	48	95	22	40	11	2	6	1	234	20.1
Mats Sundin	Toronto	82	41	53	94	6	59	7	4	8	1	281	14.6
Zigmund Palffy	NY Islanders	80	48	42	90	21	43	6	4	6	1	292	16.4
Ron Francis	Pittsburgh	81	27	63	90	7	20	10	1	2	0	183	14.8
Brendan Shanahan	Hfd.-Det.	81	47	41	88	32	131	20	3	7	2	336	14.0
Keith Tkachuk	Phoenix	81	52	34	86	-1	228	9	2	7	1	296	17.6
Peter Forsberg	Colorado	65	28	58	86	31	73	5	4	4	0	188	14.9
Pierre Turgeon	Mtl.-St.L.	78	26	59	85	8	14	5	0	7	1	216	12.0
Steve Yzerman	Detroit	81	22	63	85	22	78	8	0	3	0	232	9.5
Mark Messier	NY Rangers	71	36	48	84	12	88	7	5	9	1	227	15.9
Mike Modano	Dallas	80	35	48	83	43	42	9	5	9	2	291	12.0
Brett Hull	St. Louis	77	42	40	82	-9	10	12	2	6	2	302	13.9
Adam Oates	Bos.-Wsh.	80	22	60	82	-5	14	3	2	5	0	160	13.8
Doug Gilmour	Tor.-N.J.	81	22	60	82	2	68	4	1	1	1	143	15.4
Doug Weight	Edmonton	80	21	61	82	1	80	4	0	2	0	235	8.9
Vincent Damphousse	Montreal	82	27	54	81	-6	82	7	2	3	2	244	11.1
Mark Recchi	Montreal	82	34	46	80	-1	58	7	2	3	0	202	16.8
Eric Lindros	Philadelphia	52	32	47	79	31	136	9	0	7	2	198	16.2
Brian Leetch	NY Rangers	82	20	58	78	31	40	9	0	2	0	256	7.8
Peter Bondra	Washington	77	46	31	77	7	72	10	4	3	2	314	14.6
Tony Amonte	Chicago	81	41	36	77	35	64	9	2	4	2	266	15.4

Defensemen Scoring Leaders

Player	Team	GP	G	A	Pts	+/−	PIM	PP	SH	GW	GT	S	%
Brian Leetch	NY Rangers	82	20	58	78	31	40	9	0	2	0	256	7.8
Sandis Ozolinsh	Colorado	80	23	45	68	4	88	13	0	4	1	232	9.9
Nicklas Lidstrom	Detroit	79	15	42	57	11	30	8	0	1	0	214	7.0
Oleg Tverdovsky	Phoenix	82	10	45	55	-5	30	3	1	2	0	144	6.9
Kevin Hatcher	Pittsburgh	80	15	39	54	11	103	9	0	1	0	199	7.5
Dmitri Mironov	Pit.-Ana.	77	13	39	52	16	101	3	1	2	0	177	7.3
Ray Bourque	Boston	62	19	31	50	-11	18	8	1	3	1	230	8.3
Chris Chelios	Chicago	72	10	38	48	16	112	2	0	2	0	194	5.2
Darryl Sydor	Dallas	82	8	40	48	37	51	2	0	2	0	142	5.6
*Bryan Berard	NY Islanders	82	8	40	48	1	86	3	0	1	0	172	4.7
Steve Duchesne	Ottawa	78	19	28	47	-9	38	10	2	3	0	208	9.1
Eric Desjardins	Philadelphia	82	12	34	46	25	50	5	1	1	0	183	6.6
Robert Svehla	Florida	82	13	32	45	2	86	5	0	3	0	159	8.2
Larry Murphy	Tor.-Det.	81	9	36	45	3	20	5	0	1	1	158	5.7
*Janne Niinimaa	Philadelphia	77	4	40	44	12	58	1	0	2	0	141	2.8
Al MacInnis	St. Louis	72	13	30	43	2	65	6	1	1	0	296	4.4
Sergei Zubov	Dallas	78	13	30	43	19	24	1	0	3	0	133	9.8
Roman Hamrlik	Tampa Bay	79	12	28	40	-29	57	6	0	0	1	238	5.0
Phil Housley	Washington	77	11	29	40	-10	24	3	1	2	0	167	6.6
Fredrik Olausson	Ana.-Pit.	71	9	29	38	16	32	3	0	3	0	110	8.2
A. Karpovtsev	NY Rangers	77	9	29	38	1	59	6	1	0	0	84	10.7
Vlad. Konstantinov	Detroit	77	5	33	38	38	151	0	0	0	0	141	3.5
Garry Galley	Buffalo	71	4	34	38	10	102	1	1	1	0	84	4.8
Jason Woolley	Fla.-Pit.	60	6	30	36	4	30	2	0	1	0	86	7.0
Jyrki Lumme	Vancouver	66	11	24	35	8	32	5	0	2	0	107	10.3
Chris Pronger	St. Louis	79	11	24	35	15	143	4	0	0	0	147	7.5

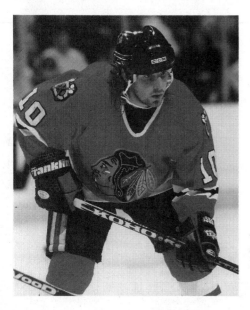

Tony Amonte led Chicago's offense all season, hitting the 40-goal mark for the first time and finishing among the League leaders in plus/minus (+35).

CONSECUTIVE SCORING STREAKS

Goals

Games	Player	Team	G
9	Jaromir Jagr	Pittsburgh	14
7	Mario Lemieux	Pittsburgh	12
6	Jaromir Jagr	Pittsburgh	9
6	Peter Bondra	Washington	8
6	Brett Hull	St. Louis	8
6	Mike Modano	Dallas	7
6	Peter Forsberg	Colorado	7
5	Vincent Damphousse	Montreal	9
5	Brendan Shanahan	Detroit	9
5	Zigmund Palffy	NY Islanders	9
5	Keith Tkachuk	Phoenix	8
5	Tony Amonte	Chicago	7
5	Pavel Bure	Vancouver	7
5	Eric Lindros	Philadelphia	6
5	Martin Rucinsky	Montreal	6
5	Adam Oates	Boston	5
5	Teemu Selanne	Anaheim	5
5	Ryan Smyth	Edmonton	5
5	Daniel Goneau	NY Rangers	5
5	Harry York	St. Louis	5

Assists

Games	Player	Team	A
14	Adam Oates	Boston	16
8	Vincent Damphousse	Montreal	14
8	Kevin Hatcher	Pittsburgh	12
8	Doug Weight	Edmonton	10
8	Doug Weight	Edmonton	10
8	Steve Yzerman	Detroit	9
8	Bernie Nicholls	San Jose	8
7	Mario Lemieux	Pittsburgh	19
7	Wayne Gretzky	NY Rangers	14
7	Brendan Shanahan	Detroit	9
7	Brian Leetch	NY Rangers	8
7	Bryan Smolinski	NY Islanders	8
6	Steve Yzerman	Detroit	11
6	Steve Yzerman	Detroit	11
6	Eric Lindros	Philadelphia	10
6	Mark Recchi	Montreal	9
6	Paul Kariya	Anaheim	9
6	Mats Sundin	Toronto	8
6	Jamie Langenbrunner	Dallas	8
6	Steve Rucchin	Anaheim	7
6	Kevin Dineen	Hartford	6
6	Cory Stillman	Calgary	6

Points

Games	Player	Team	G	A	PTS
20	Adam Oates	Boston	7	21	28
17	Eric Lindros	Philadelphia	13	16	29
15	Mario Lemieux	Pittsburgh	15	23	38
15	Wayne Gretzky	NY Rangers	7	15	22
14	Brian Leetch	NY Rangers	6	14	20
13	Jaromir Jagr	Pittsburgh	15	9	24
12	Wayne Gretzky	NY Rangers	5	19	24
12	Brett Hull	St. Louis	11	8	19
12	Teemu Selanne	Anaheim	9	10	19
12	Paul Kariya	Anaheim	10	9	19
12	Brett Hull	St. Louis	8	9	17
11	Mats Sundin	Toronto	7	9	16
11	Andrei Kovalenko	Edmonton	8	7	15
10	Peter Forsberg	Colorado	9	11	20
10	Mark Messier	NY Rangers	8	9	17
10	Bobby Holik	New Jersey	5	10	15
10	Peter Bondra	Washington	12	2	14
10	Doug Weight	Edmonton	3	11	14

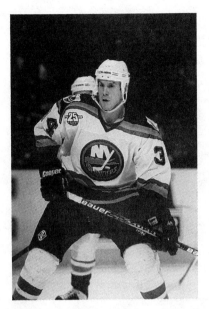

Bryan Berard's offensive prowess and defensive poise allowed him to become the first Islander since Mike Bossy to capture the Calder Trophy as the NHL's top rookie.

Individual Rookie Scoring Leaders

Rookie	Team	GP	G	A	Pts	+/–	PIM	PP	SH	GW	GT	S	%
Jarome Iginla	Calgary	82	21	29	50	–4	37	8	1	3	0	169	12.4
Bryan Berard	NY Islanders	82	8	40	48	1	86	3	0	1	0	172	4.7
Janne Niinimaa	Philadelphia	77	4	40	44	12	58	1	0	2	0	141	2.8
Jim Campbell	St. Louis	68	23	20	43	3	68	5	0	6	1	169	13.6
Sergei Berezin	Toronto	73	25	16	41	–3	2	7	0	2	0	177	14.1
Jamie Langenbrunner	Dallas	76	13	26	39	–2	51	3	0	3	0	112	11.6
Steve Sullivan	N.J.-Tor.	54	13	25	38	14	37	3	0	3	1	108	12.0
Jonas Hoglund	Calgary	68	19	16	35	–4	12	3	0	6	1	189	10.1
Mike Grier	Edmonton	79	15	17	32	7	45	4	0	2	0	89	16.9
Harry York	St. Louis	74	14	18	32	1	24	3	1	3	0	86	16.3
Denis Pederson	New Jersey	70	12	20	32	7	62	3	0	3	0	106	11.3
Ethan Moreau	Chicago	82	15	16	31	13	123	0	0	1	1	114	13.2
Andreas Dackell	Ottawa	79	12	19	31	–6	8	2	0	3	0	79	15.2
Rem Murray	Edmonton	82	11	20	31	9	16	1	0	2	0	85	12.9
Wade Redden	Ottawa	82	6	24	30	1	41	2	0	1	0	102	5.9
Daymond Langkow	Tampa Bay	79	15	13	28	1	35	3	1	1	1	170	8.8
Sergei Zholtok	Ottawa	57	12	16	28	2	19	5	0	0	0	96	12.5
Mats Lindgren	Edmonton	69	11	14	25	–7	12	2	3	1	0	71	15.5
Darren Van Impe	Anaheim	74	4	19	23	3	90	2	0	0	0	107	3.7
Lonny Bohonos	Vancouver	36	11	11	22	–3	10	2	0	1	0	67	16.4
Daniel McGillis	Edmonton	73	6	16	22	2	52	2	1	2	0	139	4.3
Stephen Guolla	San Jose	43	13	8	21	–10	14	2	0	1	1	81	16.0
Bruce Gardiner	Ottawa	67	11	10	21	4	49	0	1	2	2	94	11.7
Dainius Zubrus	Philadelphia	68	8	13	21	3	22	1	0	2	0	71	11.3
Landon Wilson	Col.-Bos.	49	8	12	20	–5	72	0	0	0	0	83	9.6
Darcy Tucker	Montreal	73	7	13	20	–5	110	1	0	3	1	62	11.3

Goal Scoring

Name	Team	GP	G
Sergei Berezin	Toronto	73	25
Jim Campbell	St. Louis	68	23
Jarome Iginla	Calgary	82	21
Jonas Hoglund	Calgary	68	19
Mike Grier	Edmonton	79	15
Daymond Langkow	Tampa Bay	79	15
Ethan Moreau	Chicago	82	15
Harry York	St. Louis	74	14

Assists

Name	Team	GP	A
Janne Niinimaa	Philadelphia	77	40
Bryan Berard	NY Islanders	82	40
Jarome Iginla	Calgary	82	29
Jamie Langenbrunner	Dallas	76	26
Steve Sullivan	N.J.-Tor.	54	25
Wade Redden	Ottawa	82	24
Jim Campbell	St. Louis	68	20
Denis Pederson	New Jersey	70	20
Rem Murray	Edmonton	82	20

Power-Play Goals

Name	Team	GP	PP
Jarome Iginla	Calgary	82	8
Sergei Berezin	Toronto	73	7
Sergei Zholtok	Ottawa	57	5
Jim Campbell	St. Louis	68	5
Mike Grier	Edmonton	79	4
Daniel Goneau	NY Rangers	41	3
Tomas Holmstrom	Detroit	47	3
Steve Sullivan	N.J.-Tor.	54	3
David Wilkie	Montreal	61	3
Jonas Hoglund	Calgary	68	3
Denis Pederson	New Jersey	70	3
Harry York	St. Louis	74	3
Jamie Langenbrunner	Dallas	76	3
Daymond Langkow	Tampa Bay	79	3
Bryan Berard	NY Islanders	82	3

Short-Handed Goals

Name	Team	GP	SH
Mats Lindgren	Edmonton	69	3
Mike Johnson	Toronto	13	1
Mark Wotton	Vancouver	36	1
Anson Carter	Boston	38	1
Cale Hulse	Calgary	63	1
Bruce Gardiner	Ottawa	67	1
Daniel McGillis	Edmonton	73	1
Harry York	St. Louis	74	1
Joel Bouchard	Calgary	76	1
Daymond Langkow	Tampa Bay	79	1
Jarome Iginla	Calgary	82	1

Game-Winning Goals

Name	Team	GP	GW
Jim Campbell	St. Louis	68	6
Jonas Hoglund	Calgary	68	6
Steve Sullivan	N.J.-Tor.	54	3
Aaron Miller	Colorado	56	3
Denis Pederson	New Jersey	70	3
Darcy Tucker	Montreal	73	3
Harry York	St. Louis	74	3
Jamie Langenbrunner	Dallas	76	3
Andreas Dackell	Ottawa	79	3
Jarome Iginla	Calgary	82	3

Game-Tying Goals

Name	Team	GP	GT
Jay Pandolfo	New Jersey	46	2
Bruce Gardiner	Ottawa	67	2
Jan Vopat	Los Angeles	33	1
Sean Pronger	Anaheim	39	1
David Nemirovsky	Florida	39	1
Mattias Timander	Boston	41	1
Stephen Guolla	San Jose	43	1
Brad Smyth	Los Angeles	52	1
Steve Sullivan	New Jersey	54	1
Steve Staios	Boston	63	1
Jim Campbell	St. Louis	68	1
Jonas Hoglund	Calgary	68	1
Darcy Tucker	Montreal	73	1
Daymond Langkow	Tampa Bay	79	1
Ethan Moreau	Chicago	82	1
Todd Simpson	Calgary	82	1

Shots

Name	Team	GP	S
Jonas Hoglund	Calgary	68	189
Sergei Berezin	Toronto	73	177
Bryan Berard	NY Islanders	82	172
Daymond Langkow	Tampa Bay	79	170
Jim Campbell	St. Louis	68	169
Jarome Iginla	Calgary	82	169
Janne Niinimaa	Philadelphia	77	141
Daniel McGillis	Edmonton	73	139
Ethan Moreau	Chicago	82	114
Jamie Langenbrunner	Dallas	76	112

Shooting Percentage
(minimum 82 shots)

Name	Team	GP	G	S	%
Mike Grier	Edmonton	79	15	89	16.9
Harry York	St. Louis	74	14	86	16.3
Sergei Berezin	Toronto	73	25	177	14.1
Jim Campbell	St. Louis	68	23	169	13.6
Ethan Moreau	Chicago	82	15	114	13.2
Rem Murray	Edmonton	82	11	85	12.9
Sergei Zholtok	Ottawa	57	12	96	12.5
Jarome Iginla	Calgary	82	21	169	12.4
Steve Sullivan	N.J.-Tor.	54	13	108	12.0
Bruce Gardiner	Ottawa	67	11	94	11.7

Penalty Minutes

Name	Team	GP	PIM
Todd Simpson	Calgary	82	208
Matt Johnson	Los Angeles	52	194
Eric Cairns	NY Rangers	40	147
Steve Webb	NY Islanders	41	144
Brantt Myhres	Tampa Bay	47	136

Plus/Minus

Name	Team	GP	+/–
Aaron Miller	Colorado	56	15
Steve Sullivan	N.J.-Tor.	54	14
Ethan Moreau	Chicago	82	13
Janne Niinimaa	Philadelphia	77	12
Rem Murray	Edmonton	82	9
Mark Wotton	Vancouver	36	8

Three-or-More-Goal Games

Player	Team	Date	Final Score	G
Tony Amonte	Chicago	Nov. 30	Chi. 5 L.A. 3	3
Tony Amonte	Chicago	Mar. 16	NYI 4 Chi. 5	3
Peter Bondra	Washington	Dec. 13	Wsh. 4 Ana. 5	3
Peter Bondra	Washington	Mar. 06	Col. 3 Wsh. 6	3
Dino Ciccarelli	Tampa Bay	Nov. 08	Pit. 5 T.B. 5	3
Wendel Clark	Toronto	Nov. 09	Edm. 3 Tor. 7	4
Mariusz Czerkawski	Edmonton	Nov. 07	Edm. 6 Bos. 0	3
Mariusz Czerkawski	Edmonton	Feb. 19	Tor. 5 Edm. 6	3
Vincent Damphousse	Montreal	Jan. 06	Hfd. 4 Mtl. 5	3
Eric Daze	Chicago	Apr. 13	Chi. 5 Dal. 2	3
Sergei Fedorov	Detroit	Dec. 26	Wsh. 4 Det. 5	5
Theoren Fleury	Calgary	Oct. 22	Col. 1 Cgy. 5	3
Peter Forsberg	Colorado	Apr. 02	Col. 5 Cgy. 1	3
Mike Gartner	Phoenix	Oct. 07	Pho. 5 Bos. 2	3
Martin Gelinas	Vancouver	Feb. 06	Van. 7 Det. 4	3
Martin Gelinas	Vancouver	Feb. 27	Pho. 2 Van. 6	4
Tony Granato	San Jose	Oct. 06	S.J. 1 Col. 6	3
Tony Granato	San Jose	Apr. 04	Col. 6 S.J. 7	3
Chris Gratton	Tampa Bay	Oct. 12	T.B. 7 Tor. 4	3
Adam Graves	NY Rangers	Mar. 14	NYR 4 Ott. 3	3
Michal Grosek	Buffalo	Dec. 04	Van. 7 Buf. 6	3
Bill Guerin	New Jersey	Dec. 31	N.J. 5 Buf. 6	3
Dale Hawerchuk	Philadelphia	Nov. 21	Pit. 3 Phi. 7	3
Brett Hull	St. Louis	Dec. 22	L.A. 4 St.L. 7	3
Brett Hull	St. Louis	Feb. 06	Dal. 4 St.L. 6	3
Jaromir Jagr	Pittsburgh	Nov. 02	Ott. 3 Pit. 7	3
Jaromir Jagr	Pittsburgh	Nov. 30	Bos. 2 Pit. 6	3
Joe Juneau	Washington	Nov. 01	Pit. 2 Wsh. 4	3
Valeri Kamensky	Colorado	Mar. 26	Col. 5 Det. 6	3
Paul Kariya	Anaheim	Jan. 10	Buf. 2 Ana. 5	3
Paul Kariya	Anaheim	Jan. 23	Ana. 3 Pho. 6	3
Derek King	NY Islanders	Jan. 24	NYI 5 Hfd. 2	3
Trent Klatt	Philadelphia	Mar. 01	Phi. 5 Bos. 5	3
Alexei Kovalev	NY Rangers	Oct. 16	Pit. 1 NYR 8	3
Eric Lacroix	Colorado	Oct. 15	Edm. 2 Col. 7	3
John LeClair	Philadelphia	Feb. 06	Mtl. 5 Phi. 9	4
John LeClair	Philadelphia	Feb. 26	Phi. 8 Ott. 5	3
Mario Lemieux	Pittsburgh	Dec. 29	Pit. 4 St.L. 0	3
Mario Lemieux	Pittsburgh	Jan. 26	Pit. 5 Mtl. 2	4
Eric Lindros	Philadelphia	Mar. 19	Phi. 6 Tor. 3	4
Al MacInnis	St. Louis	Dec. 11	St.L. 5 Dal. 5	3
Kent Manderville	Hartford	Mar. 12	Bos. 3 Hfd. 6	3
Randy McKay	New Jersey	Mar. 13	Hfd. 0 N.J. 6	3
Jim McKenzie	Phoenix	Feb. 18	L.A. 1 Pho. 6	3
Mark Messier	NY Rangers	Nov. 26	NYR 3 Pho. 1	3
Mark Messier	NY Rangers	Feb. 08	NYR 5 NYI 2	3
Alexander Mogilny	Vancouver	Dec. 15	Van. 8 St.L. 0	3
*Rem Murray	Edmonton	Oct. 24	Edm. 8 L.A. 2	3
Owen Nolan	San Jose	Oct. 27	S.J. 6 Chi. 2	3
Jeff O'Neill	Hartford	Jan. 31	Hfd. 3 Ana. 6	3
Ed Olczyk	Los Angeles	Jan. 07	Van. 2 L.A. 5	3
Zigmund Palffy	NY Islanders	Mar. 29	Bos. 2 NYI 8	3
Mark Recchi	Montreal	Nov. 21	Mtl. 6 Bos. 2	3
Dave Reid	Dallas	Jan. 08	Det. 3 Dal. 6	3
Brian Rolston	New Jersey	Nov. 16	T.B. 3 N.J. 6	3
Martin Rucinsky	Montreal	Nov. 06	Mtl. 6 Ana. 5	3
Joe Sakic	Colorado	Mar. 14	Pit. 3 Col. 6	3
Miroslav Satan	Buffalo	Apr. 04	NYR 1 Buf. 5	3
Brian Savage	Montreal	Oct. 07	Ana. 6 Mtl. 6	3
Teemu Selanne	Anaheim	Nov. 01	S.J. 3 Ana. 4	3
Brendan Shanahan	Detroit	Nov. 27	Tor. 2 Det. 5	3
Brendan Shanahan	Detroit	Feb. 08	Det. 6 Pit. 5	3
Brendan Shanahan	Detroit	Feb. 12	S.J. 1 Det. 7	3
Ray Sheppard	Florida	Nov. 26	Buf. 3 Fla. 4	3
Ray Sheppard	Florida	Dec. 22	Fla. 3 NYR 7	3
Ray Sheppard	Florida	Mar. 13	Van. 4 Fla. 5	3
Ryan Smyth	Edmonton	Oct. 08	Edm. 4 Tor. 2	3
Mats Sundin	Toronto	Dec. 21	Tor. 6 Col. 2	3
*Jaroslav Svejkovsky	Washington	Apr. 13	Wsh. 8 Buf. 3	4
German Titov	Calgary	Dec. 22	Cgy. 7 Pho. 2	3
Keith Tkachuk	Phoenix	Nov. 28	N.J. 3 Pho. 4	3
Keith Tkachuk	Phoenix	Mar. 20	Pho. 4 Chi. 2	4
Scott Young	Colorado	Nov. 09	Mtl. 2 Col. 5	3
Alexei Zhamnov	Chicago	Apr. 11	Cgy. 3 Chi. 7	3

NOTE: *74* Three-or-more-goal games recorded in 1996-97.

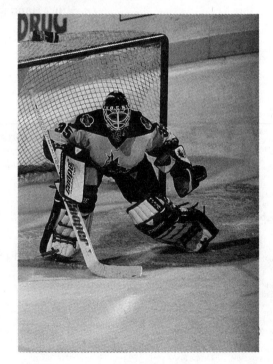

Left: The always dangerous Teemu Selanne hit the 50-goal mark for the second time in his career and proved himself to be a clutch performer with eight game-winning goals. Below: Phoenix's Nikolai Khabibulin recorded a franchise-record seven shutouts in 1996-97.

Goaltending Leaders

Minimum 25 games

Goals Against Average

Goaltender	Team	GPI	Mins	GA	Avg
Martin Brodeur	New Jersey	67	3838	120	1.88
Andy Moog	Dallas	48	2738	98	2.15
Jeff Hackett	Chicago	41	2473	89	2.16
Dominik Hasek	Buffalo	67	4037	153	2.27
J. Vanbiesbrouck	Florida	57	3347	128	2.29

Wins

Goaltender	Team	GPI	MINS	W	L	T
Patrick Roy	Colorado	62	3698	38	15	7
Martin Brodeur	New Jersey	67	3838	37	14	13
Dominik Hasek	Buffalo	67	4037	37	20	10
Mike Richter	NY Rangers	61	3598	33	22	6
Grant Fuhr	St. Louis	73	4261	33	27	11
Curtis Joseph	Edmonton	72	4100	32	29	9
Ron Hextall	Philadelphia	55	3094	31	16	5
N. Khabibulin	Phoenix	72	4091	30	33	6

Save Percentage

Goaltender	Team	GPI	MINS	GA	SA	S%	W	L	T
Dominik Hasek	Buffalo	67	4037	153	2177	.930	37	20	10
Martin Brodeur	New Jersey	67	3838	120	1633	.927	37	14	13
Jeff Hackett	Chicago	41	2473	89	1212	.927	19	18	4
Patrick Roy	Colorado	62	3698	143	1861	.923	38	15	7
Guy Hebert	Anaheim	67	3863	172	2133	.919	29	25	12
J. Vanbiesbrouck	Florida	57	3347	128	1582	.919	27	19	10
Mike Richter	NY Rangers	61	3598	161	1945	.917	33	22	6
Sean Burke	Hartford	51	2985	134	1560	.914	22	22	6
Mark Fitzpatrick	Florida	30	1680	66	771	.914	8	9	9

Shutouts

Goaltender	Team	GPI	MINS	SO	W	L	T
Martin Brodeur	New Jersey	67	3838	10	37	14	13
Patrick Roy	Colorado	62	3698	7	38	15	7
N. Khabibulin	Phoenix	72	4091	7	30	33	6
Chris Osgood	Detroit	47	2769	6	23	13	9
Curtis Joseph	Edmonton	72	4100	6	32	29	9

Team-by-Team Point Totals

1992-93 to 1996-97

(Ranked by five-year winning %)

Team	96-97	95-96	94-95	93-94	92-93	W%
Detroit	94	131	70	100	103	.655
Pittsburgh	84	102	61	101	119	.614
Que./Col.	107	104	65	76	104	.600
New Jersey	104	86	52	106	87	.572
Philadelphia	103	103	60	80	83	.564
Chicago	81	94	53	87	106	.554
NY Rangers	86	96	47	112	79	.553
Boston	61	91	57	97	109	.546
Montreal	77	90	43	96	102	.537
Calgary	73	79	55	97	97	.528
St. Louis	83	80	61	91	85	.526
Florida	89	92	46	83	–	.524
Buffalo	92	73	51	95	86	.522
Washington	75	89	52	88	93	.522
Toronto	68	80	50	98	99	.520
Min./Dallas	104	66	42	97	82	.514
Vancouver	77	79	48	85	101	.513
Anaheim	85	78	37	71	–	.458
Wpg./Pho.	83	78	39	57	87	.453
NY Islanders	70	54	35	84	87	.434
Los Angeles	67	66	41	66	88	.432
Tampa Bay	74	88	37	71	53	.425
Hartford	75	77	43	63	58	.416
Edmonton	81	68	38	64	60	.409
San Jose	62	47	42	82	24	.338
Ottawa	77	41	23	37	24	.266

Team Record When Scoring First Goal of a Game

Team	GP	FG	W	L	T
New Jersey	82	59	40	12	7
Colorado	82	46	37	5	4
Buffalo	82	46	33	6	7
Dallas	82	44	32	6	6
Philadelphia	82	39	29	5	5
Pittsburgh	82	44	29	12	3
Edmonton	82	41	28	8	5
Florida	82	43	28	7	8
St. Louis	82	47	28	13	6
Anaheim	82	49	28	11	10
Phoenix	82	37	27	7	3
Detroit	82	42	27	8	7
NY Rangers	82	37	26	9	2
Washington	82	37	25	10	2
Toronto	82	45	24	15	6
Vancouver	82	34	23	7	4
Los Angeles	82	38	23	11	4
Tampa Bay	82	38	23	7	8
Hartford	82	40	23	9	8
Montreal	82	36	22	7	7
Chicago	82	40	22	12	6
Boston	82	35	21	11	3
San Jose	82	40	21	17	2
Calgary	82	33	20	10	3
NY Islanders	82	40	20	11	9
Ottawa	82	32	19	8	5

Team Plus/Minus Differential

Team	GF	PPGF	Net GF	GA	PPGA	Net GA	Goal Differential
Dallas	252	46	206	198	51	147	+ 59
Philadelphia	274	53	221	217	49	168	+ 53
Buffalo	237	43	194	208	59	149	+ 45
New Jersey	231	40	191	182	28	154	+ 37
Detroit	253	66	187	197	46	151	+ 36
NY Rangers	258	63	195	231	69	162	+ 33
Colorado	277	83	194	205	42	163	+ 31
Chicago	223	45	178	210	59	151	+ 27
Florida	221	50	171	201	50	151	+ 20
Anaheim	245	56	189	233	62	171	+ 18
St. Louis	236	50	186	239	55	184	+ 2
Vancouver	257	51	206	273	66	207	– 1
Pittsburgh	285	74	211	280	64	216	– 5
NY Islanders	240	48	192	250	53	197	– 5
Montreal	249	53	196	276	71	205	– 9
Edmonton	252	73	179	247	59	188	– 9
Washington	214	51	163	231	54	177	– 14
Ottawa	226	56	170	234	48	186	– 16
Phoenix	240	65	175	243	47	196	– 21
Tampa Bay	217	47	170	247	55	192	– 22
Calgary	214	61	153	239	58	181	– 28
Toronto	230	48	182	273	59	214	– 32
Hartford	226	58	168	256	51	205	– 37
San Jose	211	50	161	278	66	212	– 51
Los Angeles	214	46	168	268	45	223	– 55
Boston	234	46	188	300	56	244	– 56

Team Record when Leading, Trailing, Tied

Team	Leading after 1 period W	L	T	Leading after 2 periods W	L	T	Trailing after 1 period W	L	T	Trailing after 2 periods W	L	T	Tied after 1 period W	L	T	Tied after 2 periods W	L	T
Anaheim	20	8	4	27	4	4	3	13	3	3	25	4	13	12	6	6	4	5
Boston	13	3	1	19	0	1	4	33	5	3	45	4	9	11	3	4	2	4
Buffalo	25	3	3	27	3	5	3	17	2	2	17	1	12	10	7	11	10	6
Calgary	15	6	1	22	2	1	6	21	4	4	31	3	11	14	4	6	8	5
Chicago	18	7	5	23	4	2	6	14	6	6	25	5	10	14	2	5	6	6
Colorado	23	2	4	35	4	3	8	12	2	3	16	3	18	10	3	11	4	3
Dallas	18	2	2	36	0	3	10	14	2	5	21	1	20	10	4	7	5	4
Detroit	27	4	7	33	4	8	6	12	8	2	19	4	5	10	3	3	3	6
Edmonton	23	5	2	26	3	2	3	22	3	1	26	2	10	10	4	9	8	5
Florida	15	5	6	27	4	5	3	15	7	1	19	7	17	8	6	7	5	7
Hartford	18	3	7	21	3	5	4	26	3	4	32	4	10	10	1	7	4	2
Los Angeles	18	6	0	23	2	2	3	25	3	1	37	3	8	11	4	4	4	6
Montreal	19	5	5	22	2	5	4	20	4	1	24	4	8	11	6	8	10	6
New Jersey	25	6	4	33	6	4	4	10	3	3	14	3	16	7	7	9	3	7
NY Islanders	14	7	7	23	1	7	4	22	1	2	31	3	11	12	4	4	9	2
NY Rangers	22	7	1	30	3	2	9	18	3	1	26	4	7	9	6	7	5	4
Ottawa	15	6	4	24	0	5	6	18	5	1	27	6	10	12	6	6	9	4
Philadelphia	23	3	5	30	2	3	10	13	5	7	17	6	12	8	3	8	6	4
Phoenix	25	0	1	31	1	1	7	26	3	5	29	3	6	11	3	2	7	3
Pittsburgh	18	10	2	26	4	4	10	18	4	3	25	4	10	8	2	7	9	0
San Jose	18	7	2	17	4	3	1	31	3	3	36	5	8	9	3	7	7	0
St. Louis	19	6	5	26	2	4	3	18	5	1	27	5	14	11	1	9	6	2
Tampa Bay	17	6	5	21	5	7	7	21	2	6	28	3	8	9	3	5	11	4
Toronto	23	7	4	24	4	2	1	25	1	1	29	2	6	12	3	5	11	4
Vancouver	19	3	2	29	2	1	5	23	1	3	29	1	11	14	4	3	9	5
Washington	17	7	3	28	3	4	4	20	4	0	28	3	12	13	2	5	9	2

Team Statistics

TEAMS' HOME-AND-ROAD RECORD

Northeast Division

	GP	W	L	T	GF	GA	PTS	%	GP	W	L	T	GF	GA	PTS	%
				Home								Road				
BUF	41	24	11	6	139	107	54	.659	41	16	19	6	98	101	38	.463
PIT	41	25	11	5	154	122	55	.671	41	13	25	3	131	158	29	.354
OTT	41	16	17	8	122	117	40	.488	41	15	19	7	104	117	37	.451
MTL	41	17	17	7	128	138	41	.500	41	14	19	8	121	138	36	.439
HFD	41	23	15	3	116	108	49	.598	41	9	24	8	110	148	26	.317
BOS	41	14	20	7	123	139	35	.427	41	12	27	2	111	161	26	.317
Total	246	119	91	36	782	731	274	.557	246	79	133	34	675	823	192	.390

Atlantic Division

	GP	W	L	T	GF	GA	PTS	%	GP	W	L	T	GF	GA	PTS	%
N.J.	41	23	9	9	119	85	55	.671	41	22	14	5	112	97	49	.598
PHI	41	25	11	6	135	101	52	.634	41	22	12	7	139	116	51	.622
FLA	41	21	12	8	119	97	50	.610	41	14	16	11	102	104	39	.476
NYR	41	21	14	6	139	110	48	.585	41	17	20	4	119	121	38	.463
WSH	41	17	19	5	109	109	43	.524	41	14	23	4	105	122	32	.390
T.B.	41	15	18	8	103	115	38	.463	41	17	22	2	114	132	36	.439
NYI	41	19	18	4	141	125	42	.512	41	10	23	8	99	125	28	.341
Total	287	141	100	46	865	742	328	.571	287	116	130	41	790	817	273	.476

Central Division

	GP	W	L	T	GF	GA	PTS	%	GP	W	L	T	GF	GA	PTS	%
DAL	41	25	13	3	137	103	53	.646	41	23	13	5	115	95	51	.622
DET	41	20	12	9	115	84	49	.598	41	18	14	9	138	113	45	.549
PHO	41	15	19	7	117	121	37	.451	41	23	18	0	123	122	46	.561
ST.L.	41	17	20	4	113	128	38	.463	41	19	15	7	123	111	45	.549
CHI	41	16	21	4	105	112	36	.439	41	18	14	9	118	98	45	.549
TOR	41	18	20	3	121	128	39	.476	41	12	24	5	109	145	29	.354
Total	246	111	105	30	708	676	252	.512	246	113	98	35	726	684	261	.530

Pacific Division

	GP	W	L	T	GF	GA	PTS	%	GP	W	L	T	GF	GA	PTS	%
COL	41	26	10	5	143	103	57	.695	41	23	14	4	134	102	50	.610
ANA	41	23	12	6	138	110	52	.634	41	13	21	7	107	123	33	.402
EDM	41	21	16	4	124	117	46	.561	41	15	21	5	128	130	35	.427
VAN	41	24	13	4	126	123	44	.537	41	15	23	3	131	150	33	.402
CGY	41	21	18	2	121	121	44	.537	41	11	23	7	93	118	29	.354
L.A.	41	18	16	7	119	122	43	.524	41	10	27	4	95	146	24	.293
S.J.	41	14	23	4	109	136	32	.390	41	13	24	4	102	142	30	.366
Total	287	143	112	32	880	832	318	.554	287	100	153	34	790	911	234	.408
	1066	514	408	144	3235	2981	1172	.550	1066	408	514	144	2981	3235	960	.450

TEAMS' DIVISIONAL RECORD

Northeast Division

	GP	W	L	T	GF	GA	PTS	%	GP	W	L	T	GF	GA	PTS	%
			Against Own Division								Against Other Division					
BUF	28	17	9	2	88	60	36	.643	54	23	21	10	149	148	56	.519
PIT	28	13	9	6	100	84	32	.571	54	25	27	2	185	196	52	.481
OTT	28	12	12	4	79	79	28	.500	54	19	24	11	147	155	49	.454
MTL	28	8	13	7	80	96	23	.411	54	23	23	8	169	180	54	.500
HFD	28	14	10	4	98	90	32	.571	54	18	29	7	128	166	43	.398
BOS	28	8	19	1	76	112	17	.304	54	18	28	8	158	188	44	.407
Total	168	72	72	24	521	521	168	.500	324	126	152	46	936	1033	298	.460

Atlantic Division

	GP	W	L	T	GF	GA	PTS	%	GP	W	L	T	GF	GA	PTS	%
N.J.	32	14	12	6	78	77	34	.531	50	31	11	8	153	105	70	.700
PHI	32	14	14	4	84	91	32	.500	50	31	10	9	190	126	71	.710
FLA	32	13	10	9	88	83	35	.547	50	22	18	10	133	118	54	.540
NYR	32	10	16	6	85	90	26	.406	50	28	18	4	173	141	60	.600
WSH	32	14	14	4	81	81	32	.500	50	19	26	5	133	150	43	.430
T.B.	32	14	13	5	90	85	33	.516	50	18	27	5	127	162	41	.410
NYI	32	14	14	4	92	91	32	.500	50	15	27	8	148	159	38	.380
Total	224	93	93	38	598	598	224	.500	350	164	137	49	1057	961	377	.539

Central Division

	GP	W	L	T	GF	GA	PTS	%	GP	W	L	T	GF	GA	PTS	%
DAL	28	19	9	4	93	80	36	.643	54	32	18	4	159	118	68	.630
DET	28	9	11	8	78	80	26	.464	54	29	15	10	175	117	68	.630
PHO	28	15	10	3	83	72	33	.589	54	23	27	4	157	171	50	.463
ST.L.	28	12	11	5	77	76	27	.482	54	24	23	6	159	163	56	.519
CHI	28	11	13	4	78	76	26	.464	54	23	22	9	145	134	55	.509
TOR	28	8	16	4	64	89	20	.357	54	22	28	4	166	184	48	.444
Total	168	70	70	28	473	473	168	.500	324	154	133	37	961	887	345	.532

Pacific Division

	GP	W	L	T	GF	GA	PTS	%	GP	W	L	T	GF	GA	PTS	%
COL	32	19	9	4	120	81	42	.656	50	30	15	5	157	124	65	.650
ANA	32	13	12	7	100	94	33	.516	50	23	21	6	145	139	52	.520
EDM	32	12	16	4	102	95	28	.438	50	24	21	5	150	152	53	.530
VAN	32	14	15	3	88	108	31	.484	50	21	25	4	169	165	46	.460
CGY	32	15	14	3	88	93	33	.516	50	17	27	6	126	146	40	.400
L.A.	32	12	16	4	86	100	28	.438	50	16	27	7	128	168	39	.390
S.J.	32	14	17	1	94	107	29	.453	50	13	30	7	117	171	33	.330
Total	224	99	99	26	678	678	224	.500	350	144	166	40	992	1065	328	.469

TEAM STREAKS

Consecutive Wins

Games	Team	From	To
7	Philadelphia	Dec. 6	Dec. 21
7	Dallas	Mar. 16	Apr. 2
6	Dallas	Oct. 5	Oct. 15
6	Pittsburgh	Dec. 4	Dec. 13
6	Pittsburgh	Dec. 28	Jan. 10
6	Colorado	Feb. 11	Feb. 23
5	New Jersey	Nov. 2	Nov. 12
5	Colorado	Nov. 6	Nov. 13
5	St. Louis	Nov. 8	Nov. 17
5	Dallas	Dec. 13	Dec. 21
5	NY Rangers	Dec. 13	Dec. 22
5	Colorado	Dec. 23	Jan. 2
5	Edmonton	Jan. 24	Feb. 5
5	Calgary	Feb. 7	Feb. 15
5	Los Angeles	Feb. 20	Mar. 1
5	New Jersey	Feb. 26	Mar. 5
5	New Jersey	Mar. 27	Apr. 6

Consecutive Home Wins

Games	Team	From	To
8	Philadelphia	Nov. 21	Jan. 7
6	NY Rangers	Dec. 16	Jan. 4
6	Pittsburgh	Dec. 28	Jan. 21
5	Pittsburgh	Oct. 12	Nov. 12
5	St. Louis	Nov. 3	Nov. 21
5	Edmonton	Jan. 12	Feb. 5
5	Calgary	Feb. 7	Feb. 15
5	Dallas	Feb. 14	Mar. 7
5	Tampa Bay	Feb. 20	Mar. 1
5	New Jersey	Feb. 27	Mar. 15
5	Dallas	Mar. 16	Apr. 9

Consecutive Road Wins

Games	Team	From	To
6	Pittsburgh	Nov. 22	Dec. 13
5	Philadelphia	Oct. 31	Nov. 23
5	NY Rangers	Nov. 26	Dec. 21
5	New Jersey	Dec. 10	Dec. 20
5	St. Louis	Jan. 15	Jan. 30
4	Colorado	Nov. 6	Nov. 13
4	Florida	Nov. 13	Dec. 1
4	Washington	Nov. 14	Nov. 30
4	Dallas	Dec. 15	Dec. 21
4	Pittsburgh	Dec. 19	Jan. 7
4	Philadelphia	Dec. 27	Jan. 2
4	Tampa Bay	Jan. 6	Jan. 13
4	NY Rangers	Jan. 22	Feb. 8
4	Colorado	Feb. 2	Feb. 21
4	Phoenix	Mar. 5	Mar. 14

Consecutive Undefeated

Games	Team	W	T	From	To
17	Philadelphia	14	3	Nov. 30	Jan. 7
14	Pittsburgh	12	2	Dec. 19	Jan. 21
13	New Jersey	6	7	Jan. 24	Feb. 20
12	Florida	8	4	Oct. 5	Oct. 30
12	Colorado	9	3	Dec. 23	Jan. 20
12	Buffalo	7	5	Jan. 29	Feb. 23
12	Anaheim	7	5	Feb. 22	Mar. 19
11	Colorado	9	2	Oct. 23	Nov. 13
11	Detroit	6	5	Feb. 16	Mar. 10
11	Dallas	9	2	Mar. 5	Apr. 2
10	Pittsburgh	8	2	Nov. 22	Dec. 13
7	Detroit	5	2	Oct. 19	Nov. 1
7	NY Rangers	6	1	Nov. 26	Dec. 9
7	Dallas	5	2	Dec. 8	Dec. 21
7	New Jersey	5	2	Dec. 10	Dec. 23
7	Montreal	4	3	Dec. 26	Jan. 6
7	Anaheim	5	2	Mar. 28	Apr. 11#

Consecutive Home Undefeated

Games	Team	W	T	From	To
15	New Jersey	9	6	Jan. 8	Mar. 15
14	Anaheim	10	4	Feb. 12	Apr. 9#
11	Buffalo	7	4	Jan. 29	Mar. 5
11	Dallas	10	1	Feb. 14	Apr. 9
9	Philadelphia	8	1	Nov. 16	Jan. 7
8	Colorado	6	2	Oct. 19	Nov. 22
8	Buffalo	7	1	Dec. 18	Jan. 22
8	Pittsburgh	7	1	Dec. 21	Jan. 21
8	Detroit	7	1	Feb. 12	Mar. 28
7	NY Rangers	6	1	Dec. 16	Jan. 6
7	Tampa Bay	6	1	Feb. 15	Mar. 1
6	Montreal	4	2	Oct. 5	Oct. 26
6	Ottawa	3	3	Oct. 9	Nov. 7
6	Detroit	5	1	Oct. 19	Nov. 4
6	Washington	5	1	Oct. 30	Nov. 23
6	Florida	4	2	Nov. 20	Dec. 15
6	Washington	5	1	Dec. 20	Jan. 13
6	Colorado	5	1	Dec. 23	Jan. 29
6	Tampa Bay	3	3	Dec. 26	Jan. 21
6	Philadelphia	4	2	Feb. 4	Feb. 23

Consecutive Road Undefeated

Games	Team	W	T	From	To
12	Philadelphia	8	4	Nov. 30	Jan. 29
8	Hartford	4	4	Nov. 12	Dec. 5
8	Colorado	5	3	Dec. 18	Jan. 20
7	Florida	4	3	Oct. 5	Oct. 29
7	Colorado	6	1	Oct. 23	Nov. 13
7	Dallas	6	1	Nov. 20	Dec. 21
7	Montreal	3	4	Dec. 6	Jan. 2
7	Pittsburgh	6	1	Dec. 19	Jan. 26
7	St. Louis	5	2	Jan. 15	Feb. 8
7	Detroit	3	4	Feb. 16	Mar. 10
6	Pittsburgh	6	0	Nov. 22	Dec. 13
6	New Jersey	3	3	Jan. 24	Feb. 20
6	New Jersey	4	2	Mar. 9	Apr. 8
5	Chicago	3	2	Oct. 5	Oct. 29
5	Philadelphia	5	0	Oct. 31	Nov. 23
5	NY Rangers	5	0	Nov. 26	Dec. 21
5	New Jersey	5	0	Dec. 10	Dec. 20
5	Chicago	2	3	Mar. 2	Apr. 1

TEAM PENALTIES

Abbreviations: GP – games played; **PEN** – total penalty minutes including bench minutes; **BMI** – total bench minor minutes; **AVG** – average penalty minutes/game calculated by dividing total penalty minutes by games played

Team	GP	PEN	BMI	AVG
OTT	82	1087	10	13.3
N.J.	82	1135	4	13.8
DAL	82	1325	10	16.2
TOR	82	1331	12	16.2
STL	82	1336	24	16.3
COL	82	1361	24	16.6
BOS	82	1369	4	16.7
EDM	82	1368	18	16.7
CGY	82	1444	16	17.6
MTL	82	1469	24	17.9
NYR	82	1481	14	18.1
PIT	82	1498	12	18.3
HFD	82	1513	18	18.5
DET	82	1582	12	19.3
PHO	82	1582	16	19.3
VAN	82	1607	22	19.6
FLA	82	1628	20	19.9
L.A.	82	1638	8	20.0
NYI	82	1640	18	20.0
WSH	82	1652	28	20.1
T.B.	82	1686	10	20.6
PHI	82	1699	8	20.7
ANA	82	1710	22	20.9
CHI	82	1763	14	21.5
BUF	82	1840	12	22.4
S.J.	82	2085	6	25.4
Total	**1066**	**39829**	**386**	**37.4**

Known as "The Little Tank" in Russia because of his size and solid build, Andrei Kovalenko used his physique to plow through defenders and record 14 power-play goals, the second-highest mark on the Oilers.

TEAMS' POWER-PLAY RECORD

Abbreviations: ADV – total advantages; **PPGF** – power-play goals for; **%** – calculated by dividing number of power-play goals by total advantages.

			Home					Road					Overall		
	Team	GP	ADV	PPGF	%	Team	GP	ADV	PPGF	%	Team	GP	ADV	PPGF	%
1	NYR	41	135	32	23.7	PIT	41	170	41	24.1	NYR	82	287	63	22.0
2	PIT	41	169	33	19.5	COL	41	188	41	21.8	PIT	82	339	74	21.8
3	COL	41	215	42	19.5	DET	41	187	40	21.4	COL	82	403	83	20.6
4	CGY	41	184	35	19.0	NYR	41	152	31	20.4	HFD	82	321	58	18.1
5	EDM	41	207	37	17.9	HFD	41	159	30	18.9	PHO	82	359	65	18.1
6	PHO	41	193	34	17.6	PHO	41	166	31	18.7	EDM	82	406	73	18.0
7	FLA	41	194	34	17.5	EDM	41	199	36	18.1	DET	82	368	66	17.9
8	HFD	41	162	28	17.3	OTT	41	161	29	18.0	CGY	82	361	61	16.9
9	ANA	41	168	28	16.7	VAN	41	134	24	17.9	ANA	82	333	56	16.8
10	S.J.	41	175	29	16.6	ST.L.	41	153	27	17.6	VAN	82	303	51	16.8
11	MTL	41	171	28	16.4	ANA	41	165	28	17.0	OTT	82	336	56	16.7
12	WSH	41	167	27	16.2	DAL	41	157	26	16.6	WSH	82	322	51	15.8
13	VAN	41	169	27	16.0	PHI	41	182	29	15.9	MTL	82	337	53	15.7
14	TOR	41	155	24	15.5	CHI	41	139	22	15.8	TOR	82	309	48	15.5
15	OTT	41	175	27	15.4	TOR	41	154	24	15.6	ST.L.	82	327	50	15.3
16	N.J.	41	138	21	15.2	WSH	41	155	24	15.5	BOS	82	310	46	14.8
17	T.B.	41	186	28	15.1	MTL	41	166	25	15.1	CHI	82	304	45	14.8
18	BOS	41	157	23	14.6	BOS	41	153	23	15.0	PHI	82	362	53	14.6
19	BUF	41	165	24	14.5	CGY	41	177	26	14.7	DAL	82	314	46	14.6
20	DET	41	181	26	14.4	NYI	41	179	26	14.5	S.J.	82	349	50	14.3
21	CHI	41	165	23	13.9	L.A.	41	157	22	14.0	FLA	82	352	50	14.2
22	L.A.	41	181	24	13.3	N.J.	41	150	19	12.7	NYI	82	346	48	13.9
23	PHI	41	180	24	13.3	T.B.	41	154	19	12.3	N.J.	82	288	40	13.9
24	ST.L.	41	174	23	13.2	S.J.	41	174	21	12.1	T.B.	82	340	47	13.8
25	NYI	41	167	22	13.2	BUF	41	161	19	11.8	L.A.	82	338	46	13.6
26	DAL	41	157	20	12.7	FLA	41	158	16	10.1	BUF	82	326	43	13.2
	Total	**1066**	**4490**	**723**	**16.1**		**1066**	**4250**	**699**	**16.4**		**1066**	**8740**	**1422**	**16.3**

SHORT-HANDED GOALS FOR

		Home			Road			Overall	
	Team	GP	SHGF	Team	GP	SHGF	Team	GP	SHGF
1	BUF	41	11	BOS	41	10	BUF	82	16
2	NYI	41	10	T.B.	41	9	BOS	82	15
3	PIT	41	9	DAL	41	9	NYR	82	15
4	MTL	41	7	NYR	41	8	COL	82	14
5	TOR	41	7	PHO	41	8	NYI	82	14
6	VAN	41	7	COL	41	7	T.B.	82	13
7	NYR	41	7	DET	41	7	HFD	82	12
8	CGY	41	7	S.J.	41	6	VAN	82	12
9	COL	41	7	EDM	41	6	PIT	82	11
10	HFD	41	6	PHI	41	6	PHI	82	11
11	ANA	41	6	HFD	41	6	TOR	82	11
12	ST.L.	41	5	BUF	41	5	DAL	82	11
13	BOS	41	5	VAN	41	5	CGY	82	11
14	PHI	41	5	WSH	41	5	MTL	82	10
15	OTT	41	5	NYI	41	4	DET	82	10
16	T.B.	41	4	OTT	41	4	ST.L.	82	9
17	EDM	41	3	CHI	41	4	EDM	82	9
18	L.A.	41	3	CGY	41	4	PHO	82	9
19	WSH	41	3	ST.L.	41	4	OTT	82	9
20	S.J.	41	3	TOR	41	4	ANA	82	9
21	FLA	41	3	ANA	41	3	S.J.	82	9
22	DET	41	3	MTL	41	3	WSH	82	8
23	N.J.	41	2	FLA	41	2	L.A.	82	5
24	DAL	41	2	N.J.	41	2	FLA	82	5
25	CHI	41	1	PIT	41	2	CHI	82	5
26	PHO	41	1	L.A.	41	1	N.J.	82	4
	Total	**1066**	**132**		**1066**	**135**		**1066**	**267**

TEAMS' PENALTY KILLING RECORD

Abbreviations: TSH – total times short-handed; **PPGA** – power-play goals against; **%** – calculated by dividing times short minus power-play goals against by times short.

			Home					Road					Overall		
	Team	GP	TSH	PPGA	%	Team	GP	TSH	PPGA	%	Team	GP	TSH	PPGA	%
1	COL	41	167	20	88.0	N.J.	41	123	12	90.2	N.J.	82	235	28	88.1
2	T.B.	41	188	23	87.8	PHO	41	172	20	88.4	COL	82	339	42	87.6
3	L.A.	41	175	22	87.4	PHI	41	186	23	87.6	L.A.	82	352	45	87.2
4	DET	41	159	20	87.4	COL	41	172	22	87.2	DET	82	346	46	86.7
5	N.J.	41	112	16	85.7	L.A.	41	177	23	87.0	PHO	82	334	47	85.9
6	FLA	41	166	25	84.9	WSH	41	188	25	86.7	PHI	82	342	49	85.7
7	HFD	41	153	24	84.3	DET	41	187	26	86.1	FLA	82	346	50	85.5
8	OTT	41	125	20	84.0	FLA	41	180	25	86.1	T.B.	82	361	54	84.8
9	CHI	41	175	28	84.0	ST.L.	41	164	24	85.4	WSH	82	354	54	84.7
10	BOS	41	148	24	83.8	DAL	41	157	23	85.4	HFD	82	332	51	84.6
11	VAN	41	179	29	83.8	S.J.	41	220	33	85.0	CHI	82	374	59	84.2
12	BUF	41	188	31	83.5	HFD	41	179	27	84.9	S.J.	82	409	66	83.9
13	PIT	41	169	28	83.4	CGY	41	176	27	84.7	BUF	82	364	59	83.8
14	PHI	41	156	26	83.3	NYI	41	168	26	84.5	ST.L.	82	332	55	83.4
15	PHO	41	162	27	83.3	CHI	41	199	31	84.4	NYI	82	319	55	83.4
16	EDM	41	165	28	83.0	BUF	41	176	28	84.1	DAL	82	308	51	83.4
17	TOR	41	162	28	82.7	EDM	41	173	31	82.1	CGY	82	345	58	83.2
18	WSH	41	166	29	82.5	T.B.	41	173	32	81.5	EDM	82	338	59	82.5
19	S.J.	41	189	33	82.5	MTL	41	166	31	81.3	TOR	82	328	59	82.0
20	ANA	41	160	28	82.5	TOR	41	166	31	81.3	OTT	82	265	48	81.9
21	NYI	41	151	27	82.1	ANA	41	176	34	80.7	BOS	82	308	56	81.8
22	CGY	41	169	31	81.7	OTT	41	140	28	80.0	ANA	82	336	62	81.5
23	ST.L.	41	168	31	81.5	BOS	41	160	32	80.0	PIT	82	338	64	81.1
24	DAL	41	151	28	81.5	NYR	41	178	36	79.8	VAN	82	344	66	80.8
25	NYR	41	166	33	80.1	PIT	41	169	36	78.7	NYR	82	344	69	79.9
26	MTL	41	181	40	77.9	VAN	41	165	37	77.6	MTL	82	347	71	79.5
	Total	**1066**	**4250**	**699**	**83.6**		**1066**	**4490**	**723**	**83.9**		**1066**	**8740**	**1422**	**83.7**

SHORT-HANDED GOALS AGAINST

		Home			Road			Overall	
	Team	GP	SHGA	Team	GP	SHGA	Team	GP	SHGA
1	HFD	41	2	COL	41	2	BUF	82	4
2	PHI	41	2	BUF	41	2	NYR	82	5
3	NYR	41	2	ANA	41	2	BOS	82	6
4	DET	41	2	TOR	41	2	ST.L.	82	8
5	BUF	41	2	NYR	41	3	DET	82	8
6	BOS	41	3	VAN	41	3	PHI	82	8
7	N.J.	41	4	ST.L.	41	3	TOR	82	8
8	MTL	41	4	BOS	41	3	VAN	82	8
9	CHI	41	4	NYI	41	4	NYI	82	9
10	T.B.	41	4	S.J.	41	4	T.B.	82	9
11	ST.L.	41	5	WSH	41	4	N.J.	82	9
12	EDM	41	5	DAL	41	4	CHI	82	9
13	PIT	41	5	PHO	41	5	DAL	82	9
14	DAL	41	5	T.B.	41	5	WSH	82	10
15	VAN	41	5	CHI	41	5	HFD	82	11
16	NYI	41	5	OTT	41	6	MTL	82	11
17	WSH	41	6	DET	41	6	ANA	82	11
18	TOR	41	6	N.J.	41	6	S.J.	82	11
19	OTT	41	6	L.A.	41	6	COL	82	12
20	S.J.	41	7	PHI	41	6	PIT	82	12
21	CGY	41	7	PIT	41	7	OTT	82	12
22	L.A.	41	8	MTL	41	7	EDM	82	13
23	FLA	41	9	FLA	41	8	L.A.	82	14
24	PHO	41	9	EDM	41	8	PHO	82	14
25	ANA	41	9	HFD	41	9	FLA	82	17
26	COL	41	10	CGY	41	12	CGY	82	19
	Total	**1066**	**135**		**1066**	**132**		**1066**	**267**

Overtime Results

1987-88 to 1996-97

Team	1996-97 GP	W	L	T	1995-96 GP	W	L	T	1994-95 GP	W	L	T	1993-94 GP	W	L	T	1992-93 GP	W	L	T	1991-92 GP	W	L	T	1990-91 GP	W	L	T	1989-90 GP	W	L	T	1988-89 GP	W	L	T	1987-88 GP	W	L	T
ANA	16	3	0	13	16	6	2	8	7	2	0	5	12	2	5	5																								
BOS	15	3	3	9	19	2	6	11	8	2	3	3	17	2	2	13	15	5	3	7	20	6	2	12	17	5	0	12	14	3	2	9	19	3	2	14	14	4	4	6
BUF	21	5	4	12	15	2	6	7	9	1	1	7	13	0	4	9	18	4	4	10	16	2	2	12	24	3	2	19	15	4	3	8	13	2	4	7	12	0	1	11
CGY	16	3	4	9	16	2	3	11	9	1	1	7	18	3	2	13	19	4	4	11	19	2	5	12	15	3	4	8	21	3	3	15	17	5	3	9	15	2	4	9
CHI	19	1	5	13	19	1	4	14	7	2	0	5	16	2	5	9	16	1	3	12	19	2	2	15	12	3	1	8	10	2	2	6	10	2	1	7	15	4	2	9
QUE/COL	15	2	3	10	6	1	0	5	8	0	0	8	15	3	3	9	15	4	1	10	17	0	5	12	18	1	3	14	8	0	1	7	10	2	1	7	9	2	2	5
MIN/DAL	15	4	3	8	15	1	0	14	9	0	1	8	22	6	3	13	10	0	0	10	8	0	2	6	17	0	3	14	11	3	4	4	17	0	1	16	16	1	2	13
DET	27	7	2	18	11	3	1	7	4	0	0	4	15	5	2	8	11	2	0	9	16	3	1	12	14	2	4	8	17	2	1	14	16	3	1	12	16	2	3	11
EDM	16	1	6	9	14	4	2	8	7	1	2	4	21	1	6	14	17	5	4	8	12	0	2	10	15	4	5	6	20	5	1	14	15	4	3	8	16	3	2	11
FLA	26	3	4	19	13	0	3	10	9	0	3	6	24	2	5	17																								
HFD	18	3	4	11	14	2	3	9	9	4	0	5	14	4	1	9	18	3	9	6	18	2	3	13	18	2	5	11	9	0	0	9	10	1	4	5	12	3	2	7
L.A.	14	0	3	11	23	3	2	18	9	0	0	9	18	3	3	12	13	2	1	10	16	1	1	14	16	4	2	10	12	3	2	7	14	6	1	7	12	1	3	8
MTL	21	2	4	15	15	2	3	10	10	1	2	7	19	3	2	14	14	5	3	6	20	6	3	11	17	3	3	11	17	4	2	11	11	2	0	9	16	1	2	13
N.J.	17	1	2	14	19	7	0	12	11	1	2	8	14	1	1	12	11	4	0	7	17	2	4	11	17	1	1	15	16	3	4	9	17	1	4	12	12	4	2	6
NYI	17	3	2	12	17	2	5	10	7	1	1	5	19	5	2	12	13	3	3	7	16	3	2	11	15	2	3	10	16	3	2	11	11	3	3	5	13	3	0	10
NYR	13	3	0	10	17	2	1	14	3	0	0	3	12	3	1	8	17	2	4	11	11	5	1	5	16	1	2	13	17	2	2	13	10	1	1	8	11	0	1	10
OTT	17	0	2	15	8	0	3	5	7	1	1	5	17	4	4	9	10	0	6	4																				
PHI	18	3	2	13	20	4	3	13	8	3	1	4	18	3	5	10	17	4	2	11	17	2	4	11	11	1	0	10	18	2	5	11	14	1	5	8	13	1	3	9
WPG/PHO	16	5	4	7	8	2	0	6	9	0	2	7	15	1	5	9	11	2	2	7	20	1	4	15	14	1	2	11	19	4	4	11	20	6	2	12	21	8	2	11
PIT	13	1	4	8	9	3	2	4	5	1	1	3	19	4	2	13	10	3	0	7	12	2	1	9	12	4	2	6	14	3	3	8	10	2	1	7	16	5	2	9
ST.L.	13	1	1	11	18	1	1	16	7	1	1	5	17	4	2	11	17	2	4	11	15	2	2	11	18	3	4	11	15	2	4	9	16	3	1	12	14	2	4	8
S.J.	12	3	1	8	9	1	1	7	5	1	0	4	19	2	1	16	16	3	5	2	9	1	3	5																
T.B.	16	4	2	10	18	3	3	12	7	2	2	3	18	3	4	11	14	3	4	7																				
TOR	10	1	1	8	18	4	2	12	8	0	0	8	17	4	1	12	13	1	1	11	11	4	0	7	17	4	2	11	11	3	4	4	11	1	4	6	13	1	2	10
VAN	14	5	2	7	20	1	4	15	13	0	1	12	12	5	4	3	10	1	0	9	14	4	1	12	15	3	3	9	21	2	5	14	14	2	4	8	11	0	2	9
WSH	13	2	2	9	16	4	1	11	9	0	1	8	14	2	2	10	11	2	2	7	12	2	2	8	14	4	3	7	9	2	1	6	16	2	4	10	15	2	4	9
Totals	**214**	**70**		**144**	**201**	**64**		**137**	**101**	**26**		**75**	**214**	**74**		**140**	**165**	**65**		**100**	**169**	**52**		**117**	**166**	**54**		**112**	**155**	**55**		**100**	**149**	**52**		**97**	**146**	**49**		**97**

1996-97

Home Team Wins: 37
Visiting Team Wins: 33

1996-97 Penalty Shots

Scored

Theoren Fleury (Calgary) scored against Patrick Roy (Colorado), October 22. Final score: Colorado 1 at Calgary 5.

Robert Reichel (Calgary) scored against Tom Barrasso (Pittsburgh), October 24. Final score: Pittsburgh 5 at Calgary 7.

Valeri Kamensky (Colorado) scored against Curtis Joseph (Edmonton), October 26. Final score: Colorado 4 at Edmonton 2.

Geoff Courtnall (St. Louis) scored against Jeff Hackett (Chicago), December 13. Final score: Chicago 4 at St. Louis 1.

Rob Zamuner (Tampa Bay) scored against Tommy Salo (NY Islanders), January 11. Final score: NY Islanders 4 at Tampa Bay 4.

Mike Sillinger (Vancouver) scored against Mark Fitzpatrick (Florida), January 14. Final score: Florida 4 at Vancouver 4.

John MacLean (New Jersey) scored against Dominik Hasek (Buffalo), February 27. Final score: Buffalo 1 at New Jersey 4.

Adam Deadmarsh (Colorado) scored against Jeff Hackett (Chicago), March 1. Final score: Chicago 1 at Colorado 2.

Sami Kapanen (Hartford) scored against Jim Carey (Boston), March 12. Final score: Boston 3 at Hartford 6.

Mario Lemieux (Pittsburgh) scored against John Vanbiesbrouck (Florida), April 11. Final score: Pittsburgh 2 at Florida 4.

Stopped

Mark Fitzpatrick (Florida) stopped Jaromir Jagr (Pittsburgh), November 9. Final score: Pittsburgh 2 at Florida 4.

Damian Rhodes (Ottawa) stopped Todd Marchant (Edmonton), November 13. Final score: Edmonton 4 at Ottawa 0.

Chris Osgood (Detroit) stopped Mike Hudson (Phoenix), November 18. Final score: Detroit 2 at Phoenix 2.

Jim Carey (Washington) stopped Todd Elik (Boston), November 19. Final score: Boston 2 at Washington 2.

Felix Potvin (Toronto) stopped Donald Audette (Buffalo), November 21. Final score: Toronto 3 at Buffalo 6.

Grant Fuhr (St. Louis) stopped Peter Forsberg (Colorado), December 6. Final score: St. Louis 4 at Colorado 3.

M. Shtalenkov (Anaheim) stopped Peter Bondra (Washington), December 13. Final score: Washington 4 at Anaheim 5.

Guy Hebert (Anaheim) stopped Alexandre Daigle (Ottawa), December 30. Final score: Anaheim 4 at Ottawa 3.

Olaf Kolzig (Washington) stopped Todd Marchant (Edmonton), January 26. Final score: Edmonton 3 at Washington 2.

Dominik Hasek (Buffalo) stopped Vincent Damphousse (Montreal), March 8. Final score: Buffalo 3 at Montreal 3.

Mike Richter (NY Rangers) stopped Ken Klee (Washington), March 12. Final score: Washington 2 at NY Rangers 3.

Corey Hirsch (Vancouver) stopped Rob Niedermayer (Florida), March 13. Final score: Vancouver 4 at Florida 5.

Ron Tugnutt (Ottawa) stopped Brett Harkins (Boston), March 22. Final score: Ottawa 5 at Boston 4.

Dominik Hasek (Buffalo) stopped Jason Allison (Boston), April 10. Final score: Buffalo 5 at Boston 1.

Summary

24 penalty shots resulted in 10 goals.

Guy Hebert's clutch save on Alexander Daigle's penalty shot allowed the Mighty Ducks to escape with a narrow 4-3 win over the surging Ottawa Senators on December 30, 1996.

TEAM USA WINS FIRST WORLD CUP OF HOCKEY 1996

THE 1996 WORLD CUP OF HOCKEY was a cooperative effort of the National Hockey League (NHL) and the NHL Players' Association (NHLPA), under the auspices of the International Ice Hockey Federation (IIHF). The tournament featured the world's top professional players playing on their respective national teams.and was played with NHL on-ice officials using NHL rules.

Eight national teams participated, divided into two pools. The North American pool included Canada, Russia, Slovakia and USA. The European pool included Czech Republic, Finland, Germany and Sweden. All games were played before the start of the NHL regular season.

Games were held in four European cities—Helsinki, Garmisch, Prague and Stockholm—and in five NHL venues—Montreal, New York, Ottawa, Philadelphia and Vancouver.

In the first round of the tournament, each team played the other teams in its pool. USA and Sweden were the winners of their pools and advanced to the semifinals. The second and third-place teams played in the quarterfinals, with the winners advancing to the semi-final round.

Canada and USA advanced to the best of three final. Team Canada won the opener in Philadelphia 4-3 in overtime. Team USA won games two and three by identical 5-2 scores, clinching the inaugural World Cup of Hockey.

Team USA defenseman Mathieu Schneider pursued by Team Canada center Wayne Gretzky in Game Three of the World Cup of Hockey Final won by Team USA 5-2.

1996 World Cup of Hockey Results

First Round

Aug. 26	Sweden	6	Germany	1
Aug. 27	Finland	7	Czech Republic	3
Aug. 28	Finland	8	Germany	3
Aug. 28	Sweden	3	Czech Republic	0
Aug. 28	Canada	5	Russia	3
Aug. 31	Germany	7	Czech Republic	1
Aug. 31	USA	5	Canada	3
Aug. 31	Russia	7	Slovakia	4
Sept. 1	Canada	3	Slovakia	2
Sept. 1	Sweden	5	Finland	2
Sept. 2	USA	5	Russia	2
Sept. 3	USA	9	Slovakia	3

First Round Standings

North American Pool

Team	GP	W	L	T	GF	GA	PTS
USA	3	3	0	0	19	8	6
Canada	3	2	1	0	11	10	4
Russia	3	1	2	0	12	14	2
Slovakia	3	0	3	0	9	19	0

European Pool

Team	GP	W	L	T	GF	GA	PTS
Sweden	3	3	0	0	14	3	6
Finland	3	2	1	0	17	11	4
Germany	3	1	2	0	11	15	2
Czech Republic	3	0	3	0	4	17	0

Quarterfinals

Sept. 5	Canada	4	Germany	1
Sept. 6	Russia	5	Finland	0

Semifinals

Sept. 7	Canada	3	Sweden	2	(OT)
Sept. 8	USA	5	Russia	2	

Final

Sept. 10	Canada	4	USA	3	(OT)
Sept. 12	USA	5	Canada	2	
Sept. 14	USA	5	Canada	2	

World Cup of Hockey Top Scorers

Player	Team	GP	G	A	PTS	PIM
Brett Hull	USA	7	7	4	11	4
John LeClair	USA	7	6	4	10	6
Mats Sundin	Sweden	4	4	3	7	4
Brendan Shanahan	Canada	7	3	4	7	8
Doug Weight	Canada	7	3	4	7	12
Brian Leetch	USA	7	0	7	7	4
Paul Coffey	Canada	8	0	7	7	12
Keith Tkachuk	USA	7	5	1	6	44
Theoren Fleury	Canada	8	4	2	6	8
Sergei Fedorov	Russia	5	3	3	6	2
Wayne Gretzky	Canada	8	3	3	6	2
Eric Lindros	Canada	8	3	3	6	10
Alex Mogilny	Russia	5	2	4	6	0
Mike Modano	USA	7	2	4	6	4
Tony Amonte	USA	7	2	4	6	6
Calle Johansson	Sweden	4	1	5	6	8
Teemu Selanne	Finland	4	3	2	5	0
Derian Hatcher	USA	6	3	2	5	10
Peter Draisaitl	Germany	4	1	4	5	2
Peter Forsberg	Sweden	4	1	4	5	6
Mark Messier	Canada	7	1	4	5	12
Bryan Smolinski	USA	6	0	5	5	0
Jere Lehtinen	Finland	4	2	2	4	0
Sergei Gonchar	Russia	4	2	2	4	2
Niklas Sundstrom	Sweden	4	2	2	4	0

Player	Team	GP	G	A	PTS	PIM
Pat LaFontaine	USA	5	2	2	4	2
Scott Young	USA	7	2	2	4	4
Adam Deadmarsh	USA	7	2	2	4	8
Joe Sakic	Canada	8	2	2	4	6
Juha Ylonen	Finland	4	1	3	4	0
Saku Koivu	Finland	4	1	3	4	4
Ville Peltonen	Finland	4	1	3	4	0
Mark MacKay	Germany	4	1	3	4	2
Andrei Nikolishin	Russia	4	1	3	4	4
Scott Niedermayer	Canada	8	1	3	4	6
Juha Riihijarvi	Finland	4	0	4	4	0
Igor Larionov	Russia	5	0	4	4	2
Chris Chelios	USA	7	0	4	4	10
Peter Bondra	Slovakia	3	3	0	3	2
Jyrki Lumme	Finland	4	2	1	3	4
Nicklas Lidstrom	Sweden	4	2	1	3	0
Michael Nylander	Sweden	4	2	1	3	0
Alexei Kovalev	Russia	5	2	1	3	8
Steve Yzerman	Canada	6	2	1	3	0
Mika Stromberg	Finland	3	1	2	3	2
Zigmund Palffy	Slovakia	3	1	2	3	2
Slava Kozlov	Russia	5	1	2	3	8
Sergei Nemchinov	Russia	5	1	2	3	2
Rod Brind'Amour	Canada	7	1	2	3	0
Joel Otto	USA	7	1	2	3	6

Notes

NHL Record Book

All-Time Standings of NHL Teams
(ranked by percentage)

Active Clubs

Team	Games	Wins	Losses	Ties	Goals For	Goals Against	Points	%	First Season
Montreal	4972	2610	1593	769	16843	13308	5989	.602	1917-18
Philadelphia	2358	1174	818	366	8407	7238	2714	.575	1967-68
Boston	4812	2306	1800	706	15891	14391	5318	.553	1924-25
Edmonton	1420	691	552	177	5816	5287	1559	.549	1979-80
Buffalo	2132	1004	797	331	7604	6862	2339	.549	1970-71
Calgary	1976	925	756	295	7368	6709	2145	.543	1972-73
NY Islanders	1976	898	798	280	7104	6504	2076	.525	1972-73
Florida	296	129	115	52	823	795	310	.524	1993-94
Detroit	4746	2028	1975	743	14736	14585	4799	.506	1926-27
NY Rangers	4746	2016	1989	741	14952	14983	4773	.503	1926-27
Toronto	4972	2129	2121	722	15526	15535	4980	.501	1917-18
St. Louis	2358	989	1011	358	7691	7935	2336	.495	1967-68
Chicago	4746	1964	2048	734	14386	14505	4662	.491	1926-27
Colorado	1420	593	648	179	5228	5328	1365	.481	1979-80
Washington	1820	757	829	234	6140	6473	1748	.480	1974-75
Pittsburgh	2358	964	1082	312	8369	8847	2240	.475	1967-68
Los Angeles	2358	913	1095	350	8203	8836	2176	.461	1967-68
Dallas	2358	891	1090	377	7591	8251	2159	.458	1967-68
Anaheim	296	120	145	31	833	895	271	.458	1993-94
Phoenix	1420	544	697	179	5002	5590	1267	.446	1979-80
Hartford	1420	534	709	177	4704	5345	1245	.438	1979-80
Vancouver	2132	780	1043	309	7023	7909	1869	.438	1970-71
Tampa Bay	380	140	197	43	1044	1222	323	.425	1992-93
New Jersey	1820	616	949	255	5746	6870	1487	.409	1974-75
San Jose	460	127	291	42	1281	1834	296	.322	1991-92
Ottawa	380	82	260	38	937	1491	202	.266	1992-93

Defunct Clubs

Team	Games	Wins	Losses	Ties	Goals For	Goals Against	Points	%	First Season	Last Season
Ottawa Senators	542	258	221	63	1458	1333	579	.534	1917-18	1933-34
Montreal Maroons	622	271	260	91	1474	1405	633	.509	1924-25	1937-38
NY/Brooklyn Americans	784	255	402	127	1643	2182	637	.406	1925-26	1941-42
Hamilton Tigers	126	47	78	1	414	475	95	.377	1920-21	1924-25
Cleveland Barons	160	47	87	26	470	617	120	.375	1976-77	1977-78
Pittsburgh Pirates	212	67	122	23	376	519	157	.370	1925-26	1929-30
Calif./Oakland Seals	698	182	401	115	1826	2580	479	.343	1967-68	1975-76
St. Louis Eagles	48	11	31	6	86	144	28	.292	1934-35	1934-35
Quebec Bulldogs	24	4	20	0	91	177	8	.167	1919-20	1919-20
Montreal Wanderers	6	1	5	0	17	35	2	.167	1917-18	1917-18
Philadelphia Quakers	44	4	36	4	76	184	12	.136	1930-31	1930-31

Calgary totals include Atlanta, 1972-73 to 1979-80.
Colorado totals include Quebec, 1979-80 to 1994-95.
Dallas totals include Minnesota, 1967-68 to 1992-93.
Detroit totals include Cougars, 1926-27 to 1929-30, and Falcons, 1930-31 to 1931-32.
New Jersey totals include Kansas City, 1974-75 to 1975-76, and Colorado Rockies, 1976-77 to 1981-82.
Phoenix totals include Winnipeg, 1979-80 to 1995-96.
Toronto totals include Arenas, 1917-18 to 1918-19, and St. Patricks, 1919-20 to 1925-26.

Year-By-Year Final Standings & Leading Scorers

*Stanley Cup winner

1917-18

Team	GP	W	L	T	GF	GA	PTS
Montreal	22	13	9	0	115	84	26
*Toronto	22	13	9	0	108	109	26
Ottawa	22	9	13	0	102	114	18
**Mtl. Wanderers	6	1	5	0	17	35	2

**Montreal Arena burned down and Wanderers forced to withdraw from League. Canadiens and Toronto each counted a win for defaulted games with Wanderers.

Leading Scorers

Player	Club	GP	G	A	PTS
Malone, Joe	Montreal	20	44	—	44
Denneny, Cy	Ottawa	22	36	—	36
Noble, Reg	Toronto	20	28	—	28
Lalonde, Newsy	Montreal	14	23	—	23
Denneny, Corbett	Toronto	21	20	—	20
Pitre, Didier	Montreal	19	17	—	17
Cameron, Harry	Toronto	20	17	—	17
Darragh, Jack	Ottawa	18	14	—	14
Hyland, Harry	Mtl.W., Ott.	16	14	—	14
Skinner, Alf	Toronto	19	13	—	13
Gerard, Eddie	Ottawa	21	13	—	13

1918-19

Team	GP	W	L	T	GF	GA	PTS
Ottawa	18	12	6	0	71	53	24
Montreal	18	10	8	0	88	78	20
Toronto	18	5	13	0	64	92	10

Leading Scorers

Player	Club	GP	G	A	PTS	PIM
Lalonde, Newsy	Montreal	17	21	9	30	40
Cleghorn, Odie	Montreal	17	23	6	29	33
Denneny, Cy	Ottawa	18	18	4	22	43
Nighbor, Frank	Ottawa	18	18	4	22	27
Pitre, Didier	Montreal	17	14	4	18	9
Skinner, Alf	Toronto	17	12	3	15	26
Cameron, Harry	Tor., Ott.	14	11	3	14	35
Noble, Reg	Toronto	17	11	3	14	35
Darragh, Jack	Ottawa	14	12	1	13	27
Randall, Ken	Toronto	14	7	6	13	27

1919-20

Team	GP	W	L	T	GF	GA	PTS
*Ottawa	24	19	5	0	121	64	38
Montreal	24	13	11	0	129	113	26
Toronto	24	12	12	0	119	106	24
Quebec	24	4	20	0	91	177	8

Leading Scorers

Player	Club	GP	G	A	PTS	PIM
Malone, Joe	Quebec	24	39	9	48	12
Lalonde, Newsy	Montreal	23	36	6	42	33
Denneny, Corbett	Toronto	23	23	12	35	18
Nighbor, Frank	Ottawa	23	26	7	33	18
Noble, Reg	Toronto	24	24	7	31	51
Darragh, Jack	Ottawa	22	22	5	27	22
Arbour, Amos	Montreal	20	22	4	26	10
Wilson, Cully	Toronto	23	21	5	26	79
Broadbent, Punch	Ottawa	20	19	4	23	39
Cleghorn, Odie	Montreal	21	19	3	22	30
Pitre, Didier	Montreal	22	15	7	22	6

1920-21

Team	GP	W	L	T	GF	GA	PTS
Toronto	24	15	9	0	105	100	30
*Ottawa	24	14	10	0	97	75	28
Montreal	24	13	11	0	112	99	26
Hamilton	24	6	18	0	92	132	12

Leading Scorers

Player	Club	GP	G	A	PTS	PIM
Lalonde, Newsy	Montreal	24	33	8	41	36
Denneny, Cy	Ottawa	24	34	5	39	0
Dye, Babe	Ham., Tor.	24	35	2	37	32
Malone, Joe	Hamilton	20	30	4	34	2
Cameron, Harry	Toronto	24	18	9	27	35
Noble, Reg	Toronto	24	20	6	26	54
Prodgers, Goldie	Hamilton	23	18	8	26	8
Denneny, Corbett	Toronto	20	17	6	23	27
Nighbor, Frank	Ottawa	24	18	3	21	10
Berlinquette, Louis	Montreal	24	12	9	21	24

1921-22

Team	GP	W	L	T	GF	GA	PTS
Ottawa	24	14	8	2	106	84	30
*Toronto	24	13	10	1	98	97	27
Montreal	24	12	11	1	88	94	25
Hamilton	24	7	17	0	88	105	14

Leading Scorers

Player	Club	GP	G	A	PTS	PIM
Broadbent, Punch	Ottawa	24	32	14	46	24
Denneny, Cy	Ottawa	22	27	12	39	18
Dye, Babe	Toronto	24	30	7	37	18
Malone, Joe	Hamilton	24	25	7	32	4
Cameron, Harry	Toronto	24	19	8	27	18
Denneny, Corbett	Toronto	24	19	7	26	28
Noble, Reg	Toronto	24	17	8	25	10
Cleghorn, Odie	Montreal	23	21	3	24	26
Cleghorn, Sprague	Montreal	24	17	7	24	63
Reise, Leo	Hamilton	24	9	14	23	8

1922-23

Team	GP	W	L	T	GF	GA	PTS
*Ottawa	24	14	9	1	77	54	29
Montreal	24	13	9	2	73	61	28
Toronto	24	13	10	1	82	88	27
Hamilton	24	6	18	0	81	110	12

Leading Scorers

Player	Club	GP	G	A	PTS	PIM
Dye, Babe	Toronto	22	26	11	37	19
Denneny, Cy	Ottawa	24	21	10	31	20
Adams, Jack	Toronto	23	19	9	28	42
Boucher, Billy	Montreal	24	23	4	27	52
Cleghorn, Odie	Montreal	24	19	7	26	14
Roach, Mickey	Hamilton	23	17	8	25	8
Boucher, George	Ottawa	23	15	9	24	44
Joliat, Aurel	Montreal	24	13	9	22	31
Noble, Reg	Toronto	24	12	10	22	41
Wilson, Cully	Hamilton	23	16	3	19	46

1923-24

Team	GP	W	L	T	GF	GA	PTS
Ottawa	24	16	8	0	74	54	32
*Montreal	24	13	11	0	59	48	26
Toronto	24	10	14	0	59	85	20
Hamilton	24	9	15	0	63	68	18

Leading Scorers

Player	Club	GP	G	A	PTS	PIM
Denneny, Cy	Ottawa	21	22	1	23	10
Boucher, Billy	Montreal	23	16	6	22	33
Joliat, Aurel	Montreal	24	15	5	20	19
Dye, Babe	Toronto	19	17	2	19	23
Boucher, George	Ottawa	21	14	5	19	28
Burch, Billy	Hamilton	24	16	2	18	4
Clancy, King	Ottawa	24	9	8	17	18
Adams, Jack	Toronto	22	13	3	16	49
Morenz, Howie	Montreal	24	13	3	16	20
Noble, Reg	Toronto	23	12	3	15	23

1924-25

Team	GP	W	L	T	GF	GA	PTS
Hamilton	30	19	10	1	90	60	39
Toronto	30	19	11	0	90	84	38
Montreal	30	17	11	2	93	56	36
Ottawa	30	17	12	1	83	66	35
Mtl. Maroons	30	9	19	2	45	65	20
Boston	30	6	24	0	49	119	12

Leading Scorers

Player	Club	GP	G	A	PTS	PIM
Dye, Babe	Toronto	29	38	6	44	41
Denneny, Cy	Ottawa	28	27	15	42	16
Joliat, Aurel	Montreal	24	29	11	40	85
Morenz, Howie	Montreal	30	27	7	34	31
Boucher, Billy	Montreal	30	18	13	31	92
Adams, Jack	Toronto	27	21	8	29	66
Burch, Billy	Hamilton	27	20	4	24	10
Green, Red	Hamilton	30	19	4	23	63
Herberts, Jimmy	Boston	30	17	5	22	50
Day, Hap	Toronto	26	10	12	22	27

1925-26

Team	GP	W	L	T	GF	GA	PTS
Ottawa	36	24	8	4	77	42	52
*Mtl. Maroons	36	20	11	5	91	73	45
Pittsburgh	36	19	16	1	82	70	39
Boston	36	17	15	4	92	85	38
NY Americans	36	12	20	4	68	89	28
Toronto	36	12	21	3	92	114	27
Montreal	36	11	24	1	79	108	23

Leading Scorers

Player	Club	GP	G	A	PTS	PIM
Stewart, Nels	Mtl. Maroons	36	34	8	42	119
Denneny, Cy	Ottawa	36	24	12	36	18
Cooper, Carson	Boston	36	28	3	31	10
Herberts, Jimmy	Boston	36	26	5	31	47
Morenz, Howie	Montreal	31	23	3	26	39
Adams, Jack	Toronto	36	21	5	26	52
Joliat, Aurel	Montreal	35	17	9	26	52
Burch, Billy	NY Americans	36	22	3	25	33
Smith, Hooley	Ottawa	28	16	9	25	53
Nighbor, Frank	Ottawa	35	12	13	25	40

1926-27

Canadian Division

Team	GP	W	L	T	GF	GA	PTS
*Ottawa	44	30	10	4	86	69	64
Montreal	44	28	14	2	99	67	58
Mtl. Maroons	44	20	20	4	71	68	44
NY Americans	44	17	25	2	82	91	36
Toronto	44	15	24	5	79	94	35

American Division

Team	GP	W	L	T	GF	GA	PTS
New York	44	25	13	6	95	72	56
Boston	44	21	20	3	97	89	45
Chicago	44	19	22	3	115	116	41
Pittsburgh	44	15	26	3	79	108	33
Detroit	44	12	28	4	76	105	28

Leading Scorers

Player	Club	GP	G	A	PTS	PIM
Cook, Bill	New York	44	33	4	37	58
Irvin, Dick	Chicago	43	18	18	36	34
Morenz, Howie	Montreal	44	25	7	32	49
Fredrickson, Frank	Det., Bos.	41	18	13	31	46
Dye, Babe	Chicago	41	25	5	30	14
Bailey, Ace	Toronto	42	15	13	28	82
Boucher, Frank	New York	44	13	15	28	17
Burch, Billy	NY Americans	43	19	8	27	40
Oliver, Harry	Boston	42	18	6	24	17
Keats, Gordon	Bos., Det.	42	16	8	24	52

1927-28

Canadian Division

Team	GP	W	L	T	GF	GA	PTS
Montreal	44	26	11	7	116	48	59
Mtl. Maroons	44	24	14	6	96	77	54
Ottawa	44	20	14	10	78	57	50
Toronto	44	18	18	8	89	88	44
NY Americans	44	11	27	6	63	128	28

American Division

Team	GP	W	L	T	GF	GA	PTS
Boston	44	20	13	11	77	70	51
*New York	44	19	16	9	94	79	47
Pittsburgh	44	19	17	8	67	76	46
Detroit	44	19	19	6	88	79	44
Chicago	44	7	34	3	68	134	17

Leading Scorers

Player	Club	GP	G	A	PTS	PIM
Morenz, Howie	Montreal	43	33	18	51	66
Joliat, Aurel	Montreal	44	28	11	39	105
Boucher, Frank	New York	44	23	12	35	15
Hay, George	Detroit	42	22	13	35	20
Stewart, Nels	Mtl. Maroons	41	27	7	34	104
Gagne, Art	Montreal	44	20	10	30	75
Cook, Fred	New York	44	14	14	28	45
Carson, Bill	Toronto	32	20	6	26	36
Finnigan, Frank	Ottawa	38	20	5	25	34
Cook, Bill	New York	43	18	6	24	42
Keats, Gordon	Det., Chi.	38	14	10	24	60

1928-29

Canadian Division

Team	GP	W	L	T	GF	GA	PTS
Montreal	44	22	7	15	71	43	59
NY Americans	44	19	13	12	53	53	50
Toronto	44	21	18	5	85	69	47
Ottawa	44	14	17	13	54	67	41
Mtl. Maroons	44	15	20	9	67	65	39

American Division

Team	GP	W	L	T	GF	GA	PTS
*Boston	44	26	13	5	89	52	57
New York	44	21	13	10	72	65	52
Detroit	44	19	16	9	72	63	47
Pittsburgh	44	9	27	8	46	80	26
Chicago	44	7	29	8	33	85	22

Leading Scorers

Player	Club	GP	G	A	PTS	PIM
Bailey, Ace	Toronto	44	22	10	32	78
Stewart, Nels	Mtl. Maroons	44	21	8	29	74
Cooper, Carson	Detroit	43	18	9	27	14
Morenz, Howie	Montreal	42	17	10	27	47
Blair, Andy	Toronto	44	12	15	27	41
Boucher, Frank	New York	44	10	16	26	8
Oliver, Harry	Boston	43	17	6	23	24
Cook, Bill	New York	43	15	8	23	41
Ward, Jimmy	Mtl. Maroons	43	14	8	22	46

Seven players tied with 19 points

1929-30

Canadian Division

Team	GP	W	L	T	GF	GA	PTS
Mtl. Maroons	44	23	16	5	141	114	51
*Montreal	44	21	14	9	142	114	51
Ottawa	44	21	15	8	138	118	50
Toronto	44	17	21	6	116	124	40
NY Americans	44	14	25	5	113	161	33

American Division

Team	GP	W	L	T	GF	GA	PTS
Boston	44	38	5	1	179	98	77
Chicago	44	21	18	5	117	111	47
New York	44	17	17	10	136	143	44
Detroit	44	14	24	6	117	133	34
Pittsburgh	44	5	36	3	102	185	13

Leading Scorers

Player	Club	GP	G	A	PTS	PIM
Weiland, Cooney	Boston	44	43	30	73	27
Boucher, Frank	New York	42	26	36	62	16
Clapper, Dit	Boston	44	41	20	61	48
Cook, Bill	New York	44	29	30	59	56
Kilrea, Hec	Ottawa	44	36	22	58	72
Stewart, Nels	Mtl. Maroons	44	39	16	55	81
Morenz, Howie	Montreal	44	40	10	50	72
Himes, Norm	NY Americans	44	28	22	50	15
Lamb, Joe	Ottawa	44	29	20	49	119
Gainor, Norm	Boston	42	18	31	49	39

1930-31

Canadian Division

Team	GP	W	L	T	GF	GA	PTS
*Montreal	44	26	10	8	129	89	60
Toronto	44	22	13	9	118	99	53
Mtl. Maroons	44	20	18	6	105	106	46
NY Americans	44	18	16	10	76	74	46
Ottawa	44	10	30	4	91	142	24

American Division

Team	GP	W	L	T	GF	GA	PTS
Boston	44	28	10	6	143	90	62
Chicago	44	24	17	3	108	78	51
New York	44	19	16	9	106	87	47
Detroit	44	16	21	7	102	105	39
Philadelphia	44	4	36	4	76	184	12

Leading Scorers

Player	Club	GP	G	A	PTS	PIM
Morenz, Howie	Montreal	39	28	23	51	49
Goodfellow, Ebbie	Detroit	44	25	23	48	32
Conacher, Charlie	Toronto	37	31	12	43	78
Cook, Bill	New York	43	30	12	42	39
Bailey, Ace	Toronto	40	23	19	42	46
Primeau, Joe	Toronto	38	9	32	41	18
Stewart, Nels	Mtl. Maroons	42	25	14	39	75
Boucher, Frank	New York	44	12	27	39	20
Weiland, Cooney	Boston	44	25	13	38	14
Cook, Fred	New York	44	18	17	35	72
Joliat, Aurel	Montreal	43	13	22	35	73

1931-32

Canadian Division

Team	GP	W	L	T	GF	GA	PTS
Montreal	48	25	16	7	128	111	57
*Toronto	48	23	18	7	155	127	53
Mtl. Maroons	48	19	22	7	142	139	45
NY Americans	48	16	24	8	95	142	40

American Division

Team	GP	W	L	T	GF	GA	PTS
New York	48	23	17	8	134	112	54
Chicago	48	18	19	11	86	101	47
Detroit	48	18	20	10	95	108	46
Boston	48	15	21	12	122	117	42

Leading Scorers

Player	Club	GP	G	A	PTS	PIM
Jackson, Harvey	Toronto	48	28	25	53	63
Primeau, Joe	Toronto	46	13	37	50	25
Morenz, Howie	Montreal	48	24	25	49	46
Conacher, Charlie	Toronto	44	34	14	48	66
Cook, Bill	New York	48	34	14	48	33
Trottier, Dave	Mtl. Maroons	48	26	18	44	94
Smith, Reg	Mtl. Maroons	43	11	33	44	49
Siebert, Albert	Mtl. Maroons	48	21	18	39	64
Clapper, Dit	Boston	48	17	22	39	21
Joliat, Aurel	Montreal	48	15	24	39	46

Howie Morenz, known as the Stratford Streak and the Mitchell Meteor during his career, won two scoring titles with the Canadiens thanks to his explosive speed and sizzling snapshot.

1932-33

Canadian Division

Team	GP	W	L	T	GF	GA	PTS
Toronto	48	24	18	6	119	111	54
Mtl. Maroons	48	22	20	6	135	119	50
Montreal	48	18	25	5	92	115	41
NY Americans	48	15	22	11	91	118	41
Ottawa	48	11	27	10	88	131	32

American Division

Team	GP	W	L	T	GF	GA	PTS
Boston	48	25	15	8	124	88	58
Detroit	48	25	15	8	111	93	58
*New York	48	23	17	8	135	107	54
Chicago	48	16	20	12	88	101	44

Leading Scorers

Player	Club	GP	G	A	PTS	PIM
Cook, Bill	New York	48	28	22	50	51
Jackson, Harvey	Toronto	48	27	17	44	43
Northcott, Lawrence	Mtl. Maroons	48	22	21	43	30
Smith, Reg	Mtl. Maroons	48	20	21	41	66
Haynes, Paul	Mtl. Maroons	48	16	25	41	18
Joliat, Aurel	Montreal	48	18	21	39	53
Barry, Marty	Boston	48	24	13	37	40
Cook, Fred	New York	48	22	15	37	35
Stewart, Nels	Boston	47	18	18	36	62
Morenz, Howie	Montreal	46	14	21	35	32
Gagnon, Johnny	Montreal	48	12	23	35	64
Shore, Eddie	Boston	48	8	27	35	102
Boucher, Frank	New York	47	7	28	35	4

1933-34

Canadian Division

Team	GP	W	L	T	GF	GA	PTS
Toronto	48	26	13	9	174	119	61
Montreal	48	22	20	6	99	101	50
Mtl. Maroons	48	19	18	11	117	122	49
NY Americans	48	15	23	10	104	132	40
Ottawa	48	13	29	6	115	143	32

American Division

Team	GP	W	L	T	GF	GA	PTS
Detroit	48	24	14	10	113	98	58
*Chicago	48	20	17	11	88	83	51
New York	48	21	19	8	120	113	50
Boston	48	18	25	5	111	130	41

Leading Scorers

Player	Club	GP	G	A	PTS	PIM
Conacher, Charlie	Toronto	42	32	20	52	38
Primeau, Joe	Toronto	45	14	32	46	8
Boucher, Frank	New York	48	14	30	44	4
Barry, Marty	Boston	48	27	12	39	12
Dillon, Cecil	New York	48	13	26	39	10
Stewart, Nels	Boston	48	21	17	38	68
Jackson, Harvey	Toronto	38	20	18	38	38
Joliat, Aurel	Montreal	48	22	15	37	27
Smith, Reg	Mtl. Maroons	47	18	19	37	58
Thompson, Paul	Chicago	48	20	16	36	17

1934-35

Canadian Division

Team	GP	W	L	T	GF	GA	PTS
Toronto	48	30	14	4	157	111	64
*Mtl. Maroons	48	24	19	5	123	92	53
Montreal	48	19	23	6	110	145	44
NY Americans	48	12	27	9	100	142	33
St. Louis	48	11	31	6	86	144	28

American Division

Team	GP	W	L	T	GF	GA	PTS
Boston	48	26	16	6	129	112	58
Chicago	48	26	17	5	118	88	57
New York	48	22	20	6	137	139	50
Detroit	48	19	22	7	127	114	45

Leading Scorers

Player	Club	GP	G	A	PTS	PIM
Conacher, Charlie	Toronto	47	36	21	57	24
Howe, Syd	St.L., Det.	50	22	25	47	34
Aurie, Larry	Detroit	48	17	29	46	24
Boucher, Frank	New York	48	13	32	45	2
Jackson, Harvey	Toronto	42	22	22	44	27
Lewis, Herb	Detroit	47	16	27	43	26
Chapman, Art	NY Americans	47	9	34	43	4
Barry, Marty	Boston	48	20	20	40	33
Schriner, Sweeney	NY Americans	48	18	22	40	6
Stewart, Nels	Boston	47	21	18	39	45
Thompson, Paul	Chicago	48	16	23	39	20

1935-36

Canadian Division

Team	GP	W	L	T	GF	GA	PTS
Mtl. Maroons	48	22	16	10	114	106	54
Toronto	48	23	19	6	126	106	52
NY Americans	48	16	25	7	109	122	39
Montreal	48	11	26	11	82	123	33

American Division

Team	GP	W	L	T	GF	GA	PTS
*Detroit	48	24	16	8	124	103	56
Boston	48	22	20	6	92	83	50
Chicago	48	21	19	8	93	92	50
New York	48	19	17	12	91	96	50

Leading Scorers

Player	Club	GP	G	A	PTS	PIM
Schriner, Sweeney	NY Americans	48	19	26	45	8
Barry, Marty	Detroit	48	21	19	40	16
Thompson, Paul	Chicago	45	17	23	40	19
Thoms, Bill	Toronto	48	23	15	38	29
Conacher, Charlie	Toronto	44	23	15	38	74
Smith, Reg	Mtl. Maroons	47	19	19	38	75
Romnes, Doc	Chicago	48	13	25	38	6
Chapman, Art	NY Americans	47	10	28	38	14
Lewis, Herb	Detroit	45	14	23	37	25
Northcott, Lawrence	Mtl. Maroons	48	15	21	36	41

1936-37

Canadian Division

Team	GP	W	L	T	GF	GA	PTS
Montreal	48	24	18	6	115	111	54
Mtl. Maroons	48	22	17	9	126	110	53
Toronto	48	22	21	5	119	115	49
NY Americans	48	15	29	4	122	161	34

American Division

Team	GP	W	L	T	GF	GA	PTS
*Detroit	48	25	14	9	128	102	59
Boston	48	23	18	7	120	110	53
New York	48	19	20	9	117	106	47
Chicago	48	14	27	7	99	131	35

Leading Scorers

Player	Club	GP	G	A	PTS	PIM
Schriner, Sweeney	NY Americans	48	21	25	46	17
Apps, Syl	Toronto	48	16	29	45	10
Barry, Marty	Detroit	48	17	27	44	6
Aurie, Larry	Detroit	45	23	20	43	20
Jackson, Harvey	Toronto	46	21	19	40	12
Gagnon, Johnny	Montreal	48	20	16	36	38
Gracie, Bob	Mtl. Maroons	47	11	25	36	18
Stewart, Nels	Bos., NYA	43	23	12	35	37
Thompson, Paul	Chicago	47	17	18	35	28
Cowley, Bill	Boston	46	13	22	35	4

1937-38

Canadian Division

Team	GP	W	L	T	GF	GA	PTS
Toronto	48	24	15	9	151	127	57
NY Americans	48	19	18	11	110	111	49
Montreal	48	18	17	13	123	128	49
Mtl. Maroons	48	12	30	6	101	149	30

American Division

Team	GP	W	L	T	GF	GA	PTS
Boston	48	30	11	7	142	89	67
New York	48	27	15	6	149	96	60
*Chicago	48	14	25	9	97	139	37
Detroit	48	12	25	11	99	133	35

Leading Scorers

Player	Club	GP	G	A	PTS	PIM
Drillon, Gord	Toronto	48	26	26	52	4
Apps, Syl	Toronto	47	21	29	50	9
Thompson, Paul	Chicago	48	22	22	44	14
Mantha, Georges	Montreal	47	23	19	42	12
Dillon, Cecil	New York	48	21	18	39	6
Cowley, Bill	Boston	48	17	22	39	8
Schriner, Sweeney	NY Americans	49	21	17	38	22
Thoms, Bill	Toronto	48	14	24	38	14
Smith, Clint	New York	48	14	23	37	0
Stewart, Nels	NY Americans	48	19	17	36	29
Colville, Neil	New York	45	17	19	36	11

1938-39

Team	GP	W	L	T	GF	GA	PTS
*Boston	48	36	10	2	156	76	74
New York	48	26	16	6	149	105	58
Toronto	48	19	20	9	114	107	47
NY Americans	48	17	21	10	119	157	44
Detroit	48	18	24	6	107	128	42
Montreal	48	15	24	9	115	146	39
Chicago	48	12	28	8	91	132	32

Leading Scorers

Player	Club	GP	G	A	PTS	PIM
Blake, Hector	Montreal	48	24	23	47	10
Schriner, Sweeney	NY Americans	48	13	31	44	20
Cowley, Bill	Boston	34	8	34	42	2
Smith, Clint	New York	48	21	20	41	2
Barry, Marty	Detroit	48	13	28	41	4
Apps, Syl	Toronto	44	15	25	40	4
Anderson, Tom	NY Americans	48	13	27	40	14
Gottselig, Johnny	Chicago	48	16	23	39	15
Haynes, Paul	Montreal	47	5	33	38	27
Conacher, Roy	Boston	47	26	11	37	12
Carr, Lorne	NY Americans	46	19	18	37	16
Colville, Neil	New York	48	18	19	37	12
Watson, Phil	New York	48	15	22	37	42

1939-40

Team	GP	W	L	T	GF	GA	PTS
Boston	48	31	12	5	170	98	67
*New York	48	27	11	10	136	77	64
Toronto	48	25	17	6	134	110	56
Chicago	48	23	19	6	112	120	52
Detroit	48	16	26	6	90	126	38
NY Americans	48	15	29	4	106	140	34
Montreal	48	10	33	5	90	167	25

Leading Scorers

Player	Club	GP	G	A	PTS	PIM
Schmidt, Milt	Boston	48	22	30	52	37
Dumart, Woody	Boston	48	22	21	43	16
Bauer, Bob	Boston	48	17	26	43	2
Drillon, Gord	Toronto	43	21	19	40	13
Cowley, Bill	Boston	48	13	27	40	24
Hextall, Bryan	New York	48	24	15	39	52
Colville, Neil	New York	48	19	19	38	22
Howe, Syd	Detroit	46	14	23	37	17
Blake, Hector	Montreal	48	17	19	36	48
Armstrong, Murray	NY Americans	48	16	20	36	12

1940-41

Team	GP	W	L	T	GF	GA	PTS
*Boston	48	27	8	13	168	102	67
Toronto	48	28	14	6	145	99	62
Detroit	48	21	16	11	112	102	53
New York	48	21	19	8	143	125	50
Chicago	48	16	25	7	112	139	39
Montreal	48	16	26	6	121	147	38
NY Americans	48	8	29	11	99	186	27

Leading Scorers

Player	Club	GP	G	A	PTS	PIM
Cowley, Bill	Boston	46	17	45	62	16
Hextall, Bryan	New York	48	26	18	44	16
Drillon, Gord	Toronto	42	23	21	44	2
Apps, Syl	Toronto	41	20	24	44	6
Patrick, Lynn	New York	48	20	24	44	12
Howe, Syd	Detroit	48	20	24	44	8
Colville, Neil	New York	48	14	28	42	28
Wiseman, Eddie	Boston	48	16	24	40	10
Bauer, Bobby	Boston	48	17	22	39	2
Schriner, Sweeney	Toronto	48	24	14	38	6
Conacher, Roy	Boston	40	24	14	38	7
Schmidt, Milt	Boston	44	13	25	38	23

1941-42

Team	GP	W	L	T	GF	GA	PTS
New York	48	29	17	2	177	143	60
*Toronto	48	27	18	3	158	136	57
Boston	48	25	17	6	160	118	56
Chicago	48	22	23	3	145	155	47
Detroit	48	19	25	4	140	147	42
Montreal	48	18	27	3	134	173	39
Brooklyn	48	16	29	3	133	175	35

Leading Scorers

Player	Club	GP	G	A	PTS	PIM
Hextall, Bryan	New York	48	24	32	56	30
Patrick, Lynn	New York	47	32	22	54	18
Grosso, Don	Detroit	48	23	30	53	13
Watson, Phil	New York	48	15	37	52	48
Abel, Sid	Detroit	48	18	31	49	45
Blake, Hector	Montreal	47	17	28	45	19
Thoms, Bill	Chicago	47	15	30	45	8
Drillon, Gord	Toronto	48	23	18	41	6
Apps, Syl	Toronto	38	18	23	41	0
Anderson, Tom	Brooklyn	48	12	29	41	54

1942-43

Team	GP	W	L	T	GF	GA	PTS
*Detroit	50	25	14	11	169	124	61
Boston	50	24	17	9	195	176	57
Toronto	50	22	19	9	198	159	53
Montreal	50	19	19	12	181	191	50
Chicago	50	17	18	15	179	180	49
New York	50	11	31	8	161	253	30

Leading Scorers

Player	Club	GP	G	A	PTS	PIM
Bentley, Doug	Chicago	50	33	40	73	18
Cowley, Bill	Boston	48	27	45	72	10
Bentley, Max	Chicago	47	26	44	70	2
Patrick, Lynn	New York	50	22	39	61	28
Carr, Lorne	Toronto	50	27	33	60	15
Taylor, Billy	Toronto	50	18	42	60	2
Hextall, Bryan	New York	50	27	32	59	28
Blake, Hector	Montreal	48	23	36	59	28
Lach, Elmer	Montreal	45	18	40	58	14
O'Connor, Herb	Montreal	50	15	43	58	2

1943-44

Team	GP	W	L	T	GF	GA	PTS
*Montreal	50	38	5	7	234	109	83
Detroit	50	26	18	6	214	177	58
Toronto	50	23	23	4	214	174	50
Chicago	50	22	23	5	178	187	49
Boston	50	19	26	5	223	268	43
New York	50	6	39	5	162	310	17

Leading Scorers

Player	Club	GP	G	A	PTS	PIM
Cain, Herb	Boston	48	36	46	82	4
Bentley, Doug	Chicago	50	38	39	77	22
Carr, Lorne	Toronto	50	36	38	74	9
Liscombe, Carl	Detroit	50	36	37	73	17
Lach, Elmer	Montreal	48	24	48	72	23
Smith, Clint	Chicago	50	23	49	72	4
Cowley, Bill	Boston	36	30	41	71	12
Mosienko, Bill	Chicago	50	32	38	70	10
Jackson, Art	Boston	49	28	41	69	8
Bodnar, Gus	Toronto	50	22	40	62	18

1944-45

Team	GP	W	L	T	GF	GA	PTS
Montreal	50	38	8	4	228	121	80
Detroit	50	31	14	5	218	161	67
*Toronto	50	24	22	4	183	161	52
Boston	50	16	30	4	179	219	36
Chicago	50	13	30	7	141	194	33
New York	50	11	29	10	154	247	32

Leading Scorers

Player	Club	GP	G	A	PTS	PIM
Lach, Elmer	Montreal	50	26	54	80	37
Richard, Maurice	Montreal	50	50	23	73	36
Blake, Hector	Montreal	49	29	38	67	15
Cowley, Bill	Boston	49	25	40	65	2
Kennedy, Ted	Toronto	49	29	25	54	14
Mosienko, Bill	Chicago	50	28	26	54	0
Carveth, Joe	Detroit	50	26	28	54	6
DeMarco, Albert	New York	50	24	30	54	10
Smith, Clint	Chicago	50	23	31	54	0
Howe, Syd	Detroit	46	17	36	53	6

1945-46

Team	GP	W	L	T	GF	GA	PTS
*Montreal	50	28	17	5	172	134	61
Boston	50	24	18	8	167	156	56
Chicago	50	23	20	7	200	178	53
Detroit	50	20	20	10	146	159	50
Toronto	50	19	24	7	174	185	45
New York	50	13	28	9	144	191	35

Leading Scorers

Player	Club	GP	G	A	PTS	PIM
Bentley, Max	Chicago	47	31	30	61	6
Stewart, Gaye	Toronto	50	37	15	52	8
Blake, Hector	Montreal	50	29	21	50	2
Smith, Clint	Chicago	50	26	24	50	2
Richard, Maurice	Montreal	50	27	21	48	50
Mosienko, Bill	Chicago	40	18	30	48	12
DeMarco, Albert	New York	50	20	27	47	20
Lach, Elmer	Montreal	50	13	34	47	34
Kaleta, Alex	Chicago	49	19	27	46	17
Taylor, Billy	Toronto	48	23	18	41	14
Horeck, Pete	Chicago	50	20	21	41	34

Max Bentley, who won back-to-back scoring titles in 1945-46 and 1946-47, was a stickhandling master who excelled on the powerplay.

1946-47

Team	GP	W	L	T	GF	GA	PTS
Montreal	60	34	16	10	189	138	78
*Toronto	60	31	19	10	209	172	72
Boston	60	26	23	11	190	175	63
Detroit	60	22	27	11	190	193	55
New York	60	22	32	6	167	186	50
Chicago	60	19	37	4	193	274	42

Leading Scorers

Player	Club	GP	G	A	PTS	PIM
Bentley, Max	Chicago	60	29	43	72	12
Richard, Maurice	Montreal	60	45	26	71	69
Taylor, Billy	Detroit	60	17	46	63	35
Schmidt, Milt	Boston	59	27	35	62	40
Kennedy, Ted	Toronto	60	28	32	60	27
Bentley, Doug	Chicago	52	21	34	55	18
Bauer, Bob	Boston	58	30	24	54	4
Conacher, Roy	Detroit	60	30	24	54	6
Mosienko, Bill	Chicago	59	25	27	52	2
Dumart, Woody	Boston	60	24	28	52	12

1947-48

Team	GP	W	L	T	GF	GA	PTS
*Toronto	60	32	15	13	182	143	77
Detroit	60	30	18	12	187	148	72
Boston	60	23	24	13	167	168	59
New York	60	21	26	13	176	201	55
Montreal	60	20	29	11	147	169	51
Chicago	60	20	34	6	195	225	46

Leading Scorers

Player	Club	GP	G	A	PTS	PIM
Lach, Elmer	Montreal	60	30	31	61	72
O'Connor, Buddy	New York	60	24	36	60	8
Bentley, Doug	Chicago	60	20	37	57	16
Stewart, Gaye	Tor., Chi.	61	27	29	56	83
Bentley, Max	Chi., Tor.	59	26	28	54	14
Poile, Bud	Tor., Chi.	58	25	29	54	17
Richard, Maurice	Montreal	53	28	25	53	89
Apps, Syl	Toronto	55	26	27	53	12
Lindsay, Ted	Detroit	60	33	19	52	95
Conacher, Roy	Chicago	52	22	27	49	4

1948-49

Team	GP	W	L	T	GF	GA	PTS
Detroit	60	34	19	7	195	145	75
Boston	60	29	23	8	178	163	66
Montreal	60	28	23	9	152	126	65
*Toronto	60	22	25	13	147	161	57
Chicago	60	21	31	8	173	211	50
New York	60	18	31	11	133	172	47

Leading Scorers

Player	Club	GP	G	A	PTS	PIM
Conacher, Roy	Chicago	60	26	42	68	8
Bentley, Doug	Chicago	58	23	43	66	38
Abel, Sid	Detroit	60	28	26	54	49
Lindsay, Ted	Detroit	50	26	28	54	97
Conacher, Jim	Det., Chi.	59	26	23	49	43
Ronty, Paul	Boston	60	20	29	49	11
Watson, Harry	Toronto	60	26	19	45	0
Reay, Billy	Montreal	60	22	23	45	33
Bodnar, Gus	Chicago	59	19	26	45	14
Peirson, John	Boston	59	22	21	43	45

1949-50

Team	GP	W	L	T	GF	GA	PTS
*Detroit	70	37	19	14	229	164	88
Montreal	70	29	22	19	172	150	77
Toronto	70	31	27	12	176	173	74
New York	70	28	31	11	170	189	67
Boston	70	22	32	16	198	228	60
Chicago	70	22	38	10	203	244	54

Leading Scorers

Player	Club	GP	G	A	PTS	PIM
Lindsay, Ted	Detroit	69	23	55	78	141
Abel, Sid	Detroit	69	34	35	69	46
Howe, Gordie	Detroit	70	35	33	68	69
Richard, Maurice	Montreal	70	43	22	65	114
Ronty, Paul	Boston	70	23	36	59	8
Conacher, Roy	Chicago	70	25	31	56	16
Bentley, Doug	Chicago	64	20	33	53	28
Peirson, John	Boston	57	27	25	52	49
Prystai, Metro	Chicago	65	29	22	51	31
Guidolin, Bep	Chicago	70	17	34	51	42

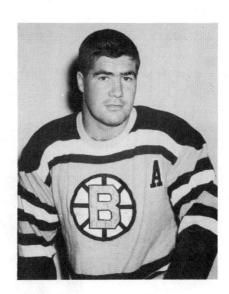

Left: Alex Delvecchio, who began his remarkable NHL career in 1950-51, finished tied for fourth spot on the NHL scoring ladder in 1952-53. Below: After making his NHL debut with Toronto, Fleming Mackell's career blossomed in Boston during the 1950s.

1950-51

Team	GP	W	L	T	GF	GA	PTS
Detroit	70	44	13	13	236	139	101
*Toronto	70	41	16	13	212	138	95
Montreal	70	25	30	15	173	184	65
Boston	70	22	30	18	178	197	62
New York	70	20	29	21	169	201	61
Chicago	70	13	47	10	171	280	36

Leading Scorers

Player	Club	GP	G	A	PTS	PIM
Howe, Gordie	Detroit	70	43	43	86	74
Richard, Maurice	Montreal	65	42	24	66	97
Bentley, Max	Toronto	67	21	41	62	34
Abel, Sid	Detroit	69	23	38	61	30
Schmidt, Milt	Boston	62	22	39	61	33
Kennedy, Ted	Toronto	63	18	43	61	32
Lindsay, Ted	Detroit	67	24	35	59	110
Sloan, Tod	Toronto	70	31	25	56	105
Kelly, Red	Detroit	70	17	37	54	24
Smith, Sid	Toronto	70	30	21	51	10
Gardner, Cal	Toronto	66	23	28	51	42

1951-52

Team	GP	W	L	T	GF	GA	PTS
*Detroit	70	44	14	12	215	133	100
Montreal	70	34	26	10	195	164	78
Toronto	70	29	25	16	168	157	74
Boston	70	25	29	16	162	176	66
New York	70	23	34	13	192	219	59
Chicago	70	17	44	9	158	241	43

Leading Scorers

Player	Club	GP	G	A	PTS	PIM
Howe, Gordie	Detroit	70	47	39	86	78
Lindsay, Ted	Detroit	70	30	39	69	123
Lach, Elmer	Montreal	70	15	50	65	36
Raleigh, Don	New York	70	19	42	61	14
Smith, Sid	Toronto	70	27	30	57	6
Geoffrion, Bernie	Montreal	67	30	24	54	66
Mosienko, Bill	Chicago	70	31	22	53	10
Abel, Sid	Detroit	62	17	36	53	32
Kennedy, Ted	Toronto	70	19	33	52	33
Schmidt, Milt	Boston	69	21	29	50	57
Peirson, John	Boston	68	20	30	50	30

1952-53

Team	GP	W	L	T	GF	GA	PTS
Detroit	70	36	16	18	222	133	90
*Montreal	70	28	23	19	155	148	75
Boston	70	28	29	13	152	172	69
Chicago	70	27	28	15	169	175	69
Toronto	70	27	30	13	156	167	67
New York	70	17	37	16	152	211	50

Leading Scorers

Player	Club	GP	G	A	PTS	PIM
Howe, Gordie	Detroit	70	49	46	95	57
Lindsay, Ted	Detroit	70	32	39	71	111
Richard, Maurice	Montreal	70	28	33	61	112
Hergesheimer, Wally	New York	70	30	29	59	10
Delvecchio, Alex	Detroit	70	16	43	59	28
Ronty, Paul	New York	70	16	38	54	20
Prystai, Metro	Detroit	70	16	34	50	12
Kelly, Red	Detroit	70	19	27	46	8
Olmstead, Bert	Montreal	69	17	28	45	83
Mackell, Fleming	Boston	65	27	17	44	63
McFadden, Jim	Chicago	70	23	21	44	29

1953-54

Team	GP	W	L	T	GF	GA	PTS
*Detroit	70	37	19	14	191	132	88
Montreal	70	35	24	11	195	141	81
Toronto	70	32	24	14	152	131	78
Boston	70	32	28	10	177	181	74
New York	70	29	31	10	161	182	68
Chicago	70	12	51	7	133	242	31

Leading Scorers

Player	Club	GP	G	A	PTS	PIM
Howe, Gordie	Detroit	70	47	34	81	109
Richard, Maurice	Montreal	70	37	30	67	112
Lindsay, Ted	Detroit	70	26	36	62	110
Geoffrion, Bernie	Montreal	54	29	25	54	87
Olmstead, Bert	Montreal	70	15	37	52	85
Kelly, Red	Detroit	62	16	33	49	18
Reibel, Earl	Detroit	69	15	33	48	18
Sandford, Ed	Boston	70	16	31	47	42
Mackell, Fleming	Boston	67	15	32	47	60
Mosdell, Ken	Montreal	67	22	24	46	64
Ronty, Paul	New York	70	13	33	46	18

1954-55

Team	GP	W	L	T	GF	GA	PTS
*Detroit	70	42	17	11	204	134	95
Montreal	70	41	18	11	228	157	93
Toronto	70	24	24	22	147	135	70
Boston	70	23	26	21	169	188	67
New York	70	17	35	18	150	210	52
Chicago	70	13	40	17	161	235	43

Leading Scorers

Player	Club	GP	G	A	PTS	PIM
Geoffrion, Bernie	Montreal	70	38	37	75	57
Richard, Maurice	Montreal	67	38	36	74	125
Beliveau, Jean	Montreal	70	37	36	73	58
Reibel, Earl	Detroit	70	25	41	66	15
Howe, Gordie	Detroit	64	29	33	62	68
Sullivan, George	Chicago	69	19	42	61	51
Olmstead, Bert	Montreal	70	10	48	58	103
Smith, Sid	Toronto	70	33	21	54	14
Mosdell, Ken	Montreal	70	22	32	54	82
Lewicki, Danny	New York	70	29	24	53	8

1955-56

Team	GP	W	L	T	GF	GA	PTS
*Montreal	70	45	15	10	222	131	100
Detroit	70	30	24	16	183	148	76
New York	70	32	28	10	204	203	74
Toronto	70	24	33	13	153	181	61
Boston	70	23	34	13	147	185	59
Chicago	70	19	39	12	155	216	50

Leading Scorers

Player	Club	GP	G	A	PTS	PIM
Beliveau, Jean	Montreal	70	47	41	88	143
Howe, Gordie	Detroit	70	38	41	79	100
Richard, Maurice	Montreal	70	38	33	71	89
Olmstead, Bert	Montreal	70	14	56	70	94
Sloan, Tod	Toronto	70	37	29	66	100
Bathgate, Andy	New York	70	19	47	66	59
Geoffrion, Bernie	Montreal	59	29	33	62	66
Reibel, Earl	Detroit	68	17	39	56	10
Delvecchio, Alex	Detroit	70	25	26	51	24
Creighton, Dave	New York	70	20	31	51	43
Gadsby, Bill	New York	70	9	42	51	84

1956-57

Team	GP	W	L	T	GF	GA	PTS
Detroit	70	38	20	12	198	157	88
*Montreal	70	35	23	12	210	155	82
Boston	70	34	24	12	195	174	80
New York	70	26	30	14	184	227	66
Toronto	70	21	34	15	174	192	57
Chicago	70	16	39	15	169	225	47

Leading Scorers

Player	Club	GP	G	A	PTS	PIM
Howe, Gordie	Detroit	70	44	45	89	72
Lindsay, Ted	Detroit	70	30	55	85	103
Beliveau, Jean	Montreal	69	33	51	84	105
Bathgate, Andy	New York	70	27	50	77	60
Litzenberger, Ed	Chicago	70	32	32	64	48
Richard, Maurice	Montreal	63	33	29	62	74
McKenney, Don	Boston	69	21	39	60	31
Moore, Dickie	Montreal	70	29	29	58	56
Richard, Henri	Montreal	63	18	36	54	71
Ullman, Norm	Detroit	64	16	36	52	47

1957-58

Team	GP	W	L	T	GF	GA	PTS
*Montreal	70	43	17	10	250	158	96
New York	70	32	25	13	195	188	77
Detroit	70	29	29	12	176	207	70
Boston	70	27	28	15	199	194	69
Chicago	70	24	39	7	163	202	55
Toronto	70	21	38	11	192	226	53

Leading Scorers

Player	Club	GP	G	A	PTS	PIM
Moore, Dickie	Montreal	70	36	48	84	65
Richard, Henri	Montreal	67	28	52	80	56
Bathgate, Andy	New York	65	30	48	78	42
Howe, Gordie	Detroit	64	33	44	77	40
Horvath, Bronco	Boston	67	30	36	66	71
Litzenberger, Ed	Chicago	70	32	30	62	63
Mackell, Fleming	Boston	70	20	40	60	72
Beliveau, Jean	Montreal	55	27	32	59	93
Delvecchio, Alex	Detroit	70	21	38	59	22
McKenney, Don	Boston	70	28	30	58	22

1958-59

Team	GP	W	L	T	GF	GA	PTS
*Montreal	70	39	18	13	258	158	91
Boston	70	32	29	9	205	215	73
Chicago	70	28	29	13	197	208	69
Toronto	70	27	32	11	189	201	65
New York	70	26	32	12	201	217	64
Detroit	70	25	37	8	167	218	58

Leading Scorers

Player	Club	GP	G	A	PTS	PIM
Moore, Dickie	Montreal	70	41	55	96	61
Beliveau, Jean	Montreal	64	45	46	91	67
Bathgate, Andy	New York	70	40	48	88	48
Howe, Gordie	Detroit	70	32	46	78	57
Litzenberger, Ed	Chicago	70	33	44	77	37
Geoffrion, Bernie	Montreal	59	22	44	66	30
Sullivan, George	New York	70	21	42	63	56
Hebenton, Andy	New York	70	33	29	62	8
McKenney, Don	Boston	70	32	30	62	20
Sloan, Tod	Chicago	59	27	35	62	79

1959-60

Team	GP	W	L	T	GF	GA	PTS
*Montreal	70	40	18	12	255	178	92
Toronto	70	35	26	9	199	195	79
Chicago	70	28	29	13	191	180	69
Detroit	70	26	29	15	186	197	67
Boston	70	28	34	8	220	241	64
New York	70	17	38	15	187	247	49

Leading Scorers

Player	Club	GP	G	A	PTS	PIM
Hull, Bobby	Chicago	70	39	42	81	68
Horvath, Bronco	Boston	68	39	41	80	60
Beliveau, Jean	Montreal	60	34	40	74	57
Bathgate, Andy	New York	70	26	48	74	28
Richard, Henri	Montreal	70	30	43	73	66
Howe, Gordie	Detroit	70	28	45	73	46
Geoffrion, Bernie	Montreal	59	30	41	71	36
McKenney, Don	Boston	70	20	49	69	28
Stasiuk, Vic	Boston	69	29	39	68	121
Prentice, Dean	New York	70	32	34	66	43

1960-61

Team	GP	W	L	T	GF	GA	PTS
Montreal	70	41	19	10	254	188	92
Toronto	70	39	19	12	234	176	90
*Chicago	70	29	24	17	198	180	75
Detroit	70	25	29	16	195	215	66
New York	70	22	38	10	204	248	54
Boston	70	15	42	13	176	254	43

Leading Scorers

Player	Club	GP	G	A	PTS	PIM
Geoffrion, Bernie	Montreal	64	50	45	95	29
Béliveau, Jean	Montreal	69	32	58	90	57
Mahovlich, Frank	Toronto	70	48	36	84	131
Bathgate, Andy	New York	70	29	48	77	22
Howe, Gordie	Detroit	64	23	49	72	30
Ullman, Norm	Detroit	70	28	42	70	34
Kelly, Red	Toronto	64	20	50	70	12
Moore, Dickie	Montreal	57	35	34	69	62
Richard, Henri	Montreal	70	24	44	68	91
Delvecchio, Alex	Detroit	70	27	35	62	26

1961-62

Team	GP	W	L	T	GF	GA	PTS
Montreal	70	42	14	14	259	166	98
*Toronto	70	37	22	11	232	180	85
Chicago	70	31	26	13	217	186	75
New York	70	26	32	12	195	207	64
Detroit	70	23	33	14	184	219	60
Boston	70	15	47	8	177	306	38

Leading Scorers

Player	Club	GP	G	A	PTS	PIM
Hull, Bobby	Chicago	70	50	34	84	35
Bathgate, Andy	New York	70	28	56	84	44
Howe, Gordie	Detroit	70	33	44	77	54
Mikita, Stan	Chicago	70	25	52	77	97
Mahovlich, Frank	Toronto	70	33	38	71	87
Delvecchio, Alex	Detroit	70	26	43	69	18
Backstrom, Ralph	Montreal	66	27	38	65	29
Ullman, Norm	Detroit	70	26	38	64	54
Hay, Bill	Chicago	60	11	52	63	34
Provost, Claude	Montreal	70	33	29	62	22

Bernie "Boom-Boom" Geoffrion, seen here eluding Leaf forechecker Parker McDonald for a close-range scoring attempt on goaltender Harry Lumley, captured the Art Ross Trophy in 1954-55.

1962-63

Team	GP	W	L	T	GF	GA	PTS
*Toronto	70	35	23	12	221	180	82
Chicago	70	32	21	17	194	178	81
Montreal	70	28	19	23	225	183	79
Detroit	70	32	25	13	200	194	77
New York	70	22	36	12	211	233	56
Boston	70	14	39	17	198	281	45

Leading Scorers

Player	Club	GP	G	A	PTS	PIM
Howe, Gordie	Detroit	70	38	48	86	100
Bathgate, Andy	New York	70	35	46	81	54
Mikita, Stan	Chicago	65	31	45	76	69
Mahovlich, Frank	Toronto	67	36	37	73	56
Richard, Henri	Montreal	67	23	50	73	57
Beliveau, Jean	Montreal	69	18	49	67	68
Bucyk, John	Boston	69	27	39	66	36
Delvecchio, Alex	Detroit	70	20	44	64	8
Hull, Bobby	Chicago	65	31	31	62	27
Oliver, Murray	Boston	65	22	40	62	38

1963-64

Team	GP	W	L	T	GF	GA	PTS
Montreal	70	36	21	13	209	167	85
Chicago	70	36	22	12	218	169	84
*Toronto	70	33	25	12	192	172	78
Detroit	70	30	29	11	191	204	71
New York	70	22	38	10	186	242	54
Boston	70	18	40	12	170	212	48

Leading Scorers

Player	Club	GP	G	A	PTS	PIM
Mikita, Stan	Chicago	70	39	50	89	146
Hull, Bobby	Chicago	70	43	44	87	50
Beliveau, Jean	Montreal	68	28	50	78	42
Bathgate, Andy	NYR, Tor.	71	19	58	77	34
Howe, Gordie	Detroit	69	26	47	73	70
Wharram, Ken	Chicago	70	39	32	71	18
Oliver, Murray	Boston	70	24	44	68	41
Goyette, Phil	New York	67	24	41	65	15
Gilbert, Rod	New York	70	24	40	64	62
Keon, Dave	Toronto	70	23	37	60	6

1964-65

Team	GP	W	L	T	GF	GA	PTS
Detroit	70	40	23	7	224	175	87
*Montreal	70	36	23	11	211	185	83
Chicago	70	34	28	8	224	176	76
Toronto	70	30	26	14	204	173	74
New York	70	20	38	12	179	246	52
Boston	70	21	43	6	166	253	48

Leading Scorers

Player	Club	GP	G	A	PTS	PIM
Mikita, Stan	Chicago	70	28	59	87	154
Ullman, Norm	Detroit	70	42	41	83	70
Howe, Gordie	Detroit	70	29	47	76	104
Hull, Bobby	Chicago	61	39	32	71	32
Delvecchio, Alex	Detroit	68	25	42	67	16
Provost, Claude	Montreal	70	27	37	64	28
Gilbert, Rod	New York	70	25	36	61	52
Pilote, Pierre	Chicago	68	14	45	59	162
Bucyk, John	Boston	68	26	29	55	24
Backstrom, Ralph	Montreal	70	25	30	55	41
Esposito, Phil	Chicago	70	23	32	55	44

1965-66

Team	GP	W	L	T	GF	GA	PTS
*Montreal	70	41	21	8	239	173	90
Chicago	70	37	25	8	240	187	82
Toronto	70	34	25	11	208	187	79
Detroit	70	31	27	12	221	194	74
Boston	70	21	43	6	174	275	48
New York	70	18	41	11	195	261	47

Leading Scorers

Player	Club	GP	G	A	PTS	PIM
Hull, Bobby	Chicago	65	54	43	97	70
Mikita, Stan	Chicago	68	30	48	78	58
Rousseau, Bobby	Montreal	70	30	48	78	20
Beliveau, Jean	Montreal	67	29	48	77	50
Howe, Gordie	Detroit	70	29	46	75	83
Ullman, Norm	Detroit	70	31	41	72	35
Delvecchio, Alex	Detroit	70	31	38	69	16
Nevin, Bob	New York	69	29	33	62	10
Richard, Henri	Montreal	62	22	39	61	47
Oliver, Murray	Boston	70	18	42	60	30

1966-67

Team	GP	W	L	T	GF	GA	PTS
Chicago	70	41	17	12	264	170	94
Montreal	70	32	25	13	202	188	77
*Toronto	70	32	27	11	204	211	75
New York	70	30	28	12	188	189	72
Detroit	70	27	39	4	212	241	58
Boston	70	17	43	10	182	253	44

Leading Scorers

Player	Club	GP	G	A	PTS	PIM
Mikita, Stan	Chicago	70	35	62	97	12
Hull, Bobby	Chicago	66	52	28	80	52
Ullman, Norm	Detroit	68	26	44	70	26
Wharram, Ken	Chicago	70	31	34	65	21
Howe, Gordie	Detroit	69	25	40	65	53
Rousseau, Bobby	Montreal	68	19	44	63	58
Esposito, Phil	Chicago	69	21	40	61	40
Goyette, Phil	New York	70	12	49	61	6
Mohns, Doug	Chicago	61	25	35	60	58
Richard, Henri	Montreal	65	21	34	55	28
Delvecchio, Alex	Detroit	70	17	38	55	10

Phil Esposito made his first appearance on the NHL's scoring leader board in 1966-67, when he finished seventh in points with 21 goals and 41 assists. Later traded to Boston, Esposito would set a single-season goal scoring record of 76 in 1970-71, a mark that would stand for 11 seasons until surpassed by Wayne Gretzky (92 goals) in 1981-82.

1967-68

East Division

Team	GP	W	L	T	GF	GA	PTS
*Montreal	74	42	22	10	236	167	94
New York	74	39	23	12	226	183	90
Boston	74	37	27	10	259	216	84
Chicago	74	32	26	16	212	222	80
Toronto	74	33	31	10	209	176	76
Detroit	74	27	35	12	245	257	66

West Division

Team	GP	W	L	T	GF	GA	PTS
Philadelphia	74	31	32	11	173	179	73
Los Angeles	74	31	33	10	200	224	72
St. Louis	74	27	31	16	177	191	70
Minnesota	74	27	32	15	191	226	69
Pittsburgh	74	27	34	13	195	216	67
Oakland	74	15	42	17	153	219	47

Leading Scorers

Player	Club	GP	G	A	PTS	PIM
Mikita, Stan	Chicago	72	40	47	87	14
Esposito, Phil	Boston	74	35	49	84	21
Howe, Gordie	Detroit	74	39	43	82	53
Ratelle, Jean	New York	74	32	46	78	18
Gilbert, Rod	New York	73	29	48	77	12
Hull, Bobby	Chicago	71	44	31	75	39
Ullman, Norm	Det., Tor.	71	35	37	72	28
Delvecchio, Alex	Detroit	74	22	48	70	14
Bucyk, John	Boston	72	30	39	69	8
Wharram, Ken	Chicago	74	27	42	69	18

1968-69

East Division

Team	GP	W	L	T	GF	GA	PTS
*Montreal	76	46	19	11	271	202	103
Boston	76	42	18	16	303	221	100
New York	76	41	26	9	231	196	91
Toronto	76	35	26	15	234	217	85
Detroit	76	33	31	12	239	221	78
Chicago	76	34	33	9	280	246	77

West Division

Team	GP	W	L	T	GF	GA	PTS
St. Louis	76	37	25	14	204	157	88
Oakland	76	29	36	11	219	251	69
Philadelphia	76	20	35	21	174	225	61
Los Angeles	76	24	42	10	185	260	58
Pittsburgh	76	20	45	11	189	252	51
Minnesota	76	18	43	5	189	270	51

Leading Scorers

Player	Club	GP	G	A	PTS	PIM
Esposito, Phil	Boston	74	49	77	126	79
Hull, Bobby	Chicago	74	58	49	107	48
Howe, Gordie	Detroit	76	44	59	103	58
Mikita, Stan	Chicago	74	30	67	97	52
Hodge, Ken	Boston	75	45	45	90	75
Cournoyer, Yvan	Montreal	76	43	44	87	31
Delvecchio, Alex	Detroit	72	25	58	83	8
Berenson, Red	St. Louis	76	35	47	82	43
Beliveau, Jean	Montreal	69	33	49	82	55
Mahovlich, Frank	Detroit	76	49	29	78	38
Ratelle, Jean	New York	75	32	46	78	26

1969-70

East Division

Team	GP	W	L	T	GF	GA	PTS
Chicago	76	45	22	9	250	170	99
*Boston	76	40	17	19	277	216	99
Detroit	76	40	21	15	246	199	95
New York	76	38	22	16	246	189	92
Montreal	76	38	22	16	244	201	92
Toronto	76	29	34	13	222	242	71

West Division

Team	GP	W	L	T	GF	GA	PTS
St. Louis	76	37	27	12	224	179	86
Pittsburgh	76	26	38	12	182	238	64
Minnesota	76	19	35	22	224	257	60
Oakland	76	22	40	14	169	243	58
Philadelphia	76	17	35	24	197	225	58
Los Angeles	76	14	52	10	168	290	38

Leading Scorers

Player	Club	GP	G	A	PTS	PIM
Orr, Bobby	Boston	76	33	87	120	125
Esposito, Phil	Boston	76	43	56	99	50
Mikita, Stan	Chicago	76	39	47	86	50
Goyette, Phil	St. Louis	72	29	49	78	16
Tkaczuk, Walt	New York	76	27	50	77	38
Ratelle, Jean	New York	75	32	42	74	28
Berenson, Red	St. Louis	67	33	39	72	38
Parise, Jean-Paul	Minnesota	74	24	48	72	72
Howe, Gordie	Detroit	76	31	40	71	58
Mahovlich, Frank	Detroit	74	38	32	70	59
Balon, Dave	New York	76	33	37	70	100
McKenzie, John	Boston	72	29	41	70	114

1970-71

East Division

Team	GP	W	L	T	GF	GA	PTS
Boston	78	57	14	7	399	207	121
New York	78	49	18	11	259	177	109
*Montreal	78	42	23	13	291	216	97
Toronto	78	37	33	8	248	211	82
Buffalo	78	24	39	15	217	291	63
Vancouver	78	24	46	8	229	296	56
Detroit	78	22	45	11	209	308	55

West Division

Team	GP	W	L	T	GF	GA	PTS
Chicago	78	49	20	9	277	184	107
St. Louis	78	34	25	19	223	208	87
Philadelphia	78	28	33	17	207	225	73
Minnesota	78	28	34	16	191	223	72
Los Angeles	78	25	40	13	239	303	63
Pittsburgh	78	21	37	20	221	240	62
California	78	20	53	5	199	320	45

Leading Scorers

Player	Club	GP	G	A	PTS	PIM
Esposito, Phil	Boston	78	76	76	152	71
Orr, Bobby	Boston	78	37	102	139	91
Bucyk, John	Boston	78	51	65	116	8
Hodge, Ken	Boston	78	43	62	105	113
Hull, Bobby	Chicago	78	44	52	96	32
Ullman, Norm	Toronto	73	34	51	85	24
Cashman, Wayne	Boston	77	21	58	79	100
McKenzie, John	Boston	65	31	46	77	120
Keon, Dave	Toronto	76	38	38	76	4
Beliveau, Jean	Montreal	70	25	51	76	40
Stanfield, Fred	Boston	75	24	52	76	12

1971-72

East Division

Team	GP	W	L	T	GF	GA	PTS
*Boston	78	54	13	11	330	204	119
New York	78	48	17	13	317	192	109
Montreal	78	46	16	16	307	205	108
Toronto	78	33	31	14	209	208	80
Detroit	78	33	35	10	261	262	76
Buffalo	78	16	43	19	203	289	51
Vancouver	78	20	50	8	203	297	48

West Division

Team	GP	W	L	T	GF	GA	PTS
Chicago	78	46	17	15	256	166	107
Minnesota	78	37	29	12	212	191	86
St. Louis	78	28	39	11	208	247	67
Pittsburgh	78	26	38	14	220	258	66
Philadelphia	78	26	38	14	200	236	66
California	78	21	39	18	216	288	60
Los Angeles	78	20	49	9	206	305	49

Leading Scorers

Player	Club	GP	G	A	PTS	PIM
Esposito, Phil	Boston	76	66	67	133	76
Orr, Bobby	Boston	76	37	80	117	106
Ratelle, Jean	New York	63	46	63	109	4
Hadfield, Vic	New York	78	50	56	106	142
Gilbert, Rod	New York	73	43	54	97	64
Mahovlich, Frank	Montreal	76	43	53	96	36
Hull, Bobby	Chicago	78	50	43	93	24
Cournoyer, Yvan	Montreal	73	47	36	83	15
Bucyk, John	Boston	78	32	51	83	4
Clarke, Bobby	Philadelphia	78	35	46	81	87
Lemaire, Jacques	Montreal	77	32	49	81	26

1972-73

East Division

Team	GP	W	L	T	GF	GA	PTS
*Montreal	78	52	10	16	329	184	120
Boston	78	51	22	5	330	235	107
NY Rangers	78	47	23	8	297	208	102
Buffalo	78	37	27	14	257	219	88
Detroit	78	37	29	12	265	243	86
Toronto	78	27	41	10	247	279	64
Vancouver	78	22	47	9	233	339	53
NY Islanders	78	12	60	6	170	347	30

West Division

Team	GP	W	L	T	GF	GA	PTS
Chicago	78	42	27	9	284	225	93
Philadelphia	78	37	30	11	296	256	85
Minnesota	78	37	30	11	254	230	85
St. Louis	78	32	34	12	233	251	76
Pittsburgh	78	32	37	9	257	265	73
Los Angeles	78	31	36	11	232	245	73
Atlanta	78	25	38	15	191	239	65
California	78	16	46	16	213	323	48

Leading Scorers

Player	Club	GP	G	A	PTS	PIM
Esposito, Phil	Boston	78	55	75	130	87
Clarke, Bobby	Philadelphia	78	37	67	104	80
Orr, Bobby	Boston	63	29	72	101	99
MacLeish, Rick	Philadelphia	78	50	50	100	69
Lemaire, Jacques	Montreal	77	44	51	95	16
Ratelle, Jean	NY Rangers	78	41	53	94	12
Redmond, Mickey	Detroit	76	52	41	93	24
Bucyk, John	Boston	78	40	53	93	12
Mahovlich, Frank	Montreal	78	38	55	93	51
Pappin, Jim	Chicago	76	41	51	92	82

1973-74

East Division

Team	GP	W	L	T	GF	GA	PTS
Boston	78	52	17	9	349	221	113
Montreal	78	45	24	9	293	240	99
NY Rangers	78	40	24	14	300	251	94
Toronto	78	35	27	16	274	230	86
Buffalo	78	32	34	12	242	250	76
Detroit	78	29	39	10	255	319	68
Vancouver	78	24	43	11	224	296	59
NY Islanders	78	19	41	18	182	247	56

West Division

Team	GP	W	L	T	GF	GA	PTS
*Philadelphia	78	50	16	12	273	164	112
Chicago	78	41	14	23	272	164	105
Los Angeles	78	33	33	12	233	231	78
Atlanta	78	30	34	14	214	238	74
Pittsburgh	78	28	41	9	242	273	65
St. Louis	78	26	40	12	206	248	64
Minnesota	78	23	38	17	235	275	63
California	78	13	55	10	195	342	36

Leading Scorers

Player	Club	GP	G	A	PTS	PIM
Esposito, Phil	Boston	78	68	77	145	58
Orr, Bobby	Boston	74	32	90	122	82
Hodge, Ken	Boston	76	50	55	105	43
Cashman, Wayne	Boston	78	30	59	89	111
Clarke, Bobby	Philadelphia	77	35	52	87	113
Martin, Rick	Buffalo	78	52	34	86	38
Apps, Syl	Pittsburgh	75	24	61	85	37
Sittler, Darryl	Toronto	78	38	46	84	55
MacDonald, Lowell	Pittsburgh	78	43	39	82	14
Park, Brad	NY Rangers	78	25	57	82	148
Hextall, Dennis	Minnesota	78	20	62	82	138

In his eight NHL seasons, Montreal's Ken Dryden captured numerous accolades and awards, including five Vezina Trophy wins and six Stanley Cup titles.

1974-75
PRINCE OF WALES CONFERENCE
Norris Division

Team	GP	W	L	T	GF	GA	PTS
Montreal	80	47	14	19	374	225	113
Los Angeles	80	42	17	21	269	185	105
Pittsburgh	80	37	28	15	326	289	89
Detroit	80	23	45	12	259	335	58
Washington	80	8	67	5	181	446	21

Adams Division

Buffalo	80	49	16	15	354	240	113
Boston	80	40	26	14	345	245	94
Toronto	80	31	33	16	280	309	78
California	80	19	48	13	212	316	51

CLARENCE CAMPBELL CONFERENCE
Patrick Division

*Philadelphia	80	51	18	11	293	181	113
NY Rangers	80	37	29	14	319	276	88
NY Islanders	80	33	25	22	264	221	88
Atlanta	80	34	31	15	243	233	83

Smythe Division

Vancouver	80	38	32	10	271	254	86
St. Louis	80	35	31	14	269	267	84
Chicago	80	37	35	8	268	241	82
Minnesota	80	23	50	7	221	341	53
Kansas City	80	15	54	11	184	328	41

Leading Scorers

Player	Club	GP	G	A	PTS	PIM
Orr, Bobby	Boston	80	46	89	135	101
Esposito, Phil	Boston	79	61	66	127	62
Dionne, Marcel	Detroit	80	47	74	121	14
Lafleur, Guy	Montreal	70	53	66	119	37
Mahovlich, Pete	Montreal	80	35	82	117	64
Clarke, Bobby	Philadelphia	80	27	89	116	125
Robert, Rene	Buffalo	74	40	60	100	75
Gilbert, Rod	NY Rangers	76	36	61	97	22
Perreault, Gilbert	Buffalo	68	39	57	96	36
Martin, Rick	Buffalo	68	52	43	95	72

1975-76
PRINCE OF WALES CONFERENCE
Norris Division

Team	GP	W	L	T	GF	GA	PTS
*Montreal	80	58	11	11	337	174	127
Los Angeles	80	38	33	9	263	265	85
Pittsburgh	80	35	33	12	339	303	82
Detroit	80	26	44	10	226	300	62
Washington	80	11	59	10	224	394	32

Adams Division

Boston	80	48	15	17	313	237	113
Buffalo	80	46	21	13	339	240	105
Toronto	80	34	31	15	294	276	83
California	80	27	42	11	250	278	65

CLARENCE CAMPBELL CONFERENCE
Patrick Division

Philadelphia	80	51	13	16	348	209	118
NY Islanders	80	42	21	17	297	190	101
Atlanta	80	35	33	12	262	237	82
NY Rangers	80	29	42	9	262	333	67

Smythe Division

Chicago	80	32	30	18	254	261	82
Vancouver	80	33	32	15	271	272	81
St. Louis	80	29	37	14	249	290	72
Minnesota	80	20	53	7	195	303	47
Kansas City	80	12	56	12	190	351	36

Leading Scorers

Player	Club	GP	G	A	PTS	PIM
Lafleur, Guy	Montreal	80	56	69	125	36
Clarke, Bobby	Philadelphia	76	30	89	119	13
Perreault, Gilbert	Buffalo	80	44	69	113	36
Barber, Bill	Philadelphia	80	50	62	112	104
Larouche, Pierre	Pittsburgh	76	53	58	111	33
Ratelle, Jean	Bos., NYR	80	36	69	105	18
Mahovlich, Pete	Montreal	80	34	71	105	76
Pronovost, Jean	Pittsburgh	80	52	52	104	24
Sittler, Darryl	Toronto	79	41	59	100	90
Apps, Syl	Pittsburgh	80	32	67	99	24

1976-77
PRINCE OF WALES CONFERENCE
Norris Division

Team	GP	W	L	T	GF	GA	PTS
*Montreal	80	60	8	12	387	171	132
Los Angeles	80	34	31	15	271	241	83
Pittsburgh	80	34	33	13	240	252	81
Washington	80	24	42	14	221	307	62
Detroit	80	16	55	9	183	309	41

Adams Division

Boston	80	49	23	8	312	240	106
Buffalo	80	48	24	8	301	220	104
Toronto	80	33	32	15	301	285	81
Cleveland	80	25	42	13	240	292	63

CLARENCE CAMPBELL CONFERENCE
Patrick Division

Philadelphia	80	48	16	16	323	213	112
NY Islanders	80	47	21	12	288	193	106
Atlanta	80	34	34	12	264	265	80
NY Rangers	80	29	37	14	272	310	72

Smythe Division

St. Louis	80	32	39	9	239	276	73
Minnesota	80	23	39	18	240	310	64
Chicago	80	26	43	11	240	298	63
Vancouver	80	25	42	13	235	294	63
Colorado	80	20	46	14	226	307	54

Leading Scorers

Player	Club	GP	G	A	PTS	PIM
Lafleur, Guy	Montreal	80	56	80	136	20
Dionne, Marcel	Los Angeles	80	53	69	122	12
Shutt, Steve	Montreal	80	60	45	105	28
MacLeish, Rick	Philadelphia	79	49	48	97	42
Perreault, Gilbert	Buffalo	80	39	56	95	30
Young, Tim	Minnesota	80	29	66	95	58
Ratelle, Jean	Boston	78	33	61	94	22
McDonald, Lanny	Toronto	80	46	44	90	77
Sittler, Darryl	Toronto	73	38	52	90	89
Clarke, Bobby	Philadelphia	80	27	63	90	71

1977-78
PRINCE OF WALES CONFERENCE
Norris Division

Team	GP	W	L	T	GF	GA	PTS
*Montreal	80	59	10	11	359	183	129
Detroit	80	32	34	14	252	266	78
Los Angeles	80	31	34	15	243	245	77
Pittsburgh	80	25	37	18	254	321	68
Washington	80	17	49	14	195	321	48

Adams Division

Boston	80	51	18	11	333	218	113
Buffalo	80	44	19	17	288	215	105
Toronto	80	41	29	10	271	237	92
Cleveland	80	22	45	13	230	325	57

CLARENCE CAMPBELL CONFERENCE
Patrick Division

NY Islanders	80	48	17	15	334	210	111
Philadelphia	80	45	20	15	296	200	105
Atlanta	80	34	27	19	274	252	87
NY Rangers	80	30	37	13	279	280	73

Smythe Division

Chicago	80	32	29	19	230	220	83
Colorado	80	19	40	21	257	305	59
Vancouver	80	20	43	17	239	320	57
St. Louis	80	20	47	13	195	304	53
Minnesota	80	18	53	9	218	325	45

Leading Scorers

Player	Club	GP	G	A	PTS	PIM
Lafleur, Guy	Montreal	79	60	72	132	26
Trottier, Bryan	NY Islanders	77	46	77	123	46
Sittler, Darryl	Toronto	80	45	72	117	100
Lemaire, Jacques	Montreal	76	36	61	97	14
Potvin, Denis	NY Islanders	80	30	64	94	81
Bossy, Mike	NY Islanders	73	53	38	91	6
O'Reilly, Terry	Boston	77	29	61	90	211
Perreault, Gilbert	Buffalo	79	41	48	89	20
Clarke, Bobby	Philadelphia	71	21	68	89	83
McDonald, Lanny	Toronto	74	47	40	87	54
Paiement, Wilf	Colorado	80	31	56	87	114

1978-79
PRINCE OF WALES CONFERENCE
Norris Division

Team	GP	W	L	T	GF	GA	PTS
*Montreal	80	52	17	11	337	204	115
Pittsburgh	80	36	31	13	281	279	85
Los Angeles	80	34	34	12	292	286	80
Washington	80	24	41	15	273	338	63
Detroit	80	23	41	16	252	295	62

Adams Division

Boston	80	43	23	14	316	270	100
Buffalo	80	36	28	16	280	263	88
Toronto	80	34	33	13	267	252	81
Minnesota	80	28	40	12	257	289	68

CLARENCE CAMPBELL CONFERENCE
Patrick Division

NY Islanders	80	51	15	14	358	214	116
Philadelphia	80	40	25	15	281	248	95
NY Rangers	80	40	29	11	316	292	91
Atlanta	80	41	31	8	327	280	90

Smythe Division

Chicago	80	29	36	15	244	277	73
Vancouver	80	25	42	13	217	291	63
St. Louis	80	18	50	12	249	348	48
Colorado	80	15	53	12	210	331	42

Leading Scorers

Player	Club	GP	G	A	PTS	PIM
Trottier, Bryan	NY Islanders	76	47	87	134	50
Dionne, Marcel	Los Angeles	80	59	71	130	30
Lafleur, Guy	Montreal	80	52	77	129	28
Bossy, Mike	NY Islanders	80	69	57	126	25
MacMillan, Bob	Atlanta	79	37	71	108	14
Chouinard, Guy	Atlanta	80	50	57	107	14
Potvin, Denis	NY Islanders	73	31	70	101	58
Federko, Bernie	St. Louis	74	31	64	95	14
Taylor, Dave	Los Angeles	78	43	48	91	124
Gillies, Clark	NY Islanders	75	35	56	91	68

A member of Buffalo's famed French Connection line in the 1970s, Rick Martin became the first member of the Sabres to eclipse the 50-goal plateau with 52 in 1973-74.

1979-80

PRINCE OF WALES CONFERENCE

Norris Division

Team	GP	W	L	T	GF	GA	PTS
Montreal	80	47	20	13	328	240	107
Los Angeles	80	30	36	14	290	313	74
Pittsburgh	80	30	37	13	251	303	73
Hartford	80	27	34	19	303	312	73
Detroit	80	26	43	11	268	306	63

Adams Division

Team	GP	W	L	T	GF	GA	PTS
Buffalo	80	47	17	16	318	201	110
Boston	80	46	21	13	310	234	105
Minnesota	80	36	28	16	311	253	88
Toronto	80	35	40	5	304	327	75
Quebec	80	25	44	11	248	313	61

CLARENCE CAMPBELL CONFERENCE

Patrick Division

Team	GP	W	L	T	GF	GA	PTS
Philadelphia	80	48	12	20	327	254	116
*NY Islanders	80	39	28	13	281	247	91
NY Rangers	80	38	32	10	308	284	86
Atlanta	80	35	32	13	282	269	83
Washington	80	27	40	13	261	293	67

Smythe Division

Team	GP	W	L	T	GF	GA	PTS
Chicago	80	34	27	19	241	250	87
St. Louis	80	34	34	12	266	278	80
Vancouver	80	27	37	16	256	281	70
Edmonton	80	28	39	13	301	322	69
Winnipeg	80	20	49	11	214	314	51
Colorado	80	19	48	13	234	308	51

Leading Scorers

Player	Club	GP	G	A	PTS	PIM
Dionne, Marcel	Los Angeles	80	53	84	137	32
Gretzky, Wayne	Edmonton	79	51	86	137	21
Lafleur, Guy	Montreal	74	50	75	125	12
Perreault, Gilbert	Buffalo	80	40	66	106	57
Rogers, Mike	Hartford	80	44	61	105	10
Trottier, Bryan	NY Islanders	78	42	62	104	68
Simmer, Charlie	Los Angeles	64	56	45	101	65
Stoughton, Blaine	Hartford	80	56	44	100	16
Sittler, Darryl	Toronto	73	40	57	97	62
MacDonald, Blair	Edmonton	80	46	48	94	6
Federko, Bernie	St. Louis	79	38	56	94	24

1980-81

PRINCE OF WALES CONFERENCE

Norris Division

Team	GP	W	L	T	GF	GA	PTS
Montreal	80	45	22	13	332	232	103
Los Angeles	80	43	24	13	337	290	99
Pittsburgh	80	30	37	13	302	345	73
Hartford	80	21	41	18	292	372	60
Detroit	80	19	43	18	252	339	56

Adams Division

Team	GP	W	L	T	GF	GA	PTS
Buffalo	80	39	20	21	327	250	99
Boston	80	37	30	13	316	272	87
Minnesota	80	35	28	17	291	263	87
Quebec	80	30	32	18	314	318	78
Toronto	80	28	37	15	322	367	71

CLARENCE CAMPBELL CONFERENCE

Patrick Division

Team	GP	W	L	T	GF	GA	PTS
*NY Islanders	80	48	18	14	355	260	110
Philadelphia	80	41	24	15	313	249	97
Calgary	80	39	27	14	329	298	92
NY Rangers	80	30	36	14	312	317	74
Washington	80	26	36	18	286	317	70

Smythe Division

Team	GP	W	L	T	GF	GA	PTS
St. Louis	80	45	18	17	352	281	107
Chicago	80	31	33	16	304	315	78
Vancouver	80	28	32	20	289	301	76
Edmonton	80	29	35	16	328	327	74
Colorado	80	22	45	13	258	344	57
Winnipeg	80	9	57	14	246	400	32

Leading Scorers

Player	Club	GP	G	A	PTS	PIM
Gretzky, Wayne	Edmonton	80	55	109	164	28
Dionne, Marcel	Los Angeles	80	58	77	135	70
Nilsson, Kent	Calgary	80	49	82	131	26
Bossy, Mike	NY Islanders	79	68	51	119	32
Taylor, Dave	Los Angeles	72	47	65	112	130
Stastny, Peter	Quebec	77	39	70	109	37
Simmer, Charlie	Los Angeles	65	56	49	105	62
Rogers, Mike	Hartford	80	40	65	105	32
Federko, Bernie	St. Louis	78	31	73	104	47
Richard, Jacques	Quebec	78	52	51	103	39
Middleton, Rick	Boston	80	44	59	103	16
Trottier, Bryan	NY Islanders	73	31	72	103	74

1981-82

CLARENCE CAMPBELL CONFERENCE

Norris Division

Team	GP	W	L	T	GF	GA	PTS
Minnesota	80	37	23	20	346	288	94
Winnipeg	80	33	33	14	319	332	80
St. Louis	80	32	40	8	315	349	72
Chicago	80	30	38	12	332	363	72
Toronto	80	20	44	16	298	380	56
Detroit	80	21	47	12	270	351	54

Smythe Division

Team	GP	W	L	T	GF	GA	PTS
Edmonton	80	48	17	15	417	295	111
Vancouver	80	30	33	17	290	286	77
Calgary	80	29	34	17	334	345	75
Los Angeles	80	24	41	15	314	369	63
Colorado	80	18	49	13	241	362	49

PRINCE OF WALES CONFERENCE

Adams Division

Team	GP	W	L	T	GF	GA	PTS
Montreal	80	46	17	17	360	223	109
Boston	80	43	27	10	323	285	96
Buffalo	80	39	26	15	307	273	93
Quebec	80	33	31	16	356	345	82
Hartford	80	21	41	18	264	351	60

Patrick Division

Team	GP	W	L	T	GF	GA	PTS
*NY Islanders	80	54	16	10	385	250	118
NY Rangers	80	39	27	14	316	306	92
Philadelphia	80	38	31	11	325	313	87
Pittsburgh	80	31	36	13	310	337	75
Washington	80	26	41	13	319	338	65

Leading Scorers

Player	Club	GP	G	A	PTS	PIM
Gretzky, Wayne	Edmonton	80	92	120	212	26
Bossy, Mike	NY Islanders	80	64	83	147	22
Stastny, Peter	Quebec	80	46	93	139	91
Maruk, Dennis	Washington	80	60	76	136	128
Trottier, Bryan	NY Islanders	80	50	79	129	88
Savard, Denis	Chicago	80	32	87	119	82
Dionne, Marcel	Los Angeles	78	50	67	117	50
Smith, Bobby	Minnesota	80	43	71	114	82
Ciccarelli, Dino	Minnesota	76	55	51	106	138
Taylor, Dave	Los Angeles	78	39	67	106	130

1982-83

CLARENCE CAMPBELL CONFERENCE

Norris Division

Team	GP	W	L	T	GF	GA	PTS
Chicago	80	47	23	10	338	268	104
Minnesota	80	40	24	16	321	290	96
Toronto	80	28	40	12	293	330	68
St. Louis	80	25	40	15	285	316	65
Detroit	80	21	44	15	263	344	57

Smythe Division

Team	GP	W	L	T	GF	GA	PTS
Edmonton	80	47	21	12	424	315	106
Calgary	80	32	34	14	321	317	78
Vancouver	80	30	35	15	303	309	75
Winnipeg	80	33	39	8	311	333	74
Los Angeles	80	27	41	12	308	365	66

PRINCE OF WALES CONFERENCE

Adams Division

Team	GP	W	L	T	GF	GA	PTS
Boston	80	50	20	10	327	228	110
Montreal	80	42	24	14	350	286	98
Buffalo	80	38	29	13	318	285	89
Quebec	80	34	34	12	343	336	80
Hartford	80	19	54	7	261	403	45

Patrick Division

Team	GP	W	L	T	GF	GA	PTS
Philadelphia	80	49	23	8	326	240	106
*NY Islanders	80	42	26	12	302	226	96
Washington	80	39	25	16	306	283	94
NY Rangers	80	35	35	10	306	287	80
New Jersey	80	17	49	14	230	338	48
Pittsburgh	80	18	53	9	257	394	45

Leading Scorers

Player	Club	GP	G	A	PTS	PIM
Gretzky, Wayne	Edmonton	80	71	125	196	59
Stastny, Peter	Quebec	75	47	77	124	78
Savard, Denis	Chicago	78	35	86	121	99
Bossy, Mike	NY Islanders	79	60	58	118	20
Dionne, Marcel	Los Angeles	80	56	51	107	22
Pederson, Barry	Boston	77	46	61	107	47
Messier, Mark	Edmonton	77	48	58	106	72
Goulet, Michel	Quebec	80	57	48	105	51
Anderson, Glenn	Edmonton	72	48	56	104	70
Nilsson, Kent	Calgary	80	46	58	104	10
Kurri, Jari	Edmonton	80	45	59	104	22

1983-84

CLARENCE CAMPBELL CONFERENCE

Norris Division

Team	GP	W	L	T	GF	GA	PTS
Minnesota	80	39	31	10	345	344	88
St. Louis	80	32	41	7	293	316	71
Detroit	80	31	42	7	298	323	69
Chicago	80	30	42	8	277	311	68
Toronto	80	26	45	9	303	387	61

Smythe Division

Team	GP	W	L	T	GF	GA	PTS
*Edmonton	80	57	18	5	446	314	119
Calgary	80	34	32	14	311	314	82
Vancouver	80	32	39	9	306	328	73
Winnipeg	80	31	38	11	340	374	73
Los Angeles	80	23	44	13	309	376	59

PRINCE OF WALES CONFERENCE

Adams Division

Team	GP	W	L	T	GF	GA	PTS
Boston	80	49	25	6	336	261	104
Buffalo	80	48	25	7	315	257	103
Quebec	80	42	28	10	360	278	94
Montreal	80	35	40	5	286	295	75
Hartford	80	28	42	10	288	320	66

Patrick Division

Team	GP	W	L	T	GF	GA	PTS
NY Islanders	80	50	26	4	357	269	104
Washington	80	48	27	5	308	226	101
Philadelphia	80	44	26	10	350	290	98
NY Rangers	80	42	29	9	314	304	93
New Jersey	80	17	56	7	231	350	41
Pittsburgh	80	16	58	6	254	390	38

Leading Scorers

Player	Club	GP	G	A	PTS	PIM
Gretzky, Wayne	Edmonton	74	87	118	205	39
Coffey, Paul	Edmonton	80	40	86	126	104
Goulet, Michel	Quebec	75	56	65	121	76
Stastny, Peter	Quebec	80	46	73	119	73
Bossy, Mike	NY Islanders	67	51	67	118	8
Pederson, Barry	Boston	80	39	77	116	64
Kurri, Jari	Edmonton	64	52	61	113	14
Trottier, Bryan	NY Islanders	68	40	71	111	59
Federko, Bernie	St. Louis	79	41	66	107	43
Middleton, Rick	Boston	80	47	58	105	14

1984-85

CLARENCE CAMPBELL CONFERENCE

Norris Division

Team	GP	W	L	T	GF	GA	PTS
St. Louis	80	37	31	12	299	288	86
Chicago	80	38	35	7	309	299	83
Detroit	80	27	41	12	313	357	66
Minnesota	80	25	43	12	268	321	62
Toronto	80	20	52	8	253	358	48

Smythe Division

Team	GP	W	L	T	GF	GA	PTS
*Edmonton	80	49	20	11	401	298	109
Winnipeg	80	43	27	10	358	332	96
Calgary	80	41	27	12	363	302	94
Los Angeles	80	34	32	14	339	326	82
Vancouver	80	25	46	9	284	401	59

PRINCE OF WALES CONFERENCE

Adams Division

Team	GP	W	L	T	GF	GA	PTS
Montreal	80	41	27	12	309	262	94
Quebec	80	41	30	9	323	275	91
Buffalo	80	38	28	14	290	237	90
Boston	80	36	34	10	303	287	82
Hartford	80	30	41	9	268	318	69

Patrick Division

Team	GP	W	L	T	GF	GA	PTS
Philadelphia	80	53	20	7	348	241	113
Washington	80	46	25	9	322	240	101
NY Islanders	80	40	34	6	345	312	86
NY Rangers	80	26	44	10	295	345	62
New Jersey	80	22	48	10	264	346	54
Pittsburgh	80	24	51	5	276	385	53

Leading Scorers

Player	Club	GP	G	A	PTS	PIM
Gretzky, Wayne	Edmonton	80	73	135	208	52
Kurri, Jari	Edmonton	73	71	64	135	30
Hawerchuk, Dale	Winnipeg	80	53	77	130	74
Dionne, Marcel	Los Angeles	80	46	80	126	46
Coffey, Paul	Edmonton	80	37	84	121	97
Bossy, Mike	NY Islanders	76	58	59	117	38
Ogrodnick, John	Detroit	79	55	50	105	30
Savard, Denis	Chicago	79	38	67	105	56
Federko, Bernie	St. Louis	76	30	73	103	27
Gartner, Mike	Washington	80	50	52	102	71

Left: Peter Stastny finished behind only Wayne Gretzky in total points during the 1980s, collecting an astounding 356 goals and 630 assists for the Quebec Nordiques. Below: Billy Smith won 57 playoff games (and four Stanley Cup titles) with the Islanders from 1980 to 1983.

1985-86
CLARENCE CAMPBELL CONFERENCE
Norris Division

Team	GP	W	L	T	GF	GA	PTS
Chicago	80	39	33	8	351	349	86
Minnesota	80	38	33	9	327	305	85
St. Louis	80	37	34	9	302	291	83
Toronto	80	25	48	7	311	386	57
Detroit	80	17	57	6	266	415	40

Smythe Division

Team	GP	W	L	T	GF	GA	PTS
Edmonton	80	56	17	7	426	310	119
Calgary	80	40	31	9	354	315	89
Winnipeg	80	26	47	7	295	372	59
Vancouver	80	23	44	13	282	333	59
Los Angeles	80	23	49	8	284	389	54

PRINCE OF WALES CONFERENCE
Adams Division

Team	GP	W	L	T	GF	GA	PTS
Quebec	80	43	31	6	330	289	92
*Montreal	80	40	33	7	330	280	87
Boston	80	37	31	12	311	288	86
Hartford	80	40	36	4	332	302	84
Buffalo	80	37	37	6	296	291	80

Patrick Division

Team	GP	W	L	T	GF	GA	PTS
Philadelphia	80	53	23	4	335	241	110
Washington	80	50	23	7	315	272	107
NY Islanders	80	39	29	12	327	284	90
NY Rangers	80	36	38	6	280	276	78
Pittsburgh	80	34	38	8	313	305	76
New Jersey	80	28	49	3	300	374	59

Leading Scorers

Player	Club	GP	G	A	PTS	PIM
Gretzky, Wayne	Edmonton	80	52	163	215	52
Lemieux, Mario	Pittsburgh	79	48	93	141	43
Coffey, Paul	Edmonton	79	48	90	138	120
Kurri, Jari	Edmonton	78	68	63	131	22
Bossy, Mike	NY Islanders	80	61	62	123	14
Stastny, Peter	Quebec	76	41	81	122	60
Savard, Denis	Chicago	80	47	69	116	111
Naslund, Mats	Montreal	80	43	67	110	16
Hawerchuk, Dale	Winnipeg	80	46	59	105	44
Broten, Neal	Minnesota	80	29	76	105	47

1986-87
CLARENCE CAMPBELL CONFERENCE
Norris Division

Team	GP	W	L	T	GF	GA	PTS
St. Louis	80	32	33	15	281	293	79
Detroit	80	34	36	10	260	274	78
Chicago	80	29	37	14	290	310	72
Toronto	80	32	42	6	286	319	70
Minnesota	80	30	40	10	296	314	70

Smythe Division

Team	GP	W	L	T	GF	GA	PTS
*Edmonton	80	50	24	6	372	284	106
Calgary	80	46	31	3	318	289	95
Winnipeg	80	40	32	8	279	271	88
Los Angeles	80	31	41	8	318	341	70
Vancouver	80	29	43	8	282	314	66

PRINCE OF WALES CONFERENCE
Adams Division

Team	GP	W	L	T	GF	GA	PTS
Hartford	80	43	30	7	287	270	93
Montreal	80	41	29	10	277	241	92
Boston	80	39	34	7	301	276	85
Quebec	80	31	39	10	267	276	72
Buffalo	80	28	44	8	280	308	64

Patrick Division

Team	GP	W	L	T	GF	GA	PTS
Philadelphia	80	46	26	8	310	245	100
Washington	80	38	32	10	285	278	86
NY Islanders	80	35	33	12	279	281	82
NY Rangers	80	34	38	8	307	323	76
Pittsburgh	80	30	38	12	297	290	72
New Jersey	80	29	45	6	293	368	64

Leading Scorers

Player	Club	GP	G	A	PTS	PIM
Gretzky, Wayne	Edmonton	79	62	121	183	28
Kurri, Jari	Edmonton	79	54	54	108	41
Lemieux, Mario	Pittsburgh	63	54	53	107	57
Messier, Mark	Edmonton	77	37	70	107	73
Gilmour, Doug	St. Louis	80	42	63	105	58
Ciccarelli, Dino	Minnesota	80	52	51	103	92
Hawerchuk, Dale	Winnipeg	80	47	53	100	54
Goulet, Michel	Quebec	75	49	47	96	61
Kerr, Tim	Philadelphia	75	58	37	95	57
Bourque, Ray	Boston	78	23	72	95	36

1987-88
CLARENCE CAMPBELL CONFERENCE
Norris Division

Team	GP	W	L	T	GF	GA	PTS
Detroit	80	41	28	11	322	269	93
St. Louis	80	34	38	8	278	294	76
Chicago	80	30	41	9	284	328	69
Toronto	80	21	49	10	273	345	52
Minnesota	80	19	48	13	242	349	51

Smythe Division

Team	GP	W	L	T	GF	GA	PTS
Calgary	80	48	23	9	397	305	105
*Edmonton	80	44	25	11	363	288	99
Winnipeg	80	33	36	11	292	310	77
Los Angeles	80	30	42	8	318	359	68
Vancouver	80	25	46	9	272	320	59

PRINCE OF WALES CONFERENCE
Adams Division

Team	GP	W	L	T	GF	GA	PTS
Montreal	80	45	22	13	298	238	103
Boston	80	44	30	6	300	251	94
Buffalo	80	37	32	11	283	305	85
Hartford	80	35	38	7	249	267	77
Quebec	80	32	43	5	271	306	69

Patrick Division

Team	GP	W	L	T	GF	GA	PTS
NY Islanders	80	39	31	10	308	267	88
Washington	80	38	33	9	281	249	85
Philadelphia	80	38	33	9	292	292	85
New Jersey	80	38	36	6	295	296	82
NY Rangers	80	36	34	10	300	283	82
Pittsburgh	80	36	35	9	319	316	81

Leading Scorers

Player	Club	GP	G	A	PTS	PIM
Lemieux, Mario	Pittsburgh	76	70	98	168	92
Gretzky, Wayne	Edmonton	64	40	109	149	24
Savard, Denis	Chicago	80	44	87	131	95
Hawerchuk, Dale	Winnipeg	80	44	77	121	59
Robitaille, Luc	Los Angeles	80	53	58	111	82
Stastny, Peter	Quebec	76	46	65	111	69
Messier, Mark	Edmonton	77	37	74	111	103
Carson, Jimmy	Los Angeles	80	55	52	107	45
Loob, Hakan	Calgary	80	50	56	106	47
Goulet, Michel	Quebec	80	48	58	106	56

1988-89

CLARENCE CAMPBELL CONFERENCE
Norris Division

Team	GP	W	L	T	GF	GA	PTS
Detroit	80	34	34	12	313	316	80
St. Louis	80	33	35	12	275	285	78
Minnesota	80	27	37	16	258	278	70
Chicago	80	27	41	12	297	335	66
Toronto	80	28	46	6	259	342	62

Smythe Division

*Calgary	80	54	17	9	354	226	117
Los Angeles	80	42	31	7	376	335	91
Edmonton	80	38	34	8	325	306	84
Vancouver	80	33	39	8	251	253	74
Winnipeg	80	26	42	12	300	355	64

PRINCE OF WALES CONFERENCE
Adams Division

Montreal	80	53	18	9	315	218	115
Boston	80	37	29	14	289	256	88
Buffalo	80	38	35	7	291	299	83
Hartford	80	37	38	5	299	290	79
Quebec	80	27	46	7	269	342	61

Patrick Division

Washington	80	41	29	10	305	259	92
Pittsburgh	80	40	33	7	347	349	87
NY Rangers	80	37	35	8	310	307	82
Philadelphia	80	36	36	8	307	285	80
New Jersey	80	27	41	12	281	325	66
NY Islanders	80	28	47	5	265	325	61

Leading Scorers

Player	Club	GP	G	A	PTS	PIM
Lemieux, Mario	Pittsburgh	76	85	114	199	100
Gretzky, Wayne	Los Angeles	78	54	114	168	26
Yzerman, Steve	Detroit	80	65	90	155	61
Nicholls, Bernie	Los Angeles	79	70	80	150	96
Brown, Rob	Pittsburgh	68	49	66	115	118
Coffey, Paul	Pittsburgh	75	30	83	113	193
Mullen, Joe	Calgary	79	51	59	110	16
Kurri, Jari	Edmonton	76	44	58	102	69
Carson, Jimmy	Edmonton	80	49	51	100	36
Robitaille, Luc	Los Angeles	78	46	52	98	65

1989-90

CLARENCE CAMPBELL CONFERENCE
Norris Division

Team	GP	W	L	T	GF	GA	PTS
Chicago	80	41	33	6	316	294	88
St. Louis	80	37	34	9	295	279	83
Toronto	80	38	38	4	337	358	80
Minnesota	80	36	40	4	284	291	76
Detroit	80	28	38	14	288	323	70

Smythe Division

Calgary	80	42	23	15	348	265	99
*Edmonton	80	38	28	14	315	283	90
Winnipeg	80	37	32	11	298	290	85
Los Angeles	80	34	39	7	338	337	75
Vancouver	80	25	41	14	245	306	64

PRINCE OF WALES CONFERENCE
Adams Division

Boston	80	46	25	9	289	232	101
Buffalo	80	45	27	8	286	248	98
Montreal	80	41	28	11	288	234	93
Hartford	80	38	33	9	275	268	85
Quebec	80	12	61	7	240	407	31

Patrick Division

NY Rangers	80	36	31	13	279	267	85
New Jersey	80	37	34	9	295	288	83
Washington	80	36	38	6	284	275	78
NY Islanders	80	31	38	11	281	288	73
Pittsburgh	80	32	40	8	318	359	72
Philadelphia	80	30	39	11	290	297	71

Leading Scorers

Player	Club	GP	G	A	PTS	PIM
Gretzky, Wayne	Los Angeles	73	40	102	142	42
Messier, Mark	Edmonton	79	45	84	129	79
Yzerman, Steve	Detroit	79	62	65	127	79
Lemieux, Mario	Pittsburgh	59	45	78	123	78
Hull, Brett	St. Louis	80	72	41	113	24
Nicholls, Bernie	L.A., NYR	79	39	73	112	86
Turgeon, Pierre	Buffalo	80	40	66	106	29
LaFontaine, Pat	NY Islanders	74	54	51	105	38
Coffey, Paul	Pittsburgh	80	29	74	103	95
Sakic, Joe	Quebec	80	39	63	102	27
Oates, Adam	St. Louis	80	23	79	102	30

1990-91

CLARENCE CAMPBELL CONFERENCE
Norris Division

Team	GP	W	L	T	GF	GA	PTS
Chicago	80	49	23	8	284	211	106
St. Louis	80	47	22	11	310	250	105
Detroit	80	34	38	8	273	298	76
Minnesota	80	27	39	14	256	266	68
Toronto	80	23	46	11	241	318	57

Smythe Division

Los Angeles	80	46	24	10	340	254	102
Calgary	80	46	26	8	344	263	100
Edmonton	80	37	37	6	272	272	80
Vancouver	80	28	43	9	243	315	65
Winnipeg	80	26	43	11	260	288	63

PRINCE OF WALES CONFERENCE
Adams Division

Boston	80	44	24	12	299	264	100
Montreal	80	39	30	11	273	249	89
Buffalo	80	31	30	19	292	278	81
Hartford	80	31	38	11	238	276	73
Quebec	80	16	50	14	236	354	46

Patrick Division

*Pittsburgh	80	41	33	6	342	305	88
NY Rangers	80	36	31	13	297	265	85
Washington	80	37	36	7	258	258	81
New Jersey	80	32	33	15	272	264	79
Philadelphia	80	33	37	10	252	267	76
NY Islanders	80	25	45	10	223	290	60

Leading Scorers

Player	Club	GP	G	A	PTS	PIM
Gretzky, Wayne	Los Angeles	78	41	122	163	16
Hull, Brett	St. Louis	78	86	45	131	22
Oates, Adam	St. Louis	61	25	90	115	29
Recchi, Mark	Pittsburgh	78	40	73	113	48
Cullen, John	Pit., Hfd.	78	39	71	110	101
Sakic, Joe	Quebec	80	48	61	109	24
Yzerman, Steve	Detroit	80	51	57	108	34
Fleury, Theo	Calgary	79	51	53	104	136
MacInnis, Al	Calgary	78	28	75	103	90
Larmer, Steve	Chicago	80	44	57	101	79

1991-92

CLARENCE CAMPBELL CONFERENCE
Norris Division

Team	GP	W	L	T	GF	GA	PTS
Detroit	80	43	25	12	320	256	98
Chicago	80	36	29	15	257	236	87
St. Louis	80	36	33	11	279	266	83
Minnesota	80	32	42	6	246	278	70
Toronto	80	30	43	7	234	294	67

Smythe Division

Vancouver	80	42	26	12	285	250	96
Los Angeles	80	35	31	14	287	296	84
Edmonton	80	36	34	10	295	297	82
Winnipeg	80	33	32	15	251	244	81
Calgary	80	31	37	12	296	305	74
San Jose	80	17	58	5	219	359	39

PRINCE OF WALES CONFERENCE
Adams Division

Montreal	80	41	28	11	267	207	93
Boston	80	36	32	12	270	275	84
Buffalo	80	31	37	12	289	299	74
Hartford	80	26	41	13	247	283	65
Quebec	80	20	48	12	255	318	52

Patrick Division

NY Rangers	80	50	25	5	321	246	105
Washington	80	45	27	8	330	275	98
*Pittsburgh	80	39	32	9	343	308	87
New Jersey	80	38	31	11	289	259	87
NY Islanders	80	34	35	11	291	299	79
Philadelphia	80	32	37	11	252	273	75

Leading Scorers

Player	Club	GP	G	A	PTS	PIM
Lemieux, Mario	Pittsburgh	64	44	87	131	94
Stevens, Kevin	Pittsburgh	80	54	69	123	254
Gretzky, Wayne	Los Angeles	74	31	90	121	34
Hull, Brett	St. Louis	73	70	39	109	48
Robitaille, Luc	Los Angeles	80	44	63	107	95
Messier, Mark	NY Rangers	79	35	72	107	76
Roenick, Jeremy	Chicago	80	53	50	103	23
Yzerman, Steve	Detroit	79	45	58	103	64
Leetch, Brian	NY Rangers	80	22	80	102	26
Oates, Adam	St. L., Bos.	80	20	79	99	22

1992-93

CLARENCE CAMPBELL CONFERENCE
Norris Division

Team	GP	W	L	T	GF	GA	PTS
Chicago	84	47	25	12	279	230	106
Detroit	84	47	28	9	369	280	103
Toronto	84	44	29	11	288	241	99
St. Louis	84	37	36	11	282	278	85
Minnesota	84	36	38	10	272	293	82
Tampa Bay	84	23	54	7	245	332	53

Smythe Division

Vancouver	84	46	29	9	346	278	101
Calgary	84	43	30	11	322	282	97
Los Angeles	84	39	35	10	338	340	88
Winnipeg	84	40	37	7	322	320	87
Edmonton	84	26	50	8	242	337	60
San Jose	84	11	71	2	218	414	24

PRINCE OF WALES CONFERENCE
Adams Division

Boston	84	51	26	7	332	268	109
Quebec	84	47	27	10	351	300	104
*Montreal	84	48	30	6	326	280	102
Buffalo	84	38	36	10	335	297	86
Hartford	84	26	52	6	284	369	58
Ottawa	84	10	70	4	202	395	24

Patrick Division

Pittsburgh	84	56	21	7	367	268	119
Washington	84	43	34	7	325	286	93
NY Islanders	84	40	37	7	335	297	87
New Jersey	84	40	37	7	308	299	87
Philadelphia	84	36	37	11	319	319	83
NY Rangers	84	34	39	11	304	308	79

Leading Scorers

Player	Club	GP	G	A	PTS	PIM
Lemieux, Mario	Pittsburgh	60	69	91	160	38
LaFontaine, Pat	Buffalo	84	53	95	148	63
Oates, Adam	Boston	84	45	97	142	32
Yzerman, Steve	Detroit	84	58	79	137	44
Selanne, Teemu	Winnipeg	84	76	56	132	45
Turgeon, Pierre	NY Islanders	83	58	74	132	26
Mogilny, Alexander	Buffalo	77	76	51	127	40
Gilmour, Doug	Toronto	83	32	95	127	100
Robitaille, Luc	Los Angeles	84	63	62	125	100
Recchi, Mark	Philadelphia	84	53	70	123	95

1993-94

EASTERN CONFERENCE
Northeast Division

Team	GP	W	L	T	GF	GA	PTS
Pittsburgh	84	44	27	13	299	285	101
Boston	84	42	29	13	289	252	97
Montreal	84	41	29	14	283	248	96
Buffalo	84	43	32	9	282	218	95
Quebec	84	34	42	8	277	292	76
Hartford	84	27	48	9	227	288	63
Ottawa	84	14	61	9	201	397	37

Atlantic Division

*NY Rangers	84	52	24	8	299	231	112
New Jersey	84	47	25	12	306	220	106
Washington	84	39	35	10	277	263	88
NY Islanders	84	36	36	12	282	264	84
Florida	84	33	34	17	233	233	83
Philadelphia	84	35	39	10	294	314	80
Tampa Bay	84	30	43	11	224	251	71

WESTERN CONFERENCE
Central Division

Detroit	84	46	30	8	356	275	100
Toronto	84	43	29	12	280	243	98
Dallas	84	42	29	13	286	265	97
St. Louis	84	40	33	11	270	283	91
Chicago	84	39	36	9	254	240	87
Winnipeg	84	24	51	9	245	344	57

Pacific Division

Calgary	84	42	29	13	302	256	97
Vancouver	84	41	40	3	279	276	85
San Jose	84	33	35	16	252	265	82
Anaheim	84	33	46	5	229	251	71
Los Angeles	84	27	45	12	294	322	66
Edmonton	84	25	45	14	261	305	64

Leading Scorers

Player	Club	GP	G	A	PTS	PIM
Gretzky, Wayne	Los Angeles	81	38	92	130	20
Fedorov, Sergei	Detroit	82	56	64	120	34
Oates, Adam	Boston	77	32	80	112	45
Gilmour, Doug	Toronto	83	27	84	111	105
Bure, Pavel	Vancouver	76	60	47	107	86
Roenick, Jeremy	Chicago	84	46	61	107	125
Recchi, Mark	Philadelphia	84	40	67	107	46
Shanahan, Brendan	St. Louis	81	52	50	102	211
Andreychuk, Dave	Toronto	83	53	46	99	98
Jagr, Jaromir	Pittsburgh	80	32	67	99	61

1994-95
EASTERN CONFERENCE
Northeast Division

Team	GP	W	L	T	GF	GA	PTS
Quebec	48	30	13	5	185	134	65
Pittsburgh	48	29	16	3	181	158	61
Boston	48	27	18	3	150	127	57
Buffalo	48	22	19	7	130	119	51
Hartford	48	19	24	5	127	141	43
Montreal	48	18	23	7	125	148	43
Ottawa	48	9	34	5	117	174	23

Atlantic Division

Team	GP	W	L	T	GF	GA	PTS
Philadelphia	48	28	16	4	150	132	60
*New Jersey	48	22	18	8	136	121	52
Washington	48	22	18	8	136	120	52
NY Rangers	48	22	23	3	139	134	47
Florida	48	20	22	6	115	127	46
Tampa Bay	48	17	28	3	120	144	37
NY Islanders	48	15	28	5	126	158	35

WESTERN CONFERENCE
Central Division

Team	GP	W	L	T	GF	GA	PTS
Detroit	48	33	11	4	180	117	70
St. Louis	48	28	15	5	178	135	61
Chicago	48	24	19	5	156	115	53
Toronto	48	21	19	8	135	146	50
Dallas	48	17	23	8	136	135	42
Winnipeg	48	16	25	7	157	177	39

Pacific Division

Team	GP	W	L	T	GF	GA	PTS
Calgary	48	24	17	7	163	135	55
Vancouver	48	18	18	12	153	148	48
San Jose	48	19	25	4	129	161	42
Los Angeles	48	16	23	9	142	174	41
Edmonton	48	17	27	4	136	183	38
Anaheim	48	16	27	5	125	164	37

Leading Scorers

Player	Club	GP	G	A	PTS	PIM
Jagr, Jaromir	Pittsburgh	48	32	38	70	37
Lindros, Eric	Philadelphia	46	29	41	70	60
Zhamnov, Alexei	Winnipeg	48	30	35	65	20
Sakic, Joe	Quebec	47	19	43	62	30
Francis, Ron	Pittsburgh	44	11	48	59	18
Fleury, Theoren	Calgary	47	29	29	58	112
Coffey, Paul	Detroit	45	14	44	58	72
Renberg, Mikael	Philadelphia	47	26	31	57	20
LeClair, John	Mtl., Phi.	46	26	28	54	30
Messier, Mark	NY Rangers	46	14	39	53	40
Oates, Adam	Boston	48	12	41	53	8

1995-96
EASTERN CONFERENCE
Northeast Division

Team	GP	W	L	T	GF	GA	PTS
Pittsburgh	82	49	29	4	362	284	102
Boston	82	40	31	11	282	269	91
Montreal	82	40	32	10	265	248	90
Hartford	82	34	39	9	237	259	77
Buffalo	82	33	42	7	247	262	73
Ottawa	82	18	59	5	191	291	41

Atlantic Division

Team	GP	W	L	T	GF	GA	PTS
Philadelphia	82	45	24	13	282	208	103
NY Rangers	82	41	27	14	272	237	96
Florida	82	41	31	10	254	234	92
Washington	82	39	32	11	234	204	89
Tampa Bay	82	38	32	12	238	248	88
New Jersey	82	37	33	12	215	202	86
NY Islanders	82	22	50	10	229	315	54

WESTERN CONFERENCE
Central Division

Team	GP	W	L	T	GF	GA	PTS
Detroit	82	62	13	7	325	181	131
Chicago	82	40	28	14	273	220	94
Toronto	82	34	36	12	247	252	80
St. Louis	82	32	34	16	219	248	80
Winnipeg	82	36	40	6	275	291	78
Dallas	82	26	42	14	227	280	66

Pacific Division

Team	GP	W	L	T	GF	GA	PTS
*Colorado	82	47	25	10	326	240	104
Calgary	82	34	37	11	241	240	79
Vancouver	82	32	35	15	278	278	79
Anaheim	82	35	39	8	234	247	78
Edmonton	82	30	44	8	240	304	68
Los Angeles	82	24	40	18	256	302	66
San Jose	82	20	55	7	252	357	47

Leading Scorers

Player	Club	GP	G	A	PTS	PIM
Lemieux, Mario	Pittsburgh	70	69	92	161	54
Jagr, Jaromir	Pittsburgh	82	62	87	149	96
Sakic, Joe	Colorado	82	51	69	120	44
Francis, Ron	Pittsburgh	77	27	92	119	56
Forsberg, Peter	Colorado	82	30	86	116	47
Lindros, Eric	Philadelphia	73	47	68	115	163
Kariya, Paul	Anaheim	82	50	58	108	20
Selanne, Teemu	Wpg., Ana.	79	40	68	108	22
Mogilny, Alexander	Vancouver	79	55	52	107	16
Fedorov, Sergei	Detroit	78	39	68	107	48

1996-97
EASTERN CONFERENCE
Northeast Division

Team	GP	W	L	T	GF	GA	PTS
Buffalo	82	40	30	12	237	208	92
Pittsburgh	82	38	36	8	285	280	84
Ottawa	82	31	36	15	226	234	77
Montreal	82	31	36	15	249	276	77
Hartford	82	32	39	11	226	256	75
Boston	82	26	47	9	234	300	61

Atlantic Division

Team	GP	W	L	T	GF	GA	PTS
New Jersey	82	45	23	14	231	182	104
Philadelphia	82	45	24	13	274	217	103
Florida	82	35	28	19	221	201	89
NY Rangers	82	38	34	10	258	231	86
Washington	82	33	40	9	214	231	75
Tampa Bay	82	32	40	10	217	247	74
NY Islanders	82	29	41	12	240	250	70

WESTERN CONFERENCE
Central Division

Team	GP	W	L	T	GF	GA	PTS
Dallas	82	48	26	8	252	198	104
*Detroit	82	38	26	18	253	197	94
Phoenix	82	38	37	7	240	243	83
St. Louis	82	36	35	11	236	239	83
Chicago	82	34	35	13	223	210	81
Toronto	82	30	44	8	230	273	68

Pacific Division

Team	GP	W	L	T	GF	GA	PTS
Colorado	82	49	24	9	277	205	107
Anaheim	82	36	33	13	245	233	85
Edmonton	82	36	37	9	252	247	81
Vancouver	82	35	40	7	257	273	77
Calgary	82	32	41	9	214	239	73
Los Angeles	82	28	43	11	214	268	67
San Jose	82	27	47	8	211	278	62

Leading Scorers

Player	Club	GP	G	A	PTS	PIM
Lemieux, Mario	Pittsburgh	76	50	72	122	65
Selanne, Teemu	Anaheim	78	51	58	109	34
Kariya, Paul	Anaheim	69	44	55	99	6
LeClair, John	Philadelphia	82	50	47	97	58
Gretzky, Wayne	NY Rangers	82	25	72	97	28
Jagr, Jaromir	Pittsburgh	63	47	48	95	40
Sundin, Mats	Toronto	82	41	53	94	59
Palffy, Zigmund	NY Islanders	80	48	42	90	43
Francis, Ron	Pittsburgh	81	27	63	90	20
Shanahan, Brendan	Hfd., Det.	81	47	41	88	131

Note: Detailed statistics for 1996-97 are listed in the Final Statistics, 1996-97 section of the **NHL Guide & Record Book. See page 121.**

Mario Lemieux celebrated his final season in style, scoring his 600th goal on February 4, 1997. Lemieux became the first player in NHL history to retire after winning the League's scoring title.

Team Records
Regular Season

FINAL STANDINGS

MOST POINTS, ONE SEASON:
132 —Montreal Canadiens, 1976-77. 60w-8L-12T. 80GP
131 —Detroit Red Wings, 1995-96. 62w-13L-7T. 82GP
129 —Montreal Canadiens, 1977-78. 59w-10L-11T. 80GP

BEST WINNING PERCENTAGE, ONE SEASON:
.875 —Boston Bruins, 1929-30. 38w-5L-1T. 77PTS in 44GP
.830 —Montreal Canadiens, 1943-44. 38w-5L-7T. 83PTS in 50GP
.825 —Montreal Canadiens, 1976-77. 60w-8L-12T. 132PTS in 80GP
.806 —Montreal Canadiens, 1977-78. 59w-10L-11T. 129PTS in 80GP
.800 —Montreal Canadiens, 1944-45. 38w-8L-4T. 80PTS in 50GP

FEWEST POINTS, ONE SEASON:
8 —Quebec Bulldogs, 1919-20. 4w-20L-0T. 24GP
10 —Toronto Arenas, 1918-19. 5w-13L-0T. 18GP
12 —Hamilton Tigers, 1920-21. 6w-18L-0T. 24GP
—Hamilton Tigers, 1922-23. 6w-18L-0T. 24GP
—Boston Bruins, 1924-25. 6w-24L-0T. 30GP
—Philadelphia Quakers, 1930-31. 4w-36L-4T. 44GP

FEWEST POINTS, ONE SEASON (MINIMUM 70-GAME SCHEDULE):
21 —Washington Capitals, 1974-75. 8w-67L-5T. 80GP
24 —Ottawa Senators, 1992-93. 10w-70L-4T. 84GP
—San Jose Sharks, 1992-93. 11w-71L-2T. 84GP
30 —NY Islanders, 1972-73. 12w-60L-6T. 78GP

WORST WINNING PERCENTAGE, ONE SEASON:
.131 —Washington Capitals, 1974-75. 8w-67L-5T. 21PTS in 80GP
.136 —Philadelphia Quakers, 1930-31. 4w-36L-4T. 12PTS in 44GP
.143 —Ottawa Senators, 1992-93. 10w-70L-4T. 24PTS in 84GP
.143 —San Jose Sharks, 1992-93. 11w-71L-2T. 24PTS in 84GP
.148 —Pittsburgh Pirates, 1929-30. 5w-36L-3T. 13PTS in 44GP

TEAM WINS

Most Wins

MOST WINS, ONE SEASON:
62 —Detroit Red Wings, 1995-96. 82GP
60 —Montreal Canadiens, 1976-77. 80GP
59 —Montreal Canadiens, 1977-78. 80GP

MOST HOME WINS, ONE SEASON:
36 —Philadelphia Flyers, 1975-76. 40GP
—Detroit Red Wings, 1995-96. 41GP
33 —Boston Bruins, 1970-71. 39GP
—Boston Bruins, 1973-74. 39GP
—Montreal Canadiens, 1976-77. 40GP
—Philadelphia Flyers, 1976-77. 40GP
—NY Islanders, 1981-82. 40GP
—Philadelphia Flyers, 1985-86. 40GP

MOST ROAD WINS, ONE SEASON:
27 —Montreal Canadiens, 1976-77. 40GP
—Montreal Canadiens, 1977-78. 40GP
26 —Boston Bruins, 1971-72. 39GP
—Montreal Canadiens, 1975-76. 40GP
—Edmonton Oilers, 1983-84. 40GP
—Detroit Red Wings, 1995-96. 41GP

Fewest Wins

FEWEST WINS, ONE SEASON:
4 —Quebec Bulldogs, 1919-20. 24GP
—Philadelphia Quakers, 1930-31. 44GP
5 —Toronto Arenas, 1918-19. 18GP
—Pittsburgh Pirates, 1929-30. 44GP

FEWEST WINS, ONE SEASON (MINIMUM 70-GAME SCHEDULE):
8 —Washington Capitals, 1974-75. 80GP
9 —Winnipeg Jets, 1980-81. 80GP
10 —Ottawa Senators, 1992-93. 84GP

FEWEST HOME WINS, ONE SEASON:
2 —Chicago Blackhawks, 1927-28. 22GP
3 —Boston Bruins, 1924-25. 15GP
—Chicago Blackhawks, 1928-29. 22GP
—Philadelphia Quakers, 1930-31. 22GP

FEWEST HOME WINS, ONE SEASON (MINIMUM 70-GAME SCHEDULE):
6 —Chicago Blackhawks, 1954-55. 35GP
—Washington Capitals, 1975-76. 40GP
7 —Boston Bruins, 1962-63. 35GP
—Washington Capitals, 1974-75. 40GP
—Winnipeg Jets, 1980-81. 40GP
—Pittsburgh Penguins, 1983-84. 40GP

FEWEST ROAD WINS, ONE SEASON:
0 —Toronto Arenas, 1918-19. 9GP
—Quebec Bulldogs, 1919-20. 12GP
—Pittsburgh Pirates, 1929-30. 22GP
1 —Hamilton Tigers, 1921-22. 12GP
—Toronto St. Patricks, 1925-26. 18GP
—Philadelphia Quakers, 1930-31. 22GP
—NY Americans, 1940-41. 24GP
—Washington Capitals, 1974-75. 40GP
* —Ottawa Senators, 1992-93. 41GP

FEWEST ROAD WINS, ONE SEASON (MINIMUM 70-GAME SCHEDULE):
1 —Washington Capitals, 1974-75. 40GP
* **—Ottawa Senators,** 1992-93. 41GP
2 —Boston Bruins, 1960-61. 35GP
—Los Angeles Kings, 1969-70. 38GP
—NY Islanders, 1972-73. 39GP
—California Seals, 1973-74. 39GP
—Colorado Rockies, 1977-78. 40GP
—Winnipeg Jets, 1980-81. 40GP
—Quebec Nordiques, 1991-92. 40GP

TEAM LOSSES

Fewest Losses

FEWEST LOSSES, ONE SEASON:
5 —Ottawa Senators, 1919-20. 24GP
—Boston Bruins, 1929-30. 44GP
—Montreal Canadiens, 1943-44. 50GP

FEWEST HOME LOSSES, ONE SEASON:
0 —Ottawa Senators, 1922-23. 12GP
—Montreal Canadiens, 1943-44. 25GP
1 —Toronto Arenas, 1917-18. 11GP
—Ottawa Senators, 1918-19. 9GP
—Ottawa Senators, 1919-20. 12GP
—Toronto St. Patricks, 1922-23. 12GP
—Boston Bruins, 1929-30. 22GP
—Boston Bruins, 1930-31. 22GP
—Montreal Canadiens, 1976-77. 40GP
—Quebec Nordiques, 1994-95. 24GP

FEWEST ROAD LOSSES, ONE SEASON:
3 —Montreal Canadiens, 1928-29. 22GP
4 —Ottawa Senators, 1919-20. 12GP
—Montreal Canadiens, 1927-28. 22GP
—Boston Bruins, 1929-30. 20GP
—Boston Bruins, 1940-41. 24GP

FEWEST LOSSES, ONE SEASON (MINIMUM 70-GAME SCHEDULE):
8 —Montreal Canadiens, 1976-77. 80GP
10 —Montreal Canadiens, 1972-73. 78GP
—Montreal Canadiens, 1977-78. 80GP
11 —Montreal Canadiens, 1975-76. 80GP

FEWEST HOME LOSSES, ONE SEASON (MINIMUM 70-GAME SCHEDULE):
1 —Montreal Canadiens, 1976-77. 40GP
2 —Montreal Canadiens, 1961-62. 35GP
—NY Rangers, 1970-71. 39GP
—Philadelphia Flyers, 1975-76. 40GP

FEWEST ROAD LOSSES, ONE SEASON (MINIMUM 70-GAME SCHEDULE):
6 —Montreal Canadiens, 1972-73. 39GP
—Montreal Canadiens, 1974-75. 40GP
—Montreal Canadiens, 1977-78. 40GP
7 —Detroit Red Wings, 1951-52. 35GP
—Montreal Canadiens, 1976-77. 40GP
—Philadelphia Flyers, 1979-80. 40GP

Most Losses

MOST LOSSES, ONE SEASON:
71 —San Jose Sharks, 1992-93. 84GP
70 —Ottawa Senators, 1992-93. 84GP
67 —Washington Capitals, 1974-75. 80GP
61 —Quebec Nordiques, 1989-90. 80GP
—Ottawa Senators, 1993-94. 84GP

MOST HOME LOSSES, ONE SEASON:
***32 —San Jose Sharks,** 1992-93. 41GP
29 —Pittsburgh Penguins, 1983-84. 40GP
* —Ottawa Senators, 1993-94. 41GP

MOST ROAD LOSSES, ONE SEASON:
***40 —Ottawa Senators,** 1992-93. 41GP
39 —Washington Capitals, 1974-75. 40GP
37 —California Seals, 1973-74. 39GP
* —San Jose Sharks, 1992-93. 41GP

* – Does not include neutral site games.

TEAM TIES

Most Ties

MOST TIES, ONE SEASON:
24 —Philadelphia Flyers, 1969-70. 76GP
23 —Montreal Canadiens, 1962-63. 70GP
—Chicago Blackhawks, 1973-74. 78GP

MOST HOME TIES, ONE SEASON:
13 —NY Rangers, 1954-55. 35GP
—**Philadelphia Flyers,** 1969-70. 38GP
—**California Seals,** 1971-72. 39GP
—**California Seals,** 1972-73. 39GP
—**Chicago Blackhawks,** 1973-74. 39GP

MOST ROAD TIES, ONE SEASON:
15 —Philadelphia Flyers, 1976-77. 40GP
14 —Montreal Canadiens, 1952-53. 35GP
—Montreal Canadiens, 1974-75. 40GP
—Philadelphia Flyers, 1975-76. 40GP

Fewest Ties

FEWEST TIES, ONE SEASON (Since 1926-27):
1 —Boston Bruins, 1929-30. 44GP
2 —NY Americans, 1926-27. 44GP
—Montreal Canadiens, 1926-27. 44GP
—Boston Bruins, 1938-39. 48GP
—NY Rangers, 1941-42. 48GP
—San Jose Sharks, 1992-93. 84GP

FEWEST TIES, ONE SEASON (MINIMUM 70-GAME SCHEDULE):
2 —San Jose Sharks, 1992-93. 84GP
3 —New Jersey Devils, 1985-86. 80GP
—Calgary Flames, 1986-87. 80GP
—Vancouver Canucks, 1993-94. 84GP

WINNING STREAKS

LONGEST WINNING STREAK, ONE SEASON:
17 Games —Pittsburgh Penguins, Mar. 9, 1993 - Apr. 10, 1993.
15 Games —NY Islanders, Jan. 21, 1982 - Feb. 20, 1982.
14 Games —Boston Bruins, Dec. 3, 1929 - Jan. 9, 1930.

LONGEST HOME WINNING STREAK, ONE SEASON:
20 Games —Boston Bruins, Dec. 3, 1929 - Mar. 18, 1930.
—**Philadelphia Flyers,** Jan. 4, 1976 - Apr. 3, 1976.

LONGEST ROAD WINNING STREAK, ONE SEASON:
10 Games —Buffalo Sabres, Dec. 10, 1983 - Jan. 23, 1984.
8 Games —Boston Bruins, Feb. 17, 1972 - Mar. 8, 1972.
—Los Angeles Kings, Dec. 18, 1974 - Jan. 16, 1975.
—Montreal Canadiens, Dec. 18, 1977 - Jan. 18, 1978.
—NY Islanders, Feb. 27, 1981 - Mar. 29, 1981.
—Montreal Canadiens, Jan. 21, 1982 - Feb. 21, 1982.
—Philadelphia Flyers, Dec. 22, 1982 - Jan. 16, 1983.
—Winnipeg Jets, Feb. 25, 1985 - Apr. 6, 1985.
—Edmonton Oilers, Dec. 9, 1986 - Jan. 17, 1987.
—Boston Bruins, Mar. 15, 1993 - Apr. 14, 1993.

LONGEST WINNING STREAK FROM START OF SEASON:
10 Games —Toronto Maple Leafs, 1993-94.
8 Games —Toronto Maple Leafs, 1934-35.
—Buffalo Sabres, 1975-76.
7 Games —Edmonton Oilers, 1983-84.
—Quebec Nordiques, 1985-86.
—Pittsburgh Penguins, 1986-87.
—Pittsburgh Penguins, 1994-95.

LONGEST HOME WINNING STREAK FROM START OF SEASON:
11 Games —Chicago Blackhawks, 1963-64.
10 Games —Ottawa Senators, 1925-26.
9 Games —Montreal Canadiens, 1953-54.
—Chicago Blackhawks, 1971-72.

LONGEST ROAD WINNING STREAK FROM START OF SEASON:
7 Games —Toronto Maple Leafs, Nov. 14, 1940 - Dec. 15, 1940.

LONGEST WINNING STREAK, INCLUDING PLAYOFFS:
15 Games —Detroit Red Wings, Feb. 27, 1955 - Apr. 5, 1955. Nine regular-season games, six playoff games.

LONGEST HOME WINNING STREAK, INCLUDING PLAYOFFS:
24 Games —Philadelphia Flyers, Jan. 4, 1976 - Apr. 25, 1976. Twenty regular-season games, four playoff games.

LONGEST ROAD WINNING STREAK, INCLUDING PLAYOFFS:
8 Games —NY Islanders, Apr. 4 - May 1, 1980. One regular season game, seven playoff games.

UNDEFEATED STREAKS

LONGEST UNDEFEATED STREAK, ONE SEASON:
35 Games —Philadelphia Flyers, Oct. 14, 1979 - Jan. 6, 1980. 25w-10T.
28 Games —Montreal Canadiens, Dec. 18, 1977 - Feb. 23, 1978. 23w-5T.
23 Games —Boston Bruins, Dec. 22, 1940 - Feb. 23, 1941. 15w-8T.
—Philadelphia Flyers, Jan. 29, 1976 - Mar. 18, 1976. 17w-6T.

LONGEST HOME UNDEFEATED STREAK, ONE SEASON:
34 Games —Montreal Canadiens, Nov. 1, 1976 - Apr. 2, 1977. 28w-6T.
27 Games —Boston Bruins, Nov. 22, 1970 - Mar. 20, 1971. 26w-1T.

LONGEST ROAD UNDEFEATED STREAK, ONE SEASON:
23 Games —Montreal Canadiens, Nov. 27, 1974 - Mar. 12, 1975. 14w-9T.
17 Games —Montreal Canadiens, Dec. 18, 1977 - Mar. 1, 1978. 14w-3T.
16 Games —Philadelphia Flyers, Oct. 20, 1979 - Jan. 6, 1980. 11w-5T.

LONGEST UNDEFEATED STREAK FROM START OF SEASON:
15 Games —Edmonton Oilers, 1984-85. 12w-3T.
14 Games —Montreal Canadiens, 1943-44. 11w-3T.
13 Games —Montreal Canadiens, 1972-73. 9w-4T.
—Pittsburgh Penguins, 1994-95. 12w-1T.

LONGEST HOME UNDEFEATED STREAK FROM START OF SEASON:
25 Games —Montreal Canadiens, Oct. 30, 1943 - Mar. 18, 1944. 22w-3T.

LONGEST ROAD UNDEFEATED STREAK FROM START OF SEASON:
15 Games —Detroit Red Wings, Oct. 18, 1951 - Dec. 20, 1951. 10w-5T.

LONGEST UNDEFEATED STREAK, INCLUDING PLAYOFFS:
21 Games —Pittsburgh Penguins, Mar. 9, 1993 - Apr. 22, 1993. 17w-1T in regular season and 3w in playoffs.

LONGEST HOME UNDEFEATED STREAK, INCLUDING PLAYOFFS:
38 Games —Montreal Canadiens, Nov. 1, 1976 - Apr. 26, 1977. 28w-6T in regular season and 4w in playoff.

LONGEST ROAD UNDEFEATED STREAK, INCLUDING PLAYOFFS:
13 Games —Montreal Canadiens, Feb. 26 - Apr. 20, 1980. 6w-4T in regular season and 3w in playoffs.
—**NY Islanders,** Mar. 16 - May 1, 1980. 3w-3T in regular season and 7w in playoffs.

LOSING STREAKS

LONGEST LOSING STREAK, ONE SEASON:
17 Games —Washington Capitals, Feb. 18, 1975 - Mar. 26, 1975.
—**San Jose Sharks,** Jan. 4, 1993 - Feb. 12, 1993.
15 Games —Philadelphia Quakers, Nov. 29, 1930 - Jan. 8, 1931.

LONGEST HOME LOSING STREAK, ONE SEASON:
11 Games —Boston Bruins, Dec. 8, 1924 - Feb. 17, 1925.
—**Washington Capitals,** Feb. 18, 1975 - Mar. 30, 1975.
—**Ottawa Senators,** Oct. 27, 1993 - Dec. 8, 1993.

LONGEST ROAD LOSING STREAK, ONE SEASON:
*38 Games —Ottawa Senators, Oct. 10, 1992 - Apr. 3, 1993.
37 Games —Washington Capitals, Oct. 9, 1974 - Mar. 26, 1975.

LONGEST LOSING STREAK FROM START OF SEASON:
11 Games —NY Rangers, 1943-44.
7 Games —Montreal Canadiens, 1938-39.
—Chicago Blackhawks, 1947-48.
—Washington Capitals, 1983-84.

LONGEST HOME LOSING STREAK FROM START OF SEASON:
8 Games —Los Angeles Kings, Oct. 13, 1971 - Nov. 6, 1971.

LONGEST ROAD LOSING STREAK FROM START OF SEASON:
*38 Games —Ottawa Senators, Oct. 10, 1992 - Apr. 3, 1993.

WINLESS STREAKS

LONGEST WINLESS STREAK, ONE SEASON:
30 Games —Winnipeg Jets, Oct. 19, 1980 - Dec. 20, 1980. 23L-7T.
27 Games —Kansas City Scouts, Feb. 12, 1976 - Apr. 4, 1976. 21L-6T.
25 Games —Washington Capitals, Nov. 29, 1975 - Jan. 21, 1976. 22L-3T.

LONGEST HOME WINLESS STREAK, ONE SEASON:
17 Games —Ottawa Senators, Oct. 28, 1995 - Jan. 27, 1996. 15L-2T.
15 Games —Chicago Blackhawks, Dec. 16, 1928 - Feb. 28, 1929. 11L-4T.
—Montreal Canadiens, Dec. 16, 1939 - Mar. 7, 1940. 12L-3T.

LONGEST ROAD WINLESS STREAK, ONE SEASON:
*38 Games —Ottawa Senators, Oct. 10, 1992 - Apr. 3, 1993. 38L-0T.
37 Games —Washington Capitals, Oct. 9, 1974 - Mar. 26, 1975. 37L-0T.

LONGEST WINLESS STREAK FROM START OF SEASON:
15 Games —NY Rangers, 1943-44. 14L-1T.
12 Games —Pittsburgh Pirates, 1927-28. 9L-3T.
11 Games —Minnesota North Stars, 1973-74. 5L-6T.
—San Jose Sharks, 1995-96. 7L-4T.

LONGEST HOME WINLESS STREAK FROM START OF SEASON:
11 Games —Pittsburgh Penguins, Oct. 8, 1983 - Nov. 19, 1983. 9L-2T.

LONGEST ROAD WINLESS STREAK FROM START OF SEASON:
*38 Games —Ottawa Senators, Oct. 10, 1992 - Apr. 3, 1993. 38L-0T.

* – Does not include neutral site games.

NON-SHUTOUT STREAKS

LONGEST NON-SHUTOUT STREAK:
   264 Games —Calgary Flames, Nov. 12, 1981 - Jan. 9, 1985.
   262 Games —Los Angeles Kings, Mar. 15, 1986 - Oct. 25, 1989.
   244 Games —Washington Capitals, Oct. 31, 1989 - Nov. 11, 1993.
   230 Games —Quebec Nordiques, Feb. 10, 1980 - Jan. 13, 1983.
   229 Games —Edmonton Oilers, Mar. 15, 1981 - Feb. 11, 1984.

LONGEST NON-SHUTOUT STREAK INCLUDING PLAYOFFS:
   264 Games —Los Angeles Kings, Mar. 15, 1986 - Apr. 6, 1989.
      (5 playoff games in 1987; 5 in 1988; 2 in 1989).
   262 Games —Chicago Blackhawks, Mar. 14, 1970 - Feb. 21, 1973. (8 playoff
      games in 1970; 18 in 1971; 8 in 1972).
   251 Games —Quebec Nordiques, Feb. 10, 1980 - Jan. 13, 1983. (5 playoff games
      in 1981; 16 in 1982).
   245 Games —Pittsburgh Penguins, Jan. 7, 1989 - Oct. 26, 1991. (11 playoff games
      in 1989; 23 in 1991).

TEAM GOALS

Most Goals

MOST GOALS, ONE SEASON:
   446 —Edmonton Oilers, 1983-84. 80GP
   426 —Edmonton Oilers, 1985-86. 80GP
   424 —Edmonton Oilers, 1982-83. 80GP
   417 —Edmonton Oilers, 1981-82. 80GP
   401 —Edmonton Oilers, 1984-85. 80GP

MOST GOALS, ONE TEAM, ONE GAME:
   16 —Montreal Canadiens, Mar. 3, 1920, at Quebec. Defeated Que. Bulldogs
      16-3.

MOST GOALS, BOTH TEAMS, ONE GAME:
   21 —Montreal Canadiens, Toronto St. Patricks, at Montreal, Jan. 10, 1920.
      Montreal won 14-7.
      —Edmonton Oilers, Chicago Blackhawks, at Chicago, Dec. 11, 1985.
      Edmonton won 12-9.
   20 —Edmonton Oilers, Minnesota North Stars, at Edmonton, Jan. 4, 1984.
      Edmonton won 12-8.
      —Toronto Maple Leafs, Edmonton Oilers, at Toronto, Jan. 8, 1986.
      Toronto won 11-9.
   19 —Montreal Wanderers, Toronto Arenas, at Montreal, Dec. 19, 1917.
      Montreal won 10-9.
      —Montreal Canadiens, Quebec Bulldogs, at Quebec, Mar. 3, 1920.
      Montreal won 16-3.
      —Montreal Canadiens, Hamilton Tigers, at Montreal, Feb. 26, 1921.
      Montreal won 13-6.
      —Boston Bruins, NY Rangers, at Boston, Mar. 4, 1944. Boston won 10-9.
      —Boston Bruins, Detroit Red Wings, at Detroit, Mar. 16, 1944.
      Detroit won 10-9.
      —Vancouver Canucks, Minnesota North Stars, at Vancouver, Oct. 7, 1983.
      Vancouver won 10-9.

MOST GOALS, ONE TEAM, ONE PERIOD:
   9 —Buffalo Sabres, Mar. 19, 1981, at Buffalo, second period during 14-4 win
      over Toronto.
   8 —Detroit Red Wings, Jan. 23, 1944, at Detroit, third period during 15-0 win
      over NY Rangers.
      —Boston Bruins, Mar. 16, 1969, at Boston, second period during 11-3 win over
      Toronto.
      —NY Rangers, Nov. 21, 1971, at New York, third period during 12-1 win over
      California.
      —Philadelphia Flyers, Mar. 31, 1973, at Philadelphia, second period during 10-2
      win over NY Islanders.
      —Buffalo Sabres, Dec. 21, 1975, at Buffalo, third period during 14-2 win over
      Washington.
      —Minnesota North Stars, Nov. 11, 1981, at Minnesota, second period during
      15-2 win over Winnipeg.
      —Pittsburgh Penguins, Dec. 17, 1991, at Pittsburgh, second period during 10-2
      win over San Jose.

MOST GOALS, BOTH TEAMS, ONE PERIOD:
   12 —Buffalo Sabres, Toronto Maple Leafs, at Buffalo, March 19, 1981, second
      period. Buffalo scored 9 goals, Toronto 3. Buffalo won 14-4.
      —Edmonton Oilers, Chicago Blackhawks, at Chicago, Dec. 11, 1985,
      second period. Edmonton scored 6 goals, Chicago 6. Edmonton won 12-9.
   10 —NY Rangers, NY Americans, at NY Americans, March 16, 1939, third period.
      NY Rangers scored 7 goals, NY Americans 3. NY Rangers won 11-5.
      —Toronto Maple Leafs, Detroit Red Wings, at Detroit, March 17, 1946, third
      period. Toronto scored 6 goals, Detroit 4. Toronto won 11-7.
      —Vancouver Canucks, Buffalo Sabres, at Buffalo, Jan. 8, 1976, third period.
      Buffalo scored 6 goals, Vancouver 4. Buffalo won 8-5.
      —Buffalo Sabres, Montreal Canadiens, at Montreal, Oct. 26, 1982, first period.
      Montreal scored 5 goals, Buffalo 5. 7-7 tie.
      —Boston Bruins, Quebec Nordiques, at Quebec, Dec. 7, 1982, second period.
      Quebec scored 6 goals, Boston 4. Quebec won 10-5.
      —Calgary Flames, Vancouver Canucks, at Vancouver, Jan. 16, 1987, first
      period. Vancouver scored 6 goals, Calgary 4. Vancouver won 9-5.
      —Winnipeg Jets, Detroit Red Wings, at Detroit, Nov. 25, 1987, third period.
      Detroit scored 7 goals, Winnipeg 3. Detroit won 10-8.
      —Chicago Blackhawks, St. Louis Blues, at St. Louis, March 15, 1988, third
      period. Chicago scored 5 goals, St. Louis 5. 7-7 tie.

MOST CONSECUTIVE GOALS, ONE TEAM, ONE GAME:
   15 —Detroit Red Wings, Jan. 23, 1944, at Detroit. Defeated NY Rangers 15-0.

Fewest Goals

FEWEST GOALS, ONE SEASON:
   33 —Chicago Blackhawks, 1928-29. 44GP
   45 —Montreal Maroons, 1924-25. 30GP
   46 —Pittsburgh Pirates, 1928-29. 44GP

FEWEST GOALS, ONE SEASON (MINIMUM 70-GAME SCHEDULE):
   133 —Chicago Blackhawks, 1953-54. 70GP
   147 —Toronto Maple Leafs, 1954-55. 70GP
      —Boston Bruins, 1955-56. 70GP
   150 —NY Rangers, 1954-55. 70GP

TEAM POWER-PLAY GOALS

MOST POWER-PLAY GOALS, ONE SEASON:
   119 —Pittsburgh Penguins, 1988-89. 80GP
   113 —Detroit Red Wings, 1992-93. 84GP
   111 —NY Rangers, 1987-88. 80GP
   110 —Pittsburgh Penguins, 1987-88. 80GP
      —Winnipeg Jets, 1987-88, 80GP

TEAM SHORTHAND GOALS

MOST SHORTHAND GOALS, ONE SEASON:
   36 —Edmonton Oilers, 1983-84. 80GP
   28 —Edmonton Oilers, 1986-87. 80GP
   27 —Edmonton Oilers, 1985-86. 80GP
      —Edmonton Oilers, 1988-89. 80GP

TEAM GOALS-PER-GAME

HIGHEST GOALS-PER-GAME AVERAGE, ONE SEASON:
   5.58 —Edmonton Oilers, 1983-84. 446G in 80GP
   5.38 —Montreal Canadiens, 1919-20. 129G in 24GP
   5.33 —Edmonton Oilers, 1985-86. 426G in 80GP
   5.30 —Edmonton Oilers, 1982-83. 424G in 80GP
   5.23 —Montreal Canadiens, 1917-18. 115G in 22GP

LOWEST GOALS-PER-GAME AVERAGE, ONE SEASON:
   .75 —Chicago Blackhawks, 1928-29. 33G in 44GP
   1.05 —Pittsburgh Pirates, 1928-29. 46G in 44GP
   1.20 —NY Americans, 1928-29. 53G in 44GP

TEAM ASSISTS

MOST ASSISTS, ONE SEASON:
   737 —Edmonton Oilers, 1985-86. 80GP
   736 —Edmonton Oilers, 1983-84. 80GP
   706 —Edmonton Oilers, 1981-82. 80GP

FEWEST ASSISTS, ONE SEASON:
   45 —NY Rangers, 1926-27. 44GP

FEWEST ASSISTS, ONE SEASON (MINIMUM 70-GAME SCHEDULE):
   206 —Chicago Blackhawks, 1953-54. 70GP

TEAM TOTAL POINTS

MOST SCORING POINTS, ONE SEASON:
   1,182 —Edmonton Oilers, 1983-84. 80GP
   1,163 —Edmonton Oilers, 1985-86. 80GP
   1,123 —Edmonton Oilers, 1981-82. 80GP

MOST SCORING POINTS, ONE TEAM, ONE GAME:
   40 —Buffalo Sabres, Dec. 21, 1975, at Buffalo. Buffalo defeated Washington
      14-2, receiving 26A.
   39 —Minnesota North Stars, Nov. 11, 1981, at Minnesota. Minnesota defeated
      Winnipeg 15-2, receiving 24A.
   37 —Detroit Red Wings, Jan. 23, 1944, at Detroit. Detroit defeated NY Rangers
      15-0, receiving 22A.
      —Toronto Maple Leafs, Mar. 16, 1957, at Toronto. Toronto defeated NY
      Rangers 14-1, receiving 23A.
      —Buffalo Sabres, Feb. 25, 1978, at Cleveland. Buffalo defeated Cleveland 13-3,
      receiving 24A.
      —Calgary Flames, Feb. 10, 1993, at Calgary. Calgary defeated San Jose 13-1,
      receiving 24A.

MOST SCORING POINTS, BOTH TEAMS, ONE GAME:
   62 —Edmonton Oilers, Chicago Blackhawks, at Chicago, Dec. 11, 1985.
      Edmonton won 12-9. Edmonton had 24A, Chicago, 17.
   53 —Quebec Nordiques, Washington Capitals, at Washington, Feb. 22, 1981.
      Quebec won 11-7. Quebec had 22A, Washington, 13.
      —Edmonton Oilers, Minnesota North Stars, at Edmonton, Jan. 4, 1984.
      Edmonton won 12-8. Edmonton had 20A, Minnesota 13.
      —Minnesota North Stars, St. Louis Blues, at St. Louis, Jan. 27, 1984. Minnesota
      won 10-8. Minnesota had 19A, St. Louis 16.
      —Toronto Maple Leafs, Edmonton Oilers, at Toronto, Jan. 8, 1986. Toronto
      won 11-9. Toronto had 17A, Edmonton 16.
   52 —Mtl. Maroons, NY Americans, at New York, Feb. 18, 1936. 8-8 tie. New York
      had 20A, Montreal 16. (3A allowed for each goal.)
      —Vancouver Canucks, Minnesota North Stars, at Vancouver, Oct. 7, 1983.
      Vancouver won 10-9. Vancouver had 16A, Minnesota 17.

MOST SCORING POINTS, ONE TEAM, ONE PERIOD:

23 —NY Rangers, Nov. 21, 1971, at New York, third period during 12-1 win over California. NY Rangers scored 8ɢ and 15ᴀ.

—Buffalo Sabres, Dec. 21, 1975, at Buffalo, third period during 14-2 win over Washington. Buffalo scored 8ɢ and 15ᴀ.

—Buffalo Sabres, March 19, 1981, at Buffalo, second period, during 14-4 win over Toronto. Buffalo scored 9ɢ and 14ᴀ.

22 —Detroit Red Wings, Jan. 23, 1944, at Detroit, third period during 15-0 win over NY Rangers. Detroit scored 8ɢ and 14ᴀ.

—Boston Bruins, March 16, 1969, at Boston, second period during 11-3 win over Toronto Maple Leafs. Boston scored 8ɢ and 14ᴀ.

—Minnesota North Stars, Nov. 11, 1981, at Minnesota, second period during 15-2 win over Winnipeg. Minnesota scored 8ɢ and 14ᴀ.

—Pittsburgh Penguins, Dec. 17, 1991, at Pittsburgh, second period during 10-2 win over San Jose. Pittsburgh scored 8ɢ and 14ᴀ.

MOST SCORING POINTS, BOTH TEAMS, ONE PERIOD:

35 —Edmonton, Oilers, Chicago Blackhawks, at Chicago, Dec. 11, 1985, second period. Edmonton had 6ɢ, 12ᴀ; Chicago, 6ɢ, 11ᴀ. Edmonton won 12-9.

31 —Buffalo Sabres, Toronto Maple Leafs, at Buffalo, March 19, 1981, second period. Buffalo had 9ɢ, 14ᴀ; Toronto, 3ɢ, 5ᴀ. Buffalo won 14-4.

29 —Winnipeg Jets, Detroit Red Wings, at Detroit, Nov. 25, 1987, third period. Detroit had 7ɢ, 13ᴀ; Winnipeg had 3ɢ, 6ᴀ. Detroit won 10-8.

—Chicago Blackhawks, St. Louis Blues, at St. Louis, March 15, 1988, third period. St. Louis had 5ɢ, 10ᴀ; Chicago had 5ɢ, 9ᴀ. 7-7 tie.

FASTEST GOALS

FASTEST SIX GOALS, BOTH TEAMS

3 Minutes, 15 Seconds — Montreal Canadiens, Toronto Maple Leafs, at Montreal, Jan. 4, 1944, first period. Montreal scored 4ɢ, Toronto 2. Montreal won 6-3.

FASTEST FIVE GOALS, BOTH TEAMS:

1 Minute, 24 Seconds — Chicago Blackhawks, Toronto Maple Leafs, at Toronto, Oct. 15, 1983, second period. Scorers: Gaston Gingras, Toronto, 16:49; Denis Savard, Chicago, 17:12; Steve Larmer, Chicago, 17:27; Savard, 17:42; John Anderson, Toronto, 18:13. Toronto won 10-8.

1 Minute, 39 Seconds — Detroit Red Wings, Toronto Maple Leafs, at Toronto, Nov. 15, 1944, third period. Scorers: Ted Kennedy, Toronto, 10:36 and 10:55; Hal Jackson, Detroit, 11:48; Steve Wochy, Detroit, 12:02; Don Grosso, Detroit, 12:15. Detroit won 8-4.

FASTEST FIVE GOALS, ONE TEAM:

2 Minutes, 7 Seconds — Pittsburgh Penguins, at Pittsburgh, Nov. 22, 1972, third period. Scorers: Bryan Hextall, 12:00; Jean Pronovost, 12:18; Al McDonough, 13:40; Ken Schinkel, 13:49; Ron Schock, 14:07. Pittsburgh defeated St. Louis 10-4.

2 Minutes, 37 Seconds — NY Islanders, at New York, Jan. 26, 1982, first period. Scorers: Duane Sutter, 1:31; John Tonelli, 2:30; Bryan Trottier, 2:46; Bryan Trottier, 3:31; Duane Sutter, 4:08. NY Islanders defeated Pittsburgh 9-2.

2 Minutes, 55 Seconds — Boston Bruins, at Boston, Dec. 19, 1974. Scorers: Bobby Schmautz, 19:13 (first period); Ken Hodge, 0:18; Phil Esposito, 0:43; Don Marcotte, 0:58; John Bucyk, 2:08 (second period). Boston defeated NY Rangers 11-3.

FASTEST FOUR GOALS, BOTH TEAMS:

53 Seconds — Chicago Blackhawks, Toronto Maple Leafs, at Toronto, Oct. 15, 1983, second period. Scorers: Gaston Gingras, Toronto, 16:49; Denis Savard, Chicago, 17:12; Steve Larmer, Chicago, 17:27; and Savard at 17:42. Toronto won 10-8.

57 Seconds — Quebec Nordiques, Detroit Red Wings, at Quebec, Jan. 27, 1990, first period. Scorers: Paul Gillis, Quebec, 18:01; Claude Loiselle, Quebec, 18:12; Joe Sakic, Quebec, 18:27; and Jimmy Carson, Detroit, 18:58. Detroit won 8-6.

1 Minute, 1 Second — Colorado Rockies, NY Rangers, at New York, Jan. 15, 1980, first period. Scorers: Doug Sulliman, NY Rangers, 7:52; Ed Johnstone, NY Rangers, 7:57; Warren Miller, NY Rangers, 8:20; Rob Ramage, Colorado, 8:53. 6-6 tie.

— Chicago Blackhawks, Toronto Maple Leafs, at Toronto, Oct. 15, 1983, second period. Scorers: Denis Savard, Chicago, 17:12; Steve Larmer, Chicago, 17:27; Savard, 17:42; John Anderson, Toronto, 18:13. Toronto won 10-8.

FASTEST FOUR GOALS, ONE TEAM:

1 Minute, 20 Seconds — Boston Bruins, at Boston, Jan. 21, 1945, second period. Scorers: Bill Thoms, 6:34; Frank Mario, 7:08 and 7:27; and Ken Smith, 7:54. Boston defeated NY Rangers 14-3.

FASTEST THREE GOALS, BOTH TEAMS:

15 Seconds — Minnesota North Stars, NY Rangers, at Minnesota, Feb. 10, 1983, second period. Scorers: Mark Pavelich, NY Rangers, 19:18; Ron Greschner, NY Rangers, 19:27; Willi Plett, Minnesota, 19:33. Minnesota won 7-5.

18 Seconds — Montreal Canadiens, NY Rangers, at Montreal, Dec. 12, 1963, first period. Scorers: Dave Balon, Montreal, 0:58; Gilles Tremblay, Montreal, 1:04; Camille Henry, NY Rangers, 1:16. Montreal won 6-4.

— California Golden Seals, Buffalo Sabres, at California, Feb. 1, 1976, third period. Scorers: Jim Moxey, California, 19:38; Wayne Merrick, California, 19:45; Danny Gare, Buffalo, 19:56. Buffalo won 9-5.

FASTEST THREE GOALS, ONE TEAM:

20 Seconds — Boston Bruins, at Boston, Feb. 25, 1971, third period. Scorers: John Bucyk, 4:50; Ed Westfall, 5:02; Ted Green, 5:10. Boston defeated Vancouver 8-3.

21 Seconds — Chicago Blackhawks, at New York, Mar. 23, 1952, third period. Bill Mosienko scored all three goals, at 6:09, 6:20 and 6:30. Chicago defeated NY Rangers 7-6.

— Washington Capitals, at Washington, Nov. 23, 1990, first period. Scorers: Michal Pivonka, 16:18; Stephen Leach, 16:29 and 16:39. Washington defeated Pittsburgh 7-3.

FASTEST THREE GOALS FROM START OF PERIOD, BOTH TEAMS:

1 Minute, 5 Seconds — Hartford Whalers, Montreal Canadiens, at Montreal, March 11, 1989, second period. Scorers: Kevin Dineen, Hartford, 0:11; Guy Carbonneau, Montreal, 0:36; Petr Svoboda, Montreal, 1:05. Montreal won 5-3.

FASTEST THREE GOALS FROM START OF PERIOD, ONE TEAM:

53 Seconds — Calgary Flames, at Calgary, Feb. 10, 1993, third period. Scorers: Gary Suter, 0:17; Chris Lindbergh, 0:40; Ron Stern, 0:53. Calgary defeated San Jose 13-1.

FASTEST TWO GOALS, BOTH TEAMS:

2 Seconds — St. Louis Blues, Boston Bruins, at Boston, Dec. 19, 1987, third period. Scorers: Ken Linseman, Boston, at 19:50; Doug Gilmour, St. Louis, at 19:52. St. Louis won 7-5.

3 Seconds — Chicago Blackhawks, Minnesota North Stars, at Minnesota, Nov. 5, 1988, third period. Scorers: Steve Thomas, Chicago, at 6:03; Dave Gagner, Minnesota, at 6:06. 5-5 tie.

FASTEST TWO GOALS, ONE TEAM:

4 Seconds — Montreal Maroons, at Montreal, Jan. 3, 1931, third period. Nels Stewart scored both goals, at 8:24 and 8:28. Mtl. Maroons defeated Boston 5-3.

— Buffalo Sabres, at Buffalo, Oct. 17, 1974, third period. Scorers: Lee Fogolin, 14:55; Don Luce, 14:59. Buffalo defeated California 6-1.

— Toronto Maple Leafs, at Quebec, Dec. 29, 1988, third period. Scorers: Ed Olczyk, 5:24; Gary Leeman, 5:28. Toronto defeated Quebec 6-5.

— Calgary Flames, at Quebec, Oct. 17, 1989, third period. Scorers: Doug Gilmour, 19:45; Paul Ranheim, 19:49. Calgary and Quebec tied 8-8.

— Winnipeg Jets, at Winnipeg, Dec. 15, 1995, second period. Deron Quint scored both goals, at 7:51 and 7:55. Winnipeg defeated Edmonton 9-4.

FASTEST TWO GOALS FROM START OF GAME, ONE TEAM:

24 Seconds — Edmonton Oilers, Mar. 28, 1982, at Los Angeles. Scorers: Mark Messier, 0:14; Dave Lumley, 0:24. Edmonton defeated Los Angeles 6-2.

29 Seconds — Pittsburgh Penguins, Dec. 6, 1980, at Pittsburgh. Scorers: George Ferguson, 0:17; Greg Malone, 0:29. Pittsburgh defeated Chicago 6-4.

32 Seconds — Calgary Flames, Mar. 11, 1987, at Hartford. Scorers: Doug Risebrough 0:09; Colin Patterson, 0:32. Calgary defeated Hartford 6-1.

FASTEST TWO GOALS FROM START OF PERIOD, BOTH TEAMS:

14 Seconds — NY Rangers, Quebec Nordiques, at Quebec, Nov. 5, 1983, third period. Scorers: Andre Savard, Quebec, 0:08; Pierre Larouche, NY Rangers, 0:14. 4-4 tie.

26 Seconds — Buffalo Sabres, St. Louis Blues, at Buffalo, Jan. 3, 1993, third period. Scorers: Alexander Mogilny, Buffalo, 0:08; Phillippe Bozon, St. Louis, 0:26. Buffalo won 6-5.

28 Seconds — Boston Bruins, Montreal Canadiens, at Montreal, Oct. 11, 1989, third period. Scorers: Jim Wiemer, Boston 0:10; Tom Chorske, Montreal 0:28. Montreal won 4-2.

FASTEST TWO GOALS FROM START OF PERIOD, ONE TEAM:

21 Seconds — Chicago Blackhawks, Nov. 5, 1983, at Minnesota, second period. Scorers: Ken Yaremchuk, 0:12; Darryl Sutter, 0:21. Minnesota defeated Chicago 10-5.

30 Seconds — Washington Capitals, Jan. 27, 1980, at Washington, second period. Scorers: Mike Gartner, 0:08; Bengt Gustafsson, 0:30. Washington defeated NY Islanders 7-1.

31 Seconds —Buffalo Sabres, Jan. 10, 1974, at Buffalo, third period. Scorers: Rene Robert, 0:21; Rick Martin, 0:31. Buffalo defeated NY Rangers 7-2.

— NY Islanders, Feb. 22, 1986, at New York, third period. Scorers: Roger Kortko, 0:10; Bob Bourne, 0:31. NY Islanders defeated Detroit 5-2.

Doug Gilmour helped the Calgary Flames earn a hard-fought 8-8 tie with Quebec on October 18, 1989 when he and Paul Ranheim combined to score two goals in only four seconds late in the third period.

50, 40, 30, 20-GOAL SCORERS

MOST 50-OR-MORE-GOAL SCORERS, ONE SEASON:

3 —**Edmonton Oilers,** 1983-84. Wayne Gretzky, 87; Glenn Anderson, 54; Jari Kurri, 52. 80GP
—**Edmonton Oilers,** 1985-86. Jari Kurri, 68; Glenn Anderson, 54; Wayne Gretzky, 52. 80GP
2 —Boston Bruins, 1970-71. Phil Esposito, 76; John Bucyk, 51. 78GP
—Boston Bruins, 1973-74. Phil Esposito, 68; Ken Hodge, 50. 78GP
—Philadelphia Flyers, 1975-76. Reggie Leach, 61; Bill Barber, 50. 80GP
—Pittsburgh Penguins, 1975-76. Pierre Larouche, 53; Jean Pronovost, 52. 80GP
—Montreal Canadiens, 1976-77. Steve Shutt, 60; Guy Lafleur, 56. 80GP
—Los Angeles Kings, 1979-80. Charlie Simmer, 56; Marcel Dionne, 53. 80GP
—Montreal Canadiens, 1979-80. Pierre Larouche, 50; Guy Lafleur, 50. 80GP
—Los Angeles Kings, 1980-81. Marcel Dionne, 58; Charlie Simmer, 56. 80GP
—Edmonton Oilers, 1981-82. Wayne Gretzky, 92; Mark Messier, 50. 80GP
—NY Islanders, 1981-82. Mike Bossy, 64; Bryan Trottier, 50. 80GP
—Edmonton Oilers, 1984-85. Wayne Gretzky, 73; Jari Kurri, 71. 80GP
—Washington Capitals, 1984-85. Bob Carpenter, 53; Mike Gartner, 50. 80GP
—Edmonton Oilers, 1986-87. Wayne Gretzky, 62; Jari Kurri, 54. 80GP
—Calgary Flames, 1987-88. Joe Nieuwendyk, 51; Hakan Loob, 50. 80GP
—Los Angeles Kings, 1987-88. Jimmy Carson, 55; Luc Robitaille, 53. 80GP
—Los Angeles Kings, 1988-89. Bernie Nicholls, 70; Wayne Gretzky, 54. 80GP
—Calgary Flames, 1988-89. Joe Nieuwendyk, 51; Joe Mullen, 51. 80GP
—Buffalo Sabres, 1992-93. Alexander Mogilny, 76; Pat LaFontaine, 53. 84GP
—Pittsburgh Penguins, 1992-93. Mario Lemieux, 69; Kevin Stevens, 55. 84GP
—St. Louis Blues, 1992-93. Brett Hull, 54; Brendan Shanahan, 51. 84GP
—St. Louis Blues, 1993-94. Brett Hull, 57; Brendan Shanahan, 52. 84GP
—Detroit Red Wings, 1993-94. Sergei Fedorov, 56; Ray Sheppard, 52. 84GP
—Pittsburgh Penguins, 1995-96. Mario Lemieux, 69; Jaromir Jagr, 62. 82GP

MOST 40-OR-MORE-GOAL SCORERS, ONE SEASON:

4 —**Edmonton Oilers,** 1982-83. Wayne Gretzky, 71; Glenn Anderson, 48; Mark Messier, 48; Jari Kurri, 45. 80GP
—**Edmonton Oilers,** 1983-84. Wayne Gretzky, 87; Glenn Anderson, 54; Jari Kurri, 52; Paul Coffey, 40. 80GP
—**Edmonton Oilers,** 1984-85. Wayne Gretzky, 73; Jari Kurri, 71; Mike Krushelnyski, 43; Glenn Anderson, 42. 80GP
—**Edmonton Oilers,** 1985-86. Jari Kurri, 68; Glenn Anderson, 54; Wayne Gretzky, 52; Paul Coffey, 48. 80GP
—**Calgary Flames,** 1987-88. Joe Nieuwendyk, 51; Hakan Loob, 50; Mike Bullard, 48; Joe Mullen, 40. 80GP
3 —Boston Bruins, 1970-71. Phil Esposito, 76; John Bucyk, 51; Ken Hodge, 43. 78GP
—NY Rangers, 1971-72. Vic Hadfield, 50; Jean Ratelle, 46; Rod Gilbert, 43. 78GP
—Buffalo Sabres, 1975-76. Danny Gare, 50; Rick Martin, 49; Gilbert Perreault, 44. 80GP
—Montreal Canadiens, 1979-80. Guy Lafleur, 50; Pierre Larouche, 50; Steve Shutt, 47. 80GP
—Buffalo Sabres, 1979-80. Danny Gare, 56; Rick Martin, 45; Gilbert Perreault, 40. 80GP
—Los Angeles Kings, 1980-81. Marcel Dionne, 58; Charlie Simmer, 56; Dave Taylor, 47. 80GP
—Los Angeles Kings, 1984-85. Marcel Dionne, 46; Bernie Nicholls, 46; Dave Taylor, 41. 80GP
—NY Islanders, 1984-85. Mike Bossy, 58; Brent Sutter, 42; John Tonelli, 42. 80GP
—Chicago Blackhawks, 1985-86. Denis Savard, 47; Troy Murray, 45; Al Secord, 40. 80GP
—Chicago Blackhawks, 1987-88. Denis Savard, 44; Rick Vaive, 43; Steve Larmer, 41. 80GP
—Edmonton Oilers, 1987-88. Craig Simpson, 43; Jari Kurri, 43; Wayne Gretzky, 40. 80GP
—Los Angeles Kings, 1988-89. Bernie Nicholls, 70; Wayne Gretzky, 54; Luc Robitaille, 46. 80GP
—Los Angeles Kings, 1990-91. Luc Robitaille, 45; Tomas Sandstrom, 45; Wayne Gretzky 41. 80GP
—Pittsburgh Penguins, 1991-92. Kevin Stevens, 54; Mario Lemieux, 44; Joe Mullen, 42. 80GP
—Pittsburgh Penguins, 1992-93. Mario Lemieux, 69; Kevin Stevens, 55; Rick Tocchet, 48. 84GP
—Calgary Flames, 1993-94. Gary Roberts, 41; Robert Reichel, 40; Theoren Fleury, 40. 84GP
—Pittsburgh Penguins, 1995-96. Mario Lemieux, 69; Jaromir Jagr, 62; Petr Nedved, 45. 82GP

MOST 30-OR-MORE GOAL SCORERS, ONE SEASON:

6 —**Buffalo Sabres,** 1974-75. Rick Martin, 52; Rene Robert, 40; Gilbert Perreault, 39; Don Luce, 33; Rick Dudley, Danny Gare, 31 each. 80GP
—**NY Islanders,** 1977-78, Mike Bossy, 53; Bryan Trottier, 46; Clark Gillies, 35; Denis Potvin, Bob Nystrom, Bob Bourne, 30 each. 80GP
—**Winnipeg Jets,** 1984-85. Dale Hawerchuk, 53; Paul MacLean, 41; Laurie Boschman, 32; Brian Mullen, 32; Doug Smail, 31; Thomas Steen, 30. 80GP
5 —Chicago Blackhawks, 1968-69. 76GP
—Boston Bruins, 1970-71. 78GP
—Montreal Canadiens, 1971-72. 78GP
—Philadelphia Flyers, 1972-73. 78GP
—Boston Bruins, 1973-74. 78GP
—Montreal Canadiens, 1974-75. 80GP
—Montreal Canadiens, 1975-76. 80GP
—Pittsburgh Penguins, 1975-76. 80GP
—NY Islanders, 1978-79. 80GP
—Detroit Red Wings, 1979-80. 80GP
—Philadelphia Flyers, 1979-80. 80GP
—NY Islanders, 1980-81. 80GP
—St. Louis Blues, 1980-81. 80GP
—Chicago Blackhawks, 1981-82. 80GP
—Edmonton Oilers, 1981-82. 80GP
—Montreal Canadiens, 1981-82. 80GP
—Quebec Nordiques, 1981-82. 80GP
—Washington Capitals, 1981-82. 80GP
—Edmonton Oilers, 1982-83. 80GP
—Edmonton Oilers, 1983-84. 80GP
—Edmonton Oilers, 1984-85. 80GP
—Los Angeles Kings, 1984-85. 80GP
—Edmonton Oilers, 1985-86. 80GP
—Edmonton Oilers, 1986-87. 80GP
—Edmonton Oilers, 1987-88. 80GP
—Edmonton Oilers, 1988-89. 80GP
—Detroit Red Wings, 1991-92. 80GP
—NY Rangers, 1991-92. 80GP
—Pittsburgh Penguins, 1991-92. 80GP
—Detroit Red Wings, 1992-93. 84GP
—Pittsburgh Penguins, 1992-93. 84GP

MOST 20-OR-MORE GOAL SCORERS, ONE SEASON:

11 —**Boston Bruins,** 1977-78; Peter McNab, 41; Terry O'Reilly, 29; Bobby Schmautz, Stan Jonathan, 27 each; Jean Ratelle, Rick Middleton, 25 each; Wayne Cashman, 24; Gregg Sheppard, 23; Brad Park, 22; Don Marcotte, Bob Miller, 20 each. 80GP
10 —Boston Bruins, 1970-71. 78GP
—Montreal Canadiens, 1974-75. 80GP
—St. Louis Blues, 1980-81. 80GP

An important cog in the explosive Edmonton Oiler machine, of the 1980s, Glenn Anderson was one of three Edmonton sharpshooters to connect for 50 goals in the 1982-83 season.

100-POINT SCORERS

MOST 100 OR-MORE-POINT SCORERS, ONE SEASON:
4 —**Boston Bruins,** 1970-71, Phil Esposito, 76G-76A-152PTS; Bobby Orr, 37G-102A-139PTS; John Bucyk, 51G-65A-116PTS; Ken Hodge, 43G-62A-105PTS. 78GP
—**Edmonton Oilers,** 1982-83, Wayne Gretzky, 71G-125A-196PTS; Mark Messier, 48G-58A-106PTS; Glenn Anderson, 48G-56A-104PTS; Jari Kurri, 45G-59A-104PTS. 80GP
—**Edmonton Oilers,** 1983-84, Wayne Gretzky, 87G-118A-205PTS; Paul Coffey, 40G-86A-126PTS; Jari Kurri, 52G-61A-113PTS; Mark Messier, 37G-64A-101PTS. 80GP
—**Edmonton Oilers,**1985-86, Wayne Gretzky, 52G-163A-215PTS; Paul Coffey, 48G-90A-138PTS; Jari Kurri, 68G-63A-131PTS; Glenn Anderson, 54G-48A-102PTS. 80GP
—**Pittsburgh Penguins,**1992-93, Mario Lemieux, 69G-91A-160PTS; Kevin Stevens, 55G-56A-111PTS; Rick Tocchet, 48G-61A-109PTS; Ron Francis, 24G-76A-100PTS. 84GP
3 —Boston Bruins, 1973-74, Phil Esposito, 68G-77A-145PTS; Bobby Orr, 32G-90A-122PTS; Ken Hodge, 50G-55A-105PTS. 78GP
—NY Islanders, 1978-79, Bryan Trottier, 47G-87A-134PTS; Mike Bossy, 69G-57A-126PTS; Denis Potvin, 31G-70A-101PTS. 80GP
—Los Angeles Kings, 1980-81, Marcel Dionne, 58G-77A-135PTS; Dave Taylor, 47 G-65A-112PTS; Charlie Simmer, 56G-49A-105PTS. 80GP
—Edmonton Oilers, 1984-85, Wayne Gretzky, 73G-135A-208PTS; Jari Kurri, 71G-64A-135PTS; Paul Coffey, 37G-84A-121PTS. 80GP
—NY Islanders, 1984-85, Mike Bossy, 58G-59A-117PTS; Brent Sutter, 42G-60A-102PTS; John Tonelli, 42G-58A-100PTS. 80GP
—Edmonton Oilers, 1986-87, Wayne Gretzky, 62G-121A-183PTS; Jari Kurri, 54G-54A-108PTS; Mark Messier, 37G-70A-107PTS. 80GP
—Pittsburgh Penguins, 1988-89, Mario Lemieux, 85G-114A-199PTS; Rob Brown, 49G-66A-115PTS; Paul Coffey, 30G-83A-113PTS. 80GP
—Pittsburgh Penguins, 1995-96, Mario Lemieux, 69G-92A-161PTS; Jaromir Jagr, 62G-87A-149PTS; Ron Francis, 27G-92A-119PTS. 82GP

SHOTS ON GOAL

MOST SHOTS, BOTH TEAMS, ONE GAME:
141 —NY Americans, Pittsburgh Pirates, Dec. 26, 1925, at New York. NY Americans, who won game 3-1, had 73 shots; Pit. Pirates, 68 shots.

MOST SHOTS, ONE TEAM, ONE GAME:
83 —**Boston Bruins,** March 4, 1941, at Boston. Boston defeated Chicago 3-2.
73 —NY Americans, Dec. 26, 1925, at New York. NY Americans defeated Pit. Pirates 3-1.
—Boston Bruins, March 21, 1991, at Boston. Boston tied Quebec 3-3.
72 —Boston Bruins, Dec. 10, 1970, at Boston. Boston defeated Buffalo 8-2.

MOST SHOTS, ONE TEAM, ONE PERIOD:
33 —**Boston Bruins,** March 4, 1941, at Boston, second period. Boston defeated Chicago 3-2.

TEAM GOALS-AGAINST

Fewest Goals-Against

FEWEST GOALS AGAINST, ONE SEASON:
42 —**Ottawa Senators,** 1925-26. 36GP
43 —Montreal Canadiens, 1928-29. 44GP
48 —Montreal Canadiens, 1923-24. 24GP
—Montreal Canadiens, 1927-28. 44GP

FEWEST GOALS AGAINST, ONE SEASON (MINIMUM 70-GAME SCHEDULE):
131 —**Toronto Maple Leafs,** 1953-54. 70GP
—**Montreal Canadiens,** 1955-56. 70GP
132 —Detroit Red Wings, 1953-54. 70GP
133 —Detroit Red Wings, 1951-52. 70GP
—Detroit Red Wings, 1952-53. 70GP

LOWEST GOALS-AGAINST-PER-GAME AVERAGE, ONE SEASON:
.98 —**Montreal Canadiens,** 1928-29. 43GA in 44GP.
1.09 —Montreal Canadiens, 1927-28. 48GA in 44GP.
1.17 —Ottawa Senators, 1925-26. 42GA in 36GP.

Most Goals-Against

MOST GOALS AGAINST, ONE SEASON:
446 —**Washington Capitals,** 1974-75. 80GP
415 —Detroit Red Wings, 1985-86. 80GP
414 —San Jose Sharks, 1992-93. 84GP
407 —Quebec Nordiques, 1989-90. 80GP
403 —Hartford Whalers, 1982-83. 80GP

HIGHEST GOALS-AGAINST-PER-GAME AVERAGE, ONE SEASON:
7.38 —**Quebec Bulldogs,** 1919-20, 177GA in 24GP.
6.20 —NY Rangers, 1943-44, 310GA in 50GP.
5.58 —Washington Capitals, 1974-75, 446GA in 80GP.

MOST POWER-PLAY GOALS AGAINST, ONE SEASON:
122 —**Chicago Blackhawks,** 1988-89. 80GP
120 —Pittsburgh Penguins, 1987-88. 80GP
115 —New Jersey Devils, 1988-89. 80GP
—Ottawa Senators, 1992-93. 84GP
114 —Los Angeles Kings, 1992-93. 84GP
113 —San Jose Sharks, 1992-93. 84GP

MOST SHORTHAND GOALS AGAINST, ONE SEASON:
22 —**Pittsburgh Penguins,** 1984-85. 80GP
—**Minnesota North Stars,** 1991-92. 80GP
—**Colorado Avalanche,** 1995-96. 82GP
21 —Calgary Flames, 1984-85. 80GP
—Pittsburgh Penguins, 1989-90. 80GP

SHUTOUTS

MOST SHUTOUTS, ONE SEASON:
22 —**Montreal Canadiens,** 1928-29. All by George Hainsworth. 44GP
16 —NY Americans, 1928-29. Roy Worters had 13; Flat Walsh 3. 44GP
15 —Ottawa Senators, 1925-26. All by Alex Connell. 36GP
—Ottawa Senators, 1927-28. All by Alex Connell. 44GP
—Boston Bruins, 1927-28. All by Hal Winkler. 44GP
—Chicago Blackhawks, 1969-70. All by Tony Esposito. 76GP

MOST CONSECUTIVE SHUTOUTS, ONE SEASON:
6 —**Ottawa Senators,** Jan. 31 - Feb. 18, 1928.

MOST CONSECUTIVE SHUTOUTS TO START SEASON:
5 —**Toronto Maple Leafs,** Nov. 13 - 22, 1930.

MOST GAMES SHUTOUT, ONE SEASON:
20 —**Chicago Blackhawks,** 1928-29. 44GP

MOST CONSECUTIVE GAMES SHUTOUT:
8 —**Chicago Blackhawks,** Feb. 7 - 28, 1929.

MOST CONSECUTIVE GAMES SHUTOUT TO START SEASON:
3 —**Montreal Maroons,** Nov. 11 - 18, 1930.

TEAM PENALTIES

MOST PENALTY MINUTES, ONE SEASON:
2,713—**Buffalo Sabres,** 1991-92. 80GP
2,670 —Pittsburgh Penguins, 1988-89. 80GP
2,663 —Chicago Blackhawks, 1991-92. 80GP
2,643 —Calgary Flames, 1991-92. 80GP
2,621 —Philadelphia Flyers, 1980-81. 80GP

MOST PENALTIES, BOTH TEAMS, ONE GAME:
85 Penalties —**Edmonton Oilers (44), Los Angeles Kings (41)** at Los Angeles, Feb. 28, 1990. Edmonton received 26 minors, 7 majors, 6 10-minute misconducts, 4 game misconducts and 1 match penalty; Los Angeles received 26 minors, 9 majors, 3 10-minute misconducts and 3 game misconducts.

MOST PENALTY MINUTES, BOTH TEAMS, ONE GAME:
406 Minutes — **Minnesota North Stars, Boston Bruins** at Boston, Feb. 26, 1981. Minnesota received 18 minors, 13 majors, 4 10-minute misconducts and 7 game misconducts; a total of 211PIM. Boston received 20 minors, 13 majors, 3 10-minute misconducts and six game misconducts; a total of 195PIM.

MOST PENALTIES, ONE TEAM, ONE GAME:
44 —**Edmonton Oilers,** Feb. 28, 1990, at Los Angeles. Edmonton received 26 minors, 7 majors, 6 10-minute misconducts, 4 game misconducts and 1 match penalty.
42 —Minnesota North Stars, Feb. 26, 1981, at Boston. Minnesota received 18 minors, 13 majors, 4 10-minute misconducts and 7 game misconducts.
—Boston Bruins, Feb. 26, 1981, at Boston vs. Minnesota. Boston received 20 minors, 13 majors, 3 10-minute misconducts and 7 game misconducts.

MOST PENALTY MINUTES, ONE TEAM, ONE GAME:
211 —**Minnesota North Stars,** Feb. 26, 1981, at Boston. Minnesota received 18 minors, 13 majors, 4 10-minute misconducts and 7 game misconducts.

MOST PENALTIES, BOTH TEAMS, ONE PERIOD:
67 —**Minnesota North Stars, Boston Bruins,** at Boston, Feb. 26, 1981, first period. Minnesota received 15 minors, 8 majors, 4 10-minute misconducts and 7 game misconducts, a total of 34 penalties. Boston had 16 minors, 8 majors, 3 10-minute misconducts and 6 game misconducts, a total of 33 penalties.

MOST PENALTY MINUTES, BOTH TEAMS, ONE PERIOD:
372 —**Los Angeles Kings, Philadelphia Flyers** at Philadelphia, March 11, 1979, first period. Philadelphia received 4 minors, 8 majors, 6 10-minute misconducts and 8 game misconducts for 188 minutes. Los Angeles received 2 minors, 8 majors, 6 10-minute misconducts and 8 game misconducts for 184 minutes.

MOST PENALTIES, ONE TEAM, ONE PERIOD:
34 —**Minnesota North Stars,** Feb. 26, 1981, at Boston, first period. 15 minors, 8 majors, 4 10-minute misconducts, 7 game misconducts.

MOST PENALTY MINUTES, ONE TEAM, ONE PERIOD:
188 —**Philadelphia Flyers,** March 11, 1979, at Philadelphia vs. Los Angeles, first period. Flyers received 4 minors, 8 majors, 6 10-minute misconducts and 8 game misconducts.

NHL Individual Scoring Records – History

Six individual scoring records stand as benchmarks in the history of the game: most goals, single-season and career; most assists, single-season and career; and most points, single-season and career. The evolution of these six records is traced here, beginning with 1917-18, the NHL's first season.

MOST GOALS, ONE SEASON

44 – Joe Malone, Montreal, 1917-18.
Scored goal #44 against Toronto's Harry Holmes on March 2, 1918 and finished season with 44 goals.

50 – Maurice Richard, Montreal, 1944-45.
Scored goal #45 against Toronto's Frank McCool on February 25, 1945 and finished the season with 50 goals.

50 – Bernie Geoffrion, Montreal, 1960-61.
Scored goal #50 against Toronto's Cesare Maniago on March 16, 1961 and finished the season with 50 goals.

50 – Bobby Hull, Chicago, 1961-62.
Scored goal #50 against NY Rangers' Gump Worsley on March 25, 1962 and finished the season with 50 goals.

54 – Bobby Hull, Chicago, 1965-66.
Scored goal #51 against NY Rangers' Cesare Maniago on March 12, 1966 and finished the season with 54 goals.

58 – Bobby Hull, Chicago, 1968-69.
Scored goal #55 against Boston's Gerry Cheevers on March 20, 1969 and finished the season with 58 goals.

76 – Phil Esposito, Boston, 1970-71.
Scored goal #59 against Los Angeles' Denis DeJordy on March 11, 1971 and finished the season with 76 goals.

92 – Wayne Gretzky, Edmonton, 1981-82.
Scored goal #77 against Buffalo's Don Edwards on February 24, 1982 and finished the season with 92 goals.

MOST ASSISTS, ONE SEASON

9 – Newsy Lalonde, Montreal, 1918-19.
14 – Leo Reise, Sr., Hamilton, 1921-22.
14 – Punch Broadbent, Ottawa, 1921-22.
15 – Cy Denneny, Ottawa, 1924-25.
18 – Dick Irvin, Chicago, 1926-27.
18 – Howie Morenz, Montreal, 1927-28.
36 – Frank Boucher, NY Rangers, 1929-30.
37 – Joe Primeau, Toronto, 1931-32.
45 – Bill Cowley, Boston, 1940-41.
45 – Bill Cowley, Boston, 1942-43.
49 – Clint Smith, Chicago, 1943-44.
54 – Elmer Lach, Montreal, 1944-45.
55 – Ted Lindsay, Detroit, 1949-50.
56 – Bert Olmstead, Montreal, 1955-56.
58 – Jean Beliveau, Montreal, 1960-61.
58 – Andy Bathgate, NY Rangers/Toronto, 1963-64.
59 – Stan Mikita, Chicago, 1964-65.
62 – Stan Mikita, Chicago, 1966-67.
77 – Phil Esposito, Boston, 1968-69.
87 – Bobby Orr, Boston, 1969-70.
102 – Bobby Orr, Boston, 1970-71.
109 – Wayne Gretzky, Edmonton, 1980-81.
120 – Wayne Gretzky, Edmonton, 1981-82.
125 – Wayne Gretzky, Edmonton, 1982-83.
135 – Wayne Gretzky, Edmonton, 1984-85.
163 – Wayne Gretzky, Edmonton, 1985-86.

MOST POINTS, ONE SEASON

44 – Joe Malone, Montreal, 1917-18.
48 – Joe Malone, Montreal, 1919-20.
51 – Howie Morenz, Montreal, 1927-28.
73 – Cooney Weiland, Boston, 1929-30.
73 – Doug Bentley, Chicago, 1942-43.
82 – Herb Cain, Boston, 1943-44.
86 – Gordie Howe, Detroit, 1950-51.
95 – Gordie Howe, Detroit, 1952-53.
96 – Dickie Moore, Montreal, 1958-59.
97 – Bobby Hull, Chicago, 1965-66.
97 – Stan Mikita, Chicago, 1966-67.
126 – Phil Esposito, Boston, 1968-69.
152 – Phil Esposito, Boston, 1970-71.
164 – Wayne Gretzky, Edmonton, 1980-81.
212 – Wayne Gretzky, Edmonton, 1981-82.
215 – Wayne Gretzky, Edmonton, 1985-86.

"Phantom" Joe Malone, shown here front row center with the Quebec Bulldogs of the National Hockey Association, led the NHL with 44 goals in 1917-18, the League's first season. Malone was a Stanley Cup winner in 1912 and 1913 with the Bulldogs. The squat trophy and the club's squat mascot are both visible in this photograph.

MOST REGULAR-SEASON GOALS, CAREER

44 – Joe Malone, 1917-18, Montreal.
Malone led the NHL in goals in the league's first season and finished with 44 goals in 22 games in 1917-18.

54 – Cy Denneny, 1918-19, Ottawa.
Denneny passed Malone during the 1918-19 season, finishing the year with a two-year total of 54 goals. He held the career goal-scoring mark until 1919-20.

146 – Joe Malone, Montreal, Quebec Bulldogs, Hamilton.
Malone passed Denneny in 1919-20 and remained the NHL's career goal-scoring leader until his retirement. He finished with a career total of 146 goals.

246 – Cy Denneny, Ottawa, Boston.
Denneny passed Malone with goal #147 in 1922-23 and remained the NHL's career goal-scoring leader until his retirement. He finished with a career total of 246 goals.

270 – Howie Morenz, Montreal, NY Rangers, Chicago.
Morenz passed Denneny with goal #247 in 1933-34 and finished his career with 270 goals.

324 – Nels Stewart, Montreal Maroons, Boston, NY Americans.
Stewart passed Morenz with goal #271 in 1936-37 and remained the NHL's career goal-scoring leader until his retirement. He finished his career with 324 goals.

544 – Maurice Richard, Montreal.
Richard passed Nels Stewart with goal #325 on Nov. 8, 1952 and remained the NHL's career goal-scoring leader until his retirement. He finished his career with 544 goals.

801 – Gordie Howe, Detroit, Hartford.
Howe passed Richard with goal #545 on Nov. 10, 1963 and remained the NHL's career goal-scoring leader until his retirement. He finished his career with 801 goals.

862 – Wayne Gretzky, Edmonton, Los Angeles, St. Louis, NY Rangers.
Gretzky passed Gordie Howe with goal #802 on March 23, 1994. He is the current career goal-scoring leader with 862.

Frank Boucher retired with a League-leading assist total of 252 in 1938. Boucher's record and his retirement remained intact for four seasons. He returned to the ice in 1943-44 and added an additional ten assists, but Bill Cowley equalled and surpassed Boucher's career mark that same season.

MOST REGULAR-SEASON POINTS, CAREER (minimum 100 points)

100 – Joe Malone, Montreal, Quebec Bulldogs, Hamilton.
In 1920-21, Malone became the first player in NHL history to record 100 points.

200 – Cy Denneny, Ottawa.
In 1923-24, Denneny became the first player in NHL history to record 200 points.

300 – Cy Denneny, Ottawa.
In 1926-27, Denneny became the first player in NHL history to record 300 points.

315 – Cy Denneny, Ottawa, Boston.
Denneny retired as the NHL's career point-scoring leader in 1929 with 315 points.

467 – Howie Morenz, Montreal, Chicago, NY Rangers.
Morenz passed Cy Denneny with point #316 in 1931-32. At the time his career ended in 1937, he was the NHL's career point-scoring leader with 467 points.

515 – Nels Stewart, Montreal Maroons, Boston, NY Americans.
Stewart passed Morenz with point #468 in 1938-39. He retired as the NHL's career point-scoring leader in 1940 with 515 points.

528 – Syd Howe, Ottawa, Philadelphia Quakers, Toronto, St. Louis Eagles, Detroit.
Howe passed Nels Stewart with point #516 on March 8, 1945. He retired as the NHL's career point-scoring leader in 1946 with 528 points.

548 – Bill Cowley, St. Louis Eagles, Boston.
Cowley passed Syd Howe with point #529 on Feb. 12, 1947. He retired as the NHL's career point-scoring leader in 1947 with 548 points.

610 – Elmer Lach, Montreal.
Lach passed Bill Cowley with point #549 on Feb. 23, 1952. He remained the NHL's career point-scoring leader until he was overtaken by Maurice Richard in 1953-54. He finished his career with 623 points.

946 – Maurice Richard, Montreal.
Richard passed teammate Elmer Lach with point #611 on Dec. 12, 1953. He remained the NHL's career point-scoring leader until he was overtaken by Gordie Howe in 1959-60. He finished his career with 965 points.

1,850 – Gordie Howe, Detroit, Hartford.
Howe passed Richard with point #947 on Jan. 16, 1960. He retired as the NHL's career point-scoring leader in 1980 with 1,850 points.

2,705 – Wayne Gretzky, Edmonton, Los Angeles, St. Louis, NY Rangers.
Gretzky passed Howe with point #1,851 on Oct. 15, 1989. He is the current career point-scoring leader with 2,705.

MOST REGULAR-SEASON ASSISTS, CAREER (minimum 100 assists)

Note: Assists were not tabulated in 1917-18, the NHL's first season. Newsy Lalonde of the Canadiens was the NHL's first career (and single-season) assist leader, recording nine in 1918-19

100 – Frank Boucher, Ottawa, NY Rangers.
In 1930-31, Boucher became the first NHL player to reach the 100-assist milestone.

262 – Frank Boucher, Ottawa, NY Rangers.
Boucher retired as the NHL's career assist leader in 1938 with 252. He returned to the NHL in 1943-44 and remained the NHL's career assist leader until he was overtaken by Bill Cowley in 1943-44. He finished his career with 262 assists.

353 – Bill Cowley, St. Louis Eagles, Boston.
Cowley passed Boucher with assist #263 in 1943-44. He retired as the NHL's career assist leader in 1947 with 353.

408 – Elmer Lach, Montreal.
Lach passed Cowley with assist #354 in 1951-52. He retired as the NHL's career assist leader in 1953 with 408.

1,049 – Gordie Howe, Detroit, Hartford.
Howe passed Lach with assist #409 in 1957-58. He retired as the NHL's career assist leader in 1980 with 1,049.

1,843 – Wayne Gretzky, Edmonton, Los Angeles, St. Louis, NY Rangers.
Gretzky passed Howe with assist #1,050 in 1988-89. He is the current career assist leader with 1,843.

Individual Records
Regular Season

SEASONS

MOST SEASONS:
26 —Gordie Howe, Detroit, 1946-47 – 1970-71; Hartford, 1979-80.
24 —Alex Delvecchio, Detroit, 1950-51 – 1973-74.
  —Tim Horton, Toronto, NY Rangers, Pittsburgh, Buffalo, 1949-50, 1951-52 – 1973-74.
23 —John Bucyk, Detroit, Boston, 1955-56 – 1977-78.
22 —Dean Prentice, NY Rangers, Boston, Detroit, Pittsburgh, Minnesota, 1952-53 – 1973-74.
  —Doug Mohns, Boston, Chicago, Minnesota, Atlanta, Washington, 1953-54 – 1974-75.
  —Stan Mikita, Chicago, 1958-59 – 1979-80.

GAMES

MOST GAMES:
1,767 —Gordie Howe, Detroit, 1946-47 – 1970-71; Hartford, 1979-80.
1,549 —Alex Delvecchio, Detroit, 1950-51 – 1973-74.
1,540 —John Bucyk, Detroit, Boston, 1955-56 – 1977-78.

MOST GAMES, INCLUDING PLAYOFFS:
1,924 —Gordie Howe, Detroit, Hartford, 1,767 regular-season and 157 playoff games.
1,670 —Alex Delvecchio, Detroit, 1,549 regular-season and 121 playoff games.
1,664 —John Bucyk, Detroit, Boston, 1,540 regular-season and 124 playoff games.

MOST CONSECUTIVE GAMES:
964 —Doug Jarvis, Montreal, Washington, Hartford, from Oct. 8, 1975 – Oct. 10, 1987.
914 —Garry Unger, Toronto, Detroit, St. Louis, Atlanta from Feb. 24, 1968 – Dec. 21, 1979.
884 —Steve Larmer, Chicago, from Oct. 6, 1982 – Apr. 16, 1993.
776 —Craig Ramsay, Buffalo, from Mar. 27, 1973 – Feb. 10, 1983.
630 —Andy Hebenton, NY Rangers, Boston, Oct. 6, 1956 – Mar. 22, 1964.

GOALS

MOST GOALS:
862 —Wayne Gretzky, Edmonton, Los Angeles, St. Louis, NY Rangers, in 18 seasons, 1,335GP.
801 —Gordie Howe, Detroit, Hartford, in 26 seasons, 1,767GP.
731 —Marcel Dionne, Detroit, Los Angeles, NY Rangers, in 18 seasons, 1,348GP.
717 —Phil Esposito, Chicago, Boston, NY Rangers, in 18 seasons, 1,282GP.
696 —Mike Gartner, Washington, Minnesota, NY Rangers, Toronto, Phoenix, in 18 seasons, 1,372GP.

MOST GOALS, INCLUDING PLAYOFFS:
984 —Wayne Gretzky, Edmonton, Los Angeles, St. Louis, NY Rangers, 862 regular-season and 122 playoff goals.
869 —Gordie Howe, Detroit, Hartford, 801 regular-season and 68 playoff goals.
778 —Phil Esposito, Chicago, Boston, NY Rangers, 717 regular-season and 61 playoff goals.
752 —Marcel Dionne, Detroit, Los Angeles, NY Rangers, 731 regular-season and 21 playoff goals.

MOST GOALS, ONE SEASON:
92 —Wayne Gretzky, Edmonton, 1981-82. 80 game schedule.
87 —Wayne Gretzky, Edmonton, 1983-84. 80 game schedule.
86 —Brett Hull, St. Louis, 1990-91. 80 game schedule.
85 —Mario Lemieux, Pittsburgh, 1988-89. 80 game schedule.
76 —Phil Esposito, Boston, 1970-71. 78 game schedule.
  —Alexander Mogilny, Buffalo, 1992-93. 84 game schedule.
  —Teemu Selanne, Winnipeg, 1992-93. 84 game schedule.
73 —Wayne Gretzky, Edmonton, 1984-85. 80 game schedule.
72 —Brett Hull, St. Louis, 1989-90. 80 game schedule.
71 —Jari Kurri, Edmonton, 1984-85. 80 game schedule.
  —Wayne Gretzky, Edmonton, 1982-83. 80 game schedule.
70 —Mario Lemieux, Pittsburgh, 1987-1988. 80 game schedule.
  —Bernie Nicholls, Los Angeles, 1988-89. 80 game schedule.
  —Brett Hull, St. Louis, 1991-92. 80 game schedule.

MOST GOALS, ONE SEASON, INCLUDING PLAYOFFS:
100 —Wayne Gretzky, Edmonton, 1983-84, 87G in 74 regular-season games and 13G in 19 playoff games.
97 —Wayne Gretzky, Edmonton, 1981-82, 92G in 80 regular-season games and 5G in 5 playoff games.
  —Mario Lemieux, Pittsburgh, 1988-89, 85G in 76 regular-season games and 12G in 11 playoff games.
  —Brett Hull, St. Louis, 1990-91, 86G in 78 regular-season games and 11G in 13 playoff games.
90 —Wayne Gretzky, Edmonton, 1984-85, 73G in 80 regular-season games and 17G in 18 playoff games.
  —Jari Kurri, Edmonton, 1984-85, 71G in 80 regular-season games and 19G in 18 playoff games.
85 —Mike Bossy, NY Islanders, 1980-81, 68G in 79 regular-season games and 17G in 18 playoff games.
  —Brett Hull, St. Louis, 1989-90, 72G in 80 regular-season games and 13G in 12 playoff games.
83 —Wayne Gretzky, Edmonton, 1982-83, 71G in 73 regular-season games and 12G in 16 playoff games.
  —Alexander Mogilny, Buffalo, 1992-93, 76G in 77 regular-season games and 7G in 7 playoff games.

MOST GOALS, 50 GAMES FROM START OF SEASON:
61 —Wayne Gretzky, Edmonton, 1981-82. Oct. 7, 1981 - Jan. 22, 1982. (80-game schedule)
  —**Wayne Gretzky,** Edmonton, 1983-84. Oct. 5, 1983 - Jan. 25, 1984. (80-game schedule)
54 —Mario Lemieux, Pittsburgh, 1988-89. Oct. 7, 1988 - Jan. 31, 1989. (80-game schedule)
53 —Wayne Gretzky, Edmonton, 1984-85. Oct. 11, 1984 - Jan. 28, 1985. (80-game schedule)
52 —Brett Hull, St. Louis, 1990-91. Oct. 4, 1990 - Jan. 26, 1991. (80-game schedule)
50 —Maurice Richard, Montreal, 1944-45. Oct. 28, 1944 - March 18, 1945. (50-game schedule)
  —Mike Bossy, NY Islanders, 1980-81. Oct. 11, 1980 - Jan. 24, 1981. (80-game schedule)
  —Brett Hull, St. Louis, 1991-92. Oct. 5, 1991 – Jan 28, 1992. (80 game schedule)

MOST GOALS, ONE GAME:
7 —Joe Malone, Que. Bulldogs, Jan. 31, 1920, at Quebec. Quebec 10, Toronto 6.
6 —Newsy Lalonde, Montreal, Jan. 10, 1920, at Montreal. Montreal 14, Toronto 7.
  —Joe Malone, Que. Bulldogs, March 10, 1920, at Quebec. Quebec 10, Ottawa 4.
  —Corb Denneny, Toronto, Jan. 26, 1921, at Toronto. Toronto 10, Hamilton 3.
  —Cy Denneny, Ottawa, Mar. 7, 1921, at Ottawa. Ottawa 12, Hamilton 5.
  —Syd Howe, Detroit, Feb. 3, 1944, at Detroit. Detroit 12, NY Rangers 2.
  —Red Berenson, St. Louis, Nov. 7, 1968, at Philadelphia. St. Louis 8, Philadelphia 0.
  —Darryl Sittler, Toronto, Feb. 7, 1976, at Toronto. Toronto 11, Boston 4.

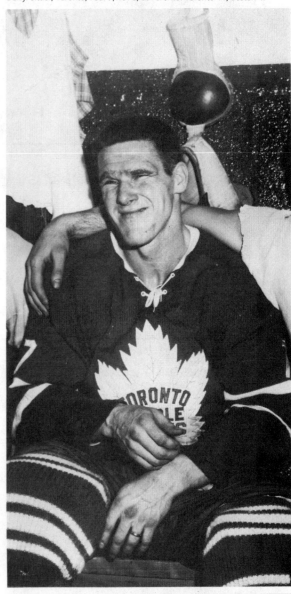

Venerable Tim Horton, seen here after the Toronto Maple Leafs downed the New York Rangers in the 1962 semi-finals, played 24 seasons in the NHL with four different teams.

One of the most spectacular performers to ever shoot, skate and score in the NHL, Bobby Orr remains the first – and only – defenseman to record 100 assists in a season, a feat he accomplished in 1970-71.

MOST GOALS, ONE ROAD GAME:
6 —**Red Berenson,** St. Louis, Nov. 7, 1968, at Philadelphia. St. Louis 8, Philadelphia 0.
5 —Joe Malone, Montreal, Dec. 19, 1917, at Ottawa. Montreal 9, Ottawa 4.
—Redvers Green, Hamilton, Dec. 5, 1924, at Toronto. Hamilton 10, Toronto 3.
—Babe Dye, Toronto, Dec. 22, 1924, at Boston. Toronto 10, Boston 2.
—Harry Broadbent, Mtl. Maroons, Jan. 7, 1925, at Hamilton. Mtl. Maroons 6, Hamilton 2.
—Don Murdoch, NY Rangers, Oct. 12, 1976, at Minnesota. NY Rangers 10, Minnesota 4.
—Tim Young, Minnesota, Jan. 15, 1979, at NY Rangers. Minnesota 8, NY Rangers 1.
—Willy Lindstrom, Winnipeg, Mar. 2, 1982, at Philadelphia. Winnipeg 7, Philadelphia 6.
—Bengt Gustafsson, Washington, Jan. 8, 1984, at Philadelphia. Washington 7, Philadelphia 1.
—Wayne Gretzky, Edmonton, Dec. 15, 1984, at St. Louis. Edmonton 8, St. Louis 2.
—Dave Andreychuk, Buffalo, Feb. 6, 1986, at Boston. Buffalo 8, Boston 6.
—Mats Sundin, Quebec, Mar. 5, 1992, at Hartford. Quebec 10, Hartford 4.
—Mario Lemieux, Pittsburgh, Apr. 9, 1993, at New York. Pittsburgh 10, NY Rangers 4.
—Mike Ricci, Quebec, Feb. 17, 1994, at San Jose. Quebec 8, San Jose 2.
—Alexei Zhamnov, Winnipeg, Apr. 1, 1995, at Los Angeles. Winnipeg 7, Los Angeles 7.

MOST GOALS, ONE PERIOD:
4 —**Harvey (Busher) Jackson,** Toronto, Nov. 20, 1934, at St. Louis, third period. Toronto 5, St. Louis Eagles 2.
—**Max Bentley,** Chicago, Jan. 28, 1943, at Chicago, third period. Chicago 10, NY Rangers 1.
—**Clint Smith,** Chicago, Mar. 4, 1945, at Chicago, third period. Chicago 6, Montreal 4.
—**Red Berenson,** St. Louis, Nov. 7, 1968, at Philadelphia, second period. St. Louis 8, Philadelphia 0.
—**Wayne Gretzky,** Edmonton, Feb. 18, 1981, at Edmonton, third period. Edmonton 9, St. Louis 2.
—**Grant Mulvey,** Chicago, Feb. 3, 1982, at Chicago, first period. Chicago 9, St. Louis 5.
—**Bryan Trottier,** NY Islanders, Feb. 13, 1982, at New York, second period. NY Islanders 8, Philadelphia 2.
—**Al Secord,** Chicago, Jan. 7, 1987, at Chicago, second period. Chicago 6, Toronto 4.
—**Joe Nieuwendyk,** Calgary, Jan. 11, 1989, at Calgary, second period. Calgary 8, Winnipeg 3.
—**Peter Bondra,** Washington, Feb. 5, 1994, at Washington, first period. Washington 6, Tampa Bay 3.
—**Mario Lemieux,** Pittsburgh, Jan. 26, 1997, at Montreal, third period. Pittsburgh 5, Montreal 2.

ASSISTS

MOST ASSISTS:
1,843 —**Wayne Gretzky,** Edmonton, Los Angeles, St. Louis, NY Rangers, in 18 seasons, 1,335GP.
1,063 —Paul Coffey, Edmonton, Pittsburgh, Los Angeles, Detroit, Hartford, Philadelphia, in 17 seasons, 1,211GP.
1,049 —Gordie Howe, Detroit, Hartford in 26 seasons, 1,767GP.
1,040 —Marcel Dionne, Detroit, Los Angeles, NY Rangers in 18 seasons, 1,348GP.
1,001 —Ray Bourque, Boston, in 18 seasons, 1,290GP.

MOST ASSISTS, INCLUDING PLAYOFFS:
2,103 —**Wayne Gretzky,** Edmonton, Los Angeles, St. Louis, NY Rangers, 1,843 regular-season and 260 playoff assists.
1,199 —Paul Coffey, Edmonton, Pittsburgh, Los Angeles, Detroit, Hartford, Philadelphia, 1,063 regular-season and 136 playoff assists.
1,163 —Mark Messier, Edmonton, NY Rangers, 977 regular-season and 186 playoff assists.
1,141 —Gordie Howe, Detroit, Hartford, 1,049 regular-season and 92 playoff assists.
1,064 —Marcel Dionne, Detroit, Los Angeles, NY Rangers, 1,040 regular-season and 24 playoff assists.

MOST ASSISTS, ONE SEASON:
163 —**Wayne Gretzky,** Edmonton, 1985-86. 80 game schedule.
135 —Wayne Gretzky, Edmonton, 1984-85. 80 game schedule.
125 —Wayne Gretzky, Edmonton, 1982-83. 80 game schedule.
122 —Wayne Gretzky, Los Angeles, 1990-91. 80 game schedule.
121 —Wayne Gretzky, Edmonton, 1986-87. 80 game schedule.
120 —Wayne Gretzky, Edmonton, 1981-82. 80 game schedule.
118 —Wayne Gretzky, Edmonton, 1983-84. 80 game schedule.
114 —Wayne Gretzky, Los Angeles, 1988-89. 80 game schedule.
—Mario Lemieux, Pittsburgh, 1988-89. 80 game schedule.
109 —Wayne Gretzky, Edmonton, 1980-81. 80 game schedule.
—Wayne Gretzky, Edmonton, 1987-88. 80 game schedule.
102 —Bobby Orr, Boston, 1970-71. 78 game schedule.
—Wayne Gretzky, Los Angeles, 1989-90. 80 game schedule.

MOST ASSISTS, ONE SEASON, INCLUDING PLAYOFFS:
174 —**Wayne Gretzky,** Edmonton, 1985-86, 163A in 80 regular-season games and 11A in 10 playoff games.
165 —Wayne Gretzky, Edmonton, 1984-85, 135A in 80 regular-season games and 30A in 18 playoff games.
151 —Wayne Gretzky, Edmonton, 1982-83, 125A in 80 regular-season games and 26A in 16 playoff games.
150 —Wayne Gretzky, Edmonton, 1986-87, 121A in 79 regular-season games and 29A in 21 playoff games.
140 —Wayne Gretzky, Edmonton, 1983-84, 118A in 74 regular-season games and 22A in 19 playoff games.
—Wayne Gretzky, Edmonton, 1987-88, 109A in 64 regular-season games and 31A in 19 playoff games.
133 —Wayne Gretzky, Los Angeles, 1990-91, 122A in 78 regular-season games and 11A in 12 playoff games.
131 —Wayne Gretzky, Los Angeles, 1988-89, 114A in 78 regular-season games and 17A in 11 playoff games.
127 —Wayne Gretzky, Edmonton, 1981-82, 120A in 80 regular-season games and 7A in 5 playoff games.
123 —Wayne Gretzky, Edmonton, 1980-81, 109A in 80 regular-season games and 14A in 9 playoff games.
121 —Mario Lemieux, Pittsburgh, 1988-89, 114A in 76 regular-season games and 7A in 11 playoff games.

MOST ASSISTS, ONE GAME:
7 —**Billy Taylor,** Detroit, Mar. 16, 1947, at Chicago. Detroit 10, Chicago 6.
—**Wayne Gretzky,** Edmonton, Feb. 15, 1980, at Edmonton. Edmonton 8, Washington 2.
—**Wayne Gretzky,** Edmonton, Dec. 11, 1985, at Chicago. Edmonton 12, Chicago 9.
—**Wayne Gretzky,** Edmonton, Feb. 14, 1986, at Edmonton. Edmonton 8, Quebec 2.
6 —Elmer Lach, Montreal, Feb. 6, 1943.
—Walter (Babe) Pratt, Toronto, Jan. 8, 1944.
—Don Grosso, Detroit, Feb. 3, 1944.
—Pat Stapleton, Chicago, Mar. 30, 1969.
—Ken Hodge, Boston, Feb. 9, 1971.
—Bobby Orr, Boston, Jan. 1, 1973.
—Ron Stackhouse, Pittsburgh, Mar. 8, 1975.
—Greg Malone, Pittsburgh, Nov. 28, 1979.
—Mike Bossy, NY Islanders, Jan. 6, 1981.
—Guy Chouinard, Calgary, Feb. 25, 1981.
—Mark Messier, Edmonton, Jan. 4, 1984.
—Patrik Sundstrom, Vancouver, Feb 29, 1984.
—Wayne Gretzky, Edmonton, Dec. 20, 1985.
—Paul Coffey, Edmonton, Mar. 14, 1986.
—Gary Suter, Calgary, Apr. 4, 1986.
—Ron Francis, Hartford, Mar. 5, 1987.
—Mario Lemieux, Pittsburgh, Oct. 15, 1988.
—Bernie Nicholls, Los Angeles, Dec. 1, 1988.
—Mario Lemieux, Pittsburgh, Dec. 31, 1988.
—Mario Lemieux, Pittsburgh, Dec. 5, 1992.
—Doug Gilmour, Toronto, Feb. 13, 1993.
—Tomas Sandstrom, Los Angeles, Oct. 9, 1993.
—Eric Lindros, Philadelphia, Feb. 26, 1997.

MOST ASSISTS, ONE ROAD GAME:
7 —**Billy Taylor,** Detroit, Mar. 16, 1947, at Chicago. Detroit 10, Chicago 6.
—**Wayne Gretzky,** Edmonton, Dec. 11, 1985, at Chicago. Edmonton 12, Chicago 9.
6 —Bobby Orr, Boston, Jan. 1, 1973, at Vancouver. Boston 8, Vancouver 2.
—Patrik Sundstrom, Vancouver, Feb. 29, 1984, at Pittsburgh. Vancouver 9, Pittsburgh 5.
—Mario Lemieux, Pittsburgh, Dec. 5, 1992, at San Jose. Pittsburgh 9, San Jose 4.
—Eric Lindros, Philadelphia, Feb. 26, 1997, at Ottawa. Philadelphia 8, Ottawa 5.

MOST ASSISTS, ONE PERIOD:
5 —**Dale Hawerchuk,** Winnipeg, Mar. 6, 1984, at Los Angeles, second period. Winnipeg 7, Los Angeles 3.
4 —Four assists have been recorded in one period on 49 occasions since Buddy O'Connor of Montreal first accomplished the feat vs. NY Rangers on Nov. 8, 1942. Most recent player, Eric Lindros of Philadelphia (Feb. 26, 1997 at Ottawa).

POINTS

MOST POINTS:
2,705 —**Wayne Gretzky,** Edmonton, Los Angeles, St. Louis, NY Rangers, in 18 seasons, 1,335GP (862G-1,843A).
1,850 —Gordie Howe, Detroit, Hartford, in 26 seasons, 1,767GP (801G-1049A).
1,771 —Marcel Dionne, Detroit, Los Angeles, NY Rangers, in 18 seasons, 1,348GP (731G-1,040A).
1,590 —Phil Esposito, Chicago, Boston, NY Rangers in 18 seasons, 1,282GP (717G-873A).
1,552 —Mark Messier, Edmonton, NY Rangers in 18 seasons, 1,272GP (575G-977A).

MOST POINTS, INCLUDING PLAYOFFS:
3,087 —**Wayne Gretzky,** Edmonton, Los Angeles, St. Louis, NY Rangers, 2,705 regular-season and 382 playoff points.
2,010 —Gordie Howe, Detroit, Hartford, 1,850 regular-season and 160 playoff assists.
1,816 —Marcel Dionne, Detroit, Los Angeles, NY Rangers, 1,771 regular-season and 45 playoff points.
1,847 —Mark Messier, Edmonton, NY Rangers, 1,552 regular-season and 295 playoff points.
1,727 —Phil Esposito, Chicago, Boston, NY Rangers, 1,590 regular-season and 137 playoff points.

MOST POINTS, ONE SEASON:
215 —**Wayne Gretzky,** Edmonton, 1985-86. 80 game schedule.
212 —Wayne Gretzky, Edmonton, 1981-82. 80 game schedule.
208 —Wayne Gretzky, Edmonton, 1984-85. 80 game schedule.
205 —Wayne Gretzky, Edmonton, 1983-84. 80 game schedule.
199 —Mario Lemieux, Pittsburgh, 1988-89. 80 game schedule.
196 —Wayne Gretzky, Edmonton, 1982-83. 80 game schedule.
183 —Wayne Gretzky, Edmonton, 1986-87. 80 game schedule.
168 —Mario Lemieux, Pittsburgh, 1987-88, 80 game schedule.
—Wayne Gretzky, Los Angeles, 1988-89. 80 game schedule.
164 —Wayne Gretzky, Edmonton, 1980-81. 80 game schedule.
163 —Wayne Gretzky, Los Angeles, 1990-91. 80 game schedule.
161 —Mario Lemieux, Pittsburgh, 1995-96. 82 game schedule.
160 —Mario Lemieux, Pittsburgh, 1992-93. 84 game schedule.

MOST POINTS, ONE SEASON, INCLUDING PLAYOFFS:
255 —**Wayne Gretzky,** Edmonton, 1984-85, 208PTS in 80 regular-season games and 47PTS in 18 playoff games.
240 —Wayne Gretzky, Edmonton, 1983-84, 205PTS in 74 regular-season games and 35PTS in 19 playoff games.
234 —Wayne Gretzky, Edmonton, 1982-83, 196PTS in 80 regular-season games and 38PTS in 16 playoff games.
—Wayne Gretzky, Edmonton, 1985-86, 215PTS in 80 regular-season games and 19PTS in 10 playoff games.
224 —Wayne Gretzky, Edmonton, 1981-82, 212PTS in 80 regular-season games and 12PTS in 5 playoff games.
218 —Mario Lemieux, Pittsburgh, 1988-89, 199PTS in 76 regular-season games and 19PTS in 11 playoff games.
217 —Wayne Gretzky, Edmonton, 1986-87, 183PTS in 79 regular-season games and 34PTS in 21 playoff games.
192 —Wayne Gretzky, Edmonton, 1987-88, 149PTS in 64 regular-season games and 43PTS in 19 playoff games.
190 —Wayne Gretzky, Los Angeles, 1988-89, 168PTS in 78 regular-season games and 22PTS in 11 playoff games.
188 —Mario Lemieux, Pittsburgh, 1995-96, 161PTS in 70 regular-season games and 27PTS in 18 playoff games.
185 —Wayne Gretzky, Edmonton, 1980-81, 164PTS in 80 regular-season games and 21PTS in 9 playoff games.

Although his NHL career was brief, Patrik Sundstrom took a leap into the record books when he notched six assists against Pittsburgh on February 29, 1984.

MOST POINTS, ONE GAME:
10 —Darryl Sittler, Toronto, Feb. 7, 1976, at Toronto, 6G-4A. Toronto 11, Boston 4.
8 —Maurice Richard, Montreal, Dec. 28, 1944, at Montreal, 5G-3A. Montreal 9, Detroit 1.
 —Bert Olmstead, Montreal, Jan. 9, 1954, at Montreal, 4G-4A. Montreal 12, Chicago 1.
 —Tom Bladon, Philadelphia, Dec. 11, 1977, at Philadelphia, 4G-4A. Philadelphia 11, Cleveland 1.
 —Bryan Trottier, NY Islanders, Dec. 23, 1978, at New York, 5G-3A. NY Islanders 9, NY Rangers 4.
 —Peter Stastny, Quebec, Feb. 22, 1981, at Washington, 4G-4A. Quebec 11, Washington 7.
 —Anton Stastny, Quebec, Feb. 22, 1981, at Washington, 3G-5A. Quebec 11, Washington 7.
 —Wayne Gretzky, Edmonton, Nov. 19, 1983, at Edmonton, 3G-5A. Edmonton 13, New Jersey 4.
 —Wayne Gretzky, Edmonton, Jan. 4, 1984, at Edmonton, 4G-4A. Edmonton 12, Minnesota 8.
 —Paul Coffey, Edmonton, Mar. 14, 1986, at Edmonton, 2G-6A. Edmonton 12, Detroit 3.
 —Mario Lemieux, Pittsburgh, Oct. 15, 1988, at Pittsburgh, 2G-6A. Pittsburgh 9, St. Louis 2.
 —Mario Lemieux, Pittsburgh, Dec. 31, 1988, at Pittsburgh, 5G-3A. Pittsburgh 8, New Jersey 6.
 —Bernie Nicholls, Los Angeles, Dec. 1, 1988, at Los Angeles, 2G-6A. Los Angeles 9, Toronto 3.

MOST POINTS, ONE ROAD GAME:
8 —Peter Stastny, Quebec, Feb. 22, 1981, at Washington, 4G-4A. Quebec 11, Washington 7.
 —**Anton Stastny,** Quebec, Feb. 22, 1981, at Washington, 3G-5A. Quebec 11, Washington 7.
7 —Billy Taylor, Detroit, Mar. 16, 1947, at Chicago, 7A. Detroit 10, Chicago 6.
 —Red Berenson, St. Louis, Nov. 7, 1968, at Philadelphia, 6G-1A. St. Louis 8, Philadelphia 0.
 —Gilbert Perreault, Buffalo, Feb. 1, 1976, at California, 2G-5A. Buffalo 9, California 5.
 —Peter Stastny, Quebec, Apr. 1, 1982, at Boston, 3G-4A. Quebec 8, Boston 5.
 —Wayne Gretzky, Edmonton, Nov. 6, 1983, at Winnipeg, 4G-3A. Edmonton 8, Winnipeg 5.
 —Patrik Sundstrom, Vancouver, Feb. 29, 1984, at Pittsburgh, 1G-6A. Vancouver 9, Pittsburgh 5.
 —Wayne Gretzky, Edmonton, Dec. 11, 1985, at Chicago. 7A. Edmonton 12, Chicago 9.
 —Mario Lemieux, Pittsburgh, Jan. 21, 1989, at Edmonton, 2G-5A. Pittsburgh 7, Edmonton 4.
 —Cam Neely, Boston, Oct. 16, 1988, at Chicago, 3G-4A. Boston 10, Chicago 3.
 —Dino Ciccarelli, Washington, Mar. 18, 1989, at Hartford, 4G-3A. Washington 8, Hartford 2.
 —Mats Sundin, Quebec, Mar. 5, 1992, at Hartford, 5G-2A. Quebec 10, Hartford 4.
 —Mario Lemieux, Pittsburgh, Dec. 5, 1992, at San Jose, 1G-6A. Pittsburgh 9, San Jose 4.
 —Eric Lindros, Philadelphia, Feb. 26, 1997, at Ottawa, 1G-6A. Philadelphia 8, Ottawa 5.

MOST POINTS, ONE PERIOD:
6 —Bryan Trottier, NY Islanders, Dec. 23, 1978, at NY Islanders, second period. 3G-3A. NY Islanders 9, NY Rangers 4.
5 —Les Cunningham, Chicago, Jan. 28, 1940, at Chicago, third period. 2G- 3A. Chicago 8, Montreal 1.
 —Max Bentley, Chicago, Jan. 28, 1943, at Chicago, third period. 4G-1A, Chicago 10, NY Rangers 1.
 —Leo Labine, Boston, Nov. 28, 1954, at Boston, second period. 3G-2A. Boston 6, Detroit 2.
 —Darryl Sittler, Toronto, Feb. 7, 1976, at Toronto, second period. 3G-2A. Toronto 11, Boston 4.
 —Grant Mulvey, Chicago, Feb. 3, 1982, at Chicago, first period. 4G-1A. Chicago 9, St. Louis 5.
 —Dale Hawerchuk, Winnipeg, Mar. 6, 1984, at Los Angeles, second period. 5A. Winnipeg 7, Los Angeles 3.
 —Jari Kurri, Edmonton, Oct. 26, 1984 at Edmonton, second period. 2G-3A. Edmonton 8, Los Angeles 2.
 —Pat Elynuik, Winnipeg, Jan. 20, 1989, at Winnipeg, second period. 2G- 3A. Winnipeg 7, Pittsburgh 3.
 —Ray Ferraro, Hartford, Dec. 9, 1989, at Hartford, first period. 3G-2A. Hartford 7, New Jersey 3.
 —Stephane Richer, Montreal, Feb. 14, 1990, at Montreal, first period. 2G- 3A. Montreal 10, Vancouver 1.
 —Cliff Ronning, Vancouver, Apr. 15, 1993, at Los Angeles, third period. 3G- 2A. Vancouver 8, Los Angeles 6.

POWER-PLAY and SHORTHAND GOALS

MOST POWER-PLAY GOALS, ONE SEASON:
34 —Tim Kerr, Philadelphia, 1985-86. 80 game schedule.
32 —Dave Andreychuk, Buffalo, Toronto, 1992-93. 84 game schedule.
31 —Joe Nieuwendyk, Calgary, 1987-88. 80 game schedule.
 —Mario Lemieux, Pittsburgh, 1988-89. 80 game schedule.
 —Mario Lemieux, Pittsburgh, 1995-96. 82 game schedule.
29 —Michel Goulet, Quebec, 1987-88. 80 game schedule.
 —Brett Hull, St. Louis, 1990-91. 80 game schedule.
 —Brett Hull, St. Louis, 1992-93. 84 game schedule.

MOST SHORTHAND GOALS, ONE SEASON:
13 —Mario Lemieux, Pittsburgh, 1988-89. 80 game schedule.
12 —Wayne Gretzky, Edmonton, 1983-84. 80 game schedule.
11 —Wayne Gretzky, Edmonton, 1984-85. 80 game schedule.
10 —Marcel Dionne, Detroit, 1974-75. 80 game schedule.
 —Mario Lemieux, Pittsburgh, 1987-88. 80 game schedule.
 —Dirk Graham, Chicago, 1988-89. 80 game schedule.

MOST SHORTHAND GOALS, ONE GAME:
3 —Theoren Fleury, Calgary, Mar. 9, 1991, at St. Louis. Calgary 8, St. Louis 4.

OVERTIME SCORING

MOST OVERTIME GOALS, CAREER:
9 —Mario Lemieux, Pittsburgh.
8 —Bob Sweeney, Boston, Buffalo, Calgary.
 —Steve Thomas, Toronto, Chicago, NY Islanders, New Jersey.
 —Tomas Sandstrom, NY Rangers, Los Angeles, Pittsburgh, Detroit.
7 —Jari Kurri, Edmonton, Los Angeles, NY Rangers, Anaheim.
 —Murray Craven, Philadelphia, Hartford, Vancouver, Chicago.
 —Stephane Richer, Montreal, New Jersey.
 —Sergei Fedorov, Detroit.
 —Mike Gartner, Washington, Minnesota, NY Rangers, Toronto, Phoenix.

MOST OVERTIME ASSISTS, CAREER:
13 —Wayne Gretzky, Edmonton, Los Angeles, St. Louis, NY Rangers.
11 —Mark Messier, Edmonton, NY Rangers.
 —Doug Gilmour, St. Louis, Calgary, Toronto, New Jersey.
 —Paul Coffey, Edmonton, Pittsburgh, Los Angeles, Detroit, Hartford, Philadelphia.
 —Adam Oates, Detroit, St. Louis, Boston, Washington.
10 —Mario Lemieux, Pittsburgh.

MOST OVERTIME POINTS, CAREER:
19 —Mario Lemieux, Pittsburgh, 9G-10A
17 —Mark Messier, Edmonton, NY Rangers. 6G-11A
15 —Wayne Gretzky, Edmonton, Los Angeles, St. Louis, NY Rangers. 2G-13A
13 —Jari Kurri, Edmonton, Los Angeles, NY Rangers, Anaheim. 7G-6A
 —Paul MacLean, Winnipeg, Detroit, St. Louis. 6G-7A
 —Dale Hawerchuk, Winnipeg, Buffalo, St. Louis, Philadelphia. 4G-9A
 —Steve Thomas, Toronto, Chicago, NY Islanders, New Jersey. 8G-5A
 —Adam Oates, Detroit, St. Louis, Boston, Washington, 2G-11A.

SCORING BY A CENTER

MOST GOALS BY A CENTER, CAREER
862 —Wayne Gretzky, Edmonton, Los Angeles, St. Louis, NY Rangers, in 18 seasons.
731 —Marcel Dionne, Detroit, Los Angeles, NY Rangers, in 18 seasons.
717 —Phil Esposito, Chicago, Boston, NY Rangers, in 18 seasons.
613 —Mario Lemieux, Pittsburgh, in 12 seasons.
575 —Mark Messier, Edmonton, NY Rangers, in 18 seasons.

MOST GOALS BY A CENTER, ONE SEASON:
92 —Wayne Gretzky, Edmonton, 1981-82. 80 game schedule.
87 —Wayne Gretzky, Edmonton, 1983-84. 80 game schedule.
85 —Mario Lemieux, Pittsburgh, 1988-89. 80 game schedule.
76 —Phil Esposito, Boston, 1970-71. 78 game schedule.
73 —Wayne Gretzky, Edmonton, 1984-85. 80 game schedule.

Dave Andreychuk used his long reach, sharp reflexes and quick hands to collect 32 power-play goals during the 1992-93 season.

MOST ASSISTS BY A CENTER, CAREER:
 1,843 —**Wayne Gretzky,** Edmonton, Los Angeles, St. Louis, NY Rangers, in 18 seasons.
 1,040 —Marcel Dionne, Detroit, Los Angeles, NY Rangers, in 18 seasons.
  977 —Mark Messier, Edmonton, NY Rangers, in 18 seasons.
  926 —Stan Mikita, Chicago, in 22 seasons.
  901 —Bryan Trottier, NY Islanders, Pittsburgh, in 18 seasons.

MOST ASSISTS BY A CENTER, ONE SEASON:
  163 —**Wayne Gretzky,** Edmonton, 1985-86. 80 game schedule.
  135 —Wayne Gretzky, Edmonton, 1984-85. 80 game schedule.
  125 —Wayne Gretzky, Edmonton, 1982-83. 80 game schedule.
  122 —Wayne Gretzky, Los Angeles, 1990-91. 80 game schedule.
  121 —Wayne Gretzky, Edmonton, 1986-87. 80 game schedule.

MOST POINTS BY A CENTER, CAREER:
 2,705 —**Wayne Gretzky,** Edmonton, Los Angeles, St. Louis, NY Rangers, in 18 seasons.
 1,771 —Marcel Dionne, Detroit, Los Angeles, NY Rangers, in 18 seasons.
 1,590 —Phil Esposito, Chicago, Boston, NY Rangers, in 18 seasons.
 1,552 —Mark Messier, Edmonton, NY Rangers, in 18 seasons.
 1,467 —Stan Mikita, Chicago, in 22 seasons.

MOST POINTS BY A CENTER, ONE SEASON:
  215 —**Wayne Gretzky,** Edmonton, 1985-86. 80 game schedule.
  212 —Wayne Gretzky, Edmonton, 1981-82. 80 game schedule.
  208 —Wayne Gretzky, Edmonton, 1984-85. 80 game schedule.
  205 —Wayne Gretzky, Edmonton, 1983-84. 80 game schedule.
  199 —Mario Lemieux, Pittsburgh, 1988-89. 80 game schedule.

SCORING BY A LEFT WING

MOST GOALS BY A LEFT WING, CAREER:
  610 —**Bobby Hull,** Chicago, Winnipeg, Hartford, in 16 seasons.
  556 —John Bucyk, Detroit, Boston, in 23 seasons.
  548 —Michel Goulet, Quebec, Chicago, in 15 seasons.
  533 —Frank Mahovlich, Toronto, Detroit, Montreal, in 18 seasons.
  503 —Dave Andreychuk, Buffalo, Toronto, New Jersey, in 15 seasons.

MOST GOALS BY A LEFT WING, ONE SEASON:
   63 —**Luc Robitaille,** Los Angeles, 1992-93. 84 game schedule.
   60 —Steve Shutt, Montreal, 1976-77. 80 game schedule.
   58 —Bobby Hull, Chicago, 1968-69. 76 game schedule.
   57 —Michel Goulet, Quebec, 1982-83. 80 game schedule.
   56 —Charlie Simmer, Los Angeles, 1979-80. 80 game schedule.
      —Charlie Simmer, Los Angeles, 1980-81. 80 game schedule.
      —Michel Goulet, Quebec, 1983-84. 80 game schedule.

MOST ASSISTS BY A LEFT WING, CAREER:
  813 —**John Bucyk,** Detroit, Boston, in 23 seasons.
  604 —Michel Goulet, Quebec, Chicago, in 15 seasons.
  579 —Brian Propp, Philadelphia, Boston, Minnesota, Hartford, in 15 seasons.
  570 —Frank Mahovlich, Toronto, Detroit, Montreal, in 18 seasons.
  561 —Dave Andreychuk, Buffalo, Toronto, New Jersey, in 15 seasons.

MOST ASSISTS BY A LEFT WING, ONE SEASON:
   70 —**Joe Juneau,** Boston, 1992-93. 84 game schedule.
   69 —Kevin Stevens, Pittsburgh, 1991-92. 80 game schedule.
   67 —Mats Naslund, Montreal, 1985-86. 80 game schedule.
   65 —John Bucyk, Boston, 1970-71. 78 game schedule.
      —Michel Goulet, Quebec, 1983-84. 80 game schedule.
   64 —Mark Messier, Edmonton, 1983-84. 80 game schedule.

MOST POINTS BY A LEFT WING, CAREER:
 1,369 —**John Bucyk,** Detroit, Boston, in 23 seasons.
 1,170 —Bobby Hull, Chicago, Winnipeg, Hartford, in 16 seasons.
 1,152 —Michel Goulet, Quebec, Chicago, in 15 seasons.
 1,103 —Frank Mahovlich, Toronto, Detroit, Montreal, in 18 seasons.
 1,004 —Brian Propp, Philadelphia, Boston, Minnesota, Hartford, in 15 seasons.

MOST POINTS BY A LEFT WING, ONE SEASON:
  125 —**Luc Robitaille,** Los Angeles, 1992-93. 84 game schedule.
  123 —Kevin Stevens, Pittsburgh, 1991-92. 80 game schedule.
  121 —Michel Goulet, Quebec, 1983-84. 80 game schedule.
  116 —John Bucyk, Boston, 1970-71. 78 game schedule.
  112 —Bill Barber, Philadelphia, 1975-76. 80 game schedule.

SCORING BY A RIGHT WING

MOST GOALS BY A RIGHT WING, CAREER:
  801 —**Gordie Howe,** Detroit, Hartford, in 26 seasons.
  696 —Mike Gartner, Washington, Minnesota, NY Rangers, Toronto, Phoenix, in 18 seasons.
  596 —Jari Kurri, Edmonton, Los Angeles, NY Rangers, Anaheim, in 16 seasons.
  586 —Dino Ciccarelli, Minnesota, Washington, Detroit, Tampa Bay, in 17 seasons.
  573 —Mike Bossy, NY Islanders, in 10 seasons.

MOST GOALS BY A RIGHT WING, ONE SEASON:
   86 —**Brett Hull,** St. Louis, 1990-91. 80 game schedule.
   76 —Alexander Mogilny, Buffalo, 1992-93. 84 game schedule.
      —Teemu Selanne, Winnipeg, 1992-93. 84 game schedule.
   72 —Brett Hull, St. Louis, 1989-90. 80 game schedule.
   71 —Jari Kurri, Edmonton, 1984-85. 80 game schedule.
   70 —Brett Hull, St. Louis, 1991-92. 80 game schedule.

MOST ASSISTS BY A RIGHT WING, CAREER:
 1,049 —**Gordie Howe,** Detroit, Hartford, in 26 seasons.
  793 —Guy Lafleur, Montreal, NY Rangers, Quebec, in 17 seasons.
  780 —Jari Kurri, Edmonton, Los Angeles, NY Rangers, Anaheim, in 16 seasons.
  638 —Dave Taylor, Los Angeles, in 17 seasons.
  624 —Andy Bathgate, NY Rangers, Toronto, Detroit, Pittsburgh in 17 seasons.

MOST ASSISTS BY A RIGHT WING, ONE SEASON:
   87 —**Jaromir Jagr,** Pittsburgh, 1995-96. 82 game schedule.
   83 —Mike Bossy, NY Islanders, 1981-82. 80 game schedule.
   80 —Guy Lafleur, Montreal, 1976-77. 80 game schedule.
   77 —Guy Lafleur, Montreal, 1978-79. 80 game schedule.

Since becoming the only defenseman to move into the NHL directly from high-school hockey in 1982, Phil Housley has 285 goals to his credit.

Before a head injury ended his career in 1994, Michel Goulet was one of the NHL's most productive left-wingers, snapping 548 pucks past enemy goaltenders during his 15-year career.

MOST POINTS BY A RIGHT WING, CAREER:
1,850 —**Gordie Howe,** Detroit, Hartford, in 26 seasons.
  1,376 —Jari Kurri, Edmonton, Los Angeles, NY Rangers, Anaheim, in 16 seasons.
  1,353 —Guy Lafleur, Montreal, NY Rangers, Quebec, in 17 seasons.
  1,308 —Mike Gartner, Washington, Minnesota, NY Rangers, Toronto, Phoenix, in 18 seasons.

MOST POINTS BY A RIGHT WING, ONE SEASON:
  149 —**Jaromir Jagr,** Pittsburgh, 1995-96. 82 game schedule.
  147 —Mike Bossy, NY Islanders, 1981-82. 80 game schedule.
  136 —Guy Lafleur, Montreal, 1976-77. 80 game schedule.
  135 —Jari Kurri, Edmonton, 1984-85. 80 game schedule.
  132 —Guy Lafleur, Montreal, 1977-78. 80 game schedule.
      —Teemu Selanne, Winnipeg, 1992-93. 84 game schedule.

SCORING BY A DEFENSEMAN

MOST GOALS BY A DEFENSEMAN, CAREER:
  381 —**Paul Coffey,** Edmonton, Pittsburgh, Los Angeles, Detroit, Hartford, Philadelphia, in 17 seasons.
  362 —Ray Bourque, Boston, in 18 seasons.
  310 —Denis Potvin, NY Islanders, in 15 seasons.
  285 —Phil Housley, Buffalo, Winnipeg, St. Louis, Calgary, New Jersey, Washington, in 15 seasons.
  270 —Bobby Orr, Boston, Chicago, in 12 seasons.

MOST GOALS BY A DEFENSEMAN, ONE SEASON:
  48 —**Paul Coffey,** Edmonton, 1985-86. 80 game schedule.
  46 —Bobby Orr, Boston, 1974-75. 80 game schedule.
  40 —Paul Coffey, Edmonton, 1983-84. 80 game schedule.
  39 —Doug Wilson, Chicago, 1981-82. 80 game schedule.
  37 —Bobby Orr, Boston, 1970-71. 78 game schedule.
     —Bobby Orr, Boston, 1971-72. 78 game schedule.
     —Paul Coffey, Edmonton, 1984-85. 80 game schedule.

MOST GOALS BY A DEFENSEMAN, ONE GAME:
  5 —**Ian Turnbull,** Toronto, Feb. 2, 1977, at Toronto. Toronto 9, Detroit 1.
  4 —Harry Cameron, Toronto, Dec. 26, 1917, at Toronto. Toronto 7, Montreal 5.
    —Harry Cameron, Montreal, Mar. 3, 1920, at Quebec City. Montreal 16, Que. Bulldogs 3.
    —Sprague Cleghorn, Montreal, Jan. 14, 1922, at Montreal. Montreal 10, Hamilton 6.
    —Johnny McKinnon, Pit. Pirates, Nov. 19, 1929, at Pittsburgh. Pit. Pirates 10, Toronto 5.
    —Hap Day, Toronto, Nov. 19, 1929, at Pittsburgh. Pit. Pirates 10, Toronto 5.
    —Tom Bladon, Philadelphia, Dec. 11, 1977, at Philadelphia. Philadelphia 11, Cleveland 1.
    —Ian Turnbull, Los Angeles, Dec. 12, 1981, at Los Angeles. Los Angeles 7, Vancouver 5.
    —Paul Coffey, Edmonton, Oct. 26, 1984, at Calgary. Edmonton 6, Calgary 5.

MOST ASSISTS BY A DEFENSEMAN, CAREER:
1,063 —**Paul Coffey,** Edmonton, Pittsburgh, Los Angeles, Detroit, Hartford, Philadelphia, in 17 seasons.
  1,001 —Ray Bourque, Boston, in 18 seasons.
   797 —Larry Murphy, Los Angeles, Washington, Minnesota, Pittsburgh, Toronto, Detroit, in 17 seasons.
   750 —Larry Robinson, Montreal, Los Angeles, in 20 seasons.
   742 —Denis Potvin, NY Islanders, in 15 seasons.

MOST ASSISTS BY A DEFENSEMAN, ONE SEASON:
  102 —**Bobby Orr,** Boston, 1970-71. 78 game schedule.
  90 —Paul Coffey, Edmonton, 1985-86. 80 game schedule.
  90 —Bobby Orr, Boston, 1973-74. 78 game schedule.
  89 —Bobby Orr, Boston, 1974-75. 80 game schedule.

MOST ASSISTS BY A DEFENSEMAN, ONE GAME:
  6 —**Babe Pratt,** Toronto, Jan. 8, 1944, at Toronto. Toronto 12, Boston 3.
    —**Pat Stapleton,** Chicago, Mar. 30, 1969, at Chicago. Chicago 9, Detroit 5.
    —**Bobby Orr,** Boston, Jan. 1, 1973, at Vancouver, Boston 8, Vancouver 2.
    —**Ron Stackhouse,** Pittsburgh, Mar. 8, 1975, at Pittsburgh. Pittsburgh 8, Philadelphia 2.
    —**Paul Coffey,** Edmonton, Mar. 14, 1986, at Edmonton. Edmonton 12, Detroit 3.
    —**Gary Suter,** Calgary, Apr. 4, 1986, at Calgary. Calgary 9, Edmonton 3.

MOST POINTS BY A DEFENSEMAN, CAREER:
1,444 —**Paul Coffey,** Edmonton, Pittsburgh, Los Angeles, Detroit, Hartford, Philadelphia in 17 seasons.
  1,363 —Ray Bourque, Boston, in 18 seasons.
  1,052 —Denis Potvin, NY Islanders, in 15 seasons.
  1,051 —Larry Murphy, Los Angeles, Washington, Minnesota, Pittsburgh, Toronto, Detroit, in 17 seasons.
   990 —Phil Housley, Buffalo, Winnipeg, St. Louis, Calgary, New Jersey, Washington, in 15 seasons.

MOST POINTS BY A DEFENSEMAN, ONE SEASON:
  139 —**Bobby Orr,** Boston, 1970-71. 78 game schedule.
  138 —Paul Coffey, Edmonton, 1985-86. 80 game schedule.
  135 —Bobby Orr, Boston, 1974-75. 80 game schedule.
  126 —Paul Coffey, Edmonton, 1983-84. 80 game schedule.
  122 —Bobby Orr, Boston, 1973-74. 78 game schedule.

MOST POINTS BY A DEFENSEMAN, ONE GAME:
  8 —**Tom Bladon,** Philadelphia, Dec. 11, 1977, at Philadelphia. 4G-4A. Philadelphia 11, Cleveland 1.
    —**Paul Coffey,** Edmonton, Mar. 14, 1986, at Edmonton. 2G-6A. Edmonton 12, Detroit 3.
  7 —Bobby Orr, Boston, Nov. 15, 1973, at Boston, 3G-4A. Boston 10, NY Rangers 2.

SCORING BY A GOALTENDER

MOST POINTS BY A GOALTENDER, CAREER:
  44 —**Grant Fuhr,** Edmonton, Toronto, Buffalo, Los Angeles, St. Louis, in 16 seasons. (44A)

MOST POINTS BY A GOALTENDER, ONE SEASON:
  14 —**Grant Fuhr,** Edmonton, 1983-84. (14A)
  9 —Curtis Joseph, St. Louis, 1991-92. (9A)
  8 —Mike Palmateer, Washington, 1980-81. (8A)
    —Grant Fuhr, Edmonton, 1987-88. (8A)
    —Ron Hextall, Philadelphia, 1988-89. (8A)
    —Tom Barrasso, Pittsburgh, 1992-93. (8A)
  7 —Ron Hextall, Philadelphia, 1987-88. (1G-6A)
    —Mike Vernon, Calgary, 1987-88. (7A)

MOST POINTS BY A GOALTENDER, ONE GAME:
  3 —**Jeff Reese,** Calgary, Feb. 10, 1993, at Calgary. Calgary 13, San Jose 1. (3A)

SCORING BY A ROOKIE

MOST GOALS BY A ROOKIE, ONE SEASON:
76 —**Teemu Selanne,** Winnipeg, 1992-93. 84 game schedule.
53 —Mike Bossy, NY Islanders, 1977-78. 80 game schedule.
51 —Joe Nieuwendyk, Calgary, 1987-88. 80 game schedule.
45 —Dale Hawerchuk, Winnipeg, 1981-82. 80 game schedule.
 —Luc Robitaille, Los Angeles, 1986-87. 80 game schedule.

MOST GOALS BY A PLAYER IN HIS FIRST NHL SEASON, ONE GAME:
5 —**Howie Meeker,** Toronto, Jan. 8, 1947, at Toronto. Toronto 10, Chicago 4.
 —**Don Murdoch,** NY Rangers, Oct. 12, 1976, at Minnesota. NY Rangers 10, Minnesota 4.

MOST GOALS BY A PLAYER IN HIS FIRST NHL GAME:
3 —**Alex Smart,** Montreal, Jan. 14, 1943, at Montreal. Montreal 5, Chicago 1.
 —**Real Cloutier,** Quebec, Oct. 10, 1979, at Quebec. Atlanta 5, Quebec 3.

MOST ASSISTS BY A ROOKIE, ONE SEASON:
70 —**Peter Stastny,** Quebec, 1980-81. 80 game schedule.
 —**Joe Juneau,** Boston, 1992-93. 84 game schedule.
63 —Bryan Trottier, NY Islanders, 1975-76. 80 game schedule.
62 —Sergei Makarov, Calgary, 1989-90. 80 game schedule.
60 —Larry Murphy, Los Angeles, 1980-81. 80 game schedule.

MOST ASSISTS BY A PLAYER IN HIS FIRST NHL SEASON, ONE GAME:
7 —**Wayne Gretzky,** Edmonton, Feb. 15, 1980, at Edmonton. Edmonton 8, Washington 2.
6 —Gary Suter, Calgary, Apr. 4, 1986, at Calgary. Calgary 9, Edmonton 3.

MOST ASSISTS BY A PLAYER IN HIS FIRST NHL GAME:
4 —**Earl (Dutch) Reibel,** Detroit, Oct. 8, 1953, at Detroit. Detroit 4, NY Rangers 1.
 —**Roland Eriksson,** Minnesota, Oct. 6, 1976, at New York. NY Rangers 6, Minnesota 5.
3 —Al Hill, Philadelphia, Feb. 14, 1977, at Philadelphia. Philadelphia 6, St. Louis 4.

MOST POINTS BY A ROOKIE, ONE SEASON:
132 —**Teemu Selanne,** Winnipeg, 1992-93, 84 game schedule.
109 —Peter Stastny, Quebec, 1980-81. 80 game schedule.
103 —Dale Hawerchuk, Winnipeg, 1981-82. 80 game schedule.
102 —Joe Juneau, Boston, 1992-93. 84 game schedule.
100 —Mario Lemieux, Pittsburgh, 1984-85. 80 game schedule.

MOST POINTS BY A PLAYER IN HIS FIRST NHL SEASON, ONE GAME:
8 —**Peter Stastny,** Quebec, Feb. 22, 1981, at Washington. 4G-4A. Quebec 11, Washington 7.
 —**Anton Stastny,** Quebec, Feb. 22, 1981, at Washington. 3G-5A. Quebec 11, Washington 7.
7 —Wayne Gretzky, Edmonton, Feb. 15, 1980, at Edmonton. 7A. Edmonton 8, Washington 2.
 —Sergei Makarov, Calgary, Feb. 25, 1990, at Calgary, 2G-5A. Calgary 10, Edmonton 4.
6 —Wayne Gretzky, Edmonton, Mar. 29, 1980, at Toronto. 2G-4A. Edmonton 8, Toronto 5.
 —Gary Suter, Calgary, Apr. 4, 1986, at Calgary. 6A. Calgary 9, Edmonton 3.

MOST POINTS BY A PLAYER IN HIS FIRST NHL GAME:
5 —**Al Hill,** Philadelphia, Feb. 14, 1977, at Philadelphia. 2G-3A. Philadelphia 6, St. Louis 4.
4 —Alex Smart, Montreal, Jan. 14, 1943, at Montreal, 3G-1A. Montreal 5, Chicago 1.
 —Earl (Dutch) Reibel, Detroit, Oct. 8, 1953, at Detroit. 4A. Detroit 4, NY Rangers 1.
 —Roland Eriksson, Minnesota, Oct. 6, 1976 at New York. 4A. NY Rangers 6, Minnesota 5.

SCORING BY A ROOKIE DEFENSEMAN

MOST GOALS BY A ROOKIE DEFENSEMAN, ONE SEASON:
23 —**Brian Leetch,** NY Rangers, 1988-89. 80 game schedule.
22 —Barry Beck, Colorado, 1977-78. 80 game schedule.
19 —Reed Larson, Detroit, 1977-78. 80 game schedule.
 —Phil Housley, Buffalo, 1982-83. 80 game schedule.

MOST ASSISTS BY A ROOKIE DEFENSEMAN, ONE SEASON:
60 —**Larry Murphy,** Los Angeles, 1980-81. 80 game schedule.
55 —Chris Chelios, Montreal, 1984-85. 80 game schedule.
50 —Stefan Persson, NY Islanders, 1977-78. 80 game schedule.
 —Gary Suter, Calgary, 1985-86, 80 game schedule.
49 —Nicklas Lidstrom, Detroit, 1991-92. 80 game schedule.

MOST POINTS BY A ROOKIE DEFENSEMAN, ONE SEASON:
76 —**Larry Murphy,** Los Angeles, 1980-81. 80 game schedule.
71 —Brian Leetch, NY Rangers, 1988-89. 80 game schedule.
68 —Gary Suter, Calgary, 1985-86. 80 game schedule.
66 —Phil Housley, Buffalo, 1982-83. 80 game schedule.
65 —Raymond Bourque, Boston, 1979-80. 80 game schedule.

Brian Leetch made an immediate impression in the NHL, establishing a rookie record for rearguards with 23 goals for the Rangers during the 1988-89 season.

PER-GAME SCORING AVERAGES

**HIGHEST GOALS-PER-GAME AVERAGE, CAREER
(AMONG PLAYERS WITH 200 OR MORE GOALS):**
.823 —Mario Lemieux, Pittsburgh, 613G, 745GP, from 1984-85 – 1996-97.
.767 —Cy Denneny, Ottawa, Boston, 250G, 326GP, from 1917-18 – 1928-29.
.762 —Mike Bossy, NY Islanders, 573G, 752GP, from 1977-78 – 1986-87.
.717 —Brett Hull, Calgary, St. Louis, 527G, 735GP, from 1986-87 – 1996-97.
.646 —Wayne Gretzky, Edmonton, Los Angeles, St. Louis, NY Rangers, 862G, 1,335GP, from 1979-80 – 1996-97.

**HIGHEST GOALS-PER-GAME AVERAGE, ONE SEASON
(AMONG PLAYERS WITH 20-OR-MORE GOALS):**
2.20 —Joe Malone, Montreal, 1917-18, with 44G in 20GP.
1.64 —Cy Denneny, Ottawa, 1917-18, with 36G in 22GP.
—Newsy Lalonde, Montreal, 1917-18, with 23G in 14GP.
1.63 —Joe Malone, Quebec, 1919-20, with 39G in 24GP.
1.57 —Newsy Lalonde, Montreal, 1919-20, with 36G in 23GP.
1.50 —Joe Malone, Hamilton, 1920-21, with 30G in 20GP.

**HIGHEST GOALS-PER-GAME AVERAGE, ONE SEASON
(AMONG PLAYERS WITH 50-OR-MORE GOALS):**
1.18 —Wayne Gretzky, Edmonton, 1983-84, with 87G in 74GP.
1.15 —Wayne Gretzky, Edmonton, 1981-82, with 92G in 80GP.
—Mario Lemieux, Pittsburgh, 1992-93, with 69G in 60GP.
1.12 —Mario Lemieux, Pittsburgh, 1988-89, with 85G in 76GP.
1.10 —Brett Hull, St. Louis, 1990-91, with 86G in 78GP.
1.02 —Cam Neely, Boston, 1993-94, with 50G in 49GP.
1.00 —Maurice Richard, Montreal, 1944-45, with 50G in 50GP.

**HIGHEST ASSIST-PER-GAME AVERAGE, CAREER
(AMONG PLAYERS WITH 300 OR MORE ASSISTS):**
1.381 —Wayne Gretzky, Edmonton, Los Angeles, St. Louis, NY Rangers, 1,843A, 1,335GP from 1979-80 – 1996-97.
1.183 —Mario Lemieux, Pittsburgh, 881A, 745GP from 1984-85 – 1996-97.
.982 —Bobby Orr, Boston, Chicago, 645A, 657GP from 1966-67 – 1978-79.
.893 —Adam Oates, Detroit, St. Louis, Boston, Washington, 738A, 826GP from 1984-85 – 1996-97.
.878 —Paul Coffey, Edmonton, Pittsburgh, Los Angeles, Detroit, 1,063A, 1,211GP from 1980-81 – 1996-97.

**HIGHEST ASSISTS-PER-GAME AVERAGE, ONE SEASON
(AMONG PLAYERS WITH 35-OR-MORE ASSISTS):**
2.04 —Wayne Gretzky, Edmonton, 1985-86, with 163A in 80GP.
1.70 —Wayne Gretzky, Edmonton, 1987-88, with 109A in 64GP.
1.69 —Wayne Gretzky, Edmonton, 1984-85, with 135A in 80GP.
1.59 —Wayne Gretzky, Edmonton, 1983-84, with 118A in 74GP.
1.56 —Wayne Gretzky, Edmonton, 1982-83, with 125A in 80GP.
1.56 —Wayne Gretzky, Los Angeles, 1990-91, with 122A in 78GP.
1.53 —Wayne Gretzky, Edmonton, 1986-87, with 121A in 79GP.
1.52 —Mario Lemieux, Pittsburgh, 1992-93, with 91A in 60GP.
1.50 —Wayne Gretzky, Edmonton, 1981-82, with 120A in 80GP.
1.50 —Mario Lemieux, Pittsburgh, 1988-89, with 114A in 76GP.

**HIGHEST POINTS-PER-GAME AVERAGE, CAREER:
(AMONG PLAYERS WITH 500 OR MORE POINTS):**
2.026 —Wayne Gretzky, Edmonton, Los Angeles, St. Louis, NY Rangers, 2,705PTS (862G-1,843A), 1,335GP from 1979-80 – 1996-97.
2.005 —Mario Lemieux, Pittsburgh, 1,494PTS (613G-881A), 745GP from 1984-85 – 1996-97.
1.497 —Mike Bossy, NY Islanders, 1,126PTS (573G-553A), 752GP from 1978-79 – 1986-87.
1.393 —Bobby Orr, Boston, Chicago, 915PTS (270G-645A), 657GP from 1966-67 – 1978-79.
1.310 —Steve Yzerman, Detroit, 1,340PTS (539G-801A), 1,023GP from 1983-84 – 1996-97.

**HIGHEST POINTS-PER-GAME AVERAGE, ONE SEASON
(AMONG PLAYERS WITH 50-OR-MORE POINTS):**
2.77 —Wayne Gretzky, Edmonton, 1983-84, with 205PTS in 74GP.
2.69 —Wayne Gretzky, Edmonton, 1985-86, with 215PTS in 80GP.
2.67 —Mario Lemieux, Pittsburgh, 1992-93, with 160PTS in 60GP.
2.65 —Wayne Gretzky, Edmonton, 1981-82, with 212PTS in 80GP.
2.62 —Mario Lemieux, Pittsburgh, 1988-89, with 199PTS in 78GP.
2.60 —Wayne Gretzky, Edmonton, 1984-85, with 208PTS in 80GP.
2.45 —Wayne Gretzky, Edmonton, 1982-83, with 196PTS in 80GP.
2.33 —Wayne Gretzky, Edmonton, 1987-88, with 149PTS in 64GP.
2.32 —Wayne Gretzky, Edmonton, 1986-87, with 183PTS in 79GP.
2.30 —Mario Lemieux, Pittsburgh, 1995-96 with 161PTS in 70GP.
2.18 —Mario Lemieux, Pittsburgh, 1987-88, with 168PTS in 77GP.
2.15 —Wayne Gretzky, Los Angeles, 1988-89, with 168PTS in 78GP.
2.09 —Wayne Gretzky, Los Angeles, 1990-91, with 163 PTS in 78GP.
2.08 —Mario Lemieux, Pittsburgh, 1989-90, with 123 PTS in 59GP.
2.05 —Wayne Gretzky, Edmonton, 1980-81, with 164PTS in 80GP.

SCORING PLATEAUS

MOST 20-OR-MORE GOAL SEASONS:
22 —Gordie Howe, Detroit, Hartford in 26 seasons.
17 —Marcel Dionne, Detroit, Los Angeles, NY Rangers, in 18 seasons.
—Mike Gartner, Washington, Minnesota, NY Rangers, Toronto, Phoenix, in 18 seasons.
16 —Phil Esposito, Chicago, Boston, NY Rangers, in 18 seasons.
—Norm Ullman, Detroit, Toronto, in 19 seasons.
—John Bucyk, Detroit, Boston, in 22 seasons.
—Wayne Gretzky, Edmonton, Los Angeles, St. Louis, NY Rangers, in 18 seasons.

MOST CONSECUTIVE 20-OR-MORE GOAL SEASONS:
22 —Gordie Howe, Detroit, 1949-50 – 1970-71.
17 —Marcel Dionne, Detroit, Los Angeles, NY Rangers, 1971-72 – 1987-88.
16 —Phil Esposito, Chicago, Boston, NY Rangers, 1964-65 – 1979-80.
15 —Mike Gartner, Washington, Minnesota, NY Rangers, Toronto, 1979-80 – 1993-94.
14 —Maurice Richard, Montreal, 1943-44 – 1956-57.
—Stan Mikita, Chicago, 1961-62 – 1974-75.
—Michel Goulet, Quebec, Chicago, 1979-80 – 1992-93.

MOST 30-OR-MORE GOAL SEASONS:
17 —Mike Gartner, Washington, Minnesota, NY Rangers, Toronto, Phoenix, in 18 seasons.
14 —Gordie Howe, Detroit, Hartford, in 26 seasons.
—Marcel Dionne, Detroit, Los Angeles, NY Rangers, in 18 seasons.
—Wayne Gretzky, Edmonton, Los Angeles, St. Louis, Phoenix, in 18 seasons.
13 —Bobby Hull, Chicago, Winnipeg, Hartford, in 16 seasons.
—Phil Esposito, Chicago, Boston, NY Rangers, in 18 seasons.

Very few players in NHL history have been as consistent as swift-skating Mike Gartner, who reached the 20 goal mark for the 17th time in 18 seasons in 1996-97. Gartner's career has taken him to Washington, Minnesota, the New York Rangers, Toronto and, most recently, Phoenix.

MOST CONSECUTIVE 30-OR-MORE GOAL SEASONS:
15 —**Mike Gartner,** Washington, Minnesota, NY Rangers, Toronto, 1979-80 – 1993-94.
13 —Bobby Hull, Chicago, 1959-60 – 1971-72.
—Phil Esposito, Boston, NY Rangers, 1967-68 – 1979-80.
—Wayne Gretzky, Edmonton, Los Angeles, 1979-80 – 1991-92.
12 —Marcel Dionne, Detroit, Los Angeles, 1974-75 – 1985-86.
10 —Darryl Sittler, Toronto, Philadelphia, 1973-74 – 1982-83.
—Mike Bossy, NY Islanders, 1977-78 – 1986-87.
—Jari Kurri, Edmonton, 1980-81 – 1989-90.

MOST 40-OR-MORE GOAL SEASONS:
12 —**Wayne Gretzky,** Edmonton, Los Angeles, St. Louis, NY Rangers, in 18 seasons.
10 —Marcel Dionne, Detroit, Los Angeles, NY Rangers, in 18 seasons.
—Mario Lemieux, Pittsburgh, in 12 seasons.
9 —Mike Bossy, NY Islanders, in 10 seasons.
—Mike Gartner, Washington, Minnesota, NY Rangers, Toronto, Phoenix, in 18 seasons.

MOST CONSECUTIVE 40-OR-MORE GOAL SEASONS:
12 —**Wayne Gretzky,** Edmonton, Los Angeles, 1979-80 – 1990-91.
9 —Mike Bossy, NY Islanders, 1977-78 – 1985-86.
8 —Luc Robitaille, Los Angeles, 1986-87 – 1993-94.
7 —Phil Esposito, Boston, 1968-69 – 1974-75.
—Michel Goulet, Quebec, 1981-82 – 1987-88.
—Jari Kurri, Edmonton, 1982-83 – 1988-89.

MOST 50-OR-MORE GOAL SEASONS:
9 —**Mike Bossy,** NY Islanders, in 10 seasons.
—Wayne Gretzky, Edmonton, Los Angeles, St. Louis, NY Rangers, in 18 seasons.
6 —Guy Lafleur, Montreal, NY Rangers, Quebec, in 17 seasons.
—Marcel Dionne, Detroit, Los Angeles, NY Rangers, in 18 seasons.
—Mario Lemieux, Pittsburgh, in 12 seasons.
5 —Bobby Hull, Chicago, Winnipeg, Hartford, in 16 seasons.
—Phil Esposito, Chicago, Boston, NY Rangers, in 18 seasons.
—Brett Hull, Calgary, St. Louis, in 11 seasons.
—Steve Yzerman, Detroit, in 14 seasons.

MOST CONSECUTIVE 50-OR-MORE GOAL SEASONS:
9 —**Mike Bossy,** NY Islanders, 1977-78 – 1985-86.
8 —Wayne Gretzky, Edmonton, 1979-80 – 1986-87.
6 —Guy Lafleur, Montreal, 1974-75 – 1979-80.
5 —Phil Esposito, Boston, 1970-71 – 1974-75.
—Marcel Dionne, Los Angeles, 1978-79 – 1982-83.
—Brett Hull, St. Louis, 1989-90 – 1993-94.

MOST 60-OR-MORE GOAL SEASONS:
5 —**Mike Bossy,** NY Islanders, in 10 seasons.
—Wayne Gretzky, Edmonton, Los Angeles, St. Louis, NY Rangers, in 18 seasons.
4 —Phil Esposito, Chicago, Boston, NY Rangers, in 18 seasons.
—Mario Lemieux, Pittsburgh, in 12 seasons.

MOST CONSECUTIVE 60-OR-MORE GOAL SEASONS:
4 —**Wayne Gretzky,** Edmonton, 1981-82 – 1984-85.
3 —Mike Bossy, NY Islanders, 1980-81 – 1982-83.
—Brett Hull, St. Louis, 1989-90 – 1991-92.
2 —Phil Esposito, Boston, 1970-71 – 1971-72, 1973-74 – 1974-75.
—Jari Kurri, Edmonton, 1984-85 – 1985-86.
—Mario Lemieux, Pittsburgh, 1987-88 – 1988-89.
—Steve Yzerman, Detroit, 1988-89 – 1989-90.
—Pavel Bure, Vancouver, 1992-93 – 1993-94.

MOST 100-OR-MORE POINT SEASONS:
15 —**Wayne Gretzky,** Edmonton, Los Angeles, St. Louis, NY Rangers, in 18 seasons.
10 —Mario Lemieux, Pittsburgh, in 12 seasons.
8 —Marcel Dionne, Detroit, Los Angeles, NY Rangers, in 18 seasons.
7 —Mike Bossy, NY Islanders, in 10 seasons.
—Peter Stastny, Quebec, New Jersey, St. Louis, in 15 seasons.

MOST CONSECUTIVE 100-OR-MORE POINT SEASONS:
13 —**Wayne Gretzky,** Edmonton, Los Angeles, 1979-80 – 1991-92.
6 —Bobby Orr, Boston, 1969-70 – 1974-75.
—Guy Lafleur, Montreal, 1974-75 – 1979-80.
—Mike Bossy, NY Islanders, 1980-81 – 1985-86.
—Peter Stastny, Quebec, 1980-81 – 1985-86.
—Mario Lemieux, Pittsburgh, 1984-85 – 1989-90.
—Steve Yzerman, Detroit, 1987-88 – 1992-93.

THREE-OR-MORE-GOAL GAMES

MOST THREE-OR-MORE GOAL GAMES, CAREER:
49 —**Wayne Gretzky,** Edmonton, Los Angeles, St. Louis, NY Rangers, in 18 seasons, 36 three-goal games, 9 four-goal games, 4 five-goal games.
39 —Mike Bossy, NY Islanders, in 10 seasons, 30 three-goal games, 9 four-goal games.
—Mario Lemieux, Pittsburgh, in 12 seasons, 26 three-goal games, 10 four-goal games and 3 five-goal games.
32 —Phil Esposito, Chicago, Boston, NY Rangers, in 18 seasons, 27 three-goal games, 5 four-goal games.
28 —Bobby Hull, Chicago, Winnipeg, Hartford, in 16 seasons, 24 three-goal games, 4 four-goal games.
—Marcel Dionne, Detroit, Los Angeles, NY Rangers, in 18 seasons, 25 three-goal games, 3 four-goal games.
26 —Cy Denneny, Ottawa in 12 seasons. 20 three-goal games, 5 four-goal games, 1 six-goal game.
—Maurice Richard, Montreal, in 18 seasons, 23 three-goal games, 2 four-goal games, 1 five-goal game.

MOST THREE-OR-MORE GOAL GAMES, ONE SEASON:
10 —**Wayne Gretzky,** Edmonton, 1981-82. 6 three-goal games, 3 four-goal games, 1 five-goal game.
—**Wayne Gretzky,** Edmonton, 1983-84. 6 three-goal games, 4 four-goal games.
9 —Mike Bossy, NY Islanders, 1980-81. 6 three-goal games, 3 four-goal games.
—Mario Lemieux, Pittsburgh, 1988-89. 7 three-goal games, 1 four-goal game, 1 five-goal game.
8 —Brett Hull, St. Louis, 1991-92. 8 three-goal games.
7 —Joe Malone, Montreal, 1917-18. 2 three-goal games, 2 four-goal games, 3 five-goal games.
—Phil Esposito, Boston, 1970-71. 7 three-goal games.
—Rick Martin, Buffalo, 1975-76. 6 three-goal games, 1 four-goal game.
—Alexander Mogilny, Buffalo, 1992-93. 5 three-goal games, 2 four-goal games.

Mike Bossy made the 14 teams that passed on him in the 1977 Amateur Draft regret their decisions when he went to on to set an NHL mark by scoring at least 50 goals in nine straight seasons.

SCORING STREAKS

LONGEST CONSECUTIVE GOAL-SCORING STREAK:
16 Games —Harry (Punch) Broadbent, Ottawa, 1921-22.
25 goals during streak.
14 Games —Joe Malone, Montreal, 1917-18. 35 goals during streak.
13 Games —Newsy Lalonde, Montreal, 1920-21. 24 goals during streak.
— Charlie Simmer, Los Angeles, 1979-80. 17 goals during streak.
12 Games —Cy Denneny, Ottawa, 1917-18: 23 goals during streak.
— Dave Lumley, Edmonton, 1981-82. 15 goals during streak.
— Mario Lemieux, Pittsburgh, 1992-93. 18 goals during streak.

LONGEST CONSECUTIVE ASSIST-SCORING STREAK:
23 Games —Wayne Gretzky, Los Angeles, 1990-91. 48A during streak.
18 Games —Adam Oates, Boston, 1992-93. 28A during streak.
17 Games —Wayne Gretzky, Edmonton, 1983-84. 38A during streak.
— Paul Coffey, Edmonton, 1985-86. 27A during streak.
— Wayne Gretzky, Los Angeles, 1989-90. 35A during streak.
15 Games —Jari Kurri, Edmonton, 1983-84. 21A during streak.
— Brian Leetch, NY Rangers, 1991-92. 23A during streak.

LONGEST CONSECUTIVE POINT SCORING STREAK:
51 Games —Wayne Gretzky, Edmonton, 1983-84. 61G-92A-153PTS during streak.
46 Games —Mario Lemieux, Pittsburgh, 1989-90. 39G-64A-103PTS during streak.
39 Games —Wayne Gretzky, Edmonton, 1985-86. 33G-75A-108PTS during streak.
30 Games —Wayne Gretzky, Edmonton, 1982-83. 24G52A-76PTS during streak.
— Mats Sundin, Quebec, 1992-93. 21G-25A-46PTS during streak.
28 Games —Guy Lafleur, Montreal, 1976-77. 19G-42A-61PTS during streak.
— Wayne Gretzky, Edmonton, 1984-85. 20G-43A-63PTS during streak.
— Mario Lemieux, Pittsburgh, 1985-86. 21G-38A-59PTS during streak.
— Paul Coffey, Edmonton, 1985-86. 16G-39A-55PTS during streak.
— Steve Yzerman, Detroit, 1988-89. 29G-36A-65PTS during streak.

LONGEST CONSECUTIVE POINT-SCORING STREAK FROM START OF SEASON:
51 Games —Wayne Gretzky, Edmonton, 1983-84. 61G-92A-153PTS during streak which was stopped by goaltender Markus Mattsson and Los Angeles on Jan. 28, 1984.

LONGEST CONSECUTIVE POINT-SCORING STREAK BY A DEFENSEMAN:
28 Games —Paul Coffey, Edmonton, 1985-86. 16G-39A-55PTS during streak.
19 Games —Ray Bourque, Boston, 1987-88. 6G-21A-27PTS during streak.
17 Games —Ray Bourque, Boston, 1984-85. 4G-24A-28PTS during streak.
— Brian Leetch, NY Rangers, 1991-92. 5G-24A-29PTS during streak.
16 Games —Gary Suter, Calgary, 1987-88. 8G-17A-25PTS during streak.
15 Games —Bobby Orr, Boston, 1970-71. 10G-23A-33PTS during streak.
— Bobby Orr, Boston, 1973-74. 8G-15A-23PTS during streak.
— Steve Duchesne, Quebec, 1992-93. 4G-17A-21PTS during streak.
— Chris Chelios, Chicago, 1995-96. 4G-16A-20PTS during streak.

FASTEST GOALS AND ASSISTS

FASTEST GOAL FROM START OF A GAME:
5 Seconds — Doug Smail, Winnipeg, Dec. 20, 1981, at Winnipeg. Winnipeg 5, St. Louis 4.
— **Bryan Trottier,** NY Islanders, Mar. 22, 1984, at Boston. NY Islanders 3, Boston 3.
— **Alexander Mogilny,** Buffalo, Dec. 21, 1991, at Toronto. Buffalo 4, Toronto 1.
6 Seconds — Henry Boucha, Detroit, Jan. 28, 1973, at Montreal. Detroit 4, Montreal 2.
— Jean Pronovost, Pittsburgh, Mar. 25, 1976, at St. Louis. St. Louis 5, Pittsburgh 2.
7 Seconds — Charlie Conacher, Toronto, Feb. 6, 1932, at Toronto. Toronto 6, Boston 0.
— Danny Gare, Buffalo, Dec. 17, 1978, at Buffalo. Buffalo 6, Vancouver 3.
— Dave Williams, Los Angeles, Feb. 14, 1987 at Los Angeles. Los Angeles 5, Harford 2.
8 Seconds — Ron Martin, NY Americans, Dec. 4, 1932, at New York. NY Americans 4, Montreal 2.
— Chuck Arnason, Colorado, Jan. 28, 1977, at Atlanta. Colorado 3, Atlanta 3.
— Wayne Gretzky, Edmonton, Dec. 14, 1983, at New York. Edmonton 9, NY Rangers 4.
— Gaetan Duchesne, Washington, Mar. 14, 1987, at St. Louis. Washington 3, St. Louis 3.
— Tim Kerr, Philadelphia, Mar. 7, 1989, at Philadelphia. Philadelphia 4, Edmonton 4.
— Grant Ledyard, Buffalo, Dec. 4, 1991, at Winnipeg. Buffalo 4, Winnipeg 4.
— Brent Sutter, Chicago, Feb. 5, 1995, at Vancouver. Chicago 9, Vancouver 4.
— Paul Kariya, Anaheim, Mar. 9, 1997, at Colorado. Anaheim 2, Colorado 2.

FASTEST GOAL FROM START OF A PERIOD:
4 Seconds — Claude Provost, Montreal, Nov. 9, 1957, at Montreal, second period. Montreal 4, Boston 2.
— **Denis Savard,** Chicago, Jan. 12, 1986, at Chicago, third period. Chicago 4, Hartford 2.

FASTEST GOAL BY A PLAYER IN HIS FIRST NHL GAME:
15 Seconds — Gus Bodnar, Toronto, Oct. 30, 1943. Toronto 5, NY Rangers 2.
18 Seconds — Danny Gare, Buffalo, Oct. 10, 1974. Buffalo 9, Boston 5.
20 Seconds — Alexander Mogilny, Buffalo, Oct. 5, 1989. Buffalo 4, Quebec 3.

FASTEST TWO GOALS:
4 Seconds — Nels Stewart, Mtl. Maroons, Jan. 3, 1931, at Montreal at 8:24 and 8:28, third period. Mtl. Maroons 5, Boston 3.
— **Deron Quint,** Winnipeg, Dec. 15, 1995, at Winnipeg at 7:51 and 7:55, second period. Winnipeg 9, Edmonton 4.
5 Seconds — Pete Mahovlich, Montreal, Feb. 20, 1971, at Montreal at 12:16 and 12:21, third period. Montreal 7, Chicago 1.
6 Seconds — Jim Pappin, Chicago, Feb. 16, 1972, at Chicago at 2:57 and 3:03, third period. Chicago 3, Philadelphia 3.
— Ralph Backstrom, Los Angeles, Nov. 2, 1972, at Los Angeles at 8:30 and 8:36, third period. Los Angeles 5, Boston 2.
— Lanny McDonald, Calgary, Mar. 22, 1984, at Calgary at 16:23 and 16:29, first period. Detroit 6, Calgary 4.
— Sylvain Turgeon, Hartford, Mar. 28, 1987, at Hartford at 13:59 and 14:05, second period. Hartford 5, Pittsburgh 4.

FASTEST THREE GOALS:
21 Seconds — Bill Mosienko, Chicago, Mar. 23, 1952, at New York, against goaltender Lorne Anderson. Mosienko scored at 6:09, 6:20 and 6:30 of third period, all with both teams at full strength. Chicago 7, NY Rangers 6.
44 Seconds — Jean Béliveau, Montreal, Nov. 5, 1955, at Montreal, against goaltender Terry Sawchuk. Béliveau scored at :42, 1:08 and 1:26 of second period, all with Montreal holding a 6-4 man advantage. Montreal 4, Boston 2.

FASTEST THREE ASSISTS:
21 Seconds — Gus Bodnar, Chicago, Mar. 23, 1952, at New York, Bodnar assisted on Bill Mosienko's three goals at 6:09, 6:20, 6:30 of third period. Chicago 7, NY Rangers 6.
44 Seconds — Bert Olmstead, Montreal, Nov. 5, 1955, at Montreal against Boston. Olmstead assisted on Jean Béliveau's three goals at :42, 1:08 and 1:26 of second period. Montreal 4, Boston 2.

SHOTS ON GOAL

MOST SHOTS ON GOAL, ONE SEASON:
550 —Phil Esposito, Boston, 1970-71. 78 game schedule.
426 —Phil Esposito, Boston, 1971-72. 78 game schedule.
414 —Bobby Hull, Chicago, 1968-69. 76 game schedule.

PENALTIES

MOST PENALTY MINUTES, CAREER:
3,966 —Dave Williams, Toronto, Vancouver, Detroit, Los Angeles, Hartford, in 14 seasons, 962GP.
3,343 —Dale Hunter, Quebec, Washington, in 17 seasons, 1,263GP.
3,146 —Tim Hunter, Calgary, Quebec, Vancouver, San Jose, in 16 seasons, 815GP.
3,078 —Marty McSorley, Pittsburgh, Edmonton, Los Angeles, NY Rangers, San Jose, in 14 seasons, 832GP.
3,043 —Chris Nilan, Montreal, NY Rangers, Boston, in 13 seasons, 688GP.

MOST PENALTY MINUTES, CAREER, INCLUDING PLAYOFFS:
4,421 —Dave Williams, Toronto, Vancouver, Detroit, Los Angeles, Hartford, 3,966 in regular-season; 455 in playoffs.
3,879 —Dale Hunter, Quebec, Washington, 3,218 in regular-season; 661 in playoffs.
3,584 —Chris Nilan, Montreal, NY Rangers, Boston, 3,043 in regular-season; 541 in playoffs.
3,437 —Tim Hunter, Calgary, Quebec, Vancouver, 3,011 regular-season; 426 in playoffs.
3,264 —Marty McSorley, Pittsburgh, Edmonton, Los Angeles, NY Rangers, 2,892 in regular-season; 372 in playoffs.

MOST PENALTY MINUTES, ONE SEASON:
472 —Dave Schultz, Philadelphia, 1974-75.
409 —Paul Baxter, Pittsburgh, 1981-82.
408 —Mike Peluso, Chicago, 1991-92.
405 —Dave Schultz, Los Angeles, Pittsburgh, 1977-78.

MOST PENALTIES, ONE GAME:
   10 —**Chris Nilan,** Boston, Mar. 31, 1991, at Boston against Hartford.
      6 minors, 2 majors, 1 10-minute misconduct, 1 game misconduct.
   9 —Jim Dorey, Toronto, Oct. 16, 1968, at Toronto against Pittsburgh. 4 minors,
      2 majors, 2 10-minute misconducts, 1 game misconduct.
   —Dave Schultz, Pittsburgh, Apr. 6, 1978, at Detroit. 5 minors,
      2 majors, 2 10-minute misconducts.
   —Randy Holt, Los Angeles, Mar. 11, 1979, at Philadelphia. 1 minor,
      3 majors, 2 10-minute misconducts, 3 game misconducts.
   —Russ Anderson, Pittsburgh, Jan. 19, 1980, at Pittsburgh.
      3 minors, 3 majors, 3 game misconducts.
   —Kim Clackson, Quebec, Mar. 8, 1981, at Quebec. 4 minors, 3 majors,
      2 game misconducts.
   —Terry O'Reilly, Boston, Dec. 19, 1984 at Hartford. 5 minors,
      3 majors, 1 game misconduct.
   —Larry Playfair, Los Angeles, Dec. 9, 1986, at NY Islanders. 6 minors,
      2 majors, 1 10-minute misconduct.
   —Marty McSorley, Los Angeles, Apr. 14, 1992, at Vancouver. 5 minors,
      2 majors, 1 10-minute misconduct, 1 game misconduct.

MOST PENALTY MINUTES, ONE GAME:
   67 —**Randy Holt,** Los Angeles, Mar. 11, 1979, at Philadelphia. 1 minor,
      3 majors, 2 10-minute misconducts, 3 game misconducts.
   55 —Frank Bathe, Philadelphia, Mar. 11, 1979, at Philadelphia.
      3 majors, 2 10-minute misconducts, 2 game misconducts.
   51 —Russ Anderson, Pittsburgh, Jan. 19, 1980, at Pittsburgh.
      3 minors, 3 majors, 3 game misconducts.

MOST PENALTIES, ONE PERIOD:
   9 —**Randy Holt,** Los Angeles, Mar. 11, 1979, at Philadelphia, first period.
      1 minor, 3 majors, 2 10-minute misconducts, 3 game misconducts.

MOST PENALTY MINUTES, ONE PERIOD:
   67 —**Randy Holt,** Los Angeles, Mar. 11, 1979, at Philadelphia, first period.
      1 minor, 3 majors, 2 10-minute misconducts, 3 game misconducts.

GOALTENDING

MOST GAMES APPEARED IN BY A GOALTENDER, CAREER:
   971 —**Terry Sawchuk,** Detroit, Boston, Toronto, Los Angeles, NY Rangers
      from 1949-50 – 1969-70.
   906 —Glenn Hall, Detroit, Chicago, St. Louis from 1952-53 – 1970-71.
   886 —Tony Esposito, Montreal, Chicago from 1968-69 – 1983-84.
   861 —Lorne "Gump" Worsley, NY Rangers, Montreal, Minnesota from
      1952-53 – 1973-74.

MOST CONSECUTIVE COMPLETE GAMES BY A GOALTENDER:
   502 —**Glenn Hall,** Detroit, Chicago. Played 502 games from beginning of 1955-56
      season - first 12 games of 1962-63. In his 503rd straight game, Nov. 7, 1962,
      at Chicago, Hall was removed from the game against Boston with a back
      injury in the first period.

MOST GAMES APPEARED IN BY A GOALTENDER, ONE SEASON:
   79 —**Grant Fuhr,** St. Louis, 1995-96.
   77 —Martin Brodeur, New Jersey, 1995-96.
   75 —Grant Fuhr, Edmonton, 1987-88.
   74 —Ed Belfour, Chicago, 1990-91.
      —Arturs Irbe, San Jose, 1993-94.
      —Felix Potvin, Toronto, 1996-97.

MOST MINUTES PLAYED BY A GOALTENDER, CAREER:
   57,184 —**Terry Sawchuk,** Detroit, Boston, Toronto, Los Angeles, NY Rangers, from
      1949-50 – 1969-70.

MOST MINUTES PLAYED BY A GOALTENDER, ONE SEASON:
   4,433 —**Martin Brodeur,** New Jersey, 1995-96.

MOST SHUTOUTS, CAREER:
   103 —**Terry Sawchuk,** Detroit, Boston, Toronto, Los Angeles, NY Rangers
      in 21 seasons.
   94 —George Hainsworth, Montreal Canadiens, Toronto in 10 seasons.
   84 —Glenn Hall, Detroit, Chicago, St. Louis in 16 seasons.

MOST SHUTOUTS, ONE SEASON:
   22 —**George Hainsworth,** Montreal, 1928-29. 44GP
   15 —Alex Connell, Ottawa, 1925-26. 36GP
      —Alex Connell, Ottawa, 1927-28. 44GP
      —Hal Winkler, Boston, 1927-28. 44GP
      —Tony Esposito, Chicago, 1969-70. 63GP
   14 —George Hainsworth, Montreal, 1926-27. 44GP

LONGEST SHUTOUT SEQUENCE BY A GOALTENDER:
461 Minutes, 29 Seconds — Alex Connell, Ottawa, 1927-28, six consecutive
   shutouts. (Forward passing not permitted in attacking zones in 1927-1928.)
343 Minutes, 5 Seconds — George Hainsworth, Montreal, 1928-29, four consecutive
   shutouts.
324 Minutes, 40 Seconds — Roy Worters, NY Americans, 1930-31, four consecutive
   shutouts.
309 Minutes, 21 Seconds — Bill Durnan, Montreal, 1948-49, four consecutive shutouts.

MOST WINS BY A GOALTENDER, CAREER:
   447 —**Terry Sawchuk,** Detroit, Boston, Toronto, Los Angeles, NY Rangaers,
      in 21 seasons. 971GP
   434 —Jacques Plante, Montreal, NY Rangers, St. Louis, Toronto, Boston,
      in 18 seasons. 837GP
   423 —Tony Esposito, Montreal, Chicago, in 16 seasons. 886GP

MOST WINS BY A GOALTENDER, ONE SEASON:
   47 —**Bernie Parent,** Philadelphia, 1973-74.
   44 —Bernie Parent, Philadelphia, 1974-75.
      —Terry Sawchuk, Detroit, 1950-51.
      —Terry Sawchuk, Detroit, 1951-52.

LONGEST WINNING STREAK BY A GOALTENDER, ONE SEASON:
   17 —**Gilles Gilbert,** Boston, 1975-76.
   14 —Don Beaupre, Minnesota, 1985-86.
      —Ross Brooks, Boston, 1973-74.
      —Tiny Thompson, Boston, 1929-30.
      —Tom Barrasso, Pittsburgh, 1992-93.

LONGEST UNDEFEATED STREAK BY A GOALTENDER, ONE SEASON:
   32 Games — Gerry Cheevers, Boston, 1971-72. 24w-8T.
   31 Games — Pete Peeters, Boston, 1982-83. 26w-5T.
   27 Games — Pete Peeters, Philadelphia, 1979-80. 22w-5T.
   23 Games — Frank Brimsek, Boston, 1940-41. 15w-8T.
      — Glenn Resch, NY Islanders, 1978-79. 15w-8T.
      — Grant Fuhr, Edmonton, 1981-82. 15w-8T.

LONGEST UNDEFEATED STREAK BY A GOALTENDER IN HIS FIRST NHL SEASON:
   23 Games — Grant Fuhr, 1981-82. 15w-8T.

LONGEST UNDEFEATED STREAK BY A GOALTENDER FROM START OF CAREER:
   16 Games — Patrick Lalime, Pittsburgh, 1996-97. 14w-2T.

MOST 40-OR-MORE WIN SEASONS BY A GOALTENDER:
   3 —**Jacques Plante,** Montreal, NY Rangers, St. Louis, Toronto, Boston
      in 18 seasons.
   2 —Terry Sawchuk, Detroit, Boston, Toronto, Los Angeles, NY Rangers
      in 21 seasons.
      —Bernie Parent, Boston, Philadelphia, Toronto in 13 seasons.
      —Ken Dryden, Montreal in 8 seasons.
      —Ed Belfour, Chicago, San Jose in 8 seasons.

MOST CONSECUTIVE 40-OR-MORE WIN SEASONS BY A GOALTENDER:
   2 —**Terry Sawchuk,** Detroit, 1950-51 – 1951-52.
      —Bernie Parent, Philadelphia, 1973-74 – 1974-75.
      —Ken Dryden, Montreal, 1975-76 – 1976-77.

MOST 30-OR-MORE WIN SEASONS BY A GOALTENDER:
   8 —**Tony Esposito,** Montreal, Chicago in 16 seasons.
   7 —Jacques Plante, Montreal, NY Rangers, St. Louis, Toronto, Boston
      in 18 seasons.
      —Ken Dryden, Montreal, in 8 seasons.
      —Patrick Roy, Montreal, Colorado in 13 seasons.
   6 —Glenn Hall, Detroit, Chicago, St. Louis in 18 seasons.

MOST CONSECUTIVE 30-OR-MORE WIN SEASONS BY A GOALTENDER:
   7 —**Tony Esposito,** Chicago, 1969-70 – 1975-76.
   6 —Jacques Plante, Montreal, 1954-55 – 1959-60.
   5 —Ken Dryden, Montreal, 1974-75 – 1978-79.
   4 —Terry Sawchuk, Detroit, 1950-51 – 1953-54.
      —Ed Giacomin, NY Rangers, 1966-67 – 1969-70.

MOST LOSSES BY A GOALTENDER, CAREER:
   353 —**Gump Worsley,** NY Rangers, Montreal, Minnesota, in 21 seasons. 861GP
   351 —Gilles Meloche, Chicago, California, Cleveland, Minnesota, Pittsburgh,
      in 18 seasons. 788GP
   330 — Terry Sawchuk, Detroit, Boston, Toronto, Los Angeles, NY Rangers,
      in 21 seasons. 971GP

MOST LOSSES BY A GOALTENDER, ONE SEASON:
   48 —**Gary Smith,** California, 1970-71.
   47 —Al Rollins, Chicago, 1953-54.

Using an aggressive crease-clearing style and a solid stand-up technique, Gerry Cheevers went 32 games without a loss during the 1971-72 season.

Active NHL Players' Three-or-More-Goal Games

Regular Season

Teams named are the ones the players were with at the time of their multiple-scoring games. Players listed alphabetically.

Bernie Nicholls has scored at least three goals in a game 18 times in his career, which began with the Los Angeles Kings in 1981-82.

Player	Team	3-Goals	4-Goals	5-Goals
Adams, Greg	Vancouver	1	1	—
Alfredsson, Daniel	Ottawa	1	—	—
Amonte, Tony	NYR, Chi	4	—	—
Andersson, Mikael	Tampa Bay	1	—	—
Andersson, Niklas	NY Islanders	1	—	—
Andreychuk, Dave	Buf., Tor.	7	2	1
Arnott, Jason	Edmonton	2	—	—
Audette, Donald	Buffalo	2	—	—
Babych, Dave	Vancouver	1	—	—
Barnes, Stu	Winnipeg	1	—	—
Barr, Dave	St.L., Det.	2	—	—
Bellows, Brian	Min., Mtl., T.B.	6	3	—
Beranek, Josef	Philadelphia	1	—	—
Bondra, Peter	Washington	5	3	1
Bourque, Phil	Pittsburgh	1	—	—
Bourque, Ray	Boston	1	—	—
Bradley, Brian	Tampa Bay	1	—	—
Brind'Amour, Rod	Philadelphia	1	—	—
Broten, Neal	Minnesota	6	—	—
Broten, Paul	NY Rangers	1	—	—
Brown, Rob	Pittsburgh	7	—	—
Buchberger, Kelly	Edmonton	1	—	—
Bure, Pavel	Vancouver	5	1	—
Burr, Shawn	Detroit	3	—	—
Burridge, Randy	Bos., Wsh.	4	—	—
Butsayev, Viacheslav	Philadelphia	1	—	—
Carbonneau, Guy	Montreal	1	1	—
Carpenter, Bob	Wsh., Bos.	2	1	—
Carson, Jimmy	L.A., Edm., Det.	9	1	—
Ciccarelli, Dino	Min., Wsh., Det., T.B.	15	4	—
Clark, Wendel	Tor., Que.	7	2	—
Coffey, Paul	Edmonton	4	1	—
Corson, Shayne	Mtl., Edm.	3	—	—
Courtnall, Geoff	Bos., Wsh., St.L.	3	—	—
Courtnall, Russ	Tor., Mtl., Min., Van.	5	—	—
Craven, Murray	Philadelphia	3	—	—
Creighton, Adam	Buf., Chi.	2	—	—
Cullen, John	Pit., Hfd.	3	—	—
Cunneyworth, R.	Pittsburgh	1	1	—
Czerkawski, Mariusz	Edmonton	2	—	—
Dahlen, Ulf	NYR, Min., S.J.	4	—	—
Daigle, Alexandre	Ottawa	1	—	—
Damphousse, V.	Tor., Edm., Mtl.	8	1	—
Dawe, Jason	Buffalo	1	—	—
Daze, Eric	Chicago	1	—	—
Dineen, Kevin	Hfd., Phi.	9	1	—
Dionne, Gilbert	Montreal	1	—	—
Donnelly, Mike	Los Angeles	2	—	—
Druce, John	Wsh., L.A.	2	—	—
Duchesne, Steve	L.A., Phi., St.L.	3	—	—
Emerson, Nelson	Winnipeg	1	—	—
Errey, Bob	Pittsburgh	1	—	—
Evason, Dean	Hartford	1	—	—
Fedorov, Sergei	Detroit	1	1	1
Ferraro, Ray	Hfd., NYI, NYR	7	1	—
Flatley, Patrick	NY Islanders	2	1	—
Fleury, Theo	Calgary	11	—	—
Forsberg, Peter	Colorado	3	—	—
Francis, Ron	Hfd., Pit.	9	1	—
Friesen, Jeff	San Jose	1	—	—
Gagner, Dave	Min., Dal.	3	1	—
Garpenlov, Johan	Det., S.J., Fla.	2	1	—
Gartner, Mike	Wsh., Min., NYR, Pho.	15	2	—
Gaudreau, Rob	San Jose	3	—	—
Gelinas, Martin	Edm., Van.	2	1	—
Gilchrist, Brent	Montreal	1	—	—
Gilmour, Doug	St.L.; Tor.	3	—	—
Granato, Tony	NYR, L.A., S.J.	6	1	—
Gratton, Chris	Tampa Bay	1	—	—
Graves, Adam	Edm., NYR	6	—	—
Green, Travis	NY Islanders	1	—	—
Gretzky, Wayne	Edm., L.A.	36	9	4
Grieve, Brent	Edmonton	1	—	—
Grosek, Michal	Buffalo	1	—	—
Guerin, Bill	New Jersey	1	—	—
Hannan, Dave	Edmonton	1	—	—
Harvey, Todd	Dallas	1	—	—
Hatcher, Kevin	Wsh., Dal.	2	—	—
Heinze, Stephen	Boston	2	—	—
Hogue, Benoit	NY Islanders	1	—	—
Holik, Bobby	New Jersey	2	—	—
Housley, Phil	Buffalo	2	—	—
Hull, Brett	Cgy., St.L.	25	2	—
Hull, Jody	Hartford	1	—	—
Hunter, Dale	Que., Wsh.	4	—	—

Player	Team	3-Goals	4-Goals	5-Goals
Jagr, Jaromir	Pittsburgh	4	—	—
Janney, Craig	Bos., St.L.	3	—	—
Juneau, Joe	Bos., Wsh.	2	—	—
Kamensky, Valeri	Colorado	3	—	—
Kariya, Paul	Anaheim	2	—	—
Khmylev, Yuri	Buffalo	1	—	—
Khristich, Dimitri	Washington	2	—	—
King, Derek	NY Islanders	5	1	—
Klatt, Trent	Philadelphia	1	—	—
Klima, Petr	Det., Edm.	6	—	—
Konowalchuk, Steve	Washington	2	—	—
Kontos, Chris	Tampa Bay	—	1	—
Korolev, Igor	Winnipeg	1	—	—
Kovalenko, Andrei	Quebec	1	—	—
Kovalev, Alexei	NY Rangers	2	—	—
Kozlov, Vyacheslav	Detroit	1	1	—
Krupp, Uwe	Quebec	1	—	—
Krygier, Todd	Washington	1	—	—
Kurri, Jari	Edm., L.A.	21	1	1
Lacroix, Eric	Colorado	1	—	—
LaFontaine, Pat	NYI, Buf.	13	—	—
Larionov, Igor	Van., S.J.	4	—	—
Larouche, Steve	Ottawa	1	—	—
Lebeau, Stephan	Montreal	1	—	—
LeClair, John	Philadelphia	5	1	—
Leeman, Gary	Tor., Cgy.	5	—	—
Lemieux, Claude	Mtl., N.J., Col.	6	—	—
Lemieux, Jocelyn	Chicago	2	—	—
Linden, Trevor	Vancouver	4	—	—
Lindros, Eric	Philadelphia	8	1	—
MacInnis, Al	Cgy., St. L.	2	—	—
MacLean, John	New Jersey	6	—	—
Manderville, Kent	Hartford	1	—	—
McKay, Randy	New Jersey	1	—	—
McKenzie, Jim	Phoenix	1	—	—
Messier, Mark	Edm., NYR	15	4	—
Miller, Kevin	Det., St.L., S.J.	4	—	—
Modano, Mike	Min., Dal.	2	1	—
Mogilny, Alexander	Buf., Van.	12	2	—
Momesso, Sergio	Montreal	1	—	—
Muller, Kirk	N.J., Mtl., Tor.	7	—	—
Murray, Rem	Edmonton	1	—	—
Murzyn, Dana	Calgary	1	—	—
Naslund, Markus	Pit., Van.	2	—	—
Nedved, Petr	Pittsburgh	—	1	—
Nemchinov, Sergei	NY Rangers	1	—	—
Nicholls, Bernie	L.A., N.J., Chi.	14	4	—
Nieuwendyk, Joe	Calgary	7	2	1
Nolan, Owen	Que., S.J.	8	1	—
Noonan, Brian	Chi., NYR	3	1	—
Nylander, Michael	Hartford	1	—	—
Oates, Adam	Boston	5	1	—
Odelein, Lyle	Montreal	1	—	—
Olczyk, Ed	Tor., NYR, Wpg., L.A.	5	—	—
Oliver, David	Edmonton	1	—	—
O'Neill, Jeff	Hartford	1	—	—
Otto, Joel	Calgary	2	—	—
Palffy, Zigmund	NY Islanders	3	—	—
Pivonka, Michal	Washington	1	—	—
Plante, Derek	Buffalo	1	—	—
Presley, Wayne	Chicago	1	—	—

Player	Team	3-Goals	4-Goals	5-Goals
Probert, Bob	Detroit	1	—	—
Quinn, Dan	Pit., Van., Ott.	5	—	—
Ranheim, Paul	Calgary	1	—	—
Recchi, Mark	Pit., Mtl.	2	—	—
Reichel, Robert	Calgary	3	—	—
Reid, Dave	Bos., Dal.	2	—	—
Renberg, Mikael	Philadelphia	1	—	—
Ricci, Mike	Quebec	—	—	1
Rice, Steven	Hartford	1	—	—
Richer, Stephane	Mtl., N.J.	8	1	—
Ridley, Mike	NYR, Wsh.	3	1	—
Roberts, Gary	Calgary	9	1	—
Robitaille, Luc	L.A., Pit.	9	3	—
Roenick, Jeremy	Chicago	4	2	—
Rolston, Brian	New Jersey	1	—	—
Ronning, Cliff	St.L., Van.	3	—	—
Rucinsky, Martin	Montreal	1	—	—
Sakic, Joe	Que., Col.	5	1	—
Sanderson, Geoff	Hartford	5	—	—
Sandstrom, Tomas	NYR, L.A.	7	1	—
Satan, Miroslav	Buffalo	1	—	—
Savage, Brian	Montreal	2	—	—
Selanne, Teemu	Wpg., Ana.	9	2	—
Semak, Alexander	New Jersey	1	—	—
Shanahan, Brendan	N.J., St.L., Hfd., Det.	10	—	—
Sheppard, Ray	Buf., Det., S.J., Fla.	11	—	—
Smolinski, Bryan	Boston	1	—	—
Smyth, Ryan	Edmonton	1	—	—
Stern, Ronnie	Calgary	1	—	—
Stevens, Kevin	Pittsburgh	8	2	—
Straka, Martin	Pittsburgh	1	—	—
Stumpel, Jozef	Boston	1	—	—
Sundin, Mats	Que., Tor.	4	—	1
Sutter, Brent	NY Islanders	6	—	—
Svejkovsky, Jaroslav	Washington	—	1	—
Sweeney, Bob	Boston	1	—	—
Thomas, Steve	Chi., NYI	4	2	—
Tikkanen, Esa	Edmonton	3	—	—
Titov, German	Calgary	2	—	—
Tkachuk, Keith	Wpg., Pho.	2	2	—
Tocchet, Rick	Phi., Pit., L.A., Bos.	12	2	—
Turcotte, Darren	NY Rangers	2	—	—
Turgeon, Pierre	Buf., NYI, Mtl.	12	—	—
Turgeon, Sylvain	Hfd., N.J., Ott.	5	—	—
Valk, Garry	Anaheim	1	—	—
Verbeek, Pat	N.J., Hfd., NYR	10	1	—
Vukota, Mick	NY Islanders	1	—	—
Weight, Doug	Edmonton	1	—	—
Wesley, Glen	Boston	1	—	—
Wiemer, Jason	Tampa Bay	1	—	—
Wood, Randy	NY Islanders	1	—	—
Yachmenev, Vitali	Los Angeles	1	—	—
Yake, Terry	Anaheim	1	—	—
Yashin, Alexei	Ottawa	3	—	—
Yegorov, Alexei	San Jose	1	—	—
Young, Scott	Que., Col.	4	—	—
Yzerman, Steve	Detroit	17	1	—
Ysebaert, Paul	Detroit	1	—	—
Zezel, Peter	Philadelphia	1	—	—
Zhamnov, Alexei	Wpg., Chi.	5	—	1

Mario Lemieux's complete career statistics can be found in the Player Register on page 335.

PITTSBURGH SUPERSTAR MARIO LEMIEUX RETIRES AFTER 12 SEASONS

Merci, Mario. 66

MARIO LEMIEUX, ONE OF THE NATIONAL HOCKEY LEAGUE's most gifted goal scorers, concluded his remarkable playing career at the end of the 1996-97 season and playoffs. An electrifying presence on the ice, he was described by Hall of Fame defenseman Bobby Orr as the most skilled player he had ever seen play.

Despite battling back injuries and Hodgkin's disease, Lemieux leaves as the NHL's sixth leading goal scorer with 613 regular-season goals. Of the players on the all-time top ten list of scorers, only Lemieux played fewer than 1,000 games. His career goals-per-game average (.823) is the highest ever recorded.

Lemieux played his entire career with Pittsburgh and is an inseparable part of the success of NHL hockey in that city. He led the Penguins to consecutive Stanley Cup championships in 1991 and 1992, winning the Conn Smythe Trophy as playoff MVP in both years.

Drafted first overall by the Penguins in 1984, Lemieux recorded his first of what would prove to be ten 100-point seasons en route to winning the Calder Trophy as the NHL's top rookie in 1984-85.

He finished his career as a six-time winner of the Art Ross Trophy as the NHL's top scorer and a three-time winner of the Hart Trophy awarded to the player judged to be most valuable to his team. He was also named to the NHL's First All-Star Team on five occasions and to the Second All-Star Team three times. He also played in eight All-Star Games.

His decision to retire after 12 seasons leaves the game and NHL fans poorer for his absence.

Of Mario Lemieux's 613 regular-season goals:

- 330 goals were scored at home
- 280 were scored on the road
- 3 were scored in neutral-site games
- 53 were unassisted
- 6 were scored on penalty shots (in eight attempts)
- 201 came on the power play
- 47 were short-handed
- 65 were game-winning goals
- 186 were scored in the first period (30.3%)
- 201 were scored in the second period (32.8%)
- 217 were scored in the third period (35.4%)
- 9 were scored in overtime (1.5%)
- 29 were scored into an empty net
- Mario Lemieux scored on 114 different goaltenders
- 110 different players were credited with assists on Lemieux's goals, led by Paul Coffey's 72.

Multiple-goal games:

- Mario Lemieux recorded two-or-more goals in 140 of his 745 regular-season games (18.8%)
- 101 were two-goal games
- Of his 39 hat tricks (tied for second-most in NHL history with Mike Bossy and second to Wayne Gretzky's 49), 26 were three-goal games, 10 were four-goal games and three were five-goal games.

NHL RECORDS

- Most shorthanded goals in one season (13)
- Most overtime goals, career (9)
- Most overtime points, career (19)
- Highest goals-per-game average, career (.823)
- Most goals in one period (4 – shared with 10 others)

PLAYOFF RECORDS

- Highest goals-per-game average, playoff career (.775)
- Most goals in one playoff game (5 – shared with 4 others)
- Most points in one playoff game (8 – shared with Patrick Sundstrom)
- Most goals in one playoff period (4 – shared with Tim Kerr)
- Most points in one playoff period (4, twice – shared with 9 others)
- Most Conn Smythe Trophy wins (2 – shared with 4 others)

ALL-STAR GAME RECORDS

- Most goals, one All-Star game (4 – '90 – shared with 3 others)
- Most points, one All-Star game (6 – '88 – 3 goals, 3 assists)
- Most points, All-Star career (20 – 11 goals, 9 assists – shared with Wayne Gretzky)

Calder Trophy winner, 1985.

PENGUINS RECORDS

- Most goals, career (613)
- Most assists, career (881)
- Most points, career (1,494)
- Most game-winning goals, career (65)
- Most shorthanded goals, career (47)
- Most shots on goal, career (3,054)
- Most hat tricks, career (39)
- Most goals, season (85 in 1988-89)
- Most assists, season (114 in 1988-89)
- Most points, season (199 in 1988-89)
- Most power-play goals, season (31 in 1995-96)
- Most overtime goals, season (2, three times – shared with Jaromir Jagr)
- Most power-play assists, season (58 in 1987-88)
- Most power-play points, season (80 in 1987-88)
- Most hat tricks, season (9 in 1988-89)
- Most consecutive games with a goal (12, Oct. 6-Nov. 1, '92)
- Most consecutive games with an assist (14, Jan. 15-Feb. 16, '86)
- Most consecutive games with a point (46, Oct. 31, '89-Feb. 11, '90)
- Most goals, game (5, three times)
- Most assists, game (6, three times – shared with Ron Stackhouse and Greg Malone)
- Most points, game (8, two times)
- Most goals, period (4, Jan. 26, '97)
- Most assists, period (4, Nov. 1, '95 – shared with Syl Apps, Paul Coffey and Ron Stackhouse)
- Most points, period (4)
- Most goals, one month (18 in March, '93)
- Most assists, one month (25 in March, '88)
- Most points, one month (38, October, '88)
- Most penalty shots attempted (8)
- Most penalty shots made (6)
- Fastest four goals by one player (14:54, Jan. 26, '97)
- Most goals in a playoff career (70)
- Most assists in a playoff career (85)
- Most points in a playoff career (155)
- Most power-play goals in a playoff career (28)
- Most shorthanded goals in a playoff career (7)
- Most assists in a playoff season (28 in 1991)
- Most points in a playoff season (44 in 1991)
- Most power-play goals in a playoff season (8 in 1992)
- Most game-winning goals in a playoff season (5, '92)
- Most shots on goal in a playoff season (93 in 1991)
- Most consecutive playoff games with a goal (7, twice)
- Most consecutive playoff games with an assist (10, April 19-May 11, '91)
- Most consecutive playoff games with a point (15, April 13-May 17, '91)
- Most playoff hat tricks (3)

Art Ross Trophy winner, 1997.

MILESTONE REGULAR-SEASON GOALS

Total goals scored each season in brackets.

#	DATE	vs.	ASSISTS	PERIOD	TIME	GOALIE	SCORE
1984-85 (43)							
1	10/11/84	at Bos.	unassisted	1	2:59	Pete Peeters	3-4
43	4/7/85	at Wsh.	Babych, Young	2	16:08	Pat Riggin	3-7

(100th point of his rookie campaign. First Penguin and 3rd NHL rookie to record 100 points.)

1985-86 (48)							
50	10/24/85	vs Tor.	Shedden, Ruskowski	3	19:08	Tim Bernhard	6-4
1986-87 (54)							
100	10/22/86	vs Buf.	Mantha, LaVallee PP	3	14:53	Jacques Cloutier	5-4 OT
1987-88 (70)							
150	10/21/87	vs N.J.	Simmer, Simpson	1	6:41	Alain Chevrier	4-5
200	3/1/88	vs Min.	Coffey	1	3:03	Don Beaupre	8-3
1988-89 (85)							
250	12/21/88	at Tor.	Errey, Quinn	1	18:08	Ken Wregget	6-1

Five-goal game:

254	12/31/88	vs N.J.	Brown	1	4:17	Bob Sauve	8-6
255	12/31/88	vs N.J.	Hillier SH	1	7:50	Bob Sauve	8-6
256	12/31/88	vs N.J.	Coffey, Dineen PP	1	10:59	Bob Sauve	8-6
257	12/31/88	vs N.J.	penalty shot	2	11:14	Chris Terreri	8-6
258	12/31/88	vs N.J.	Caufield	3	19:59	empty net	8-6

(each goal scored in a different fashion: even strength, short handed, power-play, penalty shot and empty net.)

300	4/2/89	at Phi.	Loney	OT	3:38	empty net	6-5 OT
1989-90 (45)							
317	12/6/89	vs Wsh.	Coffey, Brown PP	1	2:04	Bob Mason	5-3

(surpassing Jean Pronovost to become the Penguin's all-time leading goal scorer.)

1990-91 (19)							
350	2/14/91	vs NYI	Errey, Jagr	3	15:00	Glenn Healy	5-2
1991-92 (44)							
400	3/14/92	at Tor.	Stevens, Francis PP	2	8:01	Grant Fuhr	3-6
1992-93 (69)							
450	3/18/93	vs Wsh.	Stevens Murphy	1	1:00	Don Beaupre	7-5

Five-goal game:

471	4/9/93	at NYR	U. Samuelsson	2	4:43	Corey Hirsch	10-4
472	4/9/93	at NYR	Francis, Tocchet PP	2	8:09	Corey Hirsch	10-4
473	4/9/93	at NYR	Barrasso SH	2	16:05	Corey Hirsch	10-4
474	4/9/93	at NYR	Tocchet, Stevens	3	4:14	Mike Richter	10-4
475	4/9/93	at NYR	Stevens, Jennings	3	11:15	Mike Richter	10-4

1993-94 (17)							
1995-96 (69)							
500	10/26/95	at NYI	Sandstrom, Mironov	3	17:12	T. Soderstrom	7-5
501	10/28/95	at N.J.	Sandstrom, Jagr PP	2	7:49	Martin Brodeur	5-3

(surpassing Lanny McDonald's 500 goals)

508	11/10/95	at S.J.	Sandstrom, Maciver	3	10:31	Wade Flaherty	9-1

(surpassing Jean Beliveau's 507 goals)

513	11/30/95	at Bos.	Naslund	1	13:21	Scott Bailey	9-6

(surpassing Gilbert Perreault's 512 goals)

525	12/28/95	at Hfd.	Sandstrom, Francis PP	3	1:02	Jason Muzzatti	9-4

(surpassing Bryan Trottier's 524 goals)

534	1/16/96	vs Col.	unassisted SH	2	15:49	Patrick Roy	2-5

(surpassing Frank Mahovlich's 533 goals)

542	2/18/96	vs NYR	Sandstrom, Smolinski OT	2:17		Glenn Healy	4-3 OT

(surpassing Stan Mikita's 541 goals also establishing NHL record of 9 regular-season overtime goals)

545	2/24/96	at Mtl.	Nedved, Zubov PP	2	5:33	Jocelyn Thibault	3-7

(surpassing Maurice Richard's 544 goals)

549	3/9/96	vs N.J.	Francis, Mironov	1	6:19	Martin Brodeur	3-4 OT

(surpassing Michel Goulet's 548 goals)

550	3/13/96	at Hfd.	Francis, Mironov PP	2	4:19	Sean Burke	2-3

Five-goal game:

553	3/26/96	vs St.L	Nedved, Leroux	1	3:35	Grant Fuhr	8-4
554	3/26/96	vs St.L	Francis, Zubov PP	1	15:37	Jon Casey	8-4
555	3/26/96	vs St.L	Nedved, Jagr PP	2	8:43	Jon Casey	8-4
556	3/26/96	vs St.L	unassisted SH	2	11:15	Jon Casey	8-4
557	3/26/96	vs St.L	Francis, McLlwain	3	6:08	Jon Casey	8-4

(surpassing John Bucyk's 556 goals)

561	4/10/96	vs NYI	Jagr, Nedved PP	3	2:34	T. Soderstrom	2-6

(surpassing Guy Lafleur's 560 goals)

1996-97 (50)							
574	12/6/96	at Wsh.	Johansson, Barnes	3	3:13	Olaf Kolzig	5-3

(surpassing Mike Bossy's 573 goals)

600	2/4/97	vs Van.	Francis, Jagr	3	19:04	empty net	6-4
611	4/3/97	at Hfd.	Jagr, Olausson	3	5:28	Sean Burke	5-5

(surpassing Bobby Hull's 610 goals)

613	4/11/97	at Fla.	penalty shot	3	2:28	J. Vanbiesbrouck	2-4

MILESTONE PLAYOFF GOALS

Total goals scored each playoff year in brackets.

#	DATE	vs.	ASSISTS	PERIOD	TIME	GOALIE	SCORE
1989 (12)							
1	4/6/89	vs NYR	Barrasso	3	18:54	empty net	7-4

Five-goal game: (5th player in NHL history to score 5 goals in a playoff game.)

7	4/25/89	vs Phi.	Coffey, Stevens	1	2:15	Ron Hextall	10-7
8	4/25/89	vs Phi.	Errey, Coffey	1	3:45	Ron Hextall	10-7
9	4/25/89	vs Phi.	Cullen PP	1	6:55	Ron Hextall	10-7
10	4/25/89	vs Phi.	Quinn PP	1	17:09	Ron Hextall	10-7

(surpassing Jean Pronovost as the Penguins' all-time leading playoff goal scorer.)

11	4/25/89	vs Phi.	Errey	3	19:23	empty net	10-7
1991 (16)							
1992 (16)							

Three-goal game:

29	4/23/92	vs Wsh.	Stanton	2	17:18	Don Beaupre	6-4
30	4/23/92	vs Wsh.	Stevens, Francis PP	2	19:07	Don Beaupre	6-4
31	4/23/92	vs Wsh.	unassisted	3	19:09	empty net	6-4
1993 (8)							
50	5/10/93	vs NYI	Stevens, Tocchet	1	0:19	Glenn Healy	6-3
1994 (4)							
1996 (11)							

Three-goal game:

64	5/11/96	vs NYR	Sandstrom, Tamer SH	1	11:49	Mike Richter	7-3
65	5/11/96	vs NYR	Roche, Daigneault PP	2	9:53	Mike Richter	7-3
66	5/11/96	vs NYR	Murray, Daigneault	3	15:14	Mike Richter	7-3
1997 (3)							
70	4/26/97	at Phi.	Jagr, Francis	1	15:34	Garth Snow	3-6

REGULAR-SEASON SCORING vs. GOALTENDERS
Top Ten

	NAME	TEAM(S)	# OF GOALS	
1.	J. Vanbiesbrouck	NYR, Fla.	30	(24-NYR, 6-Fla.)
2.	Ron Hextall	Phi., Que.	19	(17-Phi., 2-Que.)
3.	Don Beaupre	Min., Wsh., Ott.	15	(4-Min., 10-Wsh., 1-Ott.)
4.	Pete Peeters	Bos., Wsh., Phi.	14	(3-Bos., 8-Wsh., 3-Phi.)
	Kelly Hrudey	NYI, L.A.	14	(13-NYI, 1-L.A.)
	Bill Ranford	Bos., Edm.	14	(10-Bos., 4-Edm.)
	Glenn Healy	L.A., NYI, NYR	14	(4-L.A., 7-NYI, 3-NYR)
8.	Sean Burke	N.J., Hfd.	13	(6-N.J., 7-Hfd.)
9.	Alain Chevrier	N.J., Chi.	11	(7-N.J., 4-Chi.)
	Bob Froese	Phi., NYR	11	(2-Phi., 9-NYR)
	Mario Gosselin	Que., Hfd.	11	(9-Que., 2-Hfd.)
	Mike Liut	Hfd.	11	
	Clint Malarchuk	Que., Wsh., Buf.	11	(2-Que., 8-Wsh., 1-Buf.)
	Ken Wregget	Tor., Phi.	11	(8-Tor., 3-Phi.)
	empty net goal		29	

PLAYOFF SCORING vs. GOALTENDERS
Top Ten

	NAME	TEAM	# OF GOALS
1.	Don Beaupre	Wsh.	11
2.	Andy Moog	Bos.	8
	Mike Richter	NYR	8
4.	Ron Hextall	Phi.	7
	Chris Terreri	N.J.	7
6.	Jon Casey	Min.	5
7.	Ed Belfour	Chi.	4
8.	Glenn Healy	NYI	3
	Garth Snow	Phi.	3
	empty net goal		6

PLAYERS ASSISTING ON LEMIEUX'S REGULAR-SEASON GOALS
Top Ten

	PLAYER	# OF ASSISTS
1.	Paul Coffey	72
2.	Jaromir Jagr	68
3.	Kevin Stevens	64
4.	Ron Francis	60
5.	Bob Errey	51
6.	Rob Brown	39
7.	Doug Bodger	31
8.	Rick Tocchet	30
9.	Moe Mantha	27
10.	Terry Ruskowski	25

PLAYERS ASSISTING ON LEMIEUX'S PLAYOFF GOALS
Top Ten

	PLAYER	# OF ASSISTS
1.	Larry Murphy	16
2.	Kevin Stevens	15
3.	Ron Francis	11
4.	Jaromir Jagr	10
5.	Paul Coffey	6
	Mark Recchi	6
	Rick Tocchet	6
8.	Petr Nedved	4
9.	Tom Barrasso	3
	Phil Bourque	3
	J.J. Daigneault	3
	Bob Errey	3
	Ulf Samuelsson	3
	Chris Tamer	3

Top 100 All-Time Goal-Scoring Leaders
Regular Season

Player	Seasons	Games	Goals	Goals per game
* 1. **Wayne Gretzky**, Edm., L.A., St.L., NYR .	18	1335	**862**	.646
2. **Gordie Howe**, Det., Hfd.	26	1767	**801**	.453
3. **Marcel Dionne**, Det., L.A., NYR	18	1348	**731**	.542
4. **Phil Esposito**, Chi., Bos., NYR	18	1282	**717**	.559
* 5. **Mike Gartner**, Wsh., Min., NYR, Tor., Pho.	18	1372	**696**	.507
6. **Mario Lemieux**, Pit.	12	745	**613**	.823
7. **Bobby Hull**, Chi., Wpg., Hfd.	16	1063	**610**	.574
* 8. **Jari Kurri**, Edm., L.A., NYR, Ana. . . .	16	1181	**596**	.505
* 9. **Dino Ciccarelli**, Min., Wsh., Det., T.B. .	17	1156	**586**	.507
* 10. **Mark Messier**, Edm., NYR	18	1272	**575**	.452
11. **Mike Bossy**, NYI.	10	752	**573**	.762
12. **Guy Lafleur**, Mtl., NYR, Que.	17	1126	**560**	.497
13. **John Bucyk**, Det., Bos.	23	1540	**556**	.361
14. **Michel Goulet**, Que., Chi.	15	1089	**548**	.503
15. **Maurice Richard**, Mtl.	18	978	**544**	.556
16. **Stan Mikita**, Chi.	22	1394	**541**	.388
* 17. **Steve Yzerman**, Det.	14	1023	**539**	.527
18. **Frank Mahovlich**, Tor., Det., Mtl.	18	1181	**533**	.451
* 19. **Brett Hull**, Cgy., St.L.	12	735	**527**	.717
20. **Bryan Trottier**, NYI, Pit.	18	1279	**524**	.410
21. **Dale Hawerchuk**, Wpg., Buf., St.L., Phi.	16	1188	**518**	.436
22. **Gilbert Perreault**, Buf.	17	1191	**512**	.430
23. **Jean Beliveau**, Mtl.	20	1125	**507**	.451
* 24. **Dave Andreychuk**, Buf., Tor., N.J. . . .	15	1083	**503**	.464
25. **Joe Mullen**, St.L., Cgy., Pit., Bos.	17	1062	**502**	.473
26. **Lanny McDonald**, Tor., Col., Cgy.	16	1111	**500**	.450
27. **Glenn Anderson**, Edm., Tor., NYR, St.L.	16	1129	**498**	.441
28. **Jean Ratelle**, NYR, Bos.	21	1281	**491**	.383
29. **Norm Ullman**, Det., Tor.	20	1410	**490**	.348
30. **Darryl Sittler**, Tor., Phi., Det.	15	1096	**484**	.442
31. **Denis Savard**, Chi., Mtl., T.B.	17	1196	**473**	.395
* 32. **Bernie Nicholls**, L.A., NYR, Edm., N.J., Chi., S.J.	16	1057	**469**	.444
* 33. **Luc Robitaille**, L.A., Pit., NYR	11	832	**462**	.555
* 34. **Brian Bellows**, Min., Mtl., T.B., Ana. . .	15	1101	**462**	.420
35. **Alex Delvecchio**, Det.	24	1549	**456**	.294
36. **Peter Stastny**, Que., N.J., St.L.	15	977	**450**	.461
37. **Rick Middleton**, NYR, Bos.	14	1005	**448**	.446
* 38. **Pat LaFontaine**, NYI, Buf.	14	798	**445**	.558
39. **Rick Vaive**, Van., Tor., Buf.	13	876	**441**	.503
40. **Steve Larmer**, Chi., NYR	15	1006	**441**	.438
41. **Dave Taylor**, L.A.	17	1111	**431**	.388
* 42. **Pat Verbeek**, N.J., Hfd., NYR, Dal. . . .	15	1065	**430**	.404
43. **Yvan Cournoyer**, Mtl.	16	968	**428**	.442
44. **Brian Propp**, Phi., Bos., Min., Hfd. . . .	15	1016	**425**	.418
45. **Steve Shutt**, Mtl., L.A.	13	930	**424**	.456
46. **Bill Barber**, Phi.	12	903	**420**	.465
47. **Garry Unger**, Tor., Det., St.L., Atl., L.A., Edm.	16	1105	**413**	.374
48. **Rod Gilbert**, NYR	18	1065	**406**	.381
* 49. **Ron Francis**, Hfd., Pit.	16	1166	**403**	.346
50. **John Ogrodnick**, Det., Que., NYR	14	928	**402**	.433
51. **Dave Keon**, Tor., Hfd.	18	1296	**396**	.306
52. **Cam Neely**, Van., Bos.	13	726	**395**	.544
53. **Pierre Larouche**, Pit., Mtl., Hfd., NYR. .	14	812	**395**	.486
54. **Bernie Geoffrion**, Mtl., NYR	16	883	**393**	.445
55. **Jean Pronovost**, Wsh., Pit., Atl.	14	998	**391**	.392
56. **Dean Prentice**, Pit., Min., Det., NYR, Bos.. .	22	1378	**391**	.284
57. **Rick Martin**, Buf., L.A.	11	685	**384**	.561
58. **Reggie Leach**, Bos., Cal., Phi., Det. . . .	13	934	**381**	.408
* 59. **Paul Coffey**, Edm., Pit., L.A., Det., Hfd., Phi.	17	1211	**381**	.315
60. **Ted Lindsay**, Det., Chi.	17	1068	**379**	.355
61. **Butch Goring**, L.A., NYI, Bos.	16	1107	**375**	.339
62. **Rick Kehoe**, Tor., Pit.	14	906	**371**	.409
63. **Tim Kerr**, Phi., NYR, Hfd.	13	655	**370**	.565
* 64. **Tomas Sandstrom**, NYR, L.A., Pit., Det. .	13	848	**370**	.436
65. **Bernie Federko**, St.L., Det.	14	1000	**369**	.369
* 66. **Doug Gilmour**, St.L., Cgy., Tor., N.J. . .	14	1062	**368**	.347
* 67. **Stephane Richer**, Mtl., N.J.	13	826	**366**	.443
68. **Jacques Lemaire**, Mtl.	12	853	**366**	.429
69. **Peter McNab**, Buf., Bos., Van., N.J. . . .	14	954	**363**	.381
* 70. **Ray Bourque**, Bos.	18	1290	**362**	.281
71. **Ivan Boldirev**, Bos., Cal., Chi., Atl., Van., Det.	15	1052	**361**	.343
* 72. **Brent Sutter**, NYI, Chi.	17	1059	**361**	.341
* 73. **Rick Tocchet**, Phi., Pit., L.A., Bos., Wsh. .	13	841	**359**	.427
* 74. **Joe Nieuwendyk**, Cgy., Dal.	11	695	**358**	.515
75. **Bobby Clarke**, Phi.	15	1144	**358**	.313
76. **Henri Richard**, Mtl.	20	1256	**358**	.285
77. **Bobby Smith**, Min., Mtl.	15	1077	**357**	.331
78. **Dennis Maruk**, Cal., Clev., Min., Wsh. . .	14	888	**356**	.401
79. **Wilf Paiement**, K.C. Col., Tor., Que., NYR, Buf., Pit.	14	946	**356**	.376

Gordie Howe used a blistering wrist shot, incredible upper body strength and rock-hard elbows to score 801 goals in his amazing 26-year career.

Player	Seasons	Games	Goals	Goals per game
80. **Mike Foligno**, Det., Buf., Tor., Fla. . . .	15	1018	**355**	.349
81. **Danny Gare**, Buf., Det., Edm.	13	827	**354**	.428
82. **Rick MacLeish**, Phi., Hfd., Pit., Det. . . .	14	846	**349**	.413
83. **Andy Bathgate**, NYR, Tor., Det., Pit. . . .	17	1069	**349**	.326
* 84. **Pierre Turgeon**, Buf., NYI, Mtl., St.L. . .	10	750	**344**	.459
* 85. **John MacLean**, N.J.	13	908	**344**	.379
86. **Charlie Simmer**, Cal., Cle., L.A., Bos., Pit.. .	14	712	**342**	.480
87. **Dave Christian**, Wpg., Wsh., Bos., St.L., Chi.. .	15	1009	**340**	.337
* 88. **Brendan Shanahan**, N.J., St.L., Hfd., Det.. .	10	713	**335**	.470
89. **Ron Ellis**, Tor.	16	1034	**332**	.321
90. **Mike Bullard**, Pit., Cgy., St.L., Phi., Tor. .	11	727	**329**	.453
* 91. **Geoff Courtnall**, Bos., Edm., Wsh., St.L., Van. .	14	939	**329**	.350
92. **Ken Hodge**, Chi., Bos., NYR	14	881	**328**	.372
* 93. **Ray Ferraro**, Hfd., NYI, NYR, L.A.	13	915	**327**	.357
* 94. **Kirk Muller**, N.J., Mtl., NYI, Tor., Fla. . .	13	962	**326**	.339
95. **John Tonelli**, NYI, Cgy., L.A., Chi., Que. .	14	1028	**325**	.316
96. **Nels Stewart**, Mtl.M., Bos., NYA	15	650	**324**	.498
97. **Paul MacLean**, St.L., Wpg., Det.	11	719	**324**	.451
98. **Pit Martin**, Det., Bos., Chi., Van.	17	1101	**324**	.294
* 99. **Kevin Dineen**, Hfd., Phi.	13	871	**323**	.371
100. **Vic Hadfield**, NYR, Pit.	16	1002	**323**	.322

Top 100 Active Goal-Scoring Leaders

Regular Season

	Player	Games	Goals	Goals per game
1.	**Wayne Gretzky**, Edm., L.A., St.L., NYR	1335	**862**	.646
2.	**Mike Gartner**, Wsh., Min., NYR, Tor., Pho.	1372	**696**	.507
3.	**Jari Kurri**, Edm., L.A., NYR, Ana.	1181	**596**	.505
4.	**Dino Ciccarelli**, Min., Wsh., Det., T.B.	1156	**586**	.507
5.	**Mark Messier**, Edm., NYR	1272	**575**	.452
6.	**Steve Yzerman**, Det.	1023	**539**	.527
7.	**Brett Hull**, Cgy., St.L.	735	**527**	.717
8.	**Dave Andreychuk**, Buf., Tor., N.J.	1083	**503**	.464
9.	**Bernie Nicholls**, L.A., NYR, Edm., N.J., Chi., S.J.	1057	**469**	.444
10.	**Luc Robitaille**, L.A., Pit., NYR	832	**462**	.555
11.	**Brian Bellows**, Min., Mtl., T.B., Ana.	1101	**462**	.420
12.	**Pat LaFontaine**, NYI, Buf.	798	**445**	.558
13.	**Pat Verbeek**, N.J., Hfd., NYR, Dal.	1065	**430**	.404
14.	**Ron Francis**, Hfd., Pit.	1166	**403**	.346
15.	**Paul Coffey**, Edm., Pit., L.A., Det., Hfd., Phi.	1211	**381**	.315
16.	**Tomas Sandstrom**, NYR, L.A., Pit., Det.	848	**370**	.436
17.	**Doug Gilmour**, St.L., Cgy., Tor., N.J.	1062	**368**	.347
18.	**Stephane Richer**, Mtl., N.J.	826	**366**	.443
19.	**Ray Bourque**, Bos.	1290	**362**	.281
20.	**Brent Sutter**, NYI, Chi.	1059	**361**	.341
21.	**Rick Tocchet**, Phi., Pit., L.A., Bos., Wsh.	841	**359**	.427
22.	**Joe Nieuwendyk**, Cgy., Dal.	695	**358**	.515
23.	**Pierre Turgeon**, Buf., NYI, Mtl., St.L.	750	**344**	.459
24.	**John MacLean**, N.J.	908	**344**	.379
25.	**Brendan Shanahan**, N.J., St.L., Hfd., Det.	713	**335**	.470
26.	**Geoff Courtnall**, Bos., Edm., Wsh., St.L., Van.	939	**329**	.350
27.	**Ray Ferraro**, Hfd., NYI, NYR, L.A.	915	**327**	.357
28.	**Kirk Muller**, N.J., Mtl., NYI, Tor., Fla.	962	**326**	.339
29.	**Kevin Dineen**, Hfd., Phi.	871	**323**	.371
30.	**Eddie Olczyk**, Chi., Tor., Wpg., NYR, L.A., Pit.	881	**319**	.362
31.	**Dale Hunter**, Que., Wsh.	1263	**313**	.248
32.	**Petr Klima**, Det., Edm., T.B., L.A., Pit.	773	**312**	.404
33.	**Steve Thomas**, Tor., Chi., NYI, N.J.	805	**310**	.385
34.	**Vincent Damphousse**, Tor., Edm., Mtl.	852	**310**	.364
35.	**Bob Carpenter**, Wsh., NYR, L.A., Bos., N.J.	1056	**309**	.293
36.	**Theoren Fleury**, Cgy.	649	**307**	.473
37.	**Joe Sakic**, Que., Colorado.	655	**307**	.469
38.	**Ray Sheppard**, Buf., NYR, Det., S.J., Fla.	625	**304**	.486
39.	**Alexander Mogilny**, Buf., Van.	536	**297**	.554
40.	**Jeremy Roenick**, Chi., Pho.	596	**296**	.497
41.	**Dave Gagner**, NYR, Min., Dal., Tor., Cgy.	799	**292**	.365
42.	**Greg Adams**, N.J., Van., Dal.	803	**292**	.364
43.	**Mike Ridley**, NYR, Wsh., Van.	866	**292**	.337
44.	**Mark Recchi**, Pit., Phi., Mtl.	628	**285**	.454
45.	**Phil Housley**, Buf., Wpg., St.L., Cgy., N.J., Wsh.	1067	**285**	.267
46.	**Wendel Clark**, Tor., Que., NYI	636	**282**	.443
47.	**Russ Courtnall**, Tor., Mtl., Min., Dal., Van., NYR	914	**279**	.305
48.	**Kevin Stevens**, Pit., Bos., L.A.	588	**278**	.473
49.	**Jimmy Carson**, L.A., Edm., Det., Van., Hfd.	626	**275**	.439
50.	**Claude Lemieux**, Mtl., N.J., Colorado.	758	**272**	.359
51.	**Sylvain Turgeon**, Hfd., N.J., Mtl., Ott.	669	**269**	.402
52.	**Jaromir Jagr**, Pit.	504	**266**	.528
53.	**Dan Quinn**, Cgy., Pit., Van., St.L., Phi., Min., Ott., L.A.	805	**266**	.330
54.	**Adam Oates**, Det., St.L., Bos., Wsh.	826	**258**	.312
55.	**Gary Roberts**, Cgy.	585	**257**	.439
56.	**Mike Modano**, Min., Dal.	581	**256**	.441
57.	**Larry Murphy**, L.A., Wsh., Min., Pit., Tor., Det.	1315	**254**	.193
58.	**Al MacInnis**, Cgy., St.L.	989	**251**	.254
59.	**Murray Craven**, Det., Phi., Hfd., Van., Chi.	942	**250**	.265
60.	**Sergei Fedorov**, Det.	506	**242**	.478
61.	**Esa Tikkanen**, Edm., NYR, St.L., N.J., Van.	797	**241**	.302
62.	**Trevor Linden**, Van.	660	**240**	.364
63.	**Guy Carbonneau**, Mtl., St.L., Dal.	1098	**239**	.218
64.	**Peter Bondra**, Wsh.	468	**233**	.498
65.	**Mats Sundin**, Que., Tor.	529	**232**	.439
66.	**Ulf Dahlen**, NYR, Min., Dal., S.J., Chi.	686	**231**	.337
67.	**Scott Mellanby**, Phi., Edm., Fla.	793	**223**	.281
68.	**Tony Granato**, NYR, L.A., S.J.	571	**216**	.378
69.	**Teemu Selanne**, Wpg., Ana.	337	**214**	.635
70.	**Derek King**, NYI, Hfd.	650	**214**	.329
71.	**Rod Brind'Amour**, St.L., Phi.	614	**213**	.347
72.	**Adam Graves**, Det., Edm., NYR	676	**209**	.309
73.	**Peter Zezel**, Phi., St.L., Wsh., Tor., Dal., N.J.	802	**208**	.259
74.	**Pavel Bure**, Van.	346	**203**	.587
75.	**Shayne Corson**, Mtl., Edm., St.L.	747	**200**	.268
76.	**Gary Leeman**, Tor., Cgy., Mtl., Van., St.L.	667	**199**	.298
77.	**Keith Tkachuk**, Wpg., Pho.	389	**196**	.504
78.	**Randy Burridge**, Bos., Wsh., L.A., Buf.	676	**195**	.288
79.	**Ron Sutter**, Phi., St.L., Que., NYI, Bos., S.J.	878	**194**	.221
80.	**Eric Lindros**, Phi.	297	**193**	.650
81.	**Joel Otto**, Cgy., Phi.	875	**192**	.219
82.	**Benoit Hogue**, Buf., NYI, Tor., Dal.	617	**191**	.310
83.	**Geoff Sanderson**, Hfd.	439	**189**	.431
84.	**Kevin Hatcher**, Wsh., Dal., Pit.	886	**189**	.213
85.	**Steve Duchesne**, L.A., Phi., Que., St.L., Ott.	765	**188**	.246

The highest-scoring European-born player in NHL history, Jari Kurri added 13 more entries to his goal-scoring ledger in 1996-97, giving him a career total of 596 regular-season goals.

	Player	Games	Goals	Goals per game
86.	**John Cullen**, Pit., Hfd., Tor., T.B.	617	**187**	.303
87.	**Adam Creighton**, Buf., Chi., NYI, T.B., St.L.	708	**187**	.264
88.	**Joe Murphy**, Det., Edm., Chi., St.L.	597	**186**	.312
89.	**Cliff Ronning**, St.L., Van., Pho.	615	**185**	.301
90.	**Randy Cunneyworth**, Buf., Pit., Wpg., Hfd., Chi., Ott.	781	**185**	.237
91.	**Brian Bradley**, Cgy., Van., Tor., T.B.	637	**180**	.283
92.	**Darren Turcotte**, NYR, Hfd., Wpg., S.J.	524	**179**	.342
93.	**Owen Nolan**, Que., Colorado, S.J.	412	**177**	.430
94.	**John LeClair**, Mtl., Phi.	425	**175**	.412
95.	**Randy Wood**, NYI, Buf., Tor., Dal.	741	**175**	.236
96.	**Shawn Burr**, Det., T.B.	814	**175**	.215
97.	**Scott Young**, Hfd., Pit., Que., Colorado.	599	**173**	.289
98.	**Craig Janney**, Bos., St.L., S.J., Wpg., Pho.	636	**173**	.272
99.	**Michal Pivonka**, Wsh.	756	**173**	.229
100.	**Tony Amonte**, NYR, Chi.	451	**172**	.381

Top 100 All-Time Assist Leaders

Regular Season

Player	Seasons	Games	Assists	Assist per game
* 1. **Wayne Gretzky**, Edm., L.A., St.L., NYR .	18	1335	**1843**	1.38
* 2. **Paul Coffey**, Edm., Pit., L.A., Det., Hfd., Phi.	17	1211	**1063**	.878
3. **Gordie Howe**, Det., Hfd.	26	1767	**1049**	.594
4. **Marcel Dionne**, Det., L.A., NYR	18	1348	**1040**	.772
* 5. **Ray Bourque**, Bos.	18	1290	**1001**	.776
* 6. **Mark Messier**, Edm., NYR	18	1272	**977**	.768
* 7. **Ron Francis**, Hfd., Pit.	16	1166	**944**	.810
8. **Stan Mikita**, Chi.	22	1394	**926**	.664
9. **Bryan Trottier**, NYI, Pit.	18	1279	**901**	.704
10. **Dale Hawerchuk**, Wpg., Buf., St.L., Phi.	16	1188	**891**	.750
11. **Mario Lemieux**, Pit.	12	745	**881**	1.18
12. **Phil Esposito**, Chi., Bos., NYR	18	1282	**873**	.681
13. **Denis Savard**, Chi., Mtl., T.B.	17	1196	**865**	.723
14. **Bobby Clarke**, Phi.	15	1144	**852**	.745
15. **Alex Delvecchio**, Det.	24	1549	**825**	.533
16. **Gilbert Perreault**, Buf.	17	1191	**814**	.683
17. **John Bucyk**, Det., Bos.	23	1540	**813**	.528
* 18. **Steve Yzerman**, Det.	14	1023	**801**	.783
* 19. **Larry Murphy**, L.A., Wsh., Min., Pit., Tor., Det.	17	1315	**797**	.606
20. **Guy Lafleur**, Mtl., NYR, Que.	17	1126	**793**	.704
21. **Peter Stastny**, Que., N.J., St.L.	15	977	**789**	.808
* 22. **Jari Kurri**, Edm., L.A., NYR, Ana.	16	1181	**780**	.660
23. **Jean Ratelle**, NYR, Bos.	21	1281	**776**	.606
24. **Bernie Federko**, St.L., Det.	14	1000	**761**	.761
* 25. **Doug Gilmour**, St.L., Cgy., Tor., N.J.	14	1062	**755**	.711
26. **Larry Robinson**, Mtl., L.A.	20	1384	**750**	.542
27. **Denis Potvin**, NYI	15	1060	**742**	.700
28. **Norm Ullman**, Det., Tor.	20	1410	**739**	.524
* 29. **Adam Oates**, Det., St.L., Bos., Wsh.	12	826	**738**	.893
30. **Jean Beliveau**, Mtl.	20	1125	**712**	.633
* 31. **Bernie Nicholls**, L.A., NYR, Edm., N.J., Chi., S.J.	16	1057	**710**	.672
* 32. **Phil Housley**, Buf., Wpg., St.L., Cgy., N.J., Wsh.	15	1067	**705**	.661
* 33. **Al MacInnis**, Cgy., St.L.	16	989	**703**	.711
34. **Henri Richard**, Mtl.	20	1256	**688**	.548
35. **Brad Park**, NYR, Bos., Det.	17	1113	**683**	.614
36. **Bobby Smith**, Min., Mtl.	15	1077	**679**	.630
* 37. **Dale Hunter**, Que., Wsh.	17	1263	**670**	.530
38. **Bobby Orr**, Bos., Chi.	12	657	**645**	.982
39. **Dave Taylor**, L.A.	17	1111	**638**	.574
40. **Darryl Sittler**, Tor., Phi., Det.	15	1096	**637**	.581
41. **Borje Salming**, Tor., Det.	17	1148	**637**	.555
42. **Neal Broten**, Min., Dal., N.J., L.A.	17	1099	**634**	.577
43. **Andy Bathgate**, NYR, Tor., Det., Pit.	17	1069	**624**	.584
44. **Rod Gilbert**, NYR	18	1065	**615**	.577
* 45. **Mike Gartner**, Wsh., Min., NYR, Tor., Pho.	18	1372	**612**	.446
46. **Michel Goulet**, Que., Chi.	15	1089	**604**	.555
47. **Glenn Anderson**, Edm., Tor., NYR, St.L.	16	1129	**601**	.532
48. **Doug Wilson**, Chi., S.J.	16	1024	**590**	.576
49. **Dave Keon**, Tor., Hfd.	18	1296	**590**	.455
* 50. **Scott Stevens**, Wsh., St.L., N.J.	15	1120	**584**	.521
51. **Brian Propp**, Phi., Bos., Min., Hfd.	15	1016	**579**	.570
* 52. **Dino Ciccarelli**, Min., Wsh., Det., T.B.	17	1156	**574**	.497
53. **Steve Larmer**, Chi., NYR	15	1006	**571**	.568
54. **Frank Mahovlich**, Tor., Det., Mtl.	18	1181	**570**	.483
* 55. **Chris Chelios**, Mtl., Chi.	14	920	**567**	.616
* 56. **Dave Babych**, Wpg., Hfd., Van.	17	1101	**566**	.514
57. **Joe Mullen**, St.L., Cgy., Pit., Bos.	17	1062	**561**	.528
* 58. **Dave Andreychuk**, Buf., Tor., N.J.	15	1083	**561**	.518
59. **Bobby Hull**, Chi., Wpg., Hfd.	16	1063	**560**	.527
60. **Mike Bossy**, NYI.	10	752	**553**	.735
61. **Thomas Steen**, Wpg.	14	950	**553**	.582
62. **Ken Linseman**, Phi., Edm., Bos., Tor.	14	860	**551**	.641
63. **Tom Lysiak**, Atl., Chi.	13	919	**551**	.600
64. **Mark Howe**, Hfd., Phi., Det.	16	929	**545**	.587
65. **Red Kelly**, Det., Tor.	20	1316	**542**	.412
66. **Rick Middleton**, NYR, Bos.	14	1005	**540**	.537
* 67. **Gary Suter**, Cgy., Chi.	12	845	**535**	.633
68. **Dennis Maruk**, Cal., Clev., Min., Wsh.	14	888	**522**	.588
* 69. **Kirk Muller**, N.J., Mtl., NYI, Tor., Fla.	13	962	**521**	.542
* 70. **Pierre Turgeon**, Buf., NYI, Mtl., St.L.	10	750	**520**	.693
71. **Wayne Cashman**, Bos.	17	1027	**516**	.502
* 72. **Brian Bellows**, Min., Mtl., T.B., Ana.	15	1101	**515**	.468
* 73. **Joe Sakic**, Que., Colorado	9	655	**513**	.783
74. **Butch Goring**, L.A., NYI, Bos.	16	1107	**513**	.463
* 75. **Vincent Damphousse**, Tor., Edm., Mtl.	11	852	**511**	.600
76. **John Tonelli**, NYI, Cgy., L.A., Chi., Que.	14	1028	**511**	.497
* 77. **Pat LaFontaine**, NYI, Buf.	14	798	**506**	.634
78. **Lanny McDonald**, Tor., Col., Cgy.	16	1111	**506**	.455
79. **Ivan Boldirev**, Bos., Cal., Chi., Atl., Van., Det.	15	1052	**505**	.480
* 80. **Brian Leetch**, NYR	10	649	**503**	.775

The backbone of the Boston Bruins back-line for the past 18 seasons, Ray Bourque is one of only five players in League history to record 1000 career assists.

Player	Seasons	Games	Assists	Assist per game
* 81. **Luc Robitaille**, L.A., Pit., NYR	11	832	**500**	.601
82. **Randy Carlyle**, Tor., Pit., Wpg.	17	1055	**499**	.473
* 83. **Craig Janney**, Bos., St.L., S.J., Wpg., Pho.	10	636	**498**	.783
84. **Pete Mahovlich**, Det., Mtl., Pit.	16	884	**485**	.549
85. **Pit Martin**, Det., Bos., Chi., Van.	17	1101	**485**	.441
86. **Ken Hodge**, Chi., Bos., NYR	14	881	**472**	.536
87. **Ted Lindsay**, Det., Chi.	17	1068	**472**	.442
88. **Jacques Lemaire**, Mtl.	12	853	**469**	.550
89. **Dean Prentice**, Pit., Min., Det., NYR, Bos.	22	1378	**469**	.340
90. **Phil Goyette**, Mtl., NYR, St.L., Buf.	16	941	**467**	.496
* 91. **Mike Ridley**, NYR, Wsh., Tor., Van.	12	866	**466**	.538
* 92. **Murray Craven**, Det., Phi., Hfd., Van., Chi.	15	942	**464**	.493
93. **Bill Barber**, Phi.	12	903	**463**	.513
94. **Reed Larson**, Det., Bos., Edm., NYI, Min., Buf.	14	904	**463**	.512
95. **Doug Mohns**, Bos., Chi., Min., Atl., Wsh.	22	1390	**462**	.332
* 96. **Brent Sutter**, NYI, Chi.	17	1059	**460**	.434
97. **Bobby Rousseau**, Mtl.	15	942	**458**	.486
98. **Wilf Paiement**, K.C. Col., Tor., Que., NYR, Buf., Pit.	14	946	**458**	.484
99. **Murray Oliver**, Det., Bos., Tor., Min.	17	1127	**454**	.403
100. **Doug Harvey**, Mtl., NYR, Det., St.L.	20	1113	**452**	.406

Top 100 Active Assist Leaders

Regular Season

	Player	Games	Assists	Assists per game
1.	Wayne Gretzky, Edm., L.A., St.L., NYR	1335	**1843**	1.381
2.	Paul Coffey, Edm., Pit., L.A., Det., Hfd., Phi.	1211	**1063**	.878
3.	Ray Bourque, Bos.	1290	**1001**	.776
4.	Mark Messier, Edm., NYR	1272	**977**	.768
5.	Ron Francis, Hfd., Pit.	1166	**944**	.810
6.	Steve Yzerman, Det.	1023	**801**	.783
7.	Larry Murphy, L.A., Wsh., Min., Pit., Tor., Det.	1315	**797**	.606
8.	Jari Kurri, Edm., L.A., NYR, Ana.	1181	**780**	.660
9.	Doug Gilmour, St.L., Cgy., Tor., N.J.	1062	**755**	.711
10.	Adam Oates, Det., St.L., Bos., Wsh.	826	**738**	.893
11.	Bernie Nicholls, L.A., NYR, Edm., N.J., Chi., S.J.	1057	**710**	.672
12.	Phil Housley, Buf., Wpg., St.L., Cgy., N.J., Wsh.	1067	**705**	.661
13.	Al MacInnis, Cgy., St.L.	989	**703**	.711
14.	Dale Hunter, Que., Wsh.	1263	**670**	.530
15.	Mike Gartner, Wsh., Min., NYR, Tor., Pho.	1372	**612**	.446
16.	Scott Stevens, Wsh., St.L., N.J.	1120	**584**	.521
17.	Dino Ciccarelli, Min., Wsh., Det., T.B.	1156	**574**	.497
18.	Chris Chelios, Mtl., Chi.	920	**567**	.616
19.	Dave Babych, Wpg., Hfd., Van.	1101	**566**	.514
20.	Dave Andreychuk, Buf., Tor., N.J.	1083	**561**	.518
21.	Gary Suter, Cgy., Chi.	845	**535**	.633
22.	Kirk Muller, N.J., Mtl., NYI, Tor., Fla.	962	**521**	.542
23.	Pierre Turgeon, Buf., NYI, Mtl., St.L.	750	**520**	.693
24.	Brian Bellows, Min., Mtl., T.B., Ana.	1101	**515**	.468
25.	Joe Sakic, Que., Colorado	655	**513**	.783
26.	Vincent Damphousse, Tor., Edm., Mtl.	852	**511**	.600
27.	Pat LaFontaine, NYI, Buf.	798	**506**	.634
28.	Brian Leetch, NYR	649	**503**	.775
29.	Luc Robitaille, L.A., Pit., NYR	832	**500**	.601
30.	Craig Janney, Bos., St.L., S.J., Wpg., Pho.	636	**498**	.783
31.	Mike Ridley, NYR, Wsh., Tor., Van.	866	**466**	.538
32.	Murray Craven, Det., Phi., Hfd., Van., Chi.	942	**464**	.493
33.	Brent Sutter, NYI, Chi.	1059	**460**	.434
34.	Pat Verbeek, N.J., Hfd., NYR, Dal.	1065	**444**	.417
35.	Tomas Sandstrom, NYR, L.A., Pit., Det.	848	**437**	.515
36.	Mark Recchi, Pit., Phi., Mtl.	628	**430**	.685
37.	James Patrick, NYR, Hfd., Cgy.	875	**428**	.489
38.	Russ Courtnall, Tor., Mtl., Min., Dal., Van., NYR	914	**428**	.468
39.	Eddie Olczyk, Chi., Tor., Wpg., NYR, L.A., Pit.	881	**424**	.481
40.	Dan Quinn, Cgy., Pit., Van., St.L., Phi., Min., Ott., L.A.	805	**419**	.520
41.	Rick Tocchet, Phi., Pit., L.A., Bos., Wsh.	841	**417**	.496
42.	Jeff Brown, Que., St.L., Van., Hfd.	687	**406**	.591
43.	Michal Pivonka, Wsh.	756	**406**	.537
44.	Garry Galley, L.A., Wsh., Bos., Phi., Buf.	889	**400**	.450
45.	Doug Bodger, Pit., Buf., S.J.	916	**399**	.436
46.	Steve Duchesne, L.A., Phi., Que., St.L., Ott.	765	**394**	.515
47.	Geoff Courtnall, Bos., Edm., Wsh., St.L., Van.	939	**392**	.417
48.	Bob Carpenter, Wsh., NYR, L.A., Bos., N.J.	1056	**391**	.370
49.	Brett Hull, Cgy., St.L.	735	**388**	.528
50.	Dave Ellett, Wpg., Tor., N.J.	941	**381**	.405
51.	Theoren Fleury, Cgy.	649	**376**	.579
52.	Bruce Driver, N.J., NYR	847	**375**	.443
53.	Jeremy Roenick, Chi., Pho.	596	**369**	.619
54.	Ray Ferraro, Hfd., NYI, NYR, L.A.	915	**368**	.402
55.	Guy Carbonneau, Mtl., St.L., Dal.	1098	**368**	.335
56.	Jaromir Jagr, Pit.	504	**367**	.728
57.	Peter Zezel, Phi., St.L., Wsh., Tor., Dal., N.J.	802	**366**	.456
58.	Esa Tikkanen, Edm., NYR, St.L., N.J., Van.	797	**365**	.458
59.	John Cullen, Pit., Hfd., Tor., T.B.	617	**363**	.588
60.	Steve Thomas, Tor., Chi., NYI, N.J.	805	**362**	.450
61.	Kevin Hatcher, Wsh., Dal., Pit.	886	**361**	.407
62.	Kevin Dineen, Hfd., Phi.	871	**356**	.409
63.	Charlie Huddy, Edm., L.A., Buf., St.L.	1017	**354**	.348
64.	Brendan Shanahan, N.J., St.L., Hfd., Det.	713	**351**	.492
65.	Dave Gagner, NYR, Min., Dal., Tor., Cgy.	799	**351**	.439
66.	Sergei Fedorov, Det.	506	**350**	.692
67.	Kevin Lowe, Edm., NYR	1247	**347**	.278
68.	John MacLean, N.J.	908	**346**	.381
69.	Rod Brind'Amour, St.L., Phi.	614	**342**	.557
70.	Joe Nieuwendyk, Cgy., Dal.	695	**341**	.491
71.	Pat Flatley, NYI, NYR	780	**340**	.436
72.	Mike Modano, Min., Dal.	581	**339**	.583
73.	Fredrik Olausson, Wpg., Edm., Ana., Pit.	711	**329**	.463
74.	Alexander Mogilny, Buf., Van.	536	**327**	.610
75.	Mats Sundin, Que., Tor.	529	**326**	.616
76.	Stephane Richer, Mtl., N.J.	826	**326**	.395
77.	Kevin Stevens, Pit., Bos., L.A.	588	**319**	.543
78.	Cliff Ronning, St.L., Van., Pho.	615	**319**	.519
79.	Brian Bradley, Cgy., Van., Tor., T.B.	637	**316**	.496
80.	Joel Otto, Cgy., Phi.	875	**309**	.353
81.	Trevor Linden, Van.	660	**308**	.467

One of the NHL's most innovative passers, Paul Coffey has collected 50 or more assists in 14 of his 17 NHL campaigns.

	Player	Games	Assists	Assists per game
82.	Greg Adams, N.J., Van., Dal.	803	**307**	.382
83.	Ron Sutter, Phi., St.L., Que., NYI, Bos., S.J.	878	**307**	.350
84.	Al Iafrate, Tor., Wsh., Bos., S.J.	778	**304**	.391
85.	Calle Johansson, Buf., Wsh.	710	**303**	.427
86.	Shayne Corson, Mtl., Edm., St.L.	747	**294**	.394
87.	Derek King, NYI, Hfd.	650	**291**	.448
88.	Jimmy Carson, L.A., Edm., Det., Van., Hfd.	626	**286**	.457
89.	Glen Wesley, Bos., Hfd.	721	**286**	.397
90.	Petr Svoboda, Mtl., Buf., Phi.	824	**282**	.342
91.	Doug Weight, NYR, Edm.	425	**276**	.649
92.	Claude Lemieux, Mtl., N.J., Colorado	758	**275**	.363
93.	Andrew Cassels, Mtl., Hfd.	498	**272**	.546
94.	Zarley Zalapski, Pit., Hfd., Cgy.	562	**271**	.482
95.	Steve Chiasson, Det., Cgy., Hfd.	657	**270**	.411
96.	Kelly Miller, NYR, Wsh.	919	**270**	.294
97.	Gary Leeman, Tor., Cgy., Mtl., Van., St.L.	667	**267**	.400
98.	Scott Mellanby, Phi., Edm., Fla.	793	**267**	.337
99.	Craig MacTavish, Bos., Edm., NYR, Phi., St.L.	1093	**267**	.244
100.	Mike Ramsey, Buf., Pit., Det.	1070	**266**	.249

Top 100 All-Time Point Leaders

Regular Season

Joe Mullen, who honed his skills playing ball hockey on the streets of New York City, is one of only 27 players in NHL history to play over 1000 games and average at least one point-per-game.

Player	Seasons	Games	Goals	Assists	Points	Points per game
* 1. Wayne Gretzky, Edm., L.A., St.L., NYR	18	1335	862	1843	**2705**	2.03
2. Gordie Howe, Det., Hfd.	26	1767	801	1049	**1850**	1.05
3. Marcel Dionne, Det., L.A., NYR	18	1348	731	1040	**1771**	1.31
4. Phil Esposito, Chi., Bos., NYR	18	1282	717	873	**1590**	1.24
* 5. Mark Messier, Edm., NYR	18	1272	575	977	**1552**	1.22
6. Mario Lemieux, Pit.	12	745	613	881	**1494**	2.01
7. Stan Mikita, Chi.	22	1394	541	926	**1467**	1.05
* 8. Paul Coffey, Edm., Pit., L.A., Det., Hfd., Phi.	17	1211	381	1063	**1444**	1.19
9. Bryan Trottier, NYI, Pit.	18	1279	524	901	**1425**	1.11
10. Dale Hawerchuk, Wpg., Buf., St.L., Phi.	16	1188	518	891	**1409**	1.19
* 11. Jari Kurri, Edm., L.A., NYR, Ana.	16	1181	596	780	**1376**	1.17
12. John Bucyk, Det., Bos.	23	1540	556	813	**1369**	.889
* 13. Ray Bourque, Bos.	18	1290	362	1001	**1363**	1.06
14. Guy Lafleur, Mtl., NYR, Que.	17	1126	560	793	**1353**	1.20
* 15. Ron Francis, Hfd., Pit.	16	1166	403	944	**1347**	1.16
* 16. Steve Yzerman, Det.	14	1023	539	801	**1340**	1.31
17. Denis Savard, Chi., Mtl., T.B.	17	1196	473	865	**1338**	1.12
18. Gilbert Perreault, Buf.	17	1191	512	814	**1326**	1.11
* 19. Mike Gartner, Wsh., Min., NYR, Tor., Pho.	18	1372	696	612	**1308**	.953
20. Alex Delvecchio, Det.	24	1549	456	825	**1281**	.827
21. Jean Ratelle, NYR, Bos.	21	1281	491	776	**1267**	.989
22. Peter Stastny, Que., N.J., St.L.	15	977	450	789	**1239**	1.27
23. Norm Ullman, Det., Tor.	20	1410	490	739	**1229**	.872
24. Jean Beliveau, Mtl.	20	1125	507	712	**1219**	1.08
25. Bobby Clarke, Phi.	15	1144	358	852	**1210**	1.06
* 26. Bernie Nicholls, L.A., NYR, Edm., N.J., Chi., S.J.	16	1057	469	710	**1179**	1.12
27. Bobby Hull, Chi., Wpg., Hfd.	16	1063	610	560	**1170**	1.10
* 28. Dino Ciccarelli, Min., Wsh., Det., T.B.	17	1156	586	574	**1160**	1.00
29. Michel Goulet, Que., Chi.	15	1089	548	604	**1152**	1.06
30. Bernie Federko, St.L., Det.	14	1000	369	761	**1130**	1.13
31. Mike Bossy, NYI	10	752	573	553	**1126**	1.50
* 32. Doug Gilmour, St.L., Cgy., Tor., N.J.	14	1062	368	755	**1123**	1.06
33. Darryl Sittler, Tor., Phi., Det.	15	1096	484	637	**1121**	1.02
34. Frank Mahovlich, Tor., Det., Mtl.	18	1181	533	570	**1103**	.934
35. Glenn Anderson, Edm., Tor., YR, St.L.	16	1129	498	601	**1099**	.973
36. Dave Taylor, L.A.	17	1111	431	638	**1069**	.962
* 37. Dave Andreychuk, Buf., Tor., N.J.	15	1083	503	561	**1064**	.982
38. Joe Mullen, St.L., Cgy., Pit., Bos.	17	1062	502	561	**1063**	1.00
39. Denis Potvin, NYI	15	1060	310	742	**1052**	.992
* 40. Larry Murphy, L.A., Wsh., Min., Pit., Tor., Det.	17	1315	254	797	**1051**	.799
41. Henri Richard, Mtl.	20	1256	358	688	**1046**	.833
42. Bobby Smith, Min., Mtl.	15	1077	357	679	**1036**	.962
43. Rod Gilbert, NYR	18	1065	406	615	**1021**	.959
44. Steve Larmer, Chi., NYR	15	1006	441	571	**1012**	1.01
45. Lanny McDonald, Tor., Col., Cgy.	16	1111	500	506	**1006**	.905
46. Brian Propp, Phi., Bos., Min., Hfd.	15	1016	425	579	**1004**	.988
* 47. Adam Oates, Det., St.L., Bos., Wsh.	12	826	258	738	**996**	1.21
* 48. Phil Housley, Buf., Wpg., St.L., Cgy., N.J., Wsh.	15	1067	285	705	**990**	.928
49. Rick Middleton, NYR, Bos.	14	1005	448	540	**988**	.983
50. Dave Keon, Tor., Hfd.	18	1296	396	590	**986**	.761
* 51. Dale Hunter, Que., Wsh.	17	1263	313	670	**983**	.778
* 52. Brian Bellows, Min., Mtl., T.B., Ana.	15	1101	462	515	**977**	.887
53. Andy Bathgate, NYR, Tor., Det., Pit.	17	1069	349	624	**973**	.910
54. Maurice Richard, Mtl.	18	978	544	421	**965**	.987
* 55. Luc Robitaille, L.A., Pit., NYR	11	832	462	500	**962**	1.16
56. Larry Robinson, Mtl., L.A.	20	1384	208	750	**958**	.692
* 57. Al MacInnis, Cgy., St.L.	16	989	251	703	**954**	.965
* 58. Pat LaFontaine, NYI, Buf.	14	798	445	506	**951**	1.19
59. Neal Broten, Min., Dal., N.J., L.A.	17	1099	289	634	**923**	.840
60. Bobby Orr, Bos., Chi.	12	657	270	645	**915**	1.39
* 61. Brett Hull, Cgy., St.L.	12	735	527	388	**915**	1.25
62. Brad Park, NYR, Bos., Det.	17	1113	213	683	**896**	.805
63. Butch Goring, L.A., NYI, Bos.	16	1107	375	513	**888**	.802
64. Bill Barber, Phi.	12	903	420	463	**883**	.978

Player	Seasons	Games	Goals	Assists	Points	Points per game
65. Dennis Maruk, Cal., Clev., Min., Wsh.	14	888	356	522	**878**	.989
* 66. Pat Verbeek, N.J., Hfd., NYR, Dal.	15	1065	430	444	**874**	.821
67. Ivan Boldirev, Bos., Cal., Chi., Atl., Van., Det.	15	1052	361	505	**866**	.823
* 68. Pierre Turgeon, Buf., NYI, Mtl., St.L.	10	750	344	520	**864**	1.15
69. Yvan Cournoyer, Mtl.	16	968	428	435	**863**	.892
70. Dean Prentice, Pit., Min., Det., NYR, Bos.	22	1378	391	469	**860**	.624
71. Ted Lindsay, Det., Chi.	17	1068	379	472	**851**	.797
* 72. Kirk Muller, N.J., Mtl., NYI, Tor., Fla.	13	962	326	521	**847**	.880
73. Tom Lysiak, Atl., Chi.	13	919	292	551	**843**	.917
74. John Tonelli, NYI, Cgy., L.A., Chi., Que.	14	1028	325	511	**836**	.813
75. Jacques Lemaire, Mtl.	12	853	366	469	**835**	.979
76. John Ogrodnick, Det., Que., NYR	14	928	402	425	**827**	.891
77. Doug Wilson, Chi., S.J.	16	1024	237	590	**827**	.808
78. Red Kelly, Det., Tor.	20	1316	281	542	**823**	.625
79. Pierre Larouche, Pit., Mtl., Hfd., NYR	14	812	395	427	**822**	1.01
80. Bernie Geoffrion, Mtl., NYR	16	883	393	429	**822**	.931
* 81. Vincent Damphousse, Tor., Edm., Mtl.	11	852	310	511	**821**	.964
* 82. Brent Sutter, NYI, Chi.	17	1059	361	460	**821**	.775
* 83. Joe Sakic, Que., Colorado	9	655	307	513	**820**	1.25
84. Steve Shutt, Mtl., L.A.	13	930	424	393	**817**	.878
85. Thomas Steen, Wpg.	14	950	264	553	**817**	.860
86. Wilf Paiement, K.C. Col., Tor., Que., NYR, Buf., Pit.	14	946	356	458	**814**	.860
87. Peter McNab, Buf., Bos., Van., N.J.	14	954	363	450	**813**	.852
88. Pit Martin, Det., Bos., Chi., Van.	17	1101	324	485	**809**	.735
* 89. Tomas Sandstrom, NYR, L.A., Pit., Det.	13	848	370	437	**807**	.952
90. Ken Linseman, Phi., Edm., Bos., Tor.	14	860	256	551	**807**	.938
91. Garry Unger, Tor., Det., St.L., Atl., L.A., Edm.	16	1105	413	391	**804**	.728
92. Ken Hodge, Chi., Bos., NYR	14	881	328	472	**800**	.908
93. Wayne Cashman, Bos.	17	1027	277	516	**793**	.772
94. Rick Vaive, Van., Tor., Chi., Buf.	13	876	441	347	**788**	.900
95. Borje Salming, Tor., Det.	17	1148	150	637	**787**	.686
* 96. Rick Tocchet, Phi., Pit., L.A., Bos., Wsh.	13	841	359	417	**776**	.923
97. Jean Pronovost, Wsh., Pit., Atl.	14	998	391	383	**774**	.776
98. Pete Mahovlich, Det., Mtl., Pit.	16	884	288	485	**773**	.874
99. Dave Christian, Wpg., Wsh., Bos., St.L., Chi.	15	1009	340	433	**773**	.766
100. Rick Kehoe, Tor., Pit.	14	906	371	396	**767**	.847

Top 100 Active Points Leaders

Regular Season

	Player	Games	Goals	Assists	Points	Points per game
1.	**Wayne Gretzky**, Edm., L.A., St.L., NYR .	1335	862	1843	**2705**	2.026
2.	**Mark Messier**, Edm., NYR	1272	575	977	**1552**	1.220
3.	**Paul Coffey**, Edm., Pit., L.A., Det., Hfd., Phi.	1211	381	1063	**1444**	1.192
4.	**Jari Kurri**, Edm., L.A., NYR, Ana.	1181	596	780	**1376**	1.165
5.	**Ray Bourque**, Bos.	1290	362	1001	**1363**	1.057
6.	**Ron Francis**, Hfd., Pit.	1166	403	944	**1347**	1.155
7.	**Steve Yzerman**, Det.	1023	539	801	**1340**	1.310
8.	**Mike Gartner**, Wsh., Min., NYR, Tor., Pho.	1372	696	612	**1308**	.953
9.	**Bernie Nicholls**, L.A., NYR, Edm., N.J., Chi., S.J.	1057	469	710	**1179**	1.115
10.	**Dino Ciccarelli**, Min., Wsh., Det., T.B. . .	1156	586	574	**1160**	1.003
11.	**Doug Gilmour**, St.L., Cgy., Tor., N.J. . . .	1062	368	755	**1123**	1.057
12.	**Dave Andreychuk**, Buf., Tor., N.J.	1083	503	561	**1064**	.982
13.	**Larry Murphy**, L.A., Wsh., Min., Pit., Tor., Det.	1315	254	797	**1051**	.799
14.	**Adam Oates**, Det., St.L., Bos., Wsh. . .	826	258	738	**996**	1.206
15.	**Phil Housley**, Buf., Wpg., St.L., Cgy., N.J., Wsh.	1067	285	705	**990**	.928
16.	**Dale Hunter**, Que., Wsh.	1263	313	670	**983**	.778
17.	**Brian Bellows**, Min., Mtl., T.B., Ana. . .	1101	462	515	**977**	.887
18.	**Luc Robitaille**, L.A., Pit., NYR	832	462	500	**962**	1.156
19.	**Al MacInnis**, Cgy., St.L.	989	251	703	**954**	.965
20.	**Pat LaFontaine**, NYI, Buf.	798	445	506	**951**	1.192
21.	**Brett Hull**, Cgy., St.L.	735	527	388	**915**	1.245
22.	**Pat Verbeek**, N.J., Hfd., NYR, Dal.	1065	430	444	**874**	.821
23.	**Pierre Turgeon**, Buf., NYI, Mtl., St.L. . . .	750	344	520	**864**	1.152
24.	**Kirk Muller**, N.J., Mtl., NYI, Tor., Fla. . . .	962	326	521	**847**	.880
25.	**Vincent Damphousse**, Tor., Edm., Mtl. . .	852	310	511	**821**	.964
26.	**Brent Sutter**, NYI, Chi.	1059	361	460	**821**	.775
27.	**Joe Sakic**, Que., Colorado.	655	307	513	**820**	1.252
28.	**Tomas Sandstrom**, NYR, L.A., Pit., Det. . .	848	370	437	**807**	.952
29.	**Rick Tocchet**, Phi., Pit., L.A., Bos., Wsh. .	841	359	417	**776**	.923
30.	**Mike Ridley**, NYR, Wsh., Tor., Van. . . .	866	292	466	**758**	.875
31.	**Scott Stevens**, Wsh., St.L., N.J.	1120	162	584	**746**	.666
32.	**Eddie Olczyk**, Chi., Tor., Wpg., NYR, L.A., Pit.	881	319	424	**743**	.843
33.	**Geoff Courtnall**, Bos., Edm., Wsh., St.L., Van.	939	329	392	**721**	.768
34.	**Chris Chelios**, Mtl., Chi.	920	153	567	**720**	.783
35.	**Mark Recchi**, Pit., Phi., Mtl.	628	285	430	**715**	1.139
36.	**Murray Craven**, Det., Phi., Hfd., Van., Chi.	942	250	464	**714**	.758
37.	**Russ Courtnall**, Tor., Mtl., Min., Dal., Van., NYR	914	279	428	**707**	.774
38.	**Dave Babych**, Wpg., Hfd., Van.	1101	140	566	**706**	.641
39.	**Gary Suter**, Cgy., Chi.	845	167	535	**702**	.831
40.	**Bob Carpenter**, Wsh., NYR, L.A., Bos., N.J.	1056	309	391	**700**	.663
41.	**Joe Nieuwendyk**, Cgy., Dal.	695	358	341	**699**	1.006
42.	**Ray Ferraro**, Hfd., NYI, NYR, L.A.	915	327	368	**695**	.760
43.	**Stephane Richer**, Mtl., N.J.	826	366	326	**692**	.838
44.	**John MacLean**, N.J.	908	344	346	**690**	.760
45.	**Brendan Shanahan**, N.J., St.L., Hfd., Det.	713	335	351	**686**	.962
46.	**Dan Quinn**, Cgy., Pit., Van., St.L., Phi., Min., Ott., L.A.	805	266	419	**685**	.851
47.	**Theoren Fleury**, Cgy.	649	307	376	**683**	1.052
48.	**Kevin Dineen**, Hfd., Phi.	871	323	356	**679**	.780
49.	**Steve Thomas**, Tor., Chi., NYI, N.J.	805	310	362	**672**	.835
50.	**Craig Janney**, Bos., St.L., S.J., Wpg., Pho.	636	173	498	**671**	1.055
51.	**Jeremy Roenick**, Chi., Pho.	596	296	369	**665**	1.116
52.	**Brian Leetch**, NYR	649	147	503	**650**	1.002
53.	**Dave Gagner**, NYR, Min., Dal., Tor., Cgy. .	799	292	351	**643**	.805
54.	**Jaromir Jagr**, Pit.	504	266	367	**633**	1.256
55.	**Alexander Mogilny**, Buf., Van.	536	297	327	**624**	1.164
56.	**Guy Carbonneau**, Mtl., St.L., Dal.	1098	239	368	**607**	.553
57.	**Esa Tikkanen**, Edm., NYR, St.L., N.J., Van.	797	241	365	**606**	.760
58.	**Greg Adams**, N.J., Van., Dal.	803	292	307	**599**	.746
59.	**Kevin Stevens**, Pit., Bos., L.A.	588	278	319	**597**	1.015
60.	**Mike Modano**, Min., Dal.	581	256	339	**595**	1.024
61.	**Sergei Fedorov**, Det.	506	242	350	**592**	1.170
62.	**Steve Duchesne**, L.A., Phi., Que., St.L., Ott.	765	188	394	**582**	.761
63.	**Michal Pivonka**, Wsh.	756	173	406	**579**	.766
64.	**Peter Zezel**, Phi., St.L., Wsh., Tor., Dal., N.J.	802	208	366	**574**	.716
65.	**Petr Klima**, Det., Edm., T.B., L.A., Pit. . . .	773	312	260	**572**	.740
66.	**Jimmy Carson**, L.A., Edm., Det., Van., Hfd.	626	275	286	**561**	.896
67.	**Mats Sundin**, Que., Tor.	529	232	326	**558**	1.055
68.	**Jeff Brown**, Que., St.L., Van., Hfd.	687	150	406	**556**	.809
69.	**Rod Brind'Amour**, St.L., Phi.	614	213	342	**555**	.904
70.	**John Cullen**, Pit., Hfd., Tor., T.B.	617	187	363	**550**	.891
71.	**Kevin Hatcher**, Wsh., Dal., Pit.	886	189	361	**550**	.621
72.	**Trevor Linden**, Van.	660	240	308	**548**	.830
73.	**James Patrick**, NYR, Hfd., Cgy.	875	120	428	**548**	.626
74.	**Claude Lemieux**, Mtl., N.J., Colorado	758	272	275	**547**	.722
75.	**Ray Sheppard**, Buf., NYR, Det., S.J., Fla. . .	625	304	238	**542**	.867
76.	**Dave Ellett**, Wpg., Tor., N.J.	941	148	381	**529**	.562
77.	**Pat Flatley**, NYI, NYR	780	170	340	**510**	.654
78.	**Gary Roberts**, Cgy.	585	257	248	**505**	.863
79.	**Derek King**, NYI, Hfd.	650	214	291	**505**	.777
80.	**Cliff Ronning**, St.L., Van., Pho.	615	185	319	**504**	.820
81.	**Joel Otto**, Cgy., Phi.	875	192	309	**501**	.573
82.	**Ron Sutter**, Phi., St.L., Que., NYI, Bos., S.J.	878	194	307	**501**	.571
83.	**Garry Galley**, L.A., Wsh., Bos., Phi., Buf. . .	889	97	400	**497**	.559
84.	**Brian Bradley**, Cgy., Van., Tor., T.B.	637	180	316	**496**	.779
85.	**Sylvain Turgeon**, Hfd., N.J., Mtl., Ott. . . .	669	269	226	**495**	.740
86.	**Shayne Corson**, Mtl., Edm., St.L.	747	200	294	**494**	.661
87.	**Doug Bodger**, Pit., Buf., S.J.	916	94	399	**493**	.538
88.	**Wendel Clark**, Tor., Que., NYI	636	282	209	**491**	.772
89.	**Scott Mellanby**, Phi., Edm., Fla.	793	223	267	**490**	.618
90.	**Ulf Dahlen**, NYR, Min., Dal., S.J., Chi. . . .	686	231	249	**480**	.700
91.	**Gary Leeman**, Tor., Cgy., Mtl., Van., St.L. .	667	199	267	**466**	.699
92.	**Bruce Driver**, N.J., NYR	847	91	375	**466**	.550
93.	**Benoit Hogue**, Buf., NYI, Tor., Dal.	617	191	263	**454**	.736
94.	**Al Iafrate**, Tor., Wsh., Bos., S.J.	778	150	304	**454**	.584
95.	**Charlie Huddy**, Edm., L.A., Buf., St.L. . . .	1017	99	354	**453**	.445
96.	**Teemu Selanne**, Wpg., Ana.	337	214	237	**451**	1.338
97.	**Kelly Miller**, NYR, Wsh.	919	172	270	**442**	.481
98.	**Randy Burridge**, Bos., Wsh., L.A., Buf. . . .	676	195	245	**440**	.651
99.	**Eric Lindros**, Phi.	297	193	243	**436**	1.468
100.	**Fredrik Olausson**, Wpg., Edm., Ana., Pit. .	711	106	329	**435**	.612

The longest-serving captain in NHL history, Steve Yzerman has collected 1340 points during his red-hot career with the Red Wings in Motown.

All-Time Games Played Leaders

Regular Season

* active player

	Player	Team	Seasons	GP
1.	Gordie Howe	Detroit	25	1,687
		Hartford	1	80
		Total	**26**	**1,767**
2.	Alex Delvecchio	Detroit	24	1,549
3.	John Bucyk	Detroit	2	104
		Boston	21	1,436
		Total	**23**	**1,540**
4.	Tim Horton	Toronto	$19\frac{3}{4}$	1,185
		NY Rangers	$1\frac{1}{4}$	93
		Pittsburgh	1	44
		Buffalo	2	124
		Total	**24**	**1,446**
5.	Harry Howell	NY Rangers	17	1,160
		California	$1\frac{1}{2}$	83
		Los Angeles	$2\frac{1}{2}$	168
		Total	**21**	**1,411**
6.	Norm Ullman	Detroit	$12\frac{1}{2}$	875
		Toronto	$7\frac{1}{2}$	535
		Total	**20**	**1,410**
7.	Stan Mikita	**Chicago**	**22**	**1,394**
8.	Doug Mohns	Boston	11	710
		Chicago	$6\frac{1}{2}$	415
		Minnesota	$2\frac{1}{2}$	162
		Atlanta	1	28
		Washington	1	75
		Total	**22**	**1,390**
9.	Larry Robinson	Montreal	17	1,202
		Los Angeles	3	182
		Total	**20**	**1,384**
10.	Dean Prentice	NY Rangers	$10\frac{1}{2}$	666
		Boston	3	170
		Detroit	$3\frac{1}{2}$	230
		Pittsburgh	2	144
		Minnesota	3	168
		Total	**22**	**1,378**
* 11.	Mike Gartner	Washington	$9\frac{3}{4}$	758
		Minnesota	1	80
		NY Rangers	4	322
		Toronto	$2\frac{1}{4}$	120
		Phoenix	1	82
		Total	**18**	**1,372**
12.	Ron Stewart	Toronto	13	838
		Boston	2	126
		St. Louis	$\frac{1}{2}$	19
		NY Rangers	4	306
		Vancouver	1	42
		NY Islanders	$\frac{1}{2}$	22
		Total	**21**	**1,353**
13.	Marcel Dionne	Detroit	4	309
		Los Angeles	$11\frac{3}{4}$	921
		NY Rangers	$2\frac{1}{4}$	118
		Total	**18**	**1,348**
* 14.	Wayne Gretzky	Edmonton	9	696
		Los Angeles	$7\frac{3}{4}$	539
		St. Louis	$\frac{1}{4}$	18
		NY Rangers	1	82
		Total	**18**	**1,335**
15.	Red Kelly	Detroit	$12\frac{1}{2}$	846
		Toronto	$7\frac{1}{2}$	470
		Total	**20**	**1,316**
* 16.	Larry Murphy	Los Angeles	$3\frac{1}{4}$	242
		Washington	$5\frac{1}{2}$	453
		Minnesota	$1\frac{3}{4}$	121
		Pittsburgh	$4\frac{1}{2}$	336
		Toronto	$1\frac{3}{4}$	151
		Detroit	$\frac{1}{4}$	12
		Total	**17**	**1,315**
17.	Dave Keon	Toronto	15	1,062
		Hartford	3	234
		Total	**18**	**1,296**
* 18.	Ray Bourque	**Boston**	**18**	**1,290**
19.	Phil Esposito	Chicago	4	235
		Boston	$8\frac{1}{4}$	625
		NY Rangers	$5\frac{1}{4}$	422
		Total	**18**	**1,282**
20.	Jean Ratelle	NY Rangers	$15\frac{1}{4}$	862
		Boston	$5\frac{3}{4}$	419
		Total	**21**	**1,281**
21.	Bryan Trottier	NY Islanders	15	1,123
		Pittsburgh	3	156
		Total	**18**	**1,279**
* 22.	Mark Messier	Edmonton	12	851
		NY Rangers	6	421
		Total	**18**	**1,272**
* 23.	Dale Hunter	Quebec	7	523
		Washington	10	740
		Total	**17**	**1,263**
24.	Henri Richard	**Montreal**	**20**	**1,256**
25.	Bill Gadsby	Chicago	$8\frac{1}{2}$	468

	Player	Team	Seasons	GP
		NY Rangers	$6\frac{1}{2}$	457
		Detroit	5	323
		Total	**20**	**1,248**
* 26.	Kevin Lowe	Edmonton	14	1,030
		NY Rangers	4	217
		Total	**18**	**1,247**
27.	Allan Stanley	NY Rangers	$6\frac{1}{4}$	307
		Chicago	$1\frac{3}{4}$	111
		Boston	2	129
		Toronto	9	633
		Philadelphia	1	64
		Total	**21**	**1,244**
28.	Eddie Westfall	Boston	11	734
		NY Islanders	7	493
		Total	**18**	**1,227**
29.	Brad McCrimmon	Boston	3	228
		Philadelphia	5	367
		Calgary	3	231
		Detroit	3	203
		Hartford	3	156
		Phoenix	1	37
		Total	**18**	**1,222**
30.	Eric Nesterenko	Toronto	5	206
		Chicago	16	1,013
		Total	**21**	**1,219**
* 31.	Paul Coffey	Edmonton	7	532
		Pittsburgh	$4\frac{3}{4}$	331
		Los Angeles	$\frac{3}{4}$	60
		Detroit	$3\frac{1}{2}$	231
		Hartford	$\frac{1}{2}$	20
		Philadelphia	$\frac{1}{2}$	37
		Total	**17**	**1,211**
32.	Marcel Pronovost	Detroit	16	983
		Toronto	5	223
		Total	**21**	**1,206**
33.	Denis Savard	Chicago	$12\frac{1}{4}$	881
		Montreal	3	210
		Tampa Bay	$1\frac{3}{4}$	105
		Total	**17**	**1,196**
34.	Gilbert Perreault	**Buffalo**	**17**	**1,191**
35.	Dale Hawerchuk	Winnipeg	9	713
		Buffalo	5	342
		St. Louis	$\frac{3}{4}$	66
		Philadelphia	$1\frac{1}{4}$	67
		Total	**16**	**1,188**
36.	George Armstrong	**Toronto**	**21**	**1,187**
37.	Frank Mahovlich	Toronto	$11\frac{3}{4}$	720
		Detroit	$2\frac{3}{4}$	198
		Montreal	$3\frac{1}{2}$	263
		Total	**18**	**1,181**
* 38.	Jari Kurri	Edmonton	10	754
		Los Angeles	$4\frac{3}{4}$	331
		NY Rangers	$\frac{1}{4}$	14
		Anaheim	1	82
		Total	**16**	**1,181**
39.	Don Marshall	Montreal	10	585
		NY Rangers	7	479
		Buffalo	1	62
		Toronto	1	50
		Total	**19**	**1,176**

	Player	Team	Seasons	GP
* 40.	Ron Francis	Hartford	$9\frac{3}{4}$	714
		Pittsburgh	$6\frac{1}{4}$	452
		Total	**16**	**1,166**
41.	Bob Gainey	**Montreal**	**16**	**1,160**
* 42.	Dino Ciccarelli	Minnesota	$8\frac{3}{4}$	602
		Washington	$3\frac{1}{4}$	223
		Detroit	4	254
		Tampa Bay	1	77
		Total	**17**	**1,156**
43.	Leo Boivin	Toronto	$3\frac{1}{4}$	137
		Boston	$11\frac{1}{2}$	717
		Detroit	$1\frac{1}{4}$	85
		Pittsburgh	$1\frac{1}{2}$	114
		Minnesota	$1\frac{1}{2}$	97
		Total	**19**	**1,150**
44.	Borje Salming	Toronto	16	1,099
		Detroit	1	49
		Total	**17**	**1,148**
45.	Bobby Clarke	**Philadelphia**	**15**	**1,144**
46.	Glenn Anderson	Edmonton	$11\frac{1}{2}$	845
		Toronto	$2\frac{3}{4}$	221
		NY Rangers	$\frac{1}{4}$	12
		St. Louis	$1\frac{1}{2}$	51
		Total	**16**	**1,129**
47.	Bob Nevin	Toronto	$5\frac{3}{4}$	250
		NY Rangers	$7\frac{1}{4}$	505
		Minnesota	2	138
		Los Angeles	3	235
		Total	**18**	**1,128**
48.	Murray Oliver	Detroit	$2\frac{1}{2}$	101
		Boston	$6\frac{1}{2}$	429
		Toronto	3	226
		Minnesota	5	371
		Total	**17**	**1,127**
49.	Guy Lafleur	Montreal	14	961
		NY Rangers	1	67
		Quebec	2	98
		Total	**17**	**1,126**
50.	Jean Beliveau	**Montreal**	**20**	**1,125**
* 51.	Scott Stevens	Washington	8	601
		St. Louis	1	78
		New Jersey	6	441
		Total	**15**	**1,120**
52.	Doug Harvey	Montreal	14	890
		NY Rangers	3	151
		Detroit	1	2
		St. Louis	1	70
		Total	**19**	**1,113**
53.	Brad Park	NY Rangers	$7\frac{1}{2}$	465
		Boston	$7\frac{1}{2}$	501
		Detroit	2	147
		Total	**17**	**1,113**
54.	Lanny McDonald	Toronto	$6\frac{1}{2}$	477
		Colorado	$1\frac{3}{4}$	142
		Calgary	$7\frac{3}{4}$	441
		Total	**16**	**1,111**
55.	Dave Taylor	Los Angeles	17	1,111
56.	Butch Goring	Los Angeles	$10\frac{3}{4}$	736
		NY Islanders	$4\frac{1}{2}$	332
		Boston	$\frac{1}{2}$	39
		Total	**16**	**1,107**

Mark Messier, who will be wearing the colors of the Vancouver Canucks in 1997-98, has never missed more than 17 games in a season since his NHL debut in 1979-80.

	Player	Team	Seasons	GP
57.	**Garry Unger**	Toronto	½	15
		Detroit	3	216
		St. Louis	8½	662
		Atlanta	1	79
		Los Angeles	¾	58
		Edmonton	2¼	75
		Total	**16**	**1,105**
58.	**Pit Martin**	Detroit	3¼	119
		Boston	1¾	111
		Chicago	10¼	740
		Vancouver	1¾	131
		Total	**17**	**1,101**
* 59.	**Brian Bellows**	Minnesota	10	753
		Montreal	3	200
		Tampa Bay	1¼	86
		Anaheim	¾	62
		Total	**15**	**1,101**
* 60.	**Dave Babych**	Winnipeg	5¼	390
		Hartford	5¾	349
		Vancouver	6	362
		Total	**17**	**1,101**
* 61.	**Neal Broten**	Minnesota	13	876
		Dallas	2	116
		New Jersey	1¾	88
		Los Angeles	¼	19
		Total	**17**	**1,099**
62.	**Jay Wells**	Los Angeles	9	604
		Philadelphia	1¾	126
		Buffalo	2	85
		NY Rangers	3¼	186
		St. Louis	1	76
		Tampa Bay	1	21
		Total	**18**	**1,098**
* 63.	**Guy Carbonneau**	Montreal	13	912
		St. Louis	1	42
		Dallas	2	144
		Total	**16**	**1,098**
64.	**Gordie Roberts**	Hartford	1½	107
		Minnesota	7	555
		Philadelphia	¼	11
		St. Louis	2½	166
		Pittsburgh	1¾	134
		Boston	2	124
		Total	**15**	**1,097**
65.	**Darryl Sittler**	Toronto	11½	844
		Philadelphia	2½	191
		Detroit	1	61
		Total	**15**	**1,096**
* 66.	**Craig Ludwig**	Montreal	8	597
		NY Islanders	1	75
		Minnesota	2	151
		Dallas	4	273
		Total	**15**	**1,096**
67.	**Craig MacTavish**	Boston	5	217
		Edmonton	8¾	701
		NY Rangers	¼	12
		Philadelphia	1¾	100
		St. Louis	1¼	63
		Total	**17**	**1,093**
68.	**Michel Goulet**	Quebec	10¾	813
		Chicago	4¼	276
		Total	**15**	**1,089**
69.	**Carol Vadnais**	Montreal	2	42
		Oakland	2	152
		California	1¾	94
		Boston	3½	263
		NY Rangers	6¾	485
		New Jersey	1	51
		Total	**17**	**1,087**
70.	**Brad Marsh**	Atlanta	2	160
		Calgary	1¼	97
		Philadelphia	6¾	514
		Toronto	2¾	181
		Detroit	1¼	75
		Ottawa	1	59
		Total	**15**	**1,086**
* 71.	**Dave Andreychuk**	Buffalo	10½	763
		Toronto	3¼	223
		New Jersey	1¼	97
		Total	**15**	**1,083**
72.	**Bob Pulford**	Toronto	14	947
		Los Angeles	2	132
		Total	**16**	**1,079**
73.	**Bobby Smith**	Minnesota	8¼	572
		Montreal	6¾	505
		Total	**15**	**1,077**
74.	**Craig Ramsay**	**Buffalo**	**14**	**1,070**
75.	**Andy Bathgate**	NY Rangers	11¾	719
		Toronto	1¼	70
		Detroit	2	130
		Pittsburgh	2	150
		Total	**17**	**1,069**
76.	**Ted Lindsay**	Detroit	14	862
		Chicago	3	206
		Total	**17**	**1,068**
77.	**Mike Ramsey**	Buffalo	13¾	911
		Pittsburgh	1¼	77
		Detroit	2	80
		Total	**17**	**1,068**
* 78.	**Phil Housley**	Buffalo	8	608
		Winnipeg	3	232
		St. Louis	1	26
		Calgary	1¾	102
		New Jersey	¼	22
		Washington	1	77
		Total	**15**	**1,067**
79.	**Terry Harper**	Montreal	10	554
		Los Angeles	3	234
		Detroit	4	252
		St. Louis	1	11
		Colorado	1	15
		Total	**19**	**1,066**
80.	**Rod Gilbert**	**NY Rangers**	**18**	**1,065**
* 81.	**Pat Verbeek**	New Jersey	7	463
		Hartford	5¾	433
		NY Rangers	1¼	88
		Dallas	1	81
		Total	**15**	**1,065**
82.	**Bobby Hull**	Chicago	15	1,036
		Winnipeg	⅔	18
		Hartford	⅓	9
		Total	**16**	**1,063**
83.	**Joe Mullen**	St. Louis	4½	301
		Calgary	4½	345
		Pittsburgh	6	379
		Boston	1	37
		Total	**16**	**1,062**
* 84.	**Doug Gilmour**	St. Louis	5	384
		Calgary	3½	266
		Toronto	5¼	392
		New Jersey	¼	20
		Total	**14**	**1,062**
85.	**Denis Potvin**	**NY Islanders**	**15**	**1,060**
* 86.	**Brent Sutter**	NY Islanders	11¼	694
		Chicago	5¾	365
		Total	**17**	**1,059**
* 87.	**Bernie Nicholls**	Los Angeles	8½	602
		NY Rangers	1¾	104
		Edmonton	1¼	95
		New Jersey	1½	84
		Chicago	2	107
		San Jose	1	65
		Total	**16**	**1,057**
88.	**Jean Guy Talbot**	Montreal	13	791
		Minnesota	¼	4
		Detroit	½	32
		St. Louis	2½	172
		Buffalo	¾	57
		Total	**17**	**1,056**
* 89.	**Bob Carpenter**	Washington	6¼	490
		NY Rangers	½	28
		Los Angeles	1¾	120
		Boston	3½	187
		New Jersey	4	231
		Total	**16**	**1,056**
90.	**Randy Carlyle**	Toronto	2	94
		Pittsburgh	5¾	397
		Winnipeg	9¼	564
		Total	**17**	**1,055**
91.	**Ivan Boldirev**	Boston	1¼	13
		California	2¾	191
		Chicago	4¾	384
		Atlanta	1	65
		Vancouver	2¾	216
		Detroit	2½	183
		Total	**15**	**1,052**
92.	**Eddie Shack**	NY Rangers	2¼	141
		Toronto	8¾	504
		Boston	2	120
		Los Angeles	1¼	84
		Buffalo	1½	111
		Pittsburgh	1¼	87
		Total	**17**	**1,047**
93.	**Rob Ramage**	Colorado	3	234
		St. Louis	5¾	441
		Calgary	1¼	80
		Toronto	2	160
		Minnesota	1	34
		Tampa Bay	¾	66
		Montreal	½	14
		Philadelphia	¾	15
		Total	**15**	**1,044**
94.	**Serge Savard**	Montreal	15	917
		Winnipeg	2	123
		Total	**17**	**1,040**
95.	**Ron Ellis**	**Toronto**	**16**	**1,034**
96.	**Harold Snepsts**	Vancouver	11¾	781
		Minnesota	1	71
		Detroit	3	120
		St. Louis	1¼	61
		Total	**17**	**1,033**
97.	**Ralph Backstrom**	Montreal	14½	844
		Los Angeles	2¼	172
		Chicago	¼	16
		Total	**17**	**1,032**
98.	**Dick Duff**	Toronto	9¾	582
		NY Rangers	¾	43
		Montreal	5	305
		Los Angeles	¾	39
		Buffalo	1¾	61
		Total	**18**	**1,030**
99.	**John Tonelli**	NY Islanders	7¾	584
		Calgary	2¼	161
		Los Angeles	3	231
		Chicago	¾	33
		Quebec	¼	19
		Total	**14**	**1,028**
100.	**Gaetan Duchesne**	Washington	6	451
		Quebec	2	150
		Minnesota	4	297
		San Jose	1¾	117
		Florida	¼	13
		Total	**14**	**1,028**
101.	**Wayne Cashman**	**Boston**	**17**	**1,027**
102.	**Doug Wilson**	Chicago	14	938
		San Jose	2	86
		Total	**16**	**1,024**
103.	**Jim Neilson**	NY Rangers	12	810
		California	2	98
		Cleveland	2	115
		Total	**16**	**1,023**
104.	**Keith Acton**	Montreal	4¼	228
		Minnesota	4¼	343
		Edmonton	1	72
		Philadelphia	4½	303
		Washington	¼	6
		NY Islanders	¾	71
		Total	**15**	**1,023**
* 105.	**Steve Yzerman**	**Detroit**	**14**	**1,023**
106.	**Don Lever**	Vancouver	7⅔	593
		Atlanta	⅓	28
		Calgary	1¼	85
		Colorado	¾	59
		New Jersey	3	216
		Buffalo	2	39
		Total	**15**	**1,020**
107.	**Mike Foligno**	Detroit	2½	186
		Buffalo	9	664
		Toronto	2¾	129
		Florida	¾	39
		Total	**15**	**1,018**
* 108.	**Charlie Huddy**	Edmonton	11	694
		Los Angeles	3¼	226
		Buffalo	2½	85
		St. Louis	¼	12
		Total	**17**	**1,017**
109.	**Phil Russell**	Chicago	6¾	504
		Atlanta	1¼	93
		Calgary	3	229
		New Jersey	2¾	172
		Buffalo	1¼	18
		Total	**15**	**1,016**
110.	**Brian Propp**	Philadelphia	10¾	790
		Boston	¼	14
		Minnesota	3	147
		Hartford	1	65
		Total	**15**	**1,016**
111.	**Laurie Boschman**	Toronto	2¾	187
		Edmonton	1	73
		Winnipeg	7¼	526
		New Jersey	2	153
		Ottawa	1	70
		Total	**14**	**1,009**
112.	**Dave Christian**	Winnipeg	4	230
		Washington	6½	504
		Boston	1½	128
		St. Louis	1	78
		Chicago	2	69
		Total	**15**	**1,009**
113.	**Dave Lewis**	NY Islanders	6¾	514
		Los Angeles	3¼	221
		New Jersey	3	209
		Detroit	2	64
		Total	**15**	**1,008**
114.	**Bob Murray**	**Chicago**	**15**	**1,008**
115.	**Jim Roberts**	Montreal	9⅔	611
		St. Louis	5⅓	395
		Total	**15**	**1,006**
116.	**Steve Larmer**	Chicago	13	891
		NY Rangers	2	115
		Total	**15**	**1,006**
117.	**Claude Provost**	**Montreal**	**15**	**1,005**
118.	**Rick Middleton**	NY Rangers	2	124
		Boston	12	881
		Total	**14**	**1,005**
119.	**Ryan Walter**	Washington	4	307
		Montreal	9	604
		Vancouver	2	92
		Total	**15**	**1,003**
120.	**Vic Hadfield**	NY Rangers	13	839
		Pittsburgh	3	163
		Total	**16**	**1,002**
121.	**Bernie Federko**	St. Louis	14	927
		Detroit	1	73
		Total	**15**	**1,000**

Goaltending Records

All-Time Shutout Leaders

Goaltender	Team	Seasons	Games	Shutouts
Terry Sawchuk	Detroit	14	734	85
(1949-1970)	Boston	2	102	11
	Toronto	3	91	4
	Los Angeles	1	36	2
	NY Rangers	1	8	1
	Total	21	971	**103**
George Hainsworth	Montreal	7½	318	75
(1926-1937)	Toronto	3½	147	19
	Total	11	465	**94**
Glenn Hall	Detroit	4	148	17
(1952-1971)	Chicago	10	618	51
	St. Louis	4	140	16
	Total	18	906	**84**
Jacques Plante	Montreal	11	556	58
(1952-1973)	NY Rangers	2	98	5
	St. Louis	2	69	10
	Toronto	2¾	106	7
	Boston	¼	8	2
	Total	18	837	**82**
Tiny Thompson	Boston	10¼	468	74
(1928-1940)	Detroit	1¾	85	7
	Total	12	553	**81**
Alex Connell	Ottawa	8	293	64
(1924-1937)	Detroit	1	48	6
	NY Americans	1	1	0
	Mtl. Maroons	2	75	11
	Total	12	417	**81**
Tony Esposito	Montreal	1	13	2
(1968-1984)	Chicago	15	873	74
	Total	16	886	**76**
Lorne Chabot	NY Rangers	2	80	21
(1926-1937)	Toronto	5	214	33
	Montreal	1	47	8
	Chicago	1	48	8
	Mtl. Maroons	1	16	2
	NY Americans	1	6	1
	Total	11	411	**73**
Harry Lumley	Detroit	6½	324	26
(1943-1960)	NY Rangers	½	1	0
	Chicago	2	134	5
	Toronto	4	267	34
	Boston	3	78	6
	Total	16	804	**71**
Roy Worters	Pittsburgh Pirates	3	123	22
(1925-1937)	NY Americans	9	360	44
	* Montreal		1	0
	Total	12	484	**66**
Turk Broda	Toronto	14	629	**62**
(1936-1952)				
John Roach	Toronto	7	222	13
(1921-1935)	NY Rangers	4	89	30
	Detroit	3	180	15
	Total	14	491	**58**
Clint Benedict	Ottawa	7	158	19
(1917-1930)	Mtl. Maroons	6	204	38
	Total	13	362	**57**

Goaltender	Team	Seasons	Games	Shutouts
Bernie Parent	Boston	2	57	1
(1965-1979)	Philadelphia	9½	486	50
	Toronto	1½	65	3
	Total	13	608	**54**
Ed Giacomin	NY Rangers	10¼	539	49
(1965-1978)	Detroit	2¾	71	5
	Total	13	610	**54**
David Kerr	Mtl. Maroons	3	101	11
(1930-1941)	NY Americans	1	1	0
	NY Rangers	7	324	40
	Total	11	426	**51**
Rogie Vachon	Montreal	5¼	206	13
(1966-1982)	Los Angeles	6¾	389	32
	Detroit	2	109	4
	Boston	2	91	2
	Total	16	795	**51**
Ken Dryden	Montreal	8	397	**46**
(1970-1979)				
Gump Worsley	NY Rangers	10	582	24
(1952-1974)	Montreal	6½	172	16
	Minnesota	4½	107	3
	Total	21	861	**43**
Charlie Gardiner	Chicago	7	316	**42**
(1927-1934)				
Frank Brimsek	Boston	9	444	35
(1938-1950)	Chicago	1	70	5
	Total	10	514	**40**
Johnny Bower	NY Rangers	3	77	5
(1953-1970)	Toronto	12	475	32
	Total	15	552	**37**
Patrick Roy	Montreal	11½	551	29
(1984-1997)	Colorado	1½	101	8
	Total	13	652	**37**
Bill Durnan	Montreal	7	383	**34**
(1943-1950)				
Eddie Johnston	Boston	11	444	27
(1962-1978)	Toronto	1	26	1
	St. Louis	3⅔	118	4
	Chicago	⅓	4	0
	Total	16	592	**32**
Ed Belfour	Chicago	7⅔	415	30
(1988-1997)	San Jose	⅓	13	1
	Total	4	428	**31**
Roger Crozier	Detroit	7	313	20
(1963-1977)	Buffalo	6	202	10
	Washington	1	3	0
	Total	14	518	**30**
Cesare Maniago	Toronto	1	7	0
(1960-1978)	Montreal	1	14	0
	NY Rangers	2	34	2
	Minnesota	9	420	26
	Vancouver	2	93	2
	Total	15	568	**30**

*Played 1 game for Canadiens in 1929-30.

Ten or More Shutouts, One Season

Number of Shutouts	Goaltender	Team	Season	Length of Schedule
22	George Hainsworth	Montreal	1928-29	44
15	Alex Connell	Ottawa	1925-26	36
	Alex Connell	Ottawa	1927-28	44
	Hal Winkler	Boston	1927-28	44
	Tony Esposito	Chicago	1969-70	76
14	George Hainsworth	Montreal	1926-27	44
13	Clint Benedict	Mtl. Maroons	1926-27	44
	Alex Connell	Ottawa	1926-27	44
	George Hainsworth	Montreal	1927-28	44
	John Roach	NY Rangers	1928-29	44
	Roy Worters	NY Americans	1928-29	44
	Harry Lumley	Toronto	1953-54	70
12	Tiny Thompson	Boston	1928-29	44
	Lorne Chabot	Toronto	1928-29	44
	Chuck Gardiner	Chicago	1930-31	44
	Terry Sawchuk	Detroit	1951-52	70
	Terry Sawchuk	Detroit	1953-54	70
	Terry Sawchuk	Detroit	1954-55	70
	Glenn Hall	Detroit	1955-56	70
	Bernie Parent	Philadelphia	1973-74	78
	Bernie Parent	Philadelphia	1974-75	80

Number of Shutouts	Goaltender	Team	Season	Length of Schedule
11	Lorne Chabot	NY Rangers	1927-28	44
	Harry Holmes	Detroit	1927-28	44
	Clint Benedict	Mtl. Maroons	1928-29	44
	Joe Miller	Pittsburgh Pirates	1928-29	44
	Tiny Thompson	Boston	1932-33	48
	Terry Sawchuk	Detroit	1950-51	70
10	Lorne Chabot	NY Rangers	1926-27	44
	Roy Worters	Pittsburgh Pirates	1927-28	44
	Clarence Dolson	Detroit	1928-29	44
	John Roach	Detroit	1932-33	48
	Chuck Gardiner	Chicago	1933-34	48
	Tiny Thompson	Boston	1935-36	48
	Frank Brimsek	Boston	1938-39	48
	Bill Durnan	Montreal	1948-49	60
	Gerry McNeil	Montreal	1952-53	70
	Harry Lumley	Toronto	1952-53	70
	Tony Esposito	Chicago	1973-74	78
	Ken Dryden	Montreal	1976-77	80
	Martin Brodeur	**New Jersey**	**1996-97**	**82**

All-Time Win Leaders

(Minimum 200 Wins)

Wins	Goaltender	GP	Dec.	Losses	Ties	%
447	Terry Sawchuk	971	950	330	173	.562
434	Jacques Plante	837	827	246	147	.614
423	Tony Esposito	886	881	306	152	.567
407	Glenn Hall	906	897	327	163	.545
355	Rogie Vachon	795	773	291	127	.541
354	* Andy Moog	671	629	192	83	.629
353	* Grant Fuhr	748	701	250	98	.573
349	* Patrick Roy	652	628	205	74	.615
334	Gump Worsley	861	831	349	148	.491
333	Harry Lumley	804	802	326	143	.504
305	Billy Smith	680	643	233	105	.556
302	Turk Broda	629	627	224	101	.562
301	* Mike Vernon	562	545	179	65	.612
295	* Tom Barrasso	602	576	218	63	.567
294	Mike Liut	663	639	271	74	.518
289	Ed Giacomin	610	592	206	97	.570
288	* John Vanbiesbrouck	657	623	256	79	.526
286	Dan Bouchard	655	631	232	113	.543
284	Tiny Thompson	553	553	194	75	.581
270	Bernie Parent	608	588	197	121	.562
270	Gilles Meloche	788	752	351	131	.446
268	* Don Beaupre	667	620	277	75	.493
267	* Kelly Hrudey	649	602	249	86	.515
265	* Ron Hextall	539	513	190	58	.573
258	Ken Dryden	397	389	57	74	.758
252	Frank Brimsek	514	514	182	80	.568
251	Johnny Bower	552	537	196	90	.551
246	George Hainsworth	465	465	145	74	.609
246	Pete Peeters	489	452	155	51	.601
236	Reggie Lemelin	507	461	162	63	.580
236	Eddie Johnston	592	573	256	81	.483
231	Glenn Resch	571	537	224	82	.507
230	Gerry Cheevers	418	407	103	74	.656
223	* Bill Ranford	573	533	243	67	.481
219	John Roach	491	491	204	68	.514
215	Greg Millen	604	588	284	89	.441
208	Bill Durnan	383	382	112	62	.626
208	Don Edwards	459	437	155	74	.561
207	* Kirk McLean	493	478	213	58	.494
206	Lorne Chabot	411	411	140	65	.580
206	Roger Crozier	518	474	198	70	.508
204	Rick Wamsley	407	381	131	46	.596
204	* Ed Belfour	428	407	147	56	.570
203	David Kerr	426	426	148	75	.565

* active player

Active Shutout Leaders

(Minimum 14 Shutouts)

Goaltender	Teams	Seasons	Games	Shutouts
Patrick Roy	Montreal, Colorado	13	652	37
Ed Belfour	Chicago, San Jose	9	428	31
John Vanbiesbrouck	NY Rangers, Florida	15	657	25
Andy Moog	Edm., Bos., Dal.	17	671	25
Tom Barrasso	Buffalo, Pittsburgh	14	602	23
Martin Brodeur	New Jersey	5	235	22
Dominik Hasek	Chicago, Buffalo	7	278	20
Grant Fuhr	Edm., Tor., Buf., L.A., St.L.	16	748	20
Kirk McLean	New Jersey, Vancouver	12	493	19
Ron Hextall	Phi., Que., NYI	11	539	19
Mike Richter	NY Rangers	8	352	18
Daren Puppa	Buf., Tor., T.B.	12	385	17
Don Beaupre	Min., Wsh., Ott., Tor.	17	667	17
Bob Essensa	Wpg., Det., Edm.	7	313	16
Jon Casey	Min., Bos., St.L.	12	425	16
Kelly Hrudey	NYI, L.A., S.J.	14	649	16
Chris Osgood	Detroit	4	157	14

Active Goaltending Leaders

(Ranked by winning percentage; minimum 250 games played)

Goaltender	Teams	Seasons	GP	Decisions	W	L	T	Winning %
Andy Moog	Edm., Bos., Dal.	17	671	629	354	192	83	.629
Patrick Roy	Montreal, Colorado	13	652	628	349	205	74	.615
Mike Vernon	Calgary, Detroit	14	562	545	301	179	65	.612
Mike Richter	NY Rangers	8	352	329	182	113	34	.605
Grant Fuhr	Edm., Tor., Buf., L.A., St.L.	16	748	701	353	250	98	.573
Ron Hextall	Phi., Que., NYI	11	539	513	265	190	58	.573
Ed Belfour	Chicago, San Jose	9	428	407	204	147	56	.570
Tom Barrasso	Buffalo, Pittsburgh	14	602	576	295	218	63	.567
Dominik Hasek	Chicago, Buffalo	7	278	265	132	98	35	.564
Curtis Joseph	St. Louis, Edmonton	8	386	370	184	141	45	.558
Daren Puppa	Buf., Tor., T.B.	12	385	354	168	139	47	.541
Felix Potvin	Toronto	6	297	287	131	114	42	.530
John Vanbiesbrouck	NY Rangers, Florida	15	657	623	288	256	79	.526
Tim Cheveldae	Det., Wpg., Bos.	9	340	322	149	136	37	.520
Jon Casey	Min., Bos., St.L.	12	425	382	170	157	55	.517
Kelly Hrudey	NYI, L.A., S.J.	14	649	602	267	249	86	.515
Mark Fitzpatrick	LA, NYI,Flo.	9	253	233	98	95	40	.506
Kirk McLean	New Jersey, Vancouver	12	493	478	207	213	58	.494
Don Beaupre	Min., Wsh., Ott., Tor.	17	667	620	268	277	75	.493
Bob Essensa	Wpg., Det., Edm.	7	313	287	124	129	34	.491
Guy Hebert	St. Louis, Anaheim	6	254	237	102	108	27	.487
Bill Ranford	Bos., Edm., Wsh.	12	573	533	223	243	67	.481
Chris Terreri	N.J., S.J., Chi.	10	343	308	129	141	38	.481
Ken Wregget	Tor., Phi., Pit.	14	504	463	198	220	45	.476
Glenn Healy	L.A., NYI, NYR	11	372	345	143	160	42	.475
Sean Burke	New Jersey, Hartford	9	418	395	162	186	47	.470
Ron Tugnutt	Que., Edm., Ana., Mtl., Ott.	9	262	232	75	132	25	.377

Goals Against Average Leaders

(minimum 13 games played, 1994-95; minimum 27 games played, 1992-93 to 1993-94, 1995-96, 1996-97; 25 games played, 1926-27 to 1991-92; 15 games played, 1917-18 to 1925-26.)

Season	Goaltender and Club	GP	Mins.	GA	SO	AVG.
1996-97	Martin Brodeur, New Jersey	67	3,838	120	10	1.88
1995-96	Ron Hextall, Philadelphia	53	3,102	112	4	2.17
1994-95	Dominik Hasek, Buffalo	41	2,416	85	5	2.11
1993-94	Dominik Hasek, Buffalo	58	3,358	109	7	1.95
1992-93	Felix Potvin, Toronto	48	2,781	116	2	2.50
1991-92	Patrick Roy, Montreal	67	3,935	155	5	2.36
1990-91	Ed Belfour, Chicago	74	4,127	170	4	2.47
1989-90	Mike Liut, Hartford, Washington	37	2,161	91	4	2.53
1988-89	Patrick Roy, Montreal	48	2,744	113	4	2.47
1987-88	Pete Peeters, Washington	35	1,896	88	2	2.78
1986-87	Brian Hayward, Montreal	37	2,178	102	1	2.81
1985-86	Bob Froese, Philadelphia	51	2,728	116	5	2.55
1984-85	Tom Barrasso, Buffalo	54	3,248	144	5	2.66
1983-84	Pat Riggin, Washington	41	2,299	102	4	2.66
1982-83	Pete Peeters, Boston	62	3,611	142	8	2.36
1981-82	Denis Herron, Montreal	27	1,547	68	3	2.64
1980-81	Richard Sevigny, Montreal	33	1,777	71	2	2.40
1979-80	Bob Sauve, Buffalo	32	1,880	74	4	2.36
1978-79	Ken Dryden, Montreal	47	2,814	108	5	2.30
1977-78	Ken Dryden, Montreal	52	3,071	105	5	2.05
1976-77	Michel Larocque, Montreal	26	1,525	53	4	2.09
1975-76	Ken Dryden, Montreal	62	3,580	121	8	2.03
1974-75	Bernie Parent, Philadelphia	68	4,041	137	12	2.03
1973-74	Bernie Parent, Philadelphia	73	4,314	136	12	1.89
1972-73	Ken Dryden, Montreal	54	3,165	119	6	2.26
1971-72	Tony Esposito, Chicago	48	2,780	82	9	1.77
1970-71	Jacques Plante, Toronto	40	2,329	73	4	1.88
1969-70	Ernie Wakely, St. Louis	30	1,651	58	4	2.11
1968-69	Jacques Plante, St. Louis	37	2,139	70	5	1.96
1967-68	Gump Worsley, Montreal	40	2,213	73	6	1.98
1966-67	Glenn Hall, Chicago	32	1,664	66	2	2.38
1965-66	Johnny Bower, Toronto	35	1,998	75	3	2.25
1964-65	Johnny Bower, Toronto	34	2,040	81	3	2.38
1963-64	Johnny Bower, Toronto	51	3,009	106	5	2.11
1962-63	Jacques Plante, Montreal	56	3,320	138	5	2.49
1961-62	Jacques Plante, Montreal	70	4,200	166	4	2.37
1960-61	Johnny Bower, Toronto	58	3,480	145	2	2.50
1959-60	Jacques Plante, Montreal	69	4,140	175	3	2.54
1958-59	Jacques Plante, Montreal	67	4,000	144	9	2.16
1957-58	Jacques Plante, Montreal	57	3,386	119	9	2.11
1956-57	Jacques Plante, Montreal	61	3,660	123	9	2.02
1955-56	Jacques Plante, Montreal	64	3,840	119	7	1.86
1954-55	Terry Sawchuk, Detroit	68	4,080	132	12	1.94
1953-54	Harry Lumley, Toronto	69	4,140	128	13	1.86
1952-53	Terry Sawchuk, Detroit	63	3,780	120	9	1.90
1951-52	Terry Sawchuk, Detroit	70	4,200	133	12	1.90
1950-51	Al Rollins, Toronto	40	2,367	70	5	1.77
1949-50	Bill Durnan, Montreal	64	3,840	141	8	2.20
1948-49	Bill Durnan, Montreal	60	3,600	126	10	2.10
1947-48	Turk Broda, Toronto	60	3,600	143	5	2.38
1946-47	Bill Durnan, Montreal	60	3,600	138	4	2.30
1945-46	Bill Durnan, Montreal	40	2,400	104	4	2.60
1944-45	Bill Durnan, Montreal	50	3,000	121	1	2.42
1943-44	Bill Durnan, Montreal	50	3,000	109	2	2.18
1942-43	Johnny Mowers, Detroit	50	3,010	124	6	2.47
1941-42	Frank Brimsek, Boston	47	2,930	115	3	2.35
1940-41	Turk Broda, Toronto	48	2,970	99	5	2.00
1939-40	Dave Kerr, NY Rangers	48	3,000	77	8	1.54
1938-39	Frank Brimsek, Boston	43	2,610	68	10	1.56
1937-38	Tiny Thompson, Boston	48	2,970	89	7	1.80
1936-37	Normie Smith, Detroit	48	2,980	102	6	2.05
1935-36	Tiny Thompson, Boston	48	2,930	82	10	1.68
1934-35	Lorne Chabot, Chicago	48	2,940	88	8	1.80
1933-34	Wilf Cude, Detroit, Montreal	30	1,920	47	5	1.47
1932-33	Tiny Thompson, Boston	48	3,000	88	11	1.76
1931-32	Chuck Gardiner, Chicago	48	2,989	92	4	1.85
1930-31	Roy Worters, NY Americans	44	2,760	74	8	1.61
1929-30	Tiny Thompson, Boston	44	2,680	98	3	2.19
1928-29	George Hainsworth, Montreal	44	2,800	43	22	0.92
1927-28	George Hainsworth, Montreal	44	2,730	48	13	1.05
1926-27	Clint Benedict, Mtl. Maroons	43	2,748	65	13	1.42
1925-26	Alex Connell, Ottawa	36	2,251	42	15	1.12
1924-25	Georges Vezina, Montreal	30	1,860	56	5	1.81
1923-24	Georges Vezina, Montreal	24	1,459	48	3	1.97
1922-23	Clint Benedict, Ottawa	24	1,478	54	4	2.19
1921-22	Clint Benedict, Ottawa	24	1,508	84	2	3.34
1920-21	Clint Benedict, Ottawa	24	1,457	75	2	3.09
1919-20	Clint Benedict, Ottawa	24	1,444	64	5	2.66
1918-19	Clint Benedict, Ottawa	18	1,113	53	2	2.86
1917-18	Georges Vezina, Montreal	21	1,282	84	1	3.93

All-Time Regular Season NHL Coaching Register

Regular Season, 1917-97

(figures in parentheses indicate ranking of top 10 in order of games coached)

Coach	Team	Games	Wins	Losses	Ties	%	Cup Wins	Seasons
Abel, Sid (6)	Chicago	140	39	79	22	.357	0	1952-54
	Detroit	811	340	339	132	.501	0	1957-68, 1969-70
	St. Louis	10	3	6	1	.350	0	1971-72
	Kansas City	3	0	3	0	.000	0	1975-76
	Total	**963**	**382**	**426**	**155**	**.477**	**0**	**1952-76**
Adams, Jack (5)	Toronto St. Pats	18	10	71	1	.583		1922-23
	Detroit	964	413	390	161	.512	3	1927-44
	Total	**982**	**423**	**397**	**162**	**.513**	**3**	**1922-44**
Allen, Keith	Philadelphia	150	51	67	32	.447	0	1967-69
Allison, Dave	Ottawa	25	2	22	1	.100	0	1995-96
Anderson, Jim	Washington	54	4	45	5	.120	0	1974-75
Angotti, Lou	St. Louis	32	6	20	6	.281	0	1973-75
	Pittsburgh	80	16	58	6	.238	0	1983-84
	Total	**112**	**22**	**78**	**12**	**.250**	**0**	**1973-84**
Arbour, Al (2)	St. Louis	107	42	40	25	.509	0	1970-71, 1971-73
	NY Islanders	1499	739	537	223	.567	4	1973-86, 1988-94
	Total	**1606**	**781**	**577**	**248**	**.564**	**4**	**1970-94**
Armstrong, George	Toronto	47	17	26	4	.404	0	1988-89
Barkley, Doug	Detroit	77	20	46	11	.331	0	1970-72, 1975-76
Beaulieu, Andre	Minnesota	32	6	23	3	.234	0	1977-78
Belisle, Danny	Washington	96	28	51	17	.380	0	1978-80
Berenson, Red	St. Louis	204	100	72	32	.569	0	1979-82
Bergeron, Michel	Quebec	634	265	283	86	.486	0	1980-87, 1989-90
	NY Rangers	158	73	67	18	.519	0	1987-89
	Total	**792**	**338**	**350**	**104**	**.492**	**0**	**1980-89**
Berry, Bob (10)	Los Angeles	240	107	94	39	.527	0	1978-81
	Montreal	223	116	71	36	.601	0	1981-84
	Pittsburgh	240	88	127	25	.419	0	1984-87
	St. Louis	157	73	63	21	.532	0	1992-94
	Total	**860**	**384**	**355**	**121**	**.517**	**0**	**1978-94**
Beverley, Nick	Toronto	17	9	6	2	.588	0	1995-96
Blackburn, Don	Hartford	140	42	63	35	.425	0	1979-81
Blair, Wren	Minnesota	147	48	65	34	.442	0	1967-70
Blake, Toe (8)	Montreal	914	500	255	159	.634	8	1955-68
Boileau, Marc	Pittsburgh	151	66	61	24	.517	0	1973-76
Boivin, Leo	St. Louis	97	28	53	16	.371	0	1975-76, 1977-78
Boucher, Frank	NY Rangers	525	179	263	83	.420	1	1939-49, 1953-54
Boucher, George	Mtl. Maroons	12	6	5	1	.542	0	1930-31
	Ottawa	48	13	29	6	.333	0	1933-34
	St.L. Eagles	35	9	20	6	.343	0	1934-35
	Boston	70	22	32	16	.429	0	1949-50
	Total	**165**	**50**	**86**	**29**	**.391**	**0**	**1930-50**
Bowman, Scott (1)	St. Louis	238	110	83	45	.557	0	1967-70, 1970-71
	Montreal	634	419	110	105	.744	5	1971-79
	Buffalo	404	210	134	60	.594	0	1979-80, 1981-85, 1985-87
	Pittsburgh	164	95	53	16	.628	1	1991-93
	Detroit	296	179	80	37	.667	1	1993-97
	Total	**1736**	**1013**	**460**	**263**	**.659**	**7**	**1967-97**
Bowness, Rick	Winnipeg	28	8	17	3	.339	0	1988-89
	Boston	80	36	32	12	.525	0	1991-92
	Ottawa	235	39	178	18	.204	0	1992-96
	NY Islanders	37	16	18	3	.473	0	1996-97
	Total	**380**	**99**	**245**	**36**	**.308**	**0**	**1991-97**
Brooks, Herb	NY Rangers	285	131	113	41	.532	0	1981-85
	Minnesota	80	19	48	13	.319	0	1987-88
	New Jersey	84	40	37	7	.518	0	1992-93
	Total	**449**	**190**	**198**	**61**	**.491**	**0**	**1981-93**
Brophy, John	Toronto	160	53	91	16	.381	0	1986-88
Burnett, George	Edmonton	35	12	20	3	.386	0	1994-95
Burns, Charlie	Minnesota	86	22	50	14	.337	0	1969-70, 1974-75
Burns, Pat	Montreal	320	174	104	42	.609	0	1988-92
	Toronto	281	133	107	41	.546	0	1992-96
	Total	**601**	**307**	**211**	**83**	**.580**	**0**	**1988-96**
Bush, Eddie	Kansas City	32	1	23	8	.156	0	1975-76
Campbell, Colin	NY Rangers	212	101	84	27	.540	0	1994-97
Carpenter, Doug	New Jersey	290	100	166	24	.386	0	1984-88
	Toronto	91	39	47	5	.456	0	1989-91
	Total	**381**	**139**	**213**	**29**	**.403**	**0**	**1984-91**
Carroll, Dick	Toronto Arenas	40	18	22	0	.450	1	1917-19
	Toronto St. Pats	24	15	9	0	.625	0	1920-21
	Total	**64**	**33**	**31**	**0**	**.516**	**1**	**1917-21**
Cashman, Wayne	NY Rangers	2	0	2	0	.000	0	1986-87
Chambers, Dave	Quebec	98	19	64	15	.270	0	1990-92
Charron, Guy	Calgary	16	6	7	3	.469	0	1991-92
Cheevers, Gerry	Boston	376	204	126	46	.604	0	1980-85
Cherry, Don	Boston	400	231	105	64	.658	0	1974-79
	Colorado	80	19	48	13	.319	0	1979-80
	Total	**480**	**250**	**153**	**77**	**.601**	**0**	**1974-80**

Coach	Team	Games	Wins	Losses	Ties	%	Cup Wins	Seasons
Clancy, King	Mtl. Maroons	18	6	11	1	.361	0	1937-38
	Toronto	235	96	94	45	.504	0	1953-56, 1966-67, 1971-72
	Total	**253**	**102**	**105**	**46**	**.494**	**0**	**1937-72**
Clapper, Dit	Boston	230	102	88	40	.530	0	1945-49
Cleghorn, Odie	Pit. Pirates	168	62	86	20	.429	0	1925-29
Colville, Neil	NY Rangers	93	26	41	26	.419	0	1950-52
Conacher, Charlie	Chicago	162	56	84	22	.414	0	1947-50
Conacher, Lionel	NY Americans	44	14	25	5	.375	0	1929-30
Constantine, Kevin	San Jose	157	55	78	24	.427	0	1993-96
Cook, Bill	NY Rangers	117	34	59	24	.393	0	1951-53
Crawford, Marc	Quebec	48	30	13	5	.677	0	1994-95
	Colorado	164	96	49	19	.643	1	1995-97
	Total	**212**	**126**	**62**	**24**	**.651**	**1**	**1994-97**
Creamer, Pierre	Pittsburgh	80	36	35	9	.506	0	1987-88
Creighton, Fred	Atlanta	348	156	136	56	.529	0	1974-79
	Boston	73	40	20	13	.637	0	1979-80
	Total	**421**	**196**	**156**	**69**	**.548**	**0**	**1974-80**
Crisp, Terry	Calgary	240	144	63	33	.669	1	1987-90
	Tampa Bay	380	140	197	43	.425	0	1992-97
	Total	**620**	**284**	**260**	**76**	**.519**	**1**	**1987-97**
Crozier, Joe	Buffalo	192	77	80	35	.492	0	1971-74
	Toronto	40	13	22	5	.388	0	1980-81
	Total	**232**	**90**	**102**	**40**	**.474**	**0**	**1971-81**
Crozier, Roger	Washington	1	0	1	0	.000	0	1981-82
Cunniff, John	Hartford	13	3	9	1	.269	0	1982-83
	New Jersey	133	59	56	18	.511	0	1989-91
	Total	**146**	**62**	**65**	**19**	**.490**	**0**	**1983-91**
Dandurand, Leo	Montreal	158	82	68	8	.544	1	1920-25, 1934-35
Day, Hap	Toronto	546	259	206	81	.549	5	1940-50
Dea, Bill	Detroit	100	32	57	11	.375	0	1975-77, 1981-82
Delvecchio, Alex	Detroit	156	53	82	21	.407	0	1973-77
Demers, Jacques	Quebec	80	25	44	11	.381	0	1979-80
	St. Louis	240	106	106	28	.500	0	1983-86
	Detroit	320	137	136	47	.502	0	1986-90
	Montreal	220	107	86	27	.548	1	1992-96
	Total	**860**	**375**	**372**	**113**	**.502**	**1**	**1979-96**
Denneny, Cy	Boston	44	26	13	5	.648	1	1928-29
	Ottawa	48	11	27	10	.333	0	1932-33
	Total	**92**	**37**	**40**	**15**	**.484**	**1**	**1928-33**
Dineen, Bill	Philadelphia	140	60	60	20	.500	0	1991-93
Dudley, Rick	Buffalo	188	85	72	31	.535	0	1989-92
Duff, Dick	Toronto	2	0	2	0	.000	0	1979-80
Dugal, Jules	Montreal	18	9	6	3	.583	0	1938-39
Duncan, Art	Detroit	33	10	21	2	.333	0	1926-27
	Toronto	47	21	16	10	.553	0	1930-32
	Total	**80**	**31**	**37**	**12**	**.463**	**0**	**1926-32**
Dutton, Red	NY Americans	336	106	180	50	.390	0	1935-42
Eddolls, Frank	Chicago	70	13	40	17	.307	0	1954-55
Esposito, Phil	NY Rangers	45	24	21	0	.533	0	1986-87, 1988-89

A stern taskmaster and a noted strategist, Rudy Pilous guided the Chicago Black Hawks to the franchise's last Stanley Cup championship in 1960-61.

Coach	Team	Games	Wins	Losses	Ties	%	Cup Wins	Seasons
Evans, Jack	California	80	27	42	11	.406	0	1975-76
	Cleveland	160	47	87	26	.375	0	1976-78
	Hartford	374	163	174	37	.485	0	1983-88
	Total	**614**	**237**	**303**	**74**	**.446**	**0**	**1975-88**
Fashoway, Gordie	Oakland	10	4	5	1	.450	0	1967-68
Ferguson, John	NY Rangers	121	43	59	19	.434	0	1975-77
	Winnipeg	14	7	6	1	.536	0	1985-86
	Total	**135**	**50**	**65**	**20**	**.444**	**0**	**1975-86**
Filion, Maurice	Quebec	6	1	3	2	.333	0	1980-81
Francis, Emile	NY Rangers	654	347	209	98	.606	0	1965-68, 1968-73, 1973-75
	St. Louis	124	46	64	14	.427	0	1976-77, 1981-83
	Total	**778**	**393**	**273**	**112**	**.577**	**0**	**1965-83**
Fredrickson, Frank	Pit. Pirates	44	5	36	3	.148	0	1929-30
Ftorek, Robbie	Los Angeles	132	65	56	11	.534	0	1987-89
Gadsby, Bill	Detroit	78	35	31	12	.526	0	1968-69
Gainey, Bob	Minnesota	244	95	119	30	.451	0	1990-93
	Dallas	171	70	71	30	.497	0	1993-96
	Total	**415**	**165**	**190**	**60**	**.470**	**0**	**1990-96**
Gardiner, Herb	Chicago	44	7	29	8	.250	0	1928-29
Gardner, Jimmy	Hamilton	30	19	10	1	.650	0	1924-25
Garvin, Ted	Detroit	11	2	8	1	.227	0	1973-74
Geoffrion, Bernie	NY Rangers	43	22	18	3	.547	0	1968-69
	Atlanta	208	77	92	39	.464	0	1972-75
	Montreal	30	15	9	6	.600	0	1979-80
	Total	**281**	**114**	**119**	**48**	**.491**	**0**	**1968-80**
Gerard, Eddie	Ottawa	22	9	13	0	.409	0	1917-18
	Mtl. Maroons	284	129	112	43	.530	1	1924-29, 1932-34
	NY Americans	102	34	50	18	.422	0	1930-32
	St.L. Eagles	13	2	11	0	.154	0	1934-35
	Total	**421**	**174**	**186**	**61**	**.486**	**1**	**1917-35**
Gill, David	Ottawa	132	64	41	27	.587	1	1926-29
Glover, Fred	California	356	96	207	53	.344	0	1968-72, 1972-74
	Los Angeles	68	18	42	8	.324	0	1971-72
	Total	**424**	**114**	**249**	**61**	**.341**	**0**	**1968-74**
Goodfellow, Ebbie	Chicago	140	30	91	19	.282	0	1950-52
Gordon, Jackie	Minnesota	289	116	123	50	.488	0	1970-74, 1974-75
Goring, Butch	Boston	93	42	38	13	.522	0	1985-87
Gorman, Tommy	NY Americans	80	31	33	16	.488	0	1925-26, 1928-29
	Chicago	73	28	28	17	.500	1	1932-34
	Mtl. Maroons	174	74	71	29	.509	1	1934-38
	Total	**327**	**133**	**132**	**62**	**.502**	**2**	**1925-38**
Gottselig, Johnny	Chicago	187	62	104	21	.388	0	1944-48
Goyette, Phil	NY Islanders	48	6	38	4	.167	0	1972-73
Green, Gary	Washington	157	50	78	29	.411	0	1979-82
Green, Pete	Ottawa	186	117	61	8	.651	3	1919-26
Green, Wilf	NY Americans	44	11	27	6	.318	0	1927-28
Green, Ted	Edmonton	188	65	102	21	.402	0	1991-94
Guidolin, Aldo	Colorado	59	12	39	8	.271	0	1978-79
Guidolin, Bep	Boston	104	72	23	9	.736	0	1972-74
	Kansas City	125	26	84	15	.268	0	1974-76
	Total	**229**	**98**	**107**	**24**	**.480**	**0**	**1972-76**
Harkness, Ned	Detroit	38	12	22	4	.368	0	1970-71
Harris, Ted	Minnesota	179	48	104	27	.344	0	1975-78
Hart, Cecil	Montreal	430	207	149	74	.567	2	1925-32, 1936-39
Hartsburg, Craig	Chicago	164	74	63	27	.534	0	1995-97
Harvey, Doug	NY Rangers	70	26	32	12	.457	0	1961-62
Hay, Don	Phoenix	82	38	37	7	.506	0	1996-97
Heffernan, Frank	Toronto St. Pats	12	5	7	0	.417	0	1919-20
Henning, Lorne	Minnesota	158	68	72	18	.487	0	1985-87
	NY Islanders	48	15	28	5	.365	0	1994-95
	Total	**206**	**83**	**100**	**23**	**.459**	**0**	**1985-95**
Hitchcock, Ken	Dallas	125	63	49	13	.556	0	1995-97
Holmgren, Paul	Philadelphia	264	107	126	31	.464	0	1988-92
	Hartford	161	54	93	14	.379	0	1992-96
	Total	**425**	**161**	**219**	**45**	**.432**	**0**	**1988-96**
Howell, Harry	Minnesota	11	3	6	2	.364	0	1978-79
Imlach, Punch (7)	Toronto	760	363	274	123	.559	4	1958-69, 1979-80
	Buffalo	119	32	62	25	.374	0	1970-72
	Total	**879**	**395**	**336**	**148**	**.534**	**4**	**1958-80**
Ingarfield, Earl	NY Islanders	30	6	22	2	.233	0	1972-73
Inglis, Bill	Buffalo	56	28	18	10	.589	0	1978-79
Irvin, Dick (3)	Chicago	114	43	56	15	.443	0	1930-31, 1955-56
	Toronto	427	216	152	59	.575	1	1931-40
	Montreal	896	431	313	152	.566	3	1940-55
	Total	**1437**	**690**	**521**	**226**	**.559**	**4**	**1930-55**
Ivan, Tommy	Detroit	470	262	118	90	.653	3	1947-54
	Chicago	103	26	56	21	.354	0	1956-58
	Total	**573**	**288**	**174**	**111**	**.599**	**3**	**1947-58**
Iverson, Emil	Chicago	71	26	28	17	.486	0	1931-33
Johnson, Bob	Calgary	400	193	155	52	.548	0	1982-87
	Pittsburgh	80	41	33	6	.550	1	1990-91
	Total	**480**	**234**	**188**	**58**	**.548**	**1**	**1982-91**
Johnson, Tom	Boston	208	142	43	23	.738	1	1970-73
Johnston, Eddie	Chicago	80	34	27	19	.544	0	1979-80
	Pittsburgh	516	232	224	60	.508	0	1980-83, 1993-97
	Total	**596**	**266**	**251**	**79**	**.513**	**0**	**1979-97**

Coach	Team	Games	Wins	Losses	Ties	%	Cup Wins	Seasons
Johnston, Marshall	California	69	13	45	11	.268	0	1973-75
	Colorado	56	15	32	9	.348	0	1981-82
	Total	**125**	**28**	**77**	**20**	**.304**	**0**	**1973-82**
Kasper, Steve	Boston	164	66	78	20	.463	0	1995-97
Keats, Duke	Detroit	11	2	7	2	.273	0	1926-27
Keenan, Mike (9)	Philadelphia	320	190	102	28	.638	0	1984-88
	Chicago	320	153	126	41	.542	0	1988-92
	NY Rangers	84	52	24	8	.667	1	1993-94
	St. Louis	163	75	66	22	.528	0	1994-97
	Total	**887**	**470**	**318**	**99**	**.586**	**1**	**1984-97**
Kelly, Pat	Colorado	101	22	54	25	.342	0	1977-79
Kelly, Red	Los Angeles	150	55	75	20	.433	0	1967-69
	Pittsburgh	274	90	132	52	.423	0	1969-73
	Toronto	318	133	123	62	.516	0	1973-77
	Totals	**742**	**278**	**330**	**134**	**.465**	**0**	**1967-77**
Kennedy, George	Montreal	64	36	28	0	.563	0	1917-20
King, Dave	Calgary	216	109	76	31	.576	0	1992-95
Kingston, George	San Jose	164	28	129	7	.192	0	1991-93
Kish, Larry	Hartford	49	12	32	5	.296	0	1982-83
Kromm, Bobby	Detroit	231	79	111	41	.431	0	1977-80
Kurtenbach, Orland	Vancouver	125	36	62	27	.396	0	1976-78
LaForge, Bill	Vancouver	20	4	14	2	.250	0	1984-85
Lalonde, Newsy	NY Americans	44	17	25	2	.409	0	1926-27
	Ottawa	88	31	45	12	.420	0	1929-31
	Montreal	112	45	53	14	.464	0	1932-35
	Totals	**244**	**93**	**123**	**28**	**.439**	**0**	**1926-35**
Laperriere, Jacques	Montreal	1	0	1	0	.000	0	1995-96
Lapointe, Ron	Quebec	89	33	50	6	.404	0	1987-89
Laycoe, Hal	Los Angeles	24	5	18	1	.229	0	1969-70
	Vancouver	156	44	96	16	.333	0	1970-72
	Totals	**180**	**49**	**114**	**17**	**.319**	**0**	**1969-72**
Lehman, Hugh	Chicago	21	3	17	1	.167	0	1927-28
Lemaire, Jacques	Montreal	97	48	37	12	.557	0	1983-85
	New Jersey	296	151	99	46	.588	1	1993-97
	Total	**393**	**199**	**136**	**58**	**.580**	**1**	**1983-97**
Lepine, Pit	Montreal	48	10	33	5	.260	0	1939-40
LeSueur, Percy	Hamilton	24	9	15	0	.375	0	1923-24
Ley, Rick	Hartford	160	69	71	20	.494	0	1989-91
	Vancouver	124	47	50	27	.488	0	1994-96
	Total	**284**	**116**	**121**	**47**	**.491**	**0**	**1989-96**
Lindsay, Ted	Detroit	20	3	14	3	.225	0	1980-81
Long, Barry	Winnipeg	205	87	93	25	.485	0	1983-86
Loughlin, Clem	Chicago	144	61	63	20	.493	0	1934-37
Low, Ron	Edmonton	177	71	88	18	.452	0	1994-97
MacDonald, Parker	Minnesota	61	20	30	11	.418	0	1973-74
	Los Angeles	42	13	24	5	.369	0	1981-82
	Total	**103**	**33**	**54**	**16**	**.398**	**0**	**1973-82**
MacLean, Doug	Florida	164	76	59	29	.552	0	1995-97
MacMillan, Billy	Colorado	80	22	45	13	.356	0	1980-81
	New Jersey	100	19	67	14	.260	0	1982-84
	Total	**180**	**41**	**112**	**27**	**.303**	**0**	**1980-83**
MacNeil, Al	Montreal	55	31	15	9	.645	1	1970-71
	Atlanta	80	35	32	13	.519	0	1979-80
	Calgary	160	68	61	31	.522	0	1980-82
	Total	**295**	**134**	**108**	**53**	**.544**	**1**	**1970-82**
Mahoney, Bill	Minnesota	93	42	39	12	.516	0	1983-85
Magnuson, Keith	Chicago	132	49	57	26	.470	0	1980-82
Maguire, Pierre	Hartford	67	23	37	7	.396	0	1993-94
Maloney, Dan	Toronto	160	45	100	15	.328	0	1984-86
	Winnipeg	212	91	93	28	.495	0	1986-89
	Total	**372**	**136**	**193**	**43**	**.423**	**0**	**1984-89**
Maloney, Phil	Vancouver	232	95	105	32	.478	0	1973-77
Mantha, Sylvio	Montreal	48	11	26	11	.344	0	1935-36
Marshall, Bert	Colorado	24	3	17	4	.208	0	1981-82
Martin, Jacques	St. Louis	160	66	71	23	.484	0	1986-88
	Ottawa	120	41	60	19	.421	0	1995-97
	Total	**280**	**107**	**131**	**42**	**.457**	**0**	**1986-97**
Maurice, Paul	Hartford	152	61	72	19	.464	0	1995-97
Maxner, Wayne	Detroit	129	34	68	27	.368	0	1980-82
McCammon, Bob	Philadelphia	218	119	68	31	.617	0	1978-79, 1981-84
	Vancouver	294	102	156	36	.408	0	1987-91
	Total	**511**	**221**	**223**	**67**	**.498**	**0**	**1978-91**
McCreary, Bill	St. Louis	24	6	14	4	.333	0	1971-72
	Vancouver	41	9	25	7	.305	0	1973-74
	California	32	8	20	4	.313	0	1974-75
	Total	**97**	**23**	**59**	**15**	**.314**	**0**	**1971-75**
McLellan, John	Toronto	295	117	136	42	.468	0	1969-73
McVie, Tom	Washington	204	49	122	33	.321	0	1975-78
	Winnipeg	105	20	67	18	.276	0	1979-80, 1980-81
	New Jersey	153	57	74	22	.444	0	1983-84, 1990-92
	Total	**462**	**126**	**263**	**73**	**.352**	**0**	**1975-92**
Meeker, Howie	Toronto	70	21	34	15	.407	0	1956-57
Melrose, Barry	Los Angeles	209	79	101	29	.447	0	1992-95
Milbury, Mike	Boston	160	90	49	21	.628	0	1989-91
	NY Islanders	127	35	73	19	.350	0	1995-97
	Total	**287**	**125**	**122**	**40**	**.505**	**0**	**1989-97**
Muckler, John	Minnesota	35	6	23	6	.257	0	1968-69
	Edmonton	160	75	65	20	.531	1	1989-91
	Buffalo	268	125	109	34	.530	0	1991-95
	Total	**463**	**206**	**197**	**60**	**.510**	**1**	**1968-95**
Muldoon, Pete	Chicago	44	19	22	3	.466	0	1926-27
Munro, Dunc	Mtl. Maroons	76	37	29	10	.553	0	1929-31
Murdoch, Bob	Chicago	80	30	41	9	.431	0	1987-88
	Winnipeg	160	63	75	22	.463	0	1989-91
	Total	**240**	**93**	**116**	**31**	**.452**	**0**	**1987-91**

Coach	Team	Games	Wins	Losses	Ties	%	Cup Wins	Seasons
Murphy, Mike	Los Angeles	65	20	37	8	.369	0	1986-88
	Toronto	82	30	44	8	.415	0	1996-97
	Total	**147**	**50**	**81**	**16**	**.395**	**0**	**1986-97**
Murray, Bryan (7)	Washington	672	343	246	83	.572	0	1981-90
	Detroit	244	124	91	29	.568	0	1990-93
	Total	**916**	**467**	**337**	**112**	**.571**	**0**	**1981-93**
Murray, Terry	Washington	325	163	134	28	.545	0	1989-94
	Philadelphia	212	118	64	30	.627	0	1994-97
	Total	**537**	**281**	**198**	**58**	**.577**	**0**	**1989-97**
Nanne, Lou	Minnesota	29	7	18	4	.310	0	1977-78
Neale, Harry	Vancouver	407	142	189	76	.442	0	1978-82
	Detroit	35	8	23	4	.286	0	1985-86
	Total	**442**	**150**	**212**	**80**	**.430**	**0**	**1978-85**
Neilson, Roger	Toronto	160	75	62	23	.541	0	1977-79
	Buffalo	80	39	20	21	.619	0	1980-81
	Vancouver	133	51	61	21	.462	0	1982-84
	Los Angeles	28	8	17	3	.339	0	1983-84
	NY Rangers	280	141	104	35	.566	0	1989-93
	Florida	132	53	56	23	.489	0	1993-95
	Total	**813**	**367**	**320**	**126**	**.529**	**0**	**1977-95**
Nolan, Ted	Buffalo	164	73	72	19	.503	0	1995-97
Nykoluk, Mike	Toronto	280	89	144	47	.402	0	1980-84
Oliver, Murray	Minnesota	41	21	12	8	.610	0	1981-83
Olmstead, Bert	Oakland	64	11	37	16	.297	0	1967-68
O'Reilly, Terry	Boston	227	115	86	26	.564	0	1986-89
Paddock, John	Winnipeg	281	106	138	37	.443	0	1991-95
Page, Pierre	Minnesota	160	63	77	20	.456	0	1988-90
	Quebec	230	98	103	29	.489	0	1991-94
	Calgary	164	66	78	20	.463	0	1995-97
	Total	**554**	**227**	**258**	**69**	**.472**	**0**	**1988-97**
Park, Brad	Detroit	45	9	34	2	.222	0	1985-86
Patrick, Craig	NY Rangers	94	37	45	12	.457	0	1980-81, 1984-85
	Pittsburgh	74	29	36	9	.453	0	1989-90, 1996-97
	Total	**168**	**66**	**81**	**21**	**.455**	**0**	**1980-97**
Patrick, Frank	Boston	96	48	36	12	.563	0	1934-36
Patrick, Lester	NY Rangers	604	281	216	107	.554	2	1926-39
Patrick, Lynn	NY Rangers	107	40	51	16	.449	0	1948-50
	Boston	310	117	130	63	.479	0	1950-55
	St. Louis	26	8	15	3	.365	0	1967-68, 1974-75, 1975-76
	Total	**443**	**165**	**186**	**82**	**.465**	**0**	**1948-76**
Patrick, Muzz	NY Rangers	135	44	65	26	.422	0	1953-55, 1962-63
Perron, Jean	Montreal	240	126	84	30	.588	1	1985-88
	Quebec	47	16	26	5	.394	0	1988-89
	Total	**287**	**142**	**110**	**35**	**.556**	**1**	**1985-89**
Perry, Don	Los Angeles	168	52	85	31	.402	0	1981-84
Pike, Alf	NY Rangers	125	36	67	22	.376	0	1959-61
Pilous, Rudy	Chicago	387	162	151	74	.514	1	1958-63
Plager, Barclay	St. Louis	178	49	96	33	.368	0	1977-80, 1982-83
Plager, Bob	St. Louis	11	4	6	1	.409	0	1992-93
Pleau, Larry	Hartford	224	81	117	26	.420	0	1980-83, 1987-89
Polano, Nick	Detroit	240	79	127	34	.400	0	1982-85
Popein, Larry	NY Rangers	41	18	14	9	.549	0	1973-74
Powers, Eddie	Toronto St. Pats	114	54	56	4	.491	1	1921-22, 1923-26
Primeau, Joe	Toronto	210	97	71	42	.562	1	1950-53
Pronovost, Marcel	Buffalo	104	52	29	23	.611	0	1977-79
	Detroit	9	2	7	0	.222	0	1979-80
	Total	**113**	**54**	**36**	**23**	**.580**	**0**	**1977-80**
Pulford, Bob	Los Angeles	396	178	150	68	.535	0	1972-77
	Chicago	375	158	155	62	.504	0	1977-79, 1981-82, 1984-87
	Total	**771**	**336**	**305**	**130**	**.520**	**0**	**1972-87**
Querrie, Charlie	Toronto St. Pats	6	3	3	0	.500	0	1922-23
Quenneville, Joel	St. Louis	40	18	15	7	.538	0	1996-97
Quinn, Mike	Quebec Bulldogs	24	4	20	0	.167	0	1919-20
Quinn, Pat	Philadelphia	262	141	73	48	.630	0	1978-82
	Los Angeles	202	75	101	26	.436	0	1984-87
	Vancouver	280	141	111	28	.554	0	1990-96
	Total	**746**	**357**	**285**	**102**	**.547**	**0**	**1978-96**
Ramsay, Craig	Buffalo	21	4	15	2	.238	0	1986-87
Reay, Billy (4)	Toronto	90	26	50	14	.367	0	1957-59
	Chicago	1012	516	335	161	.589	0	1963-77
	Total	**1102**	**542**	**385**	**175**	**.571**	**0**	**1957-77**
Regan, Larry	Los Angeles	88	27	47	14	.386	0	1970-72
Renney, Tom	Vancouver	82	35	40	7	.470	0	1996-97
Risebrough, Doug	Calgary	144	71	56	17	.552	0	1990-92
Roberts, Jim	Buffalo	45	21	16	8	.556	0	1981-82
	Hartford	80	26	41	13	.406	0	1991-92
	St. Louis	9	3	3	3	.500	0	1996-97
	Total	**134**	**50**	**60**	**24**	**.463**	**0**	**1981-97**
Robinson, Larry	Los Angeles	164	52	83	29	.405	0	1995-97
Ross, Art	Mtl. Wanderers	6	1	5	0	.167	0	1917-18
	Hamilton	24	6	18	0	.250	0	1922-23
	Boston	698	354	254	90	.572	1	1924-28, 1929-34, 1936-39, 1941-45
	Total	**728**	**361**	**277**	**90**	**.558**	**1**	**1917-45**
Ruel, Claude	Montreal	305	172	82	51	.648	1	1968-71, 1979-81
Sather, Glen	Edmonton	842	464	268	110	.616	4	1979-80, 1980-89, 1993-94
Sator, Ted	NY Rangers	99	41	48	10	.465	0	1985-87
	Buffalo	207	96	89	22	.517	0	1986-89
	Total	**306**	**137**	**137**	**32**	**.500**	**0**	**1985-88**
Savard, Andre	Quebec	24	10	13	1	.438	0	1987-88
Schinkel, Ken	Pittsburgh	203	83	92	28	.478	0	1972-74, 1975-77
Schmidt, Milt	Boston	726	245	360	121	.421	0	1954-61, 1962-66
	Washington	43	5	33	5	.174	0	1974-76
	Total	**769**	**250**	**393**	**126**	**.407**	**0**	**1954-66**
Schoenfeld, Jim	Buffalo	43	19	19	5	.500	0	1985-86
	New Jersey	124	50	59	15	.464	0	1987-90
	Washington	249	113	102	34	.522	0	1993-97
	Total	**416**	**182**	**180**	**54**	**.502**	**0**	**1985-97**
Shaughnessy, Tom	Chicago	21	10	8	3	.548	0	1929-30
Shero, Fred	Philadelphia	554	308	151	95	.642	2	1971-78
	NY Rangers	180	82	74	24	.522	0	1978-81
	Total	**734**	**390**	**225**	**119**	**.612**	**2**	**1971-81**
Simpson, Joe	NY Americans	144	42	72	30	.396	0	1932-35
Simpson, Terry	NY Islanders	187	81	82	24	.497	0	1986-89
	Winnipeg	1	0	1	0	.000	0	1992-93
	Philadelphia	84	35	39	10	.476	0	1993-94
	Winnipeg	97	43	47	7	.479	0	1994-96
	Total	**353**	**152**	**161**	**40**	**.487**	**0**	**1986-96**
Sims, Al	San Jose	82	27	47	8	.378	0	1996-97
Sinden, Harry	Boston	330	151	121	58	.545	1	1966-70, 1979-80, 1984-85
Skinner, Jimmy	Detroit	247	123	78	46	.591	1	1954-58
Smeaton, Cooper	Phi. Quakers	44	4	36	4	.136	0	1930-31
Smith, Alf	Ottawa	18	12	6	0	.667	0	1918-19
Smith, Floyd	Buffalo	241	143	62	36	.668	0	1974-77
	Toronto	68	30	33	5	.478	0	1979-80
	Total	**309**	**173**	**95**	**41**	**.626**	**0**	**1971-80**
Smith, Mike	Winnipeg	23	2	17	4	.174	0	1980-81
Smith, Ron	NY Rangers	44	15	22	7	.420	0	1992-93
Smythe, Conn	Toronto	178	72	81	25	.475	0	1926-30
Sonmor, Glen	Minnesota	417	174	161	82	.516	0	1978-83, 1984-85, 1986-87
Sproule, Harry	Toronto St. Pats	12	7	5	0	.583	0	1919-20
Stanley, Barney	Chicago	23	4	17	2	.217	0	1927-28
Stasiuk, Vic	Philadelphia	154	45	68	41	.425	0	1969-71
	California	75	21	38	16	.387	0	1971-72
	Vancouver	78	22	47	9	.340	0	1972-73
	Total	**307**	**88**	**153**	**66**	**.394**	**0**	**1969-73**
Stewart, Bill	Chicago	69	22	35	12	.406	1	1937-39
Stewart, Ron	NY Rangers	39	15	20	4	.436	0	1975-76
	Los Angeles	80	31	34	15	.481	0	1977-78
	Total	**119**	**46**	**54**	**19**	**.466**	**0**	**1975-78**
Sullivan, Red	NY Rangers	196	58	103	35	.385	0	1962-66
	Pittsburgh	150	47	79	24	.393	0	1967-69
	Washington	19	2	17	0	.105	0	1974-75
	Total	**365**	**107**	**199**	**59**	**.374**	**0**	**1962-75**
Sutherland, Bill	Winnipeg	32	7	22	3	.266	0	1979-80, 1980-81
Sutter, Brian	St. Louis	320	153	124	43	.545	0	1988-92
	Boston	216	120	73	23	.609	0	1992-95
	Total	**536**	**273**	**197**	**66**	**.571**	**0**	**1988-95**
Sutter, Darryl	Chicago	216	110	80	26	.569	0	1992-95
Talbot, Jean-Guy	St. Louis	120	52	53	15	.496	0	1972-74
	NY Rangers	80	30	37	13	.456	0	1977-78
	Total	**200**	**82**	**90**	**28**	**.480**	**0**	**1972-78**
Tessier, Orval	Chicago	213	99	93	21	.514	0	1982-85
Thompson, Paul	Chicago	272	104	127	41	.458	0	1938-45
Thompson, Percy	Hamilton	48	14	34	0	.292	0	1920-22
Tobin, Bill	Chicago	23	11	10	2	.522	0	1929-30
Tremblay, Mario	Montreal	159	71	63	25	.525	0	1995-97
Ubriaco, Gene	Pittsburgh	106	50	47	9	.514	0	1988-90
Vachon, Rogie	Los Angeles	8	4	2	2	.625	0	1983-84, 1987-88, 1994-95
Watson, Bryan	Edmonton	18	4	9	5	.361	0	1980-81
Watson, Phil	NY Rangers	294	118	124	52	.490	0	1955-60
	Boston	84	16	55	13	.268	0	1961-63
	Total	**378**	**134**	**179**	**65**	**.440**	**0**	**1955-64**
Watt, Tom	Winnipeg	181	72	85	24	.464	0	1981-84
	Vancouver	160	52	87	21	.391	0	1985-87
	Toronto	149	52	80	17	.406	0	1990-92
	Total	**490**	**176**	**252**	**62**	**.422**	**0**	**1981-92**
Webster, Tom	NY Rangers	16	5	7	4	.438	0	1986-87
	Los Angeles	240	115	94	31	.544	0	1989-92
	Total	**256**	**120**	**101**	**35**	**.537**	**0**	**1986-92**
Weiland, Cooney	Boston	96	58	20	18	.698	1	1939-41
White, Bill	Chicago	46	16	24	6	.413	0	1976-77
Wiley, Jim	San Jose	57	17	37	3	.325	0	1995-96
Wilson, Johnny	Los Angeles	52	9	34	9	.260	0	1969-70
	Detroit	145	67	56	22	.538	0	1971-73
	Colorado	80	20	46	14	.338	0	1976-77
	Pittsburgh	240	91	105	44	.471	0	1977-80
	Total	**517**	**187**	**241**	**89**	**.448**	**0**	**1969-80**
Wilson, Larry	Detroit	36	3	29	4	.139	0	1976-77
Wilson, Ron	Anaheim	296	120	145	31	.458	0	1993-97
Young, Garry	California	12	2	7	3	.292	0	1972-73
	St. Louis	98	41	41	16	.500	0	1974-76
	Total	**110**	**43**	**48**	**19**	**.477**	**0**	**1972-76**

Brad Park was one of the top-ranked rearguards of his era. He coached the Detroit Red Wings for 45 games during the 1985-86 season.

All-Time Penalty-Minute Leaders

* active player

(Regular season. Minimum 1,500 minutes)

Player	Teams	Seasons	Games	Penalty Minutes	Mins. per game
Dave Williams,	Tor., Van., Det., L.A., Hfd.	14	962	3966	4.12
*Dale Hunter,	Que., Wsh.	17	1263	3343	2.65
Tim Hunter,	Cgy., Que., Van., S.J.	16	815	3146	3.86
*Marty McSorley,	Pit., Edm., L.A., NYR, S.J.	14	832	3078	3.70
Chris Nilan,	Mtl., NYR, Bos.	13	688	3043	4.42
*Bob Probert,	Det., Chi.	11	634	2653	4.19
Willi Plett,	Atl., Cgy., Min., Bos.	13	834	2572	3.08
*Rick Tocchet,	Phi., Pit., L.A., Bos., Wsh.	13	841	2469	2.94
Basil McRae,	Que., Tor., Det., Min., T.B., St.L., Chi.	16	576	2457	4.27
*Pat Verbeek,	N.J., Hfd., NYR, Dal.	15	1065	2362	2.22
*Scott Stevens,	Wsh., St.L., N.J.	15	1120	2360	2.11
Jay Wells,	L.A., Phi., Buf., NYR, St.L., T.B.	18	1098	2359	2.15
*Joe Kocur,	Det., NYR, Van.	13	718	2340	3.26
*Dave Manson,	Chi., Edm., Wpg., Pho., Mtl.	11	763	2327	3.05
Garth Butcher,	Van., St.L., Que., Tor.	14	897	2302	2.57
*Shane Churla,	Hfd., Cgy., Min., Dal., L.A., NYR	11	488	2301	4.72
Dave Schultz,	Phi., L.A., Pit., Buf.	9	535	2294	4.29
*Craig Berube,	Phi., Tor., Cgy., Wsh.	11	645	2268	3.52
Laurie Boschman,	Tor., Edm., Wpg., N.J., Ott.	14	1009	2265	2.25
Rob Ramage,	Col., St.L., Cgy., Tor., Min., T.B., Mtl., Phi.	15	1044	2226	2.13
Bryan Watson,	Mtl., Oak., Pit., Det., St.L., Wsh.	16	878	2212	2.52
*Ulf Samuelsson,	Hfd., Pit., NYR	13	887	2174	2.45
*Ken Daneyko,	N.J.	14	873	2121	2.43
Terry O'Reilly,	Bos.	14	891	2095	2.35
Al Secord,	Bos., Chi., Tor., Phi.	12	766	2093	2.73
*Gord Donnelly,	Que., Wpg., Buf., Dal.	12	554	2069	3.74
Mike Foligno,	Det., Buf., Tor., Fla.	15	1018	2049	2.01
*Chris Chelios,	Mtl., Chi.	14	920	2038	2.22
Phil Russell,	Chi., Atl., Cgy., N.J., Buf.	15	1016	2038	2.01
*Rob Ray,	Buf.	8	506	2034	4.02
Harold Snepsts,	Van., Min., Det., St.L.	17	1033	2009	1.95
Steve Smith,	Edm., Chi.	13	702	2000	2.85
Andre Dupont,	NYR, St.L., Phi., Que.	13	800	1986	2.48
*Gino Odjick,	Van.	7	409	1946	4.76
*Ken Baumgartner,	L.A., NYI, Tor., Ana.	10	545	1926	3.53
*Todd Ewen,	St.L., Mtl., Ana., S.J.	11	518	1911	3.69
*Tie Domi,	Tor., NYR, Wpg.	8	406	1895	4.67
*Mick Vukota,	NYI	10	510	1879	3.68
*Joel Otto,	Cgy., Phi.	13	875	1856	2.12
*Mike Peluso,	Chi., Ott., N.J., St.L.	8	435	1838	4.23
Garry Howatt,	NYI, Hfd., N.J.	12	720	1836	2.55
Carol Vadnais,	Mtl., Oak., Cal., Bos., NYR, N.J.	17	1087	1813	1.67
Larry Playfair,	Buf., L.A.	12	688	1812	2.63
Ted Lindsay,	Det., Chi.	17	1068	1808	1.69
Jim Korn,	Det., Tor., Buf., N.J., Cgy.	10	597	1801	3.02
David Brown,	Phi., Edm., S.J.	14	729	1789	2.45
Brian Sutter,	St.L.	12	779	1786	2.29
*Kevin Dineen,	Hfd., Phi.	13	871	1770	2.03
*Ron Stern,	Van., Cgy.	10	493	1768	3.59
Bob McGill,	Tor., Chi., S.J., Det., NYI, Hfd.	13	705	1766	2.51
*Michel Petit,	Van., NYR, Que., Tor., Cgy., L.A., T.B., Edm., Phi.	15	795	1762	2.22
Wilf Paiement,	K.C. Col., Tor., Que., NYR, Buf., Pit.	14	946	1757	1.86
Torrie Robertson,	Wsh., Hfd., Det.	10	442	1751	3.96
Mario Marois,	NYR, Van., Que., Wpg., St.L.	15	955	1746	1.83
*Gary Roberts,	Cgy.	10	585	1736	2.97
Ken Linseman,	Phi., Edm., Bos., Tor.	14	860	1727	2.01
*Steven Finn,	Que., T.B., L.A.	12	725	1724	2.38
Jay Miller,	Bos., L.A.	7	446	1723	3.86
Randy Moller,	Que., NYR, Buf., Fla.	14	815	1692	2.08
Gordie Howe,	Det., Hfd.	26	1767	1685	.954
Paul Holmgren,	Phi., Min.	10	527	1684	3.20
*Paul Coffey,	Edm., Pit., L.A., Det., Hfd., Phi.	17	1211	1674	1.38
Gerard Gallant,	Det., T.B.	11	615	1674	2.72
Kevin McClelland,	Pit., Edm., Det., Tor., Wpg.	12	588	1672	2.84
*Kris King,	Det., NYR, Wpg., Pho.	10	648	1663	2.57
*Jeff Beukeboom,	Edm., NYR	12	696	1635	2.35
Jerry Korab,	Chi., Van., Buf., L.A.	15	975	1629	1.67
Mel Bridgman,	Phi., Cgy., N.J., Det., Van.	14	977	1625	1.66
Tim Horton,	Tor., NYR, Buf., Pit.	24	1446	1611	1.11
*Scott Mellanby,	Phi., Edm., Fla.	12	793	1607	2.03
*Shayne Corson,	Mtl., Edm., St.L.	12	747	1600	2.14
*Mark Messier,	Edm., NYR	18	1272	1596	1.26
Dave Taylor,	L.A.	17	1111	1589	1.43
Gordie Roberts,	Hfd., Min., Phi., St.L., Pit., Bos.	15	1097	1582	1.44
Paul Baxter,	Que., Pit., Cgy.	8	472	1564	3.31
*Kelly Buchberger,	Edm.	11	661	1557	2.36
*Sergio Momesso,	Mtl., St.L., Van., Tor., NYR	13	710	1557	2.19
Glen Cochrane,	Phi., Van., Chi., Edm.	10	411	1556	3.79
Stan Smyl,	Van.	13	896	1556	1.74
Mike Milbury,	Bos.	12	754	1552	2.06
Dave Hutchison,	L.A., Tor., Chi., N.J.	10	584	1550	2.65
Doug Risebrough,	Mtl., Cgy.	13	740	1542	2.08
*Wendel Clark,	Tor., Que., NYI	12	636	1539	2.42
Bill Gadsby,	Chi., NYR, Det.	20	1248	1539	1.23
*Kelly Chase,	St.L., Hfd., Tor.	8	321	1525	4.75
*Dana Murzyn,	Hfd., Cgy., Van.	12	795	1508	1.90

A rambunctious performer on the ice but a trusted confidante in the dressing room, Dale Hunter has spent a total of more than 55 hours in the penalty box during his NHL career.

Year-by-Year Individual Regular-Season Leaders

Season	Goals	G	Assists	A	Points	Pts.	Penalty Minutes	PIM
1917-18	Joe Malone	44	no assists recorded	...	Joe Malone	44	Joe Hall	60
1918-19	Newsy Lalonde	23	Newsy Lalonde	9	Newsy Lalonde	32	Joe Hall	85
1919-20	Joe Malone	39	Cy Denneny	12	Joe Malone	48	Cully Wilson	79
1920-21	Babe Dye	35	Harry Cameron	9	Newsy Lalonde	41	Bert Corbeau	86
			Louis Berlinquette	9				
			Joe Matte	9				
1921-22	Punch Broadbent	32	Punch Broadbent	14	Punch Broadbent	46	Sprague Cleghorn	63
			Leo Reise	14				
1922-23	Babe Dye	26	Edmond Bouchard	12	Babe Dye	37	Billy Boucher	52
1923-24	Cy Denneny	22	King Clancy	8	Cy Denneny	23	Bert Corbeau	55
1924-25	Babe Dye	38	Cy Denneny	15	Babe Dye	44	Billy Boucher	92
1925-26	Nels Stewart	34	Frank Nighbor	13	Nels Stewart	42	Bert Corbeau	121
1926-27	Bill Cook	33	Dick Irvin	18	Bill Cook	37	Nels Stewart	133
1927-28	Howie Morenz	33	Howie Morenz	18	Howie Morenz	51	Eddie Shore	165
1928-29	Ace Bailey	22	Frank Boucher	16	Ace Bailey	32	Red Dutton	139
1929-30	Cooney Weiland	43	Frank Boucher	36	Cooney Weiland	73	Joe Lamb	119
1930-31	Charlie Conacher	31	Joe Primeau	32	Howie Morenz	51	Harvey Rockburn	118
1931-32	Charlie Conacher	34	Joe Primeau	37	Busher Jackson	53	Red Dutton	107
	Bill Cook	34						
1932-33	Bill Cook	28	Frank Boucher	28	Bill Cook	50	Red Horner	144
1933-34	Charlie Conacher	32	Joe Primeau	32	Charlie Conacher	52	Red Horner	126 *
1934-35	Charlie Conacher	36	Art Chapman	34	Charlie Conacher	57	Red Horner	125
1935-36	Charlie Conacher	23	Art Chapman	28	Sweeney Schriner	45	Red Horner	167
	Bill Thoms	23						
1936-37	Larry Aurie	23	Syl Apps	29	Sweeney Schriner	46	Red Horner	124
	Nels Stewart	23						
1937-38	Gordie Drillon	26	Syl Apps	29	Gordie Drillon	52	Red Horner	82 *
1938-39	Roy Conacher	26	Bill Cowley	34	Toe Blake	47	Red Horner	85
1939-40	Bryan Hextall	24	Milt Schmidt	30	Milt Schmidt	52	Red Horner	87
1940-41	Bryan Hextall	26	Bill Cowley	45	Bill Cowley	62	Jimmy Orlando	99
1941-42	Lynn Patrick	32	Phil Watson	37	Bryan Hextall	56	Jimmy Orlando	81 **
1942-43	Doug Bentley	33	Bill Cowley	45	Doug Bentley	73	Jimmy Orlando	89 *
1943-44	Doug Bentley	38	Clint Smith	49	Herb Cain	82	Mike McMahon	98
1944-45	Maurice Richard	50	Elmer Lach	54	Elmer Lach	80	Pat Egan	86
1945-46	Gaye Stewart	37	Elmer Lach	34	Max Bentley	61	Jack Stewart	73
1946-47	Maurice Richard	45	Billy Taylor	46	Max Bentley	72	Gus Mortson	133
1947-48	Ted Lindsay	33	Doug Bentley	37	Elmer Lach	61	Bill Barilko	147
1948-49	Sid Abel	28	Doug Bentley	43	Roy Conacher	68	Bill Ezinicki	145
1949-50	Maurice Richard	43	Ted Lindsay	55	Ted Lindsay	78	Bill Ezinicki	144
1950-51	Gordie Howe	43	Gordie Howe	43	Gordie Howe	86	Gus Mortson	142
1951-52	Gordie Howe	47	Elmer Lach	50	Gordie Howe	86	Gus Kyle	127
1952-53	Gordie Howe	49	Gordie Howe	46	Gordie Howe	95	Maurice Richard	112
1953-54	Maurice Richard	37	Gordie Howe	48	Gordie Howe	81	Gus Mortson	132
1954-55	Maurice Richard	38	Bert Olmstead	48	Bernie Geoffrion	75	Fernie Flaman	150
	Bernie Geoffrion	38						
1955-56	Jean Beliveau	47	Bert Olmstead	56	Jean Beliveau	88	Lou Fontinato	202
1956-57	Gordie Howe	44	Ted Lindsay	55	Gordie Howe	89	Gus Mortson	147
1957-58	Dickie Moore	36	Henri Richard	52	Dickie Moore	84	Lou Fontinato	152
1958-59	Jean Beliveau	45	Dickie Moore	55	Dickie Moore	96	Ted Lindsay	184
1959-60	Bobby Hull	39	Don McKenney	49	Bobby Hull	81	Carl Brewer	150
1960-61	Bernie Geoffrion	50	Jean Beliveau	58	Bernie Geoffrion	95	Pierre Pilote	165
1961-62	Bobby Hull	50	Andy Bathgate	56	Bobby Hull	84	Lou Fontinato	167
					Andy Bathgate	84		
1962-63	Gordie Howe	38	Henri Richard	50	Gordie Howe	86	Howie Young	273
1963-64	Bobby Hull	43	Andy Bathgate	58	Stan Mikita	89	Vic Hadfield	151
1964-65	Norm Ullman	42	Stan Mikita	59	Stan Mikita	87	Carl Brewer	177
1965-66	Bobby Hull	54	Stan Mikita	48	Bobby Hull	97	Reg Fleming	166
			Bobby Rousseau	48				
			Jean Beliveau	48				
1966-67	Bobby Hull	52	Stan Mikita	62	Stan Mikita	97	John Ferguson	177
1967-68	Bobby Hull	44	Phil Esposito	49	Stan Mikita	87	Barclay Plager	153
1968-69	Bobby Hull	58	Phil Esposito	77	Phil Esposito	126	Forbes Kennedy	219
1969-70	Phil Esposito	43	Bobby Orr	87	Bobby Orr	120	Keith Magnuson	213
1970-71	Phil Esposito	76	Bobby Orr	102	Phil Esposito	152	Keith Magnuson	291
1971-72	Phil Esposito	66	Bobby Orr	80	Phil Esposito	133	Bryan Watson	212
1972-73	Phil Esposito	55	Phil Esposito	75	Phil Esposito	130	Dave Schultz	259
1973-74	Phil Esposito	68	Bobby Orr	90	Phil Esposito	145	Dave Schultz	348
1974-75	Phil Esposito	61	Bobby Orr	89	Bobby Orr	135	Dave Schultz	472
			Bobby Clarke	89				
1975-76	Reggie Leach	61	Bobby Clarke	89	Guy Lafleur	125	Steve Durbano	370
1976-77	Steve Shutt	60	Guy Lafleur	80	Guy Lafleur	136	Tiger Williams	338
1977-78	Guy Lafleur	60	Bryan Trottier	77	Guy Lafleur	132	Dave Schultz	405
1978-79	Mike Bossy	69	Bryan Trottier	87	Bryan Trottier	134	Tiger Williams	298
1979-80	Charlie Simmer	56	Wayne Gretzky	86	Marcel Dionne	137	Jimmy Mann	287
	Danny Gare	56			Wayne Gretzky	137		
	Blaine Stoughton	56						
1980-81	Mike Bossy	68	Wayne Gretzky	109	Wayne Gretzky	164	Tiger Williams	343
1981-82	Wayne Gretzky	92	Wayne Gretzky	120	Wayne Gretzky	212	Paul Baxter	409
1982-83	Wayne Gretzky	71	Wayne Gretzky	125	Wayne Gretzky	196	Randy Holt	275
1983-84	Wayne Gretzky	87	Wayne Gretzky	118	Wayne Gretzky	205	Chris Nilan	338
1984-85	Wayne Gretzky	73	Wayne Gretzky	135	Wayne Gretzky	208	Chris Nilan	358
1985-86	Jari Kurri	68	Wayne Gretzky	163	Wayne Gretzky	215	Joey Kocur	377
1986-87	Wayne Gretzky	62	Wayne Gretzky	121	Wayne Gretzky	183	Tim Hunter	375
1987-88	Mario Lemieux	70	Wayne Gretzky	109	Mario Lemieux	168	Bob Probert	398
1988-89	Mario Lemieux	85	Mario Lemieux	114	Mario Lemieux	199	Tim Hunter	375
			Wayne Gretzky	114				
1989-90	Brett Hull	72	Wayne Gretzky	102	Wayne Gretzky	142	Basil McRae	351
1990-91	Brett Hull	86	Wayne Gretzky	122	Wayne Gretzky	163	Rob Ray	350
1991-92	Brett Hull	70	Wayne Gretzky	90	Mario Lemieux	131	Mike Peluso	408
1992-93	Teemu Selanne	76	Adam Oates	97	Mario Lemeiux	160	Marty McSorley	399
	Alex Mogilny	76						
1993-94	Pavel Bure	60	Wayne Gretzky	92	Wayne Gretzky	130	Tie Domi	347
1994-95	Peter Bondra	34	Ron Francis	48	Jaromir Jagr	70	Enrico Ciccone	225
					Eric Lindros	70		
1995-96	Mario Lemieux	69	Mario Lemieux	92	Mario Lemieux	161	Matthew Barnaby	335
			Ron Francis	92				
1996-97	Keith Tkachuk	52	Mario Lemieux	72	Mario Lemieux	122	Gino Odjick	371
			Wayne Gretzky	72				

* Match Misconduct penalty not included in total penalty minutes. ** Three Match Misconduct penalties not included in total penalty minutes.
1946-47 was the first season that a Match penalty was automatically written into the player's total penalty minutes as 20 minutes.
Now all penalties, Match, Game Misconduct, and Misconduct, are written as 10 minutes.

One Season
Scoring Records

Goals-Per-Game Leaders, One Season

(Among players with 20 goals or more in one season)

Player	Team	Season	Games	Goals	Average
Joe Malone	Montreal	1917-18	20	44	2.20
Cy Denneny	Ottawa	1917-18	22	36	1.64
Newsy Lalonde	Montreal	1917-18	14	23	1.64
Joe Malone	Quebec	1919-20	24	39	1.63
Newsy Lalonde	Montreal	1919-20	23	36	1.57
Joe Malone	Hamilton	1920-21	20	30	1.50
Babe Dye	Ham., Tor.	1920-21	24	35	1.46
Cy Denneny	Ottawa	1920-21	24	34	1.42
Reg Noble	Toronto	1917-18	20	28	1.40
Newsy Lalonde	Montreal	1920-21	24	33	1.38
Odie Cleghorn	Montreal	1918-19	17	23	1.35
Harry Broadbent	Ottawa	1921-22	24	32	1.33
Babe Dye	Toronto	1924-25	29	38	1.31
Babe Dye	Toronto	1921-22	24	30	1.25
Newsy Lalonde	Montreal	1918-19	17	21	1.24
Cy Denneny	Ottawa	1921-22	22	27	1.23
Aurel Joliat	Montreal	1924-25	24	29	1.21
Wayne Gretzky	Edmonton	1983-84	74	87	1.18
Babe Dye	Toronto	1922-23	22	26	1.18
Wayne Gretzky	Edmonton	1981-82	80	92	1.15
Mario Lemieux	Pittsburgh	1992-93	60	69	1.15
Frank Nighbor	Ottawa	1919-20	23	26	1.13
Mario Lemieux	Pittsburgh	1988-89	76	85	1.12
Brett Hull	St. Louis	1990-91	78	86	1.10
Amos Arbour	Montreal	1919-20	20	22	1.10
Cy Denneny	Ottawa	1923-24	21	22	1.05
Joe Malone	Hamilton	1921-22	24	25	1.04
Billy Boucher	Montreal	1922-23	24	25	1.04
Cam Neely	Boston	1993-94	49	50	1.02
Maurice Richard	Montreal	1944-45	50	50	1.00
Howie Morenz	Montreal	1924-25	30	30	1.00
Reg Noble	Toronto	1919-20	24	24	1.00
Corbett Denneny	Toronto	1919-20	23	23	1.00
Jack Darragh	Ottawa	1919-20	22	22	1.00
Alexander Mogilny	Buffalo	1992-93	77	76	.99
Mario Lemieux	Pittsburgh	1995-96	70	69	.99
Cooney Weiland	Boston	1929-30	44	43	.98
Phil Esposito	Boston	1970-71	78	76	.97
Jari Kurri	Edmonton	1984-85	73	71	.97

Hailed as the "Babe Ruth of Hockey" in the early 1920s, Babe Dye averaged better than a goal-per-game four times between 1920-21 and 1924-25.

Assists-Per-Game Leaders, One Season

(Among players with 35 assists or more in one season)

Player	Team	Season	Games	Assists	Average
Wayne Gretzky	Edmonton	1985-86	80	163	2.04
Wayne Gretzky	Edmonton	1987-88	64	109	1.70
Wayne Gretzky	Edmonton	1984-85	80	135	1.69
Wayne Gretzky	Edmonton	1983-84	74	118	1.59
Wayne Gretzky	Edmonton	1982-83	80	125	1.56
Wayne Gretzky	Los Angeles	1990-91	78	122	1.56
Wayne Gretzky	Edmonton	1986-87	79	121	1.53
Mario Lemieux	Pittsburgh	1992-93	60	91	1.52
Wayne Gretzky	Edmonton	1981-82	80	120	1.50
Mario Lemieux	Pittsburgh	1988-89	76	114	1.50
Adam Oates	St. Louis	1990-91	61	90	1.48
Wayne Gretzky	Los Angeles	1988-89	78	114	1.46
Wayne Gretzky	Los Angeles	1989-90	73	102	1.40
Wayne Gretzky	Edmonton	1980-81	80	109	1.36
Mario Lemieux	Pittsburgh	1991-92	64	87	1.36
Mario Lemieux	Pittsburgh	1989-90	59	78	1.32
Bobby Orr	Boston	1970-71	78	102	1.31
Mario Lemieux	Pittsburgh	1995-96	70	92	1.31
Mario Lemieux	Pittsburgh	1987-88	77	98	1.27
Bobby Orr	Boston	1973-74	74	90	1.22
Wayne Gretzky	Los Angeles	1991-92	74	90	1.22
Ron Francis	Pittsburgh	1995-96	77	92	1.19
Mario Lemieux	Pittsburgh	1985-86	79	93	1.18
Bobby Clarke	Philadelphia	1975-76	76	89	1.17
Peter Stastny	Quebec	1981-82	80	93	1.16
Adam Oates	Boston	1992-93	84	97	1.15
Doug Gilmour	Toronto	1992-93	83	95	1.14
Wayne Gretzky	Los Angeles	1993-94	81	92	1.14
Paul Coffey	Edmonton	1985-86	79	90	1.14
Bobby Orr	Boston	1969-70	76	87	1.14
Bryan Trottier	NY Islanders	1978-79	76	87	1.14
Bobby Orr	Boston	1972-73	63	72	1.14
Bill Cowley	Boston	1943-44	36	41	1.14
Pat LaFontaine	Buffalo	1992-93	84	95	1.13
Steve Yzerman	Detroit	1988-89	80	90	1.13
Paul Coffey	Pittsburgh	1987-88	46	52	1.13
Bobby Orr	Boston	1974-75	80	89	1.11
Bobby Clarke	Philadelphia	1974-75	80	89	1.11
Paul Coffey	Pittsburgh	1988-89	75	83	1.11
Wayne Gretzky	Los Angeles	1992-93	45	49	1.11
Denis Savard	Chicago	1982-83	78	86	1.10
Ron Francis	Pittsburgh	1994-95	44	48	1.09
Denis Savard	Chicago	1981-82	80	87	1.09
Denis Savard	Chicago	1987-88	80	87	1.09
Wayne Gretzky	Edmonton	1979-80	79	86	1.09
Paul Coffey	Edmonton	1983-84	80	86	1.08
Elmer Lach	Montreal	1944-45	50	54	1.08
Peter Stastny	Quebec	1985-86	76	81	1.07
Jaromir Jagr	Pittsburgh	1995-96	82	87	1.06
Mark Messier	Edmonton	1989-90	79	84	1.06
Peter Forsberg	Colorado	1995-96	82	86	1.05
Paul Coffey	Edmonton	1984-85	80	84	1.05
Marcel Dionne	Los Angeles	1979-80	80	84	1.05
Bobby Orr	Boston	1971-72	76	80	1.05
Mike Bossy	NY Islanders	1981-82	80	83	1.04
Adam Oates	Boston	1993-94	77	80	1.04
Phil Esposito	Boston	1968-69	74	77	1.04
Bryan Trottier	NY Islanders	1983-84	68	71	1.04
Pete Mahovlich	Montreal	1974-75	80	82	1.03
Kent Nilsson	Calgary	1980-81	80	82	1.03
Peter Stastny	Quebec	1982-83	75	77	1.03
Doug Gilmour	Toronto	1993-94	83	84	1.01
Bernie Nicholls	Los Angeles	1988-89	79	80	1.01
Guy Lafleur	Montreal	1979-80	74	75	1.01
Guy Lafleur	Montreal	1976-77	80	80	1.00
Marcel Dionne	Los Angeles	1984-85	80	80	1.00
Brian Leetch	NY Rangers	1991-92	80	80	1.00
Bryan Trottier	NY Islanders	1977-78	77	77	1.00
Mike Bossy	NY Islanders	1983-84	67	67	1.00
Jean Ratelle	NY Rangers	1971-72	63	63	1.00
Steve Yzerman	Detroit	1993-94	58	58	1.00
Ron Francis	Hartford	1985-86	53	53	1.00
Guy Chouinard	Calgary	1980-81	52	52	1.00
Elmer Lach	Montreal	1943-44	48	48	1.00

Points-Per-Game Leaders, One Season

(Among players with 50 points or more in one season)

Player	Team	Season	Games	Points	Average	Player	Team	Season	Games	Points	Average
Wayne Gretzky	Edmonton	1983-84	74	205	2.77	Alexander Mogilny	Buffalo	1992-93	77	127	1.65
Wayne Gretzky	Edmonton	1985-86	80	215	2.69	Peter Stastny	Quebec	1982-83	75	124	1.65
Mario Lemieux	Pittsburgh	1992-93	60	160	2.67	Bobby Orr	Boston	1973-74	74	122	1.65
Wayne Gretzky	Edmonton	1981-82	80	212	2.65	Kent Nilsson	Calgary	1980-81	80	131	1.64
Mario Lemieux	Pittsburgh	1988-89	76	199	2.62	Wayne Gretzky	Los Angeles	1991-92	74	121	1.64
Wayne Gretzky	Edmonton	1984-85	80	208	2.60	Denis Savard	Chicago	1987-88	80	131	1.64
Wayne Gretzky	Edmonton	1982-83	80	196	2.45	Steve Yzerman	Detroit	1992-93	84	137	1.63
Wayne Gretzky	Edmonton	1987-88	64	149	2.33	Marcel Dionne	Los Angeles	1978-79	80	130	1.63
Wayne Gretzky	Edmonton	1986-87	79	183	2.32	Dale Hawerchuk	Winnipeg	1984-85	80	130	1.63
Mario Lemieux	Pittsburgh	1995-96	70	161	2.30	Mark Messier	Edmonton	1989-90	79	129	1.63
Mario Lemieux	Pittsburgh	1987-88	77	168	2.18	Bryan Trottier	NY Islanders	1983-84	68	111	1.63
Wayne Gretzky	Los Angeles	1988-89	78	168	2.15	Pat LaFontaine	Buffalo	1991-92	57	93	1.63
Wayne Gretzky	Los Angeles	1990-91	78	163	2.09	Charlie Simmer	Los Angeles	1980-81	65	105	1.62
Mario Lemieux	Pittsburgh	1989-90	59	123	2.08	Guy Lafleur	Montreal	1978-79	80	129	1.61
Wayne Gretzky	Edmonton	1980-81	80	164	2.05	Bryan Trottier	NY Islanders	1981-82	80	129	1.61
Mario Lemieux	Pittsburgh	1991-92	64	131	2.05	Phil Esposito	Boston	1974-75	79	127	1.61
Bill Cowley	Boston	1943-44	36	71	1.97	Steve Yzerman	Detroit	1989-90	79	127	1.61
Phil Esposito	Boston	1970-71	78	152	1.95	Peter Stastny	Quebec	1985-86	76	122	1.61
Wayne Gretzky	Los Angeles	1989-90	73	142	1.95	Mario Lemieux	Pittsburgh	**1996-97**	76	122	1.61
Steve Yzerman	Detroit	1988-89	80	155	1.94	Michel Goulet	Quebec	1983-84	75	121	1.61
Bernie Nicholls	Los Angeles	1988-89	79	150	1.90	Wayne Gretzky	Los Angeles	1993-94	81	130	1.60
Adam Oates	St. Louis	1990-91	61	115	1.89	Bryan Trottier	NY Islanders	1977-78	77	123	1.60
Phil Esposito	Boston	1973-74	78	145	1.86	Bobby Orr	Boston	1972-73	63	101	1.60
Jari Kurri	Edmonton	1984-85	73	135	1.85	Guy Chouinard	Calgary	1980-81	52	83	1.60
Mike Bossy	NY Islanders	1981-82	80	147	1.84	Elmer Lach	Montreal	1944-45	50	80	1.60
Jaromir Jagr	Pittsburgh	1995-96	82	149	1.82	Pierre Turgeon	NY Islanders	1992-93	83	132	1.59
Mario Lemieux	Pittsburgh	1985-86	79	141	1.78	Steve Yzerman	Detroit	1987-88	64	102	1.59
Bobby Orr	Boston	1970-71	78	139	1.78	Mike Bossy	NY Islanders	1978-79	80	126	1.58
Jari Kurri	Edmonton	1983-84	64	113	1.77	Paul Coffey	Edmonton	1983-84	80	126	1.58
Pat LaFontaine	Buffalo	1992-93	84	148	1.76	Marcel Dionne	Los Angeles	1984-85	80	126	1.58
Bryan Trottier	NY Islanders	1978-79	76	134	1.76	Bobby Orr	Boston	1969-70	76	120	1.58
Mike Bossy	NY Islanders	1983-84	67	118	1.76	Eric Lindros	Philadelphia	1995-96	73	115	1.58
Paul Coffey	Edmonton	1985-86	79	138	1.75	Charlie Simmer	Los Angeles	1979-80	64	101	1.58
Phil Esposito	Boston	1971-72	76	133	1.75	Teemu Selanne	Winnipeg	1992-93	84	132	1.57
Peter Stastny	Quebec	1981-82	80	139	1.74	Bobby Clarke	Philadelphia	1975-76	76	119	1.57
Wayne Gretzky	Edmonton	1979-80	79	137	1.73	Guy Lafleur	Montreal	1975-76	80	125	1.56
Jean Ratelle	NY Rangers	1971-72	63	109	1.73	Dave Taylor	Los Angeles	1980-81	72	112	1.56
Marcel Dionne	Los Angeles	1979-80	80	137	1.71	Denis Savard	Chicago	1982-83	78	121	1.55
Herb Cain	Boston	1943-44	48	82	1.71	Ron Francis	Pittsburgh	1995-96	77	119	1.55
Guy Lafleur	Montreal	1976-77	80	136	1.70	Mike Bossy	NY Islanders	1985-86	80	123	1.54
Dennis Maruk	Washington	1981-82	80	136	1.70	Bobby Orr	Boston	1971-72	76	117	1.54
Phil Esposito	Boston	1968-69	74	126	1.70	Kevin Stevens	Pittsburgh	1991-92	80	123	1.54
Guy Lafleur	Montreal	1974-75	70	119	1.70	Mike Bossy	NY Islanders	1984-85	76	117	1.54
Mario Lemieux	Pittsburgh	1986-87	63	107	1.70	Kevin Stevens	Pittsburgh	1992-93	72	111	1.54
Adam Oates	Boston	1992-93	84	142	1.69	Doug Bentley	Chicago	1943-44	50	77	1.54
Bobby Orr	Boston	1974-75	80	135	1.69	Doug Gilmour	Toronto	1992-93	83	127	1.53
Marcel Dionne	Los Angeles	1980-81	80	135	1.69	Marcel Dionne	Los Angeles	1976-77	80	122	1.53
Guy Lafleur	Montreal	1977-78	78	132	1.69	Eric Lindros	Philadelphia	**1996-97**	52	79	1.52
Guy Lafleur	Montreal	1979-80	74	125	1.69	Eric Lindros	Philadelphia	1994-95	46	70	1.52
Rob Brown	Pittsburgh	1988-89	68	115	1.69	Marcel Dionne	Detroit	1974-75	80	121	1.51
Jari Kurri	Edmonton	1985-86	78	131	1.68	Dale Hawerchuk	Winnipeg	1987-88	80	121	1.51
Brett Hull	St. Louis	1990-91	78	131	1.68	Paul Coffey	Pittsburgh	1988-89	75	113	1.51
Phil Esposito	Boston	1972-73	78	130	1.67	Jaromir Jagr	Pittsburgh	**1996-97**	63	95	1.51
Cooney Weiland	Boston	1929-30	44	73	1.66	Cam Neely	Boston	1993-94	49	74	1.51

Calgary's slick Swede Kent Nilsson (14) is seen here tripping up Flyers' forward Dave Poulin. "Magic" enjoyed the finest season of his career in 1980-81, collecting 131 points in 80 games for an average of 1.65 points-per-game.

Left: One of finest players produced by U.S. college hockey, Neal Broten – who scored 38 goals as a rookie in 1981-82 – is the only member of the gold-medal winning 1980 U.S. Olympic Team still active in the NHL. Below: Steve Larmer used the full season he spent in the AHL in 1981-82 to his advantage, refining his skills and adapting to the professional game. When he arrived in the NHL in 1982-83, he had one of the greatest rookie campaigns on record, connecting for 43 goals and winning the Calder Trophy.

Rookie Scoring Records

All-Time Top 50 Goal-Scoring Rookies

	Rookie	Team	Position	Season	GP	G	A	PTS
1.	* Teemu Selanne	Winnipeg	Right wing	1992-93	84	**76**	56	132
2.	* Mike Bossy	NY Islanders	Right wing	1977-78	73	**53**	38	91
3.	* Joe Nieuwendyk	Calgary	Center	1987-88	75	**51**	41	92
4.	* Dale Hawerchuk	Winnipeg	Center	1981-82	80	**45**	58	103
	* Luc Robitaille	Los Angeles	Left wing	1986-87	79	**45**	39	84
6.	Rick Martin	Buffalo	Left wing	1971-72	73	**44**	30	74
	Barry Pederson	Boston	Center	1981-82	80	**44**	48	92
8.	* Steve Larmer	Chicago	Right wing	1982-83	80	**43**	47	90
	* Mario Lemieux	Pittsburgh	Center	1984-85	73	**43**	57	100
10.	* Eric Lindros	Philadelphia	Center	1992-93	61	**41**	34	75
11.	Darryl Sutter	Chicago	Left wing	1980-81	76	**40**	22	62
	Sylvain Turgeon	Hartford	Left wing	1983-84	76	**40**	32	72
	Warren Young	Pittsburgh	Left wing	1984-85	80	**40**	32	72
14.	* Eric Vail	Atlanta	Left wing	1974-75	72	**39**	21	60
	Anton Stastny	Quebec	Left wing	1980-81	80	**39**	46	85
	* Peter Stastny	Quebec	Center	1980-81	77	**39**	70	109
	Steve Yzerman	Detroit	Center	1983-84	80	**39**	48	87
18.	* Gilbert Perreault	Buffalo	Center	1970-71	78	**38**	34	72
	Neal Broten	Minnesota	Center	1981-82	73	**38**	60	98
	Ray Sheppard	Buffalo	Right wing	1987-88	74	**38**	27	65
	Mikael Renberg	Philadelphia	Left wing	1993-94	83	**38**	44	82
22.	Jorgen Pettersson	St. Louis	Left wing	1980-81	62	**37**	36	73
	Jimmy Carson	Los Angeles	Centre	1986-87	80	**37**	42	79
24.	Mike Foligno	Detroit	Right wing	1979-80	80	**36**	35	71
	Mike Bullard	Pittsburgh	Center	1981-82	75	**36**	27	63
	Paul MacLean	Winnipeg	Right wing	1981-82	74	**36**	25	61
	Tony Granato	NY Rangers	Right wing	1988-89	78	**36**	27	63
28.	Marian Stastny	Quebec	Right wing	1981-82	74	**35**	54	89
	Brian Bellows	Minnesota	Right wing	1982-83	78	**35**	30	65
	Tony Amonte	NY Rangers	Right wing	1991-92	79	**35**	34	69
31.	Nels Stewart	Mtl. Maroons	Center	1925-26	36	**34**	8	42
	* Danny Grant	Minnesota	Left wing	1968-69	75	**34**	31	65
	Norm Ferguson	Oakland	Right wing	1968-69	76	**34**	20	54
	Brian Propp	Philadelphia	Left wing	1979-80	80	**34**	41	75
	Wendel Clark	Toronto	Left wing	1985-86	66	**34**	11	45
	* Pavel Bure	Vancouver	Right wing	1991-92	65	**34**	26	60
37.	* Willi Plett	Atlanta	Right wing	1976-77	64	**33**	23	56
	Dale McCourt	Detroit	Center	1977-78	76	**33**	39	72
	Mark Pavelich	NY Rangers	Center	1981-82	79	**33**	43	76
	Ron Flockhart	Philadelphia	Center	1981-82	72	**33**	39	72
	Steve Bozek	Los Angeles	Center	1981-82	71	**33**	23	56
	Jason Arnott	Edmonton	Center	1993-94	78	**33**	35	68
43.	Bill Mosienko	Chicago	Right wing	1943-44	50	**32**	38	70
	Michel Bergeron	Detroit	Right wing	1975-76	72	**32**	27	59
	* Bryan Trottier	NY Islanders	Center	1975-76	80	**32**	63	95
	Don Murdoch	NY Rangers	Right wing	1976-77	59	**32**	24	56
	Jari Kurri	Edmonton	Left wing	1980-81	75	**32**	43	75
	Bobby Carpenter	Washington	Center	1981-82	80	**32**	35	67
	Kjell Dahlin	Montreal	Right wing	1985-86	77	**32**	39	71
	Petr Klima	Detroit	Left wing	1985-86	74	**32**	24	56
	Darren Turcotte	NY Rangers	Center	1989-90	76	**32**	34	66
	Joe Juneau	Boston	Center	1992-93	84	**32**	70	102

* Calder Trophy Winner

All-Time Top 50 Point-Scoring Rookies

	Rookie	Team	Position	Season	GP	G	A	PTS
1.	* Teemu Selanne	Winnipeg	Right wing	1992-93	84	76	56	**132**
2.	* Peter Stastny	Quebec	Center	1980-81	77	39	70	**109**
3.	* Dale Hawerchuk	Winnipeg	Center	1981-82	80	45	58	**103**
4.	Joe Juneau	Boston	Center	1992-93	84	32	70	**102**
5.	* Mario Lemieux	Pittsburgh	Center	1984-85	73	43	57	**100**
6.	Neal Broten	Minnesota	Center	1981-82	73	38	60	**98**
7.	* Bryan Trottier	NY Islanders	Center	1975-76	80	32	63	**95**
8.	Barry Pederson	Boston	Center	1981-82	80	44	48	**92**
	* Joe Nieuwendyk	Calgary	Center	1987-88	75	51	41	**92**
10.	* Mike Bossy	NY Islanders	Right wing	1977-78	73	53	38	**91**
11.	* Steve Larmer	Chicago	Right wing	1982-83	80	43	47	**90**
12.	Marian Stastny	Quebec	Right wing	1981-82	74	35	54	**89**
13.	Steve Yzerman	Detroit	Center	1983-84	80	39	48	**87**
14.	* Sergei Makarov	Calgary	Right wing	1989-90	80	24	62	**86**
15.	Anton Stastny	Quebec	Left wing	1980-81	80	39	46	**85**
16.	* Luc Robitaille	Los Angeles	Left wing	1986-87	79	45	39	**84**
17.	Mikael Renberg	Philadelphia	Left wing	1993-94	83	38	44	**82**
18.	Jimmy Carson	Los Angeles	Center	1986-87	80	37	42	**79**
	Sergei Fedorov	Detroit	Center	1990-91	77	31	48	**79**
	Alexei Yashin	Ottawa	Center	1993-94	83	30	49	**79**
21.	Marcel Dionne	Detroit	Center	1971-72	78	28	49	**77**
22.	Larry Murphy	Los Angeles	Defense	1980-81	80	16	60	**76**
	Mark Pavelich	NY Rangers	Center	1981-82	79	33	43	**76**
	Dave Poulin	Philadelphia	Center	1983-84	73	31	45	**76**
25.	Brian Propp	Philadelphia	Left wing	1979-80	80	34	41	**75**
	Jari Kurri	Edmonton	Left wing	1980-81	75	32	43	**75**
	Denis Savard	Chicago	Center	1980-81	76	28	47	**75**
	Mike Modano	Minnesota	Center	1989-90	80	29	46	**75**
	Eric Lindros	Philadelphia	Center	1992-93	61	41	34	**75**
30.	Rick Martin	Buffalo	Left wing	1971-72	73	44	30	**74**
	* Bobby Smith	Minnesota	Center	1978-79	80	30	44	**74**
32.	Jorgen Pettersson	St. Louis	Left wing	1980-81	62	37	36	**73**
33.	* Gilbert Perreault	Buffalo	Center	1970-71	78	38	34	**72**
	Dale McCourt	Detroit	Center	1977-78	76	33	39	**72**
	Ron Flockhart	Philadelphia	Center	1981-82	72	33	39	**72**
	Sylvain Turgeon	Hartford	Left wing	1983-84	76	40	32	**72**
	Warren Young	Pittsburgh	Left wing	1984-85	80	40	32	**72**
	Carey Wilson	Calgary	Center	1984-85	74	24	48	**72**
	Alexei Zhamnov	Winnipeg	Center	1992-93	68	25	47	**72**
40.	Mike Foligno	Detroit	Right wing	1979-80	80	36	35	**71**
	Dave Christian	Winnipeg	Center	1980-81	80	28	43	**71**
	Mats Naslund	Montreal	Left wing	1982-83	74	26	45	**71**
	Kjell Dahlin	Montreal	Right wing	1985-86	77	32	39	**71**
	* Brian Leetch	NY Rangers	Defense	1988-89	68	23	48	**71**
45.	Bill Mosienko	Chicago	Right wing	1943-44	50	32	38	**70**
46.	Roland Eriksson	Minnesota	Center	1976-77	80	25	44	**69**
	Tony Amonte	NY Rangers	Right wing	1991-92	79	35	34	**69**
48.	Jude Drouin	Minnesota	Center	1970-71	75	16	52	**68**
	Pierre Larouche	Pittsburgh	Center	1974-75	79	31	37	**68**
	Ron Francis	Hartford	Center	1981-82	59	25	43	**68**
	* Gary Suter	Calgary	Defense	1985-86	80	18	50	**68**
	Jason Arnott	Edmonton	Center	1993-94	84	33	35	**68**

* Calder Trophy Winner

50-Goal Seasons

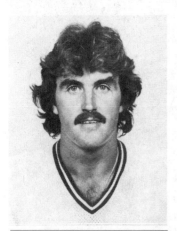

Blaine Stoughton

Marcel Dionne

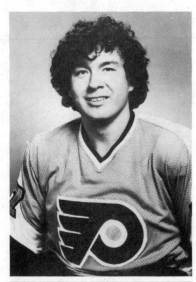

Reggie Leach

Player	Team	Date of 50th Goal	Score	at	Goaltender	Player's Game No.	Team Game No.	Total Goals	Total Games	Age When First 50th Scored (Yrs. & Mos.)
Maurice Richard	Mtl.	18-3-45	Mtl. 4	at Bos. 2	Harvey Bennett	50	50	50	50	23.7
Bernie Geoffrion	Mtl.	16-3-61	Tor. 2	at Mtl. 5	Cesare Maniago	62	68	50	64	30.1
Bobby Hull	Chi.	25-3-62	Chi. 1	at NYR 4	Gump Worsley	70	70	50	70	23.2
Bobby Hull	Chi.	2-3-66	Det. 4	at Chi. 5	Hank Bassen	52	57	54	65	
Bobby Hull	Chi.	18-3-67	Chi. 5	at Tor. 9	Bruce Gamble	63	66	52	66	
Bobby Hull	Chi.	5-3-69	NYR 4	at Chi. 4	Ed Giacomin	64	66	58	74	
Phil Esposito	Bos.	20-2-71	Bos. 4	at L.A. 5	Denis DeJordy	58	58	76	78	29.0
John Bucyk	Bos.	16-3-71	Bos. 11	at Det. 4	Roy Edwards	69	69	51	78	35.10
Phil Esposito	Bos.	20-2-72	Bos. 3	at Chi. 1	Tony Esposito	60	60	66	76	
Bobby Hull	Chi.	2-4-72	Det. 1	at Chi. 6	Andy Brown	78	78	50	78	
Vic Hadfield	NYR	2-4-72	Mtl. 6	at NYR 5	Denis DeJordy	78	78	50	78	31.6
Phil Esposito	Bos.	25-3-73	Buf. 1	at Bos. 6	Roger Crozier	75	75	55	78	
Mickey Redmond	Det.	27-3-73	Det. 8	at Tor. 1	Ron Low	73	75	52	76	25.3
Rick MacLeish	Phi.	1-4-73	Phi. 4	at Pit. 5	Cam Newton	78	78	50	78	23.2
Phil Esposito	Bos.	20-2-74	Bos. 5	at Min. 5	Cesare Maniago	56	56	68	78	
Mickey Redmond	Det.	23-3-74	NYR 3	at Det 5	Ed Giacomin	69	71	51	76	
Ken Hodge	Bos.	6-4-74	Bos. 2	at Mtl. 6	Michel Larocque	75	77	50	76	29.10
Rick Martin	Buf.	7-4-74	St. L. 2	at Buf. 5	Wayne Stephenson	78	78	52	78	22.9
Phil Esposito	Bos.	8-2-75	Bos. 8	at Det. 5	Jim Rutherford	54	54	61	79	
Guy Lafleur	Mtl.	29-3-75	K.C. 1	at Mtl. 4	Denis Herron	66	76	53	70	23.6
Danny Grant	Det.	2-4-75	Wsh. 2	at Det. 8	John Adams	78	78	50	80	29.2
Rick Martin	Buf.	3-4-75	Bos. 2	at Buf. 4	Ken Broderick	67	79	52	68	
Reggie Leach	Phi.	14-3-76	Atl. 1	at Phi. 6	Daniel Bouchard	69	69	61	80	25.11
Jean Pronovost	Pit.	24-3-76	Bos. 5	at Pit. 5	Gilles Gilbert	74	74	52	80	30.3
Guy Lafleur	Mtl.	27-3-76	K.C. 2	at Mtl. 8	Denis Herron	76	76	56	80	
Bill Barber	Phi.	3-4-76	Buf. 2	at Phi. 5	Al Smith	79	79	50	80	23.9
Pierre Larouche	Pit.	3-4-76	Wsh. 5	at Pit. 4	Ron Low	75	79	53	76	20.5
Danny Gare	Buf.	4-4-76	Tor. 2	at Buf. 5	Gord McRae	79	80	50	79	21.11
Steve Shutt	Mtl.	1-3-77	Mtl. 5	at NYI 4	Glenn Resch	65	65	60	80	24.8
Guy Lafleur	Mtl.	6-3-77	Mtl. 1	at Buf. 4	Don Edwards	68	68	56	80	
Marcel Dionne	L.A.	2-4-77	Min. 2	at L.A. 7	Pete LoPresti	79	79	53	80	25.8
Guy Lafleur	Mtl.	8-3-78	Wsh. 3	at Mtl. 4	Jim Bedard	63	65	60	78	
Mike Bossy	NYI	1-4-78	Wsh. 2	at NYI 3	Bernie Wolfe	69	76	53	73	21.2
Mike Bossy	NYI	24-2-79	Det. 1	at NYI 3	Rogie Vachon	58	58	69	80	
Marcel Dionne	L.A.	11-3-79	L.A. 3	at Phi. 6	Wayne Stephenson	68	68	59	80	
Guy Lafleur	Mtl.	31-3-79	Pit. 3	at Mtl. 5	Denis Herron	76	76	52	80	
Guy Chouinard	Atl.	6-4-79	NYR 2	at Atl. 9	John Davidson	79	79	50	80	22.5
Marcel Dionne	L.A.	12-3-80	L.A. 2	at Pit. 4	Nick Ricci	70	70	53	80	
Mike Bossy	NYI	16-3-80	NYI 6	at Chi. 1	Tony Esposito	68	71	51	75	
Charlie Simmer	L.A.	19-3-80	Det. 3	at L.A. 4	Jim Rutherford	57	73	56	64	26.0
Pierre Larouche	Mtl.	25-3-80	Chi. 4	at Mtl. 8	Tony Esposito	72	75	50	73	
Danny Gare	Buf.	27-3-80	Det. 1	at Buf. 10	Jim Rutherford	71	75	56	76	
Blaine Stoughton	Hfd.	28-3-80	Hfd. 4	at Van. 4	Glen Hanlon	75	75	56	80	27.0
Guy Lafleur	Mtl.	2-4-80	Mtl. 7	at Det. 2	Rogie Vachon	72	78	50	74	
Wayne Gretzky	Edm.	2-4-80	Min. 1	at Edm. 1	Gary Edwards	78	79	51	79	19.2
Reggie Leach	Phi.	3-4-80	Wsh. 2	at Phi. 4	empty net	75	79	50	76	
Mike Bossy	NYI	24-1-81	Que. 3	at NYI 7	Ron Grahame	50	50	68	79	
Charlie Simmer	L.A.	26-1-81	L.A. 7	at Que. 5	Michel Dion	51	51	56	65	
Marcel Dionne	L.A.	8-3-81	L.A. 4	at Wpg. 1	Markus Mattsson	68	68	58	80	
Wayne Babych	St. L.	12-3-81	St. L. 3	at Mtl. 4	Richard Sevigny	70	68	54	78	22.9
Wayne Gretzky	Edm.	15-3-81	Edm. 3	at Cgy. 3	Pat Riggin	69	69	55	80	
Rick Kehoe	Pit.	16-3-81	Pit. 7	at Edm. 6	Eddie Mio	70	70	55	80	29.7
Jacques Richard	Que.	29-3-81	Mtl. 0	at Que. 4	Richard Sevigny	76	75	52	78	28.6
Dennis Maruk	Wsh.	5-4-81	Det. 2	at Wsh. 7	Larry Lozinski	80	80	50	80	25.3
Wayne Gretzky	Edm.	30-12-81	Phi. 5	at Edm. 7	empty net	39	39	92	80	
Dennis Maruk	Wsh.	21-2-82	Wpg. 3	at Wsh. 6	Doug Soetaert	61	61	60	80	
Mike Bossy	NYI	4-3-82	Tor. 1	at NYI 10	Michel Larocque	66	66	64	80	
Dino Ciccarelli	Min.	8-3-82	St. L. 1	at Min. 8	Mike Liut	67	68	55	76	21.7
Rick Vaive	Tor.	24-3-82	St. L. 3	at Tor. 4	Mike Liut	72	75	54	77	22.10
Blaine Stoughton	Hfd.	28-3-82	Min. 5	at Hfd. 2	Gilles Meloche	76	76	52	80	
Rick Middleton	Bos.	28-3-82	Bos. 5	at Buf. 9	Paul Harrison	72	77	51	75	28.11
Marcel Dionne	L.A.	30-3-82	Cgy. 7	at L.A. 5	Pat Riggin	75	77	50	78	
Mark Messier	Edm.	31-3-82	L.A. 3	at Edm. 7	Mario Lessard	78	79	50	78	21.3
Bryan Trottier	NYI	3-4-82	Phi. 3	at NYI 6	Pete Peeters	79	79	50	80	25.9
Lanny McDonald	Cgy.	18-2-83	Cgy. 1	at Buf. 5	Bob Sauve	60	60	66	80	30.0
Wayne Gretzky	Edm.	19-2-83	Edm. 10	at Pit. 7	Nick Ricci	60	60	71	80	
Michel Goulet	Que.	5-3-83	Hfd. 3	at Que. 10	Mike Veisor	67	67	57	80	22.11
Mike Bossy	NYI	12-3-83	Wsh. 2	at NYI 6	Al Jensen	70	71	60	79	
Marcel Dionne	L.A.	17-3-83	Que. 3	at L.A. 4	Daniel Bouchard	71	71	56	80	
Al Secord	Chi.	20-3-83	Tor. 3	at Chi. 7	Mike Palmateer	73	73	54	80	25.0
Rick Vaive	Tor.	30-3-83	Tor. 4	at Det. 2	Gilles Gilbert	76	78	51	78	
Wayne Gretzky	Edm.	7-1-84	Hfd. 3	at Edm. 5	Greg Millen	42	42	87	74	
Michel Goulet	Que.	8-3-84	Que. 8	at Pit. 6	Denis Herron	63	69	56	75	
Rick Vaive	Tor.	14-3-84	Min. 3	at Tor. 3	Gilles Meloche	69	72	52	76	
Mike Bullard	Pit.	14-3-84	Pit. 6	at L.A. 7	Markus Mattsson	71	72	51	76	23.0
Jari Kurri	Edm.	15-3-84	Edm. 2	at Mtl. 3	Rick Wamsley	57	73	52	64	23.10
Glenn Anderson	Edm.	21-3-84	Hfd. 3	at Edm. 5	Greg Millen	76	76	54	80	23.6
Tim Kerr	Phi.	22-3-84	Pit. 4	at Phi. 13	Denis Herron	74	75	54	79	24.3
Mike Bossy	NYI	31-3-84	NYI 3	at Wsh. 1	Pat Riggin	67	79	51	67	

Player	Team	Date of 50th Goal	Score	Goaltender	Player's Game No.	Team Game No.	Total Goals	Total Games	Age When First 50th Scored (Yrs. & Mos.)
Wayne Gretzky	Edm.	26-1-85	Pit. 3 at Edm. 6	Denis Herron	49	49	73	80	
Jari Kurri	Edm.	3-2-85	Hfd. 3 at Edm. 6	Greg Millen	50	53	71	73	
Mike Bossy	NYI	5-3-85	Phi. 5 at NYI 4	Bob Froese	61	65	58	76	
Michel Goulet	Que.	6-3-85	Buf. 3 at Que. 4	Tom Barrasso	62	73	55	69	
Tim Kerr	Phi.	7-3-85	Wsh. 6 at Phi. 9	Pat Riggin	63	65	54	74	
John Ogrodnick	Det.	13-3-85	Det. 6 at Edm. 7	Grant Fuhr	69	69	55	79	25.9
Bob Carpenter	Wsh.	21-3-85	Wsh. 2 at Mtl. 3	Steve Penney	72	72	53	80	21.9
Dale Hawerchuk	Wpg.	29-3-85	Chi. 5 at Wpg. 5	W. Skorodenski	77	77	53	80	21.11
Mike Gartner	Wsh.	7-4-85	Pit. 3 at Wsh. 7	Brian Ford	80	80	50	80	25.5
Jari Kurri	Edm.	4-3-86	Edm. 6 at Van. 2	Richard Brodeur	63	65	68	78	
Mike Bossy	NYI	11-3-86	Cgy. 4 at NYI 8	Rejean Lemelin	67	67	61	80	
Glenn Anderson	Edm.	14-3-86	Det. 3 at Edm. 12	Greg Stefan	63	71	54	72	
Michel Goulet	Que.	17-3-86	Que. 8 at Mtl. 6	Patrick Roy	67	72	53	75	
Wayne Gretzky	Edm.	18-3-86	Wpg. 2 at Edm. 6	Brian Hayward	72	72	52	80	
Tim Kerr	Phi.	20-3-86	Pit. 1 at Phi. 5	Roberto Romano	68	72	58	76	
Wayne Gretzky	Edm.	4-2-87	Edm. 6 at Min. 5	Don Beaupre	55	55	62	79	
Dino Ciccarelli	Min.	7-3-87	Pit. 7 at Min. 3	Gilles Meloche	66	66	52	80	
Mario Lemieux	Pit.	12-3-87	Que. 3 at Pit. 6	Mario Gosselin	53	70	54	63	21.5
Tim Kerr	Phi.	17-3-87	NYR 1 at Phi. 4	J. Vanbiesbrouck	67	71	58	75	
Jari Kurri	Edm.	17-3-87	N.J. 4 at Edm. 7	Craig Billington	69	70	54	79	
Mario Lemieux	Pit.	2-2-88	Wsh. 2 at Pit. 3	Pete Peeters	51	54	70	77	
Steve Yzerman	Det.	1-3-88	Buf. 0 at Det. 4	Tom Barrasso	64	64	50	64	22.10
Joe Nieuwendyk	Cgy.	12-3-88	Buf. 4 at Cgy. 10	Tom Barrasso	66	70	51	75	21.5
Craig Simpson	Edm.	15-3-88	Buf. 4 at Edm. 6	Jacques Cloutier	71	71	56	80	21.1
Jimmy Carson	L.A.	26-3-88	Chi. 5 at L.A. 9	Darren Pang	77	77	55	88	19.8
Luc Robitaille	L.A.	1-4-88	L.A. 6 at Cgy. 3	Mike Vernon	79	79	53	80	21.10
Hakan Loob	Cgy.	3-4-88	Min. 1 at Cgy. 4	Don Beaupre	80	80	50	80	27.9
Stephane Richer	Mtl.	3-4-88	Mtl. 4 at Buf. 4	Tom Barrasso	72	80	50	72	21.10
Mario Lemieux	Pit.	20-1-89	Pit. 3 at Wpg. 7	Eldon Reddick	44	46	85	76	
Bernie Nicholls	L.A.	28-1-89	Edm. 7 at L.A. 6	Grant Fuhr	51	51	70	79	27.7
Steve Yzerman	Det.	5-2-89	Det. 6 at Wpg. 2	Eldon Reddick	55	55	65	80	
Wayne Gretzky	L.A.	4-3-89	Phi. 2 at L.A. 6	Ron Hextall	66	67	54	78	
Joe Nieuwendyk	Cgy.	21-3-89	NYI 1 at Cgy. 4	Mark Fitzpatrick	72	74	51	77	
Joe Mullen	Cgy.	31-3-89	Wpg. 1 at Cgy. 4	Bob Essensa	78	79	51	79	32.1
Brett Hull	St. L.	6-2-90	Tor. 4 at St. L. 6	Jeff Reese	54	54	72	80	25.6
Steve Yzerman	Det.	24-2-90	Det. 3 at NYI 3	Glenn Healy	63	63	62	79	
Cam Neely	Bos.	10-3-90	Bos. 3 at NYI 3	Mark Fitzpatrick	69	71	55	76	24.9
Luc Robitaille	L.A.	21-3-90	L.A. 3 at Van. 6	Kirk McLean	79	79	52	80	
Brian Bellows	Min.	22-3-90	Min. 5 at Det. 1	Tim Cheveldae	75	75	55	80	25.6
Pat LaFontaine	NYI	24-3-90	NYI 5 at Edm. 5	Bill Ranford	71	77	54	74	25.1
Stephane Richer	Mtl.	24-3-90	Mtl. 4 at Hfd. 7	Peter Sidorkiewicz	75	77	51	75	
Gary Leeman	Tor.	28-3-90	NYI 6 at Tor. 3	Mark Fitzpatrick	78	78	51	80	26.1
Brett Hull	St. L.	25-1-91	St. L. 9 at Det. 4	Dave Gagnon	49	49	86	78	
Cam Neely	Bos.	26-3-91	Bos. 7 at Que. 4	empty net	67	78	51	69	
Theoren Fleury	Cgy.	26-3-91	Van. 2 at Cgy. 7	Bob Mason	77	77	51	79	22.9
Steve Yzerman	Det.	30-3-91	NYR 5 at Det. 6	Mike Richter	79	79	51	80	
Brett Hull	St. L.	28-1-92	St. L. 3 at L.A. 3	Kelly Hrudey	50	50	70	73	
Jeremy Roenick	Chi.	7-3-92	Chi. 2 at Bos. 1	Daniel Berthiaume	67	67	53	80	22.2
Kevin Stevens	Pit.	24-3-92	Pit. 3 at Det. 4	Tim Cheveldae	74	74	54	80	26.11
Gary Roberts	Cgy.	31-3-92	Edm. 2 at Cgy. 5	Bill Ranford	73	77	53	76	25.10
Alexander Mogilny	Buf.	3-2-93	Hfd. 2 at Buf. 3	Sean Burke	46	53	76	77	23.11
Teemu Selanne	Wpg.	28-2-93	Min. 6 at Wpg. 7	Darcy Wakaluk	63	63	76	84	22.6
Pavel Bure	Van.	1-3-93	Van. 5 at Buf. 2*	Grant Fuhr	63	63	60	83	21.11
Steve Yzerman	Det.	10-3-93	Det. 6 at Edm. 3	Bill Ranford	70	70	58	84	
Luc Robitaille	L.A.	15-3-93	L.A. 4 at Buf. 2	Grant Fuhr	69	69	63	84	
Brett Hull	St. L.	20-3-93	St. L. 2 at L.A. 3	Robb Stauber	73	73	54	80	
Mario Lemieux	Pit.	21-3-93	Pit. 6 at Edm. 4**	Ron Tugnutt	48	72	69	60	
Kevin Stevens	Pit.	21-3-93	Pit. 6 at Edm. 4**	Ron Tugnutt	62	72	55	72	
Dave Andreychuk	Tor.	23-3-93	Tor. 5 at Wpg. 4	Bob Essensa	72	73	54	83	29.6
Pat LaFontaine	Buf.	28-3-93	Ott. 1 at Buf. 3	Peter Sidorkiewicz	75	75	53	84	
Pierre Turgeon	NYI	2-4-93	NYI 3 at NYR 2	Mike Richter	75	76	58	83	23.8
Mark Recchi	Phi.	3-4-93	T.B. 2 at Phi. 6	J-C Bergeron	77	77	53	84	25.2
Jeremy Roenick	Chi.	15-4-93	Tor. 2 at Chi. 3	Felix Potvin	84	84	50	84	
Brendan Shanahan	St. L.	15-4-93	T.B. 5 at St. L. 6	Pat Jablonski	71	84	51	71	24.3
Cam Neely	Bos.	7-3-94	Wsh. 3 at Bos. 6	Don Beaupre	44	66	50	49	
Sergei Fedorov	Det.	15-3-94	Van. 2 at Det. 5	Kirk McLean	67	69	56	82	24.3
Pavel Bure	Van.	23-3-94	Van. 6 at L.A. 3	empty net	65	73	60	76	
Adam Graves	NYR	23-3-94	NYR 5 at Edm. 3	Bill Ranford	74	74	51	84	25.11
Dave Andreychuk	Tor	24-3-94	S.J. 2 at Tor. 1	Arturs Irbe	73	74	53	83	
Brett Hull	St.L.	25-3-94	Dal. 3 at St.L. 5	Andy Moog	71	74	52	81	
Ray Sheppard	Det.	29-3-94	Hfd. 2 at Det. 6	Sean Burke	74	76	52	82	27.10
Brendan Shanahan	St.L.	12-4-94	St.L. 5 at Dal. 9	Andy Moog	80	83	52	81	
Mike Modano	Dal.	12-4-94	St.L. 5 at Dal. 9	Curtis Joseph	75	83	50	76	23.11
Mario Lemieux	Pit.	23-2-96	Hfd. 4 at Pit. 5	Sean Burke	50	59	69	70	
Jaromir Jagr	Pit.	23-2-96	Hfd. 4 at Pit. 5	Sean Burke	59	59	62	82	24.0
Alexander Mogilny	Van.	29-2-96	St.L. 2 at Van. 2	Grant Fuhr	60	63	55	79	
Peter Bondra	Wsh.	3-4-96	Wsh. 5 at Buf. 1	Andrei Trefilov	62	77	52	67	28.1
Joe Sakic	Col.	7-4-96	Col. 4 at Dal. 1	empty net	79	79	51	82	26.7
John LeClair	Phi.	10-4-96	Phi. 5 at N.J. 1	Corey Schwab	80	80	51	82	26.7
Keith Tkachuk	Wpg.	12-4-96	L.A. 3 at Wpg. 5	empty net	75	81	50	76	24.0
Paul Kariya	Ana.	14-4-96	Wpg. 2 at Ana. 5	N. Khabibulin	82	82	50	82	21.5
Keith Tkachuk	Pho.	6-4-97	Pho. 1 at Col. 2	Patrick Roy	78	79	52	81	
Teemu Selanne	Ana.	9-4-97	L.A. 1 at Ana. 4	empty net	77	81	51	78	
Mario Lemieux	Pit.	11-4-97	Pit. 2 at Fla. 4	J. Vanbiesbrouck	75	81	50	76	
John LeClair	Phi.	13-4-97	N.J. 4 at Phi. 5	Mike Dunham	82	82	50	82	

* neutral site game played at Hamilton; ** neutral site game played at Cleveland

Craig Simpson

Hakan Loob

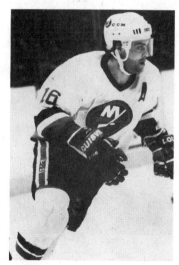

Pat LaFontaine

100-Point Seasons

Jean Ratelle

Bobby Clarke

Gilbert Perreault

Player	Team	Date of 100th Point	G or A	Score		Player's Game No.	Team Game No.	Points G - A PTS	Total Games	Age when first 100th point scored (Yrs. & Mos.)
Phil Esposito	Bos.	2-3-69	(G)	Pit. 0	at Bos. 4	60	62	49-77 — 126	74	27.1
Bobby Hull	Chi.	20-3-69	(G)	Chi. 5	at Bos. 5	71	71	58-49 — 107	76	30.2
Gordie Howe	Det.	30-3-69	(G)	Det. 5	at Chi. 9	76	76	44-59 — 103	76	41.0
Bobby Orr	Bos.	15-3-70	(G)	Det. 5	at Bos. 5	67	67	33-87 — 120	76	22.11
Phil Esposito	Bos.	6-2-71	(A)	Buf. 3	at Bos. 4	51	51	76-76 — 152	78	
Bobby Orr	Bos.	22-2-71	(A)	Bos. 4	at L.A. 5	58	58	37-102 — 139	78	
John Bucyk	Bos.	13-3-71	(G)	Bos. 6	at Van. 3	68	68	51-65 — 116	78	35.10
Ken Hodge	Bos.	21-3-71	(A)	Buf. 7	at Bos. 5	72	72	43-62 — 105	78	26.9
Jean Ratelle	NYR	18-2-72	(A)	NYR 2	at Cal. 2	58	58	46-63 — 109	63	31.4
Phil Esposito	Bos.	19-2-72	(A)	Bos. 6	at Min. 4	59	59	66-67 — 133	76	
Bobby Orr	Bos.	2-3-72	(A)	Van. 3	at Bos. 7	64	64	37-80 — 117	76	
Vic Hadfield	NYR	25-3-72	(A)	NYR 3	at Mtl. 3	74	74	50-56 — 106	78	31.5
Phil Esposito	Bos.	3-3-73	(A)	Bos. 1	at Mtl. 5	64	64	55-75 — 130	78	
Bobby Clarke	Phi.	29-3-73	(G)	Atl. 2	at Phi. 4	76	76	37-67 — 104	78	23.7
Bobby Orr	Bos.	31-3-73	(G)	Bos. 3	at Tor. 7	62	77	29-72 — 101	63	
Rick MacLeish	Phi.	1-4-73	(G)	Phi. 4	at Pit. 5	78	78	50-50 — 100	78	23.3
Phil Esposito	Bos.	13-2-74	(A)	Bos. 9	at Cal. 6	53	53	68-77 — 145	78	
Bobby Orr	Bos.	12-3-74	(A)	Buf. 0	at Bos. 4	62	66	32-90 — 122	74	
Ken Hodge	Bos.	24-3-74	(A)	Mtl. 3	at Bos. 6	72	72	50-55 — 105	76	
Phil Esposito	Bos.	8-2-75	(A)	Bos. 8	at Det. 5	54	54	61-66 — 127	79	
Bobby Orr	Bos.	13-2-75	(A)	Bos. 1	at Buf. 3	57	57	46-89 — 135	80	
Guy Lafleur	Mtl.	7-3-75	(G)	Wsh. 4	at Mtl. 8	56	66	53-66 — 119	70	24.6
Pete Mahovlich	Mtl.	9-3-75	(G)	Mtl. 5	at NYR 3	67	67	35-82 — 117	80	29.5
Marcel Dionne	Det.	9-3-75	(G)	Det. 5	at Phi. 8	67	67	47-74 — 121	80	23.7
Bobby Clarke	Phi.	22-3-75	(A)	Min. 0	at Phi. 4	72	72	27-89 — 116	80	
Rene Robert	Buf.	5-4-75	(A)	Buf. 4	at Tor. 2	74	80	40-60 — 100	74	26.4
Guy Lafleur	Mtl.	10-3-76	(A)	Mtl. 5	at Chi. 1	69	69	56-69 — 125	80	
Bobby Clarke	Phi.	11-3-76	(A)	Buf. 1	at Phi. 6	64	68	30-89 — 119	76	
Bill Barber	Phi.	18-3-76	(A)	Van. 2	at Phi. 3	71	71	50-62 — 112	80	23.8
Gilbert Perreault	Buf.	21-3-76	(A)	K.C. 1	at Buf. 3	73	73	44-69 — 113	80	25.4
Pierre Larouche	Pit.	24-3-76	(G)	Bos. 5	at Pit. 5	70	74	53-58 — 111	76	20.4
Pete Mahovlich	Mtl.	28-3-76	(A)	Mtl. 2	at Bos. 2	77	77	34-71 — 105	80	
Jean Ratelle	Bos.	30-3-76	(G)	Buf. 4	at Bos. 4	77	77	36-69 — 105	80	
Jean Pronovost	Pit.	3-4-76	(A)	Wsh. 5	at Pit. 4	79	79	52-52 — 104	80	30.4
Darryl Sittler	Tor.	3-4-76	(A)	Bos. 4	at Tor. 2	78	79	41-59 — 100	79	26.7
Guy Lafleur	Mtl.	26-2-77	(A)	Clev. 3	at Mtl. 5	63	63	56-80 — 136	80	
Marcel Dionne	L.A.	5-3-77	(G)	Pit. 3	at L.A. 3	67	67	53-69 — 122	80	
Steve Shutt	Mtl.	27-3-77	(A)	Mtl. 6	at Det. 0	77	77	60-45 — 105	80	24.9
Bryan Trottier	NYI	25-2-78	(A)	Chi. 1	at NYI 7	59	60	46-77 — 123	77	21.7
Guy Lafleur	Mtl.	28-2-78	(G)	Det. 3	at Mtl. 9	69	61	60-72 — 132	78	
Darryl Sittler	Tor.	12-3-78	(A)	Tor. 7	at Pit. 1	67	67	45-72 — 117	80	
Guy Lafleur	Mtl.	27-2-79	(A)	Mtl. 3	at NYI 7	61	61	52-77 — 129	80	
Bryan Trottier	NYI	6-3-79	(A)	Buf. 3	at NYI 2	59	63	47-87 — 134	76	
Marcel Dionne	L.A.	8-3-79	(A)	L.A. 4	at Buf. 6	66	66	59-71 — 130	80	
Mike Bossy	NYI	11-3-79	(A)	NYI 4	at Bos. 4	66	66	69-57 — 126	80	22.2
Bob MacMillan	Atl.	15-3-79	(A)	Atl. 4	at Phi. 5	68	69	37-71 — 108	79	26.6
Guy Chouinard	Atl.	30-3-79	(G)	L.A. 3	at Atl. 5	75	75	50-57 — 107	80	22.5
Denis Potvin	NYI	8-4-79	(A)	NYI 5	at NYR 2	73	80	31-70 — 101	73	25.5
Marcel Dionne	L.A.	6-2-80	(A)	L.A. 3	at Hfd. 7	53	53	53-84 — 137	80	
Guy Lafleur	Mtl.	10-2-80	(A)	Mtl. 3	at Bos. 2	55	55	50-75 — 125	74	
Wayne Gretzky	Edm.	24-2-80	(A)	Bos. 4	at Edm. 2	61	62	51-86 — 137	79	19.2
Bryan Trottier	NYI	30-3-80	(A)	NYI 9	at Que. 6	75	77	42-62 — 104	78	
Gilbert Perreault	Buf.	1-4-80	(A)	Buf. 5	at Atl. 2	77	77	40-66 — 106	80	
Mike Rogers	Hfd.	4-4-80	(A)	Que. 2	at Hfd. 9	79	79	44-61 — 105	80	25.5
Charlie Simmer	L.A.	5-4-80	(A)	Van. 5	at L.A. 3	64	80	56-45 — 101	64	26.0
Blaine Stoughton	Hfd.	6-4-80	(A)	Det. 3	at Hfd. 5	80	80	56-44 — 100	80	27.0
Wayne Gretzky	Edm.	6-2-81	(G)	Wpg. 4	at Edm. 10	53	53	55-109 — 164	80	
Marcel Dionne	L.A.	12-2-81	(A)	L.A. 5	at Chi. 5	58	58	58-77 — 135	80	
Charlie Simmer	L.A.	14-2-81	(A)	Bos. 5	at L.A. 4	59	59	56-49 — 105	65	
Kent Nilsson	Cgy.	27-2-81	(A)	Hfd. 1	at Cgy. 5	64	64	49-82 — 131	80	24.6
Mike Bossy	NYI	3-3-81	(G)	Edm. 8	at NYI 8	65	66	68-51 — 119	79	
Dave Taylor	L.A.	14-3-81	(A)	Min. 4	at L.A. 10	63	70	47-65 — 112	72	25.3
Mike Rogers	Hfd.	22-3-81	(G)	Tor. 3	at Hfd. 3	74	74	40-65 — 105	80	
Bernie Federko	St. L.	28-3-81	(A)	Buf. 4	at St. L. 7	74	76	31-73 — 104	78	24.10
Rick Middleton	Bos.	28-3-81	(A)	Chi. 2	at Bos. 5	76	76	44-59 — 103	80	27.4
Jacques Richard	Que.	29-3-81	(G)	Mtl. 0	at Que. 4	75	76	52-51 — 103	78	28.6
Bryan Trottier	NYI	29-3-81	(G)	NYI 5	at Wsh. 4	69	76	31-72 — 103	73	
Peter Stastny	Que.	29-3-81	(A)	Mtl. 0	at Que. 4	73	76	39-70 — 109	77	24.6
Wayne Gretzky	Edm.	27-12-81	(G)	L.A. 3	at Edm. 10	38	38	92-120 — 212	80	
Mike Bossy	NYI	13-2-82	(A)	Phi. 2	at NYI 8	55	55	64-83 — 147	80	
Peter Stastny	Que.	16-2-82	(A)	Wpg. 3	at Que. 7	60	60	46-93 — 139	80	
Dennis Maruk	Wsh.	20-2-82	(G)	Wsh. 3	at Min. 7	60	60	60-76 — 136	80	26.3
Bryan Trottier	NYI	23-2-82	(A)	Chi. 1	at NYI 5	61	61	50-79 — 129	80	
Denis Savard	Chi.	27-2-82	(A)	Chi. 5	at L.A. 3	64	64	32-87 — 119	80	21.1
Bobby Smith	Min.	3-3-82	(G)	Det. 4	at Min. 6	66	66	43-71 — 114	80	24.1
Marcel Dionne	L.A.	6-3-82	(G)	L.A. 6	at Hfd. 7	64	66	50-67 — 117	78	
Dave Taylor	L.A.	20-3-82	(A)	Pit. 5	at L.A. 7	71	72	39-67 — 106	78	
Dale Hawerchuk	Wpg.	24-3-82	(A)	L.A. 3	at Wpg.	74	74	45-58 — 103	80	18.11
Dino Ciccarelli	Min.	27-3-82	(G)	Min. 6	at Bos. 5	72	76	55-52 — 107	76	21.8
Glenn Anderson	Edm.	28-3-82	(G)	Edm. 6	at L.A. 2	78	78	38-67 — 105	80	21.7
Mike Rogers	NYR	2-4-82	(G)	Pit. 7	at NYR 5	79	79	38-65 — 103	80	

Player	Team	Date of 100th Point	G or A	Score		Player's Game No.	Team Game No.	Points G - A — PTS	Total Games	Age when first 100th point scored (Yrs. & Mos.)
Wayne Gretzky	Edm.	5-1-83	(A)	Edm. 8	at Wpg. 3	42	42	71-125 — 196	80	
Mike Bossy	NYI	3-3-83	(A)	Tor. 1	at NYI. 5	66	67	60-58 — 118	79	
Peter Stastny	Que.	5-3-83	(A)	Hfd. 3	at Que. 10	62	67	47-77 — 124	75	
Denis Savard	Chi.	6-3-83	(G)	Mtl. 4	at Chi. 5	65	67	35-86 — 121	78	
Mark Messier	Edm.	23-3-83	(G)	Edm. 4	at Wpg. 7	73	76	48-58 — 106	77	22.2
Barry Pederson	Bos.	26-3-83	(A)	Hfd. 4	at Bos. 7	73	76	46-61 — 107	77	22.0
Marcel Dionne	L.A.	26-3-83	(A)	Edm. 9	at L.A. 3	75	75	56-51 — 107	80	
Michel Goulet	Que.	27-3-83	(A)	Que. 6	at Buf. 6	77	77	57-48 — 105	80	22.11
Glenn Anderson	Edm.	29-3-83	(A)	Edm. 7	at Van. 4	70	78	48-56 — 104	72	
Jari Kurri	Edm.	29-3-83	(A)	Edm. 7	at Van. 4	78	78	45-59 — 104	80	22.10
Kent Nilsson	Cgy.	29-3-83	(G)	L.A. 3	at Cgy. 5	78	78	46-58 — 104	80	
Wayne Gretzky	Edm.	18-12-83	(G)	Edm. 7	at Wpg. 5	34	34	87-118 — 205	74	
Paul Coffey	Edm.	4-3-84	(A)	Mtl. 1	at Edm. 6	68	68	40-86 — 126	80	22.9
Michel Goulet	Que.	4-3-84	(A)	Que. 1	at Buf. 1	62	67	56-65 — 121	75	
Jari Kurri	Edm.	7-3-84	(G)	Chi. 4	at Edm. 7	53	69	52-61 — 113	64	
Peter Stastny	Que.	8-3-84	(A)	Que. 8	at Pit. 6	69	69	46-73 — 119	80	
Mike Bossy	NYI	8-3-84	(A)	Tor. 5	at NYI 9	56	68	51-67 — 118	67	
Barry Pederson	Bos.	14-3-84	(A)	Bos. 4	at Det. 2	71	71	39-77 — 116	80	
Bryan Trottier	NYI	18-3-84	(G)	NYI 4	at Hfd. 5	62	73	40-71 — 111	68	
Bernie Federko	St. L.	20-3-84	(A)	Wpg. 3	at St. L. 9	75	76	41-66 — 107	79	
Rick Middleton	Bos.	27-3-84	(G)	Bos. 6	at Que. 4	77	77	47-58 — 105	80	
Dale Hawerchuk	Wpg.	27-3-84	(G)	Wpg. 3	at L.A. 3	77	77	37-65 — 102	80	
Mark Messier	Edm.	27-3-84	(A)	Edm. 9	at Cgy. 2	72	79	37-64 — 101	73	
Wayne Gretzky	Edm.	29-12-84	(A)	Det. 3	at Edm. 6	35	35	73-135 — 208	80	
Jari Kurri	Edm.	29-1-85	(G)	Edm. 4	at Cgy. 2	48	51	71-64 — 135	73	
Mike Bossy	NYI	23-2-85	(G)	Bos. 1	at NYI 7	56	60	58-59 — 117	76	
Dale Hawerchuk	Wpg.	25-2-85	(A)	Wpg. 12	at NYR 5	64	64	53-77 — 130	80	
Marcel Dionne	L.A.	5-3-85	(A)	Pit. 0	at L.A. 6	66	66	46-80 — 126	80	
Brent Sutter	NYI	12-3-85	(A)	NYI 6	at St. L. 5	68	68	42-60 — 102	72	22.10
John Ogrodnick	Det.	22-3-85	(A)	NYR 3	at Det. 5	73	73	55-50 — 105	79	25.9
Paul Coffey	Edm.	26-3-85	(G)	Edm. 7	at NYI 5	74	74	37-84 — 121	80	
Denis Savard	Chi.	29-3-85	(A)	Chi. 5	at Wpg. 5	75	76	38-67 — 105	79	
Peter Stastny	Que.	2-4-85	(A)	Bos. 4	at Que. 6	74	77	32-68 — 100	75	
Bernie Federko	St. L.	4-4-85	(A)	NYR 5	at St. L. 4	74	78	30-73 — 103	76	
John Tonelli	NYI	6-4-85	(G)	NJ 5	at NYI 5	80	80	42-58 — 100	80	28.1
Paul MacLean	Wpg.	6-4-85	(A)	Wpg. 6	at Edm. 5	78	79	41-60 — 101	79	27.1
Bernie Nicholls	L.A.	6-4-85	(A)	Van. 4	at L.A. 4	80	80	46-54 — 100	80	22.9
Mike Gartner	Wsh.	7-4-85	(A)	Pit. 3	at Wsh. 7	80	80	50-52 — 102	80	25.6
Mario Lemieux	Pit.	7-4-85	(G)	Pit. 3	at Wsh. 7	73	80	43-57 — 100	73	19.6
Wayne Gretzky	Edm.	4-1-86	(A)	Hfd. 3	at Edm. 4	39	39	52-163 — 215	80	
Mario Lemieux	Pit.	15-2-86	(G)	Van. 4	at Pit. 9	55	56	48-93 — 141	79	
Paul Coffey	Edm.	19-2-86	(A)	Tor. 5	at Edm. 9	59	60	48-90 — 138	79	
Peter Stastny	Que.	1-3-86	(G)	Buf. 8	at Que. 4	66	68	41-81 — 122	80	
Jari Kurri	Edm.	2-3-86	(G)	Phi. 1	at Edm. 2	62	64	68-63 — 131	78	
Mike Bossy	NYI	8-3-86	(G)	Wsh. 6	at NYI 2	65	65	61-62 — 123	80	
Denis Savard	Chi.	12-3-86	(G)	Buf. 7	at Chi. 6	69	69	47-69 — 116	80	
Mats Naslund	Mtl.	13-3-86	(A)	Mtl. 2	at Bos. 3	70	70	43-67 — 110	80	26.4
Michel Goulet	Que.	24-3-86	(A)	Que. 1	at Min. 0	70	75	53-50 — 103	75	
Glenn Anderson	Edm.	25-3-86	(G)	Edm. 7	at Det. 2	66	74	54-48 — 102	72	
Neal Broten	Min.	26-3-86	(A)	Min. 6	at Tor. 1	76	76	29-76 — 105	80	26.4
Dale Hawerchuk	Wpg.	31-3-86	(A)	Wpg. 5	at L.A. 2	78	78	46-59 — 105	80	
Bernie Federko	St. L.	5-4-86	(G)	Chi. 5	at St. L. 7	79	79	34-68 — 102	80	
Wayne Gretzky	Edm.	11-1-87	(A)	Cgy. 3	at Edm. 5	42	42	62-121 — 183	79	
Jari Kurri	Edm.	14-3-87	(A)	Buf. 3	at Edm. 5	67	68	54-54 — 108	79	
Mario Lemieux	Pit.	18-3-87	(A)	St. L. 4	at Pit. 5	55	72	54-53 — 107	63	
Mark Messier	Edm.	19-3-87	(A)	Edm. 4	at Cgy. 5	71	71	37-70 — 107	77	
Dino Ciccarelli	Min.	30-3-87	(A)	NYR 6	at Min. 5	78	78	52-51 — 103	80	
Doug Gilmour	St. L.	2-4-87	(A)	Buf. 3	at St. L. 5	78	78	42-63 — 105	80	23.10
Dale Hawerchuk	Wpg.	5-4-87	(A)	Wpg. 3	at Cgy. 1	80	80	47-53 — 100	80	
Mario Lemieux	Pit.	20-1-88	(G)	Pit. 8	at Chi. 3	45	48	70-98 — 168	77	
Wayne Gretzky	Edm.	11-2-88	(A)	Edm. 7	at Van. 2	43	56	40-109 — 149	64	
Denis Savard	Chi.	12-2-88	(A)	St. L. 3	at Chi. 4	57	57	44-87 — 131	80	
Dale Hawerchuk	Wpg.	23-2-88	(A)	Wpg. 4	at Pit. 3	61	61	44-77 — 121	80	
Steve Yzerman	Det.	27-2-88	(A)	Det. 4	at Que. 5	63	63	50-52 — 102	64	22.10
Peter Stastny	Que.	8-3-88	(A)	Hfd. 4	at Que. 6	63	67	46-65 — 111	76	
Mark Messier	Edm.	15-3-88	(A)	Buf. 4	at Edm. 6	68	71	37-74 — 111	77	
Jimmy Carson	L.A.	26-3-88	(A)	Chi. 5	at L.A. 9	77	77	55-52 — 107	80	19.8
Hakan Loob	Cgy.	26-3-88	(A)	Van. 1	at Cgy. 6	76	76	50-56 — 106	80	27.9
Mike Bullard	Cgy.	26-3-88	(A)	Van. 1	at Cgy. 6	76	76	48-55 — 103	79	27.1
Michel Goulet	Que.	27-3-88	(A)	Pit. 6	at Que. 3	76	76	48-58 — 106	80	
Luc Robitaille	L.A.	30-3-88	(A)	Cgy. 7	at L.A. 9	78	78	53-58 — 111	80	22.1
Mario Lemieux	Pit.	31-12-88	(A)	N.J. 6	at Pit. 8	36	38	85-114 — 199	76	
Wayne Gretzky	L.A.	21-1-89	(A)	L.A. 4	at Hfd. 5	47	48	54-114 — 168	78	
Bernie Nicholls	L.A.	21-1-89	(A)	L.A. 4	at Hfd. 5	48	48	70-80 — 150	79	
Steve Yzerman	Det.	27-1-89	(G)	Tor. 1	at Det. 8	50	50	65-90 — 155	80	
Rob Brown	Pit.	16-3-89	(A)	Pit. 2	at N.J. 1	60	72	49-66 — 115	68	20.11
Paul Coffey	Pit.	20-3-89	(A)	Pit. 2	at Min. 7	69	74	30-83 — 113	75	
Joe Mullen	Cgy.	23-3-89	(A)	L.A. 2	at Cgy. 4	74	75	51-59 — 110	79	32.1
Jari Kurri	Edm.	29-3-89	(A)	Edm. 5	at Van. 2	75	79	44-58 — 102	76	
Jimmy Carson	Edm.	2-4-89	(A)	Edm. 2	at Cgy. 4	80	80	49-51 — 100	80	
Mario Lemieux	Pit.	28-1-90	(G)	Pit. 2	at Buf. 7	50	50	45-78 — 123	59	
Wayne Gretzky	L.A.	30-1-90	(A)	N.J. 2	at L.A. 5	51	51	40-102 — 142	73	
Steve Yzerman	Det.	19-2-90	(A)	Mtl. 5	at Det. 5	61	61	62-65 — 127	79	
Mark Messier	Edm.	20-2-90	(A)	Edm. 4	at Van. 2	62	62	45-84 — 129	79	
Brett Hull	St. L.	3-3-90	(A)	NYI 4	at St. L. 5	67	67	72-41 — 113	80	25.7
Bernie Nicholls	NYR	12-3-90	(A)	L.A. 6	at NYR 2	70	71	39-73 — 112	79	
Pierre Turgeon	Buf.	25-3-90	(A)	N.J. 4	at Buf. 3	76	76	40-66 — 106	80	20.7
Paul Coffey	Pit.	25-3-90	(A)	Pit. 2	at Hfd. 4	77	77	29-74 — 103	80	
Pat LaFontaine	NYI	27-3-90	(G)	Cgy. 4	at NYI 2	72	78	54-51 — 105	74	25.1

Guy Lafleur

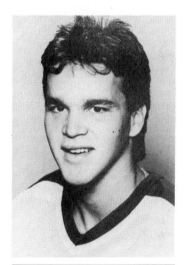

Luc Robitaille

Brett Hull

Theoren Fleury

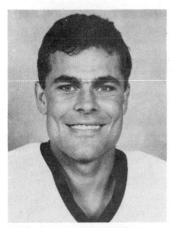

Adam Oates

Pavel Bure

Player	Team	Date of 100th Point	G or A	Score		Player's Game No.	Team Game No.	Points G - A PTS	Total Games	Age when first 100th point scored (Yrs. & Mos.)
Adam Oates	St. L.	29-3-90	(G)	Pit 4	at St. L. 5	79	79	23-79 — 102	80	27.7
Joe Sakic	Que.	31-3-90	(G)	Hfd. 3	at Que. 2	79	79	39-63 — 102	80	20.8
Ron Francis	Hfd.	31-3-90	(G)	Hfd. 3	at Que. 2	79	79	32-69 — 101	80	27.0
Luc Robitaille	L.A.	1-4-90	(A)	L.A. 4	at Cgy. 8	80	80	52-49 — 101	80	
Wayne Gretzky	L.A.	30-1-91	(A)	N.J. 4	at L.A. 2	50	51	41-122 — 163	78	
Brett Hull	St. L.	23-2-91	(G)	Bos. 2	at St. L. 9	60	62	86-45 — 131	78	
Mark Recchi	Pit.	5-3-91	(G)	Van. 1	at Pit. 4	66	67	40-73 — 113	78	23.1
Steve Yzerman	Det.	10-3-91	(G)	Det. 4	at St. L. 1	72	72	51-57 — 108	80	
John Cullen	Hfd.	16-3-91	(G)	N.J. 2	at Hfd. 6	71	71	39-71 — 110	78	26.7
Adam Oates	St. L.	17-3-91	(A)	St. L. 4	at Chi. 6	54	73	25-90 — 115	61	
Joe Sakic	Que.	19-3-91	(G)	Edm. 7	at Que. 6	74	74	48-61 — 109	80	
Steve Larmer	Chi.	24-3-91	(G)	Min. 4	at Chi. 5	76	76	44-57 — 101	80	29.9
Theoren Fleury	Cgy.	26-3-91	(G)	Van. 2	at Cgy. 7	77	77	51-53 — 104	79	22.9
Al MacInnis	Cgy.	28-3-91	(A)	Edm. 4	at Cgy. 4	78	78	28-75 — 103	78	27.8
Brett Hull	St. L.	2-3-92	(G)	St. L. 5	at Van. 3	66	66	70-39 — 109	73	
Wayne Gretzky	L.A.	3-3-92	(A)	Phi. 1	at L.A. 4	60	66	31-90 — 121	74	
Kevin Stevens	Pit.	7-3-92	(A)	Pit. 3	at L.A. 5	66	66	54-69 — 123	80	26.11
Mario Lemieux	Pit.	10-3-92	(A)	Cgy. 2	at Pit. 5	53	67	44-87 — 131	64	
Luc Robitaille	L.A.	17-3-92	(A)	Wpg. 4	at L.A. 5	73	73	44-63 — 107	80	
Mark Messier	NYR	22-3-92	(A)	N.J. 3	at NYR 6	74	75	35-72 — 107	79	
Jeremy Roenick	Chi.	29-3-92	(A)	Tor. 1	at Chi. 5	77	77	53-50 — 103	80	22.2
Steve Yzerman	Det.	14-4-92	(G)	Det. 7	at Min. 4	79	80	45-58 — 103	79	
Brian Leetch	NYR	16-4-92	(G)	Pit. 1	at NYR 7	80	80	22-80 — 102	80	24.1
Mario Lemieux	Pit.	31-12-92	(G)	Tor. 3	at Pit. 3	38	39	69-91 — 160	60	
Pat LaFontaine	Buf.	10-2-93	(A)	Buf. 6	at Wpg. 2	55	55	53-95 — 148	84	
Adam Oates	Bos.	14-2-93	(A)	Bos. 3	at T.B. 3	58	58	45-97 — 142	84	
Steve Yzerman	Det.	24-2-93	(A)	Det. 7	at Buf. 10	64	64	58-79 — 137	84	
Pierre Turgeon	NYI	28-2-93	(G)	NYI 7	at Hfd. 6	62	63	58-74 — 132	83	
Doug Gilmour	Tor.	3-3-93	(A)	Min. 1	at Tor. 3	64	64	32-95 — 127	83	
Alexander Mogilny	Buf.	5-3-93	(A)	Hfd. 4	at Buf. 2	58	65	76-51 — 127	77	24.1
Mark Recchi	Phi.	7-3-93	(G)	Phi. 3	at N.J. 7	66	66	53-70 — 123	84	
Teemu Selanne	Wpg.	9-3-93	(G)	Wpg. 4	at T.B. 2	68	68	76-56 — 132	84	22.7
Luc Robitaille	L.A.	15-3-93	(A)	L.A. 4	at Buf. 2	69	69	63-62 — 125	84	
Kevin Stevens	Pit.	23-3-93	(A)	S.J. 2	at Pit. 7	63	73	55-56 — 111	72	
Mats Sundin	Que.	27-3-93	(A)	Phi. 3	at Que. 8	71	75	47-67 — 114	80	22.1
Pavel Bure	Van.	1-4-93	(A)	Van. 5	at T.B. 3	77	77	60-50 — 110	83	22.0
Jeremy Roenick	Chi.	4-4-93	(G)	St. L. 4	at Chi. 5	79	79	50-57 — 107	84	
Craig Janney	St. L.	4-4-93	(A)	St. L. 4	at Chi. 5	79	79	24-82 — 106	84	25.7
Rick Tocchet	Pit.	7-4-93	(G)	Mtl. 3	at Pit. 4	77	81	48-61 — 109	80	28.11
Joe Sakic	Que.	8-4-93	(A)	Que. 2	at Bos. 6	75	81	48-57 — 105	78	
Ron Francis	Pit.	9-4-93	(A)	Pit. 10	at NYR 4	82	82	24-76 — 100	84	
Brett Hull	St. L.	11-4-93	(G)	Min. 1	at St. L. 5	78	82	54-47 — 101	80	
Theoren Fleury	Cgy.	11-4-93	(G)	Cgy. 3	at Van. 6	82	82	34-66 — 100	83	
Joe Juneau	Bos.	14-4-93	(A)	Bos. 4	at Ott. 2	84	84	32-70 — 102	84	25.3
Wayne Gretzky	L.A.	14-2-94	(A)	Bos. 3	at L.A. 2	56	56	38-92 — 130	81	
Sergei Fedorov	Det.	1-3-94	(A)	Cgy. 2	at Det. 5	63	63	56-64 — 120	82	24.2
Doug Gilmour	Tor.	23-3-94	(G)	Tor. 1	at Fla. 1	74	74	27-84 — 111	83	
Adma Oates	Bos.	26-3-94	(A)	Mtl. 3	at Bos. 6	68	75	32-80 — 112	77	
Mark Recchi	Phi.	27-3-94	(A)	Ana. 3	at Phi. 2	76	76	40-67 — 107	84	
Pavel Bure	Van.	28-3-94	(A)	Tor. 2	at Van. 3	68	76	60-47 — 107	76	
Brendan Shanahan	St.L.	12-4-94	(G)	St.L. 5	at Dal. 9	80	83	52-50 — 102	81	25.2
Mario Lemieux	Pit.	16-1-96	(G)	Col. 5	at Pit. 2	38	44	69-92 — 161	70	
Jaromir Jagr	Pit.	6-2-96	(G)	Bos. 5	at Pit. 6	52	52	62-87 — 149	82	23.12
Ron Francis	Pit.	9-3-96	(A)	N.J. 4	at Pit. 3	61	66	27-92 — 119	77	
Peter Forsberg	Col.	9-3-96	(A)	Col. 7	at Van. 5	68	68	30-86 — 116	82	22.7
Joe Sakic	Col.	17-3-96	(A)	Edm. 1	at Col. 8	70	70	51-69 — 120	82	
Teemu Selanne	Ana.	25-3-96	(A)	Ana. 1	at Det. 5	70	73	40-68 — 108	79	
Alexander Mogilny	Van.	25-3-96	(A)	L.A. 1	at Van. 4	72	75	55-52 — 107	79	
Eric Lindros	Phi.	25-3-96	(A)	Hfd. 0	at Phi. 3	65	73	47-68 — 115	73	23.0
Wayne Gretzky	St.L.	28-3-96	(A)	N.J. 4	at St.L. 4	76	75	23-79 — 102	80	
Doug Weight	Edm.	30-3-96	(G)	Tor. 4	at Edm. 3	76	76	25-79 — 104	82	25.3
Sergei Fedorov	Det.	2-4-96	(A)	Det. 3	at S.J. 6	72	76	39-68 — 107	78	
Paul Kariya	Ana.	7-4-96	(G)	Ana. 5	at S.J. 3	78	78	50-58 — 108	82	21.5
Mario Lemieux	Pit.	8-3-97	(A)	Phi. 2	at Pit. 3	61	65	50-72 — 122	76	
Teemu Selanne	Ana.	1-4-97	(A)	Chi. 3	at Ana. 3	74	78	51-58 — 109	78	

Washington's Peter Bondra puts the scissor hold on a perplexed Adam Graves of the New York Rangers only days before becoming the second Capital to record a five-goal game in a 6-3 win over Tampa Bay on February 5, 1994.

Five-or-more-Goal Games

Player	Team	Date	Score		Opposing Goaltender
SEVEN GOALS					
Joe Malone	Quebec Bulldogs	Jan. 31/20	Tor. 6	at Que. 10	Ivan Mitchell
SIX GOALS					
Newsy Lalonde	Montreal	Jan. 10/20	Tor. 7	at Mtl. 14	Ivan Mitchell
Joe Malone	Quebec Bulldogs	Mar. 10/20	Ott. 4	at Que. 10	Clint Benedict
Corb Denneny	Toronto St. Pats	Jan. 26/21	Ham. 3	at Tor. 10	Howard Lockhart
Cy Denneny	Ottawa Senators	Mar. 7/21	Ham. 5	at Ott. 12	Howard Lockhart
Syd Howe	Detroit	Feb. 3/44	NYR 2	at Det. 12	Ken McAuley
Red Berenson	St. Louis	Nov. 7/68	St. L. 8	at Phil 0	Doug Favell
Darryl Sittler	Toronto	Feb. 7/76	Bos. 4	at Tor. 11	Dave Reece
FIVE GOALS					
Joe Malone	Montreal	Dec. 19/17	Mtl. 7	at Ott. 4	Clint Benedict
Harry Hyland	Mtl. Wanderers	Dec. 19/17	Tor. 9	at Mtl. W. 10	Arthur Brooks
Joe Malone	Montreal	Jan. 12/18	Ott. 4	at Mtl. 9	Clint Benedict
Joe Malone	Montreal	Feb. 2/18	Tor. 2	at Mtl. 11	Harry Holmes
Mickey Roach	Toronto St. Pats	Mar. 6/20	Que. 2	at Tor. 11	Frank Brophy
Newsy Lalonde	Montreal	Feb. 16/21	Ham. 5	at Mtl. 10	Howard Lockhart
Babe Dye	Toronto St. Pats	Dec. 16/22	Mtl. 2	at Tor. 7	Georges Vezina
Redvers Green	Hamilton Tigers	Dec. 5/24	Ham. 10	at Tor. 3	John Roach
Babe Dye	Toronto St. Pats	Dec. 22/24	Tor. 10	at Bos. 1	Charlie Stewart
Harry Broadbent	Mtl. Maroons	Jan. 7/25	Mtl. 6	at Ham. 2	Vernon Forbes
Pit Lepine	Montreal	Dec. 14/29	Ott. 4	at Mtl. 6	Alex Connell
Howie Morenz	Montreal	Mar. 18/30	NYA 3	at Mtl. 8	Roy Worters
Charlie Conacher	Toronto	Jan. 19/32	NYA 3	at Tor. 11	Roy Worters
Ray Getliffe	Montreal	Feb. 6/43	Bos. 3	at Mtl. 8	Frank Brimsek
Maurice Richard	Montreal	Dec. 28/44	Det. 1	at Mtl. 9	Harry Lumley
Howie Meeker	Toronto	Jan. 8/47	Chi. 4	at Tor. 10	Paul Bibeault
Bernie Geoffrion	Montreal	Feb. 19/55	NYR 2	at Mtl. 10	Gump Worsley
Bobby Rousseau	Montreal	Feb. 1/64	Det. 3	at Mtl. 9	Roger Crozier
Yvan Cournoyer	Montreal	Feb. 15/75	Chi. 3	at Mtl. 12	Mike Veisor
Don Murdoch	NY Rangers	Oct. 12/76	NYR 10	at Min. 4	Gary Smith
Ian Turnbull	Toronto	Feb. 2/77	Det. 1	at Tor. 9	Ed Giacomin (2) / Jim Rutherford (3)
Bryan Trottier	NY Islanders	Dec. 23/78	NYR 4	at NYI 9	Wayne Thomas (4) / John Davidson (1)
Tim Young	Minnesota	Jan. 15/79	Min. 8	at NYR 1	Doug Soetaert (3) / Wayne Thomas (2)
John Tonelli	NY Islanders	Jan. 6/81	Tor. 3	at NYI 6	Jiri Crha (4) / empty net (1)
Wayne Gretzky	Edmonton	Feb. 18/81	St. L. 2	at Edm. 9	Mike Liut (3) / Ed Staniowski (2)
Wayne Gretzky	Edmonton	Dec. 30/81	Phi. 5	at Edm. 7	Pete Peeters (4) / empty net (1)
Grant Mulvey	Chicago	Feb. 3/82	St. L. 5	at Chi. 9	Mike Liut (4) / Gary Edwards (1)
Bryan Trottier	NY Islanders	Feb. 13/82	Phi. 2	at NYI 8	Pete Peeters
Willy Lindstrom	Winnipeg	Mar. 2/82	Wpg. 7	at Phi. 6	Pete Peeters
Mark Pavelich	NY Rangers	Feb. 23/83	Hfd. 3	at NYR 11	Greg Millen
Jari Kurri	Edmonton	Nov. 19/83	N.J. 4	at Edm. 13	Glenn Resch (3) / Ron Low (2)
Bengt Gustafsson	Washington	Jan. 8/84	Wsh. 7	at Phi. 1	Pelle Lindbergh
Pat Hughes	Edmonton	Feb. 3/84	Cgy. 5	at Edm. 10	Don Edwards (3) / Rejean Lemelin (2)
Wayne Gretzky	Edmonton	Dec. 15/84	Edm. 8	at St. L. 2	Rick Wamsley (4) / Mike Liut(1)
Dave Andreychuk	Buffalo	Feb. 6/86	Buf. 8	at Bos. 6	Pat Riggin (1) / Doug Keans (4)
Wayne Gretzky	Edmonton	Dec. 6/87	Min. 4	at Edm. 10	Don Beaupre (4) / Kari Takko (1)
Mario Lemieux	Pittsburgh	Dec. 31/88	N.J. 6	at Pit. 8	Bob Sauve (3) / Chris Terreri (2)
Joe Nieuwendyk	Calgary	Jan. 11/89	Wpg. 3	at Cgy. 8	Daniel Berthiaume
Mats Sundin	Quebec	Mar. 5/92	Que. 10	at Hfd. 4	Peter Sidorkiewicz (3) / Kay Whitmore (2)
Mario Lemieux	Pittsburgh	Apr. 9/93	Pit. 10	at NYR 4	Corey Hirsch (3) / Mike Richter (2)
Peter Bondra	Washington	Feb. 5/94	T.B. 3	at Wsh. 6	Darren Puppa (4) / Pat Jablonski (1)
Mike Ricci	Quebec	Feb. 17/94	Que. 8	at S.J. 2	Arturs Irbe (3) / Jimmy Waite (2)
Alexei Zhamnov	Winnipeg	Apr. 1/95	Wpg. 7	at L.A. 7	Kelly Hrudey (3) / Grant Fuhr (2)
Mario Lemieux	Pittsburgh	Mar. 26/96	St. L. 4	at Pit. 8	Grant Fuhr (1) / Jon Casey (4)
Sergei Fedorov	Detroit	Dec. 26/96	Wsh. 4	at Det. 5	Jim Carey

Players' 500th Goals

Regular Season

Player	Team	Date	Game No.		Score	Opposing Goaltender	Total Goals	Total Games
Maurice Richard	Montreal	Oct. 19/57	863	Chi. 1	at Mtl. 3	Glenn Hall	544	978
Gordie Howe	Detroit	Mar. 14/62	1,045	Det. 2	at NYR 3	Gump Worsley	801	1,767
Bobby Hull	Chicago	Feb. 21/70	861	NYR. 2	at Chi. 4	Ed Giacomin	610	1,063
Jean Béliveau	Montreal	Feb. 11/71	1,101	Min. 2	at Mtl. 6	Gilles Gilbert	507	1,125
Frank Mahovlich	Montreal	Mar. 21/73	1,105	Van. 2	at Mtl. 3	Dunc Wilson	533	1,181
Phil Esposito	Boston	Dec. 22/74	803	Det. 4	at Bos. 5	Jim Rutherford	717	1,282
John Bucyk	Boston	Oct. 30/75	1,370	St. L. 2	at Bos. 3	Yves Bélanger	556	1,540
Stan Mikita	Chicago	Feb. 27/77	1,221	Van. 4	at Chi. 3	Cesare Maniago	541	1,394
Marcel Dionne	Los Angeles	Dec. 14/82	887	L.A. 2	at Wsh. 7	Al Jensen	731	1,348
Guy Lafleur	Montreal	Dec. 20/83	918	Mtl. 6	at N.J. 0	Glenn Resch	560	1,126
Mike Bossy	NY Islanders	Jan. 2/86	647	Bos. 5	at NYI 7	empty net	573	752
Gilbert Perreault	Buffalo	Mar. 9/86	1,159	NJ 3	at Buf. 4	Alain Chevrier	512	1,191
*Wayne Gretzky	Edmonton	Nov. 22/86	575	Van. 2	at Edm. 5	empty net	862	1,335
Lanny McDonald	Calgary	Mar. 21/89	1,107	NYI 1	at Cgy. 4	Mark Fitzpatrick	500	1,111
Bryan Trottier	NY Islanders	Feb. 13/90	1,104	Cgy. 4	at NYI 2	Rick Wamsley	524	1,279
*Mike Gartner	NY Rangers	Oct. 14/91	936	Wsh. 5	at NYR 3	Mike Liut	696	1,372
Michel Goulet	Chicago	Feb. 16/92	951	Cgy. 5	at Chi. 5	Jeff Reese	548	1,089
*Jari Kurri	Los Angeles	Oct. 17/92	833	Bos. 6	at L.A. 8	empty net	596	1,181
*Dino Ciccarelli	Detroit	Jan. 8/94	946	Det. 6	at L.A. 3	Kelly Hrudey	586	1,156
Mario Lemieux	Pittsburgh	Oct. 26/95	605	Pit. 7	at NYI 5	Tommy Soderstrom	613	745
*Mark Messier	NY Rangers	Nov. 6/95	1,141	Cgy. 2	at NYR 4	Rick Tabaracci	575	1,272
*Steve Yzerman	Detroit	Jan. 17/96	906	Col. 2	at Det. 3	Patrick Roy	539	1,023
Dale Hawerchuk	St. Louis	Jan. 31/96	1,103	St. L. 4	at Tor. 0	Felix Potvin	518	1,188
*Brett Hull	St. Louis	Dec. 22/96	693	L.A. 4	at St. L. 7	Stephane Fiset	527	735
Joe Mullen	Pittsburgh	Mar. 14/97	1,052	Pit. 3	at Col. 6	Patrick Roy	502	1,062
*Dave Andreychuk	New Jersey	Mar. 15/97	1,070	Wsh. 2	at N.J. 3	Bill Ranford	503	1,083

*Active

Maurice Richard, who earned the title as the NHL's all-time leading goal-scorer on February 8, 1952, became the first NHL sniper to score 500 regular-season goals in the NHL when he put #500 past Glenn Hall on October 19, 1957.

Players' 1,000th Points

Regular Season

Player	Team	Date	Game No.	G or A	Score	Total Points G A PTS	Total Games
Gordie Howe	Detroit	Nov. 27/60	938	(A)	Tor. 0 at Det. 2	801-1,049–1,850	1,767
Jean Béliveau	Montreal	Mar. 3/68	911	(G)	Mtl. 2 at Det. 5	507-712–1,219	1,125
Alex Delvecchio	Detroit	Feb. 16/69	1,143	(A)	LA 3 at Det. 6	456-825–1,281	1,549
Bobby Hull	Chicago	Dec. 12/70	909	(A)	Minn. 3 at Chi. 5	610-560–1,170	1,063
Norm Ullman	Toronto	Oct. 16/71	1,113	(A)	NYR 5 at Tor. 3	490-739–1,229	1,410
Stan Mikita	Chicago	Oct. 15/72	924	(A)	St.L. 3 at Chi. 1	541-926–1,467	1,394
John Bucyk	Boston	Nov. 9/72	1,144	(G)	Det. 3 at Bos. 8	556-813–1,369	1,540
Frank Mahovlich	Montreal	Feb. 17/73	1,090	(A)	Phi. 7 at Mtl. 6	533-570–1,103	1,181
Henri Richard	Montreal	Dec. 20/73	1,194	(A)	Mtl. 2 at Buf. 2	358-688–1,046	1,256
Phil Esposito	Boston	Feb. 15/74	745	(A)	Bos. 4 at Van. 2	717-873–1,590	1,282
Rod Gilbert	NY Rangers	Feb. 19/77	1,027	(A)	NYR 2 at NYI 5	406-615–1,021	1,065
Jean Ratelle	Boston	Apr. 3/77	1,007	(A)	Tor. 4 at Bos. 7	491-776–1,267	1,281
Marcel Dionne	Los Angeles	Jan. 7/81	740	(G)	L.A. 5 at Hfd. 3	731-1,040–1,771	1,348
Guy Lafleur	Montreal	Mar. 4/81	720	(G)	Mtl. 9 at Wpg. 3	560-793–1,353	1,126
Bobby Clarke	Philadelphia	Mar. 19/81	922	(G)	Bos. 3 at Phi. 5	358-852–1,210	1,144
Gilbert Perreault	Buffalo	Apr. 3/82	871	(A)	Buf. 5 at Mtl.4	512-814–1,326	1,191
Darryl Sittler	Philadelphia	Jan. 20/83	927	(G)	Cgy 2 at Phi. 5	484-637–1,121	1,096
*Wayne Gretzky	Edmonton	Dec. 19/84	424	(A)	L.A. 3 at Edm. 7	862-1,843–2,705	1,335
Bryan Trottier	NY Islanders	Jan. 29/85	726	(A)	Min. 4 at NYI 4	524-901–1,425	1,279
Mike Bossy	NY Islanders	Jan. 24/86	656	(A)	NYI 7 at Wsh. 5	573-553–1,126	752
Denis Potvin	NY Islanders	Apr. 4/87	987	(G)	Buf. 6 at NYI 6	310-742–1,052	1,060
Bernie Federko	St. Louis	Mar 19/88	855	(A)	Hfd. 5 at St.L. 3	369-761–1,130	1,000
Lanny McDonald	Calgary	Mar. 7/89	1,101	(G)	Wpg. 5 at Cgy. 9	500-506–1,006	1,111
Peter Stastny	Quebec	Oct. 19/89	682	(G)	Que. 5 at Chi. 3	450-789–1,239	977
*Jari Kurri	Edmonton	Jan. 2/90	716	(A)	Edm. 6 at St.L. 4	596-780–1,376	1,181
Denis Savard	Chicago	Mar. 11/90	727	(A)	St.L. 6 at Chi. 4	473-865–1,338	1,196
*Paul Coffey	Pittsburgh	Dec. 22/90	770	(A)	Pit. 4 at NYI 3	381-1,063–1,444	1,211
*Mark Messier	Edmonton	Jan. 13/91	822	(A)	Edm. 5 at Phi. 3	575-977–1,552	1,272
Dave Taylor	Los Angeles	Feb. 5/91	930	(A)	L.A. 3 at Phi. 2	431-638–1,069	1,111
Michel Goulet	Chicago	Feb. 23/91	878	(G)	Chi. 3 at Min. 3	548-604–1,152	1,089
Dale Hawerchuk	Buffalo	Mar. 8/91	781	(G)	Chi. 5 at Buf. 3	518-891–1,409	1,188
Bobby Smith	Minnesota	Nov. 30/91	986	(A)	Min. 4 at Tor. 3	357-679–1,036	1,077
*Mike Gartner	NY Rangers	Jan. 4/92	971	(A)	NYR 4 at N.J. 6	696-612–1,308	1,372
*Ray Bourque	Boston	Feb. 29/92	933	(A)	Wsh. 5 at Bos. 5	362-1,001–1,363	1,290
Mario Lemieux	Pittsburgh	Mar. 24/92	513	(A)	Pit. 3 at Det. 4	613-881–1,494	745
Glenn Anderson	Toronto	Feb. 22/93	954	(G)	Tor. 8 at Van. 1	498-601–1,099	1,129
*Steve Yzerman	Detroit	Feb. 24/93	737	(A)	Det. 7 at Buf. 10	539-801–1,340	1,023
*Ron Francis	Pittsburgh	Oct. 28/93	893	(G)	Que. 7 at Pit. 3	403-944–1,347	1,166
*Bernie Nicholls	New Jersey	Feb. 13/94	858	(G)	N.J. 3 at T.B. 3	469-710–1,179	1,057
*Dino Ciccarelli	Detroit	Mar. 9/94	957	(G)	Det. 5 at Cgy. 1	586-574–1,160	1,156
Brian Propp	Hartford	Mar. 19/94	1,008	(G)	Hfd. 5 at Phi. 3	425-579–1,004	1,016
Joe Mullen	Pittsburgh	Feb. 7/95	935	(A)	Fla. 3 at Pit. 7	502-561–1,063	1,062
Steve Larmer	NY Rangers	Mar. 8/95	983	(A)	N.J. 4 at NYR 6	441-571–1,012	1,006
*Doug Gilmour	Toronto	Dec. 23/95	935	(A)	Edm. 1 at Tor. 6	368-755–1,123	1,062
*Larry Murphy	Toronto	Mar. 27/96	1,228	(G)	Tor. 6 at Van. 2	254-797–1,051	1,315
*Dave Andreychuk	New Jersey	Apr. 7/96	998	(G)	NYR 2 at N.J. 4	503-561–1,064	1,083

*Active

Hall of Fame center Norm Ullman recorded 1,229 points during his 20-year career.

Larry Murphy became only the fourth defenseman to reach the 1000-point milestone when he scored against the Vancouver Canucks on March 27, 1996.

Individual Awards

Hart Memorial Trophy

Art Ross Trophy

Calder Memorial Trophy

James Norris Memorial Trophy

HART MEMORIAL TROPHY

An annual award "to the player adjudged to be the most valuable to his team". Winner selected in poll by Professional Hockey Writers' Association in the 26 NHL cities at the end of the regular schedule. The winner receives $10,000 and the runners-up $6,000 and $4,000.

History: The Hart Memorial Trophy was presented by the National Hockey League in 1960 after the original Hart Trophy was retired to the Hockey Hall of Fame. The original Hart Trophy was donated to the NHL in 1923 by Dr. David A. Hart, father of Cecil Hart, former manager-coach of the Montreal Canadiens.

1996-97 Winner: **Dominik Hasek, Buffalo Sabres**
Runners-up: **Paul Kariya, Mighty Ducks of Anaheim**
                    Mario Lemieux, Pittsburgh Penguins

Goaltender Dominik Hasek of the Buffalo Sabres captured the Hart Memorial Trophy, awarded annually "to the player adjudged to be the most valuable to his team." Hasek was a top five selection on 53 of 54 ballots, attracting 50 first place votes and 519 total points. Hasek becomes the first goaltender to win the Hart Trophy since Montreal's Jacques Plante in 1962. Hasek, who also captured the Vezina Trophy as the NHL's top goaltender, was the only double winner in 1996-97.

Hasek led the NHL in save percentage for the third consecutive year in 1996-97, stopping 93% of the shots he faced. In addition, Hasek was tied for second in the League with 37 wins (37-20-10); finished fourth overall in goals-against average (2.27); and posted ten shutouts. His 37 wins accounted for 92.5% (37 of 40) of the Sabres' wins this season.

ART ROSS TROPHY

An annual award "to the player who leads the league in scoring points at the end of the regular season." The winner receives $10,000 and the runners-up $6,000 and $4,000.

History: Arthur Howie Ross, former manager-coach of Boston Bruins, presented the trophy to the National Hockey League in 1947. If two players finish the schedule with the same number of points, the trophy is awarded in the following manner: 1. Player with most goals. 2. Player with fewer games played. 3. Player scoring first goal of the season.

1996-97 Winner: **Mario Lemieux, Pittsburgh Penguins**
Runners-up: **Teemu Selanne, Mighty Ducks of Anaheim**
                    Paul Kariya, Mighty Ducks of Anaheim

Center Mario Lemieux of the Pittsburgh Penguins received his sixth career Art Ross Trophy in 1997.

Playing in his final NHL season, Lemieux recorded 122 points (50-72-122) to win the Art Ross Trophy for the second straight season. Lemieux played in 76 games in 1996-97, averaging 1.6 points per game. His 50 goals placed him tied for third in the League and his 72 assists tied him with the New York Rangers Wayne Gretzky for the most in the NHL. Lemieux, who earned his six Art Ross Trophies over the last nine years, becomes just the third player in NHL history to win the Art Ross Trophy six times, joining Wayne Gretzky (10 times) and Gordie Howe (six).

CALDER MEMORIAL TROPHY

An annual award "to the player selected as the most proficient in his first year of competition in the National Hockey League." Winner selected in poll by Professional Hockey Writers' Association at the end of the regular schedule. The winner receives $10,000 and the runners-up $6,000 and $4,000.

History: From 1936-37 until his death in 1943, Frank Calder, NHL President, bought a trophy each year to be given permanently to the outstanding rookie. After Calder's death, the NHL presented the Calder Memorial Trophy in his memory and the trophy is to be kept in perpetuity. To be eligible for the award, a player cannot have played more than 25 games in any single preceding season nor in six or more games in each of any two preceding seasons in any major professional league. Beginning in 1990-91, to be eligible for this award a player must not have attained his twenty-sixth birthday by September 15th of the season in which he is eligible.

1996-97 Winner: **Bryan Berard, New York Islanders**
Runners-up: **Jarome Iginla, Calgary Flames**
                    Jim Campbell, St. Louis Blues

Defenseman Bryan Berard of the New York Islanders was selected as the winner of the Calder Memorial Trophy, awarded "to the player selected as the most proficient in his first year of competition in the National Hockey League." Berard was a top-five selection on all 54 ballots and polled 501 points, ahead of Calgary Flames right wing Jarome Iginla (second, 372 points). Berard is the first defenseman to win the Calder Trophy since Brian Leetch of the New York Rangers earned rookie of the year honors in 1989 and the first Islanders player to win it since Mike Bossy in 1978.

Berard led all rookie defensemen and all Islanders defensemen with 48 points (8-40-48) in 82 games. He finished second in rookie scoring and was one of two Islanders players to play all 82 games. He was Ottawa's first choice, first overall, in the 1995 Entry Draft and was obtained by the Islanders via trade on Jan. 23, 1995.

JAMES NORRIS MEMORIAL TROPHY

An annual award "to the defense player who demonstrates throughout the season the greatest all-round ability in the position." Winner selected in poll by Professional Hockey Writers' Association at the end of the regular schedule. The winner receives $10,000 and the runners-up $6,000 and $4,000.

History: The James Norris Memorial Trophy was presented in 1953 by the four children of the late James Norris in memory of the former owner-president of the Detroit Red Wings.

1996-97 Winner: **Brian Leetch, New York Rangers**
Runners-up: **Vladimir Konstantinov, Detroit Red Wings**
                    Sandis Ozolinsh, Colorado Avalanche

Leetch was named on all 54 ballots, including 42 first-place votes, and earned 494 points in finishing ahead of second-place Vladimir Konstantinov of the Detroit Red Wings. Konstantinov was named on 36 of the 54 ballots and polled 178 points to finish on top of an extremely close four-man race for second, ahead of Colorado's Sandis Ozolinsh (176 points), Chicago's Chris Chelios (172) and New Jersey's Scott Stevens (171).

Leetch appeared in all 82 Rangers games this season and led all NHL defensemen in scoring with 78 points (20-58-78). The 1996-97 campaign was the fourth consecutive season in which he did not miss a game (84 games played in 1993-94, 48 games played in 1994-95 and 82 in 1995-96). Leetch finished third to Wayne Gretzky and Mark Messier in team scoring and led all Rangers in plus-minus with a plus-31 rating.

Vezina Trophy

Lady Byng Memorial Trophy

Frank J. Selke Trophy

Conn Smythe Trophy

VEZINA TROPHY

An annual award "to the goalkeeper adjudged to be the best at his position" as voted by the general managers of each of the 26 clubs. Over-all winner receives $10,000, runners-up $6,000 and $4,000.

History: Leo Dandurand, Louis Letourneau and Joe Cattarinich, former owners of the Montreal Canadiens, presented the trophy to the National Hockey League in 1926-27 in memory of Georges Vezina, outstanding goalkeeper of the Canadiens who collapsed during an NHL game on November 28, 1925, and died of tuberculosis a few months later. Until the 1981-82 season, the goalkeeper(s) of the team allowing the fewest number of goals during the regular-season were awarded the Vezina Trophy.

1996-97 Winner: **Dominik Hasek, Buffalo Sabres**
Runners-up: **Martin Brodeur, New Jersey Devils**
                Patrick Roy, Colorado Avalanche

Hasek was a runaway winner in this year's balloting, having been named on all 26 ballots and receiving 22 of 26 first place votes for a total of 120 points, ahead of second-place Martin Brodeur of the New Jersey Devils. Brodeur earned votes on 25 of 26 ballots, including three first-place votes, and finished with 73 points, well ahead of third-place Patrick Roy of the Colorado Avalanche (25 points).

Hasek led the NHL in save percentage for the third consecutive year, stopping 93.0% of the shots he faced. In addition, Hasek was tied for second in the League with 37 wins (37-20-10); finished fourth overall in goals-against average (2.27); and posted five shutouts. His 37 wins accounted for 92.5% (37 of 40) of the Sabres' wins this past season.

Hasek becomes the second three-time winner of the Vezina Trophy since the current criteria for the award were established in 1981-82, joining Patrick Roy. Hasek and Roy are the only two active goaltenders with three career Vezina Trophy wins.

CONN SMYTHE TROPHY

An annual award "to the most valuable player for his team in the playoffs." Winner selected by the Professional Hockey Writers' Association at the conclusion of the final game in the Stanley Cup Finals. The winner receives $10,000.

History: Presented by Maple Leaf Gardens Limited in 1964 to honor Conn Smythe, the former coach, manager, president and owner-governor of the Toronto Maple Leafs.

1996-97 Winner: **Mike Vernon, Detroit Red Wings**

Vernon's superb play in goal contributed to the Detroit Red Wings' 1997 Stanley Cup championship. Vernon registered 16 wins in 20 playoff games, allowed only 36 goals against and posted a goals-against average of 1.76.

LADY BYNG MEMORIAL TROPHY

An annual award "to the player adjudged to have exhibited the best type of sportsmanship and gentlemanly conduct combined with a high standard of playing ability." Winner selected by poll by Professional Hockey Writers' Association at the end of the regular schedule. The winner receives $10,000 and the runners-up $6,000 and $4,000.

History: Lady Byng, wife of Canada's Governor-General at the time, presented the Lady Byng Trophy in 1925. After Frank Boucher of New York Rangers won the award seven times in eight seasons, he was given the trophy to keep and Lady Byng donated another trophy in 1936. After Lady Byng's death in 1949, the National Hockey League presented a new trophy, changing the name to Lady Byng Memorial Trophy.

1996-97 Winner: **Paul Kariya, Mighty Ducks of Anaheim**
Runners-up: **Teemu Selanne, Mighty Ducks of Anaheim**
                Adam Oates, Boston, Washington

Kariya was named on 53 of the 54 ballots and received 492 points to easily outdistance Anaheim teammate Teemu Selanne, who finished second with 119 points. Kariya and Selanne become just the second set of teammates to finish 1-2 in Lady Byng voting since the award was first presented in 1925, following Toronto's Syl Apps and Gord Drillon in 1942. Kariya recorded 99 points (44-55-99) in 69 games this season, third among NHL scorers, and accumulated just six penalty minutes.

FRANK J. SELKE TROPHY

An annual award "to the forward who best excels in the defensive aspects of the game." Winner selected in poll by Professional Hockey Writers' Association at the end of the regular schedule. The winner receives $10,000 and the runners-up $6,000 and $4,000.

History: Presented to the National Hockey League in 1977 by the Board of Governors of the NHL in honour of Frank J. Selke, one of the great architects of NHL championship teams.

1996-97 Winner: **Michael Peca, Buffalo Sabres**
Runners-up: **Peter Forsberg, Colorado Avalanche**
                Jere Lehtinen, Dallas Stars

Peca received 284 points and was named on 40 of 54 ballots to finish well ahead of fellow first-time Selke nominees Peter Forsberg of the Colorado Avalanche (141 points) and Jere Lehtinen of the Dallas Stars (118 points).

In addition to leading all NHL players with six shorthanded goals, Peca finished the regular season as the leading plus-minus performer on the Sabres with a rating of +26. He posted 49 points (20-29-49) in 79 games, career highs in all categories, finishing fourth among Sabres in scoring. Peca becomes the first Buffalo player to win the Selke Trophy since Craig Ramsay in 1985.

WILLIAM M. JENNINGS TROPHY

An annual award "to the goalkeeper(s) having played a minimum of 25 games for the team with the fewest goals scored against it." Winners selected on regular-season play. Overall winner receives $10,000, runners-up $6,000 and $4,000.

History: The Jennings Trophy was presented in 1981-82 by the National Hockey League's Board of Governors to honor the late William M. Jennings, longtime governor and president of the New York Rangers and one of the great builders of hockey in the United States.

1996-97 Winner: **Martin Brodeur, Mike Dunham, New Jersey Devils**
Runners-up: **Chris Osgood, Mike Vernon, Detroit Red Wings**
                Andy Moog, Arturs Irbe, Dallas Stars

Brodeur and Dunham are the first netminders in Devils franchise history to capture the award, backstopping New Jersey to the League's top defensive record. The club allowed just 182 goals during the regular season, or 2.22 per game. The duo combined for 13 shutouts and 45 wins, leading New Jersey to its first ever Eastern Conference regular season title. Brodeur led the League with a 1.88 goals-against average and 10 shutouts. Dunham completed his first NHL season with a record of 8-7-1 and a 2.55 goals-against average, including two shutouts. Brodeur appeared in 67 games this season, with Dunham playing in 26.

LESTER B. PEARSON AWARD

An annual award presented to the NHL's outstanding player as selected by the members of the National Hockey League Players' Association. The winner receives $10,000.

History: The award was presented in 1970-71 by the NHLPA in honor of the late Lester B. Pearson, former Prime Minister of Canada.

1996-97 Winner: **Dominik Hasek, Buffalo Sabres**

Hasek backstopped the young Buffalo Sabres to a winning record in 1996-97. He led the NHL in save percentage (.930) and yielded just 153 goals against in 67 games played.

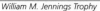

| William M. Jennings Trophy | Jack Adams Award | Bill Masterton Trophy | Lester Patrick Trophy | Lester B. Pearson Award |

JACK ADAMS AWARD

An annual award presented by the National Hockey League Broadcasters' Association to "the NHL coach adjudged to have contributed the most to his team's success." Winner selected by poll among members of the NHL Broadcasters' Association at the end of the regular season. The winner receives $1,000 from the NHLBA.

History: The award was presented by the NHL Broadcasters' Association in 1974 to commemorate the late Jack Adams, coach and general manager of the Detroit Red Wings, whose lifetime dedication to hockey serves as an inspiration to all who aspire to further the game.

1996-97 Winner: **Ted Nolan, Buffalo Sabres**
Runners-up: Ken Hitchcock, Dallas Stars
         Jacques Martin, Ottawa Senators

Nolan polled 39 of a possible 87 first place votes and 307 points overall, narrowly edging Dallas Stars head coach Ken Hitchcock, who finished with 300 points including 38 first place votes. It marked the closest race for the Jack Adams Award since Winnipeg's Bob Murdoch captured the trophy by a mere five points over Boston's Mike Milbury in 1990.

In just his second season behind the Buffalo Sabres bench, Nolan led the club to the Northeast Division title, earning a Stanley Cup playoff berth after a one-year absence. Buffalo posted a 40-30-12 record for 92 points en route to its first division title since the 1980-81 season. The Sabres finished the 1996-97 campaign with a 19-point improvement over 1995-96.

Nolan becomes the first head coach in Sabres history to capture the Jack Adams Award. The only previous Sabres coach to finish as high as second in Adams balloting was Scott Bowman, who was runner-up to Washington's Bryan Murray in 1984.

BILL MASTERTON MEMORIAL TROPHY

An annual award under the trusteeship of the Professional Hockey Writers' Association to "the National Hockey League player who best exemplifies the qualities of perseverance, sportsmanship and dedication to hockey." Winner selected by poll among the 26 chapters of the PHWA at the end of the regular season. A $2,500 grant from the PHWA is awarded annually to the Bill Masterton Scholarship Fund, based in Bloomington, MN, in the name of the Masterton Trophy winner.

History: The trophy was presented by the NHL Writers' Association in 1968 to commemorate the late William Masterton, a player of the Minnesota North Stars, who exhibited to a high degree the qualities of perseverance, sportsmanship and dedication to hockey, and who died January 15, 1968.

1996-97 Winner: **Tony Granato, San Jose Sharks**
Runners-up;   Sheldon Kennedy, Boston Bruins
         Joe Mullen, Pittsburgh Penguins

Only six months after having brain surgery to remove an abnormal collection of blood vessels in February, 1996, Granato signed with the San Jose Sharks for the 1996-97 season, his ninth in the NHL. He made an unforgettable return, skating in the Sharks' opening-night lineup on Oct. 5 before tallying a hat-trick and adding an assist in just his second game of the season at Los Angeles on Oct. 6.

Granato enjoyed an outstanding season with the Sharks, earning regular spots on the power play and penalty killing units, and concluded the year fifth on the team in scoring with 40 points (25-15-40) in 76 games played. Recognized as a popular player and outstanding role model for his younger teammates, Granato was named an alternate captain by head coach Al Sims. In recognition of his comeback, Granato was named as a Commissioner's Selection to participate in the 1997 NHL All-Star Game at San Jose Arena.

LESTER PATRICK TROPHY

An annual award "for outstanding service to hockey in the United States." Eligible recipients are players, officials, coaches, executives and referees. Winner selected by an award committee consisting of the President of the NHL, an NHL Governor, a representative of the New York Rangers, a member of the Hockey Hall of Fame Builder's section, a member of the Hockey Hall of Fame Player's section, a member of the U.S. Hockey Hall of Fame, a member of the NHL Broadcasters' Association and a member of the Professional Hockey Writers' Association. Each except the League President is rotated annually. The winner receives a miniature of the trophy.

History: Presented by the New York Rangers in 1966 to honor the late Lester Patrick, longtime general manager and coach of the New York Rangers, whose teams finished out of the playoffs only once in his first 16 years with the club.

1996-97 Winners: **Seymour H. Knox III**
         Bill Cleary
         Pat LaFontaine

Seymour H. Knox III, who passed away on May 22, 1996 was one of the most respected builders and leaders the National Hockey League has ever known. He and his brother Northrup brought NHL hockey to Buffalo in 1970 and successfully guided the franchise over the next quarter of a century.

Mr. Knox served the Sabres as their first chairman and president and represented the team on the NHL Board of Governors from its inception until his death. He was also a driving force behind the construction of the Sabres new home, Marine Midland Arena. The rink was formally dedicated to the Knox brothers upon its opening in September of 1996.

Mr. Knox was a long-time supporter of civic, philanthropic and charitable causes in the Greater Buffalo area. He was inducted into the Hockey Hall of Fame as a builder in November of 1993.

Bill Cleary, one of the most storied names in the history of United States hockey, is currently the director of athletics at Harvard University, following an outstanding playing and coaching career there. Clearly is the winningest coach in Harvard history and the winner of two ECAC championships, four Beanpot championships and 11 Ivy League titles. As a player, he also set Harvard records for most points in a single season (89) and most goals in one season (42).

Cleary was also a member of the famed 1960 United States Olympic Team that won the gold medal at Squaw Valley, CA. He is a member of the United States Hockey Hall of Fame.

LaFontaine, a native of St. Louis, MO, has amassed 951 points (445 goals, 506 assists) in 798 career games. He won the NHL's Bill Masterton Trophy in 1995 for perseverance, sportsmanship and dedication to hockey and has played in five NHL All-Star Games. At the international level he represented the United States in the 1984 Winter Olympics in Sarajevo and in the inaugural World Cup of Hockey last September.

Off the ice, LaFontaine has long been known as an enthusiastic benefactor of charitable causes in the local community. His tireless efforts, particularly with youngsters, have long been saluted both on Long Island and in Buffalo.

Mr. Knox and Mr. LaFontaine become the first members of the Sabres organization to win the Lester Patrick Award. Two players from 1980 United States Olympic Hockey Team, whose members captured the award in 1980 — Mike Ramsey and Rob McClanahan — became Sabres later in their career.

King Clancy Memorial Trophy

KING CLANCY MEMORIAL TROPHY

An annual award "to the player who best exemplifies leadership qualities on and off the ice and has made a noteworthy humanitarian contribution in his community."

History: The King Clancy Memorial Trophy was presented to the National Hockey League by the Board of Governors in 1988 to honor the late Frank "King" Clancy.

1996-97 Winner: **Trevor Linden, Vancouver Canucks**

Vancouver Canucks right wing Trevor Linden is the 1996-97 recipient of the King Clancy Trophy, awarded "to the player who best exemplifies leadership on and off the ice and who has made a noteworthy humanitarian contribution to his community."

Linden is well-known as a leader on the ice and in the dressing room, having served as the Canucks' captain since the 1991-92 season. He has also played a leading role in the Greater Vancouver community, particularly with children's charitable causes.

Linden's "Captain's Crew" program, in its second year of operation, gives children who would not otherwise have the chance the opportunity to attend an NHL game. Developed and funded by Linden, 16 children attend each Canucks game from a private suite at General Motors Place as Linden's guests. He later meets the group post-game.

Linden also acts as honourary spokesperson and is a regular visitor at Canuck Place, a hospice for terminally ill children; provides financial support, fundraising assistance and makes special unannounced visits at Ronald McDonald House; acts as a spokesperson and role model in the Youth Against Violence Program in British Columbia; supports the Canadian Cancer Society through fundraising and visits to the cancer ward at BC Children's Hospital; and sponsors several needy families at Christmas.

Linden recently received the Gillette World Champion Award, presented to the Canadian athlete demonstrating athletic excellence, sportsmanship, and humanitarian contributions as selected by a poll of over 100 Canadian journalists.

Bud Ice Plus-Minus Award

BUD ICE PLUS-MINUS AWARD

An annual award "to the player, having played a minimum of 60 games (34 games in 1994-95), who leads the League in plus/minus statistics" at the end of the regular season. Bud Ice will contribute $5,000 on behalf of the winner to the charity of his choice.

History: The award was presented to the NHL in 1996-97 by Bud Ice to recognize the League leader in plus-minus statistics. Plus-minus statistics are calculated by giving a player a "plus" when on-ice for an even-strength or shorthand goal scored by his team. He receives a "minus" when on-ice for an even-strength or shorthand goal scored by the opposing team. A plus-minus award has been presented since the 1982-83 season.

1996-97 Winner: **John LeClair, Philadelphia Flyers**

Philadelphia left wing John LeClair was the NHL's leader in +/- in 1996-97 with a total of +44 in 82 games played. The second highest +/- figure belonged to Dallas' Mike Modano who finished with a rating of +43. Tied for third were Vladimir Konstantinov of Detroit and Dave Andreychuk of New Jersey who each had a rating of +38.

Team Award

PRESIDENTS' TROPHY

An annual award to the club finishing the regular-season with the best overall record. The winner receives $200,000, to be split evenly between the team and its players.

History: Presented to the National Hockey League in 1985-86 by the NHL Board of Governors to recognize the team compiling the top regular-season record.

1996-97 Winner: **Colorado Avalanche**
Runners-up: Dallas Stars
New Jersey Devils

The Colorado Avalanche won their first Presidents' Trophy in 1996-97, compiling the NHL's best regular-season record of 49-24-9 for 107 points.

The Dallas Stars finished second with a 48-26-8 record for 104 points while the New Jersey Devils had the third-best regular-season mark with a record of 45-23-14 for 104 points.

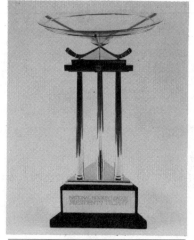

Presidents' Trophy

PRESIDENTS' TROPHY

	Winner	Runner-up
1997	Colorado Avalanche	Dallas Stars
1996	Detroit Red Wings	Colorado Avalanche
1995	Detroit Red Wings	Quebec Nordiques
1994	New York Rangers	New Jersey Devils
1993	Pittsburgh Penguins	Boston Bruins
1992	New York Rangers	Washington Capitals
1991	Chicago Blackhawks	St. Louis Blues
1990	Boston Bruins	Calgary Flames
1989	Calgary Flames	Montreal Canadiens
1988	Calgary Flames	Montreal Canadiens
1987	Edmonton Oilers	Philadelphia Flyers
1986	Edmonton Oilers	Philadelphia Flyers

MasterCard Cutting Edge Play of the Year

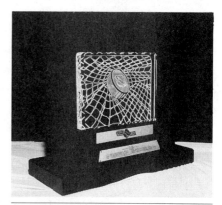

Duracell/NHL PowerPlay Award

MASTERCARD CUTTING EDGE PLAY OF THE YEAR

An acrobatic, 360-degree spinning goal by Valeri Kamensky of the Colorado Avalanche was named the MasterCard Cutting Edge Play of the Year. The award was chosen by NHL fans.

1996-97 Winner: **Goal by Valeri Kamensky, Colorado Avalanche**

In the winning play, Kamensky charged the net against the Florida Panthers to receive a centering pass from teammate Alexei Gusarov. As Gusarov's pass went behind Kamensky, Kamensky leapt into the air from one skate for a 360-degree spin. While in mid-air, Kamensky backhanded the puck past Panther goaltender John Vanbiesbrouck for a goal and the MasterCard Cutting Edge Play of the Year.

DURACELL/NHL POWERPLAY AWARD

A monthly and annual award "to the NHL team with the best monthly and yearly power play percentage." From October 1996 to April 1997, the Duracell PowerPlay Award recognized the team that displayed League-wide superiority on the power play, as calculated by dividing the number of power play goals a club scored by the number of power play opportunities it had. In addition to a monthly on-ice trophy presentation, Duracell contributed $1,000 to the winning team's charity of choice. The New York Rangers posted the best power play percentage for the 1996-97 regular season, winning the year-end Duracell/NHL PowerPlay Award. Duracell made a $3,000 contribution on behalf of the New York Rangers' charity of choice.

The 1996-97 Duracell/NHL PowerPlay Award winners are as follows:

Month	Winning Team	Power Play %
October	New York Rangers	30.6%
November	Pittsburgh Penguins	28.3%
December	Ottawa Senators	26.7%
January	Colorado Avalanche	27.5%
February	Detroit Red Wings	30.4%
March	Mighty Ducks of Anaheim	28.0%
April	New York Rangers	28.6%
Year-End	New York Rangers	22.0%

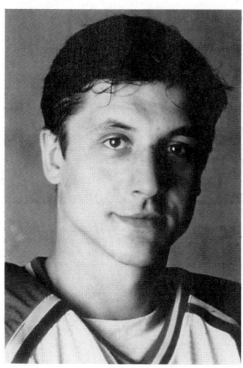

Valeri Kamensky's MasterCard Cutting Edge Play of the Year was just one of many highlight-reel goals scored by Colorado's gifted left winger. He first caught the attention of North American fans – and scored an equally brilliant goal – during Rendez-Vous 87, a two game series between the NHL All-Stars and the Soviet National Team held in Quebec City. in February of 1987.

NHL AWARD MONEY BREAKDOWN — 1996-97

(Players on each club determine how team award money is divided. All award monies are in U.S. funds.)

TEAM AWARDS

Stanley Cup Playoffs	Number of Clubs	Share Per Club	Total
Conference Quarter-Final Losers	8	$ 175,000	$1,400,000
Conference Semi-Final Losers	4	350,000	1,400,000
Conference Championship Losers	2	675,000	1,350,000
Stanley Cup Loser	1	1,075,000	1,075,000
Stanley Cup Winners	1	1,750,000	1,750,000
TOTAL PLAYOFF AWARD MONEY			$6,975,000

Final Standings, Regular Season	Number of Clubs	Share Per Club	Total
Presidents' Trophy			
Club's Share	1	$ 100,000	$ 100,000
Players' Share	1	250,000	250,000
Division Winners	4	425,000	1,700,000
Division Second Place	4	200,000	800,000
TOTAL REGULAR-SEASON AWARD MONEY			$2,850,000

INDIVIDUAL AWARDS	Winner	First Runner-up	Second Runner-up
Hart, Calder, Norris, Ross, Vezina, Byng, Selke, Jennings, Masterton Trophies	$10,000	$6,000	$4,000
King Clancy Trophy	$ 3,000	$1,000	
Conn Smythe Trophy	$10,000		
TOTAL INDIVIDUAL AWARD MONEY			$194,000

ALL-STARS	Number of winners	Per Player	Total
First Team All-Stars	6	$10,000	$ 60,000
Second Team All-Stars	6	5,000	$ 30,000
All-Star Game Winners			$250,000
TOTAL ALL-STAR AWARD MONEY			$340,000
TOTAL ALL AWARDS			**$10,359,000**

NATIONAL HOCKEY LEAGUE INDIVIDUAL AWARD WINNERS

ART ROSS TROPHY

	Winner	Runner-up
1997	Mario Lemieux, Pit.	Teemu Selanne, Ana.
1996	Mario Lemieux, Pit.	Jaromir Jagr, Pit.
1995	Jaromir Jagr, Pit.	Eric Lindros, Phi.
1994	Wayne Gretzky, L.A.	Sergei Fedorov, Det.
1993	Mario Lemieux, Pit.	Pat LaFontaine, Buf.
1992	Mario Lemieux, Pit.	Kevin Stevens, Pit.
1991	Wayne Gretzky, L.A.	Brett Hull, St.L.
1990	Wayne Gretzky, L.A.	Mark Messier, Edm.
1989	Mario Lemieux, Pit.	Wayne Gretzky, L.A.
1988	Mario Lemieux, Pit.	Wayne Gretzky, Edm.
1987	Wayne Gretzky, Edm.	Jari Kurri, Edm.
1986	Wayne Gretzky, Edm.	Mario Lemieux, Pit.
1985	Wayne Gretzky, Edm.	Jari Kurri, Edm.
1984	Wayne Gretzky, Edm.	Paul Coffey, Edm.
1983	Wayne Gretzky, Edm.	Peter Stastny, Que.
1982	Wayne Gretzky, Edm.	Mike Bossy, NYI
1981	Wayne Gretzky, Edm.	Marcel Dionne, L.A.
1980	Marcel Dionne, L.A.	Wayne Gretzky, Edm.
1979	Bryan Trottier, NYI	Marcel Dionne, L.A.
1978	Guy Lafleur, Mtl.	Bryan Trottier, NYI
1977	Guy Lafleur, Mtl.	Marcel Dionne, L.A.
1976	Guy Lafleur, Mtl.	Bobby Clarke, Phi.
1975	Bobby Orr, Bos.	Phil Esposito, Bos.
1974	Phil Esposito, Bos.	Bobby Orr, Bos.
1973	Phil Esposito, Bos.	Bobby Clarke, Phi.
1972	Phil Esposito, Bos.	Bobby Orr, Bos.
1971	Phil Esposito, Bos.	Bobby Orr, Bos.
1970	Bobby Orr, Bos.	Phil Esposito, Bos.
1969	Phil Esposito, Bos.	Bobby Hull, Chi.
1968	Stan Mikita, Chi.	Phil Esposito, Bos.
1967	Stan Mikita, Chi.	Bobby Hull, Chi.
1966	Bobby Hull, Chi.	Stan Mikita, Chi.
1965	Stan Mikita, Chi.	Norm Ullman, Det.
1964	Stan Mikita, Chi.	Bobby Hull, Chi.
1963	Gordie Howe, Det.	Andy Bathgate, NYR
1962	Bobby Hull, Chi.	Andy Bathgate, NYR
1961	Bernie Geoffrion, Mtl.	Jean Beliveau, Mtl.
1960	Bobby Hull, Chi.	Bronco Horvath, Bos.
1959	Dickie Moore, Mtl.	Jean Beliveau, Mtl.
1958	Dickie Moore, Mtl.	Henri Richard, Mtl.
1957	Gordie Howe, Det.	Ted Lindsay, Det.
1956	Jean Beliveau, Mtl.	Gordie Howe, Det.
1955	Bernie Geoffrion, Mtl.	Maurice Richard, Mtl.
1954	Gordie Howe, Det.	Maurice Richard, Mtl.
1953	Gordie Howe, Det.	Ted Lindsay, Det.
1952	Gordie Howe, Det.	Ted Lindsay, Det.
1951	Gordie Howe, Det.	Maurice Richard, Mtl.
1950	Ted Lindsay, Det.	Sid Abel, Det.
1949	Roy Conacher, Chi.	Doug Bentley, Chi.
1948	Elmer Lach, Mtl.	Buddy O'Connor, NYR
1947*	Max Bentley, Chi.	Maurice Richard, Mtl.
1946	Max Bentley, Chi.	Gaye Stewart, Tor.
1945	Elmer Lach, Mtl.	Maurice Richard, Mtl.
1944	Herbie Cain, Bos.	Doug Bentley, Chi.
1943	Doug Bentley, Chi.	Bill Cowley, Bos.
1942	Bryan Hextall, NYR	Lynn Patrick, NYR
1941	Bill Cowley, Bos.	Bryan Hextall, NYR
1940	Milt Schmidt, Bos.	Woody Dumart, Bos.
1939	Toe Blake, Mtl.	Dave Schriner, NYA
1938	Gordie Drillon, Tor.	Syl Apps, Tor.
1937	Dave Schriner, NYA	Syl Apps, Tor.
1936	Dave Schriner, NYA	Marty Barry, Det.
1935	Charlie Conacher, Tor.	Syd Howe, St.L-Det.
1934	Charlie Conacher, Tor.	Joe Primeau, Tor
1933	Bill Cook, NYR	Harvey Jackson, Tor.
1932	Harvey Jackson, Tor.	Joe Primeau, Tor.
1931	Howie Morenz, Mtl.	Ebbie Goodfellow, Det.
1930	Cooney Weiland, Bos.	Frank Boucher, NYR
1929	Ace Bailey, Tor.	Nels Stewart, Mtl.M
1928	Howie Morenz, Mtl.	Aurel Joliat, Mtl.
1927	Bill Cook, NYR	Dick Irvin, Chi.
1926	Nels Stewart, Mtl.M.	Cy Denneny, Ott.
1925	Babe Dye, Tor.	Cy Denneny, Ott.
1924	Cy Denneny, Ott.	Billy Boucher, Mtl.
1923	Babe Dye, Tor.	Cy Denneny, Ott.
1922	Punch Broadbent, Ott.	Cy Denneny, Ott.
1921	Newsy Lalonde, Mtl.	Cy Denneny, Ott.
1920	Joe Malone, Que.	Newsy Lalonde, Mtl.
1919	Newsy Lalonde, Mtl.	Odie Cleghorn, Mtl.
1918	Joe Malone, Mtl.	Cy Denneny, Ott.

* Trophy first awarded in 1948.
Scoring leaders listed from 1918 to 1947.

KING CLANCY MEMORIAL TROPHY WINNERS

1997	Trevor Linden	Vancouver
1996	Kris King	Winnipeg
1995	Joe Nieuwendyk	Calgary
1994	Adam Graves	NY Rangers
1993	Dave Poulin	Boston .
1992	Ray Bourque	Boston
1991	Dave Taylor	Los Angeles
1990	Kevin Lowe	Edmonton
1989	Bryan Trottier	NY Islanders
1988	Lanny McDonald	Calgary

HART TROPHY

	Winner	Runner-up
1997	Dominik Hasek, Buf.	Paul Kariya, Ana.
1996	Mario Lemieux, Pit.	Mark Messier, NYR
1995	Eric Lindros, Phi.	Jaromir Jagr, Pit.
1994	Sergei Fedorov, Det.	Dominik Hasek, Buf.
1993	Mario Lemieux, Pit.	Doug Gilmour, Tor.
1992	Mark Messier, NYR	Patrick Roy, Mtl.
1991	Brett Hull, St.L.	Wayne Gretzky, L.A.
1990	Mark Messier, Edm.	Ray Bourque, Bos.
1989	Wayne Gretzky, L.A.	Mario Lemieux, Pit.
1988	Mario Lemieux, Pit.	Grant Fuhr, Edm.
1987	Wayne Gretzky, Edm.	Ray Bourque, Bos.
1986	Wayne Gretzky, Edm.	Mario Lemieux, Pit.
1985	Wayne Gretzky, Edm.	Dale Hawerchuk, Wpg.
1984	Wayne Gretzky, Edm.	Rod Langway, Wsh.
1983	Wayne Gretzky, Edm.	Pete Peeters, Bos.
1982	Wayne Gretzky, Edm.	Bryan Trottier, NYI
1981	Wayne Gretzky, Edm.	Mike Liut, St.L.
1980	Wayne Gretzky, Edm.	Marcel Dionne, L.A.
1979	Bryan Trottier, NYI	Guy Lafleur, Mtl
1978	Guy Lafleur, Mtl.	Bryan Trottier, NYI
1977	Guy Lafleur, Mtl.	Bobby Clarke, Phi.
1976	Bobby Clarke, Phi.	Denis Potvin, NYI
1975	Bobby Clarke, Phi.	Rogatien Vachon, L.A.
1974	Phil Esposito, Bos.	Bernie Parent, Phi.
1973	Bobby Clarke, Phi.	Phil Esposito, Bos.
1972	Bobby Orr, Bos.	Ken Dryden, Mtl.
1971	Bobby Orr, Bos.	Phil Esposito, Bos.
1970	Bobby Orr, Bos.	Tony Esposito, Chi.
1969	Phil Esposito, Bos.	Jean Beliveau, Mtl.
1968	Stan Mikita, Chi.	Jean Beliveau, Mtl.
1967	Stan Mikita, Chi.	Ed Giacomin, NYR
1966	Bobby Hull, Chi.	Jean Beliveau, Mtl.
1965	Bobby Hull, Chi.	Norm Ullman, Det.
1964	Jean Beliveau, Mtl.	Bobby Hull, Chi.
1963	Gordie Howe, Det.	Stan Mikita, Chi.
1962	Jacques Plante, Mtl.	Doug Harvey, NYR
1961	Bernie Geoffrion, Mtl.	Johnny Bower, Tor.
1960	Gordie Howe, Det.	Bobby Hull, Chi.
1959	Andy Bathgate, NYR	Gordie Howe, Det.
1958	Gordie Howe, Det.	Andy Bathgate, NYR
1957	Gordie Howe, Det.	Jean Beliveau, Mtl.
1956	Jean Beliveau, Mtl.	Tod Sloan, Tor.
1955	Ted Kennedy, Tor.	Harry Lumley, Tor.
1954	Al Rollins, Chi.	Red Kelly, Det.
1953	Gordie Howe, Det.	Al Rollins, Chi.
1952	Gordie Howe, Det.	Elmer Lach, Mtl.
1951	Milt Schmidt, Bos.	Maurice Richard, Mtl.
1950	Charlie Rayner, NYR	Ted Kennedy, Tor.
1949	Sid Abel, Det.	Bill Durnan, Mtl.
1948	Buddy O'Connor, NYR	Frank Brimsek, Bos.
1947	Maurice Richard, Mtl.	Milt Schmidt, Bos.
1946	Max Bentley, Chi.	Gaye Stewart, Tor.
1945	Elmer Lach, Mtl.	Maurice Richard, Mtl.
1944	Babe Pratt, Tor.	Bill Cowley, Bos.
1943	Bill Cowley, Bos.	Doug Bentley, Chi.
1942	Tom Anderson, Bro.	Syl Apps, Tor.
1941	Bill Cowley, Bos.	Dit Clapper, Bos.
1940	Ebbie Goodfellow, Det.	Syl Apps, Tor.
1939	Toe Blake, Mtl.	Syl Apps, Tor.
1938	Eddie Shore, Bos.	Paul Thompson, Chi.
1937	Babe Siebert, Mtl.	Lionel Conacher, Mtl.M
1936	Eddie Shore, Bos.	Hooley Smith, Mtl.M
1935	Eddie Shore, Bos.	Charlie Conacher, Tor.
1934	Aurel Joliat, Mtl.	Lionel Conacher, Chi.
1933	Eddie Shore, Bos.	Bill Cook, NYR
1932	Howie Morenz, Mtl.	Ching Johnson, NYR
1931	Howie Morenz, Mtl.	Eddie Shore, Bos.
1930	Nels Stewart, Mtl.M.	Lionel Hitchman, Bos.
1929	Roy Worters, NYA	Ace Bailey, Tor.
1928	Howie Morenz, Mtl.	Roy Worters, Pit.
1927	Herb Gardiner, Mtl.	Bill Cook, NYR
1926	Nels Stewart, Mtl.M.	Sprague Cleghorn, Bos.
1925	Billy Burch, Ham.	Howie Morenz, Mtl.
1924	Frank Nighbor, Ott.	Sprague Cleghorn, Mtl.

FRANK J. SELKE TROPHY WINNERS

	Winner	Runner-up
1997	Michael Peca, Buf.	Peter Forsberg, Col.
1996	Sergei Fedorov, Det.	Ron Francis, Pit.
1995	Ron Francis, Pit.	Esa Tikkanen, St.L.
1994	Sergei Fedorov, Det.	Doug Gilmour, Tor.
1993	Doug Gilmour, Tor.	Dave Poulin, Bos.
1992	Guy Carbonneau, Mtl.	Sergei Fedorov, Det.
1991	Dirk Graham, Chi.	Esa Tikkanen, Edm.
1990	Rick Meagher, St.L.	Guy Carbonneau, Mtl.
1989	Guy Carbonneau, Mtl.	Esa Tikkanen, Edm.
1988	Guy Carbonneau, Mtl.	Steve Kasper, Bos.
1987	Dave Poulin, Phi.	Guy Carbonneau, Mtl.
1986	Troy Murray, Chi.	Ron Sutter, Phi.
1985	Craig Ramsay, Buf.	Doug Jarvis, Wsh.
1984	Doug Jarvis, Wsh.	Bryan Trottier, NYI
1983	Bobby Clarke, Phi.	Jari Kurri, Edm.
1982	Steve Kasper, Bos.	Bob Gainey, Mtl.
1981	Bob Gainey, Mtl.	Craig Ramsay, Buf.
1980	Bob Gainey, Mtl.	Craig Ramsay, Buf.
1979	Bob Gainey, Mtl.	Don Marcotte, Bos.
1978	Bob Gainey, Mtl.	Craig Ramsay, Buf.

1996-97 NHL Player of the Week Award Winners

Player of the Week

Week Ending	Player	Team
Oct. 14	John Vanbiesbrouck	Florida
Oct. 21	Joe Sakic	Colorado
Oct. 28	Brendan Shanahan	Detroit
Nov. 4	Zigmund Palffy	NY Islanders
Nov. 11	John LeClair	Philadelphia
Nov. 18	Greg Adams	Dallas
Nov. 25	Peter Bondra	Washington
Dec. 2	Mark Messier	NY Rangers
Dec. 9	Geoff Sanderson	Hartford
Dec. 16	Eric Lindros	Philadelphia
Dec. 23	Wayne Gretzky	NY Rangers
Dec. 30	Sergei Fedorov	Detroit
Jan. 6	Mario Lemieux	Pittsburgh
Jan. 13	Patrick Roy	Colorado
Jan. 20	Patrick Lalime	Pittsburgh
Jan. 27	Brian Leetch	NY Rangers
Feb. 3	Dominik Hasek	Buffalo
Feb. 10	Andy Moog	Dallas
Feb. 17	co-winners	
	Martin Brodeur	New Jersey
	Trevor Kidd	Calgary
Feb. 24	Daymond Langkow	Tampa Bay
Mar. 3	Stephane Fiset	Los Angeles
Mar. 10	Nikolai Khabibulin	Phoenix
Mar. 17	Pierre Turgeon	St. Louis
Mar. 24	Arturs Irbe	Dallas
Mar. 31	Zigmund Palffy	NY Islanders
Apr. 7	Keith Tkachuk	Phoenix
Apr. 14	Ron Tugnutt	Ottawa

1996-97 Player of the Month

Month	Player	Team
Oct.	John Vanbiesbrouck	Florida
Nov.	Jaromir Jagr	Pittsburgh
Dec.	Mike Richter	NY Rangers
Jan.	Mario Lemieux	Pittsburgh
Feb.	Brendan Shanahan	Detroit
Mar.	Mike Modano	Dallas
Apr.	Ron Tugnutt	Ottawa

1996-97 Rookie of the Month

Month	Player	Team
Oct.	Jim Campbell	St. Louis
Nov.	Harry York	St. Louis
Dec.	Patrick Lalime	Pittsburgh
Jan.	Patrick Lalime	Pittsburgh
Feb.	Daymond Langkow	Tampa Bay
Mar.	Steve Sullivan	Toronto
Apr.	Wade Redden	Ottawa

LADY BYNG TROPHY

	Winner	Runner-up
1996	Paul Kariya, Ana.	Teemu Selanne, Ana.
1996	Paul Kariya, Ana.	Adam Oates, Bos.
1995	Ron Francis, Pit.	Adam Oates, Bos.
1994	Wayne Gretzky, L.A.	Adam Oates, Bos.
1993	Pierre Turgeon, NYI	Adam Oates, Bos.
1992	Wayne Gretzky, L.A.	Joe Sakic, Que.
1991	Wayne Gretzky, L.A.	Brett Hull, St.L.
1990	Brett Hull, St.L.	Wayne Gretzky, L.A.
1989	Joe Mullen, Cgy.	Wayne Gretzky, L.A.
1988	Mats Naslund, Mtl.	Wayne Gretzky, Edm.
1987	Joe Mullen, Cgy.	Wayne Gretzky, Edm.
1986	Mike Bossy, NYI	Jari Kurri, Edm.
1985	Jari Kurri, Edm.	Joe Mullen, St.L.
1984	Mike Bossy, NYI	Rick Middleton, Bos.
1983	Mike Bossy, NYI	Rick Middleton, Bos.
1982	Rick Middleton, Bos.	Mike Bossy, NYI
1981	Rick Kehoe, Pit.	Wayne Gretzky, Edm.
1980	Wayne Gretzky, Edm.	Marcel Dionne, L.A.
1979	Bob MacMillan, Atl.	Marcel Dionne, L.A.
1978	Butch Goring, L.A.	Peter McNab, Bos.
1977	Marcel Dionne, L.A.	Jean Ratelle, Bos.
1976	Jean Ratelle, NYR-Bos.	Jean Pronovost, Pit.
1975	Marcel Dionne, Det.	John Bucyk, Bos.
1974	John Bucyk, Bos.	Lowell MacDonald, Pit.
1973	Gilbert Perreault, Buf.	Jean Ratelle, NYR
1972	Jean Ratelle, NYR	John Bucyk, Bos.
1971	John Bucyk, Bos.	Dave Keon, Tor.
1970	Phil Goyette, St.L.	John Bucyk, Bos.
1969	Alex Delvecchio, Det.	Ted Hampson, Oak.
1968	Stan Mikita, Chi.	John Bucyk, Bos.
1967	Stan Mikita, Chi.	Dave Keon, Tor.
1966	Alex Delvecchio, Det.	Bobby Rousseau, Mtl.
1965	Bobby Hull, Chi.	Alex Delvecchio, Det.
1964	Ken Wharram, Chi.	Dave Keon, Tor.
1963	Dave Keon, Tor.	Camille Henry, NYR
1962	Dave Keon, Tor.	Claude Provost, Mtl.
1961	Red Kelly, Tor.	Norm Ullman, Det.
1960	Don McKenney, Bos.	Andy Hebenton, NYR
1959	Alex Delvecchio, Det.	Andy Hebenton, NYR
1958	Camille Henry, NYR	Don Marshall, Mtl.
1957	Andy Hebenton, NYR	Earl Reibel, Det.
1956	Earl Reibel, Det.	Floyd Curry, Mtl.
1955	Sid Smith, Tor.	Danny Lewicki, NYR
1954	Red Kelly, Det.	Don Raleigh, NYR
1953	Red Kelly, Det.	Wally Hergesheimer, NYR
1952	Sid Smith, Tor.	Red Kelly, Det.
1951	Red Kelly, Det.	Woody Dumart, Bos.
1950	Edgar Laprade, NYR	Red Kelly, Det.
1949	Bill Quackenbush, Det.	Harry Watson, Tor.
1948	Buddy O'Connor, NYR	Syl Apps, Tor.
1947	Bobby Bauer, Bos.	Syl Apps, Tor.
1946	Toe Blake, Mtl.	Clint Smith, Chi.
1945	Bill Mosienko, Chi.	Syd Howe, Det.
1944	Clint Smith, Chi.	Herb Cain, Bos.
1943	Max Bentley, Chi.	Buddy O'Connor, Mtl.
1942	Syl Apps, Tor.	Gordie Drillon, Tor.
1941	Bobby Bauer, Bos.	Gordie Drillon, Tor.
1940	Bobby Bauer, Bos.	Clint Smith, NYR
1939	Clint Smith, NYR	Marty Barry, Det.
1938	Gordie Drillon, Tor.	Clint Smith, NYR
1937	Marty Barry, Det.	Gordie Drillon, Tor.
1936	Doc Romnes, Chi.	Dave Schriner, NYA
1935	Frank Boucher, NYR	Russ Blinco, Mtl.M
1934	Frank Boucher, NYR	Joe Primeau, Tor.
1933	Frank Boucher, NYR	Joe Primeau, Tor.
1932	Joe Primeau, Tor.	Frank Boucher, NYR
1931	Frank Boucher, NYR	Normie Himes, NYA
1930	Frank Boucher, NYR	Normie Himes, NYA
1929	Frank Boucher, NYR	Harry Darragh, Pit.
1928	Frank Boucher, NYR	George Hay, Det.
1927	Billy Burch, NYA	Dick Irvin, Chi.
1926	Frank Nighbor, Ott.	Billy Burch, NYA
1925	Frank Nighbor, Ott.	none

VEZINA TROPHY

	Winner	Runner-up
1997	Dominik Hasek, Buf.	Martin Brodeur, N.J.
1996	Jim Carey, Wsh.	Chris Osgood, Det.
1995	Dominik Hasek, Buf.	Ed Belfour, Chi.
1994	Dominik Hasek, Buf.	John Vanbiesbrouck, Fla.
1993	Ed Belfour, Chi.	Tom Barrasso, Pit.
1992	Patrick Roy, Mtl.	Kirk McLean, Van.
1991	Ed Belfour, Chi.	Patrick Roy, Mtl.
1990	Patrick Roy, Mtl.	Daren Puppa, Buf.
1989	Patrick Roy, Mtl.	Mike Vernon, Cgy.
1988	Grant Fuhr, Edm.	Tom Barrasso, Buf.
1987	Ron Hextall, Phi.	Mike Liut, Hfd.
1986	John Vanbiesbrouck, NYR	Bob Froese, Phi.
1985	Pelle Lindbergh, Phi.	Tom Barrasso, Buf.
1984	Tom Barrasso, Buf.	Rejean Lemelin, Cgy.
1983	Pete Peeters, Bos.	Roland Melanson, NYI
1982	Bill Smith, NYI	Grant Fuhr, Edm.
1981	Richard Sevigny, Mtl.	Pete Peeters, Phi.
	Denis Herron, Mtl.	Rick St. Croix, Phi.
	Michel Larocque, Mtl.	
1980	Bob Sauve, Buf.	Gerry Cheevers, Bos.
	Don Edwards, Buf.	Gilles Gilbert, Bos.
1979	Ken Dryden, Mtl.	Glenn Resch, NYI
	Michel Larocque, Mtl.	Bill Smith, NYI
1978	Ken Dryden, Mtl.	Bernie Parent, Phi.
	Michel Larocque	Wayne Stephenson, Phi.
1977	Ken Dryden, Mtl.	Glenn Resch, NYI
	Michel Larocque, Mtl.	Bill Smith, NYI
1976	Ken Dryden, Mtl.	Glenn Resch, NYI
		Bill Smith, NYI
1975	Bernie Parent, Phi.	Rogie Vachon, L.A.
		Gary Edwards, L.A.
1974	Bernie Parent, Phi. (tie)	Gilles Gilbert, Bos.
	Tony Esposito, Chi. (tie)	
1973	Ken Dryden, Mtl.	Ed Giacomin, NYR
		Gilles Villemure, NYR
1972	Tony Esposito, Chi.	Cesare Maniago, Min.
	Gary Smith, Chi.	Lorne Worsley, Min.
1971	Ed Giacomin, NYR	Tony Esposito, Chi.
	Gilles Villemure, NYR	
1970	Tony Esposito, Chi.	Jacques Plante, St.L.
		Ernie Wakely, St.L.
1969	Jacques Plante, St.L.	Ed Giacomin, NYR
	Glenn Hall, St.L.	
1968	Lorne Worsley, Mtl.	Johnny Bower, Tor.
	Rogatien Vachon, Mtl.	Bruce Gamble, Tor.
1967	Glenn Hall, Chi.	Charlie Hodge, Mtl.
	Denis Dejordy, Chi.	
1966	Lorne Worsley, Mtl.	Glenn Hall, Chi.
	Charlie Hodge, Mtl.	
1965	Terry Sawchuk, Tor.	Roger Crozier, Det.
	Johnny Bower, Tor.	
1964	Charlie Hodge, Mtl.	Glenn Hall, Chi.
1963	Glenn Hall, Chi.	Johnny Bower, Tor.
		Don Simmons, Tor.
1962	Jacques Plante, Mtl.	Johnny Bower, Tor.
1961	Johnny Bower, Tor.	Glenn Hall, Chi.
1960	Jacques Plante, Mtl.	Glenn Hall, Chi.
1959	Jacques Plante, Mtl.	Johnny Bower, Tor.
		Ed Chadwick, Tor.
1958	Jacques Plante, Mtl.	Lorne Worsley, NYR
		Marcel Paille, NYR
1957	Jacques Plante, Mtl.	Glenn Hall, Det.
1956	Jacques Plante, Mtl.	Glenn Hall, Det.
1955	Terry Sawchuk, Det.	Harry Lumley, Tor.
1954	Harry Lumley, Tor.	Terry Sawchuk, Det.
1953	Terry Sawchuk, Det.	Gerry McNeil, Mtl.
1952	Terry Sawchuk, Det.	Al Rollins, Tor.
1951	Al Rollins, Tor.	Terry Sawchuk, Det.
1950	Bill Durnan, Mtl.	Harry Lumley, Det.
1949	Bill Durnan, Mtl.	Harry Lumley, Det.
1948	Turk Broda, Tor.	Harry Lumley, Det.
1947	Bill Durnan, Mtl.	Turk Broda, Tor.
1946	Bill Durnan, Mtl.	Frank Brimsek, Bos.
1945	Bill Durnan, Mtl.	Frank McCool, Tor. (tie)
		Harry Lumley, Det. (tie)
1944	Bill Durnan, Mtl.	Paul Bibeault, Tor.
1943	Johnny Mowers, Det.	Turk Broda, Tor.
1942	Frank Brimsek, Bos.	Turk Broda, Tor.
1941	Turk Broda, Tor.	Frank Brimsek, Bos. (tie)
		Johnny Mowers, Det. (tie)
1940	Dave Kerr, NYR	Frank Brimsek, Bos.
1939	Frank Brimsek, Bos.	Dave Kerr, NYR
1938	Tiny Thompson, Bos.	Dave Kerr, NYR
1937	Normie Smith, Det.	Dave Kerr, NYR
1936	Tiny Thompson, Bos.	Mike Karakas, Chi.
1935	Lorne Chabot, Chi.	Alex Connell, Mtl.M
1934	Charlie Gardiner, Chi.	Wilf Cude, Det.
1933	Tiny Thompson, Bos.	John Roach, Det.
1932	Charlie Gardiner, Chi.	Alex Connell, Det.
1931	Roy Worters, NYA	Charlie Gardiner, Chi.
1930	Tiny Thompson, Bos.	Charlie Gardiner, Chi.
1929	George Hainsworth, Mtl.	Tiny Thompson, Bos.
1928	George Hainsworth, Mtl.	Alex Connell, Ott.
1927	George Hainsworth, Mtl.	Clint Benedict, Mtl.M

BILL MASTERTON TROPHY WINNERS

1997	Tony Granato	San Jose
1996	Gary Roberts	Calgary
1995	Pat LaFontaine	Buffalo
1994	Cam Neely	Boston
1993	Mario Lemieux	Pittsburgh
1992	Mark Fitzpatrick	NY Islanders
1991	Dave Taylor	Los Angeles
1990	Gord Kluzak	Boston
1989	Tim Kerr	Philadelphia
1988	Bob Bourne	Los Angeles
1987	Doug Jarvis	Hartford
1986	Charlie Simmer	Boston
1985	Anders Hedberg	NY Rangers
1984	Brad Park	Detroit
1983	Lanny McDonald	Calgary
1982	Glenn Resch	Colorado
1981	Blake Dunlop	St. Louis
1980	Al MacAdam	Minnesota
1979	Serge Savard	Montreal
1978	Butch Goring	Los Angeles
1977	Ed Westfall	NY Islanders
1976	Rod Gilbert	NY Rangers
1975	Don Luce	Buffalo
1974	Henri Richard	Montreal
1973	Lowell MacDonald	Pittsburgh
1972	Bobby Clarke	Phiiladelphia
1971	Jean Ratelle	NY Rangers
1970	Pit Martin	Chicago
1969	Ted Hampson	Oakland
1968	Claude Provost	Montreal

CALDER MEMORIAL TROPHY WINNERS

	Winner	Runner-up
1997	Bryan Berard, NYI	Jarome Iginla, Cgy.
1996	Daniel Alfredsson, Ott.	Eric Daze, Chi.
1995	Peter Forsberg, Que.	Jim Carey, Wsh.
1994	Martin Brodeur, N.J.	Jason Arnott, Edm.
1993	Teemu Selanne, Wpg.	Joe Juneau, Bos.
1992	Pavel Bure, Van.	Nicklas Lidstrom, Det
1991	Ed Belfour, Chi.	Sergei Fedorov, Det.
1990	Sergei Makarov, Cgy.	Mike Modano, Min.
1989	Brian Leetch, NYR	Trevor Linden, Van.
1988	Joe Nieuwendyk, Cgy.	Ray Sheppard, Buf.
1987	Luc Robitaille, L.A.	Ron Hextall, Phi.
1986	Gary Suter, Cgy.	Wendel Clark, Tor.
1985	Mario Lemieux, Pit.	Chris Chelios, Mtl.
1984	Tom Barrasso, Buf.	Steve Yzerman, Det.
1983	Steve Larmer, Chi.	Phil Housley, Buf.
1982	Dale Hawerchuk, Wpg.	Barry Pederson, Bos.
1981	Peter Stastny, Que.	Larry Murphy, L.A.
1980	Ray Bourque, Bos.	Mike Foligno, Det.
1979	Bobby Smith, Min	Ryan Walter, Wsh.
1978	Mike Bossy, NYI	Barry Beck, Col.
1977	Willi Plett, Atl.	Don Murdoch, NYR
1976	Bryan Trottier, NYI	Glenn Resch, NYI
1975	Eric Vail, Atl.	Pierre Larouche, Pit.
1974	Denis Potvin, NYI	Tom Lysiak, Atl.
1973	Steve Vickers, NYR	Bill Barber, Phi.
1972	Ken Dryden, Mtl.	Rick Martin, Buf.
1971	Gilbert Perreault, Buf.	Jude Drouin, Min.
1970	Tony Esposito, Chi.	Bill Fairbairn, NYR
1969	Danny Grant, Min.	Norm Ferguson, Oak.
1968	Derek Sanderson, Bos.	Jacques Lemaire, Mtl.
1967	Bobby Orr, Bos.	Ed Van Impe, Chi.
1966	Brit Selby, Tor.	Bert Marshall, Det.
1965	Roger Crozier, Det.	Ron Ellis, Tor.
1964	Jacques Laperriere, Mtl.	John Ferguson, Mtl.
1963	Kent Douglas, Tor.	Doug Barkley, Det.
1962	Bobby Rousseau, Mtl.	Cliff Pennington, Bos.
1961	Dave Keon, Tor.	Bob Nevin, Tor.
1960	Bill Hay, Chi.	Murray Oliver, Det.
1959	Ralph Backstrom, Mtl.	Carl Brewer, Tor.
1958	Frank Mahovlich, Tor.	Bobby Hull, Chi.
1957	Larry Regan, Bos.	Ed Chadwick, Tor.
1956	Glenn Hall, Det.	Andy Hebenton, NYR
1955	Ed Litzenberger, Chi.	Don McKenney, Bos.
1954	Camille Henry, NYR	Earl Reibel, Det.
1953	Lorne Worsley, NYR	Gordie Hannigan, Tor.
1952	Bernie Geoffrion, Mtl.	Hy Buller, NYR
1951	Terry Sawchuk, Det.	Al Rollins, Tor.
1950	Jack Gelineau, Bos.	Phil Maloney, Bos.
1949	Pentti Lund, NYR	Allan Stanley, NYR
1948	Jim McFadden, Det.	Pete Babando, Bos.
1947	Howie Meeker, Tor.	Jimmy Conacher, Det.
1946	Edgar Laprade, NYR	George Gee, Chi.
1945	Frank McCool, Tor.	Ken Smith, Bos.
1944	Gus Bodnar, Tor.	Bill Durnan, Mtl.
1943	Gaye Stewart, Tor.	Glen Harmon, Mtl.
1942	Grant Warwick, NYR	Buddy O'Connor, Mtl.
1941	Johnny Quilty, Mtl.	Johnny Mowers, Det.
1940	Kilby MacDonald, NYR	Wally Stanowski, Tor.
1939	Frank Brimsek, Bos.	Roy Conacher, Bos.
1938	Cully Dahlstrom, Chi.	Murph Chamberlain, Tor.
1937	Syl Apps, Tor.	Gordie Drillon, Tor.
1936	Mike Karakas, Chi.	Bucko McDonald, Det.
1935	Dave Schriner, NYA	Bert Connolly, NYR
1934	Russ Blinko, Mtl.M.	
1933	Carl Voss, Det.	

CONN SMYTHE TROPHY WINNERS

1997	Mike Vernon	Detroit
1996	Joe Sakic	Colorado
1995	Claude Lemieux	New Jersey
1994	Brian Leetch	NY Rangers
1993	Patrick Roy	Montreal
1992	Mario Lemieux	Pittsburgh
1991	Mario Lemieux	Pittsburgh
1990	Bill Ranford	Edmonton
1989	Al MacInnis	Calgary
1988	Wayne Gretzky	Edmonton
1987	Ron Hextall	Philadelphia
1986	Patrick Roy	Montreal
1985	Wayne Gretzky	Edmonton
1984	Mark Messier	Edmonton
1983	Bill Smith	NY Islanders
1982	Mike Bossy	NY Islanders
1981	Butch Goring	NY Islanders
1980	Bryan Trottier	NY Islanders
1979	Bob Gainey	Montreal
1978	Larry Robinson	Montreal
1977	Guy Lafleur	Montreal
1976	Reggie Leach	Philadelphia
1975	Bernie Parent	Philadelphia
1974	Bernie Parent	Philadelphia
1973	Yvan Cournoyer	Montreal
1972	Bobby Orr	Boston
1971	Ken Dryden	Montreal
1970	Bobby Orr	Boston
1969	Serge Savard	Montreal
1968	Glenn Hall	St. Louis
1967	Dave Keon	Toronto
1966	Roger Crozier	Detroit
1965	Jean Béliveau	Montreal

JAMES NORRIS TROPHY WINNERS

	Winner	Runner-up
1997	Brian Leetch, NYR	V. Konstantinov, Det.
1996	Chris Chelios, Chi.	Ray Bourque, Bos.
1995	Paul Coffey, Det.	Chris Chelios, Chi.
1994	Ray Bourque, Bos.	Scott Stevens, N.J.
1993	Chris Chelios, Chi.	Ray Bourque, Bos.
1992	Brian Leetch, NYR	Ray Bourque, Bos.
1991	Ray Bourque, Bos.	Al MacInnis, Cgy.
1990	Ray Bourque, Bos.	Al MacInnis, Cgy.
1989	Chris Chelios, Mtl	Paul Coffey, Pit.
1988	Ray Bourque, Bos.	Scott Stevens, Wsh.
1987	Ray Bourque, Bos.	Mark Howe, Phi.
1986	Paul Coffey, Edm.	Mark Howe, Phi.
1985	Paul Coffey, Edm.	Ray Bourque, Bos.
1984	Rod Langway, Wsh.	Paul Coffey, Edm.
1983	Rod Langway, Wsh.	Mark Howe, Phi.
1982	Doug Wilson, Chi.	Ray Bourque, Bos.
1981	Randy Carlyle, Pit.	Denis Potvin, NYI
1980	Larry Robinson, Mtl.	Borje Salming, Tor.
1979	Denis Potvin, NYI	Larry Robinson, Mtl.
1978	Denis Potvin, NYI	Brad Park, Bos.
1977	Larry Robinson, Mtl.	Borje Salming, Tor.
1976	Denis Potvin, NYI	Brad Park, NYR-Bos.
1975	Bobby Orr, Bos.	Denis Potvin, NYI
1974	Bobby Orr, Bos.	Brad Park, NYR
1973	Bobby Orr, Bos.	Guy Lapointe, Mtl.
1972	Bobby Orr, Bos.	Brad Park, NYR
1971	Bobby Orr, Bos.	Brad Park, NYR
1970	Bobby Orr, Bos.	Brad Park, NYR
1969	Bobby Orr, Bos.	Tim Horton, Tor.
1968	Bobby Orr, Bos.	J.C. Tremblay, Mtl
1967	Harry Howell, NYR	Pierre Pilote, Chi.
1966	Jacques Laperriere, Mtl.	Pierre Pilote, Chi.
1965	Pierre Pilote, Chi.	Jacques Laperriere, Mtl.
1964	Pierre Pilote, Chi.	Tim Horton, Tor.
1963	Pierre Pilote, Chi.	Carl Brewer, Tor.
1962	Doug Harvey, NYR	Pierre Pilote, Chi.
1961	Doug Harvey, Mtl.	Marcel Pronovost, Det.
1960	Doug Harvey, Mtl.	Allan Stanley, Tor.
1959	Tom Johnson, Mtl.	Bill Gadsby, NYR
1958	Doug Harvey, Mtl.	Bill Gadsby, NYR
1957	Doug Harvey, Mtl.	Red Kelly, Det.
1956	Doug Harvey, Mtl.	Bill Gadsby, NYR
1955	Doug Harvey, Mtl.	Red Kelly, Det.
1954	Red Kelly, Det.	Doug Harvey, Mtl.

MASTERCARD CUTTING EDGE PLAY OF THE YEAR WINNER

1997	Valeri Kamensky	Colorado
1996	Chris Osgood	Detroit

LESTER PATRICK TROPHY WINNERS

1997	Seymour H. Knox III
	Bill Cleary
	Pat LaFontaine
1996	George Gund
	Ken Morrow
	Milt Schmidt
1995	Joe Mullen
	Brian Mullen
	Bob Fleming
1994	Wayne Gretzky
	Robert Ridder
1993	*Frank Boucher
	*Mervyn (Red) Dutton
	Bruce McNall
	Gil Stein
1992	Al Arbour
	Art Berglund
	Lou Lamoriello
1991	Rod Gilbert
	Mike Ilitch
1990	Len Ceglarski
1989	Dan Kelly
	Lou Nanne
	*Lynn Patrick
	Bud Poile
1988	Keith Allen
	Fred Cusick
	Bob Johnson
1987	*Hobey Baker
	Frank Mathers
1986	John MacInnes
	Jack Riley
1985	Jack Butterfield
	Arthur M. Wirtz
1984	John A. Ziegler Jr.
	*Arthur Howie Ross
1983	Bill Torrey
1982	Emile P. Francis
1981	Charles M. Schulz
1980	Bobby Clarke
	Edward M. Snider
	Frederick A. Shero
	1980 U.S. Olympic Hockey Team
1979	Bobby Orr
1978	Phil Esposito
	Tom Fitzgerald
	William T. Tutt
	William W. Wirtz
1977	John P. Bucyk
	Murray A. Armstrong
	John Mariucci
1976	Stanley Mikita
	George A. Leader
	Bruce A. Norris
1975	Donald M. Clark
	William L. Chadwick
	Thomas N. Ivan
1974	Alex Delvecchio
	Murray Murdoch
	*Weston W. Adams, Sr.
	*Charles L. Crovat
1973	Walter L. Bush, Jr.
1972	Clarence S. Campbell
	John A. "Snooks" Kelly
	Ralph "Cooney" Weiland
	*James D. Norris
1971	William M. Jennings
	*John B. Sollenberger
	*Terrance G. Sawchuk
1970	Edward W. Shore
	*James C. V. Hendy
1969	Robert M. Hull
	*Edward J. Jeremiah
1968	Thomas F. Lockhart
	*Walter A. Brown
	*Gen. John R. Kilpatrick
1967	Gordon Howe
	*Charles F. Adams
	*James Norris, Sr.
1966	J.J. "Jack" Adams

* awarded posthumously

BUD ICE PLUS-MINUS AWARD WINNER

1997	John LeClair	Philadelphia

WILLIAM M. JENNINGS TROPHY WINNERS

	Winner	Runner-up
1997	Martin Brodeur, N.J.	Chris Osgood, Det.
	Mike Dunham	Mike Vernon
1996	Chris Osgood, Det.	Martin Brodeur, N.J.
	Mike Vernon	
1995	Ed Belfour, Chi.	Mike Vernon, Det.
		Chris Osgood
1994	Dominik Hasek, Buf.	Martin Brodeur, N.J.
	Grant Fuhr	Chris Terreri
1993	Ed Belfour, Chi.	Felix Potvin, Tor.
		Grant Fuhr
1992	Patrick Roy, Mtl.	Ed Belfour, Chi.
1991	Ed Belfour, Chi.	Patrick Roy, Mtl.
1990	Andy Moog, Bos.	Patrick Roy, Mtl.
	Rejean Lemelin	Brian Hayward
1989	Patrick Roy, Mtl.	Mike Vernon, Cgy.
	Brian Hayward	Rick Wamsley
1988	Patrick Roy, Mtl.	Clint Malarchuk, Wsh.
	Brian Hayward	Pete Peeters
1987	Patrick Roy, Mtl.	Ron Hextall, Phi.
	Brian Hayward	
1986	Bob Froese, Phi.	Al Jensen, Wsh.
	Darren Jensen	Pete Peeters
1985	Tom Barrasso, Buf.	Pat Riggin, Wsh.
	Bob Sauve	
1984	Al Jensen, Wsh.	Tom Barrasso, Buf.
	Pat Riggin	Bob Sauve
1983	Roland Melanson, NYI	Pete Peeters, Bos.
	Bill Smith	
1982	Rick Wamsley, Mtl.	Billy Smith, NYI
	Denis Herron	Roland Melanson

LESTER B. PEARSON AWARD WINNERS

1997	Dominik Hasek	Buf.
1996	Mario Lemieux	Pittsburgh
1995	Eric Lindros	Philadelphia
1994	Sergei Fedorov	Detroit
1993	Mario Lemieux	Pittsburgh
1992	Mark Messier	NY Rangers
1991	Brett Hull	St. Louis
1990	Mark Messier	Edmonton
1989	Steve Yzerman	Detroit
1988	Mario Lemieux	Pittsburgh
1987	Wayne Gretzky	Edmonton
1986	Mario Lemieux	Pittsburgh
1985	Wayne Gretzky	Edmonton
1984	Wayne Gretzky	Edmonton
1983	Wayne Gretzky	Edmonton
1982	Wayne Gretzky	Edmonton
1981	Mike Liut	St. Louis
1980	Marcel Dionne	Los Angeles
1979	Marcel Dionne	Los Angeles
1978	Guy Lafleur	Montreal
1977	Guy Lafleur	Montreal
1976	Guy Lafleur	Montreal
1975	Bobby Orr	Boston
1974	Phil Esposito	Boston
1973	Bobby Clarke	Philadelphia
1972	Jean Ratelle	NY Rangers
1971	Phil Esposito	Boston

JACK ADAMS AWARD WINNERS

	Winner	Runner-up
1997	Ted Nolan, Buf.	Ken Hitchcock, Dal.
1996	Scotty Bowman, Det.	Doug MacLean, Fla.
1995	Marc Crawford, Que.	Scotty Bowman, Det.
1994	Jacques Lemaire, N.J.	Kevin Constantine, S.J.
1993	Pat Burns, Tor.	Brian Sutter, Bos.
1992	Pat Quinn, Van.	Roger Neilson, NYR
1991	Brian Sutter, St.L.	Tom Webster, L.A.
1990	Bob Murdoch, Wpg.	Mike Milbury, Bos.
1989	Pat Burns, Mtl.	Bob McCammon, Van.
1988	Jacques Demers, Det.	Terry Crisp, Cgy.
1987	Jacques Demers, Det.	Jack Evans, Hfd.
1986	Glen Sather, Edm.	Jacques Demers, St.L.
1985	Mike Keenan, Phi.	Barry Long, Wpg.
1984	Bryan Murray, Wsh.	Scotty Bowman, Buf.
1983	Orval Tessier, Chi.	
1982	Tom Watt, Wpg.	
1981	Red Berenson, St.L.	Bob Berry, L.A.
1980	Pat Quinn, Phi.	
1979	Al Arbour, NYI	Fred Shero, NYR
1978	Bobby Kromm, Det.	Don Cherry, Bos.
1977	Scotty Bowman, Mtl.	Tom McVie, Wsh.
1976	Don Cherry, Bos.	
1975	Bob Pulford, L.A.	
1974	Fred Shero, Phi.	

NHL Amateur and Entry Draft

History

Year	Site	Date	Total Players Drafted
1963	Queen Elizabeth Hotel	June 5	21
1964	Queen Elizabeth Hotel	June 11	24
1965	Queen Elizabeth Hotel	April 27	11
1966	Mount Royal Hotel	April 25	24
1967	Queen Elizabeth Hotel	June 7	18
1968	Queen Elizabeth Hotel	June 13	24
1969	Queen Elizabeth Hotel	June 12	84
1970	Queen Elizabeth Hotel	June 11	115
1971	Queen Elizabeth Hotel	June 10	117
1972	Queen Elizabeth Hotel	June 8	152
1973	Mount Royal Hotel	May 15	168
1974	NHL Montreal Office	May 28	247
1975	NHL Montreal Office	June 3	217
1976	NHL Montreal Office	June 1	135
1977	NHL Montreal Office	June 14	185
1978	Queen Elizabeth Hotel	June 15	234
1979	Queen Elizabeth Hotel	August 9	126
1980	Montreal Forum	June 11	210
1981	Montreal Forum	June 10	211
1982	Montreal Forum	June 9	252
1983	Montreal Forum	June 8	242
1984	Montreal Forum	June 9	250
1985	Toronto Convention Centre	June 15	252
1986	Montreal Forum	June 21	252
1987	Joe Louis Sports Arena	June 13	252
1988	Montreal Forum	June 11	252
1989	Metropolitan Sports Center	June 17	252
1990	B. C. Place	June 16	250
1991	Memorial Auditorium	June 9	264
1992	Montreal Forum	June 20	264
1993	Colisée de Québec	June 26	286
1994	Hartford Civic Center	June 28-29	286
1995	Edmonton Coliseum	July 8	234
1996	Kiel Center	June 22	241
1997	Civic Arena	June 21	246

* The NHL Amateur Draft became the NHL Entry Draft in 1979

First Selections

Year	Player	Pos	Drafted By	Drafted From	Age
1969	Rejean Houle	LW	Montreal	Jr. Canadiens	19.8
1970	Gilbert Perreault	C	Buffalo	Jr. Canadiens	19.7
1971	Guy Lafleur	RW	Montreal	Quebec Remparts	19.9
1972	Billy Harris	RW	NY Islanders	Toronto Marlboros	20.4
1973	Denis Potvin	D	NY Islanders	Ottawa 67's	19.7
1974	Greg Joly	D	Washington	Regina Pats	20.0
1975	Mel Bridgman	C	Philadelphia	Victoria Cougars	20.1
1976	Rick Green	D	Washington	London Knights	20.3
1977	Dale McCourt	C	Detroit	St. Catharines Fincups	20.4
1978	Bobby Smith	C	Minnesota	Ottawa 67's	20.4
1979	Rob Ramage	D	Colorado	London Knights	20.5
1980	Doug Wickenheiser	C	Montreal	Regina Pats	19.2
1981	Dale Hawerchuk	C	Winnipeg	Cornwall Royals	18.2
1982	Gord Kluzak	D	Boston	Nanaimo Islanders	18.3
1983	Brian Lawton	C	Minnesota	Mount St. Charles HS	18.11
1984	Mario Lemieux	C	Pittsburgh	Laval Voisins	18.8
1985	Wendel Clark	LW/D	Toronto	Saskatoon Blades	18.7
1986	Joe Murphy	C	Detroit	Michigan State	18.8
1987	Pierre Turgeon	C	Buffalo	Granby Bisons	17.10
1988	Mike Modano	C	Minnesota	Prince Albert Raiders	18.0
1989	Mats Sundin	RW	Quebec	Nacka (Sweden)	18.4
1990	Owen Nolan	RW	Quebec	Cornwall Royals	18.4
1991	Eric Lindros	C	Quebec	Oshawa Generals	18.3
1992	Roman Hamrlik	D	Tampa Bay	ZPS Zlin (Czech.)	18.2
1993	Alexandre Daigle	C	Ottawa	Victoriaville Tigres	18.5
1994	Ed Jovanovski	D	Florida	Windsor Spitfires	18.0
1995	Bryan Berard	D	Ottawa	Detroit Jr. Red Wings	18.4
1996	Chris Phillips	D	Ottawa	Prince Albert Raiders	18.3
1997	Joe Thornton	C	Boston	Sault Ste. Marie	17.11

The Boston Bruins used 1997's first overall selection in the NHL Entry Draft to select center Joe Thornton of the Sault Ste. Marie Greyhounds. At 6'4", Thornton is a complete package: tough, fast and skilled. Profiles of all 26 first-round selections are found on page 204.

Draft Summary

Following is a summary of the number of players drafted from the Ontario Hockey League (OHL), Western Hockey League (WHL), Quebec Major Junior Hockey League (QMJHL), United States Colleges, United States High Schools, European Leagues and other Leagues throughout North America since 1969:

	OHL	WHL	QMJHL	US Colleges	US HS	International	Other
1969	36	20	11	7	0	1	9
1970	51	22	13	16	0	0	13
1971	41	28	13	22	0	0	13
1972	46	44	30	21	0	0	11
1973	56	49	24	25	0	0	14
1974	69	66	40	41	0	6	25
1975	55	57	28	59	0	6	12
1976	47	33	18	26	0	8	3
1977	42	44	40	49	0	5	5
1978	59	48	22	73	0	16	16
1979	48	37	19	15	0	6	1
1980	73	41	24	42	7	13	10
1981	59	37	28	21	17	32	17
1982	60	55	17	20	47	35	18
1983	57	41	24	14	35	34	37
1984	55	38	16	22	44	40	36
1985	59	47	15	20	48	31	31
1986	66	32	22	22	40	28	42
1987	32	36	17	40	69	38	20
1988	32	30	22	48	56	39	25
1989	39	44	16	48	47	38	20
1990	39	33	14	38	57	53	16
1991	43	40	25	43	37	55	21
1992	57	45	22	9	25	84	22
1993	60	44	23	17	33	78	31
1994	45	66	28	6	28	80	33
1995	54	55	35	5	2	69	14
1996	51	54	31	25	6	58	16
1997	52	63	19	26	4	63	19
Total	1483	1249	656	820	602	916	550

Total Drafted, 1969-1997:   6,276

Ontario Hockey League

Club	'69	'70	'71	'72	'73	'74	'75	'76	'77	'78	'79	'80	'81	'82	'83	'84	'85	'86	'87	'88	'89	'90	'91	'92	'93	'94	'95	'96	'97	Total
Peterborough	5	5	4	5	9	4	8	1	4	6	9	10	3	5	7	3	9	2	5	2	2	4	3	4	4	2	5	4	5	139
Oshawa	5	4	3	5	5	7	6	6	1	3	3	2	9	5	5	6	6	6	3	2	4	2	4	4	4	1	10	1	3	125
Kitchener	1	6	2	8	4	13	3	1	3	4	4	4	5	5	8	4	6	3	2	1	7	5	3	1	4	2	4	2	3	118
Ottawa	2	4	3	4	6	5	6	5	5	5	3	8	4	9	2	2	3	3	2	1	–	5	5	6	4	1	1	2	5	111
London	4	9	1	5	6	6	3	5	4	3	6	2	5	5	3	7	1	3	2	6	3	3	1	3	4	1	1	4	1	107
S.S. Marie	–	–	–	–	4	5	2	5	1	5	3	3	8	1	6	4	5	7	1	2	3	1	2	7	3	4	3	4	1	90
Sudbury	–	–	–	–	6	6	4	5	4	4	3	7	2	4	–	2	5	3	1	–	1	2	8	2	10	2	2	1	3	87
Kingston	–	–	–	–	–	4	4	6	4	9	2	8	5	2	1	3	3	4	1	1	–	2	2	3	5	2	3	4	4	82
Niagara Falls	4	2	1	4	–	–	–	–	2	3	5	8	6	6	–	–	–	–	–	–	4	4	4	4	4	3	2	6	–	72
Windsor	–	–	–	–	–	–	–	2	1	4	2	3	5	3	2	2	3	7	–	5	2	1	–	3	–	3	4	1	5	58
Guelph	–	–	–	–	–	–	–	–	–	–	–	–	–	–	1	5	3	8	2	–	4	–	–	2	2	7	5	6	1	46
North Bay	–	–	–	–	–	–	–	–	–	–	–	–	–	–	4	4	3	3	3	3	1	4	2	5	2	7	2	1	1	45
Belleville	–	–	–	–	–	–	–	–	–	–	–	–	–	–	3	4	4	5	2	–	4	2	1	4	–	3	3	–	5	40
Detroit	–	–	–	–	–	–	–	–	–	–	–	–	–	–	–	–	–	–	–	–	–	–	2	2	7	2	6	3	4	26
Owen Sound	–	–	–	–	–	–	–	–	–	–	–	–	–	–	–	–	–	–	–	–	–	1	1	2	4	3	2	3	2	18
Sarnia	–	–	–	–	–	–	–	–	–	–	–	–	–	–	–	–	–	–	–	–	–	–	–	–	–	–	1	7	2	10
Barrie	–	–	–	–	–	–	–	–	–	–	–	–	–	–	–	–	–	–	–	–	–	–	–	–	–	–	–	2	4	6
Erie	–	–	–	–	–	–	–	–	–	–	–	–	–	–	–	–	–	–	–	–	–	–	–	–	–	–	–	–	3	3
Teams no longer operating																														
Toronto	3	7	6	5	6	8	4	4	7	5	4	10	2	6	4	4	3	4	1	2	2	–	–	–	–	–	–	–	–	97
Hamilton	2	3	5	4	6	4	7	3	–	8	1	–	–	–	–	–	3	6	4	4	–	–	2	–	–	–	–	–	–	62
St. Catharines	5	5	8	5	4	7	8	4	6	–	–	–	–	–	–	–	–	–	–	–	–	–	–	–	–	–	–	–	–	52
Cornwall	–	–	–	–	–	–	–	–	–	–	–	–	–	7	4	3	2	2	3	3	2	3	3	5	–	–	–	–	–	37
Brantford	–	–	–	–	–	–	–	–	–	–	3	8	5	2	7	2	–	–	–	–	–	–	–	–	–	–	–	–	–	27
Montreal	5	6	8	1	–	–	–	–	–	–	–	–	–	–	–	–	–	–	–	–	–	–	–	–	–	–	–	–	–	20
Newmarket	–	–	–	–	–	–	–	–	–	–	–	–	–	–	–	–	–	–	–	–	–	–	–	–	3	2	–	–	–	5

Year	Total Ontario Drafted	Total Players Drafted	Ontario %
1969	36	84	42.9
1970	51	115	44.3
1971	41	117	35.0
1972	46	152	30.3
1973	56	168	33.3
1974	69	247	27.9
1975	55	217	25.3
1976	47	135	34.8
1977	42	185	22.7
1978	59	234	25.2
1979	48	126	38.1
1980	73	210	34.8
1981	59	211	28.0
1982	60	252	23.8
1983	57	242	23.6
1984	55	250	22.0
1985	59	252	23.4
1986	66	252	26.2
1987	32	252	12.7
1988	32	252	12.7
1989	39	252	15.5
1990	39	250	15.6
1991	43	264	16.3
1992	57	264	21.6
1993	60	286	21.0
1994	45	286	15.7
1995	54	234	23.1
1996	51	241	21.1
1997	52	246	21.1

Western Hockey League

Club	'69	'70	'71	'72	'73	'74	'75	'76	'77	'78	'79	'80	'81	'82	'83	'84	'85	'86	'87	'88	'89	'90	'91	'92	'93	'94	'95	'96	'97	Total
Regina	–	–	5	5	1	8	5	3	1	4	1	3	5	6	8	4	4	3	2	–	5	1	–	4	–	3	2	4	3	90
Saskatoon	1	–	1	3	8	4	5	3	4	1	2	2	3	5	5	3	1	5	4	4	3	2	2	3	2	4	2	2	2	86
Portland	–	–	–	–	–	–	–	–	4	8	7	8	6	7	7	5	2	4	3	1	4	1	1	4	4	3	2	1	3	85
Medicine Hat	–	–	–	4	6	4	5	3	5	4	–	4	2	1	2	1	6	2	5	1	4	1	3	3	1	6	2	7	2	84
Brandon	–	3	1	5	2	7	4	–	3	1	10	5	2	2	1	3	2	1	3	3	–	1	1	1	2	5	6	2	5	81
Kamloops	–	–	–	–	–	4	4	4	4	–	–	–	–	2	4	4	4	4	3	1	5	4	6	3	2	9	5	4	3	79
Lethbridge	–	–	–	–	–	–	3	2	3	5	4	1	4	7	2	1	5	1	–	3	3	4	7	3	4	3	3	1	5	74
Seattle	–	–	–	–	–	–	–	–	–	4	2	3	–	6	–	1	3	1	2	4	2	6	3	2	4	5	5	1	8	62
Prince Albert	–	–	–	–	–	–	–	–	–	–	–	–	–	4	2	2	6	6	1	3	3	4	6	2	5	3	4	3	5	59
Spokane	–	–	–	–	–	–	–	–	–	–	–	–	1	–	–	–	–	–	1	3	2	1	5	7	4	4	4	5	4	41
Swift Current	1	–	1	–	3	6	–	–	–	–	–	–	–	–	–	–	–	–	5	2	2	2	1	1	5	4	4	1	2	40
Moose Jaw	–	–	–	–	–	–	–	–	–	–	–	–	–	–	–	–	4	1	3	–	3	1	2	3	2	3	4	4	4	34
Tri-City	–	–	–	–	–	–	–	–	–	–	–	–	–	–	–	–	–	–	–	–	4	3	3	5	2	2	6	6	1	32
Red Deer	–	–	–	–	–	–	–	–	–	–	–	–	–	–	–	–	–	–	–	–	–	–	–	–	3	5	2	4	3	17
Kelowna	–	–	–	–	–	–	–	–	–	–	–	–	–	–	–	–	–	–	–	–	–	–	–	–	–	–	–	4	7	11
Prince George	–	–	–	–	–	–	–	–	–	–	–	–	–	–	–	–	–	–	–	–	–	–	–	–	–	–	2	2	2	6
Calgary	–	–	–	–	–	–	–	–	–	–	–	–	–	–	–	–	–	–	–	–	–	–	–	–	–	–	–	3	–	3
Edmonton	–	–	–	–	–	–	–	–	–	–	–	–	–	–	–	–	–	–	–	–	–	–	–	–	–	–	–	–	4	4
Teams no longer operating																														
Victoria	–	–	–	2	2	5	7	4	3	3	1	8	6	2	3	4	2	1	2	4	4	2	–	1	2	2	–	–	–	70
Calgary	3	5	2	7	4	8	4	4	4	3	–	2	5	4	3	3	3	2	–	–	–	–	–	–	–	–	–	–	–	66
New Westm'r	–	–	–	6	8	7	9	5	8	6	5	1	–	–	–	2	1	1	2	1	–	–	–	–	–	–	–	–	–	62
Flin Flon	4	4	5	2	4	7	4	3	1	5	–	–	–	–	–	–	–	–	–	–	–	–	–	–	–	–	–	–	–	39
Winnipeg	3	2	4	2	5	4	4	–	4	–	–	–	1	4	1	–	–	–	–	–	–	–	–	–	–	–	–	–	–	34
Edmonton	4	4	5	6	6	2	3	2	–	–	2	–	–	–	–	–	–	–	–	–	–	–	–	–	–	–	–	–	–	34
Billings	–	–	–	–	–	–	–	–	–	4	3	4	2	–	–	–	–	–	–	–	–	–	–	–	–	–	–	–	–	13
Estevan	4	4	4	–	–	–	–	–	–	–	–	–	–	–	–	–	–	–	–	–	–	–	–	–	–	–	–	–	–	12
Tacoma	–	–	–	–	–	–	–	–	–	–	–	–	–	–	–	–	–	–	–	–	–	–	–	3	2	5	2	–	–	12
Kelowna	–	–	–	–	–	–	–	–	–	–	–	–	–	–	2	4	5	–	–	–	–	–	–	–	–	–	–	–	–	11
Nanaimo	–	–	–	–	–	–	–	–	–	–	–	–	–	5	1	–	–	–	–	–	–	–	–	–	–	–	–	–	–	6
Vancouver	–	–	–	2	–	–	–	–	–	–	–	–	–	–	–	–	–	–	–	–	–	–	–	–	–	–	–	–	–	2

Year	Total Western Drafted	Total Players Drafted	Western %
1969	20	84	23.8
1970	22	115	19.1
1971	28	117	23.9
1972	44	152	28.9
1973	49	168	29.2
1974	66	247	26.7
1975	57	217	26.3
1976	33	135	24.4
1977	44	185	23.8
1978	48	234	20.5
1979	37	126	29.4
1980	41	210	19.5
1981	37	211	17.5
1982	55	252	21.8
1983	41	242	16.9
1984	37	250	14.8
1985	48	252	19.0
1986	32	252	12.7
1987	36	252	14.3
1988	30	252	11.9
1989	44	252	17.5
1990	33	250	13.2
1991	40	264	15.2
1992	45	264	17.0
1993	44	286	15.4
1994	66	286	23.0
1995	55	234	23.5
1996	54	241	22.4
1997	63	246	25.6

Quebec Major Junior Hockey League

Club	'69	'70	'71	'72	'73	'74	'75	'76	'77	'78	'79	'80	'81	'82	'83	'84	'85	'86	'87	'88	'89	'90	'91	'92	'93	'94	'95	'96	'97	Total
Shawinigan	3	2	1	6	1	5	3	–	3	–	–	2	2	5	5	2	–	2	1	–	2	–	2	3	1	1	2	4	1	59
Sherbrooke	–	–	2	2	4	3	7	5	6	3	4	1	5	2	–	–	–	–	–	–	–	–	–	–	3	2	4	–	1	54
Laval	–	–	–	1	–	2	1	1	4	2	1	–	–	2	1	2	–	5	3	1	3	3	4	1	2	5	4	2	1	51
Hull	–	–	–	–	–	–	3	2	2	3	–	3	1	–	3	1	–	4	3	2	2	3	3	3	3	1	3	3	–	48
Drummondville	2	4	1	4	2	1	–	–	–	–	–	–	–	–	–	1	2	2	2	4	1	–	4	2	2	1	4	3	2	44
Chicoutimi	–	–	–	–	–	1	–	–	5	1	1	3	6	1	3	–	3	1	2	2	1	1	–	1	1	3	2	–	2	40
Granby	–	–	–	–	–	–	–	–	–	–	–	–	–	2	1	3	2	2	4	–	2	–	2	–	1	5	2	3	1	30
Beauport	–	–	–	–	–	–	–	–	–	–	–	–	–	–	–	–	–	–	–	–	–	–	1	3	1	3	7	3	3	21
Victoriaville	–	–	–	–	–	–	–	–	–	–	–	–	–	–	–	–	–	–	–	4	–	1	–	2	6	1	1	3	2	20
St. Hyacinthe	–	–	–	–	–	–	–	–	–	–	–	–	–	–	–	–	–	–	–	–	–	3	1	2	1	4	–	4	–	15
Val D'Or	–	–	–	–	–	–	–	–	–	–	–	–	–	–	–	–	–	–	–	–	–	–	–	–	–	1	2	4	2	9
Halifax	–	–	–	–	–	–	–	–	–	–	–	–	–	–	–	–	–	–	–	–	–	–	–	–	–	–	3	1	3	7
Moncton	–	–	–	–	–	–	–	–	–	–	–	–	–	–	–	–	–	–	–	–	–	–	–	–	–	–	–	1	1	2
Teams no longer operating																														
Quebec	1	1	2	4	6	6	1	3	7	1	3	2	2	1	2	2	3	–	–	–	–	–	–	–	–	–	–	–	–	47
Trois Rivieres	–	1	2	2	2	2	3	2	6	3	2	2	2	1	3	–	3	–	1	3	3	1	2	1	–	–	–	–	–	47
Cornwall	2	1	2	6	4	8	1	3	1	6	1	5	5	–	–	–	–	–	–	–	–	–	–	–	–	–	–	–	–	45
Montreal	–	–	–	–	4	4	8	1	3	2	4	3	–	3	–	–	–	–	–	–	–	–	–	–	–	–	–	–	–	32
Sorel	2	3	1	3	1	8	1	1	3	–	–	–	5	–	–	–	–	–	–	–	–	–	–	–	–	–	–	–	–	28
Verdun	–	1	1	2	–	–	–	–	–	1	3	3	–	–	3	3	–	3	0	3	1	–	–	3	–	–	–	–	–	27
St. Jean	–	–	–	–	–	–	–	–	–	–	–	–	–	–	2	–	1	1	0	3	1	–	3	1	2	1	1	–	–	16
Longueuil	–	–	–	–	–	–	–	–	–	–	–	–	–	–	1	2	1	2	1	–	–	2	3	–	–	–	–	–	–	12
St. Jerome	1	–	1	–	–	–	–	–	–	–	–	–	–	–	–	–	–	–	–	–	–	–	–	–	–	–	–	–	–	2

Year	Total Quebec Drafted	Total Players Drafted	Quebec %
1969	11	84	13.1
1970	13	115	11.3
1971	13	117	11.1
1972	30	152	19.7
1973	24	168	14.3
1974	40	247	16.2
1975	28	217	12.9
1976	18	135	13.3
1977	40	185	21.6
1978	22	234	9.4
1979	19	126	15.1
1980	24	210	11.4
1981	28	211	13.3
1982	17	252	6.7
1983	24	242	9.9
1984	16	250	6.4
1985	15	252	5.9
1986	22	252	8.7
1987	17	252	6.7
1988	22	252	8.7
1989	16	252	6.3
1990	14	250	5.6
1991	25	264	9.5
1992	22	264	8.3
1993	23	286	8.0
1994	28	286	9.7
1995	35	234	14.9
1996	31	241	12.8
1997	19	246	7.7

United States Colleges

Club	'69	'70	'71	'72	'73	'74	'75	'76	'77	'78	'79	'80	'81	'82	'83	'84	'85	'86	'87	'88	'89	'90	'91	'92	'93	'94	'95	'96	'97	Total
Minnesota	1	3	2	-	-	9	4	4	5	5	2	3	1	1	1	-	-	2	1	1	1	-	-	-	-	-	2	3	2	53
Michigan	1	-	-	-	2	2	3	3	1	6	-	4	-	-	-	1	1	-	1	2	3	5	4	2	1	1	-	3	1	47
Michigan Tech	-	-	3	1	2	5	4	4	1	2	1	4	-	1	-	2	2	2	1	1	2	1	2	-	1	2	-	1	-	45
Boston U.	-	4	-	-	1	1	1	1	4	5	1	-	1	-	-	1	1	2	2	3	1	2	2	1	1	-	1	1	1	38
Denver	1	3	2	4	2	3	1	2	2	2	2	1	-	1	-	-	1	2	4	1	1	-	-	-	-	-	-	-	3	38
Wisconsin	-	1	2	4	5	4	4	2	3	-	1	-	3	2	-	1	1	-	1	-	1	-	1	-	-	-	-	-	-	36
Michigan State	-	-	1	-	1	1	1	1	-	-	-	2	-	2	-	2	-	1	1	4	4	5	4	1	1	1	-	1	1	35
North Dakota	2	3	3	1	4	2	1	-	1	2	3	3	1	-	-	1	-	-	-	2	1	1	-	-	-	-	-	-	2	33
Providence	-	-	-	-	-	3	2	3	4	-	5	4	1	2	-	1	1	-	-	-	1	-	-	-	-	-	-	-	1	28
Clarkson	-	-	2	2	1	-	2	-	2	2	1	1	1	1	1	1	-	-	1	1	1	3	2	1	1	-	-	-	-	27
New Hampshire	-	-	-	1	1	3	6	-	4	1	1	2	1	1	2	1	1	2	-	-	-	-	-	-	-	-	-	-	1	26
Cornell	-	-	2	1	1	-	1	1	1	1	-	1	1	1	-	1	2	-	1	2	5	2	-	-	-	-	-	-	1	24
Harvard	-	-	2	-	-	-	2	-	2	2	-	-	-	1	1	-	2	-	1	1	2	-	-	-	2	1	-	3	1	23
Boston College	-	1	-	-	-	-	1	1	-	5	-	2	1	1	-	-	-	1	2	-	2	-	-	-	-	-	-	2	3	22
Bowling Green	-	-	-	-	1	3	2	1	1	1	1	-	1	-	-	-	-	3	2	1	3	1	-	-	-	-	-	-	1	22
Lake Superior	-	-	-	-	1	1	1	-	3	-	-	-	-	-	1	-	3	-	3	2	3	1	-	1	-	-	1	1	-	22
Notre Dame	-	-	2	3	-	-	7	2	-	3	1	1	-	-	-	-	-	-	-	-	-	-	-	-	-	-	-	1	2	22
Colorado	2	1	-	-	1	3	1	2	2	-	1	-	-	-	3	-	1	-	1	-	-	2	-	-	-	1	-	-	-	21
W. Michigan	-	-	-	-	-	-	-	2	-	-	2	-	-	2	2	-	2	1	1	1	1	4	-	2	-	-	-	1	-	21
St. Lawrence	-	-	-	-	-	-	1	-	1	4	-	-	-	3	-	1	1	1	1	1	1	-	1	-	-	-	1	1	1	21
RPI	-	-	-	-	1	-	-	-	1	3	-	1	2	1	1	-	1	-	2	2	-	-	3	1	-	-	-	-	1	20
Northern Mich.	-	-	-	-	-	-	-	-	4	-	1	2	1	-	-	-	4	1	2	-	1	-	-	-	1	-	-	1	-	17
Vermont	-	-	-	1	-	4	-	1	1	-	1	1	-	1	1	2	-	-	1	-	-	1	-	-	1	-	1	-	1	17
Miami of Ohio	-	-	-	-	-	-	-	-	-	-	-	-	1	-	2	4	2	-	2	1	1	-	-	-	-	-	-	-	-	13
Ohio State	-	-	-	-	-	-	-	2	1	-	-	-	-	-	1	1	-	-	1	2	2	-	1	1	1	1	-	1	1	14
Maine	-	-	-	-	-	-	-	-	1	1	-	-	1	-	1	-	3	2	1	-	-	1	-	-	1	-	1	1	-	12
Minn.-Duluth	-	2	1	-	-	-	1	1	-	1	-	1	-	-	-	-	-	2	1	2	1	-	-	-	1	-	-	-	-	12
Brown	-	-	-	-	1	2	1	-	3	2	-	-	1	-	-	-	-	-	-	-	-	-	1	-	-	-	-	-	-	11
Colgate	-	-	-	-	1	-	-	-	2	1	-	-	-	-	-	-	-	1	1	2	2	-	-	-	-	-	-	-	-	10
Yale	-	-	1	-	1	-	-	2	1	-	-	1	-	-	1	-	1	-	1	1	-	-	-	-	-	-	-	-	-	10
Northeastern	-	-	-	-	-	1	-	1	-	1	-	1	1	-	1	1	-	1	-	1	-	-	-	-	-	-	-	-	-	8
Princeton	-	-	-	-	-	1	-	1	-	1	1	1	-	1	-	-	1	-	1	-	1	-	-	-	-	-	-	-	-	8
Ferris State	-	-	-	-	-	-	-	-	-	-	-	-	-	-	-	-	2	1	1	1	2	-	-	-	-	-	-	-	-	7
St. Louis	-	-	-	-	1	2	-	1	2	-	-	-	-	-	-	-	-	-	-	-	-	-	-	-	-	-	-	-	-	6
U. of Ill.-Chi.	-	-	-	-	-	-	-	-	-	-	-	-	1	-	2	1	2	-	-	-	-	-	-	-	-	-	-	-	-	6
Pennsylvania	-	-	-	1	2	1	-	-	-	1	-	-	-	-	-	-	-	-	-	-	-	-	-	-	-	-	-	-	-	5
Dartmouth	-	-	1	-	-	-	-	1	-	1	-	-	-	-	-	1	-	-	1	-	-	-	-	-	-	-	-	-	-	5
Merrimack	-	-	-	-	-	-	-	1	-	-	1	-	-	1	-	-	1	-	-	-	-	-	1	-	-	-	-	-	-	5
Union College	-	-	-	-	-	-	4	-	-	-	-	-	-	-	-	-	-	-	-	-	-	-	-	-	-	-	-	-	-	4
Lowell	-	-	-	-	-	1	1	-	1	-	1	-	-	-	1	-	-	-	-	-	-	-	-	-	-	-	-	-	-	4
Alaska-Anchorage	-	-	-	-	-	-	-	-	-	-	-	-	-	-	-	-	-	-	2	1	-	1	-	-	-	-	-	-	-	4
Babson College	-	-	-	-	-	-	-	-	-	-	-	-	-	-	-	1	-	1	1	-	-	-	-	-	-	-	-	-	-	3
St. Cloud State	-	-	-	-	-	-	-	-	-	-	-	-	-	-	-	-	-	1	-	-	-	-	-	-	-	-	-	2	-	3
Alaska-Fairbanks	-	-	-	-	-	-	-	-	-	-	-	-	-	-	-	-	-	-	-	-	1	1	-	-	-	-	-	-	-	2
Salem State	-	-	-	-	1	-	-	-	-	-	-	-	-	-	-	-	-	-	-	-	-	-	-	-	-	-	-	-	-	1
Bemidji State	-	1	-	-	-	-	-	-	-	-	-	-	-	-	-	-	-	-	-	-	-	-	-	-	-	-	-	-	-	1
San Diego U.	-	-	-	-	-	-	-	-	-	-	-	-	-	-	-	-	-	1	-	-	-	-	-	-	-	-	-	-	-	1
Greenway	-	-	-	-	-	-	-	-	-	-	-	-	-	-	-	-	-	-	-	-	-	1	-	-	-	-	-	-	-	1
St. Anselen College	-	-	-	-	-	-	-	-	-	-	-	-	-	-	-	-	-	-	-	-	-	1	-	-	-	-	-	-	-	1
Hamilton College	-	-	-	-	-	-	-	-	-	-	-	-	-	-	-	-	-	-	-	-	-	1	-	-	-	-	-	-	-	1
St. Thomas	-	-	-	-	-	-	-	-	-	-	-	-	-	-	-	-	-	-	-	-	1	-	-	-	-	-	-	-	-	1
Amer. Int'l College	-	-	-	-	-	-	-	-	-	-	-	-	-	-	-	-	-	-	-	-	1	-	-	-	-	-	-	-	-	1
Wisc.-River Falls	-	-	-	-	-	-	-	-	-	-	-	-	-	-	-	-	-	-	-	-	-	-	-	-	-	-	-	1	-	1
Army	-	-	-	-	-	-	-	-	-	-	-	-	-	-	-	-	-	-	-	-	-	-	-	-	-	-	1	-	-	1

Year	Total College Drafted	Total Players Drafted	College %
1969	7	84	8.3
1970	16	115	13.9
1971	22	117	18.8
1972	21	152	13.8
1973	25	168	14.9
1974	41	247	16.6
1975	59	217	26.7
1976	26	135	19.3
1977	49	185	26.5
1978	73	234	31.2
1979	15	126	11.9
1980	42	210	20.0
1981	21	211	10.0
1982	20	252	7.9
1983	14	242	5.8
1984	22	250	8.8
1985	20	252	7.9
1986	22	252	8.7
1987	40	252	15.9
1988	48	252	19.0
1989	48	252	19.0
1990	38	250	15.2
1991	43	264	16.3
1992	9	264	3.4
1993	17	286	5.9
1994	6	286	2.1
1995	5	234	2.1
1996	25	241	10.4
1997	26	246	10.5
Total	**820**	**6276**	**13.0**

United States High Schools (10 or more players drafted)

Club	'80	'81	'82	'83	'84	'85	'86	'87	'88	'89	'90	'91	'92	'93	'94	'95	'96	'97	Total
Northwood Prep (NY)	-	-	2	1	-	2	2	4	1	1	3	1	-	1	1	-	-	-	19
Belmont Hill (MA)	-	-	-	1	-	2	1	2	1	3	2	1	2	-	1	-	-	-	16
Cushing Acad. (MA)	-	-	-	-	1	-	-	-	3	2	3	1	-	2	2	-	1	1	16
Edina (MN)	-	1	4	2	2	-	-	1	2	2	1	-	1	-	-	-	-	-	16
Hill-Murray (MN)	-	-	-	-	3	-	3	3	-	2	3	-	-	1	-	-	-	-	15
Mount St. Charles (RI)	-	1	-	3	1	-	2	1	2	1	1	-	-	-	-	-	-	-	12
Culver Mil. Acad. (IN)	-	-	-	-	-	-	2	1	2	2	1	2	2	-	-	-	-	-	12
Catholic Memorial (MA)	-	-	-	-	-	-	2	-	1	1	2	-	-	2	1	2	-	-	11
Canterbury (CT)	-	-	-	-	-	-	2	-	3	-	2	-	2	1	-	-	-	-	10
Matignon (MA)	1	1	1	-	3	-	-	3	-	-	1	-	-	-	-	-	-	-	10
Roseau (MN)	1	-	1	1	1	-	1	-	-	1	3	1	-	-	-	-	-	-	10

Year	Total USHS Drafted	Total Players Drafted	USHS %
1980	7	210	3.3
1981	17	211	8.1
1982	47	252	18.6
1983	35	242	14.5
1984	44	250	17.6
1985	48	252	19.1
1986	40	252	15.9
1987	69	252	27.4
1988	56	252	22.2
1989	47	252	18.7
1990	57	250	22.8
1991	37	264	14.0
1992	25	264	9.5
1993	33	286	11.5
1994	28	286	9.7
1995	2	234	0.9
1996	6	241	2.4
1997	4	246	1.6
Total	**602**	**6276**	**9.6**

International

Country	'69	'70	'71	'72	'73	'74	'75	'76	'77	'78	'79	'80	'81	'82	'83	'84	'85	'86	'87	'88	'89	'90	'91	'92	'93	'94	'95	'96	'97	Total
USSR/CIS	–	–	–	–	–	–	1	–	–	2	–	–	–	3	5	1	2	1	2	11	18	14	25	45	31	35	27	17	16	256
Sweden	–	–	–	–	–	5	2	5	2	8	5	9	14	14	10	14	16	9	15	14	9	7	11	11	18	17	8	16	14	253
Czech Republic and Slovakia	–	–	–	–	–	–	–	–	–	–	–	2	1	–	4	13	8	6	11	5	8	21	9	17	15	18	21	14	17	212
Finland	1	–	–	–	–	1	3	2	3	2	–	4	12	5	9	10	4	10	6	7	3	9	6	8	9	8	12	7	11	152
Germany	–	–	–	–	–	–	–	–	–	2	–	–	2	–	1	2	1	–	1	2	–	–	1	1	3	1	1	3	1	23
Switzerland	–	–	–	–	–	–	–	1	–	–	–	–	–	–	–	–	–	–	–	–	–	–	1	–	2	1	–	1	3	9
Norway	–	–	–	–	–	–	–	–	–	–	–	–	–	–	–	–	–	–	2	–	–	2	1	–	–	–	–	–	1	6
Denmark	–	–	–	–	–	–	–	–	–	–	–	–	–	–	–	–	–	1	1	–	–	–	–	–	–	–	–	–	–	2
Scotland	–	–	–	–	–	–	–	–	–	–	–	–	–	–	–	–	–	1	–	–	–	–	–	–	–	–	–	–	–	1
Poland	–	–	–	–	–	–	–	–	–	–	–	–	–	–	–	–	–	–	–	–	–	–	1	–	–	–	–	–	–	1
Japan	–	–	–	–	–	–	–	–	–	–	–	–	–	–	–	–	–	–	–	–	–	–	–	1	–	–	–	–	–	1

Sweden

Club	'74	'75	'76	'77	'78	'79	'80	'81	'82	'83	'84	'85	'86	'87	'88	'89	'90	'91	'92	'93	'94	'95	'96	'97	Total
Djurgarden Stockholm	1	1	1	–	–	1	2	–	1	2	1	–	1	2	–	1	1	2	1	1	–	3	2	2	26
Farjestad Karlstad	–	–	–	2	2	–	1	2	1	1	1	2	–	–	–	1	–	1	2	1	–	2	–	3	22
MoDo Hockey Ornskoldsvik	–	–	1	–	–	1	–	–	1	–	2	–	–	1	–	–	–	2	2	5	–	–	3	3	21
Leksand	1	–	–	–	–	1	–	–	1	–	2	2	1	1	2	1	–	2	–	2	2	–	1		19
AIK Solna	–	–	1	–	1	1	–	2	3	1	–	4	–	–	–	–	1	1	1	–	1	–	–	1	18
Brynas Gavle	1	–	–	–	1	1	1	1	–	1	2	–	–	4	–	–	–	–	–	1	–	–	1	1	15
Sodertalje	–	–	–	–	1	–	–	1	1	1	2	2	2	–	–	2	–	–	–	1	–	–	–		13
Vastra Frolunda Goteborg	–	–	–	–	–	–	–	–	–	–	2	1	–	1	1	1	–	–	1	–	3	1	1		12
Skelleftea	–	1	1	–	–	–	–	1	1	2	1	–	–	–	1	–	–	–	–	1	–	–	–	1	10
HV 71 Jonkoping	–	–	–	–	–	–	–	1	–	–	–	–	–	1	1	–	1	–	–	–	2	–	2	1	9
Vasteras	–	–	–	–	–	–	–	–	–	–	–	–	–	–	2	2	1	1	–	1	1	–	–		8
Rogle Angelholm	–	–	–	–	–	–	–	–	–	–	–	–	–	1	2	–	–	–	–	2	2	1	–		8
Lulea	–	–	–	–	–	–	1	1	–	–	–	–	1	1	1	–	–	–	1	–	–	–	–	1	7
Sundsvall Timra[1]	–	–	–	–	–	–	1	2	–	–	–	1	1	–	–	–	–	–	–	–	1	–	–		6
Malmo	–	–	–	–	–	–	–	–	–	–	–	–	–	–	1	–	–	–	1	1	1	–	2		6
Bjorkloven Umea	–	–	–	–	–	–	2	1	–	–	–	1	–	–	1	–	–	–	–	–	–	–	–		5
Orebro	–	–	1	–	1	–	–	–	–	1	–	1	–	1	–	–	–	–	–	–	–	–	–		5
Nacka	–	–	–	–	–	–	–	–	–	–	–	–	1	–	–	1	–	–	2	–	–	–	–		4
Hammarby Stockholm	–	–	–	–	–	–	1	1	–	–	–	–	–	–	–	–	–	–	–	1	1	–	–		4
Mora	–	–	–	–	–	–	–	–	–	1	–	–	1	–	–	–	–	–	–	–	–	–	1	1	4
Falun	–	–	–	–	–	–	–	1	–	–	–	–	–	–	1	–	–	1	–	–	–	–	–		3
Team Kiruna	–	–	–	–	1	–	–	–	1	–	–	–	–	–	–	–	–	–	–	1	–	–	–		3
Boden	1	–	–	–	–	–	–	–	–	–	–	–	1	–	–	–	–	–	–	–	1	–	–		3
Pitea	–	–	–	–	–	–	–	–	1	–	–	–	–	–	–	–	1	–	–	–	1	–	–		3
Huddinge	–	–	–	–	–	–	–	–	–	–	–	–	–	–	–	–	–	1	–	–	–	–	2		3
Troja	–	–	–	–	–	–	–	–	–	–	–	1	–	–	1	–	–	–	–	–	–	–	–		2
Ostersund	–	–	–	–	–	–	–	–	–	–	–	1	–	1	–	–	–	–	–	–	–	–	–		2
Almtuna	–	–	–	–	–	–	–	–	1	–	–	–	–	–	–	–	–	–	–	–	–	–	–		1
Danderyd Hockey	–	–	–	–	–	–	–	–	–	–	–	–	–	–	–	–	1	–	–	–	–	–	–		1
Fagersta	–	–	–	–	–	–	–	–	1	–	–	–	–	–	–	–	–	–	–	–	–	–	–		1
Karskoga	–	–	–	–	1	–	–	–	–	–	–	–	–	–	–	–	–	–	–	–	–	–	–		1
Stocksund	–	–	–	–	–	–	–	–	1	–	–	–	–	–	–	–	–	–	–	–	–	–	–		1
S/G Hockey 83 Gavle	–	–	–	–	–	–	–	–	–	–	1	–	–	–	–	–	–	–	–	–	–	–	–		1
Talje	–	–	–	–	–	–	–	–	–	–	–	–	–	1	–	–	–	–	–	–	–	–	–		1
Tunabro	1	–	–	–	–	–	–	–	–	–	–	–	–	–	–	–	–	–	–	–	–	–	–		1
Uppsala	–	–	–	–	–	–	–	–	–	–	–	–	–	–	–	–	1	–	–	–	–	–	–		1
Grums	–	–	–	–	–	–	–	–	–	–	–	–	–	–	–	–	–	–	–	–	1	–	–		1
Vallentuna	–	–	–	–	–	–	–	–	–	–	–	–	–	–	–	–	–	–	–	–	–	1	–		1
Vita Hasten	–	–	–	–	–	–	–	–	–	–	–	–	–	–	–	–	–	–	–	–	–	–	1		1

Former club names: [1]–Timra

Russia/C.I.S.

Club	'74	'75	'76	'77	'78	'79	'80	'81	'82	'83	'84	'85	'86	'87	'88	'89	'90	'91	'92	'93	'94	'95	'96	'97	Total
CSKA Moscow	–	–	–	–	1	–	–	–	1	4	–	1	1	1	5	8	3	4	7	3	5	2	3	–	49
Dynamo Moscow	–	–	–	–	–	–	–	–	–	–	–	–	–	–	2	3	4	7	10	2	1	7	1	1	38
Krylja Sovetov Moscow	–	–	–	–	–	–	–	–	–	–	–	–	–	–	1	1	2	4	3	1	5	3	2	1	23
Spartak Moscow	–	–	–	–	–	–	–	–	1	–	–	1	–	1	–	–	–	1	4	–	6	1	–	–	15
Traktor Chelyabinsk	–	–	–	–	–	–	–	–	–	–	–	–	–	–	–	2	–	–	2	7	1	1	–	1	14
Sokol Kiev	–	–	–	–	–	–	–	–	–	–	1	–	–	–	1	–	1	2	3	1	–	2	–	–	11
Torpedo Yaroslavl	–	–	–	–	–	–	–	–	–	–	–	–	–	–	–	–	1	2	–	–	1	5	1	1	11
Pardaugava Riga[1]	–	1	–	–	–	–	–	–	–	–	–	–	–	–	1	2	–	1	4	1	–	–	–	–	10
Khimik Voskresensk	–	–	–	–	–	–	–	–	–	1	–	–	–	–	–	1	3	1	2	–	1	–	–	–	9
Dynamo-2 Moscow	–	–	–	–	–	–	–	–	–	–	–	–	–	–	–	–	–	–	2	1	2	–	–	3	8
Salavat Yulayev Ufa	–	–	–	–	–	–	–	–	–	–	–	–	–	–	–	–	–	–	–	2	2	1	1	1	7
Lada Togliatti	–	–	–	–	–	–	–	–	–	–	–	–	–	–	–	–	–	–	1	2	–	–	1	3	7
SKA St. Peterburg[2]	–	–	–	–	1	–	–	–	1	–	–	–	–	–	–	–	–	2	1	–	1	–	–	–	6
Torpedo Ust Kamenogorsk	–	–	–	–	–	–	–	–	–	–	–	–	–	–	–	–	–	–	1	1	2	1	–	–	5
CSKA-2 Moscow	–	–	–	–	–	–	–	–	–	–	–	–	–	–	–	–	–	–	–	–	1	–	2	2	5
Torpedo-2 Yaroslavl	–	–	–	–	–	–	–	–	–	–	–	–	–	–	–	–	–	–	–	–	–	1	2	2	5
Tivali Minsk[3]	–	–	–	–	–	–	–	–	–	–	–	–	–	–	1	–	–	–	–	2	1	–	–	–	4
Avangard Omsk	–	–	–	–	–	–	–	–	–	–	–	–	–	–	–	–	–	–	–	–	3	–	1	–	4
Severstal Cherepovets[5]	–	–	–	–	–	–	–	–	–	–	–	–	–	–	–	–	–	–	1	1	–	1	1	–	4
Kristall Elektrostal	–	–	–	–	–	–	–	–	–	–	–	–	–	–	–	–	–	–	–	3	–	–	–	–	3
Torpedo Nizhny Novgorod[4]	–	–	–	–	–	–	–	–	–	–	–	–	–	–	–	–	–	1	–	2	–	–	–	–	3
Molot Perm	–	–	–	–	–	–	–	–	–	–	–	–	–	–	–	–	–	–	–	–	1	1	–	–	2
Argus Moscow	–	–	–	–	–	–	–	–	–	–	–	–	–	–	–	–	–	–	1	–	–	–	–	–	1
Dizelist Penza	–	–	–	–	–	–	–	–	–	–	–	–	–	–	–	–	–	–	1	–	–	–	–	–	1
Dynamo Kharkov	–	–	–	–	–	–	–	–	–	–	–	–	–	–	–	1	–	–	–	–	–	–	–	–	1
Izhorets St. Peterburg	–	–	–	–	–	–	–	–	–	–	–	–	–	–	–	–	–	–	1	–	–	–	–	–	1
Khimik Novopolotsk	–	–	–	–	–	–	–	–	–	–	–	–	–	–	–	–	–	–	–	1	–	–	–	–	1
Kristall Saratov	–	–	–	–	–	–	–	–	–	–	–	–	–	–	–	–	–	–	1	–	–	–	–	–	1
Krylja Sovetov-2 Moscow	–	–	–	–	–	–	–	–	–	–	–	–	–	–	–	–	–	–	–	1	–	–	–	–	1
Itil Kazan	–	–	–	–	–	–	–	–	–	–	–	–	–	–	–	–	–	–	–	–	1	–	–	–	1
Mechel Chelyabinsk	–	–	–	–	–	–	–	–	–	–	–	–	–	–	–	–	–	–	–	–	1	–	–	–	1
CSK VVS Samara	–	–	–	–	–	–	–	–	–	–	–	–	–	–	–	–	–	–	–	–	–	1	–	–	1
Avtomobilist Yekaterinburg	–	–	–	–	–	–	–	–	–	–	–	–	–	–	–	–	–	–	–	–	–	–	1	–	1
Salavat Novoil Ufa	–	–	–	–	–	–	–	–	–	–	–	–	–	–	–	–	–	–	–	–	–	–	1	–	1
Neftekhimik Nizhnekamsk	–	–	–	–	–	–	–	–	–	–	–	–	–	–	–	–	–	–	–	–	–	–	–	1	1

Former club names: [1]–Dynamo Riga, HC Riga, [2]–SKA Leningrad, [3]–Dynamo Minsk, [4]–Torpedo Gorky, [5]–Metallurg Cherepovets

Year	Total International Drafted	Total Players Drafted	International %
1969	1	84	1.2
1970	0	115	0
1971	0	117	0
1972	0	152	0
1973	0	168	0
1974	6	247	2.4
1975	6	217	2.8
1976	8	135	5.9
1977	5	185	2.7
1978	16	234	6.8
1979	6	126	4.8
1980	13	210	6.2
1981	32	211	15.2
1982	35	252	13.9
1983	34	242	14.0
1984	40	250	17.6
1985	31	252	12.3
1986	28	252	11.1
1987	38	252	15.1
1988	39	252	15.5
1989	38	252	15.1
1990	53	250	21.2
1991	55	264	20.8
1992	84	264	31.4
1993	78	286	27.3
1994	80	286	27.9
1995	69	234	29.5
1996	58	241	24.0
1997	63	246	25.6
Total	**916**	**6276**	**14.6**

Note: Players drafted in the international category played outside North America in their draft year. European-born players drafted from the OHL, QMJHL, WHL or U.S. Colleges are not counted as International players. See Country of Origin, below.

1997 Entry Draft Analysis

Country of Origin

Country	Players Drafted
Canada	129
Russia	19
Czech Republic	16
USA	39
Finland	12
Sweden	15
Slovakia	6
Ukraine	1
Germany	2
Norway	1
Belarus	1
Latvia	1
Switzerland	3
Austria	1

Position

Position	Players Drafted
Defense	94
Center	49
Left Wing	45
Right Wing	39
Goaltender	19

Birth Year

Year	Players Drafted
1979	140
1978	68
1977	29
1976	1
1975	1
1974	2
1973	1
1971	4

Czech Republic and Slovakia

Club	'69	'70	'71	'72	'73	'74	'75	'76	'77	'78	'79	'80	'81	'82	'83	'84	'85	'86	'87	'88	'89	'90	'91	'92	'93	'94	'95	'96	'97	Total
Dukla Jihlava	–	–	–	–	–	–	–	–	–	–	–	–	–	2	4	3	1	–	3	1	1	3	2	1	1	2	2	2	–	27
Chemopetrol Litvinov[1]	–	–	–	–	–	–	–	–	–	–	–	–	–	3	1	2	–	–	–	–	2	2	1	3	2	4	2	2	2	26
HC Ceske Budejovice[6]	–	–	–	–	–	–	–	–	–	–	–	2	1	1	–	1	–	1	–	1	2	–	–	1	2	3	1	–	1	17
Sparta Praha[7]	–	–	–	–	–	–	–	–	–	–	–	–	1	–	2	1	1	1	2	1	2	–	1	1	–	1	–	–	1	15
HC Kladno	–	–	–	–	–	–	–	–	–	2	1	–	1	–	1	–	1	–	–	1	2	–	1	1	–	2	–	–	–	13
Slovan Bratislava	–	–	–	–	–	–	1	1	–	–	2	–	–	–	1	1	1	–	–	–	–	1	–	–	3	1	1	–	–	13
Dukla Trencin	–	–	–	–	–	–	–	–	–	–	–	–	–	–	–	–	1	–	–	1	1	–	2	2	2	–	–	2	1	12
ZPS Zlin[2]	–	–	–	–	–	–	–	–	–	–	–	–	–	–	–	1	–	1	1	1	–	2	2	1	–	2	–	–	1	12
HC Vitkovice[8]	–	–	–	–	–	–	1	–	–	–	1	–	–	–	–	–	–	–	–	–	1	–	1	3	1	1	1	–	–	10
HC Kosice[3]	–	–	–	–	–	–	–	–	–	–	–	1	–	2	–	2	–	1	–	–	2	–	–	–	–	–	–	1	1	10
HC Pardubice[4]	–	–	–	–	–	–	–	–	–	–	–	–	–	2	–	2	–	1	–	1	1	–	–	–	–	2	–	–	–	9
Interconex Plzen[9]	–	–	–	–	–	–	–	–	–	–	–	–	–	–	–	–	1	–	–	1	1	–	3	–	1	1	–	–	–	8
Zetor Brno	–	–	–	–	–	–	–	–	–	–	–	–	–	–	–	1	–	3	–	–	2	–	1	–	–	–	–	–	–	7
HC Olomouc[5]	–	–	–	–	–	–	–	–	–	–	–	–	–	–	–	–	–	–	–	1	–	–	2	–	1	2	–	–	–	6
Slavia Praha	–	–	–	–	–	–	–	–	–	–	–	–	–	–	1	–	–	–	–	–	–	–	–	1	–	–	–	–	4	6
AC Nitra	–	–	–	–	–	–	–	–	–	–	–	–	–	–	–	–	–	–	–	–	–	–	2	–	1	–	–	1	–	4
ZTS Martin	–	–	–	–	–	–	–	–	–	–	–	–	–	–	–	–	–	–	–	1	–	–	–	–	–	2	–	–	–	3
ZTK Zvolen	–	–	–	–	–	–	–	–	–	–	–	–	–	–	–	–	–	–	–	–	–	–	–	1	–	–	1	1	–	3
IS Banska Bystrica	–	–	–	–	–	–	–	–	–	–	–	–	–	–	–	–	–	–	–	–	–	–	–	1	–	–	1	–	–	2
Petra Vsetin	–	–	–	–	–	–	–	–	–	–	–	–	–	–	–	–	–	–	–	–	–	–	–	–	–	–	–	2	–	2
ZPA Presov	–	–	–	–	–	–	–	–	–	–	–	–	–	–	–	–	–	–	–	–	–	–	–	–	1	–	–	1	–	2
Ingstav Brno	–	–	–	–	–	–	–	–	–	–	–	–	–	–	–	–	1	–	–	–	–	–	–	–	–	–	–	–	–	1
Partizan Liptovsky Mikulas	–	–	–	–	–	–	–	–	–	–	–	–	–	–	–	–	–	–	–	–	–	1	–	–	–	–	–	–	–	1
VTJ Pisek	–	–	–	–	–	–	–	–	–	–	–	–	–	–	–	–	–	–	–	–	–	1	–	–	–	–	–	–	–	1
Banik Sokolov	–	–	–	–	–	–	–	–	–	–	–	–	–	–	–	–	–	–	–	–	–	–	–	–	–	–	–	1	–	1

Former club names: [1]–CHZ Litvinov, [2]–TJ Gottwaldov, TJ Zlin, [3]–VSZ Kosice, [4]–Tesla Pardubice, [5]–DS Olomouc, [6]–Motor Ceske Budejovice, [7]–Poldi Kladno, [8]–TJ Vitkovice, [9]–Skoda Plzen

Finland

Club	'69	'70	'71	'72	'73	'74	'75	'76	'77	'78	'79	'80	'81	'82	'83	'84	'85	'86	'87	'88	'89	'90	'91	'92	'93	'94	'95	'96	'97	Total
TPS Turku	–	–	–	–	–	–	–	–	–	–	1	6	–	–	–	1	1	–	–	–	–	–	–	–	3	2	3	1	3	21
HIFK Helsinki	1	–	–	–	–	1	–	1	–	–	–	1	1	2	2	1	–	–	2	1	–	–	–	1	–	1	1	–	1	17
Ilves Tampere	–	–	–	–	–	–	1	2	–	–	–	–	2	–	2	2	–	1	1	–	1	–	–	–	–	–	2	–	1	15
Jokerit Helsinki	–	–	–	–	–	–	–	–	–	–	2	1	–	–	1	–	–	1	–	1	1	–	2	3	–	1	–	–	1	14
Tappara Tampere	–	–	–	–	1	–	–	–	–	–	–	2	–	–	–	4	–	1	–	1	–	–	–	–	–	–	1	1	2	13
Assat Pori	–	–	–	2	–	–	–	–	–	–	–	2	–	–	2	–	–	1	–	1	–	–	1	–	1	1	–	–	1	12
Karpat Oulu	–	–	–	–	–	–	–	–	–	–	–	1	–	1	–	1	–	2	2	–	–	1	–	1	–	–	–	–	1	10
Lukko Rauma	–	–	–	–	–	2	1	–	–	–	–	–	–	2	–	1	–	1	–	1	–	1	–	–	–	–	–	–	–	9
Kiekko-Espoo	–	–	–	–	–	–	–	–	–	–	–	–	–	–	–	–	–	–	1	–	1	1	2	–	2	1	–	–	1	9
Reipas Lahti	–	–	–	–	–	–	–	–	–	1	1	1	–	–	–	–	–	–	–	–	–	2	–	1	–	–	1	–	–	7
KalPa Kuopio	–	–	–	–	–	–	–	–	–	–	–	–	–	–	–	–	–	1	–	–	–	–	–	1	2	–	–	–	–	4
HPK Hameenlinna	–	–	–	–	–	–	–	–	–	–	–	–	–	–	–	–	–	–	1	–	–	–	2	–	–	–	–	–	1	4
JyP HT Jyvaskyla	–	–	–	–	–	–	–	–	–	–	–	–	–	–	–	–	–	–	–	–	–	–	–	–	–	–	2	1	1	4
Kiekoo-67 Turku	–	–	–	–	–	–	–	–	–	–	–	–	–	–	–	–	–	–	–	–	–	–	–	–	–	3	–	–	–	3
SaiPa Lappeenranta	–	–	–	–	–	–	–	–	1	–	–	–	–	–	–	–	–	–	–	–	1	–	–	–	–	–	–	–	–	2
Sapko Savonlinna	–	–	–	–	–	–	–	–	–	–	–	–	–	–	–	–	1	1	–	–	–	–	–	–	–	–	–	–	–	2
Sport Vaasa	–	–	–	–	–	–	–	–	–	–	–	–	–	–	–	–	1	1	–	–	–	–	–	–	–	–	–	–	–	2
GrIFK Kauniainen	–	–	–	–	–	–	–	–	–	–	–	–	–	–	–	–	–	–	–	–	–	–	1	–	–	–	–	–	–	1
Koo Koo Kouvola	–	–	–	–	–	–	–	–	–	–	–	–	–	–	–	–	–	–	–	–	–	1	–	–	–	–	–	–	–	1
S-Kiekko Seinajoki	–	–	–	–	–	–	–	–	–	–	–	–	–	–	–	–	1	–	–	–	–	–	–	–	–	–	–	–	–	1
Junkkarit Kalajoki	–	–	–	–	–	–	–	–	–	–	–	–	–	–	–	–	–	–	–	–	–	–	–	–	–	–	–	1	–	1

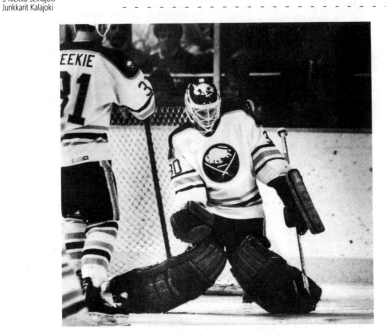

Left: On March 10, 1981, the Buffalo Sabres traded Rick Martin to Los Angeles in exchange for a first-round selection in the 1983 Entry Draft. Later, the Sabres used that pick to select Tom Barrasso, who became the first goalie in history to move directly from high-school hockey to the NHL. Below: Although John Davidson did play some time in the minors, such as this brief eight-game stint with Springfield in the closing days of his career, he became the first drafted goaltender to go directly from junior hockey to the NHL when he made his debut with the St. Louis Blues in the opener of the 1973-74 season.

First Round Draft Selections, 1997

1. BOSTON • **JOE THORNTON** • C • This 1996-97 OHL Second Team All-Star has all the physical and mental elements needed to be a dominant NHL player. At 6'4" and 198 pounds, Joe Thornton already possesses power forward size, and he has the toughness and aggressiveness to match it. Thornton also impresses with his finesse: he's fast, shifty and well-balanced, he shoots and passes intelligently and he's very creative. With his excellent work ethic and confident attitude, Thornton is a leader.

2. SAN JOSE • **PATRICK MARLEAU** • C • Patrick Marleau is a deadly attacker. His superior stick skills make him a one-on-one threat and a main cog in any power play. He is also adept at scoring short-handed. Marleau has the ability to make swift, correct decisions, and this helps him to score big goals. He's willing to fight through traffic to make plays, but his quick, fast skating helps him to avoid these situations.

3. LOS ANGELES • **OLLI JOKINEN** • C • At the age of 18, Olli Jokinen showed early maturity by becoming the first-line center on IFK Helsinki in 1996-97. Jokinen plays a determined game and always tries to improve himself. He helps his teammates with his fine playmaking ability and superior hockey sense. Always confident, Jokinen is an impact player who can change the course of a game. He played well for Finland in the 1997 World Junior Tournament, notching five goals.

4. NY ISLANDERS • **ROBERTO LUONGO** • G • This 6'3" goalie is the first netminder ever to be drafted in the top four. Like role models Patrick Roy and Martin Brodeur, Roberto Luongo plays a sound butterfly style. He blocks the lower part of the net effectively while staying upright, which leaves him in position to reach high shots. His legs and glove hand are extremely quick. He covers his angles well but knows when to make a move. Luongo is a confident, mature player.

5. NY ISLANDERS • **ERIC BREWER** • D • A two-way blueliner, Eric Brewer excels in the transition game thanks to his good puckhandling. Brewer is a fine skater – quick, with strong lateral moves, and he's dangerous on the rush. His shot is accurate and strong. He plays consistently well in his own zone, using his 6'3", 195 pound frame with vigor. Brewer works very hard and leads by example.

6. CALGARY • **DANIEL TKACZUK** • C • At age 17, Daniel Tkaczuk was the youngest OHL captain in 1996-97. Tkaczuk leads with his strong personality and his relentless, two-way game. He's an outstanding penalty killer, forechecker and face-off man, and he uses his strength and stamina to force opponents into errors. Tkaczuk is an inventive playmaker with a very high degree of hockey sense.

7. TAMPA BAY • **PAUL MARA** • D • Paul Mara's size – 6'4", 202 pounds – does not prevent him from being a mobile defenseman or a good rusher. The first American-born player taken in the draft, Mara handles the puck with flair, skates powerfully and shoots well from the point. Mara effectively shuts down opponents with his long reach and sound positional play. He is exceptionally good at reading and anticipating plays. His conditioning and stamina allow him to log a lot of ice time.

8. BOSTON • **SERGEI SAMSONOV** • LW • Sergei Samsonov showed his abundant skill winning the top forward prize at the 1997 World Junior Tournament. Samsonov is a great skater: he's quick, smooth, able to change directions instantly and highly maneuverable. His on-ice vision is very good, and he releases his shot in a split-second. He has a sound defensive game to complement his attacking style. This stocky winger has a knack for scoring flashy goals.

9. WASHINGTON • **NICHOLAS BOYNTON** • D • Nicholas Boynton is an all-around defender. In 1996-97, he led the OHL in plus-minus (+81) and averaged a point per game. Boynton is a skilled bodychecker and, at 210 pounds, he has the weight to dominate. He handles one-on-one situations confidently and skillfully. Offensively, he distinguishes himself with his accurate passes and his hard point shot. Boynton starts the transition game quickly and possesses superior vision. A complete skater, he possesses very good balance.

10. VANCOUVER • **BRAD FERENCE** • D • In 1996-97, Brad Ference finished second in voting for the WHL's top rookie and impressed everyone with his rugged play. Ference loves to hit, and he's a force in front of his own net, along the boards and in the corners. His defensive game is further elevated by his ability to skate backwards and laterally. He handles and passes the puck with ease. His biggest offensive weapon is his hard accurate point shot.

11. MONTREAL • **JASON WARD** • C • This big power forward, who doubles as a right winger, also plays a top-flight lacrosse player. Ward plays his best when he utilizes his size to create scoring chances. With his wide skating style, he is difficult to knock off-stride, and his strength allows him to handle defensemen. Scouting reports noted his high skill level and good hockey sense.

12. OTTAWA • **MARIAN HOSSA** • LW • The first Slovak chosen in the draft and the second-ranked European, Marian Hossa led his Slovak team to its league championship. He is a natural goal scorer with a flair for big goals, He has a wide array of shots, and understands how to react in one-on-one situations. He accelerates quickly and uses speed to beat opponents.

13. CHICAGO • **DANIEL CLEARY** • LW • Only the second Newfoundlander selected in the opening round, Daniel Cleary has been an OHL First Team All-Star for two consecutive seasons. A complete attacker, he was chosen as the league's best stickhandler in a poll of OHL coaches. Cleary excels in congested areas in front of the net. He is a smooth, fast skater and a well-rounded shooter. Cleary has a reputation for playing his best in big games.

14. EDMONTON • **MICHEL RIESSEN** • LW • Michel Riessen made history by becoming the first Swiss player drafted in the opening round. In 1996-97, this two-way winger scored 32 points in 38 games with Biel of the Swiss B-League. Riessen possesses good hockey sense and a natural scoring touch. At 6'2" and 185 pounds, he initiates and absorbs physical contact without difficulty. He scored four goals for Switzerland in the 1997 World Junior Championships.

15. LOS ANGELES • **MATT ZULTEK** • LW • Big and strong at 6'4" and 218 pounds, Zultek excels along the boards and in the corners. He is also a fine, smooth skater who can accelerate quickly and carry the puck with ease. He has soft hands, is an expert at deflecting pucks and has a great shot. His size belies his skating skill as he won the agility event at 1997's Top Prospects skills competition.

16. CHICAGO • **TY JONES** • RW • A power forward who models himself after Eric Lindros, Ty Jones possesses great balance and above-average skating ability. He is very good at reaching and taking possession of loose pucks. Jones handles the puck strongly, passes well and shows a good shooting touch near the net. His size allows him to check and hit effectively.

17. PITTSBURGH • **ROBERT DOME** • RW • Dome played in the IHL at the age of 16. Two years later, he is ready to join his favorite player, Jaromir Jagr, on the Penguins' attack. An excellent skater, Dome burns defensemen with his outside speed. He usually wins races for loose pucks. He knows how to get open and finishes well with a strong, fast shot. Dome backchecks readily and plays effectively along the boards and in the corners.

18. ANAHEIM • **MIKAEL HOLMQVIST** • C • The top Swedish player selected in the draft, Holmqvist is a very good playmaker who makes intelligent decisions with the puck. He is a smooth puckhandler. At 6'3" he emulates the style of Toronto's Mats Sundin and admires the creativity of Mario Lemieux. He played for Sweden at the 1997 European Junior Championships.

19. NY RANGERS • **STEFAN CHERNESKI** • RW • Stefan Cherneski is an intense competitor who will do what's necessary to win. He plays a disciplined, two-way game and stands out on special teams. Cherneski is an outstanding puckhandler with an equally high-calibre shot. A shifty skater, he is able to succeed in any situation. Deeply involved in charity work, he also was named the WHL's Scholastic Player of the Year in 1996-97.

20. FLORIDA • **MIKE BROWN** • C • Mike Brown is a hard-hitting forward who can also score. At 6'5", Brown is tough to move when planted in the opposing crease. Possessing a good stride and balance, he skates and handles the puck well and is capable of making a soft pass. Has played all three forward positions but was most effective as a center in 1996-97.

21. BUFFALO • **MIKA NORONEN** • G • Mika Noronen did not lose a game in two European Junior Championships. The tall, well-built goalie reminds some of Carolina's Sean Burke and, like Burke, he's very quick. He played five games for Tappara in Finland's SM-Liiga in 1996-97.

22. CAROLINA • **NIKOS TSELIOS** • D • A cousin of All-Star NHL defenseman Chris Chelios. Prefers to ride opponents out of the play rather than crunching them. Tselios reads the play well and readily joins the rush. He is an effective point man on the power play, making smart decisions and not taking low-percentage shots. He's agile and competes hard for loose pucks in the corners.

23. SAN JOSE • **SCOTT HANNAN** • D • Hannan is a consistent, well-rounded defenseman. He is solid defensively, rushes the puck well and can finish with a good wristshot or a slapshot. Plays with poise and confidence. He has good passing skills and is a team player with a strong work ethic. He tries to emulate New Jersey's Scott Stevens.

24. NEW JERSEY • **JEAN-FRANCOIS DAMPHOUSSE** • G • The second-ranked goalie in the draft, Damphousse plays a strong butterfly style. He reads and anticipates plays very well, even through traffic, and times his moves accurately. Damphousse drops to his knees easily and smoothly and places his stick flat on the ice to block point-blank shots. He plays his angles well, controls rebounds and owns a superior glove hand. He has a reputation as a clutch performer.

25. DALLAS • **BRENDEN MORROW** • LW • Morrow is a complete player. He admires namesake Brendan Shanahan and like Shanahan, relishes the physical side of the game. He is difficult to move from the slot and owns a powerful shot. He works hard and plays intensely in all zones. Morrow handles the puck with ease and is very creative. He is a special-teams standout.

26. COLORADO • **KEVIN GRIMES** • D • This tough, defensive blueliner excels in one-on-one situations. Grimes plays a hard-hitting style in his own end and rises to the occasion during penalty kills. He skates well and can be used as a point man on the power play. He was named best defenseman at the Four Nations tournament in Sweden in February 1997. Grimes counts Detroit's Kris Draper as a member of his extended family.

1997 Entry Draft

Transferred draft choice notation:

Example: Col.-Ana. represents a draft choice transferred
from Colorado **to** Anaheim.

Pick	Player	Claimed By	Amateur Club	Position
ROUND #1				
1	THORNTON, Joe	Bos.	Sault Ste. Marie	C
2	MARLEAU, Patrick	S.J.	Seattle	C
3	JOKINEN, Olli	L.A.	HIFK Helsinki	C
4	LUONGO, Roberto	Tor.-NYI	Val D'Or	G
5	BREWER, Eric	NYI	Prince George	D
6	TKACZUK, Daniel	Cgy.	Barrie	C
7	MARA, Paul	T.B.	Sudbury	D
8	SAMSONOV, Sergei	Car.-Bos.	Detroit	LW
9	BOYNTON, Nicholas	Wsh.	Ottawa	D
10	FERENCE, Brad	Van.	Spokane	D
11	WARD, Jason	Mtl.	Erie	C
12	HOSSA, Marian	Ott.	Dukla Trencin	RW
13	CLEARY, Daniel	Chi.	Belleville	LW
14	RIESEN, Michel	Edm.	Biel-Bienne	LW
15	ZULTEK, Matt	St.L.-Edm.-St.L.-L.A.	Ottawa	LW
16	JONES, Ty	Pho.-Chi.	Spokane	RW
17	DOME, Robert	Pit.	Long Beach/Las Vegas	RW
18	HOLMQVIST, Mikael	Ana.	Djurgarden	C
19	CHERNESKI, Stefan	NYR	Brandon	RW
20	BROWN, Mike	Fla.	Red Deer	C
21	NORONEN, Mika	Buf.	Tappara Tampere	G
22	TSELIOS, Nikos	Det.-Car.	Belleville	D
23	HANNAN, Scott	Phi.-Car.-S.J.	Kelowna	D
24	DAMPHOUSSE, J-F	N.J.	Moncton	G
25	MORROW, Brenden	Dal.	Portland	LW
26	GRIMES, Kevin	Col.	Kingston	D
ROUND #2				
27	CLYMER, Ben	Bos.	U. of Minnesota	D
28	DEFAUW, Brad	S.J.-Car.	U. of North Dakota	LW
29	BARNEY, Scott	L.A.	Peterborough	C
30	PELLETIER, Jean-Marc	Tor.-Phi.	Cornell U.	G
31	ZEHR, Jeff	NYI	Windsor	LW
32	LINDSAY, Evan	Cgy.	Prince Albert	G
33	KOS, Kyle	T.B.	Red Deer	D
34	BONNI, Ryan	Car.-Van.	Saskatoon	D
35	FORTIN, J-F	Wsh.	Sherbrooke	D
36	DRUKEN, Harold	Van.	Detroit	LW
37	BAUMGARTNER, Gregor	Mtl.	Laval	C
38	GRON, Stanislav	Ott.-N.J.	Slovan Bratislava Jr.	C
39	REICH, Jeremy	Chi.	Seattle	C
40	RENNETTE, Tyler	St.L.	North Bay	C
41	DOVIGI, Patrick	Edm.	Erie	G
42	TRIPP, John	St.L.-Cgy.	Oshawa	RW
43	GUSTAFSSON, Juha	Pho.	Kiekko-Espoo Jr.	D
44	GAFFANEY, Brian	Pit.	North Iowa Jr. A	D
45	BALMOCHNYKH, Maxim	Ana.	Lada Togliatti	LW
46	JARVIS, Wes	NYR	Kitchener	D
47	HUSELIUS, Kristian	Fla.	Farjestad Karlstad	LW
48	TALLINDER, Henrik	Buf.	AIK Solna	D
49	BUTSAYEV, Yuri	Det.	Lada Togliatti	C
50	KAVANAGH, Pat	Phi.	Peterborough	RW
51	KOKOREV, Dmitri	N.J.-Car.-Cgy.	Dynamo-2 Moscow	D
52	LYASHENKO, Roman	Dal.	Torpedo Yaroslavl	C
53	BELAK, Graham	Col.	Edmonton	D
ROUND #3				
54	KARLIN, Mattias	Bos.	Modo Ornskoldsvik	C
55	BERRY, Rick	S.J.-St.L.-Col.	Seattle	D
56	CECH, Vratislav	L.A.-Fla.	Kitchener	D
57	FARKAS, Jeff	Tor.	Boston College	C
58	HURME, Jani	N.J.-Ott.	TPS Turku	G
59	SMITH, Jarrett	NYI	Prince George	C
60	SCHUTZ, Derek	Cgy.	Spokane	C
61	ELICH, Matt	T.B.	Windsor	RW
62	MALLETTE, Kris	Car.-Phi.	Kelowna	D
63	GOREN, Lee	Wsh.-Bos.	U. of North Dakota	RW
64	TREADRICH, Kyle	Van.	Regina	LW
65	MIKKOLA, Ilkka	Mtl.	Karpat Oulu	D
66	LANGFELD, Josh	Ott.-N.J.-Ott.	Lincoln	RW
67	SOUZA, Mike	Chi.	U. of New Hampshire	LW
68	YERKOVICH, Sergei	Edm.	Las Vegas	D
69	AFINOGENOV, Maxim	St.L.-Buf.	Dynamo Moscow	RW
70	ANDERSSON, Erik	Pho.-Cgy.	U. of Denver	C
71	MELICHAR, Josef	Pit.	HC Ceske Budejovice Jr.	D
72	LEGAULT, Jay	Ana.	London	LW
73	HENRY, Burke	NYR	Brandon	D
74	SMITH, Nick	Fla.	Barrie	C
75	MARTIN, Jeff	Buf.	Windsor	C
76	SYKORA, Petr	Det.	Pojistovna Pardubice	C
77	GAINEY, Steve	Phi.-Dal.	Kamloops	C
78	NIEMINEN, Ville	N.J.-St.L.-Col.	Tappara Tampere	RW
79	SCHNABEL, Robert	Dal.-NYI	Slavia Praha Jr.	D
80	LESSARD, Francis	Col.-NYI-Cgy.-Car.	Val D'Or	D

Players selected second through tenth in the 1997 NHL Entry Draft: (All rows left to right)
Top row: 2. Patrick Marleau, C, San Jose; 3. Olli Jokinen, C, Los Angeles
Second row: 4. Roberto Luongo, G, NY Islanders; 5. Eric Brewer, D, NY Islanders
Third row: 6. Daniel Tkachuk, C, Calgary; 7. Paul Mara, D, Tampa Bay
Fourth row: 8. Sergei Samsonov, LW, Boston; 9. Nick Boynton, D, Washington
Bottom: 10. Brad Ference, D, Vancouver.

ROUND #4

81	BARTANUS, Karol	Bos.	Drummondville	RW
82	COLAGIACOMO, Adam	S.J.-NYR-S.J.	Oshawa	RW
83	CORVO, Joseph	L.A.	Western Michigan	D
84	MAIR, Adam	Tor.	Owen Sound	C
85	MIKA, Petr	NYI	Slavia Praha	LW
86	TREMBLAY, Didier	Cgy.-St.L.	Halifax	D
87	LARSEN, Brad	T.B.-Col.	Swift Current	LW
88	WILLIS, Shane	Car.	Lethbridge	RW
89	CRUICKSHANK, Curtis	Wsh.	Kingston	G
90	STANLEY, Chris	Van.	Belleville	C
91	TETRAULT, Daniel	Mtl.	Brandon	D
92	ST. CROIX, Chris	Ott.-Cgy.	Kamloops	D
93	KALLARSSON, Tomi	Chi.-S.J.-NYR	HPK Hameenlinna Jr.	D
94	ELOFSSON, Jonas	Edm.	Farjestad Karlstad	D
95	NOVOSELTSEV, Ivan	St.L.-Fla.	Krylja Sovetov Moscow	RW
96	MCCALLUM, Scott	Pho.	Tri-City	D
97	MATHIEU, Alexandre	Pit.	Halifax	C
98	HORACEK, Jan	Ana.-Col.-St.L.	Slavia Praha Jr.	D
99	BLANCHARD, Sean	NYR-L.A.	Ottawa	D
100	READY, Ryan	Fla.-Cgy.	Belleville	LW
101	THEORET, Luc	Buf.	Lethbridge	D
102	LAING, Quintin	Det.	Kelowna	LW
103	CHERNOV, Mikhail	Phi.	Torpedo-2 Yaroslavl	D
104	NEHRLING, Lucas	N.J.	Sarnia	D
105	KRISTOFFERSSON, Marcus	Dal.	Mora	RW
106	POLLOCK, Jame	Col.-St.L.	Seattle	D

ROUND #5

107	NITTEL, Adam	Bos.-S.J.	Erie	RW
108	THOMPSON, Mark	S.J.-T.B.	Regina	D
109	SULC, Jan	L.A.-T.B.	Chemopetrol Litvinov Jr.	C
110	SIMON, Benjamin	Chi.	U. of Notre Dame	C
111	MRAZEK, Frantisek	Tor.	HC Ceske Budejovice Jr.	LW
112	BETIK, Karel	NYI-T.B.	Kelowna	D
113	MOISE, Martin	Cgy.	Beauport	LW
114	DARGUZAS, David	T.B.-Van.	Edmonton	LW
115	EDINGER, Adam	Car.-NYI	Bowling Green	C
116	CAULFIELD, Kevin	Wsh.	Boston College	RW
117	COCKELL, Matt	Van.	Saskatoon	G
118	SIDULOV, Konstantin	Mtl.	Traktor Chelyabinsk	D
119	ARVEDSON, Magnus	Ott.	Farjestad Karlstad	RW
120	GARDINER, Peter	Chi.	Rensselaer	RW
121	CHIMERA, Jason	Edm.	Medicine Hat	C
122	RAZIN, Gennady	St.L.-Mtl.	Kamloops	D
123	SUTER, Curtis	Pho.	Spokane	D
124	PRATT, Harlan	Pit.	Prince Albert	D
125	VAILLANCOURT, Luc	Ana.	Beauport	G
126	MCLEAN, Jason	NYR	Moose Jaw	G
127	PARTHENAIS, Pat	Fla.	Detroit	D
128	DIROBERTO, Torrey	Buf.	Seattle	C
129	WIKSTROM, John	Det.	Lulea	D
130	CALDER, Kyle	Phi.-Chi.	Regina	C
131	BICEK, Jiri	N.J.	HC Kosice	LW
132	ELOMO, Teemu	Dal.	TPS Turku	LW
133	MISKOVICH, Aaron	Col.	Green Bay	C
134	LINDBOM, Johan	NYR	HV 71 Jonkoping	LW

ROUND #6

135	TIMOFEEV, Denis	Bos.	CSKA-2 Moscow	D
136	YORK, Michael	S.J.-NYR	Michigan State	C
137	SEELEY, Richard	L.A.	Prince Albert	D
138	GOOLDY, Eric	Tor.	Detroit	LW
139	LEAVINS, Bobby	NYI	Brandon	LW
140	DEMIDOV, Ilja	Cgy.-NYI-Cgy.	Dynamo-2 Moscow	D
141	SARNO, Peter	T.B.-Edm.	Windsor	C
142	DAFOE, Kyle	Car.	Owen Sound	D
143	PETRE, Henrik	Wsh.	Djurgarden Stockholm	D
144	COOKE, Matt	Van.	Windsor	LW
145	DESROCHES, Jonathan	Mtl.	Granby	D
146	SULLIVAN, Jeff	Ott.	Halifax	D
147	GORDON, Heath	Chi.	Green Bay	LW
148	SHAPLEY, Larry	Edm.-Van.	Welland Jr. B	D
149	BILOTTO, Nicholas	St.L.	Beauport	D
150	KATCHER, Jeff	L.A.	Brandon	D
151	FRANCZ, Robert	Pho.	Peterborough	LW
152	HAVELKA, Petr	Pit.	Sparta Praha Jr.	LW
153	SKOPINTSEV, Andrei	Ana.-T.B.	TPS Turku	D
154	DEGAGNE, Shawn	NYR	Kitchener	G
155	DELANEY, Keith	Fla.	Barrie	C
156	CAMPBELL, Brian	Buf.	Ottawa	D
157	YOUNG, B.J.	Det.	Red Deer	RW
158	FLODELL, Jordon	Phi.	Moose Jaw	D
159	GOC, Sascha	N.J.	Schwenningen	D
160	TIMKIN, Alexei	Dal.	Torpedo-2 Yaroslavl	RW
161	AEBISCHER, David	Col.	Fribourg-Gotteron	G

ROUND #7

162	TROTTIER, Joel	Bos.	Ottawa	RW
163	DUSBABEK, Joe	S.J.	U. of Notre Dame	RW
164	FEDORUK, Todd	L.A.-Phi.	Kelowna	LW
165	MARCHAND, Hugo	Tor.	Victoriaville	D
166	KNOBLAUCH, Kris	NYI	Edmonton	LW
167	RONDEAU, Jeremy	Cgy.	Swift Current	LW
168	JACK, Justin	T.B.	Kelowna	RW
169	MERRICK, Andrew	Car.-Phi.-Car.	U. of Michigan	C
170	SOMERVUORI, Eero	Wsh.-T.B.	Jokerit Helsinki	RW
171	LEROUX, Rod	Van.	Seattle	D
172	GUITE, Ben	Mtl.	U. of Maine	RW
173	BACUL, Robin	Ott.	Slavia Praha Jr.	RW
174	SMITH, Jerad	Chi.	Portland	D
175	HOLMQVIST, Johan	NYR	Brynas Gavle	G
176	OLIBRUCK, Kevin	Edm.	Peterborough	D
177	NAGY, Ladislav	St.L.	Dragon Presov	C
178	MOHAGEN, Tony	Pho.-Phi.-Ana.	Seattle	LW
179	MOORE, Mark	Pit.	Harvard U.	D
180	BAXTER, Jim	Bos.	Oshawa	D
181	SNESRUD, Mat	Ana.	North Iowa Jr. A	D
182	MOTTAU, Mike	NYR	Boston College	D
183	PALMER, Tyler	Fla.	Lake Superior	D
184	ADDUONO, Jeremy	Buf.	Sudbury	RW
185	ST. PIERRE, Samuel	T.B.	Victoriaville	RW
186	LACEBY, Mike	Det.	Kingston	C
187	HINZ, Chad	Phi.-Edm.	Moose Jaw	C
188	BENOIT, Mathieu	N.J.	Chicoutimi	RW
189	MCKERCHER, Jeff	Dal.	Barrie	D
190	THORNTON, Shawn	Col.-Tor.	Peterborough	RW

ROUND #8

191	LAAKSONEN, Antti	Bos.	U. of Denver	LW
192	SEVERSON, Cam	S.J.	Prince Albert	LW
193	KOPISCHKE, Jay	L.A.	North Iowa Jr. A	C
194	BARTLETT, Russ	Tor.	Phillips-Exeter	C
195	NORDGREN, Niklas	Car.	Modo Ornskoldsvik	LW
196	SYMINGTON, Jeremy	NYI	Petrolia Jr. B	G
197	KUBOS, Petr	Cgy.-Mtl.	Petra Vsetin	D
198	SKOLNEY, Shawn	T.B.	Seattle	D
199	FITZGERALD, Randy	Car.	Detroit	LW
200	THERRIEN, Pierre-Luc	Wsh.	Drummondville	G
201	MARTYNYUK, Denis	Van.	CSKA-2 Moscow	LW
202	SIDYAKIN, Andrei	Mtl.	Salavat Yulayev UFA	RW
203	GILLIS, Nick	Ott.	Cushing Academy	RW
204	SHIKHANOV, Sergei	Chi.	Lada Togliatti	RW
205	KERR, Chris	Edm.	Sudbury	D
206	HAGLUND, Brian	St.L.	Des Moines Jr. A	LW
207	ANDREYEV, Alexander	Pho.	Weyburn	D
208	FERENCE, Andrew	Pit.	Portland	D
209	STUSSI, Marco	Ana.	Thurgau	LW
210	PROSKURNICKI, Andrew	NYR	Sarnia	LW
211	SCHUELLER, Doug	Fla.	Twin Cities	C
212	PIROS, Kamil	Buf.	Chemopetrol Litvinov	C
213	WILEJTO, Scott	Det.	Prince Albert	D
214	KAUPPINEN, Marko	Phi.	JYP HT Jyvaskyla Jr.	D
215	CLEMMENSEN, Scott	N.J.	Des Moines Jr. A	G
216	KOMAROV, Alexei	Dal.	Dynamo-2 Moscow	D
217	SCHMIDT, Doug	Col.	Waterloo Jr. A	D

ROUND #9

218	VAN ACKER, Eric	Bos.	Chicoutimi	D
219	SMITH, Mark	S.J.	Lethbridge	C
220	BRAND, Konrad	L.A.	Medicine Hat	D
221	HEDSTROM, Jonathan	Tor.	Skelleftea	RW
222	CLARK, Ryan	NYI	Lincoln	D
223	PAUL, Dustin	Cgy.	Moose Jaw	RW
224	COMRIE, Paul	T.B.	U. of Denver	C
225	MCDONELL, Kent	Car.	Guelph	RW
226	OIKAWA, Matt	Wsh.	St. Lawrence U.	RW
227	BRADY, Peter	Van.	Powell River	G
228	YGRANES, Jarl-Espen	Mtl.	Furuset Oslo	D
229	RACHUNEK, Karel	Ott.	ZPS Zlin Jr.	D
230	FEIL, Chris	Chi.	Ohio State	G
231	FOMICHEV, Alexander	Edm.	St. Albert	G
232	PLEKHANOV, Dmitri	St.L.	Neftekhimik Nizhnekamsk	D
233	SMITH, Wyatt	Pho.	U. of Minnesota	C
234	LIND, Eric	Pit.	Avon Old Farms	D
235	DEGERMAN, Tommi	Ana.	Boston U.	LW
236	MILLER, Richard	NYR	Providence College	D
237	COTE, Benoit	Fla.	Shawinigan	C
238	KEMP, Dylan	Buf.	Lethbridge	D
239	WILLERS, Greg	Det.	Kingston	D
240	STYF, Par	Phi.	Modo Ornskoldsvik	D
241	SRDINKA, Jan	N.J.	Petra Vsetin	D
242	MCLEAN, Brett	Dal.	Kelowna	C
243	KIDNEY, Kyle	Col.	Salisbury	LW
244	IVAN, Marek	St.L.	Lethbridge	C
245	LAFLEUR, Stephen	Bos.-Col.	Belleville	D
246	HENDERSON, Jay	Col.-Bos.	Edmonton	LW

Draft Choices, 1996-69

1996

FIRST ROUND

Selection	Claimed By	Amateur Club	
1 PHILLIPS, Chris	Ott.	Prince Albert	D
2 ZYUZIN, Andrei	S.J.	Salavat Yulayev Ufa	D
3 DUMONT, Jean-Pierre	NYI	Val d'Or	RW
4 VOLCHKOV, Alexander	L.A.-Wsh.	Barrie	C
5 JACKMAN, Richard	Dal.	Sault Ste. Marie	D
6 DEVEREAUX, Boyd	Edm.	Kitchener	C
7 RASMUSSEN, Erik	Buf.	U. of Minnesota	C
8 AITKEN, Johnathan	Hfd.-Bos.	Medicine Hat	D
9 SALEI, Ruslan	Ana.	Las Vegas	D
10 WARD, Lance	N.J.	Red Deer	D
11 FOCHT, Dan	Pho.	Tri-City	D
12 HOLDEN, Josh	Van.	Regina	C
13 MORRIS, Derek	Cgy.	Regina	D
14 REASONER, Marty	St.L.-Edm.-St.L.	Boston College	C
15 ZUBRUS, Dainius	Tor.-Phi.	Pembroke	RW
16 LAROCQUE, Mario	T.B.	Hull	D
17 SVEJKOVSKY, Jaroslav	Wsh.	Tri-City	RW
18 HIGGINS, Matt	Mtl.	Moose Jaw	C
19 DESCOTEAUX, Matthieu	Bos.-Edm.	Shawinigan	D
20 NILSON, Marcus	Fla.	Djurgarden Stockholm	C
21 STURM, Marco	Chi.-S.J.	Landshut	D
22 BROWN, Jeff	NYR	Sarnia	D
23 HILLIER, Craig	Pit.	Ottawa	G
24 BRIERE, Daniel	Phi.-Pho.	Drummondville	C
25 RATCHUK, Peter	Col.	Shattuck St. Mary's	D
26 WALLIN, Jesse	Det.	Red Deer	D

ROUND # 2

Selection	Claimed By	Amateur Club	
27 SARICH, Cory	Ott.-St.L.-Buf.	Saskatoon	D
28 SKRBEK, Pavel	S.J.-N.J.-Pit.	HC Kladno	D
29 LACOUTURE, Dan	NYI	Jr. Whalers	LW
30 GREEN, Josh	L.A.	Medicine Hat	LW
31 ROYER, Remi	Dal.-Pho.- S.J.-Chi.	St-Hyacinthe	D
32 HAJT, Chris	Edm.	Guelph	D
33 VAN OENE, Darren	Buf.	Brandon	LW
34 WASYLUK, Trevor	Hfd.	Medicine Hat	LW
35 CULLEN, Matt	Ana.	St. Cloud State	C
36 POSMYK, Marek	N.J.-Tor.	Dukla Jihlava	D
37 CISAR, Marian	Pho.-L.A.	Slovan Bratislava	W
38 MASON, Wesley	Van.-N.J.	Sarnia	LW
39 BRIGLEY, Travis	Cgy.	Lethbridge	LW
40 BEGIN, Steve	St.L.-Cgy.	Val d'Or	C
41 DEWOLF, Joshua	Tor.-Pit.-N.J.	Twin Cities	D
42 PAUL, Jeff	T.B.-Chi.	Niagara Falls	D
43 BULIS, Jan	Wsh.	Barrie	C
44 GARON, Mathieu	Mtl.	Victoriaville	G
45 KUSTER, Henry	Bos.	Medicine Hat	RW
46 PETERS, Geoff	Fla.-S.J.-Chi.	Niagara Falls	C
47 DAGENAIS, Pierre	Chi.-T.B.-N.J.	Moncton	LW
48 GONEAU, Daniel	NYR	Granby	LW
49 WHITE, Colin	Pit.-N.J.	Hull	D
50 LARIVEE, Francis	Phi.-Tor.	Laval	G
51 BABENKO, Yuri	Col.	Krylja Sovetov	C
52 MILLER, Aren	Det.	Spokane	G

1995

FIRST ROUND

Selection	Claimed By	Amateur Club	
1. BERARD, Bryan	Ott.	Detroit	D
2. REDDEN, Wade	NYI	Brandon	D
3. BERG, Aki-Petteri	L.A.	Kiekko-67 Turku	D
4. KILGER, Chad	Ana.	Kingston	C
5. LANGKOW, Daymond	T.B.	Tri-City	C
6. KELLY, Steve	Edm.	Prince Albert	C
7. DOAN, Shane	Wpg.	Kamloops	RW
8. RYAN, Terry	Mtl.	Tri-City	LW
9. McLAREN, Kyle	Hfd.-Bos.	Tacoma	D
10. DVORAK, Radek	Fla.	HC Ceske Budejovice	W
11. IGINLA, Jarome	Dal.	Kamloops	C
12. RIIHIJARVI, Teemu	S.J.	Kiekko-Espoo Jr.	LW
13. GIGUERE, J-Sebastien	NYR-Hfd.	Halifax	G
14. McKEE, Jay	Van.-Buf.	Niagara Falls	D
15. WARE, Jeff	Tor.	Oshawa	D
16. BIRON, Martin	Buf.	Beauport	G
17. CHURCH, Brad	Wsh.	Prince Albert	LW
18. SYKORA, Petr	N.J.	Detroit	C
19. NABOKOV, Dmitri	Chi.	Krylja Sovetov	C
20. GAUTHIER, Denis Jr.	Cgy.	Drummondville	D
21. BROWN, Sean	Bos.	Belleville	D
22. BOUCHER, Brian	Phi.	Tri-City	G
23. ELOMO, Miika	St.L.-Wsh.	Kiekko-67 Turku	LW
24. MOROZOV, Alexei	Pit.	Krylja Sovetov	RW
25. DENIS, Marc	Col.	Chicoutimi	G
26. KUZNETSOV, Maxim	Det.	Dynamo Moscow	D

SECOND ROUND

Selection	Claimed By	Amateur Club	
27. MORO, Marc	Ott.	Kingston	D
28. HLAVAC, Jan	NYI	Sparta Praha	LW
29. WESENBERG, Brian	Ana.	Guelph	RW
30. McBAIN, Mike	T.B.	Red Deer	D
31. LARAQUE, Georges	Edm.	St-Jean	RW
32. CHOUINARD, Marc	Wpg.	Beauport	C
33. MacLEAN, Donald	L.A.	Beauport	C
34. DOIG, Jason	Mtl.-Wpg.	Laval	D
35. FEDOTOV, Sergei	Hfd.	Dynamo Moscow	D
36. MacDONALD, Aaron	Fla.	Swift Current	G
37. COTE, Patrick	Dal.	Beauport	LW
38. ROED, Peter	S.J.	White Bear Lake	C
39. DUBE, Christian	NYR	Sherbrooke	C
40. McALLISTER, Chris	Van.	Saskatoon	D
41. SMITH, Denis (D.J.)	Tor.-NYI	Windsor	D
42. DUTIAUME, Mark	Buf.	Brandon	LW
43. HAY, Dwayne	Wsh.	Guelph	LW
44. PERROTT, Nathan	N.J.	Oshawa	RW
45. LAFLAMME, Christian	Chi.	Beauport	D
46. SMIRNOV, Pavel	Cgy.	Molot Perm	RW/C
47. SCHAFER, Paxton	Bos.	Medicine Hat	G
48. KENNY, Shane	Phi.	Owen Sound	D
49. HECHT, Jochen	St.L.	Mannheim	C
50. ROSA, Pavel	Pit.-L.A.	Chemopetrol Litvinov	RW
51. BEAUDOIN, Nic	Col.	Detroit	LW
52. AUDET, Philippe	Det.	Granby	LW

1994

FIRST ROUND

Selection	Claimed By	Amateur Club	
1. JOVANOVSKI, Ed	Fla.	Windsor	D
2. TVERDOVSKY, Oleg	Ana.	Soviet Wings	D
3. BONK, Radek	Ott.	Las Vegas	C
4. BONSIGNORE, Jason	Wpg.-Edm.	Niagara Falls	C
5. O'NEILL, Jeff	Hfd.	Guelph	C
6. SMYTH, Ryan	Edm.	Moose Jaw	LW
7. STORR, Jamie	L.A.	Owen Sound	G
8. WIEMER, Jason	T.B.	Portland	LW
9. LINDROS, Brett	Que.-NYI	Kingston	RW
10. BAUMGARTNER, Nolan	Phi.-Que.- Tor.-Wsh.	Kamloops	D
11. FRIESEN, Jeff	S.J.	Regina	LW
12. BELAK, Wade	NYI-Que.	Saskatoon	D
13. OHLUND, Mattias	Van.	Pitea	D
14. MOREAU, Ethan	Chi.	Niagara Falls	LW
15. KHARLAMOV, Alexander	Wsh.	CSKA Moscow	C
16. FICHAUD, Eric	St.L.-Wsh.-Tor.	Chicoutimi	G
17. PRIMEAU, Wayne	Buf.	Owen Sound	C
18. BROWN, Brad	Mtl.	North Bay	C
19. DINGMAN, Chris	Cgy.	Brandon	LW
20. BOTTERILL, Jason	Dal.	U. of Michigan	LW
21. RYABCHIKOV, Evgeni	Bos.	Molot Perm	G
22. KEALTY, Jeffrey	Tor.-Que.	Catholic Memorial	D
23. GOLUBOVSKY, Yan	Det.	CSKA Jr. Moscow	D
24. WELLS, Chris	Pit.	Seattle	C
25. SHARIFIJANOV, Vadim	N.J.	Salavat Yulayev ufa	RW
26. CLOUTIER, Dan	NYR	Sault Ste. Marie	G

SECOND ROUND

Selection	Claimed By	Amateur Club	
27. WARRENER, Rhett	Fla.	Saskatoon	D
28. DAVIDSSON, Johan	Ana.	HV 71	C
29. NECKAR, Stanislav	Ott.	Ceske Budejovice	D
30. QUINT, Deron	Wpg.	Seattle	D
31. PODOLLAN, Jason	Hfd.-Fla.	Spokane	C
32. WATT, Mike	Edm.	Stratford Jr. B	LW
33. JOHNSON, Matt	L.A.	Peterborough	LW
34. CLOUTIER, Colin	T.B.	Brandon	C
35. MARHA, Josef	Que.	Dukla Jihlava	C
36. JOHNSON, Ryan	Phi.-Fla.	Thunder Bay Jr. A	C
37. NIKOLOV, Angel	NYI	Litvinov	D
38. HOLLAND, Jason	NYI	Kamloops	D
39. GORDON, Robb	Van.	Powell River Jr. A	C
40. LEROUX, Jean-Yves	Chi.	Beauport	LW
41. CHERREY, Scott	Wsh.	North Bay	LW
42. SCATCHARD, Dave	St.L.-Van.	Portland	C
43. BROWN, Curtis	Buf.	Moose Jaw	C
44. THEODORE, Jose	Mtl.	St-Jean	G
45. RYABYKIN, Dmitri	Cgy.	Dynamo-2	D
46. JINMAN, Lee	Dal.	North Bay	C
47. GONEAU, Daniel	Bos.	Laval	LW
48. HAGGERTY, Sean	Tor.	Detroit	LW
49. DANDENAULT, Mathieu	Det.	Sherbrooke	RW
50. PARK, Richard	Pit.	Belleville	C
51. ELIAS, Patrik	N.J.	Kladno	LW
52. VERCIK, Rudolf	NYR	Slovan Bratislava	LW

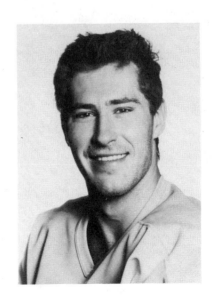

Below: A second-round selection of the Los Angeles Kings in the 1987 Entry Draft, Mark Fitzpatrick was traded to the Islanders in the deal that brought Kelly Hrudey to California on February 22, 1989. Right: Although he was drafted third overall in the 1981 Entry Draft by Washington because of his offensive skills, Bob Carpenter has transformed his game to become of the League's top defensive forwards.

1993

FIRST ROUND

Selection	Claimed By	Amateur Club	
1. DAIGLE, Alexandre	Ott.	Victoriaville	C
2. PRONGER, Chris	S.J.-Hfd.	Peterborough	D
3. GRATTON, Chris	T.B.	Kingston	C
4. KARIYA, Paul	Ana.	University of Maine	LW
5. NIEDERMAYER, Rob	Fla.	Medicine Hat	C
6. KOZLOV, Viktor	Hfd.-S.J.	Dynamo Moscow	LW
7. ARNOTT, Jason	Edm.	Oshawa	C
8. SUNDSTROM, Niklas	NYR	MoDo	LW
9. HARVEY, Todd	Dal.	Detroit	C
10. THIBAULT, Jocelyn	Phi.-Que.	Sherbrooke	G
11. WITT, Brendan	St. L.-Wsh.	Seattle	D
12. JONSSON, Kenny	Buf.-Tor.	Rogle Angelholm	D
13. PEDERSON, Denis	N.J.	Prince Albert	C
14. DEADMARSH, Adam	NYI-Que.	Portland	C
15. LINDGREN, Mats	Wpg.	Skelleftea	C
16. STAJDUHAR, Nick	L.A.-Edm.	London	D
17. ALLISON, Jason	Wsh.	London	C
18. MATTSSON, Jesper	Cgy.	Malmo	C
19. WILSON, Landon	Tor.	Dubuque Jr. A	RW
20. WILSON, Mike	Van.	Sudbury	D
21. KOIVU, Saku	Mtl.	TPS Turku	C
22. ERIKSSON, Anders	Det.	MoDo	D
23. BERTUZZI, Todd	Que.-NYI	Guelph	C
24. LECOMPTE, Eric	Chi.	Hull	LW
25. ADAMS, Kevyn	Bos.	Miami-Ohio	C
26. BERGQVIST, Stefan	Pit.	Leksand	D

SECOND ROUND

Selection	Claimed By	Amateur Club	
27. BICANEK, Radim	Ott.	Dukla Jihlava	D
28. DONOVAN, Shean	S.J.	Ottawa	RW
29. MOSS, Tyler	T.B.	Kingston	G
30. TSULYGIN, Nikolai	Ana.	Salavat Yulalev Ufa	D
31. LANGKOW, Scott	Fla.-Wpg.	Portland	G
32. PANDOLFO, Jay	Hfd.-N.J.	Boston University	LW
33. VYBORNY, David	Edm.	Sparta Praha	C
34. SOROCHAN, Lee	NYR	Lethbridge	D
35. LANGENBRUNNER, Jamie	Dal.	Cloquet	C
36. NIINIMAA, Janne	Phi.	Karpat Oulu	D
37. BETS, Maxim	St. L.	Spokane	LW
38. TSYGUROV, Denis	Buf.	Lada Togliatti	D
39. MORRISON, Brendan	N.J.	Penticton T-II Jr. A	C
40. McCABE, Bryan	NYI	Spokane	D
41. WEEKES, Kevin	Wpg.-Fla.	Owen Sound	G
42. TOPOROWSKI, Shayne	L.A.	Prince Albert	RW
43. BUDAYEV, Alexei	Wsh.-Wpg.	Kristall Elektrostal	C
44. ALLISON, Jamie	Cgy.	Detroit	D
45. KROUPA, Vlastimil	Tor.-Hfd.-S.J.	Chemopetrol Litvinov	D
46. GIRARD, Rick	Van.	Swift Current	C
47. FITZPATRICK, Rory	Mtl.	Sudbury	D
48. COLEMAN, Jonathan	Det.	Andover Academy	D
49. BUCKBERGER, Ashley	Que.	Swift Current	RW
50. MANLOW, Eric	Chi.	Kitchener	C
51. ALVEY, Matt	Bos.	Springfield Jr. B	RW
52. PITTIS, Domenic	Pit.	Lethbridge	C

1992

FIRST ROUND

Selection	Claimed By	Amateur Club	
1. HAMRLIK, Roman	T.B.	ZPS Zlin (Czech.)	D
2. YASHIN, Alexei	Ott.	Dynamo Moscow (CIS)	C
3. RATHJE, Mike	S.J.	Medicine Hat	D
4. WARRINER, Todd	Que.	Windsor	LW
5. KASPARAITIS, Darius	Tor.-NYI	Dynamo Moscow (CIS)	D
6. STILLMAN, Cory	Cgy.	Windsor	C
7. SITTLER, Ryan	Phi.	Nichols	LW
8. CONVERY, Brandon	NYI-Tor.	Sudbury	C
9. PETROVICKY, Robert	Hfd.	Dukla Trencin (Czech.)	C
10. NAZAROV, Andrei	Min.-S.J.	Dynamo Moscow	LW
11. COOPER, David	Buf.	Medicine Hat	D
12. KRIVOKRASOV, Sergei	Wpg.-Chi.	CSKA Moscow (CIS)	RW
13. HULBIG, Joe	Edm.	St. Sebastian's	LW
14. GONCHAR, Sergei	St.L.-Wsh.	Chelybinsk (CIS)	D
15. BOWEN, Jason	L.A.-Pit.-Phi.	Tri-City	LW
16. KVARTALNOV, Dmitri	Bos.	San Diego	LW
17. BAUTIN, Sergei	Chi.-Wpg.	Dynamo Moscow (CIS)	D
18. SMITH, Jason	N.J.	Regina	D
19. STRAKA, Martin	Pit.	Skoda Plzen (Czech.)	C
20. WILKIE, David	Mtl.	Kamloops	D
21. POLASEK, Libor	Van.	TJ Vitkovice (Czech.)	C
22. BOWEN, Curtis	Det.	Ottawa	LW
23. MARSHALL, Grant	Wsh.-Tor.	Ottawa	RW
24. FERRARO, Peter	NYR	Waterloo Jr. A	C

SECOND ROUND

Selection	Claimed By	Amateur Club	
25. PENNEY, Chad	Ott.	North Bay	LW
26. BANNISTER, Drew	T.B.	Sault-Ste-Marie	D
27. MIRONOV, Boris	S.J.-Chi.-Wpg.	CSKA Moscow (CIS)	D
28. BROUSSEAU, Paul	Que.	Hull	RW
29. GRONMAN, Toumas	Tor.-Que.	Tacoma	D
30. O'SULLIVAN, Chris	Cgy.	Catholic Memorial	D
31. METLYUK, Denis	Phi.	Lada Togliatti (CIS)	C
32. CAREY, Jim	NYI-Tor.-Wsh.	Catholic Memorial	G
33. BURE, Valeri	Hfd.-Mtl.	Spokane	LW
34. VARVIO, Jarkko	Min.	HPK (Finland)	RW
35. CIERNY, Jozef	Buf.	ZTK Zvolen (Czech.)	LW
36. SHANTZ, Jeff	Wpg.-Chi.	Regina	C
37. REICHEL, Martin	Edm.	Freiburg (Germany)	RW
38. KOROLEV, Igor	St.L.	Dynamo Moscow	RW
39. HOCKING, Justin	L.A.	Spokane	D
40. PECA, Mike	Bos.-Van.	Ottawa	C
41. KLIMOVICH, Sergei	Chi.	Dynamo Moscow	C
42. BRYLIN, Sergei	N.J.	CSKA Moscow (CIS)	C
43. HUSSEY, Marc	Pit.	Moose Jaw	D
44. CORPSE, Keli	Mtl.	Kingston	C
45. FOUNTAIN, Michael	Van.	Oshawa	G
46. McCARTY, Darren	Det.	Belleville	RW
47. NIKOLISHIN, Andrei	Wsh.-Hfd.	Dynamo Moscow	LW
48. NORSTROM, Mattias	NYR	AIK (Sweden)	D

1991

FIRST ROUND

Selection	Claimed By	Amateur Club	
1. LINDROS, Eric	Que.	Oshawa	C
2. FALLOON, Pat	S.J.	Spokane	RW
3. NIEDERMAYER, Scott	Tor.-N.J.	Kamloops	D
4. LACHANCE, Scott	NYI	Boston University	D
5. WARD, Aaron	Wpg.	U. of Michigan	D
6. FORSBERG, Peter	Phi.	MoDo (Sweden)	C
7. STOJANOV, Alex	Van.	Hamilton	RW
8. MATVICHUK, Richard	Min.	Saskatoon	D
9. POULIN, Patrick	Hfd.	St.-Hyacinthe	LW
10. LAPOINTE, Martin	Det.	Laval	RW
11. ROLSTON, Brian	N.J.	Detroit Comp. Jr. A	C
12. WRIGHT, Tyler	Edm.	Swift Current	C
13. BOUCHER, Phillipe	Buf.	Granby	D
14. PEAKE, Pat	Wsh.	Detroit	C
15. KOVALEV, Alexei	NYR	D'amo Moscow	RW
16. NASLUND, Markus	Pit.	MoDo	RW
17. BILODEAU, Brent	Mtl.	Seattle	D
18. MURRAY, Glen	Bos.	Sudbury	RW
19. SUNDBLAD, Niklas	Cgy.	AIK (Sweden)	RW
20. RUCINSKY, Martin	L.A.-Edm.	CHZ Litvinov (Czech.)	LW
21. HALVERSON, Trevor	St.L.-Wsh.	North Bay	LW
22. McAMMOND, Dean	Chi.	Prince Albert	C

SECOND ROUND

Selection	Claimed By	Amateur Club	
23. WHITNEY, Ray	S.J.	Spokane	C
24. CORBET, Rene	Que.	Drummondville	LW
25. LAVIGNE, Eric	Tor.-Que.-Wsh.	Hull	D
26. PALFFY, Zigmund	NYI	AC Nitra (Czech.)	LW
27. STAIOS, Steve	Wpg.-St.L.	Niagara Falls	D
28. CAMPBELL, Jim	Phi.-Mtl.	Northwood Prep	C
29. CULLIMORE, Jassen	Van.	Peterborough	D
30. OZOLINSH, Sandis	Min.-S.J.	Dynamo Riga (USSR)	D
31. HAMRLIK, Martin	Hfd.	TJ Zin (Czech.)	D
32. PUSHOR, Jamie	Det.	Lethbridge	D
33. HEXTALL, Donevan	N.J.	Prince Albert	LW
34. VERNER, Andrew	Edm.	Peterborough	G
35. DAWE, Jason	Buf.	Peterborough	LW
36. NELSON, Jeff	Wsh.	Prince Albert	C
37. WERENKA, Darcy	NYR	Lethbridge	D
38. FITZGERALD, Rusty	Pit.	Duluth East HS	C
39. POMICHTER, Michael	Mtl.-Chi.	Springfield Jr. B	C
40. STUMPEL, Jozef	Bos.	AC Nitra (Czech.)	RW
41. GROLEAU, Francois	Cgy.	Shawinigan	D
42. LEVEQUE, Guy	L.A.	Cornwall	C
43. DARBY, Craig	St.L.-Mtl.	Albany Academy	C
44. MATTHEWS, Jamie	Chi.	Sudbury	C

1990

FIRST ROUND

Selection	Claimed By	Amateur Club	
1. NOLAN, Owen	Que.	Cornwall	RW
2. NEDVED, Petr	Van.	Seattle	C
3. PRIMEAU, Keith	Det.	Niagara Falls	C
4. RICCI, Mike	Phi.	Peterborough	C
5. JAGR, Jaromir	Pit.	Poldi Kladno (Czech.)	LW
6. SCISSONS, Scott	NYI	Saskatoon	C
7. SYDOR, Darryl	L.A.	Kamloops	D
8. HATCHER, Derian	Min.	North Bay	D
9. SLANEY, John	Wsh.	Cornwall	D
10. BEREHOWSKY, Drake	Tor.	Kingston	D
11. KIDD, Trevor	N.J.-Cgy.	Brandon	G
12. STEVENSON, Turner	St.L.-Mtl.	Seattle	RW
13. STEWART, Michael	NYR	Michigan State	D
14. MAY, Brad	Wpg.-Buf.	Niagara Falls	LW
15. GREIG, Mark	Hfd.	Lethbridge	RW
16. DYKHUIS, Karl	Chi.	Hull	D
17. ALLISON, Scott	Edm.	Prince Albert	C
18. ANTOSKI, Shawn	Mtl.-St.L.-Van.	North Bay	LW
19. TKACHUK, Keith	Buf.-Wpg.	Malden Catholic	LW
20. BRODEUR, Martin	Cgy.-N.J.	St. Hyacinthe	G
21. SMOLINSKI, Bryan	Bos.	Michigan State	C

SECOND ROUND

Selection	Claimed By	Amateur Club	
22. HUGHES, Ryan	Que.	Cornell	C
23. SLEGR, Jiri	Van.	CHZ Litvinov (Czech.)	D
24. HARLOCK, David	Det.-Cgy.-N.J.	U. of Michigan	D
25. SIMON, Chris	Phi.	Ottawa	LW
26. PERREAULT, Nicolas P.	Pit.-Cgy.	Hawkesbury Jr. A	D
27. TAYLOR, Chris	NYI	London	C
28. SEMCHUK, Brandy	L.A.	Canadian National	RW
29. GOTZIAMAN, Chris	Min.-Cgy.-N.J.	Roseau	RW
30. PASMA, Rod	Wsh.	Cornwall	D
31. POTVIN, Felix	Tor.	Chicoutimi	G
32. VIITAKOSKI, Vesa	N.J.-Cgy.	SaiPa (Finland)	LW
33. JOHNSON, Craig	St.L.	Hill-Murray HS	C
34. WEIGHT, Doug	NYR	Lake Superior	C
35. MULLER, Mike	Wpg.	Wayzata	D
36. SANDERSON, Geoff	Hfd.	Swift Current	C
37. DROPPA, Ivan	Chi.	Partizan (Czech.)	D
38. LEGAULT, Alexandre	Edm.	Boston University	RW
39. KUWABARA, Ryan	Mtl.	Ottawa	RW
40. RENBERG, Mikael	Buf.-Phi.	Pitea (Sweden)	LW
41. BELZILE, Etienne	Cgy.	Cornell	D
42. SANDWITH, Terran	Bos.-Phi.	Tri-Cities	D

1989

FIRST ROUND

Selection	Claimed By	Amateur Club	
1. SUNDIN, Mats	Que.	Nacka (Sweden)	RW
2. CHYZOWSKI, Dave	NYI	Kamloops	LW
3. THORNTON, Scott	Tor.	Belleville	C
4. BARNES, Stu	Wpg.	Tri-Cities	C
5. GUERIN, Bill	N.J.	Springfield Jr. B	RW
6. BENNETT, Adam	Chi.	Sudbury	D
7. ZMOLEK, Doug	Min.	John Marshall	D
8. HERTER, Jason	Van.	U. of North Dakota	D
9. MARSHALL, Jason	St.L.	Vernon Jr. A	D
10. HOLIK, Robert	Hfd.	Dukla Jihlava (Czech.)	C
11. SILLINGER, Mike	Det.	Regina	C
12. PEARSON, Rob	Phi.-Tor.	Belleville	RW
13. VALLIS, Lindsay	NYR-Mtl.	Seattle	RW
14. HALLER, Kevin	Buf.	Regina	D
15. SOULES, Jason	Edm.	Niagara Falls	D
16. HEWARD, Jamie	Pit.	Regina	RW
17. STEVENSON, Shayne	Bos.	Kitchener	RW
18. MILLER, Jason	L.A.-Edm.-N.J.	Medicine Hat	C
19. KOLZIG, Olaf	Wsh.	Tri-Cities	G
20. RICE, Steven	Mtl.-NYR	Kitchener	RW
21. BANCROFT, Steve	Cgy.-Tor.	Belleville	D

SECOND ROUND

Selection	Claimed By	Amateur Club	
22. FOOTE, Adam	Que.	Sault Ste. Marie	D
23. GREEN, Travis	NYI	Spokane	C
24. MANDERVILLE, Kent	Tor.-Cgy.	Notre Dame Jr. A	LW
25. RATUSHNY, Dan	Wpg.	Cornell	D
26. SKALDE, Jarrod	N.J.	Oshawa	C
27. SPEER, Michael	Chi.	Guelph	D
28. CRAIG, Mike	Min.	Oshawa	RW
29. WOODWARD, Robert	Van.	Deerfield	LW
30. BRISEBOIS, Patrice	St.L.-Mtl.	Laval	D
31. CORRIVEAU, Rick	Hfd.-St.L.	London	D
32. BOUGHNER, Bob	Det.	Sault-Ste. Marie	D
33. JOHNSON, Greg	Phi.	Thunder Bay Jr. A	C
34. JUHLIN, Patrik	NYR-Phi.	Vasteras (Sweden)	LW
35. DAFOE, Byron	Buf.-Wsh.	Portland	D
36. BORGO, Richard	Edm.	Kitchener	G
37. LAUS, Paul	Pit.	Niagara Falls	D
38. PARSON, Mike	Bos.	Guelph	G
39. THOMPSON, Brent	L.A.	Medicine Hat	D
40. PROSOFSKY, Jason	Wsh.-NYR	Medicine Hat	RW
41. LAROUCHE, Steve	Mtl.	Trois-Rivieres	C
42. DRURY, Ted	Cgy.	Fairfield Prep	C

1988

FIRST ROUND

Selection	Claimed By	Amateur Club	
1. MODANO, Mike	Min.	Prince Albert	C
2. LINDEN, Trevor	Van.	Medicine Hat	RW
3. LESCHYSHYN, Curtis	Que.	Saskatoon	D
4. SHANNON, Darrin	Pit.	Windsor	LW
5. DORE, Daniel	NYR-Que.	Drummondville	RW
6. PEARSON, Scott	Tor.	Kingston	LW
7. GELINAS, Martin	L.A.	Hull	LW
8. ROENICK, Jeremy	Chi.	Thayer Academy	C
9. BRIND'AMOUR, Rod	St.L.	Notre Dame Jr. A	C
10. SELANNE, Teemu	Wpg.	Jokerit (Finland)	RW
11. GOVEDARIS, Chris	Hfd.	Toronto	LW
12. FOSTER, Corey	N.J.	Peterborough	D
13. SAVAGE, Joel	Buf.	Victoria	RW
14. BOIVIN, Claude	Phi.	Drummondville	LW
15. SAVAGE, Reginald	Wsh.	Victoriaville	C
16. CHEVELDAYOFF, Kevin	NYI	Brandon	D
17. KOCUR, Kory	Det.	Saskatoon	RW
18. CIMETTA, Robert	Bos.	Toronto	LW
19. LEROUX, Francois	Edm.	St. Jean	D
20. CHARRON, Eric	Mtl.	Trois-Rivieres	D
21. MUZZATTI, Jason	Cgy.	Michigan State	G

SECOND ROUND

Selection	Claimed By	Amateur Club	
22. MALLETTE, Troy	Min.-NYR	Sault Ste. Marie	C
23. CHRISTIAN, Jeff	Van.-N.J.	London	LW
24. FISET, Stephane	Que.	Victoriaville	G
25. MAJOR, Mark	Pit.	North Bay	D
26. DUVAL, Murray	NYR	Spokane	RW
27. DOMI, Tie	Tor.	Peterborough	RW
28. HOLDEN, Paul	L.A.	London	D
29. DOUCET, Wayne	Chi.-NYI	Hamilton	LW
30. PLAVSIC, Adrien	St.L.	U. of New Hampshire	D
31. ROMANIUK, Russell	Wpg.	St. Boniface Jr. A	LW
32. RICHTER, Barry	Hfd.	Culver Academy	D
33. ROHLIN, Leif	N.J.-Van.	Vasteras (Sweden)	D
34. ST. AMOUR, Martin	Buf.-Mtl.	Verdun	LW
35. MURRAY, Pat	Phi.	Michigan State	LW
36. TAYLOR, Tim	Wsh.	London	C
37. LEBRUN, Sean	NYI	New Westminster	LW
38. ANGLEHART, Serge	Det.	Drummondville	D
39. KOIVUNEN, Petro	Bos.-Edm.	Espoo (Finland)	C
40. GAETZ, Link	Edm.-Min.	Spokane	D
41. BARTLEY, Wade	Mtl.-St.L.-Wsh.	Dauphin Jr. A	D
42. HARKINS, Todd	Cgy.	Miami-Ohio	RW

1987

FIRST ROUND

Selection	Claimed By	Amateur Club	
1. TURGEON, Pierre	Buf.	Granby	C
2. SHANAHAN, Brendan	N.J.	London	C
3. WESLEY, Glen	Van.-Bos.	Portland	D
4. McBEAN, Wayne	Min.-L.A.	Medicine Hat	D
5. JOSEPH, Chris	Pit.	Seattle	D
6. ARCHIBALD, David	L.A.-Min.	Portland	C/LW
7. RICHARDSON, Luke	Tor.	Peterborough	D
8. WAITE, Jimmy	Chi.	Chicoutimi	G
9. FOGARTY, Bryan	Que.	Kingston	D
10. MORE, Jayson	NYR	New Westminster	D
11. RACINE, Yves	Det.	Longueuil	D
12. OSBORNE, Keith	St.L.	North Bay	RW
13. CHYNOWETH, Dean	NYI	Medicine Hat	D
14. QUINTAL, Stephane	Bos.	Granby	D
15. SAKIC, Joe	Wsh.-Que.	Swift Current	C
16. MARCHMENT, Bryan	Wpg.	Belleville	D
17. CASSELS, Andrew	Mtl.	Ottawa	C
18. HULL, Jody	Hfd.	Peterborough	RW
19. DEASLEY, Bryan	Cgy.	U. of Michigan	LW
20. RUMBLE, Darren	Phi.	Kitchener	D
21. SOBERLAK, Peter	Edm.	Swift Current	LW

SECOND ROUND

Selection	Claimed By	Amateur Club	
22. MILLER, Brad	Buf.	Regina	D
23. PERSSON, Rickard	N.J.	Ostersund (Sweden)	D
24. MURPHY, Rob	Van.	Laval	C
25. MATTEAU, Stephane	Min.-Cgy.	Hull	LW
26. TABARACCI, Richard	Pit.	Cornwall	G
27. FITZPATRICK, Mark	L.A.	Medicine Hat	G
28. MAROIS, Daniel	Tor.	Chicoutimi	RW
29. McGILL, Ryan	Chi.	Swift Current	D
30. HARDING, Jeff	Que.-Phi.	St. Michael's Jr. B	LW
31. LACROIX, Daniel	NYR	Granby	LW
32. KRUPPKE, Gordon	Det.	Prince Albert	D
33. LECLAIR, John	St.L.-Mtl.	Bellows Academy	D
34. HACKETT, Jeff	NYI	Oshawa	G
35. McCRADY, Scott	Bos.-Min.	Medicine Hat	D
36. BALLANTYNE, Jeff	Wsh.	Ottawa	D
37. ERICKSSON, Patrik	Wpg.	Brynas (Sweden)	C
38. DESJARDINS, Eric	Mtl.	Granby	D
39. BURT, Adam	Hfd.	North Bay	D
40. GRANT, Kevin	Cgy.	Kitchener	D
41. WILKIE, Bob	Phi.-Det.	Swift Current	D
42. WERENKA, Brad	Edm.	N. Michigan	D

1986

FIRST ROUND

Selection	Claimed By	Amateur Club	
1. MURPHY, Joe	Det.	Michigan State	C
2. CARSON, Jimmy	L.A.	Verdun	C
3. BRADY, Neil	N.J.	Medicine Hat	C
4. ZALAPSKI, Zarley	Pit.	Canadian National	D
5. ANDERSON, Shawn	Buf.	Canadian National	D
6. DAMPHOUSSE, Vincent	Tor.	Laval	LW
7. WOODLEY, Dan	Van.	Portland	C
8. ELYNUIK, Pat	Wpg.	Prince Albert	RW
9. LEETCH, Brian	NYR	Avon Old Farms HS	D
10. LEMIEUX, Jocelyn	St.L.	Laval	RW
11. YOUNG, Scott	Hfd.	Boston University	RW
12. BABE, Warren	Min.	Lethbridge	LW
13. JANNEY, Craig	Bos.	Boston College	C
14. SANIPASS, Everett	Chi.	Verdun	LW
15. PEDERSON, Mark	Mtl.	Medicine Hat	LW
16. PELAWA, George	Cgy.	Bemidji HS	RW
17. FITZGERALD, Tom	NYI	Austin Prep	C
18. McRAE, Ken	Que.	Sudbury	C
19. GREENLAW, Jeff	Wsh.	Canadian National	LW
20. HUFFMAN, Kerry	Phi.	Guelph	D
21. ISSEL, Kim	Edm.	Prince Albert	RW

SECOND ROUND

Selection	Claimed By	Amateur Club	
22. GRAVES, Adam	Det.	Windsor	C
23. SEPPO, Jukka	L.A.-Phi.	Sport (Finland)	LW
24. COPELAND, Todd	N.J.	Belmont Hill HS	D
25. CAPUANO, Dave	Pit.	Mt. St. Charles HS	C
26. BROWN, Greg	Buf.	St. Mark's	D
27. BRUNET, Benoit	Tor.-Mtl.	Hull	LW
28. HAWLEY, Kent	Van.-Phi.	Ottawa	C
29. NUMMINEN, Teppo	Wpg.	Tappara (Finland)	D
30. WILKINSON, Neil	NYR-Min.	Selkirk	D
31. POSMA, Mike	St.L.	Buffalo Jr. A	D
32. LaFORGE, Marc	Hfd.	Kingston	D
33. KOLSTAD, Dean	Min.	Prince Albert	D
34. TIRKKONEN, Pekka	Bos.	SaPKo (Finland)	C
35. KURZAWSKI, Mark	Chi.	Windsor	D
36. SHANNON, Darryl	Mtl.-Tor.	Windsor	D
37. GLYNN, Brian	Cgy.	Saskatoon	D
38. VASKE, Dennis	NYI	Armstrong HS	D
39. ROUTHIER, Jean-Marc	Que.	Hull	RW
40. SEFTEL, Steve	Wsh.	Kingston	LW
41. GUERARD, Stephane	Phi.-Que.	Shawinigan	D
42. NICHOLS, Jamie	Edm.	Portland	LW

1985

FIRST ROUND

Selection	Claimed By	Amateur Club	
1. CLARK, Wendel	Tor.	Saskatoon	D
2. SIMPSON, Craig	Pit.	Michigan State	C
3. WOLANIN, Craig	N.J.	Kitchener	D
4. SANDLAK, Jim	Van.	London	RW
5. MURZYN, Dana	Hfd.	Calgary	D
6. DALGARNO, Brad	Min.-NYI	Hamilton	RW
7. DAHLEN, Ulf	NYR	Ostersund (Sweden)	C
8. FEDYK, Brent	Det.	Regina	RW
9. DUNCANSON, Craig	L.A.	Sudbury	LW
10. GRATTON, Dan	Bos.-L.A.	Oshawa	C
11. MANSON, David	Chi.	Prince Albert	D
12. CHARBONNEAU, Jose	St.L.-Mtl.	Drummondville	RW
13. KING, Derek	NYI	Sault Ste. Marie	LW
14. JOHANSSON, Calle	Buf.	V. Frolunda (Sweden)	D
15. LATTA, Dave	Que.	Kitchener	LW
16. CHORSKE, Tom	Mtl.	Minneapolis SW HS	LW
17. BIOTTI, Chris	Cgy.	Belmont Hill HS	D
18. STEWART, Ryan	Wpg.	Kamloops	C
19. CORRIVEAU, Yvon	Wsh.	Toronto	LW
20. METCALFE, Scott	Edm.	Kingston	LW
21. SEABROOKE, Glen	Phi.	Peterborough	C

SECOND ROUND

Selection	Claimed By	Amateur Club	
22. SPANGLER, Ken	Tor.	Calgary	D
23. GIFFIN, Lee	Pit.	Oshawa	RW
24. BURKE, Sean	N.J.	Toronto	G
25. GAMBLE, Troy	Van.	Medicine Hat	G
26. WHITMORE, Kay	Hfd.	Peterborough	G
27. NIEUWENDYK, Joe	Min.-Cgy.	Cornell	C
28. RICHTER, Mike	NYR	Northwood Prep.	G
29. SHARPLES, Jeff	Det.	Kelowna	D
30. EDLUND, Par	L.A.	Bjorkloven (Sweden)	RW
31. COTE, Alain	Bos.	Quebec	D
32. WEINRICH, Eric	Chi.-N.J.	North Yarmouth	D
33. RICHARD, Todd	Mtl.	Armstrong HS	D
34. LAUER, Brad	NYI	Regina	RW
35. HOGUE, Benoit	Buf.	St-Jean	C
36. LAFRENIERE, Jason	Que.	Hamilton	C
37. RAGLAN, Herb	Mtl.-St.L.	Kingston	RW
38. WENAAS, Jeff	Cgy.	Medicine Hat	C
39. OHMAN, Roger	Wpg.	Leksand (Sweden)	D
40. DRUCE, John	Wsh.	Peterborough	RW
41. CARNELLEY, Todd	Edm.	Kamloops	D
42. RENDALL, Bruce	Phi.	Chatham	LW

1984

FIRST ROUND

Selection	Claimed By	Amateur Club	
1. LEMIEUX, Mario	Pit.	Laval	C
2. MULLER, Kirk	N.J.	Cdn-Nat.-Guelph	C
3. OLCZYK, Ed	L.A.-Chi.	U.S. National	RW
4. IAFRATE, Al	Tor.	U.S. National-Belleville	D
5. SVOBODA, Petr	Hfd.-Mtl.	CHZ (Czech.)	D
6. REDMOND, Craig	Chi.-L.A.	Canadian National	D
7. BURR, Shawn	Det.	Kitchener	C
8. CORSON, Shayne	St.L.-Mtl.	Brantford	C
9. BODGER, Doug	Wpg.-Pit.	Kamloops Jr. A	D
10. DAIGNEAULT, J.J.	Van.	Cdn. Nat.-Longueuil	D
11. COTE, Sylvain	Mtl.-Hfd.	Quebec	D
12. ROBERTS, Gary	Cgy.	Ottawa	LW
13. QUINN, David	Min.	Kent HS	D
14. CARKNER, Terry	NYR	Peterborough	D
15. STIENBURG, Trevor	Que.	Guelph	C
16. BELANGER, Roger	Phi.-Pit.	Kingston	D
17. HATCHER, Kevin	Wsh.	North Bay	D
18. ANDERSSON, Mikael	Buf.	V. Frolunda (Sweden)	C
19. PASIN, Dave	Bos.	Prince Albert	RW
20. MacPHERSON, Duncan	NYI	Saskatoon	D
21. ODELEIN, Selmar	Edm.	Regina	D

SECOND ROUND

Selection	Claimed By	Amateur Club	
22. SMYTH, Greg	Phi.	London	D
23. BILLINGTON, Craig	N.J.	Belleville	G
24. WILKS, Brian	L.A.	Kitchener	C
25. GILL, Todd	Tor.	Windsor	D
26. BENNING, Brian	Hfd.-St.L.	Portland	D
27. MELLANBY, Scott	Chi.-Phi.	Henry Carr Jr. B	RW
28. HOUDA, Doug	Det.	Calgary	D
29. RICHER, Stephane	St.L.-Mtl.	Granby	C
30. DOURIS, Peter	Wpg.	U. of New Hampshire	C
31. ROHLICEK, Jeff	Van.	Portland	LW
32. HRKAC, Anthony	Mtl.-St.L.	Orillia Jr. A	C
33. SABOURIN, Ken	Cgy.	Sault Ste. Marie	D
34. LEACH, Stephen	Min.-Wsh.	Matignon HS	RW
35. HELMINEN, Raimo	NYR	Ilves (Finland)	C
36. BROWN, Jeff	Que.	Sudbury	D
37. CHYCHRUN, Jeff	Phi.	Kingston	D
38. RANHEIM, Paul	Wsh.-Cgy.	Edina Hornets HS	C
39. TRAPP, Doug	Buf.	Regina	LW
40. PODLOSKI, Ray	Bos.	Portland	C
41. MELANSON, Bruce	NYI	Oshawa	RW
42. REAUGH, Daryl	Edm.	Kamloops Jr. A	G

1983

FIRST ROUND

Selection	Claimed By	Amateur Club	
1. LAWTON, Brian	Pit.-Min.	Mount St. Charles HS	C
2. TURGEON, Sylvain	Hfd.	Hull	C
3. LaFONTAINE, Pat	N.J.-NYI	Verdun	C
4. YZERMAN, Steve	Det.	Peterborough	C
5. BARRASSO, Tom	St.L.-L.A.-Buf.	Acton-Boxboro HS	G
6. MacLEAN, John	L.A.-N.J.	Oshawa	RW
7. COURTNALL, Russ	Tor.	Victoria	C
8. McBAIN, Andrew	Wpg.	North Bay	RW
9. NEELY, Cam	Van.	Portland	RW
10. LACOMBE, Normand	Cgy.-Buf.	U. of New Hampshire	RW
11. CREIGHTON, Adam	Que.-Buf.	Ottawa	C
12. GAGNER, Dave	NYR	Brantford	C
13. QUINN, Dan	Buf.-Cgy.	Belleville	C
14. DOLLAS, Bobby	Wsh.-Wpg.	Laval	D
15. ERREY, Bob	Min.-Pit.	Peterborough	LW
16. DIDUCK, Gerald	NYI	Lethbridge	D
17. TURCOTTE, Alfie	Mtl.	Portland	C
18. CASSIDY, Bruce	Chi.	Ottawa	D
19. BEUKEBOOM, Jeff	Edm.	Sault Ste. Marie	D
20. JENSEN, David	Phi.-Hfd.	Lawrence	C
21. MARKWART, Nevin	Bos.	Regina	LW

SECOND ROUND

Selection	Claimed By	Amateur Club	
22. CHARLESWORTH, Todd	Pit.	Oshawa	D
23. SIREN, Ville	Hfd.	Ilves (Finland)	D
24. EVANS, Shawn	N.J.	Peterborough	D
25. LAMBERT, Lane	Det.	Saskatoon	RW
26. LEMIEUX, Claude	St.L.-Mtl.	Trois-Rivières	RW
27. MOMESSO, Sergio	L.A.-Mtl.	Shawinigan	C
28. JACKSON, Jeff	Tor.	Brantford	LW
29. BERRY, Brad	Wpg.	St. Albert	D
30. BRUCE, Dave	Van.	Kitchener	RW
31. TUCKER, John	Cgy.-Buf.	Kitchener	C
32. HEROUX, Yves	Que.	Chicoutimi	RW
33. HEATH, Randy	NYR	Portland	LW
34. HAJDU, Richard	Wsh.-Buf.	Kamloops Jr. A	LW
35. FRANCIS, Todd	Mtl.	Brantford	RW
36. PARKS, Malcolm	Min.	St. Albert	C
37. McKECHNEY, Garnet	NYI	Kitchener	RW
38. MUSIL, Frantisek	Mtl.-Min.	Tesla (Czech.)	D
39. PRESLEY, Wayne	Chi.	Kitchener	RW
40. GOLDEN, Mike	Edm.	Reading HS	C
41. ZEZEL, Peter	Phi.	Toronto	C
42. JOHNSTON, Greg	Bos.	Toronto	RW

1982

FIRST ROUND

Selection	Claimed By	Amateur Club	
1. KLUZAK, Gord	Col.-Bos.	Nanaimo	D
2. BELLOWS, Brian	Det.-Min.	Kitchener	RW
3. NYLUND, Gary	Tor.	Portland	D
4. SUTTER, Ron	Hfd.-Phi.	Lethbridge	C
5. STEVENS, Scott	L.A.-Wsh.	Kitchener	D
6. HOUSLEY, Phil	Wsh.-Buf.	S. St. Paul HS	D
7. YAREMCHUK, Ken	Chi.	Portland	C
8. TROTTIER, Rocky	St.L.-N.J.	Nanaimo	RW
9. CYR, Paul	Cgy.-Buf.	Victoria	LW
10. SUTTER, Rich	Pit.	Lethbridge	RW
11. PETIT, Michel	Van.	Sherbrooke	D
12. KYTE, Jim	Wpg.	Cornwall	D
13. SHAW, David	Que.	Kitchener	D
14. LAWLESS, Paul	Phi.-Hfd.	Windsor	LW
15. KONTOS, Chris	NYR	Toronto	C
16. ANDREYCHUK, Dave	Buf.	Oshawa	LW
17. CRAVEN, Murray	Min.-Det.	Medicine Hat	C
18. DANEYKO, Ken	Bos.-N.J.	Seattle	D
19. HEROUX, Alain	Mtl.	Chicoutimi	LW
20. PLAYFAIR, Jim	Edm.	Portland	D
21. FLATLEY, Pat	NYI	U. of Wisconsin	RW

SECOND ROUND

Selection	Claimed By	Amateur Club	
22. CURRAN, Brian	Col.-Bos.	Portland	D
23. COURTEAU, Yves	Det.	Laval	RW
24. LEEMAN, Gary	Tor.	Regina	D
25. IHNACAK, Peter	Hfd.-Tor.	Sparta (Czech.)	C
26. ANDERSON, Mike	L.A.-Buf.	N. St. Paul HS	C
27. HEIDT, Mike	Wsh.-L.A.	Calgary	D
28. BADEAU, Rene	St.L.-Chi.	Quebec	D
29. REIERSON, Dave	Cgy.	Prince Albert	D
30. JOHANSSON, Jens	Buf.	Pitea (Sweden)	D
31. GAUVREAU, Jocelyn	Pit.-Mtl.	Granby	D
32. CARLSON, Kent	Van.-Mtl.	St. Lawrence University	D
33. MALEY, David	Wpg.-Mtl.	Edina HS	C
34. GILLIS, Paul	Que.	Niagara Falls	C
35. PATERSON, Mark	Phi.-Hfd.	Ottawa	D
36. SANDSTROM, Tomas	NYR	Farjestads (Sweden)	RW
37. KROMM, Richard	Buf.-Cgy.	Portland	LW
38. HRYNEWICH, Tim	Min.-Pit.	Sudbury	LW
39. BYERS, Lyndon	Bos.	Regina	RW
40. SANDELIN, Scott	Mtl.	Hibbing HS	D
41. GRAVES, Steve	Edm.	Sault Ste. Marie	C
42. SMITH, Vern	NYI	Lethbridge	D

1981

FIRST ROUND

Selection	Claimed By	Amateur Club	
1. HAWERCHUK, Dale	Wpg.	Cornwall	C
2. SMITH, Doug	Det.-L.A.	Ottawa	C
3. CARPENTER, Bobby	Col.-Wsh.	St. John's HS	C
4. FRANCIS, Ron	Hfd.	Sault Ste. Marie	C
5. CIRELLA, Joe	Wsh.-Col.	Oshawa	D
6. BENNING, Jim	Tor.	Portland	D
7. HUNTER, Mark	Pit.-Mtl.	Brantford	RW
8. FUHR, Grant	Edm.	Victoria	G
9. PATRICK, James	NYR	Prince Albert	D
10. BUTCHER, Garth	Van.	Regina	D
11. MOLLER, Randy	Que.	Lethbridge	D
12. TANTI, Tony	Chi.	Oshawa	RW
13. MEIGHAN, Ron	Min.	Niagara Falls	D
14. LEVEILLE, Normand	Bos.	Chicoutimi	LW
15. MacINNIS, Allan	Cgy.	Kitchener	D
16. SMITH, Steve	Phi.	Sault Ste. Marie	D
17. DUDACEK, Jiri	Buf.	Poldi Kladno (Czech.)	RW
18. DELORME, Gilbert	L.A.-Mtl.	Chicoutimi	D
19. INGMAN, Jan	Mtl.	Farjestad (Sweden)	LW
20. RUFF, Marty	St.L.	Lethbridge	D
21. BOUTILIER, Paul	NYI	Sherbrooke	D

SECOND ROUND

Selection	Claimed By	Amateur Club	
22. ARNIEL, Scott	Wpg.	Cornwall	LW
23. LOISELLE, Claude	Det.	Windsor	C
24. YAREMCHUK, Gary	Col.-Tor.	Portland	C
25. GRIFFIN, Kevin	Hfd.-Chi.	Portland	LW
26. CHERNOMAZ, Rich	Wsh.-Col.	Victoria	C
27. DONNELLY, Dave	Tor.-Min.	St. Albert	C
28. GATZOS, Steve	Pit.	Sault Ste. Marie	RW
29. STRUEBY, Todd	Edm.	Regina	LW
30. ERIXON, Jan	NYR	Skelleftea (Sweden)	RW
31. SANDS, Mike	Van.-Min.	Sudbury	G
32. ERIKSSON, Lars	Que.-Mtl.	Brynas (Sweden)	G
33. HIRSCH, Tom	Chi.-Min.	Patrick Henry HS	D
34. PREUSS, Dave	Min.	St. Thomas Academy	RW
35. DUFOUR, Luc	Bos.	Chicoutimi	RW
36. NORDIN, Hakan	Cgy.-St.L.	Farjestad (Sweden)	D
37. COSTELLO, Rich	Phi.	Natick HS	C
38. VIRTA, Hannu	Buf.	TPS (Finland)	D
39. KENNEDY, Dean	L.A.	Brandon	D
40. CHELIOS, Chris	Mtl.	Moose Jaw	D
41. WAHLSTEN, Jali	St.L.-Min.	TPS (Finland)	C
42. DINEEN, Gord	NYI	Sault Ste. Marie	D

1980

FIRST ROUND

Selection	Claimed By	Amateur Club	
1. WICKENHEISER, Doug	Col.-Mtl.	Regina	C
2. BABYCH, Dave	Wpg.	Portland	D
3. SAVARD, Denis	Que.-Chi.	Montreal	C
4. MURPHY, Larry	Det.-L.A.	Peterborough	D
5. VEITCH, Darren	Wsh.	Regina	D
6. COFFEY, Paul	Edm.	Kitchener	D
7. LANZ, Rick	Van.	Oshawa	D
8. ARTHUR, Fred	Hfd.	Cornwall	D
9. BULLARD, Mike	Pit.	Brantford	C
10. FOX, Jimmy	L.A.	Ottawa	RW
11. BLAISDELL, Mike	Tor.-Det.	Regina	RW
12. WILSON, Rik	St.L.	Kingston	D
13. CYR, Denis	Cgy.	Montreal	RW
14. MALONE, Jim	NYR	Toronto	C
15. DUPONT, Jerome	Chi.	Toronto	D
16. PALMER, Brad	Min.	Victoria	LW
17. SUTTER, Brent	NYI	Red Deer	C
18. PEDERSON, Barry	Bos.	Victoria	C
19. GAGNE, Paul	Mtl.-Col.	Windsor	LW
20. PATRICK, Steve	Buf.	Brandon	RW
21. STOTHERS, Mike	Phi.	Kingston	D

SECOND ROUND

Selection	Claimed By	Amateur Club	
22. WARD, Joe	Col.	Seattle	C
23. MANTHA, Moe	Wpg.	Toronto	D
24. ROCHEFORT, Normand	Que.	Quebec	D
25. MUNI, Craig	Det.-Tor.	Kingston	D
26. McGILL, Bob	Wsh.-Tor.	Victoria	D
27. NATTRESS, Ric	Edm.-Mtl.	Brantford	D
28. LUDZIK, Steve	Van.-Chi.	Niagara Falls	C
29. GALARNEAU, Michel	Hfd.	Hull	C
30. SOLHEIM, Ken	Pit.-Chi.	Medicine Hat	LW
31. CURTALE, Tony	L.A.-Cgy.	Brantford	D
32. LaVALLEE, Kevin	Tor.-Cgy.	Brantford	LW
33. TERRION, Greg	St.L.-L.A.	Brantford	LW
34. MORRISON, Dave	Cgy.-L.A.	Peterborough	RW
35. ALLISON, Mike	NYR	Sudbury	LW
36. DAWES, Len	Chi.	Victoria	D
37. BEAUPRE, Don	Min.	Sudbury	G
38. HRUDEY, Kelly	NYI	Medicine Hat	G
39. KONROYD, Steve	Cgy.	Oshawa	D
40. CHABOT, John	Mtl.	Hull	C
41. MOLLER, Mike	Buf.	Lethbridge	RW
42. FRASER, Jay	Phi.	Ottawa	LW

1979

FIRST ROUND

Selection	Claimed By	Amateur Club	
1. RAMAGE, Rob	Col.	London	D
2. TURNBULL, Perry	St.L.	Portland	C
3. FOLIGNO, Mike	Det.	Sudbury	RW
4. GARTNER, Mike	Wsh.	Niagara Falls	RW
5. VAIVE, Rick	Van.	Sherbrooke	RW
6. HARTSBURG, Craig	Min.	Sault St. Marie	D
7. BROWN, Keith	Chi.	Portland	D
8. BOURQUE, Raymond	L.A.-Bos.	Verdun	D
9. BOSCHMAN, Laurie	Tor.	Brandon	C
10. McCARTHY, Tom	Wsh.-Min.	Oshawa	LW
11. RAMSEY, Mike	Buf.	U. of Minnesota	D
12. REINHART, Paul	Atl.	Kitchener	D
13. SULLIMAN, Doug	NYR	Kitchener	RW
14. PROPP, Brian	Phi.	Brandon	LW
15. McCRIMMON, Brad	Bos.	Brandon	D
16. WELLS, Jay	Mtl.-L.A.	Kingston	D
17. SUTTER, Duane	NYI	Lethbridge	RW
18. ALLISON, Ray	Hfd.	Brandon	RW
19. MANN, Jimmy	Wpg.	Sherbrooke	RW
20. GOULET, Michel	Que.	Quebec	LW
21. LOWE, Kevin	Edm.	Quebec	D

SECOND ROUND

Selection	Claimed By	Amateur Club	
22. WESLEY, Blake	Col.-Phi.	Portland	D
23. PEROVICH, Mike	St.L.-Atl.	Brandon	D
24. RAUSSE, Errol	Det.-Wsh.	Seattle	LW
25. JONSSON, Tomas	Wsh.-NYI	MoDo AIK (Sweden)	D
26. ASHTON, Brent	Van.	Saskatoon	LW
27. GINGRAS, Gaston	Min.-Mtl.	Hamilton	D
28. TRIMPER, Tim	Chi.	Peterborough	LW
29. HOPKINS, Dean	L.A.	London	RW
30. HARDY, Mark	Tor.-L.A.	Montreal	D
31. MARSHALL, Paul	Wsh.-Pit.	Brantford	LW
32. RUFF, Lindy	Buf.	Lethbridge	D
33. RIGGIN, Pat	Atl.	London	G
34. HOSPODAR, Ed	NYR	Ottawa	D
35. LINDBERGH, Pelle	Phi.	AIK Solna (Sweden)	G
36. MORRISON, Doug	Bos.	Lethbridge	RW
37. NASLUND, Mats	Mtl.	Brynas IFK (Sweden)	LW
38. CARROLL, Billy	NYI	London	C
39. SMITH, Stuart	Hfd.	Peterborough	D
40. CHRISTIAN, Dave	Wpg.	U. of North Dakota	C
41. HUNTER, Dale	Que.	Sudbury	C
42. BROTEN, Neal	Min.	U. of Minnesota	C

1978

FIRST ROUND

Selection	Claimed By	Amateur Club	
1. SMITH, Bobby	Min.	Ottawa	C
2. WALTER, Ryan	Wsh.	Seattle	LW
3. BABYCH, Wayne	St.L.	Portland	RW
4. DERLAGO, Bill	Van.	Brandon	C
5. GILLIS, Mike	Col.	Kingston	LW
6. WILSON, Behn	Pit.-Phi.	Kingston	D
7. LINSEMAN, Ken	NYR-Phi.	Kingston	C
8. GEOFFRION, Danny	L.A.-Mtl.	Cornwall	RW
9. HUBER, Willie	Det.	Hamilton	D
10. HIGGINS, Tim	Chi.	Ottawa	RW
11. MARSH, Brad	Atl.	London	D
12. PETERSON, Brent	Tor.-Det.	Portland	C
13. PLAYFAIR, Larry	Buf.	Portland	D
14. LUCAS, Danny	Phi.	Sault Ste. Marie	RW
15. TAMBELLINI, Steve	NYI	Lethbridge	C
16. SECORD, Al	Bos.	Hamilton	LW
17. HUNTER, Dave	Mtl.	Sudbury	LW
18. COULIS, Tim	Wsh.	Hamilton	LW

SECOND ROUND

Selection	Claimed By	Amateur Club	
19. PAYNE, Steve	Min.	Ottawa	LW
20. MULVEY, Paul	Wsh.	Portland	RW
21. QUENNEVILLE, Joel	Tor.	Windsor	D
22. FRASER, Curt	Van.	Victoria	LW
23. MacKINNON, Paul	Wsh.	Peterborough	D
24. CHRISTOFF, Steve	Min.	U. of Minnesota	C
25. MEEKER, Mike	Pit.	Peterborough	RW
26. MALONEY, Don	NYR	Kitchener	LW
27. MALINOWSKI, Merlin	Col.	Medicine Hat	C
28. HICKS, Glenn	Det.	Flin Flon	LW
29. LECUYER, Doug	Chi.	Portland	LW
30. YAKIWCHUK, Dale	Mtl.	Portland	C
31. JENSEN, Al	Det.	Hamilton	G
32. McKEGNEY, Tony	Buf.	Kingston	LW
33. SIMURDA, Mike	Phi.	Kingston	RW
34. JOHNSTON, Randy	NYI	Peterborough	D
35. NICOLSON, Graeme	Bos.	Cornwall	D
36. CARTER, Ron	Mtl.	Sherbrooke	RW

1977

FIRST ROUND

Selection	Claimed By	Amateur Club	
1. McCOURT, Dale	Det.	St. Catharines	C
2. BECK, Barry	Col.	New Westminster	D
3. PICARD, Robert	Wsh.	Montreal	D
4. GILLIS, Jere	Van.	Sherbrooke	LW
5. CROMBEEN, Mike	Cle.	Kingston	RW
6. WILSON, Doug	Chi.	Ottawa	D
7. MAXWELL, Brad	Min.	New Westminster	D
8. DEBLOIS, Lucien	NYR	Sorel	C
9. CAMPBELL, Scott	St.L.	London	D
10. NAPIER, Mark	Atl.-Mtl.	Toronto	RW
11. ANDERSON, John	Tor.	Toronto	RW
12. JOHANSEN, Trevor	Pit.-Tor.	Toronto	D
13. DUGUAY, Ron	L.A.-NYR	Sudbury	C
14. SEILING, Ric	Buf.	St. Catharines	RW
15. BOSSY, Mike	NYI	Laval	RW
16. FOSTER, Dwight	Bos.	Kitchener	C/RW
17. McCARTHY, Kevin	Phi.	Winnipeg	D
18. DUPONT, Norm	Mtl.	Montreal	C

SECOND ROUND

Selection	Claimed By	Amateur Club	
19. SAVARD, Jean	Det.-Chi.	Quebec	C
20. ZAHARKO, Miles	Col.-Atl.	New Westminister	D
21. LOFTHOUSE, Mark	Wsh.	New Westminster	RW
22. BANDURA, Jeff	Van.	Portland	D
23. CHICOINE, Daniel	Cle.	Sherbrooke	RW
24. GLADNEY, Bob	Chi.-Tor.	Oshawa	D
25. SEMENKO, Dave	Min.	Brandon	LW
26. KEATING, Mike	NYR	St. Catherines	LW
27. LABATTE, Neil	St.L.	Toronto	D
28. LAURENCE, Don	Atl.	Kitchener	C
29. SAGANIUK, Rocky	Tor.	Lethbridge	RW
30. HAMILTON, Jim	Pit.	London	RW
31. HILL, Brian	L.A.-Atl.	Medicine Hat	RW
32. ARESHENKOFF, Ron	Buf.	Medicine Hat	C
33. TONELLI, John	NYI	Toronto	LW
34. PARRO, Dave	Bos.	Saskatoon	G
35. GORENCE, Tom	Phi.	U. of Minnesota	RW
36. LANGWAY, Rod	Mtl.	U. of New Hampshire	D

1976

FIRST ROUND

Selection	Claimed By	Amateur Club	
1. GREEN, Rick	K.C.-Wsh.	London	D
2. CHAPMAN, Blair	Pit.	Saskatoon	RW
3. SHARPLEY, Glen	Min.	Hull	C
4. WILLIAMS, Fred	Det.	Saskatoon	C
5. JOHANSSON, Bjorn	Cal.	Sweden	D
6. MURDOCH, Don	NYR	Medicine Hat	RW
7. FEDERKO, Bernie	St.L.	Saskatoon	C
8. SHAND, Dave	Van.-Atl.	Peterborough	D
9. CLOUTIER, Real	Chi.	Quebec	RW
10. PHILLIPOFF, Harold	Atl.	New Westminster	LW
11. GARDNER, Paul	Pit.-K.C.	Oshawa	C
12. LEE, Peter	Tor.-Mtl.	Ottawa	RW
13. SCHUTT, Rod	L.A.-Mtl.	Sudbury	LW
14. McKENDRY, Alex	NYI	Sudbury	LW
15. CARROLL, Greg	Buf.-Wsh.	Medicine Hat	C
16. PACHAL, Clayton	Bos.	New Westminster	C
17. SUZOR, Mark	Phi.	Kingston	D
18. BAKER, Bruce	Mtl.	Ottawa	RW

SECOND ROUND

Selection	Claimed By	Amateur Club	
19. MALONE, Greg	Wsh.-Pit.	Oshawa	C
20. SUTTER, Brian	K.C.-St.L.	Lethbridge	LW
21. CLIPPINGDALE, Steve	Min.-L.A.	New Westminster	LW
22. LARSON, Reed	Det.	U. of Minnesota	D
23. STENLUND, Vern	Cal.	London	C
24. FARRISH, Dave	NYR	Sudbury	D
25. SMRKE, John	St.L.	Toronto	LW
26. MANNO, Bob	Van.	St. Catharines	D
27. McDILL, Jeff	Chi.	Victoria	RW
28. SIMPSON, Bobby	Atl.	Sherbrooke	LW
29. MARSH, Peter	Pit.	Sherbrooke	RW
30. CARLYLE, Randy	Tor.	Sudbury	D
31. ROBERTS, Jim	L.A.-Min.	Ottawa	LW
32. KASZYCKI, Mike	NYI	Sault Ste. Marie	C
33. KOWAL, Joe	Buf.	Hamilton	LW
34. GLOECKNER, Larry	Bos.	Victoria	D
35. CALLANDER, Drew	Phi.	Regina	C
36. MELROSE, Barry	Mtl.	Kamloops	D

1975

FIRST ROUND

Selection	Claimed By	Amateur Club	
1. BRIDGMAN, Mel	Wsh.-Phi.	Victoria	C
2. DEAN, Barry	K.C.	Medicine Hat	LW
3. KLASSEN, Ralph	Cal.	Saskatoon	C
4. MAXWELL, Brian	Min.	Medicine Hat	D
5. LAPOINTE, Rick	Det.	Victoria	D
6. ASHBY, Don	Tor.	Calgary	C
7. VAYDIK, Greg	Chi.	Medicine Hat	C
8. MULHERN, Richard	Atl.	Sherbrooke	D
9. SADLER, Robin	St.L.-Mtl.	Edmonton	D
10. BLIGHT, Rick	Van.	Brandon	RW
11. PRICE, Pat	NYI	Saskatoon	D
12. DILLON, Wayne	NYR	Toronto	C
13. LAXTON, Gord	Pit.	New Westminster	G
14. HALWARD, Doug	Bos.	Peterborough	D
15. MONDOU, Pierre	L.A.-Mtl.	Montreal	C
16. YOUNG, Tim	Mtl.-L.A.	Ottawa	C
17. SAUVE, Bob	Buf.	Laval	G
18. FORSYTH, Alex	Phi.-Wsh.	Kingston	C

SECOND ROUND

19. SCAMURRA, Peter	Wsh.	Peterborough	D
20. CAIRNS, Don	K.C.	Victoria	LW
21. MARUK, Dennis	Cal.	London	C
22. ENGBLOM, Brian	Min.-Mtl.	U. of Wisconsin	D
23. ROLLINS, Jerry	Det.	Winnipeg	D
24. JARVIS, Doug	Tor.	Peterborough	C
25. ARNDT, Daniel	Chi.	Saskatoon	LW
26. BOWNESS, Rick	Atl.	Montreal	RW
27. STANIOWSKI, Ed	St.L.	Regina	G
28. GASSOFF, Brad	Van.	Kamloops	D
29. SALVIAN, David	NYI	St. Catharines	RW
30. SOETAERT, Doug	NYR	Edmonton	G
31. ANDERSON, Russ	Pit.	U. of Minnesota	D
32. SMITH, Barry	Bos.	New Westminster	C
33. BUCYK, Terry	L.A.	Lethbridge	RW
34. GREENBANK, Kelvin	Mtl.	Winnipeg	RW
35. BREITENBACH, Ken	Buf.	St. Catharines	D
36. MASTERS, Jamie	Phi.-St.L.	Ottawa	D

1974

FIRST ROUND

Selection	Claimed By	Amateur Club	
1. JOLY, Greg	Wsh.	Regina	D
2. PAIEMENT, Wilfred	K.C.	St. Catharines	RW
3. HAMPTON, Rick	Cal.	St. Catharines	D
4. GILLIES, Clark	NYI	Regina	LW
5. CONNOR, Cam	Van.-Mtl.	Flin Flon	RW
6. HICKS, Doug	Min.	Flin Flon	D
7. RISEBROUGH, Doug	St.L.-Mtl.	Kitchener	C
8. LAROUCHE, Pierre	Pit.	Sorel	C
9. LOCHEAD, Bill	Det.	Oshawa	LW
10. CHARTRAW, Rick	Atl.-Mtl.	Kitchener	D
11. FOGOLIN, Lee	Buf.	Oshawa	D
12. TREMBLAY, Mario	L.A.-Mtl.	Montreal	RW
13. VALIQUETTE, Jack	Tor.	Sault Ste. Marie	C
14. MALONEY, Dave	NYR	Kitchener	D
15. McTAVISH, Gord	Mtl.	Sudbury	C
16. MULVEY, Grant	Chi.	Calgary	RW
17. CHIPPERFIELD, Ron	Phi.-Cal.	Brandon	C
18. LARWAY, Don	Bos.	Swift Current	RW

SECOND ROUND

19. MARSON, Mike	Wsh.	Sudbury	LW
20. BURDON, Glen	K.C.	Regina	C
21. AFFLECK, Bruce	Cal.	U. of Denver	D
22. TROTTIER, Bryan	NYI	Swift Current	C
23. SEDLBAUER, Ron	Van.	Kitchener	LW
24. NANTAIS, Rick	Min.	Quebec	LW
25. HOWE, Mark	St.L.-Bos.	Toronto	D
26. HESS, Bob	Pit.-St.L.	New Westminster	D
27. COSSETTE, Jacques	Det.-Pit.	Sorel	RW
28. CHOUINARD, Guy	Atl.	Quebec	C
29. GARE, Danny	Buf.	Calgary	RW
30. MacGREGOR, Gary	L.A.-Mtl.	Cornwall	C
31. WILLIAMS, Dave	Tor.	Swift Current	LW
32. GRESCHNER, Ron	NYR	New Westminster	D
33. LUPIEN, Gilles	Mtl.	Montreal	D
34. DAIGLE, Alain	Chi.	Trois-Rivières	RW
35. McLEAN, Don	Phi.	Sudbury	D
36. STURGEON, Peter	Bos.	Kitchener	LW

1973

FIRST ROUND

Selection	Claimed By	Amateur Club	
1. POTVIN, Denis	NYI	Ottawa	D
2. LYSIAK, Tom	Cal.-Mtl.-Atl.	Medicine Hat	C
3. VERVERGAERT, Dennis	Van.	London	RW
4. McDONALD, Lanny	Tor.	Medicine Hat	RW
5. DAVIDSON, John	Atl.-Mtl.-St.L.	Calgary	G
6. SAVARD, Andre	L.A.-Bos.	Quebec	C
7. STOUGHTON, Blaine	Pit.	Flin Flon	RW
8. GAINEY, Bob	St.L.-Mtl.	Peterborough	LW
9. DAILEY, Bob	Min.-Mtl.-Van.	Toronto	D
10. NEELY, Bob	Phi.-Tor.	Peterborough	LW
11. RICHARDSON, Terry	Det.	New Westminster	G
12. TITANIC, Morris	Buf.	Sudbury	LW
13. ROTA, Darcy	Chi.	Edmonton	LW
14. MIDDLETON, Rick	NYR	Oshawa	RW
15. TURNBULL, Ian	Bos.-Tor.	Ottawa	D
16. MERCREDI, Vic	Mtl.-Atl.	New Westminster	C

SECOND ROUND

17. GOLDUP, Glen	NYI-Mtl.	Toronto	RW
18. DUNLOP, Blake	Cal.-Min.	Ottawa	C
19. BORDELEAU, Paulin	Van.	Toronto	RW
20. GOODENOUGH, Larry	Tor.-Phi.	London	D
21. VAIL, Eric	Atl.	Sudbury	LW
22. MARRIN, Peter	L.A.-Mtl.	Toronto	C
23. BIANCHIN, Wayne	Pit.	Flin Flon	LW
24. PESUT, George	St.L.	Saskatoon	D
25. ROGERS, John	Min.	Edmonton	RW
26. LEVINS, Brent	Phi.	Swift Current	
27. CAMPBELL, Colin	Det.-Pit.	Peterborough	D
28. LANDRY, Jean	Buf.	Quebec	D
29. THOMAS, Reg	Chi.	London	LW
30. HICKEY, Pat	NYR	Hamilton	LW
31. JONES, Jim	Bos.	Peterborough	RW
32. ANDRUFF, Ron	Mtl.	Flin Flon	C

1972

FIRST ROUND

Selection	Claimed By	Amateur Club	
1. HARRIS, Billy	NYI	Toronto	RW
2. RICHARD, Jacques	Atl.	Quebec	LW
3. LEVER, Don	Van.	Niagara Falls	C
4. SHUTT, Steve	L.A.-Mtl.	Toronto	LW
5. SCHOENFELD, Jim	Buf.	Niagara Falls	D
6. LAROCQUE, Michel	Cal.-Mtl.	Ottawa	G
7. BARBER, Bill	Phi.	Kitchener	LW
8. GARDNER, Dave	Pit.-Min.-Mtl.	Toronto	C
9. MERRICK, Wayne	St.L.	Ottawa	C
10. BLANCHARD, Albert	Det.-NYR	Kitchener	LW
11. FERGUSON, George	Tor.	Toronto	C
12. BYERS, Jerry	Min.	Kitchener	LW
13. RUSSELL, Phil	Chi.	Edmonton	D
14. VAN BOXMEER, John	Mtl.	Guelph	D
15. MacMILLAN, Bobby	NYR	St. Catharines	RW
16. BLOOM, Mike	Bos.	St. Catharines	LW

SECOND ROUND

17. HENNING Lorne	NYI	New Westminster	C
18. BIALOWAS, Dwight	Atl.	Regina	D
19. McSHEFFREY, Brian	Van.	Ottawa	RW
20. KOZAK, Don	L.A.	Edmonton	RW
21. SACHARUK, Larry	Buf.-NYR	Saskatoon	D
22. CASSIDY, Tom	Cal.	Kitchener	C
23. BLADON, Tom	Phi.	Edmonton	D
24. LYNCH, Jack	Pit.	Oshawa	D
25. CARRIERE, Larry	St.L.-Buf.	Loyola College	D
26. GUITE, Pierre	Det.	St. Catharines	LW
27. OSBURN, Randy	Tor.	London	LW
28. WEIR, Stan	Min.-Cal.	Medicine Hat	C
29. OGILVIE, Brian	Chi.	Edmonton	C
30. LUKOWICH, Bernie	Mtl.-Pit.	New Westminster	RW
31. VILLEMURE, Rene	NYR	Shawinigan	LW
32. ELDER, Wayne	Bos.	London	D

1971

FIRST ROUND

Selection	Claimed By	Amateur Club	
1. LAFLEUR, Guy	Cal.-Mtl.	Quebec	RW
2. DIONNE, Marcel	Det.	St. Catharines	C
3. GUEVREMONT, Jocelyn	Van.	Montreal	D
4. CARR, Gene	Pit.-St.L.	Flin Flon	C
5. MARTIN, Rick	Buf.	Montreal	LW
6. JONES, Ron	L.A.-Bos.	Edmonton	D
7. ARNASON, Chuck	Min.-Mtl.	Flin Flon	RW
8. WRIGHT, Larry	Phi.	Regina	C
9. PLANTE, Pierre	Tor.-Phi.	Drummondville	RW
10. VICKERS, Steve	St.L.-NYR	Toronto	LW
11. WILSON, Murray	Mtl.	Ottawa	LW
12. SPRING, Dan	Chi.	Edmonton	C
13. DURBANO, Steve	NYR	Toronto	D
14. O'REILLY, Terry	Bos.	Oshawa	RW

SECOND ROUND

15. BAIRD, Ken	Cal.	Flin Flon	D
16. BOUCHA, Henry	Det.	U.S. Nationals	C
17. LALONDE, Bobby	Van.	Montreal	C
18. McKENZIE, Brian	Pit.	St. Catharines	LW
19. RAMSAY, Craig	Buf.	Peterborough	LW
20. ROBINSON, Larry	L.A.-Mtl.	Kitchener	D
21. NORRISH, Rod	Min.	Regina	LW
22. KEHOE, Rick	Phi.-Tor.	Hamilton	RW
23. FORTIER, Dave	Tor.	St. Catharines	D
24. DEGUISE, Michel	St.L.-Mtl.	Sorel	G
25. FRENCH, Terry	Mtl.	Ottawa	C
26. KRYSKOW, Dave	Chi.	Edmonton	LW
27. WILLIAMS, Tom	NYR	Hamilton	LW
28. RIDLEY, Curt	Bos.	Portage	G

1970

FIRST ROUND

Selection	Claimed By	Amateur Club	
1. PERREAULT, Gilbert	Buf.	Montreal	C
2. TALLON, Dale	Van.	Toronto	D
3. LEACH, Reg	L.A.-Bos.	Flin Flon	LW
4. MacLEISH, Rick	Phi.-Bos.	Peterborough	C
5. MARTINIUK, Ray	Oak.-Mtl.	Flin Flon	G
6. LEFLEY, Chuck	Min.-Mtl.	Canadian Nationals	C
7. POLIS, Greg	Pit.	Estevan	LW
8. SITTLER, Darryl	Tor.	London	C
9. PLUMB, Ron	Bos.	Peterborough	D
10. ODDLEIFSON, Chris	St.L.-Oak.	Winnipeg	C
11. GRATTON, Norm	Mtl.-NYR	Montreal	LW
12. LAJEUNESSE, Serge	Det.	Montreal	RW
13. STEWART, Bob	Bos.	Oshawa	D
14. MALONEY, Dan	Chi.	London	LW

SECOND ROUND

15. DEADMARSH, Butch	Buf.	Brandon	LW
16. HARGREAVES, Jim	Van.	Winnipeg	D
17. HARVEY, Fred	L.A.-Min.	Hamilton	RW
18. CLEMENT, Bill	Phi.	Ottawa	C
19. LAFRAMBOISE, Pete	Oak.	Ottawa	C
20. BARRETT, Fred	Min.	Toronto	D
21. STEWART, John	Pit.	Flin Flon	LW
22. THOMPSON, Errol	Tor.	Charlottetown	LW
23. KEOGAN, Murray	St.L.	U. of Minnesota	C
24. McDONOUGH, Al	Mtl.-L.A.	St. Catharines	RW
25. MURPHY, Mike	NYR	Toronto	RW
26. GUINDON, Bobby	Det.	Montreal	LW
27. BOUCHARD, Dan	Bos.	London	G
28. ARCHAMBAULT, Mike	Chi.	Drummondville	LW

1969

FIRST ROUND

Selection	Claimed By	Amateur Club	
1. HOULE, Rejean	Mtl.	Montreal	LW
2. TARDIF, Marc	Mtl.	Montreal	LW
3. TANNAHILL, Don	Min.-Bos.	Niagara Falls	LW
4. SPRING, Frank	Pit.-Bos.	Edmonton	RW
5. REDMOND, Dick	L.A.-Mtl.-Min.	St. Catharines	D
6. CURRIER, Bob	Phi.	Cornwall	C
7. FEATHERSTONE, Tony	Oak.	Peterborough	RW
8. DUPONT, André	St.L.-NYR	Montreal	D
9. MOSER, Ernie	Det.-Tor.	Estevan	RW
10. RUTHERFORD, Jim	Det.	Hamilton	G
11. BOLDIREV, Ivan	Bos.	Oshawa	C
12. JARRY, Pierre	NYR	Ottawa	LW
13. BORDELEAU, J.-P.	Chi.	Montreal	RW
14. O'BRIEN, Dennis	Min.	St. Catharines	D

SECOND ROUND

15. KESSELL, Rick	Pit.	Oshawa	C
16. HOGANSON, Dale	L.A.	Estevan	D
17. CLARKE, Bobby	Phi.	Flin Flon	C
18. STACKHOUSE, Ron	Oak.	Peterborough	D
19. LOWE, Mike	St.L.	Loyola College	D
20. BRINDLEY, Doug	Tor.	Niagara Falls	C
21. GARWASIUK, Ron	Det.	Regina	LW
22. QUOQUOCHI, Art	Bos.	Montreal	
23. WILSON, Bert	NYR	London	LW
24. ROMANCHYCH, Larry	Chi.	Flin Flon	RW
25. GILBERT, Gilles	Min.	London	G
26. BRIERE, Michel	Pit.	Shawinigan Falls	C
27. BODDY, Greg	L.A.	Edmonton	D
28. BROSSART, Bill	Phi.	Estevan	D

Although every team passed on his services during the first round of the 1974 Amateur Draft, Bryan Trottier went on to become only the fourth player in NHL history to win two-or-more Stanley Cup titles with two-or-more teams. He won with the New York Islanders from 1980 to 1983 and with the Pittsburgh Penguins in 1991 and 1992.

NHL All-Stars

Active Players' All-Star Selection Records

GOALTENDERS

Player	First Team Selections	Second Team Selections	Total
Patrick Roy	(3) 1988-89; 1989-90; 1991-92.	(2) 1987-88; 1990-91.	5
Dominik Hasek	(3) 1993-94; 1994-95; 1996-97.	(0)	3
Ed Belfour	(2) 1990-91; 1992-93.	(1) 1994-95.	3
Tom Barrasso	(1) 1983-84.	(2) 1984-85; 1992-93.	3
Grant Fuhr	(1) 1987-88.	(1) 1981-82.	2
J.Vanbiesbrouck	(1) 1985-86.	(1) 1993-94.	2
Ron Hextall	(1) 1986-87.	(0)	1
Jim Carey	(1) 1995-96.	(0)	1
Mike Vernon	(0)	(1) 1988-89.	1
Daren Puppa	(0)	(1) 1989-90.	1
Kirk McLean	(0)	(1) 1991-92.	1
Chris Osgood	(0)	(1) 1995-96.	1
Martin Brodeur	(0)	(1) 1996-97.	1

DEFENSEMEN

Player	First Team Selections	Second Team Selections	Total
Ray Bourque	(12) 1979-80; 1981-82; 1983-84; 1984-85; 1986-87; 1987-88; 1989-90; 1990-91; 1992-93; 1993-94; 1995-96.	(5) 1980-81; 1982-83; 1985-86; 1988-89; 1994-95.	17
Paul Coffey	(4) 1984-85; 1985-86; 1988-89; 1994-95.	(4) 1981-82; 1982-83; 1983-84; 1989-90.	8
Chris Chelios	(4) 1988-89; 1992-93; 1994-95; 1995-96.	(2) 1990-91; 1996-97.	6
Al MacInnis	(2) 1989-90; 1990-91.	(3) 1986-87; 1988-89; 1993-94.	5
Brian Leetch	(2) 1991-92; 1996-97.	(3) 1990-91; 1993-94; 1995-96.	5
Scott Stevens	(2) 1987-88; 1993-94.	(2) 1991-92; 1996-97.	4
Sandis Ozolinsh	(1) 1996-97.	(0)	
Larry Murphy	(0)	(3) 1986-87; 1992-93; 1994-95.	3
Gary Suter	(0)	(1) 1987-88.	1
Phil Housley	(0)	(1) 1991-92.	1
Al Iafrate	(0)	(1) 1992-93.	1
V. Konstantinov	(0)	(1) 1995-96.	1

CENTERS

Player	First Team Selections	Second Team Selections	Total
Wayne Gretzky	(8) 1980-81; 1981-82; 1982-83; 1983-84; 1984-85; 1985-86; 1986-87; 1990-91.	(6) 1979-80; 1987-88; 1988-89; 1989-90; 1993-94; 1996-97.	14
Mark Messier	(2) 1989-90; 1991-92.	(0)	2
Eric Lindros	(1) 1994-95.	(1) 1995-96.	2
Sergei Fedorov	(1) 1993-94.	(0)	1
Adam Oates	(0)	(1) 1990-91.	1
Pat LaFontaine	(0)	(1) 1992-93.	1
Alexei Zhamnov	(0)	(1) 1994-95.	1

RIGHT WINGERS

Player	First Team Selections	Second Team Selections	Total
Jari Kurri	(2) 1984-85; 1986-87.	(3) 1983-84; 1985-86; 1988-89.	5
Brett Hull	(3) 1989-90; 1990-91; 1991-92.	(0)	3
Jaromir Jagr	(2) 1994-95; 1995-96.	(1) 1996-97.	3
Teemu Selanne	(2) 1992-93; 1996-97.	(0)	2
Alexander Mogilny	(0)	(2) 1992-93; 1995-96.	2
Pavel Bure	(1) 1993-94.	(0)	1
Mark Recchi	(0)	(1) 1991-92.	1
Theoren Fleury	(0)	(1) 1994-95.	1

LEFT WINGERS

Player	First Team Selections	Second Team Selections	Total
Luc Robitaille	(5) 1987-88; 1988-89; 1989-90; 1990-91; 1992-93.	(2) 1986-87; 1991-92.	7
Mark Messier	(2) 1981-82; 1982-83.	(1) 1983-84.	3
Kevin Stevens	(1) 1991-92.	(2) 1990-91; 1992-93.	3
John LeClair	(1) 1994-95.	(2) 1995-96; 1996-97.	3
Paul Kariya	(2) 1995-96; 1996-97.	(0)	2
Brendan Shanahan	(1) 1993-94.	(0)	1
Brian Bellows	(0)	(1) 1989-90.	1
Adam Graves	(0)	(1) 1993-94.	1
Keith Tkachuk	(0)	(1) 1994-95.	1

Leading NHL All-Stars 1930-97

Player	Pos	Team	NHL Seasons	First Team Selections	Second Team Selections	Total Selections
Howe, Gordie	RW	Detroit	26	12	9	21
* Bourque, Ray	D	Boston	18	12	5	17
Richard, Maurice	RW	Montreal	18	8	6	14
* Gretzky, Wayne	C	Edm., L.A., NYR	18	8	6	14
Hull, Bobby	LW	Chicago	16	10	2	12
Harvey, Doug	D	Mtl., NYR	19	10	1	11
Hall, Glenn	G	Det., Chi., St.L.	18	7	4	11
Beliveau, Jean	C	Montreal	20	6	4	10
Seibert, Earl	D	NYR., Chi	15	4	6	10
Orr, Bobby	D	Boston	12	8	1	9
Lindsay, Ted	LW	Detroit	17	8	1	9
Mahovlich, Frank	LW	Tor., Det., Mtl.	18	3	6	9
Shore, Eddie	D	Boston	14	7	1	8
Mikita, Stan	C	Chicago	22	6	2	8
Kelly, Red	D	Detroit	20	6	2	8
Esposito, Phil	C	Boston	18	6	2	8
Pilote, Pierre	D	Chicago	14	5	3	8
Lemieux, Mario	C	Pittsburgh	12	5	3	8
* Coffey, Paul	D	Edm., Pit., Det.	17	4	4	8
Brimsek, Frank	G	Boston	10	2	6	8
Bossy, Mike	RW	NY Islanders	10	5	3	8
* Robitaille, Luc	LW	Los Angeles	11	5	2	7
Potvin, Denis	D	NY Islanders	15	5	2	7
Park, Brad	D	NYR, Bos.	17	5	2	7
Plante, Jacques	G	Mtl., Tor.	18	3	4	7
Gadsby, Bill	D	Chi., NYR, Det.	20	3	4	7
Sawchuk, Terry	G	Detroit	21	3	4	7
Durnan, Bill	G	Montreal	7	6	0	6
Lafleur, Guy	RW	Montreal	16	6	0	6
Dryden, Ken	G	Montreal	8	5	1	6
* Chelios, Chris	D	Mtl., Chi.	14	4	2	6
Robinson, Larry	D	Montreal	20	3	3	6
Horton, Tim	D	Toronto	24	3	3	6
Salming, Borje	D	Toronto	17	1	5	6
Cowley, Bill	C	Boston	13	4	1	5
* Messier, Mark	LW/C	Edm., NYR	18	4	1	5
Jackson, Harvey	LW	Toronto	15	4	1	5
Goulet, Michel	LW	Quebec	15	3	2	5
Clapper, "Dit"	RW/D	Boston	20	3	2	5
Conacher, Charlie	RW	Toronto	12	3	2	5
Stewart, Jack	D	Detroit	12	3	2	5
Lach, Elmer	C	Montreal	14	3	2	5
Quackenbush, Bill	D	Det., Bos.	14	3	2	5
Blake, Toe	LW	Montreal	15	3	2	5
Esposito, Tony	G	Chicago	16	3	2	5
* Roy, Patrick	G	Montreal	13	2	3	5
Reardon, Ken	D	Montreal	7	2	3	5
* Kurri, Jari	RW	Edmonton	16	2	3	5
Apps, Syl	C	Toronto	10	2	3	5
Giacomin, Ed	G	NY Rangers	13	2	3	5
* MacInnis, Al	D	Calgary	16	2	3	5
Leetch, Brian	D	NY Rangers	10	2	3	5

* Active

Position Leaders in All-Star Selections

Position	Player	First Team	Second Team	Total
GOAL	Glenn Hall	7	4	11
	Frank Brimsek	2	6	8
	Jacques Plante	3	4	7
	Terry Sawchuk	3	4	7
	Bill Durnan	6	0	6
	Ken Dryden	5	1	6
DEFENSE	* Ray Bourque	12	5	17
	Doug Harvey	10	1	11
	Earl Seibert	4	6	10
	Bobby Orr	8	1	9
	Eddie Shore	7	1	8
	Red Kelly	6	2	8
	Pierre Pilote	5	3	8
	* Paul Coffey	4	4	8

Position	Player	First Team	Second Team	Total
LEFT WING	Bobby Hull	10	2	12
	Ted Lindsay	8	1	9
	Frank Mahovlich	3	6	9
	* Luc Robitaille	5	2	7
	Harvey Jackson	4	1	5
	Michel Goulet	3	2	5
	Toe Blake	3	2	5
RIGHT WING	Gordie Howe	12	9	21
	Maurice Richard	8	6	14
	Mike Bossy	5	3	8
	Guy Lafleur	6	0	6
	Charlie Conacher	3	2	5
	* Jari Kurri	2	3	5
CENTER	* Wayne Gretzky	8	6	14
	Jean Beliveau	6	4	10
	Stan Mikita	6	2	8
	Phil Esposito	6	2	8
	Mario Lemieux	5	3	8

* active player

All-Star Teams

1930-97

Voting for the NHL All-Star Team is conducted among the representatives of the Professional Hockey Writers' Association at the end of the season.

Following is a list of the First and Second All-Star Teams since their inception in 1930-31.

First Team		Second Team	First Team		Second Team	First Team		Second Team
1996-97			**1988-89**			**1986-87**		
Hasek, Dominik, Buf.	G	Brodeur, Martin, N.J.	Roy, Patrick, Mtl.	G	Vernon, Mike, Cgy.	Hextall, Ron, Phi.	G	Liut, Mike, Hfd.
Leetch, Brian, NYR	D	Chelios, Chris, Chi.	Chelios, Chris, Mtl.	D	MacInnis, Al, Cgy.	Bourque, Ray, Bos.	D	Murphy, Larry, Wsh.
Ozolinsh, Sandis, Col.	D	Stevens, Scott, N.J.	Coffey, Paul, Pit.	D	Bourque, Ray, Bos.	Howe, Mark, Phi.	D	MacInnis, Al, Cgy.
Lemieux, Mario, Pit.	C	Gretzky, Wayne, NYR	Lemieux, Mario, Pit.	C	Gretzky, Wayne, L.A.	Gretzky, Wayne, Edm.	C	Lemieux, Mario, Pit.
Selanne, Teemu, Ana.	RW	Jagr, Jaromir, Pit.	Mullen, Joe, Cgy.	RW	Kurri, Jari, Edm.	Kurri, Jari, Edm.	RW	Kerr, Tim, Phi.
Kariya, Paul, Ana.	LW	LeClair, John, Phi.	Robitaille, Luc, L.A.	LW	Gallant, Gerard, Det.	Goulet, Michel, Que.	LW	Robitaille, Luc, L.A.
1995-96			**1987-88**			**1985-86**		
Carey, Jim, Wsh.	G	Osgood, Chris, Det.	Fuhr, Grant, Edm.	G	Roy, Patrick, Mtl.	Vanbiesbrouck, J., NYR	G	Froese, Bob, Phi.
Chelios, Chris, Chi.	D	Konstantinov, V., Det.	Bourque, Ray, Bos.	D	Suter, Gary, Cgy.	Coffey, Paul, Edm.	D	Robinson, Larry, Mtl.
Bourque, Ray, Bos.	D	Leetch, Brian, NYR	Stevens, Scott, Wsh.	D	McCrimmon, Brad, Cgy.	Howe, Mark, Phi.	D	Bourque, Ray, Bos.
Lemieux, Mario, Pit.	C	Lindros, Eric, Phi.	Lemieux, Mario, Pit.	C	Gretzky, Wayne, Edm.	Gretzky, Wayne, Edm.	C	Lemieux, Mario, Pit.
Jagr, Jaromir, Pit.	RW	Mogilny, Alexander, Van.	Loob, Hakan, Cgy.	RW	Neely, Cam, Bos.	Bossy, Mike, NYI	RW	Kurri, Jari, Edm.
Kariya, Paul, Ana.	LW	LeClair, John, Phi.	Robitaille, Luc, L.A.	LW	Goulet, Michel, Que.	Goulet, Michel, Que.	LW	Naslund, Mats, Mtl.
1994-95								
Hasek, Dominik, Buf.	G	Belfour, Ed, Chi.						
Coffey, Paul, Det.	D	Bourque, Ray, Bos.						
Chelios, Chris, Chi.	D	Murphy, Larry, Pit.						
Lindros, Eric, Phi.	C	Zhamnov, Alexei, Wpg.						
Jagr, Jaromir, Pit.	RW	Fleury, Theoren, Cgy.						
LeClair, John, Mtl., Phi.	LW	Tkachuk, Keith, Wpg.						
1993-94								
Hasek, Dominik, Buf.	G	Vanbiesbrouck, John, Fla.						
Bourque, Ray, Bos.	D	MacInnis, Al, Cgy.						
Stevens, Scott, N.J.	D	Leetch, Brian, NYR						
Fedorov, Sergei, Det.	C	Gretzky, Wayne, L.A.						
Bure, Pavel, Van.	RW	Neely, Cam, Bos.						
Shanahan, Brendan, St. L.	LW	Graves, Adam, NYR						
1992-93								
Belfour, Ed, Chi.	G	Barrasso, Tom, Pit.						
Chelios, Chris, Chi.	D	Murphy, Larry, Pit.						
Bourque, Ray, Bos.	D	Iafrate, Al, Wsh.						
Lemieux, Mario, Pit.	C	LaFontaine, Pat, Buf.						
Selanne, Teemu, Wpg.	RW	Mogilny, Alexander, Buf.						
Robitaille, Luc, L.A.	LW	Stevens, Kevin, Pit.						
1991-92								
Roy, Patrick, Mtl.	G	McLean, Kirk, Van.						
Leetch, Brian, NYR	D	Housley, Phil, Wpg.						
Bourque, Ray, Bos.	D	Stevens, Scott, N.J.						
Messier, Mark, NYR	C	Lemieux, Mario, Pit.						
Hull, Brett, St. L.	RW	Recchi, Mark, Pit., Phi.						
Stevens, Kevin, Pit.	LW	Robitaille, Luc, L.A.						
1990-91								
Belfour, Ed, Chi.	G	Roy, Patrick, Mtl.						
Bourque, Ray, Bos.	D	Chelios, Chris, Chi.						
MacInnis, Al, Cgy.	D	Leetch, Brian, NYR						
Gretzky, Wayne, L.A.	C	Oates, Adam, St. L.						
Hull, Brett, St. L.	RW	Neely, Cam, Bos.						
Robitaille, Luc, L.A.	LW	Stevens, Kevin, Pit.						
1989-90								
Roy, Patrick, Mtl.	G	Puppa, Daren, Buf.						
Bourque, Ray, Bos.	D	Coffey, Paul, Pit.						
MacInnis, Al, Cgy.	D	Wilson, Doug, Chi.						
Messier, Mark, Edm.	C	Gretzky, Wayne, L.A.						
Hull, Brett, St. L.	RW	Neely, Cam, Bos.						
Robitaille, Luc, L.A.	LW	Bellows, Brian, Min.						

Scott Stevens was a solid presence along the New Jersey blueline in 1996-97, earning a berth on the NHL's Second All-Star Team.

First Team		Second Team

1984-85
First Team	Pos	Second Team
Lindbergh, Pelle, Phi.	G	Barrasso, Tom, Buf.
Coffey, Paul, Edm.	D	Langway, Rod, Wsh.
Bourque, Ray, Bos.	D	Wilson, Doug, Chi.
Gretzky, Wayne, Edm.	C	Hawerchuk, Dale, Wpg.
Kurri, Jari, Edm.	RW	Bossy, Mike, NYI
Ogrodnick, John, Det.	LW	Tonelli, John, NYI

1983-84
First Team	Pos	Second Team
Barrasso, Tom, Buf.	G	Riggin, Pat, Wsh.
Langway, Rod, Wsh.	D	Coffey, Paul, Edm.
Bourque, Ray, Bos.	D	Potvin, Denis, NYI
Gretzky, Wayne, Edm.	C	Trottier, Bryan, NYI
Bossy, Mike, NYI	RW	Kurri, Jari, Edm.
Goulet, Michel, Que.	LW	Messier, Mark, Edm.

1982-83
First Team	Pos	Second Team
Peeters, Pete, Bos.	G	Melanson, Roland, NYI
Howe, Mark, Phi.	D	Bourque, Ray, Bos.
Langway, Rod, Wsh.	D	Coffey, Paul, Edm.
Gretzky, Wayne, Edm.	C	Savard, Denis, Chi.
Bossy, Mike, NYI	RW	McDonald, Lanny, Cgy.
Messier, Mark, Edm.	LW	Goulet, Michel, Que.

1981-82
First Team	Pos	Second Team
Smith, Bill, NYI	G	Fuhr, Grant, Edm.
Wilson, Doug, Chi.	D	Coffey, Paul, Edm.
Bourque, Ray, Bos.	D	Trottier, Bryan, NYI
Gretzky, Wayne, Edm.	C	Trottier, Bryan, NYI
Bossy, Mike, NYI	RW	Middleton, Rick, Bos.
Messier, Mark, Edm.	LW	Tonelli, John, NYI

1980-81
First Team	Pos	Second Team
Liut, Mike, St.L.	G	Lessard, Mario, L.A.
Potvin, Denis, NYI	D	Robinson, Larry, Mtl.
Carlyle, Randy, Pit.	D	Bourque, Ray, Bos.
Gretzky, Wayne, Edm.	C	Dionne, Marcel, L.A.
Bossy, Mike, NYI	RW	Taylor, Dave, L.A.
Simmer, Charlie, L.A.	LW	Barber, Bill, Phi.

1979-80
First Team	Pos	Second Team
Esposito, Tony, Chi.	G	Edwards, Don, Buf.
Robinson, Larry, Mtl.	D	Salming, Borje, Tor.
Bourque, Ray, Bos.	D	Schoenfeld, Jim, Buf.
Dionne, Marcel, L.A.	C	Gretzky, Wayne, Edm.
Lafleur, Guy, Mtl.	RW	Gare, Danny, Buf.
Simmer, Charlie, L.A.	LW	Shutt, Steve, Mtl.

1978-79
First Team	Pos	Second Team
Dryden, Ken, Mtl.	G	Resch, Glenn, NYI
Potvin, Denis, NYI	D	Salming, Borje, Tor.
Robinson, Larry, Mtl.	D	Savard, Serge, Mtl.
Trottier, Bryan, NYI	C	Dionne, Marcel, L.A.
Lafleur, Guy, Mtl.	RW	Bossy, Mike, NYI
Gillies, Clark, NYI	LW	Barber, Bill, Phi.

1977-78
First Team	Pos	Second Team
Dryden, Ken, Mtl.	G	Edwards, Don, Buf.
Potvin, Denis, NYI	D	Robinson, Larry, Mtl.
Park, Brad, Bos.	D	Salming, Borje, Tor.
Trottier, Bryan, NYI	C	Sittler, Darryl, Tor.
Lafleur, Guy, Mtl.	RW	Bossy, Mike, NYI
Gillies, Clark, NYI	LW	Shutt, Steve, Mtl.

1976-77
First Team	Pos	Second Team
Dryden, Ken, Mtl.	G	Vachon, Rogatien, L.A.
Robinson, Larry, Mtl.	D	Potvin, Denis, NYI
Salming, Borje, Tor.	D	Lapointe, Guy, Mtl.
Dionne, Marcel, L.A.	C	Perreault, Gilbert, Buf.
Lafleur, Guy, Mtl.	RW	McDonald, Lanny, Tor.
Shutt, Steve, Mtl.	LW	Martin, Richard, Buf.

1975-76
First Team	Pos	Second Team
Dryden, Ken, Mtl.	G	Resch, Glenn, NYI
Potvin, Denis, NYI	D	Salming, Borje, Tor.
Park, Brad, Bos.	D	Lapointe, Guy, Mtl.
Clarke, Bobby, Phi.	C	Perreault, Gilbert, Buf.
Lafleur, Guy, Mtl.	RW	Leach, Reggie, Phi.
Barber, Bill, Phi.	LW	Martin, Richard, Buf.

1974-75
First Team	Pos	Second Team
Parent, Bernie, Phi.	G	Vachon, Rogie, L.A.
Orr, Bobby, Bos.	D	Lapointe, Guy, Mtl.
Potvin, Denis, NYI	D	Salming, Borje, Tor.
Clarke, Bobby, Phi.	C	Esposito, Phil, Bos.
Lafleur, Guy, Mtl.	RW	Robert, René, Buf.
Martin, Richard, Buf.	LW	Vickers, Steve, NYR

1973-74
First Team	Pos	Second Team
Parent, Bernie, Phi.	G	Esposito, Tony, Chi.
Orr, Bobby, Bos.	D	White, Bill, Chi.
Park, Brad, NYR	D	Ashbee, Barry, Phi.
Esposito, Phil, Bos.	C	Clarke, Bobby, Phi.
Hodge, Ken, Bos.	RW	Redmond, Mickey, Det.
Martin, Richard, Buf.	LW	Cashman, Wayne, Bos.

1972-73
First Team	Pos	Second Team
Dryden, Ken, Mtl.	G	Esposito, Tony, Chi.
Orr, Bobby, Bos.	D	Park, Brad, NYR
Lapointe, Guy, Mtl.	D	White, Bill, Chi.
Esposito, Phil, Bos.	C	Clarke, Bobby, Phi.
Redmond, Mickey, Det.	RW	Cournoyer, Yvan, Mtl.
Mahovlich, Frank, Mtl.	LW	Hull, Dennis, Chi.

1971-72
First Team	Pos	Second Team
Esposito, Tony, Chi.	G	Dryden, Ken, Mtl.
Orr, Bobby, Bos.	D	White, Bill, Chi.
Park, Brad, NYR	D	Stapleton, Pat, Chi.
Esposito, Phil, Bos.	C	Ratelle, Jean, NYR
Gilbert, Rod, NYR	RW	Cournoyer, Yvan, Mtl.
Hull, Bobby, Chi.	LW	Hadfield, Vic, NYR

1970-71
First Team	Pos	Second Team
Giacomin, Ed, NYR	G	Plante, Jacques, Tor.
Orr, Bobby, Bos.	D	Park, Brad, NYR
Tremblay, J.C., Mtl.	D	Stapleton, Pat, Chi.
Esposito, Phil, Bos.	C	Keon, Dave, Tor.
Hodge, Ken, Bos.	RW	Cournoyer, Yvan, Mtl.
Bucyk, John, Bos.	LW	Hull, Bobby, Chi.

1969-70
First Team	Pos	Second Team
Esposito, Tony, Chi.	G	Giacomin, Ed, NYR
Orr, Bobby, Bos.	D	Brewer, Carl, Det.
Park, Brad, NYR	D	Laperriere, Jacques, Mtl.
Esposito, Phil, Bos.	C	Mikita, Stan, Chi.
Howe, Gordie, Det.	RW	McKenzie, John, Bos.
Hull, Bobby, Chi.	LW	Mahovlich, Frank, Det.

1968-69
First Team	Pos	Second Team
Hall, Glenn, St.L.	G	Giacomin, Ed, NYR
Orr, Bobby, Bos.	D	Green, Ted, Bos.
Horton, Tim, Tor.	D	Harris, Ted, Mtl.
Esposito, Phil, Bos.	C	Béliveau, Jean, Mtl.
Howe, Gordie, Det.	RW	Cournoyer, Yvan, Mtl.
Hull, Bobby, Chi.	LW	Mahovlich, Frank, Det.

1967-68
First Team	Pos	Second Team
Worsley, Lorne, Mtl.	G	Giacomin, Ed, NYR
Orr, Bobby, Bos.	D	Tremblay, J.C., Mtl.
Horton, Tim, Tor.	D	Neilson, Jim, NYR
Mikita, Stan, Chi.	C	Esposito, Phil, Bos.
Howe, Gordie, Det.	RW	Gilbert, Rod, NYR
Hull, Bobby, Chi.	LW	Bucyk, John, Bos.

1966-67
First Team	Pos	Second Team
Giacomin, Ed, NYR	G	Hall, Glenn, Chi.
Pilote, Pierre, Chi.	D	Horton, Tim, Tor.
Howell, Harry, NYR	D	Orr, Bobby, Bos.
Mikita, Stan, Chi.	C	Ullman, Norm, Det.
Wharram, Ken, Chi.	RW	Howe, Gordie, Det.
Hull, Bobby, Chi.	LW	Marshall, Don, NYR

1965-66
First Team	Pos	Second Team
Hall, Glenn, Chi.	G	Worsley, Lorne, Mtl.
Laperriere, Jacques, Mtl.	D	Stanley, Allan, Tor.
Pilote, Pierre, Chi.	D	Stapleton, Pat, Chi.
Mikita, Stan, Chi.	C	Béliveau, Jean, Mtl.
Howe, Gordie, Det.	RW	Rousseau, Bobby, Mtl.
Hull, Bobby, Chi.	LW	Mahovlich, Frank, Tor.

1964-65
First Team	Pos	Second Team
Crozier, Roger, Det.	G	Hodge, Charlie, Mtl.
Pilote, Pierre, Chi.	D	Gadsby, Bill, Det.
Laperriere, Jacques, Mtl.	D	Brewer, Carl, Tor.
Ullman, Norm, Det.	C	Mikita, Stan, Chi.
Provost, Claude, Mtl.	RW	Howe, Gordie, Det.
Hull, Bobby, Chi.	LW	Mahovlich, Frank, Tor.

1963-64
First Team	Pos	Second Team
Hall, Glenn, Chi.	G	Hodge, Charlie, Mtl.
Pilote, Pierre, Chi.	D	Vasko, Elmer, Chi.
Horton, Tim, Tor.	D	Laperriere, Jacques, Mtl.
Mikita, Stan, Chi.	C	Béliveau, Jean, Mtl.
Wharram, Ken, Chi.	RW	Howe, Gordie, Det.
Hull, Bobby, Chi.	LW	Mahovlich, Frank, Tor.

1962-63
First Team	Pos	Second Team
Hall, Glenn, Chi.	G	Sawchuk, Terry, Det.
Pilote, Pierre, Chi.	D	Horton, Tim, Tor.
Brewer, Carl, Tor.	D	Vasko, Elmer, Chi.
Mikita, Stan, Chi.	C	Béliveau, Jean, Mtl.
Howe, Gordie, Det.	RW	Bathgate, Andy, NYR
Mahovlich, Frank, Tor.	LW	Hull, Bobby, Chi.

1961-62
First Team	Pos	Second Team
Plante, Jacques, Mtl.	G	Hall, Glenn, Chi.
Harvey, Doug, NYR	D	Brewer, Carl, Tor.
Talbot, Jean-Guy, Mtl.	D	Pilote, Pierre, Chi.
Mikita, Stan, Chi.	C	Keon, Dave, Tor.
Bathgate, Andy, NYR	RW	Howe, Gordie, Det.
Hull, Bobby, Chi.	LW	Mahovlich, Frank, Tor.

1960-61
First Team	Pos	Second Team
Bower, Johnny, Tor.	G	Hall, Glenn, Chi.
Harvey, Doug, Mtl.	D	Stanley, Allan, Tor.
Pronovost, Marcel, Det.	D	Pilote, Pierre, Chi.
Béliveau, Jean, Mtl.	C	Richard, Henri, Mtl.
Geoffrion, Bernie, Mtl.	RW	Howe, Gordie, Det.
Mahovlich, Frank, Tor.	LW	Moore, Dickie, Mtl.

1959-60
First Team	Pos	Second Team
Hall, Glenn, Chi.	G	Plante, Jacques, Mtl.
Harvey, Doug, Mtl.	D	Stanley, Allan, Tor.
Pronovost, Marcel, Det.	D	Pilote, Pierre, Chi.
Béliveau, Jean, Mtl.	C	Horvath, Bronco, Bos.
Howe, Gordie, Det.	RW	Geoffrion, Bernie, Mtl.
Hull, Bobby, Chi.	LW	Prentice, Dean, NYR

1958-59
First Team	Pos	Second Team
Plante, Jacques, Mtl.	G	Sawchuk, Terry, Det.
Johnson, Tom, Mtl.	D	Pronovost, Marcel, Det.
Gadsby, Bill, NYR	D	Harvey, Doug, Mtl.
Béliveau, Jean, Mtl.	C	Richard, Henri, Mtl.
Bathgate, Andy, NYR	RW	Howe, Gordie, Det.
Moore, Dickie, Mtl.	LW	Delvecchio, Alex, Det.

First Team		Second Team

1957-58

First Team		Second Team
Hall, Glenn, Chi.	G	Plante, Jacques, Mtl.
Harvey, Doug, Mtl.	D	Flaman, Fern, Bos.
Gadsby, Bill, NYR	D	Pronovost, Marcel, Det.
Richard, Henri, Mtl.	C	Béliveau, Jean, Mtl.
Howe, Gordie, Det.	RW	Bathgate, Andy, NYR
Moore, Dickie, Mtl.	LW	Henry, Camille, NYR

1956-57

Hall, Glenn, Det.	G	Plante, Jacques, Mtl.
Harvey, Doug, Mtl.	D	Flaman, Fern, Bos.
Kelly, Red, Det.	D	Gadsby, Bill, NYR
Béliveau, Jean, Mtl.	C	Litzenberger, Eddie, Chi.
Howe, Gordie, Det.	RW	Richard, Maurice, Mtl.
Lindsay, Ted, Det.	LW	Chevrefils, Real, Bos.

1955-56

Plante, Jacques, Mtl.	G	Hall, Glenn, Det.
Harvey, Doug, Mtl.	D	Kelly, Red, Det.
Gadsby, Bill, NYR	D	Johnson, Tom, Mtl.
Béliveau, Jean, Mtl.	C	Sloan, Tod, Tor.
Richard, Maurice, Mtl.	RW	Howe, Gordie, Det.
Lindsay, Ted, Det.	LW	Olmstead, Bert, Mtl.

1954-55

Lumley, Harry, Tor.	G	Sawchuk, Terry, Det.
Harvey, Doug, Mtl.	D	Goldham, Bob, Det.
Kelly, Red, Det.	D	Flaman, Fern, Bos.
Béliveau, Jean, Mtl.	C	Mosdell, Ken, Mtl.
Richard, Maurice, Mtl.	RW	Geoffrion, Bernie, Mtl.
Smith, Sid, Tor.	LW	Lewicki, Danny, NYR

1953-54

Lumley, Harry, Tor.	G	Sawchuk, Terry, Det.
Kelly, Red, Det.	D	Gadsby, Bill, Chi.
Harvey, Doug, Mtl.	D	Horton, Tim, Tor.
Mosdell, Ken, Mtl.	C	Kennedy, Ted, Tor.
Howe, Gordie, Det.	RW	Richard, Maurice, Mtl.
Lindsay, Ted, Det.	LW	Sandford, Ed, Bos.

1952-53

Sawchuk, Terry, Det.	G	McNeil, Gerry, Mtl.
Kelly, Red, Det.	D	Quackenbush, Bill, Bos.
Harvey, Doug, Mtl.	D	Gadsby, Bill, Chi.
Mackell, Fleming, Bos.	C	Delvecchio, Alex, Det.
Howe, Gordie, Det.	RW	Richard, Maurice, Mtl.
Lindsay, Ted, Det.	LW	Olmstead, Bert, Mtl.

1951-52

Sawchuk, Terry, Det.	G	Henry, Jim, Bos.
Kelly, Red, Det.	D	Buller, Hy, NYR
Harvey, Doug, Mtl.	D	Thomson, Jim, Tor.
Lach, Elmer, Mtl.	C	Schmidt, Milt, Bos.
Howe, Gordie, Det.	RW	Richard, Maurice, Mtl.
Lindsay, Ted, Det.	LW	Smith, Sid, Tor.

1950-51

Sawchuk, Terry, Det.	G	Rayner, Chuck, NYR
Kelly, Red, Det.	D	Thomson, Jim, Tor.
Quackenbush, Bill, Bos.	D	Reise, Leo, Det.
Schmidt, Milt, Bos.	C	Abel, Sid, Det.
	(tied)	Kennedy, Ted, Tor.
Howe, Gordie, Det.	RW	Richard, Maurice, Mtl.
Lindsay, Ted, Det.	LW	Smith, Sid, Tor.

1949-50

Durnan, Bill, Mtl.	G	Rayner, Chuck, NYR
Mortson, Gus, Tor.	D	Reise, Leo, Det.
Reardon, Kenny, Mtl.	D	Kelly, Red, Det.
Abel, Sid, Det.	C	Kennedy, Ted, Tor.
Richard, Maurice, Mtl.	RW	Howe, Gordie, Det.
Lindsay, Ted, Det.	LW	Leswick, Tony, NYR

1948-49

Durnan, Bill, Mtl.	G	Rayner, Chuck, NYR
Quackenbush, Bill, Det.	D	Harmon, Glen, Mtl.
Stewart, Jack, Det.	D	Reardon, Kenny, Mtl.
Abel, Sid, Det.	C	Bentley, Doug, Chi.
Richard, Maurice, Mtl.	RW	Howe, Gordie, Det.
Conacher, Roy, Chi.	LW	Lindsay, Ted, Det.

1947-48

First Team		Second Team
Broda, W. "Turk", Tor.	G	Brimsek, Frank, Bos.
Quackenbush, Bill, Det.	D	Reardon, Kenny, Mtl.
Stewart, Jack, Det.	D	Colville, Neil, NYR
Lach, Elmer, Mtl.	C	O'Connor, "Buddy", NYR
Richard, Maurice, Mtl.	RW	Poile, "Bud", Chi.
Lindsay, Ted, Det.	LW	Stewart, Gaye, Chi.

1946-47

Durnan, Bill, Mtl.	G	Brimsek, Frank, Bos.
Reardon, Kenny, Mtl.	D	Stewart, Jack, Det.
Bouchard, Emile, Mtl.	D	Quackenbush, Bill, Det.
Schmidt, Milt, Bos.	C	Bentley, Max, Chi.
Richard, Maurice, Mtl.	RW	Bauer, Bobby, Bos.
Bentley, Doug, Chi.	LW	Dumart, Woody, Bos.

1945-46

Durnan, Bill, Mtl.	G	Brimsek, Frank, Bos.
Crawford, Jack, Bos.	D	Reardon, Kenny, Mtl.
Bouchard, Emile, Mtl.	D	Stewart, Jack, Det.
Bentley, Max, Chi.	C	Lach, Elmer, Mtl.
Richard, Maurice, Mtl.	RW	Mosienko, Bill, Chi.
Stewart, Gaye, Tor.	LW	Blake, "Toe", Mtl.
Irvin, Dick, Mtl.	Coach	Gottselig, John, Chi.

1944-45

Durnan, Bill, Mtl.	G	Karakas, Mike, Chi.
Bouchard, Emile, Mtl.	D	Harmon, Glen, Mtl.
Hollett, Bill, Det.	D	Pratt, "Babe", Tor.
Lach, Elmer, Mtl.	C	Cowley, Bill, Bos.
Richard, Maurice, Mtl.	RW	Mosienko, Bill, Chi.
Blake, "Toe", Mtl.	LW	Howe, Syd, Det.
Irvin, Dick, Mtl.	Coach	Adams, Jack, Det.

1943-44

Durnan, Bill, Mtl.	G	Bibeault, Paul, Tor.
Seibert, Earl, Chi.	D	Bouchard, Emile, Mtl.
Pratt, "Babe", Tor.	D	Clapper, "Dit", Bos.
Cowley, Bill, Bos.	C	Lach, Elmer, Mtl.
Carr, Lorne, Tor.	RW	Richard, Maurice, Mtl.
Bentley, Doug, Chi.	LW	Cain, Herb, Bos.
Irvin, Dick, Mtl.	Coach	Day, "Hap", Tor.

1942-43

Mowers, Johnny, Det.	G	Brimsek, Frank, Bos.
Seibert, Earl, Chi.	D	Crawford, Jack, Bos.
Stewart, Jack, Det.	D	Hollett, Bill, Bos.
Cowley, Bill, Bos.	C	Apps, Syl, Tor.
Carr, Lorne, Tor.	RW	Hextall, Bryan, NYR
Bentley, Doug, Chi.	LW	Patrick, Lynn, NYR
Adams, Jack, Det.	Coach	Ross, Art, Bos.

1941-42

Brimsek, Frank, Bos.	G	Broda, W. "Turk", Tor.
Seibert, Earl, Chi.	D	Egan, Pat, Bro.
Anderson, Tommy, Bro.	D	McDonald, Bucko, Tor.
Apps, Syl, Tor.	C	Watson, Phil, NYR
Hextall, Bryan, NYR	RW	Drillon, Gord, Tor.
Patrick, Lynn, NYR	LW	Abel, Sid, Det.
Boucher, Frank, NYR	Coach	Thompson, Paul, Chi.

1940-41

Broda, W. "Turk", Tor.	G	Brimsek, Frank, Bos.
Clapper, "Dit", Bos.	D	Seibert, Earl, Chi.
Stanowski, Wally, Tor.	D	Heller, Ott, NYR
Cowley, Bill, Bos.	C	Apps, Syl, Tor.
Hextall, Bryan, NYR	RW	Bauer, Bobby, Bos.
Schriner, Dave, Tor.	LW	Dumart, Woody, Bos.
Weiland, "Cooney", Bos.	Coach	Irvin, Dick, Mtl.

1939-40

Kerr, Dave, NYR	G	Brimsek, Frank, Bos.
Clapper, "Dit", Bos.	D	Coulter, Art, NYR
Goodfellow, Ebbie, Det.	D	Seibert, Earl, Chi.
Schmidt, Milt, Bos.	C	Colville, Neil, NYR
Hextall, Bryan, NYR	RW	Bauer, Bobby, Bos.
Blake, "Toe", Mtl.	LW	Dumart, Woody, Bos.
Thompson, Paul, Chi.	Coach	Boucher, Frank, NYR

1938-39

First Team		Second Team
Brimsek, Frank, Bos.	G	Robertson, Earl, NYA
Shore, Eddie, Bos.	D	Seibert, Earl, Chi.
Clapper, "Dit", Bos.	D	Coulter, Art, NYR
Apps, Syl, Tor.	C	Colville, Neil, NYR
Drillon, Gord, Tor.	RW	Bauer, Bobby, Bos.
Blake, "Toe", Mtl.	LW	Gottselig, Johnny, Chi.
Ross, Art, Bos.	Coach	Dutton, "Red", NYA

1937-38

Thompson, "Tiny", Bos.	G	Kerr, Dave, NYR
Shore, Eddie, Bos.	D	Coulter, Art, NYR
Siebert, "Babe", Mtl.	D	Seibert, Earl, Chi.
Cowley, Bill, Bos.	C	Apps, Syl, Tor.
Dillon, Cecil, NYR	RW	Dillon, Cecil, NYR
Drillon, Gord, Tor.	(tied)	Drillon, Gord, Tor.
Thompson, Paul, Chi.	LW	Blake, Toe, Mtl.
Patrick, Lester, NYR	Coach	Ross, Art, Bos.

1936-37

Smith, Norm, Det.	G	Cude, Wilf, Mtl.
Siebert, "Babe", Mtl.	D	Seibert, Earl, Chi.
Goodfellow, Ebbie, Det.	D	Conacher, Lionel, Mtl. M.
Barry, Marty, Det.	C	Chapman, Art, NYA
Aurie, Larry, Det.	RW	Dillon, Cecil, NYR
Jackson, Harvey, Tor.	LW	Schriner, Dave, NYA
Adams, Jack, Det.	Coach	Hart, Cecil, Mtl.

1935-36

Thompson, "Tiny", Bos.	G	Cude, Wilf, Mtl.
Shore, Eddie, Bos.	D	Seibert, Earl, Chi.
Siebert, "Babe", Bos.	D	Goodfellow, Ebbie, Det.
Smith, "Hooley", Mtl. M.	C	Thoms, Bill, Tor.
Conacher, Charlie, Tor.	RW	Dillon, Cecil, NYR
Schriner, Dave, NYA	LW	Thompson, Paul, Chi.
Patrick, Lester, NYR	Coach	Gorman, T.P., Mtl. M.

1934-35

Chabot, Lorne, Chi.	G	Thompson, "Tiny", Bos.
Shore, Eddie, Bos.	D	Wentworth, Cy, Mtl. M.
Seibert, Earl, Chi.	D	Coulter, Art, Chi.
Boucher, Frank, NYR	C	Weiland, "Cooney", Det.
Conacher, Charlie, Tor.	RW	Clapper, "Dit", Bos.
Jackson, Harvey, Tor.	LW	Joliat, Aurel, Mtl.
Patrick, Lester, NYR	Coach	Irvin, Dick, Tor.

1933-34

Gardiner, Charlie, Chi.	G	Worters, Roy, NYA
Clancy, "King", Tor.	D	Shore, Eddie, Bos.
Conacher, Lionel, Chi.	D	Johnson, "Ching", NYR
Boucher, Frank, NYR	C	Primeau, Joe, Tor.
Conacher, Charlie, Tor.	RW	Cook, Bill, NYR
Jackson, Harvey, Tor.	LW	Joliat, Aurel, Mtl.
Patrick, Lester, NYR	Coach	Irvin, Dick, Tor.

1932-33

Roach, John Ross, Det.	G	Gardiner, Charlie, Chi.
Shore, Eddie, Bos.	D	Clancy, "King", Tor.
Johnson, "Ching", NYR	D	Conacher, Lionel, Mtl. M.
Boucher, Frank, NYR	C	Morenz, Howie, Mtl.
Cook, Bill, NYR	RW	Conacher, Charlie, Tor.
Northcott, "Baldy", Mtl M.	LW	Jackson, Harvey, Tor.
Patrick, Lester, NYR	Coach	Irvin, Dick, Tor.

1931-32

Gardiner, Charlie, Chi.	G	Worters, Roy, NYA
Shore, Eddie, Bos.	D	Mantha, Sylvio, Mtl.
Johnson, "Ching", NYR	D	Clancy, "King", Tor.
Morenz, Howie, Mtl.	C	Smith, "Hooley", Mtl. M.
Cook, Bill, NYR	RW	Conacher, Charlie, Tor.
Jackson, Harvey, Tor.	LW	Joliat, Aurel, Mtl.
Patrick, Lester, NYR	Coach	Irvin, Dick, Tor.

1930-31

Gardiner, Charlie, Chi.	G	Thompson, "Tiny", Bos.
Shore, Eddie, Bos.	D	Mantha, Sylvio, Mtl.
Clancy, "King", Tor.	D	Johnson, "Ching", NYR
Morenz, Howie, Mtl.	C	Boucher, Frank, NYR
Cook, Bill, NYR	RW	Clapper, "Dit", Bos.
Joliet, Aurel, Mtl.	LW	Cook, "Bun", NYR
Patrick, Lester, NYR	Coach	Irvin, Dick, Chi.

All-Star Game Results

Year	Venue	Score	Coaches	Attendance
1997	San Jose	Eastern 11, Western 7	Doug MacLean, Ken Hitchcock	17,422
1996	Boston	Eastern 5, Western 4	Doug MacLean, Scotty Bowman	17,565
1994	NY Rangers	Eastern 9, Western 8	Jacques Demers, Barry Melrose	18,200
1993	Montreal	Wales 16, Campbell 6	Scotty Bowman, Mike Keenan	17,137
1992	Philadelphia	Campbell 10, Wales 6	Bob Gainey, Scotty Bowman	17,380
1991	Chicago	Campbell 11, Wales 5	John Muckler, Mike Milbury	18,472
1990	Pittsburgh	Wales 12, Campbell 7	Pat Burns, Terry Crisp	16,236
1989	Edmonton	Campbell 9, Wales 5	Glen Sather, Terry O'Reilly	17,503
1988	St. Louis	Wales 6, Campbell 5 OT	Mike Keenan, Glen Sather	17,878
1986	Hartford	Wales 4, Campbell 3 OT	Mike Keenan, Glen Sather	15,100
1985	Calgary	Wales 6, Campbell 4	Al Arbour, Glen Sather	16,825
1984	New Jersey	Wales 7, Campbell 6	Al Arbour, Glen Sather	18,939
1983	NY Islanders	Campbell 9, Wales 3	Roger Neilson, Al Arbour	15,230
1982	Washington	Wales 4, Campbell 2	Al Arbour, Glen Sonmor	18,130
1981	Los Angeles	Campbell 4, Wales 1	Pat Quinn, Scotty Bowman	15,761
1980	Detroit	Wales 6, Campbell 3	Scotty Bowman, Al Arbour	21,002
1978	Buffalo	Wales 3, Campbell 2 OT	Scotty Bowman, Fred Shero	16,433
1977	Vancouver	Wales 4, Campbell 3	Scotty Bowman, Fred Shero	15,607
1976	Philadelphia	Wales 7, Campbell 5	Floyd Smith, Fred Shero	16,436
1975	Montreal	Wales 7, Campbell 1	Bep Guidolin, Fred Shero	16,080
1974	Chicago	West 6, East 4	Billy Reay, Scotty Bowman	16,426
1973	New York	East 5, West 4	Tom Johnson, Billy Reay	16,986
1972	Minnesota	East 3, West 2	Al MacNeil, Billy Reay	15,423
1971	Boston	West 2, East 1	Scotty Bowman, Harry Sinden	14,790
1970	St. Louis	East 4, West 1	Claude Ruel, Scotty Bowman	16,587
1969	Montreal	East 3, West 3	Toe Blake, Scotty Bowman	16,260
1968	Toronto	Toronto 4, All-Stars 3	Punch Imlach, Toe Blake	15,753
1967	Montreal	Montreal 3, All-Stars 0	Toe Blake, Sid Abel	14,284
1965	Montreal	All-Stars 5, Montreal 2	Billy Reay, Toe Blake	13,529
1964	Toronto	All-Stars 3, Toronto 2	Sid Abel, Punch Imlach	14,232
1963	Toronto	All-Stars 3, Toronto 3	Sid Abel, Punch Imlach	14,034
1962	Toronto	Toronto 4, All-Stars 1	Punch Imlach, Rudy Pilous	14,236
1961	Chicago	All-Stars 3, Chicago 1	Sid Abel, Rudy Pilous	14,534
1960	Montreal	All-Stars 2, Montreal 1	Punch Imlach, Toe Blake	13,949
1959	Montreal	Montreal 6, All-Stars 1	Toe Blake, Punch Imlach	13,818
1958	Montreal	Montreal 6, All-Stars 3	Toe Blake, Milt Schmidt	13,989
1957	Montreal	All-Stars 5, Montreal 3	Milt Schmidt, Toe Blake	13,003
1956	Montreal	All-Stars 1, Montreal 1	Jim Skinner, Toe Blake	13,095
1955	Detroit	Detroit 3, All-Stars 1	Jim Skinner, Dick Irvin	10,111
1954	Detroit	All-Stars 2, Detroit 2	King Clancy, Jim Skinner	10,689
1953	Montreal	All-Stars 3, Montreal 1	Lynn Patrick, Dick Irvin	14,153
1952	Detroit	1st team 1, 2nd team 1	Tommy Ivan, Dick Irvin	10,680
1951	Toronto	1st team 2, 2nd team 2	Joe Primeau, Hap Day	11,469
1950	Detroit	Detroit 7, All-Stars 1	Tommy Ivan, Lynn Patrick	9,166
1949	Toronto	All-Stars 3, Toronto 1	Tommy Ivan, Hap Day	13,541
1948	Chicago	All-Stars 3, Toronto 1	Tommy Ivan, Hap Day	12,794
1947	Toronto	All-Stars 4, Toronto 3	Dick Irvin, Hap Day	14,169

There was no All-Star contest during the calendar year of 1966 because the game was moved from the start of season to mid-season. In 1979, the Challenge Cup series between the Soviet Union and Team NHL replaced the All-Star Game. In 1987, Rendez-Vous '87, two games between the Soviet Union and Team NHL replaced the All-Star Game. Rendez-Vous '87 scores: game one, NHL All-Stars 4,

1996-97 All-Star Game Summary

January 18, 1997 at San Jose   Eastern 11, Western 7

PLAYERS ON ICE: Eastern Conference — Vanbiesbrouck, Brodeur, Hasek, Bourque, Leetch, Coffey, K. Hatcher, Lachance, Stevens, Svehla, Gretzky, Ciccarelli, Alfredsson, Bondra, Hawerchuk, Hunter, LeClair, Lemieux, Lindros, Messier, Oates, Recchi, Sanderson

Western Conference — Roy, Hebert, Moog, Chelios, Ozolinsh, D. Hatcher, MacInnis, Tverdovsky, Fetisov, Hull, Kariya, Amonte, Arnott, Bure, Fleury, Granato, Khristich, Nolan, Selanne, Sundin, Shanahan, Tkachuk, Yzerman

SUMMARY
First Period

1. Eastern	LeClair 1	(Bondra, Stevens)	8:52
2. Eastern	Lemieux 1	(Gretzky)	9:49
3. Eastern	Recchi 1	(Messier, Alfredsson)	15:32
4. Eastern	Hawerchuk 1	(Lindros, Coffey)	16:19
5. Western	Bure 1	(Sundin, Amonte)	17:36
6. Western	Kariya 1	(Bure, Ozolinsh)	18:36

PENALTIES: None.

Second Period

7. Eastern	Recchi 2	(Svehla, Messier)	1:56
8. Eastern	Sanderson 1	(Lindros)	3:21
9. Western	Bure 2	(Selanne, Fetisov)	4:40
10. Eastern	Lemieux 2	(Svehla, Ciccarelli)	6:09
11. Eastern	Messier 1	(K. Hatcher, Alfredsson)	8:45
12. Eastern	Recchi 3	(Oates, Lemieux)	10:57
13. Western	Shanahan 1	(Hull, Ozolinsh) (pp)	16:38
14. Eastern	Hawerchuk 2	(LeClair, Stevens)	17:28
15. Western	Nolan 1	(Fleury, Ozolinsh)	18:54
16. Western	Nolan 2	(Amonte)	19:02

Penalties: Coffey Eastern (hooking) 15:37

Third Period

17. Eastern	LeClair 2 (Bondra, Oates)		8:50
18. Western	Nolan 3		17:57

Penalties: K. Hatcher Eastern (hooking) 14:56

SHOTS ON GOAL BY:

Eastern	15	15	11	**41**
Western	12	13	21	**46**

	Goaltenders:	Time	SA	GA	ENG	Dec
Eastern	Vanbiesbrouck	20:00	12	2	0	
Eastern	Brodeur	20:00	13	4	0	W
Eastern	Hasek	20:00	21	1	0	
Western	Roy	20:00	15	4	0	
Western	Moog	20:00	15	6	0	L
Western	Hebert	20:00	11	1	0	

PP Conversions: Eastern 0/0; Western 1/2.

Referee: Rob Schick   Linesmen: Ron Asselstine, Bob Hodges, Leon Stickle.
Attendance: 17,422.

NHL ALL-ROOKIE TEAM

Voting for the NHL All-Rookie Team is conducted among the representatives of the Professional Hockey Writers' Association at the end of the season. The rookie all-star team was first selected for the 1982-83 season.

1996-97

Patrick Lalime, Pittsburgh	Goal
Bryan Berard, NY Islanders	Defense
Janne Niinimaa, Philadelphia	Defense
Jarome Iginla, Calgary	Forward
Jim Campbell, St. Louis	Forward
Sergei Berezin, Toronto	Forward

1995-96

Corey Hirsch, Vancouver	Goal
Ed Jovanovski, Florida	Defense
Kyle McLaren, Boston	Defense
Daniel Alfredsson, Ottawa	Forward
Eric Daze, Chicago	Forward
Petr Sykora, New Jersey	Forward

1993-94

Martin Brodeur, New Jersey	Goal
Chris Pronger, Hartford	Defense
Boris Mironov, Wpg., Edm.	Defense
Jason Arnott, Edmonton	Center
Mikael Renberg, Philadelphia	Wing
Oleg Petrov, Montreal	Wing

1991-92

Dominik Hasek, Chicago	Goal
Nicklas Lidstrom, Detroit	Defense
Vladimir Konstantinov, Detroit	Defense
Kevin Todd, New Jersey	Center
Tony Amonte, NY Rangers	Right Wing
Gilbert Dionne, Montreal	Left Wing

1994-95

Jim Carey, Washington	Goal
Chris Therien, Philadelphia	Defense
Kenny Jonsson, Toronto	Defense
Peter Forsberg, Quebec	Forward
Jeff Friesen, San Jose	Forward
Paul Kariya, Anaheim	Forward

1992-93

Felix Potvin, Toronto	Goal
Vladimir Malakhov, NY Islanders	Defense
Scott Niedermayer, New Jersey	Defense
Eric Lindros, Philadelphia	Center
Teemu Selanne, Winnipeg	Right Wing
Joe Juneau, Boston	Left Wing

1990-91

Ed Belfour, Chicago	Goal
Eric Weinrich, New Jersey	Defense
Rob Blake, Los Angeles	Defense
Sergei Fedorov, Detroit	Center
Ken Hodge, Boston	Right Wing
Jaromir Jagr, Pittsburgh	Left Wing

1989-90

Bob Essensa, Winnipeg	Goal
Brad Shaw, Hartford	Defense
Geoff Smith, Edmonton	Defense
Mike Modano, Minnesota	Center
Sergei Makarov, Calgary	Right Wing
Rod Brind'Amour, St. Louis	Left Wing

1987-88

Darren Pang, Chicago	Goal
Glen Wesley, Boston	Defense
Calle Johansson, Buffalo	Defense
Joe Nieuwendyk, Calgary	Center
Ray Sheppard, Buffalo	Right Wing
Iain Duncan, Winnipeg	Left Wing

1985-86

Patrick Roy, Montreal	Goal
Gary Suter, Calgary	Defense
Dana Murzyn, Hartford	Defense
Mike Ridley, NY Rangers	Center
Kjell Dahlin, Montreal	Right Wing
Wendel Clark, Toronto	Left Wing

1983-84

Tom Barrasso, Buffalo	Goal
Thomas Eriksson, Philadelphia	Defense
Jamie Macoun, Calgary	Defense
Steve Yzerman, Detroit	Center
Hakan Loob, Calgary	Right Wing
Sylvain Turgeon, Hartford	Left Wing

1988-89

Peter Sidorkiewicz, Hartford	Goal
Brian Leetch, NY Rangers	Defense
Zarley Zalapski, Pittsburgh	Defense
Trevor Linden, Vancouver	Center
Tony Granato, NY Rangers	Right Wing
David Volek, NY Islanders	Left Wing

1986-87

Ron Hextall, Philadelphia	Goal
Steve Duchesne, Los Angeles	Defense
Brian Benning, St. Louis	Defense
Jimmy Carson, Los Angeles	Center
Jim Sandlak, Vancouver	Right Wing
Luc Robitaille, Los Angeles	Left Wing

1984-85

Steve Penney, Montreal	Goal
Chris Chelios, Montreal	Defense
Bruce Bell, Quebec	Defense
Mario Lemieux, Pittsburgh	Center
Tomas Sandstrom, NY Rangers	Right Wing
Warren Young, Pittsburgh	Left Wing

1982-83

Pelle Lindbergh, Philadelphia	Goal
Scott Stevens, Washington	Defense
Phil Housley, Buffalo	Defense
Dan Daoust, Montreal/Toronto	Center
Steve Larmer, Chicago	Right Wing
Mats Naslund, Montreal	Left Wing

All-Star Game Records 1947 through 1997

TEAM RECORDS

MOST GOALS, BOTH TEAMS, ONE GAME:
22 — Wales 16, Campbell 6, 1993 at Montreal
19 — Wales 12, Campbell 7, 1990 at Pittsburgh
18 — East 11, West 7, 1997 at San Jose
17 — East 9, West 8, 1994 at NY Rangers
16 — Campbell 11, Wales 5, 1991 at Chicago
— Campbell 10, Wales 6, 1992 at Philadelphia
14 — Campbell 9, Wales 5, 1989 at Edmonton
13 — Wales 7, Campbell 6, 1984 at New Jersey

FEWEST GOALS, BOTH TEAMS, ONE GAME:
2 — NHL All-Stars 1, Montreal Canadiens 1, 1956 at Montreal
— First Team All-Stars 1, Second Team All-Stars 1, 1952 at Detroit
3 — West 2, East 1, 1971 at Boston
— Montreal Canadiens 3, NHL All-Stars 0, 1967 at Montreal
— NHL All-Stars 2, Montreal Canadiens 1, 1960 at Montreal

MOST GOALS, ONE TEAM, ONE GAME:
16 — Wales 16, Campbell 6, 1993 at Montreal
12 — Wales 12, Campbell 7, 1990 at Pittsburgh
11 — Campbell 11, Wales 5, 1991 at Chicago
— East 11, West 7, 1997 at San Jose
10 — Campbell 10, Wales 6, 1992 at Philadelphia

FEWEST GOALS, ONE TEAM, ONE GAME:
0 — NHL All-Stars 0, Montreal Canadiens 3, 1967 at Montreal
1 — 17 times (1981, 1975, 1971, 1970, 1962, 1961, 1960, 1959, both teams 1956, 1955, 1953, both teams 1952, 1950, 1949, 1948)

MOST SHOTS, BOTH TEAMS, ONE GAME (SINCE 1955):
102 — 1994 at NY Rangers — East 9 (56 shots),
West 8 (46 shots)
90 — 1993 at Montreal — Wales 16 (49 shots),
Campbell 6 (41 shots)
87 — 1990 at Pittsburgh — Wales 12 (45 shots),
Campbell 7 (42 shots)
— 1997 at San Jose — East 11 (41 shots),
West 7 (46 shots)
83 — 1992 at Philadelphia — Campbell 10 (42 shots),
Wales 6 (41 shots)

FEWEST SHOTS, BOTH TEAMS, ONE GAME (SINCE 1955):
52 — 1978 at Buffalo — Campbell 2 (12 shots)
Wales 3 (40 shots)
53 — 1960 at Montreal — NHL All-Stars 2 (27 shots)
Montreal Canadiens 1 (26 shots)
55 — 1956 at Montreal — NHL All-Stars 1 (28 shots)
Montreal Canadiens 1 (27 shots)
— 1971 at Boston — West 2 (28 shots)
East 1 (27 shots)

MOST SHOTS, ONE TEAM, ONE GAME (SINCE 1955):
56 — 1994 at NY Rangers — East (9-8 vs. West)
49 — 1993 at Montreal — Wales (16-6 vs. Campbell)
46 — 1994 at NY Rangers — West (8-9 vs. East)
— 1997 at San Jose — West (7-11 vs. East)
45 — 1990 at Pittsburgh — Wales (12-7 vs. Campbell)

FEWEST SHOTS, ONE TEAM, ONE GAME (SINCE 1955):
12 — 1978 at Buffalo — Campbell (2-3 vs. Wales)
17 — 1970 at St. Louis — West (1-4 vs. East)
23 — 1961 at Chicago — Chicago Black Hawks (1-3 vs. NHL All-Stars)
24 — 1976 at Philadelphia — Campbell (5-7 vs. Wales)

MOST POWER-PLAY GOALS, BOTH TEAMS, ONE GAME (SINCE 1950):
3 — 1953 at Montreal — NHL All-Stars 3 (2 power-play goals),
Montreal Canadiens 1 (1 power-play goal)
— 1954 at Detroit — NHL All-Stars 2 (1 power-play goal)
Detroit Red Wings 2 (2 power-play goals)
— 1958 at Montreal — NHL All-Stars 3 (1 power-play goal)
Montreal Canadiens 6 (2 power-play goals)

FEWEST POWER-PLAY GOALS, BOTH TEAMS, ONE GAME (SINCE 1950):
0 — 15 times (1952, 1959, 1960, 1967, 1968, 1969, 1972, 1973, 1976, 1980, 1981, 1984, 1985, 1992, 1994, 1996)

FASTEST TWO GOALS, BOTH TEAMS, FROM START OF GAME:
37 seconds — 1970 at St. Louis — Jacques Laperriere of East scored at 20 seconds and Dean Prentice of West scored at 37 seconds. Final score: East 4, West 1.
3:37 — 1993 at Montreal — Mike Gartner scored at 3:15 and at 3:37 for Wales. Final score: Wales 16, Campbell 6.
4:08 — 1963 at Toronto — Frank Mahovlich scored for Toronto Maple Leafs at 2:22 of first period and Henri Richard scored at 4:08 for NHL All-Stars. Final score: NHL All-Stars 3, Toronto Maple Leafs 3.

FASTEST TWO GOALS, BOTH TEAMS:
8 seconds — 1997 at San Jose — Owen Nolan scored at 18:54 and 19:02 of the second period for West. Final Score: East 11, West 7.
10 seconds — 1976 at Philadelphia — Dennis Ververgaert scored at 4:33 and at 4:43 of third period for Campbell. Final score: Wales 7, Campbell 5.
14 seconds — 1989 at Edmonton. Steve Yzerman and Gary Leeman scored at 17:21 and 17:35 of second period for Campbell. Final score: Campbell 9, Wales 5.

FASTEST THREE GOALS, BOTH TEAMS:
1:08 — 1993 at Montreal — all by Wales — Mike Gartner scored at 3:15 and at 3:37 of first period; Peter Bondra scored at 4:23. Final score: Wales 16, Campbell 6.
1:14 — 1994 at NY Rangers — Bob Kudelski scored at 9:46 of first period for East; Sergei Fedorov scored at 10:20 for West; Eric Lindros scored at 11:00 for East. Final score: East 9, West 8.
1:25 — 1992 at Philadelphia — Bryan Trottier scored at 4:03 of third period for Wales; Brian Bellows scored at 4:50 for Campbell; Alexander Mogilny scored at 5:28 for Wales. Final score: Campbell 10, Wales 6.

FASTEST FOUR GOALS, BOTH TEAMS:
2:24 — 1997 at San Jose — Brendan Shanahan scored at 16:38 of second period for West; Dale Hawerchuk scored at 17:28 for East; Owen Nolan scored at 18:54 and 19:02 for West. Final score: East 11, West 7.
3:04 — 1997 at San Jose — Mark Recchi scored at 15:32 of first period for East; Dale Hawerchuk scored at 16:19 for East; Pavel Bure scored at 17:36 for West; Paul Kariya scored at 18:36 for West. Final score: East 11, West 7.
3:29 — 1994 at NY Rangers — Jeremy Roenick scored at 7:31 of first period for West; Bob Kudelski scored at 9:46 for East; Sergei Fedorov scored at 10:20 for West; Eric Lindros scored at 11:00 for East. Final score: East 9, West 8.

FASTEST TWO GOALS, ONE TEAM, FROM START OF GAME:
3:37 — 1993 at Montreal — Wales — Mike Gartner scored at 3:15 and at 3:37. Final score: Wales 16, Campbell 6.
4:19 — 1980 at Detroit — Wales — Larry Robinson scored at 3:58 and Steve Payne scored at 4:19. Final score: Wales 6, Campbell 3.
4:38 — 1971 at Boston — West — Chico Maki scored at 36 seconds and Bobby Hull scored at 4:38. Final score: West 2, East 1.

FASTEST TWO GOALS, ONE TEAM:
8 seconds — 1997 at San Jose — West — Owen Nolan scored at 18:54 and at 19:02 of second period. Final score: East 11, West 7.
10 seconds — 1976 at Philadelphia — Campbell — Dennis Ververgaert scored at 4:33 and at 4:43 of third period. Final score: Wales 7, Campbell 5.
14 seconds — 1989 at Edmonton — Campbell — Steve Yzerman and Gary Leeman scored at 17:21 and 17:35 of second period. Final score: Campbell 9, Wales 5.

FASTEST THREE GOALS, ONE TEAM:
1:08 — 1993 at Montreal — Wales — Mike Gartner scored at 3:15 and 3:37 of first period; Peter Bondra scored at 4:23. Final score: Wales 16, Campbell 6.
1:32 — 1980 at Detroit — Wales — Ron Stackhouse scored at 11:40 of third period; Craig Hartsburg scored at 12:40; Reed Larson scored at 13:12. Final score: Wales 6, Campbell 3.
1:42 — 1993 at Montreal — Wales — Alexander Mogilny scored at 11:40 of first period; Pierre Turgeon scored at 13:05; Mike Gartner scored at 13:22. Final score: Wales 16, Campbell 6.

FASTEST FOUR GOALS, ONE TEAM:
4:19 — 1992 at Philadelphia — Campbell — Brian Bellows scored at 7:40 of second period; Jeremy Roenick scored at 8:13; Theoren Fleury scored at 11:06, Brett Hull scored at 11:59. Final score: Campbell 10, Wales 6.
4:26 — 1980 at Detroit — Wales — Ron Stackhouse scored at 11:40 of third period; Craig Hartsburg scored at 12:40; Reed Larson scored at 13:12; Real Cloutier scored at 16:06. Final score: Wales 6, Campbell 3.
5:34 — 1993 at Montreal — Campbell — Doug Gilmour scored at 13:57 of third period; Teemu Selanne scored at 17:03; Pavel Bure scored at 18:44 and 19:31. Final score: Wales 16, Campbell 6.

MOST GOALS, BOTH TEAMS, ONE PERIOD:
10 — 1997 at San Jose — Second period — East (6), West (4).
Final score: East 11, West 7.
9 — 1990 at Pittsburgh — First period — Wales (7), Campbell (2).
Final score: Wales 12, Campbell 7.
8 — 1992 at Philadelphia — Second period — Campbell (6), Wales (2).
Final Score: Campbell 10, Wales 6.
— 1993 at Montreal — Second period — Wales (6), Campbell (2).
Final score: Wales 16, Campbell 6.
— 1993 at Montreal — Third period — Wales (4), Campbell (4).
Final score: Wales 16, Campbell 6.

MOST GOALS, ONE TEAM, ONE PERIOD:
7 — 1990 at Pittsburgh — First period — Wales. Final score: Wales 12, Campbell 7.
6 — 1983 at NY Islanders — Third period — Campbell.
Final score: Campbell 9, Wales 3.
   — 1992 at Philadelphia — Second Period — Campbell.
Final score: Campbell 10, Wales 6.
   — 1993 at Montreal — First period — Wales.
Final score: Wales 16, Campbell 6.
   — 1993 at Montreal — Second period — Wales.
Final score: Wales 16, Campbell 6.
   — 1997 at San Jose — Second period — East.
Final score: East 11, West 7.

MOST SHOTS, BOTH TEAMS, ONE PERIOD:
39 — 1994 at NY Rangers — Second period — West (21) East (18).
Final score: East 9, West 8.
36 — 1990 at Pittsburgh — Third period — Campbell (22), Wales (14).
Final score: Wales 12, Campbell 7.
   — 1994 at NY Rangers — First period — East (19), West (17).
Final score: East 9, West 8.

MOST SHOTS, ONE TEAM, ONE PERIOD:
22 — 1990 at Pittsburgh — Third period — Campbell.
Final score: Wales 12, Campbell 7.
   — 1991 at Chicago — Third Period — Wales.
Final score: Campbell 11, Wales 5.
   — 1993 at Montreal — First period — Wales.
Final score: Wales 16, Campbell 6.

FEWEST SHOTS, BOTH TEAMS, ONE PERIOD:
9 — 1971 at Boston — Third period — East (2), West (7).
Final score: West 2, East 1.
   — 1980 at Detroit — Second period — Campbell (4), Wales (5).
Final score: Wales 6, Campbell 3.
13 — 1982 at Washington — Third period — Campbell (6), Wales (7).
Final score: Wales 4, Campbell 2.
14 — 1978 at Buffalo — First period — Campbell (7), Wales (7).
Final score: Wales 3, Campbell 2.
   — 1986 at Hartford — First period — Campbell (6), Wales (8).
Final score: Wales 4, Campbell 3.

FEWEST SHOTS, ONE TEAM, ONE PERIOD:
2 — 1971 at Boston   Third period   East
Final score: West 2, East 1
   — 1978 at Buffalo   Second period   Campbell
Final score: Wales 3, Campbell 2
3 — 1978 at Buffalo   Third period   Campbell
Final score: Wales 3, Campbell 2
4 — 1955 at Detroit   First period   NHL All-Stars
Final score: Detroit Red Wings 3, NHL All-Stars 1
4 — 1980 at Detroit   Second period   Campbell
Final score: Wales 6, Campbell 3

1949 NHL All-Stars – front row, from left: Chuck Rayner and Bob Goldham; back row, from left: Maurice Richard, Bill Quackenbush and Gordie Howe. All but Goldham are members of the Hockey Hall of Fame.

INDIVIDUAL RECORDS

Games

MOST GAMES PLAYED:
23 — Gordie Howe from 1948 through 1980
16 — Wayne Gretzky from 1980 through 1997
15 — Frank Mahovlich from 1959 through 1974
   — Ray Bourque from 1981 through 1997
14 — Paul Coffey from 1982 through 1997

Goals

MOST GOALS (CAREER):
12 — Wayne Gretzky in 16GP
11 — Mario Lemieux in 8GP
10 — Gordie Howe in 23GP
 8 — Frank Mahovlich in 15GP
 7 — Maurice Richard in 13GP

MOST GOALS, ONE GAME:
 4 — Wayne Gretzky, Campbell, 1983
    — Mario Lemieux, Wales, 1990
    — Vince Damphousse, Campbell, 1991
    — Mike Gartner, Wales, 1993
 3 — Ted Lindsay, Detroit Red Wings, 1950
    — Mario Lemieux, Wales, 1988
    — Pierre Turgeon, Wales, 1993
    — Mark Recchi, East, 1997
    — Owen Nolan, West, 1997

MOST GOALS, ONE PERIOD:
 4 — Wayne Gretzky, Campbell, Third period, 1983
 3 — Mario Lemieux, Wales, First period, 1990
    — Vince Damphousse, Campbell, Third period, 1991
    — Mike Gartner, Wales, First period, 1993
 2 — Ted Lindsay, Detroit Red Wings, First period, 1950
    — Wally Hergesheimer, NHL All-Stars, First period, 1953
    — Andy Bathgate, NHL All-Stars, Third period, 1958
    — Frank Mahovlich, Toronto Maple Leafs, First period, 1963
    — Dennis Ververgaert, Campbell, Third period, 1976
    — Richard Martin, Wales, Third period, 1977
    — Pierre Turgeon, Wales, First period, 1990
    — Luc Robitaille, Campbell, Third period, 1990
    — Theoren Fleury, Campbell, Second period, 1992
    — Brett Hull, Campbell, Second period, 1992
    — Rick Tocchet, Wales, Second period, 1993
    — Pavel Bure, Campbell, Third period, 1993
    — Mark Recchi, East, Second period, 1997
    — Owen Nolan, West, Second period, 1997

Assists

MOST ASSISTS (CAREER):
12 — Adam Oates in 5GP
11 — Ray Bourque in 15GP
   — Mark Messier in 12GP
10 — Joe Sakic in 6GP
   — Paul Coffey in 14GP

MOST ASSISTS, ONE GAME:
 5 — Mats Naslund, Wales, 1988
 4 — Ray Bourque, Wales, 1985
    — Adam Oates, Campbell, 1991
    — Adam Oates, Wales, 1993
    — Mark Recchi, Wales, 1993
    — Pierre Turgeon, East All-Stars, 1994
 3 — Dickie Moore, Montreal Canadiens, 1958
    — Doug Harvey, Montreal Canadiens, 1959
    — Guy Lafleur, Wales, 1975
    — Pete Mahovlich, Wales, 1976
    — Mark Messier, Campbell, 1983
    — Rick Vaive, Campbell, 1984
    — Mark Johnson, Wales, 1984
    — Don Maloney, Wales, 1984
    — Mike Krushelnyski, Campbell, 1985
    — Mario Lemieux, Wales, 1988
    — Brett Hull, Campbell, 1990
    — Luc Robitaille, Campbell, 1992
    — Joe Sakic, Wales, 1993
    — Sandis Ozolinsh, West, 1997

MOST ASSISTS, ONE PERIOD:
 4 — Adam Oates, Wales, First period, 1993
 3 — Mark Messier, Campbell, Third period, 1983

Points

MOST POINTS (CAREER):
20 — **Wayne Gretzky** (12G-8A in 16GP)
— **Mario Lemieux** (11G-9A in 8GP)
19 — Gordie Howe (10G-9A in 23GP)
15 — Mark Messier (4G-11A in 12GP)
14 — Ray Bourque (3G-11A in 15GP)

MOST POINTS, ONE GAME:
6 — **Mario Lemieux,** Wales, 1988 (3G-3A)
5 — Mats Naslund, Wales, 1988 (5A)
— Adam Oates, Campbell, 1991 (1G-4A)
— Mike Gartner, Wales, 1993 (4G-1A)
— Mark Recchi, Wales, 1993 (1G-4A)
— Pierre Turgeon, Wales, 1993 (3G-2A)

MOST POINTS, ONE PERIOD:
4 — **Wayne Gretzky,** Campbell, Third period, 1983 (4G)
— **Mike Gartner,** Wales, First period, 1993 (3G-1A)
— **Adam Oates,** Wales, First period, 1993 (4A)
3 — Gordie Howe, NHL All-Stars, Second period, 1965 (1G-2A)
— Pete Mahovlich, Wales, First period, 1976 (1G-2A)
— Mark Messier, Campbell, Third period, 1983 (3A)
— Mario Lemieux, Wales, Second period, 1988 (1G-2A)
— Mario Lemieux, Wales, First period, 1990 (3G)
— Vince Damphousse, Campbell, Third period, 1991 (3G)
— Mark Recchi, Wales, Second period, 1993 (1G-2A)

Power-Play Goals

MOST POWER-PLAY GOALS:
6 — **Gordie Howe** in 23GP
3 — Bobby Hull in 12GP
2 — Maurice Richard in 13GP

Fastest Goals

FASTEST GOAL FROM START OF GAME:
19 seconds — **Ted Lindsay,** Detroit Red Wings, 1950
20 seconds — Jacques Laperriere, East All-Stars, 1970
21 seconds — Mario Lemieux, Wales, 1990
36 seconds — Chico Maki, West All-Stars, 1971
37 seconds — Dean Prentice, West All-Stars, 1970

FASTEST GOAL FROM START OF A PERIOD:
19 seconds — **Ted Lindsay,** Detroit Red Wings, 1950 (first period)
— **Rick Tocchet,** Wales, 1993 (second period)
20 seconds — Jacques Laperriere, East, 1970 (first period)
21 seconds — Mario Lemieux, Wales, 1990 (first period)
26 seconds — Wayne Gretzky, Campbell, 1982 (second period)
28 seconds — Maurice Richard, NHL All-Stars, 1947 (third period)

FASTEST TWO GOALS (ONE PLAYER) FROM START OF GAME:
3:37 — **Mike Gartner,** Wales, 1993, at 3:15 and 3:37.
5:25 — Wally Hergesheimer, NHL All-Stars, 1953, at 4:06 and 5:25.
12:11 — Frank Mahovlich, Toronto, 1963, at 2:22 and 12:11.

FASTEST TWO GOALS (ONE PLAYER) FROM START OF A PERIOD:
3:37 — **Mike Gartner,** Wales, 1993, at 3:15 and 3:37 of first period.
4:43 — Dennis Ververgaert, Campbell, 1976, at 4:33 and 4:43 of third period.
4:57 — Rick Tocchet, Wales, 1993, at :19 and 4:57 of second period.

FASTEST TWO GOALS (ONE PLAYER):
8 seconds — **Owen Nolan,** West, 1997. Scored at 18:54 and 19:02 of second period.
10 seconds — Dennis Ververgaert, Campbell, 1976. Scored at 4:33 and 4:43 of third period.
22 seconds — Mike Gartner, Wales, 1993. Scored at 3:15 and 3:37 of first period.

Penalties

MOST PENALTY MINUTES:
27 — **Gordie Howe** in 23GP
21 — Gus Mortson in 9GP
16 — Harry Howell in 7GP

Goaltenders

MOST GAMES PLAYED:
13 — **Glenn Hall** from 1955-1969
11 — Terry Sawchuk from 1950-1968
8 — Jacques Plante from 1956-1970
7 — Patrick Roy from 1988-1997
6 — Tony Esposito from 1970-1980
— Ed Giacomin from 1967-1973
— Grant Fuhr from 1982-1989

MOST MINUTES PLAYED:
467 — **Terry Sawchuk** in 11GP
421 — Glenn Hall in 13GP
370 — Jacques Plante in 8GP
209 — Turk Broda in 4GP
182 — Ed Giacomin in 6GP
177 — Grant Fuhr in 6GP
165 — Tony Esposito in 6GP

MOST GOALS AGAINST:
22 — **Glenn Hall** in 13GP
21 — Mike Vernon in 5GP
— Patrick Roy in 7GP
19 — Terry Sawchuk in 11GP
18 — Jacques Plante in 8GP
— Andy Moog in 4GP

BEST GOALS-AGAINST-AVERAGE AMONG THOSE WITH AT LEAST TWO GAMES PLAYED:
0.68 — **Gilles Villemure** in 3GP
1.02 — Frank Brimsek in 2GP
1.59 — Johnny Bower in 4GP
1.64 — Lorne "Gump" Worsley in 4GP
1.98 — Gerry McNeil in 3GP
2.03 — Don Edwards in 2GP
2.44 — Terry Sawchuk in 11GP

Members of the NHL All-Stars who played the Toronto Maple Leafs in the first NHL All-Star Game, a benefit for injured Leaf Ace Bailey. The game took place on Valentines Day, 1934. Front row, from left: Howie Morenz, Aurel Joliat and Herbie Lewis and back row, from left: Lionel Conacher, Ching Johnson, and Nels Stewart.

Hockey Hall of Fame

(Year of induction is listed after each Honored Members name)

Both Steve Shutt, left, and Borje Salming were inducted into the Hockey Hall of Fame in the 1990s. Salming is the first Swedish player to win induction.

Location: BCE Place, at the corner of Front and Yonge Streets in the heart of downtown Toronto. Easy access from all major highways running into Toronto. Close to TTC and Union Station.

Telephone: administration (416) 360-7735; information (416) 360-7765.

Summer and Christmas/March break hours: Monday to Saturday 9:30 a.m. to 6 p.m.; Sunday 10:00 a.m. to 6 p.m.

Fall/Winter/Spring hours (except Christmas/March break): Monday to Friday 10 a.m. to 5 p.m.; Saturday 9:30 a.m. to 6 p.m.; Sunday 10:30 a.m. to 5 p.m.

The Hockey Hall of Fame can be booked for private functions after hours.

Website address: www.hhof.com

History: The Hockey Hall of Fame was established in 1943. Members were first honored in 1945. On August 26, 1961, the Hockey Hall of Fame opened its doors to the public in a building located on the grounds of the Canadian National Exhibition in Toronto. The Hockey Hall of Fame relocated to its new site at BCE Place and welcomed the hockey world on June 18, 1993.

Honor Roll: There are 307 Honored Members in the Hockey Hall of Fame. 209 have been inducted as players, 85 as builders and 13 as Referees/Linesmen. In addition, there are 54 media honorees.

Sponsors: Special thanks to Blockbuster Video, Bell Canada, Coca-Cola Canada, Household Finance, Ford of Canada, IBM Canada, Imperial Oil, Kodak Canada, Molson Breweries, London Life, TSN/RDS and The Toronto Sun.

PLAYERS

Abel, Sidney Gerald 1969
* Adams, John James "Jack" 1959
Apps, Charles Joseph Sylvanus "Syl" 1961
Armstrong, George Edward 1975
* Bailey, Irvine Wallace "Ace" 1975
* Bain, Donald H. "Dan" 1945
* Baker, Hobart "Hobey" 1945
Barber, William Charles "Bill" 1990
* Barry, Martin J. "Marty" 1965
Bathgate, Andrew James "Andy" 1978
* Bauer, Robert Theodore "Bobby" 1996
Béliveau, Jean Arthur 1972
* Benedict, Clinton S. 1965
* Bentley, Douglas Wagner 1964
* Bentley, Maxwell H. L. 1966
* Blake, Hector "Toe" 1966
Boivin, Leo Joseph 1986
* Boon, Richard R. "Dickie" 1952
Bossy, Michael 1991
Bouchard, Emile Joseph "Butch" 1966
* Boucher, Frank 1958
* Boucher, George "Buck" 1960
Bower, John William 1976
* Bowie, Russell 1945
Brimsek, Francis Charles 1966
* Broadbent, Harry L. "Punch" 1962
* Broda, Walter Edward "Turk" 1967
Bucyk, John Paul 1981
* Burch, Billy 1974
* Cameron, Harold Hugh "Harry" 1962
Cheevers, Gerald Michael "Gerry" 1985
* Clancy, Francis Michael "King" 1958
* Clapper, Aubrey "Dit" 1947
Clarke, Robert "Bobby" 1987
* Cleghorn, Sprague 1958
* Colville, Neil MacNeil 1967
* Conacher, Charles W. 1961
* Conacher, Lionel Pretoria 1994
* Connell, Alex 1958
* Cook, Fred "Bun" 1995
* Cook, William Osser 1952
Coulter, Arthur Edmund 1974
Cournoyer, Yvan Serge 1982
* Cowley, William Mailes 1968
* Crawford, Samuel Russell "Rusty" 1962
* Darragh, John Proctor "Jack" 1962
* Davidson, Allan M. "Scotty" 1950
* Day, Clarence Henry "Hap" 1961
Delvecchio, Alex 1977
* Denneny, Cyril "Cy" 1959
Dionne, Marcel 1992

* Drillon, Gordon Arthur 1975
* Drinkwater, Charles Graham 1950
Dryden, Kenneth Wayne 1983
Dumart, Woodrow "Woody" 1992
* Dunderdale, Thomas 1974
* Durnan, William Ronald 1964
* Dutton, Mervyn A. "Red" 1958
* Dye, Cecil Henry "Babe" 1970
Esposito, Anthony James "Tony" 1988
Esposito, Philip Anthony 1984
* Farrell, Arthur F. 1965
* Flaman, Ferdinand Charles "Fern" 1990
* Foyston, Frank 1958
* Frederickson, Frank 1958
Gadsby, William Alexander 1970
Gainey, Bob 1992
* Gardiner, Charles Robert "Chuck" 1945
* Gardiner, Herbert Martin "Herb" 1958
* Gardner, James Henry "Jimmy" 1962
Geoffrion, Jos. A. Bernard "Boom Boom" 1972
* Gerard, Eddie 1945
Giacomin, Edward "Eddie" 1987
* Gilbert, Rodrigue Gabriel "Rod" 1982
* Gilmour, Hamilton Livingstone "Billy" 1962
* Goheen, Frank Xavier "Moose" 1952
* Goodfellow, Ebenezer R. "Ebbie" 1963
* Grant, Michael "Mike" 1950
* Green, Wilfred "Shorty" 1962
* Griffis, Silas Seth "Si" 1950
* Hainsworth, George 1961
Hall, Glenn Henry 1975
* Hall, Joseph Henry 1961
* Harvey, Douglas Norman 1973
* Hay, George 1958
* Hern, William Milton "Riley" 1962
* Hextall, Bryan Aldwyn 1969
* Holmes, Harry "Hap" 1972
* Hooper, Charles Thomas "Tom" 1962
Horner, George Reginald "Red" 1965
* Horton, Miles Gilbert "Tim" 1977
Howe, Gordon 1972
Howe, Sydney Harris 1965
Howell, Henry Vernon "Harry" 1979
Hull, Robert Marvin 1983
* Hutton, John Bower "Bouse" 1962
Hyland, Harry M. 1962
* Irvin, James Dickenson "Dick" 1958
* Jackson, Harvey "Busher" 1971
* Johnson, Ernest "Moose" 1952
* Johnson, Ivan "Ching" 1958
Johnson, Thomas Christian 1970

* Joliat, Aurel 1947
* Keats, Gordon "Duke" 1958
Kelly, Leonard Patrick "Red" 1969
Kennedy, Theodore Samuel "Teeder" 1966
Keon, David Michael 1986
Lach, Elmer James 1966
Lafleur, Guy Damien 1988
* Lalonde, Edouard Charles "Newsy" 1950
Laperriere, Jacques 1987
Lapointe, Guy 1993
Laprade, Edgar 1993
* Laviolette, Jean Baptiste "Jack" 1962
Lehman, Hugh 1958
Lemaire, Jacques Gerard 1984
* LeSueur, Percy 1961
* Lewis, Herbert A. 1989
Lindsay, Robert Blake Theodore "Ted" 1966
Lumley, Harry 1980
* MacKay, Duncan "Mickey" 1952
Mahovlich, Frank William 1981
* Malone, Joseph "Joe" 1950
* Mantha, Sylvio 1960
* Marshall, John "Jack" 1965
* Maxwell, Fred G. "Steamer" 1962
McDonald, Lanny 1992
* McGee, Frank 1945
* McGimsie, William George "Billy" 1962
* McNamara, George 1958
Mikita, Stanley 1983
Moore, Richard Winston 1974
* Moran, Patrick Joseph "Paddy" 1958
* Morenz, Howie 1945
* Mosienko, William "Billy" 1965
* Nighbor, Frank 1947
* Noble, Edward Reginald "Reg" 1962
* O'Connor, Herbert William "Buddy" 1988
* Oliver, Harry 1967
Olmstead, Murray Bert "Bert" 1985
Orr, Robert Gordon 1979
Parent, Bernard Marcel 1984
Park, Douglas Bradford "Brad" 1988
* Patrick, Joseph Lynn 1980
* Patrick, Lester 1947
Perreault, Gilbert 1990
* Phillips, Tommy 1945
Pilote, Joseph Albert Pierre Paul 1975
* Pitre, Didier "Pit" 1962
* Plante, Joseph Jacques Omer 1978
Potvin, Denis 1991
* Pratt, Walter "Babe" 1966
* Primeau, A. Joseph 1963

Pronovost, Joseph René Marcel 1978
Pulford, Bob 1991
* Pulford, Harvey 1945
Quackenbush, Hubert George ''Bill'' 1976
* Rankin, Frank 1961
Ratelle, Joseph Gilbert Yvan Jean ''Jean'' 1985
Rayner, Claude Earl ''Chuck'' 1973
Reardon, Kenneth Joseph 1966
Richard, Joseph Henri 1979
Richard, Joseph Henri Maurice ''Rocket'' 1961
* Richardson, George Taylor 1950
* Roberts, Gordon 1971
Robinson, Larry 1995
* Ross, Arthur Howie 1945
* Russel, Blair 1965
* Russell, Ernest 1965
* Ruttan, J.D. ''Jack'' 1962
Salming, Borje Anders 1996
Savard, Serge A. 1986
* Sawchuk, Terrance Gordon ''Terry'' 1971
* Scanlan, Fred 1965
Schmidt, Milton Conrad ''Milt'' 1961
* Schriner, David ''Sweeney'' 1962
* Seibert, Earl Walter 1963
* Seibert, Oliver Levi 1961
* Shore, Edward W. ''Eddie'' 1947
Shutt, Stephen 1993
* Siebert, Albert C. ''Babe'' 1964
* Simpson, Harold Edward ''Bullet Joe'' 1962
Sittler, Darryl Glen 1989
* Smith, Alfred E. 1962
Smith, Clint 1991
* Smith, Reginald ''Hooley'' 1972
* Smith, Thomas James 1973
Smith, William John ''Billy'' 1993
Stanley, Allan Herbert 1981
* Stanley, Russell ''Barney'' 1962
* Stewart, John Sherratt ''Black Jack'' 1964
* Stewart, Nelson ''Nels'' 1962
* Stuart, Bruce 1961
* Stuart, Hod 1945
* Taylor, Frederic ''Cyclone'' (O.B.E.) 1947
* Thompson, Cecil R. ''Tiny'' 1959
Tretiak, Vladislav 1989
* Trihey, Col. Harry J. 1950
Ullman, Norman V. Alexander ''Norm'' 1982
* Vezina, Georges 1945
* Walker, John Phillip ''Jack'' 1960
* Walsh, Martin ''Marty'' 1962
* Watson, Harry E. 1962
* Watson, Harry 1994
* Weiland, Ralph ''Cooney'' 1971
* Westwick, Harry 1962
* Whitcroft, Fred 1962
* Wilson, Gordon Allan ''Phat'' 1962
Worsley, Lorne John ''Gump'' 1980
* Worters, Roy 1969

BUILDERS

Adams, Charles 1960
* Adams, Weston W. 1972
* Ahearn, Thomas Franklin ''Frank'' 1962
* Ahearne, John Francis ''Bunny'' 1977
* Allan, Sir Montagu (C.V.O.) 1945
Allen, Keith 1992
Arbour, Alger Joseph ''Al'' 1996
* Ballard, Harold Edwin 1977
* Bauer, Father David 1989
* Bickell, John Paris 1978
Bowman, Scott 1991
* Brown, George V. 1961
* Brown, Walter A. 1962
* Buckland, Frank 1975
Butterfield, Jack Arlington 1980
* Calder, Frank 1947
* Campbell, Angus D. 1964
* Campbell, Clarence Sutherland 1966
* Cattarinich, Joseph 1977
* Dandurand, Joseph Viateur ''Leo'' 1963
* Dilio, Francis Paul 1964
* Dudley, George S. 1958
* Dunn, James A. 1968
Eagleson, Robert Alan 1989
Francis, Emile 1982
* Gibson, Dr. John L. ''Jack'' 1976
* Gorman, Thomas Patrick ''Tommy'' 1963
* Griffiths, Frank A. 1993
* Hanley, William 1986
* Hay, Charles 1974
* Hendy, James C. 1968
* Hewitt, Foster 1965
* Hewitt, William Abraham 1947
* Hume, Fred J. 1962
* Imlach, George ''Punch'' 1984
Ivan, Thomas N. 1974
* Jennings, William M. 1975
* Johnson, Bob 1992
* Juckes, Gordon W. 1979
* Kilpatrick, Gen. John Reed 1960
* Knox, Seymour H. III 1993
* Leader, George Alfred 1969
LeBel, Robert 1970
* Lockhart, Thomas F. 1965
* Loicq, Paul 1961
* Mariucci, John 1985
Mathers, Frank 1992
* McLaughlin, Major Frederic 1963
* Milford, John ''Jake'' 1984
Molson, Hon. Hartland de Montarville 1973
* Nelson, Francis 1947
* Norris, Bruce A. 1969
* Norris, Sr., James 1958
* Norris, James Dougan 1962
* Northey, William M. 1947
* O'Brien, John Ambrose 1962
O'Neill, Brian 1994
Page, Fred 1993
* Patrick, Frank 1958
* Pickard, Allan W. 1958
* Pilous, Rudy 1985
Poile, Norman ''Bud'' 1990
Pollock, Samuel Patterson Smyth 1978
* Raymond, Sen. Donat 1958
* Robertson, John Ross 1947
* Robinson, Claude C. 1947
* Ross, Philip D. 1976
Sabetzki, Dr. Gunther 1995
* Selke, Frank J. 1960
Sinden, Harry James 1983
* Smith, Frank D. 1962
* Smythe, Conn 1958
Snider, Edward M. 1988
* Stanley of Preston, Lord (G.C.B.) 1945
* Sutherland, Cap. James T. 1947
* Tarasov, Anatoli V. 1974
Torrey, Bill 1995
* Turner, Lloyd 1958
* Tutt, William Thayer 1978
* Voss, Carl Potter 1974
* Waghorn, Fred C. 1961
* Wirtz, Arthur Michael 1971
Wirtz, William W. ''Bill'' 1976
Ziegler, John A. Jr. 1987

REFEREES/LINESMEN

Armstrong, Neil 1991
Ashley, John George 1981
Chadwick, William L. 1964
D'Amico, John 1993
* Elliott, Chaucer 1961
* Hayes, George William 1988
* Hewitson, Robert W. 1963
* Ion, Fred J. ''Mickey'' 1961
Pavelich, Matt 1987
* Rodden, Michael J. ''Mike'' 1962
* Smeaton, J. Cooper 1961
Storey, Roy Alvin ''Red'' 1967
Udvari, Frank Joseph 1973

United States
Hockey Hall of Fame

The United States Hockey Hall of Fame is located in Eveleth, Minnesota, 60 miles north of Duluth, on Highway 53. The facility is open Monday to Saturday 9 a.m. to 5 p.m. and Sundays 11 a.m to 5 p.m.; Adult $3.00; Seniors $2.00; Juniors 13-17 $2.00; and Children 6-12 $1.75; Children under 6 free.
Group rates available. Please call to confirm hours of operation: 1-800-443-7825.

The Hall was dedicated and opened on June 21, 1973, largely as the result of the work of D. Kelly Campbell, Chairman of the Eveleth Civic Association's Project H Committee. There are now 89 enshrinees consisting of 54 players, 19 coaches, 16 administrators, and one referee. New members are inducted annually in October and must have made a significant contribution toward hockey in the United States through the vehicle of their careers. Support for the Hall comes from sponsorship and membership programs, grants from the hockey community, and government agencies.

PLAYERS

* Abel, Clarence "Taffy"
* Baker, Hobart "Hobey"
  Bartholome, Earl
* Bessone, Peter
  Blake, Robert
  Boucha, Henry
  Brimsek, Frank
  Cavanough, Joe
* Chaisson, Ray
  Chase, John P.
  Christian, Roger
  Christian, William "Bill"
  Cleary, Robert
  Cleary, William
* Conroy, Anthony
  Dahlstrom, Carl "Cully"
* Desjardins, Victor
  Desmond, Richard
* Dill, Robert
  Everett, Doug
  Ftorek, Robbie
* Garrison, John B.
  Garrity, Jack
* Goheen, Frank "Moose"
  Grant, Wally
  Harding, Austin "Austie"
* Iglehart, Stewart
* Johnson, Virgil
* Karakas, Mike
  Kirrane, Jack
* Lane, Myles J.
  Langevin, David R.
  Larson, Reed
* Linder, Joseph
* LoPresti, Sam L.
* Mariucci, John
  Matchefts, John
  Mayasich, John
  McCartan, Jack
  Moe, William
  Morrow, Ken
* Moseley, Fred
* Murray, Hugh "Muzz" Sr.
* Nelson, Hubert "Hub"
  Nyrop, William D.
  Olson , Eddie
* Owen, Jr., George
* Palmer, Winthrop
  Paradise, Robert
  Purpur, Clifford "Fido"
  Riley, William
* Romnes, Elwin "Doc"
  Rondeau, Richard
  Sheehy, Timothy K.
* Williams, Thomas
* Winters, Frank "Coddy"
* Yackel, Ken

COACHES

* Almquist, Oscar
  Bessone, Amo
  Brooks, Herbert
  Ceglarski, Len
* Fullerton, James
  Gambucci, Sergio
* Gordon, Malcolm K.
  Harkness, Nevin D. "Ned"
  Heyliger, Victor
  Holt, Charles E.
  Ikola, Willard
* Jeremiah, Edward J.
* Johnson, Bob
* Kelley, John "Snooks"
  Kelley, John H. "Jack"
  Patrick, Craig
  Pleban, John "Connie"
  Riley, Jack
* Ross, Larry
* Thompson, Clifford, R.
* Stewart, William
* Winsor, Alfred "Ralph"

ADMINISTRATORS

* Brown, George V.
* Brown, Walter A.
  Bush, Walter
  Clark, Donald
  Claypool, James
* Gibson, J.C. "Doc"
* Jennings, William M.
* Kahler, Nick
* Lockhart, Thomas F.
  Marvin, Cal
  Ridder, Robert
  Schulz, Charles M.
  Trumble, Harold
* Tutt, William Thayer
  Wirtz, William W. "Bill"
* Wright, Lyle Z.

REFEREE

  Chadwick, William

*Deceased

Although Boston fans were outraged when fan favorite Tiny Thompson was replaced by rookie Frank Brimsek early in the 1938-39 season, the Eveleth, Minnesota, native quickly earned the admiration of Bruins fans by recording victories in 12 of his first 15 games, including six by shutout. He was a charter member of the U.S. Hockey Hall of Fame when the facility opened in 1973.

Results

1997 Stanley Cup Playoffs

CONFERENCE QUARTER-FINALS
(Best-of-seven series)

Eastern Conference

Series 'A'
Thu. Apr. 17	Montreal 2	at	New Jersey 5
Sat. Apr. 19	Montreal 1	at	New Jersey 4
Tue. Apr. 22	New Jersey 6	at	Montreal 4
Thu. Apr. 24	New Jersey 3	at	Montreal 4 ot
Sat. Apr. 26	Montreal 0	at	New Jersey 4

New Jersey Won Series 4-1

Series 'B'
Thu. Apr. 17	Ottawa 1	at	Buffalo 3
Sat. Apr. 19	Ottawa 3	at	Buffalo 1
Mon. Apr. 21	Buffalo 3	at	Ottawa 2
Wed. Apr. 23	Buffalo 0	at	Ottawa 1 ot
Fri. Apr. 25	Ottawa 4	at	Buffalo 1
Sun. Apr. 27	Buffalo 3	at	Ottawa 0
Tue. Apr. 29	Ottawa 2	at	Buffalo 3 ot

Buffalo Won Series 4-3

Series 'C'
Thu. Apr. 17	Pittsburgh 1	at	Philadelphia 5
Sat. Apr. 19	Pittsburgh 2	at	Philadelphia 3
Mon. Apr. 21	Philadelphia 5	at	Pittsburgh 3
Wed. Apr. 23	Philadelphia 1	at	Pittsburgh 4
Sat. Apr. 26	Pittsburgh 3	at	Philadelphia 6

Philadelphia Won Series 4-1

Series 'D'
Thu. Apr. 17	NY Rangers 0	at	Florida 3
Sun. Apr. 20	NY Rangers 3	at	Florida 0
Tue. Apr. 22	Florida 3	at	NY Rangers 4 ot
Wed. Apr. 23	Florida 2	at	NY Rangers 3
Fri. Apr. 25	NY Rangers 3	at	Florida 2 ot

NY Rangers Won Series 4-1

Western Conference

Series 'E'
Wed. Apr. 16	Chicago 0	at	Colorado 6
Fri. Apr. 18	Chicago 1	at	Colorado 3
Sun. Apr. 20	Colorado 3	at	Chicago 4 ot
Tue. Apr. 22	Colorado 3	at	Chicago 6
Thu. Apr. 24	Chicago 0	at	Colorado 7
Sat. Apr. 26	Colorado 6	at	Chicago 3

Colorado Won Series 4-2

Series 'F'
Wed. Apr. 16	Edmonton 3	at	Dallas 5
Fri. Apr. 18	Edmonton 4	at	Dallas 0
Sun. Apr. 20	Dallas 3	at	Edmonton 4 ot
Tue. Apr. 22	Dallas 4	at	Edmonton 3
Fri. Apr. 25	Edmonton 1	at	Dallas 0 ot
Sun. Apr. 27	Dallas 3	at	Edmonton 2
Tue. Apr. 29	Edmonton 4	at	Dallas 3 ot

Edmonton Won Series 4-3

Series 'G'
Wed. Apr. 16	St. Louis 2	at	Detroit 0
Fri. Apr. 18	St. Louis 1	at	Detroit 2
Sun. Apr. 20	Detroit 3	at	St. Louis 2
Tue. Apr. 22	Detroit 0	at	St. Louis 4
Fri. Apr. 25	St. Louis 2	at	Detroit 5
Sun. Apr. 27	Detroit 3	at	St. Louis 1

Detroit Won Series 4-2

Series 'H'
Wed. Apr. 16	Phoenix 2	at	Anaheim 4
Fri. Apr. 18	Phoenix 2	at	Anaheim 4
Sun. Apr. 20	Anaheim 1	at	Phoenix 4
Tue. Apr. 22	Anaheim 0	at	Phoenix 2
Thu. Apr. 24	Phoenix 5	at	Anaheim 2
Sun. Apr. 27	Anaheim 3	at	Phoenix 2 ot
Tue. Apr. 29	Phoenix 0	at	Anaheim 3

Anaheim Won Series 4-3

CONFERENCE SEMI-FINALS
(Best-of-seven series)

Eastern Conference

Series 'I'
Fri. May 2	NY Rangers 0	at	New Jersey 2
Sun. May 4	NY Rangers 2	at	New Jersey 0
Tue. May 6	New Jersey 2	at	NY Rangers 3
Thu. May 8	New Jersey 0	at	NY Rangers 3
Sun. May 11	NY Rangers 2	at	New Jersey 1 ot

NY Rangers Won Series 4-1

Series 'J'
Sat. May 3	Philadelphia 5	at	Buffalo 3
Mon. May 5	Philadelphia 2	at	Buffalo 1
Wed. May 7	Buffalo 1	at	Philadelphia 4
Fri. May 9	Buffalo 5	at	Philadelphia 4 ot
Sun. May 11	Philadelphia 6	at	Buffalo 3

Philadelphia Won Series 4-1

Western Conference

Series 'K'
Fri. May 2	Edmonton 1	at	Colorado 5
Sun. May 4	Edmonton 1	at	Colorado 4
Wed. May 7	Colorado 3	at	Edmonton 4
Fri. May 9	Colorado 3	at	Edmonton 2 ot
Sun. May 11	Edmonton 3	at	Colorado 4

Colorado Won Series 4-1

Series 'L'
Fri. May 2	Anaheim 1	at	Detroit 2 ot
Sun. May 4	Anaheim 2	at	Detroit 3 ot
Tue. May 6	Detroit 5	at	Anaheim 3
Thu. May 8	Detroit 3	at	Anaheim 2 ot

Detroit Won Series 4-0

CONFERENCE FINALS
(Best-of-seven series)

Eastern Conference

Series 'M'
Fri. May 16	NY Rangers 1	at	Philadelphia 3
Sun. May 18	NY Rangers 5	at	Philadelphia 4
Tue. May 20	Philadelphia 6	at	NY Rangers 3
Fri. May 23	Philadelphia 3	at	NY Rangers 2
Sun. May 25	NY Rangers 2	at	Philadelphia 4

Philadelphia Won Series 4-1

Western Conference

Series 'N'
Thu. May 15	Detroit 1	at	Colorado 2
Sat. May 17	Detroit 4	at	Colorado 2
Mon. May 19	Colorado 1	at	Detroit 2
Thu. May 22	Colorado 0	at	Detroit 6
Sat. May 24	Detroit 0	at	Colorado 6
Mon. May 26	Colorado 1	at	Detroit 3

Detroit Won Series 4-2

STANLEY CUP CHAMPIONSHIP
(Best-of-seven series)

Series 'O'
Sat. May 31	Detroit 4	at	Philadelphia 2
Tue. Jun. 3	Detroit 4	at	Philadelphia 2
Thu. Jun. 5	Philadelphia 1	at	Detroit 6
Sat. Jun. 7	Philadelphia 1	at	Detroit 2

Detroit Won Series 4-0

Team Playoff Records

	GP	W	L	GF	GA	%
Detroit	20	16	4	58	38	.800
Philadelphia	19	12	7	67	55	.632
Colorado	17	10	7	59	41	.588
NY Rangers	15	9	6	36	35	.600
New Jersey	10	5	5	27	21	.500
Edmonton	12	5	7	32	37	.417
Buffalo	12	5	7	27	34	.417
Anaheim	11	4	7	25	30	.364
Phoenix	7	3	4	17	17	.429
Ottawa	7	3	4	13	14	.429
Dallas	7	3	4	18	21	.429
St. Louis	6	2	4	12	13	.333
Chicago	6	2	4	14	28	.333
Florida	5	1	4	10	13	.200
Pittsburgh	5	1	4	13	20	.200
Montreal	5	1	4	11	22	.200

Individual Leaders

Abbreviations: * – rookie eligible for Calder Trophy; **A** – assists; **G** – goals; **GP** – Games Played; **OT** – overtime goals; **GW** – game-winning goals; **PIM** – penalties in minutes; **PP** – power play goals; **Pts** – points; **S** – shots on goal; **SH** – short-handed goals; **%** – percentage shots resulting in goals; **+/–** – difference between Goals For (**GF**) scored when a player is on the ice with his team at even strength or short-handed and Goals Against (**GA**) scored when the same player is on the ice with his team at even strength or on a power play.

Playoff Scoring Leaders

Player	Team	GP	G	A	Pts	+/–	PIM	PP	SH	GW	OT	S	%
Eric Lindros	Philadelphia	19	12	14	26	7	40	4	0	1	0	71	16.9
Joe Sakic	Colorado	17	8	17	25	5	14	3	0	0	0	50	16.0
Claude Lemieux	Colorado	17	13	10	23	7	32	4	0	4	0	73	17.8
Valeri Kamensky	Colorado	17	8	14	22	–1	16	5	0	2	0	49	16.3
Rod Brind'Amour	Philadelphia	19	13	8	21	9	10	4	2	1	0	65	20.0
John LeClair	Philadelphia	19	9	12	21	5	10	4	0	3	0	79	11.4
Wayne Gretzky	NY Rangers	15	10	10	20	5	2	3	0	2	0	44	22.7
Sergei Fedorov	Detroit	20	8	12	20	5	12	3	0	4	0	79	10.1
Brendan Shanahan	Detroit	20	9	8	17	8	43	2	0	2	1	82	11.0
Peter Forsberg	Colorado	14	5	12	17	–6	10	3	0	0	0	35	14.3
Sandis Ozolinsh	Colorado	17	4	13	17	–1	24	2	0	1	0	39	10.3
Vyacheslav Kozlov	Detroit	20	8	5	13	3	14	4	0	2	1	58	13.8
Paul Kariya	Anaheim	11	7	6	13	–2	4	4	0	1	1	61	11.5
Steve Yzerman	Detroit	20	7	6	13	3	4	3	0	2	0	65	10.8
*Janne Niinimaa	Philadelphia	19	1	12	13	3	16	1	0	1	0	56	1.8
Esa Tikkanen	NY Rangers	15	9	3	12	2	26	3	1	3	2	45	20.0
Igor Larionov	Detroit	20	4	8	12	8	8	3	0	1	0	29	13.8
Martin Lapointe	Detroit	20	4	8	12	8	60	1	0	1	1	37	10.8
Mark Messier	NY Rangers	15	3	9	12	2	6	0	0	1	0	43	7.0
Mikael Renberg	Philadelphia	18	5	6	11	1	4	2	0	0	0	35	14.3
Luc Robitaille	NY Rangers	15	4	7	11	7	4	0	0	0	0	43	9.3
Doug Weight	Edmonton	12	3	8	11	0	8	0	0	0	0	54	5.6
Larry Murphy	Detroit	20	2	9	11	16	8	1	0	1	0	51	3.9
Dmitri Mironov	Anaheim	11	1	10	11	0	10	1	0	0	0	36	2.8

Playoff Defensemen Scoring Leaders

Player	Team	GP	G	A	Pts	+/–	PIM	PP	SH	GW	OT	S	%
Sandis Ozolinsh	Colorado	17	4	13	17	–1	24	2	0	1	0	39	10.3
*Janne Niinimaa	Philadelphia	19	1	12	13	3	16	1	0	1	0	56	1.8
Larry Murphy	Detroit	20	2	9	11	16	8	1	0	1	0	51	3.9
Dmitri Mironov	Anaheim	11	1	10	11	0	10	1	0	0	0	36	2.8
Boris Mironov	Edmonton	12	2	8	10	–6	16	2	0	0	0	31	6.5
Brian Leetch	NY Rangers	15	2	8	10	5	6	1	0	1	0	56	3.6
Eric Desjardins	Philadelphia	19	2	8	10	9	12	0	0	0	0	49	4.1
J.J. Daigneault	Anaheim	11	2	7	9	–6	16	1	0	1	0	24	8.3
Paul Coffey	Philadelphia	17	1	8	9	–3	6	0	0	0	0	37	2.7
Nicklas Lidstrom	Detroit	20	2	6	8	12	2	0	0	0	0	79	2.5
Shawn Chambers	New Jersey	10	1	6	7	–2	6	1	0	0	0	17	5.9
Chris Therien	Philadelphia	19	1	6	7	14	6	0	0	1	0	36	2.8

GOALTENDING LEADERS

Goals Against Average

Goaltender	Team	GPI	Mins.	GA	Avg.
Martin Brodeur	New Jersey	10	659	19	1.73
Mike Vernon	Detroit	20	1229	36	1.76
Guy Hebert	Anaheim	9	534	18	2.02
Mike Richter	NY Rangers	15	939	33	2.11
Patrick Roy	Colorado	17	1034	38	2.21

Wins

Goaltender	Team	GPI	Mins.	W	L
Mike Vernon	Detroit	20	1229	16	4
Patrick Roy	Colorado	17	1034	10	7
Mike Richter	NY Rangers	15	939	9	6
Garth Snow	Philadelphia	12	699	8	4
Martin Brodeur	New Jersey	10	659	5	5
Curtis Joseph	Edmonton	12	767	5	7

Save Percentage

Goaltender	Team	GPI	Mins.	GA	SA	S%	W	L
Patrick Roy	Colorado	17	1034	38	559	.932	10	7
Mike Richter	NY Rangers	15	939	33	488	.932	9	6
Martin Brodeur	New Jersey	10	659	19	268	.929	5	5
Guy Hebert	Anaheim	9	534	18	255	.929	4	4
Mike Vernon	Detroit	20	1229	36	494	.927	16	4

Shutouts

Goaltender	Team	GPI	Mins.	SO
Mike Richter	NY Rangers	15	939	3
Patrick Roy	Colorado	17	1034	3
Grant Fuhr	St. Louis	6	357	2
Martin Brodeur	New Jersey	10	659	2
Curtis Joseph	Edmonton	12	767	2

Goal Scoring

Name	Team	GP	G
Claude Lemieux	Colorado	17	13
Rod Brind'Amour	Philadelphia	19	13
Eric Lindros	Philadelphia	19	12
Wayne Gretzky	NY Rangers	15	10
Esa Tikkanen	NY Rangers	15	9
John LeClair	Philadelphia	19	9
Brendan Shanahan	Detroit	20	9
Joe Sakic	Colorado	17	8
Valeri Kamensky	Colorado	17	8
Sergei Fedorov	Detroit	20	8
Vyacheslav Kozlov	Detroit	20	8

Assists

Name	Team	GP	A
Joe Sakic	Colorado	17	17
Valeri Kamensky	Colorado	17	14
Eric Lindros	Philadelphia	19	14
Sandis Ozolinsh	Colorado	17	13
Peter Forsberg	Colorado	14	12
John LeClair	Philadelphia	19	12
*Janne Niinimaa	Philadelphia	19	12
Sergei Fedorov	Detroit	20	12
Dmitri Mironov	Anaheim	11	10
Wayne Gretzky	NY Rangers	15	10
Claude Lemieux	Colorado	17	10

Power-play Goals

Name	Team	GP	PP
Valeri Kamensky	Colorado	17	5
Paul Kariya	Anaheim	11	4
Claude Lemieux	Colorado	17	4
Rod Brind'Amour	Philadelphia	19	4
John LeClair	Philadelphia	19	4
Eric Lindros	Philadelphia	19	4
Vyacheslav Kozlov	Detroit	20	4

Game-winning Goals

Name	Team	GP	GW
Claude Lemieux	Colorado	17	4
Sergei Fedorov	Detroit	20	4
Esa Tikkanen	NY Rangers	15	3
John LeClair	Philadelphia	19	3

Short-handed Goals

Name	Team	GP	SH
Todd Marchant	Edmonton	12	3
Tony Amonte	Chicago	6	2
Brian Rolston	New Jersey	10	2
Rod Brind'Amour	Philadelphia	19	2

Overtime Goals

Name	Team	GP	OT
Esa Tikkanen	NY Rangers	15	2
Patrice Brisebois	Montreal	3	1
Ed Ronan	Buffalo	6	1
Sergei Krivokrasov	Chicago	6	1
Daniel Alfredsson	Ottawa	7	1
Paul Kariya	Anaheim	11	1
Kelly Buchberger	Edmonton	12	1
Derek Plante	Buffalo	12	1
Todd Marchant	Edmonton	12	1
Ryan Smyth	Edmonton	12	1
Adam Graves	NY Rangers	15	1
Claude Lemieux	Colorado	17	1
Brendan Shanahan	Detroit	20	1
Vyacheslav Kozlov	Detroit	20	1
Martin Lapointe	Detroit	20	1

Shots

Name	Team	GP	S
Brendan Shanahan	Detroit	20	82
John LeClair	Philadelphia	19	79
Sergei Fedorov	Detroit	20	79
Nicklas Lidstrom	Detroit	20	79

Plus/Minus

Name	Team	GP	+/–
Larry Murphy	Detroit	20	16
Chris Therien	Philadelphia	19	14
Nicklas Lidstrom	Detroit	20	12

Team Statistics

TEAMS' HOME-AND-ROAD RECORD

				Home						Road		
	GP	W	L	GF	GA	%	GP	W	L	GF	GA	%
DET	10	9	1	31	12	.900	10	7	3	27	26	.700
PHI	10	6	4	37	28	.600	9	6	3	30	27	.667
COL	9	8	1	39	11	.889	8	2	6	20	30	.250
NYR	6	4	2	18	16	.667	9	5	4	18	19	.556
N.J.	6	4	2	16	7	.667	4	1	3	11	14	.250
EDM	5	2	3	15	16	.400	7	3	4	17	21	.429
BUF	7	2	5	15	23	.286	5	3	2	12	11	.600
ANA	6	3	3	18	17	.500	5	1	4	7	13	.200
PHO	3	2	1	8	4	.667	4	1	3	9	13	.250
OTT	3	1	2	3	6	.333	4	2	2	10	8	.500
DAL	4	1	3	8	12	.250	3	2	1	10	9	.667
ST.L.	3	1	2	7	6	.333	3	1	2	5	7	.333
CHI	3	2	1	13	12	.667	3	0	3	1	16	.000
FLA	3	1	2	5	6	.333	2	0	2	5	7	.000
PIT	2	1	1	7	6	.500	3	0	3	6	14	.000
MTL	2	1	1	8	9	.500	3	0	3	3	13	.000
Total	**82**	**48**	**34**	**248**	**191**	**.585**	**82**	**34**	**48**	**191**	**248**	**.415**

TEAM PENALTIES

Abbreviations: GP – games played; **PEN** – total penalty minutes, including bench penalties; **BMI** – total bench penalty minutes; **AVG** – average penalty minutes per game.

Team	GP	PEN	BMI	AVG
FLA	5	50	0	10.0
PHI	19	245	4	12.9
OTT	7	91	2	13.0
PIT	5	68	0	13.6
NYR	15	218	2	14.5
ANA	11	163	2	14.8
PHO	7	111	2	15.9
EDM	12	204	0	17.0
N.J.	10	186	0	18.6
BUF	12	226	6	18.8
DAL	7	136	0	19.4
MTL	5	105	0	21.0
DET	20	437	6	21.9
COL	17	380	6	22.4
CHI	6	160	0	26.7
ST.L.	6	198	0	33.0
Total	**82**	**2978**	**30**	**36.3**

TEAMS' POWER-PLAY RECORD

Abbreviations: Adv-total advantages; **PPGF**-power play goals for; **%** arrived by dividing number of power-play goals by total advantages.

		Home					Road					Overall		
	Team	GP	ADV	PPGF	%	Team	GP	ADV	PPGF	%	Team	GP	ADV	PPGF	%
1	ANA	6	19	7	36.8	FLA	2	8	3	37.5	ANA	11	39	10	25.6
2	N.J.	6	32	8	25.0	OTT	4	18	5	27.8	FLA	5	25	6	24.0
3	COL	9	53	13	24.5	COL	8	42	8	19.0	COL	17	95	21	22.1
4	PHI	10	50	12	24.0	NYR	9	32	6	18.8	N.J.	10	50	11	22.0
5	PIT	2	9	2	22.2	N.J.	4	18	3	16.7	OTT	7	35	7	20.0
6	FLA	3	17	3	17.6	PHO	4	12	2	16.7	PHI	19	94	18	19.1
7	BUF	7	29	5	17.2	DET	10	56	9	16.1	PIT	5	23	4	17.4
8	ST.L.	3	14	2	14.3	EDM	7	25	4	16.0	NYR	15	64	10	15.6
9	EDM	5	30	4	13.3	ANA	5	20	3	15.0	BUF	12	53	8	15.1
10	DET	10	61	8	13.1	PIT	3	14	2	14.3	EDM	12	55	8	14.5
11	NYR	6	32	4	12.5	PHI	9	44	6	13.6	DET	20	117	17	14.5
12	OTT	3	17	2	11.8	ST.L.	3	23	3	13.0	ST.L.	6	37	5	13.5
13	CHI	3	10	1	10.0	BUF	5	24	3	12.5	PHO	7	26	3	11.5
14	PHO	3	14	1	7.1	DAL	3	18	2	11.1	DAL	7	40	3	7.5
15	DAL	4	22	1	4.5	MTL	3	11	0	.0	CHI	6	27	1	3.7
16	MTL	2	5	0	.0	CHI	3	17	0	.0	MTL	5	16	0	.0
	Total	**82**	**414**	**73**	**17.6**		**82**	**382**	**59**	**15.4**		**82**	**796**	**132**	**16.6**

TEAMS' PENALTY KILLING RECORD

Abbreviations: TSH – Total times short-handed; **PPGA** – power-play goals against; **%** arrived by dividing times short minus power-play goals against by times short.

		Home					Road					Overall		
	Team	GP	TSH	PPGA	%	Team	GP	TSH	PPGA	%	Team	GP	TSH	PPGA	%
1	OTT	3	12	0	100.0	ANA	5	24	2	91.7	OTT	7	27	2	92.6
2	N.J.	6	20	1	95.0	COL	8	41	4	90.2	N.J.	10	37	3	91.9
3	COL	9	45	3	93.3	ST.L.	3	20	2	90.0	COL	17	86	7	91.9
4	FLA	3	13	1	92.3	N.J.	4	17	2	88.2	FLA	5	21	2	90.5
5	DET	10	53	6	88.7	FLA	2	8	1	87.5	ANA	11	45	6	86.7
6	PHO	3	15	2	86.7	PIT	3	16	2	87.5	PIT	5	29	4	86.2
7	PIT	2	13	2	84.6	OTT	4	15	2	86.7	ST.L.	6	42	6	85.7
8	ST.L.	3	22	4	81.8	EDM	7	35	5	85.7	DET	20	96	15	84.4
9	ANA	6	21	4	81.0	DAL	3	20	3	85.0	EDM	12	61	10	83.6
10	EDM	5	26	5	80.8	BUF	5	32	5	84.4	DAL	7	34	6	82.4
11	NYR	6	26	5	80.8	PHI	9	45	9	80.0	BUF	12	60	11	81.7
12	CHI	3	19	4	78.9	DET	10	43	9	79.1	NYR	15	68	14	79.4
13	DAL	4	14	3	78.6	NYR	9	42	9	78.6	PHI	19	89	19	78.7
14	BUF	7	28	6	78.6	CHI	3	26	8	69.2	PHO	7	28	6	78.6
15	PHI	10	44	10	77.3	PHO	4	13	4	69.2	CHI	6	45	12	73.3
16	MTL	2	11	3	72.7	MTL	3	17	6	64.7	MTL	5	28	9	67.9
	Total	**82**	**382**	**59**	**84.6**		**82**	**414**	**73**	**82.4**		**82**	**796**	**132**	**83.4**

SHORT-HANDED GOALS

	For			Against	
Team	Games	Goals	Team	Games	Goals
N.J.	10	3	DET	20	0
EDM	12	3	BUF	12	0
PHI	19	3	ANA	11	0
MTL	5	2	PHO	7	0
PIT	5	2	CHI	6	0
CHI	6	2	FLA	5	0
BUF	12	2	NYR	15	1
DET	20	2	EDM	12	1
DAL	7	1	OTT	7	1
NYR	15	1	DAL	7	1
FLA	5	0	ST.L.	6	1
ST.L.	6	0	N.J.	10	2
OTT	7	0	PIT	5	2
PHO	7	0	MTL	5	3
ANA	11	0	COL	17	4
COL	17	0	PHI	19	5
Total	**82**	**21**	**Total**	**82**	**21**

Steve Yzerman instructs the Motown faithful to keep their "eyes-on-the-prize" as he parades the Stanley Cup through the streets of downtown Detroit.

Stanley Cup Record Book

History: The Stanley Cup, the oldest trophy competed for by professional athletes in North America, was donated by Frederick Arthur, Lord Stanley of Preston and son of the Earl of Derby, in 1893. Lord Stanley purchased the trophy for 10 guineas ($50 at that time) for presentation to the amateur hockey champions of Canada. Since 1910, when the National Hockey Association took possession of the Stanley Cup, the trophy has been the symbol of professional hockey supremacy. It has been competed for only by NHL teams since 1926 and has been under the exclusive control of the NHL since 1946.

Stanley Cup Standings

1918-97
(ranked by Cup wins)

Teams	Cup Wins	Yrs.	Series	Wins	Losses	Games Wins	Losses	Ties	Goals For	Goals Against	Winning %
Montreal	23[1]	71	132[2]	84	47	628 377	243	8	1949	1559	.607
Toronto	13	58	96	51	45	444 210	230	4	1166	1230	.477
Detroit	8	46	83	45	38	408 206	201	1	1137	1091	.506
Boston	5	57	98	46	52	476 228	242	6	1405	1422	.485
Edmonton	5	14	39	30	9	192 125	67	0	802	616	.651
NY Rangers	4	48	86	42	44	386 183	195	8	1091	1114	.484
NY Islanders	4	17	43	30	13	218 128	90	0	748	650	.587
Chicago	3	52	89	40	49	406 187	214	5	1171	1298	.467
Philadelphia	2	23	52	31	21	269 144	125	0	869	814	.535
Pittsburgh	2	17	31	16	15	160 86	74	0	525	520	.538
Calgary[3]	1	21	32	12	20	156 69	87	0	529	573	.442
Colorado[4]	1	11	22	12	10	119 61	58	0	386	378	.513
New Jersey[5]	1	9	17	9	8	97 52	45	0	293	274	.536
St. Louis	0	27	45	18	27	236 105	131	0	681	777	.445
Buffalo	0	21	32	11	21	155 67	88	0	475	514	.432
Dallas[6]	0	20	35	15	20	187 89	98	0	609	645	.476
Los Angeles	0	19	29	10	19	142 55	87	0	459	568	.387
Vancouver	0	16	25	9	16	124 54	70	0	377	422	.435
Washington	0	14	21	7	14	116 52	64	0	381	389	.448
Phoenix[7]	0	12	14	2	12	69 22	47	0	194	270	.319
Carolina[8]	0	8	9	1	8	49 18	31	0	143	177	.367
Florida	0	2	5	3	2	27 13	14	0	71	70	.481
San Jose	0	2	4	2	2	25 11	14	0	74	112	.440
Anaheim	0	1	2	1	1	11 4	7	0	25	30	.364
Ottawa	0	1	1	0	1	7 3	4	0	13	14	.429
Tampa Bay	0	1	1	0	1	6 2	4	0	13	26	.333

[1] Montreal also won the Stanley Cup in 1916.
[2] 1919 final incomplete due to influenza epidemic.
[3] Includes totals of Atlanta 1972-80.
[4] Includes totals of Quebec 1979-95.
[5] Includes totals of Colorado Rockies 1976-82.
[6] Includes totals of Minnesota 1967-93.
[7] Includes totals of Winnipeg 1979-96.
[8] Includes totals of Hartford 1979-97.

Stanley Cup Winners Prior to Formation of NHL in 1917

Season	Champions	Manager	Coach
1916-17	Seattle Metropolitans	Pete Muldoon	Pete Muldoon
1915-16	Montreal Canadiens	George Kennedy	George Kennedy
1914-15	Vancouver Millionaires	Frank Patrick	Frank Patrick
1913-14	Toronto Blueshirts	Jack Marshall	Scotty Davidson*
1912-13**	Quebec Bulldogs	M.J. Quinn	Joe Malone*
1911-12	Quebec Bulldogs	M.J. Quinn	C. Nolan
1910-11	Ottawa Senators		Bruce Stuart*
1909-10	Montreal Wanderers	R. R. Boon	Pud Glass*
1908-09	Ottawa Senators		Bruce Stuart*
1907-08	Montreal Wanderers	R. R. Boon	Cecil Blachford
1906-07	Montreal Wanderers (March)	R. R. Boon	Cecil Blachford
1906-07	Kenora Thistles (January)	F.A. Hudson	Tommy Phillips*
1905-06	Montreal Wanderers		Cecil Blachford*
1904-05	Ottawa Silver Seven		A. T. Smith
1903-04	Ottawa Silver Seven		A. T. Smith
1902-03	Ottawa Silver Seven		A. T. Smith
1901-02	Montreal A.A.A.		C. McKerrow
1900-01	Winnipeg Victorias		D. H. Bain
1899-1900	Montreal Shamrocks		H.J. Trihey*
1898-99	Montreal Shamrocks		H.J. Trihey*
1897-98	Montreal Victorias		F. Richardson
1896-97	Montreal Victorias		Mike Grant*
1895-96	Montreal Victorias (December, 1896)		Mike Grant*
1895-96	Winnipeg Victorias (February)		J.C. G. Armytage
1894-95	Montreal Victorias		Mike Grant*
1893-94	Montreal A.A.A.		
1892-93	Montreal A.A.A.		

** Victoria defeated Quebec in challenge series. No official recognition.
* In the early years the teams were frequently run by the Captain. *Indicates Captain

Stanley Cup Winners

Year	W&L in Finals	Winner	Coach	Finalist	Coach
1997	4-0	Detroit	Scotty Bowman	Philadelphia	Terry Murray
1996	4-0	Colorado	Marc Crawford	Florida	Doug MacLean
1995	4-0	New Jersey	Jacques Lemaire	Detroit	Scotty Bowman
1994	4-3	NY Rangers	Mike Keenan	Vancouver	Pat Quinn
1993	4-1	Montreal	Jacques Demers	Los Angeles	Barry Melrose
1992	4-0	Pittsburgh	Scotty Bowman	Chicago	Mike Keenan
1991	4-2	Pittsburgh	Bob Johnson	Minnesota	Bob Gainey
1990	4-1	Edmonton	John Muckler	Boston	Mike Milbury
1989	4-2	Calgary	Terry Crisp	Montreal	Pat Burns
1988	4-0	Edmonton	Glen Sather	Boston	Terry O'Reilly
1987	4-3	Edmonton	Glen Sather	Philadelphia	Mike Keenan
1986	4-1	Montreal	Jean Perron	Calgary	Bob Johnson
1985	4-1	Edmonton	Glen Sather	Philadelphia	Mike Keenan
1984	4-1	Edmonton	Glen Sather	NY Islanders	Al Arbour
1983	4-0	NY Islanders	Al Arbour	Edmonton	Glen Sather
1982	4-0	NY Islanders	Al Arbour	Vancouver	Roger Neilson
1981	4-1	NY Islanders	Al Arbour	Minnesota	Glen Sonmor
1980	4-2	NY Islanders	Al Arbour	Philadelphia	Pat Quinn
1979	4-1	Montreal	Scotty Bowman	NY Rangers	Fred Shero
1978	4-2	Montreal	Scotty Bowman	Boston	Don Cherry
1977	4-0	Montreal	Scotty Bowman	Boston	Don Cherry
1976	4-0	Montreal	Scotty Bowman	Philadelphia	Fred Shero
1975	4-2	Philadelphia	Fred Shero	Buffalo	Floyd Smith
1974	4-2	Philadelphia	Fred Shero	Boston	Bep Guidolin
1973	4-2	Montreal	Scotty Bowman	Chicago	Billy Reay
1972	4-2	Boston	Tom Johnson	NY Rangers	Emile Francis
1971	4-3	Montreal	Al MacNeil	Chicago	Billy Reay
1970	4-0	Boston	Harry Sinden	St. Louis	Scotty Bowman
1969	4-0	Montreal	Claude Ruel	St. Louis	Scotty Bowman
1968	4-0	Montreal	Toe Blake	St. Louis	Scotty Bowman
1967	4-2	Toronto	Punch Imlach	Montreal	Toe Blake
1966	4-2	Montreal	Toe Blake	Detroit	Sid Abel
1965	4-3	Montreal	Toe Blake	Chicago	Billy Reay
1964	4-3	Toronto	Punch Imlach	Detroit	Sid Abel
1963	4-1	Toronto	Punch Imlach	Detroit	Sid Abel
1962	4-2	Toronto	Punch Imlach	Chicago	Rudy Pilous
1961	4-2	Chicago	Rudy Pilous	Detroit	Sid Abel
1960	4-0	Montreal	Toe Blake	Toronto	Punch Imlach
1959	4-1	Montreal	Toe Blake	Toronto	Punch Imlach
1958	4-2	Montreal	Toe Blake	Boston	Milt Schmidt
1957	4-1	Montreal	Toe Blake	Boston	Milt Schmidt
1956	4-1	Montreal	Toe Blake	Detroit	Jimmy Skinner
1955	4-3	Detroit	Jimmy Skinner	Montreal	Dick Irvin
1954	4-3	Detroit	Tommy Ivan	Montreal	Dick Irvin
1953	4-1	Montreal	Dick Irvin	Boston	Lynn Patrick
1952	4-0	Detroit	Tommy Ivan	Montreal	Dick Irvin
1951	4-1	Toronto	Joe Primeau	Montreal	Dick Irvin
1950	4-3	Detroit	Tommy Ivan	NY Rangers	Lynn Patrick
1949	4-0	Toronto	Hap Day	Detroit	Tommy Ivan
1948	4-0	Toronto	Hap Day	Detroit	Tommy Ivan
1947	4-2	Toronto	Hap Day	Montreal	Dick Irvin
1946	4-1	Montreal	Dick Irvin	Boston	Dit Clapper
1945	4-3	Toronto	Hap Day	Detroit	Jack Adams
1944	4-0	Montreal	Dick Irvin	Chicago	Paul Thompson
1943	4-0	Detroit	Jack Adams	Boston	Art Ross
1942	4-3	Toronto	Hap Day	Detroit	Jack Adams
1941	4-0	Boston	Cooney Weiland	Detroit	Ebbie Goodfellow
1940	4-2	NY Rangers	Frank Boucher	Toronto	Dick Irvin
1939	4-1	Boston	Art Ross	Toronto	Dick Irvin
1938	3-1	Chicago	Bill Stewart	Toronto	Dick Irvin
1937	3-2	Detroit	Jack Adams	NY Rangers	Lester Patrick
1936	3-1	Detroit	Jack Adams	Toronto	Dick Irvin
1935	3-0	Mtl. Maroons	Tommy Gorman	Toronto	Dick Irvin
1934	3-1	Chicago	Tommy Gorman	Detroit	Herbie Lewis
1933	3-1	NY Rangers	Lester Patrick	Toronto	Dick Irvin
1932	3-0	Toronto	Dick Irvin	NY Rangers	Lester Patrick
1931	3-2	Montreal	Cecil Hart	Chicago	Dick Irvin
1930	2-0	Montreal	Cecil Hart	Boston	Art Ross
1929	2-0	Boston	Cy Denneny	NY Rangers	Lester Patrick
1928	3-2	NY Rangers	Lester Patrick	Mtl. Maroons	Eddie Gerard
1927	2-0-2	Ottawa	Dave Gill	Boston	Art Ross
	The National Hockey League assumed control of Stanley Cup competition after 1926				
1926	3-1	Mtl. Maroons	Eddie Gerard	Victoria	Lester Patrick
1925	3-1	Victoria	Lester Patrick	Montreal	Leo Dandurand
1924	2-0	Montreal	Leo Dandurand	Cgy. Tigers	—
	2-0			Van. Maroons	—
1923	2-0	Ottawa	Pete Green	Edm. Eskimos	—
	3-1			Van. Maroons	—
1922	3-2	Tor. St. Pats	Eddie Powers	Van. Millionaires	Frank Patrick
1921	3-2	Ottawa	Pete Green	Van. Millionaires	Frank Patrick
1920	3-2	Ottawa	Pete Green	Seattle	—
1919	2-2-1	No decision - series between Montreal and Seattle cancelled due to influenza epidemic			
1918	3-2	Tor. Arenas	Dick Carroll	Van. Millionaires	Frank Patrick

Championship Trophies

PRINCE OF WALES TROPHY

Beginning with the 1993-94 season, the club which advances to the Stanley Cup Finals as the winner of the Eastern Conference Championship is presented with the Prince of Wales Trophy.

History: His Royal Highness, the Prince of Wales, donated the trophy to the National Hockey League in 1924. From 1927-28 through 1937-38, the award was presented to the team finishing first in the American Division of the NHL. From 1938-39, when the NHL reverted to one section, to 1966-67, it was presented to the team winning the NHL regular season championship. With expansion in 1967-68, it again became a divisional trophy, awarded to the regular season champions of the East Division through to the end of the 1973-74 season. Beginning in 1974-75, it was awarded to the regular-season winner of the conference bearing the name of the trophy. From 1981-82 to 1992-93 the trophy was presented to the playoff champion in the Wales Conference. Since 1993-94, the trophy has been presented to the playoff champion in the Eastern Conference.

1996-97 Winner: Philadelphia Flyers

The Philadelphia Flyers won their first Prince of Wales Trophy since 1987 on May 25, 1997 after defeating the New York Rangers 4-2 in game five of the Eastern Conference Championship series. Before defeating the Rangers, the Flyers had series wins over the Pittsburgh Penguins and Buffalo Sabres.

PRINCE OF WALES TROPHY WINNERS

1996-97	**Philadelphia Flyers**	1959-60	Montreal Canadiens
1995-96	Florida Panthers	1958-59	Montreal Canadiens
1994-95	New Jersey Devils	1957-58	Montreal Canadiens
1993-94	New York Rangers	1956-57	Detroit Red Wings
1992-93	Montreal Canadiens	1955-56	Montreal Canadiens
1991-92	Pittsburgh Penguins	1954-55	Detroit Red Wings
1990-91	Pittsburgh Penguins	1953-54	Detroit Red Wings
1989-90	Boston Bruins	1952-53	Detroit Red Wings
1988-89	Montreal Canadiens	1951-52	Detroit Red Wings
1987-88	Boston Bruins	1950-51	Detroit Red Wings
1986-87	Philadelphia Flyers	1949-50	Detroit Red Wings
1985-86	Montreal Canadiens	1948-49	Detroit Red Wings
1984-85	Philadelphia Flyers	1947-48	Toronto Maple Leafs
1983-84	New York Islanders	1946-47	Montreal Canadiens
1982-83	New York Islanders	1945-46	Montreal Canadiens
1981-82	New York Islanders	1944-45	Montreal Canadiens
1980-81	Montreal Canadiens	1943-44	Montreal Canadiens
1979-80	Buffalo Sabres	1942-43	Detroit Red Wings
1978-79	Montreal Canadiens	1941-42	New York Rangers
1977-78	Montreal Canadiens	1940-41	Boston Bruins
1976-77	Montreal Canadiens	1939-40	Boston Bruins
1975-76	Montreal Canadiens	1938-39	Boston Bruins
1974-75	Buffalo Sabres	1937-38	Boston Bruins
1973-74	Boston Bruins	1936-37	Detroit Red Wings
1972-73	Montreal Canadiens	1935-36	Detroit Red Wings
1971-72	Boston Bruins	1934-35	Boston Bruins
1970-71	Boston Bruins	1933-34	Detroit Red Wings
1969-70	Chicago Blackhawks	1932-33	Boston Bruins
1968-69	Montreal Canadiens	1931-32	New York Rangers
1967-68	Montreal Canadiens	1930-31	Boston Bruins
1966-67	Chicago Blackhawks	1929-30	Boston Bruins
1965-66	Montreal Canadiens	1928-29	Boston Bruins
1964-65	Detroit Red Wings	1927-28	Boston Bruins
1963-64	Montreal Canadiens	1926-27	Ottawa Senators
1962-63	Toronto Maple Leafs	1925-26	Montreal Maroons
1961-62	Montreal Canadiens	1924-25	Montreal Canadiens
1960-61	Montreal Canadiens	1923-24	Montreal Canadiens

CLARENCE S. CAMPBELL BOWL

Beginning with the 1993-94 season, the club which advances to the Stanley Cup Finals as the winner of the Western Conference Championship is presented with the Clarence S. Campbell Bowl.

History: Presented by the member clubs in 1968 for perpetual competition by the National Hockey League in recognition of the services of Clarence S. Campbell, President of the NHL from 1946 to 1977. From 1967-68 through 1973-74, the trophy was awarded to the regular season champions of the West Division. Beginning in 1974-75, it was awarded to the regular-season winner of the conference bearing the name of the trophy. From 1981-82 to 1992-93 the trophy was presented to the playoff champion in the Campbell Conference. Since 1993-94, the trophy has been presented to the playoff champion in the Western Conference. The trophy itself is a hallmark piece made of sterling silver and was crafted by a British silversmith in 1878.

1996-97 Winner: Detroit Red Wings

The Detroit Red Wings won their second Clarence S. Campbell Bowl in three seasons on May 26, 1997 after defeating the Colorado Avalanche 3-1 in game six of the Western Conference Championship series. Previous series wins had come over the St. Louis Blues and Anaheim Mighty Ducks.

CLARENCE S. CAMPBELL BOWL WINNERS

1996-97	**Detroit Red Wings**	1981-82	Vancouver Canucks
1995-96	Colorado Avalanche	1980-81	New York Islanders
1994-95	Detroit Red Wings	1979-80	Philadelphia Flyers
1993-94	Vancouver Canucks	1978-79	New York Islanders
1992-93	Los Angeles Kings	1977-78	New York Islanders
1991-92	Chicago Blackhawks	1976-77	Philadelphia Flyers
1990-91	Minnesota North Stars	1975-76	Philadelphia Flyers
1989-90	Edmonton Oilers	1974-75	Philadelphia Flyers
1988-89	Calgary Flames	1973-74	Philadelphia Flyers
1987-88	Edmonton Oilers	1972-73	Chicago Blackhawks
1986-87	Edmonton Oilers	1971-72	Chicago Blackhawks
1985-86	Calgary Flames	1970-71	Chicago Blackhawks
1984-85	Edmonton Oilers	1969-70	St. Louis Blues
1983-84	Edmonton Oilers	1968-69	St. Louis Blues
1982-83	Edmonton Oilers	1967-68	Philadelphia Flyers

Prince of Wales Trophy

Clarence S. Campbell Bowl

Stanley Cup

Stanley Cup Winners:

Rosters and Final Series Scores

1996-97 — Detroit Red Wings — Steve Yzerman (Captain), Doug Brown, Mathieu Dandenault, Kris Draper, Sergei Fedorov, Viacheslav Fetisov, Kevin Hodson, Tomas Holmstrom, Joe Kocur, Vladimir Konstantinov, Vyacheslav Kozlov, Martin Lapointe, Igor Larionov, Nicklas Lidstrom, Kirk Maltby, Darren McCarty, Larry Murphy, Chris Osgood, Jamie Pushor, Bob Rouse, Tomas Sandstrom, Brendan Shanahan, Tim Taylor, Mike Vernon, Aaron Ward, Mike Ilitch (Owner/Chairman), Marian Ilitch (Owner), Atanas Ilitch (Vice President), Christopher Ilitch (Vice President), Denise Ilitch Lites, Ronald Ilitch, Michael Ilitch, Jr., Lisa Ilitch Murray, Carole Ilitch Trepeck, Jim Devellano (Senior Vice President), Scotty Bowman (Head Coach/Director of Player Personnel), Ken Holland (Assistant General Manager), Barry Smith (Associate Coach), Dave Lewis (Associate Coach), Mike Krushelnyski (Assistant Coach). Jim Nill (Director of Player Development), Dan Belisle (Pro Scout), Mark Howe (Pro Scout), Hakan Andersson (Director of European Scouting), John Wharton (Athletic Trainer), Paul Boyer (Equipment Manager) Tim Abbott (Assistant Equipment Manager), Sergei Mnatsakanov (Masseur).
Scores: May 31 at Philadelphia — Detroit 4, Philadelphia 2; June 3 at Philadelphia — Detroit 4, Philadelphia 2; June 5 at Detroit — Detroit 6, Philadelphia 1; June 7 at Detroit — Detroit 2, Philadelphia 1.

1995-96 — Colorado Avalanche — Joe Sakic (Captain), Rene Corbet, Adam Deadmarsh, Stephane Fiset, Adam Foote, Peter Forsberg, Alexei Gusarov, Dave Hannan, Valeri Kamensky, Mike Keane, Jon Klemm, Uwe Krupp, Sylvain Lefebvre, Claude Lemieux, Curtis Leschyshyn, Troy Murray, Sandis Ozolinsh, Mike Ricci, Patrick Roy, Warren Rychel, Chris Simon, Craig Wolanin, Stephane Yelle, Scott Young, Charlie Lyons (Chairman, CEO), Pierre Lacroix (Exec. V.P., G.M.), Marc Crawford (Head Coach), Joel Quenneville (Assistant Coach), Jacques Cloutier (Assistant Coach), Francois Giguere (Assistant General Manager), Michel Goulet (Director of Player Personnel), Dave Draper (Chief Scout), Jean Martineau (Director of Public Relations), Pat Karns (Trainer), Matthew Sokolowski (Assistant Trainer), Rob McLean (Equipment Manager), Mike Kramer (Assistant Equipment Manager), Brock Gibbins (Assistant Equipment Manager), Skip Allen (Strength and Conditioning Coach), Paul Fixter (Video Coordinator), Leo Vyssokov (Massage Therapist).
Scores: June 4 at Colorado — Colorado 3, Florida 1; June 6 at Colorado — Colorado 8, Florida 1; June 8 at Florida — Colorado 3, Florida 2; June 10 at Florida — Colorado 1, Florida 0.

1994-95 — New Jersey Devils — R. Scott Stevens (Captain), Tommy Albelin, Martin Brodeur, Neil Broten, Sergei Brylin, Robert E. Carpenter, Jr., Shawn Chambers, Tom Chorske, Danton Cole, Ken Daneyko, Kevin Dean, Jim Dowd, Bruce Driver (Alternate Captain), Bill Guerin, Bobby Holik, Claude Lemieux, John MacLean (Alternate Captain), Chris McAlpine, Randy McKay, Scott Niedermayer, Mike Peluso, Stephane J.J. Richer, Brian Rolston, Chris Terreri, Valeri Zelepukin, Dr. John J. McMullen (Owner/Chairman), Peter S. McMullen (Owner), Lou Lamoriello (President/General Manager), Jacques Lemaire (Head Coach), Jacques Caron (Goaltender Coach), Dennis Gendron (Assistant Coach), Larry Robinson (Assistant Coach), Robbie Ftorek (AHL Coach), Alex Abasto (Assistant Equipment Manager), Bob Huddleston (Massage Therapist), David Nichols (Equipment Manager), Ted Schuch (Medical Trainer), Mike Vasalani (Strength Coach), David Conte (Director of Scouting) Claude Carrier (Scout), Milt Fisher (Scout), Dan Labraaten (Scout), Marcel Pronovost (Scout).
Scores: June 17 at Detroit — New Jersey 2, Detroit 1; June 20 at Detroit — New Jersey 4, Detroit 2; June 22 at New Jersey — New Jersey 5, Detroit 2; June 24 at New Jersey — New Jersey 5, Detroit 2.

1993-94 — New York Rangers — Mark Messier (Captain), Brian Leetch, Kevin Lowe, Adam Graves, Steve Larmer, Glenn Anderson, Jeff Beukeboom, Greg Gilbert, Mike Hartman, Glenn Healy, Mike Hudson, Alexander Karpovtsev, Joe Kocur, Alexei Kovalev, Nick Kypreos, Doug Lidster, Stephane Matteau, Craig MacTavish, Sergei Nemchinov, Brian Noonan, Ed Olczyk, Mike Richter, Esa Tikkanen, Jay Wells, Sergei Zubov, Neil Smith (President, General Manager and Governor), Robert Gutkowski, Stanley Jaffe, Kenneth Munoz (Governors), Larry Pleau (Assistant General Manager), Mike Keenan (Head Coach), Colin Campbell (Associate Coach), Dick Todd (Assistant Coach), Matthew Loughren (Manager, Team Operations), Barry Watkins (Director, Communications), Christer Rockstrom, Tony Feltrin, Martin Madden, Herb Hammond, Darwin Bennett (Scouts), Dave Smith, Joe Murphy, Mike Folga, Bruce Lifrieri (Trainers).
Scores: May 31 at New York — Vancouver 3, NY Rangers 2; June 2 at New York — NY Rangers 3, Vancouver 1; June 4 at Vancouver — NY Rangers 5, Vancouver 1; June 7 at Vancouver — NY Rangers 4, Vancouver 2; June 9 at New York — Vancouver 6 at NY Rangers 3; June 11 at Vancouver — Vancouver 4, NY Rangers 1; June 14 at New York — NY Rangers 3, Vancouver 2.

1992-93 — Montreal Canadiens — Guy Carbonneau (Captain), Patrick Roy, Mike Keane, Eric Desjardins, Stephan Lebeau, Mathieu Schneider, Jean-Jacques Daigneault, Denis Savard, Lyle Odelein, Todd Ewen, Kirk Muller, John LeClair, Gilbert Dionne, Benoit Brunet, Patrice Brisebois, Paul Di Pietro, Andre Racicot, Donald Dufresne, Mario Roberge, Sean Hill, Ed Ronan, Kevin Haller, Vincent Damphousse, Brian Bellows, Gary Leeman, Rob Ramage, Ronald Corey (President), Serge Savard (Managing Director & Vice-President Hockey), Jacques Demers (Head Coach), Jacques Laperriere (Assistant Coach), Charles Thiffault (Assistant Coach), Francois Allaire (Goaltending Instructor), Jean Béliveau (Senior Vice-President, Corporate Affairs), Fred Steer (Vice-President, Finance & Adminstration), Aldo Giampaolo (Vice-President, Operations), Bernard Brisset (Vice-President, Marketing & Communications), André Boudrias (Assistant to the Managing Director & Director of Scouting), Jacques Lemaire (Assistant to the Managing Director), Gaeten Lefebvre (Athletic Trainer), John Shipman (Assistant to the Athletic Trainer), Eddy Palchak (Equipment Manager), Pierre Gervais (Assistant to the Equipment Manager), Robert Boulanger (Assistant to the Equipment Manager), Pierre Ouellete (Assistant to the Equipment Manager).
Scores: June 1 at Montreal — Los Angeles 4, Montreal 1; June 2 at Montreal — Montreal 3, Los Angeles 2; June 5 at Los Angeles — Montreal 4, Los Angeles 3; June 7 at Los Angeles — Montreal 3, Los Angeles 2; June 9 at Montreal — Montreal 4, Los Angeles 1.

1991-92 — Pittsburgh Penguins — Mario Lemieux (Captain), Ron Francis, Bryan Trottier, Kevin Stevens, Bob Errey, Phil Bourque, Troy Loney, Rick Tocchet, Joe Mullen, Jaromir Jagr, Jiri Hrdina, Shawn McEachern, Ulf Samuelsson, Kjell Samuelsson, Larry Murphy, Gord Roberts, Jim Paek, Paul Stanton, Tom Barrasso, Ken Wregget, Jay Caufield, Jamie Leach, Wendell Young, Grant Jennings, Peter Taglianetti, Jock Callander, Dave Michayluk, Mike Needham, Jeff Chychrun, Ken Priestlay, Jeff Daniels, Howard Baldwin (Owner and President), Morris Belzberg (Owner), Thomas Ruta (Owner), Donn Patton (Executive Vice President and Chief Financial Officer), Paul Martha (Executive Vice President and General Counsel), Craig Patrick (Executive Vice President and General Manager), Bob Johnson (Coach), Scotty Bowman (Director of Player Development and Coach), Barry Smith, Rick Kehoe, Pierre McGuire, Gilles Meloche, Rick Paterson (Assistant Coaches), Steve Latin (Equipment Manager), Skip Thayer (Trainer), John Welday (Strength and Conditioning Coach), Greg Malone, Les Binkley, Charlie Hodge, John Gill, Ralph Cox (Scouts).
Scores: May 26 at Pittsburgh — Pittsburgh 5, Chicago 4; May 28 at Pittsburgh — Pittsburgh 3, Chicago 1; May 30 at Chicago — Pittsburgh 1, Chicago 0; June 1 at Chicago — Pittsburgh 6, Chicago 5.

1990-91 — Pittsburgh Penguins — Mario Lemieux (Captain), Paul Coffey, Randy Hillier, Bob Errey, Tom Barrasso, Phil Bourque, Jay Caufield, Ron Francis, Randy Gilhen, Jiri Hrdina, Jaromir Jagr, Grant Jennings, Troy Loney, Joe Mullen, Larry Murphy, Jim Paek, Frank Pietrangelo, Barry Pederson, Mark Recchi, Gordie Roberts, Ulf Samuelsson, Paul Stanton, Kevin Stevens, Peter Taglianetti, Bryan Trottier, Scott Young, Wendell Young, Edward J. DeBartolo, Sr. (Owner), Marie D. DeBartolo York (President), Paul Martha (Vice-President & General Counsel), Craig Patrick (General Manager), Scotty Bowman (Director of Player Development & Recruitment), Bob Johnson (Coach), Rick Kehoe (Assistant Coach), Gilles Meloche (Goaltending Coach & Scout), Rick Paterson (Assistant Coach), Barry Smith (Assistant Coach), Steve Latin (Equipment Manager), Skip Thayer (Trainer), John Welday (Strength & Conditioning Coach), Greg Malone (Scout).
Scores: May 15 at Pittsburgh — Minnesota 5, Pittsburgh 4; May 17 at Pittsburgh — Pittsburgh 4, Minnesota 1; May 19 at Minnesota — Minnesota 3, Pittsburgh 1; May 21 at Minnesota — Pittsburgh 5, Minnesota 3; May 23 at Pittsburgh — Pittsburgh 6, Minnesota 4; May 25 at Minnesota — Pittsburgh 8, Minnesota 0.

Although he missed the 1993 finals with a broken ankle, Denis Savard still managed to indulge in the traditional Stanley Cup salute when he joined his teammates on the ice following their five-game victory over Los Angeles on June 9, 1993.

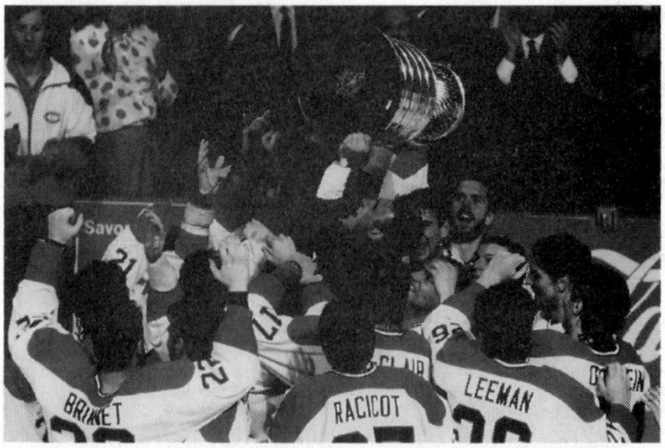

1989-90 — Edmonton Oilers — Kevin Lowe, Steve Smith, Jeff Beukeboom, Mark Lamb, Joe Murphy, Glenn Anderson, Mark Messier, Adam Graves, Craig MacTavish, Kelly Buchberger, Jari Kurri, Craig Simpson, Martin Gelinas, Randy Gregg, Charlie Huddy, Geoff Smith, Reijo Ruotsalainen, Craig Muni, Bill Ranford, Dave Brown, Eldon Reddick, Petr Klima, Esa Tikkanen, Grant Fuhr, Peter Pocklington (Owner), Glen Sather (President/General Manager), John Muckler (Coach), Ted Green (Co-Coach), Ron Low (Ass't Coach), Bruce MacGregor (Ass't General Manager), Barry Fraser (Director of Player Personnel), John Blackwell (Director of Operations, AHL), Ace Bailey, Ed Chadwick, Lorne Davis, Harry Howell, Matti Vaisanen and Albert Reeves (Scouts), Bill Tuele (Director of Public Relations), Werner Baum (Controller), Dr. Gordon Cameron (Medical Chief of Staff), Dr. David Reid (Team Physician), Barrie Stafford (Athletic Trainer), Ken Lowe (Athletic Therapist), Stuart Poirier (Massage Therapist), Lyle Kulchisky (Ass't Trainer).
Scores: May 15 at Boston — Edmonton 3, Boston 2; May 18 at Boston — Edmonton 7, Boston 2; May 20 at Edmonton — Boston 2, Edmonton 1; May 22 at Edmonton — Edmonton 5, Boston 1; May 24 at Boston — Edmonton 4, Boston 1.

1988-89 — Calgary Flames — Mike Vernon, Rick Wamsley, Al MacInnis, Brad McCrimmon, Dana Murzyn, Ric Nattress, Joe Mullen, Lanny McDonald (Co-captain), Gary Roberts, Colin Patterson, Hakan Loob, Theoren Fleury, Jiri Hrdina, Tim Hunter (Ass't. captain), Gary Suter, Mark Hunter, Jim Peplinski (Co-captain), Joe Nieuwendyk, Brian MacLellan, Joel Otto, Jamie Macoun, Doug Gilmour, Rob Ramage. Norman Green, Harley Hotchkiss, Norman Kwong, Sonia Scurfield, B.J. Seaman, D.K. Seaman (Owners), Cliff Fletcher (President and General Manager), Al MacNeil (Ass't General Manager), Al Coates (Ass't to the President), Terry Crisp (Head Coach), Doug Risebrough, Tom Watt (Ass't Coaches), Glenn Hall (Goaltending Consultant), Jim Murray (Trainer), Bob Stewart (Equipment Manager), Al Murray (Ass't Trainer).
Scores: May 14 at Calgary — Calgary 3, Montreal 2; May 17 at Calgary— Montreal 4, Calgary 2; May 19 at Montreal — Montreal 4, Calgary 3; May 21 at Montreal — Calgary 4, Montreal 2; May 23 at Calgary — Calgary 3, Montreal 2; May 25 at Montreal — Calgary 4, Montreal 2.

1987-88 — Edmonton Oilers — Keith Acton, Glenn Anderson, Jeff Beukeboom, Geoff Courtnall, Grant Fuhr, Randy Gregg, Wayne Gretzky, Dave Hannan, Charlie Huddy, Mike Krushelnyski, Jari Kurri, Normand Lacombe, Kevin Lowe, Craig MacTavish, Kevin McClelland, Marty McSorley, Mark Messier, Craig Muni, Bill Ranford, Craig Simpson, Steve Smith, Esa Tikkanen, Peter Pocklington (Owner), Glen Sather (General Manager/Coach), John Muckler (Co-Coach), Ted Green (Ass't Coach), Bruce MacGregor (Ass't General Manager), Barry Fraser (Director of Player Personnel), Bill Tuele (Director of Public Relations), Dr. Gordon Cameron (Team Physician), Peter Millar (Athletic Therapist), Barrie Stafford (Trainer), Juergen Mers (Massage Therapist), Lyle Kulchisky (Ass't Trainer).
Scores: May 18 at Edmonton — Edmonton 2, Boston 1; May 20 at Edmonton — Edmonton 4, Boston 2; May 22 at Boston — Edmonton 6, Boston 3; May 24 at Boston — Boston 3, Edmonton 3 (suspended due to power failure); May 26 at Edmonton — Edmonton 6, Boston 3.

1986-87 — Edmonton Oilers — Glenn Anderson, Jeff Beukeboom, Kelly Buchberger, Paul Coffey, Grant Fuhr, Randy Gregg, Wayne Gretzky, Charlie Huddy, Dave Hunter, Mike Krushelnyski, Jari Kurri, Moe Lemay, Kevin Lowe, Craig MacTavish, Kevin McClelland, Marty McSorley, Mark Messier, Andy Moog, Craig Muni, Kent Nilsson, Jaroslav Pouzar, Reijo Ruotsalainen, Steve Smith, Esa Tikkanen, Peter Pocklington (Owner), Glen Sather (General Manager/Coach), John Muckler (Co-Coach), Ted Green (Ass't. Coach), Ron Low (Ass't. Coach), Bruce MacGregor (Ass't. General Manager), Barry Fraser (Director of Player Personnel), Peter Millar (Athletic Therapist), Barrie Stafford (Trainer), Lyle Kulchisky (Ass't Trainer).
Scores: May 17 at Edmonton — Edmonton 4, Philadelphia 2; May 20 at Edmonton — Edmonton 3, Philadelphia 2; May 22 at Philadelphia — Philadelphia 5, Edmonton 3; May 24 at Philadelphia — Edmonton 4, Philadelphia 1; May 26 at Edmonton — Philadelphia 4, Edmonton 3; May 28 at Philadelphia — Philadelphia 3, Edmonton 2; May 31 at Edmonton — Edmonton 3, Philadelphia 1.

1985-86 — Montreal Canadiens — Bob Gainey, Doug Soetaert, Patrick Roy, Rick Green, David Maley, Ryan Walter, Serge Boisvert, Mario Tremblay, Bobby Smith, Craig Ludwig, Tom Kurvers, Kjell Dahlin, Larry Robinson, Guy Carbonneau, Chris Chelios, Petr Svoboda, Mats Naslund, Lucien DeBlois, Steve Rooney, Gaston Gingras, Mike Lalor, Chris Nilan, John Kordic, Claude Lemieux, Mike McPhee, Brian Skrudland, Stephane Richer, Ronald Corey (President), Serge Savard (General Manager), Jean Perron (Coach), Jacques Laperrière (Ass't. Coach), Jean Béliveau (Vice President), Francois-Xavier Seigneur (Vice President), Fred Steer (Vice President), Jacques Lemaire (Ass't. General Manager), André Boudrias (Ass't. General Manager), Claude Ruel, Yves Belanger (Athletic Therapist), Gaetan Lefebvre (Ass't. Athletic Therapist), Eddy Palchek (Trainer), Sylvain Toupin (Ass't. Trainer).
Scores: May 16 at Calgary — Calgary 5, Montreal 2; May 18 at Calgary — Montreal 3, Calgary 2; May 20 at Montreal — Montreal 5, Calgary 3; May 22 at Montreal — Montreal 1, Calgary 0; May 24 at Calgary — Montreal 4, Calgary 3.

1984-85 — Edmonton Oilers — Glenn Anderson, Bill Carroll, Paul Coffey, Lee Fogolin, Grant Fuhr, Randy Gregg, Wayne Gretzky, Charlie Huddy, Pat Hughes, Dave Hunter, Don Jackson, Mike Krushelnyski, Jari Kurri, Willy Lindstrom, Kevin Lowe, Dave Lumley, Kevin McClelland, Larry Melnyk, Mark Messier, Andy Moog, Mark Napier, Jaroslav Pouzar, Dave Semenko, Esa Tikkanen, Peter Pocklington (Owner), Glen Sather (General Manager/Coach), John Muckler (Ass't. Coach), Ted Green (Ass't. Coach), Bruce MacGregor (Ass't. General Manager), Barry Fraser (Director of Player Personnel/Chief Scout), Peter Millar (Athletic Therapist), Barrie Stafford, Lyle Kulchisky (Trainers)
Scores: May 21 at Philadelphia — Philadelphia 4, Edmonton 1; May 23 at Philadelphia — Edmonton 3, Philadelphia 1; May 25 at Edmonton — Edmonton 4, Philadelphia 3; May 28 at Edmonton — Edmonton 5, Philadelphia 3; May 30 at Edmonton — Edmonton 8, Philadelphia 3.

1983-84 — Edmonton Oilers — Glenn Anderson, Paul Coffey, Pat Conacher, Lee Fogolin, Grant Fuhr, Randy Gregg, Wayne Gretzky, Charlie Huddy, Pat Hughes, Dave Hunter, Don Jackson, Jari Kurri, Willy Lindstrom, Ken Linseman, Kevin Lowe, Dave Lumley, Kevin McClelland, Mark Messier, Andy Moog, Jaroslav Pouzar, Dave Semenko, Peter Pocklington (Owner), Glen Sather (General Manager/Coach), John Muckler (Ass't. Coach), Ted Green (Ass't. Coach), Bruce MacGregor (Ass't. General Manager), Barry Fraser (Director of Player Personnel/Chief Scout), Peter Millar (Athletic Therapist), Barrie Stafford (Trainer)
Scores: May 10 at New York — Edmonton 1, NY Islanders 0; May 12 at New York — NY Islanders 6, Edmonton 1; May 15 at Edmonton — Edmonton 7, NY Islanders 2; May 17 at Edmonton — Edmonton 7, NY Islanders 2; May 19 at Edmonton — Edmonton 5, NY Islanders 2.

1982-83 — New York Islanders — Mike Bossy, Bob Bourne, Paul Boutilier, Bill Carroll, Greg Gilbert, Clark Gillies, Butch Goring, Mats Hallin, Tomas Jonsson, Anders Kallur, Gord Lane, Dave Langevin, Mike McEwen, Roland Melanson, Wayne Merrick, Ken Morrow, Bob Nystrom, Stefan Persson, Denis Potvin, Bill Smith, Brent Sutter, Duane Sutter, John Tonelli, Bryan Trottier, Al Arbour (coach), Lorne Henning (ass't coach), Bill Torrey (general manager), Ron Waske, Jim Pickard (trainers)
Scores: May 10 at Edmonton — NY Islanders 2, Edmonton 0; May 12 at Edmonton — NY Islanders 6, Edmonton 3; May 14 at New York — NY Islanders 5, Edmonton 1; May 17 at New York — NY Islanders 4, Edmonton 2

1981-82 — New York Islanders — Mike Bossy, Bob Bourne, Bill Carroll, Butch Goring, Greg Gilbert, Clark Gillies, Tomas Jonsson, Anders Kallur, Gord Lane, Dave Langevin, Hector Marini, Mike McEwen, Roland Melanson, Wayne Merrick, Ken Morrow, Bob Nystrom, Stefan Persson, Denis Potvin, Bill Smith, Brent Sutter, Duane Sutter, John Tonelli, Bryan Trottier, Al Arbour (coach), Lorne Henning (ass't coach), Bill Torrey (general manager), Ron Waske, Jim Pickard (trainers)
Scores: May 8 at New York — NY Islanders 6, Vancouver 5; May 11 at New York — NY Islanders 6, Vancouver 4; May 13 at Vancouver — NY Islanders 3, Vancouver 0; May 16 at Vancouver — NY Islanders 3, Vancouver 1

1980-81 — New York Islanders — Denis Potvin, Mike McEwen, Ken Morrow, Gord Lane, Bob Lorimer, Stefan Persson, Dave Langevin, Mike Bossy, Bryan Trottier, Butch Goring, Wayne Merrick, Clark Gillies, John Tonelli, Bob Nystrom, Bill Carroll, Bob Bourne, Hector Marini, Anders Kallur, Duane Sutter, Garry Howatt, Lorne Henning, Bill Smith, Roland Melanson, Al Arbour (coach), Bill Torrey (general manager), Ron Waske, Jim Pickard (trainers).
Scores: May 12 at New York — NY Islanders 6, Minnesota 3; May 14 at New York — NY Islanders 6, Minnesota 3; May 17 at Minnesota — NY Islanders 7, Minnesota 5; May 19 at Minnesota— Minnesota 4, NY Islanders 2; May 21 at New York — NY Islanders 5, Minnesota 1.

1979-80 — New York Islanders — Gord Lane, Jean Potvin, Bob Lorimer, Denis Potvin, Stefan Persson, Ken Morrow, Dave Langevin, Duane Sutter, Garry Howatt, Clark Gillies, Lorne Henning, Wayne Merrick, Bob Bourne, Steve Tambellini, Bryan Trottier, Mike Bossy, Bob Nystrom, John Tonelli, Anders Kallur, Butch Goring, Alex McKendry, Glenn Resch, Billy Smith, Al Arbour (coach), Bill Torrey (general manager), Ron Waske, Jim Pickard (trainers).
Scores: May 13 at Philadelphia — NY Islanders 4, Philadelphia 3; May 15 at Philadelphia — Philadelphia 8, NY Islanders 3; May 17 at New York — NY Islanders 6, Philadelphia 2; May 19 at New York — NY Islanders 5, Philadelphia 2; May 22 at Philadelphia — Philadelphia 6, NY Islanders 3; May 24 at New York — NY Islanders 5, Philadelphia 4.

1978-79 — Montreal Canadiens — Ken Dryden, Larry Robinson, Serge Savard, Guy Lapointe, Brian Engblom, Gilles Lupien, Rick Chartraw, Guy Lafleur, Steve Shutt, Jacques Lemaire, Yvan Cournoyer, Réjean Houle, Pierre Mondou, Bob Gainey, Doug Jarvis, Yvon Lambert, Doug Risebrough, Pierre Larouche, Mario Tremblay, Cam Connor, Pat Hughes, Rod Langway, Mark Napier, Michel Larocque, Richard Sévigny, Scotty Bowman (coach), Irving Grundman (managing director), Eddy Palchak, Pierre Meilleur (trainers).
Scores: May 13 at Montreal — NY Rangers 4, Montreal 1; May 15 at Montreal — Montreal 6, NY Rangers 2; May 17 at New York — Montreal 4, NY Rangers 1; May 19 at New York — Montreal 4, NY Rangers 3; May 21 at Montreal — Montreal 4, NY Rangers 1.

1977-78 — Montreal Canadiens — Ken Dryden, Larry Robinson, Serge Savard, Guy Lapointe, Bill Nyrop, Pierre Bouchard, Brian Engblom, Gilles Lupien, Rick Chartraw, Guy Lafleur, Steve Shutt, Jacques Lemaire, Yvan Cournoyer, Réjean Houle, Pierre Mondou, Bob Gainey, Doug Jarvis, Yvon Lambert, Doug Risebrough, Pierre Larouche, Mario Tremblay, Michel Larocque, Murray Wilson, Scotty Bowman (coach), Sam Pollock (general manager), Eddy Palchak, Pierre Meilleur (trainers).
Scores: May 13 at Montreal — Montreal 4, Boston 1; May 16 at Montreal — Montreal 3, Boston 2; May 18 at Boston — Boston 4, Montreal 0; May 21 at Boston — Boston 4, Montreal 3; May 23 at Montreal — Montreal 4, Boston 1; May 25 at Boston — Montreal 4, Boston 1.

1976-77 — Montreal Canadiens — Ken Dryden, Guy Lapointe, Larry Robinson, Serge Savard, Jimmy Roberts, Rick Chartraw, Bill Nyrop, Pierre Bouchard, Brian Engblom, Yvan Cournoyer, Guy Lafleur, Jacques Lemaire, Steve Shutt, Pete Mahovlich, Murray Wilson, Doug Jarvis, Yvon Lambert, Bob Gainey, Doug Risebrough, Mario Tremblay, Rejean Houle, Pierre Mondou, Mike Polich, Michel Larocque, Scotty Bowman (coach), Sam Pollock (general manager), Eddy Palchak, Pierre Meilleur (trainers).
Scores: May 7 at Montreal — Montreal 7, Boston 3; May 10 at Montreal — Montreal 3, Boston 0; May 12 at Boston — Montreal 4, Boston 2; May 14 at Boston — Montreal 2, Boston 1.

1975-76 — Montreal Canadiens — Ken Dryden, Serge Savard, Guy Lapointe, Larry Robinson, Bill Nyrop, Pierre Bouchard, Jim Roberts, Guy Lafleur, Steve Shutt, Pete Mahovlich, Yvan Cournoyer, Jacques Lemaire, Yvon Lambert, Bob Gainey, Doug Jarvis, Doug Risebrough, Murray Wilson, Mario Tremblay, Rick Chartraw, Michel Larocque, Scotty Bowman (coach), Sam Pollock (general manager), Eddy Palchak, Pierre Meilleur (trainers).
Scores: May 9 at Montreal — Montreal 4, Philadelphia 3; May 11 at Montreal — Montreal 2, Philadelphia 1; May 13 at Philadelphia — Montreal 3, Philadelphia 2; May 16 at Philadelphia — Montreal 5, Philadelphia 3.

1974-75 — Philadelphia Flyers — Bernie Parent, Wayne Stephenson, Ed Van Impe, Tom Bladon, André Dupont, Joe Watson, Jim Watson, Ted Harris, Larry Goodenough, Rick MacLeish, Bobby Clarke, Bill Barber, Reggie Leach, Gary Dornhoefer, Ross Lonsberry, Bob Kelly, Terry Crisp, Don Saleski, Dave Schultz, Orest Kindrachuk, Bill Clement, Fred Shero (coach), Keith Allen (general manager), Frank Lewis, Jim McKenzie (trainers).
Scores: May 15 at Philadelphia — Philadelphia 4, Buffalo 1; May 18 at Philadelphia — Philadelphia 2, Buffalo 1; May 20 at Buffalo — Buffalo 5, Philadelphia 4; May 22 at Buffalo — Buffalo 4, Philadelphia 2; May 25 at Philadelphia — Philadelphia 5, Buffalo 1; May 27 at Buffalo — Philadelphia 2, Buffalo 0.

1973-74 — Philadelphia Flyers — Bernie Parent, Ed Van Impe, Tom Bladon, André Dupont, Joe Watson, Jim Watson, Barry Ashbee, Bill Barber, Dave Schultz, Don Saleski, Gary Dornhoefer, Terry Crisp, Bobby Clarke, Simon Nolet, Ross Lonsberry, Rick MacLeish, Bill Flett, Orest Kindrachuk, Bill Clement, Bob Kelly, Bruce Cowick, Al MacAdam, Bobby Taylor, Fred Shero (coach), Keith Allen (general manager), Frank Lewis, Jim McKenzie (trainers).
Scores: May 7 at Boston — Boston 3, Philadelphia 2; May 9 at Boston — Philadelphia 3, Boston 2; May 12 at Philadelphia — Philadelphia 4, Boston 1; May 14 at Philadelphia — Philadelphia 4, Boston 2; May 16 at Boston — Boston 5, Philadelphia 1; May 19 at Philadelphia — Philadelphia 1, Boston 0.

1972-73 — Montreal Canadiens — Ken Dryden, Guy Lapointe, Serge Savard, Larry Robinson, Jacques Laperrière, Bob Murdoch, Pierre Bouchard, Jim Roberts, Yvan Cournoyer, Frank Mahovlich, Jacques Lemaire, Pete Mahovlich, Marc Tardif, Henri Richard, Réjean Houle, Guy Lafleur, Chuck Lefley, Claude Larose, Murray Wilson, Steve Shutt, Michel Plasse, Scotty Bowman (coach), Sam Pollock (general manager), Ed Palchak, Bob Williams (trainers).
Scores: April 29 at Montreal — Montreal 8, Chicago 3; May 1 at Montreal — Montreal 4, Chicago 1; May 3 at Chicago — Chicago 7, Montreal 4; May 6 at Chicago — Montreal 4, Chicago 0; May 8 at Montreal — Chicago 8, Montreal 7; May 10 at Chicago — Montreal 6, Chicago 4.

1971-72 — Boston Bruins — Gerry Cheevers, Ed Johnston, Bobby Orr, Ted Green, Carol Vadnais, Dallas Smith, Don Awrey, Phil Esposito, Ken Hodge, John Bucyk, Mike Walton, Wayne Cashman, Garnet Bailey, Derek Sanderson, Fred Stanfield, Ed Westfall, John McKenzie, Don Marcotte, Garry Peters, Chris Hayes, Tom Johnson (coach), Milt Schmidt (general manager), Dan Canney, John Forristall (trainers).
Scores: April 30 at Boston — Boston 6, NY Rangers 5; May 2 at Boston — Boston 2, NY Rangers 1; May 4 at New York — NY Rangers 5, Boston 2; May 7 at New York — Boston 3, NY Rangers 2; May 9 at Boston — NY Rangers 3, Boston 2; May 11 at New York — Boston 3, NY Rangers 0.

1970-71 — Montreal Canadiens — Ken Dryden, Rogatien Vachon, Jacques Laperrière, Jean-Claude Tremblay, Guy Lapointe, Terry Harper, Pierre Bouchard, Jean Béliveau, Marc Tardif, Yvan Cournoyer, Réjean Houle, Claude Larose, Henri Richard, Phil Roberto, Pete Mahovlich, Leon Rochefort, John Ferguson, Bobby Sheehan, Jacques Lemaire, Frank Mahovlich, Bob Murdoch, Chuck Lefley, Al MacNeil (coach), Sam Pollock (general manager), Yvon Belanger, Ed Palchak (trainers).
Scores: May 4 at Chicago — Chicago 2, Montreal 1; May 6 at Chicago — Chicago 5, Montreal 3; May 9 at Montreal — Montreal 4, Chicago 2; May 11 at Montreal — Montreal 5, Chicago 2; May 13 at Chicago — Chicago 2, Montreal 0; May 16 at Montreal — Montreal 4, Chicago 3; May 18 at Chicago — Montreal 3, Chicago 2.

1969-70 — Boston Bruins — Gerry Cheevers, Ed Johnston, Bobby Orr, Rick Smith, Dallas Smith, Bill Speer, Gary Doak, Don Awrey, Phil Esposito, Ken Hodge, John Bucyk, Wayne Carleton, Wayne Cashman, Derek Sanderson, Fred Stanfield, Ed Westfall, John McKenzie, Jim Lorentz, Don Marcotte, Bill Lesuk, Dan Schock, Harry Sinden (coach), Milt Schmidt (general manager), Dan Canney, John Forristall (trainers).
Scores: May 3 at St. Louis — Boston 6, St. Louis 1; May 5 at St. Louis — Boston 6, St. Louis 2; May 7 at Boston — Boston 4, St. Louis 1; May 10 at Boston — Boston 4, St. Louis 3.

1968-69 — Montreal Canadiens — Lorne Worsley, Rogatien Vachon, Jacques Laperrière, Jean-Claude Tremblay, Ted Harris, Serge Savard, Terry Harper, Larry Hillman, Jean Béliveau, Ralph Backstrom, Dick Duff, Yvan Cournoyer, Claude Provost, Bobby Rousseau, Henri Richard, John Ferguson, Christian Bordeleau, Mickey Redmond, Jacques Lemaire, Lucien Grenier, Tony Esposito, Claude Ruel (coach), Sam Pollock (general manager), Larry Aubut, Eddy Palchak (trainers).
Scores: April 27 at Montreal — Montreal 3, St. Louis 1; April 29 at Montreal — Montreal 3, St. Louis 1; May 1 at St. Louis — Montreal 4, St. Louis 0; May 4 at St. Louis — Montreal 2, St. Louis 1.

1967-68 — Montreal Canadiens — Lorne Worsley, Rogatien Vachon, Jacques Laperrière, Jean-Claude Tremblay, Ted Harris, Serge Savard, Terry Harper, Carol Vadnais, Jean Béliveau, Gilles Tremblay, Ralph Backstrom, Dick Duff, Claude Larose, Yvan Cournoyer, Claude Provost, Bobby Rousseau, Henri Richard, John Ferguson, Danny Grant, Jacques Lemaire, Mickey Redmond, Toe Blake (coach), Sam Pollock (general manager), Larry Aubut, Eddy Palchak (trainers).
Scores: May 5 at St. Louis — Montreal 3, St. Louis 2; May 7 at St. Louis — Montreal 1, St. Louis 0; May 9 at Montreal — Montreal 4, St. Louis 3; May 11 at Montreal — Montreal 3, St. Louis 2.

1966-67 — Toronto Maple Leafs — Johnny Bower, Terry Sawchuk, Larry Hillman, Marcel Pronovost, Tim Horton, Bob Baun, Aut Erickson, Allan Stanley, Red Kelly, Ron Ellis, George Armstrong, Pete Stemkowski, Dave Keon, Mike Walton, Jim Pappin, Bob Pulford, Brian Conacher, Eddie Shack, Frank Mahovlich, Milan Marcetta, Larry Jeffrey, Bruce Gamble, Punch Imlach (manager-coach), Bob Haggart (trainer).
Scores: April 20 at Montreal — Toronto 2, Montreal 6; April 22 at Montreal — Toronto 3, Montreal 0; April 25 at Toronto — Toronto 3, Montreal 2; April 27 at Toronto — Toronto 2, Montreal 6; April 29 at Montreal — Toronto 4, Montreal 1; May 2 at Toronto — Toronto 3, Montreal 1.

1965-66 — Montreal Canadiens — Lorne Worsley, Charlie Hodge, Jean-Claude Tremblay, Ted Harris, Jean-Guy Talbot, Terry Harper, Jacques Laperrière, Noel Price, Jean Béliveau, Ralph Backstrom, Dick Duff, Gilles Tremblay, Claude Larose, Yvan Cournoyer, Claude Provost, Bobby Rousseau, Henri Richard, Dave Balon, John Ferguson, Leon Rochefort, Jim Roberts, Toe Blake (coch), Sam Pollock (general manager), Larry Aubut, Andy Galley (trainers).
Scores: April 24 at Montreal — Detroit 3, Montreal 2; April 26 at Montreal — Detroit 5, Montreal 2; April 28 at Detroit — Montreal 4, Detroit 2; May 1 at Detroit — Montreal 2, Detroit 1; May 3 at Montreal — Montreal 5, Detroit 1; May 5 at Detroit — Montreal 3, Detroit 2.

1964-65 — Montreal Canadiens — Lorne Worsley, Charlie Hodge, Jean-Claude Tremblay, Ted Harris, Jean-Guy Talbot, Terry Harper, Jacques Laperrière, Jean Gauthier, Noel Picard, Jean Béliveau, Ralph Backstrom, Dick Duff, Claude Larose, Yvan Cournoyer, Claude Provost, Bobby Rousseau, Henri Richard, Dave Balon, John Ferguson, Red Berenson, Jim Roberts, Toe Blake (coach), Sam Pollock (general manager), Larry Aubut, Andy Galley (trainers).
Scores: April 17 at Montreal — Montreal 3, Chicago 2; April 20 at Montreal — Montreal 2, Chicago 0; April 22 at Chicago — Montreal 1, Chicago 3; April 25 at Chicago — Montreal 1, Chicago 5; April 7 at Montreal — Montreal 6, Chicago 0; April 29 at Chicago — Montreal 1, Chicago 2; May 1 at Montreal — Montreal 4, Chicago 0.

1963-64 — Toronto Maple Leafs — Johnny Bower, Carl Brewer, Tim Horton, Bob Baun, Allan Stanley, Larry Hillman, Al Arbour, Red Kelly, Gerry Ehman, Andy Bathgate, George Armstrong, Ron Stewart, Dave Keon, Billy Harris, Don McKenney, Jim Pappin, Bob Pulford, Eddie Shack, Frank Mahovlich, Eddie Litzenberger, Punch Imlach (manager-coach), Bob Haggert (trainer).
Scores April 11 at Toronto — Toronto 3, Detroit 2; April 14 at Toronto — Toronto 3, Detroit 4; April 16 at Detroit — Toronto 3, Detroit 4; April 18 at Detroit — Toronto 4, Detroit 2; April 21 at Toronto — Toronto 1, Detroit 2; April 23 at Detroit — Toronto 4, Detroit 3; April 25 at Toronto — Toronto 4, Detroit 0.

1962-63 — Toronto Maple Leafs — Johnny Bower, Don Simmons, Carl Brewer, Tim Horton, Kent Douglas, Allan Stanley, Bob Baun, Larry Hillman, Red Kelly, Dick Duff, George Armstrong, Bob Nevin, Ron Stewart, Dave Keon, Billy Harris, Bob Pulford, Eddie Shack, Ed Litzenberger, Frank Mahovlich, John MacMillan, Punch Imlach (manager-coach), Bob Haggert (trainer).
Scores: April 9 at Toronto — Toronto 4, Detroit 2; April 11 at Toronto — Toronto 4, Detroit 2; April 14 at Detroit — Toronto 2, Detroit 3; April 16 at Detroit — Toronto 4, Detroit 2; April 18 at Toronto — Toronto 3, Detroit 1.

1961-62 — Toronto Maple Leafs — Johnny Bower, Don Simmons, Carl Brewer, Tim Horton, Bob Baun, Allan Stanley, Al Arbour, Larry Hillman, Red Kelly, Dick Duff, George Armstrong, Frank Mahovlich, Bob Nevin, Ron Stewart, Bill Harris, Bert Olmstead, Bob Pulford, Eddie Shack, Dave Keon, Ed Litzenberger, John MacMillan, Punch Imlach (manager-coach), Bob Haggert (trainer).
Scores: April 10 at Toronto — Toronto 4, Chicago 1; April 12 at Toronto — Toronto 3, Chicago 2; April 15 at Chicago — Toronto 0, Chicago 3; April 17 at Chicago — Toronto 1, Chicago 4; April 19 at Toronto —Toronto 8, Chicago 4; April 22 at Chicago — Toronto 2, Chicago 1.

1960-61 — Chicago Black Hawks — Glenn Hall, Al Arbour, Pierre Pilote, Elmer Vasko, Jack Evans, Dollard St. Laurent, Reg Fleming, Tod Sloan, Ron Murphy, Eddie Litzenberger, Bill Hay, Bobby Hull, Ab McDonald, Eric Nesterenko, Ken Wharram, Earl Balfour, Stan Mikita, Murray Balfour, Chico Maki, Wayne Hicks, Tommy Ivan (manager), Rudy Pilous (coach), Nick Garen (trainer).
Scores: April 6 at Chicago — Chicago 3, Detroit 2; April 8 at Detroit — Detroit 3, Chicago 1; April 10 at Chicago — Chicago 3, Detroit 1; April 12 at Detroit — Detroit 2, Chicago 1; April 14 at Chicago — Chicago 6, Detroit 3; April 16 at Detroit — Chicago 5, Detroit 1.

1959-60 — Montreal Canadiens — Jacques Plante, Charlie Hodge, Doug Harvey, Tom Johnson, Jean-Guy Talbot, Albert Langlois, Jean Béliveau, Marcel Bonin, Bernie Geoffrion, Phil Goyette, Bill Hicke, Don Marshall, Ab McDonald, Dickie Moore, André Pronovost, Claude Provost, Henri Richard, Maurice Richard (manager), Toe Blake (coach), Hector Dubois, Larry Aubut (trainers).
Scores: April 7 at Montreal — Montreal 4, Toronto 2; April 9 at Montreal — Montreal 2, Toronto 1; April 12 at Toronto — Montreal 5, Toronto 2; April 14 at Toronto — Montreal 4, Toronto 0.

1958-59 — Montreal Canadiens — Jacques Plante, Charlie Hodge, Doug Harvey, Tom Johnson, Bob Turner, Jean-Guy Talbot, Albert Langlois, Bernie Geoffrion, Ralph Backstrom, Bill Hicke, Maurice Richard, Dickie Moore, Claude Provost, Ab McDonald, Henri Richard, Marcel Bonin, Phil Goyette, Don Marshall, André Pronovost, Jean Béliveau, Frank Selke (manager), Toe Blake (coach), Hector Dubois, Larry Aubut (trainers).
Scores: April 9 at Montreal — Montreal 5, Toronto 3; April 11 at Montreal — Montreal 3, Toronto 1; April 14 at Toronto — Toronto 3, Montreal 2; April 16 at Toronto — Montreal 3, Toronto 2; April 18 at Montreal — Montreal 5, Toronto 3.

1957-58 — Montreal Canadiens — Jacques Plante, Gerry McNeil, Doug Harvey, Tom Johnson, Bob Turner, Dollard St-Laurent, Jean-Guy Talbot, Albert Langlois, Jean Béliveau, Bernie Geoffrion, Maurice Richard, Dickie Moore, Claude Provost, Floyd Curry, Bert Olmstead, Henri Richard, Marcel Bonin, Phil Goyette, Don Marshall, André Pronovost, Connie Broden, Frank Selke (manager), Toe Blake (coach), Hector Dubois, Larry Aubut (trainers).
Scores: April 8 at Montreal —Montreal 2, Boston 1; April 10 at Montreal — Boston 5, Montreal 2; April 13 at Boston — Montreal 3, Boston 0; April 15 at Boston — Boston 3, Montreal 1; April 17 at Montreal — Montreal 3, Boston 2; April 20 at Boston — Montreal 5, Boston 3.

George Armstrong can't help but grin as he waits for the Toronto Maple Leafs' Stanley Cup parade to wind its way around Maple Leaf Gardens on May 5, 1967.

1956-57 — Montreal Canadiens — Jacques Plante, Gerry McNeil, Doug Harvey, Tom Johnson, Bob Turner, Dollard St. Laurent, Jean-Guy Talbot, Jean Béliveau, Bernie Geoffrion, Floyd Curry, Dickie Moore, Maurice Richard, Claude Provost, Bert Olmstead, Henri Richard, Phil Goyette, Don Marshall, André Pronovost, Connie Broden, Frank Selke (manager), Toe Blake (coach), Hector Dubois, Larry Aubut (trainers).
Scores: April 6, at Montreal — Montreal 5, Boston 1; April 9, at Montreal — Montreal 1, Boston 0; April 11, at Boston — Montreal 4, Boston 2; April 14, at Boston — Boston 2, Montreal 0; April 16, at Montreal — Montreal 5, Boston 1.

1955-56 — Montreal Canadiens — Jacques Plante, Doug Harvey, Emile Bouchard, Bob Turner, Tom Johnson, Jean-Guy Talbot, Dollard St. Laurent, Jean Béliveau, Bernie Geoffrion, Bert Olmstead, Floyd Curry, Jackie Leclair, Maurice Richard, Dickie Moore, Henri Richard, Ken Mosdell, Don Marshall, Claude Provost, Frank Selke (manager), Toe Blake (coach), Hector Dubois (trainer).
Scores: March 31, at Montreal — Montreal 6, Detroit 4; April 3, at Montreal — Montreal 5, Detroit 1; April 5, at Detroit — Detroit 3, Montreal 1; April 8, at Detroit — Montreal 3, Detroit 0; April 10, at Montreal — Montreal 3, Detroit 1.

1954-55 — Detroit Red Wings — Terry Sawchuk, Red Kelly, Bob Goldham, Marcel Pronovost, Ben Woit, Jim Hay, Larry Hillman, Ted Lindsay, Tony Leswick, Gordie Howe, Alex Delvecchio, Marty Pavelich, Glen Skov, Earl Reibel, John Wilson, Bill Dineen, Vic Stasiuk, Marcel Bonin, Jack Adams (manager), Jimmy Skinner (coach), Carl Mattson (trainer).
Scores: April 3, at Detroit — Detroit 4, Montreal 2; April 5, at Detroit — Detroit 7, Montreal 1, April 7 at Montreal — Montreal 4, Detroit 2; April 9, at Montreal — Montreal 5, Detroit 3; April 10, at Detroit — Detroit 5, Montreal 1; April 12, at Montreal — Montreal 6, Detroit 3; April 14, at Detroit — Detroit 3, Montreal 1.

1953-54 — Detroit Red Wings — Terry Sawchuk, Red Kelly, Bob Goldham, Ben Woit, Marcel Pronovost, Al Arbour, Keith Allen, Ted Lindsay, Tony Leswick, Gordie Howe, Marty Pavelich, Alex Delvecchio, Metro Prystai, Glen Skov, John Wilson, Bill Dineen, Jim Peters, Earl Reibel, Vic Stasiuk, Jack Adams (manager), Tommy Ivan (coach), Carl Mattson (trainer).
Scores: April 4, at Detroit — Detroit 3, Montreal 1; April 6, at Detroit — Montreal 3, Detroit 1; April 8, at Montreal — Detroit 5, Montreal 2; April 10, at Montreal — Detroit 2, Montreal 0; April 11, at Detroit — Montreal 1, Detroit 0; April 13, at Montreal — Montreal 4, Detroit 1; April 16, at Detroit — Detroit 2, Montreal 1.

1952-53 — Montreal Canadiens — Gerry McNeil, Jacques Plante, Doug Harvey, Emile Bouchard, Tom Johnson, Dollard St. Laurent, Bud MacPherson, Maurice Richard, Elmer Lach, Bert Olmstead, Bernie Geoffrion, Floyd Curry, Paul Masnick, Billy Reay, Dickie Moore, Ken Mosdell, Dick Gamble, Johnny McCormack, Lorne Davis, Calum McKay, Eddie Mazur, Frank Selke (manager), Dick Irvin (coach), Hector Dubois (trainer).
Scores: April 9, at Montreal — Montreal 4, Boston 2; April 11, at Montreal — Boston 4, Montreal 1; April 12, at Boston — Montreal 3, Boston 0; April 14, at Boston — Montreal 7, Boston 3; April 16, at Montreal — Montreal 1, Boston 0.

1951-52 — Detroit Red Wings — Terry Sawchuk, Bob Goldham, Ben Woit, Red Kelly, Leo Reise, Marcel Pronovost, Ted Lindsay, Tony Leswick, Gordie Howe, Metro Prystai, Marty Pavelich, Sid Abel, Glen Skov, Alex Delvecchio, John Wilson, Vic Stasiuk, Larry Zeidel, Jack Adams (manager) Tommy Ivan (coach), Carl Mattson (trainer).
Scores: April 10, at Montreal — Detroit 3, Montreal 1; April 12 at Montreal — Detroit 2, Montreal 1; April 13, at Detroit — Detroit 3, Montreal 0; April 15, at Detroit — Detroit 3, Montreal 0.

1950-51 — Toronto Maple Leafs — Turk Broda, Al Rollins, Jim Thomson, Gus Mortson, Bill Barilko, Bill Juzda, Fern Flaman, Hugh Bolton, Ted Kennedy, Sid Smith, Tod Sloan, Cal Gardner, Howie Meeker, Harry Watson, Max Bentley, Joe Klukay, Danny Lewicki, Ray Timgren, Fleming Mackell, Johnny McCormack, Bob Hassard, Conn Smythe (manager), Joe Primeau (coach), Tim Daly (trainer).
Scores: April 11, at Toronto — Toronto 3, Montreal 2; April 14, at Toronto — Montreal 3, Toronto 2; April 17, at Montreal — Toronto 2, Montreal 1; April 19, at Montreal — Toronto 3, Montreal 2; April 21, at Toronto — Toronto 3, Montreal 2.

1949-50 — Detroit Red Wings — Harry Lumley, Jack Stewart, Leo Reise, Clare Martin, Al Dewsbury, Lee Fogolin, Marcel Pronovost, Red Kelly, Ted Lindsay, Sid Abel, Gordie Howe, George Gee, Jimmy Peters, Marty Pavelich, Jim McFadden, Pete Babando, Max McNab, Gerry Couture, Joe Carveth, John Wilson, Larry Wilson, Jack Adams (manager), Tommy Ivan (coach), Carl Mattson (trainer).
Scores: April 11, at Detroit — Detroit 4, NY Rangers 1; April 13, at Toronto* — NY Rangers 3, Detroit 1; April 15, at Toronto — Detroit 4, NY Rangers 0; April 18, at Detroit — NY Rangers 4, Detroit 3; April 20, at Detroit — NY Rangers 2, Detroit 1; April 22, at Detroit — Detroit 5, NY Rangers 4; April 23, at Detroit — Detroit 4, NY Rangers 3.

* Ice was unavailable in Madison Square Garden and Rangers elected to play second and third games on Toronto ice.

1948-49 — Toronto Maple Leafs — Turk Broda, Jim Thomson, Gus Mortson, Bill Barilko, Garth Boesch, Bill Juzda, Ted Kennedy, Howie Meeker, Vic Lynn, Harry Watson, Bill Ezinicki, Cal Gardner, Max Bentley, Joe Klukay, Sid Smith, Don Metz, Ray Timgren, Fleming Mackell, Harry Taylor, Bob Dawes, Tod Sloan, Conn Smythe (manager), Hap Day (coach), Tim Daly (trainer).
Scores: April 8, at Detroit — Toronto 3, Detroit 2; April 10, at Detroit — Toronto 3, Detroit 1; April 13, at Toronto — Toronto 3, Detroit 1; April 16, at Toronto — Toronto 3, Detroit 1.

1947-48 — Toronto Maple Leafs — Turk Broda, Jim Thomson, Wally Stanowski, Garth Boesch, Bill Barilko, Gus Mortson, Phil Samis, Syl Apps, Bill Ezinicki, Harry Watson, Ted Kennedy, Howie Meeker, Vic Lynn, Nick Metz, Max Bentley, Joe Klukay, Les Costello, Don Metz, Sid Smith, Conn Smythe (manager), Hap Day (coach), Tim Daly (trainer).
Scores: April 7, at Toronto — Toronto 5, Detroit 3; April 10, at Toronto — Toronto 4, Detroit 2; April 11, at Detroit — Toronto 2, Detroit 0; April 14, at Detroit — Toronto 7, Detroit 2.

Ted Lindsay puts the hug on the mug as he cradles Lord Stanley's silver chalice following the Detroit Red Wings' four-game victory over the Montreal Canadiens in the 1952 finals.

1946-47 — Toronto Maple Leafs — Turk Broda, Garth Boesch, Gus Mortson, Jim Thomson, Wally Stanowski, Bill Barilko, Harry Watson, Bud Poile, Ted Kennedy, Syl Apps, Don Metz, Nick Metz, Bill Ezinicki, Vic Lynn, Howie Meeker, Gaye Stewart, Joe Klukay, Gus Bodnar, Bob Goldham, Conn Smythe (manager), Hap Day (coach), Tim Daly (trainer).
Scores: April 8, at Montreal — Montreal 6, Toronto 0; April 10, at Montreal — Toronto 4, Montreal 0; April 12, at Toronto — Toronto 4, Montreal 2; April 15, at Toronto — Toronto 2, Montreal 1; April 17, at Montreal — Montreal 3, Toronto 1; April 19, at Toronto — Toronto 2, Montreal 1.

1945-46 — Montreal Canadiens — Elmer Lach, Toe Blake, Maurice Richard, Bob Fillion, Dutch Hiller, Murph Chamberlain, Ken Mosdell, Buddy O'Connor, Glen Harmon, Jim Peters, Emile Bouchard, Bill Reay, Ken Reardon, Leo Lamoureux, Frank Eddolls, Gerry Plamondon, Bill Durnan, Tommy Gorman (manager), Dick Irvin (coach), Ernie Cook (trainer).
Scores: March 30, at Montreal — Montreal 4, Boston 3; April 2, at Montreal — Montreal 3, Boston 2; April 4, at Boston — Montreal 4, Boston 2; April 7, at Boston — Boston 3, Montreal 2; April 9, at Montreal — Montreal 6, Boston 3.

1944-45 — Toronto Maple Leafs — Don Metz, Frank McCool, Wally Stanowski, Reg Hamilton, Elwyn Morris, Johnny McCreedy, Tommy O'Neill, Ted Kennedy, Babe Pratt, Gus Bodnar, Art Jackson, Jack McLean, Mel Hill, Nick Metz, Bob Davidson, Dave Schriner, Lorne Carr, Conn Smythe (manager), Frank Selke (business manager), Hap Day (coach), Tim Daly (trainer).
Scores: April 6, at Detroit — Toronto 1, Detroit 0; April 8, at Detroit — Toronto 2, Detroit 0; April 12, at Toronto — Toronto 1, Detroit 0; April 14, at Toronto — Detroit 5, Toronto 3; April 19, at Detroit — Detroit 2, Toronto 0; April 21, at Toronto — Detroit 1, Toronto 0; April 22, at Detroit — Toronto 2, Detroit 1.

1943-44 — Montreal Canadiens — Toe Blake, Maurice Richard, Elmer Lach, Ray Getliffe, Murph Chamberlain, Phil Watson, Emile Bouchard, Glen Harmon, Buddy O'Connor, Jerry Heffernan, Mike McMahon, Leo Lamoureux, Fernand Majeau, Bob Fillion, Bill Durnan, Tommy Gorman (manager), Dick Irvin (coach), Ernie Cook (trainer).
Scores: April 4, at Montreal — Montreal 5, Chicago 1; April 6, at Chicago — Montreal 3, Chicago 1; April 9, at Chicago — Montreal 3, Chicago 2; April 13, at Montreal — Montreal 5, Chicago 4.

1942-43 — Detroit Red Wings — Jack Stewart, Jimmy Orlando, Sid Abel, Alex Motter, Harry Watson, Joe Carveth, Mud Bruneteau, Eddie Wares, Johnny Mowers, Cully Simon, Don Grosso, Carl Liscombe, Connie Brown, Syd Howe, Les Douglas, Hal Jackson, Joe Fisher, Jack Adams (manager), Ebbie Goodfellow (playing-coach), Honey Walker (trainer).
Scores: April 1, at Detroit — Detroit 6, Boston 2; April 4, at Detroit — Detroit 4, Boston 3; April 7, at Boston — Detroit 4, Boston 0; April 8, at Boston — Detroit 2, Boston 0.

1941-42 — Toronto Maple Leafs — Wally Stanowski, Syl Apps, Bob Goldham, Gord Drillon, Hank Goldup, Ernie Dickens, Dave Schriner, Bucko McDonald, Bob Davidson, Nick Metz, Bingo Kampman, Don Metz, Gaye Stewart, Turk Broda, Johnny McCreedy, Lorne Carr, Pete Langelle, Billy Taylor, Conn Smythe (manager), Hap Day (coach), Frank Selke (business manager), Tim Daly (trainer).
Scores: April 4, at Toronto — Detroit 3, Toronto 2; April 7, at Toronto — Detroit 4, Toronto 2; April 9, at Detroit — Detroit 5, Toronto 2; April 12, at Detroit — Toronto 4, Detroit 3; April 14, at Toronto — Toronto 9, Detroit 3; April 16, at Detroit — Toronto 3, Detroit 0; April 18, at Toronto — Toronto 3, Detroit 1.

1940-41 — Boston Bruins — Bill Cowley, Des Smith, Dit Clapper, Frank Brimsek, Flash Hollett, John Crawford, Bobby Bauer, Pat McReavy, Herb Cain, Mel Hill, Milt Schmidt, Woody Dumart, Roy Conacher, Terry Reardon, Art Jackson, Eddie Wiseman, Art Ross (manager), Cooney Weiland (coach), Win Green (trainer).
Scores: April 6, at Boston — Detroit 2, Boston 3; April 8, at Boston — Detroit 1, Boston 2; April 10, at Detroit — Boston 4, Detroit 2; April 12, at Detroit — Boston 3, Detroit 1.

1939-40 — New York Rangers — Dave Kerr, Art Coulter, Ott Heller, Alex Shibicky, Mac Colville, Neil Colville, Phil Watson, Lynn Patrick, Clint Smith, Muzz Patrick, Babe Pratt, Bryan Hextall, Kilby Macdonald, Dutch Hiller, Alf Pike, Sanford Smith, Lester Patrick (manager), Frank Boucher (coach), Harry Westerby (trainer).
Scores: April 2, at New York — NY Rangers 2, Toronto 1; April 3, at New York — NY Rangers 6, Toronto 2; April 6, at Toronto — NY Rangers 1, Toronto 2; April 9, at Toronto — NY Rangers 0, Toronto 3; April 11, at Toronto — NY Rangers 2, Toronto 1; April 13, at Toronto — NY Rangers 3, Toronto 2.

1938-39 — Boston Bruins — Bobby Bauer, Mel Hill, Flash Hollett, Roy Conacher, Gord Pettinger, Milt Schmidt, Woody Dumart, Jack Crawford, Ray Getliffe, Frank Brimsek, Eddie Shore, Dit Clapper, Bill Cowley, Jack Portland, Red Hamill, Cooney Weiland, Art Ross (manager-coach), Win Green (trainer).
Scores: April 6, at Boston — Toronto 1, Boston 2; April 9, at Boston — Toronto 3, Boston 2; April 11, at Toronto — Toronto 1, Boston 3; April 13 at Toronto — Toronto 0, Boston 2; April 16, at Boston — Toronto 1, Boston 3.

1937-38 — Chicago Black Hawks — Art Wiebe, Carl Voss, Hal Jackson, Mike Karakas, Mush March, Jack Shill, Earl Seibert, Cully Dahlstrom, Alex Levinsky, Johnny Gottselig, Lou Trudel, Pete Palangio, Bill MacKenzie, Doc Romnes, Paul Thompson, Roger Jenkins, Alf Moore, Bert Connolly, Virgil Johnson, Paul Goodman, Bill Stewart (manager-coach), Eddie Froelich (trainer).
Scores: April 5, at Toronto — Chicago 3, Toronto 1; April 7, at Toronto — Chicago 1, Toronto 5; April 10 at Chicago — Chicago 2, Toronto 1; April 12, at Chicago — Chicago 4, Toronto 1.

1936-37 — Detroit Red Wings — Normie Smith, Pete Kelly, Larry Aurie, Herbie Lewis, Hec Kilrea, Mud Bruneteau, Syd Howe, Wally Kilrea, Jimmy Franks, Bucko McDonald, Gordon Pettinger, Ebbie Goodfellow, Johnny Gallagher, Ralph Bowman, Johnny Sorrell, Marty Barry, Earl Robertson, Johnny Sherf, Howard Mackie, Jack Adams (manager-coach), Honey Walker (trainer).
Scores: April 6, at New York — Detroit 1, NY Rangers 5; April 8, at Detroit — Detroit 4, NY Rangers 2; April 11, at Detroit — Detroit 0, NY Rangers 1; April 13, at Detroit — Detroit 1, NY Rangers 0; April 15, at Detroit — Detroit 3, NY Rangers 0.

1935-36 — Detroit Red Wings — Johnny Sorrell, Syd Howe, Marty Barry, Herbie Lewis, Mud Bruneteau, Wally Kilrea, Hec Kilrea, Gordon Pettinger, Bucko McDonald, Ralph Bowman, Pete Kelly, Doug Young, Ebbie Goodfellow, Normie Smith, Jack Adams (manager-coach), Honey Walker (trainer).
Scores: April 5, at Detroit — Detroit 3, Toronto 1; April 7, at Detroit — Detroit 9, Toronto 4; April 9, at Toronto — Detroit 3, Toronto 4; April 11, at Toronto — Detroit 3, Toronto 2.

1934-35 — Montreal Maroons — Marvin (Cy) Wentworth, Alex Connell, Toe Blake, Stew Evans, Earl Robinson, Bill Miller, Dave Trottier, Jimmy Ward, Larry Northcott, Hooley Smith, Russ Blinco, Allan Shields, Sammy McManus, Gus Marker, Bob Gracie, Herb Cain, Tommy Gorman (manager), Lionel Conacher (coach), Bill O'Brien (trainer).
Scores: April 4, at Toronto — Mtl. Maroons 3, Toronto 2; April 6, at Toronto — Mtl. Maroons 3, Toronto 1; April 9, at Montreal — Mtl. Maroons 4, Toronto 1.

1933-34 — Chicago Black Hawks — Taffy Abel, Lolo Couture, Lou Trudel, Lionel Conacher, Paul Thompson, Leroy Goldsworthy, Art Coulter, Roger Jenkins, Don McFayden, Tommy Cook, Doc Romnes, Johnny Gottselig, Mush March, Johnny Sheppard, Chuck Gardiner (captain), Bill Kendall, Tommy Gorman (manager-coach), Eddie Froelich (trainer).
Scores: April 3, at Detroit — Chicago 2, Detroit 1; April 5, at Detroit — Chicago 4, Detroit 1; April 8, at Chicago — Detroit 5, Chicago 2; April 10, at Chicago — Chicago 1, Detroit 0.

1932-33 — New York Rangers — Ching Johnson, Butch Keeling, Frank Boucher, Art Somers, Babe Siebert, Bun Cook, Andy Aitkenhead, Ott Heller, Ozzie Asmundson, Gord Pettinger, Doug Brennan, Cecil Dillon, Bill Cook (captain), Murray Murdoch, Earl Seibert, Lester Patrick (manager-coach), Harry Westerby (trainer).
Scores: April 4, at New York — NY Rangers 5, Toronto 1; April 8, at Toronto — NY Rangers 3, Toronto 1; April 11, at Toronto — Toronto 3, NY Rangers 2; April 13, at Toronto — NY Rangers 1, Toronto 0.

1931-32 — Toronto Maple Leafs — Charlie Conacher, Harvey Jackson, King Clancy, Andy Blair, Red Horner, Lorne Chabot, Alex Levinsky, Joe Primeau, Hal Darragh, Hal Cotton, Frank Finnigan, Hap Day, Ace Bailey, Bob Gracie, Fred Robertson, Earl Miller, Conn Smythe (manager), Dick Irvin (coach), Tim Daly (trainer).
Scores: April 5 at New York — Toronto 6, NY Rangers 4; April 7, at Boston* — Toronto 6, NY Rangers 2; April 9, at Toronto — Toronto 6, NY Rangers 4.

* Ice was unavailable in Madison Square Garden and Rangers elected to play the second game on neutral ice.

1930-31 — Montreal Canadiens — George Hainsworth, Wildor Larochelle, Marty Burke, Sylvio Mantha, Howie Morenz, Johnny Gagnon, Aurel Joliat, Armand Mondou, Pit Lepine, Albert Leduc, Georges Mantha, Art Lesieur, Nick Wasnie, Bert McCaffrey, Gus Rivers, Jean Pusie, Léo Dandurand (manager), Cecil Hart (coach), Ed Dufour (trainer).
Scores: April 3, at Chicago — Montreal 2, Chicago 1; April 5, at Chicago — Chicago 2, Montreal 1; April 9, at Montreal — Chicago 3, Montreal 2; April 11, at Montreal — Montreal 4, Chicago 2; April 14, at Montreal — Montreal 2, Chicago 0.

1929-30 — Montreal Canadiens — George Hainsworth, Marty Burke, Sylvio Mantha, Howie Morenz, Bert McCaffrey, Aurel Joliat, Albert Leduc, Pit Lepine, Wildor Larochelle, Nick Wasnie, Gerald Carson, Armand Mondou, Georges Mantha, Gus Rivers, Léo Dandurand (manager), Cecil Hart (coach), Ed Dufour (trainer).
Scores: April 1 at Boston — Montreal 3, Boston 0; April 3 at Montreal — Montreal 4, Boston 3.

1928-29 — Boston Bruins — Cecil (Tiny) Thompson, Eddie Shore, Lionel Hitchman, Perk Galbraith, Eric Pettinger, Frank Fredrickson, Mickey Mackay, Red Green, Dutch Gainor, Harry Oliver, Eddie Rodden, Dit Clapper, Cooney Weiland, Lloyd Klein, Cy Denneny, Bill Carson, George Owen, Myles Lane, Art Ross (manager-coach), Win Green (trainer).
Scores: March 28 at Boston — Boston 2, NY Rangers 0; March 29 at New York — Boston 2, NY Rangers 1.

1927-28 — New York Rangers — Lorne Chabot, Taffy Abel, Leon Bourgault, Ching Johnson, Bill Cook, Bun Cook, Frank Boucher, Billy Boyd, Murray Murdoch, Paul Thompson, Alex Gray, Joe Miller, Patsy Callighen, Lester Patrick (manager-coach), Harry Westerby (trainer).
Scores: April 5 at Montreal — Mtl. Maroons 2, NY Rangers 0; April 7 at Montreal — NY Rangers 2, Mtl. Maroons 1; April 10 at Montreal — Mtl. Maroons 2, NY Rangers 0; April 12 at Montreal — NY Rangers 1, Mtl. Maroons 0; April 14 at Montreal — NY Rangers 2, Mtl. Maroons 1.

1926-27 — Ottawa Senators — Alex Connell, King Clancy, George (Buck) Boucher, Ed Gorman, Frank Finnigan, Alex Smith, Hec Kilrea, Hooley Smith, Cy Denneny, Frank Nighbor, Jack Adams, Milt Halliday, Dave Gill (manager-coach).
Scores: April 7 at Boston — Ottawa 0, Boston 0; April 9 at Boston — Ottawa 3, Boston 1; April 11 at Ottawa — Boston 1, Ottawa 1; April 13 at Ottawa — Ottawa 3, Boston 1.

1925-26 — Montreal Maroons — Clint Benedict, Reg Noble, Frank Carson, Dunc Munro, Nels Stewart, Harry Broadbent, Babe Siebert, Dinny Dinsmore, Bill Phillips, Hobart (Hobie) Kitchen, Sammy Rothschield, Albert (Toots) Holway, Shorty Horne, Bern Brophy, Eddie Gerard (manager-coach), Bill O'Brien (trainer).
Scores: March 30 at Montreal — Mtl. Maroons 3, Victoria 0; April 1 at Montreal — Mtl. Maroons 3, Victoria 0; April 3 at Montreal — Victoria 3, Mtl. Maroons 2; April 6 at Montreal — Mtl. Maroons 2, Victoria 0.

The series in the spring of 1926 ended the annual playoffs between the champions of the East and the champions of the West. Since 1926-27 the annual playoffs in the National Hockey League have decided the Stanley Cup champions.

1924-25 — Victoria Cougars — Harry (Happy) Holmes, Clem Loughlin, Gordie Fraser, Frank Fredrickson, Jack Walker, Harold (Gizzy) Hart, Harold (Slim) Halderson, Frank Foyston, Wally Elmer, Harry Meeking, Jocko Anderson, Lester Patrick (manager-coach).
Scores: March 21 at Victoria — Victoria 5, Montreal 2; March 23 at Vancouver — Victoria 3, Montreal 1; March 27 at Victoria — Montreal 4, Victoria 2; March 30 at Victoria — Victoria 6, Montreal 1.

1923-24 — Montreal Canadiens — Georges Vezina, Sprague Cleghorn, Billy Couture, Howie Morenz, Aurel Joliat, Billy Boucher, Odie Cleghorn, Sylvio Mantha, Bobby Boucher, Billy Bell, Billy Cameron, Joe Malone, Charles Fortier, Leo Dandurand (manager-coach).
Scores: March 18 at Montreal — Montreal 3, Van. Maroons 2; March 20 at Montreal — Montreal 2, Van. Maroons 1. March 22 at Montreal — Montreal 6, Cgy. Tigers 1; March 25 at Ottawa* — Montreal 3, Cgy. Tigers 0.

* Game transferred to Ottawa to benefit from artificial ice surface.

1922-23 — Ottawa Senators — George (Buck) Boucher, Lionel Hitchman, Frank Nighbor, King Clancy, Harry Helman, Clint Benedict, Jack Darragh, Eddie Gerard, Cy Denneny, Harry Broadbent, Tommy Gorman (manager), Pete Green (coach), F. Dolan (trainer).
Scores: March 16 at Vancouver — Ottawa 1, Van. Maroons 0; March 19 at Vancouver — Van. Maroons 4, Ottawa 1; March 23 at Vancouver — Ottawa 3, Van. Maroons 2; March 26 at Vancouver — Ottawa 5, Van. Maroons 1; March 29 at Vancouver — Ottawa 2, Edm. Eskimos 1; March 31 at Vancouver — Ottawa 1, Edm. Eskimos 0.

MONTREAL MAROONS HOCKEY TEAM

WORLD'S CHAMPIONS
HOLDERS OF THE STANLEY CUP 1934-1935

TOE BLAKE   CY WENTWORTH   LIONEL CONACHER   ALEX CONNELL   STEW EVANS   EARL ROBINSON   BILL MILLER   T. GORMAN MGR.

DAVE TROTTIER   JIMMIE WARD   BALDY NORTHCOTT   HOOLEY SMITH CAPT.   RUSS BLINCO   ALLAN SHIELDS

SAMMY McMANUS   GUS MARKER   DUTCH GAINOR   BOB GRACIE   HERB CAIN   BILL McKENZIE

Shortly after the Montreal Maroons won the Stanley Cup in 1935, they sent a gangly youngster named Hec Blake (top row, far left) to the Montreal Canadiens for the rights to goalie Lorne Chabot. Hec, who was better known as "Toe", kept his foot in the door of the game long enough to win three Stanley Cup titles as a player and another eight as a coach.

1921-22 — Toronto St. Pats — Ted Stackhouse, Corb Denneny, Rod Smylie, Lloyd Andrews, John Ross Roach, Harry Cameron, Bill (Red) Stuart, Cecil (Babe) Dye, Ken Randall, Reg Noble, Eddie Gerard (borrowed for one game from Ottawa), Stan Jackson, Nolan Mitchell, Charlie Querrie (manager), Eddie Powers (coach).
Scores: March 17 at Toronto — Van. Millionaires 4, Toronto 3; March 20 at Toronto — Toronto 2, Van. Millionaires 1; March 23 at Toronto — Van. Millionaires 3, Toronto 0; March 25 at Toronto — Toronto 6, Van. Millionaires 0; March 28 at Toronto — Toronto 5, Van. Millionaires 1.

1920-21 — Ottawa Senators — Jack McKell, Jack Darragh, Morley Bruce, George (Buck) Boucher, Eddie Gerard, Clint Benedict, Sprague Cleghorn, Frank Nighbor, Harry Broadbent, Cy Denneny, Leth Graham, Tommy Gorman (manager),Pete Green (coach), F. Dolan (trainer).
Scores: March 21 at Vancouver — Van. Millionaires 2, Ottawa 1; March 24 at Vancouver — Ottawa 4, Van. Millionaires 3; March 28 at Vancouver — Ottawa 3, Van. Millionaires 2; March 31 at Vancouver — Van. Millionaires 3, Ottawa 2; April 4 at Vancouver — Ottawa 2, Van. Millionaires 1

1919-20 — Ottawa Senators — Jack McKell, Jack Darragh, Morley Bruce, Horrace Merrill, George (Buck) Boucher, Eddie Gerard, Clint Benedict, Sprague Cleghorn, Frank Nighbor, Harry Broadbent, Cy Denneny, Price, Tommy Gorman (manager), Pete Green (coach).
Scores: March 22 at Ottawa — Ottawa 3, Seattle 2; March 24 at Ottawa — Ottawa 3, Seattle 0; March 27 at Ottawa — Seattle 3, Ottawa 1; March 30 at Toronto* — Seattle 5, Ottawa 2; April 1 at Toronto* — Ottawa 6, Seattle 1.

* Games transferred to Toronto to benefit from artificial ice surface.

1918-19 — No decision, Series halted by Spanish influenza epidemic, illness of several players and death of Joe Hall of Montreal Canadiens from flu. Five games had been played when the series was halted, each team having won two and tied one. The results are shown:
Scores: March 19 at Seattle — Seattle 7, Montreal 0; March 22 at Seattle — Montreal 4, Seattle 2; March 24 at Seattle — Seattle 7, Montreal 2; March 26 at Seattle — Montreal 0, Seattle 0; March 30 at Seattle — Montreal 4, Seattle 3.

1917-18 — Toronto Arenas — Rusty Crawford, Harry Meeking, Ken Randall, Corb Denneny, Harry Cameron, Jack Adams, Alf Skinner, Harry Mummery, Harry (Happy) Holmes, Reg Noble, Sammy Hebert, Jack Marks, Jack Coughlin, Neville, Charlie Querrie (manager), Dick Carroll (coach), Frank Carroll (trainer).
Scores: March 20 at Toronto — Toronto 5, Van. Millionaires 3; March 23 at Toronto — Van. Millionaires 6, Toronto 4; March 26 at Toronto — Toronto 6, Van. Millionaires 3; March 28 at Toronto — Van. Millionaires 8, Toronto 1; March 30 at Toronto — Toronto 2, Van. Millionaires 1.

1916-17 — Seattle Metropolitans — Harry (Happy) Holmes, Ed Carpenter, Cully Wilson, Jack Walker, Bernie Morris, Frank Foyston, Roy Rickey, Jim Riley, Bobby Rowe (captain), Peter Muldoon (manager).
Scores: March 17 at Seattle — Montreal 8, Seattle 4; March 20 at Seattle — Seattle 6, Montreal 1; March 23 at Seattle — Seattle 4, Montreal 1; March 25 at Seattle — Seattle 9, Montreal 1.

1915-16 — Montreal Canadiens — Georges Vezina, Bert Corbeau, Jack Laviolette, Newsy Lalonde, Louis Berlinguette, Goldie Prodgers, Howard McNamara, Skene Ronan, Amos Arbour, Georges Poulin, Jacques Fournier, George Kennedy (manager).
Scores: March 20 at Montreal — Portland 2, Montreal 0; March 22 at Montreal — Montreal 2, Portland 1; March 25 at Montreal — Montreal 6, Portland 3; March 28 at Montreal — Portland 6, Montreal 5; March 30 at Montreal — Montreal 2, Portland 1.

1914-15 — Vancouver Millionaires — Kenny Mallen, Frank Nighbor, Fred (Cyclone) Taylor, Hughie Lehman, Lloyd Cook, Mickey MacKay, Barney Stanley, Jim Seaborn, Si Griffis (captain), Jean Matz, Frank Patrick (playing manager).
Scores: March 22 at Vancouver — Van. Millionaires 6, Ottawa 2; March 24 at Vancouver — Van. Millionaires 8, Ottawa 3; March 26 at Vancouver — Van. Millionaires 12, Ottawa 3.

1913-14 — Toronto Blueshirts — Con Corbeau, F. Roy McGiffen, Jack Walker, George McNamara, Cully Wilson, Frank Foyston, Harry Cameron, Harry (Happy) Holmes, Alan M. Davidson (captain), Harriston, Jack Marshall (playing-manager), Frank and Dick Carroll (trainers).
Scores: March 14 at Toronto — Toronto 5, Victoria 2; March 17 at Toronto — Toronto 6, Victoria 5; March 19 at Toronto — Toronto 2, Victoria 1.

1912-13 — Quebec Bulldogs — Joe Malone, Joe Hall, Paddy Moran, Harry Mummery, Tommy Smith, Jack Marks, Russell Crawford, Billy Creighton, Jeff Malone, Rocket Power, M.J. Quinn (manager), D. Beland (trainer).
Scores: March 8 at Quebec — Que. Bulldogs 14, Sydney 3; March 10 at Quebec — Que. Bulldogs 6, Sydney 2.

Victoria challenged Quebec but the Bulldogs refused to put the Stanley Cup in competition so the two teams played an exhibition series with Victoria winning two games to one by scores of 7-5, 3-6, 6-1. It was the first meeting between the Eastern champions and the Western champions. The following year, and until the Western Hockey League disbanded after the 1926 playoffs, the Cup went to the winner of the series between East and West.

1911-12 — Quebec Bulldogs — Goldie Prodgers, Joe Hall, Walter Rooney, Paddy Moran, Jack Marks, Jack McDonald, Eddie Oatman, George Leonard, Joe Malone (captain), C. Nolan (coach), M.J. Quinn (manager), D. Beland (trainer).
Scores: March 11 at Quebec — Que. Bulldogs 9, Moncton 3; March 13 at Quebec — Que. Bulldogs 8, Moncton 0.

Prior to 1912, teams could challenge the Stanley Cup champions for the title, thus there was more than one Championship Series played in most of the seasons between 1894 and 1911.

1910-11 — Ottawa Senators — Hamby Shore, Percy LeSueur, Jack Darragh, Bruce Stuart, Marty Walsh, Bruce Ridpath, Fred Lake, Albert (Dubby) Kerr, Alex Currie, Horace Gaul.
Scores: March 13 at Ottawa — Ottawa 7, Galt 4; March 16 at Ottawa — Ottawa 13, Port Arthur 4.

1909-10 — Montreal Wanderers — Cecil W. Blachford, Ernie (Moose) Johnson, Ernie Russell, Riley Hern, Harry Hyland, Jack Marshall, Frank (Pud) Glass (captain), Jimmy Gardner, R. R. Boon (manager).
Scores: March 12 at Montreal — Mtl. Wanderers 7, Berlin (Kitchener) 3.

1908-09 — Ottawa Senators — Fred Lake, Percy LeSueur, Fred (Cyclone) Taylor, H.L. (Billy) Gilmour, Albert Kerr, Edgar Dey, Marty Walsh, Bruce Stuart (captain).
Scores: Ottawa, as champions of the Eastern Canada Hockey Association took over the Stanley Cup in 1909 and, although a challenge was accepted by the Cup trustees from Winnipeg Shamrocks, games could not be arranged because of the lateness of the season. No other challenges were made in 1909. The following season — 1909-10 — however, the Senators accepted two challenges as defending Cup Champions. The first was against Galt in a two-game, total-goals series, and the second against Edmonton, also a two-game, total-goals series. Results: January 5 at Ottawa —Ottawa 12, Galt 3; January 7 at Ottawa — Ottawa 3, Galt 1. January 18 at Ottawa — Ottawa 8, Edm. Eskimos 4; January 20 at Ottawa — Ottawa 13, Edm. Eskimos 7.

1907-08 — Montreal Wanderers — Riley Hern, Art Ross, Walter Smaill, Frank (Pud) Glass, Bruce Stuart, Ernie Russell, Ernie (Moose) Johnson, Cecil Blachford (captain), Tom Hooper, Larry Gilmour, Ernie Liffiton, R.R. Boon (manager).
Scores: Wanderers accepted four challenges for the Cup: January 9 at Montreal — Mtl. Wanderers 9, Ott. Victorias 3; January 13 at Montreal — Mtl. Wanderers 13, Ott. Victorias 1; March 10 at Montreal — Mtl. Wanderers 11, Wpg. Maple Leafs 5; March 12 at Montreal — Mtl. Wanderers 9, Wpg. Maple Leafs 3; March 14 at Montreal — Mtl. Wanderers 6, Toronto (OPHL) 4. At start of following season, 1908-09, Wanderers were challenged by Edmonton. Results: December 28 at Montreal — Mtl. Wanderers 7, Edm. Eskimos 3; December 30 at Montreal — Edm. Eskimos 7, Mtl. Wanderers 6. Total goals: Mtl. Wanderers 13, Edm. Eskimos 10.

1906-07 — (March) **— Montreal Wanderers —** W. S. (Billy) Strachan, Riley Hern, Lester Patrick, Hod Stuart, Frank (Pud) Glass, Ernie Russell, Cecil Blachford (captain), Ernie (Moose) Johnson, Rod Kennedy, Jack Marshall, R.R. Boon (manager).
Scores: March 23 at Winnipeg — Mtl. Wanderers 7, Kenora 2; March 25 at Winnipeg — Kenora 6, Mtl. Wanderers 5. Total goals: Mtl. Wanderers 12, Kenora 8.

1906-07 — (January) **— Kenora Thistles —** Eddie Geroux, Art Ross, Si Griffis, Tom Hooper, Billy McGimsie, Roxy Beaudro, Tom Phillips.
Scores: January 17 at Montreal — Kenora 4, Mtl. Wanderers 2; Jan. 21 at Montreal — Kenora 8, Mtl. Wanderers 6.

1905-06 — (March) **— Montreal Wanderers —** Henri Menard, Billy Strachan, Rod Kennedy, Lester Patrick, Frank (Pud) Glass, Ernie Russell, Ernie (Moose) Johnson, Cecil Blachford (captain), Josh Arnold, R.R. Boon (manager).
Scores: March 14 at Montreal — Mtl. Wanderers 9, Ottawa 1; March 17 at Ottawa — Ottawa 9, Mtl. Wanderers 3. Total goals: Mtl. Wanderers 12, Ottawa 10. Wanderers accepted a challenge from New Glasgow, N.S., prior to the start of the 1906-07 season. Results: December 27 at Montreal — Mtl. Wanderers 10, New Glasgow 3; December 29 at Montreal — Mtl. Wanderers 7, New Glasgow 2.

1905-06 — (February) **— Ottawa Silver Seven —** Harvey Pulford (captain), Arthur Moore, Harry Westwick, Frank McGee, Alf Smith (playing coach), Billy Gilmour, Billy Hague, Percy LeSueur, Harry Smith, Tommy Smith, Dion, Ebbs.
Scores: February 27 at Ottawa — Ottawa 16, Queen's University 7; February 28 at Ottawa — Ottawa 12, Queen's University 7; March 6 at Ottawa — Ottawa 6, Smiths Falls 5; March 8 at Ottawa — Ottawa 8, Smiths Falls 2.

1904-05 — Ottawa Silver Seven — Dave Finnie, Harvey Pulford (captain), Arthur Moore, Harry Westwick, Frank McGee, Alf Smith (playing coach), Billy Gilmour, Frank White, Horace Gaul, Hamby Shore, Bones Allen.
Scores: January 13 at Ottawa — Ottawa 9, Dawson City 2; January 16 at Ottawa — Ottawa 23, Dawson City 2; March 7 at Ottawa — Rat Portage 9, Ottawa 3; March 9 at Ottawa — Ottawa 4, Rat Portage 2; March 11 at Ottawa — Ottawa 5, Rat Portage 4.

1903-04 — Ottawa Silver Seven — S.C. (Suddy) Gilmour, Arthur Moore, Frank McGee, J.B. (Bouse) Hutton, H.L. (Billy) Gilmour, Jim McGee, Harry Westwick, E. H. (Harvey) Pulford (captain), Scott, Alf Smith (playing coach).
Scores: December 30 at Ottawa — Ottawa 9, Wpg. Rowing Club 1; January 1 at Ottawa — Wpg. Rowing Club 6, Ottawa 2; January 4 at Ottawa — Ottawa 2, Wpg. Rowing Club 0. February 23 at Ottawa — Ottawa 6, Tor. Marlboros 3; February 25 at Ottawa — Ottawa 11, Tor. Marlboros 2; March 2 at Montreal — Ottawa 5, Mtl. Wanderers 5. Following the tie game, a new two-game series was ordered to be played in Ottawa but the Wanderers refused unless the tie game was replayed in Montreal. When no settlement could be reached, the series was abandoned and Ottawa retained the Cup and accepted a two-game challenge from Brandon. Results: (both games at Ottawa), March 9, Ottawa 6, Brandon 3; March 11, Ottawa 9, Brandon 3.

1902-03 — (March) **— Ottawa Silver Seven —** S.C. (Suddy) Gilmour, P.T. (Percy) Sims, J.B. (Bouse) Hutton, D.J. (Dave) Gilmour, H.L. (Billy) Gilmour, Harry Westwick, Frank McGee, F.H. Wood, A.A. Fraser, Charles D. Spittal, E.H. (Harvey) Pulford (captain), Arthur Moore, Alf Smith (coach.)
Scores: March 7 at Montreal — Ottawa 1, Mtl. Victorias 1; March 10 at Ottawa — Ottawa 8, Mtl. Victorias 0. Total goals: Ottawa 9, Mtl. Victorias 1; March 12 at Ottawa — Ottawa 6, Rat Portage 2; March 14 at Ottawa — Ottawa 4, Rat Portage 2.

1902-03 — (February) **— Montreal AAA —** Tom Hodge, R.R. (Dickie) Boon, W.C. (Billy) Nicholson, Tom Phillips, Art Hooper, W.J. (Billy) Bellingham, Charles A. Liffiton, Jack Marshall, Jim Gardner, Cecil Blachford, George Smith.
Scores: January 29 at Montreal — Mtl. AAA 8, Wpg. Victorias 1; January 31 at Montreal — Wpg. Victorias 2, Mtl. AAA 2; February 2 at Montreal — Wpg. Victorias 4, Mtl. AAA 2; February 4 at Montreal — Mtl. AAA 5, Wpg. Victorias 1.

1901-02 — (March) **— Montreal AAA —** Tom Hodge, R.R. (Dickie) Boon, William C. (Billy) Nicholson, Archie Hooper, W.J. (Billy) Bellingham, Charles A. Liffiton, Jack Marshall, Roland Elliott, Jim Gardner.
Scores: March 13 at Winnipeg — Wpg. Victorias 1, Mtl. AAA 0; March 15 at Winnipeg — Mtl. AAA 5, Wpg. Victorias 0; March 17 at Winnipeg — Mtl. AAA 2, Wpg. Victorias 1.

1901-02 — (January) **— Winnipeg Victorias —** Burke Wood, A.B. (Tony) Gingras, Charles W. Johnstone, R.M. (Rod) Flett, Magnus L. Flett, Dan Bain (captain), Fred Scanlon, F. Cadham, G. Brown.
Scores: January 21 at Winnipeg — Wpg. Victorias 5, Tor Wellingtons 3; January 23 at Winnipeg — Wpg. Victorias 5, Tor. Wellingtons 3.

1900-01 — Winnipeg Victorias — Burke Wood, Jack Marshall, A.B. (Tony) Gingras, Charles W. Johnstone, R.M. (Rod) Flett, Magnus L. Flett, Dan Bain (captain), G. Brown.
Scores: January 29 at Montreal — Wpg. Victorias 4, Mtl. Shamrocks 3; January 31 at Montreal — Wpg. Victorias 2, Mtl. Shamrocks 1.

1899-1900 — Montreal Shamrocks — Joe McKenna, Frank Tansey, Frank Wall, Art Farrell, Fred Scanlon, Harry Trihey (captain), Jack Brannen.
Scores: February 12 at Montreal — Mtl. Shamrocks 4, Wpg. Victorias 3; February 14 at Montreal — Wpg. Victorias 3, Mtl. Shamrocks 2; February 16 at Montreal — Mtl. Shamrocks 5, Wpg. Victorias 4; March 5 at Montreal — Mtl. Shamrocks 10, Halifax 2; March 7 at Montreal — Mtl. Shamrocks 11, Halifax 0.

1898-99 — (March) **— Montreal Shamrocks —** Jim McKenna, Frank Tansey, Frank Wall, Harry Trihey (captain), Art Farrell, Fred Scanlon, Jack Brannen, John Dobby, Charles Hoerner.
Scores: March 14 at Montreal — Mtl. Shamrocks 6, Queen's University 2.

1898-99 — (February) **— Montreal Victorias —** Gordon Lewis, Mike Grant, Graham Drinkwater, Cam Davidson, Bob McDougall, Ernie McLea, Frank Richardson, Jack Ewing, Russell Bowie, Douglas Acer, Fred McRobie.
Scores: February 15 at Montreal — Mtl. Victorias 2, Wpg. Victorias 1; February 18 at Montreal — Mtl. Victorias 3, Wpg. Victorias 2.

1897-98 — Montreal Victorias — Gordon Lewis, Hartland McDougall, Mike Grant, Graham Drinkwater, Cam Davidson, Bob McDougall, Ernie McLea, Frank Richardson (captain), Jack Ewing. The Victorias as champions of the Amateur Hockey Association, retained the Cup and were not called upon to defend it.

1896-97 — Montreal Victorias — Gordon Lewis, Harold Henderson, Mike Grant (captain), Cam Davidson, Graham Drinkwater, Robert McDougall, Ernie McLea, Shirley Davidson, Hartland McDougall, Jack Ewing, Percy Molson, David Gillilan, McLellan.
Scores: December 27 at Montreal — Mtl. Victorias 15, Ott. Capitals 2.

1895-96 — (December) **— Montreal Victorias —** Harold Henderson, Mike Grant (captain), Robert McDougall, Graham Drinkwater, Shirley Davidson, Ernie McLea, Robert Jones, Cam Davidson, David Gillilan, Stanley Willett.
Scores: December 30 at Winnipeg — Mtl. Victorias 6, Wpg. Victorias 5.

1895-96 — (February) **— Winnipeg Victorias —** G.H. Merritt, Rod Flett, Fred Higginbotham, Jack Armitage (captain), C.J. (Tote) Campbell, Dan Bain, Charles Johnstone, H. Howard.
Scores: February 14 at Montreal — Wpg. Victorias 2, Mtl. Victorias 0.

1894-95 — Montreal Victorias — Robert Jones, Harold Henderson, Mike Grant (captain), Shirley Davidson, Bob McDougall, Norman Rankin, Graham Drinkwater, Roland Elliot, William Pullan, Hartland McDougall, Jim Fenwick, A. McDougall. Montreal Victorias, as champions of the Amateur Hockey Association, were prepared to defend the Stanley Cup. However, the Stanley Cup trustees had already accepted a challenge match between the 1894 champion Montreal AAA and Queen's University. It was declared that if Montreal AAA defeated Queen's University, Montreal Victorias would be declared Stanley Cup champions. If Queen's University won, the Cup would go to the university club. In a game played March 9, 1895, Montreal AAA defeated Queen's University 5-1. As a result, Montreal Victorias were awarded the Stanley Cup.

1893-94 — Montreal AAA — Herbert Collins, Allan Cameron, George James, Billy Barlow, Clare Mussen, Archie Hodgson, Haviland Routh, Alex Irving, James Stewart, A.C. (Toad) Wand, A. Kingan.
Scores: March 17 at Mtl. Victorias — Mtl. AAA 3, Mtl. Victorias 2; March 22 at Montreal — Mtl. AAA 3, Ott. Capitals 1.

1892-93 — Montreal AAA — Tom Paton, James Stewart, Allan Cameron, Haviland Routh, Archie Hodgson, Billy Barlow, A.B. Kingan, G.S. Lowe.
In accordance with the terms governing the presentation of the Stanley Cup, it was awarded for the first time to the Montreal AAA as champions of the Amateur Hockey Association in 1893. Once Montreal AAA had been declared holders of the Stanley Cup, any Canadian hockey team could challenge for the trophy.

All-Time NHL Playoff Formats

1917-18 — The regular-season was split into two halves. The winners of both halves faced each other in a two-game, total-goals series for the NHL championship and the right to meet the PCHA champion in the best-of-five Stanley Cup Finals.

1918-19 — Same as 1917-18, except that the Stanley Cup Finals was extended to a best-of-seven series.

1919-20 — Same as 1917-1918, except that Ottawa won both halves of the split regular-season schedule to earn an automatic berth into the best-of-five Stanley Cup Finals against the PCHA champions.

1921-22 — The top two teams at the conclusion of the regular-season faced each other in a two-game, total-goals series for the NHL championship. The NHL champion then moved on to play the winner of the PCHA-WCHL playoff series in the best-of-five Stanley Cup Finals.

1922-23 — The top two teams at the conclusion of the regular-season faced each other in a two-game, total-goals series for the NHL championship. The NHL champion then moved on to play the PCHA champion in the best-of-three Stanley Cup Semi-Finals, and the winner of the Semi-Finals played the WCHL champion, which had been given a bye, in the best-of-three Stanley Cup Finals.

1923-24 — The top two teams at the conclusion of the regular-season faced each other in a two-game, total-goals series for the NHL championship. The NHL champion then moved to play the loser of the PCHA-WCHL playoff (the winner of the PCHA-WCHL playoff earned a bye into the Stanley Cup Finals) in the best-of-three Stanley Cup Semi-Finals. The winner of this series met the PCHA-WCHL playoff winner in the best-of-three Stanley Cup Finals.

1924-25 — The first place team (Hamilton) at the conclusion of the regular-season was supposed to play the winner of a two-game, total goals series between the second (Toronto) and third (Montreal) place clubs. However, Hamilton refused to abide by this new format, demanding greater compensation than offered by the League. Thus, Toronto and Montreal played their two-game, total-goals series, and the winner (Montreal) earned the NHL title and then played the WCHL champion (Victoria) in the best-of-five Stanley Cup Finals.

1925-26 — The format which was intended for 1924-25 went into effect. The winner of the two-game, total-goals series between the second and third place teams squared off against the first place team in the two-game, total-goals NHL championship series. The NHL champion then moved on to play the WHL champion in the best-of-five Stanley Cup Finals.

After the 1925-26 season, the NHL was the only major professional hockey league still in existence and consequently took over sole control of the Stanley Cup competition.

1926-27 — The 10-team league was divided into two divisions — Canadian and American — of five teams apiece. In each division, the winner of the two-game, total-goals series between the second and third place teams faced the first place team in a two-game, total-goals series for the division title. The two division title winners then met in the best-of-five Stanley Cup Finals.

1928-29 — Both first place teams in the two divisions played each other in a best-of-five series. Both second place teams in the two divisions played each other in a two-game, total-goals series as did the two third place teams. The winners of these latter two series then played each other in a best-of-three series for the right to meet the winner of the series between the two first place clubs. This Stanley Cup Final was a best-of-three.

Series A: First in Canadian Division versus first in American (best-of-five)
Series B: Second in Canadian Division versus second in American (two-game, total-goals)
Series C: Third in Canadian Division versus third in American (two-game, total-goals)
Series D: Winner of Series B versus winner of Series C (best-of-three)
Series E: Winner of Series A versus winner of Series D (best of three) for Stanley Cup

1931-32 — Same as 1928-29, except that Series D was changed to a two-game, total-goals format and Series E was changed to best of five.

1936-37 — Same as 1931-32, except that Series B, C, and D were each best-of-three.

1938-39 — With the NHL reduced to seven teams, the two-division system was replaced by one seven-team league. Based on final regular-season standings, the following playoff format was adopted:

Series A: First versus Second (best-of-seven)
Series B: Third versus Fourth (best-of-three)
Series C: Fifth versus Sixth (best-of-three)
Series D: Winner of Series B versus winner of Series C (best-of-three)
Series E: Winner of Series A versus winner of Series D (best-of-seven)

1942-43 — With the NHL reduced to six teams (the ''original six''), only the top four finishers qualified for playoff action. The best-of-seven Semi-Finals pitted Team #1 vs Team #3 and Team #2 vs Team #4. The winners of each Semi-Final series met in the best-of-seven Stanley Cup Finals.

1967-68 — When it doubled in size from 6 to 12 teams, the NHL once again was divided into two divisions — East and West — of six teams apiece. The top four clubs in each division qualified for the playoffs (all series were best-of-seven):

Series A; Team #1 (East) vs Team #3 (East)
Series B: Team #2 (East) vs Team #4 (East)
Series C: Team #1 (West) vs Team #3 (West)
Series D: Team #2 (West) vs Team #4 (West)
Series E: Winner of Series A vs winner of Series B
Series F: Winner of Series C vs winner of Series D
Series G: Winner of Series E vs Winner of Series F

1970-71 — Same as 1967-68 except that Series E matched the winners of Series A and D, and Series F matched the winners of Series B and C.

1971-72 — Same as 1970-71, except that Series A and C matched Team #1 vs Team #4, and Series B and D matched Team #2 vs Team #3.

1974-75 — With the League now expanded to 18 teams in four divisions, a completely new playoff format was introduced. First, the #2 and #3 teams in each of the four divisions were pooled together in the Preliminary round. These eight (#2 and #3) clubs were ranked #1 to #8 based on regular-season record:

Series A: Team #1 vs Team #8 (best-of-three)
Series B: Team #2 vs Team #7 (best-of-three)
Series C: Team #3 vs Team #6 (best-of-three)
Series D: Team #4 vs Team #5 (best-of-three)
The winners of this Preliminary round then pooled together with the four division winners, which had received byes into this Quarter-Final round. These eight teams were again ranked #1 to #8 based on regular-season record:
Series E: Team #1 vs Team #8 (best-of-seven)
Series F: Team #2 vs Team #7 (best-of-seven)
Series G: Team #3 vs Team #6 (best-of-seven)
Series H: Team #4 vs Team #5 (best-of-seven)
The four Quarter-Finals winners, which moved on to the Semi-Finals, were then ranked #1 to #4 based on regular season record:
Series I: Team #1 vs Team #4 (best-of-seven)
Series J: Team #2 vs Team #3 (best-of-seven)
Series K: Winner of Series I vs winner of Series J (best-of-seven)

1977-78 — Same as 1974-75, except that the Preliminary round consisted of the #2 teams in the four divisions and the next four teams based on regular-season record (not their standings within their divisions).

1979-80 — With the addition of four WHA franchises, the League expanded its playoff structure to include 16 of its 21 teams. The four first place teams in the four divisions automatically earned playoff berths. Among the 17 other clubs, the top 12, according to regular-season record, also earned berths. All 16 teams were then pooled together and ranked #1 to #16 based on regular-season record:

Series A: Team #1 vs Team #16 (best-of-five)
Series B: Team #2 vs Team #15 (best-of-five)
Series C: Team #3 vs Team #14 (best-of-five)
Series D: Team #4 vs Team #13 (best-of-five)
Series E: Team #5 vs Team #12 (best-of-five)
Series F: Team #6 vs Team #11 (best-of-five)
Series G: Team #7 vs Team #10 (best-of-five)
Series H: Team #8 vs Team #9 (best-of-five)
The eight Preliminary round winners, ranked #1 to #8 based on regular-season record, moved on to the Quarter-Finals:
Series I: Team #1 vs Team #8 (best-of-seven)
Series J: Team #2 vs Team #7 (best-of-seven)
Series K: Team #3 vs Team #6 (best-of-seven)
Series L: Team #4 vs Team #5 (best-of-seven)
The eight Quarter-finals winners, ranked #1 to #4 based on regular-season record, moved on to the semi-finals:
Series M: Team #1 vs Team #4 (best-of-seven)
Series N: Team #2 vs Team #3 (best-of-seven)
Series O: Winner of Series M vs winner of Series N (best-of-seven)

1981-82 — The first four teams in each division earned playoff berths. In each division, the first-place team opposed the fourth-place team and the second-place team opposed the third-place team in a best-of-five Division Semi-Final series (DSF). In each division, the two winners of the DSF met in a best-of-seven Division Final series (DF). The two winners in each conference met in a best-of-seven Conference Final series (CF). In the Prince of Wales Conference, the Adams Division winner opposed the Patrick Division winner; in the Clarence Campbell Conference, the Smythe Division winner opposed the Norris Division winner. The two CF winners met in a best-of-seven Stanley Cup Final (F) series.

1986-87 — Division Semi-Final series changed from best-of-five to best-of-seven.

1993-94 — The NHL's playoff draw conference-based rather than division-based. At the conclusion of the regular season, the top eight teams in each of the Eastern and Western Conferences qualify for the playoffs. The teams that finish in first place in each of the League's divisions are seeded first and second in each conference's playoff draw and are assured of home ice advantage in the first two playoff rounds. The remaining teams are seeded based on their regular-season point totals. In each conference, the team seeded #1 plays #8; #2 vs. #6; and #4 vs. #5. All series are best-of-seven with home ice rotating on a 2-2-1-1-1 basis, with the exception of• matchups between Central and Pacific teams. These matchups will be played on a 2-3-2 basis to reduce travel. In a 2-3-2 series, the team with the most points will have its choice to start the series at home or on the road. The Eastern Conference champion will face the Western Conference champion in the Stanley Cup Final.

1994-95 — Same as 1993-94, except that in first, second or third-round playoff series involving Central and Pacific Division teams, the team with the better record has the choice of using either a 2-3-2 or a 2-2-1-1-1 format. When a 2-3-2 format is selected, the higher-ranked team also has the choice of playing games 1, 2, 6 and 7 at home or playing games 3, 4 and 5 at home. The format for the Stanley Cup Final remains 2-2-1-1-1.

Eight years after he backstopped the Calgary Flames to the Stanley Cup title in 1989, Mike Vernon repeated the feat with a superb display of goaltending for the Detroit Red Wings in 1997. Vernon, seen here turning back Eric Lindros in game one of the Finals, held the opposition to two or fewer goals in 17 of the 20 games he started during the 1997 playoffs.

Team Records

1918-1997

GAMES PLAYED

MOST GAMES PLAYED BY ALL TEAMS, ONE PLAYOFF YEAR:
92 — 1991. There were 51 DSF, 24 DF, 11 CF and 6 F games.
90 — 1994. There were 48 CQF, 23 CSF, 12 CF and 7 F games.
87 — 1987. There were 44 DSF, 25 DF, 11 CF and 7 F games.

MOST GAMES PLAYED, ONE TEAM, ONE PLAYOFF YEAR:
26 — Philadelphia Flyers, 1987. Won DSF 4-2 against NY Rangers, DF 4-3 against NY Islanders, CF 4-2 against Montreal, and lost F 4-3 against Edmonton.
24 — Pittsburgh Penguins,1991. Won DSF 4-3 against New Jersey, DF 4-1 against Washington, CF 4-2 against Boston, and F 4-2 against Minnesota.
— Los Angeles Kings, 1993. Won DSF 4-2 against Calgary, DF 4-2 against Vancouver, CF 4-3 against Toronto, and lost F 4-1 against Montreal.
— Vancouver Canucks, 1994. Won CQF 4-3 against Calgary, CSF 4-1 against Dallas, CF 4-1 against Toronto, and lost F 4-3 against NY Rangers.

PLAYOFF APPEARANCES

MOST STANLEY CUP CHAMPIONSHIPS:
23 — Montreal Canadiens 1924-30-31-44-46-53-56-57-58-59-60-65-66-68-69-71-73-76-77-78-79-86-93
13 — Toronto Maple Leafs 1918-22-32-42-45-47-48-49-51-62-63-64-67
8 — Detroit Red Wings 1936-37-43-50-52-54-55-97

MOST CONSECUTIVE STANLEY CUP CHAMPIONSHIPS:
5 — Montreal Canadiens (1956-57-58-59-60)
4 — Montreal Canadiens (1976-77-78-79)
— NY Islanders (1980-81-82-83)

MOST FINAL SERIES APPEARANCES:
32 — Montreal Canadiens in 80-year history.
21 — Toronto Maple Leafs in 80-year history.
20 — Detroit Red Wings in 71-year history.

MOST CONSECUTIVE FINAL SERIES APPEARANCES:
10 — Montreal Canadiens (1951-60, inclusive)
5 — Montreal Canadiens, (1965-69, inclusive)
— NY Islanders, (1980-84, inclusive)

MOST YEARS IN PLAYOFFS:
71 — Montreal Canadiens in 80-year history.
58 — Toronto Maple Leafs in 80-year history.
57 — Boston Bruins in 73-year history.

MOST CONSECUTIVE PLAYOFF APPEARANCES:
29 — Boston Bruins (1968-96, inclusive)
28 — Chicago Blackhawks (1970-97, inclusive)
24 — Montreal Canadiens (1971-94, inclusive)
21 — Montreal Canadiens (1949-69, inclusive)
20 — Detroit Red Wings (1939-58, inclusive)

TEAM WINS

MOST HOME WINS, ONE TEAM, ONE PLAYOFF YEAR:
11 — Edmonton Oilers, 1988
10 — Edmonton Oilers, 1985 in 10 home-ice games.
— Montreal Canadiens, 1986
— Montreal Canadiens, 1993

MOST ROAD WINS, ONE TEAM, ONE PLAYOFF YEAR:
10 — New Jersey Devils, 1995. Won three at Boston in CQF; two at Pittsburgh in CSF; three at Philadelphia in CF; and two at Detroit in F series.
8 — NY Islanders, 1980. Won two at Los Angeles in PR; three at Boston in QF; two at Buffalo in SF; and one at Philadelphia in F series.
— Philadelphia Flyers, 1987. Won two at NY Rangers in DSF; two at NY Islanders in DF; three at Montreal in CF; and one at Edmonton in F series.
— Edmonton Oilers, 1990. Won one at Winnipeg in DSF; two at Los Angeles in DF; two at Chicago in CF and three at Boston in F series.
— Pittsburgh Penguins, 1992. Won two at Washington in DSF; two at NY Rangers in DF; two at Boston in CF; and two at Chicago in F series.
— Vancouver Canucks, 1994. Won three at Calgary in CQF; two at Dallas in CSF; one at Toronto in CF; and two at NY Rangers in F series.
— Colorado Avalanche, 1996. Won three at Vancouver in CQF; two at Chicago in CSF; two at Detroit in CF; and two at Florida in F series.

MOST ROAD WINS, ALL TEAMS, ONE PLAYOFF YEAR:
46 — 1987. Of 87 games played, road teams won 46 (22 DSF, 14 DF, 8 CF and 2 Stanley Cup final).

MOST OVERTIME WINS, ONE TEAM, ONE PLAYOFF YEAR:
10 — Montreal Canadiens, 1993. Two against Quebec in the DSF; three against Buffalo in the DF; two against NY Islanders in the CF; and three against Los Angeles in the F. Montreal played 20 games.
6 — NY Islanders, 1980. One against Los Angeles in the PR; two against Boston in the QF; one against Buffalo in the SF; and two against Philadelphia in the F. Islanders played 21 games.
— Vancouver Canucks, 1994. Three against Calgary in the CQF; one against Dallas in the CSF; one against Toronto in the CF; and one against NY Rangers in the F. Vancouver played 24 games.

MOST OVERTIME WINS AT HOME, ONE TEAM, ONE PLAYOFF YEAR:
4 — St. Louis Blues, 1968. Won one vs. Philadelphia in QF and three vs. Minnesota in SF.
— Montreal Canadiens, 1993. Won one vs. Quebec in DSF, one vs. Buffalo in DF, one vs. NY Islanders in CF and one vs. Los Angeles in F series.

MOST OVERTIME WINS ON THE ROAD, ONE TEAM, ONE PLAYOFF YEAR:
6 — Montreal Canadiens, 1993. Won one vs. Quebec in DSF, two vs. Buffalo in DF, one vs. NY Islanders in CF and two vs. Los Angeles in F series.

TEAM LOSSES

MOST LOSSES, ONE TEAM, ONE PLAYOFF YEAR:
11 — Philadelphia Flyers, 1987. Lost two vs. NY Rangers in DSF; three vs. NY Islanders in DF; two vs. Montreal in CF; and four vs. Edmonton in F series.

MOST HOME LOSSES, ONE TEAM, ONE PLAYOFF YEAR:
6 — Philadelphia Flyers, 1987. Lost one vs. NY Rangers in DSF; two vs. NY Islanders in DF; two vs. Montreal in CF; and one vs. Edmonton in F series.

MOST ROAD LOSSES, ONE TEAM, ONE PLAYOFF YEAR:
6 — St. Louis Blues, 1968. Lost two at Philadelphia in QF; two at Minnesota in SF; and two at Montreal in F series.
— **St. Louis Blues, 1970.** Lost two at Minnesota in QF; two at Pittsburgh in SF; and two at Boston in F series.
— **NY Islanders, 1984.** Lost one at NY Rangers in DSF; two at Montreal in CF; and three at Edmonton in F series.
— **Los Angeles Kings, 1993.** Lost one at Calgary in DSF; one at Vancouver in DF; two at Toronto in CF; and two at Montreal in F series.

MOST OVERTIME LOSSES, ONE TEAM, ONE PLAYOFF YEAR:
4 — St. Louis Blues, 1968. Lost one vs. Philadelphia in QF; one vs. Minnesota in SF; and two vs. Montreal in F series.
— **Los Angeles Kings, 1991.** Lost one vs. Vancouver in DSF; and three vs. Edmonton in DF series.
— **Los Angeles Kings, 1993.** Lost one vs. Toronto in CF; and three vs. Montreal in F series.
— **Philadelphia Flyers, 1996.** Lost two vs. Tampa Bay in CQF; and two vs. Florida in CSF series.

MOST OVERTIME LOSSES AT HOME, ONE TEAM, ONE PLAYOFF YEAR:
2 — Two overtime losses at home by one team in one playoff year has occurred 33 times. The Dallas Stars are the most recent team to equal this mark when they lost twice in overtime at home to the Edmonton Oilers in the 1997 Stanley Cup CQF series.

MOST OVERTIME LOSSES ON THE ROAD, ONE TEAM, ONE PLAYOFF YEAR:
3 — Los Angeles Kings, 1991. Lost one at Vancouver in DSF; and two at Edmonton in DF series.
— **St. Louis Blues, 1996.** Lost two at Toronto in CQF; and one at Detroit in CSF series.

PLAYOFF WINNING STREAKS

LONGEST PLAYOFF WINNING STREAK:
14 — Pittsburgh Penguins. Streak started May 9, 1992, at Pittsburgh with a 5-4 win in fourth game of a DF series against NY Rangers, won by Pittsburgh 4-2. Continued with a four-game sweep over Boston in the 1992 CF and a four-game win over Chicago in the 1992 F. Pittsburgh then won the first three games of the 1993 DSF versus New Jersey. New Jersey ended the streak April 25, 1993, at New Jersey with a 4-1 win.
12 — Edmonton Oilers. Streak began May 15, 1984 at Edmonton with a 7-2 win over NY Islanders in third game of F series, and ended May 9, 1985 when Chicago defeated Edmonton 5-2 at Chicago. Included in the streak were three wins over the NY Islanders, in 1984, three over Los Angeles, four over Winnipeg and two over Chicago, all in 1985.

MOST CONSECUTIVE WINS, ONE TEAM, ONE PLAYOFF YEAR:
11 — Chicago Blackhawks in 1992. Chicago won last three games of best-of-seven DSF against St. Louis to win series 4-2 and then defeated Detroit 4-0 in best-of-seven DF and Edmonton 4-0 in best-of-seven CF.
— **Pittsburgh Penguins** in 1992. Pittsburgh won last three games of best-of-seven DF against NY Rangers to win series 4-2 and then defeated Boston 4-0 in best-of-seven CF and Chicago 4-0 in best-of-seven F.
— **Montreal Canadiens** in 1993. Montreal won last four games of best-of-seven DSF against Quebec to win series 4-2, defeated Buffalo 4-0 in best-of-seven DF and won first three games of CF against NY Islanders.

PLAYOFF LOSING STREAKS

LONGEST PLAYOFF LOSING STREAK:
16 Games — Chicago Blackhawks. Streak started in 1975 QF against Buffalo when Chicago lost last two games. Then Chicago lost four games to Montreal in 1976 QF; two games to NY Islanders in 1977 PR; four games to Boston in 1978 QF and four games to NY Islanders in 1979 QF. Streak ended on April 8, 1980 when Chicago defeated St. Louis 3-2 in the opening game of their 1980 PR series.
12 Games — Toronto Maple Leafs. Streak started on April 16, 1979 as Toronto lost four straight games in a QF series against Montreal. Continued with three-game PR defeats versus Philadelphia and NY Islanders in 1980 and 1981 respectively. Toronto failed to qualify for the 1982 playoffs and lost the first two games of a 1983 DSF against Minnesota. Toronto ended the streak with a 6-3 win against the North Stars on April 9, 1983.

Left: Guy Carbonneau, Larry Robinson and Chris Chelios celebrate the Montreal Canadiens' impending Stanley Cup championship during the 1986 playoffs. Below: Ed Belfour played a major role in the Chicago Blackhawks' miracle run during the 1992 playoffs. With Belfour shutting down the opposition, the Hawks won 11 straight games against St. Louis, Detroit and Edmonton on their way to a berth in the Stanley Cup Finals.

MOST GOALS IN A SERIES, ONE TEAM

MOST GOALS, ONE TEAM, ONE PLAYOFF SERIES:
44 — **Edmonton Oilers** in 1985 CF. Edmonton won best-of-seven series 4-2, outscoring Chicago 44-25.
35 — Edmonton Oilers in 1983 DF. Edmonton won best-of-seven series 4-1, outscoring Calgary 35-13.
— Calgary Flames in 1995 CQF. Calgary lost best-of-seven series 3-4, outscoring San Jose 35-26.

MOST GOALS, ONE TEAM, TWO-GAME SERIES:
11 — **Buffalo Sabres** in 1977 PR. Buffalo won best-of-three series 2-0, outscoring Minnesota 11-3.
— Toronto Maple Leafs in 1978 PR. Toronto won best-of-three series 2-0, outscoring Los Angeles 11-3.
10 — Boston Bruins in 1927 QF. Boston won two-game total goal series 10-5.

MOST GOALS, ONE TEAM, THREE-GAME SERIES:
23 — **Chicago Blackhawks** in 1985 DSF. Chicago won best-of-five series 3-0, outscoring Detroit 23-8.
20 — Minnesota North Stars in 1981 PR. Minnesota won best-of-five series 3-0, outscoring Boston 20-13.
— NY Islanders in 1981 PR. New York won best-of-five series 3-0, outscoring Toronto 20-4.

MOST GOALS, ONE TEAM, FOUR-GAME SERIES:
28 — **Boston Bruins** in 1972 SF. Boston won best-of-seven series 4-0, outscoring St. Louis 28-8.

MOST GOALS, ONE TEAM, FIVE-GAME SERIES:
35 — **Edmonton Oilers** in 1983 DF. Edmonton won best-of-seven series 4-1, outscoring Calgary 35-13.
32 — Edmonton Oilers in 1987 DSF. Edmonton won best-of-seven series 4-1, outscoring Los Angeles 32-20.
28 — NY Rangers in 1979 QF. NY Rangers won best-of-seven series 4-1, outscoring Philadelphia 28-8.
27 — Philadelphia Flyers in 1980 SF. Philadelphia won best-of-seven series 4-1, outscoring Minnesota 27-14.
— Los Angeles Kings, in 1982 DSF. Los Angeles won best-of-five series 3-2, outscoring Edmonton 27-23.

MOST GOALS, ONE TEAM, SIX-GAME SERIES:
44 — **Edmonton Oilers** in 1985 CF. Edmonton won best-of-seven series 4-2, outscoring Chicago 44-25.
33 — Chicago Blackhawks in 1985 DF. Chicago won best-of-seven series 4-2, outscoring Minnesota 33-29.
— Montreal Canadiens in 1973 F. Montreal won best-of-seven series 4-2, outscoring Chicago 33-23.
— Los Angeles Kings in 1993 DSF. Los Angeles won best-of-seven series 4-2, outscoring Calgary 33-28.

MOST GOALS, ONE TEAM, SEVEN-GAME SERIES:
35 — **Calgary Flames** in 1995 CQF. Calgary lost best-of-seven series 3-4, outscoring San Jose 35-26.
33 — Philadelphia Flyers in 1976 QF. Philadelphia won best-of-seven series 4-3, outscoring Toronto 33-23.
— Boston Bruins in 1983 DF. Boston won best-of-seven series 4-3, outscoring Buffalo 33-23.
— Edmonton Oilers in 1984 DF. Edmonton won best-of-seven series 4-3, outscoring Calgary 33-27.

FEWEST GOALS IN A SERIES, ONE TEAM

FEWEST GOALS, ONE TEAM, TWO-GAME SERIES:
0 — **NY Americans** in 1929 SF. Lost two-game total-goal series 1-0 against NY Rangers.
— **Chicago Blackhawks** in 1935 SF. Lost two-game total-goal series 1-0 against Mtl. Maroons.
— **Mtl. Maroons** in 1937 SF. Lost best-of-three series 2-0 to NY Rangers while being outscored 5-0.
— **NY Americans** in 1939 QF. Lost best-of-three series 2-0 to Toronto while being outscored 6-0.

FEWEST GOALS, ONE TEAM, THREE-GAME SERIES:
1 — **Mtl. Maroons** in 1936 SF. Lost best-of-five series 3-0 to Detroit and were outscored 6-1.

FEWEST GOALS, ONE TEAM, FOUR-GAME SERIES:
2 — **Boston Bruins** in 1935 SF. Toronto won best-of-five series 3-1, outscoring Boston 7-2.
— **Montreal Canadiens** in 1952 F. Detroit won best-of-seven series 4-0, outscoring Montreal 11-2.

FEWEST GOALS, ONE TEAM, FIVE-GAME SERIES:
5 — **NY Rangers** in 1928 F. NY Rangers won best-of-five series 3-2, while being outscored by Mtl. Maroons 6-5.
— **Boston Bruins** in 1995 CQF. New Jersey won best-of-seven series 4-1, while outscoring Boston 14-5.
— **New Jersey Devils** in 1997 CSF. NY Rangers won best-of-seven series 4-1, while outscoring New Jersey 10-5.

FEWEST GOALS, ONE TEAM, SIX-GAME SERIES:
5 — **Boston Bruins** in 1951 SF. Toronto won best-of-seven series 4-1 with 1 tie, outscoring Boston 17-5.

FEWEST GOALS, ONE TEAM, SEVEN-GAME SERIES:
9 — **Toronto Maple Leafs,** in 1945 F. Toronto won best-of- seven series 4-3; teams tied in scoring 9-9.
— **Detroit Red Wings,** in 1945 F. Toronto won best-of-seven series 4-3; teams tied in scoring 9-9.

Ian Turnbull assisted on four of the Toronto Maple Leafs' record 11 goals in their two-game sweep of the Los Angeles in the 1978 Preliminary Round.

MOST GOALS IN A SERIES, BOTH TEAMS

MOST GOALS, BOTH TEAMS, ONE PLAYOFF SERIES:
69 — **Edmonton Oilers, Chicago Blackhawks** in 1985 CF. Edmonton won best-of-seven series 4-2, outscoring Chicago 44-25.
62 — Chicago Blackhawks, Minnesota North Stars in 1985 DF. Chicago won best-of-seven series 4-2, outscoring Minnesota 33-29.
61 — Los Angeles Kings, Calgary Flames in 1993 DSF. Los Angeles won best-of-seven series 4-2, outscoring Calgary 33-28.
— San Jose Sharks, Calgary Flames in 1995 CQF. San Jose won best-of-seven series 4-3, while being outscored 35-26.

MOST GOALS, BOTH TEAMS, TWO-GAME SERIES:
17 — **Toronto St. Patricks, Montreal Canadiens** in 1918 NHL F. Toronto won two-game total goal series 10-7.
15 — Boston Bruins, Chicago Blackhawks in 1927 QF. Boston won two-game total goal series 10-5.
— Pittsburgh Penguins, St. Louis Blues in 1975 PR. Pittsburgh won best-of-three series 2-0, outscoring St. Louis 9-6.

MOST GOALS, BOTH TEAMS, THREE-GAME SERIES:
33 — **Minnesota North Stars, Boston Bruins** in 1981 PR. Minnesota won best-of-five series 3-0, outscoring Boston 20-13.
31 — Chicago Blackhawks, Detroit Red Wings in 1985 DSF. Chicago won best-of-five series 3-0, outscoring Detroit 23-8.
28 — Toronto Maple Leafs, NY Rangers in 1932 F. Toronto won best-of-five series 3-0, outscoring New York 18-10.

MOST GOALS, BOTH TEAMS, FOUR-GAME SERIES:
36 — **Boston Bruins, St. Louis Blues** in 1972 SF. Boston won best-of-seven series 4-0, outscoring St. Louis 28-8.
— **Edmonton Oilers, Chicago Blackhawks** in 1983 CF. Edmonton won best-of-seven series 4-0, outscoring Chicago 25-11.
— **Minnesota North Stars, Toronto Maple Leafs** in 1983 DSF. Minnesota won best-of-five series 3-1; teams tied in scoring 18-18.
35 — NY Rangers, Los Angeles Kings in 1981 PR. NY Rangers won best-of-five series 3-1, outscoring Los Angeles 23-12.

MOST GOALS, BOTH TEAMS, FIVE-GAME SERIES:
  52 — **Edmonton Oilers, Los Angeles Kings** in 1987 DSF. Edmonton won
    best-of-seven series 4-1, outscoring Los Angeles 32-20.
  50 — Los Angeles Kings, Edmonton Oilers in 1982 DSF. Los Angeles won best-of-five
    series 3-2, outscoring Edmonton 27-23.
  48 — Edmonton Oilers, Calgary Flames in 1983 DF. Edmonton won best-of-seven
    series 4-1, outscoring Calgary 35-13.
      — Calgary Flames, Los Angeles Kings in 1988 DSF. Calgary won best-of-seven
    series 4-1, outscoring Los Angeles 30-18.

MOST GOALS, BOTH TEAMS, SIX-GAME SERIES:
  69 — **Edmonton Oilers, Chicago Blackhawks** in 1985 CF. Edmonton won
    best-of-seven series 4-2, outscoring Chicago 44-25.
  62 — Chicago Blackhawks, Minnesota North Stars in 1985 DF. Chicago won
    best-of-seven series 4-2, outscoring Minnesota 33-29.
  61 — Los Angeles Kings, Calgary Flames in 1993 DSF. Los Angeles won best-of-seven
    series 4-2, outscoring Calgary 33-28.

MOST GOALS, BOTH TEAMS, SEVEN-GAME SERIES:
  61 — **San Jose Sharks, Calgary Flames** in 1995 CQF. San Jose won best-of-seven
    series 4-3, while being outscored 35-26.
  60 — Edmonton Oilers, Calgary Flames in 1984 DF. Edmonton won best-of-seven
    series 4-3, outscoring Calgary 33-27.

FEWEST GOALS IN A SERIES, BOTH TEAMS

FEWEST GOALS, BOTH TEAMS, TWO-GAME SERIES:
  1 — **NY Rangers, NY Americans,** in 1929 SF. NY Rangers defeated NY Americans
    1-0 in two-game, total-goal series.
      — **Mtl. Maroons, Chicago Blackhawks** in 1935 SF. Mtl. Maroons defeated
    Chicago 1-0 in two-game, total-goal series.

FEWEST GOALS, BOTH TEAMS, THREE-GAME SERIES:
  7 — **Boston Bruins, Montreal Canadiens** in 1929 SF. Boston won best-of-five
    series 3-0, outscoring Montreal 5-2.
      — **Detroit Red Wings, Mtl. Maroons** in 1936 SF. Detroit won best-of-five series
    3-0, outscoring Mtl. Maroons 6-1.

FEWEST GOALS, BOTH TEAMS, FOUR-GAME SERIES:
  9 — **Toronto Maple Leafs, Boston Bruins** in 1935 SF. Toronto won best-of-five
    series 3-1, outscoring Boston 7-2.

FEWEST GOALS, BOTH TEAMS, FIVE-GAME SERIES:
  11 — **NY Rangers, Mtl. Maroons** in 1928 F. NY Rangers won best-of-five series
    3-2, while being outscored by Mtl. Maroons 6-5.

FEWEST GOALS, BOTH TEAMS, SIX-GAME SERIES:
  22 — **Toronto Maple Leafs, Boston Bruins** in 1951 SF. Toronto won best-of-seven
    series 4-1 with 1 tie, outscoring Boston 17-5.

FEWEST GOALS, BOTH TEAMS, SEVEN-GAME SERIES:
  18 — **Toronto Maple Leafs, Detroit Red Wings** in 1945 F. Toronto won
    best-of-seven series 4-3; teams tied in scoring 9-9.

MOST GOALS IN A GAME OR PERIOD

MOST GOALS, ONE TEAM, ONE GAME:
  13 — **Edmonton Oilers** at Edmonton, April 9, 1987. Edmonton 13, Los Angeles 3.
    Edmonton won best-of-seven DSF 4-1.
  12 — Los Angeles Kings at Los Angeles, April 10, 1990. Los Angeles 12, Calgary 4.
    Los Angeles won best-of-seven DSF 4-2.
  11 — Montreal Canadiens at Montreal, March 30, 1944. Montreal 11, Toronto 0.
    Canadiens won best-of-seven SF 4-1.
      — Edmonton Oilers at Edmonton, May 4, 1985. Edmonton 11, Chicago 2.
    Edmonton won best-of-seven CF 4-2.

*A power-play specialist, Clark Gillies scored three of the New York
Islanders' then-record 31 powerplay markers in the 1981 playoffs.*

MOST GOALS, ONE TEAM, ONE PERIOD:
  7 — **Montreal Canadiens,** March 30, 1944, at Montreal in third period, during
    11-0 win against Toronto.

MOST GOALS, BOTH TEAMS, ONE GAME:
  18 — **Los Angeles Kings, Edmonton Oilers** at Edmonton, April 7, 1982.
    Los Angeles 10, Edmonton 8. Los Angeles won best-of-five DSF 3-2.
  17 — Pittsburgh Penguins, Philadelphia Flyers at Pittsburgh, April 25, 1989.
    Pittsburgh 10, Philadelphia 7. Philadelphia won best-of-seven DF 4-3.
  16 — Edmonton Oilers, Los Angeles Kings at Edmonton, April 9, 1987.
    Edmonton 13, Los Angeles 3. Edmonton won best-of-seven DSF 4-1.
      — Los Angeles Kings, Calgary Flames at Los Angeles, April 10, 1990.
    Los Angeles 12, Calgary 4. Los Angeles won best-of-seven DF 4-2.

MOST GOALS, BOTH TEAMS, ONE PERIOD:
  9 — **NY Rangers, Philadelphia Flyers,** April 24, 1979, at Philadelphia, third
    period. NY Rangers won 8-3, scoring six of nine third-period goals.
      — **Los Angeles Kings, Calgary Flames,** at Los Angeles, April 10, 1990, second
    period. Los Angeles won game 12-4, scoring five of nine second-period goals.
  8 — Chicago Blackhawks, Montreal Canadiens, at Montreal, May 8, 1973, second
    period. Chicago won 8-7, scoring five of eight second-period goals.
      — Chicago Blackhawks, Edmonton Oilers, at Chicago, May 12, 1985, first period.
    Chicago won 8-6, scoring five of eight first-period goals.
      — Edmonton Oilers, Winnipeg Jets, at Edmonton, April 6, 1988, third period.
    Edmonton won 7-4, scoring six of eight third period goals.
      — Hartford Whalers, Montreal Canadiens, at Hartford, April 10, 1988, third
    period. Hartford won 7-5, scoring five of eight third period goals.
      — Vancouver Canucks, NY Rangers, at New York, June 9, 1994, third period.
    Vancouver won 6-3, scoring five of eight third period goals.

TEAM POWER-PLAY GOALS

MOST POWER-PLAY GOALS BY ALL TEAMS, ONE PLAYOFF YEAR:
  199 — **1988** in 83 games.

MOST POWER-PLAY GOALS, ONE TEAM, ONE PLAYOFF YEAR:
  35 — **Minnesota North Stars,** 1991 in 23 games.
  32 — Edmonton Oilers, 1988 in 18 games.
  31 — NY Islanders, 1981, in 18 games.

MOST POWER-PLAY GOALS, ONE TEAM, ONE SERIES:
  15 — **NY Islanders** in 1980 F against Philadelphia. NY Islanders won series 4-2.
      — **Minnesota North Stars** in 1991 DSF against Chicago. Minnesota won series
    4-2.
  13 — NY Islanders in 1981 QF against Edmonton. NY Islanders won series 4-2.
      — Calgary Flames in 1986 CF against St. Louis. Calgary won series 4-3.
  12 — Toronto Maple Leafs in 1976 QF series won by Philadelphia 4-3.

MOST POWER-PLAY GOALS, BOTH TEAMS, ONE SERIES:
  21 — **NY Islanders, Philadelphia Flyers** in 1980 F, won by NY Islanders 4-2.
    NY Islanders had 15 and Flyers 6.
      — **NY Islanders, Edmonton Oilers** in 1981 QF, won by NY Islanders 4-2.
    NY Islanders had 13 and Edmonton 8.
      — **Philadelphia Flyers, Pittsburgh Penguins** in 1989 DF, won by Philadelphia
    4-3. Philadelphia had 11 and Pittsburgh 10.
      — **Minnesota North Stars, Chicago Blackhawks** in 1991 DSF, won by
    Minnesota 4-2. Minnesota had 15 and Chicago 6.
  20 — Toronto Maple Leafs, Philadelphia Flyers in 1976 QF series won by Philadelphia
    4-3. Toronto had 12 and Philadelphia 8.

MOST POWER-PLAY GOALS, ONE TEAM, ONE GAME:
  6 — **Boston Bruins,** April 2, 1969, at Boston against Toronto. Boston won 10-0.

MOST POWER-PLAY GOALS, BOTH TEAMS, ONE GAME:
  8 — **Minnesota North Stars, St. Louis Blues,** April 24, 1991 at Minnesota.
    Minnesota had 4, St. Louis 4. Minnesota won 8-4.
  7 — Minnesota North Stars, Edmonton Oilers, April 28, 1984 at Minnesota.
    Minnesota had 4, Edmonton 3. Edmonton won 8-5.
      — Philadelphia Flyers, NY Rangers, April 13, 1985 at New York. Philadelphia
    had 4, NY Rangers 3. Philadelphia won 6-5.
      — Edmonton Oilers, Chicago Blackhawks, May 14, 1985 at Edmonton. Chicago
    had 5, Edmonton 2. Edmonton won 10-5.
      — Edmonton Oilers, Los Angeles Kings, April 9, 1987 at Edmonton. Edmonton
    had 5, Los Angeles 2. Edmonton won 13-3.
      — Vancouver Canucks, Calgary Flames, April 9, 1989 at Vancouver. Vancouver
    had 4, Calgary 3. Vancouver won 5-3.

MOST POWER-PLAY GOALS, ONE TEAM, ONE PERIOD:
  4 — **Toronto Maple Leafs,** March 26, 1936, second period against Boston at
    Toronto. Toronto won 8-3.
      — **Minnesota North Stars,** April 28, 1984, second period against Edmonton at
    Minnesota. Edmonton won 8-5.
      — **Boston Bruins,** April 11, 1991, third period against Hartford at Boston. Boston
    won 6-1.
      — **Minnesota North Stars,** April 24, 1991, second period against St. Louis at
    Minnesota. Minnesota won 8-4.

MOST POWER-PLAY GOALS, BOTH TEAMS, ONE PERIOD:
  5 — **Minnesota North Stars, Edmonton Oilers,** April 28, 1984, second period, at
    Minnesota. Minnesota had 4 and Edmonton 1. Edmonton won 8-5.
      — **Vancouver Canucks, Calgary Flames,** April 9, 1989, third period at
    Vancouver. Vancouver had 3 and Calgary 2. Vancouver won 5-3.
      — **Minnesota North Stars, St. Louis Blues,** April 24, 1991, second period, at
    Minnesota. Minnesota had 4 and St. Louis 1. Minnesota won 8-4.

TEAM SHORTHAND GOALS

MOST SHORTHAND GOALS BY ALL TEAMS, ONE PLAYOFF YEAR:
  33 — **1988,** in 83 games.

MOST SHORTHAND GOALS, ONE TEAM, ONE PLAYOFF YEAR:
10 — Edmonton Oilers, 1983, in 16 games.
9 — NY Islanders, 1981, in 19 games.
8 — Philadelphia Flyers, 1989, in 19 games.

MOST SHORTHAND GOALS, ONE TEAM, ONE SERIES:
6 — **Calgary Flames** in 1995 against San Jose in best-of-seven CQF won by San Jose 4-3.
— **Vancouver Canucks** in 1995 against St. Louis in best-of-seven CQF won by Vancouver 4-3.
5 — **Edmonton Oilers** in 1983 against Calgary in best-of-seven DF won by Edmonton 4-1.
— **NY Rangers** in 1979 against Philadelphia in best-of-seven QF, won by NY Rangers 4-1.

MOST SHORTHAND GOALS, BOTH TEAMS, ONE SERIES:
7 — **Boston Bruins (4), NY Rangers (3),** in 1958 SF won by Boston 4-2.
— **Edmonton Oilers (5), Calgary Flames (2),** in 1983 DF won by Edmonton 4-1.
— **Vancouver Canucks (6), St. Louis Blues (1),** in 1995 CQF won by Vancouver 4-3.

MOST SHORTHAND GOALS, ONE TEAM, ONE GAME:
3 — **Boston Bruins,** April 11, 1981, at Minnesota. Minnesota won 6-3.
— **NY Islanders,** April 17, 1983, at NY Rangers. NY Rangers won 7-6.
— **Toronto Maple Leafs,** May 8, 1994, at San Jose. Toronto won 8-3.

MOST SHORTHAND GOALS, BOTH TEAMS, ONE GAME:
4 — **NY Islanders, NY Rangers,** April 17, 1983, at NY Rangers. NY Islanders had 3 shorthand goals, NY Rangers 1. NY Rangers won 7-6.
— **Boston Bruins, Minnesota North Stars,** April 11, 1981, at Minnesota. Boston had 3 shorthand goals, Minnesota 1. Minnesota won 6-3.
— **San Jose Sharks, Toronto Maple Leafs,** May 8, 1994, at San Jose. Toronto had 3 shorthand goals, San Jose 1. Toronto won 8-3.
3 — Toronto Maple Leafs, Detroit Red Wings, April 5, 1947, at Toronto. Toronto had 2 shorthand goals, Detroit 1. Toronto won 6-1.
— NY Rangers, Boston Bruins, April 1, 1958, at Boston. NY Rangers had 2 shorthand goals, Boston 1. NY Rangers won 5-2.
— Minnesota North Stars, Philadelphia Flyers, May 4, 1980, at Minnesota. Minnesota had 2 shorthand goals, Philadelphia 1. Philadelphia won 5-3.
— Edmonton Oilers, Winnipeg Jets, April 9, 1988, at Winnipeg. Winnipeg had 2 shorthand goals, Edmonton 1. Winnipeg won 6-4.
— New Jersey Devils, NY Islanders, April 14, 1988, at New Jersey. NY Islanders had 2 shorthand goals, New Jersey 1. New Jersey won 6-5.
— Montreal Canadiens, New Jersey Devils, April 17, 1997, at New Jersey. Montreal had 2 shorthand goals, New Jersey 1. New Jersey won 5-2

MOST SHORTHAND GOALS, ONE TEAM, ONE PERIOD:
2 — **Toronto Maple Leafs,** April 5, 1947, at Toronto against Detroit, first period. Toronto won 6-1.
— **Toronto Maple Leafs,** April 13, 1965, at Toronto against Montreal, first period. Montreal won 4-3.
— **Boston Bruins,** April 20, 1969, at Boston against Montreal, first period. Boston won 3-2.
— **Boston Bruins,** April 8, 1970, at Boston against NY Rangers, second period. Boston won 8-2.
— **Boston Bruins,** April 30, 1972, at Boston against NY Rangers, first period. Boston won 6-5.
— **Chicago Blackhawks,** May 3, 1973, at Chicago against Montreal, first period. Chicago won 7-4.
— **Montreal Canadiens,** April 23, 1978, at Detroit, first period. Montreal won 8-0.
— **NY Islanders,** April 8, 1980, at New York against Los Angeles, second period. NY Islanders won 8-1.
— **Los Angeles Kings,** April 9, 1980, at NY Islanders, first period. Los Angeles won 6-3.
— **Boston Bruins,** April 13, 1980, at Pittsburgh, second period. Boston won 8-3.
— **Minnesota North Stars,** May 4, 1980, at Minnesota against Philadelphia, second period. Philadelphia won 5-3.
— **Boston Bruins,** April 11, 1981, at Minnesota, third period. Minnesota won 6-3.
— **NY Islanders,** May 12, 1981, at New York against Minnesota, first period. NY Islanders won 6-3.
— **Montreal Canadiens,** April 7, 1982, at Montreal against Quebec, third period. Montreal won 5-1.
— **Edmonton Oilers,** April 24, 1983, at Edmonton against Chicago, third period. Edmonton won 8-4.
— **Winnipeg Jets,** April 14, 1985, at Calgary, second period. Winnipeg won 5-3.
— **Boston Bruins,** April 6, 1988, at Boston against Buffalo, first period. Boston won 7-3.
— **NY Islanders,** April 14, 1988, at New Jersey, third period. New Jersey won 6-5.
— **Detroit Red Wings,** April 29, 1993, at Toronto, second period. Detroit won 7-3.
— **Toronto Maple Leafs,** May 8, 1994, at San Jose, third period. Toronto won 8-3.
— **Calgary Flames,** May 11, 1995, at San Jose, first period. Calgary won 9-2.
— **Vancouver Canucks,** May 15, 1995 at St. Louis, second period. Vancouver won 6-5.
— **Montreal Canadiens,** April 17, 1997, at New Jersey, second period. New Jersey won 5-2.
— **Philadelphia Flyers,** April 26, 1997, at Philadelphia against Pittsburgh, first period. Philadelphia won 6-3.

MOST SHORTHAND GOALS, BOTH TEAMS, ONE PERIOD:
3 — **Toronto Maple Leafs, Detroit Red Wings,** April 5, 1947, at Toronto, first period. Toronto had 2 shorthand goals, Detroit 1. Toronto won 6-1.
— **Toronto Maple Leafs, San Jose Sharks,** May 8, 1994, at San Jose, third period. Toronto had 2 shorthand goals, San Jose 1. Toronto won 8-3.

FASTEST GOALS

FASTEST FIVE GOALS, BOTH TEAMS:
3 Minutes, 6 Seconds — Chicago Blackhawks, Minnesota North Stars, at Chicago April 21, 1985. Keith Brown scored for Chicago at 1:12, second period; Ken Yaremchuk, Chicago, 1:27; Dino Ciccarelli, Minnesota, 2:48; Tony McKegney, Minnesota, 4:07; and Curt Fraser, Chicago, 4:18. Chicago won 6-2 and best-of-seven DF 4-2.
3 Minutes, 20 Seconds — Minnesota North Stars, Philadelphia Flyers, at Philadelphia, April 29, 1980. Paul Shmyr scored for Minnesota at 13:20, first period; Steve Christoff, Minnesota, 13:59; Ken Linseman, Philadelphia, 14:54; Tom Gorence, Philadelphia, 15:36; and Linseman, 16:40. Minnesota won 6-5. Philadelphia won best-of-seven SF 4-1.
4 Minutes, 19 Seconds — Toronto Maple Leafs, NY Rangers at Toronto, April 9, 1932. Ace Bailey scored for Toronto at 15:07, third period; Fred Cook, NY Rangers, 16:32; Bob Gracie, Toronto, 17:36; Frank Boucher, NY Rangers, 18:26 and again at 19:26. Toronto won 6-4 and best-of-five F 3-0.

FASTEST FIVE GOALS, ONE TEAM:
3 Minutes, 36 Seconds — Montreal Canadiens at Montreal, March 30, 1944, against Toronto. Toe Blake scored at 7:58 of third period and again at 8:37; Maurice Richard, 9:17; Ray Getliffe, 10:33; and Buddy O'Connor, 11:34. Canadiens won 11-0 and best-of-seven SF 4-1.

FASTEST FOUR GOALS, BOTH TEAMS:
1 Minute, 33 Seconds — Philadelphia Flyers, Toronto Maple Leafs at Philadelphia, April 20, 1976. Don Saleski of Philadelphia scored at 10:04 of second period; Bob Neely, Toronto, 10:42; Gary Dornhoefer, Philadelphia, 11:24; and Don Saleski, 11:37. Philadelphia won 7-1 and best-of-seven QF series 4-3.
1 minute, 34 seconds — Montreal Canadiens, Calgary Flames at Montreal, May 20, 1986. Joel Otto of Calgary scored at 17:59 of first period; Bobby Smith, Montreal, 18:25; Mats Naslund, Montreal, 19:17; and Bob Gainey, Montreal, 19:33. Montreal won 5-3 and best-of-seven F series 4-1.
1 Minute, 38 Seconds — Boston Bruins, Philadelphia Flyers at Philadelphia, April 26, 1977. Gregg Sheppard of Boston scored at 14:01 of second period; Mike Milbury, Boston, 15:01; Gary Dornhoefer, Philadelphia, 15:16; and Jean Ratelle, Boston, 15:39. Boston won 5-4 and best-of-seven SF series 4-0.

FASTEST FOUR GOALS, ONE TEAM:
2 Minutes, 35 Seconds — Montreal Canadiens at Montreal, March 30, 1944, against Toronto. Toe Blake scored at 7:58 of third period and again at 8:37; Maurice Richard, 9:17; Ray Getliffe, 10:33. Montreal won 11-0 and best-of-seven SF 4-1.

FASTEST THREE GOALS, BOTH TEAMS:
21 Seconds — Edmonton Oilers, Chicago Blackhawks at Edmonton, May 7, 1985. Behn Wilson scored for Chicago at 19:22 of third period, Jari Kurri at 19:36 and Glenn Anderson at 19:43 for Edmonton. Edmonton won 7-3 and best-of-seven CF 4-2.
30 Seconds — Chicago Blackhawks, Pittsburgh Penguins at Chicago, June 1, 1992. Dirk Graham scored for Chicago at 6:21 of first period, Kevin Stevens for Pittsburgh at 6:33 and Graham for Chicago at 6:51. Pittsburgh won 6-5 and best-of-seven F 4-0.
31 Seconds — Edmonton Oilers, Philadelphia Flyers at Edmonton, May 25, 1985. Wayne Gretzky scored for Edmonton at 1:10 and 1:25 of first period, Derrick Smith scored for Philadelphia at 1:41. Edmonton won 4-3 and best-of-seven F 4-1.

FASTEST THREE GOALS, ONE TEAM:
23 Seconds — Toronto Maple Leafs at Toronto, April 12, 1979, against Atlanta. Darryl Sittler scored at 4:04 of first period and again at 4:16 and Ron Ellis at 4:27. Leafs won 7-4 and best-of-three PR 2-0.
38 Seconds — NY Rangers at New York, April 12, 1986 against Philadelphia. Jim Wiemer scored at 12:29 of third period, Bob Brooke at 12:43 and Ron Greschner at 13:07. NY Rangers won 5-2 and best-of-five DSF 3-2.
56 Seconds — Montreal Canadiens at Detroit, April 6, 1954. Dickie Moore scored at 15:03 of first period, Maurice Richard at 15:28 and again at 15:59. Montreal won 3-1. Detroit won best-of-seven F 4-3.

FASTEST TWO GOALS, BOTH TEAMS:
5 Seconds — Pittsburgh Penguins, Buffalo Sabres at Buffalo, April 14, 1979. Gilbert Perreault scored for Buffalo at 12:59 and Jim Hamilton for Pittsburgh at 13:04 of first period. Pittsburgh won 4-3 and best-of-three PR 2-0.
8 Seconds — Minnesota North Stars, St. Louis Blues at Minnesota, April 9, 1989. Bernie Federko scored for St. Louis at 2:28 of third period and Perry Berezan at 2:36 for Minnesota. Minnesota won 5-4. St. Louis won best-of-seven DSF 4-1.
9 Seconds — NY Islanders, Washington Capitals at Washington, April 10, 1986. Bryan Trottier scored for New York at 18:26 of second period and Scott Stevens at 18:35 for Washington. Washington won 5-2, and best-of-five DSF 3-0.
10 Seconds — Washington Capitals, New Jersey Devils at New Jersey, April 5, 1990. Pat Conacher scored for New Jersey at 8:02 of second period and Dale Hunter at 8:12 for Washington. Washington won 5-4, and best-of-seven DSF 4-2.
— Calgary Flames, Edmonton Oilers at Edmonton, April 8, 1991. Joe Nieuwendyk scored for Calgary at 2:03 of first period and Esa Tikkanen at 2:13 for Edmonton. Edmonton won 4-3, and best-of-seven DSF 4-3.

FASTEST TWO GOALS, ONE TEAM:
5 Seconds — Detroit Red Wings at Detroit, April 11, 1965, against Chicago. Norm Ullman scored at 17:35 and 17:40, second period. Detroit won 4-2. Chicago won best-of-seven SF 4-3.

The Atlanta Flames were burned early and often by Darryl Sittler and the Toronto Maple Leafs in game two of their Preliminary Round series on April 12, 1979. Sittler scored at 4:04 and 4:16 and Ron Ellis connected at 4:27 to give the Leafs three goals in 32 seconds, a record first-period explosion.

OVERTIME

SHORTEST OVERTIME:
9 Seconds — Montreal Canadiens, Calgary Flames, at Calgary, May 18, 1986. Montreal won 3-2 on Brian Skrudland's goal and captured the best-of-seven F 4-1.
11 Seconds — NY Islanders, NY Rangers, at NY Rangers, April 11, 1975. NY Islanders won 4-3 on Jean-Paul Parise's goal and captured the best-of-three PR 2-1.

LONGEST OVERTIME:
116 Minutes, 30 Seconds — Detroit Red Wings, Mtl. Maroons at Montreal, March 24, 25, 1936. Detroit 1, Mtl. Maroons 0. Mud Bruneteau scored, assisted by Hec Kilrea, at 16:30 of sixth overtime period, or after 176 minutes, 30 seconds from start of game, which ended at 2:25 a.m. Detroit won best-of-five SF 3-0.

MOST OVERTIME GAMES, ONE PLAYOFF YEAR:
28 — 1993. Of 85 games played, 28 went into overtime.
19 — 1996. Of 86 games played, 19 went into overtime.
18 — 1994. Of 90 games played, 18 went into overtime.
— 1995. Of 81 games played, 18 went into overtime.

FEWEST OVERTIME GAMES, ONE PLAYOFF YEAR:
0 — 1963. None of the 16 games went into overtime, the only year since 1926 that no overtime was required in any playoff series.

MOST OVERTIME GAMES, ONE SERIES:
5 — Toronto Maple Leafs, Montreal Canadiens in 1951. Toronto defeated Montreal 4-1 in best-of-seven F.
4 — Toronto Maple Leafs, Boston Bruins in 1933. Toronto won best-of-five SF 3-2.
— Boston Bruins, NY Rangers in 1939. Boston won best-of-seven SF 4-3.
— St. Louis Blues, Minnesota North Stars in 1968. St. Louis won best-of-seven SF 4-3.

THREE-OR-MORE GOAL GAMES

MOST THREE-OR-MORE GOAL GAMES BY ALL TEAMS, ONE PLAYOFF YEAR:
12 — **1983** in 66 games.
— **1988** in 83 games.
11 — 1985 in 70 games.
— 1992 in 86 games.

MOST THREE-OR-MORE GOAL GAMES, ONE TEAM, ONE PLAYOFF YEAR:
6 — Edmonton Oilers in 16 games, 1983.
— **Edmonton Oilers in 18 games, 1985.**

SHUTOUTS

MOST SHUTOUTS, ONE PLAYOFF YEAR, ALL TEAMS:
18 — 1997. Of 82 games played, Colorado and NY Rangers had 3 each, Edmonton, New Jersey, and St. Louis had 2 each, while Anaheim, Buffalo, Detroit, Florida, Ottawa and Phoenix had 1 each.
16 — 1994. Of 90 games played, NY Rangers and Vancouver had 4 each, Toronto had 3, Buffalo had 2, while Washington, Detroit and New Jersey had 1 each.

FEWEST SHUTOUTS, ONE PLAYOFF YEAR, ALL TEAMS:
0 — 1959. 18 games played.

MOST SHUTOUTS, BOTH TEAMS, ONE SERIES:
5 — 1945 F, Toronto Maple Leafs, Detroit Red Wings. Toronto had 3 shutouts, Detroit 2. Toronto won best-of-seven series 4-3.
— **1950 SF, Toronto Maple Leafs, Detroit Red Wings.** Toronto had 3 shutouts, Detroit 2. Detroit won best-of-seven series 4-3.

TEAM PENALTIES

FEWEST PENALTIES, BOTH TEAMS, BEST-OF-SEVEN SERIES:
19 — Detroit Red Wings, Toronto Maple Leafs in 1945 F, won by Toronto 4-3. Detroit received 10 minors, Toronto had 9 minors.

FEWEST PENALTIES, ONE TEAM, BEST-OF-SEVEN SERIES:
9 — Toronto Maple Leafs in 1945 F, won by Toronto 4-3 against Detroit.

MOST PENALTIES, BOTH TEAMS, ONE SERIES:
219 — New Jersey Devils, Washington Capitals in 1988 DF won by New Jersey 4-3. New Jersey received 98 minors, 11 majors, 9 misconducts and 1 match penalty. Washington received 80 minors, 11 majors, 8 misconducts and 1 match penalty.

MOST PENALTY MINUTES, BOTH TEAMS, ONE SERIES:
656 — New Jersey Devils, Washington Capitals in 1988 DF won by New Jersey 4-3. New Jersey had 351 minutes; Washington 305.

MOST PENALTIES, ONE TEAM, ONE SERIES:
119 — New Jersey Devils in 1988 DF versus Washington. New Jersey received 98 minors, 11 majors, 9 misconducts and 1 match penalty.

MOST PENALTY MINUTES, ONE TEAM, ONE SERIES:
351 — New Jersey Devils in 1988 DF versus Washington. Series won by New Jersey 4-3.

MOST PENALTIES, BOTH TEAMS, ONE GAME:
66 — Detroit Red Wings, St. Louis Blues, at St. Louis, April 12, 1991. Detroit received 33 penalties; St. Louis had 33. St. Louis won 6-1.
62 — New Jersey Devils, Washington Capitals, at New Jersey, April 22, 1988. New Jersey received 32 penalties; Washington 30. New Jersey won 10-4.

MOST PENALTY MINUTES, BOTH TEAMS, ONE GAME:
298 Minutes — Detroit Red Wings, St. Louis Blues, at St. Louis, April 12, 1991. Detroit received 33 penalties for 152 minutes; St. Louis 33 penalties for 146 minutes. St. Louis won 6-1.
267 Minutes — NY Rangers, Los Angeles Kings, at Los Angeles, April 9, 1981. NY Rangers received 31 penalties for 142 minutes; Los Angeles 28 penalties for 125 minutes. Los Angeles won 5-4.

MOST PENALTIES, ONE TEAM, ONE GAME:
33 — Detroit Red Wings, at St. Louis, April 12,1991. St. Louis won 6-1.
— **St. Louis Blues,** at St. Louis, April 12, 1991. St. Louis won 6-1.
32 — New Jersey Devils, at Washington, April 22,1988. New Jersey won 10-4.
31 — NY Rangers, at Los Angeles, April 9, 1981. Los Angeles won 5-4.
30 — Philadelphia Flyers, at Toronto, April 15, 1976. Toronto won 5-4.

MOST PENALTY MINUTES, ONE TEAM, ONE GAME:
152 — Detroit Red Wings, at St. Louis, April 12, 1991. St. Louis won 6-1.
146 — St. Louis Blues, at St. Louis, April 12, 1991. St. Louis won 6-1.
142 — NY Rangers, at Los Angeles, April 9, 1981. Los Angeles won 5-4.

MOST PENALTIES, BOTH TEAMS, ONE PERIOD:
43 — NY Rangers, Los Angeles Kings, April 9, 1981, at Los Angeles, first period. NY Rangers had 24 penalties; Los Angeles 19. Los Angeles won 5-4.

MOST PENALTY MINUTES, BOTH TEAMS, ONE PERIOD:
248 — NY Islanders, Boston Bruins, April 17, 1980, first period, at Boston. Each team received 124 minutes. Islanders won 5-4.

MOST PENALTIES, ONE TEAM, ONE PERIOD: (AND) MOST PENALTY MINUTES, ONE TEAM, ONE PERIOD:
24 Penalties; 125 Minutes — NY Rangers, April 9, 1981, at Los Angeles, first period. Los Angeles won 5-4.

Individual Records

GAMES PLAYED

MOST YEARS IN PLAYOFFS:
20 — Gordie Howe, Detroit, Hartford (1947-58 incl.; 60-61; 63-66 incl.; 70 & 80)
— **Larry Robinson, Montreal, Los Angeles** (1973-92 incl.)
19 — Red Kelly, Detroit, Toronto
18 — Stan Mikita, Chicago
— Henri Richard, Montreal

MOST CONSECUTIVE YEARS IN PLAYOFFS:
20 — Larry Robinson, Montreal, Los Angeles (1973-1992, inclusive).
17 — Brad Park, NY Rangers, Boston, Detroit (1969-1985, inclusive).
— Ray Bourque, Boston (1980-96, inclusive).
16 — Jean Beliveau, Montreal (1954-69, inclusive).
— Bob Gainey, Montreal (1974-89, inclusive).
— Dale Hunter, Quebec, Washington (1981-96, inclusive)

MOST PLAYOFF GAMES:
236 — Mark Messier, Edmonton, NY Rangers
227 — Larry Robinson, Montreal, Los Angeles
225 — Glenn Anderson, Edmonton, Toronto, NY Rangers, St. Louis
221 — Bryan Trottier, NY Islanders, Pittsburgh
213 — Kevin Lowe, Edmonton, NY Rangers

GOALS

MOST GOALS IN PLAYOFFS (CAREER):
122 — Wayne Gretzky, Edmonton, Los Angeles, St. Louis, NY Rangers
109 — Mark Messier, Edmonton, NY Rangers
106 — Jari Kurri, Edmonton, Los Angeles, NY Rangers, Anaheim
93 — Glenn Anderson, Edmonton, Toronto, NY Rangers, St. Louis
85 — Mike Bossy, NY Islanders

MOST GOALS, ONE PLAYOFF YEAR:
19 — Reggie Leach, Philadelphia, 1976. 16 games.
— **Jari Kurri, Edmonton,** 1985. 18 games.
18 — Joe Sakic, Colorado, 1996. 22 games.
17 — Newsy Lalonde, Montreal, 1919. 10 games.
— Mike Bossy, NY Islanders, 1981. 18 games.
— Steve Payne, Minnesota, 1981. 19 games.
— Mike Bossy, NY Islanders, 1982. 19 games.
— Mike Bossy, NY Islanders, 1983. 19 games
— Wayne Gretzky, Edmonton, 1985. 18 games.
— Kevin Stevens, Pittsburgh, 1991. 24 games.

MOST GOALS IN ONE SERIES (OTHER THAN FINAL):
12 — Jari Kurri, Edmonton, in 1985 CF, 6 games vs. Chicago.
11 — Newsy Lalonde, Montreal, in 1919 NHL F, 5 games vs. Ottawa.
10 — Tim Kerr, Philadelphia, in 1989 DF, 7 games vs. Pittsburgh.
9 — Reggie Leach, Philadelphia, in 1976 SF, 5 games vs. Boston.
— Bill Barber, Philadelphia, in 1980 SF, 5 games vs. Minnesota.
— Mike Bossy, NY Islanders, in 1983 CF, 6 games vs. Boston.
— Mario Lemieux, Pittsburgh, in 1989 DF, 7 games vs. Philadelphia.

MOST GOALS IN FINAL SERIES:
9 — Babe Dye, Toronto, in 1922, 5 games vs. Van. Millionaires.
8 — Alf Skinner, Toronto, in 1918, 5 games vs. Van. Millionaires.
7 — Jean Beliveau, Montreal, in 1956, 5 games vs. Detroit.
— Mike Bossy, NY Islanders, in 1982, 4 games vs. Vancouver.
— Wayne Gretzky, Edmonton, in 1985, 5 games vs. Philadelphia.

MOST GOALS, ONE GAME:
5 — Newsy Lalonde, Montreal, March 1, 1919, at Montreal. Final score: Montreal 6, Ottawa 3.
— **Maurice Richard, Montreal,** March 23, 1944, at Montreal. Final score: Montreal 5, Toronto 1.
— **Darryl Sittler, Toronto,** April 22, 1976, at Toronto. Final score: Toronto 8, Philadelphia 5.
— **Reggie Leach, Philadelphia,** May 6, 1976, at Philadelphia. Final score: Philadelphia 6, Boston 3.
— **Mario Lemieux, Pittsburgh,** April 25, 1989 at Pittsburgh. Final score: Pittsburgh 10, Philadelphia 7.

MOST GOALS, ONE PERIOD:
4 — Tim Kerr, Philadelphia, April 13, 1985, at New York vs. NY Rangers, second period. Final score: Philadelphia 6, NY Rangers 5.
— **Mario Lemieux, Pittsburgh,** April 25, 1989, at Pittsburgh vs. Philadelphia, first period. Final score: Pittsburgh 10, Philadelphia 7.

ASSISTS

MOST ASSISTS IN PLAYOFFS (CAREER):
260 — Wayne Gretzky, Edmonton, Los Angeles, St. Louis, NY Rangers
186 — Mark Messier, Edmonton, NY Rangers
136 — Paul Coffey, Edmonton, Pittsburgh, Los Angeles, Detroit, Philadelphia
127 — Jari Kurri, Edmonton, Los Angeles, NY Rangers, Anaheim
121 — Glenn Anderson, Edmonton, Toronto, NY Rangers, St. Louis

MOST ASSISTS, ONE PLAYOFF YEAR:
31 — Wayne Gretzky, Edmonton, 1988. 19 games.
30 — Wayne Gretzky, Edmonton, 1985. 18 games.
29 — Wayne Gretzky, Edmonton, 1987. 21 games.
28 — Mario Lemieux, Pittsburgh, 1991. 23 games.
26 — Wayne Gretzky, Edmonton, 1983. 16 games.

MOST ASSISTS IN ONE SERIES (OTHER THAN FINAL):
14 — Rick Middleton, Boston, in 1983 DF, 7 games vs. Buffalo.
— **Wayne Gretzky, Edmonton,** in 1985 CF, 6 games vs. Chicago.
13 — Wayne Gretzky, Edmonton, in 1987 DSF, 5 games vs. Los Angeles.
— Doug Gilmour, Toronto, in 1994 CSF, 7 games vs. San Jose.
11 — Mark Messier, Edmonton, in 1989 DSF, 7 games vs. Los Angeles.
— Al MacInnis, Calgary, in 1984 DF, 7 games vs. Edmonton.
— Mike Ridley, Washington, in 1992 DSF, 7 games vs. Pittsburgh.
— Ron Francis, Pittsburgh, in 1995 CQF, 7 games vs. Washington.
10 — Fleming Mackell, Boston, in 1958 SF, 6 games vs. NY Rangers.
— Stan Mikita, Chicago, in 1962 SF, 6 games vs. Montreal.
— Bob Bourne, NY Islanders, in 1983 DF, 6 games vs. NY Rangers.
— Wayne Gretzky, Edmonton, in 1988 DSF, 5 games vs. Winnipeg.
— Mario Lemieux, Pittsburgh, in 1992 DSF, 6 games vs. Washington.

MOST ASSISTS IN FINAL SERIES:
10 — Wayne Gretzky, Edmonton, in 1988, 4 games plus suspended game vs. Boston.
9 — Jacques Lemaire, Montreal, in 1973, 6 games vs. Chicago.
— Wayne Gretzky, Edmonton, in 1987, 7 games vs. Philadelphia.
— Larry Murphy, Pittsburgh, in 1991, 6 games vs. Minnesota.

MOST ASSISTS, ONE GAME:
6 — Mikko Leinonen, NY Rangers, April 8, 1982, at New York. Final score: NY Rangers 7, Philadelphia 3.
— **Wayne Gretzky, Edmonton,** April 9, 1987, at Edmonton. Final score: Edmonton 13, Los Angeles 3.
5 — Toe Blake, Montreal, March 23, 1944, at Montreal. Final score: Montreal 5, Toronto 1.
— Maurice Richard, Montreal, March 27, 1956, at Montreal. Final score: Montreal 7, NY Rangers 0.
— Bert Olmstead, Montreal, March 30, 1957, at Montreal. Final score: Montreal 8, NY Rangers 3.
— Don McKenney, Boston, April 5, 1958, at Boston. Final score: Boston 8, NY Rangers 2.
— Stan Mikita, Chicago, April 4, 1973, at Chicago. Final score: Chicago 7, St. Louis 1.
— Wayne Gretzky, Edmonton, April 8, 1981, at Montreal. Final score: Edmonton 6, Montreal 3.
— Paul Coffey, Edmonton, May 14, 1985, at Edmonton. Final score: Edmonton 10, Chicago 5.
— Doug Gilmour, St. Louis, April 15, 1986, at Minnesota. Final score: St. Louis 6, Minnesota 3.
— Risto Siltanen, Quebec, April 14, 1987 at Hartford. Final score: Quebec 7, Hartford 5.
— Patrik Sundstrom, New Jersey, April 22, 1988, at New Jersey. Final score: New Jersey 10, Washington 4.

MOST ASSISTS, ONE PERIOD:
3 — Three assists by one player in one period of a playoff game has been recorded on 66 occasions. Rod Brind'Amour of the Philadelphia Flyers is the most recent to equal this mark with 3 assists in the second period at Buffalo, May 11, 1997. Final score: Philadelphia 6, Buffalo 3.
Wayne Gretzky has had 3 assists in one period 5 times; Ray Bourque, 3 times; Toe Blake, Jean Beliveau, Doug Harvey and Bobby Orr, twice. Nick Metz of Toronto was the first player to be credited with 3 assists in one period of a playoff game Mar. 21, 1941 at Toronto vs. Boston.

POINTS

MOST POINTS IN PLAYOFFS (CAREER):
382 — Wayne Gretzky, Edmonton, Los Angeles, St. Louis, NY Rangers, 122G, 260A
295 — Mark Messier, Edmonton, NY Rangers, 109G, 186A
233 — Jari Kurri, Edmonton, Los Angeles, NY Rangers, Anaheim, 106G, 127A
214 — Glenn Anderson, Edmonton, Toronto, NY Rangers, St. Louis, 93G, 121A
195 — Paul Coffey, Edmonton, Pittsburgh, Los Angeles, Detroit, Philadelphia, 59G, 136A

MOST POINTS, ONE PLAYOFF YEAR:
47 — Wayne Gretzky, Edmonton, in 1985. 17 goals, 30 assists in 18 games.
44 — Mario Lemieux, Pittsburgh, in 1991. 16 goals, 28 assists in 23 games.
43 — Wayne Gretzky, Edmonton, in 1988. 12 goals, 31 assists in 19 games.
40 — Wayne Gretzky, Los Angeles, in 1993. 15 goals, 25 assists in 24 games.
38 — Wayne Gretzky, Edmonton, in 1983. 12 goals, 26 assists in 16 games.

MOST POINTS IN ONE SERIES (OTHER THAN FINAL):
19 — Rick Middleton, Boston, in 1983 DF, 7 games vs. Buffalo. 5 goals, 14 assists.
18 — Wayne Gretzky, Edmonton, in 1985 CF, 6 games vs. Chicago. 4 goals, 14 assists.
17 — Mario Lemieux, Pittsburgh, in 1992 DSF, 6 games vs. Washington. 7 goals, 10 assists.
16 — Barry Pederson, Boston, in 1983 DF, 7 games vs. Buffalo. 7 goals, 9 assists.
— Doug Gilmour, Toronto, in 1994 CSF, 7 games vs. San Jose. 3 goals, 13 assists.
15 — Jari Kurri, Edmonton, in 1985 CF, 6 games vs. Chicago. 12 goals, 3 assists.
— Wayne Gretzky, Edmonton, in 1987 DSF, 5 games vs. Los Angeles. 2 goals, 13 assists.
— Tim Kerr, Philadelphia, in 1989 DF, 7 games vs. Pittsburgh. 10 goals, 5 assists.
— Mario Lemieux, Pittsburgh, in 1991 CF, 6 games vs. Boston. 6 goals, 9 assists.

MOST POINTS IN FINAL SERIES:

13 — **Wayne Gretzky, Edmonton,** in 1988, 4 games plus suspended game vs. Boston. 3 goals, 10 assists.

12 — Gordie Howe, Detroit, in 1955, 7 games vs. Montreal. 5 goals, 7 assists.
— Yvan Cournoyer, Montreal, in 1973, 6 games vs. Chicago. 6 goals, 6 assists.
— Jacques Lemaire, Montreal, in 1973, 6 games vs. Chicago. 3 goals, 9 assists.
— Mario Lemieux, Pittsburgh, in 1991, 5 games vs. Minnesota. 5 goals, 7 assists.

MOST POINTS, ONE GAME:

8 — **Patrik Sundstrom, New Jersey,** April 22, 1988 at New Jersey during 10-4 win over Washington. Sundstrom had 3 goals, 5 assists.
— **Mario Lemieux, Pittsburgh,** April 25, 1989 at Pittsburgh during 10-7 win over Philadelphia. Lemieux had 5 goals, 3 assists.

7 — Wayne Gretzky, Edmonton, April 17, 1983 at Calgary during 10-2 win. Gretzky had 4 goals, 3 assists.
— Wayne Gretzky, Edmonton, April 25,1985 at Winnipeg during 8-3 win. Gretzky had 3 goals, 4 assists.
— Wayne Gretzky, Edmonton, April 9, 1987, at Edmonton during 13-3 win over Los Angeles. Gretzky had 1 goal, 6 assists.

6 — Dickie Moore, Montreal, March 25, 1954, at Montreal during 8-1 win over Boston. Moore had 2 goals, 4 assists.
— Phil Esposito, Boston, April 2, 1969, at Boston during 10-0 win over Toronto. Esposito had 4 goals, 2 assists.
— Darryl Sittler, Toronto, April 22, 1976, at Toronto during 8-5 win over Philadelphia. Sittler had 5 goals, 1 assist.
— Guy Lafleur, Montreal, April 11, 1977, at Montreal during 7-2 victory vs. St. Louis. Lafleur had 3 goals, 3 assists.
— Mikko-Leinonen, NY Rangers, April 8, 1982, at New York during 7-3 win over Philadelphia. Leinonen had 6 assists.
— Paul Coffey, Edmonton, May 14, 1985 at Edmonton during 10-5 win over Chicago. Coffey had 1 goal, 5 assists.
— John Anderson, Hartford, April 12, 1986 at Hartford during 9-4 win over Quebec. Anderson had 2 goals, 4 assists.
— Mario Lemieux, Pittsburgh, April 23, 1992 at Pittsburgh during 6-4 win over Washington. Lemieux had 3 goals, 3 assists.

MOST POINTS, ONE PERIOD:

4 — **Maurice Richard, Montreal,** March 29, 1945, at Montreal vs. Toronto. Third period, 3 goals, 1 assist. Final score: Montreal 10, Toronto 3.
— **Dickie Moore, Montreal,** March 25, 1954, at Montreal vs. Boston. First period, 2 goals, 2 assists. Final score: Montreal 8, Boston 1.
— **Barry Pederson, Boston,** April 8, 1982, at Boston vs. Buffalo. Second period, 3 goals, 1 assist. Final score: Boston 7, Buffalo 3.
— **Peter McNab, Boston,** April 11, 1982, at Buffalo. Second period, 1 goal, 3 assists. Final score: Boston 5, Buffalo 2.
— **Tim Kerr, Philadelphia,** April 13, 1985 at New York. Second period, 4 goals. Final score: Philadelphia 6, Rangers 5.
— **Ken Linseman, Boston,** April 14, 1985 at Boston vs. Montreal. Second period, 2 goals, 2 assists. Final score: Boston 7, Montreal 6.
— **Wayne Gretzky, Edmonton,** April 12, 1987, at Los Angeles. Third period, 1 goal, 3 assists. Final score: Edmonton 6, Los Angeles 3.
— **Glenn Anderson, Edmonton,** April 6, 1988, at Edmonton vs. Winnipeg. Third period, 3 goals, 1 assist. Final score: Edmonton 7, Winnipeg 4.
— **Mario Lemieux, Pittsburgh,** April 25, 1989, at Pittsburgh vs. Philadelphia. First period, 4 goals. Final score: Pittsburgh 10, Philadelphia 7.
— **Dave Gagner, Minnesota,** April 8, 1991, at Minnesota vs. Chicago. First period, 2 goals, 2 assists. Final score: Chicago 6, Minnesota 5.
— **Mario Lemieux, Pittsburgh,** April 23, 1992, at Pittsburgh vs. Washington. Second period, 2 goals, 2 assists. Final score: Pittsburgh 6, Washington 4.

POWER-PLAY GOALS

MOST POWER-PLAY GOALS IN PLAYOFFS (CAREER):

35 — **Mike Bossy, NY Islanders**

34 — Dino Ciccarelli, Minnesota, Washington, Detroit
— Wayne Gretzky, Edmonton, Los Angeles, St. Louis, NY Rangers
28 — Mario Lemieux, Pittsburgh
27 — Denis Potvin, NY Islanders

MOST POWER-PLAY GOALS, ONE PLAYOFF YEAR:

9 — **Mike Bossy, NY Islanders,** 1981. 18 games against Toronto, Edmonton, NY Rangers and Minnesota.
— **Cam Neely, Boston,** 1991. 19 games against Hartford, Montreal, Pittsburgh.

8 — Tim Kerr, Philadelphia, 1989. 19 games.
— John Druce, Washington, 1990. 15 games.
— Brian Propp, Minnesota, 1991. 23 games.
— Mario Lemieux, Pittsburgh, 1992. 15 games.

MOST POWER-PLAY GOALS, ONE PLAYOFF SERIES:

6 — **Chris Kontos, Los Angeles,** 1989, DSF vs. Edmonton, won by Los Angeles 4-3.

5 — Andy Bathgate, Detroit, 1966, SF vs. Chicago, won by Detroit 4-2.
— Denis Potvin, NY Islanders, 1981, QF vs. Edmonton, won by NY Islanders 4-2.
— Ken Houston, Calgary, 1981, QF vs. Philadelphia, won by Calgary 4-3.
— Rick Vaive, Chicago, 1988, DSF vs. St. Louis, won by St. Louis 4-1.
— Tim Kerr, Philadelphia, 1989, DF vs. Pittsburgh, won by Philadelphia 4-3.
— Mario Lemieux, Pittsburgh, 1989, DF vs. Philadelphia won by Philadelphia 4-3.
— John Druce, Washington, 1990, DF vs. NY Rangers won by Washington 4-1.
— Pat LaFontaine, Buffalo, 1992, DSF vs. Boston won by Boston 4-3.
— Adam Graves, NY Rangers, 1996, CQF vs Montreal, won by NY Rangers 4-2.

MOST POWER-PLAY GOALS, ONE GAME:

3 — **Syd Howe, Detroit,** March 23, 1939, at Detroit vs. Montreal. Detroit won 7-3.
— **Sid Smith, Toronto,** April 10, 1949, at Detroit. Toronto won 3-1.
— **Phil Esposito, Boston,** April 2, 1969, at Boston vs. Toronto. Boston won 10-0.
— **John Bucyk, Boston,** April 21, 1974, at Boston vs. Chicago. Boston won 8-6.
— **Denis Potvin, NY Islanders,** April 17, 1981, at New York vs. Edmonton. NY Islanders won 6-3.
— **Tim Kerr, Philadelphia,** April 13, 1985, at NY Rangers. Philadelphia won 6-5.
— **Jari Kurri, Edmonton,** April 9, 1987, at Edmonton vs. Los Angeles. Edmonton won 13-3.
— **Mark Johnson, New Jersey,** April 22, 1988, at New Jersey vs. Washington. New Jersey won 10-4.
— **Dino Ciccarelli, Detroit,** April 29, 1993, at Toronto. Detroit won 7-3.
— **Dino Ciccarelli, Detroit,** May 11, 1995, at Dallas. Detroit won 5-1.
— **Valeri Kamensky, Colorado,** April 24, 1997, at Colorado vs. Chicago. Colorado won 7-0.

MOST POWER-PLAY GOALS, ONE PERIOD:

3 — **Tim Kerr, Philadelphia,** April 13, 1985 at New York, second period in 6-5 win vs. NY Rangers.

2 — Two power-play goals have been scored by one player in one period on 52 occasions. Charlie Conacher of Toronto was the first to score two power-play goals in one period, setting the mark on March 26, 1936. Rod Brind'Amour of the Philadelphia Flyers is the most recent to equal this mark with two power-play goals in the first period at Philadelphia, June 3, 1997. Final score: Detroit 4, Philadelphia 2.

SHORTHAND GOALS

MOST SHORTHAND GOALS IN PLAYOFFS (CAREER):

14 — **Mark Messier, Edmonton, NY Rangers**

11 — Wayne Gretzky, Edmonton, Los Angeles, St. Louis
10 — Jari Kurri, Edmonton, Los Angeles, NY Rangers
8 — Ed Westfall, Boston, NY Islanders
— Hakan Loob, Calgary

MOST SHORTHAND GOALS, ONE PLAYOFF YEAR:

3 — **Derek Sanderson, Boston,** 1969. 1 against Toronto in QF, won by Boston 4-0; 2 against Montreal in SF, won by Montreal, 4-2.
— **Bill Barber, Philadelphia,** 1980. All against Minnesota in SF, won by Philadelphia 4-1.
— **Lorne Henning, NY Islanders,** 1980. 1 against Boston in QF won by NY Islanders 4-1; 1 against Buffalo in SF, won by NY Islanders 4-2, 1 against Philadelphia in F, won by NY Islanders 4-2.
— **Wayne Gretzky, Edmonton,** 1983. 2 against Winnipeg in DSF won by Edmonton 3-0; 1 against Calgary in DF, won by Edmonton 4-1.
— **Wayne Presley, Chicago,** 1989. All against Detroit in DSF won by Chicago 4-2.
— **Todd Marchant, Edmonton,** 1997. 1 against Dallas in CQF won by Edmonton 4-3; 2 against Colorado in CSF won by Colorado 4-1.

MOST SHORTHAND GOALS, ONE PLAYOFF SERIES:

3 — **Bill Barber, Philadelphia,** 1980, SF vs. Minnesota, won by Philadelphia 4-1.
— **Wayne Presley, Chicago,** 1989, DSF vs. Detroit, won by Chicago 4-2.

2 — Mac Colville, NY Rangers, 1940, SF vs. Boston, won by NY Rangers 4-2.
— Jerry Toppazzini, Boston, 1958, SF vs. NY Rangers, won by Boston 4-2.
— Dave Keon, Toronto, 1963, F vs. Detroit, won by Toronto 4-1.
— Bob Pulford, Toronto, 1964, F vs. Detroit, won by Toronto 4-3.
— Serge Savard, Montreal, 1968, F vs. St. Louis, won by Montreal 4-0.
— Derek Sanderson, Boston, 1969, SF vs. Montreal, won by Montreal 4-2.
— Bryan Trottier, NY Islanders, 1980, PR vs. Los Angeles, won by NY Islanders 3-1.
— Bobby Lalonde, Boston, 1981, PR vs. Minnesota, won by Minnesota 3-0.
— Butch Goring, NY Islanders, 1981, SF vs. NY Rangers, won by NY Islanders 4-0.
— Wayne Gretzky, Edmonton, 1983, DSF vs. Winnipeg, won by Edmonton 3-0.
— Mark Messier, Edmonton, 1983, DF vs. Calgary, won by Edmonton 4-1.
— Jari Kurri, Edmonton, 1983, CF vs. Chicago, won by Edmonton 4-0.
— Wayne Gretzky, Edmonton, 1985, DF vs. Winnipeg, won by Edmonton 4-0.
— Kevin Lowe, Edmonton, 1987, F vs. Philadelphia, won by Edmonton 4-3.
— Bob Gould, Washington, 1988, DSF vs. Philadelphia, won by Washington 4-3.
— Dave Poulin, Philadelphia, 1989, DF vs. Pittsburgh, won by Philadelphia 4-3.
— Russ Courtnall, Montreal, 1991, DF vs. Boston, won by Boston 4-3.
— Sergei Fedorov, Detroit, 1992 DSF vs. Minnesota, won by Detroit 4-3.
— Mark Messier, NY Rangers, 1992, DSF vs. New Jersey, won by NY Rangers 4-3.
— Tom Fitzgerald, NY Islanders, 1993, DF vs. Pittsburgh, won by NY Islanders 4-3.
— Mark Osborne, Toronto, 1994, CSF vs. San Jose, won by Toronto 4-3.
— Tony Amonte, Chicago, 1997, CQF vs. Colorado, won by Colorado 4-2.
— Brian Rolston, New Jersey, 1997, CQF vs. Montreal, won by New Jersey 4-1.
— Rod Brind'Amour, Philadelphia, 1997, CQF vs. Pittsburgh, won by Philadelphia 4-1.
— Todd Marchant, Edmonton, 1997, CSF vs. Colorado, won by Colorado 4-1

MOST SHORTHAND GOALS, ONE GAME:

2 — **Dave Keon, Toronto,** April 18, 1963, at Toronto, in 3-1 win vs. Detroit.
— **Bryan Trottier, NY Islanders,** April 8, 1980 at New York, in 8-1 win vs. Los Angeles.
— **Bobby Lalonde, Boston,** April 11, 1981 at Minnesota, in 6-3 win by Minnesota.
— **Wayne Gretzky, Edmonton,** April 6, 1983 at Edmonton, in 6-3 win vs. Winnipeg.
— **Jari Kurri, Edmonton,** April 24, 1983, at Edmonton, in 8-3 win vs. Chicago.
— **Mark Messier, NY Rangers,** April 21, 1992, at New York, in 7-3 loss vs. New Jersey.
— **Tom Fitzgerald, NY Islanders,** May 8, 1993, at Long Island, in 6-5 win vs. Pittsburgh.
— **Rod Brind'Amour, Philadelphia,** April 26, 1997, at Philadelphia, in 6-3 win vs. Pittsburgh.

Doug Risebrough had reason to smile during the 1978 playoffs. He and teammate Bob Gainey each scored a shorthanded goal for the Montreal Canadiens in the first period of their 8-0 victory over Detroit on April 23, 1978.

MOST SHORTHAND GOALS, ONE PERIOD:
2 — **Bryan Trottier, NY Islanders,** April 8, 1980, second period at New York in 8-1 win vs. Los Angeles.
— **Bobby Lalonde, Boston,** April 11, 1981, third period at Minnesota in 6-3 win by Minnesota.
— **Jari Kurri, Edmonton,** April 24, 1983, third period at Edmonton in 8-4 win vs. Chicago.
— **Rod Brind'Amour, Philadelphia,** April 26, 1997, first period at Philadelphia in 6-3 win vs. Pittsburgh.

GAME-WINNING GOALS

MOST GAME-WINNING GOALS IN PLAYOFFS (CAREER):
24 — **Wayne Gretzky, Edmonton, Los Angeles, St. Louis, NY Rangers**
18 — Maurice Richard, Montreal
— Claude Lemieux, Montreal, New Jersey, Colorado
17 — Mike Bossy, NY Islanders
— Glenn Anderson, Edmonton, Toronto, NY Rangers, St. Louis

MOST GAME-WINNING GOALS, ONE PLAYOFF YEAR:
6 — **Joe Sakic, Colorado,** 1996. 22 games.
5 — Mike Bossy, NY Islanders, 1983. 19 games.
— Jari Kurri, Edmonton, 1987. 21 games.
— Bobby Smith, Minnesota, 1991. 23 games.
— Mario Lemieux, Pittsburgh, 1992. 15 games.

MOST GAME-WINNING GOALS, ONE PLAYOFF SERIES:
4 — **Mike Bossy, NY Islanders,** 1983, CF vs. Boston, won by NY Islanders 4-2.

OVERTIME GOALS

MOST OVERTIME GOALS IN PLAYOFFS (CAREER):
6 — **Maurice Richard, Montreal** (1 in 1946; 3 in 1951; 1 in 1957; 1 in 1958.)
5 — Glenn Anderson, Edmonton, Toronto, NY Rangers, St. Louis
4 — Bob Nystrom, NY Islanders
— Dale Hunter, Quebec, Washington
— Wayne Gretzky, Edmonton, Los Angeles
— Stephane Richer, Montreal, New Jersey
— Joe Murphy, Edmonton, Chicago
— Esa Tikkanen, Edmonton, NY Rangers
3 — Mel Hill, Boston
— Rene Robert, Buffalo
— Danny Gare, Buffalo
— Jacques Lemaire, Montreal
— Bobby Clarke, Philadelphia
— Terry O'Reilly, Boston
— Mike Bossy, NY Islanders
— Steve Payne, Minnesota
— Ken Morrow, NY Islanders
— Lanny McDonald, Toronto, Calgary
— Peter Stastny, Quebec
— Dino Ciccarelli, Minnesota, Washington
— Russ Courtnall, Montreal
— Kirk Muller, Montreal
— Doug Gilmour, St. Louis, Calgary, Toronto
— Greg Adams, Vancouver
— Claude Lemieux, Montreal, Colorado
— Mike Gartner, Washington, Toronto

MOST OVERTIME GOALS, ONE PLAYOFF YEAR:
3 — **Mel Hill, Boston,** 1939. All against NY Rangers in best-of-seven SF, won by Boston 4-3.
— **Maurice Richard, Montreal,** 1951. 2 against Detroit in best-of-seven SF, won by Montreal 4-2; 1 against Toronto best-of-seven F, won by Toronto 4-1.

MOST OVERTIME GOALS, ONE PLAYOFF SERIES:
3 — **Mel Hill, Boston,** 1939, SF vs. NY Rangers, won by Boston 4-3. Hill scored at 59:25 of overtime March 21 for a 2-1 win; at 8:24, March 23 for a 3-2 win; and at 48:00, April 2 for a 2-1 win.

SCORING BY A DEFENSEMAN

MOST GOALS BY A DEFENSEMAN, ONE PLAYOFF YEAR:
12 — Paul Coffey, Edmonton, 1985. 18 games.
11 — Brian Leetch, NY Rangers, 1994. 23 games.
 9 — Bobby Orr, Boston, 1970. 14 games.
   — Brad Park, Boston, 1978. 15 games.
 8 — Denis Potvin, NY Islanders, 1981. 18 games.
   — Raymond Bourque, Boston, 1983. 17 games.
   — Denis Potvin, NY Islanders, 1983. 20 games.
   — Paul Coffey, Edmonton, 1984. 19 games.

MOST GOALS BY A DEFENSEMAN, ONE GAME:
 3 — **Bobby Orr, Boston,** April 11, 1971 at Montreal. Final score: Boston 5, Montreal 2.
   — **Dick Redmond, Chicago,** April 4, 1973 at Chicago. Final score: Chicago 7, St. Louis 1.
   — **Denis Potvin, NY Islanders,** April 17, 1981 at New York. Final score: NY Islanders 6, Edmonton 3.
   — **Paul Reinhart, Calgary,** April 14, 1983 at Edmonton. Final score: Edmonton 6, Calgary 3.
   — **Paul Reinhart, Calgary,** April 8, 1984 at Vancouver. Final score: Calgary 5, Vancouver 1.
   — **Doug Halward, Vancouver,** April 7, 1984 at Vancouver. Final score: Vancouver 7, Calgary 0.
   — **Al Iafrate, Washington,** April 26, 1993 at Washington. Final score: Washington 6, NY Islanders 4.
   — **Eric Desjardins, Montreal,** June 3, 1993 at Montreal. Final score: Montreal 3, Los Angeles 2.
   — **Gary Suter, Chicago,** April 24, 1994, at Chicago. Final score: Chicago 4, Toronto 3.
   — **Brian Leetch, NY Rangers,** May 22, 1995 at Philadelphia. Final score: Philadelphia 4, NY Rangers 3.

MOST ASSISTS BY A DEFENSEMAN, ONE PLAYOFF YEAR:
25 — Paul Coffey, Edmonton, 1985. 18 games.
24 — Al MacInnis, Calgary, 1989. 22 games.
23 — Brian Leetch, NY Rangers, 1994. 23 games.
19 — Bobby Orr, Boston, 1972. 15 games.
18 — Ray Bourque, Boston, 1988. 23 games.
   — Ray Bourque, Boston, 1991. 19 games.
   — Larry Murphy, Pittsburgh, 1991. 23 games.

MOST ASSISTS BY A DEFENSEMAN, ONE GAME:
 5 — **Paul Coffey, Edmonton,** May 14, 1985 at Edmonton vs. Chicago. Edmonton won 10-5.
   — Risto Siltanen, Quebec, April 14, 1987 at Hartford. Quebec won 7-5.

MOST POINTS BY A DEFENSEMAN, ONE PLAYOFF YEAR:
37 — Paul Coffey, Edmonton, in 1985. 12 goals, 25 assists in 18 games.
34 — Brian Leetch, NY Rangers, in 1994. 11 goals, 23 assists in 23 games.
31 — Al MacInnis, Calgary, in 1989. 7 goals, 24 assists in 22 games.
25 — Denis Potvin, NY Islanders, in 1981. 8 goals, 17 assists in 18 games.
   — Ray Bourque, Boston, in 1991. 7 goals, 18 assists in 19 games.

MOST POINTS BY A DEFENSEMAN, ONE GAME:
 6 — **Paul Coffey, Edmonton,** May 14, 1985 at Edmonton vs. Chicago. 1 goal, 5 assists. Edmonton won 10-5.
 5 — Eddie Bush, Detroit, April 9, 1942, at Detroit vs. Toronto. 1 goal, 4 assists. Detroit won 5-2.
   — Bob Dailey, Philadelphia, May 1, 1980, at Philadelphia vs. Minnesota. 1 goal, 4 assists. Philadelphia won 7-0.
   — Denis Potvin, NY Islanders, April 17, 1981, at New York vs. Edmonton. 3 goals, 2 assists. NY Islanders won 6-3.
   — Risto Siltanen, Quebec, April 14, 1987 at Hartford. 5 assists. Quebec won 7-5.

SCORING BY A ROOKIE

MOST GOALS BY A ROOKIE, ONE PLAYOFF YEAR:
14 — Dino Ciccarelli, Minnesota, 1981. 19 games.
11 — Jeremy Roenick, Chicago, 1990. 20 games.
10 — Claude Lemieux, Montreal, 1986. 20 games.
 9 — Pat Flatley, NY Islanders, 1984. 21 games
 8 — Steve Christoff, Minnesota, 1980. 14 games.
   — Brad Palmer, Minnesota, 1981. 19 games.
   — Mike Krushelnyski, Boston, 1983. 17 games.
   — Bob Joyce, Boston, 1988. 23 games.

MOST POINTS BY A ROOKIE, ONE PLAYOFF YEAR:
21 — Dino Ciccarelli, Minnesota, in 1981. 14 goals, 7 assists in 19 games.
20 — Don Maloney, NY Rangers, in 1979. 7 goals, 13 assists in 18 games.

THREE-OR-MORE-GOAL GAMES

MOST THREE-OR-MORE-GOAL GAMES IN PLAYOFFS (CAREER):
10 — Wayne Gretzky, Edmonton, Los Angeles, NY Rangers. Eight three-goal games; two four-goal games.
 7 — Maurice Richard, Montreal. Four three-goal games; two four-goal games; one five-goal game.
   — Jari Kurri, Edmonton. Six three-goal games; one four-goal game.
 6 — Dino Ciccarelli, Minnesota, Washington, Detroit. Five three-goal games; one four-goal game.
 5 — Mike Bossy, NY Islanders. Four three-goal games; one four-goal game.

MOST THREE-OR-MORE-GOAL GAMES, ONE PLAYOFF YEAR:
 4 — **Jari Kurri, Edmonton,** 1985. 1 four-goal game, 3 three-goal games.
 3 — Mark Messier, Edmonton, 1983. 3 three-goal games.
   — Mike Bossy, NY Islanders, 1983. 1 four-goal game, 2 three-goal games
 2 — Newsy Lalonde, Montreal, 1919. 1 five-goal game, 1 four-goal game.
   — Maurice Richard, Montreal, 1944. 1 five-goal game; 1 four-goal game.
   — Doug Bentley, Chicago, 1944. 2 three-goal games.
   — Norm Ullman, Detroit, 1964. 2 three-goal games.
   — Phil Esposito, Boston, 1970. 2 three-goal games.
   — Pit Martin, Chicago, 1973. 2 three-goal games.
   — Rick MacLeish, Philadelphia, 1975. 2 three-goal games.
   — Lanny McDonald, Toronto, 1977. 1 three-goal game; 1 four-goal game.
   — Wayne Gretzky, Edmonton, 1981. 2 three-goal games.
   — Wayne Gretzky, Edmonton, 1983. 2 four-goal games.
   — Wayne Gretzky, Edmonton, 1985. 2 three-goal games.
   — Petr Klima, Detroit, 1988. 2 three-goal games.
   — Cam Neely, Boston, 1991. 2 three-goal games.
   — Wayne Gretzky, NY Rangers, 1997. 2 three-goal games.

MOST THREE-OR-MORE-GOAL GAMES, ONE PLAYOFF SERIES:
 3 — **Jari Kurri, Edmonton** 1985, CF vs. Chicago won by Edmonton 4-2. Kurri scored 3 G May 7 at Edmonton in 7-3 win, 3 G May 14 in 10-5 win and 4 G May 16 at Chicago in 8-2 win.
 2 — Doug Bentley, Chicago, 1944, SF vs. Detroit, won by Chicago 4-1. Bentley scored 3 G Mar. 28 at Chicago in 7-1 win and 3 G Mar. 30 at Detroit in 5-2 win.
   — Norm Ullman, Detroit, 1964, SF vs. Chicago, won by Detroit 4-3. Ullman scored 3 G Mar. 29 at Chicago in 7-1 win and 3 G April 7 at Detroit in 7-2 win.
   — Mark Messier, Edmonton, 1983, DF vs. Calgary won by Edmonton 4-1. Messier scored 4 G April 14 at Edmonton in 6-3 win and 3 G-April 17 at Calgary in 10-2 win.
   — Mike Bossy, NY Islanders, 1983, CF vs. Boston won by NY Islanders 4-2. Bossy scored 3 G May 3 at New York in 8-3 win and 4 G on May 7 at New York in 8-4 win.

SCORING STREAKS

LONGEST CONSECUTIVE GOAL-SCORING STREAK, ONE PLAYOFF YEAR:
9 Games — Reggie Leach, Philadelphia, 1976. Streak started April 17 at Toronto and ended May 9 at Montreal. He scored one goal in each of seven games; two in one game; and five in another; a total of 14 goals.

LONGEST CONSECUTIVE POINT-SCORING STREAK, ONE PLAYOFF YEAR:
18 games — Bryan Trottier, NY Islanders, 1981. 11 goals, 18 assists, 29 points.
17 games — Wayne Gretzky, Edmonton, 1988. 12 goals, 29 assists, 41 points.
   — Al MacInnis, Calgary, 1989. 7 goals, 19 assists, 24 points.

LONGEST CONSECUTIVE POINT-SCORING STREAK, MORE THAN ONE PLAYOFF YEAR:
27 games — Bryan Trottier, NY Islanders, 1980, 1981 and 1982. 7 games in 1980 (3 G, 5 A, 8 PTS), 18 games in 1981 (11 G, 18 A, 29 PTS), and two games in 1982 (2 G, 3 A, 5 PTS). Total points, 42.
19 games — Wayne Gretzky, Edmonton, Los Angeles, 1988 and 1989. 17 games in 1988 (12 G, 29 A, 41 PTS with Edmonton), 2 games in 1989 (1 G, 2 A, 3 PTS with Los Angeles). Total points, 44.
18 games — Phil Esposito, Boston, 1970 and 1971. 13 G, 20 A, 33 PTS.

FASTEST GOALS

FASTEST GOAL FROM START OF GAME:
6 Seconds — Don Kozak, Los Angeles, April 17, 1977, at Los Angeles vs. Boston and goaltender Gerry Cheevers. Los Angeles won 7-4.
7 Seconds — Bob Gainey, Montreal, May 5, 1971, at New York vs. NY Islanders and goaltender Glenn Resch. Montreal won 2-1.
   — Terry Murray, Philadelphia, April 12, 1981, at Quebec vs. goaltender Dan Bouchard. Quebec won 4-3 in overtime.
8 Seconds — Stan Smyl, Vancouver, April 7, 1982, at Vancouver vs. Calgary and goaltender Pat Riggin. Vancouver won 5-3.

FASTEST GOAL FROM START OF PERIOD (OTHER THAN FIRST):
6 Seconds — Pelle Eklund, Philadelphia, April 25, 1989, at Pittsburgh vs. goaltender Tom Barrasso, second period. Pittsburgh won 10-7.
9 Seconds — Bill Collins, Minnesota, April 9, 1968, at Minnesota vs. Los Angeles and goaltender Wayne Rutledge, third period. Minnesota won 7-5.
   — Dave Balon, Minnesota, April 25, 1968, at St. Louis vs. goaltender Glenn Hall, third period. Minnesota won 5-1.
   — Murray Oliver, Minnesota, April 8, 1971, at St. Louis vs. goaltender Ernie Wakely, third period. St. Louis won 4-2.
   — Clark Gillies, NY Islanders, April 15, 1977, at Buffalo vs. goaltender Don Edwards, third period. NY Islanders won 4-3.
   — Eric Vail, Atlanta, April 11, 1978, at Atlanta vs. Detroit and goaltender Ron Low, third period. Detroit won 5-3.
   — Stan Smyl, Vancouver, April 10, 1979, at Philadelphia vs. goaltender Wayne Stephenson, third period. Vancouver won 3-2.
   — Wayne Gretzky, Edmonton, April 6, 1983, at Edmonton vs. Winnipeg and goaltender Brian Hayward, third period. Edmonton won 6-3.
   — Mark Messier, Edmonton, April 16, 1984, at Calgary vs. goaltender Don Edwards, third period. Edmonton won 5-3.
   — Brian Skrudland, Montreal, May 18, 1986 at Calgary and goaltender Mike Vernon, overtime. Montreal won 3-2.

FASTEST TWO GOALS:
5 Seconds — Norm Ullman, Detroit, at Detroit, April 11, 1965, vs. Chicago and goaltender Glenn Hall. Ullman scored at 17:35 and 17:40 of second period. Detroit won 4-2.

FASTEST TWO GOALS FROM START OF A GAME:
1 Minute, 8 Seconds — Dick Duff, Toronto, April 9, 1963 at Toronto vs. Detroit and goaltender Terry Sawchuk. Duff scored at 49 seconds and 1:08. Final score: Toronto 4, Detroit 2.

FASTEST TWO GOALS FROM START OF A PERIOD:
35 Seconds — Pat LaFontaine, NY Islanders, May 19, 1984 at Edmonton vs. goaltender Andy Moog. LaFontaine scored at 13 and 35 seconds of third period. Final score: Edmonton 5, NY Islanders 2.

PENALTIES

MOST PENALTY MINUTES IN PLAYOFFS (CAREER):
661 — Dale Hunter, Quebec, Washington
541 — Chris Nilan, Montreal, NY Rangers, Boston
466 — Willi Plett, Atlanta, Calgary, Minnesota, Boston
455 — Dave Williams, Toronto, Vancouver, Los Angeles
442 — Glenn Anderson, Edmonton, Toronto, NY Rangers, St. Louis

MOST PENALTIES, ONE GAME:
8 — Forbes Kennedy, Toronto, April 2, 1969, at Boston. Four minors, 2 majors, 1 10-minute misconduct, 1 game misconduct. Final score: Boston 10, Toronto 0.
— Kim Clackson, Pittsburgh, April 14, 1980, at Boston. Five minors, 2 majors, 1 10-minute misconduct. Final score: Boston 6, Pittsburgh 2

MOST PENALTY MINUTES, ONE GAME:
42 — Dave Schultz, Philadelphia, April 22, 1976, at Toronto. One minor, 2 majors, 1 10-minute misconduct and 2 game-misconducts. Final score: Toronto 8, Philadelphia 5.

MOST PENALTIES, ONE PERIOD AND MOST PENALTY MINUTES, ONE PERIOD:
6 Penalties; 39 Minutes — Ed Hospodar, NY Rangers, April 9, 1981, at Los Angeles, first period. Two minors, 1 major, 1 10-minute misconduct, 2 game misconducts. Final score: Los Angeles 5, NY Rangers 4.

GOALTENDING

MOST PLAYOFF GAMES APPEARED IN BY A GOALTENDER (CAREER):
153 — Patrick Roy, Montreal, Colorado
132 — Bill Smith, Los Angeles, NY Islanders
127 — Grant Fuhr, Edmonton, Toronto, Buffalo, St. Louis
123 — Andy Moog, Edmonton, Boston, Dallas
— Mike Vernon, Calgary, Detroit

MOST MINUTES PLAYED BY A GOALTENDER (CAREER):
9,452 — Patrick Roy, Montreal, Colorado
7,645 — Bill Smith, Los Angeles, NY Islanders
7,428 — Grant Fuhr, Edmonton, Toronto, Buffalo, St. Louis
7,308 — Mike Vernon, Calgary, Detroit
6,978 — Andy Moog, Edmonton, Boston, Dallas

MOST MINUTES PLAYED BY A GOALTENDER, ONE PLAYOFF YEAR:
1,544 — Kirk McLean, Vancouver, 1994. 24 games.
1,540 — Ron Hextall, Philadelphia, 1987. 26 games.
1,477 — Mike Richter, NY Rangers, 1994. 23 games.
1,454 — Patrick Roy, Colorado, 1996. 22 games.
1,401 — Bill Ranford, Edmonton, 1990. 22 games.

MOST SHUTOUTS IN PLAYOFFS (CAREER):
15 — Clint Benedict, Ottawa, Mtl. Maroons
14 — Jacques Plante, Montreal, St. Louis
13 — Turk Broda, Toronto
12 — Terry Sawchuk, Detroit, Toronto, Los Angeles

MOST SHUTOUTS, ONE PLAYOFF YEAR:
4 — Clint Benedict, Mtl. Maroons, 1926. 8 games.
— Clint Benedict, Mtl. Maroons, 1928. 9 games.
— Dave Kerr, NY Rangers, 1937. 9 games.
— Frank McCool, Toronto, 1945. 13 games.
— Terry Sawchuk, Detroit, 1952. 8 games.
— Bernie Parent, Philadelphia, 1975. 17 games.
— Ken Dryden, Montreal, 1977. 14 games.
— Mike Richter, NY Rangers, 1994. 23 games.
— Kirk McLean, Vancouver, 1994. 24 games.

MOST WINS BY A GOALTENDER, (CAREER):
96 — Patrick Roy, Montreal, Colorado
88 — Bill Smith, Los Angeles, NY Islanders
80 — Ken Dryden, Montreal
— Grant Fuhr, Edmonton, Buffalo, St. Louis

MOST WINS BY A GOALTENDER, ONE PLAYOFF YEAR:
16 — Grant Fuhr, Edmonton, 1988. 19 games.
— Mike Vernon, Calgary, 1989. 22 games.
— Bill Ranford, Edmonton, 1990. 22 games.
— Tom Barrasso, Pittsburgh, 1992. 21 games.
— Patrick Roy, Montreal, 1993. 20 games.
— Mike Richter, NY Rangers, 1994. 23 games.
— Martin Brodeur, New Jersey, 1995. 20 games.
— Patrick Roy, Colorado, 1996. 22 games.
— Mike Vernon, Detroit, 1997. 20 games.

MOST CONSECUTIVE WINS BY A GOALTENDER, ONE PLAYOFF YEAR:
11 — Ed Belfour, Chicago, 1992. 3 wins against St. Louis in DSF, won by Chicago 4-2; 4 wins against Detroit in DF, won by Chicago 4-0; and 4 wins against Edmonton in CF, won by Chicago 4-0.
— Tom Barrasso, Pittsburgh, 1992. 3 wins against NY Rangers in DF, won by Pittsburgh 4-2; 4 wins against Boston in CF, won by Pittsburgh 4-0; and 4 wins against Chicago in F, won by Pittsburgh 4-0.
— Patrick Roy, Montreal, 1993. 4 wins against Quebec in DSF, won by Montreal 4-2; 4 wins against Buffalo in DF, won by Montreal 4-0; and 3 wins against NY Islanders in CF, won by Montreal 4-1.

LONGEST SHUTOUT SEQUENCE:
248 Minutes, 32 Seconds — Norm Smith, Detroit, 1936. In best-of-five SF, Smith shut out Mtl. Maroons 1-0, March 24, in 116:30 overtime; shut out Maroons 3-0 in second game, March 26; and was scored against at 12:02 of first period, March 29, by Gus Marker. Detroit won SF 3-0.

MOST CONSECUTIVE SHUTOUTS:
3 — Clint Benedict, Mtl. Maroons, 1926. Benedict shut out Ottawa 1-0, Mar. 27; he then shut out Victoria twice, 3-0, Mar. 30; 3-0, Apr. 1. Mtl. Maroons won NHL F vs. Ottawa 2 goals to 1 and won the best-of-five F vs. Victoria 3-1.
— John Roach, NY Rangers, 1929. Roach shut out NY Americans twice, 0-0, Mar. 19; 1-0, Mar. 21; he then shut out Toronto 1-0, Mar. 24. NY Rangers won QF vs. NY Americans 1 goal to 0 and won the best-of-three SF vs. Toronto 2-0.
— Frank McCool, Toronto, 1945. McCool shut out Detroit 1-0, April 6; 2-0, April 8; 1-0, April 12. Toronto won the best-of-seven F 4-3.

Early Playoff Records

1893-1918
Team Records

MOST GOALS, BOTH TEAMS, ONE GAME:
25 — Ottawa Silver Seven, Dawson City at Ottawa, Jan. 16, 1905. Ottawa 23, Dawson City 2. Ottawa won best-of-three series 2-0.

MOST GOALS, ONE TEAM, ONE GAME:
23 — Ottawa Silver Seven at Ottawa, Jan. 16, 1905. Ottawa defeated Dawson City 23-2.

MOST GOALS, BOTH TEAMS, BEST-OF-THREE SERIES:
42 — Ottawa Silver Seven, Queen's University at Ottawa, 1906. Ottawa defeated Queen's 16-7, Feb. 27, and 12-7, Feb. 28.

MOST GOALS, ONE TEAM, BEST-OF-THREE SERIES:
32 — Ottawa Silver Seven in 1905 at Ottawa. Defeated Dawson City 9-2, Jan. 13, and 23-2, Jan. 16.

MOST GOALS, BOTH TEAMS, BEST-OF-FIVE SERIES:
39 — Toronto Arenas, Vancouver Millionaires at Toronto, 1918. Toronto won 5-3, Mar. 20; 6-3, Mar. 26; 2-1, Mar. 30. Vancouver won 6-4, Mar. 23, and 8-1, Mar. 28. Toronto scored 18 goals; Vancouver 21.

MOST GOALS, ONE TEAM, BEST-OF-FIVE SERIES:
26 — Vancouver Millionaires in 1915 at Vancouver. Defeated Ottawa Senators 6-2, Mar. 22; 8-3, Mar. 24; and 12-3 Mar. 26.

Individual Records

MOST GOALS IN PLAYOFFS:
63 — Frank McGee, Ottawa Silver Seven, in 22 playoff games. Seven goals in four games, 1903; 21 goals in eight games, 1904; 18 goals in four games, 1905; 17 goals in six games, 1906.

MOST GOALS, ONE PLAYOFF SERIES:
15 — Frank McGee, Ottawa Silver Seven, in two games in 1905 at Ottawa. Scored one goal, Jan. 13, in 9-2 victory over Dawson City and 14 goals, Jan. 16, in 23-2 victory.

MOST GOALS, ONE PLAYOFF GAME:
14 — Frank McGee, Ottawa Silver Seven, Jan. 16, 1905 at Ottawa in 23-2 victory over Dawson City.

FASTEST THREE GOALS:
40 Seconds — Marty Walsh, Ottawa Senators, at Ottawa, March 16, 1911, at 3:00, 3:10, and 3:40 of third period. Ottawa defeated Port Arthur 13-4.

One of the game's most creative and productive post-season performers, Rick Middleton (16) rattled opposition goaltenders for 45 goals in 114 playoff games during his career.

All-Time Playoff Goal Leaders since 1918
(40 or more goals)

Player	Teams	Yrs.	GP	G
* Wayne Gretzky	Edm., L.A., St.L.	16	208	122
* Mark Messier	Edm., NYR	17	236	109
* Jari Kurri	Edm., L.A., NYR, Ana.	14	196	106
Glenn Anderson	Edm., Tor., NYR, St.L.	15	225	93
Mike Bossy	NY Islanders	10	129	85
Maurice Richard	Montreal	15	133	82
Jean Beliveau	Montreal	17	162	79
* Dino Ciccarelli	Min., Wsh., Det.	14	141	73
Bryan Trottier	NYI, Pit.	17	221	71
Mario Lemieux	Pittsburgh	7	89	70
* Claude Lemieux	Mtl., N.J., Col.	12	172	70
* Esa Tikkanen	Edm., NYR, St.L., Van.	12	165	69
Gordie Howe	Det., Hfd.	20	157	68
Denis Savard	Chi., Mtl.	16	169	66
* Brett Hull	Cgy., St.L.	12	98	66
Yvan Cournoyer	Montreal	12	147	64
Brian Propp	Phi., Bos., Min.	13	160	64
Bobby Smith	Min., Mtl.	13	184	64
Bobby Hull	Chi., Hfd.	14	119	62
Phil Esposito	Chi., Bos., NYR	15	130	61
Jacques Lemaire	Montreal	11	145	61
Joe Mullen	St.L., Cgy., Pit.	15	143	60
Stan Mikita	Chicago	18	155	59
Guy Lafleur	Mtl, NYR	14	128	58
Bernie Geoffrion	Mtl., NYR	16	132	58
* Paul Coffey	Edm., Pit., L.A., Det., Phi.	15	189	59
Cam Neely	Van., Bos.	9	93	57
Steve Larmer	Chi., NYR	13	140	56
Denis Potvin	NY Islanders	14	185	56
Rick Middleton	Phi., Pit., Det.	11	114	54
Bill Barber	Philadelphia	11	129	53
* Stephane Richer	Mtl., N.J.	11	128	52
Frank Mahovlich	Tor., Det., Mtl.	14	137	51
Steve Shutt	Mtl., L.A.	12	99	50
* Doug Gilmour	St.L., Cgy., Tor., N.J.	13	146	49
Henri Richard	Montreal	18	180	49
Reggie Leach	Bos., Phi.	8	94	47
Ted Lindsay	Det., Chi.	16	133	47
Clark Gillies	NYI, Buf.	13	164	47
* Jaromir Jagr	Pit.	7	98	46
* Luc Robitaille	L.A., Pit., NYR	10	111	46
* Steve Yzerman	Detroit	12	113	46
Dickie Moore	Mtl., Tor., St.L.	14	135	46
Rick Middleton	NYR, Bos.	12	114	45
* Brian Bellows	Min., Mtl., T.B., Ana.	12	122	45
Lanny McDonald	Tor., Cgy.	13	117	44
* Kevin Stevens	Pit.	6	86	43
Ken Linseman	Phi., Edm., Bos.	11	113	43
* Bernie Nicholls	L.A., NYR, Edm., N.J., Chi.	12	112	42
* Mike Gartner	Wsh., Min., NYR, Tor., Pho.	14	117	42
Bobby Clarke	Philadelphia	13	136	42
* Rick Tocchet	Phi., Pit., L.A., Bos.	9	108	41
John Bucyk	Det., Bos.	14	124	41
* Dale Hunter	Que., Wsh.	16	146	41
Tim Kerr	Phi., NYR	10	81	40
Peter McNab	Bos., Van.	10	107	40
Bob Bourne	NYI, L.A.	13	139	40
John Tonelli	NYI, Cgy., L.A.	13	172	40

* — Active player.

All-Time Playoff Assist Leaders since 1918
(60 or more assists)

Player	Teams	Yrs.	GP	A
* Wayne Gretzky	Edm., L.A., St.L.	16	208	260
* Mark Messier	Edm., NYR	17	236	186
* Paul Coffey	Edm., Pit., L.A., Det., Phi.	15	189	136
* Jari Kurri	Edm., L.A., NYR, Ana.	14	196	127
Glenn Anderson	Edm., Tor., NYR, St.L.	15	225	121
Larry Robinson	Mtl., L.A.	20	227	116
* Doug Gilmour	St.L., Cgy., Tor., N.J.	13	146	115
Bryan Trottier	NYI, Pit.	17	221	113
* Ray Bourque	Boston	17	162	112
Denis Savard	Chi., Mtl.	16	169	109
Denis Potvin	NY Islanders	14	185	108
Jean Beliveau	Montreal	17	162	97
* Larry Murphy	L.A., Wsh., Min., Pit., Tor., Det.	16	168	97
Bobby Smith	Min., Mtl.	13	184	96
Gordie Howe	Det., Hfd.	20	157	92
Stan Mikita	Chicago	18	155	91
Brad Park	NYR, Bos., Det.	17	161	90
* Adam Oates	Det., St.L., Bos.	10	105	89
* Chris Chelios	Mtl., Chi.	14	163	88
* Al MacInnis	Cgy., St.L.	13	121	88
Mario Lemieux	Pittsburgh	7	89	85
Brian Propp	Phi., Bos., Min.	13	160	84
* Craig Janney	Bos., St. L., S.J., Wpg., Pho.	10	114	83
Henri Richard	Montreal	18	180	80
Jacques Lemaire	Montreal	11	145	78
Ken Linseman	Phi., Edm., Bos.	11	113	77
* Ron Francis	Hfd., Pit.	12	124	77
Bobby Clarke	Philadelphia	13	136	77
Guy Lafleur	Mtl, NYR	14	128	76
Phil Esposito	Chi., Bos., NYR	15	130	76
Mike Bossy	NY Islanders	10	129	75
Steve Larmer	Chi., NYR	13	140	75
John Tonelli	NYI, Cgy., L.A.	13	172	75
Peter Stastny	Que., N.J., St.L.	12	93	72
* Sergei Fedorov	Detroit	7	88	70
Gilbert Perreault	Buffalo	11	90	70
* Scott Stevens	Wsh., St. L., N.J.	14	142	70
Dale Hawerchuk	Wpg., Buf., Phi.	15	97	69
Alex Delvecchio	Detroit	14	121	69
* Dale Hunter	Que., Wsh.	16	146	69
* Bernie Nicholls	L.A., NYR, Edm., N.J., Chi.	12	112	67
Bobby Hull	Chi., Hfd.	14	119	67
Frank Mahovlich	Tor., Det., Mtl.	14	137	67
Bobby Orr	Boston	8	74	66
Bernie Federko	St. Louis	11	91	66
Jean Ratelle	NYR, Bos.	15	123	66
* Charlie Huddy	Edm., L.A., Buf., St.L.	14	183	66
* Steve Yzerman	Detroit	12	113	65
Dickie Moore	Mtl., Tor., St.L.	14	135	64
Doug Harvey	Mtl., NYR, St.L.	15	137	64
* Brian Bellows	Min., Mtl., T.B., Ana.	12	122	64
* Neal Broten	Min., Dal., N.J.	13	135	63
Yvan Cournoyer	Montreal	12	147	63
John Bucyk	Det., Bos.	14	124	62
* Brian Leetch	NY Rangers	7	82	61
Doug Wilson	Chicago	12	95	61
Bernie Geoffrion	Mtl., NYR	16	132	60

All-Time Playoff Point Leaders since 1918
(100 or more points)

Player	Teams	Yrs.	GP	G	A	Pts.
* Wayne Gretzky	Edm., L.A., St.L., NYR	16	208	122	260	382
* Mark Messier	Edm., NYR	17	236	109	186	295
Jari Kurri	Edm., L.A., NYR, Ana.	14	196	106	127	233
Glenn Anderson	Edm., Tor., NYR, St.L.	15	225	93	121	214
* Paul Coffey	Edm., Pit., L.A., Det., Phi.	15	189	59	136	195
Bryan Trottier	NYI, Pit.	17	221	71	113	184
Jean Beliveau	Montreal	17	162	79	97	176
Denis Savard	Chi., Mtl.	16	169	66	109	175
* Doug Gilmour	St.L., Cgy., Tor., N.J.	13	146	49	115	164
Denis Potvin	NY Islanders	14	185	56	108	164
Mike Bossy	NY Islanders	10	129	85	75	160
Gordie Howe	Det., Hfd.	20	157	68	92	160
Bobby Smith	Min., Mtl.	13	184	64	96	160
Mario Lemieux	Pittsburgh	7	89	70	85	155
Stan Mikita	Chicago	18	155	59	91	150
Brian Propp	Phi., Bos., Min.	13	160	64	84	148
* Ray Bourque	Boston	17	162	34	112	146
Larry Robinson	Mtl., L.A.	20	227	28	116	144
Jacques Lemaire	Montreal	11	145	61	78	139
Phil Esposito	Chi., Bos., NYR	15	130	61	76	137
Guy Lafleur	Mtl, NYR	14	128	58	76	134
Steve Larmer	Chi., NYR	13	140	56	75	131
Bobby Hull	Chi., Hfd.	14	119	62	67	129
* Larry Murphy	L.A., Wsh., Min., Pit., Tor., Det.	16	168	32	97	129
Henri Richard	Montreal	18	180	49	80	129
Yvan Cournoyer	Montreal	12	147	64	63	127
* Claude Lemieux	Mtl., N.J., Col.	12	172	70	57	127
Maurice Richard	Montreal	15	133	82	44	126
* Esa Tikkanen	Edm., NYR, St.L., Van.	12	165	69	57	126
Brad Park	NYR, Bos., Det.	17	161	35	90	125
* Adam Oates	Det., St.L., Bos.	10	105	32	89	121
Ken Linseman	Phi., Edm., Bos.	11	113	43	77	120
Bobby Clarke	Philadelphia	13	136	42	77	119
Bernie Geoffrion	Mtl., NYR	16	132	58	60	118
Frank Mahovlich	Tor., Det., Mtl.	14	137	51	67	118
* Dino Ciccarelli	Min., Wsh., Det.	14	141	73	45	118
* Al MacInnis	Cgy., St.L.	13	121	30	88	118
* Ron Francis	Hfd., Pit.	12	124	39	77	116
* Chris Chelios	Mtl., Chi.	14	163	28	88	116
John Tonelli	NYI, Cgy., L.A.	13	172	40	75	115
* Brett Hull	Cgy., St.L.	12	98	66	48	114
* Steve Yzerman	Detroit	12	113	46	65	111
Dickie Moore	Mtl., Tor., St.L.	14	135	46	64	110
* Dale Hunter	Que., Wsh.	16	146	41	69	110
* Bernie Nicholls	L.A., NYR, Edm., N.J., Chi.	12	112	42	67	109
* Brian Bellows	Min., Mtl., T.B., Ana.	12	122	45	64	109
Bill Barber	Philadelphia	11	129	53	55	108
Rick MacLeish	Phi., Pit., Det.	11	114	54	53	107
* Craig Janney	Bos., St. L., S.J., Wpg., Pho.	10	114	24	83	107
Joe Mullen	St.L., Cgy., Pit.	15	143	60	46	106
Peter Stastny	Que., N.J., St.L.	12	93	33	72	105
Alex Delvecchio	Detroit	14	121	35	69	104
Gilbert Perreault	Buffalo	11	90	33	70	103
* Luc Robitaille	L.A., Pit., NYR	10	111	46	57	103
John Bucyk	Det., Bos.	14	124	41	62	103
Bernie Federko	St. Louis	11	91	35	66	101
* Kevin Stevens	Pit.	6	86	43	57	100
Rick Middleton	NYR, Bos.	12	114	45	55	100

Three-or-more-Goal Games, Playoffs 1918 –1997

Player	Team	Date	City	Total Goals	Opposing Goaltender	Score	
Wayne Gretzky (10)	Edm.	Apr. 11/81	Edm.	3	Richard Sevigny	Edm. 6	Mtl. 2
		Apr. 19/81	Edm.	3	Billy Smith	Edm. 5	NYI 2
		Apr. 6/83	Edm.	4	Brian Hayward	Edm. 6	Wpg. 3
		Apr. 17/83	Cgy.	4	Rejean Lemelin	Edm. 10	Cgy. 2
		Apr. 25/85	Wpg.	3	Bryan Hayward (2)		
					Marc Behrend (1)	Edm. 8	Wpg. 3
		May 25/85	Edm.	3	Pelle Lindbergh	Edm. 4	Phi. 3
		Apr. 24/86	Cgy.	3	Mike Vernon	Edm. 7	Cgy. 4
	L.A.	May 29/93	Tor.	3	Felix Potvin	L.A. 5	Tor. 4
	NYR	Apr. 23/97	NYR	3	John Vanbiesbrouck	NYR 3	Fla. 2
		May 18/97	Phi.	3	Garth Snow	NYR 5	Phi. 4
Maurice Richard (7)	Mtl.	Mar. 23/44	Mtl.	5	Paul Bibeault	Mtl. 5	Tor. 1
		Apr. 7/44	Chi.	3	Mike Karakas	Mtl. 3	Chi. 1
		Mar. 29/45	Mtl.	4	Frank McCool	Mtl. 10	Tor. 3
		Apr. 14/53	Bos.	3	Gord Henry	Mtl. 7	Bos. 3
		Mar. 20/56	Mtl.	3	Lorne Worsley	Mtl. 7	NYR 1
		Apr. 6/57	Mtl.	4	Don Simmons	Mtl. 5	Bos. 1
		Apr. 1/58	Det.	3	Terry Sawchuk	Mtl. 4	Det. 3
Jari Kurri (7)	Edm.	Apr. 4/84	Edm.	3	Doug Soetaert (1)		
					Mike Veisor (2)	Edm. 9	Wpg. 2
		Apr. 25/85	Wpg.	3	Bryan Hayward (2)		
					Marc Behrend (1)	Edm. 8	Wpg. 3
		May 7/85	Edm.	3	Murray Bannerman	Edm. 7	Chi. 3
		May 14/85	Edm.	3	Murray Bannerman	Edm. 10	Chi. 5
		May 16/85	Chi.	4	Murray Bannerman	Edm. 8	Chi. 2
		Apr. 9/87	Edm.	4	Roland Melanson (2)		
					Daren Eliot (2)	Edm. 13	L.A. 3
		May 18/90	Bos.	3	Andy Moog (2)		
					Rejean Lemelin (1)	Edm. 7	Bos. 2
Dino Ciccarelli (6)	Min.	May 5/81	Min.	3	Pat Riggin	Min. 7	Cgy. 4
		Apr. 10/82	Min.	3	Murray Bannerman	Min. 7	Chi. 1
	Wsh.	Apr. 5/90	N.J.	3	Sean Burke	Wsh. 5	N.J. 4
		Apr. 25/92	Pit.	4	Tom Barrasso (1)		
					Ken Wregget (3)	Wsh. 7	Pit. 2
	Det.	Apr. 29/93	Tor.	3	Felix Potvin (2)		
					Daren Puppa (1)	Det. 7	Tor. 3
		May 11/95	Dal.	3	Andy Moog (2)		
					Darcy Wakaluk (1)	Det. 5	Dal. 1
Mike Bossy (5)	NYI	Apr. 16/79	NYI	3	Tony Esposito	NYI 6	Chi. 2
		May 8/82	NYI	3	Richard Brodeur	NYI 6	Van. 5
		Apr. 10/83	Wsh.	3	Al Jensen	NYI 6	Wsh. 3
		May 3/83	NYI	3	Pete Peeters	NYI 8	Bos. 3
		May 7/83	NYI	4	Pete Peeters	NYI 8	Bos. 4
Phil Esposito (4)	Bos.	Apr. 2/69	Bos.	4	Bruce Gamble	Bos. 10	Tor. 0
		Apr. 8/70	Bos.	3	Ed Giacomin	Bos. 8	NYR 2
		Apr. 19/70	Chi.	3	Tony Esposito	Bos. 6	Chi. 3
		Apr. 8/75	Bos.	3	Tony Esposito (2)		
					Michel Dumas (1)	Bos. 8	Chi. 2
Mark Messier (4)	Edm.	Apr. 14/83	Edm.	4	Rejean Lemelin	Edm. 6	Cgy. 3
		Apr. 17/83	Cgy.	3	Rejean Lemelin (1)	Edm. 10	Cgy. 2
					Don Edwards (2)		
		Apr. 26/83	Edm.	3	Murray Bannerman	Edm. 8	Chi. 2
	NYR	May 25/94	N.J.	3	Martin Brodeur (2)	NYR 4	N.J. 2
					ENG (1)		
Bernie Geoffrion (3)	Mtl.	Mar. 27/52	Mtl.	3	Jim Henry	Mtl. 4	Bos. 0
		Apr. 7/55	Mtl.	3	Terry Sawchuk	Mtl. 4	Det. 2
		Mar. 30/57	Mtl.	3	Lorne Worsley	Mtl. 8	NYR 3
Norm Ullman (3)	Det.	Mar. 29/64	Chi.	3	Glenn Hall	Det. 5	Chi. 4
		Apr. 7/64	Det.	3	Glenn Hall (2)		
					Denis DeJordy (1)	Det. 7	Chi. 2
		Apr. 11/65	Det.	3	Glenn Hall	Det. 4	Chi. 2
John Bucyk (3)	Bos.	May 3/70	St. L.	3	Jacques Plante (1)		
					Ernie Wakely (2)	Bos. 6	St. L. 1
		Apr. 20/72	Bos.	3	Jacques Caron (1)		
					Ernie Wakely (2)	Bos. 10	St. L. 2
		Apr. 21/74	Bos.	3	Tony Esposito	Bos. 8	Chi. 6
Rick MacLeish (3)	Phi.	Apr. 11/74	Phi.	3	Phil Myre	Phi. 5	Atl. 1
		Apr. 13/75	Phi.	3	Gord McRae	Phi. 6	Tor. 3
		May 13/75	Phi.	3	Glenn Resch	Phi. 4	NYI 1
Denis Savard (3)	Chi.	Apr. 19/82	Chi.	3	Mike Liut	Chi. 7	StL. 4
		Apr. 10/86	Chi.	4	Ken Wregget	Tor. 6	Chi. 4
		Apr. 9/88	St. L.	3	Greg Millen	Chi. 6	St. L. 3
Tim Kerr (3)	Phi.	Apr. 13/85	NYR	4	Glen Hanlon	Phi. 6	NYR 5
		Apr. 20/87	Phi.	3	Kelly Hrudey	Phi. 4	NYI 2
		Apr. 19/89	Pit.	3	Tom Barrasso	Phi. 4	Pit. 2
Cam Neely (3)	Bos.	Apr. 9/87	Mtl.	3	Patrick Roy	Mtl. 4	Bos. 3
		Apr. 5/91	Bos.	3	Peter Sidorkiewicz	Bos. 4	Hfd. 3
		Apr. 25/91	Bos.	3	Patrick Roy	Bos. 4	Mtl. 1
Petr Klima (3)	Det.	Apr. 7/88	Tor.	3	Alan Bester (2)		
					Ken Wregett (1)	Det. 6	Tor. 2
		Apr. 21/88	St. L.	3	Greg Millen	Det. 6	St. L. 0
	Edm.	May 4/91	Edm.	3	Jon Casey	Edm. 7	Min. 2
Esa Tikkanen (3)	Edm.	May 22/88	Edm.	3	Rejean Lemelin	Edm. 6	Bos. 3
		Apr. 16/91	Cgy.	3	Mike Vernon	Edm. 5	Cgy. 4
		Apr. 26/92	L.A.	3	Kelly Hrudey	Edm. 5	L.A. 2
Steve Yzerman (3)	Det.	Apr. 6/89	Det.	3	Alain Chevrier	Chi. 5	Det. 4
		Apr. 4/91	St. L.	3	Vincent Riendeau (2)	Det. 6	St. L. 3
					Pat Jablonski (1)		
		May 8/96	St.L.	3	Jon Casey	St.L. 5	Det. 4
Mario Lemieux (3)	Pit.	Apr. 25/89	Pit.	5	Ron Hextall	Pit. 10	Phi. 7
		Apr. 23/92	Pit.	3	Don Beaupre	Pit. 6	Wsh. 4
		May 11/96	Pit.	3	Mike Richter	Pit. 7	NYR 3

Player	Team	Date	City	Total Goals	Opposing Goaltender	Score	
Mike Gartner (3)	NYR	Apr. 13/90	NYR	3	Mark Fitzpatrick (2)		
					Glenn Healy (1)	NYR 6	NYI 5
		Apr. 27/92	NYR	3	Chris Terreri	NYR 8	N.J. 5
	Tor.	Apr. 25/96	Tor.	3	Jon Casey	Tor. 5	St.L. 4
Newsy Lalonde (2)	Mtl.	Mar. 1/19	Mtl.	5	Clint Benedict	Mtl. 6	Ott. 3
		Mar. 22/19	Sea.	4	Harry Holmes	Mtl. 4	Sea. 2
Howie Morenz (2)	Mtl.	Mar. 22/24	Mtl.	3	Charles Reid	Mtl. 6	Cgy.T. 1
		Mar. 27/25	Mtl.	3	Harry Holmes	Mtl. 4	Vic. 2
Toe Blake (2)	Mtl.	Mar. 22/38	Mtl.	3	Mike Karakas	Mtl. 6	Chi. 4
		Mar. 26/46	Chi.	3	Mike Karakas	Mtl. 7	Chi. 2
Doug Bentley (2)	Chi.	Mar. 28/44	Chi.	3	Connie Dion	Chi. 7	Det. 1
		Mar. 30/44	Det.	3	Connie Dion	Chi. 5	Det. 2
Ted Kennedy (2)	Tor.	Apr. 14/45	Tor.	3	Harry Lumley	Det. 5	Tor. 3
		Mar. 27/48	Tor.	4	Frank Brimsek	Tor. 5	Bos. 3
Bobby Hull (2)	Chi.	Apr. 7/63	Det.	3	Terry Sawchuk	Det. 7	Chi. 4
		Apr. 9/72	Pit.	3	Jim Rutherford	Chi. 6	Pit. 5
F. St. Marseille (2)	St. L.	Apr. 28/70	St. L.	3	Al Smith	St. L. 5	Pit. 0
		Apr. 6/72	Min.	3	Cesare Maniago	Min. 6	St. L. 5
Pit Martin (2)	Chi.	Apr. 4/73	Chi.	3	W. Stephenson	Chi. 7	St. L. 1
		May 10/73	Chi.	3	Ken Dryden	Mtl. 6	Chi. 4
Yvan Cournoyer (2)	Mtl.	Apr. 5/73	Mtl.	3	Dave Dryden	Mtl. 7	Buf. 3
		Apr. 11/74	Mtl.	3	Ed Giacomin	Mtl. 4	NYR 1
Guy Lafleur (2)	Mtl.	May 1/75	Mtl.	3	Roger Crozier (1)		
					Gerry Desjardins (2)	Mtl. 7	Buf. 0
		Apr. 11/77	Mtl.	3	Ed Staniowski	Mtl. 7	St. L. 2
Lanny McDonald (2)	Tor.	Apr. 9/77	Pit.	3	Denis Herron	Tor. 5	Pit. 2
		Apr. 17/77	Tor.	4	W. Stephenson	Phi. 6	Tor. 5
Butch Goring (2)	L.A.	Apr. 9/77	L.A.	3	Phil Myre	L.A. 4	Atl. 2
	NYI	May 17/81	Min.	3	Gilles Meloche	NYI 7	Min. 5
Bryan Trottier (2)	NYI	Apr. 8/80	NYI	3	Doug Keans	NYI 8	L.A. 1
		Apr. 9/81	NYI	3	Michel Larocque	NYI 5	Tor. 1
Bill Barber (2)	Phi.	May 4/80	Min.	4	Gilles Meloche	Phi. 5	Min. 3
		Apr. 9/81	Phi.	3	Dan Bouchard	Phi. 8	Que. 5
Brian Propp (2)	Phi.	Apr. 22/81	Phi.	3	Pat Riggin	Phi. 9	Cgy. 4
		Apr. 21/85	Phi.	3	Billy Smith	Phi. 5	NYI 2
Paul Reinhart (2)	Cgy	Apr. 14/83	Edm.	3	Andy Moog	Edm. 6	Cgy. 3
		Apr. 8/84	Van	3	Richard Brodeur	Cgy. 5	Van. 1
Peter Stastny (2)	Que.	Apr. 5/83	Bos.	3	Pete Peeters	Bos. 4	Que. 3
		Apr. 11/87	Que.	3	Mike Liut (2)		
					Steve Weeks (1)	Que. 5	Hfd. 1
Glenn Anderson (2)	Edm.	Apr. 26/83	Edm.	4	Murray Bannerman	Edm. 8	Chi. 2
		Apr. 6/88	Wpg.	3	Daniel Berthiaume	Edm. 7	Wpg. 4
Michel Goulet (2)	Que.	Apr. 23/85	Que.	3	Steve Penney	Que. 7	Mtl. 6
		Apr. 12/87	Que.	3	Mike Liut	Que. 4	Hfd. 1
Peter Zezel (2)	Phi.	Apr. 13/86	NYR	3	J. Vanbiesbrouck	Phi. 7	NYR 1
	St. L.	Apr. 11/89	St. L.	3	Jon Casey (2)		
					Kari Takko (1)	St. L. 6	Min. 1
Geoff Courtnall (2)	Van.	Apr. 4/91	L.A.	3	Kelly Hrudey	Van. 6	L.A. 5
		Apr. 30/92	Van.	3	Rick Tabaracci	Van. 5	Win. 0
Joe Sakic (2)	Que.	May 6/95	Que.	3	Mike Richter	Que. 5	NYR 4
	Col.	Apr. 25/96	Col.	3	Corey Hirsch	Col. 5	Van. 4
Harry Meeking	Tor.	Mar. 11/18	Tor.	3	Georges Vezina	Tor. 7	Mtl. 3
Alf Skinner	Tor.	Mar. 23/18	Tor.	3	Hugh Lehman	Van.M. 6	Tor. 4
Joe Malone	Mtl.	Feb. 23/19	Mtl.	3	Clint Benedict	Mtl. 8	Ott. 4
Odie Cleghorn	Mtl.	Feb. 27/19	Ott.	3	Clint Benedict	Mtl. 5	Ott. 3
Jack Darragh	Ott.	Apr. 1/20	Tor.	3	Harry Holmes	Ott. 6	Sea. 1
George Boucher	Ott.	Mar. 10/21	Ott.	3	Jake Forbes	Ott. 5	Tor. 0
Babe Dye	Tor.	Mar. 28/22	Tor.	4	Hugh Lehman	Tor. 5	Van.M. 1
Perk Galbraith	Bos.	Mar. 31/27	Bos.	3	Hugh Lehman	Bos. 4	Chi. 4
Busher Jackson	Tor.	Apr. 5/32	NYR	3	John Ross Roach	Tor. 6	NYR 4
Frank Boucher	NYR	Apr. 9/32	Tor.	3	Lorne Chabot	Tor. 6	NYR 4
Charlie Conacher	Tor.	Mar. 26/36	Tor.	3	Tiny Thompson	Tor. 8	Bos. 3
Syd Howe	Det.	Mar. 23/39	Det.	3	Claude Bourque	Det. 7	Mtl. 3
Bryan Hextall	NYR	Apr. 3/40	NYR	3	Turk Broda	NYR 6	Tor. 2
Joe Benoit	Mtl.	Mar. 22/41	Mtl.	3	Sam LoPresti	Mtl. 4	Chi. 3
Syl Apps	Tor.	Mar. 25/41	Tor.	3	Frank Brimsek	Tor. 7	Bos. 2
Jack McGill	Bos.	Mar. 29/42	Bos.	3	Johnny Mowers	Det. 6	Bos. 4
Don Metz	Tor.	Apr. 14/42	Tor.	3	Johnny Mowers	Tor. 9	Det. 3
Mud Bruneteau	Det.	Apr. 1/43	Det.	3	Frank Brimsek	Det. 6	Bos. 2
Don Grosso	Det.	Apr. 7/43	Bos.	3	Frank Brimsek	Det. 4	Bos. 0
Carl Liscombe	Det.	Apr. 3/45	Bos.	4	Paul Bibeault	Det. 5	Bos. 3
Billy Reay	Mtl.	Apr. 1/47	Bos.	4	Frank Brimsek	Mtl. 5	Bos. 1
Gerry Plamondon	Mtl.	Mar. 24/49	Det.	3	Harry Lumley	Mtl. 4	Det. 3
Sid Smith	Tor.	Apr. 10/49	Det.	3	Harry Lumley	Tor. 3	Det. 1
Pentti Lund	NYR	Apr. 2/50	NYR	3	Bill Durnan	NYR 4	Mtl. 1
Ted Lindsay	Det.	Apr. 5/55	Det.	4	Charlie Hodge (1)		
					Jacques Plante (3)	Det. 7	Mtl. 1
Gordie Howe	Det.	Apr. 10/55	Det.	3	Jacques Plante	Det. 5	Mtl. 1
Phil Goyette	Mtl.	Mar. 25/58	Mtl.	3	Terry Sawchuk	Mtl. 8	Det. 1
Jerry Toppazzini	Bos.	Apr. 5/58	Bos.	3	Lorne Worsley	Bos. 8	NYR 2
Bob Pulford	Tor.	Apr. 19/62	Tor.	3	Glenn Hall	Tor. 8	Chi. 4
Dave Keon	Tor.	Apr. 9/64	Mtl.	3	Charlie Hodge	Tor. 3	Mtl. 1
Henri Richard	Mtl.	Apr. 20/67	Mtl.	3	Terry Sawchuk (2)		
					Johnny Bower (1)	Mtl. 6	Tor. 2
Rosaire Paiement	Phi.	Apr. 13/68	Phi.	3	Glenn Hall (1)		
					Seth Martin (2)	Phi. 6	St. L. 1
Jean Beliveau	Mtl.	Apr. 20/68	Mtl.	3	Denis DeJordy	Mtl. 4	Chi. 1
Red Berenson	St. L.	Apr. 15/69	St. L.	3	Gerry Desjardins	St. L. 4	L.A. 0
Ken Schinkel	Pit.	Apr. 11/70	Oak.	3	Gary Smith	Pit. 5	Oak. 2
Jim Pappin	Chi.	Apr. 11/71	Phi.	3	Bruce Gamble	Chi. 6	Phi. 2
Bobby Orr	Bos.	Apr. 11/71	Mtl.	3	Ken Dryden	Bos. 5	Mtl. 2
Jacques Lemaire	Mtl.	Apr. 20/71	Mtl.	3	Lorne Worsley	Mtl. 7	Min. 2

Player	Team	Date	City	Total Goals	Opposing Goaltender	Score	
Vic Hadfield	NYR	Apr. 22/71	NYR	3	Tony Esposito	NYR 4	Chi. 1
Fred Stanfield	Bos.	Apr. 18/72	Bos.	3	Jacques Caron	Bos. 6	St. L. 1
Ken Hodge	Bos.	Apr. 30/72	Bos.	3	Ed Giacomin	Bos. 6	NYR 5
Steve Vickers	NYR	Apr. 10/73	Bos.	3	Ross Brooks (2)		
					Ed Johnston (1)	NYR 6	Bos. 3
Dick Redmond	Chi.	Apr. 4/73	Chi.	3	Wayne Stephenson	Chi. 7	St. L. 1
Tom Williams	L.A.	Apr. 14/74	L.A.	3	Mike Veisor	L.A. 5	Chi. 1
Marcel Dionne	L.A.	Apr. 15/76	L.A.	3	Gilles Gilbert	L.A. 6	Bos. 4
Don Saleski	Phi.	Apr. 20/76	Phi.	3	Wayne Thomas	Phi. 7	Tor. 1
Darryl Sittler	Tor.	Apr. 22/76	Tor.	5	Bernie Parent	Tor. 8	Phi. 5
Reggie Leach	Phi.	May 6/76	Phi.	5	Gilles Gilbert	Phi. 6	Bos. 3
Jim Lorentz	Buf.	Apr. 7/77	Min.	3	Pete LoPresti (2)		
					Gary Smith (1)	Buf. 7	Min. 1
Bobby Schmautz	Bos.	Apr. 11/77	Bos.	3	Rogatien Vachon	Bos. 8	L.A. 3
Billy Harris	NYI	Apr. 23/77	Mtl.	3	Ken Dryden	Mtl. 4	NYI 3
George Ferguson	Tor.	Apr. 11/78	Tor.	3	Rogatien Vachon	Tor. 7	L.A. 3
Jean Ratelle	Bos.	May 3/79	Bos.	3	Ken Dryden	Bos. 4	Mtl. 3
Stan Jonathan	Bos.	May 8/79	Bos.	3	Ken Dryden	Bos. 5	Mtl. 2
Ron Duguay	NYR	Apr. 20/80	NYR	3	Pete Peeters	NYR 4	Phi. 2
Steve Shutt	Mtl.	Apr. 22/80	Mtl.	3	Gilles Meloche	Mtl. 6	Min. 2
Gilbert Perreault	Buf.	May 6/80	NYI	3	Billy Smith (2)		
					ENG (1)	Buf. 7	NYI 4
Paul Holmgren	Phi.	May 15/80	Phil	3	Billy Smith	Phi. 8	NYI 3
Steve Payne	Min.	Apr. 8/81	Bos.	3	Rogatien Vachon	Min. 5	Bos. 4
Denis Potvin	NYI	Apr. 17/81	NYI	3	Andy Moog	NYI 6	Edm. 3
Barry Pederson	Bos.	Apr. 8/82	Bos.	3	Don Edwards	Bos. 7	Buf. 3
Duane Sutter	NYI	Apr. 15/83	NYI	3	Glen Hanlon	NYI 5	NYR 0
Doug Halward	Van.	Apr. 7/84	Van.	3	Rejean Lemelin (2)		
					Don Edwards (1)	Van. 7	Cgy. 0
Jorgen Pettersson	St. L.	Apr. 8/84	Det.	3	Ed Mio	St. L. 3	Det. 2
Clark Gillies	NYI	May 12/84	NYI	3	Grant Fuhr	NYI 6	Edm. 1
Ken Linseman	Bos.	Apr. 14/85	Bos.	3	Steve Penney	Bos. 7	Mtl. 6
Dave Andreychuk	Buf.	Apr. 14/85	Buf.	3	Dan Bouchard	Que. 4	Buf. 7
Greg Paslawski	StL.	Apr. 15/86	Min.	3	Don Beaupre	St. L. 6	Min. 3
Doug Risebrough	Cgy.	May 4/86	Cgy.	3	Rick Wamsley	Cgy. 8	St. L. 2
Mike McPhee	Mtl.	Apr. 11/87	Bos.	3	Doug Keans	Mtl. 5	Bos. 4
John Ogrodnick	Que.	Apr. 14/87	Hfd.	3	Mike Liut	Que. 7	Hfd. 5
Pelle Eklund	Phi.	May 10/87	Mtl.	3	Patrick Roy (1)		
					Bryan Hayward (2)	Phi. 6	Mtl. 3
John Tucker	Buf.	Apr. 9/88	Bos.	4	Andy Moog	Buf. 6	Bos. 2
Tony Hrkac	St. L.	Apr. 10/88	St. L.	4	Darren Pang	St. L. 6	Chi. 5
Hakan Loob	Cgy.	Apr. 10/88	Cgy.	3	Glenn Healy	Cgy. 7	L.A. 3
Ed Olczyk	Tor.	Apr. 12/88	Tor.	3	Greg Stefan (2)		
					Glen Hanlon (1)	Tor. 6	Det. 5
Aaron Broten	N.J.	Apr. 20/88	N.J.	3	Pete Peeters	N.J. 5	Wsh. 2
Mark Johnson	N.J.	Apr. 22/88	Wsh.	4	Pete Peeters	N.J. 10	Wsh. 4
Patrik Sundstrom	N.J.	Apr. 22/88	Wsh.	3	Pete Peeters (2)		
					Clint Malarchuk (1)	N.J. 10	Wsh. 4
Bob Brooke	Min.	Apr. 5/89	St. L.	3	Greg Millen	St. L. 4	Min. 3
Chris Kontos	L.A.	Apr. 6/89	L.A.	3	Grant Fuhr	L.A. 5	Edm. 2
Wayne Presley	Chi.	Apr. 13/89	Chi.	3	Greg Stefan (1)		
					Glen Hanlon (2)	Chi. 7	Det. 1
Tony Granato	L.A.	Apr. 10/90	L.A.	3	Mike Vernon (1)		
					Rick Wamsley (2)	L.A. 12	Cgy. 4
Tomas Sandstrom	L.A.	Apr. 10/90	L.A.	3	Mike Vernon (1)		
					Rick Wamsley (2)	L.A. 12	Cgy. 4
Dave Taylor	L.A.	Apr. 10/90	L.A.	3	Mike Vernon (1)		
					Rick Wamsley (2)	L.A. 12	Cgy. 4
Bernie Nicholls	NYR	Apr. 19/90	NYR	3	Mike Liut	NYR 7	Wsh. 3
John Druce	Wsh.	Apr. 21/90	NYR	3	John Vanbiesbrouck	Wsh. 6	NYR 3
Adam Oates	St. L.	Apr. 12/91	St. L.	3	Tim Chevaldae	St. L. 6	Det. 1
Luc Robitaille	L.A.	Apr. 26/91	L.A.	3	Grant Fuhr	L.A. 5	Edm. 2
Ron Francis	Pit.	May 9/92	Pit.	3	Mike Richter (2)		
					John V'brouck (1)	Pit. 5	NYR. 4
Dirk Graham	Chi.	June 1/92	Chi.	3	Tom Barrasso	Pit. 5	Chi. 2
Joe Murphy	Edm.	May 6/92	Edm.	3	Kirk McLean	Edm. 5	Van. 2
Ray Sheppard	Det.	Apr. 24/92	Min.	3	Jon Casey	Min. 5	Det. 2
Kevin Stevens	Pit.	May 21/92	Bos.	4	Andy Moog	Pit. 5	Bos. 2
Pavel Bure	Van.	Apr. 28/92	Wpg.	3	Rick Tabaracci	Van. 8	Wpg. 3
Brian Noonan	Chi.	Apr. 18/93	Chi.	3	Curtis Joseph	St. L. 4	Chi. 3
Dale Hunter	Wsh.	Apr. 20/93	Wsh.	3	Glenn Healy	NYI 5	Wsh. 4
Teemu Selanne	Wpg.	Apr. 23/93	Wpg.	3	Kirk McLean	Wpg. 5	Van. 4
Ray Ferraro	NYI	Apr. 26/93	Wsh.	4	Don Beaupre	Wsh. 6	NYI 4
Al Iafrate	Wsh.	Apr. 26/93	Wsh.	3	Glenn Healy (2)		
					Mark Fitzpatrick (1)	Wsh. 6	NYI 4
Paul Di Pietro	Mtl.	Apr. 28/93	Mtl.	3	Ron Hextall	Mtl. 6	Que. 2
Wendel Clark	Tor.	May 27/93	L.A.	3	Kelly Hrudey	L.A. 5	Tor. 4
Eric Desjardins	Mtl.	Jun. 3/93	Mtl.	3	Kelly Hrudey	Mtl. 3	L.A. 2
Tony Amonte	Chi.	Apr. 23/94	Chi.	4	Felix Potvin	Chi. 5	Tor. 4
Gary Suter	Chi.	Apr. 24/94	Chi.	3	Felix Potvin	Chi. 4	Tor. 3
Ulf Dahlen	S.J.	May 6/94	S.J.	3	Felix Potvin	S.J. 5	Tor. 2
Mike Sullivan	Cgy.	May 11/95	S.J.	3	Arturs Irbe (2)		
					Wade Flaherty (1)	Cgy. 9	S.J. 2
Theoren Fleury	Cgy.	May 13/95	S.J.	4	Arturs Irbe (3)		
					ENG (1)	Cgy. 6	S.J. 4
Brendan Shanahan	St. L.	May 13/95	Van.	3	Kirk McLean	St. L. 5	Van. 2
John LeClair	Phi.	May 21/95	Phi.	3	Mike Richter	Phi. 5	NYR 4
Brian Leetch	NYR	May 22/95	Phi.	3	Ron Hextall	Phi. 4	NYR 3
Trevor Linden	Van.	Apr. 25/96	Col.	3	Patrick Roy	Col. 5	Van. 4
Jaromir Jagr	Pit.	May 11/96	Pit.	3	Mike Richter	Pit. 7	NYR 3
Peter Forsberg	Col.	Jun. 6/96	Col.	3	John Vanbiesbrouck	Col. 8	Fla. 1
Valeri Zelepukin	N.J.	Apr. 22/97	Mtl.	3	Jocelyn Thibault	N.J. 6	Mtl. 4
Valeri Kamensky	Col.	Apr. 24/97	Col.	3	Jeff Hackett (2)		
					Chris Terreri (1)	Col. 7	Chi. 0
Eric Lindros	Phi.	May 20/97	NYR	3	Mike Richter	Phi. 6	NYR 3

Leading Playoff Scorers, 1918–1997

Season	Player and Club	Games Played	Goals	Assists	Points
1996-97	Eric Lindros, Philadelphia	19	12	14	26
1995-96	Joe Sakic, Colorado	22	18	16	34
1994-95	Sergei Fedorov, Detroit	17	7	17	24
1993-94	Brian Leetch, NY Rangers	23	11	23	34
1992-93	Wayne Gretzky, Los Angeles	24	15	25	40
1991-92	Mario Lemieux, Pittsburgh	15	16	18	34
1990-91	Mario Lemieux, Pittsburgh	23	16	28	44
1989-90	Craig Simpson, Edmonton	22	16	15	31
	Mark Messier, Edmonton	22	9	22	31
1988-89	Al MacInnis, Calgary	22	7	24	31
1987-88	Wayne Gretzky, Edmonton	19	12	31	43
1986-87	Wayne Gretzky, Edmonton	21	5	29	34
1985-86	Doug Gilmour, St. Louis	19	9	12	21
	Bernie Federko, St. Louis	19	7	14	21
1984-85	Wayne Gretzky, Edmonton	18	17	30	47
1983-84	Wayne Gretzky, Edmonton	19	13	22	35
1982-83	Wayne Gretzky, Edmonton	16	12	26	38
1981-82	Bryan Trottier, NY Islanders	19	6	23	29
1980-81	Mike Bossy, NY Islanders	18	17	18	35
1979-80	Bryan Trottier, NY Islanders	21	12	17	29
1978-79	Jacques Lemaire, Montreal	16	11	12	23
	Guy Lafleur, Montreal	16	10	13	23
1977-78	Guy Lafleur, Montreal	15	10	11	21
	Larry Robinson, Montreal	15	4	17	21
1976-77	Guy Lafleur, Montreal	14	9	17	26
1975-76	Reggie Leach, Philadelphia	16	19	5	24
1974-75	Rick MacLeish, Philadelphia	17	11	9	20
1973-74	Rick MacLeish, Philadelphia	17	13	9	22
1972-73	Yvan Cournoyer, Montreal	17	15	10	25
1971-72	Phil Esposito, Boston	15	9	15	24
	Bobby Orr, Boston	15	5	19	24
1970-71	Frank Mahovlich, Montreal	20	14	13	27
1969-70	Phil Esposito, Boston	14	13	14	27
1968-69	Phil Esposito, Boston	10	8	10	18
1967-68	Bill Goldsworthy, Minnesota	14	8	7	15
1966-67	Jim Pappin, Toronto	12	7	8	15
1965-66	Norm Ullman, Detroit	12	6	9	15
1964-65	Bobby Hull, Chicago	14	10	7	17
1963-64	Gordie Howe, Detroit	14	9	10	19
1962-63	Gordie Howe, Detroit	11	7	9	16
	Norm Ullman, Detroit	11	4	12	16
1961-62	Stan Mikita, Chicago	12	6	15	21
1960-61	Gordie Howe, Detroit	11	4	11	15
	Pierre Pilote, Chicago	12	3	12	15
1959-60	Henri Richard, Montreal	8	3	9	12
	Bernie Geoffrion, Montreal	8	2	10	12
1958-59	Dickie Moore, Montreal	11	5	12	17
1957-58	Fleming Mackell, Boston	12	5	14	19
1956-57	Bernie Geoffrion, Montreal	11	11	7	18
1955-56	Jean Béliveau, Montreal	10	12	7	19
1954-55	Gordie Howe, Detroit	11	9	11	20
1953-54	Dickie Moore, Montreal	11	5	8	13
1952-53	Ed Sanford, Boston	11	8	3	11
1951-52	Ted Lindsay, Detroit	8	5	2	7
	Floyd Curry, Montreal	11	4	3	7
	Metro Prystai, Detroit	8	2	5	7
	Gordie Howe, Detroit	8	2	5	7
1950-51	Maurice Richard, Montreal	11	9	4	13
	Max Bentley, Toronto	11	2	11	13
1949-50	Pentti Lund, NY Rangers	12	6	5	11
1948-49	Gordie Howe, Detroit	11	8	3	11
1947-48	Ted Kennedy, Toronto	9	8	6	14
1946-47	Maurice Richard, Montreal	10	6	5	11
1945-46	Elmer Lach, Montreal	9	5	12	17
1944-45	Joe Carveth, Detroit	14	5	6	11
1943-44	Toe Blake, Montreal	9	7	11	18
1942-43	Carl Liscombe, Detroit	10	6	8	14
1941-42	Don Grosso, Detroit	12	8	6	14
1940-41	Milt Schmidt, Boston	11	5	6	11
1939-40	Phil Watson, NY Rangers	12	3	6	9
	Neil Colville, NY Rangers	12	2	7	9
1938-39	Bill Cowley, Boston	12	3	11	14
1937-38	Johnny Gottselig, Chicago	10	5	3	8
1936-37	Marty Barry, Detroit	10	4	7	11
1935-36	Buzz Boll, Toronto	9	7	3	10
1934-35	Baldy Northcott, Mtl. Maroons	7	4	1	5
	Harvey Jackson, Toronto	7	3	2	5
	Marvin Wentworth, Mtl. Maroons	7	3	2	5
1933-34	Larry Aurie, Detroit	9	3	7	10
1932-33	Cecil Dillon, NY Rangers	8	8	2	10
1931-32	Frank Boucher, NY Rangers	7	3	6	9
1930-31	Cooney Weiland, Boston	5	6	3	9
1929-30	Marty Barry, Boston	6	3	3	6
	Cooney Weiland, Boston	6	1	5	6
1928-29	Andy Blair, Toronto	4	3	0	3
	Butch Keeling, NY Rangers	6	3	0	3
	Ace Bailey, Toronto	4	1	2	3
1927-28	Frank Boucher, NY Rangers	9	7	3	10
1926-27	Harry Oliver, Boston	8	4	2	6
	Perk Galbraith, Boston	8	3	3	6
	Frank Fredrickson, Boston	8	2	4	6
1925-26	Nels Stewart, Mtl. Maroons	8	6	3	9
1924-25	Howie Morenz, Montreal	6	7	1	8
1923-24	Howie Morenz, Montreal	6	7	2	9
1922-23	Punch Broadbent, Ottawa	8	6	1	7
1921-22	Babe Dye, Toronto	7	11	2	13
1920-21	Cy Denneny, Ottawa	7	4	2	6
1919-20	Frank Nighbor, Ottawa	5	6	1	7
	Jack Darragh, Ottawa	5	5	2	7
1918-19	Newsy Lalonde, Montreal	10	17	1	18
1917-18	Alf Skinner, Toronto	7	8	1	9

Overtime Games since 1918

Abbreviations: Teams/Cities: — **Ana.** - Anaheim; **Atl.** - Atlanta; **Bos.** - Boston; **Buf.** - Buffalo; **Cgy.** - Calgary; **Cgy. T.** - Calgary Tigers (Western Canada Hockey League); **Chi.** - Chicago; **Col.** - Colorado; **Dal.** - Dallas; **Det.** - Detroit; **Edm.** - Edmonton; **Edm. E.** - Edmonton Eskimos (WCHL); **Fla.** - Florida; **Hfd.** - Hartford; **K.C.** - Kansas City; **L.A.** - Los Angeles; **Min.** - Minnesota; **Mtl.** - Montreal; **Mtl.M.** - Montreal Maroons; **N.J.** - New Jersey; **NYA** - NY Americans; **NYI** - New York Islanders; **NYR** - New York Rangers; **Oak.** - Oakland; **Ott.** - Ottawa; **Phi.** - Philadelphia; **Pho.** - Phoenix; **Pit.** - Pittsburgh; **Que.** - Quebec; **St. L.** - St. Louis; **Sea.** - Seattle Metropolitans (Pacific Coast Hockey Association); **S.J.** - San Jose; **T.B.** - Tampa Bay; **Tor.** - Toronto; **Van.** - Vancouver; **Van. M** - Vancouver Millionaires (PCHA); **Vic.** - Victoria Cougars (WCHL); **Wpg.** - Winnipeg; **Wsh.** - Washington.

SERIES — **CF** - conference final; **CSF** - conference semi-final; **CQF** - conference quarter-final; **DF** - division final; **DSF** - division semi-final; **F** - final; **PR** - preliminary round; **QF** - quarter final; **SF** - semi-final.

Date	City	Series	Score	Scorer		Overtime	Series Winner
Mar. 26/19	Sea.	F	Mtl. 0	Sea. 0	no scorer	20:00	
Mar. 30/19	Sea.	F	Mtl. 4	Sea. 3	Odie Cleghorn	15:57	
Mar. 20/22	Tor.	F	Tor 2	Van.M. 1	Babe Dye	4:50	Tor.
Mar. 29/23	Van.	F	Ott. 2	Edm.E. 1	Cy Denneny	2:08	Ott.
Mar. 31/27	Mtl.	QF	Mtl. 1	Mtl. M. 0	Howie Morenz	12:05	Mtl.
Apr. 7/27	Bos.	F	Ott. 0	Bos. 0	no scorer	20:00	Ott.
Apr. 11/27	Ott.	F	Bos. 1	Ott. 1	no scorer	20:00	Ott.
Apr. 3/28	Mtl.	QF	Mtl. M. 1	Mtl. 0	Russ Oatman	8:20	Mtl. M.
Apr. 7/28	Mtl.	F	NYR 2	Mtl. M. 1	Frank Boucher	7:05	NYR
Mar. 21/29	NY	QF	NYR 1	NYA 0	Butch Keeling	29:50	NYR
Mar. 26/29	Tor.	SF	NYR 2	Tor. 1	Frank Boucher	2:03	NYR
Mar. 20/30	Mtl.	SF	Bos. 2	Mtl. M. 1	Harry Oliver	45:35	Bos.
Mar. 25/30	Bos.	SF	Mtl. M. 1	Bos. 0	Archie Wilcox	26:27	Bos.
Mar. 26/30	Mtl.	QF	Chi. 2	Mtl. 2	Howie Morenz (Mtl.)	51:43	Mtl.
Mar. 28/30	Mtl.	SF	Mtl. 2	NYR 1	Gus Rivers	68:52	Mtl.
Mar. 24/31	Bos.	SF	Bos. 5	Mtl. 4	Cooney Weiland	18:56	Mtl.
Mar. 26/31	Chi.	QF	Chi. 2	Tor. 1	Steward Adams	19:20	Chi.
Mar. 28/31	Mtl.	SF	Mtl. 4	Bos. 3	Georges Mantha	5:10	Mtl.
Apr. 1/31	Mtl.	SF	Mtl. 3	Bos. 2	Wildor Larochelle	19:00	Mtl.
Apr. 5/31	Chi.	F	Chi. 2	Mtl. 1	Johnny Gottselig	24:50	Mtl.
Apr. 9/31	Mtl.	F	Chi. 3	Mtl. 2	Cy Wentworth	53:50	Mtl.
Mar. 26/32	Mtl.	SF	NYR 4	Mtl. 3	Fred Cook	59:32	NYR
Apr. 2/32	Tor.	SF	Tor. 3	Mtl. M. 2	Bob Gracie	17:59	Tor.
Mar. 25/33	Bos.	SF	Bos. 2	Tor. 1	Marty Barry	14:14	Tor.
Mar. 28/33	Bos.	SF	Tor. 1	Bos. 0	Busher Jackson	15:03	Tor.
Mar. 30/33	Tor.	SF	Bos. 2	Tor. 1	Eddie Shore	4:23	Tor.
Apr. 3/33	Tor.	SF	Tor. 1	Bos. 0	Ken Doraty	104:46	Tor.
Apr. 13/33	Tor.	F	NYR 1	Tor. 0	Bill Cook	7:33	NYR
Mar. 22/34	Tor.	SF	Det. 2	Tor. 1	Herbie Lewis	1:33	Det.
Mar. 25/34	Chi.	QF	Chi. 1	Mtl. 1	Mush March (Chi)	11:05	Chi.
Apr. 3/34	Det.	F	Chi. 2	Det. 1	Paul Thompson	21:10	Chi.
Apr. 10/34	Chi.	F	Chi. 1	Det. 0	Mush March	30:05	Chi.
Mar. 23/35	Bos.	SF	Bos. 1	Tor. 0	Dit Clapper	33:26	Tor.
Mar. 26/35	Chi.	QF	Mtl. M. 1	Chi. 0	Baldy Northcott	4:02	Mtl. M.
Mar. 30/35	Tor.	SF	Tor. 2	Bos. 1	Pep Kelly	1:36	Tor.
Apr. 4/35	Tor.	F	Mtl. M. 3	Tor. 2	Dave Trottier	5:28	Mtl. M.
Mar. 24/36	Mtl.	SF	Det. 1	Mtl. M. 0	Mud Bruneteau	116:30	Det.
Apr. 9/36	Tor.	F	Tor. 4	Det. 3	Buzz Boll	0:31	Det.
Mar. 25/37	NY	QF	NYR 2	Tor. 1	Babe Pratt	13:05	NYR
Apr. 1/37	Mtl.	SF	Det. 2	Mtl. 1	Hec Kilrea	51:49	Det.
Mar. 22/38	NY	QF	NYA 2	NYR 1	Johnny Sorrell	21:25	NYA
Mar. 24/38	Tor.	SF	Tor. 1	Bos. 0	George Parsons	21:31	Tor.
Mar. 26/38	Mtl.	QF	Chi. 3	Mtl. 2	Paul Thompson	11:49	Chi.
Mar. 27/38	NY	QF	NYA 3	NYR 2	Lorne Carr	60:40	NYA
Mar. 29/38	Bos.	SF	Tor. 3	Bos. 2	Gord Drillon	10:04	Tor.
Mar. 31/38	Chi.	SF	Chi. 1	NYA 0	Cully Dahlstrom	33:01	Chi.
Mar. 21/39	NY	SF	Bos. 2	NYR 1	Mel Hill	59:25	Bos.
Mar. 23/39	Bos.	SF	Bos. 3	NYR 2	Mel Hill	8:24	Bos.
Mar. 26/39	Det.	QF	Det. 1	Mtl. 0	Marty Barry	7:47	Det.
Mar. 30/39	Bos.	SF	NYR 2	Bos. 1	Clint Smith	17:19	Bos.
Apr. 1/39	Tor.	SF	Tor. 5	Det. 4	Gord Drillon	5:42	Tor.
Apr. 2/39	Bos.	SF	Bos. 2	NYR 1	Mel Hill	48:00	Bos.
Apr. 9/39	Bos.	F	Tor. 3	Bos. 2	Doc Romnes	10:38	Bos.
Mar. 19/40	Det.	QF	Det. 2	NYA 1	Syd Howe	0:25	Det.
Mar. 19/40	Tor.	QF	Tor. 3	Chi. 2	Syl Apps	6:35	Tor.
Apr. 2/40	NY	F	NYR 2	Tor. 1	Alf Pike	15:30	NYR
Apr. 11/40	Tor.	F	NYR 2	Tor. 1	Muzz Patrick	31:43	NYR
Apr. 13/40	Tor.	F	NYR 3	Tor. 2	Bryan Hextall	2:07	NYR
Mar. 20/41	Det.	QF	Det. 2	NYR 1	Gus Giesebrecht	12:01	Det.
Mar. 22/41	Mtl.	QF	Mtl. 4	Chi. 3	Charlie Sands	34:04	Chi.
Mar. 29/41	Bos.	SF	Tor. 2	Bos. 1	Pete Langelle	17:31	Bos.
Mar. 30/41	Chi.	SF	Det. 2	Chi. 1	Gus Giesebrecht	9:15	Det.
Mar. 22/42	Chi.	QF	Bos. 2	Chi. 1	Des Smith	6:51	Bos.
Mar. 21/43	Bos.	SF	Bos. 5	Mtl. 4	Don Gallinger	12:30	Bos.
Mar. 23/43	Det.	SF	Tor. 3	Det. 2	Jack McLean	70:18	Det.
Mar. 25/43	Mtl.	SF	Bos. 3	Mtl. 2	Harvey Jackson	3:20	Bos.
Mar. 30/43	Tor.	SF	Det. 3	Tor. 2	Adam Brown	9:21	Det.
Mar. 30/43	Bos.	SF	Bos. 5	Mtl. 4	Ab DeMarco	3:41	Bos.
Apr. 13/44	Mtl.	F	Mtl. 5	Chi. 4	Toe Blake	9:12	Mtl.
Mar. 27/45	Tor.	SF	Tor. 4	Mtl. 3	Gus Bodnar	12:36	Tor.
Mar. 29/45	Det.	SF	Det. 3	Bos. 2	Mud Bruneteau	17:12	Det.
Apr. 21/45	Tor.	F	Det. 1	Tor. 0	Ed Bruneteau	14:16	Tor.
Mar. 28/46	Bos.	SF	Bos. 4	Det. 3	Don Gallinger	9:51	Bos.
Mar. 30/46	Mtl.	F	Mtl. 4	Bos. 3	Maurice Richard	9:08	Mtl.
Apr. 2/46	Mtl.	F	Mtl. 3	Bos. 2	Jim Peters	16:55	Mtl.
Apr. 7/46	Bos.	F	Bos. 3	Mtl. 2	Terry Reardon	15:13	Mtl.
Mar. 26/47	Tor.	SF	Tor. 3	Det. 2	Howie Meeker	3:05	Tor.
Mar. 27/47	Mtl.	SF	Mtl. 2	Bos. 1	Ken Mosdell	5:38	Mtl.
Apr. 3/47	Mtl.	SF	Mtl. 4	Bos. 3	John Quilty	36:40	Mtl.
Apr. 15/47	Tor.	F	Tor. 2	Mtl. 1	Syl Apps	16:36	Tor.
Mar. 24/48	Tor.	SF	Tor. 5	Bos. 4	Nick Metz	17:03	Tor.
Mar. 22/49	Det.	SF	Det. 2	Mtl. 1	Max McNab	44:52	Det.
Mar. 24/49	Det.	SF	Mtl. 4	Det. 3	Gerry Plamondon	2:59	Det.
Mar. 26/49	Tor.	SF	Bos. 5	Tor. 4	Woody Dumart	16:14	Tor.
Apr. 8/49	Det.	F	Tor. 3	Det. 2	Joe Klukay	17:31	Tor.
Apr. 4/50	Tor.	SF	Det. 2	Tor. 1	Leo Reise	20:38	Det.
Apr. 4/50	Mtl.	SF	Mtl. 3	NYR 2	Elmer Lach	15:19	NYR
Apr. 9/50	Det.	SF	Det. 1	Tor. 0	Leo Reise	8:39	Det.
Apr. 18/50	Det.	F	NYR 4	Det. 3	Don Raleigh	8:34	Det.
Apr. 20/50	Det.	F	NYR 2	Det. 1	Don Raleigh	1:38	Det.
Apr. 23/50	Det.	F	Det. 4	NYR 3	Pete Babando	28:31	Det.
Mar. 27/51	Det.	SF	Mtl. 3	Det. 2	Maurice Richard	61:09	Mtl.
Mar. 29/51	Det.	SF	Mtl. 1	Det. 0	Maurice Richard	42:20	Mtl.
Mar. 31/51	Tor.	SF	Bos. 1	Tor. 1	no scorer	20:00	Tor.
Apr. 11/51	Tor.	F	Tor. 3	Mtl. 2	Sid Smith	5:51	Tor.
Apr. 14/51	Tor.	F	Mtl. 3	Tor. 2	Maurice Richard	2:55	Tor.
Apr. 17/51	Mtl.	F	Tor. 2	Mtl. 1	Ted Kennedy	4:47	Tor.
Apr. 19/51	Mtl.	F	Tor. 3	Mtl. 2	Harry Watson	5:15	Tor.
Apr. 21/51	Tor.	F	Tor. 3	Mtl. 2	Bill Barilko	2:53	Tor.
Apr. 6/52	Bos.	SF	Mtl. 3	Bos. 2	Paul Masnick	27:49	Mtl.
Mar. 29/53	Bos.	SF	Bos. 2	Det. 1	Jack McIntyre	12:29	Bos.
Mar. 29/53	Chi.	SF	Chi. 2	Mtl. 1	Al Dewsbury	5:18	Mtl.
Apr. 16/53	Mtl.	F	Mtl. 1	Bos. 0	Elmer Lach	1:22	Mtl.
Apr. 1/54	Det.	SF	Det. 4	Tor. 3	Ted Lindsay	21:01	Det.
Apr. 11/54	Det.	F	Mtl. 1	Det. 0	Ken Mosdell	5:45	Det.
Apr. 16/54	Det.	F	Det. 2	Mtl. 1	Tony Leswick	4:29	Det.
Mar. 29/55	Bos.	SF	Mtl. 4	Bos. 3	Don Marshall	3:05	Mtl.
Mar. 24/56	Tor.	SF	Det. 5	Tor. 4	Ted Lindsay	4:22	Det.
Mar. 28/57	NY	SF	NYR 4	Mtl. 3	Andy Hebenton	13:38	Mtl.
Apr. 4/57	Mtl.	SF	Mtl. 4	NYR 3	Maurice Richard	1:11	Mtl.
Mar. 27/58	NY	SF	Bos. 4	NYR 3	Jerry Toppazzini	4:46	Bos.
Mar. 30/58	Det.	SF	Mtl. 2	Det. 1	André Pronovost	11:52	Mtl.
Apr. 17/58	Mtl.	F	Mtl. 3	Bos. 2	Maurice Richard	5:45	Mtl.
Mar. 28/59	Tor.	SF	Tor. 3	Bos. 2	Gerry Ehman	5:02	Tor.
Mar. 31/59	Tor.	SF	Tor. 3	Bos. 2	Frank Mahovlich	11:21	Tor.
Apr. 14/59	Tor.	F	Tor. 3	Mtl. 2	Dick Duff	10:06	Mtl.
Mar. 26/60	Mtl.	SF	Mtl. 4	Chi. 3	Doug Harvey	8:38	Mtl.
Mar. 27/60	Det.	SF	Tor. 5	Det. 4	Frank Mahovlich	43:00	Tor.
Mar. 29/60	Det.	SF	Det. 2	Tor. 1	Gerry Melnyk	1:54	Tor.
Mar. 22/61	Tor.	SF	Tor. 3	Det. 2	George Armstrong	24:51	Det.
Mar. 26/61	Chi.	SF	Chi. 2	Mtl. 1	Murray Balfour	52:12	Chi.
Apr. 5/62	Tor.	SF	Tor. 3	NYR 2	Red Kelly	24:23	Tor.
Apr. 2/64	Det.	SF	Chi. 3	Det. 2	Murray Balfour	8:21	Det.
Apr. 14/64	Tor.	F	Det. 4	Tor. 3	Larry Jeffrey	7:52	Tor.
Apr. 23/64	Det.	F	Tor. 4	Det. 3	Bobby Baun	1:43	Tor.
Apr. 6/65	Tor.	SF	Tor. 3	Mtl. 2	Dave Keon	4:17	Mtl.
Apr. 13/65	Tor.	SF	Mtl. 4	Tor. 3	Claude Provost	16:33	Mtl.
May 5/66	Det.	F	Mtl. 3	Det. 2	Henri Richard	2:20	Mtl.
Apr. 13/67	NY	SF	Mtl. 2	NYR 1	John Ferguson	6:28	Mtl.
Apr. 25/67	Tor.	F	Tor. 3	Mtl. 2	Bob Pulford	28:26	Tor.
Apr. 10/68	St. L.	QF	St. L. 3	Phi. 2	Larry Keenan	24:10	St. L.
Apr. 16/68	St. L.	QF	Phi. 2	St. L. 1	Don Blackburn	31:18	St. L.
Apr. 16/68	Min.	QF	Min. 4	L.A. 3	Milan Marcetta	9:11	Min.
Apr. 22/68	Min.	SF	Min. 3	St. L. 2	Parker MacDonald	3:41	St. L.
Apr. 27/68	St. L.	SF	St. L. 4	Min. 3	Gary Sabourin	1:32	St. L.
Apr. 28/68	Mtl.	SF	Mtl. 4	Chi. 3	Jacques Lemaire	2:14	Mtl.
Apr. 29/68	St. L.	SF	St. L. 3	Min. 2	Bill McCreary	17:27	St. L.
May 3/68	St. L.	SF	St. L. 2	Min. 1	Ron Schock	22:50	St. L.
May 5/68	St. L.	F	Mtl. 3	St. L. 2	Jacques Lemaire	1:41	Mtl.
May 9/68	Mtl.	F	Mtl. 4	St. L. 3	Bobby Rousseau	1:13	Mtl.
Apr. 2/69	Oak.	QF	L.A. 5	Oak. 4	Ted Irvine	0:19	L.A.
Apr. 10/69	Mtl.	SF	Mtl. 3	Bos. 2	Ralph Backstrom	0:42	Mtl.
Apr. 13/69	Mtl.	SF	Mtl. 4	Bos. 3	Mickey Redmond	4:55	Mtl.
Apr. 24/69	Bos.	SF	Mtl. 2	Bos. 1	Jean Béliveau	31:28	Mtl.
Apr. 12/70	Oak.	QF	Pit. 3	Oak. 2	Michel Briere	8:28	Pit.
May 10/70	Bos.	F	Bos. 4	St. L. 3	Bobby Orr	0:40	Bos.
Apr. 15/71	Tor.	QF	NYR 2	Tor. 1	Bob Nevin	9:07	NYR
Apr. 18/71	Chi.	SF	NYR 2	Chi. 1	Pete Stemkowski	1:37	Chi.
Apr. 27/71	Chi.	SF	Chi. 3	NYR 2	Bobby Hull	6:35	Chi.
Apr. 29/71	NY	SF	NYR 3	Chi. 2	Pete Stemkowski	41:29	Chi.
May 4/71	Chi.	F	Chi. 2	Mtl. 1	Jim Pappin	21:11	Mtl.
Apr. 6/72	Bos.	QF	Tor. 4	Bos. 3	Jim Harrison	2:58	Bos.
Apr. 6/72	Min.	QF	Min. 6	St. L. 5	Bill Goldsworthy	1:36	St. L.
Apr. 9/72	Pit.	QF	Chi. 6	Pit. 5	Pit Martin	0:12	Chi.
Apr. 16/72	Min.	QF	St. L. 2	Min. 1	Kevin O'Shea	10:07	St. L.
Apr. 1/73	Mtl.	QF	Buf. 3	Mtl. 2	René Robert	9:18	Mtl.
Apr. 10/73	Phi.	QF	Phi. 3	Min. 2	Gary Dornhoefer	8:35	Phi.
Apr. 14/73	Mtl.	SF	Phi. 5	Mtl. 4	Rick MacLeish	2:56	Mtl.
Apr. 17/73	Mtl.	SF	Mtl. 4	Phi. 3	Larry Robinson	6:45	Mtl.
Apr. 14/74	Tor.	QF	Bos. 4	Tor. 3	Ken Hodge	1:27	Bos.
Apr. 14/74	Atl.	QF	Phi. 4	Atl. 3	Dave Schultz	5:40	Phi.
Apr. 16/74	Mtl.	QF	NYR 3	Mtl. 2	Ron Harris	4:07	NYR
Apr. 23/74	Chi.	SF	Chi. 4	Bos. 3	Jim Pappin	3:48	Bos.
Apr. 28/74	NY	SF	NYR 2	Phi. 1	Rod Gilbert	4:20	Phi.
May 9/74	Bos.	F	Phi. 3	Bos. 2	Bobby Clarke	12:01	Phi.
Apr. 8/75	L.A.	PR	L.A. 3	Tor. 2	Mike Murphy	8:53	Tor.
Apr. 10/75	Tor.	PR	Tor. 3	L.A. 2	Blaine Stoughton	10:19	Tor.
Apr. 10/75	Chi.	PR	Chi. 4	Bos. 3	Ivan Boldirev	7:33	Chi.
Apr. 11/75	NY	PR	NYI 4	NYR 3	Jean-Paul Parise	0:11	NYI
Apr. 19/75	Tor.	QF	Phi. 4	Tor. 3	André Dupont	1:45	Phi.
Apr. 17/75	Chi.	QF	Chi. 5	Buf. 4	Stan Mikita	2:31	Buf.
Apr. 22/75	Mtl.	QF	Mtl. 5	Van. 4	Guy Lafleur	17:06	Mtl.
May 1/75	Phi.	SF	Phi. 5	NYI 4	Bobby Clarke	2:56	Phi.
May 7/75	NYI	SF	NYI 4	Phi. 3	Jude Drouin	1:53	Phi.
Apr. 27/75	Buf.	SF	Buf. 6	Mtl. 5	Danny Gare	4:42	Buf.
May 6/75	Buf.	SF	Buf. 5	Mtl. 4	René Robert	5:56	Buf.
May 20/75	Buf.	F	Buf. 5	Phi. 4	René Robert	18:29	Phi.
Apr. 8/76	Buf.	PR	Buf. 3	St. L. 2	Danny Gare	11:43	Buf.
Apr. 9/76	Buf.	PR	Buf. 2	St. L. 1	Don Luce	14:27	Buf.
Apr. 13/76	Bos.	QF	L.A. 3	Bos. 2	Butch Goring	0:27	Bos.
Apr. 13/76	Buf.	QF	Buf. 3	NYI 2	Danny Gare	14:04	NYI
Apr. 22/76	L.A.	QF	L.A. 4	Bos. 3	Butch Goring	18:28	Bos.
Apr. 29/76	Phi.	SF	Phi. 2	Bos. 1	Reggie Leach	13:38	Phi.
Apr. 15/77	Tor.	QF	Phi. 4	Tor. 3	Rick MacLeish	2:55	Phi.
Apr. 17/77	Tor.	QF	Phi. 6	Tor. 5	Reggie Leach	19:10	Phi.
Apr. 24/77	Phi.	SF	Bos. 4	Phi. 3	Rick Middleton	2:57	Bos.
Apr. 26/77	Phi.	SF	Bos. 5	Phi. 4	Terry O'Reilly	30:07	Bos.
May 3/77	Mtl.	SF	NYI 4	Mtl. 3	Billy Harris	3:58	Mtl.
May 14/77	Bos.	F	Mtl. 2	Bos. 1	Jacques Lemaire	4:32	Mtl.

Date	City	Series	Score		Scorer	Overtime	Series Winner
Apr. 11/78	Phi.	PR	Phi. 3	Col. 2	Mel Bridgman	0:23	Phi.
Apr. 13/78	NY	PR	NYR 4	Buf. 3	Don Murdoch	1:37	Buf.
Apr. 19/78	Bos.	QF	Bos. 4	Chi. 3	Terry O'Reilly	1:50	Bos.
Apr. 19/78	NYI	QF	NYI 3	Tor. 2	Mike Bossy	2:50	Tor.
Apr. 21/78	Chi.	QF	Bos. 4	Chi. 3	Peter McNab	10:17	Bos.
Apr. 25/78	NYI	QF	NYI 2	Tor. 1	Bob Nystrom	8:02	Tor.
Apr. 29/78	NYI	QF	Tor. 2	NYI 1	Lanny McDonald	4:13	Tor.
May 2/78	Bos.	SF	Bos. 3	Phi. 2	Rick Middleton	1:43	Bos.
May 16/78	Mtl.	F	Mtl. 3	Bos. 2	Guy Lafleur	13:09	Mtl.
May 21/78	Bos.	F	Bos. 4	Mtl. 3	Bobby Schmautz	6:22	Mtl.
Apr. 12/79	L.A.	PR	NYR 2	L.A. 1	Phil Esposito	6:11	NYR
Apr. 14/79	Buf.	PR	Pit. 4	Buf. 3	George Ferguson	0:47	Pit.
Apr. 16/79	Phi.	QF	Phi. 3	NYR 2	Ken Linseman	0:44	NYR
Apr. 18/79	NYI	QF	NYI 1	Chi. 0	Mike Bossy	2:31	NYI
Apr. 21/79	Tor.	QF	Mtl. 4	Tor. 3	Cam Connor	25:25	Mtl.
Apr. 22/79	Tor.	QF	Mtl. 5	Tor. 4	Larry Robinson	4:14	Mtl.
Apr. 28/79	NYI	SF	NYI 4	NYR 3	Denis Potvin	8:02	NYR
May 3/79	NY	SF	NYI 3	NYR 2	Bob Nystrom	3:40	NYR
May 3/79	Bos.	SF	Bos. 4	Mtl. 3	Jean Ratelle	3:46	Mtl.
May 10/79	Mtl.	SF	Mtl. 5	Bos. 4	Yvon Lambert	9:33	Mtl.
May 19/79	NY	F	Mtl. 4	NYR 3	Serge Savard	7:25	Mtl.
Apr. 8/80	NY	PR	NYR 2	Atl. 1	Steve Vickers	0:33	NYR
Apr. 8/80	Phi.	PR	Phi. 4	Edm. 3	Bobby Clarke	8:06	Phi.
Apr. 8/80	Chi.	PR	Chi. 3	St. L. 2	Doug Lecuyer	12:34	Chi.
Apr. 11/80	Hfd.	PR	Mtl. 4	Hfd. 3	Yvon Lambert	0:29	Mtl.
Apr. 11/80	Tor.	PR	Min. 4	Tor. 3	Al MacAdam	0:32	Min.
Apr. 11/80	L.A.	PR	NYI 4	L.A. 3	Ken Morrow	6:55	NYI
Apr. 11/80	Edm.	PR	Phi. 3	Edm. 2	Ken Linseman	23:56	Phi.
Apr. 16/80	Bos.	QF	NYI 2	Bos. 1	Clark Gillies	1:02	NYI
Apr. 17/80	Bos.	QF	NYI 5	Bos. 4	Bob Bourne	1:24	NYI
Apr. 21/80	NYI	QF	Bos. 4	NYI 3	Terry O'Reilly	17:13	NYI
May 1/80	Buf.	SF	NYI 2	Buf. 1	Bob Nystrom	21:20	NYI
May 13/80	Phi.	F	NYI 4	Phi. 3	Denis Potvin	4:07	NYI
May 24/80	NYI	F	NYI 5	Phi. 4	Bob Nystrom	7:11	NYI
Apr. 8/81	Buf.	PR	Buf. 3	Van. 2	Alan Haworth	5:00	Buf.
Apr. 8/81	Bos.	PR	Min. 5	Bos. 4	Steve Payne	3:34	Min.
Apr. 11/81	Chi.	PR	Cgy. 5	Chi. 4	Willi Plett	35:17	Cgy.
Apr. 12/81	Que.	PR	Que. 4	Phi. 3	Dale Hunter	0:37	Phi.
Apr. 14/81	St. L.	PR	St. L 4	Pit. 3	Mike Crombeen	25:16	St. L.
Apr. 16/81	Buf.	QF	Min. 4	Buf. 3	Steve Payne	0:22	Min.
Apr. 20/81	Min.	QF	Buf. 5	Min. 4	Craig Ramsay	16:32	Min.
Apr. 20/81	Edm.	QF	NYI 5	Edm. 4	Ken Morrow	5:41	NYI
Apr. 7/82	Min.	DSF	Chi. 3	Min. 2	Greg Fox	3:34	Chi.
Apr. 8/82	Edm.	DSF	Edm. 3	L.A. 2	Wayne Gretzky	6:20	L.A.
Apr. 8/82	Van.	DSF	Van. 2	Cgy. 1	Dave Williams	14:20	Van.
Apr. 10/82	Pit.	DSF	Pit. 2	NYI 1	Rick Kehoe	4:14	NYI
Apr. 10/82	L.A.	DSF	L.A. 6	Edm. 5	Daryl Evans	2:35	L.A.
Apr. 13/82	Mtl.	DSF	Que. 3	Mtl. 2	Dale Hunter	0:22	Que.
Apr. 13/82	NYI	DSF	NYI 4	Pit. 3	John Tonelli	6:19	NYI
Apr. 16/82	Van.	DF	L.A. 3	Van. 2	Steve Bozek	4:33	Van.
Apr. 18/82	Que.	DF	Que. 3	Bos. 2	Wilf Paiement	11:44	Que.
Apr. 18/82	NY	DF	NYI 4	NYR 3	Bryan Trottier	3:00	NYI
Apr. 18/82	L.A.	DF	Van. 4	L.A. 3	Colin Campbell	1:23	Van.
Apr. 21/82	St. L.	DF	St. L 3	Chi. 2	Bernie Federko	3:28	Chi.
Apr. 23/82	Que.	DF	Bos. 6	Que. 5	Peter McNab	10:54	Que.
Apr. 27/82	Chi.	CF	Van. 2	Chi. 1	Jim Nill	28:58	Van.
May 1/82	Que.	CF	NYI 5	Que. 4	Wayne Merrick	16:52	NYI
May 8/82	NYI	F	NYI 6	Van. 5	Mike Bossy	19:58	NYI
May 5/82	Bos.	DSF	Bos. 4	Que. 3	Barry Pederson	1:46	Bos.
Apr. 6/83	Cgy.	DSF	Cgy. 4	Van. 3	Eddy Beers	12:27	Cgy.
Apr. 7/83	Min.	DSF	Min. 5	Tor. 4	Bobby Smith	5:03	Min.
Apr. 10/83	Tor.	DSF	Min. 5	Tor. 4	Dino Ciccarelli	8:05	Min.
Apr. 10/83	Van.	DSF	Cgy. 4	Van. 3	Greg Meredith	1:06	Cgy.
Apr. 18/83	Min.	DF	Chi. 4	Min. 3	Rich Preston	10:34	Chi.
Apr. 24/83	Bos.	DF	Bos. 3	Buf. 2	Brad Park	1:52	Bos.
Apr. 5/84	Edm.	DSF	Edm. 5	Wpg. 4	Randy Gregg	0:21	Edm.
Apr. 7/84	Det.	DSF	St. L 4	Det. 3	Mark Reeds	37:07	St. L.
Apr. 8/84	Det.	DSF	St. L 3	Det. 2	Jorgen Pettersson	2:42	St. L.
Apr. 10/84	NYI	DSF	NYI 3	NYR 2	Ken Morrow	8:56	NYI
Apr. 13/84	Min.	DF	St. L 4	Min. 3	Doug Gilmour	16:16	Min.
Apr. 13/84	Edm.	DF	Cgy. 6	Edm. 5	Carey Wilson	3:42	Edm.
Apr. 13/84	NYI	DF	NYI 5	Wsh. 4	Anders Kallur	7:35	NYI
Apr. 16/84	Mtl.	DF	Que. 4	Mtl. 3	Bo Berglund	3:00	Mtl.
Apr. 20/84	Cgy.	DF	Cgy. 5	Edm. 4	Lanny McDonald	1:04	Edm.
Apr. 22/84	Min.	DF	Min. 4	St. L 3	Steve Payne	6:00	Min.
Apr. 10/85	Phi.	DSF	Phi. 5	NYR 4	Mark Howe	8:01	Phi.

Overtime heroes – Left: Montreal's Claude Lemieux scored his first overtime goal in game seven of the Adams Division Finals to eliminate the Hartford Whalers on April 29, 1986. Lemieux recorded a second overtime marker six days later and then had to wait 11 years before adding another as a member of the Colorado Avalanche vs. Edmonton on May 9, 1997. Below: Bob Nystrom delivers the knockout punch for the New York Islanders as he chips the puck past Philadelphia's Pete Peeters to bring the Stanley Cup to Long Island for the first time in franchise history.

Date	City	Series	Score	Scorer		Overtime	Series Winner
Apr. 10/85	Wsh.	DSF	Wsh. 4	NYI 3	Alan Haworth	2:28	NYI
Apr. 10/85	Edm.	DSF	Edm. 3	L.A. 2	Lee Fogolin	3:01	Edm.
Apr. 10/85	Wpg.	DSF	Wpg. 5	Cgy. 4	Brian Mullen	7:56	Wpg.
Apr. 11/85	Wsh.	DSF	Wsh. 2	NYI 1	Mike Gartner	21:23	NYI
Apr. 13/85	L.A.	DSF	Edm. 4	L.A. 3	Glenn Anderson	0:46	Edm.
Apr. 18/85	Mtl.	DF	Que. 2	Mtl. 1	Mark Kumpel	12:23	Que.
Apr. 23/85	Que.	DF	Que. 7	Mtl. 6	Dale Hunter	18:36	Que.
May 2/85	Mtl.	DF	Que. 3	Mtl. 2	Peter Stastny	2:22	Que.
Apr. 25/85	Min.	DF	Chi. 7	Min. 6	Darryl Sutter	21:57	Chi.
Apr. 28/85	Chi.	DF	Min. 5	Chi. 4	Dennis Maruk	1:14	Chi.
Apr. 30/85	Min.	DF	Chi. 6	Min. 5	Darryl Sutter	15:41	Chi.
May 5/85	Que.	CF	Que. 2	Phi. 1	Peter Stastny	6:20	Phi.
Apr. 9/86	Que.	DSF	Hfd. 3	Que. 2	Sylvain Turgeon	2:36	Hfd.
Apr. 12/86	Wpg.	DSF	Cgy. 4	Wpg. 3	Lanny McDonald	8:25	Cgy.
Apr. 17/86	Wsh.	DF	NYR 4	Wsh. 3	Brian MacLellan	1:16	NYR
Apr. 20/86	Edm.	DF	Edm. 6	Cgy. 5	Glenn Anderson	1:04	Cgy.
Apr. 23/86	Hfd.	DF	Hfd. 2	Mtl. 1	Kevin Dineen	1:07	Mtl.
Apr. 23/86	NYR	DF	NYR 6	Wsh. 5	Bob Brooke	2:40	NYR
Apr. 26/86	St L.	DF	St L. 4	Tor. 3	Mark Reeds	7:11	St L.
Apr. 29/86	Mtl.	DF	Mtl. 2	Hfd. 1	Claude Lemieux	5:55	Mtl.
May 5/86	NYR	CF	Mtl. 4	NYR 3	Claude Lemieux	9:41	Mtl.
May 12/86	St L.	CF	St L. 6	Cgy. 5	Doug Wickenheiser	7:30	Cgy.
May 18/86	Cgy.	F	Mtl. 3	Cgy. 2	Brian Skrudland	0:09	Mtl.
Apr. 8/87	Hfd.	DSF	Hfd. 3	Que. 2	Paul MacDermid	2:20	Que.
Apr. 9/87	Mtl.	DSF	Mtl. 4	Bos. 3	Mats Naslund	2:38	Mtl.
Apr. 9/87	St. L.	DSF	Tor. 3	St. L. 2	Rick Lanz	10:17	Tor.
Apr. 11/87	Wpg.	DSF	Cgy. 3	Wpg. 2	Mike Bullard	3:53	Wpg.
Apr. 11/87	Chi.	DSF	Det. 4	Chi. 3	Shawn Burr	4:51	Det.
Apr. 16/87	Que.	DSF	Que. 5	Hfd. 4	Peter Stastny	6:05	Que.
Apr. 18/87	Wsh.	DSF	NYI 3	Wsh. 2	Pat LaFontaine	68:47	NYI
Apr. 21/87	Edm.	DF	Edm. 3	Wpg. 2	Glenn Anderson	0:36	Edm.
Apr. 26/87	Que.	DF	Mtl. 3	Que. 2	Mats Naslund	5:30	Mtl.
Apr. 27/87	Tor.	DF	Tor. 3	Det. 2	Mike Allison	9:31	Det.
May 4/87	Phi.	CF	Phi. 4	Mtl. 3	Ilkka Sinislao	9:11	Phi.
May 20/87	Edm.	F	Edm. 3	Phi. 2	Jari Kurri	6:50	Edm.
Apr. 6/88	NYI	DSF	NYI 4	N.J. 3	Pat LaFontaine	6:11	N.J.
Apr. 10/88	Phi.	DSF	Phi. 5	Wsh. 4	Murray Craven	1:18	Wsh.
Apr. 10/88	N.J.	DSF	NYI 5	N.J. 4	Brent Sutter	15:07	N.J.
Apr. 10/88	Buf.	DSF	Buf. 6	Bos. 5	John Tucker	5:32	Bos.
Apr. 12/88	Det.	DSF	Tor. 6	Det. 5	Ed Olczyk	0:34	Det.
Apr. 16/88	Wsh.	DSF	Wsh. 5	Phi. 4	Dale Hunter	5:57	Wsh.
Apr. 21/88	Cgy.	DF	Edm. 5	Cgy. 4	Wayne Gretzky	7:54	Edm.
May 4/88	Bos.	CF	N.J. 3	Bos. 2	Doug Brown	17:46	Bos.
May 9/88	Det.	CF	Edm. 4	Det. 3	Jari Kurri	11:02	Edm.
Apr. 5/89	St. L.	DSF	St. L. 4	Min. 3	Brett Hull	11:55	St. L.
Apr. 5/89	Cgy.	DSF	Van. 4	Cgy. 3	Paul Reinhart	2:47	Cgy.
Apr. 6/89	St. L.	DSF	St. L. 4	Min. 3	Rick Meagher	5:30	St. L.
Apr. 6/89	Det.	DSF	Chi. 5	Det. 4	Duane Sutter	14:36	Chi.
Apr. 8/89	Hfd.	DSF	Mtl. 5	Hfd. 4	Stephane Richer	5:01	Mtl.
Apr. 8/89	Phi.	DSF	Wsh. 4	Phi. 3	Kelly Miller	0:51	Phi.
Apr. 9/89	Hfd.	DSF	Mtl. 4	Hfd. 3	Russ Courtnall	15:12	Mtl.
Apr. 15/89	Cgy.	DSF	Cgy. 4	Van. 3	Joel Otto	19:21	Cgy.
Apr. 18/89	Cgy.	DF	Cgy. 4	L.A. 3	Doug Gilmour	7:47	Cgy.
Apr. 19/89	Mtl.	DF	Mtl. 3	Bos. 2	Bobby Smith	12:24	Mtl.
Apr. 20/89	St. L.	DF	St. L. 5	Chi. 4	Tony Hrkac	33:49	Chi.
Apr. 21/89	Phi.	DF	Pit. 4	Phi. 3	Phil Bourque	12:08	Phi.
May 8/89	Chi.	CF	Cgy. 2	Chi. 1	Al MacInnis	15:05	Cgy.
May 9/89	Mtl.	CF	Phi. 2	Mtl. 1	Dave Poulin	5:02	Mtl.
May 19/89	Mtl.	F	Mtl. 4	Cgy. 3	Ryan Walter	38:08	Cgy.
Apr. 5/90	N.J.	DSF	Wsh. 5	N.J. 4	Dino Ciccarelli	5:34	Wsh.
Apr. 6/90	Edm.	DSF	Edm. 3	Wpg. 2	Mark Lamb	4:21	Edm.
Apr. 8/90	Tor.	DSF	St. L. 6	Tor. 5	Sergio Momesso	6:04	St. L.
Apr. 8/90	L.A.	DSF	L.A. 2	Cgy. 1	Tony Granato	8:37	L.A.
Apr. 9/90	Mtl.	DSF	Mtl. 2	Buf. 1	Brian Skrudland	12:35	Mtl.
Apr. 9/90	NYI	DSF	NYI 4	NYR 3	Brent Sutter	20:59	NYR
Apr. 10/90	Wpg.	DSF	Wpg. 4	Edm. 3	Dave Ellett	21:08	Edm.
Apr. 14/90	L.A.	DSF	L.A. 4	Cgy. 3	Mike Krushelnyski	23:14	L.A.
Apr. 15/90	Hfd.	DSF	Hfd. 3	Bos. 2	Kevin Dineen	12:30	Bos.
Apr. 21/90	Bos.	DF	Bos. 5	Mtl. 4	Garry Galley	3:42	Bos.
Apr. 24/90	L.A.	DF	Edm. 6	L.A. 5	Joe Murphy	4:42	Edm.
Apr. 25/90	Wsh.	DF	Wsh. 4	NYR 3	Rod Langway	0:34	Wsh.
Apr. 27/90	NYR	DF	Wsh. 2	NYR 1	John Druce	6:48	Wsh.
May 15/90	Bos.	F	Edm. 3	Bos. 2	Petr Klima	55:13	Edm.
Apr. 4/91	Chi.	DSF	Min. 4	Chi. 3	Brian Propp	4:14	Min.
Apr. 5/91	Pit.	DSF	Pit. 5	N.J. 4	Jaromir Jagr	8:52	Pit.
Apr. 6/91	L.A.	DSF	L.A. 3	Van. 2	Wayne Gretzky	11:08	L.A.
Apr. 8/91	Van.	DSF	Van. 2	L.A. 1	Cliff Ronning	3:12	L.A.
Apr. 11/91	NYR	DSF	Wsh. 5	NYR 4	Dino Ciccarelli	6:44	Wsh.
Apr. 11/91	Mtl.	DSF	Mtl. 4	Buf. 3	Russ Courtnall	5:56	Mtl.
Apr. 14/91	Edm.	DSF	Cgy. 2	Edm. 1	Theo Fleury	4:40	Edm.
Apr. 16/91	Cgy.	DSF	Edm. 5	Cgy. 4	Esa Tikkanen	6:58	Edm.
Apr. 18/91	L.A.	DF	L.A. 4	Edm. 3	Luc Robitaille	2:13	Edm.
Apr. 19/91	Bos.	DF	Mtl. 4	Bos. 3	Stephane Richer	0:27	Bos.
Apr. 19/91	Pit.	DF	Pit. 7	Wsh. 6	Kevin Stevens	8:10	Pit.
Apr. 20/91	L.A.	DF	Edm. 4	L.A. 3	Petr Klima	24:48	Edm.
Apr. 22/91	Edm.	DF	Edm. 4	L.A. 3	Esa Tikkanen	20:48	Edm.
Apr. 27/91	Mtl.	DF	Mtl. 3	Bos. 2	Shayne Corson	17:47	Bos.
Apr. 28/91	Edm.	DF	Edm. 4	L.A. 3	Craig MacTavish	16:57	Edm.
May 3/91	Bos.	CF	Bos. 5	Pit. 4	Vladimir Ruzicka	8:14	Pit.
Apr. 21/92	Bos.	DSF	Bos. 3	Buf. 2	Adam Oates	11:14	Bos.
Apr. 22/92	Min.	DSF	Det. 5	Min. 4	Yves Racine	1:15	Det.
Apr. 22/92	St. L.	DSF	St. L. 5	Chi. 4	Brett Hull	23:33	Chi.
Apr. 25/92	Buf.	DSF	Bos. 5	Buf. 4	Ted Donato	2:08	Bos.
Apr. 28/92	Min.	DSF	Det. 1	Min. 0	Sergei Fedorov	16:13	Det.
Apr. 29/92	Hfd.	DSF	Hfd. 2	Mtl. 1	Yvon Corriveau	0:24	Mtl.
May 1/92	Mtl.	DSF	Mtl. 3	Hfd. 2	Russ Courtnall	25:26	Mtl.
May 3/92	Van.	DF	Edm. 4	Van. 3	Joe Murphy	8:36	Edm.
May 5/92	Mtl.	DF	Bos. 3	Mtl. 2	Peter Douris	3:12	Bos.
May 7/92	Pit.	DF	NYR 6	Pit. 5	Kris King	1:29	Pit.
May 9/92	Pit.	DF	Pit. 5	NYR 4	Ron Francis	2:47	Pit.
May 17/92	Pit.	CF	Pit. 4	Bos. 3	Jaromir Jagr	9:44	Pit.
May 20/92	Edm.	CF	Chi. 4	Edm. 3	Jeremy Roenick	2:45	Chi.
Apr. 18/93	Bos.	DSF	Buf. 5	Bos. 4	Bob Sweeney	11:03	Buf.
Apr. 18/93	Que.	DSF	Que. 3	Mtl. 2	Scott Young	16:49	Mtl.
Apr. 20/93	Wsh.	DSF	NYI 5	Wsh. 4	Brian Mullen	34:50	NYI
Apr. 22/93	Mtl.	DSF	Mtl. 2	Que. 1	Vincent Damphousse	10:30	Mtl.
Apr. 22/93	Buf.	DSF	Buf. 4	Bos. 3	Yuri Khmylev	1:05	Buf.
Apr. 22/93	NYI	DSF	NYI 4	Wsh. 3	Ray Ferraro	4:46	NYI
Apr. 24/93	Buf.	DSF	Buf. 6	Bos. 5	Brad May	4:48	Buf.
Apr. 24/93	NYI	DSF	NYI 4	Wsh. 3	Ray Ferraro	25:40	NYI
Apr. 25/93	St. L.	DSF	St. L. 4	Chi. 3	Craig Janney	10:43	St. L.
Apr. 26/93	Que.	DSF	Mtl. 5	Que. 4	Kirk Muller	8:17	Mtl.
Apr. 27/93	Det.	DSF	Tor. 5	Det. 4	Mike Foligno	2:05	Tor.
Apr. 27/93	Van.	DSF	Wpg. 4	Van. 3	Teemu Selanne	6:18	Van.
Apr. 29/93	Wpg.	DSF	Van. 4	Wpg. 3	Greg Adams	4:30	Van.
May 1/93	Det.	DSF	Tor. 4	Det. 3	Nikolai Borschevsky	2:35	Tor.
May 3/93	Tor.	DF	Tor. 2	St. L. 1	Doug Gilmour	23:16	Tor.
May 4/93	Mtl.	DF	Mtl. 4	Buf. 3	Guy Carbonneau	2:50	Mtl.
May 5/93	Tor.	DF	St. L. 2	Tor. 1	Jeff Brown	23:03	Tor.
May 6/93	Buf.	DF	Mtl. 4	Buf. 3	Gilbert Dionne	8:28	Mtl.
May 8/93	Buf.	DF	Mtl. 4	Buf. 3	Kirk Muller	11:37	Mtl.
May 11/93	Van.	DF	L.A. 4	Van. 3	Gary Shuchuk	26:31	L.A.
May 14/93	Pit.	DF	NYI 4	Pit. 3	Dave Volek	5:16	NYI
May 18/93	Mtl.	CF	Mtl. 4	NYI 3	Stephan Lebeau	26:21	Mtl.
May 20/93	NYI	CF	Mtl. 2	NYI 1	Guy Carbonneau	12:34	Mtl.
May 25/93	Tor.	CF	Tor. 3	L.A. 2	Glenn Anderson	19:20	L.A.
May 27/93	L.A.	CF	L.A. 5	Tor. 4	Wayne Gretzky	1:41	L.A.
Jun. 3/93	Mtl.	F	Mtl. 3	L.A. 2	Eric Desjardins	0:51	Mtl.
Jun. 5/93	L.A.	F	Mtl. 4	L.A. 3	John LeClair	0:34	Mtl.
Jun. 7/93	L.A.	F	Mtl. 3	L.A. 2	John LeClair	14:37	Mtl.
Apr. 20/94	Tor.	CQF	Tor. 1	Chi. 0	Todd Gill	2:15	Tor.
Apr. 22/94	St. L.	CQF	Dal. 5	St. L. 4	Paul Cavallini	8:34	Dal.
Apr. 24/94	Chi.	CQF	Chi. 4	Tor. 3	Jeremy Roenick	1:23	Tor.
Apr. 25/94	Bos.	CQF	Mtl. 2	Bos. 1	Kirk Muller	17:18	Bos.
Apr. 26/94	Cgy.	CQF	Van. 2	Cgy. 1	Geoff Courtnall	7:15	Van.
Apr. 27/94	Buf.	CQF	Buf. 1	N.J. 0	Dave Hannan	65:43	N.J.
Apr. 28/94	Van.	CQF	Van. 3	Cgy. 2	Trevor Linden	16:43	Van.
Apr. 30/94	Cgy.	CQF	Van. 4	Cgy. 3	Pavel Bure	22:20	Van.
May 3/94	N.J.	CSF	Bos. 6	N.J. 5	Don Sweeney	9:08	N.J.
May 7/94	Bos.	CSF	N.J. 5	Bos. 4	Stephane Richer	14:19	N.J.
May 8/94	Van.	CSF	Van. 2	Dal. 1	Sergio Momesso	11:01	Van.
May 12/94	Tor.	CSF	Tor. 3	S.J. 2	Mike Gartner	8:53	Tor.
May 15/94	NYR	CF	N.J. 4	NYR 3	Stephane Richer	35:23	NYR
May 16/94	Tor.	CF	Tor. 3	Van. 2	Peter Zezel	16:55	Van.
May 19/94	N.J.	CF	NYR 3	N.J. 2	Stephane Matteau	26:13	NYR
May 24/94	Van.	CF	Van. 4	Tor. 3	Greg Adams	20:14	Van.
May 27/94	NYR	CF	NYR 2	N.J. 1	Stephane Matteau	24:24	NYR
May 31/94	NYR	F	Van. 3	NYR 2	Greg Adams	19:26	NYR
May 7/95	Phi.	CQF	Phi. 4	Buf. 3	Karl Dykhuis	10:06	Phi.
May 9/95	Cgy.	CQF	S.J. 5	Cgy. 4	Ulf Dahlen	12:21	S.J.
May 12/95	NYR	CQF	NYR 3	Que. 2	Steve Larmer	8:09	NYR
May 12/95	N.J.	CQF	N.J. 1	Bos. 0	Randy McKay	8:51	N.J.
May 14/95	Pit.	CQF	Pit. 6	Wsh. 5	Luc Robitaille	4:30	Pit.
May 15/95	St. L.	CQF	Van. 6	St. L. 5	Cliff Ronning	1:48	Van.
May 17/95	Tor.	CQF	Tor. 5	Chi. 4	Randy Wood	10:00	Chi.
May 19/95	Cgy.	CQF	S.J. 5	Cgy. 4	Ray Whitney	21:54	S.J.
May 21/95	Phi.	CSF	Phi. 5	NYR 4	Eric Desjardins	7:03	Phi.
May 21/95	Chi.	CSF	Chi. 2	Van. 1	Joe Murphy	9:04	Chi.
May 22/95	Phi.	CSF	Phi. 4	NYR 3	Kevin Haller	0:25	Phi.
May 25/95	Van.	CSF	Chi. 3	Van. 2	Chris Chelios	6:22	Chi.
May 26/95	N.J.	CSF	N.J. 2	Pit. 1	Neal Broten	18:36	N.J.
May 27/95	Van.	CSF	Chi. 4	Van. 3	Chris Chelios	5:35	Chi.
Jun. 1/95	Det.	CF	Det. 2	Chi. 1	Nicklas Lidstrom	1:01	Det.
Jun. 6/95	Chi.	CF	Det. 4	Chi. 3	Vladimir Konstantinov	29:25	Det.
Jun. 7/95	N.J.	CF	Phi. 3	N.J. 2	Eric Lindros	4:19	N.J.
Jun. 11/95	Det.	CF	Det. 2	Chi. 1	Vyacheslav Kozlov	22:25	Det.
Apr. 16/96	NYR	CQF	Mtl. 3	NYR 2	Vincent Damphousse	5:04	NYR
Apr. 18/96	Tor.	CQF	Tor. 5	St. L. 4	Mats Sundin	4:02	St. L.
Apr. 18/96	Phi.	CQF	T.B. 2	Phi. 1	Brian Bellows	9:05	Phi.
Apr. 21/96	St. L.	CQF	St. L. 3	Tor. 2	Glenn Anderson	1:24	St. L.
Apr. 21/96	T.B.	CQF	T.B. 5	Phi. 4	Alexander Selivanov	2:04	Phi.
Apr. 23/96	Cgy.	CQF	Chi. 2	Cgy. 1	Joe Murphy	50:02	Chi.
Apr. 24/96	Wsh.	CQF	Pit. 3	Wsh. 2	Petr Nedved	79:15	Pit.
Apr. 25/96	Col.	CQF	Col. 5	Van. 4	Joe Sakic	0:51	Col.
Apr. 25/96	Tor.	CQF	Tor. 5	St. L. 4	Mike Gartner	7:31	St. L.
May 2/96	Col.	CSF	Chi. 3	Col. 2	Jeremy Roenick	6:29	Col.
May 6/96	Chi.	CSF	Chi. 4	Col. 3	Sergei Krivokrasov	0:46	Col.
May 8/96	St. L.	CSF	St. L. 5	Det. 4	Igor Kravchuk	3:23	Det.
May 8/96	Chi.	CSF	Col. 3	Chi. 2	Joe Sakic	44:33	Col.
May 9/96	Fla.	CSF	Fla. 4	Phi. 3	Dave Lowry	4:06	Fla.
May 12/96	Phi.	CSF	Fla. 2	Phi. 1	Mike Hough	28:05	Fla.
May 13/96	Chi.	CSF	Col. 4	Chi. 3	Sandis Ozolinsh	25:18	Col.
May 16/96	Det.	CSF	Det. 1	St. L. 0	Steve Yzerman	21:15	Det.
May 19/96	Det.	CF	Col. 3	Det. 2	Mike Keane	17:31	Col.
Jun. 10/96	Fla.	F	Col. 1	Fla. 0	Uwe Krupp	44:31	Col.
Apr. 20/97	Chi.	CQF	Chi. 4	Col. 3	Sergei Krivokrasov	31:03	Col.
Apr. 20/97	Edm.	CQF	Edm. 4	Dal. 3	Kelly Buchberger	9:15	Edm.
Apr. 22/97	NYR	CQF	NYR 4	Fla. 3	Esa Tikkanen	16:29	NYR
Apr. 23/97	Ott.	CQF	Ott. 1	Buf. 0	Daniel Alfredsson	2:34	Buf.
Apr. 24/97	Mtl.	CQF	Mtl. 4	N.J. 3	Patrice Brisebois	47:37	N.J.
Apr. 25/97	Fla.	CQF	NYR 3	Fla. 2	Esa Tikkanen	12:02	NYR
Apr. 25/97	Dal.	CQF	Edm. 1	Dal. 0	Ryan Smyth	20:22	Edm.
Apr. 27/97	Pho.	CQF	Ana. 3	Pho. 2	Paul Kariya	7:29	Ana.
Apr. 29/97	Buf.	CQF	Buf. 3	Ott. 2	Derek Plante	5:24	Buf.
Apr. 29/97	Dal.	CQF	Edm. 4	Dal. 3	Todd Marchant	12:26	Edm.
May 2/97	Det.	CSF	Det. 2	Ana. 1	Martin Lapointe	0:59	Det.
May 4/97	Det.	CSF	Det. 3	Ana. 2	Vyacheslav Kozlov	41:31	Det.
May 8/97	Ana.	CSF	Det. 3	Ana. 2	Brendan Shanahan	37:03	Det.
May 9/97	Phi.	CSF	Buf. 5	Phi. 4	Ed Ronan	6:24	Phi.
May 9/97	Edm.	CSF	Col. 3	Edm. 2	Claude Lemieux	8:35	Col.
May 11/97	N.J.	CSF	NYR 2	N.J. 1	Adam Graves	14:08	NYR

The Exorcist and the Architect: Mike Keenan, left, helped "exorcise" the Broadway Blues' 54-year curse by guiding the New York Rangers to the Stanley Cup title in 1994, while Glen Sather, right, designed and built five Stanley Cup championship teams in Edmonton.

Stanley Cup Coaching Records

Coaches listed in order of total games coached in playoffs. Minimum: 65 games.

Coach	Team	Years	Series	Series W	L	G	Games W	L	T	Cups	%
Bowman, Scott	St. Louis	4	10	6	4	52	26	26	0	0	.500
	Montreal	8	19	16	3	98	70	28	0	5	.714
	Buffalo	5	8	3	5	36	18	18	0	0	.500
	Pittsburgh	2	6	5	1	33	23	10	0	1	.696
	Detroit	4	12	9	3	64	41	23	0	1	.641
	Total	**23**	**55**	**39**	**16**	**283**	**178**	**105**	**0**	**7**	**.629**
Arbour, Al	St. Louis	1	2	1	1	11	4	7	0	0	.364
	NY Islanders	15	40	29	11	198	119	79	0	4	.601
	Total	**16**	**42**	**30**	**12**	**209**	**123**	**86**	**0**	**4**	**.589**
Irvin, Dick	Chicago	1	3	2	1	9	5	3	1	0	.611
	Toronto	9	20	12	8	66	33	32	1	1	.508
	Montreal	14	22	11	11	115	62	53	0	3	.539
	Total	**24**	**45**	**25**	**20**	**190**	**100**	**88**	**2**	**4**	**.532**
Keenan, Mike	Philadelphia	4	10	6	4	57	32	25	0	0	.561
	Chicago	4	11	7	4	60	33	27	0	0	.550
	NY Rangers	1	4	4	0	23	16	7	0	1	.695
	St. Louis	2	3	1	2	20	10	10	0	0	.500
	Total	**11**	**28**	**18**	**10**	**160**	**91**	**69**	**0**	**1**	**.569**
Sather, Glen	Edmonton	10	27	21	6	*126	89	37	0	4	.706
Blake, Toe	Montreal	13	23	18	5	119	82	37	0	8	.689
Reay, Billy	Chicago	12	22	10	12	117	57	60	0	0	.487
Shero, Fred	Philadelphia	6	16	12	4	83	48	35	0	2	.578
	NY Rangers	2	5	3	2	25	13	12	0	0	.520
	Total	**8**	**21**	**15**	**6**	**108**	**61**	**47**	**0**	**2**	**.565**
Adams, Jack	Detroit	15	27	15	12	105	52	52	1	3	.500
Quinn, Pat	Philadelphia	3	8	5	3	39	22	17	0	0	.564
	Los Angeles	1	1	0	1	3	0	3	0	0	.000
	Vancouver	5	10	5	5	61	31	30	0	0	.508
	Total	**9**	**19**	**10**	**9**	**103**	**53**	**50**	**0**	**0**	**.515**
Burns, Pat	Montreal	4	10	6	4	56	30	26	0	0	.535
	Toronto	3	7	4	3	46	23	23	0	0	.500
	Total	**7**	**17**	**10**	**7**	**102**	**53**	**49**	**0**	**0**	**.519**
Demers, Jacques	St. Louis	3	6	3	3	33	16	17	0	0	.485
	Detroit	3	7	4	3	38	20	18	0	0	.526
	Montreal	2	5	4	1	27	19	8	0	1	.704
	Total	**8**	**18**	**11**	**7**	**98**	**55**	**43**	**0**	**1**	**.561**
Francis, Emile	NY Rangers	9	14	5	9	75	34	41	0	0	.453
	St. Louis	3	4	1	3	18	6	12	0	0	.333
	Total	**12**	**18**	**6**	**12**	**93**	**40**	**53**	**0**	**0**	**.430**
Imlach, Punch	Toronto	11	17	10	7	92	44	48	0	4	.478
Murray, Terry	Washington	4	7	3	4	39	18	21	0	0	.462
	Philadelphia	3	9	6	3	46	28	18	0	0	.609
	Total	**7**	**16**	**9**	**7**	**85**	**46**	**39**	**0**	**0**	**.541**
Day, Hap	Toronto	9	14	10	4	80	49	31	0	5	.613
Murray, Bryan	Washington	7	10	3	7	53	24	29	0	0	.452
	Detroit	3	4	1	3	25	10	15	0	0	.400
	Total	**10**	**14**	**4**	**10**	**78**	**34**	**44**	**0**	**0**	**.435**
Lemaire, Jacques	Montreal	2	5	3	2	27	15	12	0	0	.555
	New Jersey	3	9	7	2	50	32	18	0	1	.640
	Total	**5**	**14**	**10**	**4**	**77**	**47**	**30**	**0**	**1**	**.610**
Johnson, Bob	Calgary	5	10	5	5	52	25	27	0	0	.481
	Pittsburgh	1	4	4	0	24	16	8	0	1	.666
	Total	**6**	**14**	**9**	**5**	**76**	**41**	**35**	**0**	**1**	**.539**
Abel, Sid	Chicago	1	1	0	1	7	3	4	0	0	.429
	Detroit	8	12	4	8	69	29	40	0	0	.420
	Total	**9**	**13**	**4**	**9**	**76**	**32**	**44**	**0**	**0**	**.421**
Ross, Art	Boston	12	19	9	10	70	32	33	5	1	.493
Bergeron, Michel	Quebec	7	13	6	7	68	31	37	0	0	.456
Muckler, John	Edmonton	2	7	6	1	40	25	15	0	1	.625
	Buffalo	4	5	1	4	27	11	16	0	0	.407
	Total	**6**	**12**	**7**	**5**	**67**	**36**	**31**	**0**	**1**	**.537**
Ivan, Tommy	Detroit	7	12	8	4	67	36	31	0	3	.537
Neilson, Roger	Toronto	2	5	3	2	19	8	11	0	0	.421
	Buffalo	1	2	1	1	8	4	4	0	0	.500
	Vancouver	2	5	3	2	21	12	9	0	0	.571
	NY Rangers	2	3	1	2	19	8	11	0	0	.421
	Total	**7**	**15**	**8**	**7**	**67**	**32**	**35**	**0**	**0**	**.473**
Pulford, Bob	Los Angeles	4	6	2	4	26	11	15	0	0	.423
	Chicago	5	9	4	5	41	17	24	0	0	.415
	Total	**9**	**15**	**6**	**9**	**67**	**28**	**39**	**0**	**0**	**.418**
Patrick, Lester	NY Rangers	12	24	14	10	65	31	26	8	2	.538

* Does not include suspended game, May 24, 1988.

Penalty Shots in Stanley Cup Playoff Games

Date	Player	Goaltender	Scored		Final Score			Series
Mar. 25/37	Lionel Conacher, Mtl. Maroons	Tiny Thompson, Boston	No	Mtl. M.	0	at	Bos. 4	QF
Apr. 15/37	Alex Shibicky, NY Rangers	Earl Robertson, Detroit	No	NYR	0	at	Det. 3	F
Apr. 13/44	Virgil Johnson, Chicago	Bill Durnan, Montreal	No	Chi.	4	at	Mtl. 5*	F
Apr. 9/68	Wayne Connelly, Minnesota	Terry Sawchuk, Los Angeles	Yes	L.A.	5	at	Min. 7	QF
Apr. 27/68	Jim Roberts, St. Louis	Cesare Maniago, Minnesota	No	St. L.	4	at	Min. 3	SF
May 16/71	Frank Mahovlich, Montreal	Tony Esposito, Chicago	No	Chi.	3	at	Mtl. 4	F
May 7/75	Bill Barber, Philadelphia	Glenn Resch, NY Islanders	No	Phi.	3	at	NYI 4*	SF
Apr. 20/79	Mike Walton, Chicago	Glenn Resch, NY Islanders	No	NYI	4	at	Chi. 0	QF
Apr. 9/81	Peter McNab, Boston	Don Beaupre, Minnesota	No	Min.	5	at	Bos. 4*	PR
Apr. 17/81	Anders Hedberg, NY Rangers	Mike Liut, St. Louis	Yes	NYR	6	at	St. L. 4	QF
Apr. 9/83	Denis Potvin, NY Islanders	Pat Riggin, Washington	No	NYI	6	at	Wsh. 2	DSF
Apr. 28/84	Wayne Gretzky, Edmonton	Don Beaupre, Minnesota	Yes	Edm.	8	at	Min. 5	CF
May 1/84	Mats Naslund, Montreal	Bill Smith, NY Islanders	No	Mtl.	1	at	NYI 3	CF
Apr. 14/85	Bob Carpenter, Washington	Bill Smith, NY Islanders	No	Wsh.	4	at	NYI. 6	DF
May 28/85	Ron Sutter, Philadelphia	Grant Fuhr, Edmonton	No	Phi.	3	at	Edm. 5	F
May 30/85	Dave Poulin, Philadelphia	Grant Fuhr, Edmonton	No	Phi.	3	at	Edm. 8	F
Apr. 9/88	John Tucker, Buffalo	Andy Moog, Boston	Yes	Bos.	2	at	Buf. 6	DSF
Apr. 9/88	Petr Klima, Detroit	Allan Bester, Toronto	Yes	Det.	6	at	Tor. 3	DSF
Apr. 8/89	Neal Broten, Minnesota	Greg Millen, St. Louis	Yes	St. L.	5	at	Min. 3	DSF
Apr. 4/90	Al MacInnis, Calgary	Kelly Hrudey, Los Angeles	Yes	L.A.	5	at	Cgy. 3	DSF
Apr. 5/90	Randy Wood, NY Islanders	Mike Richter, NY Rangers	No	NYI	1	at	NYR 2	DSF
May 3/90	Kelly Miller, Washington	Andy Moog, Boston	No	Wsh.	3	at	Bos. 5	CF
May 18/90	Petr Klima, Edmonton	Rejean Lemelin, Boston	No	Edm.	7	at	Bos. 2	F
Apr. 6/91	Basil McRae, Minnesota	Ed Belfour, Chicago	Yes	Min.	2	at	Chi. 5	DSF
Apr. 10/91	Steve Duchesne, Los Angeles	Kirk McLean, Vancouver	Yes	L.A.	6	at	Van. 5	DSF
May 11/92	Jaromir Jagr, Pittsburgh	John Vanbiesbrouck, NYR	Yes	Pit.	3	at	NYR 2	DF
May 13/92	Shawn McEachern, Pittsburgh	John Vanbiesbrouck, NYR	No	NYR	1	at	Pit. 5	DF
June 7/94	Pavel Bure, Vancouver	Mike Richter, NYR	No	NYR	4	at	Van. 2	F
May 9/95	Patrick Poulin, Chicago	Felix Potvin, Toronto	No	Tor.	3	at	Chi. 0	CQF
May 10/95	Michal Pivonka, Washington	Tom Barrasso, Pittsburgh	No	Pit.	2	at	Wsh. 6	CQF
Apr. 24/96	Joe Juneau, Washington	Ken Wregget, Pittsburgh	No	Pit.	3	at	Wsh. 2**	CQF
May 11/97	Eric Lindros, Philadelphia	Steve Shields, Buffalo	Yes	Phi.	6	at	Buf. 3	CSF

* Game was decided in overtime, but shot taken during regulation time.
** Shot taken in overtime.

Ten Longest Overtime Games

Date	City	Series	Score				Scorer	Overtime	Series Winner
Mar. 24/36	Mtl.	SF	Det. 1		Mtl. M. 0		Mud Bruneteau	116:30	Det.
Apr. 3/33	Tor.	SF	Tor. 1		Bos. 0		Ken Doraty	104:46	Tor.
Apr. 24/96	Wsh.	CQF	Pit. 3		Wsh. 2		Petr Nedved	79:15	Pit.
Mar. 23/43	Det.	SF	Tor. 3		Det. 2		Jack McLean	70:18	Det.
Mar. 28/30	Mtl.	SF	Mtl. 2		NYR 1		Gus Rivers	68:52	Mtl.
Apr. 18/87	Wsh.	DSF	NYI 3		Wsh. 2		Pat LaFontaine	68:47	NYI
Apr. 27/94	Buf.	CQF	Buf. 1		N.J. 0		Dave Hannan	65:43	N.J.
Mar. 27/51	Det.	SF	Mtl. 3		Det. 2		Maurice Richard	61:09	Mtl.
Mar. 27/38	NY	QF	NYA 3		NYR 2		Lorne Carr	60:40	NYA
Mar. 26/32	Mtl.	SF	NYR 4		Mtl. 3		Fred Cook	59:32	NYR

Overtime Record of Current Teams

(Listed by number of OT games played)

Team	Overall				Home				Last OT Game	Road				Last OT Game
	GP	W	L	T	GP	W	L	T		GP	W	L	T	
Montreal	117	68	47	2	54	36	17	1	Apr. 24/97	63	32	30	1	Apr. 16/96
Boston	93	36	54	3	43	20	22	1	May 9/94	50	16	32	2	May 12/94
Toronto	90	46	43	1	57	30	26	1	Apr. 25/96	33	16	17	0	Apr. 21/96
NY Rangers	63	30	33	0	27	12	15	0	Apr. 22/97	36	18	18	0	May 11/97
Chicago	62	30	30	2	30	16	13	1	Apr. 20/97	32	14	17	1	May 2/96
Detroit	60	29	31	0	37	15	22	0	May 4/97	23	14	9	0	May 8/97
Philadelphia	43	22	21	0	19	11	8	0	May 9/97	24	11	13	0	May 9/96
NY Islanders	38	29	9	0	17	14	3	0	May 20/93	21	15	6	0	May 18/93
St. Louis	38	21	17	0	19	15	4	0	May 8/96	19	6	13	0	May 16/96
Buffalo	31	16	15	0	18	12	6	0	Apr. 29/97	13	4	9	0	May 9/97
* Dallas	31	12	19	0	16	5	11	0	Apr. 29/97	15	7	8	0	Apr. 20/97
Edmonton	31	20	11	0	16	10	6	0	May 9/97	15	10	5	0	Apr. 29/97
Los Angeles	30	12	18	0	16	8	8	0	Jun. 7/93	14	4	10	0	Jun. 3/93
** Calgary	30	11	19	0	14	4	10	0	Apr. 23/96	16	7	9	0	Apr. 28/94
Vancouver	29	13	16	0	12	5	7	0	May 27/95	17	8	9	0	Apr. 25/96
*** Colorado	28	16	12	0	13	7	6	0	May 2/96	15	9	6	0	May 9/97
Washington	19	8	11	0	8	4	4	0	Apr. 24/96	11	4	7	0	May 14/95
Pittsburgh	17	10	7	0	9	6	3	0	May 14/95	8	4	4	0	Apr. 24/96
**** New Jersey	17	5	12	0	8	2	6	0	May 11/97	9	3	6	0	Apr. 24/97
Hartford	11	5	6	0	7	4	3	0	Apr. 29/92	4	1	3	0	May 1/92
Phoenix	10	4	6	0	6	2	4	0	Apr. 27/97	4	2	2	0	Apr. 27/93
Florida	5	2	3	0	3	1	2	0	Apr. 25/97	2	1	1	0	Apr. 22/97
Anaheim	4	1	3	0	1	0	1	0	May 8/97	3	1	2	0	May 4/97
San Jose	3	2	1	0	0	0	0	0		3	2	1	0	May 19/95
Tampa Bay	2	2	0	0	1	1	0	0	Apr. 21/96	1	1	0	0	Apr. 18/96

* Totals include those of Minnesota 1967-93.
** Totals include those of Atlanta 1972-80.
*** Totals include those of Quebec 1979-95.
**** Totals include those of Kansas City and Colorado 1974-82.

An injury to Dominik Hasek during the 1997 playoffs thrust Steve Shields (above) into the spotlight and the rookie responded with a solid performance. He probably wished he was somewhere else, however, when he had to face Eric Lindros in a one-on-one battle during game five of the Eastern Conference Semi-final between the Sabres and the Flyers. In the only penalty shot awarded in the 1997 playoffs, Lindros calmly fired the puck past Shields to give the Flyers a commanding 3-0 lead en route to a 6-3 win and a five-game series victory.

Key to Player and Goaltender Registers

Demographics: Position, shooting side (catching hand for goaltenders), height, weight, place and date of birth are found on first line. Draft information, if any, is located on second line.

Major Junior, NCAA, minor pro, senior European and NHL clubs form a permanent part of each player's data panel. If a player sees action with more than one club in any of the above categories, a separate line is included for each one.

High school, prep school, Tier II junior, European junior and U.S. junior listings are deleted if a player accumulates two or more years of Major Junior, NCAA or senior European experience.

Canadian and U.S. National and Olympic Team statistics are also listed. For Europeans, Olympic Team participation is included as a separate line if a player joins an NHL club at the conclusion of the Games.

Some data is unavailable at press time. Readers are encouraged to contribute.
See page 5 for contact names and addresses.

Player's NHL organization as of August 22, 1997. This includes players under contract, unsigned draft choices and other players on reserve lists. Free agents as of August 22, 1997 show a blank here.

The complete career data panels of players with NHL experience who announced their retirement before the start of the 1997-98 season are included in the 1997-98 Player Register. These newly-retired players also show a blank here.

Each NHL club's minor-pro affiliates are listed at the bottom of this page.

Footnotes are listed below player's year-by-year data and indicate league awards and all-star selections. Letter corresponding to footnote is placed beside the season in which awards or all-star selections were received.

PLAYER, JOHN SAMPLE   (PLAY-uhr) **PHO.**

Center. Shoots left, 6'1", 200 lbs.   Born, Moncton, N.B., April 14, 1974.
(Pittsburgh's 3rd choice, 62nd overall in the 1992 Entry Draft).

			Regular Season					Playoffs				
Season	Club	League	GP	G	A	TP	PIM	GP	G	A	TP	PIM
1991-92	Brandon	WHL	66	15	13	28	17	4	3		4	6
1992-93	Brandon	WHL	72	36	30	66	72	12	4	5	9	12
1993-94ab	Brandon	WHL	70	47	59	106	83	16	*16	8	*24	14
1994-95	**Pittsburgh**	**NHL**	10	1	2	3	6	....	....	....	....	....
	Cleveland	IHL	64	31	22	53	71	5	3	2	5	8
1995-96	**Montreal**	**NHL**	24	7	6	13	42	1	0	0	0	0
	Fredericton	AHL	47	41	31	72	106	....	....	....	....	....
1996-97	**Detroit**	**NHL**	68	27	35	62	88	14	4	6	10	12 ♦
	NHL Totals		102	35	43	78	136	15	4	6	10	12

a WHL East Second All-Star Team (1994)
b Won Stafford Smythe Memorial Trophy (Memorial Cup MVP) (1994)

Traded to **Montreal** by **Pittsburgh** for Montreal's third round choice in 1996 Entry Draft, June 14, 1995. Traded to **Detroit** by **Montreal** for Bill Winger, June 17, 1996. Signed as a free agent by **Phoenix**, August 23, 1997.

Member of Stanley Cup-winning team.

Asterisk (*) indicates league leader in this statistical category.

All trades, free agent signings and other transactions involving NHL clubs are listed in chronological order. Players selected by NHL clubs after re-entering the NHL Entry Draft are noted here. NHL All-Star Game appearances are listed above trade notes.

NHL Clubs and Minor-League Affiliates 1997-98

NHL CLUB	MINOR LEAGUE AFFILIATE
Anaheim	Cincinnati Mighty Ducks (AHL)
	Fort Wayne Komets (IHL)
	Long Beach Ice Dogs (IHL)
Boston	Providence Bruins (AHL)
	Charlotte Checkers (ECHL)
Buffalo	Rochester Americans (AHL)
	South Carolina Stingrays (ECHL)
Calgary	Saint John Flames (AHL)
	Roanoke Express (ECHL)
Carolina	The Beast of New Haven (AHL)
	Richmond Renegades (ECHL)
Chicago	Indianapolis Ice (IHL)
	Columbus Chill (ECHL)
Colorado	Hershey Bears (AHL)
Dallas	Michigan K-Wings (IHL)
	Dayton Bombers (ECHL)
Detroit	Adirondack Red Wings (AHL)
	Toledo Storm (ECHL)
Edmonton	Hamilton Bulldogs (AHL)
	Wheeling Nailers (ECHL)
Florida	The Beast of New Haven (AHL)
	Tallahassie Tiger-Sharks (ECHL)
	Port Huron Border Cats (UHL)
Los Angeles	Fredericton Canadiens (AHL)
	Springfield Falcons (AHL)
	Long Beach Ice Dogs (IHL)
	Utah Grizzlies (IHL)

NHL CLUB	MINOR LEAGUE AFFILIATE
Montreal	Fredericton Canadiens (AHL)
	New Orleans Brass (ECHL)
New Jersey	Albany River Rats (AHL)
	Raleigh IceCaps (ECHL)
NY Islanders	Kentucky Thoroughblades (AHL)
	Utah Grizzlies (IHL)
NY Rangers	Hartford Wolf Pack (AHL)
Ottawa	Worcester IceCats (AHL)
	Detroit Vipers (IHL)
Philadelphia	Philadelphia Phantoms (AHL)
	Johnstown Chiefs (ECHL)
Phoenix	Springfield Falcons (AHL)
	Las Vegas Thunder (IHL)
Pittsburgh	Syracuse Crunch (AHL)
St. Louis	Worcester IceCats (AHL)
	Baton Rouge Kingfish (ECHL)
San Jose	Kentucky Thoroughblades (IHL)
	Louisville River Frogs (ECHL)
Tampa Bay	Adirondack Red Wings (AHL)
	Chesapeake Icebreakers (ECHL)
Toronto	St. John's Maple Leafs (AHL)
Vancouver	Syracuse Crunch (AHL)
Washington	Portland Pirates (AHL)
	Hampton Roads Admirals (ECHL)

Pronunciation of Player Names

United Press International phonetic style.

AY	long A as in mate
A	short A as in cat
AI	nasal A as on air
AH	short A as in father
AW	broad A as in talk
EE	long E as in meat
EH	short E as in get
UH	hollow E as in "the"
AY	French long E with acute accent as in Pathe
IH	middle E as in pretty
EW	EW dipthong as in few
IGH	long I as in time
EE	French long I as in machine
IH	short I as in pity
OH	long O as in note
AH	short O as in hot
AW	broad O as in fought
OI	OI dipthong as in noise
OO	long double OO as in fool
UH	short double O as in ouch
OW	OW dipthong as in how
EW	long U as in mule
OO	long U as in rule
U	middle U as in put
UH	short U as in shut or hurt
K	hard C as in cat
S	soft C as in cease
SH	soft CH as in machine
CH	hard CH or TCH as in catch
Z	hard S as in decrease
S	soft S as in sun
G	hard G as in gang
J	soft G as in general
ZH	soft J as in French version of Joliet
KH	gutteral CH as in Scottish version of Loch

Late Additions to Player Register

NORRIS, WARREN   TOR.

Center. Shoots left. 6'1", 185 lbs.   Born, St. John's, Nfld., September 19, 1974.

				Regular Season					Playoffs			
Season	Club	Lea	GP	G	A	TP	PIM	GP	G	A	TP	PIM
1993-94	Massachusetts	H.E.	29	20	27	47	12	....	....	....	....	....
1994-95	Massachusetts	H.E.	35	13	8	21	12	....	....	....	....	....
1995-96	Massachusetts	H.E.	33	20	20	40	64	....	....	....	....	....
1996-96	Massachusetts	H.E.	35	20	26	46	48	....	....	....	....	....
	St. John's	AHL	9	1	0	1	4	....	....	....	....	....

Signed as a free agent by **Toronto**, April 10, 1997.

WHITE, COLIN   N.J.

Defense. Shoots left. 6'3", 190 lbs.   Born, New Glasgow, N.S., December 12, 1977.
(New Jersey's 5th choice, 49th overall, in 1996 Entry Draft).

				Regular Season					Playoffs			
Season	Club	Lea	GP	G	A	TP	PIM	GP	G	A	TP	PIM
1994-95	Laval	QMJHL	7	0	1	1	32	....	....	....	....	....
	Hull	QMJHL	5	0	1	1	4	12	0	0	0	23
1995-96	Hull	QMJHL	62	2	8	10	303	18	0	4	4	42
1996-97	Hull	QMJHL	63	3	12	15	297	14	3	12	15	65

Trade Notes and Free Agent Signings

Forwards and Defensemen

CASSELS, ANDREW Traded to Calgary by Carolina with Jean-Sebastien Giguere for Gary Roberts and Trevor Kidd, August 25, 1997.

CHARRON, ERIC Traded to Calgary by Washington for future considerations, September 4, 1997.

CZERKAWSKI, MARIUSZ Traded to NY Islanders by Edmonton for Dan Lacouture, August 25, 1997.

DEBRUSK, LOUIE Signed as a free agent by Tampa Bay, August 26, 1997.

DUCHESNE, STEVE Traded to St. Louis by Ottawa for Igor Kravchuk, August 25, 1997.

KHRISTICH, DIMITRI Traded to Boston by Los Angeles with Byron Dafoe for Jozef Stumpel, Sandy Moger and Boston's fourth round choice in 1998 Entry Draft, August 29, 1997.

KRAVCHUK, IGOR Traded to Ottawa by St. Louis for Steve Duchesne, August 25, 1997.

LACOUTURE, DAN Traded to Edmonton by NY Islanders for Mariusz Czerkawski, August 25, 1997.

MOGER, SANDY Traded to Los Angeles by Boston with Jozef Stumpel and Boston's fourth round choice in 1998 Entry Draft for Dimitri Khristich and Byron Dafoe, August 29, 1997.

ROBERTS, GARY Traded to Carolina by Calgary with Trevor Kidd for Andrew Cassels and Jean-Sebastien Giguere, August 25, 1997.

ROBITAILLE, LUC Traded to Los Angeles by NY Rangers for Kevin Stevens, August 28, 1997.

STEVENS, KEVIN Traded to NY Rangers by Los Angeles for Luc Robitaille, August 28, 1997.

STUMPEL, JOZEF Traded to Los Angeles by Boston with Sandy Moger and Boston's fourth round choice in 1998 Entry Draft for Dimitri Khristich and Byron Dafoe, August 29, 1997.

TIKKANEN, ESA Signed as a free agent by Florida, September 5, 1997.

TOPOROWSKI, SHAYNE Signed as a free agent by St. Louis, August 29, 1997.

Goaltenders

DAFOE, BYRON Traded to Boston by Los Angeles with Dimitri Khristich for Jozef Stumpel, Sandy Moger and Boston's fourth round choice in 1998 Entry Draft, August 29, 1997.

GIGUERE, JEAN-SEBASTIEN Traded to Calgary by Carolina with Andrew Cassels for Gary Roberts and Trevor Kidd, August 25, 1997.

KIDD, TREVOR Traded to Carolina by Calgary with Gary Roberts for Andrew Cassels and Jean-Sebastien Giguere, August 25, 1997.

Note:

The spelling of the last name of Tampa Bay center Vadim Yepanchintsev has been changed to **EPACHINTSEV**. He is listed in the Player Register as Yepanchintsev. He is listed in Tampa Bay's roster on page 106 as Epachintsev.

1997-98 Player Register

Note: The 1997-98 Player Register lists forwards and defensemen only. Goaltenders are listed separately. The Player Register lists every skater who appeared in an NHL game in the 1996-97 season, every skater drafted in the first six rounds of the 1997 Entry Draft, players on NHL Reserve Lists and other players. Trades and roster changes are current as of August 22, 1997.

Abbreviations: A – assists; **G** – goals; **GP** – games played; **Lea** – league; **PIM** – penalties in minutes; **TP** – total points; ***** – league-leading total; **♦** – member of Stanley Cup-winning team.

Pronunciations courtesy of the NHL Broadcasters' Association and Igor Kuperman, Phoenix Coyotes

Goaltender Register begins on page 437.

LEAGUES:

ACHL	Atlantic Coast Hockey League
AHL	American Hockey League
AJHL	Alberta Junior Hockey League
Alp.	Alpenliga
AUAA	Atlantic Universities Athletic Association
BCJHL	British Columbia Junior Hockey League
CCHA	Central Collegiate Hockey Association
CHL	Central Hockey League
CIAU	Canadian Interuniversity Athletic Union
COJHL	Central Ontario Junior Hockey League
ColHL	Colonial Hockey League
CWUAA	Canada West Universities Athletic Association
ECAC	Eastern Collegiate Athletic Association
ECHL	East Coast Hockey League
EJHL	Eastern Junior Hockey League
G.N.	Great Northern
GPAC	Great Plains Athletic Conference
H.E.	Hockey East
HS	High School
IHL	International Hockey League
Jr.	Junior
MJHA	(New York) Metropolitan Junior Hockey Association
MJHL	Manitoba Junior Hockey League
NAJHL	North American Junior Hockey League
NCAA	National Collegiate Athletic Association
NCHA	Northern Collegiate Hockey Association
NHL	**National Hockey League**
OHA	Ontario Hockey Association
OHL	Ontario Hockey League
OMJHL	Ontario Major Junior Hockey League
OPJHL	Ontario Provincial Junior Hockey League
OUAA	Ontario Universities Athletic Association
QJHL	Quebec Junior Hockey League
QMJHL	Quebec Major Junior Hockey League
SJHL	Saskatchewan Junior Hockey League
SOHL	Southern Ontario Hockey League
USHL	United States Hockey League (Junior A)
WCHA	Western Collegiate Hockey Association
WHA	World Hockey Association
WHL	Western Hockey League

AALTO, ANTTI — (AL-toh, AN-tee) — ANA.

Center. Shoots left. 6'2", 190 lbs.   Born, Lappeenranta, Finland, March 4, 1975.
(Anaheim's 6th choice, 134th overall, in 1993 Entry Draft).

			Regular Season					Playoffs				
Season	Club	Lea	GP	G	A	TP	PIM	GP	G	A	TP	PIM
1991-92	SaiPa	Fin. 2	20	6	6	12	20	....	....	....	....	....
1992-93	SaiPa	Fin. 2	23	6	8	14	14	....	....	....	....	....
	TPS	Fin.	1	0	0	0	0	....	....	....	....	....
1993-94	TPS	Fin.	33	5	9	14	16	10	1	1	2	4
1994-95	TPS	Fin.	44	11	7	18	18	5	0	1	1	2
1995-96	TPS	Fin.	40	15	16	31	22	11	3	5	8	14
	Kiekko-67	Fin. 2	2	0	2	2	2	....	....	....	....	....
1996-97	TPS	Fin.	44	15	19	34	60	11	5	6	11	31

ABRAHAMSSON, ELIAS — (AH-brah-ham-suhn, eh-LEE-ahs) — BOS.

Defense. Shoots left. 6'3", 227 lbs.   Born, Uppsala, Sweden, June 15, 1977.
(Boston's 6th choice, 132nd overall, in 1996 Entry Draft).

			Regular Season					Playoffs				
Season	Club	Lea	GP	G	A	TP	PIM	GP	G	A	TP	PIM
1994-95	Halifax	QMJHL	25	0	3	3	41	....	....	....	....	....
1995-96	Halifax	QMJHL	64	3	11	14	268	6	2	2	4	8
1996-97	Halifax	QMJHL	30	4	10	14	231	18	4	9	13	74

ADAMS, CRAIG — CAR.

Right wing. Shoots right. 6', 200 lbs.   Born, Calgary, Alta., April 26, 1977.
(Hartford's 9th choice, 223rd overall, in 1996 Entry Draft).

			Regular Season					Playoffs				
Season	Club	Lea	GP	G	A	TP	PIM	GP	G	A	TP	PIM
1995-96	Harvard	ECAC	34	8	9	17	56	....	....	....	....	....
1996-97	Harvard	ECAC	32	6	4	10	36	....	....	....	....	....

ADAMS, GREG — DAL.

Left wing. Shoots left. 6'3", 195 lbs.   Born, Nelson, B.C., August 1, 1963.

			Regular Season					Playoffs				
Season	Club	Lea	GP	G	A	TP	PIM	GP	G	A	TP	PIM
1982-83	N. Arizona	NCAA	29	14	21	35	19	....	....	....	....	....
1983-84	N. Arizona	NCAA	26	44	29	73	24	....	....	....	....	....
1984-85	**New Jersey**	**NHL**	**36**	**12**	**9**	**21**	**14**	....	....	....	....	....
	Maine	AHL	41	15	20	35	12	11	3	4	7	0
1985-86	**New Jersey**	**NHL**	**78**	**35**	**42**	**77**	**30**	....	....	....	....	....
1986-87	**New Jersey**	**NHL**	**72**	**20**	**27**	**47**	**19**	....	....	....	....	....
1987-88	**Vancouver**	**NHL**	**80**	**36**	**40**	**76**	**30**	....	....	....	....	....
1988-89	**Vancouver**	**NHL**	**61**	**19**	**14**	**33**	**24**	**7**	**2**	**3**	**5**	**2**
1989-90	**Vancouver**	**NHL**	**65**	**30**	**20**	**50**	**18**	....	....	....	....	....
1990-91	**Vancouver**	**NHL**	**55**	**21**	**24**	**45**	**10**	**5**	**0**	**0**	**0**	**2**
1991-92	**Vancouver**	**NHL**	**76**	**30**	**27**	**57**	**26**	**6**	**0**	**2**	**2**	**4**
1992-93	**Vancouver**	**NHL**	**53**	**25**	**31**	**56**	**14**	**12**	**7**	**6**	**13**	**6**
1993-94	**Vancouver**	**NHL**	**68**	**13**	**24**	**37**	**20**	**23**	**6**	**8**	**14**	**2**
1994-95	**Vancouver**	**NHL**	**31**	**5**	**10**	**15**	**12**	....	....	....	....	....
	Dallas	**NHL**	**12**	**3**	**3**	**6**	**4**	**5**	**2**	**0**	**2**	**0**
1995-96	**Dallas**	**NHL**	**66**	**22**	**21**	**43**	**33**	....	....	....	....	....
1996-97	**Dallas**	**NHL**	**50**	**21**	**15**	**36**	**2**	**3**	**0**	**1**	**1**	**0**
	NHL Totals		**803**	**292**	**307**	**599**	**256**	**61**	**17**	**20**	**37**	**16**

Played in NHL All-Star Game (1988)

Signed as a free agent by **New Jersey**, June 25, 1984. Traded to **Vancouver** by **New Jersey** with Kirk McLean for Patrik Sundstrom and Vancouver's fourth round choice (Matt Ruchty) in 1988 Entry Draft, September 10, 1987. Traded to **Dallas** by **Vancouver** with Dan Kesa and Vancouver's fifth round choice (later traded to Los Angeles — Los Angeles selected Jason Morgan) in 1995 Entry Draft for Russ Courtnall, April 7, 1995.

ADAMS, KEVYN — TOR.

Center. Shoots right. 6'1", 182 lbs.   Born, Washington, D.C., October 8, 1974.
(Boston's 1st choice, 25th overall, in 1993 Entry Draft).

			Regular Season					Playoffs				
Season	Club	Lea	GP	G	A	TP	PIM	GP	G	A	TP	PIM
1992-93	Miami-Ohio	CCHA	40	17	15	32	18	....	....	....	....	....
1993-94	Miami-Ohio	CCHA	36	15	28	43	24	....	....	....	....	....
1994-95a	Miami-Ohio	CCHA	38	20	29	49	30	....	....	....	....	....
1995-96	Miami-Ohio	CCHA	36	17	30	47	30	....	....	....	....	....
1996-97	Grand Rapids	IHL	82	22	25	47	47	5	1	1	2	4

a CCHA Second All-Star Team (1995)

Signed as a free agent by **Toronto**, August 7, 1997.

AFANASIEV, EUGENY — (ah-fah-NAH-see-ehv) — DET.

Left wing. Shoots left. 6'2", 180 lbs.   Born, Voronezh, USSR, February 2, 1978.
(Detroit's 9th choice, 241st overall, in 1996 Entry Draft).

			Regular Season					Playoffs				
Season	Club	Lea	GP	G	A	TP	PIM	GP	G	A	TP	PIM
1995-96	Detroit L.C.	Midget	36	16	18	34	78	....	....	....	....	....
1996-97	Gaylord	Jr. A.	28	1	4	5	69	....	....	....	....	....

AFINOGENOV, MAXIM — (ah-fihn-ah-GEHN-ahf) — BUF.

Right wing. Shoots left. 6', 185 lbs.   Born, Moscow, Russia, September 4, 1979.
(Buffalo's 3rd choice, 69th overall, in 1997 Entry Draft).

			Regular Season					Playoffs				
Season	Club	Lea	GP	G	A	TP	PIM	GP	G	A	TP	PIM
1995-96	Mosc. D'amo 2	Rus. 2			UNAVAILABLE			....	....	....	....	....
	Moscow D'amo	CIS	1	0	0	0	0	....	....	....	....	....
1996-97	Moscow D'amo	Rus.	29	6	5	11	10	4	0	2	2	0

AHMAOJA, TIMO — (ahkh-mah-OH-yah) — ANA.

Defense. Shoots right. 6'1", 180 lbs.   Born, Jyvaskyla, Finland, August 8, 1978.
(Anaheim's 5th choice, 172nd overall, in 1996 Entry Draft).

			Regular Season					Playoffs				
Season	Club	Lea	GP	G	A	TP	PIM	GP	G	A	TP	PIM
1995-96	JyP HT	Fin.	4	0	0	0	4	....	....	....	....	....
	JyP HT	Fin. Jr.	28	0	7	7	16	6	1	0	1	2
1996-97	JyP HT	Fin.	35	0	4	4	8	....	....	....	....	....
	JyP HT	Fin. Jr.	19	4	5	9	24	....	....	....	....	....

AITKEN, JOHNATHAN — BOS.

Defense. Shoots left. 6'4", 205 lbs.   Born, Edmonton, Alta., May 24, 1978.
(Boston's 1st choice, 8th overall, in 1996 Entry Draft).

			Regular Season					Playoffs				
Season	Club	Lea	GP	G	A	TP	PIM	GP	G	A	TP	PIM
1994-95	Medicine Hat	WHL	53	0	5	5	71	5	0	0	0	0
1995-96	Medicine Hat	WHL	71	6	14	20	131	5	1	0	1	6
1996-97	Brandon	WHL	65	4	18	22	211	6	0	0	0	4

AIVAZOFF, MICAH (A-vuh-zahf, MIGH-kuh)

Center. Shoots left. 6', 195 lbs. Born, Powell River, B.C., May 4, 1969.
(Los Angeles' 6th choice, 109th overall, in 1988 Entry Draft).

			Regular Season					Playoffs				
Season	Club	Lea	GP	G	A	TP	PIM	GP	G	A	TP	PIM
1986-87	Victoria	WHL	72	18	39	57	112	5	1	0	1	2
1987-88	Victoria	WHL	69	26	57	83	79	8	3	4	7	14
1988-89	Victoria	WHL	70	35	65	100	136	8	5	7	12	2
1989-90	New Haven	AHL	77	20	39	59	71	....	....	....	....	....
1990-91	New Haven	AHL	79	11	29	40	84	....	....	....	....	....
1991-92	Adirondack	AHL	61	9	20	29	50	19	2	8	10	25
1992-93	Adirondack	AHL	79	32	53	85	100	11	8	6	14	10
1993-94	**Detroit**	**NHL**	**59**	**4**	**4**	**8**	**38**	....	....	....	....	....
1994-95	**Edmonton**	**NHL**	**21**	**0**	**1**	**1**	**2**	....	....	....	....	....
1995-96	**NY Islanders**	**NHL**	**12**	**0**	**1**	**1**	**6**	....	....	....	....	....
	Utah	IHL	59	14	21	35	58	22	3	5	8	33
1996-97	Binghamton	AHL	75	12	36	48	70	4	1	1	2	0
	NHL Totals		**92**	**4**	**6**	**10**	**46**	....	....	....	....	....

Signed as a free agent by **Detroit**, March 18, 1993. Claimed by **Pittsburgh** from **Detroit** in NHL Waiver Draft, January 18, 1995. Claimed by **Edmonton** from **Pittsburgh** in NHL Waiver Draft, January 18, 1995. Signed as a free agent by **NY Islanders**, August 23, 1995. Signed as a free agent by **NY Rangers**, August 23, 1996.

ALBELIN, TOMMY (AL-buh-LEEN) CGY.

Defense. Shoots left. 6'1", 190 lbs. Born, Stockholm, Sweden, May 21, 1964.
(Quebec's 7th choice, 152nd overall, in 1983 Entry Draft).

			Regular Season					Playoffs				
Season	Club	Lea	GP	G	A	TP	PIM	GP	G	A	TP	PIM
1982-83	Djurgarden	Swe.	19	2	5	7	4	6	1	0	1	2
1983-84	Djurgarden	Swe.	30	9	5	14	26	4	0	1	1	2
1984-85	Djurgarden	Swe.	32	9	8	17	22	8	2	1	3	4
1985-86	Djurgarden	Swe.	35	4	8	12	26	....	....	....	....	....
1986-87	Djurgarden	Swe.	33	7	5	12	49	2	0	0	0	0
1987-88	**Quebec**	**NHL**	**60**	**3**	**23**	**26**	**47**	....	....	....	....	....
1988-89	**Quebec**	**NHL**	**14**	**2**	**4**	**6**	**27**	....	....	....	....	....
	Halifax	AHL	8	2	5	7	4	....	....	....	....	....
	New Jersey	**NHL**	**46**	**7**	**24**	**31**	**40**	....	....	....	....	....
1989-90	**New Jersey**	**NHL**	**68**	**6**	**23**	**29**	**63**	....	....	....	....	....
1990-91	**New Jersey**	**NHL**	**47**	**2**	**12**	**14**	**44**	**3**	**0**	**1**	**1**	**2**
	Utica	AHL	14	4	2	6	10	....	....	....	....	....
1991-92	**New Jersey**	**NHL**	**19**	**0**	**4**	**4**	**4**	**1**	**1**	**1**	**2**	**0**
	Utica	AHL	11	4	6	10	4	....	....	....	....	....
1992-93	**New Jersey**	**NHL**	**36**	**1**	**5**	**6**	**14**	**5**	**2**	**0**	**2**	**0**
1993-94	**New Jersey**	**NHL**	**62**	**2**	**17**	**19**	**36**	**20**	**2**	**5**	**7**	**14**
	Albany	AHL	4	0	2	2	17	....	....	....	....	....
1994-95	**New Jersey**	**NHL**	**48**	**5**	**10**	**15**	**20**	**20**	**1**	**7**	**8**	**2** ♦
1995-96	**New Jersey**	**NHL**	**53**	**1**	**12**	**13**	**14**	....	....	....	....	....
	Calgary	**NHL**	**20**	**0**	**1**	**1**	**4**	**4**	**0**	**0**	**0**	**0**
1996-97	**Calgary**	**NHL**	**72**	**4**	**11**	**15**	**14**	....	....	....	....	....
	NHL Totals		**545**	**33**	**146**	**179**	**327**	**53**	**6**	**14**	**20**	**18**

Traded to **New Jersey** by **Quebec** for New Jersey's fourth round choice (Niclas Andersson) in 1989 Entry Draft, December 12, 1988. Traded to **Calgary** by **New Jersey** with Cale Hulse and Jocelyn Lemieux for Phil Housley and Dan Keczmer, February 26, 1996.

ALDOUS, CHRIS MTL.

Defense. Shoots left. 6'3", 181 lbs. Born, Massena, NY, November 19, 1975.
(Montreal's 12th choice, 252nd overall, in 1994 Entry Draft).

			Regular Season					Playoffs				
Season	Club	Lea	GP	G	A	TP	PIM	GP	G	A	TP	PIM
1994-95	RPI	ECAC	31	0	1	1	4	....	....	....	....	....
1995-96	RPI	ECAC	35	1	3	4	26	....	....	....	....	....
1996-97	RPI	ECAC	36	3	13	16	18	....	....	....	....	....

ALFREDSSON, DANIEL (AHL-frehd-suhn) OTT.

Right wing. Shoots right. 5'11", 200 lbs. Born, Goteborg, Sweden, December 11, 1972.
(Ottawa's 5th choice, 133rd overall, in 1994 Entry Draft).

			Regular Season					Playoffs				
Season	Club	Lea	GP	G	A	TP	PIM	GP	G	A	TP	PIM
1991-92	Molndal	Swe. 2	32	12	8	20	43	....	....	....	....	....
1992-93	V. Frolunda	Swe.	20	1	5	6	8	....	....	....	....	....
1993-94	V. Frolunda	Swe.	39	20	10	30	18	4	1	1	2	....
1994-95	V. Frolunda	Swe.	22	7	11	18	22	....	....	....	....	....
1995-96ab	**Ottawa**	**NHL**	**82**	**26**	**35**	**61**	**28**	....	....	....	....	....
1996-97	**Ottawa**	**NHL**	**76**	**24**	**47**	**71**	**30**	**7**	**5**	**2**	**7**	**6**
	NHL Totals		**158**	**50**	**82**	**132**	**58**	**7**	**5**	**2**	**7**	**6**

a NHL All-Rookie Team (1996)
b Won Calder Memorial Trophy (1996)

Played in NHL All-Star Game (1996, 1997)

ALINC, JAN (AH-lihnch, YAHN) PIT.

Center. Shoots left. 6'2", 190 lbs. Born, Most, Czech., May 27, 1972.
(Pittsburgh's 7th choice, 163rd overall, in 1992 Entry Draft).

			Regular Season					Playoffs				
Season	Club	Lea	GP	G	A	TP	PIM	GP	G	A	TP	PIM
1990-91	Litvinov	Czech.	7	1	1	2	....	....	....	....	....	....
1991-92	Litvinov	Czech.	45	21	16	37	24	....	....	....	....	....
1992-93	Litvinov	Czech.	36	16	13	29	....	....	....	....	....	....
1993-94	Litvinov	Czech.	36	16	25	41	....	4	1	4	5	....
1994-95	Litvinov	Czech.	42	16	32	48	50	4	3	2	5	2
1995-96	Litvinov	Czech.	38	15	29	44	....	16	2	5	7	....
1996-97	Assat	Fin.	47	9	16	25	16	4	0	4	4	2

ALLAN, CHAD VAN.

Defense. Shoots left. 6'1", 192 lbs. Born, Saskatoon, Sask., July 12, 1976.
(Vancouver's 4th choice, 65th overall, in 1994 Entry Draft).

			Regular Season					Playoffs				
Season	Club	Lea	GP	G	A	TP	PIM	GP	G	A	TP	PIM
1991-92	Saskatoon	WHL	1	0	0	0	2	....	....	....	....	....
1992-93	Saskatoon	WHL	69	2	10	12	67	9	0	0	0	25
1993-94	Saskatoon	WHL	70	6	16	22	123	16	1	1	2	21
1994-95a	Saskatoon	WHL	63	14	29	43	95	9	0	3	3	2
1995-96b	Saskatoon	WHL	57	8	30	38	106	4	0	0	0	5
1996-97	Syracuse	AHL	73	3	10	13	83	3	0	1	1	0

a WHL East First All-Star Team (1995)
b WHL East Second All-Star Team (1996)

ALLEN, CHRIS FLA.

Defense. Shoots right. 6'2", 193 lbs. Born, Chatham, Ont., May 8, 1978.
(Florida's 2nd choice, 60th overall, in 1996 Entry Draft).

			Regular Season					Playoffs				
Season	Club	Lea	GP	G	A	TP	PIM	GP	G	A	TP	PIM
1994-95	Kingston	OHL	43	3	5	8	15	2	0	0	0	0
1995-96	Kingston	OHL	55	21	18	39	58	6	0	2	2	8
1996-97	Kingston	OHL	61	14	29	43	81	5	1	2	3	4
	Carolina	AHL	9	0	0	0	2	....	....	....	....	....

ALLEN, PETER S.J.

Defense. Shoots right. 6'2", 195 lbs. Born, Calgary, Alta., March 6, 1970.
(Boston's 1st choice, 24th overall, in 1991 Supplemental Draft).

			Regular Season					Playoffs				
Season	Club	Lea	GP	G	A	TP	PIM	GP	G	A	TP	PIM
1989-90	Yale	ECAC	26	2	4	6	16	....	....	....	....	....
1990-91	Yale	ECAC	17	0	6	6	14	....	....	....	....	....
1991-92	Yale	ECAC	26	5	13	18	26	....	....	....	....	....
1992-93	Yale	ECAC	30	3	15	18	32	....	....	....	....	....
1993-94	Richmond	ECHL	52	2	16	18	62	....	....	....	....	....
	P.E.I.	AHL	6	0	1	1	6	....	....	....	....	....
1994-95	Cdn. National	....	52	5	15	20	36	....	....	....	....	....
1995-96	**Pittsburgh**	**NHL**	**8**	**0**	**0**	**0**	**8**	....	....	....	....	....
	Cleveland	IHL	65	3	45	48	55	3	0	0	0	2
1996-97	Cleveland	IHL	81	14	31	45	75	14	0	6	6	24
	NHL Totals		**8**	**0**	**0**	**0**	**8**	....	....	....	....	....

Signed as a free agent by **Pittsburgh**, August 10, 1995. Signed as a free agent by **San Jose**, August 15, 1997.

ALLISON, JAMIE CGY.

Defense. Shoots left. 6'1", 190 lbs. Born, Lindsay, Ont., May 13, 1975.
(Calgary's 2nd choice, 44th overall, in 1993 Entry Draft).

			Regular Season					Playoffs				
Season	Club	Lea	GP	G	A	TP	PIM	GP	G	A	TP	PIM
1991-92	Windsor	OHL	59	4	8	12	70	4	1	1	2	2
1992-93	Detroit	OHL	61	0	13	13	64	15	2	5	7	23
1993-94	Detroit	OHL	40	2	22	24	69	17	2	9	11	35
1994-95	Detroit	OHL	50	1	14	15	119	18	2	7	9	35
	Calgary	**NHL**	**1**	**0**	**0**	**0**	**0**	....	....	....	....	....
1995-96	Saint John	AHL	71	3	16	19	223	14	0	2	2	16
1996-97	**Calgary**	**NHL**	**20**	**0**	**0**	**0**	**35**	....	....	....	....	....
	Saint John	AHL	46	3	6	9	139	5	0	1	1	4
	NHL Totals		**21**	**0**	**0**	**0**	**35**	....	....	....	....	....

ALLISON, JASON BOS.

Center. Shoots right. 6'3", 205 lbs. Born, North York, Ont., May 29, 1975.
(Washington's 2nd choice, 17th overall, in 1993 Entry Draft).

			Regular Season					Playoffs				
Season	Club	Lea	GP	G	A	TP	PIM	GP	G	A	TP	PIM
1991-92	London	OHL	65	11	19	30	15	7	0	0	0	0
1992-93	London	OHL	66	42	76	118	50	12	7	13	20	8
1993-94	**Washington**	**NHL**	**2**	**0**	**1**	**1**	**0**	....	....	....	....	....
abc	London	OHL	56	55	87	*142	68	5	2	13	15	13
	Portland	AHL	....	....	....	....	....	6	2	1	3	0
1994-95	London	OHL	15	15	21	36	43	....	....	....	....	....
	Washington	**NHL**	**12**	**2**	**1**	**3**	**6**	....	....	....	....	....
	Portland	AHL	8	5	4	9	2	7	3	8	11	2
1995-96	**Washington**	**NHL**	**19**	**0**	**3**	**3**	**2**	....	....	....	....	....
	Portland	AHL	57	28	41	69	42	6	1	6	7	9
1996-97	**Washington**	**NHL**	**53**	**5**	**17**	**22**	**25**	....	....	....	....	....
	Boston	**NHL**	**19**	**3**	**9**	**12**	**9**	....	....	....	....	....
	NHL Totals		**105**	**10**	**31**	**41**	**42**	....	....	....	....	....

a OHL First All-Star Team (1994)
b Canadian Major Junior First All-Star Team (1994)
c Canadian Major Junior Player of the Year (1994)

Traded to **Boston** by **Washington** with Jim Carey, Anson Carter, Washington's third round choice (Lee Goren) in 1997 Entry Draft and a conditional choice in 1998 Entry Draft for Bill Ranford, Adam Oates and Rick Tocchet, March 1, 1997.

ALVEY, MATT BOS.

Right wing. Shoots right. 6'5", 200 lbs. Born, Troy, NY, May 15, 1975.
(Boston's 2nd choice, 51st overall, in 1993 Entry Draft).

			Regular Season					Playoffs				
Season	Club	Lea	GP	G	A	TP	PIM	GP	G	A	TP	PIM
1993-94	Lake Superior	CCHA	41	6	8	14	16	....	....	....	....	....
1994-95	Lake Superior	CCHA	25	4	7	11	32	....	....	....	....	....
1995-96	Lake Superior	CCHA	39	14	8	22	40	....	....	....	....	....
1996-97	Lake Superior	CCHA	18	10	8	18	49	....	....	....	....	....
	Pensacola	ECHL	7	1	2	3	0	3	0	0	0	4

AMONTE, TONY (eh-MAHN-tee) CHI.

Right wing. Shoots left. 6', 195 lbs. Born, Hingham, MA, August 2, 1970.
(NY Rangers' 3rd choice, 68th overall, in 1988 Entry Draft).

			Regular Season					Playoffs				
Season	Club	Lea	GP	G	A	TP	PIM	GP	G	A	TP	PIM
1989-90	Boston U.	H.E.	41	25	33	58	52	....	....	....	....	....
1990-91ab	Boston U.	H.E.	38	31	37	68	82	....	....	....	....	....
	NY Rangers	**NHL**	....	....	....	....	....	**2**	**0**	**2**	**2**	**2**
1991-92c	**NY Rangers**	**NHL**	**79**	**35**	**34**	**69**	**55**	**13**	**3**	**6**	**9**	**2**
1992-93	**NY Rangers**	**NHL**	**83**	**33**	**43**	**76**	**49**	....	....	....	....	....
1993-94	**NY Rangers**	**NHL**	**72**	**16**	**22**	**38**	**31**	....	....	....	....	....
	Chicago	**NHL**	**7**	**1**	**3**	**4**	**6**	**6**	**4**	**2**	**6**	**4**
1994-95	Fassa	Italy	14	22	16	38	10	....	....	....	....	....
	Chicago	**NHL**	**48**	**15**	**20**	**35**	**41**	**16**	**3**	**3**	**6**	**10**
1995-96	**Chicago**	**NHL**	**81**	**31**	**32**	**63**	**62**	**7**	**2**	**4**	**6**	**6**
1996-97	**Chicago**	**NHL**	**81**	**41**	**36**	**77**	**64**	**6**	**4**	**2**	**6**	**8**
	NHL Totals		**451**	**172**	**190**	**362**	**308**	**50**	**16**	**19**	**35**	**32**

a Hockey East Second All-Star Team (1991)
b NCAA Final Four All-Tournament Team (1991)
c NHL/Upper Deck All-Rookie Team (1992)

Played in NHL All-Star Game (1997)

Traded to **Chicago** by **NY Rangers** with the rights to Matt Oates for Stephane Matteau and Brian Noonan, March 21, 1994.

ANDERSON, CRAIG NYR

Defense. Shoots left. 6'1", 171 lbs.   Born, Minneapolis, MN, January 6, 1976.
(NY Rangers' 10th choice, 208th overall, in 1994 Entry Draft).

			Regular Season					Playoffs				
Season	Club	Lea	GP	G	A	TP	PIM	GP	G	A	TP	PIM
1995-96	U. Wisconsin	WCHA	16	1	3	4	2	....	....	....	....	....
1996-97	U. Wisconsin	WCHA	34	3	8	11	22	....	....	....	....	....

ANDERSON, GLENN •

Right wing. Shoots left. 6'1", 190 lbs.   Born, Vancouver, B.C., October 2, 1960.
(Edmonton's 3rd choice, 69th overall, in 1979 Entry Draft).

			Regular Season					Playoffs				
Season	Club	Lea	GP	G	A	TP	PIM	GP	G	A	TP	PIM
1978-79	U. of Denver	WCHA	40	26	29	55	58	....	....	....	....	....
1979-80	Seattle	WHL	7	5	5	10	4	....	....	....	....	....
	Cdn. National	....	49	21	21	42	46	....	....	....	....	....
1980-81	Edmonton	NHL	58	30	23	53	24	9	5	7	12	12
1981-82	Edmonton	NHL	80	38	67	105	71	5	2	5	7	8
1982-83	Edmonton	NHL	72	48	56	104	70	16	10	10	20	32
1983-84	Edmonton	NHL	80	54	45	99	65	19	6	11	17	33 ♦
1984-85	Edmonton	NHL	80	42	39	81	69	18	10	16	26	38 ♦
1985-86	Edmonton	NHL	72	54	48	102	90	10	8	3	11	14
1986-87	Edmonton	NHL	80	35	38	73	65	21	14	13	27	59 ♦
1987-88	Edmonton	NHL	80	38	50	88	58	19	9	16	25	49 ♦
1988-89	Edmonton	NHL	79	16	48	64	93	7	1	2	3	8
1989-90	Edmonton	NHL	73	34	38	72	107	22	10	12	22	20 ♦
1990-91	Edmonton	NHL	74	24	31	55	59	18	6	7	13	41
1991-92	Toronto	NHL	72	24	33	57	100	....	....	....	....	....
1992-93	Toronto	NHL	76	22	43	65	117	21	7	11	18	31
1993-94	Toronto	NHL	73	17	18	35	·50	....	....	....	....	....
	NY Rangers	NHL	12	4	2	6	12	23	3	3	6	42 ♦
1994-95	Augsburg	Ger.	5	6	2	8	10	....	....	....	....	....
	Lukko	Fin.	4	1	1	2	0	....	....	....	....	....
	Cdn. National	....	26	11	8	19	40	....	....	....	....	....
	St. Louis	NHL	36	12	14	26	37	6	1	1	2	*49
1995-96	Cdn. National	....	11	4	4	8	39	....	....	....	....	....
	Augsburg	Ger.	9	5	3	8	48	....	....	....	....	....
	Edmonton	NHL	17	4	6	10	27	....	....	....	....	....
	St. Louis	NHL	15	2	2	4	6	11	1	4	5	6
1996-97	Chaux	Switz.	23	14	15	29	103	....	....	....	....	....
	NHL Totals		**1129**	**498**	**601**	**1099**	**1120**	**225**	**93**	**121**	**214**	**442**

Played in NHL All-Star Game (1984-86, 1988)

Traded to **Toronto** by **Edmonton** with Grant Fuhr and Craig Berube for Vincent Damphousse, Peter Ing, Scott Thornton, Luke Richardson, future considerations and cash, September 19, 1991. Traded to **NY Rangers** by **Toronto** with the rights to Scott Malone and Toronto's fourth round choice (Alexander Korobolin) in 1994 Entry Draft for Mike Gartner, March 21, 1994. Signed as a free agent by **St. Louis**, February 13, 1995. Signed as a free agent by **Vancouver**, January 22, 1996. Claimed on waivers by **Edmonton** from **Vancouver**, January 25, 1996. Claimed on waivers by **St. Louis** from **Edmonton**, March 12, 1996.

ANDERSON, MICHAEL WSH.

Right wing. Shoots right. 6'1", 186 lbs.   Born, Edina, MN, December 24, 1976.
(Washington's 10th choice, 180th overall, in 1996 Entry Draft).

			Regular Season					Playoffs				
Season	Club	Lea	GP	G	A	TP	PIM	GP	G	A	TP	PIM
1995-96	U. Minnesota	WCHA	28	3	6	9	51	....	....	....	....	....
1996-97	U. Minnesota	WCHA	42	9	11	20	46	....	....	....	....	....

ANDERSON, SHAWN

Defense. Shoots left. 6'1", 200 lbs.   Born, Montreal, Que., February 7, 1968.
(Buffalo's 1st choice, 5th overall, in 1986 Entry Draft).

			Regular Season					Playoffs				
Season	Club	Lea	GP	G	A	TP	PIM	GP	G	A	TP	PIM
1985-86	Maine	H.E.	16	5	8	13	22 •	....	....	....	....	....
	Cdn. National	....	33	2	6	8	16	....	....	....	....	....
1986-87	Buffalo	NHL	41	2	11	13	23	....	....	....	....	....
	Rochester	AHL	15	2	5	7	11	....	....	....	....	....
1987-88	Buffalo	NHL	23	1	2	3	17	....	....	....	....	....
	Rochester	AHL	22	5	16	21	19	6	0	0	0	0
1988-89	Buffalo	NHL	33	2	10	12	18	5	0	1	1	4
	Rochester	AHL	31	5	14	19	24	....	....	....	....	....
1989-90	Buffalo	NHL	16	1	3	4	8	....	....	....	....	....
	Rochester	AHL	39	2	16	18	41	9	1	0	1	4
1990-91	Quebec	NHL	31	3	10	13	21	....	....	....	....	....
	Halifax	AHL	4	0	1	1	2	....	....	....	....	....
1991-92	Weiswasser	Ger.	38	7	15	22	83	....	....	....	....	....
1992-93	Washington	NHL	60	2	6	8	18	6	0	0	0	0
	Baltimore	AHL	10	1	5	6	8	....	....	....	....	....
1993-94	Washington	NHL	50	0	9	9	12	8	1	0	1	12
1994-95	Philadelphia	NHL	1	0	0	0	0	....	....	....	....	....
	Hershey	AHL	31	9	21	30	18	6	2	3	5	19
1995-96	Milwaukee	IHL	79	22	39	61	68	5	0	7	7	0
1996-97	Wedemark	Ger.	8	1	0	1	4	....	....	....	....	....
	Utah	IHL	31	2	12	14	21	....	....	....	....	....
	Manitoba	IHL	17	2	7	9	5	....	....	....	....	....
	NHL Totals		**255**	**11**	**51**	**62**	**117**	**19**	**1**	**1**	**2**	**16**

Traded to **Washington** by **Buffalo** for Bill Houlder, September 30, 1990. Claimed by **Quebec** from **Washington** in NHL Waiver Draft, October 1, 1990. Traded to **Winnipeg** by **Quebec** for Sergei Kharin, October 22, 1991. Traded to **Washington** by **Winnipeg** for future considerations, October 23, 1991. Signed as a free agent by **Philadelphia**, August 16, 1994.

ANDERSSON, ERIK CGY.

Center. Shoots left. 6'3", 210 lbs.   Born, Stockholm, Sweden, August 19, 1971.
(Los Angeles' 5th choice, 112th overall, in 1990 Entry Draft).

			Regular Season					Playoffs				
Season	Club	Lea	GP	G	A	TP	PIM	GP	G	A	TP	PIM
1989-90	Danderyd	Swe. 2	30	14	5	19	16	....	....	....	....	....
1990-91	AIK	Swe.	32	1	1	2	10	....	....	....	....	....
1991-92	AIK	Swe.	3	0	0	0	0	....	....	....	....	....
1992-93					DID NOT PLAY							
1993-94	U. of Denver	WCHA	38	10	20	30	26	....	....	....	....	....
1994-95	U. of Denver	WCHA	42	12	19	31	42	....	....	....	....	....
1995-96	U. of Denver	WCHA	39	12	35	47	40	....	....	....	....	....
1996-97	U. of Denver	WCHA	39	17	17	34	42	....	....	....	....	....

Re-entered NHL Entry Draft, **Calgary's** 6th choice, 70th overall, in 1997 Entry Draft.

ANDERSSON, MIKAEL (AN-duhr-suhn) T.B.

Left wing. Shoots left. 5'11", 185 lbs.   Born, Malmo, Sweden, May 10, 1966.
(Buffalo's 1st choice, 18th overall, in 1984 Entry Draft).

			Regular Season					Playoffs				
Season	Club	Lea	GP	G	A	TP	PIM	GP	G	A	TP	PIM
1982-83	V. Frolunda	Swe.	1	1	0	1	0	....	....	....	....	....
1983-84	V. Frolunda	Swe.	18	0	3	3	6	....	....	....	....	....
1984-85	V. Frolunda	Swe. 2	30	16	11	27	18	6	3	2	5	2
1985-86	Buffalo	NHL	32	1	9	10	4	....	....	....	....	....
	Rochester	AHL	20	10	4	14	6	....	....	....	....	....
1986-87	Buffalo	NHL	16	0	3	3	0	....	....	....	....	....
	Rochester	AHL	42	6	20	26	14	9	1	2	3	2
1987-88	Buffalo	NHL	37	3	20	23	10	1	1	0	1	0
	Rochester	AHL	35	12	24	36	16	....	....	....	....	....
1988-89	Buffalo	NHL	14	0	1	1	4	....	....	....	....	....
	Rochester	AHL	56	18	33	51	12	....	....	....	....	....
1989-90	Hartford	NHL	50	13	24	37	6	5	0	3	3	2
1990-91	Hartford	NHL	41	4	7	11	8	....	....	....	....	....
	Springfield	AHL	26	7	22	29	10	18	*10	8	18	12
1991-92	Hartford	NHL	74	18	29	47	14	7	0	2	2	6
1992-93	Tampa Bay	NHL	77	16	11	27	14	....	....	....	....	....
1993-94	Tampa Bay	NHL	76	13	12	25	23	....	....	....	....	....
1994-95	V. Frolunda	Swe.	7	1	0	1	31	....	....	....	....	....
	Tampa Bay	NHL	36	4	7	11	4	....	....	....	....	....
1995-96	Tampa Bay	NHL	64	8	11	19	2	6	1	1	2	0
1996-97	Tampa Bay	NHL	70	5	14	19	8	....	....	....	....	....
	NHL Totals		**587**	**85**	**148**	**233**	**97**	**19**	**2**	**6**	**8**	**8**

Claimed by **Hartford** from **Buffalo** in NHL Waiver Draft, October 2, 1989. Signed as a free agent by **Tampa Bay**, June 29, 1992.

ANDERSSON, NIKLAS (AN-duhr-suhn)

Left wing. Shoots left. 5'9", 175 lbs.   Born, Kungalv, Sweden, May 20, 1971.
(Quebec's 5th choice, 68th overall, in 1989 Entry Draft).

			Regular Season					Playoffs				
Season	Club	Lea	GP	G	A	TP	PIM	GP	G	A	TP	PIM
1987-88	V. Frolunda	Swe. 2	15	5	5	10	6	8	6	4	10	4
1988-89	V. Frolunda	Swe. 2	30	13	24	37	24	....	....	....	....	....
1989-90	V. Frolunda	Swe.	38	10	21	31	14	....	....	....	....	....
1990-91	V. Frolunda	Swe.	22	6	10	16	16	....	....	....	....	....
1991-92	Halifax	AHL	57	8	26	34	41	....	....	....	....	....
1992-93	Quebec	NHL	3	0	1	1	2	....	....	....	....	....
	Halifax	AHL	76	32	50	82	42	....	....	....	....	....
1993-94	Cornwall	AHL	42	18	34	52	8	....	....	....	....	....
1994-95	Denver	IHL	66	22	39	61	28	15	8	13	21	10
1995-96	NY Islanders	NHL	47	14	12	26	12	....	....	....	....	....
	Utah	IHL	30	13	22	35	25	....	....	....	....	....
1996-97	NY Islanders	NHL	74	12	31	43	57	....	....	....	....	....
	NHL Totals		**124**	**26**	**44**	**70**	**71**					

Signed as a free agent by **NY Islanders**, July 15, 1994.

ANDERSSON-JUNKKA, JONAS PIT.

Defense. Shoots right. 6'2", 170 lbs.   Born, Kiruna, Sweden, May 4, 1975.
(Pittsburgh's 4th choice, 104th overall, in 1993 Entry Draft).

			Regular Season					Playoffs				
Season	Club	Lea	GP	G	A	TP	PIM	GP	G	A	TP	PIM
1991-92	Kiruna	Swe. 2	1	0	0	0	0	....	....	....	....	....
1992-93	Kiruna	Swe. 2	30	3	7	10	32	....	....	....	....	....
1993-94	Kiruna	Swe. 2	32	6	10	16	84	....	....	....	....	....
1994-95	V. Frolunda	Swe.	19	0	2	2	2	....	....	....	....	....
1995-96	V. Frolunda	Swe.	31	3	1	4	20	13	1	0	1	6
1996-97	MoDo	Swe.	12	1	3	4	10	....	....	....	....	....

ANDREWS, DARYL N.J.

Defense. Shoots left. 6'2", 205 lbs.   Born, Campbell River, B.C., April 27, 1977.
(New Jersey's 11th choice, 173rd overall, in 1996 Entry Draft).

			Regular Season					Playoffs				
Season	Club	Lea	GP	G	A	TP	PIM	GP	G	A	TP	PIM
1995-96	Melfort	Jr. A	55	2	12	14	51	....	....	....	....	....
1996-97	W. Michigan	CCHA	37	6	20	26	86	....	....	....	....	....

ANDREYCHUK, DAVE (AN-druh-chuhk) N.J.

Left wing. Shoots right. 6'4", 220 lbs.   Born, Hamilton, Ont., September 29, 1963.
(Buffalo's 3rd choice, 16th overall, in 1982 Entry Draft).

			Regular Season					Playoffs				
Season	Club	Lea	GP	G	A	TP	PIM	GP	G	A	TP	PIM
1980-81	Oshawa	OHA	67	22	22	44	80	10	3	2	5	20
1981-82	Oshawa	OHL	67	57	43	100	71	3	1	4	5	16
1982-83	Buffalo	NHL	43	14	23	37	16	4	1	0	1	4
	Oshawa	OHL	14	8	24	32	6	....	....	....	....	....
1983-84	Buffalo	NHL	78	38	42	80	42	2	0	1	1	2
1984-85	Buffalo	NHL	64	31	30	61	54	5	4	2	6	4
1985-86	Buffalo	NHL	80	36	51	87	61	....	....	....	....	....
1986-87	Buffalo	NHL	77	25	48	73	46	....	....	....	....	....
1987-88	Buffalo	NHL	80	30	48	78	112	6	2	4	6	0
1988-89	Buffalo	NHL	56	28	24	52	40	5	0	3	3	0
1989-90	Buffalo	NHL	73	40	42	82	42	6	2	5	7	2
1990-91	Buffalo	NHL	80	36	33	69	32	6	2	2	4	8
1991-92	Buffalo	NHL	80	41	50	91	71	7	1	3	4	12
1992-93	Buffalo	NHL	52	29	32	61	48	....	....	....	....	....
	Toronto	NHL	31	25	13	38	8	21	12	7	19	35
1993-94	Toronto	NHL	83	53	46	99	98	18	5	5	10	16
1994-95	Toronto	NHL	48	22	16	38	34	7	3	2	5	25
1995-96	Toronto	NHL	61	20	24	44	54	....	....	....	....	....
	New Jersey	NHL	15	8	5	13	10	....	....	....	....	....
1996-97	New Jersey	NHL	82	27	34	61	48	1	0	0	0	0
	NHL Totals		**1083**	**503**	**561**	**1064**	**816**	**88**	**32**	**34**	**66**	**108**

Played in NHL All-Star Game (1990, 1994)

Traded to **Toronto** by **Buffalo** with Daren Puppa and Buffalo's first round choice (Kenny Jonsson) in 1993 Entry Draft for Grant Fuhr and Toronto's fifth round choice (Kevin Popp) in 1995 Entry Draft, February 2, 1993. Traded to **New Jersey** by **Toronto** for New Jersey's second round choice (Marek Posmyk) in 1996 Entry Draft and a conditional choice in 1998 or 1999 Entry Draft, March 13, 1996.

ANDRUSAK, GREG (AN-druh-sak)

Defense. Shoots right. 6'1", 190 lbs. Born, Cranbrook, B.C., November 14, 1969.
(Pittsburgh's 5th choice, 88th overall, in 1988 Entry Draft).

			Regular Season					Playoffs				
Season	Club	Lea	GP	G	A	TP	PIM	GP	G	A	TP	PIM
1987-88	Minn.-Duluth	WCHA	37	4	5	9	42	....	....	....	....	....
1988-89	Minn.-Duluth	WCHA	35	4	8	12	74	....	....	....	....	....
	Cdn. National	....	2	0	0	0	0	....	....	....	....	....
1989-90	Minn.-Duluth	WCHA	35	5	29	34	74	....	....	....	....	....
1990-91	Cdn. National	....	53	4	11	15	34	....	....	....	....	....
1991-92a	Minn.-Duluth	WCHA	36	7	27	34	125	....	....	....	....	....
1992-93	Cleveland	IHL	55	3	22	25	78	2	0	0	0	2
	Muskegon	ColHL	2	0	3	3	7	....	....	....	....	....
1993-94	**Pittsburgh**	**NHL**	**3**	**0**	**0**	**0**	**2**	....	....	....	....	....
	Cleveland	IHL	69	13	26	39	109	....	....	....	....	....
1994-95	Detroit	IHL	37	5	26	31	50	....	....	....	....	....
	Pittsburgh	**NHL**	**7**	**0**	**4**	**4**	**6**	....	....	....	....	....
	Cleveland	IHL	8	0	8	8	14	....	....	....	....	....
1995-96	**Pittsburgh**	**NHL**	**2**	**0**	**0**	**0**	**0**	....	....	....	....	....
	Detroit	IHL	58	6	30	36	128	....	....	....	....	....
	Minnesota	IHL	5	0	4	4	8	....	....	....	....	....
1996-97	Eisbaren	Ger.	45	5	17	22	170	8	1	1	2	20
	NHL Totals		**12**	**0**	**4**	**4**	**8**	....	....	....	....	....

a WCHA First All-Star Team (1992)

ANGER, NIKLAS (AN-guhr) MTL.

Right wing. Shoots left. 6'1", 185 lbs. Born, Gavle, Sweden, July 31, 1977.
(Montreal's 5th choice, 112th overall, in 1995 Entry Draft).

			Regular Season					Playoffs				
Season	Club	Lea	GP	G	A	TP	PIM	GP	G	A	TP	PIM
1994-95	Djurgarden	Swe. Jr.	30	14	12	26	26	....	....	....	....	....
	Djurgarden	Swe.	1	0	0	0	0	....	....	....	....	....
1995-96	Djurgarden	Swe.	10	0	0	0	2	....	....	....	....	....
1996-97	Djurgarden	Swe.	4	0	0	0	0	....	....	....	....	....
	Arlanda	Swe. 2	16	5	9	14	6	....	....	....	....	....
	Linkoping	Swe. 2	7	2	1	3	10	....	....	....	....	....

ANISIMOV, ARTEM (ah-NIH-sih-mohv) PHI.

Defense. Shoots left. 6'1", 187 lbs. Born, Kazan, USSR, July 27, 1976.
(Philadelphia's 1st choice, 62nd overall, in 1994 Entry Draft).

			Regular Season					Playoffs				
Season	Club	Lea	GP	G	A	TP	PIM	GP	G	A	TP	PIM
1993-94	Kazan	CIS	38	0	1	1	12	5	0	0	0	0
1994-95	Kazan	CIS	46	3	2	5	55	1	0	0	0	0
1995-96	Kazan	CIS	30	0	2	2	8	....	....	....	....	....
1996-97	Kazan	Rus.	5	0	1	1	2	....	....	....	....	....

ANTIPOV, VLADIMIR (an-TIH-pahv) TOR.

Right wing. Shoots left. 5'11", 180 lbs. Born, Appatity, USSR, January 17, 1978.
(Toronto's 6th choice, 103rd overall, in 1996 Entry Draft).

			Regular Season					Playoffs				
Season	Club	Lea	GP	G	A	TP	PIM	GP	G	A	TP	PIM
1995-96	Yaroslavl 2	CIS 2	39	14	11	25	....	....	....	....	....	....
1996-97	Yaroslavl	Rus.	27	6	4	10	22	2	0	0	0	0
	Yaroslavl 2	Rus. 3	14	3	4	7	26	....	....	....	....	....

ANTONIN, JIRI EDM.

Defense. Shoots left. 6'3", 207 lbs. Born, Pardubice, Czech., November 15, 1975.
(Edmonton's 8th choice, 213th overall, in 1995 Entry Draft).

			Regular Season					Playoffs				
Season	Club	Lea	GP	G	A	TP	PIM	GP	G	A	TP	PIM
1995-96	Pardubice	Czech.	20	1	1	2	....	....	....	....	....	....
1996-97	Brno	Czech. 2	26	0	3	3	....	....	....	....	....	....

ANTOSKI, SHAWN (an-TAW-skee) ANA.

Left wing. Shoots left. 6'4", 235 lbs. Born, Brantford, Ont., March 25, 1970.
(Vancouver's 2nd choice, 18th overall, in 1990 Entry Draft).

			Regular Season					Playoffs				
Season	Club	Lea	GP	G	A	TP	PIM	GP	G	A	TP	PIM
1987-88	North Bay	OHL	52	3	4	7	163	....	....	....	....	....
1988-89	North Bay	OHL	57	6	21	27	201	9	5	3	8	24
1989-90	North Bay	OHL	59	25	31	56	201	5	1	2	3	17
1990-91	**Vancouver**	**NHL**	**2**	**0**	**0**	**0**	**0**	....	....	....	....	....
	Milwaukee	IHL	62	17	7	24	330	5	1	2	3	10
1991-92	**Vancouver**	**NHL**	**4**	**0**	**0**	**0**	**29**	....	....	....	....	....
	Milwaukee	IHL	52	17	16	33	346	5	2	0	2	20
1992-93	**Vancouver**	**NHL**	**2**	**0**	**0**	**0**	**0**	....	....	....	....	....
	Hamilton	AHL	41	3	4	7	172	....	....	....	....	....
1993-94	**Vancouver**	**NHL**	**55**	**1**	**2**	**3**	**190**	**16**	**0**	**1**	**1**	**36**
1994-95	**Vancouver**	**NHL**	**7**	**0**	**0**	**0**	**46**	....	....	....	....	....
	Philadelphia	**NHL**	**25**	**0**	**0**	**0**	**61**	**13**	**0**	**1**	**1**	**10**
1995-96	**Philadelphia**	**NHL**	**64**	**1**	**3**	**4**	**204**	**7**	**1**	**1**	**2**	**28**
1996-97	**Pittsburgh**	**NHL**	**13**	**0**	**0**	**0**	**49**	....	....	....	....	....
	Anaheim	**NHL**	**2**	**0**	**0**	**0**	**2**	....	....	....	....	....
	NHL Totals		**174**	**2**	**5**	**7**	**581**	**36**	**1**	**3**	**4**	**74**

Traded to **Philadelphia** by **Vancouver** for Josef Beranek, February 15, 1995. Signed as a free agent by **Pittsburgh**, July 31, 1996. Traded to **Anaheim** by **Pittsburgh** with Dmitri Mironov for Alex Hicks and Fredrik Olausson, November 19, 1996.

ARCHAMBAULT, DANIEL (ahr-sham-BOH) MTL.

Defense. Shoots left. 6', 200 lbs. Born, Ste-Agathe, Que., March 28, 1978.
(Montreal's 6th choice, 127th overall, in 1996 Entry Draft).

			Regular Season					Playoffs				
Season	Club	Lea	GP	G	A	TP	PIM	GP	G	A	TP	PIM
1994-95	Val d'Or	QMJHL	54	3	1	4	165	....	....	....	....	....
1995-96	Val d'Or	QMJHL	43	1	12	13	254	13	1	1	2	74
1996-97	Val d'Or	QMJHL	38	3	9	12	229	10	0	1	1	29

ARCHIBALD, DAVE

Center/Left wing. Shoots left. 6'1", 210 lbs. Born, Chilliwack, B.C., April 14, 1969.
(Minnesota's 1st choice, 6th overall, in 1987 Entry Draft).

			Regular Season					Playoffs				
Season	Club	Lea	GP	G	A	TP	PIM	GP	G	A	TP	PIM
1984-85	Portland	WHL	47	7	11	18	10	3	0	2	2	0
1985-86	Portland	WHL	70	29	35	64	56	15	6	7	13	11
1986-87	Portland	WHL	65	50	57	107	40	20	10	18	28	11
1987-88	**Minnesota**	**NHL**	**78**	**13**	**20**	**33**	**26**	....	....	....	....	....
1988-89	**Minnesota**	**NHL**	**72**	**14**	**19**	**33**	**14**	**5**	**0**	**1**	**1**	**0**
1989-90	**Minnesota**	**NHL**	**12**	**1**	**5**	**6**	**6**	....	....	....	....	....
	NY Rangers	**NHL**	**19**	**2**	**3**	**5**	**6**	....	....	....	....	....
	Flint	IHL	41	14	38	52	16	4	3	2	5	0
1990-91	Cdn. National	....	29	19	12	31	20	....	....	....	....	....
1991-92	Cdn. National	....	58	20	43	63	64	....	....	....	....	....
	Cdn. Olympic	....	8	7	1	8	18	....	....	....	....	....
	Bolzano	....	5	4	3	7	16	7	8	5	13	7
1992-93	Binghamton	AHL	8	6	3	9	10	....	....	....	....	....
	Ottawa	**NHL**	**44**	**9**	**6**	**15**	**32**	....	....	....	....	....
1993-94	**Ottawa**	**NHL**	**33**	**10**	**8**	**18**	**14**	....	....	....	....	....
1994-95	**Ottawa**	**NHL**	**14**	**2**	**2**	**4**	**19**	....	....	....	....	....
1995-96	**Ottawa**	**NHL**	**44**	**6**	**4**	**10**	**18**	....	....	....	....	....
	Utah	IHL	19	1	4	5	10	....	....	....	....	....
1996-97	**NY Islanders**	**NHL**	**7**	**0**	**0**	**0**	**4**	....	....	....	....	....
	Frankfurt	Ger.	34	10	19	29	48	9	4	2	6	16
	NHL Totals		**323**	**57**	**67**	**124**	**139**	**5**	**0**	**1**	**1**	**0**

Traded to **NY Rangers** by **Minnesota** for Jayson More, November 1, 1989. Traded to **Ottawa** by **NY Rangers** for Ottawa's fifth round choice (later traded to Los Angeles — Los Angeles selected Frederick Beaubien) in 1993 Entry Draft, November 5, 1992. Signed as a free agent by **NY Islanders**, October 10, 1996

ARMSTRONG, CHRIS FLA.

Defense. Shoots left. 6', 198 lbs. Born, Regina, Sask., June 26, 1975.
(Florida's 3rd choice, 57th overall, in 1993 Entry Draft).

			Regular Season					Playoffs				
Season	Club	Lea	GP	G	A	TP	PIM	GP	G	A	TP	PIM
1991-92	Moose Jaw	WHL	43	2	7	9	19	4	0	0	0	0
1992-93	Moose Jaw	WHL	67	9	35	44	104	....	....	....	....	....
1993-94ab	Moose Jaw	WHL	64	13	55	68	54	....	....	....	....	....
	Cincinnati	IHL	1	0	0	0	0	10	1	3	4	2
1994-95c	Moose Jaw	WHL	66	17	54	71	61	10	2	12	14	22
	Cincinnati	IHL	....	....	....	....	....	9	1	3	4	10
1995-96	Carolina	AHL	78	9	33	42	65	....	....	....	....	....
1996-97	Carolina	AHL	66	9	23	32	38	....	....	....	....	....

a WHL East First All-Star Team (1994)
b Canadian Major Junior Second All-Star Team (1994)
c WHL East Second All-Star Team (1995)

ARMSTRONG, DEREK OTT.

Center. Shoots right. 5'11", 188 lbs. Born, Ottawa, Ont., April 23, 1973.
(NY Islanders' 5th choice, 128th overall, in 1992 Entry Draft).

			Regular Season					Playoffs				
Season	Club	Lea	GP	G	A	TP	PIM	GP	G	A	TP	PIM
1991-92	Sudbury	OHL	66	31	54	85	22	9	2	2	4	2
1992-93	Sudbury	OHL	66	44	62	106	56	14	9	10	19	26
1993-94	**NY Islanders**	**NHL**	**1**	**0**	**0**	**0**	**0**	....	....	....	....	....
	Salt Lake	IHL	76	23	35	58	61	....	....	....	....	....
1994-95	Denver	IHL	59	13	18	31	65	6	0	2	2	0
1995-96	**NY Islanders**	**NHL**	**19**	**1**	**3**	**4**	**14**	....	....	....	....	....
	Worcester	AHL	51	11	15	26	33	4	2	1	3	0
1996-97	**NY Islanders**	**NHL**	**50**	**6**	**7**	**13**	**33**	....	....	....	....	....
	Utah	IHL	17	4	8	12	10	6	0	4	4	4
	NHL Totals		**70**	**7**	**10**	**17**	**47**	....	....	....	....	....

Signed as a free agent by **Ottawa**, July 28, 1997.

ARNOTT, JASON (AHR-nawt) EDM.

Center. Shoots right. 6'3", 220 lbs. Born, Collingwood, Ont., October 11, 1974.
(Edmonton's 1st choice, 7th overall, in 1993 Entry Draft).

			Regular Season					Playoffs				
Season	Club	Lea	GP	G	A	TP	PIM	GP	G	A	TP	PIM
1991-92	Oshawa	OHL	57	9	15	24	12	....	....	....	....	....
1992-93	Oshawa	OHL	56	41	57	98	74	13	9	9	18	20
1993-94a	**Edmonton**	**NHL**	**78**	**33**	**35**	**68**	**104**	....	....	....	....	....
1994-95	**Edmonton**	**NHL**	**42**	**15**	**22**	**37**	**128**	....	....	....	....	....
1995-96	**Edmonton**	**NHL**	**64**	**28**	**31**	**59**	**87**	....	....	....	....	....
1996-97	**Edmonton**	**NHL**	**67**	**19**	**38**	**57**	**92**	**12**	**3**	**6**	**9**	**18**
	NHL Totals		**251**	**95**	**126**	**221**	**411**	**12**	**3**	**6**	**9**	**18**

a NHL/Upper Deck All-Rookie Team (1994)

Played in NHL All-Star Game (1997)

ARVEDSON, MAGNUS (AHR-vehd-suhn, MAGH-nuhs) OTT.

Center. Shoots left. 6'2", 198 lbs. Born, Karlstad, Swe., November 25, 1971.
(Ottawa's 4th choice, 119th overall, in 1997 Entry Draft).

			Regular Season					Playoffs				
Season	Club	Lea	GP	G	A	TP	PIM	GP	G	A	TP	PIM
1991-92	Orebro	Swe. 2	32	12	21	33	30	7	4	4	8	4
1992-93	Orebro	Swe. 2	36	11	18	29	34	6	2	1	3	0
1993-94	Farjestad	Swe.	16	1	7	8	10	....	....	....	....	....
1994-95	Farjestad	Swe.	36	1	6	7	45	4	0	0	0	6
1995-96	Farjestad	Swe.	40	10	14	24	40	8	0	3	3	10
1996-97	Farjestad	Swe.	48	13	11	24	36	14	4	7	11	8

ASHAM, ARRON (ASH-uhm, AIR-uhn) MTL.

Right wing. Shoots right. 5'10", 170 lbs. Born, Portage La Prairie, Man., April 13, 1978.
(Montreal's 3rd choice, 71st overall, in 1996 Entry Draft).

			Regular Season					Playoffs				
Season	Club	Lea	GP	G	A	TP	PIM	GP	G	A	TP	PIM
1994-95	Red Deer	WHL	62	11	16	27	126	....	....	....	....	....
1995-96	Red Deer	WHL	70	32	45	77	174	10	6	3	9	20
1996-97	Red Deer	WHL	67	45	51	96	149	16	12	14	26	36

ASTLEY, MARK

Defense. Shoots left. 5'11", 185 lbs. Born, Calgary, Alta., March 30, 1969.
(Buffalo's 9th choice, 194th overall, in 1989 Entry Draft).

			Regular Season					Playoffs				
Season	Club	Lea	GP	G	A	TP	PIM	GP	G	A	TP	PIM
1988-89	Lake Superior	CCHA	42	3	12	15	26	....	....	....	....	....
1989-90	Lake Superior	CCHA	43	7	25	32	29	....	....	....	....	....
1990-91a	Lake Superior	CCHA	45	19	27	46	50	....	....	....	....	....
1991-92bcd	Lake Superior	CCHA	39	11	36	47	65	....	....	....	....	....
	Cdn. National	....	11	2	2	4	6	....	....	....	....	....
1992-93	Lugano	Switz.	30	10	12	22	57	....	....	....	....	....
	Cdn. National	....	22	4	14	18	14	....	....	....	....	....
1993-94	Ambri	Switz.	23	5	9	14	17	....	....	....	....	....
	Cdn. National	....	13	4	8	12	6	....	....	....	....	....
	Cdn. Olympic	....	8	0	1	1	4	....	....	....	....	....
	Buffalo	**NHL**	**1**	**0**	**0**	**0**	**0**	....	....	....	....	....
1994-95	Rochester	AHL	46	5	24	29	49	3	0	2	2	2
	Buffalo	**NHL**	**14**	**2**	**1**	**3**	**12**	**2**	**0**	**0**	**0**	**0**
1995-96	**Buffalo**	**NHL**	**60**	**2**	**18**	**20**	**80**	....	....	....	....	....
1996-97	Phoenix	IHL	52	6	11	17	43	....	....	....	....	....
	NHL Totals		**75**	**4**	**19**	**23**	**92**	**2**	**0**	**0**	**0**	**0**

a CCHA Second All-Star Team (1991)
b CCHA First All-Star Team (1992)
c NCAA West First All-American Team (1992)
d NCAA All-Tournament Team (1992)

Signed as a free agent by **Los Angeles**, September 6, 1996.

ATCHEYNUM, BLAIR (ATCH-uh-num) ST.L.

Right wing. Shoots right. 6'2", 210 lbs. Born, Estevan, Sask., April 20, 1969.
(Hartford's 2nd choice, 52nd overall, in 1989 Entry Draft).

			Regular Season					Playoffs				
Season	Club	Lea	GP	G	A	TP	PIM	GP	G	A	TP	PIM
1985-86	Saskatoon	WHL	19	1	4	5	22	....	....	....	....	....
1986-87	Saskatoon	WHL	21	0	4	4	4	....	....	....	....	....
	Swift Current	WHL	5	2	1	3	0	....	....	....	....	....
	Moose Jaw	WHL	12	3	0	3	2	....	....	....	....	....
1987-88	Moose Jaw	WHL	60	32	16	48	52	....	....	....	....	....
1988-89a	Moose Jaw	WHL	71	70	68	138	70	7	2	5	7	13
1989-90	Binghamton	AHL	78	20	21	41	45	....	....	....	....	....
1990-91	Springfield	AHL	72	25	27	52	42	13	0	6	6	6
1991-92	Springfield	AHL	62	16	21	37	64	6	1	1	2	2
1992-93	**Ottawa**	**NHL**	**4**	**0**	**1**	**1**	**0**	....	....	....	....	....
	New Haven	AHL	51	16	18	34	47	....	....	....	....	....
1993-94	Columbus	ECHL	16	15	12	27	10	....	....	....	....	....
	Portland	AHL	2	0	0	0	0	....	....	....	....	....
	Springfield	AHL	40	18	22	40	13	6	0	2	2	0
1994-95	Minnesota	IHL	17	4	6	10	7	....	....	....	....	....
	Worcester	AHL	55	17	29	46	26	....	....	....	....	....
1995-96	Cape Breton	AHL	79	30	42	72	65	....	....	....	....	....
1996-97b	Hershey	AHL	77	42	45	87	57	13	6	11	17	6
	NHL Totals		**4**	**0**	**1**	**1**	**0**	....	....	....	....	....

a WHL First All-Star Team (1989)
b AHL First All-Star Team (1997)

Claimed by **Ottawa** from **Hartford** in Expansion Draft, June 18, 1992. Signed as a free agent by **St. Louis**, August 12, 1997.

AUBIN, SERGE (oh-BEHN) PIT.

Center. Shoots left. 6'1", 194 lbs. Born, Val d'Or, Que., February 15, 1975.
(Pittsburgh's 9th choice, 161st overall, in 1994 Entry Draft).

			Regular Season					Playoffs				
Season	Club	Lea	GP	G	A	TP	PIM	GP	G	A	TP	PIM
1992-93	Drummondville	QMJHL	65	16	34	50	30	8	0	1	1	16
1993-94	Granby	QMJHL	63	42	32	74	80	7	2	3	5	8
1994-95	Granby	QMJHL	60	37	73	110	55	11	8	15	23	4
1995-96	Hampton Rds.	ECHL	62	24	62	86	74	3	1	4	5	10
	Cleveland	IHL	2	0	0	0	0	2	0	0	0	0
1996-97	Cleveland	IHL	57	9	16	25	38	2	0	0	0	0

AUCOIN, ADRIAN (oh-KWEHN) VAN.

Defense. Shoots right. 6'1", 194 lbs. Born, Ottawa, Ont., July 3, 1973.
(Vancouver's 7th choice, 117th overall, in 1992 Entry Draft).

			Regular Season					Playoffs				
Season	Club	Lea	GP	G	A	TP	PIM	GP	G	A	TP	PIM
1991-92	Boston U.	H.E.	32	2	10	12	60	....	....	....	....	....
1992-93	Cdn. National	....	42	8	10	18	71	....	....	....	....	....
1993-94	Cdn. National	....	59	5	12	17	80	....	....	....	....	....
	Cdn. Olympic	....	4	0	0	0	2	....	....	....	....	....
	Hamilton	AHL	13	1	2	3	19	4	0	2	2	6
1994-95	Syracuse	AHL	71	13	18	31	52	....	....	....	....	....
	Vancouver	**NHL**	**1**	**1**	**0**	**1**	**0**	**4**	**1**	**0**	**1**	**0**
1995-96	**Vancouver**	**NHL**	**49**	**4**	**14**	**18**	**34**	**6**	**0**	**0**	**0**	**2**
	Syracuse	AHL	29	5	13	18	47	....	....	....	....	....
1996-97	**Vancouver**	**NHL**	**70**	**5**	**16**	**21**	**63**	....	....	....	....	....
	NHL Totals		**120**	**10**	**30**	**40**	**97**	**10**	**1**	**0**	**1**	**2**

AUDET, PHILIPPE (aw-DEHT) DET.

Left wing. Shoots left. 6'2", 175 lbs. Born, Ottawa, Ont., June 4, 1977.
(Detroit's 2nd choice, 52nd overall, in 1995 Entry Draft).

			Regular Season					Playoffs				
Season	Club	Lea	GP	G	A	TP	PIM	GP	G	A	TP	PIM
1994-95	Granby	QMJHL	62	19	17	36	93	13	2	5	7	10
1995-96a	Granby	QMJHL	67	40	43	83	162	21	12	18	30	32
1996-97b	Granby	QMJHL	67	52	56	108	138	4	4	1	5	35
	Adirondack	AHL	3	1	1	2	0	1	1	0	1	0

a Memorial Cup All-Star Team (1996)
b QMJHL First All-Star Team (1997)

AUDETTE, DONALD (aw-DEHT) BUF.

Right wing. Shoots right. 5'8", 184 lbs. Born, Laval, Que., September 23, 1969.
(Buffalo's 8th choice, 183rd overall, in 1989 Entry Draft).

			Regular Season					Playoffs				
Season	Club	Lea	GP	G	A	TP	PIM	GP	G	A	TP	PIM
1986-87	Laval	QMJHL	66	17	22	39	36	14	2	6	8	10
1987-88	Laval	QMJHL	63	48	61	109	56	14	7	12	19	20
1988-89a	Laval	QMJHL	70	76	85	161	123	17	17	12	29	43
1989-90bc	Rochester	AHL	70	42	46	88	78	15	9	8	17	29
	Buffalo	**NHL**	....	....	....	....	....	**2**	**0**	**0**	**0**	**0**
1990-91	**Buffalo**	**NHL**	**8**	**4**	**3**	**7**	**4**	....	....	....	....	....
	Rochester	AHL	5	4	0	4	2	....	....	....	....	....
1991-92	**Buffalo**	**NHL**	**63**	**31**	**17**	**48**	**75**	....	....	....	....	....
1992-93	**Buffalo**	**NHL**	**44**	**12**	**7**	**19**	**51**	**8**	**2**	**2**	**4**	**6**
	Rochester	AHL	6	8	4	12	10	....	....	....	....	....
1993-94	**Buffalo**	**NHL**	**77**	**29**	**30**	**59**	**41**	**7**	**0**	**1**	**1**	**6**
1994-95	**Buffalo**	**NHL**	**46**	**24**	**13**	**37**	**27**	**5**	**1**	**1**	**2**	**4**
1995-96	**Buffalo**	**NHL**	**23**	**12**	**13**	**25**	**18**	....	....	....	....	....
1996-97	**Buffalo**	**NHL**	**73**	**28**	**22**	**50**	**48**	**11**	**4**	**5**	**9**	**6**
	NHL Totals		**334**	**140**	**105**	**245**	**264**	**33**	**7**	**9**	**16**	**22**

a QMJHL First All-Star Team (1989)
b AHL First All-Star Team (1990)
c Won Dudley "Red" Garret Memorial Trophy (Top Rookie - AHL) (1990)

AUGER, VINCENT (OH-zhay, VIHN-cehnt) COL.

Center. Shoots left. 5'10", 175 lbs. Born, Quebec, Que., March 7, 1975.
(Quebec's 11th choice, 231st overall, in 1993 Entry Draft).

			Regular Season					Playoffs				
Season	Club	Lea	GP	G	A	TP	PIM	GP	G	A	TP	PIM
1993-94	Cornell	ECAC	29	11	13	24	33	....	....	....	....	....
1994-95					DID NOT PLAY							
1995-96	Cornell	ECAC	23	5	15	20	22	....	....	....	....	....
1996-97	Cornell	ECAC	26	11	7	18	36	....	....	....	....	....

AUGUSTA, PATRIK (ah-GOOS-tuh, pa-TREEK)

Right wing. Shoots left. 5'10", 170 lbs. Born, Jihlava, Czech., November 13, 1969.
(Toronto's 8th choice, 149th overall, in 1992 Entry Draft).

			Regular Season					Playoffs				
Season	Club	Lea	GP	G	A	TP	PIM	GP	G	A	TP	PIM
1988-89	Dukla Jihlava	Czech.	15	3	1	4	4	....	....	....	....	....
1989-90	Dukla Jihlava	Czech.	46	12	12	24	....	....	....	....	....	....
1990-91	Dukla Jihlava	Czech.	51	20	23	43	....	....	....	....	....	....
1991-92	Dukla Jihlava	Czech.	42	16	16	32	26	....	....	....	....	....
1992-93	St. John's	AHL	75	32	45	77	74	8	3	3	6	23
1993-94	**Toronto**	**NHL**	**2**	**0**	**0**	**0**	**0**	....	....	....	....	....
a	St. John's	AHL	77	*53	43	96	105	11	4	8	12	4
1994-95	St. John's	AHL	71	37	32	69	98	4	2	0	2	7
1995-96	Los Angeles	IHL	79	34	51	85	83	....	....	....	....	....
1996-97b	Long Beach	IHL	82	45	42	87	96	18	4	4	8	33
	NHL Totals		**2**	**0**	**0**	**0**	**0**	....	....	....	....	....

a AHL Second All-Star Team (1994)
b IHL Second All-Star Team (1997)

AXELSSON, PER-JOHAN (AHX-ehl-suhn, PAIR, YEW-hahn) BOS.

Left wing. Shoots left. 6'1", 174 lbs. Born, Kungalv, Sweden, February 26, 1975.
(Boston's 7th choice, 177th overall, in 1995 Entry Draft).

			Regular Season					Playoffs				
Season	Club	Lea	GP	G	A	TP	PIM	GP	G	A	TP	PIM
1993-94	V. Frolunda	Swe.	11	0	0	0	4	4	0	0	0	0
1994-95	V. Frolunda	Swe.	8	2	1	3	6	....	....	....	....	....
1995-96	V. Frolunda	Swe.	36	15	5	20	10	13	3	0	3	10
1996-97	V. Frolunda	Swe.	50	19	15	34	34	3	0	2	2	0

BABARIKO, JEVGENI (boh-bah-RIH-koh) VAN.

Center. Shoots left. 6'1", 183 lbs. Born, Gorky, USSR, March 3, 1974.
(Vancouver's 6th choice, 176th overall, in 1993 Entry Draft).

			Regular Season					Playoffs				
Season	Club	Lea	GP	G	A	TP	PIM	GP	G	A	TP	PIM
1991-92	Torpedo Niz.	CIS	17	5	0	5	4	....	....	....	....	....
1992-93	Torpedo Niz.	CIS	13	1	0	1	4	....	....	....	....	....
1993-94	Torpedo Niz.	CIS	44	3	5	8	12	....	....	....	....	....
1994-95	Torpedo Niz.	CIS	41	10	4	14	12	5	0	2	2	0
1995-96	Torpedo Niz.	CIS	49	16	18	34	20	3	2	1	3	2
1996-97	Torpedo Niz.	Rus.	24	2	4	6	16	....	....	....	....	....

BABENKO, YURI (bah-BEHN-koh) COL.

Center. Shoots left. 6', 185 lbs. Born, Penza, USSR, January 2, 1978.
(Colorado's 2nd choice, 51st overall, in 1996 Entry Draft).

			Regular Season					Playoffs				
Season	Club	Lea	GP	G	A	TP	PIM	GP	G	A	TP	PIM
1995-96	Soviet Wings	CIS	21	0	0	0	16	....	....	....	....	....
1996-97	Soviet Wings	Rus.	4	1	0	1	4	....	....	....	....	....
	Soviet Wings 2	Rus. 3	26	8	10	18	24	....	....	....	....	....
	CSKA	Rus. 2	24	3	3	6	12	....	....	....	....	....

BABYCH, DAVE (BAB-itch) VAN.

Defense. Shoots left. 6'2", 215 lbs. Born, Edmonton, Alta., May 23, 1961.
(Winnipeg's 1st choice, 2nd overall, in 1980 Entry Draft).

			Regular Season					Playoffs				
Season	Club	Lea	GP	G	A	TP	PIM	GP	G	A	TP	PIM
1978-79	Portland	WHL	67	20	59	79	63	25	7	22	29	22
1979-80a	Portland	WHL	50	22	60	82	71	8	1	10	11	2
1980-81	**Winnipeg**	**NHL**	**69**	**6**	**38**	**44**	**90**	....	....	....	....	....
1981-82	**Winnipeg**	**NHL**	**79**	**19**	**49**	**68**	**92**	**4**	**1**	**2**	**3**	**29**
1982-83	**Winnipeg**	**NHL**	**79**	**13**	**61**	**74**	**56**	**3**	**0**	**0**	**0**	**0**
1983-84	**Winnipeg**	**NHL**	**66**	**18**	**39**	**57**	**62**	**3**	**1**	**1**	**2**	**0**
1984-85	**Winnipeg**	**NHL**	**78**	**13**	**49**	**62**	**78**	**8**	**2**	**7**	**9**	**6**
1985-86	**Winnipeg**	**NHL**	**19**	**4**	**12**	**16**	**14**	....	....	....	....	....
	Hartford	**NHL**	**62**	**10**	**43**	**53**	**36**	**8**	**1**	**3**	**4**	**14**
1986-87	**Hartford**	**NHL**	**66**	**8**	**33**	**41**	**44**	**6**	**1**	**1**	**2**	**14**
1987-88	**Hartford**	**NHL**	**71**	**14**	**36**	**50**	**54**	**6**	**3**	**2**	**5**	**2**
1988-89	**Hartford**	**NHL**	**70**	**6**	**41**	**47**	**54**	**4**	**1**	**5**	**6**	**2**
1989-90	**Hartford**	**NHL**	**72**	**6**	**37**	**43**	**62**	**7**	**1**	**2**	**3**	**0**
1990-91	**Hartford**	**NHL**	**8**	**0**	**6**	**6**	**4**	....	....	....	....	....
1991-92	**Vancouver**	**NHL**	**75**	**5**	**24**	**29**	**63**	**13**	**2**	**6**	**8**	**10**
1992-93	**Vancouver**	**NHL**	**43**	**3**	**16**	**19**	**44**	**12**	**2**	**5**	**7**	**6**
1993-94	**Vancouver**	**NHL**	**73**	**4**	**28**	**32**	**52**	**24**	**3**	**5**	**8**	**12**
1994-95	**Vancouver**	**NHL**	**40**	**3**	**11**	**14**	**18**	**11**	**2**	**2**	**4**	**14**
1995-96	**Vancouver**	**NHL**	**53**	**3**	**21**	**24**	**38**	....	....	....	....	....
1996-97	**Vancouver**	**NHL**	**78**	**5**	**22**	**27**	**38**	....	....	....	....	....
	NHL Totals		**1101**	**140**	**566**	**706**	**899**	**109**	**20**	**41**	**61**	**109**

a WHL First All-Star Team (1980)

Played in NHL All-Star Game (1983, 1984)

Traded to **Hartford** by **Winnipeg** for Ray Neufeld, November 21, 1985. Claimed by **Minnesota** from **Hartford** in Expansion Draft, May 30, 1991. Traded to **Vancouver** by **Minnesota** for Tom Kurvers, June 22, 1991.

BAKER, JAMIE TOR.

Center. Shoots left. 6', 195 lbs. Born, Ottawa, Ont., August 31, 1966.
(Quebec's 2nd choice, 8th overall, in 1988 Supplemental Draft).

			Regular Season					Playoffs				
Season	Club	Lea	GP	G	A	TP	PIM	GP	G	A	TP	PIM
1985-86	St. Lawrence	ECAC	31	9	16	25	52	....	....	....	....	....
1986-87	St. Lawrence	ECAC	32	8	24	32	59	....	....	....	....	....
1987-88	St. Lawrence	ECAC	34	26	24	50	38	....	....	....	....	....
1988-89	St. Lawrence	ECAC	13	11	16	27	16	....	....	....	....	....
1989-90	**Quebec**	**NHL**	**1**	**0**	**0**	**0**	**0**	....	....	....	....	....
	Halifax	AHL	74	17	43	60	47	6	0	0	0	7
1990-91	**Quebec**	**NHL**	**18**	**2**	**0**	**2**	**8**	....	....	....	....	....
	Halifax	AHL	50	14	22	36	85	....	....	....	....	....
1991-92	**Quebec**	**NHL**	**52**	**7**	**10**	**17**	**32**	....	....	....	....	....
	Halifax	AHL	9	5	0	5	12	....	....	....	....	....
1992-93	**Ottawa**	**NHL**	**76**	**19**	**29**	**48**	**54**	....	....	....	....	....
1993-94	**San Jose**	**NHL**	**65**	**12**	**5**	**17**	**38**	**14**	**3**	**2**	**5**	**30**
1994-95	**San Jose**	**NHL**	**43**	**7**	**4**	**11**	**22**	**11**	**2**	**2**	**4**	**12**
1995-96	**San Jose**	**NHL**	**77**	**16**	**17**	**33**	**79**	....	....	....	....	....
1996-97	**Toronto**	**NHL**	**58**	**8**	**8**	**16**	**28**	....	....	....	....	....
	NHL Totals		**390**	**71**	**73**	**144**	**261**	**25**	**5**	**4**	**9**	**42**

Signed as a free agent by **Ottawa**, September 2, 1992. Signed as a free agent by **San Jose**, September 11, 1993. Traded to **Toronto** by **San Jose** with San Jose's fifth round choice (Peter Cava) in 1996 Entry Draft for Todd Gill, June 14, 1996.

BALMOCHNYKH, MAXIM (bahl-MAWCH-nihky, mahx-EEM) ANA.

Left wing. Shoots left. 6', 185 lbs. Born, Lipetsk, USSR, March 7, 1979.
(Anaheim's 2nd choice, 45th overall, in 1997 Entry Draft).

			Regular Season					Playoffs				
Season	Club	Lea	GP	G	A	TP	PIM	GP	G	A	TP	PIM
1994-95	Lipetsk	CIS 2	3	0	1	1	4	....	....	....	....	....
1995-96	Lipetsk	CIS 2	40	15	5	20	60	....	....	....	....	....
1996-97	Lada Togliatti	Rus.	18	6	1	7	22	....	....	....	....	....

BANCROFT, STEVE

Defense. Shoots left. 6'1", 214 lbs. Born, Toronto, Ont., October 6, 1970.
(Toronto's 3rd choice, 21st overall, in 1989 Entry Draft).

			Regular Season					Playoffs				
Season	Club	Lea	GP	G	A	TP	PIM	GP	G	A	TP	PIM
1987-88	Belleville	OHL	56	1	8	9	42	....	....	....	....	....
1988-89	Belleville	OHL	66	7	30	37	99	5	0	2	2	10
1989-90	Belleville	OHL	53	10	33	43	135	11	3	9	12	38
1990-91	Newmarket	AHL	9	0	3	3	22	....	....	....	....	....
	Maine	AHL	53	2	12	14	46	2	0	0	0	2
1991-92	Maine	AHL	26	1	3	4	45	....	....	....	....	....
	Indianapolis	IHL	36	8	23	31	49	....	....	....	....	....
1992-93	**Chicago**	**NHL**	**1**	**0**	**0**	**0**	**0**	....	....	....	....	....
	Indianapolis	IHL	53	10	35	45	138	....	....	....	....	....
	Moncton	AHL	21	3	13	16	16	5	0	0	0	16
1993-94	Cleveland	IHL	33	2	12	14	58	....	....	....	....	....
1994-95	Detroit	IHL	6	1	3	4	0	....	....	....	....	....
	Fort Wayne	IHL	50	7	17	24	100	....	....	....	....	....
	St. John's	AHL	4	2	0	2	2	5	0	3	3	8
1995-96	Los Angeles	IHL	15	3	10	13	22	....	....	....	....	....
	Chicago	IHL	64	9	41	50	91	9	1	7	8	22
1996-97	Chicago	IHL	39	6	10	16	66	....	....	....	....	....
	Las Vegas	IHL	36	9	28	37	64	3	0	0	0	2
	NHL Totals		**1**	**0**	**0**	**0**	**0**	....	....	....	....	....

Traded to **Boston** by **Toronto** for Rob Cimetta, November 9, 1990. Traded to **Chicago** by **Boston** with Boston's eleventh round choice (later traded to Winnipeg — Winnipeg selected Russel Hewson) in 1993 Entry Draft for Chicago's eleventh round choice (Eugene Pavlov) in 1992 Entry Draft, January 9, 1992. Traded to **Winnipeg** by **Chicago** with future considerations for Troy Murray, February 21, 1993. Claimed by **Florida** from **Winnipeg** in Expansion Draft, June 24, 1993. Signed as a free agent by **Pittsburgh**, August 2, 1993.

BANHAM, FRANK ANA.

Right wing. Shoots right. 6', 190 lbs. Born, Calahoo, Alta., April 14, 1975.
(Washington's 4th choice, 147th overall, in 1993 Entry Draft).

			Regular Season					Playoffs				
Season	Club	Lea	GP	G	A	TP	PIM	GP	G	A	TP	PIM
1992-93	Saskatoon	WHL	71	29	33	62	55	9	2	7	9	8
1993-94	Saskatoon	WHL	65	28	39	67	99	16	8	11	19	36
1994-95	Saskatoon	WHL	70	50	39	89	63	8	2	6	8	12
1995-96a	Saskatoon	WHL	72	*83	69	152	116	4	6	0	6	2
	Baltimore	AHL	9	1	4	5	0	7	1	1	2	2
1996-97	**Anaheim**	**NHL**	**3**	**0**	**0**	**0**	**0**	....	....	....	....	....
	Baltimore	AHL	21	11	13	24	4	....	....	....	....	....
	NHL Totals		**3**	**0**	**0**	**0**	**0**	....	....	....	....	....

a WHL East First All-Star Team (1996)

Signed as a free agent by **Anaheim**, January 27, 1996.

BANNISTER, DREW EDM.

Defense. Shoots right. 6'2", 200 lbs. Born, Belleville, Ont., September 4, 1974.
(Tampa Bay's 2nd choice, 26th overall, in 1992 Entry Draft).

			Regular Season					Playoffs				
Season	Club	Lea	GP	G	A	TP	PIM	GP	G	A	TP	PIM
1990-91	S.S. Marie	OHL	41	2	8	10	51	4	0	0	0	0
1991-92	S.S. Marie	OHL	64	4	21	25	122	16	3	10	13	36
1992-93a	S.S. Marie	OHL	59	5	28	33	114	18	2	7	9	12
1993-94b	S.S. Marie	OHL	58	7	43	50	108	14	6	9	15	20
1994-95	Atlanta	IHL	72	5	7	12	74	5	0	2	2	22
1995-96	**Tampa Bay**	**NHL**	**13**	**0**	**1**	**1**	**4**	....	....	....	....	....
	Atlanta	IHL	61	3	13	16	105	3	0	0	0	4
1996-97	**Tampa Bay**	**NHL**	**64**	**4**	**13**	**17**	**44**	....	....	....	....	....
	Edmonton	**NHL**	**1**	**0**	**1**	**1**	**0**	**12**	**0**	**0**	**0**	**30**
	NHL Totals		**78**	**4**	**15**	**19**	**48**	**12**	**0**	**0**	**0**	**30**

a Memorial Cup All-Star Team (1993)
b OHL Second All-Star Team (1994)

Traded to **Edmonton** by **Tampa Bay** with Tampa Bay's sixth round choice (Peter Sarno) in 1997 Entry Draft for Jeff Norton, March 18, 1997.

BARNABY, MATTHEW BUF.

Right wing. Shoots left. 6', 188 lbs. Born, Ottawa, Ont., May 4, 1973.
(Buffalo's 5th choice, 83rd overall, in 1992 Entry Draft).

			Regular Season					Playoffs				
Season	Club	Lea	GP	G	A	TP	PIM	GP	G	A	TP	PIM
1990-91	Beauport	QMJHL	52	9	5	14	262	....	....	....	....	....
1991-92	Beauport	QMJHL	63	29	37	66	*476	....	....	....	....	....
1992-93	**Buffalo**	**NHL**	**2**	**1**	**0**	**1**	**10**	**1**	**0**	**1**	**1**	**4**
	Victoriaville	QMJHL	65	44	67	111	*448	6	2	4	6	44
1993-94	**Buffalo**	**NHL**	**35**	**2**	**4**	**6**	**106**	**3**	**0**	**0**	**0**	**17**
	Rochester	AHL	42	10	32	42	153	....	....	....	....	....
1994-95	Rochester	AHL	56	21	29	50	274	....	....	....	....	....
	Buffalo	**NHL**	**23**	**1**	**1**	**2**	**116**	....	....	....	....	....
1995-96	**Buffalo**	**NHL**	**73**	**15**	**16**	**31**	***335**	....	....	....	....	....
1996-97	**Buffalo**	**NHL**	**68**	**19**	**24**	**43**	**249**	**8**	**0**	**4**	**4**	**36**
	NHL Totals		**201**	**38**	**45**	**83**	**816**	**12**	**0**	**5**	**5**	**57**

BARNES, STU PIT.

Center. Shoots right. 5'11", 174 lbs. Born, Spruce Grove, Alta., December 25, 1970.
(Winnipeg's 1st choice, 4th overall, in 1989 Entry Draft).

			Regular Season					Playoffs				
Season	Club	Lea	GP	G	A	TP	PIM	GP	G	A	TP	PIM
1987-88	N. Westminster	WHL	71	37	64	101	88	5	2	3	5	6
1988-89a	Tri-City	WHL	70	59	82	141	117	7	6	5	11	10
1989-90	Tri-City	WHL	63	52	92	144	165	7	1	5	6	26
1990-91	Cdn. National	....	53	22	27	49	68	....	....	....	....	....
1991-92	**Winnipeg**	**NHL**	**46**	**8**	**9**	**17**	**26**	....	....	....	....	....
	Moncton	AHL	30	13	19	32	10	11	3	9	12	6
1992-93	**Winnipeg**	**NHL**	**38**	**12**	**10**	**22**	**10**	**6**	**1**	**3**	**4**	**2**
	Moncton	AHL	42	23	31	54	58	....	....	....	....	....
1993-94	**Winnipeg**	**NHL**	**18**	**5**	**4**	**9**	**8**	....	....	....	....	....
	Florida	**NHL**	**59**	**18**	**20**	**38**	**30**	....	....	....	....	....
1994-95	**Florida**	**NHL**	**41**	**10**	**19**	**29**	**8**	....	....	....	....	....
1995-96	**Florida**	**NHL**	**72**	**19**	**25**	**44**	**46**	**22**	**6**	**10**	**16**	**4**
1996-97	**Florida**	**NHL**	**19**	**2**	**8**	**10**	**10**	....	....	....	....	....
	Pittsburgh	**NHL**	**62**	**17**	**22**	**39**	**16**	**5**	**0**	**1**	**1**	**0**
	NHL Totals		**355**	**91**	**117**	**208**	**154**	**33**	**7**	**14**	**21**	**6**

a WHL West Second All-Star Team (1989)

Traded to **Florida** by **Winnipeg** with St. Louis' sixth round choice (previously acquired by Winnipeg — later traded to Edmonton — later traded to Winnipeg — Winnipeg selected Chris Kibermanis) in 1994 Entry Draft for Randy Gilhen, November 25, 1993. Traded to **Pittsburgh** by **Florida** with Jason Woolley for Chris Wells, November 19, 1996.

BARNEY, SCOTT L.A.

Center. Shoots right. 6'4", 198 lbs. Born, Oshawa, Ont., March 27, 1979.
(Los Angeles' 3rd choice, 29th overall, in 1997 Entry Draft).

			Regular Season					Playoffs				
Season	Club	Lea	GP	G	A	TP	PIM	GP	G	A	TP	PIM
1995-96	Peterborough	OHL	60	22	24	46	52	24	6	8	14	38
1996-97	Peterborough	OHL	64	21	33	54	110	9	0	3	3	16

BARON, MURRAY — PHO.

Defense. Shoots left. 6'3", 215 lbs. Born, Prince George, B.C., June 1, 1967.
(Philadelphia's 7th choice, 167th overall, in 1986 Entry Draft).

			Regular Season					Playoffs				
Season	Club	Lea	GP	G	A	TP	PIM	GP	G	A	TP	PIM
1986-87	North Dakota	WCHA	41	4	10	14	62	....	....	....	....	....
1987-88	North Dakota	WCHA	41	1	10	11	95	....	....	....	....	....
1988-89	North Dakota	WCHA	40	2	6	8	92	....	....	....	....	....
	Hershey	AHL	9	0	3	3	8	....	....	....	....	....
1989-90	Philadelphia	NHL	16	2	2	4	12	....	....	....	....	....
	Hershey	AHL	50	0	10	10	101	....	....	....	....	....
1990-91	Philadelphia	NHL	67	8	8	16	74	....	....	....	....	....
	Hershey	AHL	6	2	3	5	0	....	....	....	....	....
1991-92	St. Louis	NHL	67	3	8	11	94	2	0	0	0	2
1992-93	St. Louis	NHL	53	2	2	4	59	11	0	0	0	12
1993-94	St. Louis	NHL	77	5	9	14	123	4	0	0	0	10
1994-95	St. Louis	NHL	39	0	5	5	93	7	1	1	2	2
1995-96	St. Louis	NHL	82	2	9	11	190	13	1	0	1	20
1996-97	St. Louis	NHL	11	0	2	2	11	....	....	....	....	....
	Montreal	NHL	60	1	5	6	107	....	....	....	....	....
	Phoenix	NHL	8	0	0	0	4	1	0	0	0	0
	NHL Totals		480	23	50	73	767	38	2	1	3	46

Traded to **St. Louis** by **Philadelphia** with Ron Sutter for Dan Quinn and Rod Brind'Amour, September 22, 1991. Traded to **Montreal** by **St. Louis** with Shayne Corson and St. Louis' fifth round choice (Gennady Razin) in 1997 Entry Draft for Pierre Turgeon, Rory Fitzpatrick and Craig Conroy, October 29, 1996. Traded to **Phoenix** by **Montreal** with Chris Murray for Dave Manson, March 18, 1997.

BARR, DAVE

Right wing. Shoots right. 6'1", 195 lbs. Born, Toronto, Ont., November 30, 1960.

			Regular Season					Playoffs				
Season	Club	Lea	GP	G	A	TP	PIM	GP	G	A	TP	PIM
1979-80	Lethbridge	WHL	60	16	38	54	47	....	....	....	....	....
1980-81	Lethbridge	WHL	72	26	62	88	106	10	4	10	14	4
1981-82	Boston	NHL	2	0	0	0	0	5	1	0	1	0
	Erie	AHL	76	18	48	66	29	....	....	....	....	....
1982-83	Boston	NHL	10	1	1	2	7	10	0	0	0	2
	Baltimore	AHL	72	27	51	78	67	....	....	....	....	....
1983-84	NY Rangers	NHL	6	0	0	0	2	....	....	....	....	....
	Tulsa	CHL	50	28	37	65	24	....	....	....	....	....
	St. Louis	NHL	1	0	0	0	0	....	....	....	....	....
1984-85	St. Louis	NHL	75	16	18	34	32	2	0	0	0	2
1985-86	St. Louis	NHL	72	13	38	51	70	11	1	1	2	14
1986-87	St. Louis	NHL	2	0	0	0	0	....	....	....	....	....
	Hartford	NHL	30	2	4	6	19	....	....	....	....	....
	Detroit	NHL	37	13	13	26	49	13	1	0	1	14
1987-88	Detroit	NHL	51	14	26	40	58	16	5	7	12	22
1988-89	Detroit	NHL	73	27	32	59	69	6	3	1	4	6
1989-90	Detroit	NHL	62	10	25	35	45	....	....	....	....	....
	Adirondack	AHL	9	1	14	15	17	....	....	....	....	....
1990-91	Detroit	NHL	70	18	22	40	55	....	....	....	....	....
1991-92	New Jersey	NHL	41	6	12	18	32	....	....	....	....	....
	Utica	AHL	1	0	0	0	7	....	....	....	....	....
1992-93	New Jersey	NHL	62	6	8	14	61	5	1	0	1	6
1993-94	Dallas	NHL	20	2	5	7	21	3	0	1	1	4
	Kalamazoo	IHL	4	3	2	5	5	....	....	....	....	....
1994-95	Kalamazoo	IHL	66	18	41	59	77	16	1	4	5	8
1995-96	Orlando	IHL	82	38	62	100	87	23	8	13	21	14
1996-97	Orlando	IHL	50	15	29	44	29	9	2	3	5	8
	NHL Totals		614	128	204	332	520	71	12	10	22	70

Signed as a free agent by **Boston**, September 28, 1981. Traded to **NY Rangers** by **Boston** for Dave Silk, October 5, 1983. Traded to **St. Louis** by **NY Rangers** with NY Rangers' third round choice (Alan Perry) in the 1984 Entry Draft for Larry Patey and Bob Brooke, March 5, 1984. Traded to **Hartford** by **St. Louis** for Tim Bothwell, October 21, 1986. Traded to **Detroit** by **Hartford** for Randy Ladouceur, January 12, 1987. Acquired by **New Jersey** from **Detroit** with Randy McKay as compensation for Detroit's signing of free agent Troy Crowder, September 9, 1991. Signed as a free agent by **Dallas**, August 28, 1993.

BARRIE, LEN

Center. Shoots left. 6', 200 lbs. Born, Kimberley, B.C., June 4, 1969.
(Edmonton's 7th choice, 124th overall, in 1988 Entry Draft).

			Regular Season					Playoffs				
Season	Club	Lea	GP	G	A	TP	PIM	GP	G	A	TP	PIM
1985-86	Calgary	WHL	32	3	0	3	18	....	....	....	....	....
1986-87	Calgary	WHL	34	13	13	26	81	....	....	....	....	....
	Victoria	WHL	34	7	6	13	92	5	0	1	1	15
1987-88	Victoria	WHL	70	37	49	86	192	8	2	0	2	29
1988-89	Victoria	WHL	67	39	48	87	157	7	5	2	7	23
1989-90	Philadelphia	NHL	1	0	0	0	0	....	....	....	....	....
a	Kamloops	WHL	70	*85	*100	*185	108	17	*14	23	*37	24
1990-91	Hershey	AHL	63	26	32	58	60	7	4	0	4	12
1991-92	Hershey	AHL	75	42	43	85	78	3	0	2	2	32
1992-93	Philadelphia	NHL	8	2	2	4	9	....	....	....	....	....
	Hershey	AHL	61	31	45	76	162	....	....	....	....	....
1993-94	Florida	NHL	2	0	0	0	0	....	....	....	....	....
b	Cincinnati	IHL	77	45	71	116	246	11	8	13	21	60
1994-95	Cleveland	IHL	28	13	30	43	137	....	....	....	....	....
	Pittsburgh	NHL	48	3	11	14	66	4	1	0	1	8
1995-96	Pittsburgh	NHL	5	0	0	0	18	....	....	....	....	....
	Cleveland	IHL	55	29	43	72	178	3	2	3	5	6
1996-97	San Antonio	IHL	57	26	40	66	196	9	5	5	10	20
	NHL Totals		64	5	13	18	93	4	1	0	1	8

a WHL West First All-Star Team (1990)
b IHL Second All-Star Team (1994)

Signed as a free agent by **Philadelphia**, February 28, 1990. Signed as a free agent by **Florida**, July 20, 1993. Signed as a free agent by **Pittsburgh**, August 15, 1994.

BARTANUS, KAROL (bahr-TAHN-uhs, KAHR-uhl) — BOS.

Right wing. Shoots left. 6'2", 185 lbs. Born, Liptovsky Mikulas, Slovakia, June 9, 1978.
(Boston's 6th choice, 81st overall, in 1997 Entry Draft).

			Regular Season					Playoffs				
Season	Club	Lea	GP	G	A	TP	PIM	GP	G	A	TP	PIM
1995-96	Lip. Mikulas	Slo. Jr.	35	46	24	70	....	....	....	....	....	....
	HK Mikulus	Slovak	15	2	1	3	0	....	....	....	....	....
1996-97	Drummondville	QMJHL	61	40	44	84	115	8	1	2	3	20

BASSEN, BOB — DAL.

Center. Shoots left. 5'10", 185 lbs. Born, Calgary, Alta., May 6, 1965.

			Regular Season					Playoffs				
Season	Club	Lea	GP	G	A	TP	PIM	GP	G	A	TP	PIM
1982-83	Medicine Hat	WHL	4	3	2	5	0	3	0	0	0	4
1983-84	Medicine Hat	WHL	72	29	29	58	93	14	5	11	16	12
1984-85a	Medicine Hat	WHL	65	32	50	82	143	10	2	8	10	39
1985-86	NY Islanders	NHL	11	2	1	3	6	3	0	1	1	0
	Springfield	AHL	54	13	21	34	111	....	....	....	....	....
1986-87	NY Islanders	NHL	77	7	10	17	89	14	1	2	3	21
1987-88	NY Islanders	NHL	77	6	16	22	99	6	0	1	1	23
1988-89	NY Islanders	NHL	19	1	4	5	21	....	....	....	....	....
	Chicago	NHL	49	4	12	16	62	10	1	1	2	34
1989-90	Chicago	NHL	6	1	1	2	8	1	0	0	0	2
b	Indianapolis	IHL	73	22	32	54	179	12	3	8	11	33
1990-91	St. Louis	NHL	79	16	18	34	183	13	1	3	4	24
1991-92	St. Louis	NHL	79	7	25	32	167	6	0	2	2	4
1992-93	St. Louis	NHL	53	9	10	19	63	11	0	0	0	10
1993-94	St. Louis	NHL	46	2	7	9	44	....	....	....	....	....
	Quebec	NHL	37	11	8	19	55	....	....	....	....	....
1994-95	Quebec	NHL	47	12	15	27	33	5	2	4	6	0
1995-96	Dallas	NHL	13	0	1	1	15	....	....	....	....	....
	Michigan	IHL	1	0	0	0	4	....	....	....	....	....
1996-97	Dallas	NHL	46	5	7	12	41	7	3	1	4	4
	NHL Totals		639	83	135	218	886	76	8	15	23	122

a WHL First All-Star Team (1985)
b IHL First All-Star Team (1990)

Signed as a free agent by **NY Islanders**, October 19, 1984. Traded to **Chicago** by **NY Islanders** with Steve Konroyd for Marc Bergevin and Gary Nylund, November 25, 1988. Claimed by **St. Louis** from **Chicago** in NHL Waiver Draft, October 1, 1990. Traded to **Quebec** by **St. Louis** with Garth Butcher and Ron Sutter for Steve Duchesne and Denis Chasse, January 23, 1994. Signed as a free agent by **Dallas**, August 10, 1995.

BATES, SHAWN — BOS.

Center. Shoots right. 5'11", 205 lbs. Born, Melrose, MA, April 3, 1975.
(Boston's 4th choice, 103rd overall, in 1993 Entry Draft).

			Regular Season					Playoffs				
Season	Club	Lea	GP	G	A	TP	PIM	GP	G	A	TP	PIM
1993-94	Boston U.	H.E.	41	10	19	29	24	....	....	....	....	....
1994-95a	Boston U.	H.E.	38	18	12	30	48	....	....	....	....	....
1995-96	Boston U.	H.E.	40	28	22	50	54	....	....	....	....	....
1996-97	Boston U.	H.E.	41	17	18	35	64	....	....	....	....	....

a NCAA Final Four All-Tournament Team (1995)

BATHERSON, NORM — WSH.

Left wing. Shoots left. 6'1", 198 lbs. Born, North Sydney, N.S., March 27, 1969.

			Regular Season					Playoffs				
Season	Club	Lea	GP	G	A	TP	PIM	GP	G	A	TP	PIM
1992-93	Acadia	AUAA	20	16	21	37	44	....	....	....	....	....
1993-94	P.E.I.	AHL	67	14	23	37	85	....	....	....	....	....
1994-95	Portland	AHL	77	27	34	61	64	7	3	4	7	4
1995-96	Portland	AHL	45	6	21	27	72	24	11	8	19	16
1996-97	Portland	AHL	53	15	28	43	43	5	2	1	3	0

Signed as a free agent by **Washington**, August 21, 1995.

BATTAGLIA, BATES — CAR.

Left wing. Shoots left. 6'2", 185 lbs. Born, Chicago, IL, December 13, 1975.
(Anaheim's 6th choice, 132nd overall, in 1994 Entry Draft).

			Regular Season					Playoffs				
Season	Club	Lea	GP	G	A	TP	PIM	GP	G	A	TP	PIM
1994-95	Lake Superior	CCHA	38	6	14	20	34	....	....	....	....	....
1995-96	Lake Superior	CCHA	40	13	22	35	48	....	....	....	....	....
1996-97	Lake Superior	CCHA	38	12	27	39	80	....	....	....	....	....

Traded to **Hartford** by **Anaheim** with Anaheim's fourth round choice in 1998 Entry Draft for Mark Janssens, March 18, 1997.

BATTAGLIA, DOUG — DET.

Left wing. Shoots left. 6'1", 185 lbs. Born, Newmarket, Ont., October 26, 1975.
(Detroit's 5th choice, 127th overall, in 1994 Entry Draft).

			Regular Season					Playoffs				
Season	Club	Lea	GP	G	A	TP	PIM	GP	G	A	TP	PIM
1994-95	RPI	ECAC	34	1	4	5	57	....	....	....	....	....
1995-96	RPI	ECAC	33	5	5	10	37	....	....	....	....	....
1996-97	RPI	ECAC	36	19	11	30	50	....	....	....	....	....

BATYRSHIN, RUSLAN (ba-TEER-shihn) — L.A.

Defense. Shoots left. 6'1", 185 lbs. Born, Moscow, USSR, February 19, 1975.
(Winnipeg's 4th choice, 79th overall, in 1993 Entry Draft).

			Regular Season					Playoffs				
Season	Club	Lea	GP	G	A	TP	PIM	GP	G	A	TP	PIM
1991-92	Mosc. D'amo 2	CIS 3	40	0	2	2	52	....	....	....	....	....
1992-93	Mosc. D'amo 2	CIS 2				UNAVAILABLE						
1993-94	Moscow D'amo	CIS	10	0	0	0	10	3	0	0	0	22
1994-95	Moscow D'amo	CIS	36	2	2	4	65	12	1	1	2	6
1995-96	Los Angeles	NHL	2	0	0	0	6	....	....	....	....	....
	Phoenix	IHL	71	1	9	10	144	2	0	0	0	2
1996-97	Phoenix	IHL	59	3	4	7	123	....	....	....	....	....
	NHL Totals		2	0	0	0	6	....	....	....	....	....

Rights traded to **Los Angeles** by **Winnipeg** with Winnipeg's second round choice (Marian Cisar) in 1996 Entry Draft for Brent Thompson and future considerations, August 8, 1994.

BAUMGARTNER, GREGOR — MTL.

Left wing. Shoots left. 6', 170 lbs. Born, Leoben, Austria, July 13, 1979.
(Montreal's 2nd choice, 37th overall, in 1997 Entry Draft).

			Regular Season					Playoffs				
Season	Club	Lea	GP	G	A	TP	PIM	GP	G	A	TP	PIM
1994-95	Clarkson	CCHA	7	0	1	1	0	....	....	....	....	....
1995-96	Gatineau	Midget	15	8	11	19	6	....	....	....	....	....
1996-97	Laval	QMJHL	68	19	45	64	15	3	0	0	0	0

BAUMGARTNER, KEN — BOS.

Left wing. Shoots left. 6'1", 205 lbs. Born, Flin Flon, Man., March 11, 1966.
(Buffalo's 12th choice, 245th overall, in 1985 Entry Draft).

			Regular Season					Playoffs				
Season	Club	Lea	GP	G	A	TP	PIM	GP	G	A	TP	PIM
1984-85	Prince Albert	WHL	60	3	9	12	252	13	1	3	4	89
1985-86	Prince Albert	WHL	70	4	23	27	277	20	3	9	12	112
1986-87	New Haven	AHL	13	0	3	3	99	6	0	0	0	60
1987-88	**Los Angeles**	**NHL**	**30**	**2**	**3**	**5**	**189**	**5**	**0**	**1**	**1**	**28**
	New Haven	AHL	48	1	5	6	181	....	....	....	....	....
1988-89	**Los Angeles**	**NHL**	**49**	**1**	**3**	**4**	**288**	**5**	**0**	**0**	**0**	**8**
	New Haven	AHL	10	1	3	4	26	....	....	....	....	....
1989-90	**Los Angeles**	**NHL**	**12**	**1**	**0**	**1**	**28**	....	....	....	....	....
	NY Islanders	**NHL**	**53**	**0**	**5**	**5**	**194**	**4**	**0**	**0**	**0**	**27**
1990-91	**NY Islanders**	**NHL**	**78**	**1**	**6**	**7**	**282**	....	....	....	....	....
1991-92	**NY Islanders**	**NHL**	**44**	**0**	**1**	**1**	**202**	....	....	....	....	....
	Toronto	**NHL**	**11**	**0**	**0**	**0**	**23**	....	....	....	....	....
1992-93	**Toronto**	**NHL**	**63**	**1**	**0**	**1**	**155**	**7**	**1**	**0**	**1**	**0**
1993-94	**Toronto**	**NHL**	**64**	**4**	**4**	**8**	**185**	**10**	**0**	**0**	**0**	**18**
1994-95	**Toronto**	**NHL**	**2**	**0**	**0**	**0**	**5**	....	....	....	....	....
1995-96	**Toronto**	**NHL**	**60**	**2**	**3**	**5**	**152**	....	....	....	....	....
	Anaheim	**NHL**	**12**	**0**	**1**	**1**	**41**	....	....	....	....	....
1996-97	**Anaheim**	**NHL**	**67**	**0**	**11**	**11**	**182**	**11**	**0**	**1**	**1**	**11**
	NHL Totals		**545**	**12**	**37**	**49**	**1926**	**42**	**1**	**2**	**3**	**92**

Traded to **Los Angeles** by **Buffalo** with Sean McKenna and Larry Playfair for Brian Engblom and Doug Smith, January 29, 1986. Traded to **NY Islanders** by **Los Angeles** with Hubie McDonough for Mikko Makela, November 29, 1989. Traded to **Toronto** by **NY Islanders** with Dave McLlwain for Daniel Marois and Claude Loiselle, March 10, 1992. Traded to **Anaheim** by **Toronto** for Winnipeg's fourth round choice (previously acquired by Anaheim — later traded to Montreal — Montreal selected Kim Staal) in 1996 Entry Draft, March 20, 1996. Signed as a free agent by **Boston**, July 14, 1997.

BAUMGARTNER, NOLAN — WSH.

Defense. Shoots right. 6'1", 200 lbs. Born, Calgary, Alta., March 23, 1976.
(Washington's 1st choice, 10th overall, in 1994 Entry Draft).

			Regular Season					Playoffs				
Season	Club	Lea	GP	G	A	TP	PIM	GP	G	A	TP	PIM
1992-93	Kamloops	WHL	43	0	5	5	30	11	1	1	2	0
1993-94a	Kamloops	WHL	69	13	42	55	109	19	3	14	17	33
1994-95abcd	Kamloops	WHL	62	8	36	44	71	21	4	13	17	16
1995-96b	Kamloops	WHL	28	13	15	28	45	16	1	9	10	26
	Washington	**NHL**	**1**	**0**	**0**	**0**	**0**	**1**	**0**	**0**	**0**	**10**
1996-97	Portland	AHL	8	2	2	4	4	....	....	....	....	....
	NHL Totals		**1**	**0**	**0**	**0**	**0**	**1**	**0**	**0**	**0**	**10**

a Memorial Cup All-Star Team (1994, 1995)
b WHL West First All-Star Team (1995, 1996)
c Canadian Major Junior First All-Star Team (1995)
d Canadian Major Junior Defenseman of the Year (1995)

BAWA, ROBIN — (BAH-wah)

Right wing. Shoots right. 6'2", 214 lbs. Born, Chemainus, B.C., March 26, 1966.

			Regular Season					Playoffs				
Season	Club	Lea	GP	G	A	TP	PIM	GP	G	A	TP	PIM
1982-83	Kamloops	WHL	66	10	24	34	17	7	1	2	3	0
1983-84	Kamloops	WHL	64	16	28	44	40	13	4	2	6	4
1984-85	Kamloops	WHL	52	6	19	25	45	15	4	9	13	14
1985-86	Kamloops	WHL	63	29	43	72	78	16	5	13	18	4
1986-87a	Kamloops	WHL	62	57	56	113	91	13	6	7	13	22
1987-88	Fort Wayne	IHL	55	12	27	39	239	6	1	3	4	24
1988-89	Baltimore	AHL	75	23	24	47	205	....	....	....	....	....
1989-90	**Washington**	**NHL**	**5**	**1**	**0**	**1**	**6**	....	....	....	....	....
	Baltimore	AHL	61	7	18	25	189	11	1	2	3	49
1990-91	Fort Wayne	IHL	72	21	26	47	381	18	4	4	8	87
1991-92	**Vancouver**	**NHL**	**2**	**0**	**0**	**0**	**0**	**1**	**0**	**0**	**0**	**0**
	Milwaukee	IHL	70	27	14	41	238	5	2	2	4	8
1992-93	Hamilton	AHL	23	3	4	7	58	....	....	....	....	....
	San Jose	**NHL**	**42**	**5**	**0**	**5**	**47**	....	....	....	....	....
	Kansas City	IHL	5	2	0	2	20	....	....	....	....	....
1993-94	**Anaheim**	**NHL**	**12**	**0**	**1**	**1**	**7**	....	....	....	....	....
	San Diego	IHL	25	6	15	21	54	6	0	0	0	52
1994-95	Kalamazoo	IHL	71	22	12	34	184	....	....	....	....	....
	Milwaukee	IHL	4	1	1	2	19	15	1	5	6	48
1995-96	San Francisco	IHL	77	23	25	48	234	4	0	2	2	4
1996-97	Fort Wayne	IHL	54	10	23	33	181	....	....	....	....	....
	NHL Totals		**61**	**6**	**1**	**7**	**60**	**1**	**0**	**0**	**0**	**0**

a WHL West All-Star Team (1987)

Signed as a free agent by **Washington**, May 22, 1987. Traded to **Vancouver** by **Washington** for cash, July 31, 1991. Traded to **San Jose** by **Vancouver** for Rick Lessard, December 15, 1992. Claimed by **Anaheim** from **San Jose** in Expansion Draft, June 24, 1993. Signed as a free agent by **Dallas**, July 22, 1994.

BEARDSMORE, COLIN — DET.

Center. Shoots left. 6'1", 194 lbs. Born, Peterborough, Ont., February 7, 1978.
(Detroit's 7th choice, 189th overall, in 1996 Entry Draft).

			Regular Season					Playoffs				
Season	Club	Lea	GP	G	A	TP	PIM	GP	G	A	TP	PIM
1995-96	North Bay	OHL	65	12	12	24	27	....	....	....	....	....
1996-97	North Bay	OHL	40	21	21	42	19	....	....	....	....	....
	Owen Sound	OHL	30	7	13	20	29	4	0	2	2	8

BEAUDOIN, NIC — (BOH-dwehn) COL.

Left wing. Shoots left. 6'3", 205 lbs. Born, Ottawa, Ont., December 25, 1976.
(Colorado's 2nd choice, 51st overall, in 1995 Entry Draft).

			Regular Season					Playoffs				
Season	Club	Lea	GP	G	A	TP	PIM	GP	G	A	TP	PIM
1993-94	Detroit	OHL	63	9	18	27	32	17	1	2	3	13
1994-95	Detroit	OHL	11	1	3	4	16	21	5	7	12	16
1995-96	Detroit	OHL	60	26	33	59	78	16	8	10	18	35
1996-97	Hershey	AHL	34	4	3	7	51	....	....	....	....	....

BEAUFAIT, MARK

Center. Shoots right. 5'9", 170 lbs. Born, Livonia, MI, May 13, 1970.
(San Jose's 2nd choice, 7th overall, in 1991 Supplemental Draft).

			Regular Season					Playoffs				
Season	Club	Lea	GP	G	A	TP	PIM	GP	G	A	TP	PIM
1988-89	N. Michigan	WCHA	11	2	1	3	2	....	....	....	....	....
1989-90	N. Michigan	WCHA	34	10	14	24	12	....	....	....	....	....
1990-91	N. Michigan	WCHA	47	19	30	49	18	....	....	....	....	....
1991-92	N. Michigan	WCHA	39	31	44	75	43	....	....	....	....	....
1992-93	**San Jose**	**NHL**	**5**	**1**	**0**	**1**	**0**	....	....	....	....	....
	Kansas City	IHL	66	19	40	59	22	9	1	1	2	8
1993-94	U.S. National	....	51	22	29	51	36	....	....	....	....	....
	U.S. Olympic	....	8	1	4	5	2	....	....	....	....	....
	Kansas City	IHL	21	12	9	21	18	....	....	....	....	....
1994-95	San Diego	IHL	68	24	39	63	22	5	2	2	4	2
1995-96	Orlando	IHL	77	30	79	109	87	22	9	*19	*28	22
1996-97a	Orlando	IHL	80	26	65	91	63	10	5	8	13	18
	NHL Totals		**5**	**1**	**0**	**1**	**0**	....	....	....	....	....

a IHL Second All-Star Team (1997)

BEDDOES, CLAYTON — OTT.

Center. Shoots left. 5'11", 190 lbs. Born, Bentley, Alta., November 10, 1970.

			Regular Season					Playoffs				
Season	Club	Lea	GP	G	A	TP	PIM	GP	G	A	TP	PIM
1990-91	Lake Superior	CCHA	45	14	28	42	26	....	....	....	....	....
1991-92	Lake Superior	CCHA	38	14	26	40	24	....	....	....	....	....
1992-93	Lake Superior	CCHA	43	18	40	58	30	....	....	....	....	....
1993-94ab	Lake Superior	CCHA	44	23	31	54	56	....	....	....	....	....
1994-95	Providence	AHL	65	16	20	36	39	13	3	1	4	18
1995-96	**Boston**	**NHL**	**39**	**1**	**6**	**7**	**44**	....	....	....	....	....
	Providence	AHL	32	10	15	25	24	4	2	3	5	0
1996-97	**Boston**	**NHL**	**21**	**1**	**2**	**3**	**13**	....	....	....	....	....
	Providence	AHL	36	11	23	34	60	7	2	0	2	4
	NHL Totals		**60**	**2**	**8**	**10**	**57**	....	....	....	....	....

a CCHA Second All-Star Team (1994)
b NCAA West Second All-American Team (1994)

Signed as a free agent by **Boston**, June 2, 1994. Signed as a free agent by **Ottawa**, July 28, 1997.

BEERS, BOB

Defense. Shoots right. 6'2", 200 lbs. Born, Pittsburgh, PA, May 20, 1967.
(Boston's 10th choice, 210th overall, in 1985 Entry Draft).

			Regular Season					Playoffs				
Season	Club	Lea	GP	G	A	TP	PIM	GP	G	A	TP	PIM
1985-86	N. Arizona	NCAA	28	11	39	50	96	....	....	....	....	....
1986-87	U. of Maine	H.E.	38	0	13	13	45	....	....	....	....	....
1987-88	U. of Maine	H.E.	41	3	11	14	72	....	....	....	....	....
1988-89ab	U. of Maine	H.E.	44	10	27	37	53	....	....	....	....	....
1989-90	**Boston**	**NHL**	**3**	**0**	**1**	**1**	**6**	**14**	**1**	**1**	**2**	**18**
	Maine	AHL	74	7	36	43	63	....	....	....	....	....
1990-91	**Boston**	**NHL**	**16**	**0**	**1**	**1**	**10**	**6**	**0**	**0**	**0**	**4**
	Maine	AHL	36	2	16	18	21	....	....	....	....	....
1991-92	**Boston**	**NHL**	**31**	**0**	**5**	**5**	**29**	**1**	**0**	**0**	**0**	**0**
	Maine	AHL	33	6	23	29	24	....	....	....	....	....
1992-93	Providence	AHL	6	1	2	3	10	....	....	....	....	....
	Tampa Bay	**NHL**	**64**	**12**	**24**	**36**	**70**	....	....	....	....	....
	Atlanta	IHL	1	0	0	0	0	....	....	....	....	....
1993-94	**Tampa Bay**	**NHL**	**16**	**1**	**5**	**6**	**12**	....	....	....	....	....
	Edmonton	**NHL**	**66**	**10**	**27**	**37**	**74**	....	....	....	....	....
1994-95	**NY Islanders**	**NHL**	**22**	**2**	**7**	**9**	**6**	....	....	....	....	....
1995-96	**NY Islanders**	**NHL**	**13**	**0**	**5**	**5**	**10**	....	....	....	....	....
	Utah	IHL	65	6	36	42	54	22	1	12	13	16
1996-97	**Boston**	**NHL**	**27**	**3**	**4**	**7**	**8**	....	....	....	....	....
	Providence	AHL	45	10	12	22	18	....	....	....	....	....
	NHL Totals		**258**	**28**	**79**	**107**	**225**	**21**	**1**	**1**	**2**	**22**

a Hockey East Second All-Star Team (1989)
b NCAA East Second All-American Team (1989)

Traded to **Tampa Bay** by **Boston** for Stephane Richer, October 28, 1992. Traded to **Edmonton** by **Tampa Bay** for Chris Joseph, November 11, 1993. Signed as a free agent by **NY Islanders**, August 29, 1994. Signed as a free agent by **Boston**, August 5, 1996.

BEGIN, STEVE — (bay-ZHIN) CGY.

Center. Shoots left. 5'11", 180 lbs. Born, Trois-Rivieres, Que., June 14, 1978.
(Calgary's 3rd choice, 40th overall, in 1996 Entry Draft).

			Regular Season					Playoffs				
Season	Club	Lea	GP	G	A	TP	PIM	GP	G	A	TP	PIM
1995-96	Val d'Or	QMJHL	64	13	23	36	218	13	1	3	4	33
1996-97	Val d'Or	QMJHL	58	13	33	46	229	10	0	3	3	8
	Saint John	AHL	....	....	....	....	....	4	0	2	2	6

BEKAR, DEREK — ST.L.

Center. Shoots left. 6'3", 185 lbs. Born, Burnaby, B.C., September 15, 1975.
(St. Louis' 6th choice, 205th overall, in 1995 Entry Draft).

			Regular Season					Playoffs				
Season	Club	Lea	GP	G	A	TP	PIM	GP	G	A	TP	PIM
1995-96	N. Hampshire	H.E.	34	15	18	33	4	....	....	....	....	....
1996-97	N. Hampshire	H.E.	39	18	21	39	34	....	....	....	....	....

BELAK, GRAHAM — (BEE-lak) COL.

Defense. Shoots left. 6'4", 210 lbs. Born, Battleford, Sask., August 1, 1979.
(Colorado's 2nd choice, 53rd overall, in 1997 Entry Draft).

			Regular Season					Playoffs				
Season	Club	Lea	GP	G	A	TP	PIM	GP	G	A	TP	PIM
1995-96	N. Battleford	Midget	55	3	14	17	110	....	....	....	....	....
1996-97	Edmonton	WHL	61	3	5	8	251	....	....	....	....	....

BELAK, WADE — (BEE-lak) COL.

Defense. Shoots right. 6'4", 213 lbs. Born, Saskatoon, Sask., July 3, 1976.
(Quebec's 1st choice, 12th overall, in 1994 Entry Draft).

			Regular Season					Playoffs				
Season	Club	Lea	GP	G	A	TP	PIM	GP	G	A	TP	PIM
1992-93	N. Battleford	Midget	50	5	15	20	146	....	....	....	....	....
	Saskatoon	WHL	7	0	0	0	23	7	0	0	0	0
1993-94	Saskatoon	WHL	69	4	13	17	226	16	2	2	4	43
1994-95	Saskatoon	WHL	72	4	14	18	290	9	0	0	0	36
	Cornwall	AHL	....	....	....	....	....	11	1	2	3	40
1995-96	Saskatoon	WHL	63	3	15	18	207	4	0	0	0	9
	Cornwall	AHL	5	0	0	0	18	2	0	0	0	2
1996-97	**Colorado**	**NHL**	**5**	**0**	**0**	**0**	**11**	....	....	....	....	....
	Hershey	AHL	65	1	7	8	320	16	0	1	1	61
	NHL Totals		**5**	**0**	**0**	**0**	**11**	....	....	....	....	....

BELANGER, ERIC (buh-LAWN-zhay) L.A.

Center. Shoots left. 5'11", 170 lbs. Born, Sherbrooke, Que., December 16, 1977.
(Los Angeles' 5th choice, 96th overall, in 1996 Entry Draft).

			Regular Season					Playoffs				
Season	Club	Lea	GP	G	A	TP	PIM	GP	G	A	TP	PIM
1994-95	Beauport	QMJHL	71	12	28	40	24	18	5	9	14	25
1995-96	Beauport	QMJHL	59	35	38	83	18	20	13	14	27	6
1996-97	Beauport	QMJHL	21	10	30	40	22	....	....	....	....	....
	Rimouski	QMJHL	29	23	41	64	34	4	2	3	5	10

BELANGER, JESSE (buh-LAWN-zhay)

Center. Shoots right. 6'1", 190 lbs. Born, St. Georges de Beauce, Que., June 15, 1969.

			Regular Season					Playoffs				
Season	Club	Lea	GP	G	A	TP	PIM	GP	G	A	TP	PIM
1987-88	Granby	QMJHL	69	33	43	76	10	5	3	3	6	0
1988-89	Granby	QMJHL	67	40	63	103	26	4	0	5	5	0
1989-90	Granby	QMJHL	67	53	54	107	53	....	....	....	....	....
1990-91	Fredericton	AHL	75	40	58	98	30	6	2	4	6	0
1991-92	Montreal	NHL	4	0	0	0	0	....	....	....	....	....
	Fredericton	AHL	65	30	41	71	26	7	3	3	6	2
1992-93	Montreal	NHL	19	4	2	6	4	9	0	1	1	0 ♦
	Fredericton	AHL	39	19	32	51	24	....	....	....	....	....
1993-94	Florida	NHL	70	17	33	50	16	....	....	....	....	....
1994-95	Florida	NHL	47	15	14	29	18	....	....	....	....	....
1995-96	Florida	NHL	63	17	21	38	10	....	....	....	....	....
	Vancouver	NHL	9	3	0	3	4	3	0	2	2	2
1996-97	Edmonton	NHL	6	0	0	0	0	....	....	....	....	....
	Hamilton	AHL	6	4	3	7	0	....	....	....	....	....
	Quebec	IHL	47	34	28	62	18	9	3	5	8	13
	NHL Totals		218	56	70	126	52	12	0	3	3	2

Signed as a free agent by **Montreal**, October 3, 1990. Claimed by **Florida** from **Montreal** in Expansion Draft, June 24, 1993. Traded to **Vancouver** by **Florida** for Vancouver's third round choice (Oleg Kvasha) in 1996 Entry Draft and future considerations, March 20, 1996. Signed as a free agent by **Edmonton**, September 16, 1996.

BELANGER, KEN (buh-LAWN-zhay) NYI

Left wing. Shoots left. 6'4", 225 lbs. Born, Sault Ste. Marie, Ont., May 14, 1974.
(Hartford's 7th choice, 153rd overall, in 1992 Entry Draft).

			Regular Season					Playoffs				
Season	Club	Lea	GP	G	A	TP	PIM	GP	G	A	TP	PIM
1991-92	Ottawa	OHL	51	4	4	8	174	11	0	0	0	24
1992-93	Ottawa	OHL	34	6	12	18	139	....	....	....	....	....
	Guelph	OHL	29	10	14	24	86	5	2	1	3	14
1993-94	Guelph	OHL	55	11	22	33	185	9	2	3	5	30
1994-95	St. John's	AHL	47	5	5	10	246	4	0	0	0	30
	Toronto	NHL	3	0	0	0	9	....	....	....	....	....
1995-96	St. John's	AHL	40	16	14	30	222	....	....	....	....	....
	NY Islanders	NHL	7	0	0	0	27	....	....	....	....	....
1996-97	NY Islanders	NHL	18	0	2	2	102	....	....	....	....	....
	Kentucky	AHL	38	10	12	22	164	4	0	1	1	27
	NHL Totals		28	0	2	2	138	....	....	....	....	....

Traded to **Toronto** by **Hartford** for Toronto's ninth round choice (Matt Ball) in 1994 Entry Draft, March 18, 1994. Traded to **NY Islanders** by **Toronto** with Damian Rhodes for future considerations, January 23, 1996.

BELLOWS, BRIAN

Left wing. Shoots right. 5'11", 210 lbs. Born, St. Catharines, Ont., September 1, 1964.
(Minnesota's 1st choice, 2nd overall, in 1982 Entry Draft).

			Regular Season					Playoffs				
Season	Club	Lea	GP	G	A	TP	PIM	GP	G	A	TP	PIM
1980-81	Kitchener	OHA	66	49	67	116	23	16	14	13	27	13
1981-82ab	Kitchener	OHL	47	45	52	97	23	15	16	13	29	11
1982-83	Minnesota	NHL	78	35	30	65	27	9	5	4	9	18
1983-84	Minnesota	NHL	78	41	42	83	66	16	2	12	14	6
1984-85	Minnesota	NHL	78	26	36	62	72	9	2	4	6	9
1985-86	Minnesota	NHL	77	31	48	79	46	5	5	0	5	16
1986-87	Minnesota	NHL	65	26	27	53	34	....	....	....	....	....
1987-88	Minnesota	NHL	77	40	41	81	81	....	....	....	....	....
1988-89	Minnesota	NHL	60	23	27	50	55	5	2	3	5	8
1989-90c	Minnesota	NHL	80	55	44	99	72	7	4	3	7	10
1990-91	Minnesota	NHL	80	35	40	75	43	23	10	19	29	30
1991-92	Minnesota	NHL	80	30	45	75	41	7	4	4	8	14
1992-93	Montreal	NHL	82	40	48	88	44	18	6	9	15	18 ♦
1993-94	Montreal	NHL	77	33	38	71	36	6	1	2	3	2
1994-95	Montreal	NHL	41	8	8	16	8	....	....	....	....	....
1995-96	Tampa Bay	NHL	79	23	26	49	39	6	2	0	2	4
1996-97	Tampa Bay	NHL	7	1	2	3	0	....	....	....	....	....
	Anaheim	NHL	62	15	13	28	22	11	2	4	6	2
	NHL Totals		1101	462	515	977	686	122	45	64	109	137

a OHL First All-Star Team (1982)
b Won George Parsons Trophy (Memorial Cup Tournament Most Sportsmanlike Player) (1982)
c NHL Second All-Star Team (1990)

Played in NHL All-Star Game (1984, 1988, 1992)

Traded to **Montreal** by **Minnesota** for Russ Courtnall, August 31, 1992. Traded to **Tampa Bay** by **Montreal** for Marc Bureau, June 30, 1995. Traded to **Anaheim** by **Tampa Bay** for Anaheim's sixth round choice (Andrei Skopintsev) in 1997 Entry Draft, November 19, 1996.

BERANEK, JOSEF (buh-RAH-nehk, JOH-sehf) PIT.

Left wing. Shoots left. 6'2", 190 lbs. Born, Litvinov, Czechoslovakia, October 25, 1969.
(Edmonton's 3rd choice, 78th overall, in 1989 Entry Draft).

			Regular Season					Playoffs				
Season	Club	Lea	GP	G	A	TP	PIM	GP	G	A	TP	PIM
1987-88	Litvinov	Czech.	14	7	4	11	12	....	....	....	....	....
1988-89	Litvinov	Czech.	32	18	10	28	47	....	....	....	....	....
1989-90	Dukla Trencin	Czech.	49	19	23	42	....	....	....	....	....	....
1990-91	Litvinov	Czech.	58	29	31	60	98	....	....	....	....	....
1991-92	Edmonton	NHL	58	12	16	28	18	12	2	1	3	0
1992-93	Edmonton	NHL	26	2	6	8	28	....	....	....	....	....
	Cape Breton	AHL	6	1	2	3	8	....	....	....	....	....
	Philadelphia	NHL	40	13	12	25	50	....	....	....	....	....
1993-94	Philadelphia	NHL	80	28	21	49	85	....	....	....	....	....
1994-95	Vsetin	Czech.	16	7	7	14	26	....	....	....	....	....
	Philadelphia	NHL	14	5	5	10	2	....	....	....	....	....
	Vancouver	NHL	37	8	13	21	28	11	1	1	2	12
1995-96	Vancouver	NHL	61	6	14	20	60	3	2	1	3	0
1996-97	Vsetin	Czech.	39	19	24	43	115	3	3	2	5	4
	Pittsburgh	NHL	8	3	1	4	4	5	0	0	0	2
	NHL Totals		324	77	88	165	275	31	5	3	8	14

Traded to **Philadelphia** by **Edmonton** with Greg Hawgood for Brian Benning, January 16, 1993. Traded to **Vancouver** by **Philadelphia** for Shawn Antoski, February 15, 1995. Traded to **Pittsburgh** by **Vancouver** for future considerations, March 18, 1997.

BERARD, BRYAN NYI

Defense. Shoots left. 6'1", 190 lbs. Born, Woonsocket, RI, March 5, 1977.
(Ottawa's 1st choice, 1st overall, in 1995 Entry Draft).

			Regular Season					Playoffs				
Season	Club	Lea	GP	G	A	TP	PIM	GP	G	A	TP	PIM
1994-95abc	Detroit	OHL	58	20	55	75	97	21	4	20	24	38
1995-96abd	Detroit	OHL	56	31	58	89	116	17	7	18	25	41
1996-97ef	NY Islanders	NHL	82	8	40	48	86	....	....	....	....	....
	NHL Totals		82	8	40	48	86	....	....	....	....	....

a OHL First All-Star Team (1995, 1996)
b Canadian Major Junior First All-Star Team (1995, 1996)
c Canadian Major Junior Rookie of the Year (1995)
d Canadian Major Junior Defenseman of the Year (1996)
e NHL All-Rookie Team (1997)
f Won Calder Memorial Trophy (1997)

Traded to **NY Islanders** by **Ottawa** with Don Beaupre and Martin Straka for Damian Rhodes and Wade Redden, January 23, 1996.

BEREHOWSKY, DRAKE (beh-reh-HOW-skee)

Defense. Shoots right. 6'1", 211 lbs. Born, Toronto, Ont., January 3, 1972.
(Toronto's 1st choice, 10th overall, in 1990 Entry Draft).

			Regular Season					Playoffs				
Season	Club	Lea	GP	G	A	TP	PIM	GP	G	A	TP	PIM
1988-89	Kingston	OHL	63	7	39	46	85	....	....	....	....	....
	Cdn. National	....	1	0	0	0	0	....	....	....	....	....
1989-90	Kingston	OHL	9	3	11	14	28	....	....	....	....	....
1990-91	Toronto	NHL	8	0	1	1	25	....	....	....	....	....
	Kingston	OHL	13	5	13	18	38	....	....	....	....	....
	North Bay	OHL	26	7	23	30	51	10	2	7	9	21
1991-92	Toronto	NHL	1	0	0	0	0	....	....	....	....	....
ab	North Bay	OHL	62	19	63	82	147	21	7	24	31	22
	St. John's	AHL	....	....	....	....	....	6	0	5	5	21
1992-93	Toronto	NHL	41	4	15	19	61	....	....	....	....	....
	St. John's	AHL	28	10	17	27	38	....	....	....	....	....
1993-94	Toronto	NHL	49	2	8	10	63	....	....	....	....	....
	St. John's	AHL	18	3	12	15	40	....	....	....	....	....
1994-95	Toronto	NHL	25	0	2	2	15	....	....	....	....	....
	Pittsburgh	NHL	4	0	0	0	13	1	0	0	0	0
1995-96	Pittsburgh	NHL	1	0	0	0	0	....	....	....	....	....
	Cleveland	IHL	74	6	28	34	141	3	0	3	3	6
1996-97	Carolina	AHL	49	2	15	17	55	....	....	....	....	....
	San Antonio	IHL	16	3	4	7	36	....	....	....	....	....
	NHL Totals		129	6	26	32	177	1	0	0	0	0

a Canadian Major Junior Defenseman of the Year (1992)
b OHL First All-Star Team (1992)

Traded to **Pittsburgh** by **Toronto** for Grant Jennings, April 7, 1995.

BERENZWEIG, ANDY NYI

Defense. Shoots left. 6'2", 195 lbs. Born, Chicago, IL, August 8, 1977.
(NY Islanders' 5th choice, 109th overall, in 1996 Entry Draft).

			Regular Season					Playoffs				
Season	Club	Lea	GP	G	A	TP	PIM	GP	G	A	TP	PIM
1995-96	U. of Michigan	CCHA	42	4	8	12	4	....	....	....	....	....
1996-97	U. of Michigan	CCHA	38	7	12	19	49	....	....	....	....	....

BEREZIN, SERGEI (BEH-reh-zihn) TOR.

Right wing. Shoots right. 5'10", 187 lbs. Born, Voskresensk, USSR, November 5, 1971.
(Toronto's 8th choice, 256th overall, in 1994 Entry Draft).

			Regular Season					Playoffs				
Season	Club	Lea	GP	G	A	TP	PIM	GP	G	A	TP	PIM
1990-91	Khimik	USSR	30	6	2	8	4	....	....	....	....	....
1991-92	Khimik	CIS	36	7	5	12	10	....	....	....	....	....
1992-93	Khimik	CIS	38	9	3	12	12	2	1	0	1	0
1993-94	Khimik	CIS	40	31	10	41	16	3	2	0	2	2
1994-95	Koln	Ger.	43	38	19	57	8	18	17	8	25	14
1995-96	Koln	Ger.	45	49	31	80	8	14	13	9	22	10
1996-97a	Toronto	NHL	73	25	16	41	2	....	....	....	....	....
	NHL Totals		73	25	16	41	2	....	....	....	....	....

a NHL All-Rookie Team (1997)

BERG, AKI-PETTERI L.A.

Defense. Shoots left. 6'3", 198 lbs. Born, Turku, Finland, February 28, 1977.
(Los Angeles' 1st choice, 3rd overall, in 1995 Entry Draft).

			Regular Season					Playoffs				
Season	Club	Lea	GP	G	A	TP	PIM	GP	G	A	TP	PIM
1993-94	TPS	Fin.	6	0	6	6	4	....	....	....	....	....
1994-95	TPS	Fin.	5	0	0	0	4	....	....	....	....	....
	Kiekko-67	Fin. 2	28	3	9	12	34	....	....	....	....	....
1995-96	Los Angeles	NHL	51	0	7	7	29	....	....	....	....	....
	Phoenix	IHL	20	0	3	3	18	2	0	0	0	4
1996-97	Los Angeles	NHL	41	2	6	8	24	....	....	....	....	....
	Phoenix	IHL	23	1	3	4	21	....	....	....	....	....
	NHL Totals		92	2	13	15	53	....	....	....	....	....

BERG, BILL NYR

Left wing. Shoots left. 6'1", 205 lbs. Born, St. Catharines, Ont., October 21, 1967.
(NY Islanders' 3rd choice, 59th overall, in 1986 Entry Draft).

			Regular Season					Playoffs				
Season	Club	Lea	GP	G	A	TP	PIM	GP	G	A	TP	PIM
1985-86	Toronto	OHL	64	3	35	38	143	4	0	0	0	19
	Springfield	AHL	4	1	1	2	4	....	....	....	....	....
1986-87	Toronto	OHL	57	3	15	18	138	....	....	....	....	....
1987-88	Springfield	AHL	76	6	26	32	148	....	....	....	....	....
	Peoria	IHL	5	0	1	1	8	7	0	3	3	31
1988-89	NY Islanders	NHL	7	1	2	3	10	....	....	....	....	....
	Springfield	AHL	69	17	32	49	122	....	....	....	....	....
1989-90	Springfield	AHL	74	12	42	54	74	15	5	12	17	35
1990-91	NY Islanders	NHL	78	9	14	23	67	....	....	....	....	....
1991-92	NY Islanders	NHL	47	5	9	14	28	....	....	....	....	....
	Capital Dist.	AHL	3	0	2	2	16	....	....	....	....	....
1992-93	NY Islanders	NHL	22	6	3	9	49	....	....	....	....	....
	Toronto	NHL	58	7	8	15	54	21	1	1	2	18
1993-94	Toronto	NHL	83	8	11	19	93	18	1	2	3	10
1994-95	Toronto	NHL	32	5	1	6	26	7	0	1	1	4
1995-96	Toronto	NHL	23	1	1	2	33	....	....	....	....	....
	NY Rangers	NHL	18	2	1	3	8	10	1	0	1	0
1996-97	NY Rangers	NHL	67	8	6	14	37	3	0	0	0	2
	NHL Totals		435	52	56	108	405	59	3	4	7	34

Claimed on waivers by **Toronto** from **NY Islanders**, December 3, 1992. Traded to **NY Rangers** by **Toronto** for Nick Kypreos, February 29, 1996.

BERG, REGGIE — TOR.

Center. Shoots left. 5'10", 180 lbs. Born, Coon Rapids, MN, September 18, 1976.
(Toronto's 12th choice, 178th overall, in 1996 Entry Draft).

			Regular Season					Playoffs				
Season	Club	Lea	GP	G	A	TP	PIM	GP	G	A	TP	PIM
1995-96	U. Minnesota	WCHA	40	23	11	34	69	....	....	....	....	....
1996-97	U. Minnesota	WCHA	38	11	26	37	48	....	....	....	....	....

BERGEVIN, MARC (BUHR-zheh-vihn) — ST.L.

Defense. Shoots left. 6'1", 197 lbs. Born, Montreal, Que., August 11, 1965.
(Chicago's 3rd choice, 59th overall, in 1983 Entry Draft).

			Regular Season					Playoffs				
Season	Club	Lea	GP	G	A	TP	PIM	GP	G	A	TP	PIM
1982-83	Chicoutimi	QMJHL	64	3	27	30	113	....	....	....	....	....
1983-84	Chicoutimi	QMJHL	70	10	35	45	125	....	....	....	....	....
	Springfield	AHL	7	0	1	1	2	....	....	....	....	....
1984-85	Chicago	NHL	60	0	6	6	54	6	0	3	3	2
	Springfield	AHL	....	....	....	....	....	4	0	0	0	0
1985-86	Chicago	NHL	71	7	7	14	60	3	0	0	0	0
1986-87	Chicago	NHL	66	4	10	14	66	3	1	0	1	2
1987-88	Chicago	NHL	58	1	6	7	85	....	....	....	....	....
	Saginaw	IHL	10	2	7	9	20	....	....	....	....	....
1988-89	Chicago	NHL	11	0	0	0	18	....	....	....	....	....
	NY Islanders	NHL	58	2	13	15	62	....	....	....	....	....
1989-90	NY Islanders	NHL	18	0	4	4	30	....	....	....	....	....
	Springfield	AHL	47	7	16	23	66	17	2	11	13	16
1990-91	Capital Dist.	AHL	7	0	5	5	6	....	....	....	....	....
	Hartford	NHL	4	0	0	0	4	....	....	....	....	....
	Springfield	AHL	58	4	23	27	85	18	0	7	7	26
1991-92	Hartford	NHL	75	7	17	24	64	5	0	0	0	2
1992-93	Tampa Bay	NHL	78	2	12	14	66	....	....	....	....	....
1993-94	Tampa Bay	NHL	83	1	15	16	87	....	....	....	....	....
1994-95	Tampa Bay	NHL	44	2	4	6	51	....	....	....	....	....
1995-96	Detroit	NHL	70	1	9	10	33	17	1	0	1	14
1996-97	St. Louis	NHL	82	0	4	4	53	6	1	0	1	8
	NHL Totals		778	27	107	134	733	40	3	3	6	28

Traded to **NY Islanders** by **Chicago** with Gary Nylund for Steve Konroyd and Bob Bassen, November 25, 1988. Traded to **Hartford** by **NY Islanders** for Hartford's fifth round choice (Ryan Duthie) in 1992 Entry Draft, October 30, 1990. Signed as a free agent by **Tampa Bay**, July 9, 1992. Traded to **Detroit** by **Tampa Bay** with Ben Hankinson for Shawn Burr and Detroit's third round choice (later traded to Boston — Boston selected Jason Doyle) in 1996 Entry Draft, August 17, 1995. Signed as a free agent by **St. Louis**, July 31, 1996.

BERGKVIST, STEFAN — PIT.

Defense. Shoots left. 6'2", 224 lbs. Born, Leksand, Sweden, March 10, 1975.
(Pittsburgh's 1st choice, 26th overall, in 1993 Entry Draft).

			Regular Season					Playoffs				
Season	Club	Lea	GP	G	A	TP	PIM	GP	G	A	TP	PIM
1992-93	Leksand	Swe.	15	0	0	0	6	....	....	....	....	....
1993-94	Leksand	Swe.	6	0	0	0	0	....	....	....	....	....
1994-95	London	OHL	64	3	17	20	93	4	0	0	0	5
1995-96	Pittsburgh	NHL	2	0	0	0	2	4	0	0	0	2
	Cleveland	IHL	61	2	8	10	58	3	0	0	0	14
1996-97	Pittsburgh	NHL	5	0	0	0	7	....	....	....	....	....
	Cleveland	IHL	33	0	1	1	54	4	0	0	0	0
	NHL Totals		7	0	0	0	9	4	0	0	0	2

BERGMAN, PETER — PIT.

Center. Shoots left. 6'1", 195 lbs. Born, Regina, Sask., April 14, 1978.
(Pittsburgh's 6th choice, 150th overall, in 1996 Entry Draft).

			Regular Season					Playoffs				
Season	Club	Lea	GP	G	A	TP	PIM	GP	G	A	TP	PIM
1995-96	Kamloops	WHL	53	8	7	15	23	10	1	2	3	10
1996-97	Kamloops	WHL	3	0	1	1	4	....	....	....	....	....
	Calgary	WHL	61	10	17	27	57	....	....	....	....	....

BERRY, BRAD

Defense. Shoots left. 6'2", 190 lbs. Born, Bashaw, Alta., April 1, 1965.
(Winnipeg's 3rd choice, 29th overall, in 1983 Entry Draft).

			Regular Season					Playoffs				
Season	Club	Lea	GP	G	A	TP	PIM	GP	G	A	TP	PIM
1983-84	North Dakota	WCHA	32	2	7	9	8	....	....	....	....	....
1984-85	North Dakota	WCHA	40	4	26	30	26	....	....	....	....	....
1985-86	North Dakota	WCHA	40	6	29	35	26	....	....	....	....	....
	Winnipeg	NHL	13	1	0	1	10	3	0	0	0	0
1986-87	Winnipeg	NHL	52	2	8	10	60	7	0	1	1	14
1987-88	Winnipeg	NHL	48	0	6	6	75	....	....	....	....	....
	Moncton	AHL	10	1	3	4	14	....	....	....	....	....
1988-89	Winnipeg	NHL	38	0	9	9	45	....	....	....	....	....
	Moncton	AHL	38	3	16	19	39	....	....	....	....	....
1989-90	Winnipeg	NHL	12	1	2	3	6	1	0	0	0	0
	Moncton	AHL	38	1	9	10	58	....	....	....	....	....
1990-91	Brynas	Swe.	38	3	1	4	38	....	....	....	....	....
	Cdn. National	....	4	0	1	1	0	....	....	....	....	....
1991-92	Minnesota	NHL	7	0	0	0	6	2	0	0	0	2
	Kalamazoo	IHL	65	5	18	23	90	5	2	0	2	6
1992-93	Minnesota	NHL	63	0	3	3	109	....	....	....	....	....
1993-94	Dallas	NHL	8	0	0	0	12	....	....	....	....	....
	Kalamazoo	IHL	45	3	19	22	91	1	0	0	0	0
1994-95	Kalamazoo	IHL	65	4	11	15	146	1	0	0	0	0
1995-96	Michigan	IHL	80	4	13	17	73	10	0	5	5	12
1996-97	Michigan	IHL	77	4	7	11	68	4	0	0	0	4
	NHL Totals		241	4	28	32	323	13	0	1	1	16

Signed as a free agent by **Minnesota**, October 4, 1991.

BERRY, RICK — COL.

Defense. Shoots left. 6'1", 192 lbs. Born, Brandon, Man., November 4, 1978.
(Colorado's 3rd choice, 55th overall, in 1997 Entry Draft).

			Regular Season					Playoffs				
Season	Club	Lea	GP	G	A	TP	PIM	GP	G	A	TP	PIM
1995-96	Seattle	WHL	59	4	9	13	103	1	0	0	0	0
1996-97	Seattle	WHL	72	12	21	33	125	15	3	7	10	23

BERTRAND, ERIC — N.J.

Left wing. Shoots left. 6'1", 205 lbs. Born, St. Ephrem, Que., April 16, 1975.
(New Jersey's 9th choice, 207th overall, in 1994 Entry Draft).

			Regular Season					Playoffs				
Season	Club	Lea	GP	G	A	TP	PIM	GP	G	A	TP	PIM
1992-93	Granby	QMJHL	64	10	15	25	82	....	....	....	....	....
1993-94	Granby	QMJHL	60	11	15	26	151	6	1	0	1	18
1994-95	Granby	QMJHL	56	14	26	40	268	13	3	8	11	50
1995-96	Albany	AHL	70	16	13	29	199	4	0	0	0	6
1996-97	Albany	AHL	77	16	27	43	204	8	3	3	6	15

BERTUZZI, TODD (buhr-TOO-zee) — NYI

Center. Shoots left. 6'3", 224 lbs. Born, Sudbury, Ont., February 2, 1975.
(NY Islanders' 1st choice, 23rd overall, in 1993 Entry Draft).

			Regular Season					Playoffs				
Season	Club	Lea	GP	G	A	TP	PIM	GP	G	A	TP	PIM
1991-92	Guelph	OHL	47	7	14	21	145	....	....	....	....	....
1992-93	Guelph	OHL	59	27	32	59	164	5	2	2	4	6
1993-94	Guelph	OHL	61	28	54	82	165	9	2	6	8	30
1994-95a	Guelph	OHL	62	54	65	119	58	14	*15	18	33	41
1995-96	NY Islanders	NHL	76	18	21	39	83	....	....	....	....	....
1996-97	NY Islanders	NHL	64	10	13	23	68	....	....	....	....	....
	Utah	IHL	13	5	5	10	16	....	....	....	....	....
	NHL Totals		140	28	34	62	151	....	....	....	....	....

a OHL Second All-Star team (1995)

BERUBE, CRAIG (buh-ROO-bee) — WSH.

Left wing. Shoots left. 6'1", 205 lbs. Born, Calahoo, Alta., December 17, 1965.

			Regular Season					Playoffs				
Season	Club	Lea	GP	G	A	TP	PIM	GP	G	A	TP	PIM
1982-83	Kamloops	WHL	4	0	0	0	0	....	....	....	....	....
1983-84	N. Westminster	WHL	70	11	20	31	104	8	1	2	3	5
1984-85	N. Westminster	WHL	70	25	44	69	191	10	3	2	5	4
1985-86	Kamloops	WHL	32	17	14	31	119	....	....	....	....	....
	Medicine Hat	WHL	34	14	16	30	95	25	7	8	15	102
1986-87	Philadelphia	NHL	7	0	0	0	57	5	0	0	0	17
	Hershey	AHL	63	7	17	24	325	....	....	....	....	....
1987-88	Philadelphia	NHL	27	3	2	5	108	....	....	....	....	....
	Hershey	AHL	31	5	9	14	119	....	....	....	....	....
1988-89	Philadelphia	NHL	53	1	1	2	199	16	0	0	0	56
	Hershey	AHL	7	0	2	2	19	....	....	....	....	....
1989-90	Philadelphia	NHL	74	4	14	18	291	....	....	....	....	....
1990-91	Philadelphia	NHL	74	8	9	17	293	....	....	....	....	....
1991-92	Toronto	NHL	40	5	7	12	109	....	....	....	....	....
	Calgary	NHL	36	1	4	5	155	....	....	....	....	....
1992-93	Calgary	NHL	77	4	8	12	209	6	0	1	1	21
1993-94	Washington	NHL	84	7	7	14	305	8	0	0	0	21
1994-95	Washington	NHL	43	2	4	6	173	7	0	0	0	29
1995-96	Washington	NHL	50	2	10	12	151	2	0	0	0	19
1996-97	Washington	NHL	80	4	3	7	218	....	....	....	....	....
	NHL Totals		645	41	69	110	2268	44	0	1	1	163

Signed as a free agent by **Philadelphia**, March 19, 1986. Traded to **Edmonton** by **Philadelphia** with Craig Fisher and Scott Mellanby for Dave Brown, Corey Foster and Jari Kurri, May 30, 1991. Traded to **Toronto** by **Edmonton** with Grant Fuhr and Glenn Anderson for Vincent Damphousse, Peter Ing, Scott Thornton, Luke Richardson, future considerations and cash, September 19, 1991. Traded to **Calgary** by **Toronto** with Alexander Godynyuk, Gary Leeman, Michel Petit and Jeff Reese for Doug Gilmour, Jamie Macoun, Ric Nattress, Rick Wamsley and Kent Manderville, January 2, 1992. Traded to **Washington** by **Calgary** for Washington's fifth round choice (Darryl Lafrance) in 1993 Entry Draft, June 26, 1993.

BETIK, KAREL (BEH-tihk, KAHR-ehl) — T.B.

Defense. Shoots left. 6'2", 208 lbs. Born, Karvina, Czech., October 28, 1978.
(Tampa Bay's 6th choice, 112th overall, in 1997 Entry Draft).

			Regular Season					Playoffs				
Season	Club	Lea	GP	G	A	TP	PIM	GP	G	A	TP	PIM
1995-96	Vitkovice	Czech. Jr.	48	3	12	15	88	....	....	....	....	....
1996-97	Kelowna	WHL	56	3	10	13	76	6	1	1	2	2

BEUKEBOOM, JEFF (BOO-kuh-BOOM) — NYR

Defense. Shoots right. 6'5", 230 lbs. Born, Ajax, Ont., March 28, 1965.
(Edmonton's 1st choice, 19th overall, in 1983 Entry Draft).

			Regular Season					Playoffs				
Season	Club	Lea	GP	G	A	TP	PIM	GP	G	A	TP	PIM
1982-83	S.S. Marie	OHL	70	0	25	25	143	16	1	4	5	46
1983-84	S.S. Marie	OHL	61	6	30	36	178	16	1	7	8	43
1984-85a	S.S. Marie	OHL	37	4	20	24	85	16	4	6	10	47
1985-86	Nova Scotia	AHL	77	9	20	29	175	....	....	....	....	....
	Edmonton	NHL	....	....	....	....	....	1	0	0	0	4
1986-87	Edmonton	NHL	44	3	8	11	124	....	....	....	....	.... ♦
	Nova Scotia	AHL	14	1	7	8	35	....	....	....	....	....
1987-88	Edmonton	NHL	73	5	20	25	201	7	0	0	0	16 ♦
1988-89	Edmonton	NHL	36	0	5	5	94	1	0	0	0	2
	Cape Breton	AHL	8	0	4	4	36	....	....	....	....	....
1989-90	Edmonton	NHL	46	1	12	13	86	2	0	0	0	0 ♦
1990-91	Edmonton	NHL	67	3	7	10	150	18	1	3	4	28
1991-92	Edmonton	NHL	18	0	5	5	78	....	....	....	....	....
	NY Rangers	NHL	56	1	10	11	122	13	2	3	5	47
1992-93	NY Rangers	NHL	82	2	17	19	153	....	....	....	....	....
1993-94	NY Rangers	NHL	68	8	8	16	170	22	0	6	6	50 ♦
1994-95	NY Rangers	NHL	44	1	3	4	70	9	0	0	0	10
1995-96	NY Rangers	NHL	82	3	11	14	220	11	0	3	3	6
1996-97	NY Rangers	NHL	80	3	9	12	167	15	0	1	1	34
	NHL Totals		696	30	115	145	1635	99	3	16	19	197

a OHL First All-Star Team (1985)

Traded to **NY Rangers** by **Edmonton** for David Shaw, November 12, 1991.

BIALOWAS, FRANK (bigh-uh-LOH-uhs) **PHI.**

Left wing. Shoots left. 5'11", 220 lbs. Born, Winnipeg, Man., September 25, 1970.

			Regular Season					Playoffs				
Season	Club	Lea	GP	G	A	TP	PIM	GP	G	A	TP	PIM
1991-92	Roanoke	ECHL	23	4	2	6	150	3	0	0	0	4
1992-93	Richmond	ECHL	60	3	18	21	261	1	0	0	0	2
	St. John's	AHL	7	1	0	1	28	1	0	0	0	0
1993-94	St. John's	AHL	69	2	8	10	352	7	0	3	3	25
	Toronto	**NHL**	**3**	**0**	**0**	**0**	**12**	....	....	....	....	....
1994-95	St. John's	AHL	51	2	3	5	277	4	0	0	0	12
1995-96	Portland	AHL	65	4	3	7	211	7	0	0	0	42
1996-97	Philadelphia	AHL	67	7	6	13	254	6	0	2	2	41
	NHL Totals		**3**	**0**	**0**	**0**	**12**	....	....	....	....	....

Signed as a free agent by **Toronto**, March 20, 1994. Signed as a free agent by **Washington**, September 8, 1995. Traded to **Philadelphia** by **Washington** for future considerations, July 18, 1996.

BICANEK, RADIM (BEE-chah-nehk) **OTT.**

Defense. Shoots left. 6'1", 195 lbs. Born, Uherske Hradiste, Czech., January 18, 1975.
(Ottawa's 2nd choice, 27th overall, in 1993 Entry Draft).

			Regular Season					Playoffs				
Season	Club	Lea	GP	G	A	TP	PIM	GP	G	A	TP	PIM
1992-93	Dukla Jihlava	Czech.	43	2	3	5	....	....	....	....	....	....
1993-94	Belleville	OHL	63	16	27	43	49	12	2	8	10	21
1994-95	Belleville	OHL	49	13	26	39	61	16	6	5	11	30
	Ottawa	**NHL**	**6**	**0**	**0**	**0**	**0**	....	....	....	....	....
	P.E.I.	AHL	....	....	....	....	....	3	0	1	1	0
1995-96	P.E.I.	AHL	74	7	19	26	87	5	0	2	2	6
1996-97	**Ottawa**	**NHL**	**21**	**0**	**1**	**1**	**8**	**7**	**0**	**0**	**0**	**8**
	Worcester	AHL	44	1	15	16	22	....	....	....	....	....
	NHL Totals		**27**	**0**	**1**	**1**	**8**	**7**	**0**	**0**	**0**	**8**

BICEK, JIRI (bee-CHEHK, YEH-ree) **N.J.**

Left wing. Shoots left. 5'11", 183 lbs. Born, Kosice, Czech., December 3, 1978.
(New Jersey's 4th choice, 131st overall, in 1997 Entry Draft).

			Regular Season					Playoffs				
Season	Club	Lea	GP	G	A	TP	PIM	GP	G	A	TP	PIM
1995-96	Kosice	Slovak	30	10	15	25	16	9	2	4	6	0
1996-97	Kosice	Slovak	44	11	14	25	20	7	1	3	4	....

BIENVENUE, DANIEL (bee-ehn-veh-nyoo) **BUF.**

Left wing. Shoots left. 6', 196 lbs. Born, Val d'Or, Que., June 10, 1977.
(Buffalo's 8th choice, 123rd overall, in 1995 Entry Draft).

			Regular Season					Playoffs				
Season	Club	Lea	GP	G	A	TP	PIM	GP	G	A	TP	PIM
1993-94	Chicoutimi	QMJHL	42	2	7	9	4	....	....	....	....	....
1994-95	Val d'Or	QMJHL	67	27	14	41	40	....	....	....	....	....
1995-96	Val d'Or	QMJHL	67	30	42	72	65	13	6	1	7	0
1996-97	Val d'Or	QMJHL	20	4	4	8	22	13	6	6	12	19

BIGGS, DON

Center. Shoots right. 5'8", 185 lbs. Born, Mississauga, Ont., April 7, 1965.
(Minnesota's 9th choice, 156th overall, in 1983 Entry Draft).

			Regular Season					Playoffs				
Season	Club	Lea	GP	G	A	TP	PIM	GP	G	A	TP	PIM
1982-83	Oshawa	OHL	70	22	53	75	145	16	3	6	9	17
1983-84	Oshawa	OHL	58	31	60	91	149	7	4	4	8	18
1984-85	**Minnesota**	**NHL**	**1**	**0**	**0**	**0**	**0**	....	....	....	....	....
	Springfield	AHL	6	0	3	3	0	2	1	0	1	0
	Oshawa	OHL	60	48	69	117	105	5	3	4	7	6
1985-86	Springfield	AHL	28	15	16	31	46	....	....	....	....	....
	Nova Scotia	AHL	47	6	23	29	36	....	....	....	....	....
1986-87	Nova Scotia	AHL	80	22	25	47	165	5	1	2	3	4
1987-88	Hershey	AHL	77	38	41	79	151	12	5	*11	*16	22
1988-89	Hershey	AHL	76	36	67	103	158	11	5	9	14	30
1989-90	**Philadelphia**	**NHL**	**11**	**2**	**0**	**2**	**8**	....	....	....	....	....
	Hershey	AHL	66	39	53	92	125	....	....	....	....	....
1990-91	Rochester	AHL	65	31	57	88	115	15	9	*14	*23	14
1991-92	Binghamton	AHL	74	32	50	82	122	11	3	7	10	8
1992-93abc	Binghamton	AHL	78	54	*84	*138	112	14	3	9	12	32
1993-94	Cincinnati	IHL	80	30	59	89	128	11	8	9	17	29
1994-95	Cincinnati	IHL	77	27	49	76	152	10	1	9	10	29
1995-96	Cincinnati	IHL	82	27	57	84	160	17	9	10	19	24
1996-97	Cincinnati	IHL	82	25	41	66	128	3	1	2	3	19
	NHL Totals		**12**	**2**	**0**	**2**	**8**	....	....	....	....	....

a Won Les Cunningham Plaque (MVP - AHL) (1993)
b Won John B. Sollenberger Trophy (Top Scorer - AHL) (1993)
c AHL First All-Star Team (1993)

Traded to **Edmonton** by **Minnesota** with Gord Sherven for Marc Habscheid, Don Barber and Emanuel Viveiros, December 20, 1985. Signed as a free agent by **Philadelphia**, July 17, 1987. Traded to **NY Rangers** by **Philadelphia** for future considerations, August 8, 1991.

BILOTTO, NICHOLAS (BIHL-awt-oh) **ST.L.**

Defense. Shoots right. 6'2", 198 lbs. Born, Montreal, Que., February 24, 1979.
(St. Louis' 5th choice, 149th overall, in 1997 Entry Draft).

			Regular Season					Playoffs				
Season	Club	Lea	GP	G	A	TP	PIM	GP	G	A	TP	PIM
1996-97	Beauport	QMJHL	29	3	2	5	28	4	0	1	1	2

BLACK, JAMES **CHI.**

Center. Shoots left. 6', 202 lbs. Born, Regina, Sask., August 15, 1969.
(Hartford's 4th choice, 94th overall, in 1989 Entry Draft).

			Regular Season					Playoffs				
Season	Club	Lea	GP	G	A	TP	PIM	GP	G	A	TP	PIM
1987-88	Portland	WHL	72	30	50	80	50	....	....	....	....	....
1988-89	Portland	WHL	71	45	51	96	57	19	13	6	19	28
1989-90	**Hartford**	**NHL**	**1**	**0**	**0**	**0**	**0**	....	....	....	....	....
	Binghamton	AHL	80	37	35	72	34	....	....	....	....	....
1990-91	**Hartford**	**NHL**	**1**	**0**	**0**	**0**	**0**	....	....	....	....	....
	Springfield	AHL	79	35	61	96	34	18	9	9	18	6
1991-92	**Hartford**	**NHL**	**30**	**4**	**6**	**10**	**10**	....	....	....	....	....
	Springfield	AHL	47	15	25	40	33	10	3	2	5	18
1992-93	**Minnesota**	**NHL**	**10**	**2**	**1**	**3**	**4**	....	....	....	....	....
	Kalamazoo	IHL	63	25	45	70	40	....	....	....	....	....
1993-94	**Dallas**	**NHL**	**13**	**2**	**3**	**5**	**2**	....	....	....	....	....
	Buffalo	**NHL**	**2**	**0**	**0**	**0**	**0**	....	....	....	....	....
	Rochester	AHL	45	19	32	51	28	4	2	3	5	0
1994-95	Las Vegas	IHL	78	29	44	73	54	10	1	6	7	4
1995-96	**Chicago**	**NHL**	**13**	**3**	**3**	**6**	**16**	**8**	**1**	**0**	**1**	**2**
	Indianapolis	IHL	67	32	50	82	56	....	....	....	....	....
1996-97	**Chicago**	**NHL**	**64**	**12**	**11**	**23**	**20**	**5**	**1**	**1**	**2**	**2**
	NHL Totals		**134**	**23**	**24**	**47**	**52**	**13**	**2**	**1**	**3**	**4**

Traded to **Minnesota** by **Hartford** for Mark Janssens, September 3, 1992. Traded to **Buffalo** by **Dallas** with Dallas' seventh round choice (Steve Webb) in 1994 Entry Draft for Gord Donnelly, December 15, 1993. Signed as a free agent by **Chicago**, September 18, 1995.

BLACK, JESSE **L.A.**

Defense. Shoots right. 6'4", 197 lbs. Born, Thunder Bay, Ont., June 23, 1978.
(Los Angeles' 6th choice, 120th overall, in 1996 Entry Draft).

			Regular Season					Playoffs				
Season	Club	Lea	GP	G	A	TP	PIM	GP	G	A	TP	PIM
1995-96	Niagara Falls	OHL	59	1	3	4	27	10	0	2	2	0
1996-97	Erie	OHL	60	1	12	13	102	5	0	1	1	0

BLAKE, ROB **L.A.**

Defense. Shoots right. 6'3", 215 lbs. Born, Simcoe, Ont., December 10, 1969.
(Los Angeles' 4th choice, 70th overall, in 1988 Entry Draft).

			Regular Season					Playoffs				
Season	Club	Lea	GP	G	A	TP	PIM	GP	G	A	TP	PIM
1987-88	Bowling Green	CCHA	43	5	8	13	88	....	....	....	....	....
1988-89a	Bowling Green	CCHA	46	11	21	32	140	....	....	....	....	....
1989-90bc	Bowling Green	CCHA	42	23	36	59	140	....	....	....	....	....
	Los Angeles	**NHL**	**4**	**0**	**0**	**0**	**4**	**8**	**1**	**3**	**4**	**4**
1990-91d	**Los Angeles**	**NHL**	**75**	**12**	**34**	**46**	**125**	**12**	**1**	**4**	**5**	**26**
1991-92	**Los Angeles**	**NHL**	**57**	**7**	**13**	**20**	**102**	**6**	**2**	**1**	**3**	**12**
1992-93	**Los Angeles**	**NHL**	**76**	**16**	**43**	**59**	**152**	**23**	**4**	**6**	**10**	**46**
1993-94	**Los Angeles**	**NHL**	**84**	**20**	**48**	**68**	**137**	....	....	....	....	....
1994-95	**Los Angeles**	**NHL**	**24**	**4**	**7**	**11**	**38**	....	....	....	....	....
1995-96	**Los Angeles**	**NHL**	**6**	**1**	**2**	**3**	**8**	....	....	....	....	....
1996-97	**Los Angeles**	**NHL**	**62**	**8**	**23**	**31**	**82**	....	....	....	....	....
	NHL Totals		**388**	**68**	**170**	**238**	**648**	**49**	**8**	**14**	**22**	**88**

a CCHA Second All-Star Team (1989)
b CCHA First All-Star Team (1990)
c NCAA West First All-American Team (1990)
d NHL/Upper Deck All-Rookie Team (1991)

Played in NHL All-Star Game (1994)

BLANCHARD, SEAN **L.A.**

Defense. Shoots left. 6', 201 lbs. Born, Sudbury, Ont., March 29, 1978.
(Los Angeles' 5th choice, 99th overall, in 1997 Entry Draft).

			Regular Season					Playoffs				
Season	Club	Lea	GP	G	A	TP	PIM	GP	G	A	TP	PIM
1994-95	Ottawa	OHL	59	2	5	7	24	....	....	....	....	....
1995-96	Ottawa	OHL	64	7	29	36	49	4	1	3	4	7
1996-97abc	Ottawa	OHL	66	11	57	68	64	24	3	15	18	34

a OHL First All-Star Team (1997)
b Canadian Major Junior First All-Star Team (1997)
c Canadian Major Junior Defenseman of the Year (1997)

BLOEMBERG, JEFF (BLOOM-buhrg)

Defense. Shoots right. 6'2", 205 lbs. Born, Listowel, Ont., January 31, 1968.
(NY Rangers' 5th choice, 93rd overall, in 1986 Entry Draft).

			Regular Season					Playoffs				
Season	Club	Lea	GP	G	A	TP	PIM	GP	G	A	TP	PIM
1985-86	North Bay	OHL	60	2	11	13	76	8	1	2	3	9
1986-87	North Bay	OHL	60	5	13	18	91	21	1	6	7	13
1987-88	Colorado	IHL	5	0	0	0	0	11	1	0	1	8
	North Bay	OHL	46	9	26	35	60	4	1	4	5	2
1988-89	**NY Rangers**	**NHL**	**9**	**0**	**0**	**0**	**0**	....	....	....	....	....
	Denver	IHL	64	7	22	29	55	1	0	0	0	0
1989-90	**NY Rangers**	**NHL**	**28**	**3**	**3**	**6**	**25**	**7**	**0**	**3**	**3**	**5**
	Flint	IHL	41	7	14	21	24	....	....	....	....	....
1990-91	**NY Rangers**	**NHL**	**3**	**0**	**2**	**2**	**0**	....	....	....	....	....
a	Binghamton	AHL	77	16	46	62	28	10	0	6	6	10
1991-92	**NY Rangers**	**NHL**	**3**	**0**	**1**	**1**	**0**	....	....	....	....	....
	Binghamton	AHL	66	6	41	47	22	11	1	10	11	10
1992-93	Cape Breton	AHL	76	6	45	51	34	16	5	10	15	10
1993-94	Springfield	AHL	78	8	28	36	36	6	0	3	3	8
1994-95	Adirondack	AHL	44	5	19	24	10	4	0	0	0	0
1995-96	Adirondack	AHL	72	10	28	38	32	3	0	1	1	4
1996-97	Adirondack	AHL	69	5	31	36	24	4	0	3	3	2
	NHL Totals		**43**	**3**	**6**	**9**	**25**	**7**	**0**	**3**	**3**	**5**

a AHL Second All-Star Team (1991)

Claimed by **Tampa Bay** from **NY Rangers** in Expansion Draft, June 18, 1992. Traded to **Edmonton** by **Tampa Bay** for future considerations, September 25, 1992. Signed as a free agent by **Hartford**, August 9, 1993. Signed as a free agent by **Detroit**, May 9, 1995.

BLOUIN, SYLVAIN (bluh-WEHN) NYR

Left wing. Shoots left. 6'2", 207 lbs. Born, Montreal, Que., May 21, 1974.
(NY Rangers' 5th choice, 104th overall, in 1994 Entry Draft).

			Regular Season					Playoffs				
Season	Club	Lea	GP	G	A	TP	PIM	GP	G	A	TP	PIM
1991-92	Laval	QMJHL	28	0	0	0	23	9	0	0	0	35
1992-93	Laval	QMJHL	68	0	10	10	373	13	1	0	1	*66
1993-94	Laval	QMJHL	62	18	22	40	*492	21	4	13	17	*177
1994-95	Chicago	IHL	1	0	0	0	2	....	....	....	....	....
	Charlotte	ECHL	50	5	7	12	280	3	0	0	0	6
	Binghamton	AHL	10	1	0	1	46	2	0	0	0	24
1995-96	Binghamton	AHL	71	5	8	13	*352	4	0	3	3	4
1996-97	**NY Rangers**	**NHL**	**6**	**0**	**0**	**0**	**18**	....	....	....	....	....
	Binghamton	AHL	62	13	17	30	301	4	2	1	3	16
	NHL Totals		**6**	**0**	**0**	**0**	**18**	....	....	....	....	....

BODGER, DOUG S.J.

Defense. Shoots left. 6'2", 210 lbs. Born, Chemainus, B.C., June 18, 1966.
(Pittsburgh's 2nd choice, 9th overall, in 1984 Entry Draft).

			Regular Season					Playoffs				
Season	Club	Lea	GP	G	A	TP	PIM	GP	G	A	TP	PIM
1982-83a	Kamloops	WHL	72	26	66	92	98	7	0	5	5	2
1983-84	Kamloops	WHL	70	21	77	98	90	17	2	15	17	12
1984-85	**Pittsburgh**	**NHL**	**65**	**5**	**26**	**31**	**67**	....	....	....	....	....
1985-86	**Pittsburgh**	**NHL**	**79**	**4**	**33**	**37**	**63**	....	....	....	....	....
1986-87	**Pittsburgh**	**NHL**	**76**	**11**	**38**	**49**	**52**	....	....	....	....	....
1987-88	**Pittsburgh**	**NHL**	**69**	**14**	**31**	**45**	**103**	....	....	....	....	....
1988-89	**Pittsburgh**	**NHL**	**10**	**1**	**4**	**5**	**7**	....	....	....	....	....
	Buffalo	**NHL**	**61**	**7**	**40**	**47**	**52**	**5**	**1**	**1**	**2**	**11**
1989-90	**Buffalo**	**NHL**	**71**	**12**	**36**	**48**	**64**	**6**	**1**	**5**	**6**	**6**
1990-91	**Buffalo**	**NHL**	**58**	**5**	**23**	**28**	**54**	**4**	**0**	**1**	**1**	**0**
1991-92	**Buffalo**	**NHL**	**73**	**11**	**35**	**46**	**108**	**7**	**2**	**1**	**3**	**2**
1992-93	**Buffalo**	**NHL**	**81**	**9**	**45**	**54**	**87**	**8**	**2**	**3**	**5**	**0**
1993-94	**Buffalo**	**NHL**	**75**	**7**	**32**	**39**	**76**	**7**	**0**	**3**	**3**	**6**
1994-95	**Buffalo**	**NHL**	**44**	**3**	**17**	**20**	**47**	**5**	**0**	**4**	**4**	**0**
1995-96	**Buffalo**	**NHL**	**16**	**0**	**5**	**5**	**18**	....	....	....	....	....
	San Jose	**NHL**	**57**	**4**	**19**	**23**	**50**	....	....	....	....	....
1996-97	**San Jose**	**NHL**	**81**	**1**	**15**	**16**	**64**	....	....	....	....	....
	NHL Totals		**916**	**94**	**399**	**493**	**912**	**42**	**6**	**18**	**24**	**25**

a WHL Second All-Star Team (1983)

Traded to **Buffalo** by **Pittsburgh** wih Darrin Shannon for Tom Barrasso and Buffalo's third round choice (Joe Dziedzic) in 1990 Entry Draft, November 12, 1988. Traded to **San Jose** by **Buffalo** for an optional first round choice in 1996 Entry Draft, Philadelphia's fourth round choice (previously acquired by San Jose — Buffalo selected Mike Martone) in 1996 Entry Draft, Vaclav Varada and Martin Spanhel, November 16, 1995.

BODTKER, STEWART (BAWD-kuhr) VAN.

Center. Shoots right. 6'1", 185 lbs. Born, Vancouver, B.C., September 15, 1976.
(Vancouver's 7th choice, 174th overall, in 1995 Entry Draft).

			Regular Season					Playoffs				
Season	Club	Lea	GP	G	A	TP	PIM	GP	G	A	TP	PIM
1994-95	Colorado	WCHA	27	6	4	10	22	....	....	....	....	....
1995-96	Colorado	WCHA	42	6	7	13	40	....	....	....	....	....
1996-97	Colorado	WCHA	43	19	17	36	71	....	....	....	....	....

BOGAS, CHRIS (BOH-GUHS) TOR.

Defense. Shoots right. 6', 192 lbs. Born, Cleveland, OH, November 12, 1976.
(Toronto's 10th choice, 148th overall, in 1996 Entry Draft).

			Regular Season					Playoffs				
Season	Club	Lea	GP	G	A	TP	PIM	GP	G	A	TP	PIM
1995-96	Michigan State	CCHA	39	1	19	20	55	....	....	....	....	....
1996-97	Michigan State	CCHA	40	7	4	11	58	....	....	....	....	....

BOGUNIECKI, ERIC (BOH-guhn-ih-kee)

Center. Shoots right. 5'8", 192 lbs. Born, New Haven, CT, May 6, 1975.
(St. Louis' 6th choice, 193rd overall, in 1993 Entry Draft).

			Regular Season					Playoffs				
Season	Club	Lea	GP	G	A	TP	PIM	GP	G	A	TP	PIM
1993-94	N. Hampshire	H.E.	40	17	16	33	66	....	....	....	....	....
1994-95	N. Hampshire	H.E.	34	12	16	28	62	....	....	....	....	....
1995-96	N. Hampshire	H.E.	32	23	28	51	46	....	....	....	....	....
1996-97a	N. Hampshire	H.E.	36	26	31	57	58	....	....	....	....	....

a Hockey East All-Star Team (1997)

BOHONOS, LONNY (boh-HOH-nohz) VAN.

Right wing. Shoots right. 5'11", 190 lbs. Born, Winnipeg, Man., May 20, 1973.

			Regular Season					Playoffs				
Season	Club	Lea	GP	G	A	TP	PIM	GP	G	A	TP	PIM
1991-92	Moose Jaw	WHL	8	1	1	2	0	....	....	....	....	....
1992-93	Seattle	WHL	46	13	13	26	27	....	....	....	....	....
	Portland	WHL	27	20	17	37	16	15	8	13	21	19
1993-94ab	Portland	WHL	70	*62	*90	*152	80	10	8	11	19	13
1994-95	Syracuse	AHL	67	30	45	75	71	....	....	....	....	....
1995-96	**Vancouver**	**NHL**	**3**	**0**	**1**	**1**	**0**	....	....	....	....	....
	Syracuse	AHL	74	40	39	79	82	16	14	8	22	16
1996-97	**Vancouver**	**NHL**	**36**	**11**	**11**	**22**	**10**	....	....	....	....	....
	Syracuse	AHL	41	22	30	52	28	3	2	2	4	4
	NHL Totals		**39**	**11**	**12**	**23**	**10**	....	....	....	....	....

a WHL West First All-Star Team (1994)
b Canadian Major Junior First All-Star Team (1994)

Signed as a free agent by **Vancouver**, May 31, 1994.

BOIKOV, ALEXANDER (bohy-KAHV) S.J.

Defense. Shoots left. 6', 180 lbs. Born, Chelyabinsk, USSR, February 7, 1975.

			Regular Season					Playoffs				
Season	Club	Lea	GP	G	A	TP	PIM	GP	G	A	TP	PIM
1993-94	Victoria	WHL	70	4	31	35	250	....	....	....	....	....
1994-95	Prince George	WHL	46	5	23	28	115	....	....	....	....	....
	Tri-City	WHL	24	3	13	16	63	17	1	7	8	30
1995-96	Tri-City	WHL	71	3	49	52	230	11	2	4	6	28
1996-97	Kentucky	AHL	61	1	19	20	182	4	0	1	1	4

Signed as a free agent by **San Jose**, April 22, 1996.

BOILEAU, PATRICK WSH.

Defense. Shoots right. 6', 190 lbs. Born, Montreal, Que., February 22, 1975.
(Washington's 3rd choice, 69th overall, in 1993 Entry Draft).

			Regular Season					Playoffs				
Season	Club	Lea	GP	G	A	TP	PIM	GP	G	A	TP	PIM
1992-93	Laval	QMJHL	69	4	19	23	73	13	1	2	3	10
1993-94	Laval	QMJHL	64	13	57	70	56	21	1	7	8	24
1994-95	Laval	QMJHL	38	8	25	33	46	20	4	16	20	24
1995-96	Portland	AHL	78	10	28	38	41	19	1	3	4	12
1996-97	**Washington**	**NHL**	**1**	**0**	**0**	**0**	**0**	....	....	....	....	....
	Portland	AHL	67	16	28	44	63	5	1	1	2	4
	NHL Totals		**1**	**0**	**0**	**0**	**0**	....	....	....	....	....

BOISVENUE, MARTIN PHI.

Center. Shoots left. 6', 192 lbs. Born, Cornwall, Ont., April 24, 1977.

			Regular Season					Playoffs				
Season	Club	Lea	GP	G	A	TP	PIM	GP	G	A	TP	PIM
1995-96	Val D'Or	QMJHL	37	9	13	22	24	13	2	8	10	4
1996-97	Val D'Or	QMJHL	28	7	12	19	54	....	....	....	....	....

Signed as a free agent by **Philadelphia**, October 2, 1996.

BOLIBRUCK, KEVIN EDM.

Defense. Shoots left. 6'1", 197 lbs. Born, Peterborough, Ont., February 8, 1977.
(Ottawa's 4th choice, 89th overall, in 1995 Entry Draft).

			Regular Season					Playoffs				
Season	Club	Lea	GP	G	A	TP	PIM	GP	G	A	TP	PIM
1994-95	Peterborough	OHL	66	2	16	18	88	11	1	1	2	14
1995-96a	Peterborough	OHL	57	6	21	27	105	24	3	6	9	46
1996-97	Peterborough	OHL	46	4	26	30	63	11	3	3	6	14

a OHL First All-Star Team (1996)

Rights traded to **Chicago** by **Ottawa** with Denis Chasse and Ottawa's sixth round choice in 1998 Entry Draft for Mike Prokopec, March 18, 1997. Re-entered NHL Entry Draft, **Edmonton's** 7th choice, 176th overall, in 1997 Entry Draft.

BOMBARDIR, BRAD (bawm-bahr-DEER) N.J.

Defense. Shoots left. 6'2", 190 lbs. Born, Powell River, B.C., May 5, 1972.
(New Jersey's 5th choice, 56th overall, in 1990 Entry Draft).

			Regular Season					Playoffs				
Season	Club	Lea	GP	G	A	TP	PIM	GP	G	A	TP	PIM
1990-91	North Dakota	WCHA	33	3	6	9	18	....	....	....	....	....
1991-92	North Dakota	WCHA	35	3	14	17	54	....	....	....	....	....
1992-93	North Dakota	WCHA	38	8	15	23	34	....	....	....	....	....
1993-94	North Dakota	WCHA	38	5	17	22	38	....	....	....	....	....
1994-95	Albany	AHL	77	5	22	27	22	14	0	3	3	6
1995-96a	Albany	AHL	80	6	25	31	63	3	0	1	1	4
1996-97	Albany	AHL	32	0	8	8	6	16	1	3	4	8

a AHL Second All-Star Team (1996)

BONDRA, PETER WSH.

Right wing. Shoots left. 6'1", 200 lbs. Born, Luck, USSR, February 7, 1968.
(Washington's 9th choice, 156th overall, in 1990 Entry Draft).

			Regular Season					Playoffs				
Season	Club	Lea	GP	G	A	TP	PIM	GP	G	A	TP	PIM
1986-87	VSZ Kosice	Czech.	32	4	5	9	24	....	....	....	....	....
1987-88	VSZ Kosice	Czech.	45	27	11	38	20	....	....	....	....	....
1988-89	VSZ Kosice	Czech.	40	30	10	40	20	....	....	....	....	....
1989-90	VSZ Kosice	Czech.	49	36	19	55	....	....	....	....	....	....
1990-91	**Washington**	**NHL**	**54**	**12**	**16**	**28**	**47**	**4**	**0**	**1**	**1**	**2**
1991-92	**Washington**	**NHL**	**71**	**28**	**28**	**56**	**42**	**7**	**6**	**2**	**8**	**4**
1992-93	**Washington**	**NHL**	**83**	**37**	**48**	**85**	**70**	**6**	**0**	**6**	**6**	**0**
1993-94	**Washington**	**NHL**	**69**	**24**	**19**	**43**	**40**	**9**	**2**	**4**	**6**	**4**
1994-95	Kosice	Slov.	2	1	0	1	0	....	....	....	....	....
	Washington	**NHL**	**47**	***34**	**9**	**43**	**24**	**7**	**5**	**3**	**8**	**10**
1995-96	Detroit	IHL	7	8	1	9	0	....	....	....	....	....
	Washington	**NHL**	**67**	**52**	**28**	**80**	**40**	**6**	**3**	**2**	**5**	**8**
1996-97	**Washington**	**NHL**	**77**	**46**	**31**	**77**	**72**	....	....	....	....	....
	NHL Totals		**468**	**233**	**179**	**412**	**335**	**39**	**16**	**18**	**34**	**28**

Played in NHL All-Star Game (1993, 1996, 1997)

BONIN, BRIAN PIT.

Center. Shoots left. 5'10", 185 lbs. Born, St. Paul, MN, November 28, 1973.
(Pittsburgh's 9th choice, 211th overall, in 1992 Entry Draft).

			Regular Season					Playoffs				
Season	Club	Lea	GP	G	A	TP	PIM	GP	G	A	TP	PIM
1992-93	U. Minnesota	WCHA	38	10	18	28	10	....	....	....	....	....
1993-94	U. Minnesota	WCHA	42	24	20	44	14	....	....	....	....	....
1994-95ab	U. Minnesota	WCHA	44	32	31	*63	28	....	....	....	....	....
1995-96abc	U. Minnesota	WCHA	42	34	*47	*81	30	....	....	....	....	....
1996-97	Cleveland	IHL	60	13	26	39	18	1	1	0	1	0

a WCHA First All-Star Team (1995, 1996)
b NCAA West First All-American Team (1995, 1996)
c Won Hobey Baker Memorial Award (Top U.S. Collegiate Player) (1996)

BONK, RADEK (BOHNK) OTT.

Center. Shoots left. 6'3", 205 lbs. Born, Krnov, Czech., January 9, 1976.
(Ottawa's 1st choice, 3rd overall, in 1994 Entry Draft).

			Regular Season					Playoffs				
Season	Club	Lea	GP	G	A	TP	PIM	GP	G	A	TP	PIM
1992-93	ZPS Zlin	Czech.	30	5	5	10	10	....	....	....	....	....
1993-94a	Las Vegas	IHL	76	42	45	87	208	5	1	2	3	10
1994-95	Las Vegas	IHL	33	7	13	20	62	....	....	....	....	....
	Ottawa	**NHL**	**42**	**3**	**8**	**11**	**28**	....	....	....	....	....
	P.E.I.	AHL	....	....	....	....	....	1	0	0	0	0
1995-96	**Ottawa**	**NHL**	**76**	**16**	**19**	**35**	**36**	....	....	....	....	....
1996-97	**Ottawa**	**NHL**	**53**	**5**	**13**	**18**	**14**	**7**	**0**	**1**	**1**	**4**
	NHL Totals		**171**	**24**	**40**	**64**	**78**	**7**	**0**	**1**	**1**	**4**

a Won Garry F. Longman Memorial Trophy (Top Rookie - IHL) (1994)

BONNI, RYAN (baw-NEE) VAN.

Defense. Shoots left. 6'4", 190 lbs. Born, Winnipeg, Man., February 18, 1979.
(Vancouver's 2nd choice, 34th overall, in 1997 Entry Draft).

			Regular Season					Playoffs				
Season	Club	Lea	GP	G	A	TP	PIM	GP	G	A	TP	PIM
1995-96	Saskatoon	WHL	63	1	7	8	78	3	0	0	0	0
1996-97	Saskatoon	WHL	69	11	19	30	219	....	....	....	....	....

BONSIGNORE, JASON (bohn-SEE-nohr) **EDM.**

Center. Shoots right. 6'4", 220 lbs. Born, Rochester, NY, April 15, 1976.
(Edmonton's 1st choice, 4th overall, in 1994 Entry Draft).

			Regular Season					Playoffs				
Season	Club	Lea	GP	G	A	TP	PIM	GP	G	A	TP	PIM
1992-93	Newmarket	OHL	66	22	20	42	6	7	0	3	3	0
1993-94	Newmarket	OHL	17	7	17	24	22	....	....	....	....	....
	U.S. National	....	5	0	2	2	0	....	....	....	....	....
	Niagara Falls	OHL	41	15	47	62	41	....	....	....	....	....
1994-95	Niagara Falls	OHL	26	12	21	33	51	....	....	....	....	....
	Sudbury	OHL	23	15	14	29	45	17	13	10	23	12
	Edmonton	**NHL**	**1**	**1**	**0**	**1**	**0**	....	....	....	....	....
1995-96	**Edmonton**	**NHL**	**20**	**0**	**2**	**2**	**4**	....	....	....	....	....
	Sudbury	OHL	18	10	16	26	37	....	....	....	....	....
	Cape Breton	AHL	12	1	4	5	12	....	....	....	....	....
1996-97	Hamilton	AHL	78	21	33	54	78	7	0	0	0	4
	NHL Totals		**21**	**1**	**2**	**3**	**4**	....	....	....	....	....

BONVIE, DENNIS **EDM.**

Right wing/Defense. Shoots right. 5'11", 205 lbs. Born, Antigonish, N.S., July 23, 1973.

			Regular Season					Playoffs				
Season	Club	Lea	GP	G	A	TP	PIM	GP	G	A	TP	PIM
1991-92	Kitchener	OHL	7	1	1	2	23	....	....	....	....	....
	North Bay	OHL	49	0	12	12	261	21	0	1	1	91
1992-93	North Bay	OHL	64	3	21	24	*316	5	0	0	0	34
1993-94	Cape Breton	AHL	63	1	10	11	278	4	0	0	0	11
1994-95	Cape Breton	AHL	74	5	15	20	422	....	....	....	....	....
	Edmonton	**NHL**	**2**	**0**	**0**	**0**	**0**	....	....	....	....	....
1995-96	**Edmonton**	**NHL**	**8**	**0**	**0**	**0**	**47**	....	....	....	....	....
	Cape Breton	AHL	38	13	14	27	269	....	....	....	....	....
1996-97	Hamilton	AHL	73	9	20	29	*522	22	3	11	14	*91
	NHL Totals		**10**	**0**	**0**	**0**	**47**	....	....	....	....	....

Signed as a free agent by **Edmonton**, August 25, 1994.

BOOTLAND, NICK **DAL.**

Left wing. Shoots left. 6', 210 lbs. Born, Shelbourne, Ont., July 31, 1978.
(Dallas' 8th choice, 220th overall, in 1996 Entry Draft).

			Regular Season					Playoffs				
Season	Club	Lea	GP	G	A	TP	PIM	GP	G	A	TP	PIM
1995-96	Guelph	OHL	54	8	7	15	90	16	1	0	1	21
1996-97	Guelph	OHL	64	35	23	58	117	18	11	7	18	36

BORDELEAU, SEBASTIEN (BOHR-duh-loh) **MTL.**

Center. Shoots right. 5'11", 187 lbs. Born, Vancouver, B.C., February 15, 1975.
(Montreal's 3rd choice, 73rd overall, in 1993 Entry Draft).

			Regular Season					Playoffs				
Season	Club	Lea	GP	G	A	TP	PIM	GP	G	A	TP	PIM
1991-92	Hull	QMJHL	62	26	32	58	91	5	0	3	3	23
1992-93	Hull	QMJHL	60	18	39	57	95	10	3	8	11	20
1993-94	Hull	QMJHL	60	26	57	83	147	17	6	14	20	26
1994-95a	Hull	QMJHL	68	52	76	128	142	18	*13	19	*32	25
	Fredericton	AHL	....	....	....	....	....	1	0	0	0	0
1995-96	**Montreal**	**NHL**	**4**	**0**	**0**	**0**	**0**	....	....	....	....	....
	Fredericton	AHL	43	17	29	46	68	7	0	2	2	8
1996-97	**Montreal**	**NHL**	**28**	**2**	**9**	**11**	**2**	....	....	....	....	....
	Fredericton	AHL	33	17	21	38	50	....	....	....	....	....
	NHL Totals		**32**	**2**	**9**	**11**	**2**	....	....	....	....	....

a QMJHL First All-Star Team (1995)

BORSATO, LUCIANO (bohr-SAH-toh, LOO-chee-AH-noh)

Center. Shoots right. 5'11", 190 lbs. Born, Richmond Hill, Ont., January 7, 1966.
(Winnipeg's 7th choice, 135th overall, in 1984 Entry Draft).

			Regular Season					Playoffs				
Season	Club	Lea	GP	G	A	TP	PIM	GP	G	A	TP	PIM
1984-85	Clarkson	ECAC	33	15	17	32	37	....	....	....	....	....
1985-86	Clarkson	ECAC	28	14	17	31	44	....	....	....	....	....
1986-87	Clarkson	ECAC	31	16	41	57	55	....	....	....	....	....
1987-88ab	Clarkson	ECAC	33	15	29	44	38	....	....	....	....	....
	Moncton	AHL	3	1	1	2	0	....	....	....	....	....
1988-89	Moncton	AHL	6	2	5	7	4	....	....	....	....	....
	Tappara	Fin.	44	31	36	67	69	7	0	3	3	4
1989-90	Moncton	AHL	1	1	0	1	0	....	....	....	....	....
1990-91	**Winnipeg**	**NHL**	**1**	**0**	**1**	**1**	**2**	....	....	....	....	....
	Moncton	AHL	41	14	24	38	40	9	3	7	10	22
1991-92	**Winnipeg**	**NHL**	**56**	**15**	**21**	**36**	**45**	**1**	**0**	**0**	**0**	**0**
	Moncton	AHL	14	2	7	9	39	....	....	....	....	....
1992-93	**Winnipeg**	**NHL**	**67**	**15**	**20**	**35**	**38**	**6**	**1**	**0**	**1**	**4**
1993-94	**Winnipeg**	**NHL**	**75**	**5**	**13**	**18**	**28**	....	....	....	....	....
1994-95	**Winnipeg**	**NHL**	**4**	**0**	**0**	**0**	**0**	....	....	....	....	....
	Springfield	AHL	22	9	11	20	14	....	....	....	....	....
1995-96	Koln	Ger.	49	25	36	61	52	12	6	8	14	28
1996-97	Koln	Ger.	23	13	21	34	32	4	2	3	5	0
	NHL Totals		**203**	**35**	**55**	**90**	**113**	**7**	**1**	**0**	**1**	**4**

a ECAC Second All-Star Team (1988)
b NCAA East Second All-American Team (1988)

BORSCHEVSKY, NIKOLAI (bohr-SHEHV-skee)

Right wing. Shoots left. 5'9", 180 lbs. Born, Tomsk, USSR, January 12, 1965.
(Toronto's 3rd choice, 77th overall, in 1992 Entry Draft).

			Regular Season					Playoffs				
Season	Club	Lea	GP	G	A	TP	PIM	GP	G	A	TP	PIM
1983-84	Moscow D'amo	USSR	34	4	5	9	4	....	....	....	....	....
1984-85	Moscow D'amo	USSR	34	5	9	14	6	....	....	....	....	....
1985-86	Moscow D'amo	USSR	31	6	4	10	4	....	....	....	....	....
1986-87	Moscow D'amo	USSR	28	1	4	5	8	....	....	....	....	....
1987-88	Moscow D'amo	USSR	37	11	7	18	6	....	....	....	....	....
1988-89	Moscow D'amo	USSR	43	7	8	15	18	....	....	....	....	....
1989-90	Spartak	USSR	48	17	25	42	8	....	....	....	....	....
1990-91	Spartak	USSR	45	19	16	35	16	....	....	....	....	....
1991-92	Spartak	CIS	40	25	14	39	16	....	....	....	....	....
1992-93	**Toronto**	**NHL**	**78**	**34**	**40**	**74**	**28**	**16**	**2**	**7**	**9**	**0**
1993-94	**Toronto**	**NHL**	**45**	**14**	**20**	**34**	**10**	**15**	**2**	**2**	**4**	**4**
1994-95	Spartak	CIS	9	5	1	6	14	....	....	....	....	....
	Toronto	**NHL**	**19**	**0**	**5**	**5**	**0**	....	....	....	....	....
	Calgary	**NHL**	**8**	**0**	**5**	**5**	**0**	....	....	....	....	....
1995-96	**Dallas**	**NHL**	**12**	**1**	**3**	**4**	**6**	....	....	....	....	....
	Koln	Ger.	8	0	4	4	27	8	2	2	4	4
1996-97	Spartak	Rus.	42	15	*29	*44	52	....	....	....	....	....
	NHL Totals		**162**	**49**	**73**	**122**	**44**	**31**	**4**	**9**	**13**	**4**

Traded to **Calgary** by **Toronto** for Calgary's sixth round choice (Chris Bogas) in 1996 Entry Draft, April 6, 1995. Signed as a free agent by **Dallas**, September 13, 1995.

BOTTERILL, JASON (BOH-tuhr-ihl) **DAL.**

Left wing. Shoots left. 6'3", 205 lbs. Born, Edmonton, Alta., May 19, 1976.
(Dallas' 1st choice, 20th overall, in 1994 Entry Draft).

			Regular Season					Playoffs				
Season	Club	Lea	GP	G	A	TP	PIM	GP	G	A	TP	PIM
1993-94	U. of Michigan	CCHA	36	20	19	39	94	....	....	....	....	....
1994-95	U. of Michigan	CCHA	34	14	14	28	117	....	....	....	....	....
1995-96a	U. of Michigan	CCHA	37	*32	25	57	*143	....	....	....	....	....
1996-97b	U. of Michigan	CCHA	42	*37	24	61	129	....	....	....	....	....

a CCHA Second All-Star Team (1996)
b NCAA West Second All-American Team (1977)

BOUCHARD, FREDERIC **DAL.**

Defense. Shoots right. 6', 181 lbs. Born, Beauport, Que., July 30, 1976.

			Regular Season					Playoffs				
Season	Club	Lea	GP	G	A	TP	PIM	GP	G	A	TP	PIM
1993-94	Granby	QMJHL	45	1	9	10	67	7	1	3	4	8
1994-95	Granby	QMJHL	70	17	49	66	190	13	3	6	9	20
1995-96	Granby	QMJHL	43	13	37	50	152	....	....	....	....	....
	St-Hyacinthe	QMJHL	23	7	10	17	48	12	3	8	11	38
1996-97a	Rouyn-Noranda	QMJHL	6	1	5	6	6	....	....	....	....	....
	Chicoutimi	QMJHL	50	33	62	95	87	21	22	29	51	42

a QMJHL Second All-Star Team (1997)

Signed as a free agent by **Dallas**, August 14, 1997.

BOUCHARD, JOEL (BOO-shahrd) **CGY.**

Defense. Shoots left. 6', 190 lbs. Born, Montreal, Que., January 23, 1974.
(Calgary's 7th choice, 129th overall, in 1992 Entry Draft).

			Regular Season					Playoffs				
Season	Club	Lea	GP	G	A	TP	PIM	GP	G	A	TP	PIM
1990-91	Longueuil	QMJHL	53	3	19	22	34	8	1	0	1	11
1991-92	Verdun	QMJHL	70	9	20	29	55	19	1	7	8	20
1992-93	Verdun	QMJHL	60	10	49	59	126	4	0	2	2	4
1993-94a	Verdun	QMJHL	60	15	55	70	62	4	1	0	1	6
	Saint John	AHL	1	0	0	0	0	2	0	0	0	0
1994-95	Saint John	AHL	77	6	25	31	63	5	1	0	1	4
	Calgary	**NHL**	**2**	**0**	**0**	**0**	**0**	....	....	....	....	....
1995-96	**Calgary**	**NHL**	**4**	**0**	**0**	**0**	**4**	....	....	....	....	....
	Saint John	AHL	74	8	25	33	104	16	1	4	5	10
1996-97	**Calgary**	**NHL**	**76**	**4**	**5**	**9**	**49**	....	....	....	....	....
	NHL Totals		**82**	**4**	**5**	**9**	**53**	....	....	....	....	....

a QMJHL First All-Star Team (1994)

BOUCHER, PHILIPPE (boo-SHAY, fihl-EEP) **L.A.**

Defense. Shoots right. 6'3", 190 lbs. Born, St. Apollinaire, Que., March 24, 1973.
(Buffalo's 1st choice, 13th overall, in 1991 Entry Draft).

			Regular Season					Playoffs				
Season	Club	Lea	GP	G	A	TP	PIM	GP	G	A	TP	PIM
1990-91ab	Granby	QMJHL	69	21	46	67	92	....	....	....	....	....
1991-92	Granby	QMJHL	49	22	37	59	47	....	....	....	....	....
b	Laval	QMJHL	16	7	11	18	36	10	5	6	11	8
1992-93	**Buffalo**	**NHL**	**18**	**0**	**4**	**4**	**14**	....	....	....	....	....
	Laval	QMJHL	16	12	15	27	37	13	6	15	21	12
	Rochester	AHL	5	4	3	7	8	3	0	1	1	2
1993-94	**Buffalo**	**NHL**	**38**	**6**	**8**	**14**	**29**	**7**	**1**	**1**	**2**	**2**
	Rochester	AHL	31	10	22	32	51	....	....	....	....	....
1994-95	Rochester	AHL	43	14	27	41	26	....	....	....	....	....
	Buffalo	**NHL**	**9**	**1**	**4**	**5**	**0**	....	....	....	....	....
	Los Angeles	**NHL**	**6**	**1**	**0**	**1**	**4**	....	....	....	....	....
1995-96	**Los Angeles**	**NHL**	**53**	**7**	**16**	**23**	**31**	....	....	....	....	....
	Phoenix	IHL	10	4	3	7	4	....	....	....	....	....
1996-97	**Los Angeles**	**NHL**	**60**	**7**	**18**	**25**	**25**	....	....	....	....	....
	NHL Totals		**184**	**22**	**50**	**72**	**103**	**7**	**1**	**1**	**2**	**2**

a Canadian Major Junior Rookie of the Year (1991)
b QMJHL Second All-Star Team (1991, 1992)

Traded to **Los Angeles** by **Buffalo** with Denis Tsygurov and Grant Fuhr for Alexei Zhitnik, Robb Stauber, Charlie Huddy and Los Angeles' fifth round choice (Marian Menhart) in 1995 Entry Draft, February 14, 1995.

BOUGHNER, BOB (BOOG-nuhr) **BUF.**

Defense. Shoots right. 6', 206 lbs. Born, Windsor, Ont., March 8, 1971.
(Detroit's 2nd choice, 32nd overall, in 1989 Entry Draft).

			Regular Season					Playoffs				
Season	Club	Lea	GP	G	A	TP	PIM	GP	G	A	TP	PIM
1988-89	S.S. Marie	OHL	64	6	15	21	182	....	....	....	....	....
1989-90	S.S. Marie	OHL	49	7	23	30	122	....	....	....	....	....
1990-91	S.S. Marie	OHL	64	13	33	46	156	14	2	9	11	35
1991-92	Toledo	ECHL	28	3	10	13	79	5	2	0	2	15
	Adirondack	AHL	1	0	0	0	7	....	....	....	....	....
1992-93	Adirondack	AHL	69	1	16	17	190	....	....	....	....	....
1993-94	Adirondack	AHL	72	8	14	22	292	10	1	1	2	18
1994-95	Cincinnati	IHL	81	2	14	16	192	10	0	0	0	18
1995-96	Carolina	AHL	46	2	15	17	127	....	....	....	....	....
	Buffalo	**NHL**	**31**	**0**	**1**	**1**	**104**	....	....	....	....	....
1996-97	**Buffalo**	**NHL**	**77**	**1**	**7**	**8**	**225**	**11**	**0**	**1**	**1**	**9**
	NHL Totals		**108**	**1**	**8**	**9**	**329**	**11**	**0**	**1**	**1**	**9**

Signed as a free agent by **Florida**, July 25, 1994. Traded to **Buffalo** by **Florida** for Buffalo's third round choice (Chris Allen) in 1996 Entry Draft, February 1, 1996.

BOULERICE, JESSE (BOO-luhr-ighs) **PHI.**

Defense. Shoots right. 6'1", 214 lbs. Born, Plattsburgh, NY, August 10, 1978.
(Philadelphia's 4th choice, 133rd overall, in 1996 Entry Draft).

			Regular Season					Playoffs				
Season	Club	Lea	GP	G	A	TP	PIM	GP	G	A	TP	PIM
1995-96	Detroit	OHL	64	2	5	7	150	16	0	0	0	12
1996-97	Detroit	OHL	33	10	14	24	209	....	....	....	....	....

BOULTON, ERIC **NYR**

Left wing. Shoots left. 6', 201 lbs. Born, Halifax, N.S., August 17, 1976.
(NY Rangers' 12th choice, 234th overall, in 1994 Entry Draft).

			Regular Season					Playoffs				
Season	Club	Lea	GP	G	A	TP	PIM	GP	G	A	TP	PIM
1993-94	Oshawa	OHL	45	4	3	7	149	5	0	0	0	16
1994-95	Oshawa	OHL	27	7	5	12	125	....	....	....	....	....
	Sarnia	OHL	24	3	7	10	134	4	0	1	1	10
1995-96	Sarnia	OHL	66	14	29	43	243	9	0	3	3	29
1996-97	Binghamton	AHL	23	2	3	5	67	3	0	0	0	4
	Charlotte	ECHL	44	14	11	25	325	3	0	1	1	6

BOUMEDIENNE, JOSEF (BOO-mih-dyehn) **N.J.**

Defense. Shoots left. 6'1", 190 lbs. Born, Stockholm, Sweden, January 12, 1978.
(New Jersey's 7th choice, 91st overall, in 1996 Entry Draft).

			Regular Season					Playoffs				
Season	**Club**	**Lea**	**GP**	**G**	**A**	**TP**	**PIM**	**GP**	**G**	**A**	**TP**	**PIM**
1995-96	Huddinge	Swe. Jr.	25	2	4	6	66	....	....	....	....	....
	Huddinge	Swe. 2	7	0	0	0	14	....	....	....	....	....
1996-97	Sodertalje	Swe.	32	1	1	2	32	....	....	....	....	....

BOURQUE, PHIL (BOHRK)

Left wing. Shoots left. 6'1", 196 lbs. Born, Chelmsford, MA, June 8, 1962.

			Regular Season					Playoffs				
Season	**Club**	**Lea**	**GP**	**G**	**A**	**TP**	**PIM**	**GP**	**G**	**A**	**TP**	**PIM**
1980-81	Kingston	OHL	47	4	4	8	46	6	0	0	0	10
1981-82	Kingston	OHL	67	11	40	51	111	4	0	0	0	0
1982-83	Baltimore	AHL	65	1	15	16	93	....	....	....	....	....
1983-84	**Pittsburgh**	**NHL**	**5**	**0**	**1**	**1**	**12**	....	....	....	....	....
	Baltimore	AHL	58	5	17	22	96	....	....	....	....	....
1984-85	Baltimore	AHL	79	6	15	21	164	13	2	5	7	23
1985-86	**Pittsburgh**	**NHL**	**4**	**0**	**0**	**0**	**2**	....	....	....	....	....
	Baltimore	AHL	74	8	18	26	226	....	....	....	....	....
1986-87	**Pittsburgh**	**NHL**	**22**	**2**	**3**	**5**	**32**	....	....	....	....	....
	Baltimore	AHL	49	15	16	31	183	....	....	....	....	....
1987-88	**Pittsburgh**	**NHL**	**21**	**4**	**12**	**16**	**20**	....	....	....	....	....
ab	Muskegon	IHL	52	16	36	52	66	6	1	2	3	16
1988-89	**Pittsburgh**	**NHL**	**80**	**17**	**26**	**43**	**97**	**11**	**4**	**1**	**5**	**66**
1989-90	**Pittsburgh**	**NHL**	**76**	**22**	**17**	**39**	**108**	....	....	....	....	....
1990-91	**Pittsburgh**	**NHL**	**78**	**20**	**14**	**34**	**106**	**24**	**6**	**7**	**13**	**16 ♦**
1991-92	**Pittsburgh**	**NHL**	**58**	**10**	**16**	**26**	**58**	**21**	**3**	**4**	**7**	**25 ♦**
1992-93	**NY Rangers**	**NHL**	**55**	**6**	**14**	**20**	**39**	....	....	....	....	....
1993-94	**NY Rangers**	**NHL**	**16**	**0**	**1**	**1**	**8**	....	....	....	....	....
	Ottawa	**NHL**	**11**	**2**	**3**	**5**	**0**	....	....	....	....	....
1994-95	**Ottawa**	**NHL**	**38**	**4**	**3**	**7**	**20**	....	....	....	....	....
1995-96	**Ottawa**	**NHL**	**13**	**1**	**1**	**2**	**14**	....	....	....	....	....
	Detroit	IHL	36	4	13	17	70	10	1	3	4	10
1996-97	Chicago	IHL	77	7	14	21	50	4	0	2	2	2
	NHL Totals		**477**	**88**	**111**	**199**	**516**	**56**	**13**	**12**	**25**	**107**

a IHL First All-Star Team (1988)
b Won Governor's Trophy (Outstanding Defenseman - IHL) (1988)

Signed as a free agent by **Pittsburgh**, October 4, 1982. Signed as a free agent by **NY Rangers**, August 31, 1992. Traded to **Ottawa** by **NY Rangers** for future considerations, March 21, 1994.

BOURQUE, RAY (BOHRK) **BOS.**

Defense. Shoots left. 5'11", 219 lbs. Born, Montreal, Que., December 28, 1960.
(Boston's 1st choice, 8th overall, in 1979 Entry Draft).

			Regular Season					Playoffs				
Season	**Club**	**Lea**	**GP**	**G**	**A**	**TP**	**PIM**	**GP**	**G**	**A**	**TP**	**PIM**
1976-77	Sorel	QJHL	69	12	36	48	61	....	....	....	....	....
1977-78	Verdun	QJHL	72	22	57	79	90	4	2	1	3	0
1978-79	Verdun	QJHL	63	22	71	93	44	11	3	16	19	18
1979-80ab	**Boston**	**NHL**	**80**	**17**	**48**	**65**	**73**	**10**	**2**	**9**	**11**	**27**
1980-81c	**Boston**	**NHL**	**67**	**27**	**29**	**56**	**96**	**3**	**0**	**1**	**1**	**2**
1981-82b	**Boston**	**NHL**	**65**	**17**	**49**	**66**	**51**	**9**	**1**	**5**	**6**	**16**
1982-83c	**Boston**	**NHL**	**65**	**22**	**51**	**73**	**20**	**17**	**8**	**15**	**23**	**10**
1983-84b	**Boston**	**NHL**	**78**	**31**	**65**	**96**	**57**	**3**	**0**	**2**	**2**	**0**
1984-85b	**Boston**	**NHL**	**73**	**20**	**66**	**86**	**53**	**5**	**0**	**3**	**3**	**4**
1985-86c	**Boston**	**NHL**	**74**	**19**	**58**	**77**	**68**	**3**	**0**	**0**	**0**	**0**
1986-87bd	**Boston**	**NHL**	**78**	**23**	**72**	**95**	**36**	**4**	**1**	**2**	**3**	**0**
1987-88bd	**Boston**	**NHL**	**78**	**17**	**64**	**81**	**72**	**23**	**3**	**18**	**21**	**26**
1988-89c	**Boston**	**NHL**	**60**	**18**	**43**	**61**	**52**	**10**	**0**	**4**	**4**	**6**
1989-90bd	**Boston**	**NHL**	**76**	**19**	**65**	**84**	**50**	**17**	**5**	**12**	**17**	**16**
1990-91bd	**Boston**	**NHL**	**76**	**21**	**73**	**94**	**75**	**19**	**7**	**18**	**25**	**12**
1991-92be	**Boston**	**NHL**	**80**	**21**	**60**	**81**	**56**	**12**	**3**	**6**	**9**	**12**
1992-93b	**Boston**	**NHL**	**78**	**19**	**63**	**82**	**40**	**4**	**1**	**0**	**1**	**2**
1993-94bd	**Boston**	**NHL**	**72**	**20**	**71**	**91**	**58**	**13**	**2**	**8**	**10**	**0**
1994-95c	**Boston**	**NHL**	**46**	**12**	**31**	**43**	**20**	**5**	**0**	**3**	**3**	**0**
1995-96b	**Boston**	**NHL**	**82**	**20**	**62**	**82**	**58**	**5**	**1**	**6**	**7**	**2**
1996-97	**Boston**	**NHL**	**62**	**19**	**31**	**50**	**18**	....	....	....	....	....
	NHL Totals		**1290**	**362**	**1001**	**1363**	**953**	**162**	**34**	**112**	**146**	**135**

a Won Calder Memorial Trophy (1980)
b NHL First All-Star Team (1980, 1982, 1984, 1985, 1987, 1988, 1990, 1991, 1992, 1993, 1994, 1996)
c NHL Second All-Star Team (1981, 1983, 1986, 1989, 1995)
d Won James Norris Memorial Trophy (1987, 1988, 1990, 1991, 1994)
e Won King Clancy Memorial Trophy (1992)

Played in NHL All-Star Game (1981-86, 1988-94, 1996, 1997)

BOWEN, CURTIS (BOW-ehn)

Left wing. Shoots left. 6'1", 195 lbs. Born, Kenora, Ont., March 24, 1974.
(Detroit's 1st choice, 22nd overall, in 1992 Entry Draft).

			Regular Season					Playoffs				
Season	**Club**	**Lea**	**GP**	**G**	**A**	**TP**	**PIM**	**GP**	**G**	**A**	**TP**	**PIM**
1990-91	Ottawa	OHL	42	12	14	26	31	....	....	....	....	....
1991-92	Ottawa	OHL	65	31	45	76	94	11	3	7	10	11
1992-93	Ottawa	OHL	21	9	19	28	51	....	....	....	....	....
1993-94	Ottawa	OHL	52	25	37	62	98	17	8	13	21	14
1994-95	Adirondack	AHL	64	6	11	17	71	4	0	2	2	4
1995-96	Cdn. National	....	31	8	8	16	48	....	....	....	....	....
	Adirondack	AHL	3	0	0	0	0	....	....	....	....	....
1996-97	Adirondack	AHL	78	11	11	22	110	4	0	0	0	2

BOWEN, JASON (BOW-ehn) **PHI.**

Left wing. Shoots left. 6'4", 215 lbs. Born, Port Alice, B.C., November 9, 1973.
(Philadelphia's 2nd choice, 15th overall, in 1992 Entry Draft).

			Regular Season					Playoffs				
Season	**Club**	**Lea**	**GP**	**G**	**A**	**TP**	**PIM**	**GP**	**G**	**A**	**TP**	**PIM**
1989-90	Tri-City	WHL	61	8	5	13	129	7	0	3	3	4
1990-91	Tri-City	WHL	60	7	13	20	252	6	2	2	4	18
1991-92	Tri-City	WHL	19	5	3	8	135	5	0	1	1	42
1992-93	**Philadelphia**	**NHL**	**7**	**1**	**0**	**1**	**2**	....	....	....	....	....
	Tri-City	WHL	62	10	12	22	219	3	1	1	2	18
1993-94	**Philadelphia**	**NHL**	**56**	**1**	**5**	**6**	**87**	....	....	....	....	....
1994-95	Hershey	AHL	55	5	5	10	116	6	0	0	0	46
	Philadelphia	**NHL**	**4**	**0**	**0**	**0**	**0**	....	....	....	....	....
1995-96	**Philadelphia**	**NHL**	**2**	**0**	**0**	**0**	**2**	....	....	....	....	....
	Hershey	AHL	72	6	7	13	128	4	2	0	2	13
1996-97	**Philadelphia**	**NHL**	**4**	**0**	**1**	**1**	**8**	....	....	....	....	....
	Philadelphia	AHL	61	10	12	22	160	6	0	1	1	10
	NHL Totals		**73**	**2**	**6**	**8**	**99**	....	....	....	....	....

BOYER, ZAC (BOH-yuhr)

Right wing. Shoots right. 6'1", 199 lbs. Born, Inuvik, N.W.T., October 25, 1971.
(Chicago's 4th choice, 88th overall, in 1991 Entry Draft).

			Regular Season					Playoffs				
Season	**Club**	**Lea**	**GP**	**G**	**A**	**TP**	**PIM**	**GP**	**G**	**A**	**TP**	**PIM**
1988-89	Kamloops	WHL	42	10	17	27	22	16	9	8	17	10
1989-90	Kamloops	WHL	71	24	47	71	163	17	4	4	8	8
1990-91	Kamloops	WHL	64	45	60	105	58	12	6	10	16	8
1991-92	Kamloops	WHL	70	40	69	109	90	17	9	*20	*29	16
1992-93	Indianapolis	IHL	59	7	14	21	26	....	....	....	....	....
1993-94	Indianapolis	IHL	54	13	12	25	67	....	....	....	....	....
1994-95	Kalamazoo	IHL	22	9	7	16	22	15	3	9	12	8
	Dallas	**NHL**	**1**	**0**	**0**	**0**	**0**	**2**	**0**	**0**	**0**	**0**
1995-96	**Dallas**	**NHL**	**2**	**0**	**0**	**0**	**0**	....	....	....	....	....
	Michigan	IHL	67	24	27	51	58	10	11	6	17	0
1996-97	Orlando	IHL	80	25	49	74	63	3	0	1	1	2
	NHL Totals		**3**	**0**	**0**	**0**	**0**	**2**	**0**	**0**	**0**	**0**

Signed as a free agent by **Dallas**, July 25, 1994.

BOYNTON, NICHOLAS (BOHYN-tuhn) **WSH.**

Defense. Shoots right. 6'2", 210 lbs. Born, Etobicoke, Ont., January 14, 1979.
(Washington's 1st choice, 9th overall, in 1997 Entry Draft).

			Regular Season					Playoffs				
Season	**Club**	**Lea**	**GP**	**G**	**A**	**TP**	**PIM**	**GP**	**G**	**A**	**TP**	**PIM**
1995-96	Ottawa	OHL	64	10	14	24	90	4	0	3	3	10
1996-97	Ottawa	OHL	63	13	51	64	143	24	4	24	28	38

BRADLEY, BRIAN **T.B.**

Center. Shoots right. 5'10", 177 lbs. Born, Kitchener, Ont., January 21, 1965.
(Calgary's 2nd choice, 51st overall, in 1983 Entry Draft).

			Regular Season					Playoffs				
Season	**Club**	**Lea**	**GP**	**G**	**A**	**TP**	**PIM**	**GP**	**G**	**A**	**TP**	**PIM**
1982-83	London	OHL	67	37	82	119	37	3	1	0	1	0
1983-84	London	OHL	49	40	60	100	24	4	2	4	6	0
1984-85	London	OHL	32	27	49	76	22	8	5	10	15	4
1985-86	**Calgary**	**NHL**	**5**	**0**	**1**	**1**	**0**	**1**	**0**	**0**	**0**	**0**
	Moncton	AHL	59	23	42	65	40	10	6	9	15	4
1986-87	**Calgary**	**NHL**	**40**	**10**	**18**	**28**	**16**	....	....	....	....	....
	Moncton	AHL	20	12	16	28	8	....	....	....	....	....
1987-88	Cdn. National	....	47	18	19	37	42	....	....	....	....	....
	Cdn. Olympic	....	7	0	4	4	0	....	....	....	....	....
	Vancouver	**NHL**	**11**	**3**	**5**	**8**	**6**	....	....	....	....	....
1988-89	**Vancouver**	**NHL**	**71**	**18**	**27**	**45**	**42**	**7**	**3**	**4**	**7**	**10**
1989-90	**Vancouver**	**NHL**	**67**	**19**	**29**	**48**	**65**	....	....	....	....	....
1990-91	**Vancouver**	**NHL**	**44**	**11**	**20**	**31**	**42**	....	....	....	....	....
	Toronto	**NHL**	**26**	**0**	**11**	**11**	**20**	....	....	....	....	....
1991-92	**Toronto**	**NHL**	**59**	**10**	**21**	**31**	**48**	....	....	....	....	....
1992-93	**Tampa Bay**	**NHL**	**80**	**42**	**44**	**86**	**92**	....	....	....	....	....
1993-94	**Tampa Bay**	**NHL**	**78**	**24**	**40**	**64**	**56**	....	....	....	....	....
1994-95	**Tampa Bay**	**NHL**	**46**	**13**	**27**	**40**	**42**	....	....	....	....	....
1995-96	**Tampa Bay**	**NHL**	**75**	**23**	**56**	**79**	**77**	**5**	**0**	**3**	**3**	**6**
1996-97	**Tampa Bay**	**NHL**	**35**	**7**	**17**	**24**	**16**	....	....	....	....	....
	NHL Totals		**637**	**180**	**316**	**496**	**522**	**13**	**3**	**7**	**10**	**16**

Played in NHL All-Star Game (1993, 1994)

Traded to **Vancouver** by **Calgary** with Peter Bakovic and Kevin Guy for Craig Coxe, March 6, 1988. Traded to **Toronto** by **Vancouver** for Tom Kurvers, January 12, 1991. Claimed by **Tampa Bay** from **Toronto** in Expansion Draft, June 18, 1992.

BRADLEY, E.J. **PHI.**

Center. Shoots left. 5'10", 182 lbs. Born, New Hyde Park, NY, January 2, 1975.
(Philadelphia's 9th choice, 226th overall, in 1993 Entry Draft).

			Regular Season					Playoffs				
Season	**Club**	**Lea**	**GP**	**G**	**A**	**TP**	**PIM**	**GP**	**G**	**A**	**TP**	**PIM**
1994-95	U. Wisconsin	WCHA	40	3	4	7	22	....	....	....	....	....
1995-96	U. Wisconsin	WCHA	26	1	6	7	39	....	....	....	....	....
1996-97	U. Wisconsin	WCHA	38	8	12	20	60	....	....	....	....	....

BRADLEY, MATT **S.J.**

Right wing. Shoots right. 6'1", 168 lbs. Born, Stittsville, Ont., June 13, 1978.
(San Jose's 4th choice, 102nd overall, in 1996 Entry Draft).

			Regular Season					Playoffs				
Season	**Club**	**Lea**	**GP**	**G**	**A**	**TP**	**PIM**	**GP**	**G**	**A**	**TP**	**PIM**
1995-96	Kingston	OHL	55	10	14	24	17	6	0	1	1	6
1996-97	Kingston	OHL	65	24	24	48	41	5	0	4	4	2
	Kentucky	AHL	1	0	1	1	0	....	....	....	....	....

BRADY, NEIL

Center. Shoots left. 6'2", 200 lbs. Born, Montreal, Que., April 12, 1968.
(New Jersey's 1st choice, 3rd overall, in 1986 Entry Draft).

			Regular Season					Playoffs				
Season	**Club**	**Lea**	**GP**	**G**	**A**	**TP**	**PIM**	**GP**	**G**	**A**	**TP**	**PIM**
1984-85	Calgary	Midget	37	25	50	75	75	....	....	....	....	....
	Medicine Hat	WHL	....	....	....	....	....	3	0	0	0	2
1985-86	Medicine Hat	WHL	72	21	60	81	104	21	9	11	20	23
1986-87	Medicine Hat	WHL	57	19	64	83	126	18	1	4	5	25
1987-88	Medicine Hat	WHL	61	16	35	51	110	15	0	3	3	19
1988-89	Utica	AHL	75	16	21	37	56	4	0	3	3	0
1989-90	**New Jersey**	**NHL**	**19**	**1**	**4**	**5**	**13**	....	....	....	....	....
	Utica	AHL	38	10	13	23	21	5	0	1	1	10
1990-91	**New Jersey**	**NHL**	**3**	**0**	**0**	**0**	**0**	....	....	....	....	....
	Utica	AHL	77	33	63	96	91	....	....	....	....	....
1991-92	**New Jersey**	**NHL**	**7**	**1**	**0**	**1**	**4**	....	....	....	....	....
	Utica	AHL	33	12	30	42	28	....	....	....	....	....
1992-93	**Ottawa**	**NHL**	**55**	**7**	**17**	**24**	**57**	....	....	....	....	....
	New Haven	AHL	8	6	3	9	2	....	....	....	....	....
1993-94	Kalamazoo	IHL	43	10	16	26	188	5	1	1	2	10
	Dallas	**NHL**	**5**	**0**	**1**	**1**	**21**	....	....	....	....	....
1994-95	Kalamazoo	IHL	70	13	45	58	140	15	5	14	19	22
1995-96	Michigan	IHL	61	14	20	34	127	10	1	4	5	8
1996-97	Michigan	IHL	76	13	20	33	62	4	1	0	1	0
	NHL Totals		**89**	**9**	**22**	**31**	**95**	....	....	....	....	....

Traded to **Ottawa** by **New Jersey** for future considerations, September 3, 1992. Signed as a free agent by **Dallas**, December 3, 1993.

BRAND, AARON TOR.

Center. Shoots left. 6', 190 lbs. Born, Toronto, Ont., June 14, 1975.

				Regular Season				Playoffs			
Season	Club	Lea	GP	G	A	TP	PIM	GP	G	A	TP	PIM
1993-94	Newmarket	OHL	65	19	45	64	55	....	....	....	....	....
1994-95	Sarnia	OHL	66	33	42	75	58	3	0	2	2	4
1995-96a	Sarnia	OHL	66	46	*73	*119	110	10	7	11	18	18
	St. John's	AHL	1	0	1	1	0	4	0	0	0	4
1996-97	St. John's	AHL	75	15	25	40	80	11	3	2	5	2

a OHL Second All-Star Team (1996)

Signed as a free agent by **Toronto**, March 21, 1997.

BRASHEAR, DONALD (bra-SHEER) VAN.

Left wing. Shoots left. 6'2", 220 lbs. Born, Bedford, IN, January 7, 1972.

				Regular Season				Playoffs			
Season	Club	Lea	GP	G	A	TP	PIM	GP	G	A	TP	PIM
1989-90	Longueuil	QMJHL	64	.12	14	26	169	7	0	0	0	11
1990-91	Longueuil	QMJHL	68	12	26	38	195	8	0	3	3	33
1991-92	Verdun	QMJHL	65	18	24	42	283	18	4	2	6	98
1992-93	Fredericton	AHL	76	11	3	14	261	5	0	0	0	8
1993-94	**Montreal**	**NHL**	14	2	2	4	34	2	0	0	0	0
	Fredericton	AHL	62	38	28	66	250	....	....	....	....	....
1994-95	Fredericton	AHL	29	10	9	19	182	17	7	5	12	77
	Montreal	**NHL**	20	1	1	2	63	....	....	....	....	....
1995-96	**Montreal**	**NHL**	67	0	4	4	223	6	0	0	0	2
1996-97	**Montreal**	**NHL**	10	0	0	0	38	....	....	....	....	....
	Vancouver	**NHL**	59	8	5	13	207	....	....	....	....	....
	NHL Totals		170	11	12	23	565	8	0	0	0	2

Signed as a free agent by **Montreal**, July 28, 1992. Traded to **Vancouver** by **Montreal** for Jassen Cullimore, November 13, 1996.

BRENNAN, RICH S.J.

Defense. Shoots right. 6'2", 200 lbs. Born, Schenectady, NY, November 26, 1972.
(Quebec's 3rd choice, 46th overall, in 1991 Entry Draft).

				Regular Season				Playoffs			
Season	Club	Lea	GP	G	A	TP	PIM	GP	G	A	TP	PIM
1991-92	Boston U.	H.E.	30	4	13	17	50	....	....	....	....	....
1992-93	Boston U.	H.E.	40	9	11	20	68	....	....	....	....	....
1993-94ab	Boston U.	H.E.	41	8	27	35	82	....	....	....	....	....
1994-95	Boston U.	H.E.	31	5	22	27	56	....	....	....	....	....
1995-96	Brantford	ColHL	5	1	2	3	2	....	....	....	....	....
	Cornwall	AHL	36	4	8	12	61	7	0	0	0	6
1996-97	**Colorado**	**NHL**	2	0	0	0	0	....	....	....	....	....
	Hershey	AHL	74	11	45	56	88	23	2	16	18	22
	NHL Totals		2	0	0	0	0	....	....	....	....	....

a Hockey East First All-Star Team (1994)
b NCAA East Second All-American Team (1994)

Signed as a free agent by **San Jose**, July 9, 1997.

BREWER, ERIC NYI

Defense. Shoots left. 6'3", 195 lbs. Born, Vernon, B.C., April 17, 1979.
(NY Islanders' 2nd choice, 5th overall, in 1997 Entry Draft).

				Regular Season				Playoffs			
Season	Club	Lea	GP	G	A	TP	PIM	GP	G	A	TP	PIM
1995-96	Prince George	WHL	63	4	10	14	25	....	....	....	....	....
1996-97	Prince George	WHL	71	5	24	29	81	15	2	4	6	16

BRIERE, DANIEL (bree-AIR) PHO.

Center. Shoots left. 5'9", 160 lbs. Born, Gatineau, Que., October 6, 1977.
(Phoenix's 2nd choice, 24th overall, in 1996 Entry Draft).

				Regular Season				Playoffs			
Season	Club	Lea	GP	G	A	TP	PIM	GP	G	A	TP	PIM
1994-95	Drummondville	QMJHL	72	51	72	123	54	4	2	3	5	2
1995-96a	Drummondville	QMJHL	67	*67	*96	*163	84	6	6	12	18	8
1996-97a	Drummondville	QMJHL	59	52	78	130	94	8	7	7	14	14

a QMJHL Second All-Star Team (1996, 1997)

BRIGLEY, TRAVIS CGY.

Left wing. Shoots left. 6'1", 190 lbs. Born, Coronation, Alta., June 16, 1977.
(Calgary's 2nd choice, 39th overall, in 1996 Entry Draft).

				Regular Season				Playoffs			
Season	Club	Lea	GP	G	A	TP	PIM	GP	G	A	TP	PIM
1993-94	Lethbridge	WHL	1	0	0	0	0	....	....	....	....	....
1994-95	Lethbridge	WHL	64	14	18	32	14	....	....	....	....	....
1995-96	Lethbridge	WHL	69	34	43	77	94	4	2	3	5	8
1996-97	Lethbridge	WHL	71	43	47	90	56	19	9	9	18	31

BRIMANIS, ARIS (brih-MAN-ihs, AR-ihs) PHI.

Defense. Shoots right. 6'3", 210 lbs. Born, Cleveland, OH, March 14, 1972.
(Philadelphia's 3rd choice, 86th overall, in 1991 Entry Draft).

				Regular Season				Playoffs			
Season	Club	Lea	GP	G	A	TP	PIM	GP	G	A	TP	PIM
1990-91	Bowling Green	CCHA	38	3	6	9	42	....	....	....	....	....
1991-92	Bowling Green	CCHA	32	2	9	11	38	....	....	....	....	....
1992-93	Brandon	WHL	71	8	50	58	110	4	2	1	3	7
1993-94	**Philadelphia**	**NHL**	1	0	0	0	0	....	....	....	....	....
	Hershey	AHL	75	8	15	23	65	11	2	3	5	12
1994-95	Hershey	AHL	76	8	17	25	68	6	1	1	2	14
1995-96	**Philadelphia**	**NHL**	17	0	2	2	12	....	....	....	....	....
	Hershey	AHL	54	9	22	31	64	5	1	2	3	4
1996-97	**Philadelphia**	**NHL**	3	0	1	1	0	....	....	....	....	....
	Philadelphia	AHL	65	14	18	32	69	10	2	2	4	13
	NHL Totals		21	0	3	3	12	....	....	....	....	....

BRIND'AMOUR, ROD (BRIHND-uh-MOHR) PHI.

Center. Shoots left. 6'1", 202 lbs. Born, Ottawa, Ont., August 9, 1970.
(St. Louis' 1st choice, 9th overall, in 1988 Entry Draft).

				Regular Season				Playoffs			
Season	Club	Lea	GP	G	A	TP	PIM	GP	G	A	TP	PIM
1988-89	Michigan State	CCHA	42	27	32	59	63	....	....	....	....	....
	St. Louis	**NHL**	....	....	....	....	....	5	2	0	2	4
1989-90a	**St. Louis**	**NHL**	79	26	35	61	46	12	5	8	13	6
1990-91	**St. Louis**	**NHL**	78	17	32	49	93	13	2	5	7	10
1991-92	**Philadelphia**	**NHL**	80	33	44	77	100	....	....	....	....	....
1992-93	**Philadelphia**	**NHL**	81	37	49	86	89	....	....	....	....	....
1993-94	**Philadelphia**	**NHL**	84	35	62	97	85	....	....	....	....	....
1994-95	**Philadelphia**	**NHL**	48	12	27	39	33	15	6	9	15	8
1995-96	**Philadelphia**	**NHL**	82	26	61	87	110	12	2	5	7	6
1996-97	**Philadelphia**	**NHL**	82	27	32	59	41	19	*13	8	21	10
	NHL Totals		614	213	342	555	597	76	30	35	65	44

a NHL All-Rookie Team (1990)

Played in NHL All-Star Game (1992)

Traded to **Philadelphia** by **St. Louis** with Dan Quinn for Ron Sutter and Murray Baron, September 22, 1991.

BRISEBOIS, PATRICE (BREES-bwah, pa-TREEZ) MTL.

Defense. Shoots right. 6'1", 188 lbs. Born, Montreal, Que., January 27, 1971.
(Montreal's 2nd choice, 30th overall, in 1989 Entry Draft).

				Regular Season				Playoffs			
Season	Club	Lea	GP	G	A	TP	PIM	GP	G	A	TP	PIM
1987-88	Laval	QMJHL	48	10	34	44	95	6	0	2	2	2
1988-89	Laval	QMJHL	50	20	45	65	95	17	8	14	22	45
1989-90a	Laval	QMJHL	56	18	70	88	108	13	7	9	16	26
1990-91	**Montreal**	**NHL**	10	0	2	2	4	....	....	....	....	....
bcd	Drummondville	QMJHL	54	17	44	61	72	14	6	18	24	49
1991-92	**Montreal**	**NHL**	26	2	8	10	20	11	2	4	6	6
	Fredericton	AHL	53	12	27	39	51	....	....	....	....	....
1992-93	**Montreal**	**NHL**	70	10	21	31	79	20	0	4	4	18 ♦
1993-94	**Montreal**	**NHL**	53	2	21	23	63	7	0	4	4	6
1994-95	**Montreal**	**NHL**	35	4	8	12	26	....	....	....	....	....
1995-96	**Montreal**	**NHL**	69	9	27	36	65	6	1	2	3	6
1996-97	**Montreal**	**NHL**	49	2	13	15	24	3	1	1	2	24
	NHL Totals		312	29	100	129	281	47	4	15	19	60

a QMJHL Second All-Star Team (1990)
b Canadian Major Junior Defenseman of the Year (1991)
c QMJHL First All-Star Team (1991)
d Memorial Cup All-Star Team (1991)

BRISKE, BYRON (BRIHS-kee) ANA.

Defense. Shoots right. 6'3", 195 lbs. Born, Humboldt, Sask., January 23, 1976.
(Anaheim's 4th choice, 80th overall, in 1994 Entry Draft).

				Regular Season				Playoffs			
Season	Club	Lea	GP	G	A	TP	PIM	GP	G	A	TP	PIM
1992-93	Victoria	WHL	66	1	10	11	110	....	....	....	....	....
1993-94	Red Deer	WHL	61	6	21	27	174	....	....	....	....	....
1994-95	Red Deer	WHL	48	4	17	21	116	....	....	....	....	....
	Tri-City	WHL	15	0	1	1	22	13	0	0	0	18
1995-96	Tri-City	WHL	72	15	38	53	189	11	0	5	5	36
1996-97	Baltimore	AHL	69	0	6	6	131	1	0	0	0	0

BROS, MICHAL (BROHSH, MEE-khahl) S.J.

Center. Shoots right. 6'1", 195 lbs. Born, Olomouc, Czech., January 25, 1976.
(San Jose's 6th choice, 130th overall, in 1995 Entry Draft).

				Regular Season				Playoffs			
Season	Club	Lea	GP	G	A	TP	PIM	GP	G	A	TP	PIM
1994-95	Olomouc	Czech. Jr.	34	29	32	61	....	....	....	....	....	....
1995-96	Olomouc	Czech.	35	8	11	19	....	4	2	0	2	....
1996-97	Olomouc	Czech.	50	13	14	27	28	....	....	....	....	....

BROSSEAU, DAVID NYR

Center. Shoots right. 6'1", 190 lbs. Born, Montreal, Que., January 16, 1976.
(NY Rangers' 8th choice, 156th overall, in 1994 Entry Draft).

				Regular Season				Playoffs			
Season	Club	Lea	GP	G	A	TP	PIM	GP	G	A	TP	PIM
1992-93	Shawinigan	QMJHL	56	5	4	9	28	....	....	....	....	....
1993-94	Shawinigan	QMJHL	65	27	26	53	62	5	3	0	3	2
1994-95	Shawinigan	QMJHL	39	28	20	48	65	....	....	....	....	....
	Granby	QMJHL	26	9	6	15	37	13	2	2	4	4
1995-96	Granby	QMJHL	63	32	33	65	115	21	*22	12	34	30
1996-97	Binghamton	AHL	2	0	0	0	0	1	0	0	0	0
	Charlotte	ECHL	68	37	18	55	65	3	1	3	4	12

BROTEN, NEAL (BRAH-tuhn)

Center. Shoots left. 5'9", 175 lbs. Born, Roseau, MN, November 29, 1959.
(Minnesota's 3rd choice, 42nd overall, in 1979 Entry Draft).

			Regular Season					Playoffs				
Season	Club	Lea	GP	G	A	TP	PIM	GP	G	A	TP	PIM
1978-79	U. Minnesota	WCHA	40	21	50	71	18	....	....	....	....	....
1979-80	U.S. National	....	55	25	30	55	20	....	....	....	....	....
	U.S. Olympic	....	7	2	1	3	2	....	....	....	....	....
1980-81ab	U. Minnesota	WCHA	36	17	54	71	56	....	....	....	....	....
	Minnesota	**NHL**	**3**	**2**	**0**	**2**	**12**	**19**	**1**	**7**	**8**	**9**
1981-82	**Minnesota**	**NHL**	**73**	**38**	**60**	**98**	**42**	**4**	**0**	**2**	**2**	**0**
1982-83	**Minnesota**	**NHL**	**79**	**32**	**45**	**77**	**43**	**9**	**1**	**6**	**7**	**10**
1983-84	**Minnesota**	**NHL**	**76**	**28**	**61**	**89**	**43**	**16**	**5**	**5**	**10**	**4**
1984-85	**Minnesota**	**NHL**	**80**	**19**	**37**	**56**	**39**	**9**	**2**	**5**	**7**	**10**
1985-86	**Minnesota**	**NHL**	**80**	**29**	**76**	**105**	**47**	**5**	**3**	**2**	**5**	**2**
1986-87	**Minnesota**	**NHL**	**46**	**18**	**35**	**53**	**33**	....	....	....	....	....
1987-88	**Minnesota**	**NHL**	**54**	**9**	**30**	**39**	**32**	....	....	....	....	....
1988-89	**Minnesota**	**NHL**	**68**	**18**	**38**	**56**	**57**	**5**	**2**	**2**	**4**	**4**
1989-90	**Minnesota**	**NHL**	**80**	**23**	**62**	**85**	**45**	**7**	**2**	**2**	**4**	**18**
1990-91	**Minnesota**	**NHL**	**79**	**13**	**56**	**69**	**26**	**23**	**9**	**13**	**22**	**6**
1991-92	Preussen	Ger.	8	3	5	8	2	....	....	....	....	....
	Minnesota	**NHL**	**76**	**8**	**26**	**34**	**16**	**7**	**1**	**5**	**6**	**2**
1992-93	**Minnesota**	**NHL**	**82**	**12**	**21**	**33**	**22**	....	....	....	....	....
1993-94	**Dallas**	**NHL**	**79**	**17**	**35**	**52**	**62**	**9**	**2**	**1**	**3**	**6**
1994-95	**Dallas**	**NHL**	**17**	**0**	**4**	**4**	**4**	....	....	....	....	....
	New Jersey	**NHL**	**30**	**8**	**20**	**28**	**20**	**20**	**7**	**12**	**19**	**6** ♦
1995-96	**New Jersey**	**NHL**	**55**	**7**	**16**	**23**	**14**	....	....	....	....	....
1996-97	**New Jersey**	**NHL**	**3**	**0**	**1**	**1**	**0**	....	....	....	....	....
	Los Angeles	**NHL**	**19**	**0**	**4**	**4**	**0**	....	....	....	....	....
	Phoenix	IHL	11	3	3	6	4	....	....	....	....	....
	Dallas	**NHL**	**20**	**8**	**7**	**15**	**12**	**2**	**0**	**1**	**1**	**0**
	NHL Totals		**1099**	**289**	**634**	**923**	**569**	**135**	**35**	**63**	**98**	**77**

a WCHA First All-Star Team (1981)
b Won Hobey Baker Memorial Award (Top U.S. Collegiate Player) (1981)

Played in NHL All-Star Game (1983, 1986)

Traded to **New Jersey** by **Dallas** for Corey Millen, February 27, 1995. Traded to **Los Angeles** by **New Jersey** for future considerations, November 22, 1996. Claimed on waivers by **Dallas** from **Los Angeles**, January 28, 1997.

BROTEN, PAUL (BRAH-tuhn)

Right wing. Shoots right. 5'11", 188 lbs. Born, Roseau, MN, October 27, 1965.
(NY Rangers' 3rd choice, 77th overall, in 1984 Entry Draft).

			Regular Season					Playoffs				
Season	Club	Lea	GP	G	A	TP	PIM	GP	G	A	TP	PIM
1984-85	U. Minnesota	WCHA	44	8	8	16	26	....	....	....	....	....
1985-86	U. Minnesota	WCHA	38	6	16	22	24	....	....	....	....	....
1986-87	U. Minnesota	WCHA	48	17	22	39	52	....	....	....	....	....
1987-88	U. Minnesota	WCHA	38	18	21	39	42	....	....	....	....	....
1988-89	Denver	IHL	77	28	31	59	133	4	0	2	2	6
1989-90	**NY Rangers**	**NHL**	**32**	**5**	**3**	**8**	**26**	**6**	**1**	**1**	**2**	**2**
	Flint	IHL	28	17	9	26	55	....	....	....	....	....
1990-91	**NY Rangers**	**NHL**	**28**	**4**	**6**	**10**	**18**	**5**	**0**	**0**	**0**	**2**
	Binghamton	AHL	8	2	2	4	4	....	....	....	....	....
1991-92	**NY Rangers**	**NHL**	**74**	**13**	**15**	**28**	**102**	**13**	**1**	**2**	**3**	**10**
1992-93	**NY Rangers**	**NHL**	**60**	**5**	**9**	**14**	**48**	....	....	....	....	....
1993-94	**Dallas**	**NHL**	**64**	**12**	**12**	**24**	**30**	**9**	**1**	**1**	**2**	**2**
1994-95	**Dallas**	**NHL**	**47**	**7**	**9**	**16**	**36**	**5**	**1**	**2**	**3**	**2**
1995-96	**St. Louis**	**NHL**	**17**	**0**	**1**	**1**	**4**	....	....	....	....	....
	Worcester	AHL	50	22	21	43	42	3	0	0	0	0
1996-97	Fort Wayne	IHL	59	19	28	47	82	....	....	....	....	....
	NHL Totals		**322**	**46**	**55**	**101**	**264**	**38**	**4**	**6**	**10**	**18**

Claimed by **Dallas** from **NY Rangers** in NHL Waiver Draft, October 3, 1993. Traded to **St. Louis** by **Dallas** for Guy Carbonneau, October 2, 1995.

BROUSSEAU, PAUL

Right wing. Shoots right. 6'2", 203 lbs. Born, Pierrefonds, Que., September 18, 1973.
(Quebec's 2nd choice, 28th overall, in 1992 Entry Draft).

			Regular Season					Playoffs				
Season	Club	Lea	GP	G	A	TP	PIM	GP	G	A	TP	PIM
1989-90	Chicoutimi	QMJHL	57	17	24	41	32	7	0	3	3	0
1990-91	Trois-Rivières	QMJHL	67	30	66	96	48	6	3	2	5	2
1991-92	Hull	QMJHL	57	35	61	96	54	6	3	5	8	10
1992-93	Hull	QMJHL	59	27	48	75	49	10	7	8	15	6
1993-94	Cornwall	AHL	69	18	26	44	35	1	0	0	0	0
1994-95	Cornwall	AHL	57	19	17	36	29	7	2	1	3	10
1995-96	**Colorado**	**NHL**	**8**	**1**	**1**	**2**	**2**	....	....	....	....	....
	Cornwall	AHL	63	21	22	43	60	8	4	0	4	2
1996-97	**Tampa Bay**	**NHL**	**6**	**0**	**0**	**0**	**0**	....	....	....	....	....
	Adirondack	AHL	66	35	31	66	25	4	1	2	3	0
	NHL Totals		**14**	**1**	**1**	**2**	**2**	....	....	....	....	....

Signed as a free agent by **Tampa Bay**, September 10, 1996.

BROWN, BOBBY CGY.

Center. Shoots right. 6', 200 lbs. Born, Winnipeg, Man., September 26, 1975.

			Regular Season					Playoffs				
Season	Club	Lea	GP	G	A	TP	PIM	GP	G	A	TP	PIM
1992-93	Brandon	WHL	5	1	1	2	0	....	....	....	....	....
1993-94	Brandon	WHL	71	18	19	37	138	14	5	0	5	12
1994-95	Brandon	WHL	72	23	28	51	128	18	3	3	6	31
1995-96	Brandon	WHL	59	42	46	88	106	19	14	13	27	38
1996-97	Roanoke	ECHL	39	9	14	23	61	....	....	....	....	....
	Baton Rouge	ECHL	24	7	8	15	26	....	....	....	....	....

Signed as a free agent by **Calgary**, August 6, 1996.

BROWN, BRAD MTL.

Defense. Shoots right. 6'3", 220 lbs. Born, Baie Verte, Nfld., December 27, 1975.
(Montreal's 1st choice, 18th overall, in 1994 Entry Draft).

			Regular Season					Playoffs				
Season	Club	Lea	GP	G	A	TP	PIM	GP	G	A	TP	PIM
1991-92	North Bay	OHL	49	2	9	11	170	18	0	6	6	43
1992-93	North Bay	OHL	61	4	9	13	228	2	0	2	2	13
1993-94	North Bay	OHL	66	8	24	32	196	18	3	12	15	33
1994-95	North Bay	OHL	64	8	38	46	172	6	1	4	5	8
1995-96	Barrie	OHL	27	3	13	16	82	....	....	....	....	....
	Fredericton	AHL	38	0	3	3	148	10	2	1	3	6
1996-97	**Montreal**	**NHL**	**8**	**0**	**0**	**0**	**22**	....	....	....	....	....
	Fredericton	AHL	64	3	7	10	368	....	....	....	....	....
	NHL Totals		**8**	**0**	**0**	**0**	**22**	....	....	....	....	....

BROWN, CURTIS BUF.

Center. Shoots left. 6', 190 lbs. Born, Unity, Sask., February 12, 1976.
(Buffalo's 2nd choice, 43rd overall, in 1994 Entry Draft).

			Regular Season					Playoffs				
Season	Club	Lea	GP	G	A	TP	PIM	GP	G	A	TP	PIM
1992-93	Moose Jaw	WHL	71	13	16	29	30	....	....	....	....	....
1993-94	Moose Jaw	WHL	72	27	38	65	82	....	....	....	....	....
1994-95a	Moose Jaw	WHL	70	51	53	104	63	10	8	7	15	20
	Buffalo	**NHL**	**1**	**1**	**1**	**2**	**2**	....	....	....	....	....
1995-96	Moose Jaw	WHL	25	20	18	38	30	....	....	....	....	....
b	Prince Albert	WHL	19	12	21	33	8	18	10	15	25	18
	Buffalo	**NHL**	**4**	**0**	**0**	**0**	**0**	....	....	....	....	....
	Rochester	AHL	....	....	....	....	....	12	0	1	1	2
1996-97	**Buffalo**	**NHL**	**28**	**4**	**3**	**7**	**18**	....	....	....	....	....
	Rochester	AHL	51	22	21	43	30	10	4	6	10	4
	NHL Totals		**33**	**5**	**4**	**9**	**20**	....	....	....	....	....

a WHL East First All-Star Team (1995)
b WHL East Second All-Star Team (1996)

BROWN, DOUG DET.

Right wing. Shoots right. 5'10", 185 lbs. Born, Southborough, MA, June 12, 1964.

			Regular Season					Playoffs				
Season	Club	Lea	GP	G	A	TP	PIM	GP	G	A	TP	PIM
1982-83	Boston College	ECAC	22	9	8	17	0	....	....	....	....	....
1983-84	Boston College	ECAC	38	11	10	21	6	....	....	....	....	....
1984-85a	Boston College	H.E.	45	37	31	68	10	....	....	....	....	....
1985-86a	Boston College	H.E.	38	16	40	56	16	....	....	....	....	....
1986-87	**New Jersey**	**NHL**	**4**	**0**	**1**	**1**	**0**	....	....	....	....	....
	Maine	AHL	73	24	34	58	15	....	....	....	....	....
1987-88	**New Jersey**	**NHL**	**70**	**14**	**11**	**25**	**20**	**19**	**5**	**1**	**6**	**6**
	Utica	AHL	2	0	2	2	2	....	....	....	....	....
1988-89	**New Jersey**	**NHL**	**63**	**15**	**10**	**25**	**15**	....	....	....	....	....
	Utica	AHL	4	1	4	5	0	....	....	....	....	....
1989-90	**New Jersey**	**NHL**	**69**	**14**	**20**	**34**	**16**	**6**	**0**	**1**	**1**	**2**
1990-91	**New Jersey**	**NHL**	**58**	**14**	**16**	**30**	**4**	**7**	**2**	**2**	**4**	**2**
1991-92	**New Jersey**	**NHL**	**71**	**11**	**17**	**28**	**27**	....	....	....	....	....
1992-93	**New Jersey**	**NHL**	**15**	**0**	**5**	**5**	**2**	....	....	....	....	....
	Utica	AHL	25	11	17	28	8	....	....	....	....	....
1993-94	**Pittsburgh**	**NHL**	**77**	**18**	**37**	**55**	**18**	**6**	**0**	**0**	**0**	**2**
1994-95	**Detroit**	**NHL**	**45**	**9**	**12**	**21**	**16**	**18**	**4**	**8**	**12**	**2**
1995-96	**Detroit**	**NHL**	**62**	**12**	**15**	**27**	**4**	**13**	**3**	**3**	**6**	**4**
1996-97	**Detroit**	**NHL**	**49**	**6**	**7**	**13**	**8**	**14**	**3**	**3**	**6**	**2** ♦
	NHL Totals		**583**	**113**	**151**	**264**	**130**	**83**	**17**	**18**	**35**	**20**

a Hockey East First All-Star Team (1985, 1986)

Signed as a free agent by **New Jersey**, August 6, 1986. Signed as a free agent by **Pittsburgh**, September 28, 1993. Claimed by **Detroit** from **Pittsburgh** in NHL Waiver Draft, January 18, 1995.

BROWN, JEFF CAR.

Defense. Shoots right. 6'1", 204 lbs. Born, Ottawa, Ont., April 30, 1966.
(Quebec's 2nd choice, 36th overall, in 1984 Entry Draft).

			Regular Season					Playoffs				
Season	Club	Lea	GP	G	A	TP	PIM	GP	G	A	TP	PIM
1982-83	Sudbury	OHL	65	9	37	46	39	....	....	....	....	....
1983-84	Sudbury	OHL	68	17	60	77	39	....	....	....	....	....
1984-85	Sudbury	OHL	56	16	48	64	26	....	....	....	....	....
1985-86	**Quebec**	**NHL**	**8**	**3**	**2**	**5**	**6**	**1**	**0**	**0**	**0**	**0**
a	Sudbury	OHL	45	22	28	50	24	4	0	2	2	11
	Fredericton	AHL	....	....	....	....	....	1	0	1	1	0
1986-87	**Quebec**	**NHL**	**44**	**7**	**22**	**29**	**16**	**13**	**3**	**3**	**6**	**2**
	Fredericton	AHL	26	2	14	16	16	....	....	....	....	....
1987-88	**Quebec**	**NHL**	**78**	**16**	**36**	**52**	**64**	....	....	....	....	....
1988-89	**Quebec**	**NHL**	**78**	**21**	**47**	**68**	**62**	....	....	....	....	....
1989-90	**Quebec**	**NHL**	**29**	**6**	**10**	**16**	**18**	....	....	....	....	....
	St. Louis	**NHL**	**48**	**10**	**28**	**38**	**37**	**12**	**2**	**10**	**12**	**4**
1990-91	**St. Louis**	**NHL**	**67**	**12**	**47**	**59**	**39**	**13**	**3**	**9**	**12**	**6**
1991-92	**St. Louis**	**NHL**	**80**	**20**	**39**	**59**	**38**	**6**	**2**	**1**	**3**	**2**
1992-93	**St. Louis**	**NHL**	**71**	**25**	**53**	**78**	**58**	**11**	**3**	**8**	**11**	**6**
1993-94	**St. Louis**	**NHL**	**63**	**13**	**47**	**60**	**46**	....	....	....	....	....
	Vancouver	**NHL**	**11**	**1**	**5**	**6**	**10**	**24**	**6**	**9**	**15**	**37**
1994-95	**Vancouver**	**NHL**	**33**	**8**	**23**	**31**	**16**	**5**	**1**	**3**	**4**	**2**
1995-96	**Vancouver**	**NHL**	**28**	**1**	**16**	**17**	**18**	....	....	....	....	....
	Hartford	**NHL**	**48**	**7**	**31**	**38**	**38**	....	....	....	....	....
1996-97	**Hartford**	**NHL**	**1**	**0**	**0**	**0**	**0**	....	....	....	....	....
	NHL Totals		**687**	**150**	**406**	**556**	**466**	**85**	**20**	**43**	**63**	**59**

a OHL First All-Star Team (1986)

Traded to **St Louis** by **Quebec** for Tony Hrkac and Greg Millen, December 13, 1989. Traded to **Vancouver** by **St. Louis** with Bret Hedican and Nathan Lafayette for Craig Janney, March 21, 1994. Traded to **Hartford** by **Vancouver** with Vancouver's third round choice in 1998 Entry Draft for Jim Dowd, Frantisek Kucera and Hartford's second round choice (Ryan Bonni) in 1997 Entry Draft, December 19, 1995.

BROWN, JEFF NYR

Defense. Shoots right. 6'1", 215 lbs. Born, Mississauga, Ont., April 24, 1978.
(NY Rangers' 1st choice, 22nd overall, in 1996 Entry Draft).

			Regular Season					Playoffs				
Season	Club	Lea	GP	G	A	TP	PIM	GP	G	A	TP	PIM
1994-95	Sarnia	OHL	58	2	14	16	52	4	0	2	2	2
1995-96	Sarnia	OHL	65	8	20	28	111	10	1	2	3	12
1996-97	Sarnia	OHL	35	5	14	19	60	....	....	....	....	....
	London	OHL	28	1	17	18	32	....	....	....	....	....

BROWN, KEVIN — CAR.

Right wing. Shoots right. 6'1", 212 lbs. Born, Birmingham, England, May 11, 1974.
(Los Angeles' 3rd choice, 87th overall, in 1992 Entry Draft).

			Regular Season					Playoffs				
Season	Club	Lea	GP	G	A	TP	PIM	GP	G	A	TP	PIM
1991-92	Belleville	OHL	66	24	24	48	52	5	1	4	5	8
1992-93a	Belleville	OHL	6	2	5	7	4	....	....	....	....	....
	Detroit	OHL	56	48	86	134	76	15	10	18	28	18
1993-94bc	Detroit	OHL	57	54	81	135	85	17	14	*26	*40	28
1994-95	Phoenix	IHL	48	19	31	50	64	....	....	....	....	....
	Los Angeles	**NHL**	**23**	**2**	**3**	**5**	**18**	....	....	....	....	....
1995-96	**Los Angeles**	**NHL**	**7**	**1**	**0**	**1**	**4**	....	....	....	....	....
	Phoenix	IHL	45	10	16	26	39	....	....	....	....	....
	P.E.I.	AHL	8	3	6	9	2	3	1	3	4	0
1996-97	**Hartford**	**NHL**	**11**	**0**	**4**	**4**	**6**	....	....	....	....	....
	Springfield	AHL	48	32	16	48	45	17	*11	6	17	24
	NHL Totals		**41**	**3**	**7**	**10**	**28**	....	....	....	....	....

a OHL Second All-Star Team (1993)
b OHL First All-Star Team (1994)
c Canadian Major Junior Second All-Star Team (1994)

Traded to **Ottawa** by **Los Angeles** for Jaroslav Modry and Ottawa's eighth round choice (Stephen Valiquette) in 1996 Entry Draft, March 20, 1996. Traded to **Anaheim** by **Ottawa** for Mike Maneluk, July 1, 1996. Traded to **Hartford** by **Anaheim** for the rights to Espen Knutsen, October 1, 1996.

BROWN, MIKE — FLA.

Center. Shoots left. 6'5", 185 lbs. Born, Surrey, B.C., April 27, 1979.
(Florida's 1st choice, 20th overall, in 1997 Entry Draft).

			Regular Season					Playoffs				
Season	Club	Lea	GP	G	A	TP	PIM	GP	G	A	TP	PIM
1995-96	Red Deer	WHL	62	4	5	9	125	10	0	0	0	18
1996-97	Red Deer	WHL	70	19	13	32	243	16	1	2	3	47

BROWN, ROB

Right wing. Shoots left. 5'11", 185 lbs. Born, Kingston, Ont., April 10, 1968.
(Pittsburgh's 4th choice, 67th overall, in 1986 Entry Draft).

			Regular Season					Playoffs				
Season	Club	Lea	GP	G	A	TP	PIM	GP	G	A	TP	PIM
1984-85	Kamloops	WHL	60	29	50	79	95	15	8	8	26	28
1985-86a	Kamloops	WHL	69	58	*115	*173	171	16	*18	*28	*46	14
1986-87ab	Kamloops	WHL	63	*76	*136	*212	101	5	6	5	11	6
1987-88	**Pittsburgh**	**NHL**	**51**	**24**	**20**	**44**	**56**	....	....	....	....	....
1988-89	**Pittsburgh**	**NHL**	**68**	**49**	**66**	**115**	**118**	**11**	**5**	**3**	**8**	**22**
1989-90	**Pittsburgh**	**NHL**	**80**	**33**	**47**	**80**	**102**	....	....	....	....	....
1990-91	**Pittsburgh**	**NHL**	**25**	**6**	**10**	**16**	**31**	....	....	....	....	....
	Hartford	**NHL**	**44**	**18**	**24**	**42**	**101**	**5**	**1**	**0**	**1**	**7**
1991-92	**Hartford**	**NHL**	**42**	**16**	**15**	**31**	**39**	....	....	....	....	....
	Chicago	**NHL**	**25**	**5**	**11**	**16**	**34**	**8**	**2**	**4**	**6**	**4**
1992-93	**Chicago**	**NHL**	**15**	**1**	**6**	**7**	**33**	....	....	....	....	....
	Indianapolis	IHL	19	14	19	33	32	2	0	1	1	2
1993-94	**Dallas**	**NHL**	**1**	**0**	**0**	**0**	**0**	....	....	....	....	....
cde	Kalamazoo	IHL	79	42	*113	*155	188	5	1	3	4	6
1994-95f	Phoenix	IHL	69	34	73	107	135	9	4	12	16	0
	Los Angeles	**NHL**	**2**	**0**	**0**	**0**	**0**	....	....	....	....	....
1995-96cd	Chicago	IHL	79	52	*91	*143	100	9	4	11	15	6
1996-97cd	Chicago	IHL	76	37	*80	*117	98	4	2	4	6	16
	NHL Totals		**353**	**152**	**199**	**351**	**514**	**24**	**8**	**7**	**15**	**33**

a WHL First All-Star Team (1986, 1987)
b Canadian Major Junior Player of the Year (1987)
c IHL First All-Star Team (1994, 1996, 1997)
d Won Leo P. Lamoureux Memorial Trophy (Top Scorer - IHL) (1994, 1996, 1997)
e Won James Gatschene Memorial Trophy (MVP - IHL) (1994)
f IHL Second All-Star Team (1995)

Played in NHL All-Star Game (1989)

Traded to **Hartford** by **Pittsburgh** for Scott Young, December 21, 1990. Traded to **Chicago** by **Hartford** for Steve Konroyd, January 24, 1992. Signed as a free agent by **Dallas**, August 12, 1993. Signed as a free agent by **Los Angeles**, June 14, 1994.

BROWN, SEAN — EDM.

Defense. Shoots left. 6'2", 205 lbs. Born, Oshawa, Ont., November 5, 1976.
(Boston's 2nd choice, 21st overall, in 1995 Entry Draft).

			Regular Season					Playoffs				
Season	Club	Lea	GP	G	A	TP	PIM	GP	G	A	TP	PIM
1993-94	Belleville	OHL	28	1	2	3	53	8	0	0	0	17
1994-95	Belleville	OHL	58	2	16	18	200	16	4	2	6	*67
1995-96	Belleville	OHL	37	10	23	33	150	....	....	....	....	....
a	Sarnia	OHL	26	8	17	25	112	10	1	0	1	38
1996-97	**Edmonton**	**NHL**	**5**	**0**	**0**	**0**	**4**	....	....	....	....	....
	Hamilton	AHL	61	1	7	8	238	19	1	0	1	47
	NHL Totals		**5**	**0**	**0**	**0**	**4**	....	....	....	....	....

a OHL Second All-Star Team (1996)

Traded to **Edmonton** by **Boston** with Mariusz Czerkawski and Boston's first round choice (Matthieu Descoteaux) in 1996 Entry Draft for Bill Ranford, January 11, 1996.

BROWN, THOMAS — BOS.

Defense. Shoots right. 6'4", 200 lbs. Born, Hamilton, Ont., November 11, 1977.
(Boston's 8th choice, 182nd overall, in 1996 Entry Draft).

			Regular Season					Playoffs				
Season	Club	Lea	GP	G	A	TP	PIM	GP	G	A	TP	PIM
1994-95	Sarnia	OHL	53	0	3	3	17	....	....	....	....	....
1995-96	Sarnia	OHL	61	2	5	7	49	10	0	0	0	8
1996-97	Sarnia	OHL	1	0	0	0	4	....	....	....	....	....
	Sudbury	OHL	65	1	13	14	104	....	....	....	....	....

BRUCE, DAVID

Left wing. Shoots right. 5'11", 190 lbs. Born, Thunder Bay, Ont., October 7, 1964.
(Vancouver's 2nd choice, 30th overall, in 1983 Entry Draft).

			Regular Season					Playoffs				
Season	Club	Lea	GP	G	A	TP	PIM	GP	G	A	TP	PIM
1982-83	Kitchener	OHL	67	36	35	71	199	12	7	9	16	27
1983-84	Kitchener	OHL	62	52	40	92	203	10	5	8	13	20
1984-85	Fredericton	AHL	56	14	11	25	104	5	0	0	0	37
1985-86	**Vancouver**	**NHL**	**12**	**0**	**1**	**1**	**14**	**1**	**0**	**0**	**0**	**0**
	Fredericton	AHL	66	25	16	41	151	2	0	1	1	12
1986-87	**Vancouver**	**NHL**	**50**	**9**	**7**	**16**	**109**	....	....	....	....	....
	Fredericton	AHL	17	7	6	13	73	....	....	....	....	....
1987-88	**Vancouver**	**NHL**	**28**	**7**	**3**	**10**	**57**	....	....	....	....	....
	Fredericton	AHL	30	27	18	45	115	....	....	....	....	....
1988-89	**Vancouver**	**NHL**	**53**	**7**	**7**	**14**	**65**	....	....	....	....	....
1989-90a	Milwaukee	IHL	68	40	35	75	148	6	5	3	8	0
1990-91	**St. Louis**	**NHL**	**12**	**1**	**2**	**3**	**14**	**2**	**0**	**0**	**0**	**2**
ab	Peoria	IHL	60	*64	52	116	78	18	*18	11	*29	40
1991-92	**San Jose**	**NHL**	**60**	**22**	**16**	**38**	**46**	....	....	....	....	....
	Kansas City	IHL	7	5	5	10	6	....	....	....	....	....
1992-93	**San Jose**	**NHL**	**17**	**2**	**3**	**5**	**33**	....	....	....	....	....
1993-94	**San Jose**	**NHL**	**2**	**0**	**0**	**0**	**0**	....	....	....	....	....
	Kansas City	IHL	72	40	24	64	115	....	....	....	....	....
1994-95	Kansas City	IHL	63	33	25	58	80	....	....	....	....	....
1995-96	Kansas City	IHL	62	27	26	53	84	1	0	0	0	8
1996-97	Kansas City	IHL	79	45	24	69	90	3	0	0	0	2
	NHL Totals		**234**	**48**	**39**	**87**	**338**	**3**	**0**	**0**	**0**	**2**

a IHL First All-Star Team (1990, 1991)
b Won James Gatschene Memorial Trophy (MVP - IHL) (1991)

Signed as a free agent by **St. Louis**, July 6, 1990. Claimed by **San Jose** from **St. Louis** in Expansion Draft, May 30, 1991.

BRUININKS, BRETT (broo-IHN-kihs) PHI.

Right wing. Shoots right. 6'4", 235 lbs. Born, Minneapolis, MN, March 10, 1972.

			Regular Season					Playoffs				
Season	Club	Lea	GP	G	A	TP	PIM	GP	G	A	TP	PIM
1992-93	Notre Dame	CCHA	36	9	7	16	98	....	....	....	....	....
1993-94	Notre Dame	CCHA	42	9	7	16	89	....	....	....	....	....
1994-95	Notre Dame	CCHA	42	10	3	13	103	....	....	....	....	....
1995-96	Notre Dame	CCHA	40	10	5	15	74	....	....	....	....	....
1996-97	Philadelphia	AHL	45	3	2	5	54	4	1	1	2	2

Signed as a free agent by **Philadelphia**, October 3, 1996.

BRULE, STEVE (broo-LAY) N.J.

Center. Shoots right. 5'11", 185 lbs. Born, Montreal, Que., January 15, 1975.
(New Jersey's 6th choice, 143rd overall, in 1993 Entry Draft).

			Regular Season					Playoffs				
Season	Club	Lea	GP	G	A	TP	PIM	GP	G	A	TP	PIM
1992-93	St-Jean	QMJHL	70	33	47	80	46	4	0	0	0	9
1993-94	St-Jean	QMJHL	66	41	64	105	46	5	2	1	3	0
1994-95a	St-Jean	QMJHL	69	44	64	108	42	7	3	4	7	8
	Albany	AHL	3	1	4	5	0	14	9	5	14	4
1995-96	Albany	AHL	80	30	21	51	37	4	0	0	0	17
1996-97	Albany	AHL	79	28	48	76	27	16	7	7	14	12

a QMJHL Second All-Star Team (1995)

BRUNET, BENOIT (broo-NAY, BEHN-wah) MTL.

Left wing. Shoots left. 5'11", 195 lbs. Born, Pointe-Claire, Que., August 24, 1968.
(Montreal's 2nd choice, 27th overall, in 1986 Entry Draft).

			Regular Season					Playoffs				
Season	Club	Lea	GP	G	A	TP	PIM	GP	G	A	TP	PIM
1985-86	Hull	QMJHL	71	33	37	70	81	....	....	....	....	....
1986-87a	Hull	QMJHL	60	43	67	110	105	6	7	5	12	8
1987-88	Hull	QMJHL	62	54	89	143	131	10	3	10	13	11
1988-89	**Montreal**	**NHL**	**2**	**0**	**1**	**1**	**0**	....	....	....	....	....
b	Sherbrooke	AHL	73	41	76	117	95	6	2	0	2	4
1989-90	Sherbrooke	AHL	72	32	35	67	82	12	8	7	15	20
1990-91	**Montreal**	**NHL**	**17**	**1**	**3**	**4**	**0**	....	....	....	....	....
	Fredericton	AHL	24	13	18	31	16	6	5	6	11	2
1991-92	**Montreal**	**NHL**	**18**	**4**	**6**	**10**	**14**	....	....	....	....	....
	Fredericton	AHL	6	7	9	16	27	....	....	....	....	....
1992-93	**Montreal**	**NHL**	**47**	**10**	**15**	**25**	**19**	**20**	**2**	**8**	**10**	**8** ♦
1993-94	**Montreal**	**NHL**	**71**	**10**	**20**	**30**	**20**	**7**	**1**	**4**	**5**	**16**
1994-95	**Montreal**	**NHL**	**45**	**7**	**18**	**25**	**16**	....	....	....	....	....
1995-96	**Montreal**	**NHL**	**26**	**7**	**8**	**15**	**17**	**3**	**0**	**2**	**2**	**0**
	Fredericton	AHL	3	2	1	3	6	....	....	....	....	....
1996-97	**Montreal**	**NHL**	**39**	**10**	**13**	**23**	**14**	**4**	**1**	**3**	**4**	**4**
	NHL Totals		**265**	**49**	**84**	**133**	**100**	**34**	**4**	**17**	**21**	**28**

a QMJHL Second All-Star Team (1987)
b AHL First All-Star Team (1989)

BRUNETTE, ANDREW (broo-NEHT) WSH.

Left wing. Shoots left. 6', 212 lbs. Born, Sudbury, Ont., August 24, 1973.
(Washington's 6th choice, 174th overall, in 1993 Entry Draft).

			Regular Season					Playoffs				
Season	Club	Lea	GP	G	A	TP	PIM	GP	G	A	TP	PIM
1990-91	Owen Sound	OHL	63	15	20	35	15	....	....	....	....	....
1991-92	Owen Sound	OHL	66	51	47	98	42	5	5	0	5	8
1992-93ab	Owen Sound	OHL	66	*62	*100	*162	91	8	8	6	14	16
1993-94	Portland	AHL	23	9	11	20	10	2	0	1	1	0
	Providence	AHL	3	0	0	0	0	....	....	....	....	....
	Hampton	ECHL	20	12	18	30	32	7	7	6	13	18
1994-95c	Portland	AHL	79	30	50	80	53	7	3	3	6	10
1995-96	**Washington**	**NHL**	**11**	**3**	**3**	**6**	**0**	**6**	**1**	**3**	**4**	**0**
	Portland	AHL	69	28	66	94	125	20	11	18	29	15
1996-97	**Washington**	**NHL**	**23**	**4**	**7**	**11**	**12**	....	....	....	....	....
	Portland	AHL	50	22	51	73	48	5	1	2	3	0
	NHL Totals		**34**	**7**	**10**	**17**	**12**	**6**	**1**	**3**	**4**	**0**

a OHL First All-Star Team (1993)
b Canadian Major Junior Second All-Star Team (1993)
c AHL Second All-Star Team (1995)

BRYLIN, SERGEI (BRIH-lin) N.J.

Center. Shoots left. 5'10", 190 lbs. Born, Moscow, USSR, January 13, 1974.
(New Jersey's 2nd choice, 42nd overall, in 1992 Entry Draft).

			Regular Season					Playoffs				
Season	Club	Lea	GP	G	A	TP	PIM	GP	G	A	TP	PIM
1991-92	CSKA	CIS	44	1	6	7	4	....	....	....	....	....
1992-93	CSKA	CIS	42	5	4	9	36	....	....	....	....	....
1993-94	CSKA	CIS	39	4	6	10	36	3	1	0	1	2
	Russian Pen's	IHL	13	4	5	9	18	....	....	....	....	....
1994-95	Albany	AHL	63	19	35	54	78	....	....	....	....	....
	New Jersey	NHL	26	6	8	14	8	12	1	2	3	4 ◆
1995-96	New Jersey	NHL	50	4	5	9	26	....	....	....	....	....
1996-97	New Jersey	NHL	29	2	2	4	20	....	....	....	....	....
	Albany	AHL	43	17	24	41	38	16	4	8	12	12
	NHL Totals		105	12	15	27	54	12	1	2	3	4

BUCHBERGER, KELLY (BUK-buhr-guhr) EDM.

Right wing. Shoots left. 6'2", 200 lbs. Born, Langenburg, Sask., December 2, 1966.
(Edmonton's 8th choice, 188th overall, in 1985 Entry Draft).

			Regular Season					Playoffs				
Season	Club	Lea	GP	G	A	TP	PIM	GP	G	A	TP	PIM
1984-85	Moose Jaw	WHL	51	12	17	29	114	....	....	....	....	....
1985-86	Moose Jaw	WHL	72	14	22	36	206	13	11	4	15	37
1986-87	Nova Scotia	AHL	70	12	20	32	257	5	0	1	1	23
	Edmonton	NHL	....	....	....	....	....	3	0	1	1	5 ◆
1987-88	Edmonton	NHL	19	1	0	1	81	....	....	....	....	....
	Nova Scotia	AHL	49	21	23	44	206	2	0	0	0	11
1988-89	Edmonton	NHL	66	5	9	14	234	....	....	....	....	....
1989-90	Edmonton	NHL	55	2	6	8	168	19	0	5	5	13 ◆
1990-91	Edmonton	NHL	64	3	1	4	160	12	2	1	3	25
1991-92	Edmonton	NHL	79	20	24	44	157	16	1	4	5	32
1992-93	Edmonton	NHL	83	12	18	30	133	....	....	....	....	....
1993-94	Edmonton	NHL	84	3	18	21	199	....	....	....	....	....
1994-95	Edmonton	NHL	48	7	17	24	82	....	....	....	....	....
1995-96	Edmonton	NHL	82	11	14	25	184	....	....	....	....	....
1996-97	Edmonton	NHL	81	8	30	38	159	12	5	2	7	16
	NHL Totals		661	72	137	209	1557	62	8	13	21	91

BUCKBERGER, ASHLEY (BUK-buhr-guhr) FLA.

Right wing. Shoots right. 6'2", 206 lbs. Born, Esterhazy, Sask., February 19, 1975.
(Quebec's 3rd choice, 49th overall, in 1993 Entry Draft).

			Regular Season					Playoffs				
Season	Club	Lea	GP	G	A	TP	PIM	GP	G	A	TP	PIM
1991-92	Swift Current	WHL	67	23	22	45	38	8	2	1	3	2
1992-93	Swift Current	WHL	72	23	44	67	41	17	6	7	13	6
1993-94	Swift Current	WHL	67	42	45	87	42	7	0	1	1	6
1994-95	Swift Current	WHL	53	23	37	60	51	....	....	....	....	....
	Kamloops	WHL	21	9	13	22	13	19	7	11	18	22
1995-96	Carolina	AHL	67	8	9	17	25	....	....	....	....	....
1996-97	Carolina	AHL	69	8	10	18	24	....	....	....	....	....

Signed as a free agent by **Florida**, July 27, 1995.

BUCKLEY, BRENDAN ANA.

Defense. Shoots right. 6'2", 190 lbs. Born, Boston, MA, February 26, 1977.
(Anaheim's 3rd choice, 117th overall, in 1996 Entry Draft).

			Regular Season					Playoffs				
Season	Club	Lea	GP	G	A	TP	PIM	GP	G	A	TP	PIM
1995-96	Boston College	H.E.	34	0	4	4	72	....	....	....	....	....
1996-97	Boston College	H.E.	38	2	6	8	90	....	....	....	....	....

BUCKLEY, TOM CAR.

Center. Shoots left. 6'1", 204 lbs. Born, Buffalo, NY, May 26, 1976.
(Hartford's 4th choice, 187th overall, in 1994 Entry Draft).

			Regular Season					Playoffs				
Season	Club	Lea	GP	G	A	TP	PIM	GP	G	A	TP	PIM
1994-95	Detroit	OHL	64	30	36	66	49	21	10	9	19	8
1995-96	Detroit	OHL	66	29	43	72	31	17	6	20	26	20
1996-97	Springfield	AHL	62	7	12	19	39	3	0	0	0	4
	Richmond	ECHL	3	0	0	0	14	....	....	....	....	....

BULIS, JAN (BOO-lihs, YAHN) WSH.

Center. Shoots left. 6', 194 lbs. Born, Pardubice, Czech., March 18, 1978.
(Washington's 3rd choice, 43rd overall, in 1996 Entry Draft).

			Regular Season					Playoffs				
Season	Club	Lea	GP	G	A	TP	PIM	GP	G	A	TP	PIM
1995-96	Barrie	OHL	59	29	30	59	22	7	2	3	5	2
1996-97	Barrie	OHL	64	42	61	103	42	9	3	7	10	10

BURE, PAVEL (boo-RAY) VAN.

Right wing. Shoots left. 5'10", 189 lbs. Born, Moscow, USSR, March 31, 1971.
(Vancouver's 4th choice, 113th overall, in 1989 Entry Draft).

			Regular Season					Playoffs				
Season	Club	Lea	GP	G	A	TP	PIM	GP	G	A	TP	PIM
1987-88	CSKA	USSR	5	1	1	2	0	....	....	....	....	....
1988-89a	CSKA	USSR	32	17	9	26	8	....	....	....	....	....
1989-90	CSKA	USSR	46	14	10	24	20	....	....	....	....	....
1990-91	CSKA	USSR	44	35	11	46	24	....	....	....	....	....
1991-92b	Vancouver	NHL	65	34	26	60	30	13	6	4	10	14
1992-93	Vancouver	NHL	83	60	50	110	69	12	5	7	12	8
1993-94c	Vancouver	NHL	76	*60	47	107	86	24	*16	15	31	40
1994-95	Landshut	Ger.	1	3	0	3	2	....	....	....	....	....
	Spartak	CIS	1	2	0	2	2	....	....	....	....	....
	Vancouver	NHL	44	20	23	43	47	11	7	6	13	10
1995-96	Vancouver	NHL	15	6	7	13	8	....	....	....	....	....
1996-97	Vancouver	NHL	63	23	32	55	40	....	....	....	....	....
	NHL Totals		346	203	185	388	280	60	34	32	66	72

a Named Soviet National League Rookie-of-the-Year (1989)
b Won Calder Memorial Trophy (1992)
c NHL First All-Star Team (1994)

Played in NHL All-Star Game (1993, 1994, 1997)

BURE, VALERI (boo-RAY) MTL.

Right wing. Shoots right. 5'10", 168 lbs. Born, Moscow, USSR, June 13, 1974.
(Montreal's 2nd choice, 33rd overall, in 1992 Entry Draft).

			Regular Season					Playoffs				
Season	Club	Lea	GP	G	A	TP	PIM	GP	G	A	TP	PIM
1990-91	CSKA	USSR	3	0	0	0	0	....	....	....	....	....
1991-92	Spokane	WHL	53	27	22	49	78	10	11	6	17	10
1992-93a	Spokane	WHL	66	68	79	147	49	9	6	11	17	14
1993-94b	Spokane	WHL	59	40	62	102	48	3	5	3	8	2
1994-95	Fredericton	AHL	45	23	25	48	32	....	....	....	....	....
	Montreal	NHL	24	3	1	4	6	....	....	....	....	....
1995-96	Montreal	NHL	77	22	20	42	28	6	0	1	1	6
1996-97	Montreal	NHL	64	14	21	35	6	5	0	1	1	2
	NHL Totals		165	39	42	81	40	11	0	2	2	8

a WHL West First All-Star Team (1993)
b WHL West Second All-Star Team (1994)

BUREAU, MARC (BEWR-oh) MTL.

Center. Shoots right. 6'1", 198 lbs. Born, Trois-Rivières, Que., May 19, 1966.

			Regular Season					Playoffs				
Season	Club	Lea	GP	G	A	TP	PIM	GP	G	A	TP	PIM
1983-84	Chicoutimi	QMJHL	56	6	16	22	14	....	....	....	....	....
1984-85	Chicoutimi	QMJHL	41	30	25	55	15	....	....	....	....	....
	Granby	QMJHL	27	20	45	65	14	....	....	....	....	....
1985-86	Granby	QMJHL	19	6	17	23	36	....	....	....	....	....
	Chicoutimi	QMJHL	44	30	45	75	33	9	3	7	10	10
1986-87	Longueuil	QMJHL	66	54	58	112	68	20	17	20	37	12
1987-88	Salt Lake	IHL	69	7	20	27	86	7	0	3	3	8
1988-89	Salt Lake	IHL	76	28	36	64	119	14	7	5	12	31
1989-90	Calgary	NHL	5	0	0	0	4	....	....	....	....	....
a	Salt Lake	IHL	67	43	48	91	173	11	4	8	12	0
1990-91	Calgary	NHL	5	0	0	0	2	....	....	....	....	....
a	Salt Lake	IHL	54	40	48	88	101	....	....	....	....	....
	Minnesota	NHL	9	0	6	6	4	23	3	2	5	20
1991-92	Minnesota	NHL	46	6	4	10	50	5	0	0	0	14
	Kalamazoo	IHL	7	2	8	10	2	....	....	....	....	....
1992-93	Tampa Bay	NHL	63	10	21	31	111	....	....	....	....	....
1993-94	Tampa Bay	NHL	75	8	7	15	30	....	....	....	....	....
1994-95	Tampa Bay	NHL	48	2	12	14	30	....	....	....	....	....
1995-96	Montreal	NHL	65	3	7	10	46	6	1	1	2	4
1996-97	Montreal	NHL	43	6	9	15	16	....	....	....	....	....
	NHL Totals		359	35	66	101	293	34	4	3	7	38

a IHL Second All-Star Team (1990, 1991)

Signed as a free agent by **Calgary**, May 19, 1987. Traded to **Minnesota** by **Calgary** for Minnesota's third round choice (Sandy McCarthy) in 1991 Entry Draft, March 5, 1991. Claimed on waivers by **Tampa Bay** from **Minnesota**, October 16, 1992. Traded to **Montreal** by **Tampa Bay** for Brian Bellows, June 30, 1995.

BURR, SHAWN S.J.

Left wing/Center. Shoots left. 6'1", 200 lbs. Born, Sarnia, Ont., July 1, 1966.
(Detroit's 1st choice, 7th overall, in 1984 Entry Draft).

			Regular Season					Playoffs				
Season	Club	Lea	GP	G	A	TP	PIM	GP	G	A	TP	PIM
1983-84	Kitchener	OHL	68	41	44	85	50	16	5	12	17	22
1984-85	Detroit	NHL	9	0	0	0	2	....	....	....	....	....
	Adirondack	AHL	4	0	0	0	2	....	....	....	....	....
	Kitchener	OHL	48	24	42	66	50	4	3	3	6	2
1985-86	Detroit	NHL	5	1	0	1	4	....	....	....	....	....
	Adirondack	AHL	3	2	2	4	2	17	5	7	12	32
a	Kitchener	OHL	59	60	67	127	104	5	2	3	5	8
1986-87	Detroit	NHL	80	22	25	47	107	16	7	2	9	20
1987-88	Detroit	NHL	78	17	23	40	97	9	3	1	4	14
1988-89	Detroit	NHL	79	19	27	46	78	6	1	2	3	6
1989-90	Detroit	NHL	76	24	32	56	82	....	....	....	....	....
	Adirondack	AHL	3	4	2	6	2	....	....	....	....	....
1990-91	Detroit	NHL	80	20	30	50	112	7	0	4	4	15
1991-92	Detroit	NHL	79	19	32	51	118	11	1	5	6	10
1992-93	Detroit	NHL	80	10	25	35	74	7	2	1	3	2
1993-94	Detroit	NHL	51	10	12	22	31	7	2	0	2	6
1994-95	Detroit	NHL	42	6	8	14	60	16	0	2	2	6
1995-96	Tampa Bay	NHL	81	13	15	28	119	6	0	2	2	8
1996-97	Tampa Bay	NHL	74	14	21	35	106	....	....	....	....	....
	NHL Totals		814	175	250	425	990	85	16	19	35	87

a OHL Second All-Star Team (1986)

Traded to **Tampa Bay** by **Detroit** with Detroit's third round choice (later traded to Boston — Boston selected Jason Doyle) in 1996 Entry Draft for Marc Bergevin and Ben Hankinson, August 17, 1995. Traded to **San Jose** by **Tampa Bay** for San Jose's fifth round choice (Mark Thompson) in 1997 Entry Draft, June 21, 1997.

BURRIDGE, RANDY BUF.

Left wing. Shoots left. 5'9", 188 lbs. Born, Fort Erie, Ont., January 7, 1966.
(Boston's 7th choice, 157th overall, in 1985 Entry Draft).

			Regular Season					Playoffs				
Season	Club	Lea	GP	G	A	TP	PIM	GP	G	A	TP	PIM
1983-84	Peterborough	OHL	55	6	7	13	44	8	3	2	5	7
1984-85	Peterborough	OHL	66	49	57	106	88	17	9	16	25	18
1985-86	Boston	NHL	52	17	25	42	28	3	0	4	4	12
	Peterborough	OHL	17	15	11	26	23	3	1	3	4	2
	Moncton	AHL	....	....	....	....	....	3	0	2	2	2
1986-87	Boston	NHL	23	1	4	5	16	2	1	0	1	2
	Moncton	AHL	47	26	41	67	139	3	1	2	3	30
1987-88	Boston	NHL	79	27	28	55	105	23	2	10	12	16
1988-89	Boston	NHL	80	31	30	61	39	10	5	2	7	6
1989-90	Boston	NHL	63	17	15	32	47	21	4	11	15	14
1990-91	Boston	NHL	62	15	13	28	40	19	0	3	3	39
1991-92	Washington	NHL	66	23	44	67	50	2	0	1	1	0
1992-93	Washington	NHL	4	0	0	0	0	4	1	0	1	0
	Baltimore	AHL	2	0	1	1	2	....	....	....	....	....
1993-94	Washington	NHL	78	25	17	42	73	11	0	2	2	12
1994-95	Washington	NHL	2	0	0	0	2	....	....	....	....	....
	Los Angeles	NHL	38	4	15	19	8	....	....	....	....	....
1995-96	Buffalo	NHL	74	25	33	58	30	....	....	....	....	....
1996-97	Buffalo	NHL	55	10	21	31	20	12	5	1	6	2
	NHL Totals		676	195	245	440	458	107	18	34	52	103

Played in NHL All-Star Game (1992)

Traded to **Washington** by **Boston** for Stephen Leach, June 21, 1991. Traded to **Los Angeles** by **Washington** for Warren Rychel, February 10, 1995. Signed as a free agent by **Buffalo**, October 5, 1995.

BURT, ADAM — CAR.

Defense. Shoots left. 6'2", 207 lbs. Born, Detroit, MI, January 15, 1969.
(Hartford's 2nd choice, 39th overall, in 1987 Entry Draft).

			Regular Season					Playoffs				
Season	Club	Lea	GP	G	A	TP	PIM	GP	G	A	TP	PIM
1985-86	North Bay	OHL	49	0	11	11	81	10	0	0	0	24
1986-87	North Bay	OHL	57	4	27	31	138	24	1	6	7	68
1987-88	Binghamton	AHL	....	....	....	....	....	2	1	1	2	0
a	North Bay	OHL	66	17	53	70	176	2	0	3	3	6
1988-89	**Hartford**	**NHL**	**5**	**0**	**0**	**0**	**6**	....	....	....	....	....
	Binghamton	AHL	5	0	2	2	13	....	....	....	....	....
	North Bay	OHL	23	4	11	15	45	12	2	12	14	12
1989-90	**Hartford**	**NHL**	**63**	**4**	**8**	**12**	**105**	**2**	**0**	**0**	**0**	**0**
1990-91	**Hartford**	**NHL**	**42**	**2**	**7**	**9**	**63**	....	....	....	....	....
	Springfield	AHL	9	1	3	4	22	....	....	....	....	....
1991-92	**Hartford**	**NHL**	**66**	**9**	**15**	**24**	**93**	**2**	**0**	**0**	**0**	**0**
1992-93	**Hartford**	**NHL**	**65**	**6**	**14**	**20**	**116**	....	....	....	....	....
1993-94	**Hartford**	**NHL**	**63**	**1**	**17**	**18**	**75**	....	....	....	....	....
1994-95	**Hartford**	**NHL**	**46**	**7**	**11**	**18**	**65**	....	....	....	....	....
1995-96	**Hartford**	**NHL**	**78**	**4**	**9**	**13**	**121**	....	....	....	....	....
1996-97	**Hartford**	**NHL**	**71**	**2**	**11**	**13**	**79**	....	....	....	....	....
	NHL Totals		**499**	**35**	**92**	**127**	**723**	**4**	**0**	**0**	**0**	**0**

a OHL Second All-Star Team (1988)

BUTENSCHON, SVEN (BUH-tehn-shohn) — PIT.

Defense. Shoots left. 6'5", 201 lbs. Born, Itzehoe, West Germany, March 22, 1976.
(Pittsburgh's 3rd choice, 57th overall, in 1994 Entry Draft).

			Regular Season					Playoffs				
Season	Club	Lea	GP	G	A	TP	PIM	GP	G	A	TP	PIM
1993-94	Brandon	WHL	70	3	19	22	51	4	0	0	0	6
1994-95	Brandon	WHL	21	1	5	6	44	18	1	2	3	11
1995-96	Brandon	WHL	70	4	37	41	99	19	1	12	13	18
1996-97	Cleveland	IHL	75	3	12	15	68	10	0	1	1	4

BUTSAYEV, VIACHESLAV (boot-SIGH-yehf)

Center. Shoots left. 6'2", 200 lbs. Born, Togliatti, USSR, June 13, 1970.
(Philadelphia's 10th choice, 109th overall, in 1990 Entry Draft).

			Regular Season					Playoffs				
Season	Club	Lea	GP	G	A	TP	PIM	GP	G	A	TP	PIM
1989-90	CSKA	USSR	48	14	4	18	30	....	....	....	....	....
1990-91	CSKA	USSR	46	14	9	23	32	....	....	....	....	....
1991-92	CSKA	CIS	36	12	13	25	26	....	....	....	....	....
1992-93	CSKA	CIS	5	3	4	7	6	....	....	....	....	....
	Philadelphia	**NHL**	**52**	**2**	**14**	**16**	**61**	....	....	....	....	....
	Hershey	AHL	24	8	10	18	51	....	....	....	....	....
1993-94	**Philadelphia**	**NHL**	**47**	**12**	**9**	**21**	**58**	....	....	....	....	....
	San Jose	**NHL**	**12**	**0**	**2**	**2**	**10**	....	....	....	....	....
1994-95	Togliatti	CIS	9	2	6	8	6	....	....	....	....	....
	San Jose	**NHL**	**6**	**2**	**0**	**2**	**0**	....	....	....	....	....
	Kansas City	IHL	13	3	4	7	12	3	0	0	0	2
1995-96	**Anaheim**	**NHL**	**7**	**1**	**0**	**1**	**0**	....	....	....	....	....
	Baltimore	AHL	62	23	42	65	70	12	4	8	12	28
1996-97	Farjestad	Swe.	40	6	7	13	108	8	3	4	7	41
	NHL Totals		**124**	**17**	**25**	**42**	**129**	....	....	....	....	....

Traded to **San Jose** by **Philadelphia** for Rob Zettler, February 1, 1994. Signed as a free agent by **Anaheim**, October 19, 1995.

BUTSAYEV, YURI — DET.

Center. Shoots left. 6'1", 183 lbs. Born, Togliatti, USSR, October 11, 1978.
(Detroit's 1st choice, 49th overall, in 1997 Entry Draft).

			Regular Season					Playoffs				
Season	Club	Lea	GP	G	A	TP	PIM	GP	G	A	TP	PIM
1995-96	Togliatti 2	CIS 2				UNAVAILABLE						
	Togliatti	CIS	1	0	0	0	0	....	....	....	....	....
1996-97	Togliatti	Rus.	42	13	11	24	38	11	2	2	4	8

BUTZ, ROB — TOR.

Left wing. Shoots left. 6'3", 191 lbs. Born, Dewberry, Alta., February 24, 1975.

			Regular Season					Playoffs				
Season	Club	Lea	GP	G	A	TP	PIM	GP	G	A	TP	PIM
1992-93	Victoria	WHL	67	7	11	18	64	....	....	....	....	....
1993-94	Victoria	WHL	72	24	24	48	161	....	....	....	....	....
	St. John's	AHL	5	0	0	0	26	....	....	....	....	....
1994-95	Prince George	WHL	32	12	18	30	83	....	....	....	....	....
	Tri-City	WHL	17	4	8	12	38	17	4	5	9	22
1995-96	St. John's	AHL	74	10	20	30	127	4	1	0	1	4
1996-97	St. John's	AHL	60	16	21	37	131	8	2	1	3	15

Signed as a free agent by **Toronto**, April 1, 1993.

BUZEK, PETR (BOO-zehk) — DAL.

Defense. Shoots left. 6', 205 lbs. Born, Jihlava, Czech., April 26, 1977.
(Dallas' 3rd choice, 63rd overall, in 1995 Entry Draft).

			Regular Season					Playoffs				
Season	Club	Lea	GP	G	A	TP	PIM	GP	G	A	TP	PIM
1993-94	Dukla Jihlava	Czech.	3	0	0	0	....	....	....	....	....	....
1994-95	Dukla Jihlava	Czech.	43	2	5	7	47	2	0	0	0	2
1995-96						DID NOT PLAY – INJURED						
1996-97	Michigan	IHL	67	4	6	10	48	....	....	....	....	....

BYLSMA, DAN (BEEL-smah) — L.A.

Left wing. Shoots left. 6'2", 215 lbs. Born, Grand Haven, MI, September 19, 1970.
(Winnipeg's 7th choice, 109th overall, in 1989 Entry Draft).

			Regular Season					Playoffs				
Season	Club	Lea	GP	G	A	TP	PIM	GP	G	A	TP	PIM
1988-89	Bowling Green	CCHA	32	3	7	10	10	....	....	....	....	....
1989-90	Bowling Green	CCHA	44	13	17	30	30	....	....	....	....	....
1990-91	Bowling Green	CCHA	40	9	12	21	48	....	....	....	....	....
1991-92	Bowling Green	CCHA	34	11	14	25	24	....	....	....	....	....
1992-93	Greensboro	ECHL	60	25	35	60	66	1	0	1	1	10
	Rochester	AHL	2	0	1	1	0	....	....	....	....	....
1993-94	Greensboro	ECHL	25	14	16	30	52	....	....	....	....	....
	Albany	AHL	3	0	1	1	2	....	....	....	....	....
	Moncton	AHL	50	12	16	28	25	21	3	4	7	31
1994-95	Phoenix	IHL	81	19	23	42	41	9	4	4	8	4
1995-96	**Los Angeles**	**NHL**	**4**	**0**	**0**	**0**	**0**	....	....	....	....	....
	Phoenix	IHL	78	22	20	42	48	4	1	0	1	2
1996-97	**Los Angeles**	**NHL**	**79**	**3**	**6**	**9**	**32**	....	....	....	....	....
	NHL Totals		**83**	**3**	**6**	**9**	**32**	....	....	....	....	....

Signed as a free agent by **Los Angeles**, July 7, 1994.

CABANA, CLINT — VAN.

Defense. Shoots right. 6'2", 192 lbs. Born, Bonnyville, Alta., April 28, 1978.
(Vancouver's 7th choice, 175th overall, in 1996 Entry Draft).

			Regular Season					Playoffs				
Season	Club	Lea	GP	G	A	TP	PIM	GP	G	A	TP	PIM
1994-95	Medicine Hat	WHL	49	0	1	1	68	....	....	....	....	....
1995-96	Medicine Hat	WHL	71	1	11	12	156	5	0	1	1	35
1996-97	Medicine Hat	WHL	4	0	1	1	10	....	....	....	....	....
	Edmonton	WHL	67	3	12	15	302	....	....	....	....	....

CAIRNS, ERIC — NYR

Defense. Shoots left. 6'5", 230 lbs. Born, Oakville, Ont., June 27, 1974.
(NY Rangers' 3rd choice, 72nd overall, in 1992 Entry Draft).

			Regular Season					Playoffs				
Season	Club	Lea	GP	G	A	TP	PIM	GP	G	A	TP	PIM
1991-92	Detroit	OHL	64	1	11	12	232	7	0	0	0	31
1992-93	Detroit	OHL	64	3	13	16	194	15	0	3	3	24
1993-94	Detroit	OHL	59	7	35	42	204	17	0	4	4	46
1994-95	Birmingham	ECHL	11	1	3	4	49	....	....	....	....	....
	Binghamton	AHL	27	0	3	3	134	9	1	1	2	28
1995-96	Binghamton	AHL	46	1	13	14	192	4	0	0	0	37
	Charlotte	ECHL	6	0	1	1	34	....	....	....	....	....
1996-97	**NY Rangers**	**NHL**	**40**	**0**	**1**	**1**	**147**	**3**	**0**	**0**	**0**	**0**
	Binghamton	AHL	10	1	1	2	96	....	....	....	....	....
	NHL Totals		**40**	**0**	**1**	**1**	**147**	**3**	**0**	**0**	**0**	**0**

CALDER, KYLE — CHI.

Center. Shoots left. 5'11", 180 lbs. Born, Mannville, Alta., January 5, 1979.
(Chicago's 7th choice, 130th overall, in 1997 Entry Draft).

			Regular Season					Playoffs				
Season	Club	Lea	GP	G	A	TP	PIM	GP	G	A	TP	PIM
1995-96	Regina	WHL	27	1	7	8	10	11	0	0	0	0
1996-97	Regina	WHL	62	25	34	59	17	5	3	0	3	6

CALLAHAN, BRIAN — PIT.

Center. Shoots left. 6'1", 190 lbs. Born, Melrose, MA, July 13, 1974.
(Pittsburgh's 10th choice, 235th overall, in 1992 Entry Draft).

			Regular Season					Playoffs				
Season	Club	Lea	GP	G	A	TP	PIM	GP	G	A	TP	PIM
1993-94	Boston College	H.E.	36	11	11	22	58	....	....	....	....	....
1994-95	Boston College	H.E.	34	10	1	11	58	....	....	....	....	....
1995-96	Boston College	H.E.	36	14	8	22	38	....	....	....	....	....
1996-97	Boston College	H.E.	38	19	19	38	70	....	....	....	....	....

CALOUN, JAN (CHAH-loon) — S.J.

Right wing. Shoots right. 5'10", 190 lbs. Born, Usti-Nad-Labem, Czech., December 20, 1972.
(San Jose's 4th choice, 75th overall, in 1992 Entry Draft).

			Regular Season					Playoffs				
Season	Club	Lea	GP	G	A	TP	PIM	GP	G	A	TP	PIM
1990-91	Litvinov	Czech.	50	28	19	47	12	....	....	....	....	....
1991-92	Litvinov	Czech.	46	39	13	52	24	....	....	....	....	....
1992-93	Litvinov	Czech.	47	45	22	67	....	....	....	....	....	....
1993-94	Litvinov	Czech.	38	25	17	42	....	4	2	2	4	....
1994-95	Kansas City	IHL	76	34	39	73	50	21	13	10	23	18
1995-96	**San Jose**	**NHL**	**11**	**8**	**3**	**11**	**0**	....	....	....	....	....
	Kansas City	IHL	61	38	30	68	58	5	0	1	1	6
1996-97	**San Jose**	**NHL**	**2**	**0**	**0**	**0**	**0**	....	....	....	....	....
a	Kentucky	AHL	66	43	43	86	68	4	0	1	1	4
	NHL Totals		**13**	**8**	**3**	**11**	**0**	....	....	....	....	....

a AHL Second All-Star Team (1997)

CAMPBELL, BRIAN — BUF.

Defense. Shoots left. 5'11", 185 lbs. Born, Strathroy, Ont., May 23, 1979.
(Buffalo's 7th choice, 156th overall, in 1997 Entry Draft).

			Regular Season					Playoffs				
Season	Club	Lea	GP	G	A	TP	PIM	GP	G	A	TP	PIM
1995-96	Ottawa	OHL	66	5	22	27	23	4	0	1	1	2
1996-97	Ottawa	OHL	66	7	36	43	12	24	2	11	13	8

CAMPBELL, ED — NYR

Defense. Shoots left. 6'2", 212 lbs. Born, Worcester, MA, November 26, 1974.
(NY Rangers' 9th choice, 190th overall, in 1993 Entry Draft).

			Regular Season					Playoffs				
Season	Club	Lea	GP	G	A	TP	PIM	GP	G	A	TP	PIM
1993-94	Lowell	H.E.	40	8	16	24	114	....	....	....	....	....
1994-95	Lowell	H.E.	34	6	24	30	105	....	....	....	....	....
1995-96	Lowell	H.E.	39	6	33	39	*107	....	....	....	....	....
1996-97	Binghamton	AHL	74	5	17	22	108	4	0	0	0	2

CAMPBELL, JIM — ST.L.

Center. Shoots right. 6'2", 185 lbs. Born, Worcester, MA, April 3, 1973.
(Montreal's 2nd choice, 28th overall, in 1991 Entry Draft).

			Regular Season					Playoffs				
Season	Club	Lea	GP	G	A	TP	PIM	GP	G	A	TP	PIM
1991-92	Hull	QMJHL	64	41	44	85	51	6	7	3	10	8
1992-93	Hull	QMJHL	50	42	29	71	66	8	11	4	15	43
1993-94	U.S. National	....	56	24	33	57	59	....	....	....	....	....
	U.S. Olympic	....	8	0	0	0	6	....	....	....	....	....
	Fredericton	AHL	19	6	17	23	6	....	....	....	....	....
1994-95	Fredericton	AHL	77	27	24	51	103	12	0	7	7	8
1995-96	Fredericton	AHL	44	28	23	51	24	....	....	....	....	....
	Anaheim	**NHL**	**16**	**2**	**3**	**5**	**36**	....	....	....	....	....
	Baltimore	AHL	16	13	7	20	8	12	7	5	12	10
1996-97a	**St. Louis**	**NHL**	**68**	**23**	**20**	**43**	**68**	**4**	**1**	**0**	**1**	**6**
	NHL Totals		**84**	**25**	**23**	**48**	**104**	**4**	**1**	**0**	**1**	**6**

a NHL All-Rookie Team (1997)

Traded to **Anaheim** by **Montreal** for Robert Dirk, January 21, 1996. Signed as a free agent by **St. Louis**, July 11, 1996.

CARBONNEAU, GUY (KAR-buhn-oh, GEE) DAL.

Center. Shoots right. 5'11", 186 lbs. Born, Sept-Iles, Que., March 18, 1960.
(Montreal's 4th choice, 44th overall, in 1979 Entry Draft).

			Regular Season					Playoffs				
Season	Club	Lea	GP	G	A	TP	PIM	GP	G	A	TP	PIM
1976-77	Chicoutimi	QJHL	59	9	20	29	8	4	1	0	1	0
1977-78	Chicoutimi	QJHL	70	28	55	83	60	....	....	....	....	....
1978-79	Chicoutimi	QJHL	72	62	79	141	47	4	2	1	3	4
1979-80	Chicoutimi	QJHL	72	72	110	182	66	12	9	15	24	28
	Nova Scotia	AHL	....	....	....	....	....	2	1	1	2	2
1980-81	**Montreal**	**NHL**	**2**	**0**	**1**	**1**	**0**	....	....	....	....	....
	Nova Scotia	AHL	78	35	53	88	87	6	1	3	4	9
1981-82	Nova Scotia	AHL	77	27	67	94	124	9	2	7	9	8
1982-83	**Montreal**	**NHL**	**77**	**18**	**29**	**47**	**68**	**3**	**0**	**0**	**0**	**2**
1983-84	**Montreal**	**NHL**	**78**	**24**	**30**	**54**	**75**	**15**	**4**	**3**	**7**	**12**
1984-85	**Montreal**	**NHL**	**79**	**23**	**34**	**57**	**43**	**12**	**4**	**3**	**7**	**8**
1985-86	**Montreal**	**NHL**	**80**	**20**	**36**	**56**	**57**	**20**	**7**	**5**	**12**	**35** ♦
1986-87	**Montreal**	**NHL**	**79**	**18**	**27**	**45**	**68**	**17**	**3**	**8**	**11**	**20**
1987-88a	**Montreal**	**NHL**	**80**	**17**	**21**	**38**	**61**	**11**	**0**	**4**	**4**	**2**
1988-89a	**Montreal**	**NHL**	**79**	**26**	**30**	**56**	**44**	**21**	**4**	**5**	**9**	**10**
1989-90	**Montreal**	**NHL**	**68**	**19**	**36**	**55**	**37**	**11**	**2**	**3**	**5**	**6**
1990-91	**Montreal**	**NHL**	**78**	**20**	**24**	**44**	**63**	**13**	**1**	**5**	**6**	**10**
1991-92a	**Montreal**	**NHL**	**72**	**18**	**21**	**39**	**39**	**11**	**1**	**1**	**2**	**6**
1992-93	**Montreal**	**NHL**	**61**	**4**	**13**	**17**	**20**	**20**	**3**	**3**	**6**	**10** ♦
1993-94	**Montreal**	**NHL**	**79**	**14**	**24**	**38**	**48**	**7**	**1**	**3**	**4**	**4**
1994-95	**St. Louis**	**NHL**	**42**	**5**	**11**	**16**	**16**	**7**	**1**	**2**	**3**	**6**
1995-96	**Dallas**	**NHL**	**71**	**8**	**15**	**23**	**38**	....	....	....	....	....
1996-97	**Dallas**	**NHL**	**73**	**5**	**16**	**21**	**36**	**7**	**0**	**1**	**1**	**6**
	NHL Totals		**1098**	**239**	**368**	**607**	**713**	**175**	**31**	**46**	**77**	**137**

a Won Frank J. Selke Trophy (1988, 1989, 1992)

Traded to **St. Louis** by **Montreal** for Jim Montgomery, August 19, 1994. Traded to **Dallas** by **St. Louis** for Paul Broten, October 2, 1995.

CARDARELLI, JOE T.B.

Left winger. Shoots left. 6', 203 lbs. Born, Vancouver, B.C., June 13, 1977.
(Tampa Bay's 7th choice, 186th overall, in 1995 Entry Draft).

			Regular Season					Playoffs				
Season	Club	Lea	GP	G	A	TP	PIM	GP	G	A	TP	PIM
1993-94	Spokane	WHL	51	7	11	18	9	2	0	0	0	0
1994-95	Spokane	WHL	71	27	22	49	20	11	4	9	13	0
1995-96	Spokane	WHL	44	25	19	44	21	18	4	0	4	4
1996-97	Spokane	WHL	66	34	37	71	39	9	6	1	7	0

CARKNER, TERRY FLA.

Defense. Shoots left. 6'3", 210 lbs. Born, Smiths Falls, Ont., March 7, 1966.
(NY Rangers' 1st choice, 14th overall, in 1984 Entry Draft).

			Regular Season					Playoffs				
Season	Club	Lea	GP	G	A	TP	PIM	GP	G	A	TP	PIM
1983-84	Peterborough	OHL	58	4	19	23	77	8	0	6	6	13
1984-85a	Peterborough	OHL	64	14	47	61	125	17	2	10	12	11
1985-86b	Peterborough	OHL	54	12	32	44	106	16	1	7	8	17
1986-87	**NY Rangers**	**NHL**	**52**	**2**	**13**	**15**	**118**	**1**	**0**	**0**	**0**	**0**
	New Haven	AHL	12	2	6	8	56	3	1	0	1	0
1987-88	**Quebec**	**NHL**	**63**	**3**	**24**	**27**	**159**	....	....	....	....	....
1988-89	**Philadelphia**	**NHL**	**78**	**11**	**32**	**43**	**149**	**19**	**1**	**5**	**6**	**28**
1989-90	**Philadelphia**	**NHL**	**63**	**4**	**18**	**22**	**169**	....	....	....	....	....
1990-91	**Philadelphia**	**NHL**	**79**	**7**	**25**	**32**	**204**	....	....	....	....	....
1991-92	**Philadelphia**	**NHL**	**73**	**4**	**12**	**16**	**195**	....	....	....	....	....
1992-93	**Philadelphia**	**NHL**	**83**	**3**	**16**	**19**	**150**	....	....	....	....	....
1993-94	**Detroit**	**NHL**	**68**	**1**	**6**	**7**	**130**	**7**	**0**	**0**	**0**	**4**
1994-95	**Detroit**	**NHL**	**20**	**1**	**2**	**3**	**21**	....	....	....	....	....
1995-96	**Florida**	**NHL**	**73**	**3**	**10**	**13**	**80**	**22**	**0**	**4**	**4**	**10**
1996-97	**Florida**	**NHL**	**70**	**0**	**14**	**14**	**96**	**5**	**0**	**0**	**0**	**6**
	NHL Totals		**722**	**39**	**172**	**211**	**1471**	**54**	**1**	**9**	**10**	**48**

a OHL Second All-Star Team (1985)
b OHL First All-Star Team (1986)

Traded to **Quebec** by **NY Rangers** with Jeff Jackson for John Ogrodnick and David Shaw, September 30, 1987. Traded to **Philadelphia** by **Quebec** for Greg Smyth and Philadelphia's third round choice (John Tanner) in the 1989 Entry Draft, July 25, 1988. Traded to **Detroit** by **Philadelphia** for Yves Racine and Detroit's fourth round choice (Sebastien Vallee) in 1994 Entry Draft, October 5, 1993. Signed as a free agent by **Florida**, August 8, 1995.

CARNEY, KEITH CHI.

Defense. Shoots left. 6'2", 205 lbs. Born, Providence, RI, February 3, 1970.
(Buffalo's 3rd choice, 76th overall, in 1988 Entry Draft).

			Regular Season					Playoffs				
Season	Club	Lea	GP	G	A	TP	PIM	GP	G	A	TP	PIM
1988-89	U. of Maine	H.E.	40	4	22	26	24	....	....	....	....	....
1989-90ab	U. of Maine	H.E.	41	3	41	44	43	....	....	....	....	....
1990-91cd	U. of Maine	H.E.	40	7	49	56	38	....	....	....	....	....
1991-92	U.S. National	....	49	2	17	19	16	....	....	....	....	....
	Buffalo	**NHL**	**14**	**1**	**2**	**3**	**18**	**7**	**0**	**3**	**3**	**0**
	Rochester	AHL	24	1	10	11	2	2	0	2	2	0
1992-93	**Buffalo**	**NHL**	**30**	**2**	**4**	**6**	**55**	**8**	**0**	**3**	**3**	**6**
	Rochester	AHL	41	5	21	26	32	....	....	....	....	....
1993-94	**Buffalo**	**NHL**	**7**	**1**	**3**	**4**	**4**	....	....	....	....	....
	Chicago	**NHL**	**30**	**3**	**5**	**8**	**35**	**6**	**0**	**1**	**1**	**4**
	Indianapolis	IHL	28	0	14	14	20	....	....	....	....	....
1994-95	**Chicago**	**NHL**	**18**	**1**	**0**	**1**	**11**	**4**	**0**	**1**	**1**	**0**
1995-96	**Chicago**	**NHL**	**82**	**5**	**14**	**19**	**94**	**10**	**0**	**3**	**3**	**4**
1996-97	**Chicago**	**NHL**	**81**	**3**	**15**	**18**	**62**	**6**	**1**	**1**	**2**	**2**
	NHL Totals		**262**	**16**	**43**	**59**	**279**	**41**	**1**	**12**	**13**	**16**

a Hockey East Second All-Star Team (1990)
b NCAA East Second All-American Team (1990)
c Hockey East First All-Star Team (1991)
d NCAA East First All-American Team (1991)

Traded to **Chicago** by **Buffalo** with Buffalo's sixth round choice (Marc Magliarditi) in 1995 Entry Draft for Craig Muni and Chicago's fifth round choice (Daniel Bienvenue) in 1995 Entry Draft, October 26, 1993.

CARPENTER, BOB N.J.

Center. Shoots left. 6', 200 lbs. Born, Beverly, MA, July 13, 1963.
(Washington's 1st choice, 3rd overall, in 1981 Entry Draft).

			Regular Season					Playoffs				
Season	Club	Lea	GP	G	A	TP	PIM	GP	G	A	TP	PIM
1980-81	St. John's	HS	18	14	24	38	....	....	....	....	....	....
1981-82	**Washington**	**NHL**	**80**	**32**	**35**	**67**	**69**	....	....	....	....	....
1982-83	**Washington**	**NHL**	**80**	**32**	**37**	**69**	**64**	**4**	**1**	**0**	**1**	**2**
1983-84	**Washington**	**NHL**	**80**	**28**	**40**	**68**	**51**	**8**	**2**	**1**	**3**	**25**
1984-85	**Washington**	**NHL**	**80**	**53**	**42**	**95**	**87**	**5**	**1**	**4**	**5**	**8**
1985-86	**Washington**	**NHL**	**80**	**27**	**29**	**56**	**105**	**9**	**5**	**4**	**9**	**12**
1986-87	**Washington**	**NHL**	**22**	**5**	**7**	**12**	**21**	....	....	....	....	....
	NY Rangers	**NHL**	**28**	**2**	**8**	**10**	**20**	....	....	....	....	....
	Los Angeles	**NHL**	**10**	**2**	**3**	**5**	**6**	**5**	**1**	**2**	**3**	**2**
1987-88	**Los Angeles**	**NHL**	**71**	**19**	**33**	**52**	**84**	**5**	**1**	**1**	**2**	**0**
1988-89	**Los Angeles**	**NHL**	**39**	**11**	**15**	**26**	**16**	....	....	....	....	....
	Boston	**NHL**	**18**	**5**	**9**	**14**	**10**	**8**	**1**	**1**	**2**	**4**
1989-90	**Boston**	**NHL**	**80**	**25**	**31**	**56**	**97**	**21**	**4**	**6**	**10**	**39**
1990-91	**Boston**	**NHL**	**29**	**8**	**8**	**16**	**22**	**1**	**0**	**1**	**1**	**2**
1991-92	**Boston**	**NHL**	**60**	**25**	**23**	**48**	**46**	**8**	**0**	**1**	**1**	**6**
1992-93	**Washington**	**NHL**	**68**	**11**	**17**	**28**	**65**	**6**	**1**	**4**	**5**	**6**
1993-94	**New Jersey**	**NHL**	**76**	**10**	**23**	**33**	**51**	**20**	**1**	**7**	**8**	**20**
1994-95	**New Jersey**	**NHL**	**41**	**5**	**11**	**16**	**19**	**17**	**1**	**4**	**5**	**6** ♦
1995-96	**New Jersey**	**NHL**	**52**	**5**	**5**	**10**	**14**	....	....	....	....	....
1996-97	**New Jersey**	**NHL**	**62**	**4**	**15**	**19**	**14**	**10**	**1**	**2**	**3**	**2**
	NHL Totals		**1056**	**309**	**391**	**700**	**861**	**127**	**20**	**38**	**58**	**134**

Played in NHL All-Star Game (1985)

Traded to **NY Rangers** by **Washington** with Washington's second round choice (Jason Prosofsky) in 1989 Entry Draft for Bob Crawford, Kelly Miller and Mike Ridley, January 1, 1987. Traded to **Los Angeles** by **NY Rangers** with Tom Laidlaw for Jeff Crossman, Marcel Dionne and Los Angeles' third round choice (later traded to Minnesota — Minnesota selected Murray Garbutt) in 1989 Entry Draft. Traded to **Boston** by **Los Angeles** for Steve Kasper, January 23, 1989. Signed as a free agent by **Washington**, June 30, 1992. Signed as a free agent by **New Jersey**, September 30, 1993.

CARSON, JIMMY

Center. Shoots right. 6'1", 200 lbs. Born, Southfield, MI, July 20, 1968.
(Los Angeles' 1st choice, 2nd overall, in 1986 Entry Draft).

			Regular Season					Playoffs				
Season	Club	Lea	GP	G	A	TP	PIM	GP	G	A	TP	PIM
1984-85	Verdun	QMJHL	68	44	72	116	12	14	9	17	26	12
1985-86a	Verdun	QMJHL	69	70	83	153	46	5	2	6	8	0
1986-87b	**Los Angeles**	**NHL**	**80**	**37**	**42**	**79**	**22**	**5**	**1**	**2**	**3**	**6**
1987-88	**Los Angeles**	**NHL**	**80**	**55**	**52**	**107**	**45**	**5**	**5**	**3**	**8**	**4**
1988-89	**Edmonton**	**NHL**	**80**	**49**	**51**	**100**	**36**	**7**	**2**	**1**	**3**	**6**
1989-90	**Edmonton**	**NHL**	**4**	**1**	**2**	**3**	**0**	....	....	....	....	....
	Detroit	**NHL**	**44**	**20**	**16**	**36**	**8**	....	....	....	....	....
1990-91	**Detroit**	**NHL**	**64**	**21**	**25**	**46**	**28**	**7**	**2**	**1**	**3**	**4**
1991-92	**Detroit**	**NHL**	**80**	**34**	**35**	**69**	**30**	**11**	**2**	**3**	**5**	**0**
1992-93	**Detroit**	**NHL**	**52**	**25**	**26**	**51**	**18**	....	....	....	....	....
	Los Angeles	**NHL**	**34**	**12**	**10**	**22**	**14**	**18**	**5**	**4**	**9**	**2**
1993-94	**Los Angeles**	**NHL**	**25**	**4**	**7**	**11**	**2**	....	....	....	....	....
	Vancouver	**NHL**	**34**	**7**	**10**	**17**	**22**	**2**	**0**	**1**	**1**	**0**
1994-95	**Hartford**	**NHL**	**38**	**9**	**10**	**19**	**29**	....	....	....	....	....
1995-96	**Hartford**	**NHL**	**11**	**1**	**0**	**1**	**0**	....	....	....	....	....
	Lausanne	Switz.	13	3	4	7	14	....	....	....	....	....
1996-97	Detroit	IHL	18	7	16	23	4	13	4	6	10	12
	NHL Totals		**626**	**275**	**286**	**561**	**254**	**55**	**17**	**15**	**32**	**22**

a QMJHL Second All-Star Team (1986)
b Named to NHL All-Rookie Team (1987)

Played in NHL All-Star Game (1989)

Traded to **Edmonton** by **Los Angeles** with Martin Gelinas, Los Angeles' first round choices in 1989 (later traded to New Jersey — New Jersey selected Jason Miller), 1991 (Martin Rucinsky) and 1993 (Nick Stajduhar) Entry Drafts and cash for Wayne Gretzky, Mike Krushelnyski and Marty McSorley, August 9, 1988. Traded to **Detroit** by **Edmonton** with Kevin McClelland and Edmonton's fifth round choice (later traded to Montreal — Montreal selected Brad Layzell) in 1991 Entry Draft for Petr Klima, Joe Murphy, Adam Graves and Jeff Sharples, November 2, 1989. Traded to **Los Angeles** by **Detroit** with Marc Potvin and Gary Shuchuk for Paul Coffey, Sylvain Couturier and Jim Hiller, January 29, 1993. Traded to **Vancouver** by **Los Angeles** for Dixon Ward, January 8, 1994. Signed as a free agent by **Hartford**, July 15, 1994.

CARTER, ANSON BOS.

Center. Shoots right. 6'1", 175 lbs. Born, Toronto, Ont., June 6, 1974.
(Quebec's 10th choice, 220th overall, in 1992 Entry Draft).

			Regular Season					Playoffs				
Season	Club	Lea	GP	G	A	TP	PIM	GP	G	A	TP	PIM
1992-93	Michigan State	CCHA	34	15	7	22	20	....	....	....	....	....
1993-94a	Michigan State	CCHA	39	30	24	54	36	....	....	....	....	....
1994-95ab	Michigan State	CCHA	39	34	17	51	40	....	....	....	....	....
1995-96c	Michigan State	CCHA	42	23	20	43	36	....	....	....	....	....
1996-97	**Washington**	**NHL**	**19**	**3**	**2**	**5**	**7**	....	....	....	....	....
	Portland	AHL	27	19	19	38	11	....	....	....	....	....
	Boston	**NHL**	**19**	**8**	**5**	**13**	**2**	....	....	....	....	....
	NHL Totals		**38**	**11**	**7**	**18**	**9**	....	....	....	....	....

a CCHA First All-Star Team (1994, 1995)
b NCAA West Second All-American Team (1995)
c CCHA Second All-Star Team (1996)

Traded to **Washington** by **Colorado** for Washington's fourth round choice (Ben Storey) in 1996 Entry Draft, April 3, 1996. Traded to **Boston** by **Washington** with Jim Carey, Jason Allison, Washington's third round choice (Lee Goren) in 1997 Entry Draft and a conditional choice in 1998 Entry Draft for Bill Ranford, Adam Oates and Rick Tocchet, March 1, 1997.

CARTER, SHAWN TOR.

Center. Shoots left. 6'2", 210 lbs. Born, Eagle River, WI, April 16, 1973.

			Regular Season					Playoffs				
Season	Club	Lea	GP	G	A	TP	PIM	GP	G	A	TP	PIM
1992-93	U. Wisconsin	WCHA	5	1	0	1	4	....	....	....	....	....
1993-94	U. Wisconsin	WCHA	16	2	2	4	24	....	....	....	....	....
1994-95	U. Wisconsin	WCHA	43	15	13	28	98	....	....	....	....	....
1995-96	U. Wisconsin	WCHA	40	17	28	45	50	....	....	....	....	....
1996-97	Orlando	IHL	53	22	25	47	40	....	....	....	....	....
	St. John's	AHL	18	5	6	11	15	7	1	2	3	6

Signed as a free agent by **Toronto**, February 14, 1997.

CASSELMAN, MIKE

Center. Shoots left. 5'11", 190 lbs. Born, Morrisburg, Ont., August 23, 1968.
(Detroit's 1st choice, 3rd overall, in 1990 Supplemental Draft).

			Regular Season					Playoffs				
Season	Club	Lea	GP	G	A	TP	PIM	GP	G	A	TP	PIM
1987-88	Clarkson	ECAC	24	4	1	5	....	....	....	....	....	....
1988-89	Clarkson	ECAC	31	3	14	17	....	....	....	....	....	....
1989-90	Clarkson	ECAC	34	22	21	43	69	....	....	....	....	....
1990-91	Clarkson	ECAC	40	19	35	54	44	....	....	....	....	....
1991-92a	Toledo	ECHL	61	39	60	99	83	5	0	1	1	6
	Adirondack	AHL	1	0	0	0	0	....	....	....	....	....
1992-93	Adirondack	AHL	60	12	19	31	27	8	3	3	6	0
	Toledo	ECHL	3	0	1	1	2	....	....	....	....	....
1993-94	Adirondack	AHL	77	17	38	55	34	12	2	4	6	10
1994-95	Adirondack	AHL	60	17	43	60	42	4	0	0	0	2
1995-96	**Florida**	**NHL**	**3**	**0**	**0**	**0**	**0**	....	....	....	....	....
	Carolina	AHL	70	34	68	102	46	....	....	....	....	....
1996-97	Cincinnati	IHL	68	30	34	64	54	3	1	0	1	2
	NHL Totals		**3**	**0**	**0**	**0**	**0**	....	....	....	....	....

a ECHL Second All-Star Team (1992)

Signed as a free agent by **Florida**, October 31, 1995.

CASSELS, ANDREW (KAS-uhls) CAR.

Center. Shoots left. 5'11", 177 lbs. Born, Bramalea, Ont., July 23, 1969.
(Montreal's 1st choice, 17th overall, in 1987 Entry Draft).

			Regular Season					Playoffs				
Season	Club	Lea	GP	G	A	TP	PIM	GP	G	A	TP	PIM
1986-87	Ottawa	OHL	66	26	66	92	28	11	5	9	14	7
1987-88a	Ottawa	OHL	61	48	*103	*151	39	16	8	*24	*32	13
1988-89a	Ottawa	OHL	56	37	97	134	66	12	5	10	15	10
1989-90	**Montreal**	**NHL**	**6**	**2**	**0**	**2**	**2**	....	....	....	....	....
	Sherbrooke	AHL	55	22	45	67	25	12	2	11	13	6
1990-91	**Montreal**	**NHL**	**54**	**6**	**19**	**25**	**20**	**8**	**0**	**2**	**2**	**2**
1991-92	**Hartford**	**NHL**	**67**	**11**	**30**	**41**	**18**	**7**	**2**	**4**	**6**	**6**
1992-93	**Hartford**	**NHL**	**84**	**21**	**64**	**85**	**62**	....	....	....	....	....
1993-94	**Hartford**	**NHL**	**79**	**16**	**42**	**58**	**37**	....	....	....	....	....
1994-95	**Hartford**	**NHL**	**46**	**7**	**30**	**37**	**18**	....	....	....	....	....
1995-96	**Hartford**	**NHL**	**81**	**20**	**43**	**63**	**39**	....	....	....	....	....
1996-97	**Hartford**	**NHL**	**81**	**22**	**44**	**66**	**46**	....	....	....	....	....
	NHL Totals		**498**	**105**	**272**	**377**	**242**	**15**	**2**	**6**	**8**	**8**

a OHL First All-Star Team (1988,1989)

Traded to **Hartford** by **Montreal** for Hartford's second round choice (Valeri Bure) in 1992 Entry Draft, September 17, 1991.

CAULFIELD, KEVIN WSH.

Right wing. Shoots right. 6'2", 210 lbs. Born, Boston, MA, January 7, 1978.
(Washington's 4th choice, 116th overall, in 1997 Entry Draft).

			Regular Season					Playoffs				
Season	Club	Lea	GP	G	A	TP	PIM	GP	G	A	TP	PIM
1996-97	Boston College	H.E.	38	5	10	15	90	....	....	....	....	....

CAVA, PETER (KAH-va) TOR.

Center. Shoots left. 5'11", 175 lbs. Born, Thunder Bay, Ont., February 14, 1978.
(Toronto's 7th choice, 110th overall, in 1996 Entry Draft).

			Regular Season					Playoffs				
Season	Club	Lea	GP	G	A	TP	PIM	GP	G	A	TP	PIM
1995-96	S.S. Marie	OHL	40	14	17	31	44	4	1	1	2	4
1996-97	S.S. Marie	OHL	55	14	36	50	64	11	5	4	9	27

CAVANAGH, CHAD WSH.

Center. Shoots left. 5'11", 166 lbs. Born, Peterborough, Ont., February 13, 1978.
(Washington's 12th choice, 232nd overall, in 1996 Entry Draft).

			Regular Season					Playoffs				
Season	Club	Lea	GP	G	A	TP	PIM	GP	G	A	TP	PIM
1995-96	London	OHL	65	14	17	31	55	....	....	....	....	....
1996-97	London	OHL	1	0	0	0	2	....	....	....	....	....
	Detroit	OHL	37	11	17	28	31	....	....	....	....	....
	Sudbury	OHL	27	5	9	14	14	....	....	....	....	....

CECH, VRATISLAV (CHEHKH) FLA.

Defense. Shoots left. 6'3", 196 lbs. Born, Tabor, Czech., January 28, 1979.
(Florida's 3rd choice, 56th overall, in 1997 Entry Draft).

			Regular Season					Playoffs				
Season	Club	Lea	GP	G	A	TP	PIM	GP	G	A	TP	PIM
1995-96	HC Brno	Czech. Jr.	37	10	13	23	....	....	....	....	....	....
1996-97	Kitchener	OHL	57	5	19	24	72	13	1	2	3	12

CERVEN, MARTIN (CHEHR-vehn) PHI.

Center. Shoots left. 6'4", 200 lbs. Born, Trencin, Czech., March 7, 1977.
(Edmonton's 6th choice, 161st overall, in 1995 Entry Draft).

			Regular Season					Playoffs				
Season	Club	Lea	GP	G	A	TP	PIM	GP	G	A	TP	PIM
1994-95	Dukla Trencin	Slo. Jr.	22	8	3	11	....	....	....	....	....	....
1995-96	Spokane	WHL	40	9	9	18	42	....	....	....	....	....
	Seattle	WHL	27	6	14	20	10	5	1	2	3	0
1996-97	Seattle	WHL	72	27	25	52	64	15	2	6	8	14

Traded to **Philadelphia** by **Edmonton** for Philadelphia's seventh round choice (Chad Hinz) in 1997 Entry Draft, June 18, 1997.

CHAMBERS, SHAWN DAL.

Defense. Shoots left. 6'2", 200 lbs. Born, Sterling Hts., MI, October 11, 1966.
(Minnesota's 1st choice, 4th overall, in 1987 Supplemental Draft).

			Regular Season					Playoffs				
Season	Club	Lea	GP	G	A	TP	PIM	GP	G	A	TP	PIM
1985-86	Alaska-Fair.	G.N.	25	15	21	36	34	....	....	....	....	....
1986-87	Alaska-Fair.	G.N.	28	11	19	30	....	....	....	....	....	....
	Seattle	WHL	28	8	25	33	58	....	....	....	....	....
	Fort Wayne	IHL	12	2	6	8	0	10	1	4	5	5
1987-88	**Minnesota**	**NHL**	**19**	**1**	**7**	**8**	**21**	....	....	....	....	....
	Kalamazoo	IHL	19	1	6	7	22	....	....	....	....	....
1988-89	**Minnesota**	**NHL**	**72**	**5**	**19**	**24**	**80**	**3**	**0**	**2**	**2**	**0**
1989-90	**Minnesota**	**NHL**	**78**	**8**	**18**	**26**	**81**	**7**	**2**	**1**	**3**	**10**
1990-91	**Minnesota**	**NHL**	**29**	**1**	**3**	**4**	**24**	**23**	**0**	**7**	**7**	**16**
	Kalamazoo	IHL	3	1	1	2	0	....	....	....	....	....
1991-92	**Washington**	**NHL**	**2**	**0**	**0**	**0**	**2**	....	....	....	....	....
	Baltimore	AHL	5	2	3	5	9	....	....	....	....	....
1992-93	**Tampa Bay**	**NHL**	**55**	**10**	**29**	**39**	**36**	....	....	....	....	....
	Atlanta	IHL	6	0	2	2	18	....	....	....	....	....
1993-94	**Tampa Bay**	**NHL**	**66**	**11**	**23**	**34**	**23**	....	....	....	....	....
1994-95	**Tampa Bay**	**NHL**	**24**	**2**	**12**	**14**	**6**	....	....	....	....	....
	New Jersey	**NHL**	**21**	**2**	**5**	**7**	**6**	**20**	**4**	**5**	**9**	**2** ♦
1995-96	**New Jersey**	**NHL**	**64**	**2**	**21**	**23**	**18**	....	....	....	....	....
1996-97	**New Jersey**	**NHL**	**73**	**4**	**17**	**21**	**19**	**10**	**1**	**6**	**7**	**6**
	NHL Totals		**503**	**46**	**154**	**200**	**316**	**63**	**7**	**21**	**28**	**34**

Traded to **Washington** by **Minnesota** for Steve Maltais and Trent Klatt, June 21, 1991. Claimed by **Tampa Bay** from **Washington** in Expansion Draft, June 18, 1992. Traded to **New Jersey** by **Tampa Bay** with Danton Cole for Alexander Semak and Ben Hankinson, March 14, 1995. Signed as a free agent by **Dallas**, July 17, 1997.

CHARA, ZDENO (KHAH-rah, ZDEH-noh) NYI

Defense. Shoots left. 6'8", 231 lbs. Born, Trencin, Czech., March 18, 1977.
(NY Islanders' 3rd choice, 56th overall, in 1996 Entry Draft).

			Regular Season					Playoffs				
Season	Club	Lea	GP	G	A	TP	PIM	GP	G	A	TP	PIM
1994-95	Trencin	Slo. Jr.	2	0	0	0	0	....	....	....	....	....
	Trencin	Slo. Jr. B	30	22	22	44	113	....	....	....	....	....
1995-96	Trencin	Slo. Jr.	22	1	13	14	80	....	....	....	....	....
	Piestany	Slo. 2	10	1	3	4	10	....	....	....	....	....
	Sparta	Czech. Jr.	15	1	2	3	42	....	....	....	....	....
	Sparta	Czech.	1	0	0	0	0	....	....	....	....	....
1996-97	Prince George	WHL	49	3	19	22	120	15	1	7	8	45

CHARRON, ERIC (shah-ROHN) WSH.

Defense. Shoots left. 6'3", 192 lbs. Born, Verdun, Que., January 14, 1970.
(Montreal's 1st choice, 20th overall, in 1988 Entry Draft).

			Regular Season					Playoffs				
Season	Club	Lea	GP	G	A	TP	PIM	GP	G	A	TP	PIM
1987-88	Trois-Rivières	QMJHL	67	3	13	16	135	....	....	....	....	....
1988-89	Trois-Rivières	QMJHL	38	2	16	18	111	....	....	....	....	....
	Verdun	QMJHL	28	2	15	17	66	....	....	....	....	....
	Sherbrooke	AHL	1	0	0	0	0	....	....	....	....	....
1989-90	St-Hyacinthe	QMJHL	68	13	38	51	152	11	3	4	7	67
	Sherbrooke	AHL	....	....	....	....	....	2	0	0	0	0
1990-91	Fredericton	AHL	71	1	11	12	108	2	1	0	1	29
1991-92	Fredericton	AHL	59	2	11	13	98	6	1	0	1	4
1992-93	**Montreal**	**NHL**	**3**	**0**	**0**	**0**	**2**	....	....	....	....	....
	Fredericton	AHL	54	3	13	16	93	....	....	....	....	....
	Atlanta	IHL	11	0	2	2	12	3	0	1	1	6
1993-94	**Tampa Bay**	**NHL**	**4**	**0**	**0**	**0**	**2**	....	....	....	....	....
	Atlanta	IHL	66	5	18	23	144	14	1	4	5	28
1994-95	**Tampa Bay**	**NHL**	**45**	**1**	**4**	**5**	**26**	....	....	....	....	....
1995-96	**Tampa Bay**	**NHL**	**14**	**0**	**0**	**0**	**18**	....	....	....	....	....
	Washington	**NHL**	**4**	**0**	**1**	**1**	**4**	**6**	**0**	**0**	**0**	**8**
	Portland	AHL	45	0	8	8	88	20	1	1	2	33
1996-97	**Washington**	**NHL**	**25**	**1**	**1**	**2**	**20**	....	....	....	....	....
	Portland	AHL	29	6	8	14	55	5	0	3	3	0
	NHL Totals		**95**	**2**	**6**	**8**	**72**	**6**	**0**	**0**	**0**	**8**

Traded to **Tampa Bay** by **Montreal** with Alain Cote and future considerations (Donald Dufresne, June 18, 1993) for Rob Ramage, March 20, 1993. Traded to **Washington** by **Tampa Bay** for Washington's seventh round choice (Eero Somervuori) in 1997 Entry Draft, November 16, 1995.

CHASE, KELLY TOR.

Right wing. Shoots right. 5'11", 193 lbs. Born, Porcupine Plain, Sask., October 25, 1967.

			Regular Season					Playoffs				
Season	Club	Lea	GP	G	A	TP	PIM	GP	G	A	TP	PIM
1985-86	Saskatoon	WHL	57	7	18	25	172	10	3	4	7	37
1986-87	Saskatoon	WHL	68	17	29	46	285	11	2	8	10	37
1987-88	Saskatoon	WHL	70	21	34	55	*343	9	3	5	8	32
1988-89	Peoria	IHL	38	14	7	21	278	....	....	....	....	....
1989-90	**St. Louis**	**NHL**	**43**	**1**	**3**	**4**	**244**	**9**	**1**	**0**	**1**	**46**
	Peoria	IHL	10	1	2	3	76	....	....	....	....	....
1990-91	**St. Louis**	**NHL**	**2**	**1**	**0**	**1**	**15**	**6**	**0**	**0**	**0**	**18**
	Peoria	IHL	61	20	34	54	406	10	4	3	7	61
1991-92	**St. Louis**	**NHL**	**46**	**1**	**2**	**3**	**264**	**1**	**0**	**0**	**0**	**7**
1992-93	**St. Louis**	**NHL**	**49**	**2**	**5**	**7**	**204**	....	....	....	....	....
1993-94	**St. Louis**	**NHL**	**68**	**2**	**5**	**7**	**278**	**4**	**0**	**1**	**1**	**6**
1994-95	**Hartford**	**NHL**	**28**	**0**	**4**	**4**	**141**	....	....	....	....	....
1995-96	**Hartford**	**NHL**	**55**	**2**	**4**	**6**	**230**	....	....	....	....	....
1996-97	**Hartford**	**NHL**	**28**	**1**	**2**	**3**	**122**	....	....	....	....	....
	Toronto	**NHL**	**2**	**0**	**0**	**0**	**27**	....	....	....	....	....
	NHL Totals		**321**	**10**	**25**	**35**	**1525**	**20**	**1**	**1**	**2**	**77**

Signed as a free agent by **St. Louis**, February 23, 1988. Claimed by **Hartford** from **St. Louis** in NHL Waiver Draft, January 18, 1995. Traded to **Toronto** by **Hartford** for Toronto's eighth round choice in 1998 Entry Draft, March 18, 1997.

CHASSE, DENIS (shah-SAY)

Right wing. Shoots right. 6'2", 200 lbs. Born, Montreal, Que., February 7, 1970.

			Regular Season					Playoffs				
Season	Club	Lea	GP	G	A	TP	PIM	GP	G	A	TP	PIM
1987-88	St-Jean	QMJHL	13	0	1	1	2	1	0	0	0	0
1988-89	Verdun	QMJHL	38	12	12	24	61	....	....	....	....	....
	Drummondville	QMJHL	30	15	16	31	77	3	0	2	2	28
1989-90	Drummondville	QMJHL	34	14	29	43	85	....	....	....	....	....
	Chicoutimi	QMJHL	33	19	27	46	105	7	7	4	11	50
1990-91	Drummondville	QMJHL	62	47	54	101	246	13	9	11	20	56
1991-92	Halifax	AHL	73	26	35	61	254	....	....	....	....	....
1992-93	Halifax	AHL	75	35	41	76	242	....	....	....	....	....
1993-94	Cornwall	AHL	48	27	39	66	194	....	....	....	....	....
	St. Louis	**NHL**	**3**	**0**	**1**	**1**	**15**	....	....	....	....	....
1994-95	**St. Louis**	**NHL**	**47**	**7**	**9**	**16**	**133**	**7**	**1**	**7**	**8**	**23**
1995-96	**St. Louis**	**NHL**	**42**	**3**	**0**	**3**	**108**	....	....	....	....	....
	Worcester	AHL	3	0	0	0	6	....	....	....	....	....
	Washington	**NHL**	**3**	**0**	**0**	**0**	**5**	....	....	....	....	....
	Winnipeg	**NHL**	**15**	**0**	**0**	**0**	**12**	....	....	....	....	....
1996-97	**Ottawa**	**NHL**	**22**	**1**	**4**	**5**	**19**	....	....	....	....	....
	Detroit	IHL	9	2	1	3	33	....	....	....	....	....
	Indianapolis	IHL	3	0	0	0	10	4	1	1	2	23
	NHL Totals		**132**	**11**	**14**	**25**	**292**	**7**	**1**	**7**	**8**	**23**

Signed as a free agent by **Quebec**, May 14, 1991. Traded to **St. Louis** by **Quebec** with Steve Duchesne for Garth Butcher, Ron Sutter and Bob Bassen, January 23, 1994. Traded to **Washington** by **St. Louis** for Rob Pearson, January 29, 1996. Traded to **Winnipeg** by **Washington** for Stewart Malgunas, February 15, 1996. Traded to **Chicago** by **Ottawa** with the rights to Kevin Bolibruck and Ottawa's sixth round choice in 1998 Entry Draft for Mike Prokopec, March 18, 1997.

CHEBATURKIN, VLADIMIR (cheh-bah-TOOR-kihn) NYI

Defense. Shoots left. 6'2", 213 lbs. Born, Tyumen, USSR, April 23, 1975.
(NY Islanders' 3rd choice, 66th overall, in 1993 Entry Draft).

			Regular Season					Playoffs				
Season	Club	Lea	GP	G	A	TP	PIM	GP	G	A	TP	PIM
1993-94	Elektrostal	CIS 2	42	4	4	8	38	....	....	....	....	....
1994-95	Elektrostal	CIS	52	2	6	8	90	....	....	....	....	....
1995-96	Elektrostal	CIS	44	1	6	7	30	1	0	0	0	0
1996-97	Utah	IHL	68	0	4	4	34	....	....	....	....	....

CHELIOS, CHRIS (CHELL-EE-ohs) CHI.

Defense. Shoots right. 6'1", 190 lbs. Born, Chicago, IL, January 25, 1962.
(Montreal's 5th choice, 40th overall, in 1981 Entry Draft).

			Regular Season					Playoffs				
Season	Club	Lea	GP	G	A	TP	PIM	GP	G	A	TP	PIM
1981-82	U. Wisconsin	WCHA	43	6	43	49	50	....	....	....	....	....
1982-83ab	U. Wisconsin	WCHA	26	9	17	26	50	....	....	....	....	....
1983-84	U.S. National	....	60	14	35	49	58	....	....	....	....	....
	U.S. Olympic	....	6	0	4	4	8	....	....	....	....	....
	Montreal	**NHL**	**12**	**0**	**2**	**2**	**12**	**15**	**1**	**9**	**10**	**17**
1984-85c	**Montreal**	**NHL**	**74**	**9**	**55**	**64**	**87**	**9**	**2**	**8**	**10**	**17**
1985-86	**Montreal**	**NHL**	**41**	**8**	**26**	**34**	**67**	**20**	**2**	**9**	**11**	**49** ♦
1986-87	**Montreal**	**NHL**	**71**	**11**	**33**	**44**	**124**	**17**	**4**	**9**	**13**	**38**
1987-88	**Montreal**	**NHL**	**71**	**20**	**41**	**61**	**172**	**11**	**3**	**1**	**4**	**29**
1988-89de	**Montreal**	**NHL**	**80**	**15**	**58**	**73**	**185**	**21**	**4**	**15**	**19**	**28**
1989-90	**Montreal**	**NHL**	**53**	**9**	**22**	**31**	**136**	**5**	**0**	**1**	**1**	**8**
1990-91f	**Chicago**	**NHL**	**77**	**12**	**52**	**64**	**192**	**6**	**1**	**7**	**8**	**46**
1991-92	**Chicago**	**NHL**	**80**	**9**	**47**	**56**	**245**	**18**	**6**	**15**	**21**	**37**
1992-93de	**Chicago**	**NHL**	**84**	**15**	**58**	**73**	**282**	**4**	**0**	**2**	**2**	**14**
1993-94	**Chicago**	**NHL**	**76**	**16**	**44**	**60**	**212**	**6**	**1**	**1**	**2**	**8**
1994-95	Biel	Switz.	3	0	3	3	4	....	....	....	....	....
d	**Chicago**	**NHL**	**48**	**5**	**33**	**38**	**72**	**16**	**4**	**7**	**11**	**12**
1995-96de	**Chicago**	**NHL**	**81**	**14**	**58**	**72**	**140**	**9**	**0**	**3**	**3**	**8**
1996-97f	**Chicago**	**NHL**	**72**	**10**	**38**	**48**	**112**	**6**	**0**	**1**	**1**	**8**
	NHL Totals		**920**	**153**	**567**	**720**	**2038**	**163**	**28**	**88**	**116**	**319**

a WCHA Second All-Star Team (1983)
b NCAA All-Tournament Team (1983)
c NHL All-Rookie Team (1985)
d NHL First All-Star Team (1989, 1993, 1995, 1996)
e Won James Norris Memorial Trophy (1989, 1993, 1996)
f NHL Second All-Star Team (1991, 1997)

Played in NHL All-Star Game (1985, 1990-94, 1996, 1997)

Traded to **Chicago** by **Montreal** with Montreal's second round choice (Michael Pomichter) in 1991 Entry Draft for Denis Savard, June 29, 1990.

CHEREDARYK, STEVE (shair-a-DAIR-ehk) MTL.

Defense. Shoots left. 6'2", 197 lbs. Born, Calgary, Alta., November 20, 1975.
(Winnipeg's 4th choice, 82nd overall, in 1994 Entry Draft).

			Regular Season					Playoffs				
Season	Club	Lea	GP	G	A	TP	PIM	GP	G	A	TP	PIM
1992-93	Medicine Hat	WHL	67	1	9	10	88	10	0	1	1	16
1993-94	Medicine Hat	WHL	72	3	35	38	151	3	0	1	1	9
1994-95	Medicine Hat	WHL	70	3	26	29	193	5	0	1	1	13
	Springfield	AHL	3	0	1	1	0	....	....	....	....	....
1995-96	Springfield	AHL	32	0	1	1	36	....	....	....	....	....
	Knoxville	ECHL	13	0	10	10	72	6	2	4	6	12
1996-97	Springfield	AHL	46	1	2	3	69	....	....	....	....	....
	Fredericton	AHL	14	0	1	1	24	....	....	....	....	....
	Mississippi	ECHL	9	0	1	1	33	....	....	....	....	....

Traded to **Montreal** by **Phoenix** for Pat Jablonski, March 18, 1997.

CHERNESKI, STEFAN (chuhr-NEHS-kee) NYR

Right wing. Shoots left. 6', 195 lbs. Born, Winnipeg, Man., September 19, 1978.
(NY Rangers' 1st choice, 19th overall, in 1997 Entry Draft).

			Regular Season					Playoffs				
Season	Club	Lea	GP	G	A	TP	PIM	GP	G	A	TP	PIM
1995-96	Brandon	WHL	58	8	21	29	62	19	3	1	4	11
1996-97	Brandon	WHL	56	39	29	68	83	....	....	....	....	....

CHERNOV, MIHAIL PHI.

Defense. Shoots right. 6'2", 196 lbs. Born, Prokopjevsk, USSR, November 11, 1978.
(Philadelphia's 4th choice, 103rd overall, in 1997 Entry Draft).

			Regular Season					Playoffs				
Season	Club	Lea	GP	G	A	TP	PIM	GP	G	A	TP	PIM
1996-97	Yaroslavl 2	Rus. 3	33	4	2	6	40	....	....	....	....	....
	Yaroslavl	Rus.	5	0	0	0	0	....	....	....	....	....

CHERVYAKOV, DENIS (CHAIR-vuh-kahf)

Defense. Shoots left. 6', 185 lbs. Born, Leningrad, USSR, April 20, 1970.
(Boston's 9th choice, 256th overall, in 1992 Entry Draft).

			Regular Season					Playoffs				
Season	Club	Lea	GP	G	A	TP	PIM	GP	G	A	TP	PIM
1990-91	Leningrad	USSR	28	2	1	3	40	....	....	....	....	....
1991-92	Riga	CIS	14	0	1	1	12	....	....	....	....	....
1992-93	**Boston**	**NHL**	**2**	**0**	**0**	**0**	**2**	....	....	....	....	....
	Providence	AHL	48	4	12	16	99	....	....	....	....	....
	Atlanta	IHL	1	0	0	0	0	....	....	....	....	....
1993-94	Providence	AHL	58	2	16	18	128	....	....	....	....	....
1994-95	Providence	AHL	65	1	18	19	130	10	0	2	2	14
1995-96	Providence	AHL	64	3	7	10	58	4	1	0	1	21
1996-97	Kentucky	AHL	52	2	11	13	78	....	....	....	....	....
	NHL Totals		**2**	**0**	**0**	**0**	**2**	....	....	....	....	....

Signed as a free agent by **NY Islanders**, September 12, 1996.

CHIASSON, STEVE (CHAY-sahn) CAR.

Defense. Shoots left. 6'1", 205 lbs. Born, Barrie, Ont., April 14, 1967.
(Detroit's 3rd choice, 50th overall, in 1985 Entry Draft).

			Regular Season					Playoffs				
Season	Club	Lea	GP	G	A	TP	PIM	GP	G	A	TP	PIM
1984-85	Guelph	OHL	61	8	22	30	139	....	....	....	....	....
1985-86a	Guelph	OHL	54	12	30	42	126	18	10	10	20	37
1986-87	**Detroit**	**NHL**	**45**	**1**	**4**	**5**	**73**	**2**	**0**	**0**	**0**	**19**
1987-88	**Detroit**	**NHL**	**29**	**2**	**9**	**11**	**57**	**9**	**2**	**2**	**4**	**31**
	Adirondack	AHL	23	6	11	17	58	....	....	....	....	....
1988-89	**Detroit**	**NHL**	**65**	**12**	**35**	**47**	**149**	**5**	**2**	**1**	**3**	**6**
1989-90	**Detroit**	**NHL**	**67**	**14**	**28**	**42**	**114**	....	....	....	....	....
1990-91	**Detroit**	**NHL**	**42**	**3**	**17**	**20**	**80**	**5**	**3**	**1**	**4**	**19**
1991-92	**Detroit**	**NHL**	**62**	**10**	**24**	**34**	**136**	**11**	**1**	**5**	**6**	**12**
1992-93	**Detroit**	**NHL**	**79**	**12**	**50**	**62**	**155**	**7**	**2**	**2**	**4**	**19**
1993-94	**Detroit**	**NHL**	**82**	**13**	**33**	**46**	**122**	**7**	**2**	**3**	**5**	**2**
1994-95	**Calgary**	**NHL**	**45**	**2**	**23**	**25**	**39**	**7**	**1**	**2**	**3**	**9**
1995-96	**Calgary**	**NHL**	**76**	**8**	**25**	**33**	**62**	**4**	**2**	**1**	**3**	**0**
1996-97	**Calgary**	**NHL**	**47**	**5**	**11**	**16**	**32**	....	....	....	....	....
	Hartford	**NHL**	**18**	**3**	**11**	**14**	**7**	....	....	....	....	....
	NHL Totals		**657**	**85**	**270**	**355**	**1026**	**57**	**15**	**17**	**32**	**117**

a Won Stafford Smythe Memorial Trophy (Memorial Cup Tournament MVP) (1986)

Played in NHL All-Star Game (1993)

Traded to **Calgary** by **Detroit** for Mike Vernon, June 29, 1994. Traded to **Hartford** by **Calgary** with Colorado's third round choice (previously acquired by Calgary — Carolina selected Francis Lessard) in 1997 Entry Draft for Hnat Domenichelli, Glen Featherstone, New Jersey's second round choice (previously acquired by Hartford — Calgary selected Dimitri Kokorev) in 1997 Entry Draft and Vancouver's third round choice (previously acquired by Hartford) in 1998 Entry Draft, March 5, 1997.

CHIMERA, JASON (CHIHM-air-a) EDM.

Center. Shoots left. 6', 160 lbs. Born, Edmonton, Alta., May 2, 1979.
(Edmonton's 5th choice, 121st overall, in 1997 Entry Draft).

			Regular Season					Playoffs				
Season	Club	Lea	GP	G	A	TP	PIM	GP	G	A	TP	PIM
1995-96	SSAC Edmonton	Midget	34	23	24	47	44	....	....	....	....	....
1996-97	Medicine Hat	WHL	71	16	23	39	64	4	0	1	1	4

CHORSKE, TOM (CHOHR-skee) OTT.

Right wing. Shoots right. 6'1", 205 lbs. Born, Minneapolis, MN, September 18, 1966.
(Montreal's 2nd choice, 16th overall, in 1985 Entry Draft).

			Regular Season					Playoffs				
Season	Club	Lea	GP	G	A	TP	PIM	GP	G	A	TP	PIM
1985-86	U. Minnesota	WCHA	39	6	4	10	16	....	....	....	....	....
1986-87	U. Minnesota	WCHA	47	20	22	42	20	....	....	....	....	....
1987-88	U.S. National	....	36	9	16	25	24	....	....	....	....	....
1988-89a	U. Minnesota	WCHA	37	25	24	49	28	....	....	....	....	....
1989-90	**Montreal**	**NHL**	**14**	**3**	**1**	**4**	**2**	....	....	....	....	....
	Sherbrooke	AHL	59	22	24	46	54	12	4	4	8	8
1990-91	**Montreal**	**NHL**	**57**	**9**	**11**	**20**	**32**	....	....	....	....	....
1991-92	**New Jersey**	**NHL**	**76**	**19**	**17**	**36**	**32**	**7**	**0**	**3**	**3**	**4**
1992-93	**New Jersey**	**NHL**	**50**	**7**	**12**	**19**	**25**	**1**	**0**	**0**	**0**	**0**
	Utica	AHL	6	1	4	5	2	....	....	....	....	....
1993-94	**New Jersey**	**NHL**	**76**	**21**	**20**	**41**	**32**	**20**	**4**	**3**	**7**	**0**
1994-95	Milan Devils	Italy	7	11	5	16	6	....	....	....	....	....
	New Jersey	**NHL**	**42**	**10**	**8**	**18**	**16**	**17**	**1**	**5**	**6**	**4** ♦
1995-96	**Ottawa**	**NHL**	**72**	**15**	**14**	**29**	**21**	....	....	....	....	....
1996-97	**Ottawa**	**NHL**	**68**	**18**	**8**	**26**	**16**	**5**	**0**	**1**	**1**	**2**
	NHL Totals		**455**	**102**	**91**	**193**	**176**	**50**	**5**	**12**	**17**	**10**

a WCHA First All-Star Team (1989)

Traded to **New Jersey** by **Montreal** with Stephane Richer for Kirk Muller and Roland Melanson, September 20, 1991. Claimed on waivers by **Ottawa** from **New Jersey**, October 5, 1995.

CHOUINARD, MARC (shwee-NAHR) ANA.

Center. Shoots right. 6'5", 187 lbs. Born, Charlesbourg, Ont., May 5, 1977.
(Winnipeg's 2nd choice, 32nd overall, in 1995 Entry Draft).

			Regular Season					Playoffs				
Season	Club	Lea	GP	G	A	TP	PIM	GP	G	A	TP	PIM
1993-94	Beauport	QMJHL	62	11	19	30	23	13	2	5	7	2
1994-95	Beauport	QMJHL	68	24	40	64	32	18	1	6	7	4
1995-96	Beauport	QMJHL	30	14	21	35	19	....	....	....	....	....
	Halifax	QMJHL	24	6	12	18	17	6	2	1	3	2
1996-97	Halifax	QMJHL	63	24	49	73	74	18	9	16	25	12

Traded to **Anaheim** by **Winnipeg** with Teemu Selanne and Winnipeg's fourth round choice (later traded to Toronto — later traded to Montreal — Montreal selected Kim Staal) in 1996 Entry Draft for Chad Kilger, Oleg Tverdovsky and Anaheim's third round choice (Per-Anton Ludstrom) in 1996 Entry Draft, February 7, 1996.

CHRISTIAN, JEFF — PHO.

Left wing. Shoots left. 6'2", 210 lbs. Born, Burlington, Ont., July 30, 1970.
(New Jersey's 2nd choice, 23rd overall, in 1988 Entry Draft).

			Regular Season					Playoffs				
Season	Club	Lea	GP	G	A	TP	PIM	GP	G	A	TP	PIM
1987-88	London	OHL	64	15	29	44	154	9	1	5	6	27
1988-89	London	OHL	60	27	30	57	221	20	3	4	7	56
1989-90	London	OHL	18	14	7	21	64	....	....	....	....	....
	Owen Sound	OHL	37	19	26	45	145	10	6	7	13	43
1990-91	Utica	AHL	80	24	42	66	165	....	....	....	....	....
1991-92	**New Jersey**	**NHL**	**2**	**0**	**0**	**0**	**2**	....	....	....	....	....
	Utica	AHL	76	27	24	51	198	4	0	0	0	16
1992-93	Utica	AHL	22	4	6	10	39	....	....	....	....	....
	Hamilton	AHL	11	2	5	7	35	....	....	....	....	....
	Cincinnati	IHL	36	5	12	17	113	....	....	....	....	....
1993-94	Albany	AHL	76	34	43	77	227	5	1	2	3	19
1994-95	**Pittsburgh**	**NHL**	**1**	**0**	**0**	**0**	**0**	....	....	....	....	....
	Cleveland	IHL	56	13	24	37	126	2	0	1	1	8
1995-96	**Pittsburgh**	**NHL**	**3**	**0**	**0**	**0**	**2**	....	....	....	....	....
	Cleveland	IHL	66	23	32	55	131	3	0	1	1	8
1996-97	**Pittsburgh**	**NHL**	**11**	**2**	**2**	**4**	**13**	....	....	....	....	....
	Cleveland	IHL	69	40	40	80	262	12	6	8	14	44
	NHL Totals		**17**	**2**	**2**	**4**	**17**	....	....	....	....	....

Signed as a free agent by **Pittsburgh**, August 2, 1994. Signed as a free agent by **Phoenix**, July 28, 1997.

CHRISTIE, RYAN — DAL.

Left wing. Shoots left. 6'2", 175 lbs. Born, Beamsville, Ont., July 3, 1978.
(Dallas' 4th choice, 112th overall, in 1996 Entry Draft).

			Regular Season					Playoffs				
Season	Club	Lea	GP	G	A	TP	PIM	GP	G	A	TP	PIM
1995-96	Owen Sound	OHL	66	29	17	46	93	6	1	1	2	0
1996-97	Owen Sound	OHL	66	23	29	52	136	4	1	1	2	8

CHURCH, BRAD — WSH.

Left wing. Shoots left. 6'1", 210 lbs. Born, Dauphin, Man., November 14, 1976.
(Washington's 1st choice, 17th overall, in 1995 Entry Draft).

			Regular Season					Playoffs				
Season	Club	Lea	GP	G	A	TP	PIM	GP	G	A	TP	PIM
1993-94	Prince Albert	WHL	71	33	20	53	197	....	....	....	....	....
1994-95	Prince Albert	WHL	62	26	24	50	184	15	6	9	15	32
1995-96	Prince Albert	WHL	69	42	46	88	123	18	15	*20	*35	74
1996-97	Portland	AHL	50	4	8	12	92	1	0	0	0	0

CHURLA, SHANE (CHUHR-lah) — NYR

Right wing. Shoots right. 6'1", 200 lbs. Born, Fernie, B.C., June 24, 1965.
(Hartford's 4th choice, 110th overall, in 1985 Entry Draft).

			Regular Season					Playoffs				
Season	Club	Lea	GP	G	A	TP	PIM	GP	G	A	TP	PIM
1983-84	Medicine Hat	WHL	48	3	7	10	115	14	1	5	6	41
1984-85	Medicine Hat	WHL	70	14	20	34	370	9	1	0	1	55
1985-86	Binghamton	AHL	52	4	10	14	306	3	0	0	0	22
1986-87	**Hartford**	**NHL**	**20**	**0**	**1**	**1**	**78**	**2**	**0**	**0**	**0**	**42**
	Binghamton	AHL	24	1	5	6	249	....	....	....	....	....
1987-88	**Hartford**	**NHL**	**2**	**0**	**0**	**0**	**14**	....	....	....	....	....
	Binghamton	AHL	25	5	8	13	168	....	....	....	....	....
	Calgary	**NHL**	**29**	**1**	**5**	**6**	**132**	**7**	**0**	**1**	**1**	**17**
1988-89	**Calgary**	**NHL**	**5**	**0**	**0**	**0**	**25**	....	....	....	....	....
	Salt Lake	IHL	32	3	13	16	278	....	....	....	....	....
	Minnesota	**NHL**	**13**	**1**	**0**	**1**	**54**	....	....	....	....	....
1989-90	**Minnesota**	**NHL**	**53**	**2**	**3**	**5**	**292**	**7**	**0**	**0**	**0**	**44**
1990-91	**Minnesota**	**NHL**	**40**	**2**	**2**	**4**	**286**	**22**	**2**	**1**	**3**	**90**
1991-92	**Minnesota**	**NHL**	**57**	**4**	**1**	**5**	**278**	....	....	....	....	....
1992-93	**Minnesota**	**NHL**	**73**	**5**	**16**	**21**	**286**	....	....	....	....	....
1993-94	**Dallas**	**NHL**	**69**	**6**	**7**	**13**	**333**	**9**	**1**	**3**	**4**	**35**
1994-95	**Dallas**	**NHL**	**27**	**1**	**3**	**4**	**186**	**5**	**0**	**0**	**0**	**20**
1995-96	**Dallas**	**NHL**	**34**	**3**	**4**	**7**	**168**	....	....	....	....	....
	Los Angeles	**NHL**	**11**	**1**	**2**	**3**	**37**	....	....	....	....	....
	NY Rangers	**NHL**	**10**	**0**	**0**	**0**	**26**	**11**	**2**	**2**	**4**	**14**
1996-97	**NY Rangers**	**NHL**	**45**	**0**	**1**	**1**	**106**	**15**	**0**	**0**	**0**	**20**
	NHL Totals		**488**	**26**	**45**	**71**	**2301**	**78**	**5**	**7**	**12**	**282**

Traded to **Calgary** by **Hartford** with Dana Murzyn for Neil Sheehy, Carey Wilson, and the rights to Lane MacDonald, January 3, 1988. Traded to **Minnesota** by **Calgary** with Perry Berezan for Brian MacLellan and Minnesota's fourth round choice (Robert Reichel) in 1989 Entry Draft, March 4, 1989. Claimed by **San Jose** from **Minnesota** in Dispersal Draft, May 30, 1991. Traded to **Minnesota** by **San Jose** for Kelly Kisio, June 3, 1991. Traded to **Los Angeles** by **Dallas** with Doug Zmolek for Darryl Sydor and Los Angeles' fifth round choice (Ryan Christie) in 1996 Entry Draft, February 17, 1996. Traded to **NY Rangers** by **Los Angeles** with Marty McSorley and Jari Kurri for Ray Ferraro, Ian Laperriere, Mattias Norstrom, Nathan Lafayette and NY Rangers' fourth round choice (Sean Blanchard) in 1997 Entry Draft, March 14, 1996.

CHYNOWETH, DEAN (shih-NOWTH) — BOS.

Defense. Shoots right. 6'1", 191 lbs. Born, Calgary, Alta., October 30, 1968.
(NY Islanders' 1st choice, 13th overall, in 1987 Entry Draft).

			Regular Season					Playoffs				
Season	Club	Lea	GP	G	A	TP	PIM	GP	G	A	TP	PIM
1985-86	Medicine Hat	WHL	69	3	12	15	208	17	3	2	5	52
1986-87	Medicine Hat	WHL	67	3	18	21	285	13	4	2	6	28
1987-88	Medicine Hat	WHL	64	1	21	22	274	16	0	6	6	*87
1988-89	**NY Islanders**	**NHL**	**6**	**0**	**0**	**0**	**48**	....	....	....	....	....
1989-90	**NY Islanders**	**NHL**	**20**	**0**	**2**	**2**	**39**	....	....	....	....	....
	Springfield	AHL	40	0	7	7	98	17	0	4	4	36
1990-91	**NY Islanders**	**NHL**	**25**	**1**	**1**	**2**	**59**	....	....	....	....	....
	Capital Dist.	AHL	44	1	5	6	176	....	....	....	....	....
1991-92	**NY Islanders**	**NHL**	**11**	**1**	**0**	**1**	**23**	....	....	....	....	....
	Capital Dist.	AHL	43	4	6	10	164	6	1	1	2	39
1992-93	Capital Dist.	AHL	52	3	10	13	197	4	0	1	1	9
1993-94	**NY Islanders**	**NHL**	**39**	**0**	**4**	**4**	**122**	**2**	**0**	**0**	**0**	**2**
	Salt Lake	IHL	5	0	1	1	33	....	....	....	....	....
1994-95	**NY Islanders**	**NHL**	**32**	**0**	**2**	**2**	**77**	....	....	....	....	....
1995-96	**NY Islanders**	**NHL**	**14**	**0**	**1**	**1**	**40**	....	....	....	....	....
	Boston	**NHL**	**35**	**2**	**5**	**7**	**88**	**4**	**0**	**0**	**0**	**24**
1996-97	**Boston**	**NHL**	**57**	**0**	**3**	**3**	**171**	....	....	....	....	....
	Providence	AHL	2	0	0	0	13	....	....	....	....	....
	NHL Totals		**239**	**4**	**18**	**22**	**667**	**6**	**0**	**0**	**0**	**26**

Traded to **Boston** by **NY Islanders** for Boston's fifth round choice (Petr Sachl) in 1996 Entry Draft, December 9, 1995.

CHYZOWSKI, DAVE (chih-ZOW-skee)

Left wing. Shoots left. 6'1", 190 lbs. Born, Edmonton, Alta., July 11, 1971.
(NY Islanders' 1st choice, 2nd overall, in 1989 Entry Draft).

			Regular Season					Playoffs				
Season	Club	Lea	GP	G	A	TP	PIM	GP	G	A	TP	PIM
1987-88	Kamloops	WHL	66	16	17	33	117	18	2	4	6	26
1988-89a	Kamloops	WHL	68	56	48	104	139	16	15	13	28	32
1989-90	**NY Islanders**	**NHL**	**34**	**8**	**6**	**14**	**45**	....	....	....	....	....
	Springfield	AHL	4	0	0	0	7	....	....	....	....	....
	Kamloops	WHL	4	5	2	7	17	17	11	6	17	46
1990-91	**NY Islanders**	**NHL**	**56**	**5**	**9**	**14**	**61**	....	....	....	....	....
	Capital Dist.	AHL	7	3	6	9	22	....	....	....	....	....
1991-92	**NY Islanders**	**NHL**	**12**	**1**	**1**	**2**	**17**	....	....	....	....	....
	Capital Dist.	AHL	55	15	18	33	121	6	1	1	2	23
1992-93	Capital Dist.	AHL	66	15	21	36	177	3	2	0	2	0
1993-94	**NY Islanders**	**NHL**	**3**	**1**	**0**	**1**	**4**	**2**	**0**	**0**	**0**	**0**
	Salt Lake	IHL	66	27	13	40	151	....	....	....	....	....
1994-95	**NY Islanders**	**NHL**	**13**	**0**	**0**	**0**	**11**	....	....	....	....	....
	Kalamazoo	IHL	4	0	4	4	8	16	9	5	14	27
1995-96	Adirondack	AHL	80	44	39	83	160	3	0	0	0	6
1996-97	**Chicago**	**NHL**	**8**	**0**	**0**	**0**	**6**	....	....	....	....	....
	Indianapolis	IHL	76	34	40	74	261	4	0	2	2	38
	NHL Totals		**126**	**15**	**16**	**31**	**144**	**2**	**0**	**0**	**0**	**0**

a WHL West All-Star Team (1989)

Signed as a free agent by **Detroit**, August 29, 1995. Signed as a free agent by **Chicago**, September 26, 1996.

CIAVAGLIA, PETER (see-a-VIHG-lee-a)

Center. Shoots left. 5'10", 173 lbs. Born, Albany, NY, July 15, 1969.
(Calgary's 8th choice, 145th overall, in 1987 Entry Draft).

			Regular Season					Playoffs				
Season	Club	Lea	GP	G	A	TP	PIM	GP	G	A	TP	PIM
1987-88	Harvard	ECAC	30	10	23	33	16	....	....	....	....	....
1988-89a	Harvard	ECAC	34	15	48	63	36	....	....	....	....	....
1989-90	Harvard	ECAC	28	17	18	35	22	....	....	....	....	....
1990-91ab	Harvard	ECAC	27	24	*38	*62	2	....	....	....	....	....
1991-92	**Buffalo**	**NHL**	**2**	**0**	**0**	**0**	**0**	....	....	....	....	....
	Rochester	AHL	77	37	61	98	16	6	2	5	7	6
1992-93	**Buffalo**	**NHL**	**3**	**0**	**0**	**0**	**0**	....	....	....	....	....
	Rochester	AHL	64	35	67	102	32	17	9	16	25	12
1993-94	Leksand	Swe.	39	14	18	32	34	4	1	2	3	0
	U.S. National	....	18	2	9	11	6	....	....	....	....	....
	U.S. Olympic	....	8	2	4	6	0	....	....	....	....	....
1994-95	Detroit	IHL	73	22	59	81	83	5	1	1	2	6
1995-96	Detroit	IHL	75	22	56	78	38	12	6	11	17	12
1996-97	Detroit	IHL	72	21	51	72	54	21	*14	19	*33	32
	NHL Totals		**5**	**0**	**0**	**0**	**0**	....	....	....	....	....

a ECAC Second All-Star Team (1989, 1991)
b NCAA East Second All-American Team (1991)

Signed as a free agent by **Buffalo**, August 30, 1991.

CICCARELLI, DINO (sih-sih-REHL-ee) — T.B.

Right wing. Shoots right. 5'10", 185 lbs. Born, Sarnia, Ont., February 8, 1960.

			Regular Season					Playoffs				
Season	Club	Lea	GP	G	A	TP	PIM	GP	G	A	TP	PIM
1977-78a	London	OHA	68	72	70	142	49	9	6	10	16	6
1978-79	London	OHA	30	8	11	19	35	7	3	5	8	0
1979-80	London	OHA	62	50	53	103	72	5	2	6	8	15
1980-81	**Minnesota**	**NHL**	**32**	**18**	**12**	**30**	**29**	**19**	**14**	**7**	**21**	**25**
	Oklahoma City	CHL	48	32	25	57	45	....	....	....	....	....
1981-82	**Minnesota**	**NHL**	**76**	**55**	**51**	**106**	**138**	**4**	**3**	**1**	**4**	**2**
1982-83	**Minnesota**	**NHL**	**77**	**37**	**38**	**75**	**94**	**9**	**4**	**6**	**10**	**11**
1983-84	**Minnesota**	**NHL**	**79**	**38**	**33**	**71**	**58**	**16**	**4**	**5**	**9**	**27**
1984-85	**Minnesota**	**NHL**	**51**	**15**	**17**	**32**	**41**	**9**	**3**	**3**	**6**	**8**
1985-86	**Minnesota**	**NHL**	**75**	**44**	**45**	**89**	**51**	**5**	**0**	**1**	**1**	**6**
1986-87	**Minnesota**	**NHL**	**80**	**52**	**51**	**103**	**88**	....	....	....	....	....
1987-88	**Minnesota**	**NHL**	**67**	**41**	**45**	**86**	**79**	....	....	....	....	....
1988-89	**Minnesota**	**NHL**	**65**	**32**	**27**	**59**	**64**	....	....	....	....	....
	Washington	**NHL**	**11**	**12**	**3**	**15**	**12**	**6**	**3**	**3**	**6**	**12**
1989-90	**Washington**	**NHL**	**80**	**41**	**38**	**79**	**122**	**8**	**8**	**3**	**11**	**6**
1990-91	**Washington**	**NHL**	**54**	**21**	**18**	**39**	**66**	**11**	**5**	**4**	**9**	**22**
1991-92	**Washington**	**NHL**	**78**	**38**	**38**	**76**	**78**	**7**	**5**	**4**	**9**	**14**
1992-93	**Detroit**	**NHL**	**82**	**41**	**56**	**97**	**81**	**7**	**4**	**2**	**6**	**16**
1993-94	**Detroit**	**NHL**	**66**	**28**	**29**	**57**	**73**	**7**	**5**	**2**	**7**	**14**
1994-95	**Detroit**	**NHL**	**42**	**16**	**27**	**43**	**39**	**16**	**9**	**2**	**11**	**22**
1995-96	**Detroit**	**NHL**	**64**	**22**	**21**	**43**	**99**	**17**	**6**	**2**	**8**	**26**
1996-97	**Tampa Bay**	**NHL**	**77**	**35**	**25**	**60**	**116**	....	....	....	....	....
	NHL Totals		**1156**	**586**	**574**	**1160**	**1328**	**141**	**73**	**45**	**118**	**211**

a OHA Second All-Star Team (1978)

Played in NHL All-Star Game (1982, 1983, 1989, 1997)

Signed as a free agent by **Minnesota**, September 28, 1979. Traded to **Washington** by **Minnesota** with Bob Rouse for Mike Gartner and Larry Murphy, March 7, 1989. Traded to **Detroit** by **Washington** for Kevin Miller, June 20, 1992. Traded to **Tampa Bay** by **Detroit** for a conditional choice in 1998 Entry Draft, August 27, 1996.

CICCONE, ENRICO (CHIH-koh-nee) CAR.

Defense. Shoots left. 6'5", 220 lbs. Born, Montreal, Que., April 10, 1970.
(Minnesota's 5th choice, 92nd overall, in 1990 Entry Draft).

			Regular Season					Playoffs				
Season	Club	Lea	GP	G	A	TP	PIM	GP	G	A	TP	PIM
1987-88	Shawinigan	QMJHL	61	2	12	14	324	....	....	....	....	....
1988-89	Shawinigan	QMJHL	34	7	11	18	132	....	....	....	....	....
	Trois-Rivières	QMJHL	24	0	7	7	153	....	....	....	....	....
1989-90	Trois-Rivières	QMJHL	40	4	24	28	227	3	0	0	0	15
1990-91	Kalamazoo	IHL	57	4	9	13	384	4	0	1	1	32
1991-92	**Minnesota**	**NHL**	**11**	**0**	**0**	**0**	**48**	....	....	....	....	....
	Kalamazoo	IHL	53	4	16	20	406	10	0	1	1	58
1992-93	**Minnesota**	**NHL**	**31**	**0**	**1**	**1**	**115**	....	....	....	....	....
	Kalamazoo	IHL	13	1	3	4	50	....	....	....	....	....
	Hamilton	AHL	6	1	3	4	44	....	....	....	....	....
1993-94	**Washington**	**NHL**	**46**	**1**	**1**	**2**	**174**	....	....	....	....	....
	Portland	AHL	6	0	0	0	27	....	....	....	....	....
	Tampa Bay	**NHL**	**11**	**0**	**1**	**1**	**52**	....	....	....	....	....
1994-95	**Tampa Bay**	**NHL**	**41**	**2**	**4**	**6**	***225**	....	....	....	....	....
1995-96	**Tampa Bay**	**NHL**	**55**	**2**	**3**	**5**	**258**	....	....	....	....	....
	Chicago	**NHL**	**11**	**0**	**1**	**1**	**48**	**9**	**1**	**0**	**1**	**30**
1996-97	**Chicago**	**NHL**	**67**	**2**	**2**	**4**	**233**	**4**	**0**	**0**	**0**	**18**
	NHL Totals		**273**	**7**	**13**	**20**	**1153**	**13**	**1**	**0**	**1**	**48**

Traded to **Washington** by **Dallas** to complete June 20, 1993 trade which sent Paul Cavallini to Dallas for future considerations, June 25, 1993. Traded to **Tampa Bay** by **Washington** with Washington's third round choice (later traded to Anaheim — Anaheim selected Craig Reichert) in 1994 Entry Draft and the return of future draft choices transferred in the Pat Elynuik trade for Joe Reekie, March 21, 1994. Traded to **Chicago** by **Tampa Bay** with Tampa Bay's second round choice (Jeff Paul) in 1996 Entry Draft for Patrick Poulin, Igor Ulanov and Chicago's second round choice (later traded to New Jersey — New Jersey selected Pierre Dagenais) in 1996 Entry Draft, March 20, 1996. Traded to **Carolina** by **Chicago** for Ryan Risidore and Carolina's fifth round choice in 1998 Entry Draft, July 25, 1997.

CIERNIK, IVAN (CHAIR-nihk, ee-VAHN) OTT.

Left wing. Shoots left. 6'1", 198 lbs. Born, Levice, Czech., October 30, 1977.
(Ottawa's 6th choice, 216th overall, in 1996 Entry Draft).

			Regular Season					Playoffs				
Season	Club	Lea	GP	G	A	TP	PIM	GP	G	A	TP	PIM
1994-95	Nitra	Slo. Jr.	30	22	15	37	36	....	....	....	....	....
	Nitra	Slovak	7	1	0	1	2	....	....	....	....	....
1995-96	Nitra	Slovak	35	9	7	16	36	8	3	3	6	....
1996-97	Nitra	Slovak	41	11	19	30	....	....	....	....	....	....

CIERNY, JOZEF (chee-ER-nee) EDM.

Left wing. Shoots left. 6'2", 185 lbs. Born, Zvolen, Czech., May 13, 1974.
(Buffalo's 2nd choice, 35th overall, in 1992 Entry Draft).

			Regular Season					Playoffs				
Season	Club	Lea	GP	G	A	TP	PIM	GP	G	A	TP	PIM
1991-92	ZTK Zvolen	Czech.2	26	10	3	13	8	....	....	....	....	....
1992-93	Rochester	AHL	54	27	27	54	36	....	....	....	....	....
1993-94	**Edmonton**	**NHL**	**1**	**0**	**0**	**0**	**0**	....	....	....	....	....
	Cape Breton	AHL	73	30	27	57	88	4	1	1	2	4
1994-95	Cape Breton	AHL	73	28	24	52	58	....	....	....	....	....
1995-96	Detroit	IHL	20	2	5	7	16	....	....	....	....	....
	Los Angeles	IHL	43	23	16	39	36	....	....	....	....	....
1996-97	Long Beach	IHL	68	27	27	54	106	16	8	5	13	7
	NHL Totals		**1**	**0**	**0**	**0**	**0**	....	....	....	....	....

Traded to **Edmonton** by **Buffalo** with Buffalo's fourth round choice (Jussi Tarvainen) in 1994 Entry Draft for Craig Simpson, September 1, 1993.

CIGER, ZDENO (SEE-gu, ZDEH-noh) EDM.

Left wing. Shoots left. 6'1", 190 lbs. Born, Martin, Czech., October 19, 1969.
(New Jersey's 3rd choice, 54th overall, in 1988 Entry Draft).

			Regular Season					Playoffs				
Season	Club	Lea	GP	G	A	TP	PIM	GP	G	A	TP	PIM
1987-88	Dukla Trencin	Czech.	8	3	4	7	2	....	....	....	....	....
1988-89	Dukla Trencin	Czech.	43	18	13	31	18	....	....	....	....	....
1989-90	Dukla Trencin	Czech.	53	18	28	46	....	....	....	....	....	....
1990-91	**New Jersey**	**NHL**	**45**	**8**	**17**	**25**	**8**	**6**	**0**	**2**	**2**	**4**
	Utica	AHL	8	5	4	9	2	....	....	....	....	....
1991-92	**New Jersey**	**NHL**	**20**	**6**	**5**	**11**	**10**	**7**	**2**	**4**	**6**	**0**
1992-93	**New Jersey**	**NHL**	**27**	**4**	**8**	**12**	**2**	....	....	....	....	....
	Edmonton	**NHL**	**37**	**9**	**15**	**24**	**6**	....	....	....	....	....
1993-94	**Edmonton**	**NHL**	**84**	**22**	**35**	**57**	**8**	....	....	....	....	....
1994-95	Dukla Trencin	Slovak	34	23	25	48	8	9	2	9	11	2
	Edmonton	**NHL**	**5**	**2**	**2**	**4**	**0**	....	....	....	....	....
1995-96	**Edmonton**	**NHL**	**78**	**31**	**39**	**70**	**41**	....	....	....	....	....
1996-97	Bratislava	Slovak	44	26	27	53	....	2	1	3	4	....
	NHL Totals		**296**	**82**	**121**	**203**	**75**	**13**	**2**	**6**	**8**	**4**

Traded to **Edmonton** by **New Jersey** with Kevin Todd for Bernie Nicholls, January 13, 1993.

CISAR, MARIAN (SIH-sahr) L.A.

Right wing. Shoots right. 6', 176 lbs. Born, Bratislava, Czech., February 25, 1978.
(Los Angeles' 2nd choice, 37th overall, in 1996 Entry Draft).

			Regular Season					Playoffs				
Season	Club	Lea	GP	G	A	TP	PIM	GP	G	A	TP	PIM
1994-95	Bratislava	Slo. Jr.	38	42	28	70	16	....	....	....	....	....
1995-96	Bratislava	Slo. Jr.	16	26	17	43	2	....	....	....	....	....
	Bratislava	Slovak	13	3	3	6	0	6	3	0	3	0
1996-97	Spokane	WHL	70	31	35	66	52	9	6	2	8	4

CLARK, BRETT MTL.

Defense. Shoots left. 6', 175 lbs. Born, Moosomin, Sask., December 23, 1976.
(Montreal's 7th choice, 154th overall, in 1996 Entry Draft).

			Regular Season					Playoffs				
Season	Club	Lea	GP	G	A	TP	PIM	GP	G	A	TP	PIM
1995-96	Maine	H.E.	39	7	31	38	22	....	....	....	....	....
1996-97	Cdn. National	....	57	6	21	27	52	....	....	....	....	....

CLARK, CHRIS CGY.

Right wing. Shoots right. 6', 190 lbs. Born, Manchester, CT, March 8, 1976.
(Calgary's 3rd choice, 77th overall, in 1994 Entry Draft).

			Regular Season					Playoffs				
Season	Club	Lea	GP	G	A	TP	PIM	GP	G	A	TP	PIM
1994-95	Clarkson	ECAC	32	12	11	23	92	....	....	....	....	....
1995-96	Clarkson	ECAC	38	10	8	18	108	....	....	....	....	....
1996-97	Clarkson	ECAC	37	23	25	48	*86	....	....	....	....	....

CLARK, JUSTIN COL.

Right wing. Shoots right. 6'3", 220 lbs. Born, Madison, WI, January 29, 1977.
(Colorado's 13th choice, 240th overall, in 1996 Entry Draft).

			Regular Season					Playoffs				
Season	Club	Lea	GP	G	A	TP	PIM	GP	G	A	TP	PIM
1995-96	U. of Michigan	CCHA	11	1	2	3	2	....	....	....	....	....
1996-97	U. of Michigan	CCHA	30	3	4	7	38	....	....	....	....	....

CLARK, WENDEL TOR.

Left wing. Shoots left. 5'11", 194 lbs. Born, Kelvington, Sask., October 25, 1966.
(Toronto's 1st choice, 1st overall, in 1985 Entry Draft).

			Regular Season					Playoffs				
Season	Club	Lea	GP	G	A	TP	PIM	GP	G	A	TP	PIM
1983-84	Saskatoon	WHL	72	23	45	68	225	....	....	....	....	....
1984-85a	Saskatoon	WHL	64	32	55	87	253	3	3	3	6	7
1985-86b	**Toronto**	**NHL**	**66**	**34**	**11**	**45**	**227**	**10**	**5**	**1**	**6**	**47**
1986-87	**Toronto**	**NHL**	**80**	**37**	**23**	**60**	**271**	**13**	**6**	**5**	**11**	**38**
1987-88	**Toronto**	**NHL**	**28**	**12**	**11**	**23**	**80**	....	....	....	....	....
1988-89	**Toronto**	**NHL**	**15**	**7**	**4**	**11**	**66**	....	....	....	....	....
1989-90	**Toronto**	**NHL**	**38**	**18**	**8**	**26**	**116**	**5**	**1**	**1**	**2**	**19**
1990-91	**Toronto**	**NHL**	**63**	**18**	**16**	**34**	**152**	....	....	....	....	....
1991-92	**Toronto**	**NHL**	**43**	**19**	**21**	**40**	**123**	....	....	....	....	....
1992-93	**Toronto**	**NHL**	**66**	**17**	**22**	**39**	**193**	**21**	**10**	**10**	**20**	**51**
1993-94	**Toronto**	**NHL**	**64**	**46**	**30**	**76**	**115**	**18**	**9**	**7**	**16**	**24**
1994-95	**Quebec**	**NHL**	**37**	**12**	**18**	**30**	**45**	**6**	**1**	**2**	**3**	**6**
1995-96	**NY Islanders**	**NHL**	**58**	**24**	**19**	**43**	**60**	....	....	....	....	....
	Toronto	**NHL**	**13**	**8**	**7**	**15**	**16**	**6**	**2**	**2**	**4**	**2**
1996-97	**Toronto**	**NHL**	**65**	**30**	**19**	**49**	**75**	....	....	....	....	....
	NHL Totals		**636**	**282**	**209**	**491**	**1539**	**79**	**34**	**28**	**62**	**187**

a WHL East First All-Star Team (1985)
b NHL All-Rookie Team (1986)

Played in NHL All-Star Game (1986)

Traded to **Quebec** by **Toronto** with Sylvain Lefebvre, Landon Wilson and Toronto's first round choice (Jeffrey Kealty) in 1994 Entry Draft for Mats Sundin, Garth Butcher, Todd Warriner and Philadelphia's first round choice (previously acquired by Quebec — later traded to Washington — Washington selected Nolan Baumgartner) in 1994 Entry Draft, June 28, 1994. Traded to **NY Islanders** by **Colorado** for Claude Lemieux, October 3, 1995. Traded to **Toronto** by **NY Islanders** with Mathieu Schneider and D.J. Smith for Darby Hendrickson, Sean Haggerty, Kenny Jonsson and Toronto's first round choice (Roberto Luongo) in 1997 Entry Draft, March 13, 1996.

CLEARY, DANIEL (KLIH-ree) CHI.

Left wing. Shoots left. 6', 203 lbs. Born, Carbonear, Nfld., December 18, 1978.
(Chicago's 1st choice, 13th overall, in 1997 Entry Draft).

			Regular Season					Playoffs				
Season	Club	Lea	GP	G	A	TP	PIM	GP	G	A	TP	PIM
1994-95	Belleville	OHL	62	26	55	81	62	16	7	10	17	23
1995-96a	Belleville	OHL	64	53	62	115	74	14	10	17	27	40
1996-97a	Belleville	OHL	64	32	48	80	88	6	3	4	7	6

a OHL First All-Star Team (1996, 1997)

CLOUTIER, COLIN (klootz-YAY) T.B.

Center. Shoots left. 6'3", 224 lbs. Born, Winnipeg, Man., January 27, 1976.
(Tampa Bay's 2nd choice, 34th overall, in 1994 Entry Draft).

			Regular Season					Playoffs				
Season	Club	Lea	GP	G	A	TP	PIM	GP	G	A	TP	PIM
1992-93	Brandon	WHL	60	11	15	26	138	4	0	0	0	18
1993-94	Brandon	WHL	30	10	13	23	102	11	2	5	7	23
1994-95	Brandon	WHL	47	16	27	43	170	16	5	6	11	47
1995-96	Brandon	WHL	39	9	19	28	84	....	....	....	....	....
	Lethbridge	WHL	14	5	10	15	39	3	2	2	4	19
1996-97	Adirondack	AHL	52	5	15	20	127	2	0	0	0	0

CLOUTIER, SYLVAIN (klootz-YAY) DET.

Center. Shoots left. 6', 195 lbs. Born, Mont-Laurier, Que., February 13, 1974.
(Detroit's 3rd choice, 70th overall, in 1992 Entry Draft).

			Regular Season					Playoffs				
Season	Club	Lea	GP	G	A	TP	PIM	GP	G	A	TP	PIM
1991-92	Guelph	OHL	62	35	31	66	74	....	....	....	....	....
1992-93	Guelph	OHL	44	26	29	55	78	5	0	5	5	14
1993-94	Guelph	OHL	66	45	71	116	127	9	7	9	16	32
	Adirondack	AHL	2	0	2	2	2	....	....	....	....	....
1994-95	Adirondack	AHL	71	7	26	33	144	....	....	....	....	....
1995-96	Adirondack	AHL	65	11	17	28	118	3	0	0	0	4
	Toledo	ECHL	6	4	2	6	4	....	....	....	....	....
1996-97	Adirondack	AHL	77	13	36	49	190	4	0	2	2	4

CLYMER, BEN BOS.

Defense. Shoots left. 6'1", 195 lbs. Born, Edina, MN, April 11, 1978.
(Boston's 3rd choice, 27th overall, in 1997 Entry Draft).

			Regular Season					Playoffs				
Season	Club	Lea	GP	G	A	TP	PIM	GP	G	A	TP	PIM
1995-96	Jefferson	HS	23	12	34	46	34	....	....	....	....	....
1996-97	U. Minnesota	WCHA	29	7	13	20	64	....	....	....	....	....

COFFEY, PAUL — PHI.

Defense. Shoots left. 6', 190 lbs. Born, Weston, Ont., June 1, 1961.
(Edmonton's 1st choice, 6th overall, in the 1980 Draft).

			Regular Season					Playoffs				
Season	Club	Lea	GP	G	A	TP	PIM	GP	G	A	TP	PIM
1978-79	S.S. Marie	OHA	68	17	72	89	103	....	....	....	....	....
1979-80a	S.S. Marie	OHA	23	10	21	31	63	....	....	....	....	....
	Kitchener	OHA	52	19	52	71	130	....	....	....	....	....
1980-81	**Edmonton**	**NHL**	**74**	**9**	**23**	**32**	**130**	**9**	**4**	**3**	**7**	**22**
1981-82b	**Edmonton**	**NHL**	**80**	**29**	**60**	**89**	**106**	**5**	**1**	**1**	**2**	**6**
1982-83b	**Edmonton**	**NHL**	**80**	**29**	**67**	**96**	**87**	**16**	**7**	**7**	**14**	**14**
1983-84b	**Edmonton**	**NHL**	**80**	**40**	**86**	**126**	**104**	**19**	**8**	**14**	**22**	**21 ♦**
1984-85cd	**Edmonton**	**NHL**	**80**	**37**	**84**	**121**	**97**	**18**	**12**	**25**	**37**	**44 ♦**
1985-86cd	**Edmonton**	**NHL**	**79**	**48**	**90**	**138**	**120**	**10**	**1**	**9**	**10**	**30**
1986-87	**Edmonton**	**NHL**	**59**	**17**	**50**	**67**	**49**	**17**	**3**	**8**	**11**	**30 ♦**
1987-88	**Pittsburgh**	**NHL**	**46**	**15**	**52**	**67**	**93**	....	....	....	....	....
1988-89d	**Pittsburgh**	**NHL**	**75**	**30**	**83**	**113**	**195**	**11**	**2**	**13**	**15**	**31**
1989-90b	**Pittsburgh**	**NHL**	**80**	**29**	**74**	**103**	**95**	....	....	....	....	....
1990-91	**Pittsburgh**	**NHL**	**76**	**24**	**69**	**93**	**128**	**12**	**2**	**9**	**11**	**6 ♦**
1991-92	**Pittsburgh**	**NHL**	**54**	**10**	**54**	**64**	**62**	....	....	....	....	....
	Los Angeles	**NHL**	**10**	**1**	**4**	**5**	**25**	**6**	**4**	**3**	**7**	**2**
1992-93	**Los Angeles**	**NHL**	**50**	**8**	**49**	**57**	**50**	....	....	....	....	....
	Detroit	**NHL**	**30**	**4**	**26**	**30**	**27**	**7**	**2**	**9**	**11**	**2**
1993-94	**Detroit**	**NHL**	**80**	**14**	**63**	**77**	**106**	**7**	**1**	**6**	**7**	**8**
1994-95cd	**Detroit**	**NHL**	**45**	**14**	**44**	**58**	**72**	**18**	**6**	**12**	**18**	**10**
1995-96	**Detroit**	**NHL**	**76**	**14**	**60**	**74**	**90**	**17**	**5**	**9**	**14**	**30**
1996-97	**Hartford**	**NHL**	**20**	**3**	**5**	**8**	**18**	....	....	....	....	....
	Philadelphia	**NHL**	**37**	**6**	**20**	**26**	**20**	**17**	**1**	**8**	**9**	**6**
	NHL Totals		**1211**	**381**	**1063**	**1444**	**1674**	**189**	**59**	**136**	**195**	**262**

a OHA Second All-Star Team (1980)
b NHL Second All-Star Team (1982, 1983, 1984, 1990)
c Won James Norris Memorial Trophy (1985, 1986, 1995)
d NHL First All-Star Team (1985, 1986, 1989, 1995)

Played in NHL All-Star Game (1982-86, 1988-94, 1996, 1997)

Traded to **Pittsburgh** by **Edmonton** with Dave Hunter and Wayne Van Dorp for Craig Simpson, Dave Hannan, Moe Mantha and Chris Joseph, November 24, 1987. Traded to **Los Angeles** by **Pittsburgh** for Brian Benning, Jeff Chychrun and Los Angeles' first round choice (later traded to Philadelphia — Philadelphia selected Jason Bowen) in 1992 Entry Draft, February 19, 1992. Traded to **Detroit** by **Los Angeles** with Sylvain Couturier and Jim Hiller for Jimmy Carson, Marc Potvin and Gary Shuchuk, January 29, 1993. Traded to **Hartford** by **Detroit** with Keith Primeau and Detroit's first round choice (Nikos Tselios) in 1997 Entry Draft for Brendan Shanahan and Brian Glynn, October 9, 1996. Traded to **Philadelphia** by **Hartford** with Hartford's third round choice (Kris Mallette) in 1997 Entry Draft for Kevin Haller, Philadelphia's first round choice (later traded to San Jose — San Jose selected Scott Hannan) in 1997 Entry Draft and Hartford's seventh round choice (previously acquired by Philadelphia — Carolina selected Andrew Merrick) in 1997 Entry Draft, December 15, 1996.

COLAGIACOMO, ADAM (coh-lah-JAH-coh-moh) — S.J.

Right wing. Shoots right. 6'2", 206 lbs. Born, Toronto, Ont., March 17, 1979.
(San Jose's 3rd choice, 82nd overall, in 1997 Entry Draft).

			Regular Season					Playoffs				
Season	Club	Lea	GP	G	A	TP	PIM	GP	G	A	TP	PIM
1995-96	London	OHL	66	28	38	66	88	....	....	....	....	....
1996-97	London	OHL	26	11	11	22	37	....	....	....	....	....
	Oshawa	OHL	23	14	10	24	32	13	1	5	6	4

COLE, DANTON

Center/Right wing. Shoots right. 5'11", 185 lbs. Born, Pontiac, MI, January 10, 1967.
(Winnipeg's 6th choice, 123rd overall, in 1985 Entry Draft).

			Regular Season					Playoffs				
Season	Club	Lea	GP	G	A	TP	PIM	GP	G	A	TP	PIM
1985-86	Michigan State	CCHA	43	11	10	21	22	....	....	....	....	....
1986-87	Michigan State	CCHA	44	9	15	24	16	....	....	....	....	....
1987-88	Michigan State	CCHA	46	20	36	56	38	....	....	....	....	....
1988-89	Michigan State	CCHA	47	29	33	62	46	....	....	....	....	....
1989-90	**Winnipeg**	**NHL**	**2**	**1**	**1**	**2**	**0**	....	....	....	....	....
	Moncton	AHL	80	31	42	73	18	....	....	....	....	....
1990-91	**Winnipeg**	**NHL**	**66**	**13**	**11**	**24**	**24**	....	....	....	....	....
	Moncton	AHL	3	1	1	2	0	....	....	....	....	....
1991-92	**Winnipeg**	**NHL**	**52**	**7**	**5**	**12**	**32**	....	....	....	....	....
1992-93	**Tampa Bay**	**NHL**	**67**	**12**	**15**	**27**	**23**	....	....	....	....	....
	Atlanta	IHL	1	1	0	1	2	....	....	....	....	....
1993-94	**Tampa Bay**	**NHL**	**81**	**20**	**23**	**43**	**32**	....	....	....	....	....
1994-95	**Tampa Bay**	**NHL**	**26**	**3**	**3**	**6**	**6**	....	....	....	....	....
	New Jersey	**NHL**	**12**	**1**	**2**	**3**	**8**	**1**	**0**	**0**	**0**	**0 ♦**
1995-96	**NY Islanders**	**NHL**	**10**	**1**	**0**	**1**	**0**	....	....	....	....	....
	Utah	IHL	34	28	15	43	22	....	....	....	....	....
	Chicago	**NHL**	**2**	**0**	**0**	**0**	**0**	....	....	....	....	....
	Indianapolis	IHL	32	9	13	22	20	5	1	5	6	8
1996-97	Krefeld	Ger.	28	7	12	19	14	....	....	....	....	....
	Grand Rapids	IHL	35	8	18	26	24	5	3	1	4	2
	NHL Totals		**318**	**58**	**60**	**118**	**125**	**1**	**0**	**0**	**0**	**0**

Traded to **Tampa Bay** by **Winnipeg** for future considerations, June 19, 1992. Traded to **New Jersey** by **Tampa Bay** with Shawn Chambers for Alexander Semak and Ben Hankinson, March 14, 1995. Signed as a free agent by **NY Islanders**, August 26, 1995. Traded to **Chicago** by **NY Islanders** for Bob Halkidis, February 2, 1996.

COLEMAN, JON — DET.

Defense. Shoots right. 6'1", 190 lbs. Born, Boston, MA, March 9, 1975.
(Detroit's 2nd choice, 48th overall, in 1993 Entry Draft).

			Regular Season					Playoffs				
Season	Club	Lea	GP	G	A	TP	PIM	GP	G	A	TP	PIM
1993-94	Boston U.	H.E.	29	1	14	15	26	....	....	....	....	....
1994-95	Boston U.	H.E.	40	5	23	28	42	....	....	....	....	....
1995-96ab	Boston U.	H.E.	40	7	31	38	58	....	....	....	....	....
1996-97ac	Boston U.	H.E.	39	5	27	32	20	....	....	....	....	....

a Hockey East All-Star Team (1996, 1997)
b NCAA East Second All-American Team (1996)
c NCAA East First All-American Team (1997)

COLES, BRUCE — PHI.

Left wing. Shoots left. 5'9", 183 lbs. Born, Montreal, Que., January 12, 1968.
(Montreal's 1st choice, 23rd overall, in 1990 Supplemental Draft).

			Regular Season					Playoffs				
Season	Club	Lea	GP	G	A	TP	PIM	GP	G	A	TP	PIM
1987-89	RPI	ECAC	32	16	23	39	48	....	....	....	....	....
1988-89	RPI	ECAC	27	8	14	22	66	....	....	....	....	....
1989-90	RPI	ECAC	34	*28	24	52	142	....	....	....	....	....
1990-91	RPI	ECAC	31	23	29	52	145	....	....	....	....	....
1991-92	Winston-Salem	ECHL	16	2	6	8	37	....	....	....	....	....
	Johnstown	ECHL	43	32	45	77	113	6	3	1	4	12
1992-93	Johnstown	ECHL	28	28	26	54	61	5	1	3	4	29
	Cdn. National	....	27	9	22	31	20	....	....	....	....	....
	Providence	AHL	2	0	0	0	0	....	....	....	....	....
1993-94	Johnstown	ECHL	24	23	20	43	56	3	0	1	1	10
1994-95	Johnstown	ECHL	29	20	25	45	56	....	....	....	....	....
	Hershey	AHL	51	16	25	41	73	6	1	5	6	14
1995-96	Hershey	AHL	68	23	29	52	75	5	2	2	4	6
1996-97	Philadelphia	AHL	79	31	49	80	152	10	2	5	7	28

Signed as a free agent by **Philadelphia**, May 31, 1995

CONN, ROB

Left/Right wing. Shoots right. 6'2", 200 lbs. Born, Calgary, Alta., September 3, 1968.

			Regular Season					Playoffs				
Season	Club	Lea	GP	G	A	TP	PIM	GP	G	A	TP	PIM
1988-89	Alaska-Anch.	G.N.	33	21	17	38	46	....	....	....	....	....
1989-90	Alaska-Anch.	G.N.	34	27	21	48	46	....	....	....	....	....
1990-91	Alaska-Anch.	G.N.	43	28	32	60	53	....	....	....	....	....
1991-92	**Chicago**	**NHL**	**2**	**0**	**0**	**0**	**2**	....	....	....	....	....
	Indianapolis	IHL	72	19	16	35	100	....	....	....	....	....
1992-93	Indianapolis	IHL	75	13	14	27	81	5	0	1	1	6
1993-94	Indianapolis	IHL	51	16	11	27	46	....	....	....	....	....
1994-95	Indianapolis	IHL	10	4	4	8	11	....	....	....	....	....
	Albany	AHL	68	35	32	67	76	14	4	6	10	16
1995-96	**Buffalo**	**NHL**	**28**	**2**	**5**	**7**	**18**	....	....	....	....	....
	Rochester	AHL	36	22	15	37	40	19	7	6	13	10
1996-97	Indianapolis	IHL	72	25	32	57	81	4	0	0	0	8
	NHL Totals		**30**	**2**	**5**	**7**	**20**	....	....	....	....	....

Signed as a free agent by **Chicago**, July 31, 1991. Traded to **New Jersey** by **Chicago** for Dean Malkoc, January 30, 1995. Claimed by **Buffalo** from **New Jersey** in NHL Waiver Draft, October 2, 1995. Signed as a free agent by **Chicago**, September 26, 1996.

CONROY, AL

Center. Shoots right. 5'8", 170 lbs. Born, Calgary, Alta., January 17, 1966.

			Regular Season					Playoffs				
Season	Club	Lea	GP	G	A	TP	PIM	GP	G	A	TP	PIM
1986-87	Rapperswill	Switz.	36	30	32	62	0	....	....	....	....	....
	Rochester	AHL	13	4	4	8	40	13	1	3	4	50
1987-88	Varese	Italy	36	25	39	64	....	....	....	....	....	....
	Adirondack	AHL	13	5	8	13	20	11	1	3	4	41
1988-89	Dortmund	W. Ger.	46	53	78	131	....	....	....	....	....	....
1989-90	Adirondack	AHL	77	23	33	56	147	5	0	0	0	20
1990-91	Adirondack	AHL	80	26	39	65	172	2	1	1	2	0
1991-92	**Philadelphia**	**NHL**	**31**	**2**	**9**	**11**	**74**	....	....	....	....	....
	Hershey	AHL	47	17	28	45	90	6	4	2	6	12
1992-93	**Philadelphia**	**NHL**	**21**	**3**	**2**	**5**	**17**	....	....	....	....	....
	Hershey	AHL	60	28	32	60	130	....	....	....	....	....
1993-94	**Philadelphia**	**NHL**	**62**	**4**	**3**	**7**	**65**	....	....	....	....	....
1994-95	Detroit	IHL	71	18	40	58	151	....	....	....	....	....
	Houston	IHL	9	3	4	7	17	4	1	2	3	8
1995-96	Houston	IHL	82	24	38	62	134	....	....	....	....	....
1996-97	Houston	IHL	70	15	32	47	171	13	4	10	14	26
	NHL Totals		**114**	**9**	**14**	**23**	**156**	....	....	....	....	....

Signed as a free agent by **Detroit**, August 16, 1989. Signed as a free agent by **Philadelphia**, August 21, 1991.

CONROY, CRAIG — ST.L.

Center. Shoots right. 6'2", 198 lbs. Born, Potsdam, NY, September 4, 1971.
(Montreal's 7th choice, 123rd overall, in 1990 Entry Draft).

			Regular Season					Playoffs				
Season	Club	Lea	GP	G	A	TP	PIM	GP	G	A	TP	PIM
1990-91	Clarkson	ECAC	40	8	21	29	24	....	....	....	....	....
1991-92	Clarkson	ECAC	31	19	17	36	36	....	....	....	....	....
1992-93	Clarkson	ECAC	35	10	23	33	26	....	....	....	....	....
1993-94abc	Clarkson	ECAC	34	26	*40	*66	46	....	....	....	....	....
1994-95	Fredericton	AHL	55	26	18	44	29	11	7	3	10	6
	Montreal	**NHL**	**6**	**1**	**0**	**1**	**0**	....	....	....	....	....
1995-96	**Montreal**	**NHL**	**7**	**0**	**0**	**0**	**2**	....	....	....	....	....
	Fredericton	AHL	67	31	38	69	65	10	5	7	12	6
1996-97	Fredericton	AHL	9	10	6	16	10	....	....	....	....	....
	St. Louis	**NHL**	**61**	**6**	**11**	**17**	**43**	**6**	**0**	**0**	**0**	**8**
	Worcester	AHL	5	5	6	11	2	....	....	....	....	....
	NHL Totals		**74**	**7**	**11**	**18**	**45**	**6**	**0**	**0**	**0**	**8**

a ECAC First All-Star Team (1994)
b NCAA East First All-American Team (1994)
c NCAA Final Four All-Tournament Team (1994)

Traded to **St. Louis** by **Montreal** with Pierre Turgeon and Rory Fitzpatrick for Murray Baron, Shayne Corson and St. Louis' fifth round choice (Gennady Razin) in 1997 Entry Draft, October 29, 1996.

CONVERY, BRANDON — TOR.

Center. Shoots right. 6'1", 182 lbs. Born, Kingston, Ont., February 4, 1974.
(Toronto's 1st choice, 8th overall, in 1992 Entry Draft).

			Regular Season					Playoffs				
Season	Club	Lea	GP	G	A	TP	PIM	GP	G	A	TP	PIM
1990-91	Sudbury	OHL	56	26	22	48	18	5	1	1	2	2
1991-92	Sudbury	OHL	44	40	26	66	44	5	3	2	5	4
1992-93	Sudbury	OHL	7	7	9	16	6	....	....	....	....	....
	Niagara Falls	OHL	51	38	39	77	24	4	1	3	4	4
	St. John's	AHL	3	0	0	0	0	5	0	1	1	0
1993-94	Niagara Falls	OHL	29	24	29	53	30	....	....	....	....	....
	Belleville	OHL	23	16	19	35	22	12	4	10	14	13
	St. John's	AHL	....	....	....	....	....	1	0	0	0	0
1994-95	St. John's	AHL	76	34	37	71	43	5	2	2	4	4
1995-96	**Toronto**	**NHL**	**11**	**5**	**2**	**7**	**4**	**5**	**0**	**0**	**0**	**2**
	St. John's	AHL	57	22	23	45	28	....	....	....	....	....
1996-97	**Toronto**	**NHL**	**39**	**2**	**8**	**10**	**20**	....	....	....	....	....
	St. John's	AHL	25	14	14	28	15	....	....	....	....	....
	NHL Totals		**50**	**7**	**10**	**17**	**24**	**5**	**0**	**0**	**0**	**2**

COOKE, MATT — VAN.

Left wing. Shoots left. 5'11", 192 lbs. Born, Belleville, Ont., September 7, 1978.
(Vancouver's 7th choice, 144th overall, in 1997 Entry Draft).

			Regular Season					Playoffs				
Season	Club	Lea	GP	G	A	TP	PIM	GP	G	A	TP	PIM
1995-96	Windsor	OHL	61	8	11	19	102	7	1	3	4	6
1996-97	Windsor	OHL	65	45	50	95	146	5	5	5	10	10

COOPER, DAVID — TOR.

Defense. Shoots left. 6'2", 204 lbs. Born, Ottawa, Ont., November 2, 1973.
(Buffalo's 1st choice, 11th overall, in 1992 Entry Draft).

			Regular Season					Playoffs				
Season	Club	Lea	GP	G	A	TP	PIM	GP	G	A	TP	PIM
1989-90	Medicine Hat	WHL	61	4	11	15	65	3	0	2	2	2
1990-91	Medicine Hat	WHL	64	12	31	43	66	11	1	3	4	23
1991-92a	Medicine Hat	WHL	72	17	47	64	176	4	1	4	5	8
1992-93	Medicine Hat	WHL	63	15	50	65	88	10	2	2	4	32
	Rochester	AHL	....	....	....	....	....	2	0	0	0	2
1993-94	Rochester	AHL	68	10	25	35	82	4	1	1	2	2
1994-95	Rochester	AHL	21	2	4	6	48	....	....	....	....	....
	S. Carolina	ECHL	39	9	19	28	90	9	3	8	11	24
1995-96	Rochester	AHL	67	9	18	27	79	8	0	1	1	12
1996-97	**Toronto**	**NHL**	**19**	**3**	**3**	**6**	**16**	....	....	....	....	....
	St. John's	AHL	44	16	19	35	65	....	....	....	....	....
	NHL Totals		**19**	**3**	**3**	**6**	**16**	....	....	....	....	....

a WHL East First All-Star Team (1992)

Signed as a free agent by **Toronto**, September 26, 1996.

COPELAND, ADAM — EDM.

Right wing. Shoots right. 6'1", 185 lbs. Born, St. Catharines, Ont., June 5, 1976.
(Edmonton's 6th choice, 79th overall, in 1994 Entry Draft).

			Regular Season					Playoffs				
Season	Club	Lea	GP	G	A	TP	PIM	GP	G	A	TP	PIM
1994-95	Miami-Ohio	CCHA	39	6	4	10	28	....	....	....	....	....
1995-96	Miami-Ohio	CCHA	36	10	4	14	38	....	....	....	....	....
1996-97	Miami-Ohio	CCHA	40	18	22	40	62	....	....	....	....	....

CORBET, RENE (cohr-BAY, ruh-NAY) — COL.

Left wing. Shoots left. 6', 187 lbs. Born, Victoriaville, Que., June 25, 1973.
(Quebec's 2nd choice, 24th overall, in 1991 Entry Draft).

			Regular Season					Playoffs				
Season	Club	Lea	GP	G	A	TP	PIM	GP	G	A	TP	PIM
1990-91	Drummondville	QMJHL	45	25	40	65	34	14	11	6	17	15
1991-92	Drummondville	QMJHL	56	46	50	96	90	4	1	2	3	17
1992-93ab	Drummondville	QMJHL	63	*79	69	*148	143	10	7	13	20	16
1993-94	**Quebec**	**NHL**	**9**	**1**	**1**	**2**	**0**	....	....	....	....	....
c	Cornwall	AHL	68	37	40	77	56	13	7	2	9	18
1994-95	Cornwall	AHL	65	33	24	57	79	12	2	8	10	27
	Quebec	**NHL**	**8**	**0**	**3**	**3**	**2**	**2**	**0**	**1**	**1**	**0**
1995-96	**Colorado**	**NHL**	**33**	**3**	**6**	**9**	**33**	**8**	**3**	**2**	**5**	**2** ♦
	Cornwall	AHL	9	5	6	11	10	....	....	....	....	....
1996-97	**Colorado**	**NHL**	**76**	**12**	**15**	**27**	**67**	**17**	**2**	**2**	**4**	**27**
	NHL Totals		**126**	**16**	**25**	**41**	**102**	**27**	**5**	**5**	**10**	**29**

a QMJHL First All-Star Team (1993)
b Canadian Major Junior First All-Star Team (1993)
c Won Dudley "Red" Garrett Memorial Trophy (Top Rookie - AHL) (1994)

CORKUM, BOB (KOHR-kuhm) — PHO.

Center. Shoots right. 6'2", 210 lbs. Born, Salisbury, MA, December 18, 1967.
(Buffalo's 3rd choice, 47th overall, in 1986 Entry Draft).

			Regular Season					Playoffs				
Season	Club	Lea	GP	G	A	TP	PIM	GP	G	A	TP	PIM
1985-86	U. of Maine	H.E.	39	7	26	33	53	....	....	....	....	....
1986-87	U. of Maine	H.E.	35	18	11	29	24	....	....	....	....	....
1987-88	U. of Maine	H.E.	40	14	18	32	64	....	....	....	....	....
1988-89	U. of Maine	H.E.	45	17	31	48	64	....	....	....	....	....
1989-90	**Buffalo**	**NHL**	**8**	**2**	**0**	**2**	**4**	**5**	**1**	**0**	**1**	**4**
	Rochester	AHL	43	8	11	19	45	12	2	5	7	16
1990-91	Rochester	AHL	69	13	21	34	77	15	4	4	8	4
1991-92	**Buffalo**	**NHL**	**20**	**2**	**4**	**6**	**21**	**4**	**1**	**0**	**1**	**0**
	Rochester	AHL	52	16	12	28	47	8	0	6	6	8
1992-93	**Buffalo**	**NHL**	**68**	**6**	**4**	**10**	**38**	**5**	**0**	**0**	**0**	**2**
1993-94	**Anaheim**	**NHL**	**76**	**23**	**28**	**51**	**18**	....	....	....	....	....
1994-95	**Anaheim**	**NHL**	**44**	**10**	**9**	**19**	**25**	....	....	....	....	....
1995-96	**Anaheim**	**NHL**	**48**	**5**	**7**	**12**	**26**	....	....	....	....	....
	Philadelphia	**NHL**	**28**	**4**	**3**	**7**	**8**	**12**	**1**	**2**	**3**	**6**
1996-97	**Phoenix**	**NHL**	**80**	**9**	**11**	**20**	**40**	**7**	**2**	**2**	**4**	**4**
	NHL Totals		**372**	**61**	**66**	**127**	**180**	**33**	**5**	**4**	**9**	**16**

Claimed by **Anaheim** from **Buffalo** in Expansion Draft, June 24, 1993. Traded to **Philadelphia** by **Anaheim** for Chris Herperger and Winnipeg's seventh round choice (previously acquired by Philadelphia) in 1997 Entry Draft, February 6, 1996. Claimed by **Phoenix** from **Philadelphia** in NHL Waiver Draft, September 30, 1996.

CORNFORTH, MARK — BOS.

Defense. Shoots left. 6'1", 193 lbs. Born, Montreal, Que., November 13, 1972.

			Regular Season					Playoffs				
Season	Club	Lea	GP	G	A	TP	PIM	GP	G	A	TP	PIM
1991-92	Merrimack	H.E.	23	1	9	10	20	....	....	....	....	....
1992-93	Merrimack	H.E.	36	3	18	21	27	....	....	....	....	....
1993-94	Merrimack	H.E.	37	5	13	18	29	....	....	....	....	....
1994-95	Merrimack	H.E.	30	8	20	28	43	....	....	....	....	....
	Syracuse	AHL	2	0	1	1	2	....	....	....	....	....
1995-96	**Boston**	**NHL**	**6**	**0**	**0**	**0**	**4**	....	....	....	....	....
	Providence	AHL	65	5	10	15	117	4	0	0	0	4
1996-97	Providence	AHL	61	8	12	20	47	....	....	....	....	....
	Cleveland	IHL	13	1	4	5	25	14	1	3	4	29
	NHL Totals		**6**	**0**	**0**	**0**	**4**	....	....	....	....	....

Signed as a free agent by **Boston**, October 6, 1995.

CORSO, DANIEL — ST.L.

Center. Shoots left. 5'9", 155 lbs. Born, Montreal, Que., April 3, 1978.
(St. Louis' 5th choice, 169th overall, in 1996 Entry Draft).

			Regular Season					Playoffs				
Season	Club	Lea	GP	G	A	TP	PIM	GP	G	A	TP	PIM
1994-95	Victoriaville	QMJHL	65	27	26	53	6	4	2	5	7	2
1995-96	Victoriaville	QMJHL	65	49	65	114	77	12	6	7	13	4
1996-97	Victoriaville	QMJHL	54	51	68	119	50	....	....	....	....	....

CORSON, SHAYNE — MTL.

Left wing. Shoots left. 6'1", 200 lbs. Born, Midland, Ont., August 13, 1966.
(Montreal's 2nd choice, 8th overall, in 1984 Entry Draft).

			Regular Season					Playoffs				
Season	Club	Lea	GP	G	A	TP	PIM	GP	G	A	TP	PIM
1983-84	Brantford	OHL	66	25	46	71	165	6	4	1	5	26
1984-85	Hamilton	OHL	54	27	63	90	154	11	3	7	10	19
1985-86	**Montreal**	**NHL**	**3**	**0**	**0**	**0**	**2**	....	....	....	....	....
	Hamilton	OHL	47	41	57	98	153	....	....	....	....	....
1986-87	**Montreal**	**NHL**	**55**	**12**	**11**	**23**	**144**	**17**	**6**	**5**	**11**	**30**
1987-88	**Montreal**	**NHL**	**71**	**12**	**27**	**39**	**152**	**3**	**1**	**0**	**1**	**12**
1988-89	**Montreal**	**NHL**	**80**	**26**	**24**	**50**	**193**	**21**	**4**	**5**	**9**	**65**
1989-90	**Montreal**	**NHL**	**76**	**31**	**44**	**75**	**144**	**11**	**2**	**8**	**10**	**20**
1990-91	**Montreal**	**NHL**	**71**	**23**	**24**	**47**	**138**	**13**	**9**	**6**	**15**	**36**
1991-92	**Montreal**	**NHL**	**64**	**17**	**36**	**53**	**118**	**10**	**2**	**5**	**7**	**15**
1992-93	**Edmonton**	**NHL**	**80**	**16**	**31**	**47**	**209**	....	....	....	....	....
1993-94	**Edmonton**	**NHL**	**64**	**25**	**29**	**54**	**118**	....	....	....	....	....
1994-95	**Edmonton**	**NHL**	**48**	**12**	**24**	**36**	**86**	....	....	....	....	....
1995-96	**St. Louis**	**NHL**	**77**	**18**	**28**	**46**	**192**	**13**	**8**	**6**	**14**	**22**
1996-97	**St. Louis**	**NHL**	**11**	**2**	**1**	**3**	**24**	....	....	....	....	....
	Montreal	**NHL**	**47**	**6**	**15**	**21**	**80**	**5**	**1**	**0**	**1**	**4**
	NHL Totals		**747**	**200**	**294**	**494**	**1600**	**93**	**33**	**35**	**68**	**204**

Played in NHL All-Star Game (1990, 1994)

Traded to **Edmonton** by **Montreal** with Brent Gilchrist and Vladimir Vujtek for Vincent Damphousse and Edmonton's fourth round choice (Adam Wiesel) in 1993 Entry Draft, August 27, 1992. Signed as a free agent by **St. Louis**, July 28, 1995. Traded to **Montreal** by **St. Louis** with Murray Baron and St. Louis' fifth round choice (Gennady Razin) in 1997 Entry Draft for Pierre Turgeon, Rory Fitzpatrick and Craig Conroy, October 29, 1996.

CORVO, JOSEPH — L.A.

Defense. Shoots right. 6', 201 lbs. Born, Oak Park, IL, June 20, 1977.
(Los Angeles' 4th choice, 83rd overall, in 1997 Entry Draft).

			Regular Season					Playoffs				
Season	Club	Lea	GP	G	A	TP	PIM	GP	G	A	TP	PIM
1995-96	W. Michigan	CCHA	41	5	25	30	38	....	....	....	....	....
1996-97	W. Michigan	CCHA	32	12	21	33	85	....	....	....	....	....

COTE, PATRICK — DAL.

Left wing. Shoots left. 6'3", 199 lbs. Born, Lasalle, Que., January 24, 1975.
(Dallas' 2nd choice, 37th overall, in 1995 Entry Draft).

			Regular Season					Playoffs				
Season	Club	Lea	GP	G	A	TP	PIM	GP	G	A	TP	PIM
1993-94	Beauport	QMJHL	48	2	4	6	230	12	1	0	1	61
1994-95	Beauport	QMJHL	56	20	20	40	314	17	8	8	16	115
1995-96	**Dallas**	**NHL**	**2**	**0**	**0**	**0**	**5**	....	....	....	....	....
	Michigan	IHL	57	4	6	10	239	3	0	0	0	2
1996-97	**Dallas**	**NHL**	**3**	**0**	**0**	**0**	**27**	....	....	....	....	....
	Michigan	IHL	58	14	10	24	237	4	2	0	2	6
	NHL Totals		**5**	**0**	**0**	**0**	**32**	....	....	....	....	....

COTE, SYLVAIN (KOH-tay) — WSH.

Defense. Shoots right. 6', 190 lbs. Born, Quebec City, Que., January 19, 1966.
(Hartford's 1st choice, 11th overall, in 1984 Entry Draft).

			Regular Season					Playoffs				
Season	Club	Lea	GP	G	A	TP	PIM	GP	G	A	TP	PIM
1982-83	Quebec	QMJHL	66	10	24	34	50	....	....	....	....	....
1983-84	Quebec	QMJHL	66	15	50	65	89	5	1	1	2	0
1984-85	**Hartford**	**NHL**	**67**	**3**	**9**	**12**	**17**	....	....	....	....	....
1985-86	**Hartford**	**NHL**	**2**	**0**	**0**	**0**	**0**	....	....	....	....	....
a	Hull	QMJHL	26	10	33	43	14	13	6	*28	34	22
	Binghamton	AHL	12	2	4	6	0	....	....	....	....	....
1986-87	**Hartford**	**NHL**	**67**	**2**	**8**	**10**	**20**	**2**	**0**	**2**	**2**	**2**
1987-88	**Hartford**	**NHL**	**67**	**7**	**21**	**28**	**30**	**6**	**1**	**1**	**2**	**4**
1988-89	**Hartford**	**NHL**	**78**	**8**	**9**	**17**	**49**	**3**	**0**	**1**	**1**	**4**
1989-90	**Hartford**	**NHL**	**28**	**4**	**2**	**6**	**14**	**5**	**0**	**0**	**0**	**2**
1990-91	**Hartford**	**NHL**	**73**	**7**	**12**	**19**	**17**	**6**	**0**	**2**	**2**	**2**
1991-92	**Washington**	**NHL**	**78**	**11**	**29**	**40**	**31**	**7**	**1**	**2**	**3**	**4**
1992-93	**Washington**	**NHL**	**77**	**21**	**29**	**50**	**34**	**6**	**1**	**1**	**2**	**4**
1993-94	**Washington**	**NHL**	**84**	**16**	**35**	**51**	**66**	**9**	**1**	**8**	**9**	**6**
1994-95	**Washington**	**NHL**	**47**	**5**	**14**	**19**	**53**	**7**	**1**	**3**	**4**	**2**
1995-96	**Washington**	**NHL**	**81**	**5**	**33**	**38**	**40**	**6**	**2**	**0**	**2**	**12**
1996-97	**Washington**	**NHL**	**57**	**6**	**18**	**24**	**28**	....	....	....	....	....
	NHL Totals		**806**	**95**	**219**	**314**	**399**	**57**	**7**	**20**	**27**	**42**

a QMJHL First All-Star Team (1986).

Traded to **Washington** by **Hartford** for Washington's second round choice (Andrei Nikolishin) in 1992 Entry Draft, September 8, 1991.

COURTNALL, GEOFF — ST.L.

Left wing. Shoots left. 6'1", 195 lbs. Born, Duncan, B.C., August 18, 1962.

			Regular Season					Playoffs				
Season	Club	Lea	GP	G	A	TP	PIM	GP	G	A	TP	PIM
1980-81	Victoria	WHL	11	3	4	7	6	15	2	1	3	7
1981-82	Victoria	WHL	72	35	57	90	100	4	1	0	1	2
1982-83	Victoria	WHL	71	41	73	114	186	12	6	7	13	42
1983-84	**Boston**	**NHL**	**4**	**0**	**0**	**0**	**0**	....	....	....	....	....
	Hershey	AHL	74	14	12	26	51	....	....	....	....	....
1984-85	**Boston**	**NHL**	**64**	**12**	**16**	**28**	**82**	**5**	**0**	**2**	**2**	**7**
	Hershey	AHL	9	8	4	12	4	....	....	....	....	....
1985-86	**Boston**	**NHL**	**64**	**21**	**16**	**37**	**61**	**3**	**0**	**0**	**0**	**2**
	Moncton	AHL	12	8	8	16	6	....	....	....	....	....
1986-87	**Boston**	**NHL**	**65**	**13**	**23**	**36**	**117**	**1**	**0**	**0**	**0**	**0**
1987-88	**Boston**	**NHL**	**62**	**32**	**26**	**58**	**108**	....	....	....	....	....
	Edmonton	**NHL**	**12**	**4**	**4**	**8**	**15**	**19**	**0**	**3**	**3**	**23** ♦
1988-89	**Washington**	**NHL**	**79**	**42**	**38**	**80**	**112**	**6**	**2**	**5**	**7**	**12**
1989-90	**Washington**	**NHL**	**80**	**35**	**39**	**74**	**104**	**15**	**4**	**9**	**13**	**32**
1990-91	**St. Louis**	**NHL**	**66**	**27**	**30**	**57**	**56**	....	....	....	....	....
	Vancouver	**NHL**	**11**	**6**	**2**	**8**	**8**	**6**	**3**	**5**	**8**	**4**
1991-92	**Vancouver**	**NHL**	**70**	**23**	**34**	**57**	**116**	**12**	**6**	**8**	**14**	**20**
1992-93	**Vancouver**	**NHL**	**84**	**31**	**46**	**77**	**167**	**12**	**4**	**10**	**14**	**12**
1993-94	**Vancouver**	**NHL**	**82**	**26**	**44**	**70**	**123**	**24**	**9**	**10**	**19**	**51**
1994-95	**Vancouver**	**NHL**	**45**	**16**	**18**	**34**	**81**	**11**	**4**	**2**	**6**	**34**
1995-96	**St. Louis**	**NHL**	**69**	**24**	**16**	**40**	**101**	**13**	**0**	**3**	**3**	**14**
1996-97	**St. Louis**	**NHL**	**82**	**17**	**40**	**57**	**86**	**6**	**3**	**1**	**4**	**23**
	NHL Totals		**939**	**329**	**392**	**721**	**1337**	**133**	**35**	**58**	**93**	**234**

Signed as a free agent by **Boston**, July 6, 1983. Traded to **Edmonton** by **Boston** with Bill Ranford and future considerations for Andy Moog, March 8, 1988. Rights traded to **Washington** by **Edmonton** for Greg C. Adams, July 22, 1988. Traded to **St. Louis** by **Washington** for Peter Zezel and Mike Lalor, July 13, 1990. Traded to **Vancouver** by **St. Louis** with Robert Dirk, Sergio Momesso, Cliff Ronning and St. Louis' fifth round choice (Brian Loney) in 1992 Entry Draft for Dan Quinn and Garth Butcher, March 5, 1991. Signed as a free agent by **St. Louis**, July 14, 1995.

COURTNALL, RUSS

Right wing. Shoots right. 5'11", 185 lbs. Born, Duncan, B.C., June 2, 1965.
(Toronto's 1st choice, 7th overall, in 1983 Entry Draft).

			Regular Season					Playoffs				
Season	Club	Lea	GP	G	A	TP	PIM	GP	G	A	TP	PIM
1982-83	Victoria	WHL	60	36	61	97	33	12	11	7	18	6
1983-84	Victoria	WHL	32	29	37	66	63	....	....	....	....	....
	Cdn. National	....	16	4	7	11	10	....	....	....	....	....
	Cdn. Olympic	....	7	1	3	4	2	....	....	....	....	....
	Toronto	**NHL**	**14**	**3**	**9**	**12**	**6**	....	....	....	....	....
1984-85	**Toronto**	**NHL**	**69**	**12**	**10**	**22**	**44**	....	....	....	....	....
1985-86	**Toronto**	**NHL**	**73**	**22**	**38**	**60**	**52**	**10**	**3**	**6**	**9**	**8**
1986-87	**Toronto**	**NHL**	**79**	**29**	**44**	**73**	**90**	**13**	**3**	**4**	**7**	**11**
1987-88	**Toronto**	**NHL**	**65**	**23**	**26**	**49**	**47**	**6**	**2**	**1**	**3**	**0**
1988-89	**Toronto**	**NHL**	**9**	**1**	**1**	**2**	**4**	....	....	....	....	....
	Montreal	**NHL**	**64**	**22**	**17**	**39**	**15**	**21**	**8**	**5**	**13**	**18**
1989-90	**Montreal**	**NHL**	**80**	**27**	**32**	**59**	**27**	**11**	**5**	**1**	**6**	**10**
1990-91	**Montreal**	**NHL**	**79**	**26**	**50**	**76**	**29**	**13**	**8**	**3**	**11**	**7**
1991-92	**Montreal**	**NHL**	**27**	**7**	**14**	**21**	**6**	**10**	**1**	**1**	**2**	**4**
1992-93	**Minnesota**	**NHL**	**84**	**36**	**43**	**79**	**49**	....	....	....	....	....
1993-94	**Dallas**	**NHL**	**84**	**23**	**57**	**80**	**59**	**9**	**1**	**8**	**9**	**0**
1994-95	**Dallas**	**NHL**	**32**	**7**	**10**	**17**	**13**	....	....	....	....	....
	Vancouver	**NHL**	**13**	**4**	**14**	**18**	**4**	**11**	**4**	**8**	**12**	**21**
1995-96	**Vancouver**	**NHL**	**81**	**26**	**39**	**65**	**40**	**6**	**1**	**3**	**4**	**2**
1996-97	**Vancouver**	**NHL**	**47**	**9**	**19**	**28**	**24**	....	....	....	....	....
	NY Rangers	**NHL**	**14**	**2**	**5**	**7**	**2**	**15**	**3**	**4**	**7**	**0**
	NHL Totals		**914**	**279**	**428**	**707**	**511**	**125**	**39**	**44**	**83**	**81**

Played in NHL All-Star Game (1994)

Traded to **Montreal** by **Toronto** for John Kordic and Montreal's sixth round choice (Michael Doers) in 1989 Entry Draft, November 7, 1988. Traded to **Minnesota** by **Montreal** for Brian Bellows, August 31, 1992. Traded to **Vancouver** by **Dallas** for Greg Adams, Dan Kesa and Vancouver's fifth round choice (later traded to Los Angeles — Los Angeles selected Jason Morgan) in 1995 Entry Draft, April 7, 1995. Traded to **NY Rangers** by **Vancouver** with Esa Tikkanen for Sergei Nemchinov and Brian Noonan, March 8, 1997.

COURVILLE, LARRY (KOOR-vihl) VAN.

Left wing. Shoots left. 6'1", 180 lbs. Born, Timmins, Ont., April 2, 1975.
(Winnipeg's 6th choice, 119th overall, in 1993 Entry Draft).

			Regular Season					Playoffs				
Season	Club	Lea	GP	G	A	TP	PIM	GP	G	A	TP	PIM
1991-92	Cornwall	OHL	60	8	12	20	80	6	0	0	0	8
1992-93	Newmarket	OHL	64	21	18	39	181	7	0	6	6	14
1993-94	Newmarket	OHL	39	20	19	39	134	....	....	....	....	....
	Moncton	AHL	8	2	0	2	37	10	2	2	4	27
1994-95a	Sarnia	OHL	16	9	9	18	58	....	....	....	....	....
	Oshawa	OHL	28	25	30	55	72	7	4	10	14	10
1995-96	**Vancouver**	**NHL**	**3**	**1**	**0**	**1**	**0**	....	....	....	....	....
	Syracuse	AHL	71	17	32	49	127	14	5	3	8	10
1996-97	**Vancouver**	**NHL**	**19**	**0**	**2**	**2**	**11**	....	....	....	....	....
	Syracuse	AHL	54	20	24	44	103	3	0	1	1	20
	NHL Totals		**22**	**1**	**2**	**3**	**11**	....	....	....	....	....

a OHL Second All-Star Team (1995)

Re-entered NHL Entry Draft, **Vancouver's** 2nd choice, 61st overall in 1995 Entry Draft.

COUTURE, ALEXANDRE (koo-TUHR) FLA.

Defense. Shoots right. 6'4", 197 lbs. Born, Hamnord, Que., December 18, 1977.
(Florida's 7th choice, 183rd overall, in 1996 Entry Draft).

			Regular Season					Playoffs				
Season	Club	Lea	GP	G	A	TP	PIM	GP	G	A	TP	PIM
1994-95	Victoriaville	QMJHL	24	4	7	11	4	4	1	2	3	2
1995-96	Victoriaville	QMJHL	67	3	10	13	121	11	0	0	0	10
1996-97	Victoriaville	QMJHL	47	2	12	14	113	5	0	1	1	4

COUTURIER, SYLVAIN (koo-TOOR-ee-yah, SIHL-vay)

Center. Shoots left. 6'2", 205 lbs. Born, Greenfield Park, Que., April 23, 1968.
(Los Angeles' 3rd choice, 65th overall, in 1986 Entry Draft).

			Regular Season					Playoffs				
Season	Club	Lea	GP	G	A	TP	PIM	GP	G	A	TP	PIM
1985-86	Laval	QMJHL	68	21	37	58	64	14	1	7	8	28
1986-87	Laval	QMJHL	67	39	51	90	77	13	12	14	26	19
1987-88	Laval	QMJHL	67	70	67	137	115	....	....	....	....	....
1988-89	**Los Angeles**	**NHL**	**16**	**1**	**3**	**4**	**2**	....	....	....	....	....
	New Haven	AHL	44	18	20	38	33	10	2	2	4	11
1989-90	New Haven	AHL	50	9	8	17	47	....	....	....	....	....
1990-91	**Los Angeles**	**NHL**	**3**	**0**	**1**	**1**	**0**	....	....	....	....	....
	Phoenix	IHL	66	50	37	87	49	10	8	2	10	10
1991-92	**Los Angeles**	**NHL**	**14**	**3**	**1**	**4**	**2**	....	....	....	....	....
	Phoenix	IHL	39	19	20	39	68	....	....	....	....	....
1992-93	Phoenix	IHL	38	23	16	39	63	....	....	....	....	....
	Adirondack	AHL	29	17	17	34	12	11	3	5	8	10
	Fort Wayne	IHL	....	....	....	....	....	4	2	3	5	2
1993-94	Milwaukee	IHL	80	41	51	92	123	4	1	2	3	2
1994-95	Milwaukee	IHL	77	31	41	72	77	15	1	4	5	10
1995-96	Milwaukee	IHL	82	33	52	85	60	5	1	0	1	2
1996-97	Milwaukee	IHL	79	26	24	50	42	3	0	1	1	2
	NHL Totals		**33**	**4**	**5**	**9**	**4**	....	....	....	....	....

Traded to **Detroit** by **Los Angeles** with Paul Coffey and Jim Hiller for Jimmy Carson, Marc Potvin and Gary Shuchuk, January 29, 1993.

COWAN, JEFF CGY.

Left wing. Shoots left. 6'2", 185 lbs. Born, Scarborough, Ont., September 27, 1976.

			Regular Season					Playoffs				
Season	Club	Lea	GP	G	A	TP	PIM	GP	G	A	TP	PIM
1993-94	Guelph	OHL	17	1	0	1	5	....	....	....	....	....
1994-95	Guelph	OHL	51	10	7	17	14	14	1	1	2	0
1995-96	Barrie	OHL	66	38	14	52	29	5	1	2	3	6
1996-97	Saint John	AHL	22	5	5	10	8	....	....	....	....	....
	Roanoke	ECHL	47	21	13	34	42	....	....	....	....	....

Signed as a free agent by **Calgary**, October 2, 1995.

CRAIG, MIKE

Right wing. Shoots right. 6'1", 180 lbs. Born, St. Mary's, Ont., June 6, 1971.
(Minnesota's 2nd choice, 28th overall, in 1989 Entry Draft).

			Regular Season					Playoffs				
Season	Club	Lea	GP	G	A	TP	PIM	GP	G	A	TP	PIM
1987-88	Oshawa	OHL	61	6	10	16	39	7	7	0	1	11
1988-89	Oshawa	OHL	63	36	36	72	34	6	3	1	4	6
1989-90	Oshawa	OHL	43	36	40	76	85	17	10	16	26	46
1990-91	**Minnesota**	**NHL**	**39**	**8**	**4**	**12**	**32**	**10**	**1**	**1**	**2**	**20**
1991-92	**Minnesota**	**NHL**	**67**	**15**	**16**	**31**	**155**	**4**	**1**	**0**	**1**	**7**
1992-93	**Minnesota**	**NHL**	**70**	**15**	**23**	**38**	**106**	....	....	....	....	....
1993-94	**Dallas**	**NHL**	**72**	**13**	**24**	**37**	**139**	**4**	**0**	**0**	**0**	**2**
1994-95	**Toronto**	**NHL**	**37**	**5**	**5**	**10**	**12**	**2**	**0**	**1**	**1**	**2**
1995-96	**Toronto**	**NHL**	**70**	**8**	**12**	**20**	**42**	**6**	**0**	**0**	**0**	**18**
1996-97	**Toronto**	**NHL**	**65**	**7**	**13**	**20**	**62**	....	....	....	....	....
	NHL Totals		**420**	**71**	**97**	**168**	**548**	**26**	**2**	**2**	**4**	**49**

Signed as a free agent by **Toronto**, July 29, 1994.

CRAIGHEAD, JOHN

Right wing. Shoots right. 6', 195 lbs. Born, Vancouver, B.C., November 23, 1971.

			Regular Season					Playoffs				
Season	Club	Lea	GP	G	A	TP	PIM	GP	G	A	TP	PIM
1990-91	Br. Columbia	Jr. A	25	21	23	44	120	....	....	....	....	....
1991-92	W. Palm Beach	SHL	39	12	17	29	160	....	....	....	....	....
1992-93					UNAVAILABLE							
1993-94	Huntington	ECHL	9	4	2	6	44	....	....	....	....	....
	Richmond	ECHL	28	18	12	30	89	....	....	....	....	....
1994-95	Detroit	IHL	44	5	7	12	285	3	0	1	1	4
1995-96	Detroit	IHL	63	7	9	16	368	10	2	3	5	28
1996-97	**Toronto**	**NHL**	**5**	**0**	**0**	**0**	**10**	....	....	....	....	....
	St. John's	AHL	53	9	10	19	318	7	1	1	2	22
	NHL Totals		**5**	**0**	**0**	**0**	**10**	....	....	....	....	....

Signed as a free agent by **Toronto**, July 22, 1996.

CRAIGWELL, DALE

Center. Shoots left. 5'11", 180 lbs. Born, Toronto, Ont., April 24, 1971.
(San Jose's 11th choice, 199th overall, in 1991 Entry Draft).

			Regular Season					Playoffs				
Season	Club	Lea	GP	G	A	TP	PIM	GP	G	A	TP	PIM
1988-89	Oshawa	OHL	55	9	14	23	15	....	....	....	....	....
1989-90	Oshawa	OHL	64	22	41	63	39	17	7	7	14	11
1990-91	Oshawa	OHL	56	27	68	95	34	16	7	16	23	9
1991-92	**San Jose**	**NHL**	**32**	**5**	**11**	**16**	**8**	....	....	....	....	....
	Kansas City	IHL	48	6	19	25	29	12	4	7	11	4
1992-93	**San Jose**	**NHL**	**8**	**3**	**1**	**4**	**4**	....	....	....	....	....
	Kansas City	IHL	60	15	38	53	24	12	*7	5	12	2
1993-94	**San Jose**	**NHL**	**58**	**3**	**6**	**9**	**16**	....	....	....	....	....
	Kansas City	IHL	5	3	1	4	0	....	....	....	....	....
1994-95					DID NOT PLAY – INJURED							
1995-96	San Francisco	IHL	75	11	49	60	38	4	2	0	2	0
1996-97	Kansas City	IHL	82	17	51	68	34	3	1	0	1	0
	NHL Totals		**98**	**11**	**18**	**29**	**28**	....	....	....	....	....

CRAVEN, MURRAY S.J.

Left wing. Shoots left. 6'2", 185 lbs. Born, Medicine Hat, Alta., July 20, 1964.
(Detroit's 1st choice, 17th overall, in 1982 Entry Draft).

			Regular Season					Playoffs				
Season	Club	Lea	GP	G	A	TP	PIM	GP	G	A	TP	PIM
1980-81	Medicine Hat	WHL	69	5	10	15	18	5	0	0	0	2
1981-82	Medicine Hat	WHL	72	35	46	81	49	....	....	....	....	....
1982-83	**Detroit**	**NHL**	**31**	**4**	**7**	**11**	**6**	....	....	....	....	....
	Medicine Hat	WHL	28	17	29	46	35	....	....	....	....	....
1983-84	**Detroit**	**NHL**	**15**	**0**	**4**	**4**	**6**	....	....	....	....	....
	Medicine Hat	WHL	48	38	56	94	53	4	5	3	8	4
1984-85	**Philadelphia**	**NHL**	**80**	**26**	**35**	**61**	**30**	**19**	**4**	**6**	**10**	**11**
1985-86	**Philadelphia**	**NHL**	**78**	**21**	**33**	**54**	**34**	**5**	**0**	**3**	**3**	**4**
1986-87	**Philadelphia**	**NHL**	**77**	**19**	**30**	**49**	**38**	**12**	**3**	**1**	**4**	**9**
1987-88	**Philadelphia**	**NHL**	**72**	**30**	**46**	**76**	**58**	**7**	**2**	**5**	**7**	**4**
1988-89	**Philadelphia**	**NHL**	**51**	**9**	**28**	**37**	**52**	**1**	**0**	**0**	**0**	**0**
1989-90	**Philadelphia**	**NHL**	**76**	**25**	**50**	**75**	**42**	....	....	....	....	....
1990-91	**Philadelphia**	**NHL**	**77**	**19**	**47**	**66**	**53**	....	....	....	....	....
1991-92	**Philadelphia**	**NHL**	**12**	**3**	**3**	**6**	**8**	....	....	....	....	....
	Hartford	**NHL**	**61**	**24**	**30**	**54**	**38**	**7**	**3**	**3**	**6**	**6**
1992-93	**Hartford**	**NHL**	**67**	**25**	**42**	**67**	**20**	....	....	....	....	....
	Vancouver	**NHL**	**10**	**0**	**10**	**10**	**12**	**12**	**4**	**6**	**10**	**4**
1993-94	**Vancouver**	**NHL**	**78**	**15**	**40**	**55**	**30**	**22**	**4**	**9**	**13**	**18**
1994-95	**Chicago**	**NHL**	**16**	**4**	**3**	**7**	**2**	**16**	**5**	**5**	**10**	**4**
1995-96	**Chicago**	**NHL**	**66**	**18**	**29**	**47**	**36**	**9**	**1**	**4**	**5**	**2**
1996-97	**Chicago**	**NHL**	**75**	**8**	**27**	**35**	**12**	**2**	**0**	**0**	**0**	**2**
	NHL Totals		**942**	**250**	**464**	**714**	**477**	**112**	**26**	**42**	**68**	**64**

Traded to **Philadelphia** by **Detroit** with Joe Paterson for Darryl Sittler, October 10, 1984. Traded to **Hartford** by **Philadelphia** with Philadelphia's fourth round choice (Kevin Smyth) in 1992 Entry Draft for Kevin Dineen, November 13, 1991. Traded to **Vancouver** by **Hartford** with Vancouver's fifth round choice (previously acquired by Hartford — Vancouver selected Scott Walker) in 1993 Entry Draft for Robert Kron, Vancouver's third round choice (Marek Malik) in 1993 Entry Draft and future considerations (Jim Sandlak, May 17, 1993), March 22, 1993. Traded to **Chicago** by **Vancouver** for Christian Ruutu, March 10, 1995. Traded to **San Jose** by **Chicago** for the rights to Petri Varis and San Jose's sixth round choice in 1998 Entry Draft, July 25, 1997.

CRAWFORD, GLENN N.J.

Center. Shoots left. 5'11", 175 lbs. Born, Orillia, Ont., February 27, 1978.
(New Jersey's 9th choice, 118th overall, in 1996 Entry Draft).

			Regular Season					Playoffs				
Season	Club	Lea	GP	G	A	TP	PIM	GP	G	A	TP	PIM
1994-95	Windsor	OHL	61	5	11	16	17	10	2	5	7	8
1995-96	Windsor	OHL	65	26	33	59	44	7	4	4	8	6
1996-97	Windsor	OHL	53	11	40	51	36	5	3	1	4	0

CREIGHTON, ADAM (KRAY-ton)

Center. Shoots left. 6'5", 220 lbs. Born, Burlington, Ont., June 2, 1965.
(Buffalo's 3rd choice, 11th overall, in 1983 Entry Draft).

			Regular Season					Playoffs				
Season	Club	Lea	GP	G	A	TP	PIM	GP	G	A	TP	PIM
1981-82	Ottawa	OHL	60	15	27	42	73	17	7	1	8	40
1982-83	Ottawa	OHL	68	44	46	90	88	9	0	2	2	12
1983-84	**Buffalo**	**NHL**	**7**	**2**	**2**	**4**	**4**	....	....	....	....	....
a	Ottawa	OHL	56	42	49	91	79	13	16	11	27	28
1984-85	**Buffalo**	**NHL**	**30**	**2**	**8**	**10**	**33**	....	....	....	....	....
	Rochester	AHL	6	5	3	8	2	5	2	1	3	20
	Ottawa	OHL	10	4	14	18	23	5	6	2	8	11
1985-86	**Buffalo**	**NHL**	**19**	**1**	**1**	**2**	**2**	....	....	....	....	....
	Rochester	AHL	32	17	21	38	27	....	....	....	....	....
1986-87	**Buffalo**	**NHL**	**56**	**18**	**22**	**40**	**26**	....	....	....	....	....
1987-88	**Buffalo**	**NHL**	**36**	**10**	**17**	**27**	**87**	....	....	....	....	....
1988-89	**Buffalo**	**NHL**	**24**	**7**	**10**	**17**	**44**	....	....	....	....	....
	Chicago	**NHL**	**43**	**15**	**14**	**29**	**92**	**15**	**5**	**6**	**11**	**44**
1989-90	**Chicago**	**NHL**	**80**	**34**	**36**	**70**	**224**	**20**	**3**	**6**	**9**	**59**
1990-91	**Chicago**	**NHL**	**72**	**22**	**29**	**51**	**135**	**6**	**0**	**1**	**1**	**10**
1991-92	**Chicago**	**NHL**	**11**	**6**	**6**	**12**	**16**	....	....	....	....	....
	NY Islanders	**NHL**	**66**	**15**	**9**	**24**	**102**	....	....	....	....	....
1992-93	**Tampa Bay**	**NHL**	**83**	**19**	**20**	**39**	**110**	....	....	....	....	....
1993-94	**Tampa Bay**	**NHL**	**53**	**10**	**10**	**20**	**37**	....	....	....	....	....
1994-95	**St. Louis**	**NHL**	**48**	**14**	**20**	**34**	**74**	**7**	**2**	**0**	**2**	**16**
1995-96	**St. Louis**	**NHL**	**61**	**11**	**10**	**21**	**78**	**13**	**1**	**1**	**2**	**8**
1996-97	**Chicago**	**NHL**	**19**	**1**	**2**	**3**	**13**	....	....	....	....	....
	Indianapolis	IHL	6	1	7	8	11	....	....	....	....	....
	NHL Totals		**708**	**187**	**216**	**403**	**1077**	**61**	**11**	**14**	**25**	**137**

a Won Stafford Smythe Memorial Trophy (Memorial Cup Tournament MVP) (1984)

Traded to **Chicago** by **Buffalo** for Rick Vaive, December 26, 1988. Traded to **NY Islanders** by **Chicago** with Steve Thomas for Brent Sutter and Brad Lauer, October 25, 1991. Claimed by **Tampa Bay** from **NY Islanders** in NHL Waiver Draft, October 4, 1992. Traded to **St. Louis** by **Tampa Bay** for Tom Tilley, October 6, 1994. Signed as a free agent by **Chicago**, October 9, 1996.

CREURER, TROY (KRUH-yuhr) VAN.

Defense. Shoots left. 6'1", 190 lbs. Born, Weyburn, Sask., May 2, 1975.
(Vancouver's 5th choice, 158th overall, in 1993 Entry Draft).

			Regular Season					Playoffs				
Season	Club	Lea	GP	G	A	TP	PIM	GP	G	A	TP	PIM
1993-94	St. Lawrence	ECAC	31	5	10	15	22	....	....	....	....	....
1994-95	St. Lawrence	ECAC	33	1	11	12	30	....	....	....	....	....
1995-96	St. Lawrence	ECAC	35	2	15	17	24	....	....	....	....	....
1996-97	St. Lawrence	ECAC	33	3	8	11	12	....	....	....	....	....

CRONAN, EARL MTL.

Left wing. Shoots left. 6'1", 210 lbs. Born, Warwick, RI, January 2, 1973.
(Montreal's 11th choice, 212th overall, in 1992 Entry Draft).

			Regular Season					Playoffs				
Season	Club	Lea	GP	G	A	TP	PIM	GP	G	A	TP	PIM
1992-93	Colgate	ECAC	33	8	9	17	40	....	....	....	....	....
1993-94	Colgate	ECAC	32	14	17	31	80	....	....	....	....	....
1994-95	Colgate	ECAC	37	21	20	41	81	....	....	....	....	....
1995-96	Colgate	ECAC	32	9	12	21	28	....	....	....	....	....
1996-97	Fredericton	AHL	50	5	3	8	33	....	....	....	....	....

CRONIN, SHAWN (kroh-NIHN)

Defense. Shoots left. 6'2", 225 lbs. Born, Joliet, IL, August 20, 1963.

			Regular Season					Playoffs				
Season	Club	Lea	GP	G	A	TP	PIM	GP	G	A	TP	PIM
1982-83	Ill.-Chicago	CCHA	36	1	5	6	52	....	....	....	....	....
1983-84	Ill.-Chicago	CCHA	32	0	4	4	41	....	....	....	....	....
1984-85	Ill.-Chicago	CCHA	31	2	6	8	52	....	....	....	....	....
1985-86	Ill.-Chicago	CCHA	35	3	8	11	70	....	....	....	....	....
1986-87	Salt Lake	IHL	53	8	16	24	118	....	....	....	....	....
	Binghamton	AHL	12	0	1	1	60	10	0	0	0	41
1987-88	Binghamton	AHL	65	3	8	11	212	4	0	0	0	15
1988-89	**Washington**	**NHL**	**1**	**0**	**0**	**0**	**0**	....	....	....	....	....
	Baltimore	AHL	75	3	9	12	267	....	....	....	....	....
1989-90	**Winnipeg**	**NHL**	**61**	**0**	**4**	**4**	**243**	**5**	**0**	**0**	**0**	**7**
1990-91	**Winnipeg**	**NHL**	**67**	**1**	**5**	**6**	**189**	....	....	....	....	....
1991-92	**Winnipeg**	**NHL**	**65**	**0**	**4**	**4**	**271**	**4**	**0**	**0**	**0**	**6**
1992-93	**Philadelphia**	**NHL**	**35**	**2**	**1**	**3**	**37**	....	....	....	....	....
	Hershey	AHL	7	0	1	1	12	....	....	....	....	....
1993-94	**San Jose**	**NHL**	**34**	**0**	**2**	**2**	**76**	**14**	**1**	**0**	**1**	**20**
1994-95	**San Jose**	**NHL**	**29**	**0**	**2**	**2**	**61**	**9**	**0**	**0**	**0**	**5**
1995-96	Fort Wayne	IHL	48	0	1	1	120	5	0	0	0	8
1996-97	Fort Wayne	IHL	13	0	1	1	27	....	....	....	....	....
	NHL Totals		**292**	**3**	**18**	**21**	**877**	**32**	**1**	**0**	**1**	**38**

Signed as a free agent by **Hartford**, March, 1986. Signed as a free agent by **Washington**, June 6, 1988. Signed as a free agent by **Philadelphia**, June 12, 1989. Traded to **Winnipeg** by **Philadelphia** for future considerations (Keith Acton and Pete Peeters were traded to Philadelphia for Toronto's fifth round choice (previously acquired by Philadelphia — Winnipeg selected Juha Ylonen), October 3, 1989), July 21, 1989. Traded to **Quebec** by **Winnipeg** for Dan Lambert, August 25, 1992. Claimed by **Philadelphia** from **Quebec** in NHL Waiver Draft, October 4, 1992. Traded to **San Jose** by **Philadelphia** for cash, August 5, 1993.

CROSS, CORY T.B.

Defense. Shoots left. 6'5", 212 lbs. Born, Lloydminster, Alta., January 3, 1971.
(Tampa Bay's 1st choice, 1st overall, in 1992 Supplemental Draft).

			Regular Season					Playoffs				
Season	Club	Lea	GP	G	A	TP	PIM	GP	G	A	TP	PIM
1989-90	U. of Alberta	CWUAA	UNAVAILABLE									
1990-91	U. of Alberta	CWUAA	20	2	5	7	16	....	....	....	....	....
1991-92	U. of Alberta	CWUAA	41	4	11	15	82	....	....	....	....	....
1992-93	U. of Alberta	CWUAA	43	11	28	39	105	....	....	....	....	....
	Atlanta	IHL	7	0	1	1	2	4	0	0	0	6
1993-94	**Tampa Bay**	**NHL**	**5**	**0**	**0**	**0**	**6**	....	....	....	....	....
	Atlanta	IHL	70	4	14	18	72	9	1	2	3	14
1994-95	Atlanta	IHL	41	5	10	15	67	....	....	....	....	....
	Tampa Bay	**NHL**	**43**	**1**	**5**	**6**	**41**	....	....	....	....	....
1995-96	**Tampa Bay**	**NHL**	**75**	**2**	**14**	**16**	**66**	**6**	**0**	**0**	**0**	**22**
1996-97	**Tampa Bay**	**NHL**	**72**	**4**	**5**	**9**	**95**	....	....	....	....	....
	NHL Totals		**195**	**7**	**24**	**31**	**208**	**6**	**0**	**0**	**0**	**22**

CROWDER, TROY

Right wing. Shoots right. 6'4", 220 lbs. Born, Sudbury, Ont., May 3, 1968.
(New Jersey's 6th choice, 108th overall, in 1986 Entry Draft).

			Regular Season					Playoffs				
Season	Club	Lea	GP	G	A	TP	PIM	GP	G	A	TP	PIM
1985-86	Hamilton	OHL	56	4	4	8	178	....	....	....	....	....
1986-87	Belleville	OHL	21	5	5	10	52	....	....	....	....	....
	North Bay	OHL	35	6	11	17	90	23	3	9	12	99
1987-88	North Bay	OHL	9	1	2	3	44	....	....	....	....	....
	Belleville	OHL	46	12	27	39	103	6	2	3	5	24
	Utica	AHL	3	0	0	0	36	....	....	....	....	....
	New Jersey	**NHL**	....	....	....	....	....	**1**	**0**	**0**	**0**	**12**
1988-89	Utica	AHL	62	6	4	10	152	2	0	0	0	25
1989-90	**New Jersey**	**NHL**	**10**	**0**	**0**	**0**	**23**	**2**	**0**	**0**	**0**	**10**
	Nashville	ECHL	3	0	0	0	15	....	....	....	....	....
1990-91	**New Jersey**	**NHL**	**59**	**6**	**3**	**9**	**182**	....	....	....	....	....
1991-92	**Detroit**	**NHL**	**7**	**0**	**0**	**0**	**35**	**1**	**0**	**0**	**0**	**0**
1992-93			DID NOT PLAY – INJURED									
1993-94			DID NOT PLAY – INJURED									
1994-95	**Los Angeles**	**NHL**	**29**	**1**	**2**	**3**	**99**	....	....	....	....	....
1995-96	**Los Angeles**	**NHL**	**15**	**1**	**0**	**1**	**42**	....	....	....	....	....
1996-97	**Vancouver**	**NHL**	**30**	**1**	**2**	**3**	**52**	....	....	....	....	....
	Syracuse	AHL	2	0	0	0	0	....	....	....	....	....
	NHL Totals		**150**	**9**	**7**	**16**	**433**	**4**	**0**	**0**	**0**	**22**

Signed as a free agent by **Detroit**, August 27, 1991. Signed as a free agent by **Los Angeles**, August 31, 1994. Signed as a free agent by **Vancouver**, October 4, 1996.

CROWE, PHILIP OTT.

Left wing. Shoots left. 6'2", 230 lbs. Born, Nanton, Alta., April 14, 1970.

			Regular Season					Playoffs				
Season	Club	Lea	GP	G	A	TP	PIM	GP	G	A	TP	PIM
1991-92	Adirondack	AHL	6	1	0	1	29	....	....	....	....	....
	Columbus	ECHL	32	4	7	11	145	....	....	....	....	....
	Toledo	ECHL	2	0	0	0	0	5	0	0	0	58
1992-93	Phoenix	IHL	53	3	3	6	190	....	....	....	....	....
1993-94	Fort Wayne	IHL	5	0	1	1	26	....	....	....	....	....
	Phoenix	IHL	2	0	0	0	0	....	....	....	....	....
	Los Angeles	**NHL**	**31**	**0**	**2**	**2**	**77**	....	....	....	....	....
1994-95	Hershey	AHL	46	11	6	17	132	6	0	1	1	19
1995-96	**Philadelphia**	**NHL**	**16**	**1**	**1**	**2**	**28**	....	....	....	....	....
	Hershey	AHL	39	6	8	14	105	5	1	2	3	19
1996-97	**Ottawa**	**NHL**	**26**	**0**	**1**	**1**	**30**	**3**	**0**	**0**	**0**	**16**
	Detroit	IHL	41	7	7	14	83	....	....	....	....	....
	NHL Totals		**73**	**1**	**4**	**5**	**135**	**3**	**0**	**0**	**0**	**16**

Signed as a free agent by **Los Angeles**, November 8, 1993. Signed as a free agent by **Philadelphia**, July 19, 1994. Signed as a free agent by **Ottawa**, July 29, 1996.

CROWLEY, MIKE ANA.

Defense. Shoots left. 5'11", 175 lbs. Born, Bloomington, MN, July 4, 1975.
(Philadelphia's 5th choice, 140th overall, in 1993 Entry Draft).

			Regular Season					Playoffs				
Season	Club	Lea	GP	G	A	TP	PIM	GP	G	A	TP	PIM
1994-95	U. Minnesota	WCHA	41	11	27	38	60	....	....	....	....	....
1995-96ab	U. Minnesota	WCHA	42	17	46	63	28	....	....	....	....	....
1996-97ab	U. Minnesota	WCHA	42	9	*47	*56	24	....	....	....	....	....

a WCHA First All-Star Team (1996, 1997)
b NCAA West First All-American Team (1996, 1997)

Traded to **Anaheim** by **Philadelphia** with Anatoli Semenov for Brian Wesenberg, March 19, 1996.

CROWLEY, TED PHO.

Defense. Shoots right. 6'2", 188 lbs. Born, Concord, MA, May 3, 1970.
(Toronto's 4th choice, 69th overall, in 1988 Entry Draft).

			Regular Season					Playoffs				
Season	Club	Lea	GP	G	A	TP	PIM	GP	G	A	TP	PIM
1989-90	Boston College	H.E.	39	7	24	31	34	....	....	....	....	....
1990-91ab	Boston College	H.E.	39	12	24	36	61	....	....	....	....	....
1991-92	U.S. National	....	42	6	7	13	65	....	....	....	....	....
	St. John's	AHL	29	5	4	9	33	10	3	1	4	11
1992-93	St. John's	AHL	79	19	38	57	41	9	2	2	4	4
1993-94	U.S. National	....	48	9	13	22	80	....	....	....	....	....
	U.S. Olympic	....	8	0	2	2	8	....	....	....	....	....
	Hartford	**NHL**	**21**	**1**	**2**	**3**	**10**	....	....	....	....	....
1994-95	Chicago	IHL	53	8	23	31	68	....	....	....	....	....
	Houston	IHL	23	4	9	13	35	3	0	1	1	0
1995-96	Providence	AHL	72	12	30	42	47	4	1	2	3	2
1996-97	Cincinnati	IHL	39	9	9	18	24	....	....	....	....	....
	Phoenix	IHL	30	5	8	13	21	....	....	....	....	....
	NHL Totals		**21**	**1**	**2**	**3**	**10**	....	....	....	....	....

a Hockey East First All-Star Team (1991)
b NCAA East Second All-American Team (1991)

Traded to **Hartford** by **Toronto** for Mark Greig and Hartford's sixth round choice (later traded to NY Rangers — NY Rangers selected Yuri Litvinov) in 1994 Entry Draft, January 25, 1994. Signed as a free agent by **Boston**, August 9, 1995. Signed as a free agent by **Phoenix**, June 27, 1997.

CROZIER, GREG PIT.

Left wing. Shoots left. 6'4", 200 lbs. Born, Calgary, Alta., July 6, 1976.
(Pittsburgh's 4th choice, 73rd overall, in 1994 Entry Draft).

			Regular Season					Playoffs				
Season	Club	Lea	GP	G	A	TP	PIM	GP	G	A	TP	PIM
1995-96	U. of Michigan	CCHA	42	14	10	24	46	....	....	....	....	....
1996-97	U. of Michigan	CCHA	31	5	15	20	45	....	....	....	....	....

CULLEN, JOHN — T.B.

Center. Shoots right. 5'10", 180 lbs. Born, Puslinch, Ont., August 2, 1964.
(Buffalo's 2nd choice, 10th overall, in 1986 Supplemental Draft).

			Regular Season					Playoffs				
Season	Club	Lea	GP	G	A	TP	PIM	GP	G	A	TP	PIM
1983-84	Boston U.	ECAC	40	23	33	56	28	....	....	....	....	....
1984-85a	Boston U.	H.E.	41	27	32	59	46	....	....	....	....	....
1985-86ab	Boston U.	H.E.	43	25	49	74	54	....	....	....	....	....
1986-87c	Boston U.	H.E.	36	23	29	52	35	....	....	....	....	....
1987-88defg	Flint	IHL	81	48	*109	*157	113	16	11	*15	26	16
1988-89	**Pittsburgh**	**NHL**	**79**	**12**	**37**	**49**	**112**	**11**	**3**	**6**	**9**	**28**
1989-90	**Pittsburgh**	**NHL**	**72**	**32**	**60**	**92**	**138**	....	....	....	....	....
1990-91	**Pittsburgh**	**NHL**	**65**	**31**	**63**	**94**	**83**	....	....	....	....	....
	Hartford	**NHL**	**13**	**8**	**8**	**16**	**18**	**6**	**2**	**7**	**9**	**10**
1991-92	**Hartford**	**NHL**	**77**	**26**	**51**	**77**	**141**	**7**	**2**	**1**	**3**	**12**
1992-93	**Hartford**	**NHL**	**19**	**5**	**4**	**9**	**58**	....	....	....	....	....
	Toronto	**NHL**	**47**	**13**	**28**	**41**	**53**	**12**	**2**	**3**	**5**	**0**
1993-94	**Toronto**	**NHL**	**53**	**13**	**17**	**30**	**67**	**3**	**0**	**0**	**0**	**0**
1994-95	**Pittsburgh**	**NHL**	**46**	**13**	**24**	**37**	**66**	**9**	**0**	**2**	**2**	**8**
1995-96	**Tampa Bay**	**NHL**	**76**	**16**	**34**	**50**	**65**	**5**	**3**	**3**	**6**	**0**
1996-97	**Tampa Bay**	**NHL**	**70**	**18**	**37**	**55**	**95**	....	....	....	....	....
	NHL Totals		**617**	**187**	**363**	**550**	**896**	**53**	**12**	**22**	**34**	**58**

a Hockey East First All-Star Team (1985, 1986)
b NCAA East Second All-American Team (1986)
c Hockey East Second All-Star Team (1987)
d IHL First All-Star Team (1988)
e Won James Gatschene Memorial Trophy (MVP - IHL) (1988)
f Shared Garry F. Longman Memorial Trophy (Top Rookie - IHL) with Ed Belfour (1988)
g Won Leo P. Lamoureux Memorial Trophy (Top Scorer - IHL) (1988)

Played in NHL All-Star Game (1991, 1992)

Signed as a free agent by **Pittsburgh**, June 21, 1988. Traded to **Hartford** by **Pittsburgh** with Jeff Parker and Zarley Zalapski for Ron Francis, Grant Jennings and Ulf Samuelsson, March 4, 1991. Traded to **Toronto** by **Hartford** for future considerations, November 24, 1992. Signed as a free agent by **Pittsburgh**, August 3, 1994. Signed as a free agent by **Tampa Bay**, September 11, 1995.

CULLEN, MATT — ANA.

Center. Shoots left. 6'1", 195 lbs. Born, Virginia, MN, November 2, 1976.
(Anaheim's 2nd choice, 35th overall, in 1996 Entry Draft).

			Regular Season					Playoffs				
Season	Club	Lea	GP	G	A	TP	PIM	GP	G	A	TP	PIM
1995-96	St. Cloud	WCHA	39	12	29	41	28	....	....	....	....	....
1996-97a	St. Cloud	WCHA	36	15	30	45	70	....	....	....	....	....
	Baltimore	AHL	6	3	3	6	7	3	0	2	2	0

a WCHA Second All-Star Team (1997)

CULLIMORE, JASSEN (KUHL-ih-mohr) — MTL.

Defense. Shoots left. 6'5", 225 lbs. Born, Simcoe, Ont., December 4, 1972.
(Vancouver's 2nd choice, 29th overall, in 1991 Entry Draft).

			Regular Season					Playoffs				
Season	Club	Lea	GP	G	A	TP	PIM	GP	G	A	TP	PIM
1989-90	Peterborough	OHL	59	2	6	8	61	11	0	2	2	8
1990-91	Peterborough	OHL	62	8	16	24	74	4	1	0	1	7
1991-92a	Peterborough	OHL	54	9	37	46	65	10	3	6	9	8
1992-93	Hamilton	AHL	56	5	7	12	60	....	....	....	....	....
1993-94	Hamilton	AHL	71	8	20	28	86	3	0	1	1	2
1994-95	Syracuse	AHL	33	2	7	9	66	....	....	....	....	....
	Vancouver	**NHL**	**34**	**1**	**2**	**3**	**39**	**11**	**0**	**0**	**0**	**12**
1995-96	**Vancouver**	**NHL**	**27**	**1**	**1**	**2**	**21**	....	....	....	....	....
1996-97	**Vancouver**	**NHL**	**3**	**0**	**0**	**0**	**2**	....	....	....	....	....
	Montreal	**NHL**	**49**	**2**	**6**	**8**	**42**	**2**	**0**	**0**	**0**	**2**
	NHL Totals		**113**	**4**	**9**	**13**	**104**	**13**	**0**	**0**	**0**	**14**

a OHL Second All-Star Team (1992)

Traded to **Montreal** by **Vancouver** for Donald Brashear, November 13, 1996.

CUMMINS, JIM — CHI.

Right wing. Shoots right. 6'2", 219 lbs. Born, Dearborn, MI, May 17, 1970.
(NY Rangers' 5th choice, 67th overall, in 1989 Entry Draft).

			Regular Season					Playoffs				
Season	Club	Lea	GP	G	A	TP	PIM	GP	G	A	TP	PIM
1988-89	Michigan State	CCHA	30	3	8	11	98	....	....	....	....	....
1989-90	Michigan State	CCHA	41	8	7	15	94	....	....	....	....	....
1990-91	Michigan State	CCHA	34	9	6	15	110	....	....	....	....	....
1991-92	**Detroit**	**NHL**	**1**	**0**	**0**	**0**	**7**	....	....	....	....	....
	Adirondack	AHL	65	7	13	20	338	5	0	0	0	19
1992-93	**Detroit**	**NHL**	**7**	**1**	**1**	**2**	**58**	....	....	....	....	....
	Adirondack	AHL	43	16	4	20	179	9	3	1	4	4
1993-94	**Philadelphia**	**NHL**	**22**	**1**	**2**	**3**	**71**	....	....	....	....	....
	Hershey	AHL	17	6	6	12	70	....	....	....	....	....
	Tampa Bay	**NHL**	**4**	**0**	**0**	**0**	**13**	....	....	....	....	....
	Atlanta	IHL	7	4	5	9	14	13	1	2	3	90
1994-95	**Tampa Bay**	**NHL**	**10**	**1**	**0**	**1**	**41**	....	....	....	....	....
	Chicago	**NHL**	**27**	**3**	**1**	**4**	**117**	**14**	**1**	**1**	**2**	**4**
1995-96	**Chicago**	**NHL**	**52**	**2**	**4**	**6**	**180**	**10**	**0**	**0**	**0**	**2**
1996-97	**Chicago**	**NHL**	**65**	**6**	**6**	**12**	**199**	**6**	**0**	**0**	**0**	**24**
	NHL Totals		**188**	**14**	**14**	**28**	**686**	**30**	**1**	**1**	**2**	**30**

Traded to **Detroit** by **NY Rangers** with Kevin Miller and Dennis Vial for Joey Kocur and Per Djoos, March 5, 1991. Traded to **Philadelphia** by **Detroit** with Philadelphia's fourth round choice (previously acquired by Detroit — later traded to Boston — Boston selected Charles Paquette) in 1993 Entry Draft for Greg Johnson and Philadelphia's fifth round choice (Frederic Deschenes) in 1994 Entry Draft, June 20, 1993. Traded to **Tampa Bay** by **Philadelphia** with Philadelphia's fourth round choice in 1995 Entry Draft for Rob DiMaio, March 18, 1994. Traded to **Chicago** by **Tampa Bay** with Tom Tilley and Jeff Buchanan for Paul Ysebaert and Rich Sutter, February 22, 1995.

CUNNEYWORTH, RANDY — OTT.

Left wing. Shoots left. 6', 198 lbs. Born, Etobicoke, Ont., May 10, 1961.
(Buffalo's 9th choice, 167th overall, in 1980 Entry Draft).

			Regular Season					Playoffs				
Season	Club	Lea	GP	G	A	TP	PIM	GP	G	A	TP	PIM
1979-80	Ottawa	OHA	63	16	25	41	145	11	0	1	1	13
1980-81	**Buffalo**	**NHL**	**1**	**0**	**0**	**0**	**2**	....	....	....	....	....
	Rochester	AHL	1	0	1	1	2	....	....	....	....	....
	Ottawa	OHA	67	54	74	128	240	15	5	8	13	35
1981-82	**Buffalo**	**NHL**	**20**	**2**	**4**	**6**	**47**	....	....	....	....	....
	Rochester	AHL	57	12	15	27	86	9	4	0	4	30
1982-83	Rochester	AHL	78	23	33	56	111	16	4	4	8	35
1983-84	Rochester	AHL	54	18	17	35	85	17	5	5	10	55
1984-85	Rochester	AHL	72	30	38	68	148	5	2	1	3	16
1985-86	**Pittsburgh**	**NHL**	**75**	**15**	**30**	**45**	**74**	....	....	....	....	....
1986-87	**Pittsburgh**	**NHL**	**79**	**26**	**27**	**53**	**142**	....	....	....	....	....
1987-88	**Pittsburgh**	**NHL**	**71**	**35**	**39**	**74**	**141**	....	....	....	....	....
1988-89	**Pittsburgh**	**NHL**	**70**	**25**	**19**	**44**	**156**	**11**	**3**	**5**	**8**	**26**
1989-90	**Winnipeg**	**NHL**	**28**	**5**	**6**	**11**	**34**	....	....	....	....	....
	Hartford	**NHL**	**43**	**9**	**9**	**18**	**41**	**4**	**0**	**0**	**0**	**2**
1990-91	**Hartford**	**NHL**	**32**	**9**	**5**	**14**	**49**	**1**	**0**	**0**	**0**	**0**
	Springfield	AHL	2	0	0	0	5	....	....	....	....	....
1991-92	**Hartford**	**NHL**	**39**	**7**	**10**	**17**	**71**	**7**	**3**	**0**	**3**	**9**
1992-93	**Hartford**	**NHL**	**39**	**5**	**4**	**9**	**63**	....	....	....	....	....
1993-94	**Hartford**	**NHL**	**63**	**9**	**8**	**17**	**87**	....	....	....	....	....
	Chicago	**NHL**	**16**	**4**	**3**	**7**	**13**	**6**	**0**	**0**	**0**	**8**
1994-95	**Ottawa**	**NHL**	**48**	**5**	**5**	**10**	**68**	....	....	....	....	....
1995-96	**Ottawa**	**NHL**	**81**	**17**	**19**	**36**	**130**	....	....	....	....	....
1996-97	**Ottawa**	**NHL**	**76**	**12**	**24**	**36**	**99**	**7**	**1**	**1**	**2**	**10**
	NHL Totals		**781**	**185**	**212**	**397**	**1217**	**36**	**7**	**6**	**13**	**55**

Traded to **Pittsburgh** by **Buffalo** with Mike Moller for Pat Hughes, October 4, 1985. Traded to **Winnipeg** by **Pittsburgh** with Rick Tabaracci and Dave McLlwain for Jim Kyte, Andrew McBain and Randy Gilhen, June 17, 1989. Traded to **Hartford** by **Winnipeg** for Paul MacDermid, December 13, 1989. Traded to **Chicago** by **Hartford** with Gary Suter and Hartford's third round choice (later traded to Vancouver — Vancouver selected Larry Courville) in 1995 Entry Draft for Frantisek Kucera and Jocelyn Lemieux, March 11, 1994. Signed as a free agent by **Ottawa**, July 15, 1994.

CURRIE, DAN

Left wing. Shoots left. 6'2", 195 lbs. Born, Burlington, Ont., March 15, 1968.
(Edmonton's 4th choice, 84th overall, in 1986 Entry Draft).

			Regular Season					Playoffs				
Season	Club	Lea	GP	G	A	TP	PIM	GP	G	A	TP	PIM
1985-86	S.S. Marie	OHL	66	21	24	45	37	....	....	....	....	....
1986-87	S.S. Marie	OHL	66	31	52	83	53	4	2	1	3	2
1987-88	Nova Scotia	AHL	3	4	2	6	0	5	4	3	7	0
	S.S. Marie	OHL	57	50	59	109	53	6	3	9	12	4
1988-89	Cape Breton	AHL	77	29	36	65	29	....	....	....	....	....
1989-90	Cape Breton	AHL	77	36	40	76	28	6	4	4	8	0
1990-91	**Edmonton**	**NHL**	**5**	**0**	**0**	**0**	**0**	....	....	....	....	....
	Cape Breton	AHL	71	47	45	92	51	4	3	1	4	8
1991-92	**Edmonton**	**NHL**	**7**	**1**	**0**	**1**	**0**	....	....	....	....	....
a	Cape Breton	AHL	66	*50	42	92	39	5	4	5	9	4
1992-93	**Edmonton**	**NHL**	**5**	**0**	**0**	**0**	**4**	....	....	....	....	....
b	Cape Breton	AHL	75	57	41	98	73	16	7	4	11	29
1993-94	**Los Angeles**	**NHL**	**5**	**1**	**1**	**2**	**0**	....	....	....	....	....
	Phoenix	IHL	74	37	49	86	96	....	....	....	....	....
1994-95	Phoenix	IHL	16	2	6	8	8	....	....	....	....	....
	Minnesota	IHL	54	18	35	53	34	3	0	0	0	2
1995-96	Chicago	IHL	79	39	34	73	53	9	5	4	9	12
1996-97	Chicago	IHL	55	18	10	28	18	....	....	....	....	....
	Fort Wayne	IHL	24	10	12	22	6	....	....	....	....	....
	NHL Totals		**22**	**2**	**1**	**3**	**4**	....	....	....	....	....

a AHL Second All-Star Team (1992)
b AHL First All-Star Team (1993)

Signed as a free agent by **Los Angeles**, July 16, 1993.

CURTIN, LUKE — COL.

Left wing. Shoots left. 6'2", 190 lbs. Born, St. Paul, MN, September 23, 1977.
(Colorado's 6th choice, 134th overall, in 1996 Entry Draft).

			Regular Season					Playoffs				
Season	Club	Lea	GP	G	A	TP	PIM	GP	G	A	TP	PIM
1994-95	Langley	Jr. A	59	26	47	73	49	....	....	....	....	....
	Tacoma	WHL	1	0	0	0	0	4	1	1	2	2
1995-96	Kelowna	WHL	69	21	26	47	39	6	3	2	5	6
1996-97	Kelowna	WHL	47	23	37	60	36	6	3	3	6	4

CYRENNE, CORY (suh-REEN) — S.J.

Center. Shoots left. 5'9", 170 lbs. Born, Winnipeg, Man., August 25, 1977.
(San Jose's 7th choice, 191st overall, in 1996 Entry Draft).

			Regular Season					Playoffs				
Season	Club	Lea	GP	G	A	TP	PIM	GP	G	A	TP	PIM
1995-96	Brandon	WHL	69	38	59	97	58	19	6	14	20	18
1996-97	Brandon	WHL	55	26	56	82	23	6	3	3	6	0

CZERKAWSKI, MARIUSZ (chehr-KAWV-skee) — EDM.

Right wing. Shoots left. 6', 195 lbs. Born, Radomsko, Poland, April 13, 1972.
(Boston's 5th choice, 106th overall, in 1991 Entry Draft).

			Regular Season					Playoffs				
Season	Club	Lea	GP	G	A	TP	PIM	GP	G	A	TP	PIM
1990-91	GKS Tychy	Poland	24	25	15	40	....	....	....	....	....	....
1991-92	Djurgarden	Swe.	39	8	5	13	4	3	0	0	0	2
1992-93	Hammarby	Swe. 2	32	39	30	69	74	....	....	....	....	....
1993-94	Djurgarden	Swe.	39	13	21	34	20	6	3	1	4	2
	Boston	**NHL**	**4**	**2**	**1**	**3**	**0**	**13**	**3**	**3**	**6**	**4**
1994-95	Kiekko-Espoo	Fin.	7	9	3	12	10	....	....	....	....	....
	Boston	**NHL**	**47**	**12**	**14**	**26**	**31**	**5**	**1**	**0**	**1**	**0**
1995-96	**Boston**	**NHL**	**33**	**5**	**6**	**11**	**10**	....	....	....	....	....
	Edmonton	**NHL**	**37**	**12**	**17**	**29**	**8**	....	....	....	....	....
1996-97	**Edmonton**	**NHL**	**76**	**26**	**21**	**47**	**16**	**12**	**2**	**1**	**3**	**10**
	NHL Totals		**197**	**57**	**59**	**116**	**65**	**30**	**6**	**4**	**10**	**14**

Traded to **Edmonton** by **Boston** with Sean Brown and Boston's first round choice (Matthieu Descoteaux) in 1996 Entry Draft for Bill Ranford, January 11, 1996.

DACKELL, ANDREAS (DA-kuhl, an-DRAY-uhs) OTT.

Right wing. Shoots right. 5'11", 191 lbs. Born, Gavle, Sweden, December 29, 1972.
(Ottawa's 3rd choice, 136th overall, in 1996 Entry Draft).

			Regular Season					Playoffs				
Season	Club	Lea	GP	G	A	TP	PIM	GP	G	A	TP	PIM
1990-91	Brynas	Swe.	3	0	1	1	2	....	....	....	....	....
1991-92	Brynas	Swe.	4	0	0	0	2	2	0	1	1	4
1992-93	Brynas	Swe.	40	12	15	27	12	10	4	5	9	2
1993-94	Brynas	Swe.	38	12	17	29	47	7	2	2	4	8
1994-95	Brynas	Swe.	39	17	16	33	34	14	3	3	6	14
1995-96	Brynas	Swe.	22	6	6	12	8	....	....	....	....	....
1996-97	**Ottawa**	**NHL**	**79**	**12**	**19**	**31**	**8**	**7**	**1**	**0**	**1**	**0**
	NHL Totals		**79**	**12**	**19**	**31**	**8**	**7**	**1**	**0**	**1**	**0**

DAFOE, KYLE CAR.

Defense. Shoots right. 6'5", 195 lbs. Born, Charlottetown, P.E.I., January 11, 1979.
(Carolina's 5th choice, 142nd overall, in 1997 Entry Draft).

			Regular Season					Playoffs				
Season	Club	Lea	GP	G	A	TP	PIM	GP	G	A	TP	PIM
1996-97	Owen Sound	OHL	41	1	2	58	3	....	....	....	....	....

DAGENAIS, PIERRE (da-ZHUH-nay) N.J.

Left wing. Shoots left. 6'3", 185 lbs. Born, Blainville, Que., March 4, 1978.
(New Jersey's 4th choice, 47th overall, in 1996 Entry Draft).

			Regular Season					Playoffs				
Season	Club	Lea	GP	G	A	TP	PIM	GP	G	A	TP	PIM
1995-96	Moncton	QMJHL	67	43	25	68	59	....	....	....	....	....
1996-97	Moncton	QMJHL	6	4	2	6	0	....	....	....	....	....
	Laval	QMJHL	37	16	14	30	40	....	....	....	....	....
	Rouyn-Noranda	QMJHL	27	21	8	29	22	....	....	....	....	....

DAHL, KEVIN (DAHL)

Defense. Shoots right. 5'11", 190 lbs. Born, Regina, Sask., December 30, 1968.
(Montreal's 12th choice, 230th overall, in 1988 Entry Draft).

			Regular Season					Playoffs				
Season	Club	Lea	GP	G	A	TP	PIM	GP	G	A	TP	PIM
1986-87	Bowling Green	CCHA	32	2	6	8	54	....	....	....	....	....
1987-88	Bowling Green	CCHA	44	2	23	25	78	....	....	....	....	....
1988-89	Bowling Green	CCHA	46	9	26	35	51	....	....	....	....	....
1989-90	Bowling Green	CCHA	43	8	22	30	74	....	....	....	....	....
1990-91	Fredericton	AHL	32	1	15	16	45	9	0	1	1	11
	Winston-Salem	ECHL	36	7	17	24	58	....	....	....	....	....
1991-92	Cdn. National	....	45	2	15	17	44	....	....	....	....	....
	Cdn. Olympic	....	8	2	0	2	6	....	....	....	....	....
	Salt Lake	IHL	13	0	2	2	12	5	0	0	0	13
1992-93	**Calgary**	**NHL**	**61**	**2**	**9**	**11**	**56**	**6**	**0**	**2**	**2**	**8**
1993-94	**Calgary**	**NHL**	**33**	**0**	**3**	**3**	**23**	**6**	**0**	**0**	**0**	**4**
	Saint John	AHL	2	0	0	0	0	....	....	....	....	....
1994-95	**Calgary**	**NHL**	**34**	**4**	**8**	**12**	**38**	**3**	**0**	**0**	**0**	**0**
1995-96	**Calgary**	**NHL**	**32**	**1**	**1**	**2**	**26**	**1**	**0**	**0**	**0**	**0**
	Saint John	AHL	23	4	11	15	37	....	....	....	....	....
1996-97	**Phoenix**	**NHL**	**2**	**0**	**0**	**0**	**0**	....	....	....	....	....
	Las Vegas	IHL	73	10	21	31	101	3	0	0	0	2
	NHL Totals		**162**	**7**	**21**	**28**	**143**	**16**	**0**	**2**	**2**	**12**

Signed as a free agent by **Calgary**, July 27, 1991. Signed as a free agent by **Phoenix**, September 4, 1996.

DAHLEN, ULF (DAH-lehn) CHI.

Right wing. Shoots left. 6'2", 195 lbs. Born, Ostersund, Sweden, January 12, 1967.
(NY Rangers' 1st choice, 7th overall, in 1985 Entry Draft).

			Regular Season					Playoffs				
Season	Club	Lea	GP	G	A	TP	PIM	GP	G	A	TP	PIM
1983-84	Ostersund	Swe. 2	36	15	11	26	10	....	....	....	....	....
1984-85	Ostersund	Swe. 2	36	33	26	59	20	....	....	....	....	....
1985-86	Bjorkloven	Swe.	22	4	3	7	8	....	....	....	....	....
1986-87	Bjorkloven	Swe.	31	9	12	21	20	6	6	2	8	4
1987-88	**NY Rangers**	**NHL**	**70**	**29**	**23**	**52**	**26**	....	....	....	....	....
	Colorado	IHL	2	2	2	4	0	....	....	....	....	....
1988-89	**NY Rangers**	**NHL**	**56**	**24**	**19**	**43**	**50**	**4**	**0**	**0**	**0**	**0**
1989-90	**NY Rangers**	**NHL**	**63**	**18**	**18**	**36**	**30**	....	....	....	....	....
	Minnesota	**NHL**	**13**	**2**	**4**	**6**	**0**	**7**	**1**	**4**	**5**	**2**
1990-91	**Minnesota**	**NHL**	**66**	**21**	**18**	**39**	**6**	**15**	**2**	**6**	**8**	**4**
1991-92	**Minnesota**	**NHL**	**79**	**36**	**30**	**66**	**10**	**7**	**0**	**3**	**3**	**2**
1992-93	**Minnesota**	**NHL**	**83**	**35**	**39**	**74**	**6**	....	....	....	....	....
1993-94	**Dallas**	**NHL**	**65**	**19**	**38**	**57**	**10**	....	....	....	....	....
	San Jose	**NHL**	**13**	**6**	**6**	**12**	**0**	**14**	**6**	**2**	**8**	**0**
1994-95	**San Jose**	**NHL**	**46**	**11**	**23**	**34**	**11**	**11**	**5**	**4**	**9**	**0**
1995-96	**San Jose**	**NHL**	**59**	**16**	**12**	**28**	**27**	....	....	....	....	....
1996-97	**San Jose**	**NHL**	**43**	**8**	**11**	**19**	**8**	....	....	....	....	....
	Chicago	**NHL**	**30**	**6**	**8**	**14**	**10**	**5**	**0**	**1**	**1**	**0**
	NHL Totals		**686**	**231**	**249**	**480**	**194**	**63**	**14**	**20**	**34**	**8**

Traded to **Minnesota** by **NY Rangers** with Los Angeles' fourth round choice (previously acquired by NY Rangers — Minnesota selected Cal McGowan) in 1990 Entry Draft and future considerations for Mike Gartner, March 6, 1990. Traded to **San Jose** by **Dallas** with Dallas' seventh round choice (Brad Mehalko) in 1995 Entry Draft for Doug Zmolek, Mike Lalor and cash, March 19, 1994. Traded to **Chicago** by **San Jose** with Chris Terreri, Michal Sykora and a conditional choice in 1998 Entry Draft for Ed Belfour, January 25, 1997.

DAHLQUIST, CHRIS (DAHL-kwist)

Defense. Shoots left. 6'1", 195 lbs. Born, Fridley, MN, December 14, 1962.

			Regular Season					Playoffs				
Season	Club	Lea	GP	G	A	TP	PIM	GP	G	A	TP	PIM
1981-82	Lake Superior	CCHA	39	4	10	14	62	....	....	....	....	....
1982-83	Lake Superior	CCHA	35	0	12	12	63	....	....	....	....	....
1983-84	Lake Superior	CCHA	40	4	19	23	76	....	....	....	....	....
1984-85	Lake Superior	CCHA	32	4	10	14	18	....	....	....	....	....
1985-86	**Pittsburgh**	**NHL**	**5**	**1**	**2**	**3**	**2**	....	....	....	....	....
	Baltimore	AHL	65	4	21	25	64	....	....	....	....	....
1986-87	**Pittsburgh**	**NHL**	**19**	**0**	**1**	**1**	**20**	....	....	....	....	....
	Baltimore	AHL	51	1	16	17	50	....	....	....	....	....
1987-88	**Pittsburgh**	**NHL**	**44**	**3**	**6**	**9**	**69**	....	....	....	....	....
1988-89	**Pittsburgh**	**NHL**	**43**	**1**	**5**	**6**	**42**	**2**	**0**	**0**	**0**	**0**
	Muskegon	IHL	10	3	6	9	14	....	....	....	....	....
1989-90	**Pittsburgh**	**NHL**	**62**	**4**	**10**	**14**	**56**	....	....	....	....	....
	Muskegon	IHL	6	1	1	2	8	....	....	....	....	....
1990-91	**Pittsburgh**	**NHL**	**22**	**1**	**2**	**3**	**30**	....	....	....	....	....
	Minnesota	**NHL**	**42**	**2**	**6**	**8**	**33**	**23**	**1**	**6**	**7**	**20**
1991-92	**Minnesota**	**NHL**	**74**	**1**	**13**	**14**	**68**	**7**	**0**	**0**	**0**	**6**
1992-93	**Calgary**	**NHL**	**74**	**3**	**7**	**10**	**66**	**6**	**3**	**1**	**4**	**4**
1993-94	**Calgary**	**NHL**	**77**	**1**	**11**	**12**	**52**	**1**	**0**	**0**	**0**	**0**
1994-95	**Ottawa**	**NHL**	**46**	**1**	**7**	**8**	**36**	....	....	....	....	....
1995-96	**Ottawa**	**NHL**	**24**	**1**	**1**	**2**	**14**	....	....	....	....	....
	Cincinnati	IHL	38	4	8	12	50	2	1	3	4	0
1996-97	Las Vegas	IHL	18	1	4	5	26	....	....	....	....	....
	NHL Totals		**532**	**19**	**71**	**90**	**488**	**39**	**4**	**7**	**11**	**30**

Signed as a free agent by **Pittsburgh**, May 7, 1985. Traded to **Minnesota** by **Pittsburgh** with Jim Johnson for Larry Murphy and Peter Taglianetti, December 11, 1990. Claimed by **Calgary** from **Minnesota** in NHL Waiver Draft, October 4, 1992. Signed as a free agent by **Ottawa**, July 4, 1994.

DAIGLE, ALEXANDRE (DAYG) OTT.

Center. Shoots left. 6', 195 lbs. Born, Montreal, Que., February 7, 1975.
(Ottawa's 1st choice, 1st overall, in 1993 Entry Draft).

			Regular Season					Playoffs				
Season	Club	Lea	GP	G	A	TP	PIM	GP	G	A	TP	PIM
1991-92ab	Victoriaville	QMJHL	66	35	75	110	63	....	....	....	....	....
1992-93c	Victoriaville	QMJHL	53	45	92	137	85	6	5	6	11	4
1993-94	**Ottawa**	**NHL**	**84**	**20**	**31**	**51**	**40**	....	....	....	....	....
1994-95	Victoriaville	QMJHL	18	14	20	34	16	....	....	....	....	....
	Ottawa	**NHL**	**47**	**16**	**21**	**37**	**14**	....	....	....	....	....
1995-96	**Ottawa**	**NHL**	**50**	**5**	**12**	**17**	**24**	....	....	....	....	....
1996-97	**Ottawa**	**NHL**	**82**	**26**	**25**	**51**	**33**	**7**	**0**	**0**	**0**	**2**
	NHL Totals		**263**	**67**	**89**	**156**	**111**	**7**	**0**	**0**	**0**	**2**

a QMJHL Second All-Star Team (1992)
b Canadian Major Junior Rookie of the Year (1992)
c QMJHL First All-Star Team (1993)

DAIGNEAULT, JEAN-JACQUES (J.J.) (DAYN-yoh) ANA.

Defense. Shoots left. 5'10", 186 lbs. Born, Montreal, Que., October 12, 1965.
(Vancouver's 1st choice, 10th overall, in 1984 Entry Draft).

			Regular Season					Playoffs				
Season	Club	Lea	GP	G	A	TP	PIM	GP	G	A	TP	PIM
1981-82	Laval	QMJHL	64	4	25	29	41	18	1	3	4	2
1982-83a	Longueuil	QMJHL	70	26	58	84	58	15	4	11	15	35
1983-84	Cdn. National	....	55	5	14	19	40	....	....	....	....	....
	Cdn. Olympic	....	7	1	1	2	0	....	....	....	....	....
	Longueuil	QMJHL	10	2	11	13	6	14	3	13	16	30
1984-85	**Vancouver**	**NHL**	**67**	**4**	**23**	**27**	**69**	....	....	....	....	....
1985-86	**Vancouver**	**NHL**	**64**	**5**	**23**	**28**	**45**	**3**	**0**	**2**	**2**	**0**
1986-87	**Philadelphia**	**NHL**	**77**	**6**	**16**	**22**	**56**	**9**	**1**	**0**	**1**	**0**
1987-88	**Philadelphia**	**NHL**	**28**	**2**	**2**	**4**	**12**	....	....	....	....	....
	Hershey	AHL	10	1	5	6	8	....	....	....	....	....
1988-89	Hershey	AHL	12	0	10	10	13	....	....	....	....	....
	Sherbrooke	AHL	63	10	33	43	48	6	1	3	4	2
1989-90	**Montreal**	**NHL**	**36**	**2**	**10**	**12**	**14**	**9**	**0**	**0**	**0**	**2**
	Sherbrooke	AHL	28	8	19	27	18	....	....	....	....	....
1990-91	**Montreal**	**NHL**	**51**	**3**	**16**	**19**	**31**	**5**	**0**	**1**	**1**	**0**
1991-92	**Montreal**	**NHL**	**79**	**4**	**14**	**18**	**36**	**11**	**0**	**3**	**3**	**4**
1992-93	**Montreal**	**NHL**	**66**	**8**	**10**	**18**	**57**	**20**	**1**	**3**	**4**	**22 ♦**
1993-94	**Montreal**	**NHL**	**68**	**2**	**12**	**14**	**73**	**7**	**0**	**1**	**1**	**12**
1994-95	**Montreal**	**NHL**	**45**	**3**	**5**	**8**	**40**	....	....	....	....	....
1995-96	**Montreal**	**NHL**	**7**	**0**	**1**	**1**	**6**	....	....	....	....	....
	St. Louis	**NHL**	**37**	**1**	**3**	**4**	**24**	....	....	....	....	....
	Worcester	IHL	9	1	10	11	10	....	....	....	....	....
	Pittsburgh	**NHL**	**13**	**3**	**3**	**6**	**23**	**17**	**1**	**9**	**10**	**36**
1996-97	**Pittsburgh**	**NHL**	**53**	**3**	**14**	**17**	**36**	....	....	....	....	....
	Anaheim	**NHL**	**13**	**2**	**9**	**11**	**22**	**11**	**2**	**7**	**9**	**16**
	NHL Totals		**704**	**48**	**161**	**209**	**544**	**92**	**5**	**26**	**31**	**92**

a QMJHL First All-Star Team (1983)

Traded to **Philadelphia** by **Vancouver** with Vancouver's second round choice (Kent Hawley) in 1986 Entry Draft for Dave Richter, Rich Sutter and Vancouver's third round choice (previously acquired by Philadelphia — Vancouver selected Don Gibson) in 1986 Entry Draft, June 6, 1986. Traded to **Montreal** by **Philadelphia** for Scott Sandelin, November 7, 1988. Traded to **St. Louis** by **Montreal** for Pat Jablonski, November 7, 1995. Traded to **Pittsburgh** by **St. Louis** for Pittsburgh's sixth round choice (Stephen Wagner) in 1996 Entry Draft, March 20, 1996. Traded to **Anaheim** by **Pittsburgh** for Garry Valk, February 21, 1997.

DALE, ANDREW L.A.

Center. Shoots left. 6'1", 196 lbs. Born, Sudbury, Ont., February 16, 1976.
(Los Angeles' 6th choice, 189th overall, in 1994 Entry Draft).

			Regular Season					Playoffs				
Season	Club	Lea	GP	G	A	TP	PIM	GP	G	A	TP	PIM
1993-94	Sudbury	OHL	53	8	13	21	21	9	0	3	3	4
1994-95	Sudbury	OHL	65	21	30	51	99	18	2	9	11	37
1995-96	Sudbury	OHL	40	32	24	56	47	....	....	....	....	....
	Kitchener	OHL	24	12	21	33	28	12	5	5	10	25
1996-97	Mississippi	ECHL	19	6	9	15	16	2	0	1	1	0
	Phoenix	IHL	32	7	6	13	19	....	....	....	....	....

DAMPHOUSSE, VINCENT (DAHM-fooz) MTL.

Center. Shoots left. 6'1", 195 lbs. Born, Montreal, Que., December 17, 1967.
(Toronto's 1st choice, 6th overall, in 1986 Entry Draft).

Season	Club	Lea	Regular Season					Playoffs				
			GP	G	A	TP	PIM	GP	G	A	TP	PIM
1983-84	Laval	QMJHL	66	29	36	65	25	....	....	....	....	....
1984-85	Laval	QMJHL	68	35	68	103	62	....	....	....	....	....
1985-86a	Laval	QMJHL	69	45	110	155	70	14	9	27	36	12
1986-87	**Toronto**	**NHL**	**80**	**21**	**25**	**46**	**26**	**12**	**1**	**5**	**6**	**8**
1987-88	**Toronto**	**NHL**	**75**	**12**	**36**	**48**	**40**	**6**	**0**	**1**	**1**	**10**
1988-89	**Toronto**	**NHL**	**80**	**26**	**42**	**68**	**75**	....	....	....	....	....
1989-90	**Toronto**	**NHL**	**80**	**33**	**61**	**94**	**56**	**5**	**0**	**2**	**2**	**2**
1990-91	**Toronto**	**NHL**	**79**	**26**	**47**	**73**	**65**	....	....	....	....	....
1991-92	**Edmonton**	**NHL**	**80**	**38**	**51**	**89**	**53**	**16**	**6**	**8**	**14**	**8**
1992-93	**Montreal**	**NHL**	**84**	**39**	**58**	**97**	**98**	**20**	**11**	**12**	**23**	**16** ♦
1993-94	**Montreal**	**NHL**	**84**	**40**	**51**	**91**	**75**	**7**	**1**	**2**	**3**	**8**
1994-95	Ratingen	Ger.	11	5	7	12	24	....	....	....	....	....
	Montreal	**NHL**	**48**	**10**	**30**	**40**	**42**	....	....	....	....	....
1995-96	**Montreal**	**NHL**	**80**	**38**	**56**	**94**	**158**	**6**	**4**	**4**	**8**	**0**
1996-97	**Montreal**	**NHL**	**82**	**27**	**54**	**81**	**82**	**5**	**0**	**0**	**0**	**2**
	NHL Totals		**852**	**310**	**511**	**821**	**770**	**77**	**23**	**34**	**57**	**54**

a QMJHL Second All-Star Team (1986)

Played in NHL All-Star Game (1991, 1992)

Traded to **Edmonton** by **Toronto** with Peter Ing, Scott Thornton, Luke Richardson, future considerations and cash for Grant Fuhr, Glenn Anderson and Craig Berube, September 19, 1991. Traded to **Montreal** by **Edmonton** with Edmonton's fourth round choice (Adam Wiesel) in 1993 Entry Draft for Shayne Corson, Brent Gilchrist and Vladimir Vujtek, August 27, 1992.

DANDENAULT, MATHIEU (DAHN-deh-noh) DET.

Right wing. Shoots right. 6', 174 lbs. Born, Sherbrooke, Que., February 3, 1976.
(Detroit's 2nd choice, 49th overall, in 1994 Entry Draft).

Season	Club	Lea	Regular Season					Playoffs				
			GP	G	A	TP	PIM	GP	G	A	TP	PIM
1993-94	Sherbrooke	QMJHL	67	17	36	53	67	12	4	10	14	12
1994-95	Sherbrooke	QMJHL	67	37	70	107	76	7	1	7	8	10
1995-96	**Detroit**	**NHL**	**34**	**5**	**7**	**12**	**6**	....	....	....	....	....
	Adirondack	AHL	4	0	0	0	0	....	....	....	....	....
1996-97	**Detroit**	**NHL**	**65**	**3**	**9**	**12**	**28**	....	....	....	....	.... ♦
	NHL Totals		**99**	**8**	**16**	**24**	**34**	....	....	....	....	....

DANEYKO, KEN (DAN-ee-KOH) N.J.

Defense. Shoots left. 6'1", 215 lbs. Born, Windsor, Ont., April 17, 1964.
(New Jersey's 2nd choice, 18th overall, in 1982 Entry Draft).

Season	Club	Lea	Regular Season					Playoffs				
			GP	G	A	TP	PIM	GP	G	A	TP	PIM
1980-81	Spokane	WHL	62	6	13	19	140	4	0	0	0	6
1981-82	Spokane	WHL	26	1	11	12	147	....	....	....	....	....
	Seattle	WHL	38	1	22	23	151	14	1	9	10	49
1982-83	Seattle	WHL	69	17	43	60	150	4	1	3	4	14
1983-84	**New Jersey**	**NHL**	**11**	**1**	**4**	**5**	**17**	....	....	....	....	....
	Kamloops	WH	19	6	28	34	52	17	4	9	13	28
1984-85	**New Jersey**	**NHL**	**1**	**0**	**0**	**0**	**10**	....	....	....	....	....
	Maine	AHL	80	4	9	13	206	11	1	3	4	36
1985-86	**New Jersey**	**NHL**	**44**	**0**	**10**	**10**	**100**	....	....	....	....	....
	Maine	AHL	21	3	2	5	75	....	....	....	....	....
1986-87	**New Jersey**	**NHL**	**79**	**2**	**12**	**14**	**183**	....	....	....	....	....
1987-88	**New Jersey**	**NHL**	**80**	**5**	**7**	**12**	**239**	**20**	**1**	**6**	**7**	**83**
1988-89	**New Jersey**	**NHL**	**80**	**5**	**5**	**10**	**283**	....	....	....	....	....
1989-90	**New Jersey**	**NHL**	**74**	**6**	**15**	**21**	**219**	**6**	**2**	**0**	**2**	**21**
1990-91	**New Jersey**	**NHL**	**80**	**4**	**16**	**20**	**249**	**7**	**0**	**1**	**1**	**10**
1991-92	**New Jersey**	**NHL**	**80**	**1**	**7**	**8**	**170**	**7**	**0**	**3**	**3**	**16**
1992-93	**New Jersey**	**NHL**	**84**	**2**	**11**	**13**	**236**	**5**	**0**	**0**	**0**	**8**
1993-94	**New Jersey**	**NHL**	**78**	**1**	**9**	**10**	**176**	**20**	**0**	**1**	**1**	**45**
1994-95	**New Jersey**	**NHL**	**25**	**1**	**2**	**3**	**54**	**20**	**1**	**0**	**1**	**22** ♦
1995-96	**New Jersey**	**NHL**	**80**	**2**	**4**	**6**	**115**	....	....	....	....	....
1996-97	**New Jersey**	**NHL**	**77**	**2**	**7**	**9**	**70**	**10**	**0**	**0**	**0**	**28**
	NHL Totals		**873**	**32**	**109**	**141**	**2121**	**95**	**4**	**11**	**15**	**233**

DANIELS, JEFF CAR.

Left wing. Shoots left. 6'1", 200 lbs. Born, Oshawa, Ont., June 24, 1968.
(Pittsburgh's 6th choice, 109th overall, in 1986 Entry Draft).

Season	Club	Lea	Regular Season					Playoffs				
			GP	G	A	TP	PIM	GP	G	A	TP	PIM
1984-85	Oshawa	OHL	59	7	11	18	16	....	....	....	....	....
1985-86	Oshawa	OHL	62	13	19	32	23	6	0	1	1	0
1986-87	Oshawa	OHL	54	14	9	23	22	15	3	2	5	5
1987-88	Oshawa	OHL	64	29	39	68	59	4	2	3	5	0
1988-89	Muskegon	IHL	58	21	21	42	58	11	3	5	8	11
1989-90	Muskegon	IHL	80	30	47	77	39	6	1	1	2	7
1990-91	**Pittsburgh**	**NHL**	**11**	**0**	**2**	**2**	**2**	....	....	....	....	....
	Muskegon	IHL	62	23	29	52	18	5	1	3	4	2
1991-92	**Pittsburgh**	**NHL**	**2**	**0**	**0**	**0**	**0**	....	....	....	....	....
	Muskegon	IHL	44	19	16	35	38	10	5	4	9	9
1992-93	**Pittsburgh**	**NHL**	**58**	**5**	**4**	**9**	**14**	**12**	**3**	**2**	**5**	**0**
	Cleveland	IHL	3	2	1	3	0	....	....	....	....	....
1993-94	**Pittsburgh**	**NHL**	**63**	**3**	**5**	**8**	**20**	....	....	....	....	....
	Florida	**NHL**	**7**	**0**	**0**	**0**	**0**	....	....	....	....	....
1994-95	**Florida**	**NHL**	**3**	**0**	**0**	**0**	**0**	....	....	....	....	....
	Detroit	IHL	25	8	12	20	6	5	1	0	1	0
1995-96	Springfield	AHL	72	22	20	42	32	10	3	0	3	2
1996-97	**Hartford**	**NHL**	**10**	**0**	**2**	**2**	**0**	....	....	....	....	....
	Springfield	AHL	38	18	14	32	19	16	7	3	10	4
	NHL Totals		**154**	**8**	**13**	**21**	**36**	**12**	**3**	**2**	**5**	**0**

Traded to **Florida** by **Pittsburgh** for Greg Hawgood, March 19, 1994. Signed as a free agent by **Hartford**, August 18, 1995.

DANIELS, SCOTT PHI.

Left wing. Shoots left. 6'3", 214 lbs. Born, Prince Albert, Sask., September 19, 1969.
(Hartford's 6th choice, 136th overall, in 1989 Entry Draft).

Season	Club	Lea	Regular Season					Playoffs				
			GP	G	A	TP	PIM	GP	G	A	TP	PIM
1986-87	Kamloops	WHL	43	6	4	10	68	....	....	....	....	....
	N. Westminster	WHL	19	4	7	11	30	....	....	....	....	....
1987-88	N. Westminster	WHL	37	6	11	17	157	....	....	....	....	....
	Regina	WHL	19	2	3	5	83	....	....	....	....	....
1988-89	Regina	WHL	64	21	26	47	241	....	....	....	....	....
1989-90	Regina	WHL	52	28	31	59	171	....	....	....	....	....
1990-91	Springfield	AHL	40	2	6	8	121	....	....	....	....	....
	Louisville	ECHL	9	5	3	8	34	1	0	2	2	0
1991-92	Springfield	AHL	54	7	15	22	213	10	0	0	0	32
1992-93	**Hartford**	**NHL**	**1**	**0**	**0**	**0**	**19**	....	....	....	....	....
	Springfield	AHL	60	11	12	23	181	12	2	7	9	12
1993-94	Springfield	AHL	52	9	11	20	185	6	0	1	1	53
1994-95	Springfield	AHL	48	9	5	14	277	....	....	....	....	....
	Hartford	**NHL**	**12**	**0**	**2**	**2**	**55**	....	....	....	....	....
1995-96	**Hartford**	**NHL**	**53**	**3**	**4**	**7**	**254**	....	....	....	....	....
	Springfield	AHL	6	4	1	5	17	....	....	....	....	....
1996-97	**Philadelphia**	**NHL**	**56**	**5**	**3**	**8**	**237**	....	....	....	....	....
	NHL Totals		**122**	**8**	**9**	**17**	**565**	....	....	....	....	....

Signed as a free agent by **Philadelphia**, June 27, 1996.

DARBY, CRAIG PHI.

Center. Shoots right. 6'3", 200 lbs. Born, Oneida, NY, September 26, 1972.
(Montreal's 3rd choice, 43rd overall, in 1991 Entry Draft).

Season	Club	Lea	Regular Season					Playoffs				
			GP	G	A	TP	PIM	GP	G	A	TP	PIM
1991-92	Providence	H.E.	35	17	24	41	47	....	....	....	....	....
1992-93	Providence	H.E.	35	11	21	32	62	....	....	....	....	....
1993-94	Fredericton	AHL	66	23	33	56	51	....	....	....	....	....
1994-95	Fredericton	AHL	64	21	47	68	82	....	....	....	....	....
	Montreal	**NHL**	**10**	**0**	**2**	**2**	**0**	....	....	....	....	....
	NY Islanders	**NHL**	**3**	**0**	**0**	**0**	**0**	....	....	....	....	....
1995-96	**NY Islanders**	**NHL**	**10**	**0**	**2**	**2**	**0**	....	....	....	....	....
	Worcester	AHL	68	22	28	50	47	4	1	1	2	2
1996-97	**Philadelphia**	**NHL**	**9**	**1**	**4**	**5**	**2**	....	....	....	....	....
	Philadelphia	AHL	59	26	33	59	24	10	3	6	9	0
	NHL Totals		**32**	**1**	**8**	**9**	**2**	....	....	....	....	....

Traded to **NY Islanders** by **Montreal** with Kirk Muller and Mathieu Schneider for Pierre Turgeon and Vladimir Malakhov, April 5, 1995. Claimed on waivers by **Philadelphia** from **NY Islanders**, June 4, 1996.

DARGUZAS, DAVID (DAHR-goo-suhs) VAN.

Center. Shoots left. 6'2", 205 lbs. Born, Maple Ridge, Alta., January 20, 1979.
(Vancouver's 6th choice, 114th overall, in 1997 Entry Draft).

Season	Club	Lea	Regular Season					Playoffs				
			GP	G	A	TP	PIM	GP	G	A	TP	PIM
1995-96	Brandon	WHL	47	3	9	12	51	3	0	0	0	0
1996-97	Edmonton	WHL	71	23	32	55	124	....	....	....	....	....

DARLING, DION MTL.

Defense. Shoots left. 6'3", 220 lbs. Born, Edmonton, Alta., October 22, 1974.
(Montreal's 7th choice, 125th overall, in 1993 Entry Draft).

Season	Club	Lea	Regular Season					Playoffs				
			GP	G	A	TP	PIM	GP	G	A	TP	PIM
1991-92	St. Albert	AJHL	29	5	15	20	101	....	....	....	....	....
1992-93	Spokane	WHL	69	1	4	5	168	9	0	1	1	14
1993-94	Spokane	WHL	45	1	8	9	190	....	....	....	....	....
	Moose Jaw	WHL	23	4	6	10	96	....	....	....	....	....
	Wheeling	ECHL	3	0	1	1	7	9	0	1	1	14
1994-95	Fredericton	AHL	51	0	2	2	153	....	....	....	....	....
	Wheeling	ECHL	4	0	0	0	24	....	....	....	....	....
1995-96	Fredericton	AHL	74	3	2	5	215	6	0	0	0	5
1996-97	Fredericton	AHL	58	2	6	8	150	....	....	....	....	....

DAVIDSON, MATT BUF.

Right wing. Shoots right. 6'2", 190 lbs. Born, Flin Flon, Man., August 9, 1977.
(Buffalo's 5th choice, 94th overall, in 1995 Entry Draft).

Season	Club	Lea	Regular Season					Playoffs				
			GP	G	A	TP	PIM	GP	G	A	TP	PIM
1993-94	Portland	WHL	59	4	12	16	18	10	0	0	0	4
1994-95	Portland	WHL	72	17	20	37	51	9	1	3	4	0
1995-96	Portland	WHL	70	24	26	50	96	7	2	2	4	2
1996-97	Portland	WHL	72	44	27	71	47	6	0	1	1	2

DAVIDSSON, JOHAN (DAH-vihd-suhn) ANA.

Center. Shoots right. 5'11", 170 lbs. Born, Jonkoping, Sweden, January 6, 1976.
(Anaheim's 2nd choice, 28th overall, in 1994 Entry Draft).

Season	Club	Lea	Regular Season					Playoffs				
			GP	G	A	TP	PIM	GP	G	A	TP	PIM
1992-93	HV 71	Swe.	8	1	0	1	0	....	....	....	....	....
1993-94	HV 71	Swe.	38	2	5	7	4	....	....	....	....	....
1994-95	HV 71	Swe.	37	4	7	11	20	13	3	2	5	0
1995-96	HV 71	Swe.	39	7	11	18	20	4	0	2	2	0
1996-97	HV 71	Swe.	50	18	21	39	18	5	0	3	3	2

DAVIS, JUSTIN WSH.

Right wing. Shoots right. 6'2", 175 lbs. Born, Burlington, Ont., March 1, 1978.
(Washington's 7th choice, 85th overall, in 1996 Entry Draft).

Season	Club	Lea	Regular Season					Playoffs				
			GP	G	A	TP	PIM	GP	G	A	TP	PIM
1995-96	Kingston	OHL	64	30	18	48	20	6	2	3	5	0
1996-97	Kingston	OHL	35	8	17	25	17	....	....	....	....	....
	S.S. Marie	OHL	20	1	5	6	2	3	0	1	1	0

DAVIS, RYAN BUF.

Right wing. Shoots right. 6'2", 185 lbs. Born, Hamilton, Ont., February 16, 1978.
(Buffalo's 8th choice, 142nd overall, in 1996 Entry Draft).

Season	Club	Lea	Regular Season					Playoffs				
			GP	G	A	TP	PIM	GP	G	A	TP	PIM
1995-96	Owen Sound	OHL	60	11	9	20	62	5	1	0	1	5
1996-97	Owen Sound	OHL	61	23	20	43	112	4	1	2	3	4

DAW, JEFF — EDM.

Center. Shoots right. 6'3", 190 lbs. Born, Carlisle, Ont., February 28, 1972.

			Regular Season					Playoffs				
Season	Club	Lea	GP	G	A	TP	PIM	GP	G	A	TP	PIM
1992-93	Lowell	H.E.	37	12	18	30	14	....	....	....	....	....
1993-94	Lowell	H.E.	40	6	12	18	12	....	....	....	....	....
1994-95	Lowell	H.E.	40	27	15	42	24	....	....	....	....	....
1995-96	Lowell	H.E.	40	23	28	51	10	....	....	....	....	....
1996-97	Wheeling	ECHL	13	3	8	11	26	....	....	....	....	....
	Hamilton	AHL	56	11	8	19	39	19	4	5	9	0

Signed as a free agent by **Edmonton**, August 1, 1996.

DAWE, JASON (DAW) — BUF.

Left wing. Shoots left. 5'10", 189 lbs. Born, North York, Ont., May 29, 1973.
(Buffalo's 2nd choice, 35th overall, in 1991 Entry Draft).

			Regular Season					Playoffs				
Season	Club	Lea	GP	G	A	TP	PIM	GP	G	A	TP	PIM
1989-90	Peterborough	OHL	50	15	18	33	19	12	4	7	11	4
1990-91	Peterborough	OHL	66	43	27	70	43	4	3	1	4	0
1991-92	Peterborough	OHL	66	53	55	108	55	4	5	0	5	0
1992-93abc	Peterborough	OHL	59	58	68	126	80	21	18	33	51	18
	Rochester	AHL	....	....	....	....	....	3	1	0	1	0
1993-94	**Buffalo**	**NHL**	**32**	**6**	**7**	**13**	**12**	**6**	**0**	**1**	**1**	**6**
	Rochester	AHL	48	22	14	36	44	....	....	....	....	....
1994-95	Rochester	AHL	44	27	19	46	24	....	....	....	....	....
	Buffalo	**NHL**	**42**	**7**	**4**	**11**	**19**	**5**	**2**	**1**	**3**	**6**
1995-96	**Buffalo**	**NHL**	**67**	**25**	**25**	**50**	**33**	....	....	....	....	....
	Rochester	AHL	7	5	4	9	2	....	....	....	....	....
1996-97	**Buffalo**	**NHL**	**81**	**22**	**26**	**48**	**32**	**11**	**2**	**1**	**3**	**6**
	NHL Totals		**222**	**60**	**62**	**122**	**96**	**22**	**4**	**3**	**7**	**18**

a OHL First All-Star Team (1993)
b Canadian Major Junior Second All-Star Team (1993)
c Won George Parsons Trophy (Memorial Cup Tournament Most Sportsmanlike Player) (1993)

DAZE, ERIC (dah-ZAY) — CHI.

Left wing. Shoots left. 6'6", 222 lbs. Born, Montreal, Que., July 2, 1975.
(Chicago's 5th choice, 90th overall, in 1993 Entry Draft).

			Regular Season					Playoffs				
Season	Club	Lea	GP	G	A	TP	PIM	GP	G	A	TP	PIM
1992-93	Beauport	QMJHL	68	19	36	55	24	....	....	....	....	....
1993-94a	Beauport	QMJHL	66	59	48	107	31	15	16	8	24	2
1994-95ab	Beauport	QMJHL	57	54	45	99	20	16	9	12	21	23
	Chicago	**NHL**	**4**	**1**	**1**	**2**	**2**	**16**	**0**	**1**	**1**	**4**
1995-96c	**Chicago**	**NHL**	**80**	**30**	**23**	**53**	**18**	**10**	**3**	**5**	**8**	**0**
1996-97	**Chicago**	**NHL**	**71**	**22**	**19**	**41**	**16**	**6**	**2**	**1**	**3**	**2**
	NHL Totals		**155**	**53**	**43**	**96**	**36**	**32**	**5**	**7**	**12**	**6**

a QMJHL First All-Star Team (1994, 1995)
b Canadian Major Junior Most Sportsmanlike Player of the Year (1995)
c NHL All-Rookie Team (1996)

DEADMARSH, ADAM — COL.

Center. Shoots right. 6', 195 lbs. Born, Trail, B.C., May 10, 1975.
(Quebec's 2nd choice, 14th overall, in 1993 Entry Draft).

			Regular Season					Playoffs				
Season	Club	Lea	GP	G	A	TP	PIM	GP	G	A	TP	PIM
1991-92	Portland	WHL	68	30	30	60	81	6	3	3	6	13
1992-93	Portland	WHL	58	33	36	69	126	16	7	8	15	29
1993-94	Portland	WHL	65	43	56	99	212	10	9	8	17	33
1994-95	Portland	WHL	29	28	20	48	129	....	....	....	....	....
	Quebec	**NHL**	**48**	**9**	**8**	**17**	**56**	**6**	**0**	**1**	**1**	**0**
1995-96	**Colorado**	**NHL**	**78**	**21**	**27**	**48**	**142**	**22**	**5**	**12**	**17**	**25 ♦**
1996-97	**Colorado**	**NHL**	**78**	**33**	**27**	**60**	**136**	**17**	**3**	**6**	**9**	**24**
	NHL Totals		**204**	**63**	**62**	**125**	**334**	**45**	**8**	**19**	**27**	**49**

DEAN, KEVIN — N.J.

Defense. Shoots left. 6'3", 200 lbs. Born, Madison, WI, April 1, 1969.
(New Jersey's 4th choice, 86th overall, in 1987 Entry Draft).

			Regular Season					Playoffs				
Season	Club	Lea	GP	G	A	TP	PIM	GP	G	A	TP	PIM
1987-88	N. Hampshire	H.E.	27	1	6	7	34	....	....	....	....	....
1988-89	N. Hampshire	H.E.	34	1	12	13	28	....	....	....	....	....
1989-90	N. Hampshire	H.E.	39	2	6	8	42	....	....	....	....	....
1990-91	N. Hampshire	H.E.	31	10	12	22	22	....	....	....	....	....
	Utica	AHL	7	0	1	1	2	....	....	....	....	....
1991-92	Utica	AHL	23	0	3	3	6	....	....	....	....	....
	Cincinnati	ECHL	30	3	22	25	43	9	1	6	7	8
1992-93	Cincinnati	IHL	13	2	1	3	15	....	....	....	....	....
	Utica	AHL	57	2	16	18	76	5	1	0	1	8
1993-94	Albany	AHL	70	9	33	42	92	5	0	2	2	7
1994-95a	Albany	AHL	68	5	37	42	66	8	0	4	4	4
	New Jersey	**NHL**	**17**	**0**	**1**	**1**	**4**	**3**	**0**	**2**	**2**	**0 ♦**
1995-96	**New Jersey**	**NHL**	**41**	**0**	**6**	**6**	**28**	....	....	....	....	....
	Albany	AHL	1	1	0	1	2	....	....	....	....	....
1996-97	**New Jersey**	**NHL**	**28**	**2**	**4**	**6**	**6**	**1**	**1**	**0**	**1**	**0**
	Albany	AHL	2	0	1	1	4	....	....	....	....	....
	NHL Totals		**86**	**2**	**11**	**13**	**38**	**4**	**1**	**2**	**3**	**0**

a AHL First All-Star Team (1995)

DEBRUSK, LOUIE (dah-BRUHSK)

Left wing. Shoots left. 6'2", 215 lbs. Born, Cambridge, Ont., March 19, 1971.
(NY Rangers' 4th choice, 49th overall, in 1989 Entry Draft).

			Regular Season					Playoffs				
Season	Club	Lea	GP	G	A	TP	PIM	GP	G	A	TP	PIM
1988-89	London	OHL	59	11	11	22	149	19	1	1	2	43
1989-90	London	OHL	61	21	19	40	198	6	2	2	4	24
1990-91	London	OHL	61	31	33	64	*223	7	2	2	4	14
	Binghamton	AHL	2	0	0	0	7	2	0	0	0	9
1991-92	**Edmonton**	**NHL**	**25**	**2**	**1**	**3**	**124**	....	....	....	....	....
	Cape Breton	AHL	28	2	2	4	73	....	....	....	....	....
1992-93	**Edmonton**	**NHL**	**51**	**8**	**2**	**10**	**205**	....	....	....	....	....
1993-94	**Edmonton**	**NHL**	**48**	**4**	**6**	**10**	**185**	....	....	....	....	....
	Cape Breton	AHL	5	3	1	4	58	....	....	....	....	....
1994-95	**Edmonton**	**NHL**	**34**	**2**	**0**	**2**	**93**	....	....	....	....	....
1995-96	**Edmonton**	**NHL**	**38**	**1**	**3**	**4**	**96**	....	....	....	....	....
1996-97	**Edmonton**	**NHL**	**32**	**2**	**0**	**2**	**94**	**6**	**0**	**0**	**0**	**4**
	NHL Totals		**228**	**19**	**12**	**31**	**797**	**6**	**0**	**0**	**0**	**4**

Traded to **Edmonton** by **NY Rangers** with Bernie Nicholls and Steven Rice for Mark Messier and future considerations, October 4, 1991.

DEFAUW, BRAD — CAR.

Left wing. Shoots left. 6'2", 210 lbs. Born, Edina, MN, November 10, 1977.
(Carolina's 2nd choice, 28th overall, in 1997 Entry Draft).

			Regular Season					Playoffs				
Season	Club	Lea	GP	G	A	TP	PIM	GP	G	A	TP	PIM
1995-96	Apple Valley	HS	28	21	34	55	14	....	....	....	....	....
1996-97	North Dakota	WCHA	37	7	6	13	39	....	....	....	....	....

DELANEY, KEITH — FLA.

Center. Shoots left. 6'1", 196 lbs. Born, Labrador City, Nfld., May 7, 1979.
(Florida's 7th choice, 155th overall, in 1997 Entry Draft).

			Regular Season					Playoffs				
Season	Club	Lea	GP	G	A	TP	PIM	GP	G	A	TP	PIM
1995-96	St. Paul's	HS	36	25	51	76	....	....	....	....	....	....
1996-97	Barrie	OHL	64	5	5	10	19	9	0	1	1	0

DELISLE, JONATHAN — MTL.

Right wing. Shoots right. 5'10", 186 lbs. Born, Ste-Anne-des-Plaines, Que., June 30, 1977.
(Montreal's 4th choice, 86th overall, in 1995 Entry Draft).

			Regular Season					Playoffs				
Season	Club	Lea	GP	G	A	TP	PIM	GP	G	A	TP	PIM
1993-94	Verdun	QMJHL	61	16	17	33	130	4	0	1	1	14
1994-95	Hull	QMJHL	60	21	38	59	218	19	11	8	19	43
1995-96	Hull	QMJHL	62	31	57	88	193	18	6	13	19	64
1996-97	Hull	QMJHL	61	35	54	89	228	14	11	13	24	46

DELISLE, XAVIER — T.B.

Center. Shoots right. 5'11", 182 lbs. Born, Quebec City, Que., May 24, 1977.
(Tampa Bay's 5th choice, 157th overall, in 1996 Entry Draft).

			Regular Season					Playoffs				
Season	Club	Lea	GP	G	A	TP	PIM	GP	G	A	TP	PIM
1993-94	Granby	QMJHL	46	11	22	33	25	7	2	0	2	0
1994-95	Granby	QMJHL	72	18	36	54	48	13	2	6	8	4
1995-96ab	Granby	QMJHL	67	45	75	120	45	20	13	*27	*40	12
1996-97	Granby	QMJHL	59	36	56	92	20	5	1	4	5	6

a QMJHL Second All-Star Team (1996)
b Memorial Cup All-Star Team (1996)

DELMORE, ANDY — PHI.

Defense. Shoots right. 6'1", 192 lbs. Born, LaSalle, Ont., December 26, 1976.

			Regular Season					Playoffs				
Season	Club	Lea	GP	G	A	TP	PIM	GP	G	A	TP	PIM
1993-94	North Bay	OHL	45	2	7	9	33	17	0	0	0	2
1994-95	North Bay	OHL	40	2	14	16	21	....	....	....	....	....
	Sarnia	OHL	27	5	13	18	27	3	0	0	0	2
1995-96	Sarnia	OHL	64	21	38	59	45	10	3	7	10	2
1996-97a	Sarnia	OHL	64	18	60	78	39	12	2	10	12	10
	Fredericton	AHL	4	0	1	1	0	....	....	....	....	....

a OHL First All-Star Team (1997)

Signed as a free agent by **Philadelphia**, June 9, 1997.

DEMARTINIS, LUCIO — TOR.

Left wing. Shoots left. 6'2", 182 lbs. Born, Montreal, Que., July 31, 1978.
(Toronto's 11th choice, 151st overall, in 1996 Entry Draft).

			Regular Season					Playoffs				
Season	Club	Lea	GP	G	A	TP	PIM	GP	G	A	TP	PIM
1995-96	Shawinigan	QMJHL	57	10	4	14	91	....	....	....	....	....
1996-97	Val d'Or	QMJHL	66	15	21	36	46	13	3	3	6	6

DEMIDOV, ILJA (deh-MEE-dahf, ihl-YA) — CGY.

Defense. Shoots left. 6'3", 185 lbs. Born, Moscow, USSR, April 14, 1979.
(Calgary's 10th choice, 140th overall, in 1997 Entry Draft).

			Regular Season					Playoffs				
Season	Club	Lea	GP	G	A	TP	PIM	GP	G	A	TP	PIM
1995-96	Mosc. D'amo 2	CIS 2	10	0	14	14	....	....	....	....	....	....
1996-97	Mosc. D'amo 2	Rus. 3	32	1	0	1	60	....	....	....	....	....

DEMITRA, PAVOL (deh-MIHT-rah) — ST.L.

Left wing. Shoots left. 6', 189 lbs. Born, Dubnica, Czech., November 29, 1974.
(Ottawa's 9th choice, 227th overall, in 1993 Entry Draft).

			Regular Season					Playoffs				
Season	Club	Lea	GP	G	A	TP	PIM	GP	G	A	TP	PIM
1991-92	Spartak Dubnica	Czech. 2	28	13	10	23	12	....	....	....	....	....
1992-93	Dukla Trencin	Czech.	46	10	18	28	....	....	....	....	....	....
	CAPEH Dubnica	Czech. 2	4	3	0	3	....	....	....	....	....	....
1993-94	**Ottawa**	**NHL**	**12**	**1**	**1**	**2**	**4**	....	....	....	....	....
	P.E.I.	AHL	41	18	23	41	8	....	....	....	....	....
1994-95	P.E.I.	AHL	61	26	48	74	23	5	0	7	7	0
	Ottawa	**NHL**	**16**	**4**	**3**	**7**	**0**	....	....	....	....	....
1995-96	**Ottawa**	**NHL**	**31**	**7**	**10**	**17**	**6**	....	....	....	....	....
	P.E.I.	AHL	48	28	53	81	44	....	....	....	....	....
1996-97	Dukla Trencin	Slovak	1	1	1	2	....	....	....	....	....	....
	Las Vegas	IHL	22	8	13	21	10	....	....	....	....	....
	St. Louis	**NHL**	**8**	**3**	**0**	**3**	**2**	**6**	**1**	**3**	**4**	**6**
	Grand Rapids	IHL	42	20	30	50	24	....	....	....	....	....
	NHL Totals		**67**	**15**	**14**	**29**	**12**	**6**	**1**	**3**	**4**	**6**

Traded to **St. Louis** by **Ottawa** for Christer Olsson, November 27, 1996.

DEMPSEY, NATHAN — TOR.

Left wing. Shoots left. 6', 170 lbs. Born, Spruce Grove, Alta., July 14, 1974.
(Toronto's 11th choice, 148th overall, in 1992 Entry Draft).

			Regular Season					Playoffs				
Season	Club	Lea	GP	G	A	TP	PIM	GP	G	A	TP	PIM
1991-92	Regina	WHL	70	4	22	26	72	....	....	....	....	....
1992-93	Regina	WHL	72	12	29	41	95	13	3	8	11	14
	St. John's	AHL	....	....	....	....	....	2	0	0	0	0
1993-94a	Regina	WHL	56	14	36	50	100	4	0	0	0	4
1994-95	St. John's	AHL	74	7	30	37	91	5	1	0	1	11
1995-96	St. John's	AHL	73	5	15	20	103	4	1	0	1	9
1996-97	**Toronto**	**NHL**	**14**	**1**	**1**	**2**	**2**	....	....	....	....	....
	St. John's	AHL	52	8	18	26	108	6	1	0	1	4
	NHL Totals		**14**	**1**	**1**	**2**	**2**	....	....	....	....	....

a WHL East Second All-Star Team (1994)

DESCOTEAUX, MATTHIEU (DAY-koh-toh) EDM.

Defense. Shoots left. 6'3", 220 lbs. Born, Pierreville, Que., September 23, 1977.
(Edmonton's 2nd choice, 19th overall, in 1996 Entry Draft).

			Regular Season					Playoffs				
Season	Club	Lea	GP	G	A	TP	PIM	GP	G	A	TP	PIM
1994-95	Shawinigan	QMJHL	50	3	2	5	28	15	1	1	2	19
1995-96	Shawinigan	QMJHL	69	2	13	15	129	6	0	0	0	6
1996-97	Shawinigan	QMJHL	38	6	18	24	121	....	....	....	....	....
	Hull	QMJHL	32	6	19	25	34	14	1	8	9	29

DESJARDINS, ERIC (deh-ZHAHR-dai) PHI.

Defense. Shoots right. 6'1", 200 lbs. Born, Rouyn, Que., June 14, 1969.
(Montreal's 3rd choice, 38th overall, in 1987 Entry Draft).

			Regular Season					Playoffs				
Season	Club	Lea	GP	G	A	TP	PIM	GP	G	A	TP	PIM
1986-87a	Granby	QMJHL	66	14	24	38	178	8	3	2	5	10
1987-88	Sherbrooke	AHL	3	0	0	0	6	4	0	2	2	2
b	Granby	QMJHL	62	18	49	67	138	5	0	3	3	10
1988-89	**Montreal**	**NHL**	**36**	**2**	**12**	**14**	**26**	**14**	**1**	**1**	**2**	**6**
1989-90	**Montreal**	**NHL**	**55**	**3**	**13**	**16**	**51**	**6**	**0**	**0**	**0**	**10**
1990-91	**Montreal**	**NHL**	**62**	**7**	**18**	**25**	**27**	**13**	**1**	**4**	**5**	**8**
1991-92	**Montreal**	**NHL**	**77**	**6**	**32**	**38**	**50**	**11**	**3**	**3**	**6**	**4**
1992-93	**Montreal**	**NHL**	**82**	**13**	**32**	**45**	**98**	**20**	**4**	**10**	**14**	**23 ♦**
1993-94	**Montreal**	**NHL**	**84**	**12**	**23**	**35**	**97**	**7**	**0**	**2**	**2**	**4**
1994-95	**Montreal**	**NHL**	**9**	**0**	**6**	**6**	**2**	....	....	....	....	....
	Philadelphia	**NHL**	**34**	**5**	**18**	**23**	**12**	**15**	**4**	**4**	**8**	**10**
1995-96	**Philadelphia**	**NHL**	**80**	**7**	**40**	**47**	**45**	**12**	**0**	**6**	**6**	**2**
1996-97	**Philadelphia**	**NHL**	**82**	**12**	**34**	**46**	**50**	**19**	**2**	**8**	**10**	**12**
	NHL Totals		**601**	**67**	**228**	**295**	**458**	**117**	**15**	**38**	**53**	**79**

a QMJHL Second All-Star Team (1987)
b QMJHL First All-Star Team (1988)

Played in NHL All-Star Game (1992, 1996)

Traded to **Philadelphia** by **Montreal** with Gilbert Dionne and John LeClair for Mark Recchi and Philadelphia's third round choice (Martin Hohenberger) in 1995 Entry Draft, February 9, 1995.

DESROCHES, JONATHAN (deh-ROHSH) MTL.

Defense. Shoots left. 6', 206 lbs. Born, Granby, Que., May 23, 1979.
(Montreal's 7th choice, 145th overall, in 1997 Entry Draft).

			Regular Season					Playoffs				
Season	Club	Lea	GP	G	A	TP	PIM	GP	G	A	TP	PIM
1995-96	Granby	QMJHL	44	1	6	7	38	11	0	0	0	2
1996-97	Granby	QMJHL	58	7	15	22	36	5	0	1	1	2

DESSNER, JEFF NYR

Defense. Shoots left. 6'2", 177 lbs. Born, Skokie, IL, April 16, 1977.
(NY Rangers' 6th choice, 185th overall, in 1996 Entry Draft).

			Regular Season					Playoffs				
Season	Club	Lea	GP	G	A	TP	PIM	GP	G	A	TP	PIM
1995-96	Taft	HS	23	12	25	37	....	....	....	....	....	....
1996-97	DID NOT PLAY – INJURED											

DEULING, JARRETT

Left wing. Shoots left. 6', 202 lbs. Born, Vernon, B.C., March 4, 1974.
(NY Islanders' 2nd choice, 56th overall, in 1992 Entry Draft).

			Regular Season					Playoffs				
Season	Club	Lea	GP	G	A	TP	PIM	GP	G	A	TP	PIM
1990-91	Kamloops	WHL	48	4	12	16	43	12	5	2	7	7
1991-92	Kamloops	WHL	68	28	26	54	79	17	10	6	16	18
1992-93	Kamloops	WHL	68	31	32	63	93	13	6	7	13	14
1993-94	Kamloops	WHL	70	44	59	103	171	18	*13	8	21	43
1994-95	Worcester	AHL	63	11	8	19	37	....	....	....	....	....
1995-96	**NY Islanders**	**NHL**	**14**	**0**	**1**	**1**	**11**	....	....	....	....	....
	Worcester	AHL	57	16	7	23	57	4	1	2	3	2
1996-97	**NY Islanders**	**NHL**	**1**	**0**	**0**	**0**	**0**	....	....	....	....	....
	Kentucky	AHL	58	15	31	46	57	4	3	0	3	8
	NHL Totals		**15**	**0**	**1**	**1**	**11**					

DEVEREAUX, BOYD (DEH-vuhr-oh) EDM.

Center. Shoots left. 6'2", 195 lbs. Born, Seaforth, Ont., April 16, 1978.
(Edmonton's 1st choice, 6th overall, in 1996 Entry Draft).

			Regular Season					Playoffs				
Season	Club	Lea	GP	G	A	TP	PIM	GP	G	A	TP	PIM
1995-96a	Kitchener	OHL	66	20	38	58	35	12	3	7	10	4
1996-97	Kitchener	OHL	54	28	41	69	37	13	4	11	15	8
	Hamilton	AHL	....	....	....	....	....	1	0	1	1	0

a Canadian Major Junior Scholastic Player of the Year (1996)

de VRIES, GREG (deh-VREES) EDM.

Defense. Shoots left. 6'3", 218 lbs. Born, Sundridge, Ont., January 4, 1973.

			Regular Season					Playoffs				
Season	Club	Lea	GP	G	A	TP	PIM	GP	G	A	TP	PIM
1991-92	Bowling Green	CCHA	24	0	3	3	20	....	....	....	....	....
1992-93	Niagara Falls	OHL	62	3	23	26	86	4	0	1	1	6
1993-94	Niagara Falls	OHL	64	5	40	45	135	....	....	....	....	....
	Cape Breton	AHL	9	0	0	0	11	1	0	0	0	0
1994-95	Cape Breton	AHL	77	5	19	24	68	....	....	....	....	....
1995-96	**Edmonton**	**NHL**	**13**	**1**	**1**	**2**	**12**	....	....	....	....	....
	Cape Breton	AHL	58	9	30	39	174	....	....	....	....	....
1996-97	**Edmonton**	**NHL**	**37**	**0**	**4**	**4**	**52**	**12**	**0**	**1**	**1**	**8**
	Hamilton	AHL	34	4	14	18	26	....	....	....	....	....
	NHL Totals		**50**	**1**	**5**	**6**	**64**	**12**	**0**	**1**	**1**	**8**

Signed as a free agent by **Edmonton**, March 20, 1994.

DEWOLF, JOSHUA N.J.

Defense. Shoots left. 6'2", 190 lbs. Born, Bloomington, MN, July 25, 1977.
(New Jersey's 3rd choice, 41st overall, in 1996 Entry Draft).

			Regular Season					Playoffs				
Season	Club	Lea	GP	G	A	TP	PIM	GP	G	A	TP	PIM
1995-96	Twin Cities	Jr. A	40	11	15	26	38	....	....	....	....	....
1996-97	St. Cloud	WCHA	31	3	11	14	62	....	....	....	....	....

DEYELL, MARK (digh-EHL) TOR.

Center. Shoots right. 6', 180 lbs. Born, Regina, Sask., March 26, 1976.
(Toronto's 4th choice, 126th overall, in 1994 Entry Draft).

			Regular Season					Playoffs				
Season	Club	Lea	GP	G	A	TP	PIM	GP	G	A	TP	PIM
1993-94	Saskatoon	WHL	66	17	36	53	52	16	5	2	7	20
1994-95	Saskatoon	WHL	70	34	68	102	56	10	2	5	7	14
1995-96a	Saskatoon	WHL	69	61	*98	*159	122	4	0	5	5	8
1996-97	St. John's	AHL	58	15	27	42	30	10	1	5	6	6

a WHL East First All-Star Team (1996)

DHADPHALE, ANIKET (dahd-FAH-lee, AN-ih-keht) S.J.

Center. Shoots left. 6'3", 185 lbs. Born, Ann Arbor, MI, April 26, 1976.
(San Jose's 11th choice, 245th overall, in 1994 Entry Draft).

			Regular Season					Playoffs				
Season	Club	Lea	GP	G	A	TP	PIM	GP	G	A	TP	PIM
1995-96	Notre Dame	CCHA	34	13	7	20	34	....	....	....	....	....
1996-97	Notre Dame	CCHA	34	5	16	21	20	....	....	....	....	....

DIDUCK, GERALD (DIH-duhk) PHO.

Defense. Shoots right. 6'2", 217 lbs. Born, Edmonton, Alta., April 6, 1965.
(NY Islanders' 2nd choice, 16th overall, in 1983 Entry Draft).

			Regular Season					Playoffs				
Season	Club	Lea	GP	G	A	TP	PIM	GP	G	A	TP	PIM
1981-82	Lethbridge	WHL	71	1	15	16	81	12	0	3	3	27
1982-83	Lethbridge	WHL	67	8	16	24	151	20	3	12	15	49
1983-84	Lethbridge	WHL	65	10	24	34	133	5	1	4	5	27
	Indianapolis	IHL	....	....	....	....	....	10	1	6	7	19
1984-85	**NY Islanders**	**NHL**	**65**	**2**	**8**	**10**	**80**	....	....	....	....	....
1985-86	**NY Islanders**	**NHL**	**10**	**1**	**2**	**3**	**2**	....	....	....	....	....
	Springfield	AHL	61	6	14	20	173	....	....	....	....	....
1986-87	**NY Islanders**	**NHL**	**30**	**2**	**3**	**5**	**67**	**14**	**0**	**1**	**1**	**35**
	Springfield	AHL	45	6	8	14	120	....	....	....	....	....
1987-88	**NY Islanders**	**NHL**	**68**	**7**	**12**	**19**	**113**	**6**	**1**	**0**	**1**	**42**
1988-89	**NY Islanders**	**NHL**	**65**	**11**	**21**	**32**	**155**	....	....	....	....	....
1989-90	**NY Islanders**	**NHL**	**76**	**3**	**17**	**20**	**163**	**5**	**0**	**0**	**0**	**12**
1990-91	**Montreal**	**NHL**	**32**	**1**	**2**	**3**	**39**	....	....	....	....	....
	Vancouver	**NHL**	**31**	**3**	**7**	**10**	**66**	**6**	**1**	**0**	**1**	**11**
1991-92	**Vancouver**	**NHL**	**77**	**6**	**21**	**27**	**229**	**5**	**0**	**0**	**0**	**10**
1992-93	**Vancouver**	**NHL**	**80**	**6**	**14**	**20**	**171**	**12**	**4**	**2**	**6**	**12**
1993-94	**Vancouver**	**NHL**	**55**	**1**	**10**	**11**	**72**	**24**	**1**	**7**	**8**	**22**
1994-95	**Vancouver**	**NHL**	**22**	**1**	**3**	**4**	**15**	....	....	....	....	....
	Chicago	**NHL**	**13**	**1**	**0**	**1**	**48**	**16**	**1**	**3**	**4**	**22**
1995-96	**Hartford**	**NHL**	**79**	**1**	**9**	**10**	**88**	....	....	....	....	....
1996-97	**Hartford**	**NHL**	**56**	**1**	**10**	**11**	**40**	....	....	....	....	....
	Phoenix	**NHL**	**11**	**1**	**2**	**3**	**23**	**7**	**0**	**0**	**0**	**10**
	NHL Totals		**770**	**48**	**141**	**189**	**1371**	**95**	**8**	**13**	**21**	**176**

Traded to **Montreal** by **NY Islanders** for Craig Ludwig, September 4, 1990. Traded to **Vancouver** by **Montreal** for Vancouver's fourth round choice (Vladimir Vujtek) in 1991 Entry Draft, January 12, 1991. Traded to **Chicago** by **Vancouver** for Bogdan Savenko and Hartford's third round choice (previously acquired by Chicago — Vancouver selected Larry Courville) in 1995 Entry Draft, April 7, 1995. Signed as a free agent by **Hartford**, August 24, 1995. Traded to **Phoenix** by **Hartford** for Chris Murray, March 18, 1997.

DiMAIO, ROB (duh-MIGH-oh) BOS.

Center. Shoots right. 5'10", 190 lbs. Born, Calgary, Alta., February 19, 1968.
(NY Islanders' 6th choice, 118th overall, in 1987 Entry Draft).

			Regular Season					Playoffs				
Season	Club	Lea	GP	G	A	TP	PIM	GP	G	A	TP	PIM
1986-87	Medicine Hat	WHL	70	27	43	70	130	20	7	11	18	46
1987-88a	Medicine Hat	WHL	54	47	43	90	120	14	12	19	*31	59
1988-89	**NY Islanders**	**NHL**	**16**	**1**	**0**	**1**	**30**	....	....	....	....	....
	Springfield	AHL	40	13	18	31	67	....	....	....	....	....
1989-90	**NY Islanders**	**NHL**	**7**	**0**	**0**	**0**	**2**	**1**	**1**	**0**	**1**	**4**
	Springfield	AHL	54	25	27	52	69	16	4	7	11	45
1990-91	**NY Islanders**	**NHL**	**1**	**0**	**0**	**0**	**0**	....	....	....	....	....
	Capital Dist.	AHL	12	3	4	7	22	....	....	....	....	....
1991-92	**NY Islanders**	**NHL**	**50**	**5**	**2**	**7**	**43**	....	....	....	....	....
1992-93	**Tampa Bay**	**NHL**	**54**	**9**	**15**	**24**	**62**	....	....	....	....	....
1993-94	**Tampa Bay**	**NHL**	**39**	**8**	**7**	**15**	**40**	....	....	....	....	....
	Philadelphia	**NHL**	**14**	**3**	**5**	**8**	**6**	....	....	....	....	....
1994-95	**Philadelphia**	**NHL**	**36**	**3**	**1**	**4**	**53**	**15**	**2**	**4**	**6**	**4**
1995-96	**Philadelphia**	**NHL**	**59**	**6**	**15**	**21**	**58**	**3**	**0**	**0**	**0**	**0**
1996-97	**Boston**	**NHL**	**72**	**13**	**15**	**28**	**82**	....	....	....	....	....
	NHL Totals		**348**	**48**	**60**	**108**	**376**	**19**	**3**	**4**	**7**	**8**

a Won Stafford Smythe Memorial Trophy (Memorial Cup Tournament MVP) (1988)

Claimed by **Tampa Bay** from **NY Islanders** in Expansion Draft, June 18, 1992. Traded to **Philadelphia** by **Tampa Bay** for Jim Cummins and Philadelphia's fourth round choice in 1995 Entry Draft, March 18, 1994. Claimed by **San Jose** from **Philadelphia** in NHL Waiver Draft, September 30, 1996. Traded to **Boston** by **San Jose** for Boston's fifth round choice (Adam Nittel) in 1997 Entry Draft, September 30, 1996.

DINEEN, GORD

Defense. Shoots right. 6', 195 lbs.   Born, Quebec City, Que., September 21, 1962.
(NY Islanders' 2nd choice, 42nd overall, in 1981 Entry Draft).

			Regular Season					Playoffs				
Season	Club	Lea	GP	G	A	TP	PIM	GP	G	A	TP	PIM
1980-81	S.S. Marie	OHA	68	4	26	30	158	19	1	7	8	58
1981-82	S.S. Marie	OHL	68	9	45	54	185	13	1	2	3	52
1982-83	**NY Islanders**	**NHL**	**2**	**0**	**0**	**0**	**4**	....	....	....	....	....
abc	Indianapolis	CHL	73	10	47	57	78	13	2	10	12	29
1983-84	**NY Islanders**	**NHL**	**43**	**1**	**11**	**12**	**32**	9	1	1	2	28
	Indianapolis	CHL	26	4	13	17	63	....	....	....	....	....
1984-85	**NY Islanders**	**NHL**	**48**	**1**	**12**	**13**	**89**	10	0	0	0	26
	Springfield	AHL	25	1	8	9	46	....	....	....	....	....
1985-86	**NY Islanders**	**NHL**	**57**	**1**	**8**	**9**	**81**	3	0	0	0	2
	Springfield	AHL	11	2	3	5	20	....	....	....	....	....
1986-87	**NY Islanders**	**NHL**	**71**	**4**	**10**	**14**	**110**	7	0	4	4	4
1987-88	**NY Islanders**	**NHL**	**57**	**4**	**12**	**16**	**62**	....	....	....	....	....
	Minnesota	**NHL**	**13**	**1**	**1**	**2**	**21**	....	....	....	....	....
1988-89	**Minnesota**	**NHL**	**2**	**0**	**1**	**1**	**2**	....	....	....	....	....
	Kalamazoo	IHL	25	2	6	8	49	....	....	....	....	....
	Pittsburgh	**NHL**	**38**	**1**	**2**	**3**	**42**	11	0	2	2	8
1989-90	**Pittsburgh**	**NHL**	**69**	**1**	**8**	**9**	**125**	....	....	....	....	....
1990-91	**Pittsburgh**	**NHL**	**9**	**0**	**0**	**0**	**4**	....	....	....	....	....
	Muskegon	IHL	40	1	14	15	57	5	0	2	2	0
1991-92	**Pittsburgh**	**NHL**	**1**	**0**	**0**	**0**	**0**	....	....	....	....	....
d	Muskegon	IHL	79	8	37	45	83	14	2	4	6	33
1992-93	**Ottawa**	**NHL**	**32**	**2**	**4**	**6**	**30**	....	....	....	....	....
	San Diego	IHL	41	6	23	29	36	....	....	....	....	....
1993-94	**Ottawa**	**NHL**	**77**	**0**	**21**	**21**	**89**	....	....	....	....	....
	San Diego	IHL	3	0	0	0	2	....	....	....	....	....
1994-95	Denver	IHL	68	5	27	32	75	17	1	6	7	8
	NY Islanders	**NHL**	**9**	**0**	**0**	**0**	**2**	....	....	....	....	....
1995-96	Utah	IHL	82	1	17	18	89	22	0	3	3	14
1996-97	Utah	IHL	81	5	29	34	62	7	0	3	3	4
	NHL Totals		**528**	**16**	**90**	**106**	**693**	**40**	**1**	**7**	**8**	**68**

a   CHL First All-Star Team (1983)
b   Won Bob Gassoff Trophy (CHL's Most Improved Defenseman) (1983)
c   Won Bobby Orr Trophy (CHL's Top Defenseman) (1983)
d   IHL First All-Star Team (1992)

Traded to **Minnesota** by **NY Islanders** for Chris Pryor and future considerations, March 8, 1988. Traded to **Pittsburgh** by **Minnesota** with Scott Bjugstad for Ville Siren and Steve Gotaas, December 17, 1988. Signed as a free agent by **Ottawa**, August 31, 1992. Signed as a free agent by **NY Islanders**, July 26, 1994.

DINEEN, KEVIN   CAR.

Right wing. Shoots right. 5'11", 190 lbs.   Born, Quebec City, Que., October 28, 1963.
(Hartford's 3rd choice, 56th overall, in 1982 Entry Draft).

			Regular Season					Playoffs				
Season	Club	Lea	GP	G	A	TP	PIM	GP	G	A	TP	PIM
1981-82	U. of Denver	WCHA	26	10	10	20	70	....	....	....	....	....
1982-83	U. of Denver	WCHA	36	16	13	29	108	....	....	....	....	....
1983-84	Cdn. National	....	52	5	11	16	2	....	....	....	....	....
	Cdn Olympic	....	7	0	0	0	0	....	....	....	....	....
1984-85	**Hartford**	**NHL**	**57**	**25**	**16**	**41**	**120**	....	....	....	....	....
	Binghamton	AHL	25	15	8	23	41	....	....	....	....	....
1985-86	**Hartford**	**NHL**	**57**	**33**	**35**	**68**	**124**	10	6	7	13	18
1986-87	**Hartford**	**NHL**	**78**	**40**	**39**	**79**	**110**	6	2	1	3	31
1987-88	**Hartford**	**NHL**	**74**	**25**	**25**	**50**	**217**	6	4	4	8	8
1988-89	**Hartford**	**NHL**	**79**	**45**	**44**	**89**	**167**	4	1	0	1	10
1989-90	**Hartford**	**NHL**	**67**	**25**	**41**	**66**	**164**	6	3	2	5	18
1990-91a	**Hartford**	**NHL**	**61**	**17**	**30**	**47**	**104**	6	1	0	1	16
1991-92	**Hartford**	**NHL**	**16**	**4**	**2**	**6**	**23**	....	....	....	....	....
	Philadelphia	**NHL**	**64**	**26**	**30**	**56**	**130**	....	....	....	....	....
1992-93	**Philadelphia**	**NHL**	**83**	**35**	**28**	**63**	**201**	....	....	....	....	....
1993-94	**Philadelphia**	**NHL**	**71**	**19**	**23**	**42**	**113**	....	....	....	....	....
1994-95	Houston	IHL	17	6	4	10	42	....	....	....	....	....
	Philadelphia	**NHL**	**40**	**8**	**5**	**13**	**39**	15	6	4	10	18
1995-96	**Philadelphia**	**NHL**	**26**	**0**	**2**	**2**	**50**	....	....	....	....	....
	Hartford	**NHL**	**20**	**2**	**7**	**9**	**67**	....	....	....	....	....
1996-97	**Hartford**	**NHL**	**78**	**19**	**29**	**48**	**141**	....	....	....	....	....
	NHL Totals		**871**	**323**	**356**	**679**	**1770**	**53**	**23**	**18**	**41**	**119**

a   Won Bud Light/NHL Man of the Year Award (1991)
Played in NHL All-Star Game (1988, 1989)

Traded to **Philadelphia** by **Hartford** for Murray Craven and Philadelphia's fourth round choice (Kevin Smyth) in 1992 Entry Draft, November 13, 1991. Traded to **Hartford** by **Philadelphia** for a conditional choice in 1997 Entry Draft, December 28, 1995.

DINGMAN, CHRIS   CGY.

Left wing. Shoots left. 6'4", 225 lbs.   Born, Edmonton, Alta., July 6, 1976.
(Calgary's 1st choice, 19th overall, in 1994 Entry Draft).

			Regular Season					Playoffs				
Season	Club	Lea	GP	G	A	TP	PIM	GP	G	A	TP	PIM
1992-93	Brandon	WHL	50	10	17	27	64	4	0	0	0	0
1993-94	Brandon	WHL	45	21	20	41	77	13	1	7	8	39
1994-95	Brandon	WHL	66	40	43	83	201	3	1	0	1	9
1995-96	Brandon	WHL	40	16	29	45	109	19	12	11	23	60
	Saint John	AHL	....	....	....	....	....	1	0	0	0	0
1996-97	Saint John	AHL	71	5	6	11	195	....	....	....	....	....

DIONNE, GILBERT   (dee-AHN, ZHIHL-bair)

Left wing. Shoots left. 6', 194 lbs.   Born, Drummondville, Que., September 19, 1970.
(Montreal's 5th choice, 81st overall, in 1990 Entry Draft).

			Regular Season					Playoffs				
Season	Club	Lea	GP	G	A	TP	PIM	GP	G	A	TP	PIM
1988-89	Kitchener	OHL	66	11	33	44	13	5	1	1	2	4
1989-90	Kitchener	OHL	64	48	57	105	85	17	13	10	23	22
1990-91	**Montreal**	**NHL**	**2**	**0**	**0**	**0**	**0**	....	....	....	....	....
	Fredericton	AHL	77	40	47	87	62	9	6	5	11	8
1991-92a	**Montreal**	**NHL**	**39**	**21**	**13**	**34**	**10**	11	3	4	7	10
	Fredericton	AHL	29	19	27	46	20	....	....	....	....	....
1992-93	**Montreal**	**NHL**	**75**	**20**	**28**	**48**	**63**	20	6	6	12	20 ◆
	Fredericton	AHL	3	4	3	7	0	....	....	....	....	....
1993-94	**Montreal**	**NHL**	**74**	**19**	**26**	**45**	**31**	5	1	2	3	0
1994-95	**Montreal**	**NHL**	**6**	**0**	**3**	**3**	**2**	....	....	....	....	....
	Philadelphia	**NHL**	**20**	**0**	**6**	**6**	**2**	3	0	0	0	4
1995-96	**Philadelphia**	**NHL**	**2**	**0**	**1**	**1**	**0**	....	....	....	....	....
	Florida	**NHL**	**5**	**1**	**2**	**3**	**0**	....	....	....	....	....
b	Carolina	AHL	55	43	58	101	29	....	....	....	....	....
1996-97	Carolina	AHL	72	41	47	88	69	....	....	....	....	....
	NHL Totals		**223**	**61**	**79**	**140**	**108**	**39**	**10**	**12**	**22**	**34**

a   NHL/Upper Deck All-Rookie Team (1992)
b   AHL Second All-Star Team (1996)

Traded to **Philadelphia** by **Montreal** with Eric Desjardins and John LeClair for Mark Recchi and Philadelphia's third round choice (Martin Hohenberger) in 1995 Entry draft, February 9, 1995. Signed as a free agent by **Florida**, January 29, 1996.

DI PIETRO, PAUL   (dee-pee-AY-troh)

Center. Shoots right. 5'9", 181 lbs.   Born, Sault Ste. Marie, Ont., September 8, 1970.
(Montreal's 6th choice, 102nd overall, in 1990 Entry Draft).

			Regular Season					Playoffs				
Season	Club	Lea	GP	G	A	TP	PIM	GP	G	A	TP	PIM
1986-87	Sudbury	OHL	49	5	11	16	13	....	....	....	....	....
1987-88	Sudbury	OHL	63	25	42	67	27	....	....	....	....	....
1988-89	Sudbury	OHL	57	31	48	79	27	....	....	....	....	....
1989-90	Sudbury	OHL	66	56	63	119	57	7	3	6	9	7
1990-91	Fredericton	AHL	78	39	31	70	38	9	5	6	11	2
1991-92	**Montreal**	**NHL**	**33**	**4**	**6**	**10**	**25**	....	....	....	....	....
	Fredericton	AHL	43	26	31	57	52	7	3	4	7	8
1992-93	**Montreal**	**NHL**	**29**	**4**	**13**	**17**	**14**	17	8	5	13	8 ◆
	Fredericton	AHL	26	8	16	24	16	....	....	....	....	....
1993-94	**Montreal**	**NHL**	**70**	**13**	**20**	**33**	**37**	7	2	4	6	2
1994-95	**Montreal**	**NHL**	**22**	**4**	**5**	**9**	**4**	....	....	....	....	....
	Toronto	**NHL**	**12**	**1**	**1**	**2**	**6**	7	1	1	2	0
1995-96	**Toronto**	**NHL**	**20**	**4**	**4**	**8**	**4**	....	....	....	....	....
	St. John's	AHL	2	2	2	4	0	....	....	....	....	....
	Houston	IHL	36	18	23	41	44	....	....	....	....	....
	Las Vegas	IHL	13	5	6	11	10	13	4	8	12	16
1996-97	**Los Angeles**	**NHL**	**6**	**1**	**0**	**1**	**6**	....	....	....	....	....
	Phoenix	IHL	33	9	20	29	32	....	....	....	....	....
	Cincinnati	IHL	32	15	14	29	28	3	1	1	2	2
	NHL Totals		**192**	**31**	**49**	**80**	**96**	**31**	**11**	**10**	**21**	**10**

Traded to **Toronto** by **Montreal** for a conditional fourth round draft choice (Phoenix's 1996 choice - previously acquired by Toronto - Montreal selected Kim Staal), April 6, 1995. Signed as a free agent by **Los Angeles**, July 23, 1996.

DIRK, ROBERT

Defense. Shoots left. 6'4", 210 lbs.   Born, Regina, Sask., August 20, 1966.
(St. Louis' 4th choice, 53rd overall, in 1984 Entry Draft).

			Regular Season					Playoffs				
Season	Club	Lea	GP	G	A	TP	PIM	GP	G	A	TP	PIM
1982-83	Regina	WHL	1	0	0	0	0	....	....	....	....	....
1983-84	Regina	WHL	62	2	10	12	64	23	1	12	13	24
1984-85	Regina	WHL	69	10	34	44	97	8	0	0	0	4
1985-86	Regina	WHL	72	19	60	79	140	10	3	5	8	8
1986-87	Peoria	IHL	76	5	17	22	155	....	....	....	....	....
1987-88	**St. Louis**	**NHL**	**7**	**0**	**1**	**1**	**16**	6	0	1	1	2
	Peoria	IHL	54	4	21	25	126	....	....	....	....	....
1988-89	**St. Louis**	**NHL**	**9**	**0**	**1**	**1**	**11**	....	....	....	....	....
	Peoria	IHL	22	0	2	2	54	....	....	....	....	....
1989-90	**St. Louis**	**NHL**	**37**	**1**	**1**	**2**	**128**	3	0	0	0	0
	Peoria	IHL	24	1	2	3	79	....	....	....	....	....
1990-91	**St. Louis**	**NHL**	**41**	**1**	**3**	**4**	**100**	....	....	....	....	....
	Peoria	IHL	3	0	0	0	2	....	....	....	....	....
	Vancouver	**NHL**	**11**	**1**	**0**	**1**	**20**	6	0	0	0	13
1991-92	**Vancouver**	**NHL**	**72**	**2**	**7**	**9**	**126**	13	0	0	0	20
1992-93	**Vancouver**	**NHL**	**69**	**4**	**8**	**12**	**150**	9	0	0	0	6
1993-94	**Vancouver**	**NHL**	**65**	**2**	**3**	**5**	**105**	....	....	....	....	....
	Chicago	**NHL**	**6**	**0**	**0**	**0**	**26**	2	0	0	0	15
1994-95	**Anaheim**	**NHL**	**38**	**1**	**3**	**4**	**56**	....	....	....	....	....
1995-96	**Anaheim**	**NHL**	**44**	**1**	**2**	**3**	**42**	....	....	....	....	....
	Montreal	**NHL**	**3**	**0**	**0**	**0**	**6**	....	....	....	....	....
1996-97	Detroit	IHL	48	2	8	10	36	....	....	....	....	....
	Chicago	IHL	31	1	5	6	26	3	0	0	0	0
	NHL Totals		**402**	**13**	**29**	**42**	**786**	**39**	**0**	**1**	**1**	**56**

Traded to **Vancouver** by **St. Louis** with Geoff Courtnall, Sergio Momesso, Cliff Ronning and St. Louis' fifth round choice (Brian Loney) in 1992 Entry Draft for Dan Quinn and Garth Butcher, March 5, 1991. Traded to **Chicago** by **Vancouver** for Chicago's fourth round choice (Mike Dubinsky) in 1994 Entry Draft, March 21, 1994. Traded to **Anaheim** by **Chicago** for Tampa Bay's fourth round choice (previously acquired by Anaheim — Chicago selected Chris Van Dyk) in 1995 Entry Draft, July 12, 1994. Traded to **Montreal** by **Anaheim** for Jim Campbell, January 21, 1996.

DIROBERTO, TORREY   (DIH-raw-buhr-toh)   BUF.

Center. Shoots left. 5'11", 180 lbs.   Born, New York, NY, April 17, 1978.
(Buffalo's 6th choice, 128th overall, in 1997 Entry Draft).

			Regular Season					Playoffs				
Season	Club	Lea	GP	G	A	TP	PIM	GP	G	A	TP	PIM
1995-96	Seattle	WHL	70	16	19	35	118	5	0	2	2	8
1996-97	Seattle	WHL	72	37	44	81	91	15	9	5	14	8

DOAN, SHANE (DOHN) PHO.

Right wing. Shoots right. 6'1", 215 lbs. Born, Halkirk, Alta., October 10, 1976.
(Winnipeg's 1st choice, 7th overall, in 1995 Entry Draft).

			Regular Season					Playoffs				
Season	**Club**	**Lea**	**GP**	**G**	**A**	**TP**	**PIM**	**GP**	**G**	**A**	**TP**	**PIM**
1992-93	Kamloops	WHL	51	7	12	19	65	13	0	1	1	8
1993-94	Kamloops	WHL	52	24	24	48	88	....	....	....	....	....
1994-95ab	Kamloops	WHL	71	37	57	94	106	21	6	10	16	16
1995-96	**Winnipeg**	**NHL**	**74**	**7**	**10**	**17**	**101**	**6**	**0**	**0**	**0**	**6**
1996-97	**Phoenix**	**NHL**	**63**	**4**	**8**	**12**	**49**	**4**	**0**	**0**	**0**	**2**
	NHL Totals		**137**	**11**	**18**	**29**	**150**	**10**	**0**	**0**	**0**	**8**

a Memorial Cup All-Star Team (1995)
b Won Stafford Smythe Memorial Trophy (Memorial Cup Tournament MVP) (1995)

DOIG, JASON (DOHYG) PHO.

Defense. Shoots right. 6'3", 216 lbs. Born, Montreal, Que., January 29, 1977.
(Winnipeg's 3rd choice, 34th overall, in 1995 Entry Draft).

			Regular Season					Playoffs				
Season	**Club**	**Lea**	**GP**	**G**	**A**	**TP**	**PIM**	**GP**	**G**	**A**	**TP**	**PIM**
1993-94	St-Jean	QMJHL	63	8	17	25	65	5	0	2	2	2
1994-95	Laval	QMJHL	55	13	42	55	259	20	4	13	17	39
1995-96	**Winnipeg**	**NHL**	**15**	**1**	**1**	**2**	**28**	....	....	....	....	....
	Laval	QMJHL	5	3	6	9	20	....	....	....	....	....
a	Granby	QMJHL	24	4	30	34	91	20	10	22	32	*110
	Springfield	AHL	5	0	0	0	28	....	....	....	....	....
1996-97	Granby	QMJHL	39	14	33	47	211	5	0	4	4	27
	Springfield	AHL	5	0	3	3	2	17	1	4	5	37
	Las Vegas	IHL	6	0	1	1	19	....	....	....	....	....
	NHL Totals		**15**	**1**	**1**	**2**	**28**	....	....	....	....	....

a Memorial Cup All-Star Team (1996)

DOLLAS, BOBBY (DAW-luhs) ANA.

Defense. Shoots left. 6'2", 212 lbs. Born, Montreal, Que., January 31, 1965.
(Winnipeg's 2nd choice, 14th overall, in 1983 Entry Draft).

			Regular Season					Playoffs				
Season	**Club**	**Lea**	**GP**	**G**	**A**	**TP**	**PIM**	**GP**	**G**	**A**	**TP**	**PIM**
1940-41	Kansas City	AHA	24	5	8	13	12	....	....	....	....	....
1982-83a	Laval	QMJHL	63	16	45	61	144	11	5	5	10	23
1983-84	**Winnipeg**	**NHL**	**1**	**0**	**0**	**0**	**0**	....	....	....	....	....
	Laval	QMJHL	54	12	33	45	80	14	1	8	9	23
1984-85	**Winnipeg**	**NHL**	**9**	**0**	**0**	**0**	**0**	....	....	....	....	....
	Sherbrooke	AHL	8	1	3	4	4	17	3	6	9	17
1985-86	**Winnipeg**	**NHL**	**46**	**0**	**5**	**5**	**66**	**3**	**0**	**0**	**0**	**2**
	Sherbrooke	AHL	25	4	7	11	29	....	....	....	....	....
1986-87	Sherbrooke	AHL	75	6	18	24	87	16	2	4	6	13
1987-88	**Quebec**	**NHL**	**9**	**0**	**0**	**0**	**2**	....	....	....	....	....
	Moncton	AHL	26	4	10	14	20	....	....	....	....	....
	Fredericton	AHL	33	4	8	12	27	15	2	2	4	24
1988-89	**Quebec**	**NHL**	**16**	**0**	**3**	**3**	**16**	....	....	....	....	....
	Halifax	AHL	57	5	19	24	65	4	1	0	1	14
1989-90	Cdn. National	....	68	8	29	37	60	....	....	....	....	....
1990-91	**Detroit**	**NHL**	**56**	**3**	**5**	**8**	**20**	**7**	**1**	**0**	**1**	**13**
1991-92	**Detroit**	**NHL**	**27**	**3**	**1**	**4**	**20**	**2**	**0**	**1**	**1**	**0**
	Adirondack	AHL	19	1	6	7	33	18	7	4	11	22
1992-93	**Detroit**	**NHL**	**6**	**0**	**0**	**0**	**2**	....	....	....	....	....
c	Adirondack	AHL	64	7	36	43	54	11	3	8	11	8
1993-94	**Anaheim**	**NHL**	**77**	**9**	**11**	**20**	**55**	....	....	....	....	....
1994-95	**Anaheim**	**NHL**	**45**	**7**	**13**	**20**	**12**	....	....	....	....	....
1995-96	**Anaheim**	**NHL**	**82**	**8**	**22**	**30**	**64**	....	....	....	....	....
1996-97	**Anaheim**	**NHL**	**79**	**4**	**14**	**18**	**55**	**11**	**0**	**0**	**0**	**4**
	NHL Totals		**453**	**34**	**74**	**108**	**312**	**23**	**1**	**1**	**2**	**19**

a QMJHL Second All-Star Team (1983)
b Won Eddie Shore Plaque (AHL's Outstanding Defenseman) (1993)
c AHL First All-Star Team (1993)

Traded to **Quebec** by **Winnipeg** for Stu Kulak, December 17, 1987. Signed as a free agent by **Detroit**, October 18, 1990. Claimed by **Anaheim** from **Detroit** in Expansion Draft, June 24, 1993.

DOME, ROBERT (doh-MAY) PIT.

Right wing. Shoots left. 6', 214 lbs. Born, Skalica, Czech., January 29, 1979.
(Pittsburgh's 1st choice, 17th overall, in 1997 Entry Draft).

			Regular Season					Playoffs				
Season	**Club**	**Lea**	**GP**	**G**	**A**	**TP**	**PIM**	**GP**	**G**	**A**	**TP**	**PIM**
1995-96	Utah	IHL	56	10	9	19	28	....	....	....	....	....
1996-97	Long Beach	IHL	13	4	6	10	14	....	....	....	....	....
	Las Vegas	IHL	43	10	7	17	22	....	....	....	....	....

DOMENICHELLI, HNAT (daw-mehn-ih-CHEHL-ee, NAT) CGY.

Center. Shoots left. 6', 175 lbs. Born, Edmonton, Alta., February 17, 1976.
(Hartford's 2nd choice, 83rd overall, in 1994 Entry Draft).

			Regular Season					Playoffs				
Season	**Club**	**Lea**	**GP**	**G**	**A**	**TP**	**PIM**	**GP**	**G**	**A**	**TP**	**PIM**
1992-93	Kamloops	WHL	45	12	8	20	15	11	1	1	2	2
1993-94	Kamloops	WHL	69	27	40	67	31	19	10	12	22	0
1994-95a	Kamloops	WHL	72	52	62	114	34	19	9	9	18	9
1995-96bc	Kamloops	WHL	62	59	89	148	37	16	7	9	16	29
1996-97	**Hartford**	**NHL**	**13**	**2**	**1**	**3**	**7**	....	....	....	....	....
	Springfield	AHL	39	24	24	48	12	....	....	....	....	....
	Calgary	**NHL**	**10**	**1**	**2**	**3**	**2**	....	....	....	....	....
	Saint John	AHL	1	1	1	2	0	5	5	0	5	2
	NHL Totals		**23**	**3**	**3**	**6**	**9**	....	....	....	....	....

a WHL West Second All-Star Team (1995)
b WHL West First All-Star Team (1996)
c Canadian Major Junior First All-Star Team (1996)

Traded to **Calgary** by **Hartford** with Glen Featherstone, New Jersey's second round choice (previously acquired by Hartford — Calgary selected Dimitri Kokorev) in 1997 Entry Draft and Vancouver's third round choice (previously acquired by Hartford) in 1998 Entry Draft for Steve Chiasson and Colorado's third round choice (previously acquired by Calgary — Carolina selected Francis Lessard) in 1997 Entry Draft, March 5, 1997.

DOMI, TIE (DOH-mee) TOR.

Right wing. Shoots right. 5'10", 200 lbs. Born, Windsor, Ont., November 1, 1969.
(Toronto's 2nd choice, 27th overall, in 1988 Entry Draft).

			Regular Season					Playoffs				
Season	**Club**	**Lea**	**GP**	**G**	**A**	**TP**	**PIM**	**GP**	**G**	**A**	**TP**	**PIM**
1986-87	Peterborough	OHL	18	1	1	2	79	....	....	....	....	....
1987-88	Peterborough	OHL	60	22	21	43	292	12	3	9	12	24
1988-89	Peterborough	OHL	43	14	16	30	175	17	10	9	19	70
1989-90	**Toronto**	**NHL**	**2**	**0**	**0**	**0**	**42**	....	....	....	....	....
	Newmarket	AHL	57	14	11	25	285	....	....	....	....	....
1990-91	**NY Rangers**	**NHL**	**28**	**1**	**0**	**1**	**185**	....	....	....	....	....
	Binghamton	AHL	25	11	6	17	219	7	3	2	5	16
1991-92	**NY Rangers**	**NHL**	**42**	**2**	**4**	**6**	**246**	**6**	**1**	**1**	**2**	**32**
1992-93	**NY Rangers**	**NHL**	**12**	**2**	**0**	**2**	**95**	....	....	....	....	....
	Winnipeg	**NHL**	**49**	**3**	**10**	**13**	**249**	**6**	**1**	**0**	**1**	**23**
1993-94	**Winnipeg**	**NHL**	**81**	**8**	**11**	**19**	***347**	....	....	....	....	....
1994-95	**Winnipeg**	**NHL**	**31**	**4**	**4**	**8**	**128**	....	....	....	....	....
	Toronto	**NHL**	**9**	**0**	**1**	**1**	**31**	**7**	**1**	**0**	**1**	**0**
1995-96	**Toronto**	**NHL**	**72**	**7**	**6**	**13**	**297**	**6**	**0**	**2**	**2**	**4**
1996-97	**Toronto**	**NHL**	**80**	**11**	**17**	**28**	**275**	....	....	....	....	....
	NHL Totals		**406**	**38**	**53**	**91**	**1895**	**25**	**3**	**3**	**6**	**59**

Traded to **NY Rangers** by **Toronto** with Mark LaForest for Greg Johnston, June 28, 1990. Traded to **Winnipeg** by **NY Rangers** with Kris King for Ed Olczyk, December 28, 1992. Traded to **Toronto** by **Winnipeg** for Mike Eastwood and Toronto's third round choice (Brad Isbister) in 1995 Entry Draft, April 7, 1995.

DONATO, TED (duh-NAH-toh) BOS.

Left wing. Shoots left. 5'10", 183 lbs. Born, Boston, MA, April 28, 1969.
(Boston's 6th choice, 98th overall, in 1987 Entry Draft).

			Regular Season					Playoffs				
Season	**Club**	**Lea**	**GP**	**G**	**A**	**TP**	**PIM**	**GP**	**G**	**A**	**TP**	**PIM**
1987-88	Harvard	ECAC	28	12	14	26	24	....	....	....	....	....
1988-89	Harvard	ECAC	34	14	37	51	30	....	....	....	....	....
1989-90	Harvard	ECAC	16	5	6	11	34	....	....	....	....	....
1990-91a	Harvard	ECAC	27	19	*37	56	26	....	....	....	....	....
1991-92	U.S. National	....	52	11	22	33	24	....	....	....	....	....
	U.S. Olympic	....	8	4	3	7	8	....	....	....	....	....
	Boston	**NHL**	**10**	**1**	**2**	**3**	**8**	**15**	**3**	**4**	**7**	**4**
1992-93	**Boston**	**NHL**	**82**	**15**	**20**	**35**	**61**	**4**	**0**	**1**	**1**	....
1993-94	**Boston**	**NHL**	**84**	**22**	**32**	**54**	**59**	**13**	**4**	**2**	**6**	**10**
1994-95	TuTo	Fin.	14	5	5	10	47	....	....	....	....	....
	Boston	**NHL**	**47**	**10**	**10**	**20**	**10**	**5**	**0**	**0**	**0**	**4**
1995-96	**Boston**	**NHL**	**82**	**23**	**26**	**49**	**46**	**5**	**1**	**2**	**3**	**2**
1996-97	**Boston**	**NHL**	**67**	**25**	**26**	**51**	**37**	....	....	....	....	....
	NHL Totals		**372**	**96**	**116**	**212**	**221**	**42**	**8**	**9**	**17**	**20**

a ECAC First All-Star Team (1991)

DONNELLY, GORD

Defense. Shoots right. 6'1", 202 lbs. Born, Montreal, Que., April 5, 1962.
(St. Louis' 3rd choice, 62nd overall, in 1981 Entry Draft).

			Regular Season					Playoffs				
Season	**Club**	**Lea**	**GP**	**G**	**A**	**TP**	**PIM**	**GP**	**G**	**A**	**TP**	**PIM**
1980-81	Sherbrooke	QMJHL	67	15	23	38	252	14	1	2	3	35
1981-82	Sherbrooke	QMJHL	60	8	41	49	250	22	2	7	9	106
1982-83	Salt Lake	CHL	67	3	12	15	222	6	1	1	2	8
1983-84	**Quebec**	**NHL**	**38**	**0**	**5**	**5**	**60**	....	....	....	....	....
	Fredericton	AHL	30	2	3	5	146	7	1	1	2	43
1984-85	**Quebec**	**NHL**	**22**	**0**	**0**	**0**	**33**	....	....	....	....	....
	Fredericton	AHL	42	1	5	6	134	6	0	1	1	25
1985-86	**Quebec**	**NHL**	**36**	**2**	**2**	**4**	**85**	**1**	**0**	**0**	**0**	**0**
	Fredericton	AHL	38	3	5	8	103	5	0	0	0	33
1986-87	**Quebec**	**NHL**	**38**	**0**	**2**	**2**	**143**	**13**	**0**	**0**	**0**	**53**
1987-88	**Quebec**	**NHL**	**63**	**4**	**3**	**7**	**301**	....	....	....	....	....
1988-89	**Quebec**	**NHL**	**16**	**4**	**0**	**4**	**46**	....	....	....	....	....
	Winnipeg	**NHL**	**57**	**6**	**10**	**16**	**228**	....	....	....	....	....
1989-90	**Winnipeg**	**NHL**	**55**	**3**	**3**	**6**	**222**	**6**	**0**	**1**	**1**	**8**
1990-91	**Winnipeg**	**NHL**	**57**	**3**	**4**	**7**	**265**	....	....	....	....	....
1991-92	**Winnipeg**	**NHL**	**4**	**0**	**0**	**0**	**11**	....	....	....	....	....
	Buffalo	**NHL**	**67**	**2**	**3**	**5**	**305**	**6**	**0**	**1**	**1**	**0**
1992-93	**Buffalo**	**NHL**	**60**	**3**	**8**	**11**	**221**	....	....	....	....	....
1993-94	**Buffalo**	**NHL**	**7**	**0**	**0**	**0**	**31**	....	....	....	....	....
	Dallas	**NHL**	**18**	**0**	**1**	**1**	**66**	....	....	....	....	....
1994-95	Kalamazoo	IHL	7	2	2	4	18	....	....	....	....	....
	Dallas	**NHL**	**16**	**1**	**0**	**1**	**52**	....	....	....	....	....
1995-96	Houston	IHL	73	3	4	7	333	....	....	....	....	....
1996-97	Houston	IHL	5	0	0	0	25	....	....	....	....	....
	Chicago	IHL	59	3	5	8	144	4	0	2	2	28
	NHL Totals		**554**	**28**	**41**	**69**	**2069**	**26**	**0**	**2**	**2**	**61**

Rights transferred to **Quebec** by **St. Louis** with rights to Claude Julien when St. Louis signed Jacques Demers as coach, August 19, 1983. Traded to **Winnipeg** by **Quebec** for Mario Marois, December 6, 1988. Traded to **Buffalo** by **Winnipeg** with Dave McLlwain, Winnipeg's fifth round choice (Yuri Khmylev) in 1992 Entry Draft and future considerations for Darrin Shannon, Mike Hartman and Dean Kennedy, October 11, 1991. Traded to **Dallas** by **Buffalo** for James Black and Dallas' seventh round choice (Steve Webb) in 1994 Entry Draft, December 15, 1993.

DONNELLY, MIKE

Left wing. Shoots left. 5'11", 185 lbs. Born, Detroit, MI, October 10, 1963.

			Regular Season					Playoffs				
Season	Club	Lea	GP	G	A	TP	PIM	GP	G	A	TP	PIM
1982-83	Michigan State	CCHA	24	7	13	20	8	....	....	....	....	....
1983-84	Michigan State	CCHA	44	18	14	32	40	....	....	....	....	....
1984-85	Michigan State	CCHA	44	26	21	47	48	....	....	....	....	....
1985-86ab	Michigan State	CCHA	44	*59	38	97	65	....	....	....	....	....
1986-87	NY Rangers	NHL	5	1	1	2	0	....	....	....	....	....
	New Haven	AHL	58	27	34	61	52	7	2	0	2	9
1987-88	NY Rangers	NHL	17	2	2	4	8	....	....	....	....	....
	Colorado	IHL	8	7	11	18	15	....	....	....	....	....
	Buffalo	NHL	40	6	8	14	44	....	....	....	....	....
1988-89	Buffalo	NHL	22	4	6	10	10	....	....	....	....	....
	Rochester	AHL	53	32	37	69	53	....	....	....	....	....
1989-90	Buffalo	NHL	12	1	2	3	8	....	....	....	....	....
	Rochester	AHL	68	43	55	98	71	16	*12	7	19	9
1990-91	Los Angeles	NHL	53	7	5	12	41	12	5	4	9	6
	New Haven	AHL	18	10	6	16	2	....	....	....	....	....
1991-92	Los Angeles	NHL	80	29	16	45	20	6	1	0	1	4
1992-93	Los Angeles	NHL	84	29	40	69	45	24	6	7	13	14
1993-94	Los Angeles	NHL	81	21	21	42	34	....	....	....	....	....
1994-95	Los Angeles	NHL	9	1	1	2	4	....	....	....	....	....
	Dallas	NHL	35	11	14	25	29	5	0	1	1	6
1995-96	Dallas	NHL	24	2	5	7	10	....	....	....	....	....
	Michigan	IHL	21	8	15	23	20	8	3	0	3	10
1996-97	NY Islanders	NHL	3	0	0	0	2	....	....	....	....	....
	Utah	IHL	14	7	2	9	33	....	....	....	....	....
	Detroit	IHL	19	4	4	8	12	....	....	....	....	....
	NHL Totals		**465**	**114**	**121**	**235**	**255**	**47**	**12**	**12**	**24**	**30**

a CCHA First All-Star Team (1986)
b NCAA West First All-American Team (1986)

Signed as a free agent by **NY Rangers**, August 15, 1986. Traded to **Buffalo** by **NY Rangers** with Rangers' fifth round choice (Alexander Mogilny) in 1988 Entry Draft for Paul Cyr and Buffalo's tenth round choice (Eric Fenton) in 1988 Entry Draft, December 31, 1987. Traded to **Los Angeles** by **Buffalo** for Mikko Makela, September 30, 1990. Traded to **Dallas** by **Los Angeles** with Los Angeles' seventh round choice (Eoin McInerney) in 1996 Entry Draft for Dallas' fourth round choice (later traded to Washington — Washington selected Justin Davis) in 1996 Entry Draft, February 17, 1995. Signed as a free agent by **NY Islanders**, August 19, 1996.

DONOVAN, SHEAN — S.J.

Right wing. Shoots right. 6'2", 200 lbs. Born, Timmins, Ont., January 22, 1975.
(San Jose's 2nd choice, 28th overall, in 1993 Entry Draft).

			Regular Season					Playoffs				
Season	Club	Lea	GP	G	A	TP	PIM	GP	G	A	TP	PIM
1991-92	Ottawa	OHL	58	11	8	19	14	11	1	0	1	5
1992-93	Ottawa	OHL	66	29	23	52	33	....	....	....	....	....
1993-94	Ottawa	OHL	62	35	49	84	63	17	10	11	21	14
1994-95	Ottawa	OHL	29	22	19	41	41	....	....	....	....	....
	San Jose	NHL	14	0	0	0	6	7	0	1	1	6
	Kansas City	IHL	5	0	2	2	7	14	5	3	8	23
1995-96	San Jose	NHL	74	13	8	21	39	....	....	....	....	....
	Kansas City	IHL	4	0	0	0	8	5	0	0	0	8
1996-97	San Jose	NHL	73	9	6	15	42	....	....	....	....	....
	Kentucky	AHL	3	1	3	4	18	....	....	....	....	....
	NHL Totals		**161**	**22**	**14**	**36**	**87**	**7**	**0**	**1**	**1**	**6**

DOURIS, PETER — (DOOR-ihs) DAL.

Right wing. Shoots right. 6'1", 195 lbs. Born, Toronto, Ont., February 19, 1966.
(Winnipeg's 1st choice, 30th overall, in 1984 Entry Draft).

			Regular Season					Playoffs				
Season	Club	Lea	GP	G	A	TP	PIM	GP	G	A	TP	PIM
1983-84	N. Hampshire	ECAC	37	19	15	34	14	....	....	....	....	....
1984-85	N. Hampshire	H.E.	42	27	24	51	34	....	....	....	....	....
1985-86	Winnipeg	NHL	11	0	0	0	0	....	....	....	....	....
	Cdn. Olympic	....	33	16	7	23	18	....	....	....	....	....
1986-87	Winnipeg	NHL	6	0	0	0	0	....	....	....	....	....
	Sherbrooke	AHL	62	14	28	42	24	17	7	*15	*22	16
1987-88	Winnipeg	NHL	4	0	2	2	0	1	0	0	0	0
	Moncton	AHL	73	42	37	79	53	....	....	....	....	....
1988-89	Peoria	IHL	81	28	41	69	32	4	1	2	3	0
1989-90	Boston	NHL	36	5	6	11	15	8	0	1	1	8
	Maine	AHL	38	17	20	37	14	....	....	....	....	....
1990-91	Boston	NHL	39	5	2	7	9	7	0	1	1	6
	Maine	AHL	35	16	15	31	9	2	3	0	3	2
1991-92	Boston	NHL	54	10	13	23	10	7	2	3	5	0
	Maine	AHL	12	4	3	7	2	....	....	....	....	....
1992-93	Boston	NHL	19	4	4	8	4	4	1	0	1	0
	Providence	AHL	50	29	26	55	12	....	....	....	....	....
1993-94	Anaheim	NHL	74	12	22	34	21	....	....	....	....	....
1994-95	Anaheim	NHL	46	10	11	21	12	....	....	....	....	....
1995-96	Anaheim	NHL	31	8	7	15	9	....	....	....	....	....
1996-97	Milwaukee	IHL	80	36	36	72	14	3	2	2	4	2
	NHL Totals		**320**	**54**	**67**	**121**	**80**	**27**	**3**	**5**	**8**	**14**

Traded to **St. Louis** by **Winnipeg** for Kent Carlson and St. Louis' twelfth round choice (Sergei Kharin) in 1989 Entry Draft and St. Louis' fourth round choice (Scott Levins) in 1990 Entry Draft, September 29, 1988. Signed as a free agent by **Boston**, June 27, 1989. Signed as a free agent by **Anaheim**, July 22, 1993. Signed as a free agent by **Dallas**, July 16, 1997.

DOWD, JIM — (DOWD) CGY.

Center. Shoots right. 6'1", 190 lbs. Born, Brick, NJ, December 25, 1968.
(New Jersey's 7th choice, 149th overall, in 1987 Entry Draft).

			Regular Season					Playoffs				
Season	Club	Lea	GP	G	A	TP	PIM	GP	G	A	TP	PIM
1987-88	Lake Superior	CCHA	45	18	27	45	16	....	....	....	....	....
1988-89	Lake Superior	CCHA	46	24	35	59	40	....	....	....	....	....
1989-90ab	Lake Superior	CCHA	46	25	*67	92	30	....	....	....	....	....
1990-91cd	Lake Superior	CCHA	44	24	*54	*78	53	....	....	....	....	....
1991-92	New Jersey	NHL	1	0	0	0	0	....	....	....	....	....
	Utica	AHL	78	17	42	59	47	4	2	2	4	4
1992-93	New Jersey	NHL	1	0	0	0	0	....	....	....	....	....
	Utica	AHL	78	27	45	72	62	5	1	7	8	10
1993-94	New Jersey	NHL	15	5	10	15	0	19	2	6	8	8
	Albany	AHL	58	26	37	63	76	....	....	....	....	....
1994-95	New Jersey	NHL	10	1	4	5	0	11	2	1	3	8 ♦
1995-96	New Jersey	NHL	28	4	9	13	17	....	....	....	....	....
	Vancouver	NHL	38	1	6	7	6	1	0	0	0	0
1996-97	NY Islanders	NHL	3	0	0	0	0	....	....	....	....	....
	Utah	IHL	48	10	21	31	27	....	....	....	....	....
	Saint John	AHL	24	5	11	16	18	5	1	2	3	0
	NHL Totals		**96**	**11**	**29**	**40**	**23**	**31**	**4**	**7**	**11**	**16**

a CCHA Second All-Star Team (1990)
b NCAA West Second All-American Team (1990)
c CCHA First All-Star Team (1991)
d NCAA West First All-American Team (1991)

Traded to **Hartford** by **New Jersey** with New Jersey's second round choice (later traded to Calgary – Calgary selected Dmitri Kokorev) in 1997 Entry Draft for Jocelyn Lemieux and Hartford's second round choice in 1998 Entry Draft, December 19, 1995. Traded to **Vancouver** by **Hartford** with Frantisek Kucera and Hartford's second round choice (Ryan Bonni) in 1997 Entry Draft for Jeff Brown and Vancouver's third round choice in 1998 Entry Draft, December 19, 1995. Claimed by **NY Islanders** from **Vancouver** in NHL Waiver Draft, September 30, 1996. Signed as a free agent by **Calgary**, August, 1997.

DOYLE, JASON — BOS.

Right wing. Shoots right. 6'1", 200 lbs. Born, Toronto, Ont., May 15, 1978.
(Boston's 4th choice, 80th overall, in 1996 Entry Draft).

			Regular Season					Playoffs				
Season	Club	Lea	GP	G	A	TP	PIM	GP	G	A	TP	PIM
1994-95	London	OHL	45	4	10	14	7	4	1	1	2	0
1995-96	London	OHL	21	11	5	16	24	....	....	....	....	....
	S.S. Marie	OHL	44	17	17	34	30	4	1	1	2	6
1996-97	S.S. Marie	OHL	5	0	1	1	5	....	....	....	....	....
	Owen Sound	OHL	58	13	15	28	33	4	1	1	2	4

DOYLE, TREVOR — FLA.

Defense. Shoots right. 6'3", 212 lbs. Born, Ottawa, Ont., January 1, 1974.
(Florida's 9th choice, 161st overall, in 1993 Entry Draft).

			Regular Season					Playoffs				
Season	Club	Lea	GP	G	A	TP	PIM	GP	G	A	TP	PIM
1991-92	Kingston	OHL	26	0	1	1	19	....	....	....	....	....
1992-93	Kingston	OHL	62	1	8	9	148	16	2	3	5	25
1993-94	Kingston	OHL	53	2	12	14	246	3	0	0	0	4
1994-95	Cincinnati	IHL	52	0	3	3	139	6	0	0	0	13
1995-96	Carolina	AHL	48	1	2	3	117	....	....	....	....	....
1996-97	Carolina	AHL	47	3	10	13	288	....	....	....	....	....

DRAKE, DALLAS — PHO.

Center. Shoots left. 6', 180 lbs. Born, Trail, B.C., February 4, 1969.
(Detroit's 6th choice, 116th overall, in 1989 Entry Draft).

			Regular Season					Playoffs				
Season	Club	Lea	GP	G	A	TP	PIM	GP	G	A	TP	PIM
1988-89	N. Michigan	WCHA	38	17	22	39	22	....	....	....	....	....
1989-90	N. Michigan	WCHA	46	13	24	37	42	....	....	....	....	....
1990-91	N. Michigan	WCHA	44	22	36	58	89	....	....	....	....	....
1991-92ab	N. Michigan	WCHA	38	*39	41	*80	46	....	....	....	....	....
1992-93	Detroit	NHL	72	18	26	44	93	7	3	3	6	6
1993-94	Detroit	NHL	47	10	22	32	37	....	....	....	....	....
	Adirondack	AHL	1	2	0	2	0	....	....	....	....	....
	Winnipeg	NHL	15	3	5	8	12	....	....	....	....	....
1994-95	Winnipeg	NHL	43	8	18	26	30	....	....	....	....	....
1995-96	Winnipeg	NHL	69	19	20	39	36	3	0	0	0	0
1996-97	Phoenix	NHL	63	17	19	36	52	7	0	1	1	2
	NHL Totals		**309**	**75**	**110**	**185**	**260**	**17**	**3**	**4**	**7**	**8**

a WCHA First All-Star Team (1992)
b NCAA West First All-American Team (1992)

Traded to **Winnipeg** by **Detroit** with Tim Cheveldae for Bob Essensa and Sergei Bautin, March 8, 1994.

DRAPEAU, ETIENNE — (dra-POH, eh-TYEHN) MTL.

Center. Shoots left. 6'1", 180 lbs. Born, Quebec City, Que., January 10, 1978.
(Montreal's 5th choice, 99th overall, in 1996 Entry Draft).

			Regular Season					Playoffs				
Season	Club	Lea	GP	G	A	TP	PIM	GP	G	A	TP	PIM
1994-95	Halifax	QMJHL	63	26	35	61	121	7	2	2	4	20
1995-96	Halifax	QMJHL	42	10	25	35	98	....	....	....	....	....
	Beauport	QMJHL	28	8	12	20	37	20	8	7	15	66
1996-97	Beauport	QMJHL	46	14	31	45	42	....	....	....	....	....
	Drummondville	QMJHL	21	10	15	25	32	8	3	6	9	9

DRAPER, KRIS — DET.

Center. Shoots left. 5'11", 185 lbs. Born, Toronto, Ont., May 24, 1971.
(Winnipeg's 4th choice, 62nd overall, in 1989 Entry Draft).

			Regular Season					Playoffs				
Season	Club	Lea	GP	G	A	TP	PIM	GP	G	A	TP	PIM
1988-89	Cdn. National	....	60	11	15	26	16	....	....	....	....	....
1989-90	Cdn. National	....	61	12	22	34	44	....	....	....	....	....
1990-91	Winnipeg	NHL	3	1	0	1	5	....	....	....	....	....
	Ottawa	OHL	39	19	42	61	35	17	8	11	19	20
	Moncton	AHL	7	2	1	3	2	....	....	....	....	....
1991-92	Winnipeg	NHL	10	2	0	2	2	2	0	0	0	0
	Moncton	AHL	61	11	18	29	113	4	0	1	1	6
1992-93	Winnipeg	NHL	7	0	0	0	2	....	....	....	....	....
	Moncton	AHL	67	12	23	35	40	5	2	2	4	18
1993-94	Detroit	NHL	39	5	8	13	31	7	2	2	4	4
	Adirondack	AHL	46	20	23	43	49	....	....	....	....	....
1994-95	Detroit	NHL	36	2	6	8	22	18	4	1	5	12
1995-96	Detroit	NHL	52	7	9	16	32	18	4	2	6	18
1996-97	Detroit	NHL	76	8	5	13	73	20	2	4	6	12 ♦
	NHL Totals		**223**	**25**	**28**	**53**	**167**	**65**	**12**	**9**	**21**	**46**

Traded to **Detroit** by **Winnipeg** for future considerations, June 30, 1993.

DRIVER, BRUCE — NYR

Defense. Shoots left. 6', 185 lbs. Born, Toronto, Ont., April 29, 1962.
(Colorado's 6th choice, 108th overall, in 1981 Entry Draft).

			Regular Season					Playoffs				
Season	Club	Lea	GP	G	A	TP	PIM	GP	G	A	TP	PIM
1980-81	U. Wisconsin	WCHA	42	5	15	20	42	....	....	....	....	....
1981-82ab	U. Wisconsin	WCHA	46	7	37	44	84	....	....	....	....	....
1982-83c	U. Wisconsin	WCHA	49	19	42	61	100	....	....	....	....	....
1983-84	Cdn. National	....	61	11	17	28	44	....	....	....	....	....
	Cdn. Olympic	....	7	3	1	4	10	....	....	....	....	....
	New Jersey	NHL	4	0	2	2	0	....	....	....	....	....
	Maine	AHL	12	2	6	8	15	16	0	10	10	8
1984-85	New Jersey	NHL	67	9	23	32	36	....	....	....	....	....
1985-86	New Jersey	NHL	40	3	15	18	32	....	....	....	....	....
	Maine	AHL	15	4	7	11	16	....	....	....	....	....
1986-87	New Jersey	NHL	74	6	28	34	36	....	....	....	....	....
1987-88	New Jersey	NHL	74	15	40	55	68	20	3	7	10	14
1988-89	New Jersey	NHL	27	1	15	16	24	....	....	....	....	....
1989-90	New Jersey	NHL	75	7	46	53	63	6	1	5	6	6
1990-91	New Jersey	NHL	73	9	36	45	62	7	1	2	3	12
1991-92	New Jersey	NHL	78	7	35	42	66	7	0	4	4	2
1992-93	New Jersey	NHL	83	14	40	54	66	5	1	3	4	4
1993-94	New Jersey	NHL	66	8	24	32	63	20	3	5	8	12
1994-95	New Jersey	NHL	41	4	12	16	18	17	1	6	7	8 ♦
1995-96	NY Rangers	NHL	66	3	34	37	42	11	0	7	7	4
1996-97	NY Rangers	NHL	79	5	25	30	48	15	0	1	1	2
	NHL Totals		847	91	375	466	624	108	10	40	50	64

a WCHA First All-Star Team (1982)
b NCAA All-Tournament Team (1982)
c WCHA Second All-Star Team (1983)

Signed as a free agent by **NY Rangers**, September 28, 1995.

DROLET, JIMMY — MTL.

Defense. Shoots left. 6', 187 lbs. Born, Vanier, Que., February 19, 1976.
(Montreal's 7th choice, 122nd overall, in 1994 Entry Draft).

			Regular Season					Playoffs				
Season	Club	Lea	GP	G	A	TP	PIM	GP	G	A	TP	PIM
1993-94	St-Hyacinthe	QMJHL	72	10	46	56	93	7	1	7	8	10
1994-95	St-Hyacinthe	QMJHL	68	9	27	36	126	5	0	2	2	12
1995-96	St-Hyacinthe	QMJHL	33	4	27	31	65	....	....	....	....	....
	Granby	QMJHL	29	4	26	30	70	21	7	18	25	28
1996-97	Fredericton	AHL	57	3	2	5	43	....	....	....	....	....

DROPPA, IVAN

Defense. Shoots left. 6'2", 209 lbs. Born, Liptovsky Mikulas, Czech., February 1, 1972.
(Chicago's 2nd choice, 37th overall, in 1990 Entry Draft).

			Regular Season					Playoffs				
Season	Club	Lea	GP	G	A	TP	PIM	GP	G	A	TP	PIM
1990-91	VSZ Kosice	Czech.	54	1	7	8	12	....	....	....	....	....
1991-92	VSZ Kosice	Czech.	43	4	9	13	24	....	....	....	....	....
1992-93	Indianapolis	IHL	77	14	29	43	92	5	0	1	1	2
1993-94	Chicago	NHL	12	0	1	1	12	....	....	....	....	....
	Indianapolis	IHL	55	9	10	19	71	....	....	....	....	....
1994-95	Indianapolis	IHL	67	5	28	33	91	....	....	....	....	....
1995-96	Chicago	NHL	7	0	0	0	2	....	....	....	....	....
	Indianapolis	IHL	72	6	30	36	71	3	0	1	1	2
1996-97	Indianapolis	IHL	26	1	13	14	44	....	....	....	....	....
	Carolina	AHL	47	4	22	26	48	....	....	....	....	....
	NHL Totals		19	0	1	1	14	....	....	....	....	....

Traded to **Florida** by **Chicago** for Alain Nasreddine and a conditional choice in 1999 Entry Draft, December 18, 1996.

DROUIN, P.C. — (droo-IHN) BOS.

Left wing. Shoots left. 6'2", 208 lbs. Born, St. Lambert, Que., April 22, 1974.

			Regular Season					Playoffs				
Season	Club	Lea	GP	G	A	TP	PIM	GP	G	A	TP	PIM
1992-93	Cornell	ECAC	23	3	6	9	30	....	....	....	....	....
1993-94	Cornell	ECAC	21	6	13	19	32	....	....	....	....	....
1994-95	Cornell	ECAC	26	4	16	20	48	....	....	....	....	....
1995-96	Cornell	ECAC	31	18	14	32	60	....	....	....	....	....
1996-97	Boston	NHL	3	0	0	0	0	....	....	....	....	....
	Providence	AHL	42	12	11	23	10	....	....	....	....	....
	NHL Totals		3	0	0	0	0	....	....	....	....	....

Signed as a free agent by **Boston**, October 14, 1996.

DRUCE, JOHN — (DROOS) PHI.

Right wing. Shoots right. 6'2", 195 lbs. Born, Peterborough, Ont., February 23, 1966.
(Washington's 2nd choice, 40th overall, in 1985 Entry Draft).

			Regular Season					Playoffs				
Season	Club	Lea	GP	G	A	TP	PIM	GP	G	A	TP	PIM
1984-85	Peterborough	OHL	54	12	14	26	90	17	6	2	8	21
1985-86	Peterborough	OHL	49	22	24	46	84	16	0	5	5	34
1986-87	Binghamton	AHL	77	13	9	22	131	12	0	3	3	28
1987-88	Binghamton	AHL	68	32	29	61	82	1	0	0	0	0
1988-89	Washington	NHL	48	8	7	15	62	1	0	0	0	0
	Baltimore	AHL	16	2	11	13	10	....	....	....	....	....
1989-90	Washington	NHL	45	8	3	11	52	15	14	3	17	23
	Baltimore	AHL	26	15	16	31	38	....	....	....	....	....
1990-91	Washington	NHL	80	22	36	58	46	11	1	1	2	7
1991-92	Washington	NHL	67	19	18	37	39	7	1	0	1	2
1992-93	Winnipeg	NHL	50	6	14	20	37	2	0	0	0	0
1993-94	Los Angeles	NHL	55	14	17	31	50	....	....	....	....	....
	Phoenix	IHL	8	5	6	11	9	....	....	....	....	....
1994-95	Los Angeles	NHL	43	15	5	20	20	....	....	....	....	....
1995-96	Los Angeles	NHL	64	9	12	21	14	....	....	....	....	....
	Philadelphia	NHL	13	4	4	8	13	2	0	2	2	2
1996-97	Philadelphia	NHL	43	7	8	15	12	13	1	0	1	2
	NHL Totals		508	112	124	236	345	51	17	6	23	36

Traded to **Winnipeg** by **Washington** with Toronto's fourth round choice (previously acquired by Washington — later traded to Detroit — Detroit selected John Jakopin) in 1993 Entry Draft for Pat Elynuik, October 1, 1992. Signed as a free agent by Los Angeles, August 2, 1993. Traded to **Philadelphia** by **Los Angeles** with Los Angeles' seventh round choice (Todd Fedoruk) in 1997 Entry Draft for Los Angeles' fourth round choice (previously acquired by Philadelphia — Los Angeles selected Mikael Simons) in 1996 Entry Draft, March 19, 1996.

DRUKEN, HAROLD — VAN.

Center. Shoots left. 5'11", 194 lbs. Born, St. John's, Nfld., January 26, 1979.
(Vancouver's 3rd choice, 36th overall, in 1997 Entry Draft).

			Regular Season					Playoffs				
Season	Club	Lea	GP	G	A	TP	PIM	GP	G	A	TP	PIM
1996-97	Detroit	OHL	63	27	31	58	14	5	3	2	5	0

DRURY, CHRIS — COL.

Center. Shoots right. 5'10", 180 lbs. Born, Trumbull, CT, August 20, 1976.
(Quebec's 5th choice, 72nd overall, in 1994 Entry Draft).

			Regular Season					Playoffs				
Season	Club	Lea	GP	G	A	TP	PIM	GP	G	A	TP	PIM
1994-95	Boston U.	H.E.	39	12	15	27	38	....	....	....	....	....
1995-96ab	Boston U.	H.E.	37	35	33	*68	46	....	....	....	....	....
1996-97acd	Boston U.	H.E.	41	*38	24	62	64	....	....	....	....	....

a Hockey East All-Star Team (1996, 1997)
b NCAA East Second All-American Team (1996)
c NCAA East First All-American Team (1997)
d NCAA Final Four All-Tournament Team (1997)

DRURY, TED — (DROO-ree) ANA.

Center. Shoots left. 6', 185 lbs. Born, Boston, MA, September 13, 1971.
(Calgary's 2nd choice, 42nd overall, in 1989 Entry Draft).

			Regular Season					Playoffs				
Season	Club	Lea	GP	G	A	TP	PIM	GP	G	A	TP	PIM
1989-90	Harvard	ECAC	17	9	13	22	10	....	....	....	....	....
1990-91	Harvard	ECAC	25	18	18	36	22	....	....	....	....	....
1991-92	U.S. National	....	53	11	23	34	30	....	....	....	....	....
	U.S. Olympic	....	7	1	1	2	0	....	....	....	....	....
1992-93ab	Harvard	ECAC	31	22	*41	*63	28	....	....	....	....	....
1993-94	Calgary	NHL	34	5	7	12	26	....	....	....	....	....
	U.S. National	....	11	1	4	5	11	....	....	....	....	....
	U.S. Olympic	....	7	1	2	3	2	....	....	....	....	....
	Hartford	NHL	16	1	5	6	10	....	....	....	....	....
1994-95	Hartford	NHL	34	3	6	9	21	....	....	....	....	....
	Springfield	AHL	2	0	1	1	0	....	....	....	....	....
1995-96	Ottawa	NHL	42	9	7	16	54	....	....	....	....	....
1996-97	Anaheim	NHL	73	9	9	18	54	10	1	0	1	4
	NHL Totals		199	27	34	61	165	10	1	0	1	4

a ECAC First All-Star Team (1993)
b NCAA East First All-America Team (1993)

Traded to **Hartford** by **Calgary** with Gary Suter and Paul Ranheim for James Patrick, Zarley Zalapski and Michael Nylander, March 10, 1994. Claimed by **Ottawa** from **Hartford** in NHL Waiver Draft, October 2, 1995. Traded to **Anaheim** by **Ottawa** with the rights to Marc Moro for Jason York and Shaun Van Allen, October 1, 1996.

DUBE, CHRISTIAN — (doo-BAY) NYR

Center. Shoots right. 5'11", 170 lbs. Born, Sherbrooke, Que., April 25, 1977.
(NY Rangers' 1st choice, 39th overall, in 1995 Entry Draft).

			Regular Season					Playoffs				
Season	Club	Lea	GP	G	A	TP	PIM	GP	G	A	TP	PIM
1993-94	Sherbrooke	QMJHL	72	31	41	72	22	11	3	2	5	8
1994-95	Sherbrooke	QMJHL	71	36	65	101	43	7	1	7	8	8
1995-96abc	Sherbrooke	QMJHL	62	52	93	145	105	7	5	5	10	6
1996-97	NY Rangers	NHL	27	1	1	2	4	3	0	0	0	0
d	Hull	QMJHL	19	15	22	37	37	14	7	16	23	14
	NHL Totals		27	1	1	2	4	3	0	0	0	0

a QMJHL First All-Star Team (1996)
b Canadian Major Junior First All-Star Team (1996)
c Canadian Major Junior Player of the Year (1996)
d Won Stafford Smythe Memorial Trophy (Memorial Cup Tournament MVP) (1997)

DUBINSKY, STEVE — (doo-BIHN-skee) CHI.

Center. Shoots left. 6', 190 lbs. Born, Montreal, Que., July 9, 1970.
(Chicago's 9th choice, 226th overall, in 1990 Entry Draft).

			Regular Season					Playoffs				
Season	Club	Lea	GP	G	A	TP	PIM	GP	G	A	TP	PIM
1989-90	Clarkson	ECAC	35	7	10	17	24	....	....	....	....	....
1990-91	Clarkson	ECAC	39	13	23	36	26	....	....	....	....	....
1991-92	Clarkson	ECAC	32	20	31	51	40	....	....	....	....	....
1992-93	Clarkson	ECAC	35	18	26	44	58	....	....	....	....	....
1993-94	Chicago	NHL	27	2	6	8	16	6	0	0	0	10
	Indianapolis	IHL	54	15	25	40	63	....	....	....	....	....
1994-95	Indianapolis	IHL	62	16	11	27	29	....	....	....	....	....
	Chicago	NHL	16	0	0	0	8	....	....	....	....	....
1995-96	Chicago	NHL	43	2	3	5	14	....	....	....	....	....
	Indianapolis	IHL	16	8	8	16	10	....	....	....	....	....
1996-97	Chicago	NHL	5	0	0	0	0	4	1	0	1	4
	Indianapolis	IHL	77	32	40	72	53	1	3	1	4	0
	NHL Totals		91	4	9	13	38	10	1	0	1	14

DUCE, BRYAN — N.J.

Right wing. Shoots right. 6', 190 lbs. Born, Thunder Bay, Ont., January 15, 1978.

			Regular Season					Playoffs				
Season	Club	Lea	GP	G	A	TP	PIM	GP	G	A	TP	PIM
1995-96	Kitchener	OHL	55	14	9	23	16	11	0	0	0	2
1996-97	Kitchener	OHL	62	27	30	57	36	11	5	3	8	2

Signed as a free agent by **New Jersey**, August 12, 1997.

DUCHESNE, STEVE (doo-SHAYN) OTT.

Defense. Shoots left. 5'11", 195 lbs. Born, Sept-Iles, Que., June 30, 1965.

			Regular Season					Playoffs				
Season	Club	Lea	GP	G	A	TP	PIM	GP	G	A	TP	PIM
1983-84	Drummondville	QMJHL	67	1	34	35	79	....	....	....	....	....
1984-85a	Drummondville	QMJHL	65	22	54	76	94	5	4	7	11	8
1985-86	New Haven	AHL	75	14	35	49	76	5	0	2	2	9
1986-87b	**Los Angeles**	**NHL**	**75**	**13**	**25**	**38**	**74**	**5**	**2**	**2**	**4**	**4**
1987-88	**Los Angeles**	**NHL**	**71**	**16**	**39**	**55**	**109**	**5**	**1**	**3**	**4**	**14**
1988-89	**Los Angeles**	**NHL**	**79**	**25**	**50**	**75**	**92**	**11**	**4**	**4**	**8**	**12**
1989-90	**Los Angeles**	**NHL**	**79**	**20**	**42**	**62**	**36**	**10**	**2**	**9**	**11**	**6**
1990-91	**Los Angeles**	**NHL**	**78**	**21**	**41**	**62**	**66**	**12**	**4**	**8**	**12**	**8**
1991-92	**Philadelphia**	**NHL**	**78**	**18**	**38**	**56**	**86**	....	....	....	....	....
1992-93	**Quebec**	**NHL**	**82**	**20**	**62**	**82**	**57**	**6**	**0**	**5**	**5**	**6**
1993-94	**St. Louis**	**NHL**	**36**	**12**	**19**	**31**	**14**	**4**	**0**	**2**	**2**	**2**
1994-95	**St. Louis**	**NHL**	**47**	**12**	**26**	**38**	**36**	**7**	**0**	**4**	**4**	**2**
1995-96	**Ottawa**	**NHL**	**62**	**12**	**24**	**36**	**42**	....	....	....	....	....
1996-97	**Ottawa**	**NHL**	**78**	**19**	**28**	**47**	**38**	**7**	**1**	**4**	**5**	**0**
	NHL Totals		**765**	**188**	**394**	**582**	**650**	**67**	**14**	**41**	**55**	**54**

a QMJHL First All-Star Team (1985)
b NHL All-Rookie Team (1987)

Played in NHL All-Star Game (1989, 1990, 1993)

Signed as a free agent by **Los Angeles,** October 1, 1984. Traded to **Philadelphia** by **Los Angeles** with Steve Kasper and Los Angeles' fourth round choice (Aris Brimanis) in 1991 Entry Draft for Jari Kurri and Jeff Chychrun, May 30, 1991. Traded to **Quebec** by **Philadelphia** with Peter Forsberg, Kerry Huffman, Mike Ricci, Ron Hextall, Chris Simon, Philadelphia's first round choice in the 1993 (Jocelyn Thibault) and 1994 (later traded to Toronto — later traded to Washington — Washington selected Nolan Baumgartner) Entry Drafts and cash for Eric Lindros, June 30, 1992. Traded to **St. Louis** by **Quebec** with Denis Chasse for Garth Butcher, Ron Sutter and Bob Bassen, January 23, 1994. Traded to **Ottawa** by **St. Louis** for Ottawa's second round choice (later traded to Buffalo — Buffalo selected Cory Sarich) in 1996 Entry Draft, August 4, 1995.

DUERDEN, DAVE FLA.

Left wing. Shoots left. 6'2", 201 lbs. Born, Oshawa, Ont., April 11, 1977.
(Florida's 4th choice, 80th overall, in 1995 Entry Draft).

			Regular Season					Playoffs				
Season	Club	Lea	GP	G	A	TP	PIM	GP	G	A	TP	PIM
1994-95	Peterborough	OHL	66	20	33	53	21	11	6	2	8	6
1995-96	Peterborough	OHL	66	35	35	70	47	24	14	13	27	16
1996-97a	Peterborough	OHL	66	36	48	84	34	4	2	4	6	0

a OHL Second All-Star Team (1997)

DUFRESNE, DONALD (doo-FRAYN, DOH-nal)

Defense. Shoots right. 6'1", 206 lbs. Born, Quebec City, Que., April 10, 1967.
(Montreal's 8th choice, 117th overall, in 1985 Entry Draft).

			Regular Season					Playoffs				
Season	Club	Lea	GP	G	A	TP	PIM	GP	G	A	TP	PIM
1983-84	Trois-Rivières	QMJHL	67	7	12	19	97	....	....	....	....	....
1984-85	Trois-Rivières	QMJHL	65	5	30	35	112	7	1	3	4	12
1985-86a	Trois-Rivières	QMJHL	63	8	32	40	160	1	0	0	0	0
1986-87a	Trois-Rivières	QMJHL	51	5	21	26	79	....	....	....	....	....
	Longueuil	QMJHL	16	0	8	8	18	20	1	8	9	38
1987-88	Sherbrooke	AHL	47	1	8	9	107	6	1	0	1	34
1988-89	**Montreal**	**NHL**	**13**	**0**	**1**	**1**	**43**	**6**	**1**	**1**	**2**	**4**
	Sherbrooke	AHL	47	0	12	12	170	....	....	....	....	....
1989-90	**Montreal**	**NHL**	**18**	**0**	**4**	**4**	**23**	**10**	**0**	**1**	**1**	**18**
	Sherbrooke	AHL	38	2	11	13	104	....	....	....	....	....
1990-91	**Montreal**	**NHL**	**53**	**2**	**13**	**15**	**55**	**10**	**0**	**1**	**1**	**21**
	Fredericton	AHL	10	1	4	5	35	1	0	0	0	0
1991-92	**Montreal**	**NHL**	**3**	**0**	**0**	**0**	**2**	....	....	....	....	....
	Fredericton	AHL	31	8	12	20	60	7	0	0	0	10
1992-93	**Montreal**	**NHL**	**32**	**1**	**2**	**3**	**32**	**2**	**0**	**0**	**0**	**0** ♦
1993-94	**Tampa Bay**	**NHL**	**51**	**2**	**6**	**8**	**48**	....	....	....	....	....
	Los Angeles	**NHL**	**9**	**0**	**0**	**0**	**10**	....	....	....	....	....
1994-95	**St. Louis**	**NHL**	**22**	**0**	**3**	**3**	**10**	**3**	**0**	**0**	**0**	**4**
1995-96	**St. Louis**	**NHL**	**3**	**0**	**0**	**0**	**4**	....	....	....	....	....
	Worcester	AHL	13	1	1	2	14	....	....	....	....	....
	Edmonton	**NHL**	**42**	**1**	**6**	**7**	**16**	....	....	....	....	....
1996-97	**Edmonton**	**NHL**	**22**	**0**	**1**	**1**	**15**	**3**	**0**	**0**	**0**	**0**
	NHL Totals		**268**	**6**	**36**	**42**	**258**	**34**	**1**	**3**	**4**	**47**

a QMJHL Second All-Star Team (1986, 1987)

Traded to **Tampa Bay** by **Montreal** to complete March 20, 1993 trade in which Rob Ramage was traded to Montreal for Eric Charron, Alain Cote and future considerations, June 20, 1993. Traded to **Los Angeles** by **Tampa Bay** for Los Angeles' sixth round choice (Daniel Juden) in 1994 Entry Draft, March 19, 1994. Claimed by **St. Louis** from **Los Angeles** in NHL Waiver Draft, January 18, 1995. Traded to **Edmonton** by **St. Louis** with Jeff Norton for Igor Kravchuk and Ken Sutton, January 4, 1996.

DUMONT, JEAN-PIERRE NYI

Right wing. Shoots left. 6'1", 187 lbs. Born, Montreal, Que., April 1, 1978.
(NY Islanders' 1st choice, 3rd overall, in 1996 Entry Draft).

			Regular Season					Playoffs				
Season	Club	Lea	GP	G	A	TP	PIM	GP	G	A	TP	PIM
1993-94	Val d'Or	QMJHL	25	9	11	20	10	....	....	....	....	....
1994-95	Val d'Or	QMJHL	48	5	14	19	24	....	....	....	....	....
1995-96	Val d'Or	QMJHL	66	48	57	105	109	13	12	8	20	22
1996-97a	Val d'Or	QMJHL	62	44	64	108	86	13	9	7	16	12

a QMJHL Second All-Star Team (1997)

DUNCANSON, CRAIG

Left wing. Shoots left. 6', 190 lbs. Born, Sudbury, Ont., March 17, 1967.
(Los Angeles' 1st choice, 9th overall, in 1985 Entry Draft).

			Regular Season					Playoffs				
Season	Club	Lea	GP	G	A	TP	PIM	GP	G	A	TP	PIM
1983-84	Sudbury	OHL	62	38	38	76	176	....	....	....	....	....
1984-85	Sudbury	OHL	53	35	28	63	129	....	....	....	....	....
1985-86	**Los Angeles**	**NHL**	**2**	**0**	**1**	**1**	**0**	....	....	....	....	....
	Sudbury	OHL	21	12	17	29	55	....	....	....	....	....
	Cornwall	OHL	40	31	50	81	135	6	4	7	11	2
	New Haven	AHL	....	....	....	....	....	2	0	0	0	5
1986-87	**Los Angeles**	**NHL**	**2**	**0**	**0**	**0**	**24**	....	....	....	....	....
	Cornwall	OHL	52	22	45	67	88	5	4	3	7	20
1987-88	**Los Angeles**	**NHL**	**9**	**0**	**0**	**0**	**12**	....	....	....	....	....
	New Haven	AHL	57	15	25	40	170	....	....	....	....	....
1988-89	**Los Angeles**	**NHL**	**5**	**0**	**0**	**0**	**0**	....	....	....	....	....
	New Haven	AHL	69	25	39	64	200	17	4	8	12	60
1989-90	**Los Angeles**	**NHL**	**10**	**3**	**2**	**5**	**9**	....	....	....	....	....
	New Haven	AHL	51	17	30	47	152	....	....	....	....	....
1990-91	**Winnipeg**	**NHL**	**7**	**2**	**0**	**2**	**16**	....	....	....	....	....
	Moncton	AHL	58	16	34	50	107	9	3	11	14	31
1991-92	Baltimore	AHL	46	20	26	46	98	....	....	....	....	....
	Moncton	AHL	19	12	9	21	6	11	6	4	10	10
1992-93	**NY Rangers**	**NHL**	**3**	**0**	**1**	**1**	**0**	....	....	....	....	....
	Binghamton	AHL	69	35	59	94	126	14	7	5	12	9
1993-94	Binghamton	AHL	70	25	44	69	83	....	....	....	....	....
1994-95	Binghamton	AHL	62	21	43	64	105	11	4	4	8	16
1995-96	Orlando	IHL	79	19	24	43	123	22	3	10	13	16
1996-97	Fort Wayne	IHL	61	14	24	38	64	....	....	....	....	....
	Cincinnati	IHL	21	3	11	14	19	3	1	1	2	0
	NHL Totals		**38**	**5**	**4**	**9**	**61**	....	....	....	....	....

Traded to **Minnesota** by **Los Angeles** for Daniel Berthiaume, September 6, 1990. Traded to **Winnipeg** by **Minnesota** for Brian Hunt, September 6, 1990. Traded to **Washington** by **Winnipeg** with Brent Hughes and Simon Wheeldon for Bob Joyce, Tyler Larter and Kent Paynter, May 21, 1991. Signed as a free agent by **NY Rangers**, September 4, 1992.

DUTIAUME, MARK BUF.

Left wing. Shoots left. 6', 200 lbs. Born, Winnipeg, Man., January 31, 1977.
(Buffalo's 3rd choice, 42nd overall, in 1995 Entry Draft).

			Regular Season					Playoffs				
Season	Club	Lea	GP	G	A	TP	PIM	GP	G	A	TP	PIM
1993-94	Tri-City	WHL	3	2	0	2	0	....	....	....	....	....
	Brandon	WHL	55	4	7	11	43	12	0	2	2	6
1994-95	Brandon	WHL	62	23	21	44	80	17	1	2	3	33
1995-96	Brandon	WHL	7	0	4	4	6	9	2	1	3	12
1996-97	Brandon	WHL	48	12	11	23	73	6	2	2	4	13
	Rochester	AHL	6	1	1	2	0	....	....	....	....	....

DVORAK, RADEK (duh-VOHR-ak) FLA.

Left wing. Shoots right. 6'2", 187 lbs. Born, Tabor, Czech., March 9, 1977.
(Florida's 1st choice, 10th overall, in 1995 Entry Draft).

			Regular Season					Playoffs				
Season	Club	Lea	GP	G	A	TP	PIM	GP	G	A	TP	PIM
1993-94	Budejovice	Czech.	8	0	0	0	0	....	....	....	....	....
1994-95	Budejovice	Czech.	10	3	5	8	2	9	5	1	6	....
1995-96	**Florida**	**NHL**	**77**	**13**	**14**	**27**	**20**	**16**	**1**	**3**	**4**	**0**
1996-97	**Florida**	**NHL**	**78**	**18**	**21**	**39**	**30**	**3**	**0**	**0**	**0**	**0**
	NHL Totals		**155**	**31**	**35**	**66**	**50**	**19**	**1**	**3**	**4**	**0**

DWYER, GORDIE ST.L.

Left wing. Shoots left. 6'2", 190 lbs. Born, Dalhousie, NB, January 25, 1978.
(St. Louis' 2nd choice, 67th overall, in 1996 Entry Draft).

			Regular Season					Playoffs				
Season	Club	Lea	GP	G	A	TP	PIM	GP	G	A	TP	PIM
1994-95	Hull	QMJHL	57	3	7	10	204	17	1	3	4	54
1995-96	Hull	QMJHL	25	5	9	14	199	....	....	....	....	....
	Laval	QMJHL	22	5	17	22	72	....	....	....	....	....
	Beauport	QMJHL	22	4	9	13	87	20	3	5	8	104
1996-97	Drummondville	QMJHL	66	21	48	69	393	8	6	1	7	39

DYKHUIS, KARL (DIGH-kowz) T.B.

Defense. Shoots left. 6'3", 205 lbs. Born, Sept-Iles, Que., July 8, 1972.
(Chicago's 1st choice, 16th overall, in 1990 Entry Draft).

			Regular Season					Playoffs				
Season	Club	Lea	GP	G	A	TP	PIM	GP	G	A	TP	PIM
1988-89	Hull	QMJHL	63	2	29	31	59	9	1	9	10	6
1989-90a	Hull	QMJHL	69	10	46	56	119	11	2	5	7	2
1990-91	Cdn. National	....	37	2	9	11	16	....	....	....	....	....
	Longueuil	QMJHL	3	1	4	5	6	8	2	5	7	6
1991-92	**Chicago**	**NHL**	**6**	**1**	**3**	**4**	**4**	....	....	....	....	....
	Cdn. National	....	19	1	2	3	16	....	....	....	....	....
	Verdun	QMJHL	29	5	19	24	55	17	0	12	12	14
1992-93	**Chicago**	**NHL**	**12**	**0**	**5**	**5**	**0**	....	....	....	....	....
	Indianapolis	IHL	59	5	18	23	76	5	1	1	2	8
1993-94	Indianapolis	IHL	73	7	25	32	132	....	....	....	....	....
1994-95	Indianapolis	IHL	52	2	21	23	63	....	....	....	....	....
	Hershey	AHL	1	0	0	0	0	....	....	....	....	....
	Philadelphia	**NHL**	**33**	**2**	**6**	**8**	**37**	**15**	**4**	**4**	**8**	**14**
1995-96	**Philadelphia**	**NHL**	**82**	**5**	**15**	**20**	**101**	**12**	**2**	**2**	**4**	**22**
1996-97	**Philadelphia**	**NHL**	**62**	**4**	**15**	**19**	**35**	**18**	**0**	**3**	**3**	**2**
	NHL Totals		**195**	**12**	**44**	**56**	**177**	**45**	**6**	**9**	**15**	**38**

a QMJHL First All-Star Team (1990)

Traded to **Philadelphia** by **Chicago** for Bob Wilkie and a possible conditional choice in 1997 Entry Draft, February 16, 1995. Traded to **Tampa Bay** by **Philadelphia** with Mikael Renberg for Philadelphia's first round choices in 1998, 1999, 2000, and 2001 Entry Drafts (previously acquired by Tampa Bay), August 20, 1997.

DZIEDZIC, JOE (zehd-ZIHK) PIT.

Left wing. Shoots left. 6'3", 227 lbs. Born, Minneapolis, MN, December 18, 1971.
(Pittsburgh's 2nd choice, 61st overall, in 1990 Entry Draft).

			Regular Season					Playoffs				
Season	Club	Lea	GP	G	A	TP	PIM	GP	G	A	TP	PIM
1990-91	U. Minnesota	WCHA	20	6	4	10	26	....	....	....	....	....
1991-92	U. Minnesota	WCHA	34	8	9	17	68	....	....	....	....	....
1992-93	U. Minnesota	WCHA	41	11	14	25	62	....	....	....	....	....
1993-94	U. Minnesota	WCHA	18	7	10	17	48	....	....	....	....	....
1994-95	Cleveland	IHL	68	15	15	30	74	4	1	0	1	10
1995-96	**Pittsburgh**	**NHL**	**69**	**5**	**5**	**10**	**68**	**16**	**1**	**2**	**3**	**19**
1996-97	**Pittsburgh**	**NHL**	**59**	**9**	**9**	**18**	**63**	**5**	**0**	**1**	**1**	**4**
	NHL Totals		**128**	**14**	**14**	**28**	**131**	**21**	**1**	**3**	**4**	**23**

EAGLES, MIKE — WSH.

Center/Left wing. Shoots left. 5'10", 190 lbs. Born, Sussex, N.B., March 7, 1963.
(Quebec's 5th choice, 116th overall, in 1981 Entry Draft).

			Regular Season					Playoffs				
Season	Club	Lea	GP	G	A	TP	PIM	GP	G	A	TP	PIM
1980-81	Kitchener	OHA	56	11	27	38	64	18	4	2	6	36
1981-82	Kitchener	OHL	62	26	40	66	148	15	3	11	14	27
1982-83	**Quebec**	**NHL**	**2**	**0**	**0**	**0**	**2**	....	....	....	....	....
	Kitchener	OHL	58	26	36	62	133	12	5	7	12	27
1983-84	Fredericton	AHL	68	13	29	42	85	4	0	0	0	5
1984-85	Fredericton	AHL	36	4	20	24	80	3	0	0	0	2
1985-86	**Quebec**	**NHL**	**73**	**11**	**12**	**23**	**49**	**3**	**0**	**0**	**0**	**2**
1986-87	**Quebec**	**NHL**	**73**	**13**	**19**	**32**	**55**	**4**	**1**	**0**	**1**	**10**
1987-88	**Quebec**	**NHL**	**76**	**10**	**10**	**20**	**74**	....	....	....	....	....
1988-89	**Chicago**	**NHL**	**47**	**5**	**11**	**16**	**44**	....	....	....	....	....
1989-90	**Chicago**	**NHL**	**23**	**1**	**2**	**3**	**34**	....	....	....	....	....
	Indianapolis	IHL	24	11	13	24	47	13	*10	10	20	34
1990-91	**Winnipeg**	**NHL**	**44**	**0**	**9**	**9**	**79**	....	....	....	....	....
	Indianapolis	IHL	25	15	14	29	47	....	....	....	....	....
1991-92	**Winnipeg**	**NHL**	**65**	**7**	**10**	**17**	**118**	**7**	**0**	**0**	**0**	**8**
1992-93	**Winnipeg**	**NHL**	**84**	**8**	**18**	**26**	**131**	**5**	**0**	**1**	**1**	**6**
1993-94	**Winnipeg**	**NHL**	**73**	**4**	**8**	**12**	**96**	....	....	....	....	....
1994-95	**Winnipeg**	**NHL**	**27**	**2**	**1**	**3**	**40**	....	....	....	....	....
	Washington	**NHL**	**13**	**1**	**3**	**4**	**8**	**7**	**0**	**2**	**2**	**4**
1995-96	**Washington**	**NHL**	**70**	**4**	**7**	**11**	**75**	**6**	**1**	**1**	**2**	**2**
1996-97	**Washington**	**NHL**	**70**	**1**	**7**	**8**	**42**	....	....	....	....	....
	NHL Totals		**740**	**67**	**117**	**184**	**847**	**32**	**2**	**4**	**6**	**32**

Traded to **Chicago** by **Quebec** for Bob Mason, July 5, 1988. Traded to **Winnipeg** by **Chicago** for Winnipeg's fourth round choice (Igor Kravchuk) in 1991 Entry Draft, December 14, 1990. Traded to **Washington** by **Winnipeg** with Igor Ulanov for Washington's third (later traded to Dallas — Dallas selected Sergei Gusev) and fifth (Brian Elder) round choices in 1995 Entry Draft, April 7, 1995.

EAKINS, DALLAS (EE-kins) — FLA.

Defense. Shoots left. 6'2", 195 lbs. Born, Dade City, FL, February 27, 1967.
(Washington's 11th choice, 208th overall, in 1985 Entry Draft).

			Regular Season					Playoffs				
Season	Club	Lea	GP	G	A	TP	PIM	GP	G	A	TP	PIM
1984-85	Peterborough	OHL	48	0	8	8	96	7	0	0	0	18
1985-86	Peterborough	OHL	60	6	16	22	134	16	0	1	1	30
1986-87	Peterborough	OHL	54	3	11	14	145	12	1	4	5	37
1987-88	Peterborough	OHL	64	11	27	38	129	12	3	12	15	16
1988-89	Baltimore	AHL	62	0	10	10	139	....	....	....	....	....
1989-90	Moncton	AHL	75	2	11	13	189	....	....	....	....	....
1990-91	Moncton	AHL	75	1	12	13	132	9	0	1	1	44
1991-92	Moncton	AHL	67	3	13	16	136	11	2	1	3	16
1992-93	**Winnipeg**	**NHL**	**14**	**0**	**2**	**2**	**38**	....	....	....	....	....
	Moncton	AHL	55	4	6	10	132	....	....	....	....	....
1993-94	**Florida**	**NHL**	**1**	**0**	**0**	**0**	**0**	....	....	....	....	....
	Cincinnati	IHL	80	1	18	19	143	8	0	1	1	41
1994-95	Cincinnati	IHL	59	6	12	18	69	....	....	....	....	....
	Florida	**NHL**	**17**	**0**	**1**	**1**	**35**	....	....	....	....	....
1995-96	**St. Louis**	**NHL**	**16**	**0**	**1**	**1**	**34**	....	....	....	....	....
	Worcester	AHL	4	0	0	0	12	....	....	....	....	....
	Winnipeg	**NHL**	**2**	**0**	**0**	**0**	**0**	....	....	....	....	....
1996-97	**Phoenix**	**NHL**	**4**	**0**	**0**	**0**	**10**	....	....	....	....	....
	Springfield	AHL	38	6	7	13	63	....	....	....	....	....
	NY Rangers	**NHL**	**3**	**0**	**0**	**0**	**6**	**4**	**0**	**0**	**0**	**4**
	Binghamton	AHL	19	1	7	8	15	....	....	....	....	....
	NHL Totals		**57**	**0**	**4**	**4**	**123**	**4**	**0**	**0**	**0**	**4**

Signed as a free agent by **Winnipeg**, October 17, 1989. Signed as a free agent by **Florida**, July 8, 1993. Traded to **St. Louis** by **Florida** for St. Louis' fourth round choice (Ivan Novoseltsev) in 1997 Entry Draft, September 28, 1995. Claimed on waivers by **Winnipeg** from **St. Louis**, March 20, 1996. Traded to **NY Rangers** by **Phoenix** with Mike Eastwood for Jayson More, February 6, 1997. Signed as a free agent by **Florida**, July 30, 1997.

EASTWOOD, MIKE — NYR

Center. Shoots right. 6'3", 205 lbs. Born, Ottawa, Ont., July 1, 1967.
(Toronto's 5th choice, 91st overall, in 1987 Entry Draft).

			Regular Season					Playoffs				
Season	Club	Lea	GP	G	A	TP	PIM	GP	G	A	TP	PIM
1987-88	W. Michigan	CCHA	42	5	8	13	14	....	....	....	....	....
1988-89	W. Michigan	CCHA	40	10	13	23	87	....	....	....	....	....
1989-90	W. Michigan	CCHA	40	25	27	52	36	....	....	....	....	....
1990-91a	W. Michigan	CCHA	42	29	32	61	84	....	....	....	....	....
1991-92	**Toronto**	**NHL**	**9**	**0**	**2**	**2**	**4**	....	....	....	....	....
	St. John's	AHL	61	18	25	43	28	16	9	10	19	16
1992-93	**Toronto**	**NHL**	**12**	**1**	**6**	**7**	**21**	**10**	**1**	**2**	**3**	**8**
	St. John's	AHL	60	24	35	59	32	....	....	....	....	....
1993-94	**Toronto**	**NHL**	**54**	**8**	**10**	**18**	**28**	**18**	**3**	**2**	**5**	**12**
1994-95	**Toronto**	**NHL**	**36**	**5**	**5**	**10**	**32**	....	....	....	....	....
	Winnipeg	**NHL**	**13**	**3**	**6**	**9**	**4**	....	....	....	....	....
1995-96	**Winnipeg**	**NHL**	**80**	**14**	**14**	**28**	**20**	**6**	**0**	**1**	**1**	**2**
1996-97	**Phoenix**	**NHL**	**33**	**1**	**3**	**4**	**4**	....	....	....	....	....
	NY Rangers	**NHL**	**27**	**1**	**7**	**8**	**10**	**15**	**1**	**2**	**3**	**22**
	NHL Totals		**264**	**33**	**53**	**86**	**123**	**49**	**5**	**7**	**12**	**44**

a CCHA Second All-Star Team (1991)

Traded to **Winnipeg** by **Toronto** with Toronto's third round choice (Brad Isbister) in 1995 Entry Draft for Tie Domi, April 7, 1995. Traded to **NY Rangers** by **Phoenix** with Dallas Eakins for Jayson More, February 6, 1997.

EDINGER, ADAM — NYI

Center. Shoots left. 6'2", 210 lbs. Born, Toledo, OH, September 21, 1977.
(NY Islanders' 7th choice, 115th overall, in 1997 Entry Draft).

			Regular Season					Playoffs				
Season	Club	Lea	GP	G	A	TP	PIM	GP	G	A	TP	PIM
1995-96	Leamington	Jr. B	45	45	50	95	120	....	....	....	....	....
1996-97	Bowling Green	CCHA	34	11	18	29	42	....	....	....	....	....

EGELAND, ALLAN — T.B.

Center. Shoots left. 6', 184 lbs. Born, Lethbridge, Alta., January 31, 1973.
(Tampa Bay's 3rd choice, 55th overall, in 1993 Entry Draft).

			Regular Season					Playoffs				
Season	Club	Lea	GP	G	A	TP	PIM	GP	G	A	TP	PIM
1990-91	Lethbridge	WHL	67	2	16	18	57	9	0	0	0	0
1991-92	Tacoma	WHL	72	35	39	74	135	4	0	1	1	18
1992-93a	Tacoma	WHL	71	56	57	113	119	7	9	7	16	18
1993-94b	Tacoma	WHL	70	47	76	123	204	8	5	3	8	26
1994-95	Atlanta	IHL	60	8	16	24	112	5	0	1	1	16
1995-96	**Tampa Bay**	**NHL**	**5**	**0**	**0**	**0**	**2**	....	....	....	....	....
	Atlanta	IHL	68	22	22	44	182	3	0	1	1	0
1996-97	**Tampa Bay**	**NHL**	**4**	**0**	**0**	**0**	**5**	....	....	....	....	....
	Adirondack	AHL	52	18	32	50	184	2	0	1	1	4
	NHL Totals		**9**	**0**	**0**	**0**	**7**	....	....	....	....	....

a WHL West First All-Star Team (1993)
b WHL West Second All-Star Team (1994)

EISENHUT, NEIL (IGHS-ihn-huht)

Center. Shoots left. 6'1", 190 lbs. Born, Osoyoos, B.C., February 9, 1967.
(Vancouver's 11th choice, 238th overall, in 1987 Entry Draft).

			Regular Season					Playoffs				
Season	Club	Lea	GP	G	A	TP	PIM	GP	G	A	TP	PIM
1987-88	North Dakota	WCHA	42	12	20	32	14	....	....	....	....	....
1988-89	North Dakota	WCHA	41	22	16	38	20	....	....	....	....	....
1989-90	North Dakota	WCHA	45	22	32	54	46	....	....	....	....	....
1990-91	North Dakota	WCHA	20	9	15	24	10	....	....	....	....	....
1991-92	Milwaukee	IHL	76	13	23	36	26	2	1	2	3	0
1992-93	Hamilton	AHL	72	22	40	62	41	....	....	....	....	....
1993-94	**Vancouver**	**NHL**	**13**	**1**	**3**	**4**	**21**	....	....	....	....	....
	Hamilton	AHL	60	17	36	53	30	4	1	4	5	0
1994-95	Saint John	AHL	75	16	39	55	30	5	1	1	2	6
	Calgary	**NHL**	**3**	**0**	**0**	**0**	**0**	....	....	....	....	....
1995-96	Orlando	IHL	59	10	18	28	30	....	....	....	....	....
	Binghamton	AHL	10	3	3	6	2	4	3	2	5	0
1996-97	Flint	ColHL	21	10	33	43	20	5	1	4	5	8
	Binghamton	AHL	55	25	26	51	16	4	1	2	3	0
	NHL Totals		**16**	**1**	**3**	**4**	**21**	....	....	....	....	....

Signed as a free agent by **Calgary**, June 16, 1994.

EKLUND, PER — DET.

Left wing. Shoots left. 5'11", 196 lbs. Born, Sollentuna, Sweden, July 9, 1970.
(Detroit's 8th choice, 182nd overall, in 1995 Entry Draft).

			Regular Season					Playoffs				
Season	Club	Lea	GP	G	A	TP	PIM	GP	G	A	TP	PIM
1991-92	Vasby	Swe. 2	29	13	24	37	26	....	....	....	....	....
1992-93	Huddinge	Swe. 2	36	22	23	45	14	....	....	....	....	....
1993-94	Huddinge	Swe. 2	35	20	11	31	40	....	....	....	....	....
1994-95	Djurgarden	Swe.	40	19	10	29	20	3	1	1	2	4
1995-96	Djurgarden	Swe.	39	17	10	27	10	1	0	0	0	0
1996-97	Djurgarden	Swe.	50	20	16	36	14	4	1	0	1	0
	Leksand	Swe.	36	6	15	21	10	9	2	5	7	4

EKMAN, NILS (EHK-mahn) — CGY.

Left wing. Shoots left. 5'11", 175 lbs. Born, Stockholm, Sweden, March 11, 1976.
(Calgary's 6th choice, 107th overall, in 1994 Entry Draft).

			Regular Season					Playoffs				
Season	Club	Lea	GP	G	A	TP	PIM	GP	G	A	TP	PIM
1993-94	Hammarby	Swe. 2	18	7	2	9	4	....	....	....	....	....
1994-95	Hammarby	Swe. 2	29	10	7	17	18	....	....	....	....	....
1995-96	Hammarby	Swe. 2	26	9	7	16	53	1	0	0	0	0
1996-97	Kiekko-Espoo	Fin.	50	24	19	43	60	4	2	0	2	4

ELFRING, CALVIN — COL.

Defense. Shoots left. 6', 170 lbs. Born, Lethbridge, Alta., April 23, 1976.
(Quebec's 9th choice, 165th overall, in 1994 Entry Draft).

			Regular Season					Playoffs				
Season	Club	Lea	GP	G	A	TP	PIM	GP	G	A	TP	PIM
1994-95	Colorado	WCHA	43	3	23	26	34	....	....	....	....	....
1995-96	Colorado	WCHA	42	10	24	34	32	....	....	....	....	....
1996-97	Colorado	WCHA	44	9	22	31	26	....	....	....	....	....

ELIAS, PATRIK (EH-lih-ahsh) — N.J.

Left wing. Shoots left. 6', 175 lbs. Born, Trebic, Czech., April 13, 1976.
(New Jersey's 2nd choice, 51st overall, in 1994 Entry Draft).

			Regular Season					Playoffs				
Season	Club	Lea	GP	G	A	TP	PIM	GP	G	A	TP	PIM
1992-93	Kladno	Czech.	2	0	0	0	....	....	....	....	....	....
1993-94	Kladno	Czech.	15	1	2	3	....	11	2	2	4	....
1994-95	Kladno	Czech.	28	4	3	7	37	7	1	2	3	12
1995-96	**New Jersey**	**NHL**	**1**	**0**	**0**	**0**	**0**	....	....	....	....	....
	Albany	AHL	74	27	36	63	83	4	1	1	2	2
1996-97	**New Jersey**	**NHL**	**17**	**2**	**3**	**5**	**2**	**8**	**2**	**3**	**5**	**4**
	Albany	AHL	57	24	43	67	76	6	1	2	3	8
	NHL Totals		**18**	**2**	**3**	**5**	**2**	**8**	**2**	**3**	**5**	**4**

ELICH, MATT — T.B.

Right wing. Shoots right. 6'3", 187 lbs. Born, Detroit, MI, September 22, 1979.
(Tampa Bay's 3rd choice, 61st overall, in 1997 Entry Draft).

			Regular Season					Playoffs				
Season	Club	Lea	GP	G	A	TP	PIM	GP	G	A	TP	PIM
1995-96	Windsor	OHL	52	10	2	12	17	5	1	0	1	2
1996-97	Windsor	OHL	58	15	13	28	19	5	0	1	1	6

ELIK, TODD (EHL-ihk)

Center. Shoots left. 6'2", 195 lbs. Born, Brampton, Ont., April 15, 1966.

			Regular Season					Playoffs				
Season	Club	Lea	GP	G	A	TP	PIM	GP	G	A	TP	PIM
1984-85	Kingston	OHL	34	14	11	25	6	....	....	....	....	....
	North Bay	OHL	23	4	6	10	2	4	2	0	2	0
1985-86	North Bay	OHL	40	12	34	46	20	10	7	6	13	0
1986-87	U. of Regina	CWUAA	27	26	34	60	137	....	....	....	....	....
	Cdn. National	....	1	0	0	0	0	....	....	....	....	....
1987-88	Colorado	IHL	81	44	56	100	83	12	8	12	20	9
1988-89	Denver	IHL	28	20	15	35	22	....	....	....	....	....
	New Haven	AHL	43	11	25	36	31	17	10	12	22	44
1989-90	**Los Angeles**	**NHL**	**48**	**10**	**23**	**33**	**41**	**10**	**3**	**9**	**12**	**10**
	New Haven	AHL	32	20	23	43	42	....	....	....	....	....
1990-91	**Los Angeles**	**NHL**	**74**	**21**	**37**	**58**	**58**	**12**	**2**	**7**	**9**	**6**
1991-92	**Minnesota**	**NHL**	**62**	**14**	**32**	**46**	**125**	**5**	**1**	**1**	**2**	**2**
1992-93	**Minnesota**	**NHL**	**46**	**13**	**18**	**31**	**48**	....	....	....	....	....
	Edmonton	**NHL**	**14**	**1**	**9**	**10**	**8**	....	....	....	....	....
1993-94	**Edmonton**	**NHL**	**4**	**0**	**0**	**0**	**6**	....	....	....	....	....
	San Jose	**NHL**	**75**	**25**	**41**	**66**	**89**	**14**	**5**	**5**	**10**	**12**
1994-95	**San Jose**	**NHL**	**22**	**7**	**10**	**17**	**18**	....	....	....	....	....
	St. Louis	**NHL**	**13**	**2**	**4**	**6**	**4**	**7**	**4**	**3**	**7**	**2**
1995-96	**Boston**	**NHL**	**59**	**13**	**33**	**46**	**40**	**4**	**0**	**2**	**2**	**16**
	Providence	AHL	7	2	7	9	10	....	....	....	....	....
1996-97	**Boston**	**NHL**	**31**	**4**	**12**	**16**	**16**	....	....	....	....	....
	Providence	AHL	37	16	29	45	63	10	1	6	7	33
	NHL Totals		**448**	**110**	**219**	**329**	**453**	**52**	**15**	**27**	**42**	**48**

Signed as a free agent by **NY Rangers**, February 26, 1988. Traded to **Los Angeles** by **NY Rangers** with Igor Liba, Michael Boyce and future considerations for Dean Kennedy and Denis Larocque, December 12, 1988. Traded to **Minnesota** by **Los Angeles** for Randy Gilhen, Charlie Huddy, Jim Thomson and NY Rangers' fourth round choice (previously acquired by Minnesota — Los Angeles selected Alexei Zhitnik) in 1991 Entry Draft, June 22, 1991. Traded to **Edmonton** by **Minnesota** for Brent Gilchrist, March 5, 1993. Claimed on waivers by **San Jose** from **Edmonton**, October 26, 1993. Traded to **St. Louis** by **San Jose** for Kevin Miller, March 23, 1995. Signed as a free agent by **Boston**, August 8, 1995.

ELLETT, DAVE BOS.

Defense. Shoots left. 6'2", 205 lbs. Born, Cleveland, OH, March 30, 1964.
(Winnipeg's 3rd choice, 75th overall, in 1982 Entry Draft).

			Regular Season					Playoffs				
Season	Club	Lea	GP	G	A	TP	PIM	GP	G	A	TP	PIM
1982-83	Bowling Green	CCHA	40	4	13	17	34	....	....	....	....	....
1983-84ab	Bowling Green	CCHA	43	15	39	54	96	....	....	....	....	....
1984-85	**Winnipeg**	**NHL**	**80**	**11**	**27**	**38**	**85**	**8**	**1**	**5**	**6**	**4**
1985-86	**Winnipeg**	**NHL**	**80**	**15**	**31**	**46**	**96**	**3**	**0**	**1**	**1**	**0**
1986-87	**Winnipeg**	**NHL**	**78**	**13**	**31**	**44**	**53**	**10**	**0**	**8**	**8**	**2**
1987-88	**Winnipeg**	**NHL**	**68**	**13**	**45**	**58**	**106**	**5**	**1**	**2**	**3**	**10**
1988-89	**Winnipeg**	**NHL**	**75**	**22**	**34**	**56**	**62**	....	....	....	....	....
1989-90	**Winnipeg**	**NHL**	**77**	**17**	**29**	**46**	**96**	**7**	**2**	**0**	**2**	**6**
1990-91	**Winnipeg**	**NHL**	**17**	**4**	**7**	**11**	**6**	....	....	....	....	....
	Toronto	**NHL**	**60**	**8**	**30**	**38**	**69**	....	....	....	....	....
1991-92	**Toronto**	**NHL**	**79**	**18**	**33**	**51**	**95**	....	....	....	....	....
1992-93	**Toronto**	**NHL**	**70**	**6**	**34**	**40**	**46**	**21**	**4**	**8**	**12**	**8**
1993-94	**Toronto**	**NHL**	**68**	**7**	**36**	**43**	**42**	**18**	**3**	**15**	**18**	**31**
1994-95	**Toronto**	**NHL**	**33**	**5**	**10**	**15**	**26**	**7**	**0**	**2**	**2**	**0**
1995-96	**Toronto**	**NHL**	**80**	**3**	**19**	**22**	**59**	**6**	**0**	**0**	**0**	**4**
1996-97	**Toronto**	**NHL**	**56**	**4**	**10**	**14**	**34**	....	....	....	....	....
	New Jersey	**NHL**	**20**	**2**	**5**	**7**	**6**	**10**	**0**	**3**	**3**	**10**
	NHL Totals		**941**	**148**	**381**	**529**	**881**	**95**	**11**	**44**	**55**	**75**

a CCHA Second All-Star Team (1984)
b Named to NCAA All-Tournament Team (1984)

Played in NHL All-Star Game (1989, 1992)

Traded to **Toronto** by **Winnipeg** with Paul Fenton for Ed Olczyk and Mark Osborne, November 10, 1990. Traded to **New Jersey** by **Toronto** with Doug Gilmour and a conditional draft choice for Jason Smith, Steve Sullivan and the rights to Alyn McCauley, February 25, 1997. Signed as a free agent by **Boston**, July 29, 1997.

ELOFSSON, JONAS (EHL-uhf-suhn, YEW-nuhs) EDM.

Defense. Shoots left. 6'1", 180 lbs. Born, Ulricehamn, Sweden, January 31, 1979.
(Edmonton's 4th choice, 94th overall, in 1997 Entry Draft).

			Regular Season					Playoffs				
Season	Club	Lea	GP	G	A	TP	PIM	GP	G	A	TP	PIM
1995-96	Farjestad	Swe. Jr.	26	6	11	17	18	....	....	....	....	....
1996-97	Farjestad	Swe.	3	0	0	0	0	5	0	1	1	0

ELOMO, MIIKA (eh-LOH-moh, MEE-ka) WSH.

Left wing. Shoots left. 6', 180 lbs. Born, Turku, Finland, April 21, 1977.
(Washington's 2nd choice, 23rd overall, in 1995 Entry Draft).

			Regular Season					Playoffs				
Season	Club	Lea	GP	G	A	TP	PIM	GP	G	A	TP	PIM
1994-95	Kiekko-67	Fin. 2	14	9	2	11	39	....	....	....	....	....
	TPS	Fin. Jr.	14	3	8	11	24	....	....	....	....	....
1995-96	TPS	Fin. Jr.	6	0	2	2	18	....	....	....	....	....
	Kiekko-67	Fin. 2	21	9	6	15	100	....	....	....	....	....
	TPS	Fin.	10	1	1	2	8	3	0	0	0	2
1996-97	Portland	AHL	52	8	9	17	37	....	....	....	....	....

ELOMO, TEEMU (eh-LOH-moh, TEE-moo) DAL.

Left wing. Shoots left. 5'11", 176 lbs. Born, Turku, Finland, January 13, 1979.
(Dallas' 5th choice, 132nd overall, in 1997 Entry Draft).

			Regular Season					Playoffs				
Season	Club	Lea	GP	G	A	TP	PIM	GP	G	A	TP	PIM
1996-97	TPS	Fin. Jr.	9	6	2	8	16	....	....	....	....	....
	Kiekko-67	Fin. 2	15	4	3	7	24	....	....	....	....	....
	TPS	Fin.	6	0	1	1	0	3	0	0	0	2

ELYNUIK, PAT (EL-ih-NYUK)

Right wing. Shoots right. 6', 185 lbs. Born, Foam Lake, Sask., October 30, 1967.
(Winnipeg's 1st choice, 8th overall, in 1986 Entry Draft).

			Regular Season					Playoffs				
Season	Club	Lea	GP	G	A	TP	PIM	GP	G	A	TP	PIM
1984-85	Prince Albert	WHL	70	23	20	43	54	13	9	3	12	7
1985-86a	Prince Albert	WHL	68	53	53	106	62	20	7	9	16	17
1986-87a	Prince Albert	WHL	64	51	62	113	40	8	5	5	10	12
1987-88	**Winnipeg**	**NHL**	**13**	**1**	**3**	**4**	**12**	....	....	....	....	....
	Moncton	AHL	30	11	18	29	35	....	....	....	....	....
1988-89	**Winnipeg**	**NHL**	**56**	**26**	**25**	**51**	**29**	....	....	....	....	....
	Moncton	AHL	7	8	2	10	2	....	....	....	....	....
1989-90	**Winnipeg**	**NHL**	**80**	**32**	**42**	**74**	**83**	**7**	**2**	**4**	**6**	**2**
1990-91	**Winnipeg**	**NHL**	**80**	**31**	**34**	**65**	**73**	....	....	....	....	....
1991-92	**Winnipeg**	**NHL**	**60**	**25**	**25**	**50**	**65**	**7**	**2**	**2**	**4**	**4**
1992-93	**Washington**	**NHL**	**80**	**22**	**35**	**57**	**66**	**6**	**2**	**3**	**5**	**19**
1993-94	**Washington**	**NHL**	**4**	**1**	**1**	**2**	**0**	....	....	....	....	....
	Tampa Bay	**NHL**	**63**	**12**	**14**	**26**	**64**	....	....	....	....	....
1994-95	**Ottawa**	**NHL**	**41**	**3**	**7**	**10**	**51**	....	....	....	....	....
1995-96	**Ottawa**	**NHL**	**29**	**1**	**2**	**3**	**16**	....	....	....	....	....
	Fort Wayne	IHL	42	22	28	50	43	....	....	....	....	....
1996-97	Michigan	IHL	81	24	34	58	62	4	1	0	1	0
	NHL Totals		**506**	**154**	**188**	**342**	**459**	**20**	**6**	**9**	**15**	**25**

a WHL East All-Star Team (1986, 1987)

Traded to **Washington** by **Winnipeg** for John Druce and Toronto's fourth round choice (previously acquired by Washington — later traded to Detroit — Detroit selected John Jakopin) in 1993 Entry Draft, October 1, 1992. Signed as a free agent by **Ottawa**, June 22, 1994. Traded to **Tampa Bay** by **Washington** for future draft choices, October 22, 1993. Signed as a free agent by **Ottawa**, June 21, 1994. Signed as a free agent by **Dallas**, September 6, 1996.

EMERSON, NELSON CAR.

Right wing. Shoots right. 5'11", 175 lbs. Born, Hamilton, Ont., August 17, 1967.
(St. Louis' 2nd choice, 44th overall, in 1985 Entry Draft).

			Regular Season					Playoffs				
Season	Club	Lea	GP	G	A	TP	PIM	GP	G	A	TP	PIM
1986-87	Bowling Green	CCHA	45	26	35	61	28	....	....	....	....	....
1987-88ab	Bowling Green	CCHA	45	34	49	83	54	....	....	....	....	....
1988-89c	Bowling Green	CCHA	44	22	46	68	46	....	....	....	....	....
1989-90bd	Bowling Green	CCHA	44	30	52	82	42	....	....	....	....	....
	Peoria	IHL	3	1	1	2	0	....	....	....	....	....
1990-91	**St. Louis**	**NHL**	**4**	**0**	**3**	**3**	**2**	....	....	....	....	....
ef	Peoria	IHL	73	36	79	115	91	17	9	12	21	16
1991-92	**St. Louis**	**NHL**	**79**	**23**	**36**	**59**	**66**	**6**	**3**	**3**	**6**	**21**
1992-93	**St. Louis**	**NHL**	**82**	**22**	**51**	**73**	**62**	**11**	**1**	**6**	**7**	**6**
1993-94	**Winnipeg**	**NHL**	**83**	**33**	**41**	**74**	**80**	....	....	....	....	....
1994-95	**Winnipeg**	**NHL**	**48**	**14**	**23**	**37**	**26**	....	....	....	....	....
1995-96	**Hartford**	**NHL**	**81**	**29**	**29**	**58**	**78**	....	....	....	....	....
1996-97	**Hartford**	**NHL**	**66**	**9**	**29**	**38**	**34**	....	....	....	....	....
	NHL Totals		**443**	**130**	**212**	**342**	**348**	**17**	**4**	**9**	**13**	**27**

a NCAA West Second All-American Team (1988)
b CCHA First All-Star Team (1988, 1990)
c CCHA Second All-Star Team (1989)
d NCAA West First All-American Team (1990)
e IHL First All-Star Team (1991)
f Won Garry F. Longman Memorial Trophy (Top Rookie - IHL) (1991)

Traded to **Winnipeg** by **St. Louis** with Stephane Quintal for Phil Housley, September 24, 1993. Traded to **Hartford** by **Winnipeg** for Darren Turcotte, October 6, 1995.

EMMA, DAVID

Center. Shoots left. 5'11", 180 lbs. Born, Cranston, RI, January 14, 1969.
(New Jersey's 6th choice, 110th overall, in 1989 Entry Draft).

			Regular Season					Playoffs				
Season	Club	Lea	GP	G	A	TP	PIM	GP	G	A	TP	PIM
1987-88	Boston College	H.E.	30	19	16	35	30	....	....	....	....	....
1988-89	Boston College	H.E.	36	20	31	51	36	....	....	....	....	....
1989-90ab	Boston College	H.E.	42	38	34	*72	46	....	....	....	....	....
1990-91abcd	Boston College	H.E.	39	*35	46	*81	44	....	....	....	....	....
1991-92	U.S. National	....	55	15	16	31	32	....	....	....	....	....
	U.S. Olympic	....	6	0	1	1	6	....	....	....	....	....
	Utica	AHL	15	4	7	11	12	4	1	1	2	2
1992-93	**New Jersey**	**NHL**	**2**	**0**	**0**	**0**	**0**	....	....	....	....	....
	Utica	AHL	61	21	40	61	47	5	2	1	3	6
1993-94	**New Jersey**	**NHL**	**15**	**5**	**5**	**10**	**2**	....	....	....	....	....
	Albany	AHL	56	26	29	55	53	5	1	2	3	8
1994-95	**New Jersey**	**NHL**	**6**	**0**	**1**	**1**	**0**	....	....	....	....	....
	Albany	AHL	1	0	0	0	0	....	....	....	....	....
1995-96	Detroit	IHL	79	30	32	62	75	11	5	2	7	2
1996-97	**Boston**	**NHL**	**5**	**0**	**0**	**0**	**0**	....	....	....	....	....
	Providence	AHL	53	10	18	28	24	....	....	....	....	....
	Phoenix	IHL	8	0	4	4	4	....	....	....	....	....
	NHL Totals		**28**	**5**	**6**	**11**	**2**	....	....	....	....	....

a Hockey East First All-Star Team (1990, 1991)
b NCAA East First All-American Team (1990, 1991)
c Hockey East Player of the Year (1991)
d Won Hobey Baker Memorial Award (Top U.S. Collegiate Player) (1991)

Signed as a free agent by **Boston**, August 27, 1996.

ENGBLOM, DAVID DET.

Center. Shoots left. 6'1", 183 lbs. Born, Vallentuna, Sweden, June 2, 1977.
(Detroit's 10th choice, 234th overall, in 1995 Entry Draft).

			Regular Season					Playoffs				
Season	Club	Lea	GP	G	A	TP	PIM	GP	G	A	TP	PIM
1993-94	Vallentuna	Swe. 2	27	0	0	0	4	....	....	....	....	....
1994-95	Vallentuna	Swe. 2	32	1	4	5	12	....	....	....	....	....
1995-96	AIK	Swe.	39	0	4	4	6	....	....	....	....	....
1996-97	AIK	Swe.	39	3	1	4	10	7	0	1	1	0

ENGLEHART, BRAD ANA.

Center. Shoots left. 5'11", 180 lbs. Born, Woodstock, N.B., September 16, 1975.
(Anaheim's 8th choice, 184th overall, in 1994 Entry Draft).

			Regular Season					Playoffs				
Season	Club	Lea	GP	G	A	TP	PIM	GP	G	A	TP	PIM
1994-95	U. Wisconsin	WCHA	29	6	6	12	42	....	....	....	....	....
1995-96	U. Wisconsin	WCHA	39	6	7	13	67	....	....	....	....	....
1996-97	U. Wisconsin	WCHA	35	17	19	36	89	....	....	....	....	....

ERIKSSON, ANDERS — DET.

Defense. Shoots left. 6'3", 218 lbs. Born, Bollnas, Sweden, January 9, 1975.
(Detroit's 1st choice, 22nd overall, in 1993 Entry Draft).

			Regular Season					Playoffs				
Season	Club	Lea	GP	G	A	TP	PIM	GP	G	A	TP	PIM
1992-93	MoDo	Swe.	20	0	2	2	2	1	0	0	0	0
1993-94	MoDo	Swe.	38	2	8	10	42	11	0	0	0	8
1994-95	MoDo	Swe.	39	3	6	9	54	....	....	....	....	....
1995-96	**Detroit**	**NHL**	**1**	**0**	**0**	**0**	**2**	**3**	**0**	**0**	**0**	**0**
	Adirondack	AHL	75	6	36	42	64	3	0	0	0	0
1996-97	**Detroit**	**NHL**	**23**	**0**	**6**	**6**	**10**	....	....	....	....	....
	Adirondack	AHL	44	3	25	28	36	4	0	1	1	4
	NHL Totals		**24**	**0**	**6**	**6**	**12**	**3**	**0**	**0**	**0**	**0**

ERREY, BOB — (AIRY) DAL.

Left wing. Shoots left. 5'10", 185 lbs. Born, Montreal, Que., September 21, 1964.
(Pittsburgh's 1st choice, 15th overall, in 1983 Entry Draft).

			Regular Season					Playoffs				
Season	Club	Lea	GP	G	A	TP	PIM	GP	G	A	TP	PIM
1981-82	Peterborough	OHL	68	29	31	60	39	9	3	1	4	9
1982-83a	Peterborough	OHL	67	53	47	100	74	4	1	3	4	7
1983-84	**Pittsburgh**	**NHL**	**65**	**9**	**13**	**22**	**29**	....	....	....	....	....
1984-85	**Pittsburgh**	**NHL**	**16**	**0**	**2**	**2**	**7**	....	....	....	....	....
	Baltimore	AHL	59	17	24	41	14	8	3	4	7	11
1985-86	**Pittsburgh**	**NHL**	**37**	**11**	**6**	**17**	**8**	....	....	....	....	....
	Baltimore	AHL	18	8	7	15	28	....	....	....	....	....
1986-87	**Pittsburgh**	**NHL**	**72**	**16**	**18**	**34**	**46**	....	....	....	....	....
1987-88	**Pittsburgh**	**NHL**	**17**	**3**	**6**	**9**	**18**	....	....	....	....	....
1988-89	**Pittsburgh**	**NHL**	**76**	**26**	**32**	**58**	**124**	**11**	**1**	**2**	**3**	**12**
1989-90	**Pittsburgh**	**NHL**	**78**	**20**	**19**	**39**	**109**	....	....	....	....	....
1990-91	**Pittsburgh**	**NHL**	**79**	**20**	**22**	**42**	**115**	**24**	**5**	**2**	**7**	**29 ♦**
1991-92	**Pittsburgh**	**NHL**	**78**	**19**	**16**	**35**	**119**	**14**	**3**	**0**	**3**	**10 ♦**
1992-93	**Pittsburgh**	**NHL**	**54**	**8**	**6**	**14**	**76**	....	....	....	....	....
	Buffalo	**NHL**	**8**	**1**	**3**	**4**	**4**	**4**	**0**	**1**	**1**	**10**
1993-94	**San Jose**	**NHL**	**64**	**12**	**18**	**30**	**126**	**14**	**3**	**2**	**5**	**10**
1994-95	**San Jose**	**NHL**	**13**	**2**	**2**	**4**	**27**	....	....	....	....	....
	Detroit	**NHL**	**30**	**6**	**11**	**17**	**31**	**18**	**1**	**5**	**6**	**30**
1995-96	**Detroit**	**NHL**	**71**	**11**	**21**	**32**	**66**	**14**	**0**	**4**	**4**	**8**
1996-97	**Detroit**	**NHL**	**36**	**1**	**2**	**3**	**27**	....	....	....	....	....
	San Jose	**NHL**	**30**	**3**	**6**	**9**	**20**	....	....	....	....	....
	NHL Totals		**824**	**168**	**203**	**371**	**952**	**99**	**13**	**16**	**29**	**109**

a OHL First All-Star Team (1983)

Traded to **Buffalo** by **Pittsburgh** for Mike Ramsey, March 22, 1993. Signed as a free agent by **San Jose**, August 17, 1993. Traded to **Detroit** by **San Jose** for Detroit's fifth round choice (Michal Bros) in 1995 Entry Draft, February 27, 1995. Claimed on waivers by **San Jose** from **Detroit**, February 8, 1997. Signed as a free agent by **Dallas**, July 28, 1997.

ESAU, LEONARD — (EE-saw)

Defense. Shoots right. 6'3", 190 lbs. Born, Meadow Lake, Sask., June 3, 1968.
(Toronto's 5th choice, 86th overall, in 1988 Entry Draft).

			Regular Season					Playoffs				
Season	Club	Lea	GP	G	A	TP	PIM	GP	G	A	TP	PIM
1988-89	St. Cloud	NCAA	35	12	27	39	69	....	....	....	....	....
1989-90	St. Cloud	NCAA	29	8	11	19	83	....	....	....	....	....
1990-91	Newmarket	AHL	76	4	14	18	28	....	....	....	....	....
1991-92	**Toronto**	**NHL**	**2**	**0**	**0**	**0**	**0**	....	....	....	....	....
	St. John's	AHL	78	9	29	38	68	13	0	2	2	14
1992-93	**Quebec**	**NHL**	**4**	**0**	**1**	**1**	**2**	....	....	....	....	....
	Halifax	AHL	75	11	31	42	79	....	....	....	....	....
1993-94	**Calgary**	**NHL**	**6**	**0**	**3**	**3**	**7**	....	....	....	....	....
	Saint John	AHL	75	12	36	48	129	7	2	2	4	6
1994-95	Saint John	AHL	54	13	27	40	73	5	0	2	2	0
	Edmonton	**NHL**	**14**	**0**	**6**	**6**	**15**	....	....	....	....	....
	Calgary	**NHL**	**1**	**0**	**0**	**0**	**0**	....	....	....	....	....
1995-96	Cincinnati	IHL	82	15	21	36	150	17	5	6	11	26
1996-97	Milwaukee	IHL	49	6	16	22	70	....	....	....	....	....
	Detroit	IHL	30	6	8	14	36	13	1	4	5	38
	NHL Totals		**27**	**0**	**10**	**10**	**24**	....	....	....	....	....

Traded to **Quebec** by **Toronto** for Ken McRae, July 21, 1992. Signed as a free agent by **Calgary**, September 6, 1993. Claimed by **Edmonton** from **Calgary** in NHL Waiver Draft, January 18, 1995. Claimed on waivers by **Calgary** from **Edmonton**, March 7, 1995. Signed as a free agent by **Florida**, August 31, 1995.

EVASON, DEAN — (EH-vih-suhn)

Center. Shoots right. 5'10", 180 lbs. Born, Flin Flon, Man., August 22, 1964.
(Washington's 3rd choice, 89th overall, in 1982 Entry Draft).

			Regular Season					Playoffs				
Season	Club	Lea	GP	G	A	TP	PIM	GP	G	A	TP	PIM
1980-81	Spokane	WHL	3	1	1	2	0	....	....	....	....	....
1981-82	Spokane	WHL	26	8	14	22	65	....	....	....	....	....
	Kamloops	WHL	44	21	55	76	47	4	2	1	3	0
1982-83	Kamloops	WHL	70	71	93	164	102	7	5	7	12	18
1983-84	**Washington**	**NHL**	**2**	**0**	**0**	**0**	**2**	....	....	....	....	....
a	Kamloops	WHL	57	49	88	137	89	17	*21	20	41	33
1984-85	**Washington**	**NHL**	**15**	**3**	**4**	**7**	**2**	....	....	....	....	....
	Hartford	**NHL**	**2**	**0**	**0**	**0**	**0**	....	....	....	....	....
	Binghamton	AHL	65	27	49	76	38	8	3	5	8	9
1985-86	**Hartford**	**NHL**	**55**	**20**	**28**	**48**	**65**	**10**	**1**	**4**	**5**	**10**
	Binghamton	AHL	26	9	17	26	29	....	....	....	....	....
1986-87	**Hartford**	**NHL**	**80**	**22**	**37**	**59**	**67**	**5**	**3**	**2**	**5**	**35**
1987-88	**Hartford**	**NHL**	**77**	**10**	**18**	**28**	**115**	**6**	**1**	**1**	**2**	**2**
1988-89	**Hartford**	**NHL**	**67**	**11**	**17**	**28**	**60**	**4**	**1**	**2**	**3**	**10**
1989-90	**Hartford**	**NHL**	**78**	**18**	**25**	**43**	**138**	**7**	**2**	**2**	**4**	**22**
1990-91	**Hartford**	**NHL**	**75**	**6**	**23**	**29**	**170**	**6**	**0**	**4**	**4**	**29**
1991-92	**San Jose**	**NHL**	**74**	**11**	**15**	**26**	**99**	....	....	....	....	....
1992-93	**San Jose**	**NHL**	**84**	**12**	**19**	**31**	**132**	....	....	....	....	....
1993-94	**Dallas**	**NHL**	**80**	**11**	**33**	**44**	**66**	**9**	**0**	**2**	**2**	**12**
1994-95	**Dallas**	**NHL**	**47**	**8**	**7**	**15**	**48**	**5**	**1**	**2**	**3**	**12**
1995-96	**Calgary**	**NHL**	**67**	**7**	**7**	**14**	**38**	**3**	**0**	**1**	**1**	**0**
1996-97	Cdn. National	....	56	25	46	71	106	....	....	....	....	....
	Zug	Switz.	3	0	1	1	2	4	0	2	2	4
	NHL Totals		**803**	**139**	**233**	**372**	**1002**	**55**	**9**	**20**	**29**	**132**

a WHL First All-Star Team, West Division (1984)

Traded to **Hartford** by **Washington** with Peter Sidorkiewicz for David Jensen, March 12, 1985. Traded to **San Jose** by **Hartford** for Dan Keczmer, October 2, 1991. Traded to **Dallas** by **San Jose** for San Jose's sixth round choice (previously acquired by Dallas — San Jose selected Petri Varis) in 1993 Entry Draft, June 26, 1993. Signed as a free agent by **Calgary**, August 1, 1995.

EWEN, TODD — (YOO-ihn) S.J.

Right wing. Shoots right. 6'2", 230 lbs. Born, Saskatoon, Sask., March 22, 1966.
(Edmonton's 9th choice, 168th overall, in 1984 Entry Draft).

			Regular Season					Playoffs				
Season	Club	Lea	GP	G	A	TP	PIM	GP	G	A	TP	PIM
1982-83	Kamloops	WHL	3	0	0	0	2	2	0	0	0	0
1983-84	N. Westminster	WHL	68	11	13	24	176	7	2	1	3	15
1984-85	N. Westminster	WHL	56	11	20	31	304	10	1	8	9	60
1985-86	N. Westminster	WHL	60	28	24	52	289	....	....	....	....	....
	Maine	AHL	....	....	....	....	....	3	0	0	0	7
1986-87	**St. Louis**	**NHL**	**23**	**2**	**0**	**2**	**84**	**4**	**0**	**0**	**0**	**23**
	Peoria	IHL	16	3	3	6	110	....	....	....	....	....
1987-88	**St. Louis**	**NHL**	**64**	**4**	**2**	**6**	**227**	**6**	**0**	**0**	**0**	**21**
1988-89	**St. Louis**	**NHL**	**34**	**4**	**5**	**9**	**171**	**2**	**0**	**0**	**0**	**21**
1989-90	**St. Louis**	**NHL**	**3**	**0**	**0**	**0**	**11**	....	....	....	....	....
	Peoria	IHL	2	0	0	0	12	....	....	....	....	....
	Montreal	**NHL**	**41**	**4**	**6**	**10**	**158**	**10**	**0**	**0**	**0**	**4**
1990-91	**Montreal**	**NHL**	**28**	**3**	**2**	**5**	**128**	....	....	....	....	....
1991-92	**Montreal**	**NHL**	**46**	**1**	**2**	**3**	**130**	**3**	**0**	**0**	**0**	**18**
1992-93	**Montreal**	**NHL**	**75**	**5**	**9**	**14**	**193**	**1**	**0**	**0**	**0**	**0 ♦**
1993-94	**Anaheim**	**NHL**	**76**	**9**	**9**	**18**	**272**	....	....	....	....	....
1994-95	**Anaheim**	**NHL**	**24**	**0**	**0**	**0**	**90**	....	....	....	....	....
1995-96	**Anaheim**	**NHL**	**53**	**4**	**3**	**7**	**285**	....	....	....	....	....
1996-97	**San Jose**	**NHL**	**51**	**0**	**2**	**2**	**162**	....	....	....	....	....
	NHL Totals		**518**	**36**	**40**	**76**	**1911**	**26**	**0**	**0**	**0**	**87**

Traded to **St. Louis** by **Edmonton** for Shawn Evans, October 15, 1986. Traded to **Montreal** by **St. Louis** for future considerations, December 12, 1989. Traded to **Anaheim** by **Montreal** with Patrik Carnback for Anaheim's third round choice (Chris Murray) in 1994 Entry Draft, August 10, 1993. Signed as a free agent by **San Jose**, September 4, 1996.

FAIRCHILD, KELLY — TOR.

Center. Shoots left. 5'11", 180 lbs. Born, Hibbing, MN, April 9, 1973.
(Los Angeles' 7th choice, 152nd overall, in 1991 Entry Draft).

			Regular Season					Playoffs				
Season	Club	Lea	GP	G	A	TP	PIM	GP	G	A	TP	PIM
1991-92	U. Wisconsin	WCHA	37	11	10	21	45	....	....	....	....	....
1992-93	U. Wisconsin	WCHA	42	25	29	54	54	....	....	....	....	....
1993-94a	U. Wisconsin	WCHA	42	20	44	*64	81	....	....	....	....	....
1994-95	St. John's	AHL	53	27	23	50	51	4	0	2	2	4
1995-96	**Toronto**	**NHL**	**1**	**0**	**1**	**1**	**2**	....	....	....	....	....
	St. John's	AHL	78	29	49	78	85	2	0	1	1	4
1996-97	**Toronto**	**NHL**	**22**	**0**	**2**	**2**	**2**	....	....	....	....	....
	St. John's	AHL	29	9	22	31	36	....	....	....	....	....
	Orlando	IHL	25	9	6	15	20	9	6	5	11	16
	NHL Totals		**23**	**0**	**3**	**3**	**4**	....	....	....	....	....

a WCHA First All-Star Team (1994)

Traded to **Toronto** by **Los Angeles** with Dixon Ward, Guy Leveque and Shayne Toporowski for Eric Lacroix, Chris Snell and Toronto's fourth round choice (Eric Belanger) in 1996 Entry Draft, October 3, 1994.

FALLOON, PAT — (fah-LOON) PHI.

Right wing. Shoots right. 5'11", 190 lbs. Born, Foxwarren, Man., September 22, 1972.
(San Jose's 1st choice, 2nd overall, in 1991 Entry Draft).

			Regular Season					Playoffs				
Season	Club	Lea	GP	G	A	TP	PIM	GP	G	A	TP	PIM
1988-89	Spokane	WHL	72	22	56	78	41	....	....	....	....	....
1989-90	Spokane	WHL	71	60	64	124	48	6	5	8	13	4
1990-91abcd	Spokane	WHL	61	64	74	138	33	15	10	14	24	10
1991-92	**San Jose**	**NHL**	**79**	**25**	**34**	**59**	**16**	....	....	....	....	....
1992-93	**San Jose**	**NHL**	**41**	**14**	**14**	**28**	**12**	....	....	....	....	....
1993-94	**San Jose**	**NHL**	**83**	**22**	**31**	**53**	**18**	**14**	**1**	**2**	**3**	**6**
1994-95	**San Jose**	**NHL**	**46**	**12**	**7**	**19**	**25**	**11**	**3**	**1**	**4**	**0**
1995-96	**San Jose**	**NHL**	**9**	**3**	**0**	**3**	**4**	....	....	....	....	....
	Philadelphia	**NHL**	**62**	**22**	**26**	**48**	**6**	**12**	**3**	**2**	**5**	**2**
1996-97	**Philadelphia**	**NHL**	**52**	**11**	**12**	**23**	**10**	**14**	**3**	**1**	**4**	**2**
	NHL Totals		**372**	**109**	**124**	**233**	**91**	**51**	**10**	**6**	**16**	**10**

a WHL West First All-Star Team (1991)
b Canadian Major Junior Most Sportsmanlike Player of the Year (1991)
c Memorial Cup All-Star Team (1991)
d Won Stafford Smythe Memorial Trophy (Memorial Cup Tournament MVP) (1991)

Traded to **Philadelphia** by **San Jose** for Martin Spanhel, Philadelphia's first round choice (later traded to Phoenix — Phoenix selected Daniel Briere) in 1996 Entry Draft and Philadelphia's fourth round choice (later traded to Buffalo — Buffalo selected Mike Martone), in 1996 Entry Draft, November 16, 1995.

FARKAS, JEFF — (FAHR-kuhs) TOR.

Center. Shoots left. 6'1", 173 lbs. Born, Amherst, MA, January 24, 1978.
(Toronto's 1st choice, 57th overall, in 1997 Entry Draft).

			Regular Season					Playoffs				
Season	Club	Lea	GP	G	A	TP	PIM	GP	G	A	TP	PIM
1996-97	Boston College	H.E.	35	13	23	36	34	....	....	....	....	....

FAUST, ANDRE

Center. Shoots left. 5'11", 191 lbs. Born, Joliette, Que., October 7, 1969.
(New Jersey's 8th choice, 173rd overall, in 1989 Entry Draft).

			Regular Season					Playoffs				
Season	Club	Lea	GP	G	A	TP	PIM	GP	G	A	TP	PIM
1988-89	Princeton	ECAC	27	15	24	39	28	....	....	....	....	....
1989-90a	Princeton	ECAC	22	9	28	37	20	....	....	....	....	....
1990-91	Princeton	ECAC	26	15	22	37	51	....	....	....	....	....
1991-92a	Princeton	ECAC	27	14	21	35	38	....	....	....	....	....
1992-93	**Philadelphia**	**NHL**	**10**	**2**	**2**	**4**	**4**	....	....	....	....	....
	Hershey	AHL	62	26	25	51	71	....	....	....	....	....
1993-94	**Philadelphia**	**NHL**	**37**	**8**	**5**	**13**	**10**	....	....	....	....	....
	Hershey	AHL	13	6	7	13	10	10	4	3	7	26
1994-95	Hershey	AHL	55	12	28	40	72	6	1	5	6	12
1995-96	Springfield	AHL	50	19	19	38	40	10	5	2	7	6
1996-97	Augsburg	Ger.	46	21	19	40	84	4	3	1	4	2
	NHL Totals		**47**	**10**	**7**	**17**	**14**	....	....	....	....	....

a ECAC Second All-Star Team (1990, 1992)

Signed as a free agent by **Philadelphia**, October 5, 1992. Traded to **Winnipeg** by **Philadelphia** for Winnipeg's seventh round choice in 1997 Entry Draft, September 20, 1995.

FEATHERSTONE, GLEN

Defense. Shoots left. 6'4", 209 lbs. Born, Toronto, Ont., July 8, 1968.
(St. Louis' 4th choice, 73rd overall, in 1986 Entry Draft).

			Regular Season					Playoffs				
Season	Club	Lea	GP	G	A	TP	PIM	GP	G	A	TP	PIM
1985-86	Windsor	OHL	49	0	6	6	135	14	1	1	2	23
1986-87	Windsor	OHL	47	6	11	17	154	14	2	6	8	19
1987-88	Windsor	OHL	53	7	27	34	201	12	6	9	15	47
1988-89	**St. Louis**	**NHL**	**18**	**0**	**2**	**2**	**22**	**6**	**0**	**0**	**0**	**25**
	Peoria	IHL	37	5	19	24	97	....	....	....	....	....
1989-90	**St. Louis**	**NHL**	**58**	**0**	**12**	**12**	**145**	**12**	**0**	**2**	**2**	**47**
	Peoria	IHL	15	1	4	5	43	....	....	....	....	....
1990-91	**St. Louis**	**NHL**	**68**	**5**	**15**	**20**	**204**	**9**	**0**	**0**	**0**	**31**
1991-92	**Boston**	**NHL**	**7**	**1**	**0**	**1**	**20**	....	....	....	....	....
1992-93	**Boston**	**NHL**	**34**	**5**	**5**	**10**	**102**	....	....	....	....	....
	Providence	AHL	8	3	4	7	60	....	....	....	....	....
1993-94	**Boston**	**NHL**	**58**	**1**	**8**	**9**	**152**	**1**	**0**	**0**	**0**	**0**
1994-95	**NY Rangers**	**NHL**	**6**	**1**	**0**	**1**	**18**	....	....	....	....	....
	Hartford	**NHL**	**13**	**1**	**1**	**2**	**32**	....	....	....	....	....
1995-96	**Hartford**	**NHL**	**68**	**2**	**10**	**12**	**138**	....	....	....	....	....
1996-97	**Hartford**	**NHL**	**41**	**2**	**5**	**7**	**87**	....	....	....	....	....
	Calgary	**NHL**	**13**	**1**	**3**	**4**	**19**	....	....	....	....	....
	NHL Totals		**384**	**19**	**61**	**80**	**939**	**28**	**0**	**2**	**2**	**103**

Signed as a free agent by **Boston**, July 25, 1991. Traded to **NY Rangers** by **Boston** for Daniel Lacroix, August 19, 1994. Traded to **Hartford** by **NY Rangers** with Michael Stewart, NY Rangers' first round choice (Jean-Sebastien Giguere) in 1995 Entry Draft and fourth round choice (Steve Wasylko) in 1996 Entry Draft for Pat Verbeek, March 23, 1995. Traded to **Calgary** by **Hartford** with Hnat Domenichelli, New Jersey's second round choice (previously acquired by Hartford — Calgary selected Dimitri Kokorev) in 1997 Entry Draft and Vancouver's third round choice (previously acquired by Hartford) in 1998 Entry Draft for Steve Chiasson and Colorado's third round choice (previously acquired by Calgary — Carolina selected Francis Lessard) in 1997 Entry Draft, March 5, 1997.

FEDOROV, SERGEI (FEH-duh-rahf) DET.

Center. Shoots left. 6'1", 200 lbs. Born, Pskov, USSR, December 13, 1969.
(Detroit's 4th choice, 74th overall, in 1989 Entry Draft).

			Regular Season					Playoffs				
Season	Club	Lea	GP	G	A	TP	PIM	GP	G	A	TP	PIM
1986-87	CSKA	USSR	29	6	6	12	12	....	....	....	....	....
1987-88	CSKA	USSR	48	7	9	16	20	....	....	....	....	....
1988-89	CSKA	USSR	44	9	8	17	35	....	....	....	....	....
1989-90	CSKA	USSR	48	19	10	29	22	....	....	....	....	....
1990-91a	**Detroit**	**NHL**	**77**	**31**	**48**	**79**	**66**	**7**	**1**	**5**	**6**	**4**
1991-92	**Detroit**	**NHL**	**80**	**32**	**54**	**86**	**72**	**11**	**5**	**5**	**10**	**8**
1992-93	**Detroit**	**NHL**	**73**	**34**	**53**	**87**	**72**	**7**	**3**	**6**	**9**	**23**
1993-94bcde	**Detroit**	**NHL**	**82**	**56**	**64**	**120**	**34**	**7**	**1**	**7**	**8**	**6**
1994-95	**Detroit**	**NHL**	**42**	**20**	**30**	**50**	**24**	**17**	**7**	***17**	***24**	**6**
1995-96c	**Detroit**	**NHL**	**78**	**39**	**68**	**107**	**48**	**19**	**2**	***18**	**20**	**10**
1996-97	**Detroit**	**NHL**	**74**	**30**	**33**	**63**	**30**	**20**	**8**	**12**	**20**	**12 ♦**
	NHL Totals		**506**	**242**	**350**	**592**	**346**	**88**	**27**	**70**	**97**	**69**

a NHL/Upper Deck All-Rookie Team (1991)
b NHL First All-Star Team (1994)
c Won Frank J. Selke Trophy (1994, 1996)
d Won Lester B. Pearson Award (1994)
e Won Hart Trophy (1994)

Played in NHL All-Star Game (1992, 1994, 1996)

FEDOTOV, SERGEI (feh-DAW-tahf) CAR.

Defense. Shoots left. 6'1", 185 lbs. Born, Moscow, USSR, January 24, 1977.
(Hartford's 2nd choice, 35th overall, in 1995 Entry Draft).

			Regular Season					Playoffs				
Season	Club	Lea	GP	G	A	TP	PIM	GP	G	A	TP	PIM
1994-95	Moscow D'amo	CIS	8	0	0	0	2	....	....	....	....	....
1995-96	Magnitogorsk	CIS	7	0	0	0	2	....	....	....	....	....
	Moscow D'amo	CIS	4	0	0	0	24	....	....	....	....	....
	Saratov	CIS	41	4	8	12	30	....	....	....	....	....
1996-97	Saratov	Rus.	38	2	11	13	64	5	0	1	1	8
	Detroit	OHL	52	10	27	37	60	5	0	2	2	9

FEDYK, BRENT (FEH-dihk)

Left wing. Shoots right. 6', 194 lbs. Born, Yorkton, Sask., March 8, 1967.
(Detroit's 1st choice, 8th overall, in 1985 Entry Draft).

			Regular Season					Playoffs				
Season	Club	Lea	GP	G	A	TP	PIM	GP	G	A	TP	PIM
1983-84	Regina	WHL	63	15	28	43	30	23	8	7	15	6
1984-85	Regina	WHL	66	35	35	70	48	8	5	4	9	0
1985-86	Regina	WHL	50	43	34	77	47	5	0	1	1	0
1986-87	Regina	WHL	12	9	6	15	9	....	....	....	....	....
	Seattle	WHL	13	5	11	16	9	....	....	....	....	....
	Portland	WHL	11	5	4	9	6	14	5	6	11	0
1987-88	**Detroit**	**NHL**	**2**	**0**	**1**	**1**	**2**	....	....	....	....	....
	Adirondack	AHL	34	9	11	20	22	5	0	2	2	6
1988-89	**Detroit**	**NHL**	**5**	**2**	**0**	**2**	**0**	....	....	....	....	....
	Adirondack	AHL	66	40	28	68	33	15	7	8	15	23
1989-90	**Detroit**	**NHL**	**27**	**1**	**4**	**5**	**6**	....	....	....	....	....
	Adirondack	AHL	33	14	15	29	24	6	2	1	3	4
1990-91	**Detroit**	**NHL**	**67**	**16**	**19**	**35**	**38**	**6**	**1**	**0**	**1**	**2**
1991-92	**Detroit**	**NHL**	**61**	**5**	**8**	**13**	**42**	**1**	**0**	**0**	**0**	**2**
	Adirondack	AHL	1	0	2	2	0	....	....	....	....	....
1992-93	**Philadelphia**	**NHL**	**74**	**21**	**38**	**59**	**48**	....	....	....	....	....
1993-94	**Philadelphia**	**NHL**	**72**	**20**	**18**	**38**	**74**	....	....	....	....	....
1994-95	**Philadelphia**	**NHL**	**30**	**8**	**4**	**12**	**14**	**9**	**2**	**2**	**4**	**8**
1995-96	**Philadelphia**	**NHL**	**24**	**10**	**5**	**15**	**24**	....	....	....	....	....
	Dallas	**NHL**	**41**	**10**	**9**	**19**	**30**	....	....	....	....	....
1996-97	Michigan	IHL	9	1	2	3	4	....	....	....	....	....
	NHL Totals		**403**	**93**	**106**	**199**	**278**	**16**	**3**	**2**	**5**	**12**

Traded to **Philadelphia** by **Detroit** for Philadelphia's fourth round choice (later traded to Boston — Boston selected Charles Paquette) in 1993 Entry Draft, October 1, 1992. Traded to **Dallas** by **Philadelphia** for Trent Klatt, December 13, 1995.

FERENCE, BRAD (fuhr-EHNS) VAN.

Defense. Shoots right. 6'3", 185 lbs. Born, Calgary, Alta., April 2, 1979.
(Vancouver's 1st choice, 10th overall, in 1997 Entry Draft).

			Regular Season					Playoffs				
Season	Club	Lea	GP	G	A	TP	PIM	GP	G	A	TP	PIM
1995-96	Spokane	WHL	5	0	2	2	18	....	....	....	....	....
1996-97	Spokane	WHL	67	6	20	26	324	9	0	4	4	21

FERGUSON, CRAIG FLA.

Right wing. Shoots left. 5'11", 190 lbs. Born, Castro Valley, CA, April 8, 1970.
(Montreal's 7th choice, 146th overall, in 1989 Entry Draft).

			Regular Season					Playoffs				
Season	Club	Lea	GP	G	A	TP	PIM	GP	G	A	TP	PIM
1988-89	Yale	ECAC	24	11	6	17	20	....	....	....	....	....
1989-90	Yale	ECAC	28	6	13	19	36	....	....	....	....	....
1990-91	Yale	ECAC	29	11	10	21	34	....	....	....	....	....
1991-92	Yale	ECAC	27	9	16	25	26	....	....	....	....	....
1992-93	Fredericton	AHL	55	15	13	28	20	5	0	1	1	2
	Wheeling	ECHL	9	6	5	11	24	....	....	....	....	....
1993-94	**Montreal**	**NHL**	**2**	**0**	**1**	**1**	**0**	....	....	....	....	....
	Fredericton	AHL	57	29	32	61	60	....	....	....	....	....
1994-95	Fredericton	AHL	80	27	35	62	62	17	6	2	8	6
	Montreal	**NHL**	**1**	**0**	**0**	**0**	**0**	....	....	....	....	....
1995-96	**Montreal**	**NHL**	**10**	**1**	**0**	**1**	**2**	....	....	....	....	....
	Calgary	**NHL**	**8**	**0**	**0**	**0**	**4**	....	....	....	....	....
	Saint John	AHL	18	5	13	18	8	....	....	....	....	....
	Phoenix	IHL	31	6	9	15	25	4	0	2	2	6
1996-97	**Florida**	**NHL**	**3**	**0**	**0**	**0**	**0**	....	....	....	....	....
	Carolina	AHL	74	29	41	70	57	....	....	....	....	....
	NHL Totals		**24**	**1**	**1**	**2**	**6**	....	....	....	....	....

Traded to **Calgary** by **Montreal** with Yves Sarault for Calgary's eighth round choice (Petr Kubos) in 1997 Entry Draft, November 26, 1995. Traded to **Los Angeles** by **Calgary** for Pat Conacher, February 10, 1996. Signed as a free agent by **Florida**, July 24, 1996.

FERGUSON, SCOTT EDM.

Defense. Shoots left. 6'1", 195 lbs. Born, Camrose, Alta., January 6, 1973.

			Regular Season					Playoffs				
Season	Club	Lea	GP	G	A	TP	PIM	GP	G	A	TP	PIM
1990-91	Kamloops	WHL	4	0	0	0	0	....	....	....	....	....
1991-92	Kamloops	WHL	62	4	10	14	138	12	0	2	2	21
1992-93	Kamloops	WHL	71	4	19	23	206	13	0	2	2	24
1993-94a	Kamloops	WHL	68	5	49	54	180	19	5	11	16	48
1994-95	Cape Breton	AHL	58	4	6	10	103	....	....	....	....	....
	Wheeling	ECHL	5	1	5	6	16	....	....	....	....	....
1995-96	Cape Breton	AHL	80	5	16	21	196	....	....	....	....	....
1996-97	Hamilton	AHL	74	6	14	20	115	21	5	7	12	59

a WHL West Second All-Star Team (1994)

Signed as a free agent by **Edmonton**, June 2, 1994.

FERRARO, CHRIS NYR

Right wing. Shoots right. 5'10", 185 lbs. Born, Port Jefferson, NY, January 24, 1973.
(NY Rangers' 4th choice, 85th overall, in 1992 Entry Draft).

			Regular Season					Playoffs				
Season	Club	Lea	GP	G	A	TP	PIM	GP	G	A	TP	PIM
1992-93	U. of Maine	H.E.	39	25	26	51	46	....	....	....	....	....
1993-94	U. of Maine	H.E.	4	0	1	1	8	....	....	....	....	....
	U.S. National	....	48	8	34	42	58	....	....	....	....	....
1994-95	Atlanta	IHL	54	13	14	27	72	....	....	....	....	....
	Binghamton	AHL	13	6	4	10	38	10	2	3	5	16
1995-96	**NY Rangers**	**NHL**	**2**	**1**	**0**	**1**	**0**	....	....	....	....	....
	Binghamton	AHL	77	32	67	99	208	4	4	2	6	13
1996-97	**NY Rangers**	**NHL**	**12**	**1**	**1**	**2**	**6**	....	....	....	....	....
	Binghamton	AHL	53	29	34	63	94	....	....	....	....	....
	NHL Totals		**14**	**2**	**1**	**3**	**6**	....	....	....	....	....

FERRARO, PETER NYR

Center. Shoots right. 5'10", 185 lbs. Born, Port Jefferson, NY, January 24, 1973.
(NY Rangers' 1st choice, 24th overall, in 1992 Entry Draft).

			Regular Season					Playoffs				
Season	Club	Lea	GP	G	A	TP	PIM	GP	G	A	TP	PIM
1992-93	U. of Maine	H.E.	36	18	32	50	106	....	....	....	....	....
1993-94	U. of Maine	H.E.	4	3	6	9	16	....	....	....	....	....
	U.S. National	....	60	30	34	64	87	....	....	....	....	....
	U.S. Olympic	....	8	6	0	6	6	....	....	....	....	....
1994-95	Atlanta	IHL	61	15	24	39	118	....	....	....	....	....
	Binghamton	AHL	12	2	6	8	67	11	4	3	7	51
1995-96	**NY Rangers**	**NHL**	**5**	**0**	**1**	**1**	**0**	....	....	....	....	....
a	Binghamton	AHL	68	48	53	101	157	4	1	6	7	22
1996-97	**NY Rangers**	**NHL**	**2**	**0**	**0**	**0**	**0**	**2**	**0**	**0**	**0**	**0**
	Binghamton	AHL	75	38	39	77	171	4	3	1	4	18
	NHL Totals		**7**	**0**	**1**	**1**	**0**	**2**	**0**	**0**	**0**	**0**

a AHL First All-Star Team (1996)

FERRARO, RAY L.A.

Center. Shoots left. 5'10", 185 lbs. Born, Trail, B.C., August 23, 1964.
(Hartford's 5th choice, 88th overall, in 1982 Entry Draft).

			Regular Season					Playoffs				
Season	Club	Lea	GP	G	A	TP	PIM	GP	G	A	TP	PIM
1982-83	Portland	WHL	50	41	49	90	39	14	14	10	24	13
1983-84a	Brandon	WHL	72	*108	84	*192	84	11	13	15	28	20
1984-85	**Hartford**	**NHL**	**44**	**11**	**17**	**28**	**40**	....	....	....	....	....
	Binghamton	AHL	37	20	13	33	29	....	....	....	....	....
1985-86	**Hartford**	**NHL**	**76**	**30**	**47**	**77**	**57**	**10**	**3**	**6**	**9**	**4**
1986-87	**Hartford**	**NHL**	**80**	**27**	**32**	**59**	**42**	**6**	**1**	**1**	**2**	**8**
1987-88	**Hartford**	**NHL**	**68**	**21**	**29**	**50**	**81**	**6**	**1**	**1**	**2**	**6**
1988-89	**Hartford**	**NHL**	**80**	**41**	**35**	**76**	**86**	**4**	**2**	**0**	**2**	**4**
1989-90	**Hartford**	**NHL**	**79**	**25**	**29**	**54**	**109**	**7**	**0**	**3**	**3**	**2**
1990-91	**Hartford**	**NHL**	**15**	**2**	**5**	**7**	**18**	....	....	....	....	....
	NY Islanders	**NHL**	**61**	**19**	**16**	**35**	**52**	....	....	....	....	....
1991-92	**NY Islanders**	**NHL**	**80**	**40**	**40**	**80**	**92**	....	....	....	....	....
1992-93	**NY Islanders**	**NHL**	**46**	**14**	**13**	**27**	**40**	**18**	**13**	**7**	**20**	**18**
	Capital Dist.	AHL	1	0	2	2	2	....	....	....	....	....
1993-94	**NY Islanders**	**NHL**	**82**	**21**	**32**	**53**	**83**	**4**	**1**	**0**	**1**	**6**
1994-95	**NY Islanders**	**NHL**	**47**	**22**	**21**	**43**	**30**	....	....	....	....	....
1995-96	**NY Rangers**	**NHL**	**65**	**25**	**29**	**54**	**82**	....	....	....	....	....
	Los Angeles	**NHL**	**11**	**4**	**2**	**6**	**10**	....	....	....	....	....
1996-97	**Los Angeles**	**NHL**	**81**	**25**	**21**	**46**	**112**	....	....	....	....	....
	NHL Totals		**915**	**327**	**368**	**695**	**934**	**55**	**21**	**18**	**39**	**48**

a WHL First All-Star Team (1984)

Played in NHL All-Star Game (1992)

Traded to **NY Islanders** by **Hartford** for Doug Crossman, November 13, 1990. Signed as a free agent by **NY Rangers**, August 9, 1995. Traded to **Los Angeles** by **NY Rangers** with Ian Laperriere, Mattias Norstrom, Nathan Lafayette and NY Rangers' fourth round choice (Sean Blanchard) in 1997 Entry Draft for Marty McSorley, Jari Kurri and Shane Churla, March 14, 1996.

FETISOV, VIACHESLAV (feh-TEE-sahf) DET.

Defense. Shoots left. 6'1", 220 lbs. Born, Moscow, USSR, April 20, 1958.
(New Jersey's 6th choice, 150th overall, in 1983 Entry Draft).

			Regular Season					Playoffs				
Season	Club	Lea	GP	G	A	TP	PIM	GP	G	A	TP	PIM
1974-75	CSKA	USSR	1	0	0	0	0	....	....	....	....	....
1976-77	CSKA	USSR	28	3	4	7	14	....	....	....	....	....
1977-78a	CSKA	USSR	35	9	18	27	46	....	....	....	....	....
1978-79	CSKA	USSR	29	10	19	29	40	....	....	....	....	....
1979-80	CSKA	USSR	37	10	14	24	46	....	....	....	....	....
1980-81	CSKA	USSR	48	13	16	29	44	....	....	....	....	....
1981-82ac	CSKA	USSR	46	15	26	41	20	....	....	....	....	....
1982-83a	CSKA	USSR	43	6	17	23	46	....	....	....	....	....
1983-84ab	CSKA	USSR	44	19	30	49	38	....	....	....	....	....
1984-85a	CSKA	USSR	20	13	12	25	6	....	....	....	....	....
1985-86abc	CSKA	USSR	40	15	19	34	12	....	....	....	....	....
1986-87ab	CSKA	USSR	39	13	20	33	18	....	....	....	....	....
1987-88ab	CSKA	USSR	46	18	17	35	26	....	....	....	....	....
1988-89	CSKA	USSR	23	9	8	17	18	....	....	....	....	....
1989-90	**New Jersey**	**NHL**	**72**	**8**	**34**	**42**	**52**	**6**	**0**	**2**	**2**	**10**
1990-91	**New Jersey**	**NHL**	**67**	**3**	**16**	**19**	**62**	**7**	**0**	**0**	**0**	**17**
	Utica	AHL	1	1	1	2	0	....	....	....	....	....
1991-92	**New Jersey**	**NHL**	**70**	**3**	**23**	**26**	**108**	**6**	**0**	**3**	**3**	**8**
1992-93	**New Jersey**	**NHL**	**76**	**4**	**23**	**27**	**158**	**5**	**0**	**2**	**2**	**4**
1993-94	**New Jersey**	**NHL**	**52**	**1**	**14**	**15**	**30**	**14**	**1**	**0**	**1**	**8**
1994-95	Spartak	CIS	1	0	1	1	4	....	....	....	....	....
	New Jersey	**NHL**	**4**	**0**	**1**	**1**	**0**	....	....	....	....	....
	Detroit	**NHL**	**14**	**3**	**11**	**14**	**2**	**18**	**0**	**8**	**8**	**14**
1995-96	**Detroit**	**NHL**	**69**	**7**	**35**	**42**	**96**	**19**	**1**	**4**	**5**	**34**
1996-97	**Detroit**	**NHL**	**64**	**5**	**23**	**28**	**76**	**20**	**0**	**4**	**4**	**42 ♦**
	NHL Totals		**488**	**34**	**180**	**214**	**584**	**95**	**2**	**23**	**25**	**137**

a Soviet National League All-Star Team (1979, 1980, 1982-88)
b Leningradskaya-Pravda Trophy (Top Scoring Defenseman) (1984, 1986-88)
c Soviet Player of the Year (1982, 1986, 1988)

Played in NHL All-Star Game (1997)

Traded to **Detroit** by **New Jersey** for Detroit's third round choice (David Gosselin) in 1995 Entry Draft, April 3, 1995.

FILATOV, ANATOLI (fih-LAH-tohv) S.J.

Right wing. Shoots right. 5'10", 180 lbs. Born, Kamenogorsk, USSR, April 28, 1975.
(San Jose's 9th choice, 158th overall, in 1993 Entry Draft).

			Regular Season					Playoffs				
Season	Club	Lea	GP	G	A	TP	PIM	GP	G	A	TP	PIM
1992-93	Kamenogorsk	CIS	17	4	0	4	14	....	....	....	....	....
1993-94	Kamenogorsk	CIS	20	3	3	6	22	....	....	....	....	....
1994-95	Kamenogorsk	CIS	33	6	6	12	30	....	....	....	....	....
	Niagara Falls	OHL	12	2	3	5	6	....	....	....	....	....
1995-96	Kamenogorsk	CIS	48	9	15	24	78	....	....	....	....	....
1996-97	Kamenogorsk	Rus. 2	25	14	14	28	28	....	....	....	....	....

FINLEY, JEFF NYR

Defense. Shoots left. 6'2", 205 lbs. Born, Edmonton, Alta., April 14, 1967.
(NY Islanders' 4th choice, 55th overall, in 1985 Entry Draft).

			Regular Season					Playoffs				
Season	Club	Lea	GP	G	A	TP	PIM	GP	G	A	TP	PIM
1983-84	Portland	WHL	5	0	0	0	5	5	0	1	1	4
1984-85	Portland	WHL	69	6	44	50	57	6	1	2	3	2
1985-86	Portland	WHL	70	11	59	70	83	15	1	7	8	16
1986-87	Portland	WHL	72	13	53	66	113	20	1	*21	22	27
1987-88	**NY Islanders**	**NHL**	**10**	**0**	**5**	**5**	**15**	**1**	**0**	**0**	**0**	**2**
	Springfield	AHL	52	5	18	23	50	....	....	....	....	....
1988-89	**NY Islanders**	**NHL**	**4**	**0**	**0**	**0**	**6**	....	....	....	....	....
	Springfield	AHL	65	3	16	19	55	....	....	....	....	....
1989-90	**NY Islanders**	**NHL**	**11**	**0**	**1**	**1**	**0**	**5**	**0**	**2**	**2**	**2**
	Springfield	AHL	57	1	15	16	41	13	1	4	5	23
1990-91	**NY Islanders**	**NHL**	**11**	**0**	**0**	**0**	**4**	....	....	....	....	....
	Capital Dist.	AHL	67	10	34	44	34	....	....	....	....	....
1991-92	**NY Islanders**	**NHL**	**51**	**1**	**10**	**11**	**26**	....	....	....	....	....
	Capital Dist.	AHL	20	1	9	10	6	....	....	....	....	....
1992-93	Capital Dist.	AHL	61	6	29	35	34	4	0	1	1	0
1993-94	**Philadelphia**	**NHL**	**55**	**1**	**8**	**9**	**24**	....	....	....	....	....
1994-95	Hershey	AHL	36	2	9	11	33	6	0	1	1	8
1995-96	**Winnipeg**	**NHL**	**65**	**1**	**5**	**6**	**81**	**6**	**0**	**0**	**0**	**4**
	Springfield	AHL	14	3	12	15	22	....	....	....	....	....
1996-97	**Phoenix**	**NHL**	**65**	**3**	**7**	**10**	**40**	**1**	**0**	**0**	**0**	**2**
	NHL Totals		**272**	**6**	**36**	**42**	**196**	**13**	**0**	**2**	**2**	**10**

Traded to **Ottawa** by **NY Islanders** for Chris Luongo, June 30, 1993. Signed as a free agent by **Philadelphia**, July 30, 1993. Traded to **Winnipeg** by **Philadelphia** for Russ Romaniuk, June 27, 1995. Signed as a free agent by **NY Rangers**, July 16, 1997.

FINN, STEVEN L.A.

Defense. Shoots left. 6', 191 lbs. Born, Laval, Que., August 20, 1966.
(Quebec's 3rd choice, 57th overall, in 1984 Entry Draft).

			Regular Season					Playoffs				
Season	Club	Lea	GP	G	A	TP	PIM	GP	G	A	TP	PIM
1982-83	Laval	QMJHL	69	7	30	37	108	6	0	2	2	6
1983-84	Laval	QMJHL	68	7	39	46	159	14	1	6	7	27
1984-85a	Laval	QMJHL	61	20	33	53	169	....	....	....	....	....
	Fredericton	AHL	4	0	0	0	14	6	1	1	2	4
1985-86	**Quebec**	**NHL**	**17**	**0**	**1**	**1**	**28**	....	....	....	....	....
	Laval	QMJHL	29	4	15	19	111	14	6	16	22	57
1986-87	**Quebec**	**NHL**	**36**	**2**	**5**	**7**	**40**	**13**	**0**	**2**	**2**	**29**
	Fredericton	AHL	38	7	19	26	73	....	....	....	....	....
1987-88	**Quebec**	**NHL**	**75**	**3**	**7**	**10**	**198**	....	....	....	....	....
1988-89	**Quebec**	**NHL**	**77**	**2**	**6**	**8**	**235**	....	....	....	....	....
1989-90	**Quebec**	**NHL**	**64**	**3**	**9**	**12**	**208**	....	....	....	....	....
1990-91	**Quebec**	**NHL**	**71**	**6**	**13**	**19**	**228**	....	....	....	....	....
1991-92	**Quebec**	**NHL**	**65**	**4**	**7**	**11**	**194**	....	....	....	....	....
1992-93	**Quebec**	**NHL**	**80**	**5**	**9**	**14**	**160**	**6**	**0**	**1**	**1**	**8**
1993-94	**Quebec**	**NHL**	**80**	**4**	**13**	**17**	**159**	....	....	....	....	....
1994-95	**Quebec**	**NHL**	**40**	**0**	**3**	**3**	**64**	**4**	**0**	**1**	**1**	**2**
1995-96	**Tampa Bay**	**NHL**	**16**	**0**	**0**	**0**	**24**	....	....	....	....	....
	Los Angeles	**NHL**	**50**	**3**	**2**	**5**	**102**	....	....	....	....	....
1996-97	**Los Angeles**	**NHL**	**54**	**2**	**3**	**5**	**84**	....	....	....	....	....
	NHL Totals		**725**	**34**	**78**	**112**	**1724**	**23**	**0**	**4**	**4**	**39**

a QMJHL Second All-Star Team (1985)

Traded to **Tampa Bay** by **Colorado** for Tampa Bay's fourth round choice (Brad Larsen) in 1997 Entry Draft, October 5, 1995. Traded to **Los Angeles** by **Tampa Bay** for Michel Petit, November 13, 1995.

FINNSTROM, JOHAN (FIHN-struhm) CGY.

Defense. Shoots left. 6'3", 205 lbs. Born, Broby, Sweden, March 27, 1976.
(Calgary's 5th choice, 97th overall, in 1994 Entry Draft).

			Regular Season					Playoffs				
Season	Club	Lea	GP	G	A	TP	PIM	GP	G	A	TP	PIM
1993-94	Rogle	Swe.	7	1	1	2	2	....	....	....	....	....
1994-95	Rogle	Swe.	19	0	0	0	10	....	....	....	....	....
1995-96	Rogle	Swe.	18	0	0	0	10	....	....	....	....	....
1996-97	Rogle	Swe. 2	31	1	5	6	59	....	....	....	....	....

FIORENTINO, PETER NYR

Defense. Shoots right. 6'1", 205 lbs. Born, Niagara Falls, Ont., December 22, 1968.
(NY Rangers' 11th choice, 215th overall, in 1988 Entry Draft).

			Regular Season					Playoffs				
Season	Club	Lea	GP	G	A	TP	PIM	GP	G	A	TP	PIM
1985-86	S.S. Marie	OHL	58	1	6	7	87	....	....	....	....	....
1986-87	S.S. Marie	OHL	64	1	12	13	187	....	....	....	....	....
1987-88	S.S. Marie	OHL	65	5	27	32	252	6	2	2	4	21
1988-89	S.S. Marie	OHL	55	5	24	29	220	....	....	....	....	....
	Denver	IHL	10	0	0	0	39	4	0	0	0	24
1989-90	Flint	IHL	64	2	7	9	302	....	....	....	....	....
1990-91	Binghamton	AHL	55	2	11	13	361	1	0	0	0	0
1991-92	**NY Rangers**	**NHL**	**1**	**0**	**0**	**0**	**0**	....	....	....	....	....
	Binghamton	AHL	70	2	11	13	340	5	0	1	1	24
1992-93	Binghamton	AHL	64	9	5	14	286	13	0	3	3	22
1993-94	Binghamton	AHL	68	7	15	22	220	....	....	....	....	....
1994-95	Binghamton	AHL	66	9	16	25	183	2	0	1	1	11
1995-96	Las Vegas	IHL	54	5	7	12	192	....	....	....	....	....
	Indianapolis	IHL	10	0	0	0	27	5	0	0	0	2
1996-97	Binghamton	AHL	63	1	10	11	191	4	0	2	2	0
	NHL Totals		**1**	**0**	**0**	**0**	**0**	....	....	....	....	....

FISHER, CRAIG

Center. Shoots left. 6'3", 180 lbs. Born, Oshawa, Ont., June 30, 1970.
(Philadelphia's 3rd choice, 56th overall, in 1988 Entry Draft).

			Regular Season					Playoffs				
Season	Club	Lea	GP	G	A	TP	PIM	GP	G	A	TP	PIM
1988-89	Miami-Ohio	CCHA	37	22	20	42	37	....	....	....	....	....
1989-90a	Miami-Ohio	CCHA	39	37	29	66	38	....	....	....	....	....
	Philadelphia	**NHL**	**2**	**0**	**0**	**0**	**0**	....	....	....	....	....
1990-91	**Philadelphia**	**NHL**	**2**	**0**	**0**	**0**	**0**	....	....	....	....	....
	Hershey	AHL	77	43	36	79	46	7	5	3	8	2
1991-92	Cape Breton	AHL	60	20	25	45	28	1	0	0	0	0
1992-93	Cape Breton	AHL	75	32	29	61	74	1	0	0	0	2
1993-94	Cape Breton	AHL	16	5	5	10	11	....	....	....	....	....
	Winnipeg	**NHL**	**4**	**0**	**0**	**0**	**2**	....	....	....	....	....
	Moncton	AHL	46	26	35	61	36	21	11	11	22	28
1994-95	Indianapolis	IHL	77	53	40	93	65	....	....	....	....	....
1995-96b	Orlando	IHL	82	*74	56	130	81	14	10	7	17	6
1996-97	Utah	IHL	15	6	7	13	4	....	....	....	....	....
	Florida	**NHL**	**4**	**0**	**0**	**0**	**0**	....	....	....	....	....
	Carolina	AHL	42	33	29	62	16	....	....	....	....	....
	NHL Totals		**12**	**0**	**0**	**0**	**2**	....	....	....	....	....

a CCHA First All-Star Team (1990)
b IHL First All-Star Team (1996)

Traded to **Edmonton** by **Philadelphia** with Scott Mellanby and Craig Berube for Dave Brown, Corey Foster and Jari Kurri, May 30, 1991. Traded to **Winnipeg** by **Edmonton** for cash, December 9, 1993. Signed as a free agent by **Chicago**, June 9, 1994. Signed as a free agent by **NY Islanders**, July 29, 1996. Traded to **Florida** by **NY Islanders** for cash, December 7, 1996.

FITZGERALD, RUSTY PIT.

Center. Shoots left. 6'1", 210 lbs. Born, Minneapolis, MN, October 4, 1972.
(Pittsburgh's 2nd choice, 38th overall, in 1991 Entry Draft).

			Regular Season					Playoffs				
Season	Club	Lea	GP	G	A	TP	PIM	GP	G	A	TP	PIM
1991-92	Minn.-Duluth	WCHA	37	9	11	20	40	....	....	....	....	....
1992-93	Minn.-Duluth	WCHA	39	24	23	47	48	....	....	....	....	....
1993-94	Minn.-Duluth	WCHA	37	11	25	36	59	....	....	....	....	....
1994-95	Minn.-Duluth	WCHA	34	16	22	38	50	....	....	....	....	....
	Cleveland	IHL	2	0	1	1	0	3	3	0	3	6
	Pittsburgh	**NHL**	**4**	**1**	**0**	**1**	**0**	**5**	**0**	**0**	**0**	**4**
1995-96	**Pittsburgh**	**NHL**	**21**	**1**	**2**	**3**	**12**	....	....	....	....	....
	Cleveland	IHL	46	17	19	36	90	1	0	0	0	2
1996-97			DID NOT PLAY – INJURED									
	NHL Totals		**25**	**2**	**2**	**4**	**12**	**5**	**0**	**0**	**0**	**4**

FITZGERALD, TOM

Right wing/Center. Shoots right. 6'1", 191 lbs. Born, Melrose, MA, August 28, 1968.
(NY Islanders' 1st choice, 17th overall, in 1986 Entry Draft).

			Regular Season					Playoffs				
Season	Club	Lea	GP	G	A	TP	PIM	GP	G	A	TP	PIM
1986-87	Providence	H.E.	27	8	14	22	22	....	....	....	....	....
1987-88	Providence	H.E.	36	19	15	34	50	....	....	....	....	....
1988-89	**NY Islanders**	**NHL**	**23**	**3**	**5**	**8**	**10**	....	....	....	....	....
	Springfield	AHL	61	24	18	42	43	....	....	....	....	....
1989-90	**NY Islanders**	**NHL**	**19**	**2**	**5**	**7**	**4**	**4**	**1**	**0**	**1**	**4**
	Springfield	AHL	53	30	23	53	32	14	2	9	11	13
1990-91	**NY Islanders**	**NHL**	**41**	**5**	**5**	**10**	**24**	....	....	....	....	....
	Capital Dist.	AHL	27	7	7	14	50	....	....	....	....	....
1991-92	**NY Islanders**	**NHL**	**45**	**6**	**11**	**17**	**28**	....	....	....	....	....
	Capital Dist.	AHL	4	1	1	2	4	....	....	....	....	....
1992-93	**NY Islanders**	**NHL**	**77**	**9**	**18**	**27**	**34**	**18**	**2**	**5**	**7**	**18**
1993-94	**Florida**	**NHL**	**83**	**18**	**14**	**32**	**54**	....	....	....	....	....
1994-95	**Florida**	**NHL**	**48**	**3**	**13**	**16**	**31**	....	....	....	....	....
1995-96	**Florida**	**NHL**	**82**	**13**	**21**	**34**	**75**	**22**	**4**	**4**	**8**	**34**
1996-97	**Florida**	**NHL**	**71**	**10**	**14**	**24**	**64**	**5**	**0**	**1**	**1**	**0**
	NHL Totals		**489**	**69**	**106**	**175**	**324**	**49**	**7**	**10**	**17**	**56**

Claimed by **Florida** from **NY Islanders** in Expansion Draft, June 24, 1993.

FITZPATRICK, RORY — ST.L.

Defense. Shoots right. 6'1", 205 lbs. Born, Rochester, NY, January 11, 1975.
(Montreal's 2nd choice, 47th overall, in 1993 Entry Draft).

			Regular Season					Playoffs				
Season	**Club**	**Lea**	**GP**	**G**	**A**	**TP**	**PIM**	**GP**	**G**	**A**	**TP**	**PIM**
1992-93	Sudbury	OHL	58	4	20	24	68	14	0	0	0	17
1993-94	Sudbury	OHL	65	12	34	46	112	10	2	5	7	10
1994-95	Sudbury	OHL	56	12	36	48	72	18	3	15	18	21
	Fredericton	AHL	....	....	....	....	....	10	1	2	3	5
1995-96	**Montreal**	**NHL**	**42**	**0**	**2**	**2**	**18**	**6**	**1**	**1**	**2**	**0**
	Fredericton	AHL	18	4	6	10	36	....	....	....	....	....
1996-97	**Montreal**	**NHL**	**6**	**0**	**1**	**1**	**6**	....	....	....	....	....
	St. Louis	**NHL**	**2**	**0**	**0**	**0**	**2**	....	....	....	....	....
	Worcester	AHL	49	4	13	17	78	5	1	2	3	0
	NHL Totals		**50**	**0**	**3**	**3**	**26**	**6**	**1**	**1**	**2**	**0**

Traded to **St. Louis** by **Montreal** with Pierre Turgeon and Craig Conroy for Murray Baron, Shayne Corson and St. Louis' fifth round choice (Gennady Razin) in 1997 Entry Draft, October 29, 1996.

FLATLEY, PAT — (FLAT-lee)

Right wing. Shoots right. 6'2", 197 lbs. Born, Toronto, Ont., October 3, 1963.
(NY Islanders' 1st choice, 21st overall, in 1982 Entry Draft).

			Regular Season					Playoffs				
Season	**Club**	**Lea**	**GP**	**G**	**A**	**TP**	**PIM**	**GP**	**G**	**A**	**TP**	**PIM**
1981-82	U. Wisconsin	WCHA	17	10	9	19	40	....	....	....	....	....
1982-83ab	U. Wisconsin	WCHA	26	17	24	41	48	....	....	....	....	....
1983-84	Cdn. National	....	57	31	17	48	136	....	....	....	....	....
	Cdn. Olympic	....	7	3	3	6	70	....	....	....	....	....
	NY Islanders	**NHL**	**16**	**2**	**7**	**9**	**6**	**21**	**9**	**6**	**15**	**14**
1984-85	**NY Islanders**	**NHL**	**78**	**20**	**31**	**51**	**106**	**4**	**1**	**0**	**1**	**6**
1985-86	**NY Islanders**	**NHL**	**73**	**18**	**34**	**52**	**66**	**3**	**0**	**0**	**0**	**21**
1986-87	**NY Islanders**	**NHL**	**63**	**16**	**35**	**51**	**81**	**11**	**3**	**2**	**5**	**6**
1987-88	**NY Islanders**	**NHL**	**40**	**9**	**15**	**24**	**28**	....	....	....	....	....
1988-89	**NY Islanders**	**NHL**	**41**	**10**	**15**	**25**	**31**	....	....	....	....	....
	Springfield	AHL	2	1	1	2	2	....	....	....	....	....
1989-90	**NY Islanders**	**NHL**	**62**	**17**	**32**	**49**	**101**	**5**	**3**	**0**	**3**	**2**
1990-91	**NY Islanders**	**NHL**	**56**	**20**	**25**	**45**	**74**	....	....	....	....	....
1991-92	**NY Islanders**	**NHL**	**38**	**8**	**28**	**36**	**31**	....	....	....	....	....
1992-93	**NY Islanders**	**NHL**	**80**	**13**	**47**	**60**	**63**	**15**	**2**	**7**	**9**	**12**
1993-94	**NY Islanders**	**NHL**	**64**	**12**	**30**	**42**	**40**	....	....	....	....	....
1994-95	**NY Islanders**	**NHL**	**45**	**7**	**20**	**27**	**12**	....	....	....	....	....
1995-96	**NY Islanders**	**NHL**	**56**	**8**	**9**	**17**	**21**	....	....	....	....	....
1996-97	**NY Rangers**	**NHL**	**68**	**10**	**12**	**22**	**26**	**11**	**0**	**0**	**0**	**14**
	NHL Totals		**780**	**170**	**340**	**510**	**686**	**70**	**18**	**15**	**33**	**75**

a WCHA First All-Star Team (1983)
b Named to NCAA All-Tournament Team (1983)

Signed as a free agent by **NY Rangers**, September 26, 1996.

FLEURY, THEOREN — (FLUH-ree, THAIR-ihn) CGY.

Right wing. Shoots right. 5'6", 160 lbs. Born, Oxbow, Sask., June 29, 1968.
(Calgary's 9th choice, 166th overall, in 1987 Entry Draft).

			Regular Season					Playoffs				
Season	**Club**	**Lea**	**GP**	**G**	**A**	**TP**	**PIM**	**GP**	**G**	**A**	**TP**	**PIM**
1984-85	Moose Jaw	WHL	71	29	46	75	82	....	....	....	....	....
1985-86	Moose Jaw	WHL	72	43	65	108	124	....	....	....	....	....
1986-87	Moose Jaw	WHL	66	61	68	129	110	9	7	9	16	34
1987-88	Moose Jaw	WHL	65	68	92	*160	235	....	....	....	....	....
	Salt Lake	IHL	2	3	4	7	7	8	11	5	16	16
1988-89	**Calgary**	**NHL**	**36**	**14**	**20**	**34**	**46**	**22**	**5**	**6**	**11**	**24 ♦**
	Salt Lake	IHL	40	37	37	74	81	....	....	....	....	....
1989-90	**Calgary**	**NHL**	**80**	**31**	**35**	**66**	**157**	**6**	**2**	**3**	**5**	**10**
1990-91a	**Calgary**	**NHL**	**79**	**51**	**53**	**104**	**136**	**7**	**2**	**5**	**7**	**14**
1991-92	**Calgary**	**NHL**	**80**	**33**	**40**	**73**	**133**	....	....	....	....	....
1992-93	**Calgary**	**NHL**	**83**	**34**	**66**	**100**	**88**	**6**	**5**	**7**	**12**	**27**
1993-94	**Calgary**	**NHL**	**83**	**40**	**45**	**85**	**186**	**7**	**6**	**4**	**10**	**5**
1994-95	Tappara	Fin.	10	8	9	17	22	....	....	....	....	....
b	**Calgary**	**NHL**	**47**	**29**	**29**	**58**	**112**	**7**	**7**	**7**	**14**	**2**
1995-96	**Calgary**	**NHL**	**80**	**46**	**50**	**96**	**112**	**4**	**2**	**1**	**3**	**14**
1996-97	**Calgary**	**NHL**	**81**	**29**	**38**	**67**	**104**	....	....	....	....	....
	NHL Totals		**649**	**307**	**376**	**683**	**1074**	**59**	**29**	**33**	**62**	**96**

a Co-winner of Alka-Seltzer Plus Award with Marty McSorley (1991)
b NHL Second All-Star Team (1995)

Played in NHL All-Star Game (1991, 1992, 1996, 1997)

FLICHEL, MARTY — (FLICK-ehl) DAL.

Right wing. Shoots left. 5'11", 175 lbs. Born, Hodgeville, Sask., March 6, 1976.
(Dallas' 6th choice, 228th overall, in 1994 Entry Draft).

			Regular Season					Playoffs				
Season	**Club**	**Lea**	**GP**	**G**	**A**	**TP**	**PIM**	**GP**	**G**	**A**	**TP**	**PIM**
1992-93	Tacoma	WHL	61	21	20	41	19	7	0	0	0	8
1993-94	Tacoma	WHL	72	27	48	75	69	8	1	4	5	13
1994-95	Tacoma	WHL	67	25	53	78	81	4	2	3	5	8
1995-96	Kelowna	WHL	69	28	79	107	107	6	1	6	7	10
1996-97	Dayton	ECHL	28	17	16	33	24	2	0	1	1	4
	Michigan	IHL	19	2	3	5	10	....	....	....	....	....

FLINTON, ERIC

Left wing. Shoots left. 6'2", 200 lbs. Born, William Lake, B.C., February 2, 1972.
(Ottawa's 1st choice, 1st overall, in 1993 Supplemental Draft).

			Regular Season					Playoffs				
Season	**Club**	**Lea**	**GP**	**G**	**A**	**TP**	**PIM**	**GP**	**G**	**A**	**TP**	**PIM**
1991-92	N. Hampshire	H.E.	36	6	4	10	10	....	....	....	....	....
1992-93	N. Hampshire	H.E.	37	18	18	36	14	....	....	....	....	....
1993-94	N. Hampshire	H.E.	40	16	25	41	36	....	....	....	....	....
1994-95a	N. Hampshire	H.E.	36	22	23	45	44	....	....	....	....	....
1995-96	Charlotte	ECHL	69	20	26	46	29	16	5	8	13	4
1996-97	Binghamton	AHL	68	6	18	24	22	4	0	0	0	2

a Hockey East Second All-Star Team (1995)

Signed as a free agent by **NY Rangers**, September 12, 1995.

FLODELL, JORDON — (FLOH-dehl) PHI.

Defense. Shoots right. 6'2", 198 lbs. Born, Melfort, Sask., April 28, 1979.
(Philadelphia's 5th choice, 158th overall, in 1997 Entry Draft).

			Regular Season					Playoffs				
Season	**Club**	**Lea**	**GP**	**G**	**A**	**TP**	**PIM**	**GP**	**G**	**A**	**TP**	**PIM**
1995-96	Moose Jaw	WHL	17	0	0	0	7	....	....	....	....	....
1996-97	Moose Jaw	WHL	39	0	3	3	48	12	0	3	3	8

FOCHT, DAN — (FOHKT) PHO.

Defense. Shoots left. 6'6", 226 lbs. Born, Regina, Sask., December 31, 1977.
(Phoenix's 1st choice, 11th overall, in 1996 Entry Draft).

			Regular Season					Playoffs				
Season	**Club**	**Lea**	**GP**	**G**	**A**	**TP**	**PIM**	**GP**	**G**	**A**	**TP**	**PIM**
1995-96	Tri-City	WHL	63	6	12	18	161	11	1	1	2	23
1996-97	Tri-City	WHL	28	0	5	5	92	....	....	....	....	....
	Regina	WHL	22	2	2	4	59	5	0	2	2	8
	Springfield	AHL	1	0	0	0	2	....	....	....	....	....

FOOTE, ADAM — COL.

Defense. Shoots right. 6'1", 202 lbs. Born, Toronto, Ont., July 10, 1971.
(Quebec's 2nd choice, 22nd overall, in 1989 Entry Draft).

			Regular Season					Playoffs				
Season	**Club**	**Lea**	**GP**	**G**	**A**	**TP**	**PIM**	**GP**	**G**	**A**	**TP**	**PIM**
1988-89	S.S. Marie	OHL	66	7	32	39	120	....	....	....	....	....
1989-90	S.S. Marie	OHL	61	12	43	55	199	....	....	....	....	....
1990-91a	S.S. Marie	OHL	59	18	51	69	93	14	5	12	17	28
1991-92	**Quebec**	**NHL**	**46**	**2**	**5**	**7**	**44**	....	....	....	....	....
	Halifax	AHL	6	0	1	1	2	....	....	....	....	....
1992-93	**Quebec**	**NHL**	**81**	**4**	**12**	**16**	**168**	**6**	**0**	**1**	**1**	**2**
1993-94	**Quebec**	**NHL**	**45**	**2**	**6**	**8**	**67**	....	....	....	....	....
1994-95	**Quebec**	**NHL**	**35**	**0**	**7**	**7**	**52**	**6**	**0**	**1**	**1**	**14**
1995-96	**Colorado**	**NHL**	**73**	**5**	**11**	**16**	**88**	**22**	**1**	**3**	**4**	**36 ♦**
1996-97	**Colorado**	**NHL**	**78**	**2**	**19**	**21**	**135**	**17**	**0**	**4**	**4**	**62**
	NHL Totals		**358**	**15**	**60**	**75**	**554**	**51**	**1**	**9**	**10**	**114**

a OHL First All-Star Team (1991)

FORBES, COLIN — PHI.

Left wing. Shoots left. 6'3", 205 lbs. Born, New Westminster, B.C., February 16, 1976.
(Philadelphia's 5th choice, 166th overall, in 1994 Entry Draft).

			Regular Season					Playoffs				
Season	**Club**	**Lea**	**GP**	**G**	**A**	**TP**	**PIM**	**GP**	**G**	**A**	**TP**	**PIM**
1994-95	Portland	WHL	72	24	31	55	108	9	1	3	4	10
1995-96	Portland	WHL	72	33	44	77	137	7	2	5	7	14
	Hershey	AHL	2	1	0	1	2	4	0	2	2	2
1996-97	**Philadelphia**	**NHL**	**3**	**1**	**0**	**1**	**0**	**3**	**0**	**0**	**0**	**0**
	Philadelphia	AHL	74	21	28	49	108	10	5	5	10	33
	NHL Totals		**3**	**1**	**0**	**1**	**0**	**3**	**0**	**0**	**0**	**0**

FORSANDER, JOHAN — (fohr-SAHN-duhr, YOO-hahn) DET.

Left wing. Shoots left. 6'1", 174 lbs. Born, Jonkoping, Sweden, April 28, 1978.
(Detroit's 3rd choice, 108th overall, in 1996 Entry Draft).

			Regular Season					Playoffs				
Season	**Club**	**Lea**	**GP**	**G**	**A**	**TP**	**PIM**	**GP**	**G**	**A**	**TP**	**PIM**
1995-96	HV 71	Swe. Jr.	27	15	8	23	12	....	....	....	....	....
	HV 71	Swe.	6	0	0	0	0	3	0	0	0	2
1996-97	HV 71	Swe.	44	3	2	5	6	5	0	0	0	0

FORSBERG, PETER — (FOHRS-buhrg) COL.

Center. Shoots left. 6', 190 lbs. Born, Ornskoldsvik, Sweden, July 20, 1973.
(Philadelphia's 1st choice, 6th overall, in 1991 Entry Draft).

			Regular Season					Playoffs				
Season	**Club**	**Lea**	**GP**	**G**	**A**	**TP**	**PIM**	**GP**	**G**	**A**	**TP**	**PIM**
1990-91	MoDo	Swe.	23	7	10	17	22	....	....	....	....	....
1991-92	MoDo	Swe.	39	9	18	27	78	....	....	....	....	....
1992-93	MoDo	Swe.	39	23	24	47	92	3	4	1	5	0
1993-94	MoDo	Swe.	39	18	26	44	82	11	9	7	16	14
1994-95	MoDo	Swe.	11	5	9	14	20	....	....	....	....	....
ab	**Quebec**	**NHL**	**47**	**15**	**35**	**50**	**16**	**6**	**2**	**4**	**6**	**4**
1995-96	**Colorado**	**NHL**	**82**	**30**	**86**	**116**	**47**	**22**	**10**	**11**	**21**	**18 ♦**
1996-97	**Colorado**	**NHL**	**65**	**28**	**58**	**86**	**73**	**14**	**5**	**12**	**17**	**10**
	NHL Totals		**194**	**73**	**179**	**252**	**136**	**42**	**17**	**27**	**44**	**32**

a NHL/Upper Deck All-Rookie Team (1995)
b Won Calder Memorial Trophy (1995)

Played in NHL All-Star Game (1996)

Traded to **Quebec** by **Philadelphia** with Steve Duchesne, Kerry Huffman, Mike Ricci, Ron Hextall, Chris Simon, Philadelphia's first round choice in the 1993 (Jocelyn Thibault) and 1994 (later traded to Toronto — later traded to Washington — Washington selected Nolan Baumgartner) Entry Drafts and cash for Eric Lindros, June 30, 1992.

FORTIN, JEAN-FRANCOIS — (fohr-TEHN) WSH.

Defense. Shoots right. 6'2", 190 lbs. Born, Laval, Que., March 15, 1979.
(Washington's 2nd choice, 35th overall, in 1997 Entry Draft).

			Regular Season					Playoffs				
Season	**Club**	**Lea**	**GP**	**G**	**A**	**TP**	**PIM**	**GP**	**G**	**A**	**TP**	**PIM**
1995-96	Sherbrooke	QMJHL	69	7	15	22	40	7	2	6	8	2
1996-97	Sherbrooke	QMJHL	59	7	30	37	89	2	0	1	1	14

FOSTER, COREY

Defense. Shoots left. 6'3", 204 lbs. Born, Ottawa, Ont., October 27, 1969.
(New Jersey's 1st choice, 12th overall, in 1988 Entry Draft).

			Regular Season					Playoffs				
Season	**Club**	**Lea**	**GP**	**G**	**A**	**TP**	**PIM**	**GP**	**G**	**A**	**TP**	**PIM**
1986-87	Peterborough	OHL	30	3	4	7	4	1	0	0	0	0
1987-88	Peterborough	OHL	66	13	31	44	58	11	5	9	14	13
1988-89	**New Jersey**	**NHL**	**2**	**0**	**0**	**0**	**0**	....	....	....	....	....
	Peterborough	OHL	55	14	42	56	42	17	1	17	18	12
1989-90	Cape Breton	AHL	54	7	17	24	32	1	0	0	0	0
1990-91	Cape Breton	AHL	67	14	11	25	51	4	2	4	6	4
1991-92	**Philadelphia**	**NHL**	**25**	**3**	**4**	**7**	**20**	....	....	....	....	....
	Hershey	AHL	19	5	9	14	26	6	1	1	2	5
1992-93	Hershey	AHL	80	9	25	34	102	....	....	....	....	....
1993-94	Hershey	AHL	66	21	37	58	96	9	2	5	7	10
1994-95	P.E.I.	AHL	78	13	34	47	61	11	2	5	7	12
1995-96	**Pittsburgh**	**NHL**	**11**	**2**	**2**	**4**	**2**	**3**	**0**	**0**	**0**	**4**
	Cleveland	IHL	61	10	36	46	93	....	....	....	....	....
1996-97	**NY Islanders**	**NHL**	**7**	**0**	**0**	**0**	**2**	....	....	....	....	....
	Cleveland	IHL	51	5	29	34	71	14	0	9	9	22
	NHL Totals		**45**	**5**	**6**	**11**	**24**	**3**	**0**	**0**	**0**	**4**

Traded to **Edmonton** by **New Jersey** for Edmonton's first round choice (Jason Miller) in 1989 Entry Draft, June 17, 1989. Traded to **Philadelphia** by **Edmonton** with Dave Brown and Jari Kurri for Craig Fisher, Scott Mellanby and Craig Berube, May 30, 1991. Signed as a free agent by **Ottawa**, June 20, 1994. Signed as a free agent by **Pittsburgh**, August 7, 1995. Claimed by **NY Islanders** from **Pittsburgh** in NHL Waiver Draft, September 30, 1996.

FRANCIS, RON — PIT.

Center. Shoots left. 6'3", 200 lbs. Born, Sault Ste. Marie, Ont., March 1, 1963.
(Hartford's 1st choice, 4th overall, in 1981 Entry Draft).

			Regular Season					Playoffs				
Season	Club	Lea	GP	G	A	TP	PIM	GP	G	A	TP	PIM
1980-81	S.S. Marie	OHA	64	26	43	69	33	19	7	8	15	34
1981-82	**Hartford**	**NHL**	**59**	**25**	**43**	**68**	**51**	....	....	....	....	....
	S.S. Marie	OHL	25	18	30	48	46	....	....	....	....	....
1982-83	**Hartford**	**NHL**	**79**	**31**	**59**	**90**	**60**	....	....	....	....	....
1983-84	**Hartford**	**NHL**	**72**	**23**	**60**	**83**	**45**	....	....	....	....	....
1984-85	**Hartford**	**NHL**	**80**	**24**	**57**	**81**	**66**	....	....	....	....	....
1985-86	**Hartford**	**NHL**	**53**	**24**	**53**	**77**	**24**	**10**	**1**	**2**	**3**	**4**
1986-87	**Hartford**	**NHL**	**75**	**30**	**63**	**93**	**45**	**6**	**2**	**2**	**4**	**6**
1987-88	**Hartford**	**NHL**	**80**	**25**	**50**	**75**	**87**	**6**	**2**	**5**	**7**	**2**
1988-89	**Hartford**	**NHL**	**69**	**29**	**48**	**77**	**36**	**4**	**0**	**2**	**2**	**0**
1989-90	**Hartford**	**NHL**	**80**	**32**	**69**	**101**	**73**	**7**	**3**	**3**	**6**	**8**
1990-91	**Hartford**	**NHL**	**67**	**21**	**55**	**76**	**51**	....	....	....	....	....
	Pittsburgh	**NHL**	**14**	**2**	**9**	**11**	**21**	**24**	**7**	**10**	**17**	**24 ♦**
1991-92	**Pittsburgh**	**NHL**	**70**	**21**	**33**	**54**	**30**	**21**	**8**	***19**	**27**	**6 ♦**
1992-93	**Pittsburgh**	**NHL**	**84**	**24**	**76**	**100**	**68**	**12**	**6**	**11**	**17**	**19**
1993-94	**Pittsburgh**	**NHL**	**82**	**27**	**66**	**93**	**62**	**6**	**0**	**2**	**2**	**6**
1994-95abc	**Pittsburgh**	**NHL**	**44**	**11**	***48**	**59**	**18**	**12**	**6**	**13**	**19**	**4**
1995-96	**Pittsburgh**	**NHL**	**77**	**27**	***92**	**119**	**56**	**11**	**3**	**6**	**9**	**4**
1996-97	**Pittsburgh**	**NHL**	**81**	**27**	**63**	**90**	**20**	**5**	**1**	**2**	**3**	**2**
	NHL Totals		**1166**	**403**	**944**	**1347**	**813**	**124**	**39**	**77**	**116**	**85**

a Won Alka-Seltzer Plus Award (1995)
b Won Frank J. Selke Trophy (1995)
c Won Lady Byng Trophy (1995)

Played in NHL All-Star Game (1983, 1985, 1990, 1996)

Traded to **Pittsburgh** by **Hartford** with Grant Jennings and Ulf Samuelsson for John Cullen, Jeff Parker and Zarley Zalapski, March 4, 1991.

FRANCZ, ROBERT — (FRANZ) PHO.

Left wing. Shoots left. 6'1", 194 lbs. Born, Bad Muskau, East Germany, March 30, 1978.
(Phoenix's 4th choice, 151st overall, in 1997 Entry Draft).

			Regular Season					Playoffs				
Season	Club	Lea	GP	G	A	TP	PIM	GP	G	A	TP	PIM
1995-96	Augsburg	Ger. Jr.	7	1	1	2	62	....	....	....	....	....
	Augsburg	Ger.	36	0	1	1	43	6	0	0	0	0
1996-97	Peterborough	OHL	60	9	21	30	149	8	1	1	2	17

FRASER, IAIN

Center. Shoots left. 5'10", 175 lbs. Born, Scarborough, Ont., August 10, 1969.
(NY Islanders' 12th choice, 233rd overall, in 1989 Entry Draft).

			Regular Season					Playoffs				
Season	Club	Lea	GP	G	A	TP	PIM	GP	G	A	TP	PIM
1986-87	Oshawa	OHL	5	1	2	3	0	....	....	....	....	....
1987-88	Oshawa	OHL	16	4	4	8	22	6	2	3	5	2
1988-89	Oshawa	OHL	62	33	57	90	87	6	2	8	10	12
1989-90ab	Oshawa	OHL	56	40	65	105	75	17	10	*22	32	8
1990-91	Capital Dist.	AHL	32	5	13	18	16	....	....	....	....	....
	Richmond	ECHL	3	1	1	2	0	....	....	....	....	....
1991-92	Capital Dist.	AHL	45	9	11	20	24	....	....	....	....	....
1992-93	**NY Islanders**	**NHL**	**7**	**2**	**2**	**4**	**2**	....	....	....	....	....
c	Capital Dist.	AHL	74	41	69	110	16	4	0	1	1	0
1993-94	**Quebec**	**NHL**	**60**	**17**	**20**	**37**	**23**	....	....	....	....	....
1994-95	**Dallas**	**NHL**	**4**	**0**	**0**	**0**	**0**	....	....	....	....	....
	Edmonton	**NHL**	**9**	**3**	**0**	**3**	**0**	....	....	....	....	....
	Denver	IHL	1	0	0	0	0	....	....	....	....	....
1995-96	**Winnipeg**	**NHL**	**12**	**1**	**1**	**2**	**4**	**4**	**0**	**0**	**0**	**0**
	Springfield	AHL	53	24	47	71	27	6	0	6	6	2
1996-97	**San Jose**	**NHL**	**2**	**0**	**0**	**0**	**2**	....	....	....	....	....
	Kentucky	AHL	57	27	33	60	24	....	....	....	....	....
	NHL Totals		**94**	**23**	**23**	**46**	**31**	**4**	**0**	**0**	**0**	**0**

a Memorial Cup All-Star Team (1990)
b Won Stafford Smythe Memorial Trophy (Memorial Cup Tournament MVP) (1990)
c AHL Second All-Star Team (1993)

Signed as a free agent by **Quebec**, August 3, 1993. Traded to **Dallas** by **Quebec** for Dallas' seventh round choice (Dan Hinote) in 1996 Entry Draft, January 31, 1995. Claimed on waivers by **Edmonton** from **Dallas**, March 3, 1995. Signed as a free agent by **Winnipeg**, October 11, 1995. Signed as a free agent by **San Jose**, September 1, 1996.

FRASER, SCOTT

Center. Shoots right. 6'1", 178 lbs. Born, Moncton, N.B., May 3, 1972.
(Montreal's 12th choice, 193rd overall, in 1991 Entry Draft).

			Regular Season					Playoffs				
Season	Club	Lea	GP	G	A	TP	PIM	GP	G	A	TP	PIM
1990-91	Dartmouth	ECAC	24	10	10	20	30	....	....	....	....	....
1991-92	Dartmouth	ECAC	24	11	7	18	60	....	....	....	....	....
1992-93	Cdn. National	....	5	1	0	1	0	....	....	....	....	....
a	Dartmouth	ECAC	26	21	23	44	13	....	....	....	....	....
1993-94	Dartmouth	ECAC	24	17	13	30	34	....	....	....	....	....
	Cdn. National		4	0	1	1	4	....	....	....	....	....
1994-95	Fredericton	AHL	65	23	25	48	36	16	3	5	8	14
	Wheeling	ECHL	8	4	2	6	8	....	....	....	....	....
1995-96	**Montreal**	**NHL**	**15**	**2**	**0**	**2**	**4**	....	....	....	....	....
	Fredericton	AHL	58	37	37	74	43	10	9	7	16	2
1996-97	Fredericton	AHL	7	3	8	11	0	....	....	....	....	....
	Carolina	AHL	18	9	19	28	12	....	....	....	....	....
	San Antonio	IHL	8	0	1	1	2	....	....	....	....	....
	NHL Totals		**15**	**2**	**0**	**2**	**4**	....	....	....	....	....

a ECAC Second All-Star Team (1993)

Traded to **Calgary** by **Montreal** for David Ling and Calgary's sixth round choice in 1998 Entry Draft, October 24, 1996.

FREADRICH, KYLE — (FREE-drihk) VAN.

Left wing. Shoots left. 6'6", 225 lbs. Born, Edmonton, Alta., December 28, 1978.
(Vancouver's 4th choice, 64th overall, in 1997 Entry Draft).

			Regular Season					Playoffs				
Season	Club	Lea	GP	G	A	TP	PIM	GP	G	A	TP	PIM
1996-97	Prince George	WHL	12	0	0	0	12	....	....	....	....	....
	Regina	WHL	50	1	3	4	152	4	0	0	0	8

FREER, MARK — (FRIHR)

Center. Shoots left. 5'10", 180 lbs. Born, Peterborough, Ont., July 14, 1968.

			Regular Season					Playoffs				
Season	Club	Lea	GP	G	A	TP	PIM	GP	G	A	TP	PIM
1985-86	Peterborough	OHL	65	16	28	44	24	14	3	4	7	13
1986-87	**Philadelphia**	**NHL**	**1**	**0**	**1**	**1**	**0**	....	....	....	....	....
	Peterborough	OHL	65	39	43	82	44	12	2	6	8	5
1987-88	**Philadelphia**	**NHL**	**1**	**0**	**0**	**0**	**0**	....	....	....	....	....
	Peterborough	OHL	63	38	70	108	63	12	5	12	17	4
1988-89	**Philadelphia**	**NHL**	**5**	**0**	**1**	**1**	**0**	....	....	....	....	....
	Hershey	AHL	75	30	49	79	77	12	4	6	10	2
1989-90	**Philadelphia**	**NHL**	**2**	**0**	**0**	**0**	**0**	....	....	....	....	....
	Hershey	AHL	65	28	36	64	31	....	....	....	....	....
1990-91	Hershey	AHL	77	18	44	62	45	7	1	3	4	17
1991-92	**Philadelphia**	**NHL**	**50**	**6**	**7**	**13**	**18**	....	....	....	....	....
	Hershey	AHL	31	13	11	24	38	6	0	3	3	2
1992-93	**Ottawa**	**NHL**	**63**	**10**	**14**	**24**	**39**	....	....	....	....	....
1993-94	**Calgary**	**NHL**	**2**	**0**	**0**	**0**	**4**	....	....	....	....	....
	Saint John	AHL	77	33	53	86	45	7	2	4	6	16
1994-95	Houston	IHL	80	38	42	80	54	4	0	1	1	4
1995-96	Houston	IHL	80	22	31	53	67	....	....	....	....	....
1996-97	Houston	IHL	81	21	36	57	43	12	2	3	5	4
	NHL Totals		**124**	**16**	**23**	**39**	**61**	....	....	....	....	....

Signed as a free agent by **Philadelphia**, October 7, 1986. Claimed by **Ottawa** from **Philadelphia** in Expansion Draft, June 18, 1992. Signed as a free agent by **Calgary**, August 10, 1993.

FRIEDMAN, DOUG — EDM.

Left wing. Shoots left. 6'1", 195 lbs. Born, Cape Elizabeth, ME, September 1, 1971.
(Quebec's 11th choice, 222nd overall, in 1991 Entry Draft).

			Regular Season					Playoffs				
Season	Club	Lea	GP	G	A	TP	PIM	GP	G	A	TP	PIM
1990-91	Boston U.	H.E.	36	6	6	12	37	....	....	....	....	....
1991-92	Boston U.	H.E.	34	11	8	19	42	....	....	....	....	....
1992-93	Boston U.	H.E.	38	17	24	41	62	....	....	....	....	....
1993-94	Boston U.	H.E.	41	9	23	32	110	....	....	....	....	....
1994-95	Cornwall	AHL	55	6	9	15	56	3	0	0	0	0
1995-96	Cornwall	AHL	80	12	22	34	178	8	1	1	2	17
1996-97	Hershey	AHL	61	12	21	33	245	23	6	9	15	49

Signed as a free agent by **Edmonton**, July 14, 1997.

FRIESEN, JEFF — (FREE-zuhn) S.J.

Center. Shoots left. 6', 190 lbs. Born, Meadow Lake, Sask., August 5, 1976.
(San Jose's 1st choice, 11th overall, in 1994 Entry Draft).

			Regular Season					Playoffs				
Season	Club	Lea	GP	G	A	TP	PIM	GP	G	A	TP	PIM
1991-92	Regina	WHL	4	3	1	4	2	....	....	....	....	....
1992-93a	Regina	WHL	70	45	38	83	23	13	7	10	17	8
1993-94	Regina	WHL	66	51	67	118	48	4	3	2	5	2
1994-95	Regina	WHL	25	21	23	44	22	....	....	....	....	....
b	**San Jose**	**NHL**	**48**	**15**	**10**	**25**	**14**	**11**	**1**	**5**	**6**	**4**
1995-96	**San Jose**	**NHL**	**79**	**15**	**31**	**46**	**42**	....	....	....	....	....
1996-97	**San Jose**	**NHL**	**82**	**28**	**34**	**62**	**75**	....	....	....	....	....
	NHL Totals		**209**	**58**	**75**	**133**	**131**	**11**	**1**	**5**	**6**	**4**

a Canadian Major Junior Rookie of the Year (1993)
b NHL/Upper Deck All-Rookie Team (1995)

FRYLEN, EDVIN — (FRYUH-lehn) ST.L.

Defense. Shoots left. 6', 211 lbs. Born, Jarfalla, Sweden, December 23, 1975.
(St. Louis' 3rd choice, 120th overall, in 1994 Entry Draft).

			Regular Season					Playoffs				
Season	Club	Lea	GP	G	A	TP	PIM	GP	G	A	TP	PIM
1991-92	Vasteras	Swe.	2	0	0	0	0	....	....	....	....	....
1992-93	Vasteras	Swe.	29	0	2	2	14	3	0	0	0	0
1993-94	Vasteras	Swe.	32	1	0	1	26	....	....	....	....	....
1994-95	Vasteras	Swe.	25	2	1	3	14	4	0	0	0	4
1995-96	Vasteras	Swe.	39	8	5	13	16	....	....	....	....	....
1996-97	Vasteras	Swe.	47	8	3	11	32	....	....	....	....	....

GAFFANEY, BRIAN — PIT.

Defense. Shoots left. 6'5", 205 lbs. Born, Alexandria, MN, October 4, 1977.
(Pittsburgh's 2nd choice, 44th overall, in 1997 Entry Draft).

			Regular Season					Playoffs				
Season	Club	Lea	GP	G	A	TP	PIM	GP	G	A	TP	PIM
1996-97	North Iowa	Jr. A	48	8	13	21	49	....	....	....	....	....

GAFFNEY, MIKE — OTT.

Defense. Shoots right. 6'1", 202 lbs. Born, Worchester, MA, June 19, 1976.
(Ottawa's 4th choice, 131st overall, in 1994 Entry Draft).

			Regular Season					Playoffs				
Season	Club	Lea	GP	G	A	TP	PIM	GP	G	A	TP	PIM
1994-95	Massachusetts	H.E.	33	1	4	5	38	....	....	....	....	....
1995-96	Massachusetts	H.E.	33	0	6	6	41	....	....	....	....	....
1996-97	Massachusetts	H.E.	34	7	13	20	49	....	....	....	....	....

GAGNER, DAVE (GAH-nyay) FLA.

Center. Shoots left. 5'10", 180 lbs. Born, Chatham, Ont., December 11, 1964.
(NY Rangers' 1st choice, 12th overall, in 1983 Entry Draft).

			Regular Season					Playoffs				
Season	Club	Lea	GP	G	A	TP	PIM	GP	G	A	TP	PIM
1981-82	Brantford	OHL	68	30	46	76	31	11	3	6	9	6
1982-83a	Brantford	OHL	70	55	66	121	57	8	5	5	10	4
1983-84	Cdn. National	....	50	19	18	37	26	....	....	....	....	....
	Cdn. Olympic	....	7	5	2	7	6	....	....	....	....	....
	Brantford	OHL	12	7	13	20	4	6	0	4	4	6
1984-85	**NY Rangers**	**NHL**	**38**	**6**	**6**	**12**	**16**	....	....	....	....	....
	New Haven	AHL	38	13	20	33	23	....	....	....	....	....
1985-86	**NY Rangers**	**NHL**	**32**	**4**	**6**	**10**	**19**	....	....	....	....	....
	New Haven	AHL	16	10	11	21	11	4	1	2	3	2
1986-87	**NY Rangers**	**NHL**	**10**	**1**	**4**	**5**	**12**	....	....	....	....	....
	New Haven	AHL	56	22	41	63	50	7	1	5	6	18
1987-88	**Minnesota**	**NHL**	**51**	**8**	**11**	**19**	**55**	....	....	....	....	....
	Kalamazoo	IHL	14	16	10	26	26	....	....	....	....	....
1988-89	**Minnesota**	**NHL**	**75**	**35**	**43**	**78**	**104**	....	....	....	....	....
	Kalamazoo	IHL	1	0	1	1	4	....	....	....	....	....
1989-90	**Minnesota**	**NHL**	**79**	**40**	**38**	**78**	**54**	**7**	**2**	**3**	**5**	**16**
1990-91	**Minnesota**	**NHL**	**73**	**40**	**42**	**82**	**114**	**23**	**12**	**15**	**27**	**28**
1991-92	**Minnesota**	**NHL**	**78**	**31**	**40**	**71**	**107**	**7**	**2**	**4**	**6**	**8**
1992-93	**Minnesota**	**NHL**	**84**	**33**	**43**	**76**	**143**	....	....	....	....	....
1993-94	**Dallas**	**NHL**	**76**	**32**	**29**	**61**	**83**	**9**	**5**	**1**	**6**	**2**
1994-95	Courmaosta	Italy	3	0	0	0	0	....	....	....	....	....
	Courmaosta	Euro.	1	0	4	4	0	....	....	....	....	....
	Dallas	**NHL**	**48**	**14**	**28**	**42**	**42**	**5**	**1**	**1**	**2**	**4**
1995-96	**Dallas**	**NHL**	**45**	**14**	**13**	**27**	**44**	....	....	....	....	....
	Toronto	**NHL**	**28**	**7**	**15**	**22**	**59**	**6**	**0**	**2**	**2**	**6**
1996-97	**Calgary**	**NHL**	**82**	**27**	**33**	**60**	**48**	....	....	....	....	....
	NHL Totals		**799**	**292**	**351**	**643**	**900**	**57**	**22**	**26**	**48**	**64**

a OHL Second All-Star Team (1983)

Played in NHL All-Star Game (1991)

Traded to **Minnesota** by **NY Rangers** with Jay Caulfield for Jari Gronstrand and Paul Boutilier, October 8, 1987. Traded to **Toronto** by **Dallas** with Dallas' sixth round choice (Dmitriy Yakushin) in 1996 Entry Draft for Benoit Hogue and Randy Wood, January 29, 1996. Traded to **Calgary** by **Toronto** for Calgary's third round choice (Mike Lankshear) in 1996 Entry Draft, June 22, 1996. Signed as a free agent by **Florida**, July 12, 1997.

GAGNON, SEAN PHO.

Defense. Shoots Left. 6'2", 210 lbs. Born, Sault Ste. Marie, Ont., September 11, 1973.

			Regular Season					Playoffs				
Season	Club	Lea	GP	G	A	TP	PIM	GP	G	A	TP	PIM
1991-92	Sudbury	OHL	44	3	4	7	60	5	0	1	1	0
1992-93	Sudbury	OHL	6	1	1	2	16	....	....	....	....	....
	Ottawa	OHL	33	2	10	12	68	....	....	....	....	....
	S.S. Marie	OHL	24	1	5	6	65	15	2	2	4	25
1993-94	S.S. Marie	OHL	42	4	12	16	147	14	1	1	2	52
1994-95	Dayton	ECHL	68	9	23	32	339	8	0	3	3	69
1995-96	Dayton	ECHL	68	7	22	29	326	3	0	1	1	33
1996-97	Fort Wayne	IHL	72	7	7	14	457	....	....	....	....	....

Signed as a free agent by **Phoenix**, May 14, 1997.

GAINEY, STEVE DAL.

Center. Shoots left. 6', 180 lbs. Born, Montreal, Que., January 26, 1979.
(Dallas' 3rd choice, 77th overall, in 1997 Entry Draft).

			Regular Season					Playoffs				
Season	Club	Lea	GP	G	A	TP	PIM	GP	G	A	TP	PIM
1995-96	Kamloops	WHL	49	1	4	5	40	3	0	0	0	0
1996-97	Kamloops	WHL	60	9	18	27	60	2	0	0	0	9

GALANOV, MAXIM (gah-LAH-nahf, mahx-EEM) NYR

Defense. Shoots left. 6'1", 195 lbs. Born, Krasnoyarsk, USSR, March 13, 1974.
(NY Rangers' 3rd choice, 61st overall, in 1993 Entry Draft).

			Regular Season					Playoffs				
Season	Club	Lea	GP	G	A	TP	PIM	GP	G	A	TP	PIM
1992-93	Togliatti	CIS	41	4	2	6	12	10	1	1	2	12
1993-94	Togliatti	CIS	7	1	0	1	4	12	1	0	1	8
1994-95	Togliatti	CIS	45	5	6	11	54	9	0	1	1	12
1995-96	Binghamton	AHL	72	17	36	53	24	4	1	1	2	0
1996-97	Binghamton	AHL	73	13	30	43	30	3	0	0	0	2

GALLANT, CHESTER PHI.

Right wing. Shoots right. 6'1", 184 lbs. Born, Thunder Bay, Ont., December 22, 1977.
(Philadelphia's 2nd choice, 64th overall, in 1996 Entry Draft).

			Regular Season					Playoffs				
Season	Club	Lea	GP	G	A	TP	PIM	GP	G	A	TP	PIM
1994-95	Sudbury	OHL	37	3	5	8	63	....	....	....	....	....
	Niagara Falls	OHL	26	3	5	8	70	6	1	0	1	19
1995-96	Niagara Falls	OHL	66	10	20	30	178	10	2	0	2	18
1996-97	Erie	OHL	56	7	15	22	183	5	1	0	1	8

GALLEY, GARRY L.A.

Defense. Shoots left. 6', 204 lbs. Born, Montreal, Que., April 16, 1963.
(Los Angeles' 4th choice, 100th overall, in 1983 Entry Draft).

			Regular Season					Playoffs				
Season	Club	Lea	GP	G	A	TP	PIM	GP	G	A	TP	PIM
1981-82	Bowling Green	CCHA	42	3	36	39	48	....	....	....	....	....
1982-83	Bowling Green	CCHA	40	17	29	46	40	....	....	....	....	....
1983-84ab	Bowling Green	CCHA	44	15	52	67	61	....	....	....	....	....
1984-85	**Los Angeles**	**NHL**	**78**	**8**	**30**	**38**	**82**	**3**	**1**	**0**	**1**	**2**
1985-86	**Los Angeles**	**NHL**	**49**	**9**	**13**	**22**	**46**	....	....	....	....	....
	New Haven	AHL	4	2	6	8	6	....	....	....	....	....
1986-87	**Los Angeles**	**NHL**	**30**	**5**	**11**	**16**	**57**	....	....	....	....	....
	Washington	**NHL**	**18**	**1**	**10**	**11**	**10**	**2**	**0**	**0**	**0**	**0**
1987-88	**Washington**	**NHL**	**58**	**7**	**23**	**30**	**44**	**13**	**2**	**4**	**6**	**13**
1988-89	**Boston**	**NHL**	**78**	**8**	**22**	**30**	**80**	**9**	**0**	**1**	**1**	**33**
1989-90	**Boston**	**NHL**	**71**	**8**	**27**	**35**	**75**	**21**	**3**	**3**	**6**	**34**
1990-91	**Boston**	**NHL**	**70**	**6**	**21**	**27**	**84**	**16**	**1**	**5**	**6**	**17**
1991-92	**Boston**	**NHL**	**38**	**2**	**12**	**14**	**83**	....	....	....	....	....
	Philadelphia	**NHL**	**39**	**3**	**15**	**18**	**34**	....	....	....	....	....
1992-93	**Philadelphia**	**NHL**	**83**	**13**	**49**	**62**	**115**	....	....	....	....	....
1993-94	**Philadelphia**	**NHL**	**81**	**10**	**60**	**70**	**91**	....	....	....	....	....
1994-95	**Philadelphia**	**NHL**	**33**	**2**	**20**	**22**	**20**	....	....	....	....	....
	Buffalo	**NHL**	**14**	**1**	**9**	**10**	**10**	**5**	**0**	**3**	**3**	**4**
1995-96	**Buffalo**	**NHL**	**78**	**10**	**44**	**54**	**81**	....	....	....	....	....
1996-97	**Buffalo**	**NHL**	**71**	**4**	**34**	**38**	**102**	**12**	**0**	**6**	**6**	**14**
	NHL Totals		**889**	**97**	**400**	**497**	**1014**	**81**	**7**	**22**	**29**	**117**

a CCHA First All-Star Team (1984)
b NCAA All-American (1984)

Played in NHL All-Star Game (1991, 1994)

Traded to **Washington** by **Los Angeles** for Al Jensen, February 14, 1987. Signed as a free agent by **Boston**, July 8, 1988. Traded to **Philadelphia** by **Boston** with Wes Walz and Boston's third round choice (Milos Holan) in 1993 Entry Draft for Gord Murphy, Brian Dobbin, Philadelphia's third round choice (Sergei Zholtok) in 1992 Entry Draft and Philadelphia's fourth round choice (Charles Paquette) in 1993 Entry Draft, January 2, 1992. Traded to **Buffalo** by **Philadelphia** for Petr Svoboda, April 7, 1995. Signed as a free agent by **Los Angeles**, July 15, 1997.

GARANIN, YEVGENY (gah-RAH-nihn) PHO.

Center. Shoots left. 6'4", 191 lbs. Born, Voskresensk, USSR, August 3, 1973.
(Winnipeg's 9th choice, 228th overall, in 1992 Entry Draft).

			Regular Season					Playoffs				
Season	Club	Lea	GP	G	A	TP	PIM	GP	G	A	TP	PIM
1991-92	Khimik	CIS	1	1	0	1	0	....	....	....	....	....
1992-93	Khimik	CIS	34	5	4	9	10	1	0	0	0	2
1993-94	Khimik	CIS	46	6	4	10	12	3	0	0	0	0
1994-95	Khimik	CIS	50	19	8	27	6	2	0	0	0	0
1995-96	Khimik	CIS	50	14	12	26	12	....	....	....	....	....
1996-97	Khimik	Rus.	36	10	12	22	4	1	1	0	1	0

GARDINER, BRUCE OTT.

Center. Shoots right. 6'1", 193 lbs. Born, Barrie, Ont., February 11, 1971.
(St. Louis' 6th choice, 131st overall, in 1991 Entry Draft).

			Regular Season					Playoffs				
Season	Club	Lea	GP	G	A	TP	PIM	GP	G	A	TP	PIM
1990-91	Colgate	ECAC	27	4	9	13	72	....	....	....	....	....
1991-92	Colgate	ECAC	23	7	8	15	77	....	....	....	....	....
1992-93	Colgate	ECAC	33	17	12	29	64	....	....	....	....	....
1993-94a	Colgate	ECAC	33	23	23	46	68	....	....	....	....	....
	Peoria	IHL	3	0	0	0	0	....	....	....	....	....
1994-95	P.E.I.	AHL	72	17	20	37	132	7	4	1	5	4
1995-96	P.E.I.	AHL	38	11	13	24	87	5	2	4	6	4
1996-97	**Ottawa**	**NHL**	**67**	**11**	**10**	**21**	**49**	**7**	**0**	**1**	**1**	**2**
	NHL Totals		**67**	**11**	**10**	**21**	**49**	**7**	**0**	**1**	**1**	**2**

a ECAC Second All-Star Team (1994)

Signed as a free agent by **Ottawa**, June 14, 1994.

GARDINER, PETER CHI.

Right wing. Shoots right. 6'5", 220 lbs. Born, Toronto, Ont., September 29, 1977.
(Chicago's 6th choice, 120th overall, in 1997 Entry Draft).

			Regular Season					Playoffs				
Season	Club	Lea	GP	G	A	TP	PIM	GP	G	A	TP	PIM
1996-97	RPI	ECAC	36	10	21	31	47	....	....	....	....	....

GARPENLOV, JOHAN (GAHR-pehn-LAHV, YOH-hahn) FLA.

Left wing. Shoots left. 5'11", 184 lbs. Born, Stockholm, Sweden, March 21, 1968.
(Detroit's 5th choice, 85th overall, in 1986 Entry Draft).

			Regular Season					Playoffs				
Season	Club	Lea	GP	G	A	TP	PIM	GP	G	A	TP	PIM
1986-87	Djurgarden	Swe.	29	5	8	13	22	2	0	0	0	0
1987-88	Djurgarden	Swe.	30	7	10	17	12	3	1	3	4	4
1988-89	Djurgarden	Swe.	36	12	19	31	20	8	3	4	7	10
1989-90	Djurgarden	Swe.	39	20	13	33	35	8	2	4	6	4
1990-91	**Detroit**	**NHL**	**71**	**18**	**22**	**40**	**18**	**6**	**0**	**1**	**1**	**4**
1991-92	**Detroit**	**NHL**	**16**	**1**	**1**	**2**	**4**	....	....	....	....	....
	Adirondack	AHL	9	3	3	6	6	....	....	....	....	....
	San Jose	**NHL**	**12**	**5**	**6**	**11**	**4**	....	....	....	....	....
1992-93	**San Jose**	**NHL**	**79**	**22**	**44**	**66**	**56**	....	....	....	....	....
1993-94	**San Jose**	**NHL**	**80**	**18**	**35**	**53**	**28**	**14**	**4**	**6**	**10**	**6**
1994-95	**San Jose**	**NHL**	**13**	**1**	**1**	**2**	**2**	....	....	....	....	....
	Florida	**NHL**	**27**	**3**	**9**	**12**	**0**	....	....	....	....	....
1995-96	**Florida**	**NHL**	**82**	**23**	**28**	**51**	**36**	**20**	**4**	**2**	**6**	**8**
1996-97	**Florida**	**NHL**	**53**	**11**	**25**	**36**	**47**	**4**	**2**	**0**	**2**	**4**
	NHL Totals		**433**	**102**	**171**	**273**	**195**	**44**	**10**	**9**	**19**	**22**

Traded to **San Jose** by **Detroit** for Bob McGill and Vancouver's eighth round choice (previously acquired by Detroit — San Jose selected C.J. Denomme) in 1992 Entry Draft, March 9, 1992. Traded to **Florida** by **San Jose** for a conditional choice in 1998 Entry Draft, March 3, 1995.

GARTNER, MIKE — PHO.

Right wing. Shoots right. 6', 187 lbs. Born, Ottawa, Ont., October 29, 1959.
(Washington's 1st choice, 4th overall, in 1979 Entry Draft).

			Regular Season					Playoffs				
Season	Club	Lea	GP	G	A	TP	PIM	GP	G	A	TP	PIM
1976-77	Niagara Falls	OHA	62	33	42	75	125	....	....	....	....	....
1977-78a	Niagara Falls	OHA	64	41	49	90	56	....	....	....	....	....
1978-79	Cincinnati	WHA	78	27	25	52	123	3	0	2	2	2
1979-80	Washington	NHL	77	36	32	68	66	....	....	....	....	....
1980-81	Washington	NHL	80	48	46	94	100	....	....	....	....	....
1981-82	Washington	NHL	80	35	45	80	121	....	....	....	....	....
1982-83	Washington	NHL	73	38	38	76	54	4	0	0	0	4
1983-84	Washington	NHL	80	40	45	85	90	8	3	7	10	16
1984-85	Washington	NHL	80	50	52	102	71	5	4	3	7	9
1985-86	Washington	NHL	74	35	40	75	63	9	2	10	12	4
1986-87	Washington	NHL	78	41	32	73	61	7	4	3	7	14
1987-88	Washington	NHL	80	48	33	81	73	14	3	4	7	14
1988-89	Washington	NHL	56	26	29	55	71	....	....	....	....	....
	Minnesota	NHL	13	7	7	14	2	5	0	0	0	6
1989-90	Minnesota	NHL	67	34	36	70	32	....	....	....	....	....
	NY Rangers	NHL	12	11	5	16	6	10	5	3	8	12
1990-91	NY Rangers	NHL	79	49	20	69	53	6	1	1	2	0
1991-92	NY Rangers	NHL	76	40	41	81	55	13	8	8	16	4
1992-93	NY Rangers	NHL	84	45	23	68	59	....	....	....	....	....
1993-94	NY Rangers	NHL	71	28	24	52	58	....	....	....	....	....
	Toronto	NHL	10	6	6	12	4	18	5	6	11	14
1994-95	Toronto	NHL	38	12	8	20	6	5	2	2	4	2
1995-96	Toronto	NHL	82	35	19	54	52	6	4	1	5	4
1996-97	Phoenix	NHL	82	32	31	63	38	7	1	2	3	4
	NHL Totals		1372	696	612	1308	1135	117	42	50	92	107

a OHA First All-Star Team (1978)

Played in NHL All-Star Game (1981, 1985, 1986, 1988, 1990, 1993, 1996)

Traded to **Minnesota** by **Washington** with Larry Murphy for Dino Ciccarelli and Bob Rouse, March 7, 1989. Traded to **NY Rangers** by **Minnesota** for Ulf Dahlen, Los Angeles' fourth round choice (previously acquired by NY Rangers — Minnesota selected Cal McGowan) in 1990 Entry Draft and future considerations, March 6, 1990. Traded to **Toronto** by **NY Rangers** for Glenn Anderson, the rights to Scott Malone and Toronto's fourth round choice (Alexander Korobolin) in 1994 Entry Draft, March 21, 1994. Traded to **Phoenix** by **Toronto** for Chicago's fourth round choice (previously acquired by Phoenix — Toronto selected Vladimir Antipov) in 1996 Entry Draft, June 22, 1996.

GASKINS, JON — EDM.

Defense. Shoots left. 6'3", 205 lbs. Born, Dallas, TX, January 11, 1976.
(Edmonton's 8th choice, 110th overall, in 1994 Entry Draft).

			Regular Season					Playoffs				
Season	Club	Lea	GP	G	A	TP	PIM	GP	G	A	TP	PIM
1994-95	Michigan State	CCHA	28	1	5	6	18	....	....	....	....	....
1995-96	Michigan State	CCHA	17	0	1	1	4	....	....	....	....	....
1996-97	Michigan State	CCHA	40	1	5	6	12	....	....	....	....	....

GAUDREAU, ROB — (GUH-droh)

Right wing. Shoots right. 5'11", 185 lbs. Born, Lincoln, RI, January 20, 1970.
(Pittsburgh's 8th choice, 172nd overall, in 1988 Entry Draft).

			Regular Season					Playoffs				
Season	Club	Lea	GP	G	A	TP	PIM	GP	G	A	TP	PIM
1988-89	Providence	H.E.	42	28	29	57	32	....	....	....	....	....
1989-90	Providence	H.E.	32	20	18	38	12	....	....	....	....	....
1990-91a	Providence	H.E.	36	34	27	61	20	....	....	....	....	....
1991-92bc	Providence	H.E.	36	21	34	55	22	....	....	....	....	....
1992-93	San Jose	NHL	59	23	20	43	18	....	....	....	....	....
	Kansas City	IHL	19	8	6	14	6	....	....	....	....	....
1993-94	San Jose	NHL	84	15	20	35	28	14	2	0	2	0
1994-95	Ottawa	NHL	36	5	9	14	8	....	....	....	....	....
1995-96	Ottawa	NHL	52	8	5	13	15	....	....	....	....	....
	P.E.I.	AHL	3	2	0	2	4	....	....	....	....	....
1996-97	Chaux	Switz.	37	19	23	42	62	....	....	....	....	....
	NHL Totals		231	51	54	105	69	14	2	0	2	0

a Hockey East Second All-Star Team (1991)
b NCAA East Second All-American Team (1992)
c Hockey East First All-Star Team (1992)

Rights traded to **Minnesota** by **Pittsburgh** for Richard Zemlak, November 1, 1988. Claimed by **San Jose** from **Minnesota** in Dispersal Draft, May 30, 1991. Claimed by **Ottawa** from **San Jose** in NHL Waiver Draft, January 18, 1995.

GAUTHIER, DENIS — (GOH-tyay) CGY.

Defense. Shoots left. 6'2", 195 lbs. Born, Montreal, Que., October 1, 1976.
(Calgary's 1st choice, 20th overall, in 1995 Entry Draft).

			Regular Season					Playoffs				
Season	Club	Lea	GP	G	A	TP	PIM	GP	G	A	TP	PIM
1992-93	Drummondville	QMJHL	60	1	7	8	136	10	0	5	5	40
1993-94	Drummondville	QMJHL	60	0	7	7	176	9	2	0	2	41
1994-95	Drummondville	QMJHL	64	9	31	40	190	4	0	5	5	12
1995-96ab	Drummondville	QMJHL	53	25	49	74	140	6	4	4	8	32
	Saint John	AHL	5	2	0	2	8	16	1	6	7	20
1996-97	Saint John	AHL	73	3	28	31	74	5	0	0	0	6

a QMJHL First All-Star Team (1996)
b Canadian Major Junior First All-Star Team (1996)

GAVEY, AARON — (GAY-vee) CGY.

Center. Shoots left. 6'1", 194 lbs. Born, Sudbury, Ont., February 22, 1974.
(Tampa Bay's 4th choice, 74th overall, in 1992 Entry Draft).

			Regular Season					Playoffs				
Season	Club	Lea	GP	G	A	TP	PIM	GP	G	A	TP	PIM
1991-92	S.S. Marie	OHL	48	7	11	18	27	19	5	1	6	10
1992-93	S.S. Marie	OHL	62	45	39	84	116	18	5	9	14	36
1993-94	S.S. Marie	OHL	60	42	60	102	116	14	11	10	21	22
1994-95	Atlanta	IHL	66	18	17	35	85	5	0	1	1	9
1995-96	Tampa Bay	NHL	73	8	4	12	56	6	0	0	0	4
1996-97	Tampa Bay	NHL	16	1	2	3	12	....	....	....	....	....
	Calgary	NHL	41	7	9	16	34	....	....	....	....	....
	NHL Totals		130	16	15	31	102	6	0	0	0	4

Traded to **Calgary** by **Tampa Bay** for Rick Tabaracci, November 19, 1996.

GELINAS, MARTIN — (ZHEHL-in-nuh, MAHR-ta) VAN.

Left wing. Shoots left. 5'11", 195 lbs. Born, Shawinigan, Que., June 5, 1970.
(Los Angeles' 1st choice, 7th overall, in 1988 Entry Draft).

			Regular Season					Playoffs				
Season	Club	Lea	GP	G	A	TP	PIM	GP	G	A	TP	PIM
1987-88ab	Hull	QMJHL	65	63	68	131	74	17	15	18	33	32
1988-89	Edmonton	NHL	6	1	2	3	0	....	....	....	....	....
	Hull	QMJHL	41	38	39	77	31	9	5	4	9	14
1989-90	Edmonton	NHL	46	17	8	25	30	20	2	3	5	6 ♦
1990-91	Edmonton	NHL	73	20	20	40	34	18	3	6	9	25
1991-92	Edmonton	NHL	68	11	18	29	62	15	1	3	4	10
1992-93	Edmonton	NHL	65	11	12	23	30	....	....	....	....	....
1993-94	Quebec	NHL	31	6	6	12	8	....	....	....	....	....
	Vancouver	NHL	33	8	8	16	26	24	5	4	9	14
1994-95	Vancouver	NHL	46	13	10	23	36	3	0	1	1	0
1995-96	Vancouver	NHL	81	30	26	56	59	6	1	1	2	12
1996-97	Vancouver	NHL	74	35	33	68	42	....	....	....	....	....
	NHL Totals		523	152	143	295	327	86	12	18	30	67

a Canadian Major Junior Rookie of the Year (1988)
b Won George Parsons Trophy (Memorial Cup Tournament Most Sportsmanlike Player) (1988)

Traded to **Edmonton** by **Los Angeles** with Jimmy Carson and Los Angeles' first round choices in 1989 (acquired by New Jersey — New Jersey selected Jason Miller), 1991 (Martin Rucinsky) and 1993 (Nick Stajduhar) Entry Drafts and cash for Wayne Gretzky, Mike Krushelnyski and Marty McSorley, August 9, 1988. Traded to **Quebec** by **Edmonton** with Edmonton's sixth round choice (Nicholas Checco) in 1993 Entry Draft for Scott Pearson, June 20, 1993. Claimed on waivers by **Vancouver** from **Quebec**, January 15, 1994.

GENDRON, MARTIN — (ZHEHN-drawn) WSH.

Right wing. Shoots right. 5'9", 190 lbs. Born, Valleyfield, Que., February 15, 1974.
(Washington's 4th choice, 71st overall, in 1992 Entry Draft).

			Regular Season					Playoffs				
Season	Club	Lea	GP	G	A	TP	PIM	GP	G	A	TP	PIM
1990-91	St-Hyacinthe	QMJHL	55	34	23	57	33	4	1	2	3	0
1991-92a	St-Hyacinthe	QMJHL	69	*71	66	137	45	6	7	4	11	14
1992-93bc	St-Hyacinthe	QMJHL	63	73	61	134	44	....	....	....	....	....
	Baltimore	AHL	10	1	2	3	2	3	0	0	0	0
1993-94	Cdn. National	....	19	4	5	9	2	....	....	....	....	....
	Hull	QMJHL	37	39	36	75	18	20	*21	17	38	8
1994-95	Portland	AHL	72	36	32	68	54	4	5	1	6	2
	Washington	NHL	8	2	1	3	2	....	....	....	....	....
1995-96	Washington	NHL	20	2	1	3	8	....	....	....	....	....
	Portland	AHL	48	38	29	67	39	22	*15	18	33	8
1996-97	Las Vegas	IHL	81	51	39	90	20	3	2	1	3	0
	NHL Totals		28	4	2	6	10	....	....	....	....	....

a QMJHL First All-Star Team (1992)
b QMJHL Second All-Star Team (1993)
c Canadian Major Junior First All-Star Team (1993)

GERIS, DAVE — FLA.

Defense. Shoots left. 6'5", 240 lbs. Born, North Bay, Ont., June 7, 1976.
(Florida's 6th choice, 105th overall, in 1994 Entry Draft).

			Regular Season					Playoffs				
Season	Club	Lea	GP	G	A	TP	PIM	GP	G	A	TP	PIM
1993-94	Windsor	OHL	63	0	6	6	121	3	0	0	0	6
1994-95	Windsor	OHL	65	5	11	16	135	10	1	6	7	21
1995-96	Windsor	OHL	64	8	20	28	205	7	1	0	1	20
1996-97	Port Huron	ColHL	42	1	7	8	117	5	0	1	1	0
	Carolina	AHL	28	1	1	2	59	....	....	....	....	....

GERNANDER, KEN — (guhr-NAN-duhr) NYR

Center. Shoots left. 5'10", 180 lbs. Born, Coleraine, MN, June 30, 1969.
(Winnipeg's 4th choice, 96th overall, in 1987 Entry Draft).

			Regular Season					Playoffs				
Season	Club	Lea	GP	G	A	TP	PIM	GP	G	A	TP	PIM
1987-88	U. Minnesota	WCHA	44	14	14	28	14	....	....	....	....	....
1988-89	U. Minnesota	WCHA	44	9	11	20	2	....	....	....	....	....
1989-90	U. Minnesota	WCHA	44	32	17	49	24	....	....	....	....	....
1990-91	U. Minnesota	WCHA	44	23	20	43	24	....	....	....	....	....
1991-92	Fort Wayne	IHL	13	7	6	13	2	....	....	....	....	....
	Moncton	AHL	43	8	18	26	9	8	1	1	2	2
1992-93	Moncton	AHL	71	18	29	47	20	5	1	4	5	0
1993-94	Moncton	AHL	71	22	25	47	12	19	6	1	7	0
1994-95	Binghamton	AHL	80	28	25	53	24	11	2	2	4	6
1995-96	NY Rangers	NHL	10	2	3	5	4	6	0	0	0	0
a	Binghamton	AHL	63	44	29	73	38	....	....	....	....	....
1996-97	Binghamton	AHL	46	13	18	31	30	2	0	1	1	0
	NY Rangers	NHL	....	....	....	....	....	9	0	0	0	0
	NHL Totals		10	2	3	5	4	15	0	0	0	0

a Won Fred Hunt Memorial Trophy (Sportsmanship - AHL) (1996)

Signed as a free agent by **NY Rangers**, July 4, 1994.

GILCHRIST, BRENT — DET.

Left wing. Shoots left. 5'11", 180 lbs. Born, Moose Jaw, Sask., April 3, 1967.
(Montreal's 6th choice, 79th overall, in 1985 Entry Draft).

			Regular Season					Playoffs				
Season	Club	Lea	GP	G	A	TP	PIM	GP	G	A	TP	PIM
1983-84	Kelowna	WHL	69	16	11	27	16	....	....	....	....	....
1984-85	Kelowna	WHL	51	35	38	73	58	6	5	2	7	8
1985-86	Spokane	WHL	52	45	45	90	57	9	6	7	13	19
1986-87	Spokane	WHL	46	45	55	100	71	5	2	7	9	6
	Sherbrooke	AHL	....	....	....	....	....	10	2	7	9	2
1987-88	Sherbrooke	AHL	77	26	48	74	83	6	1	3	4	6
1988-89	Montreal	NHL	49	8	16	24	16	9	1	1	2	10
	Sherbrooke	AHL	7	6	5	11	7	....	....	....	....	....
1989-90	Montreal	NHL	57	9	15	24	28	8	2	0	2	2
1990-91	Montreal	NHL	51	6	9	15	10	13	5	3	8	6
1991-92	Montreal	NHL	79	23	27	50	57	11	2	4	6	6
1992-93	Edmonton	NHL	60	10	10	20	47	....	....	....	....	....
	Minnesota	NHL	8	0	1	1	2	....	....	....	....	....
1993-94	Dallas	NHL	76	17	14	31	31	9	3	1	4	2
1994-95	Dallas	NHL	32	9	4	13	16	5	0	1	1	2
1995-96	Dallas	NHL	77	20	22	42	36	....	....	....	....	....
1996-97	Dallas	NHL	67	10	20	30	24	6	2	2	4	2
	NHL Totals		556	112	138	250	267	61	15	12	27	30

Traded to **Edmonton** by **Montreal** with Shayne Corson and Vladimir Vujtek for Vincent Damphousse and Edmonton's fourth round choice (Adam Wiesel) in 1993 Entry Draft, August 27, 1992. Traded to **Minnesota** by **Edmonton** for Todd Elik, March 5, 1993. Signed as a free agent by **Detroit**, August 1, 1997.

GILHEN, RANDY (GIHL-uhn)

Center. Shoots left. 6', 190 lbs. Born, Zweibrucken, W. Germany, June 13, 1963.
(Hartford's 6th choice, 109th overall, in 1982 Entry Draft).

			Regular Season					Playoffs				
Season	Club	Lea	GP	G	A	TP	PIM	GP	G	A	TP	PIM
1980-81	Saskatoon	WHL	68	10	5	15	154	....	....	....	....	....
1981-82	Saskatoon	WHL	25	15	9	24	45	....	....	....	....	....
	Winnipeg	WHL	36	26	28	54	42	....	....	....	....	....
1982-83	**Hartford**	**NHL**	**2**	**0**	**1**	**1**	**0**	....	....	....	....	....
	Winnipeg	WHL	71	57	44	101	84	3	2	2	4	0
1983-84	Binghamton	AHL	73	8	12	20	72	....	....	....	....	....
1984-85	Salt Lake	IHL	57	20	20	40	28	....	....	....	....	....
	Binghamton	AHL	18	3	3	6	9	8	4	1	5	16
1985-86	Fort Wayne	IHL	82	44	40	84	48	15	10	8	18	6
1986-87	**Winnipeg**	**NHL**	**2**	**0**	**0**	**0**	**0**	....	....	....	....	....
	Sherbrooke	AHL	75	36	29	65	44	17	7	13	20	10
1987-88	**Winnipeg**	**NHL**	**13**	**3**	**2**	**5**	**15**	**4**	**1**	**0**	**1**	**10**
	Moncton	AHL	68	40	47	87	51	....	....	....	....	....
1988-89	**Winnipeg**	**NHL**	**64**	**5**	**3**	**8**	**38**	....	....	....	....	....
1989-90	**Pittsburgh**	**NHL**	**61**	**5**	**11**	**16**	**54**	....	....	....	....	....
1990-91	**Pittsburgh**	**NHL**	**72**	**15**	**10**	**25**	**51**	**16**	**1**	**0**	**1**	**14 ♦**
1991-92	**Los Angeles**	**NHL**	**33**	**3**	**6**	**9**	**14**	....	....	....	....	....
	NY Rangers	**NHL**	**40**	**7**	**7**	**14**	**14**	**13**	**1**	**2**	**3**	**2**
1992-93	**NY Rangers**	**NHL**	**33**	**3**	**2**	**5**	**8**	....	....	....	....	....
	Tampa Bay	**NHL**	**11**	**0**	**2**	**2**	**6**	....	....	....	....	....
1993-94	**Florida**	**NHL**	**20**	**4**	**4**	**8**	**16**	....	....	....	....	....
	Winnipeg	**NHL**	**40**	**3**	**3**	**6**	**34**	....	....	....	....	....
1994-95	**Winnipeg**	**NHL**	**44**	**5**	**6**	**11**	**52**	....	....	....	....	....
1995-96	**Winnipeg**	**NHL**	**22**	**2**	**3**	**5**	**12**	....	....	....	....	....
1996-97	Manitoba	IHL	79	21	24	45	101	....	....	....	....	....
	NHL Totals		**457**	**55**	**60**	**115**	**314**	**33**	**3**	**2**	**5**	**26**

Signed as a free agent by **Winnipeg**, November 8, 1985. Traded to **Pittsburgh** by **Winnipeg** with Jim Kyte and Andrew McBain for Randy Cunneyworth, Rick Tabaracci and Dave McLlwain, June 17, 1989. Claimed by **Minnesota** from **Pittsburgh** in Expansion Draft, May 30, 1991. Traded to **Los Angeles** by **Minnesota** with Charlie Huddy, Jim Thomson and NY Rangers' fourth round choice (previously acquired by Minnesota — Los Angeles selected Alexei Zhitnik) in 1991 Entry Draft for Todd Elik, June 22, 1991. Traded to **NY Rangers** by **Los Angeles** for Corey Millen, December 23, 1991. Traded to **Tampa Bay** by **NY Rangers** for Mike Hartman, March 22, 1993. Claimed by **Florida** from **Tampa Bay** in Expansion Draft, June 24, 1993. Traded to **Winnipeg** by **Florida** for Stu Barnes and St. Louis' sixth round choice (previously acquired by Winnipeg — later traded to Edmonton — later traded to Winnipeg — Winnipeg selected Chris Kibermanis) in 1994 Entry Draft, November 25, 1993.

GILL, HAL (GIHL) BOS.

Defense. Shoots left. 6'6", 200 lbs. Born, Concord, MA, April 6, 1975.
(Boston's 8th choice, 207th overall, in 1993 Entry Draft).

			Regular Season					Playoffs				
Season	Club	Lea	GP	G	A	TP	PIM	GP	G	A	TP	PIM
1993-94	Providence	H.E.	31	1	2	3	26	....	....	....	....	....
1994-95	Providence	H.E.	26	1	3	4	22	....	....	....	....	....
1995-96	Providence	H.E.	39	5	12	17	54	....	....	....	....	....
1996-97	Providence	H.E.	35	5	16	21	52	....	....	....	....	....

GILL, TODD (GIHL) S.J.

Defense. Shoots left. 6', 180 lbs. Born, Cardinal, Ont., November 9, 1965.
(Toronto's 2nd choice, 25th overall, in 1984 Entry Draft).

			Regular Season					Playoffs				
Season	Club	Lea	GP	G	A	TP	PIM	GP	G	A	TP	PIM
1982-83	Windsor	OHL	70	12	24	36	108	3	0	0	0	11
1983-84	Windsor	OHL	68	9	48	57	184	3	1	1	2	10
1984-85	**Toronto**	**NHL**	**10**	**1**	**0**	**1**	**13**	....	....	....	....	....
	Windsor	OHL	53	17	40	57	148	4	0	1	1	14
1985-86	**Toronto**	**NHL**	**15**	**1**	**2**	**3**	**28**	**1**	**0**	**0**	**0**	**0**
	St. Catharines	AHL	58	8	25	33	90	10	1	6	7	17
1986-87	**Toronto**	**NHL**	**61**	**4**	**27**	**31**	**92**	**13**	**2**	**2**	**4**	**42**
	Newmarket	AHL	11	1	8	9	33	....	....	....	....	....
1987-88	**Toronto**	**NHL**	**65**	**8**	**17**	**25**	**131**	**6**	**1**	**3**	**4**	**20**
	Newmarket	AHL	2	0	1	1	2	....	....	....	....	....
1988-89	**Toronto**	**NHL**	**59**	**11**	**14**	**25**	**72**	....	....	....	....	....
1989-90	**Toronto**	**NHL**	**48**	**1**	**14**	**15**	**92**	**5**	**0**	**3**	**3**	**16**
1990-91	**Toronto**	**NHL**	**72**	**2**	**22**	**24**	**113**	....	....	....	....	....
1991-92	**Toronto**	**NHL**	**74**	**2**	**15**	**17**	**91**	....	....	....	....	....
1992-93	**Toronto**	**NHL**	**69**	**11**	**32**	**43**	**66**	**21**	**1**	**10**	**11**	**26**
1993-94	**Toronto**	**NHL**	**45**	**4**	**24**	**28**	**44**	**18**	**1**	**5**	**6**	**37**
1994-95	**Toronto**	**NHL**	**47**	**7**	**25**	**32**	**64**	**7**	**0**	**3**	**3**	**6**
1995-96	**Toronto**	**NHL**	**74**	**7**	**18**	**25**	**116**	**6**	**0**	**0**	**0**	**24**
1996-97	**San Jose**	**NHL**	**79**	**0**	**21**	**21**	**101**	....	....	....	....	....
	NHL Totals		**718**	**59**	**231**	**290**	**1023**	**77**	**5**	**26**	**31**	**171**

Traded to **San Jose** by **Toronto** for Jamie Baker and San Jose's fifth round choice (Peter Cava) in 1996 Entry Draft, June 14, 1996.

GILLAM, SEAN DET.

Defense. Shoots right. 6'2", 187 lbs. Born, Lethbridge, Alta., May 7, 1976.
(Detroit's 3rd choice, 75th overall, in 1994 Entry Draft).

			Regular Season					Playoffs				
Season	Club	Lea	GP	G	A	TP	PIM	GP	G	A	TP	PIM
1992-93	Spokane	WHL	70	6	27	33	121	10	0	2	2	10
1993-94	Spokane	WHL	70	7	17	24	106	3	0	0	0	6
1994-95a	Spokane	WHL	72	16	40	56	192	11	0	3	3	33
1995-96a	Spokane	WHL	69	11	58	69	123	18	2	12	14	26
1996-97	Adirondack	AHL	64	1	7	8	50	....	....	....	....	....

a WHL West Second All-Star Team (1995, 1996)

GILMOUR, DOUG N.J.

Center. Shoots left. 5'11", 172 lbs. Born, Kingston, Ont., June 25, 1963.
(St. Louis' 4th choice, 134th overall, in 1982 Entry Draft).

			Regular Season					Playoffs				
Season	Club	Lea	GP	G	A	TP	PIM	GP	G	A	TP	PIM
1981-82	Cornwall	OHL	67	46	73	119	42	5	6	9	15	2
1982-83a	Cornwall	OHL	68	70	*107	*177	62	8	8	10	18	16
1983-84	**St. Louis**	**NHL**	**80**	**25**	**28**	**53**	**57**	**11**	**2**	**9**	**11**	**10**
1984-85	**St. Louis**	**NHL**	**78**	**21**	**36**	**57**	**49**	**3**	**1**	**1**	**2**	**2**
1985-86	**St. Louis**	**NHL**	**74**	**25**	**28**	**53**	**41**	**19**	**9**	**12**	***21**	**25**
1986-87	**St. Louis**	**NHL**	**80**	**42**	**63**	**105**	**58**	**6**	**2**	**2**	**4**	**16**
1987-88	**St. Louis**	**NHL**	**72**	**36**	**50**	**86**	**59**	**10**	**3**	**14**	**17**	**18**
1988-89	**Calgary**	**NHL**	**72**	**26**	**59**	**85**	**44**	**22**	**11**	**11**	**22**	**20 ♦**
1989-90	**Calgary**	**NHL**	**78**	**24**	**67**	**91**	**54**	**6**	**3**	**1**	**4**	**8**
1990-91	**Calgary**	**NHL**	**78**	**20**	**61**	**81**	**144**	**7**	**1**	**1**	**2**	**0**
1991-92	**Calgary**	**NHL**	**38**	**11**	**27**	**38**	**46**	....	....	....	....	....
	Toronto	**NHL**	**40**	**15**	**34**	**49**	**32**	....	....	....	....	....
1992-93b	**Toronto**	**NHL**	**83**	**32**	**95**	**127**	**100**	**21**	**10**	***25**	**35**	**30**
1993-94	**Toronto**	**NHL**	**83**	**27**	**84**	**111**	**105**	**18**	**6**	**22**	**28**	**42**
1994-95	Rapperswil	Switz.	9	2	13	15	16	....	....	....	....	....
	Toronto	**NHL**	**44**	**10**	**23**	**33**	**26**	**7**	**0**	**6**	**6**	**6**
1995-96	**Toronto**	**NHL**	**81**	**32**	**40**	**72**	**77**	**6**	**1**	**7**	**8**	**12**
1996-97	**Toronto**	**NHL**	**61**	**15**	**45**	**60**	**46**	....	....	....	....	....
	New Jersey	**NHL**	**20**	**7**	**15**	**22**	**22**	**10**	**0**	**4**	**4**	**14**
	NHL Totals		**1062**	**368**	**755**	**1123**	**960**	**146**	**49**	**115**	**164**	**203**

a OHL First All-Star Team (1983)
b Won Frank J. Selke Trophy (1993)

Played in NHL All-Star Game (1993, 1994)

Traded to **Calgary** by **St. Louis** with Mark Hunter, Steve Bozek and Michael Dark for Mike Bullard, Craig Coxe and Tim Corkery, September 6, 1988. Traded to **Toronto** by **Calgary** with Jamie Macoun, Ric Nattress, Kent Manderville and Rick Wamsley for Gary Leeman, Alexander Godynyuk, Jeff Reese, Michel Petit and Craig Berube, January 2, 1992. Traded to **New Jersey** by **Toronto** with Dave Ellett and a conditional draft choice for Jason Smith, Steve Sullivan and the rights to Alyn McCauley, February 25, 1997.

GIRARD, RICK

Center. Shoots left. 5'11", 175 lbs. Born, Edmonton, Alta., May 1, 1974.
(Vancouver's 2nd choice, 46th overall, in 1993 Entry Draft).

			Regular Season					Playoffs				
Season	Club	Lea	GP	G	A	TP	PIM	GP	G	A	TP	PIM
1991-92	Swift Current	WHL	45	14	17	31	6	8	2	0	2	2
1992-93ab	Swift Current	WHL	72	71	70	141	25	17	9	17	26	10
1993-94a	Swift Current	WHL	58	40	49	89	43	7	1	8	9	6
	Hamilton	AHL	1	1	1	2	0	....	....	....	....	....
1994-95	Syracuse	AHL	26	10	13	23	22	....	....	....	....	....
1995-96	Syracuse	AHL	67	15	21	36	32	16	9	8	17	16
1996-97	Syracuse	AHL	66	19	28	47	20	1	1	1	2	2

a WHL East First All-Star Team (1993, 1994)
b Canadian Major Junior Sportsmanlike Player of the Year (1993)

GIROUX, RAYMOND (jih-ROO) PHI.

Defense. Shoots left. 6', 180 lbs. Born, North Bay, Ont., July 20, 1976.
(Philadelphia's 7th choice, 202nd overall, in 1994 Entry Draft).

			Regular Season					Playoffs				
Season	Club	Lea	GP	G	A	TP	PIM	GP	G	A	TP	PIM
1994-95	Yale	ECAC	27	1	3	4	8	....	....	....	....	....
1995-96	Yale	ECAC	30	3	16	19	36	....	....	....	....	....
1996-97	Yale	ECAC	32	9	12	21	38	....	....	....	....	....

GLYNN, BRIAN (GLIHN)

Defense. Shoots left. 6'4", 218 lbs. Born, Iserlohn, West Germany, November 23, 1967.
(Calgary's 2nd choice, 37th overall, in 1986 Entry Draft).

			Regular Season					Playoffs				
Season	Club	Lea	GP	G	A	TP	PIM	GP	G	A	TP	PIM
1984-85	Saskatoon	WHL	12	1	0	1	2	3	0	0	0	0
1985-86	Saskatoon	WHL	66	7	25	32	131	13	0	3	3	30
1986-87	Saskatoon	WHL	44	2	26	28	163	11	1	3	4	19
1987-88	**Calgary**	**NHL**	**67**	**5**	**14**	**19**	**87**	**1**	**0**	**0**	**0**	**0**
1988-89	**Calgary**	**NHL**	**9**	**0**	**1**	**1**	**19**	....	....	....	....	....
	Salt Lake	IHL	31	3	10	13	105	14	3	7	10	31
1989-90	**Calgary**	**NHL**	**1**	**0**	**0**	**0**	**0**	....	....	....	....	....
ab	Salt Lake	IHL	80	17	44	61	164	....	....	....	....	....
1990-91	Salt Lake	IHL	8	1	3	4	18	....	....	....	....	....
	Minnesota	**NHL**	**66**	**8**	**11**	**19**	**83**	**23**	**2**	**6**	**8**	**18**
1991-92	**Minnesota**	**NHL**	**37**	**2**	**12**	**14**	**24**	....	....	....	....	....
	Edmonton	**NHL**	**25**	**2**	**6**	**8**	**6**	**16**	**4**	**1**	**5**	**12**
1992-93	**Edmonton**	**NHL**	**64**	**4**	**12**	**16**	**60**	....	....	....	....	....
1993-94	**Ottawa**	**NHL**	**48**	**2**	**13**	**15**	**41**	....	....	....	....	....
	Vancouver	**NHL**	**16**	**0**	**0**	**0**	**12**	**17**	**0**	**3**	**3**	**10**
1994-95	**Hartford**	**NHL**	**43**	**1**	**6**	**7**	**32**	....	....	....	....	....
1995-96	**Hartford**	**NHL**	**54**	**0**	**4**	**4**	**44**	....	....	....	....	....
1996-97	**Hartford**	**NHL**	**1**	**1**	**0**	**1**	**2**	....	....	....	....	....
	San Antonio	IHL	62	13	11	24	46	9	2	6	8	4
	NHL Totals		**431**	**25**	**79**	**104**	**410**	**57**	**6**	**10**	**16**	**40**

a IHL First All-Star Team (1990)
b Won Governors' Trophy (Outstanding Defenseman - IHL) (1990)

Traded to **Minnesota** by **Calgary** for Frantisek Musil, October 26, 1990. Traded to **Edmonton** by **Minnesota** for David Shaw, January 21, 1992. Traded to **Ottawa** by **Edmonton** for Ottawa's eighth round choice (Rob Quinn) in 1994 Entry Draft, September 15, 1993. Claimed on waivers by **Vancouver** from **Ottawa**, February 5, 1994. Claimed by **Hartford** from **Vancouver** in NHL Waiver Draft, January 18, 1995. Traded to **Detroit** by **Hartford** with Brendan Shanahan for Paul Coffey, Keith Primeau and Detroit's first round choice (Nikos Tselios) in 1997 Entry Draft, October 9, 1996.

GOC, SASCHA (GAWCH, SA-shah) N.J.

Defense. Shoots right. 6'2", 196 lbs. Born, Calw, Germany, April 17, 1979.
(New Jersey's 5th choice, 159th overall, in 1997 Entry Draft).

			Regular Season					Playoffs				
Season	Club	Lea	GP	G	A	TP	PIM	GP	G	A	TP	PIM
1995-96	Schwenningen	Ger. Jr.	11	3	6	9	77	....	....	....	....	....
	Schwenningen	Ger.	1	0	0	0	0	....	....	....	....	....
1996-97	Schwenningen	Ger.	41	3	1	4	28	5	0	0	0	0

GODYNYUK, ALEXANDER (goh-dih-NYOOK) ST.L.

Defense. Shoots left. 6', 207 lbs. Born, Kiev, Ukraine, January 27, 1970.
(Toronto's 5th choice, 115th overall, in 1990 Entry Draft).

			Regular Season					Playoffs				
Season	Club	Lea	GP	G	A	TP	PIM	GP	G	A	TP	PIM
1986-87	Sokol Kiev	USSR	9	0	1	1	2	....	....	....	....	....
1987-88	Sokol Kiev	USSR	2	0	0	0	2	....	....	....	....	....
1988-89	Sokol Kiev	USSR	30	3	3	6	12	....	....	....	....	....
1989-90	Sokol Kiev	USSR	37	3	2	5	31	....	....	....	....	....
1990-91	Sokol Kiev	USSR	19	3	1	4	20	....	....	....	....	....
	Toronto	**NHL**	**18**	**0**	**3**	**3**	**16**	....	....	....	....	....
	Newmarket	AHL	11	0	1	1	29	....	....	....	....	....
1991-92	**Toronto**	**NHL**	**31**	**3**	**6**	**9**	**59**	....	....	....	....	....
	Calgary	**NHL**	**6**	**0**	**1**	**1**	**4**	....	....	....	....	....
	Salt Lake	IHL	17	2	1	3	24	....	....	....	....	....
1992-93	**Calgary**	**NHL**	**27**	**3**	**4**	**7**	**19**	....	....	....	....	....
1993-94	**Florida**	**NHL**	**26**	**0**	**10**	**10**	**35**	....	....	....	....	....
	Hartford	**NHL**	**43**	**3**	**9**	**12**	**40**	....	....	....	....	....
1994-95	**Hartford**	**NHL**	**14**	**0**	**0**	**0**	**8**	....	....	....	....	....
1995-96	**Hartford**	**NHL**	**3**	**0**	**0**	**0**	**2**	....	....	....	....	....
	Springfield	AHL	14	1	3	4	19	....	....	....	....	....
	Detroit	IHL	7	0	3	3	12	....	....	....	....	....
	Minnesota	IHL	45	9	17	26	81	....	....	....	....	....
1996-97	**Hartford**	**NHL**	**55**	**1**	**6**	**7**	**41**	....	....	....	....	....
	NHL Totals		**223**	**10**	**39**	**49**	**224**	....	....	....	....	....

Traded to **Calgary** by **Toronto** with Craig Berube, Gary Leeman, Michel Petit and Jeff Reese for Doug Gilmour, Jamie Macoun, Ric Nattress, Rick Wamsley and Kent Manderville, January 2, 1992. Claimed by **Florida** from **Calgary** in Expansion Draft, June 24, 1993. Traded to **Hartford** by **Florida** for Jim McKenzie, December 16, 1993. Traded to **St. Louis** by **Carolina** with Carolina's sixth round choice in 1998 Entry Draft for Stephen Leach, June 27, 1997.

GOLDMANN, ERICH (GOHLD-mahn, AIR-ihkh) OTT.

Defense. Shoots left. 6'3", 196 lbs. Born, Dingolfing, West Germany, April 7, 1976.
(Ottawa's 5th choice, 212th overall, in 1996 Entry Draft).

			Regular Season					Playoffs				
Season	Club	Lea	GP	G	A	TP	PIM	GP	G	A	TP	PIM
1993-94	Landshut	Ger.	33	0	0	0	4	7	0	0	0	0
1994-95	Mannheim	Ger.	31	0	0	0	22	10	1	0	1	2
1995-96	Mannheim	Ger.	47	0	3	3	40	8	0	0	0	4
1996-97	Kaufbeuren	Ger.	44	2	4	6	58	6	1	0	1	2

GOLOKHVASTOV, KONSTANTIN (goh-lohkh-VAS-tahf) T.B.

Right wing. Shoots right. 6'1", 185 lbs. Born, Dneprodzerzinsk, USSR, February 6, 1977.
(Tampa Bay's 4th choice, 108th overall, in 1995 Entry Draft).

			Regular Season					Playoffs				
Season	Club	Lea	GP	G	A	TP	PIM	GP	G	A	TP	PIM
1994-95	Moscow D'amo	CIS	6	0	0	0	2	....	....	....	....	....
1995-96	Nizhnekamsk	CIS	21	6	1	7	2	....	....	....	....	....
1996-97	Moscow D'amo	Rus.				DID NOT PLAY						

GOLUBOVSKY, YAN (goh-luh-BOHV-skee) DET.

Defense. Shoots right. 6'3", 183 lbs. Born, Novosibirsk, USSR, March 9, 1976.
(Detroit's 1st choice, 23rd overall, in 1994 Entry Draft).

			Regular Season					Playoffs				
Season	Club	Lea	GP	G	A	TP	PIM	GP	G	A	TP	PIM
1993-94	Mosc. D'amo 2	CIS 3				UNAVAILABLE						
	Russian Pen's	IHL	8	0	0	0	23	....	....	....	....	....
1994-95	Adirondack	AHL	57	4	2	6	39	....	....	....	....	....
1995-96	Adirondack	AHL	71	5	16	21	97	3	0	0	0	2
1996-97	Adirondack	AHL	62	2	11	13	67	4	0	0	0	0

GONCHAR, SERGEI (gohn-CHAR) WSH.

Defense. Shoots left. 6'2", 212 lbs. Born, Chelyabinsk, USSR, April 13, 1974.
(Washington's 1st choice, 14th overall, in 1992 Entry Draft).

			Regular Season					Playoffs				
Season	Club	Lea	GP	G	A	TP	PIM	GP	G	A	TP	PIM
1991-92	Chelyabinsk	CIS	31	1	0	1	6	....	....	....	....	....
1992-93	Moscow D'amo	CIS	31	1	3	4	70	10	0	0	0	12
1993-94	Moscow D'amo	CIS	44	4	5	9	36	10	0	3	3	14
	Portland	AHL	....	....	....	....	....	2	0	0	0	0
1994-95	Portland	AHL	61	10	32	42	67	....	....	....	....	....
	Washington	**NHL**	**31**	**2**	**5**	**7**	**22**	**7**	**2**	**2**	**4**	**2**
1995-96	**Washington**	**NHL**	**78**	**15**	**26**	**41**	**60**	**6**	**2**	**4**	**6**	**4**
1996-97	**Washington**	**NHL**	**57**	**13**	**17**	**30**	**36**	....	....	....	....	....
	NHL Totals		**166**	**30**	**48**	**78**	**118**	**13**	**4**	**6**	**10**	**6**

GONEAU, DANIEL (guh-NOH) NYR

Left wing. Shoots left. 6', 194 lbs. Born, Montreal, Que., January 16, 1976.
(Boston's 2nd choice, 47th overall, in 1994 Entry Draft).

			Regular Season					Playoffs				
Season	Club	Lea	GP	G	A	TP	PIM	GP	G	A	TP	PIM
1992-93	Laval	QMJHL	62	16	25	41	44	13	0	4	4	4
1993-94	Laval	QMJHL	68	29	57	86	81	19	8	21	29	45
1994-95	Laval	QMJHL	56	16	31	47	78	20	5	10	15	33
1995-96a	Granby	QMJHL	67	54	51	105	115	21	11	22	33	40
1996-97	**NY Rangers**	**NHL**	**41**	**10**	**3**	**13**	**10**	....	....	....	....	....
	Binghamton	AHL	39	15	15	30	10	....	....	....	....	....
	NHL Totals		**41**	**10**	**3**	**13**	**10**	....	....	....	....	....

a QMJHL First All-Star Team (1996)

Re-entered NHL Entry Draft, **NY Rangers'** 2nd choice, 48th overall in 1996 Entry Draft.

GOOLDY, ERIC TOR.

Left wing. Shoots left. 6'2", 200 lbs. Born, Utica, NY, February 10, 1979.
(Toronto's 4th choice, 138th overall, in 1997 Entry Draft).

			Regular Season					Playoffs				
Season	Club	Lea	GP	G	A	TP	PIM	GP	G	A	TP	PIM
1996-97	Detroit	OHL	66	7	11	18	131	5	0	1	1	15

GORBACHEV, SERGEI (gohr-buh-CHEHF) DAL.

Right wing. Shoots left. 6'1", 185 lbs. Born, Saratov, USSR, October 24, 1975.
(San Jose's 7th choice, 167th overall, in 1994 Entry Draft).

			Regular Season					Playoffs				
Season	Club	Lea	GP	G	A	TP	PIM	GP	G	A	TP	PIM
1993-94	Moscow D'amo	CIS 2	2	0	0	0	0	....	....	....	....	....
1994-95	Moscow D'amo	CIS	4	0	1	1	2	....	....	....	....	....
1995-96	Saratov	CIS				DID NOT PLAY						
1996-97	Yaroslavl	Rus.	28	2	4	6	53	9	0	2	2	6

Traded to **Dallas** by **San Jose** for Dallas' fifth round choice in 1998 Entry Draft, August 15, 1996.

GORDON, HEATH CHI.

Left wing. Shoots left. 6'2", 197 lbs. Born, Boston, MA, May 28, 1978.
(Chicago's 8th choice, 147th overall, in 1997 Entry Draft).

			Regular Season					Playoffs				
Season	Club	Lea	GP	G	A	TP	PIM	GP	G	A	TP	PIM
1995-96	Cushing Acad.	HS	37	34	37	71	120	....	....	....	....	....
1996-97	Green Bay	Jr. A	52	16	28	44	71	....	....	....	....	....

GORDON, RHETT PHO.

Right wing. Shoots right. 5'11", 175 lbs. Born, Regina, Sask., August 26, 1976.

			Regular Season					Playoffs				
Season	Club	Lea	GP	G	A	TP	PIM	GP	G	A	TP	PIM
1992-93	Regina	WHL	2	1	0	1	2	4	0	0	0	0
1993-94	Regina	WHL	60	19	28	47	14	4	0	0	0	7
1994-95	Regina	WHL	71	36	43	79	64	4	2	2	4	0
1995-96a	Regina	WHL	66	53	50	103	68	11	9	4	13	10
	Springfield	AHL	2	0	0	0	2	1	0	0	0	0
1996-97	Springfield	AHL	54	11	11	22	54	8	1	2	3	6

a WHL West First All-Star Team (1996)

Signed as a free agent by **Winnipeg**, September 29, 1994.

GORDON, ROBB VAN.

Center. Shoots right. 5'11", 190 lbs. Born, Murrayville, B.C., January 13, 1976.
(Vancouver's 2nd choice, 39th overall, in 1994 Entry Draft).

			Regular Season					Playoffs				
Season	Club	Lea	GP	G	A	TP	PIM	GP	G	A	TP	PIM
1994-95	U. of Michigan	CCHA	39	15	26	41	72	....	....	....	....	....
1995-96	Kelowna	WHL	58	51	63	114	84	6	3	6	9	19
1996-97	Syracuse	AHL	63	11	14	25	72	3	0	0	0	7

GOREN, LEE BOS.

Right wing. Shoots right. 6'3", 190 lbs. Born, Winnipeg, Man., December 26, 1977.
(Boston's 5th choice, 63rd overall, in 1997 Entry Draft).

			Regular Season					Playoffs				
Season	Club	Lea	GP	G	A	TP	PIM	GP	G	A	TP	PIM
1995-96	Minote	Jr. A	64	31	55	86	....	....	....	....	....	....
1996-97	North Dakota	WCHA				DID NOT PLAY						

GORENKO, DMITRI (goh-REHN-koh) CAR.

Left wing. Shoots left. 6', 165 lbs. Born, Barnaul, USSR, February 13, 1975.
(Hartford's 6th choice, 214th overall, in 1993 Entry Draft).

			Regular Season					Playoffs				
Season	Club	Lea	GP	G	A	TP	PIM	GP	G	A	TP	PIM
1991-92	CSKA	CIS	14	0	1	1	6	....	....	....	....	....
1992-93	CSKA	CIS	42	3	0	3	20	....	....	....	....	....
1993-94	CSKA	CIS	40	5	1	6	28	3	1	0	1	2
1994-95	CSKA	CIS	33	5	2	7	35	....	....	....	....	....
1995-96	Omsk	CIS	37	4	2	6	14	3	0	1	1	0
1996-97	Omsk	Rus.	11	0	1	1	8	....	....	....	....	....

GOROKHOV, ILJA (goh-ROH-khahf, ihl-YA) NYR

Defense. Shoots right. 6', 185 lbs. Born, Yaroslavl, USSR, August 23, 1977.
(NY Rangers' 8th choice, 195th overall, in 1995 Entry Draft).

			Regular Season					Playoffs				
Season	Club	Lea	GP	G	A	TP	PIM	GP	G	A	TP	PIM
1994-95	Yaroslavl	CIS	1	0	0	0	0	....	....	....	....	....
1995-96	Yaroslavl	CIS	43	0	3	3	10	2	0	0	0	0
1996-97	Las Vegas	IHL	1	0	0	0	0	....	....	....	....	....
	Yaroslavl	Rus.	22	1	1	2	6	9	1	0	1	2

GOVEDARIS, CHRIS (goh-va-DAIR-us)

Left wing. Shoots left. 6', 200 lbs. Born, Toronto, Ont., February 2, 1970.
(Hartford's 1st choice, 11th overall, in 1988 Entry Draft).

			Regular Season					Playoffs				
Season	Club	Lea	GP	G	A	TP	PIM	GP	G	A	TP	PIM
1986-87	Toronto	OHL	64	36	28	64	148	....	....	....	....	....
1987-88	Toronto	OHL	62	42	38	80	118	4	2	1	3	10
1988-89	Toronto	OHL	49	41	38	79	117	6	2	3	5	0
1989-90	**Hartford**	**NHL**	**12**	**0**	**1**	**1**	**6**	**2**	**0**	**0**	**0**	**2**
	Binghamton	AHL	14	3	3	6	4	....	....	....	....	....
	Hamilton	OHL	23	11	21	32	53	....	....	....	....	....
1990-91	**Hartford**	**NHL**	**14**	**1**	**3**	**4**	**4**	....	....	....	....	....
	Springfield	AHL	56	26	36	62	133	9	2	5	7	36
1991-92	Springfield	AHL	43	14	25	39	55	11	3	2	5	25
1992-93	**Hartford**	**NHL**	**7**	**1**	**0**	**1**	**0**	....	....	....	....	....
	Springfield	AHL	65	31	24	55	58	15	7	4	11	18
1993-94	**Toronto**	**NHL**	**12**	**2**	**2**	**4**	**14**	**2**	**0**	**0**	**0**	**0**
	St. John's	AHL	62	35	35	70	76	11	6	5	11	22
1994-95	Milwaukee	IHL	54	34	25	59	71	....	....	....	....	....
	Adirondack	AHL	24	19	11	30	34	4	2	1	3	10
1995-96	Minnesota	IHL	81	31	36	67	133	....	....	....	....	....
1996-97	Eisbaren	Ger.	48	24	22	46	115	8	4	2	6	10
	NHL Totals		**45**	**4**	**6**	**10**	**24**	**4**	**0**	**0**	**0**	**2**

Signed as a free agent by **Toronto**, September 16, 1993. Signed as a free agent by **Winnipeg**, August 14, 1995.

GRACHEV, VLADIMIR (grah-CHEHF) NYI

Left wing. Shoots left. 6', 178 lbs. Born, Moscow, USSR, January 28, 1973.
(NY Islanders' 6th choice, 152nd overall, in 1992 Entry Draft).

			Regular Season					Playoffs				
Season	Club	Lea	GP	G	A	TP	PIM	GP	G	A	TP	PIM
1991-92	Mosc. D'amo 2	CIS 3	62	13	3	16	26	....	....	....	....	....
1992-93	Moscow D'amo	CIS	33	2	1	3	26	7	0	0	0	2
1993-94	Moscow D'amo	CIS	36	4	3	7	10	6	0	0	0	4
1994-95	Moscow D'amo	CIS	48	13	8	21	20	14	7	2	9	10
1995-96	Moscow D'amo	CIS	44	5	9	14	16	11	2	1	3	2
1996-97	Moscow D'amo	Rus.	35	2	8	10	14	4	0	2	2	2

GRANATO, TONY (gruh-NA-toh) S.J.

Left wing. Shoots right. 5'10", 185 lbs. Born, Downers Grove, IL, June 25, 1964.
(NY Rangers' 5th choice, 120th overall, in 1982 Entry Draft).

			Regular Season					Playoffs				
Season	Club	Lea	GP	G	A	TP	PIM	GP	G	A	TP	PIM
1983-84	U. Wisconsin	WCHA	35	14	17	31	48	....	....	....	....	....
1984-85	U. Wisconsin	WCHA	42	33	34	67	94	....	....	....	....	....
1985-86	U. Wisconsin	WCHA	33	25	24	49	36	....	....	....	....	....
1986-87ab	U. Wisconsin	WCHA	42	28	45	73	64	....	....	....	....	....
1987-88	U.S. National	....	49	40	31	71	55	....	....	....	....	....
	U.S. Olympic	....	6	1	7	8	4	....	....	....	....	....
	Colorado	IHL	22	13	14	27	36	8	9	4	13	16
1988-89c	**NY Rangers**	**NHL**	**78**	**36**	**27**	**63**	**140**	**4**	**1**	**1**	**2**	**21**
1989-90	**NY Rangers**	**NHL**	**37**	**7**	**18**	**25**	**77**	....	....	....	....	....
	Los Angeles	**NHL**	**19**	**5**	**6**	**11**	**45**	**10**	**5**	**4**	**9**	**12**
1990-91	**Los Angeles**	**NHL**	**68**	**30**	**34**	**64**	**154**	**12**	**1**	**4**	**5**	**28**
1991-92	**Los Angeles**	**NHL**	**80**	**39**	**29**	**68**	**187**	**6**	**1**	**5**	**6**	**10**
1992-93	**Los Angeles**	**NHL**	**81**	**37**	**45**	**82**	**171**	**24**	**6**	**11**	**17**	**50**
1993-94	**Los Angeles**	**NHL**	**50**	**7**	**14**	**21**	**150**	....	....	....	....	....
1994-95	**Los Angeles**	**NHL**	**33**	**13**	**11**	**24**	**68**	....	....	....	....	....
1995-96	**Los Angeles**	**NHL**	**49**	**17**	**18**	**35**	**46**	....	....	....	....	....
1996-97d	**San Jose**	**NHL**	**76**	**25**	**15**	**40**	**159**	....	....	....	....	....
	NHL Totals		**571**	**216**	**217**	**433**	**1197**	**56**	**14**	**25**	**39**	**121**

a WCHA Second All-Star Team (1987)
b NCAA West Second All-American Team (1987)
c NHL All-Rookie Team (1989)
d Won Bill Masterton Memorial Trophy (1997)

Played in NHL All-Star Game (1997)

Traded to **Los Angeles** by **NY Rangers** with Tomas Sandstrom for Bernie Nicholls, January 20, 1990. Signed as a free agent by **San Jose**, September 1, 1996.

GRAND PIERRE, JEAN-LUC BUF.

Defense. Shoots left. 6'3", 207 lbs. Born, Montreal, Que., February 2, 1977.
(St. Louis' 5th choice, 179th overall, in 1995 Entry Draft).

			Regular Season					Playoffs				
Season	Club	Lea	GP	G	A	TP	PIM	GP	G	A	TP	PIM
1994-95	Val d'Or	QMJHL	59	10	13	23	126	....	....	....	....	....
1995-96	Val d'Or	QMJHL	67	13	21	34	209	13	1	4	5	47
1996-97	Val d'Or	QMJHL	58	9	24	33	186	13	5	8	13	46

Traded to **Buffalo** by **St. Louis** with Ottawa's second round choice (previously acquired by St. Louis — Buffalo selected Cory Sarich) in 1996 Entry Draft and St. Louis' third round choice (Maxim Afinogenov) in 1997 Entry Draft for Yuri Khmylev and Buffalo's eighth round choice (Andrei Podkonicky) in 1996 Entry Draft, March 20, 1996.

GRATTON, BENOIT (grah-TOHN) WSH.

Left wing. Shoots left. 5'10", 163 lbs. Born, Montreal, Que., December 28, 1976.
(Washington's 6th choice, 105th overall, in 1995 Entry Draft).

			Regular Season					Playoffs				
Season	Club	Lea	GP	G	A	TP	PIM	GP	G	A	TP	PIM
1993-94	Laval	QMJHL	51	9	14	23	70	20	2	1	3	19
1994-95	Laval	QMJHL	71	30	58	88	199	20	8	*21	29	42
1995-96	Laval	QMJHL	38	21	39	60	130	....	....	....	....	....
	Granby	QMJHL	27	12	46	58	97	21	13	26	39	68
1996-97	Portland	AHL	76	6	40	46	140	5	2	1	3	14

GRATTON, CHRIS (GRA-tuhn) PHI.

Center. Shoots left. 6'4", 218 lbs. Born, Brantford, Ont., July 5, 1975.
(Tampa Bay's 1st choice, 3rd overall, in 1993 Entry Draft).

			Regular Season					Playoffs				
Season	Club	Lea	GP	G	A	TP	PIM	GP	G	A	TP	PIM
1991-92	Kingston	OHL	62	27	29	66	37	....	....	....	....	....
1992-93	Kingston	OHL	58	55	54	109	125	16	11	18	29	42
1993-94	**Tampa Bay**	**NHL**	**84**	**13**	**29**	**42**	**123**	....	....	....	....	....
1994-95	**Tampa Bay**	**NHL**	**46**	**7**	**20**	**27**	**89**	....	....	....	....	....
1995-96	**Tampa Bay**	**NHL**	**82**	**17**	**21**	**38**	**105**	**6**	**0**	**2**	**2**	**27**
1996-97	**Tampa Bay**	**NHL**	**82**	**30**	**32**	**62**	**201**	....	....	....	....	....
	NHL Totals		**294**	**67**	**102**	**169**	**518**	**6**	**0**	**2**	**2**	**27**

Signed as a free agent by **Philadelphia**, August 14, 1997.

GRAVES, ADAM NYR

Center. Shoots left. 6', 210 lbs. Born, Toronto, Ont., April 12, 1968.
(Detroit's 2nd choice, 22nd overall, in 1986 Entry Draft).

			Regular Season					Playoffs				
Season	Club	Lea	GP	G	A	TP	PIM	GP	G	A	TP	PIM
1985-86	Windsor	OHL	62	27	37	64	35	16	5	11	16	10
1986-87	Windsor	OHL	66	45	55	100	70	14	9	8	17	32
	Adirondack	AHL	....	....	....	....	....	5	0	1	1	0
1987-88	**Detroit**	**NHL**	**9**	**0**	**1**	**1**	**8**	....	....	....	....	....
	Windsor	OHL	37	28	32	60	107	12	14	18	*32	16
1988-89	**Detroit**	**NHL**	**56**	**7**	**5**	**12**	**60**	**5**	**0**	**0**	**0**	**4**
	Adirondack	AHL	14	10	11	21	28	14	11	7	18	17
1989-90	**Detroit**	**NHL**	**13**	**0**	**1**	**1**	**13**	....	....	....	....	....
	Edmonton	**NHL**	**63**	**9**	**12**	**21**	**123**	**22**	**5**	**6**	**11**	**17** ♦
1990-91	**Edmonton**	**NHL**	**76**	**7**	**18**	**25**	**127**	**18**	**2**	**4**	**6**	**22**
1991-92	**NY Rangers**	**NHL**	**80**	**26**	**33**	**59**	**139**	**10**	**5**	**3**	**8**	**22**
1992-93	**NY Rangers**	**NHL**	**84**	**36**	**29**	**65**	**148**	....	....	....	....	....
1993-94ab	**NY Rangers**	**NHL**	**84**	**52**	**27**	**79**	**127**	**23**	**10**	**7**	**17**	**24** ♦
1994-95	**NY Rangers**	**NHL**	**47**	**17**	**14**	**31**	**51**	**10**	**4**	**4**	**8**	**8**
1995-96	**NY Rangers**	**NHL**	**82**	**22**	**36**	**58**	**100**	**10**	**7**	**1**	**8**	**4**
1996-97	**NY Rangers**	**NHL**	**82**	**33**	**28**	**61**	**66**	**15**	**2**	**1**	**3**	**12**
	NHL Totals		**676**	**209**	**204**	**413**	**962**	**113**	**35**	**26**	**61**	**113**

a NHL Second All-Star Team (1994)
b Won King Clancy Memorial Trophy (1994)

Played in NHL All-Star Game (1994)

Traded to **Edmonton** by **Detroit** with Petr Klima, Joe Murphy and Jeff Sharples for Jimmy Carson, Kevin McClelland and Edmonton's fifth round choice (later traded to Montreal — Montreal selected Brad Layzell) in 1991 Entry Draft, November 2, 1989. Signed as a free agent by **NY Rangers**, September 3, 1991.

GREEN, JOSH L.A.

Left wing. Shoots left. 6'3", 197 lbs. Born, Camrose, Alta., November 16, 1977.
(Los Angeles' 1st choice, 30th overall, in 1996 Entry Draft).

			Regular Season					Playoffs				
Season	Club	Lea	GP	G	A	TP	PIM	GP	G	A	TP	PIM
1993-94	Medicine Hat	WHL	63	22	22	44	43	3	0	0	0	4
1994-95	Medicine Hat	WHL	68	32	23	55	64	5	5	1	6	2
1995-96	Medicine Hat	WHL	46	18	25	43	55	5	2	2	4	4
1996-97	Medicine Hat	WHL	51	25	32	57	61	....	....	....	....	....
	Swift Current	WHL	23	10	15	25	33	10	9	7	16	19

GREEN, TRAVIS NYI

Center. Shoots right. 6'1", 193 lbs. Born, Castlegar, B.C., December 20, 1970.
(NY Islanders' 2nd choice, 23rd overall, in 1989 Entry Draft).

			Regular Season					Playoffs				
Season	Club	Lea	GP	G	A	TP	PIM	GP	G	A	TP	PIM
1986-87	Spokane	WHL	64	8	17	25	27	3	0	0	0	0
1987-88	Spokane	WHL	72	33	54	87	42	15	10	10	20	13
1988-89	Spokane	WHL	75	51	51	102	79	....	....	....	....	....
1989-90	Spokane	WHL	50	45	44	89	80	....	....	....	....	....
	Medicine Hat	WHL	25	15	24	39	19	3	0	0	0	2
1990-91	Capital Dist.	AHL	73	21	34	55	26	....	....	....	....	....
1991-92	Capital Dist.	AHL	71	23	27	50	10	7	0	4	4	21
1992-93	**NY Islanders**	**NHL**	**61**	**7**	**18**	**25**	**43**	**12**	**3**	**1**	**4**	**6**
	Capital Dist.	AHL	20	12	11	23	39	....	....	....	....	....
1993-94	**NY Islanders**	**NHL**	**83**	**18**	**22**	**40**	**44**	**4**	**0**	**0**	**0**	**2**
1994-95	**NY Islanders**	**NHL**	**42**	**5**	**7**	**12**	**25**	....	....	....	....	....
1995-96	**NY Islanders**	**NHL**	**69**	**25**	**45**	**70**	**42**	....	....	....	....	....
1996-97	**NY Islanders**	**NHL**	**79**	**23**	**41**	**64**	**38**	....	....	....	....	....
	NHL Totals		**334**	**78**	**133**	**211**	**192**	**16**	**3**	**1**	**4**	**8**

GREIG, MARK (GREG)

Right wing. Shoots right. 5'11", 190 lbs. Born, High River, Alta., January 25, 1970.
(Hartford's 1st choice, 15th overall, in 1990 Entry Draft).

			Regular Season					Playoffs				
Season	Club	Lea	GP	G	A	TP	PIM	GP	G	A	TP	PIM
1987-88	Lethbridge	WHL	65	9	18	27	38	....	....	....	....	....
1988-89	Lethbridge	WHL	71	36	72	108	113	8	5	5	10	16
1989-90a	Lethbridge	WHL	65	55	80	135	149	18	11	21	32	35
1990-91	**Hartford**	**NHL**	**4**	**0**	**0**	**0**	**0**	....	....	....	....	....
	Springfield	AHL	73	32	55	87	73	17	2	6	8	22
1991-92	**Hartford**	**NHL**	**17**	**0**	**5**	**5**	**6**	....	....	....	....	....
	Springfield	AHL	50	20	27	47	38	9	1	1	2	20
1992-93	**Hartford**	**NHL**	**22**	**1**	**7**	**8**	**27**	....	....	....	....	....
	Springfield	AHL	55	20	38	58	86	....	....	....	....	....
1993-94	**Hartford**	**NHL**	**31**	**4**	**5**	**9**	**31**	....	....	....	....	....
	Springfield	AHL	4	0	4	4	21	....	....	....	....	....
	Toronto	**NHL**	**13**	**2**	**2**	**4**	**10**	....	....	....	....	....
	St. John's	AHL	9	4	6	10	0	11	4	2	6	26
1994-95	Saint John	AHL	67	31	50	81	82	2	0	1	1	0
	Calgary	**NHL**	**8**	**1**	**1**	**2**	**2**	....	....	....	....	....
1995-96	Atlanta	IHL	71	25	48	73	104	3	2	1	3	4
1996-97	Quebec	IHL	5	1	2	3	0	....	....	....	....	....
	Houston	IHL	59	12	30	42	59	13	5	8	13	2
	NHL Totals		**95**	**8**	**20**	**28**	**76**	....	....	....	....	....

a WHL East First All-Star Team (1990)

Traded to **Toronto** by **Hartford** with Hartford's sixth round choice (later traded to NY Rangers — NY Rangers selected Yuri Litvinov) in 1994 Entry Draft for Ted Crowley, January 25, 1994. Signed as a free agent by **Calgary**, August 9, 1994.

GRETZKY, BRENT (GRETZ-kee)

Center. Shoots left. 5'10", 160 lbs. Born, Brantford, Ont., February 20, 1972.
(Tampa Bay's 3rd choice, 49th overall, in 1992 Entry Draft).

			Regular Season					Playoffs				
Season	Club	Lea	GP	G	A	TP	PIM	GP	G	A	TP	PIM
1989-90	Belleville	OHL	66	15	32	47	30	11	0	0	0	0
1990-91	Belleville	OHL	66	26	56	82	25	6	3	3	6	2
1991-92	Belleville	OHL	62	43	78	121	37	....	....	....	....	....
1992-93	Atlanta	IHL	77	20	34	54	84	9	3	2	5	8
1993-94	**Tampa Bay**	**NHL**	**10**	**1**	**2**	**3**	**2**	....	....	....	....	....
	Atlanta	IHL	54	17	23	40	30	14	1	1	2	2
1994-95	Atlanta	IHL	67	19	32	51	42	5	4	1	5	4
	Tampa Bay	**NHL**	**3**	**0**	**1**	**1**	**0**	....	....	....	....	....
1995-96	St. John's	AHL	68	13	28	41	40	4	0	6	6	0
1996-97	Las Vegas	IHL	40	5	12	17	8	....	....	....	....	....
	Quebec	IHL	1	0	0	0	0	....	....	....	....	....
	Pensacola	ECHL	22	9	15	24	4	12	5	8	13	4
	NHL Totals		**13**	**1**	**3**	**4**	**2**	....	....	....	....	....

Signed as a free agent by **Toronto**, September 20, 1995.

GRETZKY, WAYNE

(GRETZ-kee) **NYR**

Center. Shoots left. 6', 185 lbs.   Born, Brantford, Ont., January 26, 1961.

			Regular Season					Playoffs				
Season	Club	Lea	GP	G	A	TP	PIM	GP	G	A	TP	PIM
1976-77	Peterborough	OHA	3	0	3	3	0	....	....	....	....	....
1977-78a	S.S. Marie	OHA	64	70	112	182	14	13	6	20	26	0
1978-79	Indianapolis	WHA	8	3	3	6	0	....	....	....	....	....
bc	Edmonton	WHA	72	43	61	104	19	13	*10	10	*20	2
1979-80def	Edmonton	NHL	79	51	*86	*137	21	3	2	1	3	0
1980-81 dghij	Edmonton	NHL	80	55	*109	*164	28	9	7	14	21	4
1981-82 dghijklp	Edmonton	NHL	80	*92	*120	*212	26	5	5	7	12	8
1982-83 dghilmn	Edmonton	NHL	80	*71	*125	*196	59	16	12	*26	*38	4
1983-84 dghlp	Edmonton	NHL	74	*87	*118	*205	39	19	13	*22	*35	12 ♦
1984-85 dghilmnopq	Edmonton	NHL	80	*73	*135	*208	52	18	17	*30	*47	4 ♦
1985-86 dghijq	Edmonton	NHL	80	52	*163	*215	46	10	8	11	19	2
1986-87 dghlpq	Edmonton	NHL	79	*62	*121	*183	28	21	5	*29	*34	6 ♦
1987-88fmo	Edmonton	NHL	64	40	*109	149	24	19	12	*31	*43	16 ♦
1988-89dfr	Los Angeles	NHL	78	54	*114	168	26	11	5	17	22	0
1989-90fh	Los Angeles	NHL	73	40	*102	*142	42	7	3	7	10	0
1990-91egh	Los Angeles	NHL	78	41	*122	*163	16	12	4	11	15	2
1991-92e	Los Angeles	NHL	74	31	*90	121	34	6	2	5	7	2
1992-93	Los Angeles	NHL	45	16	49	65	6	24	*15	*25	*40	4
1993-94efhs	Los Angeles	NHL	81	38	*92	*130	20	....	....	....	....	....
1994-95	Los Angeles	NHL	48	11	37	48	6	....	....	....	....	....
1995-96	Los Angeles	NHL	62	15	66	81	32	....	....	....	....	....
	St. Louis	NHL	18	8	13	21	2	13	2	14	16	0
1996-97f	NY Rangers	NHL	82	25	*72	97	28	15	10	10	20	2
	NHL Totals		**1335**	***862**	***1843**	***2705**	**535**	**208**	***122**	***260**	***382**	**66**

a OHA Second All-Star Team (1978)
b WHA Second All-Star Team (1979)
c Named WHA's Rookie of the Year (1979)
d Won Hart Trophy (1980, 1981, 1982, 1983, 1984, 1985, 1986, 1987, 1989)
e Won Lady Byng Trophy (1980, 1991, 1992, 1994)
f NHL Second All-Star Team (1980, 1988, 1989, 1990, 1994, 1997)
g NHL First All-Star Team (1981, 1982, 1983, 1984, 1985, 1986, 1987, 1991)
h Won Art Ross Trophy (1981, 1982, 1983, 1984, 1985, 1986, 1987, 1990, 1991, 1994)
i NHL record for assists in regular season (1981, 1982, 1983, 1985, 1986)
j NHL record for points in regular season (1981, 1982, 1986)
k NHL record for goals in regular season (1982)
l Won Lester B. Pearson Award (1982, 1983, 1984, 1985, 1987)
m NHL record for assists in one playoff year (1983, 1985, 1988)
n NHL record for points in one playoff year (1983, 1985)
o Won Conn Smythe Trophy (1985, 1988)
p NHL Plus/Minus Leader (1982, 1984, 1985, 1987)
q Selected Chrysler-Dodge/NHL Performer of the Year (1985, 1986, 1987)
r Won Dodge Performance of the Year Award (1989)
s Won Lester Patrick Trophy (1994)

Played in NHL All-Star Game (1980-1986, 1988-94, 1996, 1997)

Reclaimed by **Edmonton** as an under-age junior prior to Expansion Draft, June 9, 1979. Claimed as priority selection by **Edmonton**, June 9, 1979. Traded to **Los Angeles** by **Edmonton** with Mike Krushelnyski and Marty McSorley for Jimmy Carson, Martin Gelinas, Los Angeles' first round choices in 1989 (acquired by New Jersey — New Jersey selected Jason Miller), 1991 (Martin Rucinsky) and 1993 (Nick Stajduhar) Entry Drafts and cash, August 9, 1988. Traded to **St. Louis** by **Los Angeles** for Craig Johnson, Patrice Tardif, Roman Vopat, St. Louis fifth round choice (Peter Hogan) in 1996 Entry Draft and first round choice (Matt Zultek) in 1997 Entry Draft, February 27, 1996. Signed as a free agent by **NY Rangers**, July 21, 1996.

GRIER, MICHAEL

(GREER) **EDM.**

Right wing. Shoots right. 6'1", 225 lbs.   Born, Detroit, MI, January 5, 1975.
(St. Louis' 7th choice, 219th overall, in 1993 Entry Draft).

			Regular Season					Playoffs				
Season	Club	Lea	GP	G	A	TP	PIM	GP	G	A	TP	PIM
1993-94	Boston U.	H.E.	39	9	9	18	56	....	....	....	....	....
1994-95ab	Boston U.	H.E.	37	*29	26	55	85	....	....	....	....	....
1995-96	Boston U.	H.E.	38	21	25	46	82	....	....	....	....	....
1996-97	Edmonton	NHL	79	15	17	32	45	12	3	1	4	4
	NHL Totals		**79**	**15**	**17**	**32**	**45**	**12**	**3**	**1**	**4**	**4**

a Hockey East First All-Star Team (1995)
b NCAA East First All-American Team (1995)

Rights traded to **Edmonton** by **St. Louis** with Curtis Joseph for St. Louis' first round choices (previously acquired by Edmonton) in 1996 (Marty Reasoner) and 1997 (later traded to Los Angeles — Los Angeles selected Matt Zultek) Entry Drafts, August 4, 1995.

GRIEVE, BRENT

Left wing. Shoots left. 6'1", 202 lbs.   Born, Oshawa, Ont., May 9, 1969.
(NY Islanders' 4th choice, 65th overall, in 1989 Entry Draft).

			Regular Season					Playoffs				
Season	Club	Lea	GP	G	A	TP	PIM	GP	G	A	TP	PIM
1986-87	Oshawa	OHL	60	9	19	28	102	24	3	8	11	22
1987-88	Oshawa	OHL	55	19	20	39	122	7	0	1	1	8
1988-89	Oshawa	OHL	49	34	33	67	105	6	4	3	7	4
1989-90	Oshawa	OHL	62	46	47	93	125	17	10	10	20	26
1990-91	Capital Dist.	AHL	61	14	13	27	80	....	....	....	....	....
	Kansas City	IHL	5	2	2	4	2	....	....	....	....	....
1991-92	Capital Dist.	AHL	74	34	32	66	84	7	3	1	4	16
1992-93	Capital Dist.	AHL	79	34	28	62	122	4	1	1	2	10
1993-94	**NY Islanders**	**NHL**	3	0	0	0	7	....	....	....	....	....
	Salt Lake	IHL	22	9	5	14	30	....	....	....	....	....
	Edmonton	**NHL**	24	13	5	18	14	....	....	....	....	....
	Cape Breton	AHL	20	10	11	21	14	4	2	4	6	16
1994-95	**Chicago**	**NHL**	24	1	5	6	23	....	....	....	....	....
1995-96	**Chicago**	**NHL**	28	2	4	6	28	....	....	....	....	....
	Indianapolis	IHL	24	9	10	19	16	....	....	....	....	....
	Phoenix	IHL	13	8	11	19	14	4	2	1	3	18
1996-97	**Los Angeles**	**NHL**	18	4	2	6	15	....	....	....	....	....
	Phoenix	IHL	31	10	14	24	51	....	....	....	....	....
	NHL Totals		**97**	**20**	**16**	**36**	**87**	....	....	....	....	....

Traded to **Edmonton**, by **NY Islanders** for Marc Laforge, December 15, 1993. Signed as a free agent by **Chicago**, July 7, 1994. Signed as a free agent by **Los Angeles**, August 2, 1996.

GRIMES, KEVIN

COL.

Defense. Shoots left. 6'2", 202 lbs.   Born, Ottawa, Ont., August 19, 1979.
(Colorado's 1st choice, 26th overall, in 1997 Entry Draft).

			Regular Season					Playoffs				
Season	Club	Lea	GP	G	A	TP	PIM	GP	G	A	TP	PIM
1995-96	Cumberland	Jr. A	51	2	10	12	220	....	....	....	....	....
1996-97	Kingston	OHL	57	2	12	14	188	1	0	0	0	0

GRIMSON, STU

CAR.

Left wing. Shoots left. 6'5", 227 lbs.   Born, Kamloops, B.C., May 20, 1965.
(Detroit's 11th choice, 186th overall, in 1983 Entry Draft).

			Regular Season					Playoffs				
Season	Club	Lea	GP	G	A	TP	PIM	GP	G	A	TP	PIM
1982-83	Regina	WHL	48	0	1	1	105	5	0	0	0	14
1983-84	Regina	WHL	63	8	8	16	131	21	0	1	1	29
1984-85	Regina	WHL	71	24	32	56	248	8	1	2	3	14
1985-86	U. Manitoba	CWUAA	12	7	4	11	113	3	1	1	2	20
1986-87	U. Manitoba	CWUAA	29	8	8	16	67	14	4	2	6	28
1987-88	Salt Lake	IHL	38	9	5	14	268	....	....	....	....	....
1988-89	**Calgary**	**NHL**	1	0	0	0	5	....	....	....	....	....
	Salt Lake	IHL	72	9	18	27	397	14	2	3	5	86
1989-90	**Calgary**	**NHL**	3	0	0	0	17	....	....	....	....	....
	Salt Lake	IHL	62	8	8	16	319	4	0	0	0	8
1990-91	**Chicago**	**NHL**	35	0	1	1	183	5	0	0	0	46
1991-92	**Chicago**	**NHL**	54	2	2	4	234	14	0	1	1	10
	Indianapolis	IHL	5	1	1	2	17	....	....	....	....	....
1992-93	**Chicago**	**NHL**	78	1	1	2	193	2	0	0	0	4
1993-94	**Anaheim**	**NHL**	77	1	5	6	199	....	....	....	....	....
1994-95	**Anaheim**	**NHL**	31	0	1	1	110	....	....	....	....	....
	Detroit	**NHL**	11	0	0	0	37	11	1	0	1	26
1995-96	**Detroit**	**NHL**	56	0	1	1	128	2	0	0	0	0
1996-97	**Detroit**	**NHL**	1	0	0	0	0	....	....	....	....	....
	Hartford	**NHL**	75	2	2	4	218	....	....	....	....	....
	NHL Totals		**422**	**6**	**13**	**19**	**1324**	**34**	**1**	**1**	**2**	**86**

Re-entered NHL Entry Draft. **Calgary's** 8th choice, 143rd overall, in 1985 Entry Draft.
Claimed on conditional waivers by **Chicago** from **Calgary**, October 1, 1990. Claimed by **Anaheim** from **Chicago** in Expansion Draft, June 24, 1993. Traded to **Detroit** by **Anaheim** with Mark Ferner and Anaheim's sixth round choice (Magnus Nilsson) in 1996 Entry Draft for Mike Sillinger and Jason York, April 4, 1995. Claimed on waivers by **Hartford** from **Detroit**, October 13, 1996.

GROLEAU, FRANCOIS

MTL.

Defense. Shoots left. 6', 197 lbs.   Born, Longueuil, Que., January 23, 1973.
(Calgary's 2nd choice, 41st overall, in 1991 Entry Draft).

			Regular Season					Playoffs				
Season	Club	Lea	GP	G	A	TP	PIM	GP	G	A	TP	PIM
1989-90a	Shawinigan	QMJHL	65	11	54	65	80	6	0	1	1	12
1990-91	Shawinigan	QMJHL	70	9	60	69	70	6	0	3	3	2
1991-92b	Shawinigan	QMJHL	65	8	70	78	74	10	5	15	20	8
1992-93	St-Jean	QMJHL	48	7	38	45	66	4	0	1	1	14
1993-94	Saint John	AHL	73	8	14	22	49	7	0	1	1	2
1994-95	Saint John	AHL	65	6	34	40	28	....	....	....	....	....
	Cornwall	AHL	8	1	2	3	7	14	2	7	9	16
1995-96	**Montreal**	**NHL**	2	0	1	1	2	....	....	....	....	....
	San Francisco	IHL	63	6	26	32	60	....	....	....	....	....
	Fredericton	AHL	12	3	5	8	10	10	1	6	7	14
1996-97	**Montreal**	**NHL**	5	0	0	0	4	....	....	....	....	....
	Fredericton	AHL	47	8	24	32	43	....	....	....	....	....
	NHL Totals		**7**	**0**	**1**	**1**	**6**	....	....	....	....	....

a QMJHL Second All-Star Team (1990)
b QMJHL First All-Star Team (1992)

Traded to **Quebec** by **Calgary** for Ed Ward, March 23, 1995. Signed as a free agent by **Montreal**, June 17, 1995.

GRON, STANISLAV

(GRAHN) **N.J.**

Center. Shoots left. 6'1", 189 lbs.   Born, Bratislava, Czech., October 28, 1978.
(New Jersey's 2nd choice, 38th overall, in 1997 Entry Draft).

			Regular Season					Playoffs				
Season	Club	Lea	GP	G	A	TP	PIM	GP	G	A	TP	PIM
1996-97	Bratislava	Slovak	7	0	0	0	....	....	....	....	....	....
	Bratislava	Slo. Jr.	22	20	16	36	....	....	....	....	....	....

GRONMAN, TUOMAS

(GROHN-mahn) **CHI.**

Defense. Shoots right. 6'3", 219 lbs.   Born, Viitasaari, Finland, March 22, 1974.
(Quebec's 3rd choice, 29th overall, in 1992 Entry Draft).

			Regular Season					Playoffs				
Season	Club	Lea	GP	G	A	TP	PIM	GP	G	A	TP	PIM
1991-92	Tacoma	WHL	61	5	18	23	102	4	0	1	1	2
1992-93	Lukko	Fin.	45	2	11	13	46	3	1	0	1	2
1993-94	Lukko	Fin.	44	4	12	16	60	9	0	1	1	14
1994-95	TPS	Fin.	47	4	20	24	66	13	2	2	4	43
1995-96	TPS	Fin.	32	5	7	12	85	11	1	4	5	16
1996-97	**Chicago**	**NHL**	16	0	1	1	13	....	....	....	....	....
	Indianapolis	IHL	51	5	16	21	89	4	1	1	2	6
	NHL Totals		**16**	**0**	**1**	**1**	**13**	....	....	....	....	....

Rights traded to **Chicago** by **Colorado** for Chicago's second round choice in 1998 Entry Draft, July 10, 1996.

GROSEK, MICHAL

(GROH-shehk) **BUF.**

Left wing. Shoots right. 6'2", 207 lbs.   Born, Vyskov, Czech., June 1, 1975.
(Winnipeg's 7th choice, 145th overall, in 1993 Entry Draft).

			Regular Season					Playoffs				
Season	Club	Lea	GP	G	A	TP	PIM	GP	G	A	TP	PIM
1992-93	ZPS Zlin	Czech.	17	1	3	4	....	....	....	....	....	....
1993-94	**Winnipeg**	**NHL**	3	1	0	1	0	....	....	....	....	....
	Tacoma	WHL	30	25	20	45	106	7	2	2	4	30
	Moncton	AHL	20	1	2	3	47	2	0	0	0	0
1994-95	Springfield	AHL	45	10	22	32	98	....	....	....	....	....
	Winnipeg	**NHL**	24	2	2	4	21	....	....	....	....	....
1995-96	**Winnipeg**	**NHL**	1	0	0	0	0	....	....	....	....	....
	Buffalo	**NHL**	22	6	4	10	31	....	....	....	....	....
	Springfield	AHL	39	16	19	35	68	....	....	....	....	....
1996-97	**Buffalo**	**NHL**	82	15	21	36	71	12	3	3	6	8
	NHL Totals		**132**	**24**	**27**	**51**	**123**	**12**	**3**	**3**	**6**	**8**

Traded to **Buffalo** by **Winnipeg** with Darryl Shannon for Craig Muni, February 15, 1996.

GRUDEN, JOHN

Defense. Shoots left. 6', 190 lbs. Born, Virginia, MN, June 4, 1970.
(Boston's 7th choice, 168th overall, in 1990 Entry Draft).

			Regular Season					Playoffs				
Season	Club	Lea	GP	G	A	TP	PIM	GP	G	A	TP	PIM
1990-91	Ferris State	CCHA	37	4	11	15	27	....	....	....	....	....
1991-92	Ferris State	CCHA	37	9	14	23	24	....	....	....	....	....
1992-93	Ferris State	CCHA	41	16	14	30	58	....	....	....	....	....
1993-94ab	Ferris State	CCHA	38	11	25	36	52	....	....	....	....	....
	Boston	**NHL**	**7**	**0**	**1**	**1**	**2**	....	....	....	....	....
1994-95	**Boston**	**NHL**	**38**	**0**	**6**	**6**	**22**	....	....	....	....	....
	Providence	AHL	1	0	1	1	0	....	....	....	....	....
1995-96	**Boston**	**NHL**	**14**	**0**	**0**	**0**	**4**	**3**	**0**	**1**	**1**	**0**
	Providence	AHL	39	5	19	24	29	....	....	....	....	....
1996-97	Providence	AHL	78	18	27	45	52	10	3	6	9	4
	NHL Totals		**59**	**0**	**7**	**7**	**28**	**3**	**0**	**1**	**1**	**0**

a CCHA First All-Star Team (1994)
b NCAA West First All-American Team (1994)

GUERIN, BILL (GAIR-ihn) N.J.

Right wing. Shoots right. 6'2", 210 lbs. Born, Wilbraham, MA, November 9, 1970.
(New Jersey's 1st choice, 5th overall, in 1989 Entry Draft).

			Regular Season					Playoffs				
Season	Club	Lea	GP	G	A	TP	PIM	GP	G	A	TP	PIM
1989-90	Boston College	H.E.	39	14	11	25	54	....	....	....	....	....
1990-91	Boston College	H.E.	38	26	19	45	102	....	....	....	....	....
	U.S. National	....	46	12	15	27	67	....	....	....	....	....
1991-92	**New Jersey**	**NHL**	**5**	**0**	**1**	**1**	**9**	**6**	**3**	**0**	**3**	**4**
	Utica	AHL	22	13	10	23	6	4	1	3	4	14
1992-93	**New Jersey**	**NHL**	**65**	**14**	**20**	**34**	**63**	**5**	**1**	**1**	**2**	**4**
	Utica	AHL	18	10	7	17	47	....	....	....	....	....
1993-94	**New Jersey**	**NHL**	**81**	**25**	**19**	**44**	**101**	**17**	**2**	**1**	**3**	**35**
1994-95	**New Jersey**	**NHL**	**48**	**12**	**13**	**25**	**72**	**20**	**3**	**8**	**11**	**30** ♦
1995-96	**New Jersey**	**NHL**	**80**	**23**	**30**	**53**	**116**	....	....	....	....	....
1996-97	**New Jersey**	**NHL**	**82**	**29**	**18**	**47**	**95**	**8**	**2**	**1**	**3**	**18**
	NHL Totals		**361**	**103**	**101**	**204**	**456**	**56**	**11**	**11**	**22**	**91**

GUNKO, YURI (goon-KOH, YOO-ree) ST.L.

Defense. Shoots left. 6'1", 187 lbs. Born, Kiev, USSR, February 28, 1972.
(St. Louis' 11th choice, 230th overall, in 1992 Entry Draft).

			Regular Season					Playoffs				
Season	Club	Lea	GP	G	A	TP	PIM	GP	G	A	TP	PIM
1990-91	Sokol Kiev	USSR	14	0	0	0	8	....	....	....	....	....
1991-92	Sokol Kiev	CIS	22	1	0	1	16	....	....	....	....	....
1992-93	Sokol Kiev	CIS	40	2	3	5	28	....	....	....	....	....
1993-94	Sokol Kiev	CIS	42	0	8	8	28	....	....	....	....	....
1994-95	Sokol Kiev	CIS	25	4	0	4	18	....	....	....	....	....
1995-96	Kazan	CIS	41	1	2	3	22	5	1	0	1	4
1996-97	Kazan	Rus.	42	6	7	13	42	3	1	0	1	4

GUOLLA, STEPHEN (GUH-wah-lah) S.J.

Left wing. Shoots left. 6', 180 lbs. Born, Scarborough, Ont., March 15, 1973.
(Ottawa's 1st choice, 3rd overall, in 1994 Supplemental Draft).

			Regular Season					Playoffs				
Season	Club	Lea	GP	G	A	TP	PIM	GP	G	A	TP	PIM
1991-92	Michigan State	CCHA	33	4	9	13	8	....	....	....	....	....
1992-93	Michigan State	CCHA	39	19	35	54	6	....	....	....	....	....
1993-94ab	Michigan State	CCHA	41	23	46	69	16	....	....	....	....	....
1994-95	Michigan State	CCHA	40	16	35	51	16	....	....	....	....	....
1995-96	P.E.I.	AHL	72	32	48	80	28	3	0	0	0	0
1996-97	**San Jose**	**NHL**	**43**	**13**	**8**	**21**	**14**	....	....	....	....	....
	Kentucky	AHL	34	22	22	44	10	4	2	1	3	0
	NHL Totals		**43**	**13**	**8**	**21**	**14**	....	....	....	....	....

a CCHA Second All-Star Team (1994)
b NCAA West Second All-American Team (1994)

Signed as a free agent by **San Jose**, August 22, 1996.

GUREN, MILOSLAV (GOO-rihn) MTL.

Defense. Shoots left. 6'2", 215 lbs. Born, Uherske. Hradiste, Czech., September 24, 1976.
(Montreal's 2nd choice, 60th overall, in 1995 Entry Draft).

			Regular Season					Playoffs				
Season	Club	Lea	GP	G	A	TP	PIM	GP	G	A	TP	PIM
1993-94	ZPS Zlin	Czech.	22	1	5	6	....	3	0	0	0	....
1994-95	ZPS Zlin	Czech.	32	3	7	10	10	12	1	0	1	6
1995-96	ZPS Zlin	Czech.	28	1	2	3	....	7	1	0	1	....
1996-97	Fredericton	AHL	79	6	26	32	26	....	....	....	....	....

GUSAROV, ALEXEI (goo-SAH-rahf) COL.

Defense. Shoots left. 6'3", 185 lbs. Born, Leningrad, USSR, July 8, 1964.
(Quebec's 11th choice, 213th overall, in 1988 Entry Draft).

			Regular Season					Playoffs				
Season	Club	Lea	GP	G	A	TP	PIM	GP	G	A	TP	PIM
1981-82	SKA Leningrad	USSR	20	1	2	3	16	....	....	....	....	....
1982-83	SKA Leningrad	USSR	42	2	1	3	32	....	....	....	....	....
1983-84	SKA Leningrad	USSR	43	2	3	5	32	....	....	....	....	....
1984-85	CSKA	USSR	36	3	2	5	26	....	....	....	....	....
1985-86	CSKA	USSR	40	3	5	8	30	....	....	....	....	....
1986-87	CSKA	USSR	38	4	7	11	24	....	....	....	....	....
1987-88	CSKA	USSR	39	3	2	5	28	....	....	....	....	....
1988-89	CSKA	USSR	42	5	4	9	37	....	....	....	....	....
1989-90	CSKA	USSR	42	4	7	11	42	....	....	....	....	....
1990-91	CSKA	USSR	15	0	0	0	12	....	....	....	....	....
	Quebec	**NHL**	**36**	**3**	**9**	**12**	**12**	....	....	....	....	....
	Halifax	AHL	2	0	3	3	2	....	....	....	....	....
1991-92	**Quebec**	**NHL**	**68**	**5**	**18**	**23**	**22**	....	....	....	....	....
	Halifax	AHL	3	0	0	0	0	....	....	....	....	....
1992-93	**Quebec**	**NHL**	**79**	**8**	**22**	**30**	**57**	**5**	**0**	**1**	**1**	**0**
1993-94	**Quebec**	**NHL**	**76**	**5**	**20**	**25**	**38**	....	....	....	....	....
1994-95	**Quebec**	**NHL**	**14**	**1**	**2**	**3**	**6**	....	....	....	....	....
1995-96	**Colorado**	**NHL**	**65**	**5**	**15**	**20**	**56**	**21**	**0**	**9**	**9**	**12** ♦
1996-97	**Colorado**	**NHL**	**58**	**2**	**12**	**14**	**28**	**17**	**0**	**3**	**3**	**14**
	NHL Totals		**396**	**29**	**98**	**127**	**219**	**43**	**0**	**13**	**13**	**26**

GUSEV, SERGEY (GOO-sehv) DAL.

Defense. Shoots left. 6'1", 195 lbs. Born, Nizhny Tagil, USSR, July 31, 1975.
(Dallas' 4th choice, 69th overall, in 1995 Entry Draft).

			Regular Season					Playoffs				
Season	Club	Lea	GP	G	A	TP	PIM	GP	G	A	TP	PIM
1994-95	CSK Samara	CIS	50	3	5	8	58	....	....	....	....	....
1995-96	Michigan	IHL	73	11	17	28	76	....	....	....	....	....
1996-97	Michigan	IHL	51	7	8	15	44	4	0	4	4	6

GUSMANOV, RAVIL (goos-MAN-ohv) CGY.

Left wing. Shoots left. 6'3", 185 lbs. Born, Naberezhnye Chelny, USSR, July 25, 1972.
(Winnipeg's 5th choice, 93rd overall, in 1993 Entry Draft).

			Regular Season					Playoffs				
Season	Club	Lea	GP	G	A	TP	PIM	GP	G	A	TP	PIM
1990-91	Chelyabinsk	USSR	15	0	0	0	10	....	....	....	....	....
1991-92	Chelyabinsk	CIS	38	4	4	8	20	....	....	....	....	....
1992-93	Chelyabinsk	CIS	39	15	8	23	30	8	4	0	4	2
1993-94	Chelyabinsk	CIS	43	18	9	27	51	6	4	3	7	10
1994-95	Springfield	AHL	72	18	15	33	14	....	....	....	....	....
1995-96	**Winnipeg**	**NHL**	**4**	**0**	**0**	**0**	**0**	....	....	....	....	....
	Springfield	AHL	60	36	32	68	20	....	....	....	....	....
	Indianapolis	IHL	11	6	10	16	4	5	2	3	5	4
1996-97	Indianapolis	IHL	60	21	27	48	14	....	....	....	....	....
	Saint John	AHL	12	4	4	8	2	3	0	1	1	2
	NHL Totals		**4**	**0**	**0**	**0**	**0**	....	....	....	....	....

Traded to **Chicago** by **Winnipeg** for Chicago's fourth round choice (later traded to Toronto — Toronto selected Vladimir Antipov) in 1996 Entry Draft, March 20, 1996. Traded to **Calgary** by **Chicago** for Marc Hussey, March 18, 1997.

GUSTAFSSON, JUHA (GOOS-tahf-suhn, YOO-huh) PHO.

Defense. Shoots left. 6'2", 194 lbs. Born, Espoo, Finland, April 26, 1979.
(Phoenix's 1st choice, 43rd overall, in 1997 Entry Draft).

			Regular Season					Playoffs				
Season	Club	Lea	GP	G	A	TP	PIM	GP	G	A	TP	PIM
1995-96	Kiekko-Espoo	Fin.	1	0	0	0	0	....	....	....	....	....
	Kiekko-Espoo	Fin. Jr.	33	1	5	6	28	4	0	0	0	2
1996-97	Kiekko-Espoo	Fin. Jr.	32	1	3	4	30	....	....	....	....	....
	Kiekko-Espoo	Fin.	3	0	0	0	0	3	0	0	0	0

GUSTAFSSON, PER (GOOS-tahf-suhn) TOR.

Defense. Shoots left. 6'2", 190 lbs. Born, Osterham, Sweden, June 6, 1970.
(Florida's 10th choice, 261st overall, in 1994 Entry Draft).

			Regular Season					Playoffs				
Season	Club	Lea	GP	G	A	TP	PIM	GP	G	A	TP	PIM
1993-94	HV 71	Swe.	34	9	7	16	10	....	....	....	....	....
1994-95	HV 71	Swe.	38	10	6	16	14	13	7	5	12	8
1995-96	HV 71	Swe.	34	8	13	21	12	4	3	1	4	2
1996-97	**Florida**	**NHL**	**58**	**7**	**22**	**29**	**22**	....	....	....	....	....
	NHL Totals		**58**	**7**	**22**	**29**	**22**	....	....	....	....	....

Traded to **Toronto** by **Florida** for Mike Lankshear, June 13, 1997.

GUZIOR, RUSSELL (GUHZ-ee-or) MTL.

Center. Shoots right. 5'10", 165 lbs. Born, Chicago, IL, January 12, 1974.
(Montreal's 13th choice, 281st overall, in 1993 Entry Draft).

			Regular Season					Playoffs				
Season	Club	Lea	GP	G	A	TP	PIM	GP	G	A	TP	PIM
1993-94	Providence	H.E.	34	9	13	22	8	....	....	....	....	....
1994-95	Providence	H.E.	9	1	7	8	10	....	....	....	....	....
1995-96	Providence	H.E.	38	20	17	37	24	....	....	....	....	....
1996-97	Providence	H.E.	35	12	28	40	30	....	....	....	....	....

HAGGERTY, SEAN NYI

Left wing. Shoots left. 6'1", 186 lbs. Born, Rye, NY, February 11, 1976.
(Toronto's 2nd choice, 48th overall, in 1994 Entry Draft).

			Regular Season					Playoffs				
Season	Club	Lea	GP	G	A	TP	PIM	GP	G	A	TP	PIM
1993-94	Detroit	OHL	60	31	32	63	21	17	9	10	19	11
1994-95a	Detroit	OHL	61	40	49	89	37	21	13	24	37	18
1995-96	**Toronto**	**NHL**	**1**	**0**	**0**	**0**	**0**	....	....	....	....	....
b	Detroit	OHL	66	*60	51	111	78	17	15	9	24	30
	Worcester	AHL	....	....	....	....	....	1	0	0	0	2
1996-97	Kentucky	AHL	77	13	22	35	60	4	1	0	1	4
	NHL Totals		**1**	**0**	**0**	**0**	**0**	....	....	....	....	....

a Memorial Cup All-Star Team (1995)
b OHL Second All-Star Team (1996)

Traded to **NY Islanders** by **Toronto** with Darby Hendrickson, Kenny Jonsson and Toronto's first round choice (Roberto Luongo) in 1997 Entry Draft for Wendel Clark, Mathieu Schneider and D.J. Smith, March 13, 1996.

HAJT, CHRIS (HIGHT) EDM.

Defense. Shoots left. 6'3", 206 lbs. Born, Saskatoon, Sask., July 5, 1978.
(Edmonton's 3rd choice, 32nd overall, in 1996 Entry Draft).

			Regular Season					Playoffs				
Season	Club	Lea	GP	G	A	TP	PIM	GP	G	A	TP	PIM
1994-95	Guelph	OHL	57	1	7	8	35	14	0	2	2	9
1995-96	Guelph	OHL	63	8	27	35	69	16	0	6	6	13
1996-97	Guelph	OHL	58	11	15	26	62	18	0	8	8	25

HAKANEN, TIMO (HAW-kan-en, TEE-moo) S.J.

Center. Shoots left. 6'2", 195 lbs. Born, Pori, Finland, March 26, 1977.
(San Jose's 7th choice, 140th overall, in 1995 Entry Draft).

			Regular Season					Playoffs				
Season	Club	Lea	GP	G	A	TP	PIM	GP	G	A	TP	PIM
1995-96	Assat	Fin. Jr.	28	8	24	32	6	....	....	....	....	....
	Assat	Fin.	12	0	2	2	0	3	0	0	0	0
1996-97	Assat	Fin. Jr.	20	10	12	22	22	....	....	....	....	....
	Assat	Fin.	22	0	2	2	2	2	0	0	0	0

HAKANSSON, MIKAEL (HAK-ahn-suhn) TOR.

Center. Shoots left. 6'1", 196 lbs. Born, Stockholm, Sweden, May 31, 1974.
(Toronto's 7th choice, 125th overall, in 1992 Entry Draft).

			Regular Season					Playoffs				
Season	Club	Lea	GP	G	A	TP	PIM	GP	G	A	TP	PIM
1990-91	Nacka	Swe. 2	27	2	5	7	6	....	....	....	....	....
1991-92	Nacka	Swe. 2	29	3	15	18	24	....	....	....	....	....
1992-93	Djurgarden	Swe.	40	0	1	1	6	3	0	0	0	0
1993-94	Djurgarden	Swe.	37	3	3	6	12	4	0	0	0	0
1994-95	MoDo	Swe.	37	3	7	10	16	....	....	....	....	....
1995-96	MoDo	Swe.	40	8	4	12	18	8	2	0	2	0
1996-97	Djurgarden	Swe.	48	8	12	20	12	4	0	0	0	0

HALFNIGHT, ASHLIN (HAF-night, ASH-lihn) CAR.

Defense. Shoots left. 6', 180 lbs. Born, Toronto, Ont., March 14, 1975.
(Hartford's 5th choice, 213th overall, in 1994 Entry Draft).

			Regular Season					Playoffs				
Season	Club	Lea	GP	G	A	TP	PIM	GP	G	A	TP	PIM
1992-93	Cdn. National	....	3	1	0	1	2	....	....	....	....	....
1993-94	Harvard	ECAC	30	2	8	10	24	....	....	....	....	....
1994-95	Harvard	ECAC	24	5	15	20	42	....	....	....	....	....
1995-96	Harvard	ECAC	30	2	10	12	12	....	....	....	....	....
1996-97	Harvard	ECAC	31	6	6	12	50	....	....	....	....	....

HALKIDIS, BOB (hal-KEE-dihs)

Defense. Shoots left. 5'11", 205 lbs. Born, Toronto, Ont., March 5, 1966.
(Buffalo's 4th choice, 81st overall, in 1984 Entry Draft).

			Regular Season					Playoffs				
Season	Club	Lea	GP	G	A	TP	PIM	GP	G	A	TP	PIM
1983-84	London	OHL	51	9	22	31	123	8	0	2	2	27
1984-85a	London	OHL	62	14	50	64	154	8	3	6	9	22
	Buffalo	**NHL**	....	....	....	....	....	**4**	**0**	**0**	**0**	**19**
1985-86	**Buffalo**	**NHL**	**37**	**1**	**9**	**10**	**115**	....	....	....	....	....
1986-87	**Buffalo**	**NHL**	**6**	**1**	**1**	**2**	**19**	....	....	....	....	....
	Rochester	AHL	59	1	8	9	144	8	0	0	0	43
1987-88	**Buffalo**	**NHL**	**30**	**0**	**3**	**3**	**115**	**4**	**0**	**0**	**0**	**22**
	Rochester	AHL	15	2	5	7	50	....	....	....	....	....
1988-89	**Buffalo**	**NHL**	**16**	**0**	**1**	**1**	**66**	....	....	....	....	....
	Rochester	AHL	16	0	6	6	64	....	....	....	....	....
1989-90	Rochester	AHL	18	1	13	14	70	....	....	....	....	....
	Los Angeles	**NHL**	**20**	**0**	**4**	**4**	**56**	**8**	**0**	**1**	**1**	**8**
	New Haven	AHL	30	3	17	20	67	....	....	....	....	....
1990-91	**Los Angeles**	**NHL**	**34**	**1**	**3**	**4**	**133**	**3**	**0**	**0**	**0**	**0**
	New Haven	AHL	7	1	3	4	10	....	....	....	....	....
	Phoenix	IHL	4	1	5	6	6	....	....	....	....	....
1991-92	**Toronto**	**NHL**	**46**	**3**	**3**	**6**	**145**	....	....	....	....	....
1992-93	St. John's	AHL	29	2	13	15	61	....	....	....	....	....
	Milwaukee	IHL	26	0	9	9	79	5	0	1	1	27
1993-94	**Detroit**	**NHL**	**28**	**1**	**4**	**5**	**93**	**1**	**0**	**0**	**0**	**2**
	Adirondack	AHL	15	0	6	6	46	....	....	....	....	....
1994-95	**Detroit**	**NHL**	**4**	**0**	**1**	**1**	**6**	....	....	....	....	....
	Tampa Bay	**NHL**	**27**	**1**	**3**	**4**	**40**	....	....	....	....	....
1995-96	**Tampa Bay**	**NHL**	**3**	**0**	**0**	**0**	**7**	....	....	....	....	....
	Atlanta	IHL	21	1	7	8	62	....	....	....	....	....
	NY Islanders	**NHL**	**5**	**0**	**0**	**0**	**30**	....	....	....	....	....
	Indianapolis	IHL	3	0	2	2	8	....	....	....	....	....
	Utah	IHL	27	0	7	7	72	12	1	1	2	36
1996-97	Carolina	AHL	41	5	13	18	47	....	....	....	....	....
	NHL Totals		**256**	**8**	**32**	**40**	**825**	**20**	**0**	**1**	**1**	**51**

a OHL First All-Star Team (1985)

Traded to **Los Angeles** by **Buffalo** with future considerations for Dale DeGray and future considerations, November 24, 1989. Signed as a free agent by **Toronto**, July 24, 1991. Signed as a free agent by **Detroit**, September 2, 1993. Claimed on waivers by **Tampa Bay** from **Detroit**, February 10, 1995. Claimed on waivers by **Chicago** from **Tampa Bay**, December 6, 1995. Traded to **NY Islanders** by **Chicago** for Danton Cole, February 2, 1996. Signed as a free agent by **Florida**, July 25, 1996.

HALKO, STEVEN CAR.

Defense. Shoots right. 6'1", 195 lbs. Born, Etobicoke, Ont., March 8, 1974.
(Hartford's 10th choice, 225th overall, in 1992 Entry Draft).

			Regular Season					Playoffs				
Season	Club	Lea	GP	G	A	TP	PIM	GP	G	A	TP	PIM
1992-93	U. of Michigan	CCHA	39	1	12	13	12	....	....	....	....	....
1993-94	U. of Michigan	CCHA	41	2	13	15	32	....	....	....	....	....
1994-95a	U. of Michigan	CCHA	39	2	14	16	20	....	....	....	....	....
1995-96a	U. of Michigan	CCHA	43	4	16	20	32	....	....	....	....	....
1996-97	Springfield	AHL	70	1	5	6	37	11	0	2	2	8

a CCHA Second All-Star Team (1995, 1996)

HALL, TODD NYR

Defense. Shoots left. 6'1", 212 lbs. Born, Hamden, CT, January 22, 1973.
(Hartford's 3rd choice, 53rd overall, in 1991 Entry Draft).

			Regular Season					Playoffs				
Season	Club	Lea	GP	G	A	TP	PIM	GP	G	A	TP	PIM
1991-92	Boston College	H.E.	33	2	10	12	14	....	....	....	....	....
1992-93	Boston College	H.E.	34	2	10	12	22	....	....	....	....	....
1993-94	N. Hampshire	H.E.			DID NOT PLAY							
1994-95	N. Hampshire	H.E.	36	8	18	26	16	....	....	....	....	....
1995-96a	N. Hampshire	H.E.	31	4	26	30	10	....	....	....	....	....
1996-97	Binghamton	AHL	40	3	7	10	12	4	0	1	1	0
	Charlotte	ECHL	13	0	2	2	8	....	....	....	....	....

a Hockey East All-Star Team (1996)

Signed as a free agent by **NY Rangers**, June 12, 1997.

HALLER, KEVIN (HAHL-ehr) CAR.

Defense. Shoots left. 6'2", 195 lbs. Born, Trochu, Alta., December 5, 1970.
(Buffalo's 1st choice, 14th overall, in 1989 Entry Draft).

			Regular Season					Playoffs				
Season	Club	Lea	GP	G	A	TP	PIM	GP	G	A	TP	PIM
1988-89	Regina	WHL	72	10	31	41	99	....	....	....	....	....
1989-90	**Buffalo**	**NHL**	**2**	**0**	**0**	**0**	**0**	....	....	....	....	....
a	Regina	WHL	58	16	37	53	93	11	2	9	11	16
1990-91	**Buffalo**	**NHL**	**21**	**1**	**8**	**9**	**20**	**6**	**1**	**4**	**5**	**10**
	Rochester	AHL	52	2	8	10	53	10	2	1	3	6
1991-92	**Buffalo**	**NHL**	**58**	**6**	**15**	**21**	**75**	....	....	....	....	....
	Rochester	AHL	4	0	0	0	18	....	....	....	....	....
	Montreal	**NHL**	**8**	**2**	**2**	**4**	**17**	**9**	**0**	**0**	**0**	**6**
1992-93	**Montreal**	**NHL**	**73**	**11**	**14**	**25**	**117**	**17**	**1**	**6**	**7**	**16** ♦
1993-94	**Montreal**	**NHL**	**68**	**4**	**9**	**13**	**118**	**7**	**1**	**1**	**2**	**19**
1994-95	**Philadelphia**	**NHL**	**36**	**2**	**8**	**10**	**48**	**15**	**4**	**4**	**8**	**10**
1995-96	**Philadelphia**	**NHL**	**69**	**5**	**9**	**14**	**92**	**6**	**0**	**1**	**1**	**8**
1996-97	**Philadelphia**	**NHL**	**27**	**0**	**5**	**5**	**37**	....	....	....	....	....
	Hartford	**NHL**	**35**	**2**	**6**	**8**	**48**	....	....	....	....	....
	NHL Totals		**397**	**33**	**76**	**109**	**572**	**60**	**7**	**16**	**23**	**69**

a WHL East First All-Star Team (1990)

Traded to **Montreal** by **Buffalo** for Petr Svoboda, March 10, 1992. Traded to **Philadelphia** by **Montreal** for Yves Racine, June 29, 1994. Traded to **Hartford** by **Philadelphia** with Philadelphia's first round choice (later traded to San Jose — San Jose selected Scott Hannan) in 1997 Entry Draft and Hartford's seventh round choice (previously acquired by Philadelphia — Carolina selected Andrew Merrick) in 1997 Entry Draft for Paul Coffey and Hartford's third round choice (Kris Mallette) in 1997 Entry Draft, December 15, 1996.

HAMEL, DENIS (ha-MEHL, deh-NEE) BUF.

Left wing. Shoots left. 6'2", 200 lbs. Born, Lachute, Que., May 10, 1977.
(St. Louis' 5th choice, 153rd overall, in 1995 Entry Draft).

			Regular Season					Playoffs				
Season	Club	Lea	GP	G	A	TP	PIM	GP	G	A	TP	PIM
1994-95	Chicoutimi	QMJHL	66	15	12	27	155	12	2	0	2	27
1995-96	Chicoutimi	QMJHL	65	40	49	89	199	17	10	14	24	64
1996-97	Chicoutimi	QMJHL	70	50	50	100	357	20	15	10	25	58

Traded to **Buffalo** by **St. Louis** for Charlie Huddy and Buffalo's seventh round choice (Daniel Corso) in 1996 Entry Draft, March 19, 1996.

HAMILTON, HUGH CAR.

Defense. Shoots left. 6'1", 175 lbs. Born, Saskatoon, Sask., February 11, 1977.
(Hartford's 5th choice, 113th overall, in 1995 Entry Draft).

			Regular Season					Playoffs				
Season	Club	Lea	GP	G	A	TP	PIM	GP	G	A	TP	PIM
1993-94	Spokane	WHL	64	5	9	14	70	3	0	0	0	0
1994-95	Spokane	WHL	60	5	28	33	102	11	3	5	8	16
1995-96	Spokane	WHL	72	11	49	60	92	18	3	5	8	26
1996-97a	Spokane	WHL	57	8	37	45	69	9	1	6	7	14

a WHL West Second All-Star Team (1997)

HAMRLIK, MARTIN (HAHM-reh-lik)

Defense. Shoots right. 5'11", 185 lbs. Born, Gottwaldov, Czech., May 6, 1973.
(Hartford's 2nd choice, 31st overall, in 1991 Entry Draft).

			Regular Season					Playoffs				
Season	Club	Lea	GP	G	A	TP	PIM	GP	G	A	TP	PIM
1989-90	TJ Zlin	Czech.	11	2	0	2	....	....	....	....	....	....
1990-91	TJ Zlin	Czech.	50	8	14	22	44	....	....	....	....	....
1991-92	ZPS Zlin	Czech.	4	0	2	2	23	....	....	....	....	....
1992-93	Ottawa	OHL	26	4	11	15	41	....	....	....	....	....
	Springfield	AHL	8	1	3	4	16	....	....	....	....	....
1993-94	Springfield	AHL	1	0	0	0	0	....	....	....	....	....
	Peoria	IHL	47	1	11	12	61	6	0	1	1	2
1994-95	Peoria	IHL	77	5	13	18	120	3	0	0	0	2
1995-96	Peoria	IHL	65	6	25	31	91	....	....	....	....	....
1996-97	Long Beach	IHL	64	3	14	17	110	....	....	....	....	....
	Orlando	IHL	16	3	3	6	21	10	1	6	7	10

Traded to **St. Louis** by **Hartford** for cash, November 12, 1993.

HAMRLIK, ROMAN (HAHM-reh-lik) T.B.

Defense. Shoots left. 6'2", 202 lbs. Born, Gottwaldov, Czech., April 12, 1974.
(Tampa Bay's 1st choice, 1st overall, in 1992 Entry Draft).

			Regular Season					Playoffs				
Season	Club	Lea	GP	G	A	TP	PIM	GP	G	A	TP	PIM
1990-91	TJ Zlin	Czech.	14	2	2	4	18	....	....	....	....	....
1991-92	ZPS Zlin	Czech.	34	5	5	10	50	....	....	....	....	....
1992-93	**Tampa Bay**	**NHL**	**67**	**6**	**15**	**21**	**71**	....	....	....	....	....
	Atlanta	IHL	2	1	1	2	2	....	....	....	....	....
1993-94	**Tampa Bay**	**NHL**	**64**	**3**	**18**	**21**	**135**	....	....	....	....	....
1994-95	ZPS Zlin	Czech.	2	1	0	1	10	....	....	....	....	....
	Tampa Bay	**NHL**	**48**	**12**	**11**	**23**	**86**	....	....	....	....	....
1995-96	**Tampa Bay**	**NHL**	**82**	**16**	**49**	**65**	**103**	**5**	**0**	**1**	**1**	**4**
1996-97	**Tampa Bay**	**NHL**	**79**	**12**	**28**	**40**	**57**	....	....	....	....	....
	NHL Totals		**340**	**49**	**121**	**170**	**452**	**5**	**0**	**1**	**1**	**4**

Played in NHL All-Star Game (1996)

HANDZUS, MICHAL (HAHND-zuhs, MEE-chal) ST.L.

Center. Shoots left. 6'3", 191 lbs. Born, Banska Bystrica, Czech., March 11, 1977.
(St. Louis' 3rd choice, 101st overall, in 1995 Entry Draft).

			Regular Season					Playoffs				
Season	Club	Lea	GP	G	A	TP	PIM	GP	G	A	TP	PIM
1994-95	B. Bystrica	Slov. 2	22	15	14	29	10	....	....	....	....	....
1995-96	B. Bystrica	Slovak	19	3	1	4	8	....	....	....	....	....
1996-97	Poprad	Slovak	44	15	18	33	....	....	....	....	....	....

HANKINSON, BEN (HAN-kihn-suhn)

Right wing. Shoots right. 6'2", 210 lbs. Born, Edina, MN, May 1, 1969.
(New Jersey's 5th choice, 107th overall, in 1987 Entry Draft).

			Regular Season					Playoffs				
Season	Club	Lea	GP	G	A	TP	PIM	GP	G	A	TP	PIM
1987-88	U. Minnesota	WCHA	24	4	7	11	36	....	....	....	....	....
1988-89	U. Minnesota	WCHA	43	7	11	18	115	....	....	....	....	....
1989-90a	U. Minnesota	WCHA	46	25	41	66	34	....	....	....	....	....
1990-91	U. Minnesota	WCHA	43	19	21	40	133	....	....	....	....	....
1991-92	Utica	AHL	77	17	16	33	186	4	3	1	4	2
1992-93	**New Jersey**	**NHL**	**4**	**2**	**1**	**3**	**9**	....	....	....	....	....
	Utica	AHL	75	35	27	62	145	5	2	2	4	6
1993-94	**New Jersey**	**NHL**	**13**	**1**	**0**	**1**	**23**	**2**	**1**	**0**	**1**	**4**
	Albany	AHL	29	9	14	23	80	5	3	1	4	6
1994-95	**New Jersey**	**NHL**	**8**	**0**	**0**	**0**	**7**	....	....	....	....	....
	Albany	AHL	1	1	0	1	6	....	....	....	....	....
	Tampa Bay	**NHL**	**18**	**0**	**2**	**2**	**6**	....	....	....	....	....
1995-96	Adirondack	AHL	75	25	21	46	210	3	0	0	0	8
1996-97	Grand Rapids	IHL	68	16	13	29	219	5	2	2	4	4
	NHL Totals		**43**	**3**	**3**	**6**	**45**	**2**	**1**	**0**	**1**	**4**

a WCHA First All-Star Team (1990)

Traded to **Tampa Bay** by **New Jersey** with Alexander Semak for Shawn Chambers and Danton Cole, March 14, 1995. Traded to **Detroit** by **Tampa Bay** with Marc Bergevin for Shawn Burr and Detroit's third round choice (later traded to Boston — Boston selected Jason Doyle) in 1996 Entry Draft, August 17, 1995.

HANKINSON, CASEY (HAN-kihn-suhn) CHI.

Left wing. Shoots left. 6'1", 187 lbs. Born, Edina, MN, May 8, 1976.
(Chicago's 9th choice, 201st overall, in 1995 Entry Draft).

			Regular Season					Playoffs				
Season	Club	Lea	GP	G	A	TP	PIM	GP	G	A	TP	PIM
1994-95	U. Minnesota	WCHA	33	7	1	8	86	....	....	....	....	....
1995-96	U. Minnesota	WCHA	39	16	19	35	101	....	....	....	....	....
1996-97	U. Minnesota	WCHA	42	17	24	41	79	....	....	....	....	....

HANNAN, DAVE

Center. Shoots left. 5'10", 180 lbs. Born, Sudbury, Ont., November 26, 1961.
(Pittsburgh's 9th choice, 196th overall, in 1981 Entry Draft).

			Regular Season					Playoffs				
Season	Club	Lea	GP	G	A	TP	PIM	GP	G	A	TP	PIM
1979-80	S.S. Marie	OHA	28	11	10	21	31	....	....	....	....	....
	Brantford	OHA	25	5	10	15	26	....	....	....	....	....
1980-81	Brantford	OHA	56	46	35	81	155	6	2	4	6	20
1981-82	**Pittsburgh**	**NHL**	**1**	**0**	**0**	**0**	**0**	....	....	....	....	....
	Erie	AHL	76	33	37	70	129	....	....	....	....	....
1982-83	**Pittsburgh**	**NHL**	**74**	**11**	**22**	**33**	**127**	....	....	....	....	....
	Baltimore	AHL	5	2	2	4	13	....	....	....	....	....
1983-84	**Pittsburgh**	**NHL**	**24**	**2**	**3**	**5**	**33**	....	....	....	....	....
	Baltimore	AHL	47	18	24	42	98	10	2	6	8	27
1984-85	**Pittsburgh**	**NHL**	**30**	**6**	**7**	**13**	**43**	....	....	....	....	....
	Baltimore	AHL	49	20	25	45	91	....	....	....	....	....
1985-86	**Pittsburgh**	**NHL**	**75**	**17**	**18**	**35**	**91**	....	....	....	....	....
1986-87	**Pittsburgh**	**NHL**	**58**	**10**	**15**	**25**	**56**	....	....	....	....	....
1987-88	**Pittsburgh**	**NHL**	**21**	**4**	**3**	**7**	**23**	....	....	....	....	....
	Edmonton	**NHL**	**51**	**9**	**11**	**20**	**43**	**12**	**1**	**1**	**2**	**8 ♦**
1988-89	**Pittsburgh**	**NHL**	**72**	**10**	**20**	**30**	**157**	**8**	**0**	**1**	**1**	**4**
1989-90	**Toronto**	**NHL**	**39**	**6**	**9**	**15**	**55**	**3**	**1**	**0**	**1**	**4**
1990-91	**Toronto**	**NHL**	**74**	**11**	**23**	**34**	**82**	....	....	....	....	....
1991-92	**Toronto**	**NHL**	**35**	**2**	**2**	**4**	**16**	....	....	....	....	....
	Cdn. National	....	3	0	0	0	2	....	....	....	....	....
	Cdn. Olympic	....	8	3	5	8	8	....	....	....	....	....
	Buffalo	**NHL**	**12**	**2**	**4**	**6**	**48**	**7**	**2**	**0**	**2**	**2**
1992-93	**Buffalo**	**NHL**	**55**	**5**	**15**	**20**	**43**	**8**	**1**	**1**	**2**	**18**
1993-94	**Buffalo**	**NHL**	**83**	**6**	**15**	**21**	**53**	**7**	**1**	**0**	**1**	**6**
1994-95	**Buffalo**	**NHL**	**42**	**4**	**12**	**16**	**32**	**5**	**0**	**2**	**2**	**2**
1995-96	**Buffalo**	**NHL**	**57**	**6**	**10**	**16**	**30**	....	....	....	....	....
	Colorado	**NHL**	**4**	**1**	**0**	**1**	**2**	**13**	**0**	**2**	**2**	**2 ♦**
1996-97	**Ottawa**	**NHL**	**34**	**2**	**2**	**4**	**8**	....	....	....	....	....
	NHL Totals		**841**	**114**	**191**	**305**	**942**	**63**	**6**	**7**	**13**	**46**

Traded to **Edmonton** by **Pittsburgh** with Craig Simpson, Moe Mantha and Chris Joseph for Paul Coffey, Dave Hunter and Wayne Van Dorp, November 24, 1987. Claimed by **Pittsburgh** from **Edmonton** in NHL Waiver Draft, October 3, 1988. Claimed by **Toronto** from **Pittsburgh** in NHL Waiver Draft, October 2, 1989. Traded to **Buffalo** by **Toronto** for Minnesota's fifth round choice (previously acquired by Buffalo — Toronto selected Chris Deruiter) in 1992 Entry Draft, March 10, 1992. Traded to **Colorado** by **Buffalo** for Colorado's sixth round choice (Darren Mortier) in 1996 Entry Draft, March 20, 1996. Signed as a free agent by **Ottawa**, September 13, 1996.

HANNAN, SCOTT — S.J.

Defense. Shoots left. 6'1", 210 lbs. Born, Richmond, B.C., January 23, 1979.
(San Jose's 2nd choice, 23rd overall, in 1997 Entry Draft).

			Regular Season					Playoffs				
Season	Club	Lea	GP	G	A	TP	PIM	GP	G	A	TP	PIM
1994-95	Tacoma	WHL	2	0	0	0	0	....	....	....	....	....
1995-96	Kelowna	WHL	69	4	5	9	76	6	0	1	1	4
1996-97	Kelowna	WHL	70	17	26	43	101	6	0	0	0	8

HANSEN, TAVIS — PHO.

Center. Shoots right. 6'1", 180 lbs. Born, Prince Albert, Sask., June 17, 1975.
(Winnipeg's 3rd choice, 58th overall, in 1994 Entry Draft).

			Regular Season					Playoffs				
Season	Club	Lea	GP	G	A	TP	PIM	GP	G	A	TP	PIM
1993-94	Tacoma	WHL	71	23	31	54	122	8	1	3	4	17
1994-95	Tacoma	WHL	71	32	41	73	142	4	1	1	2	8
	Winnipeg	**NHL**	**1**	**0**	**0**	**0**	**0**	....	....	....	....	....
1995-96	Springfield	AHL	67	6	16	22	85	5	1	2	3	2
1996-97	**Phoenix**	**NHL**	**1**	**0**	**0**	**0**	**0**	....	....	....	....	....
	Springfield	AHL	12	3	1	4	23	....	....	....	....	....
	NHL Totals		**2**	**0**	**0**	**0**	**0**	....	....	....	....	....

HARDY, FRANCOIS — OTT.

Defense. Shoots left. 6'2", 185 lbs. Born, Les Saules, Que., July 6, 1978.
(Ottawa's 4th choice, 163rd overall, in 1996 Entry Draft).

			Regular Season					Playoffs				
Season	Club	Lea	GP	G	A	TP	PIM	GP	G	A	TP	PIM
1995-96	Val d'Or	QMJHL	55	2	3	5	93	3	0	0	0	4
1996-97	Val d'Or	QMJHL	57	2	10	12	120	13	1	1	2	20

HARKINS, BRETT

Left wing. Shoots left. 6'1", 185 lbs. Born, North Ridgeville, OH, July 2, 1970.
(NY Islanders' 9th choice, 133rd overall, in 1989 Entry Draft).

			Regular Season					Playoffs				
Season	Club	Lea	GP	G	A	TP	PIM	GP	G	A	TP	PIM
1989-90	Bowling Green	CCHA	41	11	43	54	45	....	....	....	....	....
1990-91	Bowling Green	CCHA	40	22	38	60	30	....	....	....	....	....
1991-92	Bowling Green	CCHA	34	8	39	47	32	....	....	....	....	....
1992-93	Bowling Green	CCHA	35	19	28	47	28	....	....	....	....	....
1993-94	Adirondack	AHL	80	22	47	69	23	10	1	5	6	4
1994-95	Providence	AHL	80	23	*69	92	32	13	8	14	22	4
	Boston	**NHL**	**1**	**0**	**1**	**1**	**0**	....	....	....	....	....
1995-96	**Florida**	**NHL**	**8**	**0**	**3**	**3**	**6**	....	....	....	....	....
	Carolina	AHL	55	23	*71	94	44	....	....	....	....	....
1996-97	**Boston**	**NHL**	**44**	**4**	**14**	**18**	**8**	....	....	....	....	....
	Providence	AHL	28	9	31	40	32	10	2	10	12	0
	NHL Totals		**53**	**4**	**18**	**22**	**14**	....	....	....	....	....

Signed as a free agent by **Boston**, July 1, 1994. Signed as a free agent by **Florida**, July 24, 1995. Signed as a free agent by **Boston**, September 4, 1996.

HARKINS, TODD

Center. Shoots right. 6'3", 210 lbs. Born, Cleveland, OH, October 8, 1968.
(Calgary's 2nd choice, 42nd overall, in 1988 Entry Draft).

			Regular Season					Playoffs				
Season	Club	Lea	GP	G	A	TP	PIM	GP	G	A	TP	PIM
1987-88	Miami-Ohio	CCHA	34	9	7	16	133	....	....	....	....	....
1988-89	Miami-Ohio	CCHA	36	8	7	15	77	....	....	....	....	....
1989-90	Miami-Ohio	CCHA	40	27	17	44	78	....	....	....	....	....
1990-91	Salt Lake	IHL	79	15	27	42	113	3	0	0	0	0
1991-92	**Calgary**	**NHL**	**5**	**0**	**0**	**0**	**7**	....	....	....	....	....
	Salt Lake	IHL	72	32	30	62	67	5	1	1	2	6
1992-93	**Calgary**	**NHL**	**15**	**2**	**3**	**5**	**22**	....	....	....	....	....
	Salt Lake	IHL	53	13	21	34	90	....	....	....	....	....
1993-94	Saint John	AHL	38	13	9	22	64	....	....	....	....	....
	Hartford	**NHL**	**28**	**1**	**0**	**1**	**49**	....	....	....	....	....
	Springfield	AHL	1	0	3	3	0	....	....	....	....	....
1994-95	Chicago	IHL	52	18	25	43	136	....	....	....	....	....
	Houston	IHL	25	9	10	19	77	4	1	1	2	28
1995-96	Carolina	AHL	69	27	28	55	172	....	....	....	....	....
1996-97	Fort Wayne	IHL	60	12	13	25	131	....	....	....	....	....
	Phoenix	IHL	16	4	3	7	24	....	....	....	....	....
	NHL Totals		**48**	**3**	**3**	**6**	**78**	....	....	....	....	....

Traded to **Hartford** by **Calgary** for Scott Morrow, January 24, 1994. Signed as a free agent by **Florida**, June 6, 1995.

HARLOCK, DAVID

Defense. Shoots left. 6'2", 205 lbs. Born, Toronto, Ont., March 16, 1971.
(New Jersey's 2nd choice, 24th overall, in 1990 Entry Draft).

			Regular Season					Playoffs				
Season	Club	Lea	GP	G	A	TP	PIM	GP	G	A	TP	PIM
1989-90	U. of Michigan	CCHA	42	2	13	15	44	....	....	....	....	....
1990-91	U. of Michigan	CCHA	39	2	8	10	70	....	....	....	....	....
1991-92	U. of Michigan	CCHA	44	1	6	7	80	....	....	....	....	....
1992-93	U. of Michigan	CCHA	38	3	9	12	58	....	....	....	....	....
	Cdn. National	....	4	0	0	0	2	....	....	....	....	....
1993-94	Cdn. National	....	41	0	3	3	28	....	....	....	....	....
	Cdn. Olympic	....	8	0	0	0	8	....	....	....	....	....
	Toronto	**NHL**	**6**	**0**	**0**	**0**	**0**	....	....	....	....	....
	St. John's	AHL	10	0	3	3	2	9	0	0	0	6
1994-95	St. John's	AHL	58	0	6	6	44	5	0	0	0	0
	Toronto	**NHL**	**1**	**0**	**0**	**0**	**0**	....	....	....	....	....
1995-96	**Toronto**	**NHL**	**1**	**0**	**0**	**0**	**0**	....	....	....	....	....
	St. John's	AHL	77	0	12	12	92	4	0	1	1	2
1996-97	San Antonio	IHL	69	3	10	13	82	9	0	0	0	10
	NHL Totals		**8**	**0**	**0**	**0**	**0**	....	....	....	....	....

Signed as a free agent by **Toronto**, August 20, 1993.

HARLTON, TYLER — ST.L.

Defense. Shoots left. 6'3", 201 lbs. Born, Pense, Sask., January 11, 1976.
(St. Louis' 2nd choice, 94th overall, in 1994 Entry Draft).

			Regular Season					Playoffs				
Season	Club	Lea	GP	G	A	TP	PIM	GP	G	A	TP	PIM
1994-95	Michigan State	CCHA	39	1	3	4	55	....	....	....	....	....
1995-96	Michigan State	CCHA	39	1	6	7	51	....	....	....	....	....
1996-97	Michigan State	CCHA	39	2	9	11	75	....	....	....	....	....

HARTMAN, MIKE

Left wing. Shoots left. 6', 190 lbs. Born, Detroit, MI, February 7, 1967.
(Buffalo's 8th choice, 131st overall, in 1986 Entry Draft).

			Regular Season					Playoffs				
Season	Club	Lea	GP	G	A	TP	PIM	GP	G	A	TP	PIM
1984-85	Belleville	OHL	49	13	12	25	119	....	....	....	....	....
1985-86	Belleville	OHL	4	2	1	3	5	....	....	....	....	....
	North Bay	OHL	53	19	16	35	205	10	2	4	6	34
1986-87	**Buffalo**	**NHL**	**17**	**3**	**3**	**6**	**69**	....	....	....	....	....
	North Bay	OHL	32	15	24	39	144	19	7	8	15	88
1987-88	**Buffalo**	**NHL**	**18**	**3**	**1**	**4**	**90**	**6**	**0**	**0**	**0**	**35**
	Rochester	AHL	57	13	14	27	283	4	1	0	1	22
1988-89	**Buffalo**	**NHL**	**70**	**8**	**9**	**17**	**316**	**5**	**0**	**0**	**0**	**34**
1989-90	**Buffalo**	**NHL**	**60**	**11**	**10**	**21**	**211**	**6**	**0**	**0**	**0**	**18**
1990-91	**Buffalo**	**NHL**	**60**	**9**	**3**	**12**	**204**	**2**	**0**	**0**	**0**	**17**
1991-92	**Winnipeg**	**NHL**	**75**	**4**	**4**	**8**	**264**	**2**	**0**	**0**	**0**	**2**
1992-93	**Tampa Bay**	**NHL**	**58**	**4**	**4**	**8**	**154**	....	....	....	....	....
	NY Rangers	**NHL**	**3**	**0**	**0**	**0**	**6**	....	....	....	....	....
1993-94	**NY Rangers**	**NHL**	**35**	**1**	**1**	**2**	**70**	....	....	....	....	....
1994-95	**NY Rangers**	**NHL**	**1**	**0**	**0**	**0**	**4**	....	....	....	....	....
	Detroit	IHL	6	1	0	1	52	1	0	0	0	0
1995-96	Orlando	IHL	77	14	10	24	243	21	2	2	4	31
1996-97	Hershey	AHL	42	5	8	13	116	1	0	0	0	0
	NHL Totals		**397**	**43**	**35**	**78**	**1388**	**21**	**0**	**0**	**0**	**106**

Traded to **Winnipeg** by **Buffalo** with Darrin Shannon and Dean Kennedy for Dave McLlwain, Gord Donnelly, Winnipeg's fifth round choice (Yuri Khmylev) in 1992 Entry Draft and future considerations, October 11, 1991. Claimed by **Tampa Bay** from **Winnipeg** in Expansion Draft, June 18, 1992. Traded to **NY Rangers** by **Tampa Bay** for Randy Gilhen, March 22, 1993. Signed as a free agent by **Colorado**, September 26, 1996.

HARVEY, TODD — DAL.

Center. Shoots right. 6', 195 lbs. Born, Hamilton, Ont., February 17, 1975.
(Dallas' 1st choice, 9th overall, in 1993 Entry Draft).

			Regular Season					Playoffs				
Season	Club	Lea	GP	G	A	TP	PIM	GP	G	A	TP	PIM
1991-92	Detroit	OHL	58	21	43	64	141	7	3	5	8	30
1992-93	Detroit	OHL	55	50	50	100	83	15	9	12	21	39
1993-94	Detroit	OHL	49	34	51	85	75	17	10	12	22	26
1994-95	Detroit	OHL	11	8	14	22	12	....	....	....	....	....
	Dallas	**NHL**	**40**	**11**	**9**	**20**	**67**	**5**	**0**	**0**	**0**	**8**
1995-96	**Dallas**	**NHL**	**69**	**9**	**20**	**29**	**136**	....	....	....	....	....
	Michigan	IHL	5	1	3	4	8	....	....	....	....	....
1996-97	**Dallas**	**NHL**	**71**	**9**	**22**	**31**	**142**	**7**	**0**	**1**	**1**	**10**
	NHL Totals		**180**	**29**	**51**	**80**	**345**	**12**	**0**	**1**	**1**	**18**

HATCHER, DERIAN — DAL.

Defense. Shoots left. 6'5", 225 lbs. Born, Sterling Heights, MI, June 4, 1972.
(Minnesota's 1st choice, 8th overall, in 1990 Entry Draft).

			Regular Season					Playoffs				
Season	Club	Lea	GP	G	A	TP	PIM	GP	G	A	TP	PIM
1989-90	North Bay	OHL	64	14	38	52	81	5	2	3	5	8
1990-91	North Bay	OHL	64	13	49	62	163	10	2	10	12	28
1991-92	**Minnesota**	**NHL**	**43**	**8**	**4**	**12**	**88**	**5**	**0**	**2**	**2**	**8**
1992-93	**Minnesota**	**NHL**	**67**	**4**	**15**	**19**	**178**	....	....	....	....	....
	Kalamazoo	IHL	2	1	2	3	21	....	....	....	....	....
1993-94	**Dallas**	**NHL**	**83**	**12**	**19**	**31**	**211**	**9**	**0**	**2**	**2**	**14**
1994-95	**Dallas**	**NHL**	**43**	**5**	**11**	**16**	**105**	....	....	....	....	....
1995-96	**Dallas**	**NHL**	**79**	**8**	**23**	**31**	**129**	....	....	....	....	....
1996-97	**Dallas**	**NHL**	**63**	**3**	**19**	**22**	**97**	**7**	**0**	**2**	**2**	**20**
	NHL Totals		**378**	**40**	**91**	**131**	**808**	**21**	**0**	**6**	**6**	**42**

Played in NHL All-Star Game (1997)

HATCHER, KEVIN — PIT.

Defense. Shoots right. 6'4", 225 lbs. Born, Detroit, MI, September 9, 1966.
(Washington's 1st choice, 17th overall, in 1984 Entry Draft).

			Regular Season					Playoffs				
Season	Club	Lea	GP	G	A	TP	PIM	GP	G	A	TP	PIM
1983-84	North Bay	OHL	67	10	39	49	61	4	2	2	4	11
1984-85	**Washington**	**NHL**	**2**	**1**	**0**	**1**	**0**	**1**	**0**	**0**	**0**	**0**
a	North Bay	OHL	58	26	37	63	75	8	3	8	11	9
1985-86	**Washington**	**NHL**	**79**	**9**	**10**	**19**	**119**	**9**	**1**	**1**	**2**	**19**
1986-87	**Washington**	**NHL**	**78**	**8**	**16**	**24**	**144**	**7**	**1**	**0**	**1**	**20**
1987-88	**Washington**	**NHL**	**71**	**14**	**27**	**41**	**137**	**14**	**5**	**7**	**12**	**55**
1988-89	**Washington**	**NHL**	**62**	**13**	**27**	**40**	**101**	**6**	**1**	**4**	**5**	**20**
1989-90	**Washington**	**NHL**	**80**	**13**	**41**	**54**	**102**	**11**	**0**	**8**	**8**	**32**
1990-91	**Washington**	**NHL**	**79**	**24**	**50**	**74**	**69**	**11**	**3**	**3**	**6**	**8**
1991-92	**Washington**	**NHL**	**79**	**17**	**37**	**54**	**105**	**7**	**2**	**4**	**6**	**19**
1992-93	**Washington**	**NHL**	**83**	**34**	**45**	**79**	**114**	**6**	**0**	**1**	**1**	**14**
1993-94	**Washington**	**NHL**	**72**	**16**	**24**	**40**	**108**	**11**	**3**	**4**	**7**	**37**
1994-95	**Dallas**	**NHL**	**47**	**10**	**19**	**29**	**66**	**5**	**2**	**1**	**3**	**2**
1995-96	**Dallas**	**NHL**	**74**	**15**	**26**	**41**	**58**	....	....	....	....	....
1996-97	**Pittsburgh**	**NHL**	**80**	**15**	**39**	**54**	**103**	**5**	**1**	**1**	**2**	**4**
	NHL Totals		**886**	**189**	**361**	**550**	**1226**	**93**	**19**	**34**	**53**	**230**

a OHL Second All-Star Team (1985)

Played in NHL All-Star Game (1990, 1991, 1992, 1996, 1997)

Traded to **Dallas** by **Washington** for Mark Tinordi and Rick Mrozik, January 18, 1995. Traded to **Pittsburgh** by **Dallas** for Sergei Zubov, June 22, 1996.

HAUER, BRETT (HOW-uhr)

Defense. Shoots right. 6'2", 200 lbs. Born, Richfield, MN, July 11, 1971.
(Vancouver's 3rd choice, 71st overall, in 1989 Entry Draft).

			Regular Season					Playoffs				
Season	Club	Lea	GP	G	A	TP	PIM	GP	G	A	TP	PIM
1989-90	Minn.-Duluth	WCHA	37	2	6	8	44	....	....	....	....	....
1990-91	Minn.-Duluth	WCHA	30	1	7	8	54	....	....	....	....	....
1991-92	Minn.-Duluth	WCHA	33	8	14	22	40	....	....	....	....	....
1992-93ab	Minn.-Duluth	WCHA	40	10	46	56	52	....	....	....	....	....
1993-94	U.S. National	....	57	6	14	20	88	....	....	....	....	....
	U.S. Olympic	....	8	0	0	0	10	....	....	....	....	....
	Las Vegas	IHL	21	0	7	7	8	1	0	0	0	0
1994-95	AIK	Swe.	37	1	3	4	38	....	....	....	....	....
1995-96	**Edmonton**	**NHL**	**29**	**4**	**2**	**6**	**30**	....	....	....	....	....
	Cape Breton	AHL	17	3	5	8	29	....	....	....	....	....
1996-97	Chicago	IHL	81	10	30	40	50	4	2	0	2	4
	NHL Totals		**29**	**4**	**2**	**6**	**30**	....	....	....	....	....

a WCHA First All-Star Team (1993)
b NCAA West First All-American Team (1993)

Traded to **Edmonton** by **Vancouver** for a conditional draft choice, August 24, 1995.

HAVELKA, PETR (huh-VEHL-kah) — PIT.

Left wing. Shoots left. 6'2", 187 lbs. Born, Most, Czech., March 4, 1979.
(Pittsburgh's 6th choice, 152nd overall, in 1997 Entry Draft).

			Regular Season					Playoffs				
Season	Club	Lea	GP	G	A	TP	PIM	GP	G	A	TP	PIM
1995-96	Sparta Praha	Czech. Jr.	40	15	10	25	....	....	....	....	....	....
1996-97	Sparta Praha	Czech. Jr.	22	14	13	27	....	....	....	....	....	....
	Sparta Praha	Czech.	....	....	....	....	....	1	0	0	0	0

HAWERCHUK, DALE (HOW-uhr-CHUHK)

Center. Shoots left. 5'11", 190 lbs. Born, Toronto, Ont., April 4, 1963.
(Winnipeg's 1st choice, 1st overall, in 1981 Entry Draft).

			Regular Season					Playoffs				
Season	Club	Lea	GP	G	A	TP	PIM	GP	G	A	TP	PIM
1979-80a	Cornwall	QJHL	72	37	66	103	21	18	20	25	45	0
1980-81bcd	Cornwall	QJHL	72	81	102	183	69	19	15	20	35	8
1981-82e	**Winnipeg**	**NHL**	**80**	**45**	**58**	**103**	**47**	**4**	**1**	**7**	**8**	**5**
1982-83	**Winnipeg**	**NHL**	**79**	**40**	**51**	**91**	**31**	**3**	**1**	**4**	**5**	**8**
1983-84	**Winnipeg**	**NHL**	**80**	**37**	**65**	**102**	**73**	**3**	**1**	**1**	**2**	**0**
1984-85f	**Winnipeg**	**NHL**	**80**	**53**	**77**	**130**	**74**	**3**	**2**	**1**	**3**	**4**
1985-86	**Winnipeg**	**NHL**	**80**	**46**	**59**	**105**	**44**	**3**	**0**	**3**	**3**	**0**
1986-87	**Winnipeg**	**NHL**	**80**	**47**	**53**	**100**	**52**	**10**	**5**	**8**	**13**	**4**
1987-88	**Winnipeg**	**NHL**	**80**	**44**	**77**	**121**	**59**	**5**	**3**	**4**	**7**	**16**
1988-89	**Winnipeg**	**NHL**	**75**	**41**	**55**	**96**	**28**	....	....	....	....	....
1989-90	**Winnipeg**	**NHL**	**79**	**26**	**55**	**81**	**60**	**7**	**3**	**5**	**8**	**2**
1990-91	**Buffalo**	**NHL**	**80**	**31**	**58**	**89**	**32**	**6**	**2**	**4**	**6**	**10**
1991-92	**Buffalo**	**NHL**	**77**	**23**	**75**	**98**	**27**	**7**	**2**	**5**	**7**	**0**
1992-93	**Buffalo**	**NHL**	**81**	**16**	**80**	**96**	**52**	**8**	**5**	**9**	**14**	**2**
1993-94	**Buffalo**	**NHL**	**81**	**35**	**51**	**86**	**91**	**7**	**0**	**7**	**7**	**4**
1994-95	**Buffalo**	**NHL**	**23**	**5**	**11**	**16**	**2**	**2**	**0**	**0**	**0**	**0**
1995-96	**St. Louis**	**NHL**	**66**	**13**	**28**	**41**	**22**	....	....	....	....	....
	Philadelphia	**NHL**	**16**	**4**	**16**	**20**	**4**	**12**	**3**	**6**	**9**	**12**
1996-97	**Philadelphia**	**NHL**	**51**	**12**	**22**	**34**	**32**	**17**	**2**	**5**	**7**	**0**
	NHL Totals		**1188**	**518**	**891**	**1409**	**730**	**97**	**30**	**69**	**99**	**67**

a Won George Parsons Trophy (Memorial Cup Tournament Most Sportsmanlike Player) (1980)
b QMJHL First All-Star Team (1981)
c Canadian Major Junior Player of the Year (1981)
d Won Stafford Smythe Memorial Trophy (Memorial Cup Tournament MVP) (1981)
e Won Calder Memorial Trophy (1982)
f NHL Second All-Star Team (1985)

Played in NHL All-Star Game (1982, 1985, 1986, 1988, 1997)

Traded to **Buffalo** by **Winnipg** with Winnipeg's first round choice (Brad May) in 1990 Entry Draft and future considerations for Phil Housley, Scott Arniel, Jeff Parker and Buffalo's first round choice (Keith Tkachuk) in 1990 Entry Draft, June 16, 1990. Signed as a free agent by **St. Louis**, September 8, 1995. Traded to **Philadelphia** by **St. Louis** for Craig MacTavish, March 15, 1996.

HAWGOOD, GREG (HAW-guhd)

Defense. Shoots left. 5'10", 190 lbs. Born, Edmonton, Alta., August 10, 1968.
(Boston's 9th choice, 202nd overall, in 1986 Entry Draft).

			Regular Season					Playoffs				
Season	Club	Lea	GP	G	A	TP	PIM	GP	G	A	TP	PIM
1983-84	Kamloops	WHL	49	10	23	33	39	....	....	....	....	....
1984-85	Kamloops	WHL	66	25	40	65	72	....	....	....	....	....
1985-86a	Kamloops	WHL	71	34	85	119	86	16	9	22	31	16
1986-87a	Kamloops	WHL	61	30	93	123	139	....	....	....	....	....
1987-88	**Boston**	**NHL**	**1**	**0**	**0**	**0**	**0**	**3**	**1**	**0**	**1**	**0**
ab	Kamloops	WHL	63	48	85	133	142	16	10	16	26	33
1988-89	**Boston**	**NHL**	**56**	**16**	**24**	**40**	**84**	**10**	**0**	**2**	**2**	**2**
	Maine	AHL	21	2	9	11	41	....	....	....	....	....
1989-90	**Boston**	**NHL**	**77**	**11**	**27**	**38**	**76**	**15**	**1**	**3**	**4**	**12**
1990-91	Asiago	Italy	2	3	0	3	9	....	....	....	....	....
	Edmonton	**NHL**	**6**	**0**	**1**	**1**	**6**	....	....	....	....	....
	Maine	AHL	5	0	1	1	13	....	....	....	....	....
	Cape Breton	AHL	55	10	32	42	73	4	0	3	3	23
1991-92	**Edmonton**	**NHL**	**20**	**2**	**11**	**13**	**22**	**13**	**0**	**3**	**3**	**23**
cd	Cape Breton	AHL	56	20	55	75	26	3	2	2	4	0
1992-93	**Edmonton**	**NHL**	**29**	**5**	**13**	**18**	**35**	....	....	....	....	....
	Philadelphia	**NHL**	**40**	**6**	**22**	**28**	**39**	....	....	....	....	....
1993-94	**Philadelphia**	**NHL**	**19**	**3**	**12**	**15**	**19**	....	....	....	....	....
	Florida	**NHL**	**33**	**2**	**14**	**16**	**9**	....	....	....	....	....
	Pittsburgh	**NHL**	**12**	**1**	**2**	**3**	**8**	**1**	**0**	**0**	**0**	**0**
1994-95	**Pittsburgh**	**NHL**	**21**	**1**	**4**	**5**	**25**	....	....	....	....	....
	Cleveland	IHL	....	....	....	....	....	3	1	0	1	4
1995-96ef	Las Vegas	IHL	78	20	65	85	101	15	5	11	16	24
1996-97	**San Jose**	**NHL**	**63**	**6**	**12**	**18**	**69**	....	....	....	....	....
	NHL Totals		**377**	**53**	**142**	**195**	**392**	**42**	**2**	**8**	**10**	**37**

a WHL West All-Star Team (1986, 1987, 1988)
b Canadian Major Junior Defenseman of the Year (1988)
c AHL First All-Star Team (1992)
d Won Eddie Shore Plaque (Top Defenseman - AHL) (1992)
e IHL First All-Star Team (1996)
f Won Governors' Trophy (Top Defenseman - IHL) (1996)

Traded to **Edmonton** by **Boston** for Vladimir Ruzicka, October 22, 1990. Traded to **Philadelphia** by **Edmonton** with Josef Beranek for Brian Benning, January 16, 1993. Traded to **Florida** by **Philadelphia** for cash, November 30, 1993. Traded to **Pittsburgh** by **Florida** for Jeff Daniels, March 19, 1994. Signed as a free agent by **San Jose**, September 25, 1996.

HAWKINS, TODD

Left/Right wing. Shoots right. 6'1", 195 lbs. Born, Kingston, Ont., August 2, 1966.
(Vancouver's 10th choice, 217th overall, in 1986 Entry Draft).

			Regular Season					Playoffs				
Season	Club	Lea	GP	G	A	TP	PIM	GP	G	A	TP	PIM
1984-85	Belleville	OHL	58	7	16	23	117	12	1	0	1	10
1985-86	Belleville	OHL	60	14	13	27	172	24	9	7	16	60
1986-87	Belleville	OHL	60	47	40	87	187	6	3	5	8	16
1987-88	Flint	IHL	50	13	13	26	337	16	3	5	8	*174
	Fredericton	AHL	2	0	4	4	11	....	....	....	....	....
1988-89	**Vancouver**	**NHL**	**4**	**0**	**0**	**0**	**9**	....	....	....	....	....
	Milwaukee	IHL	63	12	14	26	307	9	1	0	1	33
1989-90	**Vancouver**	**NHL**	**4**	**0**	**0**	**0**	**6**	....	....	....	....	....
	Milwaukee	IHL	61	23	17	40	273	5	4	1	5	19
1990-91	Newmarket	AHL	22	2	5	7	66	....	....	....	....	....
	Milwaukee	IHL	39	9	11	20	134	....	....	....	....	....
1991-92	**Toronto**	**NHL**	**2**	**0**	**0**	**0**	**0**	....	....	....	....	....
	St. John's	AHL	66	30	27	57	139	7	1	0	1	10
1992-93	St. John's	AHL	72	21	41	62	103	9	1	3	4	10
1993-94	Cleveland	IHL	76	19	14	33	115	....	....	....	....	....
1994-95	Cleveland	IHL	4	2	0	2	29	....	....	....	....	....
	Minnesota	IHL	47	10	8	18	95	3	0	1	1	12
1995-96	Cincinnati	IHL	73	16	12	28	65	17	7	4	11	32
1996-97	Cincinnati	IHL	81	13	13	26	162	3	0	1	1	2
	NHL Totals		**10**	**0**	**0**	**0**	**15**	....	....	....	....	....

Traded to **Toronto** by **Vancouver** for Brian Blad, January 22, 1991. Signed as a free agent by **Pittsburgh**, August 20, 1993.

HAY, DWAYNE — WSH.

Left wing. Shoots left. 6'1", 183 lbs. Born, London, Ont., February 11, 1977.
(Washington's 3rd choice, 43rd overall, in 1995 Entry Draft).

			Regular Season					Playoffs				
Season	Club	Lea	GP	G	A	TP	PIM	GP	G	A	TP	PIM
1994-95	Guelph	OHL	65	26	28	54	37	14	5	7	12	6
1995-96	Guelph	OHL	60	28	30	58	49	16	4	9	13	18
1996-97	Guelph	OHL	32	17	17	34	21	11	4	6	10	0

HEALEY, PAUL — PHI.

Right wing. Shoots right. 6'2", 196 lbs. Born, Edmonton, Alta., March 20, 1975.
(Philadelphia's 7th choice, 192nd overall, in 1993 Entry Draft).

			Regular Season					Playoffs				
Season	Club	Lea	GP	G	A	TP	PIM	GP	G	A	TP	PIM
1992-93	Prince Albert	WHL	72	12	20	32	66	....	....	....	....	....
1993-94	Prince Albert	WHL	63	23	26	49	70	....	....	....	....	....
1994-95a	Prince Albert	WHL	71	43	50	93	67	12	3	4	7	2
1995-96	Hershey	AHL	60	7	15	22	35	....	....	....	....	....
1996-97	**Philadelphia**	**NHL**	**2**	**0**	**0**	**0**	**0**	....	....	....	....	....
	Philadelphia	AHL	64	21	19	40	56	10	4	1	5	10
	NHL Totals		**2**	**0**	**0**	**0**	**0**	....	....	....	....	....

a WHL East Second All-Star Team (1995)

HECHT, JOCHEN — ST.L.

Center. Shoots left. 6'1", 180 lbs. Born, Mannheim, Germany, June 21, 1977.
(St. Louis' 1st choice, 49th overall, in 1995 Entry Draft).

			Regular Season					Playoffs				
Season	Club	Lea	GP	G	A	TP	PIM	GP	G	A	TP	PIM
1994-95	Mannheim	Ger.	43	11	12	23	68	10	5	4	9	12
1995-96	Mannheim	Ger.	44	12	16	28	68	8	3	2	5	6
1996-97	Mannheim	Ger.	46	21	21	42	36	9	3	3	6	4

HEDICAN, BRET (HEH-dih-kan) VAN.

Defense. Shoots left. 6'2", 195 lbs. Born, St. Paul, MN, August 10, 1970.
(St. Louis' 10th choice, 198th overall, in 1988 Entry Draft).

			Regular Season					Playoffs				
Season	Club	Lea	GP	G	A	TP	PIM	GP	G	A	TP	PIM
1988-89	St. Cloud	NCAA	28	5	3	8	28	....	....	....	....	....
1989-90	St. Cloud	NCAA	36	4	17	21	37	....	....	....	....	....
1990-91a	St. Cloud	WCHA	41	21	26	47	26	....	....	....	....	....
1991-92	U.S. National	....	54	1	8	9	59	....	....	....	....	....
	U.S. Olympic	....	8	0	0	0	4	....	....	....	....	....
	St. Louis	**NHL**	**4**	**1**	**0**	**1**	**0**	**5**	**0**	**0**	**0**	**0**
1992-93	**St. Louis**	**NHL**	**42**	**0**	**8**	**8**	**30**	**10**	**0**	**0**	**0**	**14**
	Peoria	IHL	19	0	8	8	10	....	....	....	....	....
1993-94	**St. Louis**	**NHL**	**61**	**0**	**11**	**11**	**64**	....	....	....	....	....
	Vancouver	**NHL**	**8**	**0**	**1**	**1**	**0**	**24**	**1**	**6**	**7**	**16**
1994-95	**Vancouver**	**NHL**	**45**	**2**	**11**	**13**	**34**	**11**	**0**	**2**	**2**	**6**
1995-96	**Vancouver**	**NHL**	**77**	**6**	**23**	**29**	**83**	**6**	**0**	**1**	**1**	**10**
1996-97	**Vancouver**	**NHL**	**67**	**4**	**15**	**19**	**51**	....	....	....	....	....
	NHL Totals		**304**	**13**	**69**	**82**	**262**	**56**	**1**	**9**	**10**	**46**

a WCHA First All-Star Team (1991)

Traded to **Vancouver** by **St. Louis** with Jeff Brown and Nathan Lafayette for Craig Janney, March 21, 1994.

HEINZE, STEPHEN (HIGHNS) BOS.

Right wing. Shoots right. 5'11", 202 lbs. Born, Lawrence, MA, January 30, 1970.
(Boston's 2nd choice, 60th overall, in 1988 Entry Draft).

			Regular Season					Playoffs				
Season	Club	Lea	GP	G	A	TP	PIM	GP	G	A	TP	PIM
1988-89	Boston College	H.E.	36	26	23	49	26	....	....	....	....	....
1989-90ab	Boston College	H.E.	40	27	36	63	41	....	....	....	....	....
1990-91	Boston College	H.E.	35	21	26	47	35	....	....	....	....	....
1991-92	U.S. National	....	49	18	15	33	38	....	....	....	....	....
	U.S. Olympic	....	8	1	3	4	8	....	....	....	....	....
	Boston	**NHL**	**14**	**3**	**4**	**7**	**6**	**7**	**0**	**3**	**3**	**17**
1992-93	**Boston**	**NHL**	**73**	**18**	**13**	**31**	**24**	**4**	**1**	**1**	**2**	**2**
1993-94	**Boston**	**NHL**	**77**	**10**	**11**	**21**	**32**	**13**	**2**	**3**	**5**	**7**
1994-95	**Boston**	**NHL**	**36**	**7**	**9**	**16**	**23**	**5**	**0**	**0**	**0**	**0**
1995-96	**Boston**	**NHL**	**76**	**16**	**12**	**28**	**43**	**5**	**1**	**1**	**2**	**4**
1996-97	**Boston**	**NHL**	**30**	**17**	**8**	**25**	**27**	....	....	....	....	....
	NHL Totals		**306**	**71**	**57**	**128**	**155**	**34**	**4**	**8**	**12**	**30**

a Hockey East First All-Star Team (1990)
b NCAA East First All-American Team (1990)

HEJDUK, MILAN (HEHI-duhk) COL.

Right wing. Shoots right. 5'11", 163 lbs. Born, Usti-nad-Labem, Czech., February 14, 1976.
(Quebec's 6th choice, 87th overall, in 1994 Entry Draft).

			Regular Season					Playoffs				
Season	Club	Lea	GP	G	A	TP	PIM	GP	G	A	TP	PIM
1993-94	Pardubice	Czech.	22	6	3	9	....	10	5	1	6	....
1994-95	Pardubice	Czech.	43	11	13	24	6	6	3	1	4	0
1995-96	Pardubice	Czech.	37	13	7	20	....	....	....	....	....	....
1996-97	Pardubice	Czech.	51	27	11	38	10	10	6	0	6	27

HELENIUS, SAMI (huh-LEHN-ee-uhs) CGY.

Defense. Shoots left. 6'5", 225 lbs. Born, Helsinki, Finland, January 22, 1974.
(Calgary's 5th choice, 102nd overall, in 1992 Entry Draft).

			Regular Season					Playoffs				
Season	Club	Lea	GP	G	A	TP	PIM	GP	G	A	TP	PIM
1992-93	Jokerit	Fin.	1	0	0	0	0	....	....	....	....	....
1993-94	Reipas	Fin.	37	2	3	5	46	....	....	....	....	....
1994-95	Saint John	AHL	69	2	5	7	217	....	....	....	....	....
1995-96	Saint John	AHL	68	0	3	3	231	10	0	0	0	9
1996-97	**Calgary**	**NHL**	**3**	**0**	**1**	**1**	**0**	....	....	....	....	....
	Saint John	AHL	72	5	10	15	218	2	0	0	0	0
	NHL Totals		**3**	**0**	**1**	**1**	**0**	....	....	....	....	....

HELMER, BRYAN N.J.

Defense. Shoots right. 6'1", 200 lbs. Born, Sault Ste. Marie, Ont., July 15, 1972.

			Regular Season					Playoffs				
Season	Club	Lea	GP	G	A	TP	PIM	GP	G	A	TP	PIM
1993-94	Albany	AHL	65	4	19	23	79	5	0	0	0	9
1994-95	Albany	AHL	77	7	36	43	101	7	1	0	1	0
1995-96	Albany	AHL	80	14	30	44	107	4	2	0	2	6
1996-97	Albany	AHL	77	12	27	39	113	16	1	7	8	10

Signed as a free agent by **New Jersey**, July 10, 1994.

HEMENWAY, KEN PHI.

Defense. Shoots right. 6'1", 187 lbs. Born, Boston, MA, August 1, 1975.
(Philadelphia's 11th choice, 270th overall, in 1993 Entry Draft).

			Regular Season					Playoffs				
Season	Club	Lea	GP	G	A	TP	PIM	GP	G	A	TP	PIM
1994-95	Boston College	H.E.	32	4	6	10	24	....	....	....	....	....
1995-96	Boston College	H.E.	36	12	13	25	26	....	....	....	....	....
1996-97	Boston College	H.E.	38	3	17	20	52	....	....	....	....	....

HENDRICKSON, DARBY TOR.

Center. Shoots left. 6', 185 lbs. Born, Richfield, MN, August 28, 1972.
(Toronto's 3rd choice, 73rd overall, in 1990 Entry Draft).

			Regular Season					Playoffs				
Season	Club	Lea	GP	G	A	TP	PIM	GP	G	A	TP	PIM
1991-92	U. Minnesota	WCHA	41	25	28	53	61	....	....	....	....	....
1992-93	U. Minnesota	WCHA	31	12	15	27	35	....	....	....	....	....
1993-94	U.S. National	....	59	12	16	28	30	....	....	....	....	....
	U.S. Olympic	....	8	0	0	0	6	....	....	....	....	....
	St. John's	AHL	6	4	1	5	4	3	1	1	2	0
	Toronto	**NHL**	....	....	....	....	....	**2**	**0**	**0**	**0**	**0**
1994-95	St. John's	AHL	59	16	20	36	48	....	....	....	....	....
	Toronto	**NHL**	**8**	**0**	**1**	**1**	**4**	....	....	....	....	....
1995-96	**Toronto**	**NHL**	**46**	**6**	**6**	**12**	**47**	....	....	....	....	....
	NY Islanders	**NHL**	**16**	**1**	**4**	**5**	**33**	....	....	....	....	....
1996-97	**Toronto**	**NHL**	**64**	**11**	**6**	**17**	**47**	....	....	....	....	....
	St. John's	AHL	12	5	4	9	21	....	....	....	....	....
	NHL Totals		**134**	**18**	**17**	**35**	**131**	**2**	**0**	**0**	**0**	**0**

Traded to **NY Islanders** by **Toronto** with Sean Haggerty, Kenny Jonsson and Toronto's first round choice (Roberto Luongo) in 1997 Entry Draft for Wendel Clark, Mathieu Schneider and D.J. Smith, March 13, 1996. Traded to **Toronto** by **NY Islanders** for a conditional choice in 1998 Entry Draft, October 10, 1996.

HENRY, BURKE NYR

Defense. Shoots left. 6'2", 190 lbs. Born, Ste. Rose, Man., January 21, 1979.
(NY Rangers' 3rd choice, 73rd overall, in 1997 Entry Draft).

			Regular Season					Playoffs				
Season	Club	Lea	GP	G	A	TP	PIM	GP	G	A	TP	PIM
1995-96	Brandon	WHL	50	6	11	17	58	19	0	4	4	19
1996-97	Brandon	WHL	55	6	25	31	81	6	1	3	4	4

HERBERS, IAN

Defense. Shoots left. 6'4", 225 lbs. Born, Jasper, Alta., July 18, 1967.
(Buffalo's 11th choice, 190th overall, in 1987 Entry Draft).

			Regular Season					Playoffs				
Season	Club	Lea	GP	G	A	TP	PIM	GP	G	A	TP	PIM
1984-85	Kelowna	WHL	68	3	14	17	120	6	0	1	1	9
1985-86	Spokane	WHL	29	1	6	7	85	....	....	....	....	....
	Lethbridge	WHL	32	1	4	5	109	10	1	0	1	37
1986-87	Swift Current	WHL	72	5	8	13	230	4	1	1	2	12
1987-88	Swift Current	WHL	56	5	14	19	238	4	0	2	2	4
1988-89	U. of Alberta	CWUAA	47	4	22	26	137	....	....	....	....	....
1989-90	U. of Alberta	CWUAA	45	5	31	36	83	....	....	....	....	....
1990-91a	U. of Alberta	CWUAA	45	6	24	30	87	....	....	....	....	....
1991-92a	U. of Alberta	CWUAA	43	14	34	48	86	....	....	....	....	....
1992-93	Cape Breton	AHL	77	7	15	22	129	10	0	1	1	16
1993-94	**Edmonton**	**NHL**	**22**	**0**	**2**	**2**	**32**	....	....	....	....	....
	Cape Breton	AHL	53	7	16	23	122	5	0	3	3	12
1994-95	Cape Breton	AHL	36	1	11	12	104	....	....	....	....	....
	Detroit	IHL	37	1	5	6	46	5	1	1	2	6
1995-96	Detroit	IHL	73	3	11	14	140	12	3	5	8	29
1996-97	Detroit	IHL	67	3	16	19	129	21	0	4	4	34
	NHL Totals		**22**	**0**	**2**	**2**	**32**	....	....	....	....	....

a CIAU All-Canadian Team (1991, 1992)

Signed as a free agent by **Edmonton**, September 9, 1992.

HERPERGER, CHRIS

Left wing. Shoots left. 6', 190 lbs. Born, Esterhazy, Sask., February 24, 1974.
(Philadelphia's 10th choice, 223rd overall, in 1992 Entry Draft).

			Regular Season					Playoffs				
Season	Club	Lea	GP	G	A	TP	PIM	GP	G	A	TP	PIM
1990-91	Swift Current	WHL	10	0	1	1	5	....	....	....	....	....
1991-92	Swift Current	WHL	72	14	19	33	44	8	0	1	1	9
1992-93	Swift Current	WHL	20	9	7	16	31	....	....	....	....	....
	Seattle	WHL	46	20	11	31	30	5	1	1	2	6
1993-94	Seattle	WHL	71	44	51	95	110	9	12	10	22	12
1994-95a	Seattle	WHL	59	49	52	101	106	4	4	0	4	6
	Hershey	AHL	4	0	0	0	0	....	....	....	....	....
1995-96	Hershey	AHL	46	8	12	20	36	....	....	....	....	....
	Baltimore	AHL	21	2	3	5	17	9	2	3	5	6
1996-97	Baltimore	AHL	67	19	22	41	88	3	0	0	0	0

a WHL West Second All-Star Team (1995)

Traded to **Anaheim** by **Philadelphia** with Winnipeg's seventh round choice (previously acquired by Philadelphia — Anaheim selected Tony Mohagen) in 1997 Entry Draft for Bob Corkum, February 6, 1996.

HERR, MATT WSH.

Center. Shoots left. 6'1", 180 lbs. Born, Hackensack, NJ, May 26, 1976.
(Washington's 4th choice, 93rd overall, in 1994 Entry Draft).

			Regular Season					Playoffs				
Season	Club	Lea	GP	G	A	TP	PIM	GP	G	A	TP	PIM
1994-95	U. of Michigan	CCHA	37	11	8	19	51	....	....	....	....	....
1995-96	U. of Michigan	CCHA	40	18	13	31	55	....	....	....	....	....
1996-97	U. of Michigan	CCHA	43	29	23	52	67	....	....	....	....	....

HERTER, JASON

Defense. Shoots right. 6'1", 190 lbs. Born, Hafford, Sask., October 2, 1970.
(Vancouver's 1st choice, 8th overall, in 1989 Entry Draft).

			Regular Season					Playoffs				
Season	Club	Lea	GP	G	A	TP	PIM	GP	G	A	TP	PIM
1988-89	North Dakota	WCHA	41	8	24	32	62	....	....	....	....	....
1989-90a	North Dakota	WCHA	38	11	39	50	40	....	....	....	....	....
1990-91a	North Dakota	WCHA	39	11	26	37	52	....	....	....	....	....
1991-92	Milwaukee	IHL	56	7	18	25	34	1	0	0	0	2
1992-93	Hamilton	AHL	70	7	16	23	68	....	....	....	....	....
1993-94	Kalamazoo	IHL	68	14	28	42	92	5	3	0	3	14
1994-95	Kalamazoo	IHL	60	12	20	32	70	16	2	8	10	10
1995-96	**NY Islanders**	**NHL**	**1**	**0**	**1**	**1**	**0**	....	....	....	....	....
	Utah	IHL	74	14	31	45	58	20	4	10	14	8
1996-97	Kansas City	IHL	71	9	26	35	62	3	0	1	1	0
	NHL Totals		**1**	**0**	**1**	**1**	**0**	....	....	....	....	....

a WCHA Second All-Star Team (1990, 1991)

Signed as a free agent by **Dallas**, August 6, 1993. Traded to **NY Islanders** by **Dallas** for cash, September 21, 1995.

HEWARD, JAMIE PHI.

Defense. Shoots right. 6'2", 207 lbs. Born, Regina, Sask., March 30, 1971.
(Pittsburgh's 1st choice, 16th overall, in 1989 Entry Draft).

			Regular Season					Playoffs				
Season	Club	Lea	GP	G	A	TP	PIM	GP	G	A	TP	PIM
1987-88	Regina	WHL	68	10	17	27	17	4	1	1	2	2
1988-89	Regina	WHL	52	31	28	59	29	....	....	....	....	....
1989-90	Regina	WHL	72	14	44	58	42	11	2	2	4	10
1990-91a	Regina	WHL	71	23	61	84	41	8	2	9	11	6
1991-92	Muskegon	IHL	54	6	21	27	37	14	1	4	5	4
1992-93	Cleveland	IHL	58	9	18	27	64	....	....	....	....	....
1993-94	Cleveland	IHL	73	8	16	24	72	....	....	....	....	....
1994-95	Cdn. National	....	51	11	35	46	32	....	....	....	....	....
1995-96	**Toronto**	**NHL**	**5**	**0**	**0**	**0**	**0**	....	....	....	....	....
b	St. John's	AHL	73	22	34	56	33	3	1	1	2	6
1996-97	**Toronto**	**NHL**	**20**	**1**	**4**	**5**	**6**	....	....	....	....	....
	St. John's	AHL	27	8	19	27	26	9	1	3	4	6
	NHL Totals		**25**	**1**	**4**	**5**	**6**	....	....	....	....	....

a WHL East First All-Star Team (1991)
b AHL First All-Star Team (1996)

Signed as a free agent by **Toronto**, May 4, 1995. Signed as a free agent by **Philadelphia**, July 31, 1997.

HICKS, ALEX — PIT.

Left wing. Shoots left. 6'1", 195 lbs. Born, Calgary, Alta., September 4, 1969.

			Regular Season					Playoffs				
Season	Club	Lea	GP	G	A	TP	PIM	GP	G	A	TP	PIM
1988-89	Wisc.-Eau Claire	NCHA	30	21	26	47	42	....	....	....	....	....
1989-90	Wisc.-Eau Claire	NCHA	34	31	48	79	30	....	....	....	....	....
1990-91	Wisc.-Eau Claire	NCHA	26	22	35	57	43	....	....	....	....	....
1991-92	Wisc.-Eau Claire	NCHA	26	24	42	66	63	....	....	....	....	....
1992-93	Toledo	ECHL	50	26	34	60	100	16	5	10	15	79
	Adirondack	AHL	3	0	0	0	0	....	....	....	....	....
1993-94	Toledo	ECHL	60	31	49	80	240	14	10	10	20	56
	Adirondack	AHL	8	1	3	4	2	5	0	2	2	2
1994-95	Las Vegas	IHL	79	24	42	66	212	9	2	4	6	47
1995-96	**Anaheim**	**NHL**	**64**	**10**	**11**	**21**	**37**	....	....	....	....	....
	Baltimore	AHL	13	2	10	12	23	....	....	....	....	....
1996-97	**Anaheim**	**NHL**	**18**	**2**	**6**	**8**	**14**	....	....	....	....	....
	Pittsburgh	**NHL**	**55**	**5**	**15**	**20**	**76**	**5**	**0**	**1**	**1**	**2**
	NHL Totals		**137**	**17**	**32**	**49**	**127**	**5**	**0**	**1**	**1**	**2**

Signed as a free agent by **Anaheim**, August 17, 1995. Traded to **Pittsburgh** by **Anaheim** with Fredrik Olausson for Shawn Antoski and Dmitri Mironov, November 19, 1996.

HIGGINS, MATT — MTL.

Center. Shoots left. 6'2", 170 lbs. Born, Calgary, Alta., October 29, 1977.
(Montreal's 1st choice, 18th overall, in 1996 Entry Draft).

			Regular Season					Playoffs				
Season	Club	Lea	GP	G	A	TP	PIM	GP	G	A	TP	PIM
1993-94	Moose Jaw	WHL	64	6	10	16	10	....	....	....	....	....
1994-95	Moose Jaw	WHL	72	36	34	70	26	10	1	2	3	2
1995-96	Moose Jaw	WHL	67	30	33	63	43	....	....	....	....	....
1996-97	Moose Jaw	WHL	71	33	57	90	51	12	3	5	8	2

HILL, SEAN — (HIHL, SHAWN) OTT.

Defense. Shoots right. 6', 203 lbs. Born, Duluth, MN, February 14, 1970.
(Montreal's 9th choice, 167th overall, in 1988 Entry Draft).

			Regular Season					Playoffs				
Season	Club	Lea	GP	G	A	TP	PIM	GP	G	A	TP	PIM
1988-89	U. Wisconsin	WCHA	45	2	23	25	69	....	....	....	....	....
1989-90a	U. Wisconsin	WCHA	42	14	39	53	78	....	....	....	....	....
1990-91ab	U. Wisconsin	WCHA	37	19	32	51	122	....	....	....	....	....
	Montreal	**NHL**	....	....	....	....	....	**1**	**0**	**0**	**0**	**0**
	Fredericton	AHL	....	....	....	....	....	3	0	2	2	2
1991-92	Fredericton	AHL	42	7	20	27	65	7	1	3	4	6
	U.S. National	....	12	4	3	7	16	....	....	....	....	....
	U.S. Olympic	....	8	2	0	2	6	....	....	....	....	....
	Montreal	**NHL**	....	....	....	....	....	**4**	**1**	**0**	**1**	**2**
1992-93	**Montreal**	**NHL**	**31**	**2**	**6**	**8**	**54**	**3**	**0**	**0**	**0**	**4** ♦
	Fredericton	AHL	6	1	3	4	10	....	....	....	....	....
1993-94	**Anaheim**	**NHL**	**68**	**7**	**20**	**27**	**78**	....	....	....	....	....
1994-95	**Ottawa**	**NHL**	**45**	**1**	**14**	**15**	**30**	....	....	....	....	....
1995-96	**Ottawa**	**NHL**	**80**	**7**	**14**	**21**	**94**	....	....	....	....	....
1996-97	**Ottawa**	**NHL**	**5**	**0**	**0**	**0**	**4**	....	....	....	....	....
	NHL Totals		**229**	**17**	**54**	**71**	**260**	**8**	**1**	**0**	**1**	**6**

a WCHA Second All-Star Team (1990, 1991)
b NCAA West Second All-American Team (1991)

Claimed by **Anaheim** from **Montreal** in Expansion Draft, June 24, 1993. Traded to **Ottawa** by **Anaheim** with Anaheim's ninth round choice (Frederic Cassivi) in 1994 Entry Draft for Ottawa's third round choice (later traded to Tampa Bay — Tampa Bay selected Vadim Epanchintsev) in 1994 Entry Draft, June 29, 1994.

HINOTE, DAN — COL.

Right wing. Shoots right. 6', 187 lbs. Born, Leesburg, FL, January 30, 1977.
(Colorado's 9th choice, 167th overall, in 1996 Entry Draft).

			Regular Season					Playoffs				
Season	Club	Lea	GP	G	A	TP	PIM	GP	G	A	TP	PIM
1995-96	Army	NCAA	33	20	24	44	20	....	....	....	....	....
1996-97	Army	NCAA	34	21	24	45	22	....	....	....	....	....

HIRVONEN, TOMI — (HIHR-voh-nehn) COL.

Center. Shoots left. 5'11", 180 lbs. Born, Tampere, Finland, January 11, 1977.
(Colorado's 8th choice, 207th overall, in 1995 Entry Draft).

			Regular Season					Playoffs				
Season	Club	Lea	GP	G	A	TP	PIM	GP	G	A	TP	PIM
1995-96	Ilves	Fin. Jr.	12	7	12	19	45	....	....	....	....	....
	Koo-Vee	Fin. 2	7	4	1	5	26	....	....	....	....	....
	Ilves	Fin.	28	1	0	1	24	....	....	....	....	....
1996-97	Ilves	Fin.	40	0	7	7	22	6	0	0	0	4

HLAVAC, JAN — (huh-LAH-vahch, YAHN) NYI

Left wing. Shoots left. 6', 183 lbs. Born, Prague, Czech., September 20, 1976.
(NY Islanders' 2nd choice, 28th overall, in 1995 Entry Draft).

			Regular Season					Playoffs				
Season	Club	Lea	GP	G	A	TP	PIM	GP	G	A	TP	PIM
1993-94	HC Sparta	Czech.	9	1	1	2	....	....	....	....	....	....
1994-95	HC Sparta	Czech.	38	7	6	13	18	5	0	2	2	0
1995-96	HC Sparta	Czech.	34	8	5	13	....	12	1	2	3	....
1996-97	HC Sparta	Czech.	38	8	13	21	24	10	5	2	7	2

HLUSHKO, TODD — (huh-LUSH-koh) CGY.

Center. Shoots left. 5'11", 185 lbs. Born, Toronto, Ont., February 7, 1970.
(Washington's 14th choice, 240th overall, in 1989 Entry Draft).

			Regular Season					Playoffs				
Season	Club	Lea	GP	G	A	TP	PIM	GP	G	A	TP	PIM
1988-89	Guelph	OHL	66	28	18	46	71	7	5	3	8	18
1989-90	Owen Sound	OHL	25	9	17	26	31	....	....	....	....	....
	London	OHL	40	27	17	44	39	6	2	4	6	10
1990-91	Baltimore	AHL	66	9	14	23	55	....	....	....	....	....
1991-92	Baltimore	AHL	74	16	35	51	113	....	....	....	....	....
1992-93	Cdn. National	....	58	22	26	48	10	....	....	....	....	....
1993-94	Cdn. National	....	55	22	6	28	61	....	....	....	....	....
	Cdn. Olympic	....	8	5	0	5	6	....	....	....	....	....
	Philadelphia	**NHL**	**2**	**1**	**0**	**1**	**0**	....	....	....	....	....
	Hershey	AHL	9	6	0	6	4	6	2	1	3	4
1994-95	Saint John	AHL	46	22	10	32	36	4	2	2	4	22
	Calgary	**NHL**	**2**	**0**	**1**	**1**	**2**	**1**	**0**	**0**	**0**	**2**
1995-96	**Calgary**	**NHL**	**4**	**0**	**0**	**0**	**6**	....	....	....	....	....
	Saint John	AHL	35	14	13	27	70	16	8	1	9	26
1996-97	**Calgary**	**NHL**	**58**	**7**	**11**	**18**	**49**	....	....	....	....	....
	NHL Totals		**66**	**8**	**12**	**20**	**57**	**1**	**0**	**0**	**0**	**2**

Signed as a free agent by **Philadelphia**, March 7, 1994. Signed as a free agent by **Calgary**, June 17, 1994.

HOCKING, JUSTIN — OTT.

Defense. Shoots right. 6'4", 205 lbs. Born, Stettler, Alta., January 9, 1974.
(Los Angeles' 1st choice, 39th overall, in 1992 Entry Draft).

			Regular Season					Playoffs				
Season	Club	Lea	GP	G	A	TP	PIM	GP	G	A	TP	PIM
1991-92	Spokane	WHL	71	4	6	10	309	10	0	3	3	28
1992-93	Spokane	WHL	16	0	1	1	75	....	....	....	....	....
	Medicine Hat	WHL	54	1	9	10	119	10	0	1	1	13
1993-94	**Los Angeles**	**NHL**	**1**	**0**	**0**	**0**	**0**	....	....	....	....	....
a	Medicine Hat	WHL	68	7	26	33	236	3	0	0	0	6
	Phoenix	IHL	3	0	0	0	15	....	....	....	....	....
1994-95	Syracuse	AHL	7	0	0	0	24	....	....	....	....	....
	Portland	AHL	9	0	1	1	34	....	....	....	....	....
	Knoxville	ECHL	20	0	6	6	70	4	0	0	0	26
	Phoenix	IHL	20	1	1	2	50	1	0	0	0	0
1995-96	P.E.I.	AHL	74	4	8	12	251	4	0	2	2	5
1996-97	Worcester	AHL	68	1	10	11	198	5	0	3	3	2
	NHL Totals		**1**	**0**	**0**	**0**	**0**	....	....	....	....	....

a WHL East Second All-Star Team (1994)

Claimed by **Ottawa** from **Los Angeles** in NHL Waiver Draft, October 2, 1995.

HOGAN, PETER — L.A.

Defense. Shoots right. 6'2", 167 lbs. Born, Oshawa, Ont., January 10, 1978.
(Los Angeles' 7th choice, 123rd overall, in 1996 Entry Draft).

			Regular Season					Playoffs				
Season	Club	Lea	GP	G	A	TP	PIM	GP	G	A	TP	PIM
1995-96	Oshawa	OHL	66	3	25	28	54	5	2	0	2	2
1996-97	Oshawa	OHL	65	13	37	50	56	18	1	11	12	22

HOGARDH, PETER — (HOH-gahrd) NYI

Center. Shoots left. 5'10", 183 lbs. Born, Snotorp, Sweden, May 25, 1976.
(NY Islanders' 9th choice, 203rd overall, in 1994 Entry Draft).

			Regular Season					Playoffs				
Season	Club	Lea	GP	G	A	TP	PIM	GP	G	A	TP	PIM
1993-94	V. Frolunda	Swe.	16	1	0	1	2	....	....	....	....	....
1994-95	V. Frolunda	Swe.	4	0	0	0	0	....	....	....	....	....
	V. Frolunda	Swe. 2	13	1	4	5	4	....	....	....	....	....
1995-96	V. Frolunda	Swe.	27	0	2	2	6	....	....	....	....	....
1996-97	Kiekko-Espoo	Fin.	20	6	6	12	10	4	4	1	5	0
	Lukko	Fin.	11	0	1	1	0	....	....	....	....	....

HOGLUND, JONAS — CGY.

Left wing. Shoots right. 6'3", 200 lbs. Born, Hammaro, Swe., August 29, 1972.
(Calgary's 11th choice, 222nd overall, in 1992 Entry Draft).

			Regular Season					Playoffs				
Season	Club	Lea	GP	G	A	TP	PIM	GP	G	A	TP	PIM
1988-89	Farjestad	Swe.	1	0	0	0	0	....	....	....	....	....
1989-90	Farjestad	Swe.	1	0	0	0	0	....	....	....	....	....
1990-91	Farjestad	Swe.	40	5	5	10	4	8	1	0	1	0
1991-92	Farjestad	Swe.	40	14	11	25	6	6	2	4	6	2
1992-93	Farjestad	Swe.	40	13	13	26	14	3	1	0	1	0
1993-94	Farjestad	Swe.	22	7	2	9	10	....	....	....	....	....
1994-95	Farjestad	Swe.	40	14	12	26	16	4	3	2	5	0
1995-96	Farjestad	Swe.	40	32	11	43	18	8	2	1	3	6
1996-97	**Calgary**	**NHL**	**68**	**19**	**16**	**35**	**12**	....	....	....	....	....
	NHL Totals		**68**	**19**	**16**	**35**	**12**	....	....	....	....	....

HOGUE, BENOIT — (HOHG) DAL.

Center. Shoots left. 5'10", 194 lbs. Born, Repentigny, Que., October 28, 1966.
(Buffalo's 2nd choice, 35th overall, in 1985 Entry Draft).

			Regular Season					Playoffs				
Season	Club	Lea	GP	G	A	TP	PIM	GP	G	A	TP	PIM
1983-84	St-Jean	QMJHL	59	14	11	25	42	....	....	....	....	....
1984-85	St-Jean	QMJHL	63	46	44	90	92	....	....	....	....	....
1985-86	St-Jean	QMJHL	65	54	54	108	115	9	6	4	10	26
1986-87	Rochester	AHL	52	14	20	34	52	12	5	4	9	8
1987-88	**Buffalo**	**NHL**	**3**	**1**	**1**	**2**	**0**	....	....	....	....	....
	Rochester	AHL	62	24	31	55	141	7	6	1	7	46
1988-89	**Buffalo**	**NHL**	**69**	**14**	**30**	**44**	**120**	**5**	**0**	**0**	**0**	**17**
1989-90	**Buffalo**	**NHL**	**45**	**11**	**7**	**18**	**79**	**3**	**0**	**0**	**0**	**10**
1990-91	**Buffalo**	**NHL**	**76**	**19**	**28**	**47**	**76**	**5**	**3**	**1**	**4**	**10**
1991-92	**Buffalo**	**NHL**	**3**	**0**	**1**	**1**	**0**	....	....	....	....	....
	NY Islanders	**NHL**	**72**	**30**	**45**	**75**	**67**	....	....	....	....	....
1992-93	**NY Islanders**	**NHL**	**70**	**33**	**42**	**75**	**108**	**18**	**6**	**6**	**12**	**31**
1993-94	**NY Islanders**	**NHL**	**83**	**36**	**33**	**69**	**73**	**4**	**0**	**1**	**1**	**4**
1994-95	**NY Islanders**	**NHL**	**33**	**6**	**4**	**10**	**34**	....	....	....	....	....
	Toronto	**NHL**	**12**	**3**	**3**	**6**	**0**	**7**	**0**	**0**	**0**	**6**
1995-96	**Toronto**	**NHL**	**44**	**12**	**25**	**37**	**68**	....	....	....	....	....
	Dallas	**NHL**	**34**	**7**	**20**	**27**	**36**	....	....	....	....	....
1996-97	**Dallas**	**NHL**	**73**	**19**	**24**	**43**	**54**	**7**	**2**	**2**	**4**	**6**
	NHL Totals		**617**	**191**	**263**	**454**	**715**	**49**	**11**	**10**	**21**	**84**

Traded to **NY Islanders** by **Buffalo** with Pierre Turgeon, Uwe Krupp and Dave McLlwain for Pat Lafontaine, Randy Hillier, Randy Wood and NY Islanders' fourth round choice (Dean Melanson) in 1992 Entry Draft, October 25, 1991. Traded to **Toronto** by **NY Islanders** with NY Islanders' third round choice (Ryan Pepperall) in 1995 Entry Draft and fifth round choice (Brandon Sugden) in 1996 Entry Draft for Eric Fichaud, April 6, 1995. Traded to **Dallas** by **Toronto** with Randy Wood for Dave Gagner and Dallas' sixth round choice (Dmitriy Yakushin) in 1996 Entry Draft, January 29, 1996.

HOHENBERGER, MARTIN — MTL.

Left wing. Shoots left. 6'1", 205 lbs. Born, Villach, Austria, January 29, 1977.
(Montreal's 3rd choice, 74th overall, in 1995 Entry Draft).

			Regular Season					Playoffs				
Season	Club	Lea	GP	G	A	TP	PIM	GP	G	A	TP	PIM
1993-94	Victoria	WHL	61	3	13	16	82	....	....	....	....	....
1994-95	Prince George	WHL	47	10	21	31	81	....	....	....	....	....
1995-96	Prince George	WHL	37	10	19	29	19	....	....	....	....	....
	Lethbridge	WHL	20	5	1	6	21	4	0	3	3	4
1996-97	Lethbridge	WHL	57	26	33	59	74	19	7	13	20	15

HOLDEN, JOSH — VAN.

Center. Shoots left. 5'11", 187 lbs. Born, Calgary, Alta., January 18, 1978.
(Vancouver's 1st choice, 12th overall, in 1996 Entry Draft).

			Regular Season					Playoffs				
Season	Club	Lea	GP	G	A	TP	PIM	GP	G	A	TP	PIM
1994-95	Regina	WHL	62	20	23	43	45	4	3	1	4	0
1995-96	Regina	WHL	70	57	55	112	105	11	4	5	9	23
1996-97	Regina	WHL	58	49	49	98	148	5	3	2	5	10

HOLIK, BOBBY (HOH-leek) N.J.

Left wing. Shoots right. 6'3", 220 lbs. Born, Jihlava, Czech., January 1, 1971.
(Hartford's 1st choice, 10th overall, in 1989 Entry Draft).

			Regular Season					Playoffs				
Season	Club	Lea	GP	G	A	TP	PIM	GP	G	A	TP	PIM
1987-88	Dukla Jihlava	Czech.	31	5	9	14	16	....	....	....	....	....
1988-89	Dukla Jihlava	Czech.	24	7	10	17	32	....	....	....	....	....
1989-90	Dukla Jihlava	Czech.	42	15	26	41	....	....	....	....	....	....
1990-91	**Hartford**	**NHL**	**78**	**21**	**22**	**43**	**113**	**6**	**0**	**0**	**0**	**7**
1991-92	**Hartford**	**NHL**	**76**	**21**	**24**	**45**	**44**	**7**	**0**	**1**	**1**	**6**
1992-93	**New Jersey**	**NHL**	**61**	**20**	**19**	**39**	**76**	**5**	**1**	**1**	**2**	**6**
	Utica	AHL	1	0	0	0	2	....	....	....	....	....
1993-94	**New Jersey**	**NHL**	**70**	**13**	**20**	**33**	**72**	**20**	**0**	**3**	**3**	**6**
1994-95	**New Jersey**	**NHL**	**48**	**10**	**10**	**20**	**18**	**20**	**4**	**4**	**8**	**22 ♦**
1995-96	**New Jersey**	**NHL**	**63**	**13**	**17**	**30**	**58**	....	....	....	....	....
1996-97	**New Jersey**	**NHL**	**82**	**23**	**39**	**62**	**54**	**10**	**2**	**3**	**5**	**4**
	NHL Totals		**478**	**121**	**151**	**272**	**435**	**68**	**7**	**12**	**19**	**51**

Traded to **New Jersey** by **Hartford** with Hartford's second round choice (Jay Pandolfo) in 1993 Entry Draft and future considerations for Sean Burke and Eric Weinrich, August 28, 1992.

HOLLAND, JASON NYI

Defense. Shoots right. 6'2", 193 lbs. Born, Morinville, Alta., April 30, 1976.
(NY Islanders' 2nd choice, 38th overall, in 1994 Entry Draft).

			Regular Season					Playoffs				
Season	Club	Lea	GP	G	A	TP	PIM	GP	G	A	TP	PIM
1992-93	Kamloops	WHL	4	0	0	0	2	....	....	....	....	....
1993-94	Kamloops	WHL	59	14	15	29	80	18	2	3	5	4
1994-95	Kamloops	WHL	71	9	32	41	65	21	2	7	9	9
1995-96a	Kamloops	WHL	63	24	33	57	98	16	4	9	13	22
1996-97	**NY Islanders**	**NHL**	**4**	**1**	**0**	**1**	**0**	....	....	....	....	....
	Kentucky	AHL	72	14	25	39	46	4	0	2	2	0
	NHL Totals		**4**	**1**	**0**	**1**	**0**	....	....	....	....	....

a WHL West First All-Star Team (1996)

HOLLINGER, TERRY ST.L.

Defense. Shoots left. 6'1", 200 lbs. Born, Regina, Sask., February 24, 1971.
(St. Louis' 7th choice, 153rd overall, in 1991 Entry Draft).

			Regular Season					Playoffs				
Season	Club	Lea	GP	G	A	TP	PIM	GP	G	A	TP	PIM
1987-88	Regina	WHL	7	1	1	2	4	....	....	....	....	....
1988-89	Regina	WHL	65	2	27	29	49	....	....	....	....	....
1989-90	Regina	WHL	70	14	43	57	40	11	1	3	4	10
1990-91	Regina	WHL	8	1	6	7	6	....	....	....	....	....
	Lethbridge	WHL	62	9	32	41	113	16	3	14	17	22
1991-92	Lethbridge	WHL	65	23	62	85	155	5	1	2	3	13
	Peoria	IHL	1	0	2	2	0	5	0	1	1	0
1992-93	Peoria	IHL	72	2	28	30	67	4	1	1	2	0
1993-94	**St. Louis**	**NHL**	**2**	**0**	**0**	**0**	**0**	....	....	....	....	....
	Peoria	IHL	78	12	31	43	96	6	0	3	3	31
1994-95	Peoria	IHL	69	7	25	32	137	4	2	4	6	8
	St. Louis	**NHL**	**5**	**0**	**0**	**0**	**2**	....	....	....	....	....
1995-96a	Rochester	AHL	62	5	50	55	71	19	3	11	14	12
1996-97b	Rochester	AHL	73	12	51	63	54	10	2	7	9	27
	NHL Totals		**7**	**0**	**0**	**0**	**2**	....	....	....	....	....

a AHL Second All-Star Team (1996)
b AHL First All-Star Team (1997)

Signed as a free agent by **Buffalo**, August 23, 1995. Signed as a free agent by **St. Louis**, July 16, 1997.

HOLMQVIST, MIKAEL (HOHLM-kvihst) ANA.

Center. Shoots left. 6'3", 189 lbs. Born, Stockholm, Sweden, June 8, 1979.
(Anaheim's 1st choice, 18th overall, in 1997 Entry Draft).

			Regular Season					Playoffs				
Season	Club	Lea	GP	G	A	TP	PIM	GP	G	A	TP	PIM
1995-96	Djurgarden	Swe. Jr.	24	7	2	9	4	....	....	....	....	....
1996-97	Djurgarden	Swe. Jr.				UNAVAILABLE						
	Djurgarden	Swe.	9	0	0	0	0	....	....	....	....	....

HOLMSTROM, TOMAS (HOHLM-struhm) DET.

Left wing. Shoots left. 6', 200 lbs. Born, Pitea, Sweden, January 23, 1973.
(Detroit's 9th choice, 257th overall, in 1994 Entry Draft).

			Regular Season					Playoffs				
Season	Club	Lea	GP	G	A	TP	PIM	GP	G	A	TP	PIM
1994-95	Lulea	Swe.	40	14	14	28	56	....	....	....	....	....
1995-96	Lulea	Swe.	34	12	11	23	78	11	6	2	8	22
1996-97	**Detroit**	**NHL**	**47**	**6**	**3**	**9**	**33**	**1**	**0**	**0**	**0**	**0 ♦**
	Adirondack	AHL	6	3	1	4	7	....	....	....	....	....
	NHL Totals		**47**	**6**	**3**	**9**	**33**	**1**	**0**	**0**	**0**	**0**

HOLZINGER, BRIAN (HOHL-zihn-guhr) BUF.

Center. Shoots right. 5'11", 190 lbs. Born, Parma, OH, October 10, 1972.
(Buffalo's 7th choice, 124th overall, in 1991 Entry Draft).

			Regular Season					Playoffs				
Season	Club	Lea	GP	G	A	TP	PIM	GP	G	A	TP	PIM
1991-92	Bowling Green	CCHA	30	14	8	22	36	....	....	....	....	....
1992-93a	Bowling Green	CCHA	41	31	26	57	44	....	....	....	....	....
1993-94	Bowling Green	CCHA	38	22	15	37	24	....	....	....	....	....
1994-95bcd	Bowling Green	CCHA	38	35	33	68	42	....	....	....	....	....
	Buffalo	**NHL**	**4**	**0**	**3**	**3**	**0**	**4**	**2**	**1**	**3**	**2**
1995-96	**Buffalo**	**NHL**	**58**	**10**	**10**	**20**	**37**	....	....	....	....	....
	Rochester	AHL	17	10	11	21	14	19	10	14	24	10
1996-97	**Buffalo**	**NHL**	**81**	**22**	**29**	**51**	**54**	**12**	**2**	**5**	**7**	**8**
	NHL Totals		**143**	**32**	**42**	**74**	**91**	**16**	**4**	**6**	**10**	**10**

a CCHA Second All-Star Team (1993)
b CCHA First All-Star Team (1995)
c NCAA West First All-American Team (1995)
d Won Hobey Baker Memorial Award (Top U.S. Collegiate Player) (1995)

HOPE, JARED TOR.

Center. Shoots left. 6'1", 170 lbs. Born, Camrose, Alta., February 14, 1978.
(Toronto's 14th choice, 230th overall, in 1996 Entry Draft).

			Regular Season					Playoffs				
Season	Club	Lea	GP	G	A	TP	PIM	GP	G	A	TP	PIM
1995-96	Spokane	WHL	5	1	0	1	5	....	....	....	....	....
1996-97	Edmonton	WHL	11	0	4	4	9	....	....	....	....	....

HORACEK, JAN (HOHR-uh-chehk) ST.L.

Defense. Shoots right. 6'3", 198 lbs. Born, Benesov, Czech., May 22, 1979.
(St. Louis' 3rd choice, 98th overall, in 1997 Entry Draft).

			Regular Season					Playoffs				
Season	Club	Lea	GP	G	A	TP	PIM	GP	G	A	TP	PIM
1996-97	Slavia Praha	Czech. Jr.	25	4	14	18	....	....	....	....	....	....
	Slavia Praha	Czech.	9	0	0	0	6	3	0	0	0	0
	HC Beroun	Czech. 2	2	0	0	0	....	....	....	....	....	....

HOSSA, MARIAN (HOH-sah) OTT.

Left wing. Shoots left. 6'1", 185 lbs. Born, Stara Lubovna, Czech., January 12, 1979.
(Ottawa's 1st choice, 12th overall, in 1997 Entry Draft).

			Regular Season					Playoffs				
Season	Club	Lea	GP	G	A	TP	PIM	GP	G	A	TP	PIM
1995-96	Dukla Trencin	Slo. Jr.	53	42	49	91	26	....	....	....	....	....
1996-97	Dukla Trencin	Slovak	46	25	19	44	33	7	5	5	10	....

HOUDA, DOUG (HOO-duh)

Defense. Shoots right. 6'2", 190 lbs. Born, Blairmore, Alta., June 3, 1966.
(Detroit's 2nd choice, 28th overall, in 1984 Entry Draft).

			Regular Season					Playoffs				
Season	Club	Lea	GP	G	A	TP	PIM	GP	G	A	TP	PIM
1982-83	Calgary	WHL	71	5	23	28	99	16	1	3	4	44
1983-84	Calgary	WHL	69	6	30	36	195	4	0	0	0	7
1984-85a	Calgary	WHL	65	20	54	74	182	8	3	4	7	29
1985-86	**Detroit**	**NHL**	**6**	**0**	**0**	**0**	**4**	....	....	....	....	....
	Calgary	WHL	16	4	10	14	60	....	....	....	....	....
	Medicine Hat	WHL	35	9	23	32	80	25	4	19	23	64
1986-87	Adirondack	AHL	77	6	23	29	142	11	1	8	9	50
1987-88	**Detroit**	**NHL**	**11**	**1**	**1**	**2**	**10**	....	....	....	....	....
b	Adirondack	AHL	71	10	32	42	169	11	0	3	3	44
1988-89	**Detroit**	**NHL**	**57**	**2**	**11**	**13**	**67**	**6**	**0**	**1**	**1**	**0**
	Adirondack	AHL	7	0	3	3	8	....	....	....	....	....
1989-90	**Detroit**	**NHL**	**73**	**2**	**9**	**11**	**127**	....	....	....	....	....
1990-91	**Detroit**	**NHL**	**22**	**0**	**4**	**4**	**43**	....	....	....	....	....
	Adirondack	AHL	38	9	17	26	67	....	....	....	....	....
	Hartford	**NHL**	**19**	**1**	**2**	**3**	**41**	**6**	**0**	**0**	**0**	**8**
1991-92	**Hartford**	**NHL**	**56**	**3**	**6**	**9**	**125**	**6**	**0**	**2**	**2**	**13**
1992-93	**Hartford**	**NHL**	**60**	**2**	**6**	**8**	**167**	....	....	....	....	....
1993-94	**Hartford**	**NHL**	**7**	**0**	**0**	**0**	**23**	....	....	....	....	....
	Los Angeles	**NHL**	**54**	**2**	**6**	**8**	**165**	....	....	....	....	....
1994-95	**Buffalo**	**NHL**	**28**	**1**	**2**	**3**	**68**	....	....	....	....	....
1995-96	**Buffalo**	**NHL**	**38**	**1**	**3**	**4**	**52**	....	....	....	....	....
	Rochester	AHL	21	1	6	7	41	19	3	5	8	30
1996-97	**NY Islanders**	**NHL**	**70**	**2**	**8**	**10**	**99**	....	....	....	....	....
	Utah	IHL	3	0	0	0	7	....	....	....	....	....
	NHL Totals		**501**	**17**	**58**	**75**	**991**	**18**	**0**	**3**	**3**	**21**

a WHL East Second All-Star Team (1985)
b AHL First All-Star Team (1988)

Traded to **Hartford** by **Detroit** for Doug Crossman, February 20, 1991. Traded to **Los Angeles** by **Hartford** for Marc Potvin, November 3, 1993. Traded to **Buffalo** by **Los Angeles** for Sean O'Donnell, July 26, 1994. Signed as a free agent by **NY Islanders**, October 26, 1996.

HOUDE, ERIC MTL.

Center. Shoots left. 5'11", 185 lbs. Born, Montreal, Que., December 19, 1976.
(Montreal's 9th choice, 216th overall, in 1995 Entry Draft).

			Regular Season					Playoffs				
Season	Club	Lea	GP	G	A	TP	PIM	GP	G	A	TP	PIM
1993-94	St-Jean	QMJHL	71	16	16	32	14	5	1	1	2	4
1994-95	St-Jean	QMJHL	40	10	13	23	23	....	....	....	....	....
	Halifax	QMJHL	28	13	23	36	8	3	2	1	3	4
1995-96	Halifax	QMJHL	69	40	48	88	35	6	3	4	7	2
1996-97	**Montreal**	**NHL**	**13**	**0**	**2**	**2**	**2**	....	....	....	....	....
	Fredericton	AHL	66	30	36	66	20	....	....	....	....	....
	NHL Totals		**13**	**0**	**2**	**2**	**2**	....	....	....	....	....

HOUGH, MIKE (HUHF) NYI

Left wing. Shoots left. 6'1", 197 lbs. Born, Montreal, Que., February 6, 1963.
(Quebec's 7th choice, 181st overall, in 1982 Entry Draft).

			Regular Season					Playoffs				
Season	Club	Lea	GP	G	A	TP	PIM	GP	G	A	TP	PIM
1981-82	Kitchener	OHL	58	14	24	38	172	14	4	1	5	16
1982-83	Kitchener	OHL	61	17	27	44	156	12	5	4	9	30
1983-84	Fredericton	AHL	69	11	16	27	142	1	0	0	0	7
1984-85	Fredericton	AHL	76	21	27	48	49	6	1	1	2	2
1985-86	Fredericton	AHL	74	21	33	54	68	6	0	3	3	8
1986-87	**Quebec**	**NHL**	**56**	**6**	**8**	**14**	**79**	**9**	**0**	**3**	**3**	**26**
	Fredericton	AHL	10	1	3	4	20	....	....	....	....	....
1987-88	**Quebec**	**NHL**	**17**	**3**	**2**	**5**	**2**	....	....	....	....	....
	Fredericton	AHL	46	16	25	41	133	15	4	8	12	55
1988-89	**Quebec**	**NHL**	**46**	**9**	**10**	**19**	**39**	....	....	....	....	....
	Halifax	AHL	22	11	10	21	87	....	....	....	....	....
1989-90	**Quebec**	**NHL**	**43**	**13**	**13**	**26**	**84**	....	....	....	....	....
1990-91	**Quebec**	**NHL**	**63**	**13**	**20**	**33**	**111**	....	....	....	....	....
1991-92	**Quebec**	**NHL**	**61**	**16**	**22**	**38**	**77**	....	....	....	....	....
1992-93	**Quebec**	**NHL**	**77**	**8**	**22**	**30**	**69**	**6**	**0**	**1**	**1**	**2**
1993-94	**Florida**	**NHL**	**78**	**6**	**23**	**29**	**62**	....	....	....	....	....
1994-95	**Florida**	**NHL**	**48**	**6**	**7**	**13**	**38**	....	....	....	....	....
1995-96	**Florida**	**NHL**	**64**	**7**	**16**	**23**	**37**	**22**	**4**	**1**	**5**	**8**
1996-97	**Florida**	**NHL**	**69**	**8**	**6**	**14**	**48**	**5**	**1**	**0**	**1**	**2**
	NHL Totals		**622**	**95**	**149**	**244**	**646**	**42**	**5**	**5**	**10**	**38**

Traded to **Washington** by **Quebec** for Reggie Savage and Paul MacDermid, June 20, 1993. Claimed by **Florida** from **Washington** in Expansion Draft, June 24, 1993. Signed as a free agent by **NY Islanders**, July 21, 1997.

HOULDER, BILL (HOHL-duhr) S.J.

Defense. Shoots left. 6'2", 211 lbs. Born, Thunder Bay, Ont., March 11, 1967.
(Washington's 4th choice, 82nd overall, in 1985 Entry Draft).

			Regular Season					Playoffs				
Season	Club	Lea	GP	G	A	TP	PIM	GP	G	A	TP	PIM
1984-85	North Bay	OHL	66	4	20	24	37	8	0	0	0	2
1985-86	North Bay	OHL	59	5	30	35	97	10	1	6	7	12
1986-87	North Bay	OHL	62	17	51	68	68	22	4	19	23	20
1987-88	Washington	NHL	30	1	2	3	10	....	....	....	....	....
	Fort Wayne	IHL	43	10	14	24	32	....	....	....	....	....
1988-89	Washington	NHL	8	0	3	3	4	....	....	....	....	....
	Baltimore	AHL	65	10	36	46	50	....	....	....	....	....
1989-90	Washington	NHL	41	1	11	12	28	....	....	....	....	....
	Baltimore	AHL	26	3	7	10	12	7	0	2	2	2
1990-91	Buffalo	NHL	7	0	2	2	4	....	....	....	....	....
a	Rochester	AHL	69	13	53	66	28	15	5	13	18	4
1991-92	Buffalo	NHL	10	1	0	1	8	....	....	....	....	....
	Rochester	AHL	42	8	26	34	16	16	5	6	11	4
1992-93	Buffalo	NHL	15	3	5	8	6	8	0	2	2	4
bc	San Diego	IHL	64	24	48	72	39	....	....	....	....	....
1993-94	Anaheim	NHL	80	14	25	39	40	....	....	....	....	....
1994-95	St. Louis	NHL	41	5	13	18	20	4	1	1	2	0
1995-96	Tampa Bay	NHL	61	5	23	28	22	6	0	1	1	4
1996-97	Tampa Bay	NHL	79	4	21	25	30	....	....	....	....	....
	NHL Totals		372	34	105	139	172	18	1	4	5	8

a AHL First All-Star Team (1991)
b Won Governor's Trophy (Outstanding Defenseman - IHL) (1993)
c IHL First All-Star Team (1993)

Traded to **Buffalo** by **Washington** for Shawn Anderson, September 30, 1990. Claimed by **Anaheim** from **Buffalo** in Expansion Draft, June 24, 1993. Traded to **St. Louis** by **Anaheim** for Jason Marshall, August 29, 1994. Signed as a free agent by **Tampa Bay**, July 26, 1995. Signed as a free agent by **San Jose**, July 16, 1997.

HOULE, JEAN-FRANCOIS (HOOL) MTL.

Left wing. Shoots left. 5'9", 175 lbs. Born, Charlesbourg, Que., January 14, 1975.
(Montreal's 5th choice, 99th overall, in 1993 Entry Draft).

			Regular Season					Playoffs				
Season	Club	Lea	GP	G	A	TP	PIM	GP	G	A	TP	PIM
1993-94	Clarkson	ECAC	34	6	19	25	20	....	....	....	....	....
1994-95	Clarkson	ECAC	34	8	11	19	42	....	....	....	....	....
1995-96	Clarkson	ECAC	38	14	15	29	46	....	....	....	....	....
1996-97	Clarkson	ECAC	37	21	*36	57	40	....	....	....	....	....

HOUSE, BOBBY N.J.

Right wing. Shoots right. 6'1", 200 lbs. Born, Whitehorse, Yukon, January 7, 1973.
(Chicago's 4th choice, 66th overall, in 1991 Entry Draft).

			Regular Season					Playoffs				
Season	Club	Lea	GP	G	A	TP	PIM	GP	G	A	TP	PIM
1989-90	Spokane	WHL	64	18	16	34	74	5	0	0	0	6
1990-91	Spokane	WHL	38	11	19	30	63	....	....	....	....	....
	Brandon	WHL	23	18	7	25	14	....	....	....	....	....
1991-92	Brandon	WHL	71	35	42	77	133	....	....	....	....	....
1992-93a	Brandon	WHL	61	57	39	96	87	4	2	2	4	0
1993-94	Indianapolis	IHL	42	10	8	18	51	....	....	....	....	....
	Flint	ColHL	4	3	3	6	0	....	....	....	....	....
1994-95	Columbus	ECHL	9	11	6	17	2	....	....	....	....	....
	Indianapolis	IHL	26	2	3	5	26	....	....	....	....	....
	Albany	AHL	26	4	7	11	12	8	1	1	2	0
1995-96	Albany	AHL	77	37	49	86	57	4	0	0	0	4
1996-97	Albany	AHL	68	18	16	34	65	16	3	2	5	23

a WHL East Second All-Star Team (1993)

Traded to **New Jersey** by **Chicago** for cash, May 21, 1996.

HOUSLEY, PHIL (HOWZ-lee) WSH.

Defense. Shoots left. 5'10", 185 lbs. Born, St. Paul, MN, March 9, 1964.
(Buffalo's 1st choice, 6th overall, in 1982 Entry Draft).

			Regular Season					Playoffs				
Season	Club	Lea	GP	G	A	TP	PIM	GP	G	A	TP	PIM
1981-82	South St. Paul	HS	22	31	34	65	18	....	....	....	....	....
1982-83a	Buffalo	NHL	77	19	47	66	39	10	3	4	7	2
1983-84	Buffalo	NHL	75	31	46	77	33	3	0	0	0	6
1984-85	Buffalo	NHL	73	16	53	69	28	5	3	2	5	2
1985-86	Buffalo	NHL	79	15	47	62	54	....	....	....	....	....
1986-87	Buffalo	NHL	78	21	46	67	57	....	....	....	....	....
1987-88	Buffalo	NHL	74	29	37	66	96	6	2	4	6	6
1988-89	Buffalo	NHL	72	26	44	70	47	5	1	3	4	2
1989-90	Buffalo	NHL	80	21	60	81	32	6	1	4	5	4
1990-91	Winnipeg	NHL	78	23	53	76	24	....	....	....	....	....
1991-92b	Winnipeg	NHL	74	23	63	86	92	7	1	4	5	0
1992-93	Winnipeg	NHL	80	18	79	97	52	6	0	7	7	2
1993-94	St. Louis	NHL	26	7	15	22	12	4	2	1	3	4
1994-95	Grasshoppers	Switz. 2	10	6	8	14	34	....	....	....	....	....
	Calgary	NHL	43	8	35	43	18	7	0	9	9	0
1995-96	Calgary	NHL	59	16	36	52	22	....	....	....	....	....
	New Jersey	NHL	22	1	15	16	8	....	....	....	....	....
1996-97	Washington	NHL	77	11	29	40	24	....	....	....	....	....
	NHL Totals		1067	285	705	990	638	59	13	38	51	28

a NHL All-Rookie Team (1983)
b NHL Second All-Star Team (1992)

Played in NHL All-Star Game (1984, 1989-93)

Traded to **Winnipeg** by **Buffalo** with Scott Arniel, Jeff Parker and Buffalo's first round choice (Keith Tkachuk) in 1990 Entry Draft for Dale Hawerchuk, Winnipeg's first round choice (Brad May) in 1990 Entry Draft and future considerations, June 16, 1990. Traded to **St. Louis** by **Winnipeg** for Nelson Emerson and Stephane Quintal, September 24, 1993. Traded to **Calgary** by **St. Louis** with St. Louis' second round choice (Steve Begin) in 1996 Entry Draft and second round choice (John Tripp) in 1997 Entry Draft for Al MacInnis and Calgary's fourth round choice (Didier Tremblay) in 1997 Entry Draft, July 4, 1994. Traded to **New Jersey** by **Calgary** with Dan Keczmer for Tommy Albelin, Cale Hulse and Jocelyn Lemieux, February 26, 1996. Signed as a free agent by **Washington**, July 22, 1996.

HRDINA, JAN (rih-DEE-nah) PIT.

Center. Shoots right. 6', 190 lbs. Born, Hradec Kralove, Czech., February 5, 1976.
(Pittsburgh's 4th choice, 128th overall, in 1995 Entry Draft).

			Regular Season					Playoffs				
Season	Club	Lea	GP	G	A	TP	PIM	GP	G	A	TP	PIM
1993-94	Stadion	Czech.	23	1	5	6	....	4	0	1	1	....
1994-95	Seattle	WHL	69	41	59	100	79	4	0	1	1	8
1995-96	Seattle	WHL	30	19	28	47	37	....	....	....	....	....
	Spokane	WHL	18	10	16	26	25	18	5	14	19	49
1996-97	Cleveland	IHL	68	23	31	54	82	13	1	2	3	8

HRKAC, TONY (HUHR-kuhz) DAL.

Center. Shoots left. 5'11", 170 lbs. Born, Thunder Bay, Ont., July 7, 1966.
(St. Louis' 2nd choice, 32nd overall, in 1984 Entry Draft).

			Regular Season					Playoffs				
Season	Club	Lea	GP	G	A	TP	PIM	GP	G	A	TP	PIM
1984-85	North Dakota	WCHA	36	18	36	54	16	....	....	....	....	....
1985-86	Cdn. National	....	62	19	30	49	36	....	....	....	....	....
1986-87abcd	North Dakota	WCHA	48	46	79	125	48	....	....	....	....	....
	St. Louis	NHL	....	....	....	....	....	3	0	0	0	0
1987-88	St. Louis	NHL	67	11	37	48	22	10	6	1	7	4
1988-89	St. Louis	NHL	70	17	28	45	8	4	1	1	2	0
1989-90	St. Louis	NHL	28	5	12	17	8	....	....	....	....	....
	Quebec	NHL	22	4	8	12	2	....	....	....	....	....
	Halifax	AHL	20	12	21	33	4	6	5	9	14	4
1990-91	Quebec	NHL	70	16	32	48	16	....	....	....	....	....
	Halifax	AHL	3	4	1	5	2	....	....	....	....	....
1991-92	San Jose	NHL	22	2	10	12	4	....	....	....	....	....
	Chicago	NHL	18	1	2	3	6	3	0	0	0	2
1992-93efg	Indianapolis	IHL	80	45	*87	*132	70	5	0	2	2	2
1993-94	St. Louis	NHL	36	6	5	11	8	4	0	0	0	0
	Peoria	IHL	45	30	51	81	25	1	1	2	3	0
1994-95	Milwaukee	IHL	71	24	67	91	26	15	4	9	13	16
1995-96	Milwaukee	IHL	43	14	28	42	18	5	1	3	4	4
1996-97	Milwaukee	IHL	81	27	61	88	20	3	1	1	2	2
	NHL Totals		333	62	134	196	74	24	7	2	9	6

a WCHA First All-Star Team (1987)
b NCAA West First All-American Team (1987)
c NCAA All-Tournament Team, Tournament MVP (1987)
d Won 1987 Hobey Baker Memorial Award (Top U.S. Collegiate Player) (1987)
e Won James Gatschene Memorial Trophy (MVP - IHL) (1993)
f Won Leo P. Lamoureux Memorial Trophy (Leading Scorer - IHL) (1993)
g IHL First All-Star Team (1993)

Traded to **Quebec** by **St. Louis** with Greg Millen for Jeff Brown, December 13, 1989. Traded to **San Jose** by **Quebec** for Greg Paslawski, May 31, 1991. Traded to **Chicago** by **San Jose** for future considerations, February 7, 1992. Signed as a free agent by **St. Louis**, July 30, 1993. Signed as a free agent by **Dallas**, August 12, 1997.

HRUSKA, DAVID (huhr-OOSH-kah, dah-VEED) OTT.

Right wing. Shoots right. 6', 189 lbs. Born, Sokolov, Czech., January 8, 1977.
(Ottawa's 6th choice, 131st overall, in 1995 Entry Draft).

			Regular Season					Playoffs				
Season	Club	Lea	GP	G	A	TP	PIM	GP	G	A	TP	PIM
1995-96	Red Deer	WHL	28	14	14	28	6	....	....	....	....	....
	Vsetin	Czech.	5	1	0	1	....	1	0	0	0	....
1996-97	Vsetin	Czech.	20	4	2	6	4	6	2	4	6	0
	Sokolov	Czech. 2	4	3	0	3	....	....	....	....	....	....

HUARD, BILL (HYOO-ahrd) EDM.

Left wing. Shoots left. 6'1", 215 lbs. Born, Welland, Ont., June 24, 1967.

			Regular Season					Playoffs				
Season	Club	Lea	GP	G	A	TP	PIM	GP	G	A	TP	PIM
1986-87	Peterborough	OHL	61	14	11	25	61	12	5	2	7	19
1987-88	Peterborough	OHL	66	28	33	61	132	12	7	8	15	33
1988-89	Carolina	ECHL	40	27	21	48	177	10	7	2	9	70
1989-90	Utica	AHL	27	1	7	8	67	5	0	1	1	33
	Nashville	ECHL	34	24	27	51	212	....	....	....	....	....
1990-91	Utica	AHL	72	11	16	27	359	....	....	....	....	....
1991-92	Utica	AHL	62	9	11	20	233	4	1	1	2	4
1992-93	Boston	NHL	2	0	0	0	0	....	....	....	....	....
	Providence	AHL	72	18	19	37	302	6	3	0	3	9
1993-94	Ottawa	NHL	63	2	2	4	162	....	....	....	....	....
1994-95	Ottawa	NHL	26	1	1	2	64	....	....	....	....	....
	Quebec	NHL	7	2	2	4	13	1	0	0	0	0
1995-96	Dallas	NHL	51	6	6	12	176	....	....	....	....	....
	Michigan	IHL	12	1	1	2	74	....	....	....	....	....
1996-97	Dallas	NHL	40	5	6	11	105	....	....	....	....	....
	NHL Totals		189	16	17	33	520	1	0	0	0	0

Signed as a free agent by **New Jersey**, October 1, 1989. Signed as a free agent by **Boston**, December 4, 1992. Signed as a free agent by **Ottawa**, June 30, 1993. Traded to **Quebec** by **Ottawa** for Mika Stromberg and Colorado's fourth round choice (Kevin Boyd) in 1995 Entry Draft, April 7, 1995. Claimed by **Dallas** from **Colorado** in NHL Waiver Draft, October 2, 1995. Signed as a free agent by **Edmonton**, July 22, 1997.

HUDDY, CHARLIE (HUH-dee)

Defense. Shoots left. 6', 210 lbs. Born, Oshawa, Ont., June 2, 1959.

			Regular Season					Playoffs				
Season	Club	Lea	GP	G	A	TP	PIM	GP	G	A	TP	PIM
1977-78	Oshawa	OHA	59	17	18	35	81	6	2	1	3	10
1978-79	Oshawa	OHA	64	20	38	58	108	5	3	4	7	12
1979-80	Houston	CHL	79	14	34	48	46	6	1	0	1	2
1980-81	Edmonton	NHL	12	2	5	7	6	....	....	....	....	....
	Wichita	CHL	47	8	36	44	71	17	3	11	14	10
1981-82	Edmonton	NHL	41	4	11	15	46	5	1	2	3	14
	Wichita	CHL	32	7	19	26	51	....	....	....	....	....
1982-83a	Edmonton	NHL	76	20	37	57	58	15	1	6	7	10
1983-84	Edmonton	NHL	75	8	34	42	43	12	1	9	10	8 ♦
1984-85	Edmonton	NHL	80	7	44	51	46	18	3	17	20	17 ♦
1985-86	Edmonton	NHL	76	6	35	41	55	7	0	2	2	0
1986-87	Edmonton	NHL	58	4	15	19	35	21	1	7	8	21 ♦
1987-88	Edmonton	NHL	77	13	28	41	71	13	4	5	9	10 ♦
1988-89	Edmonton	NHL	76	11	33	44	52	7	2	0	2	4
1989-90	Edmonton	NHL	70	1	23	24	56	22	0	6	6	11 ♦
1990-91	Edmonton	NHL	53	5	22	27	32	18	3	7	10	10
1991-92	Los Angeles	NHL	56	4	19	23	43	6	1	1	2	10
1992-93	Los Angeles	NHL	82	2	25	27	64	23	1	4	5	12
1993-94	Los Angeles	NHL	79	5	13	18	71	....	....	....	....	....
1994-95	Los Angeles	NHL	9	0	1	1	6	....	....	....	....	....
	Buffalo	NHL	32	2	4	6	36	3	0	0	0	0
1995-96	Buffalo	NHL	52	5	5	10	59	....	....	....	....	....
	St. Louis	NHL	12	0	0	0	6	13	1	0	1	8
1996-97	Buffalo	NHL	1	0	0	0	0	....	....	....	....	....
	Rochester	AHL	63	6	8	14	36	4	0	0	0	0
	NHL Totals		1017	99	354	453	785	183	19	66	85	135

a NHL Plus/Minus Leader (1983)

Signed as a free agent by **Edmonton**, September 14, 1979. Claimed by **Minnesota** from **Edmonton** in Expansion Draft, May 30, 1991. Traded to **Los Angeles** by **Minnesota** with Randy Gilhen, Jim Thomson and NY Rangers' fourth round choice (previously acquired by Minnesota — Los Angeles selected Alexei Zhitnik) in 1991 Entry Draft for Todd Elik, June 22, 1991. Traded to **Buffalo** by **Los Angeles** with Alexei Zhitnik, Robb Stauber and Los Angeles' fifth round choice (Marian Menhart) in 1995 Entry Draft for Philippe Boucher, Denis Tsygurov and Grant Fuhr, February 14, 1995. Traded to **St. Louis** by **Buffalo** with Buffalo's seventh round choice (Daniel Corso) in 1996 Entry Draft for Denis Hamel, March 19, 1996. Signed as a free agent by **Buffalo**, September 26, 1996.

HUDSON, MIKE

Center/Left wing. Shoots left. 6'1", 205 lbs. Born, Guelph, Ont., February 6, 1967.
(Chicago's 6th choice, 140th overall, in 1986 Entry Draft).

			Regular Season					Playoffs				
Season	Club	Lea	GP	G	A	TP	PIM	GP	G	A	TP	PIM
1984-85	Hamilton	OHL	50	10	12	22	13	....	....	....	....	....
1985-86	Hamilton	OHL	7	3	2	5	4	....	....	....	....	....
	Sudbury	OHL	59	35	42	77	20	4	2	5	7	7
1986-87	Sudbury	OHL	63	40	57	97	18	....	....	....	....	....
1987-88	Saginaw	IHL	75	18	30	48	44	10	2	3	5	20
1988-89	**Chicago**	**NHL**	41	7	16	23	20	10	1	2	3	18
	Saginaw	IHL	30	15	17	32	10	....	....	....	....	....
1989-90	**Chicago**	**NHL**	49	9	12	21	56	4	0	0	0	2
1990-91	**Chicago**	**NHL**	55	7	9	16	62	6	0	2	2	8
	Indianapolis	IHL	3	1	2	3	0	....	....	....	....	....
1991-92	**Chicago**	**NHL**	76	14	15	29	92	16	3	5	8	26
1992-93	**Chicago**	**NHL**	36	1	6	7	44	....	....	....	....	....
	Edmonton	**NHL**	5	0	1	1	2	....	....	....	....	....
1993-94	**NY Rangers**	**NHL**	48	4	7	11	47	....	....	....	....	.... ♦
1994-95	**Pittsburgh**	**NHL**	40	2	9	11	34	11	0	0	0	6
1995-96	**Toronto**	**NHL**	27	2	0	2	29	....	....	....	....	....
	St. Louis	**NHL**	32	3	12	15	26	2	0	1	1	4
1996-97	Phoenix	IHL	33	6	9	15	10	....	....	....	....	....
	Phoenix	**NHL**	7	0	0	0	2	....	....	....	....	....
	NHL Totals		416	49	87	136	414	49	4	10	14	64

Traded to **Edmonton** by **Chicago** for Craig Muni, March 22, 1993. Claimed by **NY Rangers** from **Edmonton** in NHL Waiver Draft, October 3, 1993. Claimed by **Pittsburgh** from **NY Rangers** in NHL Waiver Draft, January 18, 1995. Signed as a free agent by **Toronto**, September 22, 1995. Claimed on waivers by **St. Louis** from **Toronto**, January 4, 1996. Signed as a free agent by **Phoenix**, November 12, 1996.

HUFFMAN, KERRY

Defense. Shoots left. 6'2", 200 lbs. Born, Peterborough, Ont., January 3, 1968.
(Philadelphia's 1st choice, 20th overall, in 1986 Entry Draft).

			Regular Season					Playoffs				
Season	Club	Lea	GP	G	A	TP	PIM	GP	G	A	TP	PIM
1985-86a	Guelph	OHL	56	3	24	27	35	20	1	10	11	10
1986-87	**Philadelphia**	**NHL**	9	0	0	0	2	....	....	....	....	....
	Hershey	AHL	3	0	1	1	0	4	0	0	0	0
b	Guelph	OHL	44	4	31	35	20	5	0	2	2	8
1987-88	**Philadelphia**	**NHL**	52	6	17	23	34	2	0	0	0	0
1988-89	**Philadelphia**	**NHL**	29	0	11	11	31	....	....	....	....	....
	Hershey	AHL	29	2	13	15	16	....	....	....	....	....
1989-90	**Philadelphia**	**NHL**	43	1	12	13	34	....	....	....	....	....
1990-91	**Philadelphia**	**NHL**	10	1	2	3	10	....	....	....	....	....
	Hershey	AHL	45	5	29	34	20	7	1	2	3	0
1991-92	**Philadelphia**	**NHL**	60	14	18	32	41	....	....	....	....	....
1992-93	**Quebec**	**NHL**	52	4	18	22	54	3	0	0	0	0
1993-94	**Quebec**	**NHL**	28	0	6	6	28	....	....	....	....	....
	Ottawa	**NHL**	34	4	8	12	12	....	....	....	....	....
1994-95	**Ottawa**	**NHL**	37	2	4	6	46	....	....	....	....	....
1995-96	**Ottawa**	**NHL**	43	4	11	15	63	....	....	....	....	....
	Philadelphia	**NHL**	4	1	1	2	6	6	0	0	0	2
1996-97	Las Vegas	IHL	44	5	19	24	38	3	0	0	0	2
	NHL Totals		401	37	108	145	361	11	0	0	0	2

a Won George Parsons Trophy (Memorial Cup Tournament Most Sportsmanlike Player) (1986)
b OHL First All-Star Team (1987)

Traded to **Quebec** by **Philadelphia** with Peter Forsberg, Steve Duchesne, Mike Ricci, Ron Hextall, Chris Simon, Philadelphia's first round choice in the 1993 (Jocelyn Thibault) and 1994 (later traded to Toronto — later traded to Washington — Washington selected Nolan Baumgartner) — Entry Drafts and cash for Eric Lindros, June 30, 1992. Claimed on waivers by **Ottawa** from **Quebec**, January 15, 1994. Traded to **Philadelphia** by **Ottawa** for future considerations, March 19, 1996.

HUGHES, BRENT

Left wing. Shoots left. 5'11", 195 lbs. Born, New Westminster, B.C., April 5, 1966.

			Regular Season					Playoffs				
Season	Club	Lea	GP	G	A	TP	PIM	GP	G	A	TP	PIM
1983-84	N. Westminster	WHL	67	21	18	39	133	9	2	2	4	27
1984-85	N. Westminster	WHL	64	25	32	57	135	11	2	1	3	37
1985-86	N. Westminster	WHL	71	28	52	80	180	....	....	....	....	....
1986-87	N. Westminster	WHL	8	5	4	9	22	....	....	....	....	....
	Victoria	WHL	61	38	61	99	146	5	4	1	5	8
1987-88	Moncton	AHL	73	13	19	32	206	....	....	....	....	....
1988-89	**Winnipeg**	**NHL**	28	3	2	5	82	....	....	....	....	....
	Moncton	AHL	54	34	34	68	286	10	9	4	13	40
1989-90	**Winnipeg**	**NHL**	11	1	2	3	33	....	....	....	....	....
	Moncton	AHL	65	31	29	60	277	....	....	....	....	....
1990-91	Moncton	AHL	63	21	22	43	144	3	0	0	0	7
1991-92	Baltimore	AHL	55	25	29	54	190	....	....	....	....	....
	Boston	**NHL**	8	1	1	2	38	10	2	0	2	20
	Maine	AHL	12	6	4	10	34	....	....	....	....	....
1992-93	**Boston**	**NHL**	62	5	4	9	191	1	0	0	0	2
1993-94	**Boston**	**NHL**	77	13	11	24	143	13	2	1	3	27
	Providence	AHL	6	2	5	7	4	....	....	....	....	....
1994-95	**Boston**	**NHL**	44	6	6	12	139	5	0	0	0	4
1995-96	**Buffalo**	**NHL**	76	5	10	15	148	....	....	....	....	....
1996-97	**NY Islanders**	**NHL**	51	7	3	10	57	....	....	....	....	....
	Utah	IHL	5	2	2	4	11	....	....	....	....	....
	NHL Totals		357	41	39	80	831	29	4	1	5	53

Signed as a free agent by **Winnipeg**, June 13, 1988. Traded to **Washington** by **Winnipeg** with Craig Duncanson and Simon Wheeldon for Bob Joyce, Tyler Larter and Kent Paynter, May 21, 1991. Traded to **Boston** by **Washington** with future considerations for John Byce and Dennis Smith, February 24, 1992. Claimed By **Buffalo** from **Boston** in NHL Waiver Draft, October 2, 1995. Signed as a free agent by **NY Islanders**, August 9, 1996.

HULBIG, JOE (HUHL-bihg) EDM.

Left wing. Shoots left. 6'3", 215 lbs. Born, Norwood, MA, September 29, 1973.
(Edmonton's 1st choice, 13th overall, in 1992 Entry Draft).

			Regular Season					Playoffs				
Season	Club	Lea	GP	G	A	TP	PIM	GP	G	A	TP	PIM
1992-93	Providence	H.E.	26	3	13	16	22	....	....	....	....	....
1993-94	Providence	H.E.	28	6	4	10	36	....	....	....	....	....
1994-95	Providence	H.E.	37	14	21	35	36	....	....	....	....	....
1995-96	Providence	H.E.	31	14	22	36	56	....	....	....	....	....
1996-97	**Edmonton**	**NHL**	6	0	0	0	0	6	0	1	1	2
	Hamilton	AHL	73	18	28	46	59	16	6	10	16	6
	NHL Totals		6	0	0	0	0	6	0	1	1	2

HULL, BRETT ST.L.

Right wing. Shoots right. 5'10", 201 lbs. Born, Belleville, Ont., August 9, 1964.
(Calgary's 6th choice, 117th overall, in 1984 Entry Draft).

			Regular Season					Playoffs				
Season	Club	Lea	GP	G	A	TP	PIM	GP	G	A	TP	PIM
1984-85	Minn.-Duluth	WCHA	48	32	28	60	24	....	....	....	....	....
1985-86a	Minn.-Duluth	WCHA	42	52	32	84	46	....	....	....	....	....
	Calgary	**NHL**	....	....	....	....	....	2	0	0	0	0
1986-87	**Calgary**	**NHL**	5	1	0	1	0	4	2	1	3	0
bc	Moncton	AHL	67	50	42	92	16	3	2	2	4	2
1987-88	**Calgary**	**NHL**	52	26	24	50	12	....	....	....	....	....
	St. Louis	**NHL**	13	6	8	14	4	10	7	2	9	4
1988-89	**St. Louis**	**NHL**	78	41	43	84	33	10	5	5	10	6
1989-90def	**St. Louis**	**NHL**	80	*72	41	113	24	12	13	8	21	17
1990-91 dfghi	**St. Louis**	**NHL**	78	*86	45	131	22	13	11	8	19	4
1991-92d	**St. Louis**	**NHL**	73	*70	39	109	48	6	4	4	8	4
1992-93	**St. Louis**	**NHL**	80	54	47	101	41	11	8	5	13	2
1993-94	**St. Louis**	**NHL**	81	57	40	97	38	4	2	1	3	0
1994-95	**St. Louis**	**NHL**	48	29	21	50	10	7	6	2	8	0
1995-96	**St. Louis**	**NHL**	70	43	40	83	30	13	6	5	11	10
1996-97	**St. Louis**	**NHL**	77	42	40	82	10	6	2	7	9	2
	NHL Totals		735	527	388	915	272	98	66	48	114	49

a WCHA First All-Star Team (1986)
b AHL First All-Star Team (1987)
c Won Dudley "Red" Garrett Memorial Trophy (Top Rookie - AHL) (1987)
d NHL First All-Star Team (1990, 1991, 1992)
e Won Lady Byng Trophy (1990)
f Won Dodge Ram Tough Award (1990, 1991)
g Won Hart Memorial Trophy (1991)
h Won Lester B. Pearson Award (1991)
i Won ProSet/NHL Player of the Year Award (1991)

Played in NHL All-Star Game (1989, 1990, 1992-94, 1996, 1997)

Traded to **St. Louis** by **Calgary** with Steve Bozek for Rob Ramage and Rick Wamsley, March 7, 1988.

HULL, JODY FLA.

Right wing. Shoots right. 6'2", 195 lbs. Born, Cambridge, Ont., February 2, 1969.
(Hartford's 1st choice, 18th overall, in 1987 Entry Draft).

			Regular Season					Playoffs				
Season	Club	Lea	GP	G	A	TP	PIM	GP	G	A	TP	PIM
1985-86	Peterborough	OHL	61	20	22	42	29	16	1	5	6	4
1986-87	Peterborough	OHL	49	18	34	52	22	12	4	9	13	14
1987-88a	Peterborough	OHL	60	50	44	94	33	12	10	8	18	8
1988-89	**Hartford**	**NHL**	60	16	18	34	10	1	0	0	0	2
1989-90	**Hartford**	**NHL**	38	7	10	17	21	5	0	1	1	2
	Binghamton	AHL	21	7	10	17	6	....	....	....	....	....
1990-91	**NY Rangers**	**NHL**	47	5	8	13	10	....	....	....	....	....
1991-92	**NY Rangers**	**NHL**	3	0	0	0	2	....	....	....	....	....
	Binghamton	AHL	69	34	31	65	28	11	5	2	7	4
1992-93	**Ottawa**	**NHL**	69	13	21	34	14	....	....	....	....	....
1993-94	**Florida**	**NHL**	69	13	13	26	8	....	....	....	....	....
1994-95	**Florida**	**NHL**	46	11	8	19	8	....	....	....	....	....
1995-96	**Florida**	**NHL**	78	20	17	37	25	14	3	2	5	0
1996-97	**Florida**	**NHL**	67	10	6	16	4	5	0	0	0	0
	NHL Totals		477	95	101	196	102	25	3	3	6	4

a OHL Second All-Star Team (1988)

Traded to **NY Rangers** by **Hartford** for Carey Wilson and NY Rangers' third round choice (Mikael Nylander) in the 1991 Entry Draft, July 9, 1990. Traded to **Ottawa** by **NY Rangers** for future considerations, July 28, 1992. Signed as a free agent by **Florida**, August 10, 1993.

HULSE, CALE (HULS) CGY.

Defense. Shoots right. 6'3", 210 lbs. Born, Edmonton, Alta., November 10, 1973.
(New Jersey's 3rd choice, 66th overall, in 1992 Entry Draft).

			Regular Season					Playoffs				
Season	Club	Lea	GP	G	A	TP	PIM	GP	G	A	TP	PIM
1991-92	Portland	WHL	70	4	18	22	250	6	0	2	2	27
1992-93	Portland	WHL	72	10	26	36	284	16	4	4	8	65
1993-94	Albany	AHL	79	7	14	21	186	5	0	3	3	11
1994-95	Albany	AHL	77	5	13	18	215	12	1	1	2	17
1995-96	**New Jersey**	**NHL**	8	0	0	0	15	....	....	....	....	....
	Albany	AHL	42	4	23	27	107	....	....	....	....	....
	Calgary	**NHL**	3	0	0	0	5	1	0	0	0	0
	Saint John	AHL	13	2	7	9	39	....	....	....	....	....
1996-97	**Calgary**	**NHL**	63	1	6	7	91	....	....	....	....	....
	NHL Totals		74	1	6	7	111	1	0	0	0	0

Traded to **Calgary** by **New Jersey** with Tommy Albelin and Jocelyn Lemieux for Phil Housley and Dan Keczmer, February 26, 1996.

HUNT, GORDON DET.

Center. Shoots left. 6'5", 200 lbs. Born, Greenwich, CT, July 15, 1975.
(Detroit's 12th choice, 282nd overall, in 1993 Entry Draft).

			Regular Season					Playoffs				
Season	Club	Lea	GP	G	A	TP	PIM	GP	G	A	TP	PIM
1993-94	Ferris State	CCHA	37	2	3	5	42	....	....	....	....	....
1994-95	Ferris State	CCHA	29	8	7	15	47	....	....	....	....	....
1995-96	Ferris State	CCHA	35	12	11	23	62	....	....	....	....	....
1996-97	Ferris State	CCHA	36	12	16	28	73	....	....	....	....	....

HUNTER, DALE — WSH.

Center. Shoots left. 5'10", 198 lbs. Born, Petrolia, Ont., July 31, 1960.
(Quebec's 2nd choice, 41st overall, in 1979 Entry Draft).

			Regular Season					Playoffs				
Season	Club	Lea	GP	G	A	TP	PIM	GP	G	A	TP	PIM
1977-78	Kitchener	OHA	68	22	42	64	115	....	....	....	....	....
1978-79	Sudbury	OHA	59	42	68	110	188	10	4	12	16	47
1979-80	Sudbury	OHA	61	34	51	85	189	9	6	9	15	45
1980-81	**Quebec**	**NHL**	**80**	**19**	**44**	**63**	**226**	**5**	**4**	**2**	**6**	**34**
1981-82	**Quebec**	**NHL**	**80**	**22**	**50**	**72**	**272**	**16**	**3**	**7**	**10**	**52**
1982-83	**Quebec**	**NHL**	**80**	**17**	**46**	**63**	**206**	**4**	**2**	**1**	**3**	**24**
1983-84	**Quebec**	**NHL**	**77**	**24**	**55**	**79**	**232**	**9**	**2**	**3**	**5**	**41**
1984-85	**Quebec**	**NHL**	**80**	**20**	**52**	**72**	**209**	**17**	**4**	**6**	**10**	***97**
1985-86	**Quebec**	**NHL**	**80**	**28**	**42**	**70**	**265**	**3**	**0**	**0**	**0**	**15**
1986-87	**Quebec**	**NHL**	**46**	**10**	**29**	**39**	**135**	**13**	**1**	**7**	**8**	**56**
1987-88	**Washington**	**NHL**	**79**	**22**	**37**	**59**	**240**	**14**	**7**	**5**	**12**	**98**
1988-89	**Washington**	**NHL**	**80**	**20**	**37**	**57**	**219**	**6**	**0**	**4**	**4**	**29**
1989-90	**Washington**	**NHL**	**80**	**23**	**39**	**62**	**233**	**15**	**4**	**8**	**12**	**61**
1990-91	**Washington**	**NHL**	**76**	**16**	**30**	**46**	**234**	**11**	**1**	**9**	**10**	**41**
1991-92	**Washington**	**NHL**	**80**	**28**	**50**	**78**	**205**	**7**	**1**	**4**	**5**	**16**
1992-93	**Washington**	**NHL**	**84**	**20**	**59**	**79**	**198**	**6**	**7**	**1**	**8**	**35**
1993-94	**Washington**	**NHL**	**52**	**9**	**29**	**38**	**131**	**7**	**0**	**3**	**3**	**14**
1994-95	**Washington**	**NHL**	**45**	**8**	**15**	**23**	**101**	**7**	**4**	**4**	**8**	**24**
1995-96	**Washington**	**NHL**	**82**	**13**	**24**	**37**	**112**	**6**	**1**	**5**	**6**	**24**
1996-97	**Washington**	**NHL**	**82**	**14**	**32**	**46**	**125**	....	....	....	....	....
	NHL Totals		**1263**	**313**	**670**	**983**	**3343**	**146**	**41**	**69**	**110**	**661**

Played in NHL All-Star Game (1997)

Traded to **Washington** by **Quebec** with Clint Malarchuk for Gaetan Duchesne, Alan Haworth, and Washington's first round choice (Joe Sakic) in 1987 Entry Draft, June 13, 1987.

HUNTER, TIM

Right wing. Shoots right. 6'2", 202 lbs. Born, Calgary, Alta., September 10, 1960.
(Atlanta's 4th choice, 54th overall, in 1979 Entry Draft).

			Regular Season					Playoffs				
Season	Club	Lea	GP	G	A	TP	PIM	GP	G	A	TP	PIM
1979-80	Seattle	WHL	72	14	53	67	311	12	1	2	3	41
1980-81	Birmingham	CHL	58	3	5	8	*236	....	....	....	....	....
	Nova Scotia	AHL	17	0	0	0	62	6	0	1	1	45
1981-82	**Calgary**	**NHL**	**2**	**0**	**0**	**0**	**9**	....	....	....	....	....
	Oklahoma City	CHL	55	4	12	16	222	....	....	....	....	....
1982-83	**Calgary**	**NHL**	**16**	**1**	**0**	**1**	**54**	**9**	**1**	**0**	**1**	***70**
	Colorado	CHL	46	5	12	17	225	....	....	....	....	....
1983-84	**Calgary**	**NHL**	**43**	**4**	**4**	**8**	**130**	**7**	**0**	**0**	**0**	**21**
1984-85	**Calgary**	**NHL**	**71**	**11**	**11**	**22**	**259**	**4**	**0**	**0**	**0**	**24**
1985-86	**Calgary**	**NHL**	**66**	**8**	**7**	**15**	**291**	**19**	**0**	**3**	**3**	**108**
1986-87	**Calgary**	**NHL**	**73**	**6**	**15**	**21**	***361**	**6**	**0**	**0**	**0**	**51**
1987-88	**Calgary**	**NHL**	**68**	**8**	**5**	**13**	**337**	**9**	**4**	**0**	**4**	**32**
1988-89	**Calgary**	**NHL**	**75**	**3**	**9**	**12**	***375**	**19**	**0**	**4**	**4**	**32** ♦
1989-90	**Calgary**	**NHL**	**67**	**2**	**3**	**5**	**279**	**6**	**0**	**0**	**0**	**4**
1990-91	**Calgary**	**NHL**	**34**	**5**	**2**	**7**	**143**	**7**	**0**	**0**	**0**	**10**
1991-92	**Calgary**	**NHL**	**30**	**1**	**3**	**4**	**167**	....	....	....	....	....
1992-93	**Quebec**	**NHL**	**48**	**5**	**3**	**8**	**94**	....	....	....	....	....
	Vancouver	**NHL**	**26**	**0**	**4**	**4**	**99**	**11**	**0**	**0**	**0**	**26**
1993-94	**Vancouver**	**NHL**	**56**	**3**	**4**	**7**	**171**	**24**	**0**	**0**	**0**	**26**
1994-95	**Vancouver**	**NHL**	**34**	**3**	**2**	**5**	**120**	**11**	**0**	**0**	**0**	**22**
1995-96	**Vancouver**	**NHL**	**60**	**2**	**0**	**2**	**122**	....	....	....	....	....
1996-97	**San Jose**	**NHL**	**46**	**0**	**4**	**4**	**135**	....	....	....	....	....
	NHL Totals		**815**	**62**	**76**	**138**	**3146**	**132**	**5**	**7**	**12**	**426**

Claimed by **Tampa Bay** from **Calgary** in Expansion Draft, June 18, 1992. Traded to **Quebec** by **Tampa Bay** for future considerations (Martin Simard, September 14, 1992), June 19, 1992. Claimed on waivers by **Vancouver** from **Quebec**, February 12, 1993. Signed as a free agent by **San Jose**, July 23, 1996.

HURLBUT, MIKE — BUF.

Defense. Shoots left. 6'2", 200 lbs. Born, Massena, NY, October 7, 1966.
(NY Rangers' 1st choice, 5th overall, in 1988 Supplemental Draft).

			Regular Season					Playoffs				
Season	Club	Lea	GP	G	A	TP	PIM	GP	G	A	TP	PIM
1985-86	St. Lawrence	ECAC	25	2	10	12	40	....	....	....	....	....
1986-87	St. Lawrence	ECAC	35	8	15	23	44	....	....	....	....	....
1987-88	St. Lawrence	ECAC	38	6	12	18	18	....	....	....	....	....
1988-89ab	St. Lawrence	ECAC	36	8	25	33	30	....	....	....	....	....
	Denver	IHL	8	0	2	2	13	4	1	2	3	2
1989-90	Flint	IHL	74	3	34	37	38	3	0	1	1	2
1990-91	San Diego	IHL	2	1	0	1	0	....	....	....	....	....
	Binghamton	AHL	33	2	11	13	27	3	0	1	1	0
1991-92	Binghamton	AHL	79	16	39	55	64	11	2	7	9	8
1992-93	**NY Rangers**	**NHL**	**23**	**1**	**8**	**9**	**16**	....	....	....	....	....
	Binghamton	AHL	45	11	25	36	46	14	2	5	7	12
1993-94	**Quebec**	**NHL**	**1**	**0**	**0**	**0**	**0**	....	....	....	....	....
	Cornwall	AHL	77	13	33	46	100	13	3	7	10	12
1994-95c	Cornwall	AHL	74	11	49	60	69	3	1	0	1	15
1995-96	Minnesota	IHL	22	1	4	5	22	....	....	....	....	....
	Houston	IHL	38	3	12	15	33	....	....	....	....	....
1996-97	Houston	IHL	70	11	24	35	62	13	5	8	13	12
	NHL Totals		**24**	**1**	**8**	**9**	**16**	....	....	....	....	....

a ECAC First All-Star Team (1989)
b NCAA East First All-American Team (1989)
c AHL Second All-Star Team (1995)

Traded to **Quebec** by **NY Rangers** for Alexander Karpovtsev, September 7, 1993. Signed as a free agent by **Buffalo**, August 11, 1997.

HURLEY, MIKE — DAL.

Right wing. Shoots right. 5'11", 173 lbs. Born, Charlottetown, P.E.I., November 17, 1977.
(Dallas' 3rd choice, 90th overall, in 1996 Entry Draft).

			Regular Season					Playoffs				
Season	Club	Lea	GP	G	A	TP	PIM	GP	G	A	TP	PIM
1994-95	Tri-City	WHL	47	2	4	6	10	10	0	1	1	0
1995-96	Tri-City	WHL	65	32	13	45	34	11	0	3	3	6
1996-97	Tri-City	WHL	59	36	22	58	54	....	....	....	....	....

HUSCROFT, JAMIE — (HUHS-krawft) — T.B.

Defense. Shoots right. 6'2", 200 lbs. Born, Creston, B.C., January 9, 1967.
(New Jersey's 9th choice, 171st overall, in 1985 Entry Draft).

			Regular Season					Playoffs				
Season	Club	Lea	GP	G	A	TP	PIM	GP	G	A	TP	PIM
1983-84	Seattle	WHL	63	0	12	12	77	5	0	0	0	15
1984-85	Seattle	WHL	69	3	13	16	273	....	....	....	....	....
1985-86	Seattle	WHL	66	6	20	26	394	5	0	1	1	18
1986-87	Seattle	WHL	21	1	18	19	99	....	....	....	....	....
	Medicine Hat	WHL	35	4	21	25	170	20	0	3	3	*125
1987-88	Utica	AHL	71	5	7	12	316	....	....	....	....	....
	Flint	IHL	3	1	0	1	2	16	0	1	1	110
1988-89	**New Jersey**	**NHL**	**15**	**0**	**2**	**2**	**51**	....	....	....	....	....
	Utica	AHL	41	2	10	12	215	5	0	0	0	40
1989-90	**New Jersey**	**NHL**	**42**	**2**	**3**	**5**	**149**	**5**	**0**	**0**	**0**	**16**
	Utica	AHL	22	3	6	9	122	....	....	....	....	....
1990-91	**New Jersey**	**NHL**	**8**	**0**	**1**	**1**	**27**	**3**	**0**	**0**	**0**	**6**
	Utica	AHL	59	3	15	18	339	....	....	....	....	....
1991-92	Utica	AHL	50	4	7	11	224	....	....	....	....	....
1992-93	Providence	AHL	69	2	15	17	257	2	0	1	1	6
1993-94	**Boston**	**NHL**	**36**	**0**	**1**	**1**	**144**	**4**	**0**	**0**	**0**	**9**
	Providence	AHL	32	1	10	11	157	....	....	....	....	....
1994-95	**Boston**	**NHL**	**34**	**0**	**6**	**6**	**103**	**5**	**0**	**0**	**0**	**11**
1995-96	**Calgary**	**NHL**	**70**	**3**	**9**	**12**	**162**	**4**	**0**	**1**	**1**	**4**
1996-97	**Calgary**	**NHL**	**39**	**0**	**4**	**4**	**117**	....	....	....	....	....
	Tampa Bay	**NHL**	**13**	**0**	**1**	**1**	**34**	....	....	....	....	....
	NHL Totals		**257**	**5**	**27**	**32**	**787**	**21**	**0**	**1**	**1**	**46**

Signed as a free agent by **Boston**, July 23, 1992. Signed as a free agent by **Calgary**, August 22, 1995. Traded to **Tampa Bay** by **Calgary** for Tyler Moss, March 18, 1997.

HUSELIUS, KRISTIAN — (hoo-SAY-lee-oos) — FLA.

Left wing. Shoots left. 6'1", 183 lbs. Born, Stockholm, Sweden, November 10, 1978.
(Florida's 2nd choice, 47th overall, in 1997 Entry Draft).

			Regular Season					Playoffs				
Season	Club	Lea	GP	G	A	TP	PIM	GP	G	A	TP	PIM
1996-97	Farjestad	Swe.	13	2	0	2	4	5	1	0	1	0

HUSKA, RYAN — (HUHS-kuh) — CHI.

Left wing. Shoots left. 6'2", 194 lbs. Born, Cranbrook, B.C., July 2, 1975.
(Chicago's 4th choice, 76th overall, in 1993 Entry Draft).

			Regular Season					Playoffs				
Season	Club	Lea	GP	G	A	TP	PIM	GP	G	A	TP	PIM
1991-92	Kamloops	WHL	44	4	5	9	23	6	0	1	1	0
1992-93	Kamloops	WHL	68	17	15	32	50	13	2	6	8	4
1993-94	Kamloops	WHL	69	23	31	54	66	19	9	5	14	23
1994-95	Kamloops	WHL	66	27	40	67	78	17	7	8	15	12
1995-96	Indianapolis	IHL	28	2	3	5	15	5	1	1	2	27
1996-97	Indianapolis	IHL	80	18	12	30	100	4	0	0	0	4

HUSSEY, MARC — CHI.

Defense. Shoots right. 6'4", 210 lbs. Born, Chatham, N.B., January 22, 1974.
(Pittsburgh's 2nd choice, 43rd overall, in 1992 Entry Draft).

			Regular Season					Playoffs				
Season	Club	Lea	GP	G	A	TP	PIM	GP	G	A	TP	PIM
1990-91	Moose Jaw	WHL	68	5	8	13	67	8	2	2	4	7
1991-92	Moose Jaw	WHL	72	7	27	34	203	4	1	1	2	0
1992-93	Moose Jaw	WHL	68	12	28	40	121	....	....	....	....	....
1993-94	Moose Jaw	WHL	17	4	5	9	33	....	....	....	....	....
	Tri-City	WHL	16	3	6	9	26	....	....	....	....	....
	Medicine Hat	WHL	41	6	24	30	90	3	0	1	1	4
1994-95	St. John's	AHL	11	0	1	1	20	....	....	....	....	....
	Cdn. National	....	36	2	7	9	42	....	....	....	....	....
1995-96	Saint John	AHL	68	10	21	31	120	5	0	0	0	8
1996-97	Saint John	AHL	46	6	18	24	62	....	....	....	....	....
	Utah	IHL	8	0	1	1	6	....	....	....	....	....
	Indianapolis	IHL	14	0	2	2	17	4	0	1	1	10

Signed as a free agent by **Calgary**, March 10, 1996. Traded to **Chicago** by **Calgary** for Ravil Gusmanov, March 18, 1997.

HUTCHINS, TONY — ST.L.

Center. Shoots left. 6', 196 lbs. Born, Wolfeboro, NH, January 11, 1977.
(St. Louis' 9th choice, 203rd overall, in 1996 Entry Draft).

			Regular Season					Playoffs				
Season	Club	Lea	GP	G	A	TP	PIM	GP	G	A	TP	PIM
1995-96	Lawrence Ac.	HS	27	18	20	38	22	....	....	....	....	....
1996-97	Boston College	H.E.	26	8	0	8	10	....	....	....	....	....

IAFRATE, AL — (IGH-uh-FRAY-tee) — S.J.

Defense. Shoots left. 6'3", 235 lbs. Born, Dearborn, MI, March 21, 1966.
(Toronto's 1st choice, 4th overall, in 1984 Entry Draft).

			Regular Season					Playoffs				
Season	Club	Lea	GP	G	A	TP	PIM	GP	G	A	TP	PIM
1983-84a	U.S. National	....	55	4	17	21	26	....	....	....	....	....
	U.S. Olympic	....	6	0	0	0	2	....	....	....	....	....
	Belleville	OHL	10	2	4	6	2	3	0	1	1	5
1984-85	**Toronto**	**NHL**	**68**	**5**	**16**	**21**	**51**	....	....	....	....	....
1985-86	**Toronto**	**NHL**	**65**	**8**	**25**	**33**	**40**	**10**	**0**	**3**	**3**	**4**
1986-87	**Toronto**	**NHL**	**80**	**9**	**21**	**30**	**55**	**13**	**1**	**3**	**4**	**11**
1987-88	**Toronto**	**NHL**	**77**	**22**	**30**	**52**	**80**	**6**	**3**	**4**	**7**	**6**
1988-89	**Toronto**	**NHL**	**65**	**13**	**20**	**33**	**72**	....	....	....	....	....
1989-90	**Toronto**	**NHL**	**75**	**21**	**42**	**63**	**135**	....	....	....	....	....
1990-91	**Toronto**	**NHL**	**42**	**3**	**15**	**18**	**113**	....	....	....	....	....
	Washington	**NHL**	**30**	**6**	**8**	**14**	**124**	**10**	**1**	**3**	**4**	**22**
1991-92	**Washington**	**NHL**	**78**	**17**	**34**	**51**	**180**	**7**	**4**	**2**	**6**	**14**
1992-93a	**Washington**	**NHL**	**81**	**25**	**41**	**66**	**169**	**6**	**6**	**0**	**6**	**4**
1993-94	**Washington**	**NHL**	**67**	**10**	**35**	**45**	**143**	....	....	....	....	....
	Boston	**NHL**	**12**	**5**	**8**	**13**	**20**	**13**	**3**	**1**	**4**	**6**
1994-95			DID NOT PLAY – INJURED									
1995-96			DID NOT PLAY – INJURED									
1996-97	**San Jose**	**NHL**	**38**	**6**	**9**	**15**	**91**	....	....	....	....	....
	NHL Totals		**778**	**150**	**304**	**454**	**1273**	**65**	**18**	**16**	**34**	**67**

a NHL Second All-Star Team (1993)

Played in NHL All-Star Game (1988, 1990, 1993, 1994)

Traded to **Washington** by **Toronto** for Peter Zezel and Bob Rouse, January 16, 1991. Traded to **Boston** by **Washington** for Joe Juneau, March 21, 1994. Traded to **San Jose** by **Boston** for Jeff Odgers and Pittsburgh's fifth round choice (previously acquired by San Jose – Boston selected Elias Abrahamsson) in 1996 Entry Draft, June 21, 1996.

IGINLA, JAROME (ih-GIHN-lah, jah-ROHM) CGY.

Right wing. Shoots right. 6'1", 193 lbs. Born, Edmonton, Alta., July 1, 1977.
(Dallas' 1st choice, 11th overall, in 1995 Entry Draft).

			Regular Season					Playoffs				
Season	Club	Lea	GP	G	A	TP	PIM	GP	G	A	TP	PIM
1993-94	Kamloops	WHL	48	6	23	39	33	19	3	6	9	10
1994-95a	Kamloops	WHL	72	33	38	71	111	21	7	11	18	34
1995-96bc	Kamloops	WHL	63	63	73	136	120	16	16	13	29	44
	Calgary	**NHL**	....	....	....	....	....	**2**	**1**	**1**	**2**	**0**
1996-97d	**Calgary**	**NHL**	**82**	**21**	**29**	**50**	**37**	....	....	....	....	....
	NHL Totals		**82**	**21**	**29**	**50**	**37**	**2**	**1**	**1**	**2**	**0**

a Won George Parsons Trophy (Memorial Cup Tournament Most Sportsmanlike Player) (1995)
b WHL West First All-Star Team (1996)
c Canadian Major Junior First All-Star Team (1996)
d NHL All-Rookie Team (1997)

Traded to **Calgary** by **Dallas** with Corey Millen for Joe Nieuwendyk, December 19, 1995.

IGNATOV, NIKOLAI (ihg-NAH-tahv) T.B.

Defense. Shoots left. 6'2", 200 lbs. Born, Moscow, USSR, April 22, 1978.
(Tampa Bay's 4th choice, 152nd overall, in 1996 Entry Draft).

			Regular Season					Playoffs				
Season	Club	Lea	GP	G	A	TP	PIM	GP	G	A	TP	PIM
1995-96	CSKA 2	CIS 2				UNAVAILABLE						
1996-97	CSKA	Rus. 2	61	2	7	9	22	....	....	....	....	....

INTRANUOVO, RALPH (ihn-trah-NOO-voh) EDM.

Center. Shoots left. 5'8", 185 lbs. Born, East York, Ont., December 11, 1973.
(Edmonton's 5th choice, 96th overall, in 1992 Entry Draft).

			Regular Season					Playoffs				
Season	Club	Lea	GP	G	A	TP	PIM	GP	G	A	TP	PIM
1990-91	S.S. Marie	OHL	63	25	42	67	22	14	7	13	20	17
1991-92	S.S. Marie	OHL	65	50	63	113	44	18	10	14	24	12
1992-93ab	S.S. Marie	OHL	54	31	47	78	61	18	10	16	26	30
1993-94	Cape Breton	AHL	66	21	31	52	39	4	1	2	3	2
1994-95c	Cape Breton	AHL	70	46	47	93	62	....	....	....	....	....
	Edmonton	**NHL**	**1**	**0**	**1**	**1**	**0**	....	....	....	....	....
1995-96	**Edmonton**	**NHL**	**13**	**1**	**2**	**3**	**4**	....	....	....	....	....
	Cape Breton	AHL	52	34	39	73	84	....	....	....	....	....
1996-97	**Toronto**	**NHL**	**3**	**0**	**1**	**1**	**0**	....	....	....	....	....
	Edmonton	**NHL**	**5**	**1**	**0**	**1**	**0**	....	....	....	....	....
c	Hamilton	AHL	68	36	40	76	88	22	8	4	12	30
	NHL Totals		**22**	**2**	**4**	**6**	**4**	....	....	....	....	....

a Memorial Cup All-Star Team (1993)
b Won Stafford Smythe Memorial Trophy (Memorial Cup Tournament MVP) (1993)
c AHL Second All-Star Team (1995, 1997)

Claimed by **Toronto** from **Edmonton** in NHL Waiver Draft, September 30, 1996. Claimed on waivers by **Edmonton** from **Toronto**, October 25, 1996.

IRVING, JOEL MTL.

Center. Shoots right. 6'3", 190 lbs. Born, Lumsden, Sask., January 2, 1976.
(Montreal's 8th choice, 148th overall, in 1994 Entry Draft).

			Regular Season					Playoffs				
Season	Club	Lea	GP	G	A	TP	PIM	GP	G	A	TP	PIM
1994-95	W. Michigan	CCHA	30	2	3	5	20	....	....	....	....	....
1995-96	W. Michigan	CCHA	39	7	6	13	58	....	....	....	....	....
1996-97	W. Michigan	CCHA	34	8	11	19	62	....	....	....	....	....

ISBISTER, BRAD PHO.

Right wing. Shoots right. 6'2", 198 lbs. Born, Edmonton, Alta., May 7, 1977.
(Winnipeg's 4th choice, 67th overall, in 1995 Entry Draft).

			Regular Season					Playoffs				
Season	Club	Lea	GP	G	A	TP	PIM	GP	G	A	TP	PIM
1993-94	Portland	WHL	64	7	10	17	45	10	0	2	2	0
1994-95	Portland	WHL	67	16	20	36	123	....	....	....	....	....
1995-96	Portland	WHL	71	45	44	89	184	7	2	4	6	20
1996-97a	Portland	WHL	24	15	18	33	45	6	2	1	3	16
	Springfield	AHL	7	3	1	4	14	9	1	2	3	10

a WHL West Second All-Star Team (1997)

JACKMAN, RICHARD DAL.

Defense. Shoots right. 6'2", 180 lbs. Born, Toronto, Ont., June 28, 1978.
(Dallas' 1st choice, 5th overall, in 1996 Entry Draft).

			Regular Season					Playoffs				
Season	Club	Lea	GP	G	A	TP	PIM	GP	G	A	TP	PIM
1995-96	S.S. Marie	OHL	66	13	29	42	97	4	1	0	1	15
1996-97	S.S. Marie	OHL	53	13	34	47	116	10	2	6	8	24

JACKSON, DANE NYI

Right wing. Shoots right. 6'1", 200 lbs. Born, Castlegar, B.C., May 17, 1970.
(Vancouver's 3rd choice, 44th overall, in 1988 Entry Draft).

			Regular Season					Playoffs				
Season	Club	Lea	GP	G	A	TP	PIM	GP	G	A	TP	PIM
1988-89	North Dakota	WCHA	30	4	5	9	33	....	....	....	....	....
1989-90	North Dakota	WCHA	44	15	11	26	56	....	....	....	....	....
1990-91	North Dakota	WCHA	37	17	9	26	79	....	....	....	....	....
1991-92	North Dakota	WCHA	39	23	19	42	81	....	....	....	....	....
1992-93	Hamilton	AHL	68	23	20	43	59	....	....	....	....	....
1993-94	**Vancouver**	**NHL**	**12**	**5**	**1**	**6**	**9**	....	....	....	....	....
	Hamilton	AHL	60	25	35	60	75	4	2	2	4	16
1994-95	Syracuse	AHL	78	30	28	58	162	....	....	....	....	....
	Vancouver	**NHL**	**3**	**1**	**0**	**1**	**4**	**6**	**0**	**0**	**0**	**10**
1995-96	**Buffalo**	**NHL**	**22**	**5**	**4**	**9**	**41**	....	....	....	....	....
	Rochester	AHL	50	27	19	46	132	19	4	6	10	53
1996-97	Rochester	AHL	78	24	34	58	111	10	7	4	11	14
	NHL Totals		**37**	**11**	**5**	**16**	**54**	**6**	**0**	**0**	**0**	**10**

Signed as a free agent by **Buffalo**, September 20, 1995. Signed as a free agent by **NY Islanders**, July 21, 1997.

JACQUES, ALEXANDRE DET.

Center. Shoots right. 5'11", 165 lbs. Born, Laval, Que., September 27, 1977.
(Detroit's 6th choice, 162nd overall, in 1996 Entry Draft).

			Regular Season					Playoffs				
Season	Club	Lea	GP	G	A	TP	PIM	GP	G	A	TP	PIM
1994-95	Shawinigan	QMJHL	71	9	8	17	18	14	8	5	13	8
1995-96	Shawinigan	QMJHL	60	25	32	57	57	6	3	2	5	2
1996-97	Shawinigan	QMJHL	70	41	60	101	46	7	3	3	6	2

JAGR, JAROMIR (YAH-guhr) PIT.

Right wing. Shoots left. 6'2", 216 lbs. Born, Kladno, Czech., February 15, 1972.
(Pittsburgh's 1st choice, 5th overall, in 1990 Entry Draft).

			Regular Season					Playoffs				
Season	Club	Lea	GP	G	A	TP	PIM	GP	G	A	TP	PIM
1988-89	Kladno	Czech.	39	8	10	18	4	....	....	....	....	....
1989-90	Kladno	Czech.	51	30	29	59	....	....	....	....	....	....
1990-91a	**Pittsburgh**	**NHL**	**80**	**27**	**30**	**57**	**42**	**24**	**3**	**10**	**13**	**6 ♦**
1991-92	**Pittsburgh**	**NHL**	**70**	**32**	**37**	**69**	**34**	**21**	**11**	**13**	**24**	**6 ♦**
1992-93	**Pittsburgh**	**NHL**	**81**	**34**	**60**	**94**	**61**	**12**	**5**	**4**	**9**	**23**
1993-94	**Pittsburgh**	**NHL**	**80**	**32**	**67**	**99**	**61**	**6**	**2**	**4**	**6**	**16**
1994-95	Kladno	Czech.	11	8	14	22	10	....	....	....	....	....
	Bolzano	Euro.	5	8	8	16	4	....	....	....	....	....
	Bolzano	Italy	1	0	0	0	0	....	....	....	....	....
	Schalke	Ger. 2	1	1	10	11	0	....	....	....	....	....
bc	**Pittsburgh**	**NHL**	**48**	**32**	**38**	***70**	**37**	**12**	**10**	**5**	**15**	**6**
1995-96b	**Pittsburgh**	**NHL**	**82**	**62**	**87**	**149**	**96**	**18**	**11**	**12**	**23**	**18**
1996-97d	**Pittsburgh**	**NHL**	**63**	**47**	**48**	**95**	**40**	**5**	**4**	**4**	**8**	**4**
	NHL Totals		**504**	**266**	**367**	**633**	**371**	**98**	**46**	**52**	**98**	**79**

a NHL/Upper Deck All-Rookie Team (1991)
b NHL First All-Star Team (1995, 1996)
c Won Art Ross Trophy (1995)
d NHL Second All-Star Team (1997)

Played in NHL All-Star Game (1992, 1993, 1996)

JAKOPIN, JOHN FLA.

Defense. Shoots right. 6'5", 220 lbs. Born, Toronto, Ont., May 16, 1975.
(Detroit's 4th choice, 97th overall, in 1993 Entry Draft).

			Regular Season					Playoffs				
Season	Club	Lea	GP	G	A	TP	PIM	GP	G	A	TP	PIM
1993-94	Merrimack	H.E.	36	2	8	10	64	....	....	....	....	....
1994-95	Merrimack	H.E.	37	4	10	14	42	....	....	....	....	....
1995-96	Merrimack	H.E.	32	10	15	25	68	....	....	....	....	....
1996-97	Merrimack	H.E.	31	4	12	16	68	....	....	....	....	....
	Adirondack	AHL	3	0	0	0	9	....	....	....	....	....

Signed as a free agent by **Florida**, May 14, 1997.

JANNEY, CRAIG PHO.

Center. Shoots left. 6'1", 190 lbs. Born, Hartford, CT, September 26, 1967.
(Boston's 1st choice, 13th overall, in 1986 Entry Draft).

			Regular Season					Playoffs				
Season	Club	Lea	GP	G	A	TP	PIM	GP	G	A	TP	PIM
1985-86	Boston College	H.E.	34	13	14	27	8	....	....	....	....	....
1986-87ab	Boston College	H.E.	37	26	55	81	6	....	....	....	....	....
1987-88	U.S. National	....	52	26	44	70	6	....	....	....	....	....
	U.S. Olympic	....	5	3	1	4	2	....	....	....	....	....
	Boston	**NHL**	**15**	**7**	**9**	**16**	**0**	**23**	**6**	**10**	**16**	**11**
1988-89	**Boston**	**NHL**	**62**	**16**	**46**	**62**	**12**	**10**	**4**	**9**	**13**	**21**
1989-90	**Boston**	**NHL**	**55**	**24**	**38**	**62**	**4**	**18**	**3**	**19**	**22**	**2**
1990-91	**Boston**	**NHL**	**77**	**26**	**66**	**92**	**8**	**18**	**4**	**18**	**22**	**11**
1991-92	**Boston**	**NHL**	**53**	**12**	**39**	**51**	**20**	....	....	....	....	....
	St. Louis	**NHL**	**25**	**6**	**30**	**36**	**2**	**6**	**0**	**6**	**6**	**0**
1992-93	**St. Louis**	**NHL**	**84**	**24**	**82**	**106**	**12**	**11**	**2**	**9**	**11**	**0**
1993-94	**St. Louis**	**NHL**	**69**	**16**	**68**	**84**	**24**	**4**	**1**	**3**	**4**	**0**
1994-95	**St. Louis**	**NHL**	**8**	**2**	**5**	**7**	**0**	....	....	....	....	....
	San Jose	**NHL**	**27**	**5**	**15**	**20**	**10**	**11**	**3**	**4**	**7**	**4**
1995-96	**San Jose**	**NHL**	**71**	**13**	**49**	**62**	**26**	....	....	....	....	....
	Winnipeg	**NHL**	**13**	**7**	**13**	**20**	**0**	**6**	**1**	**2**	**3**	**0**
1996-97	**Phoenix**	**NHL**	**77**	**15**	**38**	**53**	**26**	**7**	**0**	**3**	**3**	**4**
	NHL Totals		**636**	**173**	**498**	**671**	**144**	**114**	**24**	**83**	**107**	**53**

a Hockey East First All-Star Team (1987)
b NCAA East First All-American Team (1987)

Traded to **St. Louis** by **Boston** with Stephane Quintal for Adam Oates, February 7, 1992. Acquired by **Vancouver** from **St. Louis** with St. Louis' second round choice (Dave Scathard) in 1994 Entry Draft as compensation for St. Louis' signing of free agent Petr Nedved, March 14, 1994. Traded to **St. Louis** by **Vancouver** for Jeff Brown, Bret Hedican and Nathan Lafayette, March 21, 1994. Traded to **San Jose** by **St. Louis** with cash for Jeff Norton and a conditional choice in 1997 Entry Draft, March 6, 1995. Traded to **Winnipeg** by **San Jose** for Darren Turcotte and Dallas' second round choice (previously acquired by Winnipeg — later traded to Chicago — Chicago selected Remi Royer) in 1996 Entry Draft, March 18, 1996.

JANSSENS, MARK ANA.

Center. Shoots left. 6'3", 212 lbs. Born, Surrey, B.C., May 19, 1968.
(NY Rangers' 4th choice, 72nd overall, in 1986 Entry Draft).

			Regular Season					Playoffs				
Season	Club	Lea	GP	G	A	TP	PIM	GP	G	A	TP	PIM
1984-85	Regina	WHL	70	8	22	30	51	....	....	....	....	....
1985-86	Regina	WHL	71	25	38	63	146	9	0	2	2	17
1986-87	Regina	WHL	68	24	38	62	209	3	0	1	1	14
1987-88	**NY Rangers**	**NHL**	**1**	**0**	**0**	**0**	**0**	....	....	....	....	....
	Colorado	IHL	6	2	2	4	24	12	3	2	5	20
	Regina	WHL	71	39	51	90	202	4	3	4	7	6
1988-89	**NY Rangers**	**NHL**	**5**	**0**	**0**	**0**	**0**	....	....	....	....	....
	Denver	IHL	38	19	19	38	104	4	3	0	3	18
1989-90	**NY Rangers**	**NHL**	**80**	**5**	**8**	**13**	**161**	**9**	**2**	**1**	**3**	**10**
1990-91	**NY Rangers**	**NHL**	**67**	**9**	**7**	**16**	**172**	**6**	**3**	**0**	**3**	**6**
1991-92	**NY Rangers**	**NHL**	**4**	**0**	**0**	**0**	**5**	....	....	....	....	....
	Binghamton	AHL	55	10	23	33	109	....	....	....	....	....
	Minnesota	**NHL**	**3**	**0**	**0**	**0**	**0**	....	....	....	....	....
	Kalamazoo	IHL	2	0	0	0	2	11	1	2	3	22
1992-93	**Hartford**	**NHL**	**76**	**12**	**17**	**29**	**237**	....	....	....	....	....
1993-94	**Hartford**	**NHL**	**84**	**2**	**10**	**12**	**137**	....	....	....	....	....
1994-95	**Hartford**	**NHL**	**46**	**2**	**5**	**7**	**93**	....	....	....	....	....
1995-96	**Hartford**	**NHL**	**81**	**2**	**7**	**9**	**155**	....	....	....	....	....
1996-97	**Hartford**	**NHL**	**54**	**2**	**4**	**6**	**90**	....	....	....	....	....
	Anaheim	**NHL**	**12**	**0**	**2**	**2**	**47**	**11**	**0**	**0**	**0**	**15**
	NHL Totals		**513**	**34**	**60**	**94**	**1097**	**26**	**5**	**1**	**6**	**31**

Traded to **Minnesota** by **NY Rangers** for Mario Thyer and Minnesota's third round choice (Maxim Galanov) in 1993 Entry Draft, March 10, 1992. Traded to **Hartford** by **Minnesota** for James Black, September 3, 1992. Traded to **Anaheim** by **Hartford** for Bates Battaglia and Anaheim's fourth round choice in 1998 Entry Draft, March 18, 1997.

JANTUNEN, MARKO (YAN-too-nehn) CGY.

Center. Shoots left. 5'10", 185 lbs. Born, Lahti, Finland, February 14, 1971.
(Calgary's 12th choice, 239th overall, in 1991 Entry Draft).

			Regular Season					Playoffs				
Season	Club	Lea	GP	G	A	TP	PIM	GP	G	A	TP	PIM
1990-91	Reipas	Fin.	39	9	20	29	20	....	....	....	....	....
1991-92	Reipas	Fin.	42	10	14	24	46	....	....	....	....	....
1992-93	KalPa	Fin.	48	21	27	48	63	....	....	....	....	....
1993-94	TPS	Fin.	48	29	29	58	22	11	2	6	8	12
1994-95	V. Frolunda	Swe.	22	15	8	23	22	....	....	....	....	....
1995-96	V. Frolunda	Swe.	40	17	14	31	66	13	8	8	16	10
1996-97	**Calgary**	**NHL**	**3**	**0**	**0**	**0**	**0**	....	....	....	....	....
	Saint John	AHL	23	8	16	24	18	....	....	....	....	....
	V. Frolunda	Swe.	13	4	7	11	16	3	2	0	2	16
	NHL Totals		**3**	**0**	**0**	**0**	**0**	....	....	....	....	....

JARVIS, WES NYR

Defense. Shoots left. 6'4", 203 lbs. Born, Toronto, Ont., April 16, 1979.
(NY Rangers' 2nd choice, 46th overall, in 1997 Entry Draft).

			Regular Season					Playoffs				
Season	Club	Lea	GP	G	A	TP	PIM	GP	G	A	TP	PIM
1995-96	Gloucester	Jr. A	43	3	6	9	73	....	....	....	....	....
1996-97	Kitchener	OHL	56	4	8	12	108	13	0	4	4	25

JENNINGS, GRANT

Defense. Shoots left. 6'3", 210 lbs. Born, Hudson Bay, Sask., May 5, 1965.

			Regular Season					Playoffs				
Season	Club	Lea	GP	G	A	TP	PIM	GP	G	A	TP	PIM
1983-84	Saskatoon	WHL	64	5	13	18	102	....	....	....	....	....
1984-85	Saskatoon	WHL	47	10	24	34	134	2	1	0	1	2
1985-86	Binghamton	AHL	51	0	4	4	109	....	....	....	....	....
1986-87	Fort Wayne	IHL	3	0	0	0	0	....	....	....	....	....
	Binghamton	AHL	47	1	5	6	125	13	0	2	2	17
1987-88	**Washington**	**NHL**	....	....	....	....	....	**1**	**0**	**0**	**0**	**0**
	Binghamton	AHL	56	2	12	14	195	3	1	0	1	15
1988-89	**Hartford**	**NHL**	**55**	**3**	**10**	**13**	**159**	**4**	**1**	**0**	**1**	**17**
	Binghamton	AHL	2	0	0	0	2	....	....	....	....	....
1989-90	**Hartford**	**NHL**	**64**	**3**	**6**	**9**	**171**	**7**	**0**	**0**	**0**	**13**
1990-91	**Hartford**	**NHL**	**44**	**1**	**4**	**5**	**82**	....	....	....	....	....
	Pittsburgh	**NHL**	**13**	**1**	**3**	**4**	**26**	**13**	**1**	**1**	**2**	**16 ♦**
1991-92	**Pittsburgh**	**NHL**	**53**	**4**	**5**	**9**	**104**	**10**	**0**	**0**	**0**	**12 ♦**
1992-93	**Pittsburgh**	**NHL**	**58**	**0**	**5**	**5**	**65**	**12**	**0**	**0**	**0**	**8**
1993-94	**Pittsburgh**	**NHL**	**61**	**2**	**4**	**6**	**126**	**3**	**0**	**0**	**0**	**2**
1994-95	**Pittsburgh**	**NHL**	**25**	**0**	**4**	**4**	**36**	....	....	....	....	....
	Toronto	**NHL**	**10**	**0**	**2**	**2**	**7**	**4**	**0**	**0**	**0**	**0**
1995-96	**Buffalo**	**NHL**	**6**	**0**	**0**	**0**	**28**	....	....	....	....	....
	Rochester	AHL	9	0	1	1	28	....	....	....	....	....
	Atlanta	IHL	3	0	0	0	19	3	0	0	0	20
1996-97	Quebec	IHL	42	2	10	12	79	....	....	....	....	....
	NHL Totals		**389**	**14**	**43**	**57**	**804**	**54**	**2**	**1**	**3**	**68**

Signed as a free agent by **Washington**, June 25, 1985. Traded to **Hartford** by **Washington** with Ed Kastelic for Mike Millar and Neil Sheehy, July 6, 1988. Traded to **Pittsburgh** by **Hartford** with Ron Francis and Ulf Samuelsson for John Cullen, Jeff Parker and Zarley Zalapski, March 4, 1991. Traded to **Toronto** by **Pittsburgh** for Drake Berehowsky, April 7, 1995. Signed as a free agent by **Buffalo**, September 20, 1995.

JINDRICH, ROBERT (IHN-drihkh) S.J.

Defense. Shoots left. 5'11", 187 lbs. Born, Plzen, Czech., November 14, 1976.
(San Jose's 10th choice, 168th overall, in 1995 Entry Draft).

			Regular Season					Playoffs				
Season	Club	Lea	GP	G	A	TP	PIM	GP	G	A	TP	PIM
1993-94	Plzen	Czech.	18	0	2	2	....	....	....	....	....	....
1994-95	Plzen	Czech.	11	1	0	1	4	....	....	....	....	....
1995-96	Plzen	Czech.	37	1	3	4	....	3	0	0	0	....
1996-97	Plzen	Czech.	49	7	9	16	44	....	....	....	....	....

JINMAN, LEE (JIHN-muhn) DAL.

Center. Shoots right. 5'10", 160 lbs. Born, Toronto, Ont., January 10, 1976.
(Dallas' 2nd choice, 46th overall, in 1994 Entry Draft).

			Regular Season					Playoffs				
Season	Club	Lea	GP	G	A	TP	PIM	GP	G	A	TP	PIM
1993-94	North Bay	OHL	66	31	66	97	33	18	*18	19	37	8
1994-95	North Bay	OHL	63	39	65	104	41	6	5	5	10	4
1995-96	North Bay	OHL	38	19	33	52	23	....	....	....	....	....
	Detroit	OHL	26	10	35	45	26	17	6	15	21	16
1996-97	Michigan	IHL	81	17	40	57	65	4	1	1	2	2

JOHANSSON, ANDREAS (yoh-HAHN-suhn, ahn-DRAY-uhs) PIT.

Center. Shoots left. 6', 205 lbs. Born, Hofors, Sweden, May 19, 1973.
(NY Islanders' 7th choice, 136th overall, in 1991 Entry Draft).

			Regular Season					Playoffs				
Season	Club	Lea	GP	G	A	TP	PIM	GP	G	A	TP	PIM
1990-91	Falun	Swe. 2	31	12	10	22	38	....	....	....	....	....
1991-92	Farjestad	Swe.	30	3	1	4	10	6	0	0	0	4
1992-93	Farjestad	Swe.	38	4	7	11	38	2	0	0	0	0
1993-94	Farjestad	Swe.	20	3	6	9	6	....	....	....	....	....
1994-95	Farjestad	Swe.	36	9	10	19	42	4	0	0	0	10
1995-96	**NY Islanders**	**NHL**	**3**	**0**	**1**	**1**	**0**	....	....	....	....	....
	Worcester	AHL	29	5	5	10	32	....	....	....	....	....
	Utah	IHL	22	4	13	17	28	12	0	5	5	6
1996-97	**NY Islanders**	**NHL**	**15**	**2**	**2**	**4**	**0**	....	....	....	....	....
	Pittsburgh	**NHL**	**27**	**2**	**7**	**9**	**20**	....	....	....	....	....
	Cleveland	IHL	10	2	4	6	42	11	1	5	6	8
	NHL Totals		**45**	**4**	**10**	**14**	**20**	....	....	....	....	....

Traded to **Pittsburgh** by **NY Islanders** with Darius Kasparaitis for Bryan Smolinski, November 17, 1996.

JOHANSSON, CALLE (yoh-HAHN-suhn, KAL-ee) WSH.

Defense. Shoots left. 5'11", 200 lbs. Born, Goteborg, Sweden, February 14, 1967.
(Buffalo's 1st choice, 14th overall, in 1985 Entry Draft).

			Regular Season					Playoffs				
Season	Club	Lea	GP	G	A	TP	PIM	GP	G	A	TP	PIM
1983-84	V. Frolunda	Swe.	28	4	4	8	10	....	....	....	....	....
1984-85	V. Frolunda	Swe.2	25	8	13	21	16	6	1	2	3	4
1985-86	Bjorkloven	Swe.	17	1	2	3	4	....	....	....	....	....
1986-87	Bjorkloven	Swe.	30	2	13	15	20	6	1	3	4	6
1987-88a	**Buffalo**	**NHL**	**71**	**4**	**38**	**42**	**37**	**6**	**0**	**1**	**1**	**0**
1988-89	**Buffalo**	**NHL**	**47**	**2**	**11**	**13**	**33**	....	....	....	....	....
	Washington	**NHL**	**12**	**1**	**7**	**8**	**4**	**6**	**1**	**2**	**3**	**0**
1989-90	**Washington**	**NHL**	**70**	**8**	**31**	**39**	**25**	**15**	**1**	**6**	**7**	**4**
1990-91	**Washington**	**NHL**	**80**	**11**	**41**	**52**	**23**	**10**	**2**	**7**	**9**	**8**
1991-92	**Washington**	**NHL**	**80**	**14**	**42**	**56**	**49**	**7**	**0**	**5**	**5**	**4**
1992-93	**Washington**	**NHL**	**77**	**7**	**38**	**45**	**56**	**6**	**0**	**5**	**5**	**4**
1993-94	**Washington**	**NHL**	**84**	**9**	**33**	**42**	**59**	**6**	**1**	**3**	**4**	**4**
1994-95	Kloten	Switz.	5	1	2	3	8	....	....	....	....	....
	Washington	**NHL**	**46**	**5**	**26**	**31**	**35**	**7**	**3**	**1**	**4**	**0**
1995-96	**Washington**	**NHL**	**78**	**10**	**25**	**35**	**50**	....	....	....	....	....
1996-97	**Washington**	**NHL**	**65**	**6**	**11**	**17**	**16**	....	....	....	....	....
	NHL Totals		**710**	**77**	**303**	**380**	**387**	**63**	**8**	**30**	**38**	**24**

a NHL All-Rookie Team (1988)

Traded to **Washington** by **Buffalo** with Buffalo's second round choice (Byron Dafoe) in 1989 Entry Draft for Clint Malarchuk, Grant Ledyard and Washington's sixth round choice (Brian Holzinger) in 1991 Entry Draft, March 7, 1989.

JOHANSSON, DANIEL (yoh-HAHN-suhn) NYI

Defense. Shoots right. 5'11", 180 lbs. Born, Glimakra, Sweden, September 10, 1974.
(NY Islanders' 9th choice, 222nd overall, in 1993 Entry Draft).

			Regular Season					Playoffs				
Season	Club	Lea	GP	G	A	TP	PIM	GP	G	A	TP	PIM
1991-92	Rogle	Swe. 2	33	4	9	13	30	....	....	....	....	....
1992-93	Rogle	Swe.	28	2	4	6	20	....	....	....	....	....
1993-94	Rogle	Swe.	37	5	10	15	34	3	0	0	0	0
1994-95	Rogle	Swe.	22	4	2	6	16	....	....	....	....	....
1995-96	HV 71	Swe.	40	3	5	8	24	4	0	1	1	0
1996-97	HV 71	Swe.	50	8	7	15	30	5	0	1	1	2

JOHANSSON, MATHIAS (yoh-HAHN-suhn) CGY.

Center. Shoots left. 6'2", 190 lbs. Born, Oskarshamn, Sweden, February 22, 1974.
(Calgary's 3rd choice, 54th overall, in 1992 Entry Draft).

			Regular Season					Playoffs				
Season	Club	Lea	GP	G	A	TP	PIM	GP	G	A	TP	PIM
1990-91	Farjestad	Swe.	3	0	0	0	0	....	....	....	....	....
1991-92	Farjestad	Swe.	16	0	0	0	2	1	0	0	0	0
1992-93	Farjestad	Swe.	11	2	1	3	4	3	0	0	0	0
1993-94	Farjestad	Swe.	16	2	1	3	4	....	....	....	....	....
1994-95	Farjestad	Swe.	40	7	8	15	30	4	4	3	7	2
1995-96	Farjestad	Swe.	40	8	21	29	10	8	2	1	3	4
1996-97	Farjestad	Swe.	48	12	15	27	14	14	4	4	8	12

JOHANSSON, TOBIAS (yoh-HAHN-suhn) ANA.

Left wing. Shoots left. 5'11", 180 lbs. Born, Malmo, Sweden, October 22, 1977.
(Anaheim's 7th choice, 224th overall, in 1996 Entry Draft).

			Regular Season					Playoffs				
Season	Club	Lea	GP	G	A	TP	PIM	GP	G	A	TP	PIM
1995-96	Malmo	Swe. Jr.	30	7	13	20	38	....	....	....	....	....
1996-97	Malmo	Swe. Jr.	15	6	8	14	63	....	....	....	....	....

JOHNSON, ANDY CHI.

Defense. Shoots left. 6'3", 188 lbs. Born, Fredericton, N.B., March 6, 1978.
(Chicago's 4th choice, 130th overall, in 1996 Entry Draft).

			Regular Season					Playoffs				
Season	Club	Lea	GP	G	A	TP	PIM	GP	G	A	TP	PIM
1995-96	Peterborough	OHL	54	0	4	4	57	22	0	6	6	21
1996-97	Peterborough	OHL	57	4	24	28	82	7	1	2	3	10

JOHNSON, CLINT PIT.

Left wing. Shoots left. 6'2", 200 lbs. Born, Duluth, MN, April 7, 1976.
(Pittsburgh's 7th choice, 128th overall, in 1994 Entry Draft).

			Regular Season					Playoffs				
Season	Club	Lea	GP	G	A	TP	PIM	GP	G	A	TP	PIM
1993-94	Duluth-East	HS	28	30	31	61	....	....	....	....	....	....
1994-95	St. Paul	USHL	14	0	3	3	8	....	....	....	....	....
1995-96	U. Minnesota	WCHA	1	0	0	0	0	....	....	....	....	....
1996-97						DID NOT PLAY						

JOHNSON, CRAIG L.A.

Left wing/Center. Shoots left. 6'2", 197 lbs. Born, St. Paul, MN, March 8, 1972.
(St. Louis' 1st choice, 33rd overall, in 1990 Entry Draft).

			Regular Season					Playoffs				
Season	Club	Lea	GP	G	A	TP	PIM	GP	G	A	TP	PIM
1990-91	U. Minnesota	WCHA	33	13	18	31	34	....	....	....	....	....
1991-92	U. Minnesota	WCHA	41	17	38	55	66	....	....	....	....	....
1992-93	U. Minnesota	WCHA	42	22	24	46	70	....	....	....	....	....
1993-94	U.S. National	....	54	25	26	51	64	....	....	....	....	....
	U.S. Olympic	....	8	0	4	4	4	....	....	....	....	....
1994-95	Peoria	IHL	16	2	6	8	25	9	0	4	4	10
	St. Louis	**NHL**	**15**	**3**	**3**	**6**	**6**	**1**	**0**	**0**	**0**	**2**
1995-96	**St. Louis**	**NHL**	**49**	**8**	**7**	**15**	**30**	....	....	....	....	....
	Worcester	AHL	5	3	0	3	2	....	....	....	....	....
	Los Angeles	**NHL**	**11**	**5**	**4**	**9**	**6**	....	....	....	....	....
1996-97	**Los Angeles**	**NHL**	**31**	**4**	**3**	**7**	**26**	....	....	....	....	....
	NHL Totals		**106**	**20**	**17**	**37**	**68**	**1**	**0**	**0**	**0**	**2**

Traded to **Los Angeles** by **St. Louis** with Patrice Tardif, Roman Vopat, St. Louis fifth round choice (Peter Hogan) in 1996 Entry Draft and first round choice (Matt Zultek) in 1997 Entry Draft for Wayne Gretzky, February 27, 1996.

JOHNSON, GREG — PIT.

Center. Shoots left. 5'10", 185 lbs. Born, Thunder Bay, Ont., March 16, 1971.
(Philadelphia's 1st choice, 33rd overall, in 1989 Entry Draft).

			Regular Season					Playoffs				
Season	Club	Lea	GP	G	A	TP	PIM	GP	G	A	TP	PIM
1989-90	North Dakota	WCHA	44	17	38	55	11	....	....	....	....	....
1990-91ab	North Dakota	WCHA	38	18	*61	79	6	....	....	....	....	....
1991-92ac	North Dakota	WCHA	39	20	*54	74	8	....	....	....	....	....
1992-93ab	North Dakota	WCHA	34	19	45	64	18	....	....	....	....	....
	Cdn. National	....	23	6	14	20	2	....	....	....	....	....
1993-94	**Detroit**	**NHL**	**52**	**6**	**11**	**17**	**22**	**7**	**2**	**2**	**4**	**2**
	Cdn. National	....	6	2	6	8	4	....	....	....	....	....
	Cdn. Olympic	....	8	0	3	3	0	....	....	....	....	....
	Adirondack	AHL	3	2	4	6	0	4	0	4	4	2
1994-95	**Detroit**	**NHL**	**22**	**3**	**5**	**8**	**14**	**1**	**0**	**0**	**0**	**0**
1995-96	**Detroit**	**NHL**	**60**	**18**	**22**	**40**	**30**	**13**	**3**	**1**	**4**	**8**
1996-97	**Detroit**	**NHL**	**43**	**6**	**10**	**16**	**12**	....	....	....	....	....
	Pittsburgh	**NHL**	**32**	**7**	**9**	**16**	**14**	**5**	**1**	**0**	**1**	**2**
	NHL Totals		**209**	**40**	**57**	**97**	**92**	**26**	**6**	**3**	**9**	**12**

a WCHA First All-Star Team (1991, 1993)
b NCAA West First All-American Team (1991, 1993)
c NCAA West Second All-American Team (1992)

Traded to **Detroit** by **Philadelphia** with Philadelphia's fifth round choice (Frederic Deschenes) in 1994 Entry Draft for Jim Cummins and Philadelphia's fourth round choice (previously acquired by Detroit — later traded to Boston — Boston selected Charles Paquette) in 1993 Entry Draft, June 20, 1993. Traded to **Pittsburgh** by **Detroit** for Tomas Sandstrom, January 27, 1997.

JOHNSON, JIM — PHO.

Defense. Shoots left. 6'1", 190 lbs. Born, New Hope, MN, August 9, 1962.

			Regular Season					Playoffs				
Season	Club	Lea	GP	G	A	TP	PIM	GP	G	A	TP	PIM
1981-82	Minn.-Duluth	WCHA	40	0	10	10	62	....	....	....	....	....
1982-83	Minn.-Duluth	WCHA	44	3	18	21	118	....	....	....	....	....
1983-84	Minn.-Duluth	WCHA	43	3	13	16	116	....	....	....	....	....
1984-85	Minn.-Duluth	WCHA	47	7	29	36	49	....	....	....	....	....
1985-86	**Pittsburgh**	**NHL**	**80**	**3**	**26**	**29**	**115**	....	....	....	....	....
1986-87	**Pittsburgh**	**NHL**	**80**	**5**	**25**	**30**	**116**	....	....	....	....	....
1987-88	**Pittsburgh**	**NHL**	**55**	**1**	**12**	**13**	**87**	....	....	....	....	....
1988-89	**Pittsburgh**	**NHL**	**76**	**2**	**14**	**16**	**163**	**11**	**0**	**5**	**5**	**44**
1989-90	**Pittsburgh**	**NHL**	**75**	**3**	**13**	**16**	**154**	....	....	....	....	....
1990-91	**Pittsburgh**	**NHL**	**24**	**0**	**5**	**5**	**23**	....	....	....	....	....
	Minnesota	**NHL**	**44**	**1**	**9**	**10**	**100**	**14**	**0**	**1**	**1**	**52**
1991-92	**Minnesota**	**NHL**	**71**	**4**	**10**	**14**	**102**	**7**	**1**	**3**	**4**	**18**
1992-93	**Minnesota**	**NHL**	**79**	**3**	**20**	**23**	**105**	....	....	....	....	....
1993-94	**Dallas**	**NHL**	**53**	**0**	**7**	**7**	**51**	....	....	....	....	....
	Washington	**NHL**	**8**	**0**	**0**	**0**	**12**	....	....	....	....	....
1994-95	**Washington**	**NHL**	**47**	**0**	**13**	**13**	**43**	**7**	**0**	**2**	**2**	**8**
1995-96	**Washington**	**NHL**	**66**	**2**	**4**	**6**	**34**	**6**	**0**	**0**	**0**	**6**
1996-97	**Phoenix**	**NHL**	**55**	**3**	**7**	**10**	**74**	**6**	**0**	**0**	**0**	**4**
	NHL Totals		**813**	**27**	**165**	**192**	**1179**	**51**	**1**	**11**	**12**	**132**

Signed as a free agent by **Pittsburgh**, June 9, 1985. Traded to **Minnesota** by **Pittsburgh** with Chris Dahlquist for Larry Murphy and Peter Taglianetti, December 11, 1990. Traded to **Washington** by **Dallas** for Alan May and Washington's seventh round choice (Jeff Dewar) in 1995 Entry Draft, March 21, 1994. Signed as a free agent by **Phoenix**, July 6, 1996.

JOHNSON, MATT — L.A.

Left wing. Shoots left. 6'5", 230 lbs. Born, Welland, Ont., November 23, 1975.
(Los Angeles' 2nd choice, 33rd overall, in 1994 Entry Draft).

			Regular Season					Playoffs				
Season	Club	Lea	GP	G	A	TP	PIM	GP	G	A	TP	PIM
1992-93	Peterborough	OHL	66	8	17	25	211	16	1	1	2	56
1993-94	Peterborough	OHL	50	13	24	37	233	....	....	....	....	....
1994-95	Peterborough	OHL	14	1	2	3	43	....	....	....	....	....
	Los Angeles	**NHL**	**14**	**1**	**0**	**1**	**102**	....	....	....	....	....
1995-96	**Los Angeles**	**NHL**	**1**	**0**	**0**	**0**	**5**	....	....	....	....	....
	Phoenix	IHL	29	4	4	8	87	....	....	....	....	....
1996-97	**Los Angeles**	**NHL**	**52**	**1**	**3**	**4**	**194**	....	....	....	....	....
	NHL Totals		**67**	**2**	**3**	**5**	**301**	....	....	....	....	....

JOHNSON, MIKE — TOR.

Right wing. Shoots right. 6'2", 190 lbs. Born, Scarborough, Ont., October 3, 1974.

			Regular Season					Playoffs				
Season	Club	Lea	GP	G	A	TP	PIM	GP	G	A	TP	PIM
1993-94	Bowling Green	CCHA	38	6	14	20	18	....	....	....	....	....
1994-95	Bowling Green	CCHA	37	16	33	49	35	....	....	....	....	....
1995-96	Bowling Green	CCHA	30	12	19	31	22	....	....	....	....	....
1996-97	Bowling Green	CCHA	38	30	32	62	46	....	....	....	....	....
	Toronto	**NHL**	**13**	**2**	**2**	**4**	**4**	....	....	....	....	....
	NHL Totals		**13**	**2**	**2**	**4**	**4**	....	....	....	....	....

Signed as a free agent by **Toronto**, March 16, 1997.

JOHNSON, RYAN — FLA.

Center. Shoots left. 6'2", 185 lbs. Born, Thunder Bay, Ont., June 14, 1976.
(Florida's 4th choice, 36th overall, in 1994 Entry Draft).

			Regular Season					Playoffs				
Season	Club	Lea	GP	G	A	TP	PIM	GP	G	A	TP	PIM
1994-95	North Dakota	WCHA	38	6	22	28	39	....	....	....	....	....
1995-96	North Dakota	WCHA	21	2	17	19	14	....	....	....	....	....
	Cdn. National	....	28	5	12	17	14	....	....	....	....	....
1996-97	Carolina	AHL	79	18	24	42	28	....	....	....	....	....

JOHNSSON, KIM — (YAWN-suhn) NYR

Defense. Shoots left. 6'1", 175 lbs. Born, Malmo, Sweden, March 16, 1976.
(NY Rangers' 15th choice, 286th overall, in 1994 Entry Draft).

			Regular Season					Playoffs				
Season	Club	Lea	GP	G	A	TP	PIM	GP	G	A	TP	PIM
1993-94	Malmo	Swe.	2	0	0	0	0	....	....	....	....	....
1994-95	Malmo	Swe.	13	0	0	0	4	1	0	0	0	0
1995-96	Malmo	Swe.	38	2	0	2	30	4	0	1	1	8
1996-97	Malmo	Swe.	49	4	9	13	42	4	0	0	0	2

JOKINEN, OLLI — (YOH-kih-nihn, OH-lee) L.A.

Center. Shoots left. 6'2", 198 lbs. Born, Kuopio, Finland, December 5, 1978.
(Los Angeles' 1st choice, 3rd overall, in 1997 Entry Draft).

			Regular Season					Playoffs				
Season	Club	Lea	GP	G	A	TP	PIM	GP	G	A	TP	PIM
1995-96	KalPa	Fin. Jr.	25	20	14	34	47	7	4	4	8	20
	KalPa	Fin.	15	1	1	2	2	....	....	....	....	....
1996-97	HIFK	Fin.	50	14	27	41	88	....	....	....	....	....

JOMPHE, JEAN-FRANCOIS — (ZHOHMF) ANA.

Center. Shoots left. 6'1", 195 lbs. Born, Harve' St. Pierre, Que., December 28, 1972.

			Regular Season					Playoffs				
Season	Club	Lea	GP	G	A	TP	PIM	GP	G	A	TP	PIM
1990-91	Shawinigan	QMJHL	42	17	22	39	14	6	2	1	3	2
1991-92	Shawinigan	QMJHL	44	28	33	61	69	10	6	10	16	10
1992-93	Sherbrooke	QMJHL	60	43	43	86	86	15	10	13	23	18
1993-94	San Diego	IHL	29	2	3	5	12	....	....	....	....	....
	Greensboro	ECHL	25	9	9	18	41	1	1	0	1	0
1994-95	Cdn. National	....	52	33	25	58	85	....	....	....	....	....
1995-96	**Anaheim**	**NHL**	**31**	**2**	**12**	**14**	**39**	....	....	....	....	....
	Baltimore	AHL	47	21	34	55	75	....	....	....	....	....
1996-97	**Anaheim**	**NHL**	**64**	**7**	**14**	**21**	**53**	....	....	....	....	....
	NHL Totals		**95**	**9**	**26**	**35**	**92**	....	....	....	....	....

Signed as a free agent by **Anaheim**, September 7, 1993

JONES, KEITH — COL.

Right wing. Shoots left. 6'2", 200 lbs. Born, Brantford, Ont., November 8, 1968.
(Washington's 7th choice, 141st overall, in 1988 Entry Draft).

			Regular Season					Playoffs				
Season	Club	Lea	GP	G	A	TP	PIM	GP	G	A	TP	PIM
1988-89	W. Michigan	CCHA	37	9	12	21	51	....	....	....	....	....
1989-90	W. Michigan	CCHA	40	19	18	37	82	....	....	....	....	....
1990-91	W. Michigan	CCHA	41	30	19	49	106	....	....	....	....	....
1991-92a	W. Michigan	CCHA	35	25	31	56	77	....	....	....	....	....
	Baltimore	AHL	6	2	4	6	0	....	....	....	....	....
1992-93	**Washington**	**NHL**	**71**	**12**	**14**	**26**	**124**	**6**	**0**	**0**	**0**	**10**
	Baltimore	AHL	8	7	3	10	4	....	....	....	....	....
1993-94	**Washington**	**NHL**	**68**	**16**	**19**	**35**	**149**	**11**	**0**	**1**	**1**	**36**
	Portland	AHL	6	5	7	12	4	....	....	....	....	....
1994-95	**Washington**	**NHL**	**40**	**14**	**6**	**20**	**65**	**7**	**4**	**4**	**8**	**22**
1995-96	**Washington**	**NHL**	**68**	**18**	**23**	**41**	**103**	**2**	**0**	**0**	**0**	**7**
1996-97	**Washington**	**NHL**	**11**	**2**	**3**	**5**	**13**	....	....	....	....	....
	Colorado	**NHL**	**67**	**23**	**20**	**43**	**105**	**6**	**3**	**3**	**6**	**4**
	NHL Totals		**325**	**85**	**85**	**170**	**559**	**32**	**7**	**8**	**15**	**79**

a CCHA First All-Star Team (1992)

Traded to **Colorado** by **Washington** with Washington's first and fourth round choices in 1998 Entry Draft for Curtis Leschyshyn and Chris Simon, November 2, 1996.

JONES, TY — CHI.

Right wing. Shoots right. 6'3", 210 lbs. Born, Richland, WA, February 22, 1979.
(Chicago's 2nd choice, 16th overall, in 1997 Entry Draft).

			Regular Season					Playoffs				
Season	Club	Lea	GP	G	A	TP	PIM	GP	G	A	TP	PIM
1995-96	Spokane	WHL	34	1	0	1	77	3	0	0	0	6
1996-97	Spokane	WHL	67	20	34	54	202	9	2	4	6	10

JONSSON, HANS — (YAWN-suhn) PIT.

Defense. Shoots left. 6'1", 183 lbs. Born, Jarved, Sweden, August 2, 1973.
(Pittsburgh's 11th choice, 286th overall, in 1993 Entry Draft).

			Regular Season					Playoffs				
Season	Club	Lea	GP	G	A	TP	PIM	GP	G	A	TP	PIM
1991-92	MoDo	Swe.	6	0	1	1	4	....	....	....	....	....
1992-93	MoDo	Swe.	40	2	2	4	24	3	0	1	1	2
1993-94	MoDo	Swe.	23	4	1	5	18	10	0	1	1	12
1994-95	MoDo	Swe.	39	4	6	10	30	....	....	....	....	....
1995-96	MoDo	Swe.	36	10	6	16	30	8	2	1	3	24
1996-97	MoDo	Swe.	27	7	5	12	18	....	....	....	....	....

JONSSON, JORGEN — (YAWN-suhn) CGY.

Left wing. Shoots left. 6', 185 lbs. Born, Angelholm, Sweden, September 29, 1972.
(Calgary's 11th choice, 227th overall, in 1994 Entry Draft).

			Regular Season					Playoffs				
Season	Club	Lea	GP	G	A	TP	PIM	GP	G	A	TP	PIM
1992-93	Rogle	Swe.	40	17	11	28	28	....	....	....	....	....
1993-94	Rogle	Swe.	40	17	14	31	46	....	....	....	....	....
1994-95	Rogle	Swe.	22	4	6	10	18	....	....	....	....	....
1995-96	Farjestad	Swe.	39	11	15	26	36	8	0	4	4	6
1996-97	Farjestad	Swe.	49	12	21	33	58	14	9	5	14	14

JONSSON, KENNY — (YAWN-suhn) NYI

Defense. Shoots left. 6'3", 195 lbs. Born, Angelholm, Sweden, October 6, 1974.
(Toronto's 1st choice, 12th overall, in 1993 Entry Draft).

			Regular Season					Playoffs				
Season	Club	Lea	GP	G	A	TP	PIM	GP	G	A	TP	PIM
1991-92	Rogle	Swe. 2	30	4	11	15	24	....	....	....	....	....
1992-93a	Rogle	Swe.	39	3	10	13	42	....	....	....	....	....
1993-94	Rogle	Swe.	36	4	13	17	40	3	1	1	2	2
1994-95	Rogle	Swe.	8	3	1	4	20	....	....	....	....	....
	St. John's	AHL	10	2	5	7	2	....	....	....	....	....
b	**Toronto**	**NHL**	**39**	**2**	**7**	**9**	**16**	**4**	**0**	**0**	**0**	**0**
1995-96	**Toronto**	**NHL**	**50**	**4**	**22**	**26**	**22**	....	....	....	....	....
	NY Islanders	**NHL**	**16**	**0**	**4**	**4**	**10**	....	....	....	....	....
1996-97	**NY Islanders**	**NHL**	**81**	**3**	**18**	**21**	**24**	....	....	....	....	....
	NHL Totals		**186**	**9**	**51**	**60**	**72**	**4**	**0**	**0**	**0**	**0**

a Swedish Rookie of the Year (1993)
b NHL/Upper Deck All-Rookie Team (1995)

Traded to **NY Islanders** by **Toronto** with Sean Haggerty, Darby Hendrickson and Toronto's first round choice (Roberto Luongo) in 1997 Entry Draft for Wendel Clark, Mathieu Schneider and D.J. Smith, March 13, 1996.

JOSEPH, CHRIS

Defense. Shoots right. 6'2", 202 lbs.   Born, Burnaby, B.C., September 10, 1969.
(Pittsburgh's 1st choice, 5th overall, in 1987 Entry Draft).

			Regular Season					Playoffs				
Season	Club	Lea	GP	G	A	TP	PIM	GP	G	A	TP	PIM
1985-86	Seattle	WHL	72	4	8	12	50	5	0	3	3	12
1986-87	Seattle	WHL	67	13	45	58	155	....	....	....	....	....
1987-88	**Pittsburgh**	**NHL**	**17**	**0**	**4**	**4**	**12**	....	....	....	....	....
	Seattle	WHL	23	5	14	19	49	....	....	....	....	....
	Edmonton	**NHL**	**7**	**0**	**4**	**4**	**6**	....	....	....	....	....
	Nova Scotia	AHL	8	0	2	2	8	4	0	0	0	9
1988-89	**Edmonton**	**NHL**	**44**	**4**	**5**	**9**	**54**	....	....	....	....	....
	Cape Breton	AHL	5	1	1	2	18	....	....	....	....	....
1989-90	**Edmonton**	**NHL**	**4**	**0**	**2**	**2**	**2**	....	....	....	....	....
	Cape Breton	AHL	61	10	20	30	69	6	2	1	3	4
1990-91	**Edmonton**	**NHL**	**49**	**5**	**17**	**22**	**59**	....	....	....	....	....
1991-92	**Edmonton**	**NHL**	**7**	**0**	**0**	**0**	**8**	**5**	**1**	**3**	**4**	**2**
	Cape Breton	AHL	63	14	29	43	72	5	0	2	2	8
1992-93	**Edmonton**	**NHL**	**33**	**2**	**10**	**12**	**48**	....	....	....	....	....
1993-94	**Edmonton**	**NHL**	**10**	**1**	**1**	**2**	**28**	....	....	....	....	....
	Tampa Bay	**NHL**	**66**	**10**	**19**	**29**	**108**	....	....	....	....	....
1994-95	**Pittsburgh**	**NHL**	**33**	**5**	**10**	**15**	**46**	**10**	**1**	**1**	**2**	**12**
1995-96	**Pittsburgh**	**NHL**	**70**	**5**	**14**	**19**	**71**	**15**	**1**	**0**	**1**	**8**
1996-97	**Vancouver**	**NHL**	**63**	**3**	**13**	**16**	**62**	....	....	....	....	....
	NHL Totals		**403**	**35**	**99**	**134**	**504**	**30**	**3**	**4**	**7**	**22**

Traded to **Edmonton** by **Pittsburgh** with Craig Simpson, Dave Hannan and Moe Mantha for Paul Coffey, Dave Hunter and Wayne Van Dorp, November 24, 1987. Traded to **Tampa Bay** by **Edmonton** for Bob Beers, November 11, 1993. Claimed by **Pittsburgh** from **Tampa Bay** in NHL Waiver Draft, January 18, 1995. Claimed by **Vancouver** from **Pittsburgh** in NHL Waiver Draft, September 30, 1996.

JOVANOVSKI, ED   (joh-van-OHV-skee)   **FLA.**

Defense. Shoots left. 6'2", 205 lbs.   Born, Windsor, Ont., June 26, 1976.
(Florida's 1st choice, 1st overall, in 1994 Entry Draft).

			Regular Season					Playoffs				
Season	Club	Lea	GP	G	A	TP	PIM	GP	G	A	TP	PIM
1993-94a	Windsor	OHL	62	15	36	51	221	4	0	0	0	15
1994-95b	Windsor	OHL	50	23	42	65	198	9	2	7	9	39
1995-96c	**Florida**	**NHL**	**70**	**10**	**11**	**21**	**137**	**22**	**1**	**8**	**9**	**52**
1996-97	**Florida**	**NHL**	**61**	**7**	**16**	**23**	**172**	**5**	**0**	**0**	**0**	**4**
	NHL Totals		**131**	**17**	**27**	**44**	**309**	**27**	**1**	**8**	**9**	**56**

a OHL Second All-Star Team (1994)
b OHL First All-Star Team (1995)
c NHL All-Rookie Team (1996)

JUDEN, DANIEL   **T.B.**

Right wing. Shoots right. 6'3", 190 lbs.   Born, Beverly, MA, April 17, 1976.
(Tampa Bay's 5th choice, 137th overall, in 1994 Entry Draft).

			Regular Season					Playoffs				
Season	Club	Lea	GP	G	A	TP	PIM	GP	G	A	TP	PIM
1994-95	Massachusetts	H.E.	3	0	0	0	0	....	....	....	....	....
1995-96	Massachusetts	H.E.	32	3	1	4	16	....	....	....	....	....
1996-97	Massachusetts	H.E.	33	6	9	15	38	....	....	....	....	....

JUHLIN, PATRIK   (ew-LEEN)

Left wing. Shoots left. 6', 194 lbs.   Born, Huddinge, Sweden, April 24, 1970.
(Philadelphia's 2nd choice, 34th overall, in 1989 Entry Draft).

			Regular Season					Playoffs				
Season	Club	Lea	GP	G	A	TP	PIM	GP	G	A	TP	PIM
1988-89	Vasteras	Swe. 2	30	29	13	42	....	....	....	....	....	....
1989-90	Vasteras	Swe.	35	10	13	23	18	2	0	0	0	0
1990-91	Vasteras	Swe.	40	13	9	22	24	4	3	1	4	0
1991-92	Vasteras	Swe.	39	15	12	27	40	....	....	....	....	....
1992-93	Vasteras	Swe.	34	14	12	26	22	3	0	1	1	2
1993-94	Vasteras	Swe.	40	15	16	31	20	4	1	1	2	2
1994-95	Vasteras	Swe.	11	5	9	14	8	....	....	....	....	....
	Philadelphia	**NHL**	**42**	**4**	**3**	**7**	**6**	**13**	**1**	**0**	**1**	**2**
1995-96	**Philadelphia**	**NHL**	**14**	**3**	**3**	**6**	**17**	....	....	....	....	....
	Hershey	AHL	14	5	2	7	8	1	0	0	0	0
1996-97a	Philadelphia	AHL	78	31	60	91	24	9	7	6	13	4
	NHL Totals		**56**	**7**	**6**	**13**	**23**	**13**	**1**	**0**	**1**	**2**

a AHL First All-Star Team (1997)

JUNEAU, JOE   (ZHOO-noh, ZHOH-ay)   **WSH.**

Center. Shoots left. 6', 195 lbs.   Born, Pont-Rouge, Que., January 5, 1968.
(Boston's 3rd choice, 81st overall, in 1988 Entry Draft).

			Regular Season					Playoffs				
Season	Club	Lea	GP	G	A	TP	PIM	GP	G	A	TP	PIM
1987-88	RPI	ECAC	31	16	29	45	18	....	....	....	....	....
1988-89	RPI	ECAC	30	12	23	35	40	....	....	....	....	....
1989-90a	RPI	ECAC	34	18	*52	*70	31	....	....	....	....	....
	Cdn. National	....	3	0	2	2	4	....	....	....	....	....
1990-91bc	RPI	ECAC	29	23	40	63	68	....	....	....	....	....
	Cdn. National	....	7	2	3	5	0	....	....	....	....	....
1991-92	Cdn. National	....	60	20	49	69	35	....	....	....	....	....
	Cdn. Olympic	....	8	6	9	15	4	....	....	....	....	....
	Boston	**NHL**	**14**	**5**	**14**	**19**	**4**	**15**	**4**	**8**	**12**	**21**
1992-93d	**Boston**	**NHL**	**84**	**32**	**70**	**102**	**33**	**4**	**2**	**4**	**6**	**6**
1993-94	**Boston**	**NHL**	**63**	**14**	**58**	**72**	**35**	....	....	....	....	....
	Washington	**NHL**	**11**	**5**	**8**	**13**	**6**	**11**	**4**	**5**	**9**	**6**
1994-95	**Washington**	**NHL**	**44**	**5**	**38**	**43**	**8**	**7**	**2**	**6**	**8**	**2**
1995-96	**Washington**	**NHL**	**80**	**14**	**50**	**64**	**30**	**5**	**0**	**7**	**7**	**6**
1996-97	**Washington**	**NHL**	**58**	**15**	**27**	**42**	**8**	....	....	....	....	....
	NHL Totals		**354**	**90**	**265**	**355**	**124**	**42**	**12**	**30**	**42**	**41**

a NCAA East First All-American Team (1990)
b ECAC Second All-Star Team (1991)
c NCAA East Second All-American Team (1991)
d NHL/Upper Deck All-Rookie Team (1993)

Traded to **Washington** by **Boston** for Al Iafrate, March 21, 1994.

KABERLE, TOMAS   (ka-buhr-LAY)   **TOR.**

Defense. Shoots left. 6'1", 178 lbs.   Born, Rakovnik, Czech., March 2, 1978.
(Toronto's 13th choice, 204th overall, in 1996 Entry Draft).

			Regular Season					Playoffs				
Season	Club	Lea	GP	G	A	TP	PIM	GP	G	A	TP	PIM
1995-96	Poldi Kladno	Czech. Jr.	23	6	13	19	....	....	....	....	....	....
	Poldi Kladno	Czech.	23	0	1	1	2	2	0	0	0	0
1996-97	Poldi Kladno	Czech.	49	0	5	5	26	3	0	0	0	0

KALLARSSON, TOMI   (KAL-ahr-suhn)   **NYR**

Defense. Shoots left. 6'3", 194 lbs.   Born, Lempaala, Finland, March 15, 1979.
(NY Rangers' 4th choice, 93rd overall, in 1997 Entry Draft).

			Regular Season					Playoffs				
Season	Club	Lea	GP	G	A	TP	PIM	GP	G	A	TP	PIM
1996-97	HPK	Fin. Jr.	31	1	3	4	26	....	....	....	....	....

KALLIO, TOMI   (KAL-ee-oh)   **COL.**

Left wing. Shoots left. 6'1", 176 lbs.   Born, Turku, Finland, January 27, 1977.
(Colorado's 4th choice, 81st overall, in 1995 Entry Draft).

			Regular Season					Playoffs				
Season	Club	Lea	GP	G	A	TP	PIM	GP	G	A	TP	PIM
1994-95	TPS	Fin. Jr.	14	5	12	17	24	....	....	....	....	....
	Kiekko-67	Fin. 2	25	8	5	13	16	7	3	1	4	6
1995-96	TPS	Fin. Jr.	8	8	3	11	14	....	....	....	....	....
	Kiekko-67	Fin. 2	29	10	11	21	28	....	....	....	....	....
	TPS	Fin.	8	2	3	5	10	4	0	0	0	2
1996-97	TPS	Fin.	47	9	10	19	18	8	2	0	2	2

KALMIKOV, KONSTANTIN   (kahl-mih-KAHV)   **TOR.**

Left wing. Shoots right. 6'4", 205 lbs.   Born, Kharkov, USSR, June 14, 1978.
(Toronto's 4th choice, 68th overall, in 1996 Entry Draft).

			Regular Season					Playoffs				
Season	Club	Lea	GP	G	A	TP	PIM	GP	G	A	TP	PIM
1994-95	Druzhba-78	Midget	65	51	55	106	45	....	....	....	....	....
1995-96	Flint	ColHL	38	4	12	16	16	....	....	....	....	....
	Detroit	ColHL	5	0	1	1	0	....	....	....	....	....
1996-97	Sudbury	OHL	66	22	34	56	25	....	....	....	....	....
	St. John's	AHL	2	0	0	0	0	....	....	....	....	....

KAMENSKY, VALERI   (kah-MEHN-skee)   **COL.**

Left wing. Shoots right. 6'2", 198 lbs.   Born, Voskresensk, USSR, April 18, 1966.
(Quebec's 8th choice, 129th overall, in 1988 Entry Draft).

			Regular Season					Playoffs				
Season	Club	Lea	GP	G	A	TP	PIM	GP	G	A	TP	PIM
1982-83	Khimik	USSR	5	0	0	0	0	....	....	....	....	....
1983-84	Khimik	USSR	20	2	2	4	6	....	....	....	....	....
1984-85	Khimik	USSR	45	9	3	12	24	....	....	....	....	....
1985-86	CSKA	USSR	40	15	9	24	8	....	....	....	....	....
1986-87	CSKA	USSR	37	13	8	21	16	....	....	....	....	....
1987-88	CSKA	USSR	51	26	20	46	40	....	....	....	....	....
1988-89	CSKA	USSR	40	18	10	28	30	....	....	....	....	....
1989-90	CSKA	USSR	45	19	18	37	40	....	....	....	....	....
1990-91	CSKA	USSR	46	20	26	46	66	....	....	....	....	....
1991-92	**Quebec**	**NHL**	**23**	**7**	**14**	**21**	**14**	....	....	....	....	....
1992-93	**Quebec**	**NHL**	**32**	**15**	**22**	**37**	**14**	**6**	**0**	**1**	**1**	**6**
1993-94	**Quebec**	**NHL**	**76**	**28**	**37**	**65**	**42**	....	....	....	....	....
1994-95	Ambri	Switz.	12	13	6	19	2	....	....	....	....	....
	Quebec	**NHL**	**40**	**10**	**20**	**30**	**22**	**2**	**1**	**0**	**1**	**0**
1995-96	**Colorado**	**NHL**	**81**	**38**	**47**	**85**	**85**	**22**	**10**	**12**	**22**	**28** ◆
1996-97	**Colorado**	**NHL**	**68**	**28**	**38**	**66**	**38**	**17**	**8**	**14**	**22**	**16**
	NHL Totals		**320**	**126**	**178**	**304**	**215**	**47**	**19**	**27**	**46**	**50**

KAMINSKI, ERIK   **OTT.**

Right wing. Shoots right. 6'3", 205 lbs.   Born, Hudson, OH, March 23, 1976.
(Ottawa's 9th choice, 231st overall, in 1995 Entry Draft).

			Regular Season					Playoffs				
Season	Club	Lea	GP	G	A	TP	PIM	GP	G	A	TP	PIM
1995-96	Northeastern	H.E.	34	5	8	13	30	....	....	....	....	....
1996-97	Northeastern	H.E.	34	11	7	18	30	....	....	....	....	....

KAMINSKI, KEVIN   (kah-MIHN-skee)   **WSH.**

Center. Shoots left. 5'10", 190 lbs.   Born, Churchbridge, Sask., March 13, 1969.
(Minnesota's 3rd choice, 48th overall, in 1987 Entry Draft).

			Regular Season					Playoffs				
Season	Club	Lea	GP	G	A	TP	PIM	GP	G	A	TP	PIM
1986-87	Saskatoon	WHL	67	26	44	70	325	11	5	6	11	45
1987-88	Saskatoon	WHL	55	38	61	99	247	10	5	7	12	37
1988-89	**Minnesota**	**NHL**	**1**	**0**	**0**	**0**	**0**	....	....	....	....	....
	Saskatoon	WHL	52	25	43	68	199	8	4	9	13	25
1989-90	**Quebec**	**NHL**	**1**	**0**	**0**	**0**	**0**	....	....	....	....	....
	Halifax	AHL	19	3	4	7	128	2	0	0	0	5
1990-91	Halifax	AHL	7	1	0	1	44	....	....	....	....	....
	Fort Wayne	IHL	56	9	15	24	*455	19	4	2	6	*169
1991-92	**Quebec**	**NHL**	**5**	**0**	**0**	**0**	**45**	....	....	....	....	....
	Halifax	AHL	63	18	27	45	329	....	....	....	....	....
1992-93	Halifax	AHL	79	27	37	64	*345	....	....	....	....	....
1993-94	**Washington**	**NHL**	**13**	**0**	**5**	**5**	**87**	....	....	....	....	....
	Portland	AHL	39	10	22	32	263	16	4	5	9	*91
1994-95	Portland	AHL	34	15	20	35	292	....	....	....	....	....
	Washington	**NHL**	**27**	**1**	**1**	**2**	**102**	**5**	**0**	**0**	**0**	**36**
1995-96	**Washington**	**NHL**	**54**	**1**	**2**	**3**	**164**	**3**	**0**	**0**	**0**	**16**
1996-97	**Washington**	**NHL**	**38**	**1**	**2**	**3**	**130**	....	....	....	....	....
	NHL Totals		**139**	**3**	**10**	**13**	**528**	**8**	**0**	**0**	**0**	**52**

Traded to **Quebec** by **Minnesota** for Gaetan Duchesne, June 19, 1989. Traded to **Washington** by **Quebec** for Mark Matier, June 15, 1993.

KAMINSKY, YAN   (kah-MIHN-skee)

Right wing. Shoots left. 6'1", 176 lbs.   Born, Penza, USSR, July 28, 1971.
(Winnipeg's 4th choice, 99th overall, in 1991 Entry Draft).

			Regular Season					Playoffs				
Season	Club	Lea	GP	G	A	TP	PIM	GP	G	A	TP	PIM
1989-90	Moscow D'amo	USSR	6	1	0	1	4	....	....	....	....	....
1990-91	Moscow D'amo	USSR	25	10	5	15	2	....	....	....	....	....
1991-92	Moscow D'amo	CIS	42	9	7	16	22	....	....	....	....	....
1992-93	Moscow D'amo	CIS	39	15	14	29	12	10	2	5	7	8
1993-94	**Winnipeg**	**NHL**	**1**	**0**	**0**	**0**	**0**	....	....	....	....	....
	Moncton	AHL	33	9	13	22	6	....	....	....	....	....
	NY Islanders	**NHL**	**23**	**2**	**1**	**3**	**4**	**2**	**0**	**0**	**0**	**4**
1994-95	Denver	IHL	38	17	16	33	14	15	6	6	12	0
	NY Islanders	**NHL**	**2**	**1**	**1**	**2**	**0**	....	....	....	....	....
1995-96	Utah	IHL	16	3	3	6	8	21	3	5	8	4
1996-97	Utah	IHL	77	28	27	55	18	7	1	4	5	0
	NHL Totals		**26**	**3**	**2**	**5**	**4**	**2**	**0**	**0**	**0**	**4**

Traded to **NY Islanders** by **Winnipeg** for Wayne McBean, February 1, 1994.

KANE, BOYD — PIT.

Left wing. Shoots left. 6'1", 207 lbs. Born, Swift Current, Sask., April 18, 1978.
(Pittsburgh's 3rd choice, 72nd overall, in 1996 Entry Draft).

			Regular Season					Playoffs				
Season	Club	Lea	GP	G	A	TP	PIM	GP	G	A	TP	PIM
1994-95	Regina	WHL	25	6	5	11	6	4	0	0	0	0
1995-96	Regina	WHL	72	21	42	63	155	11	5	7	12	12
1996-97	Regina	WHL	66	25	50	75	154	5	1	1	2	15

KAPANEN, SAMI — (KA-pah-nehn) CAR.

Left wing. Shoots left. 5'10", 170 lbs. Born, Vantaa, Finland, June 14, 1973.
(Hartford's 4th choice, 87th overall, in 1995 Entry Draft).

			Regular Season					Playoffs				
Season	Club	Lea	GP	G	A	TP	PIM	GP	G	A	TP	PIM
1990-91	KalPa	Fin.	14	1	2	3	2	8	2	1	3	2
1991-92	KalPa	Fin.	42	15	10	25	8	....	....	....	....	....
1992-93	KalPa	Fin.	37	4	17	21	12	....	....	....	....	....
1993-94	KalPa	Fin.	48	23	32	55	16	....	....	....	....	....
1994-95	HIFK	Fin.	49	14	28	42	42	3	0	0	0	0
1995-96	**Hartford**	**NHL**	**35**	**5**	**4**	**9**	**6**	....	....	....	....	....
	Springfield	AHL	28	14	17	31	4	3	1	2	3	0
1996-97	**Hartford**	**NHL**	**45**	**13**	**12**	**25**	**2**	....	....	....	....	....
	NHL Totals		**80**	**18**	**16**	**34**	**8**	....	....	....	....	....

KARALAHTI, JERE — (kar-ah-LAHKH-tee, YEH-reh) L.A.

Defense. Shoots right. 6'2", 185 lbs. Born, Helsinki, Finland, March 25, 1975.
(Los Angeles' 7th choice, 146th overall, in 1993 Entry Draft).

			Regular Season					Playoffs				
Season	Club	Lea	GP	G	A	TP	PIM	GP	G	A	TP	PIM
1993-94	HIFK	Fin.	46	1	10	11	36	3	0	0	0	6
1994-95	HIFK	Fin.	37	1	7	8	42	3	0	0	0	0
1995-96	HIFK	Fin.	36	4	6	10	102	3	0	0	0	4
1996-97	HIFK	Fin.	18	3	5	8	20	....	....	....	....	....

KARIYA, PAUL — (kah-REE-ah) ANA.

Left wing. Shoots left. 5'11", 175 lbs. Born, Vancouver, B.C., October 16, 1974.
(Anaheim's 1st choice, 4th overall, in 1993 Entry Draft).

			Regular Season					Playoffs				
Season	Club	Lea	GP	G	A	TP	PIM	GP	G	A	TP	PIM
1992-93abcd	U. of Maine	H.E.	36	24	*69	*93	12	....	....	....	....	....
1993-94	U. of Maine	H.E.	12	8	16	24	4	....	....	....	....	....
	Cdn. National	....	23	7	34	41	2	....	....	....	....	....
	Cdn. Olympic	....	8	3	4	7	2	....	....	....	....	....
1994-95e	**Anaheim**	**NHL**	**47**	**18**	**21**	**39**	**4**	....	....	....	....	....
1995-96fg	**Anaheim**	**NHL**	**82**	**50**	**58**	**108**	**20**	....	....	....	....	....
1996-97fg	**Anaheim**	**NHL**	**69**	**44**	**55**	**99**	**6**	**11**	**7**	**6**	**13**	**4**
	NHL Totals		**198**	**112**	**134**	**246**	**30**	**11**	**7**	**6**	**13**	**4**

a Hockey East First All-Star Team (1993)
b NCAA East First All-American Team (1993)
c NCAA Final Four All-Tournament Team (1993)
d Won Hobey Baker Memorial Award (Top U.S. Collegiate Player) (1993)
e NHL/Upper Deck All-Rookie Team (1995)
f NHL First All-Star Team (1996, 1997)
g Won Lady Byng Trophy (1996, 1997)

Played in NHL All-Star Game (1996, 1997)

KARLIN, MATTIAS — (KAR-lihn) BOS.

Center/right wing. Shoots left. 5'11", 183 lbs. Born, Ornskoldsvik, Sweden, July 4, 1979.
(Boston's 4th choice, 54th overall, in 1997 Entry Draft).

			Regular Season					Playoffs				
Season	Club	Lea	GP	G	A	TP	PIM	GP	G	A	TP	PIM
1995-96	MoDo	Swe. Jr.	30	12	23	35	16	....	....	....	....	....
1996-97	MoDo	Swe. Jr.			UNAVAILABLE							
	MoDo	Swe.	6	0	0	0	0	....	....	....	....	....

KARLSSON, ANDREAS — CGY.

Center. Shoots left. 6'2", 180 lbs. Born, Leksand, Sweden, August 19, 1975.
(Calgary's 8th choice, 148th overall, in 1993 Entry Draft).

			Regular Season					Playoffs				
Season	Club	Lea	GP	G	A	TP	PIM	GP	G	A	TP	PIM
1992-93	Leksand	Swe.	13	0	0	0	6	....	....	....	....	....
1993-94	Leksand	Swe.	21	0	0	0	10	3	0	0	0	0
1994-95	Leksand	Swe.	24	7	8	15	0	4	0	1	1	0
1995-96	Leksand	Swe.	40	10	13	23	10	....	....	....	....	....
1996-97	Leksand	Swe.	49	13	11	24	39	9	2	0	2	2

KARPA, DAVE — ANA.

Defense. Shoots right. 6'1", 210 lbs. Born, Regina, Sask., May 7, 1971.
(Quebec's 4th choice, 68th overall, in 1991 Entry Draft).

			Regular Season					Playoffs				
Season	Club	Lea	GP	G	A	TP	PIM	GP	G	A	TP	PIM
1990-91	Ferris State	CCHA	41	6	19	25	109	....	....	....	....	....
1991-92	Ferris State	CCHA	34	7	12	19	124	....	....	....	....	....
	Quebec	**NHL**	**4**	**0**	**0**	**0**	**14**	....	....	....	....	....
	Halifax	AHL	2	0	0	0	4	....	....	....	....	....
1992-93	**Quebec**	**NHL**	**12**	**0**	**1**	**1**	**13**	**3**	**0**	**0**	**0**	**0**
	Halifax	AHL	71	4	27	31	167	....	....	....	....	....
1993-94	**Quebec**	**NHL**	**60**	**5**	**12**	**17**	**148**	....	....	....	....	....
	Cornwall	AHL	1	0	0	0	0	12	2	2	4	27
1994-95	**Quebec**	**NHL**	**2**	**0**	**0**	**0**	**0**	....	....	....	....	....
	Cornwall	AHL	6	0	2	2	19	....	....	....	....	....
	Anaheim	**NHL**	**26**	**1**	**5**	**6**	**91**	....	....	....	....	....
1995-96	**Anaheim**	**NHL**	**72**	**3**	**16**	**19**	**270**	....	....	....	....	....
1996-97	**Anaheim**	**NHL**	**69**	**2**	**11**	**13**	**210**	**8**	**1**	**1**	**2**	**20**
	NHL Totals		**245**	**11**	**45**	**56**	**746**	**11**	**1**	**1**	**2**	**20**

Traded to **Anaheim** by **Quebec** for Anaheim's fourth round choice (later traded to St. Louis — St. Louis selected Jan Horacek) in 1997 Entry Draft, March 9, 1995.

KARPOV, VALERI — (KAHR-pahf) CGY.

Right wing. Shoots left. 5'10", 176 lbs. Born, Chelyabinsk, USSR, August 5, 1971.
(Anaheim's 3rd choice, 56th overall, in 1993 Entry Draft).

			Regular Season					Playoffs				
Season	Club	Lea	GP	G	A	TP	PIM	GP	G	A	TP	PIM
1988-89	Chelyabinsk	USSR	5	0	0	0	0	....	....	....	....	....
1989-90	Chelyabinsk	USSR	24	1	2	3	6	....	....	....	....	....
1990-91	Chelyabinsk	USSR	25	8	4	12	15	....	....	....	....	....
1991-92	Chelyabinsk	CIS	44	16	10	26	34	....	....	....	....	....
1992-93	CSKA	CIS	9	2	6	8	0	....	....	....	....	....
a	Chelyabinsk	CIS	29	10	15	25	6	8	0	1	1	10
1993-94	Chelyabinsk	CIS	32	13	16	29	....	6	2	5	7	2
1994-95	Chelyabinsk	CIS	10	6	8	14	8	....	....	....	....	....
	Anaheim	**NHL**	**30**	**4**	**7**	**11**	**6**	....	....	....	....	....
	San Diego	IHL	5	3	3	6	0	....	....	....	....	....
1995-96	**Anaheim**	**NHL**	**37**	**9**	**8**	**17**	**10**	....	....	....	....	....
1996-97	**Anaheim**	**NHL**	**9**	**1**	**0**	**1**	**16**	....	....	....	....	....
	Baltimore	AHL	10	4	8	12	8	....	....	....	....	....
	Long Beach	IHL	30	18	17	35	19	18	8	7	15	18
	NHL Totals		**76**	**14**	**15**	**29**	**32**	....	....	....	....	....

a CIS All-Star Team (1993)

Signed as a free agent by **Calgary**, August, 1997.

KARPOVTSEV, ALEXANDER — (kar-POHV-tzehv) NYR

Defense. Shoots right. 6'1", 205 lbs. Born, Moscow, USSR, April 7, 1970.
(Quebec's 7th choice, 158th overall, in 1990 Entry Draft).

			Regular Season					Playoffs				
Season	Club	Lea	GP	G	A	TP	PIM	GP	G	A	TP	PIM
1987-88	Moscow D'amo	USSR	2	0	1	1	10	....	....	....	....	....
1989-90	Moscow D'amo	USSR	35	1	1	2	27	....	....	....	....	....
1990-91	Moscow D'amo	USSR	40	0	5	5	15	....	....	....	....	....
1991-92	Moscow D'amo	CIS	35	4	2	6	26	....	....	....	....	....
1992-93	Moscow D'amo	CIS	36	3	11	14	100	7	2	1	3	0
1993-94	**NY Rangers**	**NHL**	**67**	**3**	**15**	**18**	**58**	**17**	**0**	**4**	**4**	**12** ♦
1994-95	Moscow D'amo	CIS	13	0	2	2	10	....	....	....	....	....
	NY Rangers	**NHL**	**47**	**4**	**8**	**12**	**30**	**8**	**1**	**0**	**1**	**0**
1995-96	**NY Rangers**	**NHL**	**40**	**2**	**16**	**18**	**26**	**6**	**0**	**1**	**1**	**4**
1996-97	**NY Rangers**	**NHL**	**77**	**9**	**29**	**38**	**59**	**13**	**1**	**3**	**4**	**20**
	NHL Totals		**231**	**18**	**68**	**86**	**173**	**44**	**2**	**8**	**10**	**36**

Traded to **NY Rangers** by **Quebec** for Mike Hurlbut, September 7, 1993.

KASPARAITIS, DARIUS — (KAZ-puhr-IGH-tihz) PIT.

Defense. Shoots left. 5'10", 205 lbs. Born, Elektrenai, USSR, October 16, 1972.
(NY Islanders' 1st choice, 5th overall, in 1992 Entry Draft).

			Regular Season					Playoffs				
Season	Club	Lea	GP	G	A	TP	PIM	GP	G	A	TP	PIM
1988-89	Moscow D'amo	USSR	3	0	0	0	0	....	....	....	....	....
1989-90	Moscow D'amo	USSR	1	0	0	0	0	....	....	....	....	....
1990-91	Moscow D'amo	USSR	17	0	1	1	10	....	....	....	....	....
1991-92	Moscow D'amo	CIS	31	2	10	12	14	....	....	....	....	....
1992-93	Moscow D'amo	CIS	7	1	3	4	8	....	....	....	....	....
	NY Islanders	**NHL**	**79**	**4**	**17**	**21**	**166**	**18**	**0**	**5**	**5**	**31**
1993-94	**NY Islanders**	**NHL**	**76**	**1**	**10**	**11**	**142**	**4**	**0**	**0**	**0**	**8**
1994-95	**NY Islanders**	**NHL**	**13**	**0**	**1**	**1**	**22**	....	....	....	....	....
1995-96	**NY Islanders**	**NHL**	**46**	**1**	**7**	**8**	**93**	....	....	....	....	....
1996-97	**NY Islanders**	**NHL**	**18**	**0**	**5**	**5**	**16**	....	....	....	....	....
	Pittsburgh	**NHL**	**57**	**2**	**16**	**18**	**84**	**5**	**0**	**0**	**0**	**6**
	NHL Totals		**289**	**8**	**56**	**64**	**523**	**27**	**0**	**5**	**5**	**45**

Traded to **Pittsburgh** by **NY Islanders** with Andreas Johansson for Bryan Smolinski, November 17, 1996.

KATCHER, JEFF — L.A.

Defense. Shoots right. 6'4", 178 lbs. Born, Winnipeg, Man., April 16, 1979.
(Los Angeles' 7th choice, 150th overall, in 1997 Entry Draft).

			Regular Season					Playoffs				
Season	Club	Lea	GP	G	A	TP	PIM	GP	G	A	TP	PIM
1996-97	Brandon	WHL	48	2	2	4	31	....	....	....	....	....

KAVANAGH, PAT — PHI.

Right wing. Shoots right. 6'3", 192 lbs. Born, Ottawa, Ont., March 14, 1979.
(Philadelphia's 2nd choice, 50th overall, in 1997 Entry Draft).

			Regular Season					Playoffs				
Season	Club	Lea	GP	G	A	TP	PIM	GP	G	A	TP	PIM
1996-97	Peterborough	OHL	43	6	8	14	53	11	1	1	2	12

KAZAKEVICH, MIKHAIL — (kah-zak-KAY-vihch) PIT.

Left wing. Shoots left. 6'1", 187 lbs. Born, Murmansk, USSR, January 14, 1976.
(Pittsburgh's 13th choice, 258th overall, in 1994 Entry Draft).

			Regular Season					Playoffs				
Season	Club	Lea	GP	G	A	TP	PIM	GP	G	A	TP	PIM
1992-93	Yaroslavl	CIS	7	0	1	1	0	3	0	0	0	0
1993-94	Yaroslavl	CIS	4	0	0	0	2	....	....	....	....	....
1994-95	Yaroslavl	CIS	11	1	3	4	2	....	....	....	....	....
1995-96	Moncton	QMJHL	41	7	13	20	16	....	....	....	....	....
	Shawinigan	QMJHL	14	1	3	4	8	4	0	1	1	2
1996-97	Khimik	Rus.	1	0	0	0	0	....	....	....	....	....

KEALTY, JEFF — COL.

Defense. Shoots left. 6'4", 175 lbs. Born, Boston, MA, April 9, 1976.
(Quebec's 2nd choice, 22nd overall, in 1994 Entry Draft).

			Regular Season					Playoffs				
Season	Club	Lea	GP	G	A	TP	PIM	GP	G	A	TP	PIM
1994-95	Boston U.	H.E.	25	0	5	5	29	....	....	....	....	....
1995-96	Boston U.	H.E.	35	4	14	18	38	....	....	....	....	....
1996-97	Boston U.	H.E.	40	4	9	13	42	....	....	....	....	....

KEANE, MIKE — NYR

Right wing. Shoots right. 6', 185 lbs. Born, Winnipeg, Man., May 29, 1967.

			Regular Season					Playoffs				
Season	Club	Lea	GP	G	A	TP	PIM	GP	G	A	TP	PIM
1984-85	Moose Jaw	WHL	65	17	26	43	141	....	....	....	....	....
1985-86	Moose Jaw	WHL	67	34	49	83	162	13	6	8	14	9
1986-87	Moose Jaw	WHL	53	25	45	70	107	9	3	9	12	11
	Sherbrooke	AHL	....	....	....	....	....	9	2	2	4	16
1987-88	Sherbrooke	AHL	78	25	43	68	70	6	1	1	2	18
1988-89	Montreal	NHL	69	16	19	35	69	21	4	3	7	17
1989-90	Montreal	NHL	74	9	15	24	78	11	0	1	1	8
1990-91	Montreal	NHL	73	13	23	36	50	12	3	2	5	6
1991-92	Montreal	NHL	67	11	30	41	64	8	1	1	2	16
1992-93	Montreal	NHL	77	15	45	60	95	19	2	13	15	6 ◆
1993-94	Montreal	NHL	80	16	30	46	119	6	3	1	4	4
1994-95	Montreal	NHL	48	10	10	20	15	....	....	....	....	....
1995-96	Montreal	NHL	18	0	7	7	6	....	....	....	....	....
	Colorado	NHL	55	10	10	20	40	22	3	2	5	16 ◆
1996-97	Colorado	NHL	81	10	17	27	63	17	3	1	4	24
	NHL Totals		642	110	206	316	599	116	19	24	43	97

Signed as a free agent by **Montreal**, September 25, 1985. Traded to **Colorado** by **Montreal** with Patrick Roy for Andrei Kovalenko, Martin Rucinsky and Jocelyn Thibault, December 6, 1995. Signed as a free agent by **NY Rangers**, July 30, 1997.

KECZMER, DAN — (KEHS-muhr) — DAL.

Defense. Shoots left. 6'1", 190 lbs. Born, Mt. Clemens, MI, May 25, 1968.
(Minnesota's 11th choice, 201st overall, in 1986 Entry Draft).

			Regular Season					Playoffs				
Season	Club	Lea	GP	G	A	TP	PIM	GP	G	A	TP	PIM
1986-87	Lake Superior	CCHA	38	3	5	8	26	....	....	....	....	....
1987-88	Lake Superior	CCHA	41	2	15	17	34	....	....	....	....	....
1988-89	Lake Superior	CCHA	46	3	26	29	68	....	....	....	....	....
1989-90a	Lake Superior	CCHA	43	13	23	36	48	....	....	....	....	....
1990-91	Minnesota	NHL	9	0	1	1	6	....	....	....	....	....
	Kalamazoo	IHL	60	4	20	24	60	9	1	2	3	10
1991-92	U.S. National	....	51	3	11	14	56	....	....	....	....	....
	Hartford	NHL	1	0	0	0	0	....	....	....	....	....
	Springfield	AHL	18	3	4	7	10	4	0	0	0	6
1992-93	Hartford	NHL	23	4	4	8	28	....	....	....	....	....
	Springfield	AHL	37	1	13	14	38	12	0	4	4	14
1993-94	Hartford	NHL	12	0	1	1	12	....	....	....	....	....
	Springfield	AHL	7	0	1	1	4	....	....	....	....	....
	Calgary	NHL	57	1	20	21	48	3	0	0	0	4
1994-95	Calgary	NHL	28	2	3	5	10	7	0	1	1	2
1995-96	Calgary	NHL	13	0	0	0	14	....	....	....	....	....
	Saint John	AHL	22	3	11	14	14	....	....	....	....	....
	Albany	AHL	17	0	4	4	4	1	0	0	0	0
1996-97	Dallas	NHL	13	0	1	1	6	....	....	....	....	....
	Michigan	IHL	42	3	17	20	24	....	....	....	....	....
	NHL Totals		156	7	30	37	124	10	0	1	1	6

a CCHA Second All-Star Team (1990)

Claimed by **San Jose** from **Minnesota** in Dispersal Draft, May 30, 1991. Traded to **Hartford** by **San Jose** for Dean Evason, October 2, 1991. Traded to **Calgary** by **Hartford** for Jeff Reese, November 19, 1993. Traded to **New Jersey** by **Calgary** with Phil Housley for Tommy Albelin, Cale Hulse and Jocelyn Lemieux, February 26, 1996. Signed as a free agent by **Dallas**, August 19, 1996.

KELLEHER, CHRIS — PIT.

Defense. Shoots left. 6'1", 215 lbs. Born, Cambridge, MA, March 23, 1975.
(Pittsburgh's 5th choice, 130th overall, in 1993 Entry Draft).

			Regular Season					Playoffs				
Season	Club	Lea	GP	G	A	TP	PIM	GP	G	A	TP	PIM
1994-95	Boston U.	H.E.	35	3	17	20	62	....	....	....	....	....
1995-96	Boston U.	H.E.	37	7	18	25	43	....	....	....	....	....
1996-97a	Boston U.	H.E.	39	10	24	34	54	....	....	....	....	....

a NCAA East Second All-American Team (1997)

KELLETT, KEVIN — ANA.

Defense. Shoots right. 6', 196 lbs. Born, Prince Albert, Sask., July 23, 1978.
(Anaheim's 6th choice, 198th overall, in 1996 Entry Draft).

			Regular Season					Playoffs				
Season	Club	Lea	GP	G	A	TP	PIM	GP	G	A	TP	PIM
1994-95	Prince Albert	WHL	8	0	1	1	6	....	....	....	....	....
1995-96	Prince Albert	WHL	62	0	5	5	71	18	0	0	0	19
1996-97	Prince Albert	WHL	69	8	16	24	165	1	0	1	1	0

KELLY, STEVE — EDM.

Center. Shoots left. 6'1", 190 lbs. Born, Vancouver, B.C., October 26, 1976.
(Edmonton's 1st choice, 6th overall, in 1995 Entry Draft).

			Regular Season					Playoffs				
Season	Club	Lea	GP	G	A	TP	PIM	GP	G	A	TP	PIM
1992-93	Prince Albert	WHL	65	11	9	20	75	....	....	....	....	....
1993-94	Prince Albert	WHL	65	19	42	61	106	....	....	....	....	....
1994-95	Prince Albert	WHL	68	31	41	72	153	15	7	9	16	35
1995-96	Prince Albert	WHL	70	27	74	101	203	18	13	18	31	47
1996-97	Edmonton	NHL	8	1	0	1	6	6	0	0	0	2
	Hamilton	AHL	48	9	29	38	111	11	3	3	6	24
	NHL Totals		8	1	0	1	6	6	0	0	0	2

KENADY, CHRIS — ST.L.

Right wing. Shoots right. 6'2", 195 lbs. Born, Mound, MN, April 10, 1973.
(St. Louis' 8th choice, 175th overall, in 1991 Entry Draft).

			Regular Season					Playoffs				
Season	Club	Lea	GP	G	A	TP	PIM	GP	G	A	TP	PIM
1991-92	U. of Denver	WCHA	36	8	5	13	56	....	....	....	....	....
1992-93	U. of Denver	WCHA	38	8	16	24	95	....	....	....	....	....
1993-94	U. of Denver	WCHA	37	14	11	25	125	....	....	....	....	....
1994-95	U. of Denver	WCHA	39	21	17	38	113	....	....	....	....	....
1995-96	Worcester	AHL	43	9	10	19	58	2	0	0	0	0
1996-97	Worcester	AHL	73	23	26	49	131	5	0	1	1	2

KENNEDY, MIKE — TOR.

Center. Shoots right. 6'1", 195 lbs. Born, Vancouver, B.C., April 13, 1972.
(Minnesota's 5th choice, 97th overall, in 1991 Entry Draft).

			Regular Season					Playoffs				
Season	Club	Lea	GP	G	A	TP	PIM	GP	G	A	TP	PIM
1989-90	U.B.C.	CIAU	9	5	7	12	0	....	....	....	....	....
1990-91	U.B.C.	CIAU	28	17	17	34	18	....	....	....	....	....
1991-92a	Seattle	WHL	71	42	47	89	134	15	11	6	17	20
1992-93	Kalamazoo	IHL	77	21	30	51	39	....	....	....	....	....
1993-94	Kalamazoo	IHL	63	20	18	38	42	3	1	2	3	2
1994-95	Kalamazoo	IHL	42	20	28	48	29	....	....	....	....	....
	Dallas	NHL	44	6	12	18	33	5	0	0	0	9
1995-96	Dallas	NHL	61	9	17	26	48	....	....	....	....	....
1996-97	Dallas	NHL	24	1	6	7	13	....	....	....	....	....
	Michigan	IHL	2	0	1	1	2	....	....	....	....	....
	NHL Totals		129	16	35	51	94	5	0	0	0	9

a WHL West Second All-Star Team (1982)

Signed as a free agent by **Toronto**, July 2, 1997.

KENNEDY, SHELDON

Right wing. Shoots right. 5'10", 180 lbs. Born, Elkhorn, Man., June 15, 1969.
(Detroit's 5th choice, 80th overall, in 1988 Entry Draft).

			Regular Season					Playoffs				
Season	Club	Lea	GP	G	A	TP	PIM	GP	G	A	TP	PIM
1986-87	Swift Current	WHL	49	23	41	64	43	4	0	3	3	4
1987-88	Swift Current	WHL	59	53	64	117	45	10	8	9	17	12
1988-89a	Swift Current	WHL	51	58	48	106	92	12	9	15	24	22
1989-90	Detroit	NHL	20	2	7	9	10	....	....	....	....	....
	Adirondack	AHL	26	11	15	26	35	....	....	....	....	....
1990-91	Detroit	NHL	7	1	0	1	12	....	....	....	....	....
	Adirondack	AHL	11	1	3	4	8	....	....	....	....	....
1991-92	Detroit	NHL	27	3	8	11	24	....	....	....	....	....
	Adirondack	AHL	46	25	24	49	56	16	5	9	14	12
1992-93	Detroit	NHL	68	19	11	30	46	7	1	1	2	2
1993-94	Detroit	NHL	61	6	7	13	30	7	1	2	3	0
1994-95	Calgary	NHL	30	7	8	15	45	7	3	1	4	16
1995-96	Calgary	NHL	41	3	7	10	36	3	1	0	1	2
	Saint John	AHL	3	4	0	4	8	....	....	....	....	....
1996-97	Boston	NHL	56	8	10	18	30	....	....	....	....	....
	Providence	AHL	3	0	1	1	2	....	....	....	....	....
	NHL Totals		310	49	58	107	233	24	6	4	10	20

a Memorial Cup All-Star Team (1989)

Traded to **Winnipeg** by **Detroit** for Winnipeg's third round choice (Darryl Laplante) in 1995 Entry Draft, May 25, 1994. Claimed by **Calgary** from **Winnipeg** in NHL Waiver Draft, January 18, 1995. Signed as free agent by **Boston**, August 7, 1996.

KESA, DAN — (KEH-suh)

Right wing. Shoots right. 6', 198 lbs. Born, Vancouver, B.C., November 23, 1971.
(Vancouver's 5th choice, 95th overall, in 1991 Entry Draft).

			Regular Season					Playoffs				
Season	Club	Lea	GP	G	A	TP	PIM	GP	G	A	TP	PIM
1990-91	Prince Albert	WHL	69	30	23	53	116	3	1	1	2	0
1991-92	Prince Albert	WHL	62	46	51	97	201	10	9	10	19	27
1992-93	Hamilton	AHL	62	16	24	40	76	....	....	....	....	....
1993-94	Vancouver	NHL	19	2	4	6	18	....	....	....	....	....
	Hamilton	AHL	53	37	33	70	33	4	1	4	5	4
1994-95	Syracuse	AHL	70	34	44	78	81	....	....	....	....	....
1995-96	Dallas	NHL	3	0	0	0	0	....	....	....	....	....
	Michigan	IHL	15	4	11	15	33	....	....	....	....	....
	Springfield	AHL	22	10	5	15	13	....	....	....	....	....
	Detroit	IHL	27	9	6	15	22	12	6	4	10	4
1996-97	Detroit	IHL	60	22	21	43	19	20	7	5	12	20
	NHL Totals		22	2	4	6	18	....	....	....	....	....

Traded by **Dallas** by **Vancouver** with Greg Adams and Vancouver's fifth round choice (later traded to Los Angeles — Los Angeles selected Jason Morgan) in 1995 Entry Draft for Russ Courtnall, April 7, 1995. Traded to **Hartford** by **Dallas** with a conditional draft choice in 1997 Entry Draft for Robert Petrovicky, November 29, 1995.

KHARLAMOV, ALEXANDER — (khahr-LAH-mohv) — WSH.

Center. Shoots left. 5'10", 180 lbs. Born, Moscow, USSR, September 23, 1975.
(Washington's 2nd choice, 15th overall, in 1994 Entry Draft).

			Regular Season					Playoffs				
Season	Club	Lea	GP	G	A	TP	PIM	GP	G	A	TP	PIM
1992-93	CSKA	CIS	42	8	4	12	12	....	....	....	....	....
1993-94	CSKA	CIS	46	8	8	16	26	3	1	0	1	2
	Russian Pen's	IHL	12	2	2	4	4	....	....	....	....	....
1994-95	CSKA	CIS	45	8	4	12	12	....	....	....	....	....
1995-96	Portland	AHL	65	14	18	32	35	14	2	3	5	8
1996-97	Portland	AHL	56	9	15	24	28	....	....	....	....	....

KHMYLEV, YURI — (kheh-meh-LUHV)

Left wing. Shoots right. 6'1", 189 lbs. Born, Moscow, USSR, August 9, 1964.
(Buffalo's 7th choice, 108th overall, in 1992 Entry Draft).

			Regular Season					Playoffs				
Season	Club	Lea	GP	G	A	TP	PIM	GP	G	A	TP	PIM
1981-82	Soviet Wings	USSR	8	2	2	4	2	....	....	....	....	....
1982-83	Soviet Wings	USSR	51	9	7	16	14	....	....	....	....	....
1983-84	Soviet Wings	USSR	43	7	8	15	10	....	....	....	....	....
1984-85	Soviet Wings	USSR	30	11	4	15	24	....	....	....	....	....
1985-86	Soviet Wings	USSR	40	24	9	33	22	....	....	....	....	....
1986-87	Soviet Wings	USSR	40	15	15	30	48	....	....	....	....	....
1987-88	Soviet Wings	USSR	48	21	8	29	46	....	....	....	....	....
1988-89	Soviet Wings	USSR	44	16	18	34	38	....	....	....	....	....
1989-90	Soviet Wings	USSR	44	14	13	27	30	....	....	....	....	....
1990-91	Soviet Wings	USSR	45	25	14	39	26	....	....	....	....	....
1991-92	Soviet Wings	CIS	42	19	17	36	20	....	....	....	....	....
1992-93	Buffalo	NHL	68	20	19	39	28	8	4	3	7	4
1993-94	Buffalo	NHL	72	27	31	58	49	7	3	1	4	8
1994-95	Soviet Wings	IHL	11	2	2	4	4	....	....	....	....	....
	Buffalo	NHL	48	8	17	25	14	5	0	1	1	8
1995-96	Buffalo	NHL	66	8	20	28	40	....	....	....	....	....
	St. Louis	NHL	7	0	1	1	0	6	1	1	2	4
1996-97	St. Louis	NHL	2	1	0	1	2	....	....	....	....	....
	Quebec	IHL	15	1	7	8	4	....	....	....	....	....
	Hamilton	AHL	52	5	19	24	43	22	6	7	13	12
	NHL Totals		263	64	88	152	133	26	8	6	14	24

Traded to **St. Louis** by **Buffalo** with Buffalo's eighth round choice (Andrei Podkonicky) in 1996 Entry Draft for Jean-Luc Grand Pierre, Ottawa's second round choice (previously acquired by St. Louis — Buffalo selected Cory Sarich) in 1996 Entry Draft and St. Louis' third round choice (Maxim Afinogenov) in 1997 Entry Draft, March 20, 1996.

KHRISTICH, DIMITRI (KRIH-stihch) L.A.

Left wing/Center. Shoots right. 6'2", 195 lbs. Born, Kiev, USSR, July 23, 1969.
(Washington's 6th choice, 120th overall, in 1988 Entry Draft).

			Regular Season					Playoffs				
Season	Club	Lea	GP	G	A	TP	PIM	GP	G	A	TP	PIM
1985-86	Sokol Kiev	USSR	4	0	0	0	0	....	....	....	....	....
1986-87	Sokol Kiev	USSR	20	3	0	3	4	....	....	....	....	....
1987-88	Sokol Kiev	USSR	37	9	1	10	18	....	....	....	....	....
1988-89	Sokol Kiev	USSR	42	17	10	27	15	....	....	....	....	....
1989-90	Sokol Kiev	USSR	47	14	22	36	32	....	....	....	....	....
1990-91	Sokol Kiev	USSR	28	10	12	22	20	....	....	....	....	....
	Washington	NHL	40	13	14	27	21	11	1	3	4	6
	Baltimore	AHL	3	0	0	0	0	....	....	....	....	....
1991-92	Washington	NHL	80	36	37	73	35	7	3	2	5	15
1992-93	Washington	NHL	64	31	35	66	28	6	2	5	7	2
1993-94	Washington	NHL	83	29	29	58	73	11	2	3	5	10
1994-95	Washington	NHL	48	12	14	26	41	7	1	4	5	0
1995-96	Los Angeles	NHL	76	27	37	64	44	....	....	....	....	....
1996-97	Los Angeles	NHL	75	19	37	56	38	....	....	....	....	....
	NHL Totals		466	167	203	370	280	42	9	17	26	33

Played in NHL All-Star Game (1997)

Traded to **Los Angeles** by **Washington** with Byron Dafoe for Los Angeles' first round choice (Alexander Volchkov) and Dallas' fourth round choice (previously acquired by Los Angeles – Washington selected Justin Davis) in 1996 Entry Draft, July 8, 1995.

KILGER, CHAD (KIHL-guhr) PHO.

Center. Shoots left. 6'3", 204 lbs. Born, Cornwall, Ont., November 27, 1976.
(Anaheim's 1st choice, 4th overall, in 1995 Entry Draft).

			Regular Season					Playoffs				
Season	Club	Lea	GP	G	A	TP	PIM	GP	G	A	TP	PIM
1993-94	Kingston	OHL	66	17	35	52	23	6	7	2	9	8
1994-95	Kingston	OHL	65	42	53	95	95	6	5	2	7	10
1995-96	Anaheim	NHL	45	5	7	12	22	....	....	....	....	....
	Winnipeg	NHL	29	2	3	5	12	4	1	0	1	0
1996-97	Phoenix	NHL	24	4	3	7	13	....	....	....	....	....
	Springfield	AHL	52	17	28	45	36	16	5	7	12	56
	NHL Totals		98	11	13	24	47	4	1	0	1	0

Traded to **Winnipeg** by **Anaheim** with Oleg Tverdovsky and Anaheim's third round choice (Per-Anton Lundstrom) in 1996 Entry Draft for Teemu Selanne, Marc Chouinard and Winnipeg's fourth round choice (later traded to Toronto — later traded to Montreal — Montreal selected Kim Staal) in 1996 Entry Draft, February 7, 1996.

KIMBLE, DARIN PHO.

Right wing. Shoots right. 6'2", 210 lbs. Born, Lucky Lake, Sask., November 22, 1968.
(Quebec's 5th choice, 66th overall, in 1988 Entry Draft).

			Regular Season					Playoffs				
Season	Club	Lea	GP	G	A	TP	PIM	GP	G	A	TP	PIM
1985-86	Calgary	WHL	37	14	8	22	93	....	....	....	....	....
	N. Westminster	WHL	11	1	1	2	22	....	....	....	....	....
	Brandon	WHL	15	1	6	7	39	....	....	....	....	....
1986-87	Prince Albert	WHL	68	17	13	30	190	....	....	....	....	....
1987-88	Prince Albert	WHL	67	35	36	71	307	10	3	2	5	4
1988-89	Quebec	NHL	26	3	1	4	149	....	....	....	....	....
	Halifax	AHL	39	8	6	14	188	....	....	....	....	....
1989-90	Quebec	NHL	44	5	5	10	185	....	....	....	....	....
	Halifax	AHL	18	6	6	12	37	6	1	1	2	61
1990-91	Quebec	NHL	35	2	5	7	114	....	....	....	....	....
	Halifax	AHL	7	1	4	5	20	....	....	....	....	....
	St. Louis	NHL	26	1	1	2	128	13	0	0	0	38
1991-92	St. Louis	NHL	46	1	3	4	166	5	0	0	0	7
1992-93	Boston	NHL	55	7	3	10	177	4	0	0	0	2
	Providence	AHL	12	1	4	5	34	....	....	....	....	....
1993-94	Chicago	NHL	65	4	2	6	133	1	0	0	0	5
1994-95	Chicago	NHL	14	0	0	0	30	....	....	....	....	....
1995-96	Indianapolis	IHL	9	1	0	1	15	....	....	....	....	....
	Albany	AHL	60	4	15	19	144	3	0	0	0	2
1996-97	Manitoba	IHL	39	3	4	7	115	....	....	....	....	....
	Kansas City	IHL	33	9	9	18	106	2	0	0	0	0
	NHL Totals		311	23	20	43	1082	23	0	0	0	52

Traded to **St. Louis** by **Quebec** for Herb Raglan, Tony Twist and Andy Rymsha, February 4, 1991. Traded to **Tampa Bay** by **St. Louis** with Pat Jablonski and Steve Tuttle for future considerations, June 19, 1992. Traded to **Boston** by **Tampa Bay** with future considerations for Ken Hodge and Matt Hervey, September 4, 1992. Signed as a free agent by **Florida**, July 9, 1993. Traded to **Chicago** by **Florida** for Keith Brown, September 30, 1993. Traded to **New Jersey** by **Chicago** for Michael Vukonich and Bill H. Armstrong, November 1, 1995. Signed as a free agent by **Phoenix**, July 28, 1997.

KING, DEREK TOR.

Left wing. Shoots left. 6', 212 lbs. Born, Hamilton, Ont., February 11, 1967.
(NY Islanders' 2nd choice, 13th overall, in 1985 Entry Draft).

			Regular Season					Playoffs				
Season	Club	Lea	GP	G	A	TP	PIM	GP	G	A	TP	PIM
1984-85	S.S. Marie	OHL	63	35	38	73	106	16	3	13	16	11
1985-86	S.S. Marie	OHL	25	12	17	29	33	....	....	....	....	....
	Oshawa	OHL	19	8	13	21	15	6	3	2	5	13
1986-87	NY Islanders	NHL	2	0	0	0	0	....	....	....	....	....
a	Oshawa	OHL	57	53	53	106	74	17	14	10	24	40
1987-88	NY Islanders	NHL	55	12	24	36	30	5	0	2	2	2
	Springfield	AHL	10	7	6	13	6	....	....	....	....	....
1988-89	NY Islanders	NHL	60	14	29	43	14	....	....	....	....	....
	Springfield	AHL	4	4	0	4	0	....	....	....	....	....
1989-90	NY Islanders	NHL	46	13	27	40	20	4	0	0	0	4
	Springfield	AHL	21	11	12	23	33	....	....	....	....	....
1990-91	NY Islanders	NHL	66	19	26	45	44	....	....	....	....	....
1991-92	NY Islanders	NHL	80	40	38	78	46	....	....	....	....	....
1992-93	NY Islanders	NHL	77	38	38	76	47	18	3	11	14	14
1993-94	NY Islanders	NHL	78	30	40	70	59	4	0	1	1	0
1994-95	NY Islanders	NHL	43	10	16	26	41	....	....	....	....	....
1995-96	NY Islanders	NHL	61	12	20	32	23	....	....	....	....	....
1996-97	NY Islanders	NHL	70	23	30	53	20	....	....	....	....	....
	Hartford	NHL	12	3	3	6	2	....	....	....	....	....
	NHL Totals		650	214	291	505	346	31	3	14	17	20

a OHL First All-Star Team (1987)

Traded to **Hartford** by **NY Islanders** for Hartford's fifth round choice (Adam Edinger) in 1997 Entry Draft, March 18, 1997. Signed as a free agent by **Toronto**, July 4, 1997.

KING, KRIS TOR.

Left wing. Shoots left. 5'11", 208 lbs. Born, Bracebridge, Ont., February 18, 1966.
(Washington's 4th choice, 80th overall, in 1984 Entry Draft).

			Regular Season					Playoffs				
Season	Club	Lea	GP	G	A	TP	PIM	GP	G	A	TP	PIM
1983-84	Peterborough	OHL	62	13	18	31	168	8	3	3	6	14
1984-85	Peterborough	OHL	61	18	35	53	222	16	2	8	10	28
1985-86	Peterborough	OHL	58	19	40	59	254	8	4	0	4	21
1986-87	Binghamton	AHL	7	0	0	0	18	....	....	....	....	....
	Peterborough	OHL	46	23	33	56	160	12	5	8	13	41
1987-88	Detroit	NHL	3	1	0	1	2	....	....	....	....	....
	Adirondack	AHL	76	21	32	53	337	10	4	4	8	53
1988-89	Detroit	NHL	55	2	3	5	168	2	0	0	0	2
1989-90	NY Rangers	NHL	68	6	7	13	286	10	0	1	1	38
1990-91	NY Rangers	NHL	72	11	14	25	154	6	2	0	2	36
1991-92	NY Rangers	NHL	79	10	9	19	224	13	4	1	5	14
1992-93	NY Rangers	NHL	30	0	3	3	67	....	....	....	....	....
	Winnipeg	NHL	48	8	8	16	136	6	1	1	2	4
1993-94	Winnipeg	NHL	83	4	8	12	205	....	....	....	....	....
1994-95	Winnipeg	NHL	48	4	2	6	85	....	....	....	....	....
1995-96a	Winnipeg	NHL	81	9	11	20	151	5	0	1	1	4
1996-97	Phoenix	NHL	81	3	11	14	185	7	0	0	0	17
	NHL Totals		648	58	76	134	1663	49	7	4	11	115

a Won King Clancy Memorial Trophy (1996)

Signed as a free agent by **Detroit**, March 23, 1987. Traded to **NY Rangers** by **Detroit** for Chris McRae and Detroit's fifth round choice (previously acquired by NY Rangers — Detroit selected Tony Burns) in 1990 Entry Draft, September 7, 1989. Traded to **Winnipeg** by **NY Rangers** with Tie Domi for Ed Olczyk, December 28, 1992. Signed as a free agent by **Toronto**, July 23, 1997.

KING, STEVEN

Right wing. Shoots right. 6', 195 lbs. Born, Greenwich, RI, July 22, 1969.
(NY Rangers' 1st choice, 21st overall, in 1991 Supplemental Draft).

			Regular Season					Playoffs				
Season	Club	Lea	GP	G	A	TP	PIM	GP	G	A	TP	PIM
1989-90	Brown	ECAC	27	19	8	27	53	....	....	....	....	....
1990-91	Brown	ECAC	27	19	15	34	76	....	....	....	....	....
1991-92	Binghamton	AHL	66	27	15	42	56	10	2	0	2	14
1992-93	NY Rangers	NHL	24	7	5	12	16	....	....	....	....	....
	Binghamton	AHL	53	35	33	68	100	14	7	9	16	26
1993-94	Anaheim	NHL	36	8	3	11	44	....	....	....	....	....
1994-95			DID NOT PLAY – INJURED									
1995-96	Anaheim	NHL	7	2	0	2	15	....	....	....	....	....
	Baltimore	AHL	68	40	21	61	95	12	7	5	12	20
1996-97	Philadelphia	AHL	39	17	10	27	47	....	....	....	....	....
	Michigan	IHL	39	15	11	26	39	4	1	2	3	12
	NHL Totals		67	17	8	25	75	....	....	....	....	....

Claimed by **Anaheim** from **NY Rangers** in Expansion Draft, June 24, 1993. Signed as a free agent by **Philadelphia**, July 31, 1996.

KINNEAR, GEORDIE N.J.

Defense. Shoots left. 6'1", 200 lbs. Born, Simcoe, Ont., July 9, 1973.
(New Jersey's 7th choice, 162nd overall, in 1992 Entry Draft).

			Regular Season					Playoffs				
Season	Club	Lea	GP	G	A	TP	PIM	GP	G	A	TP	PIM
1990-91	Peterborough	OHL	37	1	0	1	76	2	0	0	0	10
1991-92	Peterborough	OHL	63	5	16	21	195	10	0	2	2	36
1992-93	Peterborough	OHL	58	6	22	28	161	19	1	5	6	43
1993-94	Albany	AHL	59	3	12	15	197	5	0	0	0	21
1994-95	Albany	AHL	68	5	11	16	136	9	1	1	2	7
1995-96	Albany	AHL	73	4	7	11	170	4	0	1	1	2
1996-97	Albany	AHL	59	2	9	11	175	10	0	1	1	15

KIPRUSOFF, MARKO (KIHP-ruh-sohf)

Defense. Shoots left. 6', 195 lbs. Born, Turku, Finland, June 6, 1972.
(Montreal's 4th choice, 70th overall, in 1994 Entry Draft).

			Regular Season					Playoffs				
Season	Club	Lea	GP	G	A	TP	PIM	GP	G	A	TP	PIM
1990-91	TPS	Fin.	3	0	0	0	0	....	....	....	....	....
1991-92	TPS	Fin.	23	0	2	2	0	....	....	....	....	....
	HPK	Fin.	3	0	0	0	0	....	....	....	....	....
1992-93	TPS	Fin.	43	3	7	10	14	12	2	3	5	6
1993-94	TPS	Fin.	48	5	19	24	8	11	0	6	6	4
1994-95	TPS	Fin.	50	10	21	31	16	13	0	9	9	2
1995-96	Montreal	NHL	24	0	4	4	8	....	....	....	....	....
	Fredericton	AHL	28	4	10	14	2	10	2	5	7	2
1996-97	Malmo	Swe.	50	10	18	28	24	4	0	0	0	0
	NHL Totals		24	0	4	4	8	....	....	....	....	....

KLATT, TRENT (KLAT) PHI.

Right wing. Shoots right. 6'1", 205 lbs. Born, Robbinsdale, MN, January 30, 1971.
(Washington's 5th choice, 82nd overall, in 1989 Entry Draft).

			Regular Season					Playoffs				
Season	Club	Lea	GP	G	A	TP	PIM	GP	G	A	TP	PIM
1989-90	U. Minnesota	WCHA	38	22	14	36	16	....	....	....	....	....
1990-91	U. Minnesota	WCHA	39	16	28	44	58	....	....	....	....	....
1991-92	U. Minnesota	WCHA	41	27	36	63	76	....	....	....	....	....
	Minnesota	NHL	1	0	0	0	0	6	0	0	0	2
1992-93	Minnesota	NHL	47	4	19	23	38	....	....	....	....	....
	Kalamazoo	IHL	31	8	11	19	18	....	....	....	....	....
1993-94	Dallas	NHL	61	14	24	38	30	9	2	1	3	4
	Kalamazoo	IHL	6	3	2	5	4	....	....	....	....	....
1994-95	Dallas	NHL	47	12	10	22	26	5	1	0	1	0
1995-96	Dallas	NHL	22	4	4	8	23	....	....	....	....	....
	Michigan	IHL	2	1	2	3	5	....	....	....	....	....
	Philadelphia	NHL	49	3	8	11	21	12	4	1	5	0
1996-97	Philadelphia	NHL	76	24	21	45	20	19	4	3	7	12
	NHL Totals		303	61	86	147	158	51	11	5	16	18

Traded to **Minnesota** by **Washington** with Steve Maltais for Shawn Chambers, June 21, 1991. Traded to **Philadelphia** by **Dallas** for Brent Fedyk, December 13, 1995.

KLEE, KEN — WSH.

Right wing. Shoots right. 6'1", 205 lbs. Born, Indianapolis, IN, April 24, 1971.
(Washington's 11th choice, 177th overall, in 1990 Entry Draft).

			Regular Season					Playoffs				
Season	Club	Lea	GP	G	A	TP	PIM	GP	G	A	TP	PIM
1989-90	Bowling Green	CCHA	39	0	5	5	52	....	....	....	....	....
1990-91	Bowling Green	CCHA	37	7	28	35	50	....	....	....	....	....
1991-92	Bowling Green	CCHA	10	0	1	1	14	....	....	....	....	....
1992-93	Baltimore	AHL	77	4	14	18	93	7	0	1	1	15
1993-94	Portland	AHL	65	2	9	11	87	17	1	2	3	14
1994-95	Portland	AHL	49	5	7	12	89	....	....	....	....	....
	Washington	**NHL**	**23**	**3**	**1**	**4**	**41**	**7**	**0**	**0**	**0**	**4**
1995-96	**Washington**	**NHL**	**66**	**8**	**3**	**11**	**60**	**1**	**0**	**0**	**0**	**0**
1996-97	**Washington**	**NHL**	**80**	**3**	**8**	**11**	**115**	....	....	....	....	....
	NHL Totals		**169**	**14**	**12**	**26**	**216**	**8**	**0**	**0**	**0**	**4**

KLEMM, JON — COL.

Defense. Shoots right. 6'3", 200 lbs. Born, Cranbrook, B.C., January 8, 1970.

			Regular Season					Playoffs				
Season	Club	Lea	GP	G	A	TP	PIM	GP	G	A	TP	PIM
1988-89	Seattle	WHL	2	1	1	2	0	....	....	....	....	....
	Spokane	WHL	66	6	34	40	42	....	....	....	....	....
1989-90	Spokane	WHL	66	3	28	31	100	6	1	1	2	5
1990-91	Spokane	WHL	72	7	58	65	65	15	3	6	9	8
1991-92	**Quebec**	**NHL**	**4**	**0**	**1**	**1**	**0**	....	....	....	....	....
	Halifax	AHL	70	6	13	19	40	....	....	....	....	....
1992-93	Halifax	AHL	80	3	20	23	32	....	....	....	....	....
1993-94	**Quebec**	**NHL**	**7**	**0**	**0**	**0**	**4**	....	....	....	....	....
	Cornwall	AHL	66	4	26	30	78	13	1	2	3	6
1994-95	Cornwall	AHL	65	6	13	19	84	....	....	....	....	....
	Quebec	**NHL**	**4**	**1**	**0**	**1**	**2**	....	....	....	....	....
1995-96	**Colorado**	**NHL**	**56**	**3**	**12**	**15**	**20**	**15**	**2**	**1**	**3**	**0** ♦
1996-97	**Colorado**	**NHL**	**80**	**9**	**15**	**24**	**37**	**17**	**1**	**1**	**2**	**6**
	NHL Totals		**151**	**13**	**28**	**41**	**63**	**32**	**3**	**2**	**5**	**6**

Signed as a free agent by **Quebec**, May 14, 1991.

KLEVAKIN, DMITRI (kleh-VAH-kihn) — T.B.

Right wing. Shoots left. 5'11", 163 lbs. Born, Angarsk, USSR, February 20, 1976.
(Tampa Bay's 4th choice, 86th overall, in 1994 Entry Draft).

			Regular Season					Playoffs				
Season	Club	Lea	GP	G	A	TP	PIM	GP	G	A	TP	PIM
1992-93	Spartak	CIS	8	1	1	2	0	....	....	....	....	....
1993-94	Spartak	CIS	42	6	3	9	6	4	1	0	1	0
1994-95	Spartak	CIS	52	12	10	22	4	....	....	....	....	....
1995-96	Spartak	CIS	49	8	15	23	54	5	3	0	3	0
1996-97	Spartak	Rus.	41	5	12	17	35	....	....	....	....	....

KLIMA, PETR (KLEE-muh)

Right/Left wing. Shoots right. 6', 190 lbs. Born, Chomutov, Czech., December 23, 1964.
(Detroit's 5th choice, 86th overall, in 1983 Entry Draft).

			Regular Season					Playoffs				
Season	Club	Lea	GP	G	A	TP	PIM	GP	G	A	TP	PIM
1981-82	Litvinov	Czech.	18	7	3	10	8	....	....	....	....	....
1982-83	Litvinov	Czech.	44	19	17	36	74	....	....	....	....	....
1983-84	Dukla Jihlava	Czech.	41	20	16	36	46	....	....	....	....	....
1984-85	Dukla Jihlava	Czech.	35	23	22	45	76	....	....	....	....	....
1985-86	**Detroit**	**NHL**	**74**	**32**	**24**	**56**	**16**	....	....	....	....	....
1986-87	**Detroit**	**NHL**	**77**	**30**	**23**	**53**	**42**	**13**	**1**	**2**	**3**	**4**
1987-88	**Detroit**	**NHL**	**78**	**37**	**25**	**62**	**46**	**12**	**10**	**8**	**18**	**10**
1988-89	**Detroit**	**NHL**	**51**	**25**	**16**	**41**	**44**	**6**	**2**	**4**	**6**	**19**
	Adirondack	AHL	5	5	1	6	4	....	....	....	....	....
1989-90	**Detroit**	**NHL**	**13**	**5**	**5**	**10**	**6**	....	....	....	....	....
	Edmonton	**NHL**	**63**	**25**	**28**	**53**	**66**	**21**	**5**	**0**	**5**	**8** ♦
1990-91	**Edmonton**	**NHL**	**70**	**40**	**28**	**68**	**113**	**18**	**7**	**6**	**13**	**16**
1991-92	**Edmonton**	**NHL**	**57**	**21**	**13**	**34**	**52**	**15**	**1**	**4**	**5**	**8**
1992-93	**Edmonton**	**NHL**	**68**	**32**	**16**	**48**	**100**	....	....	....	....	....
1993-94	**Tampa Bay**	**NHL**	**75**	**28**	**27**	**55**	**76**	....	....	....	....	....
1994-95	Wolfsburg	Ger. 2	12	27	11	38	28	....	....	....	....	....
	ZPS Zlin	Czech.	1	1	0	1	0	....	....	....	....	....
	Tampa Bay	**NHL**	**47**	**13**	**13**	**26**	**26**	....	....	....	....	....
1995-96	**Tampa Bay**	**NHL**	**67**	**22**	**30**	**52**	**68**	**4**	**2**	**0**	**2**	**14**
1996-97	**Los Angeles**	**NHL**	**8**	**0**	**4**	**4**	**2**	....	....	....	....	....
	Pittsburgh	**NHL**	**9**	**1**	**3**	**4**	**4**	....	....	....	....	....
	Cleveland	IHL	19	7	14	21	6	....	....	....	....	....
	Edmonton	**NHL**	**16**	**1**	**5**	**6**	**6**	**6**	**0**	**0**	**0**	**4**
	NHL Totals		**773**	**312**	**260**	**572**	**667**	**95**	**28**	**24**	**52**	**83**

Traded to **Edmonton** by **Detroit** with Joe Murphy, Adam Graves and Jeff Sharples for Jimmy Carson, Kevin McClelland and Edmonton's fifth round choice (later traded to Montreal — Montreal selected Brad Layzell) in 1991 Entry Draft, November 2, 1989. Traded to **Tampa Bay** by **Edmonton** for Tampa Bay's third round choice (Brad Symes) in 1994 Entry Draft, June 16, 1993. Traded to **Los Angeles** by **Tampa Bay** for Los Angeles' fifth round choice (Jan Sulc) in 1997 Entry Draft, August 22, 1996. Traded to **Pittsburgh** by **Los Angeles** for a conditional choice in 1997 Entry Draft, October 25, 1996. Signed as a free agent by **Edmonton**, February 26, 1997.

KLIMENTIEV, SERGEI (klih-MEHN-tyehv) — BUF.

Defense. Shoots left. 5'11", 200 lbs. Born, Kiev, USSR, April 5, 1975.
(Buffalo's 4th choice, 121st overall, in 1994 Entry Draft).

			Regular Season					Playoffs				
Season	Club	Lea	GP	G	A	TP	PIM	GP	G	A	TP	PIM
1991-92	SVSM Kiev	CIS 3	42	4	15	19	....	....	....	....	....	....
1992-93	Sokol Kiev	CIS	3	0	0	0	4	1	0	0	0	0
1993-94	Medicine Hat	WHL	72	16	26	42	165	3	0	0	0	4
1994-95	Medicine Hat	WHL	71	19	45	64	146	5	4	2	6	14
	Rochester	AHL	7	0	0	0	8	1	0	0	0	0
1995-96	Rochester	AHL	70	7	29	36	74	19	2	8	10	16
1996-97	Rochester	AHL	77	14	28	42	114	10	1	4	5	28

KLIMOVICH, SERGEI (klee-MOH-vich) — CHI.

Center. Shoots right. 6'3", 189 lbs. Born, Novosibirsk, USSR, March 8, 1974.
(Chicago's 3rd choice, 41st overall, in 1992 Entry Draft).

			Regular Season					Playoffs				
Season	Club	Lea	GP	G	A	TP	PIM	GP	G	A	TP	PIM
1991-92	Moscow D'amo	CIS	3	0	0	0	0	....	....	....	....	....
1992-93	Moscow D'amo	CIS	30	4	1	5	14	10	1	0	1	2
1993-94	Moscow D'amo	CIS	39	7	4	11	14	12	2	3	5	6
1994-95	Moscow D'amo	CIS	4	1	0	1	2	....	....	....	....	....
	Indianapolis	IHL	71	14	30	44	20	....	....	....	....	....
1995-96	Indianapolis	IHL	68	17	21	38	28	5	1	1	2	6
1996-97	**Chicago**	**NHL**	**1**	**0**	**0**	**0**	**2**	....	....	....	....	....
	Indianapolis	IHL	75	20	37	57	98	3	1	2	3	0
	NHL Totals		**1**	**0**	**0**	**0**	**2**	....	....	....	....	....

KNIPSCHEER, FRED (kuh-NIHP-sheer)

Center. Shoots left. 5'11", 185 lbs. Born, Ft. Wayne, IN, September 3, 1969.

			Regular Season					Playoffs				
Season	Club	Lea	GP	G	A	TP	PIM	GP	G	A	TP	PIM
1990-91	St. Cloud	WCHA	40	9	10	19	57	....	....	....	....	....
1991-92	St. Cloud	WCHA	33	15	17	32	48	....	....	....	....	....
1992-93ab	St. Cloud	WCHA	36	34	26	60	68	....	....	....	....	....
1993-94	**Boston**	**NHL**	**11**	**3**	**2**	**5**	**14**	**12**	**2**	**1**	**3**	**6**
	Providence	AHL	62	26	13	39	50	....	....	....	....	....
1994-95	Providence	AHL	71	29	34	63	81	....	....	....	....	....
	Boston	**NHL**	**16**	**3**	**1**	**4**	**2**	**4**	**0**	**0**	**0**	**0**
1995-96	**St. Louis**	**NHL**	**1**	**0**	**0**	**0**	**2**	....	....	....	....	....
	Worcester	AHL	68	36	37	73	93	3	0	0	0	2
1996-97	Phoenix	IHL	24	5	11	16	19	....	....	....	....	....
	Indianapolis	IHL	41	10	9	19	46	4	0	2	2	10
	NHL Totals		**28**	**6**	**3**	**9**	**18**	**16**	**2**	**1**	**3**	**6**

a WCHA First All-Star Team (1993)
b NCAA West Second All-American Team (1993)

Signed as a free agent by **Boston**, April 30, 1993. Traded to **St. Louis** by **Boston** for Rick Zombo, October 2, 1995. Signed as a free agent by **Chicago**, August 16, 1996.

KNUBLE, MICHAEL (NOO-buhl) — DET.

Right wing. Shoots right. 6'3", 208 lbs. Born, Toronto, Ont., July 4, 1972.
(Detroit's 4th choice, 76th overall, in 1991 Entry Draft).

			Regular Season					Playoffs				
Season	Club	Lea	GP	G	A	TP	PIM	GP	G	A	TP	PIM
1991-92	U. of Michigan	CCHA	43	7	8	15	48	....	....	....	....	....
1992-93	U. of Michigan	CCHA	39	26	16	42	57	....	....	....	....	....
1993-94a	U. of Michigan	CCHA	41	32	26	58	71	....	....	....	....	....
1994-95ab	U. of Michigan	CCHA	34	*38	22	60	62	....	....	....	....	....
	Adirondack	AHL	....	....	....	....	....	3	0	0	0	0
1995-96	Adirondack	AHL	80	22	23	45	59	3	1	0	1	0
1996-97	**Detroit**	**NHL**	**9**	**1**	**0**	**1**	**0**	....	....	....	....	....
	Adirondack	AHL	68	28	35	63	54	....	....	....	....	....
	NHL Totals		**9**	**1**	**0**	**1**	**0**	....	....	....	....	....

a CCHA Second All-Star Team (1994, 1995)
b NCAA West Second All-American Team (1995)

KNUTSEN, ESPEN (kuh-NOOT-suhn) — ANA.

Center. Shoots left. 5'11", 180 lbs. Born, Oslo, Norway, January 12, 1972.
(Hartford's 9th choice, 204th overall, in 1990 Entry Draft).

			Regular Season					Playoffs				
Season	Club	Lea	GP	G	A	TP	PIM	GP	G	A	TP	PIM
1989-90	Valerengen	Nor.	34	22	26	48	....	....	....	....	....	....
1990-91	Valerengen	Nor.	31	30	24	54	42	5	3	4	7	....
1991-92	Valerengen	Nor.	30	28	26	54	37	8	7	8	15	....
1992-93	Valerengen	Nor.	13	11	13	24	4	....	....	....	....	....
1993-94	Valerengen	Nor.	38	32	26	58	20	....	....	....	....	....
1994-95	Djurgarden	Swe.	30	6	14	20	18	3	0	1	1	0
1995-96	Djurgarden	Swe.	32	10	23	33	50	4	1	0	1	2
1996-97	Djurgarden	Swe.	39	16	33	49	20	4	2	4	6	6

Rights traded to **Anaheim** by **Hartford** for Kevin Brown, October 1, 1996.

KOCUR, JOE (KOH-suhr) — DET.

Right wing. Shoots right. 6', 205 lbs. Born, Calgary, Alta., December 21, 1964.
(Detroit's 6th choice, 88th overall, in 1983 Entry Draft).

			Regular Season					Playoffs				
Season	Club	Lea	GP	G	A	TP	PIM	GP	G	A	TP	PIM
1982-83	Saskatoon	WHL	62	23	17	40	289	6	2	3	5	25
1983-84	Saskatoon	WHL	69	40	41	81	258	....	....	....	....	....
	Adirondack	AHL	....	....	....	....	....	5	0	0	0	20
1984-85	**Detroit**	**NHL**	**17**	**1**	**0**	**1**	**64**	**3**	**1**	**0**	**1**	**5**
	Adirondack	AHL	47	12	7	19	171	....	....	....	....	....
1985-86	**Detroit**	**NHL**	**59**	**9**	**6**	**15**	***377**	....	....	....	....	....
	Adirondack	AHL	9	6	2	8	34	....	....	....	....	....
1986-87	**Detroit**	**NHL**	**77**	**9**	**9**	**18**	**276**	**16**	**2**	**3**	**5**	**71**
1987-88	**Detroit**	**NHL**	**63**	**7**	**7**	**14**	**263**	**10**	**0**	**1**	**1**	**13**
1988-89	**Detroit**	**NHL**	**60**	**9**	**9**	**18**	**213**	**3**	**0**	**1**	**1**	**6**
1989-90	**Detroit**	**NHL**	**71**	**16**	**20**	**36**	**268**	....	....	....	....	....
1990-91	**Detroit**	**NHL**	**52**	**5**	**4**	**9**	**253**	....	....	....	....	....
	NY Rangers	**NHL**	**5**	**0**	**0**	**0**	**36**	**6**	**0**	**2**	**2**	**21**
1991-92	**NY Rangers**	**NHL**	**51**	**7**	**4**	**11**	**121**	**12**	**1**	**1**	**2**	**38**
1992-93	**NY Rangers**	**NHL**	**65**	**3**	**6**	**9**	**131**	....	....	....	....	....
1993-94	**NY Rangers**	**NHL**	**71**	**2**	**1**	**3**	**129**	**20**	**1**	**1**	**2**	**17** ♦
1994-95	**NY Rangers**	**NHL**	**48**	**1**	**2**	**3**	**71**	**10**	**0**	**0**	**0**	**8**
1995-96	**NY Rangers**	**NHL**	**38**	**1**	**2**	**3**	**49**	....	....	....	....	....
	Vancouver	**NHL**	**7**	**0**	**1**	**1**	**19**	**1**	**0**	**0**	**0**	**0**
1996-97	San Antonio	IHL	5	1	1	2	24	....	....	....	....	....
	Detroit	**NHL**	**34**	**2**	**1**	**3**	**70**	**19**	**1**	**3**	**4**	**22** ♦
	NHL Totals		**718**	**72**	**72**	**144**	**2340**	**100**	**6**	**12**	**18**	**201**

Traded to **NY Rangers** by **Detroit** with Per Djoos for Kevin Miller, Jim Cummins and Dennis Vial, March 5, 1991. Traded to **Vancouver** by **NY Rangers** for Kay Whitmore, March 20, 1996. Signed as a free agent by **Detroit**, December 27, 1996.

KOHN, LADISLAV (KOHN) — CGY.

Right wing. Shoots left. 5'10", 180 lbs. Born, Uherske Hradiste, Czech., March 4, 1975.
(Calgary's 9th choice, 175th overall, in 1994 Entry Draft).

			Regular Season					Playoffs				
Season	Club	Lea	GP	G	A	TP	PIM	GP	G	A	TP	PIM
1993-94	Brandon	WHL	2	0	0	0	0	....	....	....	....	....
	Swift Current	WHL	69	33	35	68	68	7	5	4	9	8
1994-95	Swift Current	WHL	65	32	60	92	122	6	2	6	8	14
	Saint John	AHL	1	0	0	0	0	....	....	....	....	....
1995-96	**Calgary**	**NHL**	**5**	**1**	**0**	**1**	**2**	....	....	....	....	....
	Saint John	AHL	73	28	45	73	97	16	6	5	11	12
1996-97	Saint John	AHL	76	28	29	57	81	5	0	0	0	0
	NHL Totals		**5**	**1**	**0**	**1**	**2**	....	....	....	....	....

KOIVU, SAKU (KOY-voo, SA-koo) — MTL.

Center. Shoots left. 5'9", 175 lbs. Born, Turku, Finland, November 23, 1974.
(Montreal's 1st choice, 21st overall, in 1993 Entry Draft).

			Regular Season					Playoffs				
Season	Club	Lea	GP	G	A	TP	PIM	GP	G	A	TP	PIM
1992-93	TPS	Fin.	46	3	7	10	28	11	3	2	5	2
1993-94	TPS	Fin.	47	23	30	53	42	11	4	8	12	16
1994-95	TPS	Fin.	45	27	47	74	73	13	7	10	17	16
1995-96	**Montreal**	**NHL**	**82**	**20**	**25**	**45**	**40**	**6**	**3**	**1**	**4**	**8**
1996-97	**Montreal**	**NHL**	**50**	**17**	**39**	**56**	**38**	**5**	**1**	**3**	**4**	**10**
	NHL Totals		**132**	**37**	**64**	**101**	**78**	**11**	**4**	**4**	**8**	**18**

KOKOREV, DMITRI (KOH-koh-rehf) CGY.

Defense. Shoots left. 6'3", 198 lbs. Born, Moscow, USSR, January 9, 1979.
(Calgary's 4th choice, 51st overall, in 1997 Entry Draft).

			Regular Season					Playoffs				
Season	Club	Lea	GP	G	A	TP	PIM	GP	G	A	TP	PIM
1996-97	Mosc. D'amo 2	Rus. 3	27	2	4	6	24	....	....	....	....	....
	Moscow D'amo	Rus.	1	0	0	0	0	....	....	....	....	....

KOLESAR, MARK (kohl-UH-sahr) TOR.

Left wing. Shoots right. 6'1", 188 lbs. Born, Brampton, Ont., January 23, 1973.

			Regular Season					Playoffs				
Season	Club	Lea	GP	G	A	TP	PIM	GP	G	A	TP	PIM
1991-92	Brandon	WHL	56	6	7	13	36	....	....	....	....	....
1992-93	Brandon	WHL	68	27	33	60	110	4	0	0	0	4
1993-94	Brandon	WHL	59	29	37	66	131	14	8	3	11	48
1994-95	St. John's	AHL	65	12	18	30	62	5	1	0	1	2
1995-96	**Toronto**	**NHL**	**21**	**2**	**2**	**4**	**14**	**3**	**1**	**0**	**1**	**2**
	St. John's	AHL	52	22	13	35	47	....	....	....	....	....
1996-97	**Toronto**	**NHL**	**7**	**0**	**0**	**0**	**0**	....	....	....	....	....
	St. John's	AHL	62	22	28	50	64	10	1	3	4	6
	NHL Totals		**28**	**2**	**2**	**4**	**14**	**3**	**1**	**0**	**1**	**2**

Signed as a free agent by **Toronto**, May 24, 1994.

KOLKUNOV, ALEXEI (kohl-koo-NAHV) PIT.

Center. Shoots right. 6'2", 185 lbs. Born, Belgorod, USSR, February 3, 1977.
(Pittsburgh's 5th choice, 154th overall, in 1995 Entry Draft).

			Regular Season					Playoffs				
Season	Club	Lea	GP	G	A	TP	PIM	GP	G	A	TP	PIM
1994-95	Soviet Wings	CIS	7	0	0	0	0	4	1	0	1	0
1995-96	Soviet Wings	CIS	43	9	3	12	35	....	....	....	....	....
1996-97	Soviet Wings	Rus.	44	9	16	25	36	2	0	0	0	4

KOMARNISKI, ZENITH (KOH-mahr-NIHS-kee, ZEE-nihth) VAN.

Defense. Shoots left. 6', 192 lbs. Born, Edmonton, Alta., August 13, 1978.
(Vancouver's 2nd choice, 75th overall, in 1996 Entry Draft).

			Regular Season					Playoffs				
Season	Club	Lea	GP	G	A	TP	PIM	GP	G	A	TP	PIM
1994-95	Tri-City	WHL	66	5	19	24	110	17	1	2	3	47
1995-96	Tri-City	WHL	42	5	21	26	85	....	....	....	....	....
1996-97a	Tri-City	WHL	58	12	44	56	112	....	....	....	....	....

a WHL West First All-Star Team (1997)

KONDRASHKIN, SERGEI (kohn-DRAHSH-kihn) NYR

Right wing. Shoots left. 6', 192 lbs. Born, Cherepovets, USSR, April 2, 1975.
(NY Rangers' 7th choice, 162nd overall, in 1993 Entry Draft).

			Regular Season					Playoffs				
Season	Club	Lea	GP	G	A	TP	PIM	GP	G	A	TP	PIM
1992-93	Cherepovets	CIS	41	7	3	10	8	....	....	....	....	....
1993-94	Cherepovets	CIS	41	7	2	9	26	....	....	....	....	....
1994-95	Cherepovets	CIS	51	7	2	9	22	....	....	....	....	....
1995-96	Cherepovets	CIS	28	2	1	3	8	3	1	0	1	2
1996-97	Cherepovets	Rus.	33	7	2	9	8	....	....	....	....	....

KONOWALCHUK, STEVE (kahn-uh-WAHL-chuhk) WSH.

Center. Shoots left. 6'1", 195 lbs. Born, Salt Lake City, UT, November 11, 1972.
(Washington's 5th choice, 58th overall, in 1991 Entry Draft).

			Regular Season					Playoffs				
Season	Club	Lea	GP	G	A	TP	PIM	GP	G	A	TP	PIM
1990-91	Portland	WHL	72	43	49	92	78	....	....	....	....	....
1991-92	**Washington**	**NHL**	**1**	**0**	**0**	**0**	**0**	....	....	....	....	....
	Baltimore	AHL	3	1	1	2	0	....	....	....	....	....
a	Portland	WHL	64	51	53	104	95	6	3	6	9	12
1992-93	**Washington**	**NHL**	**36**	**4**	**7**	**11**	**16**	**2**	**0**	**1**	**1**	**0**
	Baltimore	AHL	37	18	28	46	74	....	....	....	....	....
1993-94	**Washington**	**NHL**	**62**	**12**	**14**	**26**	**33**	**11**	**0**	**1**	**1**	**10**
	Portland	AHL	8	11	4	15	4	....	....	....	....	....
1994-95	**Washington**	**NHL**	**46**	**11**	**14**	**25**	**44**	**7**	**2**	**5**	**7**	**12**
1995-96	**Washington**	**NHL**	**70**	**23**	**22**	**45**	**92**	**2**	**0**	**2**	**2**	**0**
1996-97	**Washington**	**NHL**	**78**	**17**	**25**	**42**	**67**	....	....	....	....	....
	NHL Totals		**293**	**67**	**82**	**149**	**252**	**22**	**2**	**9**	**11**	**22**

a WHL First All-Star Team (1992)

KONSTANTINOV, VLADIMIR (kohn-stahn-TEE-nahf) DET.

Defense. Shoots right. 5'11", 190 lbs. Born, Murmansk, USSR, March 19, 1967.
(Detroit's 12th choice, 221st overall, in 1989 Entry Draft).

			Regular Season					Playoffs				
Season	Club	Lea	GP	G	A	TP	PIM	GP	G	A	TP	PIM
1984-85	CSKA	USSR	40	1	4	5	10	....	....	....	....	....
1985-86	CSKA	USSR	26	4	3	7	12	....	....	....	....	....
1986-87	CSKA	USSR	35	2	2	4	19	....	....	....	....	....
1987-88	CSKA	USSR	50	3	6	9	32	....	....	....	....	....
1988-89	CSKA	USSR	37	7	8	15	20	....	....	....	....	....
1989-90	CSKA	USSR	47	14	14	28	44	....	....	....	....	....
1990-91	CSKA	USSR	45	5	12	17	42	....	....	....	....	....
1991-92a	**Detroit**	**NHL**	**79**	**8**	**26**	**34**	**172**	**11**	**0**	**1**	**1**	**16**
1992-93	**Detroit**	**NHL**	**82**	**5**	**17**	**22**	**137**	**7**	**0**	**1**	**1**	**8**
1993-94	**Detroit**	**NHL**	**80**	**12**	**21**	**33**	**138**	**7**	**0**	**2**	**2**	**4**
1994-95	Wedemark	Ger. 2	15	13	17	30	51	....	....	....	....	....
	Detroit	**NHL**	**47**	**3**	**11**	**14**	**101**	**18**	**1**	**1**	**2**	**22**
1995-96bc	**Detroit**	**NHL**	**81**	**14**	**20**	**34**	**139**	**19**	**4**	**5**	**9**	**28**
1996-97	**Detroit**	**NHL**	**77**	**5**	**33**	**38**	**151**	**20**	**0**	**4**	**4**	**29** ♦
	NHL Totals		**446**	**47**	**128**	**175**	**838**	**82**	**5**	**14**	**19**	**107**

a NHL/Upper Deck All-Rookie Team (1992)
b NHL Second All-Star Team (1996)
c Won Alka-Seltzer Plus Award (1996)

KONTOS, CHRIS (KONN-tohs)

Left wing/Center. Shoots left. 6'1", 195 lbs. Born, Toronto, Ont., December 10, 1963.
(NY Rangers' 1st choice, 15th overall, in 1982 Entry Draft).

			Regular Season					Playoffs				
Season	Club	Lea	GP	G	A	TP	PIM	GP	G	A	TP	PIM
1980-81	Sudbury	OHA	57	17	27	44	36	....	....	....	....	....
1981-82	Sudbury	OHL	12	6	6	12	18	....	....	....	....	....
	Toronto	OHL	59	36	56	92	68	10	7	9	16	2
1982-83	**NY Rangers**	**NHL**	**44**	**8**	**7**	**15**	**33**	....	....	....	....	....
	Toronto	OHL	28	21	33	54	23	....	....	....	....	....
1983-84	**NY Rangers**	**NHL**	**6**	**0**	**1**	**1**	**8**	....	....	....	....	....
	Tulsa	CHL	21	5	13	18	8	....	....	....	....	....
1984-85	**NY Rangers**	**NHL**	**28**	**4**	**8**	**12**	**24**	....	....	....	....	....
	New Haven	AHL	48	19	24	43	30	....	....	....	....	....
1985-86	Ilves	Fin.	36	16	15	31	30	....	....	....	....	....
	New Haven	AHL	21	8	15	23	12	5	4	2	6	4
1986-87	**Pittsburgh**	**NHL**	**31**	**8**	**9**	**17**	**6**	....	....	....	....	....
	New Haven	AHL	36	14	17	31	29	....	....	....	....	....
1987-88	**Pittsburgh**	**NHL**	**36**	**1**	**7**	**8**	**12**	....	....	....	....	....
	Muskegon	IHL	10	3	6	9	8	....	....	....	....	....
	Los Angeles	**NHL**	**6**	**2**	**10**	**12**	**2**	**4**	**1**	**0**	**1**	**4**
	New Haven	AHL	16	8	16	24	4	....	....	....	....	....
1988-89	EHC Kloten	Swiss	36	33	22	55	....	6	6	2	8	....
	Los Angeles	**NHL**	**7**	**2**	**1**	**3**	**2**	**11**	**9**	**0**	**9**	**8**
1989-90	**Los Angeles**	**NHL**	**6**	**2**	**2**	**4**	**4**	**5**	**1**	**0**	**1**	**0**
	New Haven	AHL	42	10	20	30	25	....	....	....	....	....
1990-91	Phoenix	IHL	69	26	36	62	19	11	9	12	21	0
1991-92	Cdn. National	....	26	10	10	20	4	....	....	....	....	....
1992-93	**Tampa Bay**	**NHL**	**66**	**27**	**24**	**51**	**12**	....	....	....	....	....
1993-94	Cdn. National	....	35	16	16	32	12	....	....	....	....	....
	Cdn. Olympic	....	8	3	1	4	2	....	....	....	....	....
1994-95	Skelleftea	Swe.	36	21	27	48	30	5	2	3	5	4
	Cdn. National	....	3	0	1	1	4	....	....	....	....	....
1995-96	Cincinnati	IHL	81	26	44	70	13	17	5	8	13	0
1996-97	Cincinnati	IHL	11	1	3	4	4	....	....	....	....	....
	Quebec	IHL	19	8	3	11	0	....	....	....	....	....
	Manitoba	IHL	40	17	18	35	12	....	....	....	....	....
	NHL Totals		**230**	**54**	**69**	**123**	**103**	**20**	**11**	**0**	**11**	**12**

Traded to **Pittsburgh** by **NY Rangers** for Ron Duguay, January 21, 1987. Traded to **Los Angeles** by **Pittsburgh** with Pittsburgh's sixth round choice (Micah Aivazoff) in 1988 Entry Draft for Bryan Erickson, February 5, 1988. Signed as a free agent by **Tampa Bay**, July 21, 1992. Signed as a free agent by **Florida**, July 7, 1995.

KORDIC, DAN PHI.

Left wing. Shoots left. 6'5", 234 lbs. Born, Edmonton, Alta., April 18, 1971.
(Philadelphia's 9th choice, 88th overall, in 1990 Entry Draft).

			Regular Season					Playoffs				
Season	Club	Lea	GP	G	A	TP	PIM	GP	G	A	TP	PIM
1987-88	Medicine Hat	WHL	63	1	5	6	75	....	....	....	....	....
1988-89	Medicine Hat	WHL	70	1	13	14	190	....	....	....	....	....
1989-90	Medicine Hat	WHL	59	4	12	16	182	3	0	0	0	9
1990-91	Medicine Hat	WHL	67	8	15	23	150	12	2	6	8	42
1991-92	**Philadelphia**	**NHL**	**46**	**1**	**3**	**4**	**126**	....	....	....	....	....
1992-93	Hershey	AHL	14	0	2	2	17	....	....	....	....	....
1993-94	**Philadelphia**	**NHL**	**4**	**0**	**0**	**0**	**5**	....	....	....	....	....
	Hershey	AHL	64	0	4	4	164	11	0	3	3	26
1994-95	Hershey	AHL	37	0	2	2	121	6	0	1	1	21
1995-96	**Philadelphia**	**NHL**	**9**	**1**	**0**	**1**	**31**	....	....	....	....	....
	Hershey	AHL	52	2	6	8	101	....	....	....	....	....
1996-97	**Philadelphia**	**NHL**	**75**	**1**	**4**	**5**	**210**	**12**	**1**	**0**	**1**	**22**
	NHL Totals		**134**	**3**	**7**	**10**	**372**	**12**	**1**	**0**	**1**	**22**

KOROBOLIN, ALEXANDER (koh-roh-BOH-lihn) NYR

Defense. Shoots left. 6'2", 189 lbs. Born, Chelyabinsk, USSR, March 12, 1976.
(NY Rangers' 4th choice, 100th overall, in 1994 Entry Draft).

			Regular Season					Playoffs				
Season	Club	Lea	GP	G	A	TP	PIM	GP	G	A	TP	PIM
1993-94	Chelyabinsk	CIS	32	0	0	0	30	....	....	....	....	....
1994-95	Chelyabinsk	CIS 2				UNAVAILABLE						
1995-96	Chelyabinsk	CIS 2				UNAVAILABLE						
1996-97	Chelyabinsk	Rus. 2	60	2	7	9	54	....	....	....	....	....

KOROLEV, EVGENY (koh-roh-LEHV) NYI

Defense. Shoots left. 6'1", 186 lbs. Born, Moscow, USSR, July 24, 1978.
(NY Islanders' 9th choice, 192nd overall, in 1996 Entry Draft).

			Regular Season					Playoffs				
Season	Club	Lea	GP	G	A	TP	PIM	GP	G	A	TP	PIM
1995-96	Peterborough	OHL	60	2	12	14	60	6	0	0	0	2
1996-97	Peterborough	OHL	64	5	17	22	60	11	1	1	2	8

KOROLEV, IGOR (koh-roh-LEHV)

Right wing. Shoots left. 6'1", 187 lbs. Born, Moscow, USSR, September 6, 1970.
(St. Louis' 1st choice, 38th overall, in 1992 Entry Draft).

			Regular Season					Playoffs				
Season	Club	Lea	GP	G	A	TP	PIM	GP	G	A	TP	PIM
1988-89	Moscow D'amo	USSR	1	0	0	0	2	....	....	....	....	....
1989-90	Moscow D'amo	USSR	17	3	2	5	2	....	....	....	....	....
1990-91	Moscow D'amo	USSR	38	12	4	16	12	....	....	....	....	....
1991-92	Moscow D'amo	CIS	39	15	12	27	16	....	....	....	....	....
1992-93	Moscow D'amo	CIS	5	1	2	3	4	....	....	....	....	....
	St. Louis	**NHL**	**74**	**4**	**23**	**27**	**20**	**3**	**0**	**0**	**0**	**0**
1993-94	**St. Louis**	**NHL**	**73**	**6**	**10**	**16**	**40**	**2**	**0**	**0**	**0**	**0**
1994-95	Moscow D'amo	CIS	13	4	6	10	18	....	....	....	....	....
	Winnipeg	**NHL**	**45**	**8**	**22**	**30**	**10**	....	....	....	....	....
1995-96	**Winnipeg**	**NHL**	**73**	**22**	**29**	**51**	**42**	**6**	**0**	**3**	**3**	**0**
1996-97	**Phoenix**	**NHL**	**41**	**3**	**7**	**10**	**28**	**1**	**0**	**0**	**0**	**0**
	Michigan	IHL	4	2	2	4	0	....	....	....	....	....
	Phoenix	IHL	4	2	6	8	4	....	....	....	....	....
	NHL Totals		**306**	**43**	**91**	**134**	**140**	**12**	**0**	**3**	**3**	**0**

Claimed by **Winnipeg** from **St. Louis** in NHL Waiver Draft, January 18, 1995.

KOROLYUK, ALEXANDER (koh-roh-LYUHK) S.J.

Center. Shoots left. 5'9", 170 lbs. Born, Moscow, USSR, January 15, 1976.
(San Jose's 6th choice, 141st overall, in 1994 Entry Draft).

			Regular Season					Playoffs				
Season	Club	Lea	GP	G	A	TP	PIM	GP	G	A	TP	PIM
1993-94	Soviet Wings	CIS	22	4	4	8	20	3	1	0	1	4
1994-95	Soviet Wings	CIS	52	16	13	29	62	4	1	2	3	4
1995-96	Soviet Wings	CIS	50	30	19	49	77	....	....	....	....	....
1996-97	Soviet Wings	Rus.	17	8	5	13	46	....	....	....	....	....
	Manitoba	IHL	42	20	16	36	71	....	....	....	....	....

KOS, KYLE (KOHS) T.B.

Defense. Shoots left. 6'3", 184 lbs. Born, Hope, B.C., May 25, 1979.
(Tampa Bay's 2nd choice, 33rd overall, in 1997 Entry Draft).

			Regular Season					Playoffs				
Season	Club	Lea	GP	G	A	TP	PIM	GP	G	A	TP	PIM
1996-97	Red Deer	WHL	64	2	18	20	40	10	0	0	0	8

KOVALENKO, ANDREI (koh-vah-LEHN-koh) EDM.

Right wing. Shoots left. 5'10", 215 lbs. Born, Balakovo, USSR, June 7, 1970.
(Quebec's 6th choice, 148th overall, in 1990 Entry Draft).

			Regular Season					Playoffs				
Season	Club	Lea	GP	G	A	TP	PIM	GP	G	A	TP	PIM
1988-89	CSKA	USSR	10	1	0	1	0	....	....	....	....	....
1989-90	CSKA	USSR	48	8	5	13	20	....	....	....	....	....
1990-91	CSKA	USSR	45	13	8	21	26	....	....	....	....	....
1991-92	CSKA	CIS	44	19	13	32	32	....	....	....	....	....
1992-93	CSKA	CIS	3	3	1	4	4	....	....	....	....	....
	Quebec	**NHL**	**81**	**27**	**41**	**68**	**57**	**4**	**1**	**0**	**1**	**2**
1993-94	**Quebec**	**NHL**	**58**	**16**	**17**	**33**	**46**	....	....	....	....	....
1994-95	Togliatti	CIS	11	9	2	11	14	....	....	....	....	....
	Quebec	**NHL**	**45**	**14**	**10**	**24**	**31**	**6**	**0**	**1**	**1**	**2**
1995-96	**Colorado**	**NHL**	**26**	**11**	**11**	**22**	**16**	....	....	....	....	....
	Montreal	**NHL**	**51**	**17**	**17**	**34**	**33**	**6**	**0**	**0**	**0**	**6**
1996-97	**Edmonton**	**NHL**	**74**	**32**	**27**	**59**	**81**	**12**	**4**	**3**	**7**	**6**
	NHL Totals		**335**	**117**	**123**	**240**	**264**	**28**	**5**	**4**	**9**	**16**

Traded to **Montreal** by **Colorado** with Martin Rucinsky and Jocelyn Thibault for Patrick Roy and Mike Keane, December 6, 1995. Traded to **Edmonton** by **Montreal** for Scott Thornton, September 6, 1996.

KOVALEV, ALEXEI (koh-VAH-lehv) NYR

Right wing. Shoots left. 6', 210 lbs. Born, Togliatti, USSR, February 24, 1973.
(NY Rangers' 1st choice, 15th overall, in 1991 Entry Draft).

			Regular Season					Playoffs				
Season	Club	Lea	GP	G	A	TP	PIM	GP	G	A	TP	PIM
1989-90	Moscow D'amo	USSR	1	0	0	0	0	....	....	....	....	....
1990-91	Moscow D'amo	USSR	18	1	2	3	4	....	....	....	....	....
1991-92	Moscow D'amo	CIS	33	16	9	25	20	....	....	....	....	....
1992-93	**NY Rangers**	**NHL**	**65**	**20**	**18**	**38**	**79**	....	....	....	....	....
	Binghamton	AHL	13	13	11	24	35	9	3	5	8	14
1993-94	**NY Rangers**	**NHL**	**76**	**23**	**33**	**56**	**154**	**23**	**9**	**12**	**21**	**18** ♦
1994-95	Togliatti	CIS	12	8	8	16	49	....	....	....	....	....
	NY Rangers	**NHL**	**48**	**13**	**15**	**28**	**30**	**10**	**4**	**7**	**11**	**10**
1995-96	**NY Rangers**	**NHL**	**81**	**24**	**34**	**58**	**98**	**11**	**3**	**4**	**7**	**14**
1996-97	**NY Rangers**	**NHL**	**45**	**13**	**22**	**35**	**42**	....	....	....	....	....
	NHL Totals		**315**	**93**	**122**	**215**	**403**	**44**	**16**	**23**	**39**	**42**

KOVESHNIKOV, ANATOLI (koh-VEHSH-nih-kahv) DAL.

Right wing. Shoots left. 6'2", 187 lbs. Born, Kiev, USSR, May 31, 1973.
(Dallas' 8th choice, 193rd overall, in 1995 Entry Draft).

			Regular Season					Playoffs				
Season	Club	Lea	GP	G	A	TP	PIM	GP	G	A	TP	PIM
1992-93	Sokol Kiev	CIS	23	1	0	1	4	3	0	0	0	0
1993-94	Sokol Kiev	CIS	34	2	2	4	16	....	....	....	....	....
1994-95	Sokol Kiev	CIS	51	8	0	8	10	....	....	....	....	....
1995-96	Sokol Kiev	CIS	36	4	2	6	45	....	....	....	....	....
	Lada Togliatti	CIS	9	0	1	1	6	4	1	0	1	2
1996-97	Yaroslavl	Rus.	31	3	6	9	63	9	0	1	1	22

KOZLOV, VIKTOR (KAHS-lahf) S.J.

Left wing. Shoots right. 6'5", 225 lbs. Born, Togliatti, USSR, February 14, 1975.
(San Jose's 1st choice, 6th overall, in 1993 Entry Draft).

			Regular Season					Playoffs				
Season	Club	Lea	GP	G	A	TP	PIM	GP	G	A	TP	PIM
1990-91	Togliatti	USSR 2	2	2	0	2	0	....	....	....	....	....
1991-92	Togliatti	CIS	3	0	0	0	0	....	....	....	....	....
1992-93	Moscow D'amo	CIS	30	6	5	11	4	10	3	0	3	0
1993-94	Moscow D'amo	CIS	42	16	9	25	14	7	3	2	5	0
1994-95	Moscow D'amo	CIS	3	1	1	2	2	....	....	....	....	....
	San Jose	**NHL**	**16**	**2**	**0**	**2**	**2**	....	....	....	....	....
	Kansas City	IHL	4	1	1	2	0	13	4	5	9	12
1995-96	**San Jose**	**NHL**	**62**	**6**	**13**	**19**	**6**	....	....	....	....	....
	Kansas City	IHL	15	4	7	11	12	....	....	....	....	....
1996-97	**San Jose**	**NHL**	**78**	**16**	**25**	**41**	**40**	....	....	....	....	....
	NHL Totals		**156**	**24**	**38**	**62**	**48**	....	....	....	....	....

KOZLOV, VYACHESLAV (KAHS-lahf, VYACH-ih-slav) DET.

Center. Shoots left. 5'10", 180 lbs. Born, Voskresensk, USSR, May 3, 1972.
(Detroit's 2nd choice, 45th overall, in 1990 Entry Draft).

			Regular Season					Playoffs				
Season	Club	Lea	GP	G	A	TP	PIM	GP	G	A	TP	PIM
1987-88	Khimik	USSR	2	0	0	0	0	....	....	....	....	....
1988-89	Khimik	USSR	14	0	1	1	2	....	....	....	....	....
1989-90	Khimik	USSR	45	14	12	26	38	....	....	....	....	....
1990-91	Khimik	USSR	45	11	13	24	46	....	....	....	....	....
1991-92	CSKA	CIS	11	6	5	11	12	....	....	....	....	....
	Detroit	**NHL**	**7**	**0**	**2**	**2**	**2**	....	....	....	....	....
1992-93	**Detroit**	**NHL**	**17**	**4**	**1**	**5**	**14**	**4**	**0**	**2**	**2**	**2**
	Adirondack	AHL	45	23	36	59	54	4	1	1	2	4
1993-94	**Detroit**	**NHL**	**77**	**34**	**39**	**73**	**50**	**7**	**2**	**5**	**7**	**12**
	Adirondack	AHL	3	0	1	1	15	....	....	....	....	....
1994-95	CSKA	CIS	10	3	4	7	14	....	....	....	....	....
	Detroit	**NHL**	**46**	**13**	**20**	**33**	**45**	**18**	**9**	**7**	**16**	**10**
1995-96	**Detroit**	**NHL**	**82**	**36**	**37**	**73**	**70**	**19**	**5**	**7**	**12**	**10**
1996-97	**Detroit**	**NHL**	**75**	**23**	**22**	**45**	**46**	**20**	**8**	**5**	**13**	**14** ♦
	NHL Totals		**304**	**110**	**121**	**231**	**227**	**68**	**24**	**26**	**50**	**48**

KOZYREV, ANDREI (KOH-zih-rehf) CHI.

Defense. Shoots left. 6'1", 200 lbs. Born, Tomsk, USSR, June 17, 1973.
(Chicago's 7th choice, 236th overall, in 1996 Entry Draft).

			Regular Season					Playoffs				
Season	Club	Lea	GP	G	A	TP	PIM	GP	G	A	TP	PIM
1993-94	Cherepovets	CIS	43	0	2	2	84	2	0	0	0	0
1994-95	Cherepovets	CIS	40	0	0	0	36	....	....	....	....	....
1995-96	Cherepovets	CIS	52	2	0	2	55	4	0	0	0	4
1996-97	Cherepovets	Rus.	24	1	0	1	40	1	0	0	0	25

KRAFT, RYAN S.J.

Center. Shoots left. 5'9", 181 lbs. Born, Bottineau, ND, November 7, 1975.
(San Jose's 11th choice, 194th overall, in 1995 Entry Draft).

			Regular Season					Playoffs				
Season	Club	Lea	GP	G	A	TP	PIM	GP	G	A	TP	PIM
1994-95	U. Minnesota	WCHA	44	13	33	46	44	....	....	....	....	....
1995-96	U. Minnesota	WCHA	41	13	24	37	24	....	....	....	....	....
1996-97	U. Minnesota	WCHA	42	25	21	46	37	....	....	....	....	....

KRAVCHUK, IGOR (krahv-CHOOK) ST.L.

Defense. Shoots left. 6'1", 200 lbs. Born, Ufa, USSR, September 13, 1966.
(Chicago's 5th choice, 71st overall, in 1991 Entry Draft).

			Regular Season					Playoffs				
Season	Club	Lea	GP	G	A	TP	PIM	GP	G	A	TP	PIM
1982-83	Yulayev	USSR	10	0	0	0	0	....	....	....	....	....
	Yulayev	USSR 2	....	....	....	....	....	....	....	....	....	....
1984-85	Yulayev	USSR 2	50	3	2	5	22	....	....	....	....	....
1985-86	Yulayev	USSR	21	2	2	4	6	....	....	....	....	....
1986-87	Yulayev	USSR	22	0	1	1	8	....	....	....	....	....
1987-88	CSKA	USSR	48	1	8	9	12	....	....	....	....	....
1988-89	CSKA	USSR	22	3	3	6	2	....	....	....	....	....
1989-90	CSKA	USSR	48	1	3	4	16	....	....	....	....	....
1990-91	CSKA	USSR	41	6	5	11	16	....	....	....	....	....
1991-92	CSKA	CIS	30	3	8	11	6	....	....	....	....	....
	Chicago	**NHL**	**18**	**1**	**8**	**9**	**4**	**18**	**2**	**6**	**8**	**8**
1992-93	**Chicago**	**NHL**	**38**	**6**	**9**	**15**	**30**	....	....	....	....	....
	Edmonton	**NHL**	**17**	**4**	**8**	**12**	**2**	....	....	....	....	....
1993-94	**Edmonton**	**NHL**	**81**	**12**	**38**	**50**	**16**	....	....	....	....	....
1994-95	**Edmonton**	**NHL**	**36**	**7**	**11**	**18**	**29**	....	....	....	....	....
1995-96	**Edmonton**	**NHL**	**26**	**4**	**4**	**8**	**10**	....	....	....	....	....
	St. Louis	**NHL**	**40**	**3**	**12**	**15**	**24**	**10**	**1**	**5**	**6**	**4**
1996-97	**St. Louis**	**NHL**	**82**	**4**	**24**	**28**	**35**	**2**	**0**	**0**	**0**	**2**
	NHL Totals		**338**	**41**	**114**	**155**	**150**	**30**	**3**	**11**	**14**	**14**

Traded to **Edmonton** by **Chicago** with Dean McAmmond for Joe Murphy, February 24, 1993. Traded to **St. Louis** by **Edmonton** with Ken Sutton for Jeff Norton and Donald Dufresne, January 4, 1996.

KRISTOFFERSON, MARC DAL.

Defense. Shoots left. 6'3", 200 lbs. Born, Ostersund, Sweden, January 22, 1979.
(Dallas' 4th choice, 105th overall, in 1997 Entry Draft).

			Regular Season					Playoffs				
Season	Club	Lea	GP	G	A	TP	PIM	GP	G	A	TP	PIM
1996-97	Mora	Swe. 2	33	1	5	6	26	....	....	....	....	....

KRIVCHENKOV, ALEXEI (krihv-chehn-KOHV) PIT.

Defense. Shoots left. 6', 190 lbs. Born, Novosibirsk, USSR, June 11, 1974.
(Pittsburgh's 5th choice, 76th overall, in 1994 Entry Draft).

			Regular Season					Playoffs				
Season	Club	Lea	GP	G	A	TP	PIM	GP	G	A	TP	PIM
1993-94	Sibir Novosibirsk	CIS 2	37	1	3	4	48	....	....	....	....	....
	CSKA	CIS	4	0	0	0	2	3	0	0	0	0
1994-95	CSKA	CIS	46	1	4	5	43	2	0	0	0	0
1995-96	Hampton Rds.	ECHL	16	3	3	6	28	....	....	....	....	....
	Cleveland	IHL	37	1	4	5	30	....	....	....	....	....
1996-97	Johnstown	ECHL	5	1	1	2	24	....	....	....	....	....
	Hampton Rds.	ECHL	36	3	23	26	57	6	1	2	3	18
	Long Beach	IHL	7	0	3	3	10	....	....	....	....	....

KRIVOKRASOV, SERGEI (krih-vuh-KRA-sahf) CHI.

Right wing. Shoots left. 5'11", 185 lbs. Born, Angarsk, USSR, April 15, 1974.
(Chicago's 1st choice, 12th overall, in 1992 Entry Draft).

			Regular Season					Playoffs				
Season	Club	Lea	GP	G	A	TP	PIM	GP	G	A	TP	PIM
1990-91	CSKA	USSR	41	4	0	4	8	....	....	....	....	....
1991-92	CSKA	CIS	42	10	8	18	35	....	....	....	....	....
1992-93	**Chicago**	**NHL**	**4**	**0**	**0**	**0**	**2**	....	....	....	....	....
	Indianapolis	IHL	78	36	33	69	157	5	3	1	4	2
1993-94	**Chicago**	**NHL**	**9**	**1**	**0**	**1**	**4**	....	....	....	....	....
	Indianapolis	IHL	53	19	26	45	145	....	....	....	....	....
1994-95	Indianapolis	IHL	29	12	15	27	41	....	....	....	....	....
	Chicago	**NHL**	**41**	**12**	**7**	**19**	**33**	**10**	**0**	**0**	**0**	**8**
1995-96	**Chicago**	**NHL**	**46**	**6**	**10**	**16**	**32**	**5**	**1**	**0**	**1**	**2**
	Indianapolis	IHL	9	4	5	9	28	....	....	....	....	....
1996-97	**Chicago**	**NHL**	**67**	**13**	**11**	**24**	**42**	**6**	**1**	**0**	**1**	**4**
	NHL Totals		**167**	**32**	**28**	**60**	**113**	**21**	**2**	**0**	**2**	**14**

KRIZ, PAVEL (KRIHZH) CHI.

Defense. Shoots right. 6'1", 205 lbs. Born, Kladno, Czech., January 2, 1977.
(Chicago's 5th choice, 97th overall, in 1995 Entry Draft).

			Regular Season					Playoffs				
Season	Club	Lea	GP	G	A	TP	PIM	GP	G	A	TP	PIM
1994-95	Tri-City	WHL	68	6	34	40	47	17	5	12	17	6
1995-96	Saskatoon	WHL	71	11	52	63	96	4	0	2	2	0
1996-97	Pardubice	Czech.	37	0	7	7	63	8	0	1	1	8

KRON, ROBERT (KROHN) CAR.

Left wing. Shoots left. 5'11", 185 lbs. Born, Brno, Czech., February 27, 1967.
(Vancouver's 5th choice, 88th overall, in 1985 Entry Draft).

			Regular Season					Playoffs				
Season	Club	Lea	GP	G	A	TP	PIM	GP	G	A	TP	PIM
1983-84	Ingstav Brno	Czech. 2	3	0	1	1	0	....	....	....	....	....
1984-85	Zetor Brno	Czech.	40	6	8	14	6	....	....	....	....	....
1985-86	Zetor Brno	Czech.	44	5	6	11	....	....	....	....	....	....
1986-87	Zetor Brno	Czech.	34	18	11	29	10	....	....	....	....	....
1987-88	Zetor Brno	Czech.	44	14	7	21	30	....	....	....	....	....
1988-89	Dukla Trencin	Czech.	43	28	19	47	26	....	....	....	....	....
1989-90	Dukla Trencin	Czech.	39	22	22	44	....	....	....	....	....	....
1990-91	**Vancouver**	**NHL**	**76**	**12**	**20**	**32**	**21**	....	....	....	....	....
1991-92	**Vancouver**	**NHL**	**36**	**2**	**2**	**4**	**2**	**11**	**1**	**2**	**3**	**2**
1992-93	**Vancouver**	**NHL**	**32**	**10**	**11**	**21**	**14**	....	....	....	....	....
	Hartford	**NHL**	**13**	**4**	**2**	**6**	**4**	....	....	....	....	....
1993-94	**Hartford**	**NHL**	**77**	**24**	**26**	**50**	**8**	....	....	....	....	....
1994-95	**Hartford**	**NHL**	**37**	**10**	**8**	**18**	**10**	....	....	....	....	....
1995-96	**Hartford**	**NHL**	**77**	**22**	**28**	**50**	**6**	....	....	....	....	....
1996-97	**Hartford**	**NHL**	**68**	**10**	**12**	**22**	**10**	....	....	....	....	....
	NHL Totals		**416**	**94**	**109**	**203**	**75**	**11**	**1**	**2**	**3**	**2**

Traded to **Hartford** by **Vancouver** with Vancouver's third round choice (Marek Malik) in 1993 Entry Draft and future considerations (Jim Sandlak, May 17, 1993) for Murray Craven and Vancouver's fifth round choice (previously acquired by Hartford — Vancouver selected Scott Walker) in 1993 Entry Draft, March 22, 1993.

KROPAC, RADOSLAV (KRO-pahch) NYR

Right wing. Shoots left. 6', 187 lbs. Born, Bratislava, Czech., April 5, 1975.
(NY Rangers' 13th choice, 260th overall, in 1994 Entry Draft).

			Regular Season					Playoffs				
Season	Club	Lea	GP	G	A	TP	PIM	GP	G	A	TP	PIM
1993-94	Bratislava	Slovak	33	7	6	13	12	....	....	....	....	....
1994-95	Bratislava	Slovak	35	17	8	25	38	7	1	2	3	4
1995-96	Bratislava	Slovak	31	5	9	14	8	13	4	3	7	....
1996-97	Bratislava	Slovak	43	8	7	15	....	2	1	1	2	....

KROUPA, VLASTIMIL (KROO-pah, VLAS-tuh-meel) N.J.

Defense. Shoots left. 6'3", 205 lbs. Born, Most, Czech., April 27, 1975.
(San Jose's 3rd choice, 45th overall, in 1993 Entry Draft).

			Regular Season					Playoffs				
Season	Club	Lea	GP	G	A	TP	PIM	GP	G	A	TP	PIM
1992-93	Litvinov	Czech.	9	0	1	1	....	....	....	....	....	....
1993-94	**San Jose**	**NHL**	**27**	**1**	**3**	**4**	**20**	**14**	**1**	**2**	**3**	**21**
	Kansas City	IHL	39	3	12	15	12	....	....	....	....	....
1994-95	Kansas City	IHL	51	4	8	12	49	12	2	4	6	22
	San Jose	**NHL**	**14**	**0**	**2**	**2**	**16**	**6**	**0**	**0**	**0**	**4**
1995-96	**San Jose**	**NHL**	**27**	**1**	**7**	**8**	**18**	....	....	....	....	....
	Kansas City	IHL	39	5	22	27	44	5	0	1	1	6
1996-97	**San Jose**	**NHL**	**35**	**2**	**6**	**8**	**12**	....	....	....	....	....
	Kentucky	AHL	5	0	3	3	0	....	....	....	....	....
	NHL Totals		**103**	**4**	**18**	**22**	**66**	**20**	**1**	**2**	**3**	**25**

Traded to **New Jersey** by **San Jose** for New Jersey's third round choice in 1998 Entry Draft, August 22, 1997.

KRUPP, UWE (KROOP, OO-VAY) COL.

Defense. Shoots right. 6'6", 235 lbs. Born, Cologne, West Germany, June 24, 1965.
(Buffalo's 13th choice, 214th overall, in 1983 Entry Draft).

			Regular Season					Playoffs				
Season	Club	Lea	GP	G	A	TP	PIM	GP	G	A	TP	PIM
1982-83	Koln	W. Ger.	11	0	0	0	0	....	....	....	....	....
1983-84	Koln	W. Ger.	26	0	4	4	22	....	....	....	....	....
1984-85	Koln	W. Ger.	39	11	8	19	36	....	....	....	....	....
1985-86	Koln	W. Ger.	45	10	21	31	83	....	....	....	....	....
1986-87	**Buffalo**	**NHL**	**26**	**1**	**4**	**5**	**23**	....	....	....	....	....
	Rochester	AHL	42	3	19	22	50	17	1	11	12	16
1987-88	**Buffalo**	**NHL**	**75**	**2**	**9**	**11**	**151**	**6**	**0**	**0**	**0**	**15**
1988-89	**Buffalo**	**NHL**	**70**	**5**	**13**	**18**	**55**	**5**	**0**	**1**	**1**	**4**
1989-90	**Buffalo**	**NHL**	**74**	**3**	**20**	**23**	**85**	**6**	**0**	**0**	**0**	**4**
1990-91	**Buffalo**	**NHL**	**74**	**12**	**32**	**44**	**66**	**6**	**1**	**1**	**2**	**6**
1991-92	**Buffalo**	**NHL**	**8**	**2**	**0**	**2**	**6**	....	....	....	....	....
	NY Islanders	**NHL**	**59**	**6**	**29**	**35**	**43**	....	....	....	....	....
1992-93	**NY Islanders**	**NHL**	**80**	**9**	**29**	**38**	**67**	**18**	**1**	**5**	**6**	**12**
1993-94	**NY Islanders**	**NHL**	**41**	**7**	**14**	**21**	**30**	**4**	**0**	**1**	**1**	**4**
1994-95	Landshut	Ger.	5	1	2	3	6	....	....	....	....	....
	Quebec	**NHL**	**44**	**6**	**17**	**23**	**20**	**5**	**0**	**2**	**2**	**2**
1995-96	**Colorado**	**NHL**	**6**	**0**	**3**	**3**	**4**	**22**	**4**	**12**	**16**	**33 ♦**
1996-97	**Colorado**	**NHL**	**60**	**4**	**17**	**21**	**48**	....	....	....	....	....
	NHL Totals		**617**	**57**	**187**	**244**	**598**	**72**	**6**	**22**	**28**	**80**

Played in NHL All-Star Game (1991)

Traded to **NY Islanders** by **Buffalo** with Pierre Turgeon, Benoit Hogue and Dave McLlwain for Pat Lafontaine, Randy Hillier, Randy Wood and NY Islanders' fourth round choice (Dean Melanson) in 1992 Entry Draft, October 25, 1991. Traded to **Quebec** by **NY Islanders** with NY Islanders' first round choice (Wade Belak) in 1994 Entry Draft for Ron Sutter and Quebec's first round choice (Brett Lindros) in 1994 Entry Draft, June 28, 1994.

KRUSE, PAUL (KROOZ) NYI

Left wing. Shoots left. 6', 202 lbs. Born, Merritt, B.C., March 15, 1970.
(Calgary's 6th choice, 83rd overall, in 1990 Entry Draft).

			Regular Season					Playoffs				
Season	Club	Lea	GP	G	A	TP	PIM	GP	G	A	TP	PIM
1988-89	Kamloops	WHL	68	8	15	23	209	....	....	....	....	....
1989-90	Kamloops	WHL	67	22	23	45	291	17	3	5	8	79
1990-91	**Calgary**	**NHL**	**1**	**0**	**0**	**0**	**7**	....	....	....	....	....
	Salt Lake	IHL	83	24	20	44	313	4	1	1	2	4
1991-92	**Calgary**	**NHL**	**16**	**3**	**1**	**4**	**65**	....	....	....	....	....
	Salt Lake	IHL	57	14	15	29	267	5	1	2	3	19
1992-93	**Calgary**	**NHL**	**27**	**2**	**3**	**5**	**41**	....	....	....	....	....
	Salt Lake	IHL	35	1	4	5	206	....	....	....	....	....
1993-94	**Calgary**	**NHL**	**68**	**3**	**8**	**11**	**185**	**7**	**0**	**0**	**0**	**14**
1994-95	**Calgary**	**NHL**	**45**	**11**	**5**	**16**	**141**	**7**	**4**	**2**	**6**	**10**
1995-96	**Calgary**	**NHL**	**75**	**3**	**12**	**15**	**145**	**3**	**0**	**0**	**0**	**4**
1996-97	**Calgary**	**NHL**	**14**	**2**	**0**	**2**	**30**	....	....	....	....	....
	NY Islanders	**NHL**	**48**	**4**	**2**	**6**	**111**	....	....	....	....	....
	NHL Totals		**294**	**28**	**31**	**59**	**725**	**17**	**4**	**2**	**6**	**28**

Traded to **NY Islanders** by **Calgary** for Colorado's third round choice (previously acquired by NY Islanders — later traded to Hartford — Carolina selected Francis Lessard) in 1997 Entry Draft, November 27, 1996.

KRYGIER, TODD (KREE-guhr) WSH.

Left wing. Shoots left. 6', 185 lbs. Born, Chicago Heights, IL, October 12, 1965.
(Hartford's 1st choice, 16th overall, in 1988 Supplemental Draft).

			Regular Season					Playoffs				
Season	Club	Lea	GP	G	A	TP	PIM	GP	G	A	TP	PIM
1984-85	U. Connecticut	NCAA	14	14	11	25	12	....	....	....	....	....
1985-86	U. Connecticut	NCAA	32	29	27	56	46	....	....	....	....	....
1986-87	U. Connecticut	NCAA	28	24	24	48	44	....	....	....	....	....
1987-88	U. Connecticut	NCAA	27	32	39	71	28	....	....	....	....	....
	New Haven	AHL	13	1	5	6	34	....	....	....	....	....
1988-89	Binghamton	AHL	76	26	42	68	77	....	....	....	....	....
1989-90	**Hartford**	**NHL**	**58**	**18**	**12**	**30**	**52**	**7**	**2**	**1**	**3**	**4**
	Binghamton	AHL	12	1	9	10	16	....	....	....	....	....
1990-91	**Hartford**	**NHL**	**72**	**13**	**17**	**30**	**95**	**6**	**0**	**2**	**2**	**0**
1991-92	**Washington**	**NHL**	**67**	**13**	**17**	**30**	**107**	**5**	**2**	**1**	**3**	**4**
1992-93	**Washington**	**NHL**	**77**	**11**	**12**	**23**	**60**	**6**	**1**	**1**	**2**	**4**
1993-94	**Washington**	**NHL**	**66**	**12**	**18**	**30**	**60**	**5**	**2**	**0**	**2**	**10**
1994-95	**Anaheim**	**NHL**	**35**	**11**	**11**	**22**	**10**	....	....	....	....	....
1995-96	**Anaheim**	**NHL**	**60**	**9**	**28**	**37**	**70**	....	....	....	....	....
	Washington	**NHL**	**16**	**6**	**5**	**11**	**12**	**6**	**2**	**0**	**2**	**12**
1996-97	**Washington**	**NHL**	**47**	**5**	**11**	**16**	**37**	....	....	....	....	....
	NHL Totals		**498**	**98**	**131**	**229**	**503**	**35**	**9**	**5**	**14**	**34**

Traded to **Washington** by **Hartford** for future considerations (Washington's fourth round choice — later traded to Calgary — Calgary selected Jason Smith in 1993 Entry Draft), October 3, 1991. Traded to **Anaheim** by **Washington** for Anaheim's fourth round choice (later traded to Dallas — Dallas selected Mike Hurley) in 1996 Entry Draft, February 2, 1995. Traded to **Washington** by **Anaheim** for Mike Torchia, March 8, 1996.

KUBA, FILIP (KOO-bah, FIHL-ihp) FLA.

Defense. Shoots left. 6'3", 202 lbs. Born, Ostrava, Czech., December 29, 1976.
(Florida's 8th choice, 192nd overall, in 1995 Entry Draft).

			Regular Season					Playoffs				
Season	Club	Lea	GP	G	A	TP	PIM	GP	G	A	TP	PIM
1994-95	Vitkovice	Czech. Jr.	35	10	15	25	....	....	....	....	....	....
	Vitkovice	Czech.	....	....	....	....	....	4	0	0	0	2
1995-96	Vitkovice	Czech.	19	0	1	1	....	....	....	....	....	....
1996-97	Carolina	AHL	51	0	12	12	38	....	....	....	....	....

KUBINA, PAVEL (koo-BEE-nuh) T.B.

Defense. Shoots right. 6'3", 213 lbs. Born, Celadna, Czech., April 15, 1977.
(Tampa Bay's 6th choice, 179th overall, in 1996 Entry Draft).

			Regular Season					Playoffs				
Season	Club	Lea	GP	G	A	TP	PIM	GP	G	A	TP	PIM
1993-94	Vitkovice	Czech. Jr.	35	4	3	7	....	....	....	....	....	....
	Vitkovice	Czech.	1	0	0	0	....	....	....	....	....	....
1994-95	Vitkovice	Czech. Jr.	20	6	10	16	....	....	....	....	....	....
	Vitkovice	Czech.	8	2	0	2	10	4	0	0	0	0
1995-96	Vitkovice	Czech.	33	3	4	7	32	4	0	0	0	0
	Vitkovice	Czech. Jr.	16	5	10	15	....	....	....	....	....	....
1996-97	Vitkovice	Czech.	1	0	0	0	0	....	....	....	....	....
	Moose Jaw	WHL	61	12	32	44	116	11	2	5	7	27

KUCERA, FRANTISEK (koo-CHAIR-uh)

Defense. Shoots right. 6'2", 205 lbs. Born, Prague, Czech., February 3, 1968.
(Chicago's 3rd choice, 77th overall, in 1986 Entry Draft).

			Regular Season					Playoffs				
Season	Club	Lea	GP	G	A	TP	PIM	GP	G	A	TP	PIM
1985-86	Sparta Praha	Czech.	15	0	0	0	....	....	....	....	....	....
1986-87	Sparta Praha	Czech.	40	5	2	7	14	....	....	....	....	....
1987-88	Sparta Praha	Czech.	46	7	2	9	30	....	....	....	....	....
1988-89	Dukla Jihlava	Czech.	45	10	9	19	28	....	....	....	....	....
1989-90	Dukla Jihlava	Czech.	43	9	10	19	....	....	....	....	....	....
1990-91	**Chicago**	**NHL**	**40**	**2**	**12**	**14**	**32**	....	....	....	....	....
	Indianapolis	IHL	35	8	19	27	23	7	0	1	1	15
1991-92	**Chicago**	**NHL**	**61**	**3**	**10**	**13**	**36**	**6**	**0**	**0**	**0**	**0**
	Indianapolis	IHL	7	1	2	3	4	....	....	....	....	....
1992-93	**Chicago**	**NHL**	**71**	**5**	**14**	**19**	**59**	....	....	....	....	....
1993-94	**Chicago**	**NHL**	**60**	**4**	**13**	**17**	**34**	....	....	....	....	....
	Hartford	**NHL**	**16**	**1**	**3**	**4**	**14**	....	....	....	....	....
1994-95	Sparta Praha	Czech.	16	1	2	3	14	....	....	....	....	....
	Hartford	**NHL**	**48**	**3**	**17**	**20**	**30**	....	....	....	....	....
1995-96	**Hartford**	**NHL**	**30**	**2**	**6**	**8**	**10**	....	....	....	....	....
	Vancouver	**NHL**	**24**	**1**	**0**	**1**	**10**	**6**	**0**	**1**	**1**	**0**
1996-97	**Vancouver**	**NHL**	**2**	**0**	**0**	**0**	**0**	....	....	....	....	....
	Syracuse	AHL	42	6	29	35	36	....	....	....	....	....
	Houston	IHL	12	0	3	3	20	....	....	....	....	....
	Philadelphia	**NHL**	**2**	**0**	**0**	**0**	**2**	....	....	....	....	....
	Philadelphia	AHL	9	1	5	6	2	10	1	6	7	20
	NHL Totals		**354**	**21**	**75**	**96**	**227**	**12**	**0**	**1**	**1**	**0**

Traded to **Hartford** by **Chicago** with Jocelyn Lemieux for Gary Suter, Randy Cunneyworth and Hartford's third round choice (later traded to Vancouver — Vancouver selected Larry Courville) in 1995 Entry Draft, March 11, 1994. Traded to **Vancouver** by **Hartford** with Jim Dowd and Hartford's second round choice (Ryan Bonni) in 1997 Entry Draft for Jeff Brown and Vancouver's third round choice in 1998 Entry Draft, December 19, 1995. Traded to **Philadelphia** by **Vancouver** for future considerations, March 18, 1997.

KUCHARCIK, TOMAS (koo-HAHR-chihk) TOR.

Center. Shoots left. 6'2", 200 lbs. Born, Vlasim, Czech., May 10, 1970.
(Toronto's 11th choice, 167th overall, in 1991 Entry Draft).

			Regular Season					Playoffs				
Season	Club	Lea	GP	G	A	TP	PIM	GP	G	A	TP	PIM
1990-91	Dukla Jihlava	Czech.	30	10	6	16	6	....	....	....	....	....
1991-92	Dukla Jihlava	Czech.	45	16	23	39	24	....	....	....	....	....
1992-93	Dukla Jihlava	Czech.	39	17	20	37	....	....	....	....	....	....
1993-94	Skoda Plzen	Czech.	32	10	10	20	0	....	....	....	....	....
	St. John's	AHL	8	2	3	5	4	10	3	4	7	2
1994-95	Plzen	Czech.	40	14	4	18	22	3	0	0	0	14
1995-96	ZPS Plzen	Czech.	17	5	6	11	....	....	....	....	....	....
	Slavia Praha	Czech.	23	5	6	11	....	7	3	2	5	....
1996-97	Slavia Praha	Czech.	49	15	31	46	24	3	0	1	1	4

KUDASHOV, ALEXEI (koo-dah-SHOV)

Center. Shoots right. 6', 183 lbs. Born, Elektrostal, USSR, July 21, 1971.
(Toronto's 3rd choice, 102nd overall, in 1991 Entry Draft).

			Regular Season					Playoffs				
Season	Club	Lea	GP	G	A	TP	PIM	GP	G	A	TP	PIM
1989-90	Soviet Wings	USSR	45	0	5	5	14	....	....	....	....	....
1990-91	Soviet Wings	USSR	45	9	5	14	10	....	....	....	....	....
1991-92	Soviet Wings	CIS	42	9	16	25	14	....	....	....	....	....
1992-93	Soviet Wings	CIS	41	8	20	28	24	7	1	3	4	4
1993-94	Soviet Wings	CIS	1	2	0	2	0	....	....	....	....	....
	Toronto	**NHL**	**25**	**1**	**0**	**1**	**4**	....	....	....	....	....
	Rus. Olympic	....	8	1	2	3	4	....	....	....	....	....
	St. John's	AHL	27	7	15	22	21	....	....	....	....	....
1994-95	St. John's	AHL	75	25	54	79	17	5	1	4	5	2
1995-96	Carolina	AHL	33	7	22	29	18	....	....	....	....	....
	Dusseldorf	Ger.	9	7	8	15	4	13	5	5	10	14
1996-97	Dusseldorf	Ger.	48	13	16	29	16	4	3	1	4	2
	NHL Totals		**25**	**1**	**0**	**1**	**4**	....	....	....	....	....

Signed as a free agent by **Florida**, September 10, 1995.

KUKI, ARTO (KUH-kee) MTL.

Center. Shoots left. 6'3", 205 lbs. Born, Espoo, Finland, February 22, 1976.
(Montreal's 6th choice, 96th overall, in 1994 Entry Draft).

			Regular Season					Playoffs				
Season	Club	Lea	GP	G	A	TP	PIM	GP	G	A	TP	PIM
1994-95	Kiekko-Espoo	Fin.	4	0	1	1	0	....	....	....	....	....
1995-96	Kiekko-Espoo	Fin.	47	6	3	9	16	....	....	....	....	....
1996-97	Kiekko-Espoo	Fin.	50	6	15	21	20	4	0	1	1	2

KURRI, JARI (KUHR-ree, YAH-ree) COL.

Right wing. Shoots right. 6'1", 195 lbs. Born, Helsinki, Finland, May 18, 1960.
(Edmonton's 3rd choice, 69th overall, in 1980 Entry Draft).

			Regular Season					Playoffs				
Season	Club	Lea	GP	G	A	TP	PIM	GP	G	A	TP	PIM
1977-78	Jokerit	Fin.	29	2	9	11	12	....	....	....	....	....
1978-79	Jokerit	Fin.	33	16	14	30	12	....	....	....	....	....
1979-80	Jokerit	Fin.	33	23	16	39	22	6	7	2	9	13
1980-81	Edmonton	NHL	75	32	43	75	40	9	5	7	12	4
1981-82	Edmonton	NHL	71	32	54	86	32	5	2	5	7	10
1982-83	Edmonton	NHL	80	45	59	104	22	16	8	15	23	8
1983-84a	Edmonton	NHL	64	52	61	113	14	19	*14	14	28	13 ♦
1984-85bc	Edmonton	NHL	73	71	64	135	30	18	*19	12	31	6 ♦
1985-86a	Edmonton	NHL	78	*68	63	131	22	10	2	10	12	4
1986-87c	Edmonton	NHL	79	54	54	108	41	21	*15	10	25	20 ♦
1987-88	Edmonton	NHL	80	43	53	96	30	19	*14	17	31	12 ♦
1988-89a	Edmonton	NHL	76	44	58	102	69	7	3	5	8	6
1989-90	Edmonton	NHL	78	33	60	93	48	22	10	15	25	18 ♦
1990-91	Milan Devils	Italy	30	27	48	75	6	10	10	12	22	2
1991-92	Los Angeles	NHL	73	23	37	60	24	4	1	2	3	4
1992-93	Los Angeles	NHL	82	27	60	87	38	24	9	8	17	12
1993-94	Los Angeles	NHL	81	31	46	77	48	....	....	....	....	....
1994-95	Jokerit	Fin.	20	10	9	19	10	....	....	....	....	....
	Los Angeles	NHL	38	10	19	29	24	....	....	....	....	....
1995-96	Los Angeles	NHL	57	17	23	40	37	....	....	....	....	....
	NY Rangers	NHL	14	1	4	5	2	11	3	5	8	2
1996-97	Anaheim	NHL	82	13	22	35	12	11	1	2	3	4
	NHL Totals		1181	596	780	1376	533	196	106	127	233	123

a NHL Second All-Star Team (1984, 1986, 1989)
b Won Lady Byng Memorial Trophy (1985)
c NHL First All-Star Team (1985, 1987)

Played in NHL All-Star Game (1983, 1985, 1986, 1988-90, 1993)

Traded to **Philadelphia** by **Edmonton** with Dave Brown and Corey Foster for Craig Fisher, Scott Mellanby and Craig Berube, May 30, 1991. Traded to **Los Angeles** by **Philadelphia** with Jeff Chychrun for Steve Duchesne, Steve Kasper and Los Angeles' fourth round choice (Aris Brimanis) in 1991 Entry Draft, May 30, 1991. Traded to **NY Rangers** by **Los Angeles** with Marty McSorley and Shane Churla for Ray Ferraro, Ian Laperriere, Mattias Norstrom, Nathan Lafayette and NY Rangers' fourth round choice (Sean Blanchard) in 1997 Entry Draft, March 14, 1996. Signed as a free agent by **Anaheim**, September 10, 1996. Signed as a free agent by **Colorado**, July 11, 1997.

KUSTER, HENRY (KOO-stuhr) BOS.

Right wing. Shoots right. 6', 195 lbs. Born, Edmonton, Alta., November 11, 1977.
(Boston's 2nd choice, 45th overall, in 1996 Entry Draft).

			Regular Season					Playoffs				
Season	Club	Lea	GP	G	A	TP	PIM	GP	G	A	TP	PIM
1993-94	Medicine Hat	WHL	67	14	27	41	26	3	0	0	0	2
1994-95	Medicine Hat	WHL	71	28	26	54	61	5	1	3	4	6
1995-96	Medicine Hat	WHL	72	35	43	78	54	1	0	0	0	0
1996-97	Medicine Hat	WHL	72	26	35	61	47	4	0	1	1	4

KUZNETSOV, MAXIM (kooz-NEHT-zahv) DET.

Defense. Shoots left. 6'5", 198 lbs. Born, Pavlodar, USSR, March 24, 1977.
(Detroit's 1st choice, 26th overall, in 1995 Entry Draft).

			Regular Season					Playoffs				
Season	Club	Lea	GP	G	A	TP	PIM	GP	G	A	TP	PIM
1994-95	Moscow D'amo	CIS	11	0	0	0	8	....	....	....	....	....
1995-96	Moscow D'amo	CIS	9	1	1	2	22	4	0	0	0	0
1996-97	Moscow D'amo	Rus.	23	0	2	2	16	....	....	....	....	....
	Adirondack	AHL	2	0	1	1	6	2	0	0	0	0

KUZNIK, GREG CAR.

Defense. Shoots left. 6', 182 lbs. Born, Prince George, B.C., June 12, 1978.
(Hartford's 7th choice, 171st overall, in 1996 Entry Draft).

			Regular Season					Playoffs				
Season	Club	Lea	GP	G	A	TP	PIM	GP	G	A	TP	PIM
1995-96	Seattle	WHL	70	2	13	15	149	5	0	0	0	6
1996-97	Seattle	WHL	70	4	9	13	161	14	0	2	2	26

KVASHA, OLEG (kuh-VAH-shah) FLA.

Left wing. Shoots right. 6'5", 205 lbs. Born, Moscow, USSR, July 26, 1978.
(Florida's 3rd choice, 65th overall, in 1996 Entry Draft).

			Regular Season					Playoffs				
Season	Club	Lea	GP	G	A	TP	PIM	GP	G	A	TP	PIM
1995-96	CSKA	CIS	38	2	3	5	14	2	0	0	0	0
1996-97	CSKA	Rus. 2	44	20	22	42	115	....	....	....	....	....

KWIATKOWSKI, JOEL (KWEE-at-KOW-skee) DAL.

Defense. Shoots left. 6'2", 200 lbs. Born, Maymont, Sask., March 22, 1977.
(Dallas' 7th choice, 194th overall, in 1996 Entry Draft).

			Regular Season					Playoffs				
Season	Club	Lea	GP	G	A	TP	PIM	GP	G	A	TP	PIM
1995-96	Prince George	WHL	72	12	28	40	133	....	....	....	....	....
1996-97a	Prince George	WHL	72	15	37	52	94	15	4	2	6	24

a WHL West Second All-Star Team (1997)

KYPREOS, NICK (KIH-pree-ohz) TOR.

Left wing. Shoots left. 6', 205 lbs. Born, Toronto, Ont., June 4, 1966.

			Regular Season					Playoffs				
Season	Club	Lea	GP	G	A	TP	PIM	GP	G	A	TP	PIM
1983-84	North Bay	OHL	51	12	11	23	36	4	3	2	5	9
1984-85	North Bay	OHL	64	41	36	77	71	8	2	2	4	15
1985-86a	North Bay	OHL	64	62	35	97	112	....	....	....	....	....
1986-87	Hershey	AHL	10	0	1	1	4	....	....	....	....	....
b	North Bay	OHL	46	49	41	90	54	24	11	5	16	78
1987-88	Hershey	AHL	71	24	20	44	101	12	0	2	2	17
1988-89	Hershey	AHL	28	12	15	27	19	12	4	5	9	11
1989-90	Washington	NHL	31	5	4	9	82	7	1	0	1	15
	Baltimore	AHL	14	6	5	11	6	7	4	1	5	17
1990-91	Washington	NHL	79	9	9	18	196	9	0	1	1	38
1991-92	Washington	NHL	65	4	6	10	206	....	....	....	....	....
1992-93	Hartford	NHL	75	17	10	27	325	....	....	....	....	....
1993-94	Hartford	NHL	10	0	0	0	37	....	....	....	....	....
	NY Rangers	NHL	46	3	5	8	102	3	0	0	0	2 ♦
1994-95	NY Rangers	NHL	40	1	3	4	93	10	0	2	2	6
1995-96	NY Rangers	NHL	42	3	4	7	77	....	....	....	....	....
	Toronto	NHL	19	1	1	2	30	5	0	0	0	4
1996-97	Toronto	NHL	35	3	2	5	62	....	....	....	....	....
	St. John's	AHL	4	0	0	0	4	....	....	....	....	....
	NHL Totals		442	46	44	90	1210	34	1	3	4	65

a OHL First All-Star Team (1986)
b OHL Second All-Star Team (1987)

Signed as a free agent by **Philadelphia,** September 30, 1984. Claimed by **Washington** from **Philadelphia** in NHL Waiver Draft, October 2, 1989. Traded to **Hartford** by **Washington** for Mark Hunter and future considerations (Yvon Corriveau, August 20, 1992), June 15, 1992. Traded to **NY Rangers** by **Hartford** with Steve Larmer, Barry Richter and Hartford's sixth round choice (Yuri Litvinov) in 1994 Entry Draft for Darren Turcotte and James Patrick, November 2, 1993. Traded to **Toronto** by **NY Rangers** for Bill Berg, February 29, 1996.

KYTE, JIM (KITE)

Defense. Shoots left. 6'5", 210 lbs. Born, Ottawa, Ont., March 21, 1964.
(Winnipeg's 1st choice, 12th overall, in 1982 Entry Draft).

			Regular Season					Playoffs				
Season	Club	Lea	GP	G	A	TP	PIM	GP	G	A	TP	PIM
1981-82	Cornwall	OHL	52	4	13	17	148	5	0	0	0	10
1982-83	Winnipeg	NHL	2	0	0	0	0	....	....	....	....	....
	Cornwall	OHL	65	6	30	36	195	8	0	2	2	24
1983-84	Winnipeg	NHL	58	1	2	3	55	3	0	0	0	11
1984-85	Winnipeg	NHL	71	0	3	3	111	8	0	0	0	14
1985-86	Winnipeg	NHL	71	1	3	4	126	3	0	0	0	12
1986-87	Winnipeg	NHL	72	5	5	10	162	10	0	4	4	36
1987-88	Winnipeg	NHL	51	1	3	4	128	....	....	....	....	....
1988-89	Winnipeg	NHL	74	3	9	12	190	....	....	....	....	....
1989-90	Pittsburgh	NHL	56	3	1	4	125	....	....	....	....	....
1990-91	Pittsburgh	NHL	1	0	0	0	2	....	....	....	....	....
	Muskegon	IHL	25	2	5	7	157	....	....	....	....	....
	Calgary	NHL	42	0	9	9	153	7	0	0	0	7
1991-92	Calgary	NHL	21	0	1	1	107	....	....	....	....	....
	Salt Lake	IHL	6	0	1	1	9	....	....	....	....	....
1992-93	Ottawa	NHL	4	0	1	1	4	....	....	....	....	....
	New Haven	AHL	63	6	18	24	163	....	....	....	....	....
1993-94	Las Vegas	IHL	75	2	16	18	246	4	0	1	1	51
1994-95	Las Vegas	IHL	76	3	17	20	195	....	....	....	....	....
	San Jose	NHL	18	2	5	7	33	11	0	2	2	14
1995-96	San Jose	NHL	57	1	7	8	146	....	....	....	....	....
1996-97	Kansas City	IHL	76	3	8	11	259	3	0	0	0	2
	NHL Totals		598	17	49	66	1342	42	0	6	6	94

Traded to **Pittsburgh** by **Winnipeg** with Andrew McBain and Randy Gilhen for Randy Cunneyworth, Rick Tabaracci and Dave McLlwain, June 17, 1989. Traded to **Calgary** by **Pittsburgh** for Jiri Hrdina, December 13, 1990. Signed as a free agent by **Ottawa**, September 10, 1992. Signed as a free agent by **San Jose**, March 31, 1995.

LABELLE, MARC OTT.

Left wing. Shoots left. 6'1", 215 lbs. Born, Maniwaki, Que., December 20, 1969.

			Regular Season					Playoffs				
Season	Club	Lea	GP	G	A	TP	PIM	GP	G	A	TP	PIM
1987-88	Victoriaville	QMJHL	63	11	14	25	236	5	2	4	6	20
1988-89	Victoriaville	QMJHL	62	9	26	35	202	15	6	3	9	30
1989-90	Victoriaville	QMJHL	56	18	21	39	192	16	4	8	12	42
1990-91	Fredericton	AHL	25	1	4	5	95	4	0	2	2	25
	Richmond	ECHL	5	1	1	2	37	....	....	....	....	....
1991-92	Fredericton	AHL	62	7	10	17	238	3	0	0	0	6
1992-93	San Diego	IHL	5	0	2	2	5	....	....	....	....	....
	New Haven	AHL	31	5	4	9	124	....	....	....	....	....
	Thunder Bay	ColHL	9	0	5	5	17	7	0	1	1	11
1993-94	Cincinnati	IHL	37	2	1	3	133	4	0	1	1	6
1994-95	Cincinnati	IHL	54	3	4	7	173	8	0	0	0	7
1995-96	Cincinnati	IHL	57	6	11	17	218	....	....	....	....	....
	Milwaukee	IHL	20	5	3	8	50	5	1	1	2	4
1996-97	Dallas	NHL	9	0	0	0	46	....	....	....	....	....
	Milwaukee	IHL	14	1	1	2	33	....	....	....	....	....
	Michigan	IHL	46	4	7	11	148	3	0	0	0	6
	NHL Totals		9	0	0	0	46	....	....	....	....	....

Signed as a free agent by **Montreal**, January 21, 1991. Signed as a free agent by **Ottawa**, July 30, 1992. Claimed by **Florida** from **Ottawa** in Expansion Draft, June 24, 1993. Signed as a free agent by **Dallas**, April 15, 1996. Signed as a free agent by **Ottawa**, July 14, 1997.

LABRAATEN, JAN (la-BRA-tuhn) CGY.

Left wing. Shoots right. 6'2", 198 lbs. Born, Karlstad, Sweden, February 17, 1977.
(Calgary's 4th choice, 98th overall, in 1995 Entry Draft).

			Regular Season					Playoffs				
Season	Club	Lea	GP	G	A	TP	PIM	GP	G	A	TP	PIM
1994-95	Farjestad	Swe. Jr.	25	10	6	16	20	....	....	....	....	....
	Farjestad	Swe.	2	0	1	1	2	1	0	0	0	0
1995-96	Farjestad	Swe.	4	0	0	0	0	....	....	....	....	....
1996-97	Orebro	Swe. 2	30	9	6	15	51	....	....	....	....	....

LACHANCE, BOB ST.L.

Right wing. Shoots right. 5'11", 180 lbs. Born, Northampton, MA, February 1, 1974.
(St. Louis' 5th choice, 134th overall, in 1992 Entry Draft).

			Regular Season					Playoffs				
Season	Club	Lea	GP	G	A	TP	PIM	GP	G	A	TP	PIM
1992-93	Boston U.	H.E.	33	4	10	14	24	....	....	....	....	....
1993-94	Boston U.	H.E.	32	13	19	32	42	....	....	....	....	....
1994-95	Boston U.	H.E.	37	12	29	41	51	....	....	....	....	....
1995-96	Boston U.	H.E.	39	15	37	52	67	....	....	....	....	....
	Worcester	AHL	7	1	0	1	6	....	....	....	....	....
1996-97	Worcester	AHL	74	21	35	56	66	5	0	2	2	4

LACHANCE, SCOTT — NYI

Defense. Shoots left. 6'1", 196 lbs. Born, Charlottesville, VA, October 22, 1972.
(NY Islanders' 1st choice, 4th overall, in 1991 Entry Draft).

			Regular Season					Playoffs				
Season	Club	Lea	GP	G	A	TP	PIM	GP	G	A	TP	PIM
1990-91	Boston U.	H.E.	31	5	19	24	48	....	....	....	....	....
1991-92	U.S. National	....	36	1	10	11	34	....	....	....	....	....
	U.S. Olympic	....	8	0	1	1	6	....	....	....	....	....
	NY Islanders	NHL	17	1	4	5	9	....	....	....	....	....
1992-93	NY Islanders	NHL	75	7	17	24	67	....	....	....	....	....
1993-94	NY Islanders	NHL	74	3	11	14	70	3	0	0	0	0
1994-95	NY Islanders	NHL	26	6	7	13	26	....	....	....	....	....
1995-96	NY Islanders	NHL	55	3	10	13	54	....	....	....	....	....
1996-97	NY Islanders	NHL	81	3	11	14	47	....	....	....	....	....
	NHL Totals		328	23	60	83	273	3	0	0	0	0

Played in NHL All-Star Game (1997)

LACOUTURE, DAN (la-koo-TUHR) — NYI

Left wing. Shoots left. 6'2", 201 lbs. Born, Hyannis, MA, April 18, 1977.
(NY Islanders' 2nd choice, 29th overall, in 1996 Entry Draft).

			Regular Season					Playoffs				
Season	Club	Lea	GP	G	A	TP	PIM	GP	G	A	TP	PIM
1995-96	Jr. Whalers	Jr. B	42	36	48	84	102	....	....	....	....	....
1996-97	Boston U.	H.E.	31	13	12	25	18	....	....	....	....	....

LACROIX, DANIEL (luh-KWAH) — PHI.

Left wing. Shoots left. 6'2", 205 lbs. Born, Montreal, Que., March 11, 1969.
(NY Rangers' 2nd choice, 31st overall, in 1987 Entry Draft).

			Regular Season					Playoffs				
Season	Club	Lea	GP	G	A	TP	PIM	GP	G	A	TP	PIM
1986-87	Granby	QMJHL	54	9	16	25	311	8	1	2	3	22
1987-88	Granby	QMJHL	58	24	50	74	468	5	0	4	4	12
1988-89	Granby	QMJHL	70	45	49	94	320	4	1	1	2	57
	Denver	IHL	2	0	1	1	0	2	0	1	1	0
1989-90	Flint	IHL	61	12	16	28	128	4	2	0	2	24
1990-91	Binghamton	AHL	54	7	12	19	237	5	1	0	1	24
1991-92	Binghamton	AHL	52	12	20	32	149	11	2	4	6	28
1992-93	Binghamton	AHL	73	21	22	43	255	....	....	....	....	....
1993-94	NY Rangers	NHL	4	0	0	0	0	....	....	....	....	....
	Binghamton	AHL	59	20	23	43	278	....	....	....	....	....
1994-95	Providence	AHL	40	15	11	26	266	....	....	....	....	....
	Boston	NHL	23	1	0	1	38	....	....	....	....	....
	NY Rangers	NHL	1	0	0	0	0	....	....	....	....	....
1995-96	NY Rangers	NHL	25	2	2	4	30	....	....	....	....	....
	Binghamton	AHL	26	12	15	27	155	....	....	....	....	....
1996-97	Philadelphia	NHL	74	7	1	8	163	12	0	1	1	22
	NHL Totals		127	10	3	13	231	12	0	1	1	22

Traded to **Boston** by **NY Rangers** for Glen Featherstone, August 19, 1994. Claimed on waivers by **NY Rangers** from **Boston**, March 23, 1995. Signed as a free agent by **Philadelphia**, July 18, 1996.

LACROIX, ERIC (luh-KWAH) — COL.

Left wing. Shoots left. 6'1", 205 lbs. Born, Montreal, Que., July 15, 1971.
(Toronto's 6th choice, 136th overall, in 1990 Entry Draft).

			Regular Season					Playoffs				
Season	Club	Lea	GP	G	A	TP	PIM	GP	G	A	TP	PIM
1990-91	St. Lawrence	ECAC	35	13	11	24	35	....	....	....	....	....
1991-92	St. Lawrence	ECAC	34	11	20	31	40	....	....	....	....	....
1992-93	St. John's	AHL	76	15	19	34	59	9	5	3	8	4
1993-94	Toronto	NHL	3	0	0	0	2	2	0	0	0	0
	St. John's	AHL	59	17	22	39	69	11	5	3	8	6
1994-95	St. John's	AHL	1	0	0	0	2	....	....	....	....	....
	Phoenix	IHL	25	7	1	8	31	....	....	....	....	....
	Los Angeles	NHL	45	9	7	16	54	....	....	....	....	....
1995-96	Los Angeles	NHL	72	16	16	32	110	....	....	....	....	....
1996-97	Colorado	NHL	81	18	18	36	26	17	1	4	5	19
	NHL Totals		201	43	41	84	192	19	1	4	5	19

Traded to **Los Angeles** by **Toronto** with Chris Snell and Toronto's fourth round choice (Eric Belanger) in 1996 Entry Draft for Dixon Ward, Guy Leveque, Kelly Fairchild and Shayne Toporowski, October 3, 1994. Traded to **Colorado** by **Los Angeles** with Los Angeles' first round choice in 1998 Entry Draft for Stephane Fiset and Colorado's first round choice in 1998 Entry Draft, June 20, 1996.

LAFAYETTE, NATHAN (LAH-fay-eht) — L.A.

Center. Shoots right. 6'1", 200 lbs. Born, New Westminster, B.C., February 17, 1973.
(St. Louis' 3rd choice, 65th overall, in 1991 Entry Draft).

			Regular Season					Playoffs				
Season	Club	Lea	GP	G	A	TP	PIM	GP	G	A	TP	PIM
1989-90	Kingston	OHL	53	6	8	14	14	7	0	1	1	0
1990-91	Kingston	OHL	35	13	13	26	10	....	....	....	....	....
	Cornwall	OHL	28	16	22	38	25	....	....	....	....	....
1991-92a	Cornwall	OHL	66	28	45	73	26	6	2	5	7	15
1992-93	Newmarket	OHL	58	49	38	87	26	7	4	5	9	19
1993-94	St. Louis	NHL	38	2	3	5	14	....	....	....	....	....
	Peoria	IHL	27	13	11	24	20	....	....	....	....	....
	Vancouver	NHL	11	1	1	2	4	20	2	7	9	4
1994-95	Syracuse	AHL	27	9	9	18	10	....	....	....	....	....
	Vancouver	NHL	27	4	4	8	2	....	....	....	....	....
	NY Rangers	NHL	12	0	0	0	0	8	0	0	0	2
1995-96	NY Rangers	NHL	5	0	0	0	2	....	....	....	....	....
	Binghamton	AHL	57	21	27	48	32	....	....	....	....	....
	Los Angeles	NHL	12	2	4	6	6	....	....	....	....	....
1996-97	Los Angeles	NHL	15	1	3	4	8	....	....	....	....	....
	Phoenix	IHL	31	2	5	7	16	....	....	....	....	....
	Syracuse	AHL	26	14	11	25	18	3	1	0	1	2
	NHL Totals		120	10	15	25	36	28	2	7	9	6

a Canadian Major Junior Scholastic Player of the Year (1992)

Traded to **Vancouver** by **St. Louis** with Jeff Brown and Bret Hedican for Craig Janney, March 21, 1994. Traded to **NY Rangers** by **Vancouver** for Corey Hirsch, April 7, 1995. Traded to **Los Angeles** by **NY Rangers** with Ray Ferraro, Mattias Norstrom, Ian Laperriere and NY Rangers' fourth round choice (Sean Blanchard) in 1997 Entry Draft for Marty McSorley, Jari Kurri and Shane Churla, March 14, 1996.

LAFLAMME, CHRISTIAN (lah-FLAM) — CHI.

Defense. Shoots right. 6'1", 202 lbs. Born, St. Charles, Que., November 24, 1976.
(Chicago's 2nd choice, 45th overall, in 1995 Entry Draft).

			Regular Season					Playoffs				
Season	Club	Lea	GP	G	A	TP	PIM	GP	G	A	TP	PIM
1992-93	Verdun	QMJHL	69	2	17	19	85	3	0	2	2	6
1993-94	Verdun	QMJHL	72	4	34	38	85	4	0	3	3	4
1994-95a	Beauport	QMJHL	67	6	41	47	82	8	1	4	5	6
1995-96	Beauport	QMJHL	41	13	23	36	63	20	7	17	24	32
1996-97	Chicago	NHL	4	0	1	1	2	....	....	....	....	....
	Indianapolis	IHL	62	5	15	20	60	4	1	1	2	16
	NHL Totals		4	0	1	1	2	....	....	....	....	....

a QMJHL Second All-Star Team (1995)

LaFONTAINE, PAT (luh-FAHN-tayn) — BUF.

Center. Shoots right. 5'10", 182 lbs. Born, St. Louis, MO, February 22, 1965.
(NY Islanders' 1st choice, 3rd overall, in 1983 Entry Draft).

			Regular Season					Playoffs				
Season	Club	Lea	GP	G	A	TP	PIM	GP	G	A	TP	PIM
1982-83ab	Verdun	QMJHL	70	*104	*130	*234	10	15	11	*24	*35	4
1983-84	U.S. National	....	58	56	55	111	22	....	....	....	....	....
	U.S. Olympic	....	6	5	5	10	0	....	....	....	....	....
	NY Islanders	NHL	15	13	6	19	6	16	3	6	9	8
1984-85	NY Islanders	NHL	67	19	35	54	32	9	1	2	3	4
1985-86	NY Islanders	NHL	65	30	23	53	43	3	1	0	1	0
1986-87	NY Islanders	NHL	80	38	32	70	70	14	5	7	12	10
1987-88	NY Islanders	NHL	75	47	45	92	52	6	4	5	9	8
1988-89	NY Islanders	NHL	79	45	43	88	26	....	....	....	....	....
1989-90c	NY Islanders	NHL	74	54	51	105	38	2	0	1	1	0
1990-91	NY Islanders	NHL	75	41	44	85	42	....	....	....	....	....
1991-92	Buffalo	NHL	57	46	47	93	98	7	8	3	11	4
1992-93d	Buffalo	NHL	84	53	95	148	63	7	2	10	12	0
1993-94	Buffalo	NHL	16	5	13	18	2	....	....	....	....	....
1994-95e	Buffalo	NHL	22	12	15	27	4	5	2	2	4	2
1995-96	Buffalo	NHL	76	40	51	91	36	....	....	....	....	....
1996-97	Buffalo	NHL	13	2	6	8	4	....	....	....	....	....
	NHL Totals		798	445	506	951	516	69	26	36	62	36

a QMJHL First All-Star Team (1983)
b Canadian Major Junior Player of the Year (1983)
c Won Dodge Performer of the Year Award (1990)
d NHL Second All-Star Team (1993)
e Won Bill Masterton Memorial Trophy (1995)

Played in NHL All-Star Game (1988-91, 1993)

Traded to **Buffalo** by **NY Islanders** with Randy Hillier, Randy Wood and NY Islanders' fourth round choice (Dean Melanson) in 1992 Entry Draft for Pierre Turgeon, Uwe Krupp, Benoit Hogue and Dave McLlwain, October 25, 1991.

LAFRANCE, BRANDON — EDM.

Right wing. Shoots right. 6'1", 190 lbs. Born, Ottawa, Ont., November 1, 1976.
(Edmonton's 8th choice, 170th overall, in 1996 Entry Draft).

			Regular Season					Playoffs				
Season	Club	Lea	GP	G	A	TP	PIM	GP	G	A	TP	PIM
1995-96	Ohio State	CCHA	32	11	5	16	34	....	....	....	....	....
1996-97	Ohio State	CCHA	37	9	6	15	38	....	....	....	....	....

LAHEY, MATTHEW — WSH.

Left wing. Shoots left. 6'1", 230 lbs. Born, Nepean, Ont., October 12, 1977.
(Washington's 8th choice, 126th overall, in 1996 Entry Draft).

			Regular Season					Playoffs				
Season	Club	Lea	GP	G	A	TP	PIM	GP	G	A	TP	PIM
1994-95	Peterborough	OHL	63	6	6	12	87	11	1	1	2	18
1995-96	Peterborough	OHL	60	20	15	35	117	24	4	5	9	38
1996-97	Peterborough	OHL	28	11	14	25	76	....	....	....	....	....
	S.S. Marie	OHL	22	14	13	27	37	11	5	3	8	32

LAING, QUINTIN — DET.

Left wing. Shoots left. 6'2", 175 lbs. Born, Rosetown, Sask., June 8, 1979.
(Detroit's 3rd choice, 102nd overall, in 1997 Entry Draft).

			Regular Season					Playoffs				
Season	Club	Lea	GP	G	A	TP	PIM	GP	G	A	TP	PIM
1995-96	Saskatoon	Midget	44	18	12	30	20	....	....	....	....	....
1996-97	Kelowna	WHL	63	13	24	37	54	1	0	0	0	0

LAKOVIC, SASHA (LA-koh-vik) — N.J.

Left wing. Shoots left. 6', 205 lbs. Born, Vancouver, B.C., September 7, 1971.

			Regular Season					Playoffs				
Season	Club	Lea	GP	G	A	TP	PIM	GP	G	A	TP	PIM
1993-94	Toledo	ECHL	24	5	10	15	198	....	....	....	....	....
	Chatham	ColHL	13	11	7	18	61	....	....	....	....	....
1994-95	Tulsa	CHL	40	20	24	44	214	5	1	3	4	88
1995-96	Las Vegas	IHL	49	1	2	3	416	13	1	1	2	*57
1996-97	Calgary	NHL	19	0	1	1	54	....	....	....	....	....
	St. John	AHL	18	1	8	9	182	....	....	....	....	....
	Las Vegas	IHL	10	0	0	0	81	2	0	0	0	14
	NHL Totals		19	0	1	1	54	....	....	....	....	....

Signed as a free agent by **Calgary**, October 10, 1996. Signed as a free agent by **New Jersey**, August, 1997.

LALOR, MIKE (LAH-luhr)

Defense. Shoots left. 6', 200 lbs. Born, Buffalo, NY, March 8, 1963.

			Regular Season					Playoffs				
Season	Club	Lea	GP	G	A	TP	PIM	GP	G	A	TP	PIM
1981-82	Brantford	OHL	64	3	13	16	114	11	0	6	6	11
1982-83	Brantford	OHL	65	10	30	40	113	8	1	3	4	20
1983-84	Nova Scotia	AHL	67	5	11	16	80	12	0	2	2	13
1984-85	Sherbrooke	AHL	79	9	23	32	114	17	3	5	8	36
1985-86	**Montreal**	**NHL**	**62**	**3**	**5**	**8**	**56**	**17**	**1**	**2**	**3**	**29 ♦**
1986-87	**Montreal**	**NHL**	**57**	**0**	**10**	**10**	**47**	**13**	**2**	**1**	**3**	**29**
1987-88	**Montreal**	**NHL**	**66**	**1**	**10**	**11**	**113**	**11**	**0**	**0**	**0**	**11**
1988-89	**Montreal**	**NHL**	**12**	**1**	**4**	**5**	**15**	....	....	....	....	....
	St. Louis	**NHL**	**36**	**1**	**14**	**15**	**54**	**10**	**1**	**1**	**2**	**14**
1989-90	**St. Louis**	**NHL**	**78**	**0**	**16**	**16**	**81**	**12**	**0**	**2**	**2**	**31**
1990-91	**Washington**	**NHL**	**68**	**1**	**5**	**6**	**61**	**10**	**1**	**2**	**3**	**22**
1991-92	**Washington**	**NHL**	**64**	**5**	**7**	**12**	**64**	....	....	....	....	....
	Winnipeg	**NHL**	**15**	**2**	**3**	**5**	**14**	**7**	**0**	**0**	**0**	**19**
1992-93	**Winnipeg**	**NHL**	**64**	**1**	**8**	**9**	**76**	**4**	**0**	**2**	**2**	**4**
1993-94	**San Jose**	**NHL**	**23**	**0**	**2**	**2**	**8**	....	....	....	....	....
	Dallas	**NHL**	**12**	**0**	**1**	**1**	**6**	**5**	**0**	**0**	**0**	**6**
1994-95	**Dallas**	**NHL**	**12**	**0**	**0**	**0**	**9**	**3**	**0**	**0**	**0**	**2**
	Kalamazoo	IHL	5	0	1	1	11	....	....	....	....	....
1995-96	**Dallas**	**NHL**	**63**	**1**	**2**	**3**	**31**	....	....	....	....	....
	San Francisco	IHL	12	2	2	4	6	....	....	....	....	....
1996-97	**Dallas**	**NHL**	**55**	**1**	**1**	**2**	**42**	....	....	....	....	....
	NHL Totals		**687**	**17**	**88**	**105**	**677**	**92**	**5**	**10**	**15**	**167**

Signed as a free agent by **Montreal**, September, 1983. Traded to **St. Louis** by **Montreal** with Montreal's first round choice (later traded to Vancouver — Vancouver selected Shawn Antoski) in 1990 Entry Draft for St. Louis' first round choice (Turner Stevenson) in 1990 Entry Draft, January 16, 1989. Traded to **Washington** by **St. Louis** with Peter Zezel for Geoff Courtnall, July 13, 1990. Traded to **Winnipeg** by **Washington** for Paul MacDermid, March 2, 1992. Signed as a free agent by **San Jose**, August 13, 1993. Traded to **Dallas** by **San Jose** with Doug Zmolek and cash for Ulf Dahlen and Dallas' seventh round choice (Brad Mehalko) in 1995 Entry Draft, March 19, 1994.

LAMB, MARK

Center. Shoots left. 5'9", 180 lbs. Born, Ponteix, Sask., August 3, 1964.
(Calgary's 5th choice, 72nd overall, in 1982 Entry Draft).

			Regular Season					Playoffs				
Season	Club	Lea	GP	G	A	TP	PIM	GP	G	A	TP	PIM
1981-82	Billings	WHL	72	45	56	101	46	5	4	6	10	4
1982-83	Nanaimo	WHL	30	14	37	51	16	....	....	....	....	....
	Medicine Hat	WHL	46	22	43	65	33	5	3	2	5	4
	Colorado	CHL	....	....	....	....	....	6	0	2	2	0
1983-84a	Medicine Hat	WHL	72	59	77	136	30	14	12	11	23	6
1984-85	Moncton	AHL	80	23	49	72	53	....	....	....	....	....
1985-86	**Calgary**	**NHL**	**1**	**0**	**0**	**0**	**0**	....	....	....	....	....
	Moncton	AHL	79	26	50	76	51	10	2	6	8	17
1986-87	**Detroit**	**NHL**	**22**	**2**	**1**	**3**	**8**	**11**	**0**	**0**	**0**	**11**
	Adirondack	AHL	49	14	36	50	45	....	....	....	....	....
1987-88	**Edmonton**	**NHL**	**2**	**0**	**0**	**0**	**0**	....	....	....	....	....
	Nova Scotia	AHL	69	27	61	88	45	5	0	5	5	6
1988-89	**Edmonton**	**NHL**	**20**	**2**	**8**	**10**	**14**	**6**	**0**	**2**	**2**	**8**
	Cape Breton	AHL	54	33	49	82	29	....	....	....	....	....
1989-90	**Edmonton**	**NHL**	**58**	**12**	**16**	**28**	**42**	**22**	**6**	**11**	**17**	**2 ♦**
1990-91	**Edmonton**	**NHL**	**37**	**4**	**8**	**12**	**25**	**15**	**0**	**5**	**5**	**20**
1991-92	**Edmonton**	**NHL**	**59**	**6**	**22**	**28**	**46**	**16**	**1**	**1**	**2**	**10**
1992-93	**Ottawa**	**NHL**	**71**	**7**	**19**	**26**	**64**	....	....	....	....	....
1993-94	**Ottawa**	**NHL**	**66**	**11**	**18**	**29**	**56**	....	....	....	....	....
	Philadelphia	**NHL**	**19**	**1**	**6**	**7**	**16**	....	....	....	....	....
1994-95	**Philadelphia**	**NHL**	**8**	**0**	**2**	**2**	**2**	....	....	....	....	....
	Montreal	**NHL**	**39**	**1**	**0**	**1**	**18**	....	....	....	....	....
1995-96	**Montreal**	**NHL**	**1**	**0**	**0**	**0**	**0**	....	....	....	....	....
	Houston	IHL	67	17	60	77	65	....	....	....	....	....
1996-97	Houston	IHL	81	25	53	78	83	13	3	12	15	10
	NHL Totals		**403**	**46**	**100**	**146**	**291**	**70**	**7**	**19**	**26**	**51**

a WHL East First All-Star Team (1984)

Signed as a free agent by **Detroit**, July 28, 1986. Claimed by **Edmonton** from **Detroit** in NHL Waiver Draft, October 5, 1987. Claimed by **Ottawa** from **Edmonton** in Expansion Draft, June 18, 1992. Traded to **Philadelphia** by **Ottawa** for Claude Boivin and Kirk Daubenspeck, March 5, 1994. Traded to **Montreal** by **Philadelphia** for cash, February 10, 1995.

LAMBERT, DAN (lahm-BAIR)

Defense. Shoots left. 5'8", 177 lbs. Born, St. Boniface, Man., January 12, 1970.
(Quebec's 8th choice, 106th overall, in 1989 Entry Draft).

			Regular Season					Playoffs				
Season	Club	Lea	GP	G	A	TP	PIM	GP	G	A	TP	PIM
1986-87	Swift Current	WHL	68	13	53	66	95	4	1	1	2	9
1987-88	Swift Current	WHL	69	20	63	83	120	10	2	10	12	45
1988-89abc	Swift Current	WHL	57	25	77	102	158	12	9	19	28	12
1989-90a	Swift Current	WHL	50	17	51	68	119	4	2	3	5	12
1990-91	**Quebec**	**NHL**	**1**	**0**	**0**	**0**	**0**	....	....	....	....	....
	Halifax	AHL	30	7	13	20	20	....	....	....	....	....
	Fort Wayne	IHL	49	10	27	37	65	19	4	10	14	20
1991-92	**Quebec**	**NHL**	**28**	**6**	**9**	**15**	**22**	....	....	....	....	....
	Halifax	AHL	47	3	28	31	33	....	....	....	....	....
1992-93	Moncton	AHL	73	11	30	41	100	5	1	2	3	2
1993-94	HIFK	Fin.	13	1	2	3	8	....	....	....	....	....
	Fort Wayne	IHL	62	10	27	37	138	18	3	12	15	20
1994-95	San Diego	IHL	70	6	19	25	95	5	0	5	5	10
1995-96d	Los Angeles	IHL	81	22	65	87	121	....	....	....	....	....
1996-97	Long Beach	IHL	71	15	50	65	70	18	2	8	10	8
	NHL Totals		**29**	**6**	**9**	**15**	**22**	....	....	....	....	....

a WHL East First All-Star Team (1989, 1990)
b Memorial Cup All-Star Team (1989)
c Won Stafford Smythe Memorial Trophy (Memorial Cup Tournament MVP) (1989)
d IHL Second All-Star Team (1996)

Traded to **Winnipeg** by **Quebec** for Shawn Cronin, August 25, 1992.

LAMBERT, DENNY (lahm-BAIR) OTT.

Left wing. Shoots left. 5'11", 200 lbs. Born, Wawa, Ont., January 7, 1970.

			Regular Season					Playoffs				
Season	Club	Lea	GP	G	A	TP	PIM	GP	G	A	TP	PIM
1988-89	S.S. Marie	OHL	61	14	15	29	203	....	....	....	....	....
1989-90	S.S. Marie	OHL	61	23	29	52	276	....	....	....	....	....
1990-91	S.S. Marie	OHL	59	28	39	67	169	14	7	9	16	48
1991-92	San Diego	IHL	71	17	14	31	229	3	0	0	0	10
	St. Thomas	ColHL	5	2	6	8	9	....	....	....	....	....
1992-93	San Diego	IHL	56	18	12	30	277	14	1	1	2	44
1993-94	San Diego	IHL	79	13	14	27	314	6	1	0	1	55
1994-95	San Diego	IHL	75	25	35	60	222	....	....	....	....	....
	Anaheim	**NHL**	**13**	**1**	**3**	**4**	**4**	....	....	....	....	....
1995-96	**Anaheim**	**NHL**	**33**	**0**	**8**	**8**	**55**	....	....	....	....	....
	Baltimore	AHL	44	14	28	42	126	12	3	9	12	39
1996-97	**Ottawa**	**NHL**	**80**	**4**	**16**	**20**	**217**	**6**	**0**	**1**	**1**	**9**
	NHL Totals		**126**	**5**	**27**	**32**	**276**	**6**	**0**	**1**	**1**	**9**

Signed as a free agent by **Anaheim**, August 16, 1993. Signed as a free agent by **Ottawa**, July 29, 1996.

LANDRY, ERIC CGY.

Center. Shoots left. 5'11", 185 lbs. Born, Gatineau, Que., January 20, 1975.

			Regular Season					Playoffs				
Season	Club	Lea	GP	G	A	TP	PIM	GP	G	A	TP	PIM
1993-94	St-Hyacinthe	QMJHL	69	42	34	76	128	7	4	2	6	13
1994-95	St-Hyacinthe	QMJHL	68	38	36	74	249	5	2	1	3	10
1995-96	Cape Breton	AHL	74	19	33	52	187	....	....	....	....	....
1996-97	Hamilton	AHL	74	15	17	32	139	22	6	7	13	43

Signed as a free agent by **Calgary**, August 6, 1997.

LANE, CHRIS BOS.

Defense. Shoots right. 6'1", 192 lbs. Born, Edmonton, Alta., February 16, 1978.
(Boston's 7th choice, 155th overall, in 1996 Entry Draft).

			Regular Season					Playoffs				
Season	Club	Lea	GP	G	A	TP	PIM	GP	G	A	TP	PIM
1995-96	Spokane	WHL	50	1	2	3	40	17	0	1	1	4
1996-97	Spokane	WHL	62	2	8	10	59	....	....	....	....	....

LANG, ROBERT (LUHNG)

Center. Shoots right. 6'2", 200 lbs. Born, Teplice, Czech., December 19, 1970.
(Los Angeles' 6th choice, 133rd overall, in 1990 Entry Draft).

			Regular Season					Playoffs				
Season	Club	Lea	GP	G	A	TP	PIM	GP	G	A	TP	PIM
1988-89	Litvinov	Czech.	7	3	2	5	0	....	....	....	....	....
1989-90	Litvinov	Czech.	39	11	10	21	....	....	....	....	....	....
1990-91	Litvinov	Czech.	56	26	26	52	38	....	....	....	....	....
1991-92	Litvinov	Czech.	43	12	31	43	34	....	....	....	....	....
1992-93	**Los Angeles**	**NHL**	**11**	**0**	**5**	**5**	**2**	....	....	....	....	....
	Phoenix	IHL	38	9	21	30	20	....	....	....	....	....
1993-94	**Los Angeles**	**NHL**	**32**	**9**	**10**	**19**	**10**	....	....	....	....	....
	Phoenix	IHL	44	11	24	35	34	....	....	....	....	....
1994-95	Litvinov	Czech.	16	4	19	23	28	....	....	....	....	....
	Los Angeles	**NHL**	**36**	**4**	**8**	**12**	**4**	....	....	....	....	....
1995-96	**Los Angeles**	**NHL**	**68**	**6**	**16**	**22**	**10**	....	....	....	....	....
1996-97	HC Sparta	Czech.	38	14	27	41	30	5	1	2	3	4
	NHL Totals		**147**	**19**	**39**	**58**	**26**	....	....	....	....	....

LANGDON, DARREN NYR

Left wing. Shoots left. 6'1", 200 lbs. Born, Deer Lake, Nfld., January 8, 1971.

			Regular Season					Playoffs				
Season	Club	Lea	GP	G	A	TP	PIM	GP	G	A	TP	PIM
1991-92	Summerside	MJHL	44	34	49	83	441	....	....	....	....	....
1992-93	Binghamton	AHL	18	3	4	7	115	8	0	1	1	14
	Dayton	ECHL	54	23	22	45	429	3	0	1	1	40
1993-94	Binghamton	AHL	54	2	7	9	327	....	....	....	....	....
1994-95	Binghamton	AHL	55	6	14	20	296	11	1	3	4	*84
	NY Rangers	**NHL**	**18**	**1**	**1**	**2**	**62**	....	....	....	....	....
1995-96	**NY Rangers**	**NHL**	**64**	**7**	**4**	**11**	**175**	**2**	**0**	**0**	**0**	**0**
	Binghamton	AHL	1	0	0	0	12	....	....	....	....	....
1996-97	**NY Rangers**	**NHL**	**60**	**3**	**6**	**9**	**195**	**10**	**0**	**0**	**0**	**2**
	NHL Totals		**142**	**11**	**11**	**22**	**432**	**12**	**0**	**0**	**0**	**2**

Signed as a free agent by **NY Rangers**, August 16, 1993.

LANGENBRUNNER, JAMIE (lan-gehn-BROO-nuhr) DAL.

Center. Shoots right. 5'11", 185 lbs. Born, Duluth, MN, July 24, 1975.
(Dallas' 2nd choice, 35th overall, in 1993 Entry Draft).

			Regular Season					Playoffs				
Season	Club	Lea	GP	G	A	TP	PIM	GP	G	A	TP	PIM
1993-94	Peterborough	OHL	62	33	58	91	53	7	4	6	10	2
1994-95	Peterborough	OHL	62	42	57	99	84	11	8	14	22	12
	Dallas	**NHL**	**2**	**0**	**0**	**0**	**2**	....	....	....	....	....
	Kalamazoo	IHL	....	....	....	....	....	11	1	3	4	2
1995-96	**Dallas**	**NHL**	**12**	**2**	**2**	**4**	**6**	....	....	....	....	....
	Michigan	IHL	59	25	40	65	129	10	3	10	13	8
1996-97	**Dallas**	**NHL**	**76**	**13**	**26**	**39**	**51**	**5**	**1**	**1**	**2**	**14**
	NHL Totals		**90**	**15**	**28**	**43**	**59**	**5**	**1**	**1**	**2**	**14**

LANGFELD, JOSH OTT.

Right wing. Shoots right. 6'3", 205 lbs. Born, Fridley, MN, July 17, 1977.
(Ottawa's 3rd choice, 66th overall, in 1997 Entry Draft).

			Regular Season					Playoffs				
Season	Club	Lea	GP	G	A	TP	PIM	GP	G	A	TP	PIM
1996-97	Lincoln	Jr. A	38	35	23	58	100	....	....	....	....	....

LANGKOW, DAYMOND (LAING-kow) T.B.

Center. Shoots left. 5'11", 175 lbs. Born, Edmonton, Alta, September 27, 1976.
(Tampa Bay's 1st choice, 5th overall, in 1995 Entry Draft).

			Regular Season					Playoffs				
Season	**Club**	**Lea**	**GP**	**G**	**A**	**TP**	**PIM**	**GP**	**G**	**A**	**TP**	**PIM**
1992-93	Tri-City	WHL	64	22	42	64	100	4	1	0	1	4
1993-94	Tri-City	WHL	61	40	43	83	174	4	2	2	4	15
1994-95ab	Tri-City	WHL	72	*67	73	*140	142	17	12	15	27	52
1995-96c	Tri-City	WHL	48	30	61	91	103	11	14	13	27	20
	Tampa Bay	**NHL**	**4**	**0**	**1**	**1**	**0**	....	....	....	....	....
1996-97	**Tampa Bay**	**NHL**	**79**	**15**	**13**	**28**	**35**	....	....	....	....	....
	Adirondack	AHL	2	1	1	2	0	....	....	....	....	....
	NHL Totals		**83**	**15**	**14**	**29**	**35**	....	....	....	....	....

a WHL West First All-Star Team (1995)
b Canadian Major Junior First All-Star Team (1995)
c WHL West Second All-Star Team (1996)

LANK, JEFF PHI.

Defense. Shoots left. 6'3", 205 lbs. Born, Indian Head, Sask., March 1, 1975.
(Montreal's 6th choice, 113th overall, in 1993 Entry Draft).

			Regular Season					Playoffs				
Season	**Club**	**Lea**	**GP**	**G**	**A**	**TP**	**PIM**	**GP**	**G**	**A**	**TP**	**PIM**
1991-92	Prince Albert	WHL	56	2	8	10	26	9	0	0	0	2
1992-93	Prince Albert	WHL	63	1	11	12	60	....	....	....	....	....
1993-94	Prince Albert	WHL	72	9	38	47	62	....	....	....	....	....
1994-95	Prince Albert	WHL	68	12	25	37	60	13	2	10	12	8
1995-96	Hershey	AHL	72	7	13	20	70	5	0	0	0	8
1996-97	Philadelphia	AHL	44	2	12	14	49	7	2	1	3	4

Re-entered NHL Entry Draft, **Philadelphia's** 9th choice, 230th overall in 1995 Entry Draft.

LANKSHEAR, MIKE FLA.

Defense. Shoots left. 6'2", 185 lbs. Born, Calgary, Alta., September 8, 1978.
(Toronto's 3rd choice, 66th overall, in 1996 Entry Draft).

			Regular Season					Playoffs				
Season	**Club**	**Lea**	**GP**	**G**	**A**	**TP**	**PIM**	**GP**	**G**	**A**	**TP**	**PIM**
1995-96	Guelph	OHL	63	8	20	28	73	15	2	6	8	19
1996-97	Guelph	OHL	52	6	27	33	36	18	0	10	10	10

Traded to **Florida** by **Toronto** for Per Gustafsson, June 12, 1997.

LAPERRIERE, DANIEL (luh-PAIR-ee-YAIR)

Defense. Shoots left. 6'1", 195 lbs. Born, Laval, Que., March 28, 1969.
(St. Louis' 4th choice, 93rd overall, in 1989 Entry Draft).

			Regular Season					Playoffs				
Season	**Club**	**Lea**	**GP**	**G**	**A**	**TP**	**PIM**	**GP**	**G**	**A**	**TP**	**PIM**
1988-89	St. Lawrence	ECAC	28	0	7	7	10	....	....	....	....	....
1989-90	St. Lawrence	ECAC	31	6	19	25	16	....	....	....	....	....
1990-91a	St. Lawrence	ECAC	34	7	31	38	18	....	....	....	....	....
1991-92bc	St. Lawrence	ECAC	32	8	*45	53	36	....	....	....	....	....
1992-93	**St. Louis**	**NHL**	**5**	**0**	**1**	**1**	**0**	....	....	....	....	....
	Peoria	IHL	54	4	20	24	28	....	....	....	....	....
1993-94	**St. Louis**	**NHL**	**20**	**1**	**3**	**4**	**8**	....	....	....	....	....
	Peoria	IHL	56	10	37	47	16	6	0	2	2	2
1994-95	Peoria	IHL	65	19	33	52	42	....	....	....	....	....
	St. Louis	**NHL**	**4**	**0**	**0**	**0**	**15**	....	....	....	....	....
	Ottawa	**NHL**	**13**	**1**	**1**	**2**	**0**	....	....	....	....	....
1995-96	**Ottawa**	**NHL**	**6**	**0**	**0**	**0**	**4**	....	....	....	....	....
	P.E.I.	AHL	15	2	7	9	4	....	....	....	....	....
	Atlanta	IHL	15	4	9	13	4	....	....	....	....	....
	Kansas City	IHL	23	2	6	8	11	5	0	1	1	0
1996-97	Portland	AHL	69	14	26	40	33	5	0	2	2	2
	NHL Totals		**48**	**2**	**5**	**7**	**27**	....	....	....	....	....

a ECAC Second All-Star Team (1991)
b ECAC First All-Star Team (1992)
c NCAA East First All-American Team (1992)

Traded to **Ottawa** by **St. Louis** with St. Louis' ninth round choice (Erik Kaminski) in 1995 Entry Draft for Ottawa's ninth round choice (Libor Zabransky) in 1995 Entry Draft, April 7, 1995. Signed as a free agent by **Washington**, July 12, 1996.

LAPERRIERE, IAN (luh-PAIR-ee-YAIR, EE-ihn) L.A.

Center. Shoots right. 6'1", 195 lbs. Born, Montreal, Que., January 19, 1974.
(St. Louis' 6th choice, 158th overall, in 1992 Entry Draft).

			Regular Season					Playoffs				
Season	**Club**	**Lea**	**GP**	**G**	**A**	**TP**	**PIM**	**GP**	**G**	**A**	**TP**	**PIM**
1990-91	Drummondville	QMJHL	65	19	29	48	117	14	2	9	11	48
1991-92	Drummondville	QMJHL	70	28	49	77	160	4	2	2	4	9
1992-93a	Drummondville	QMJHL	60	44	*96	140	188	10	6	13	19	20
1993-94	**St. Louis**	**NHL**	**1**	**0**	**0**	**0**	**0**	....	....	....	....	....
	Drummondville	QMJHL	62	41	72	113	150	9	4	6	10	35
	Peoria	IHL	....	....	....	....	....	5	1	3	4	2
1994-95	Peoria	IHL	51	16	32	48	111	....	....	....	....	....
	St. Louis	**NHL**	**37**	**13**	**14**	**27**	**85**	**7**	**0**	**4**	**4**	**21**
1995-96	**St. Louis**	**NHL**	**33**	**3**	**6**	**9**	**87**	....	....	....	....	....
	Worcester	AHL	3	2	1	3	22	....	....	....	....	....
	NY Rangers	**NHL**	**28**	**1**	**2**	**3**	**53**	....	....	....	....	....
	Los Angeles	**NHL**	**10**	**2**	**3**	**5**	**15**	....	....	....	....	....
1996-97	**Los Angeles**	**NHL**	**62**	**8**	**15**	**23**	**102**	....	....	....	....	....
	NHL Totals		**171**	**27**	**40**	**67**	**342**	**7**	**0**	**4**	**4**	**21**

a QMJHL Second All-Star Team (1993)

Traded to **NY Rangers** by **St. Louis** for Stephane Matteau, December 28, 1995. Traded to **Los Angeles** by **NY Rangers** with Ray Ferraro, Mattias Norstrom, Nathan Lafayette and NY Rangers' fourth round choice (Sean Blanchard) in 1997 Entry Draft for Marty McSorley, Jari Kurri and Shane Churla, March 14, 1996.

LAPLANTE, DARRYL DET.

Center. Shoots left. 6'1", 185 lbs. Born, Calgary, Alta., March 28, 1977.
(Detroit's 3rd choice, 58th overall, in 1995 Entry Draft).

			Regular Season					Playoffs				
Season	**Club**	**Lea**	**GP**	**G**	**A**	**TP**	**PIM**	**GP**	**G**	**A**	**TP**	**PIM**
1994-95	Moose Jaw	WHL	71	22	24	46	66	10	2	2	4	7
1995-96	Moose Jaw	WHL	72	42	40	82	76	....	....	....	....	....
1996-97	Moose Jaw	WHL	69	38	42	80	79	12	2	4	6	15

LAPLANTE, MIKE ANA.

Defense. Shoots left. 6'2", 190 lbs. Born, Calgary, Alta., July 12, 1975.
(Anaheim's 6th choice, 159th overall, in 1995 Entry Draft).

			Regular Season					Playoffs				
Season	**Club**	**Lea**	**GP**	**G**	**A**	**TP**	**PIM**	**GP**	**G**	**A**	**TP**	**PIM**
1994-95	Calgary	Jr. A	54	6	28	34	262	....	....	....	....	....
	North Bay	OHL	2	0	0	0	0	....	....	....	....	....
1995-96	North Bay	OHL	1	0	0	0	0	....	....	....	....	....
	U. Wisconsin	WCHA	33	0	10	10	66	....	....	....	....	....
1996-97	U. Wisconsin	WCHA	32	0	3	3	58	....	....	....	....	....

LAPOINTE, CLAUDE (luh-PWAH, KLOHD) NYI

Center. Shoots left. 5'9", 181 lbs. Born, Lachine, Que., October 11, 1968.
(Quebec's 12th choice, 234th overall, in 1988 Entry Draft).

			Regular Season					Playoffs				
Season	**Club**	**Lea**	**GP**	**G**	**A**	**TP**	**PIM**	**GP**	**G**	**A**	**TP**	**PIM**
1986-87	Trois-Rivières	QMJHL	70	47	57	104	123	....	....	....	....	....
1987-88	Laval	QMJHL	69	37	83	120	143	13	2	17	19	53
1988-89	Laval	QMJHL	63	32	72	104	158	17	5	14	19	66
1989-90	Halifax	AHL	63	18	19	37	51	6	1	1	2	34
1990-91	**Quebec**	**NHL**	**13**	**2**	**2**	**4**	**4**	....	....	....	....	....
	Halifax	AHL	43	17	17	34	46	....	....	....	....	....
1991-92	**Quebec**	**NHL**	**78**	**13**	**20**	**33**	**86**	....	....	....	....	....
1992-93	**Quebec**	**NHL**	**74**	**10**	**26**	**36**	**98**	**6**	**2**	**4**	**6**	**8**
1993-94	**Quebec**	**NHL**	**59**	**11**	**17**	**28**	**70**	....	....	....	....	....
1994-95	**Quebec**	**NHL**	**29**	**4**	**8**	**12**	**41**	**5**	**0**	**0**	**0**	**8**
1995-96	**Colorado**	**NHL**	**3**	**0**	**0**	**0**	**0**	....	....	....	....	....
	Calgary	**NHL**	**32**	**4**	**5**	**9**	**20**	**2**	**0**	**0**	**0**	**0**
	Saint John	AHL	12	5	3	8	10	....	....	....	....	....
1996-97	**NY Islanders**	**NHL**	**73**	**13**	**5**	**18**	**49**	....	....	....	....	....
	Utah	IHL	9	7	6	13	14	....	....	....	....	....
	NHL Totals		**361**	**57**	**83**	**140**	**368**	**13**	**2**	**4**	**6**	**16**

Traded to **Calgary** by **Colorado** for Calgary's seventh round choice (Samuel Pahlsson) in 1996 Entry Draft, November 1, 1995. Signed as a free agent by **NY Islanders**, August 14, 1996.

LAPOINTE, MARTIN (luh-POYNT, MAHR-tai) DET.

Right wing. Shoots right. 5'11", 200 lbs. Born, Ville Ste. Pierre, Que., September 12, 1973.
(Detroit's 1st choice, 10th overall, in 1991 Entry Draft).

			Regular Season					Playoffs				
Season	**Club**	**Lea**	**GP**	**G**	**A**	**TP**	**PIM**	**GP**	**G**	**A**	**TP**	**PIM**
1989-90a	Laval	QMJHL	65	42	54	96	77	14	8	17	25	54
1990-91b	Laval	QMJHL	64	44	54	98	66	13	7	14	21	26
1991-92	**Detroit**	**NHL**	**4**	**0**	**1**	**1**	**5**	**3**	**0**	**1**	**1**	**4**
	Laval	QMJHL	31	25	30	55	84	10	4	10	14	32
	Adirondack	AHL	....	....	....	....	....	8	2	2	4	4
1992-93	**Detroit**	**NHL**	**3**	**0**	**0**	**0**	**0**	....	....	....	....	....
ac	Laval	QMJHL	35	38	51	89	41	13	*13	*17	*30	22
	Adirondack	AHL	8	1	2	3	9	....	....	....	....	....
1993-94	**Detroit**	**NHL**	**50**	**8**	**8**	**16**	**55**	**4**	**0**	**0**	**0**	**6**
	Adirondack	AHL	28	25	21	46	47	4	1	1	2	8
1994-95	Adirondack	AHL	39	29	16	45	80	....	....	....	....	....
	Detroit	**NHL**	**39**	**4**	**6**	**10**	**73**	**2**	**0**	**1**	**1**	**8**
1995-96	**Detroit**	**NHL**	**58**	**6**	**3**	**9**	**93**	**11**	**1**	**2**	**3**	**12**
1996-97	**Detroit**	**NHL**	**78**	**16**	**17**	**33**	**167**	**20**	**4**	**8**	**12**	**60** ♦
	NHL Totals		**232**	**34**	**35**	**69**	**393**	**40**	**5**	**12**	**17**	**90**

a QMJHL First All-Star Team (1990, 1993)
b QMJHL Second All-Star Team (1991)
c Memorial Cup All-Star Team (1993)

LARAQUE, GEORGES EDM.

Right wing. Shoots right. 6'3", 235 lbs. Born, Montreal, Que., December 7, 1976.
(Edmonton's 2nd choice, 31st overall, in 1995 Entry Draft).

			Regular Season					Playoffs				
Season	**Club**	**Lea**	**GP**	**G**	**A**	**TP**	**PIM**	**GP**	**G**	**A**	**TP**	**PIM**
1993-94	St-Jean	QMJHL	70	11	11	22	142	4	0	0	0	7
1994-95	St-Jean	QMJHL	62	19	22	41	259	7	1	1	2	42
1995-96	Laval	QMJHL	11	8	13	21	76	....	....	....	....	....
	St-Hyacinthe	QMJHL	8	3	4	7	59	....	....	....	....	....
	Granby	QMJHL	22	9	7	16	125	18	7	6	13	104
1996-97	Hamilton	AHL	73	14	20	34	179	15	1	3	4	12

LARIONOV, IGOR (LAIR-ee-AH-nohv) DET.

Center. Shoots left. 5'9", 170 lbs. Born, Voskresensk, USSR, December 3, 1960.
(Vancouver's 11th choice, 214th overall, in 1985 Entry Draft).

			Regular Season					Playoffs				
Season	**Club**	**Lea**	**GP**	**G**	**A**	**TP**	**PIM**	**GP**	**G**	**A**	**TP**	**PIM**
1977-78	Khimik	USSR	6	3	0	3	4	....	....	....	....	....
1978-79	Khimik	USSR	32	3	4	7	12	....	....	....	....	....
1979-80	Khimik	USSR	42	11	7	18	24	....	....	....	....	....
1980-81	Khimik	USSR	43	22	23	45	36	....	....	....	....	....
1981-82	CSKA	USSR	46	31	22	53	6	....	....	....	....	....
1982-83a	CSKA	USSR	44	20	19	39	20	....	....	....	....	....
1983-84	CSKA	USSR	43	15	26	41	30	....	....	....	....	....
1984-85	CSKA	USSR	40	18	28	46	20	....	....	....	....	....
1985-86a	CSKA	USSR	40	21	31	52	33	....	....	....	....	....
1986-87a	CSKA	USSR	39	20	26	46	34	....	....	....	....	....
1987-88ab	CSKA	USSR	51	25	32	57	54	....	....	....	....	....
1988-89	CSKA	USSR	31	15	12	27	22	....	....	....	....	....
1989-90	**Vancouver**	**NHL**	**74**	**17**	**27**	**44**	**20**	....	....	....	....	....
1990-91	**Vancouver**	**NHL**	**64**	**13**	**21**	**34**	**14**	**6**	**1**	**0**	**1**	**6**
1991-92	**Vancouver**	**NHL**	**72**	**21**	**44**	**65**	**54**	**13**	**3**	**7**	**10**	**4**
1992-93	Lugano	Switz.	24	10	19	29	44	....	....	....	....	....
1993-94	**San Jose**	**NHL**	**60**	**18**	**38**	**56**	**40**	**14**	**5**	**13**	**18**	**10**
1994-95	**San Jose**	**NHL**	**33**	**4**	**20**	**24**	**14**	**11**	**1**	**8**	**9**	**2**
1995-96	**San Jose**	**NHL**	**4**	**1**	**1**	**2**	**0**	....	....	....	....	....
	Detroit	**NHL**	**69**	**21**	**50**	**71**	**34**	**19**	**6**	**7**	**13**	**6**
1996-97	**Detroit**	**NHL**	**64**	**12**	**42**	**54**	**26**	**20**	**4**	**8**	**12**	**8** ♦
	NHL Totals		**440**	**107**	**243**	**350**	**202**	**83**	**20**	**43**	**63**	**36**

a Soviet National League All-Star (1983, 1986-88)
b Soviet Player of the Year (1988)

Claimed by **San Jose** from **Vancouver** in NHL Waiver Draft, October 4, 1992. Traded to **Detroit** by **San Jose** with a conditional draft choice in 1998 Entry Draft for Ray Sheppard, October 24, 1995.

LAROCQUE, MARIO (luh-RAWK) T.B.

Defense. Shoots left. 6'2", 182 lbs. Born, Montreal, Que., April 24, 1978.
(Tampa Bay's 1st choice, 16th overall, in 1996 Entry Draft).

			Regular Season					Playoffs				
Season	**Club**	**Lea**	**GP**	**G**	**A**	**TP**	**PIM**	**GP**	**G**	**A**	**TP**	**PIM**
1995-96	Hull	QMJHL	68	7	19	26	196	14	2	5	7	16
1996-97	Hull	QMJHL	64	14	36	50	155	14	2	6	8	36

LAROSE, GUY (luh-ROHS)

Center. Shoots left. 5'9", 180 lbs. Born, Hull, Que., August 31, 1967.
(Buffalo's 11th choice, 224th overall, in 1985 Entry Draft).

			Regular Season					Playoffs				
Season	Club	Lea	GP	G	A	TP	PIM	GP	G	A	TP	PIM
1984-85	Guelph	OHL	58	30	30	60	63	....	....	....	....	....
1985-86	Guelph	OHL	37	12	36	48	55	....	....	....	....	....
	Ottawa	OHL	28	19	25	44	63	....	....	....	....	....
1986-87	Ottawa	OHL	66	28	49	77	77	11	2	8	10	27
1987-88	Moncton	AHL	77	22	31	53	127	....	....	....	....	....
1988-89	**Winnipeg**	**NHL**	**3**	**0**	**1**	**1**	**6**	....	....	....	....	....
	Moncton	AHL	72	32	27	59	176	10	4	4	8	37
1989-90	Moncton	AHL	79	44	26	70	232	....	....	....	....	....
1990-91	**Winnipeg**	**NHL**	**7**	**0**	**0**	**0**	**8**	....	....	....	....	....
	Moncton	AHL	35	14	10	24	60	....	....	....	....	....
	Binghamton	AHL	34	21	15	36	48	10	8	5	13	37
1991-92	Binghamton	AHL	30	10	11	21	36	....	....	....	....	....
	Toronto	**NHL**	**34**	**9**	**5**	**14**	**27**	....	....	....	....	....
	St. John's	AHL	15	7	7	14	26	....	....	....	....	....
1992-93	**Toronto**	**NHL**	**9**	**0**	**0**	**0**	**8**	....	....	....	....	....
	St. John's	AHL	5	0	1	1	8	9	5	2	7	6
1993-94	**Toronto**	**NHL**	**10**	**1**	**2**	**3**	**10**	....	....	....	....	....
	St. John's	AHL	23	13	16	29	41	....	....	....	....	....
	Calgary	**NHL**	**7**	**0**	**1**	**1**	**4**	....	....	....	....	....
	Saint John	AHL	15	11	11	22	20	7	3	2	5	22
1994-95	Providence	AHL	68	25	33	58	93	12	4	6	10	22
	Boston	**NHL**	....	....	....	....	....	**4**	**0**	**0**	**0**	**0**
1995-96	Detroit	IHL	50	28	15	43	53	....	....	....	....	....
	Las Vegas	IHL	25	10	22	32	54	15	3	6	9	14
1996-97	Houston	IHL	79	29	25	54	108	13	6	7	13	12
	NHL Totals		**70**	**10**	**9**	**19**	**63**	**4**	**0**	**0**	**0**	**0**

Signed as a free agent by **Winnipeg**, July 16, 1987. Traded to **NY Rangers** by **Winnipeg** for Rudy Poeschek, January 22, 1991. Traded to **Toronto** by **NY Rangers** for Mike Stevens, December 26, 1991. Claimed on waivers by **Calgary** from **Toronto**, January 1, 1994. Signed as a free agent by **Boston**, July 11, 1994.

LAROUCHE, STEVE (luh-ROOSH)

Center. Shoots right. 6', 180 lbs. Born, Rouyn, Que., April 14, 1971.
(Montreal's 3rd choice, 41st overall, in 1989 Entry Draft).

			Regular Season					Playoffs				
Season	Club	Lea	GP	G	A	TP	PIM	GP	G	A	TP	PIM
1987-88	Trois-Rivières	QMJHL	66	11	29	40	25	....	....	....	....	....
1988-89	Trois-Rivières	QMJHL	70	51	102	153	53	4	4	2	6	6
1989-90a	Trois-Rivières	QMJHL	60	55	90	145	40	7	3	5	8	8
	Cdn. National	....	1	1	0	1	0	....	....	....	....	....
1990-91	Chicoutimi	QMJHL	45	35	41	76	64	17	*13	*20	*33	20
1991-92	Fredericton	AHL	74	21	35	56	41	7	1	0	1	0
1992-93	Fredericton	AHL	77	27	65	92	52	5	2	5	7	6
1993-94	Atlanta	IHL	80	43	53	96	73	14	*16	10	*26	16
1994-95bcd	P.E.I.	AHL	70	*53	48	101	54	2	1	0	1	0
	Ottawa	**NHL**	**18**	**8**	**7**	**15**	**6**	....	....	....	....	....
1995-96	**NY Rangers**	**NHL**	**1**	**0**	**0**	**0**	**0**	....	....	....	....	....
	Binghamton	AHL	39	20	46	66	47	....	....	....	....	....
	Los Angeles	**NHL**	**7**	**1**	**2**	**3**	**4**	....	....	....	....	....
	Phoenix	IHL	33	19	17	36	14	4	0	1	1	8
1996-97e	Quebec	IHL	79	49	53	102	78	9	3	10	13	18
	NHL Totals		**26**	**9**	**9**	**18**	**10**	....	....	....	....	....

a QMJHL Second All-Star Team (1990)
b AHL First All-Star Team (1995)
c Won Fred Hunt Memorial Trophy (Sportsmanship - AHL) (1995)
d Won Les Cunningham Plaque (MVP - AHL) (1995)
e IHL First All-Star Team (1997)

Signed as a free agent by **Ottawa**, September 11, 1994. Traded to **NY Rangers** by **Ottawa** for Jean-Yves Roy, October 5, 1995. Traded to **Los Angeles** by **NY Rangers** for Chris Snell, January 14, 1996.

LARSEN, BRAD COL.

Left wing. Shoots left. 5'11", 212 lbs. Born, Nakusp, B.C., January 28, 1977.
(Ottawa's 3rd choice, 53rd overall, in 1995 Entry Draft).

			Regular Season					Playoffs				
Season	Club	Lea	GP	G	A	TP	PIM	GP	G	A	TP	PIM
1993-94	Swift Current	WHL	64	15	18	33	32	7	1	2	3	4
1994-95	Swift Current	WHL	62	24	33	57	73	6	0	1	1	2
1995-96	Swift Current	WHL	51	30	47	77	67	6	3	2	5	13
1996-97a	Swift Current	WHL	61	36	46	82	61	....	....	....	....	....

a WHL East Second All-Star Team (1997)

Rights traded to **Colorado** by **Ottawa** for Janne Laukkanen, January 26, 1996. Re-entered NHL Entry Draft, **Colorado's** 5th choice, 87th overall, in 1997 Entry Draft.

LAUER, BRAD (LAU-er)

Left wing. Shoots left. 6', 195 lbs. Born, Humboldt, Sask., October 27, 1966.
(NY Islanders' 3rd choice, 34th overall, in 1985 Entry Draft).

			Regular Season					Playoffs				
Season	Club	Lea	GP	G	A	TP	PIM	GP	G	A	TP	PIM
1983-84	Regina	WHL	60	5	7	12	51	16	0	1	1	24
1984-85	Regina	WHL	72	33	46	79	57	8	6	6	12	9
1985-86	Regina	WHL	57	36	38	74	69	10	4	5	9	2
1986-87	**NY Islanders**	**NHL**	**61**	**7**	**14**	**21**	**65**	**6**	**2**	**0**	**2**	**4**
1987-88	**NY Islanders**	**NHL**	**69**	**17**	**18**	**35**	**67**	**5**	**3**	**1**	**4**	**4**
1988-89	**NY Islanders**	**NHL**	**14**	**3**	**2**	**5**	**2**	....	....	....	....	....
	Springfield	AHL	8	1	5	6	0	....	....	....	....	....
1989-90	**NY Islanders**	**NHL**	**63**	**6**	**18**	**24**	**19**	**4**	**0**	**2**	**2**	**10**
	Springfield	AHL	7	4	2	6	0	....	....	....	....	....
1990-91	**NY Islanders**	**NHL**	**44**	**4**	**8**	**12**	**45**	....	....	....	....	....
	Capital Dist.	AHL	11	5	11	16	14	....	....	....	....	....
1991-92	**NY Islanders**	**NHL**	**8**	**1**	**0**	**1**	**2**	....	....	....	....	....
	Chicago	**NHL**	**6**	**0**	**0**	**0**	**4**	**7**	**1**	**1**	**2**	**2**
	Indianapolis	IHL	57	24	30	54	46	....	....	....	....	....
1992-93	**Chicago**	**NHL**	**7**	**0**	**1**	**1**	**2**	....	....	....	....	....
a	Indianapolis	IHL	62	*50	41	91	80	5	3	1	4	6
1993-94	**Ottawa**	**NHL**	**30**	**2**	**5**	**7**	**6**	....	....	....	....	....
	Las Vegas	IHL	32	21	21	42	30	4	1	0	1	2
1994-95	Cleveland	IHL	51	32	27	59	48	4	4	2	6	6
1995-96	**Pittsburgh**	**NHL**	**21**	**4**	**1**	**5**	**6**	**12**	**1**	**1**	**2**	**4**
	Cleveland	IHL	53	25	27	52	44	....	....	....	....	....
1996-97	Cleveland	IHL	64	27	21	48	61	14	4	6	10	8
	NHL Totals		**323**	**44**	**67**	**111**	**218**	**34**	**7**	**5**	**12**	**24**

a IHL First All-Star Team (1993)

Traded to **Chicago** by **NY Islanders** with Brent Sutter for Adam Creighton and Steve Thomas, October 25, 1991. Signed as a free agent by **Ottawa**, January 3, 1994. Signed as a free agent by **Pittsburgh**, August 10, 1995.

LAUKKANEN, JANNE (LOW-kah-nehn) OTT.

Defense. Shoots left. 6', 180 lbs. Born, Lahti, Finland, March 19, 1970.
(Quebec's 8th choice, 156th overall, in 1991 Entry Draft).

			Regular Season					Playoffs				
Season	Club	Lea	GP	G	A	TP	PIM	GP	G	A	TP	PIM
1989-90	Ilves	Fin.	39	5	6	11	10	....	....	....	....	....
1990-91	Reipas	Fin.	44	8	14	22	56	....	....	....	....	....
1991-92	HPK	Fin.	43	5	14	19	62	....	....	....	....	....
1992-93	HPK	Fin.	47	8	21	29	76	12	1	4	5	10
1993-94	HPK	Fin.	48	5	24	29	46	....	....	....	....	....
1994-95	Cornwall	AHL	55	8	26	34	41	....	....	....	....	....
	Quebec	**NHL**	**11**	**0**	**3**	**3**	**4**	**6**	**1**	**0**	**1**	**2**
1995-96	**Colorado**	**NHL**	**3**	**1**	**0**	**1**	**0**	....	....	....	....	....
	Cornwall	AHL	35	7	20	27	60	....	....	....	....	....
	Ottawa	**NHL**	**20**	**0**	**2**	**2**	**14**	....	....	....	....	....
1996-97	**Ottawa**	**NHL**	**76**	**3**	**18**	**21**	**76**	**7**	**0**	**1**	**1**	**6**
	NHL Totals		**110**	**4**	**23**	**27**	**94**	**13**	**1**	**1**	**2**	**8**

Traded to **Ottawa** by **Colorado** for the rights to Brad Larsen, January 26, 1996.

LAUS, PAUL (LOWZ) FLA.

Defense. Shoots right. 6'1", 216 lbs. Born, Beamsville, Ont., September 26, 1970.
(Pittsburgh's 2nd choice, 37th overall, in 1989 Entry Draft).

			Regular Season					Playoffs				
Season	Club	Lea	GP	G	A	TP	PIM	GP	G	A	TP	PIM
1987-88	Hamilton	OHL	56	1	9	10	171	14	0	0	0	28
1988-89	Niagara Falls	OHL	49	1	10	11	225	15	0	5	5	56
1989-90	Niagara Falls	OHL	60	13	35	48	231	16	6	16	22	71
1990-91	Albany	IHL	7	0	0	0	7	....	....	....	....	....
	Knoxville	ECHL	20	6	12	18	83	....	....	....	....	....
	Muskegon	IHL	35	3	4	7	103	4	0	0	0	13
1991-92	Muskegon	IHL	75	0	21	21	248	14	2	5	7	70
1992-93	Cleveland	IHL	76	8	18	26	427	4	1	0	1	27
1993-94	**Florida**	**NHL**	**39**	**2**	**0**	**2**	**109**	....	....	....	....	....
1994-95	**Florida**	**NHL**	**37**	**0**	**7**	**7**	**138**	....	....	....	....	....
1995-96	**Florida**	**NHL**	**78**	**3**	**6**	**9**	**236**	**21**	**2**	**6**	**8**	***62**
1996-97	**Florida**	**NHL**	**77**	**0**	**12**	**12**	**313**	**5**	**0**	**1**	**1**	**4**
	NHL Totals		**231**	**5**	**25**	**30**	**796**	**26**	**2**	**7**	**9**	**66**

Claimed by **Florida** from **Pittsburgh** in Expansion Draft, June 24, 1993.

LAWRENCE, MARK NYI

Right wing. Shoots right. 6'4", 215 lbs. Born, Burlington, Ont., January 27, 1972.
(Minnesota's 6th choice, 118th overall, in 1991 Entry Draft).

			Regular Season					Playoffs				
Season	Club	Lea	GP	G	A	TP	PIM	GP	G	A	TP	PIM
1988-89	Niagara Falls	OHL	63	9	27	36	142	....	....	....	....	....
1989-90	Niagara Falls	OHL	54	15	18	33	123	16	2	5	7	42
1990-91	Detroit	OHL	66	27	38	65	53	....	....	....	....	....
1991-92	Detroit	OHL	28	19	26	45	54	....	....	....	....	....
	North Bay	OHL	24	13	14	27	21	21	*23	12	35	36
1992-93	Dayton	ECHL	20	8	14	22	46	....	....	....	....	....
	Kalamazoo	IHL	57	22	13	35	47	....	....	....	....	....
1993-94	Kalamazoo	IHL	64	17	20	37	90	....	....	....	....	....
1994-95	Kalamazoo	IHL	77	21	29	50	92	16	3	7	10	28
	Dallas	**NHL**	**2**	**0**	**0**	**0**	**0**	....	....	....	....	....
1995-96	**Dallas**	**NHL**	**13**	**0**	**1**	**1**	**17**	....	....	....	....	....
	Michigan	IHL	55	15	14	29	92	10	3	4	7	30
1996-97	Michigan	IHL	68	15	21	36	141	4	0	0	0	18
	NHL Totals		**15**	**0**	**1**	**1**	**17**	....	....	....	....	....

Signed as a free agent by **NY Islanders**, July 29, 1997.

LEACH, STEPHEN CAR.

Right wing. Shoots right. 5'11", 197 lbs. Born, Cambridge, MA, January 16, 1966.
(Washington's 2nd choice, 34th overall, in 1984 Entry Draft).

			Regular Season					Playoffs				
Season	Club	Lea	GP	G	A	TP	PIM	GP	G	A	TP	PIM
1984-85	N. Hampshire	H.E.	41	12	25	37	53	....	....	....	....	....
1985-86	N. Hampshire	H.E.	25	22	6	28	30	....	....	....	....	....
	Washington	**NHL**	**11**	**1**	**1**	**2**	**2**	**6**	**0**	**1**	**1**	**0**
1986-87	**Washington**	**NHL**	**15**	**1**	**0**	**1**	**6**	....	....	....	....	....
	Binghamton	AHL	54	18	21	39	39	13	3	1	4	6
1987-88	**Washington**	**NHL**	**8**	**1**	**1**	**2**	**17**	**9**	**2**	**1**	**3**	**0**
	U.S. National	....	49	26	20	46	30	....	....	....	....	....
	U.S. Olympic	....	6	1	2	3	0	....	....	....	....	....
1988-89	**Washington**	**NHL**	**74**	**11**	**19**	**30**	**94**	**6**	**1**	**0**	**1**	**12**
1989-90	**Washington**	**NHL**	**70**	**18**	**14**	**32**	**104**	**14**	**2**	**2**	**4**	**8**
1990-91	**Washington**	**NHL**	**68**	**11**	**19**	**30**	**99**	**9**	**1**	**2**	**3**	**8**
1991-92	**Boston**	**NHL**	**78**	**31**	**29**	**60**	**147**	**15**	**4**	**0**	**4**	**10**
1992-93	**Boston**	**NHL**	**79**	**26**	**25**	**51**	**126**	**4**	**1**	**1**	**2**	**2**
1993-94	**Boston**	**NHL**	**42**	**5**	**10**	**15**	**74**	**5**	**0**	**1**	**1**	**2**
1994-95	**Boston**	**NHL**	**35**	**5**	**6**	**11**	**68**	....	....	....	....	....
1995-96	**Boston**	**NHL**	**59**	**9**	**13**	**22**	**86**	....	....	....	....	....
	St. Louis	**NHL**	**14**	**2**	**4**	**6**	**22**	**11**	**3**	**2**	**5**	**10**
1996-97	**St. Louis**	**NHL**	**17**	**2**	**1**	**3**	**24**	**6**	**0**	**0**	**0**	**33**
	NHL Totals		**570**	**123**	**142**	**265**	**869**	**85**	**14**	**10**	**24**	**85**

Traded to **Boston** by **Washington** for Randy Burridge, June 21, 1991. Traded to **St. Louis** by **Boston** for Kevin Sawyer and Steve Staios, March 8, 1996. Traded to **Carolina** by **St. Louis** for Alexander Godynyuk and Carolina's sixth round choice in 1998 Entry Draft, June 27, 1997.

LEAVINS, BOBBY NYI

Left wing. Shoots left. 6'11", 190 lbs. Born, Saskatoon, Sask., February 14, 1979.
(NY Islanders' 8th choice, 139th overall, in 1997 Entry Draft).

			Regular Season					Playoffs				
Season	Club	Lea	GP	G	A	TP	PIM	GP	G	A	TP	PIM
1995-96	Brandon	WHL	1	0	0	0	0	....	....	....	....	....
1996-97	Brandon	WHL	59	5	6	11	42	3	0	0	0	2

LEBEAU, STEPHAN (leh-BOH)

Center. Shoots right. 5'10", 173 lbs. Born, St. Jerome, Que., February 28, 1968.

			Regular Season					Playoffs				
Season	Club	Lea	GP	G	A	TP	PIM	GP	G	A	TP	PIM
1984-85	Shawinigan	QMJHL	66	41	38	79	18	9	4	5	9	4
1985-86	Shawinigan	QMJHL	72	69	77	146	22	5	4	2	6	4
1986-87a	Shawinigan	QMJHL	65	77	90	167	60	14	9	20	29	20
1987-88a	Shawinigan	QMJHL	67	*94	94	188	66	11	17	9	26	10
	Sherbrooke	AHL	....	....	....	....	....	1	0	1	1	0
1988-89	**Montreal**	**NHL**	**1**	**0**	**1**	**1**	**2**	....	....	....	....	....
bcde	Sherbrooke	AHL	78	*70	64	*134	47	6	1	4	5	8
1989-90	**Montreal**	**NHL**	**57**	**15**	**20**	**35**	**11**	**2**	**3**	**0**	**3**	**0**
1990-91	**Montreal**	**NHL**	**73**	**22**	**31**	**53**	**24**	**7**	**2**	**1**	**3**	**2**
1991-92	**Montreal**	**NHL**	**77**	**27**	**31**	**58**	**14**	**8**	**1**	**3**	**4**	**4**
1992-93	**Montreal**	**NHL**	**71**	**31**	**49**	**80**	**20**	**13**	**3**	**3**	**6**	**6** ♦
1993-94	**Montreal**	**NHL**	**34**	**9**	**7**	**16**	**8**	....	....	....	....	....
	Anaheim	**NHL**	**22**	**6**	**4**	**10**	**14**	....	....	....	....	....
1994-95	**Anaheim**	**NHL**	**38**	**8**	**16**	**24**	**12**	....	....	....	....	....
1995-96	Lugano	Switz.	36	25	28	53	10	4	2	2	4	0
1996-97	Lugano	Switz.	18	14	12	26	12	....	....	....	....	....
	NHL Totals		**373**	**118**	**159**	**277**	**105**	**30**	**9**	**7**	**16**	**12**

a QMJHL Second All-Star Team (1987, 1988)
b AHL First All-Star Team (1989)
c Won Dudley "Red" Garrett Memorial Trophy (Top Rookie - AHL) (1989)
d Won John B. Sollenberger Trophy (Top Scorer - AHL) (1989)
e Won Les Cunningham Plaque (MVP - AHL) (1989)

Signed as a free agent by **Montreal**, September 27, 1986. Traded to **Anaheim** by **Montreal** for Ron Tugnutt, February 20, 1994.

LEBLANC, JOHN (leh-BLAHNK)

Right wing. Shoots left. 6'1", 190 lbs. Born, Campbellton, N.B., January 21, 1964.

			Regular Season					Playoffs				
Season	Club	Lea	GP	G	A	TP	PIM	GP	G	A	TP	PIM
1983-84	Hull	QMJHL	69	39	35	74	32	....	....	....	....	....
1984-85	New Brunswick	AUAA	24	25	34	59	32	....	....	....	....	....
1985-86a	New Brunswick	AUAA	24	38	28	66	35	....	....	....	....	....
1986-87	**Vancouver**	**NHL**	**2**	**1**	**0**	**1**	**0**	....	....	....	....	....
	Fredericton	AHL	75	40	30	70	27	....	....	....	....	....
1987-88	**Vancouver**	**NHL**	**41**	**12**	**10**	**22**	**18**	....	....	....	....	....
	Fredericton	AHL	35	26	25	51	54	15	6	7	13	34
1988-89	Milwaukee	IHL	61	39	31	70	42	....	....	....	....	....
	Edmonton	**NHL**	**2**	**1**	**0**	**1**	**0**	**1**	**0**	**0**	**0**	**0**
	Cape Breton	AHL	3	4	0	4	0	....	....	....	....	....
1989-90	Cape Breton	AHL	77	*54	34	88	50	6	4	0	4	4
1990-91					DID NOT PLAY							
1991-92	**Winnipeg**	**NHL**	**16**	**6**	**1**	**7**	**6**	....	....	....	....	....
	Moncton	AHL	56	31	22	53	24	10	3	2	5	8
1992-93	**Winnipeg**	**NHL**	**3**	**0**	**0**	**0**	**2**	....	....	....	....	....
	Moncton	AHL	77	48	40	88	29	5	2	1	3	6
1993-94	**Winnipeg**	**NHL**	**17**	**6**	**2**	**8**	**2**	....	....	....	....	....
	Moncton	AHL	41	25	26	51	38	20	3	6	9	6
1994-95	Springfield	AHL	65	39	34	73	32	....	....	....	....	....
	Winnipeg	**NHL**	**2**	**0**	**0**	**0**	**0**	....	....	....	....	....
1995-96	Orlando	IHL	60	22	24	46	20	....	....	....	....	....
	Fort Wayne	IHL	16	12	11	23	4	5	0	2	2	14
1996-97	Fort Wayne	IHL	77	30	31	61	22	....	....	....	....	....
	NHL Totals		**83**	**26**	**13**	**39**	**28**	**1**	**0**	**0**	**0**	**0**

a Canadian University Player of the Year (1986)

Signed as a free agent by **Vancouver**, April 12, 1986. Traded to **Edmonton** by **Vancouver** with Vancouver's fifth round choice (Peter White) in 1989 Entry Draft for Doug Smith and Gregory C. Adams, March 7, 1989. Traded to **Winnipeg** by **Edmonton** with Edmonton's tenth round choice (Teemu Numminen) in 1992 Entry Draft for Winnipeg's fifth round choice (Ryan Haggerty) in 1991 Entry Draft, June 12, 1991.

LeBOUTILLIER, PETER (lih-BOO-tihl-eer) ANA.

Right wing. Shoots right. 6'1", 205 lbs. Born, Minnedosa, Man., January 11, 1975.
(NY Islanders' 6th choice, 144th overall, in 1993 Entry Draft).

			Regular Season					Playoffs				
Season	Club	Lea	GP	G	A	TP	PIM	GP	G	A	TP	PIM
1992-93	Red Deer	WHL	67	8	26	34	284	2	0	1	1	5
1993-94	Red Deer	WHL	66	19	20	39	300	2	0	1	1	4
1994-95	Red Deer	WHL	59	27	16	43	159	....	....	....	....	....
1995-96	Baltimore	AHL	68	7	9	16	228	11	0	0	0	33
1996-97	**Anaheim**	**NHL**	**23**	**1**	**0**	**1**	**121**	....	....	....	....	....
	Baltimore	AHL	47	6	12	18	175	....	....	....	....	....
	NHL Totals		**23**	**1**	**0**	**1**	**121**	....	....	....	....	....

Re-entered NHL Entry Draft, **Anaheim's** 5th choice, 133rd overall, in 1995 Entry Draft.

LeCLAIR, JOHN (luh-KLAIR) PHI.

Left wing. Shoots left. 6'3", 226 lbs. Born, St. Albans, VT, July 5, 1969.
(Montreal's 2nd choice, 33rd overall, in 1987 Entry Draft).

			Regular Season					Playoffs				
Season	Club	Lea	GP	G	A	TP	PIM	GP	G	A	TP	PIM
1987-88	U. of Vermont	ECAC	31	12	22	34	62	....	....	....	....	....
1988-89	U. of Vermont	ECAC	18	9	12	21	40	....	....	....	....	....
1989-90	U. of Vermont	ECAC	10	10	6	16	38	....	....	....	....	....
1990-91a	U. of Vermont	ECAC	33	25	20	45	58	....	....	....	....	....
	Montreal	**NHL**	**10**	**2**	**5**	**7**	**2**	**3**	**0**	**0**	**0**	**0**
1991-92	**Montreal**	**NHL**	**59**	**8**	**11**	**19**	**14**	**8**	**1**	**1**	**2**	**4**
	Fredericton	AHL	8	7	7	14	10	2	0	0	0	4
1992-93	**Montreal**	**NHL**	**72**	**19**	**25**	**44**	**33**	**20**	**4**	**6**	**10**	**14** ♦
1993-94	**Montreal**	**NHL**	**74**	**19**	**24**	**43**	**32**	**7**	**2**	**1**	**3**	**8**
1994-95b	**Montreal**	**NHL**	**9**	**1**	**4**	**5**	**10**	....	....	....	....	....
	Philadelphia	**NHL**	**37**	**25**	**24**	**49**	**20**	**15**	**5**	**7**	**12**	**4**
1995-96c	**Philadelphia**	**NHL**	**82**	**51**	**46**	**97**	**64**	**11**	**6**	**5**	**11**	**6**
1996-97cd	**Philadelphia**	**NHL**	**82**	**50**	**47**	**97**	**58**	**19**	**9**	**12**	**21**	**10**
	NHL Totals		**425**	**175**	**186**	**361**	**233**	**83**	**27**	**32**	**59**	**46**

a ECAC Second All-Star Team (1991)
b NHL First All-Star Team (1995)
c NHL Second All-Star Team (1996, 1997)
d Won Bud Ice Plus/Minus Award (1997)

Played in NHL All-Star Game (1996, 1997)

Traded to **Philadelphia** by **Montreal** with Eric Desjardins and Gilbert Dionne for Mark Recchi and Philadelphia's third round choice (Martin Hohenberger) in 1995 Entry Draft, February 9, 1995.

LECLERC, MIKE ANA.

Left wing. Shoots left. 6'1", 205 lbs. Born, Winnipeg, Man., November 10, 1976.
(Anaheim's 3rd choice, 55th overall, in 1995 Entry Draft).

			Regular Season					Playoffs				
Season	Club	Lea	GP	G	A	TP	PIM	GP	G	A	TP	PIM
1992-93	Victoria	WHL	70	4	11	15	118	....	....	....	....	....
1993-94	Victoria	WHL	68	29	11	40	112	....	....	....	....	....
1994-95	Prince George	WHL	43	20	36	56	78	....	....	....	....	....
	Brandon	WHL	23	5	8	13	50	18	10	6	16	33
1995-96a	Brandon	WHL	71	58	53	111	161	19	6	19	25	25
1996-97	**Anaheim**	**NHL**	**5**	**1**	**1**	**2**	**0**	**1**	**0**	**0**	**0**	**0**
	Baltimore	AHL	71	29	27	56	134	....	....	....	....	....
	NHL Totals		**5**	**1**	**1**	**2**	**0**	**1**	**0**	**0**	**0**	**0**

a WHL East Second All-Star Team (1996)

LECOMPTE, ERIC (luh-COMP) CHI.

Left wing. Shoots left. 6'4", 190 lbs. Born, Montreal, Que., April 4, 1975.
(Chicago's 1st choice, 24th overall, in 1993 Entry Draft).

			Regular Season					Playoffs				
Season	Club	Lea	GP	G	A	TP	PIM	GP	G	A	TP	PIM
1991-92	Hull	QMJHL	60	16	17	33	138	6	1	0	1	4
1992-93	Hull	QMJHL	66	33	38	71	149	10	4	4	8	52
1993-94	Hull	QMJHL	62	39	49	88	171	20	10	10	20	68
1994-95	Hull	QMJHL	12	11	9	20	58	....	....	....	....	....
	St-Jean	QMJHL	18	9	10	19	54	....	....	....	....	....
	Sherbrooke	QMJHL	34	22	29	51	111	4	2	2	4	4
	Indianapolis	IHL	3	2	0	2	2	....	....	....	....	....
1995-96	Indianapolis	IHL	79	24	20	44	131	....	....	....	....	....
1996-97	Worcester	AHL	8	0	1	1	4	....	....	....	....	....
	Indianapolis	IHL	35	2	3	5	74	....	....	....	....	....
	Fort Wayne	IHL	14	1	2	3	62	....	....	....	....	....

LEDYARD, GRANT VAN.

Defense. Shoots left. 6'2", 195 lbs. Born, Winnipeg, Man., November 19, 1961.

			Regular Season					Playoffs				
Season	Club	Lea	GP	G	A	TP	PIM	GP	G	A	TP	PIM
1980-81	Saskatoon	WHL	71	9	28	37	148	....	....	....	....	....
1981-82	Fort Garry	MJHL	63	25	45	70	150	....	....	....	....	....
1982-83	Tulsa	CHL	80	13	29	42	115	....	....	....	....	....
1983-84a	Tulsa	CHL	58	9	17	26	71	9	5	4	9	10
1984-85	**NY Rangers**	**NHL**	**42**	**8**	**12**	**20**	**53**	**3**	**0**	**2**	**2**	**4**
	New Haven	AHL	36	6	20	26	18	....	....	....	....	....
1985-86	**NY Rangers**	**NHL**	**27**	**2**	**9**	**11**	**20**	....	....	....	....	....
	Los Angeles	**NHL**	**52**	**7**	**18**	**25**	**78**	....	....	....	....	....
1986-87	**Los Angeles**	**NHL**	**67**	**14**	**23**	**37**	**93**	**5**	**0**	**0**	**0**	**10**
1987-88	**Los Angeles**	**NHL**	**23**	**1**	**7**	**8**	**52**	....	....	....	....	....
	New Haven	AHL	3	2	1	3	4	....	....	....	....	....
	Washington	**NHL**	**21**	**4**	**3**	**7**	**14**	**14**	**1**	**0**	**1**	**30**
1988-89	**Washington**	**NHL**	**61**	**3**	**11**	**14**	**43**	....	....	....	....	....
	Buffalo	**NHL**	**13**	**1**	**5**	**6**	**8**	**5**	**1**	**2**	**3**	**2**
1989-90	**Buffalo**	**NHL**	**67**	**2**	**13**	**15**	**37**	....	....	....	....	....
1990-91	**Buffalo**	**NHL**	**60**	**8**	**23**	**31**	**46**	**6**	**3**	**3**	**6**	**10**
1991-92	**Buffalo**	**NHL**	**50**	**5**	**16**	**21**	**45**	....	....	....	....	....
1992-93	**Buffalo**	**NHL**	**50**	**2**	**14**	**16**	**45**	**8**	**0**	**0**	**0**	**8**
	Rochester	AHL	5	0	2	2	8	....	....	....	....	....
1993-94	**Dallas**	**NHL**	**84**	**9**	**37**	**46**	**42**	**9**	**1**	**2**	**3**	**6**
1994-95	**Dallas**	**NHL**	**38**	**5**	**13**	**18**	**20**	**3**	**0**	**0**	**0**	**2**
1995-96	**Dallas**	**NHL**	**73**	**5**	**19**	**24**	**20**	....	....	....	....	....
1996-97	**Dallas**	**NHL**	**67**	**1**	**15**	**16**	**61**	**7**	**0**	**2**	**2**	**0**
	NHL Totals		**795**	**77**	**238**	**315**	**677**	**60**	**6**	**11**	**17**	**72**

a Won Bob Gassoff Trophy (CHL's Most Improved Defenseman) (1984)

Signed as a free agent by **NY Rangers**, July 7, 1982. Traded to **Los Angeles** by **NY Rangers** with Roland Melanson for Los Angeles' fourth round choice (Mike Sullivan) in 1987 Entry Draft and Brian MacLellan, December 7, 1985. Traded to **Washington** by **Los Angeles** for Craig Laughlin, February 9, 1988. Traded to **Buffalo** by **Washington** with Clint Malarchuk and Washington's sixth round choice (Brian Holzinger) in 1991 Entry Draft for Calle Johansson and Buffalo's second round choice (Byron Dafoe) in 1989 Entry Draft, March 7, 1989. Signed as a free agent by **Dallas**, August 12, 1993. Signed as a free agent by **Vancouver**, July 17, 1997.

LEEMAN, GARY

Right wing. Shoots right. 5'11", 175 lbs. Born, Toronto, Ont., February 19, 1964.
(Toronto's 2nd choice, 24th overall, in 1982 Entry Draft).

			Regular Season					Playoffs				
Season	Club	Lea	GP	G	A	TP	PIM	GP	G	A	TP	PIM
1981-82	Regina	WHL	72	19	41	60	112	3	2	2	4	0
1982-83a	Regina	WHL	63	24	62	86	88	5	1	5	6	4
	Toronto	**NHL**	....	....	....	....	....	**2**	**0**	**0**	**0**	**0**
1983-84	**Toronto**	**NHL**	**52**	**4**	**8**	**12**	**31**	....	....	....	....	....
1984-85	**Toronto**	**NHL**	**53**	**5**	**26**	**31**	**72**	....	....	....	....	....
	St. Catharines	AHL	7	2	2	4	11	....	....	....	....	....
1985-86	**Toronto**	**NHL**	**53**	**9**	**23**	**32**	**20**	**10**	**2**	**10**	**12**	**2**
	St. Catharines	AHL	25	15	13	28	6	....	....	....	....	....
1986-87	**Toronto**	**NHL**	**80**	**21**	**31**	**52**	**66**	**5**	**0**	**1**	**1**	**14**
1987-88	**Toronto**	**NHL**	**80**	**30**	**31**	**61**	**62**	**2**	**2**	**0**	**2**	**2**
1988-89	**Toronto**	**NHL**	**61**	**32**	**43**	**75**	**66**	....	....	....	....	....
1989-90	**Toronto**	**NHL**	**80**	**51**	**44**	**95**	**63**	**5**	**3**	**3**	**6**	**16**
1990-91	**Toronto**	**NHL**	**52**	**17**	**12**	**29**	**39**	....	....	....	....	....
1991-92	**Toronto**	**NHL**	**34**	**7**	**13**	**20**	**44**	....	....	....	....	....
	Calgary	**NHL**	**29**	**2**	**7**	**9**	**27**	....	....	....	....	....
1992-93	**Calgary**	**NHL**	**30**	**9**	**5**	**14**	**10**	....	....	....	....	....
	Montreal	**NHL**	**20**	**6**	**12**	**18**	**14**	**11**	**1**	**2**	**3**	**2** ♦
1993-94	**Montreal**	**NHL**	**31**	**4**	**11**	**15**	**17**	**1**	**0**	**0**	**0**	**0**
	Fredericton	AHL	23	18	8	26	16	....	....	....	....	....
1994-95	**Vancouver**	**NHL**	**10**	**2**	**0**	**2**	**0**	....	....	....	....	....
1995-96	Gardena	Italy	20	7	12	19	59	7	2	4	6	12
1996-97	**St. Louis**	**NHL**	**2**	**0**	**1**	**1**	**0**	....	....	....	....	....
	Worcester	AHL	24	9	7	16	41	....	....	....	....	....
	Utah	IHL	15	6	1	7	20	4	0	3	3	4
	NHL Totals		**667**	**199**	**267**	**466**	**531**	**36**	**8**	**16**	**24**	**36**

a WHL First All-Star Team (1983)

Played in NHL All-Star Game (1989)

Traded to **Calgary** by **Toronto** with Craig Berube, Alexander Godynyuk, Michel Petit and Jeff Reese for Doug Gilmour, Jamie Macoun, Ric Nattress, Rick Wamsley and Kent Manderville, January 2, 1992. Traded to **Montreal** by **Calgary** for Brian Skrudland, January 28, 1993. Signed as a free agent by **Vancouver**, January 18, 1995. Signed as a free agent by **St. Louis**, September 26, 1996.

LEETCH, BRIAN — NYR

Defense. Shoots left. 5'11", 190 lbs. Born, Corpus Christi, TX, March 3, 1968.
(NY Rangers' 1st choice, 9th overall, in 1986 Entry Draft).

Season	Club	Lea	Regular Season GP	G	A	TP	PIM	Playoffs GP	G	A	TP	PIM
1986-87ab	Boston College	H.E.	37	9	38	47	10	....	....	....	....	....
1987-88	U.S. National	....	50	13	61	74	38	....	....	....	....	....
	U.S. Olympic	....	6	1	5	6	4	....	....	....	....	....
	NY Rangers	**NHL**	**17**	**2**	**12**	**14**	**0**	....	....	....	....	....
1988-89cd	**NY Rangers**	**NHL**	**68**	**23**	**48**	**71**	**50**	**4**	**3**	**2**	**5**	**2**
1989-90	**NY Rangers**	**NHL**	**72**	**11**	**45**	**56**	**26**	....	....	....	....	....
1990-91e	**NY Rangers**	**NHL**	**80**	**16**	**72**	**88**	**42**	**6**	**1**	**3**	**4**	**0**
1991-92fg	**NY Rangers**	**NHL**	**80**	**22**	**80**	**102**	**26**	**13**	**4**	**11**	**15**	**4**
1992-93	**NY Rangers**	**NHL**	**36**	**6**	**30**	**36**	**26**	....	....	....	....	....
1993-94eh	**NY Rangers**	**NHL**	**84**	**23**	**56**	**79**	**67**	**23**	**11**	***23**	***34**	**6** ♦
1994-95	**NY Rangers**	**NHL**	**48**	**9**	**32**	**41**	**18**	**10**	**6**	**8**	**14**	**8**
1995-96e	**NY Rangers**	**NHL**	**82**	**15**	**70**	**85**	**30**	**11**	**1**	**6**	**7**	**4**
1996-97fg	**NY Rangers**	**NHL**	**82**	**20**	**58**	**78**	**40**	**15**	**2**	**8**	**10**	**6**
	NHL Totals		**649**	**147**	**503**	**650**	**325**	**82**	**28**	**61**	**89**	**30**

a Hockey East First All-Star Team (1987)
b NCAA East First All-American Team (1987)
c NHL All-Rookie Team (1989)
d Won Calder Memorial Trophy (1989)
e NHL Second All-Star Team (1991, 1994, 1996)
f Won James Norris Memorial Trophy (1992, 1997)
g NHL First All-Star Team (1992, 1997)
h Won Conn Smythe Trophy (1994)

Played in NHL All-Star Game (1990-92, 1994, 1996, 1997)

LEFEBVRE, CHRISTIAN (luh-FAHV) — CGY.

Defense. Shoots left. 6'5", 212 lbs. Born, Montreal, Que., March 3, 1978.
(Calgary's 6th choice, 94th overall, in 1996 Entry Draft).

Season	Club	Lea	Regular Season GP	G	A	TP	PIM	Playoffs GP	G	A	TP	PIM
1994-95	Granby	QMJHL	24	1	1	2	11	4	0	0	0	0
1995-96	Granby	QMJHL	36	4	6	10	41	20	2	2	4	30
1996-97			DID NOT PLAY									

LEFEBVRE, SYLVAIN (luh-FAYV) — COL.

Defense. Shoots left. 6'2", 205 lbs. Born, Richmond, Que., October 14, 1967.

Season	Club	Lea	Regular Season GP	G	A	TP	PIM	Playoffs GP	G	A	TP	PIM
1984-85	Laval	QMJHL	66	7	5	12	31	....	....	....	....	....
1985-86	Laval	QMJHL	71	8	17	25	48	14	1	0	1	25
1986-87	Laval	QMJHL	70	10	36	46	44	15	1	6	7	12
1987-88	Sherbrooke	AHL	79	3	24	27	73	6	2	3	5	4
1988-89a	Sherbrooke	AHL	77	15	32	47	119	6	1	3	4	4
1989-90	**Montreal**	**NHL**	**68**	**3**	**10**	**13**	**61**	**6**	**0**	**0**	**0**	**2**
1990-91	**Montreal**	**NHL**	**63**	**5**	**18**	**23**	**30**	**11**	**1**	**0**	**1**	**6**
1991-92	**Montreal**	**NHL**	**69**	**3**	**14**	**17**	**91**	**2**	**0**	**0**	**0**	**2**
1992-93	**Toronto**	**NHL**	**81**	**2**	**12**	**14**	**90**	**21**	**3**	**3**	**6**	**20**
1993-94	**Toronto**	**NHL**	**84**	**2**	**9**	**11**	**79**	**18**	**0**	**3**	**3**	**16**
1994-95	**Quebec**	**NHL**	**48**	**2**	**11**	**13**	**17**	**6**	**0**	**2**	**2**	**2**
1995-96	**Colorado**	**NHL**	**75**	**5**	**11**	**16**	**49**	**22**	**0**	**5**	**5**	**12** ♦
1996-97	**Colorado**	**NHL**	**71**	**2**	**11**	**13**	**30**	**17**	**0**	**0**	**0**	**25**
	NHL Totals		**559**	**24**	**96**	**120**	**447**	**103**	**4**	**13**	**17**	**85**

a AHL Second All-Star Team (1989)

Signed as a free agent by **Montreal**, September 24, 1986. Traded to **Toronto** by **Montreal** for Toronto's third round choice (Martin Belanger) in 1994 Entry Draft, August 20, 1992. Traded to **Quebec** by **Toronto** with Wendel Clark, Landon Wilson and Toronto's first round choice (Jeffrey Kealty) in 1994 Entry Draft for Mats Sundin, Garth Butcher, Todd Warriner and Philadelphia's first round choice (previously acquired by Quebec — later traded to Washington — Washington selected Nolan Baumgartner) in 1994 Entry Draft, June 28, 1994.

LEGAULT, JAY (LEH-goh) — ANA.

Left wing. Shoots left. 6'4", 192 lbs. Born, Peterborough, Ont., May 15, 1979.
(Anaheim's 3rd choice, 72nd overall, in 1997 Entry Draft).

Season	Club	Lea	Regular Season GP	G	A	TP	PIM	Playoffs GP	G	A	TP	PIM
1995-96	Oshawa	OHL	61	2	11	13	37	5	0	1	1	8
1996-97	Oshawa	OHL	39	13	26	39	50	....	....	....	....	....
	London	OHL	28	6	13	19	37	....	....	....	....	....

LEGG, MIKE — N.J.

Right wing. Shoots right. 5'11", 175 lbs. Born, London, Ont., May 25, 1975.
(New Jersey's 11th choice, 273rd overall, in 1993 Entry Draft).

Season	Club	Lea	Regular Season GP	G	A	TP	PIM	Playoffs GP	G	A	TP	PIM
1993-94	U. of Michigan	CCHA	37	10	13	23	20	....	....	....	....	....
1994-95	U. of Michigan	CCHA	39	14	23	37	22	....	....	....	....	....
1995-96	U. of Michigan	CCHA	42	15	25	40	24	....	....	....	....	....
1996-97	U. of Michigan	CCHA	41	21	34	55	16	....	....	....	....	....

LEHTERA, TERO (LEHKH-tuh-rah) — FLA.

Left wing. Shoots right. 6', 185 lbs. Born, Espoo, Finland, April 21, 1972.
(Florida's 9th choice, 235th overall, in 1994 Entry Draft).

Season	Club	Lea	Regular Season GP	G	A	TP	PIM	Playoffs GP	G	A	TP	PIM
1993-94	Espoo	Fin.	48	19	27	46	2	....	....	....	....	....
1994-95	Malmo	Swe.	37	12	11	23	10	9	0	1	1	0
1995-96	Jokerit	Fin.	48	11	12	23	27	11	2	5	7	2
1996-97	Jokerit	Fin.	47	11	10	21	4	9	2	3	5	0

LEHTINEN, JERE (lehkh-TIH-nehn) — DAL.

Right wing. Shoots right. 6', 192 lbs. Born, Espoo, Finland, June 24, 1973.
(Minnesota's 3rd choice, 88th overall, in 1992 Entry Draft).

Season	Club	Lea	Regular Season GP	G	A	TP	PIM	Playoffs GP	G	A	TP	PIM
1990-91	Espoo	Fin. 2	32	15	9	24	12	....	....	....	....	....
1991-92	Espoo	Fin. 2	43	32	17	49	6	....	....	....	....	....
1992-93	Kiekko-Espoo	Fin.	45	13	14	27	6	....	....	....	....	....
1993-94	TPS	Fin.	42	19	20	39	6	11	11	2	13	2
1994-95	TPS	Fin.	39	19	23	42	33	13	8	6	14	4
1995-96	**Dallas**	**NHL**	**57**	**6**	**22**	**28**	**16**	....	....	....	....	....
	Michigan	IHL	1	1	0	1	0	....	....	....	....	....
1996-97	**Dallas**	**NHL**	**63**	**16**	**27**	**43**	**2**	**7**	**2**	**2**	**4**	**0**
	NHL Totals		**120**	**22**	**49**	**71**	**18**	**7**	**2**	**2**	**4**	**0**

LEMIEUX, CLAUDE (lehm-YOO) — COL.

Right wing. Shoots right. 6'1", 215 lbs. Born, Buckingham, Que., July 16, 1965.
(Montreal's 2nd choice, 26th overall, in 1983 Entry Draft).

Season	Club	Lea	Regular Season GP	G	A	TP	PIM	Playoffs GP	G	A	TP	PIM
1982-83	Trois-Rivières	QMJHL	62	28	38	66	187	4	1	0	1	30
1983-84	**Montreal**	**NHL**	**8**	**1**	**1**	**2**	**12**	....	....	....	....	....
	Verdun	QMJHL	51	41	45	86	225	9	8	12	20	63
	Nova Scotia	AHL	....	....	....	....	....	2	1	0	1	0
1984-85	**Montreal**	**NHL**	**1**	**0**	**1**	**1**	**7**	....	....	....	....	....
a	Verdun	QMJHL	52	58	66	124	152	14	23	17	40	38
1985-86	**Montreal**	**NHL**	**10**	**1**	**2**	**3**	**22**	**20**	**10**	**6**	**16**	**68** ♦
	Sherbrooke	AHL	58	21	32	53	145	....	....	....	....	....
1986-87	**Montreal**	**NHL**	**76**	**27**	**26**	**53**	**156**	**17**	**4**	**9**	**13**	**41**
1987-88	**Montreal**	**NHL**	**78**	**31**	**30**	**61**	**137**	**11**	**3**	**2**	**5**	**20**
1988-89	**Montreal**	**NHL**	**69**	**29**	**22**	**51**	**136**	**18**	**4**	**3**	**7**	**58**
1989-90	**Montreal**	**NHL**	**39**	**8**	**10**	**18**	**106**	**11**	**1**	**3**	**4**	**38**
1990-91	**New Jersey**	**NHL**	**78**	**30**	**17**	**47**	**105**	**7**	**4**	**0**	**4**	**34**
1991-92	**New Jersey**	**NHL**	**74**	**41**	**27**	**68**	**109**	**7**	**4**	**3**	**7**	**26**
1992-93	**New Jersey**	**NHL**	**77**	**30**	**51**	**81**	**155**	**5**	**2**	**0**	**2**	**19**
1993-94	**New Jersey**	**NHL**	**79**	**18**	**26**	**44**	**86**	**20**	**7**	**11**	**18**	**44**
1994-95b	**New Jersey**	**NHL**	**45**	**6**	**13**	**19**	**86**	**20**	***13**	**3**	**16**	**20** ♦
1995-96	**Colorado**	**NHL**	**79**	**39**	**32**	**71**	**117**	**19**	**5**	**7**	**12**	**55** ♦
1996-97	**Colorado**	**NHL**	**45**	**11**	**17**	**28**	**43**	**17**	***13**	**10**	**23**	**32**
	NHL Totals		**758**	**272**	**275**	**547**	**1277**	**172**	**70**	**57**	**127**	**455**

a QMJHL First All-Star Team (1985)
b Won Conn Smythe Trophy (1995)

Traded to **New Jersey** by **Montreal** for Sylvain Turgeon, September 4, 1990. Traded to **NY Islanders** by **New Jersey** for Steve Thomas, October 3, 1995. Traded to **Colorado** by **NY Islanders** for Wendel Clark, October 3, 1995.

LEMIEUX, JOCELYN (lehm-YOO) — PHO.

Right wing. Shoots left. 5'10", 200 lbs. Born, Mont-Laurier, Que., November 18, 1967.
(St. Louis' 1st choice, 10th overall, in 1986 Entry Draft).

Season	Club	Lea	Regular Season GP	G	A	TP	PIM	Playoffs GP	G	A	TP	PIM
1984-85	Laval	QMJHL	68	13	19	32	92	....	....	....	....	....
1985-86a	Laval	QMJHL	71	57	68	125	131	14	9	15	24	37
1986-87	**St. Louis**	**NHL**	**53**	**10**	**8**	**18**	**94**	**5**	**0**	**1**	**1**	**6**
1987-88	**St. Louis**	**NHL**	**23**	**1**	**0**	**1**	**42**	**5**	**0**	**0**	**0**	**15**
	Peoria	IHL	8	0	5	5	35	....	....	....	....	....
1988-89	**Montreal**	**NHL**	**1**	**0**	**1**	**1**	**0**	....	....	....	....	....
	Sherbrooke	AHL	73	25	28	53	134	4	3	1	4	6
1989-90	**Montreal**	**NHL**	**34**	**4**	**2**	**6**	**61**	....	....	....	....	....
	Chicago	**NHL**	**39**	**10**	**11**	**21**	**47**	**18**	**1**	**8**	**9**	**28**
1990-91	**Chicago**	**NHL**	**67**	**6**	**7**	**13**	**119**	**4**	**0**	**0**	**0**	**0**
1991-92	**Chicago**	**NHL**	**78**	**6**	**10**	**16**	**80**	**18**	**3**	**1**	**4**	**33**
1992-93	**Chicago**	**NHL**	**81**	**10**	**21**	**31**	**111**	**4**	**1**	**0**	**1**	**2**
1993-94	**Chicago**	**NHL**	**66**	**12**	**8**	**20**	**63**	....	....	....	....	....
	Hartford	**NHL**	**16**	**6**	**1**	**7**	**19**	....	....	....	....	....
1994-95	**Hartford**	**NHL**	**41**	**6**	**5**	**11**	**32**	....	....	....	....	....
1995-96	**Hartford**	**NHL**	**29**	**1**	**2**	**3**	**31**	....	....	....	....	....
	New Jersey	**NHL**	**18**	**0**	**1**	**1**	**4**	....	....	....	....	....
	Calgary	**NHL**	**20**	**4**	**4**	**8**	**10**	**4**	**0**	**0**	**0**	**0**
1996-97	Long Beach	IHL	28	4	10	14	54	....	....	....	....	....
	Phoenix	**NHL**	**2**	**1**	**0**	**1**	**0**	**2**	**0**	**0**	**0**	**4**
	NHL Totals		**568**	**77**	**81**	**158**	**713**	**60**	**5**	**10**	**15**	**88**

a QMJHL First All-Star Team (1986)

Traded to **Montreal** by **St. Louis** with Darrell May and St. Louis' second round choice (Patrice Brisebois) in the 1989 Entry Draft for Sergio Momesso and Vincent Riendeau, August 9, 1988. Traded to **Chicago** by **Montreal** for Chicago's third round choice (Charles Poulin) in 1990 Entry Draft, January 5, 1990. Traded to **Hartford** by **Chicago** with Frantisek Kucera for Gary Suter, Randy Cunneyworth and Hartford's third round choice (later traded to Vancouver — Vancouver selected Larry Courville) in 1995 Entry Draft, March 11, 1994. Traded to **New Jersey** by **Hartford** with Hartford's second round choice in 1998 Entry Draft for Jim Dowd and New Jersey's second round choice (later traded to Calgary — Calgary selected Dmitri Kokorev) in 1997 Entry Draft, December 19, 1995. Traded to **Calgary** by **New Jersey** with Tommy Albelin and Cale Hulse for Phil Housley and Dan Keczmer, February 26, 1996. Signed as a free agent by **Phoenix**, March 18, 1997.

LEMIEUX, MARIO (lehm-YOO)

Center. Shoots right. 6'4", 225 lbs. Born, Montreal, Que., October 5, 1965.
(Pittsburgh's 1st choice, 1st overall, in 1984 Entry Draft).

Season	Club	Lea	Regular Season GP	G	A	TP	PIM	Playoffs GP	G	A	TP	PIM
1981-82	Laval	QMJHL	64	30	66	96	22	18	5	9	14	31
1982-83a	Laval	QMJHL	66	84	100	184	76	12	14	18	32	18
1983-84bc	Laval	QMJHL	70	*133	*149	*282	92	14	*29	*23	*52	29
1984-85de	**Pittsburgh**	**NHL**	**73**	**43**	**57**	**100**	**54**	....	....	....	....	....
1985-86fg	**Pittsburgh**	**NHL**	**79**	**48**	**93**	**141**	**43**	....	....	....	....	....
1986-87f	**Pittsburgh**	**NHL**	**63**	**54**	**53**	**107**	**57**	....	....	....	....	....
1987-88 ghijkl	**Pittsburgh**	**NHL**	**77**	***70**	**98**	***168**	**92**	....	....	....	....	....
1988-89ijlm	**Pittsburgh**	**NHL**	**76**	***85**	***114**	***199**	**100**	**11**	**12**	**7**	**19**	**16**
1989-90	**Pittsburgh**	**NHL**	**59**	**45**	**78**	**123**	**78**	....	....	....	....	....
1990-91n	**Pittsburgh**	**NHL**	**26**	**19**	**26**	**45**	**30**	**23**	**16**	***28**	***44**	**16** ♦
1991-92fino	**Pittsburgh**	**NHL**	**64**	**44**	**87**	***131**	**94**	**15**	***16**	**18**	***34**	**2** ♦
1992-93 ghijpq	**Pittsburgh**	**NHL**	**60**	**69**	**91**	***160**	**38**	**11**	**8**	**10**	**18**	**10**
1993-94	**Pittsburgh**	**NHL**	**22**	**17**	**20**	**37**	**32**	**6**	**4**	**3**	**7**	**2**
1994-95			DID NOT PLAY									
1995-96ghij	**Pittsburgh**	**NHL**	**70**	***69**	***92**	***161**	**54**	**18**	**11**	**16**	**27**	**33**
1996-97ij	**Pittsburgh**	**NHL**	**76**	**50**	***72**	***122**	**65**	**5**	**3**	**3**	**6**	**4**
	NHL Totals		**745**	**613**	**881**	**1494**	**737**	**89**	**70**	**85**	**155**	**83**

a QMJHL Second All-Star Team (1983)
b QMJHL First All-Star Team (1984)
c Canadian Major Junior Player of the Year (1984)
d Won Calder Memorial Trophy (1985)
e NHL All-Rookie Team (1985)
f NHL Second All-Star Team (1986, 1987, 1992)
g Won Lester B. Pearson Award (1986, 1988, 1993, 1996)
h Won Hart Trophy (1988, 1993, 1996)
i Won Art Ross Trophy (1988, 1989, 1992, 1993, 1996, 1997)
j NHL First All-Star Team (1988, 1989, 1993, 1996, 1997)
k Won Dodge Performance of the Year Award (1988)
l Won Dodge Performer of the Year Award (1988, 1989)
m Won Dodge Ram Tough Award (1989)
n Won Conn Smythe Trophy (1991, 1992)
o Won ProSet/NHL Player of the Year Award (1992)
p Won Bill Masterton Memorial Trophy (1993)
q Won Alka-Seltzer Plus Award (1993)

Played in NHL All-Star Game (1985, 1986, 1988-90, 1992, 1996, 1997)

LENT, NICHOLAS — PHO.

Right wing. Shoots right. 6'3", 210 lbs. Born, Boston, MA, June 10, 1977.
(Phoenix's 7th choice, 200th overall, in 1996 Entry Draft).

			Regular Season					Playoffs				
Season	Club	Lea	GP	G	A	TP	PIM	GP	G	A	TP	PIM
1995-96	Omaha	USHL	42	7	9	16	65	6	2	1	3	8
1996-97	Providence	H.E.	27	6	6	12	16	....	....	....	....	....

LEROUX, FRANCOIS (leh-ROO) — PIT.

Defense. Shoots left. 6'6", 235 lbs. Born, Ste.-Adele, Que., April 18, 1970.
(Edmonton's 1st choice, 19th overall, in 1988 Entry Draft).

			Regular Season					Playoffs				
Season	Club	Lea	GP	G	A	TP	PIM	GP	G	A	TP	PIM
1987-88	St-Jean	QMJHL	58	3	8	11	143	7	2	0	2	21
1988-89	**Edmonton**	**NHL**	**2**	**0**	**0**	**0**	**0**	....	....	....	....	....
	St-Jean	QMJHL	57	8	34	42	185	....	....	....	....	....
1989-90	**Edmonton**	**NHL**	**3**	**0**	**1**	**1**	**0**	....	....	....	....	....
	Victoriaville	QMJHL	54	4	33	37	169	....	....	....	....	....
1990-91	**Edmonton**	**NHL**	**1**	**0**	**2**	**2**	**0**	....	....	....	....	....
	Cape Breton	AHL	71	2	7	9	124	4	0	1	1	19
1991-92	**Edmonton**	**NHL**	**4**	**0**	**0**	**0**	**7**	....	....	....	....	....
	Cape Breton	AHL	61	7	22	29	114	5	0	0	0	8
1992-93	**Edmonton**	**NHL**	**1**	**0**	**0**	**0**	**4**	....	....	....	....	....
	Cape Breton	AHL	55	10	24	34	139	16	0	5	5	29
1993-94	**Ottawa**	**NHL**	**23**	**0**	**1**	**1**	**70**	....	....	....	....	....
	P.E.I.	AHL	25	4	6	10	52	....	....	....	....	....
1994-95	P.E.I.	AHL	45	4	14	18	137	....	....	....	....	....
	Pittsburgh	**NHL**	**40**	**0**	**2**	**2**	**114**	**12**	**0**	**2**	**2**	**14**
1995-96	**Pittsburgh**	**NHL**	**66**	**2**	**9**	**11**	**161**	**18**	**1**	**1**	**2**	**20**
1996-97	**Pittsburgh**	**NHL**	**59**	**0**	**3**	**3**	**81**	**3**	**0**	**0**	**0**	**0**
	NHL Totals		**199**	**2**	**18**	**20**	**437**	**33**	**1**	**3**	**4**	**34**

Claimed on waivers by **Ottawa** from **Edmonton**, October 6, 1993. Claimed by **Pittsburgh** from **Ottawa** in NHL Waiver Draft, January 18, 1995.

LEROUX, JEAN-YVES (leh-ROO) — CHI.

Left wing. Shoots left. 6'2", 211 lbs. Born, Montreal, Que., June 24, 1976.
(Chicago's 2nd choice, 40th overall, in 1994 Entry Draft).

			Regular Season					Playoffs				
Season	Club	Lea	GP	G	A	TP	PIM	GP	G	A	TP	PIM
1992-93	Beauport	QMJHL	62	20	25	45	33	....	....	....	....	....
1993-94a	Beauport	QMJHL	45	14	25	39	43	15	7	6	13	33
1994-95	Beauport	QMJHL	59	19	33	52	125	17	4	6	10	39
1995-96	Beauport	QMJHL	54	41	41	82	176	20	5	18	23	20
1996-97	**Chicago**	**NHL**	**1**	**0**	**1**	**1**	**5**	....	....	....	....	....
	Indianapolis	IHL	69	14	17	31	112	4	1	0	1	2
	NHL Totals		**1**	**0**	**1**	**1**	**5**	....	....	....	....	....

a QMJHL Second All-Star Team (1994)

LESCHYSHYN, CURTIS (luh-SIH-shuhn) — CAR.

Defense. Shoots left. 6'1", 205 lbs. Born, Thompson, Man., September 21, 1969.
(Quebec's 1st choice, 3rd overall, in 1988 Entry Draft).

			Regular Season					Playoffs				
Season	Club	Lea	GP	G	A	TP	PIM	GP	G	A	TP	PIM
1986-87	Saskatoon	WHL	70	14	26	40	107	11	1	5	6	14
1987-88	Saskatoon	WHL	56	14	41	55	86	10	2	5	7	16
1988-89	**Quebec**	**NHL**	**71**	**4**	**9**	**13**	**71**	....	....	....	....	....
1989-90	**Quebec**	**NHL**	**68**	**2**	**6**	**8**	**44**	....	....	....	....	....
1990-91	**Quebec**	**NHL**	**55**	**3**	**7**	**10**	**49**	....	....	....	....	....
1991-92	**Quebec**	**NHL**	**42**	**5**	**12**	**17**	**42**	....	....	....	....	....
	Halifax	AHL	6	0	2	2	4	....	....	....	....	....
1992-93	**Quebec**	**NHL**	**82**	**9**	**23**	**32**	**61**	**6**	**1**	**1**	**2**	**6**
1993-94	**Quebec**	**NHL**	**72**	**5**	**17**	**22**	**65**	....	....	....	....	....
1994-95	**Quebec**	**NHL**	**44**	**2**	**13**	**15**	**20**	**3**	**0**	**1**	**1**	**4**
1995-96	**Colorado**	**NHL**	**77**	**4**	**15**	**19**	**73**	**17**	**1**	**2**	**3**	**8** ♦
1996-97	**Colorado**	**NHL**	**11**	**0**	**5**	**5**	**6**	....	....	....	....	....
	Washington	**NHL**	**2**	**0**	**0**	**0**	**2**	....	....	....	....	....
	Hartford	**NHL**	**64**	**4**	**13**	**17**	**30**	....	....	....	....	....
	NHL Totals		**588**	**38**	**120**	**158**	**463**	**26**	**2**	**4**	**6**	**18**

Traded to **Washington** by **Colorado** with Chris Simon for Keith Jones, Washington's first and fourth round choices in 1998 Entry Draft, November 2, 1996. Traded to **Hartford** by **Washington** for Andrei Nikolishin, November 9, 1996.

LESSARD, FRANCIS (leh-SAHR) — CAR.

Defense. Shoots right. 6'2", 184 lbs. Born, Montreal, Que., May 30, 1979.
(Carolina's 3rd choice, 80th overall, in 1997 Entry Draft).

			Regular Season					Playoffs				
Season	Club	Lea	GP	G	A	TP	PIM	GP	G	A	TP	PIM
1995-96	Laval	Midget	41	5	7	12	73	....	....	....	....	....
1996-97	Val d'Or	QMJHL	66	1	9	10	287	....	....	....	....	....

LETOWSKI, TREVOR (leh-TOW-skee) — PHO.

Center. Shoots right. 5'10", 170 lbs. Born, Thunder Bay, Ont., April 5, 1977.
(Phoenix's 6th choice, 174th overall, in 1996 Entry Draft).

			Regular Season					Playoffs				
Season	Club	Lea	GP	G	A	TP	PIM	GP	G	A	TP	PIM
1994-95	Sarnia	OHL	66	22	19	41	33	4	0	1	1	9
1995-96	Sarnia	OHL	66	36	63	99	66	10	9	5	14	10
1996-97	Sarnia	OHL	55	35	73	108	51	12	9	12	21	20

LEVINS, SCOTT — PHO.

Center/Right wing. Shoots right. 6'4", 210 lbs. Born, Spokane, WA, January 30, 1970.
(Winnipeg's 4th choice, 75th overall, in 1990 Entry Draft).

			Regular Season					Playoffs				
Season	Club	Lea	GP	G	A	TP	PIM	GP	G	A	TP	PIM
1989-90a	Tri-Cities	WHL	71	25	37	62	132	6	2	3	5	18
1990-91	Moncton	AHL	74	12	26	38	133	4	0	0	0	4
1991-92	Moncton	AHL	69	15	18	33	271	11	3	4	7	30
1992-93	**Winnipeg**	**NHL**	**9**	**0**	**1**	**1**	**18**	....	....	....	....	....
	Moncton	AHL	54	22	26	48	158	5	1	3	4	14
1993-94	**Florida**	**NHL**	**29**	**5**	**6**	**11**	**69**	....	....	....	....	....
	Ottawa	**NHL**	**33**	**3**	**5**	**8**	**93**	....	....	....	....	....
1994-95	**Ottawa**	**NHL**	**24**	**5**	**6**	**11**	**51**	....	....	....	....	....
	P.E.I.	AHL	6	0	4	4	14	....	....	....	....	....
1995-96	**Ottawa**	**NHL**	**27**	**0**	**2**	**2**	**80**	....	....	....	....	....
	Detroit	IHL	9	0	0	0	9	....	....	....	....	....
1996-97	Springfield	AHL	68	24	23	47	267	11	5	4	9	37
	NHL Totals		**122**	**13**	**20**	**33**	**311**	....	....	....	....	....

a WHL West Second All-Star Team (1990)

Claimed by **Florida** from **Winnipeg** in Expansion Draft, June 24, 1993. Traded to **Ottawa** by **Florida** with Evgeny Davydov, Florida's sixth round choice (Mike Gaffney) in 1994 Entry Draft and Dallas' fourth round choice (previously acquired by Florida — Ottawa selected Kevin Bolibruck) in 1995 Entry Draft for Bob Kudelski, January 6, 1994. Signed as a free agent by **Phoenix**, October 3, 1996.

LIBBY, JEFF — NYI

Defense. Shoots left. 6'3", 215 lbs. Born, Waterville, ME, March 1, 1974.

			Regular Season					Playoffs				
Season	Club	Lea	GP	G	A	TP	PIM	GP	G	A	TP	PIM
1994-95	U. of Maine	H.E.	22	2	4	6	6	....	....	....	....	....
1995-96	U. of Maine	H.E.	39	0	9	9	42	....	....	....	....	....
1996-97	U. of Maine	H.E.	34	6	25	31	41	....	....	....	....	....

Signed as a free agent by **NY Islanders**, May 12, 1997.

LIDSTER, DOUG — NYR

Defense. Shoots right. 6'1", 190 lbs. Born, Kamloops, B.C., October 18, 1960.
(Vancouver's 6th choice, 133rd overall, in 1980 Entry Draft).

			Regular Season					Playoffs				
Season	Club	Lea	GP	G	A	TP	PIM	GP	G	A	TP	PIM
1977-78	Seattle	WHL	2	0	0	0	0	....	....	....	....	....
1978-79	Kamloops	BCJHL	59	36	47	83	50	....	....	....	....	....
1979-80	Colorado	WCHA	39	18	25	43	52	....	....	....	....	....
1980-81	Colorado	WCHA	36	10	30	40	54	....	....	....	....	....
1981-82	Colorado	WCHA	36	13	22	35	32	....	....	....	....	....
1982-83	Colorado	WCHA	34	15	41	56	30	....	....	....	....	....
1983-84	Cdn. National	....	59	6	20	26	28	....	....	....	....	....
	Cdn. Olympic	....	7	0	2	2	2	....	....	....	....	....
	Vancouver	**NHL**	**8**	**0**	**0**	**0**	**4**	**2**	**0**	**1**	**1**	**0**
1984-85	**Vancouver**	**NHL**	**78**	**6**	**24**	**30**	**55**	....	....	....	....	....
1985-86	**Vancouver**	**NHL**	**78**	**12**	**16**	**28**	**56**	**3**	**0**	**1**	**1**	**2**
1986-87	**Vancouver**	**NHL**	**80**	**12**	**51**	**63**	**40**	....	....	....	....	....
1987-88	**Vancouver**	**NHL**	**64**	**4**	**32**	**36**	**105**	....	....	....	....	....
1988-89	**Vancouver**	**NHL**	**63**	**5**	**17**	**22**	**78**	**7**	**1**	**1**	**2**	**9**
1989-90	**Vancouver**	**NHL**	**80**	**8**	**28**	**36**	**36**	....	....	....	....	....
1990-91	**Vancouver**	**NHL**	**78**	**6**	**32**	**38**	**77**	**6**	**0**	**2**	**2**	**6**
1991-92	**Vancouver**	**NHL**	**66**	**6**	**23**	**29**	**39**	**11**	**1**	**2**	**3**	**11**
1992-93	**Vancouver**	**NHL**	**71**	**6**	**19**	**25**	**36**	**12**	**0**	**3**	**3**	**8**
1993-94	**NY Rangers**	**NHL**	**34**	**0**	**2**	**2**	**33**	**9**	**2**	**0**	**2**	**10** ♦
1994-95	**St. Louis**	**NHL**	**37**	**2**	**7**	**9**	**12**	**4**	**0**	**0**	**0**	**2**
1995-96	**NY Rangers**	**NHL**	**59**	**5**	**9**	**14**	**50**	**7**	**1**	**0**	**1**	**6**
1996-97	**NY Rangers**	**NHL**	**48**	**3**	**4**	**7**	**24**	**15**	**1**	**5**	**6**	**8**
	NHL Totals		**844**	**75**	**264**	**339**	**645**	**76**	**6**	**15**	**21**	**62**

Traded to **NY Rangers** by **Vancouver** to complete June 20, 1993 trade which sent John Vanbiesbrouck to Vancouver for future considerations, June 25, 1993. Traded to **St. Louis** by **NY Rangers** with Esa Tikkanen for Petr Nedved, July 24, 1994. Traded to **NY Rangers** by **St. Louis** for Jay Wells, July 28, 1995.

LIDSTROM, NICKLAS (LID-struhm) — DET.

Defense. Shoots left. 6'2", 185 lbs. Born, Vasteras, Sweden, April 28, 1970.
(Detroit's 3rd choice, 53rd overall, in 1989 Entry Draft).

			Regular Season					Playoffs				
Season	Club	Lea	GP	G	A	TP	PIM	GP	G	A	TP	PIM
1987-88	Vasteras	Swe. 2	3	0	0	0	....	....	....	....	....	....
1988-89	Vasteras	Swe.	19	0	2	2	4	....	....	....	....	....
1989-90	Vasteras	Swe.	39	8	8	16	14	2	0	1	1	2
1990-91	Vasteras	Swe.	38	4	19	23	2	4	0	0	0	4
1991-92a	**Detroit**	**NHL**	**80**	**11**	**49**	**60**	**22**	**11**	**1**	**2**	**3**	**0**
1992-93	**Detroit**	**NHL**	**84**	**7**	**34**	**41**	**28**	**7**	**1**	**0**	**1**	**0**
1993-94	**Detroit**	**NHL**	**84**	**10**	**46**	**56**	**26**	**7**	**3**	**2**	**5**	**0**
1994-95	Vasteras	Swe.	13	2	10	12	4	....	....	....	....	....
	Detroit	**NHL**	**43**	**10**	**16**	**26**	**6**	**18**	**4**	**12**	**16**	**8**
1995-96	**Detroit**	**NHL**	**81**	**17**	**50**	**67**	**20**	**19**	**5**	**9**	**14**	**10**
1996-97	**Detroit**	**NHL**	**79**	**15**	**42**	**57**	**30**	**20**	**2**	**6**	**8**	**2** ♦
	NHL Totals		**451**	**70**	**237**	**307**	**132**	**82**	**16**	**31**	**47**	**20**

a NHL/Upper Deck All-Rookie Team (1992)

Played in NHL All-Star Game (1996)

LIEVERS, BRETT

Center. Shoots right. 6'1", 185 lbs. Born, Syracuse, NY, June 18, 1971.
(NY Ranger's 13th choice, 223rd overall, in 1990 Entry Draft).

			Regular Season					Playoffs				
Season	Club	Lea	GP	G	A	TP	PIM	GP	G	A	TP	PIM
1990-91	St. Cloud	WCHA	40	14	18	32	4	....	....	....	....	....
1991-92	St. Cloud	WCHA	16	2	10	12	2	....	....	....	....	....
1992-93						DID NOT PLAY						
1993-94	St. Cloud	WCHA	32	16	16	32	6	....	....	....	....	....
1994-95	St. Cloud	WCHA	38	21	27	48	8	....	....	....	....	....
1995-96	Utah	IHL	79	36	27	63	42	20	10	3	13	6
1996-97	Utah	IHL	74	22	26	48	11	7	2	0	2	0

Signed as a free agent by **Ottawa**, July 29, 1996.

LILLEY, JOHN

Right wing. Shoots right. 5'9", 170 lbs. Born, Wakefield, MA, August 3, 1972.
(Winnipeg's 8th choice, 140th overall, in 1990 Entry Draft).

			Regular Season					Playoffs				
Season	Club	Lea	GP	G	A	TP	PIM	GP	G	A	TP	PIM
1991-92	Boston U.	H.E.	23	9	9	18	43	....	....	....	....	....
1992-93	Boston U.	H.E.	4	0	1	1	13	....	....	....	....	....
	Seattle	WHL	45	22	28	50	55	5	1	3	4	9
1993-94	U.S. National	....	58	27	23	50	117	....	....	....	....	....
	U.S. Olympic	....	8	3	1	4	4	....	....	....	....	....
	Anaheim	**NHL**	**13**	**1**	**6**	**7**	**8**	....	....	....	....	....
	San Diego	IHL	2	2	1	3	0	....	....	....	....	....
1994-95	San Diego	IHL	45	9	15	24	71	2	0	0	0	2
	Anaheim	**NHL**	**9**	**2**	**2**	**4**	**5**	....	....	....	....	....
1995-96	**Anaheim**	**NHL**	**1**	**0**	**0**	**0**	**0**	....	....	....	....	....
	Baltimore	AHL	12	2	4	6	34	....	....	....	....	....
	Los Angeles	IHL	64	12	20	32	112	....	....	....	....	....
1996-97	Rochester	AHL	1	0	2	2	15	....	....	....	....	....
	Providence	AHL	63	12	23	35	130	10	3	0	3	24
	Detroit	IHL	1	0	0	0	2	....	....	....	....	....
	NHL Totals		**23**	**3**	**8**	**11**	**13**	....	....	....	....	....

Signed as a free agent by **Anaheim**, March 9, 1994.

LIND, JUHA — DAL.

Center. Shoots left. 5'11", 178 lbs. Born, Helsinki, Finland, January 2, 1974.
(Minnesota's 6th choice, 178th overall, in 1992 Entry Draft).

			Regular Season					Playoffs				
Season	Club	Lea	GP	G	A	TP	PIM	GP	G	A	TP	PIM
1991-92	Jokerit	Fin. Jr.	28	16	24	40	10	....	....	....	....	....
1992-93	Vantaa	Fin. 2	25	8	12	20	8	....	....	....	....	....
	Jokerit	Fin.	6	0	0	0	2	1	0	0	0	0
1993-94	Jokerit	Fin.	47	17	11	28	37	11	2	5	7	4
1994-95	Jokerit	Fin.	50	10	8	18	12	11	1	2	3	6
1995-96	Jokerit	Fin.	50	15	22	37	32	11	4	5	9	4
1996-97	Jokerit	Fin.	50	16	22	38	28	9	5	3	8	0

LINDBOM, JOHAN (LIHND-buhm, YOO-hahn) — NYR

Left wing. Shoots left. 6'2", 216 lbs. Born, Alvesta, Sweden, July 8, 1971.
(NY Rangers' 6th choice, 134th overall, in 1997 Entry Draft).

			Regular Season					Playoffs				
Season	Club	Lea	GP	G	A	TP	PIM	GP	G	A	TP	PIM
1991-92	Tyringe	Swe. 2	30	10	11	21	68	....	....	....	....	....
1992-93	Troja-Ljungby	Swe. 2	30	10	16	26	20	10	6	3	9	18
1993-94	Troja-Ljungby	Swe. 2	33	16	11	27	30	11	6	6	12	2
1994-95	HV 71	Swe.	39	9	7	16	30	13	2	5	7	12
1995-96	HV 71	Swe.	37	12	14	26	30	4	0	0	0	4
1996-97	HV 71	Swe.	49	20	14	34	26	5	1	0	1	6

LINDEN, JAMIE

Right wing. Shoots right. 6'3", 185 lbs. Born, Medicine Hat, Alta., July 19, 1972.

			Regular Season					Playoffs				
Season	Club	Lea	GP	G	A	TP	PIM	GP	G	A	TP	PIM
1988-89	Portland	WHL	1	0	1	1	0	....	....	....	....	....
1989-90	Portland	WHL	67	5	7	12	124	....	....	....	....	....
1990-91	Portland	WHL	2	0	1	1	6	....	....	....	....	....
	Prince Albert	WHL	64	9	12	21	114	3	0	0	0	0
1992-93	Spokane	WHL	15	3	1	4	58	....	....	....	....	....
	Medicine Hat	WHL	50	9	9	18	147	10	1	6	7	15
1993-94	Cincinnati	IHL	47	1	5	6	55	2	0	0	0	2
	Birmingham	ECHL	16	3	7	10	38	....	....	....	....	....
1994-95	Cincinnati	IHL	51	3	6	9	173	....	....	....	....	....
	Florida	**NHL**	**4**	**0**	**0**	**0**	**17**	....	....	....	....	....
1995-96	Carolina	AHL	50	4	8	12	92	....	....	....	....	....
1996-97	Carolina	AHL	3	0	0	0	5	....	....	....	....	....
	Grand Rapids	IHL	48	8	8	16	138	5	1	1	2	4
	NHL Totals		**4**	**0**	**0**	**0**	**17**	....	....	....	....	....

Signed as a free agent by **Florida**, October 4, 1993.

LINDEN, TREVOR — VAN.

Center/Right wing. Shoots right. 6'4", 210 lbs. Born, Medicine Hat, Alta., April 11, 1970.
(Vancouver's 1st choice, 2nd overall, in 1988 Entry Draft).

			Regular Season					Playoffs				
Season	Club	Lea	GP	G	A	TP	PIM	GP	G	A	TP	PIM
1986-87	Medicine Hat	WHL	72	14	22	36	59	20	5	4	9	17
1987-88	Medicine Hat	WHL	67	46	64	110	76	16	*13	12	25	19
1988-89a	**Vancouver**	**NHL**	**80**	**30**	**29**	**59**	**41**	**7**	**3**	**4**	**7**	**8**
1989-90	**Vancouver**	**NHL**	**73**	**21**	**30**	**51**	**43**	....	....	....	....	....
1990-91	**Vancouver**	**NHL**	**80**	**33**	**37**	**70**	**65**	**6**	**0**	**7**	**7**	**2**
1991-92	**Vancouver**	**NHL**	**80**	**31**	**44**	**75**	**101**	**13**	**4**	**8**	**12**	**6**
1992-93	**Vancouver**	**NHL**	**84**	**33**	**39**	**72**	**64**	**12**	**5**	**8**	**13**	**16**
1993-94	**Vancouver**	**NHL**	**84**	**32**	**29**	**61**	**73**	**24**	**12**	**13**	**25**	**18**
1994-95	**Vancouver**	**NHL**	**48**	**18**	**22**	**40**	**40**	**11**	**2**	**6**	**8**	**12**
1995-96	**Vancouver**	**NHL**	**82**	**33**	**47**	**80**	**42**	**6**	**4**	**4**	**8**	**6**
1996-97b	**Vancouver**	**NHL**	**49**	**9**	**31**	**40**	**27**	....	....	....	....	....
	NHL Totals		**660**	**240**	**308**	**548**	**496**	**79**	**30**	**50**	**80**	**68**

a NHL All-Rookie Team (1989)
b Won King Clancy Memorial Trophy (1997)

Played in NHL All-Star Game (1991, 1992)

LINDGREN, MATS (LIHND-gruhn) — EDM.

Center. Shoots left. 6'2", 200 lbs. Born, Skelleftea, Sweden, October 1, 1974.
(Winnipeg's 1st choice, 15th overall, in 1993 Entry Draft).

			Regular Season					Playoffs				
Season	Club	Lea	GP	G	A	TP	PIM	GP	G	A	TP	PIM
1991-92	Skelleftea	Swe. 2	29	14	8	22	14	....	....	....	....	....
1992-93	Skelleftea	Swe. 2	32	20	14	34	18	....	....	....	....	....
1993-94	Farjestad	Swe.	22	11	6	17	26	....	....	....	....	....
1994-95	Farjestad	Swe.	37	17	15	32	20	3	0	0	0	4
1995-96	Cape Breton	AHL	13	7	5	12	6	....	....	....	....	....
1996-97	**Edmonton**	**NHL**	**69**	**11**	**14**	**25**	**12**	**12**	**0**	**4**	**4**	**0**
	Hamilton	AHL	9	6	7	13	6	....	....	....	....	....
	NHL Totals		**69**	**11**	**14**	**25**	**12**	**12**	**0**	**4**	**4**	**0**

Traded to **Edmonton** by **Winnipeg** with Boris Mironov, Winnipeg's first round choice (Jason Bonsignore) in 1994 Entry Draft and Florida's fourth round choice (previously acquired by Winnipeg — Edmonton selected Adam Copeland) in 1994 Entry Draft for Dave Manson and St. Louis' sixth round choice (previously acquired by Edmonton — Winnipeg selected Chris Kibermanis) in 1994 Entry Draft, March 15, 1994.

LINDQVIST, FREDRIK (LIHND-kvihst) — N.J.

Center. Shoots left. 5'11", 176 lbs. Born, Sodertalje, Sweden, June 21, 1973.
(New Jersey's 4th choice, 55th overall, in 1991 Entry Draft).

			Regular Season					Playoffs				
Season	Club	Lea	GP	G	A	TP	PIM	GP	G	A	TP	PIM
1989-90	Huddinge	Swe. 2	2	0	0	0	0	....	....	....	....	....
1990-91	Djurgarden	Swe.	28	6	4	10	0	7	1	0	1	2
1991-92	Djurgarden	Swe.	39	9	6	15	14	10	1	1	2	2
1992-93	Djurgarden	Swe.	39	9	11	20	8	4	1	2	3	2
1993-94	Djurgarden	Swe.	25	5	8	13	8	6	2	1	3	2
1994-95	Djurgarden	Swe.	40	11	16	27	14	3	0	0	0	2
1995-96	Djurgarden	Swe.	33	12	19	31	16	1	0	0	0	0
1996-97	Djurgarden	Swe.	44	19	28	47	20	4	0	3	3	2

LINDROS, ERIC (LIHND-rahz) — PHI.

Center. Shoots right. 6'4", 236 lbs. Born, London, Ont., February 28, 1973.
(Quebec's 1st choice, 1st overall, in 1991 Entry Draft).

			Regular Season					Playoffs				
Season	Club	Lea	GP	G	A	TP	PIM	GP	G	A	TP	PIM
1988-89	Cdn. National	....	2	1	0	1	0	....	....	....	....	....
1989-90	Det. Comp.	USHL	14	23	29	52	123	....	....	....	....	....
	Cdn. National	....	3	1	0	1	4	....	....	....	....	....
a	Oshawa	OHL	25	17	19	36	61	17	18	18	36	76
1990-91bc	Oshawa	OHL	57	*71	78	*149	189	16	*18	20	*38	*93
1991-92	Oshawa	OHL	13	9	22	31	54	....	....	....	....	....
	Cdn. National	....	24	19	16	35	34	....	....	....	....	....
	Cdn. Olympic	....	8	5	6	11	6	....	....	....	....	....
1992-93d	**Philadelphia**	**NHL**	**61**	**41**	**34**	**75**	**147**	....	....	....	....	....
1993-94	**Philadelphia**	**NHL**	**65**	**44**	**53**	**97**	**103**	....	....	....	....	....
1994-95efg	**Philadelphia**	**NHL**	**46**	**29**	**41**	***70**	**60**	**12**	**4**	**11**	**15**	**18**
1995-96h	**Philadelphia**	**NHL**	**73**	**47**	**68**	**115**	**163**	**12**	**6**	**6**	**12**	**43**
1996-97	**Philadelphia**	**NHL**	**52**	**32**	**47**	**79**	**136**	**19**	**12**	**14**	***26**	**40**
	NHL Totals		**297**	**193**	**243**	**436**	**609**	**43**	**22**	**31**	**53**	**101**

a Memorial Cup All-Star Team (1990)
b OHL First All-Star Team (1991)
c Canadian Major Junior Player of the Year (1991)
d NHL/Upper Deck All-Rookie Team (1993)
e NHL First All-Star Team (1995)
f Won Lester B. Pearson Award (1995)
g Won Hart Trophy (1995)
h NHL Second All-Star Team (1996)

Played in NHL All-Star Game (1994, 1996, 1997)

Traded to **Philadelphia** by **Quebec** for Peter Forsberg, Steve Duchesne, Kerry Huffman, Mike Ricci, Ron Hextall, Chris Simon, Philadelphia's first round choice in the 1993 (Jocelyn Thibault) and 1994 (later traded to Toronto — later traded to Washington — Washington selected Nolan Baumgartner) Entry Drafts and cash, June 30, 1992.

LINDSAY, BILL — FLA.

Left wing. Shoots left. 5'11", 190 lbs. Born, Big Fork, MT, May 17, 1971.
(Quebec's 6th choice, 103rd overall, in 1991 Entry Draft).

			Regular Season					Playoffs				
Season	Club	Lea	GP	G	A	TP	PIM	GP	G	A	TP	PIM
1990-91	Tri-Cities	WHL	63	46	47	93	151	5	3	6	9	10
1991-92	**Quebec**	**NHL**	**23**	**2**	**4**	**6**	**14**	....	....	....	....	....
a	Tri-Cities	WHL	42	34	59	93	111	3	2	3	5	16
1992-93	**Quebec**	**NHL**	**44**	**4**	**9**	**13**	**16**	....	....	....	....	....
	Halifax	AHL	20	11	13	24	18	....	....	....	....	....
1993-94	**Florida**	**NHL**	**84**	**6**	**6**	**12**	**97**	....	....	....	....	....
1994-95	**Florida**	**NHL**	**48**	**10**	**9**	**19**	**46**	....	....	....	....	....
1995-96	**Florida**	**NHL**	**73**	**12**	**22**	**34**	**57**	**22**	**5**	**5**	**10**	**18**
1996-97	**Florida**	**NHL**	**81**	**11**	**23**	**34**	**120**	**3**	**0**	**1**	**1**	**8**
	NHL Totals		**353**	**45**	**73**	**118**	**350**	**25**	**5**	**6**	**11**	**26**

a WHL West Second All-Star Team (1992)

Claimed by **Florida** from **Quebec** in Expansion Draft, June 24, 1993.

LING, DAVID — MTL.

Right wing. Shoots right. 5'9", 185 lbs. Born, Halifax, N.S., January 9, 1975.
(Quebec's 9th choice, 179th overall, in 1993 Entry Draft).

			Regular Season					Playoffs				
Season	Club	Lea	GP	G	A	TP	PIM	GP	G	A	TP	PIM
1992-93	Kingston	OHL	64	17	46	63	275	16	3	12	15	*72
1993-94	Kingston	OHL	61	37	40	77	*254	6	4	2	6	16
1994-95abc	Kingston	OHL	62	*61	74	135	136	6	7	8	15	12
1995-96	Saint John	AHL	75	24	32	56	179	9	0	5	5	12
1996-97	Saint John	AHL	5	0	2	2	19	....	....	....	....	....
	Montreal	**NHL**	**2**	**0**	**0**	**0**	**0**	....	....	....	....	....
	Fredericton	AHL	48	22	36	58	229	....	....	....	....	....
	NHL Totals		**2**	**0**	**0**	**0**	**0**	....	....	....	....	....

a OHL First All-Star Team (1995)
b Canadian Major Junior First All-Star Team (1995)
c Canadian Junior Player of the Year (1995)

Traded to **Calgary** by **Colorado** with Colorado's ninth round choice (Steve Shirreffs) in 1995 Entry Draft for Calgary's ninth round choice (Chris George) in 1995 Entry Draft, July 7, 1995. Traded to **Montreal** by **Calgary** with Calgary's sixth round choice in 1998 Entry Draft for Scott Fraser, October 24, 1996.

LINTNER, RICHARD (LIHNT-nuhr) — PHO.

Defense. Shoots right. 6'3", 194 lbs. Born, Trencin, Czech., November 15, 1977.
(Phoenix's 4th choice, 119th overall, in 1996 Entry Draft).

			Regular Season					Playoffs				
Season	Club	Lea	GP	G	A	TP	PIM	GP	G	A	TP	PIM
1994-95	Dukla Trencin	Slo. Jr.	42	12	13	25	20	....	....	....	....	....
1995-96	Dukla Trencin	Slo. Jr.	30	15	17	32	210	....	....	....	....	....
	Dukla Trencin	Slovak	2	0	0	0	0	....	....	....	....	....
1996-97	Spisska	Slovak	35	2	1	3	....	....	....	....	....	....

LIPIANSKY, JAN (LIH-pyahn-skee) — PHI.

Left wing. Shoots left. 6'2", 187 lbs. Born, Bratislava, Czech., July 23, 1974.
(Philadelphia's 10th choice, 270th overall, in 1994 Entry Draft).

			Regular Season					Playoffs				
Season	Club	Lea	GP	G	A	TP	PIM	GP	G	A	TP	PIM
1993-94	Bratislava	Slovak	32	11	5	16	12	....	....	....	....	....
1994-95	Hershey	AHL	7	0	0	0	2	....	....	....	....	....
	Bratislava	Slovak	12	8	7	15	4	8	0	2	2	6
1995-96	Bratislava	Slovak	33	14	6	20	8	13	5	4	9	....
1996-97	Bratislava	Slovak	45	18	19	37	....	2	2	1	3	....

LIPUMA, CHRIS (lih-POO-muh)

Defense. Shoots left. 6', 183 lbs. Born, Bridgeview, IL, March 23, 1971.

			Regular Season					Playoffs				
Season	Club	Lea	GP	G	A	TP	PIM	GP	G	A	TP	PIM
1990-91	Kitchener	OHL	61	6	30	36	145	4	0	1	1	4
1991-92	Kitchener	OHL	61	13	59	72	115	14	4	9	13	34
1992-93	**Tampa Bay**	**NHL**	**15**	**0**	**5**	**5**	**34**	....	....	....	....	....
	Atlanta	IHL	66	4	14	18	379	9	1	1	2	35
1993-94	**Tampa Bay**	**NHL**	**27**	**0**	**4**	**4**	**77**	....	....	....	....	....
	Atlanta	IHL	42	2	10	12	254	11	1	1	2	28
1994-95	Atlanta	IHL	41	5	12	17	191	....	....	....	....	....
	Tampa Bay	**NHL**	**1**	**0**	**0**	**0**	**0**	....	....	....	....	....
	Nashville	ECHL	1	0	0	0	0	....	....	....	....	....
1995-96	**Tampa Bay**	**NHL**	**21**	**0**	**0**	**0**	**13**	....	....	....	....	....
	Atlanta	IHL	48	5	11	16	146	....	....	....	....	....
1996-97	**San Jose**	**NHL**	**8**	**0**	**0**	**0**	**22**	....	....	....	....	....
	Kentucky	AHL	48	6	17	23	93	4	0	3	3	6
	NHL Totals		**72**	**0**	**9**	**9**	**146**	....	....	....	....	....

Signed as a free agent by **Tampa Bay**, June 29, 1992. Signed as a free agent by **San Jose**, August 23, 1996. Claimed on waivers by **New Jersey** from **San Jose**, March 18, 1997.

LOACH, LONNIE (LOHCH)

Left wing. Shoots left. 5'10", 181 lbs. Born, New Liskeard, Ont., April 14, 1968.
(Chicago's 4th choice, 98th overall, in 1986 Entry Draft).

			Regular Season					Playoffs				
Season	Club	Lea	GP	G	A	TP	PIM	GP	G	A	TP	PIM
1985-86	Guelph	OHL	65	41	42	83	63	20	7	8	15	16
1986-87	Guelph	OHL	56	31	24	55	42	5	2	1	3	2
1987-88	Guelph	OHL	66	43	49	92	75	....	....	....	....	....
1988-89	Flint	IHL	41	22	26	48	30	....	....	....	....	....
	Saginaw	IHL	32	7	6	13	27	....	....	....	....	....
1989-90	Indianapolis	IHL	3	0	0	0	0	....	....	....	....	....
	Cdn. National	....	9	3	1	4	2	....	....	....	....	....
	Fort Wayne	IHL	54	15	33	48	40	5	4	2	6	15
1990-91ab	Fort Wayne	IHL	81	55	76	*131	45	19	5	11	16	13
1991-92	Adirondack	AHL	67	37	49	86	69	19	*13	4	17	10
1992-93	**Ottawa**	**NHL**	**3**	**0**	**0**	**0**	**0**	....	....	....	....	....
	Los Angeles	**NHL**	**50**	**10**	**13**	**23**	**27**	**1**	**0**	**0**	**0**	**0**
	Phoenix	IHL	4	2	3	5	10	....	....	....	....	....
1993-94	**Anaheim**	**NHL**	**3**	**0**	**0**	**0**	**2**	....	....	....	....	....
	San Diego	IHL	74	42	49	91	65	9	4	10	14	6
1994-95	San Diego	IHL	13	3	10	13	21	....	....	....	....	....
	Detroit	IHL	64	32	43	75	45	3	2	1	3	2
1995-96	Detroit	IHL	79	35	51	86	75	11	1	5	6	8
1996-97	San Antonio	IHL	70	24	37	61	45	9	1	3	4	10
	NHL Totals		**56**	**10**	**13**	**23**	**29**	**1**	**0**	**0**	**0**	**0**

a IHL Second All-Star Team (1991)
b Won Leo P. Lamoureux Memorial Trophy (Leading Scorer - IHL) (1991)

Signed as a free agent by **Detroit**, June 7, 1991. Claimed by **Ottawa** from **Detroit** in Expansion Draft, June 18, 1992. Claimed on waivers by **Los Angeles** from **Ottawa**, October 21, 1992. Claimed by **Anaheim** from **Los Angeles** in Expansion Draft, June 24, 1993.

LOEWEN, DARCY (LOH-wihn)

Left wing. Shoots left. 5'10", 185 lbs. Born, Calgary, Alta., February 26, 1969.
(Buffalo's 2nd choice, 55th overall, in 1988 Entry Draft).

			Regular Season					Playoffs				
Season	Club	Lea	GP	G	A	TP	PIM	GP	G	A	TP	PIM
1986-87	Spokane	WHL	68	15	25	40	129	5	0	0	0	16
1987-88	Spokane	WHL	72	30	44	74	231	15	7	5	12	54
1988-89	Spokane	WHL	60	31	27	58	194	....	....	....	....	....
	Cdn. National	....	2	0	0	0	0	....	....	....	....	....
1989-90	**Buffalo**	**NHL**	**4**	**0**	**0**	**0**	**4**	....	....	....	....	....
	Rochester	AHL	50	7	11	18	193	5	1	0	1	6
1990-91	**Buffalo**	**NHL**	**6**	**0**	**0**	**0**	**8**	....	....	....	....	....
	Rochester	AHL	71	13	15	28	130	15	1	5	6	14
1991-92	**Buffalo**	**NHL**	**2**	**0**	**0**	**0**	**2**	....	....	....	....	....
	Rochester	AHL	73	11	20	31	193	4	0	1	1	8
1992-93	**Ottawa**	**NHL**	**79**	**4**	**5**	**9**	**145**	....	....	....	....	....
1993-94	**Ottawa**	**NHL**	**44**	**0**	**3**	**3**	**52**	....	....	....	....	....
1994-95	Las Vegas	IHL	64	9	21	30	183	7	1	1	2	16
1995-96	Las Vegas	IHL	72	14	23	37	198	....	....	....	....	....
1996-97	Las Vegas	IHL	76	14	19	33	177	3	0	0	0	0
	NHL Totals		**135**	**4**	**8**	**12**	**211**	....	....	....	....	....

Claimed by **Ottawa** from **Buffalo** in Expansion Draft, June 18, 1992.

LONEY, BRIAN (LOH-nee)

Right wing. Shoots right. 6'2", 200 lbs. Born, Winnipeg, Man., August 9, 1972.
(Vancouver's 6th choice, 110th overall, in 1992 Entry Draft).

			Regular Season					Playoffs				
Season	Club	Lea	GP	G	A	TP	PIM	GP	G	A	TP	PIM
1991-92	Ohio State	CCHA	37	21	34	55	109	....	....	....	....	....
1992-93	Red Deer	WHL	66	39	36	75	147	4	1	1	2	19
	Cdn. National	....	1	0	1	1	0	....	....	....	....	....
	Hamilton	AHL	3	0	2	2	0	....	....	....	....	....
1993-94	Hamilton	AHL	67	18	16	34	76	4	0	0	0	8
1994-95	Syracuse	AHL	67	23	17	40	98	....	....	....	....	....
1995-96	**Vancouver**	**NHL**	**12**	**2**	**3**	**5**	**6**	....	....	....	....	....
	Syracuse	AHL	48	34	17	51	157	14	3	8	11	20
1996-97	Syracuse	AHL	76	19	39	58	123	3	0	0	0	0
	NHL Totals		**12**	**2**	**3**	**5**	**6**	....	....	....	....	....

LONG, ANDREW FLA.

Right wing. Shoots right. 6'2", 181 lbs. Born, Toronto, Ont., August 10, 1978.
(Florida's 5th choice, 129th overall, in 1996 Entry Draft).

			Regular Season					Playoffs				
Season	Club	Lea	GP	G	A	TP	PIM	GP	G	A	TP	PIM
1994-95	Guelph	OHL	36	1	6	7	9	....	....	....	....	....
1995-96	Guelph	OHL	48	8	10	18	16	10	0	1	1	4
1996-97	Guelph	OHL	42	10	36	46	30	13	2	10	12	6

LONGO, CHRIS

Right wing. Shoots right. 5'11", 187 lbs. Born, Belleville, Ont., January 5, 1972.
(Washington's 3rd choice, 51st overall, in 1990 Entry Draft).

			Regular Season					Playoffs				
Season	Club	Lea	GP	G	A	TP	PIM	GP	G	A	TP	PIM
1989-90	Peterborough	OHL	66	33	41	74	48	11	2	3	5	14
1990-91	Peterborough	OHL	64	30	38	68	68	4	1	0	1	0
1991-92	Peterborough	OHL	25	5	14	19	16	10	5	6	11	16
1992-93	Baltimore	AHL	74	7	18	25	52	7	0	1	1	0
1993-94	Portland	AHL	69	6	19	25	69	17	2	4	6	11
1994-95	Portland	AHL	57	8	13	21	33	2	0	0	0	0
1995-96	Asiago	Italy	30	22	28	50	60	....	....	....	....	....
1996-97	Springfield	AHL	71	9	22	31	24	17	1	4	5	4

Signed as a free agent by **Hartford**, October 1, 1996.

LOVEN, FREDERIK (LUH-vehn) PHO.

Center. Shoots left. 6'2", 187 lbs. Born, Stockholm, Sweden, March 14, 1977.
(Winnipeg's 10th choice, 189th overall, in 1995 Entry Draft).

			Regular Season					Playoffs				
Season	Club	Lea	GP	G	A	TP	PIM	GP	G	A	TP	PIM
1994-94	Djurgarden	Swe. Jr.	29	6	10	16	14	....	....	....	....	....
1995-96	Djurgarden	Swe.	4	0	0	0	0	4	0	0	0	0
1996-97	Djurgarden	Swe.	7	0	0	0	0	....	....	....	....	....
	Djurgarden	Swe. Jr.	4	2	2	4	8	....	....	....	....	....
	Arlanda	Swe. 2	5	0	3	3	4	....	....	....	....	....

LOW, REED (LOH) ST.L.

Right wing. Shoots right. 6'4", 220 lbs. Born, Moose Jaw, Sask., June 21, 1976.
(St. Louis' 7th choice, 177th overall, in 1996 Entry Draft).

			Regular Season					Playoffs				
Season	Club	Lea	GP	G	A	TP	PIM	GP	G	A	TP	PIM
1995-96	Moose Jaw	WHL	61	12	7	19	221	....	....	....	....	....
1996-97	Moose Jaw	WHL	62	16	11	27	228	12	2	1	3	50

LOWE, KEVIN (LOH) EDM.

Defense. Shoots left. 6'2", 200 lbs. Born, Lachute, Que., April 15, 1959.
(Edmonton's 1st choice, 21st overall, in 1979 Entry Draft).

			Regular Season					Playoffs				
Season	Club	Lea	GP	G	A	TP	PIM	GP	G	A	TP	PIM
1977-78	Quebec	QJHL	64	13	52	65	86	4	1	2	3	6
1978-79a	Quebec	QJHL	68	26	60	86	120	6	1	7	8	36
1979-80	**Edmonton**	**NHL**	**64**	**2**	**19**	**21**	**70**	**3**	**0**	**1**	**1**	**0**
1980-81	**Edmonton**	**NHL**	**79**	**10**	**24**	**34**	**94**	**9**	**0**	**2**	**2**	**11**
1981-82	**Edmonton**	**NHL**	**80**	**9**	**31**	**40**	**63**	**5**	**0**	**3**	**3**	**0**
1982-83	**Edmonton**	**NHL**	**80**	**6**	**34**	**40**	**43**	**16**	**1**	**8**	**9**	**10**
1983-84	**Edmonton**	**NHL**	**80**	**4**	**42**	**46**	**59**	**19**	**3**	**7**	**10**	**16** ♦
1984-85	**Edmonton**	**NHL**	**80**	**4**	**21**	**25**	**104**	**16**	**0**	**5**	**5**	**8** ♦
1985-86	**Edmonton**	**NHL**	**74**	**2**	**16**	**18**	**90**	**10**	**1**	**3**	**4**	**15**
1986-87	**Edmonton**	**NHL**	**77**	**8**	**29**	**37**	**94**	**21**	**2**	**4**	**6**	**22** ♦
1987-88	**Edmonton**	**NHL**	**70**	**9**	**15**	**24**	**89**	**19**	**0**	**2**	**2**	**26** ♦
1988-89	**Edmonton**	**NHL**	**76**	**7**	**18**	**25**	**98**	**7**	**1**	**2**	**3**	**4**
1989-90bc	**Edmonton**	**NHL**	**78**	**7**	**26**	**33**	**140**	**20**	**0**	**2**	**2**	**10** ♦
1990-91	**Edmonton**	**NHL**	**73**	**3**	**13**	**16**	**113**	**14**	**1**	**1**	**2**	**14**
1991-92	**Edmonton**	**NHL**	**55**	**2**	**8**	**10**	**107**	**11**	**0**	**3**	**3**	**16**
1992-93	**NY Rangers**	**NHL**	**49**	**3**	**12**	**15**	**58**	....	....	....	....	....
1993-94	**NY Rangers**	**NHL**	**71**	**5**	**14**	**19**	**70**	**22**	**1**	**0**	**1**	**20** ♦
1994-95	**NY Rangers**	**NHL**	**44**	**1**	**7**	**8**	**58**	**10**	**0**	**1**	**1**	**12**
1995-96	**NY Rangers**	**NHL**	**53**	**1**	**5**	**6**	**76**	**10**	**0**	**4**	**4**	**4**
1996-97	**Edmonton**	**NHL**	**64**	**1**	**13**	**14**	**50**	**1**	**0**	**0**	**0**	**0**
	NHL Totals		**1247**	**84**	**347**	**431**	**1476**	**213**	**10**	**48**	**58**	**188**

a QMJHL Second All-Star Team (1979)
b Won Bud Man of the Year Award (1990)
c Won King Clancy Memorial Trophy (1990)

Played in NHL All-Star Game (1984-86, 1988-90, 1993)

Traded to **NY Rangers** by **Edmonton** for Roman Oksiuta and NY Rangers' third round choice (Alexander Kerch) in 1993 Entry Draft, December 11, 1992. Signed as a free agent by **Edmonton**, September 28, 1996.

LOWRY, DAVE FLA.

Left wing. Shoots left. 6'1", 200 lbs. Born, Sudbury, Ont., February 14, 1965.
(Vancouver's 6th choice, 110th overall, in 1983 Entry Draft).

			Regular Season					Playoffs				
Season	Club	Lea	GP	G	A	TP	PIM	GP	G	A	TP	PIM
1982-83	London	OHL	42	11	16	27	48	3	0	0	0	14
1983-84	London	OHL	66	29	47	76	125	8	6	6	12	41
1984-85a	London	OHL	61	60	60	120	94	8	6	5	11	10
1985-86	**Vancouver**	**NHL**	**73**	**10**	**8**	**18**	**143**	**3**	**0**	**0**	**0**	**0**
1986-87	**Vancouver**	**NHL**	**70**	**8**	**10**	**18**	**176**	....	....	....	....	....
1987-88	**Vancouver**	**NHL**	**22**	**1**	**3**	**4**	**38**	....	....	....	....	....
	Fredericton	AHL	46	18	27	45	59	14	7	3	10	72
1988-89	**St. Louis**	**NHL**	**21**	**3**	**3**	**6**	**11**	**10**	**0**	**5**	**5**	**4**
	Peoria	IHL	58	31	35	66	45	....	....	....	....	....
1989-90	**St. Louis**	**NHL**	**78**	**19**	**6**	**25**	**75**	**12**	**2**	**1**	**3**	**39**
1990-91	**St. Louis**	**NHL**	**79**	**19**	**21**	**40**	**168**	**13**	**1**	**4**	**5**	**35**
1991-92	**St. Louis**	**NHL**	**75**	**7**	**13**	**20**	**77**	**6**	**0**	**1**	**1**	**20**
1992-93	**St. Louis**	**NHL**	**58**	**5**	**8**	**13**	**101**	**11**	**2**	**0**	**2**	**14**
1993-94	**Florida**	**NHL**	**80**	**15**	**22**	**37**	**64**	....	....	....	....	....
1994-95	**Florida**	**NHL**	**45**	**10**	**10**	**20**	**25**	....	....	....	....	....
1995-96	**Florida**	**NHL**	**63**	**10**	**14**	**24**	**36**	**22**	**10**	**7**	**17**	**39**
1996-97	**Florida**	**NHL**	**77**	**15**	**14**	**29**	**51**	**5**	**0**	**0**	**0**	**0**
	NHL Totals		**741**	**122**	**132**	**254**	**965**	**82**	**15**	**18**	**33**	**151**

a OHL First All-Star Team (1985)

Traded to **St. Louis** by **Vancouver** for Ernie Vargas, September 29, 1988. Claimed by **Florida** from **St. Louis** in Expansion Draft, June 24, 1993.

LUCHINKIN, SERGEI (loo-CHIHN-kihn) DAL.

Right wing. Shoots left. 5'11", 172 lbs. Born, Dmitrov, USSR, October 16, 1976.
(Dallas' 9th choice, 202nd overall, in 1995 Entry Draft).

			Regular Season					Playoffs				
Season	Club	Lea	GP	G	A	TP	PIM	GP	G	A	TP	PIM
1994-95	Moscow D'amo	CIS	6	1	0	1	4	....	....	....	....	....
1995-96	Moscow D'amo	CIS	21	6	2	8	14	10	0	1	1	6
1996-97	Moscow D'amo	Rus.	18	1	5	6	4	....	....	....	....	....

LUDWIG, CRAIG
9LUHD-wihg) **DAL.**

Defense. Shoots left. 6'3", 220 lbs. Born, Rhinelander, WI, March 15, 1961.
(Montreal's 5th choice, 61st overall, in 1980 Entry Draft).

			Regular Season					Playoffs				
Season	Club	Lea	GP	G	A	TP	PIM	GP	G	A	TP	PIM
1979-80	North Dakota	WCHA	33	1	8	9	32	....	....	....	....	....
1980-81	North Dakota	WCHA	34	4	8	12	48	....	....	....	....	....
1981-82	North Dakota	WCHA	37	4	17	21	42	....	....	....	....	....
1982-83	**Montreal**	**NHL**	**80**	**0**	**25**	**25**	**59**	**3**	**0**	**0**	**0**	**2**
1983-84	**Montreal**	**NHL**	**80**	**7**	**18**	**25**	**52**	**15**	**0**	**3**	**3**	**23**
1984-85	**Montreal**	**NHL**	**72**	**5**	**14**	**19**	**90**	**12**	**0**	**2**	**2**	**6**
1985-86	**Montreal**	**NHL**	**69**	**2**	**4**	**6**	**63**	**20**	**0**	**1**	**1**	**48 ♦**
1986-87	**Montreal**	**NHL**	**75**	**4**	**12**	**16**	**105**	**17**	**2**	**3**	**5**	**30**
1987-88	**Montreal**	**NHL**	**74**	**4**	**10**	**14**	**69**	**11**	**1**	**1**	**2**	**6**
1988-89	**Montreal**	**NHL**	**74**	**3**	**13**	**16**	**73**	**21**	**0**	**2**	**2**	**24**
1989-90	**Montreal**	**NHL**	**73**	**1**	**15**	**16**	**108**	**11**	**0**	**1**	**1**	**16**
1990-91	**NY Islanders**	**NHL**	**75**	**1**	**8**	**9**	**77**	....	....	....	....	....
1991-92	**Minnesota**	**NHL**	**73**	**2**	**9**	**11**	**54**	**7**	**0**	**1**	**1**	**19**
1992-93	**Minnesota**	**NHL**	**78**	**1**	**10**	**11**	**153**	....	....	....	....	....
1993-94	**Dallas**	**NHL**	**84**	**1**	**13**	**14**	**123**	**9**	**0**	**3**	**3**	**8**
1994-95	**Dallas**	**NHL**	**47**	**2**	**7**	**9**	**61**	**4**	**0**	**1**	**1**	**2**
1995-96	**Dallas**	**NHL**	**65**	**1**	**2**	**3**	**70**	....	....	....	....	....
1996-97	**Dallas**	**NHL**	**77**	**2**	**11**	**13**	**62**	**7**	**0**	**2**	**2**	**18**
	NHL Totals		**1096**	**36**	**171**	**207**	**1219**	**137**	**3**	**20**	**23**	**202**

Traded to **NY Islanders** by **Montreal** for Gerald Diduck, September 4, 1990. Traded to **Minnesota** by **NY Islanders** for Tom Kurvers, June 22, 1991.

LUHNING, WARREN
NYI

Right wing. Shoots right. 6'2", 185 lbs. Born, Edmonton, Alta., July 3, 1975.
(NY Islanders' 4th choice, 92nd overall, in 1993 Entry Draft).

			Regular Season					Playoffs				
Season	Club	Lea	GP	G	A	TP	PIM	GP	G	A	TP	PIM
1993-94	U. of Michigan	CCHA	38	13	6	19	83	....	....	....	....	....
1994-95	U. of Michigan	CCHA	36	17	23	40	80	....	....	....	....	....
1995-96	U. of Michigan	CCHA	40	20	32	52	123	....	....	....	....	....
1996-97	U. of Michigan	CCHA	43	22	23	45	106	....	....	....	....	....

LUKOWICH, BRAD
(loo-KUH-wihch) **DAL.**

Defense. Shoots left. 6'1", 170 lbs. Born, Cranbrook, B.C., August 12, 1976.
(NY Islanders' 4th choice, 90th overall, in 1994 Entry Draft).

			Regular Season					Playoffs				
Season	Club	Lea	GP	G	A	TP	PIM	GP	G	A	TP	PIM
1992-93	Kamloops	WHL	1	0	0	0	0	....	....	....	....	....
1993-94	Kamloops	WHL	42	5	11	16	166	16	0	1	1	35
1994-95	Kamloops	WHL	63	10	35	45	125	18	0	7	7	21
1995-96	Kamloops	WHL	65	14	55	69	114	13	2	10	12	29
1996-97	Michigan	IHL	69	2	6	8	77	4	0	1	1	2

Traded to **Dallas** by **NY Islanders** for Dallas' third round choice (Robert Schnabel) in 1997 Entry Draft, June 1, 1996.

LUMME, JYRKI
(LOO-mee, YUHR-kee) **VAN.**

Defense. Shoots left. 6'1", 205 lbs. Born, Tampere, Finland, July 16, 1966.
(Montreal's 3rd choice, 57th overall, in 1986 Entry Draft).

			Regular Season					Playoffs				
Season	Club	Lea	GP	G	A	TP	PIM	GP	G	A	TP	PIM
1984-85	KooVee	Fin. 3	30	6	4	10	44	....	....	....	....	....
1985-86	Ilves	Fin.	31	1	4	5	4	....	....	....	....	....
1986-87	Ilves	Fin.	43	12	12	24	52	4	0	1	1	2
1987-88	Ilves	Fin.	43	8	22	30	75	....	....	....	....	....
1988-89	**Montreal**	**NHL**	**21**	**1**	**3**	**4**	**10**	....	....	....	....	....
	Sherbrooke	AHL	26	4	11	15	10	6	1	3	4	4
1989-90	**Montreal**	**NHL**	**54**	**1**	**19**	**20**	**41**	....	....	....	....	....
	Vancouver	**NHL**	**11**	**3**	**7**	**10**	**8**	....	....	....	....	....
1990-91	**Vancouver**	**NHL**	**80**	**5**	**27**	**32**	**59**	**6**	**2**	**3**	**5**	**0**
1991-92	**Vancouver**	**NHL**	**75**	**12**	**32**	**44**	**65**	**13**	**2**	**3**	**5**	**4**
1992-93	**Vancouver**	**NHL**	**74**	**8**	**36**	**44**	**55**	**12**	**0**	**5**	**5**	**6**
1993-94	**Vancouver**	**NHL**	**83**	**13**	**42**	**55**	**50**	**24**	**2**	**11**	**13**	**16**
1994-95	Ilves	Fin.	12	4	4	8	24	....	....	....	....	....
	Vancouver	**NHL**	**36**	**5**	**12**	**17**	**26**	**11**	**2**	**6**	**8**	**8**
1995-96	**Vancouver**	**NHL**	**80**	**17**	**37**	**54**	**50**	**6**	**1**	**3**	**4**	**2**
1996-97	**Vancouver**	**NHL**	**66**	**11**	**24**	**35**	**32**	....	....	....	....	....
	NHL Totals		**580**	**76**	**239**	**315**	**396**	**72**	**9**	**31**	**40**	**36**

Traded to **Vancouver** by **Montreal** for St. Louis' second round choice (previously acquired by Vancouver — Montreal selected Craig Darby) in 1991 Entry Draft, March 6, 1990.

LUNDSTROM, PER-ANTON
PHO.

Defense. Shoots left. 6'2", 185 lbs. Born, Umea, Sweden, September 29, 1977.
(Phoenix's 3rd choice, 62nd overall, in 1996 Entry Draft).

			Regular Season					Playoffs				
Season	Club	Lea	GP	G	A	TP	PIM	GP	G	A	TP	PIM
1995-96	MoDo	Swe. Jr.	25	3	3	6	28	2	1	0	1	4
	MoDo	Swe.	19	1	1	2	29	4	0	0	0	2
1996-97	MoDo	Swe.	35	0	0	0	42	....	....	....	....	....

LUONGO, CHRIS
(loo-WAHN-goh)

Defense. Shoots right. 5'10", 206 lbs. Born, Detroit, MI, March 17, 1967.
(Detroit's 5th choice, 92nd overall, in 1985 Entry Draft).

			Regular Season					Playoffs				
Season	Club	Lea	GP	G	A	TP	PIM	GP	G	A	TP	PIM
1985-86	Michigan State	CCHA	38	1	5	6	29	....	....	....	....	....
1986-87a	Michigan State	CCHA	27	4	16	20	38	....	....	....	....	....
1987-88	Michigan State	CCHA	45	3	15	18	49	....	....	....	....	....
1988-89b	Michigan State	CCHA	47	4	21	25	42	....	....	....	....	....
1989-90	Adirondack	AHL	53	9	14	23	37	3	0	0	0	0
	Phoenix	IHL	23	5	9	14	41	....	....	....	....	....
1990-91	**Detroit**	**NHL**	**4**	**0**	**1**	**1**	**4**	....	....	....	....	....
	Adirondack	AHL	76	14	25	39	71	2	0	0	0	7
1991-92	Adirondack	AHL	80	6	20	26	60	19	3	5	8	10
1992-93	**Ottawa**	**NHL**	**76**	**3**	**9**	**12**	**68**	....	....	....	....	....
	New Haven	AHL	7	0	2	2	2	....	....	....	....	....
1993-94	**NY Islanders**	**NHL**	**17**	**1**	**3**	**4**	**13**	....	....	....	....	....
	Salt Lake	IHL	51	9	31	40	54	....	....	....	....	....
1994-95	Denver	IHL	41	1	14	15	26	....	....	....	....	....
	NY Islanders	**NHL**	**47**	**1**	**3**	**4**	**36**	....	....	....	....	....
1995-96	**NY Islanders**	**NHL**	**74**	**3**	**7**	**10**	**55**	....	....	....	....	....
1996-97	Milwaukee	IHL	81	10	35	45	69	2	0	0	0	0
	NHL Totals		**218**	**8**	**23**	**31**	**176**	....	....	....	....	....

a Named to NCAA All-Tournament Team (1987)
b CCHA Second All-Star Team (1989)

Signed as a free agent by **Ottawa**, September 9, 1992. Traded to **NY Islanders** by **Ottawa** for Jeff Finley, June 30, 1993.

LYASHENKO, ROMAN
(LIGH-a-SHEHN-koh) **DAL.**

Center. Shoots right. 6', 174 lbs. Born, Murmansk, Russia, May 2, 1979.
(Dallas' 2nd choice, 52nd overall, in 1997 Entry Draft).

			Regular Season					Playoffs				
Season	Club	Lea	GP	G	A	TP	PIM	GP	G	A	TP	PIM
1995-96	Yaroslavl 2	CIS 2	60	7	10	17	12	....	....	....	....	....
1996-97	Yaroslavl	Rus.	42	5	7	12	16	9	3	0	3	6
	Yaroslavl 2	Rus. 3	2	1	1	2	8	....	....	....	....	....

LYDMAN, TONI
(LEED-man) **CGY.**

Defense. Shoots left. 6'1", 183 lbs. Born, Lahti, Finland, September 25, 1977.
(Calgary's 5th choice, 89th overall, in 1996 Entry Draft).

			Regular Season					Playoffs				
Season	Club	Lea	GP	G	A	TP	PIM	GP	G	A	TP	PIM
1995-96	Reipas	Fin. Jr.	9	2	2	4	6	....	....	....	....	....
	Reipas	Fin. 2	39	5	2	7	30	3	0	1	1	0
1996-97	Tappara	Fin.	49	1	2	3	65	3	0	0	0	6

MacDONALD, CRAIG
CAR.

Center. Shoots left. 6'2", 180 lbs. Born, Antigonish, N.S., April 7, 1977.
(Hartford's 3rd choice, 88th overall, in 1996 Entry Draft).

			Regular Season					Playoffs				
Season	Club	Lea	GP	G	A	TP	PIM	GP	G	A	TP	PIM
1995-96	Harvard	ECAC	34	7	10	17	10	....	....	....	....	....
1996-97	Harvard	ECAC	32	6	10	16	20	....	....	....	....	....

MacDONALD, DOUG

Left wing. Shoots left. 6', 192 lbs. Born, Assiniboia, Sask., February 8, 1969.
(Buffalo's 3rd choice, 77th overall, in 1989 Entry Draft).

			Regular Season					Playoffs				
Season	Club	Lea	GP	G	A	TP	PIM	GP	G	A	TP	PIM
1988-89	U. Wisconsin	WCHA	44	23	25	48	50	....	....	....	....	....
1989-90	U. Wisconsin	WCHA	44	16	35	51	52	....	....	....	....	....
1990-91	U. Wisconsin	WCHA	31	20	26	46	50	....	....	....	....	....
1991-92	U. Wisconsin	WCHA	29	14	25	39	58	....	....	....	....	....
1992-93	**Buffalo**	**NHL**	**5**	**1**	**0**	**1**	**2**	....	....	....	....	....
	Rochester	AHL	64	25	33	58	58	7	0	2	2	4
1993-94	**Buffalo**	**NHL**	**4**	**0**	**0**	**0**	**0**	....	....	....	....	....
	Rochester	AHL	63	25	19	44	46	4	1	1	2	8
1994-95	Rochester	AHL	58	21	25	46	73	5	0	1	1	0
	Buffalo	**NHL**	**2**	**0**	**0**	**0**	**0**	....	....	....	....	....
1995-96	Cincinnati	IHL	71	19	40	59	66	15	1	3	4	14
1996-97	Cincinnati	IHL	65	20	34	54	36	3	0	0	0	0
	NHL Totals		**11**	**1**	**0**	**1**	**2**	....	....	....	....	....

MacDONALD, JASON

Right wing. Shoots right. 6', 195 lbs. Born, Charlottetown, P.E.I., April 1, 1974.
(Detroit's 5th choice, 142nd overall, in 1992 Entry Draft).

			Regular Season					Playoffs				
Season	Club	Lea	GP	G	A	TP	PIM	GP	G	A	TP	PIM
1990-91	North Bay	OHL	57	12	15	27	126	10	3	3	6	15
1991-92	North Bay	OHL	17	5	8	13	50	....	....	....	....	....
	Owen Sound	OHL	42	17	19	36	129	5	0	3	3	16
1992-93	Owen Sound	OHL	56	46	43	89	197	8	6	5	11	28
1993-94a	Owen Sound	OHL	66	55	61	116	177	9	7	11	18	36
	Adirondack	AHL	....	....	....	....	....	1	0	0	0	0
1994-95	Adirondack	AHL	68	14	21	35	238	4	0	0	0	2
1995-96	Adirondack	AHL	43	9	13	22	99	....	....	....	....	....
	Toledo	ECHL	9	5	5	10	26	9	3	1	4	39
1996-97	Adirondack	AHL	1	0	0	0	2	....	....	....	....	....
	Fredericton	AHL	63	22	25	47	189	....	....	....	....	....

a OHL Second All-Star Team (1994)

Traded to **Montreal** by **Detroit** for cash, November 8, 1996.

MacINNIS, AL
ST.L.

Defense. Shoots right. 6'2", 196 lbs. Born, Inverness, N.S., July 11, 1963.
(Calgary's 1st choice, 15th overall, in 1981 Entry Draft).

			Regular Season					Playoffs				
Season	Club	Lea	GP	G	A	TP	PIM	GP	G	A	TP	PIM
1980-81	Kitchener	OHA	47	11	28	39	59	18	4	12	16	20
1981-82	**Calgary**	**NHL**	**2**	**0**	**0**	**0**	**0**	....	....	....	....	....
a	Kitchener	OHL	59	25	50	75	145	15	5	10	15	44
1982-83	**Calgary**	**NHL**	**14**	**1**	**3**	**4**	**9**	....	....	....	....	....
a	Kitchener	OHL	51	38	46	84	67	8	3	8	11	9
1983-84	**Calgary**	**NHL**	**51**	**11**	**34**	**45**	**42**	**11**	**2**	**12**	**14**	**13**
	Colorado	CHL	19	5	14	19	22	....	....	....	....	....
1984-85	**Calgary**	**NHL**	**67**	**14**	**52**	**66**	**75**	**4**	**1**	**2**	**3**	**8**
1985-86	**Calgary**	**NHL**	**77**	**11**	**57**	**68**	**76**	**21**	**4**	***15**	**19**	**30**
1986-87b	**Calgary**	**NHL**	**79**	**20**	**56**	**76**	**97**	**4**	**1**	**0**	**1**	**0**
1987-88	**Calgary**	**NHL**	**80**	**25**	**58**	**83**	**114**	**7**	**3**	**6**	**9**	**18**
1988-89bc	**Calgary**	**NHL**	**79**	**16**	**58**	**74**	**126**	**22**	**7**	***24**	***31**	**46 ♦**
1989-90d	**Calgary**	**NHL**	**79**	**28**	**62**	**90**	**82**	**6**	**2**	**3**	**5**	**8**
1990-91d	**Calgary**	**NHL**	**78**	**28**	**75**	**103**	**90**	**7**	**2**	**3**	**5**	**8**
1991-92	**Calgary**	**NHL**	**72**	**20**	**57**	**77**	**83**	....	....	....	....	....
1992-93	**Calgary**	**NHL**	**50**	**11**	**43**	**54**	**61**	**6**	**1**	**6**	**7**	**10**
1993-94b	**Calgary**	**NHL**	**75**	**28**	**54**	**82**	**95**	**7**	**2**	**6**	**8**	**12**
1994-95	**St. Louis**	**NHL**	**32**	**8**	**20**	**28**	**43**	**7**	**1**	**5**	**6**	**10**
1995-96	**St. Louis**	**NHL**	**82**	**17**	**44**	**61**	**88**	**13**	**3**	**4**	**7**	**20**
1996-97	**St. Louis**	**NHL**	**72**	**13**	**30**	**43**	**65**	**6**	**1**	**2**	**3**	**4**
	NHL Totals		**989**	**251**	**703**	**954**	**1146**	**121**	**30**	**88**	**118**	**187**

a OHL First All-Star Team (1982, 1983)
b NHL Second All-Star Team (1987, 1989, 1994)
c Won Conn Smythe Trophy (1989)
d NHL First All-Star Team (1990, 1991)

Played in NHL All-Star Game (1985, 1988, 1990-92, 1994, 1996, 1997)

Traded to **St. Louis** by **Calgary** with Calgary's fourth round choice (Didier Tremblay) in 1997 Entry Draft for Phil Housley, St. Louis' second round choice (Steve Begin) in 1996 Entry Draft and second round choice (John Tripp) in 1997 Entry Draft, July 4, 1994.

MacISAAC, DAVE
PHI.

Defense. Shoots left. 6'2", 225 lbs. Born, Arlington, MA, April 23, 1972.

			Regular Season					Playoffs				
Season	Club	Lea	GP	G	A	TP	PIM	GP	G	A	TP	PIM
1992-93	Maine	H.E.	35	5	32	37	14	....	....	....	....	....
1993-94	Maine	H.E.	31	4	20	24	22	....	....	....	....	....
1994-95	Maine	H.E.	44	5	13	18	44	....	....	....	....	....
	Milwaukee	IHL	2	0	0	0	5	9	0	2	2	2
1995-96	Milwaukee	IHL	71	7	16	23	165	....	....	....	....	....
1996-97	Philadelphia	AHL	61	3	15	18	187	10	0	1	1	31

Signed as a free agent by **Philadelphia**, July 30, 1996.

MACIVER, NORM (mac-IGH-ver) PHO.

Defense. Shoots left. 5'11", 180 lbs. Born, Thunder Bay, Ont., September 8, 1964.

			Regular Season					Playoffs				
Season	Club	Lea	GP	G	A	TP	PIM	GP	G	A	TP	PIM
1982-83	Minn.-Duluth	WCHA	45	1	26	27	40	6	0	2	2	2
1983-84a	Minn.-Duluth	WCHA	31	13	28	41	28	8	1	10	11	8
1984-85bc	Minn.-Duluth	WCHA	47	14	47	61	63	10	3	3	6	6
1985-86bc	Minn.-Duluth	WCHA	42	11	51	62	36	4	2	3	5	2
1986-87	**NY Rangers**	**NHL**	**3**	**0**	**1**	**1**	**0**	....	....	....	....	....
	New Haven	AHL	71	6	30	36	73	7	0	0	0	9
1987-88	**NY Rangers**	**NHL**	**37**	**9**	**15**	**24**	**14**	....	....	....	....	....
	Colorado	IHL	27	6	20	26	22	....	....	....	....	....
1988-89	**NY Rangers**	**NHL**	**26**	**0**	**10**	**10**	**14**	....	....	....	....	....
	Hartford	**NHL**	**37**	**1**	**22**	**23**	**24**	**1**	**0**	**0**	**0**	**2**
1989-90	Binghamton	AHL	2	0	0	0	0	....	....	....	....	....
	Edmonton	**NHL**	**1**	**0**	**0**	**0**	**0**	....	....	....	....	....
	Cape Breton	AHL	68	13	37	50	55	6	0	7	7	10
1990-91	**Edmonton**	**NHL**	**21**	**2**	**5**	**7**	**14**	**18**	**0**	**4**	**4**	**8**
de	Cape Breton	AHL	56	13	46	59	60	....	....	....	....	....
1991-92	**Edmonton**	**NHL**	**57**	**6**	**34**	**40**	**38**	**13**	**1**	**2**	**3**	**10**
1992-93	**Ottawa**	**NHL**	**80**	**17**	**46**	**63**	**84**	....	....	....	....	....
1993-94	**Ottawa**	**NHL**	**53**	**3**	**20**	**23**	**26**	....	....	....	....	....
1994-95	**Ottawa**	**NHL**	**28**	**4**	**7**	**11**	**10**	....	....	....	....	....
	Pittsburgh	**NHL**	**13**	**0**	**9**	**9**	**6**	**12**	**1**	**4**	**5**	**8**
1995-96	**Pittsburgh**	**NHL**	**32**	**2**	**21**	**23**	**32**	....	....	....	....	....
	Winnipeg	**NHL**	**39**	**5**	**25**	**30**	**26**	**6**	**1**	**0**	**1**	**2**
1996-97	**Phoenix**	**NHL**	**32**	**4**	**9**	**13**	**24**	....	....	....	....	....
	NHL Totals		**459**	**53**	**224**	**277**	**312**	**50**	**3**	**10**	**13**	**30**

a WCHA Second All-Star Team (1984)
b WCHA First All-Star Team (1985, 1986)
c NCAA West First All-American Team (1985, 1986)
d AHL First All-Star Team (1991)
e Won Eddie Shore Plaque (Top Defenseman - AHL) (1991)

Signed as a free agent by **NY Rangers**, September 8, 1986. Traded to **Hartford** by **NY Rangers** with Brian Lawton and Don Maloney for Carey Wilson and Hartford's fifth round choice (Lubos Rob) in 1990 Entry Draft, December 26, 1988. Traded to **Edmonton** by **Hartford** for Jim Ennis, October 10, 1989. Claimed by **Ottawa** from **Edmonton** in NHL Waiver Draft, October 4, 1992. Traded to **Pittsburgh** by **Ottawa** with Troy Murray for Martin Straka, April 7, 1995. Traded to **Winnipeg** by **Pittsburgh** for Neil Wilkinson, December 28, 1995.

MACKINNON, STEPHEN OTT.

Left wing. Shoots left. 6'4", 200 lbs. Born, Lowell, MA, August 20, 1976.
(Ottawa's 9th choice, 237th overall, in 1994 Entry Draft).

			Regular Season					Playoffs				
Season	Club	Lea	GP	G	A	TP	PIM	GP	G	A	TP	PIM
1995-96	Massachusetts	H.E.	18	1	0	1	61	....	....	....	....	....
1996-97	Massachusetts	H.E.	34	14	12	26	52	....	....	....	....	....

MacLEAN, DONALD L.A.

Center. Shoots left. 6'2", 174 lbs. Born, Sydney, N.S., January 14, 1977.
(Los Angeles' 2nd choice, 33rd overall, in 1995 Entry Draft).

			Regular Season					Playoffs				
Season	Club	Lea	GP	G	A	TP	PIM	GP	G	A	TP	PIM
1994-95	Beauport	QMJHL	64	15	27	42	37	17	4	4	8	6
1995-96	Beauport	QMJHL	1	0	1	1	0	....	....	....	....	....
	Laval	QMJHL	21	17	11	28	29	....	....	....	....	....
	Hull	QMJHL	39	26	34	60	44	17	6	7	13	14
1996-97	Hull	QMJHL	69	34	47	81	67	14	11	10	21	39

MacLEAN, JOHN N.J.

Right wing. Shoots right. 6', 210 lbs. Born, Oshawa, Ont., November 20, 1964.
(New Jersey's 1st choice, 6th overall, in 1983 Entry Draft).

			Regular Season					Playoffs				
Season	Club	Lea	GP	G	A	TP	PIM	GP	G	A	TP	PIM
1981-82	Oshawa	OHL	67	17	22	39	197	12	3	6	9	63
1982-83	Oshawa	OHL	66	47	51	98	138	17	*18	20	*38	35
1983-84	**New Jersey**	**NHL**	**23**	**1**	**0**	**1**	**10**	....	....	....	....	....
	Oshawa	OHL	30	23	36	59	58	7	2	5	7	18
1984-85	**New Jersey**	**NHL**	**61**	**13**	**20**	**33**	**44**	....	....	....	....	....
1985-86	**New Jersey**	**NHL**	**74**	**21**	**36**	**57**	**112**	....	....	....	....	....
1986-87	**New Jersey**	**NHL**	**80**	**31**	**36**	**67**	**120**	....	....	....	....	....
1987-88	**New Jersey**	**NHL**	**76**	**23**	**16**	**39**	**147**	**20**	**7**	**11**	**18**	**60**
1988-89	**New Jersey**	**NHL**	**74**	**42**	**45**	**87**	**122**	....	....	....	....	....
1989-90	**New Jersey**	**NHL**	**80**	**41**	**38**	**79**	**80**	**6**	**4**	**1**	**5**	**12**
1990-91	**New Jersey**	**NHL**	**78**	**45**	**33**	**78**	**150**	**7**	**5**	**3**	**8**	**20**
1991-92			DID NOT PLAY – INJURED									
1992-93	**New Jersey**	**NHL**	**80**	**24**	**24**	**48**	**102**	**5**	**0**	**1**	**1**	**10**
1993-94	**New Jersey**	**NHL**	**80**	**37**	**33**	**70**	**95**	**20**	**6**	**10**	**16**	**22**
1994-95	**New Jersey**	**NHL**	**46**	**17**	**12**	**29**	**32**	**20**	**5**	**13**	**18**	**14 ♦**
1995-96	**New Jersey**	**NHL**	**76**	**20**	**28**	**48**	**91**	....	....	....	....	....
1996-97	**New Jersey**	**NHL**	**80**	**29**	**25**	**54**	**49**	**10**	**4**	**5**	**9**	**4**
	NHL Totals		**908**	**344**	**346**	**690**	**1154**	**88**	**31**	**44**	**75**	**142**

Played in NHL All-Star Game (1989, 1991)

MACNEIL, IAN CAR.

Center. Shoots left. 6'2", 171 lbs. Born, Halifax, N.S., April 27, 1977.
(Hartford's 3rd choice, 85th overall, in 1995 Entry Draft).

			Regular Season					Playoffs				
Season	Club	Lea	GP	G	A	TP	PIM	GP	G	A	TP	PIM
1994-95	Oshawa	OHL	60	7	21	28	62	7	0	2	2	0
1995-96	Oshawa	OHL	49	15	17	32	54	5	1	2	3	8
1996-97	Oshawa	OHL	64	23	20	43	96	18	2	3	5	37

MacNEVIN, JOSH N.J.

Defense. Shoots right. 6'2", 185 lbs. Born, Calgary, Alta., July 14, 1977.
(New Jersey's 8th choice, 101st overall, in 1996 Entry Draft).

			Regular Season					Playoffs				
Season	Club	Lea	GP	G	A	TP	PIM	GP	G	A	TP	PIM
1995-96	Vernon	Jr. A	51	13	45	58	54	....	....	....	....	....
1996-97	Providence	H.E.	30	5	9	14	18	....	....	....	....	....

MACOUN, JAMIE (muh-KOW-uhn) TOR.

Defense. Shoots left. 6'2", 200 lbs. Born, Newmarket, Ont., August 17, 1961.

			Regular Season					Playoffs				
Season	Club	Lea	GP	G	A	TP	PIM	GP	G	A	TP	PIM
1980-81	Ohio State	CCHA	38	9	20	29	83	....	....	....	....	....
1981-82	Ohio State	CCHA	25	2	18	20	89	....	....	....	....	....
1982-83	Ohio State	CCHA	19	6	21	27	54	....	....	....	....	....
	Calgary	**NHL**	**22**	**1**	**4**	**5**	**25**	**9**	**0**	**2**	**2**	**8**
1983-84a	**Calgary**	**NHL**	**72**	**9**	**23**	**32**	**97**	**11**	**1**	**0**	**1**	**0**
1984-85	**Calgary**	**NHL**	**70**	**9**	**30**	**39**	**67**	**4**	**1**	**0**	**1**	**4**
1985-86	**Calgary**	**NHL**	**77**	**11**	**21**	**32**	**81**	**22**	**1**	**6**	**7**	**23**
1986-87	**Calgary**	**NHL**	**79**	**7**	**33**	**40**	**111**	**3**	**0**	**1**	**1**	**8**
1987-88			DID NOT PLAY – INJURED									
1988-89	**Calgary**	**NHL**	**72**	**8**	**19**	**27**	**76**	**22**	**3**	**6**	**9**	**30 ♦**
1989-90	**Calgary**	**NHL**	**78**	**8**	**27**	**35**	**70**	**6**	**0**	**3**	**3**	**10**
1990-91	**Calgary**	**NHL**	**79**	**7**	**15**	**22**	**84**	**7**	**0**	**1**	**1**	**4**
1991-92	**Calgary**	**NHL**	**37**	**2**	**12**	**14**	**53**	....	....	....	....	....
	Toronto	**NHL**	**39**	**3**	**13**	**16**	**18**	....	....	....	....	....
1992-93	**Toronto**	**NHL**	**77**	**4**	**15**	**19**	**55**	**21**	**0**	**6**	**6**	**36**
1993-94	**Toronto**	**NHL**	**82**	**3**	**27**	**30**	**115**	**18**	**1**	**1**	**2**	**12**
1994-95	**Toronto**	**NHL**	**46**	**2**	**8**	**10**	**75**	**7**	**1**	**2**	**3**	**8**
1995-96	**Toronto**	**NHL**	**82**	**0**	**8**	**8**	**87**	**6**	**0**	**2**	**2**	**8**
1996-97	**Toronto**	**NHL**	**73**	**1**	**10**	**11**	**93**	....	....	....	....	....
	NHL Totals		**985**	**75**	**265**	**340**	**1107**	**136**	**8**	**30**	**38**	**151**

a NHL All-Rookie Team (1984)

Signed as a free agent by **Calgary**, January 30, 1983. Traded to **Toronto** by **Calgary** with Doug Gilmour, Ric Natress, Kent Manderville and Rick Wamsley for Gary Leeman, Alexander Godynyuk, Jeff Reese, Michel Petit and Craig Berube, January 2, 1992.

MacTAVISH, CRAIG

Center. Shoots left. 6'1", 195 lbs. Born, London, Ont., August 15, 1958.
(Boston's 9th choice, 153rd overall, in 1978 Amateur Draft).

			Regular Season					Playoffs				
Season	Club	Lea	GP	G	A	TP	PIM	GP	G	A	TP	PIM
1978-79	Lowell	ECAC	....	....	....	....	....	....	....	....	....	....
1979-80	**Boston**	**NHL**	**46**	**11**	**17**	**28**	**8**	**10**	**2**	**3**	**5**	**7**
	Binghamton	AHL	34	17	15	32	29	....	....	....	....	....
1980-81	**Boston**	**NHL**	**24**	**3**	**5**	**8**	**13**	....	....	....	....	....
	Springfield	AHL	53	19	24	43	81	7	5	4	9	8
1981-82	**Boston**	**NHL**	**2**	**0**	**1**	**1**	**0**	....	....	....	....	....
	Erie	AHL	72	23	32	55	37	....	....	....	....	....
1982-83	**Boston**	**NHL**	**75**	**10**	**20**	**30**	**18**	**17**	**3**	**1**	**4**	**18**
1983-84	**Boston**	**NHL**	**70**	**20**	**23**	**43**	**35**	**1**	**0**	**0**	**0**	**0**
1984-85			DID NOT PLAY									
1985-86	**Edmonton**	**NHL**	**74**	**23**	**24**	**47**	**70**	**10**	**4**	**4**	**8**	**11**
1986-87	**Edmonton**	**NHL**	**79**	**20**	**19**	**39**	**55**	**21**	**1**	**9**	**10**	**16 ♦**
1987-88	**Edmonton**	**NHL**	**80**	**15**	**17**	**32**	**47**	**19**	**0**	**1**	**1**	**31 ♦**
1988-89	**Edmonton**	**NHL**	**80**	**21**	**31**	**52**	**55**	**7**	**0**	**1**	**1**	**8**
1989-90	**Edmonton**	**NHL**	**80**	**21**	**22**	**43**	**89**	**22**	**2**	**6**	**8**	**29 ♦**
1990-91	**Edmonton**	**NHL**	**80**	**17**	**15**	**32**	**76**	**18**	**3**	**3**	**6**	**20**
1991-92	**Edmonton**	**NHL**	**80**	**12**	**18**	**30**	**98**	**16**	**3**	**0**	**3**	**28**
1992-93	**Edmonton**	**NHL**	**82**	**10**	**20**	**30**	**110**	....	....	....	....	....
1993-94	**Edmonton**	**NHL**	**66**	**16**	**10**	**26**	**80**	....	....	....	....	....
	NY Rangers	**NHL**	**12**	**4**	**2**	**6**	**11**	**23**	**1**	**4**	**5**	**22 ♦**
1994-95	**Philadelphia**	**NHL**	**45**	**3**	**9**	**12**	**23**	**15**	**1**	**4**	**5**	**20**
1995-96	**Philadelphia**	**NHL**	**55**	**5**	**8**	**13**	**62**	....	....	....	....	....
	St. Louis	**NHL**	**13**	**0**	**1**	**1**	**8**	**13**	**0**	**2**	**2**	**6**
1996-97	**St. Louis**	**NHL**	**50**	**2**	**5**	**7**	**33**	**1**	**0**	**0**	**0**	**2**
	NHL Totals		**1093**	**213**	**267**	**480**	**891**	**193**	**20**	**38**	**58**	**218**

Played in NHL All-Star Game (1996)

Signed as a free agent by **Edmonton,** February 1, 1985. Traded to **NY Rangers** by **Edmonton** for Todd Marchant, March 21, 1994. Signed as a free agent by **Philadelphia**, July 6, 1994. Traded to **St. Louis** by **Philadelphia** for Dale Hawerchuk, March 15, 1996.

MADDEN, JOHN N.J.

Left wing. Shoots left. 5'11", 185 lbs. Born, Barrie, Ont., May 4, 1975.

			Regular Season					Playoffs				
Season	Club	Lea	GP	G	A	TP	PIM	GP	G	A	TP	PIM
1993-94	U. of Michigan	CCHA	36	6	11	17	14	....	....	....	....	....
1994-95	U. of Michigan	CCHA	39	21	22	43	8	....	....	....	....	....
1995-96	U. of Michigan	CCHA	43	27	30	57	45	....	....	....	....	....
1996-97ab	U. of Michigan	CCHA	42	26	37	63	56	....	....	....	....	....

a CCHA First All-Star Team (1997)
b NCAA West First All-American Team (1997)

Signed as a free agent by **New Jersey**, June 26, 1997.

MADER, MIKE PHO.

Defense. Shoots right. 6'2", 180 lbs. Born, Manchester, CT, November 7, 1975.
(Winnipeg's 10th choice, 238th overall, in 1994 Entry Draft).

			Regular Season					Playoffs				
Season	Club	Lea	GP	G	A	TP	PIM	GP	G	A	TP	PIM
1994-95	Providence	H.E.	29	1	5	6	26	....	....	....	....	....
1995-96	Providence	H.E.	37	3	6	9	33	....	....	....	....	....
1996-97	Providence	H.E.	35	4	10	14	48	....	....	....	....	....

MAIR, ADAM TOR.

Center. Shoots right. 6', 189 lbs. Born, Hamilton, Ont., February 15, 1979.
(Toronto's 2nd choice, 84th overall, in 1997 Entry Draft).

			Regular Season					Playoffs				
Season	Club	Lea	GP	G	A	TP	PIM	GP	G	A	TP	PIM
1995-96	Owen Sound	OHL	62	12	15	27	63	6	0	0	0	2
1996-97	Owen Sound	OHL	65	16	35	51	113	4	1	0	1	2

MAJOR, MARK

Left wing. Shoots left. 6'3", 223 lbs. Born, Toronto, Ont., March 20, 1970.
(Pittsburgh's 2nd choice, 25th overall, in 1988 Entry Draft).

			Regular Season					Playoffs				
Season	**Club**	**Lea**	**GP**	**G**	**A**	**TP**	**PIM**	**GP**	**G**	**A**	**TP**	**PIM**
1987-88	North Bay	OHL	57	16	17	33	272	4	0	2	2	8
1988-89	North Bay	OHL	11	3	2	5	58	....	....	....	....	....
	Kingston	OHL	53	22	29	51	193	....	....	....	....	....
1989-90	Kingston	OHL	62	29	32	61	168	6	3	3	6	12
1990-91	Muskegon	IHL	60	8	10	18	160	5	0	0	0	0
1991-92	Muskegon	IHL	80	13	18	31	302	12	1	3	4	29
1992-93	Cleveland	IHL	82	13	15	28	155	3	0	0	0	0
1993-94	Providence	AHL	61	17	9	26	176	....	....	....	....	....
1994-95	Detroit	IHL	78	17	19	36	229	5	0	1	1	23
1995-96	Adirondack	AHL	78	10	19	29	234	3	0	0	0	21
1996-97	**Detroit**	**NHL**	**2**	**0**	**0**	**0**	**5**	....	....	....	....	....
	Adirondack	AHL	78	17	18	35	213	4	0	0	0	13
	NHL Totals		**2**	**0**	**0**	**0**	**5**	....	....	....	....	....

Signed as a free agent by **Boston**, July 22, 1993. Signed as a free agent by **Detroit**, June 26, 1995.

MAKAROV, SERGEI (muh-KAH-rov)

Right wing. Shoots left. 5'11", 185 lbs. Born, Chelyabinsk, USSR, June 19, 1958.
(Calgary's 14th choice, 231st overall, in 1983 Entry Draft).

			Regular Season					Playoffs				
Season	**Club**	**Lea**	**GP**	**G**	**A**	**TP**	**PIM**	**GP**	**G**	**A**	**TP**	**PIM**
1976-77	Chelyabinsk	USSR	11	1	0	1	4	....	....	....	....	....
1977-78	Chelyabinsk	USSR	36	18	13	31	10	....	....	....	....	....
1978-79a	CSKA	USSR	44	18	21	39	12	....	....	....	....	....
1979-80bc	CSKA	USSR	44	29	39	68	16	....	....	....	....	....
1980-81ab	CSKA	USSR	49	42	37	79	22	....	....	....	....	....
1981-82ab	CSKA	USSR	46	32	43	75	18	....	....	....	....	....
1982-83a	CSKA	USSR	30	25	17	42	6	....	....	....	....	....
1983-84ab	CSKA	USSR	44	36	37	73	28	....	....	....	....	....
1984-85abc	CSKA	USSR	40	26	39	65	28	....	....	....	....	....
1985-86ab	CSKA	USSR	40	30	32	62	28	....	....	....	....	....
1986-87ab	CSKA	USSR	40	21	32	53	26	....	....	....	....	....
1987-88ab	CSKA	USSR	51	23	45	68	50	....	....	....	....	....
1988-89bc	CSKA	USSR	44	21	33	54	42	....	....	....	....	....
1989-90de	**Calgary**	**NHL**	**80**	**24**	**62**	**86**	**55**	**6**	**0**	**6**	**6**	**0**
1990-91	**Calgary**	**NHL**	**78**	**30**	**49**	**79**	**44**	**3**	**1**	**0**	**1**	**0**
1991-92	**Calgary**	**NHL**	**68**	**22**	**48**	**70**	**60**	....	....	....	....	....
1992-93	**Calgary**	**NHL**	**71**	**18**	**39**	**57**	**40**	....	....	....	....	....
1993-94	**San Jose**	**NHL**	**80**	**30**	**38**	**68**	**78**	**14**	**8**	**2**	**10**	**4**
1994-95	**San Jose**	**NHL**	**43**	**10**	**14**	**24**	**40**	**11**	**3**	**3**	**6**	**4**
1995-96						DID NOT PLAY						
1996-97	**Dallas**	**NHL**	**4**	**0**	**0**	**0**	**0**	....	....	....	....	....
	Fribourg	Switz.	5	3	2	5	2	1	0	0	0	0
	NHL Totals		**424**	**134**	**250**	**384**	**317**	**34**	**12**	**11**	**23**	**8**

a Soviet National League All-Star (1981-88)
b Izvestia Trophy - leading scorer (1980-82, 1984-89)
c Soviet Player of the Year (1980, 1985, 1989)
d NHL All-Rookie Team (1990)
e Won Calder Memorial Trophy (1990)

Traded to **Hartford** by **Calgary** for future considerations (Washington's fourth round choice — previously acquired by Hartford — Calgary selected Jason Smith — in 1993 Entry Draft, June 26, 1993), June 20, 1993. Traded to **San Jose** by **Hartford** with Hartford's first (Viktor Kozlov) and third (Ville Peltonen) round choices in 1993 Entry Draft and Toronto's second round choice (previously acquired by Hartford — San Jose selected Vlastimil Kroupa) in 1993 Entry Draft for San Jose's first round choice (Chris Pronger) in 1993 Entry Draft, June 26, 1993. Signed as a free agent by **Dallas**, November 1, 1996.

MAKINEN, MARKO (mya-KIH-nehn) S.J.

Right wing. Shoots right. 6'5", 200 lbs. Born, Turku, Finland, March 31, 1977.
(San Jose's 3rd choice, 64th overall, in 1995 Entry Draft).

			Regular Season					Playoffs				
Season	**Club**	**Lea**	**GP**	**G**	**A**	**TP**	**PIM**	**GP**	**G**	**A**	**TP**	**PIM**
1994-95	TPS	Fin. Jr.	26	7	1	8	34	....	....	....	....	....
	Kiekko-67	Fin. 2	4	0	0	0	6	....	....	....	....	....
1995-96	TPS	Fin. Jr.	11	5	1	6	28	....	....	....	....	....
	Kiekko-67	Fin. Jr.	4	4	2	6	12	....	....	....	....	....
	Kiekko-67	Fin. 2	21	6	2	8	98	6	2	2	4	6
1996-97	Kiekko-Espoo	Fin.	15	2	1	3	34	4	0	0	0	0
	Kiekko-67	Fin. 2	30	2	8	10	63	....	....	....	....	....

MALAKHOV, VLADIMIR (mah-LAH-kahf) MTL.

Defense. Shoots left. 6'3", 220 lbs. Born, Sverdlovsk, USSR, August 30, 1968.
(NY Islanders' 12th choice, 191st overall, in 1989 Entry Draft).

			Regular Season					Playoffs				
Season	**Club**	**Lea**	**GP**	**G**	**A**	**TP**	**PIM**	**GP**	**G**	**A**	**TP**	**PIM**
1986-87	Spartak	USSR	22	0	1	1	12	....	....	....	....	....
1987-88	Spartak	USSR	28	2	2	4	26	....	....	....	....	....
1988-89	CSKA	USSR	34	6	2	8	16	....	....	....	....	....
1989-90	CSKA	USSR	48	2	10	12	34	....	....	....	....	....
1990-91	CSKA	USSR	46	5	13	18	22	....	....	....	....	....
1991-92	CSKA	CIS	40	1	9	10	12	....	....	....	....	....
1992-93a	**NY Islanders**	**NHL**	**64**	**14**	**38**	**52**	**59**	**17**	**3**	**6**	**9**	**12**
	Capital Dist.	AHL	3	2	1	3	11	....	....	....	....	....
1993-94	**NY Islanders**	**NHL**	**76**	**10**	**47**	**57**	**80**	**4**	**0**	**0**	**0**	**6**
1994-95	**NY Islanders**	**NHL**	**26**	**3**	**13**	**16**	**32**	....	....	....	....	....
	Montreal	**NHL**	**14**	**1**	**4**	**5**	**14**	....	....	....	....	....
1995-96	**Montreal**	**NHL**	**61**	**5**	**23**	**28**	**79**	....	....	....	....	....
1996-97	**Montreal**	**NHL**	**65**	**10**	**20**	**30**	**43**	**5**	**0**	**0**	**0**	**6**
	NHL Totals		**306**	**43**	**145**	**188**	**307**	**26**	**3**	**6**	**9**	**24**

a NHL/Upper Deck All-Rookie Team (1993)

Traded to **Montreal** by **NY Islanders** with Pierre Turgeon for Kirk Muller, Mathieu Schneider and Craig Darby, April 5, 1995.

MALGUNAS, STEWART (mal-GOO-nuhs) WSH.

Defense. Shoots left. 6', 200 lbs. Born, Prince George, B.C., April 21, 1970.
(Detroit's 3rd choice, 66th overall, in 1990 Entry Draft).

			Regular Season					Playoffs				
Season	**Club**	**Lea**	**GP**	**G**	**A**	**TP**	**PIM**	**GP**	**G**	**A**	**TP**	**PIM**
1987-88	N. Westminster	WHL	6	0	0	0	0	....	....	....	....	....
1988-89	Seattle	WHL	72	11	41	52	51	....	....	....	....	....
1989-90a	Seattle	WHL	63	15	48	63	116	13	2	9	11	32
1990-91	Adirondack	AHL	78	5	19	24	70	2	0	0	0	4
1991-92	Adirondack	AHL	69	4	28	32	82	18	2	6	8	28
1992-93	Adirondack	AHL	45	3	12	15	39	11	3	3	6	8
1993-94	**Philadelphia**	**NHL**	**67**	**1**	**3**	**4**	**86**	....	....	....	....	....
1994-95	**Philadelphia**	**NHL**	**4**	**0**	**0**	**0**	**4**	....	....	....	....	....
	Hershey	AHL	32	3	5	8	28	6	2	1	3	31
1995-96	**Winnipeg**	**NHL**	**29**	**0**	**1**	**1**	**32**	....	....	....	....	....
	Washington	**NHL**	**1**	**0**	**0**	**0**	**0**	....	....	....	....	....
	Portland	AHL	16	2	5	7	18	13	1	3	4	19
1996-97	**Washington**	**NHL**	**6**	**0**	**0**	**0**	**2**	....	....	....	....	....
	Portland	AHL	68	6	12	18	59	5	0	0	0	8
	NHL Totals		**107**	**1**	**4**	**5**	**124**	....	....	....	....	....

a WHL West First All-Star Team (1990)

Traded to **Philadelphia** by **Detroit** for Philadelphia's fifth round choice (David Arsenault) in 1995 Entry Draft, September 9, 1993. Signed as a free agent by **Winnipeg**, August 9, 1995. Traded to **Washington** by **Winnipeg** for Denis Chasse, February 15, 1996.

MALIK, MAREK (MAW-leck) CAR.

Defense. Shoots left. 6'5", 190 lbs. Born, Ostrava, Czech., June 24, 1975.
(Hartford's 2nd choice, 72nd overall, in 1993 Entry Draft).

			Regular Season					Playoffs				
Season	**Club**	**Lea**	**GP**	**G**	**A**	**TP**	**PIM**	**GP**	**G**	**A**	**TP**	**PIM**
1992-93	TJ Vitkovice Jr.	Czech.	20	5	10	15	16	....	....	....	....	....
1993-94	TJ Vitkovice	Czech.	38	3	3	6	0	3	0	1	1	0
1994-95	Springfield	AHL	58	11	30	41	91	....	....	....	....	....
	Hartford	**NHL**	**1**	**0**	**1**	**1**	**0**	....	....	....	....	....
1995-96	**Hartford**	**NHL**	**7**	**0**	**0**	**0**	**4**	....	....	....	....	....
	Springfield	AHL	68	8	14	22	135	8	1	3	4	20
1996-97	**Hartford**	**NHL**	**47**	**1**	**5**	**6**	**50**	....	....	....	....	....
	Springfield	AHL	3	0	3	3	4	....	....	....	....	....
	NHL Totals		**55**	**1**	**6**	**7**	**54**	....	....	....	....	....

MALKOC, DEAN (mal-KAWK) BOS.

Defense. Shoots left. 6'3", 215 lbs. Born, Vancouver, B.C., January 26, 1970.
(New Jersey's 7th choice, 95th overall, in 1990 Entry Draft).

			Regular Season					Playoffs				
Season	**Club**	**Lea**	**GP**	**G**	**A**	**TP**	**PIM**	**GP**	**G**	**A**	**TP**	**PIM**
1989-90	Kamloops	WHL	48	3	18	21	209	17	0	3	3	56
1990-91	Kamloops	WHL	8	1	4	5	47	....	....	....	....	....
	Swift Current	WHL	56	10	23	33	248	3	0	2	2	5
	Utica	AHL	1	0	0	0	0	....	....	....	....	....
1991-92	Utica	AHL	66	1	11	12	274	4	0	2	2	6
1992-93	Utica	AHL	73	5	19	24	255	5	0	1	1	8
1993-94	Albany	AHL	79	0	9	9	296	5	0	0	0	21
1994-95	Albany	AHL	9	0	1	1	52	....	....	....	....	....
	Indianapolis	IHL	62	1	3	4	193	....	....	....	....	....
1995-96	**Vancouver**	**NHL**	**41**	**0**	**2**	**2**	**136**	....	....	....	....	....
1996-97	**Boston**	**NHL**	**33**	**0**	**0**	**0**	**70**	....	....	....	....	....
	Providence	AHL	4	0	2	2	28	....	....	....	....	....
	NHL Totals		**74**	**0**	**2**	**2**	**206**	....	....	....	....	....

Traded to **Chicago** by **New Jersey** for Rob Conn, January 30, 1995. Signed as a free agent by **Vancouver**, September 8, 1995. Claimed by **Boston** from **Vancouver** in NHL Waiver Draft, September 30, 1996.

MALLETTE, KRIS (muh-LEHT) PHI.

Defense. Shoots right. 6'3", 220 lbs. Born, North Bay, Ont., January 19, 1979.
(Philadelphia's 3rd choice, 62nd overall, in 1997 Entry Draft).

			Regular Season					Playoffs				
Season	**Club**	**Lea**	**GP**	**G**	**A**	**TP**	**PIM**	**GP**	**G**	**A**	**TP**	**PIM**
1996-97	Kelowna	WHL	67	0	3	3	206	6	0	0	0	8

MALLETTE, TROY (muh-LEHT)

Left wing. Shoots left. 6'2", 210 lbs. Born, Sudbury, Ont., February 25, 1970.
(NY Rangers' 1st choice, 22nd overall, in 1988 Entry Draft).

			Regular Season					Playoffs				
Season	**Club**	**Lea**	**GP**	**G**	**A**	**TP**	**PIM**	**GP**	**G**	**A**	**TP**	**PIM**
1986-87	S.S. Marie	OHL	65	20	25	45	157	4	0	2	2	12
1987-88	S.S. Marie	OHL	62	18	30	48	186	6	1	3	4	12
1988-89	S.S. Marie	OHL	64	39	37	76	172	....	....	....	....	....
1989-90	**NY Rangers**	**NHL**	**79**	**13**	**16**	**29**	**305**	**10**	**2**	**2**	**4**	**81**
1990-91	**NY Rangers**	**NHL**	**71**	**12**	**10**	**22**	**252**	**5**	**0**	**0**	**0**	**18**
1991-92	**Edmonton**	**NHL**	**15**	**1**	**3**	**4**	**36**	....	....	....	....	....
	New Jersey	**NHL**	**17**	**3**	**4**	**7**	**43**	....	....	....	....	....
1992-93	**New Jersey**	**NHL**	**34**	**4**	**3**	**7**	**56**	....	....	....	....	....
	Utica	AHL	5	3	3	6	17	....	....	....	....	....
1993-94	**Ottawa**	**NHL**	**82**	**7**	**16**	**23**	**166**	....	....	....	....	....
1994-95	**Ottawa**	**NHL**	**23**	**3**	**5**	**8**	**35**	....	....	....	....	....
	P.E.I.	AHL	5	1	5	6	9	....	....	....	....	....
1995-96	**Ottawa**	**NHL**	**64**	**2**	**3**	**5**	**171**	....	....	....	....	....
1996-97	**Boston**	**NHL**	**68**	**6**	**8**	**14**	**155**	....	....	....	....	....
	NHL Totals		**453**	**51**	**68**	**119**	**1219**	**15**	**2**	**2**	**4**	**99**

Acquired by **Edmonton** from **NY Rangers** as compensation for NY Rangers' signing of free agent Adam Graves, September 12, 1991. Traded to **New Jersey** by **Edmonton** for David Maley, January 12, 1992. Traded to **Ottawa** by **New Jersey** with Craig Billington and New Jersey's fourth round choice (Cosmo Dupaul) in 1993 Entry Draft for Peter Sidorkiewicz and future considerations (Mike Peluso, June 26, 1993), June 20, 1993. Signed as a free agent by **Boston**, July 24, 1996.

MALTAIS, STEVE (MAHL-tay)

Left wing. Shoots left. 6'2", 205 lbs. Born, Arvida, Que., January 25, 1969.
(Washington's 2nd choice, 57th overall, in 1987 Entry Draft).

			Regular Season					Playoffs				
Season	Club	Lea	GP	G	A	TP	PIM	GP	G	A	TP	PIM
1986-87	Cornwall	OHL	65	32	12	44	29	5	0	0	0	2
1987-88	Cornwall	OHL	59	39	46	85	30	11	9	6	15	33
1988-89	Cornwall	OHL	58	53	70	123	67	18	14	16	30	16
	Fort Wayne	IHL	....	....	....	....	....	4	2	1	3	0
1989-90	**Washington**	**NHL**	**8**	**0**	**0**	**0**	**2**	**1**	**0**	**0**	**0**	**0**
	Baltimore	AHL	67	29	37	66	54	12	6	10	16	6
1990-91	**Washington**	**NHL**	**7**	**0**	**0**	**0**	**2**	....	....	....	....	....
	Baltimore	AHL	73	36	43	79	97	6	1	4	5	10
1991-92	**Minnesota**	**NHL**	**12**	**2**	**1**	**3**	**2**	....	....	....	....	....
	Kalamazoo	IHL	48	25	31	56	51	....	....	....	....	....
	Halifax	AHL	10	3	3	6	0	....	....	....	....	....
1992-93	**Tampa Bay**	**NHL**	**63**	**7**	**13**	**20**	**35**	....	....	....	....	....
	Atlanta	IHL	16	14	10	24	22	....	....	....	....	....
1993-94	**Detroit**	**NHL**	**4**	**0**	**1**	**1**	**0**	....	....	....	....	....
	Adirondack	AHL	73	35	49	84	79	12	5	11	16	14
1994-95a	Chicago	IHL	79	*57	40	97	145	3	1	1	2	0
1995-96b	Chicago	IHL	81	56	66	122	161	9	7	7	14	20
1996-97b	Chicago	IHL	81	*60	54	114	62	4	2	0	2	4
	NHL Totals		**94**	**9**	**15**	**24**	**41**	**1**	**0**	**0**	**0**	**0**

a IHL First All-Star Team (1995)
b IHL Second All-Star Team (1996, 1997)

Traded to **Minnesota** by **Washington** with Trent Klatt for Shawn Chambers, June 21, 1991. Traded to **Quebec** by **Minnesota** for Kip Miller, March 8, 1992. Claimed by **Tampa Bay** from **Quebec** in Expansion Draft, June 18, 1992. Traded to **Detroit** by **Tampa Bay** for Dennis Vial, June 8, 1993.

MALTBY, KIRK DET.

Right wing. Shoots right. 6', 180 lbs. Born, Guelph, Ont., December 22, 1972.
(Edmonton's 4th choice, 65th overall, in 1992 Entry Draft).

			Regular Season					Playoffs				
Season	Club	Lea	GP	G	A	TP	PIM	GP	G	A	TP	PIM
1989-90	Owen Sound	OHL	61	12	15	27	90	12	1	6	7	15
1990-91	Owen Sound	OHL	66	34	32	66	100	....	....	....	....	....
1991-92	Owen Sound	OHL	66	50	41	91	99	5	3	3	6	18
1992-93	Cape Breton	AHL	73	22	23	45	130	16	3	3	6	45
1993-94	**Edmonton**	**NHL**	**68**	**11**	**8**	**19**	**74**	....	....	....	....	....
1994-95	**Edmonton**	**NHL**	**47**	**8**	**3**	**11**	**49**	....	....	....	....	....
1995-96	**Edmonton**	**NHL**	**49**	**2**	**6**	**8**	**61**	....	....	....	....	....
	Cape Breton	AHL	4	1	2	3	6	....	....	....	....	....
	Detroit	**NHL**	**6**	**1**	**0**	**1**	**6**	**8**	**0**	**1**	**1**	**4**
1996-97	**Detroit**	**NHL**	**66**	**3**	**5**	**8**	**75**	**20**	**5**	**2**	**7**	**24 ♦**
	NHL Totals		**236**	**25**	**22**	**47**	**265**	**28**	**5**	**3**	**8**	**28**

Traded to **Detroit** by **Edmonton** for Dan McGillis, March 20, 1996.

MANDERVILLE, KENT CAR.

Left wing. Shoots left. 6'3", 210 lbs. Born, Edmonton, Alta., April 12, 1971.
(Calgary's 1st choice, 24th overall, in 1989 Entry Draft).

			Regular Season					Playoffs				
Season	Club	Lea	GP	G	A	TP	PIM	GP	G	A	TP	PIM
1989-90	Cornell	ECAC	26	11	15	26	28	....	....	....	....	....
1990-91	Cornell	ECAC	28	17	14	31	60	....	....	....	....	....
	Cdn. National	....	3	1	2	3	0	....	....	....	....	....
1991-92	Cdn. National	....	63	16	24	40	78	....	....	....	....	....
	Cdn. Olympic	....	8	1	2	3	0	....	....	....	....	....
	Toronto	**NHL**	**15**	**0**	**4**	**4**	**0**	....	....	....	....	....
	St. John's	AHL	....	....	....	....	....	12	5	9	14	14
1992-93	**Toronto**	**NHL**	**18**	**1**	**1**	**2**	**17**	**18**	**1**	**0**	**1**	**8**
	St. John's	AHL	56	19	28	47	86	2	0	2	2	0
1993-94	**Toronto**	**NHL**	**67**	**7**	**9**	**16**	**63**	**12**	**1**	**0**	**1**	**4**
1994-95	**Toronto**	**NHL**	**36**	**0**	**1**	**1**	**22**	**7**	**0**	**0**	**0**	**6**
1995-96	**Edmonton**	**NHL**	**37**	**3**	**5**	**8**	**38**	....	....	....	....	....
	St. John's	AHL	27	16	12	28	26	....	....	....	....	....
1996-97	**Hartford**	**NHL**	**44**	**6**	**5**	**11**	**18**	....	....	....	....	....
	Springfield	AHL	23	5	20	25	18	....	....	....	....	....
	NHL Totals		**217**	**17**	**25**	**42**	**158**	**37**	**2**	**0**	**2**	**18**

Traded to **Toronto** by **Calgary** with Doug Gilmour, Jamie Macoun, Rick Wamsley and Ric Nattress for Gary Leeman, Alexander Godynyuk, Jeff Reese, Michel Petit and Craig Berube, January 2, 1992. Traded to **Edmonton** by **Toronto** for Peter White and Edmonton's fourth round choice (Jason Sessa) in 1996 Entry Draft, December 4, 1995. Signed as a free agent by **Hartford**, October 2, 1996.

MANELUK, MIKE OTT.

Left wing. Shoots right. 5'11", 188 lbs. Born, Winnipeg, Man., October 1, 1973.

			Regular Season					Playoffs				
Season	Club	Lea	GP	G	A	TP	PIM	GP	G	A	TP	PIM
1991-92	Brandon	WHL	68	23	30	53	102	....	....	....	....	....
1992-93	Brandon	WHL	72	36	51	87	75	4	2	1	3	2
1993-94	Brandon	WHL	63	50	47	97	112	13	11	3	14	23
	San Diego	IHL	....	....	....	....	....	1	0	0	0	0
1994-95	Cdn. National	....	44	36	24	60	34	....	....	....	....	....
	San Diego	IHL	10	0	1	1	4	....	....	....	....	....
1995-96	Baltimore	AHL	74	33	38	71	73	6	4	3	7	14
1996-97	Worcester	AHL	70	27	27	54	89	5	1	2	3	14

Signed as a free agent by **Anaheim**, January 28, 1994. Traded to **Ottawa** by **Anaheim** for Kevin Brown, July 1, 1996.

MANLOW, ERIC CHI.

Center. Shoots left. 6', 190 lbs. Born, Belleville, Ont., April 7, 1975.
(Chicago's 2nd choice, 50th overall, in 1993 Entry Draft).

			Regular Season					Playoffs				
Season	Club	Lea	GP	G	A	TP	PIM	GP	G	A	TP	PIM
1991-92	Kitchener	OHL	59	12	20	32	17	14	2	5	7	10
1992-93	Kitchener	OHL	53	26	21	47	31	4	0	1	1	2
1993-94	Kitchener	OHL	49	28	32	60	25	3	0	1	1	4
1994-95	Kitchener	OHL	44	25	29	54	26	....	....	....	....	....
	Detroit	OHL	16	4	16	20	11	21	11	10	21	18
1995-96	Indianapolis	IHL	75	6	11	17	32	4	0	1	1	4
1996-97	Baltimore	AHL	36	6	6	12	13	3	0	0	0	0
	Columbus	ECHL	32	18	18	36	20	....	....	....	....	....

MANN, CAMERON BOS.

Right wing. Shoots right. 6', 194 lbs. Born, Thompson, Man., April 20, 1977.
(Boston's 5th choice, 99th overall, in 1995 Entry Draft).

			Regular Season					Playoffs				
Season	Club	Lea	GP	G	A	TP	PIM	GP	G	A	TP	PIM
1993-94	Peterborough	OHL	49	8	17	25	18	7	1	1	2	2
1994-95	Peterborough	OHL	64	19	24	43	40	11	3	8	11	4
1995-96abc	Peterborough	OHL	66	42	60	102	108	24	*27	16	*43	33
1996-97a	Peterborough	OHL	51	33	50	83	91	11	10	18	28	16

a OHL First All-Star Team (1996, 1997)
b Memorial Cup All-Star Team (1996)
c Won Stafford Smythe Memorial Trophy (Memorial Cup Tournament MVP) (1996)

MANSON, DAVE MTL.

Defense. Shoots left. 6'2", 202 lbs. Born, Prince Albert, Sask., January 27, 1967.
(Chicago's 1st choice, 11th overall, in 1985 Entry Draft).

			Regular Season					Playoffs				
Season	Club	Lea	GP	G	A	TP	PIM	GP	G	A	TP	PIM
1983-84	Prince Albert	WHL	70	2	7	9	233	5	0	0	0	4
1984-85	Prince Albert	WHL	72	8	30	38	247	13	1	0	1	34
1985-86	Prince Albert	WHL	70	14	34	48	177	20	1	8	9	63
1986-87	**Chicago**	**NHL**	**63**	**1**	**8**	**9**	**146**	**3**	**0**	**0**	**0**	**10**
1987-88	**Chicago**	**NHL**	**54**	**1**	**6**	**7**	**185**	**5**	**0**	**0**	**0**	**27**
	Saginaw	IHL	6	0	3	3	37	....	....	....	....	....
1988-89	**Chicago**	**NHL**	**79**	**18**	**36**	**54**	**352**	**16**	**0**	**8**	**8**	**84**
1989-90	**Chicago**	**NHL**	**59**	**5**	**23**	**28**	**301**	**20**	**2**	**4**	**6**	**46**
1990-91	**Chicago**	**NHL**	**75**	**14**	**15**	**29**	**191**	**6**	**0**	**1**	**1**	**36**
1991-92	**Edmonton**	**NHL**	**79**	**15**	**32**	**47**	**220**	**16**	**3**	**9**	**12**	**44**
1992-93	**Edmonton**	**NHL**	**83**	**15**	**30**	**45**	**210**	....	....	....	....	....
1993-94	**Edmonton**	**NHL**	**57**	**3**	**13**	**16**	**140**	....	....	....	....	....
	Winnipeg	**NHL**	**13**	**1**	**4**	**5**	**51**	....	....	....	....	....
1994-95	**Winnipeg**	**NHL**	**44**	**3**	**15**	**18**	**139**	....	....	....	....	....
1995-96	**Winnipeg**	**NHL**	**82**	**7**	**23**	**30**	**205**	**6**	**2**	**1**	**3**	**30**
1996-97	**Phoenix**	**NHL**	**66**	**3**	**17**	**20**	**164**	....	....	....	....	....
	Montreal	**NHL**	**9**	**1**	**1**	**2**	**23**	**5**	**0**	**0**	**0**	**17**
	NHL Totals		**763**	**87**	**223**	**310**	**2327**	**77**	**7**	**23**	**30**	**294**

Played in NHL All-Star Game (1989, 1993)

Traded to **Edmonton** by **Chicago** with Chicago's third round choice (Kirk Maltby) in 1992 Entry Draft for Steve Smith, October 2, 1991. Traded to **Winnipeg** by **Edmonton** with St. Louis' sixth round choice (previously acquired by Edmonton — Winnipeg selected Chris Kibermanis) in 1994 Entry Draft for Boris Mironov, Mats Lindgren, Winnipeg's first round choice (Jason Bonsignore) in 1994 Entry Draft and Florida's fourth round choice (previously acquired by Winnipeg — Edmonton selected Adam Copeland) in 1994 Entry Draft, March 15, 1994. Traded to **Montreal** by **Phoenix** for Murray Baron and Chris Murray, March 18, 1997.

MARA, PAUL (MA-rah) T.B.

Defense. Shoots left. 6'4", 202 lbs. Born, Ridgewood, NJ, September 7, 1979.
(Tampa Bay's 1st choice, 7th overall, in 1997 Entry Draft).

			Regular Season					Playoffs				
Season	Club	Lea	GP	G	A	TP	PIM	GP	G	A	TP	PIM
1996-97	Sudbury	OHL	44	9	34	43	61	....	....	....	....	....

MARA, ROB (MA-rah) CHI.

Right wing. Shoots right. 6'1", 175 lbs. Born, Boston, MA, September 25, 1975.
(Chicago's 11th choice, 263rd overall, in 1994 Entry Draft).

			Regular Season					Playoffs				
Season	Club	Lea	GP	G	A	TP	PIM	GP	G	A	TP	PIM
1994-95	Colgate	ECAC	33	6	8	14	33	....	....	....	....	....
1995-96	Colgate	ECAC	33	8	6	14	36	....	....	....	....	....
1996-97	Colgate	ECAC	32	18	15	33	44	....	....	....	....	....

MARCHANT, TERRY (mahr-SHAHNT) EDM.

Left wing. Shoots left. 6'2", 205 lbs. Born, Buffalo, NY, February 24, 1976.
(Edmonton's 9th choice, 136th overall, in 1994 Entry Draft).

			Regular Season					Playoffs				
Season	Club	Lea	GP	G	A	TP	PIM	GP	G	A	TP	PIM
1994-95	Lake Superior	CCHA	23	2	5	7	12	....	....	....	....	....
1995-96	Lake Superior	CCHA	36	8	5	13	15	....	....	....	....	....
1996-97	Lake Superior	CCHA	38	12	14	26	26	....	....	....	....	....

MARCHANT, TODD (mahr-SHAHNT) EDM.

Center. Shoots left. 5'10", 175 lbs. Born, Buffalo, NY, August 12, 1973.
(NY Rangers' 8th choice, 164th overall, in 1993 Entry Draft).

			Regular Season					Playoffs				
Season	Club	Lea	GP	G	A	TP	PIM	GP	G	A	TP	PIM
1991-92	Clarkson	ECAC	32	20	12	32	32	....	....	....	....	....
1992-93a	Clarkson	ECAC	33	18	28	46	38	....	....	....	....	....
1993-94	U.S. National	....	59	28	39	67	48	....	....	....	....	....
	U.S. Olympic	....	8	1	1	2	6	....	....	....	....	....
	NY Rangers	**NHL**	**1**	**0**	**0**	**0**	**0**	....	....	....	....	....
	Binghamton	AHL	8	2	7	9	6	....	....	....	....	....
	Edmonton	**NHL**	**3**	**0**	**1**	**1**	**2**	....	....	....	....	....
	Cape Breton	AHL	3	1	4	5	2	5	1	1	2	0
1994-95	Cape Breton	AHL	38	22	25	47	25	....	....	....	....	....
	Edmonton	**NHL**	**45**	**13**	**14**	**27**	**32**	....	....	....	....	....
1995-96	**Edmonton**	**NHL**	**81**	**19**	**19**	**38**	**66**	....	....	....	....	....
1996-97	**Edmonton**	**NHL**	**79**	**14**	**19**	**33**	**44**	**12**	**4**	**2**	**6**	**12**
	NHL Totals		**209**	**46**	**53**	**99**	**144**	**12**	**4**	**2**	**6**	**12**

a ECAC Second All-Star Team (1993)

Traded to **Edmonton** by **NY Rangers** for Craig MacTavish, March 21, 1994.

MARCHMENT, BRYAN (MAHRCH-mehnt) EDM.

Defense. Shoots left. 6'1", 205 lbs. Born, Scarborough, Ont., May 1, 1969.
(Winnipeg's 1st choice, 16th overall, in 1987 Entry Draft).

			Regular Season					Playoffs				
Season	Club	Lea	GP	G	A	TP	PIM	GP	G	A	TP	PIM
1985-86	Belleville	OHL	57	5	15	20	225	21	0	7	7	83
1986-87	Belleville	OHL	52	6	38	44	238	6	0	4	4	17
1987-88	Belleville	OHL	56	7	51	58	200	6	1	3	4	19
1988-89	**Winnipeg**	**NHL**	**2**	**0**	**0**	**0**	**2**	....	....	....	....	....
a	Belleville	OHL	43	14	36	50	118	5	0	1	1	12
1989-90	**Winnipeg**	**NHL**	**7**	**0**	**2**	**2**	**28**	....	....	....	....	....
	Moncton	AHL	56	4	19	23	217	....	....	....	....	....
1990-91	**Winnipeg**	**NHL**	**28**	**2**	**2**	**4**	**91**	....	....	....	....	....
	Moncton	AHL	33	2	11	13	101	....	....	....	....	....
1991-92	**Chicago**	**NHL**	**58**	**5**	**10**	**15**	**168**	**16**	**1**	**0**	**1**	**36**
1992-93	**Chicago**	**NHL**	**78**	**5**	**15**	**20**	**313**	**4**	**0**	**0**	**0**	**12**
1993-94	**Chicago**	**NHL**	**13**	**1**	**4**	**5**	**42**	....	....	....	....	....
	Hartford	**NHL**	**42**	**3**	**7**	**10**	**124**	....	....	....	....	....
1994-95	**Edmonton**	**NHL**	**40**	**1**	**5**	**6**	**184**	....	....	....	....	....
1995-96	**Edmonton**	**NHL**	**78**	**3**	**15**	**18**	**202**	....	....	....	....	....
1996-97	**Edmonton**	**NHL**	**71**	**3**	**13**	**16**	**132**	**3**	**0**	**0**	**0**	**4**
	NHL Totals		**417**	**23**	**73**	**96**	**1286**	**23**	**1**	**0**	**1**	**52**

a OHL Second All-Star Team (1989)

Traded to **Chicago** by **Winnipeg** with Chris Norton for Troy Murray and Warren Rychel, July 22, 1991. Traded to **Hartford** by **Chicago** with Steve Larmer for Eric Weinrich and Patrick Poulin, November 2, 1993. Acquired by **Edmonton** from **Hartford** as compensation for Hartford's signing of free agent Steven Rice, August 30, 1994.

MARHA, JOSEF (MAHR-hah) COL.

Center. Shoots left. 6', 176 lbs. Born, Havlickuv Brod, Czech., June 2, 1976.
(Quebec's 3rd choice, 35th overall, in 1994 Entry Draft).

			Regular Season					Playoffs				
Season	Club	Lea	GP	G	A	TP	PIM	GP	G	A	TP	PIM
1992-93	Dukla Jihlava	Czech.	7	2	2	4	....	....	....	....	....	....
1993-94	Dukla Jihlava	Czech.	41	7	2	9	....	3	0	1	1	....
1994-95	Dukla Jihlava	Czech.	35	3	7	10	6	....	....	....	....	....
1995-96	**Colorado**	**NHL**	**2**	**0**	**1**	**1**	**0**	....	....	....	....	....
	Cornwall	AHL	74	18	30	48	30	8	1	2	3	10
1996-97	**Colorado**	**NHL**	**6**	**0**	**1**	**1**	**0**	....	....	....	....	....
	Hershey	AHL	67	23	49	72	44	19	6	*16	*22	10
	NHL Totals		**8**	**0**	**2**	**2**	**0**	....	....	....	....	....

MARINUCCI, CHRIS (mair-ihn-OO-chee)

Center. Shoots left. 6', 188 lbs. Born, Grand Rapids, MN, December 29, 1971.
(NY Islanders' 4th choice, 90th overall, in 1990 Entry Draft).

			Regular Season					Playoffs				
Season	Club	Lea	GP	G	A	TP	PIM	GP	G	A	TP	PIM
1990-91	Minn.-Duluth	WCHA	36	6	10	16	20	....	....	....	....	....
1991-92	Minn.-Duluth	WCHA	37	6	13	19	41	....	....	....	....	....
1992-93a	Minn. Duluth	WCHA	40	35	42	77	52	....	....	....	....	....
1993-94bcd	Minn.-Duluth	WCHA	38	*30	31	61	65	....	....	....	....	....
1994-95	Denver	IHL	74	29	40	69	42	14	3	4	7	12
	NY Islanders	**NHL**	**12**	**1**	**4**	**5**	**2**	....	....	....	....	....
1995-96	Utah	IHL	8	3	5	8	8	....	....	....	....	....
1996-97	Utah	IHL	21	3	13	16	6	....	....	....	....	....
	Los Angeles	**NHL**	**1**	**0**	**0**	**0**	**0**	....	....	....	....	....
	Phoenix	IHL	62	23	29	52	26	....	....	....	....	....
	NHL Totals		**13**	**1**	**4**	**5**	**2**	....	....	....	....	....

a WCHA Second All-Star Team (1993)
b WCHA First All-Star Team (1994)
c NCAA West First All-American Team (1994)
d Won Hobey Baker Memorial Award (Top U.S. Collegiate Player) (1994)

Traded to **Los Angeles** by **NY Islanders** for Nick Vachon, November 19, 1996.

MARKKANEN, MIKKO (MAHR-kah-nehn, MEE-koh) S.J.

Right wing. Shoots right. 5'9", 165 lbs. Born, Turku, Finland, January 9, 1977.
(San Jose's 12th choice, 220th overall, in 1995 Entry Draft).

			Regular Season					Playoffs				
Season	Club	Lea	GP	G	A	TP	PIM	GP	G	A	TP	PIM
1994-95	TPS	Fin. Jr.	32	10	8	18	28	....	....	....	....	....
	Kiekko-67	Fin. 2	1	0	1	1	0	....	....	....	....	....
1995-96	TPS	Fin. Jr.	7	2	3	5	16	....	....	....	....	....
	Kiekko-67	Fin. 2	38	9	11	20	34	6	1	1	2	6
1996-97	Kiekko-67	Fin. 2	43	15	3	18	51	....	....	....	....	....

MARKOV, DANIIL TOR.

Defense. Shoots left. 5'11", 176 lbs. Born, Moscow, USSR, July 11, 1976.
(Toronto's 7th choice, 223rd overall, in 1995 Entry Draft).

			Regular Season					Playoffs				
Season	Club	Lea	GP	G	A	TP	PIM	GP	G	A	TP	PIM
1993-94	Spartak	CIS	13	1	0	1	6	1	0	0	0	0
1994-95	Spartak	CIS	39	0	1	1	36	....	....	....	....	....
1995-96	Spartak	CIS	38	2	0	2	12	2	0	0	0	2
1996-97	Spartak	Rus.	39	3	6	9	41	....	....	....	....	....
	St. John's	AHL	10	2	4	6	18	11	2	6	8	14

MARLEAU, DOMINIC (mahr-LOH)

Defense. Shoots right. 6'2", 195 lbs. Born, Lasalle, Que., February 11, 1977.
(Dallas' 6th choice, 141st overall, in 1995 Entry Draft).

			Regular Season					Playoffs				
Season	Club	Lea	GP	G	A	TP	PIM	GP	G	A	TP	PIM
1993-94	Victoriaville	QMJHL	67	2	10	12	45	5	0	1	1	4
1994-95	Victoriaville	QMJHL	63	3	13	16	78	3	0	0	0	11
1995-96	Victoriaville	QMJHL	6	0	2	2	7	....	....	....	....	....
	Laval	QMJHL	27	0	6	6	41	....	....	....	....	....
	Beauport	QMJHL	18	2	3	5	22	19	0	3	3	6
1996-97	Beauport	QMJHL	54	5	8	13	73	4	0	2	2	2

MARLEAU, PATRICK S.J.

Center. Shoots left. 6'2", 190 lbs. Born, Swift Current, Sask., September 15, 1979.
(San Jose's 1st choice, 2nd overall, in 1997 Entry Draft).

			Regular Season					Playoffs				
Season	Club	Lea	GP	G	A	TP	PIM	GP	G	A	TP	PIM
1995-96	Seattle	WHL	72	32	42	74	22	5	3	4	7	4
1996-97a	Seattle	WHL	71	51	74	125	37	15	7	16	23	12

a WHL West First All-Star Team (1997)

MARSH, KEVIN CAR.

Left wing. Shoots left. 5'10", 175 lbs. Born, Edmonton, Alta., June 30, 1978.
(Hartford's 8th choice, 197th overall, in 1996 Entry Draft).

			Regular Season					Playoffs				
Season	Club	Lea	GP	G	A	TP	PIM	GP	G	A	TP	PIM
1995-96	Calgary	WHL	58	24	27	51	32	....	....	....	....	....
1996-97	Calgary	WHL	40	10	26	36	24	....	....	....	....	....
	Kelowna	WHL	22	5	7	12	20	6	0	0	0	2

MARSHALL, GRANT DAL.

Right wing. Shoots right. 6'1", 193 lbs. Born, Mississauga, Ont., June 9, 1973.
(Toronto's 2nd choice, 23rd overall, in 1992 Entry Draft).

			Regular Season					Playoffs				
Season	Club	Lea	GP	G	A	TP	PIM	GP	G	A	TP	PIM
1990-91	Ottawa	OHL	26	6	11	17	25	1	0	0	0	0
1991-92	Ottawa	OHL	61	32	51	83	132	11	6	11	17	11
1992-93	Ottawa	OHL	30	14	29	43	83	....	....	....	....	....
	Newmarket	OHL	31	11	25	36	89	7	4	7	11	20
	St. John's	AHL	2	0	0	0	0	2	0	0	0	2
1993-94	St. John's	AHL	67	11	29	40	155	11	1	5	6	17
1994-95	Kalamazoo	IHL	61	17	29	46	96	16	9	3	12	27
	Dallas	**NHL**	**2**	**0**	**1**	**1**	**0**	....	....	....	....	....
1995-96	**Dallas**	**NHL**	**70**	**9**	**19**	**28**	**111**	....	....	....	....	....
1996-97	**Dallas**	**NHL**	**56**	**6**	**4**	**10**	**98**	**5**	**0**	**2**	**2**	**8**
	NHL Totals		**128**	**15**	**24**	**39**	**209**	**5**	**0**	**2**	**2**	**8**

Acquired by **Dallas** from **Toronto** with Peter Zezel as compensation for Toronto's signing of free agent Mike Craig, August 10, 1994.

MARSHALL, JASON ANA.

Defense. Shoots right. 6'2", 200 lbs. Born, Cranbrook, B.C., February 22, 1971.
(St. Louis' 1st choice, 9th overall, in 1989 Entry Draft).

			Regular Season					Playoffs				
Season	Club	Lea	GP	G	A	TP	PIM	GP	G	A	TP	PIM
1988-89	Cdn. National	....	2	0	1	1	0	....	....	....	....	....
1989-90	Cdn. National	....	73	1	11	12	57	....	....	....	....	....
1990-91	Tri-Cities	WHL	59	10	34	44	236	7	1	2	3	20
	Peoria	IHL	....	....	....	....	....	18	0	1	1	48
1991-92	**St. Louis**	**NHL**	**2**	**1**	**0**	**1**	**4**	....	....	....	....	....
	Peoria	IHL	78	4	18	22	178	10	0	1	1	16
1992-93	Peoria	IHL	77	4	16	20	229	4	0	0	0	20
1993-94	Cdn. National	....	41	3	10	13	60	....	....	....	....	....
	Peoria	IHL	20	1	1	2	72	3	2	0	2	2
1994-95	San Diego	IHL	80	7	18	25	218	5	0	1	1	8
	Anaheim	**NHL**	**1**	**0**	**0**	**0**	**0**	....	....	....	....	....
1995-96	**Anaheim**	**NHL**	**24**	**0**	**1**	**1**	**42**	....	....	....	....	....
	Baltimore	AHL	57	1	13	14	150	....	....	....	....	....
1996-97	**Anaheim**	**NHL**	**73**	**1**	**9**	**10**	**140**	**7**	**0**	**1**	**1**	**4**
	NHL Totals		**100**	**2**	**10**	**12**	**186**	**7**	**0**	**1**	**1**	**4**

Traded to **Anaheim** by **St. Louis** for Bill Houlder, August 29, 1994.

MARTIN, CRAIG

Right wing. Shoots right. 6'2", 215 lbs. Born, Amherst, N.S., January 21, 1971.
(Winnipeg's 6th choice, 98th overall, in 1990 Entry Draft).

			Regular Season					Playoffs				
Season	Club	Lea	GP	G	A	TP	PIM	GP	G	A	TP	PIM
1989-90	Hull	QMJHL	66	14	31	45	299	11	2	1	3	65
1990-91	Hull	QMJHL	18	5	6	11	87	....	....	....	....	....
	St-Hyacinthe	QMJHL	36	8	9	17	166	....	....	....	....	....
1991-92	Moncton	AHL	11	1	1	2	70	....	....	....	....	....
	Fort Wayne	IHL	24	0	0	0	115	....	....	....	....	....
1992-93	Moncton	AHL	64	5	13	18	198	5	0	1	1	22
1993-94	Adirondack	AHL	76	15	24	39	297	12	2	2	4	63
1994-95	**Winnipeg**	**NHL**	**20**	**0**	**1**	**1**	**19**	....	....	....	....	....
	Springfield	AHL	6	0	1	1	21	....	....	....	....	....
1995-96	Springfield	AHL	48	6	5	11	245	8	0	1	1	34
1996-97	**Florida**	**NHL**	**1**	**0**	**0**	**0**	**5**	....	....	....	....	....
	Carolina	AHL	44	1	2	3	239	....	....	....	....	....
	San Antonio	IHL	15	3	3	6	99	6	0	1	1	25
	NHL Totals		**21**	**0**	**1**	**1**	**24**	....	....	....	....	....

Signed as a free agent by **Detroit**, July 28, 1993. Claimed on waivers by **Winnipeg** from **Detroit**, January 20, 1995. Signed as a free agent by **Florida**, August 1, 1996.

MARTIN, JEFF BUF.

Center. Shoots left. 6'1", 177 lbs. Born, Stratford, Ont., April 26, 1979.
(Buffalo's 4th choice, 75th overall, in 1997 Entry Draft).

			Regular Season					Playoffs				
Season	Club	Lea	GP	G	A	TP	PIM	GP	G	A	TP	PIM
1995-96	Windsor	OHL	63	9	5	14	8	7	1	1	2	4
1996-97	Windsor	OHL	65	24	23	47	37	5	2	0	2	2

MARTIN, JUSTIN L.A.

Right wing. Shoots right. 6'4", 210 lbs. Born, Syracuse, NY, May 1, 1975.
(Los Angeles' 8th choice, 172nd overall, in 1993 Entry Draft).

			Regular Season					Playoffs				
Season	Club	Lea	GP	G	A	TP	PIM	GP	G	A	TP	PIM
1994-95	Vermont	ECAC	23	4	2	6	20	....	....	....	....	....
1995-96	Vermont	ECAC	28	1	0	1	20	....	....	....	....	....
1996-97	Vermont	ECAC	35	3	6	9	49	....	....	....	....	....

MARTIN, MATT TOR.

Defense. Shoots left. 6'3", 205 lbs. Born, Hamden, CT, April 30, 1971.
(Toronto's 4th choice, 66th overall, in 1989 Entry Draft).

			Regular Season					Playoffs				
Season	Club	Lea	GP	G	A	TP	PIM	GP	G	A	TP	PIM
1990-91	U. of Maine	H.E.	35	3	12	15	48	....	....	....	....	....
1991-92	U. of Maine	H.E.	30	4	14	18	46	....	....	....	....	....
1992-93	U. of Maine	H.E.	44	6	26	32	88	....	....	....	....	....
	St. John's	AHL	2	0	0	0	2	9	1	5	6	4
1993-94	U.S. National	....	39	7	8	15	127	....	....	....	....	....
	U.S. Olympic	....	8	0	2	2	8	....	....	....	....	....
	Toronto	**NHL**	**12**	**0**	**1**	**1**	**6**	....	....	....	....	....
	St. John's	AHL	12	1	5	6	9	11	1	5	6	33
1994-95	St. John's	AHL	49	2	16	18	54	....	....	....	....	....
	Toronto	**NHL**	**15**	**0**	**0**	**0**	**13**	....	....	....	....	....
1995-96	**Toronto**	**NHL**	**13**	**0**	**0**	**0**	**14**	....	....	....	....	....
1996-97	**Toronto**	**NHL**	**36**	**0**	**4**	**4**	**38**	....	....	....	....	....
	St. John's	AHL	12	1	3	4	4	....	....	....	....	....
	NHL Totals		**76**	**0**	**5**	**5**	**71**	....	....	....	....	....

MARTIN, MIKE — NYR

Defense. Shoots right. 6'2", 204 lbs. Born, Stratford, Ont., October 27, 1976.
(NY Rangers' 2nd choice, 65th overall, in 1995 Entry Draft).

			Regular Season					Playoffs				
Season	Club	Lea	GP	G	A	TP	PIM	GP	G	A	TP	PIM
1992-93	Windsor	OHL	61	2	7	9	80	....	....	....	....	....
1993-94	Windsor	OHL	64	2	29	31	94	4	1	2	3	4
1994-95	Windsor	OHL	53	9	28	37	79	10	1	3	4	21
1995-96	Windsor	OHL	65	19	48	67	128	7	0	6	6	14
1996-97	Binghamton	AHL	62	2	7	9	45	3	0	1	1	2

MARTINS, STEVE — CAR.

Center. Shoots left. 5'9", 175 lbs. Born, Gatineau, Que., April 13, 1972.
(Hartford's 1st choice, 5th overall, in 1994 Supplemental Draft).

			Regular Season					Playoffs				
Season	Club	Lea	GP	G	A	TP	PIM	GP	G	A	TP	PIM
1991-92	Harvard	ECAC	20	13	14	27	26	....	....	....	....	....
1992-93	Harvard	ECAC	18	6	8	14	40	....	....	....	....	....
1993-94abc	Harvard	ECAC	32	25	35	60	*93	....	....	....	....	....
1994-95	Harvard	ECAC	28	15	23	38	93	....	....	....	....	....
1995-96	**Hartford**	**NHL**	**23**	**1**	**3**	**4**	**8**	....	....	....	....	....
	Springfield	AHL	30	9	20	29	10	....	....	....	....	....
1996-97	**Hartford**	**NHL**	**2**	**0**	**1**	**1**	**0**	....	....	....	....	....
	Springfield	AHL	63	12	31	43	78	17	1	3	4	26
	NHL Totals		**25**	**1**	**4**	**5**	**8**	....	....	....	....	....

a ECAC First All-Star Team (1994)
b NCAA East First All-American Team (1994)
c NCAA Final Four All-Tournament Team (1994)

MARTONE, MIKE — BUF.

Defense. Shoots right. 6'2", 200 lbs. Born, Sault Ste. Marie, Ont., September 26, 1977.
(Buffalo's 6th choice, 106th overall, in 1996 Entry Draft).

			Regular Season					Playoffs				
Season	Club	Lea	GP	G	A	TP	PIM	GP	G	A	TP	PIM
1994-95	Peterborough	OHL	62	3	9	12	99	10	0	2	2	4
1995-96	Peterborough	OHL	64	3	12	15	127	24	7	5	12	37
1996-97	Peterborough	OHL	50	9	21	30	104	10	0	6	6	30

MASON, WES — N.J.

Left wing. Shoots left. 6'2", 180 lbs. Born, Windsor, Ont., December 12, 1977.
(New Jersey's 2nd choice, 38th overall, in 1996 Entry Draft).

			Regular Season					Playoffs				
Season	Club	Lea	GP	G	A	TP	PIM	GP	G	A	TP	PIM
1994-95	Sarnia	OHL	38	1	8	9	50	2	0	0	0	9
1995-96	Sarnia	OHL	63	23	45	68	97	10	3	2	5	16
1996-97	Sarnia	OHL	66	45	46	91	72	12	7	11	18	10

MASTAD, MILT — (MIHZ-tahd) BOS.

Defense. Shoots left. 6'4", 233 lbs. Born, Regina, Sask., March 5, 1975.
(Boston's 6th choice, 155th overall, in 1993 Entry Draft).

			Regular Season					Playoffs				
Season	Club	Lea	GP	G	A	TP	PIM	GP	G	A	TP	PIM
1992-93	Seattle	WHL	60	1	1	2	123	5	0	1	1	14
1993-94	Seattle	WHL	29	1	3	4	59	....	....	....	....	....
	Moose Jaw	WHL	41	2	8	10	74	....	....	....	....	....
1994-95	Moose Jaw	WHL	68	1	8	9	155	5	0	0	0	6
1995-96	Providence	AHL	18	0	2	2	52	....	....	....	....	....
1996-97	Providence	AHL	33	0	2	2	106	....	....	....	....	....
	Charlotte	ECHL	9	0	0	0	25	3	0	1	1	4

MATHIEU, ALEXANDRE — (mah-TYOO) PIT.

Defense. Shoots left. 6'2", 180 lbs. Born, Repentigny, Que., February 12, 1979.
(Pittsburgh's 4th choice, 97th overall, in 1997 Entry Draft).

			Regular Season					Playoffs				
Season	Club	Lea	GP	G	A	TP	PIM	GP	G	A	TP	PIM
1995-96	Laval	Midget	44	6	24	30	24	....	....	....	....	....
1996-97	Halifax	QMJHL	70	12	22	34	16	18	2	5	7	2

MATSOS, DAVID — T.B.

Left wing. Shoots left. 6'1", 201 lbs. Born, Burlington, Ont., November 12, 1973.

			Regular Season					Playoffs				
Season	Club	Lea	GP	G	A	TP	PIM	GP	G	A	TP	PIM
1989-90	S.S. Marie	OHL	53	2	5	7	31	....	....	....	....	....
1990-91	S.S. Marie	OHL	60	10	16	26	41	14	2	5	7	10
1991-92	S.S. Marie	OHL	61	23	22	45	34	19	4	5	9	6
1992-93	S.S. Marie	OHL	56	31	28	59	27	18	9	8	17	16
1993-94	Western Ont.	OUAA	37	25	16	41	26	....	....	....	....	....
1994-95	Western Ont.	OUAA	33	15	16	31	25	....	....	....	....	....
1995-96	Cdn. National	....	43	18	15	33	37	....	....	....	....	....
1996-97	Adirondack	AHL	56	20	12	32	21	4	0	1	1	0

Signed as a free agent by **Tampa Bay**, May 1, 1996.

MATTE, CHRISTIAN — COL.

Right wing. Shoots right. 5'11", 166 lbs. Born, Hull, Que., January 20, 1975.
(Quebec's 8th choice, 153rd overall, in 1993 Entry Draft).

			Regular Season					Playoffs				
Season	Club	Lea	GP	G	A	TP	PIM	GP	G	A	TP	PIM
1992-93	Granby	QMJHL	68	17	36	53	59	....	....	....	....	....
1993-94a	Granby	QMJHL	59	50	47	97	103	7	5	5	10	12
	Cornwall	AHL	1	0	0	0	0	....	....	....	....	....
1994-95	Granby	QMJHL	66	50	66	116	86	13	11	7	18	12
	Cornwall	AHL	....	....	....	....	....	3	0	1	1	2
1995-96	Cornwall	AHL	64	20	32	52	51	7	1	1	2	6
1996-97	**Colorado**	**NHL**	**5**	**1**	**1**	**2**	**0**	....	....	....	....	....
	Hershey	AHL	49	18	18	36	78	22	8	3	11	25
	NHL Totals		**5**	**1**	**1**	**2**	**0**	....	....	....	....	....

a QMJHL Second All-Star Team (1994)

MATTEAU, STEPHANE — (mah-TOH) S.J.

Left wing. Shoots left. 6'3", 215 lbs. Born, Rouyn-Noranda, Que., September 2, 1969.
(Calgary's 2nd choice, 25th overall, in 1987 Entry Draft).

			Regular Season					Playoffs				
Season	Club	Lea	GP	G	A	TP	PIM	GP	G	A	TP	PIM
1985-86	Hull	QMJHL	60	6	8	14	19	4	0	0	0	0
1986-87	Hull	QMJHL	69	27	48	75	113	8	3	7	10	8
1987-88	Hull	QMJHL	57	17	40	57	179	18	5	14	19	94
1988-89	Hull	QMJHL	59	44	45	89	202	9	8	6	14	30
	Salt Lake	IHL	....	....	....	....	....	9	0	4	4	13
1989-90	Salt Lake	IHL	81	23	35	58	130	10	6	3	9	38
1990-91	**Calgary**	**NHL**	**78**	**15**	**19**	**34**	**93**	**5**	**0**	**1**	**1**	**0**
1991-92	**Calgary**	**NHL**	**4**	**1**	**0**	**1**	**19**	....	....	....	....	....
	Chicago	**NHL**	**20**	**5**	**8**	**13**	**45**	**18**	**4**	**6**	**10**	**24**
1992-93	**Chicago**	**NHL**	**79**	**15**	**18**	**33**	**98**	**3**	**0**	**1**	**1**	**2**
1993-94	**Chicago**	**NHL**	**65**	**15**	**16**	**31**	**55**	....	....	....	....	....
	NY Rangers	**NHL**	**12**	**4**	**3**	**7**	**2**	**23**	**6**	**3**	**9**	**20** ◆
1994-95	**NY Rangers**	**NHL**	**41**	**3**	**5**	**8**	**25**	**9**	**0**	**1**	**1**	**10**
1995-96	**NY Rangers**	**NHL**	**32**	**4**	**2**	**6**	**22**	....	....	....	....	....
	St. Louis	**NHL**	**46**	**7**	**13**	**20**	**65**	**11**	**0**	**2**	**2**	**8**
1996-97	**St. Louis**	**NHL**	**74**	**16**	**20**	**36**	**50**	**5**	**0**	**0**	**0**	**0**
	NHL Totals		**451**	**85**	**104**	**189**	**474**	**74**	**10**	**14**	**24**	**64**

Traded to **Chicago** by **Calgary** for Trent Yawney, December 16, 1991. Traded to **NY Rangers** by **Chicago** with Brian Noonan for Tony Amonte and the rights to Matt Oates, March 21, 1994. Traded to **St. Louis** by **NY Rangers** for Ian Laperriere, December 28, 1995. Traded to **San Jose** by **St. Louis** for Darren Turcotte, July 24, 1997.

MATTSSON, JESPER — (MAT-suhn) CGY.

Center. Shoots right. 6', 185 lbs. Born, Malmo, Sweden, May 13, 1975.
(Calgary's 1st choice, 18th overall, in 1993 Entry Draft).

			Regular Season					Playoffs				
Season	Club	Lea	GP	G	A	TP	PIM	GP	G	A	TP	PIM
1991-92	Malmo	Swe.	24	0	1	1	2	....	....	....	....	....
1992-93	Malmo	Swe.	40	9	8	17	14	5	0	0	0	0
1993-94	Malmo	Swe.	40	3	6	9	14	9	1	2	3	2
1994-95	Malmo	Swe.	37	9	6	15	18	9	2	0	2	18
1995-96	Saint John	AHL	73	12	26	38	18	9	1	1	2	2
1996-97	Saint John	AHL	72	22	18	40	32	3	1	1	2	0

MATVICHUK, RICHARD — (MAT-vih-chuhk) DAL.

Defense. Shoots left. 6'2", 200 lbs. Born, Edmonton, Alta., February 5, 1973.
(Minnesota's 1st choice, 8th overall, in 1991 Entry Draft).

			Regular Season					Playoffs				
Season	Club	Lea	GP	G	A	TP	PIM	GP	G	A	TP	PIM
1989-90	Saskatoon	WHL	56	8	24	32	126	10	2	8	10	16
1990-91	Saskatoon	WHL	68	13	36	49	117	....	....	....	....	....
1991-92a	Saskatoon	WHL	58	14	40	54	126	22	1	9	10	61
1992-93	**Minnesota**	**NHL**	**53**	**2**	**3**	**5**	**26**	....	....	....	....	....
	Kalamazoo	IHL	3	0	1	1	6	....	....	....	....	....
1993-94	**Dallas**	**NHL**	**25**	**0**	**3**	**3**	**22**	**7**	**1**	**1**	**2**	**12**
	Kalamazoo	IHL	43	8	17	25	84	....	....	....	....	....
1994-95	**Dallas**	**NHL**	**14**	**0**	**2**	**2**	**14**	**5**	**0**	**2**	**2**	**4**
	Kalamazoo	IHL	17	0	6	6	16	....	....	....	....	....
1995-96	**Dallas**	**NHL**	**73**	**6**	**16**	**22**	**71**	....	....	....	....	....
1996-97	**Dallas**	**NHL**	**57**	**5**	**7**	**12**	**87**	**7**	**0**	**1**	**1**	**20**
	NHL Totals		**222**	**13**	**31**	**44**	**220**	**19**	**1**	**4**	**5**	**36**

a WHL East First All-Star Team (1992)

MAUDIE, BOB — NYR

Center. Shoots left. 5'11", 180 lbs. Born, Cranbrook, B.C., September 17, 1976.
(NY Rangers' 9th choice, 221st overall, in 1995 Entry Draft).

			Regular Season					Playoffs				
Season	Club	Lea	GP	G	A	TP	PIM	GP	G	A	TP	PIM
1992-93	Kamloops	WHL	38	1	5	6	24	3	0	0	0	0
1993-94	Kamloops	WHL	65	11	13	24	29	19	1	1	2	2
1994-95	Kamloops	WHL	67	9	29	38	34	21	1	2	3	8
1995-96	Kamloops	WHL	67	39	62	101	77	16	8	11	19	16
1996-97	Binghamton	AHL	19	0	3	3	6	2	0	0	0	0
	Charlotte	ECHL	6	1	1	2	4	....	....	....	....	....

MAY, ALAN

Right wing. Shoots right. 6'1", 200 lbs. Born, Swan Hills, Alta., January 14, 1965.

			Regular Season					Playoffs				
Season	Club	Lea	GP	G	A	TP	PIM	GP	G	A	TP	PIM
1985-86	Medicine Hat	WHL	6	1	0	1	25	....	....	....	....	....
	N. Westminster	WHL	32	8	9	17	81	....	....	....	....	....
1986-87	Springfield	AHL	4	0	2	2	11	....	....	....	....	....
	Carolina	ACHL	42	23	14	37	310	5	2	2	4	57
1987-88	**Boston**	**NHL**	**3**	**0**	**0**	**0**	**15**	....	....	....	....	....
	Maine	AHL	61	14	11	25	257	....	....	....	....	....
	Nova Scotia	AHL	13	4	1	5	54	4	0	0	0	51
1988-89	**Edmonton**	**NHL**	**3**	**1**	**0**	**1**	**7**	....	....	....	....	....
	Cape Breton	AHL	50	12	13	25	214	....	....	....	....	....
	New Haven	AHL	12	2	8	10	99	16	6	3	9	*105
1989-90	**Washington**	**NHL**	**77**	**7**	**10**	**17**	**339**	**15**	**0**	**0**	**0**	**37**
1990-91	**Washington**	**NHL**	**67**	**4**	**6**	**10**	**264**	**11**	**1**	**1**	**2**	**37**
1991-92	**Washington**	**NHL**	**75**	**6**	**9**	**15**	**221**	**7**	**0**	**0**	**0**	**0**
1992-93	**Washington**	**NHL**	**83**	**6**	**10**	**16**	**268**	**6**	**0**	**1**	**1**	**6**
1993-94	**Washington**	**NHL**	**43**	**4**	**7**	**11**	**97**	....	....	....	....	....
	Dallas	**NHL**	**8**	**1**	**0**	**1**	**18**	**1**	**0**	**0**	**0**	**0**
1994-95	**Dallas**	**NHL**	**27**	**1**	**1**	**2**	**106**	....	....	....	....	....
	Calgary	**NHL**	**7**	**1**	**2**	**3**	**13**	....	....	....	....	....
1995-96	Orlando	IHL	4	0	0	0	11	....	....	....	....	....
	Detroit	IHL	17	2	5	7	49	....	....	....	....	....
	Utah	IHL	53	13	12	25	108	14	1	2	3	14
1996-97	Houston	IHL	82	7	11	18	270	13	1	2	3	28
	NHL Totals		**393**	**31**	**45**	**76**	**1348**	**40**	**1**	**2**	**3**	**80**

Signed as a free agent by **Boston**, October 30, 1987. Traded to **Edmonton** by **Boston** for Moe Lemay, March 8, 1988. Traded to **Los Angeles** by **Edmonton** with Jim Wiemer for Brian Wilks and John English, March 7, 1989. Traded to **Washington** by **Los Angeles** for Washington's fifth round choice (Thomas Newman) in 1989 Entry Draft, June 17, 1989. Traded to **Dallas** by **Washington** with Washington's seventh round choice (Jeff Dewar) in 1995 Entry Draft for Jim Johnson, March 21, 1994. Traded to **Calgary** by **Dallas** for Calgary's eighth round choice (Sergei Luchinkin) in 1995 Entry Draft, April 7, 1995.

MAY, BRAD — BUF.

Left wing. Shoots left. 6'1", 206 lbs. Born, Toronto, Ont., November 29, 1971.
(Buffalo's 1st choice, 14th overall, in 1990 Entry Draft).

			Regular Season					Playoffs				
Season	Club	Lea	GP	G	A	TP	PIM	GP	G	A	TP	PIM
1988-89	Niagara Falls	OHL	65	8	14	22	304	17	0	1	1	55
1989-90a	Niagara Falls	OHL	61	32	58	90	223	16	9	13	22	64
1990-91a	Niagara Falls	OHL	34	37	32	69	93	14	11	14	25	53
1991-92	**Buffalo**	**NHL**	**69**	**11**	**6**	**17**	**309**	**7**	**1**	**4**	**5**	**2**
1992-93	**Buffalo**	**NHL**	**82**	**13**	**13**	**26**	**242**	**8**	**1**	**1**	**2**	**14**
1993-94	**Buffalo**	**NHL**	**84**	**18**	**27**	**45**	**171**	**7**	**0**	**2**	**2**	**9**
1994-95	**Buffalo**	**NHL**	**33**	**3**	**3**	**6**	**87**	**4**	**0**	**0**	**0**	**2**
1995-96	**Buffalo**	**NHL**	**79**	**15**	**29**	**44**	**295**	....	....	....	....	....
1996-97	**Buffalo**	**NHL**	**42**	**3**	**4**	**7**	**106**	**10**	**1**	**1**	**2**	**32**
	NHL Totals		**389**	**63**	**82**	**145**	**1210**	**36**	**3**	**8**	**11**	**59**

a OHL Second All-Star Team (1990, 1991)

MAYERS, JAMAL — ST.L.

Center. Shoots right. 6', 190 lbs. Born, Toronto, Ont., October 24, 1974.
(St. Louis' 3rd choice, 89th overall, in 1993 Entry Draft).

			Regular Season					Playoffs				
Season	Club	Lea	GP	G	A	TP	PIM	GP	G	A	TP	PIM
1992-93	W. Michigan	CCHA	38	8	17	25	26	....	....	....	....	....
1993-94	W. Michigan	CCHA	40	17	32	49	40	....	....	....	....	....
1994-95	W. Michigan	CCHA	39	13	32	45	40	....	....	....	....	....
1995-96	W. Michigan	CCHA	38	17	22	39	75	....	....	....	....	....
1996-97	**St. Louis**	**NHL**	**6**	**0**	**1**	**1**	**2**	....	....	....	....	....
	Worcester	AHL	62	12	14	26	104	5	4	5	9	4
	NHL Totals		**6**	**0**	**1**	**1**	**2**	....	....	....	....	....

McALLISTER, CHRIS — VAN.

Defense. Shoots left. 6'7", 225 lbs. Born, Saskatoon, Sask., June 16, 1975.
(Vancouver's 2nd choice, 40th overall, in 1995 Entry Draft).

			Regular Season					Playoffs				
Season	Club	Lea	GP	G	A	TP	PIM	GP	G	A	TP	PIM
1993-94	Saskatoon	WHL	2	0	0	0	5	....	....	....	....	....
1994-95	Saskatoon	WHL	65	2	8	10	134	10	0	0	0	28
1995-96	Syracuse	AHL	68	0	2	2	142	16	0	0	0	34
1996-97	Syracuse	AHL	43	3	1	4	108	3	0	0	0	6

McALPINE, CHRIS — ST.L.

Defense. Shoots right. 6', 210 lbs. Born, Roseville, MN, December 1, 1971.
(New Jersey's 10th choice, 137th overall, in 1990 Entry Draft).

			Regular Season					Playoffs				
Season	Club	Lea	GP	G	A	TP	PIM	GP	G	A	TP	PIM
1990-91	U. Minnesota	WCHA	38	7	9	16	112	....	....	....	....	....
1991-92	U. Minnesota	WCHA	39	3	9	12	126	....	....	....	....	....
1992-93	U. Minnesota	WCHA	41	14	9	23	82	....	....	....	....	....
1993-94ab	U. Minnesota	WCHA	36	12	18	30	121	....	....	....	....	....
1994-95	Albany	AHL	48	4	18	22	49	....	....	....	....	....
	New Jersey	**NHL**	**24**	**0**	**3**	**3**	**17**	....	....	....	....	.... ♦
1995-96	Albany	AHL	57	5	14	19	72	4	0	0	0	13
1996-97	Albany	AHL	44	1	9	10	48	....	....	....	....	....
	St. Louis	**NHL**	**15**	**0**	**0**	**0**	**24**	**4**	**0**	**1**	**1**	**0**
	NHL Totals		**39**	**0**	**3**	**3**	**41**	**4**	**0**	**1**	**1**	**0**

a WCHA First All-Star Team (1994)
b NCAA West Second All-American Team (1994)

Traded to **St. Louis** by **New Jersey** with New Jersey's ninth round choice in 1999 Entry Draft for Peter Zezel, February 11, 1997.

McAMMOND, DEAN — EDM.

Center. Shoots left. 5'11", 185 lbs. Born, Grand Cache, Alta., June 15, 1973.
(Chicago's 1st choice, 22nd overall, in 1991 Entry Draft).

			Regular Season					Playoffs				
Season	Club	Lea	GP	G	A	TP	PIM	GP	G	A	TP	PIM
1989-90	Prince Albert	WHL	53	11	11	22	49	14	2	3	5	18
1990-91	Prince Albert	WHL	71	33	35	68	108	2	0	1	1	6
1991-92	**Chicago**	**NHL**	**5**	**0**	**2**	**2**	**0**	**3**	**0**	**0**	**0**	**2**
	Prince Albert	WHL	63	37	54	91	189	10	12	11	23	26
1992-93	Prince Albert	WHL	30	19	29	48	44	....	....	....	....	....
	Swift Current	WHL	18	10	13	23	24	17	*16	19	35	20
1993-94	**Edmonton**	**NHL**	**45**	**6**	**21**	**27**	**16**	....	....	....	....	....
	Cape Breton	AHL	28	9	12	21	38	....	....	....	....	....
1994-95	**Edmonton**	**NHL**	**6**	**0**	**0**	**0**	**0**	....	....	....	....	....
1995-96	**Edmonton**	**NHL**	**53**	**15**	**15**	**30**	**23**	....	....	....	....	....
	Cape Breton	AHL	22	9	15	24	55	....	....	....	....	....
1996-97	**Edmonton**	**NHL**	**57**	**12**	**17**	**29**	**28**	....	....	....	....	....
	NHL Totals		**166**	**33**	**55**	**88**	**67**	**3**	**0**	**0**	**0**	**2**

Traded to **Edmonton** by **Chicago** with Igor Kravchuk for Joe Murphy, February 24, 1993.

McBAIN, JASON — CAR.

Defense. Shoots left. 6'2", 180 lbs. Born, Ilion, NY, April 12, 1974.
(Hartford's 5th choice, 81st overall, in 1992 Entry Draft).

			Regular Season					Playoffs				
Season	Club	Lea	GP	G	A	TP	PIM	GP	G	A	TP	PIM
1990-91	Lethbridge	WHL	52	2	7	9	39	1	0	0	0	0
1991-92	Lethbridge	WHL	13	0	1	1	12	....	....	....	....	....
	Portland	WHL	54	9	23	32	95	6	1	0	1	13
1992-93	Portland	WHL	71	9	35	44	76	16	2	12	14	14
1993-94	Portland	WHL	63	15	51	66	86	10	2	7	9	14
1994-95	Springfield	AHL	77	16	28	44	92	....	....	....	....	....
1995-96	**Hartford**	**NHL**	**3**	**0**	**0**	**0**	**0**	....	....	....	....	....
	Springfield	AHL	73	11	33	44	43	8	1	1	2	2
1996-97	**Hartford**	**NHL**	**6**	**0**	**0**	**0**	**0**	....	....	....	....	....
	Springfield	AHL	58	8	26	34	40	16	0	8	8	12
	NHL Totals		**9**	**0**	**0**	**0**	**0**	....	....	....	....	....

McBAIN, MIKE — T.B.

Defense. Shoots left. 6'1", 191 lbs. Born, Kimberley, B.C., January 12, 1977.
(Tampa Bay's 2nd choice, 30th overall, in 1995 Entry Draft).

			Regular Season					Playoffs				
Season	Club	Lea	GP	G	A	TP	PIM	GP	G	A	TP	PIM
1993-94	Red Deer	WHL	58	4	13	17	41	4	0	0	0	0
1994-95	Red Deer	WHL	68	6	28	34	55	....	....	....	....	....
1995-96	Red Deer	WHL	68	7	34	41	68	10	1	7	8	10
1996-97	Red Deer	WHL	59	14	35	49	55	15	1	6	7	9

McCABE, BRYAN — NYI

Defense. Shoots left. 6'1", 204 lbs. Born, St. Catharines, Ont., June 8, 1975.
(NY Islanders' 2nd choice, 40th overall, in 1993 Entry Draft).

			Regular Season					Playoffs				
Season	Club	Lea	GP	G	A	TP	PIM	GP	G	A	TP	PIM
1991-92	Medicine Hat	WHL	68	6	24	30	157	4	0	0	0	6
1992-93	Medicine Hat	WHL	14	0	13	13	83	....	....	....	....	....
a	Spokane	WHL	46	3	44	47	134	6	1	5	6	28
1993-94	Spokane	WHL	64	22	62	84	218	3	0	4	4	4
1994-95	Spokane	WHL	42	14	39	53	115	....	....	....	....	....
bc	Brandon	WHL	20	6	10	16	38	18	4	13	17	59
1995-96	**NY Islanders**	**NHL**	**82**	**7**	**16**	**23**	**156**	....	....	....	....	....
1996-97	**NY Islanders**	**NHL**	**82**	**8**	**20**	**28**	**165**	....	....	....	....	....
	NHL Totals		**164**	**15**	**36**	**51**	**321**	....	....	....	....	....

a WHL West Second All-Star Team (1993)
b WHL East First All-Star Team (1995)
c Memorial Cup All-Star Team (1995)

McCALLUM, SCOTT — PHO.

Defense. Shoots left. 6'3", 218 lbs. Born, Dauphin, Man., February 15, 1979.
(Phoenix's 2nd choice, 96th overall, in 1997 Entry Draft).

			Regular Season					Playoffs				
Season	Club	Lea	GP	G	A	TP	PIM	GP	G	A	TP	PIM
1995-96	Tri-City	WHL	45	1	1	2	27	6	0	0	0	0
1996-97	Tri-City	WHL	56	1	16	17	119	....	....	....	....	....

McCAMBRIDGE, KEITH — CGY.

Defense. Shoots left. 6'2", 205 lbs. Born, Thompson, Man., February 1, 1974.
(Calgary's 10th choice, 201st overall, in 1994 Entry Draft).

			Regular Season					Playoffs				
Season	Club	Lea	GP	G	A	TP	PIM	GP	G	A	TP	PIM
1991-92	Swift Current	WHL	72	1	4	5	84	8	0	0	0	2
1992-93	Swift Current	WHL	70	0	6	6	87	17	0	1	1	27
1993-94	Swift Current	WHL	71	0	10	10	179	7	0	0	0	4
1994-95	Swift Current	WHL	48	5	7	12	120	....	....	....	....	....
	Kamloops	WHL	21	0	6	6	90	21	0	5	5	49
1995-96	Saint John	AHL	48	1	3	4	89	16	0	0	0	6
1996-97	Saint John	AHL	56	2	1	3	109	....	....	....	....	....

McCARTHY, SANDY — CGY.

Right wing. Shoots right. 6'3", 225 lbs. Born, Toronto, Ont., June 15, 1972.
(Calgary's 3rd choice, 52nd overall, in 1991 Entry Draft).

			Regular Season					Playoffs				
Season	Club	Lea	GP	G	A	TP	PIM	GP	G	A	TP	PIM
1989-90	Laval	QMJHL	65	10	11	21	269	14	3	3	6	60
1990-91	Laval	QMJHL	68	21	19	40	297	13	6	5	11	67
1991-92	Laval	QMJHL	62	39	51	90	326	8	4	5	9	81
1992-93	Salt Lake	IHL	77	18	20	38	220	....	....	....	....	....
1993-94	**Calgary**	**NHL**	**79**	**5**	**5**	**10**	**173**	**7**	**0**	**0**	**0**	**34**
1994-95	**Calgary**	**NHL**	**37**	**5**	**3**	**8**	**101**	**6**	**0**	**1**	**1**	**17**
1995-96	**Calgary**	**NHL**	**75**	**9**	**7**	**16**	**173**	**4**	**0**	**0**	**0**	**10**
1996-97	**Calgary**	**NHL**	**33**	**3**	**5**	**8**	**113**	....	....	....	....	....
	NHL Totals		**224**	**22**	**20**	**42**	**560**	**17**	**0**	**1**	**1**	**61**

McCARTY, DARREN — DET.

Right wing. Shoots right. 6'1", 210 lbs. Born, Burnaby, B.C., April 1, 1972.
(Detroit's 2nd choice, 46th overall, in 1992 Entry Draft).

			Regular Season					Playoffs				
Season	Club	Lea	GP	G	A	TP	PIM	GP	G	A	TP	PIM
1989-90	Belleville	OHL	63	12	15	27	142	11	1	1	2	21
1990-91	Belleville	OHL	60	30	37	67	151	6	2	2	4	13
1991-92a	Belleville	OHL	65	*55	72	127	177	5	1	4	5	13
1992-93	Adirondack	AHL	73	17	19	36	278	11	0	1	1	33
1993-94	**Detroit**	**NHL**	**67**	**9**	**17**	**26**	**181**	**7**	**2**	**2**	**4**	**8**
1994-95	**Detroit**	**NHL**	**31**	**5**	**8**	**13**	**88**	**18**	**3**	**2**	**5**	**14**
1995-96	**Detroit**	**NHL**	**63**	**15**	**14**	**29**	**158**	**19**	**3**	**2**	**5**	**20**
1996-97	**Detroit**	**NHL**	**68**	**19**	**30**	**49**	**126**	**20**	**3**	**4**	**7**	**34** ♦
	NHL Totals		**229**	**48**	**69**	**117**	**553**	**64**	**11**	**10**	**21**	**76**

a OHL First All-Star Team (1992)

McCAULEY, ALYN — TOR.

Center. Shoots left. 5'11", 185 lbs. Born, Brockville, Ont., May 29, 1977.
(New Jersey's 5th choice, 79th overall, in 1995 Entry Draft).

			Regular Season					Playoffs				
Season	Club	Lea	GP	G	A	TP	PIM	GP	G	A	TP	PIM
1993-94	Ottawa	OHL	38	13	23	36	10	13	5	14	19	4
1994-95	Ottawa	OHL	65	16	38	54	20	....	....	....	....	....
1995-96a	Ottawa	OHL	55	34	48	82	24	2	0	0	0	0
1996-97abc	Ottawa	OHL	50	*56	56	112	16	22	14	22	36	14
	St. John's	AHL	....	....	....	....	....	3	0	1	1	0

a OHL First All-Star Team (1996, 1997)
b Canadian Major Junior First All-Star Team (1997)
c Canadian Major Junior Player of the Year (1997)

Rights traded to **Toronto** by **New Jersey** with Jason Smith and Steve Sullivan for Doug Gilmour, Dave Ellett and a conditional draft choice, February 25, 1997.

McCAULEY, BILL — BOS.

Center. Shoots left. 6'1", 195 lbs. Born, Detroit, MI, April 20, 1975.
(Florida's 6th choice, 83rd overall, in 1993 Entry Draft).

			Regular Season					Playoffs				
Season	Club	Lea	GP	G	A	TP	PIM	GP	G	A	TP	PIM
1992-93	Detroit	OHL	65	13	37	50	24	15	1	4	5	6
1993-94	Detroit	OHL	59	18	39	57	51	16	4	7	11	25
1994-95	Detroit	OHL	66	41	61	102	43	21	12	*27	*39	12
1995-96	Providence	AHL	62	11	17	28	71	....	....	....	....	....
1996-97	Providence	AHL	19	2	3	5	10	....	....	....	....	....
	Charlotte	ECHL	38	8	20	28	39	3	1	1	2	8

Re-entered NHL Entry Draft, **Boston's** 4th choice, 73rd overall in 1995 Entry Draft.

McCLEARY, TRENT — BOS.

Right wing. Shoots right. 6', 180 lbs. Born, Swift Current, Sask., September 8, 1972.

			Regular Season					Playoffs				
Season	Club	Lea	GP	G	A	TP	PIM	GP	G	A	TP	PIM
1989-90	Swift Current	WHL	70	3	15	18	43	4	1	0	1	0
1990-91	Swift Current	WHL	70	16	24	40	53	3	0	0	0	2
1991-92	Swift Current	WHL	72	23	22	45	240	8	1	2	3	16
1992-93	Swift Current	WHL	63	17	33	50	138	17	5	4	9	16
	New Haven	AHL	2	1	0	1	6	....	....	....	....	....
1993-94	P.E.I.	AHL	4	0	0	0	6	....	....	....	....	....
	Thunder Bay	ColHL	51	23	17	40	123	9	2	11	13	15
1994-95	P.E.I.	AHL	51	9	20	29	60	9	2	3	5	26
1995-96	**Ottawa**	**NHL**	**75**	**4**	**10**	**14**	**68**	....	....	....	....	....
1996-97	**Boston**	**NHL**	**59**	**3**	**5**	**8**	**33**	....	....	....	....	....
	NHL Totals		**134**	**7**	**15**	**22**	**101**	....	....	....	....	....

Signed as a free agent by **Ottawa**, October 9, 1992. Traded to **Boston** by **Ottawa** with Ottawa's third round choice (Eric Naud) in 1996 Entry Draft for Shawn McEachern, June 22, 1996.

McCOSH, SHAWN — PHI.

Center. Shoots right. 6', 197 lbs. Born, Oshawa, Ont., June 5, 1969.
(Detroit's 5th choice, 95th overall, in 1989 Entry Draft).

			Regular Season					Playoffs				
Season	Club	Lea	GP	G	A	TP	PIM	GP	G	A	TP	PIM
1986-87	Hamilton	OHL	50	11	17	28	49	6	1	0	1	2
1987-88	Hamilton	OHL	64	17	36	53	96	14	6	8	14	14
1988-89	Niagara Falls	OHL	56	41	62	103	75	14	4	13	17	23
1989-90	Niagara Falls	OHL	9	6	10	16	24	....	....	....	....	....
	Hamilton	OHL	39	24	28	52	65	....	....	....	....	....
1990-91	New Haven	AHL	66	16	21	37	104	....	....	....	....	....
1991-92	**Los Angeles**	**NHL**	**4**	**0**	**0**	**0**	**4**	....	....	....	....	....
	Phoenix	IHL	71	21	32	53	118	....	....	....	....	....
	New Haven	AHL	....	....	....	....	....	5	0	1	1	0
1992-93	New Haven	AHL	46	22	32	54	54	....	....	....	....	....
	Phoenix	IHL	22	9	8	17	36	....	....	....	....	....
1993-94	Binghamton	AHL	75	31	44	75	68	....	....	....	....	....
1994-95	Binghamton	AHL	67	23	60	83	73	8	3	9	12	6
	NY Rangers	**NHL**	**5**	**1**	**0**	**1**	**2**	....	....	....	....	....
1995-96	Hershey	AHL	71	31	52	83	82	5	1	5	6	8
1996-97	Philadelphia	AHL	79	30	51	81	110	10	3	9	12	23
	NHL Totals		**9**	**1**	**0**	**1**	**6**	....	....	....	....	....

Traded to **Los Angeles** by **Detroit** for Los Angeles' eighth round choice (Justin Krall) in 1992 Entry Draft, August 15, 1990. Traded to **Ottawa** by **Los Angeles** with Bob Kudelski for Marc Fortier and Jim Thomson, December 19, 1992. Signed as a free agent by **NY Rangers**, July 30, 1993. Signed as a free agent by **Philadelphia**, July 31, 1995.

McCRIMMON, BRAD

Defense. Shoots left. 5'11", 197 lbs. Born, Dodsland, Sask., March 29, 1959.
(Boston's 2nd choice, 15th overall, in 1979 Entry Draft).

			Regular Season					Playoffs				
Season	Club	Lea	GP	G	A	TP	PIM	GP	G	A	TP	PIM
1977-78a	Brandon	WHL	65	19	78	97	245	8	2	11	13	20
1978-79a	Brandon	WHL	66	24	74	98	139	22	9	19	28	34
1979-80	**Boston**	**NHL**	**72**	**5**	**11**	**16**	**94**	**10**	**1**	**1**	**2**	**28**
1980-81	**Boston**	**NHL**	**78**	**11**	**18**	**29**	**148**	**3**	**0**	**1**	**1**	**2**
1981-82	**Boston**	**NHL**	**78**	**1**	**8**	**9**	**83**	**2**	**0**	**0**	**0**	**2**
1982-83	**Philadelphia**	**NHL**	**79**	**4**	**21**	**25**	**61**	**3**	**0**	**0**	**0**	**4**
1983-84	**Philadelphia**	**NHL**	**71**	**0**	**24**	**24**	**76**	**1**	**0**	**0**	**0**	**4**
1984-85	**Philadelphia**	**NHL**	**66**	**8**	**35**	**43**	**81**	**11**	**2**	**1**	**3**	**15**
1985-86	**Philadelphia**	**NHL**	**80**	**13**	**43**	**56**	**85**	**5**	**2**	**0**	**2**	**2**
1986-87	**Philadelphia**	**NHL**	**71**	**10**	**29**	**39**	**52**	**26**	**3**	**5**	**8**	**30**
1987-88bc	**Calgary**	**NHL**	**80**	**7**	**35**	**42**	**98**	**9**	**2**	**3**	**5**	**22**
1988-89	**Calgary**	**NHL**	**72**	**5**	**17**	**22**	**96**	**22**	**0**	**3**	**3**	**30** ♦
1989-90	**Calgary**	**NHL**	**79**	**4**	**15**	**19**	**78**	**6**	**0**	**2**	**2**	**8**
1990-91	**Detroit**	**NHL**	**64**	**0**	**13**	**13**	**81**	**7**	**1**	**1**	**2**	**21**
1991-92	**Detroit**	**NHL**	**79**	**7**	**22**	**29**	**118**	**11**	**0**	**1**	**1**	**8**
1992-93	**Detroit**	**NHL**	**60**	**1**	**14**	**15**	**71**	....	....	....	....	....
1993-94	**Hartford**	**NHL**	**65**	**1**	**5**	**6**	**72**	....	....	....	....	....
1994-95	**Hartford**	**NHL**	**33**	**0**	**1**	**1**	**42**	....	....	....	....	....
1995-96	**Hartford**	**NHL**	**58**	**3**	**6**	**9**	**62**	....	....	....	....	....
1996-97	**Phoenix**	**NHL**	**37**	**1**	**5**	**6**	**18**	....	....	....	....	....
	NHL Totals		**1222**	**81**	**322**	**403**	**1416**	**116**	**11**	**18**	**29**	**176**

a WHL First All-Star Team (1978, 1979)
b NHL Second All-Star Team (1988)
c NHL Plus/Minus Leader (1988)

Played in NHL All-Star Game (1988)

Traded to **Philadelphia** by **Boston** for Pete Peeters, June 9, 1982. Traded to **Calgary** by **Philadelphia** for Calgary's third round choice (Dominic Roussel) in 1988 Entry Draft and first round choice (later traded to Toronto — Toronto selected Steve Bancroft) in 1989 Entry Draft, August 26, 1987. Traded to **Detroit** by **Calgary** for Detroit's second round choice (later traded to New Jersey — New Jersey selected David Harlock) in 1990 Entry Draft, June 15, 1990. Traded to **Hartford** by **Detroit** for Detroit's sixth round choice (previously acquired by Hartford — Detroit selected Tim Spitzig) in 1993 Entry Draft, June 1, 1993. Signed as a free agent by **Phoenix**, July 16, 1996.

McEACHERN, SHAWN (muh-GEH-kruhn) — OTT.

Left wing. Shoots left. 5'11", 195 lbs. Born, Waltham, MA, February 28, 1969.
(Pittsburgh's 6th choice, 110th overall, in 1987 Entry Draft).

			Regular Season					Playoffs				
Season	Club	Lea	GP	G	A	TP	PIM	GP	G	A	TP	PIM
1988-89	Boston U.	H.E.	36	20	28	48	32	....	....	....	....	....
1989-90a	Boston U.	H.E.	43	25	31	56	78	....	....	....	....	....
1990-91bc	Boston U.	H.E.	41	34	48	82	43	....	....	....	....	....
1991-92	U.S. National	....	57	26	23	49	38	....	....	....	....	....
	U.S. Olympic	....	8	1	0	1	10	....	....	....	....	....
	Pittsburgh	**NHL**	**15**	**0**	**4**	**4**	**0**	**19**	**2**	**7**	**9**	**4** ♦
1992-93	**Pittsburgh**	**NHL**	**84**	**28**	**33**	**61**	**46**	**12**	**3**	**2**	**5**	**10**
1993-94	**Los Angeles**	**NHL**	**49**	**8**	**13**	**21**	**24**	....	....	....	....	....
	Pittsburgh	**NHL**	**27**	**12**	**9**	**21**	**10**	**6**	**1**	**0**	**1**	**2**
1994-95	Kiekko-Espoo	Fin.	8	1	3	4	6	....	....	....	....	....
	Pittsburgh	**NHL**	**44**	**13**	**13**	**26**	**22**	**11**	**0**	**2**	**2**	**8**
1995-96	**Boston**	**NHL**	**82**	**24**	**29**	**53**	**34**	**5**	**2**	**1**	**3**	**8**
1996-97	**Ottawa**	**NHL**	**65**	**11**	**20**	**31**	**18**	**7**	**2**	**0**	**2**	**8**
	NHL Totals		**366**	**96**	**121**	**217**	**154**	**60**	**10**	**12**	**22**	**40**

a Hockey East Second All-Star Team (1990)
b Hockey East First All-Star Team (1991)
c NCAA East First All-American Team (1991)

Traded to **Los Angeles** by **Pittsburgh** for Marty McSorley, August 27, 1993. Traded to **Pittsburgh** by **Los Angeles** with Tomas Sandstrom for Marty McSorley and Jim Paek, February 16, 1994. Traded to **Boston** by **Pittsburgh** with Kevin Stevens for Glen Murray, Bryan Smolinski and Boston's third round choice (Boyd Kane) in 1996 Entry Draft, August 2, 1995. Traded to **Ottawa** by **Boston** for Trent McCleary and Ottawa's third round choice (Eric Naud) in 1996 Entry Draft, June 22, 1996.

McGILLIS, DANIEL — EDM.

Defense. Shoots left. 6'2", 225 lbs. Born, Hawkesbury, Ont., July 1, 1972.
(Detroit's 10th choice, 238th overall, in 1992 Entry Draft).

			Regular Season					Playoffs				
Season	Club	Lea	GP	G	A	TP	PIM	GP	G	A	TP	PIM
1992-93	Northeastern	H.E.	35	5	12	17	42	....	....	....	....	....
1993-94	Northeastern	H.E.	38	4	25	29	82	....	....	....	....	....
1994-95a	Northeastern	H.E.	34	9	22	31	70	....	....	....	....	....
1995-96bc	Northeastern	H.E.	34	12	24	36	50	....	....	....	....	....
1996-97	**Edmonton**	**NHL**	**73**	**6**	**16**	**22**	**52**	**12**	**0**	**5**	**5**	**24**
	NHL Totals		**73**	**6**	**16**	**22**	**52**	**12**	**0**	**5**	**5**	**24**

a Hockey East Second All-Star Team (1995)
b Hockey East All-Star Team (1996)
c NCAA East First All-American Team (1996)

Traded to **Edmonton** by **Detroit** for Kirk Maltby, March 20, 1996.

McINNIS, MARTY — CGY.

Center. Shoots right. 5'11", 183 lbs. Born, Hingham, MA., June 2, 1970.
(NY Islanders' 10th choice, 163rd overall, in 1988 Entry Draft).

			Regular Season					Playoffs				
Season	Club	Lea	GP	G	A	TP	PIM	GP	G	A	TP	PIM
1988-89	Boston College	H.E.	39	13	19	32	8	....	....	....	....	....
1989-90	Boston College	H.E.	41	24	29	53	43	....	....	....	....	....
1990-91	Boston College	H.E.	38	21	36	57	40	....	....	....	....	....
1991-92	U.S. National	....	54	15	19	34	20	....	....	....	....	....
	U.S. Olympic	....	8	6	2	8	4	....	....	....	....	....
	NY Islanders	**NHL**	**15**	**3**	**5**	**8**	**0**	....	....	....	....	....
1992-93	**NY Islanders**	**NHL**	**56**	**10**	**20**	**30**	**24**	**3**	**0**	**1**	**1**	**0**
	Capital Dist.	AHL	10	4	12	16	2	....	....	....	....	....
1993-94	**NY Islanders**	**NHL**	**81**	**25**	**31**	**56**	**24**	**4**	**0**	**0**	**0**	**0**
1994-95	**NY Islanders**	**NHL**	**41**	**9**	**7**	**16**	**8**	....	....	....	....	....
1995-96	**NY Islanders**	**NHL**	**74**	**12**	**34**	**46**	**39**	....	....	....	....	....
1996-97	**NY Islanders**	**NHL**	**70**	**20**	**22**	**42**	**20**	....	....	....	....	....
	Calgary	**NHL**	**10**	**3**	**4**	**7**	**2**	....	....	....	....	....
	NHL Totals		**347**	**82**	**123**	**205**	**117**	**7**	**0**	**1**	**1**	**0**

Traded to **Calgary** by **NY Islanders** with Tyrone Garner and Calgary's sixth round choice (previously acquired by NY Islanders — Calgary selected Ilja Demidov) in 1997 Entry Draft for Robert Reichel, March 18, 1997.

McINTYRE, IAN

Defense. Shoots left. 6', 187 lbs. Born, Montreal, Que., February 12, 1974.
(Quebec's 5th choice, 76th overall, in 1992 Entry Draft).

			Regular Season					Playoffs				
Season	Club	Lea	GP	G	A	TP	PIM	GP	G	A	TP	PIM
1994-95	Beauport	QMJHL	56	10	33	43	149	18	1	4	5	49
1995-96	Syracuse	AHL	57	6	7	13	108	2	0	0	0	0
1996-97	Syracuse	AHL	40	3	12	15	57	....	....	....	....	....

Signed as a free agent by **Vancouver**, April 22, 1996.

McKAY, RANDY — N.J.

Right wing. Shoots right. 6'1", 210 lbs. Born, Montreal, Que., January 25, 1967.
(Detroit's 6th choice, 113th overall, in 1985 Entry Draft).

			Regular Season					Playoffs				
Season	Club	Lea	GP	G	A	TP	PIM	GP	G	A	TP	PIM
1984-85	Michigan Tech	WCHA	25	4	5	9	32	....	....	....	....	....
1985-86	Michigan Tech	WCHA	40	12	22	34	46	....	....	....	....	....
1986-87	Michigan Tech	WCHA	39	5	11	16	46	....	....	....	....	....
1987-88	Michigan Tech	WCHA	41	17	24	41	70	....	....	....	....	....
	Adirondack	AHL	10	0	3	3	12	6	0	4	4	0
1988-89	**Detroit**	**NHL**	**3**	**0**	**0**	**0**	**0**	**2**	**0**	**0**	**0**	**2**
	Adirondack	AHL	58	29	34	63	170	14	4	7	11	60
1989-90	**Detroit**	**NHL**	**33**	**3**	**6**	**9**	**51**	....	....	....	....	....
	Adirondack	AHL	36	16	23	39	99	6	3	0	3	35
1990-91	**Detroit**	**NHL**	**47**	**1**	**7**	**8**	**183**	**5**	**0**	**1**	**1**	**41**
1991-92	**New Jersey**	**NHL**	**80**	**17**	**16**	**33**	**246**	**7**	**1**	**3**	**4**	**10**
1992-93	**New Jersey**	**NHL**	**73**	**11**	**11**	**22**	**206**	**5**	**0**	**0**	**0**	**16**
1993-94	**New Jersey**	**NHL**	**78**	**12**	**15**	**27**	**244**	**20**	**1**	**2**	**3**	**24**
1994-95	**New Jersey**	**NHL**	**33**	**5**	**7**	**12**	**44**	**19**	**8**	**4**	**12**	**11** ♦
1995-96	**New Jersey**	**NHL**	**76**	**11**	**10**	**21**	**145**	....	....	....	....	....
1996-97	**New Jersey**	**NHL**	**77**	**9**	**18**	**27**	**109**	**10**	**1**	**1**	**2**	**0**
	NHL Totals		**500**	**69**	**90**	**159**	**1228**	**68**	**11**	**11**	**22**	**104**

Acquired by **New Jersey** from **Detroit** with Dave Barr as compensation for Detroit's signing of free agent Troy Crowder, September 9, 1991.

McKEE, JAY — BUF.

Defense. Shoots left. 6'3", 195 lbs. Born, Kingston, Ont., September 8, 1977.
(Buffalo's 1st choice, 14th overall, in 1995 Entry Draft).

			Regular Season					Playoffs				
Season	Club	Lea	GP	G	A	TP	PIM	GP	G	A	TP	PIM
1993-94	Sudbury	OHL	51	0	1	1	51	3	0	0	0	0
1994-95	Sudbury	OHL	39	6	6	12	91	....	....	....	....	....
	Niagara Falls	OHL	26	3	13	16	60	6	2	3	5	10
1995-96	**Buffalo**	**NHL**	**1**	**0**	**1**	**1**	**2**	....	....	....	....	....
a	Niagara Falls	OHL	64	5	41	46	129	10	1	5	6	16
	Rochester	AHL	4	0	1	1	15	....	....	....	....	....
1996-97	**Buffalo**	**NHL**	**43**	**1**	**9**	**10**	**35**	**3**	**0**	**0**	**0**	**0**
	Rochester	AHL	7	2	5	7	4	....	....	....	....	....
	NHL Totals		**44**	**1**	**10**	**11**	**37**	**3**	**0**	**0**	**0**	**0**

a OHL Second All-Star Team (1996)

McKENNA, STEVE — L.A.

Left wing. Shoots left. 6'8", 247 lbs. Born, Toronto, Ont., August 21, 1973.

			Regular Season					Playoffs				
Season	Club	Lea	GP	G	A	TP	PIM	GP	G	A	TP	PIM
1993-94	Merrimack	H.E.	37	1	2	3	74	....	....	....	....	....
1994-95	Merrimack	H.E.	37	1	9	10	74	....	....	....	....	....
1995-96	Merrimack	H.E.	33	3	11	14	67	....	....	....	....	....
1996-97	**Los Angeles**	**NHL**	**9**	**0**	**0**	**0**	**37**	....	....	....	....	....
	Phoenix	IHL	66	6	5	11	187	....	....	....	....	....
	NHL Totals		**9**	**0**	**0**	**0**	**37**	....	....	....	....	....

Signed as a free agent by **Los Angeles**, May 23, 1996.

McKENZIE, JIM — PHO.

Left wing. Shoots left. 6'3", 205 lbs. Born, Gull Lake, Sask., November 3, 1969.
(Hartford's 3rd choice, 73rd overall, in 1989 Entry Draft).

			Regular Season					Playoffs				
Season	Club	Lea	GP	G	A	TP	PIM	GP	G	A	TP	PIM
1985-86	Moose Jaw	WHL	3	0	2	2	0	....	....	....	....	....
1986-87	Moose Jaw	WHL	65	5	3	8	125	9	0	0	0	7
1987-88	Moose Jaw	WHL	62	1	17	18	134	....	....	....	....	....
1988-89	Victoria	WHL	67	15	27	42	176	8	1	4	5	30
1989-90	**Hartford**	**NHL**	**5**	**0**	**0**	**0**	**4**	....	....	....	....	....
	Binghamton	AHL	56	4	12	16	149	....	....	....	....	....
1990-91	**Hartford**	**NHL**	**41**	**4**	**3**	**7**	**108**	**6**	**0**	**0**	**0**	**8**
	Springfield	AHL	24	3	4	7	102	....	....	....	....	....
1991-92	**Hartford**	**NHL**	**67**	**5**	**1**	**6**	**87**	....	....	....	....	....
1992-93	**Hartford**	**NHL**	**64**	**3**	**6**	**9**	**202**	....	....	....	....	....
1993-94	**Hartford**	**NHL**	**26**	**1**	**2**	**3**	**67**	....	....	....	....	....
	Dallas	**NHL**	**34**	**2**	**3**	**5**	**63**	....	....	....	....	....
	Pittsburgh	**NHL**	**11**	**0**	**0**	**0**	**16**	**3**	**0**	**0**	**0**	**0**
1994-95	**Pittsburgh**	**NHL**	**39**	**2**	**1**	**3**	**63**	**5**	**0**	**0**	**0**	**4**
1995-96	**Winnipeg**	**NHL**	**73**	**4**	**2**	**6**	**202**	**1**	**0**	**0**	**0**	**2**
1996-97	**Phoenix**	**NHL**	**65**	**5**	**3**	**8**	**200**	**7**	**0**	**0**	**0**	**2**
	NHL Totals		**425**	**26**	**21**	**47**	**1012**	**22**	**0**	**0**	**0**	**16**

Traded to **Florida** by **Hartford** for Alexander Godynyuk, December 16, 1993. Traded to **Dallas** by **Florida** for Dallas' fourth round choice (later traded to Ottawa — Ottawa selected Kevin Bolibruck) in 1995 Entry Draft, December 16, 1993. Traded to **Pittsburgh** by **Dallas** for Mike Needham, March 21, 1994. Signed as a free agent by **NY Islanders**, August 2, 1995. Claimed by **Winnipeg** from **NY Islanders** in NHL Waiver Draft, October 2, 1995.

McKIE, RYAN — NYR

Defense. Shoots right. 6'2", 198 lbs. Born, Kenora, Ont., March 30, 1978.
(NY Rangers' 7th choice, 211th overall, in 1996 Entry Draft).

			Regular Season					Playoffs				
Season	Club	Lea	GP	G	A	TP	PIM	GP	G	A	TP	PIM
1995-96	London	OHL	65	2	7	9	64	....	....	....	....	....
1996-97	London	OHL	33	2	6	8	40	....	....	....	....	....
	Sudbury	OHL	30	2	7	9	27	....	....	....	....	....

McLAREN, KYLE — BOS.

Defense. Shoots left. 6'4", 219 lbs. Born, Humbolt, Sask., June 18, 1977.
(Boston's 1st choice, 9th overall, in 1995 Entry Draft).

			Regular Season					Playoffs				
Season	Club	Lea	GP	G	A	TP	PIM	GP	G	A	TP	PIM
1993-94	Tacoma	WHL	62	1	9	10	53	6	1	4	5	6
1994-95	Tacoma	WHL	47	13	19	32	68	4	1	1	2	4
1995-96a	**Boston**	**NHL**	**74**	**5**	**12**	**17**	**73**	**5**	**0**	**0**	**0**	**14**
1996-97	**Boston**	**NHL**	**58**	**5**	**9**	**14**	**54**	....	....	....	....	....
	NHL Totals		**132**	**10**	**21**	**31**	**127**	**5**	**0**	**0**	**0**	**14**

a NHL All-Rookie Team (1996)

McLAREN, STEVE — CHI.

Defense. Shoots left. 6', 194 lbs. Born, Owen Sound, Ont., February 3, 1975.
(Chicago's 3rd choice, 85th overall, in 1994 Entry Draft).

			Regular Season					Playoffs				
Season	Club	Lea	GP	G	A	TP	PIM	GP	G	A	TP	PIM
1993-94	North Bay	OHL	55	2	15	17	130	18	0	3	3	50
1994-95	North Bay	OHL	27	3	10	13	119	6	2	1	3	23
1995-96	Indianapolis	IHL	54	1	2	3	170	3	0	0	0	2
1996-97	Indianapolis	IHL	63	2	5	7	309	4	0	0	0	10

McLLWAIN, DAVE — (MA-kuhl-WAYN)

Center/Right wing. Shoots left. 6', 185 lbs. Born, Seaforth, Ont., January 9, 1967.
(Pittsburgh's 9th choice, 172nd overall, in 1986 Entry Draft).

			Regular Season					Playoffs				
Season	Club	Lea	GP	G	A	TP	PIM	GP	G	A	TP	PIM
1984-85	Kitchener	OHL	61	13	21	34	29	....	....	....	....	....
1985-86	Kitchener	OHL	13	7	7	14	12	....	....	....	....	....
	North Bay	OHL	51	30	28	58	25	10	4	4	8	2
1986-87a	North Bay	OHL	60	46	73	119	35	24	7	18	25	40
1987-88	**Pittsburgh**	**NHL**	**66**	**11**	**8**	**19**	**40**	....	....	....	....	....
	Muskegon	IHL	9	4	6	10	23	6	2	3	5	8
1988-89	**Pittsburgh**	**NHL**	**24**	**1**	**2**	**3**	**4**	**3**	**0**	**1**	**1**	**0**
	Muskegon	IHL	46	37	35	72	51	7	8	2	10	6
1989-90	**Winnipeg**	**NHL**	**80**	**25**	**26**	**51**	**60**	**7**	**0**	**1**	**1**	**2**
1990-91	**Winnipeg**	**NHL**	**60**	**14**	**11**	**25**	**46**	....	....	....	....	....
1991-92	**Winnipeg**	**NHL**	**3**	**1**	**1**	**2**	**2**	....	....	....	....	....
	Buffalo	**NHL**	**5**	**0**	**0**	**0**	**2**	....	....	....	....	....
	NY Islanders	**NHL**	**54**	**8**	**15**	**23**	**28**	....	....	....	....	....
	Toronto	**NHL**	**11**	**1**	**2**	**3**	**4**	....	....	....	....	....
1992-93	**Toronto**	**NHL**	**66**	**14**	**4**	**18**	**30**	**4**	**0**	**0**	**0**	**0**
1993-94	**Ottawa**	**NHL**	**66**	**17**	**26**	**43**	**48**	....	....	....	....	....
1994-95	**Ottawa**	**NHL**	**43**	**5**	**6**	**11**	**22**	....	....	....	....	....
1995-96	**Ottawa**	**NHL**	**1**	**0**	**1**	**1**	**2**	....	....	....	....	....
	Cleveland	IHL	60	30	45	75	80	....	....	....	....	....
	Pittsburgh	**NHL**	**18**	**2**	**4**	**6**	**4**	**6**	**0**	**0**	**0**	**0**
1996-97	**NY Islanders**	**NHL**	**4**	**1**	**1**	**2**	**0**	....	....	....	....	....
	Cleveland	IHL	63	29	46	75	85	14	8	15	23	6
	NHL Totals		**501**	**100**	**107**	**207**	**292**	**20**	**0**	**2**	**2**	**2**

a OHL Second All-Star Team (1987)

Traded to **Winnipeg** by **Pittsburgh** with Randy Cunneyworth and Rick Tabaracci for Jim Kyte, Andrew McBain and Randy Gilhen, June 17, 1989. Traded to **Buffalo** by **Winnipeg** with Gord Donnelly, Winnipeg's fifth round choice (Yuri Khmylev) in 1992 Entry Draft and future considerations for Darrin Shannon, Mike Hartman and Dean Kennedy, October 11, 1991. Traded to **NY Islanders** by **Buffalo** with Pierre Turgeon, Uwe Krupp and Benoit Hogue for Pat Lafontaine, Randy Hillier, Randy Wood and NY Islanders' fourth round choice (Dean Melanson) in 1992 Entry Draft, October 25, 1991. Traded to **Toronto** by **NY Islanders** with Ken Baumgartner for Daniel Marois and Claude Loiselle, March 10, 1992. Claimed by **Ottawa** from **Toronto** in NHL Waiver Draft, October 3, 1993. Traded to **Pittsburgh** by **Ottawa** for Pittsburgh's eighth round choice (Erich Goldmann) in 1996 Entry Draft, March 1, 1996. Signed as a free agent by **NY Islanders**, July 29, 1996.

McMAHON, MARK — (muhk-MAN) CAR.

Defense. Shoots left. 6'1", 179 lbs. Born, Geralton, Ont., February 10, 1978.
(Hartford's 5th choice, 116th overall, in 1996 Entry Draft).

			Regular Season					Playoffs				
Season	Club	Lea	GP	G	A	TP	PIM	GP	G	A	TP	PIM
1995-96	Kitchener	OHL	55	1	8	9	105	5	0	1	1	17
1996-97	Kitchener	OHL	63	4	18	22	155	13	0	6	6	31

McNEIL, SHAWN — WSH.

Center. Shoots left. 5'11", 175 lbs. Born, Pembroke, Ont., March 17, 1978.
(Washington's 6th choice, 78th overall, in 1996 Entry Draft).

			Regular Season					Playoffs				
Season	Club	Lea	GP	G	A	TP	PIM	GP	G	A	TP	PIM
1993-94	Kamloops	WHL	1	0	0	0	0	....	....	....	....	....
1994-95	Kamloops	WHL	43	4	3	7	11	9	0	1	1	0
1995-96	Kamloops	WHL	67	15	30	45	24	16	4	12	16	17
1996-97	Kamloops	WHL	70	38	47	85	37	5	1	3	4	2

McRAE, BASIL — (muh-KRAY, BA-zihl)

Left wing. Shoots left. 6'2", 210 lbs. Born, Beaverton, Ont., January 5, 1961.
(Quebec's 3rd choice, 87th overall, in 1980 Entry Draft).

			Regular Season					Playoffs				
Season	Club	Lea	GP	G	A	TP	PIM	GP	G	A	TP	PIM
1979-80	London	OHA	67	24	36	60	116	5	0	0	0	18
1980-81	London	OHA	65	29	23	52	266	....	....	....	....	....
1981-82	**Quebec**	**NHL**	**20**	**4**	**3**	**7**	**69**	**9**	**1**	**0**	**1**	**34**
	Fredericton	AHL	47	11	15	26	175	....	....	....	....	....
1982-83	**Quebec**	**NHL**	**22**	**1**	**1**	**2**	**59**	....	....	....	....	....
	Fredericton	AHL	53	22	19	41	146	12	1	5	6	75
1983-84	**Toronto**	**NHL**	**3**	**0**	**0**	**0**	**19**	....	....	....	....	....
	St. Catharines	AHL	78	14	25	39	187	6	0	0	0	40
1984-85	**Toronto**	**NHL**	**1**	**0**	**0**	**0**	**0**	....	....	....	....	....
	St. Catharines	AHL	72	30	25	55	186	....	....	....	....	....
1985-86	**Detroit**	**NHL**	**4**	**0**	**0**	**0**	**5**	....	....	....	....	....
	Adirondack	AHL	69	22	30	52	259	17	5	4	9	101
1986-87	**Detroit**	**NHL**	**36**	**2**	**2**	**4**	**193**	....	....	....	....	....
	Quebec	**NHL**	**33**	**9**	**5**	**14**	**149**	**13**	**3**	**1**	**4**	***99**
1987-88	**Minnesota**	**NHL**	**80**	**5**	**11**	**16**	**382**	....	....	....	....	....
1988-89	**Minnesota**	**NHL**	**78**	**12**	**19**	**31**	**365**	**5**	**0**	**0**	**0**	**58**
1989-90	**Minnesota**	**NHL**	**66**	**9**	**17**	**26**	***351**	**7**	**1**	**0**	**1**	**24**
1990-91	**Minnesota**	**NHL**	**40**	**1**	**3**	**4**	**224**	**22**	**1**	**1**	**2**	***94**
1991-92	**Minnesota**	**NHL**	**59**	**5**	**8**	**13**	**245**	....	....	....	....	....
1992-93	**Tampa Bay**	**NHL**	**14**	**2**	**3**	**5**	**71**	....	....	....	....	....
	St. Louis	**NHL**	**33**	**1**	**3**	**4**	**98**	**11**	**0**	**1**	**1**	**24**
1993-94	**St. Louis**	**NHL**	**40**	**1**	**2**	**3**	**103**	**2**	**0**	**0**	**0**	**12**
1994-95	**St. Louis**	**NHL**	**21**	**0**	**5**	**5**	**72**	**7**	**2**	**1**	**3**	**4**
	Peoria	IHL	2	0	0	0	12	....	....	....	....	....
1995-96	**St. Louis**	**NHL**	**18**	**1**	**1**	**2**	**40**	**2**	**0**	**0**	**0**	**0**
1996-97	**Chicago**	**NHL**	**8**	**0**	**0**	**0**	**12**	....	....	....	....	....
	NHL Totals		**576**	**53**	**83**	**136**	**2457**	**78**	**8**	**4**	**12**	**349**

Traded to **Toronto** by **Quebec** for Richard Turmel, August 12, 1983. Signed as a free agent by **Detroit**, July 17, 1985. Traded to **Quebec** by **Detroit** with John Ogrodnick and Doug Shedden for Brent Ashton, Gilbert Delorme and Mark Kumpel, January 17, 1987. Signed as a free agent by **Minnesota**, June 29, 1987. Claimed by **Tampa Bay** from **Minnesota** in Expansion Draft, June 18, 1992. Traded to **St. Louis** by **Tampa Bay** with Doug Crossman and Tampa Bay's fourth round choice (Andrei Petrakov) in 1996 Entry Draft for Jason Ruff and future considerations, January 28, 1993. Signed as a free agent by **Chicago**, October 9, 1996.

McSORLEY, MARTY — S.J.

Defense. Shoots right. 6'1", 235 lbs. Born, Hamilton, Ont., May 18, 1963.

			Regular Season					Playoffs				
Season	Club	Lea	GP	G	A	TP	PIM	GP	G	A	TP	PIM
1981-82	Belleville	OHL	58	6	13	19	234	....	....	....	....	....
1982-83	Belleville	OHL	70	10	41	51	183	4	0	0	0	7
	Baltimore	AHL	2	0	0	0	22	....	....	....	....	....
1983-84	**Pittsburgh**	**NHL**	**72**	**2**	**7**	**9**	**224**	....	....	....	....	....
1984-85	**Pittsburgh**	**NHL**	**15**	**0**	**0**	**0**	**15**	....	....	....	....	....
	Baltimore	AHL	58	6	24	30	154	14	0	7	7	47
1985-86	**Edmonton**	**NHL**	**59**	**11**	**12**	**23**	**265**	**8**	**0**	**2**	**2**	**50**
	Nova Scotia	AHL	9	2	4	6	34	....	....	....	....	....
1986-87	**Edmonton**	**NHL**	**41**	**2**	**4**	**6**	**159**	**21**	**4**	**3**	**7**	**65 ♦**
	Nova Scotia	AHL	7	2	2	4	48	....	....	....	....	....
1987-88	**Edmonton**	**NHL**	**60**	**9**	**17**	**26**	**223**	**16**	**0**	**3**	**3**	**67 ♦**
1988-89	**Los Angeles**	**NHL**	**66**	**10**	**17**	**27**	**350**	**11**	**0**	**2**	**2**	**33**
1989-90	**Los Angeles**	**NHL**	**75**	**15**	**21**	**36**	**322**	**10**	**1**	**3**	**4**	**18**
1990-91a	**Los Angeles**	**NHL**	**61**	**7**	**32**	**39**	**221**	**12**	**0**	**0**	**0**	**58**
1991-92	**Los Angeles**	**NHL**	**71**	**7**	**22**	**29**	**268**	**6**	**1**	**0**	**1**	**21**
1992-93	**Los Angeles**	**NHL**	**81**	**15**	**26**	**41**	***399**	**24**	**4**	**6**	**10**	***60**
1993-94	**Pittsburgh**	**NHL**	**47**	**3**	**18**	**21**	**139**	....	....	....	....	....
	Los Angeles	**NHL**	**18**	**4**	**6**	**10**	**55**	....	....	....	....	....
1994-95	**Los Angeles**	**NHL**	**41**	**3**	**18**	**21**	**83**	....	....	....	....	....
1995-96	**Los Angeles**	**NHL**	**59**	**10**	**21**	**31**	**148**	....	....	....	....	....
	NY Rangers	**NHL**	**9**	**0**	**2**	**2**	**21**	**4**	**0**	**0**	**0**	**0**
1996-97	**San Jose**	**NHL**	**57**	**4**	**12**	**16**	**186**	....	....	....	....	....
	NHL Totals		**832**	**102**	**235**	**337**	**3078**	**112**	**10**	**19**	**29**	**372**

a Co-winner of Alka-Seltzer Plus Award with Theoren Fleury (1991)

Signed as a free agent by **Pittsburgh**, July 30, 1982. Traded to **Edmonton** by **Pittsburgh** with Tim Hrynewich and future considerations (Craig Muni, October 6, 1986) for Gilles Meloche, September 12, 1985. Traded to **Los Angeles** by **Edmonton** with Wayne Gretzky and Mike Krushelnyski for Jimmy Carson, Martin Gelinas, Los Angeles' first round choices in 1989 (acquired by New Jersey — New Jersey selected Jason Miller), 1991 (Martin Rucinsky) and 1993 (Nick Stajduhar) Entry Drafts and cash, August 9, 1988. Traded to **Pittsburgh** by **Los Angeles**, for Shawn McEachern, August 27, 1993. Traded to **Los Angeles** by **Pittsburgh** with Jim Paek for Tomas Sandstrom and Shawn McEachern, February 16, 1994. Traded to **NY Rangers** by **Los Angeles** with Jari Kurri and Shane Churla for Ray Ferraro, Ian Laperriere, Mattias Norstrom, Nathan Lafayette and NY Rangers' fourth round choice (Sean Blanchard) in 1997 Entry Draft, March 14, 1996. Traded to **San Jose** by **NY Rangers** for Jayson More, Brian Swanson and a conditional choice in 1998 Entry Draft, August 20, 1996.

McTAVISH, DALE — CGY.

Center. Shoots left. 6'1", 200 lbs. Born, Eganville, Ont., February 28, 1972.

			Regular Season					Playoffs				
Season	Club	Lea	GP	G	A	TP	PIM	GP	G	A	TP	PIM
1995-96	Cdn. National	....	53	24	32	56	91	....	....	....	....	....
	Saint John	AHL	4	2	3	5	5	15	5	4	9	15
1996-97	**Calgary**	**NHL**	**9**	**1**	**2**	**3**	**2**	....	....	....	....	....
	Saint John	AHL	53	16	21	37	65	3	0	1	1	0
	NHL Totals		**9**	**1**	**2**	**3**	**2**	....	....	....	....	....

Signed as a free agent by **Calgary**, August 1, 1996.

MELANSON, DEAN (meh-LAHN-suhn)

Defense. Shoots right. 5'11", 211 lbs. Born, Antigonish, N.S., November 19, 1973.
(Buffalo's 4th choice, 80th overall, in 1992 Entry Draft).

			Regular Season					Playoffs				
Season	Club	Lea	GP	G	A	TP	PIM	GP	G	A	TP	PIM
1990-91	St-Hyacinthe	QMJHL	69	10	17	27	110	4	0	1	1	2
1991-92	St-Hyacinthe	QMJHL	42	8	19	27	158	6	1	2	3	25
1992-93	Rochester	AHL	8	0	1	1	6	14	1	6	7	18
	St. Hyacinthe	QMJHL	57	13	29	42	253	....	....	....	....	....
1993-94	Rochester	AHL	80	1	21	22	138	4	0	1	1	2
1994-95	Rochester	AHL	43	4	7	11	84	....	....	....	....	....
	Buffalo	**NHL**	**5**	**0**	**0**	**0**	**4**	....	....	....	....	....
1995-96	Rochester	AHL	70	3	13	16	204	14	3	3	6	22
1996-97	Quebec	IHL	72	3	21	24	95	7	0	2	2	12
	NHL Totals		**5**	**0**	**0**	**0**	**4**	....	....	....	....	....

MELENOVSKY, MAREK (meh-leh-NAHF-skee) TOR.

Center. Shoots left. 5'9", 176 lbs. Born, Humpolec, Czech., March 30, 1977.
(Toronto's 5th choice, 171st overall, in 1995 Entry Draft).

			Regular Season					Playoffs				
Season	Club	Lea	GP	G	A	TP	PIM	GP	G	A	TP	PIM
1993-94	Dukla Jihlava	Czech.	1	0	0	0	....	....	....	....	....	....
1994-95	Dukla Jihlava	Czech. Jr	28	23	11	34	....	....	....	....	....	....
	Dukla Jihlava	Czech.	3	0	0	0	0	5	1	3	4	0
1995-96	Dukla Jihlava	Czech.	33	3	3	6	....	5	1	2	3	....
1996-97	Dukla Jihlava	Czech.	46	5	13	18	22	....	....	....	....	....
	St. John's	AHL	2	1	2	3	0	2	0	0	0	0

MELICHAR, JOSEF (mehl-ee-KHAHR, YOH-sehf) PIT.

Defense. Shoots left. 6'3", 198 lbs. Born, Budejovice, Czech., January 20, 1979.
(Pittsburgh's 3rd choice, 71st overall, in 1997 Entry Draft).

			Regular Season					Playoffs				
Season	Club	Lea	GP	G	A	TP	PIM	GP	G	A	TP	PIM
1995-96	Budejovice	Czech. Jr.	38	3	4	7	....	....	....	....	....	....
1996-97	Budejovice	Czech. Jr.	41	2	3	5	10	....	....	....	....	....

MELLANBY, SCOTT FLA.

Right wing. Shoots right. 6'1", 199 lbs. Born, Montreal, Que., June 11, 1966.
(Philadelphia's 2nd choice, 27th overall, in 1984 Entry Draft).

			Regular Season					Playoffs				
Season	Club	Lea	GP	G	A	TP	PIM	GP	G	A	TP	PIM
1984-85	U. Wisconsin	WCHA	40	14	24	38	60	....	....	....	....	....
1985-86	U. Wisconsin	WCHA	32	21	23	44	89	....	....	....	....	....
	Philadelphia	**NHL**	**2**	**0**	**0**	**0**	**0**	....	....	....	....	....
1986-87	**Philadelphia**	**NHL**	**71**	**11**	**21**	**32**	**94**	**24**	**5**	**5**	**10**	**46**
1987-88	**Philadelphia**	**NHL**	**75**	**25**	**26**	**51**	**185**	**7**	**0**	**1**	**1**	**16**
1988-89	**Philadelphia**	**NHL**	**76**	**21**	**29**	**50**	**183**	**19**	**4**	**5**	**9**	**28**
1989-90	**Philadelphia**	**NHL**	**57**	**6**	**17**	**23**	**77**	....	....	....	....	....
1990-91	**Philadelphia**	**NHL**	**74**	**20**	**21**	**41**	**155**	....	....	....	....	....
1991-92	**Edmonton**	**NHL**	**80**	**23**	**27**	**50**	**197**	**16**	**2**	**1**	**3**	**29**
1992-93	**Edmonton**	**NHL**	**69**	**15**	**17**	**32**	**147**	....	....	....	....	....
1993-94	**Florida**	**NHL**	**80**	**30**	**30**	**60**	**149**	....	....	....	....	....
1994-95	**Florida**	**NHL**	**48**	**13**	**12**	**25**	**90**	....	....	....	....	....
1995-96	**Florida**	**NHL**	**79**	**32**	**38**	**70**	**160**	**22**	**3**	**6**	**9**	**44**
1996-97	**Florida**	**NHL**	**82**	**27**	**29**	**56**	**170**	**5**	**0**	**2**	**2**	**4**
	NHL Totals		**793**	**223**	**267**	**490**	**1607**	**93**	**14**	**20**	**34**	**167**

Played in NHL All-Star Game (1996)

Traded to **Edmonton** by **Philadelphia** with Craig Fisher and Craig Berube for Dave Brown, Corey Foster and Jari Kurri, May 30, 1991. Claimed by **Florida** from **Edmonton** in Expansion Draft, June 24, 1993.

MELOCHE, ERIC PIT.

Right wing. Shoots right. 5'11", 195 lbs. Born, Montreal, Que., May 1, 1976.
(Pittsburgh's 7th choice, 186th overall, in 1996 Entry Draft).

			Regular Season					Playoffs				
Season	Club	Lea	GP	G	A	TP	PIM	GP	G	A	TP	PIM
1995-96	Cornwall	Jr. A	64	68	53	121	162	....	....	....	....	....
1996-97	Ohio State	CCHA	39	12	11	23	78	....	....	....	....	....

MELYAKOV, IGOR (mehl-yuh-KAHF) L.A.

Left wing. Shoots left. 5'10", 176 lbs. Born, Lipetsk, USSR, December 23, 1976.
(Los Angeles' 6th choice, 137th overall, in 1995 Entry Draft).

			Regular Season					Playoffs				
Season	Club	Lea	GP	G	A	TP	PIM	GP	G	A	TP	PIM
1993-94	Yaroslavl	CIS	39	4	3	7	10	4	0	0	0	0
1994-95	Yaroslavl	CIS	50	6	8	14	34	4	0	1	1	0
1995-96	Yaroslavl	CIS	39	5	1	6	6	3	0	0	0	2
1996-97	Yaroslavl	Rus.	8	0	0	0	0	....	....	....	....	....
	Torpedo Niz.	Rus.	12	2	3	5	10	....	....	....	....	....

MESSIER, ERIC COL.

Defense. Shoots left. 6'2", 200 lbs. Born, Drummondville, Que., October 29, 1973.

			Regular Season					Playoffs				
Season	Club	Lea	GP	G	A	TP	PIM	GP	G	A	TP	PIM
1991-92	Trois-Rivieres	QMJHL	58	2	10	12	28	15	2	2	4	13
1992-93	Sherbrooke	QMJHL	51	4	17	21	82	15	0	4	4	18
1993-94a	Sherbrooke	QMJHL	67	4	24	28	69	12	1	7	8	14
1994-95					UNAVAILABLE							
1995-96	Cornwall	AHL	72	5	9	14	111	8	1	1	2	20
1996-97	**Colorado**	**NHL**	**21**	**0**	**0**	**0**	**4**	**6**	**0**	**0**	**0**	**4**
	Hershey	AHL	55	16	26	42	69	5	2	4	6	12
	NHL Totals		**21**	**0**	**0**	**0**	**4**	**6**	**0**	**0**	**0**	**4**

a QMJHL Second All-Star Team (1994)

Signed as a free agent by **Colorado**, June 14, 1996.

MESSIER, JOBY (MEHS-see-ay)

Defense. Shoots right. 6', 200 lbs. Born, Regina, Sask., March 2, 1970.
(NY Rangers' 7th choice, 118th overall, in 1989 Entry Draft).

			Regular Season					Playoffs				
Season	Club	Lea	GP	G	A	TP	PIM	GP	G	A	TP	PIM
1988-89	Michigan State	CCHA	39	2	10	12	66	....	....	....	....	....
1989-90	Michigan State	CCHA	42	1	11	12	58	....	....	....	....	....
1990-91	Michigan State	CCHA	39	5	11	16	71	....	....	....	....	....
1991-92ab	Michigan State	CCHA	41	13	15	28	81	....	....	....	....	....
1992-93	**NY Rangers**	**NHL**	**11**	**0**	**0**	**0**	**6**	....	....	....	....	....
	Binghamton	AHL	60	5	16	21	63	14	1	1	2	6
1993-94	**NY Rangers**	**NHL**	**4**	**0**	**2**	**2**	**0**	....	....	....	....	....
	Binghamton	AHL	42	6	14	20	58	....	....	....	....	....
1994-95	Binghamton	AHL	25	2	9	11	36	1	0	0	0	0
	NY Rangers	**NHL**	**10**	**0**	**2**	**2**	**18**	....	....	....	....	....
1995-96						DID NOT PLAY – INJURED						
1996-97	Utah	IHL	44	6	20	26	41	7	0	1	1	10
	NHL Totals		**25**	**0**	**4**	**4**	**24**	....	....	....	....	....

a CCHA First All-Star Team (1992)
b NCAA West First All-American Team (1992)

Signed as a free agent by **NY Islanders**, September 26, 1995.

MESSIER, MARK (MEHS-see-ay) VAN.

Center. Shoots left. 6'1", 205 lbs. Born, Edmonton, Alta., January 18, 1961.
(Edmonton's 2nd choice, 48th overall, in 1979 Entry Draft).

			Regular Season					Playoffs				
Season	Club	Lea	GP	G	A	TP	PIM	GP	G	A	TP	PIM
1977-78	Portland	WHL	....	....	....	....	....	7	4	1	5	2
1978-79	Indianapolis	WHA	5	0	0	0	0	....	....	....	....	....
	Cincinnati	WHA	47	1	10	11	58	....	....	....	....	....
1979-80	**Edmonton**	**NHL**	**75**	**12**	**21**	**33**	**120**	**3**	**1**	**2**	**3**	**2**
	Houston	CHL	4	0	3	3	4	....	....	....	....	....
1980-81	**Edmonton**	**NHL**	**72**	**23**	**40**	**63**	**102**	**9**	**2**	**5**	**7**	**13**
1981-82a	**Edmonton**	**NHL**	**78**	**50**	**38**	**88**	**119**	**5**	**1**	**2**	**3**	**8**
1982-83a	**Edmonton**	**NHL**	**77**	**48**	**58**	**106**	**72**	**15**	**15**	**6**	**21**	**14**
1983-84bc	**Edmonton**	**NHL**	**73**	**37**	**64**	**101**	**165**	**19**	**8**	**18**	**26**	**19** ♦
1984-85	**Edmonton**	**NHL**	**55**	**23**	**31**	**54**	**57**	**18**	**12**	**13**	**25**	**12** ♦
1985-86	**Edmonton**	**NHL**	**63**	**35**	**49**	**84**	**68**	**10**	**4**	**6**	**10**	**18**
1986-87	**Edmonton**	**NHL**	**77**	**37**	**70**	**107**	**73**	**21**	**12**	**16**	**28**	**16** ♦
1987-88	**Edmonton**	**NHL**	**77**	**37**	**74**	**111**	**103**	**19**	**11**	**23**	**34**	**29** ♦
1988-89	**Edmonton**	**NHL**	**72**	**33**	**61**	**94**	**130**	**7**	**1**	**11**	**12**	**8**
1989-90ade	**Edmonton**	**NHL**	**79**	**45**	**84**	**129**	**79**	**22**	**9**	***22**	**31**	**20** ♦
1990-91	**Edmonton**	**NHL**	**53**	**12**	**52**	**64**	**34**	**18**	**4**	**11**	**15**	**16**
1991-92ade	**NY Rangers**	**NHL**	**79**	**35**	**72**	**107**	**76**	**11**	**7**	**7**	**14**	**6**
1992-93	**NY Rangers**	**NHL**	**75**	**25**	**66**	**91**	**72**	....	....	....	....	....
1993-94	**NY Rangers**	**NHL**	**76**	**26**	**58**	**84**	**76**	**23**	**12**	**18**	**30**	**33** ♦
1994-95	**NY Rangers**	**NHL**	**46**	**14**	**39**	**53**	**40**	**10**	**3**	**10**	**13**	**8**
1995-96	**NY Rangers**	**NHL**	**74**	**47**	**52**	**99**	**122**	**11**	**4**	**7**	**11**	**16**
1996-97	**NY Rangers**	**NHL**	**71**	**36**	**48**	**84**	**88**	**15**	**3**	**9**	**12**	**6**
	NHL Totals		**1272**	**575**	**977**	**1552**	**1596**	***236**	**109**	**186**	**295**	**244**

a NHL First All-Star Team (1982, 1983, 1990, 1992)
b NHL Second All-Star Team (1984)
c Won Conn Smythe Trophy (1984)
d Won Hart Trophy (1990, 1992)
e Won Lester B. Pearson Award (1990, 1992)

Played in NHL All-Star Game (1982-86, 1988-92, 1994, 1996, 1997)

Traded to **NY Rangers** by **Edmonton** with future considerations for Bernie Nicholls, Steven Rice and Louie DeBrusk, October 4, 1991. Signed as a free agent by **Vancouver**, July 28, 1997.

METHOT, FRANCOIS BUF.

Center. Shoots right. 6', 175 lbs. Born, Montreal, Que., April 26, 1978.
(Buffalo's 4th choice, 54th overall, in 1996 Entry Draft).

			Regular Season					Playoffs				
Season	Club	Lea	GP	G	A	TP	PIM	GP	G	A	TP	PIM
1994-95	St-Hyacinthe	QMJHL	60	14	38	52	22	5	0	1	1	0
1995-96	St-Hyacinthe	QMJHL	68	32	62	94	22	12	6	6	12	4
1996-97	Rouyn-Noranda	QMJHL	47	21	30	51	22	....	....	....	....	....
	Shawinigan	QMJHL	18	8	17	25	2	7	2	6	8	2

MIETTINEN, TOMMI (mih-EHT-tih-nehn) ANA.

Center. Shoots left. 5'10", 165 lbs. Born, Kuopio, Finland, December 3, 1975.
(Anaheim's 9th choice, 236th overall, in 1994 Entry Draft).

			Regular Season					Playoffs				
Season	Club	Lea	GP	G	A	TP	PIM	GP	G	A	TP	PIM
1992-93	KalPa	Fin.	14	0	0	0	0	....	....	....	....	....
1993-94	KalPa	Fin.	47	5	7	12	14	....	....	....	....	....
1994-95	KalPa	Fin.	48	13	16	29	26	3	1	1	2	2
1995-96	TPS	Fin.	36	3	10	13	10	10	2	1	3	29
1996-97	TPS	Fin.	41	6	15	21	6	12	3	4	7	8

MIKA, PETR (MEE-kah) NYI

Left wing. Shoots right. 6'4", 194 lbs. Born, Prague, Czech., February 12, 1979.
(NY Islanders' 6th choice, 85th overall, in 1997 Entry Draft).

			Regular Season					Playoffs				
Season	Club	Lea	GP	G	A	TP	PIM	GP	G	A	TP	PIM
1996-97	Slavia Praha	Czech. Jr.	15	8	0	8	....	....	....	....	....	....
	HC Beroun	Czech. 2	9	1	0	1	....	....	....	....	....	....
	Slavia Praha	Czech.	20	1	2	3	6	....	....	....	....	....

MIKESCH, JEFF (MIHK-ihsh) DET.

Center. Shoots left. 6', 175 lbs. Born, Hancook, MI, April 11, 1975.
(Detroit's 8th choice, 231st overall, in 1994 Entry Draft).

			Regular Season					Playoffs				
Season	Club	Lea	GP	G	A	TP	PIM	GP	G	A	TP	PIM
1993-94	Michigan Tech	WCHA	41	9	4	13	80	....	....	....	....	....
1994-95	Michigan Tech	WCHA	36	9	8	17	83	....	....	....	....	....
1995-96	Michigan Tech	WCHA	41	13	13	26	66	....	....	....	....	....
1996-97	Michigan Tech	WCHA	36	10	11	21	84	....	....	....	....	....

MIKKOLA, ILKKA (mih-KOHLA-, IHL-ka) MTL.

Defense. Shoots left. 6', 189 lbs. Born, Oulu, Finland, January 18, 1979.
(Montreal's 3rd choice, 65th overall, in 1997 Entry Draft).

			Regular Season					Playoffs				
Season	Club	Lea	GP	G	A	TP	PIM	GP	G	A	TP	PIM
1995-96	Karpat	Fin. Jr.	21	2	3	5	20	....	....	....	....	....
	Karpat	Fin. 2	10	0	4	4	29	2	0	0	0	2
1996-97	Karpat	Fin. 2	40	7	12	19	32	6	0	0	0	4

MILLAR, CRAIG — EDM.

Defense. Shoots left. 6'2", 200 lbs. Born, Winnipeg, Man., May 10, 1977.
(Buffalo's 10th choice, 225th overall, in 1994 Entry Draft).

			Regular Season					Playoffs				
Season	Club	Lea	GP	G	A	TP	PIM	GP	G	A	TP	PIM
1992-93	Swift Current	WHL	43	2	1	3	8	....	....	....	....	....
1993-94	Swift Current	WHL	66	2	9	11	53	7	0	3	3	4
1994-95	Swift Current	WHL	72	8	42	50	80	6	1	1	2	10
1995-96a	Swift Current	WHL	72	31	46	77	151	6	1	0	1	22
1996-97	Rochester	AHL	64	7	18	25	65	....	....	....	....	....
	Edmonton	**NHL**	**1**	**0**	**0**	**0**	**2**	....	....	....	....	....
	Hamilton	AHL	10	1	3	4	10	22	4	4	8	21
	NHL Totals		**1**	**0**	**0**	**0**	**2**	....	....	....	....	....

a WHL East First All-Star Team (1996)

Traded to **Edmonton** by **Buffalo** with Barrie Moore for Miroslav Satan, March 18, 1997.

MILLEN, COREY

Center. Shoots right. 5'7", 170 lbs. Born, Cloquet, MN, March 30, 1964.
(NY Rangers' 3rd choice, 57th overall, in 1982 Entry Draft).

			Regular Season					Playoffs				
Season	Club	Lea	GP	G	A	TP	PIM	GP	G	A	TP	PIM
1982-83	U. Minnesota	WCHA	21	14	15	29	18	....	....	....	....	....
1983-84	U.S. National	....	45	15	11	26	10	....	....	....	....	....
	U.S. Olympic	....	6	0	0	0	2	....	....	....	....	....
1984-85	U. Minnesota	WCHA	38	28	36	64	60	....	....	....	....	....
1985-86ab	U. Minnesota	WCHA	48	41	42	83	64	....	....	....	....	....
1986-87bc	U. Minnesota	WCHA	42	36	29	65	62	....	....	....	....	....
1987-88	U.S. National	....	47	41	43	84	26	....	....	....	....	....
	U.S. Olympic	....	6	6	5	11	4	....	....	....	....	....
1988-89	Ambri	Switz.	36	32	22	54	18	6	4	3	7	0
1989-90	**NY Rangers**	**NHL**	**4**	**0**	**0**	**0**	**2**	....	....	....	....	....
	Flint	IHL	11	4	5	9	2	....	....	....	....	....
1990-91	**NY Rangers**	**NHL**	**4**	**3**	**1**	**4**	**0**	**6**	**1**	**2**	**3**	**0**
	Binghamton	AHL	40	19	37	56	68	6	0	7	7	6
1991-92	**NY Rangers**	**NHL**	**11**	**1**	**4**	**5**	**10**	....	....	....	....	....
	Binghamton	AHL	15	8	7	15	44	....	....	....	....	....
	Los Angeles	**NHL**	**46**	**20**	**21**	**41**	**44**	**6**	**0**	**1**	**1**	**6**
1992-93	**Los Angeles**	**NHL**	**42**	**23**	**16**	**39**	**42**	**23**	**2**	**4**	**6**	**12**
1993-94	**New Jersey**	**NHL**	**78**	**20**	**30**	**50**	**52**	**7**	**1**	**0**	**1**	**2**
1994-95	**New Jersey**	**NHL**	**17**	**2**	**3**	**5**	**8**	....	....	....	....	....
	Dallas	**NHL**	**28**	**3**	**15**	**18**	**28**	**5**	**1**	**0**	**1**	**2**
1995-96	**Dallas**	**NHL**	**13**	**3**	**4**	**7**	**8**	....	....	....	....	....
	Michigan	IHL	11	8	11	19	14	....	....	....	....	....
	Calgary	**NHL**	**31**	**4**	**10**	**14**	**10**	....	....	....	....	....
1996-97	**Calgary**	**NHL**	**61**	**11**	**15**	**26**	**32**	....	....	....	....	....
	NHL Totals		**335**	**90**	**119**	**209**	**236**	**47**	**5**	**7**	**12**	**22**

a NCAA West Second All-American Team (1986)
b WCHA Second All-Star Team (1986, 1987)
c Named to NCAA All-Tournament Team (1987)

Traded to **Los Angeles** by **NY Rangers** for Randy Gilhen, December 23, 1991. Traded to **New Jersey** by **Los Angeles** for New Jersey's fifth round choice (Jason Saal) in 1993 Entry Draft, June 26, 1993. Traded to **Dallas** by **New Jersey** for Neal Broten, February 27, 1995. Traded to **Calgary** by **Dallas** with Jarome Iginla for Joe Nieuwendyk, December 19, 1995.

MILLER, AARON — COL.

Defense. Shoots right. 6'3", 197 lbs. Born, Buffalo, NY, August 11, 1971.
(NY Rangers' 6th choice, 88th overall, in 1989 Entry Draft).

			Regular Season					Playoffs				
Season	Club	Lea	GP	G	A	TP	PIM	GP	G	A	TP	PIM
1989-90	U. of Vermont	ECAC	31	1	15	16	24	....	....	....	....	....
1990-91	U. of Vermont	ECAC	30	3	7	10	22	....	....	....	....	....
1991-92	U. of Vermont	ECAC	31	3	16	19	28	....	....	....	....	....
1992-93ab	U. of Vermont	ECAC	30	4	13	17	16	....	....	....	....	....
1993-94	**Quebec**	**NHL**	**1**	**0**	**0**	**0**	**0**	....	....	....	....	....
	Cornwall	AHL	64	4	10	14	49	13	0	2	2	10
1994-95	Cornwall	AHL	76	4	18	22	69	....	....	....	....	....
	Quebec	**NHL**	**9**	**0**	**3**	**3**	**6**	....	....	....	....	....
1995-96	**Colorado**	**NHL**	**5**	**0**	**0**	**0**	**0**	....	....	....	....	....
	Cornwall	AHL	62	4	23	27	77	8	0	1	1	6
1996-97	**Colorado**	**NHL**	**56**	**5**	**12**	**17**	**15**	**17**	**1**	**2**	**3**	**10**
	NHL Totals		**71**	**5**	**15**	**20**	**21**	**17**	**1**	**2**	**3**	**10**

a ECAC First All-Star Team (1993)
b NCAA East Second All-American Team (1993)

Traded to **Quebec** by **NY Rangers** with NY Rangers' fifth round choice (Bill Lindsay) in 1991 Entry Draft for Joe Cirella, January 17, 1991.

MILLER, KELLY — WSH.

Left wing. Shoots left. 5'11", 197 lbs. Born, Lansing, MI, March 3, 1963.
(NY Rangers' 9th choice, 183rd overall, in 1982 Entry Draft).

			Regular Season					Playoffs				
Season	Club	Lea	GP	G	A	TP	PIM	GP	G	A	TP	PIM
1981-82	Michigan State	CCHA	38	11	18	29	17	....	....	....	....	....
1982-83	Michigan State	CCHA	36	16	19	35	12	....	....	....	....	....
1983-84	Michigan State	CCHA	46	28	21	49	12	....	....	....	....	....
1984-85ab	Michigan State	CCHA	43	27	23	50	21	....	....	....	....	....
	NY Rangers	**NHL**	**5**	**0**	**2**	**2**	**2**	**3**	**0**	**0**	**0**	**2**
1985-86	**NY Rangers**	**NHL**	**74**	**13**	**20**	**33**	**52**	**16**	**3**	**4**	**7**	**4**
1986-87	**NY Rangers**	**NHL**	**38**	**6**	**14**	**20**	**22**	....	....	....	....	....
	Washington	**NHL**	**39**	**10**	**12**	**22**	**26**	**7**	**2**	**2**	**4**	**0**
1987-88	**Washington**	**NHL**	**80**	**9**	**23**	**32**	**35**	**14**	**4**	**4**	**8**	**10**
1988-89	**Washington**	**NHL**	**78**	**19**	**21**	**40**	**45**	**6**	**1**	**0**	**1**	**2**
1989-90	**Washington**	**NHL**	**80**	**18**	**22**	**40**	**49**	**15**	**3**	**5**	**8**	**23**
1990-91	**Washington**	**NHL**	**80**	**24**	**26**	**50**	**29**	**11**	**4**	**2**	**6**	**6**
1991-92	**Washington**	**NHL**	**78**	**14**	**38**	**52**	**49**	**7**	**1**	**2**	**3**	**4**
1992-93	**Washington**	**NHL**	**84**	**18**	**27**	**45**	**32**	**6**	**0**	**3**	**3**	**2**
1993-94	**Washington**	**NHL**	**84**	**14**	**25**	**39**	**32**	**11**	**2**	**7**	**9**	**0**
1994-95	**Washington**	**NHL**	**48**	**10**	**13**	**23**	**6**	**7**	**0**	**3**	**3**	**4**
1995-96	**Washington**	**NHL**	**74**	**7**	**13**	**20**	**30**	**6**	**0**	**1**	**1**	**4**
1996-97	**Washington**	**NHL**	**77**	**10**	**14**	**24**	**33**	....	....	....	....	....
	NHL Totals		**919**	**172**	**270**	**442**	**442**	**109**	**20**	**33**	**53**	**61**

a CCHA First All-Star Team (1985)
b NCAA West First All-American Team (1985)

Traded to **Washington** by **NY Rangers** with Bob Crawford and Mike Ridley for Bob Carpenter and Washington's second round choice (Jason Prosofsky) in 1989 Entry Draft, January 1, 1987.

MILLER, KEVIN — CHI.

Center. Shoots right. 5'11", 190 lbs. Born, Lansing, MI, September 2, 1965.
(NY Rangers' 10th choice, 202nd overall, in 1984 Entry Draft).

			Regular Season					Playoffs				
Season	Club	Lea	GP	G	A	TP	PIM	GP	G	A	TP	PIM
1984-85	Michigan State	CCHA	44	11	29	40	84	....	....	....	....	....
1985-86	Michigan State	CCHA	45	19	52	71	112	....	....	....	....	....
1986-87	Michigan State	CCHA	42	25	56	81	63	....	....	....	....	....
1987-88	Michigan State	CCHA	9	6	3	9	18	....	....	....	....	....
	U.S. National	....	48	31	32	63	33	....	....	....	....	....
	U.S. Olympic	....	5	1	3	4	4	....	....	....	....	....
1988-89	**NY Rangers**	**NHL**	**24**	**3**	**5**	**8**	**2**	....	....	....	....	....
	Denver	IHL	55	29	47	76	19	4	2	1	3	2
1989-90	**NY Rangers**	**NHL**	**16**	**0**	**5**	**5**	**2**	**1**	**0**	**0**	**0**	**0**
	Flint	IHL	48	19	23	42	41	....	....	....	....	....
1990-91	**NY Rangers**	**NHL**	**63**	**17**	**27**	**44**	**63**	....	....	....	....	....
	Detroit	**NHL**	**11**	**5**	**2**	**7**	**4**	**7**	**3**	**2**	**5**	**20**
1991-92	**Detroit**	**NHL**	**80**	**20**	**26**	**46**	**53**	**9**	**0**	**2**	**2**	**4**
1992-93	**Washington**	**NHL**	**10**	**0**	**3**	**3**	**35**	....	....	....	....	....
	St. Louis	**NHL**	**72**	**24**	**22**	**46**	**65**	**10**	**0**	**3**	**3**	**11**
1993-94	**St. Louis**	**NHL**	**75**	**23**	**25**	**48**	**83**	**3**	**1**	**0**	**1**	**4**
1994-95	**St. Louis**	**NHL**	**15**	**2**	**5**	**7**	**0**	....	....	....	....	....
	San Jose	**NHL**	**21**	**6**	**7**	**13**	**13**	**6**	**0**	**0**	**0**	**2**
1995-96	**San Jose**	**NHL**	**68**	**22**	**20**	**42**	**41**	....	....	....	....	....
	Pittsburgh	**NHL**	**13**	**6**	**5**	**11**	**4**	**18**	**3**	**2**	**5**	**8**
1996-97	**Chicago**	**NHL**	**69**	**14**	**17**	**31**	**41**	**6**	**0**	**1**	**1**	**0**
	NHL Totals		**537**	**142**	**169**	**311**	**406**	**60**	**7**	**10**	**17**	**49**

Traded to **Detroit** by **NY Rangers** with Jim Cummins and Dennis Vial for Joey Kocur and Per Djoos, March 5, 1991. Traded to **Washington** by **Detroit** for Dino Ciccarelli, June 20, 1992. Traded to **St. Louis** by **Washington** for Paul Cavallini, November 2, 1992. Traded to **San Jose** by **St. Louis** for Todd Elik, March 23, 1995. Traded to **Pittsburgh** by **San Jose** for Pittsburgh's fifth round choice (later traded to Boston — Boston selected Elias Abrahamsson) in 1996 Entry Draft and future considerations, March 20, 1996. Signed as a free agent by **Chicago**, July 18, 1996.

MILLER, KIP

Center. Shoots left. 5'10", 190 lbs. Born, Lansing, MI, June 11, 1969.
(Quebec's 4th choice, 72nd overall, in 1987 Entry Draft).

			Regular Season					Playoffs				
Season	Club	Lea	GP	G	A	TP	PIM	GP	G	A	TP	PIM
1986-87	Michigan State	CCHA	41	20	19	39	92	....	....	....	....	....
1987-88	Michigan State	CCHA	39	16	25	41	51	....	....	....	....	....
1988-89ab	Michigan State	CCHA	47	32	45	77	94	....	....	....	....	....
1989-90abc	Michigan State	CCHA	45	*48	53	*101	60	....	....	....	....	....
1990-91	**Quebec**	**NHL**	**13**	**4**	**3**	**7**	**7**	....	....	....	....	....
	Halifax	AHL	66	36	33	69	40	....	....	....	....	....
1991-92	**Quebec**	**NHL**	**36**	**5**	**10**	**15**	**12**	....	....	....	....	....
	Halifax	AHL	24	9	17	26	8	....	....	....	....	....
	Minnesota	**NHL**	**3**	**1**	**2**	**3**	**2**	....	....	....	....	....
	Kalamazoo	IHL	6	1	8	9	4	12	3	9	12	12
1992-93	Kalamazoo	IHL	61	17	39	56	59	....	....	....	....	....
1993-94	**San Jose**	**NHL**	**11**	**2**	**2**	**4**	**6**	....	....	....	....	....
	Kansas City	IHL	71	38	54	92	51	....	....	....	....	....
1994-95	Denver	IHL	71	46	60	106	54	17	*15	14	29	8
	NY Islanders	**NHL**	**8**	**0**	**1**	**1**	**0**	....	....	....	....	....
1995-96	**Chicago**	**NHL**	**10**	**1**	**4**	**5**	**2**	....	....	....	....	....
	Indianapolis	IHL	73	32	59	91	46	5	2	6	8	2
1996-97	Chicago	IHL	43	11	41	52	32	....	....	....	....	....
	Indianapolis	IHL	37	17	24	41	18	4	2	2	4	2
	NHL Totals		**81**	**13**	**22**	**35**	**29**	....	....	....	....	....

a CCHA First All-Star Team (1989, 1990)
b NCAA West First All-American Team (1989, 1990)
c Won Hobey Baker Memorial Award (Top U.S. Collegiate Player) (1990)

Traded to **Minnesota** by **Quebec** for Steve Maltais, March 8, 1992. Signed as a free agent by **San Jose**, August 10, 1993. Signed as a free agent by **NY Islanders**, July 7, 1994. Signed as a free agent by **Chicago**, July 21, 1995.

MILLER, TODD — NYI

Center. Shoots right. 6', 174 lbs. Born, Elliot Lake, Ont., May 24, 1978.
(NY Islanders' 7th choice, 138th overall, in 1996 Entry Draft).

			Regular Season					Playoffs				
Season	Club	Lea	GP	G	A	TP	PIM	GP	G	A	TP	PIM
1995-96	Sarnia	OHL	62	12	16	28	44	1	0	0	0	0
1996-97	Sarnia	OHL	19	6	13	19	14	....	....	....	....	....
	Owen Sound	OHL	17	2	6	8	10	....	....	....	....	....

MILLS, CRAIG — CHI.

Right wing. Shoots right. 6', 190 lbs. Born, Toronto, Ont., August 27, 1976.
(Winnipeg's 5th choice, 108th overall, in 1994 Entry Draft).

			Regular Season					Playoffs				
Season	Club	Lea	GP	G	A	TP	PIM	GP	G	A	TP	PIM
1993-94	Belleville	OHL	63	15	18	33	88	12	2	1	3	11
1994-95	Belleville	OHL	62	39	41	80	104	13	7	9	16	8
1995-96	**Winnipeg**	**NHL**	**4**	**0**	**2**	**2**	**0**	**1**	**0**	**0**	**0**	**0**
	Belleville	OHL	48	10	19	29	113	14	4	5	9	32
	Springfield	AHL	....	....	....	....	....	2	0	0	0	0
1996-97	Indianapolis	IHL	80	12	7	19	199	4	0	0	0	4
	NHL Totals		**4**	**0**	**2**	**2**	**0**	**1**	**0**	**0**	**0**	**0**

Traded to **Chicago** by **Phoenix** with Alexei Zhamnov and Phoenix's first round choice (Ty Jones) in 1997 Entry Draft for Jeremy Roenick, August 16, 1996.

MIRONOV, BORIS (mih-RAH-nahf) EDM.

Defense. Shoots right. 6'3", 220 lbs. Born, Moscow, USSR, March 21, 1972.
(Winnipeg's 2nd choice, 27th overall, in 1992 Entry Draft).

			Regular Season					Playoffs				
Season	Club	Lea	GP	G	A	TP	PIM	GP	G	A	TP	PIM
1988-89	CSKA	USSR	1	0	0	0	0	....	....	....	....	....
1989-90	CSKA	USSR	7	0	0	0	0	....	....	....	....	....
1990-91	CSKA	USSR	36	1	5	6	16	....	....	....	....	....
1991-92	CSKA	CIS	36	2	1	3	22	....	....	....	....	....
1992-93	CSKA	CIS	19	0	5	5	20	....	....	....	....	....
1993-94a	**Winnipeg**	**NHL**	**65**	**7**	**22**	**29**	**96**	....	....	....	....	....
	Edmonton	**NHL**	**14**	**0**	**2**	**2**	**14**	....	....	....	....	....
1994-95	**Edmonton**	**NHL**	**29**	**1**	**7**	**8**	**40**	....	....	....	....	....
	Cape Breton	AHL	4	2	5	7	23	....	....	....	....	....
1995-96	**Edmonton**	**NHL**	**78**	**8**	**24**	**32**	**101**	....	....	....	....	....
1996-97	**Edmonton**	**NHL**	**55**	**6**	**26**	**32**	**85**	**12**	**2**	**8**	**10**	**16**
	NHL Totals		**241**	**22**	**81**	**103**	**336**	**12**	**2**	**8**	**10**	**16**

a NHL/Upper Deck All-Rookie Team (1994)

Traded to **Edmonton** by **Winnipeg** with Mats Lindgren, Winnipeg's first round choice (Jason Bonsignore) in 1994 Entry Draft and Florida's fourth round choice (previously acquired by Winnipeg — Edmonton selected Adam Copeland) in 1994 Entry Draft for Dave Manson and St. Louis' sixth round choice (previously acquired by Edmonton — Winnipeg selected Chris Kibermanis) in 1994 Entry Draft, March 15, 1994.

MIRONOV, DMITRI (mih-RAWN-ohv) ANA.

Defense. Shoots right. 6'3", 215 lbs. Born, Moscow, USSR, December 25, 1965.
(Toronto's 9th choice, 160th overall, in 1991 Entry Draft).

			Regular Season					Playoffs				
Season	Club	Lea	GP	G	A	TP	PIM	GP	G	A	TP	PIM
1985-86	CSKA	USSR	9	0	1	1	8	....	....	....	....	....
1986-87	CSKA	USSR	20	1	3	4	10	....	....	....	....	....
1987-88	Soviet Wings	USSR	44	12	6	18	30	....	....	....	....	....
1988-89	Soviet Wings	USSR	44	5	6	11	44	....	....	....	....	....
1989-90	Soviet Wings	USSR	45	4	11	15	34	....	....	....	....	....
1990-91	Soviet Wings	USSR	45	16	12	28	22	....	....	....	....	....
1991-92	Soviet Wings	CIS	35	15	16	31	62	....	....	....	....	....
	Toronto	**NHL**	**7**	**1**	**0**	**1**	**0**	....	....	....	....	....
1992-93	**Toronto**	**NHL**	**59**	**7**	**24**	**31**	**40**	**14**	**1**	**2**	**3**	**2**
1993-94	**Toronto**	**NHL**	**76**	**9**	**27**	**36**	**78**	**18**	**6**	**9**	**15**	**6**
1994-95	**Toronto**	**NHL**	**33**	**5**	**12**	**17**	**28**	**6**	**2**	**1**	**3**	**2**
1995-96	**Pittsburgh**	**NHL**	**72**	**3**	**31**	**34**	**88**	**15**	**0**	**1**	**1**	**10**
1996-97	**Pittsburgh**	**NHL**	**15**	**1**	**5**	**6**	**24**	....	....	....	....	....
	Anaheim	**NHL**	**62**	**12**	**34**	**46**	**77**	**11**	**1**	**10**	**11**	**10**
	NHL Totals		**324**	**38**	**133**	**171**	**335**	**64**	**10**	**23**	**33**	**30**

Traded to **Pittsburgh** by **Toronto** with Toronto's second round choice (later traded to New Jersey — New Jersey selected Joshua Dewolf) in 1996 Entry Draft for Larry Murphy, July 8, 1995. Traded to **Anaheim** by **Pittsburgh** with Shawn Antoski for Alex Hicks and Fredrik Olausson, November 19, 1996.

MISKOVICH, AARON (MIHS-kuh-vihch) COL.

Center. Shoots left. 5'10", 185 lbs. Born, Grand Rapids, MN, April 28, 1978.
(Colorado's 6th choice, 133rd overall, in 1997 Entry Draft).

			Regular Season					Playoffs				
Season	Club	Lea	GP	G	A	TP	PIM	GP	G	A	TP	PIM
1996-97	Green Bay	USHL	14	4	9	13	14	....	....	....	....	....

MITCHELL, WILLIE N.J.

Defense. Shoots left. 6'3", 210 lbs. Born, Ft. McNeill, B.C., April 23, 1977.
(New Jersey's 12th choice, 199th overall, in 1996 Entry Draft).

			Regular Season					Playoffs				
Season	Club	Lea	GP	G	A	TP	PIM	GP	G	A	TP	PIM
1995-96	Melfort	Jr. A	19	2	6	8	0	14	0	2	2	12
1996-97	Melfort	Jr. A	64	14	42	56	227	4	0	1	1	23

MODANO, MIKE (moh-DAN-oh) DAL.

Center. Shoots left. 6'3", 200 lbs. Born, Livonia, MI, June 7, 1970.
(Minnesota's 1st choice, 1st overall, in 1988 Entry Draft).

			Regular Season					Playoffs				
Season	Club	Lea	GP	G	A	TP	PIM	GP	G	A	TP	PIM
1986-87	Prince Albert	WHL	70	32	30	62	96	8	1	4	5	4
1987-88	Prince Albert	WHL	65	47	80	127	80	9	7	11	18	18
1988-89a	Prince Albert	WHL	41	39	66	105	74	....	....	....	....	....
	Minnesota	**NHL**	....	....	....	....	....	**2**	**0**	**0**	**0**	**0**
1989-90b	**Minnesota**	**NHL**	**80**	**29**	**46**	**75**	**63**	**7**	**1**	**1**	**2**	**12**
1990-91	**Minnesota**	**NHL**	**79**	**28**	**36**	**64**	**65**	**23**	**8**	**12**	**20**	**16**
1991-92	**Minnesota**	**NHL**	**76**	**33**	**44**	**77**	**46**	**7**	**3**	**2**	**5**	**4**
1992-93	**Minnesota**	**NHL**	**82**	**33**	**60**	**93**	**83**	....	....	....	....	....
1993-94	**Dallas**	**NHL**	**76**	**50**	**43**	**93**	**54**	**9**	**7**	**3**	**10**	**16**
1994-95	**Dallas**	**NHL**	**30**	**12**	**17**	**29**	**8**	....	....	....	....	....
1995-96	**Dallas**	**NHL**	**78**	**36**	**45**	**81**	**63**	....	....	....	....	....
1996-97	**Dallas**	**NHL**	**80**	**35**	**48**	**83**	**42**	**7**	**4**	**1**	**5**	**0**
	NHL Totals		**581**	**256**	**339**	**595**	**424**	**55**	**23**	**19**	**42**	**48**

a WHL East All-Star Team (1989)
b NHL All-Rookie Team (1990)

Played in NHL All-Star Game (1993)

MODIN, FREDRIK (muh-DEEN) TOR.

Left wing. Shoots left. 6'3", 222 lbs. Born, Sundsvall, Sweden, October 8, 1974.
(Toronto's 3rd choice, 64th overall, in 1994 Entry Draft).

			Regular Season					Playoffs				
Season	Club	Lea	GP	G	A	TP	PIM	GP	G	A	TP	PIM
1991-92	Sundsvall	Swe. 2	11	1	0	1	0	....	....	....	....	....
1992-93	Sundsvall	Swe. 2	30	5	7	12	12	....	....	....	....	....
1993-94	Sundsvall	Swe. 2	30	16	15	31	36	....	....	....	....	....
1994-95	Brynas	Swe.	38	9	10	19	33	14	4	4	8	6
1995-96	Brynas	Swe.	22	4	8	12	22	....	....	....	....	....
1996-97	**Toronto**	**NHL**	**76**	**6**	**7**	**13**	**24**	....	....	....	....	....
	NHL Totals		**76**	**6**	**7**	**13**	**24**	....	....	....	....	....

MODRY, JAROSLAV (MOHD-ree) L.A.

Defense. Shoots left. 6'2", 195 lbs. Born, Ceske-Budejovice, Czech., February 27, 1971.
(New Jersey's 11th choice, 179th overall, in 1990 Entry Draft).

			Regular Season					Playoffs				
Season	Club	Lea	GP	G	A	TP	PIM	GP	G	A	TP	PIM
1987-88	Budejovice	Czech.	3	0	0	0	0	....	....	....	....	....
1988-89	Budejovice	Czech.	28	0	1	1	8	....	....	....	....	....
1989-90	Budejovice	Czech.	41	2	2	4	....	....	....	....	....	....
1990-91	Dukla Trencin	Czech.	33	1	9	10	6	....	....	....	....	....
1991-92	Dukla Trencin	Czech.	18	0	4	4	6	....	....	....	....	....
	Budejovice	Czech. 2	14	4	10	14	....	....	....	....	....	....
1992-93	Utica	AHL	80	7	35	42	62	5	0	2	2	2
1993-94	**New Jersey**	**NHL**	**41**	**2**	**15**	**17**	**18**	....	....	....	....	....
	Albany	AHL	19	1	5	6	25	....	....	....	....	....
1994-95	Budejovice	Czech.	19	1	3	4	30	....	....	....	....	....
	New Jersey	**NHL**	**11**	**0**	**0**	**0**	**0**	....	....	....	....	....
	Albany	AHL	18	5	6	11	14	14	3	3	6	4
1995-96	**Ottawa**	**NHL**	**64**	**4**	**14**	**18**	**38**	....	....	....	....	....
	Los Angeles	**NHL**	**9**	**0**	**3**	**3**	**6**	....	....	....	....	....
1996-97	**Los Angeles**	**NHL**	**30**	**3**	**3**	**6**	**25**	....	....	....	....	....
	Phoenix	IHL	23	3	12	15	17	....	....	....	....	....
	Utah	IHL	11	1	4	5	20	7	0	1	1	6
	NHL Totals		**155**	**9**	**35**	**44**	**87**	....	....	....	....	....

Traded to **Ottawa** by **New Jersey** for Ottawa's fourth round choice (Alyn McCauley) in 1995 Entry Draft, July 8, 1995. Traded to **Los Angeles** by **Ottawa** with Ottawa's eighth round choice (Stephen Valiquette) in 1996 Entry Draft for Kevin Brown, March 20, 1996.

MOGER, SANDY (MOH-guhr) BOS.

Center. Shoots right. 6'3", 214 lbs. Born, 100 Mile House, B.C., March 21, 1969.
(Vancouver's 7th choice, 176th overall, in 1989 Entry Draft).

			Regular Season					Playoffs				
Season	Club	Lea	GP	G	A	TP	PIM	GP	G	A	TP	PIM
1988-89	Lake Superior	CCHA	21	3	5	8	26	....	....	....	....	....
1989-90	Lake Superior	CCHA	46	17	15	32	76	....	....	....	....	....
1990-91	Lake Superior	CCHA	45	27	21	48	*172	....	....	....	....	....
1991-92a	Lake Superior	CCHA	38	24	24	48	93	....	....	....	....	....
1992-93	Hamilton	AHL	78	23	26	49	57	....	....	....	....	....
1993-94	Hamilton	AHL	29	9	8	17	41	....	....	....	....	....
1994-95	Providence	AHL	63	32	29	61	105	....	....	....	....	....
	Boston	**NHL**	**18**	**2**	**6**	**8**	**6**	....	....	....	....	....
1995-96	**Boston**	**NHL**	**80**	**15**	**14**	**29**	**65**	**5**	**2**	**2**	**4**	**12**
1996-97	**Boston**	**NHL**	**34**	**10**	**3**	**13**	**45**	....	....	....	....	....
	Providence	AHL	3	0	2	2	19	....	....	....	....	....
	NHL Totals		**132**	**27**	**23**	**50**	**116**	**5**	**2**	**2**	**4**	**12**

a CCHA Second All-Star Team (1992)

Signed as a free agent by **Boston**, June 22, 1994.

MOGILNY, ALEXANDER (moh-GIHL-nee) VAN.

Right wing. Shoots left. 5'11", 187 lbs. Born, Khabarovsk, USSR, February 18, 1969.
(Buffalo's 4th choice, 89th overall, in 1988 Entry Draft).

			Regular Season					Playoffs				
Season	Club	Lea	GP	G	A	TP	PIM	GP	G	A	TP	PIM
1986-87	CSKA	USSR	28	15	1	16	4	....	....	....	....	....
1987-88	CSKA	USSR	39	12	8	20	14	....	....	....	....	....
1988-89	CSKA	USSR	31	11	11	22	24	....	....	....	....	....
1989-90	**Buffalo**	**NHL**	**65**	**15**	**28**	**43**	**16**	**4**	**0**	**1**	**1**	**2**
1990-91	**Buffalo**	**NHL**	**62**	**30**	**34**	**64**	**16**	**6**	**0**	**6**	**6**	**2**
1991-92	**Buffalo**	**NHL**	**67**	**39**	**45**	**84**	**73**	**2**	**0**	**2**	**2**	**0**
1992-93a	**Buffalo**	**NHL**	**77**	***76**	**51**	**127**	**40**	**7**	**7**	**3**	**10**	**6**
1993-94	**Buffalo**	**NHL**	**66**	**32**	**47**	**79**	**22**	**7**	**4**	**2**	**6**	**6**
1994-95	Spartak	CIS	1	0	1	1	0	....	....	....	....	....
	Buffalo	**NHL**	**44**	**19**	**28**	**47**	**36**	**5**	**3**	**2**	**5**	**2**
1995-96a	**Vancouver**	**NHL**	**79**	**55**	**52**	**107**	**16**	**6**	**1**	**8**	**9**	**8**
1996-97	**Vancouver**	**NHL**	**76**	**31**	**42**	**73**	**18**	....	....	....	....	....
	NHL Totals		**536**	**297**	**327**	**624**	**237**	**37**	**15**	**24**	**39**	**26**

a NHL Second All-Star Team (1993, 1996)

Played in NHL All-Star Game (1992-94, 1996)

Traded to **Vancouver** by **Buffalo** with Buffalo's fifth round choice (Todd Norman) in 1995 Entry Draft for Mike Peca, Mike Wilson and Vancouver's first round choice (Jay McKee) in 1995 Entry Draft, July 8, 1995.

MOISE, MARTIN (MOIZ) CGY.

Left wing. Shoots left. 6', 197 lbs. Born, Valleyfield, Que., January 18, 1979.
(Calgary's 9th choice, 113th overall, in 1997 Entry Draft).

			Regular Season					Playoffs				
Season	Club	Lea	GP	G	A	TP	PIM	GP	G	A	TP	PIM
1995-96	St-Hyacinthe	QMJHL	67	6	19	25	11	10	1	1	2	0
1996-97	Beauport	QMJHL	70	21	23	44	23	4	4	1	5	0

MOMESSO, SERGIO (moh-MESS-oh)

Left wing. Shoots left. 6'3", 215 lbs. Born, Montreal, Que., September 4, 1965.
(Montreal's 3rd choice, 27th overall, in 1983 Entry Draft).

			Regular Season					Playoffs				
Season	Club	Lea	GP	G	A	TP	PIM	GP	G	A	TP	PIM
1982-83	Shawinigan	QMJHL	70	27	42	69	93	10	5	4	9	55
1983-84	**Montreal**	**NHL**	**1**	**0**	**0**	**0**	**0**	....	....	....	....	....
	Shawinigan	QMJHL	68	42	88	130	235	6	4	4	8	13
	Nova Scotia	AHL	....	....	....	....	....	8	0	2	2	4
1984-85a	Shawinigan	QMJHL	64	56	90	146	216	8	7	8	15	17
1985-86	**Montreal**	**NHL**	**24**	**8**	**7**	**15**	**46**	....	....	....	....	....
1986-87	**Montreal**	**NHL**	**59**	**14**	**17**	**31**	**96**	**11**	**1**	**3**	**4**	**31**
	Sherbrooke	AHL	6	1	6	7	10	....	....	....	....	....
1987-88	**Montreal**	**NHL**	**53**	**7**	**14**	**21**	**101**	**6**	**0**	**2**	**2**	**16**
1988-89	**St. Louis**	**NHL**	**53**	**9**	**17**	**26**	**139**	**10**	**2**	**5**	**7**	**24**
1989-90	**St. Louis**	**NHL**	**79**	**24**	**32**	**56**	**199**	**12**	**3**	**2**	**5**	**63**
1990-91	**St. Louis**	**NHL**	**59**	**10**	**18**	**28**	**131**	....	....	....	....	....
	Vancouver	**NHL**	**11**	**6**	**2**	**8**	**43**	**6**	**0**	**3**	**3**	**25**
1991-92	**Vancouver**	**NHL**	**58**	**20**	**23**	**43**	**198**	**13**	**0**	**5**	**5**	**30**
1992-93	**Vancouver**	**NHL**	**84**	**18**	**20**	**38**	**200**	**12**	**3**	**0**	**3**	**30**
1993-94	**Vancouver**	**NHL**	**68**	**14**	**13**	**27**	**149**	**24**	**3**	**4**	**7**	**56**
1994-95	Milan Devils	Euro.	2	2	3	5	0	....	....	....	....	....
	Milan Devils	Italy	2	1	4	5	2	....	....	....	....	....
	Vancouver	**NHL**	**48**	**10**	**15**	**25**	**65**	**11**	**3**	**1**	**4**	**16**
1995-96	**Toronto**	**NHL**	**54**	**7**	**8**	**15**	**112**	....	....	....	....	....
	NY Rangers	**NHL**	**19**	**4**	**4**	**8**	**30**	**11**	**3**	**1**	**4**	**14**
1996-97	**NY Rangers**	**NHL**	**9**	**0**	**0**	**0**	**11**	....	....	....	....	....
	St. Louis	**NHL**	**31**	**1**	**3**	**4**	**37**	**3**	**0**	**0**	**0**	**6**
	NHL Totals		**710**	**152**	**193**	**345**	**1557**	**119**	**18**	**26**	**44**	**311**

a QMJHL First All-Star Team (1985)

Traded to **St. Louis** by **Montreal** with Vincent Riendeau for Jocelyn Lemieux, Darrell May and St. Louis' second round choice (Patrice Brisebois) in the 1989 Entry Draft, August 9, 1988. Traded to **Vancouver** by **St. Louis** with Geoff Courtnall, Robert Dirk, Cliff Ronning and St. Louis' fifth round choice (Brian Loney) in 1992 Entry Draft for Dan Quinn and Garth Butcher, March 5, 1991. Traded to **Toronto** by **Vancouver** for Mike Ridley, July 8, 1995. Traded by **NY Rangers** by **Toronto** for Wayne Presley, February 29, 1996. Traded to **St. Louis** by **NY Rangers** for Brian Noonan, November 13, 1996.

MONTGOMERY, JIM PHI.

Center. Shoots right. 5'10", 185 lbs. Born, Montreal, Que., June 30, 1969.

			Regular Season					Playoffs				
Season	Club	Lea	GP	G	A	TP	PIM	GP	G	A	TP	PIM
1989-90	U. of Maine	H.E.	45	26	34	60	35	....	....	....	....	....
1990-91	U. of Maine	H.E.	43	24	*57	81	44	....	....	....	....	....
1991-92a	U. of Maine	H.E.	37	21	44	65	46	....	....	....	....	....
1992-93bcde	U. of Maine	H.E.	45	32	63	95	40	....	....	....	....	....
1993-94	**St. Louis**	**NHL**	**67**	**6**	**14**	**20**	**44**	....	....	....	....	....
	Peoria	IHL	12	7	8	15	10	....	....	....	....	....
1994-95	**Montreal**	**NHL**	**5**	**0**	**0**	**0**	**2**	....	....	....	....	....
	Philadelphia	**NHL**	**8**	**1**	**1**	**2**	**6**	**7**	**1**	**0**	**1**	**2**
	Hershey	AHL	16	8	6	14	14	6	3	2	5	25
1995-96	**Philadelphia**	**NHL**	**5**	**1**	**2**	**3**	**9**	**1**	**0**	**0**	**0**	**0**
f	Hershey	AHL	78	34	*71	105	95	4	3	2	5	6
1996-97	Koln	Ger.	50	12	35	47	111	4	0	1	1	6
	NHL Totals		**85**	**8**	**17**	**25**	**61**	**8**	**1**	**0**	**1**	**2**

a Hockey East Second All-Star Team (1992)
b Hockey East First All-Star Team (1993)
c NCAA East Second All-American Team (1993)
d NCAA Final Four All-Tournament Team (1993)
e NCAA Final Four Tournament Most Valuable Player (1993)
f AHL Second All-Star Team (1996)

Signed as a free agent by **St. Louis**, June 2, 1993. Traded to **Montreal** by **St. Louis** for Guy Carbonneau, August 19, 1994. Claimed on waivers by **Philadelphia** from **Montreal**, February 10, 1995.

MOORE, BARRIE EDM.

Left wing. Shoots left. 5'11", 175 lbs. Born, London, Ont., May 22, 1975.
(Buffalo's 7th choice, 220th overall, in 1993 Entry Draft).

			Regular Season					Playoffs				
Season	Club	Lea	GP	G	A	TP	PIM	GP	G	A	TP	PIM
1991-92	Sudbury	OHL	62	15	38	53	57	11	0	7	7	12
1992-93	Sudbury	OHL	57	13	26	39	71	14	4	3	7	19
1993-94	Sudbury	OHL	65	36	49	85	69	10	3	5	8	14
1994-95	Sudbury	OHL	60	47	42	89	67	18	*15	14	29	24
1995-96	**Buffalo**	**NHL**	**3**	**0**	**0**	**0**	**0**	....	....	....	....	....
	Rochester	AHL	64	26	30	56	40	18	3	6	9	18
1996-97	**Buffalo**	**NHL**	**31**	**2**	**6**	**8**	**18**	....	....	....	....	....
	Rochester	AHL	32	14	15	29	14	....	....	....	....	....
	Edmonton	**NHL**	**4**	**0**	**0**	**0**	**0**	....	....	....	....	....
	Hamilton	AHL	9	5	2	7	0	22	2	6	8	15
	NHL Totals		**38**	**2**	**6**	**8**	**18**	....	....	....	....	....

Traded to **Edmonton** by **Buffalo** with Craig Millar for Miroslav Satan, March 18, 1997.

MORAN, IAN (moh-RAN) PIT.

Defense. Shoots right. 5'11", 195 lbs. Born, Cleveland, OH, August 24, 1972.
(Pittsburgh's 6th choice, 107th overall, in 1990 Entry Draft).

			Regular Season					Playoffs				
Season	Club	Lea	GP	G	A	TP	PIM	GP	G	A	TP	PIM
1991-92	Boston College	H.E.	30	2	16	18	44	....	....	....	....	....
1992-93	Boston College	H.E.	31	8	12	20	32	....	....	....	....	....
1993-94	U.S. National	....	50	8	15	23	69	....	....	....	....	....
	Cleveland	IHL	33	5	13	18	39	....	....	....	....	....
1994-95	Cleveland	IHL	64	7	31	38	94	4	0	1	1	2
	Pittsburgh	**NHL**	....	....	....	....	....	**8**	**0**	**0**	**0**	**0**
1995-96	**Pittsburgh**	**NHL**	**51**	**1**	**1**	**2**	**47**	....	....	....	....	....
1996-97	**Pittsburgh**	**NHL**	**36**	**4**	**5**	**9**	**22**	**5**	**1**	**2**	**3**	**4**
	Cleveland	IHL	36	6	23	29	26	....	....	....	....	....
	NHL Totals		**87**	**5**	**6**	**11**	**69**	**13**	**1**	**2**	**3**	**4**

MORE, JAYSON (MOHR) PHO.

Defense. Shoots right. 6'2", 210 lbs. Born, Souris, Man., January 12, 1969.
(NY Rangers' 1st choice, 10th overall, in 1987 Entry Draft).

			Regular Season					Playoffs				
Season	Club	Lea	GP	G	A	TP	PIM	GP	G	A	TP	PIM
1984-85	Lethbridge	WHL	71	3	9	12	101	4	1	0	1	7
1985-86	Lethbridge	WHL	61	7	18	25	155	9	0	2	2	36
1986-87	Brandon	WHL	21	4	6	10	62	....	....	....	....	....
	N. Westminster	WHL	43	4	23	27	155	....	....	....	....	....
1987-88a	N. Westminster	WHL	70	13	47	60	270	5	0	2	2	26
1988-89	**NY Rangers**	**NHL**	**1**	**0**	**0**	**0**	**0**	....	....	....	....	....
	Denver	IHL	62	7	15	22	138	3	0	1	1	26
1989-90	Flint	IHL	9	1	5	6	41	....	....	....	....	....
	Minnesota	**NHL**	**5**	**0**	**0**	**0**	**16**	....	....	....	....	....
	Kalamazoo	IHL	64	9	25	34	316	10	0	3	3	13
1990-91	Kalamazoo	IHL	10	0	5	5	46	....	....	....	....	....
	Fredericton	AHL	57	7	17	24	152	9	1	1	2	34
1991-92	**San Jose**	**NHL**	**46**	**4**	**13**	**17**	**85**	....	....	....	....	....
	Kansas City	IHL	2	0	2	2	4	....	....	....	....	....
1992-93	**San Jose**	**NHL**	**73**	**5**	**6**	**11**	**179**	....	....	....	....	....
1993-94	**San Jose**	**NHL**	**49**	**1**	**6**	**7**	**63**	**13**	**0**	**2**	**2**	**32**
	Kansas City	IHL	2	1	0	1	25	....	....	....	....	....
1994-95	**San Jose**	**NHL**	**45**	**0**	**6**	**6**	**71**	**11**	**0**	**4**	**4**	**6**
1995-96	**San Jose**	**NHL**	**74**	**2**	**7**	**9**	**147**	....	....	....	....	....
1996-97	**NY Rangers**	**NHL**	**14**	**0**	**1**	**1**	**25**	....	....	....	....	....
	Phoenix	**NHL**	**23**	**1**	**6**	**7**	**37**	**7**	**0**	**0**	**0**	**7**
	NHL Totals		**330**	**13**	**45**	**58**	**623**	**31**	**0**	**6**	**6**	**45**

a WHL All-Star Team (1988)

Traded to **Minnesota** by **NY Rangers** for Dave Archibald, November 1, 1989. Traded to **Montreal** by **Minnesota** for Brian Hayward, November 7, 1990. Claimed by **San Jose** from **Montreal** in Expansion Draft, May 30, 1991. Traded to **NY Rangers** by **San Jose** with Brian Swanson and a conditional choice in 1998 Entry Draft for Marty McSorley, August 20, 1996. Traded to **Phoenix** by **NY Rangers** for Mike Eastwood and Dallas Eakins, February 6, 1997.

MOREAU, ETHAN (moh-ROH, EE-than) CHI.

Left wing. Shoots left. 6'2", 205 lbs. Born, Huntsville, Ont., September 22, 1975.
(Chicago's 1st choice, 14th overall, in 1994 Entry Draft).

			Regular Season					Playoffs				
Season	Club	Lea	GP	G	A	TP	PIM	GP	G	A	TP	PIM
1991-92	Niagara Falls	OHL	62	20	35	55	39	17	4	6	10	4
1992-93	Niagara Falls	OHL	65	32	41	73	69	4	0	3	3	4
1993-94	Niagara Falls	OHL	59	44	54	98	100	....	....	....	....	....
1994-95	Niagara Falls	OHL	39	25	41	66	69	....	....	....	....	....
	Sudbury	OHL	23	13	17	30	22	18	6	12	18	26
1995-96	**Chicago**	**NHL**	**8**	**0**	**1**	**1**	**4**	....	....	....	....	....
	Indianapolis	IHL	71	21	20	41	126	5	4	0	4	8
1996-97	**Chicago**	**NHL**	**82**	**15**	**16**	**31**	**123**	**6**	**1**	**0**	**1**	**9**
	NHL Totals		**90**	**15**	**17**	**32**	**127**	**6**	**1**	**0**	**1**	**9**

MORGAN, JASON L.A.

Center. Shoots left. 6'1", 185 lbs. Born, St. John's, Nfld., October 9, 1976.
(Los Angeles' 5th choice, 118th overall, in 1995 Entry Draft).

			Regular Season					Playoffs				
Season	Club	Lea	GP	G	A	TP	PIM	GP	G	A	TP	PIM
1993-94	Kitchener	OHL	65	6	15	21	16	5	1	0	1	0
1994-95	Kitchener	OHL	35	3	15	18	25	....	....	....	....	....
	Kingston	OHL	20	0	3	3	14	6	0	2	2	0
1995-96	Kingston	OHL	66	16	38	54	50	6	1	2	3	0
1996-97	**Los Angeles**	**NHL**	**3**	**0**	**0**	**0**	**0**	....	....	....	....	....
	Phoenix	IHL	57	3	6	9	29	....	....	....	....	....
	Mississippi	ECHL	6	3	0	3	0	3	1	1	2	6
	NHL Totals		**3**	**0**	**0**	**0**	**0**	....	....	....	....	....

MORIN, OLIVIER MTL.

Center. Shoots right. 6'1", 176 lbs. Born, Montreal, Que., April 2, 1978.

			Regular Season					Playoffs				
Season	Club	Lea	GP	G	A	TP	PIM	GP	G	A	TP	PIM
1995-96	Chicoutimi	QMJHL	68	17	32	49	102	17	6	5	11	51
1996-97	Chicoutimi	QMJHL	70	22	44	66	152	21	5	8	13	24

Signed as a free agent by **Montreal**, October 3, 1996.

MORO, MARC ANA.

Defense. Shoots left. 6'1", 220 lbs. Born, Toronto, Ont., July 17, 1977.
(Ottawa's 2nd choice, 27th overall, in 1995 Entry Draft).

			Regular Season					Playoffs				
Season	Club	Lea	GP	G	A	TP	PIM	GP	G	A	TP	PIM
1993-94	Kingston	OHL	43	0	3	3	81	....	....	....	....	....
1994-95	Kingston	OHL	64	4	12	16	255	6	0	0	0	23
1995-96	Kingston	OHL	66	4	17	21	261	6	0	0	0	12
	P.E.I.	AHL	2	0	0	0	7	2	0	0	0	4
1996-97	Kingston	OHL	37	4	8	12	97	....	....	....	....	....
	S.S. Marie	OHL	26	0	5	5	74	11	1	6	7	38

Rights traded to **Anaheim** by **Ottawa** with Ted Drury for Jason York and Shaun Van Allen, October 1, 1996.

MOROZOV, ALEXEI (moh-ROH-zohv) PIT.

Right wing. Shoots left. 6'1", 180 lbs. Born, Moscow, USSR, February 16, 1977.
(Pittsburgh's 1st choice, 24th overall, in 1995 Entry Draft).

			Regular Season					Playoffs				
Season	Club	Lea	GP	G	A	TP	PIM	GP	G	A	TP	PIM
1993-94	Soviet Wings	CIS	7	0	0	0	0	3	0	0	0	2
1994-95	Soviet Wings	CIS	48	15	12	27	53	4	0	3	3	0
1995-96	Soviet Wings	CIS	47	13	9	22	26	....	....	....	....	....
1996-97	Soviet Wings	Rus.	44	21	11	32	32	2	0	1	1	2

MOROZOV, VALENTIN (moh-ROH-zohv) PIT.

Center. Shoots left. 5'11", 176 lbs. Born, Moscow, USSR, June 1, 1975.
(Pittsburgh's 8th choice, 154th overall, in 1994 Entry Draft).

			Regular Season					Playoffs				
Season	Club	Lea	GP	G	A	TP	PIM	GP	G	A	TP	PIM
1992-93	CSKA	CIS	17	0	0	0	6	....	....	....	....	....
1993-94	CSKA	CIS	18	4	1	5	8	3	0	1	1	0
1994-95	CSKA	CIS	47	9	4	13	10	2	2	0	2	0
1995-96	CSKA	CIS	51	30	11	41	28	3	1	0	1	2
1996-97	CSKA	Rus.	22	8	5	13	8	....	....	....	....	....
	CSKA	Rus. 2	4	2	1	3	0	....	....	....	....	....

MORRIS, DEREK — CGY.

Defense. Shoots right. 5'11", 180 lbs. Born, Edmonton, Alta., August 24, 1978.
(Calgary's 1st choice, 13th overall, in 1996 Entry Draft).

			Regular Season					Playoffs				
Season	Club	Lea	GP	G	A	TP	PIM	GP	G	A	TP	PIM
1995-96	Regina	WHL	67	8	44	52	70	11	1	7	8	26
1996-97a	Regina	WHL	67	18	57	75	180	5	0	3	3	9
	Saint John	AHL	7	0	3	3	7	5	0	3	3	7

a WHL East First All-Star Team (1997)

MORRISON, BRENDAN — N.J.

Center. Shoots left. 5'11", 175 lbs. Born, N. Vancouver, B.C., August 12, 1975.
(New Jersey's 3rd choice, 39th overall, in 1993 Entry Draft).

			Regular Season					Playoffs				
Season	Club	Lea	GP	G	A	TP	PIM	GP	G	A	TP	PIM
1993-94	U. of Michigan	CCHA	38	20	28	48	24	....	....	....	....	....
1994-95ab	U. of Michigan	CCHA	39	23	*53	*76	42	....	....	....	....	....
1995-96ab	U. of Michigan	CCHA	35	28	44	*72	41	....	....	....	....	....
1996-97abc	U. of Michigan	CCHA	43	31	*57	*88	52	....	....	....	....	....

a CCHA First All-Star Team (1995, 1996, 1997)
b NCAA West First All-American Team (1995, 1996, 1997)
c Won Hobey Baker Memorial Award (Top U.S. Collegiate Player) (1997)

MORROW, BRENDEN — DAL.

Left wing. Shoots left. 5'11", 196 lbs. Born, Carlisle, Sask., January 16, 1979.
(Dallas' 1st choice, 25th overall, in 1997 Entry Draft).

			Regular Season					Playoffs				
Season	Club	Lea	GP	G	A	TP	PIM	GP	G	A	TP	PIM
1995-96	Portland	WHL	65	13	12	25	61	7	0	0	0	8
1996-97	Portland	WHL	71	39	49	88	178	6	2	1	3	4

MORTIER, DARREN — BUF.

Center. Shoots right. 6'1", 175 lbs. Born, Sarnia, Ont., May 4, 1977.
(Buffalo's 9th choice, 161st overall, in 1996 Entry Draft).

			Regular Season					Playoffs				
Season	Club	Lea	GP	G	A	TP	PIM	GP	G	A	TP	PIM
1994-95	Sarnia	OHL	42	10	5	15	6	2	0	0	0	9
1995-96	Sarnia	OHL	63	20	22	42	26	10	1	6	7	0
1996-97	Sarnia	OHL	61	22	28	50	47	12	2	4	6	8

MOSER, JAY

Defense. Shoots left. 6'2", 170 lbs. Born, Cottage Grove, MN, December 26, 1972.
(Boston's 7th choice, 172nd overall, in 1991 Entry Draft).

			Regular Season					Playoffs				
Season	Club	Lea	GP	G	A	TP	PIM	GP	G	A	TP	PIM
1991-92	St. Cloud	WCHA	35	3	9	12	40	....	....	....	....	....
1992-93	St. Cloud	WCHA	33	2	9	11	77	....	....	....	....	....
1993-94			DID NOT PLAY									
1994-95	U. Minnesota	WCHA	13	1	5	6	29	....	....	....	....	....
1995-96	U. Minnesota	WCHA	21	10	9	19	18	....	....	....	....	....
1996-97	Providence	AHL	12	0	2	2	8	....	....	....	....	....
	S. Carolina	ECHL	41	19	30	49	32	....	....	....	....	....
	Rochester	AHL	22	4	9	13	4	9	1	1	2	4

MRAZEK, FRANTISEK (muh-RA-zehk) — TOR.

Left wing. Shoots left. 6'4", 211 lbs. Born, Ceske-Budejovice, Czech., May 16, 1979.
(Toronto's 3rd choice, 111th overall, in 1997 Entry Draft).

			Regular Season					Playoffs				
Season	Club	Lea	GP	G	A	TP	PIM	GP	G	A	TP	PIM
1996-97	Budejovice	Czech. Jr.	40	18	15	33	....	....	....	....	....	....

MROZIK, RICK (muh-ROH-zihk) — WSH.

Defense. Shoots left. 6'2", 185 lbs. Born, Duluth, MN, January 2, 1975.
(Dallas' 4th choice, 136th overall, in 1993 Entry Draft).

			Regular Season					Playoffs				
Season	Club	Lea	GP	G	A	TP	PIM	GP	G	A	TP	PIM
1993-94	Minn.-Duluth	WCHA	38	2	9	11	38	....	....	....	....	....
1994-95	Minn.-Duluth	WCHA	3	0	0	0	2	....	....	....	....	....
1995-96	Minn. Duluth	WCHA	35	3	19	22	63	....	....	....	....	....
1996-97a	Minn. Duluth	WCHA	38	11	23	34	56	....	....	....	....	....

a WCHA Second All-Star Team (1997)

Traded to **Washington** by **Dallas** with Mark Tinordi for Kevin Hatcher, January 18, 1995.

MUCKALT, BILL (MUH-kawlt) — VAN.

Right wing. Shoots right. 6', 190 lbs. Born, Williams Lake, B.C., July 15, 1974.
(Vancouver's 9th choice, 221st overall, in 1994 Entry Draft).

			Regular Season					Playoffs				
Season	Club	Lea	GP	G	A	TP	PIM	GP	G	A	TP	PIM
1994-95	U. of Michigan	CCHA	39	19	18	37	42	....	....	....	....	....
1995-96	U. of Michigan	CCHA	41	28	30	58	34	....	....	....	....	....
1996-97	U. of Michigan	CCHA	36	26	38	64	69	....	....	....	....	....

MUIR, BRYAN — EDM.

Defense. Shoots left. 6'4", 220 lbs. Born, Winnipeg, Man., June 8, 1973.

			Regular Season					Playoffs				
Season	Club	Lea	GP	G	A	TP	PIM	GP	G	A	TP	PIM
1992-93	N. Hampshire	H.E.	26	1	2	3	24	....	....	....	....	....
1993-94	N. Hampshire	H.E.	40	0	4	4	48	....	....	....	....	....
1994-95	N. Hampshire	H.E.	28	9	9	18	46	....	....	....	....	....
1995-96	Cdn. National	....	42	6	12	18	38	....	....	....	....	....
	Edmonton	**NHL**	**5**	**0**	**0**	**0**	**6**	....	....	....	....	....
1996-97	Hamilton	AHL	75	8	16	24	80	14	0	5	5	12
	Edmonton	**NHL**	....	....	....	....	....	**5**	**0**	**0**	**0**	**4**
	NHL Totals		**5**	**0**	**0**	**0**	**6**	**5**	**0**	**0**	**0**	**4**

Signed as a free agent by **Edmonton**, April 30, 1996.

MULHERN, RYAN

Center. Shoots right. 6'1", 180 lbs. Born, Philadelphia, PA, January 11, 1973.
(Calgary's 8th choice, 174th overall, in 1992 Entry Draft).

			Regular Season					Playoffs				
Season	Club	Lea	GP	G	A	TP	PIM	GP	G	A	TP	PIM
1992-93	Brown	ECAC	31	15	9	24	46	....	....	....	....	....
1993-94	Brown	ECAC	27	18	17	35	48	....	....	....	....	....
1994-95	Brown	ECAC	30	18	16	34	*108	....	....	....	....	....
1995-96	Brown	ECAC	32	10	16	26	78	....	....	....	....	....
1996-97	Hampton Rds.	ECHL	40	22	16	38	52	....	....	....	....	....
	Portland	AHL	38	19	15	34	16	5	1	1	2	2

Signed as a free agent by **Washington**, March 17, 1997.

MULLEN, JOE

Right wing. Shoots right. 5'9", 180 lbs. Born, New York, NY, February 26, 1957.

			Regular Season					Playoffs				
Season	Club	Lea	GP	G	A	TP	PIM	GP	G	A	TP	PIM
1977-78a	Boston College	ECAC	34	34	34	68	12	....	....	....	....	....
1978-79a	Boston College	ECAC	25	32	24	56	8	....	....	....	....	....
1979-80bc	Salt Lake	CHL	75	40	32	72	21	13	*9	11	20	0
	St. Louis	**NHL**	....	....	....	....	....	**1**	**0**	**0**	**0**	**0**
1980-81de	Salt Lake	CHL	80	59	58	*117	8	17	11	9	20	0
1981-82	**St. Louis**	**NHL**	**45**	**25**	**34**	**59**	**4**	**10**	**7**	**11**	**18**	**4**
	Salt Lake	CHL	27	21	27	48	12	....	....	....	....	....
1982-83	**St. Louis**	**NHL**	**49**	**17**	**30**	**47**	**6**	....	....	....	....	....
1983-84	**St. Louis**	**NHL**	**80**	**41**	**44**	**85**	**19**	**6**	**2**	**0**	**2**	**0**
1984-85	**St. Louis**	**NHL**	**79**	**40**	**52**	**92**	**6**	**3**	**0**	**0**	**0**	**0**
1985-86	**St. Louis**	**NHL**	**48**	**28**	**24**	**52**	**10**	....	....	....	....	....
	Calgary	**NHL**	**29**	**16**	**22**	**38**	**11**	**21**	***12**	**7**	**19**	**4**
1986-87f	**Calgary**	**NHL**	**79**	**47**	**40**	**87**	**14**	**6**	**2**	**1**	**3**	**0**
1987-88	**Calgary**	**NHL**	**80**	**40**	**44**	**84**	**30**	**7**	**2**	**4**	**6**	**10**
1988-89fgh	**Calgary**	**NHL**	**79**	**51**	**59**	**110**	**16**	**21**	***16**	**8**	**24**	**4** ♦
1989-90	**Calgary**	**NHL**	**78**	**36**	**33**	**69**	**24**	**6**	**3**	**0**	**3**	**0**
1990-91	**Pittsburgh**	**NHL**	**47**	**17**	**22**	**39**	**6**	**22**	**8**	**9**	**17**	**4** ♦
1991-92	**Pittsburgh**	**NHL**	**77**	**42**	**45**	**87**	**30**	**9**	**3**	**1**	**4**	**4** ♦
1992-93	**Pittsburgh**	**NHL**	**72**	**33**	**37**	**70**	**14**	**12**	**4**	**2**	**6**	**6**
1993-94	**Pittsburgh**	**NHL**	**84**	**38**	**32**	**70**	**41**	**6**	**1**	**0**	**1**	**2**
1994-95i	**Pittsburgh**	**NHL**	**45**	**16**	**21**	**37**	**6**	**12**	**0**	**3**	**3**	**4**
1995-96	**Boston**	**NHL**	**37**	**8**	**7**	**15**	**0**	....	....	....	....	....
1996-97	**Pittsburgh**	**NHL**	**54**	**7**	**15**	**22**	**4**	**1**	**0**	**0**	**0**	**0**
	NHL Totals		**1062**	**502**	**561**	**1063**	**241**	**143**	**60**	**46**	**106**	**42**

a ECAC First All-Star Team (1978, 1979)
b CHL Second All-Star Team (1980)
c Won Ken McKenzie Trophy (CHL's Top Rookie) (1980)
d CHL First All-Star Team (1981)
e Won Tommy Ivan Trophy (CHL's Most Valuable Player) (1981)
f Won Lady Byng Trophy (1987, 1989)
g NHL First All-Star Team (1989)
h NHL Plus/Minus Leader (1989)
i Won Lester Patrick Trophy (1995)

Played in NHL All-Star Game (1989, 1990, 1994)

Signed as a free agent by **St. Louis,** August 16, 1979. Traded to **Calgary** by **St. Louis** with Terry Johnson and Rik Wilson for Ed Beers, Charles Bourgeois and Gino Cavallini, February 1, 1986. Traded to **Pittsburgh** by **Calgary** for Pittsburgh's second round choice (Nicolas Perreault) in 1990 Entry Draft, June 16, 1990. Signed as a free agent by **Boston**, September 13, 1995. Signed as a free agent by **Pittsburgh**, September 5, 1996.

MULLER, KIRK — FLA.

Left wing. Shoots left. 6', 205 lbs. Born, Kingston, Ont., February 8, 1966.
(New Jersey's 1st choice, 2nd overall, in 1984 Entry Draft).

			Regular Season					Playoffs				
Season	Club	Lea	GP	G	A	TP	PIM	GP	G	A	TP	PIM
1981-82	Kingston	OHL	67	12	39	51	27	4	5	1	6	4
1982-83	Guelph	OHL	66	52	60	112	41	....	....	....	....	....
1983-84	Guelph	OHL	49	31	63	94	27	....	....	....	....	....
	Cdn. National	....	15	2	2	4	6	....	....	....	....	....
	Cdn. Olympic	....	6	2	1	3	0	....	....	....	....	....
1984-85	**New Jersey**	**NHL**	**80**	**17**	**37**	**54**	**69**	....	....	....	....	....
1985-86	**New Jersey**	**NHL**	**77**	**25**	**41**	**66**	**45**	....	....	....	....	....
1986-87	**New Jersey**	**NHL**	**79**	**26**	**50**	**76**	**75**	....	....	....	....	....
1987-88	**New Jersey**	**NHL**	**80**	**37**	**57**	**94**	**114**	**20**	**4**	**8**	**12**	**37**
1988-89	**New Jersey**	**NHL**	**80**	**31**	**43**	**74**	**119**	....	....	....	....	....
1989-90	**New Jersey**	**NHL**	**80**	**30**	**56**	**86**	**74**	**6**	**1**	**3**	**4**	**11**
1990-91	**New Jersey**	**NHL**	**80**	**19**	**51**	**70**	**76**	**7**	**0**	**2**	**2**	**10**
1991-92	**Montreal**	**NHL**	**78**	**36**	**41**	**77**	**86**	**11**	**4**	**3**	**7**	**31**
1992-93	**Montreal**	**NHL**	**80**	**37**	**57**	**94**	**77**	**20**	**10**	**7**	**17**	**18** ♦
1993-94	**Montreal**	**NHL**	**76**	**23**	**34**	**57**	**96**	**7**	**6**	**2**	**8**	**4**
1994-95	**Montreal**	**NHL**	**33**	**8**	**11**	**19**	**33**	....	....	....	....	....
	NY Islanders	**NHL**	**12**	**3**	**5**	**8**	**14**	....	....	....	....	....
1995-96	**NY Islanders**	**NHL**	**15**	**4**	**3**	**7**	**15**	....	....	....	....	....
	Toronto	**NHL**	**36**	**9**	**16**	**25**	**42**	**6**	**3**	**2**	**5**	**0**
1996-97	**Toronto**	**NHL**	**66**	**20**	**17**	**37**	**85**	....	....	....	....	....
	Florida	**NHL**	**10**	**1**	**2**	**3**	**4**	**5**	**1**	**2**	**3**	**4**
	NHL Totals		**962**	**326**	**521**	**847**	**1024**	**82**	**29**	**29**	**58**	**115**

Played in NHL All-Star Game (1985, 1986, 1988, 1990, 1992, 1993)

Traded to **Montreal** by **New Jersey** with Roland Melanson for Stephane Richer and Tom Chorske, September 20, 1991. Traded to **NY Islanders** by **Montreal** with Mathieu Schneider and Craig Darby for Pierre Turgeon and Vladimir Malakhov, April 5, 1995. Traded to **Toronto** by **NY Islanders** with Don Beaupre for future considerations, January 23, 1996. Traded to **Florida** by **Toronto** for Jason Podollan, March 18, 1997.

MUNI, CRAIG (MYOO-ne)

Defense. Shoots left. 6'3", 208 lbs. Born, Toronto, Ont., July 19, 1962.
(Toronto's 1st choice, 25th overall, in 1980 Entry Draft).

			Regular Season					Playoffs				
Season	Club	Lea	GP	G	A	TP	PIM	GP	G	A	TP	PIM
1980-81	Kingston	OHA	38	2	14	16	65	....	....	....	....	....
	Windsor	OHA	25	5	11	16	41	11	1	4	5	14
	New Brunswick	AHL	....	....	....	....	....	2	0	1	1	10
1981-82	**Toronto**	**NHL**	**3**	**0**	**0**	**0**	**2**	....	....	....	....	....
	Windsor	OHL	49	5	32	37	92	9	2	3	5	16
	Cincinnati	CHL	....	....	....	....	....	3	0	2	2	2
1982-83	**Toronto**	**NHL**	**2**	**0**	**1**	**1**	**0**	....	....	....	....	....
	St. Catharines	AHL	64	6	32	38	52	....	....	....	....	....
1983-84	St. Catharines	AHL	64	4	16	20	79	7	0	1	1	0
1984-85	**Toronto**	**NHL**	**8**	**0**	**0**	**0**	**0**	....	....	....	....	....
	St. Catharines	AHL	68	7	17	24	54	....	....	....	....	....
1985-86	**Toronto**	**NHL**	**6**	**0**	**1**	**1**	**4**	....	....	....	....	....
	St. Catharines	AHL	73	3	34	37	91	13	0	5	5	16
1986-87	**Edmonton**	**NHL**	**79**	**7**	**22**	**29**	**85**	**14**	**0**	**2**	**2**	**17 ♦**
1987-88	**Edmonton**	**NHL**	**72**	**4**	**15**	**19**	**77**	**19**	**0**	**4**	**4**	**31 ♦**
1988-89	**Edmonton**	**NHL**	**69**	**5**	**13**	**18**	**71**	**7**	**0**	**3**	**3**	**8**
1989-90	**Edmonton**	**NHL**	**71**	**5**	**12**	**17**	**81**	**22**	**0**	**3**	**3**	**16 ♦**
1990-91	**Edmonton**	**NHL**	**76**	**1**	**9**	**10**	**77**	**18**	**0**	**3**	**3**	**20**
1991-92	**Edmonton**	**NHL**	**54**	**2**	**5**	**7**	**34**	**3**	**0**	**0**	**0**	**2**
1992-93	**Edmonton**	**NHL**	**72**	**0**	**11**	**11**	**67**	....	....	....	....	....
	Chicago	**NHL**	**9**	**0**	**0**	**0**	**8**	**4**	**0**	**0**	**0**	**2**
1993-94	**Chicago**	**NHL**	**9**	**0**	**4**	**4**	**4**	....	....	....	....	....
	Buffalo	**NHL**	**73**	**2**	**8**	**10**	**62**	**7**	**0**	**0**	**0**	**4**
1994-95	**Buffalo**	**NHL**	**40**	**0**	**6**	**6**	**36**	**5**	**0**	**1**	**1**	**2**
1995-96	**Buffalo**	**NHL**	**47**	**0**	**4**	**4**	**69**	....	....	....	....	....
	Winnipeg	**NHL**	**25**	**1**	**3**	**4**	**37**	**6**	**0**	**1**	**1**	**2**
1996-97	**Pittsburgh**	**NHL**	**64**	**0**	**4**	**4**	**36**	**3**	**0**	**0**	**0**	**0**
	NHL Totals		**779**	**27**	**118**	**145**	**750**	**108**	**0**	**17**	**17**	**104**

Signed as a free agent by **Edmonton**, August 18, 1986. Sold to **Buffalo** by **Edmonton**, October 2, 1986. Traded to **Pittsburgh** by **Buffalo** for future considerations, October 3, 1986. Traded to **Edmonton** by **Pittsburgh** to complete September 11, 1985 trade which sent Gilles Meloche to Pittsburgh for Tim Hrynewich, Marty McSorley and future considerations, October 6, 1986. Traded to **Chicago** by **Edmonton** for Mike Hudson, March 22, 1993. Traded to **Buffalo** by **Chicago** with Chicago's fifth round choice (Daniel Bienvenue) in 1995 Entry Draft for Keith Carney and Buffalo's sixth round choice (Marc Magliarditi) in 1995 Entry Draft, October 26, 1993. Traded to **Winnipeg** by **Buffalo** for Darryl Shannon and Michael Grosek, February 15, 1996. Signed as a free agent by **Pittsburgh**, October 2, 1996.

MURPHY, BURKE — CGY.

Left wing. Shoots left. 6', 180 lbs. Born, Gloucester, Ont., June 5, 1973.
(Calgary's 11th choice, 278th overall, in 1993 Entry Draft).

			Regular Season					Playoffs				
Season	Club	Lea	GP	G	A	TP	PIM	GP	G	A	TP	PIM
1992-93	St. Lawrence	ECAC	32	19	10	29	32	....	....	....	....	....
1993-94	St. Lawrence	ECAC	30	20	17	37	42	....	....	....	....	....
1994-95a	St. Lawrence	ECAC	33	27	23	50	61	....	....	....	....	....
1995-96bc	St. Lawrence	ECAC	35	*33	25	58	37	....	....	....	....	....
1996-97	Saint John	AHL	54	8	18	26	20	....	....	....	....	....

a ECAC Second All-Star Team (1995)
b ECAC First All-Star Team (1996)
c NCAA East Second All-American Team (1996)

MURPHY, GORD — FLA.

Defense. Shoots right. 6'2", 191 lbs. Born, Willowdale, Ont., March 23, 1967.
(Philadelphia's 10th choice, 189th overall, in 1985 Entry Draft).

			Regular Season					Playoffs				
Season	Club	Lea	GP	G	A	TP	PIM	GP	G	A	TP	PIM
1984-85	Oshawa	OHL	59	3	12	15	25	....	....	....	....	....
1985-86	Oshawa	OHL	64	7	15	22	56	6	1	1	2	6
1986-87	Oshawa	OHL	56	7	30	37	95	24	6	16	22	22
1987-88	Hershey	AHL	62	8	20	28	44	12	0	8	8	12
1988-89	**Philadelphia**	**NHL**	**75**	**4**	**31**	**35**	**68**	**19**	**2**	**7**	**9**	**13**
1989-90	**Philadelphia**	**NHL**	**75**	**14**	**27**	**41**	**95**	....	....	....	....	....
1990-91	**Philadelphia**	**NHL**	**80**	**11**	**31**	**42**	**58**	....	....	....	....	....
1991-92	**Philadelphia**	**NHL**	**31**	**2**	**8**	**10**	**33**	....	....	....	....	....
	Boston	**NHL**	**42**	**3**	**6**	**9**	**51**	**15**	**1**	**0**	**1**	**12**
1992-93	**Boston**	**NHL**	**49**	**5**	**12**	**17**	**62**	....	....	....	....	....
	Providence	AHL	2	1	3	4	2	....	....	....	....	....
1993-94	**Florida**	**NHL**	**84**	**14**	**29**	**43**	**71**	....	....	....	....	....
1994-95	**Florida**	**NHL**	**46**	**6**	**16**	**22**	**24**	....	....	....	....	....
1995-96	**Florida**	**NHL**	**70**	**8**	**22**	**30**	**30**	**14**	**0**	**4**	**4**	**6**
1996-97	**Florida**	**NHL**	**80**	**8**	**15**	**23**	**51**	**5**	**0**	**5**	**5**	**4**
	NHL Totals		**632**	**75**	**197**	**272**	**543**	**53**	**3**	**16**	**19**	**35**

Traded to **Boston** by **Philadelphia** with Brian Dobbin, Philadelphia's third round choice (Sergei Zholtok) in 1992 Entry Draft and Philadelphia's fourth round choice (Charles Paquette) in 1993 Entry Draft, for Garry Galley, Wes Walz and Boston's third round choice (Milos Holan) in 1993 Entry Draft, January 2, 1992. Traded to **Dallas** by **Boston** for future considerations (Jon Casey traded to Boston for Andy Moog, June 25, 1993), June 20, 1993. Claimed by **Florida** from **Dallas** in Expansion Draft, June 24, 1993.

MURPHY, JOE — ST.L.

Right wing. Shoots left. 6'1", 190 lbs. Born, London, Ont., October 16, 1967.
(Detroit's 1st choice, 1st overall, in 1986 Entry Draft).

			Regular Season					Playoffs				
Season	Club	Lea	GP	G	A	TP	PIM	GP	G	A	TP	PIM
1985-86	Michigan State	CCHA	35	24	37	61	50	....	....	....	....	....
	Cdn. National	....	8	3	3	6	2	....	....	....	....	....
1986-87	**Detroit**	**NHL**	**5**	**0**	**1**	**1**	**2**	....	....	....	....	....
	Adirondack	AHL	71	21	38	59	61	10	2	1	3	33
1987-88	**Detroit**	**NHL**	**50**	**10**	**9**	**19**	**37**	**8**	**0**	**1**	**1**	**6**
	Adirondack	AHL	6	5	6	11	4	....	....	....	....	....
1988-89	**Detroit**	**NHL**	**26**	**1**	**7**	**8**	**28**	....	....	....	....	....
	Adirondack	AHL	47	31	35	66	66	16	6	11	17	17
1989-90	**Detroit**	**NHL**	**9**	**3**	**1**	**4**	**4**	....	....	....	....	....
	Edmonton	**NHL**	**62**	**7**	**18**	**25**	**56**	**22**	**6**	**8**	**14**	**16 ♦**
1990-91	**Edmonton**	**NHL**	**80**	**27**	**35**	**62**	**35**	**15**	**2**	**5**	**7**	**14**
1991-92	**Edmonton**	**NHL**	**80**	**35**	**47**	**82**	**52**	**16**	**8**	**16**	**24**	**12**
1992-93	**Chicago**	**NHL**	**19**	**7**	**10**	**17**	**18**	**4**	**0**	**0**	**0**	**8**
1993-94	**Chicago**	**NHL**	**81**	**31**	**39**	**70**	**111**	**6**	**1**	**3**	**4**	**25**
1994-95	**Chicago**	**NHL**	**40**	**23**	**18**	**41**	**89**	**16**	**9**	**3**	**12**	**29**
1995-96	**Chicago**	**NHL**	**70**	**22**	**29**	**51**	**86**	**10**	**6**	**2**	**8**	**33**
1996-97	**St. Louis**	**NHL**	**75**	**20**	**25**	**45**	**69**	**6**	**1**	**1**	**2**	**10**
	NHL Totals		**597**	**186**	**239**	**425**	**587**	**103**	**33**	**39**	**72**	**153**

Traded to **Edmonton** by **Detroit** with Petr Klima, Adam Graves and Jeff Sharples for Jimmy Carson, Kevin McClelland and Edmonton's fifth round choice (later traded to Montreal — Montreal selected Brad Layzell) in 1991 Entry Draft, November 2, 1989. Traded to **Chicago** by **Edmonton** for Igor Kravchuk and Dean McAmmond, February 24, 1993. Signed as a free agent by **St. Louis**, July 8, 1996.

MURPHY, LARRY — DET.

Defense. Shoots right. 6'2", 210 lbs. Born, Scarborough, Ont., March 8, 1961.
(Los Angeles' 1st choice, 4th overall, in 1980 Entry Draft).

			Regular Season					Playoffs				
Season	Club	Lea	GP	G	A	TP	PIM	GP	G	A	TP	PIM
1978-79	Peterborough	OHA	66	6	21	27	82	19	1	9	10	42
1979-80a	Peterborough	OHA	68	21	68	89	88	14	4	13	17	20
1980-81	**Los Angeles**	**NHL**	**80**	**16**	**60**	**76**	**79**	**4**	**3**	**0**	**3**	**2**
1981-82	**Los Angeles**	**NHL**	**79**	**22**	**44**	**66**	**95**	**10**	**2**	**8**	**10**	**12**
1982-83	**Los Angeles**	**NHL**	**77**	**14**	**48**	**62**	**81**	....	....	....	....	....
1983-84	**Los Angeles**	**NHL**	**6**	**0**	**3**	**3**	**0**	....	....	....	....	....
	Washington	**NHL**	**72**	**13**	**33**	**46**	**50**	**8**	**0**	**3**	**3**	**6**
1984-85	**Washington**	**NHL**	**79**	**13**	**42**	**55**	**51**	**5**	**2**	**3**	**5**	**0**
1985-86	**Washington**	**NHL**	**78**	**21**	**44**	**65**	**50**	**9**	**1**	**5**	**6**	**6**
1986-87b	**Washington**	**NHL**	**80**	**23**	**58**	**81**	**39**	**7**	**2**	**2**	**4**	**6**
1987-88	**Washington**	**NHL**	**79**	**8**	**53**	**61**	**72**	**13**	**4**	**4**	**8**	**33**
1988-89	**Washington**	**NHL**	**65**	**7**	**29**	**36**	**70**	....	....	....	....	....
	Minnesota	**NHL**	**13**	**4**	**6**	**10**	**12**	**5**	**0**	**2**	**2**	**8**
1989-90	**Minnesota**	**NHL**	**77**	**10**	**58**	**68**	**44**	**7**	**1**	**2**	**3**	**31**
1990-91	**Minnesota**	**NHL**	**31**	**4**	**11**	**15**	**38**	....	....	....	....	....
	Pittsburgh	**NHL**	**44**	**5**	**23**	**28**	**30**	**23**	**5**	**18**	**23**	**44 ♦**
1991-92	**Pittsburgh**	**NHL**	**77**	**21**	**56**	**77**	**48**	**21**	**6**	**10**	**16**	**19 ♦**
1992-93b	**Pittsburgh**	**NHL**	**83**	**22**	**63**	**85**	**73**	**12**	**2**	**11**	**13**	**10**
1993-94	**Pittsburgh**	**NHL**	**84**	**17**	**56**	**73**	**44**	**6**	**0**	**5**	**5**	**0**
1994-95b	**Pittsburgh**	**NHL**	**48**	**13**	**25**	**38**	**18**	**12**	**2**	**13**	**15**	**0**
1995-96	**Toronto**	**NHL**	**82**	**12**	**49**	**61**	**34**	**6**	**0**	**2**	**2**	**4**
1996-97	**Toronto**	**NHL**	**69**	**7**	**32**	**39**	**20**	....	....	....	....	....
	Detroit	**NHL**	**12**	**2**	**4**	**6**	**0**	**20**	**2**	**9**	**11**	**8 ♦**
	NHL Totals		**1315**	**254**	**797**	**1051**	**948**	**168**	**32**	**97**	**129**	**189**

a OHA First All-Star Team (1980)
b NHL Second All-Star Team (1987, 1993, 1995)

Played in NHL All-Star Game (1994, 1996)

Traded to **Washington** by **Los Angeles** for Ken Houston and Brian Engblom, October 18, 1983. Traded to **Minnesota** by **Washington** with Mike Gartner for Dino Ciccarelli and Bob Rouse, March 7, 1989. Traded to **Pittsburgh** by **Minnesota** with Peter Taglianetti for Chris Dahlquist and Jim Johnson, December 11, 1990. Traded to **Toronto** by **Pittsburgh** for Dmitri Mironov and Toronto's second round choice (later traded to New Jersey — New Jersey selected Joshua Dewolf) in 1996 Entry Draft, July 8, 1995. Traded to **Detroit** by **Toronto** for future considerations, March 18, 1997.

MURPHY, MARK — TOR.

Left wing. Shoots left. 5'11", 200 lbs. Born, Stoughton, MA, August 6, 1976.
(Toronto's 6th choice, 197th overall, in 1995 Entry Draft).

			Regular Season					Playoffs				
Season	Club	Lea	GP	G	A	TP	PIM	GP	G	A	TP	PIM
1995-96	Stratford	Jr. B	1	0	0	0	0	....	....	....	....	....
	RPI	ECAC	32	1	1	2	50	....	....	....	....	....
1996-97	RPI	ECAC	34	9	18	27	56	....	....	....	....	....

MURRAY, CHRIS — CAR.

Right wing. Shoots right. 6'2", 209 lbs. Born, Port Hardy, B.C., October 25, 1974.
(Montreal's 3rd choice, 54th overall, in 1994 Entry Draft).

			Regular Season					Playoffs				
Season	Club	Lea	GP	G	A	TP	PIM	GP	G	A	TP	PIM
1991-92	Kamloops	WHL	33	1	1	2	218	5	0	0	0	10
1992-93	Kamloops	WHL	62	6	10	16	217	13	0	4	4	34
1993-94	Kamloops	WHL	59	14	16	30	260	15	4	2	6	*107
1994-95	Fredericton	AHL	55	6	12	18	234	12	1	1	2	50
	Montreal	**NHL**	**3**	**0**	**0**	**0**	**4**	....	....	....	....	....
1995-96	**Montreal**	**NHL**	**48**	**3**	**4**	**7**	**163**	**4**	**0**	**0**	**0**	**4**
	Fredericton	AHL	30	13	13	26	217	....	....	....	....	....
1996-97	**Montreal**	**NHL**	**56**	**4**	**2**	**6**	**114**	....	....	....	....	....
	Hartford	**NHL**	**8**	**1**	**1**	**2**	**10**	....	....	....	....	....
	NHL Totals		**115**	**8**	**7**	**15**	**291**	**4**	**0**	**0**	**0**	**4**

Traded to **Phoenix** by **Montreal** with Murray Baron for Dave Manson, March 18, 1997. Traded to **Hartford** by **Phoenix** for Gerald Diduck, March 18, 1997.

MURRAY, GLEN — L.A.

Right wing. Shoots right. 6'2", 220 lbs. Born, Halifax, N.S., November 1, 1972.
(Boston's 1st choice, 18th overall, in 1991 Entry Draft).

			Regular Season					Playoffs				
Season	Club	Lea	GP	G	A	TP	PIM	GP	G	A	TP	PIM
1989-90	Sudbury	OHL	62	8	28	36	17	7	0	0	0	4
1990-91	Sudbury	OHL	66	27	38	65	82	5	8	4	12	10
1991-92	**Boston**	**NHL**	**5**	**3**	**1**	**4**	**0**	**15**	**4**	**2**	**6**	**10**
	Sudbury	OHL	54	37	47	84	93	11	7	4	11	18
1992-93	**Boston**	**NHL**	**27**	**3**	**4**	**7**	**8**	....	....	....	....	....
	Providence	AHL	48	30	26	56	42	6	1	4	5	4
1993-94	**Boston**	**NHL**	**81**	**18**	**13**	**31**	**48**	**13**	**4**	**5**	**9**	**14**
1994-95	**Boston**	**NHL**	**35**	**5**	**2**	**7**	**46**	**2**	**0**	**0**	**0**	**2**
1995-96	**Pittsburgh**	**NHL**	**69**	**14**	**15**	**29**	**57**	**18**	**2**	**6**	**8**	**10**
1996-97	**Pittsburgh**	**NHL**	**66**	**11**	**11**	**22**	**24**	....	....	....	....	....
	Los Angeles	**NHL**	**11**	**5**	**3**	**8**	**8**	....	....	....	....	....
	NHL Totals		**294**	**59**	**49**	**108**	**191**	**48**	**10**	**13**	**23**	**36**

Traded to **Pittsburgh** by **Boston** with Bryan Smolinski and Boston's third round choice (Boyd Kane) in 1996 Entry Draft for Kevin Stevens and Shawn McEachern, August 2, 1995. Traded to **Los Angeles** by **Pittsburgh** for Ed Olczyk, March 18, 1997.

MURRAY, MARTY — CGY.

Center. Shoots left. 5'9", 175 lbs. Born, Deloraine, Man., February 16, 1975.
(Calgary's 5th choice, 96th overall, in 1993 Entry Draft).

			Regular Season					Playoffs				
Season	Club	Lea	GP	G	A	TP	PIM	GP	G	A	TP	PIM
1991-92	Brandon	WHL	68	20	36	56	22	....	....	....	....	....
1992-93	Brandon	WHL	67	29	65	94	50	4	1	3	4	0
1993-94ab	Brandon	WHL	64	43	71	114	33	14	6	14	20	14
1994-95a	Brandon	WHL	65	40	*88	128	53	18	9	*20	29	16
1995-96	**Calgary**	**NHL**	**15**	**3**	**3**	**6**	**0**	....	....	....	....	....
	Saint John	AHL	58	25	31	56	20	14	2	4	6	4
1996-97	**Calgary**	**NHL**	**2**	**0**	**0**	**0**	**4**	....	....	....	....	....
	Saint John	AHL	67	19	39	58	40	5	2	3	5	4
	NHL Totals		**17**	**3**	**3**	**6**	**4**	....	....	....	....	....

a WHL East First All-Star Team (1994, 1995)
b Canadian Major Junior Second All-Star Team (1994)

MURRAY, REM — EDM.

Left wing. Shoots left. 6'2", 195 lbs. Born, Stratford, Ont., October 9, 1972.
(Los Angeles' 5th choice, 135th overall, in 1992 Entry Draft).

			Regular Season					Playoffs				
Season	Club	Lea	GP	G	A	TP	PIM	GP	G	A	TP	PIM
1991-92	Michigan State	CCHA	41	12	36	48	16	....	....	....	....	....
1992-93	Michigan State	CCHA	40	22	35	57	24	....	....	....	....	....
1993-94	Michigan State	CCHA	41	16	38	54	18	....	....	....	....	....
1994-95a	Michigan State	CCHA	40	20	36	56	21	....	....	....	....	....
1995-96	Cape Breton	AHL	79	31	59	90	40	....	....	....	....	....
1996-97	**Edmonton**	**NHL**	**82**	**11**	**20**	**31**	**16**	**12**	**1**	**2**	**3**	**4**
	NHL Totals		**82**	**11**	**20**	**31**	**16**	**12**	**1**	**2**	**3**	**4**

a CCHA Second All-Star Team (1995)

Signed as a free agent by **Edmonton**, September 19, 1995.

MURRAY, ROB — PHO.

Center. Shoots right. 6'1", 180 lbs. Born, Toronto, Ont., April 4, 1967.
(Washington's 3rd choice, 61st overall, in 1985 Entry Draft).

			Regular Season					Playoffs				
Season	Club	Lea	GP	G	A	TP	PIM	GP	G	A	TP	PIM
1984-85	Peterborough	OHL	63	12	9	21	155	17	2	7	9	45
1985-86	Peterborough	OHL	52	14	18	32	125	16	1	2	3	50
1986-87	Peterborough	OHL	62	17	37	54	204	3	1	4	5	8
1987-88	Fort Wayne	IHL	80	12	21	33	139	6	0	2	2	16
1988-89	Baltimore	AHL	80	11	23	34	235	....	....	....	....	....
1989-90	**Washington**	**NHL**	**41**	**2**	**7**	**9**	**58**	**9**	**0**	**0**	**0**	**18**
	Baltimore	AHL	23	5	4	9	63	....	....	....	....	....
1990-91	**Washington**	**NHL**	**17**	**0**	**3**	**3**	**19**	....	....	....	....	....
	Baltimore	AHL	48	6	20	26	177	4	0	0	0	12
1991-92	**Winnipeg**	**NHL**	**9**	**0**	**1**	**1**	**18**	....	....	....	....	....
	Moncton	AHL	60	16	15	31	247	8	0	1	1	56
1992-93	**Winnipeg**	**NHL**	**10**	**1**	**0**	**1**	**6**	....	....	....	....	....
	Moncton	AHL	56	16	21	37	147	3	0	0	0	6
1993-94	**Winnipeg**	**NHL**	**6**	**0**	**0**	**0**	**2**	....	....	....	....	....
	Moncton	AHL	69	25	32	57	280	21	2	3	5	60
1994-95	Springfield	AHL	78	16	38	54	373	....	....	....	....	....
	Winnipeg	**NHL**	**10**	**0**	**2**	**2**	**2**	....	....	....	....	....
1995-96	**Winnipeg**	**NHL**	**1**	**0**	**0**	**0**	**2**	....	....	....	....	....
	Springfield	AHL	74	10	28	38	263	10	1	6	7	32
1996-97	Springfield	AHL	78	16	27	43	234	17	2	3	5	66
	NHL Totals		**94**	**3**	**13**	**16**	**107**	**9**	**0**	**0**	**0**	**18**

Claimed by **Minnesota** from **Washington** in Expansion Draft, May 30, 1991. Traded to **Winnipeg** by **Minnesota** with future considerations for Winnipeg's seventh round choice (Geoff Finch) in 1991 Entry Draft and future considerations, May 31, 1991.

MURRAY, TROY

Center. Shoots right. 6'1", 195 lbs. Born, Calgary, Alta., July 31, 1962.
(Chicago's 6th choice, 57th overall, in 1980 Entry Draft).

			Regular Season					Playoffs				
Season	Club	Lea	GP	G	A	TP	PIM	GP	G	A	TP	PIM
1980-81a	North Dakota	WCHA	38	33	45	78	28	....	....	....	....	....
1981-82a	North Dakota	WCHA	26	13	17	30	62	....	....	....	....	....
	Chicago	**NHL**	**1**	**0**	**0**	**0**	**0**	**7**	**1**	**0**	**1**	**5**
1982-83	**Chicago**	**NHL**	**54**	**8**	**8**	**16**	**27**	**2**	**0**	**0**	**0**	**0**
1983-84	**Chicago**	**NHL**	**61**	**15**	**15**	**30**	**45**	**5**	**1**	**0**	**1**	**7**
1984-85	**Chicago**	**NHL**	**80**	**26**	**40**	**66**	**82**	**15**	**5**	**14**	**19**	**24**
1985-86b	**Chicago**	**NHL**	**80**	**45**	**54**	**99**	**94**	**2**	**0**	**0**	**0**	**2**
1986-87	**Chicago**	**NHL**	**77**	**28**	**43**	**71**	**59**	**4**	**0**	**0**	**0**	**5**
1987-88	**Chicago**	**NHL**	**79**	**22**	**36**	**58**	**96**	**5**	**1**	**0**	**1**	**8**
1988-89	**Chicago**	**NHL**	**79**	**21**	**30**	**51**	**113**	**16**	**3**	**6**	**9**	**25**
1989-90	**Chicago**	**NHL**	**68**	**17**	**38**	**55**	**86**	**20**	**4**	**4**	**8**	**22**
1990-91	**Chicago**	**NHL**	**75**	**14**	**23**	**37**	**74**	**6**	**0**	**1**	**1**	**12**
1991-92	**Winnipeg**	**NHL**	**74**	**17**	**30**	**47**	**69**	**7**	**0**	**0**	**0**	**2**
1992-93	**Winnipeg**	**NHL**	**29**	**3**	**4**	**7**	**34**	....	....	....	....	....
	Chicago	**NHL**	**22**	**1**	**3**	**4**	**25**	**4**	**0**	**0**	**0**	**2**
1993-94	**Chicago**	**NHL**	**12**	**0**	**1**	**1**	**6**	....	....	....	....	....
	Indianapolis	IHL	8	3	3	6	12	....	....	....	....	....
	Ottawa	**NHL**	**15**	**2**	**3**	**5**	**4**	....	....	....	....	....
1994-95	**Ottawa**	**NHL**	**33**	**4**	**10**	**14**	**16**	....	....	....	....	....
	Pittsburgh	**NHL**	**13**	**0**	**2**	**2**	**23**	**12**	**2**	**1**	**3**	**12**
1995-96	**Colorado**	**NHL**	**63**	**7**	**14**	**21**	**22**	**8**	**0**	**0**	**0**	**19** ♦
1996-97	Chicago	IHL	81	21	29	50	63	4	0	2	2	2
	NHL Totals		**915**	**230**	**354**	**584**	**875**	**113**	**17**	**26**	**43**	**145**

a WCHA Second All-Star Team (1981, 1982)
b Won Frank J. Selke Memorial Trophy (1986)

Traded to **Winnipeg** by **Chicago** with Warren Rychel for Bryan Marchment and Chris Norton, July 22, 1991. Traded to **Chicago** by **Winnipeg** for Steve Bancroft and future considerations, February 21, 1993. Traded to **Ottawa** by **Chicago** with Chicago's eleventh round choice (Antti Tormanen) in 1994 Entry Draft for Ottawa's eleventh round choice (Rob Mara) in 1994 Entry Draft, March 11, 1994. Traded to **Pittsburgh** by **Ottawa** with Norm Maciver for Martin Straka, April 7, 1995. Signed as a free agent by **Colorado**, August 7, 1995.

MURZYN, DANA — (MUHR-zihn) — VAN.

Defense. Shoots left. 6'2", 200 lbs. Born, Calgary, Alta., December 9, 1966.
(Hartford's 1st choice, 5th overall, in 1985 Entry Draft).

			Regular Season					Playoffs				
Season	Club	Lea	GP	G	A	TP	PIM	GP	G	A	TP	PIM
1983-84	Calgary	WHL	65	11	20	31	135	2	0	0	0	10
1984-85a	Calgary	WHL	72	32	60	92	233	8	1	11	12	16
1985-86b	**Hartford**	**NHL**	**78**	**3**	**23**	**26**	**125**	**4**	**0**	**0**	**0**	**10**
1986-87	**Hartford**	**NHL**	**74**	**9**	**19**	**28**	**95**	**6**	**2**	**1**	**3**	**29**
1987-88	**Hartford**	**NHL**	**33**	**1**	**6**	**7**	**45**	....	....	....	....	....
	Calgary	**NHL**	**41**	**6**	**5**	**11**	**94**	**5**	**2**	**0**	**2**	**13**
1988-89	**Calgary**	**NHL**	**63**	**3**	**19**	**22**	**142**	**21**	**0**	**3**	**3**	**20** ♦
1989-90	**Calgary**	**NHL**	**78**	**7**	**13**	**20**	**140**	**6**	**2**	**2**	**4**	**2**
1990-91	**Calgary**	**NHL**	**19**	**0**	**2**	**2**	**30**	....	....	....	....	....
	Vancouver	**NHL**	**10**	**1**	**0**	**1**	**8**	**6**	**0**	**1**	**1**	**8**
1991-92	**Vancouver**	**NHL**	**70**	**3**	**11**	**14**	**147**	**1**	**0**	**0**	**0**	**15**
1992-93	**Vancouver**	**NHL**	**79**	**5**	**11**	**16**	**196**	**12**	**3**	**2**	**5**	**18**
1993-94	**Vancouver**	**NHL**	**80**	**6**	**14**	**20**	**109**	**7**	**0**	**0**	**0**	**4**
1994-95	**Vancouver**	**NHL**	**40**	**0**	**8**	**8**	**129**	**8**	**0**	**1**	**1**	**22**
1995-96	**Vancouver**	**NHL**	**69**	**2**	**10**	**12**	**130**	**6**	**0**	**0**	**0**	**25**
1996-97	**Vancouver**	**NHL**	**61**	**1**	**7**	**8**	**118**	....	....	....	....	....
	NHL Totals		**795**	**47**	**148**	**195**	**1508**	**82**	**9**	**10**	**19**	**166**

a WHL East First All-Star Team, (1985)
b NHL All-Rookie Team (1986)

Traded to **Calgary** by **Hartford** with Shane Churla for Neil Sheehy, Carey Wilson and the rights to Lane MacDonald, January 3, 1988. Traded to **Vancouver** by **Calgary** for Ron Stern, Kevan Guy and future considerations, March 5, 1991.

MUSIL, FRANK — (moo-SIHL) — OTT.

Defense. Shoots left. 6'3", 215 lbs. Born, Pardubice, Czech., December 17, 1964.
(Minnesota's 3rd choice, 38th overall, in 1983 Entry Draft).

			Regular Season					Playoffs				
Season	Club	Lea	GP	G	A	TP	PIM	GP	G	A	TP	PIM
1980-81	Pardubice	Czech.	2	0	0	0	0	....	....	....	....	....
1981-82	Pardubice	Czech.	35	1	3	4	34	....	....	....	....	....
1982-83	Pardubice	Czech.	33	1	2	3	44	....	....	....	....	....
1983-84	Pardubice	Czech.	37	4	8	12	72	....	....	....	....	....
1984-85	Dukla Jihlava	Czech.	44	4	6	10	76	....	....	....	....	....
1985-86	Dukla Jihlava	Czech.	34	4	7	11	42	....	....	....	....	....
1986-87	**Minnesota**	**NHL**	**72**	**2**	**9**	**11**	**148**	....	....	....	....	....
1987-88	**Minnesota**	**NHL**	**80**	**9**	**8**	**17**	**213**	....	....	....	....	....
1988-89	**Minnesota**	**NHL**	**55**	**1**	**19**	**20**	**54**	**5**	**1**	**1**	**2**	**4**
1989-90	**Minnesota**	**NHL**	**56**	**2**	**8**	**10**	**109**	**4**	**0**	**0**	**0**	**14**
1990-91	**Minnesota**	**NHL**	**8**	**0**	**2**	**2**	**23**	....	....	....	....	....
	Calgary	**NHL**	**67**	**7**	**14**	**21**	**160**	**7**	**0**	**0**	**0**	**10**
1991-92	**Calgary**	**NHL**	**78**	**4**	**8**	**12**	**103**	....	....	....	....	....
1992-93	**Calgary**	**NHL**	**80**	**6**	**10**	**16**	**131**	**6**	**1**	**1**	**2**	**7**
1993-94	**Calgary**	**NHL**	**75**	**1**	**8**	**9**	**50**	**7**	**0**	**1**	**1**	**4**
1994-95	Sparta Praha	Czech.	19	1	4	5	50	....	....	....	....	....
	Saxonia	Ger.	1	0	0	0	2	....	....	....	....	....
	Calgary	**NHL**	**35**	**0**	**5**	**5**	**61**	**5**	**0**	**1**	**1**	**0**
1995-96	Karlovy Vary	Czech. 2	16	7	4	11	16	....	....	....	....	....
	Ottawa	**NHL**	**65**	**1**	**3**	**4**	**85**	....	....	....	....	....
1996-97	**Ottawa**	**NHL**	**57**	**0**	**5**	**5**	**58**	....	....	....	....	....
	NHL Totals		**728**	**33**	**99**	**132**	**1195**	**34**	**2**	**4**	**6**	**39**

Traded to **Calgary** by **Minnesota** for Brian Glynn, October 26, 1990. Traded to **Ottawa** by **Calgary** for Ottawa's fourth round choice (Chris St. Croix) in 1997 Entry Draft, October 7, 1995.

MUZECHKA, MIKE — (muh-ZEHCH-kah) — NYI

Defense. Shoots left. 6'2", 200 lbs. Born, Edmonton, Alta., February 1, 1978.
(NY Islanders' 10th choice, 218th overall, in 1996 Entry Draft).

			Regular Season					Playoffs				
Season	Club	Lea	GP	G	A	TP	PIM	GP	G	A	TP	PIM
1994-95	Prince Albert	WHL	1	0	0	0	0	....	....	....	....	....
1995-96	Calgary	WHL	69	1	8	9	91	....	....	....	....	....
1996-97	Portland	WHL	65	1	8	9	74	6	1	1	2	4

MYHRES, BRANTT — (MIGH-uhrs) — EDM.

Right wing. Shoots right. 6'4", 222 lbs. Born, Edmonton, Alta., March 18, 1974.
(Tampa Bay's 6th choice, 97th overall, in 1992 Entry Draft).

			Regular Season					Playoffs				
Season	Club	Lea	GP	G	A	TP	PIM	GP	G	A	TP	PIM
1990-91	Portland	WHL	59	2	7	9	125	....	....	....	....	....
1991-92	Portland	WHL	4	0	2	2	22	....	....	....	....	....
	Lethbridge	WHL	53	4	11	15	359	5	0	0	0	36
1992-93	Lethbridge	WHL	64	13	35	48	277	3	0	0	0	11
1993-94	Lethbridge	WHL	34	10	21	31	103	....	....	....	....	....
	Spokane	WHL	27	10	22	32	139	3	1	4	5	7
	Atlanta	IHL	2	0	0	0	17	....	....	....	....	....
1994-95	Atlanta	IHL	40	5	5	10	213	....	....	....	....	....
	Tampa Bay	**NHL**	**15**	**2**	**0**	**2**	**81**	....	....	....	....	....
1995-96	Atlanta	IHL	12	0	2	2	58	....	....	....	....	....
1996-97	**Tampa Bay**	**NHL**	**47**	**3**	**1**	**4**	**136**	....	....	....	....	....
	San Antonio	IHL	12	0	0	0	98	....	....	....	....	....
	NHL Totals		**62**	**5**	**1**	**6**	**217**	....	....	....	....	....

Traded to **Edmonton** by **Tampa Bay** with a conditional draft choice for Vladimir Vujtek and Edmonton's third round choice in 1998 Entry Draft, July 16, 1997.

MYRVOLD, ANDERS — (MYOOR-vohld) — BOS.

Defense. Shoots left. 6'2", 200 lbs. Born, Lorenskog, Norway, August 12, 1975.
(Quebec's 6th choice, 127th overall, in 1993 Entry Draft).

			Regular Season					Playoffs				
Season	Club	Lea	GP	G	A	TP	PIM	GP	G	A	TP	PIM
1992-93	Farjestad	Swe.	2	0	0	0	0	....	....	....	....	....
1993-94	Grum	Swe. 2	24	1	0	1	59	....	....	....	....	....
1994-95	Laval	QMJHL	64	14	50	64	173	20	4	10	14	68
	Cornwall	AHL	....	....	....	....	....	3	0	1	1	2
1995-96	**Colorado**	**NHL**	**4**	**0**	**1**	**1**	**6**	....	....	....	....	....
	Cornwall	AHL	70	5	24	29	125	5	1	0	1	19
1996-97	Hershey	AHL	20	0	3	3	16	....	....	....	....	....
	Boston	**NHL**	**9**	**0**	**2**	**2**	**4**	....	....	....	....	....
	Providence	AHL	53	6	15	21	107	10	0	1	1	6
	NHL Totals		**13**	**0**	**3**	**3**	**10**	....	....	....	....	....

Traded to **Boston** by **Colorado** with Landon Wilson for Boston's first round choice in 1998 Entry Draft, November 22, 1996.

NABOKOV, DMITRI — (nuh-BAW-kahv) — CHI.

Center. Shoots right. 6'2", 209 lbs. Born, Novosibirsk, USSR, January 4, 1977.
(Chicago's 1st choice, 19th overall, in 1995 Entry Draft).

			Regular Season					Playoffs				
Season	Club	Lea	GP	G	A	TP	PIM	GP	G	A	TP	PIM
1993-94	Soviet Wings	CIS	17	0	2	2	6	3	0	0	0	0
1994-95	Soviet Wings	CIS	49	15	12	27	32	4	5	0	5	6
1995-96	Soviet Wings	CIS	50	12	14	26	51	....	....	....	....	....
1996-97	Soviet Wings	Rus.	1	0	0	0	0	....	....	....	....	....
a	Regina	WHL	50	39	56	95	61	5	2	3	5	2
	Indianapolis	IHL	2	0	0	0	0	....	....	....	....	....

a WHL East Second All-Star Team (1997)

NAMESTNIKOV, YEVGENY — (nah-MEST-nih-kov, yev-GAIN-ee) — NYI

Defense. Shoots right. 5'11", 190 lbs. Born, Arzamis-Ig, USSR, October 9, 1971.
(Vancouver's 6th choice, 117th overall, in 1991 Entry Draft).

			Regular Season					Playoffs				
Season	Club	Lea	GP	G	A	TP	PIM	GP	G	A	TP	PIM
1988-89	Torpedo Gorky	USSR	2	0	0	0	2	....	....	....	....	....
1989-90	Torpedo Gorky	USSR	23	0	0	0	25	....	....	....	....	....
1990-91	Torpedo Niz.	USSR	42	1	2	3	49	....	....	....	....	....
1991-92	CSKA	CIS	42	1	1	2	47	....	....	....	....	....
1992-93	CSKA	CIS	42	5	5	10	68	....	....	....	....	....
1993-94	**Vancouver**	**NHL**	**17**	**0**	**5**	**5**	**10**	....	....	....	....	....
	Hamilton	AHL	59	7	27	34	97	4	0	2	2	19
1994-95	Syracuse	AHL	59	11	22	33	59	....	....	....	....	....
	Vancouver	**NHL**	**16**	**0**	**3**	**3**	**4**	**1**	**0**	**0**	**0**	**2**
1995-96	Syracuse	AHL	59	13	34	47	85	15	1	8	9	16
	Vancouver	**NHL**	....	....	....	....	....	**1**	**0**	**0**	**0**	**0**
1996-97	**Vancouver**	**NHL**	**2**	**0**	**0**	**0**	**4**	....	....	....	....	....
	Syracuse	AHL	55	9	37	46	73	3	2	0	2	0
	NHL Totals		**35**	**0**	**8**	**8**	**18**	**2**	**0**	**0**	**0**	**2**

Signed as a free agent by **NY Islanders**, July 21, 1997.

NASH, TYSON — VAN.

Left wing. Shoots left. 6', 185 lbs.   Born, Edmonton, Alta., March 11, 1975.
(Vancouver's 10th choice, 247th overall, in 1994 Entry Draft).

			Regular Season					Playoffs				
Season	Club	Lea	GP	G	A	TP	PIM	GP	G	A	TP	PIM
1991-92	Kamloops	WHL	33	1	6	7	62	4	0	0	0	0
1992-93	Kamloops	WHL	61	10	16	26	78	13	3	2	5	32
1993-94	Kamloops	WHL	65	20	36	56	135	16	3	4	7	12
1994-95	Kamloops	WHL	63	34	41	75	70	21	10	7	17	30
1995-96	Syracuse	AHL	50	4	7	11	58	4	0	0	0	11
	Raleigh	ECHL	6	1	1	2	8	....	....	....	....	....
1996-97	Syracuse	AHL	77	17	17	34	105	3	0	2	2	0

NASLUND, MARKUS (NAZ-luhnd) VAN.

Right wing. Shoots left. 6', 186 lbs.   Born, Ornskoldsvik, Sweden, July 30, 1973.
(Pittsburgh's 1st choice, 16th overall, in 1991 Entry Draft).

			Regular Season					Playoffs				
Season	Club	Lea	GP	G	A	TP	PIM	GP	G	A	TP	PIM
1990-91	MoDo	Swe.	32	10	9	19	14	....	....	....	....	....
1991-92	MoDo	Swe.	39	22	18	40	54	....	....	....	....	....
1992-93	MoDo	Swe.	39	22	17	39	67	3	3	2	5	0
1993-94	**Pittsburgh**	**NHL**	**71**	**4**	**7**	**11**	**27**	....	....	....	....	....
	Cleveland	IHL	5	1	6	7	4	....	....	....	....	....
1994-95	**Pittsburgh**	**NHL**	**14**	**2**	**2**	**4**	**2**	....	....	....	....	....
	Cleveland	IHL	7	3	4	7	6	4	1	3	4	8
1995-96	**Pittsburgh**	**NHL**	**66**	**19**	**33**	**52**	**36**	....	....	....	....	....
	Vancouver	NHL	10	3	0	3	6	6	1	2	3	8
1996-97	**Vancouver**	**NHL**	**78**	**21**	**20**	**41**	**30**	....	....	....	....	....
	NHL Totals		**239**	**49**	**62**	**111**	**101**	**6**	**1**	**2**	**3**	**8**

Traded to **Vancouver** by **Pittsburgh** for Alek Stojanov, March 20, 1996.

NASREDDINE, ALAIN (NAS-ruh-deen, AL-ay) CHI.

Defense. Shoots left. 6'1", 201 lbs.   Born, Montreal, Que., July 10, 1975.
(Florida's 8th choice, 135th overall, in 1993 Entry Draft).

			Regular Season					Playoffs				
Season	Club	Lea	GP	G	A	TP	PIM	GP	G	A	TP	PIM
1991-92	Drummondville	QMJHL	61	1	9	10	78	4	0	0	0	17
1992-93	Drummondville	QMJHL	64	0	14	14	137	10	0	1	1	36
1993-94	Chicoutimi	QMJHL	60	3	24	27	218	26	2	10	12	118
1994-95a	Chicoutimi	QMJHL	67	8	31	39	342	13	3	5	8	40
1995-96	Carolina	AHL	63	0	5	5	245	....	....	....	....	....
1996-97	Carolina	AHL	26	0	4	4	109	....	....	....	....	....
	Indianapolis	IHL	49	0	2	2	248	4	1	1	2	27

a QMJHL Second All-Star Team (1995)
Traded to **Chicago** by **Florida** with a conditional choice in 1999 Entry Draft for Ivan Droppa, December 18, 1996.

NAUD, ERIC (NOH) BOS.

Left wing. Shoots left. 6'1", 187 lbs.   Born, Lasarre, Que., October 2, 1977.
(Boston's 3rd choice, 53rd overall, in 1996 Entry Draft).

			Regular Season					Playoffs				
Season	Club	Lea	GP	G	A	TP	PIM	GP	G	A	TP	PIM
1995-96	Laval	QMJHL	9	4	3	7	37	....	....	....	....	....
	St-Hyacinthe	QMJHL	54	7	18	25	193	12	1	2	3	19
1996-97	Rouyn-Noranda	QMJHL	34	8	11	19	159	....	....	....	....	....
	Hull	QMJHL	2	0	0	0	15	12	4	2	6	73

NAUMENKO, NICK (NAH-mehn-koh) ST.L.

Defense. Shoots right. 5'11", 180 lbs.   Born, Chicago, IL, July 7, 1974.
(St. Louis' 9th choice, 182nd overall, in 1992 Entry Draft).

			Regular Season					Playoffs				
Season	Club	Lea	GP	G	A	TP	PIM	GP	G	A	TP	PIM
1992-93	North Dakota	WCHA	38	10	24	34	26	....	....	....	....	....
1993-94	North Dakota	WCHA	32	4	22	26	22	....	....	....	....	....
1994-95a	North Dakota	WCHA	39	13	26	39	78	....	....	....	....	....
1995-96a	North Dakota	WCHA	37	11	30	41	32	....	....	....	....	....
1996-97	Worcester	AHL	54	6	22	28	72	1	0	0	0	0

a WCHA First All-Star Team (1995, 1996)

NAZAROV, ANDREI (nah-ZAH-rohv) S.J.

Left wing. Shoots right. 6'5", 230 lbs.   Born, Chelyabinsk, USSR, May 22, 1974.
(San Jose's 2nd choice, 10th overall, in 1992 Entry Draft).

			Regular Season					Playoffs				
Season	Club	Lea	GP	G	A	TP	PIM	GP	G	A	TP	PIM
1991-92	Moscow D'amo	CIS	2	1	0	1	2	....	....	....	....	....
1992-93	Moscow D'amo	CIS	42	8	2	10	79	10	1	1	2	8
1993-94	Moscow D'amo	CIS	6	2	2	4	0	....	....	....	....	....
	San Jose	**NHL**	**1**	**0**	**0**	**0**	**0**	....	....	....	....	....
	Kansas City	IHL	71	15	18	33	64	....	....	....	....	....
1994-95	Kansas City	IHL	43	15	10	25	55	....	....	....	....	....
	San Jose	**NHL**	**26**	**3**	**5**	**8**	**94**	**6**	**0**	**0**	**0**	**9**
1995-96	**San Jose**	**NHL**	**42**	**7**	**7**	**14**	**62**	....	....	....	....	....
	Kansas City	IHL	27	4	6	10	118	2	0	0	0	2
1996-97	**San Jose**	**NHL**	**60**	**12**	**15**	**27**	**222**	....	....	....	....	....
	Kentucky	AHL	3	1	2	3	4	....	....	....	....	....
	NHL Totals		**129**	**22**	**27**	**49**	**378**	**6**	**0**	**0**	**0**	**9**

NDUR, RUMUN (nih-DOOR, ROO-muhn) BUF.

Defense. Shoots left. 6'2", 200 lbs.   Born, Zaria, Nigeria, July 7, 1975.
(Buffalo's 3rd choice, 69th overall, in 1994 Entry Draft).

			Regular Season					Playoffs				
Season	Club	Lea	GP	G	A	TP	PIM	GP	G	A	TP	PIM
1992-93	Guelph	OHL	22	1	3	4	30	4	0	1	1	4
1993-94	Guelph	OHL	61	6	33	39	176	9	4	1	5	24
1994-95	Guelph	OHL	63	10	21	31	187	14	0	4	4	28
1995-96	Rochester	AHL	73	2	12	14	306	17	1	2	3	33
1996-97	**Buffalo**	**NHL**	**2**	**0**	**0**	**0**	**2**	....	....	....	....	....
	Rochester	AHL	68	5	11	16	282	10	3	1	4	21
	NHL Totals		**2**	**0**	**0**	**0**	**2**	....	....	....	....	....

NECKAR, STANISLAV (NEHTS-kahrzh) OTT.

Defense. Shoots left. 6'1", 212 lbs.   Born, Ceske Budejovice, Czech., December 22, 1975.
(Ottawa's 2nd choice, 29th overall, in 1994 Entry Draft).

			Regular Season					Playoffs				
Season	Club	Lea	GP	G	A	TP	PIM	GP	G	A	TP	PIM
1992-93	Budejovice	Czech.	42	2	9	11	12	....	....	....	....	....
1993-94	Budejovice	Czech.	12	3	2	5	2	3	0	0	0	....
1994-95	Detroit	IHL	15	2	2	4	15	....	....	....	....	....
	Ottawa	**NHL**	**48**	**1**	**3**	**4**	**37**	....	....	....	....	....
1995-96	**Ottawa**	**NHL**	**82**	**3**	**9**	**12**	**54**	....	....	....	....	....
1996-97	**Ottawa**	**NHL**	**5**	**0**	**0**	**0**	**2**	....	....	....	....	....
	NHL Totals		**135**	**4**	**12**	**16**	**93**	....	....	....	....	....

NEDVED, PETR (NEHD-VEHD) PIT.

Center. Shoots left. 6'3", 195 lbs.   Born, Liberec, Czech., December 9, 1971.
(Vancouver's 1st choice, 2nd overall, in 1990 Entry Draft).

			Regular Season					Playoffs				
Season	Club	Lea	GP	G	A	TP	PIM	GP	G	A	TP	PIM
1989-90a	Seattle	WHL	71	65	80	145	80	11	4	9	13	2
1990-91	**Vancouver**	**NHL**	**61**	**10**	**6**	**16**	**20**	**6**	**0**	**1**	**1**	**0**
1991-92	**Vancouver**	**NHL**	**77**	**15**	**22**	**37**	**36**	**10**	**1**	**4**	**5**	**16**
1992-93	**Vancouver**	**NHL**	**84**	**38**	**33**	**71**	**96**	**12**	**2**	**3**	**5**	**2**
1993-94	Cdn. National	....	17	19	12	31	16	....	....	....	....	....
	Cdn. Olympic	....	8	5	1	6	6	....	....	....	....	....
	St. Louis	**NHL**	**19**	**6**	**14**	**20**	**8**	**4**	**0**	**1**	**1**	**4**
1994-95	**NY Rangers**	**NHL**	**46**	**11**	**12**	**23**	**26**	**10**	**3**	**2**	**5**	**6**
1995-96	**Pittsburgh**	**NHL**	**80**	**45**	**54**	**99**	**68**	**18**	**10**	**10**	**20**	**16**
1996-97	**Pittsburgh**	**NHL**	**74**	**33**	**38**	**71**	**66**	**5**	**1**	**2**	**3**	**12**
	NHL Totals		**441**	**158**	**179**	**337**	**320**	**65**	**17**	**23**	**40**	**56**

a Canadian Major Junior Rookie of the Year (1990)
Signed as a free agent by **St. Louis**, March 5, 1994. Traded to **NY Rangers** by **St. Louis** for Esa Tikkanen and Doug Lidster, July 24, 1994. Traded to **Pittsburgh** by **NY Rangers** with Sergei Zubov for Luc Robitaille and Ulf Samuelsson, August 31, 1995.

NEDVED, ZDENEK (NEHD-VEHD) TOR.

Right wing. Shoots left. 6', 180 lbs.   Born, Lany, Czech., March 3, 1975.
(Toronto's 3rd choice, 123rd overall, in 1993 Entry Draft).

			Regular Season					Playoffs				
Season	Club	Lea	GP	G	A	TP	PIM	GP	G	A	TP	PIM
1991-92	Kladno	Czech.	19	15	12	27	22	....	....	....	....	....
1992-93	Sudbury	OHL	18	3	9	12	6	....	....	....	....	....
1993-94	Sudbury	OHL	60	50	50	100	42	10	7	8	15	10
1994-95	Sudbury	OHL	59	47	51	98	36	18	12	16	28	16
	Toronto	**NHL**	**1**	**0**	**0**	**0**	**2**	....	....	....	....	....
1995-96	**Toronto**	**NHL**	**7**	**1**	**1**	**2**	**6**	....	....	....	....	....
	St. John's	AHL	41	13	14	27	22	4	2	0	2	0
1996-97	**Toronto**	**NHL**	**23**	**3**	**5**	**8**	**6**	....	....	....	....	....
	St. John's	AHL	51	9	25	34	34	7	2	2	4	6
	NHL Totals		**31**	**4**	**6**	**10**	**14**	....	....	....	....	....

NEHRLING, LUCAS N.J.

Defense. Shoots right. 6'4", 195 lbs.   Born, Peterborough, Ont., August 14, 1979.
(New Jersey's 3rd choice, 104th overall, in 1997 Entry Draft).

			Regular Season					Playoffs				
Season	Club	Lea	GP	G	A	TP	PIM	GP	G	A	TP	PIM
1996-97	Sarnia	OHL	63	3	12	15	74	12	0	2	2	23

NELSON, JEFF WSH.

Center. Shoots left. 6', 190 lbs.   Born, Prince Albert, Sask., December 18, 1972.
(Washington's 4th choice, 36th overall, in 1991 Entry Draft).

			Regular Season					Playoffs				
Season	Club	Lea	GP	G	A	TP	PIM	GP	G	A	TP	PIM
1989-90	Prince Albert	WHL	72	28	69	97	79	14	2	11	13	10
1990-91a	Prince Albert	WHL	72	46	74	120	58	3	1	1	2	4
1991-92a	Prince Albert	WHL	64	48	65	113	84	9	7	14	21	18
1992-93	Baltimore	AHL	72	14	38	52	12	7	1	3	4	2
1993-94	Portland	AHL	80	34	73	107	92	17	10	5	15	20
1994-95	Portland	AHL	64	33	50	83	57	7	1	4	5	8
	Washington	**NHL**	**10**	**1**	**0**	**1**	**2**	....	....	....	....	....
1995-96	**Washington**	**NHL**	**33**	**0**	**7**	**7**	**16**	**3**	**0**	**0**	**0**	**4**
	Portland	AHL	39	15	32	47	62	....	....	....	....	....
1996-97	Grand Rapids	IHL	82	34	55	89	85	5	0	4	4	4
	NHL Totals		**43**	**1**	**7**	**8**	**18**	**3**	**0**	**0**	**0**	**4**

a WHL East Second All-Star Team (1991, 1992)

NEMCHINOV, SERGEI (nehm-CHEE-nahf, SAIR-gay) NYI

Center. Shoots left. 6', 200 lbs.   Born, Moscow, USSR, January 14, 1964.
(NY Rangers' 14th choice, 244th overall, in 1990 Entry Draft).

			Regular Season					Playoffs				
Season	Club	Lea	GP	G	A	TP	PIM	GP	G	A	TP	PIM
1981-82	Soviet Wings	USSR	15	1	0	1	0	....	....	....	....	....
1982-83	CSKA	USSR	11	0	0	0	2	....	....	....	....	....
1983-84	CSKA	USSR	20	6	5	11	4	....	....	....	....	....
1984-85	CSKA	USSR	31	2	4	6	4	....	....	....	....	....
1985-86	Soviet Wings	USSR	39	7	12	19	28	....	....	....	....	....
1986-87	Soviet Wings	USSR	40	13	9	22	24	....	....	....	....	....
1987-88	Soviet Wings	USSR	48	17	11	28	26	....	....	....	....	....
1988-89	Soviet Wings	USSR	43	15	14	29	28	....	....	....	....	....
1989-90	Soviet Wings	USSR	48	17	16	33	34	....	....	....	....	....
1990-91	Soviet Wings	USSR	46	21	24	45	30	....	....	....	....	....
1991-92	**NY Rangers**	**NHL**	**73**	**30**	**28**	**58**	**15**	**13**	**1**	**4**	**5**	**8**
1992-93	**NY Rangers**	**NHL**	**81**	**23**	**31**	**54**	**34**	....	....	....	....	....
1993-94	**NY Rangers**	**NHL**	**76**	**22**	**27**	**49**	**36**	**23**	**2**	**5**	**7**	**6 ◆**
1994-95	**NY Rangers**	**NHL**	**47**	**7**	**6**	**13**	**16**	**10**	**4**	**5**	**9**	**2**
1995-96	**NY Rangers**	**NHL**	**78**	**17**	**15**	**32**	**38**	**6**	**0**	**1**	**1**	**2**
1996-97	**NY Rangers**	**NHL**	**63**	**6**	**13**	**19**	**12**	....	....	....	....	....
	Vancouver	NHL	6	2	3	5	4	....	....	....	....	....
	NHL Totals		**424**	**107**	**123**	**230**	**155**	**52**	**7**	**15**	**22**	**18**

Traded to **Vancouver** by **NY Rangers** with Brian Noonan for Esa Tikkanen and Russ Courtnall, March 8, 1997. Signed as a free agent by **NY Islanders**, July 10, 1997.

NEMECEK, JAN

(NEHM-eh-chehk, YAHN)　　L.A.

Defense. Shoots right. 6'1", 194 lbs.　Born, Pisek, Czech., February 14, 1976.
(Los Angeles' 7th choice, 215th overall, in 1994 Entry Draft).

			Regular Season					Playoffs			
Season	Club	Lea	GP	G	A	TP	PIM	GP	G	A	TP	PIM
1992-93	Budejovice	Czech.	15	0	0	0		....	....	....	....	....
1993-94	Budejovice	Czech.	16	0	1	1	16	....	....	....	....	....
1994-95	Hull	QMJHL	49	10	16	26	48	21	5	9	14	10
1995-96a	Hull	QMJHL	57	17	49	66	58	17	2	13	15	10
1996-97	Mississippi	ECHL	20	3	9	12	16	3	0	0	0	4
	Phoenix	IHL	24	1	1	2	2	....	....	....	....	....

a QMJHL Second All-Star Team (1996)

NEMIROVSKY, DAVID

(neh-mih-ROHV-skee)　　FLA.

Right wing. Shoots right. 6'1", 192 lbs.　Born, Toronto, Ont., August 1, 1976.
(Florida's 5th choice, 84th overall, in 1994 Entry Draft).

			Regular Season					Playoffs			
Season	Club	Lea	GP	G	A	TP	PIM	GP	G	A	TP	PIM
1993-94	Ottawa	OHL	64	21	31	52	18	17	10	10	20	2
1994-95	Ottawa	OHL	59	27	29	56	25	....	....	....	....	....
1995-96	Florida	NHL	9	0	2	2	2	....	....	....	....	....
	Sarnia	OHL	26	18	27	45	14	10	8	8	16	6
	Carolina	AHL	5	1	2	3	0	....	....	....	....	....
1996-97	Florida	NHL	39	7	7	14	32	3	1	0	1	0
	Carolina	AHL	34	21	21	42	18	....	....	....	....	....
	NHL Totals		48	7	9	16	34	3	1	0	1	0

NICHOL, SCOTT

BUF.

Center. Shoots right. 5'8", 160 lbs.　Born, Edmonton, Alta., December 31, 1974.
(Buffalo's 9th choice, 272nd overall, in 1993 Entry Draft).

			Regular Season					Playoffs			
Season	Club	Lea	GP	G	A	TP	PIM	GP	G	A	TP	PIM
1992-93	Portland	WHL	67	31	33	64	146	16	8	8	16	41
1993-94	Portland	WHL	65	40	53	93	144	10	3	8	11	16
1994-95	Rochester	AHL	71	11	16	27	136	5	0	3	3	14
1995-96	Buffalo	NHL	2	0	0	0	10	....	....	....	....	....
	Rochester	AHL	62	14	18	32	170	19	7	6	13	36
1996-97	Rochester	AHL	68	22	21	43	133	10	2	1	3	26
	NHL Totals		2	0	0	0	10	....	....	....	....	....

NICHOLLS, BERNIE

(NICK-els)　　S.J.

Center. Shoots right. 6', 185 lbs.　Born, Haliburton, Ont., June 24, 1961.
(Los Angeles' 6th choice, 73rd overall, in 1980 Entry Draft).

			Regular Season					Playoffs			
Season	Club	Lea	GP	G	A	TP	PIM	GP	G	A	TP	PIM
1979-80	Kingston	OHA	68	36	43	79	85	3	1	0	1	10
1980-81	Kingston	OHA	65	63	89	152	109	14	8	10	18	17
1981-82	Los Angeles	NHL	22	14	18	32	27	10	4	0	4	23
	New Haven	AHL	55	41	30	71	31	....	....	....	....	....
1982-83	Los Angeles	NHL	71	28	22	50	124	....	....	....	....	....
1983-84	Los Angeles	NHL	78	41	54	95	83	....	....	....	....	....
1984-85	Los Angeles	NHL	80	46	54	100	76	3	1	1	2	9
1985-86	Los Angeles	NHL	80	36	61	97	78	....	....	....	....	....
1986-87	Los Angeles	NHL	80	33	48	81	101	5	2	5	7	6
1987-88	Los Angeles	NHL	65	32	46	78	114	5	2	6	8	11
1988-89	Los Angeles	NHL	79	70	80	150	96	11	7	9	16	12
1989-90	Los Angeles	NHL	47	27	48	75	66	....	....	....	....	....
	NY Rangers	NHL	32	12	25	37	20	10	7	5	12	16
1990-91	NY Rangers	NHL	71	25	48	73	96	5	4	3	7	8
1991-92	NY Rangers	NHL	1	0	0	0	0	....	....	....	....	....
	Edmonton	NHL	49	20	29	49	60	16	8	11	19	25
1992-93	Edmonton	NHL	46	8	32	40	40	....	....	....	....	....
	New Jersey	NHL	23	5	15	20	40	5	0	0	0	6
1993-94	New Jersey	NHL	61	19	27	46	86	16	4	9	13	28
1994-95	Chicago	NHL	48	22	29	51	32	16	1	11	12	8
1995-96	Chicago	NHL	59	19	41	60	60	10	2	7	9	4
1996-97	San Jose	NHL	65	12	33	45	63	....	....	....	....	....
	NHL Totals		1057	469	710	1179	1262	112	42	67	109	156

Played in NHL All-Star Game (1984, 1989, 1990)

Traded to **NY Rangers** by **Los Angeles** for Tomas Sandstrom and Tony Granato, January 20, 1990. Traded to **Edmonton** by **NY Rangers** with Steven Rice and Louie DeBrusk for Mark Messier and future considerations, October 4, 1991. Traded to **New Jersey** by **Edmonton** for Zdeno Ciger and Kevin Todd, January 13, 1993. Signed as a free agent by **Chicago**, July 14, 1994. Signed as a free agent by **San Jose**, August 5, 1996.

NICKULAS, ERIC

BOS.

Center. Shoots right. 5'11", 190 lbs.　Born, Cape Cod, MA, March 25, 1975.
(Boston's 3rd choice, 99th overall, in 1994 Entry Draft).

			Regular Season					Playoffs			
Season	Club	Lea	GP	G	A	TP	PIM	GP	G	A	TP	PIM
1994-95	N. Hampshire	H.E.	33	15	9	24	32	....	....	....	....	....
1995-96	N. Hampshire	H.E.	34	26	12	38	66	....	....	....	....	....
1996-97	N. Hampshire	H.E.	39	29	22	51	80	....	....	....	....	....

NIECKAR, BARRY

(NIGH-kahr)　　ANA.

Left wing. Shoots left. 6'3", 205 lbs.　Born, Rama, Sask., December 16, 1967.

			Regular Season					Playoffs			
Season	Club	Lea	GP	G	A	TP	PIM	GP	G	A	TP	PIM
1991-92	Phoenix	IHL	5	0	0	0	9	....	....	....	....	....
	Raleigh	ECHL	46	10	18	28	229	4	4	0	4	22
1992-93	Hartford	NHL	2	0	0	0	2	....	....	....	....	....
	Springfield	AHL	21	2	4	6	65	6	1	0	1	14
1993-94	Springfield	AHL	30	0	2	2	67	....	....	....	....	....
	Raleigh	ECHL	18	4	6	10	126	15	5	7	12	51
1994-95	Saint John	AHL	65	8	7	15	*491	4	0	0	0	22
	Calgary	NHL	3	0	0	0	12	....	....	....	....	....
1995-96	Utah	IHL	53	9	15	24	194	....	....	....	....	....
	Peoria	IHL	10	3	3	6	72	12	4	6	10	48
1996-97	Anaheim	NHL	2	0	0	0	5	....	....	....	....	....
	Long Beach	IHL	63	3	10	13	386	5	0	0	0	22
	NHL Totals		7	0	0	0	19	....	....	....	....	....

Signed as a free agent by **Hartford**, September 25, 1992. Signed as a free agent by **Calgary**, February 11, 1995. Signed as a free agent by **NY Islanders**, August 8, 1995. Signed as a free agent by **Anaheim**, October 2, 1996.

NIEDERMAYER, ROB

(nee-duhr-MIGH-uhr)　　FLA.

Center. Shoots left. 6'2", 201 lbs.　Born, Cassiar, B.C., December 28, 1974.
(Florida's 1st choice, 5th overall, in 1993 Entry Draft).

			Regular Season					Playoffs			
Season	Club	Lea	GP	G	A	TP	PIM	GP	G	A	TP	PIM
1990-91	Medicine Hat	WHL	71	24	26	50	8	12	3	7	10	2
1991-92	Medicine Hat	WHL	71	32	46	78	77	4	2	3	5	2
1992-93a	Medicine Hat	WHL	52	43	34	77	67	....	....	....	....	....
1993-94	Florida	NHL	65	9	17	26	51	....	....	....	....	....
1994-95	Medicine Hat	WHL	13	9	15	24	14	....	....	....	....	....
	Florida	NHL	48	4	6	10	36	....	....	....	....	....
1995-96	Florida	NHL	82	26	35	61	107	22	5	3	8	12
1996-97	Florida	NHL	60	14	24	38	54	5	2	1	3	6
	NHL Totals		255	53	82	135	248	27	7	4	11	18

a WHL East First All-Star Team (1993)

NIEDERMAYER, SCOTT

(NEE-duhr-MIGH-uhr)　　N.J.

Defense. Shoots left. 6', 200 lbs.　Born, Edmonton, Alta., August 31, 1973.
(New Jersey's 1st choice, 3rd overall, in 1991 Entry Draft).

			Regular Season					Playoffs			
Season	Club	Lea	GP	G	A	TP	PIM	GP	G	A	TP	PIM
1989-90	Kamloops	WHL	64	14	55	69	64	17	2	14	16	35
1990-91ab	Kamloops	WHL	57	26	56	82	52	....	....	....	....	....
1991-92	New Jersey	NHL	4	0	1	1	2	....	....	....	....	....
acd	Kamloops	WHL	35	7	32	39	61	17	9	14	23	28
1992-93e	New Jersey	NHL	80	11	29	40	47	5	0	3	3	2
1993-94	New Jersey	NHL	81	10	36	46	42	20	2	2	4	8
1994-95	New Jersey	NHL	48	4	15	19	18	20	4	7	11	10 ♦
1995-96	New Jersey	NHL	79	8	25	33	46	....	....	....	....	....
1996-97	New Jersey	NHL	81	5	30	35	64	10	2	4	6	6
	NHL Totals		373	38	136	174	219	55	8	16	24	26

a WHL West First All-Star Team (1991, 1992)
b Canadian Major Junior Scholastic Player of the Year (1991)
c Memorial Cup All-Star Team (1992)
d Won Stafford Smythe Memorial Trophy (Memorial Cup Tournament MVP) (1992)
e NHL/Upper Deck All-Rookie Team (1993)

NIELSEN, JEFF

ANA.

Right wing. Shoots right. 6', 200 lbs.　Born, Grand Rapids, MN, September 20, 1971.
(NY Rangers' 4th choice, 69th overall, in 1990 Entry Draft).

			Regular Season					Playoffs			
Season	Club	Lea	GP	G	A	TP	PIM	GP	G	A	TP	PIM
1990-91	U. Minnesota	WCHA	45	11	14	25	50	....	....	....	....	....
1991-92	U. Minnesota	WCHA	41	14	14	28	70	....	....	....	....	....
1992-93	U. Minnesota	WCHA	42	21	20	41	80	....	....	....	....	....
1993-94a	U. Minnesota	WCHA	41	29	16	45	94	....	....	....	....	....
1994-95	Binghamton	AHL	76	24	13	37	139	7	0	0	0	22
1995-96	Binghamton	AHL	64	22	20	42	56	4	1	1	2	4
1996-97	NY Rangers	NHL	2	0	0	0	2	....	....	....	....	....
	Binghamton	AHL	76	27	26	53	71	4	0	0	0	7
	NHL Totals		2	0	0	0	2	....	....	....	....	....

a WCHA Second All-Star Team (1994)

Signed as a free agent by **Anaheim**, August 11, 1997.

NIELSEN, KIRK

BOS.

Right wing. Shoots right. 6'1", 205 lbs.　Born, Grand Rapids, MN, October 19, 1973.
(Philadelphia's 1st choice, 10th overall, in 1994 Supplemental Draft).

			Regular Season					Playoffs			
Season	Club	Lea	GP	G	A	TP	PIM	GP	G	A	TP	PIM
1992-93	Harvard	ECAC	30	2	2	4	38	....	....	....	....	....
1993-94	Harvard	ECAC	32	6	9	15	41	....	....	....	....	....
1994-95	Harvard	ECAC	30	13	8	21	24	....	....	....	....	....
1995-96	Harvard	ECAC	31	12	16	28	66	....	....	....	....	....
1996-97	Providence	AHL	68	12	23	35	30	9	2	1	3	2

Signed as a free agent by **Boston**, June 7, 1996.

NIEMI, ANTTI-JUSSI

(nee-mee, AN-tee-YOO-see)　　OTT.

Defense. Shoots left. 6'1", 183 lbs.　Born, Vantaa, Finland, September 22, 1977.
(Ottawa's 2nd choice, 81st overall, in 1996 Entry Draft).

			Regular Season					Playoffs			
Season	Club	Lea	GP	G	A	TP	PIM	GP	G	A	TP	PIM
1995-96	Jokerit	Fin. Jr.	34	11	18	29	56	8	0	4	4	39
	Jarvenpaa	Fin. 2	4	0	2	2	8	....	....	....	....	....
	Jokerit	Fin.	6	0	2	2	6	1	0	0	0	0
1996-97	Jokerit	Fin.	44	2	9	11	38	9	0	2	2	2

NIEMINEN, VILLE

(nee-EHM-ih-nehn, VIHL-ee)　　COL.

Right wing. Shoots left. 5'11", 205 lbs.　Born, Tampere, Finland, April 6, 1977.
(Colorado's 4th choice, 78th overall, in 1997 Entry Draft).

			Regular Season					Playoffs			
Season	Club	Lea	GP	G	A	TP	PIM	GP	G	A	TP	PIM
1994-95	Tappara	Fin. Jr.	16	11	21	32	47	....	....	....	....	....
	Tappara	Fin.	16	0	0	0	0	....	....	....	....	....
1995-96	Tappara	Fin. Jr.	20	20	23	43	63	....	....	....	....	....
	Tappara	Fin.	4	0	1	1	8	....	....	....	....	....
	KooVee	Fin. 2	7	2	1	3	4	....	....	....	....	....
1996-97	Tappara	Fin.	49	10	13	23	120	3	1	0	1	8

NIEUWENDYK, JOE (NOO-ihn-DIGHK) DAL.

Center. Shoots left. 6'1", 195 lbs. Born, Oshawa, Ont., September 10, 1966.
(Calgary's 2nd choice, 27th overall, in 1985 Entry Draft).

			Regular Season					Playoffs				
Season	Club	Lea	GP	G	A	TP	PIM	GP	G	A	TP	PIM
1984-85	Cornell	ECAC	29	21	24	45	30	....	....	....	....	....
1985-86ab	Cornell	ECAC	29	26	28	54	67	....	....	....	....	....
1986-87ab	Cornell	ECAC	23	26	26	52	26	....	....	....	....	....
	Cdn. National	....	5	2	0	2	0	....	....	....	....	....
	Calgary	**NHL**	**9**	**5**	**1**	**6**	**0**	**6**	**2**	**2**	**4**	**0**
1987-88cde	**Calgary**	**NHL**	**75**	**51**	**41**	**92**	**23**	**8**	**3**	**4**	**7**	**2**
1988-89	**Calgary**	**NHL**	**77**	**51**	**31**	**82**	**40**	**22**	**10**	**4**	**14**	**10 ♦**
1989-90	**Calgary**	**NHL**	**79**	**45**	**50**	**95**	**40**	**6**	**4**	**6**	**10**	**4**
1990-91	**Calgary**	**NHL**	**79**	**45**	**40**	**85**	**36**	**7**	**4**	**1**	**5**	**10**
1991-92	**Calgary**	**NHL**	**69**	**22**	**34**	**56**	**55**	....	....	....	....	....
1992-93	**Calgary**	**NHL**	**79**	**38**	**37**	**75**	**52**	**6**	**3**	**6**	**9**	**10**
1993-94	**Calgary**	**NHL**	**64**	**36**	**39**	**75**	**51**	**6**	**2**	**2**	**4**	**0**
1994-95f	**Calgary**	**NHL**	**46**	**21**	**29**	**50**	**33**	**5**	**4**	**3**	**7**	**0**
1995-96	**Dallas**	**NHL**	**52**	**14**	**18**	**32**	**41**	....	....	....	....	....
1996-97	**Dallas**	**NHL**	**66**	**30**	**21**	**51**	**32**	**7**	**2**	**2**	**4**	**6**
	NHL Totals		**695**	**358**	**341**	**699**	**403**	**73**	**34**	**30**	**64**	**42**

a NCAA East First All-American Team (1986, 1987)
b ECAC First All-Star Team (1986, 1987)
c Won Calder Memorial Trophy (1988)
d NHL All-Rookie Team (1988)
e Won Dodge Ram Tough Award (1988)
f Won King Clancy Memorial Trophy (1995)

Played in NHL All-Star Game (1988-90, 1994)

Traded to **Dallas** by **Calgary** for Corey Millen and Jarome Iginla, December 19, 1995.

NIINIMAA, JANNE (nihn-EE-mah, YAH-nee) PHI.

Defense. Shoots left. 6'1", 220 lbs. Born, Raahe, Finland, May 22, 1975.
(Philadelphia's 1st choice, 36th overall, in 1993 Entry Draft).

			Regular Season					Playoffs				
Season	Club	Lea	GP	G	A	TP	PIM	GP	G	A	TP	PIM
1991-92	Karpat	Fin. 2	41	2	11	13	49	....	....	....	....	....
1992-93	Karpat	Fin. 2	29	2	3	5	14	....	....	....	....	....
1993-94	Jokerit	Fin.	45	3	8	11	24	12	1	1	2	4
1994-95	Jokerit	Fin.	42	7	10	17	36	10	1	4	5	35
1995-96	Jokerit	Fin.	49	5	15	20	79	11	0	2	2	12
1996-97a	**Philadelphia**	**NHL**	**77**	**4**	**40**	**44**	**58**	**19**	**1**	**12**	**13**	**16**
	NHL Totals		**77**	**4**	**40**	**44**	**58**	**19**	**1**	**12**	**13**	**16**

a NHL All-Rookie Team (1997)

NIKOLISHIN, ANDREI (nee-koh-LEE-shin) WSH.

Left wing. Shoots left. 5'11", 180 lbs. Born, Vorkuta, USSR, March 25, 1973.
(Hartford's 2nd choice, 47th overall, in 1992 Entry Draft).

			Regular Season					Playoffs				
Season	Club	Lea	GP	G	A	TP	PIM	GP	G	A	TP	PIM
1990-91	Moscow D'amo	USSR	2	0	0	0	0	....	....	....	....	....
1991-92	Moscow D'amo	CIS	18	1	0	1	4	....	....	....	....	....
1992-93	Moscow D'amo	CIS	42	5	7	12	30	10	2	1	3	8
1993-94	Moscow D'amo	CIS	41	8	12	20	30	9	1	3	4	4
1994-95	Moscow D'amo	CIS	12	7	2	9	6	....	....	....	....	....
	Hartford	**NHL**	**39**	**8**	**10**	**18**	**10**	....	....	....	....	....
1995-96	**Hartford**	**NHL**	**61**	**14**	**37**	**51**	**34**	....	....	....	....	....
1996-97	**Hartford**	**NHL**	**12**	**2**	**5**	**7**	**2**	....	....	....	....	....
	Washington	**NHL**	**59**	**7**	**14**	**21**	**30**	....	....	....	....	....
	NHL Totals		**171**	**31**	**66**	**97**	**76**	....	....	....	....	....

Traded to **Washington** by **Hartford** for Curtis Leschyshyn, November 9, 1996.

NIKOLOV, ANGEL (NIH-koh-lohv) S.J.

Defense. Shoots left. 6'1", 178 lbs. Born, Most, Czech., November 18, 1975.
(San Jose's 2nd choice, 37th overall, in 1994 Entry Draft).

			Regular Season					Playoffs				
Season	Club	Lea	GP	G	A	TP	PIM	GP	G	A	TP	PIM
1993-94	Litvinov	Czech.	10	2	2	4	....	3	0	0	0	....
1994-95	Litvinov	Czech.	41	1	4	5	18	4	0	0	0	27
1995-96	Litvinov	Czech.	40	1	7	8	....	10	0	1	1	....
1996-97	Litvinov	Czech.	47	0	9	9	44	....	....	....	....	....

NIKULIN, IGOR (nih-KOO-lihn) ANA.

Right wing. Shoots left. 6'1", 200 lbs. Born, Cherepovets, USSR, August 26, 1972.
(Anaheim's 4th choice, 107th overall, in 1995 Entry Draft).

			Regular Season					Playoffs				
Season	Club	Lea	GP	G	A	TP	PIM	GP	G	A	TP	PIM
1992-93	Cherepovets	CIS	42	11	11	22	22	....	....	....	....	....
1993-94	Cherepovets	CIS	44	14	15	29	52	2	1	0	1	0
1994-95	Cherepovets	CIS	52	14	12	26	28	....	....	....	....	....
1995-96	Cherepovets	CIS	47	20	13	33	28	4	1	0	1	0
	Baltimore	AHL	4	2	2	4	2	....	....	....	....	....
1996-97	Baltimore	AHL	61	27	25	52	14	3	2	1	3	2
	Fort Wayne	IHL	10	1	2	3	4	....	....	....	....	....
	Anaheim	**NHL**	....	....	....	....	....	**1**	**0**	**0**	**0**	**0**
	NHL Totals		**0**	**0**	**0**	**0**	**0**	**1**	**0**	**0**	**0**	**0**

NILSSON, MAGNUS DET.

Right wing. Shoots left. 6'1", 187 lbs. Born, Finspang, Sweden, February 1, 1978.
(Detroit's 5th choice, 144th overall, in 1996 Entry Draft).

			Regular Season					Playoffs				
Season	Club	Lea	GP	G	A	TP	PIM	GP	G	A	TP	PIM
1995-96	Vita Hasten	Swe. 2	28	3	3	6	16	....	....	....	....	....
1996-97	Malmo	Swe. Jr.	14	10	9	19	45	....	....	....	....	....
	Malmo	Swe.	12	0	0	0	0	....	....	....	....	....

NILSSON, MARCUS FLA.

Left wing. Shoots right. 6'1", 183 lbs. Born, Stockholm, Sweden, March 1, 1978.
(Florida's 1st choice, 20th overall, in 1996 Entry Draft).

			Regular Season					Playoffs				
Season	Club	Lea	GP	G	A	TP	PIM	GP	G	A	TP	PIM
1995-96	Djurgarden	Swe. Jr.	25	19	17	36	46	2	1	1	2	12
	Djurgarden	Swe.	12	0	0	0	0	1	0	0	0	0
1996-97	Djurgarden	Swe.	37	0	3	3	33	4	0	0	0	0

NITTEL, ADAM (nih-TEHL) S.J.

Right wing. Shoots right. 6', 215 lbs. Born, Kitchener, Ont., July 17, 1978.
(San Jose's 4th choice, 107th overall, in 1997 Entry Draft).

			Regular Season					Playoffs				
Season	Club	Lea	GP	G	A	TP	PIM	GP	G	A	TP	PIM
1996-97	Erie	OHL	46	8	11	19	194	....	....	....	....	....

NOBLE, STEVE ST.L.

Center. Shoots left. 6'1", 185 lbs. Born, Sault Ste. Marie, Ont., July 17, 1976.
(St. Louis' 5th choice, 198th overall, in 1994 Entry Draft).

			Regular Season					Playoffs				
Season	Club	Lea	GP	G	A	TP	PIM	GP	G	A	TP	PIM
1994-95	Notre Dame	CCHA	37	6	8	14	25	....	....	....	....	....
1995-96	Notre Dame	CCHA	36	5	15	20	48	....	....	....	....	....
1996-97	Notre Dame	CCHA	34	9	7	16	34	....	....	....	....	....

NOLAN, DOUG TOR.

Left wing. Shoots left. 6'1", 185 lbs. Born, Quincy, MA, January 5, 1976.
(Toronto's 9th choice, 282nd overall, in 1994 Entry Draft).

			Regular Season					Playoffs				
Season	Club	Lea	GP	G	A	TP	PIM	GP	G	A	TP	PIM
1995-96	Lowell	H.E.	30	1	1	2	23	....	....	....	....	....
1996-97	Lowell	H.E.	38	10	14	24	66	....	....	....	....	....

NOLAN, OWEN S.J.

Right wing. Shoots right. 6'1", 201 lbs. Born, Belfast, Ireland, February 12, 1972.
(Quebec's 1st choice, 1st overall, in 1990 Entry Draft).

			Regular Season					Playoffs				
Season	Club	Lea	GP	G	A	TP	PIM	GP	G	A	TP	PIM
1988-89	Cornwall	OHL	62	34	25	59	213	18	5	11	16	41
1989-90a	Cornwall	OHL	58	51	59	110	240	6	7	5	12	26
1990-91	**Quebec**	**NHL**	**59**	**3**	**10**	**13**	**109**	....	....	....	....	....
	Halifax	AHL	6	4	4	8	11	....	....	....	....	....
1991-92	**Quebec**	**NHL**	**75**	**42**	**31**	**73**	**183**	....	....	....	....	....
1992-93	**Quebec**	**NHL**	**73**	**36**	**41**	**77**	**185**	**5**	**1**	**0**	**1**	**2**
1993-94	**Quebec**	**NHL**	**6**	**2**	**2**	**4**	**8**	....	....	....	....	....
1994-95	**Quebec**	**NHL**	**46**	**30**	**19**	**49**	**46**	**6**	**2**	**3**	**5**	**6**
1995-96	**Colorado**	**NHL**	**9**	**4**	**4**	**8**	**9**	....	....	....	....	....
	San Jose	**NHL**	**72**	**29**	**32**	**61**	**137**	....	....	....	....	....
1996-97	**San Jose**	**NHL**	**72**	**31**	**32**	**63**	**155**	....	....	....	....	....
	NHL Totals		**412**	**177**	**171**	**348**	**832**	**11**	**3**	**3**	**6**	**8**

a OHL First All-Star Team (1990)

Played in NHL All-Star Game (1992, 1996, 1997)

Traded to **San Jose** by **Colorado** for Sandis Ozolinsh, October 26, 1995.

NOONAN, BRIAN VAN.

Right wing. Shoots right. 6'1", 200 lbs. Born, Boston, MA, May 29, 1965.
(Chicago's 10th choice, 179th overall, in 1983 Entry Draft).

			Regular Season					Playoffs				
Season	Club	Lea	GP	G	A	TP	PIM	GP	G	A	TP	PIM
1984-85	N. Westminster	WHL	72	50	66	116	76	11	8	7	15	4
1985-86	Nova Scotia	AHL	2	0	0	0	0	....	....	....	....	....
	Saginaw	IHL	76	39	39	78	69	11	6	3	9	6
1986-87	Nova Scotia	AHL	70	25	26	51	30	5	3	1	4	4
1987-88	**Chicago**	**NHL**	**77**	**10**	**20**	**30**	**44**	**3**	**0**	**0**	**0**	**4**
1988-89	**Chicago**	**NHL**	**45**	**4**	**12**	**16**	**28**	**1**	**0**	**0**	**0**	**0**
	Saginaw	IHL	19	18	13	31	36	1	0	0	0	0
1989-90	**Chicago**	**NHL**	**8**	**0**	**2**	**2**	**6**	....	....	....	....	....
a	Indianapolis	IHL	56	40	36	76	85	14	6	9	15	20
1990-91	**Chicago**	**NHL**	**7**	**0**	**4**	**4**	**2**	....	....	....	....	....
b	Indianapolis	IHL	59	38	53	91	67	7	6	4	10	18
1991-92	**Chicago**	**NHL**	**65**	**19**	**12**	**31**	**81**	**18**	**6**	**9**	**15**	**30**
1992-93	**Chicago**	**NHL**	**63**	**16**	**14**	**30**	**82**	**4**	**3**	**0**	**3**	**4**
1993-94	**Chicago**	**NHL**	**64**	**14**	**21**	**35**	**57**	....	....	....	....	....
	NY Rangers	**NHL**	**12**	**4**	**2**	**6**	**12**	**22**	**4**	**7**	**11**	**17 ♦**
1994-95	**NY Rangers**	**NHL**	**45**	**14**	**13**	**27**	**26**	**5**	**0**	**0**	**0**	**8**
1995-96	**St. Louis**	**NHL**	**81**	**13**	**22**	**35**	**84**	**13**	**4**	**1**	**5**	**10**
1996-97	**St. Louis**	**NHL**	**13**	**2**	**5**	**7**	**0**	....	....	....	....	....
	NY Rangers	**NHL**	**44**	**6**	**9**	**15**	**28**	....	....	....	....	....
	Vancouver	**NHL**	**16**	**4**	**8**	**12**	**6**	....	....	....	....	....
	NHL Totals		**540**	**106**	**144**	**250**	**456**	**66**	**17**	**17**	**34**	**73**

a IHL Second All-Star Team (1990)
b IHL First All-Star Team (1991)

Traded to **NY Rangers** by **Chicago** with Stephane Matteau for Tony Amonte and the rights to Matt Oates, March 21, 1994. Signed as a free agent by **St. Louis**, July 24, 1995. Traded to **NY Rangers** by **St. Louis** for Sergio Momesso, November 13, 1996. Traded to **Vancouver** by **NY Rangers** with Sergei Nemchinov for Esa Tikkanen and Russ Courtnall, March 8, 1997.

NORRIS, CLAYTON

Right wing. Shoots right. 6'2", 205 lbs. Born, Edmonton, Alta., March 8, 1972.
(Philadelphia's 5th choice, 116th overall, in 1991 Entry Draft).

			Regular Season					Playoffs				
Season	Club	Lea	GP	G	A	TP	PIM	GP	G	A	TP	PIM
1988-89	Medicine Hat	WHL	66	4	9	13	122	3	0	0	0	2
1989-90	Medicine Hat	WHL	72	13	18	31	176	3	0	0	0	15
1990-91	Medicine Hat	WHL	71	26	27	53	165	12	5	4	9	41
1991-92a	Medicine Hat	WHL	69	26	39	65	300	2	0	0	0	9
1992-93	Medicine Hat	WHL	41	21	16	37	128	10	3	2	5	14
	Hershey	AHL	4	0	0	0	5	....	....	....	....	....
	Roanoke	ECHL	4	0	0	0	0	....	....	....	....	....
1993-94	Hershey	AHL	62	8	10	18	217	10	1	0	1	18
1994-95	Hershey	AHL	76	12	21	33	287	4	0	0	0	8
1995-96	Hershey	AHL	57	8	8	16	163	5	0	1	1	4
1996-97	Philadelphia	AHL	1	0	0	0	17	....	....	....	....	....
	Orlando	IHL	69	9	9	18	261	10	2	3	5	17

a WHL East Second All-Star Team (1992)

NORRIS, DWAYNE

Right wing. Shoots right. 5'10", 175 lbs. Born, St. John's, Nfld., January 8, 1970.
(Quebec's 5th choice, 127th overall, in 1990 Entry Draft).

			Regular Season					Playoffs				
Season	Club	Lea	GP	G	A	TP	PIM	GP	G	A	TP	PIM
1988-89	Michigan State	CCHA	40	16	21	37	32	....	....	....	....	....
1989-90	Michigan State	CCHA	33	18	25	43	30	....	....	....	....	....
1990-91	Michigan State	CCHA	40	26	25	51	60	....	....	....	....	....
1991-92ab	Michigan State	CCHA	41	40	38	78	58	....	....	....	....	....
1992-93	Halifax	AHL	50	25	28	53	62	....	....	....	....	....
1993-94	Cdn. National	....	48	18	14	32	22	....	....	....	....	....
	Cdn. Olympic	....	8	2	2	4	4	....	....	....	....	....
	Quebec	**NHL**	**4**	**1**	**1**	**2**	**4**	....	....	....	....	....
	Cornwall	AHL	9	2	9	11	0	13	7	4	11	17
1994-95c	Cornwall	AHL	60	30	43	73	61	12	7	8	15	4
	Quebec	**NHL**	**13**	**1**	**2**	**3**	**2**	....	....	....	....	....
1995-96	Los Angeles	IHL	14	7	16	23	22	....	....	....	....	....
	Anaheim	**NHL**	**3**	**0**	**1**	**1**	**2**	....	....	....	....	....
d	Baltimore	AHL	62	31	55	86	16	12	6	9	15	12
1996-97	Koln	Ger.	49	16	28	44	24	4	3	0	3	0
	NHL Totals		**20**	**2**	**4**	**6**	**8**	....	....	....	....	....

a CCHA First All-Star Team (1992)
b NCAA West First All-American Team (1992)
c AHL First All-Star Team (1995)
d AHL Second All-Star Team (1996)

Signed as a free agent by **Anaheim**, November 3, 1995.

NORSTROM, MATTIAS — L.A.

Defense. Shoots left. 6'1", 205 lbs. Born, Stockholm, Sweden, January 2, 1972.
(NY Rangers' 2nd choice, 48th overall, in 1992 Entry Draft).

			Regular Season					Playoffs				
Season	Club	Lea	GP	G	A	TP	PIM	GP	G	A	TP	PIM
1991-92	AIK	Swe.	39	4	3	7	28	3	0	2	2	2
1992-93	AIK	Swe.	22	0	1	1	16	....	....	....	....	....
1993-94	**NY Rangers**	**NHL**	**9**	**0**	**2**	**2**	**6**	....	....	....	....	....
	Binghamton	AHL	55	1	9	10	70	....	....	....	....	....
1994-95	Binghamton	AHL	63	9	10	19	91	....	....	....	....	....
	NY Rangers	**NHL**	**9**	**0**	**3**	**3**	**2**	**3**	**0**	**0**	**0**	**0**
1995-96	**NY Rangers**	**NHL**	**25**	**2**	**1**	**3**	**22**	....	....	....	....	....
	Los Angeles	**NHL**	**11**	**0**	**1**	**1**	**18**	....	....	....	....	....
1996-97	**Los Angeles**	**NHL**	**80**	**1**	**21**	**22**	**84**	....	....	....	....	....
	NHL Totals		**134**	**3**	**28**	**31**	**132**	**3**	**0**	**0**	**0**	**0**

Traded to **Los Angeles** by **NY Rangers** with Ray Ferraro, Ian Laperriere, Nathan Lafayette and NY Rangers' fourth round choice (Sean Blanchard) in 1997 Entry Draft for Marty McSorley, Jari Kurri and Shane Churla, March 14, 1996.

NORTON, BRAD — EDM.

Defense. Shoots left. 6'4", 225 lbs. Born, Cambridge, MA, February 13, 1975.
(Edmonton's 9th choice, 215th overall, in 1993 Entry Draft).

			Regular Season					Playoffs				
Season	Club	Lea	GP	G	A	TP	PIM	GP	G	A	TP	PIM
1994-95	Massachusetts	H.E.	30	0	6	6	89	....	....	....	....	....
1995-96	Massachusetts	H.E.	34	4	12	16	99	....	....	....	....	....
1996-97	Massachusetts	H.E.	35	2	16	18	88	....	....	....	....	....

NORTON, JEFF — T.B.

Defense. Shoots left. 6'2", 200 lbs. Born, Acton, MA, November 25, 1965.
(NY Islanders' 3rd choice, 62nd overall, in 1984 Entry Draft).

			Regular Season					Playoffs				
Season	Club	Lea	GP	G	A	TP	PIM	GP	G	A	TP	PIM
1984-85	U. of Michigan	CCHA	37	8	16	24	103	....	....	....	....	....
1985-86	U. of Michigan	CCHA	37	15	30	45	99	....	....	....	....	....
1986-87a	U. of Michigan	CCHA	39	12	36	48	92	....	....	....	....	....
1987-88	U.S. National	....	54	7	22	29	52	....	....	....	....	....
	U.S. Olympic	....	6	0	4	4	4	....	....	....	....	....
	NY Islanders	**NHL**	**15**	**1**	**6**	**7**	**14**	**3**	**0**	**2**	**2**	**13**
1988-89	**NY Islanders**	**NHL**	**69**	**1**	**30**	**31**	**74**	....	....	....	....	....
1989-90	**NY Islanders**	**NHL**	**60**	**4**	**49**	**53**	**65**	**4**	**1**	**3**	**4**	**17**
1990-91	**NY Islanders**	**NHL**	**44**	**3**	**25**	**28**	**16**	....	....	....	....	....
1991-92	**NY Islanders**	**NHL**	**28**	**1**	**18**	**19**	**18**	....	....	....	....	....
1992-93	**NY Islanders**	**NHL**	**66**	**12**	**38**	**50**	**45**	**10**	**1**	**1**	**2**	**4**
1993-94	**San Jose**	**NHL**	**64**	**7**	**33**	**40**	**36**	**14**	**1**	**5**	**6**	**20**
1994-95	**San Jose**	**NHL**	**20**	**1**	**9**	**10**	**39**	....	....	....	....	....
	St. Louis	**NHL**	**28**	**2**	**18**	**20**	**33**	**7**	**1**	**1**	**2**	**11**
1995-96	**St. Louis**	**NHL**	**36**	**4**	**7**	**11**	**26**	....	....	....	....	....
	Edmonton	**NHL**	**30**	**4**	**16**	**20**	**16**	....	....	....	....	....
1996-97	**Edmonton**	**NHL**	**62**	**2**	**11**	**13**	**42**	....	....	....	....	....
	Tampa Bay	**NHL**	**13**	**0**	**5**	**5**	**16**	....	....	....	....	....
	NHL Totals		**535**	**42**	**265**	**307**	**440**	**38**	**4**	**12**	**16**	**65**

a CCHA Second All-Star Team (1987)

Traded to **San Jose** by **NY Islanders** for San Jose's third round choice (Jason Strudwick) in 1994 Entry Draft, June 20, 1993. Traded to **St. Louis** by **San Jose** with a conditional choice in 1997 Entry Draft for Craig Janney and cash, March 6, 1995. Traded to **Edmonton** by **St. Louis** with Donald Dufresne for Igor Kravchuk and Ken Sutton, January 4, 1996. Traded to **Tampa Bay** by **Edmonton** for Drew Bannister and Tampa Bay's sixth round choice (Peter Sarno) in 1997 Entry Draft, March 18, 1997.

NOVOSELTSEV, IVAN (noh-voh-SEHLT-sehv, ee-VAHN) — FLA.

Right wing. Shoots left. 6'1", 183 lbs. Born, Golitsino, USSR, January 23, 1979.
(Florida's 5th choice, 95th overall, in 1997 Entry Draft).

			Regular Season					Playoffs				
Season	Club	Lea	GP	G	A	TP	PIM	GP	G	A	TP	PIM
1995-96	Soviet Wings	CIS	1	0	0	0	2	....	....	....	....	....
1996-97	Soviet Wings	Rus.	30	0	3	3	18	2	0	0	0	4
	Sov. Wings 2	Rus. 3	19	5	3	8	39	....	....	....	....	....

NUMMINEN, TEPPO (NOO-mih-nehn, TEH-poh) — PHO.

Defense. Shoots right. 6'1", 190 lbs. Born, Tampere, Finland, July 3, 1968.
(Winnipeg's 2nd choice, 29th overall, in 1986 Entry Draft).

			Regular Season					Playoffs				
Season	Club	Lea	GP	G	A	TP	PIM	GP	G	A	TP	PIM
1985-86	Tappara	Fin.	31	2	4	6	6	8	0	0	0	0
1986-87	Tappara	Fin.	44	9	9	18	16	9	4	1	5	4
1987-88	Tappara	Fin.	40	10	10	20	29	10	6	6	12	6
1988-89	**Winnipeg**	**NHL**	**69**	**1**	**14**	**15**	**36**	....	....	....	....	....
1989-90	**Winnipeg**	**NHL**	**79**	**11**	**32**	**43**	**20**	**7**	**1**	**2**	**3**	**10**
1990-91	**Winnipeg**	**NHL**	**80**	**8**	**25**	**33**	**28**	....	....	....	....	....
1991-92	**Winnipeg**	**NHL**	**80**	**5**	**34**	**39**	**32**	**7**	**0**	**0**	**0**	**0**
1992-93	**Winnipeg**	**NHL**	**66**	**7**	**30**	**37**	**33**	**6**	**1**	**1**	**2**	**2**
1993-94	**Winnipeg**	**NHL**	**57**	**5**	**18**	**23**	**28**	....	....	....	....	....
1994-95	TuTo	Fin.	12	3	8	11	4	....	....	....	....	....
	Winnipeg	**NHL**	**42**	**5**	**16**	**21**	**16**	....	....	....	....	....
1995-96	**Winnipeg**	**NHL**	**74**	**11**	**43**	**54**	**22**	**6**	**0**	**0**	**0**	**2**
1996-97	**Phoenix**	**NHL**	**82**	**2**	**25**	**27**	**28**	**7**	**3**	**3**	**6**	**0**
	NHL Totals		**629**	**55**	**237**	**292**	**243**	**33**	**5**	**6**	**11**	**14**

NURMINEN, KAI (NUHR-mih-nehn, KIGH)

Left wing. Shoots left. 6'1", 198 lbs. Born, Turku, Finland, March 29, 1969.
(Los Angeles' 9th choice, 193rd overall, in 1996 Entry Draft).

			Regular Season					Playoffs				
Season	Club	Lea	GP	G	A	TP	PIM	GP	G	A	TP	PIM
1990-91	TuTo	Fin. 2	33	26	20	46	14	....	....	....	....	....
1991-92	Kiekko-67	Fin. 2	44	44	19	63	34	....	....	....	....	....
1992-93	TPS	Fin.	31	4	6	10	13	7	1	2	3	0
	Kiekko-67	Fin. 2	8	6	4	10	2	....	....	....	....	....
1993-94	TPS	Fin.	45	23	12	35	20	11	0	3	3	4
1994-95	HPK	Fin.	49	30	25	55	40	....	....	....	....	....
1995-96	HV 71	Fin.	40	31	24	55	30	4	3	1	4	8
1996-97	**Los Angeles**	**NHL**	**67**	**16**	**11**	**27**	**22**	....	....	....	....	....
	NHL Totals		**67**	**16**	**11**	**27**	**22**	....	....	....	....	....

NUUTINEN, SAMI (NOO-tih-nehn) — EDM.

Defense. Shoots left. 6'1", 189 lbs. Born, Espoo, Finland, June 11, 1971.
(Edmonton's 11th choice, 248th overall, in 1990 Entry Draft).

			Regular Season					Playoffs				
Season	Club	Lea	GP	G	A	TP	PIM	GP	G	A	TP	PIM
1988-89	Espoo	Fin. 2	39	18	10	28	46	....	....	....	....	....
1989-90	Espoo	Fin. 2	40	8	15	23	....	....	....	....	....	....
1990-91	K-Kissat	Fin. 2	3	1	0	1	0	....	....	....	....	....
	HIFK	Fin.	27	1	3	4	6	3	0	0	0	0
1991-92	HIFK	Fin.	44	5	6	11	10	9	0	1	1	4
1992-93	Kiekko-Espoo	Fin.	48	7	11	18	59	....	....	....	....	....
1993-94	Kiekko-Espoo	Fin.	46	9	15	24	36	....	....	....	....	....
1994-95	Kiekko-Espoo	Fin.	50	8	24	32	38	4	0	1	1	0
1995-96	Kiekko-Espoo	Fin.	49	7	7	14	54	....	....	....	....	....
1996-97	Vasteras	Swe.	50	7	7	14	22	....	....	....	....	....

NYLANDER, MICHAEL (NEE-lan-duhr) — CGY.

Center. Shoots left. 5'11", 190 lbs. Born, Stockholm, Sweden, October 3, 1972.
(Hartford's 4th choice, 59th overall, in 1991 Entry Draft).

			Regular Season					Playoffs				
Season	Club	Lea	GP	G	A	TP	PIM	GP	G	A	TP	PIM
1989-90	Huddinge	Swe. 2	31	7	15	22	4	....	....	....	....	....
1990-91	Huddinge	Swe. 2	33	14	20	34	10	....	....	....	....	....
1991-92	AIK	Swe.	40	11	17	28	30	3	1	4	5	4
1992-93	**Hartford**	**NHL**	**59**	**11**	**22**	**33**	**36**	....	....	....	....	....
	Springfield	AHL	....	....	....	....	....	3	3	3	6	2
1993-94	**Hartford**	**NHL**	**58**	**11**	**33**	**44**	**24**	....	....	....	....	....
	Springfield	AHL	4	0	9	9	0	....	....	....	....	....
	Calgary	**NHL**	**15**	**2**	**9**	**11**	**6**	**3**	**0**	**0**	**0**	**0**
1994-95	JyP HT	Fin.	16	11	19	30	63	....	....	....	....	....
	Calgary	**NHL**	**6**	**0**	**1**	**1**	**2**	**6**	**0**	**6**	**6**	**2**
1995-96	**Calgary**	**NHL**	**73**	**17**	**38**	**55**	**20**	**4**	**0**	**0**	**0**	**0**
1996-97	Lugano	Switz.	36	12	43	55	28	8	3	8	11	8
	NHL Totals		**211**	**41**	**103**	**144**	**88**	**13**	**0**	**6**	**6**	**2**

Traded to **Calgary** by **Hartford** with James Patrick and Zarley Zalapski for Gary Suter, Paul Ranheim and Ted Drury, March 10, 1994.

OATES, ADAM — WSH.

Center. Shoots right. 5'11", 185 lbs. Born, Weston, Ont., August 27, 1962.

			Regular Season					Playoffs				
Season	Club	Lea	GP	G	A	TP	PIM	GP	G	A	TP	PIM
1982-83	RPI	ECAC	22	9	33	42	8	....	....	....	....	....
1983-84	RPI	ECAC	38	26	57	83	15	....	....	....	....	....
1984-85ab	RPI	ECAC	38	31	60	91	29	....	....	....	....	....
1985-86	**Detroit**	**NHL**	**38**	**9**	**11**	**20**	**10**	....	....	....	....	....
	Adirondack	AHL	34	18	28	46	4	17	7	14	21	4
1986-87	**Detroit**	**NHL**	**76**	**15**	**32**	**47**	**21**	**16**	**4**	**7**	**11**	**6**
1987-88	**Detroit**	**NHL**	**63**	**14**	**40**	**54**	**20**	**16**	**8**	**12**	**20**	**6**
1988-89	**Detroit**	**NHL**	**69**	**16**	**62**	**78**	**14**	**6**	**0**	**8**	**8**	**2**
1989-90	**St. Louis**	**NHL**	**80**	**23**	**79**	**102**	**30**	**12**	**2**	**12**	**14**	**4**
1990-91c	**St. Louis**	**NHL**	**61**	**25**	**90**	**115**	**29**	**13**	**7**	**13**	**20**	**10**
1991-92	**St. Louis**	**NHL**	**54**	**10**	**59**	**69**	**12**	....	....	....	....	....
	Boston	**NHL**	**26**	**10**	**20**	**30**	**10**	**15**	**5**	**14**	**19**	**4**
1992-93	**Boston**	**NHL**	**84**	**45**	***97**	**142**	**32**	**4**	**0**	**9**	**9**	**4**
1993-94	**Boston**	**NHL**	**77**	**32**	**80**	**112**	**45**	**13**	**3**	**9**	**12**	**8**
1994-95	**Boston**	**NHL**	**48**	**12**	**41**	**53**	**8**	**5**	**1**	**0**	**1**	**2**
1995-96	**Boston**	**NHL**	**70**	**25**	**67**	**92**	**18**	**5**	**2**	**5**	**7**	**2**
1996-97	**Boston**	**NHL**	**63**	**18**	**52**	**70**	**10**	....	....	....	....	....
	Washington	**NHL**	**17**	**4**	**8**	**12**	**4**	....	....	....	....	....
	NHL Totals		**826**	**258**	**738**	**996**	**263**	**105**	**32**	**89**	**121**	**48**

a ECAC First All-Star Team (1985)
b Named to NCAA All-American Team (1985)
c NHL Second All-Star Team (1991)

Played in NHL All-Star Game (1991-94, 1997)

Signed as a free agent by **Detroit,** June 28, 1985. Traded to **St. Louis** by **Detroit** with Paul MacLean for Bernie Federko and Tony McKegney, June 15, 1989. Traded to **Boston** by **St. Louis** for Craig Janney and Stephane Quintal, February 7, 1992. Traded to **Washington** by **Boston** with Bill Ranford and Rick Tocchet for Jim Carey, Anson Carter, Jason Allison, Washington's third round choice (Lee Goren) in 1997 Entry Draft and a conditional choice in 1998 Entry Draft, March 1, 1997.

O'BRIEN, SEAN — L.A.

Left wing. Shoots left. 6'1", 200 lbs. Born, Belmont, MA, February 9, 1972.

			Regular Season					Playoffs				
Season	Club	Lea	GP	G	A	TP	PIM	GP	G	A	TP	PIM
1990-91	Princeton	ECAC	24	0	6	6	12	....	....	....	....	....
1991-92	Princeton	ECAC	27	3	10	13	38	....	....	....	....	....
1992-93	Princeton	ECAC	29	2	22	24	54	....	....	....	....	....
1993-94	Princeton	ECAC	28	8	15	23	40	....	....	....	....	....
1994-95	Richmond	ECHL	52	5	18	23	147	17	2	5	7	77
	Houston	IHL	13	2	1	3	23	....	....	....	....	....
1995-96	Las Vegas	IHL	1	0	0	0	2	....	....	....	....	....
	Utah	IHL	7	2	2	4	12	....	....	....	....	....
	Houston	IHL	4	0	1	1	12	....	....	....	....	....
	Tallahasee	ECHL	54	9	19	28	179	8	0	2	2	23
1996-97	Tallahassee	ECHL	10	7	3	10	29	....	....	....	....	....
	Utah	IHL	50	21	10	31	135	....	....	....	....	....
	Phoenix	IHL	10	3	3	6	20	....	....	....	....	....

Signed as a free agent by **Los Angeles**, June 26, 1997.

O'CONNELL, ALBERT — NYI

Left wing. Shoots left. 6', 188 lbs. Born, Cambridge, MA, May 20, 1976.
(NY Islanders' 6th choice, 116th overall, in 1994 Entry Draft).

			Regular Season					Playoffs				
Season	Club	Lea	GP	G	A	TP	PIM	GP	G	A	TP	PIM
1995-96	Boston U.	H.E.	38	9	8	17	34	....	....	....	....	....
1996-97	Boston U.	H.E.	41	12	12	24	72	....	....	....	....	....

ODELEIN, LYLE — (OH-duh-LIGHN) — N.J.

Defense. Shoots right. 5'11", 210 lbs. Born, Quill Lake, Sask., July 21, 1968.
(Montreal's 8th choice, 141st overall, in 1986 Entry Draft).

			Regular Season					Playoffs				
Season	Club	Lea	GP	G	A	TP	PIM	GP	G	A	TP	PIM
1985-86	Moose Jaw	WHL	67	9	37	46	117	13	1	6	7	34
1986-87	Moose Jaw	WHL	59	9	50	59	70	9	2	5	7	26
1987-88	Moose Jaw	WHL	63	15	43	58	166	....	....	....	....	....
1988-89	Sherbrooke	AHL	33	3	4	7	120	3	0	2	2	5
	Peoria	IHL	36	2	8	10	116	....	....	....	....	....
1989-90	**Montreal**	**NHL**	**8**	**0**	**2**	**2**	**33**	....	....	....	....	....
	Sherbrooke	AHL	68	7	24	31	265	12	6	5	11	79
1990-91	**Montreal**	**NHL**	**52**	**0**	**2**	**2**	**259**	**12**	**0**	**0**	**0**	**54**
1991-92	**Montreal**	**NHL**	**71**	**1**	**7**	**8**	**212**	**7**	**0**	**0**	**0**	**11**
1992-93	**Montreal**	**NHL**	**83**	**2**	**14**	**16**	**205**	**20**	**1**	**5**	**6**	**30** ♦
1993-94	**Montreal**	**NHL**	**79**	**11**	**29**	**40**	**276**	**7**	**0**	**0**	**0**	**17**
1994-95	**Montreal**	**NHL**	**48**	**3**	**7**	**10**	**152**	....	....	....	....	....
1995-96	**Montreal**	**NHL**	**79**	**3**	**14**	**17**	**230**	**6**	**1**	**1**	**2**	**6**
1996-97	**New Jersey**	**NHL**	**79**	**3**	**13**	**16**	**110**	**10**	**2**	**2**	**4**	**19**
	NHL Totals		**499**	**23**	**88**	**111**	**1477**	**62**	**4**	**8**	**12**	**137**

Traded to **New Jersey** by **Montreal** for Stephane Richer, August 22, 1996.

ODGERS, JEFF — (AWD-juhrs) — BOS.

Right wing. Shoots right. 6', 200 lbs. Born, Spy Hill, Sask., May 31, 1969.

			Regular Season					Playoffs				
Season	Club	Lea	GP	G	A	TP	PIM	GP	G	A	TP	PIM
1986-87	Brandon	WHL	70	7	14	21	150	....	....	....	....	....
1987-88	Brandon	WHL	70	17	18	35	202	4	1	1	2	14
1988-89	Brandon	WHL	71	31	29	60	277	....	....	....	....	....
1989-90	Brandon	WHL	64	37	28	65	209	....	....	....	....	....
1990-91	Kansas City	IHL	77	12	19	31	318	....	....	....	....	....
1991-92	**San Jose**	**NHL**	**61**	**7**	**4**	**11**	**217**	....	....	....	....	....
	Kansas City	IHL	12	2	2	4	56	4	2	1	3	0
1992-93	**San Jose**	**NHL**	**66**	**12**	**15**	**27**	**253**	....	....	....	....	....
1993-94	**San Jose**	**NHL**	**81**	**13**	**8**	**21**	**222**	**11**	**0**	**0**	**0**	**11**
1994-95	**San Jose**	**NHL**	**48**	**4**	**3**	**7**	**117**	**11**	**1**	**1**	**2**	**23**
1995-96	**San Jose**	**NHL**	**78**	**12**	**4**	**16**	**192**	....	....	....	....	....
1996-97	**Boston**	**NHL**	**80**	**7**	**8**	**15**	**197**	....	....	....	....	....
	NHL Totals		**414**	**55**	**42**	**97**	**1198**	**22**	**1**	**1**	**2**	**34**

Signed as a free agent by **San Jose**, September 3, 1991. Traded to **Boston** by **San Jose** with Pittsburgh's fifth round choice (previously acquired by San Jose — Boston selected Elias Abrahamsson) in 1996 Entry Draft for Al Iafrate, June 21, 1996.

ODJICK, GINO — (OH-jihk) — VAN.

Left wing. Shoots left. 6'3", 210 lbs. Born, Maniwaki, Que., September 7, 1970.
(Vancouver's 5th choice, 86th overall, in 1990 Entry Draft).

			Regular Season					Playoffs				
Season	Club	Lea	GP	G	A	TP	PIM	GP	G	A	TP	PIM
1988-89	Laval	QMJHL	50	9	15	24	278	16	0	9	9	129
1989-90	Laval	QMJHL	51	12	26	38	280	....	....	....	....	....
1990-91	**Vancouver**	**NHL**	**45**	**7**	**1**	**8**	**296**	**6**	**0**	**0**	**0**	**18**
	Milwaukee	IHL	17	7	3	10	102	....	....	....	....	....
1991-92	**Vancouver**	**NHL**	**65**	**4**	**6**	**10**	**348**	**4**	**0**	**0**	**0**	**6**
1992-93	**Vancouver**	**NHL**	**75**	**4**	**13**	**17**	**370**	**1**	**0**	**0**	**0**	**0**
1993-94	**Vancouver**	**NHL**	**76**	**16**	**13**	**29**	**271**	**10**	**0**	**0**	**0**	**18**
1994-95	**Vancouver**	**NHL**	**23**	**4**	**5**	**9**	**109**	**5**	**0**	**0**	**0**	**47**
1995-96	**Vancouver**	**NHL**	**55**	**3**	**4**	**7**	**181**	**6**	**3**	**1**	**4**	**6**
1996-97	**Vancouver**	**NHL**	**70**	**5**	**8**	**13**	***371**	....	....	....	....	....
	NHL Totals		**409**	**43**	**50**	**93**	**1946**	**32**	**3**	**1**	**4**	**95**

O'DONNELL, SEAN — L.A.

Defense. Shoots left. 6'3", 225 lbs. Born, Ottawa, Ont., October 13, 1971.
(Buffalo's 6th choice, 123rd overall, in 1991 Entry Draft).

			Regular Season					Playoffs				
Season	Club	Lea	GP	G	A	TP	PIM	GP	G	A	TP	PIM
1990-91	Sudbury	OHL	66	8	23	31	114	5	1	4	5	10
1991-92	Rochester	AHL	73	4	9	13	193	16	1	2	3	21
1992-93	Rochester	AHL	74	3	18	21	203	17	1	6	7	38
1993-94	Rochester	AHL	64	2	10	12	242	4	0	1	1	21
1994-95	Phoenix	IHL	61	2	18	20	132	9	0	1	1	21
	Los Angeles	**NHL**	**15**	**0**	**2**	**2**	**49**	....	....	....	....	....
1995-96	**Los Angeles**	**NHL**	**71**	**2**	**5**	**7**	**127**	....	....	....	....	....
1996-97	**Los Angeles**	**NHL**	**55**	**5**	**12**	**17**	**144**	....	....	....	....	....
	NHL Totals		**141**	**7**	**19**	**26**	**320**	....	....	....	....	....

Traded to **Los Angeles** by **Buffalo** for Doug Houda, July 26, 1994.

ODUYA, FREDRIK — (oh-DOO-yuh) — S.J.

Defense. Shoots left. 6'3", 200 lbs. Born, Stockholm, Sweden, May 31, 1975.
(San Jose's 8th choice, 154th overall, in 1993 Entry Draft).

			Regular Season					Playoffs				
Season	Club	Lea	GP	G	A	TP	PIM	GP	G	A	TP	PIM
1992-93	Guelph	OHL	23	2	4	6	29	....	....	....	....	....
	Ottawa	OHL	17	0	3	3	70	....	....	....	....	....
1993-94	Ottawa	OHL	51	11	12	23	181	17	0	3	3	22
1994-95	Ottawa	OHL	61	2	13	15	175	....	....	....	....	....
1995-96	Kansas City	IHL	56	2	6	8	235	3	0	0	0	2
1996-97	Kentucky	AHL	69	2	9	11	241	....	....	....	....	....

O'GRADY, MIKE — FLA.

Defense. Shoots left. 6'3", 227 lbs. Born, Neilburg, Sask., March 22, 1977.
(Florida's 3rd choice, 62nd overall, in 1995 Entry Draft).

			Regular Season					Playoffs				
Season	Club	Lea	GP	G	A	TP	PIM	GP	G	A	TP	PIM
1993-94	Saskatoon	WHL	13	0	1	1	29	....	....	....	....	....
1994-95	Saskatoon	WHL	39	0	7	7	157	....	....	....	....	....
	Lethbridge	WHL	21	1	2	3	124	....	....	....	....	....
1995-96	Lethbridge	WHL	61	2	9	11	242	4	1	0	1	8
1996-97	Lethbridge	WHL	61	8	25	33	262	18	1	5	6	41

OHLUND, MATTIAS — (OH-luhnd) — VAN.

Defense. Shoots left. 6'3", 209 lbs. Born, Pitea, Sweden, September 9, 1976.
(Vancouver's 1st choice, 13th overall, in 1994 Entry Draft).

			Regular Season					Playoffs				
Season	Club	Lea	GP	G	A	TP	PIM	GP	G	A	TP	PIM
1992-93	Pitea	Swe. 2	22	0	6	6	16	....	....	....	....	....
1993-94	Pitea	Swe. 2	28	7	10	17	62	....	....	....	....	....
1994-95	Lulea	Swe.	34	6	10	16	34	9	4	0	4	16
1995-96	Lulea	Swe.	38	4	10	14	26	13	1	0	1	47
1996-97	Lulea	Swe.	47	7	9	16	38	10	1	2	3	8

OKSIUTA, ROMAN — (ohk-SEW-tah) — PIT.

Right wing. Shoots left. 6'3", 230 lbs. Born, Murmansk, USSR, August 21, 1970.
(NY Rangers' 11th choice, 202nd overall, in 1989 Entry Draft).

			Regular Season					Playoffs				
Season	Club	Lea	GP	G	A	TP	PIM	GP	G	A	TP	PIM
1987-88	Khimik	USSR	11	1	0	1	4	....	....	....	....	....
1988-89	Khimik	USSR	34	13	3	16	14	....	....	....	....	....
1989-90	Khimik	USSR	37	13	6	19	16	....	....	....	....	....
1990-91	Khimik	USSR	41	12	8	20	24	....	....	....	....	....
1991-92	Khimik	CIS	42	24	20	44	28	....	....	....	....	....
1992-93	Khimik	CIS	20	11	2	13	42	....	....	....	....	....
	Cape Breton	AHL	43	26	25	51	22	16	9	19	28	12
1993-94	**Edmonton**	**NHL**	**10**	**1**	**2**	**3**	**4**	....	....	....	....	....
	Cape Breton	AHL	47	31	22	53	90	4	2	2	4	22
1994-95	Cape Breton	AHL	25	9	7	16	20	....	....	....	....	....
	Edmonton	**NHL**	**26**	**11**	**2**	**13**	**8**	....	....	....	....	....
	Vancouver	**NHL**	**12**	**5**	**2**	**7**	**2**	**10**	**2**	**3**	**5**	**0**
1995-96	**Vancouver**	**NHL**	**56**	**16**	**23**	**39**	**42**	....	....	....	....	....
	Anaheim	**NHL**	**14**	**7**	**5**	**12**	**18**	....	....	....	....	....
1996-97	**Anaheim**	**NHL**	**28**	**6**	**7**	**13**	**22**	....	....	....	....	....
	Pittsburgh	**NHL**	**7**	**0**	**0**	**0**	**4**	....	....	....	....	....
	NHL Totals		**153**	**46**	**41**	**87**	**100**	**10**	**2**	**3**	**5**	**0**

Traded to **Edmonton** by **NY Rangers** with NY Rangers' third round choice (Alexander Kerch) in 1993 Entry Draft for Kevin Lowe, December 11, 1992. Traded to **Vancouver** by **Edmonton** for Jiri Slegr, April 7, 1995. Traded to **Anaheim** by **Vancouver** for Mike Sillinger, March 15, 1996. Traded to **Pittsburgh** by **Anaheim** for Richard Park, March 18, 1997.

OLAUSSON, FREDRIK — (OHL-ah-suhn) — PIT.

Defense. Shoots right. 6'2", 195 lbs. Born, Dadesjo, Sweden, October 5, 1966.
(Winnipeg's 4th choice, 81st overall, in 1985 Entry Draft).

			Regular Season					Playoffs				
Season	Club	Lea	GP	G	A	TP	PIM	GP	G	A	TP	PIM
1982-83	Nybro	Swe. 2	31	4	4	8	12	....	....	....	....	....
1983-84	Nybro	Swe. 2	28	8	14	22	32	....	....	....	....	....
1984-85	Farjestad	Swe.	29	5	12	17	22	3	1	0	1	0
1985-86	Farjestad	Swe.	33	4	12	16	22	8	3	2	5	6
1986-87	**Winnipeg**	**NHL**	**72**	**7**	**29**	**36**	**24**	**10**	**2**	**3**	**5**	**4**
1987-88	**Winnipeg**	**NHL**	**38**	**5**	**10**	**15**	**18**	**5**	**1**	**1**	**2**	**0**
1988-89	**Winnipeg**	**NHL**	**75**	**15**	**47**	**62**	**32**	....	....	....	....	....
1989-90	**Winnipeg**	**NHL**	**77**	**9**	**46**	**55**	**32**	**7**	**0**	**2**	**2**	**2**
1990-91	**Winnipeg**	**NHL**	**71**	**12**	**29**	**41**	**24**	....	....	....	....	....
1991-92	**Winnipeg**	**NHL**	**77**	**20**	**42**	**62**	**34**	**7**	**1**	**5**	**6**	**4**
1992-93	**Winnipeg**	**NHL**	**68**	**16**	**41**	**57**	**22**	**6**	**0**	**2**	**2**	**2**
1993-94	**Winnipeg**	**NHL**	**18**	**2**	**5**	**7**	**10**	....	....	....	....	....
	Edmonton	**NHL**	**55**	**9**	**19**	**28**	**20**	....	....	....	....	....
1994-95	Ehrwald	Aus.	10	4	3	7	8	....	....	....	....	....
	Edmonton	**NHL**	**33**	**0**	**10**	**10**	**20**	....	....	....	....	....
1995-96	**Edmonton**	**NHL**	**20**	**0**	**6**	**6**	**14**	....	....	....	....	....
	Anaheim	**NHL**	**36**	**2**	**16**	**18**	**24**	....	....	....	....	....
1996-97	**Anaheim**	**NHL**	**20**	**2**	**9**	**11**	**8**	....	....	....	....	....
	Pittsburgh	**NHL**	**51**	**7**	**20**	**27**	**24**	**4**	**0**	**1**	**1**	**0**
	NHL Totals		**711**	**106**	**329**	**435**	**306**	**39**	**4**	**14**	**18**	**12**

Traded to **Edmonton** by **Winnipeg** with Winnipeg's seventh round choice (Curtis Sheptak) in 1994 Entry Draft for Edmonton's third round choice (Tavis Hansen) in 1994 Entry Draft, December 6, 1993. Claimed on waivers by **Anaheim** from **Edmonton**, January 16, 1996. Traded to **Pittsburgh** by **Anaheim** with Alex Hicks for Shawn Antoski and Dmitri Mironov, November 19, 1996.

OLCZYK, EDDIE (OHL-chehk) PIT.

Center. Shoots left. 6'1", 205 lbs. Born, Chicago, IL, August 16, 1966.
(Chicago's 1st choice, 3rd overall, in 1984 Entry Draft).

			Regular Season					Playoffs				
Season	Club	Lea	GP	G	A	TP	PIM	GP	G	A	TP	PIM
1983-84	U.S. National	....	62	21	47	68	36	....	....	....	....	....
1984-85	Chicago	NHL	70	20	30	50	67	15	6	5	11	11
1985-86	Chicago	NHL	79	29	50	79	47	3	0	0	0	0
1986-87	Chicago	NHL	79	16	35	51	119	4	1	1	2	4
1987-88	Toronto	NHL	80	42	33	75	55	6	5	4	9	2
1988-89	Toronto	NHL	80	38	52	90	75	....	....	....	....	....
1989-90	Toronto	NHL	79	32	56	88	78	5	1	2	3	14
1990-91	Toronto	NHL	18	4	10	14	13	....	....	....	....	....
	Winnipeg	NHL	61	26	31	57	69	....	....	....	....	....
1991-92	Winnipeg	NHL	64	32	33	65	67	6	2	1	3	4
1992-93	Winnipeg	NHL	25	8	12	20	26	....	....	....	....	....
	NY Rangers	NHL	46	13	16	29	26	....	....	....	....	....
1993-94	NY Rangers	NHL	37	3	5	8	28	1	0	0	0	0 ♦
1994-95	NY Rangers	NHL	20	2	1	3	4	....	....	....	....	....
	Winnipeg	NHL	13	2	8	10	8	....	....	....	....	....
1995-96	Winnipeg	NHL	51	27	22	49	65	6	1	2	3	6
1996-97	Los Angeles	NHL	67	21	23	44	45	....	....	....	....	....
	Pittsburgh	NHL	12	4	7	11	6	5	1	0	1	12
	NHL Totals		881	319	424	743	798	51	17	15	32	53

Traded to **Toronto** by **Chicago** with Al Secord for Rick Vaive, Steve Thomas and Bob McGill, September 3, 1987. Traded to **Winnipeg** by **Toronto** with Mark Osborne for Dave Ellett and Paul Fenton, November 10, 1990. Traded to **NY Rangers** by **Winnipeg** for Kris King and Tie Domi, December 28, 1992. Traded to **Winnipeg** by **NY Rangers** for Winnipeg's fifth round choice (Alexei Vasiliev) in 1995 Entry Draft, April 7, 1995. Signed as a free agent by **Los Angeles**, July 8, 1996. Traded to **Pittsburgh** by **Los Angeles** for Glen Murray, March 18, 1997.

OLIVER, DAVID

Right wing. Shoots right. 6', 190 lbs. Born, Sechelt, B.C., April 17, 1971.
(Edmonton's 7th choice, 144th overall, in 1991 Entry Draft).

			Regular Season					Playoffs				
Season	Club	Lea	GP	G	A	TP	PIM	GP	G	A	TP	PIM
1990-91	U. of Michigan	CCHA	27	13	11	24	34	....	....	....	....	....
1991-92	U. of Michigan	CCHA	44	31	27	58	32	....	....	....	....	....
1992-93a	U. of Michigan	CCHA	40	35	20	55	18	....	....	....	....	....
1993-94bc	U. of Michigan	CCHA	41	28	40	68	16	....	....	....	....	....
1994-95	Cape Breton	AHL	32	11	18	29	8	....	....	....	....	....
	Edmonton	NHL	44	16	14	30	20	....	....	....	....	....
1995-96	Edmonton	NHL	80	20	19	39	34	....	....	....	....	....
1996-97	Edmonton	NHL	17	1	2	3	4	....	....	....	....	....
	NY Rangers	NHL	14	2	1	3	4	3	0	0	0	0
	NHL Totals		155	39	36	75	62	3	0	0	0	0

a CCHA Second All-Star Team (1993)
b CCHA First All-Star Team (1994)
c NCAA West First All-American Team (1994)

Claimed on waivers by **NY Rangers** from **Edmonton**, February 21, 1997.

OLIWA, KRZYSZTOF (oh-LEE-vuh, KHRIH-stahf) N.J.

Left wing. Shoots left. 6'5", 235 lbs. Born, Tychy, Poland, April 12, 1973.
(New Jersey's 4th choice, 65th overall, in 1993 Entry Draft).

			Regular Season					Playoffs				
Season	Club	Lea	GP	G	A	TP	PIM	GP	G	A	TP	PIM
1991-92	GKS Tychy	Poland	10	3	7	10	6	....	....	....	....	....
1992-93	Welland	Jr. B	30	13	21	34	127	....	....	....	....	....
1993-94	Albany	AHL	33	2	4	6	151	....	....	....	....	....
	Raleigh	ECHL	15	0	2	2	65	9	0	0	0	35
1994-95	Albany	AHL	20	1	1	2	77	....	....	....	....	....
	Saint John	AHL	14	1	4	5	79	....	....	....	....	....
	Raleigh	ECHL	5	0	2	2	32	....	....	....	....	....
	Detroit	IHL	4	0	1	1	24	....	....	....	....	....
1995-96	Albany	AHL	51	5	11	16	217	....	....	....	....	....
	Raleigh	ECHL	9	1	0	1	53	....	....	....	....	....
1996-97	New Jersey	NHL	1	0	0	0	5	....	....	....	....	....
	Albany	AHL	60	13	14	27	322	15	7	1	8	49
	NHL Totals		1	0	0	0	5	....	....	....	....	....

OLSON, BOYD MTL.

Center. Shoots left. 6'1", 173 lbs. Born, Edmonton, Alta., April 4, 1976.
(Montreal's 6th choice, 138th overall, in 1995 Entry Draft).

			Regular Season					Playoffs				
Season	Club	Lea	GP	G	A	TP	PIM	GP	G	A	TP	PIM
1993-94	Tri-City	WHL	2	0	1	1	0	....	....	....	....	....
1994-95	Tri-City	WHL	69	16	16	32	87	17	6	2	8	22
1995-96	Tri-City	WHL	62	13	12	25	105	11	1	4	5	16
	Fredericton	AHL	....	....	....	....	....	2	1	0	1	0
1996-97	Fredericton	AHL	74	8	12	20	43	....	....	....	....	....

OLSSON, CHRISTER (OOL-suhn)

Defense. Shoots left. 5'11", 190 lbs. Born, Arboga, Sweden, July 24, 1970.
(St. Louis' 10th choice, 275th overall, in 1993 Entry Draft).

			Regular Season					Playoffs				
Season	Club	Lea	GP	G	A	TP	PIM	GP	G	A	TP	PIM
1991-92	Mora	Swe. 2	36	6	10	16	38	....	....	....	....	....
1992-93	Brynas	Swe.	22	4	4	8	18	....	....	....	....	....
1993-94	Brynas	Swe.	38	7	3	10	50	7	0	3	3	6
1994-95	Brynas	Swe.	39	6	5	11	18	14	1	3	4	8
1995-96	St. Louis	NHL	26	2	8	10	14	3	0	0	0	0
	Worcester	AHL	39	7	7	14	22	....	....	....	....	....
1996-97	St. Louis	NHL	5	0	1	1	0	....	....	....	....	....
	Worcester	AHL	2	0	0	0	0	....	....	....	....	....
	Ottawa	NHL	25	2	3	5	10	....	....	....	....	....
	NHL Totals		56	4	12	16	24	3	0	0	0	0

Traded to **Ottawa** by **St. Louis** for Pavol Demitra, November 27, 1996.

O'NEILL, JEFF CAR.

Center. Shoots right. 6'1", 190 lbs. Born, Richmond Hill, Ont., February 23, 1976.
(Hartford's 1st choice, 5th overall, in 1994 Entry Draft).

			Regular Season					Playoffs				
Season	Club	Lea	GP	G	A	TP	PIM	GP	G	A	TP	PIM
1992-93	Guelph	OHL	65	32	47	79	88	5	2	2	4	6
1993-94	Guelph	OHL	66	45	81	126	95	9	2	11	13	31
1994-95a	Guelph	OHL	57	43	81	124	56	14	8	18	26	34
1995-96	Hartford	NHL	65	8	19	27	40	....	....	....	....	....
1996-97	Hartford	NHL	72	14	16	30	40	....	....	....	....	....
	Springfield	AHL	1	0	0	0	0	....	....	....	....	....
	NHL Totals		137	22	35	57	80	....	....	....	....	....

a OHL First All-Star Team (1995)

OREKHOVSKY, OLEG (oh-reh-KHOHV-skee) WSH.

Defense. Shoots right. 6', 183 lbs. Born, Krasnoyarsk, USSR, November 3, 1977.
(Washington's 11th choice, 206th overall, in 1996 Entry Draft).

			Regular Season					Playoffs				
Season	Club	Lea	GP	G	A	TP	PIM	GP	G	A	TP	PIM
1994-95	Moscow D'amo	CIS	30	0	1	1	18	....	....	....	....	....
1995-96	Moscow D'amo	CIS	22	1	2	3	14	8	0	0	0	6
1996-97	Moscow D'amo	Rus.	32	4	2	6	16	4	2	1	3	2

ORSZAGH, VLADIMIR (OHR-sahk) NYI

Right wing. Shoots left. 5'11", 173 lbs. Born, Banska Bystrica, Czech., May 24, 1977.
(NY Islanders' 4th choice, 106th overall, in 1995 Entry Draft).

			Regular Season					Playoffs				
Season	Club	Lea	GP	G	A	TP	PIM	GP	G	A	TP	PIM
1994-95	B. Bystrica	Slov. 2	38	18	12	30	....	....	....	....	....	....
1995-96	B. Bystrica	Slovak	31	9	5	14	22	....	....	....	....	....
1996-97	Utah	IHL	68	12	15	27	30	3	0	1	1	4

O'SULLIVAN, CHRIS CGY.

Defense. Shoots left. 6'2", 185 lbs. Born, Dorchester, MA, May 15, 1974.
(Calgary's 2nd choice, 30th overall, in 1992 Entry Draft).

			Regular Season					Playoffs				
Season	Club	Lea	GP	G	A	TP	PIM	GP	G	A	TP	PIM
1992-93	Boston U.	H.E.	5	0	2	2	4	....	....	....	....	....
1993-94	Boston U.	H.E.	32	5	18	23	25	....	....	....	....	....
1994-95abcd	Boston U.	H.E.	40	23	33	56	48	....	....	....	....	....
1995-96	Boston U.	H.E.	37	12	35	47	50	....	....	....	....	....
1996-97	Calgary	NHL	27	2	8	10	2	....	....	....	....	....
	Saint John	AHL	29	3	8	11	17	5	0	4	4	0
	NHL Totals		27	2	8	10	2	....	....	....	....	....

a Hockey East First All-Star Team (1995)
b NCAA East Second All-American Team (1995)
c NCAA Final Four All-Tournament Team (1995)
d NCAA Final Four Tournament Most Valuable Player (1995)

OTTO, JOEL PHI.

Center. Shoots right. 6'4", 220 lbs. Born, Elk River, MN, October 29, 1961.

			Regular Season					Playoffs				
Season	Club	Lea	GP	G	A	TP	PIM	GP	G	A	TP	PIM
1980-81	Bemidji State	NCAA	23	5	11	16	10	....	....	....	....	....
1981-82	Bemidji State	NCAA	31	19	33	52	24	....	....	....	....	....
1982-83	Bemidji State	NCAA	37	33	28	61	68	....	....	....	....	....
1983-84	Bemidji State	NCAA	31	32	43	75	32	....	....	....	....	....
1984-85	Calgary	NHL	17	4	8	12	30	3	2	1	3	10
	Moncton	AHL	56	27	36	63	89	....	....	....	....	....
1985-86	Calgary	NHL	79	25	34	59	188	22	5	10	15	80
1986-87	Calgary	NHL	68	19	31	50	185	2	0	2	2	6
1987-88	Calgary	NHL	62	13	39	52	194	9	3	2	5	26
1988-89	Calgary	NHL	72	23	30	53	213	22	6	13	19	46 ♦
1989-90	Calgary	NHL	75	13	20	33	116	6	2	2	4	2
1990-91	Calgary	NHL	76	19	20	39	183	7	1	2	3	8
1991-92	Calgary	NHL	78	13	21	34	161	....	....	....	....	....
1992-93	Calgary	NHL	75	19	33	52	150	6	4	2	6	4
1993-94	Calgary	NHL	81	11	12	23	92	3	0	1	1	4
1994-95	Calgary	NHL	47	8	13	21	130	7	0	3	3	2
1995-96	Philadelphia	NHL	67	12	29	41	115	12	3	4	7	11
1996-97	Philadelphia	NHL	78	13	19	32	99	18	1	5	6	8
	NHL Totals		875	192	309	501	1856	117	27	47	74	207

Signed as a free agent by **Calgary**, September 11, 1984. Signed as a free agent by **Philadelphia**, July 31, 1995.

OZOLINSH, SANDIS (OH-zoh-LIHNCH, SAN-dihz) COL.

Defense. Shoots left. 6'1", 195 lbs. Born, Riga, Latvia, August 3, 1972.
(San Jose's 3rd choice, 30th overall, in 1991 Entry Draft).

			Regular Season					Playoffs				
Season	Club	Lea	GP	G	A	TP	PIM	GP	G	A	TP	PIM
1990-91	Riga	USSR	44	0	3	3	51	....	....	....	....	....
1991-92	Riga	CIS	30	6	0	6	42	....	....	....	....	....
	Kansas City	IHL	34	6	9	15	20	15	2	5	7	22
1992-93	San Jose	NHL	37	7	16	23	40	....	....	....	....	....
1993-94	San Jose	NHL	81	26	38	64	24	14	0	10	10	8
1994-95	San Jose	NHL	48	9	16	25	30	11	3	2	5	6
1995-96	San Francisco	IHL	2	1	0	1	0	....	....	....	....	....
	San Jose	NHL	7	1	3	4	4	....	....	....	....	....
	Colorado	NHL	66	13	37	50	50	22	5	14	19	16 ♦
1996-97a	Colorado	NHL	80	23	45	68	88	17	4	13	17	24
	NHL Totals		319	79	155	234	236	64	12	39	51	54

NHL First All-Star Team (1997)

Played in NHL All-Star Game (1994, 1997)

Traded to **Colorado** by **San Jose** for Owen Nolan, October 26, 1995.

PADEN, KEVIN EDM.

Center/Left wing. Shoots left. 6'3", 190 lbs. Born, Woodhaven, MI, February 12, 1975.
(Edmonton's 4th choice, 59th overall, in 1993 Entry Draft).

			Regular Season					Playoffs				
Season	Club	Lea	GP	G	A	TP	PIM	GP	G	A	TP	PIM
1992-93	Detroit	OHL	54	14	9	23	41	15	1	1	2	2
1993-94	Detroit	OHL	38	10	19	29	54	....	....	....	....	....
	Windsor	OHL	24	8	11	19	30	4	0	1	1	4
1994-95	Windsor	OHL	57	15	24	39	50	....	....	....	....	....
1995-96	Cape Breton	AHL	1	1	0	1	0	....	....	....	....	....
	Tallahassee	ECHL	23	3	10	13	49	....	....	....	....	....
	Huntington	ECHL	32	4	5	9	52	....	....	....	....	....
1996-97	Nashville	CHL	23	7	9	16	58	....	....	....	....	....
	Huntington	ECHL	13	7	5	12	26	....	....	....	....	....

PAEK, JIM (PAK)

Defense. Shoots left. 6'1", 195 lbs. Born, Seoul, South Korea, April 7, 1967.
(Pittsburgh's 9th choice, 170th overall, in 1985 Entry Draft).

			Regular Season					Playoffs				
Season	Club	Lea	GP	G	A	TP	PIM	GP	G	A	TP	PIM
1984-85	Oshawa	OHL	54	2	13	15	57	5	1	0	1	9
1985-86	Oshawa	OHL	64	5	21	26	122	6	0	1	1	9
1986-87	Oshawa	OHL	57	5	17	22	75	26	1	14	15	43
1987-88	Muskegon	IHL	82	7	52	59	141	6	0	0	0	29
1988-89	Muskegon	IHL	80	3	54	57	96	14	1	10	11	24
1989-90	Muskegon	IHL	81	9	41	50	115	15	1	10	11	41
1990-91	Cdn. National	....	48	2	12	14	24	....	....	....	....	....
	Pittsburgh	**NHL**	**3**	**0**	**0**	**0**	**9**	**8**	**1**	**0**	**1**	**2 ♦**
1991-92	**Pittsburgh**	**NHL**	**49**	**1**	**7**	**8**	**36**	**19**	**0**	**4**	**4**	**6 ♦**
1992-93	**Pittsburgh**	**NHL**	**77**	**3**	**15**	**18**	**64**	....	....	....	....	....
1993-94	**Pittsburgh**	**NHL**	**41**	**0**	**4**	**4**	**8**	....	....	....	....	....
	Los Angeles	**NHL**	**18**	**1**	**1**	**2**	**10**	....	....	....	....	....
1994-95	**Ottawa**	**NHL**	**29**	**0**	**2**	**2**	**28**	....	....	....	....	....
1995-96	Houston	IHL	25	2	5	7	20	....	....	....	....	....
	Minnesota	IHL	42	1	11	12	54	....	....	....	....	....
1996-97	Manitoba	IHL	9	0	2	2	12	....	....	....	....	....
	Cleveland	IHL	74	3	25	28	36	14	0	1	1	2
	NHL Totals		**217**	**5**	**29**	**34**	**155**	**27**	**1**	**4**	**5**	**8**

Traded to **Los Angeles** by **Pittsburgh** with Marty McSorley for Tomas Sandstrom and Shawn McEachern, February 16, 1994. Traded to **Ottawa** by **Los Angeles** for Ottawa's seventh round choice (Benoit Larose) in 1995 Entry Draft, June 26, 1994.

PAHLSSON, SAMUAL — COL.

Center. Shoots left. 5'11", 187 lbs. Born, Borgsjo, Sweden, December 17, 1977.
(Colorado's 10th choice, 176th overall, in 1996 Entry Draft).

			Regular Season					Playoffs				
Season	Club	Lea	GP	G	A	TP	PIM	GP	G	A	TP	PIM
1994-95	MoDo	Swe.	1	0	0	0	0	....	....	....	....	....
	MoDo	Swe. Jr.	30	10	11	21	26	....	....	....	....	....
1995-96	MoDo	Swe.	36	1	3	4	8	4	0	0	0	0
	MoDo	Swe. Jr.	5	2	6	8	2	....	....	....	....	....
1996-97	MoDo	Swe.	49	8	9	17	83	....	....	....	....	....

PALFFY, ZIGMUND (PAHL-fee) — NYI

Left wing. Shoots left. 5'10", 183 lbs. Born, Skalica, Czech., May 5, 1972.
(NY Islanders' 2nd choice, 26th overall, in 1991 Entry Draft).

			Regular Season					Playoffs				
Season	Club	Lea	GP	G	A	TP	PIM	GP	G	A	TP	PIM
1990-91	Nitra	Czech.	50	34	16	50	18	....	....	....	....	....
1991-92	Dukla Trencin	Czech.	45	41	33	74	36	....	....	....	....	....
1992-93	Dukla Trencin	Czech.	43	38	41	79	....	....	....	....	....	....
1993-94	**NY Islanders**	**NHL**	**5**	**0**	**0**	**0**	**0**	....	....	....	....	....
	Salt Lake	IHL	57	25	32	57	83	....	....	....	....	....
1994-95	Denver	IHL	33	20	23	43	40	....	....	....	....	....
	NY Islanders	**NHL**	**33**	**10**	**7**	**17**	**6**	....	....	....	....	....
1995-96	**NY Islanders**	**NHL**	**81**	**43**	**44**	**87**	**56**	....	....	....	....	....
1996-97	Dukla Trencin	Slovak	1	0	0	0		....	....	....	....	....
	NY Islanders	**NHL**	**80**	**48**	**42**	**90**	**43**	....	....	....	....	....
	NHL Totals		**199**	**101**	**93**	**194**	**105**	....	....	....	....	....

PANDOLFO, JAY (pan-DAHL-foh) — N.J.

Left wing. Shoots left. 6'1", 195 lbs. Born, Winchester, MA, December 27, 1974.
(New Jersey's 2nd choice, 32nd overall, in 1993 Entry Draft).

			Regular Season					Playoffs				
Season	Club	Lea	GP	G	A	TP	PIM	GP	G	A	TP	PIM
1992-93	Boston U.	H.E.	37	16	22	38	16	....	....	....	....	....
1993-94	Boston U.	H.E.	37	17	25	42	27	....	....	....	....	....
1994-95	Boston U.	H.E.	20	7	13	20	6	....	....	....	....	....
1995-96ab	Boston U.	H.E.	39	*38	29	67	6	....	....	....	....	....
	Albany	AHL	5	3	1	4	0	3	0	0	0	0
1996-97	**New Jersey**	**NHL**	**46**	**6**	**8**	**14**	**6**	**6**	**0**	**1**	**1**	**0**
	Albany	AHL	12	3	9	12	0	....	....	....	....	....
	NHL Totals		**46**	**6**	**8**	**14**	**6**	**6**	**0**	**1**	**1**	**0**

a Hockey East All-Star Team (1996)
b NCAA East First All-American Team (1996)

PAQUETTE, CHARLES (pa-KEHT) — BOS.

Defense. Shoots left. 6'1", 220 lbs. Born, Lachute, Que., June 17, 1975.
(Boston's 3rd choice, 88th overall, in 1993 Entry Draft).

			Regular Season					Playoffs				
Season	Club	Lea	GP	G	A	TP	PIM	GP	G	A	TP	PIM
1991-92	Trois-Rivieres	QMJHL	60	1	7	8	101	6	0	0	0	2
1992-93	Sherbrooke	QMJHL	54	2	5	7	104	15	0	0	0	33
1993-94	Sherbrooke	QMJHL	63	5	14	19	165	8	0	2	2	15
1994-95a	Sherbrooke	QMJHL	53	15	26	41	186	5	1	1	2	18
1995-96	Providence	AHL	11	0	1	1	8	4	0	1	1	4
	Charlotte	ECHL	45	4	5	9	114	3	0	1	1	6
1996-97	Providence	AHL	18	0	3	3	25	6	0	0	0	8

a QMJHL First All-Star Team (1995)

PARK, RICHARD — ANA.

Center. Shoots right. 5'11", 190 lbs. Born, Seoul, S. Korea, May 27, 1976.
(Pittsburgh's 2nd choice, 50th overall, in 1994 Entry Draft).

			Regular Season					Playoffs				
Season	Club	Lea	GP	G	A	TP	PIM	GP	G	A	TP	PIM
1992-93	Belleville	OHL	66	23	38	61	38	5	0	0	0	14
1993-94	Belleville	OHL	59	27	49	76	70	12	3	5	8	18
1994-95	Belleville	OHL	45	28	51	79	35	16	9	18	27	12
	Pittsburgh	**NHL**	**1**	**0**	**1**	**1**	**2**	**3**	**0**	**0**	**0**	**2**
1995-96	**Pittsburgh**	**NHL**	**56**	**4**	**6**	**10**	**36**	**1**	**0**	**0**	**0**	**0**
	Belleville	OHL	6	7	6	13	2	14	18	12	30	10
1996-97	**Pittsburgh**	**NHL**	**1**	**0**	**0**	**0**	**0**	....	....	....	....	....
	Cleveland	IHL	50	12	15	27	30	....	....	....	....	....
	Anaheim	**NHL**	**11**	**1**	**1**	**2**	**10**	**11**	**0**	**1**	**1**	**2**
	NHL Totals		**69**	**5**	**8**	**13**	**48**	**15**	**0**	**1**	**1**	**4**

Traded to **Anaheim** by **Pittsburgh** for Roman Oksiuta, March 18, 1997.

PARKER, SCOTT — N.J.

Right wing. Shoots right. 6'4", 220 lbs. Born, Hanford, CA, January 29, 1978.
(New Jersey's 6th choice, 63rd overall, in 1996 Entry Draft).

			Regular Season					Playoffs				
Season	Club	Lea	GP	G	A	TP	PIM	GP	G	A	TP	PIM
1995-96	Kelowna	WHL	64	3	4	7	159	6	0	0	0	12
1996-97	Kelowna	WHL	68	18	8	26	*330	6	0	2	2	4

PARRISH, MARK — COL.

Left wing. Shoots right. 6', 182 lbs. Born, Edina, MN, February 2, 1977.
(Colorado's 3rd choice, 79th overall, in 1996 Entry Draft).

			Regular Season					Playoffs				
Season	Club	Lea	GP	G	A	TP	PIM	GP	G	A	TP	PIM
1995-96	St. Cloud	WCHA	39	15	13	28	30	....	....	....	....	....
1996-97a	St. Cloud	WCHA	35	*27	15	42	60	....	....	....	....	....

a NCAA West Second All-American Team (1997)

PARTHENAIS, PAT (PAR-thehn-ay) — FLA.

Defense. Shoots left. 6'4", 212 lbs. Born, Rochester, NY, July 17, 1979.
(Florida's 6th choice, 127th overall, in 1997 Entry Draft).

			Regular Season					Playoffs				
Season	Club	Lea	GP	G	A	TP	PIM	GP	G	A	TP	PIM
1996-97	Detroit	OHL	58	0	4	4	88	5	0	0	0	5

PATRICK, JAMES — CGY.

Defense. Shoots right. 6'2", 198 lbs. Born, Winnipeg, Man., June 14, 1963.
(NY Rangers' 1st choice, 9th overall, in 1981 Entry Draft).

			Regular Season					Playoffs				
Season	Club	Lea	GP	G	A	TP	PIM	GP	G	A	TP	PIM
1981-82ab	North Dakota	WCHA	42	5	24	29	26	....	....	....	....	....
1982-83cd	North Dakota	WCHA	36	12	36	48	29	....	....	....	....	....
1983-84	Cdn. National	....	63	7	24	31	52	....	....	....	....	....
	Cdn. Olympic	....	7	0	3	3	4	....	....	....	....	....
	NY Rangers	**NHL**	**12**	**1**	**7**	**8**	**2**	**5**	**0**	**3**	**3**	**2**
1984-85	**NY Rangers**	**NHL**	**75**	**8**	**28**	**36**	**71**	**3**	**0**	**0**	**0**	**4**
1985-86	**NY Rangers**	**NHL**	**75**	**14**	**29**	**43**	**88**	**16**	**1**	**5**	**6**	**34**
1986-87	**NY Rangers**	**NHL**	**78**	**10**	**45**	**55**	**62**	**6**	**1**	**2**	**3**	**2**
1987-88	**NY Rangers**	**NHL**	**70**	**17**	**45**	**62**	**52**	....	....	....	....	....
1988-89	**NY Rangers**	**NHL**	**68**	**11**	**36**	**47**	**41**	**4**	**0**	**1**	**1**	**2**
1989-90	**NY Rangers**	**NHL**	**73**	**14**	**43**	**57**	**50**	**10**	**3**	**8**	**11**	**0**
1990-91	**NY Rangers**	**NHL**	**74**	**10**	**49**	**59**	**58**	**6**	**0**	**0**	**0**	**6**
1991-92	**NY Rangers**	**NHL**	**80**	**14**	**57**	**71**	**54**	**13**	**0**	**7**	**7**	**12**
1992-93	**NY Rangers**	**NHL**	**60**	**5**	**21**	**26**	**61**	....	....	....	....	....
1993-94	**NY Rangers**	**NHL**	**6**	**0**	**3**	**3**	**2**	....	....	....	....	....
	Hartford	**NHL**	**47**	**8**	**20**	**28**	**32**	....	....	....	....	....
	Calgary	**NHL**	**15**	**2**	**2**	**4**	**6**	**7**	**0**	**1**	**1**	**6**
1994-95	**Calgary**	**NHL**	**43**	**0**	**10**	**10**	**14**	**5**	**0**	**1**	**1**	**0**
1995-96	**Calgary**	**NHL**	**80**	**3**	**32**	**35**	**30**	**4**	**0**	**0**	**0**	**2**
1996-97	**Calgary**	**NHL**	**19**	**3**	**1**	**4**	**6**	....	....	....	....	....
	NHL Totals		**875**	**120**	**428**	**548**	**629**	**79**	**5**	**28**	**33**	**70**

a WCHA Second All-Star Team (1982)
b NCAA All-Tournament Team (1982)
c WCHA First All-Star Team (1983)
d NCAA West All American (1983)

Traded to **Hartford** by **NY Rangers** with Darren Turcotte for Steve Larmer, Nick Kypreos, Barry Richter and Hartford's sixth round choice (Yuri Litvinov) in 1994 Entry Draft, November 2, 1993. Traded to **Calgary** by **Hartford** with Zarley Zalapski and Michael Nylander for Gary Suter, Paul Ranheim and Ted Drury, March 10, 1994.

PATTERSON, ED

Right wing. Shoots right. 6'2", 213 lbs. Born, Delta, B.C., November 14, 1972.
(Pittsburgh's 7th choice, 148th overall, in 1991 Entry Draft).

			Regular Season					Playoffs				
Season	Club	Lea	GP	G	A	TP	PIM	GP	G	A	TP	PIM
1988-89	Seattle	WHL	46	4	6	10	55	....	....	....	....	....
1989-90	Seattle	WHL	18	9	2	11	19	....	....	....	....	....
	Swift Current	WHL	15	1	3	4	0	4	0	0	0	2
1990-91	Swift Current	WHL	7	2	7	9	0	....	....	....	....	....
	Kamloops	WHL	55	14	33	47	134	5	0	0	0	7
1991-92	Kamloops	WHL	38	19	25	44	120	1	0	0	0	0
1992-93	Cleveland	IHL	63	4	16	20	131	3	1	1	2	2
1993-94	**Pittsburgh**	**NHL**	**27**	**3**	**1**	**4**	**10**	....	....	....	....	....
	Cleveland	IHL	55	21	32	53	73	....	....	....	....	....
1994-95	Cleveland	IHL	58	13	17	30	93	4	1	2	3	6
1995-96	**Pittsburgh**	**NHL**	**35**	**0**	**2**	**2**	**38**	....	....	....	....	....
1996-97	**Pittsburgh**	**NHL**	**6**	**0**	**0**	**0**	**8**	....	....	....	....	....
	Cleveland	IHL	40	6	12	18	75	13	2	4	6	61
	NHL Totals		**68**	**3**	**3**	**6**	**56**	....	....	....	....	....

PAUL, JEFF — CHI.

Defense. Shoots right. 6'3", 203 lbs. Born, London, Ont., March 1, 1978.
(Chicago's 2nd choice, 42nd overall, in 1996 Entry Draft).

			Regular Season					Playoffs				
Season	Club	Lea	GP	G	A	TP	PIM	GP	G	A	TP	PIM
1994-95	Niagara Falls	OHL	57	3	10	13	64	6	0	2	2	0
1995-96	Niagara Falls	OHL	48	1	7	8	81	10	0	4	4	37
1996-97	Erie	OHL	60	4	23	27	152	5	2	0	2	12

PAYETTE, ANDRE — PHI.

Center. Shoots left. 6'2", 205 lbs. Born, Cornwall, Ont., July 29, 1976.
(Philadelphia's 9th choice, 244th overall, in 1994 Entry Draft).

			Regular Season					Playoffs				
Season	Club	Lea	GP	G	A	TP	PIM	GP	G	A	TP	PIM
1993-94	S.S. Marie	OHL	40	2	3	5	98	....	....	....	....	....
1994-95	S.S. Marie	OHL	50	15	15	30	177	....	....	....	....	....
1995-96	S.S. Marie	OHL	57	20	19	39	257	4	0	0	0	5
1996-97	S.S. Marie	OHL	4	3	0	3	19	....	....	....	....	....
	Kingston	OHL	29	10	13	23	143	2	0	0	0	2

PAYNE, DAVIS

Left wing. Shoots left. 6'2", 205 lbs. Born, Port Alberni, B.C., September 24, 1970.
(Edmonton's 6th choice, 140th overall, in 1989 Entry Draft).

			Regular Season					Playoffs				
Season	Club	Lea	GP	G	A	TP	PIM	GP	G	A	TP	PIM
1988-89	Michigan Tech	WCHA	35	5	3	8	39					
1989-90	Michigan Tech	WCHA	30	11	10	21	81					
1990-91	Michigan Tech	WCHA	41	15	20	35	82					
1991-92	Michigan Tech	WCHA	24	6	1	7	71					
1992-93	Greensboro	ECHL	57	15	20	35	178	1	0	0	0	4
1993-94	Greensboro	ECHL	36	17	17	34	139	8	2	1	3	27
	Phoenix	IHL	22	6	3	9	51					
	Rochester	AHL	2	0	0	0	5	3	0	2	2	0
1994-95	Greensboro	ECHL	62	25	36	61	195	17	7	10	17	38
	Providence	AHL	2	1	0	1	0					
1995-96	**Boston**	**NHL**	**7**	**0**	**0**	**0**	**7**					
	Providence	AHL	51	17	22	39	72	4	1	4	5	2
1996-97	**Boston**	**NHL**	**15**	**0**	**1**	**1**	**7**					
	Providence	AHL	57	18	15	33	104					
	NHL Totals		**22**	**0**	**1**	**1**	**14**					

Signed as a free agent by **Boston**, September 6, 1995.

PEAKE, PAT — WSH.

Center. Shoots right. 6'1", 195 lbs. Born, Rochester, MI, May 28, 1973.
(Washington's 1st choice, 14th overall, in 1991 Entry Draft).

			Regular Season					Playoffs				
Season	Club	Lea	GP	G	A	TP	PIM	GP	G	A	TP	PIM
1990-91	Detroit	OHL	63	39	51	90	54					
1991-92	Detroit	OHL	53	41	52	93	44	7	8	9	17	10
	Baltimore	AHL	3	1	0	1	4					
1992-93abc	Detroit	OHL	46	58	78	136	64	2	1	3	4	2
1993-94	**Washington**	**NHL**	**49**	**11**	**18**	**29**	**39**	**8**	**0**	**1**	**1**	**8**
	Portland	AHL	4	0	5	5	2					
1994-95	**Washington**	**NHL**	**18**	**0**	**4**	**4**	**12**					
	Portland	AHL	5	1	3	4	2	4	0	3	3	6
1995-96	**Washington**	**NHL**	**62**	**17**	**19**	**36**	**46**	**5**	**2**	**1**	**3**	**12**
1996-97	**Washington**	**NHL**	**4**	**0**	**0**	**0**	**4**					
	Portland	AHL	3	0	2	2	0					
	NHL Totals		**133**	**28**	**41**	**69**	**101**	**13**	**2**	**2**	**4**	**20**

a Canadian Major Junior Player of the Year (1993)
b Canadian Major Junior First All-Star Team (1993)
c OHL First All-Star Team (1993)

PEARSON, ROB

Right wing. Shoots right. 6'3", 198 lbs. Born, Oshawa, Ont., March 8, 1971.
(Toronto's 2nd choice, 12th overall, in 1989 Entry Draft).

			Regular Season					Playoffs				
Season	Club	Lea	GP	G	A	TP	PIM	GP	G	A	TP	PIM
1988-89	Belleville	OHL	26	8	12	20	51					
1989-90	Belleville	OHL	58	48	40	88	174	11	5	5	10	26
1990-91	Belleville	OHL	10	6	3	9	27					
a	Oshawa	OHL	41	57	52	109	76	16	16	17	33	39
	Newmarket	AHL	3	0	0	0	29					
1991-92	**Toronto**	**NHL**	**47**	**14**	**10**	**24**	**58**					
	St. John's	AHL	27	15	14	29	107	13	5	4	9	40
1992-93	**Toronto**	**NHL**	**78**	**23**	**14**	**37**	**211**	**14**	**2**	**2**	**4**	**31**
1993-94	**Toronto**	**NHL**	**67**	**12**	**18**	**30**	**189**	**14**	**1**	**0**	**1**	**32**
1994-95	**Washington**	**NHL**	**32**	**0**	**6**	**6**	**96**	**3**	**1**	**0**	**1**	**17**
1995-96	Portland	AHL	44	18	24	42	143					
	St. Louis	**NHL**	**27**	**6**	**4**	**10**	**54**	**2**	**0**	**0**	**0**	**14**
1996-97	**St. Louis**	**NHL**	**18**	**1**	**2**	**3**	**37**					
	Worcester	AHL	46	11	16	27	199	5	3	0	3	16
	NHL Totals		**269**	**56**	**54**	**110**	**645**	**33**	**4**	**2**	**6**	**94**

a OHL First All-Star Team (1991)

Traded to **Washington** by **Toronto** with Philadelphia's first round choice (previously acquired by Toronto — Washington selected Nolan Baumgartner) in 1994 Entry Draft for Mike Ridley and St. Louis' first round choice (previously acquired by Washington — Toronto selected Eric Fichaud) in 1994 Entry Draft, June 28, 1994. Traded to **St. Louis** by **Washington** for Denis Chasse, January 29, 1996.

PEARSON, SCOTT

Left wing. Shoots left. 6'1", 205 lbs. Born, Cornwall, Ont., December 19, 1969.
(Toronto's 1st choice, 6th overall, in 1988 Entry Draft).

			Regular Season					Playoffs				
Season	Club	Lea	GP	G	A	TP	PIM	GP	G	A	TP	PIM
1986-87	Kingston	OHL	62	30	24	54	101	9	3	3	6	42
1987-88	Kingston	OHL	46	26	32	58	117					
1988-89	**Toronto**	**NHL**	**9**	**0**	**1**	**1**	**2**					
	Kingston	OHL	13	9	8	17	34					
	Niagara Falls	OHL	32	26	34	60	90	17	14	10	24	53
1989-90	**Toronto**	**NHL**	**41**	**5**	**10**	**15**	**90**	**2**	**2**	**0**	**2**	**10**
	Newmarket	AHL	18	12	11	23	64					
1990-91	**Toronto**	**NHL**	**12**	**0**	**0**	**0**	**20**					
	Quebec	**NHL**	**35**	**11**	**4**	**15**	**86**					
	Halifax	AHL	24	12	15	27	44					
1991-92	**Quebec**	**NHL**	**10**	**1**	**2**	**3**	**14**					
	Halifax	AHL	5	2	1	3	4					
1992-93	**Quebec**	**NHL**	**41**	**13**	**1**	**14**	**95**	**3**	**0**	**0**	**0**	**0**
	Halifax	AHL	5	3	1	4	25					
1993-94	**Edmonton**	**NHL**	**72**	**19**	**18**	**37**	**165**					
1994-95	**Edmonton**	**NHL**	**28**	**1**	**4**	**5**	**54**					
	Buffalo	**NHL**	**14**	**2**	**1**	**3**	**20**	**5**	**0**	**0**	**0**	**4**
1995-96	**Buffalo**	**NHL**	**27**	**4**	**0**	**4**	**67**					
	Rochester	AHL	26	8	8	16	113					
1996-97	**Toronto**	**NHL**	**1**	**0**	**0**	**0**	**2**					
	St. John's	AHL	14	5	2	7	26	9	5	2	7	14
	NHL Totals		**290**	**56**	**41**	**97**	**615**	**10**	**2**	**0**	**2**	**14**

Traded to **Quebec** by **Toronto** with Toronto's second round choices in 1991 (later traded to Washington — Washington selected Eric Lavigne) and 1992 (Tuomas Gronman) Entry Drafts for Aaron Broten, Lucien Deblois and Michel Petit, November 17, 1990. Traded to **Edmonton** by **Quebec** for Martin Gelinas and Edmonton's sixth round choice (Nicholas Checco) in 1993 Entry Draft, June 20, 1993. Traded to **Buffalo** by **Edmonton** for Ken Sutton, April 7, 1995. Signed as a free agent by **Toronto**, July 24, 1996.

PECA, MICHAEL — (PEH-kuh) BUF.

Center. Shoots right. 5'11", 181 lbs. Born, Toronto, Ont., March 26, 1974.
(Vancouver's 2nd choice, 40th overall, in 1992 Entry Draft).

			Regular Season					Playoffs				
Season	Club	Lea	GP	G	A	TP	PIM	GP	G	A	TP	PIM
1990-91	Sudbury	OHL	62	14	27	41	24	5	1	0	1	7
1991-92	Sudbury	OHL	39	16	34	50	61					
	Ottawa	OHL	27	8	17	25	32	11	6	10	16	6
1992-93	Ottawa	OHL	55	38	64	102	80					
	Hamilton	AHL	9	6	3	9	11					
1993-94	**Vancouver**	**NHL**	**4**	**0**	**0**	**0**	**2**					
	Ottawa	OHL	55	50	63	113	101	17	7	22	29	30
1994-95	Syracuse	AHL	35	10	24	34	75					
	Vancouver	**NHL**	**33**	**6**	**6**	**12**	**30**	**5**	**0**	**1**	**1**	**8**
1995-96	**Buffalo**	**NHL**	**68**	**11**	**20**	**31**	**67**					
1996-97a	**Buffalo**	**NHL**	**79**	**20**	**29**	**49**	**80**	**10**	**0**	**2**	**2**	**8**
	NHL Totals		**184**	**37**	**55**	**92**	**179**	**15**	**0**	**3**	**3**	**16**

a Won Frank J. Selke Trophy (1997)

Traded to **Buffalo** by **Vancouver** with Mike Wilson and Vancouver's first round choice (Jay McKee) in 1995 Entry Draft for Alexander Mogilny and Buffalo's fifth round choice (Todd Norman) in 1995 Entry Draft, July 8, 1995.

PEDERSON, DENIS — N.J.

Center. Shoots right. 6'2", 190 lbs. Born, Prince Albert, Sask., September 10, 1975.
(New Jersey's 1st choice, 13th overall, in 1993 Entry Draft).

			Regular Season					Playoffs				
Season	Club	Lea	GP	G	A	TP	PIM	GP	G	A	TP	PIM
1991-92	Prince Albert	Midget	21	33	25	58	40					
	Prince Albert	WHL	10	0	0	0	6	7	0	1	1	13
1992-93	Prince Albert	WHL	72	33	40	73	134					
1993-94a	Prince Albert	WHL	71	53	45	98	157					
1994-95	Prince Albert	WHL	63	30	38	68	122	15	11	14	25	14
	Albany	AHL	....	....	....	....	....	3	0	0	0	2
1995-96	**New Jersey**	**NHL**	**10**	**3**	**1**	**4**	**0**					
	Albany	AHL	68	28	43	71	104	4	1	2	3	0
1996-97	**New Jersey**	**NHL**	**70**	**12**	**20**	**32**	**62**	**9**	**0**	**0**	**0**	**2**
	Albany	AHL	3	1	3	4	7					
	NHL Totals		**80**	**15**	**21**	**36**	**62**	**9**	**0**	**0**	**0**	**2**

a WHL East Second All-Star Team (1994)

PEDERSON, TOM

Defense. Shoots right. 5'9", 175 lbs. Born, Bloomington, MN, January 14, 1970.
(Minnesota's 12th choice, 217th overall, in 1989 Entry Draft).

			Regular Season					Playoffs				
Season	Club	Lea	GP	G	A	TP	PIM	GP	G	A	TP	PIM
1988-89	U. Minnesota	WCHA	36	4	20	24	40					
1989-90	U. Minnesota	WCHA	43	8	30	38	58					
1990-91	U. Minnesota	WCHA	36	12	20	32	46					
1991-92	U.S. National	....	44	3	11	14	41					
	Kansas City	IHL	20	6	9	15	16	13	1	6	7	14
1992-93	**San Jose**	**NHL**	**44**	**7**	**13**	**20**	**31**					
	Kansas City	IHL	26	6	15	21	10	12	1	6	7	2
1993-94	**San Jose**	**NHL**	**74**	**6**	**19**	**25**	**31**	**14**	**1**	**6**	**7**	**2**
	Kansas City	IHL	7	3	1	4	0					
1994-95	**San Jose**	**NHL**	**47**	**5**	**11**	**16**	**31**	**10**	**0**	**5**	**5**	**8**
1995-96	**San Jose**	**NHL**	**60**	**1**	**4**	**5**	**40**					
1996-97	Seibu Tetsudo	Japan	30	10	28	38	....					
	Toronto	**NHL**	**15**	**1**	**2**	**3**	**9**					
	St. John's	AHL	1	0	4	4	2					
	Utah	IHL	10	1	2	3	8	7	1	3	4	4
	NHL Totals		**240**	**20**	**49**	**69**	**142**	**24**	**1**	**11**	**12**	**10**

Claimed by **San Jose** from **Minnesota** in Dispersal Draft, May 30, 1991. Signed as a free agent by **Toronto**, December 11, 1996.

PELLERIN, SCOTT — (PEHL-ih-rihn) ST.L.

Left wing. Shoots left. 5'11", 180 lbs. Born, Shediac, N.B., January 9, 1970.
(New Jersey's 4th choice, 47th overall, in 1989 Entry Draft).

			Regular Season					Playoffs				
Season	Club	Lea	GP	G	A	TP	PIM	GP	G	A	TP	PIM
1988-89	U. of Maine	H.E.	45	29	33	62	92					
1989-90	U. of Maine	H.E.	42	22	34	56	68					
1990-91	U. of Maine	H.E.	43	23	25	48	60					
1991-92abc	U. of Maine	H.E.	37	*32	25	57	54					
	Utica	AHL	....	....	....	....	....	3	1	0	1	0
1992-93	**New Jersey**	**NHL**	**45**	**10**	**11**	**21**	**41**					
	Utica	AHL	27	15	18	33	33	2	0	1	1	0
1993-94	**New Jersey**	**NHL**	**1**	**0**	**0**	**0**	**2**					
	Albany	AHL	73	28	46	74	84	5	2	1	3	11
1994-95	Albany	AHL	74	23	33	56	95	14	6	4	10	8
1995-96	**New Jersey**	**NHL**	**6**	**2**	**1**	**3**	**0**					
	Albany	AHL	75	35	47	82	142	4	0	3	3	10
1996-97	**St. Louis**	**NHL**	**54**	**8**	**10**	**18**	**35**	**6**	**0**	**0**	**0**	**6**
	Worcester	AHL	24	10	16	26	37					
	NHL Totals		**106**	**20**	**22**	**42**	**78**	**6**	**0**	**0**	**0**	**6**

a Won Hobey Baker Memorial Award (Top U.S. Collegiate Player) (1992)
b Hockey East First All-Star Team (1992)
c NCAA East First All-American Team (1992)

Signed as a free agent by **St. Louis**, July 10, 1996.

PELTONEN, VILLE — (PEHL-TOH-ner) S.J.

Left wing. Shoots left. 5'11", 180 lbs. Born, Vantaa, Finland, May 24, 1973.
(San Jose's 4th choice, 58th overall, in 1993 Entry Draft).

			Regular Season					Playoffs				
Season	Club	Lea	GP	G	A	TP	PIM	GP	G	A	TP	PIM
1991-92	HIFK	Fin.	6	0	0	0	0					
1992-93	HIFK	Fin.	46	13	24	37	16	4	0	2	2	2
1993-94	HIFK	Fin.	43	16	22	38	14	3	0	0	0	2
1994-95	HIFK	Fin.	45	20	16	36	16	3	0	0	0	0
1995-96	**San Jose**	**NHL**	**31**	**2**	**11**	**13**	**14**					
	Kansas City	IHL	29	5	13	18	8					
1996-97	**San Jose**	**NHL**	**28**	**2**	**3**	**5**	**0**					
	Kentucky	AHL	40	22	30	52	21					
	NHL Totals		**59**	**4**	**14**	**18**	**14**					

PELUSO, MIKE

(puh-LOO-soh) **NYR**

Left wing. Shoots left. 6'4", 225 lbs. Born, Pengilly, MN, November 8, 1965.
(New Jersey's 10th choice, 190th overall, in 1984 Entry Draft).

			Regular Season					Playoffs				
Season	Club	Lea	GP	G	A	TP	PIM	GP	G	A	TP	PIM
1985-86	Alaska-Anch.	G.N.	32	2	11	13	59	....	....	....	....	....
1986-87	Alaska-Anch.	G.N.	30	5	21	26	68	....	....	....	....	....
1987-88	Alaska-Anch.	G.N.	35	4	33	37	76	....	....	....	....	....
1988-89	Alaska-Anch.	G.N.	33	10	27	37	75	....	....	....	....	....
1989-90	**Chicago**	**NHL**	**2**	**0**	**0**	**0**	**15**	....	....	....	....	....
	Indianapolis	IHL	75	7	10	17	279	14	0	1	1	58
1990-91	**Chicago**	**NHL**	**53**	**6**	**1**	**7**	**320**	**3**	**0**	**0**	**0**	**2**
	Indianapolis	IHL	6	2	1	3	21	5	0	2	2	40
1991-92	**Chicago**	**NHL**	**63**	**6**	**3**	**9**	***408**	**17**	**1**	**2**	**3**	**8**
	Indianapolis	IHL	4	0	1	1	15	....	....	....	....	....
1992-93	**Ottawa**	**NHL**	**81**	**15**	**10**	**25**	**318**	....	....	....	....	....
1993-94	**New Jersey**	**NHL**	**69**	**4**	**16**	**20**	**238**	**17**	**1**	**0**	**1**	***64**
1994-95	**New Jersey**	**NHL**	**46**	**2**	**9**	**11**	**167**	**20**	**1**	**2**	**3**	**8** ♦
1995-96	**New Jersey**	**NHL**	**57**	**3**	**8**	**11**	**146**	....	....	....	....	....
1996-97	**New Jersey**	**NHL**	**20**	**0**	**2**	**2**	**68**	....	....	....	....	....
	St. Louis	**NHL**	**44**	**2**	**3**	**5**	**158**	**5**	**0**	**0**	**0**	**25**
	NHL Totals		**435**	**38**	**52**	**90**	**1838**	**62**	**3**	**4**	**7**	**107**

Signed as a free agent by **Chicago**, September 7, 1989. Claimed by **Ottawa** from **Chicago** in Expansion Draft, June 18, 1992. Traded to **New Jersey** by **Ottawa** to complete June 20, 1993 trade which sent Craig Billington, Troy Mallette and New Jersey's fourth round choice (Cosmo Dupaul) in 1993 Entry Draft to Ottawa for Peter Sidorkiewicz and future considerations, June 26, 1993. Traded to **St. Louis** by **New Jersey** with Ricard Persson for Ken Sutton and St. Louis' second round choice in 1999 Entry Draft, November 26, 1996. Acquired by **NY Rangers** from **St. Louis** as compensation for St. Louis' hiring of Larry Pleau, June 21, 1997.

PEPPERALL, COLIN

NYR

Left wing. Shoots left. 5'10", 160 lbs. Born, Niagara Falls, Ont., April 28, 1978.
(NY Rangers' 4th choice, 131st overall, in 1996 Entry Draft).

			Regular Season					Playoffs				
Season	Club	Lea	GP	G	A	TP	PIM	GP	G	A	TP	PIM
1995-96	Niagara Falls	OHL	66	26	26	52	47	10	3	4	7	8
1996-97	Erie	OHL	66	36	36	72	39	5	3	2	5	2

PEPPERALL, RYAN

TOR.

Right wing. Shoots right. 6'1", 185 lbs. Born, Niagara Falls, Ont., January 26, 1977.
(Toronto's 2nd choice, 54th overall, in 1995 Entry Draft).

			Regular Season					Playoffs				
Season	Club	Lea	GP	G	A	TP	PIM	GP	G	A	TP	PIM
1994-95	Kitchener	OHL	62	17	16	33	86	5	2	2	4	8
1995-96	Kitchener	OHL	66	31	26	57	173	12	3	4	7	34
1996-97	Kitchener	OHL	65	35	36	71	201	13	9	6	15	17

PERREAULT, YANIC

(puh-ROH, YAH-nihk) **L.A.**

Center. Shoots left. 5'11", 182 lbs. Born, Sherbrooke, Que., April 4, 1971.
(Toronto's 1st choice, 47th overall, in 1991 Entry Draft).

			Regular Season					Playoffs				
Season	Club	Lea	GP	G	A	TP	PIM	GP	G	A	TP	PIM
1988-89a	Trois-Rivières	QMJHL	70	53	55	108	48	....	....	....	....	....
1989-90	Trois-Rivières	QMJHL	63	51	63	114	75	7	6	5	11	19
1990-91b	Trois-Rivières	QMJHL	67	*87	98	*185	103	6	4	7	11	6
1991-92	St. John's	AHL	62	38	38	76	19	16	7	8	15	4
1992-93	St. John's	AHL	79	49	46	95	56	9	4	5	9	2
1993-94	**Toronto**	**NHL**	**13**	**3**	**3**	**6**	**0**	....	....	....	....	....
	St. John's	AHL	62	45	60	105	38	11	*12	6	18	14
1994-95	Phoenix	IHL	68	51	48	99	52	....	....	....	....	....
	Los Angeles	**NHL**	**26**	**2**	**5**	**7**	**20**	....	....	....	....	....
1995-96	**Los Angeles**	**NHL**	**78**	**25**	**24**	**49**	**16**	....	....	....	....	....
1996-97	**Los Angeles**	**NHL**	**41**	**11**	**14**	**25**	**20**	....	....	....	....	....
	NHL Totals		**158**	**41**	**46**	**87**	**56**	....	....	....	....	....

a Canadian Major Junior Rookie of the Year (1989)
b QMJHL First All-Star Team (1991)

Traded to **Los Angeles** by **Toronto** for Los Angeles' fourth round choice (later traded to Philadelphia — later traded to Los Angeles — Los Angeles selected Mikael Simons) in 1996 Entry Draft, July 11, 1994.

PERSHIN, EDUARD

(PEHR-shihn, ehd-WUHRD) **T.B.**

Right wing. Shoots left. 6', 191 lbs. Born, Nizhnekamsk, USSR, September 1, 1977.
(Tampa Bay's 5th choice, 134th overall, in 1995 Entry Draft).

			Regular Season					Playoffs				
Season	Club	Lea	GP	G	A	TP	PIM	GP	G	A	TP	PIM
1994-95	Moscow D'amo	CIS	4	1	1	2	2	3	0	0	0	2
1995-96	Moscow D'amo	CIS	38	4	10	14	18	2	0	0	0	0
1996-97	Moscow D'amo	Rus.	31	4	9	13	16	3	0	2	2	0

PERSSON, RICARD

ST.L.

Defense. Shoots left. 6'2", 205 lbs. Born, Ostersund, Sweden, August 24, 1969.
(New Jersey's 2nd choice, 23rd overall, in 1987 Entry Draft).

			Regular Season					Playoffs				
Season	Club	Lea	GP	G	A	TP	PIM	GP	G	A	TP	PIM
1985-86	Ostersund	Swe. 2	24	2	2	4	16	....	....	....	....	....
1986-87	Ostersund	Swe. 2	31	10	11	21	28	....	....	....	....	....
1987-88	Leksand	Swe.	31	2	0	2	8	2	0	1	1	2
1988-89	Leksand	Swe.	33	2	4	6	28	9	0	1	1	6
1989-90	Leksand	Swe.	43	9	10	19	62	3	0	0	0	6
1990-91	Leksand	Swe.	37	6	9	15	42	....	....	....	....	....
1991-92	Leksand	Swe.	21	0	7	7	28	....	....	....	....	....
1992-93	Leksand	Swe.	36	7	15	22	63	2	0	2	2	0
1993-94	Malmo	Swe.	40	11	9	20	38	11	2	0	2	12
1994-95	Malmo	Swe.	31	3	13	16	38	9	0	2	2	8
	Albany	AHL	3	0	0	0	0	9	3	5	8	7
1995-96	**New Jersey**	**NHL**	**12**	**2**	**1**	**3**	**8**	....	....	....	....	....
	Albany	AHL	67	15	31	46	59	4	0	0	0	7
1996-97	**New Jersey**	**NHL**	**1**	**0**	**0**	**0**	**0**	....	....	....	....	....
	Albany	AHL	13	1	4	5	8	....	....	....	....	....
	St. Louis	**NHL**	**53**	**4**	**8**	**12**	**45**	**6**	**0**	**0**	**0**	**27**
	NHL Totals		**66**	**6**	**9**	**15**	**53**	**6**	**0**	**0**	**0**	**27**

Traded to **St. Louis** by **New Jersey** with Mike Peluso for Ken Sutton and St. Louis' second round choice in 1999 Entry Draft, November 26, 1996.

PETERS, GEOFF

CHI.

Center. Shoots left. 6', 180 lbs. Born, Hamilton, Ont., April 30, 1978.
(Chicago's 3rd choice, 46th overall, in 1996 Entry Draft).

			Regular Season					Playoffs				
Season	Club	Lea	GP	G	A	TP	PIM	GP	G	A	TP	PIM
1994-95	Niagara Falls	OHL	57	11	9	20	37	6	2	0	2	4
1995-96	Niagara Falls	OHL	64	25	34	59	51	10	4	4	8	8
1996-97	Erie	OHL	28	12	10	22	39	5	1	3	4	7

PETERSON, BRENT

T.B.

Left wing. Shoots left. 6'3", 200 lbs. Born, Calgary, Alta., July 20, 1972.
(Tampa Bay's 1st choice, 3rd overall, in 1993 Supplemental Draft).

			Regular Season					Playoffs				
Season	Club	Lea	GP	G	A	TP	PIM	GP	G	A	TP	PIM
1991-92	Michigan Tech	WCHA	39	11	9	20	18	....	....	....	....	....
1992-93	Michigan Tech	WCHA	37	24	18	42	32	....	....	....	....	....
1993-94	Michigan Tech	WCHA	43	25	21	46	30	....	....	....	....	....
1994-95	Michigan Tech	WCHA	39	20	16	36	27	....	....	....	....	....
1995-96	Atlanta	IHL	69	9	19	28	33	3	0	0	0	0
1996-97	**Tampa Bay**	**NHL**	**17**	**2**	**0**	**2**	**4**	....	....	....	....	....
	Adirondack	AHL	52	22	23	45	56	4	3	1	4	2
	NHL Totals		**17**	**2**	**0**	**2**	**4**	....	....	....	....	....

PETERSON, KYLE

EDM.

Center. Shoots left. 6'4", 220 lbs. Born, Calgary, Alta., April 17, 1974.
(Minnesota's 5th choice, 154th overall, in 1992 Entry Draft).

			Regular Season					Playoffs				
Season	Club	Lea	GP	G	A	TP	PIM	GP	G	A	TP	PIM
1993-94	Michigan Tech	WCHA	45	5	9	14	82	....	....	....	....	....
1994-95	Michigan Tech	WCHA	36	7	11	18	52	....	....	....	....	....
1995-96	Michigan Tech	WCHA	23	8	7	15	18	....	....	....	....	....
1996-97	Michigan Tech	WCHA	38	15	10	25	44	....	....	....	....	....

Signed as a free agent by **Edmonton**, June 5, 1997.

PETERSON, MATT

ANA.

Defense. Shoots left. 6'1", 190 lbs. Born, Maple Grove, MN, February 15, 1975.
(Anaheim's 7th choice, 160th overall, in 1993 Entry Draft).

			Regular Season					Playoffs				
Season	Club	Lea	GP	G	A	TP	PIM	GP	G	A	TP	PIM
1994-95	U. Wisconsin	WCHA	20	0	0	0	10	....	....	....	....	....
1995-96	U. Wisconsin	WCHA	21	0	0	0	24	....	....	....	....	....
1996-97	U. Wisconsin	WCHA	32	2	1	3	22	....	....	....	....	....

PETIT, MICHEL

(puh-TEE)

Defense. Shoots right. 6'1", 205 lbs. Born, St. Malo, Que., February 12, 1964.
(Vancouver's 1st choice, 11th overall, in 1982 Entry Draft).

			Regular Season					Playoffs				
Season	Club	Lea	GP	G	A	TP	PIM	GP	G	A	TP	PIM
1981-82a	Sherbrooke	QMJHL	63	10	39	49	106	22	5	20	25	24
1982-83	**Vancouver**	**NHL**	**2**	**0**	**0**	**0**	**0**	....	....	....	....	....
a	St-Jean	QMJHL	62	19	67	86	196	3	0	0	0	35
1983-84	Cdn. National	....	19	3	10	13	58	....	....	....	....	....
	Vancouver	**NHL**	**44**	**6**	**9**	**15**	**53**	**1**	**0**	**0**	**0**	**0**
1984-85	**Vancouver**	**NHL**	**69**	**5**	**26**	**31**	**127**	....	....	....	....	....
1985-86	**Vancouver**	**NHL**	**32**	**1**	**6**	**7**	**27**	....	....	....	....	....
	Fredericton	AHL	25	0	13	13	79	....	....	....	....	....
1986-87	**Vancouver**	**NHL**	**69**	**12**	**13**	**25**	**131**	....	....	....	....	....
1987-88	**Vancouver**	**NHL**	**10**	**0**	**3**	**3**	**35**	....	....	....	....	....
	NY Rangers	**NHL**	**64**	**9**	**24**	**33**	**223**	....	....	....	....	....
1988-89	**NY Rangers**	**NHL**	**69**	**8**	**25**	**33**	**154**	**4**	**0**	**2**	**2**	**27**
1989-90	**Quebec**	**NHL**	**63**	**12**	**24**	**36**	**215**	....	....	....	....	....
1990-91	**Quebec**	**NHL**	**19**	**4**	**7**	**11**	**47**	....	....	....	....	....
	Toronto	**NHL**	**54**	**9**	**19**	**28**	**132**	....	....	....	....	....
1991-92	**Toronto**	**NHL**	**34**	**1**	**13**	**14**	**85**	....	....	....	....	....
	Calgary	**NHL**	**36**	**3**	**10**	**13**	**79**	....	....	....	....	....
1992-93	**Calgary**	**NHL**	**35**	**3**	**9**	**12**	**54**	....	....	....	....	....
1993-94	**Calgary**	**NHL**	**63**	**2**	**21**	**23**	**110**	....	....	....	....	....
1994-95	**Los Angeles**	**NHL**	**40**	**5**	**12**	**17**	**84**	....	....	....	....	....
1995-96	**Los Angeles**	**NHL**	**9**	**0**	**1**	**1**	**27**	....	....	....	....	....
	Tampa Bay	**NHL**	**45**	**4**	**7**	**11**	**108**	**6**	**0**	**0**	**0**	**20**
1996-97	**Edmonton**	**NHL**	**18**	**2**	**4**	**6**	**20**	....	....	....	....	....
	Philadelphia	**NHL**	**20**	**0**	**3**	**3**	**51**	**3**	**0**	**0**	**0**	**6**
	NHL Totals		**795**	**86**	**236**	**322**	**1762**	**14**	**0**	**2**	**2**	**53**

a QMJHL First All-Star Team (1982, 1983)

Traded to **NY Rangers** by **Vancouver** for Willie Huber and Larry Melnyk, November 4, 1987. Traded to **Quebec** by **NY Rangers** for Randy Moller, October 5, 1989. Traded to **Toronto** by **Quebec** with Aaron Broten and Lucien Deblois for Scott Pearson and Toronto's second round choices in 1991 (later traded to Washington — Washington selected Eric Lavigne) and 1992 (Tuomas Gronman) Entry Drafts, November 17, 1990. Traded to **Calgary** by **Toronto** with Craig Berube, Alexander Godynyuk, Gary Leeman and Jeff Reese for Doug Gilmour, Jamie Macoun, Ric Nattress, Rick Wamsley and Kent Manderville, January 2, 1992. Signed as a free agent by **Los Angeles**, June 16, 1994. Traded to **Tampa Bay** by **Los Angeles** for Steven Finn, November 13, 1995. Signed as a free agent by **Edmonton**, October 24, 1996. Claimed on waivers by **Philadelphia** from **Edmonton**, January 17, 1997.

PETRAKOV, ANDREI

(peh-trah-KAHF) **ST.L.**

Right wing. Shoots left. 6', 198 lbs. Born, Sverdlovsk, USSR, April 26, 1976.
(St. Louis' 4th choice, 97th overall, in 1996 Entry Draft).

			Regular Season					Playoffs				
Season	Club	Lea	GP	G	A	TP	PIM	GP	G	A	TP	PIM
1992-93	Yekaterinburg	CIS	5	0	0	0	0	1	0	0	0	0
1993-94	Yekaterinburg	CIS	35	4	2	6	10	....	....	....	....	....
1994-95	Yekaterinburg	CIS	11	1	1	2	6	1	0	0	0	0
1995-96	Yekaterinburg	CIS 2	52	17	6	23	14	....	....	....	....	....
1996-97	Yekaterinburg	Rus.	14	6	1	7	6	....	....	....	....	....
	Magnitogorsk	Rus.	18	4	0	4	8	6	0	0	0	0

PETRE, HENRIK

(PEH-treh) **WSH.**

Defense. Shoots left. 6'1", 187 lbs. Born, Stockholm, Sweden, April 9, 1979.
(Washington's 5th choice, 143rd overall, in 1997 Entry Draft).

			Regular Season					Playoffs				
Season	Club	Lea	GP	G	A	TP	PIM	GP	G	A	TP	PIM
1995-96	Djurgarden	Swe. Jr.	21	6	4	10	8	....	....	....	....	....
1996-97	Djurgarden	Swe. Jr.				UNAVAILABLE						

PETRILAINEN, PASI (peh-trih-LAI-nehn, PAH-see) N.J.

Defense. Shoots left. 5'10", 185 lbs. Born, Tampere, Finland, May 5, 1978.
(New Jersey's 14th choice, 225th overall, in 1996 Entry Draft).

			Regular Season					Playoffs				
Season	**Club**	**Lea**	**GP**	**G**	**A**	**TP**	**PIM**	**GP**	**G**	**A**	**TP**	**PIM**
1994-95	Tappara	Fin.	25	3	0	3	14	....	....	....	....	....
	Tappara	Fin. Jr.	14	3	4	7	6	....	....	....	....	....
1995-96	Tappara	Fin.	40	0	4	4	18	4	0	0	0	2
	Tappara	Fin. Jr.	5	0	2	2	4	....	....	....	....	....
1996-97	Tappara	Fin.	43	2	9	11	46	3	0	0	0	2

PETROCHININ, EVGENY (peht-roh-CHIH-nihn) DAL.

Defense. Shoots left. 6'2", 190 lbs. Born, Murmansk, USSR, February 7, 1976.
(Dallas' 5th choice, 150th overall, in 1994 Entry Draft).

			Regular Season					Playoffs				
Season	**Club**	**Lea**	**GP**	**G**	**A**	**TP**	**PIM**	**GP**	**G**	**A**	**TP**	**PIM**
1993-94	Spartak	CIS	2	0	0	0	0	....	....	....	....	....
1994-95	Spartak	CIS	45	0	2	2	14	....	....	....	....	....
1995-96	Spartak	CIS	50	5	17	22	18	5	3	0	3	0
1996-97	Spartak	Rus.	32	5	6	11	52	....	....	....	....	....

PETROV, SERGEI (PEH-trahf) CHI.

Left wing. Shoots left. 5'11", 185 lbs. Born, Leningrad, USSR, January 22, 1975.
(Chicago's 9th choice, 206th overall, in 1993 Entry Draft).

			Regular Season					Playoffs				
Season	**Club**	**Lea**	**GP**	**G**	**A**	**TP**	**PIM**	**GP**	**G**	**A**	**TP**	**PIM**
1993-94	Minn.-Duluth	WCHA	28	2	4	6	26	....	....	....	....	....
1994-95	Minn.-Duluth	WCHA	30	6	6	12	46	....	....	....	....	....
1995-96					DID NOT PLAY							
1996-97	Minn.-Duluth	WCHA	35	5	12	17	26	....	....	....	....	....

PETROVICKY, ROBERT (PEHT-roh-VEETS-kee) ST.L.

Center. Shoots left. 5'11", 172 lbs. Born, Kosice, Czech., October 26, 1973.
(Hartford's 1st choice, 9th overall, in 1992 Entry Draft).

			Regular Season					Playoffs				
Season	**Club**	**Lea**	**GP**	**G**	**A**	**TP**	**PIM**	**GP**	**G**	**A**	**TP**	**PIM**
1990-91	Dukla Trencin	Czech.	33	9	14	23	12	....	....	....	....	....
1991-92	Dukla Trencin	Czech.	46	25	36	61	28	....	....	....	....	....
1992-93	**Hartford**	**NHL**	**42**	**3**	**6**	**9**	**45**	....	....	....	....	....
	Springfield	AHL	16	5	3	8	39	15	5	6	11	14
1993-94	Dukla Trencin	Slovak	1	0	0	0	0	....	....	....	....	....
	Hartford	**NHL**	**33**	**6**	**5**	**11**	**39**	....	....	....	....	....
	Springfield	AHL	30	16	8	24	39	4	0	2	2	4
1994-95	Springfield	AHL	74	30	52	82	121	....	....	....	....	....
	Hartford	**NHL**	**2**	**0**	**0**	**0**	**0**	....	....	....	....	....
1995-96	Springfield	AHL	9	4	8	12	18	....	....	....	....	....
	Detroit	IHL	12	5	3	8	16	....	....	....	....	....
	Dallas	**NHL**	**5**	**1**	**1**	**2**	**0**	....	....	....	....	....
	Michigan	IHL	50	23	23	46	63	7	3	1	4	16
1996-97	**St. Louis**	**NHL**	**44**	**7**	**12**	**19**	**10**	**2**	**0**	**0**	**0**	**0**
	Worcester	AHL	12	5	4	9	19	....	....	....	....	....
	NHL Totals		**126**	**17**	**24**	**41**	**94**	**2**	**0**	**0**	**0**	**0**

Traded to **Dallas** by **Hartford** for Dan Kesa and a conditional choice in 1997 Entry Draft, November 29, 1995. Signed as a free agent by **St. Louis**, September 6, 1996.

PETROVICKY, RONALD (PEHT-roh-VEETS-kee) CGY.

Right wing. Shoots right. 5'11", 185 lbs. Born, Zilina, Czech., February 15, 1977.
(Calgary's 9th choice, 228th overall, in 1996 Entry Draft).

			Regular Season					Playoffs				
Season	**Club**	**Lea**	**GP**	**G**	**A**	**TP**	**PIM**	**GP**	**G**	**A**	**TP**	**PIM**
1993-94	Dukla Trencin	Slo. Jr.	36	28	27	55	42	....	....	....	....	....
	Dukla Trencin	Slovak	1	0	0	0	0	....	....	....	....	....
1994-95	Tri-City	WHL	39	4	11	15	86	....	....	....	....	....
	Prince George	WHL	21	4	6	10	37	....	....	....	....	....
1995-96	Prince George	WHL	39	19	21	40	61	....	....	....	....	....
1996-97	Prince George	WHL	72	32	37	69	119	15	4	9	13	31

PETRUNIN, ANDREI (puh-TROO-nihn) CAR.

Right wing. Shoots left. 5'9", 169 lbs. Born, Moscow, USSR, February 2, 1978.
(Hartford's 2nd choice, 61st overall, in 1996 Entry Draft).

			Regular Season					Playoffs				
Season	**Club**	**Lea**	**GP**	**G**	**A**	**TP**	**PIM**	**GP**	**G**	**A**	**TP**	**PIM**
1994-95	CSKA	CIS	7	0	1	1	0	2	0	0	0	0
1995-96	CSKA	CIS	52	12	8	20	22	2	0	0	0	2
1996-97	CSKA	Rus. 2	55	36	32	68	73	....	....	....	....	....

PHILLIPS, CHRIS OTT.

Defense. Shoots left. 6'2", 200 lbs. Born, Fort McMurray, Alta., March 9, 1978.
(Ottawa's 1st choice, 1st overall, in 1996 Entry Draft).

			Regular Season					Playoffs				
Season	**Club**	**Lea**	**GP**	**G**	**A**	**TP**	**PIM**	**GP**	**G**	**A**	**TP**	**PIM**
1995-96	Prince Albert	WHL	61	10	30	40	97	18	2	12	14	30
1996-97ab	Prince Albert	WHL	32	3	23	26	58	....	....	....	....	....
	Lethbridge	WHL	26	4	18	22	28	19	4	*21	25	20

a WHL East First All-Star Team (1997)
b Canadian Major Junior First All-Star Team (1997)

PHILLIPS, GREG L.A.

Center. Shoots right. 6'2", 192 lbs. Born, Winnipeg, Man., March 27, 1978.
(Los Angeles' 3rd choice, 57th overall, in 1996 Entry Draft).

			Regular Season					Playoffs				
Season	**Club**	**Lea**	**GP**	**G**	**A**	**TP**	**PIM**	**GP**	**G**	**A**	**TP**	**PIM**
1994-95	Saskatoon	WHL	64	3	5	8	94	10	0	0	0	4
1995-96	Saskatoon	WHL	67	21	24	45	132	4	1	2	3	2
1996-97	Saskatoon	WHL	34	17	19	36	64	....	....	....	....	....

PICARD, MICHEL (PEE-cahr)

Left wing. Shoots left. 5'11", 190 lbs. Born, Beauport, Que., November 7, 1969.
(Hartford's 8th choice, 178th overall, in 1989 Entry Draft).

			Regular Season					Playoffs				
Season	**Club**	**Lea**	**GP**	**G**	**A**	**TP**	**PIM**	**GP**	**G**	**A**	**TP**	**PIM**
1986-87	Trois-Rivières	QMJHL	66	33	35	68	53	....	....	....	....	....
1987-88	Trois-Rivières	QMJHL	69	40	55	95	71	....	....	....	....	....
1988-89	Trois-Rivières	QMJHL	66	59	81	140	170	4	1	3	4	2
1989-90	Binghamton	AHL	67	16	24	40	98	....	....	....	....	....
1990-91	**Hartford**	**NHL**	**5**	**1**	**0**	**1**	**2**	....	....	....	....	....
a	Springfield	AHL	77	*56	40	96	61	18	8	13	21	18
1991-92	**Hartford**	**NHL**	**25**	**3**	**5**	**8**	**6**	....	....	....	....	....
	Springfield	AHL	40	21	17	38	44	11	2	0	2	34
1992-93	**San Jose**	**NHL**	**25**	**4**	**0**	**4**	**24**	....	....	....	....	....
	Kansas City	IHL	33	7	10	17	51	12	3	2	5	20
1993-94b	Portland	AHL	61	41	44	85	99	17	11	10	21	22
1994-95a	P.E.I.	AHL	57	32	57	89	58	8	4	4	8	6
	Ottawa	**NHL**	**24**	**5**	**8**	**13**	**14**	....	....	....	....	....
1995-96	**Ottawa**	**NHL**	**17**	**2**	**6**	**8**	**10**	....	....	....	....	....
	P.E.I.	AHL	55	37	45	82	79	5	5	1	6	2
1996-97	V. Frolunda	Swe.	3	0	1	1	0	....	....	....	....	....
c	Grand Rapids	IHL	82	46	55	101	58	5	2	0	2	10
	NHL Totals		**96**	**15**	**19**	**34**	**56**	....	....	....	....	....

a AHL First All-Star Team (1991, 1995)
b AHL Second All-Star Team (1994)
c IHL First All-Star Team (1997)

Traded to **San Jose** by **Hartford** for future considerations (Yvon Corriveau, January 21, 1993), October 9, 1992. Signed as a free agent by **Ottawa**, June 16, 1994. Traded to **Washington** by **Ottawa** for cash, May 21, 1996.

PILON, RICHARD (PEE-lahn) NYI

Defense. Shoots left. 6', 205 lbs. Born, Saskatoon, Sask., April 30, 1968.
(NY Islanders' 9th choice, 143rd overall, in 1986 Entry Draft).

			Regular Season					Playoffs				
Season	**Club**	**Lea**	**GP**	**G**	**A**	**TP**	**PIM**	**GP**	**G**	**A**	**TP**	**PIM**
1986-87	Prince Albert	WHL	68	4	21	25	192	7	1	6	7	17
1987-88	Prince Albert	WHL	65	13	34	47	177	9	0	6	6	38
1988-89	**NY Islanders**	**NHL**	**62**	**0**	**14**	**14**	**242**	....	....	....	....	....
1989-90	**NY Islanders**	**NHL**	**14**	**0**	**2**	**2**	**31**	....	....	....	....	....
1990-91	**NY Islanders**	**NHL**	**60**	**1**	**4**	**5**	**126**	....	....	....	....	....
1991-92	**NY Islanders**	**NHL**	**65**	**1**	**6**	**7**	**183**	....	....	....	....	....
1992-93	**NY Islanders**	**NHL**	**44**	**1**	**3**	**4**	**164**	**15**	**0**	**0**	**0**	**50**
	Capital Dist.	AHL	6	0	1	1	8	....	....	....	....	....
1993-94	**NY Islanders**	**NHL**	**28**	**1**	**4**	**5**	**75**	....	....	....	....	....
	Salt Lake	IHL	2	0	0	0	8	....	....	....	....	....
1994-95	**NY Islanders**	**NHL**	**20**	**1**	**1**	**2**	**40**	....	....	....	....	....
1995-96	**NY Islanders**	**NHL**	**27**	**0**	**3**	**3**	**72**	....	....	....	....	....
1996-97	**NY Islanders**	**NHL**	**52**	**1**	**4**	**5**	**179**	....	....	....	....	....
	NHL Totals		**372**	**6**	**41**	**47**	**1112**	**15**	**0**	**0**	**0**	**50**

PISANI, FERNANDO EDM.

Center/left wing. Shoots left. 6'1", 180 lbs. Born, Edmonton, Alta., December 27, 1976.
(Edmonton's 9th choice, 195th overall, in 1996 Entry Draft).

			Regular Season					Playoffs				
Season	**Club**	**Lea**	**GP**	**G**	**A**	**TP**	**PIM**	**GP**	**G**	**A**	**TP**	**PIM**
1995-96	St. Albert	Jr. A.	58	40	63	103	134	18	7	22	29	28
1996-97	Providence	H.E.	35	12	18	30	36	....	....	....	....	....

PITLICK, LANCE (PIHT-lihk) OTT.

Defense. Shoots right. 6', 203 lbs. Born, Minneapolis, MN, November 5, 1967.
(Minnesota's 10th choice, 108th overall, in 1986 Entry Draft).

			Regular Season					Playoffs				
Season	**Club**	**Lea**	**GP**	**G**	**A**	**TP**	**PIM**	**GP**	**G**	**A**	**TP**	**PIM**
1986-87	U. Minnesota	WCHA	45	0	9	9	88	....	....	....	....	....
1987-88	U. Minnesota	WCHA	38	3	9	12	76	....	....	....	....	....
1988-89	U. Minnesota	WCHA	47	4	9	13	95	....	....	....	....	....
1989-90	U. Minnesota	WCHA	14	3	2	5	26	....	....	....	....	....
1990-91	Hershey	AHL	64	6	15	21	75	3	0	0	0	9
1991-92	U.S. National	....	19	0	1	1	38	....	....	....	....	....
	Hershey	AHL	4	0	0	0	6	3	0	0	0	4
1992-93	Hershey	AHL	53	5	10	15	77	....	....	....	....	....
1993-94	Hershey	AHL	58	4	13	17	93	11	1	0	1	11
1994-95	P.E.I.	AHL	61	8	19	27	55	11	1	4	5	10
	Ottawa	**NHL**	**15**	**0**	**1**	**1**	**6**	....	....	....	....	....
1995-96	**Ottawa**	**NHL**	**28**	**1**	**6**	**7**	**20**	....	....	....	....	....
	P.E.I.	AHL	29	4	10	14	39	5	0	0	0	0
1996-97	**Ottawa**	**NHL**	**66**	**5**	**5**	**10**	**91**	**7**	**0**	**0**	**0**	**4**
	NHL Totals		**109**	**6**	**12**	**18**	**117**	**7**	**0**	**0**	**0**	**4**

Signed as a free agent by **Philadelphia**, September 5, 1990. Signed as a free agent by **Ottawa**, June 22, 1994.

PITTIS, DOMENIC PIT.

Center. Shoots left. 5'11", 190 lbs. Born, Calgary, Alta., October 1, 1974.
(Pittsburgh's 2nd choice, 52nd overall, in 1993 Entry Draft).

			Regular Season					Playoffs				
Season	**Club**	**Lea**	**GP**	**G**	**A**	**TP**	**PIM**	**GP**	**G**	**A**	**TP**	**PIM**
1991-92	Lethbridge	WHL	65	6	17	23	48	5	0	2	2	4
1992-93	Lethbridge	WHL	66	46	73	119	69	4	3	3	6	8
1993-94a	Lethbridge	WHL	72	58	69	127	93	8	4	11	15	16
1994-95	Cleveland	IHL	62	18	32	50	66	3	0	2	2	2
1995-96	Cleveland	IHL	74	10	28	38	100	3	0	0	0	2
1996-97	**Pittsburgh**	**NHL**	**1**	**0**	**0**	**0**	**0**	....	....	....	....	....
	Long Beach	IHL	65	23	43	66	91	18	5	9	14	26
	NHL Totals		**1**	**0**	**0**	**0**	**0**	....	....	....	....	....

a WHL East Second All-Star Team (1994)

PIVONKA, MICHAL (pih-VAHN-kuh) WSH.

Center. Shoots left. 6'2", 195 lbs. Born, Kladno, Czech., January 28, 1966.
(Washington's 3rd choice, 59th overall, in 1984 Entry Draft).

			Regular Season					Playoffs				
Season	Club	Lea	GP	G	A	TP	PIM	GP	G	A	TP	PIM
1984-85	Dukla Jihlava	Czech.	33	8	11	19	18	....	....	....	....	....
1985-86	Dukla Jihlava	Czech.	42	5	13	18	18	....	....	....	....	....
1986-87	**Washington**	**NHL**	73	18	25	43	41	7	1	1	2	2
1987-88	**Washington**	**NHL**	71	11	23	34	28	14	4	9	13	4
1988-89	**Washington**	**NHL**	52	8	19	27	30	6	3	1	4	10
	Baltimore	AHL	31	12	24	36	19	....	....	....	....	....
1989-90	**Washington**	**NHL**	77	25	39	64	54	11	0	2	2	6
1990-91	**Washington**	**NHL**	79	20	50	70	34	11	2	3	5	8
1991-92	**Washington**	**NHL**	80	23	57	80	47	7	1	5	6	13
1992-93	**Washington**	**NHL**	69	21	53	74	66	6	0	2	2	0
1993-94	**Washington**	**NHL**	82	14	36	50	38	7	4	4	8	4
1994-95	Klagenfurt	Aus.	7	2	4	6	4	....	....	....	....	....
	Washington	**NHL**	46	10	23	33	50	7	1	4	5	21
1995-96	Detroit	IHL	7	1	9	10	19	....	....	....	....	....
	Washington	**NHL**	73	16	65	81	36	6	3	2	5	18
1996-97	**Washington**	**NHL**	54	7	16	23	22	....	....	....	....	....
	NHL Totals		756	173	406	579	446	82	19	33	52	86

PLANTE, DAN (PLAHNT) NYI

Right wing. Shoots right. 5'11", 202 lbs. Born, Hayward, WI, October 5, 1971.
(NY Islanders' 3rd choice, 48th overall, in 1990 Entry Draft).

			Regular Season					Playoffs				
Season	Club	Lea	GP	G	A	TP	PIM	GP	G	A	TP	PIM
1990-91	U. Wisconsin	WCHA	33	1	2	3	54	....	....	....	....	....
1991-92	U. Wisconsin	WCHA	36	13	13	26	107	....	....	....	....	....
1992-93	U. Wisconsin	WCHA	42	26	31	57	142	....	....	....	....	....
1993-94	**NY Islanders**	**NHL**	12	0	1	1	4	1	1	0	1	2
	Salt Lake	IHL	66	7	17	24	148	....	....	....	....	....
1994-95	Denver	IHL	2	0	0	0	4	....	....	....	....	....
1995-96	**NY Islanders**	**NHL**	73	5	3	8	50	....	....	....	....	....
1996-97	**NY Islanders**	**NHL**	67	4	9	13	75	....	....	....	....	....
	NHL Totals		152	9	13	22	129	1	1	0	1	2

PLANTE, DEREK (PLAHNT) BUF.

Center. Shoots left. 5'11", 181 lbs. Born, Cloquet, MN, January 17, 1971.
(Buffalo's 7th choice, 161st overall, in 1989 Entry Draft).

			Regular Season					Playoffs				
Season	Club	Lea	GP	G	A	TP	PIM	GP	G	A	TP	PIM
1989-90	Minn.-Duluth	WCHA	28	10	11	21	12	....	....	....	....	....
1990-91	Minn.-Duluth	WCHA	36	23	20	43	6	....	....	....	....	....
1991-92a	Minn.-Duluth	WCHA	37	27	36	63	28	....	....	....	....	....
1992-93bc	Minn.-Duluth	WCHA	37	*36	*56	*92	30	....	....	....	....	....
1993-94	**Buffalo**	**NHL**	77	21	35	56	24	7	1	0	1	0
	U.S. National	....	2	0	1	1	0	....	....	....	....	....
1994-95	**Buffalo**	**NHL**	47	3	19	22	12	....	....	....	....	....
1995-96	**Buffalo**	**NHL**	76	23	33	56	28	....	....	....	....	....
1996-97	**Buffalo**	**NHL**	82	27	26	53	24	12	4	6	10	4
	NHL Totals		282	74	113	187	88	19	5	6	11	4

a WCHA Second All-Star Team (1992)
b WCHA First All-Star Team (1993)
c NCAA West First All-American Team (1993)

PLAVSIC, ADRIEN (PLAV-sihk)

Defense. Shoots left. 6'1", 200 lbs. Born, Montreal, Que., January 13, 1970.
(St. Louis' 2nd choice, 30th overall, in 1988 Entry Draft).

			Regular Season					Playoffs				
Season	Club	Lea	GP	G	A	TP	PIM	GP	G	A	TP	PIM
1987-88	N. Hampshire	H.E.	30	5	6	11	45	....	....	....	....	....
1988-89	Cdn. National	....	62	5	10	15	25	....	....	....	....	....
1989-90	**St. Louis**	**NHL**	4	0	1	1	2	....	....	....	....	....
	Peoria	IHL	51	7	14	21	87	....	....	....	....	....
	Vancouver	**NHL**	11	3	2	5	8	....	....	....	....	....
	Milwaukee	IHL	3	1	2	3	14	6	1	3	4	6
1990-91	**Vancouver**	**NHL**	48	2	10	12	62	....	....	....	....	....
1991-92	Cdn. National	....	38	7	8	15	44	....	....	....	....	....
	Cdn. Olympic	....	8	0	2	2	0	....	....	....	....	....
	Vancouver	**NHL**	16	1	9	10	14	13	1	7	8	4
1992-93	**Vancouver**	**NHL**	57	6	21	27	53	....	....	....	....	....
1993-94	**Vancouver**	**NHL**	47	1	9	10	6	....	....	....	....	....
	Hamilton	AHL	2	0	0	0	0	....	....	....	....	....
1994-95	**Vancouver**	**NHL**	3	0	1	1	4	....	....	....	....	....
	Tampa Bay	**NHL**	15	2	1	3	4	....	....	....	....	....
1995-96	**Tampa Bay**	**NHL**	7	1	2	3	6	....	....	....	....	....
	Atlanta	IHL	68	5	34	39	32	3	0	1	1	4
1996-97	**Anaheim**	**NHL**	6	0	0	0	2	....	....	....	....	....
	Long Beach	IHL	69	7	28	35	86	18	0	9	9	10
	NHL Totals		214	16	56	72	161	13	1	7	8	4

Traded to **Vancouver** by **St. Louis** with Montreal's first round choice (previously acquired by St. Louis — Vancouver selected Shawn Antoski) in 1990 Entry Draft and St. Louis' second round choice (later traded to Montreal — Montreal selected Craig Darby) in 1991 Entry Draft for Rich Sutter, Harold Snepsts and St. Louis' second round choice (previously acquired by Vancouver — St. Louis selected Craig Johnson) in 1990 Entry Draft, March 6, 1990. Traded to **Tampa Bay** by **Vancouver** for Tampa Bay's fifth round choice (David Darguzas) in 1997 Entry Draft, March 23, 1995. Signed as a free agent by **Anaheim**, September 6, 1996.

POAPST, STEVE (POHPST) WSH.

Defense. Shoots left. 6', 200 lbs. Born, Cornwall, Ont., January 3, 1969.

			Regular Season					Playoffs				
Season	Club	Lea	GP	G	A	TP	PIM	GP	G	A	TP	PIM
1987-88	Colgate	ECAC	32	3	13	16	22	....	....	....	....	....
1988-89	Colgate	ECAC	30	0	5	5	38	....	....	....	....	....
1989-90	Colgate	ECAC	38	4	15	19	54	....	....	....	....	....
1990-91	Colgate	ECAC	32	6	15	21	43	....	....	....	....	....
1991-92	Hampton Rds.	ECHL	55	8	20	28	29	14	1	4	5	12
1992-93a	Hampton Rds.	ECHL	63	10	35	45	57	4	0	1	1	4
	Baltimore	AHL	7	0	1	1	4	7	0	3	3	6
1993-94	Portland	AHL	78	14	21	35	47	12	0	3	3	8
1994-95	Portland	AHL	71	8	22	30	60	7	0	1	1	16
1995-96	**Washington**	**NHL**	3	1	0	1	0	6	0	0	0	0
	Portland	AHL	70	10	24	34	79	20	2	6	8	16
1996-97	Portland	AHL	47	1	20	21	34	5	0	1	1	6
	NHL Totals		3	1	0	1	0	6	0	0	0	0

a ECHL First All-Star Team (1993)

Signed as a free agent by **Washington**, February 4, 1995.

PODEIN, SHJON (poh-DEEN, SHAWN) PHI.

Left wing. Shoots left. 6'2", 200 lbs. Born, Rochester, MN, March 5, 1968.
(Edmonton's 9th choice, 166th overall, in 1988 Entry Draft).

			Regular Season					Playoffs				
Season	Club	Lea	GP	G	A	TP	PIM	GP	G	A	TP	PIM
1987-88	Minn.-Duluth	WCHA	30	4	4	8	48	....	....	....	....	....
1988-89	Minn.-Duluth	WCHA	36	7	5	12	46	....	....	....	....	....
1989-90	Minn.-Duluth	WCHA	35	21	18	39	36	....	....	....	....	....
1990-91	Cape Breton	AHL	63	14	15	29	65	4	0	0	0	5
1991-92	Cape Breton	AHL	80	30	24	54	46	5	3	1	4	2
1992-93	**Edmonton**	**NHL**	40	13	6	19	25	....	....	....	....	....
	Cape Breton	AHL	38	18	21	39	32	9	2	2	4	29
1993-94	**Edmonton**	**NHL**	28	3	5	8	8	....	....	....	....	....
	Cape Breton	AHL	5	4	4	8	4	....	....	....	....	....
1994-95	**Philadelphia**	**NHL**	44	3	7	10	33	15	1	3	4	10
1995-96	**Philadelphia**	**NHL**	79	15	10	25	89	12	1	2	3	50
1996-97	**Philadelphia**	**NHL**	82	14	18	32	41	19	4	3	7	16
	NHL Totals		273	48	46	94	196	46	6	8	14	76

Signed as a free agent by **Philadelphia**, July 27, 1994.

PODKONICKY, ANDREJ (pohd-koh-NIHTZ-kee) ST.L.

Center. Shoots left. 6', 174 lbs. Born, Zvolen, Czech., May 9, 1978.
(St. Louis' 8th choice, 196th overall, in 1996 Entry Draft).

			Regular Season					Playoffs				
Season	Club	Lea	GP	G	A	TP	PIM	GP	G	A	TP	PIM
1994-95	Zvolen	Slov. 2	17	0	4	4	6	....	....	....	....	....
1995-96	Zvolen	Slov. 2	38	18	12	30	18	....	....	....	....	....
1996-97	Portland	WHL	71	25	46	71	127	6	1	1	2	8

PODOLLAN, JASON (poh-DOH-luhn) TOR.

Right wing. Shoots right. 6'1", 192 lbs. Born, Vernon, B.C., February 18, 1976.
(Florida's 3rd choice, 31st overall, in 1994 Entry Draft).

			Regular Season					Playoffs				
Season	Club	Lea	GP	G	A	TP	PIM	GP	G	A	TP	PIM
1991-92	Spokane	WHL	2	0	0	0	2	10	3	1	4	16
1992-93	Spokane	WHL	72	36	33	69	108	10	4	4	8	14
1993-94	Spokane	WHL	69	29	37	66	108	3	3	0	3	2
1994-95	Spokane	WHL	72	43	41	84	102	11	5	7	12	18
	Cincinnati	IHL	....	....	....	....	....	3	0	0	0	2
1995-96a	Spokane	WHL	56	37	25	62	103	18	*21	12	33	28
1996-97	**Florida**	**NHL**	19	1	1	2	4	....	....	....	....	....
	Carolina	AHL	39	21	25	46	36	....	....	....	....	....
	Toronto	**NHL**	10	0	3	3	6	....	....	....	....	....
	St. John's	AHL	....	....	....	....	....	11	2	3	5	6
	NHL Totals		29	1	4	5	10	....	....	....	....	....

a WHL West Second All-Star Team (1996)

Traded to **Toronto** by **Florida** for Kirk Muller, March 18, 1997.

POESCHEK, RUDY (POH-shehk) ST.L.

Right wing/Defense. Shoots right. 6'2", 218 lbs. Born, Kamloops, B.C., September 29, 1966.
(NY Rangers' 12th choice, 238th overall, in 1985 Entry Draft).

			Regular Season					Playoffs				
Season	Club	Lea	GP	G	A	TP	PIM	GP	G	A	TP	PIM
1983-84	Kamloops	WHL	47	3	9	12	93	8	0	2	2	7
1984-85	Kamloops	WHL	34	6	7	13	100	15	0	3	3	56
1985-86	Kamloops	WHL	32	3	13	16	92	16	3	7	10	40
1986-87	Kamloops	WHL	54	13	18	31	153	15	2	4	6	37
1987-88	**NY Rangers**	**NHL**	1	0	0	0	2	....	....	....	....	....
	Colorado	IHL	82	7	31	38	210	12	2	2	4	31
1988-89	**NY Rangers**	**NHL**	52	0	2	2	199	....	....	....	....	....
	Colorado	IHL	2	0	0	0	6	....	....	....	....	....
1989-90	**NY Rangers**	**NHL**	15	0	0	0	55	....	....	....	....	....
	Flint	IHL	38	8	13	21	109	4	0	0	0	16
1990-91	Binghamton	AHL	38	1	3	4	162	....	....	....	....	....
	Winnipeg	**NHL**	1	0	0	0	5	....	....	....	....	....
	Moncton	AHL	23	2	4	6	67	9	1	1	2	41
1991-92	**Winnipeg**	**NHL**	4	0	0	0	17	....	....	....	....	....
	Moncton	AHL	63	4	18	22	170	11	0	2	2	48
1992-93	St. John's	AHL	78	7	24	31	189	9	0	4	4	13
1993-94	**Tampa Bay**	**NHL**	71	3	6	9	118	....	....	....	....	....
1994-95	**Tampa Bay**	**NHL**	25	1	1	2	92	....	....	....	....	....
1995-96	**Tampa Bay**	**NHL**	57	1	3	4	88	3	0	0	0	12
1996-97	**Tampa Bay**	**NHL**	60	0	6	6	120	....	....	....	....	....
	NHL Totals		286	5	18	23	696	3	0	0	0	12

Traded to **Winnipeg** by **NY Rangers** for Guy Larose, January 22, 1991. Signed as a free agent by **Toronto**, July 8, 1992. Signed as a free agent by **Tampa Bay**, August 10, 1993. Signed as a free agent by **St. Louis**, July 31, 1997.

POIRIER, GAETAN (pwuh-RAY, GAY-tehn) FLA.

Left wing. Shoots left. 6'2", 200 lbs. Born, Moncton, N.B., December 28, 1976.
(Florida's 6th choice, 156th overall, in 1996 Entry Draft).

			Regular Season					Playoffs				
Season	Club	Lea	GP	G	A	TP	PIM	GP	G	A	TP	PIM
1994-95	Merrimack	H.E.	32	8	6	14	38	....	....	....	....	....
1995-96	Merrimack	H.E.	33	10	14	24	52	....	....	....	....	....
1996-97	Carolina	AHL	66	5	13	18	66	....	....	....	....	....

POLLOCK, JAME ST.L.

Defense. Shoots right. 6'1", 190 lbs. Born, Quebec City, Que., June 16, 1979.
(St. Louis' 4th choice, 106th overall, in 1997 Entry Draft).

			Regular Season					Playoffs				
Season	Club	Lea	GP	G	A	TP	PIM	GP	G	A	TP	PIM
1995-96	Seattle	WHL	32	0	1	1	15	....	....	....	....	....
1996-97	Seattle	WHL	66	15	19	34	94	15	3	5	8	16

POPOVIC, PETER (puh-PUH-vihch) MTL.

Defense. Shoots left. 6'6", 235 lbs. Born, Koping, Sweden, February 10, 1968.
(Montreal's 5th choice, 93rd overall, in 1988 Entry Draft).

			Regular Season					Playoffs				
Season	Club	Lea	GP	G	A	TP	PIM	GP	G	A	TP	PIM
1986-87	Vasteras	Swe. 2	24	1	2	3	10	....	....	....	....	....
1987-88	Vasteras	Swe. 2	28	3	17	20	16	....	....	....	....	....
1988-89	Vasteras	Swe.	22	1	4	5	32	....	....	....	....	....
1989-90	Vasteras	Swe.	30	2	10	12	24	2	0	1	1	2
1990-91	Vasteras	Swe.	40	3	2	5	62	4	0	0	0	4
1991-92	Vasteras	Swe.	34	7	10	17	30	....	....	....	....	....
1992-93	Vasteras	Swe.	39	6	12	18	46	3	0	1	1	2
1993-94	**Montreal**	**NHL**	**47**	**2**	**12**	**14**	**26**	**6**	**0**	**1**	**1**	**0**
1994-95	Vasteras	Swe.	11	0	3	3	10	....	....	....	....	....
	Montreal	**NHL**	**33**	**0**	**5**	**5**	**8**	....	....	....	....	....
1995-96	**Montreal**	**NHL**	**76**	**2**	**12**	**14**	**69**	**6**	**0**	**2**	**2**	**4**
1996-97	**Montreal**	**NHL**	**78**	**1**	**13**	**14**	**32**	**3**	**0**	**0**	**0**	**2**
	NHL Totals		**234**	**5**	**42**	**47**	**135**	**15**	**0**	**3**	**3**	**6**

POSMYK, MAREK (PAWZ-mihk) TOR.

Defense. Shoots right. 6'5", 220 lbs. Born, Jihlava, Czech., September 15, 1978.
(Toronto's 1st choice, 36th overall, in 1996 Entry Draft).

			Regular Season					Playoffs				
Season	Club	Lea	GP	G	A	TP	PIM	GP	G	A	TP	PIM
1994-95	Dukla Jihlava	Czech. Jr.	16	1	3	4	....	....	....	....	....	....
1995-96	Dukla Jihlava	Czech. Jr.	16	6	5	11	....	....	....	....	....	....
	Dukla Jihlava	Czech.	18	1	2	3	....	1	0	0	0	....
1996-97	Dukla Jihlava	Czech.	24	1	7	8	44	....	....	....	....	....
	St. John's	AHL	2	0	0	0	2	....	....	....	....	....

POTAPOV, VLADIMIR (poh-TAH-pohv) PHO.

Right wing. Shoots left. 6'2", 187 lbs. Born, Murmansk, USSR, June 21, 1975.
(Winnipeg's 10th choice, 217th overall, in 1993 Entry Draft).

			Regular Season					Playoffs				
Season	Club	Lea	GP	G	A	TP	PIM	GP	G	A	TP	PIM
1993-94	Elektrostal	CIS 2	41	3	3	6	4	....	....	....	....	....
1994-95	Elektrostal	CIS	51	4	7	11	24	....	....	....	....	....
1995-96	Moscow D'amo	CIS	25	1	0	1	8	....	....	....	....	....
1996-97	Moscow D'amo	Rus.	8	0	0	0	0	....	....	....	....	....
	Ufa Salavat	Rus.	2	0	0	0	0	....	....	....	....	....
	Opava	Czech.	7	1	0	1	0	....	....	....	....	....

POTI, TOM (POH-tee) EDM.

Defense. Shoots left. 6'2", 185 lbs. Born, Worcester, MA, March 22, 1977.
(Edmonton's 4th choice, 59th overall, in 1996 Entry Draft).

			Regular Season					Playoffs				
Season	Club	Lea	GP	G	A	TP	PIM	GP	G	A	TP	PIM
1995-96	Cushing Aca.	HS	29	14	59	73	18	....	....	....	....	....
1996-97a	Boston U.	H.E.	38	4	17	21	54	....	....	....	....	....

a NCAA Final Four All-Tournament Team (1997)

POTOMSKI, BARRY S.J.

Left wing. Shoots left. 6'2", 215 lbs. Born, Windsor, Ont., November 24, 1972.

			Regular Season					Playoffs				
Season	Club	Lea	GP	G	A	TP	PIM	GP	G	A	TP	PIM
1989-90	London	OHL	9	0	2	2	18	....	....	....	....	....
1990-91	London	OHL	65	14	17	31	202	7	0	2	2	10
1991-92	London	OHL	61	19	32	51	224	10	5	1	6	22
1992-93	Erie	ECHL	5	1	1	2	31	....	....	....	....	....
	Toledo	ECHL	43	5	18	23	184	14	5	2	7	73
1993-94	Toledo	ECHL	13	9	4	13	81	....	....	....	....	....
	Adirondack	AHL	50	9	5	14	224	11	1	1	2	44
1994-95	Phoenix	IHL	42	5	6	11	171	....	....	....	....	....
1995-96	**Los Angeles**	**NHL**	**33**	**3**	**2**	**5**	**104**	....	....	....	....	....
	Phoenix	IHL	24	5	2	7	74	3	1	0	1	8
1996-97	**Los Angeles**	**NHL**	**26**	**3**	**2**	**5**	**93**	....	....	....	....	....
	Phoenix	IHL	28	2	11	13	58	....	....	....	....	....
	NHL Totals		**59**	**6**	**4**	**10**	**197**	....	....	....	....	....

Signed as a free agent by **Los Angeles**, July 7, 1994. Signed as a free agent by **San Jose**, August 15, 1997.

POTVIN, MARC (PAHT-vahn)

Right wing. Shoots right. 6'1", 200 lbs. Born, Ottawa, Ont., January 29, 1967.
(Detroit's 9th choice, 169th overall, in 1986 Entry Draft).

			Regular Season					Playoffs				
Season	Club	Lea	GP	G	A	TP	PIM	GP	G	A	TP	PIM
1986-87	Bowling Green	CCHA	43	5	15	20	74	....	....	....	....	....
1987-88	Bowling Green	CCHA	45	15	21	36	80	....	....	....	....	....
1988-89	Bowling Green	CCHA	46	23	12	35	63	....	....	....	....	....
1989-90	Bowling Green	CCHA	40	19	17	36	72	....	....	....	....	....
	Adirondack	AHL	5	2	1	3	9	4	0	1	1	23
1990-91	**Detroit**	**NHL**	**9**	**0**	**0**	**0**	**55**	**6**	**0**	**0**	**0**	**32**
	Adirondack	AHL	63	9	13	22	*365	....	....	....	....	....
1991-92	**Detroit**	**NHL**	**5**	**1**	**0**	**1**	**52**	**1**	**0**	**0**	**0**	**0**
	Adirondack	AHL	51	13	16	29	314	19	5	4	9	57
1992-93	Adirondack	AHL	37	8	12	20	109	....	....	....	....	....
	Los Angeles	**NHL**	**20**	**0**	**1**	**1**	**61**	**1**	**0**	**0**	**0**	**0**
1993-94	**Los Angeles**	**NHL**	**3**	**0**	**0**	**0**	**26**	....	....	....	....	....
	Hartford	**NHL**	**51**	**2**	**3**	**5**	**246**	....	....	....	....	....
1994-95	**Boston**	**NHL**	**6**	**0**	**1**	**1**	**4**	....	....	....	....	....
	Providence	AHL	21	4	14	18	84	12	2	4	6	25
1995-96	**Boston**	**NHL**	**27**	**0**	**0**	**0**	**12**	**5**	**0**	**1**	**1**	**18**
	Providence	AHL	48	9	9	18	118	....	....	....	....	....
1996-97	Portland	AHL	71	17	15	32	222	5	0	0	0	12
	NHL Totals		**121**	**3**	**5**	**8**	**456**	**13**	**0**	**1**	**1**	**50**

Traded to **Los Angeles** by **Detroit** with Jimmy Carson and Gary Shuchuk for Paul Coffey, Sylvain Couturier and Jim Hiller, January 29, 1993. Traded to **Hartford** by **Los Angeles** for Doug Houda, November 3, 1993. Signed as a free agent by **Boston**, June 29, 1994.

POULIN, PATRICK (poo-LIHN) T.B.

Left wing. Shoots left. 6'1", 210 lbs. Born, Vanier, Que., April 23, 1973.
(Hartford's 1st choice, 9th overall, in 1991 Entry Draft).

			Regular Season					Playoffs				
Season	Club	Lea	GP	G	A	TP	PIM	GP	G	A	TP	PIM
1989-90	St-Hyacinthe	QMJHL	60	25	26	51	55	12	1	9	10	5
1990-91	St-Hyacinthe	QMJHL	56	32	38	70	82	4	0	2	2	23
1991-92	**Hartford**	**NHL**	**1**	**0**	**0**	**0**	**2**	**7**	**2**	**1**	**3**	**0**
a	St-Hyacinthe	QMJHL	56	52	86	*138	58	5	2	2	4	4
	Springfield	AHL	....	....	....	....	....	1	0	0	0	0
1992-93	**Hartford**	**NHL**	**81**	**20**	**31**	**51**	**37**	....	....	....	....	....
1993-94	**Hartford**	**NHL**	**9**	**2**	**1**	**3**	**11**	....	....	....	....	....
	Chicago	**NHL**	**58**	**12**	**13**	**25**	**40**	**4**	**0**	**0**	**0**	**0**
1994-95	**Chicago**	**NHL**	**45**	**15**	**15**	**30**	**53**	**16**	**4**	**1**	**5**	**8**
1995-96	**Chicago**	**NHL**	**38**	**7**	**8**	**15**	**16**	....	....	....	....	....
	Indianapolis	IHL	1	0	1	1	0	....	....	....	....	....
	Tampa Bay	**NHL**	**8**	**0**	**1**	**1**	**0**	**2**	**0**	**0**	**0**	**0**
1996-97	**Tampa Bay**	**NHL**	**73**	**12**	**14**	**26**	**56**	....	....	....	....	....
	NHL Totals		**313**	**68**	**83**	**151**	**215**	**29**	**6**	**2**	**8**	**8**

a QMJHL First All-Star Team (1992)

Traded to **Chicago** by **Hartford** with Eric Weinrich for Steve Larmer and Bryan Marchment, November 2, 1993. Traded to **Tampa Bay** by **Chicago** with Igor Ulanov and Chicago's second round choice (later traded to New Jersey — New Jersey selected Pierre Dagenais) in 1996 Entry Draft for Enrico Ciccone and Tampa Bay's second round choice (Jeff Paul) in 1996 Entry Draft, March 20, 1996.

PRATT, HARLAN PIT.

Defense. Shoots right. 6'1", 202 lbs. Born, Fort McMurray, Alta., December 10, 1978.
(Pittsburgh's 5th choice, 124th overall, in 1997 Entry Draft).

			Regular Season					Playoffs				
Season	Club	Lea	GP	G	A	TP	PIM	GP	G	A	TP	PIM
1995-96	Red Deer	WHL	60	2	3	5	22	10	0	0	0	4
1996-97	Red Deer	WHL	2	0	0	0	2	....	....	....	....	....
	Prince Albert	WHL	65	7	26	33	49	4	1	1	2	4

PRATT, NOLAN CAR.

Defense. Shoots left. 6'2", 195 lbs. Born, Fort McMurray, Alta., August 14, 1975.
(Hartford's 4th choice, 115th overall, in 1993 Entry Draft).

			Regular Season					Playoffs				
Season	Club	Lea	GP	G	A	TP	PIM	GP	G	A	TP	PIM
1991-92	Portland	WHL	22	2	9	11	13	6	1	3	4	12
1992-93	Portland	WHL	70	4	19	23	97	16	2	7	9	31
1993-94	Portland	WHL	72	4	32	36	105	10	1	2	3	14
1994-95	Portland	WHL	72	6	37	43	196	9	1	6	7	10
1995-96	Springfield	AHL	62	2	6	8	72	2	0	0	0	0
	Richmond	ECHL	4	1	0	1	2	....	....	....	....	....
1996-97	**Hartford**	**NHL**	**9**	**0**	**2**	**2**	**6**	....	....	....	....	....
	Springfield	AHL	66	1	18	19	127	17	0	3	3	18
	NHL Totals		**9**	**0**	**2**	**2**	**6**	....	....	....	....	....

PRESLEY, WAYNE

Right wing. Shoots right. 5'11", 195 lbs. Born, Dearborn, MI, March 23, 1965.
(Chicago's 2nd choice, 39th overall, in 1983 Entry Draft).

			Regular Season					Playoffs				
Season	Club	Lea	GP	G	A	TP	PIM	GP	G	A	TP	PIM
1982-83	Kitchener	OHL	70	39	48	87	99	12	1	4	5	9
1983-84a	Kitchener	OHL	70	63	76	139	156	16	12	16	28	38
1984-85	**Chicago**	**NHL**	**3**	**0**	**1**	**1**	**0**	....	....	....	....	....
	Kitchener	OHL	31	25	21	46	77	....	....	....	....	....
	S.S. Marie	OHL	11	5	9	14	14	16	13	9	22	13
1985-86	**Chicago**	**NHL**	**38**	**7**	**8**	**15**	**38**	**3**	**0**	**0**	**0**	**0**
	Nova Scotia	AHL	29	6	9	15	22	....	....	....	....	....
1986-87	**Chicago**	**NHL**	**80**	**32**	**29**	**61**	**114**	**4**	**1**	**0**	**1**	**9**
1987-88	**Chicago**	**NHL**	**42**	**12**	**10**	**22**	**52**	**5**	**0**	**0**	**0**	**4**
1988-89	**Chicago**	**NHL**	**72**	**21**	**19**	**40**	**100**	**14**	**7**	**5**	**12**	**18**
1989-90	**Chicago**	**NHL**	**49**	**6**	**7**	**13**	**69**	**19**	**9**	**6**	**15**	**29**
1990-91	**Chicago**	**NHL**	**71**	**15**	**19**	**34**	**122**	**6**	**0**	**1**	**1**	**38**
1991-92	**San Jose**	**NHL**	**47**	**8**	**14**	**22**	**76**	....	....	....	....	....
	Buffalo	**NHL**	**12**	**2**	**2**	**4**	**57**	**7**	**3**	**3**	**6**	**14**
1992-93	**Buffalo**	**NHL**	**79**	**15**	**17**	**32**	**96**	**8**	**1**	**0**	**1**	**6**
1993-94	**Buffalo**	**NHL**	**65**	**17**	**8**	**25**	**103**	**7**	**2**	**1**	**3**	**14**
1994-95	**Buffalo**	**NHL**	**46**	**14**	**5**	**19**	**41**	**5**	**3**	**1**	**4**	**8**
1995-96	**NY Rangers**	**NHL**	**61**	**4**	**6**	**10**	**71**	....	....	....	....	....
	Toronto	**NHL**	**19**	**2**	**2**	**4**	**14**	**5**	**0**	**0**	**0**	**2**
1996-97	St. John's	AHL	2	0	0	0	0	....	....	....	....	....
	Detroit	IHL	42	7	16	23	80	18	0	4	4	50
	NHL Totals		**684**	**155**	**147**	**302**	**953**	**83**	**26**	**17**	**43**	**142**

a OHL First All-Star Team (1984)

Traded to **San Jose** by **Chicago** for San Jose's third round choice (Bogdan Savenko) in 1993 Entry Draft, September 20, 1991. Traded to **Buffalo** by **San Jose** for Dave Snuggerud, March 9, 1992. Signed as a free agent by **NY Rangers**, August 31, 1995. Traded to **Toronto** by **NY Rangers** for Sergio Momesso, February 29, 1996.

PRIER, BOB (PRIGH-uhr) BOS.

Right wing. Shoots right. 6'1", 210 lbs. Born, Pembroke, Ont., August 5, 1976.
(Boston's 9th choice, 208th overall, in 1996 Entry Draft).

			Regular Season					Playoffs				
Season	Club	Lea	GP	G	A	TP	PIM	GP	G	A	TP	PIM
1995-96	St. Lawrence	ECAC	32	10	8	18	31	....	....	....	....	....
1996-97	St. Lawrence	ECAC	33	15	9	24	14	....	....	....	....	....

PRIMEAU, KEITH (PREE-moh) CAR.

Center. Shoots left. 6'4", 210 lbs. Born, Toronto, Ont., November 24, 1971.
(Detroit's 1st choice, 3rd overall, in 1990 Entry Draft).

			Regular Season					Playoffs				
Season	Club	Lea	GP	G	A	TP	PIM	GP	G	A	TP	PIM
1987-88	Hamilton	OHL	47	6	6	12	69	....	....	....	....	....
1988-89	Niagara Falls	OHL	48	20	35	55	56	17	9	16	25	12
1989-90a	Niagara Falls	OHL	65	*57	70	*127	97	16	*16	17	*33	49
1990-91	**Detroit**	**NHL**	**58**	**3**	**12**	**15**	**106**	**5**	**1**	**1**	**2**	**25**
	Adirondack	AHL	6	3	5	8	8	....	....	....	....	....
1991-92	**Detroit**	**NHL**	**35**	**6**	**10**	**16**	**83**	**11**	**0**	**0**	**0**	**14**
	Adirondack	AHL	42	21	24	45	89	9	1	7	8	27
1992-93	**Detroit**	**NHL**	**73**	**15**	**17**	**32**	**152**	**7**	**0**	**2**	**2**	**26**
1993-94	**Detroit**	**NHL**	**78**	**31**	**42**	**73**	**173**	**7**	**0**	**2**	**2**	**6**
1994-95	**Detroit**	**NHL**	**45**	**15**	**27**	**42**	**99**	**17**	**4**	**5**	**9**	**45**
1995-96	**Detroit**	**NHL**	**74**	**27**	**25**	**52**	**168**	**17**	**1**	**4**	**5**	**28**
1996-97	**Hartford**	**NHL**	**75**	**26**	**25**	**51**	**161**	....	....	....	....	....
	NHL Totals		**438**	**123**	**158**	**281**	**942**	**64**	**6**	**14**	**20**	**144**

a OHL Second All-Star Team (1990)

Traded to **Hartford** by **Detroit** with Paul Coffey and Detroit's first round choice (Nikos Tselios) in 1997 Entry Draft for Brendan Shanahan and Brian Glynn, October 9, 1996.

PRIMEAU, WAYNE (PREE-moh) BUF.

Center. Shoots left. 6'3", 193 lbs. Born, Scarborough, Ont., June 4, 1976.
(Buffalo's 1st choice, 17th overall, in 1994 Entry Draft).

			Regular Season					Playoffs				
Season	Club	Lea	GP	G	A	TP	PIM	GP	G	A	TP	PIM
1992-93	Owen Sound	OHL	66	10	27	37	108	8	1	4	5	0
1993-94	Owen Sound	OHL	65	25	50	75	75	9	1	6	7	8
1994-95	Owen Sound	OHL	66	34	62	96	84	10	4	9	13	15
	Buffalo	**NHL**	**1**	**1**	**0**	**1**	**0**	....	....	....	....	....
1995-96	**Buffalo**	**NHL**	**2**	**0**	**0**	**0**	**0**	....	....	....	....	....
	Owen Sound	OHL	28	15	29	44	52	....	....	....	....	....
	Oshawa	OHL	24	12	13	25	33	3	2	3	5	2
	Rochester	AHL	8	2	3	5	6	17	3	1	4	11
1996-97	**Buffalo**	**NHL**	**45**	**2**	**4**	**6**	**64**	**9**	**0**	**0**	**0**	**6**
	Rochester	AHL	24	9	5	14	27	1	0	0	0	0
	NHL Totals		**48**	**3**	**4**	**7**	**64**	**9**	**0**	**0**	**0**	**6**

PROBERT, BOB (PROH-buhrt) CHI.

Left wing. Shoots left. 6'3", 225 lbs. Born, Windsor, Ont., June 5, 1965.
(Detroit's 3rd choice, 46th overall, in 1983 Entry Draft).

			Regular Season					Playoffs				
Season	Club	Lea	GP	G	A	TP	PIM	GP	G	A	TP	PIM
1982-83	Brantford	OHL	51	12	16	28	133	8	2	2	4	23
1983-84	Brantford	OHL	65	35	28	63	189	6	0	3	3	16
1984-85	S.S. Marie	OHL	44	20	52	72	172	15	6	11	17	60
	Hamilton	OHL	4	0	1	1	21	....	....	....	....	....
1985-86	**Detroit**	**NHL**	**44**	**8**	**13**	**21**	**186**	....	....	....	....	....
	Adirondack	AHL	32	12	15	27	152	10	2	3	5	68
1986-87	**Detroit**	**NHL**	**63**	**13**	**11**	**24**	**221**	**16**	**3**	**4**	**7**	**63**
	Adirondack	AHL	7	1	4	5	15	....	....	....	....	....
1987-88	**Detroit**	**NHL**	**74**	**29**	**33**	**62**	***398**	**16**	**8**	**13**	**21**	**51**
1988-89	**Detroit**	**NHL**	**25**	**4**	**2**	**6**	**106**	....	....	....	....	....
1989-90	**Detroit**	**NHL**	**4**	**3**	**0**	**3**	**21**	....	....	....	....	....
1990-91	**Detroit**	**NHL**	**55**	**16**	**23**	**39**	**315**	**6**	**1**	**2**	**3**	**50**
1991-92	**Detroit**	**NHL**	**63**	**20**	**24**	**44**	**276**	**11**	**1**	**6**	**7**	**28**
1992-93	**Detroit**	**NHL**	**80**	**14**	**29**	**43**	**292**	**7**	**0**	**3**	**3**	**10**
1993-94	**Detroit**	**NHL**	**66**	**7**	**10**	**17**	**275**	**7**	**1**	**1**	**2**	**8**
1994-95						DID NOT PLAY						
1995-96	**Chicago**	**NHL**	**78**	**19**	**21**	**40**	**237**	**10**	**0**	**2**	**2**	**23**
1996-97	**Chicago**	**NHL**	**82**	**9**	**14**	**23**	**326**	**6**	**2**	**1**	**3**	**41**
	NHL Totals		**634**	**142**	**180**	**322**	**2653**	**79**	**16**	**32**	**48**	**274**

Played in NHL All-Star Game (1988)

Signed as a free agent by **Chicago**, July 23, 1994.

PROCHAZKA, LIBOR (proh-HAHZ-kah) ST.L.

Defense. Shoots right. 6', 185 lbs. Born, Vlasim, Czech., April 25, 1974.
(St. Louis' 8th choice, 245th overall, in 1993 Entry Draft).

			Regular Season					Playoffs				
Season	Club	Lea	GP	G	A	TP	PIM	GP	G	A	TP	PIM
1991-92	Poldi Kladno	Czech.	7	0	0	0	0	....	....	....	....	....
1992-93	Poldi Kladno	Czech.	34	2	2	4	....	....	....	....	....	....
1993-94	Poldi Kladno	Czech.	41	4	7	11	....	8	0	3	3	....
1994-95	Poldi Kladno	Czech.	40	4	16	20	81	11	2	1	3	14
1995-96	Poldi Kladno	Czech.	38	6	10	16	....	8	2	1	3	....
1996-97	Poldi Kladno	Czech.	49	4	15	19	108	3	0	0	0	4

PROCHAZKA, MARTIN (pro-HAHS-kah) TOR.

Right wing. Shoots right. 5'11", 180 lbs. Born, Slany, Czech., March 3, 1972.
(Toronto's 8th choice, 135th overall, in 1991 Entry Draft).

			Regular Season					Playoffs				
Season	Club	Lea	GP	G	A	TP	PIM	GP	G	A	TP	PIM
1989-90	Poldi Kladno	Czech.	49	18	12	30	....	....	....	....	....	....
1990-91	Poldi Kladno	Czech.	50	19	10	29	21	....	....	....	....	....
1991-92	Dukla Jihlava	Czech.	44	18	11	29	2	....	....	....	....	....
1992-93	Poldi Kladno	Czech.	46	26	12	38	....	....	....	....	....	....
1993-94	Poldi Kladno	Czech.	43	24	16	40	0	2	2	0	2	....
1994-95	Poldi Kladno	Czech.	41	25	33	58	18	11	8	4	12	4
1995-96	Poldi Kladno	Czech.	37	15	27	42	....	8	2	4	6	....
1996-97	AIK	Swe.	49	16	23	39	38	7	2	3	5	8

PROKOPEC, MIKE (PROH-koh-pehk) OTT.

Right wing. Shoots right. 6'2", 190 lbs. Born, Toronto, Ont., May 17, 1974.
(Chicago's 7th choice, 161st overall, in 1992 Entry Draft).

			Regular Season					Playoffs				
Season	Club	Lea	GP	G	A	TP	PIM	GP	G	A	TP	PIM
1991-92	Cornwall	OHL	59	12	15	27	75	6	0	0	0	0
1992-93	Newmarket	OHL	40	6	14	20	70	....	....	....	....	....
	Guelph	OHL	28	10	14	24	27	5	1	0	1	14
1993-94	Guelph	OHL	66	52	58	110	93	9	12	4	16	17
1994-95	Indianapolis	IHL	70	21	12	33	80	....	....	....	....	....
1995-96	**Chicago**	**NHL**	**9**	**0**	**0**	**0**	**5**	....	....	....	....	....
	Indianapolis	IHL	67	18	22	40	131	5	2	0	2	4
1996-97	**Chicago**	**NHL**	**6**	**0**	**0**	**0**	**6**	....	....	....	....	....
	Indianapolis	IHL	57	13	18	31	143	....	....	....	....	....
	Detroit	IHL	3	2	0	2	4	8	2	1	3	14
	NHL Totals		**15**	**0**	**0**	**0**	**11**	....	....	....	....	....

Traded to **Ottawa** by **Chicago** for Denis Chasse, the rights to Kevin Bolibruck and Ottawa's sixth round choice in 1998 Entry Draft, March 18, 1997.

PRONGER, CHRIS (PRAHN-guhr) ST.L.

Defense. Shoots left. 6'5", 220 lbs. Born, Dryden, Ont., October 10, 1974.
(Hartford's 1st choice, 2nd overall, in 1993 Entry Draft).

			Regular Season					Playoffs				
Season	Club	Lea	GP	G	A	TP	PIM	GP	G	A	TP	PIM
1991-92	Peterborough	OHL	63	17	45	62	90	10	1	8	9	28
1992-93abc	Peterborough	OHL	61	15	62	77	108	21	15	25	40	51
1993-94d	**Hartford**	**NHL**	**81**	**5**	**25**	**30**	**113**	....	....	....	....	....
1994-95	**Hartford**	**NHL**	**43**	**5**	**9**	**14**	**54**	....	....	....	....	....
1995-96	**St. Louis**	**NHL**	**78**	**7**	**18**	**25**	**110**	**13**	**1**	**5**	**6**	**16**
1996-97	**St. Louis**	**NHL**	**79**	**11**	**24**	**35**	**143**	**6**	**1**	**1**	**2**	**22**
	NHL Totals		**281**	**28**	**76**	**104**	**420**	**19**	**2**	**6**	**8**	**38**

a OHL First All-Star Team (1993)
b Canadian Major Junior First All-Star Team (1993)
c Canadian Major Junior Defenseman of the Year (1993)
d NHL/Upper Deck All-Rookie Team (1994)

Traded to **St. Louis** by **Hartford** for Brendan Shanahan, July 27, 1995.

PRONGER, SEAN (PRAHN-guhr) ANA.

Center. Shoots left. 6'2", 205 lbs. Born, Dryden, Ont., November 30, 1972.
(Vancouver's 3rd choice, 51st overall, in 1991 Entry Draft).

			Regular Season					Playoffs				
Season	Club	Lea	GP	G	A	TP	PIM	GP	G	A	TP	PIM
1990-91	Bowling Green	CCHA	40	3	7	10	30	....	....	....	....	....
1991-92	Bowling Green	CCHA	34	9	7	16	28	....	....	....	....	....
1992-93	Bowling Green	CCHA	39	23	23	46	35	....	....	....	....	....
1993-94	Bowling Green	CCHA	38	17	17	34	38	....	....	....	....	....
1994-95	Knoxville	ECHL	34	18	23	41	55	....	....	....	....	....
	Greensboro	ECHL	2	0	2	2	0	....	....	....	....	....
	San Diego	IHL	8	0	0	0	2	....	....	....	....	....
1995-96	**Anaheim**	**NHL**	**7**	**0**	**1**	**1**	**6**	....	....	....	....	....
	Baltimore	AHL	72	16	17	33	61	12	3	7	10	16
1996-97	**Anaheim**	**NHL**	**39**	**7**	**7**	**14**	**20**	**9**	**0**	**2**	**2**	**4**
	Baltimore	AHL	41	26	17	43	17	....	....	....	....	....
	NHL Totals		**46**	**7**	**8**	**15**	**26**	**9**	**0**	**2**	**2**	**4**

Signed as a free agent by **Anaheim**, February 14, 1995.

PROSOFSKY, TYLER (proh-SAHV-skee) VAN.

Center. Shoots left. 5'11", 193 lbs. Born, Saskatoon, Sask., February 19, 1976.
(Chicago's 7th choice, 170th overall, in 1994 Entry Draft).

			Regular Season					Playoffs				
Season	Club	Lea	GP	G	A	TP	PIM	GP	G	A	TP	PIM
1992-93	Tacoma	WHL	62	10	9	19	79	7	0	0	0	5
1993-94	Tacoma	WHL	70	20	22	42	132	8	1	1	2	23
1994-95	Tacoma	WHL	71	20	27	47	161	4	0	1	1	21
1995-96	Kelowna	WHL	63	35	40	75	148	6	4	3	7	30
1996-97	Kelowna	WHL	3	2	2	4	11	6	5	2	7	24

Re-entered NHL Entry Draft, **Vancouver's** 4th choice, 121st overall, in 1996 Entry Draft.

PROSPAL, VACLAV (PRAWS-pahl, VAHT-slahv) PHI.

Center. Shoots left. 6'2", 185 lbs. Born, Ceske-Budejovice, Czech., February 17, 1975.
(Philadelphia's 2nd choice, 71st overall, in 1993 Entry Draft).

			Regular Season					Playoffs				
Season	Club	Lea	GP	G	A	TP	PIM	GP	G	A	TP	PIM
1992-93	Budejovice	Czech. Jr.	32	26	31	57	24	....	....	....	....	....
1993-94	Hershey	AHL	55	14	21	35	38	2	0	0	0	2
1994-95	Hershey	AHL	69	13	32	45	36	2	1	0	1	4
1995-96	Hershey	AHL	68	15	36	51	59	5	2	4	6	2
1996-97	**Philadelphia**	**NHL**	**18**	**5**	**10**	**15**	**4**	**5**	**1**	**3**	**4**	**4**
a	Philadelphia	AHL	63	32	63	95	70	....	....	....	....	....
	NHL Totals		**18**	**5**	**10**	**15**	**4**	**5**	**1**	**3**	**4**	**4**

a AHL First All-Star Team (1997)

PROTSENKO, BORIS (proht-SEHN-koh) PIT.

Right wing. Shoots right. 6', 185 lbs. Born, Kiev, USSR, August 21, 1978.
(Pittsburgh's 4th choice, 77th overall, in 1996 Entry Draft).

			Regular Season					Playoffs				
Season	Club	Lea	GP	G	A	TP	PIM	GP	G	A	TP	PIM
1995-96	Calgary	WHL	71	46	29	75	68	....	....	....	....	....
1996-97	Calgary	WHL	67	35	32	67	136	....	....	....	....	....

PRPIC, JOEL (puhr-PIHCH) BOS.

Center. Shoots left. 6'6", 200 lbs. Born, Sudbury, Ont., September 25, 1974.
(Boston's 9th choice, 233rd overall, in 1993 Entry Draft).

			Regular Season					Playoffs				
Season	Club	Lea	GP	G	A	TP	PIM	GP	G	A	TP	PIM
1993-94	St. Lawrence	ECAC	31	2	4	6	90	....	....	....	....	....
1994-95	St. Lawrence	ECAC	32	7	10	17	62	....	....	....	....	....
1995-96	St. Lawrence	ECAC	32	3	10	13	77	....	....	....	....	....
1996-97	St. Lawrence	ECAC	34	10	8	18	57	....	....	....	....	....

PURINTON, DALE NYR

Defense. Shoots left. 6'2", 190 lbs. Born, Fort Wayne, IN, October 11, 1976.
(NY Rangers' 5th choice, 117th overall, in 1995 Entry Draft).

			Regular Season					Playoffs				
Season	Club	Lea	GP	G	A	TP	PIM	GP	G	A	TP	PIM
1994-95	Tacoma	WHL	65	0	8	8	291	3	0	0	0	13
1995-96	Kelowna	WHL	22	1	4	5	88	....	....	....	....	....
	Lethbridge	WHL	37	3	6	9	144	4	1	1	2	25
1996-97	Lethbridge	WHL	51	6	26	32	254	18	3	5	8	*88

Signed as a free agent by **NY Rangers**, August 19, 1997.

PUSHOR, JAMIE (PUH-shohr) DET.

Defense. Shoots right. 6'3", 192 lbs. Born, Lethbridge, Alta., February 11, 1973.
(Detroit's 2nd choice, 32nd overall, in 1991 Entry Draft).

			Regular Season					Playoffs				
Season	Club	Lea	GP	G	A	TP	PIM	GP	G	A	TP	PIM
1989-90	Lethbridge	WHL	10	0	2	2	2	....	....	....	....	....
1990-91	Lethbridge	WHL	71	1	13	14	193	....	....	....	....	....
1991-92	Lethbridge	WHL	49	2	15	17	232	5	0	0	0	33
1992-93	Lethbridge	WHL	72	6	22	28	200	4	0	1	1	9
1993-94	Adirondack	AHL	73	1	17	18	124	12	0	0	0	22
1994-95	Adirondack	AHL	58	2	11	13	129	4	0	1	1	0
1995-96	**Detroit**	**NHL**	**5**	**0**	**1**	**1**	**17**	....	....	....	....	....
	Adirondack	AHL	65	2	16	18	126	3	0	0	0	5
1996-97	**Detroit**	**NHL**	**75**	**4**	**7**	**11**	**129**	**5**	**0**	**1**	**1**	**5** ♦
	NHL Totals		**80**	**4**	**8**	**12**	**146**	**5**	**0**	**1**	**1**	**5**

PYLNER, ROMAN (PIHL-nuhr) COL.

Center. Shoots left. 6', 196 lbs. Born, Most, Czech., January 8, 1978.
(Colorado's 11th choice, 188th overall, in 1996 Entry Draft).

			Regular Season					Playoffs				
Season	Club	Lea	GP	G	A	TP	PIM	GP	G	A	TP	PIM
1995-96	Litvinov	Czech. Jr.	40	19	23	42	....	....	....	....	....	....
1996-97	Calgary	WHL	22	0	4	4	34	....	....	....	....	....
	Tri-City	WHL	26	5	9	14	39	....	....	....	....	....

PYSZ, PATRIK (PIHSH) CHI.

Center. Shoots left. 5'11", 187 lbs. Born, Novy Targ, Poland, January 15, 1975.
(Chicago's 6th choice, 102nd overall, in 1993 Entry Draft).

			Regular Season					Playoffs				
Season	Club	Lea	GP	G	A	TP	PIM	GP	G	A	TP	PIM
1992-93	Augsburg	Ger. 2	36	7	5	12	12	8	2	1	3	0
1993-94	Augsburg	Ger. 2	41	7	20	27	....	9	5	5	10	8
1994-95	Augsburg	Ger.	41	5	13	18	61	5	0	2	2	6
1995-96	Mannheim	Ger.	50	14	24	38	50	8	0	2	2	26
1996-97	Columbus	ECHL	36	7	9	16	29	2	0	0	0	0

QUINN, DAN

Center. Shoots left. 5'11", 182 lbs. Born, Ottawa, Ont., June 1, 1965.
(Calgary's 1st choice, 13th overall, in 1983 Entry Draft).

			Regular Season					Playoffs				
Season	Club	Lea	GP	G	A	TP	PIM	GP	G	A	TP	PIM
1981-82	Belleville	OHL	67	19	32	51	41	....	....	....	....	....
1982-83	Belleville	OHL	70	59	88	147	27	4	2	6	8	2
1983-84	**Calgary**	**NHL**	**54**	**19**	**33**	**52**	**20**	**8**	**3**	**5**	**8**	**4**
	Belleville	OHL	24	23	36	59	12	....	....	....	....	....
1984-85	**Calgary**	**NHL**	**74**	**20**	**38**	**58**	**22**	**3**	**0**	**0**	**0**	**0**
1985-86	**Calgary**	**NHL**	**78**	**30**	**42**	**72**	**44**	**18**	**8**	**7**	**15**	**10**
1986-87	**Calgary**	**NHL**	**16**	**3**	**6**	**9**	**14**	....	....	....	....	....
	Pittsburgh	**NHL**	**64**	**28**	**43**	**71**	**40**	....	....	....	....	....
1987-88	**Pittsburgh**	**NHL**	**70**	**40**	**39**	**79**	**50**	....	....	....	....	....
1988-89	**Pittsburgh**	**NHL**	**79**	**34**	**60**	**94**	**102**	**11**	**6**	**3**	**9**	**10**
1989-90	**Pittsburgh**	**NHL**	**41**	**9**	**20**	**29**	**22**	....	....	....	....	....
	Vancouver	**NHL**	**37**	**16**	**18**	**34**	**27**	....	....	....	....	....
1990-91	**Vancouver**	**NHL**	**64**	**18**	**31**	**49**	**46**	....	....	....	....	....
	St. Louis	**NHL**	**14**	**4**	**7**	**11**	**20**	**13**	**4**	**7**	**11**	**32**
1991-92	**Philadelphia**	**NHL**	**67**	**11**	**26**	**37**	**26**	....	....	....	....	....
1992-93	**Minnesota**	**NHL**	**11**	**0**	**4**	**4**	**6**	....	....	....	....	....
1993-94	Bern	Switz.	25	13	18	31	56	....	....	....	....	....
	Ottawa	**NHL**	**13**	**7**	**0**	**7**	**6**	....	....	....	....	....
1994-95	Zug	Switz.	7	7	6	13	26	....	....	....	....	....
	Los Angeles	**NHL**	**44**	**14**	**17**	**31**	**32**	....	....	....	....	....
1995-96	**Ottawa**	**NHL**	**28**	**6**	**18**	**24**	**24**	....	....	....	....	....
	Detroit	IHL	4	0	5	5	2	....	....	....	....	....
	Philadelphia	**NHL**	**35**	**7**	**14**	**21**	**22**	**12**	**1**	**4**	**5**	**6**
1996-97	**Pittsburgh**	**NHL**	**16**	**0**	**3**	**3**	**10**	....	....	....	....	....
	NHL Totals		**805**	**266**	**419**	**685**	**533**	**65**	**22**	**26**	**48**	**62**

Traded to **Pittsburgh** by **Calgary** for Mike Bullard, November 12, 1986. Traded to **Vancouver** by **Pittsburgh** with Dave Capuano and Andrew McBain for Rod Buskas, Barry Pederson and Tony Tanti, January 8, 1990. Traded to **St. Louis** by **Vancouver** with Garth Butcher for Geoff Courtnall, Robert Dirk, Sergio Momesso, Cliff Ronning and St. Louis' fifth round choice (Brian Loney) in 1992 Entry Draft, March 5, 1991. Traded to **Philadelphia** by **St. Louis** with Rod Brind'Amour for Ron Sutter and Murray Baron, September 22, 1991. Signed as a free agent by **Minnesota**, October 4, 1992. Signed as a free agent by **Ottawa**, March 15, 1994. Signed as a free agent by **Los Angeles**, September 3, 1994. Signed as a free agent by **Ottawa**, August 1, 1995. Traded to **Philadelphia** by **Ottawa** for cash, January 23, 1996. Signed as a free agent by **Pittsburgh**, July 17, 1996.

QUINT, DERON (KWIHNT) PHO.

Defense. Shoots left. 6'1", 182 lbs. Born, Durham, NH, March 12, 1976.
(Winnipeg's 1st choice, 30th overall, in 1994 Entry Draft).

			Regular Season					Playoffs				
Season	Club	Lea	GP	G	A	TP	PIM	GP	G	A	TP	PIM
1993-94	Seattle	WHL	63	15	29	44	47	9	4	12	16	8
1994-95a	Seattle	WHL	65	29	60	89	82	3	1	2	3	6
1995-96	**Winnipeg**	**NHL**	**51**	**5**	**13**	**18**	**22**	....	....	....	....	....
	Springfield	AHL	11	2	3	5	4	10	2	3	5	6
	Seattle	WHL	....	....	....	....	....	5	4	1	5	6
1996-97	**Phoenix**	**NHL**	**27**	**3**	**11**	**14**	**4**	**7**	**0**	**2**	**2**	**0**
	Springfield	AHL	43	6	18	24	20	12	2	7	9	4
	NHL Totals		**78**	**8**	**24**	**32**	**26**	**7**	**0**	**2**	**2**	**0**

a WHL West First All-Star Team (1995)

QUINTAL, STEPHANE (KAYN-tahl) MTL.

Defense. Shoots right. 6'3", 225 lbs. Born, Boucherville, Que., October 22, 1968.
(Boston's 2nd choice, 14th overall, in 1987 Entry Draft).

			Regular Season					Playoffs				
Season	Club	Lea	GP	G	A	TP	PIM	GP	G	A	TP	PIM
1985-86	Granby	QMJHL	67	2	17	19	144	....	....	....	....	....
1986-87a	Granby	QMJHL	67	13	41	54	178	8	0	9	9	10
1987-88	Hull	QMJHL	38	13	23	36	138	19	7	12	19	30
1988-89	**Boston**	**NHL**	**26**	**0**	**1**	**1**	**29**	....	....	....	....	....
	Maine	AHL	16	4	10	14	28	....	....	....	....	....
1989-90	**Boston**	**NHL**	**38**	**2**	**2**	**4**	**22**	....	....	....	....	....
	Maine	AHL	37	4	16	20	27	....	....	....	....	....
1990-91	**Boston**	**NHL**	**45**	**2**	**6**	**8**	**89**	**3**	**0**	**1**	**1**	**7**
	Maine	AHL	23	1	5	6	30	....	....	....	....	....
1991-92	**Boston**	**NHL**	**49**	**4**	**10**	**14**	**77**	....	....	....	....	....
	St. Louis	**NHL**	**26**	**0**	**6**	**6**	**32**	**4**	**1**	**2**	**3**	**6**
1992-93	**St. Louis**	**NHL**	**75**	**1**	**10**	**11**	**100**	**9**	**0**	**0**	**0**	**8**
1993-94	**Winnipeg**	**NHL**	**81**	**8**	**18**	**26**	**119**	....	....	....	....	....
1994-95	**Winnipeg**	**NHL**	**43**	**6**	**17**	**23**	**78**	....	....	....	....	....
1995-96	**Montreal**	**NHL**	**68**	**2**	**14**	**16**	**117**	**6**	**0**	**1**	**1**	**6**
1996-97	**Montreal**	**NHL**	**71**	**7**	**15**	**22**	**100**	**5**	**0**	**1**	**1**	**6**
	NHL Totals		**522**	**32**	**99**	**131**	**763**	**27**	**1**	**5**	**6**	**33**

a QMJHL First All-Star Team (1987)

Traded to **St. Louis** by **Boston** with Craig Janney for Adam Oates, February 7, 1992. Traded to **Winnipeg** by **St. Louis** with Nelson Emerson for Phil Housley, September 24, 1993. Traded to **Montreal** by **Winnipeg** for Montreal's second round choice (Jason Doig) in 1995 Entry Draft, July 8, 1995.

RABY, MATTHIEU (RAY-bee) T.B.

Defense. Shoots right. 6'2", 204 lbs. Born, Hull, Que., January 19, 1975.
(Tampa Bay's 7th choice, 159th overall, in 1993 Entry Draft).

			Regular Season					Playoffs				
Season	Club	Lea	GP	G	A	TP	PIM	GP	G	A	TP	PIM
1992-93	Victoriaville	QMJHL	53	2	2	4	103	2	0	0	0	0
1993-94	Victoriaville	QMJHL	67	3	7	10	264	5	0	0	0	22
1994-95	Victoriaville	QMJHL	38	5	11	16	238	....	....	....	....	....
	Sherbrooke	QMJHL	25	2	2	4	106	7	0	1	1	24
1995-96	Nashville	ECHL	62	4	11	15	256	5	0	0	0	28
	Atlanta	IHL	5	0	0	0	15	....	....	....	....	....
1996-97	Adirondack	AHL	13	0	0	0	28	....	....	....	....	....
	Wheeling	ECHL	39	5	3	8	130	3	0	1	1	6

RACINE, YVES (ruh-SEEN, EEV) T.B.

Defense. Shoots left. 6', 205 lbs. Born, Matane, Que., February 7, 1969.
(Detroit's 1st choice, 11th overall, in 1987 Entry Draft).

			Regular Season					Playoffs				
Season	Club	Lea	GP	G	A	TP	PIM	GP	G	A	TP	PIM
1986-87	Longueuil	QMJHL	70	7	43	50	50	20	3	11	14	14
1987-88a	Victoriaville	QMJHL	69	10	84	94	150	5	0	0	0	13
	Adirondack	AHL	....	....	....	....	....	9	4	2	6	2
1988-89a	Victoriaville	QMJHL	63	23	85	108	95	16	3	*30	*33	41
	Adirondack	AHL	....	....	....	....	....	2	1	1	2	0
1989-90	**Detroit**	**NHL**	**28**	**4**	**9**	**13**	**23**	....	....	....	....	....
	Adirondack	AHL	46	8	27	35	31	....	....	....	....	....
1990-91	**Detroit**	**NHL**	**62**	**7**	**40**	**47**	**33**	**7**	**2**	**0**	**2**	**0**
	Adirondack	AHL	16	3	9	12	10	....	....	....	....	....
1991-92	**Detroit**	**NHL**	**61**	**2**	**22**	**24**	**94**	**11**	**2**	**1**	**3**	**10**
1992-93	**Detroit**	**NHL**	**80**	**9**	**31**	**40**	**80**	**7**	**1**	**3**	**4**	**27**
1993-94	**Philadelphia**	**NHL**	**67**	**9**	**43**	**52**	**48**	....	....	....	....	....
1994-95	**Montreal**	**NHL**	**47**	**4**	**7**	**11**	**42**	....	....	....	....	....
1995-96	**Montreal**	**NHL**	**25**	**0**	**3**	**3**	**26**	....	....	....	....	....
	San Jose	**NHL**	**32**	**1**	**16**	**17**	**28**	....	....	....	....	....
1996-97	Kentucky	AHL	4	0	1	1	2	....	....	....	....	....
	Quebec	IHL	6	0	4	4	4	....	....	....	....	....
	Calgary	**NHL**	**46**	**1**	**15**	**16**	**24**	....	....	....	....	....
	NHL Totals		**448**	**37**	**186**	**223**	**398**	**25**	**5**	**4**	**9**	**37**

a QMJHL First-All Star Team (1988, 1989)

Traded to **Philadelphia** by **Detroit** with Detroit's fourth round choice (Sebastien Vallee) in 1994 Entry Draft for Terry Carkner, October 5, 1993. Traded to **Montreal** by **Philadelphia** for Kevin Haller, June 29, 1994. Claimed on waivers by **San Jose** from **Montreal**, January 23, 1996. Traded to **Calgary** by **San Jose** for cash, December 17, 1996. Signed as a free agent by **Tampa Bay**, July 16, 1997.

RAGNARSSON, MARCUS (RAG-nahr-suhn) S.J.

Defense. Shoots left. 6'1", 215 lbs. Born, Ostervala, Sweden, August 13, 1971.
(San Jose's 5th choice, 99th overall, in 1992 Entry Draft).

			Regular Season					Playoffs				
Season	Club	Lea	GP	G	A	TP	PIM	GP	G	A	TP	PIM
1989-90	Djurgarden	Swe.	13	0	2	2	0	1	0	0	0	0
1990-91	Djurgarden	Swe.	35	4	1	5	12	7	0	0	0	6
1991-92	Djurgarden	Swe.	40	8	5	13	14	10	0	1	1	4
1992-93	Djurgarden	Swe.	35	3	3	6	53	6	0	3	3	8
1993-94	Djurgarden	Swe.	19	0	4	4	24	....	....	....	....	....
1994-95	Djurgarden	Swe.	38	7	9	16	20	3	0	0	0	4
1995-96	**San Jose**	**NHL**	**71**	**8**	**31**	**39**	**42**	....	....	....	....	....
1996-97	**San Jose**	**NHL**	**69**	**3**	**14**	**17**	**63**	....	....	....	....	....
	NHL Totals		**140**	**11**	**45**	**56**	**105**	....	....	....	....	....

RAJAMAKI, TOMMI (righ-YAH-ma-kee) TOR.

Defense. Shoots left. 6'2", 180 lbs. Born, Pori, Finland, February 29, 1976.
(Toronto's 6th choice, 178th overall, in 1994 Entry Draft).

			Regular Season					Playoffs				
Season	Club	Lea	GP	G	A	TP	PIM	GP	G	A	TP	PIM
1994-95	Assat Jr.	Fin.	29	11	17	28	30	....	....	....	....	....
	Assat	Fin.	12	4	1	5	8	7	0	1	1	2
1995-96	Assat	Fin.	45	5	2	7	26	3	0	0	0	6
1996-97	Assat	Fin.	46	0	1	1	16	4	0	0	0	2

RAJNOHA, PAVEL (righ-NOH-kha) CGY.

Defense. Shoots right. 6', 185 lbs. Born, Gottwaldov, Czech., February 23, 1974.
(Calgary's 8th choice, 150th overall, in 1992 Entry Draft).

			Regular Season					Playoffs				
Season	Club	Lea	GP	G	A	TP	PIM	GP	G	A	TP	PIM
1990-91	TJ Zlin	Czech.	6	0	0	0	4	....	....	....	....	....
1991-92	ZPS Zlin	Czech.	24	0	1	1	4	....	....	....	....	....
1992-93	ZPS Zlin	Czech.	26	2	1	3	....	....	....	....	....	....
1993-94	ZPS Zlin	Czech.	28	2	1	3	0	3	0	4	4	....
1994-95	ZPS Zlin	Czech.	29	0	6	6	22	....	....	....	....	....
1995-96	Dukla Jihlava	Czech.	38	0	2	2	....	8	0	0	0	....
1996-97	ZPS Zlin	Czech.	32	6	5	11	4	....	....	....	....	....

RAKHMATULLIN, ASKHAT (rahkh-ma-TOO-lihn, ahs-KHAHT) CAR.

Left wing. Shoots left. 5'11", 165 lbs. Born, Ufa, USSR, May 31, 1978.
(Hartford's 10th choice, 231st overall, in 1996 Entry Draft).

			Regular Season					Playoffs				
Season	Club	Lea	GP	G	A	TP	PIM	GP	G	A	TP	PIM
1996-97	Ufa Salavat	Rus.	28	1	3	4	8	3	0	0	0	0

RAMSAY, BRUCE ST.L.

Left wing. Shoots left. 6', 180 lbs. Born, Dryden, Ont., May 13, 1969.

			Regular Season					Playoffs				
Season	Club	Lea	GP	G	A	TP	PIM	GP	G	A	TP	PIM
1991-92	Thunder Bay	ColHL	54	7	16	23	313	12	1	2	3	55
1992-93	Thunder Bay	ColHL	52	3	16	19	234	....	....	....	....	....
1993-94	Thunder Bay	ColHL	63	9	22	31	313	8	1	2	3	45
1994-95	Thunder Bay	ColHL	62	14	29	43	462	11	0	3	3	83
	P.E.I.	AHL	2	0	1	1	10	1	0	0	0	2
1995-96	Thunder Bay	ColHL	56	6	15	21	400	18	2	3	5	142
	Milwaukee	IHL	3	0	0	0	5	....	....	....	....	....
1996-97	Thunder Bay	ColHL	9	6	4	10	71	....	....	....	....	....
	Grand Rapids	IHL	66	3	5	8	306	4	0	0	0	2

Signed as a free agent by **St. Louis**, July 31, 1997.

RAMSEY, MIKE

Defense. Shoots left. 6'3", 195 lbs. Born, Minneapolis, MN, December 3, 1960.
(Buffalo's 1st choice, 11th overall, in 1979 Entry Draft).

			Regular Season					Playoffs				
Season	Club	Lea	GP	G	A	TP	PIM	GP	G	A	TP	PIM
1978-79	U. Minnesota	WCHA	26	6	11	17	30	....	....	....	....	....
1979-80	U.S. National	....	56	11	22	33	55	....	....	....	....	....
	U.S. Olympic	....	7	0	2	2	8	....	....	....	....	....
	Buffalo	**NHL**	**13**	**1**	**6**	**7**	**6**	**13**	**1**	**2**	**3**	**12**
1980-81	**Buffalo**	**NHL**	**72**	**3**	**14**	**17**	**56**	**8**	**0**	**3**	**3**	**20**
1981-82	**Buffalo**	**NHL**	**80**	**7**	**23**	**30**	**56**	**4**	**1**	**1**	**2**	**14**
1982-83	**Buffalo**	**NHL**	**77**	**8**	**30**	**38**	**55**	**10**	**4**	**4**	**8**	**15**
1983-84	**Buffalo**	**NHL**	**72**	**9**	**22**	**31**	**82**	**3**	**0**	**1**	**1**	**6**
1984-85	**Buffalo**	**NHL**	**79**	**8**	**22**	**30**	**102**	**5**	**0**	**1**	**1**	**23**
1985-86	**Buffalo**	**NHL**	**76**	**7**	**21**	**28**	**117**	....	....	....	....	....
1986-87	**Buffalo**	**NHL**	**80**	**8**	**31**	**39**	**109**	....	....	....	....	....
1987-88	**Buffalo**	**NHL**	**63**	**5**	**16**	**21**	**77**	**6**	**0**	**3**	**3**	**29**
1988-89	**Buffalo**	**NHL**	**56**	**2**	**14**	**16**	**84**	**5**	**1**	**0**	**1**	**11**
1989-90	**Buffalo**	**NHL**	**73**	**4**	**21**	**25**	**47**	**6**	**0**	**1**	**1**	**8**
1990-91	**Buffalo**	**NHL**	**71**	**6**	**14**	**20**	**46**	**5**	**1**	**0**	**1**	**12**
1991-92	**Buffalo**	**NHL**	**66**	**3**	**14**	**17**	**67**	**7**	**0**	**2**	**2**	**8**
1992-93	**Buffalo**	**NHL**	**33**	**2**	**8**	**10**	**20**	....	....	....	....	....
	Pittsburgh	**NHL**	**12**	**1**	**2**	**3**	**8**	**12**	**0**	**6**	**6**	**4**
1993-94	**Pittsburgh**	**NHL**	**65**	**2**	**2**	**4**	**22**	**1**	**0**	**0**	**0**	**0**
1994-95	**Detroit**	**NHL**	**33**	**1**	**2**	**3**	**23**	**15**	**0**	**1**	**1**	**4**
1995-96	**Detroit**	**NHL**	**47**	**2**	**4**	**6**	**35**	**15**	**0**	**4**	**4**	**10**
1996-97	**Detroit**	**NHL**	**2**	**0**	**0**	**0**	**0**	....	....	....	....	....
	NHL Totals		**1070**	**79**	**266**	**345**	**1012**	**115**	**8**	**29**	**37**	**176**

Played in NHL All-Star Game (1982, 1983, 1985, 1986)

Traded to **Pittsburgh** by **Buffalo** for Bob Errey, March 22, 1993. Signed as a free agent by **Detroit**, August 3, 1994.

RANDALL, BRYAN — EDM.

Center. Shoots left. 6'3", 190 lbs. Born, Winnipeg, Man., August 8, 1978.
(Edmonton's 6th choice, 141st overall, in 1996 Entry Draft).

			Regular Season					Playoffs				
Season	Club	Lea	GP	G	A	TP	PIM	GP	G	A	TP	PIM
1995-96	Medicine Hat	WHL	64	4	5	9	51	5	0	0	0	7
1996-97	Medicine Hat	WHL	2	0	0	0	7	....	....	....	....	....
	Regina	WHL	48	5	18	23	55	2	0	1	1	2

RANHEIM, PAUL (RAN-highm) — CAR.

Left wing. Shoots right. 6'1", 210 lbs. Born, St. Louis, MO, January 25, 1966.
(Calgary's 3rd choice, 38th overall, in 1984 Entry Draft).

			Regular Season					Playoffs				
Season	Club	Lea	GP	G	A	TP	PIM	GP	G	A	TP	PIM
1984-85	U. Wisconsin	WCHA	42	11	11	22	40	....	....	....	....	....
1985-86	U. Wisconsin	WCHA	33	17	17	34	34	....	....	....	....	....
1986-87a	U. Wisconsin	WCHA	42	24	35	59	54	....	....	....	....	....
1987-88bc	U. Wisconsin	WCHA	44	36	26	62	63	....	....	....	....	....
1988-89	**Calgary**	**NHL**	**5**	**0**	**0**	**0**	**0**	....	....	....	....	....
de	Salt Lake	IHL	75	*68	29	97	16	14	5	5	10	8
1989-90	**Calgary**	**NHL**	**80**	**26**	**28**	**54**	**23**	**6**	**1**	**3**	**4**	**2**
1990-91	**Calgary**	**NHL**	**39**	**14**	**16**	**30**	**4**	**7**	**2**	**2**	**4**	**0**
1991-92	**Calgary**	**NHL**	**80**	**23**	**20**	**43**	**32**	....	....	....	....	....
1992-93	**Calgary**	**NHL**	**83**	**21**	**22**	**43**	**26**	**6**	**0**	**1**	**1**	**0**
1993-94	**Calgary**	**NHL**	**67**	**10**	**14**	**24**	**20**	....	....	....	....	....
	Hartford	**NHL**	**15**	**0**	**3**	**3**	**2**	....	....	....	....	....
1994-95	**Hartford**	**NHL**	**47**	**6**	**14**	**20**	**10**	....	....	....	....	....
1995-96	**Hartford**	**NHL**	**73**	**10**	**20**	**30**	**14**	....	....	....	....	....
1996-97	**Hartford**	**NHL**	**67**	**10**	**11**	**21**	**18**	....	....	....	....	....
	NHL Totals		**556**	**120**	**148**	**268**	**149**	**19**	**3**	**6**	**9**	**2**

a WCHA Second All-Star Team (1987)
b NCAA West First All-American Team (1988)
c WCHA First All-Star Team (1988)
d IHL Second All-Star Team (1989)
e Won Garry F. Longman Memorial Trophy (Top Rookie - IHL) (1989)

Traded to **Hartford** by **Calgary** with Gary Suter and Ted Drury for James Patrick, Zarley Zalapski and Michael Nylander, March 10, 1994.

RASMUSSEN, ERIK (RAS-moo-suhn) — BUF.

Center. Shoots left. 6'2", 193 lbs. Born, Minneapolis, MN, March 28, 1977.
(Buffalo's 1st choice, 7th overall, in 1996 Entry Draft).

			Regular Season					Playoffs				
Season	Club	Lea	GP	G	A	TP	PIM	GP	G	A	TP	PIM
1995-96	U. Minnesota	WCHA	40	16	32	48	55	....	....	....	....	....
1996-97	U. Minnesota	WCHA	34	15	12	27	*123	....	....	....	....	....

RATCHUK, PETER (RAT-chuhk) — COL.

Defense. Shoots left. 6', 175 lbs. Born, Buffalo, NY, September 10, 1977.
(Colorado's 1st choice, 25th overall, in 1996 Entry Draft).

			Regular Season					Playoffs				
Season	Club	Lea	GP	G	A	TP	PIM	GP	G	A	TP	PIM
1995-96	Shattuck	HS	35	22	28	50	24	....	....	....	....	....
1996-97	Bowling Green	CCHA	35	9	12	21	14	....	....	....	....	....

RATHJE, MIKE (RATH-jee) — S.J.

Defense. Shoots left. 6'6", 220 lbs. Born, Mannville, Alta., May 11, 1974.
(San Jose's 1st choice, 3rd overall, in 1992 Entry Draft).

			Regular Season					Playoffs				
Season	Club	Lea	GP	G	A	TP	PIM	GP	G	A	TP	PIM
1990-91	Medicine Hat	WHL	64	1	16	17	28	12	0	4	4	2
1991-92a	Medicine Hat	WHL	67	11	23	34	109	4	0	1	1	2
1992-93a	Medicine Hat	WHL	57	12	37	49	103	10	3	3	6	12
	Kansas City	IHL	....	....	....	....	....	5	0	0	0	12
1993-94	**San Jose**	**NHL**	**47**	**1**	**9**	**10**	**59**	**1**	**0**	**0**	**0**	**0**
	Kansas City	IHL	6	0	2	2	0	....	....	....	....	....
1994-95	**San Jose**	**NHL**	**42**	**2**	**7**	**9**	**29**	**11**	**5**	**2**	**7**	**4**
	Kansas City	IHL	6	0	1	1	7	....	....	....	....	....
1995-96	**San Jose**	**NHL**	**27**	**0**	**7**	**7**	**14**	....	....	....	....	....
	Kansas City	IHL	36	6	11	17	34	....	....	....	....	....
1996-97	**San Jose**	**NHL**	**31**	**0**	**8**	**8**	**21**	....	....	....	....	....
	NHL Totals		**147**	**3**	**31**	**34**	**123**	**12**	**5**	**2**	**7**	**4**

a WHL East Second All-Star Team (1992, 1993)

RAY, ROB — BUF.

Right wing. Shoots left. 6', 203 lbs. Born, Belleville, Ont., June 8, 1968.
(Buffalo's 5th choice, 97th overall, in 1988 Entry Draft).

			Regular Season					Playoffs				
Season	Club	Lea	GP	G	A	TP	PIM	GP	G	A	TP	PIM
1985-86	Cornwall	OHL	53	6	13	19	253	6	0	0	0	26
1986-87	Cornwall	OHL	46	17	20	37	158	5	1	1	2	16
1987-88	Cornwall	OHL	61	11	41	52	179	11	2	3	5	33
1988-89	Rochester	AHL	74	11	18	29	*446	....	....	....	....	....
1989-90	**Buffalo**	**NHL**	**27**	**2**	**1**	**3**	**99**	....	....	....	....	....
	Rochester	AHL	43	2	13	15	335	17	1	3	4	115
1990-91	**Buffalo**	**NHL**	**66**	**8**	**8**	**16**	***350**	**6**	**1**	**1**	**2**	**56**
	Rochester	AHL	8	1	1	2	15	....	....	....	....	....
1991-92	**Buffalo**	**NHL**	**63**	**5**	**3**	**8**	**354**	**7**	**0**	**0**	**0**	**2**
1992-93	**Buffalo**	**NHL**	**68**	**3**	**2**	**5**	**211**	....	....	....	....	....
1993-94	**Buffalo**	**NHL**	**82**	**3**	**4**	**7**	**274**	**7**	**1**	**0**	**1**	**43**
1994-95	**Buffalo**	**NHL**	**47**	**0**	**3**	**3**	**173**	**5**	**0**	**0**	**0**	**14**
1995-96	**Buffalo**	**NHL**	**71**	**3**	**6**	**9**	**287**	....	....	....	....	....
1996-97	**Buffalo**	**NHL**	**82**	**7**	**3**	**10**	**286**	**12**	**0**	**1**	**1**	**28**
	NHL Totals		**506**	**31**	**30**	**61**	**2034**	**37**	**2**	**2**	**4**	**143**

RAZIN, GENNADY (RAH-zihn, gen-AH-dee) — MTL.

Defense. Shoots left. 6'3", 175 lbs. Born, Kharkov, USSR, February 3, 1978.
(Montreal's 6th choice, 122nd overall, in 1997 Entry Draft).

			Regular Season					Playoffs				
Season	Club	Lea	GP	G	A	TP	PIM	GP	G	A	TP	PIM
1995-96	St. Albert	Jr. A	54	3	16	19	113	18	1	10	11	8
1996-97	Kamloops	WHL	63	7	19	26	56	3	0	0	0	4

READY, RYAN — CGY.

Left wing. Shoots left. 6'2", 185 lbs. Born, Peterborough, Ont., November 7, 1978.
(Calgary's 8th choice, 100th overall, in 1997 Entry Draft).

			Regular Season					Playoffs				
Season	Club	Lea	GP	G	A	TP	PIM	GP	G	A	TP	PIM
1995-96	Belleville	OHL	63	5	13	18	54	10	0	2	2	2
1996-97	Belleville	OHL	66	23	24	47	102	6	1	3	4	4

REASONER, MARTY — ST.L.

Center. Shoots left. 6'1", 185 lbs. Born, Rochester, NY, February 26, 1977.
(St. Louis' 1st choice, 14th overall, in 1996 Entry Draft).

			Regular Season					Playoffs				
Season	Club	Lea	GP	G	A	TP	PIM	GP	G	A	TP	PIM
1995-96	Boston College	H.E.	34	16	29	45	32	....	....	....	....	....
1996-97a	Boston College	H.E.	35	20	24	44	31	....	....	....	....	....

a Hockey East All-Star Team (1997)

RECCHI, MARK (REH-kee) — MTL.

Right wing. Shoots left. 5'10", 180 lbs. Born, Kamloops, B.C., February 1, 1968.
(Pittsburgh's 4th choice, 67th overall, in 1988 Entry Draft).

			Regular Season					Playoffs				
Season	Club	Lea	GP	G	A	TP	PIM	GP	G	A	TP	PIM
1985-86	N. Westminster	WHL	72	21	40	61	55	....	....	....	....	....
1986-87	Kamloops	WHL	40	26	50	76	63	13	3	16	19	17
1987-88a	Kamloops	WHL	62	61	*93	154	75	17	10	*21	*31	18
1988-89	**Pittsburgh**	**NHL**	**15**	**1**	**1**	**2**	**0**	....	....	....	....	....
b	Muskegon	IHL	63	50	49	99	86	14	7	*14	*21	28
1989-90	**Pittsburgh**	**NHL**	**74**	**30**	**37**	**67**	**44**	....	....	....	....	....
	Muskegon	IHL	4	7	4	11	2	....	....	....	....	....
1990-91	**Pittsburgh**	**NHL**	**78**	**40**	**73**	**113**	**48**	**24**	**10**	**24**	**34**	**33** ♦
1991-92	**Pittsburgh**	**NHL**	**58**	**33**	**37**	**70**	**78**	....	....	....	....	....
c	**Philadelphia**	**NHL**	**22**	**10**	**17**	**27**	**18**	....	....	....	....	....
1992-93	**Philadelphia**	**NHL**	**84**	**53**	**70**	**123**	**95**	....	....	....	....	....
1993-94	**Philadelphia**	**NHL**	**84**	**40**	**67**	**107**	**46**	....	....	....	....	....
1994-95	**Philadelphia**	**NHL**	**10**	**2**	**3**	**5**	**12**	....	....	....	....	....
	Montreal	**NHL**	**39**	**14**	**29**	**43**	**16**	....	....	....	....	....
1995-96	**Montreal**	**NHL**	**82**	**28**	**50**	**78**	**69**	**6**	**3**	**3**	**6**	**0**
1996-97	**Montreal**	**NHL**	**82**	**34**	**46**	**80**	**58**	**5**	**4**	**2**	**6**	**2**
	NHL Totals		**628**	**285**	**430**	**715**	**484**	**35**	**17**	**29**	**46**	**35**

a WHL West All-Star Team (1988)
b IHL Second All-Star Team (1989)
c NHL Second All-Star Team (1992)

Played in NHL All-Star Game (1991, 1993, 1994, 1997)

Traded to **Philadelphia** by **Pittsburgh** with Brian Benning and Los Angeles' first round choice (previously acquired by Pittsburgh — Philadelphia selected Jason Bowen) in 1992 Entry Draft for Rick Tocchet, Kjell Samuelsson, Ken Wregget and Philadelphia's third round choice (Dave Roche) in 1993 Entry Draft, February 19, 1992. Traded to **Montreal** by **Philadelphia** with Philadelphia's third round choice (Martin Hohenberger) in 1995 Entry Draft for Eric Desjardins, Gilbert Dionne and John LeClair, February 9, 1995.

REDDEN, WADE — OTT.

Defense. Shoots left. 6'2", 193 lbs. Born, Lloydminster, Sask., June 12, 1977.
(NY Islanders' 1st choice, 2nd overall, in 1995 Entry Draft).

			Regular Season					Playoffs				
Season	Club	Lea	GP	G	A	TP	PIM	GP	G	A	TP	PIM
1993-94	Brandon	WHL	63	4	35	39	98	14	2	4	6	10
1994-95a	Brandon	WHL	64	14	46	60	83	18	5	10	15	8
1995-96bc	Brandon	WHL	51	9	45	54	55	19	5	10	15	19
1996-97	**Ottawa**	**NHL**	**82**	**6**	**24**	**30**	**41**	**7**	**1**	**3**	**4**	**2**
	NHL Totals		**82**	**6**	**24**	**30**	**41**	**7**	**1**	**3**	**4**	**2**

a WHL East Second All-Star Team (1995)
b WHL East First All-Star Team (1996)
c Memorial Cup All-Star Team (1996)

Traded to **Ottawa** by **NY Islanders** with Damian Rhodes for Don Beaupre, Martin Straka and Bryan Berard, January 23, 1996.

REEKIE, JOE (REE-kee) WSH.

Defense. Shoots left. 6'3", 220 lbs. Born, Victoria, B.C., February 22, 1965.
(Buffalo's 6th choice, 119th overall, in 1985 Entry Draft).

			Regular Season					Playoffs				
Season	Club	Lea	GP	G	A	TP	PIM	GP	G	A	TP	PIM
1982-83	North Bay	OHL	59	2	9	11	49	8	0	1	1	11
1983-84	North Bay	OHL	9	1	0	1	18	....	....	....	....	....
	Cornwall	OHL	53	6	27	33	166	3	0	0	0	4
1984-85	Cornwall	OHL	65	19	63	82	134	9	4	13	17	18
1985-86	**Buffalo**	**NHL**	**3**	**0**	**0**	**0**	**14**	....	....	....	....	....
	Rochester	AHL	77	3	25	28	178	....	....	....	....	....
1986-87	**Buffalo**	**NHL**	**56**	**1**	**8**	**9**	**82**	....	....	....	....	....
	Rochester	AHL	22	0	6	6	52	....	....	....	....	....
1987-88	**Buffalo**	**NHL**	**30**	**1**	**4**	**5**	**68**	**2**	**0**	**0**	**0**	**4**
1988-89	**Buffalo**	**NHL**	**15**	**1**	**3**	**4**	**26**	....	....	....	....	....
	Rochester	AHL	21	1	2	3	56	....	....	....	....	....
1989-90	**NY Islanders**	**NHL**	**31**	**1**	**8**	**9**	**43**	....	....	....	....	....
	Springfield	AHL	15	1	4	5	24	....	....	....	....	....
1990-91	**NY Islanders**	**NHL**	**66**	**3**	**16**	**19**	**96**	....	....	....	....	....
	Capital Dist.	AHL	2	1	0	1	0	....	....	....	....	....
1991-92	**NY Islanders**	**NHL**	**54**	**4**	**12**	**16**	**85**	....	....	....	....	....
	Capital Dist.	AHL	3	2	2	4	2	....	....	....	....	....
1992-93	**Tampa Bay**	**NHL**	**42**	**2**	**11**	**13**	**69**	....	....	....	....	....
1993-94	**Tampa Bay**	**NHL**	**73**	**1**	**11**	**12**	**127**	....	....	....	....	....
	Washington	**NHL**	**12**	**0**	**5**	**5**	**29**	**11**	**2**	**1**	**3**	**29**
1994-95	**Washington**	**NHL**	**48**	**1**	**6**	**7**	**97**	**7**	**0**	**0**	**0**	**2**
1995-96	**Washington**	**NHL**	**78**	**3**	**7**	**10**	**149**	....	....	....	....	....
1996-97	**Washington**	**NHL**	**65**	**1**	**8**	**9**	**107**	....	....	....	....	....
	NHL Totals		**573**	**19**	**99**	**118**	**992**	**20**	**2**	**1**	**3**	**35**

Traded to **NY Islanders** by **Buffalo** for NY Islanders' sixth round choice (Bill Pye) in 1989 Entry Draft, June 17, 1989. Claimed by **Tampa Bay** from **NY Islanders** in Expansion Draft, June 18, 1992. Traded to **Washington** by **Tampa Bay** for Enrico Ciccone, Washington's third round choice (later traded to Anaheim — Anaheim selected Craig Reichert) in 1994 Entry Draft and the return of future draft choices transferred in the Pat Elynuik trade, March 21, 1994.

REHNBERG, HENRIK (REHN-buhrg) N.J.

Defense. Shoots left. 6'2", 194 lbs. Born, Grava, Sweden, July 20, 1977.
(New Jersey's 6th choice, 96th overall, in 1995 Entry Draft).

			Regular Season					Playoffs				
Season	Club	Lea	GP	G	A	TP	PIM	GP	G	A	TP	PIM
1995-96	Farjestad	Swe. Jr.	21	1	4	5	38	....	....	....	....	....
	Farjestad	Swe.	4	0	0	0	0	....	....	....	....	....
1996-97	Farjestad	Swe.	42	2	3	5	38	14	1	1	2	16

REICH, JEREMY (RIGHK) CHI.

Center. Shoots left. 6'1", 185 lbs. Born, Craik, Sask., February 11, 1979.
(Chicago's 3rd choice, 39th overall, in 1997 Entry Draft).

			Regular Season					Playoffs				
Season	Club	Lea	GP	G	A	TP	PIM	GP	G	A	TP	PIM
1995-96	Seattle	WHL	65	11	11	22	88	5	0	1	1	10
1996-97	Seattle	WHL	62	19	31	50	134	15	2	5	7	36

REICHEL, MARTIN (RIGH-khul) EDM.

Right wing. Shoots left. 6'1", 183 lbs. Born, Most, Czech., November 7, 1973.
(Edmonton's 2nd choice, 37th overall, in 1992 Entry Draft).

			Regular Season					Playoffs				
Season	Club	Lea	GP	G	A	TP	PIM	GP	G	A	TP	PIM
1990-91	Freiburg	Ger.	23	7	8	15	19	....	....	....	....	....
1991-92	Freiburg	Ger.	27	15	16	31	8	4	1	1	2	4
1992-93	Freiburg	Ger.	37	13	9	22	27	9	4	4	8	11
1993-94	Rosenheim	Ger.	20	5	15	20	6	....	....	....	....	....
1994-95	Rosenheim	Ger.	43	11	26	37	36	7	3	3	6	37
1995-96	Rosenheim	Ger.	50	17	28	45	40	4	3	0	3	2
1996-97	Rosenheim	Ger.	45	8	14	22	30	3	0	0	0	4

REICHEL, ROBERT (RIGH-khul) NYI

Center. Shoots left. 5'10", 185 lbs. Born, Litvinov, Czech., June 25, 1971.
(Calgary's 5th choice, 70th overall, in 1989 Entry Draft).

			Regular Season					Playoffs				
Season	Club	Lea	GP	G	A	TP	PIM	GP	G	A	TP	PIM
1987-88	Litvinov	Czech.	36	17	10	27	8	....	....	....	....	....
1988-89	Litvinov	Czech.	44	23	25	48	32	....	....	....	....	....
1989-90	Litvinov	Czech.	52	*49	34	*83	....	....	....	....	....	....
1990-91	**Calgary**	**NHL**	**66**	**19**	**22**	**41**	**22**	**6**	**1**	**1**	**2**	**0**
1991-92	**Calgary**	**NHL**	**77**	**20**	**34**	**54**	**32**	....	....	....	....	....
1992-93	**Calgary**	**NHL**	**80**	**40**	**48**	**88**	**54**	**6**	**2**	**4**	**6**	**2**
1993-94	**Calgary**	**NHL**	**84**	**40**	**53**	**93**	**58**	**7**	**0**	**5**	**5**	**0**
1994-95	Frankfurt	Ger.	21	19	24	43	41	....	....	....	....	....
	Calgary	**NHL**	**48**	**18**	**17**	**35**	**28**	**7**	**2**	**4**	**6**	**4**
1995-96	Frankfurt	Ger.	46	47	54	101	84	3	1	3	4	0
1996-97	**Calgary**	**NHL**	**70**	**16**	**27**	**43**	**22**	....	....	....	....	....
	NY Islanders	**NHL**	**12**	**5**	**14**	**19**	**4**	....	....	....	....	....
	NHL Totals		**437**	**158**	**215**	**373**	**220**	**26**	**5**	**14**	**19**	**6**

Traded to **NY Islanders** by **Calgary** for Marty McInnis, Tyrone Garner and Calgary's sixth round choice (previously acquired by NY Islanders — Calgary selected Ilja Demidov) in 1997 Entry Draft, March 18, 1997.

REICHERT, CRAIG (RIGH-kuhrt) ANA.

Right wing. Shoots right. 6'1", 200 lbs. Born, Winnipeg, Man., May 11, 1974.
(Anaheim's 3rd choice, 67th overall, in 1994 Entry Draft).

			Regular Season					Playoffs				
Season	Club	Lea	GP	G	A	TP	PIM	GP	G	A	TP	PIM
1991-92	Spokane	WHL	68	13	20	33	86	4	1	0	1	4
1992-93	Red Deer	WHL	66	32	33	65	62	4	3	1	4	2
1993-94	Red Deer	WHL	72	52	67	119	153	4	2	2	4	8
1994-95	San Diego	IHL	49	4	12	16	28	....	....	....	....	....
1995-96	Baltimore	AHL	68	10	17	27	50	1	0	0	0	0
1996-97	**Anaheim**	**NHL**	**3**	**0**	**0**	**0**	**0**	....	....	....	....	....
	Baltimore	AHL	77	22	53	75	54	3	0	2	2	0
	NHL Totals		**3**	**0**	**0**	**0**	**0**	....	....	....	....	....

REID, DAVID DAL.

Left wing. Shoots left. 6'1", 217 lbs. Born, Toronto, Ont., May 15, 1964.
(Boston's 4th choice, 60th overall, in 1982 Entry Draft).

			Regular Season					Playoffs				
Season	Club	Lea	GP	G	A	TP	PIM	GP	G	A	TP	PIM
1981-82	Peterborough	OHL	68	10	32	42	41	9	2	3	5	11
1982-83	Peterborough	OHL	70	23	34	57	33	4	3	1	4	0
1983-84	**Boston**	**NHL**	**8**	**1**	**0**	**1**	**2**	....	....	....	....	....
	Peterborough	OHL	60	33	64	97	12	....	....	....	....	....
1984-85	**Boston**	**NHL**	**35**	**14**	**13**	**27**	**27**	**5**	**1**	**0**	**1**	**0**
	Hershey	AHL	43	10	14	24	6	....	....	....	....	....
1985-86	**Boston**	**NHL**	**37**	**10**	**10**	**20**	**10**	....	....	....	....	....
	Moncton	AHL	26	14	18	32	4	....	....	....	....	....
1986-87	**Boston**	**NHL**	**12**	**3**	**3**	**6**	**0**	**2**	**0**	**0**	**0**	**0**
	Moncton	AHL	40	12	22	34	23	5	0	1	1	0
1987-88	**Boston**	**NHL**	**3**	**0**	**0**	**0**	**0**	....	....	....	....	....
	Maine	AHL	63	21	37	58	40	10	6	7	13	0
1988-89	**Toronto**	**NHL**	**77**	**9**	**21**	**30**	**22**	....	....	....	....	....
1989-90	**Toronto**	**NHL**	**70**	**9**	**19**	**28**	**9**	**3**	**0**	**0**	**0**	**0**
1990-91	**Toronto**	**NHL**	**69**	**15**	**13**	**28**	**18**	....	....	....	....	....
1991-92	**Boston**	**NHL**	**43**	**7**	**7**	**14**	**27**	**15**	**2**	**5**	**7**	**4**
	Maine	AHL	12	1	5	6	4	....	....	....	....	....
1992-93	**Boston**	**NHL**	**65**	**20**	**16**	**36**	**10**	....	....	....	....	....
1993-94	**Boston**	**NHL**	**83**	**6**	**17**	**23**	**25**	**13**	**2**	**1**	**3**	**2**
1994-95	**Boston**	**NHL**	**38**	**5**	**5**	**10**	**10**	**5**	**0**	**0**	**0**	**0**
	Providence	AHL	7	3	0	3	0	....	....	....	....	....
1995-96	**Boston**	**NHL**	**63**	**23**	**21**	**44**	**4**	**5**	**0**	**2**	**2**	**2**
1996-97	**Dallas**	**NHL**	**82**	**19**	**20**	**39**	**10**	**7**	**1**	**0**	**1**	**4**
	NHL Totals		**685**	**141**	**165**	**306**	**174**	**55**	**6**	**8**	**14**	**12**

Signed as a free agent by **Toronto**, June 23, 1988. Signed as a free agent by **Boston**, December 1, 1991. Signed as a free agent by **Dallas**, July 11, 1996.

RENBERG, MIKAEL (REHN-buhrg) T.B.

Right wing. Shoots left. 6'2", 218 lbs. Born, Pitea, Sweden, May 5, 1972.
(Philadelphia's 3rd choice, 40th overall, in 1990 Entry Draft).

			Regular Season					Playoffs				
Season	Club	Lea	GP	G	A	TP	PIM	GP	G	A	TP	PIM
1988-89	Pitea	Swe. 2	12	6	3	9	....	....	....	....	....	....
1989-90	Pitea	Swe. 2	29	15	19	34	....	....	....	....	....	....
1990-91	Lulea	Swe.	29	11	6	17	12	5	1	1	2	4
1991-92	Lulea	Swe.	38	8	15	23	20	2	0	0	0	0
1992-93	Lulea	Swe.	39	19	13	32	61	11	4	4	8	4
1993-94a	**Philadelphia**	**NHL**	**83**	**38**	**44**	**82**	**36**	....	....	....	....	....
1994-95	Lulea	Swe.	10	9	4	13	16	....	....	....	....	....
	Philadelphia	**NHL**	**47**	**26**	**31**	**57**	**20**	**15**	**6**	**7**	**13**	**6**
1995-96	**Philadelphia**	**NHL**	**51**	**23**	**20**	**43**	**45**	**11**	**3**	**6**	**9**	**14**
1996-97	**Philadelphia**	**NHL**	**77**	**22**	**37**	**59**	**65**	**18**	**5**	**6**	**11**	**4**
	NHL Totals		**258**	**109**	**132**	**241**	**166**	**44**	**14**	**19**	**33**	**24**

a NHL/Upper Deck All-Rookie Team (1994)

Traded to **Tampa Bay** by **Philadelphia** with Karl Dykhuis for Philadelphia's first round choices in 1998, 1999, 2000 and 2001 Entry Drafts (previously acquired by Tampa Bay), August 20, 1997.

RENNETTE, TYLER ST.L.

Center. Shoots right. 6'1", 175 lbs. Born, North Bay, Ont., April 16, 1979.
(St. Louis' 1st choice, 40th overall, in 1997 Entry Draft).

			Regular Season					Playoffs				
Season	Club	Lea	GP	G	A	TP	PIM	GP	G	A	TP	PIM
1996-97	North Bay	OHL	63	24	34	58	42	....	....	....	....	....

RHEAUME, PASCAL (RAY-awm) N.J.

Center. Shoots left. 6'1", 200 lbs. Born, Quebec, Que., June 21, 1973.

			Regular Season					Playoffs				
Season	Club	Lea	GP	G	A	TP	PIM	GP	G	A	TP	PIM
1991-92	Trois Rivières	QMJHL	65	17	20	37	84	14	5	4	9	23
1992-93	Sherbrooke	QMJHL	65	28	34	62	88	14	6	5	11	31
1993-94	Albany	AHL	55	17	18	35	43	5	0	1	1	0
1994-95	Albany	AHL	78	19	25	44	46	14	3	6	9	19
1995-96	Albany	AHL	68	26	42	68	50	4	1	2	3	2
1996-97	**New Jersey**	**NHL**	**2**	**1**	**0**	**1**	**0**	....	....	....	....	....
	Albany	AHL	51	22	23	45	40	16	2	8	10	16
	NHL Totals		**2**	**1**	**0**	**1**	**0**	....	....	....	....	....

Signed as a free agent by **New Jersey**, October 1, 1992.

RICCI, MIKE (REE-CHEE) COL.

Center. Shoots left. 6', 190 lbs. Born, Scarborough, Ont., October 27, 1971.
(Philadelphia's 1st choice, 4th overall, in 1990 Entry Draft).

			Regular Season					Playoffs				
Season	Club	Lea	GP	G	A	TP	PIM	GP	G	A	TP	PIM
1987-88	Peterborough	OHL	41	24	37	61	20	8	5	5	10	4
1988-89a	Peterborough	OHL	60	54	52	106	43	17	19	16	35	18
1989-90bc	Peterborough	OHL	60	52	64	116	39	12	5	7	12	26
1990-91	**Philadelphia**	**NHL**	**68**	**21**	**20**	**41**	**64**	....	....	....	....	....
1991-92	**Philadelphia**	**NHL**	**78**	**20**	**36**	**56**	**93**	....	....	....	....	....
1992-93	**Quebec**	**NHL**	**77**	**27**	**51**	**78**	**123**	**6**	**0**	**6**	**6**	**8**
1993-94	**Quebec**	**NHL**	**83**	**30**	**21**	**51**	**113**	....	....	....	....	....
1994-95	**Quebec**	**NHL**	**48**	**15**	**21**	**36**	**40**	**6**	**1**	**3**	**4**	**8**
1995-96	**Colorado**	**NHL**	**62**	**6**	**21**	**27**	**52**	**22**	**6**	**11**	**17**	**18** ♦
1996-97	**Colorado**	**NHL**	**63**	**13**	**19**	**32**	**59**	**17**	**2**	**4**	**6**	**17**
	NHL Totals		**479**	**132**	**189**	**321**	**544**	**51**	**9**	**24**	**33**	**51**

a OHL Second All-Star Team (1989)
b Canadian Major Junior Player of the Year (1990)
c OHL First All-Star Team (1990)

Traded to **Quebec** by **Philadelphia** with Peter Forsberg, Steve Duchesne, Kerry Huffman, Ron Hextall, Chris Simon, Philadelphia's first round choice in the 1993 (Jocelyn Thibault) and 1994 (later traded to Toronto — later traded to Washington — Washington selected Nolan Baumgartner) Entry Drafts and cash for Eric Lindros, June 30, 1992.

RICE, STEVEN — CAR.

Right wing. Shoots right. 6', 217 lbs. Born, Kitchener, Ont., May 26, 1971.
(NY Rangers' 1st choice, 20th overall, in 1989 Entry Draft).

			Regular Season					Playoffs				
Season	Club	Lea	GP	G	A	TP	PIM	GP	G	A	TP	PIM
1987-88	Kitchener	OHL	59	11	14	25	43	4	0	1	1	0
1988-89	Kitchener	OHL	64	36	30	66	42	5	2	1	3	8
1989-90a	Kitchener	OHL	58	39	37	76	102	16	4	8	12	24
1990-91	**NY Rangers**	**NHL**	**11**	**1**	**1**	**2**	**4**	**2**	**2**	**1**	**3**	**6**
	Binghamton	AHL	8	4	1	5	12	5	2	0	2	2
b	Kitchener	OHL	29	30	30	60	43	6	5	6	11	2
1991-92	**Edmonton**	**NHL**	**3**	**0**	**0**	**0**	**2**	....	....	....	....	....
	Cape Breton	AHL	45	32	20	52	38	5	4	4	8	10
1992-93	**Edmonton**	**NHL**	**28**	**2**	**5**	**7**	**28**	....	....	....	....	....
c	Cape Breton	AHL	51	34	28	62	63	14	4	6	10	22
1993-94	**Edmonton**	**NHL**	**63**	**17**	**15**	**32**	**36**	....	....	....	....	....
1994-95	**Hartford**	**NHL**	**40**	**11**	**10**	**21**	**61**	....	....	....	....	....
1995-96	**Hartford**	**NHL**	**59**	**10**	**12**	**22**	**47**	....	....	....	....	....
1996-97	**Hartford**	**NHL**	**78**	**21**	**14**	**35**	**59**	....	....	....	....	....
	NHL Totals		**282**	**62**	**57**	**119**	**237**	**2**	**2**	**1**	**3**	**6**

a Memorial Cup All-Star Team (1990)
b OHL Second All-Star Team (1991)
c AHL Second All-Star Team (1993)

Traded to **Edmonton** by **NY Rangers** with Bernie Nicholls and Louie DeBrusk for Mark Messier and future considerations, October 4, 1991. Signed as a free agent by **Hartford**, August 18, 1994.

RICHARDSON, LUKE — PHI.

Defense. Shoots left. 6'4", 210 lbs. Born, Ottawa, Ont., March 26, 1969.
(Toronto's 1st choice, 7th overall, in 1987 Entry Draft).

			Regular Season					Playoffs				
Season	Club	Lea	GP	G	A	TP	PIM	GP	G	A	TP	PIM
1985-86	Peterborough	OHL	63	6	18	24	57	16	2	1	3	50
1986-87	Peterborough	OHL	59	13	32	45	70	12	0	5	5	24
1987-88	**Toronto**	**NHL**	**78**	**4**	**6**	**10**	**90**	**2**	**0**	**0**	**0**	**0**
1988-89	**Toronto**	**NHL**	**55**	**2**	**7**	**9**	**106**	....	....	....	....	....
1989-90	**Toronto**	**NHL**	**67**	**4**	**14**	**18**	**122**	**5**	**0**	**0**	**0**	**22**
1990-91	**Toronto**	**NHL**	**78**	**1**	**9**	**10**	**238**	....	....	....	....	....
1991-92	**Edmonton**	**NHL**	**75**	**2**	**19**	**21**	**118**	**16**	**0**	**5**	**5**	**45**
1992-93	**Edmonton**	**NHL**	**82**	**3**	**10**	**13**	**142**	....	....	....	....	....
1993-94	**Edmonton**	**NHL**	**69**	**2**	**6**	**8**	**131**	....	....	....	....	....
1994-95	**Edmonton**	**NHL**	**46**	**3**	**10**	**13**	**40**	....	....	....	....	....
1995-96	**Edmonton**	**NHL**	**82**	**2**	**9**	**11**	**108**	....	....	....	....	....
1996-97	**Edmonton**	**NHL**	**82**	**1**	**11**	**12**	**91**	**12**	**0**	**2**	**2**	**14**
	NHL Totals		**714**	**24**	**101**	**125**	**1186**	**35**	**0**	**7**	**7**	**81**

Traded to **Edmonton** by **Toronto** with Vincent Damphousse, Peter Ing, Scott Thornton, future considerations and cash for Grant Fuhr, Glenn Anderson and Craig Berube, September 19, 1991. Signed as a free agent by **Philadelphia**, July 23, 1997.

RICHER, STEPHANE — (REE-shay) MTL.

Right wing. Shoots right. 6'2", 215 lbs. Born, Ripon, Que., June 7, 1966.
(Montreal's 3rd choice, 29th overall, in 1984 Entry Draft).

			Regular Season					Playoffs				
Season	Club	Lea	GP	G	A	TP	PIM	GP	G	A	TP	PIM
1983-84a	Granby	QMJHL	67	39	37	76	58	3	1	1	2	4
1984-85	Granby	QMJHL	30	30	27	57	31	....	....	....	....	....
b	Chicoutimi	QMJHL	27	31	32	63	40	12	13	13	26	25
	Montreal	**NHL**	**1**	**0**	**0**	**0**	**0**	....	....	....	....	....
	Sherbrooke	AHL	....	....	....	....	....	9	6	3	9	10
1985-86	**Montreal**	**NHL**	**65**	**21**	**16**	**37**	**50**	**16**	**4**	**1**	**5**	**23** ♦
1986-87	**Montreal**	**NHL**	**57**	**20**	**19**	**39**	**80**	**5**	**3**	**2**	**5**	**0**
	Sherbrooke	AHL	12	10	4	14	11	....	....	....	....	....
1987-88	**Montreal**	**NHL**	**72**	**50**	**28**	**78**	**72**	**8**	**7**	**5**	**12**	**6**
1988-89	**Montreal**	**NHL**	**68**	**25**	**35**	**60**	**61**	**21**	**6**	**5**	**11**	**14**
1989-90	**Montreal**	**NHL**	**75**	**51**	**40**	**91**	**46**	**9**	**7**	**3**	**10**	**2**
1990-91	**Montreal**	**NHL**	**75**	**31**	**30**	**61**	**53**	**13**	**9**	**5**	**14**	**6**
1991-92	**New Jersey**	**NHL**	**74**	**29**	**35**	**64**	**25**	**7**	**1**	**2**	**3**	**0**
1992-93	**New Jersey**	**NHL**	**78**	**38**	**35**	**73**	**44**	**5**	**2**	**2**	**4**	**2**
1993-94	**New Jersey**	**NHL**	**80**	**36**	**36**	**72**	**16**	**20**	**7**	**5**	**12**	**6**
1994-95	**New Jersey**	**NHL**	**45**	**23**	**16**	**39**	**10**	**19**	**6**	**15**	**21**	**2** ♦
1995-96	**New Jersey**	**NHL**	**73**	**20**	**12**	**32**	**30**	....	....	....	....	....
1996-97	**Montreal**	**NHL**	**63**	**22**	**24**	**46**	**32**	**5**	**0**	**0**	**0**	**0**
	NHL Totals		**826**	**366**	**326**	**692**	**519**	**128**	**52**	**45**	**97**	**61**

a QMJHL Rookie of the Year (1984)
b QMJHL Second All-Star Team (1985)

Played in NHL All-Star Game (1990)

Traded to **New Jersey** by **Montreal** with Tom Chorske for Kirk Muller and Roland Melanson, September 20, 1991. Traded to **Montreal** by **New Jersey** for Lyle Odelein, August 22, 1996.

RICHTER, BARRY — (RIHK-tuhr) BOS.

Defense. Shoots left. 6'2", 200 lbs. Born, Madison, WI, September 11, 1970.
(Hartford's 2nd choice, 32nd overall, in 1988 Entry Draft).

			Regular Season					Playoffs				
Season	Club	Lea	GP	G	A	TP	PIM	GP	G	A	TP	PIM
1989-90	U. Wisconsin	WCHA	42	13	23	36	36	....	....	....	....	....
1990-91	U. Wisconsin	WCHA	43	15	20	35	42	....	....	....	....	....
1991-92a	U. Wisconsin	WCHA	39	10	25	35	62	....	....	....	....	....
1992-93bc	U. Wisconsin	WCHA	42	14	32	46	74	....	....	....	....	....
1993-94	U.S. National	....	56	7	16	23	50	....	....	....	....	....
	U.S. Olympic	....	8	0	3	3	4	....	....	....	....	....
	Binghamton	AHL	21	0	9	9	12	....	....	....	....	....
1994-95	Binghamton	AHL	73	15	41	56	54	11	4	5	9	12
1995-96	**NY Rangers**	**NHL**	**4**	**0**	**1**	**1**	**0**	....	....	....	....	....
de	Binghamton	AHL	69	20	61	81	64	3	0	3	3	0
1996-97	**Boston**	**NHL**	**50**	**5**	**13**	**18**	**32**	....	....	....	....	....
	Providence	AHL	19	2	6	8	4	10	4	4	8	4
	NHL Totals		**54**	**5**	**14**	**19**	**32**	....	....	....	....	....

a NCAA All-Tournament Team (1992)
b WCHA First All-Star Team (1993)
c NCAA West First All-American Team (1993)
d AHL First All-Star Team (1996)
e Won Eddie Shore Plaque (Outstanding Defenseman - AHL) (1996)

Traded to **NY Rangers** by **Hartford** with Steve Larmer, Nick Kypreos and Hartford's sixth round choice (Yuri Litvinov) in 1994 Entry Draft for Darren Turcotte and James Patrick, November 2, 1993. Signed as a free agent by **Boston**, July 19, 1996.

RIDLEY, MIKE

Center. Shoots left. 6', 195 lbs. Born, Winnipeg, Man., July 8, 1963.

			Regular Season					Playoffs				
Season	Club	Lea	GP	G	A	TP	PIM	GP	G	A	TP	PIM
1983-84a	U. of Manitoba	GPAC	46	39	41	80	....	....	....	....	....	....
1984-85b	U. of Manitoba	GPAC	30	29	38	67	48	....	....	....	....	....
1985-86c	**NY Rangers**	**NHL**	**80**	**22**	**43**	**65**	**69**	**16**	**6**	**8**	**14**	**26**
1986-87	**NY Rangers**	**NHL**	**38**	**16**	**20**	**36**	**20**	....	....	....	....	....
	Washington	**NHL**	**40**	**15**	**19**	**34**	**20**	**7**	**2**	**1**	**3**	**6**
1987-88	**Washington**	**NHL**	**70**	**28**	**31**	**59**	**22**	**14**	**6**	**5**	**11**	**10**
1988-89	**Washington**	**NHL**	**80**	**41**	**48**	**89**	**49**	**6**	**0**	**5**	**5**	**2**
1989-90	**Washington**	**NHL**	**74**	**30**	**43**	**73**	**27**	**14**	**3**	**4**	**7**	**8**
1990-91	**Washington**	**NHL**	**79**	**23**	**48**	**71**	**26**	**11**	**3**	**4**	**7**	**8**
1991-92	**Washington**	**NHL**	**80**	**29**	**40**	**69**	**38**	**7**	**0**	**11**	**11**	**0**
1992-93	**Washington**	**NHL**	**84**	**26**	**56**	**82**	**44**	**6**	**1**	**5**	**6**	**0**
1993-94	**Washington**	**NHL**	**81**	**26**	**44**	**70**	**24**	**11**	**4**	**6**	**10**	**6**
1994-95	**Toronto**	**NHL**	**48**	**10**	**27**	**37**	**14**	**7**	**3**	**1**	**4**	**2**
1995-96	**Vancouver**	**NHL**	**37**	**6**	**15**	**21**	**29**	**5**	**0**	**0**	**0**	**2**
1996-97	**Vancouver**	**NHL**	**75**	**20**	**32**	**52**	**42**	....	....	....	....	....
	NHL Totals		**866**	**292**	**466**	**758**	**424**	**104**	**28**	**50**	**78**	**70**

a Canadian University Player of the Year; CIAU All-Canadian, GPAC MVP and First All-Star Team (1984)
b CIAU All-Canadian, GPAC First All-Star Team (1985)
c NHL All-Rookie Team (1986)

Played in NHL All-Star Game (1989)

Signed as a free agent by **NY Rangers**, September 26, 1985. Traded to **Washington** by **NY Rangers** with Bob Crawford and Kelly Miller for Bob Carpenter and Washington's second round choice (Jason Prosofsky) in 1989 Entry Draft, January 1, 1987. Traded to **Toronto** by **Washington** with St. Louis' first round choice (previously acquired by Washington — Toronto selected Eric Fichaud) in 1994 Entry Draft for Rob Pearson and Philadelphia's first round choice (previously acquired by Toronto — Washington selected Nolan Baumgartner) in 1994 Entry Draft, June 28, 1994. Traded to **Vancouver** by **Toronto** for Sergio Momesso, July 8, 1995.

RIESEN, MICHEL — (REE-sehn, MEE-shehl) EDM.

Left wing. Shoots right. 6'2", 185 lbs. Born, Oberbalm, Switzerland, April 11, 1979.
(Edmonton's 1st choice, 14th overall, in 1997 Entry Draft).

			Regular Season					Playoffs				
Season	Club	Lea	GP	G	A	TP	PIM	GP	G	A	TP	PIM
1994-95	Biel	Switz.	12	0	2	2	0	6	2	0	2	0
1995-96	Biel	Swi. 2	34	9	6	15	2	3	1	0	1	0
1996-97	Biel	Swi. 2	38	16	16	32	49	....	....	....	....	....

RIIHIJARVI, TEEMO — (REE-ee-hee-jahr-vee) S.J.

Right wing. Shoots left. 6'6", 200 lbs. Born, Espoo, Finland, March 1, 1977.
(San Jose's 1st choice, 12th overall, in 1995 Entry Draft).

			Regular Season					Playoffs				
Season	Club	Lea	GP	G	A	TP	PIM	GP	G	A	TP	PIM
1993-94	Kiekko-Espoo	Fin.	13	1	1	2	6	....	....	....	....	....
1994-95	Kiekko-Espoo	Fin.	13	1	0	1	4	....	....	....	....	....
1995-96	Kiekko-Espoo	Fin.	2	0	0	0	0	....	....	....	....	....
	Haukat	Div. 2	4	0	0	0	2	....	....	....	....	....
	Kiekko-Espoo	Fin. Jr.	19	2	4	6	46	4	0	2	2	6
1996-97	Kiekko-Espoo	Fin.	47	3	1	4	8	4	0	0	0	2

RISIDORE, RYAN — (RIHZ-ih-daws) CHI.

Defense. Shoots left. 6'4", 195 lbs. Born, Hamilton, Ont., April 4, 1976.
(Hartford's 3rd choice, 109th overall, in 1994 Entry Draft).

			Regular Season					Playoffs				
Season	Club	Lea	GP	G	A	TP	PIM	GP	G	A	TP	PIM
1993-94	Guelph	OHL	51	2	9	11	39	9	0	0	0	12
1994-95	Guelph	OHL	65	2	30	32	102	14	2	2	4	19
1995-96	Guelph	OHL	66	12	38	50	186	16	4	5	9	*48
1996-97	Springfield	AHL	63	1	9	10	90	15	0	1	1	12

Traded to **Chicago** by **Carolina** with Carolina's fifth round choice in 1998 Entry Draft for Enrico Ciccone, July 25, 1997.

RITCHIE, BYRON — CAR.

Center. Shoots left. 5'10", 180 lbs. Born, Burnaby, B.C., April 24, 1977.
(Hartford's 6th choice, 165th overall, in 1995 Entry Draft).

			Regular Season					Playoffs				
Season	Club	Lea	GP	G	A	TP	PIM	GP	G	A	TP	PIM
1993-94	Lethbridge	WHL	44	4	11	15	44	6	0	0	0	14
1994-95	Lethbridge	WHL	58	22	28	50	132	....	....	....	....	....
1995-96a	Lethbridge	WHL	66	55	51	106	163	4	0	2	2	4
	Springfield	AHL	6	2	1	3	4	8	0	3	3	0
1996-97a	Lethbridge	WHL	63	50	76	126	115	18	*16	12	*28	28

a WHL East Second All-Star Team (1996, 1997)

RITCHLIN, SEAN — (RIHCH-lihn, SHAWN) N.J.

Right wing. Shoots right. 6', 200 lbs. Born, Rochester, NY, June 14, 1977.
(New Jersey's 10th choice, 145th overall, in 1996 Entry Draft).

			Regular Season					Playoffs				
Season	Club	Lea	GP	G	A	TP	PIM	GP	G	A	TP	PIM
1995-96	U. of Michigan	CCHA	27	7	7	14	24	....	....	....	....	....
1996-97	U. of Michigan	CCHA	38	10	10	20	48	....	....	....	....	....

RIVERS, JAMIE — ST.L.

Defense. Shoots left. 6', 190 lbs. Born, Ottawa, Ont., March 16, 1975.
(St. Louis' 2nd choice, 63rd overall, in 1993 Entry Draft).

			Regular Season					Playoffs				
Season	Club	Lea	GP	G	A	TP	PIM	GP	G	A	TP	PIM
1991-92	Sudbury	OHL	55	3	13	16	20	8	0	0	0	0
1992-93	Sudbury	OHL	62	12	43	55	20	14	7	19	26	4
1993-94ab	Sudbury	OHL	65	32	*89	121	58	10	1	9	10	14
1994-95c	Sudbury	OHL	46	9	56	65	30	18	7	26	33	22
1995-96	**St. Louis**	**NHL**	**3**	**0**	**0**	**0**	**2**	....	....	....	....	....
	Worcester	AHL	75	7	45	52	130	4	0	1	1	4
1996-97	**St. Louis**	**NHL**	**15**	**2**	**5**	**7**	**6**	....	....	....	....	....
d	Worcester	AHL	63	8	35	43	83	5	1	2	3	14
	NHL Totals		**18**	**2**	**5**	**7**	**8**	....	....	....	....	....

a OHL First All-Star Team (1994)
b Canadian Major Junior Second All-Star Team (1994)
c OHL Second All-Star Team (1995)
d AHL Second All-Star Team (1997)

RIVET, CRAIG (rih-VAY) MTL.

Defense. Shoots right. 6'1", 190 lbs.   Born, North Bay, Ont., September 13, 1974.
(Montreal's 4th choice, 68th overall, in 1992 Entry Draft).

			Regular Season					Playoffs				
Season	Club	Lea	GP	G	A	TP	PIM	GP	G	A	TP	PIM
1991-92	Kingston	OHL	66	5	21	26	97	....	....	....	....	....
1992-93	Kingston	OHL	64	19	55	74	117	16	5	7	12	39
1993-94	Kingston	OHL	61	12	52	64	100	6	0	3	3	6
	Fredericton	AHL	4	0	2	2	2	....	....	....	....	....
1994-95	Fredericton	AHL	78	5	27	32	126	12	0	4	4	17
	Montreal	**NHL**	5	0	1	1	5	....	....	....	....	....
1995-96	**Montreal**	**NHL**	19	1	4	5	54	....	....	....	....	....
	Fredericton	AHL	49	5	18	23	189	6	0	0	0	12
1996-97	**Montreal**	**NHL**	35	0	4	4	54	5	0	1	1	14
	Fredericton	AHL	23	3	12	15	99	....	....	....	....	....
	NHL Totals		59	1	9	10	113	5	0	1	1	14

ROBERTS, DAVID VAN.

Left wing. Shoots left. 6', 185 lbs.   Born, Alameda, CA, May 28, 1970.
(St. Louis' 5th choice, 114th overall, in 1989 Entry Draft).

			Regular Season					Playoffs				
Season	Club	Lea	GP	G	A	TP	PIM	GP	G	A	TP	PIM
1989-90	U. of Michigan	CCHA	42	21	32	53	46	....	....	....	....	....
1990-91ab	U. of Michigan	CCHA	43	26	45	71	58	....	....	....	....	....
1991-92	U. of Michigan	CCHA	44	16	42	58	68	....	....	....	....	....
1992-93a	U. of Michigan	CCHA	40	27	38	65	40	....	....	....	....	....
1993-94	U.S. National	....	49	17	28	45	68	....	....	....	....	....
	U.S. Olympic	....	8	1	5	6	4	....	....	....	....	....
	St. Louis	**NHL**	1	0	0	0	2	3	0	0	0	12
	Peoria	IHL	10	4	6	10	4	....	....	....	....	....
1994-95	Peoria	IHL	65	30	38	68	65	....	....	....	....	....
	St. Louis	**NHL**	19	6	5	11	10	6	0	0	0	4
1995-96	**St. Louis**	**NHL**	28	1	6	7	12	....	....	....	....	....
	Worcester	AHL	22	8	17	25	46	....	....	....	....	....
	Edmonton	**NHL**	6	2	4	6	6	....	....	....	....	....
1996-97	Vancouver	**NHL**	58	10	17	27	51	....	....	....	....	....
	NHL Totals		112	19	32	51	81	9	0	0	0	16

a CCHA Second All-Star Team (1991, 1993)
b NCAA West Second All-American Team (1991)

Traded to **Edmonton** by **St. Louis** for future considerations, March 12, 1996. Signed as a free agent by **Vancouver**, July 31, 1996.

ROBERTS, GARY CGY.

Left wing. Shoots left. 6'1", 190 lbs.   Born, North York, Ont., May 23, 1966.
(Calgary's 1st choice, 12th overall, in 1984 Entry Draft).

			Regular Season					Playoffs				
Season	Club	Lea	GP	G	A	TP	PIM	GP	G	A	TP	PIM
1982-83	Ottawa	OHL	53	12	8	20	83	5	1	0	1	19
1983-84	Ottawa	OHL	48	27	30	57	144	13	10	7	17	62
1984-85	Moncton	AHL	7	4	2	6	7	....	....	....	....	....
a	Ottawa	OHL	59	44	62	106	186	5	2	8	10	10
1985-86	Ottawa	OHL	24	26	25	51	83	....	....	....	....	....
a	Guelph	OHL	23	18	15	33	65	20	18	13	31	43
1986-87	**Calgary**	**NHL**	32	5	10	15	85	2	0	0	0	4
	Moncton	AHL	38	20	18	38	72	....	....	....	....	....
1987-88	**Calgary**	**NHL**	74	13	15	28	282	9	2	3	5	29
1988-89	**Calgary**	**NHL**	71	22	16	38	250	22	5	7	12	57 ♦
1989-90	**Calgary**	**NHL**	78	39	33	72	222	6	2	5	7	41
1990-91	**Calgary**	**NHL**	80	22	31	53	252	7	1	3	4	18
1991-92	**Calgary**	**NHL**	76	53	37	90	207	....	....	....	....	....
1992-93	**Calgary**	**NHL**	58	38	41	79	172	5	1	6	7	43
1993-94	**Calgary**	**NHL**	73	41	43	84	145	7	2	6	8	24
1994-95	**Calgary**	**NHL**	8	2	2	4	43	....	....	....	....	....
1995-96b	**Calgary**	**NHL**	35	22	20	42	78	....	....	....	....	....
1996-97					DID NOT PLAY							
	NHL Totals		585	257	248	505	1736	58	13	30	43	216

a OHL Second All-Star Team (1985, 1986)
b Won Bill Masterton Memorial Trophy (1996)
Played in NHL All-Star Game (1992, 1993)

ROBERTSSON, BERT (ROH-behrt-suhn) VAN.

Defense. Shoots left. 6'3", 205 lbs.   Born, Sodertalje, Sweden, June 30, 1974.
(Vancouver's 8th choice, 254th overall, in 1993 Entry Draft).

			Regular Season					Playoffs				
Season	Club	Lea	GP	G	A	TP	PIM	GP	G	A	TP	PIM
1992-93	Sodertalje	Swe. 2	23	2	1	3	24	....	....	....	....	....
1993-94	Sodertalje	Swe. 2	28	0	1	1	12	....	....	....	....	....
1994-95	Sodertalje	Swe. 2	23	1	2	3	24	....	....	....	....	....
1995-96	Syracuse	AHL	65	1	7	8	109	16	0	1	1	26
1996-97	Syracuse	AHL	80	4	9	13	132	3	1	0	1	4

ROBIDAS, STEPHANE (ROH-bih-dah) MTL.

Defense. Shoots right. 5'11", 192 lbs.   Born, Sherbrooke, Que., March 3, 1977.
(Montreal's 7th choice, 164th overall, in 1995 Entry Draft).

			Regular Season					Playoffs				
Season	Club	Lea	GP	G	A	TP	PIM	GP	G	A	TP	PIM
1993-94	Shawinigan	QMJHL	67	3	18	21	33	1	0	0	0	0
1994-95	Shawinigan	QMJHL	71	13	56	69	44	15	7	12	19	4
1995-96a	Shawinigan	QMJHL	67	23	56	79	53	6	1	5	6	10
1996-97a	Shawinigan	QMJHL	67	24	51	75	59	7	4	6	10	14

a QMJHL First All-Star Team (1996, 1997)

ROBINSON, JASON T.B.

Defense. Shoots left. 6'2", 190 lbs.   Born, Goderich, Ont., August 22, 1978.
(Tampa Bay's 3rd choice, 125th overall, in 1996 Entry Draft).

			Regular Season					Playoffs				
Season	Club	Lea	GP	G	A	TP	PIM	GP	G	A	TP	PIM
1995-96	Niagara Falls	OHL	51	2	4	6	100	10	0	0	0	16
1996-97	Erie	OHL	19	0	7	7	58	....	....	....	....	....

ROBITAILLE, LUC (ROH-buh-tigh) NYR

Left wing. Shoots left. 6'1", 195 lbs.   Born, Montreal, Que., February 17, 1966.
(Los Angeles' 9th choice, 171st overall, in 1984 Entry Draft).

			Regular Season					Playoffs				
Season	Club	Lea	GP	G	A	TP	PIM	GP	G	A	TP	PIM
1983-84	Hull	QMJHL	70	32	53	85	48	....	....	....	....	....
1984-85a	Hull	QMJHL	64	55	94	149	115	5	4	2	6	27
1985-86bc	Hull	QMJHL	63	68	123	191	91	15	17	27	44	28
1986-87def	**Los Angeles**	**NHL**	79	45	39	84	28	5	1	4	5	2
1987-88g	**Los Angeles**	**NHL**	80	53	58	111	82	5	2	5	7	18
1988-89g	**Los Angeles**	**NHL**	78	46	52	98	65	11	2	6	8	10
1989-90g	**Los Angeles**	**NHL**	80	52	49	101	38	10	5	5	10	10
1990-91g	**Los Angeles**	**NHL**	76	45	46	91	68	12	12	4	16	22
1991-92f	**Los Angeles**	**NHL**	80	44	63	107	95	6	3	4	7	12
1992-93g	**Los Angeles**	**NHL**	84	63	62	125	100	24	9	13	22	28
1993-94	**Los Angeles**	**NHL**	83	44	42	86	86	....	....	....	....	....
1994-95	**Pittsburgh**	**NHL**	46	23	19	42	37	12	7	4	11	26
1995-96	**NY Rangers**	**NHL**	77	23	46	69	80	11	1	5	6	8
1996-97	**NY Rangers**	**NHL**	69	24	24	48	48	15	4	7	11	4
	NHL Totals		832	462	500	962	727	111	46	57	103	140

a QMJHL Second All-Star Team (1985)
b QMJHL First All-Star Team (1986)
c Canadian Major Junior Player of the Year (1986)
d NHL All-Rookie Team (1987)
e Won Calder Memorial Trophy (1987)
f NHL Second All-Star Team (1987, 1992)
g NHL First All-Star Team (1988, 1989, 1990, 1991, 1993)
Played in NHL All-Star Game (1988-93)

Traded to **Pittsburgh** by **Los Angeles** for Rick Tocchet and Pittsburgh's second round choice (Pavel Rosa) in 1995 Entry Draft, July 29, 1994. Traded to **NY Rangers** by **Pittsburgh** with Ulf Samuelsson for Petr Nedved and Sergei Zubov, August 31, 1995.

ROBITAILLE, RANDY BOS.

Center. Shoots left. 5'11", 195 lbs.   Born, Ottawa, Ont., October 12, 1975.

			Regular Season					Playoffs				
Season	Club	Lea	GP	G	A	TP	PIM	GP	G	A	TP	PIM
1995-96	Miami-Ohio	CCHA	36	14	31	45	26	....	....	....	....	....
1996-97ab	Miami-Ohio	CCHA	39	27	34	61	44	....	....	....	....	....
	Boston	**NHL**	1	0	0	0	0	....	....	....	....	....
	NHL Totals		1	0	0	0	0					

a CCHA First All-Star Team (1997)
b NCAA West First All-American Team (1997)

Signed as a free agent by **Boston**, March 27, 1997.

ROCHE, DAVE (ROHSH) PIT.

Center. Shoots left. 6'4", 227 lbs.   Born, Lindsay, Ont., June 13, 1975.
(Pittsburgh's 3rd choice, 62nd overall, in 1993 Entry Draft).

			Regular Season					Playoffs				
Season	Club	Lea	GP	G	A	TP	PIM	GP	G	A	TP	PIM
1991-92	Peterborough	OHL	62	10	17	27	134	10	0	0	0	34
1992-93	Peterborough	OHL	56	40	60	100	105	21	14	15	29	42
1993-94	Peterborough	OHL	34	15	22	37	127	....	....	....	....	....
	Windsor	OHL	29	14	20	34	73	4	1	1	2	15
1994-95a	Windsor	OHL	66	55	59	114	180	10	9	6	15	16
1995-96	**Pittsburgh**	**NHL**	71	7	7	14	130	16	2	7	9	26
1996-97	**Pittsburgh**	**NHL**	61	5	5	10	155	....	....	....	....	....
	Cleveland	IHL	18	5	5	10	25	13	6	3	9	*87
	NHL Totals		132	12	12	24	285	16	2	7	9	26

a OHL First All-Star Team (1995)

ROCHEFORT, RICHARD N.J.

Center. Shoots right. 5'9", 180 lbs.   Born, North Bay, Ont., January 7, 1977.
(New Jersey's 9th choice, 174th overall, in 1995 Entry Draft).

			Regular Season					Playoffs				
Season	Club	Lea	GP	G	A	TP	PIM	GP	G	A	TP	PIM
1994-95	Sudbury	OHL	57	21	44	65	26	13	3	7	10	6
1995-96	Sudbury	OHL	56	25	40	65	38	....	....	....	....	....
1996-97	Sudbury	OHL	28	18	24	42	40	....	....	....	....	....
	Sarnia	OHL	18	5	23	28	23	12	3	9	12	8

ROED, PETER S.J.

Center. Shoots left. 5'10", 210 lbs.   Born, St. Paul, MN, November 15, 1976.
(San Jose's 2nd choice, 38th overall, in 1995 Entry Draft).

			Regular Season					Playoffs				
Season	Club	Lea	GP	G	A	TP	PIM	GP	G	A	TP	PIM
1995-96	Prince George	WHL	66	18	19	37	36	....	....	....	....	....
1996-97	Prince George	WHL	51	21	16	37	8	14	5	2	7	9
	Louisville	ECHL	7	1	0	1	4	....	....	....	....	....

ROENICK, JEREMY (ROH-nihk) PHO.

Center. Shoots right. 6', 170 lbs.   Born, Boston, MA, January 17, 1970.
(Chicago's 1st choice, 8th overall, in 1988 Entry Draft).

			Regular Season					Playoffs				
Season	Club	Lea	GP	G	A	TP	PIM	GP	G	A	TP	PIM
1988-89a	Hull	QMJHL	28	34	36	70	14	....	....	....	....	....
	Chicago	**NHL**	20	9	9	18	4	10	1	3	4	7
1989-90	**Chicago**	**NHL**	78	26	40	66	54	20	11	7	18	8
1990-91	**Chicago**	**NHL**	79	41	53	94	80	6	3	5	8	4
1991-92	**Chicago**	**NHL**	80	53	50	103	98	18	12	10	22	12
1992-93	**Chicago**	**NHL**	84	50	57	107	86	4	1	2	3	2
1993-94	**Chicago**	**NHL**	84	46	61	107	125	6	1	6	7	2
1994-95	Koln	Ger.	3	3	1	4	2	....	....	....	....	....
	Chicago	**NHL**	33	10	24	34	14	8	1	2	3	16
1995-96	**Chicago**	**NHL**	66	32	35	67	109	10	5	7	12	2
1996-97	**Phoenix**	**NHL**	72	29	40	69	115	6	2	4	6	4
	NHL Totals		596	296	369	665	685	88	37	46	83	57

a QMJHL Second All-Star Team (1989)
Played in NHL All-Star Game (1991-94)

Traded to **Phoenix** by **Chicago** for Alexei Zhamnov, Craig Mills and Phoenix's first round choice (Ty Jones) in 1997 Entry Draft, August 16, 1996.

ROEST, STACY (ROHST) DET.

Center. Shoots right. 5'9", 192 lbs. Born, Lethbridge, Alta., March 15, 1974.

			Regular Season					Playoffs				
Season	Club	Lea	GP	G	A	TP	PIM	GP	G	A	TP	PIM
1992-93	Medicine Hat	WHL	72	33	73	106	30	10	3	10	13	6
1993-94a	Medicine Hat	WHL	72	48	72	120	48	3	1	0	1	4
1994-95b	Medicine Hat	WHL	69	37	78	115	32	5	2	7	9	2
	Adirondack	AHL	3	0	0	0	0	....	....	....	....	....
1995-96	Adirondack	AHL	76	16	39	55	40	3	0	0	0	0
1996-97	Adirondack	AHL	78	25	41	66	30	4	1	1	2	0

a WHL East First All-Star Team (1994)
b WHL East Second All-Star Team (1995)

Signed as a free agent by **Detroit**, June 9, 1997.

ROHLIN, LEIF (roh-LEEN) VAN.

Defense. Shoots left. 6'1", 198 lbs. Born, Vasteras, Sweden, February 26, 1968.
(Vancouver's 2nd choice, 33rd overall, in 1988 Entry Draft).

			Regular Season					Playoffs				
Season	Club	Lea	GP	G	A	TP	PIM	GP	G	A	TP	PIM
1986-87	Vasteras	Swe. 2	27	2	5	7	12	12	0	2	2	8
1987-88	Vasteras	Swe. 2	30	2	15	17	46	7	0	4	4	8
1988-89	Vasteras	Swe.	22	3	7	10	18	....	....	....	....	....
1989-90	Vasteras	Swe.	32	3	6	9	40	2	0	0	0	2
1990-91	Vasteras	Swe.	40	4	10	14	46	4	0	1	1	8
1991-92	Vasteras	Swe.	39	4	6	10	52	....	....	....	....	....
1992-93	Vasteras	Swe.	37	5	7	12	24	2	0	0	0	0
1993-94	Vasteras	Swe.	40	6	14	20	26	4	0	1	1	6
1994-95	Vasteras	Swe.	39	15	15	30	46	4	2	0	2	2
1995-96	**Vancouver**	**NHL**	**56**	**6**	**16**	**22**	**32**	**5**	**0**	**0**	**0**	**0**
1996-97	**Vancouver**	**NHL**	**40**	**2**	**8**	**10**	**8**	....	....	....	....	....
	NHL Totals		**96**	**8**	**24**	**32**	**40**	**5**	**0**	**0**	**0**	**0**

ROHLOFF, JON (ROH-lohf) BOS.

Defense. Shoots right. 6', 221 lbs. Born, Mankato, MN, October 3, 1969.
(Boston's 7th choice, 186th overall, in 1988 Entry Draft).

			Regular Season					Playoffs				
Season	Club	Lea	GP	G	A	TP	PIM	GP	G	A	TP	PIM
1988-89	Minn.-Duluth	WCHA	39	1	2	3	44	....	....	....	....	....
1989-90	Minn.-Duluth	WCHA	5	0	1	1	6	....	....	....	....	....
1990-91	Minn.-Duluth	WCHA	32	6	11	17	38	....	....	....	....	....
1991-92	Minn.-Duluth	WCHA	27	9	9	18	48	....	....	....	....	....
1992-93a	Minn.-Duluth	WCHA	36	15	20	35	87	....	....	....	....	....
1993-94	Providence	AHL	55	12	23	35	59	....	....	....	....	....
1994-95	**Boston**	**NHL**	**34**	**3**	**8**	**11**	**39**	**5**	**0**	**0**	**0**	**6**
	Providence	AHL	4	2	1	3	6	....	....	....	....	....
1995-96	**Boston**	**NHL**	**79**	**1**	**12**	**13**	**59**	**5**	**1**	**2**	**3**	**2**
1996-97	**Boston**	**NHL**	**37**	**3**	**5**	**8**	**31**	....	....	....	....	....
	Providence	AHL	3	1	1	2	0	....	....	....	....	....
	NHL Totals		**150**	**7**	**25**	**32**	**129**	**10**	**1**	**2**	**3**	**8**

a WCHA Second All-Star Team (1993)

ROLSTON, BRIAN N.J.

Center. Shoots left. 6'2", 200 lbs. Born, Flint, MI, February 21, 1973.
(New Jersey's 2nd choice, 11th overall, in 1991 Entry Draft).

			Regular Season					Playoffs				
Season	Club	Lea	GP	G	A	TP	PIM	GP	G	A	TP	PIM
1991-92a	Lake Superior	CCHA	37	14	23	37	14	....	....	....	....	....
1992-93abc	Lake Superior	CCHA	39	33	31	64	20	....	....	....	....	....
1993-94	U.S. National	....	41	20	28	48	36	....	....	....	....	....
	U.S. Olympic	....	8	7	0	7	8	....	....	....	....	....
	Albany	AHL	17	5	5	10	8	5	1	2	3	0
1994-95	Albany	AHL	18	9	11	20	10	....	....	....	....	....
	New Jersey	**NHL**	**40**	**7**	**11**	**18**	**17**	**6**	**2**	**1**	**3**	**4 ♦**
1995-96	**New Jersey**	**NHL**	**58**	**13**	**11**	**24**	**8**	....	....	....	....	....
1996-97	**New Jersey**	**NHL**	**81**	**18**	**27**	**45**	**20**	**10**	**4**	**1**	**5**	**6**
	NHL Totals		**179**	**38**	**49**	**87**	**45**	**16**	**6**	**2**	**8**	**10**

a NCAA Final Four All-Tournament Team (1992, 1993)
b CCHA First All-Star Team (1993)
c NCAA West Second All-American Team (1993)

ROMANIUK, RUSSELL (ROH-muh-NUHK)

Left wing. Shoots left. 6', 195 lbs. Born, Winnipeg, Man., June 9, 1970.
(Winnipeg's 2nd choice, 31st overall, in 1988 Entry Draft).

			Regular Season					Playoffs				
Season	Club	Lea	GP	G	A	TP	PIM	GP	G	A	TP	PIM
1988-89	North Dakota	WCHA	39	17	14	31	32	....	....	....	....	....
	Cdn. National	....	3	1	0	1	0	....	....	....	....	....
1989-90	North Dakota	WCHA	45	36	15	51	54	....	....	....	....	....
1990-91a	North Dakota	WCHA	39	40	28	68	30	....	....	....	....	....
1991-92	**Winnipeg**	**NHL**	**27**	**3**	**5**	**8**	**18**	....	....	....	....	....
	Moncton	AHL	45	16	15	31	25	10	5	4	9	19
1992-93	**Winnipeg**	**NHL**	**28**	**3**	**1**	**4**	**22**	**1**	**0**	**0**	**0**	**0**
	Moncton	AHL	28	18	8	26	40	5	0	4	4	2
	Fort Wayne	IHL	4	2	0	2	7	....	....	....	....	....
1993-94	Cdn. National	....	34	8	9	17	17	....	....	....	....	....
	Winnipeg	**NHL**	**24**	**4**	**8**	**12**	**6**	....	....	....	....	....
	Moncton	AHL	18	16	8	24	24	17	2	6	8	30
1994-95	**Winnipeg**	**NHL**	**6**	**0**	**0**	**0**	**0**	....	....	....	....	....
	Springfield	AHL	17	5	7	12	29	....	....	....	....	....
1995-96	**Philadelphia**	**NHL**	**17**	**3**	**0**	**3**	**17**	**1**	**0**	**0**	**0**	**0**
	Hershey	AHL	27	19	10	29	43	....	....	....	....	....
1996-97	Manitoba	IHL	46	14	13	27	43	....	....	....	....	....
	NHL Totals		**102**	**13**	**14**	**27**	**63**	**2**	**0**	**0**	**0**	**0**

a WCHA First All-Star Team (1991)

Traded to **Philadelphia** by **Winnipeg** for Jeff Finley, June 27, 1995.

RONAN, ED (ROH-nan)

Right wing. Shoots right. 6', 197 lbs. Born, Quincy, MA, March 21, 1968.
(Montreal's 13th choice, 227th overall, in 1987 Entry Draft).

			Regular Season					Playoffs				
Season	Club	Lea	GP	G	A	TP	PIM	GP	G	A	TP	PIM
1987-88	Boston U.	H.E.	31	2	5	7	20	....	....	....	....	....
1988-89	Boston U.	H.E.	36	4	11	15	34	....	....	....	....	....
1989-90	Boston U.	H.E.	44	17	23	40	50	....	....	....	....	....
1990-91	Boston U.	H.E.	41	16	19	35	38	....	....	....	....	....
1991-92	**Montreal**	**NHL**	**3**	**0**	**0**	**0**	**0**	....	....	....	....	....
	Fredericton	AHL	78	25	34	59	82	7	5	1	6	6
1992-93	**Montreal**	**NHL**	**53**	**5**	**7**	**12**	**20**	**14**	**2**	**3**	**5**	**10 ♦**
	Fredericton	AHL	16	10	5	15	15	5	2	4	6	6
1993-94	**Montreal**	**NHL**	**61**	**6**	**8**	**14**	**42**	**7**	**1**	**0**	**1**	**0**
1994-95	**Montreal**	**NHL**	**30**	**1**	**4**	**5**	**12**	....	....	....	....	....
1995-96	**Winnipeg**	**NHL**	**17**	**0**	**0**	**0**	**16**	....	....	....	....	....
	Springfield	AHL	31	8	16	24	50	10	7	6	13	4
1996-97	**Buffalo**	**NHL**	**18**	**1**	**4**	**5**	**11**	**6**	**1**	**0**	**1**	**6**
	Rochester	AHL	47	13	21	34	62	....	....	....	....	....
	NHL Totals		**182**	**13**	**23**	**36**	**101**	**27**	**4**	**3**	**7**	**16**

Signed as a free agent by **Winnipeg**, October 13, 1995. Signed as a free agent by **Buffalo**, September 5, 1996.

RONNING, CLIFF PHO.

Center. Shoots left. 5'8", 170 lbs. Born, Burnaby, B.C., October 1, 1965.
(St. Louis' 9th choice, 134th overall, in 1984 Entry Draft).

			Regular Season					Playoffs				
Season	Club	Lea	GP	G	A	TP	PIM	GP	G	A	TP	PIM
1983-84	N. Westminster	WHL	71	69	67	136	10	9	8	13	21	10
1984-85a	N. Westminster	WHL	70	*89	108	*197	20	11	10	14	24	4
1985-86	Cdn. Olympic	....	71	55	63	118	53	....	....	....	....	....
	St. Louis	**NHL**	....	....	....	....	....	**5**	**1**	**1**	**2**	**2**
1986-87	**St. Louis**	**NHL**	**42**	**11**	**14**	**25**	**6**	**4**	**0**	**1**	**1**	**0**
	Cdn. National	....	26	17	16	33	12	....	....	....	....	....
1987-88	**St. Louis**	**NHL**	**26**	**5**	**8**	**13**	**12**	....	....	....	....	....
1988-89	**St. Louis**	**NHL**	**64**	**24**	**31**	**55**	**18**	**7**	**1**	**3**	**4**	**0**
	Peoria	IHL	12	11	20	31	8	....	....	....	....	....
1989-90	Asiago	Italy	36	67	49	116	25	6	7	12	19	4
1990-91	**St. Louis**	**NHL**	**48**	**14**	**18**	**32**	**10**	....	....	....	....	....
	Vancouver	**NHL**	**11**	**6**	**6**	**12**	**0**	**6**	**6**	**3**	**9**	**12**
1991-92	**Vancouver**	**NHL**	**80**	**24**	**47**	**71**	**42**	**13**	**8**	**5**	**13**	**6**
1992-93	**Vancouver**	**NHL**	**79**	**29**	**56**	**85**	**30**	**12**	**2**	**9**	**11**	**6**
1993-94	**Vancouver**	**NHL**	**76**	**25**	**43**	**68**	**42**	**24**	**5**	**10**	**15**	**16**
1994-95	**Vancouver**	**NHL**	**41**	**6**	**19**	**25**	**27**	**11**	**3**	**5**	**8**	**2**
1995-96	**Vancouver**	**NHL**	**79**	**22**	**45**	**67**	**42**	**6**	**0**	**2**	**2**	**6**
1996-97	**Phoenix**	**NHL**	**69**	**19**	**32**	**51**	**26**	**7**	**0**	**7**	**7**	**12**
	NHL Totals		**615**	**185**	**319**	**504**	**255**	**95**	**26**	**46**	**72**	**62**

a WHL First All-Star Team (1985)

Traded to **Vancouver** by **St. Louis** with Geoff Courtnall, Robert Dirk, Sergio Momesso and St. Louis' fifth round choice (Brian Loney) in 1992 Entry Draft for Dan Quinn and Garth Butcher, March 5, 1991. Signed as a free agent by **Phoenix**, July 1, 1996.

ROSA, PAVEL (ROHZA) L.A.

Right wing. Shoots right. 5'11", 180 lbs. Born, Most, Czech., June 7, 1977.
(Los Angeles' 3rd choice, 50th overall, in 1995 Entry Draft).

			Regular Season					Playoffs				
Season	Club	Lea	GP	G	A	TP	PIM	GP	G	A	TP	PIM
1994-95	Litvinov	Czech. Jr.	40	56	42	98	....	....	....	....	....	....
	Litvinov	Czech.	2	0	0	0	0	1	0	0	0	0
1995-96	Hull	QMJHL	61	46	70	116	39	18	14	22	36	25
1996-97ab	Hull	QMJHL	68	*63	*90	*153	66	14	18	13	31	16

a QMJHL First All-Star Team (1997)
b Canadian Major Junior First All-Star Team (1997)

ROUSE, BOB (ROWS) DET.

Defense. Shoots right. 6'1", 210 lbs. Born, Surrey, B.C., June 18, 1964.
(Minnesota's 3rd choice, 80th overall, in 1982 Entry Draft).

			Regular Season					Playoffs				
Season	Club	Lea	GP	G	A	TP	PIM	GP	G	A	TP	PIM
1980-81	Billings	WHL	70	0	13	13	116	5	0	0	0	2
1981-82	Billings	WHL	71	7	22	29	209	5	0	2	2	10
1982-83	Nanaimo	WHL	29	7	20	27	86	....	....	....	....	....
	Lethbridge	WHL	42	8	30	38	82	20	2	13	15	55
1983-84	**Minnesota**	**NHL**	**1**	**0**	**0**	**0**	**0**	....	....	....	....	....
a	Lethbridge	WHL	71	18	42	60	101	5	0	1	1	28
1984-85	**Minnesota**	**NHL**	**63**	**2**	**9**	**11**	**113**	....	....	....	....	....
	Springfield	AHL	8	0	3	3	6	....	....	....	....	....
1985-86	**Minnesota**	**NHL**	**75**	**1**	**14**	**15**	**151**	**3**	**0**	**0**	**0**	**0**
1986-87	**Minnesota**	**NHL**	**72**	**2**	**10**	**12**	**179**	....	....	....	....	....
1987-88	**Minnesota**	**NHL**	**74**	**0**	**12**	**12**	**168**	....	....	....	....	....
1988-89	**Minnesota**	**NHL**	**66**	**4**	**13**	**17**	**124**	....	....	....	....	....
	Washington	**NHL**	**13**	**0**	**2**	**2**	**36**	**6**	**2**	**0**	**2**	**4**
1989-90	**Washington**	**NHL**	**70**	**4**	**16**	**20**	**123**	**15**	**2**	**3**	**5**	**47**
1990-91	**Washington**	**NHL**	**47**	**5**	**15**	**20**	**65**	....	....	....	....	....
	Toronto	**NHL**	**13**	**2**	**4**	**6**	**10**	....	....	....	....	....
1991-92	**Toronto**	**NHL**	**79**	**3**	**19**	**22**	**97**	....	....	....	....	....
1992-93	**Toronto**	**NHL**	**82**	**3**	**11**	**14**	**130**	**21**	**3**	**8**	**11**	**29**
1993-94	**Toronto**	**NHL**	**63**	**5**	**11**	**16**	**101**	**18**	**0**	**3**	**3**	**29**
1994-95	**Detroit**	**NHL**	**48**	**1**	**7**	**8**	**36**	**18**	**0**	**3**	**3**	**8**
1995-96	**Detroit**	**NHL**	**58**	**0**	**6**	**6**	**48**	**7**	**0**	**1**	**1**	**4**
1996-97	**Detroit**	**NHL**	**70**	**4**	**9**	**13**	**58**	**20**	**0**	**0**	**0**	**55 ♦**
	NHL Totals		**894**	**36**	**158**	**194**	**1439**	**108**	**7**	**18**	**25**	**176**

a WHL East First All-Star Team (1984)

Traded to **Washington** by **Minnesota** with Dino Ciccarelli for Mike Gartner and Larry Murphy, March 7, 1989. Traded to **Toronto** by **Washington** with Peter Zezel for Al Iafrate, January 16, 1991. Signed as a free agent by **Detroit**, August 5, 1994.

ROY, ANDRE (WAH, AHN-dray) BOS.

Left wing. Shoots left. 6'3", 202 lbs. Born, Port Chester, NY, February 8, 1975.
(Boston's 5th choice, 151st overall, in 1994 Entry Draft).

			Regular Season					Playoffs				
Season	Club	Lea	GP	G	A	TP	PIM	GP	G	A	TP	PIM
1993-94	Beauport	QMJHL	33	6	7	13	125	....	....	....	....	....
	Chicoutimi	QMJHL	32	4	14	18	152	25	3	6	9	94
1994-95	Chicoutimi	QMJHL	20	15	8	23	90	....	....	....	....	....
	Drummondville	QMJHL	34	18	13	31	233	4	2	0	2	34
1995-96	**Boston**	**NHL**	**3**	**0**	**0**	**0**	**0**	....	....	....	....	....
	Providence	AHL	58	7	8	15	167	1	0	0	0	10
1996-97	**Boston**	**NHL**	**10**	**0**	**2**	**2**	**12**	....	....	....	....	....
	Providence	AHL	50	17	11	28	234	....	....	....	....	....
	NHL Totals		**13**	**0**	**2**	**2**	**12**	....	....	....	....	....

ROY, JEAN-YVES (WAH)

Right wing. Shoots left. 5'10", 180 lbs. Born, Rosemere, Que., February 17, 1969.

			Regular Season					Playoffs				
Season	Club	Lea	GP	G	A	TP	PIM	GP	G	A	TP	PIM
1989-90a	U. of Maine	H.E.	46	*39	26	65	52	....	....	....	....	....
1990-91bcd	U. of Maine	H.E.	43	37	45	82	62	....	....	....	....	....
1991-92ce	U. of Maine	H.E.	35	32	24	56	62	....	....	....	....	....
	Cdn. National	....	13	10	4	14	6	....	....	....	....	....
1992-93	Binghamton	AHL	49	13	15	28	21	14	5	2	7	4
	Cdn. National	....	23	9	6	15	35	....	....	....	....	....
1993-94	Binghamton	AHL	65	41	24	65	33	....	....	....	....	....
	Cdn. National	....	6	3	2	5	2	....	....	....	....	....
	Cdn. Olympic	....	8	1	0	1	0	....	....	....	....	....
1994-95	Binghamton	AHL	67	41	36	77	28	11	4	6	10	12
	NY Rangers	**NHL**	**3**	**1**	**0**	**1**	**2**	....	....	....	....	....
1995-96	**Ottawa**	**NHL**	**4**	**1**	**1**	**2**	**2**	....	....	....	....	....
	P.E.I.	AHL	67	40	55	95	64	5	4	8	12	6
1996-97	**Boston**	**NHL**	**52**	**10**	**15**	**25**	**22**	....	....	....	....	....
	Providence	AHL	27	9	16	25	30	10	2	7	9	2
	NHL Totals		**59**	**12**	**16**	**28**	**26**	....	....	....	....	....

a NCAA East Second All-American Team (1990)
b Hockey East First All-Star Team (1991)
c NCAA East First All-American Team (1991, 1992)
d NCAA Final Four All-Tournament Team (1991)
e Hockey East Second All-Star Team (1992)

Signed as a free agent by **NY Rangers**, July 20, 1992. Traded to **Ottawa** by **NY Rangers** for Steve Larouche, October 5, 1995. Signed as a free agent by **Boston**, July 15, 1996.

ROY, JIMMY (ROI) DAL.

Center. Shoots right. 5'11", 170 lbs. Born, Sioux Lookout, Ont., September 22, 1975.
(Dallas' 7th choice, 254th overall, in 1994 Entry Draft).

			Regular Season					Playoffs				
Season	Club	Lea	GP	G	A	TP	PIM	GP	G	A	TP	PIM
1994-95	Michigan Tech.	WCHA	38	5	11	16	62	....	....	....	....	....
1995-96	Michigan Tech	WCHA	42	17	17	34	84	....	....	....	....	....
1996-97	Cdn. National	....	55	10	17	27	82	....	....	....	....	....

ROY, STEPHANE (WAH) ST.L.

Center. Shoots left. 5'10", 173 lbs. Born, Ste-Martine, Que., January 26, 1976.
(St. Louis' 1st choice, 68th overall, in 1994 Entry Draft).

			Regular Season					Playoffs				
Season	Club	Lea	GP	G	A	TP	PIM	GP	G	A	TP	PIM
1993-94	Val d'Or	QMJHL	72	25	28	53	116	....	....	....	....	....
1994-95	Val d'Or	QMJHL	68	19	52	71	113	....	....	....	....	....
1995-96	Val d'Or	QMJHL	62	43	72	115	89	13	9	15	24	10
	Worcester	AHL	1	0	0	0	2	....	....	....	....	....
1996-97	Worcester	AHL	66	24	23	47	57	5	2	0	2	4

ROYER, REMI (ROHY-uhr) CHI.

Defense. Shoots right. 6'2", 185 lbs. Born, Donnacona, Que., February 12, 1978.
(Chicago's 1st choice, 31st overall, in 1996 Entry Draft).

			Regular Season					Playoffs				
Season	Club	Lea	GP	G	A	TP	PIM	GP	G	A	TP	PIM
1994-95	Victoriaville	QMJHL	57	3	17	20	144	4	0	1	1	7
1995-96	Victoriaville	QMJHL	43	12	14	26	209	....	....	....	....	....
	St-Hyacinthe	QMJHL	19	10	9	19	80	12	1	4	5	29
1996-97	Rouyn-Noranda	QMJHL	29	3	12	15	85	....	....	....	....	....
	Indianapolis	IHL	10	0	1	1	17	....	....	....	....	....

ROZSIVAL, MICHAL (ROH-see-vahl) PIT.

Defense. Shoots right. 6'1", 189 lbs. Born, Vlasim, Czech., September 3, 1978.
(Pittsburgh's 5th choice, 105th overall, in 1996 Entry Draft).

			Regular Season					Playoffs				
Season	Club	Lea	GP	G	A	TP	PIM	GP	G	A	TP	PIM
1994-95	Dukla Jihlava	Czech. Jr.	31	8	13	21	....	....	....	....	....	....
1995-96	Dukla Jihlava	Czech. Jr.	36	3	4	7	....	....	....	....	....	....
1996-97	Swift Current	WHL	63	8	31	39	80	10	0	6	6	15

RUCCHIN, STEVE (ROO-chihn) ANA.

Center. Shoots left. 6'3", 215 lbs. Born, London, Ont., July 4, 1971.
(Anaheim's 1st choice, 2nd overall, in 1994 Supplemental Draft).

			Regular Season					Playoffs				
Season	Club	Lea	GP	G	A	TP	PIM	GP	G	A	TP	PIM
1990-91	Western Ont.	OUAA	34	13	16	29	14	....	....	....	....	....
1991-92	Western Ont.	OUAA	37	28	34	62	36	....	....	....	....	....
1992-93	Western Ont.	OUAA	34	22	26	48	16	....	....	....	....	....
1993-94	Western Ont.	OUAA	35	30	23	53	30	....	....	....	....	....
1994-95	San Diego	IHL	41	11	15	26	14	....	....	....	....	....
	Anaheim	**NHL**	**43**	**6**	**11**	**17**	**23**	....	....	....	....	....
1995-96	**Anaheim**	**NHL**	**64**	**19**	**25**	**44**	**12**	....	....	....	....	....
1996-97	**Anaheim**	**NHL**	**79**	**19**	**48**	**67**	**24**	**8**	**1**	**2**	**3**	**10**
	NHL Totals		**186**	**44**	**84**	**128**	**59**	**8**	**1**	**2**	**3**	**10**

RUCINSKI, MIKE (roo-SIHN-skee) CAR.

Defense. Shoots left. 5'11", 179 lbs. Born, Trenton, MI, March 30, 1975.
(Hartford's 8th choice, 217th overall, in 1995 Entry Draft).

			Regular Season					Playoffs				
Season	Club	Lea	GP	G	A	TP	PIM	GP	G	A	TP	PIM
1992-93	Detroit	OHL	66	6	13	19	59	15	0	4	4	12
1993-94	Detroit	OHL	66	2	26	28	58	17	0	7	7	15
1994-95	Detroit	OHL	64	9	18	27	61	21	3	3	6	8
1995-96	Detroit	OHL	51	10	26	36	65	11	2	4	6	14
1996-97	Richmond	ECHL	61	20	23	43	85	8	2	6	8	18
	Springfield	AHL	6	0	1	1	0	....	....	....	....	....

RUCINSKY, MARTIN (roo-SHIHN-skee) MTL.

Left wing. Shoots left. 6', 198 lbs. Born, Most, Czech., March 11, 1971.
(Edmonton's 2nd choice, 20th overall, in 1991 Entry Draft).

			Regular Season					Playoffs				
Season	Club	Lea	GP	G	A	TP	PIM	GP	G	A	TP	PIM
1988-89	Litvinov	Czech.	3	1	0	1	2	....	....	....	....	....
1989-90	Litvinov	Czech.	47	17	9	26	....	....	....	....	....	....
1990-91	Litvinov	Czech.	56	24	20	44	69	....	....	....	....	....
1991-92	**Edmonton**	**NHL**	**2**	**0**	**0**	**0**	**0**	....	....	....	....	....
	Cape Breton	AHL	35	11	12	23	34	....	....	....	....	....
	Quebec	**NHL**	**4**	**1**	**1**	**2**	**2**	....	....	....	....	....
	Halifax	AHL	7	1	1	2	6	....	....	....	....	....
1992-93	**Quebec**	**NHL**	**77**	**18**	**30**	**48**	**51**	**6**	**1**	**1**	**2**	**4**
1993-94	**Quebec**	**NHL**	**60**	**9**	**23**	**32**	**58**	....	....	....	....	....
1994-95	Litvinov	Czech.	13	12	10	22	54	....	....	....	....	....
	Quebec	**NHL**	**20**	**3**	**6**	**9**	**14**	....	....	....	....	....
1995-96	Vsetin	Czech.	1	1	1	2	0	....	....	....	....	....
	Colorado	**NHL**	**22**	**4**	**11**	**15**	**14**	....	....	....	....	....
	Montreal	**NHL**	**56**	**25**	**35**	**60**	**54**	....	....	....	....	....
1996-97	**Montreal**	**NHL**	**70**	**28**	**27**	**55**	**62**	**5**	**0**	**0**	**0**	**4**
	NHL Totals		**311**	**88**	**133**	**221**	**255**	**11**	**1**	**1**	**2**	**8**

Traded to **Quebec** by **Edmonton** for Ron Tugnutt and Brad Zavisha, March 10, 1992. Traded to **Montreal** by **Colorado** with Andrei Kovalenko and Jocelyn Thibault for Patrick Roy and Mike Keane, December 6, 1995.

RUFF, JASON

Left wing. Shoots left. 6'2", 192 lbs. Born, Kelowna, B.C., January 27, 1970.
(St Louis' 3rd choice, 96th overall, in 1990 Entry Draft).

			Regular Season					Playoffs				
Season	Club	Lea	GP	G	A	TP	PIM	GP	G	A	TP	PIM
1987-88	Lethbridge	WHL	69	25	22	47	109	....	....	....	....	....
1988-89	Lethbridge	WHL	69	42	38	80	127	....	....	....	....	....
1989-90	Lethbridge	WHL	72	55	64	119	114	19	9	10	19	18
1990-91a	Lethbridge	WHL	66	61	75	136	154	16	12	17	29	18
	Peoria	IHL	....	....	....	....	....	5	0	0	0	2
1991-92	Peoria	IHL	67	27	45	72	148	10	7	7	14	19
1992-93	**St. Louis**	**NHL**	**7**	**2**	**1**	**3**	**8**	....	....	....	....	....
	Peoria	IHL	40	22	21	43	81	....	....	....	....	....
	Tampa Bay	**NHL**	**1**	**0**	**0**	**0**	**0**	....	....	....	....	....
	Atlanta	IHL	26	11	14	25	90	7	2	1	3	26
1993-94	**Tampa Bay**	**NHL**	**6**	**1**	**2**	**3**	**2**	....	....	....	....	....
	Atlanta	IHL	71	24	25	49	122	14	6	*17	23	41
1994-95	Atlanta	IHL	64	42	34	76	161	3	3	1	4	10
1995-96	Atlanta	IHL	59	39	33	72	135	2	0	0	0	16
1996-97	Quebec	IHL	80	35	50	85	93	9	8	5	13	10
	NHL Totals		**14**	**3**	**3**	**6**	**10**	....	....	....	....	....

a WHL East First All-Star Team (1991)

Traded to **Tampa Bay** by **St. Louis** with future considerations for Doug Crossman, Basil McRae and Tampa Bay's fourth round choice (Andrei Petrakov) in 1996 Entry Draft, January 28, 1993.

RUMBLE, DARREN

Defense. Shoots left. 6'1", 200 lbs. Born, Barrie, Ont., January 23, 1969.
(Philadelphia's 1st choice, 20th overall, in 1987 Entry Draft).

			Regular Season					Playoffs				
Season	Club	Lea	GP	G	A	TP	PIM	GP	G	A	TP	PIM
1986-87	Kitchener	OHL	64	11	32	43	44	4	0	1	1	9
1987-88	Kitchener	OHL	55	15	50	65	64	....	....	....	....	....
1988-89	Kitchener	OHL	46	11	28	39	25	5	1	0	1	2
1989-90	Hershey	AHL	57	2	13	15	31	....	....	....	....	....
1990-91	**Philadelphia**	**NHL**	**3**	**1**	**0**	**1**	**0**	....	....	....	....	....
	Hershey	AHL	73	6	35	41	48	3	0	5	5	2
1991-92	Hershey	AHL	79	12	54	66	118	6	0	3	3	2
1992-93	**Ottawa**	**NHL**	**69**	**3**	**13**	**16**	**61**	....	....	....	....	....
	New Haven	AHL	2	1	0	1	0	....	....	....	....	....
1993-94	**Ottawa**	**NHL**	**70**	**6**	**9**	**15**	**116**	....	....	....	....	....
	P.E.I.	AHL	3	2	0	2	0	....	....	....	....	....
1994-95a	P.E.I.	AHL	70	7	46	53	77	11	0	6	6	4
1995-96	**Philadelphia**	**NHL**	**5**	**0**	**0**	**0**	**4**	....	....	....	....	....
	Hershey	AHL	58	13	37	50	83	5	0	0	0	6
1996-97	**Philadelphia**	**NHL**	**10**	**0**	**0**	**0**	**0**	....	....	....	....	....
bc	Philadelphia	AHL	72	18	44	62	83	7	0	3	3	19
	NHL Totals		**157**	**10**	**22**	**32**	**181**	....	....	....	....	....

a AHL Second All-Star Team (1995)
b AHL First All-Star Team (1997)
c Won Eddie Shore Plaque (Outstanding Defenseman - AHL) (1997)

Claimed by **Ottawa** from **Philadelphia** in Expansion Draft, June 18, 1992. Signed as a free agent by **Philadelphia**, July 31, 1995.

RUSSELL, CAM CHI.

Defense. Shoots left. 6'4", 200 lbs. Born, Halifax, N.S., January 12, 1969.
(Chicago's 3rd choice, 50th overall, in 1987 Entry Draft).

			Regular Season					Playoffs				
Season	Club	Lea	GP	G	A	TP	PIM	GP	G	A	TP	PIM
1985-86	Hull	QMJHL	56	3	4	7	24	15	0	2	2	4
1986-87	Hull	QMJHL	66	3	16	19	119	8	0	1	1	16
1987-88	Hull	QMJHL	53	9	18	27	141	19	2	5	7	39
1988-89	Hull	QMJHL	66	8	32	40	109	9	2	6	8	6
1989-90	**Chicago**	**NHL**	**19**	**0**	**1**	**1**	**27**	**1**	**0**	**0**	**0**	**0**
	Indianapolis	IHL	46	3	15	18	114	9	0	1	1	24
1990-91	**Chicago**	**NHL**	**3**	**0**	**0**	**0**	**5**	**1**	**0**	**0**	**0**	**0**
	Indianapolis	IHL	53	5	9	14	125	6	0	2	2	30
1991-92	**Chicago**	**NHL**	**19**	**0**	**0**	**0**	**34**	**12**	**0**	**2**	**2**	**2**
	Indianapolis	IHL	41	4	9	13	78	....	....	....	....	....
1992-93	**Chicago**	**NHL**	**67**	**2**	**4**	**6**	**151**	**4**	**0**	**0**	**0**	**0**
1993-94	**Chicago**	**NHL**	**67**	**1**	**7**	**8**	**200**	....	....	....	....	....
1994-95	**Chicago**	**NHL**	**33**	**1**	**3**	**4**	**88**	**16**	**0**	**3**	**3**	**8**
1995-96	**Chicago**	**NHL**	**61**	**2**	**2**	**4**	**129**	**6**	**0**	**0**	**0**	**2**
1996-97	**Chicago**	**NHL**	**44**	**1**	**1**	**2**	**65**	**4**	**0**	**0**	**0**	**4**
	NHL Totals		**313**	**7**	**18**	**25**	**699**	**44**	**0**	**5**	**5**	**16**

RYABYKIN, DMITRI (ryah-BEE-kihn) CGY.

Defense. Shoots right. 6'1", 185 lbs. Born, Chirchik, USSR, March 24, 1976.
(Calgary's 2nd choice, 45th overall, in 1994 Entry Draft).

			Regular Season					Playoffs				
Season	Club	Lea	GP	G	A	TP	PIM	GP	G	A	TP	PIM
1994-95	Moscow D'amo	CIS	48	0	0	0	12	11	0	2	2	0
1995-96	Moscow D'amo	CIS	47	3	1	4	49	13	1	1	2	6
1996-97	Moscow D'amo	Rus.	34	1	10	11	12	4	0	0	0	8

RYAN, TERRY — MTL.

Left wing. Shoots left. 6'2", 198 lbs. Born, St. John's, Nfld., January 14, 1977.
(Montreal's 1st choice, 8th overall, in 1995 Entry Draft).

			Regular Season					Playoffs				
Season	Club	Lea	GP	G	A	TP	PIM	GP	G	A	TP	PIM
1993-94	Tri-City	WHL	61	16	17	33	176	4	0	1	1	25
1994-95a	Tri-City	WHL	70	50	60	110	207	17	12	15	27	36
1995-96	Tri-City	WHL	59	32	37	69	133	5	0	0	0	4
	Fredericton	AHL	....	....	....	....	....	3	0	0	0	2
1996-97	**Montreal**	**NHL**	**3**	**0**	**0**	**0**	**0**	....	....	....	....	....
	Red Deer	WHL	16	13	22	35	10	16	18	6	24	32
	NHL Totals		**3**	**0**	**0**	**0**	**0**	....	....	....	....	....

a WHL West Second All-Star Team (1995)

RYCHEL, WARREN — (RIGH-kuhl) ANA.

Left wing. Shoots left. 6', 205 lbs. Born, Tecumseh, Ont., May 12, 1967.

			Regular Season					Playoffs				
Season	Club	Lea	GP	G	A	TP	PIM	GP	G	A	TP	PIM
1984-85	Sudbury	OHL	35	5	8	13	74	....	....	....	....	....
	Guelph	OHL	29	1	3	4	48	....	....	....	....	....
1985-86	Guelph	OHL	38	14	5	19	119	....	....	....	....	....
	Ottawa	OHL	29	11	18	29	54	....	....	....	....	....
1986-87	Ottawa	OHL	28	11	7	18	57	....	....	....	....	....
	Kitchener	OHL	21	5	5	10	39	4	0	0	0	9
1987-88	Peoria	IHL	7	2	1	3	7	....	....	....	....	....
	Saginaw	IHL	51	2	7	9	113	1	0	0	0	0
1988-89	**Chicago**	**NHL**	**2**	**0**	**0**	**0**	**17**	....	....	....	....	....
	Saginaw	IHL	50	15	14	29	226	6	0	0	0	51
1989-90	Indianapolis	IHL	77	23	16	39	374	14	1	3	4	64
1990-91	Indianapolis	IHL	68	33	30	63	338	5	2	1	3	30
	Chicago	**NHL**	....	....	....	....	....	**3**	**1**	**3**	**4**	**2**
1991-92	Moncton	AHL	36	14	15	29	211	....	....	....	....	....
	Kalamazoo	IHL	45	15	20	35	165	8	0	3	3	51
1992-93	**Los Angeles**	**NHL**	**70**	**6**	**7**	**13**	**314**	**23**	**6**	**7**	**13**	**39**
1993-94	**Los Angeles**	**NHL**	**80**	**10**	**9**	**19**	**322**	....	....	....	....	....
1994-95	**Los Angeles**	**NHL**	**7**	**0**	**0**	**0**	**19**	....	....	....	....	....
	Toronto	**NHL**	**26**	**1**	**6**	**7**	**101**	**3**	**0**	**0**	**0**	**0**
1995-96	**Colorado**	**NHL**	**52**	**6**	**2**	**8**	**147**	**12**	**1**	**0**	**1**	**23 ♦**
1996-97	**Anaheim**	**NHL**	**70**	**10**	**7**	**17**	**218**	**11**	**0**	**2**	**2**	**19**
	NHL Totals		**307**	**33**	**31**	**64**	**1138**	**52**	**8**	**12**	**20**	**83**

Signed as a free agent by **Chicago**, September 19, 1986. Traded to **Winnipeg** by **Chicago** with Troy Murray for Bryan Marchment and Chris Norton, July 22, 1991. Traded to **Minnesota** by **Winnipeg** for Tony Joseph, December 30, 1991. Signed as a free agent by **Los Angeles**, October 1, 1992. Traded to **Washington** by **Los Angeles** for Randy Burridge, February 10, 1995. Traded to **Toronto** by **Washington** for Toronto's fourth round choice (Sebastien Charpentier) in 1995 Entry Draft, February 10, 1995. Traded to **Colorado** by **Toronto** for cash, October 2, 1995. Signed as a free agent by **Anaheim**, August 21, 1996.

SACCO, DAVID — (SAK-oh)

Right wing. Shoots right. 6', 180 lbs. Born, Malden, MA, July 31, 1970.
(Toronto's 9th choice, 195th overall, in 1988 Entry Draft).

			Regular Season					Playoffs				
Season	Club	Lea	GP	G	A	TP	PIM	GP	G	A	TP	PIM
1988-89	Boston U.	H.E.	35	14	29	43	40	....	....	....	....	....
1989-90	Boston U.	H.E.	3	0	4	4	2	....	....	....	....	....
1990-91	Boston U.	H.E.	40	21	40	61	24	....	....	....	....	....
1991-92ab	Boston U.	H.E.	34	13	32	45	30	....	....	....	....	....
1992-93ab	Boston U.	H.E.	40	25	37	62	86	....	....	....	....	....
1993-94	U.S. National	....	32	8	20	28	88	....	....	....	....	....
	U.S. Olympic	....	8	3	5	8	12	....	....	....	....	....
	Toronto	**NHL**	**4**	**1**	**1**	**2**	**4**	....	....	....	....	....
	St. John's	AHL	5	3	1	4	2	....	....	....	....	....
1994-95	San Diego	IHL	45	11	25	36	57	4	3	1	4	0
	Anaheim	**NHL**	**8**	**0**	**2**	**2**	**0**	....	....	....	....	....
1995-96	**Anaheim**	**NHL**	**23**	**4**	**10**	**14**	**18**	....	....	....	....	....
	Baltimore	AHL	25	14	16	30	18	2	0	1	1	4
1996-97	Baltimore	AHL	51	18	38	56	30	1	0	2	2	0
	NHL Totals		**35**	**5**	**13**	**18**	**22**	....	....	....	....	....

a NCAA East First All-American Team (1992, 1993)
b Hockey East First All-Star Team (1992, 1993)

Traded to **Anaheim** by **Toronto** for Terry Yake, September 28, 1994. Signed as a free agent by **NY Islanders**, September 6, 1996.

SACCO, JOE — (SAK-oh) ANA.

Left wing. Shoots left. 6'1", 195 lbs. Born, Medford, MA, February 4, 1969.
(Toronto's 4th choice, 71st overall, in 1987 Entry Draft).

			Regular Season					Playoffs				
Season	Club	Lea	GP	G	A	TP	PIM	GP	G	A	TP	PIM
1987-88	Boston U.	H.E.	34	16	20	36	40	....	....	....	....	....
1988-89	Boston U.	H.E.	33	21	19	40	66	....	....	....	....	....
1989-90	Boston U.	H.E.	44	28	24	52	70	....	....	....	....	....
1990-91	**Toronto**	**NHL**	**20**	**0**	**5**	**5**	**2**	....	....	....	....	....
	Newmarket	AHL	49	18	17	35	24	....	....	....	....	....
1991-92	U.S. National	....	50	11	26	37	61	....	....	....	....	....
	U.S. Olympic	....	8	0	2	2	0	....	....	....	....	....
	Toronto	**NHL**	**17**	**7**	**4**	**11**	**4**	....	....	....	....	....
	St. John's	AHL	....	....	....	....	....	1	1	1	2	0
1992-93	**Toronto**	**NHL**	**23**	**4**	**4**	**8**	**8**	....	....	....	....	....
	St. John's	AHL	37	14	16	30	45	7	6	4	10	2
1993-94	**Anaheim**	**NHL**	**84**	**19**	**18**	**37**	**61**	....	....	....	....	....
1994-95	**Anaheim**	**NHL**	**41**	**10**	**8**	**18**	**23**	....	....	....	....	....
1995-96	**Anaheim**	**NHL**	**76**	**13**	**14**	**27**	**40**	....	....	....	....	....
1996-97	**Anaheim**	**NHL**	**77**	**12**	**17**	**29**	**35**	**11**	**2**	**0**	**2**	**2**
	NHL Totals		**338**	**65**	**70**	**135**	**173**	**11**	**2**	**0**	**2**	**2**

Claimed by **Anaheim** from **Toronto** in Expansion Draft, June 24, 1993.

SACHL, PETER — (SAH-khuhl) NYI

Center. Shoots left. 6'1", 194 lbs. Born, Jindrichuv Hradec, Czech., December 2, 1977.
(NY Islanders' 6th choice, 128th overall, in 1996 Entry Draft).

			Regular Season					Playoffs				
Season	Club	Lea	GP	G	A	TP	PIM	GP	G	A	TP	PIM
1994-95	Budejovice	Czech. Jr.	40	6	8	14	....	....	....	....	....	....
1995-96	Budejovice	Czech. Jr.	39	19	17	36	....	....	....	....	....	....
	Budejovice	Czech.	....	....	....	....	....	2	0	0	0	....
1996-97	Budejovice	Czech.	2	0	0	0	0	....	....	....	....	....
	Tri-City	WHL	63	13	24	37	32	....	....	....	....	....

ST. CROIX, CHRIS — (SAINT KWAH) CGY.

Defense. Shoots right. 6'1", 186 lbs. Born, Voorhees, NJ, May 2, 1979.
(Calgary's 7th choice, 92nd overall, in 1997 Entry Draft).

			Regular Season					Playoffs				
Season	Club	Lea	GP	G	A	TP	PIM	GP	G	A	TP	PIM
1995-96	Kamloops	WHL	61	4	5	9	29	13	0	2	2	4
1996-97	Kamloops	WHL	67	11	39	50	67	5	0	1	1	2

SAKIC, JOE — (SAK-ihk) COL.

Center. Shoots left. 5'11", 185 lbs. Born, Burnaby, B.C., July 7, 1969.
(Quebec's 2nd choice, 15th overall, in 1987 Entry Draft).

			Regular Season					Playoffs				
Season	Club	Lea	GP	G	A	TP	PIM	GP	G	A	TP	PIM
1986-87	Swift Current	WHL	72	60	73	133	31	4	0	1	1	0
	Cdn. National	....	1	0	0	0	0	....	....	....	....	....
1987-88ab	Swift Current	WHL	64	*78	82	*160	64	10	11	13	24	12
1988-89	**Quebec**	**NHL**	**70**	**23**	**39**	**62**	**24**	....	....	....	....	....
1989-90	**Quebec**	**NHL**	**80**	**39**	**63**	**102**	**27**	....	....	....	....	....
1990-91	**Quebec**	**NHL**	**80**	**48**	**61**	**109**	**24**	....	....	....	....	....
1991-92	**Quebec**	**NHL**	**69**	**29**	**65**	**94**	**20**	....	....	....	....	....
1992-93	**Quebec**	**NHL**	**78**	**48**	**57**	**105**	**40**	**6**	**3**	**3**	**6**	**2**
1993-94	**Quebec**	**NHL**	**84**	**28**	**64**	**92**	**18**	....	....	....	....	....
1994-95	**Quebec**	**NHL**	**47**	**19**	**43**	**62**	**30**	**6**	**4**	**1**	**5**	**0**
1995-96c	**Colorado**	**NHL**	**82**	**51**	**69**	**120**	**44**	**22**	***18**	**16**	***34**	**14 ♦**
1996-97	**Colorado**	**NHL**	**65**	**22**	**52**	**74**	**34**	**17**	**8**	***17**	**25**	**14**
	NHL Totals		**655**	**307**	**513**	**820**	**261**	**51**	**33**	**37**	**70**	**30**

a Canadian Major Junior Player of the Year (1988)
b WHL East All-Star Team (1988)
c Won Conn Smythe Trophy (1996)

Played in NHL All-Star Game (1990-94, 1996)

SALEI, RUSLAN — (sah-LEE, ROOS-luhn) ANA.

Defense. Shoots left. 6'2", 205 lbs. Born, Minsk, USSR, November 2, 1974.
(Anaheim's 1st choice, 9th overall, in 1996 Entry Draft).

			Regular Season					Playoffs				
Season	Club	Lea	GP	G	A	TP	PIM	GP	G	A	TP	PIM
1992-93	Dynamo Minsk	CIS	9	1	0	1	10	....	....	....	....	....
1993-94	Tivali Minsk	CIS	39	2	3	5	50	....	....	....	....	....
1994-95	Tivali Minsk	CIS	51	4	2	6	44	....	....	....	....	....
1995-96	Las Vegas	IHL	76	7	23	30	123	15	3	7	10	18
1996-97	**Anaheim**	**NHL**	**30**	**0**	**1**	**1**	**37**	....	....	....	....	....
	Baltimore	AHL	12	1	4	5	12	....	....	....	....	....
	Las Vegas	IHL	8	0	2	2	24	3	2	1	3	6
	NHL Totals		**30**	**0**	**1**	**1**	**37**	....	....	....	....	....

SALO, SAMI — (SA-loh) OTT.

Defense. Shoots right. 6'3", 190 lbs. Born, Turku, Finland, September 2, 1974.
(Ottawa's 7th choice, 239th overall, in 1996 Entry Draft).

			Regular Season					Playoffs				
Season	Club	Lea	GP	G	A	TP	PIM	GP	G	A	TP	PIM
1994-95	TPS	Fin. Jr.	14	1	3	4	6	....	....	....	....	....
	Kiekko-67	Fin. 2	19	4	2	6	4	....	....	....	....	....
	TPS	Fin.	7	1	2	3	8	1	0	0	0	0
1995-96	TPS	Fin.	47	7	14	21	32	11	1	3	4	8
1996-97	TPS	Fin.	48	9	6	15	10	10	2	3	5	4

SAMOKHVALOV, ANDREI — ((sah-mohkh-VA-lahf) DET.

Right wing. Shoots left. 5'11", 165 lbs. Born, Ust-Kamenogorsk, USSR, May 10, 1975.
(Detroit's 9th choice, 208th overall, in 1995 Entry Draft).

			Regular Season					Playoffs				
Season	Club	Lea	GP	G	A	TP	PIM	GP	G	A	TP	PIM
1992-93	Kamenogorsk	CIS	27	6	7	13	8	1	1	1	2	0
1993-94	Kamenogorsk	CIS	33	5	5	10	16	....	....	....	....	....
1994-95	Kamenogorsk	CIS	44	13	9	22	6	2	0	0	0	2
1995-96	Kamenogorsk	CIS	49	23	8	31	20	....	....	....	....	....
1996-97	Kamenogorsk	Rus.	42	11	15	26	33	5	2	1	3	4

SAMSONOV, SERGEI — (sam-SAWN-nahf) BOS.

Left wing. Shoots right. 5'8", 184 lbs. Born, Moscow, USSR, October 27, 1978.
(Boston's 2nd choice, 8th overall, in 1997 Entry Draft).

			Regular Season					Playoffs				
Season	Club	Lea	GP	G	A	TP	PIM	GP	G	A	TP	PIM
1994-95	CSKA	CIS Jr.	50	110	72	182	....	....	....	....	....	....
	CSKA	CIS	13	2	2	4	14	2	0	0	0	0
1995-96	CSKA	CIS	51	21	17	38	12	3	1	1	2	4
1996-97a	Detroit	IHL	73	29	35	64	18	19	8	4	12	12

a Won Garry F. Longman Memorial Trophy (Top Rookie - IHL) (1997)

SAMUELSSON, KJELL (SAM-yuhl-suhn, SHEHL) PHI.

Defense. Shoots right. 6'6", 235 lbs. Born, Tyngsryd, Sweden, October 18, 1958.
(NY Rangers' 5th choice, 119th overall, in 1984 Entry Draft).

			Regular Season					Playoffs				
Season	Club	Lea	GP	G	A	TP	PIM	GP	G	A	TP	PIM
1977-78	Tyngsryd	Swe. 2	20	3	0	3	41	....	....	....	....	....
1978-79	Tyngsryd	Swe. 2	24	3	4	7	67	....	....	....	....	....
1979-80	Tyngsryd	Swe. 2	26	5	4	9	45	....	....	....	....	....
1980-81	Tyngsryd	Swe. 2	35	6	7	13	61	2	0	1	1	14
1981-82	Tyngsryd	Swe. 2	33	11	14	25	68	3	0	2	2	2
1982-83	Tyngsryd	Swe. 2	32	11	6	17	57	....	....	....	....	....
1983-84	Leksand	Swe.	36	6	6	12	59	....	....	....	....	....
1984-85	Leksand	Swe.	35	9	5	14	34	....	....	....	....	....
1985-86	NY Rangers	NHL	9	0	0	0	10	9	0	1	1	8
	New Haven	AHL	56	6	21	27	87	3	0	0	0	10
1986-87	NY Rangers	NHL	30	2	6	8	50	....	....	....	....	....
	Philadelphia	NHL	46	1	6	7	86	26	0	4	4	25
1987-88	Philadelphia	NHL	74	6	24	30	184	7	2	5	7	23
1988-89	Philadelphia	NHL	69	3	14	17	140	19	1	3	4	24
1989-90	Philadelphia	NHL	66	5	17	22	91	....	....	....	....	....
1990-91	Philadelphia	NHL	78	9	19	28	82	....	....	....	....	....
1991-92	Philadelphia	NHL	54	4	9	13	76	....	....	....	....	....
	Pittsburgh	NHL	20	1	2	3	34	15	0	3	3	12 ♦
1992-93	Pittsburgh	NHL	63	3	6	9	106	12	0	3	3	2
1993-94	Pittsburgh	NHL	59	5	8	13	118	6	0	0	0	26
1994-95	Pittsburgh	NHL	41	1	6	7	54	11	0	1	1	32
1995-96	Philadelphia	NHL	75	3	11	14	81	12	1	0	1	24
1996-97	Philadelphia	NHL	34	4	3	7	47	5	0	0	0	2
	NHL Totals		718	47	131	178	1159	122	4	20	24	178

Played in NHL All-Star Game (1988)

Traded to **Philadelphia** by **NY Rangers** with NY Rangers' second round choice (Patrik Juhlin) in 1989 Entry Draft for Bob Froese, December 18, 1986. Traded to **Pittsburgh** by **Philadelphia** with Rick Tocchet, Ken Wregget and Philadelphia's third round choice (Dave Roche) in 1993 Entry Draft for Mark Recchi, Brian Benning and Los Angeles' first round choice (previously acquired by Pittsburgh — Philadelphia selected Jason Bowen) in 1992 Entry Draft, February 19, 1992. Signed as a free agent by **Philadelphia**, August 31, 1995.

SAMUELSSON, ULF (SAM-yuhl-suhn, UHLF) NYR

Defense. Shoots left. 6'1", 205 lbs. Born, Fagersta, Sweden, March 26, 1964.
(Hartford's 4th choice, 67th overall, in 1982 Entry Draft).

			Regular Season					Playoffs				
Season	Club	Lea	GP	G	A	TP	PIM	GP	G	A	TP	PIM
1981-82	Leksand	Swe.	31	3	1	4	40	....	....	....	....	....
1982-83	Leksand	Swe.	33	9	6	15	72	....	....	....	....	....
1983-84	Leksand	Swe.	36	5	11	16	53	....	....	....	....	....
1984-85	Hartford	NHL	41	2	6	8	83	....	....	....	....	....
	Binghamton	AHL	36	5	11	16	92	....	....	....	....	....
1985-86	Hartford	NHL	80	5	19	24	174	10	1	2	3	38
1986-87	Hartford	NHL	78	2	31	33	162	5	0	1	1	41
1987-88	Hartford	NHL	76	8	33	41	159	5	0	0	0	8
1988-89	Hartford	NHL	71	9	26	35	181	4	0	2	2	4
1989-90	Hartford	NHL	55	2	11	13	177	7	1	0	1	2
1990-91	Hartford	NHL	62	3	18	21	174	....	....	....	....	....
	Pittsburgh	NHL	14	1	4	5	37	20	3	2	5	34 ♦
1991-92	Pittsburgh	NHL	62	1	14	15	206	21	0	2	2	39 ♦
1992-93	Pittsburgh	NHL	77	3	26	29	249	12	1	5	6	24
1993-94	Pittsburgh	NHL	80	5	24	29	199	6	0	1	1	18
1994-95	Leksand	Swe.	2	0	0	0	8	....	....	....	....	....
	Pittsburgh	NHL	44	1	15	16	113	7	0	2	2	8
1995-96	NY Rangers	NHL	74	1	18	19	122	11	1	5	6	16
1996-97	NY Rangers	NHL	73	6	11	17	138	15	0	2	2	30
	NHL Totals		887	49	256	305	2174	123	7	24	31	262

Traded to **Pittsburgh** by **Hartford** with Ron Francis and Grant Jennings for John Cullen, Jeff Parker and Zarley Zalapski, March 4, 1991. Traded to **NY Rangers** by **Pittsburgh** with Luc Robitaille for Petr Nedved and Sergei Zubov, August 31, 1995.

SANDBERG, OLA NYR

Defense. Shoots left. 6'1", 189 lbs. Born, Djurgarden, Sweden, February 23, 1977.
(NY Rangers' 5th choice, 158th overall, in 1996 Entry Draft).

			Regular Season					Playoffs				
Season	Club	Lea	GP	G	A	TP	PIM	GP	G	A	TP	PIM
1995-96	Djurgarden	Swe. Jr.	26	3	5	8	46	....	....	....	....	....
1996-97	Djurgarden	Swe.	4	0	0	0	0	....	....	....	....	....
	Arlanda	Swe. 2	17	1	0	1	24	....	....	....	....	....

SANDERSON, GEOFF CAR.

Left wing. Shoots left. 6', 185 lbs. Born, Hay River, N.W.T., February 1, 1972.
(Hartford's 2nd choice, 36th overall, in 1990 Entry Draft).

			Regular Season					Playoffs				
Season	Club	Lea	GP	G	A	TP	PIM	GP	G	A	TP	PIM
1988-89	Swift Current	WHL	58	17	11	28	16	12	3	5	8	6
1989-90	Swift Current	WHL	70	32	62	94	56	4	1	4	5	8
1990-91	Hartford	NHL	2	1	0	1	0	3	0	0	0	0
	Swift Current	WHL	70	62	50	112	57	3	1	2	3	4
	Springfield	AHL	....	....	....	....	....	1	0	0	0	2
1991-92	Hartford	NHL	64	13	18	31	18	7	0	1	1	2
1992-93	Hartford	NHL	82	46	43	89	28	....	....	....	....	....
1993-94	Hartford	NHL	82	41	26	67	42	....	....	....	....	....
1994-95	HPK	Fin.	12	6	4	10	24	....	....	....	....	....
	Hartford	NHL	46	18	14	32	24	....	....	....	....	....
1995-96	Hartford	NHL	81	34	31	65	40	....	....	....	....	....
1996-97	Hartford	NHL	82	36	31	67	29	....	....	....	....	....
	NHL Totals		439	189	163	352	181	10	0	1	1	2

Played in NHL All-Star Game (1994, 1997)

SANDSTROM, TOMAS (SAND-struhm) ANA.

Right wing. Shoots left. 6'2", 205 lbs. Born, Jakobstad, Finland, September 4, 1964.
(NY Rangers' 2nd choice, 36th overall, in 1982 Entry Draft).

			Regular Season					Playoffs				
Season	Club	Lea	GP	G	A	TP	PIM	GP	G	A	TP	PIM
1981-82	Fagersta	Swe. 2	32	28	11	39	74	....	....	....	....	....
1982-83	Brynas	Swe.	36	23	14	37	50	....	....	....	....	....
1983-84	Brynas	Swe.	34	19	10	29	81	....	....	....	....	....
1984-85a	NY Rangers	NHL	74	29	29	58	51	3	0	2	2	0
1985-86	NY Rangers	NHL	73	25	29	54	109	16	4	6	10	20
1986-87	NY Rangers	NHL	64	40	34	74	60	6	1	2	3	20
1987-88	NY Rangers	NHL	69	28	40	68	95	....	....	....	....	....
1988-89	NY Rangers	NHL	79	32	56	88	148	4	3	2	5	12
1989-90	NY Rangers	NHL	48	19	19	38	100	....	....	....	....	....
	Los Angeles	NHL	28	13	20	33	28	10	5	4	9	19
1990-91	Los Angeles	NHL	68	45	44	89	106	10	4	4	8	14
1991-92	Los Angeles	NHL	49	17	22	39	70	6	0	3	3	8
1992-93	Los Angeles	NHL	39	25	27	52	57	24	8	17	25	12
1993-94	Los Angeles	NHL	51	17	24	41	59	....	....	....	....	....
	Pittsburgh	NHL	27	6	11	17	24	6	0	0	0	4
1994-95	Malmo	Swe.	12	10	5	15	14	....	....	....	....	....
	Pittsburgh	NHL	47	21	23	44	42	12	3	3	6	16
1995-96	Pittsburgh	NHL	58	35	35	70	69	18	4	2	6	30
1996-97	Pittsburgh	NHL	40	9	15	24	33	....	....	....	....	....
	Detroit	NHL	34	9	9	18	36	20	0	4	4	24 ♦
	NHL Totals		848	370	437	807	1087	135	32	49	81	179

a NHL All-Rookie Team (1985)

Played in NHL All-Star Game (1988, 1991)

Traded to **Los Angeles** by **NY Rangers** with Tony Granato for Bernie Nicholls, January 20, 1990. Traded to **Pittsburgh** by **Los Angeles** with Shawn McEachern for Marty McSorley and Jim Paek, February 16, 1994. Traded to **Detroit** by **Pittsburgh** for Greg Johnson, January 27, 1997. Signed as a free agent by **Anaheim**, August 1, 1997.

SANDWITH, TERRAN EDM.

Defense. Shoots left. 6'4", 210 lbs. Born, Edmonton, Alta., April 17, 1972.
(Philadelphia's 4th choice, 42nd overall, in 1990 NHL Entry Draft).

			Regular Season					Playoffs				
Season	Club	Lea	GP	G	A	TP	PIM	GP	G	A	TP	PIM
1988-89	Tri-City	WHL	31	0	0	0	29	6	0	0	0	4
1989-90	Tri-City	WHL	70	4	14	18	92	7	0	2	2	14
1990-91	Tri-City	WHL	46	5	17	22	132	7	1	0	1	14
1991-92	Brandon	WHL	41	6	14	20	145	....	....	....	....	....
	Saskatoon	WHL	18	2	5	7	53	18	2	1	3	28
1992-93	Hershey	AHL	61	1	12	13	140	....	....	....	....	....
1993-94	Hershey	AHL	62	3	5	8	169	2	0	1	1	4
1994-95	Hershey	AHL	11	1	1	2	32	....	....	....	....	....
	Kansas City	IHL	25	0	3	3	73	....	....	....	....	....
1995-96	Cdn. National	....	47	3	12	15	63	....	....	....	....	....
	Cape Breton	AHL	5	0	2	2	4	....	....	....	....	....
1996-97	Hamilton	AHL	78	3	6	9	213	22	0	2	2	27

Signed as a free agent by **Edmonton**, April 10, 1996.

SARAULT, YVES (sah-ROH, EEV) COL.

Left wing. Shoots left. 6'1", 170 lbs. Born, Valleyfield, Que., December 23, 1972.
(Montreal's 3rd choice, 61st overall, in 1991 Entry Draft).

			Regular Season					Playoffs				
Season	Club	Lea	GP	G	A	TP	PIM	GP	G	A	TP	PIM
1989-90	Victoriaville	QMJHL	70	12	28	40	140	16	0	3	3	26
1990-91	St-Jean	QMJHL	56	22	24	46	113	....	....	....	....	....
1991-92a	St-Jean	QMJHL	50	28	38	66	96	....	....	....	....	....
a	Trois-Rivières	QMJHL	18	15	14	29	12	15	10	10	20	18
1992-93	Fredericton	AHL	59	14	17	31	41	3	0	1	1	2
	Wheeling	ECHL	2	1	3	4	0	....	....	....	....	....
1993-94	Fredericton	AHL	60	13	14	27	72	....	....	....	....	....
1994-95	Fredericton	AHL	69	24	21	45	96	13	2	1	3	33
	Montreal	NHL	8	0	1	1	0	....	....	....	....	....
1995-96	Montreal	NHL	14	0	0	0	4	....	....	....	....	....
	Calgary	NHL	11	2	1	3	4	....	....	....	....	....
	Saint John	AHL	26	10	12	22	34	16	6	2	8	33
1996-97	Colorado	NHL	28	2	1	3	6	5	0	0	0	2
	Hershey	AHL	6	2	3	5	8	....	....	....	....	....
	NHL Totals		61	4	3	7	14	5	0	0	0	2

a QMJHL Second All-Star Team (1992)

Traded to **Calgary** by **Montreal** with Craig Ferguson for Calgary's eighth round choice (Petr Kubos) in 1997 Entry Draft, November 26, 1995. Signed as a free agent by **Colorado**, September 13, 1996.

SARICH, CORY (SAHR-ihch) BUF.

Defense. Shoots right. 6'3", 175 lbs. Born, Saskatoon, Sask., August 16, 1978.
(Buffalo's 2nd choice, 27th overall, in 1996 Entry Draft).

			Regular Season					Playoffs				
Season	Club	Lea	GP	G	A	TP	PIM	GP	G	A	TP	PIM
1995-96	Saskatoon	WHL	59	5	18	23	54	3	0	0	0	4
1996-97	Saskatoon	WHL	58	6	27	33	158	....	....	....	....	....

SARNO, PETER EDM.

Center. Shoots left. 5'11", 185 lbs. Born, Toronto, Ont., July 26, 1979.
(Edmonton's 6th choice, 141st overall, in 1997 Entry Draft).

			Regular Season					Playoffs				
Season	Club	Lea	GP	G	A	TP	PIM	GP	G	A	TP	PIM
1996-97	Windsor	OHL	66	20	63	83	59	5	0	3	3	6

SATAN, MIROSLAV (SHA-tuhn) BUF.

Center. Shoots left. 6'1", 195 lbs. Born, Topolcany, Czech., October 22, 1974.
(Edmonton's 6th choice, 111th overall, in 1993 Entry Draft).

			Regular Season					Playoffs				
Season	Club	Lea	GP	G	A	TP	PIM	GP	G	A	TP	PIM
1991-92	Topocalny	Czech. 2	9	2	1	3	6	....	....	....	....	....
1992-93	Dukla Trencin	Czech.	38	11	6	17	....	....	....	....	....	....
1993-94	Dukla Trencin	Slovak	30	32	16	48	16	....	....	....	....	....
1994-95	Cape Breton	AHL	25	24	16	40	15	....	....	....	....	....
	Detroit	IHL	8	1	3	4	4	....	....	....	....	....
	San Diego	IHL	6	0	2	2	6	....	....	....	....	....
1995-96	Edmonton	NHL	62	18	17	35	22	....	....	....	....	....
1996-97	Edmonton	NHL	64	17	11	28	22	....	....	....	....	....
	Buffalo	NHL	12	8	2	10	4	7	0	0	0	0
	NHL Totals		138	43	30	73	48	7	0	0	0	0

Traded to **Buffalo** by **Edmonton** for Barrie Moore and Craig Millar, March 18, 1997.

SAVAGE, BRIAN — MTL.

Left wing. Shoots left. 6'1", 190 lbs. Born, Sudbury, Ont., February 24, 1971.
(Montreal's 11th choice, 171st overall, in 1991 Entry Draft).

			Regular Season					Playoffs				
Season	Club	Lea	GP	G	A	TP	PIM	GP	G	A	TP	PIM
1990-91	Miami-Ohio	CCHA	28	5	6	11	26	....	....	....	....	....
1991-92	Miami-Ohio	CCHA	40	24	16	40	43	....	....	....	....	....
1992-93ab	Miami-Ohio	CCHA	38	*37	21	58	44	....	....	....	....	....
	Cdn. National	....	9	3	0	3	12	....	....	....	....	....
1993-94	Cdn. National	....	51	20	26	46	38	....	....	....	....	....
	Cdn. Olympic	....	8	2	2	4	6	....	....	....	....	....
	Montreal	**NHL**	**3**	**1**	**0**	**1**	**0**	**3**	**0**	**2**	**2**	**0**
	Fredericton	AHL	17	12	15	27	4	....	....	....	....	....
1994-95	**Montreal**	**NHL**	**37**	**12**	**7**	**19**	**27**	....	....	....	....	....
1995-96	**Montreal**	**NHL**	**75**	**25**	**8**	**33**	**28**	**6**	**0**	**2**	**2**	**2**
1996-97	**Montreal**	**NHL**	**81**	**23**	**37**	**60**	**39**	**5**	**1**	**1**	**2**	**0**
	NHL Totals		**196**	**61**	**52**	**113**	**94**	**14**	**1**	**5**	**6**	**2**

a CCHA First All-Star Team (1993)
b NCAA West Second All-American Team (1993)

SAVARD, DENIS — (sa-VAHR, deh-NEE)

Center. Shoots right. 5'10", 175 lbs. Born, Pointe Gatineau, Que., February 4, 1961.
(Chicago's 1st choice, 3rd overall, in 1980 Entry Draft).

			Regular Season					Playoffs				
Season	Club	Lea	GP	G	A	TP	PIM	GP	G	A	TP	PIM
1977-78	Montreal	QJHL	72	37	79	116	22	....	....	....	....	....
1978-79	Montreal	QJHL	70	46	*112	158	88	11	5	6	11	46
1979-80a	Montreal	QJHL	72	63	118	181	93	10	7	16	23	8
1980-81	**Chicago**	**NHL**	**76**	**28**	**47**	**75**	**47**	**3**	**0**	**0**	**0**	**0**
1981-82	**Chicago**	**NHL**	**80**	**32**	**87**	**119**	**82**	**15**	**11**	**7**	**18**	**52**
1982-83b	**Chicago**	**NHL**	**78**	**35**	**86**	**121**	**99**	**13**	**8**	**9**	**17**	**22**
1983-84	**Chicago**	**NHL**	**75**	**37**	**57**	**94**	**71**	**5**	**1**	**3**	**4**	**9**
1984-85	**Chicago**	**NHL**	**79**	**38**	**67**	**105**	**56**	**15**	**9**	**20**	**29**	**20**
1985-86	**Chicago**	**NHL**	**80**	**47**	**69**	**116**	**111**	**3**	**4**	**1**	**5**	**6**
1986-87	**Chicago**	**NHL**	**70**	**40**	**50**	**90**	**108**	**4**	**1**	**0**	**1**	**12**
1987-88	**Chicago**	**NHL**	**80**	**44**	**87**	**131**	**95**	**5**	**4**	**3**	**7**	**17**
1988-89	**Chicago**	**NHL**	**58**	**23**	**59**	**82**	**110**	**16**	**8**	**11**	**19**	**10**
1989-90	**Chicago**	**NHL**	**60**	**27**	**53**	**80**	**56**	**20**	**7**	**15**	**22**	**41**
1990-91	**Montreal**	**NHL**	**70**	**28**	**31**	**59**	**52**	**13**	**2**	**11**	**13**	**35**
1991-92	**Montreal**	**NHL**	**77**	**28**	**42**	**70**	**73**	**11**	**3**	**9**	**12**	**8**
1992-93	**Montreal**	**NHL**	**63**	**16**	**34**	**50**	**90**	**14**	**0**	**5**	**5**	**4** ♦
1993-94	**Tampa Bay**	**NHL**	**74**	**18**	**28**	**46**	**106**	....	....	....	....	....
1994-95	**Tampa Bay**	**NHL**	**31**	**6**	**11**	**17**	**10**	....	....	....	....	....
	Chicago	**NHL**	**12**	**4**	**4**	**8**	**8**	**16**	**7**	**11**	**18**	**10**
1995-96	**Chicago**	**NHL**	**69**	**13**	**35**	**48**	**102**	**10**	**1**	**2**	**3**	**8**
1996-97	**Chicago**	**NHL**	**64**	**9**	**18**	**27**	**60**	**6**	**0**	**2**	**2**	**2**
	NHL Totals		**1196**	**473**	**865**	**1338**	**1336**	**169**	**66**	**109**	**175**	**256**

a QMJHL First All-Star Team (1980)
b NHL Second All-Star Team (1983)

Played in NHL All-Star Game (1982-84, 1986, 1988, 1991, 1996)

Traded to **Montreal** by **Chicago** for Chris Chelios and Montreal's second round choice (Michael Pomichter) in 1991 Entry Draft, June 29, 1990. Signed as a free agent by **Tampa Bay**, July 29, 1993. Traded to **Chicago** by **Tampa Bay** for Chicago's sixth round choice (Xavier Delisle) in 1996 Entry Draft, April 6, 1995.

SAVARD, MARC — (sa-VAHR) NYR

Center. Shoots left. 5'10", 174 lbs. Born, Ottawa, Ont., July 17, 1977.
(NY Rangers' 3rd choice, 91st overall, in 1995 Entry Draft).

			Regular Season					Playoffs				
Season	Club	Lea	GP	G	A	TP	PIM	GP	G	A	TP	PIM
1993-94	Oshawa	OHL	61	18	39	57	20	5	4	3	7	8
1994-95a	Oshawa	OHL	66	43	96	*139	78	7	5	6	11	8
1995-96	Oshawa	OHL	48	28	59	87	77	5	4	5	9	6
1996-97	Oshawa	OHL	64	43	*87	*130	94	18	13	*24	*37	20

a OHL Second All-Star Team (1995)

SAVOIA, RYAN — (sa-VOI-ah) PIT.

Center. Shoots right. 6', 195 lbs. Born, Thorold, Ont., May 6, 1973.

			Regular Season					Playoffs				
Season	Club	Lea	GP	G	A	TP	PIM	GP	G	A	TP	PIM
1994-95	Brock U.	OUAA	38	35	48	83	24	....	....	....	....	....
	Cleveland	IHL	1	0	0	0	0	....	....	....	....	....
1995-96	Cleveland	IHL	49	6	7	13	31	....	....	....	....	....
1996-97	Johnstown	ECHL	60	35	44	79	100	....	....	....	....	....
	Cleveland	IHL	4	1	0	1	2	....	....	....	....	....
	Fort Wayne	IHL	8	0	2	2	2	....	....	....	....	....

Signed as a free agent by **Pittsburgh**, April 7, 1995.

SAWYER, KEVIN — DAL.

Left wing. Shoots left. 6'2", 205 lbs. Born, Christina Lake, B.C., February 21, 1974.

			Regular Season					Playoffs				
Season	Club	Lea	GP	G	A	TP	PIM	GP	G	A	TP	PIM
1992-93	Spokane	WHL	62	4	3	7	274	8	1	1	2	13
1993-94	Spokane	WHL	60	10	15	25	350	3	0	1	1	6
1994-95	Spokane	WHL	54	7	9	16	365	11	2	0	2	58
	Peoria	IHL	....	....	....	....	....	2	0	0	0	12
1995-96	**St. Louis**	**NHL**	**6**	**0**	**0**	**0**	**23**	....	....	....	....	....
	Worcester	AHL	41	3	4	7	268	....	....	....	....	....
	Boston	**NHL**	**2**	**0**	**0**	**0**	**5**	....	....	....	....	....
	Providence	AHL	4	0	0	0	29	4	0	1	1	9
1996-97	**Boston**	**NHL**	**2**	**0**	**0**	**0**	**0**	....	....	....	....	....
	Providence	AHL	60	8	9	17	367	6	0	0	0	32
	NHL Totals		**10**	**0**	**0**	**0**	**28**	....	....	....	....	....

Signed as a free agent by **St. Louis**, February 28, 1995. Traded to **Boston** by **St. Louis** with Steve Staios for Steve Leach, March 8, 1996. Signed as a free agent by **Dallas**, August, 1997.

SCATCHARD, DAVE — (SKAT-chuhrd) VAN.

Center. Shoots right. 6'2", 200 lbs. Born, Hinton, Alta., February 20, 1976.
(Vancouver's 3rd choice, 42nd overall, in 1994 Entry Draft).

			Regular Season					Playoffs				
Season	Club	Lea	GP	G	A	TP	PIM	GP	G	A	TP	PIM
1993-94	Portland	WHL	47	9	11	20	46	10	2	1	3	4
1994-95	Portland	WHL	71	20	30	50	148	8	0	3	3	21
1995-96	Portland	WHL	59	19	28	47	146	7	1	8	9	14
	Syracuse	AHL	1	0	0	0	0	15	2	5	7	29
1996-97	Syracuse	AHL	26	8	7	15	65	....	....	....	....	....

SCHAEFER, PETER — (SHAY-fuhr) VAN.

Left wing. Shoots left. 5'11", 190 lbs. Born, Yellow Grass, Sask., July 12, 1977.
(Vancouver's 3rd choice, 66th overall, in 1995 Entry Draft).

			Regular Season					Playoffs				
Season	Club	Lea	GP	G	A	TP	PIM	GP	G	A	TP	PIM
1993-94	Brandon	WHL	2	1	0	1	0	....	....	....	....	....
1994-95	Brandon	WHL	68	27	32	59	34	18	5	3	8	18
1995-96a	Brandon	WHL	69	47	61	108	53	19	10	13	23	5
1996-97ab	Brandon	WHL	61	49	74	123	85	6	1	4	5	4
	Syracuse	AHL	5	0	3	3	0	3	1	3	4	14

a WHL East First All-Star Team (1996, 1997)
b Canadian Major Junior First All-Star Team (1997)

SCHMIDT, CHRIS — L.A.

Center. Shoots left. 6'3", 200 lbs. Born, Beaverlodge, Alta., March 1, 1976.
(Los Angeles' 4th choice, 111th overall, in 1994 Entry Draft).

			Regular Season					Playoffs				
Season	Club	Lea	GP	G	A	TP	PIM	GP	G	A	TP	PIM
1992-93	Seattle	WHL	61	6	7	13	17	5	0	1	1	0
1993-94	Seattle	WHL	68	7	17	24	26	9	3	1	4	2
1994-95	Seattle	WHL	61	21	11	32	31	3	0	0	0	0
1995-96	Seattle	WHL	61	39	23	62	135	5	1	5	6	9
1996-97	Mississippi	ECHL	18	7	7	14	35	....	....	....	....	....
	Phoenix	IHL	37	3	6	9	60	....	....	....	....	....

SCHMIDT, COLIN — EDM.

Center. Shoots left. 5'11", 185 lbs. Born, Regina, Sask., February 3, 1974.
(Edmonton's 9th choice, 190th overall, in 1992 Entry Draft).

			Regular Season					Playoffs				
Season	Club	Lea	GP	G	A	TP	PIM	GP	G	A	TP	PIM
1992-93	Colorado	WCHA	27	8	13	21	26	....	....	....	....	....
1993-94	Colorado	WCHA	38	14	22	36	49	....	....	....	....	....
1994-95a	Colorado	WCHA	43	26	31	57	61	....	....	....	....	....
1995-96a	Colorado	WCHA	41	21	37	58	101	....	....	....	....	....
1996-97	Hamilton	AHL	15	2	2	4	2	....	....	....	....	....
	Wheeling	ECHL	37	9	19	28	25	....	....	....	....	....

a WCHA Second All-Star Team (1995, 1996)

SCHNABEL, ROBERT — (SHNAH-buhl) NYI

Defense. Shoots left. 6'6", 216 lbs. Born, Prague, Czech., November 10, 1978.
(NY Islanders' 5th choice, 79th overall, in 1997 Entry Draft).

			Regular Season					Playoffs				
Season	Club	Lea	GP	G	A	TP	PIM	GP	G	A	TP	PIM
1995-96	Slavia Praha	Czech. Jr.	38	3	5	8	....	....	....	....	....	....
1996-97	Slavia Praha	Czech. Jr.	36	5	2	7	....	....	....	....	....	....
	Slavia Praha	Czech.	4	0	0	0	4	1	0	0	0	0

SCHNEIDER, ANDY — OTT.

Left wing. Shoots left. 5'9", 170 lbs. Born, Edmonton, Alta., March 29, 1972.

			Regular Season					Playoffs				
Season	Club	Lea	GP	G	A	TP	PIM	GP	G	A	TP	PIM
1990-91	Swift Current	WHL	69	12	74	86	103	3	0	0	0	2
1991-92	Swift Current	WHL	63	44	60	104	120	8	4	9	13	8
1992-93a	Swift Current	WHL	38	19	66	85	78	17	13	*26	*39	40
	New Haven	AHL	19	2	2	4	13	....	....	....	....	....
1993-94	**Ottawa**	**NHL**	**10**	**0**	**0**	**0**	**15**	....	....	....	....	....
	P.E.I.	AHL	61	15	46	61	119	....	....	....	....	....
1994-95	Leksand	Swe.	39	6	8	14	71	4	1	1	2	31
	Cdn. National	....	3	1	0	1	0	....	....	....	....	....
	P.E.I.	AHL	10	1	5	6	25	11	5	5	10	11
1995-96	Minnesota	IHL	81	12	28	40	85	....	....	....	....	....
1996-97	Manitoba	IHL	79	14	37	51	142	....	....	....	....	....
	NHL Totals		**10**	**0**	**0**	**0**	**15**	....	....	....	....	....

a WHL East Second All-Star Team (1993)

Signed as a free agent by **Ottawa**, October 9, 1992.

SCHNEIDER, MATHIEU — TOR.

Defense. Shoots left. 5'11", 192 lbs. Born, New York, NY, June 12, 1969.
(Montreal's 4th choice, 44th overall, in 1987 Entry Draft).

			Regular Season					Playoffs				
Season	Club	Lea	GP	G	A	TP	PIM	GP	G	A	TP	PIM
1986-87	Cornwall	OHL	63	7	29	36	75	5	0	0	0	22
1987-88	**Montreal**	**NHL**	**4**	**0**	**0**	**0**	**2**	....	....	....	....	....
a	Cornwall	OHL	48	21	40	61	83	11	2	6	8	14
	Sherbrooke	AHL	....	....	....	....	....	3	0	3	3	12
1988-89	Cornwall	OHL	59	16	57	73	96	18	7	20	27	30
1989-90	**Montreal**	**NHL**	**44**	**7**	**14**	**21**	**25**	**9**	**1**	**3**	**4**	**31**
	Sherbrooke	AHL	28	6	13	19	20	....	....	....	....	....
1990-91	**Montreal**	**NHL**	**69**	**10**	**20**	**30**	**63**	**13**	**2**	**7**	**9**	**18**
1991-92	**Montreal**	**NHL**	**78**	**8**	**24**	**32**	**72**	**10**	**1**	**4**	**5**	**6**
1992-93	**Montreal**	**NHL**	**60**	**13**	**31**	**44**	**91**	**11**	**1**	**2**	**3**	**16** ♦
1993-94	**Montreal**	**NHL**	**75**	**20**	**32**	**52**	**62**	**1**	**0**	**0**	**0**	**0**
1994-95	**Montreal**	**NHL**	**30**	**5**	**15**	**20**	**49**	....	....	....	....	....
	NY Islanders	**NHL**	**13**	**3**	**6**	**9**	**30**	....	....	....	....	....
1995-96	**NY Islanders**	**NHL**	**65**	**11**	**36**	**47**	**93**	....	....	....	....	....
	Toronto	**NHL**	**13**	**2**	**5**	**7**	**10**	**6**	**0**	**4**	**4**	**8**
1996-97	**Toronto**	**NHL**	**26**	**5**	**7**	**12**	**20**	....	....	....	....	....
	NHL Totals		**477**	**84**	**190**	**274**	**517**	**50**	**5**	**20**	**25**	**79**

a OHL First All-Star Team (1988)

Played in NHL All-Star Game (1996)

Traded to **NY Islanders** by **Montreal** with Kirk Muller and Craig Darby for Pierre Turgeon and Vladimir Malakhov, April 5, 1995. Traded to **Toronto** by **NY Islanders** with Wendel Clark and D.J. Smith for Darby Hendrickson, Sean Haggerty, Kenny Jonsson and Toronto's first round choice (Roberto Luongo) in 1997 Entry Draft, March 13, 1996.

SCHULTE, PAXTON (SHUHL-tee) CGY.

Left wing. Shoots left. 6'2", 217 lbs. Born, Onaway, Alta., July 16, 1972.
(Quebec's 7th choice, 124th overall, in 1992 Entry Draft).

			Regular Season					Playoffs				
Season	Club	Lea	GP	G	A	TP	PIM	GP	G	A	TP	PIM
1990-91	North Dakota	WCHA	38	2	4	6	32	....	....	....	....	....
1991-92	Spokane	WHL	70	42	42	84	222	10	2	8	10	48
1992-93	Spokane	WHL	45	38	35	73	142	10	5	6	11	12
1993-94	**Quebec**	**NHL**	**1**	**0**	**0**	**0**	**2**	....	....	....	....	....
	Cornwall	AHL	56	15	15	30	102	....	....	....	....	....
1994-95	Cornwall	AHL	74	14	22	36	217	14	3	3	6	29
1995-96	Cornwall	AHL	69	25	31	56	171	....	....	....	....	....
	Saint John	AHL	14	4	5	9	25	14	4	7	11	40
1996-97	**Calgary**	**NHL**	**1**	**0**	**0**	**0**	**2**	....	....	....	....	....
	Saint John	AHL	71	14	23	37	274	4	2	0	2	35
	NHL Totals		**2**	**0**	**0**	**0**	**4**	....	....	....	....	....

Traded to **Calgary** by **Colorado** for Vesa Viitakoski, March 19, 1996.

SCHULTZ, RAY NYI

Defense. Shoots left. 6'2", 199 lbs. Born, Red Deer, Alta., November 14, 1976.
(Ottawa's 8th choice, 184th overall, in 1995 Entry Draft).

			Regular Season					Playoffs				
Season	Club	Lea	GP	G	A	TP	PIM	GP	G	A	TP	PIM
1993-94	Tri-City	WHL	3	0	0	0	11	....	....	....	....	....
1994-95	Tri-City	WHL	63	1	8	9	209	11	0	0	0	16
1995-96	Calgary	WHL	66	3	17	20	282	....	....	....	....	....
1996-97	Calgary	WHL	32	3	17	20	141	....	....	....	....	....
	Kelowna	WHL	23	3	11	14	63	6	0	2	2	12

Signed as a free agent by **NY Islanders**, June 9, 1997.

SCHUTZ, DEREK (SHOOTS) CGY.

Center. Shoots right. 6'2", 185 lbs. Born, Yorkton, Sask., March 5, 1979.
(Calgary's 5th choice, 60th overall, in 1997 Entry Draft).

			Regular Season					Playoffs				
Season	Club	Lea	GP	G	A	TP	PIM	GP	G	A	TP	PIM
1994-95	Spokane	WHL	2	0	0	0	2	....	....	....	....	....
1995-96	Spokane	WHL	70	10	7	17	121	18	1	4	5	37
1996-97	Spokane	WHL	61	20	21	41	126	9	1	3	4	9

SCISSONS, JEFF (SKIH-zuhns) VAN.

Center. Shoots left. 6'1", 190 lbs. Born, Saskatoon, Sask., November 24, 1976.
(Vancouver's 7th choice, 201st overall, in 1996 Entry Draft).

			Regular Season					Playoffs				
Season	Club	Lea	GP	G	A	TP	PIM	GP	G	A	TP	PIM
1995-96	Vernon	Jr. A	60	26	48	74	28	....	....	....	....	....
1996-97	Minn.-Duluth	WCHA	38	3	14	17	30	....	....	....	....	....

SCORSUNE, MATTHEW (SKOHR-soon) COL.

Defense. Shoots right. 6'3", 190 lbs. Born, Morristown, NJ, June 27, 1977.
(Colorado's 12th choice, 214th overall, in 1996 Entry Draft).

			Regular Season					Playoffs				
Season	Club	Lea	GP	G	A	TP	PIM	GP	G	A	TP	PIM
1995-96	Hotchkiss	HS	24	7	22	29	24	....	....	....	....	....
1996-97	Harvard	ECAC	30	3	8	11	28	....	....	....	....	....

SECORD, BRIAN (SEE-kohrd) CAR.

Center. Shoots left. 5'11", 180 lbs. Born, Ridgetown, Ont., June 19, 1975.

			Regular Season					Playoffs				
Season	Club	Lea	GP	G	A	TP	PIM	GP	G	A	TP	PIM
1992-93	Belleville	OHL	66	16	18	34	57	7	2	0	2	11
1993-94	Belleville	OHL	66	29	40	69	56	12	2	4	6	16
1994-95	Belleville	OHL	57	29	53	82	76	10	2	5	7	4
1995-96	Belleville	OHL	27	12	17	29	50	....	....	....	....	....
	S.S. Marie	OHL	32	16	28	44	50	4	0	0	0	4
	Springfield	AHL	1	0	0	0	0	....	....	....	....	....
1996-97	Springfield	AHL	6	1	2	3	2	....	....	....	....	....
	Hamilton	AHL	3	1	1	2	0	....	....	....	....	....
	Quebec	IHL	3	1	0	1	4	....	....	....	....	....
	Richmond	ECHL	31	14	8	22	58	....	....	....	....	....
	Pensacola	ECHL	19	5	9	14	20	12	2	3	5	14

Signed as a free agent by **Hartford**, September 27, 1995.

SEELEY, RICHARD L.A.

Defense. Shoots left. 6'2", 217 lbs. Born, Powell River, B.C., April 30, 1979.
(Los Angeles' 6th choice, 137th overall, in 1997 Entry Draft).

			Regular Season					Playoffs				
Season	Club	Lea	GP	G	A	TP	PIM	GP	G	A	TP	PIM
1995-96	Powell River	Jr. A	44	1	8	9	42	....	....	....	....	....
1996-97	Lethbridge	WHL	3	0	0	0	11	....	....	....	....	....
	Prince Albert	WHL	18	0	1	1	9	4	0	0	0	2

SEIKKULA, TIMO (SAY-koo-lah, TEE-moh) PIT.

Center. Shoots left. 6'1", 187 lbs. Born, Kalajoki, Finland, May 27, 1978.
(Pittsburgh's 8th choice, 238th overall, in 1996 Entry Draft).

			Regular Season					Playoffs				
Season	Club	Lea	GP	G	A	TP	PIM	GP	G	A	TP	PIM
1994-95	Junkkarit	Fin. 2	44	1	2	3	8	....	....	....	....	....
1995-96	Junkkarit	Fin. 2	46	10	11	21	80	....	....	....	....	....
1996-97	Kiekko-67	Fin. 2	43	5	5	10	38	....	....	....	....	....

SELANNE, TEEMU (SEH-lahn-nay, TEE-moo) ANA.

Right wing. Shoots right. 6', 200 lbs. Born, Helsinki, Finland, July 3, 1970.
(Winnipeg's 1st choice, 10th overall, in 1988 Entry Draft).

			Regular Season					Playoffs				
Season	Club	Lea	GP	G	A	TP	PIM	GP	G	A	TP	PIM
1987-88	Jokerit	Fin. Jr.	33	43	23	66	18	5	4	3	7	2
	Jokerit	Fin. 2	5	1	1	2	0	....	....	....	....	....
1988-89	Jokerit	Fin. 2	34	35	33	68	12	5	7	3	10	4
1989-90	Jokerit	Fin.	11	4	8	12	0	....	....	....	....	....
1990-91	Jokerit	Fin.	42	33	25	58	12	....	....	....	....	....
1991-92	Jokerit	Fin.	44	*39	23	62	20	10	10	7	17	18
1992-93abc	**Winnipeg**	**NHL**	**84**	***76**	**56**	**132**	**45**	**6**	**4**	**2**	**6**	**2**
1993-94	**Winnipeg**	**NHL**	**51**	**25**	**29**	**54**	**22**	....	....	....	....	....
1994-95	Jokerit	Fin.	20	7	12	19	6	....	....	....	....	....
	Winnipeg	**NHL**	**45**	**22**	**26**	**48**	**2**	....	....	....	....	....
1995-96	**Winnipeg**	**NHL**	**51**	**24**	**48**	**72**	**18**	....	....	....	....	....
	Anaheim	**NHL**	**28**	**16**	**20**	**36**	**4**	....	....	....	....	....
1996-97b	**Anaheim**	**NHL**	**78**	**51**	**58**	**109**	**34**	**11**	**7**	**3**	**10**	**4**
	NHL Totals		**337**	**214**	**237**	**451**	**125**	**17**	**11**	**5**	**16**	**6**

a Won Calder Memorial Trophy (1993)
b NHL First All-Star Team (1993, 1997)
c NHL/Upper Deck All-Rookie Team (1993)

Played in NHL All-Star Game (1993, 1994, 1996, 1997)

Traded to **Anaheim** by **Winnipeg** with Marc Chouinard and Winnipeg's fourth round choice (later traded to Toronto — later traded to Montreal — Montreal selected Kim Staal) in 1996 Entry Draft for Chad Kilger, Oleg Tverdovsky and Anaheim's third round choice (Per-Anton Lundstrom) in 1996 Entry Draft, February 7, 1996.

SELIVANOV, ALEXANDER (seh-lih-VAH-nohv) T.B.

Right wing. Shoots left. 6'1", 206 lbs. Born, Moscow, USSR, March 23, 1971.
(Philadelphia's 4th choice, 140th overall, in 1994 Entry Draft).

			Regular Season					Playoffs				
Season	Club	Lea	GP	G	A	TP	PIM	GP	G	A	TP	PIM
1988-89	Spartak	USSR	1	0	0	0	0	....	....	....	....	....
1989-90	Spartak	USSR	4	0	0	0	0	....	....	....	....	....
1990-91	Spartak	USSR	21	3	1	4	6	....	....	....	....	....
1991-92	Spartak	CIS	31	6	7	13	16	....	....	....	....	....
1992-93	Spartak	CIS	42	12	19	31	66	3	2	0	2	2
1993-94	Spartak	CIS	45	30	11	41	50	6	5	1	6	2
1994-95	Atlanta	IHL	4	0	3	3	2	....	....	....	....	....
	Chicago	IHL	14	4	1	5	8	....	....	....	....	....
	Tampa Bay	**NHL**	**43**	**10**	**6**	**16**	**14**	....	....	....	....	....
1995-96	**Tampa Bay**	**NHL**	**79**	**31**	**21**	**52**	**93**	**6**	**2**	**2**	**4**	**6**
1996-97	**Tampa Bay**	**NHL**	**69**	**15**	**18**	**33**	**61**	....	....	....	....	....
	NHL Totals		**191**	**56**	**45**	**101**	**168**	**6**	**2**	**2**	**4**	**6**

Traded to **Tampa Bay** by **Philadelphia** for Philadelphia's fourth round choice (previously acquired by Tampa Bay — Philadelphia selected Radovan Somik) in 1995 Entry Draft, September 6, 1994.

SEMAK, ALEXANDER (seh-MAHK)

Center. Shoots right. 5'10", 185 lbs. Born, Ufa, USSR, February 11, 1966.
(New Jersey's 12th choice, 207th overall, in 1988 Entry Draft).

			Regular Season					Playoffs				
Season	Club	Lea	GP	G	A	TP	PIM	GP	G	A	TP	PIM
1982-83	Ufa Salavat	USSR	13	2	1	3	4	....	....	....	....	....
1983-84	Ufa Salavat	USSR 2				UNAVAILABLE						
1984-85	Ufa Salavat	USSR 2	47	19	17	36	64	....	....	....	....	....
1985-86	Ufa Salavat	USSR	22	9	7	16	22	....	....	....	....	....
1986-87	Moscow D'amo	USSR	40	20	8	28	32	....	....	....	....	....
1987-88	Moscow D'amo	USSR	47	21	14	35	40	....	....	....	....	....
1988-89	Moscow D'amo	USSR	44	18	10	28	22	....	....	....	....	....
1989-90	Moscow D'amo	USSR	43	23	11	34	33	....	....	....	....	....
1990-91	Moscow D'amo	USSR	46	17	21	38	48	....	....	....	....	....
1991-92	Moscow D'amo	CIS	26	10	13	23	26	....	....	....	....	....
	New Jersey	**NHL**	**25**	**5**	**6**	**11**	**0**	**1**	**0**	**0**	**0**	**0**
	Utica	AHL	7	3	2	5	0	....	....	....	....	....
1992-93	**New Jersey**	**NHL**	**82**	**37**	**42**	**79**	**70**	**5**	**1**	**1**	**2**	**0**
1993-94	**New Jersey**	**NHL**	**54**	**12**	**17**	**29**	**22**	**2**	**0**	**0**	**0**	**0**
1994-95	Ufa Salavat	CIS	9	9	6	15	4	....	....	....	....	....
	New Jersey	**NHL**	**19**	**2**	**6**	**8**	**13**	....	....	....	....	....
	Tampa Bay	**NHL**	**22**	**5**	**5**	**10**	**12**	....	....	....	....	....
1995-96	**NY Islanders**	**NHL**	**69**	**20**	**14**	**34**	**68**	....	....	....	....	....
1996-97	**Vancouver**	**NHL**	**18**	**2**	**1**	**3**	**2**	....	....	....	....	....
	Syracuse	AHL	23	10	14	24	12	....	....	....	....	....
	Las Vegas	IHL	13	11	13	24	10	3	0	4	4	4
	NHL Totals		**289**	**83**	**91**	**174**	**187**	**8**	**1**	**1**	**2**	**0**

Traded to **Tampa Bay** by **New Jersey** with Ben Hankinson for Shawn Chambers and Danton Cole, March 14, 1995. Traded to **NY Islanders** by **Tampa Bay** for NY Islanders' fifth round choice (Karel Betik) in 1997 Entry Draft, September 14, 1995. Claimed by **Vancouver** from **NY Islanders** in NHL Waiver Draft, September 30, 1996.

SEMENOV, ANATOLI (seh-MEH-nahf)

Center/Left wing. Shoots left. 6'2", 190 lbs. Born, Moscow, USSR, March 5, 1962.
(Edmonton's 5th choice, 120th overall, in 1989 Entry Draft).

			Regular Season					Playoffs				
Season	Club	Lea	GP	G	A	TP	PIM	GP	G	A	TP	PIM
1979-80	Moscow D'amo	USSR	8	3	0	3	2	....	....	....	....	....
1980-81	Moscow D'amo	USSR	47	18	14	32	18	....	....	....	....	....
1981-82	Moscow D'amo	USSR	44	12	14	26	28	....	....	....	....	....
1982-83	Moscow D'amo	USSR	44	22	18	40	26	....	....	....	....	....
1983-84	Moscow D'amo	USSR	19	10	5	15	14	....	....	....	....	....
1984-85	Moscow D'amo	USSR	30	17	12	29	32	....	....	....	....	....
1985-86	Moscow D'amo	USSR	32	18	17	35	19	....	....	....	....	....
1986-87	Moscow D'amo	USSR	40	15	29	44	32	....	....	....	....	....
1987-88	Moscow D'amo	USSR	32	17	8	25	22	....	....	....	....	....
1988-89	Moscow D'amo	USSR	31	9	12	21	24	....	....	....	....	....
1989-90	Moscow D'amo	USSR	48	13	20	33	16	....	....	....	....	....
	Edmonton	**NHL**	....	....	....	....	....	**2**	**0**	**0**	**0**	**0** ♦
1990-91	**Edmonton**	**NHL**	**57**	**15**	**16**	**31**	**26**	**12**	**5**	**5**	**10**	**6**
1991-92	**Edmonton**	**NHL**	**59**	**20**	**22**	**42**	**16**	**8**	**1**	**1**	**2**	**6**
1992-93	**Tampa Bay**	**NHL**	**13**	**2**	**3**	**5**	**4**	....	....	....	....	....
	Vancouver	**NHL**	**62**	**10**	**34**	**44**	**28**	**12**	**1**	**3**	**4**	**0**
1993-94	**Anaheim**	**NHL**	**49**	**11**	**19**	**30**	**12**	....	....	....	....	....
1994-95	**Anaheim**	**NHL**	**15**	**3**	**4**	**7**	**4**	....	....	....	....	....
	Philadelphia	**NHL**	**26**	**1**	**2**	**3**	**6**	**15**	**2**	**4**	**6**	**0**
1995-96	**Philadelphia**	**NHL**	**44**	**3**	**13**	**16**	**14**	....	....	....	....	....
	Anaheim	**NHL**	**12**	**1**	**9**	**10**	**10**	....	....	....	....	....
1996-97	**Buffalo**	**NHL**	**25**	**2**	**4**	**6**	**2**	....	....	....	....	....
	NHL Totals		**362**	**68**	**126**	**194**	**122**	**49**	**9**	**13**	**22**	**12**

Claimed by **Tampa Bay** from **Edmonton** in Expansion Draft, June 18, 1992. Traded to **Vancouver** by **Tampa Bay** for Dave Capuano and Vancouver's fourth round choice (later traded to New Jersey — later traded to Calgary — Calgary selected Ryan Duthie) in 1994 Entry Draft, November 3, 1992. Claimed by **Anaheim** from **Vancouver** in Expansion Draft, June 24, 1993. Traded to **Philadelphia** by **Anaheim** for Milos Holan, March 8, 1995. Traded to **Anaheim** by **Philadelphia** with Mike Crowley for Brian Wesenberg, March 19, 1996. Signed as a free agency by **Buffalo**, September 17, 1996.

SESSA, JASON (SEH-sa) TOR.

Right wing. Shoots right. 6'1", 173 lbs. Born, Long Island, NY, July 17, 1977.
(Toronto's 5th choice, 86th overall, in 1996 Entry Draft).

			Regular Season					Playoffs				
Season	Club	Lea	GP	G	A	TP	PIM	GP	G	A	TP	PIM
1995-96	Lake Superior	CCHA	30	9	5	14	12	....	....	....	....	....
1996-97a	Lake Superior	CCHA	34	22	22	44	91	....	....	....	....	....

a CCHA Second All-Star Team (1997)

SEVERYN, BRENT (SEH-vuh-rihn) COL.

Left wing. Shoots left. 6'2", 211 lbs. Born, Vegreville, Alta., February 22, 1966.

			Regular Season					Playoffs				
Season	Club	Lea	GP	G	A	TP	PIM	GP	G	A	TP	PIM
1983-84	Seattle	WHL	72	14	22	36	49	....	....	....	....	....
1984-85	Seattle	WHL	38	8	32	40	54	....	....	....	....	....
	Brandon	WHL	26	7	16	23	57	....	....	....	....	....
1985-86	Seattle	WHL	33	11	20	31	164	....	....	....	....	....
	Saskatoon	WHL	9	1	4	5	38	....	....	....	....	....
1986-87	U. of Alberta	CWUAA	43	7	19	26	171	....	....	....	....	....
1987-88	U. of Alberta	CWUAA	46	21	29	50	178	....	....	....	....	....
1988-89	Halifax	AHL	47	2	12	14	141	....	....	....	....	....
1989-90	**Quebec**	**NHL**	**35**	**0**	**2**	**2**	**42**	....	....	....	....	....
	Halifax	AHL	43	6	9	15	105	6	1	2	3	49
1990-91	Halifax	AHL	50	7	26	33	202	....	....	....	....	....
1991-92	Utica	AHL	80	11	33	44	211	4	0	1	1	4
1992-93a	Utica	AHL	77	20	32	52	240	5	0	0	0	35
1993-94	**Florida**	**NHL**	**67**	**4**	**7**	**11**	**156**	....	....	....	....	....
1994-95	**Florida**	**NHL**	**9**	**1**	**1**	**2**	**37**	....	....	....	....	....
	NY Islanders	**NHL**	**19**	**1**	**3**	**4**	**34**	....	....	....	....	....
1995-96	**NY Islanders**	**NHL**	**65**	**1**	**8**	**9**	**180**	....	....	....	....	....
1996-97	**Colorado**	**NHL**	**66**	**1**	**4**	**5**	**193**	**8**	**0**	**0**	**0**	**12**
	NHL Totals		**261**	**8**	**25**	**33**	**642**	**8**	**0**	**0**	**0**	**12**

a AHL First All-Star Team (1993)

Signed as a free agent by **Quebec**, July 15, 1988. Traded to **New Jersey** by **Quebec** for Dave Marcinyshyn, June 3, 1991. Traded to **Winnipeg** by **New Jersey** for Winnipeg's sixth round choice (Ryan Smart) in 1994 Entry Draft, September 30, 1993. Traded to **Florida** by **Winnipeg** for Milan Tichy, October 3, 1993. Traded to **NY Islanders** by **Florida** for NY Islanders' fourth round choice (Dave Duerden) in 1995 Entry Draft, March 3, 1995. Traded to **Colorado** by **NY Islanders** for Colorado's third round choice (later traded to Calgary — later traded to Hartford — Carolina selected Francis Lessard) in 1997 Entry Draft, September 4, 1996.

SEVIGNY, PIERRE (seh-VIH-nee) NYR

Left wing. Shoots left. 6', 195 lbs. Born, Trois-Rivières, Que., September 8, 1971.
(Montreal's 4th choice, 51st overall, in 1989 Entry Draft).

			Regular Season					Playoffs				
Season	Club	Lea	GP	G	A	TP	PIM	GP	G	A	TP	PIM
1988-89	Verdun	QMJHL	67	27	43	70	88	....	....	....	....	....
1989-90a	St-Hyacinthe	QMJHL	67	47	72	119	205	12	8	8	16	42
1990-91a	St-Hyacinthe	QMJHL	60	36	46	82	203	....	....	....	....	....
1991-92	Fredericton	AHL	74	22	37	59	145	7	1	1	2	26
1992-93	Fredericton	AHL	80	36	40	76	113	5	1	1	2	2
1993-94	**Montreal**	**NHL**	**43**	**4**	**5**	**9**	**42**	**3**	**0**	**1**	**1**	**0**
1994-95	**Montreal**	**NHL**	**19**	**0**	**0**	**0**	**15**	....	....	....	....	....
1995-96	Fredericton	AHL	76	39	42	81	188	10	5	9	14	20
1996-97	**Montreal**	**NHL**	**13**	**0**	**0**	**0**	**5**	....	....	....	....	....
	Fredericton	AHL	32	9	17	26	58	....	....	....	....	....
	NHL Totals		**75**	**4**	**5**	**9**	**62**	**3**	**0**	**1**	**1**	**0**

a QMJHL Second All-Star Team (1990, 1991)

Signed as a free agent by **NY Rangers**, August, 1997

SHAFIKOV, RUSLAN (SHAH-fee-kahv, roos-LAHN) PHI.

Center. Shoots right. 6'1", 176 lbs. Born, Ufa, USSR, May 11, 1976.
(Philadelphia's 8th choice, 204th overall, in 1995 Entry Draft).

			Regular Season					Playoffs				
Season	Club	Lea	GP	G	A	TP	PIM	GP	G	A	TP	PIM
1994-95	Ufa Salavat	CIS	30	2	0	2	10	7	1	1	2	4
1995-96	Ufa Salavat	CIS	51	9	2	11	18	3	0	0	0	4
1996-97	Ufa Salavat	Rus.	31	11	7	18	22	10	3	2	5	12

SHAFRANOV, KONSTANTIN (shahf-RAH-nahv) ST.L.

Right wing. Shoots left. 5'11", 176 lbs. Born, Ust-Kamenogorsk, USSR, September 11, 1968.
(St. Louis' 10th choice, 229th overall, in 1996 Entry Draft).

			Regular Season					Playoffs				
Season	Club	Lea	GP	G	A	TP	PIM	GP	G	A	TP	PIM
1989-90	Torpedo Ust.	USSR	28	6	8	14	16	....	....	....	....	....
1990-91	Torpedo Ust.	USSR	40	16	6	22	32	....	....	....	....	....
1991-92	Torpedo Ust.	CIS	36	10	6	16	40	....	....	....	....	....
1992-93	Torpedo Ust.	CIS	42	19	19	38	26	1	0	1	1	0
1993-94	Detroit	ColHL	4	3	2	5	0	....	....	....	....	....
	Torpedo Ust.	CIS	27	18	21	39	6	....	....	....	....	....
1994-95	Magnitogorsk	CIS	47	21	30	51	24	7	5	4	9	12
1995-96	Magnitogorsk	CIS	6	3	3	6	0	....	....	....	....	....
a	Ft. Wayne	IHL	74	46	28	74	26	5	1	2	3	4
1996-97	**St. Louis**	**NHL**	**5**	**2**	**1**	**3**	**0**	....	....	....	....	....
	Worcester	AHL	62	23	25	48	16	5	0	2	2	0
	NHL Totals		**5**	**2**	**1**	**3**	**0**	....	....	....	....	....

a Won Garry F. Longman Memorial Trophy (Top Rookie - IHL) (1996)

SHALDYBIN, YEVGENY (shahl-DAY-bihn, yehv-GEH-nee) BOS.

Defense. Shoots left. 6'2", 198 lbs. Born, Novosibirsk, USSR, July 29, 1975.
(Boston's 6th choice, 151st overall, in 1995 Entry Draft).

			Regular Season					Playoffs				
Season	Club	Lea	GP	G	A	TP	PIM	GP	G	A	TP	PIM
1993-94	Yaroslavl	CIS	14	0	0	0	0	....	....	....	....	....
1994-95	Yaroslavl	CIS	42	2	5	7	10	4	0	1	1	0
1995-96	Yaroslavl	CIS	41	0	2	2	10	3	0	1	1	2
1996-97	**Boston**	**NHL**	**3**	**1**	**0**	**1**	**0**	....	....	....	....	....
	Providence	AHL	69	4	13	17	28	3	0	0	0	0
	NHL Totals		**3**	**1**	**0**	**1**	**0**	....	....	....	....	....

SHANAHAN, BRENDAN DET.

Left wing. Shoots right. 6'3", 218 lbs. Born, Mimico, Ont., January 23, 1969.
(New Jersey's 1st choice, 2nd overall, in 1987 Entry Draft).

			Regular Season					Playoffs				
Season	Club	Lea	GP	G	A	TP	PIM	GP	G	A	TP	PIM
1985-86	London	OHL	59	28	34	62	70	5	5	5	10	5
1986-87	London	OHL	56	39	53	92	92	....	....	....	....	....
1987-88	**New Jersey**	**NHL**	**65**	**7**	**19**	**26**	**131**	**12**	**2**	**1**	**3**	**44**
1988-89	**New Jersey**	**NHL**	**68**	**22**	**28**	**50**	**115**	....	....	....	....	....
1989-90	**New Jersey**	**NHL**	**73**	**30**	**42**	**72**	**137**	**6**	**3**	**3**	**6**	**20**
1990-91	**New Jersey**	**NHL**	**75**	**29**	**37**	**66**	**141**	**7**	**3**	**5**	**8**	**12**
1991-92	**St. Louis**	**NHL**	**80**	**33**	**36**	**69**	**171**	**6**	**2**	**3**	**5**	**14**
1992-93	**St. Louis**	**NHL**	**71**	**51**	**43**	**94**	**174**	**11**	**4**	**3**	**7**	**18**
1993-94a	**St. Louis**	**NHL**	**81**	**52**	**50**	**102**	**211**	**4**	**2**	**5**	**7**	**4**
1994-95	Dusseldorf	Ger.	3	5	3	8	4	....	....	....	....	....
	St. Louis	**NHL**	**45**	**20**	**21**	**41**	**136**	**5**	**4**	**5**	**9**	**14**
1995-96	**Hartford**	**NHL**	**74**	**44**	**34**	**78**	**125**	....	....	....	....	....
1996-97	**Hartford**	**NHL**	**2**	**1**	**0**	**1**	**0**	....	....	....	....	....
	Detroit	**NHL**	**79**	**46**	**41**	**87**	**131**	**20**	**9**	**8**	**17**	**43** ♦
	NHL Totals		**713**	**335**	**351**	**686**	**1472**	**71**	**29**	**33**	**62**	**169**

a NHL First All-Star Team (1994)

Played in NHL All-Star Game (1994, 1996, 1997)

Signed as a free agent by **St. Louis**, July 25, 1991. Traded to **Hartford** by **St. Louis** for Chris Pronger, July 27, 1995. Traded to **Detroit** by **Hartford** with Brian Glynn for Paul Coffey, Keith Primeau and Detroit's first round choice (Nikos Tselios) in 1997 Entry Draft, October 9, 1996.

SHANNON, DARRIN PHO.

Left wing. Shoots left. 6'2", 210 lbs. Born, Barrie, Ont., December 8, 1969.
(Pittsburgh's 1st choice, 4th overall, in 1988 Entry Draft).

			Regular Season					Playoffs				
Season	Club	Lea	GP	G	A	TP	PIM	GP	G	A	TP	PIM
1986-87	Windsor	OHL	60	16	67	83	116	14	4	6	10	8
1987-88a	Windsor	OHL	43	33	41	74	49	12	6	12	18	9
1988-89	**Buffalo**	**NHL**	**3**	**0**	**0**	**0**	**0**	**2**	**0**	**0**	**0**	**0**
	Windsor	OHL	54	33	48	81	47	4	1	6	7	2
1989-90	**Buffalo**	**NHL**	**17**	**2**	**7**	**9**	**4**	**6**	**0**	**1**	**1**	**4**
	Rochester	AHL	50	20	23	43	25	9	4	1	5	2
1990-91	**Buffalo**	**NHL**	**34**	**8**	**6**	**14**	**12**	**6**	**1**	**2**	**3**	**4**
	Rochester	AHL	49	26	34	60	56	10	3	5	8	22
1991-92	**Buffalo**	**NHL**	**1**	**0**	**1**	**1**	**0**	....	....	....	....	....
	Winnipeg	**NHL**	**68**	**13**	**26**	**39**	**41**	**7**	**0**	**1**	**1**	**10**
1992-93	**Winnipeg**	**NHL**	**84**	**20**	**40**	**60**	**91**	**6**	**2**	**4**	**6**	**6**
1993-94	**Winnipeg**	**NHL**	**77**	**21**	**37**	**58**	**87**	....	....	....	....	....
1994-95	**Winnipeg**	**NHL**	**19**	**5**	**3**	**8**	**14**	....	....	....	....	....
1995-96	**Winnipeg**	**NHL**	**63**	**5**	**18**	**23**	**28**	**6**	**1**	**0**	**1**	**6**
1996-97	**Phoenix**	**NHL**	**82**	**11**	**13**	**24**	**41**	**7**	**3**	**1**	**4**	**4**
	NHL Totals		**448**	**85**	**151**	**236**	**318**	**40**	**7**	**9**	**16**	**34**

a Canadian Major Junior Scholastic Player of the Year (1988)

Traded to **Buffalo** by **Pittsburgh** with Doug Bodger for Tom Barrasso and Buffalo's third round choice (Joe Dziedzic) in 1990 Entry Draft, November 12, 1988. Traded to **Winnipeg** by **Buffalo** with Mike Hartman and Dean Kennedy for Dave McLlwain, Gord Donnelly, Winnipeg's fifth round choice (Yuri Khmylev) in 1992 Entry Draft and future considerations, October 11, 1991.

SHANNON, DARRYL — BUF.

Defense. Shoots left. 6'2", 208 lbs. Born, Barrie, Ont., June 21, 1968.
(Toronto's 2nd choice, 36th overall, in 1986 Entry Draft).

			Regular Season					Playoffs				
Season	Club	Lea	GP	G	A	TP	PIM	GP	G	A	TP	PIM
1985-86	Windsor	OHL	57	6	21	27	52	16	5	6	11	22
1986-87a	Windsor	OHL	64	23	27	50	83	14	4	8	12	18
1987-88b	Windsor	OHL	60	16	67	83	116	12	3	8	11	17
1988-89	**Toronto**	**NHL**	**14**	**1**	**3**	**4**	**6**	....	....	....	....	....
	Newmarket	AHL	61	5	24	29	37	5	0	3	3	10
1989-90	**Toronto**	**NHL**	**10**	**0**	**1**	**1**	**12**	....	....	....	....	....
	Newmarket	AHL	47	4	15	19	58	....	....	....	....	....
1990-91	**Toronto**	**NHL**	**10**	**0**	**1**	**1**	**0**	....	....	....	....	....
	Newmarket	AHL	47	2	14	16	51	....	....	....	....	....
1991-92	**Toronto**	**NHL**	**48**	**2**	**8**	**10**	**23**	....	....	....	....	....
1992-93	**Toronto**	**NHL**	**16**	**0**	**0**	**0**	**11**	....	....	....	....	....
	St. John's	AHL	7	1	1	2	4	....	....	....	....	....
1993-94	**Winnipeg**	**NHL**	**20**	**0**	**4**	**4**	**18**	....	....	....	....	....
	Moncton	AHL	37	1	10	11	62	20	1	7	8	32
1994-95	**Winnipeg**	**NHL**	**40**	**5**	**9**	**14**	**48**	....	....	....	....	....
1995-96	**Winnipeg**	**NHL**	**48**	**2**	**7**	**9**	**72**	....	....	....	....	....
	Buffalo	**NHL**	**26**	**2**	**6**	**8**	**20**	....	....	....	....	....
1996-97	**Buffalo**	**NHL**	**82**	**4**	**19**	**23**	**112**	**12**	**2**	**3**	**5**	**8**
	NHL Totals		**314**	**16**	**58**	**74**	**322**	**12**	**2**	**3**	**5**	**8**

a OHL Second All-Star Team (1987)
b OHL First All-Star Team (1988)

Signed as a free agent by **Winnipeg**, June 30, 1993. Traded to **Buffalo** by **Winnipeg** with Michal Grosek for Craig Muni, February 15, 1996.

SHANTZ, JEFF — CHI.

Center. Shoots right. 6', 185 lbs. Born, Duchess, Alta., October 10, 1973.
(Chicago's 2nd choice, 36th overall, in 1992 Entry Draft).

			Regular Season					Playoffs				
Season	Club	Lea	GP	G	A	TP	PIM	GP	G	A	TP	PIM
1990-91	Regina	WHL	69	16	21	37	22	8	2	2	4	2
1991-92	Regina	WHL	72	39	50	89	75	....	....	....	....	....
1992-93a	Regina	WHL	64	29	54	83	75	13	2	12	14	14
1993-94	**Chicago**	**NHL**	**52**	**3**	**13**	**16**	**30**	**6**	**0**	**0**	**0**	**6**
	Indianapolis	IHL	19	5	9	14	20	....	....	....	....	....
1994-95	Indianapolis	IHL	32	9	15	24	20	....	....	....	....	....
	Chicago	**NHL**	**45**	**6**	**12**	**18**	**33**	**16**	**3**	**1**	**4**	**2**
1995-96	**Chicago**	**NHL**	**78**	**6**	**14**	**20**	**24**	**10**	**2**	**3**	**5**	**6**
1996-97	**Chicago**	**NHL**	**69**	**9**	**21**	**30**	**28**	**6**	**0**	**4**	**4**	**6**
	NHL Totals		**244**	**24**	**60**	**84**	**115**	**38**	**5**	**8**	**13**	**20**

a WHL East First All-Star Team (1993)

SHAPLEY, LARRY (SHAP-lee) — VAN.

Defense. Shoots right. 6'6", 215 lbs. Born, Dunnville, Ont., February 6, 1978.
(Vancouver's 8th choice, 148th overall, in 1997 Entry Draft).

			Regular Season					Playoffs				
Season	Club	Lea	GP	G	A	TP	PIM	GP	G	A	TP	PIM
1996-97	Welland	Jr. B	35	3	10	13	270	....	....	....	....	....

SHARIFIJANOV, VADIM (shah-rih-FYAH-nohv) — N.J.

Right wing. Shoots left. 5'11", 210 lbs. Born, Ufa, USSR, December 23, 1975.
(New Jersey's 1st choice, 25th overall, in 1994 Entry Draft).

			Regular Season					Playoffs				
Season	Club	Lea	GP	G	A	TP	PIM	GP	G	A	TP	PIM
1992-93	Ufa Salavat	CIS	37	6	4	10	16	2	1	0	1	0
1993-94	Ufa Salavat	CIS	46	10	6	16	36	5	3	0	3	4
1994-95	CSKA	CIS	34	7	3	10	26	2	0	0	0	0
	Albany	AHL	1	1	1	2	0	9	3	3	6	10
1995-96	Albany	AHL	69	14	28	42	28	....	....	....	....	....
1996-97	**New Jersey**	**NHL**	**2**	**0**	**0**	**0**	**0**	....	....	....	....	....
	Albany	AHL	70	14	27	41	89	10	3	3	6	6
	NHL Totals		**2**	**0**	**0**	**0**	**0**	....	....	....	....	....

SHAW, DAVID — T.B.

Defense. Shoots right. 6'2", 205 lbs. Born, St. Thomas, Ont., May 25, 1964.
(Quebec's 1st choice, 13th overall, in 1982 Entry Draft).

			Regular Season					Playoffs				
Season	Club	Lea	GP	G	A	TP	PIM	GP	G	A	TP	PIM
1981-82	Kitchener	OHL	68	6	25	31	94	15	2	2	4	51
1982-83	**Quebec**	**NHL**	**2**	**0**	**0**	**0**	**0**	....	....	....	....	....
	Kitchener	OHL	57	18	56	74	78	12	2	10	12	18
1983-84	**Quebec**	**NHL**	**3**	**0**	**0**	**0**	**0**	....	....	....	....	....
a	Kitchener	OHL	58	14	34	48	73	16	4	9	13	12
1984-85	**Quebec**	**NHL**	**14**	**0**	**0**	**0**	**11**	....	....	....	....	....
	Fredericton	AHL	48	7	6	13	73	2	0	0	0	7
1985-86	**Quebec**	**NHL**	**73**	**7**	**19**	**26**	**78**	....	....	....	....	....
1986-87	**Quebec**	**NHL**	**75**	**0**	**19**	**19**	**69**	....	....	....	....	....
1987-88	**NY Rangers**	**NHL**	**68**	**7**	**25**	**32**	**100**	....	....	....	....	....
1988-89	**NY Rangers**	**NHL**	**63**	**6**	**11**	**17**	**88**	**4**	**0**	**2**	**2**	**30**
1989-90	**NY Rangers**	**NHL**	**22**	**2**	**10**	**12**	**22**	....	....	....	....	....
1990-91	**NY Rangers**	**NHL**	**77**	**2**	**10**	**12**	**89**	**6**	**0**	**0**	**0**	**11**
1991-92	**NY Rangers**	**NHL**	**10**	**0**	**1**	**1**	**15**	....	....	....	....	....
	Edmonton	**NHL**	**12**	**1**	**1**	**2**	**8**	....	....	....	....	....
	Minnesota	**NHL**	**37**	**0**	**7**	**7**	**49**	**7**	**2**	**2**	**4**	**10**
1992-93	**Boston**	**NHL**	**77**	**10**	**14**	**24**	**108**	**4**	**0**	**1**	**1**	**6**
1993-94	**Boston**	**NHL**	**55**	**1**	**9**	**10**	**85**	**13**	**1**	**2**	**3**	**16**
1994-95	**Boston**	**NHL**	**44**	**3**	**4**	**7**	**36**	**5**	**0**	**1**	**1**	**4**
1995-96	**Tampa Bay**	**NHL**	**66**	**1**	**11**	**12**	**64**	**6**	**0**	**1**	**1**	**4**
1996-97	**Tampa Bay**	**NHL**	**57**	**1**	**10**	**11**	**72**	....	....	....	....	....
	NHL Totals		**755**	**41**	**151**	**192**	**894**	**45**	**3**	**9**	**12**	**81**

a OHL First All-Star Team (1984)

Traded to **NY Rangers** by **Quebec** with John Ogrodnick for Jeff Jackson and Terry Carkner, September 30, 1987. Traded to **Edmonton** by **NY Rangers** for Jeff Beukeboom, November 12, 1991. Traded to **Minnesota** by **Edmonton** for Brian Glynn, January 21, 1992. Traded to **Boston** by **Minnesota** for future considerations, September 2, 1992. Traded to **Tampa Bay** by **Boston** for Detroit's third round choice (previously acquired by Tampa Bay — Boston selected Jason Doyle) in 1996 Entry Draft, August 17, 1996.

SHAW, LLOYD — ANA.

Defense. Shoots right. 6'3", 220 lbs. Born, Regina, Sask., September 26, 1976.
(Vancouver's 4th choice, 92nd overall, in 1995 Entry Draft).

			Regular Season					Playoffs				
Season	Club	Lea	GP	G	A	TP	PIM	GP	G	A	TP	PIM
1993-94	Seattle	WHL	47	0	4	4	107	8	0	0	0	23
1994-95	Seattle	WHL	66	3	12	15	313	3	0	0	0	13
1995-96	Seattle	WHL	27	0	1	1	92	....	....	....	....	....
	Red Deer	WHL	37	2	4	6	120	10	0	2	2	25
1996-97	Red Deer	WHL	66	8	16	24	257	16	0	6	6	60

Signed as a free agent by **Anaheim**, July 7, 1997.

SHEARER, ROB — COL.

Center. Shoots right. 5'10", 190 lbs. Born, Kitchener, Ont., October 19, 1976.

			Regular Season					Playoffs				
Season	Club	Lea	GP	G	A	TP	PIM	GP	G	A	TP	PIM
1993-94	Windsor	OHL	66	17	25	42	46	4	0	2	2	6
1994-95	Windsor	OHL	59	28	28	56	48	10	4	4	8	10
1995-96	Windsor	OHL	63	40	53	93	74	7	6	3	9	8
1996-97	Hershey	AHL	78	12	16	28	88	23	0	4	4	9

Signed as a free agent by **Colorado**, October 5, 1995.

SHEPPARD, RAY — FLA.

Right wing. Shoots right. 6'1", 195 lbs. Born, Pembroke, Ont., May 27, 1966.
(Buffalo's 3rd choice, 60th overall, in 1984 Entry Draft).

			Regular Season					Playoffs				
Season	Club	Lea	GP	G	A	TP	PIM	GP	G	A	TP	PIM
1983-84	Cornwall	OHL	68	44	36	80	69	....	....	....	....	....
1984-85	Cornwall	OHL	49	25	33	58	51	9	2	12	14	4
1985-86a	Cornwall	OHL	63	*81	61	*142	25	6	7	4	11	0
1986-87	Rochester	AHL	55	18	13	31	11	15	12	3	15	2
1987-88b	**Buffalo**	**NHL**	**74**	**38**	**27**	**65**	**14**	**6**	**1**	**1**	**2**	**2**
1988-89	**Buffalo**	**NHL**	**67**	**22**	**21**	**43**	**15**	**1**	**0**	**1**	**1**	**0**
1989-90	**Buffalo**	**NHL**	**18**	**4**	**2**	**6**	**0**	....	....	....	....	....
	Rochester	AHL	5	3	5	8	2	17	8	7	15	9
1990-91	**NY Rangers**	**NHL**	**59**	**24**	**23**	**47**	**21**	....	....	....	....	....
1991-92	**Detroit**	**NHL**	**74**	**36**	**26**	**62**	**27**	**11**	**6**	**2**	**8**	**4**
1992-93	**Detroit**	**NHL**	**70**	**32**	**34**	**66**	**29**	**7**	**2**	**3**	**5**	**0**
1993-94	**Detroit**	**NHL**	**82**	**52**	**41**	**93**	**26**	**7**	**2**	**1**	**3**	**4**
1994-95	**Detroit**	**NHL**	**43**	**30**	**10**	**40**	**17**	**17**	**4**	**3**	**7**	**5**
1995-96	**Detroit**	**NHL**	**5**	**2**	**2**	**4**	**2**	....	....	....	....	....
	San Jose	**NHL**	**51**	**27**	**19**	**46**	**10**	....	....	....	....	....
	Florida	**NHL**	**14**	**8**	**2**	**10**	**4**	**21**	**8**	**8**	**16**	**4**
1996-97	**Florida**	**NHL**	**68**	**29**	**31**	**60**	**4**	**5**	**2**	**0**	**2**	**0**
	NHL Totals		**625**	**304**	**238**	**542**	**169**	**75**	**25**	**19**	**44**	**19**

a OHL First All-Star Team (1986)
b NHL All-Rookie Team (1988)

Traded to **NY Rangers** by **Buffalo** for cash and future considerations, July 9, 1990. Signed as a free agent by **Detroit**, August 5, 1991. Traded to **San Jose** by **Detroit** for Igor Larionov and a conditional draft choice in 1998 Entry Draft, October 24, 1995. Traded to **Florida** by **San Jose** with San Jose's fourth round choice (Joey Tetarenko) in 1996 Entry Draft for Florida's second (later traded to Chicago — Chicago selected Geoff Peters) and fourth (Matt Bradley) round choices in 1996 Entry Draft, March 16, 1996.

SHEVALIER, JEFF (sheh-VAL-ee-ay) — L.A.

Left wing. Shoots left. 5'11", 180 lbs. Born, Mississauga, Ont., March 14, 1974.
(Los Angeles' 4th choice, 111th overall, in 1992 Entry Draft).

			Regular Season					Playoffs				
Season	Club	Lea	GP	G	A	TP	PIM	GP	G	A	TP	PIM
1991-92	North Bay	OHL	64	28	29	57	26	21	5	11	16	25
1992-93	North Bay	OHL	62	59	54	113	46	2	1	2	3	4
1993-94a	North Bay	OHL	64	52	49	101	52	17	8	14	22	18
1994-95	Phoenix	IHL	68	31	39	70	44	9	5	4	9	0
	Los Angeles	**NHL**	**1**	**1**	**0**	**1**	**0**	....	....	....	....	....
1995-96	Phoenix	IHL	79	29	38	67	72	4	2	2	4	2
1996-97	**Los Angeles**	**NHL**	**26**	**4**	**9**	**13**	**6**	....	....	....	....	....
	Phoenix	IHL	46	16	21	37	26	....	....	....	....	....
	NHL Totals		**27**	**5**	**9**	**14**	**6**	....	....	....	....	....

a OHL First All-Star Team (1994)

SHIRREFFS, STEVE — CGY.

Defense. Shoots left. 6'3", 200 lbs. Born, Boston, MA, February 18, 1976.
(Calgary's 7th choice, 233rd overall, in 1995 Entry Draft).

			Regular Season					Playoffs				
Season	Club	Lea	GP	G	A	TP	PIM	GP	G	A	TP	PIM
1995-96	Princeton	ECAC	25	0	3	3	6	....	....	....	....	....
1996-97	Princeton	ECAC	34	5	4	9	12	....	....	....	....	....

SHUCHUK, GARY (SHOO-chuhk)

Right wing. Shoots right. 5'11", 190 lbs. Born, Edmonton, Alta., February 17, 1967.
(Detroit's 1st choice, 22nd overall, in 1988 Supplemental Draft).

			Regular Season					Playoffs				
Season	Club	Lea	GP	G	A	TP	PIM	GP	G	A	TP	PIM
1986-87	U. Wisconsin	WCHA	42	19	11	30	72	....	....	....	....	....
1987-88	U. Wisconsin	WCHA	44	7	22	29	70	....	....	....	....	....
1988-89	U. Wisconsin	WCHA	46	18	19	37	102	....	....	....	....	....
1989-90ab	U. Wisconsin	WCHA	45	*41	39	*80	70	....	....	....	....	....
1990-91	**Detroit**	**NHL**	**6**	**1**	**2**	**3**	**6**	**3**	**0**	**0**	**0**	**0**
	Adirondack	AHL	59	23	24	47	32	....	....	....	....	....
1991-92	Adirondack	AHL	79	32	48	80	48	19	4	9	13	18
1992-93	Adirondack	AHL	47	24	53	77	66	....	....	....	....	....
	Los Angeles	**NHL**	**25**	**2**	**4**	**6**	**16**	**17**	**2**	**2**	**4**	**12**
1993-94	**Los Angeles**	**NHL**	**56**	**3**	**4**	**7**	**30**	....	....	....	....	....
1994-95	**Los Angeles**	**NHL**	**22**	**3**	**6**	**9**	**6**	....	....	....	....	....
	Phoenix	IHL	13	8	7	15	12	....	....	....	....	....
1995-96	**Los Angeles**	**NHL**	**33**	**4**	**10**	**14**	**12**	....	....	....	....	....
	Phoenix	IHL	33	8	21	29	76	4	1	0	1	4
1996-97	Houston	IHL	55	18	23	41	48	13	5	2	7	18
	NHL Totals		**142**	**13**	**26**	**39**	**70**	**20**	**2**	**2**	**4**	**12**

a WCHA First All-Star Team (1990)
b NCAA West First All-American Team (1990)

Traded to **Los Angeles** by **Detroit** with Jimmy Carson and Marc Potvin for Paul Coffey, Sylvain Couturier and Jim Hiller, January 29, 1993.

SIDULOV, KONSTANTIN (sih-DOO-lahf) MTL.

Defense. Shoots left. 6'1", 176 lbs. Born, Chelyabinsk, USSR, January 1, 1977.
(Montreal's 5th choice, 118th overall, in 1997 Entry Draft).

			Regular Season					Playoffs				
Season	**Club**	**Lea**	**GP**	**G**	**A**	**TP**	**PIM**	**GP**	**G**	**A**	**TP**	**PIM**
1994-95	Chelyabinsk	CIS	2	0	0	0	0	....	....	....	....	....
1995-96	Chelyabinsk	CIS	52	1	0	1	58	....	....	....	....	....
1996-97	Chelyabinsk	Rus.	42	0	0	0	28	2	0	0	0	0

SILLINGER, MIKE VAN.

Center. Shoots right. 5'10", 190 lbs. Born, Regina, Sask., June 29, 1971.
(Detroit's 1st choice, 11th overall, in 1989 Entry Draft).

			Regular Season					Playoffs				
Season	**Club**	**Lea**	**GP**	**G**	**A**	**TP**	**PIM**	**GP**	**G**	**A**	**TP**	**PIM**
1987-88	Regina	WHL	67	18	25	43	17	4	2	2	4	0
1988-89	Regina	WHL	72	53	78	131	52	....	....	....	....	....
1989-90a	Regina	WHL	70	57	72	129	41	11	12	10	22	2
	Adirondack	AHL	....	....	....	....	....	1	0	0	0	0
1990-91	**Detroit**	**NHL**	**3**	**0**	**1**	**1**	**0**	**3**	**0**	**1**	**1**	**0**
b	Regina	WHL	57	50	66	116	42	8	6	9	15	4
1991-92	Adirondack	AHL	64	25	41	66	26	15	9	*19	*28	12
	Detroit	**NHL**	....	....	....	....	....	**8**	**2**	**2**	**4**	**2**
1992-93	**Detroit**	**NHL**	**51**	**4**	**17**	**21**	**16**	....	....	....	....	....
	Adirondack	AHL	15	10	20	30	31	11	5	13	18	10
1993-94	**Detroit**	**NHL**	**62**	**8**	**21**	**29**	**10**	....	....	....	....	....
1994-95	Wien	Aus.	13	13	14	27	10	....	....	....	....	....
	Detroit	**NHL**	**13**	**2**	**6**	**8**	**2**	....	....	....	....	....
	Anaheim	**NHL**	**15**	**2**	**5**	**7**	**6**	....	....	....	....	....
1995-96	**Anaheim**	**NHL**	**62**	**13**	**21**	**34**	**32**	....	....	....	....	....
	Vancouver	**NHL**	**12**	**1**	**3**	**4**	**6**	**6**	**0**	**0**	**0**	**2**
1996-97	**Vancouver**	**NHL**	**78**	**17**	**20**	**37**	**25**	....	....	....	....	....
	NHL Totals		**296**	**47**	**94**	**141**	**97**	**17**	**2**	**3**	**5**	**4**

a WHL East Second All-Star Team (1990)
b WHL East First All-Star Team (1991)

Traded to **Anaheim** by **Detroit** with Jason York for Stu Grimson, Mark Ferner and Anaheim's sixth round choice (Magnus Nilsson) in 1996 Entry Draft, April 4, 1995. Traded to **Vancouver** by **Anaheim** for Roman Oksiuta, March 15, 1996.

SIM, JONATHAN DAL.

Center. Shoots left. 5'9", 175 lbs. Born, New Glasgow, N.S., September 29, 1977.
(Dallas' 2nd choice, 70th overall, in 1996 Entry Draft).

			Regular Season					Playoffs				
Season	**Club**	**Lea**	**GP**	**G**	**A**	**TP**	**PIM**	**GP**	**G**	**A**	**TP**	**PIM**
1994-95	Sarnia	OHL	25	9	12	21	19	4	3	2	5	2
1995-96	Sarnia	OHL	63	56	46	102	130	10	8	7	15	26
1996-97	Sarnia	OHL	64	*56	39	95	109	12	9	5	14	32

SIMARD, SEBASTIEN (see-MAHR) L.A.

Left wing. Shoots left. 6'2", 178 lbs. Born, Jonquiere, Que., February 23, 1978.
(Los Angeles' 10th choice, 219th overall, in 1996 Entry Draft).

			Regular Season					Playoffs				
Season	**Club**	**Lea**	**GP**	**G**	**A**	**TP**	**PIM**	**GP**	**G**	**A**	**TP**	**PIM**
1995-96	Drummondville	QMJHL	58	8	18	26	34	6	0	0	0	2
1996-97	Rimouski	QMJHL	24	7	10	17	6	....	....	....	....	....

SIMON, BENJAMIN CHI.

Center. Shoots left. 5'11", 178 lbs. Born, Shaker Heights, OH, June 14, 1978.
(Chicago's 5th choice, 110th overall, in 1997 Entry Draft).

			Regular Season					Playoffs				
Season	**Club**	**Lea**	**GP**	**G**	**A**	**TP**	**PIM**	**GP**	**G**	**A**	**TP**	**PIM**
1996-97	Notre Dame	CCHA	30	4	15	19	79	....	....	....	....	....

SIMON, CHRIS WSH.

Left wing. Shoots left. 6'3", 219 lbs. Born, Wawa, Ont., January 30, 1972.
(Philadelphia's 2nd choice, 25th overall, in 1990 Entry Draft).

			Regular Season					Playoffs				
Season	**Club**	**Lea**	**GP**	**G**	**A**	**TP**	**PIM**	**GP**	**G**	**A**	**TP**	**PIM**
1988-89	Ottawa	OHL	36	4	2	6	31	....	....	....	....	....
1989-90	Ottawa	OHL	57	36	38	74	146	3	2	1	3	4
1990-91	Ottawa	OHL	20	16	6	22	69	17	5	9	14	59
1991-92	Ottawa	OHL	2	1	1	2	24	....	....	....	....	....
	S.S. Marie	OHL	31	19	25	44	143	11	5	8	13	49
1992-93	**Quebec**	**NHL**	**16**	**1**	**1**	**2**	**67**	**5**	**0**	**0**	**0**	**26**
	Halifax	AHL	36	12	6	18	131	....	....	....	....	....
1993-94	**Quebec**	**NHL**	**37**	**4**	**4**	**8**	**132**	....	....	....	....	....
1994-95	**Quebec**	**NHL**	**29**	**3**	**9**	**12**	**106**	**6**	**1**	**1**	**2**	**19**
1995-96	**Colorado**	**NHL**	**64**	**16**	**18**	**34**	**250**	**12**	**1**	**2**	**3**	**11** ♦
1996-97	**Washington**	**NHL**	**42**	**9**	**13**	**22**	**165**	....	....	....	....	....
	NHL Totals		**188**	**33**	**45**	**78**	**720**	**23**	**2**	**3**	**5**	**56**

Traded to **Quebec** by **Philadelphia** with Peter Forsberg, Steve Duchesne, Kerry Huffman, Mike Ricci, Ron Hextall, Philadelphia's first round choice in the 1993 (Jocelyn Thibault) and 1994 (later traded to Toronto — later traded to Washington — Washington selected Nolan Baumgartner) Entry Drafts and cash for Eric Lindros, June 30, 1992. Traded to **Washington** by **Colorado** with Curtis Leschyshyn for Keith Jones and Washington's first and fourth round choices in 1998 Entry Draft, November 2, 1996.

SIMON, JASON COL.

Left wing. Shoots left. 6'1", 210 lbs. Born, Sarnia, Ont., March 21, 1969.
(New Jersey's 9th choice, 215th overall, in 1989 Entry Draft).

			Regular Season					Playoffs				
Season	**Club**	**Lea**	**GP**	**G**	**A**	**TP**	**PIM**	**GP**	**G**	**A**	**TP**	**PIM**
1986-87	London	OHL	33	1	2	3	33	....	....	....	....	....
	Sudbury	OHL	26	2	3	5	50	....	....	....	....	....
1987-88	Sudbury	OHL	26	5	7	12	35	....	....	....	....	....
	Hamilton	OHL	29	5	13	18	124	11	0	2	2	15
1988-89	Windsor	OHL	62	23	39	62	193	4	1	4	5	13
1989-90	Utica	AHL	16	3	4	7	28	2	0	0	0	12
	Nashville	ECHL	13	4	3	7	81	5	1	3	4	17
1990-91	Utica	AHL	50	2	12	14	189	....	....	....	....	....
	Johnstown	ECHL	22	11	9	20	55	....	....	....	....	....
1991-92	Utica	AHL	1	0	0	0	12	....	....	....	....	....
	San Diego	IHL	13	1	4	5	45	3	0	1	1	9
1992-93	Detroit	ColHL	11	7	13	20	38	....	....	....	....	....
	Flint	ColHL	44	17	32	49	202	....	....	....	....	....
1993-94	Salt Lake	IHL	50	7	7	14	*323	....	....	....	....	....
	NY Islanders	**NHL**	**4**	**0**	**0**	**0**	**34**	....	....	....	....	....
	Detroit	ColHL	13	9	16	25	87	....	....	....	....	....
1994-95	Denver	IHL	61	3	6	9	300	1	0	0	0	12
1995-96	Springfield	AHL	18	2	2	4	90	7	1	0	1	26
1996-97	**Phoenix**	**NHL**	**1**	**0**	**0**	**0**	**0**	....	....	....	....	....
	Las Vegas	IHL	64	4	3	7	402	3	0	0	0	0
	NHL Totals		**5**	**0**	**0**	**0**	**34**	....	....	....	....	....

Signed as a free agent by **NY Islanders**, January 6, 1994. Signed as a free agent by **Winnipeg**, August 9, 1995. Signed as a free agent by **Colorado**, August 20, 1997.

SIMONOV, SERGEI (SEE-muh-nahv) TOR.

Defense. Shoots left. 6'3", 194 lbs. Born, Saratov, USSR, May 20, 1974.
(Toronto's 11th choice, 221st overall, in 1992 Entry Draft).

			Regular Season					Playoffs				
Season	**Club**	**Lea**	**GP**	**G**	**A**	**TP**	**PIM**	**GP**	**G**	**A**	**TP**	**PIM**
1992-93	Saratov	CIS	40	0	2	2	34	....	....	....	....	....
1993-94	CSKA	CIS	28	0	0	0	6	....	....	....	....	....
1994-95	Magnitogorsk	CIS	44	6	3	9	8	4	0	0	0	2
1995-96	Magnitogorsk	CIS	6	0	0	0	2	....	....	....	....	....
	Saratov	CIS	10	0	0	0	6	2	0	0	0	0
1996-97	St. Petersburg	Rus.	33	2	1	3	10	....	....	....	....	....

SIMONS, MIKAEL (SIH-mawns, mih-KIGHL) L.A.

Center. Shoots left. 6'2", 194 lbs. Born, Falun, Sweden, January 15, 1978.
(Los Angeles' 4th choice, 84th overall, in 1996 Entry Draft).

			Regular Season					Playoffs				
Season	**Club**	**Lea**	**GP**	**G**	**A**	**TP**	**PIM**	**GP**	**G**	**A**	**TP**	**PIM**
1995-96	Mora	Swe. Jr.	10	4	4	8	12	....	....	....	....	....
	Mora	Swe. 2	33	6	3	9	22	6	0	2	2	2
1996-97	Mora	Swe. 2	42	13	11	24	77	....	....	....	....	....

SIMPSON, REID N.J.

Left wing. Shoots left. 6'2", 220 lbs. Born, Flin Flon, Man., May 21, 1969.
(Philadelphia's 3rd choice, 72nd overall, in 1989 Entry Draft).

			Regular Season					Playoffs				
Season	**Club**	**Lea**	**GP**	**G**	**A**	**TP**	**PIM**	**GP**	**G**	**A**	**TP**	**PIM**
1985-86	N. Westminster	WHL	2	0	0	0	0	....	....	....	....	....
1986-87	Prince Albert	WHL	47	3	8	11	105	....	....	....	....	....
1987-88	Prince Albert	WHL	72	13	14	27	164	10	1	0	1	43
1988-89	Prince Albert	WHL	59	26	29	55	264	4	2	1	3	30
1989-90	Prince Albert	WHL	29	15	17	32	121	14	4	7	11	34
	Hershey	AHL	28	2	2	4	175	....	....	....	....	....
1990-91	Hershey	AHL	54	9	15	24	183	1	0	0	0	0
1991-92	**Philadelphia**	**NHL**	**1**	**0**	**0**	**0**	**0**	....	....	....	....	....
	Hershey	AHL	60	11	7	18	145	....	....	....	....	....
1992-93	**Minnesota**	**NHL**	**1**	**0**	**0**	**0**	**5**	....	....	....	....	....
	Kalamazoo	IHL	45	5	5	10	193	....	....	....	....	....
1993-94	Kalamazoo	IHL	5	0	0	0	16	....	....	....	....	....
	Albany	AHL	37	9	5	14	135	5	1	1	2	18
1994-95	Albany	AHL	70	18	25	43	268	14	1	8	9	13
	New Jersey	**NHL**	**9**	**0**	**0**	**0**	**27**	....	....	....	....	....
1995-96	**New Jersey**	**NHL**	**23**	**1**	**5**	**6**	**79**	....	....	....	....	....
	Albany	AHL	6	1	3	4	17	....	....	....	....	....
1996-97	**New Jersey**	**NHL**	**27**	**0**	**4**	**4**	**60**	**5**	**0**	**0**	**0**	**29**
	Albany	AHL	3	0	0	0	10	....	....	....	....	....
	NHL Totals		**61**	**1**	**9**	**10**	**171**	**5**	**0**	**0**	**0**	**29**

Signed as a free agent by **Minnesota**, December 14, 1992. Traded to **New Jersey** by **Dallas** with Roy Mitchell for future considerations, March 21, 1994.

SIMPSON, TODD CGY.

Defense. Shoots left. 6'3", 215 lbs. Born, North Vancouver, B.C., May 28, 1973.

			Regular Season					Playoffs				
Season	**Club**	**Lea**	**GP**	**G**	**A**	**TP**	**PIM**	**GP**	**G**	**A**	**TP**	**PIM**
1991-92	Brown	ECAC	14	1	3	4	18	....	....	....	....	....
1992-93	Tri-City	WHL	69	5	18	23	196	4	0	0	0	13
1993-94	Tri-City	WHL	12	2	3	5	32	....	....	....	....	....
	Saskatoon	WHL	51	7	19	26	175	16	0	1	1	29
1994-95	Saint John	AHL	80	3	10	13	321	5	0	0	0	4
1995-96	**Calgary**	**NHL**	**6**	**0**	**0**	**0**	**32**	....	....	....	....	....
	Saint John	AHL	66	4	13	17	277	16	2	3	5	32
1996-97	**Calgary**	**NHL**	**82**	**1**	**13**	**14**	**208**	....	....	....	....	....
	NHL Totals		**88**	**1**	**13**	**14**	**240**	....	....	....	....	....

Signed as free agent by **Calgary**, July 6, 1994.

SINCLAIR, DARREN VAN.

Center/Left wing. Shoots left. 6', 200 lbs. Born, Brooks, Alta., August 24, 1976.

			Regular Season					Playoffs				
Season	**Club**	**Lea**	**GP**	**G**	**A**	**TP**	**PIM**	**GP**	**G**	**A**	**TP**	**PIM**
1993-94	Spokane	WHL	66	9	15	24	54	3	0	0	0	0
1994-95	Spokane	WHL	71	16	20	36	81	11	2	3	5	8
1995-96	Spokane	WHL	72	35	47	82	52	18	8	12	20	25
1996-97	Syracuse	AHL	68	12	16	28	32	3	0	2	2	0

Signed as a free agent by **Vancouver**, October 5, 1995.

SKALDE, JARROD (SKAHL-dee) **S.J.**

Center. Shoots left. 6', 175 lbs. Born, Niagara Falls, Ont., February 26, 1971.
(New Jersey's 3rd choice, 26th overall, in 1989 Entry Draft).

			Regular Season					Playoffs				
Season	**Club**	**Lea**	**GP**	**G**	**A**	**TP**	**PIM**	**GP**	**G**	**A**	**TP**	**PIM**
1987-88	Oshawa	OHL	60	12	16	28	24	7	2	1	3	2
1988-89	Oshawa	OHL	65	38	38	76	36	6	1	5	6	2
1989-90	Oshawa	OHL	62	40	52	92	66	17	10	7	17	6
1990-91	**New Jersey**	**NHL**	**1**	**0**	**1**	**1**	**0**	....	....	....	....	....
	Utica	AHL	3	3	2	5	0	....	....	....	....	....
	Oshawa	OHL	15	8	14	22	14	....	....	....	....	....
a	Belleville	OHL	40	30	52	82	21	6	9	6	15	10
1991-92	**New Jersey**	**NHL**	**15**	**2**	**4**	**6**	**4**	....	....	....	....	....
	Utica	AHL	62	20	20	40	56	4	3	1	4	8
1992-93	**New Jersey**	**NHL**	**11**	**0**	**2**	**2**	**4**	....	....	....	....	....
	Utica	AHL	59	21	39	60	76	5	0	2	2	19
	Cincinnati	IHL	4	1	2	3	4	....	....	....	....	....
1993-94	**Anaheim**	**NHL**	**20**	**5**	**4**	**9**	**10**	....	....	....	....	....
	San Diego	IHL	57	25	38	63	79	9	3	12	15	10
1994-95	Las Vegas	IHL	74	34	41	75	103	9	2	4	6	8
1995-96	Baltimore	AHL	11	2	6	8	55	....	....	....	....	....
	Calgary	**NHL**	**1**	**0**	**0**	**0**	**0**	....	....	....	....	....
	Saint John	AHL	68	27	40	67	98	16	4	9	13	6
1996-97	Saint John	AHL	65	32	36	68	94	3	0	0	0	14
	NHL Totals		**48**	**7**	**11**	**18**	**18**	....	....	....	....	....

a OHL Second All-Star Team (1991)

Claimed by **Anaheim** from **New Jersey** in Expansion Draft, June 24, 1993. Signed as a free agent by **Anaheim**, May 31, 1995. Traded to **Calgary** by **Anaheim** for Bobby Marshall, October 30, 1995. Signed as a free agent by **San Jose**, August 13, 1997.

SKOPINTSEV, ANDREI (skuh-PIHN-sehf) **T.B.**

Defense. Shoots right. 6', 185 lbs. Born, Elekrostal, USSR, September 28, 1971.
(Tampa Bay's 7th choice, 153rd overall, in 1997 Entry Draft).

			Regular Season					Playoffs				
Season	**Club**	**Lea**	**GP**	**G**	**A**	**TP**	**PIM**	**GP**	**G**	**A**	**TP**	**PIM**
1989-90	Soviet Wings	USSR	20	0	0	0	10	....	....	....	....	....
1990-91	Soviet Wings	USSR	16	0	1	1	2	....	....	....	....	....
1991-92	Soviet Wings	CIS	36	1	1	2	14	....	....	....	....	....
1992-93	Soviet Wings	CIS	12	1	0	1	4	7	1	0	1	2
1993-94	Soviet Wings	CIS	43	4	8	12	14	3	1	0	1	0
1994-95	Soviet Wings	CIS	52	8	12	20	55	4	1	1	2	0
1995-96	Augsberg	Ger.	46	10	20	30	32	7	3	2	5	22
1996-97	TPS	Fin.	46	3	6	9	80	10	1	1	2	4

SKOREPA, ZDENEK (SKOHR-zheh-pah) **N.J.**

Right wing. Shoots left. 6', 185 lbs. Born, Duchcov, Czech., August 10, 1976.
(New Jersey's 4th choice, 103rd overall, in 1994 Entry Draft).

			Regular Season					Playoffs				
Season	**Club**	**Lea**	**GP**	**G**	**A**	**TP**	**PIM**	**GP**	**G**	**A**	**TP**	**PIM**
1993-94	Litvinov	Czech.	20	4	7	11	....	4	0	0	0	....
1994-95	Litvinov	Czech.	28	3	3	6	20	3	0	0	0	2
1995-96	Kingston	OHL	37	21	18	39	13	6	5	2	7	5
1996-97	Albany	AHL	60	12	12	24	38	13	3	2	5	14

SKRBEK, PAVEL (skuhr-BEHK) **PIT.**

Defense. Shoots left. 6'3", 191 lbs. Born, Kladno, Czech., August 9, 1978.
(Pittsburgh's 2nd choice, 28th overall, in 1996 Entry Draft).

			Regular Season					Playoffs				
Season	**Club**	**Lea**	**GP**	**G**	**A**	**TP**	**PIM**	**GP**	**G**	**A**	**TP**	**PIM**
1994-95	Kladno	Czech. Jr.	29	7	6	13	....	....	....	....	....	....
1995-96	Kladno	Czech. Jr.	29	10	12	22	....	....	....	....	....	....
	Kladno	Czech.	13	0	1	1	....	5	0	0	0	....
1996-97	Kladno	Czech.	35	1	5	6	26	3	0	0	0	4

SKRLAC, ROB (SKUHR-lak) **N.J.**

Left wing. Shoots left. 6'4", 230 lbs. Born, Campbell, B.C., June 10, 1976.
(Buffalo's 11th choice, 224th overall, in 1995 Entry Draft).

			Regular Season					Playoffs				
Season	**Club**	**Lea**	**GP**	**G**	**A**	**TP**	**PIM**	**GP**	**G**	**A**	**TP**	**PIM**
1994-95	Kamloops	WHL	23	0	1	1	177	....	....	....	....	....
1995-96	Kamloops	WHL	63	1	4	5	216	13	0	0	0	52
1996-97	Kamloops	WHL	61	8	10	18	278	5	0	0	0	35

Signed as a free agent by **New Jersey**, June 17, 1997.

SKRUDLAND, BRIAN (SKROOD-luhnd) **NYR**

Center. Shoots left. 6', 195 lbs. Born, Peace River, Alta., July 31, 1963.

			Regular Season					Playoffs				
Season	**Club**	**Lea**	**GP**	**G**	**A**	**TP**	**PIM**	**GP**	**G**	**A**	**TP**	**PIM**
1980-81	Saskatoon	WHL	66	15	27	42	97	....	....	....	....	....
1981-82	Saskatoon	WHL	71	27	29	56	135	5	0	1	1	2
1982-83	Saskatoon	WHL	71	35	59	94	42	6	1	3	4	19
1983-84	Nova Scotia	AHL	56	13	12	25	55	12	2	8	10	14
1984-85a	Sherbrooke	AHL	70	22	28	50	109	17	9	8	17	23
1985-86	**Montreal**	**NHL**	**65**	**9**	**13**	**22**	**57**	**20**	**2**	**4**	**6**	**76** ♦
1986-87	**Montreal**	**NHL**	**79**	**11**	**17**	**28**	**107**	**14**	**1**	**5**	**6**	**29**
1987-88	**Montreal**	**NHL**	**79**	**12**	**24**	**36**	**112**	**11**	**1**	**5**	**6**	**24**
1988-89	**Montreal**	**NHL**	**71**	**12**	**29**	**41**	**84**	**21**	**3**	**7**	**10**	**40**
1989-90	**Montreal**	**NHL**	**59**	**11**	**31**	**42**	**56**	**11**	**3**	**5**	**8**	**30**
1990-91	**Montreal**	**NHL**	**57**	**15**	**19**	**34**	**85**	**13**	**3**	**10**	**13**	**42**
1991-92	**Montreal**	**NHL**	**42**	**3**	**3**	**6**	**36**	**11**	**1**	**1**	**2**	**20**
1992-93	**Montreal**	**NHL**	**23**	**5**	**3**	**8**	**55**	....	....	....	....	....
	Calgary	**NHL**	**16**	**2**	**4**	**6**	**10**	**6**	**0**	**3**	**3**	**12**
1993-94	**Florida**	**NHL**	**79**	**15**	**25**	**40**	**136**	....	....	....	....	....
1994-95	**Florida**	**NHL**	**47**	**5**	**9**	**14**	**88**	....	....	....	....	....
1995-96	**Florida**	**NHL**	**79**	**7**	**20**	**27**	**129**	**21**	**1**	**3**	**4**	**18**
1996-97	**Florida**	**NHL**	**51**	**5**	**13**	**18**	**48**	....	....	....	....	....
	NHL Totals		**747**	**112**	**210**	**322**	**1003**	**128**	**15**	**43**	**58**	**291**

a Won Jack A. Butterfield Trophy (AHL Playoff MVP) (1985)

Signed as a free agent by **Montreal**, September 13, 1983. Traded to **Calgary** by **Montreal** for Gary Leeman, January 28, 1993. Claimed by **Florida** from **Calgary** in Expansion Draft, June 24, 1993. Signed as a free agent by **NY Rangers**, July 7, 1997.

SLAMIAR, PETER (SLA-mih-eer) **NYR**

Left wing. Shoots right. 5'11", 174 lbs. Born, Zvolen, Czech., February 26, 1977.
(NY Rangers' 6th choice, 143rd overall, in 1995 Entry Draft).

			Regular Season					Playoffs				
Season	**Club**	**Lea**	**GP**	**G**	**A**	**TP**	**PIM**	**GP**	**G**	**A**	**TP**	**PIM**
1994-95	Zvolen	Slov. Jr.	30	19	18	37	....	....	....	....	....	....
	Zvolen	Slov. 2	11	4	1	5	....	....	....	....	....	....
1995-96	Beauport	QMJHL	37	7	10	17	40	....	....	....	....	....
	Sherbrooke	QMJHL	18	4	5	9	10	....	....	....	....	....
1996-97	B. Bystrica	Slovak	3	1	0	1	....	....	....	....	....	....
	Shawinigan	QMJHL	23	8	10	18	14	7	1	2	3	2

SLANEY, JOHN **PHO.**

Defense. Shoots left. 6', 185 lbs. Born, St. John's, Nfld., February 7, 1972.
(Washington's 1st choice, 9th overall, in 1990 Entry Draft).

			Regular Season					Playoffs				
Season	**Club**	**Lea**	**GP**	**G**	**A**	**TP**	**PIM**	**GP**	**G**	**A**	**TP**	**PIM**
1988-89	Cornwall	OHL	66	16	43	59	23	18	8	16	24	10
1989-90ab	Cornwall	OHL	64	38	59	97	68	6	0	8	8	11
1990-91c	Cornwall	OHL	34	21	25	46	28	....	....	....	....	....
1991-92	Cornwall	OHL	34	19	41	60	43	6	3	8	11	0
	Baltimore	AHL	6	2	4	6	0	....	....	....	....	....
1992-93	Baltimore	AHL	79	20	46	66	60	7	0	7	7	8
1993-94	**Washington**	**NHL**	**47**	**7**	**9**	**16**	**27**	**11**	**1**	**1**	**2**	**2**
	Portland	AHL	29	14	13	27	17	....	....	....	....	....
1994-95	**Washington**	**NHL**	**16**	**0**	**3**	**3**	**6**	....	....	....	....	....
	Portland	AHL	8	3	10	13	4	7	1	3	4	4
1995-96	**Colorado**	**NHL**	**7**	**0**	**3**	**3**	**4**	....	....	....	....	....
	Cornwall	AHL	5	0	4	4	2	....	....	....	....	....
	Los Angeles	**NHL**	**31**	**6**	**11**	**17**	**10**	....	....	....	....	....
1996-97	**Los Angeles**	**NHL**	**32**	**3**	**11**	**14**	**4**	....	....	....	....	....
	Phoenix	IHL	35	9	25	34	8	....	....	....	....	....
	NHL Totals		**133**	**16**	**37**	**53**	**51**	**11**	**1**	**1**	**2**	**2**

a OHL First All-Star Team (1990)
b Canadian Major Junior Defenseman of the Year (1990)
c OHL Second All-Star Team (1991)

Traded to **Colorado** by **Washington** for Philadelphia's third round choice (previously acquired by Colorado — Washington selected Shawn McNeil) in 1996 Entry Draft, July 12, 1995. Traded to **Los Angeles** by **Colorado** for Winnipeg's sixth round choice (previously acquired by Los Angeles — Colorado selected Brian Willsie) in 1996 Entry Draft, December 28, 1995. Signed as a free agent by **Phoenix**, August 18, 1997.

SLEGR, JIRI (SLAY-guhr, YOO-ree) **PIT.**

Defense. Shoots left. 6'1", 205 lbs. Born, Jihlava, Czech., May 30, 1971.
(Vancouver's 3rd choice, 23rd overall, in 1990 Entry Draft).

			Regular Season					Playoffs				
Season	**Club**	**Lea**	**GP**	**G**	**A**	**TP**	**PIM**	**GP**	**G**	**A**	**TP**	**PIM**
1987-88	Litvinov	Czech.	4	1	1	2	0	....	....	....	....	....
1988-89	Litvinov	Czech.	8	0	0	0	4	....	....	....	....	....
1989-90	Litvinov	Czech.	51	4	15	19	....	....	....	....	....	....
1990-91	Litvinov	Czech.	47	11	36	47	26	....	....	....	....	....
1991-92	Litvinov	Czech.	42	9	23	32	38	....	....	....	....	....
1992-93	**Vancouver**	**NHL**	**41**	**4**	**22**	**26**	**109**	**5**	**0**	**3**	**3**	**4**
	Hamilton	AHL	21	4	14	18	42	....	....	....	....	....
1993-94	**Vancouver**	**NHL**	**78**	**5**	**33**	**38**	**86**	....	....	....	....	....
1994-95	Litvinov	Czech.	11	3	10	13	80	....	....	....	....	....
	Vancouver	**NHL**	**19**	**1**	**5**	**6**	**32**	....	....	....	....	....
	Edmonton	**NHL**	**12**	**1**	**5**	**6**	**14**	....	....	....	....	....
1995-96	**Edmonton**	**NHL**	**57**	**4**	**13**	**17**	**74**	....	....	....	....	....
	Cape Breton	AHL	4	1	2	3	4	....	....	....	....	....
1996-97	Litvinov	Czech.	1	0	0	0	0	....	....	....	....	....
	Sodertalje	Swe.	30	4	14	18	62	....	....	....	....	....
	NHL Totals		**207**	**15**	**78**	**93**	**315**	**5**	**0**	**3**	**3**	**4**

Traded to **Edmonton** by **Vancouver** for Roman Oksiuta, April 7, 1995. Traded to **Pittsburgh** by **Edmonton** for Pittsburgh's third round choice in 1998 Entry Draft, August 12, 1997.

SMART, RYAN **N.J.**

Center. Shoots right. 6', 175 lbs. Born, Meadville, PA, September 22, 1975.
(New Jersey's 6th choice, 134th overall, in 1994 Entry Draft).

			Regular Season					Playoffs				
Season	**Club**	**Lea**	**GP**	**G**	**A**	**TP**	**PIM**	**GP**	**G**	**A**	**TP**	**PIM**
1994-95	Cornell	ECAC	26	13	7	20	10	....	....	....	....	....
1995-96	Cornell	ECAC	34	8	19	27	22	....	....	....	....	....
1996-97	Cornell	ECAC	35	5	12	17	20	....	....	....	....	....

SMEHLIK, RICHARD (SHMEH-lihk) **BUF.**

Defense. Shoots left. 6'3", 222 lbs. Born, Ostrava, Czech., January 23, 1970.
(Buffalo's 3rd choice, 97th overall, in 1990 Entry Draft).

			Regular Season					Playoffs				
Season	**Club**	**Lea**	**GP**	**G**	**A**	**TP**	**PIM**	**GP**	**G**	**A**	**TP**	**PIM**
1988-89	TJ Vitkovice	Czech.	38	2	5	7	12	....	....	....	....	....
1989-90	TJ Vitkovice	Czech.	51	5	4	9	....	....	....	....	....	....
1990-91	Dukla Jihlava	Czech.	58	4	3	7	22	....	....	....	....	....
1991-92	TJ Vitkovice	Czech.	47	9	10	19	42	....	....	....	....	....
1992-93	**Buffalo**	**NHL**	**80**	**4**	**27**	**31**	**59**	**8**	**0**	**4**	**4**	**2**
1993-94	**Buffalo**	**NHL**	**84**	**14**	**27**	**41**	**69**	**7**	**0**	**2**	**2**	**10**
1994-95	Vitkovice	Czech.	13	5	2	7	12	....	....	....	....	....
	Buffalo	**NHL**	**39**	**4**	**7**	**11**	**46**	**5**	**0**	**0**	**0**	**2**
1995-96			DID NOT PLAY – INJURED									
1996-97	**Buffalo**	**NHL**	**62**	**11**	**19**	**30**	**43**	**12**	**0**	**2**	**2**	**4**
	NHL Totals		**265**	**33**	**80**	**113**	**217**	**32**	**0**	**8**	**8**	**18**

SMITH, ADAM **NYR**

Defense. Shoots left. 6', 190 lbs. Born, Digby, N.S., May 24, 1976.
(NY Rangers' 3rd choice, 78th overall, in 1994 Entry Draft).

			Regular Season					Playoffs				
Season	**Club**	**Lea**	**GP**	**G**	**A**	**TP**	**PIM**	**GP**	**G**	**A**	**TP**	**PIM**
1992-93	Tacoma	WHL	67	0	12	12	43	7	0	1	1	4
1993-94	Tacoma	WHL	66	4	19	23	119	8	0	0	0	10
1994-95	Tacoma	WHL	69	2	19	21	96	4	0	1	1	9
1995-96	Kelowna	WHL	67	8	15	23	125	6	1	1	2	8
1996-97	Binghamton	AHL	56	0	8	8	59	2	0	0	0	0

SMITH, BRANDON — DET.

Defense. Shoots left. 6'1", 196 lbs. Born, Hazelton, B.C., February 25, 1973.

			Regular Season					Playoffs				
Season	Club	Lea	GP	G	A	TP	PIM	GP	G	A	TP	PIM
1989-90	Portland	WHL	59	2	17	19	16	....	....	....	....	....
1990-91	Portland	WHL	17	8	5	13	8	....	....	....	....	....
1991-92	Portland	WHL	70	12	32	44	63	....	....	....	....	....
1992-93a	Portland	WHL	72	20	54	74	38	16	4	9	13	6
1993-94a	Portland	WHL	72	19	63	82	47	10	2	10	12	8
1994-95bc	Dayton	ECHL	60	16	49	65	57	4	2	3	5	0
	Adirondack	AHL	14	1	2	3	7	3	0	0	0	2
1995-96	Adirondack	AHL	48	4	13	17	22	3	0	1	1	2
1996-97	Adirondack	AHL	80	8	26	34	30	4	0	0	0	0

a WHL West Second All-Star Team (1993, 1994)
b ECHL First All-Star Team (1995)
c Top Defenseman - ECHL (1995)

Signed as a free agent by **Detroit**, July 28, 1997.

SMITH, DAN — COL.

Defense. Shoots left. 6'2", 195 lbs. Born, Fernie, B.C., October 19, 1976.
(Colorado's 7th choice, 181st overall, in 1995 Entry Draft).

			Regular Season					Playoffs				
Season	Club	Lea	GP	G	A	TP	PIM	GP	G	A	TP	PIM
1995-96	Tri City	WHL	58	1	21	22	70	11	1	3	4	14
1996-97	Tri-City	WHL	72	5	19	24	174	....	....	....	....	....
	Hershey	AHL	8	0	1	1	6	15	0	1	1	25

SMITH, DENIS (D.J.) — TOR.

Defense. Shoots left. 6'1", 200 lbs. Born, Windsor, Ont., May 13, 1977.
(NY Islanders' 3rd choice, 41st overall, in 1995 Entry Draft).

			Regular Season					Playoffs				
Season	Club	Lea	GP	G	A	TP	PIM	GP	G	A	TP	PIM
1994-95	Windsor	OHL	61	4	13	17	201	10	1	3	4	41
1995-96	Windsor	OHL	64	14	45	59	260	7	1	7	8	23
	St. John's	AHL	1	0	0	0	0	....	....	....	....	....
1996-97	**Toronto**	**NHL**	**8**	**0**	**1**	**1**	**7**	....	....	....	....	....
a	Windsor	OHL	63	15	52	67	190	5	1	7	8	11
	St. John's	AHL	....	....	....	....	....	1	0	0	0	0
	NHL Totals		**8**	**0**	**1**	**1**	**7**	....	....	....	....	....

a OHL Second All-Star Team (1997)

Traded to **Toronto** by **NY Islanders** with Wendel Clark and Mathieu Schneider for Darby Hendrickson, Sean Haggerty, Kenny Jonsson and Toronto's first round choice (Roberto Luongo) in 1997 Entry Draft, March 13, 1996.

SMITH, GEOFF

Defense. Shoots left. 6'3", 194 lbs. Born, Edmonton, Alta., March 7, 1969.
(Edmonton's 3rd choice, 63rd overall, in 1987 Entry Draft).

			Regular Season					Playoffs				
Season	Club	Lea	GP	G	A	TP	PIM	GP	G	A	TP	PIM
1987-88	North Dakota	WCHA	42	4	12	16	34	....	....	....	....	....
1988-89	North Dakota	WCHA	9	0	1	1	8	....	....	....	....	....
	Kamloops	WHL	32	4	31	35	29	6	1	3	4	12
1989-90a	**Edmonton**	**NHL**	**74**	**4**	**11**	**15**	**52**	**3**	**0**	**0**	**0**	**0** ♦
1990-91	**Edmonton**	**NHL**	**59**	**1**	**12**	**13**	**55**	**4**	**0**	**0**	**0**	**0**
1991-92	**Edmonton**	**NHL**	**74**	**2**	**16**	**18**	**43**	**5**	**0**	**1**	**1**	**6**
1992-93	**Edmonton**	**NHL**	**78**	**4**	**14**	**18**	**30**	....	....	....	....	....
1993-94	**Edmonton**	**NHL**	**21**	**0**	**3**	**3**	**12**	....	....	....	....	....
	Florida	**NHL**	**56**	**1**	**5**	**6**	**38**	....	....	....	....	....
1994-95	**Florida**	**NHL**	**47**	**2**	**4**	**6**	**22**	....	....	....	....	....
1995-96	**Florida**	**NHL**	**31**	**3**	**7**	**10**	**20**	**1**	**0**	**0**	**0**	**2**
1996-97	**Florida**	**NHL**	**3**	**0**	**0**	**0**	**2**	....	....	....	....	....
	Carolina	AHL	27	3	4	7	20	....	....	....	....	....
	NHL Totals		**443**	**17**	**72**	**89**	**274**	**13**	**0**	**1**	**1**	**8**

a NHL All-Rookie Team (1990)

Traded to **Florida** by **Edmonton** with Edmonton's fourth round choice (David Nemirovsky) in 1994 Entry Draft for Florida's third round choice (Corey Neilson) in 1994 Entry Draft and St. Louis' sixth round choice (previously acquired by Florida — later traded to Winnipeg — Winnipeg selected Chris Kibermanis) in 1994 Entry Draft, December 6, 1993.

SMITH, JARRETT — NYI

Center. Shoots left. 6'2", 190 lbs. Born, Edmonton, Alta., June 15, 1979.
(NY Islanders' 4th choice, 59th overall, in 1997 Entry Draft).

			Regular Season					Playoffs				
Season	Club	Lea	GP	G	A	TP	PIM	GP	G	A	TP	PIM
1994-95	Prince George	WHL	1	0	0	0	0	....	....	....	....	....
1995-96	Prince George	WHL	18	2	0	2	6	....	....	....	....	....
1996-97	Prince George	WHL	67	20	22	42	58	15	2	2	4	5

SMITH, JASON — TOR.

Defense. Shoots right. 6'3", 205 lbs. Born, Calgary, Alta., November 2, 1973.
(New Jersey's 1st choice, 18th overall, in 1992 Entry Draft).

			Regular Season					Playoffs				
Season	Club	Lea	GP	G	A	TP	PIM	GP	G	A	TP	PIM
1990-91	Regina	WHL	2	0	0	0	7	4	0	0	0	2
1991-92	Regina	WHL	62	9	29	38	168	....	....	....	....	....
1992-93a	Regina	WHL	64	14	52	66	175	13	4	8	12	39
	Utica	AHL	....	....	....	....	....	1	0	0	0	2
1993-94	**New Jersey**	**NHL**	**41**	**0**	**5**	**5**	**43**	**6**	**0**	**0**	**0**	**7**
	Albany	AHL	20	6	3	9	31	....	....	....	....	....
1994-95	**New Jersey**	**NHL**	**2**	**0**	**0**	**0**	**0**	....	....	....	....	....
	Albany	AHL	7	0	2	2	15	11	2	2	4	19
1995-96	**New Jersey**	**NHL**	**64**	**2**	**1**	**3**	**86**	....	....	....	....	....
1996-97	**New Jersey**	**NHL**	**57**	**1**	**2**	**3**	**38**	....	....	....	....	....
	Toronto	**NHL**	**21**	**0**	**5**	**5**	**16**	....	....	....	....	....
	NHL Totals		**185**	**3**	**13**	**16**	**183**	**6**	**0**	**0**	**0**	**7**

a Canadian Major Junior First All-Star Team (1993).

Traded to **Toronto** by **New Jersey** with Steve Sullivan and the rights to Alyn McCauley for Doug Gilmour, Dave Ellett and a conditional draft choice, February 25, 1997.

SMITH, NICK — FLA.

Center. Shoots left. 6'1", 165 lbs. Born, Hamilton, Ont., March 23, 1979.
(Florida's 4th choice, 74th overall, in 1997 Entry Draft).

			Regular Season					Playoffs				
Season	Club	Lea	GP	G	A	TP	PIM	GP	G	A	TP	PIM
1995-96	Shelburne	Jr. A	42	13	18	31	12	....	....	....	....	....
1996-97	Barrie	OHL	63	10	18	28	15	9	3	8	11	13

SMITH, STEVE

Defense. Shoots left. 6'4", 215 lbs. Born, Glasgow, Scotland, April 30, 1963.
(Edmonton's 5th choice, 111th overall, in 1981 Entry Draft).

			Regular Season					Playoffs				
Season	Club	Lea	GP	G	A	TP	PIM	GP	G	A	TP	PIM
1980-81	London	OHA	62	4	12	16	141	....	....	....	....	....
1981-82	London	OHL	58	10	36	46	207	4	1	2	3	13
1982-83	Moncton	AHL	2	0	0	0	0	....	....	....	....	....
	London	OHL	50	6	35	41	133	3	1	0	1	10
1983-84	Moncton	AHL	64	1	8	9	176	....	....	....	....	....
1984-85	**Edmonton**	**NHL**	**2**	**0**	**0**	**0**	**2**	....	....	....	....	....
	Nova Scotia	AHL	68	2	28	30	161	5	0	3	3	40
1985-86	**Edmonton**	**NHL**	**55**	**4**	**20**	**24**	**166**	**6**	**0**	**1**	**1**	**14**
	Nova Scotia	AHL	4	0	2	2	11	....	....	....	....	....
1986-87	**Edmonton**	**NHL**	**62**	**7**	**15**	**22**	**165**	**15**	**1**	**3**	**4**	**45** ♦
1987-88	**Edmonton**	**NHL**	**79**	**12**	**43**	**55**	**286**	**19**	**1**	**11**	**12**	**55** ♦
1988-89	**Edmonton**	**NHL**	**35**	**3**	**19**	**22**	**97**	**7**	**2**	**2**	**4**	**20**
1989-90	**Edmonton**	**NHL**	**75**	**7**	**34**	**41**	**171**	**22**	**5**	**10**	**15**	**37** ♦
1990-91	**Edmonton**	**NHL**	**77**	**13**	**41**	**54**	**193**	**18**	**1**	**2**	**3**	**45**
1991-92	**Chicago**	**NHL**	**76**	**9**	**21**	**30**	**304**	**18**	**1**	**11**	**12**	**16**
1992-93	**Chicago**	**NHL**	**78**	**10**	**47**	**57**	**214**	**4**	**0**	**0**	**0**	**10**
1993-94	**Chicago**	**NHL**	**57**	**5**	**22**	**27**	**174**	....	....	....	....	....
1994-95	**Chicago**	**NHL**	**48**	**1**	**12**	**13**	**128**	**16**	**0**	**1**	**1**	**26**
1995-96	**Chicago**	**NHL**	**37**	**0**	**9**	**9**	**71**	**6**	**0**	**0**	**0**	**16**
1996-97	**Chicago**	**NHL**	**21**	**0**	**0**	**0**	**29**	**3**	**0**	**0**	**0**	**4**
	NHL Totals		**702**	**71**	**283**	**354**	**2000**	**134**	**11**	**41**	**52**	**288**

Played in NHL All-Star Game (1991)

Traded to **Chicago** by **Edmonton** for Dave Manson and Chicago's third round choice (Kirk Maltby) in 1992 Entry Draft, October 2, 1991.

SMOLINSKI, BRYAN (smoh-LIHN-skee) — NYI

Center. Shoots right. 6'1", 200 lbs. Born, Toledo, OH, December 27, 1971.
(Boston's 1st choice, 21st overall, in 1990 Entry Draft).

			Regular Season					Playoffs				
Season	Club	Lea	GP	G	A	TP	PIM	GP	G	A	TP	PIM
1989-90	Michigan State	CCHA	35	9	13	22	34	....	....	....	....	....
1990-91	Michigan State	CCHA	35	9	12	21	24	....	....	....	....	....
1991-92	Michigan State	CCHA	41	28	33	61	55	....	....	....	....	....
1992-93ab	Michigan State	CCHA	40	31	37	*68	93	....	....	....	....	....
	Boston	**NHL**	**9**	**1**	**3**	**4**	**0**	**4**	**1**	**0**	**1**	**2**
1993-94	**Boston**	**NHL**	**83**	**31**	**20**	**51**	**82**	**13**	**5**	**4**	**9**	**4**
1994-95	**Boston**	**NHL**	**44**	**18**	**13**	**31**	**31**	**5**	**0**	**1**	**1**	**4**
1995-96	**Pittsburgh**	**NHL**	**81**	**24**	**40**	**64**	**69**	**18**	**5**	**4**	**9**	**10**
1996-97	Detroit	IHL	6	5	7	12	10	....	....	....	....	....
	NY Islanders	**NHL**	**64**	**28**	**28**	**56**	**25**	....	....	....	....	....
	NHL Totals		**281**	**102**	**104**	**206**	**207**	**40**	**11**	**9**	**20**	**20**

a CCHA First All-Star Team (1993)
b NCAA West First All-American Team (1993)

Traded to **Pittsburgh** by **Boston** with Glen Murray and Boston's third round choice (Boyd Kane) in 1996 Entry Draft for Kevin Stevens and Shawn McEachern, August 2, 1995. Traded to **NY Islanders** by **Pittsburgh** for Darius Kasparaitis and Andreas Johansson, November 17, 1996.

SMYTH, BRAD (SMIHTH) — L.A.

Right wing. Shoots right. 6', 200 lbs. Born, Ottawa, Ont., March 13, 1973.

			Regular Season					Playoffs				
Season	Club	Lea	GP	G	A	TP	PIM	GP	G	A	TP	PIM
1990-91	London	OHL	29	2	6	8	22	....	....	....	....	....
1991-92	London	OHL	58	17	18	35	93	10	2	0	2	8
1992-93	London	OHL	66	54	55	109	118	12	7	8	15	25
1993-94	Cincinnati	IHL	30	7	3	10	54	....	....	....	....	....
	Birmingham	ECHL	29	26	30	56	38	10	8	8	16	19
1994-95	Springfield	AHL	3	0	0	0	7	....	....	....	....	....
	Birmingham	ECHL	36	33	35	68	52	3	5	2	7	0
	Cincinnati	IHL	26	2	11	13	34	1	0	0	0	2
1995-96	**Florida**	**NHL**	**7**	**1**	**1**	**2**	**4**	....	....	....	....	....
abc	Carolina	AHL	68	*68	58	*126	80	....	....	....	....	....
1996-97	**Florida**	**NHL**	**8**	**1**	**0**	**1**	**2**	....	....	....	....	....
	Los Angeles	**NHL**	**44**	**8**	**8**	**16**	**74**	....	....	....	....	....
	Phoenix	IHL	3	5	2	7	0	....	....	....	....	....
	NHL Totals		**59**	**10**	**9**	**19**	**80**	....	....	....	....	....

a AHL First All-Star Team (1996)
b Won John B. Sollenberger Trophy (Top Scorer - AHL) (1996)
c Won Les Cunningham Plaque (MVP - AHL) (1996)

Signed as a free agent by **Florida**, October 4, 1993. Traded to **Los Angeles** by **Florida** for Los Angeles' third round choice (Vratislav Czech) in 1997 Entry Draft, November 28, 1996.

SMYTH, GREG (SMIHTH) TOR.

Defense. Shoots right. 6'3", 212 lbs. Born, Oakville, Ont., April 23, 1966.
(Philadelphia's 1st choice, 22nd overall, in 1984 Entry Draft).

			Regular Season					Playoffs				
Season	Club	Lea	GP	G	A	TP	PIM	GP	G	A	TP	PIM
1983-84	London	OHL	64	4	21	25	252	6	1	0	1	24
1984-85	London	OHL	47	7	16	23	188	8	2	2	4	27
1985-86	Hershey	AHL	2	0	1	1	5	8	0	0	0	60
a	London	OHL	46	12	42	54	199	4	1	2	3	28
1986-87	**Philadelphia**	**NHL**	**1**	**0**	**0**	**0**	**0**	**1**	**0**	**0**	**0**	**2**
	Hershey	AHL	35	0	2	2	158	2	0	0	0	19
1987-88	**Philadelphia**	**NHL**	**48**	**1**	**6**	**7**	**192**	**5**	**0**	**0**	**0**	**38**
	Hershey	AHL	21	0	10	10	102	....	....	....	....	....
1988-89	**Quebec**	**NHL**	**10**	**0**	**1**	**1**	**70**	....	....	....	....	....
	Halifax	AHL	43	3	9	12	310	4	0	1	1	35
1989-90	**Quebec**	**NHL**	**13**	**0**	**0**	**0**	**57**	....	....	....	....	....
	Halifax	AHL	49	5	14	19	235	6	1	0	1	52
1990-91	**Quebec**	**NHL**	**1**	**0**	**0**	**0**	**0**	....	....	....	....	....
	Halifax	AHL	56	6	23	29	340	....	....	....	....	....
1991-92	**Quebec**	**NHL**	**29**	**0**	**2**	**2**	**138**	....	....	....	....	....
	Halifax	AHL	9	1	3	4	35	....	....	....	....	....
	Calgary	**NHL**	**7**	**1**	**1**	**2**	**15**	....	....	....	....	....
1992-93	**Calgary**	**NHL**	**35**	**1**	**2**	**3**	**95**	....	....	....	....	....
	Salt Lake	IHL	5	0	1	1	31	....	....	....	....	....
1993-94	**Florida**	**NHL**	**12**	**1**	**0**	**1**	**37**	....	....	....	....	....
	Toronto	**NHL**	**11**	**0**	**1**	**1**	**38**	....	....	....	....	....
	Chicago	**NHL**	**38**	**0**	**0**	**0**	**108**	**6**	**0**	**0**	**0**	**0**
1994-95	**Chicago**	**NHL**	**22**	**0**	**3**	**3**	**33**	....	....	....	....	....
	Indianapolis	IHL	2	0	0	0	0	....	....	....	....	....
1995-96	Chicago	IHL	15	1	3	4	53	....	....	....	....	....
	Los Angeles	IHL	41	2	7	9	231	....	....	....	....	....
1996-97	**Toronto**	**NHL**	**2**	**0**	**0**	**0**	**0**	....	....	....	....	....
	St. John's	AHL	43	2	4	6	273	5	0	1	1	14
	NHL Totals		**229**	**4**	**16**	**20**	**783**	**12**	**0**	**0**	**0**	**40**

a OHL Second All-Star Team (1986)

Traded to **Quebec** by **Philadelphia** with Philadelphia's third round choice (John Tanner) in the 1989 Entry Draft for Terry Carkner, July 25, 1988. Traded to **Calgary** by **Quebec** for Martin Simard, March 10, 1992. Signed as a free agent by **Florida**, August 10, 1993. Traded to **Toronto** by **Florida** for cash, December 7, 1993. Claimed on waivers by **Chicago** from **Toronto**, January 8, 1994. Signed as a free agent by **Toronto**, August 22, 1996.

SMYTH, KEVIN (SMIHTH) CAR.

Left wing. Shoots left. 6'2", 217 lbs. Born, Banff, Alta., November 22, 1973.
(Hartford's 4th choice, 79th overall, in 1992 Entry Draft).

			Regular Season					Playoffs				
Season	Club	Lea	GP	G	A	TP	PIM	GP	G	A	TP	PIM
1990-91	Moose Jaw	WHL	66	30	45	75	96	6	1	1	2	0
1991-92	Moose Jaw	WHL	71	30	55	85	114	4	1	3	4	6
1992-93	Moose Jaw	WHL	64	44	38	82	111	....	....	....	....	....
1993-94	**Hartford**	**NHL**	**21**	**3**	**2**	**5**	**10**	....	....	....	....	....
	Springfield	AHL	42	22	27	49	72	6	4	5	9	0
1994-95	Springfield	AHL	57	17	22	39	72	....	....	....	....	....
	Hartford	**NHL**	**16**	**1**	**5**	**6**	**13**	....	....	....	....	....
1995-96	**Hartford**	**NHL**	**21**	**2**	**1**	**3**	**8**	....	....	....	....	....
	Springfield	AHL	47	15	33	48	87	10	5	5	10	8
1996-97	Orlando	IHL	38	14	17	31	49	10	1	2	3	6
	NHL Totals		**58**	**6**	**8**	**14**	**31**	....	....	....	....	....

SMYTH, RYAN (SMIHTH) EDM.

Left wing. Shoots left. 6'1", 195 lbs. Born, Banff, Alta., February 21, 1976.
(Edmonton's 2nd choice, 6th overall, in 1994 Entry Draft).

			Regular Season					Playoffs				
Season	Club	Lea	GP	G	A	TP	PIM	GP	G	A	TP	PIM
1991-92	Moose Jaw	WHL	2	0	0	0	0	....	....	....	....	....
1992-93	Moose Jaw	WHL	64	19	14	33	59	....	....	....	....	....
1993-94	Moose Jaw	WHL	72	50	55	105	88	....	....	....	....	....
1994-95a	Moose Jaw	WHL	50	41	45	86	66	10	6	9	15	22
	Edmonton	**NHL**	**3**	**0**	**0**	**0**	**0**	....	....	....	....	....
1995-96	**Edmonton**	**NHL**	**48**	**2**	**9**	**11**	**28**	....	....	....	....	....
	Cape Breton	AHL	9	6	5	11	4	....	....	....	....	....
1996-97	**Edmonton**	**NHL**	**82**	**39**	**22**	**61**	**76**	**12**	**5**	**5**	**10**	**12**
	NHL Totals		**133**	**41**	**31**	**72**	**104**	**12**	**5**	**5**	**10**	**12**

a WHL East Second All-Star Team (1995)

SNELL, CHRIS

Defense. Shoots left. 5'11", 200 lbs. Born, Regina, Sask., May 12, 1971.
(Buffalo's 8th choice, 145th overall, in 1991 Entry Draft).

			Regular Season					Playoffs				
Season	Club	Lea	GP	G	A	TP	PIM	GP	G	A	TP	PIM
1989-90a	Ottawa	OHL	63	18	62	80	36	3	2	4	6	4
1990-91	Ottawa	OHL	54	23	59	82	58	17	3	14	17	8
1991-92	Rochester	AHL	65	5	27	32	66	10	2	1	3	6
1992-93	Rochester	AHL	76	14	57	71	83	17	5	8	13	39
1993-94	**Toronto**	**NHL**	**2**	**0**	**0**	**0**	**2**	....	....	....	....	....
bc	St. John's	AHL	75	22	74	96	92	11	1	15	16	10
1994-95d	Phoenix	IHL	57	15	49	64	122	....	....	....	....	....
	Los Angeles	**NHL**	**32**	**2**	**7**	**9**	**22**	....	....	....	....	....
1995-96	Phoenix	IHL	40	9	22	31	113	....	....	....	....	....
	Binghamton	AHL	32	7	25	32	48	4	2	2	4	6
1996-97e	Indianapolis	IHL	73	22	45	67	130	2	0	0	0	2
	NHL Totals		**34**	**2**	**7**	**9**	**24**	....	....	....	....	....

a OHL First All-Star Team (1990)
b AHL First All-Star Team (1994)
c Won Eddie Shore Plaque (Top Defenseman - AHL) (1994)
d IHL First All-Star Team (1995)
e IHL Second All-Star Team (1997)

Signed as a free agent by **Toronto**, August 3, 1993. Traded to **Los Angeles** by **Toronto** with Eric Lacroix and Toronto's fourth round choice (Eric Belanger) in 1996 Entry Draft for Dixon Ward, Guy Leveque and Kelly Fairchild, October 3, 1994. Traded to **NY Rangers** by **Los Angeles** for Steve Larouche, January 14, 1996. Signed as a free agent by **Chicago**, August 16, 1996.

SODERBERG, ANDERS (SOH-dehr-buhrg) BOS.

Right wing. Shoots right. 5'6", 161 lbs. Born, Ornskoldsvik, Sweden, October 7, 1975.
(Boston's 10th choice, 234th overall, in 1996 Entry Draft).

			Regular Season					Playoffs				
Season	Club	Lea	GP	G	A	TP	PIM	GP	G	A	TP	PIM
1992-93	MoDo	Swe. Jr.	13	6	12	18	2	....	....	....	....	....
	MoDo	Swe.	1	0	0	0	0	....	....	....	....	....
1993-94	MoDo	Swe. Jr.	9	8	5	13	10	....	....	....	....	....
	MoDo	Swe.	19	0	0	0	2	9	0	0	0	0
1994-95	MoDo	Swe.	38	9	14	23	2	....	....	....	....	....
1995-96	MoDo	Swe.	40	10	18	28	10	8	3	3	6	0
1996-97	MoDo	Swe.	39	9	13	22	16	....	....	....	....	....

SOLING, JONAS (SOH-lihng, YOH-nahs) VAN.

Right wing. Shoots left. 6'4", 192 lbs. Born, Stockholm, Sweden, September 7, 1978.
(Vancouver's 3rd choice, 93rd overall, in 1996 Entry Draft).

			Regular Season					Playoffs				
Season	Club	Lea	GP	G	A	TP	PIM	GP	G	A	TP	PIM
1995-96	Huddinge	Swe. Jr.	24	8	4	12	18	....	....	....	....	....
	Huddinge	Swe. 2	5	0	0	0	0	....	....	....	....	....
1996-97	Sudbury	OHL	66	18	22	40	60	....	....	....	....	....

SOMIK, RADOVAN (SAW-mihk, RAH-doh-vahn) PHI.

Left wing. Shoots right. 6'2", 194 lbs. Born, Martin, Czech., May 5, 1977.
(Philadelphia's 3rd choice, 100th overall, in 1995 Entry Draft).

			Regular Season					Playoffs				
Season	Club	Lea	GP	G	A	TP	PIM	GP	G	A	TP	PIM
1993-94	Martin	Slovak	1	0	0	0	0	....	....	....	....	....
1994-95	Martin	Slovak	25	3	0	3	39	3	1	0	1	2
1995-96	Martin	Slovak	25	3	6	9	8	9	1	0	1	....
1996-97	Martin	Slovak	35	3	5	8	....	3	0	0	0	....

SOPEL, BRENT (SOH-puhl) VAN.

Defense. Shoots right. 6'1", 190 lbs. Born, Calgary, Alta., January 7, 1977.
(Vancouver's 6th choice, 144th overall, in 1995 Entry Draft).

			Regular Season					Playoffs				
Season	Club	Lea	GP	G	A	TP	PIM	GP	G	A	TP	PIM
1993-94	Saskatoon	WHL	11	2	2	4	2	....	....	....	....	....
1994-95	Saskatoon	WHL	22	1	10	11	31	....	....	....	....	....
	Swift Current	WHL	41	4	19	23	50	3	0	3	3	0
1995-96	Swift Current	WHL	71	13	48	61	87	6	1	2	3	4
	Syracuse	AHL	1	0	0	0	0	....	....	....	....	....
1996-97	Swift Current	WHL	62	15	41	56	109	10	5	11	16	32
	Syracuse	AHL	2	0	0	0	0	3	0	0	0	0

SOROCHAN, LEE (soh-RAW-kihn) NYR

Defense. Shoots left. 5'11", 210 lbs. Born, Edmonton, Alta., September 9, 1975.
(NY Rangers' 2nd choice, 34th overall, in 1993 Entry Draft).

			Regular Season					Playoffs				
Season	Club	Lea	GP	G	A	TP	PIM	GP	G	A	TP	PIM
1991-92	Lethbridge	WHL	67	2	9	11	105	5	0	2	2	6
1992-93	Lethbridge	WHL	69	8	32	40	208	4	0	1	1	12
1993-94	Lethbridge	WHL	46	5	27	32	123	9	4	3	7	16
1994-95	Lethbridge	WHL	29	4	15	19	93	....	....	....	....	....
	Saskatoon	WHL	24	5	13	18	63	10	3	6	9	34
	Binghamton	AHL	....	....	....	....	....	8	0	0	0	11
1995-96	Binghamton	AHL	45	2	8	10	26	1	0	0	0	0
1996-97	Binghamton	AHL	77	4	27	31	160	4	0	2	2	18

SOURAY, SHELDON (SUHR-ee) N.J.

Defense. Shoots left. 6'2", 210 lbs. Born, Elk Point, Alta., July 13, 1976.
(New Jersey's 3rd choice, 71st overall, in 1994 Entry Draft).

			Regular Season					Playoffs				
Season	Club	Lea	GP	G	A	TP	PIM	GP	G	A	TP	PIM
1992-93	Tri-City	WHL	2	0	0	0	0	....	....	....	....	....
1993-94	Tri-City	WHL	42	3	6	9	122	....	....	....	....	....
1994-95	Tri-City	WHL	40	2	24	26	140	....	....	....	....	....
	Prince George	WHL	11	2	3	5	23	....	....	....	....	....
	Albany	AHL	7	0	2	2	8	....	....	....	....	....
1995-96	Prince George	WHL	32	9	18	27	91	....	....	....	....	....
a	Kelowna	WHL	27	7	20	27	94	6	0	5	5	2
	Albany	AHL	6	0	2	2	12	4	0	1	1	4
1996-97	Albany	AHL	70	2	11	13	160	16	2	3	5	47

a WHL West Second All-Star Team (1996)

SOUZA, MIKE (SOO-zah) CHI.

Left wing. Shoots left. 6'1", 190 lbs. Born, Melrose, MA, January 28, 1978.
(Chicago's 4th choice, 67th overall, in 1997 Entry Draft).

			Regular Season					Playoffs				
Season	Club	Lea	GP	G	A	TP	PIM	GP	G	A	TP	PIM
1995-96	Wakefield	HS	21	25	31	56	22	....	....	....	....	....
1996-97	New Hampshire	H.E.	39	15	11	26	20	....	....	....	....	....

SPRING, COREY T.B.

Right wing. Shoots right. 6'4", 214 lbs. Born, Cranbrook, B.C., May 31, 1971.

			Regular Season					Playoffs				
Season	Club	Lea	GP	G	A	TP	PIM	GP	G	A	TP	PIM
1991-92	Alaska-Anch.	NCAA	35	3	8	11	30	....	....	....	....	....
1992-93	Alaska-Anch.	CCHA	28	5	5	10	20	....	....	....	....	....
1993-94	Alaska-Anch.	CCHA	38	19	18	37	34	....	....	....	....	....
1994-95	Alaska-Anch.	CCHA	33	18	14	32	56	....	....	....	....	....
1995-96	Atlanta	IHL	73	14	14	28	104	2	0	0	0	0
1996-97	Adirondack	AHL	69	20	26	46	118	4	0	0	0	14

Signed as a free agent by **Tampa Bay**, July 24, 1995.

SPROULE, DOUG OTT.

Left wing. Shoots left. 6'3", 190 lbs. Born, Red Bank, NJ, February 16, 1976.
(Ottawa's 6th choice, 159th overall, in 1994 Entry Draft).

			Regular Season					Playoffs				
Season	Club	Lea	GP	G	A	TP	PIM	GP	G	A	TP	PIM
1994-95	Harvard	ECAC	30	7	2	9	28	....	....	....	....	....
1995-96	Harvard	ECAC	12	1	0	1	6	....	....	....	....	....
1996-97	Harvard	ECAC	32	6	10	16	46	....	....	....	....	....

SRDINKO, JAN — N.J.

Defense. Shoots left. 5'11", 195 lbs. Born, Vsetin, Czech., February 22, 1974.
(New Jersey's 8th choice, 241st overall, in 1997 Entry Draft).

			Regular Season					Playoffs				
Season	**Club**	**Lea**	**GP**	**G**	**A**	**TP**	**PIM**	**GP**	**G**	**A**	**TP**	**PIM**
1994-95	Vsetin	Czech.	1	0	0	0	....	....	....	....	....	....
1995-96	Vsetin	Czech.	31	0	3	3	....	9	0	0	0	....
1996-97	Vsetin	Czech.	49	2	8	10	71	10	0	3	3	29

STAAL, KIM (STOHL) — MTL.

Center. Shoots right. 6', 185 lbs. Born, Herlev, Denmark, March 10, 1978.
(Montreal's 4th choice, 92nd overall, in 1996 Entry Draft).

			Regular Season					Playoffs				
Season	**Club**	**Lea**	**GP**	**G**	**A**	**TP**	**PIM**	**GP**	**G**	**A**	**TP**	**PIM**
1995-96	Malmo	Swe. Jr.	30	24	20	44	14	....	....	....	....	....
1996-97	Malmo	Swe.	4	0	1	1	2	....	....	....	....	....
	Malmo	Swe. Jr.	3	6	4	10	2	....	....	....	....	....

STAHL, CRAIG — DET.

Right wing. Shoots right. 5'10", 193 lbs. Born, Cranbrook, B.C., March 19, 1977.
(Detroit's 8th choice, 215th overall, in 1996 Entry Draft).

			Regular Season					Playoffs				
Season	**Club**	**Lea**	**GP**	**G**	**A**	**TP**	**PIM**	**GP**	**G**	**A**	**TP**	**PIM**
1995-96	Tri-City	WHL	65	5	13	18	149	11	2	2	4	10
1996-97	Tri-City	WHL	61	21	15	36	177	....	....	....	....	....

STAIOS, STEVE (STAY-uhs) — VAN.

Defense. Shoots right. 6', 185 lbs. Born, Hamilton, Ont., July 28, 1973.
(St. Louis' 1st choice, 27th overall, in 1991 Entry Draft).

			Regular Season					Playoffs				
Season	**Club**	**Lea**	**GP**	**G**	**A**	**TP**	**PIM**	**GP**	**G**	**A**	**TP**	**PIM**
1990-91	Niagara Falls	OHL	66	17	29	46	115	12	2	3	5	10
1991-92	Niagara Falls	OHL	65	11	42	53	122	17	7	8	15	27
1992-93	Niagara Falls	OHL	12	4	14	18	30	....	....	....	....	....
	Sudbury	OHL	53	13	44	57	67	11	5	6	11	22
1993-94	Peoria	IHL	38	3	9	12	42	....	....	....	....	....
1994-95	Peoria	IHL	60	3	13	16	64	6	0	0	0	10
1995-96	Peoria	IHL	6	0	1	1	14	....	....	....	....	....
	Worcester	AHL	57	1	11	12	114	....	....	....	....	....
	Boston	**NHL**	**12**	**0**	**0**	**0**	**4**	**3**	**0**	**0**	**0**	**0**
	Providence	AHL	7	1	4	5	8	....	....	....	....	....
1996-97	**Boston**	**NHL**	**54**	**3**	**8**	**11**	**71**	....	....	....	....	....
	Vancouver	**NHL**	**9**	**0**	**6**	**6**	**20**	....	....	....	....	....
	NHL Totals		**75**	**3**	**14**	**17**	**95**	**3**	**0**	**0**	**0**	**0**

Traded to **Boston** by **St. Louis** with Kevin Sawyer for Steve Leach, March 8, 1996. Claimed on waivers by **Vancouver** from **Boston**, March 18, 1997.

STANLEY, CHRIS — VAN.

Center. Shoots left. 6'1", 200 lbs. Born, Parry Sound, Ont., June 18, 1979.
(Vancouver's 5th choice, 90th overall, in 1997 Entry Draft).

			Regular Season					Playoffs				
Season	**Club**	**Lea**	**GP**	**G**	**A**	**TP**	**PIM**	**GP**	**G**	**A**	**TP**	**PIM**
1996-97	Belleville	OHL	66	19	24	43	16	6	1	0	1	0

STAPLES, JEFF — PHI.

Defense. Shoots left. 6'2", 207 lbs. Born, Kitimat, B.C., March 4, 1975.
(Philadelphia's 10th choice, 244th overall, in 1993 Entry Draft).

			Regular Season					Playoffs				
Season	**Club**	**Lea**	**GP**	**G**	**A**	**TP**	**PIM**	**GP**	**G**	**A**	**TP**	**PIM**
1991-92	Brandon	WHL	3	0	0	0	0	....	....	....	....	....
1992-93	Brandon	WHL	40	0	5	5	114	4	0	1	1	4
1993-94	Brandon	WHL	37	0	7	7	126	....	....	....	....	....
1994-95	Brandon	WHL	57	3	16	19	176	18	0	2	2	23
1995-96	Hershey	AHL	61	7	3	10	100	5	0	1	1	0
1996-97	Philadelphia	AHL	74	4	11	15	157	8	0	2	2	10

STAPLETON, MIKE — PHO.

Center. Shoots right. 5'10", 183 lbs. Born, Sarnia, Ont., May 5, 1966.
(Chicago's 7th choice, 132nd overall, in 1984 Entry Draft).

			Regular Season					Playoffs				
Season	**Club**	**Lea**	**GP**	**G**	**A**	**TP**	**PIM**	**GP**	**G**	**A**	**TP**	**PIM**
1983-84	Cornwall	OHL	70	24	45	69	94	3	1	2	3	4
1984-85	Cornwall	OHL	56	41	44	85	68	9	2	4	6	23
1985-86	Cornwall	OHL	56	39	64	103	74	6	2	3	5	2
1986-87	**Chicago**	**NHL**	**39**	**3**	**6**	**9**	**6**	**4**	**0**	**0**	**0**	**2**
	Cdn. National	....	21	2	4	6	4	....	....	....	....	....
1987-88	**Chicago**	**NHL**	**53**	**2**	**9**	**11**	**59**	....	....	....	....	....
	Saginaw	IHL	31	11	19	30	52	10	5	6	11	10
1988-89	**Chicago**	**NHL**	**7**	**0**	**1**	**1**	**7**	....	....	....	....	....
	Saginaw	IHL	69	21	47	68	162	6	1	3	4	4
1989-90	Indianapolis	IHL	16	5	10	15	6	13	9	10	19	38
1990-91	**Chicago**	**NHL**	**7**	**0**	**1**	**1**	**2**	....	....	....	....	....
	Indianapolis	IHL	75	29	52	81	76	7	1	4	5	0
1991-92	**Chicago**	**NHL**	**19**	**4**	**4**	**8**	**8**	....	....	....	....	....
	Indianapolis	IHL	59	18	40	58	65	....	....	....	....	....
1992-93	**Pittsburgh**	**NHL**	**78**	**4**	**9**	**13**	**10**	**4**	**0**	**0**	**0**	**0**
1993-94	**Pittsburgh**	**NHL**	**58**	**7**	**4**	**11**	**18**	....	....	....	....	....
	Edmonton	**NHL**	**23**	**5**	**9**	**14**	**28**	....	....	....	....	....
1994-95	**Edmonton**	**NHL**	**46**	**6**	**11**	**17**	**21**	....	....	....	....	....
1995-96	**Winnipeg**	**NHL**	**58**	**10**	**14**	**24**	**37**	**6**	**0**	**0**	**0**	**21**
1996-97	**Phoenix**	**NHL**	**55**	**4**	**11**	**15**	**36**	**7**	**0**	**0**	**0**	**14**
	NHL Totals		**443**	**45**	**79**	**124**	**232**	**21**	**0**	**0**	**0**	**37**

Signed as a free agent by **Pittsburgh**, September 30, 1992. Claimed on waivers by **Edmonton** from **Pittsburgh**, February 19, 1994. Signed as a free agent by **Winnipeg**, August 18, 1995.

STASHENKOV, ILJA (stah-shehn-KOHV) — PHO.

Defense. Shoots left. 5'11", 178 lbs. Born, Moscow, USSR, August 26, 1974.
(Winnipeg's 11th choice, 223rd overall, in 1993 Entry Draft).

			Regular Season					Playoffs				
Season	**Club**	**Lea**	**GP**	**G**	**A**	**TP**	**PIM**	**GP**	**G**	**A**	**TP**	**PIM**
1991-92	Soviet Wings	CIS	7	0	0	0	2	....	....	....	....	....
1992-93	Soviet Wings	CIS	42	0	0	0	22	1	0	0	0	0
1993-94	Soviet Wings	CIS	46	3	0	3	10	....	....	....	....	....
1994-95	Soviet Wings	CIS	51	3	3	6	40	4	1	0	1	0
1995-96	Soviet Wings	CIS	50	5	6	11	24	....	....	....	....	....
	Springfield	AHL	1	0	0	0	2	....	....	....	....	....
1996-97	Soviet Wings	Rus.	38	2	3	5	36	2	0	1	1	4

STERN, RON — CGY.

Right wing. Shoots right. 6', 195 lbs. Born, Ste. Agathe, Que., January 11, 1967.
(Vancouver's 3rd choice, 70th overall, in 1986 Entry Draft).

			Regular Season					Playoffs				
Season	**Club**	**Lea**	**GP**	**G**	**A**	**TP**	**PIM**	**GP**	**G**	**A**	**TP**	**PIM**
1984-85	Longueuil	QMJHL	67	6	14	20	176	....	....	....	....	....
1985-86	Longueuil	QMJHL	70	39	33	72	317	....	....	....	....	....
1986-87	Longueuil	QMJHL	56	32	39	71	266	19	11	9	20	55
1987-88	**Vancouver**	**NHL**	**15**	**0**	**0**	**0**	**52**	....	....	....	....	....
	Fredericton	AHL	2	1	0	1	4	....	....	....	....	....
	Flint	IHL	55	14	19	33	294	16	8	8	16	94
1988-89	**Vancouver**	**NHL**	**17**	**1**	**0**	**1**	**49**	**3**	**0**	**1**	**1**	**17**
	Milwaukee	IHL	45	19	23	42	280	5	1	0	1	11
1989-90	**Vancouver**	**NHL**	**34**	**2**	**3**	**5**	**208**	....	....	....	....	....
	Milwaukee	IHL	26	8	9	17	165	....	....	....	....	....
1990-91	**Vancouver**	**NHL**	**31**	**2**	**3**	**5**	**171**	....	....	....	....	....
	Milwaukee	IHL	7	2	2	4	81	....	....	....	....	....
	Calgary	**NHL**	**13**	**1**	**3**	**4**	**69**	**7**	**1**	**3**	**4**	**14**
1991-92	**Calgary**	**NHL**	**72**	**13**	**9**	**22**	**338**	....	....	....	....	....
1992-93	**Calgary**	**NHL**	**70**	**10**	**15**	**25**	**207**	**6**	**0**	**0**	**0**	**43**
1993-94	**Calgary**	**NHL**	**71**	**9**	**20**	**29**	**243**	**7**	**2**	**0**	**2**	**12**
1994-95	**Calgary**	**NHL**	**39**	**9**	**4**	**13**	**163**	**7**	**3**	**1**	**4**	**8**
1995-96	**Calgary**	**NHL**	**52**	**10**	**5**	**15**	**111**	**4**	**0**	**2**	**2**	**8**
1996-97	**Calgary**	**NHL**	**79**	**7**	**10**	**17**	**157**	....	....	....	....	....
	NHL Totals		**493**	**64**	**72**	**136**	**1768**	**34**	**6**	**7**	**13**	**102**

Traded to **Calgary** by **Vancouver** with Kevan Guy for Dana Murzyn, March 5, 1991.

STEVENS, JOHN — PHI.

Defense. Shoots left. 6'1", 195 lbs. Born, Completon, N.B., May 4, 1966.
(Philadelphia's 5th choice, 47th overall, in 1984 Entry Draft).

			Regular Season					Playoffs				
Season	**Club**	**Lea**	**GP**	**G**	**A**	**TP**	**PIM**	**GP**	**G**	**A**	**TP**	**PIM**
1983-84	Oshawa	OHL	70	1	10	11	71	7	0	1	1	6
1984-85	Oshawa	OHL	44	2	10	12	61	5	0	2	2	4
	Hershey	AHL	3	0	0	0	0	....	....	....	....	....
1985-86	Oshawa	OHL	65	1	7	8	146	6	0	2	2	14
	Kalamazoo	IHL	6	0	1	1	8	6	0	3	3	9
1986-87	**Philadelphia**	**NHL**	**6**	**0**	**2**	**2**	**14**	....	....	....	....	....
	Hershey	AHL	63	1	15	16	131	3	0	0	0	7
1987-88	**Philadelphia**	**NHL**	**3**	**0**	**0**	**0**	**0**	....	....	....	....	....
	Hershey	AHL	59	1	15	16	108	....	....	....	....	....
1988-89	Hershey	AHL	78	3	13	16	129	12	1	1	2	29
1989-90	Hershey	AHL	79	3	10	13	193	....	....	....	....	....
1990-91	**Hartford**	**NHL**	**14**	**0**	**1**	**1**	**11**	....	....	....	....	....
	Springfield	AHL	65	0	12	12	139	18	0	6	6	35
1991-92	**Hartford**	**NHL**	**21**	**0**	**4**	**4**	**19**	....	....	....	....	....
	Springfield	AHL	45	1	12	13	73	11	1	3	4	27
1992-93	Springfield	AHL	74	1	19	20	111	15	0	1	1	18
1993-94	**Hartford**	**NHL**	**9**	**0**	**3**	**3**	**4**	....	....	....	....	....
	Springfield	AHL	71	3	9	12	85	3	0	0	0	0
1994-95	Springfield	AHL	79	5	15	20	122	....	....	....	....	....
1995-96	Springfield	AHL	69	0	19	19	95	10	0	1	1	31
1996-97	Philadelphia	AHL	74	2	18	20	116	10	0	2	2	8
	NHL Totals		**53**	**0**	**10**	**10**	**48**	....	....	....	....	....

Signed as a free agent by **Hartford**, July 30, 1990. Signed as a free agent by **Philadelphia**, August 6, 1996.

STEVENS, KEVIN — L.A.

Left wing. Shoots left. 6'3", 217 lbs. Born, Brockton, MA, April 15, 1965.
(Los Angeles' 6th choice, 108th overall, in 1983 Entry Draft).

			Regular Season					Playoffs				
Season	**Club**	**Lea**	**GP**	**G**	**A**	**TP**	**PIM**	**GP**	**G**	**A**	**TP**	**PIM**
1983-84	Boston College	ECAC	37	6	14	20	36	....	....	....	....	....
1984-85	Boston College	H.E.	40	13	23	36	36	....	....	....	....	....
1985-86	Boston College	H.E.	42	17	27	44	56	....	....	....	....	....
1986-87ab	Boston College	H.E.	39	35	35	70	54	....	....	....	....	....
1987-88	U.S. National	....	44	22	23	45	52	....	....	....	....	....
	U.S. Olympic	....	5	1	3	4	2	....	....	....	....	....
	Pittsburgh	**NHL**	**16**	**5**	**2**	**7**	**8**	....	....	....	....	....
1988-89	**Pittsburgh**	**NHL**	**24**	**12**	**3**	**15**	**19**	**11**	**3**	**7**	**10**	**16**
	Muskegon	IHL	45	24	41	65	113	....	....	....	....	....
1989-90	**Pittsburgh**	**NHL**	**76**	**29**	**41**	**70**	**171**	....	....	....	....	....
1990-91c	**Pittsburgh**	**NHL**	**80**	**40**	**46**	**86**	**133**	**24**	***17**	**16**	**33**	**53 ♦**
1991-92d	**Pittsburgh**	**NHL**	**80**	**54**	**69**	**123**	**254**	**21**	**13**	**15**	**28**	**28 ♦**
1992-93c	**Pittsburgh**	**NHL**	**72**	**55**	**56**	**111**	**177**	**12**	**5**	**11**	**16**	**22**
1993-94	**Pittsburgh**	**NHL**	**83**	**41**	**47**	**88**	**155**	**6**	**1**	**1**	**2**	**10**
1994-95	**Pittsburgh**	**NHL**	**27**	**15**	**12**	**27**	**51**	**12**	**4**	**7**	**11**	**21**
1995-96	**Boston**	**NHL**	**41**	**10**	**13**	**23**	**49**	....	....	....	....	....
	Los Angeles	**NHL**	**20**	**3**	**10**	**13**	**22**	....	....	....	....	....
1996-97	**Los Angeles**	**NHL**	**69**	**14**	**20**	**34**	**96**	....	....	....	....	....
	NHL Totals		**588**	**278**	**319**	**597**	**1135**	**86**	**43**	**57**	**100**	**150**

a Hockey East First All-Star Team (1987)
b NCAA East Second All-American Team (1987)
c NHL Second All-Star Team (1991, 1993)
d NHL First All-Star Team (1992)

Played in NHL All-Star Game (1991-93)

Rights traded to **Pittsburgh** by **Los Angeles** for Anders Hakansson, September 9, 1983. Traded to **Boston** by **Pittsburgh** with Shawn McEachern for Glen Murray, Bryan Smolinski and Boston's third round choice (Boyd Kane) in 1996 Entry Draft, August 2, 1995. Traded to **Los Angeles** by **Boston** for Rick Tocchet, January 25, 1996.

STEVENS, SCOTT — N.J.

Defense. Shoots left. 6'2", 215 lbs. Born, Kitchener, Ont., April 1, 1964.
(Washington's 1st choice, 5th overall, in 1982 Entry Draft).

			Regular Season					Playoffs				
Season	Club	Lea	GP	G	A	TP	PIM	GP	G	A	TP	PIM
1980-81	Kitchener	OPJHL	39	7	33	40	82	....	....	....	....	....
	Kitchener	OHA	1	0	0	0	0	....	....	....	....	....
1981-82	Kitchener	OHL	68	6	36	42	158	15	1	10	11	71
1982-83a	**Washington**	**NHL**	**77**	**9**	**16**	**25**	**195**	**4**	**1**	**0**	**1**	**26**
1983-84	**Washington**	**NHL**	**78**	**13**	**32**	**45**	**201**	**8**	**1**	**8**	**9**	**21**
1984-85	**Washington**	**NHL**	**80**	**21**	**44**	**65**	**221**	**5**	**0**	**1**	**1**	**20**
1985-86	**Washington**	**NHL**	**73**	**15**	**38**	**53**	**165**	**9**	**3**	**8**	**11**	**12**
1986-87	**Washington**	**NHL**	**77**	**10**	**51**	**61**	**283**	**7**	**0**	**5**	**5**	**19**
1987-88b	**Washington**	**NHL**	**80**	**12**	**60**	**72**	**184**	**13**	**1**	**11**	**12**	**46**
1988-89	**Washington**	**NHL**	**80**	**7**	**61**	**68**	**225**	**6**	**1**	**4**	**5**	**11**
1989-90	**Washington**	**NHL**	**56**	**11**	**29**	**40**	**154**	**15**	**2**	**7**	**9**	**25**
1990-91	**St. Louis**	**NHL**	**78**	**5**	**44**	**49**	**150**	**13**	**0**	**3**	**3**	**36**
1991-92c	**New Jersey**	**NHL**	**68**	**17**	**42**	**59**	**124**	**7**	**2**	**1**	**3**	**29**
1992-93	**New Jersey**	**NHL**	**81**	**12**	**45**	**57**	**120**	**5**	**2**	**2**	**4**	**10**
1993-94bd	**New Jersey**	**NHL**	**83**	**18**	**60**	**78**	**112**	**20**	**2**	**9**	**11**	**42**
1994-95	**New Jersey**	**NHL**	**48**	**2**	**20**	**22**	**56**	**20**	**1**	**7**	**8**	**24 ♦**
1995-96	**New Jersey**	**NHL**	**82**	**5**	**23**	**28**	**100**	....	....	....	....	....
1996-97c	**New Jersey**	**NHL**	**79**	**5**	**19**	**24**	**70**	**10**	**0**	**4**	**4**	**2**
	NHL Totals		**1120**	**162**	**584**	**746**	**2360**	**142**	**16**	**70**	**86**	**323**

a NHL All-Rookie Team (1983)
b NHL First All-Star Team (1988, 1994)
c NHL Second All-Star Team (1992, 1997)
d Won Alka-Seltzer Plus Award (1994)

Played in NHL All-Star Game (1985, 1989, 1991-94, 1996, 1997)

Signed as a free agent by **St. Louis**, July 16, 1990. Acquired by **New Jersey** from **St. Louis** as compensation for St. Louis' signing of free agent Brendan Shanahan, September 3, 1991.

STEVENSON, JEREMY — ANA.

Left wing. Shoots left. 6'2", 220 lbs. Born, San Bernadino, CA, July 28, 1974.
(Winnipeg's 3rd choice, 60th overall, in 1992 Entry Draft).

			Regular Season					Playoffs				
Season	Club	Lea	GP	G	A	TP	PIM	GP	G	A	TP	PIM
1990-91	Cornwall	OHL	58	13	20	33	124	....	....	....	....	....
1991-92	Cornwall	OHL	63	15	23	38	176	6	3	1	4	4
1992-93	Newmarket	OHL	54	28	28	56	144	5	5	1	6	28
1993-94	Newmarket	OHL	9	2	4	6	27	....	....	....	....	....
	S.S. Marie	OHL	48	18	19	37	183	14	1	1	2	23
1994-95	Greensboro	ECHL	43	14	13	27	231	17	6	11	17	64
1995-96	**Anaheim**	**NHL**	**3**	**0**	**1**	**1**	**12**	....	....	....	....	....
	Baltimore	AHL	60	11	10	21	295	12	4	2	6	23
1996-97	**Anaheim**	**NHL**	**5**	**0**	**0**	**0**	**14**	....	....	....	....	....
	Baltimore	AHL	25	8	8	16	125	3	0	0	0	8
	NHL Totals		**8**	**0**	**1**	**1**	**26**	....	....	....	....	....

Re-entered NHL Entry Draft, **Anaheim's** 10th choice, 262nd overall in 1994 Entry Draft.

STEVENSON, TURNER — MTL.

Right wing. Shoots right. 6'3", 215 lbs. Born, Prince George, B.C., May 18, 1972.
(Montreal's 1st choice, 12th overall, in 1990 Entry Draft).

			Regular Season					Playoffs				
Season	Club	Lea	GP	G	A	TP	PIM	GP	G	A	TP	PIM
1989-90	Seattle	WHL	62	29	32	61	276	13	3	2	5	35
1990-91	Seattle	WHL	57	36	27	63	222	6	1	5	6	15
	Fredericton	AHL	....	....	....	....	....	4	0	0	0	5
1991-92ab	Seattle	WHL	58	20	32	52	264	15	9	3	12	55
1992-93	**Montreal**	**NHL**	**1**	**0**	**0**	**0**	**0**	....	....	....	....	....
	Fredericton	AHL	79	25	34	59	102	5	2	3	5	11
1993-94	**Montreal**	**NHL**	**2**	**0**	**0**	**0**	**2**	**3**	**0**	**2**	**2**	**0**
	Fredericton	AHL	66	19	28	47	155	....	....	....	....	....
1994-95	Fredericton	AHL	37	12	12	24	109	....	....	....	....	....
	Montreal	**NHL**	**41**	**6**	**1**	**7**	**86**	....	....	....	....	....
1995-96	**Montreal**	**NHL**	**80**	**9**	**16**	**25**	**167**	**6**	**0**	**1**	**1**	**2**
1996-97	**Montreal**	**NHL**	**65**	**8**	**13**	**21**	**97**	**5**	**1**	**1**	**2**	**2**
	NHL Totals		**189**	**23**	**30**	**53**	**352**	**14**	**1**	**4**	**5**	**4**

a WHL West First All-Star Team (1992)
b Memorial Cup All-Star Team (1992)

STEWART, CAM

Left wing. Shoots left. 5'11", 196 lbs. Born, Kitchener, Ont., September 18, 1971.
(Boston's 2nd choice, 63rd overall, in 1990 Entry Draft).

			Regular Season					Playoffs				
Season	Club	Lea	GP	G	A	TP	PIM	GP	G	A	TP	PIM
1990-91	U. of Michigan	CCHA	44	8	24	32	122	....	....	....	....	....
1991-92	U. of Michigan	CCHA	44	13	15	28	106	....	....	....	....	....
1992-93	U. of Michigan	CCHA	39	20	39	59	69	....	....	....	....	....
1993-94	**Boston**	**NHL**	**57**	**3**	**6**	**9**	**66**	**8**	**0**	**3**	**3**	**7**
	Providence	AHL	14	3	2	5	5	....	....	....	....	....
1994-95	**Boston**	**NHL**	**5**	**0**	**0**	**0**	**2**	....	....	....	....	....
	Providence	AHL	31	13	11	24	38	9	2	5	7	0
1995-96	**Boston**	**NHL**	**6**	**0**	**0**	**0**	**0**	**5**	**1**	**0**	**1**	**2**
	Providence	AHL	54	17	25	42	39	....	....	....	....	....
1996-97	**Boston**	**NHL**	**15**	**0**	**1**	**1**	**4**	....	....	....	....	....
	Providence	AHL	18	4	3	7	37	....	....	....	....	....
	Cincinnati	IHL	7	3	2	5	8	1	0	0	0	0
	NHL Totals		**83**	**3**	**7**	**10**	**72**	**13**	**1**	**3**	**4**	**9**

STEWART, JASON — NYI

Right wing. Shoots right. 5'11", 185 lbs. Born, St. Paul, MN, April 30, 1976.
(NY Islanders' 7th choice, 142nd overall, in 1994 Entry Draft).

			Regular Season					Playoffs				
Season	Club	Lea	GP	G	A	TP	PIM	GP	G	A	TP	PIM
1994-95	St. Cloud	WCHA	28	1	3	4	16	....	....	....	....	....
1995-96	St. Cloud	WCHA	36	4	7	11	40	....	....	....	....	....
1996-97	St. Cloud	WCHA	40	6	5	11	32	....	....	....	....	....

STILLMAN, CORY — CGY.

Center. Shoots left. 6', 180 lbs. Born, Peterborough, Ont., December 20, 1973.
(Calgary's 1st choice, 6th overall, in 1992 Entry Draft).

			Regular Season					Playoffs				
Season	Club	Lea	GP	G	A	TP	PIM	GP	G	A	TP	PIM
1990-91	Windsor	OHL	64	31	70	101	31	11	3	6	9	8
1991-92	Windsor	OHL	53	29	61	90	59	7	2	4	6	8
1992-93	Peterborough	OHL	61	25	55	80	55	18	3	8	11	18
	Cdn. National	....	1	0	0	0	0	....	....	....	....	....
1993-94	Saint John	AHL	79	35	48	83	52	7	2	4	6	16
1994-95	Saint John	AHL	63	28	53	81	70	5	0	2	2	2
	Calgary	**NHL**	**10**	**0**	**2**	**2**	**2**	....	....	....	....	....
1995-96	**Calgary**	**NHL**	**74**	**16**	**19**	**35**	**41**	**2**	**1**	**1**	**2**	**0**
1996-97	**Calgary**	**NHL**	**58**	**6**	**20**	**26**	**14**	....	....	....	....	....
	NHL Totals		**142**	**22**	**41**	**63**	**57**	**2**	**1**	**1**	**2**	**0**

STOJANOV, ALEK (STOY-uh-nahf) — PIT.

Right wing. Shoots left. 6'4", 225 lbs. Born, Windsor, Ont., April 25, 1973.
(Vancouver's 1st choice, 7th overall, in 1991 Entry Draft).

			Regular Season					Playoffs				
Season	Club	Lea	GP	G	A	TP	PIM	GP	G	A	TP	PIM
1989-90	Hamilton	OHL	37	4	4	8	91	....	....	....	....	....
1990-91	Hamilton	OHL	62	25	20	45	181	4	1	1	2	14
1991-92	Guelph	OHL	33	12	15	27	91	....	....	....	....	....
1992-93	Guelph	OHL	36	27	28	55	62	....	....	....	....	....
	Newmarket	OHL	14	9	7	16	26	7	1	3	4	26
	Hamilton	AHL	4	4	0	4	0	....	....	....	....	....
1993-94	Hamilton	AHL	4	0	1	1	5	....	....	....	....	....
1994-95	Syracuse	AHL	73	18	12	30	270	....	....	....	....	....
	Vancouver	**NHL**	**4**	**0**	**0**	**0**	**13**	**5**	**0**	**0**	**0**	**2**
1995-96	**Vancouver**	**NHL**	**58**	**0**	**1**	**1**	**123**	....	....	....	....	....
	Pittsburgh	**NHL**	**10**	**1**	**0**	**1**	**7**	**9**	**0**	**0**	**0**	**19**
1996-97	**Pittsburgh**	**NHL**	**35**	**1**	**4**	**5**	**79**	....	....	....	....	....
	NHL Totals		**107**	**2**	**5**	**7**	**222**	**14**	**0**	**0**	**0**	**21**

Traded to **Pittsburgh** by **Vancouver** for Markus Naslund, March 20, 1996.

STOREY, BEN — COL.

Defense. Shoots left. 6'2", 180 lbs. Born, Ottawa, Ont., June 22, 1977.
(Colorado's 4th choice, 98th overall, in 1996 Entry Draft).

			Regular Season					Playoffs				
Season	Club	Lea	GP	G	A	TP	PIM	GP	G	A	TP	PIM
1995-96	Harvard	ECAC	33	2	11	13	44	....	....	....	....	....
1996-97	Harvard	ECAC	25	0	6	6	40	....	....	....	....	....

STORM, JIM — NYI

Left wing. Shoots left. 6'2", 200 lbs. Born, Milford, MI, February 5, 1971.
(Hartford's 5th choice, 75th overall, in 1991 Entry Draft).

			Regular Season					Playoffs				
Season	Club	Lea	GP	G	A	TP	PIM	GP	G	A	TP	PIM
1990-91	Michigan Tech	WCHA	36	16	18	34	46	....	....	....	....	....
1991-92	Michigan Tech	WCHA	39	25	33	58	12	....	....	....	....	....
1992-93	Michigan Tech	WCHA	33	22	32	54	30	....	....	....	....	....
1993-94	**Hartford**	**NHL**	**68**	**6**	**10**	**16**	**27**	....	....	....	....	....
	U.S. National	....	28	8	12	20	14	....	....	....	....	....
1994-95	**Hartford**	**NHL**	**6**	**0**	**3**	**3**	**0**	....	....	....	....	....
	Springfield	AHL	33	11	11	22	29	....	....	....	....	....
1995-96	**Dallas**	**NHL**	**10**	**1**	**2**	**3**	**17**	....	....	....	....	....
	Michigan	IHL	60	18	33	51	27	10	4	8	12	2
1996-97	Michigan	IHL	75	25	24	49	27	4	0	1	1	4
	NHL Totals		**84**	**7**	**15**	**22**	**44**	....	....	....	....	....

Signed as a free agent by **Dallas**, September 13, 1995. Signed as a free agent by **NY Islanders**, July 21, 1997.

STRAKA, JOSEF (STRAH-kuh) — CGY.

Center. Shoots right. 5'11", 183 lbs. Born, Jindrichuv Hradec, Czech., February 11, 1978.
(Calgary's 7th choice, 122nd overall, in 1996 Entry Draft).

			Regular Season					Playoffs				
Season	Club	Lea	GP	G	A	TP	PIM	GP	G	A	TP	PIM
1995-96	Litvinov	Czech.	33	5	6	11	14	15	3	1	4	....
1996-97	Litvinov	Czech.	52	14	16	30	32	....	....	....	....	....

STRAKA, MARTIN (STRAH-kuh) — PIT.

Center. Shoots left. 5'10", 178 lbs. Born, Plzen, Czech., September 3, 1972.
(Pittsburgh's 1st choice, 19th overall, in 1992 Entry Draft).

			Regular Season					Playoffs				
Season	Club	Lea	GP	G	A	TP	PIM	GP	G	A	TP	PIM
1989-90	Skoda Plzen	Czech.	1	0	3	3	....	....	....	....	....	....
1990-91	Skoda Plzen	Czech.	47	7	24	31	6	....	....	....	....	....
1991-92	Skoda Plzen	Czech.	50	27	28	55	20	....	....	....	....	....
1992-93	**Pittsburgh**	**NHL**	**42**	**3**	**13**	**16**	**29**	**11**	**2**	**1**	**3**	**2**
	Cleveland	IHL	4	4	3	7	0	....	....	....	....	....
1993-94	**Pittsburgh**	**NHL**	**84**	**30**	**34**	**64**	**24**	**6**	**1**	**0**	**1**	**2**
1994-95	Interconex Plzen	Czech.	19	10	11	21	18	....	....	....	....	....
	Pittsburgh	**NHL**	**31**	**4**	**12**	**16**	**16**	....	....	....	....	....
	Ottawa	**NHL**	**6**	**1**	**1**	**2**	**0**	....	....	....	....	....
1995-96	**Ottawa**	**NHL**	**43**	**9**	**16**	**25**	**29**	....	....	....	....	....
	NY Islanders	**NHL**	**22**	**2**	**10**	**12**	**6**	....	....	....	....	....
	Florida	**NHL**	**12**	**2**	**4**	**6**	**6**	**13**	**2**	**2**	**4**	**2**
1996-97	**Florida**	**NHL**	**55**	**7**	**22**	**29**	**12**	**4**	**0**	**0**	**0**	**0**
	NHL Totals		**295**	**58**	**112**	**170**	**122**	**34**	**5**	**3**	**8**	**6**

Traded to **Ottawa** by **Pittsburgh** for Troy Murray and Norm Maciver, April 7, 1995. Traded to **NY Islanders** by **Ottawa** with Don Beaupre and Bryan Berard for Damian Rhodes and Wade Redden, January 23, 1996. Claimed on waivers by **Florida** from **NY Islanders**, March 15, 1996. Signed as a free agent by **Pittsburgh**, August 7, 1997.

STREIT, MARTIN (STRIGHT) — PHI.

Left wing. Shoots right. 6'2", 191 lbs. Born, Vyskov, Czech., February 2, 1977.
(Philadelphia's 7th choice, 178th overall, in 1995 Entry Draft).

			Regular Season					Playoffs				
Season	Club	Lea	GP	G	A	TP	PIM	GP	G	A	TP	PIM
1995-96	Olomouc	Czech. Jr.	19	10	6	16	....	....	....	....	....	....
	Olomouc	Czech.	10	0	0	0	....	....	....	....	....	....
1996-97	Olomouc	Czech.	18	1	2	3	14	....	....	....	....	....

STROM, PETER   (STRUHM)   MTL.

Left wing. Shoots right. 6', 178 lbs.   Born, Snotorp, Sweden, January 14, 1975.
(Montreal's 10th choice, 200th overall, in 1994 Entry Draft).

			Regular Season					Playoffs				
Season	Club	Lea	GP	G	A	TP	PIM	GP	G	A	TP	PIM
1993-94	V. Frolunda	Swe.	29	0	0	0	8	....	....	....	....	....
1994-95	V. Frolunda	Swe.	16	0	3	3	10	....	....	....	....	....
	V. Frolunda	Swe. 2	12	8	10	18	10	....	....	....	....	....
1995-96	V. Frolunda	Swe.	35	7	8	15	10	13	0	3	3	0
1996-97	V. Frolunda	Swe.	49	7	16	23	24	3	0	0	0	2

STRUDWICK, JASON   NYI

Defense. Shoots left. 6'3", 207 lbs.   Born, Edmonton, Alta., July 17, 1975.
(NY Islanders' 3rd choice, 63rd overall, in 1994 Entry Draft).

			Regular Season					Playoffs				
Season	Club	Lea	GP	G	A	TP	PIM	GP	G	A	TP	PIM
1993-94	Kamloops	WHL	61	6	8	14	118	19	0	4	4	24
1994-95	Kamloops	WHL	72	3	11	14	183	21	1	1	2	39
1995-96	**NY Islanders**	**NHL**	1	0	0	0	7	....	....	....	....	....
	Worcester	AHL	60	2	7	9	119	4	0	1	1	0
1996-97	Kentucky	AHL	80	1	9	10	198	4	0	0	0	0
	NHL Totals		1	0	0	0	7					

STUMPEL, JOZEF   (STUM-puhl)   BOS.

Center. Shoots right. 6'3", 210 lbs.   Born, Nitra, Czech., July 20, 1972.
(Boston's 2nd choice, 40th overall, in 1991 Entry Draft).

			Regular Season					Playoffs				
Season	Club	Lea	GP	G	A	TP	PIM	GP	G	A	TP	PIM
1989-90	Nitra	Czech. 2	38	12	11	23	....	....	....	....	....	....
1990-91	Nitra	Czech.	49	23	22	45	14	....	....	....	....	....
1991-92	Koln	Ger.	37	20	19	39	35	....	....	....	....	....
	Boston	**NHL**	4	1	0	1	0	....	....	....	....	....
1992-93	**Boston**	**NHL**	13	1	3	4	4	....	....	....	....	....
	Providence	AHL	56	31	61	92	26	6	4	4	8	0
1993-94	**Boston**	**NHL**	59	8	15	23	14	13	1	7	8	4
	Providence	AHL	17	5	12	17	4	....	....	....	....	....
1994-95	Koln	Ger.	25	16	23	39	18	....	....	....	....	....
	Boston	**NHL**	44	5	13	18	8	5	0	0	0	0
1995-96	**Boston**	**NHL**	76	18	36	54	14	5	1	2	3	0
1996-97	**Boston**	**NHL**	78	21	55	76	14	....	....	....	....	....
	NHL Totals		274	54	122	176	54	23	2	9	11	4

STURM, MARCO   (STURHM)   S.J.

Center. Shoots left. 5'11", 178 lbs.   Born, Dingolfing, Germany, September 8, 1978.
(San Jose's 2nd choice, 21st overall, in 1996 Entry Draft).

			Regular Season					Playoffs				
Season	Club	Lea	GP	G	A	TP	PIM	GP	G	A	TP	PIM
1995-96	Landshut	Ger.	47	12	20	32	50	11	1	3	4	18
1996-97	Landshut	Ger.	46	16	27	43	40	7	1	4	5	6

SUBBOTIN, DMITRI   (soo-BOH-tihn)   NYR

Left wing. Shoots left. 6'1", 183 lbs.   Born, Tomsk, USSR, October 20, 1977.
(NY Rangers' 3rd choice, 76th overall, in 1996 Entry Draft).

			Regular Season					Playoffs				
Season	Club	Lea	GP	G	A	TP	PIM	GP	G	A	TP	PIM
1993-94	Yekaterinburg	CIS	12	0	3	3	4	....	....	....	....	....
1994-95	Yekaterinburg	CIS	52	9	6	15	75	2	0	0	0	2
1995-96	CSKA	CIS	41	6	5	11	62	3	0	0	0	0
1996-97	CSKA	Rus.	17	5	3	8	22	2	0	0	0	2
	CSKA	Rus. 2	8	1	0	1	8	....	....	....	....	....

SUGDEN, BRANDON   (SUHG-duhn)   TOR.

Defense. Shoots right. 6'2", 178 lbs.   Born, Toronto, Ont., June 23, 1978.
(Toronto's 8th choice, 111th overall, in 1996 Entry Draft).

			Regular Season					Playoffs				
Season	Club	Lea	GP	G	A	TP	PIM	GP	G	A	TP	PIM
1995-96	London	OHL	55	2	7	9	*264	....	....	....	....	....
1996-97	London	OHL	31	4	10	14	158	....	....	....	....	....
	Sudbury	OHL	20	0	4	4	70	....	....	....	....	....

SULC, JAN   (SOOLTZ, YAN)   T.B.

Center. Shoots right. 6'3", 180 lbs.   Born, Litvinov, Czech., February 17, 1979.
(Tampa Bay's 5th choice, 109th overall, in 1997 Entry Draft).

			Regular Season					Playoffs				
Season	Club	Lea	GP	G	A	TP	PIM	GP	G	A	TP	PIM
1996-97	Litvinov	Czech. Jr.	37	14	17	31	....	....	....	....	....	....

SULLIVAN, JEFF   OTT.

Defense. Shoots left. 6'1", 185 lbs.   Born, St. John's, Nfld., September 18, 1978.
(Ottawa's 5th choice, 146th overall, in 1997 Entry Draft).

			Regular Season					Playoffs				
Season	Club	Lea	GP	G	A	TP	PIM	GP	G	A	TP	PIM
1995-96	East Hants	Jr. A	52	15	20	35	270	....	....	....	....	....
1996-97	Granby	QMJHL	25	4	8	12	47	....	....	....	....	....
	Halifax	QMJHL	45	4	23	27	200	18	0	5	5	96

SULLIVAN, MIKE   BOS.

Center. Shoots left. 6'2", 190 lbs.   Born, Marshfield, MA, February 27, 1968.
(NY Rangers' 4th choice, 69th overall, in 1987 Entry Draft).

			Regular Season					Playoffs				
Season	Club	Lea	GP	G	A	TP	PIM	GP	G	A	TP	PIM
1986-87	Boston U.	H.E.	37	13	18	31	18	....	....	....	....	....
1987-88	Boston U.	H.E.	30	18	22	40	30	....	....	....	....	....
1988-89	Boston U.	H.E.	36	19	17	36	30	....	....	....	....	....
1989-90	Boston U.	H.E.	38	11	20	31	26	....	....	....	....	....
1990-91	San Diego	IHL	74	12	23	35	27	....	....	....	....	....
1991-92	**San Jose**	**NHL**	64	8	11	19	15	....	....	....	....	....
	Kansas City	IHL	10	2	8	10	8	....	....	....	....	....
1992-93	**San Jose**	**NHL**	81	6	8	14	30	....	....	....	....	....
1993-94	**San Jose**	**NHL**	26	2	2	4	4	....	....	....	....	....
	Kansas City	IHL	6	3	3	6	0	....	....	....	....	....
	Calgary	**NHL**	19	2	3	5	6	7	1	1	2	8
	Saint John	AHL	5	2	0	2	4	....	....	....	....	....
1994-95	**Calgary**	**NHL**	38	4	7	11	14	7	3	5	8	2
1995-96	**Calgary**	**NHL**	81	9	12	21	24	4	0	0	0	0
1996-97	**Calgary**	**NHL**	67	5	6	11	10	....	....	....	....	....
	Adirondack	AHL	17	1	3	4	2	....	....	....	....	....
	NHL Totals		376	36	49	85	103	18	4	6	10	10

Rights traded to **Minnesota** by NY Rangers with Paul Jerrard, the rights to Bret Barnett, and Los Angeles' third round choice (previously acquired by NY Rangers — Minnesota selected Murray Garbutt) in 1989 Entry Draft for Brian Lawton, Igor Liba and the rights to Eric Bennett, October 11, 1988. Signed as a free agent by **San Jose**, August 9, 1991. Claimed on waivers by **Calgary** from **San Jose**, January 6, 1994. Traded to **Boston** by Calgary for Boston's seventh round choice in 1998 Entry Draft, June 21, 1997.

SULLIVAN, STEVE   TOR.

Center. Shoots right. 5'9", 155 lbs.   Born, Timmins, Ont., July 6, 1974.
(New Jersey's 10th choice, 233rd overall, in 1994 Entry Draft).

			Regular Season					Playoffs				
Season	Club	Lea	GP	G	A	TP	PIM	GP	G	A	TP	PIM
1992-93	S.S. Marie	OHL	62	36	27	63	44	16	3	8	11	18
1993-94	S.S. Marie	OHL	63	51	62	113	82	14	9	16	25	22
1994-95	Albany	AHL	75	31	50	81	124	14	4	7	11	10
1995-96	**New Jersey**	**NHL**	16	5	4	9	8	....	....	....	....	....
a	Albany	AHL	53	33	42	75	127	4	3	0	3	6
1996-97	**New Jersey**	**NHL**	33	8	14	22	14	....	....	....	....	....
	Albany	AHL	15	8	7	15	16	....	....	....	....	....
	Toronto	**NHL**	21	5	11	16	23	....	....	....	....	....
	NHL Totals		70	18	29	47	45					

a   AHL First All-Star Team (1996)

Traded to **Toronto** by **New Jersey** with Jason Smith and the rights to Alyn McCauley for Doug Gilmour, Dave Ellett and a conditional draft choice, February 25, 1997.

SUNDIN, MATS   (SUHN-deen)   TOR.

Center/Right wing. Shoots right. 6'4", 215 lbs.   Born, Bromma, Sweden, February 13, 1971.
(Quebec's 1st choice, 1st overall, in 1989 Entry Draft).

			Regular Season					Playoffs				
Season	Club	Lea	GP	G	A	TP	PIM	GP	G	A	TP	PIM
1988-89	Nacka	Swe. 2	25	10	8	18	18	....	....	....	....	....
1989-90	Djurgarden	Swe.	34	10	8	18	16	8	7	0	7	4
1990-91	**Quebec**	**NHL**	80	23	36	59	58	....	....	....	....	....
1991-92	**Quebec**	**NHL**	80	33	43	76	103	....	....	....	....	....
1992-93	**Quebec**	**NHL**	80	47	67	114	96	6	3	1	4	6
1993-94	**Quebec**	**NHL**	84	32	53	85	60	....	....	....	....	....
1994-95	Djurgarden	Swe.	12	7	2	9	14	....	....	....	....	....
	Toronto	**NHL**	47	23	24	47	14	7	5	4	9	4
1995-96	**Toronto**	**NHL**	76	33	50	83	46	6	3	1	4	4
1996-97	**Toronto**	**NHL**	82	41	53	94	59	....	....	....	....	....
	NHL Totals		529	232	326	558	436	19	11	6	17	14

Played in NHL All-Star Game (1996, 1997)

Traded to **Toronto** by **Quebec** with Garth Butcher, Todd Warriner and Philadelphia's first round choice (previously acquired by Quebec — later traded to Washington — Washington selected Nolan Baumgartner) in 1994 Entry Draft for Wendel Clark, Sylvain Lefebvre, Landon Wilson and Toronto's first round choice (Jeffrey Kealty) in 1994 Entry Draft, June 28, 1994.

SUNDIN, RONNIE   (SUHN-deen)   NYR

Defense. Shoots left. 6'1", 220 lbs.   Born, Ludvika, Sweden, October 3, 1970.
(NY Rangers' 8th choice, 237th overall, in 1996 Entry Draft).

			Regular Season					Playoffs				
Season	Club	Lea	GP	G	A	TP	PIM	GP	G	A	TP	PIM
1991-92	Mora	Swe. 2	35	2	5	7	18	2	0	0	0	0
1992-93	V. Frolunda	Swe.	17	2	3	5	12	....	....	....	....	....
1993-94	V. Frolunda	Swe.	38	0	9	9	42	4	0	0	0	0
1994-95	V. Frolunda	Swe.	11	3	4	7	6	....	....	....	....	....
1995-96	V. Frolunda	Swe.	40	3	6	9	18	13	1	4	5	10
1996-97	V. Frolunda	Swe.	47	3	14	17	24	3	1	0	1	2

SUNDSTROM, NIKLAS   (SUHN-struhm)   NYR

Left wing. Shoots left. 6', 185 lbs.   Born, Ornskoldsvik, Sweden, June 6, 1975.
(NY Rangers' 1st choice, 8th overall, in 1993 Entry Draft).

			Regular Season					Playoffs				
Season	Club	Lea	GP	G	A	TP	PIM	GP	G	A	TP	PIM
1991-92	MoDo	Swe.	9	1	3	4	0	....	....	....	....	....
1992-93	MoDo	Swe.	40	7	11	18	18	3	0	0	0	0
1993-94	MoDo	Swe.	37	7	12	19	28	11	4	3	7	2
1994-95	MoDo	Swe.	33	8	13	21	30	....	....	....	....	....
1995-96	**NY Rangers**	**NHL**	82	9	12	21	14	11	4	3	7	4
1996-97	**NY Rangers**	**NHL**	82	24	28	52	20	9	0	5	5	2
	NHL Totals		164	33	40	73	34	20	4	8	12	6

SUTER, CURTIS   (SOO-tuhr)   PHO.

Defense. Shoots left. 6'4", 220 lbs.   Born, Kerrobert, Sask., August 5, 1979.
(Phoenix's 3rd choice, 123rd overall, in 1997 Entry Draft).

			Regular Season					Playoffs				
Season	Club	Lea	GP	G	A	TP	PIM	GP	G	A	TP	PIM
1996-97	Spokane	WHL	56	2	2	4	133	2	0	0	0	0

SUTER, GARY (SOO-tuhr) CHI.

Defense. Shoots left. 6', 205 lbs. Born, Madison, WI, June 24, 1964.
(Calgary's 9th choice, 180th overall, in 1984 Entry Draft).

			Regular Season					Playoffs				
Season	Club	Lea	GP	G	A	TP	PIM	GP	G	A	TP	PIM
1983-84	U. Wisconsin	WCHA	35	4	18	22	32	....	....	....	....	....
1984-85	U. Wisconsin	WCHA	39	12	39	51	110	....	....	....	....	....
1985-86ab	**Calgary**	**NHL**	**80**	**18**	**50**	**68**	**141**	**10**	**2**	**8**	**10**	**8**
1986-87	**Calgary**	**NHL**	**68**	**9**	**40**	**49**	**70**	**6**	**0**	**3**	**3**	**10**
1987-88c	**Calgary**	**NHL**	**75**	**21**	**70**	**91**	**124**	**9**	**1**	**9**	**10**	**6**
1988-89	**Calgary**	**NHL**	**63**	**13**	**49**	**62**	**78**	**5**	**0**	**3**	**3**	**10 ♦**
1989-90	**Calgary**	**NHL**	**76**	**16**	**60**	**76**	**97**	**6**	**0**	**1**	**1**	**14**
1990-91	**Calgary**	**NHL**	**79**	**12**	**58**	**70**	**102**	**7**	**1**	**6**	**7**	**12**
1991-92	**Calgary**	**NHL**	**70**	**12**	**43**	**55**	**128**	....	....	....	....	....
1992-93	**Calgary**	**NHL**	**81**	**23**	**58**	**81**	**112**	**6**	**2**	**3**	**5**	**8**
1993-94	**Calgary**	**NHL**	**25**	**4**	**9**	**13**	**20**	....	....	....	....	....
	Chicago	**NHL**	**16**	**2**	**3**	**5**	**18**	**6**	**3**	**2**	**5**	**6**
1994-95	**Chicago**	**NHL**	**48**	**10**	**27**	**37**	**42**	**12**	**2**	**5**	**7**	**10**
1995-96	**Chicago**	**NHL**	**82**	**20**	**47**	**67**	**80**	**10**	**3**	**3**	**6**	**8**
1996-97	**Chicago**	**NHL**	**82**	**7**	**21**	**28**	**70**	**6**	**1**	**4**	**5**	**8**
	NHL Totals		**845**	**167**	**535**	**702**	**1082**	**83**	**15**	**47**	**62**	**100**

a Won Calder Memorial Trophy (1986)
b NHL All-Rookie Team (1986)
c NHL Second All-Star Team (1988)

Played in NHL All-Star Game (1986, 1988, 1989, 1991)

Traded to **Hartford** by **Calgary** with Paul Ranheim and Ted Drury for James Patrick, Zarley Zalapski and Michael Nylander, March 10, 1994. Traded to **Chicago** by **Hartford** with Randy Cunneyworth and Hartford's third round choice (later traded to Vancouver — Vancouver selected Larry Courville) in 1995 Entry Draft for Frantisek Kucera and Jocelyn Lemieux, March 11, 1994.

SUTTER, BRENT (SUH-tuhr) CHI.

Center. Shoots right. 6', 188 lbs. Born, Viking, Alta., June 10, 1962.
(NY Islanders' 1st choice, 17th overall, in 1980 Entry Draft).

			Regular Season					Playoffs				
Season	Club	Lea	GP	G	A	TP	PIM	GP	G	A	TP	PIM
1979-80	Red Deer	AJHL	59	70	101	171	....	....	....	....	....	....
	Lethbridge	WHL	5	1	0	1	2	....	....	....	....	....
1980-81	**NY Islanders**	**NHL**	**3**	**2**	**2**	**4**	**0**	....	....	....	....	....
	Lethbridge	WHL	68	54	54	108	116	9	6	4	10	51
1981-82	**NY Islanders**	**NHL**	**43**	**21**	**22**	**43**	**114**	**19**	**2**	**6**	**8**	**36 ♦**
	Lethbridge	WHL	34	46	33	79	162	....	....	....	....	....
1982-83	**NY Islanders**	**NHL**	**80**	**21**	**19**	**40**	**128**	**20**	**10**	**11**	**21**	**26 ♦**
1983-84	**NY Islanders**	**NHL**	**69**	**34**	**15**	**49**	**69**	**20**	**4**	**10**	**14**	**18**
1984-85	**NY Islanders**	**NHL**	**72**	**42**	**60**	**102**	**51**	**10**	**3**	**3**	**6**	**14**
1985-86	**NY Islanders**	**NHL**	**61**	**24**	**31**	**55**	**74**	**3**	**0**	**1**	**1**	**2**
1986-87	**NY Islanders**	**NHL**	**69**	**27**	**36**	**63**	**73**	**5**	**1**	**0**	**1**	**4**
1987-88	**NY Islanders**	**NHL**	**70**	**29**	**31**	**60**	**55**	**6**	**2**	**1**	**3**	**18**
1988-89	**NY Islanders**	**NHL**	**77**	**29**	**34**	**63**	**77**	....	....	....	....	....
1989-90	**NY Islanders**	**NHL**	**67**	**33**	**35**	**68**	**65**	**5**	**2**	**3**	**5**	**2**
1990-91	**NY Islanders**	**NHL**	**75**	**21**	**32**	**53**	**49**	....	....	....	....	....
1991-92	**NY Islanders**	**NHL**	**8**	**4**	**6**	**10**	**6**	....	....	....	....	....
	Chicago	**NHL**	**61**	**18**	**32**	**50**	**30**	**18**	**3**	**5**	**8**	**22**
1992-93	**Chicago**	**NHL**	**65**	**20**	**34**	**54**	**67**	**4**	**1**	**1**	**2**	**4**
1993-94	**Chicago**	**NHL**	**73**	**9**	**29**	**38**	**43**	**6**	**0**	**0**	**0**	**2**
1994-95	**Chicago**	**NHL**	**47**	**7**	**8**	**15**	**51**	**16**	**1**	**2**	**3**	**4**
1995-96	**Chicago**	**NHL**	**80**	**13**	**27**	**40**	**56**	**10**	**1**	**1**	**2**	**6**
1996-97	**Chicago**	**NHL**	**39**	**7**	**7**	**14**	**18**	**2**	**0**	**0**	**0**	**6**
	NHL Totals		**1059**	**361**	**460**	**821**	**1026**	**144**	**30**	**44**	**74**	**164**

Played in NHL All-Star Game (1985)

Traded to **Chicago** by **NY Islanders** with Brad Lauer for Adam Creighton and Steve Thomas, October 25, 1991.

SUTTER, RON (SUH-tuhr) S.J.

Center. Shoots right. 6', 180 lbs. Born, Viking, Alta., December 2, 1963.
(Philadelphia's 1st choice, 4th overall, in 1982 Entry Draft).

			Regular Season					Playoffs				
Season	Club	Lea	GP	G	A	TP	PIM	GP	G	A	TP	PIM
1980-81	Lethbridge	WHL	72	13	32	45	152	9	2	5	7	29
1981-82	Lethbridge	WHL	59	38	54	92	207	12	6	5	11	28
1982-83	**Philadelphia**	**NHL**	**10**	**1**	**1**	**2**	**9**	....	....	....	....	....
	Lethbridge	WHL	58	35	48	83	98	20	*22	*19	*41	45
1983-84	**Philadelphia**	**NHL**	**79**	**19**	**32**	**51**	**101**	**3**	**0**	**0**	**0**	**22**
1984-85	**Philadelphia**	**NHL**	**73**	**16**	**29**	**45**	**94**	**19**	**4**	**8**	**12**	**28**
1985-86	**Philadelphia**	**NHL**	**75**	**18**	**42**	**60**	**159**	**5**	**0**	**2**	**2**	**10**
1986-87	**Philadelphia**	**NHL**	**39**	**10**	**17**	**27**	**69**	**16**	**1**	**7**	**8**	**12**
1987-88	**Philadelphia**	**NHL**	**69**	**8**	**25**	**33**	**146**	**7**	**0**	**1**	**1**	**26**
1988-89	**Philadelphia**	**NHL**	**55**	**26**	**22**	**48**	**80**	**19**	**1**	**9**	**10**	**51**
1989-90	**Philadelphia**	**NHL**	**75**	**22**	**26**	**48**	**104**	....	....	....	....	....
1990-91	**Philadelphia**	**NHL**	**80**	**17**	**28**	**45**	**92**	....	....	....	....	....
1991-92	**St. Louis**	**NHL**	**68**	**19**	**27**	**46**	**91**	**6**	**1**	**3**	**4**	**8**
1992-93	**St. Louis**	**NHL**	**59**	**12**	**15**	**27**	**99**	....	....	....	....	....
1993-94	**St. Louis**	**NHL**	**36**	**6**	**12**	**18**	**46**	....	....	....	....	....
	Quebec	**NHL**	**37**	**9**	**13**	**22**	**44**	....	....	....	....	....
1994-95	**NY Islanders**	**NHL**	**27**	**1**	**4**	**5**	**21**	....	....	....	....	....
1995-96	Phoenix	IHL	25	6	13	19	28	....	....	....	....	....
	Boston	**NHL**	**18**	**5**	**7**	**12**	**24**	**5**	**0**	**0**	**0**	**8**
1996-97	**San Jose**	**NHL**	**78**	**5**	**7**	**12**	**65**	....	....	....	....	....
	NHL Totals		**878**	**194**	**307**	**501**	**1244**	**80**	**7**	**30**	**37**	**165**

Traded to **St. Louis** by **Philadelphia** with Murray Baron for Dan Quinn and Rod Brind'Amour, September 22, 1991. Traded to **Quebec** by **St. Louis** with Garth Butcher and Bob Bassen for Steve Duchesne and Denis Chasse, January 23, 1994. Traded to **NY Islanders** by **Quebec** with Quebec's first round choice (Brett Lindros) in 1994 Entry Draft for Uwe Krupp and NY Islanders' first round choice (Wade Belak) in 1994 Entry Draft, June 28, 1994. Signed as a free agent by **Boston**, March 9, 1996. Signed as a free agent by **San Jose**, October 12, 1996.

SUTTON, KEN N.J.

Defense. Shoots left. 6', 200 lbs. Born, Edmonton, Alta., November 5, 1969.
(Buffalo's 4th choice, 98th overall, in 1989 Entry Draft).

			Regular Season					Playoffs				
Season	Club	Lea	GP	G	A	TP	PIM	GP	G	A	TP	PIM
1988-89a	Saskatoon	WHL	71	22	31	53	104	8	2	5	7	12
1989-90	Rochester	AHL	57	5	14	19	83	11	1	6	7	15
1990-91	**Buffalo**	**NHL**	**15**	**3**	**6**	**9**	**13**	**6**	**0**	**1**	**1**	**2**
	Rochester	AHL	62	7	24	31	65	3	1	1	2	14
1991-92	**Buffalo**	**NHL**	**64**	**2**	**18**	**20**	**71**	**7**	**0**	**2**	**2**	**4**
1992-93	**Buffalo**	**NHL**	**63**	**8**	**14**	**22**	**30**	**8**	**3**	**1**	**4**	**8**
1993-94	**Buffalo**	**NHL**	**78**	**4**	**20**	**24**	**71**	**4**	**0**	**0**	**0**	**2**
1994-95	**Buffalo**	**NHL**	**12**	**1**	**2**	**3**	**30**	....	....	....	....	....
	Edmonton	**NHL**	**12**	**3**	**1**	**4**	**12**	....	....	....	....	....
1995-96	**Edmonton**	**NHL**	**32**	**0**	**8**	**8**	**39**	....	....	....	....	....
	St. Louis	**NHL**	**6**	**0**	**0**	**0**	**4**	**1**	**0**	**0**	**0**	**0**
	Worcester	AHL	32	4	16	20	60	4	0	2	2	21
1996-97	Manitoba	IHL	20	3	10	13	48	....	....	....	....	....
	Albany	AHL	61	6	13	19	79	16	4	8	12	55
	NHL Totals		**282**	**21**	**69**	**90**	**270**	**26**	**3**	**4**	**7**	**16**

a Memorial Cup All-Star Team (1989)

Traded to **Edmonton** by **Buffalo** for Scott Pearson, April 7, 1995. Traded to **St. Louis** by **Edmonton** with Igor Kravchuk for Jeff Norton and Donald Dufresne, January 4, 1996. Traded to **New Jersey** by **St. Louis** with St. Louis' second round choice in 1999 Entry Draft for Mike Peluso and Ricard Persson, November 26, 1996.

SUURSOO, TOIVO (SUH-uhr-soh-oh) DET.

Left wing. Shoots right. 6', 175 lbs. Born, Tallinn, USSR, November 23, 1975.
(Detroit's 10th choice, 283rd overall, in 1994 Entry Draft).

			Regular Season					Playoffs				
Season	Club	Lea	GP	G	A	TP	PIM	GP	G	A	TP	PIM
1993-94	Soviet Wings	CIS	33	3	0	3	8	....	....	....	....	....
1994-95	Soviet Wings	CIS	47	10	5	15	36	4	0	0	0	4
1995-96	Soviet Wings	CIS	47	6	4	10	36	....	....	....	....	....
1996-97	TPS	Fin.	50	11	8	19	64	12	2	3	5	4

SVARTVADET, PER (svahrt-VAH-deht) DAL.

Center. Shoots left. 6'1", 180 lbs. Born, Solleftea, Sweden, May 17, 1975.
(Dallas' 5th choice, 139th overall, in 1993 Entry Draft).

			Regular Season					Playoffs				
Season	Club	Lea	GP	G	A	TP	PIM	GP	G	A	TP	PIM
1992-93	MoDo	Swe.	2	0	0	0	0	....	....	....	....	....
1993-94	MoDo	Swe.	36	2	1	3	4	11	0	0	0	6
1994-95	MoDo	Swe.	40	6	9	15	31	....	....	....	....	....
1995-96	MoDo	Swe.	40	9	14	23	26	8	2	3	5	0
1996-97	MoDo	Swe.	50	7	18	25	38	....	....	....	....	....

SVEHLA, ROBERT (SHVEH-lah) FLA.

Defense. Shoots right. 6'1", 190 lbs. Born, Martin, Czech., January 2, 1969.
(Calgary's 4th choice, 78th overall, in 1992 Entry Draft).

			Regular Season					Playoffs				
Season	Club	Lea	GP	G	A	TP	PIM	GP	G	A	TP	PIM
1989-90	Dukla Trencin	Czech.	29	4	3	7	....	....	....	....	....	....
1990-91	Dukla Trencin	Czech.	52	16	9	25	62	....	....	....	....	....
1991-92	Dukla Trencin	Czech.	51	23	28	51	74	....	....	....	....	....
1992-93	Malmo	Swe.	40	19	10	29	86	6	0	1	1	14
1993-94	Malmo	Swe.	37	14	25	39	127	10	5	1	6	23
1994-95	Malmo	Swe.	32	11	13	24	83	9	2	3	5	6
	Florida	**NHL**	**5**	**1**	**1**	**2**	**0**	....	....	....	....	....
1995-96	**Florida**	**NHL**	**81**	**8**	**49**	**57**	**94**	**22**	**0**	**6**	**6**	**32**
1996-97	**Florida**	**NHL**	**82**	**13**	**32**	**45**	**86**	**5**	**1**	**4**	**5**	**4**
	NHL Totals		**168**	**22**	**82**	**104**	**180**	**27**	**1**	**10**	**11**	**36**

Played in NHL All-Star Game (1997)

Traded to **Florida** by **Calgary** with Magnus Svensson for Florida's third round choice (Dmitri Vlasenkov) in 1996 Entry Draft and fourth round choice (Ryan Ready) in 1997 Entry Draft, September 29, 1994.

SVEJKOVSKY, JAROSLAV (svehzh-KOHV-skee) WSH.

Right wing. Shoots right. 5'11", 185 lbs. Born, Plzen, Czech., October 1, 1976.
(Washington's 2nd choice, 17th overall, in 1996 Entry Draft).

			Regular Season					Playoffs				
Season	Club	Lea	GP	G	A	TP	PIM	GP	G	A	TP	PIM
1993-94	Plzen	Czech.	8	0	0	0	8	....	....	....	....	....
1994-95	Tabor	Czech. 2	11	6	7	13	....	....	....	....	....	....
1995-96a	Tri-City	WHL	70	58	43	101	118	11	10	9	19	8
1996-97	**Washington**	**NHL**	**19**	**7**	**3**	**10**	**4**	....	....	....	....	....
b	Portland	AHL	54	38	28	66	56	5	2	0	2	6
	NHL Totals		**19**	**7**	**3**	**10**	**4**	....	....	....	....	....

a WHL West Second All-Star Team (1996)
b Won Dudley "Red" Garrett Memorial Trophy (Top Rookie - AHL) (1997)

SVOBODA, PETR (svah-BOH-duh) PHI.

Defense. Shoots left. 6'1", 195 lbs. Born, Most, Czech., February 14, 1966.
(Montreal's 1st choice, 5th overall, in 1984 Entry Draft).

			Regular Season					Playoffs				
Season	Club	Lea	GP	G	A	TP	PIM	GP	G	A	TP	PIM
1982-83	Litvinov	Czech.	4	0	0	0	2	....	....	....	....	....
1983-84	Litvinov	Czech.	18	3	1	4	20	....	....	....	....	....
1984-85	**Montreal**	**NHL**	**73**	**4**	**27**	**31**	**65**	**7**	**1**	**1**	**2**	**12**
1985-86	**Montreal**	**NHL**	**73**	**1**	**18**	**19**	**93**	**8**	**0**	**0**	**0**	**21 ♦**
1986-87	**Montreal**	**NHL**	**70**	**5**	**17**	**22**	**63**	**14**	**0**	**5**	**5**	**10**
1987-88	**Montreal**	**NHL**	**69**	**7**	**22**	**29**	**149**	**10**	**0**	**5**	**5**	**12**
1988-89	**Montreal**	**NHL**	**71**	**8**	**37**	**45**	**147**	**21**	**1**	**11**	**12**	**16**
1989-90	**Montreal**	**NHL**	**60**	**5**	**31**	**36**	**98**	**10**	**0**	**5**	**5**	**7**
1990-91	**Montreal**	**NHL**	**60**	**4**	**22**	**26**	**52**	**2**	**0**	**1**	**1**	**2**
1991-92	**Montreal**	**NHL**	**58**	**5**	**16**	**21**	**94**	....	....	....	....	....
	Buffalo	**NHL**	**13**	**1**	**6**	**7**	**52**	**7**	**1**	**4**	**5**	**6**
1992-93	**Buffalo**	**NHL**	**40**	**2**	**24**	**26**	**59**	....	....	....	....	....
1993-94	**Buffalo**	**NHL**	**60**	**2**	**14**	**16**	**89**	**3**	**0**	**0**	**0**	**4**
1994-95	Litvinov	Czech.	8	2	0	2	50	....	....	....	....	....
	Buffalo	**NHL**	**26**	**0**	**5**	**5**	**60**	....	....	....	....	....
	Philadelphia	**NHL**	**11**	**0**	**3**	**3**	**10**	**14**	**0**	**4**	**4**	**8**
1995-96	**Philadelphia**	**NHL**	**73**	**1**	**28**	**29**	**105**	**12**	**0**	**6**	**6**	**22**
1996-97	**Philadelphia**	**NHL**	**67**	**2**	**12**	**14**	**94**	**16**	**1**	**2**	**3**	**16**
	NHL Totals		**824**	**47**	**282**	**329**	**1230**	**124**	**4**	**44**	**48**	**136**

Traded to **Buffalo** by **Montreal** for Kevin Haller, March 10, 1992. Traded to **Philadelphia** by **Buffalo** for Garry Galley, April 7, 1995.

SWANSON, BRIAN — NYR

Center. Shoots left. 5'10", 180 lbs. Born, Anchorage, AK, March 24, 1976.
(San Jose's 5th choice, 115th overall, in 1994 Entry Draft).

			Regular Season					Playoffs				
Season	Club	Lea	GP	G	A	TP	PIM	GP	G	A	TP	PIM
1995-96a	Colorado	WCHA	40	26	33	59	24	....	....	....	....	....
1996-97b	Colorado	WCHA	43	19	32	51	47	....	....	....	....	....

a WCHA Second All-Star Team (1996)
b WCHA First All-Star Team (1997)

Traded to **NY Rangers** by **San Jose** with Jayson More and a conditional choice in 1998 Entry Draft for Marty McSorley, August 20, 1996.

SWANSON, SCOTT — WSH.

Defense. Shoots left. 6'2", 190 lbs. Born, St. Paul, MN, February 15, 1975.
(Washington's 10th choice, 225th overall, in 1995 Entry Draft).

			Regular Season					Playoffs				
Season	Club	Lea	GP	G	A	TP	PIM	GP	G	A	TP	PIM
1995-96	Omaha	USHL	1	0	0	0	0	....	....	....	....	....
a	Colorado	WCHA	42	13	35	48	16	....	....	....	....	....
1996-97	Colorado	WCHA	44	4	16	20	22	....	....	....	....	....

a WCHA Second All-Star Team (1996)

SWEENEY, BOB

Center/Right wing. Shoots right. 6'3", 200 lbs. Born, Concord, MA, January 25, 1964.
(Boston's 6th choice, 123rd overall, in 1982 Entry Draft).

			Regular Season					Playoffs				
Season	Club	Lea	GP	G	A	TP	PIM	GP	G	A	TP	PIM
1982-83	Boston College	ECAC	30	17	11	28	10	....	....	....	....	....
1983-84	Boston College	ECAC	23	14	7	21	10	....	....	....	....	....
1984-85a	Boston College	ECAC	44	32	32	64	43	....	....	....	....	....
1985-86	Boston College	H.E.	41	15	24	39	52	....	....	....	....	....
1986-87	**Boston**	**NHL**	**14**	**2**	**4**	**6**	**21**	**3**	**0**	**0**	**0**	**0**
	Moncton	AHL	58	29	26	55	81	4	0	2	2	13
1987-88	**Boston**	**NHL**	**80**	**22**	**23**	**45**	**73**	**23**	**6**	**8**	**14**	**66**
1988-89	**Boston**	**NHL**	**75**	**14**	**14**	**28**	**99**	**10**	**2**	**4**	**6**	**19**
1989-90	**Boston**	**NHL**	**70**	**22**	**24**	**46**	**93**	**20**	**0**	**2**	**2**	**30**
1990-91	**Boston**	**NHL**	**80**	**15**	**33**	**48**	**115**	**17**	**4**	**2**	**6**	**45**
1991-92	**Boston**	**NHL**	**63**	**6**	**14**	**20**	**103**	**14**	**1**	**0**	**1**	**25**
	Maine	AHL	1	1	0	1	0	....	....	....	....	....
1992-93	**Buffalo**	**NHL**	**80**	**21**	**26**	**47**	**118**	**8**	**2**	**2**	**4**	**8**
1993-94	**Buffalo**	**NHL**	**60**	**11**	**14**	**25**	**94**	**1**	**0**	**0**	**0**	**0**
1994-95	**Buffalo**	**NHL**	**45**	**5**	**4**	**9**	**18**	**5**	**0**	**0**	**0**	**4**
1995-96	**NY Islanders**	**NHL**	**66**	**6**	**6**	**12**	**59**	....	....	....	....	....
	Calgary	**NHL**	**6**	**1**	**1**	**2**	**6**	**2**	**0**	**0**	**0**	**0**
1996-97	Quebec	IHL	69	10	21	31	120	9	2	0	2	8
	NHL Totals		**639**	**125**	**163**	**288**	**799**	**103**	**15**	**18**	**33**	**197**

a ECAC Second Team All-Star (1985)

Claimed on waivers by **Buffalo** from **Boston**, October 9, 1992. Claimed by **NY Islanders** from **Buffalo** in NHL Waiver Draft, October 2, 1995. Traded to **Calgary** by **NY Islanders** for Pat Conacher and Calgary's sixth round choice (later traded back to Calgary — Calgary selected Ilja Demidov) in 1997 Entry Draft, March 20, 1996.

SWEENEY, DON — BOS.

Defense. Shoots left. 5'10", 184 lbs. Born, St. Stephen, N.B., August 17, 1966.
(Boston's 8th choice, 166th overall, in 1984 Entry Draft).

			Regular Season					Playoffs				
Season	Club	Lea	GP	G	A	TP	PIM	GP	G	A	TP	PIM
1984-85	Harvard	ECAC	29	3	7	10	30	....	....	....	....	....
1985-86	Harvard	ECAC	31	4	5	9	12	....	....	....	....	....
1986-87	Harvard	ECAC	34	7	4	11	22	....	....	....	....	....
1987-88ab	Harvard	ECAC	30	6	23	29	37	....	....	....	....	....
	Maine	AHL	....	....	....	....	....	6	1	3	4	0
1988-89	**Boston**	**NHL**	**36**	**3**	**5**	**8**	**20**	....	....	....	....	....
	Maine	AHL	42	8	17	25	24	....	....	....	....	....
1989-90	**Boston**	**NHL**	**58**	**3**	**5**	**8**	**58**	**21**	**1**	**5**	**6**	**18**
	Maine	AHL	11	0	8	8	8	....	....	....	....	....
1990-91	**Boston**	**NHL**	**77**	**8**	**13**	**21**	**67**	**19**	**3**	**0**	**3**	**25**
1991-92	**Boston**	**NHL**	**75**	**3**	**11**	**14**	**74**	**15**	**0**	**0**	**0**	**10**
1992-93	**Boston**	**NHL**	**84**	**7**	**27**	**34**	**68**	**4**	**0**	**0**	**0**	**4**
1993-94	**Boston**	**NHL**	**75**	**6**	**15**	**21**	**50**	**12**	**2**	**1**	**3**	**4**
1994-95	**Boston**	**NHL**	**47**	**3**	**19**	**22**	**24**	**5**	**0**	**0**	**0**	**4**
1995-96	**Boston**	**NHL**	**77**	**4**	**24**	**28**	**42**	**5**	**0**	**2**	**2**	**6**
1996-97	**Boston**	**NHL**	**82**	**3**	**23**	**26**	**39**	....	....	....	....	....
	NHL Totals		**611**	**40**	**142**	**182**	**442**	**81**	**6**	**8**	**14**	**71**

a NCAA East All-American Team (1988)
b ECAC First All-Star Team (1988)

SWEENEY, TIM

Left wing. Shoots left. 5'11", 185 lbs. Born, Boston, MA, April 12, 1967.
(Calgary's 7th choice, 122nd overall, in 1985 Entry Draft).

			Regular Season					Playoffs				
Season	Club	Lea	GP	G	A	TP	PIM	GP	G	A	TP	PIM
1985-86	Boston College	H.E.	32	8	4	12	8	....	....	....	....	....
1986-87	Boston College	H.E.	38	31	18	49	28	....	....	....	....	....
1987-88	Boston College	H.E.	18	9	11	20	18	....	....	....	....	....
1988-89ab	Boston College	H.E.	39	29	44	73	26	....	....	....	....	....
1989-90c	Salt Lake	IHL	81	46	51	97	32	11	5	4	9	4
1990-91	**Calgary**	**NHL**	**42**	**7**	**9**	**16**	**8**	....	....	....	....	....
	Salt Lake	IHL	31	19	16	35	8	4	3	3	6	0
1991-92	U.S. National	....	21	9	11	20	10	....	....	....	....	....
	U.S. Olympic	....	8	3	4	7	6	....	....	....	....	....
	Calgary	**NHL**	**11**	**1**	**2**	**3**	**4**	....	....	....	....	....
1992-93	**Boston**	**NHL**	**14**	**1**	**7**	**8**	**6**	**3**	**0**	**0**	**0**	**0**
d	Providence	AHL	60	41	55	96	32	3	2	2	4	0
1993-94	**Anaheim**	**NHL**	**78**	**16**	**27**	**43**	**49**	....	....	....	....	....
1994-95	**Anaheim**	**NHL**	**13**	**1**	**1**	**2**	**2**	....	....	....	....	....
	Providence	AHL	2	2	2	4	0	13	8	*17	*25	6
1995-96	**Boston**	**NHL**	**41**	**8**	**8**	**16**	**14**	**1**	**0**	**0**	**0**	**2**
	Providence	AHL	34	17	22	39	12	....	....	....	....	....
1996-97	**Boston**	**NHL**	**36**	**10**	**11**	**21**	**14**	....	....	....	....	....
	Providence	AHL	23	11	22	33	6	....	....	....	....	....
	NHL Totals		**235**	**44**	**65**	**109**	**97**	**4**	**0**	**0**	**0**	**2**

a Hockey East First All-Star Team (1989)
b NCAA East Second All-American Team (1989)
c IHL Second All-Star Team (1990)
d AHL Second All-Star Team (1993)

Signed as a free agent by **Boston**, September 16, 1992. Claimed by **Anaheim** from **Boston** in Expansion Draft, June 24, 1993. Signed as a free agent by **Boston**, August 9, 1995.

SWINSON, WES — FLA.

Defense. Shoots left. 6'2", 183 lbs. Born, Peterborough, Ont., May 26, 1975.
(Hartford's 7th choice, 240th overall, in 1993 Entry Draft).

			Regular Season					Playoffs				
Season	Club	Lea	GP	G	A	TP	PIM	GP	G	A	TP	PIM
1994-95a	Kitchener	OHL	42	12	38	50	71	....	....	....	....	....
	Kingston	OHL	20	7	20	27	16	6	2	7	9	6
1995-96	Kingston	OHL	47	15	36	51	115	6	1	3	4	18
1996-97	Tallahasee	ECHL	17	3	9	12	28	3	0	1	1	4
	Carolina	AHL	10	0	0	0	10	....	....	....	....	....

a OHL Second All-Star Team (1995)

Signed as a free agent by **Florida**, March 19, 1996.

SYDOR, DARRYL (sih-DOHR) — DAL.

Defense. Shoots left. 6', 195 lbs. Born, Edmonton, Alta., May 13, 1972.
(Los Angeles' 1st choice, 7th overall, in 1990 Entry Draft).

			Regular Season					Playoffs				
Season	Club	Lea	GP	G	A	TP	PIM	GP	G	A	TP	PIM
1988-89	Kamloops	WHL	65	12	14	26	86	15	1	4	5	19
1989-90a	Kamloops	WHL	67	29	66	95	129	17	2	9	11	28
1990-91a	Kamloops	WHL	66	27	78	105	88	12	3	*22	25	10
1991-92	**Los Angeles**	**NHL**	**18**	**1**	**5**	**6**	**22**	....	....	....	....	....
a	Kamloops	WHL	29	9	39	48	43	17	3	15	18	18
1992-93	**Los Angeles**	**NHL**	**80**	**6**	**23**	**29**	**63**	**24**	**3**	**8**	**11**	**16**
1993-94	**Los Angeles**	**NHL**	**84**	**8**	**27**	**35**	**94**	....	....	....	....	....
1994-95	**Los Angeles**	**NHL**	**48**	**4**	**19**	**23**	**36**	....	....	....	....	....
1995-96	**Los Angeles**	**NHL**	**58**	**1**	**11**	**12**	**34**	....	....	....	....	....
	Dallas	**NHL**	**26**	**2**	**6**	**8**	**41**	....	....	....	....	....
1996-97	**Dallas**	**NHL**	**82**	**8**	**40**	**48**	**51**	**7**	**0**	**2**	**2**	**0**
	NHL Totals		**396**	**30**	**131**	**161**	**341**	**31**	**3**	**10**	**13**	**16**

a WHL West First All-Star Team (1990, 1991, 1992)

Traded to **Dallas** by **Los Angeles** with Los Angeles' fifth round choice (Ryan Christie) in 1996 Entry Draft for Shane Churla and Doug Zmolek, February 17, 1996.

SYKORA, MICHAL (SEE-koh-ra) — CHI.

Defense. Shoots left. 6'5", 225 lbs. Born, Pardubice, Czech., July 5, 1973.
(San Jose's 6th choice, 123rd overall, in 1992 Entry Draft).

			Regular Season					Playoffs				
Season	Club	Lea	GP	G	A	TP	PIM	GP	G	A	TP	PIM
1990-91	Pardubice	Czech.	2	0	0	0	....	....	....	....	....	....
1991-92	Tacoma	WHL	61	13	23	36	66	4	0	2	2	2
1992-93a	Tacoma	WHL	70	23	50	73	73	7	4	8	12	2
1993-94	**San Jose**	**NHL**	**22**	**1**	**4**	**5**	**14**	....	....	....	....	....
	Kansas City	IHL	47	5	11	16	30	....	....	....	....	....
1994-95	Kansas City	IHL	36	1	10	11	30	....	....	....	....	....
	San Jose	**NHL**	**16**	**0**	**4**	**4**	**10**	....	....	....	....	....
1995-96	**San Jose**	**NHL**	**79**	**4**	**16**	**20**	**54**	....	....	....	....	....
1996-97	**San Jose**	**NHL**	**35**	**2**	**5**	**7**	**59**	....	....	....	....	....
	Chicago	**NHL**	**28**	**1**	**9**	**10**	**10**	**1**	**0**	**0**	**0**	**0**
	NHL Totals		**180**	**8**	**38**	**46**	**147**	**1**	**0**	**0**	**0**	**0**

a WHL West First All-Star Team (1993)

Traded to **Chicago** by **San Jose** with Chris Terreri, Ulf Dahlen and a conditional choice in 1998 Entry Draft for Ed Belfour, January 25, 1997.

SYKORA, PETR (SEE-koh-ra) — N.J.

Center. Shoots left. 6', 190 lbs. Born, Plzen, Czech., November 19, 1976.
(New Jersey's 1st choice, 18th overall, in 1995 Entry Draft).

			Regular Season					Playoffs				
Season	Club	Lea	GP	G	A	TP	PIM	GP	G	A	TP	PIM
1992-93	Skoda Plzen	Czech.	19	12	5	17	....	....	....	....	....	....
1993-94	Skoda Plzen	Czech.	37	10	16	26	....	4	0	1	1	....
	Cleveland	IHL	13	4	5	9	8	....	....	....	....	....
1994-95	Detroit	IHL	29	12	17	29	16	....	....	....	....	....
1995-96a	**New Jersey**	**NHL**	**63**	**18**	**24**	**42**	**32**	....	....	....	....	....
	Albany	AHL	5	4	1	5	0	....	....	....	....	....
1996-97	**New Jersey**	**NHL**	**19**	**1**	**2**	**3**	**4**	**2**	**0**	**0**	**0**	**2**
	Albany	AHL	43	20	25	45	48	4	1	4	5	2
	NHL Totals		**82**	**19**	**26**	**45**	**36**	**2**	**0**	**0**	**0**	**2**

a NHL All-Rookie Team (1996)

SYKORA, PETR — DET.

Center. Shoots right. 6'2", 180 lbs. Born, Pardubice, Czech., December 21, 1978.
(Detroit's 2nd choice, 76th overall, in 1997 Entry Draft).

			Regular Season					Playoffs				
Season	Club	Lea	GP	G	A	TP	PIM	GP	G	A	TP	PIM
1995-96	Pardubice	Czech. Jr.	26	13	9	22	....	....	....	....	....	....
1996-97	Pardubice	Czech. Jr.	12	14	4	18	....	....	....	....	....	....
	Pardubice	Czech.	29	1	3	4	4	....	....	....	....	....

SYMES, BRAD — EDM.

Defense. Shoots left. 6'2", 210 lbs. Born, Edmonton, Alta., April 26, 1976.
(Edmonton's 5th choice, 60th overall, in 1994 Entry Draft).

			Regular Season					Playoffs				
Season	Club	Lea	GP	G	A	TP	PIM	GP	G	A	TP	PIM
1992-93	Portland	WHL	68	4	2	6	107	16	0	1	1	7
1993-94	Portland	WHL	71	7	15	22	170	7	0	0	0	21
1994-95	Portland	WHL	70	8	16	24	134	9	0	2	2	27
1995-96	Portland	WHL	62	9	12	21	118	7	1	2	3	14
1996-97	Wheeling	ECHL	51	6	17	23	63	1	0	0	0	0
	Hamilton	AHL	5	0	0	0	7	....	....	....	....	....

TALLAIRE, SEAN (tuh-LAIR, SHAWN)

Right wing. Shoots right. 5'10", 185 lbs. Born, Steinbach, MN, October 3, 1973.
(Vancouver's 7th choice, 202nd overall, in 1993 Entry Draft).

			Regular Season					Playoffs				
Season	Club	Lea	GP	G	A	TP	PIM	GP	G	A	TP	PIM
1992-93	Lake Superior	CCHA	43	26	26	52	26	....	....	....	....	....
1993-94	Lake Superior	CCHA	45	23	32	55	22	....	....	....	....	....
1994-95	Lake Superior	CCHA	41	21	29	50	38	....	....	....	....	....
1995-96ab	Lake Superior	CCHA	40	*32	18	50	36	....	....	....	....	....
1996-97	Manitoba	IHL	74	21	29	50	67	....	....	....	....	....

a CCHA First All-Star Team (1996)
b NCAA West Second All-American Team (1996)

TALLINDER, HENRIK (tah-LIHN-duhr) BUF.

Defense. Shoots left. 6'3", 194 lbs. Born, Stockholm, Sweden, January 10, 1979.
(Buffalo's 2nd choice, 48th overall, in 1997 Entry Draft).

			Regular Season					Playoffs				
Season	Club	Lea	GP	G	A	TP	PIM	GP	G	A	TP	PIM
1996-97	AIK	Swe. Jr.				UNAVAILABLE						
	AIK	Swe.	1	0	0	0	0	....	....	....	....	....

TAMER, CHRIS (TAY-muhr) PIT.

Defense. Shoots left. 6'2", 212 lbs. Born, Dearborn, MI, November 17, 1970.
(Pittsburgh's 3rd choice, 68th overall, in 1990 Entry Draft).

			Regular Season					Playoffs				
Season	Club	Lea	GP	G	A	TP	PIM	GP	G	A	TP	PIM
1989-90	U. of Michigan	CCHA	42	2	7	9	147	....	....	....	....	....
1990-91	U. of Michigan	CCHA	45	8	19	27	130	....	....	....	....	....
1991-92	U. of Michigan	CCHA	43	4	15	19	125	....	....	....	....	....
1992-93	U. of Michigan	CCHA	39	5	18	23	113	....	....	....	....	....
1993-94	**Pittsburgh**	**NHL**	**12**	**0**	**0**	**0**	**9**	**5**	**0**	**0**	**0**	**2**
	Cleveland	IHL	53	1	2	3	160	....	....	....	....	....
1994-95	Cleveland	IHL	48	4	10	14	204	....	....	....	....	....
	Pittsburgh	**NHL**	**36**	**2**	**0**	**2**	**82**	**4**	**0**	**0**	**0**	**18**
1995-96	**Pittsburgh**	**NHL**	**70**	**4**	**10**	**14**	**153**	**18**	**0**	**7**	**7**	**24**
1996-97	**Pittsburgh**	**NHL**	**45**	**2**	**4**	**6**	**131**	**4**	**0**	**0**	**0**	**4**
	NHL Totals		**163**	**8**	**14**	**22**	**375**	**31**	**0**	**7**	**7**	**48**

TANCILL, CHRIS (TAN-sihl) DAL.

Center. Shoots left. 5'10", 185 lbs. Born, Livonia, MI, February 7, 1968.
(Hartford's 1st choice, 15th overall, in 1989 Supplemental Draft).

			Regular Season					Playoffs				
Season	Club	Lea	GP	G	A	TP	PIM	GP	G	A	TP	PIM
1986-87	U. Wisconsin	WCHA	40	9	23	32	26	....	....	....	....	....
1987-88	U. Wisconsin	WCHA	44	13	14	27	48	....	....	....	....	....
1988-89	U. Wisconsin	WCHA	44	20	23	43	50	....	....	....	....	....
1989-90a	U. Wisconsin	WCHA	45	39	32	71	44	....	....	....	....	....
1990-91	**Hartford**	**NHL**	**9**	**1**	**1**	**2**	**4**	....	....	....	....	....
	Springfield	AHL	72	37	35	72	46	17	8	4	12	32
1991-92	**Hartford**	**NHL**	**10**	**0**	**0**	**0**	**2**	....	....	....	....	....
b	Springfield	AHL	17	12	7	19	20	....	....	....	....	....
	Detroit	**NHL**	**1**	**0**	**0**	**0**	**0**	....	....	....	....	....
	Adirondack	AHL	50	36	34	70	42	19	7	9	16	31
1992-93	**Detroit**	**NHL**	**4**	**1**	**0**	**1**	**2**	....	....	....	....	....
b	Adirondack	AHL	68	*59	43	102	62	10	7	7	14	10
1993-94	**Dallas**	**NHL**	**12**	**1**	**3**	**4**	**8**	....	....	....	....	....
	Kalamazoo	IHL	60	41	54	95	55	5	0	2	2	8
1994-95	Kansas City	IHL	64	31	28	59	40	....	....	....	....	....
	San Jose	**NHL**	**26**	**3**	**11**	**14**	**10**	**11**	**1**	**1**	**2**	**8**
1995-96	**San Jose**	**NHL**	**45**	**7**	**16**	**23**	**20**	....	....	....	....	....
	Kansas City	IHL	27	12	16	28	18	....	....	....	....	....
1996-97	**San Jose**	**NHL**	**25**	**4**	**0**	**4**	**8**	....	....	....	....	....
	Kentucky	AHL	42	19	26	45	31	4	2	0	2	2
	NHL Totals		**132**	**17**	**31**	**48**	**54**	**11**	**1**	**1**	**2**	**8**

a NCAA All-Tournament Team, Tournament MVP (1990)
b AHL First All-Star Team (1992, 1993)

Traded to **Detroit** by **Hartford** for Daniel Shank, December 18, 1991. Signed as a free agent by **Dallas**, August 28, 1993. Signed as a free agent by **San Jose**, August 24, 1994. Signed as a free agent by **Dallas**, August, 1997.

TARDIF, PATRICE (tahr-DIHF) BUF.

Center. Shoots left. 6'2", 202 lbs. Born, Thetford Mines, Que., October 30, 1970.
(St. Louis' 2nd choice, 54th overall, in 1990 Entry Draft).

			Regular Season					Playoffs				
Season	Club	Lea	GP	G	A	TP	PIM	GP	G	A	TP	PIM
1990-91	U. of Maine	H.E.	36	13	12	25	18	....	....	....	....	....
1991-92	U. of Maine	H.E.	31	18	20	38	14	....	....	....	....	....
1992-93	U. of Maine	H.E.	45	23	25	48	22	....	....	....	....	....
1993-94	U. of Maine	H.E.	34	18	15	33	42	....	....	....	....	....
	Peoria	IHL	11	4	4	8	21	4	2	0	2	4
1994-95	Peoria	IHL	53	27	18	45	83	....	....	....	....	....
	St. Louis	**NHL**	**27**	**3**	**10**	**13**	**29**	....	....	....	....	....
1995-96	**St. Louis**	**NHL**	**23**	**3**	**0**	**3**	**12**	....	....	....	....	....
	Worcester	AHL	30	13	13	26	69	....	....	....	....	....
	Los Angeles	**NHL**	**15**	**1**	**1**	**2**	**37**	....	....	....	....	....
1996-97	Phoenix	IHL	9	0	3	3	13	....	....	....	....	....
	Detroit	IHL	66	24	23	47	70	11	0	1	1	8
	NHL Totals		**65**	**7**	**11**	**18**	**78**	....	....	....	....	....

Traded to **Los Angeles** by **St. Louis** with Craig Johnson, Roman Vopat, St. Louis fifth round choice (Peter Hogan) in 1996 Entry Draft and first round choice (Matt Zultek) in 1997 Entry Draft for Wayne Gretzky, February 27, 1996. Signed as a free agent by **Buffalo**, August 11, 1997.

TARDIF, STEVE (tahr-DIHF) CHI.

Center. Shoots left. 6'1", 180 lbs. Born, St-Agnes, Que., March 29, 1977.
(Chicago's 8th choice, 175th overall, in 1995 Entry Draft).

			Regular Season					Playoffs				
Season	Club	Lea	GP	G	A	TP	PIM	GP	G	A	TP	PIM
1993-94	Drummondville	QMJHL	71	5	16	21	117	10	0	1	1	19
1994-95	Drummondville	QMJHL	64	10	33	43	313	4	1	2	3	9
1995-96	Drummondville	QMJHL	54	17	33	50	291	6	2	3	5	58
1996-97	Drummondville	QMJHL	65	24	40	64	377	6	1	5	6	62

TARNSTROM, DICK (TAHRN-struhm) NYI

Defense. Shoots left. 6', 180 lbs. Born, Sundbyberg, Sweden, January 20, 1975.
(NY Islanders' 12th choice, 272nd overall, in 1994 Entry Draft).

			Regular Season					Playoffs				
Season	Club	Lea	GP	G	A	TP	PIM	GP	G	A	TP	PIM
1992-93	AIK	Swe.	3	0	0	0	0	....	....	....	....	....
1993-94	AIK	Swe.	33	1	4	5	....	....	....	....	....	....
1994-95	AIK	Swe.	37	8	4	12	26	....	....	....	....	....
1995-96	AIK	Swe.	40	0	5	5	32	....	....	....	....	....
1996-97	AIK	Swe.	49	5	3	8	38	7	0	1	1	6

TARVAINEN, JUSSI (tahr-VIGH-nehn) EDM.

Center. Shoots right. 6'2", 185 lbs. Born, Lahti, Finland, May 31, 1976.
(Edmonton's 7th choice, 95th overall, in 1994 Entry Draft).

			Regular Season					Playoffs				
Season	Club	Lea	GP	G	A	TP	PIM	GP	G	A	TP	PIM
1993-94	KalPa	Fin.	42	3	4	7	20	....	....	....	....	....
1994-95	KalPa	Fin.	45	10	7	17	34	3	0	0	0	2
1995-96	KalPa	Fin.	47	8	11	19	50	....	....	....	....	....
1996-97	KalPa	Fin.	49	14	26	40	62	....	....	....	....	....

TAYLOR, ANDREW

Left wing. Shoots left. 6'1", 182 lbs. Born, Stratford, Ont., January 17, 1977.
(NY Islanders' 5th choice, 158th overall, in 1995 Entry Draft).

			Regular Season					Playoffs				
Season	Club	Lea	GP	G	A	TP	PIM	GP	G	A	TP	PIM
1993-94	Kitchener	OHL	62	1	8	9	60	5	0	1	1	6
1994-95	Kitchener	OHL	42	4	5	9	65	....	....	....	....	....
	Detroit	OHL	18	2	2	4	11	9	0	0	0	7
1995-96	Detroit	OHL	63	14	24	38	82	17	2	5	7	13
1996-97	Detroit	OHL	66	32	39	71	106	5	3	0	3	8

TAYLOR, CHRIS L.A.

Center. Shoots left. 6', 189 lbs. Born, Stratford, Ont., March 6, 1972.
(NY Islanders' 2nd choice, 27th overall, in 1990 Entry Draft).

			Regular Season					Playoffs				
Season	Club	Lea	GP	G	A	TP	PIM	GP	G	A	TP	PIM
1988-89	London	OHL	62	7	16	23	52	15	0	2	2	15
1989-90	London	OHL	66	45	60	105	60	6	3	2	5	6
1990-91	London	OHL	65	50	78	128	50	7	4	8	12	6
1991-92	London	OHL	66	48	74	122	57	10	8	16	24	9
1992-93	Capital Dist.	AHL	77	19	43	62	32	4	0	1	1	2
1993-94	Salt Lake	IHL	79	21	20	41	38	....	....	....	....	....
1994-95	Denver	IHL	78	38	48	86	47	14	7	6	13	10
	NY Islanders	**NHL**	**10**	**0**	**3**	**3**	**2**	....	....	....	....	....
1995-96	**NY Islanders**	**NHL**	**11**	**0**	**1**	**1**	**2**	....	....	....	....	....
	Utah	IHL	50	18	23	41	60	22	5	11	16	26
1996-97	**NY Islanders**	**NHL**	**1**	**0**	**0**	**0**	**0**	....	....	....	....	....
	Utah	IHL	71	27	40	67	24	7	1	2	3	0
	NHL Totals		**22**	**0**	**4**	**4**	**4**	....	....	....	....	....

Signed as a free agent by **Los Angeles**, July 25, 1997.

TAYLOR, TIM DET.

Center. Shoots left. 6'1", 185 lbs. Born, Stratford, Ont., February 6, 1969.
(Washington's 2nd choice, 36th overall, in 1988 Entry Draft).

			Regular Season					Playoffs				
Season	Club	Lea	GP	G	A	TP	PIM	GP	G	A	TP	PIM
1986-87	London	OHL	34	7	9	16	11	....	....	....	....	....
1987-88	London	OHL	64	46	50	96	66	12	9	9	18	26
1988-89	London	OHL	61	34	80	114	93	21	*21	25	*46	58
1989-90	Baltimore	AHL	79	31	36	67	124	9	2	2	4	13
1990-91	Baltimore	AHL	79	25	42	67	75	5	0	1	1	4
1991-92	Baltimore	AHL	65	9	18	27	131	....	....	....	....	....
1992-93	Baltimore	AHL	41	15	16	31	49	....	....	....	....	....
	Hamilton	AHL	36	15	22	37	37	....	....	....	....	....
1993-94	**Detroit**	**NHL**	**1**	**1**	**0**	**1**	**0**	....	....	....	....	....
ab	Adirondack	AHL	79	36	*81	*117	86	12	2	10	12	12
1994-95	**Detroit**	**NHL**	**22**	**0**	**4**	**4**	**16**	**6**	**0**	**1**	**1**	**12**
1995-96	**Detroit**	**NHL**	**72**	**11**	**14**	**25**	**39**	**18**	**0**	**4**	**4**	**4**
1996-97	**Detroit**	**NHL**	**44**	**3**	**4**	**7**	**52**	**2**	**0**	**0**	**0**	**0** ♦
	NHL Totals		**139**	**15**	**22**	**37**	**107**	**26**	**0**	**5**	**5**	**16**

a AHL First All-Star Team (1994)
b Won John B. Sollenberger Trophy (Top Scorer - AHL) (1994)

Traded to **Vancouver** by **Washington** for Eric Murano, January 29, 1993. Signed as a free agent by **Detroit**, July 28, 1993.

TERTYSHNY, DMITRY (tuhr-TIHSH-nee) PHI.

Defense. Shoots left. 6'1", 176 lbs. Born, Chelyabinsk, USSR, December 26, 1976.
(Philadelphia's 4th choice, 132nd overall, in 1995 Entry Draft).

			Regular Season					Playoffs				
Season	Club	Lea	GP	G	A	TP	PIM	GP	G	A	TP	PIM
1994-95	Chelyabinsk	CIS	38	0	3	3	14	1	0	0	0	0
1995-96	Chelyabinsk	CIS	44	1	5	6	50	....	....	....	....	....
1996-97	Chelyabinsk	Rus.	40	2	5	7	32	2	0	0	0	2

TETARENKO, JOEY (teh-tar-EHN-koh) FLA.

Defense. Shoots right. 6'1", 205 lbs. Born, Prince Albert, Sask., March 3, 1978.
(Florida's 4th choice, 82nd overall, in 1996 Entry Draft).

			Regular Season					Playoffs				
Season	Club	Lea	GP	G	A	TP	PIM	GP	G	A	TP	PIM
1994-95	Portland	WHL	59	0	1	1	134	9	0	0	0	8
1995-96	Portland	WHL	71	4	11	15	190	7	0	1	1	17
1996-97	Portland	WHL	68	8	18	26	182	2	0	0	0	2

TETRAULT, DANIEL (teh-TROH) MTL.

Defense. Shoots right. 6', 198 lbs. Born, St. Boniface, Man., September 4, 1979.
(Montreal's 4th choice, 91st overall, in 1997 Entry Draft).

			Regular Season					Playoffs				
Season	Club	Lea	GP	G	A	TP	PIM	GP	G	A	TP	PIM
1995-96	Brandon	WHL	72	6	13	19	91	19	1	1	2	25
1996-97	Brandon	WHL	64	5	24	29	136	6	0	0	0	14

TEZIKOV, ALEXEI (TEH-zih-kahf) BUF.

Defense. Shoots left. 6'1", 198 lbs. Born, Togliatti, USSR, June 22, 1978.
(Buffalo's 7th choice, 115th overall, in 1996 Entry Draft).

			Regular Season					Playoffs				
Season	Club	Lea	GP	G	A	TP	PIM	GP	G	A	TP	PIM
1995-96	Lada Togliatti	CIS	14	0	0	0	8	....	....	....	....	....
1996-97	Lada Togliatti	Rus.	7	0	0	0	4	....	....	....	....	....
	Torpedo Niz.	Rus.	5	0	2	2	2	....	....	....	....	....

THEORET, LUC (THEE-ohr-eht) BUF.

Defense. Shoots left. 6'1", 197 lbs. Born, Winnipeg, Man., July 30, 1979.
(Buffalo's 5th choice, 101st overall, in 1997 Entry Draft).

			Regular Season					Playoffs				
Season	Club	Lea	GP	G	A	TP	PIM	GP	G	A	TP	PIM
1995-96	Lethbridge	WHL	47	4	13	17	41	4	0	0	0	6
1996-97	Lethbridge	WHL	43	3	7	10	51	19	1	5	6	8

THERIAULT, JOEL (TEH-ree-oh) WSH.

Defense. Shoots right. 6'3", 201 lbs. Born, Montreal, Que., October 30, 1976.
(Washington's 5th choice, 95th overall, in 1995 Entry Draft).

			Regular Season					Playoffs				
Season	Club	Lea	GP	G	A	TP	PIM	GP	G	A	TP	PIM
1993-94	St-Jean	QMJHL	57	3	0	3	63	5	0	1	1	0
1994-95	St-Jean	QMJHL	18	2	7	9	94	....	....	....	....	....
	Beauport	QMJHL	51	2	5	7	293	18	3	6	9	*162
1995-96	Halifax	QMJHL	39	5	15	20	*358	....	....	....	....	....
	Drummondville	QMJHL	24	1	5	6	*215	6	0	2	2	45
1996-97	Hampton Rds.	ECHL	50	2	4	6	206	6	0	0	0	10

THERIEN, CHRIS (TEH-ree-ehn) **PHI.**

Defense. Shoots left. 6'5", 230 lbs. Born, Ottawa, Ont., December 14, 1971.
(Philadelphia's 7th choice, 47th overall, in 1990 Entry Draft).

			Regular Season					Playoffs				
Season	Club	Lea	GP	G	A	TP	PIM	GP	G	A	TP	PIM
1990-91	Providence	H.E.	36	4	18	22	36	....	....	....	....	....
1991-92	Providence	H.E.	36	16	25	41	38	....	....	....	....	....
1992-93a	Providence	H.E.	33	8	11	19	52	....	....	....	....	....
	Cdn. National	....	8	1	4	5	8	....	....	....	....	....
1993-94	Cdn. National	....	59	7	15	22	46	....	....	....	....	....
	Cdn. Olympic	....	4	0	0	0	4	....	....	....	....	....
	Hershey	AHL	6	0	0	0	2	....	....	....	....	....
1994-95	Hershey	AHL	34	3	13	16	27	....	....	....	....	....
b	**Philadelphia**	**NHL**	**48**	**3**	**10**	**13**	**38**	**15**	**0**	**0**	**0**	**10**
1995-96	**Philadelphia**	**NHL**	**82**	**6**	**17**	**23**	**89**	**12**	**0**	**0**	**0**	**18**
1996-97	**Philadelphia**	**NHL**	**71**	**2**	**22**	**24**	**64**	**19**	**1**	**6**	**7**	**6**
	NHL Totals		**201**	**11**	**49**	**60**	**191**	**46**	**1**	**6**	**7**	**34**

a Hockey East Second All-Star Team (1993)
b NHL/Upper Deck All-Rookie Team (1995)

THIBEAULT, DAVID (TEE-boh) **S.J.**

Left wing. Shoots left. 6'1", 190 lbs. Born, Trois-Rivieres, Que., May 12, 1978.
(San Jose's 8th choice, 217th overall, in 1996 Entry Draft).

			Regular Season					Playoffs				
Season	Club	Lea	GP	G	A	TP	PIM	GP	G	A	TP	PIM
1994-95	Drummondville	QMJHL	61	10	19	29	101	4	0	0	0	0
1995-96	Drummondville	QMJHL	57	23	35	58	99	6	0	3	3	12
1996-97	Victoriaville	QMJHL	58	39	38	77	37	6	3	3	6	4

THOMAS, STEVE **N.J.**

Left wing. Shoots left. 5'11", 190 lbs. Born, Stockport, England, July 15, 1963.

			Regular Season					Playoffs				
Season	Club	Lea	GP	G	A	TP	PIM	GP	G	A	TP	PIM
1983-84	Toronto	OHL	70	51	54	105	77	....	....	....	....	....
1984-85	**Toronto**	**NHL**	**18**	**1**	**1**	**2**	**2**	....	....	....	....	....
ab	St. Catharines	AHL	64	42	48	90	56	....	....	....	....	....
1985-86	**Toronto**	**NHL**	**65**	**20**	**37**	**57**	**36**	**10**	**6**	**8**	**14**	**9**
	St. Catharines	AHL	19	18	14	32	35	....	....	....	....	....
1986-87	**Toronto**	**NHL**	**78**	**35**	**27**	**62**	**114**	**13**	**2**	**3**	**5**	**13**
1987-88	**Chicago**	**NHL**	**30**	**13**	**13**	**26**	**40**	**3**	**1**	**2**	**3**	**6**
1988-89	**Chicago**	**NHL**	**45**	**21**	**19**	**40**	**69**	**12**	**3**	**5**	**8**	**10**
1989-90	**Chicago**	**NHL**	**76**	**40**	**30**	**70**	**91**	**20**	**7**	**6**	**13**	**33**
1990-91	**Chicago**	**NHL**	**69**	**19**	**35**	**54**	**129**	**6**	**1**	**2**	**3**	**15**
1991-92	**Chicago**	**NHL**	**11**	**2**	**6**	**8**	**26**	....	....	....	....	....
	NY Islanders	**NHL**	**71**	**28**	**42**	**70**	**71**	....	....	....	....	....
1992-93	**NY Islanders**	**NHL**	**79**	**37**	**50**	**87**	**111**	**18**	**9**	**8**	**17**	**37**
1993-94	**NY Islanders**	**NHL**	**78**	**42**	**33**	**75**	**139**	**4**	**1**	**0**	**1**	**8**
1994-95	**NY Islanders**	**NHL**	**47**	**11**	**15**	**26**	**60**	....	....	....	....	....
1995-96	**New Jersey**	**NHL**	**81**	**26**	**35**	**61**	**98**	....	....	....	....	....
1996-97	**New Jersey**	**NHL**	**57**	**15**	**19**	**34**	**46**	**10**	**1**	**1**	**2**	**18**
	NHL Totals		**805**	**310**	**362**	**672**	**1032**	**96**	**31**	**35**	**66**	**149**

a Won Dudley "Red" Garrett Memorial Trophy (Top Rookie - AHL) (1985)
b AHL First All-Star Team (1985)

Signed as a free agent by **Toronto,** May 12, 1984. Traded to **Chicago** by **Toronto** with Rick Vaive and Bob McGill for Al Secord and Ed Olczyk, September 3, 1987. Traded to **NY Islanders** by **Chicago** with Adam Creighton for Brent Sutter and Brad Lauer, October 25, 1991. Traded to **New Jersey** by **NY Islanders** for Claude Lemieux, October 3, 1995.

THOMPSON, BRENT **NYR**

Defense. Shoots left. 6'2", 200 lbs. Born, Calgary, Alta., January 9, 1971.
(Los Angeles' 1st choice, 39th overall, in 1989 Entry Draft).

			Regular Season					Playoffs				
Season	Club	Lea	GP	G	A	TP	PIM	GP	G	A	TP	PIM
1988-89	Medicine Hat	WHL	72	3	10	13	160	3	0	0	0	2
1989-90	Medicine Hat	WHL	68	10	35	45	167	3	0	1	1	14
1990-91a	Medicine Hat	WHL	51	5	40	45	87	12	1	7	8	16
	Phoenix	IHL	....	....	....	....	....	4	0	1	1	6
1991-92	**Los Angeles**	**NHL**	**27**	**0**	**5**	**5**	**89**	**4**	**0**	**0**	**0**	**4**
	Phoenix	IHL	42	4	13	17	139	....	....	....	....	....
1992-93	**Los Angeles**	**NHL**	**30**	**0**	**4**	**4**	**76**	....	....	....	....	....
	Phoenix	IHL	22	0	5	5	112	....	....	....	....	....
1993-94	**Los Angeles**	**NHL**	**24**	**1**	**0**	**1**	**81**	....	....	....	....	....
	Phoenix	IHL	26	1	11	12	118	....	....	....	....	....
1994-95	**Winnipeg**	**NHL**	**29**	**0**	**0**	**0**	**78**	....	....	....	....	....
1995-96	**Winnipeg**	**NHL**	**10**	**0**	**1**	**1**	**21**	....	....	....	....	....
	Springfield	AHL	58	2	10	12	203	10	1	4	5	*55
1996-97	**Phoenix**	**NHL**	**1**	**0**	**0**	**0**	**7**	....	....	....	....	....
	Springfield	AHL	64	2	15	17	215	17	0	2	2	31
	Phoenix	IHL	12	0	1	1	67	....	....	....	....	....
	NHL Totals		**121**	**1**	**10**	**11**	**352**	**4**	**0**	**0**	**0**	**4**

a WHL East Second All-Star Team (1991)

Traded to **Winnipeg** by **Los Angeles** with future considerations for the rights to Ruslan Batyrshin and Winnipeg's second round choice (Marian Cisar) in 1996 Entry Draft, August 8, 1994. Signed as a free agent by **NY Rangers,** August, 1997.

THOMPSON, MARK **T.B.**

Defense. Shoots right. 6'6", 205 lbs. Born, St. Albert, Alta., April 26, 1979.
(Tampa Bay's 4th choice, 108th overall, in 1997 Entry Draft).

			Regular Season					Playoffs				
Season	Club	Lea	GP	G	A	TP	PIM	GP	G	A	TP	PIM
1996-97	Regina	WHL	32	1	5	6	20	3	0	1	1	2

THOMPSON, ROCKY **CGY.**

Defense. Shoots right. 6'2", 192 lbs. Born, Calgary, Alta., August 8, 1977.
(Calgary's 3rd choice, 72nd overall, in 1995 Entry Draft).

			Regular Season					Playoffs				
Season	Club	Lea	GP	G	A	TP	PIM	GP	G	A	TP	PIM
1993-94	Medicine Hat	WHL	68	1	4	5	166	3	0	0	0	2
1994-95	Medicine Hat	WHL	63	1	6	7	220	5	0	0	0	17
1995-96	Medicine Hat	WHL	71	9	20	29	260	5	2	3	5	26
	Saint John	AHL	4	0	0	0	33	....	....	....	....	....
1996-97	Medicine Hat	WHL	47	6	9	15	170	....	....	....	....	....
	Swift Current	WHL	22	3	5	8	90	10	1	2	3	22

THORNTON, JOE **BOS.**

Center. Shoots left. 6'4", 198 lbs. Born, London, Ont., July 2, 1979.
(Boston's 1st choice, 1st overall, in 1997 Entry Draft).

			Regular Season					Playoffs				
Season	Club	Lea	GP	G	A	TP	PIM	GP	G	A	TP	PIM
1995-96a	S.S. Marie	OHL	66	30	46	76	53	4	1	1	2	11
1996-97b	S.S. Marie	OHL	59	41	81	122	123	11	11	8	19	24

a Canadian Major Junior Rookie of the Year (1996)
b OHL Second All-Star Team (1997)

THORNTON, SCOTT **MTL.**

Center. Shoots left. 6'3", 210 lbs. Born, London, Ont., January 9, 1971.
(Toronto's 1st choice, 3rd overall, in 1989 Entry Draft).

			Regular Season					Playoffs				
Season	Club	Lea	GP	G	A	TP	PIM	GP	G	A	TP	PIM
1987-88	Belleville	OHL	62	11	19	30	54	6	0	1	1	2
1988-89	Belleville	OHL	59	28	34	62	103	5	1	1	2	6
1989-90	Belleville	OHL	47	21	28	49	91	11	2	10	12	15
1990-91	**Toronto**	**NHL**	**33**	**1**	**3**	**4**	**30**	....	....	....	....	....
	Newmarket	AHL	5	1	0	1	4	....	....	....	....	....
	Belleville	OHL	3	2	1	3	2	6	0	7	7	14
1991-92	**Edmonton**	**NHL**	**15**	**0**	**1**	**1**	**43**	**1**	**0**	**0**	**0**	**0**
	Cape Breton	AHL	49	9	14	23	40	5	1	0	1	8
1992-93	**Edmonton**	**NHL**	**9**	**0**	**1**	**1**	**0**	....	....	....	....	....
	Cape Breton	AHL	58	23	27	50	102	16	1	2	3	35
1993-94	**Edmonton**	**NHL**	**61**	**4**	**7**	**11**	**104**	....	....	....	....	....
	Cape Breton	AHL	2	1	1	2	31	....	....	....	....	....
1994-95	**Edmonton**	**NHL**	**47**	**10**	**12**	**22**	**89**	....	....	....	....	....
1995-96	**Edmonton**	**NHL**	**77**	**9**	**9**	**18**	**149**	....	....	....	....	....
1996-97	**Montreal**	**NHL**	**73**	**10**	**10**	**20**	**128**	**5**	**1**	**0**	**1**	**2**
	NHL Totals		**315**	**34**	**43**	**77**	**543**	**6**	**1**	**0**	**1**	**2**

Traded to **Edmonton** by **Toronto** with Vincent Damphousse, Peter Ing, Luke Richardson, future considerations and cash for Grant Fuhr, Glenn Anderson and Craig Berube, September 19, 1991. Traded to **Montreal** by **Edmonton** for Andrei Kovalenko, September 6, 1996.

THURESSON, MARCUS (TOO-reh-suhn) **S.J.**

Center. Shoots left. 6'1", 180 lbs. Born, Jonkoping, Sweden, May 31, 1971.
(NY Islanders' 11th choice, 224th overall, in 1991 Entry Draft).

			Regular Season					Playoffs				
Season	Club	Lea	GP	G	A	TP	PIM	GP	G	A	TP	PIM
1989-90	Leksand	Swe.	28	8	7	15	18	3	2	0	2	12
1990-91	Leksand	Swe.	22	3	2	5	20	....	....	....	....	....
1991-92	Leksand	Swe.	21	2	4	6	22	....	....	....	....	....
1992-93	Leksand	Swe.	31	6	10	16	22	2	2	0	2	2
1993-94	Leksand	Swe.	32	3	4	7	28	4	0	1	1	0
1994-95	Leksand	Swe.	39	3	10	13	42	4	1	0	1	0
1995-96	HV 71	Swe.	32	7	6	13	28	....	....	....	....	....
1996-97	TPS	Fin.	44	14	25	39	44	12	1	1	2	8

Rights traded to **San Jose** by **NY Islanders** for Brian Mullen, August 24, 1992.

TIILIKAINEN, JUKKA (TEE-ee-lee-kigh-nehn, yoo-KUH) **L.A.**

Left wing. Shoots left. 6', 190 lbs. Born, Espoo, Finland, April 4, 1974.
(Los Angeles' 8th choice, 255th overall, in 1992 Entry Draft).

			Regular Season					Playoffs				
Season	Club	Lea	GP	G	A	TP	PIM	GP	G	A	TP	PIM
1991-92	Kiekko	Fin. 2	1	0	0	0	0	....	....	....	....	....
1992-93	Vantaa	Fin. 2	18	7	3	10	10	....	....	....	....	....
	Kiekko	Fin.	5	0	0	0	4	....	....	....	....	....
1993-94	Kiekko-Espoo	Fin.	33	2	4	6	12	....	....	....	....	....
1994-95	TPS	Fin.	38	5	4	9	8	11	1	0	1	8
1995-96	TPS	Fin.	38	6	13	19	28	10	0	2	2	2
1996-97	Lukko	Fin.	49	15	12	27	42	....	....	....	....	....

TIKKANEN, ESA (TEE-kuh-nehn, EHZ-uh)

Left wing. Shoots left. 6'1", 190 lbs. Born, Helsinki, Finland, January 25, 1965.
(Edmonton's 4th choice, 80th overall, in 1983 Entry Draft).

			Regular Season					Playoffs				
Season	Club	Lea	GP	G	A	TP	PIM	GP	G	A	TP	PIM
1981-82	Regina	SJHL	59	38	37	75	216	....	....	....	....	....
	Regina	WHL	2	0	0	0	0	....	....	....	....	....
1982-83	HIFK	Fin. Jr.	30	34	31	65	104	4	4	3	7	10
	HIFK	Fin.	....	....	....	....	....	1	0	0	0	2
1983-84	HIFK	Fin. Jr.	6	5	9	14	13	4	4	3	7	8
	HIFK	Fin.	36	19	11	30	30	2	0	0	0	0
1984-85	HIFK	Fin.	36	21	33	54	42	....	....	....	....	....
	Edmonton	**NHL**	....	....	....	....	....	**3**	**0**	**0**	**0**	**2** ♦
1985-86	**Edmonton**	**NHL**	**35**	**7**	**6**	**13**	**28**	**8**	**3**	**2**	**5**	**7**
	Nova Scotia	AHL	15	4	8	12	17	....	....	....	....	....
1986-87	**Edmonton**	**NHL**	**76**	**34**	**44**	**78**	**120**	**21**	**7**	**2**	**9**	**22** ♦
1987-88	**Edmonton**	**NHL**	**80**	**23**	**51**	**74**	**153**	**19**	**10**	**17**	**27**	**72** ♦
1988-89	**Edmonton**	**NHL**	**67**	**31**	**47**	**78**	**92**	**7**	**1**	**3**	**4**	**12**
1989-90	**Edmonton**	**NHL**	**79**	**30**	**33**	**63**	**161**	**22**	**13**	**11**	**24**	**26** ♦
1990-91	**Edmonton**	**NHL**	**79**	**27**	**42**	**69**	**85**	**18**	**12**	**8**	**20**	**24**
1991-92	**Edmonton**	**NHL**	**40**	**12**	**16**	**28**	**44**	**16**	**5**	**3**	**8**	**8**
1992-93	**Edmonton**	**NHL**	**66**	**14**	**19**	**33**	**76**	....	....	....	....	....
	NY Rangers	**NHL**	**15**	**2**	**5**	**7**	**18**	....	....	....	....	....
1993-94	**NY Rangers**	**NHL**	**83**	**22**	**32**	**54**	**114**	**23**	**4**	**4**	**8**	**34** ♦
1994-95	HIFK	Fin.	19	2	11	13	16	....	....	....	....	....
	St. Louis	**NHL**	**43**	**12**	**23**	**35**	**22**	**7**	**2**	**2**	**4**	**20**
1995-96	**St. Louis**	**NHL**	**11**	**1**	**4**	**5**	**18**	....	....	....	....	....
	New Jersey	**NHL**	**9**	**0**	**2**	**2**	**4**	....	....	....	....	....
	Vancouver	**NHL**	**38**	**13**	**24**	**37**	**14**	**6**	**3**	**2**	**5**	**2**
1996-97	**Vancouver**	**NHL**	**62**	**12**	**15**	**27**	**66**	....	....	....	....	....
	NY Rangers	**NHL**	**14**	**1**	**2**	**3**	**6**	**15**	**9**	**3**	**12**	**26**
	NHL Totals		**797**	**241**	**365**	**606**	**1021**	**165**	**69**	**57**	**126**	**255**

Traded to **NY Rangers** by **Edmonton** for Doug Weight, March 17, 1993. Traded to **St. Louis** by **NY Rangers** with Doug Lidster for Petr Nedved, July 24, 1994. Traded to **New Jersey** by **St. Louis** for New Jersey's third round choice in 1997 Entry Draft, November 1, 1995. Traded to **Vancouver** by **New Jersey** for Vancouver's second round choice (Wesley Mason) in 1996 Entry Draft, November 23, 1995. Traded to **NY Rangers** by **Vancouver** with Russ Courtnall for Sergei Nemchinov and Brian Noonan, March 8, 1997.

TIMANDER, MATTIAS (tih-MAHN-duhr, MA-tee-uhs) BOS.

Defense. Shoots left. 6'3", 210 lbs. Born, Solleftea, Sweden, April 16, 1974.
(Boston's 7th choice, 208th overall, in 1992 Entry Draft).

			Regular Season					Playoffs				
Season	**Club**	**Lea**	**GP**	**G**	**A**	**TP**	**PIM**	**GP**	**G**	**A**	**TP**	**PIM**
1992-93	MoDo	Swe.	1	0	0	0	0	....	....	....	....	....
1993-94	MoDo	Swe.	23	2	2	4	6	11	2	0	2	10
1994-95	MoDo	Swe.	39	8	9	17	24	....	....	....	....	....
1995-96	MoDo	Swe.	37	4	10	14	34	7	1	1	2	8
1996-97	**Boston**	**NHL**	**41**	**1**	**8**	**9**	**14**	....	....	....	....	....
	Providence	AHL	32	3	11	14	20	10	1	1	2	12
	NHL Totals		**41**	**1**	**8**	**9**	**14**	....	....	....	....	....

TIMKIN, ALEXEI (TIHM-kihn) DAL.

Right wing. Shoots left. 6'2", 194 lbs. Born, Kirov, USSR, April 21, 1979.
(Dallas' 6th choice, 160th overall, in 1997 Entry Draft).

			Regular Season					Playoffs				
Season	**Club**	**Lea**	**GP**	**G**	**A**	**TP**	**PIM**	**GP**	**G**	**A**	**TP**	**PIM**
1996-97	Yaroslavl 2	Rus. 3	47	16	6	22	54	....	....	....	....	....
	Yaroslavl	Rus.	3	0	1	1	0	....	....	....	....	....

TIMOFEEV, DENIS (teh-moh-FAY-ehf) BOS.

Defense. Shoots left. 6'6", 190 lbs. Born, Moscow, USSR, January 14, 1979.
(Boston's 7th choice, 135th overall, in 1997 Entry Draft).

			Regular Season					Playoffs				
Season	**Club**	**Lea**	**GP**	**G**	**A**	**TP**	**PIM**	**GP**	**G**	**A**	**TP**	**PIM**
1996-97	CSKA	Rus. Jr.	41	6	8	14	....	....	....	....	....	....
	CSKA 2	Rus. 3	11	0	0	0	2	....	....	....	....	....

TIMONEN, KIMMO (TIH-moh-nehn) L.A.

Defense. Shoots left. 5'9", 180 lbs. Born, Kuopio, Finland, March 18, 1975.
(Los Angeles' 11th choice, 250th overall, in 1993 Entry Draft).

			Regular Season					Playoffs				
Season	**Club**	**Lea**	**GP**	**G**	**A**	**TP**	**PIM**	**GP**	**G**	**A**	**TP**	**PIM**
1991-92	KalPa	Fin.	5	0	0	0	0	....	....	....	....	....
1992-93	KalPa	Fin.	33	0	2	2	4	....	....	....	....	....
1993-94	KalPa	Fin.	46	6	7	13	55	....	....	....	....	....
1994-95	TPS	Fin.	45	3	4	7	10	13	0	1	1	6
1995-96	TPS	Fin.	48	3	21	24	22	9	1	2	3	12
1996-97	TPS	Fin.	50	10	14	24	18	12	2	7	9	8

TINORDI, MARK (tih-NOHR-dee) WSH.

Defense. Shoots left. 6'4", 213 lbs. Born, Red Deer, Alta., May 9, 1966.

			Regular Season					Playoffs				
Season	**Club**	**Lea**	**GP**	**G**	**A**	**TP**	**PIM**	**GP**	**G**	**A**	**TP**	**PIM**
1982-83	Lethbridge	WHL	64	0	4	4	50	20	1	1	2	6
1983-84	Lethbridge	WHL	72	5	14	19	53	5	0	1	1	7
1984-85	Lethbridge	WHL	58	10	15	25	134	4	0	2	2	12
1985-86	Lethbridge	WHL	58	8	30	38	139	8	1	3	4	15
1986-87	Calgary	WHL	61	29	37	66	148	....	....	....	....	....
	New Haven	AHL	2	0	0	0	2	2	0	0	0	0
1987-88	**NY Rangers**	**NHL**	**24**	**1**	**2**	**3**	**50**	....	....	....	....	....
	Colorado	IHL	41	8	19	27	150	11	1	5	6	31
1988-89	**Minnesota**	**NHL**	**47**	**2**	**3**	**5**	**107**	**5**	**0**	**0**	**0**	**0**
	Kalamazoo	IHL	10	0	0	0	35	....	....	....	....	....
1989-90	**Minnesota**	**NHL**	**66**	**3**	**7**	**10**	**240**	**7**	**0**	**1**	**1**	**16**
1990-91	**Minnesota**	**NHL**	**69**	**5**	**27**	**32**	**189**	**23**	**5**	**6**	**11**	**78**
1991-92	**Minnesota**	**NHL**	**63**	**4**	**24**	**28**	**179**	**7**	**1**	**2**	**3**	**11**
1992-93	**Minnesota**	**NHL**	**69**	**15**	**27**	**42**	**157**	....	....	....	....	....
1993-94	**Dallas**	**NHL**	**61**	**6**	**18**	**24**	**143**	....	....	....	....	....
1994-95	**Washington**	**NHL**	**42**	**3**	**9**	**12**	**71**	**1**	**0**	**0**	**0**	**2**
1995-96	**Washington**	**NHL**	**71**	**3**	**10**	**13**	**113**	**6**	**0**	**0**	**0**	**16**
1996-97	**Washington**	**NHL**	**56**	**2**	**6**	**8**	**118**	....	....	....	....	....
	NHL Totals		**568**	**44**	**133**	**177**	**1367**	**49**	**6**	**9**	**15**	**123**

Played in NHL All-Star Game (1992)

Signed as a free agent by **NY Rangers**, January 4, 1987. Traded to **Minnesota** by **NY Rangers** with Paul Jerrard, the rights to Bret Barnett and Mike Sullivan, and Los Angeles' third round choice (previously acquired by NY Rangers — Minnesota selected Murray Garbutt) in 1989 Entry Draft for Brian Lawton, Igor Liba and the rights to Eric Bennett, October 11, 1988. Traded to **Washington** by **Dallas** with Rich Mrozik for Kevin Hatcher, January 18, 1995.

TIPLER, CURTIS T.B.

Right wing. Shoots right. 6'5", 205 lbs. Born, Wainwright, Alta., May 9, 1978.
(Tampa Bay's 2nd choice, 69th overall, in 1996 Entry Draft).

			Regular Season					Playoffs				
Season	**Club**	**Lea**	**GP**	**G**	**A**	**TP**	**PIM**	**GP**	**G**	**A**	**TP**	**PIM**
1995-96	Regina	WHL	69	27	38	65	65	11	3	1	4	4
1996-97	Regina	WHL	47	18	18	36	35	5	1	2	3	4

TITOV, GERMAN (TEE-tahf, GUHR-mihn) CGY.

Center. Shoots left. 6'1", 190 lbs. Born, Moscow, USSR, October 16, 1965.
(Calgary's 10th choice, 252nd overall, in 1993 Entry Draft).

			Regular Season					Playoffs				
Season	**Club**	**Lea**	**GP**	**G**	**A**	**TP**	**PIM**	**GP**	**G**	**A**	**TP**	**PIM**
1982-83	Khimik	USSR	16	0	2	2	4	....	....	....	....	....
1983-84						DID NOT PLAY						
1984-85						DID NOT PLAY						
1985-86						DID NOT PLAY						
1986-87	Khimik	USSR	23	1	0	1	10	....	....	....	....	....
1987-88	Khimik	USSR	39	6	5	11	10	....	....	....	....	....
1988-89	Khimik	USSR	44	10	3	13	24	....	....	....	....	....
1989-90	Khimik	USSR	44	6	14	20	19	....	....	....	....	....
1990-91	Khimik	USSR	45	13	11	24	28	....	....	....	....	....
1991-92	Khimik	CIS	42	18	13	31	35	....	....	....	....	....
1992-93	TPS	Fin.	47	25	19	44	49	12	5	12	17	10
1993-94	**Calgary**	**NHL**	**76**	**27**	**18**	**45**	**28**	**7**	**2**	**1**	**3**	**4**
1994-95	TPS	Fin.	14	6	6	12	20	....	....	....	....	....
	Calgary	**NHL**	**40**	**12**	**12**	**24**	**16**	**7**	**5**	**3**	**8**	**10**
1995-96	**Calgary**	**NHL**	**82**	**28**	**39**	**67**	**24**	**4**	**0**	**2**	**2**	**0**
1996-97	**Calgary**	**NHL**	**79**	**22**	**30**	**52**	**36**	....	....	....	....	....
	NHL Totals		**277**	**89**	**99**	**188**	**104**	**18**	**7**	**6**	**13**	**14**

TJALLDEN, MIKAEL (TEE-yahl-dehn) FLA.

Defense. Shoots left. 6'2", 194 lbs. Born, Ornskoldsvik, Sweden, February 16, 1975.
(Florida's 4th choice, 67th overall, in 1993 Entry Draft).

			Regular Season					Playoffs				
Season	**Club**	**Lea**	**GP**	**G**	**A**	**TP**	**PIM**	**GP**	**G**	**A**	**TP**	**PIM**
1993-94	Sundsvall-Timra	Swe. 2	24	4	5	9	32	....	....	....	....	....
1994-95	Sundsvall-Timra	Swe. 2	21	0	9	9	20	....	....	....	....	....
1995-96	Sundsvall-Timra	Swe. 2	29	1	4	5	38	5	1	1	2	16
1996-97	V. Frolunda	Swe.	32	0	2	2	14	3	0	1	1	4

TJARNQVIST, DANIEL (TUH-yahrn-kvihst) FLA.

Defense. Shoots left. 6'2", 178 lbs. Born, Umea, Sweden, October 14, 1976.
(Florida's 5th choice, 88th overall, in 1995 Entry Draft).

			Regular Season					Playoffs				
Season	**Club**	**Lea**	**GP**	**G**	**A**	**TP**	**PIM**	**GP**	**G**	**A**	**TP**	**PIM**
1994-95	Rogle	Swe.	18	0	1	1	2	....	....	....	....	....
	Rogle	Swe. 2	15	2	3	5	0	....	....	....	....	....
1995-96	Rogle	Swe.	22	1	7	8	6	....	....	....	....	....
1996-97	Jokerit	Fin.	44	3	8	11	4	9	0	3	3	4

TKACHUK, KEITH (kuh-CHUK) PHO.

Left wing. Shoots left. 6'2", 210 lbs. Born, Melrose, MA, March 28, 1972.
(Winnipeg's 1st choice, 19th overall, in 1990 Entry Draft).

			Regular Season					Playoffs				
Season	**Club**	**Lea**	**GP**	**G**	**A**	**TP**	**PIM**	**GP**	**G**	**A**	**TP**	**PIM**
1990-91	Boston U.	H.E.	36	17	23	40	70	....	....	....	....	....
1991-92	U.S. National	....	45	10	10	20	141	....	....	....	....	....
	U.S. Olympic	....	8	1	1	2	12	....	....	....	....	....
	Winnipeg	**NHL**	**17**	**3**	**5**	**8**	**28**	**7**	**3**	**0**	**3**	**30**
1992-93	**Winnipeg**	**NHL**	**83**	**28**	**23**	**51**	**201**	**6**	**4**	**0**	**4**	**14**
1993-94	**Winnipeg**	**NHL**	**84**	**41**	**40**	**81**	**255**	....	....	....	....	....
1994-95a	**Winnipeg**	**NHL**	**48**	**22**	**29**	**51**	**152**	....	....	....	....	....
1995-96	**Winnipeg**	**NHL**	**76**	**50**	**48**	**98**	**156**	**6**	**1**	**2**	**3**	**22**
1996-97	**Phoenix**	**NHL**	**81**	***52**	**34**	**86**	**228**	**7**	**6**	**0**	**6**	**7**
	NHL Totals		**389**	**196**	**179**	**375**	**1020**	**26**	**14**	**2**	**16**	**73**

a NHL Second All-Star Team (1995)

Played in NHL All-Star Game (1997)

TKACZUK, DANIEL (kuh-CHUK) CGY.

Center. Shoots left. 6', 190 lbs. Born, Toronto, Ont., June 10, 1979.
(Calgary's 1st choice, 6th overall, in 1997 Entry Draft).

			Regular Season					Playoffs				
Season	**Club**	**Lea**	**GP**	**G**	**A**	**TP**	**PIM**	**GP**	**G**	**A**	**TP**	**PIM**
1995-96	Barrie	OHL	61	22	39	61	38	7	1	2	3	8
1996-97	Barrie	OHL	62	45	48	93	49	9	7	2	9	2

TOCCHET, RICK (TAH-keht) PHO.

Right wing. Shoots right. 6', 205 lbs. Born, Scarborough, Ont., April 9, 1964.
(Philadelphia's 5th choice, 121st overall, in 1983 Entry Draft).

			Regular Season					Playoffs				
Season	**Club**	**Lea**	**GP**	**G**	**A**	**TP**	**PIM**	**GP**	**G**	**A**	**TP**	**PIM**
1981-82	S.S. Marie	OHL	59	7	15	22	184	11	1	1	2	28
1982-83	S.S. Marie	OHL	66	32	34	66	146	16	4	13	17	67
1983-84	S.S. Marie	OHL	64	44	64	108	209	16	*22	14	*36	41
1984-85	**Philadelphia**	**NHL**	**75**	**14**	**25**	**39**	**181**	**19**	**3**	**4**	**7**	**72**
1985-86	**Philadelphia**	**NHL**	**69**	**14**	**21**	**35**	**284**	**5**	**1**	**2**	**3**	**26**
1986-87	**Philadelphia**	**NHL**	**69**	**21**	**26**	**47**	**288**	**26**	**11**	**10**	**21**	**72**
1987-88	**Philadelphia**	**NHL**	**65**	**31**	**33**	**64**	**301**	**5**	**1**	**4**	**5**	**55**
1988-89	**Philadelphia**	**NHL**	**66**	**45**	**36**	**81**	**183**	**16**	**6**	**6**	**12**	**69**
1989-90	**Philadelphia**	**NHL**	**75**	**37**	**59**	**96**	**196**	....	....	....	....	....
1990-91	**Philadelphia**	**NHL**	**70**	**40**	**31**	**71**	**150**	....	....	....	....	....
1991-92	**Philadelphia**	**NHL**	**42**	**13**	**16**	**29**	**102**	....	....	....	....	....
	Pittsburgh	**NHL**	**19**	**14**	**16**	**30**	**49**	**14**	**6**	**13**	**19**	**24** ♦
1992-93	**Pittsburgh**	**NHL**	**80**	**48**	**61**	**109**	**252**	**12**	**7**	**6**	**13**	**24**
1993-94	**Pittsburgh**	**NHL**	**51**	**14**	**26**	**40**	**134**	**6**	**2**	**3**	**5**	**20**
1994-95	**Los Angeles**	**NHL**	**36**	**18**	**17**	**35**	**70**	....	....	....	....	....
1995-96	**Los Angeles**	**NHL**	**44**	**13**	**23**	**36**	**117**	....	....	....	....	....
	Boston	**NHL**	**27**	**16**	**8**	**24**	**64**	**5**	**4**	**0**	**4**	**21**
1996-97	**Boston**	**NHL**	**40**	**16**	**14**	**30**	**67**	....	....	....	....	....
	Washington	**NHL**	**13**	**5**	**5**	**10**	**31**	....	....	....	....	....
	NHL Totals		**841**	**359**	**417**	**776**	**2469**	**108**	**41**	**48**	**89**	**383**

Played in NHL All-Star Game (1989-91, 1993)

Traded to **Pittsburgh** by **Philadelphia** with Kjell Samuelsson, Ken Wregget and Philadelphia's third round choice (Dave Roche) in 1993 Entry Draft for Mark Recchi, Brian Benning and Los Angeles' first round choice (previously acquired by Pittsburgh — Philadelphia selected Jason Bowen) in 1992 Entry Draft, February 19, 1992 Traded to **Los Angeles** by **Pittsburgh** with Pittsburgh's second round choice (Pavel Rosa) in 1995 Entry Draft for Luc Robitaille, July 29, 1994. Traded to **Boston** by **Los Angeles** for Kevin Stevens, January 25, 1996. Traded to **Washington** by **Boston** with Bill Ranford and Adam Oates for Jim Carey, Anson Carter, Jason Allison, Washington's third round choice (Lee Goren) in 1997 Entry Draft and a conditional choice in 1998 Entry Draft, March 1, 1997. Signed as a free agent by **Phoenix**, July 23, 1997.

TODD, KEVIN — ANA.

Center. Shoots left. 5'10", 180 lbs. Born, Winnipeg, Man., May 4, 1968.
(New Jersey's 7th choice, 129th overall, in 1986 Entry Draft).

			Regular Season					Playoffs				
Season	Club	Lea	GP	G	A	TP	PIM	GP	G	A	TP	PIM
1985-86	Prince Albert	WHL	55	14	25	39	19	20	7	6	13	29
1986-87	Prince Albert	WHL	71	39	46	85	92	8	2	5	7	17
1987-88	Prince Albert	WHL	72	49	72	121	83	10	8	11	19	27
1988-89	**New Jersey**	**NHL**	**1**	**0**	**0**	**0**	**0**	....	....	....	....	....
	Utica	AHL	78	26	45	71	62	4	2	0	2	6
1989-90	Utica	AHL	71	18	36	54	72	5	2	4	6	2
1990-91	**New Jersey**	**NHL**	**1**	**0**	**0**	**0**	**0**	**1**	**0**	**0**	**0**	**6**
abc	Utica	AHL	75	37	*81	*118	75	....	....	....	....	....
1991-92d	**New Jersey**	**NHL**	**80**	**21**	**42**	**63**	**69**	**7**	**3**	**2**	**5**	**8**
1992-93	**New Jersey**	**NHL**	**30**	**5**	**5**	**10**	**16**	....	....	....	....	....
	Utica	AHL	2	2	1	3	0	....	....	....	....	....
	Edmonton	**NHL**	**25**	**4**	**9**	**13**	**10**	....	....	....	....	....
1993-94	**Chicago**	**NHL**	**35**	**5**	**6**	**11**	**16**	....	....	....	....	....
	Los Angeles	**NHL**	**12**	**3**	**8**	**11**	**8**	....	....	....	....	....
1994-95	**Los Angeles**	**NHL**	**33**	**3**	**8**	**11**	**12**	....	....	....	....	....
1995-96	**Los Angeles**	**NHL**	**74**	**16**	**27**	**43**	**38**	....	....	....	....	....
1996-97	**Anaheim**	**NHL**	**65**	**9**	**21**	**30**	**44**	**4**	**0**	**0**	**0**	**2**
	NHL Totals		**356**	**66**	**126**	**192**	**213**	**12**	**3**	**2**	**5**	**16**

a AHL First All-Star Team (1991)
b Won Les Cunningham Plaque (MVP - AHL) (1991)
c Won John B. Sollenberger Trophy (Leading Scorer - AHL) (1991)
d NHL/Upper Deck All-Rookie Team (1992)

Traded to **Edmonton** by **New Jersey** with Zdeno Ciger for Bernie Nicholls, January 13, 1993. Traded to **Chicago** by **Edmonton** for Adam Bennett, October 7, 1993. Traded to **Los Angeles** by **Chicago** for Los Angeles' fourth round choice (Steve McLaren) in 1994 Entry Draft, March 21, 1994. Signed as a free agent by **Pittsburgh**, July 10, 1996. Claimed on waivers by **Anaheim** from **Pittsburgh**, October 4, 1996.

TOMLINSON, DAVE

Center. Shoots left. 5'11", 180 lbs. Born, North Vancouver, B.C., May 8, 1969.
(Toronto's 1st choice, 3rd overall, in 1989 Supplemental Draft).

			Regular Season					Playoffs				
Season	Club	Lea	GP	G	A	TP	PIM	GP	G	A	TP	PIM
1987-88	Boston U.	H.E.	34	16	20	36	28	....	....	....	....	....
1988-89	Boston U.	H.E.	34	16	30	46	40	....	....	....	....	....
1989-90	Boston U.	H.E.	43	15	22	37	53	....	....	....	....	....
1990-91	Boston U.	H.E.	41	30	30	60	55	....	....	....	....	....
1991-92	**Toronto**	**NHL**	**3**	**0**	**0**	**0**	**2**	....	....	....	....	....
	St. John's	AHL	75	23	34	57	75	12	4	5	9	6
1992-93	**Toronto**	**NHL**	**3**	**0**	**0**	**0**	**2**	....	....	....	....	....
	St. John's	AHL	70	36	48	84	115	9	1	4	5	8
1993-94	**Winnipeg**	**NHL**	**31**	**1**	**3**	**4**	**24**	....	....	....	....	....
	Moncton	AHL	39	23	23	46	38	20	6	6	12	24
1994-95	Cincinnati	IHL	78	38	72	110	79	10	7	3	10	8
	Florida	**NHL**	**5**	**0**	**0**	**0**	**0**	....	....	....	....	....
1995-96a	Cincinnati	IHL	81	39	57	96	127	17	4	12	16	18
1996-97	Mannheim	Ger.	49	19	32	51	66	9	3	4	7	6
	NHL Totals		**42**	**1**	**3**	**4**	**28**	....	....	....	....	....

a IHL Second All-Star Team (1996)

Traded to **Florida** by **Toronto** for cash, July 30, 1993. Traded to **Winnipeg** by **Florida** for Jason Cirone, August 3, 1993. Signed as a free agent by **Florida**, June 23, 1994.

TOMS, JEFF — T.B.

Left wing. Shoots left. 6'5", 205 lbs. Born, Swift Current, Sask., June 4, 1974.
(New Jersey's 9th choice, 210th overall, in 1992 Entry Draft).

			Regular Season					Playoffs				
Season	Club	Lea	GP	G	A	TP	PIM	GP	G	A	TP	PIM
1991-92	S.S. Marie	OHL	36	9	5	14	0	16	0	1	1	2
1992-93	S.S. Marie	OHL	59	16	23	39	20	16	4	4	8	7
1993-94	S.S. Marie	OHL	64	52	45	97	19	14	11	4	15	2
1994-95	Atlanta	IHL	40	7	8	15	10	4	0	0	0	4
1995-96	**Tampa Bay**	**NHL**	**1**	**0**	**0**	**0**	**0**	....	....	....	....	....
	Atlanta	IHL	68	16	18	34	18	1	0	0	0	0
1996-97	**Tampa Bay**	**NHL**	**34**	**2**	**8**	**10**	**10**	....	....	....	....	....
	Adirondack	AHL	37	11	16	27	8	4	1	2	3	0
	NHL Totals		**35**	**2**	**8**	**10**	**10**	....	....	....	....	....

Traded to **Tampa Bay** by **New Jersey** for Vancouver's fourth round choice (previously acquired by Tampa Bay — later traded to Calgary — Calgary selected Ryan Duthie) in 1994 Entry Draft, May 31, 1994.

TOPOROWSKI, SHAYNE (toh-poh-ROW-skee)

Right wing. Shoots right. 6'2", 210 lbs. Born, Paddockwood, Sask., August 6, 1975.
(Los Angeles' 1st choice, 42nd overall, in 1993 Entry Draft).

			Regular Season					Playoffs				
Season	Club	Lea	GP	G	A	TP	PIM	GP	G	A	TP	PIM
1991-92	Prince Albert	WHL	6	2	0	2	2	7	2	1	3	6
1992-93	Prince Albert	WHL	72	25	32	57	235	....	....	....	....	....
1993-94	Prince Albert	WHL	68	37	45	82	183	....	....	....	....	....
1994-95	Prince Albert	WHL	72	36	38	74	151	15	10	8	18	25
1995-96	St. John's	AHL	72	11	26	37	216	4	1	1	2	4
1996-97	**Toronto**	**NHL**	**3**	**0**	**0**	**0**	**7**	....	....	....	....	....
	St. John's	AHL	72	20	17	37	210	11	3	2	5	16
	NHL Totals		**3**	**0**	**0**	**0**	**7**	....	....	....	....	....

Traded to **Toronto** by **Los Angeles** with Dixon Ward, Guy Leveque and Kelly Fairchild for Eric Lacroix, Chris Snell and Toronto's fourth round choice (Eric Belanger) in 1996 Entry Draft, October 3, 1994.

TORMANEN, ANTTI (TOHR-mah-nehn) — OTT.

Right wing. Shoots left. 6'1", 198 lbs. Born, Espoo, Finland, September 19, 1970.
(Ottawa's 10th choice, 274th overall, in 1994 Entry Draft).

			Regular Season					Playoffs				
Season	Club	Lea	GP	G	A	TP	PIM	GP	G	A	TP	PIM
1990-91	Jokerit	Fin.	44	12	9	21	70	....	....	....	....	....
1991-92	Jokerit	Fin.	40	18	11	29	18	....	....	....	....	....
1992-93	Jokerit	Fin.	21	2	0	2	8	....	....	....	....	....
1993-94	Jokerit	Fin.	46	20	18	38	46	....	....	....	....	....
1994-95	Jokerit	Fin.	50	19	13	32	32	11	7	3	11	20
1995-96	**Ottawa**	**NHL**	**50**	**7**	**8**	**15**	**28**	....	....	....	....	....
	P.E.I.	AHL	22	6	11	17	17	5	2	3	5	2
1996-97	Jokerit	Fin.	50	18	14	32	54	9	3	5	8	10
	NHL Totals		**50**	**7**	**8**	**15**	**28**	....	....	....	....	....

TRAVERSE, PATRICK — OTT.

Defense. Shoots left. 6'3", 190 lbs. Born, Montreal, Que., March 14, 1974.
(Ottawa's 3rd choice, 50th overall, in 1992 Entry Draft).

			Regular Season					Playoffs				
Season	Club	Lea	GP	G	A	TP	PIM	GP	G	A	TP	PIM
1991-92	Shawinigan	QMJHL	59	3	11	14	12	10	0	0	0	4
1992-93	St-Jean	QMJHL	68	6	30	36	24	4	0	1	1	2
	New Haven	AHL	2	0	0	0	2	....	....	....	....	....
1993-94	St-Jean	QMJHL	66	15	37	52	30	5	0	4	4	4
	P.E.I.	AHL	3	0	1	1	2	....	....	....	....	....
1994-95	P.E.I.	AHL	70	5	13	18	19	7	0	2	2	0
1995-96	**Ottawa**	**NHL**	**5**	**0**	**0**	**0**	**2**	....	....	....	....	....
	P.E.I.	AHL	55	4	21	25	32	5	1	2	3	2
1996-97	Worcester	AHL	24	0	4	4	23	....	....	....	....	....
	Grand Rapids	IHL	10	2	1	3	10	2	0	1	1	2
	NHL Totals		**5**	**0**	**0**	**0**	**2**	....	....	....	....	....

TREBIL, DANIEL (TREH-bihl) — ANA.

Defense. Shoots right. 6'3", 210 lbs. Born, Edina, MN, April 10, 1974.
(New Jersey's 7th choice, 138th overall, in 1992 Entry Draft).

			Regular Season					Playoffs				
Season	Club	Lea	GP	G	A	TP	PIM	GP	G	A	TP	PIM
1992-93	U. Minnesota	WCHA	36	2	11	13	16	....	....	....	....	....
1993-94	U. Minnesota	WCHA	42	1	21	22	24	....	....	....	....	....
1994-95	U. Minnesota	WCHA	44	10	33	43	10	....	....	....	....	....
1995-96ab	U. Minnesota	WCHA	42	11	35	46	36	....	....	....	....	....
1996-97	**Anaheim**	**NHL**	**29**	**3**	**3**	**6**	**23**	**9**	**0**	**1**	**1**	**6**
	Baltimore	AHL	49	4	20	24	38	....	....	....	....	....
	NHL Totals		**29**	**3**	**3**	**6**	**23**	**9**	**0**	**1**	**1**	**6**

a WCHA Second All-Star Team (1996)
b NCAA West Second All-American Team (1996)

Signed as a free agent by **Anaheim**, May 30, 1996.

TREMBLAY, DIDIER (TRAHM-blay) — ST.L.

Defense. Shoots left. 6'1", 190 lbs. Born, Laval, Que., May 4, 1979.
(St. Louis' 2nd choice, 86th overall, in 1997 Entry Draft).

			Regular Season					Playoffs				
Season	Club	Lea	GP	G	A	TP	PIM	GP	G	A	TP	PIM
1995-96	Halifax	QMJHL	56	4	10	14	80	6	0	3	3	4
1996-97	Halifax	QMJHL	68	11	26	37	79	12	1	3	4	6

TREMBLAY, MICHEL (TRAHM-blay) — MTL.

Left wing. Shoots left. 6'1", 185 lbs. Born, Alma, Que., April 8, 1978.
(Montreal's 10th choice, 233rd overall, in 1996 Entry Draft).

			Regular Season					Playoffs				
Season	Club	Lea	GP	G	A	TP	PIM	GP	G	A	TP	PIM
1995-96	Shawinigan	QMJHL	52	11	11	22	52	6	0	1	1	6
1996-97	Shawinigan	QMJHL	63	14	12	26	81	7	0	4	4	8

TREMBLAY, YANNICK (TRAHM-blay) — TOR.

Defense. Shoots right. 6'2", 185 lbs. Born, Pointe-aux-Trembles, Que., November 15, 1975.
(Toronto's 4th choice, 145th overall, in 1995 Entry Draft).

			Regular Season					Playoffs				
Season	Club	Lea	GP	G	A	TP	PIM	GP	G	A	TP	PIM
1994-95	Beauport	QMJHL	70	10	32	42	22	17	6	8	14	6
1995-96	Beauport	QMJHL	61	12	33	45	42	20	3	16	19	18
	St. John's	AHL	3	0	1	1	0	....	....	....	....	....
1996-97	**Toronto**	**NHL**	**5**	**0**	**0**	**0**	**0**	....	....	....	....	....
	St. John's	AHL	67	7	25	32	34	11	2	9	11	0
	NHL Totals		**5**	**0**	**0**	**0**	**0**	....	....	....	....	....

TREPANIER, PASCAL — COL.

Defense. Shoots right. 6', 205 lbs. Born, Gaspe, Que., April 9, 1973.

			Regular Season					Playoffs				
Season	Club	Lea	GP	G	A	TP	PIM	GP	G	A	TP	PIM
1991-92	Trois-Rivieres	QMJHL	53	4	18	22	125	15	3	5	8	21
1992-93	Sherbrooke	QMJHL	59	15	33	48	130	15	5	7	12	36
1993-94	Sherbrooke	QMJHL	48	16	41	57	67	12	1	8	9	14
1994-95	Dayton	ECHL	36	16	28	44	113	9	2	4	6	20
	Kalamazoo	IHL	14	1	2	3	47	....	....	....	....	....
	Cornwall	AHL	4	0	0	0	9	14	2	7	9	32
1995-96	Cornwall	AHL	70	13	20	33	142	8	1	2	3	24
1996-97a	Hershey	AHL	73	14	39	53	151	23	6	13	19	59

a AHL Second All-Star Team (1997)

Signed as a free agent by **Colorado**, August 30, 1995.

TRIPP, JOHN — CGY.

Right wing. Shoots right. 6'2", 207 lbs. Born, Kingston, Ont., May 4, 1977.
(Colorado's 3rd choice, 77th overall, in 1995 Entry Draft).

			Regular Season					Playoffs				
Season	Club	Lea	GP	G	A	TP	PIM	GP	G	A	TP	PIM
1994-95	Oshawa	OHL	58	6	11	17	53	7	0	1	1	4
1995-96	Oshawa	OHL	56	13	14	27	95	5	1	1	2	13
1996-97	Oshawa	OHL	59	28	20	48	126	18	*16	10	26	42

Re-entered NHL Entry Draft, **Calgary's** 3rd choice, 42nd overall, in 1997 Entry Draft.

TRNKA, PAVEL (tehrn-KAH) — ANA.

Defense. Shoots left. 6'3", 200 lbs. Born, Plzen, Czech., July 27, 1976.
(Anaheim's 5th choice, 106th overall, in 1994 Entry Draft).

			Regular Season					Playoffs				
Season	Club	Lea	GP	G	A	TP	PIM	GP	G	A	TP	PIM
1993-94	Skoda Plzen	Czech.	12	0	1	1	....	....	....	....	....	....
1994-95	Kladno	Czech.	28	0	5	5	24	....	....	....	....	....
	Interconex Plzen	Czech.	6	0	0	0	0	....	....	....	....	....
1995-96	Baltimore	AHL	69	2	6	8	44	6	0	0	0	2
1996-97	Baltimore	AHL	69	6	14	20	86	3	0	0	0	2

TSELIOS, NIKOS (TSEHL-ee-ohs) — CAR.

Defense. Shoots left. 6'4", 187 lbs. Born, Oak Park, IL, January 20, 1979.
(Carolina's 1st choice, 22nd overall, in 1997 Entry Draft).

			Regular Season					Playoffs				
Season	Club	Lea	GP	G	A	TP	PIM	GP	G	A	TP	PIM
1995-96	Chicago	Midget	27	5	8	13	40	....	....	....	....	....
1996-97	Belleville	OHL	64	9	37	46	61	6	1	1	2	2

TSULYGIN, NIKOLAI
(tsoo-LEE-gihn) **ANA.**

Defense. Shoots right. 6'3", 210 lbs.   Born, Ufa, USSR, May 29, 1975.
(Anaheim's 2nd choice, 30th overall, in 1993 Entry Draft).

			Regular Season					Playoffs				
Season	Club	Lea	GP	G	A	TP	PIM	GP	G	A	TP	PIM
1992-93	Ufa Salavat	CIS	42	5	4	9	21	2	0	0	0	0
1993-94	Ufa Salavat	CIS	43	0	14	14	24	5	0	1	1	0
1994-95	CSKA	CIS	16	0	0	0	12	....	....	....	....	....
	Ufa Salavat	CIS	13	2	2	4	10	7	0	0	0	4
1995-96	Baltimore	AHL	78	3	18	21	109	12	0	5	5	18
1996-97	**Anaheim**	**NHL**	**22**	**0**	**1**	**1**	**8**	....	....	....	....	....
	Baltimore	AHL	17	4	13	17	8	3	0	0	0	0
	Fort Wayne	IHL	5	2	1	3	8	....	....	....	....	....
	NHL Totals		**22**	**0**	**1**	**1**	**8**	....	....	....	....	....

TSYBUK, EVGENY
(tsee-BUHK) **DAL.**

Defense. Shoots left. 6', 183 lbs.   Born, Chebarkul, USSR, February 2, 1978.
(Dallas' 5th choice, 113th overall, in 1996 Entry Draft).

			Regular Season					Playoffs				
Season	Club	Lea	GP	G	A	TP	PIM	GP	G	A	TP	PIM
1995-96	Yaroslavl 2	CIS 2				UNAVAILABLE						
1996-97	Lethbridge	WHL	10	0	1	1	13	....	....	....	....	....

TSYPLAKOV, VLADIMIR
(tsih-plah-KAHF) **L.A.**

Left wing. Shoots left. 6', 185 lbs.   Born, Moscow, USSR, April 18, 1969.
(Los Angeles' 4th choice, 59th overall, in 1995 Entry Draft).

			Regular Season					Playoffs				
Season	Club	Lea	GP	G	A	TP	PIM	GP	G	A	TP	PIM
1988-89	Minsk D'amo	USSR	19	6	1	7	4	....	....	....	....	....
1989-90	Minsk D'amo	USSR	47	11	6	17	20	....	....	....	....	....
1990-91	Minsk D'amo	USSR	28	6	5	11	14	....	....	....	....	....
1991-92	Minsk D'amo	CIS	29	10	9	19	16	....	....	....	....	....
1992-93	Detroit	ColHL	44	33	43	76	20	6	5	4	9	6
	Indianapolis	IHL	11	6	7	13	4	5	1	1	2	2
1993-94	Fort Wayne	IHL	63	31	32	63	51	14	6	8	14	16
1994-95	Fort Wayne	IHL	79	38	40	78	39	4	2	4	6	2
1995-96	**Los Angeles**	**NHL**	**23**	**5**	**5**	**10**	**4**	....	....	....	....	....
	Las Vegas	IHL	9	5	6	11	4	....	....	....	....	....
1996-97	**Los Angeles**	**NHL**	**67**	**16**	**23**	**39**	**12**	....	....	....	....	....
	NHL Totals		**90**	**21**	**28**	**49**	**16**	....	....	....	....	....

TUCKER, DARCY
MTL.

Center. Shoots left. 5'10", 179 lbs.   Born, Castor, Alta., March 15, 1975.
(Montreal's 8th choice, 151st overall, in 1993 Entry Draft).

			Regular Season					Playoffs				
Season	Club	Lea	GP	G	A	TP	PIM	GP	G	A	TP	PIM
1991-92	Kamloops	WHL	26	3	10	13	32	9	0	1	1	16
1992-93	Kamloops	WHL	67	31	58	89	155	13	7	6	13	34
1993-94abcd	Kamloops	WHL	66	52	88	140	143	19	9	*18	*27	43
1994-95ac	Kamloops	WHL	64	64	73	137	94	21	*16	15	*31	19
1995-96	**Montreal**	**NHL**	**3**	**0**	**0**	**0**	**0**	....	....	....	....	....
e	Fredericton	AHL	74	29	64	93	174	7	7	3	10	14
1996-97	**Montreal**	**NHL**	**73**	**7**	**13**	**20**	**110**	**4**	**0**	**0**	**0**	**0**
	NHL Totals		**76**	**7**	**13**	**20**	**110**	**4**	**0**	**0**	**0**	**0**

a   WHL West First All-Star Team (1994, 1995)
b   Canadian Major Junior First All-Star Team (1994)
c   Memorial Cup All-Star Team (1994, 1995)
d   Won Stafford Smythe Memorial Trophy (Memorial Cup Tournament MVP) (1994)
e   Won Dudley "Red" Garrett Memorial Trophy (Top Rookie - AHL) (1996)

TUOHY, JOHN
(TOO-ee) **WSH.**

Defense. Shoots left. 6'2", 190 lbs.   Born, Baldwin, NY, February 2, 1976.
(Washington's 9th choice, 223rd overall, in 1994 Entry Draft).

			Regular Season					Playoffs				
Season	Club	Lea	GP	G	A	TP	PIM	GP	G	A	TP	PIM
1994-95	Providence	H.E.	16	1	1	2	18	....	....	....	....	....
1995-96	Providence	H.E.	32	0	6	6	28	....	....	....	....	....
1996-97	Providence	H.E.	22	2	1	3	33	....	....	....	....	....

TUOMAINEN, MARKO
(TOO-oh-migh-nehn) **EDM.**

Right wing. Shoots right. 6'3", 203 lbs.   Born, Kuopio, Finland, April 25, 1972.
(Edmonton's 10th choice, 205th overall, in 1992 Entry Draft).

			Regular Season					Playoffs				
Season	Club	Lea	GP	G	A	TP	PIM	GP	G	A	TP	PIM
1989-90	KalPa	Fin.	5	0	0	0	0	....	....	....	....	....
1990-91	KalPa	Fin.	30	2	1	3	2	8	0	0	0	6
1991-92	Clarkson	ECAC	28	11	12	23	32	....	....	....	....	....
1992-93a	Clarkson	ECAC	35	25	30	55	26	....	....	....	....	....
1993-94	Clarkson	ECAC	34	23	29	52	60	....	....	....	....	....
1994-95ab	Clarkson	ECAC	37	23	38	61	34	....	....	....	....	....
	Edmonton	**NHL**	**4**	**0**	**0**	**0**	**0**	....	....	....	....	....
1995-96	Cape Breton	AHL	58	25	35	60	71	....	....	....	....	....
1996-97	Hamilton	AHL	79	31	21	52	130	22	7	5	12	4
	NHL Totals		**4**	**0**	**0**	**0**	**0**	....	....	....	....	....

a   ECAC First All-Star Team (1993, 1995)
b   NCAA East Second All-American Team (1995)

TURCOTTE, DARREN
ST.L.

Center. Shoots left. 6', 178 lbs.   Born, Boston, MA, March 2, 1968.
(NY Rangers' 6th choice, 114th overall, in 1986 Entry Draft).

			Regular Season					Playoffs				
Season	Club	Lea	GP	G	A	TP	PIM	GP	G	A	TP	PIM
1984-85	North Bay	OHL	62	33	32	65	28	8	0	2	2	0
1985-86	North Bay	OHL	62	35	37	72	35	10	3	4	7	8
1986-87	North Bay	OHL	55	30	48	78	20	18	12	8	20	6
1987-88	North Bay	OHL	32	30	33	63	16	4	3	0	3	4
	Colorado	IHL	8	4	3	7	9	6	2	6	8	8
1988-89	**NY Rangers**	**NHL**	**20**	**7**	**3**	**10**	**4**	**1**	**0**	**0**	**0**	**0**
	Denver	IHL	40	21	28	49	32	....	....	....	....	....
1989-90	**NY Rangers**	**NHL**	**76**	**32**	**34**	**66**	**32**	**10**	**1**	**6**	**7**	**4**
1990-91	**NY Rangers**	**NHL**	**74**	**26**	**41**	**67**	**37**	**6**	**1**	**2**	**3**	**0**
1991-92	**NY Rangers**	**NHL**	**71**	**30**	**23**	**53**	**57**	**8**	**4**	**0**	**4**	**6**
1992-93	**NY Rangers**	**NHL**	**71**	**25**	**28**	**53**	**40**	....	....	....	....	....
1993-94	**NY Rangers**	**NHL**	**13**	**2**	**4**	**6**	**13**	....	....	....	....	....
	Hartford	**NHL**	**19**	**2**	**11**	**13**	**4**	....	....	....	....	....
1994-95	**Hartford**	**NHL**	**47**	**17**	**18**	**35**	**22**	....	....	....	....	....
1995-96	**Winnipeg**	**NHL**	**59**	**16**	**16**	**32**	**26**	....	....	....	....	....
	San Jose	**NHL**	**9**	**6**	**5**	**11**	**4**	....	....	....	....	....
1996-97	**San Jose**	**NHL**	**65**	**16**	**21**	**37**	**16**	....	....	....	....	....
	NHL Totals		**524**	**179**	**204**	**383**	**255**	**25**	**6**	**8**	**14**	**10**

Played in NHL All-Star Game (1991)

Traded to **Hartford** by **NY Rangers** with James Patrick for Steve Larmer, Nick Kypreos, Barry Richter and Hartford's sixth round choice (Yuri Litvinov) in 1994 Entry Draft, November 2, 1993. Traded to **Winnipeg** by **Hartford** for Nelson Emerson, October 6, 1995. Traded to **San Jose** by **Winnipeg** with Dallas' second round choice (previously acquired by Winnipeg — later traded to Chicago — Chicago selected Remi Royer) in 1996 Entry Draft for Craig Janney, March 18, 1996. Traded to **St. Louis** by **San Jose** for Stephane Matteau, July 24, 1997.

TURGEON, PIERRE
(TUHR-zhaw) **ST.L.**

Center. Shoots left. 6'1", 195 lbs.   Born, Rouyn, Que., August 28, 1969.
(Buffalo's 1st choice, 1st overall, in 1987 Entry Draft).

			Regular Season					Playoffs				
Season	Club	Lea	GP	G	A	TP	PIM	GP	G	A	TP	PIM
1985-86	Granby	QMJHL	69	47	67	114	31	....	....	....	....	....
	Cdn. National		11	2	4	6	2	....	....	....	....	....
1986-87	Granby	QMJHL	58	69	85	154	8	7	9	6	15	15
1987-88	**Buffalo**	**NHL**	**76**	**14**	**28**	**42**	**34**	**6**	**4**	**3**	**7**	**4**
1988-89	**Buffalo**	**NHL**	**80**	**34**	**54**	**88**	**26**	**5**	**3**	**5**	**8**	**2**
1989-90	**Buffalo**	**NHL**	**80**	**40**	**66**	**106**	**29**	**6**	**2**	**4**	**6**	**2**
1990-91	**Buffalo**	**NHL**	**78**	**32**	**47**	**79**	**26**	**6**	**3**	**1**	**4**	**6**
1991-92	**Buffalo**	**NHL**	**8**	**2**	**6**	**8**	**4**	....	....	....	....	....
	NY Islanders	**NHL**	**69**	**38**	**49**	**87**	**16**	....	....	....	....	....
1992-93a	**NY Islanders**	**NHL**	**83**	**58**	**74**	**132**	**26**	**11**	**6**	**7**	**13**	**0**
1993-94	**NY Islanders**	**NHL**	**69**	**38**	**56**	**94**	**18**	**4**	**0**	**1**	**1**	**0**
1994-95	**NY Islanders**	**NHL**	**34**	**13**	**14**	**27**	**10**	....	....	....	....	....
	Montreal	**NHL**	**15**	**11**	**9**	**20**	**4**	....	....	....	....	....
1995-96	**Montreal**	**NHL**	**80**	**38**	**58**	**96**	**44**	**6**	**2**	**4**	**6**	**2**
1996-97	**Montreal**	**NHL**	**9**	**1**	**10**	**11**	**2**	....	....	....	....	....
	St. Louis	**NHL**	**69**	**25**	**49**	**74**	**12**	**5**	**1**	**1**	**2**	**2**
	NHL Totals		**750**	**344**	**520**	**864**	**251**	**49**	**21**	**26**	**47**	**18**

a   Won Lady Byng Memorial Trophy (1993)
Played in NHL All-Star Game (1990, 1993, 1994, 1996)

Traded to **NY Islanders** by **Buffalo** with Uwe Krupp, Benoit Hogue and Dave McLlwain for Pat Lafontaine, Randy Hillier, Randy Wood and NY Islanders' fourth round choice (Dean Melanson) in 1992 Entry Draft, October 25, 1991. Traded to **Montreal** by **NY Islanders** with Vladimir Malakhov for Kirk Muller, Mathieu Schneider and Craig Darby, April 5, 1995. Traded to **St. Louis** by **Montreal** with Rory Fitzpatrick and Craig Conroy for Murray Baron, Shayne Corson and St. Louis' fifth round choice (Gennady Razin) in 1997 Entry Draft, October 29, 1996.

TURGEON, SYLVAIN
(TUHR-zhaw)

Left wing. Shoots left. 6', 200 lbs.   Born, Noranda, Que., January 17, 1965.
(Hartford's 1st choice, 2nd overall, in 1983 Entry Draft).

			Regular Season					Playoffs				
Season	Club	Lea	GP	G	A	TP	PIM	GP	G	A	TP	PIM
1981-82	Hull	QMJHL	57	33	40	73	78	14	11	11	22	16
1982-83a	Hull	QMJHL	67	54	109	163	103	7	8	7	15	10
1983-84b	**Hartford**	**NHL**	**76**	**40**	**32**	**72**	**55**	....	....	....	....	....
1984-85	**Hartford**	**NHL**	**64**	**31**	**31**	**62**	**67**	....	....	....	....	....
1985-86	**Hartford**	**NHL**	**76**	**45**	**34**	**79**	**88**	**9**	**2**	**3**	**5**	**4**
1986-87	**Hartford**	**NHL**	**41**	**23**	**13**	**36**	**45**	**6**	**1**	**2**	**3**	**4**
1987-88	**Hartford**	**NHL**	**71**	**23**	**26**	**49**	**71**	**6**	**0**	**0**	**0**	**4**
1988-89	**Hartford**	**NHL**	**42**	**16**	**14**	**30**	**40**	**4**	**0**	**2**	**2**	**4**
1989-90	**New Jersey**	**NHL**	**72**	**30**	**17**	**47**	**81**	**1**	**0**	**0**	**0**	**0**
1990-91	**Montreal**	**NHL**	**19**	**5**	**7**	**12**	**20**	**5**	**0**	**0**	**0**	**2**
1991-92	**Montreal**	**NHL**	**56**	**9**	**11**	**20**	**39**	**5**	**1**	**0**	**1**	**4**
1992-93	**Ottawa**	**NHL**	**72**	**25**	**18**	**43**	**104**	....	....	....	....	....
1993-94	**Ottawa**	**NHL**	**47**	**11**	**15**	**26**	**52**	....	....	....	....	....
1994-95	**Ottawa**	**NHL**	**33**	**11**	**8**	**19**	**29**	....	....	....	....	....
1995-96	Houston	IHL	65	28	31	59	66	....	....	....	....	....
1996-97	Wedemark	Ger.	10	4	6	10	12	8	5	2	7	41
	NHL Totals		**669**	**269**	**226**	**495**	**691**	**36**	**4**	**7**	**11**	**22**

a   QMJHL First All-Star Team (1983)
b   NHL All-Rookie Team (1984)
Played in NHL All-Star Game (1986)

Traded to **New Jersey** by **Hartford** for Pat Verbeek, June 17, 1989. Traded to **Montreal** by **New Jersey** for Claude Lemieux, September 4, 1990. Claimed by **Ottawa** from **Montreal** in Expansion Draft, June 18, 1992.

TUZZOLINO, TONY
NYI

Right wing. Shoots right. 6'2", 180 lbs.   Born, Buffalo, NY, October 9, 1975.
(Quebec's 7th choice, 113th overall, in 1994 Entry Draft).

			Regular Season					Playoffs				
Season	Club	Lea	GP	G	A	TP	PIM	GP	G	A	TP	PIM
1993-94	Michigan State	CCHA	35	4	3	7	46	....	....	....	....	....
1994-95	Michigan State	CCHA	39	9	18	27	81	....	....	....	....	....
1995-96	Michigan State	CCHA	41	12	17	29	120	....	....	....	....	....
1996-97	Michigan State	CCHA	39	14	18	32	120	....	....	....	....	....

Signed as a free agent by **NY Islanders**, April 26, 1997.

TVERDOVSKY, OLEG (tvehr-DOHV-skee) PHO.

Defense. Shoots left. 6', 185 lbs. Born, Donetsk, USSR, May 18, 1976.
(Anaheim's 1st choice, 2nd overall, in 1994 Entry Draft).

			Regular Season					Playoffs				
Season	Club	Lea	GP	G	A	TP	PIM	GP	G	A	TP	PIM
1992-93	Soviet Wings	CIS	21	0	1	1	6	6	0	0	0	0
1993-94	Soviet Wings	CIS	46	4	10	14	22	3	1	0	1	2
1994-95	Brandon	WHL	7	1	4	5	4	....	....	....	....	....
	Anaheim	**NHL**	**36**	**3**	**9**	**12**	**14**	....	....	....	....	....
1995-96	**Anaheim**	**NHL**	**51**	**7**	**15**	**22**	**35**	....	....	....	....	....
	Winnipeg	**NHL**	**31**	**0**	**8**	**8**	**6**	**6**	**0**	**1**	**1**	**0**
1996-97	**Phoenix**	**NHL**	**82**	**10**	**45**	**55**	**30**	**7**	**0**	**1**	**1**	**0**
	NHL Totals		**200**	**20**	**77**	**97**	**85**	**13**	**0**	**2**	**2**	**0**

Played in NHL All-Star Game (1997)

Traded to **Winnipeg** by **Anaheim** with Chad Kilger and Anaheim's third round choice (Per-Anton Lundstrom) in 1996 Entry Draft for Teemu Selanne, Marc Chouinard and Winnipeg's fourth round choice (later traded to Toronto — later traded to Montreal — Montreal selected Kim Staal) in 1996 Entry Draft, February 7, 1996.

TWERDUN, CHRIS CHI.

Defense. Shoots right. 6', 200 lbs. Born, Saskatoon, Sask., February 11, 1978.
(Chicago's 6th choice, 210th overall, in 1996 Entry Draft).

			Regular Season					Playoffs				
Season	Club	Lea	GP	G	A	TP	PIM	GP	G	A	TP	PIM
1994-95	Moose Jaw	WHL	70	5	12	17	25	10	0	3	3	2
1995-96	Moose Jaw	WHL	72	5	16	21	93	....	....	....	....	....
1996-97	Moose Jaw	WHL	63	8	15	23	66	12	0	2	2	10

TWIST, TONY ST.L.

Left wing. Shoots left. 6'1", 220 lbs. Born, Sherwood Park, Alta., May 9, 1968.
(St. Louis' 9th choice, 177th overall, in 1988 Entry Draft).

			Regular Season					Playoffs				
Season	Club	Lea	GP	G	A	TP	PIM	GP	G	A	TP	PIM
1987-88	Saskatoon	WHL	55	1	8	9	226	10	1	1	2	6
1988-89	Peoria	IHL	67	3	8	11	312	....	....	....	....	....
1989-90	**St. Louis**	**NHL**	**28**	**0**	**0**	**0**	**124**	....	....	....	....	....
	Peoria	IHL	36	1	5	6	200	5	0	1	1	8
1990-91	Peoria	IHL	38	2	10	12	244	....	....	....	....	....
	Quebec	**NHL**	**24**	**0**	**0**	**0**	**104**	....	....	....	....	....
1991-92	**Quebec**	**NHL**	**44**	**0**	**1**	**1**	**164**	....	....	....	....	....
1992-93	**Quebec**	**NHL**	**34**	**0**	**2**	**2**	**64**	....	....	....	....	....
1993-94	**Quebec**	**NHL**	**49**	**0**	**4**	**4**	**101**	....	....	....	....	....
1994-95	**St. Louis**	**NHL**	**28**	**3**	**0**	**3**	**89**	**1**	**0**	**0**	**0**	**6**
1995-96	**St. Louis**	**NHL**	**51**	**3**	**2**	**5**	**100**	**10**	**1**	**1**	**2**	**16**
1996-97	**St. Louis**	**NHL**	**64**	**1**	**2**	**3**	**121**	**6**	**0**	**0**	**0**	**0**
	NHL Totals		**322**	**7**	**11**	**18**	**867**	**17**	**1**	**1**	**2**	**22**

Traded to **Quebec** by **St. Louis** with Herb Raglan and Andy Rymsha for Darin Kimble, February 4, 1991. Signed as a free agent by **St. Louis**, August 16, 1994.

ULANOV, IGOR (yoo-LAH-nahf, EE-gohr) T.B.

Defense. Shoots left. 6'1", 205 lbs. Born, Krasnokamsk, USSR, October 1, 1969.
(Winnipeg's 8th choice, 203rd overall, in 1991 Entry Draft).

			Regular Season					Playoffs				
Season	Club	Lea	GP	G	A	TP	PIM	GP	G	A	TP	PIM
1990-91	Khimik	USSR	41	2	2	4	52	....	....	....	....	....
1991-92	Khimik	CIS	27	1	4	5	24	....	....	....	....	....
	Winnipeg	**NHL**	**27**	**2**	**9**	**11**	**67**	**7**	**0**	**0**	**0**	**39**
	Moncton	AHL	3	0	1	1	16	....	....	....	....	....
1992-93	**Winnipeg**	**NHL**	**56**	**2**	**14**	**16**	**124**	**4**	**0**	**0**	**0**	**4**
	Moncton	AHL	9	1	3	4	26	....	....	....	....	....
	Fort Wayne	IHL	3	0	1	1	29	....	....	....	....	....
1993-94	**Winnipeg**	**NHL**	**74**	**0**	**17**	**17**	**165**	....	....	....	....	....
1994-95	**Winnipeg**	**NHL**	**19**	**1**	**3**	**4**	**27**	....	....	....	....	....
	Washington	**NHL**	**3**	**0**	**1**	**1**	**2**	**2**	**0**	**0**	**0**	**4**
1995-96	**Chicago**	**NHL**	**53**	**1**	**8**	**9**	**92**	....	....	....	....	....
	Indianapolis	IHL	1	0	0	0	0	....	....	....	....	....
	Tampa Bay	**NHL**	**11**	**2**	**1**	**3**	**24**	**5**	**0**	**0**	**0**	**15**
1996-97	**Tampa Bay**	**NHL**	**59**	**1**	**7**	**8**	**108**	....	....	....	....	....
	NHL Totals		**302**	**9**	**60**	**69**	**609**	**18**	**0**	**0**	**0**	**62**

Traded to **Washington** by **Winnipeg** with Mike Eagles for Washington's third (later traded to Dallas — Dallas selected Sergei Gusev) and fifth (Brian Elder) round choices in 1995 Entry Draft, April 7, 1995. Traded to **Chicago** by **Washington** for Chicago's third round choice (Dave Weninger) in 1996 Entry Draft, October 17, 1995. Traded to **Tampa Bay** by **Chicago** with Patrick Poulin and Chicago's second round choice (later traded to New Jersey — New Jersey selected Pierre Dagenais) in 1996 Entry Draft for Enrico Ciccone and Tampa Bay's second round choice (Jeff Paul) in 1996 Entry Draft, March 20, 1996.

URICK, BRIAN (YOOR-ihk) EDM.

Right wing. Shoots right. 6'1", 190 lbs. Born, Minneapolis, MN, January 25, 1977.
(Edmonton's 5th choice, 114th overall, in 1996 Entry Draft).

			Regular Season					Playoffs				
Season	Club	Lea	GP	G	A	TP	PIM	GP	G	A	TP	PIM
1995-96	Notre Dame	CCHA	36	12	15	27	66	....	....	....	....	....
1996-97	Notre Dame	CCHA	34	13	12	25	88	....	....	....	....	....

USTORF, STEFAN (OOSH-tohrf, SHTEH-fuhn)

Center. Shoots left. 6', 185 lbs. Born, Kaufbeuren, Germany, January 3, 1974.
(Washington's 3rd choice, 53rd overall, in 1992 Entry Draft).

			Regular Season					Playoffs				
Season	Club	Lea	GP	G	A	TP	PIM	GP	G	A	TP	PIM
1991-92	Kaufbeuren	Ger.	41	2	22	24	46	5	2	7	9	6
1992-93	Kaufbeuren	Ger.	37	14	18	32	32	3	1	0	1	10
1993-94	Kaufbeuren	Ger.	38	10	20	30	21	3	0	0	0	4
1994-95	Portland	AHL	63	21	38	59	51	7	1	6	7	7
1995-96	**Washington**	**NHL**	**48**	**7**	**10**	**17**	**14**	**5**	**0**	**0**	**0**	**0**
	Portland	AHL	8	1	4	5	6	....	....	....	....	....
1996-97	**Washington**	**NHL**	**6**	**0**	**0**	**0**	**2**	....	....	....	....	....
	Portland	AHL	36	7	17	24	27	....	....	....	....	....
	NHL Totals		**54**	**7**	**10**	**17**	**16**	**5**	**0**	**0**	**0**	**0**

USTUGOV, ANATOLY (oos-too-gahv) DET.

Left wing. Shoots left. 5'10", 165 lbs. Born, Usole Siberskoye, USSR, June 26, 1977.
(Detroit's 4th choice, 104th overall, in 1995 Entry Draft).

			Regular Season					Playoffs				
Season	Club	Lea	GP	G	A	TP	PIM	GP	G	A	TP	PIM
1994-95	Yaroslavl	CIS	5	0	0	0	0	....	....	....	....	....
1995-96	Yaroslavl	CIS	9	1	0	1	4	....	....	....	....	....
1996-97	Yaroslavl 2	Rus. 3	32	9	12	21	52	....	....	....	....	....
	Yaroslavl	Rus.	4	0	0	0	2	....	....	....	....	....

VACHON, NICK (VA-shawn)

Center. Shoots left. 5'10", 185 lbs. Born, Montreal, Que., July 20, 1972.
(Toronto's 11th choice, 241st overall, in 1990 Entry Draft).

			Regular Season					Playoffs				
Season	Club	Lea	GP	G	A	TP	PIM	GP	G	A	TP	PIM
1990-91	Boston U.	H.E.	8	0	1	1	4	....	....	....	....	....
1991-92	Boston U.	H.E.	16	6	7	13	10	....	....	....	....	....
	Portland	WHL	25	9	19	28	46	6	0	3	3	14
1992-93	Portland	WHL	66	33	58	91	100	16	11	7	18	34
1993-94	Atlanta	IHL	3	1	1	2	0	....	....	....	....	....
	Knoxville	ECHL	61	29	57	86	139	3	0	0	0	2
1994-95	Phoenix	IHL	64	13	26	39	137	9	1	2	3	24
1995-96	Phoenix	IHL	73	13	17	30	168	1	0	0	0	2
1996-97	Phoenix	IHL	16	3	3	6	18	....	....	....	....	....
	NY Islanders	**NHL**	**1**	**0**	**0**	**0**	**0**	....	....	....	....	....
	Utah	IHL	33	3	5	8	110	....	....	....	....	....
	Long Beach	IHL	13	1	2	3	42	18	1	2	3	43
	NHL Totals		**1**	**0**	**0**	**0**	**0**	....	....	....	....	....

Signed as a free agent by **Los Angeles**, September 12, 1995. Traded to **NY Islanders** by **Los Angeles** for Chris Marinucci, November 19, 1996.

VAIC, LUBOMIR (VIGHTZ) VAN.

Center. Shoots left. 5'9", 178 lbs. Born, Spisska Nova Ves, Czech., March 6, 1977.
(Vancouver's 8th choice, 227th overall, in 1996 Entry Draft).

			Regular Season					Playoffs				
Season	Club	Lea	GP	G	A	TP	PIM	GP	G	A	TP	PIM
1993-94	Poprad	Slovak	28	10	6	16	10	....	....	....	....	....
1994-95	Spisska N.V.	Slovak	19	5	4	9	2	....	....	....	....	....
1995-96	HC Kosice	Slovak	36	7	19	26	10	13	0	7	7	....
1996-97	HC Kosice	Slovak	36	13	12	25	....	7	2	0	2	....

VALK, GARRY (VAHLK) PIT.

Left wing. Shoots left. 6'1", 205 lbs. Born, Edmonton, Alta., November 27, 1967.
(Vancouver's 5th choice, 108th overall, in 1987 Entry Draft).

			Regular Season					Playoffs				
Season	Club	Lea	GP	G	A	TP	PIM	GP	G	A	TP	PIM
1987-88	North Dakota	WCHA	38	23	12	35	64	....	....	....	....	....
1988-89	North Dakota	WCHA	40	14	17	31	71	....	....	....	....	....
1989-90	North Dakota	WCHA	43	22	17	39	92	....	....	....	....	....
1990-91	**Vancouver**	**NHL**	**59**	**10**	**11**	**21**	**67**	**5**	**0**	**0**	**0**	**20**
	Milwaukee	IHL	10	12	4	16	13	3	0	0	0	2
1991-92	**Vancouver**	**NHL**	**65**	**8**	**17**	**25**	**56**	**4**	**0**	**0**	**0**	**5**
1992-93	**Vancouver**	**NHL**	**48**	**6**	**7**	**13**	**77**	**7**	**0**	**1**	**1**	**12**
	Hamilton	AHL	7	3	6	9	6	....	....	....	....	....
1993-94	**Anaheim**	**NHL**	**78**	**18**	**27**	**45**	**100**	....	....	....	....	....
1994-95	**Anaheim**	**NHL**	**36**	**3**	**6**	**9**	**34**	....	....	....	....	....
1995-96	**Anaheim**	**NHL**	**79**	**12**	**12**	**24**	**125**	....	....	....	....	....
1996-97	**Anaheim**	**NHL**	**53**	**7**	**7**	**14**	**53**	....	....	....	....	....
	Pittsburgh	**NHL**	**17**	**3**	**4**	**7**	**25**	....	....	....	....	....
	NHL Totals		**435**	**67**	**91**	**158**	**537**	**16**	**0**	**1**	**1**	**37**

Claimed by **Anaheim** from **Vancouver** in NHL Waiver Draft, October 3, 1993. Traded to **Pittsburgh** by **Anaheim** for Jean-Jacques Daigneault, February 21, 1997.

VAN ALLEN, SHAUN OTT.

Center. Shoots left. 6'1", 200 lbs. Born, Calgary, Alta., August 29, 1967.
(Edmonton's 5th choice, 105th overall, in 1987 Entry Draft).

			Regular Season					Playoffs				
Season	Club	Lea	GP	G	A	TP	PIM	GP	G	A	TP	PIM
1984-85	Swift Current	WHL	61	12	20	32	136	....	....	....	....	....
1985-86	Saskatoon	WHL	55	12	11	23	43	13	4	8	12	28
1986-87	Saskatoon	WHL	72	38	59	97	116	11	4	6	10	24
1987-88	Milwaukee	IHL	40	14	28	42	34	....	....	....	....	....
	Nova Scotia	AHL	19	4	10	14	17	4	1	1	2	4
1988-89	Cape Breton	AHL	76	32	42	74	81	....	....	....	....	....
1989-90	Cape Breton	AHL	61	25	44	69	83	4	0	2	2	8
1990-91	**Edmonton**	**NHL**	**2**	**0**	**0**	**0**	**0**	....	....	....	....	....
a	Cape Breton	AHL	76	25	75	100	182	4	0	1	1	8
1991-92bc	Cape Breton	AHL	77	29	*84	*113	80	5	3	7	10	14
1992-93	**Edmonton**	**NHL**	**21**	**1**	**4**	**5**	**6**	....	....	....	....	....
	Cape Breton	AHL	43	14	62	76	68	15	8	9	17	18
1993-94	**Anaheim**	**NHL**	**80**	**8**	**25**	**33**	**64**	....	....	....	....	....
1994-95	**Anaheim**	**NHL**	**45**	**8**	**21**	**29**	**32**	....	....	....	....	....
1995-96	**Anaheim**	**NHL**	**49**	**8**	**17**	**25**	**41**	....	....	....	....	....
1996-97	**Ottawa**	**NHL**	**80**	**11**	**14**	**25**	**35**	**7**	**0**	**1**	**1**	**4**
	NHL Totals		**277**	**36**	**81**	**117**	**178**	**7**	**0**	**1**	**1**	**4**

a AHL Second All-Star Team (1991)
b Won John B. Sollenberger Trophy (Top Scorer - AHL) (1992)
c AHL First All-Star Team (1992)

Signed as a free agent by **Anaheim**, July 22, 1993. Traded to **Ottawa** by **Anaheim** with Jason York for Ted Drury and the rights to Marc Moro, October 1, 1996.

VAN BRUGGEN, ANDREW WSH.

Right wing. Shoots right. 6'5", 220 lbs. Born, Iowa City, IA, April 24, 1977.
(Washington's 9th choice, 153rd overall, in 1996 Entry Draft).

			Regular Season					Playoffs				
Season	Club	Lea	GP	G	A	TP	PIM	GP	G	A	TP	PIM
1995-96	N. Michigan	WCHA	36	1	7	8	63	....	....	....	....	....
1996-97	N. Michigan	WCHA	30	3	2	5	56	....	....	....	....	....

VANDENBUSSCHE, RYAN (van-dehn-BUHSH) NYR

Right wing. Shoots right. 5'11", 187 lbs. Born, Simcoe, Ont., February 28, 1973.
(Toronto's 8th choice, 173rd overall, in 1992 Entry Draft).

			Regular Season					Playoffs				
Season	Club	Lea	GP	G	A	TP	PIM	GP	G	A	TP	PIM
1990-91	Cornwall	OHL	49	3	8	11	139	....	....	....	....	....
1991-92	Cornwall	OHL	61	13	15	28	232	6	0	2	2	9
1992-93	Newmarket	OHL	30	15	12	27	161	....	....	....	....	....
	Guelph	OHL	29	3	14	17	99	5	1	3	4	13
	St. John's	AHL	1	0	0	0	0	....	....	....	....	....
1993-94	St. John's	AHL	44	4	10	14	124	....	....	....	....	....
	Springfield	AHL	9	1	2	3	29	5	0	0	0	16
1994-95	St. John's	AHL	53	2	13	15	239	3	0	0	0	17
1995-96	Binghamton	AHL	68	3	17	20	240	4	0	0	0	9
1996-97	**NY Rangers**	**NHL**	**11**	**1**	**0**	**1**	**30**	....	....	....	....	....
	Binghamton	AHL	38	8	11	19	133	....	....	....	....	....
	NHL Totals		**11**	**1**	**0**	**1**	**30**	....	....	....	....	....

Signed as a free agent by **NY Rangers**, August 22, 1995.

VAN DRUNEN, DAVID OTT.

Defense. Shoots right. 6', 200 lbs. Born, Sherwood Park, Alta., January 31, 1976.

			Regular Season					Playoffs				
Season	Club	Lea	GP	G	A	TP	PIM	GP	G	A	TP	PIM
1993-94	Prince Albert	WHL	63	3	10	13	95	....	....	....	....	....
1994-95	Prince Albert	WHL	71	2	14	16	132	15	3	4	7	36
1995-96	Prince Albert	WHL	70	10	23	33	172	18	1	5	6	37
1996-97a	Prince Albert	WHL	72	18	47	65	218	4	0	4	4	24

WHL East Second All-Star Team (1997)

Signed as a free agent by **Ottawa**, May 2, 1997.

VAN IMPE, DARREN (van-IHMP) ANA.

Defense. Shoots left. 6'1", 195 lbs. Born, Saskatoon, Sask., May 18, 1973.
(NY Islanders' 7th choice, 170th overall, in 1993 Entry Draft).

			Regular Season					Playoffs				
Season	Club	Lea	GP	G	A	TP	PIM	GP	G	A	TP	PIM
1990-91	Prince Albert	WHL	70	15	45	60	57	3	1	1	2	2
1991-92	Prince Albert	WHL	69	9	37	46	129	8	1	5	6	10
1992-93a	Red Deer	WHL	54	23	47	70	118	4	2	5	7	16
1993-94a	Red Deer	WHL	58	20	64	84	125	4	2	4	6	6
1994-95	San Diego	IHL	76	6	17	23	74	5	0	0	0	0
	Anaheim	**NHL**	**1**	**0**	**1**	**1**	**4**	....	....	....	....	....
1995-96	**Anaheim**	**NHL**	**16**	**1**	**2**	**3**	**14**	....	....	....	....	....
	Baltimore	AHL	63	11	47	58	79	....	....	....	....	....
1996-97	**Anaheim**	**NHL**	**74**	**4**	**19**	**23**	**90**	**9**	**0**	**2**	**2**	**16**
	NHL Totals		**91**	**5**	**22**	**27**	**108**	**9**	**0**	**2**	**2**	**16**

a WHL First All-Star Team (1993, 1994)

Traded to **Anaheim** by **NY Islanders** for Anaheim's eighth round choice (Mike Broda) in 1995 Entry Draft, August 31, 1994.

VAN OENE, DARREN (van OH-uhn) BUF.

Left wing. Shoots left. 6'3", 207 lbs. Born, Edmonton, Alta., January 18, 1978.
(Buffalo's 3rd choice, 33rd overall, in 1996 Entry Draft).

			Regular Season					Playoffs				
Season	Club	Lea	GP	G	A	TP	PIM	GP	G	A	TP	PIM
1994-95	Brandon	WHL	58	5	13	18	106	18	1	1	2	34
1995-96	Brandon	WHL	47	10	18	28	126	18	1	6	7	*78
1996-97	Brandon	WHL	56	21	27	48	139	6	2	3	5	19

VAN TIGHEM, TRAVIS (van-TEE-gehm) PHI.

Defense. Shoots left. 6'1", 210 lbs. Born, Calgary, Alta, March 16, 1973.

			Regular Season					Playoffs				
Season	Club	Lea	GP	G	A	TP	PIM	GP	G	A	TP	PIM
1994-95	Michigan Tech	WCHA	36	1	3	4	66	....	....	....	....	....
1995-96	Michigan Tech	WCHA	37	4	14	18	84	....	....	....	....	....
1996-97	Michigan Tech	WCHA	30	3	9	12	86	....	....	....	....	....

Signed as a free agent by **Philadelphia**, July 17, 1997.

VARADA, VACLAV (VAH-rah-dah) BUF.

Right wing. Shoots left. 6', 200 lbs. Born, Vsetin, Czech., April 26, 1976.
(San Jose's 4th choice, 89th overall, in 1994 Entry Draft).

			Regular Season					Playoffs				
Season	Club	Lea	GP	G	A	TP	PIM	GP	G	A	TP	PIM
1992-93	Vitkovice	Czech.	1	0	0	0	....	....	....	....	....	....
1993-94	Vitkovice	Czech.	24	6	7	13	....	5	1	1	2	....
1994-95	Tacoma	WHL	68	50	38	88	108	4	4	3	7	11
1995-96	Kelowna	WHL	59	39	46	85	100	6	3	3	6	16
	Buffalo	**NHL**	**1**	**0**	**0**	**0**	**0**	....	....	....	....	....
	Rochester	AHL	5	3	0	3	4	....	....	....	....	....
1996-97	**Buffalo**	**NHL**	**5**	**0**	**0**	**0**	**2**	....	....	....	....	....
	Rochester	AHL	53	23	25	48	81	10	1	6	7	27
	NHL Totals		**6**	**0**	**0**	**0**	**2**	....	....	....	....	....

Traded to **Buffalo** by **San Jose** with Martin Spahnel, an optional first round choice in 1996 Entry Draft and Philadelphia's fourth round choice (previously acquired by San Jose — Buffalo selected Mike Martone) in 1996 Entry Draft for Doug Bodger, November 16, 1995.

VARIS, PETRI (VAH-rihs) CHI.

Left wing. Shoots left. 6'1", 200 lbs. Born, Varkaus, Finland, May 13, 1969.
(San Jose's 7th choice, 132nd overall, in 1993 Entry Draft).

			Regular Season					Playoffs				
Season	Club	Lea	GP	G	A	TP	PIM	GP	G	A	TP	PIM
1990-91	KooKoo	Fin. 2	44	20	31	51	42	....	....	....	....	....
1991-92a	Assat	Fin.	36	13	23	36	24	....	....	....	....	....
1992-93	Assat	Fin.	46	14	35	49	42	8	2	2	4	12
1993-94	Jokerit	Fin.	31	14	15	29	16	11	3	4	7	6
1994-95	Jokerit	Fin.	47	21	20	41	53	11	7	2	9	10
1995-96	Jokerit	Fin.	50	28	28	56	22	11	12	7	19	6
1996-97	Jokerit	Fin.	50	*36	23	*59	38	9	7	4	11	14

a Finnish Rookie of the Year (1992)

Rights traded to **Chicago** by **San Jose** with San Jose's sixth round choice in 1998 Entry Draft for Murray Craven, July 25, 1997.

VASILEVSKI, ALEXANDER (vah-sih-LEHV-skee)

Right wing. Shoots left. 5'11", 190 lbs. Born, Kiev, USSR, January 8, 1975.
(St. Louis' 9th choice, 271st overall, in 1993 Entry Draft).

			Regular Season					Playoffs				
Season	Club	Lea	GP	G	A	TP	PIM	GP	G	A	TP	PIM
1992-93	Victoria	WHL	71	27	25	52	52	....	....	....	....	....
1993-94	Victoria	WHL	69	34	51	85	78	....	....	....	....	....
1994-95	Prince George	WHL	48	32	34	66	52	....	....	....	....	....
	Brandon	WHL	23	6	11	17	39	18	3	6	9	34
1995-96	**St. Louis**	**NHL**	**1**	**0**	**0**	**0**	**0**	....	....	....	....	....
	Worcester	AHL	69	18	21	39	112	4	2	1	3	10
1996-97	**St. Louis**	**NHL**	**3**	**0**	**0**	**0**	**2**	....	....	....	....	....
	Worcester	AHL	61	9	23	32	100	....	....	....	....	....
	NHL Totals		**4**	**0**	**0**	**0**	**2**	....	....	....	....	....

VASILIEV, ALEXEI (vah-SEE-lee-ehf) NYR

Defense. Shoots left. 6'1", 190 lbs. Born, Yaroslavl, USSR, September 1, 1977.
(NY Rangers' 4th choice, 110th overall, in 1995 Entry Draft).

			Regular Season					Playoffs				
Season	Club	Lea	GP	G	A	TP	PIM	GP	G	A	TP	PIM
1993-94	Yaroslavl	CIS	2	0	1	1	4	....	....	....	....	....
1994-95	Yaroslavl 2	CIS 2				UNAVAILABLE						
1995-96	Yaroslavl	CIS	40	4	7	11	4	....	....	....	....	....
1996-97	Yaroslavl	Rus.	44	2	8	10	10	9	1	1	2	8

VASILIEV, ANDREI (vah-SEE-lee-ehf)

Left wing. Shoots right. 5'9", 180 lbs. Born, Voskresensk, USSR, March 30, 1972.
(NY Islanders' 11th choice, 248th overall, in 1992 Entry Draft).

			Regular Season					Playoffs				
Season	Club	Lea	GP	G	A	TP	PIM	GP	G	A	TP	PIM
1991-92	CSKA	CIS	28	7	2	9	2	....	....	....	....	....
1992-93	Khimik	CIS	34	4	8	12	20	....	....	....	....	....
1993-94	CSKA	CIS	46	17	6	23	8	3	1	0	1	0
1994-95	Denver	IHL	74	28	37	65	48	13	9	4	13	22
	NY Islanders	**NHL**	**2**	**0**	**0**	**0**	**2**	....	....	....	....	....
1995-96	**NY Islanders**	**NHL**	**10**	**2**	**5**	**7**	**2**	....	....	....	....	....
	Utah	IHL	43	26	20	46	34	22	12	4	16	18
1996-97	**NY Islanders**	**NHL**	**3**	**0**	**0**	**0**	**2**	....	....	....	....	....
	Utah	IHL	56	16	18	34	42	7	4	1	5	0
	NHL Totals		**15**	**2**	**5**	**7**	**6**	....	....	....	....	....

VASILJEVS, HERBERT (vah-SEE-lee-ehf) FLA.

Center. Shoots right. 5'11", 170 lbs. Born, Riga, USSR, May 27, 1976.

			Regular Season					Playoffs				
Season	Club	Lea	GP	G	A	TP	PIM	GP	G	A	TP	PIM
1995-96	Guelph	OHL	65	34	33	67	63	16	6	13	19	6
1996-97	Carolina	AHL	54	13	18	31	30	....	....	....	....	....
	Port Huron	ColHL	3	3	2	5	4	....	....	....	....	....

Signed as a free agent by **Florida**, October 3, 1996.

VASKE, DENNIS (VAS-kee) NYI

Defense. Shoots left. 6'2", 210 lbs. Born, Rockford, IL, October 11, 1967.
(NY Islanders' 2nd choice, 38th overall, in 1986 Entry Draft).

			Regular Season					Playoffs				
Season	Club	Lea	GP	G	A	TP	PIM	GP	G	A	TP	PIM
1986-87	Minn.-Duluth	WCHA	33	0	2	2	40	....	....	....	....	....
1987-88	Minn.-Duluth	WCHA	39	1	6	7	90	....	....	....	....	....
1988-89	Minn.-Duluth	WCHA	37	9	19	28	86	....	....	....	....	....
1989-90	Minn.-Duluth	WCHA	37	5	24	29	72	....	....	....	....	....
1990-91	**NY Islanders**	**NHL**	**5**	**0**	**0**	**0**	**2**	....	....	....	....	....
	Capital Dist.	AHL	67	10	10	20	65	....	....	....	....	....
1991-92	**NY Islanders**	**NHL**	**39**	**0**	**1**	**1**	**39**	....	....	....	....	....
	Capital Dist.	AHL	31	1	11	12	59	....	....	....	....	....
1992-93	**NY Islanders**	**NHL**	**27**	**1**	**5**	**6**	**32**	**18**	**0**	**6**	**6**	**14**
	Capital Dist.	AHL	42	4	15	19	70	....	....	....	....	....
1993-94	**NY Islanders**	**NHL**	**65**	**2**	**11**	**13**	**76**	**4**	**0**	**1**	**1**	**2**
1994-95	**NY Islanders**	**NHL**	**41**	**1**	**11**	**12**	**53**	....	....	....	....	....
1995-96	**NY Islanders**	**NHL**	**19**	**1**	**6**	**7**	**21**	....	....	....	....	....
1996-97	**NY Islanders**	**NHL**	**17**	**0**	**4**	**4**	**12**	....	....	....	....	....
	NHL Totals		**213**	**5**	**38**	**43**	**235**	**22**	**0**	**7**	**7**	**16**

VELLINGA, MIKE CHI.

Defense. Shoots right. 6'1", 218 lbs. Born, Chatham, Ont., August 19, 1978.
(Chicago's 5th choice, 184th overall, in 1996 Entry Draft).

			Regular Season					Playoffs				
Season	Club	Lea	GP	G	A	TP	PIM	GP	G	A	TP	PIM
1995-96	Guelph	OHL	57	3	8	11	32	16	2	6	8	6
1996-97	Guelph	OHL	66	6	30	36	73	18	1	9	10	34

VERBEEK, PAT (vuhr-BEEK) DAL.

Right/Left wing. Shoots right. 5'9", 192 lbs. Born, Sarnia, Ont., May 24, 1964.
(New Jersey's 3rd choice, 43rd overall, in 1982 Entry Draft).

			Regular Season					Playoffs				
Season	Club	Lea	GP	G	A	TP	PIM	GP	G	A	TP	PIM
1981-82	Sudbury	OHL	66	37	51	88	180	....	....	....	....	....
1982-83	**New Jersey**	**NHL**	**6**	**3**	**2**	**5**	**8**	....	....	....	....	....
	Sudbury	OHL	61	40	67	107	184	....	....	....	....	....
1983-84	**New Jersey**	**NHL**	**79**	**20**	**27**	**47**	**158**	....	....	....	....	....
1984-85	**New Jersey**	**NHL**	**78**	**15**	**18**	**33**	**162**	....	....	....	....	....
1985-86	**New Jersey**	**NHL**	**76**	**25**	**28**	**53**	**79**	....	....	....	....	....
1986-87	**New Jersey**	**NHL**	**74**	**35**	**24**	**59**	**120**	....	....	....	....	....
1987-88	**New Jersey**	**NHL**	**73**	**46**	**31**	**77**	**227**	**20**	**4**	**8**	**12**	**51**
1988-89	**New Jersey**	**NHL**	**77**	**26**	**21**	**47**	**189**	....	....	....	....	....
1989-90	**Hartford**	**NHL**	**80**	**44**	**45**	**89**	**228**	**7**	**2**	**2**	**4**	**26**
1990-91	**Hartford**	**NHL**	**80**	**43**	**39**	**82**	**246**	**6**	**3**	**2**	**5**	**40**
1991-92	**Hartford**	**NHL**	**76**	**22**	**35**	**57**	**243**	**7**	**0**	**2**	**2**	**12**
1992-93	**Hartford**	**NHL**	**84**	**39**	**43**	**82**	**197**	....	....	....	....	....
1993-94	**Hartford**	**NHL**	**84**	**37**	**38**	**75**	**177**	....	....	....	....	....
1994-95	**Hartford**	**NHL**	**29**	**7**	**11**	**18**	**53**	....	....	....	....	....
	NY Rangers	**NHL**	**19**	**10**	**5**	**15**	**18**	**10**	**4**	**6**	**10**	**20**
1995-96	**NY Rangers**	**NHL**	**69**	**41**	**41**	**82**	**129**	**11**	**3**	**6**	**9**	**12**
1996-97	**Dallas**	**NHL**	**81**	**17**	**36**	**53**	**128**	**7**	**1**	**3**	**4**	**16**
	NHL Totals		**1065**	**430**	**444**	**874**	**2362**	**68**	**17**	**29**	**46**	**177**

Played in NHL All-Star Game (1991, 1996)

Traded to **Hartford** by **New Jersey** for Sylvain Turgeon, June 17, 1989. Traded to **NY Rangers** by **Hartford** for Glen Featherstone, Michael Stewart, NY Rangers' first round choice (Jean-Sebastien Giguere) in 1995 Entry Draft and fourth round choice (Steve Wasylko) in 1996 Entry Draft, March 23, 1995. Signed as a free agent by **Dallas**, August 21, 1996.

VERCIK, RUDOLF (VEHR-chihk) NYR

Left wing. Shoots left. 6'1", 189 lbs. Born, Bratislava, Czech., March 19, 1976.
(NY Rangers' 2nd choice, 52nd overall, in 1994 Entry Draft).

			Regular Season					Playoffs				
Season	Club	Lea	GP	G	A	TP	PIM	GP	G	A	TP	PIM
1993-94	Bratislava	Slovak	17	1	4	5	14	....	....	....	....	....
1994-95	Bratislava	Slovak	33	14	9	23	22	....	....	....	....	....
1995-96	Bratislava	Slovak	28	7	3	10	61	13	1	0	1	....
1996-97	Bratislava	Slovak	40	8	3	11	....	2	0	0	0	....

VERTALA, TIMO (vehr-TAH-lah, TEE-moh) MTL.

Right wing. Shoots left. 6'1", 180 lbs. Born, Jyvaskyla, Finland, May 2, 1978.
(Montreal's 8th choice, 181st overall, in 1996 Entry Draft).

			Regular Season					Playoffs				
Season	Club	Lea	GP	G	A	TP	PIM	GP	G	A	TP	PIM
1995-96	JyP HT	Fin.	3	0	1	1	2	....	....	....	....	....
	JyP HT	Fin. Jr.	35	15	10	25	54	6	1	1	2	6
1996-97	JyP HT	Fin.	46	8	5	13	39	4	0	0	0	0
	JyP HT	Fin. Jr.	7	4	4	8	12	....	....	....	....	....

VIAL, DENNIS (vee-AL) OTT.

Left wing. Shoots left. 6'1", 220 lbs. Born, Sault Ste. Marie, Ont., April 10, 1969.
(NY Rangers' 5th choice, 110th overall, in 1988 Entry Draft).

			Regular Season					Playoffs				
Season	Club	Lea	GP	G	A	TP	PIM	GP	G	A	TP	PIM
1985-86	Hamilton	OHL	31	1	1	2	66	....	....	....	....	....
1986-87	Hamilton	OHL	53	1	8	9	194	8	0	0	0	8
1987-88	Hamilton	OHL	52	3	17	20	229	13	2	2	4	49
1988-89	Niagara Falls	OHL	50	10	27	37	227	15	1	7	8	44
1989-90	Flint	IHL	79	6	29	35	351	4	0	0	0	10
1990-91	**NY Rangers**	**NHL**	**21**	**0**	**0**	**0**	**61**	....	....	....	....	....
	Binghamton	AHL	40	2	7	9	250	....	....	....	....	....
	Detroit	**NHL**	**9**	**0**	**0**	**0**	**16**	....	....	....	....	....
1991-92	**Detroit**	**NHL**	**27**	**1**	**0**	**1**	**72**	....	....	....	....	....
	Adirondack	AHL	20	2	4	6	107	17	1	3	4	43
1992-93	**Detroit**	**NHL**	**9**	**0**	**1**	**1**	**20**	....	....	....	....	....
	Adirondack	AHL	30	2	11	13	177	11	1	1	2	14
1993-94	**Ottawa**	**NHL**	**55**	**2**	**5**	**7**	**214**	....	....	....	....	....
1994-95	**Ottawa**	**NHL**	**27**	**0**	**4**	**4**	**65**	....	....	....	....	....
1995-96	**Ottawa**	**NHL**	**64**	**1**	**4**	**5**	**276**	....	....	....	....	....
1996-97	**Ottawa**	**NHL**	**11**	**0**	**1**	**1**	**25**	....	....	....	....	....
	NHL Totals		**223**	**4**	**15**	**19**	**749**	....	....	....	....	....

Traded to **Detroit** by **NY Rangers** with Kevin Miller and Jim Cummins for Joey Kocur and Per Djoos, March 5, 1991. Traded to **Quebec** by **Detroit** with Doug Crossman for cash, June 15, 1992. Traded to **Detroit** by **Quebec** for cash, September 9, 1992. Traded to **Tampa Bay** by **Detroit** for Steve Maltais, June 8, 1993. Claimed by **Anaheim** from **Tampa Bay** in Expansion Draft, June 24, 1993. Claimed by **Ottawa** from **Anaheim** in Phase II of Expansion Draft, June 25, 1993.

VIITAKOSKI, VESA (VEE-ee-tah-kohs-kee)

Left wing. Shoots left. 6'3", 215 lbs. Born, Lappeenranta, Finland, February 13, 1971.
(Calgary's 3rd choice, 32nd overall, in 1990 Entry Draft).

			Regular Season					Playoffs				
Season	Club	Lea	GP	G	A	TP	PIM	GP	G	A	TP	PIM
1988-89	SaiPa	Fin.	11	4	1	5	6	....	....	....	....	....
1989-90	SaiPa	Fin.	44	24	10	34	8	....	....	....	....	....
1990-91	Tappara	Fin.	41	17	23	40	14	3	2	0	2	4
1991-92	Tappara	Fin.	44	19	19	38	39	....	....	....	....	....
1992-93	Tappara	Fin.	48	27	27	54	28	....	....	....	....	....
1993-94	**Calgary**	**NHL**	**8**	**1**	**2**	**3**	**0**	....	....	....	....	....
	Saint John	AHL	67	28	39	67	24	5	1	2	3	2
1994-95	Saint John	AHL	56	17	26	43	8	4	0	1	1	2
	Calgary	**NHL**	**10**	**1**	**2**	**3**	**6**	....	....	....	....	....
1995-96	**Calgary**	**NHL**	**5**	**0**	**0**	**0**	**2**	....	....	....	....	....
	Saint John	AHL	48	18	29	47	48	....	....	....	....	....
	Cornwall	AHL	10	7	6	13	4	8	1	3	4	2
1996-97	HV-71	Swe.	50	17	12	29	24	5	1	1	2	2
	NHL Totals		**23**	**2**	**4**	**6**	**8**	....	....	....	....	....

Traded to **Colorado** by **Calgary** for Paxton Schulte, March 19, 1996.

VIRTUE, TERRY ST.L.

Defense. Shoots right. 6', 200 lbs. Born, Scarborough, Ont., August 12, 1970.

			Regular Season					Playoffs				
Season	Club	Lea	GP	G	A	TP	PIM	GP	G	A	TP	PIM
1988-89	Victoria	WHL	8	1	1	2	13	....	....	....	....	....
1989-90	Victoria	WHL	24	1	9	10	85	....	....	....	....	....
	Tri-City	WHL	34	1	10	11	82	6	0	0	0	30
1990-91	Tri-City	WHL	11	1	8	9	24	....	....	....	....	....
	Portland	WHL	59	9	44	53	127	....	....	....	....	....
1991-92	Roanoke	ECHL	38	4	22	26	165	....	....	....	....	....
	Louisville	ECHL	23	1	15	16	58	13	0	8	8	49
1992-93	Louisville	ECHL	28	0	17	17	84	....	....	....	....	....
	Wheeling	ECHL	31	3	15	18	86	16	3	5	8	18
1993-94	Wheeling	ECHL	34	5	28	33	61	6	2	2	4	4
	Cape Breton	AHL	26	4	6	10	10	5	0	0	0	17
1994-95	Worcester	AHL	73	14	25	39	183	....	....	....	....	....
	Atlanta	IHL	1	0	0	0	2	....	....	....	....	....
1995-96	Worcester	AHL	76	7	31	38	234	4	0	0	0	4
1996-97	Worcester	AHL	80	16	26	42	220	5	0	4	4	8

Signed as a free agent by **St. Louis**, January 29, 1996.

VISHEAU, MARK (VEE-SHOO) L.A.

Defense. Shoots right. 6'6", 235 lbs. Born, Burlington, Ont., June 27, 1973.
(Winnipeg's 4th choice, 84th overall, in 1992 Entry Draft).

			Regular Season					Playoffs				
Season	Club	Lea	GP	G	A	TP	PIM	GP	G	A	TP	PIM
1990-91	London	OHL	59	4	11	15	40	7	0	1	1	6
1991-92	London	OHL	66	5	31	36	104	10	0	4	4	27
1992-93	London	OHL	62	8	52	60	88	12	0	5	5	26
1993-94	**Winnipeg**	**NHL**	**1**	**0**	**0**	**0**	**0**	....	....	....	....	....
	Moncton	AHL	48	4	5	9	58	....	....	....	....	....
1994-95	Springfield	AHL	35	0	4	4	94	....	....	....	....	....
1995-96	Cape Breton	AHL	8	0	0	0	30	....	....	....	....	....
	Minnesota	IHL	10	0	0	0	25	....	....	....	....	....
	Wheeling	ECHL	7	1	2	3	14	7	0	3	3	4
1996-97	Raleigh	ECHL	15	1	5	6	61	....	....	....	....	....
	Quebec	IHL	64	3	10	13	173	9	1	1	2	11
	NHL Totals		**1**	**0**	**0**	**0**	**0**	....	....	....	....	....

Signed as a free agent by **Los Angeles**, July 30, 1997.

VLASAK, TOMAS (VLAH-sahk) L.A.

Center. Shoots right. 5'10", 175 lbs. Born, Prague, Czech., February 1, 1975.
(Los Angeles' 6th choice, 120th overall, in 1993 Entry Draft).

			Regular Season					Playoffs				
Season	Club	Lea	GP	G	A	TP	PIM	GP	G	A	TP	PIM
1992-93	Slavia Praha	Czech. 2	31	17	6	23	....	....	....	....	....	....
1993-94	Litvinov	Czech.	41	16	11	27	0	4	0	1	1	....
1994-95	Litvinov	Czech.	35	6	14	20	4	4	0	0	0	4
1995-96	Litvinov	Czech.	35	10	22	32	....	15	5	5	10	....
1996-97	Litvinov	Czech.	52	26	34	60	16	....	....	....	....	....

VLASENKOV, DMITRI (vlah-SEHN-khahf) CGY.

Left wing. Shoots left. 5'11", 183 lbs. Born, Olenigorsk, USSR, January 1, 1978.
(Calgary's 4th choice, 73rd overall, in 1996 Entry Draft).

			Regular Season					Playoffs				
Season	Club	Lea	GP	G	A	TP	PIM	GP	G	A	TP	PIM
1995-96	Yaroslavl	CIS	17	1	1	2	4	1	0	0	0	0
1996-97	Yaroslavl 2	Rus. 3	18	10	2	12	6	....	....	....	....	....
	Yaroslavl	Rus.	28	3	2	5	10	8	1	1	2	2

VOLCHKOV, ALEXANDER (VOHLCH-kahf) WSH.

Center. Shoots left. 6'1", 194 lbs. Born, Moscow, USSR, September 25, 1977.
(Washington's 1st choice, 4th overall, in 1996 Entry Draft).

			Regular Season					Playoffs				
Season	Club	Lea	GP	G	A	TP	PIM	GP	G	A	TP	PIM
1994-95	CSKA	CIS	1	0	0	0	0	....	....	....	....	....
1995-96	Barrie	OHL	47	37	27	64	36	7	2	3	5	12
1996-97a	Barrie	OHL	56	29	53	82	76	9	6	9	15	12
	Portland	AHL	....	....	....	....	....	4	0	0	0	0

a OHL Second All-Star Team (1997)

VON STEFENELLI, PHIL

Defense. Shoots left. 6'1", 200 lbs. Born, Vancouver, B.C., April 10, 1969.
(Vancouver's 5th choice, 122nd overall, in 1988 Entry Draft).

			Regular Season					Playoffs				
Season	Club	Lea	GP	G	A	TP	PIM	GP	G	A	TP	PIM
1987-88	Boston U.	H.E.	34	3	13	16	38	....	....	....	....	....
1988-89	Boston U.	H.E.	33	2	6	8	34	....	....	....	....	....
1989-90	Boston U.	H.E.	44	8	20	28	40	....	....	....	....	....
1990-91	Boston U.	H.E.	41	7	23	30	32	....	....	....	....	....
1991-92	Milwaukee	IHL	80	2	34	36	40	5	1	2	3	2
1992-93	Hamilton	AHL	78	11	20	31	75	....	....	....	....	....
1993-94	Hamilton	AHL	80	10	31	41	89	4	1	0	1	2
1994-95	Providence	AHL	75	6	13	19	93	13	2	4	6	6
1995-96	**Boston**	**NHL**	**37**	**0**	**4**	**4**	**16**	....	....	....	....	....
	Providence	AHL	42	9	21	30	52	....	....	....	....	....
1996-97	**Ottawa**	**NHL**	**6**	**0**	**1**	**1**	**7**	....	....	....	....	....
	Detroit	IHL	67	14	26	40	86	21	2	4	6	20
	NHL Totals		**43**	**0**	**5**	**5**	**23**	....	....	....	....	....

Signed as a free agent by **Boston**, September 10, 1994. Signed as a free agent by **Ottawa**, July 17, 1996.

VOPAT, JAN (VOH-paht) L.A.

Defense. Shoots left. 6', 205 lbs. Born, Most, Czech., March 22, 1973.
(Hartford's 3rd choice, 57th overall, in 1992 Entry Draft).

			Regular Season					Playoffs				
Season	Club	Lea	GP	G	A	TP	PIM	GP	G	A	TP	PIM
1990-91	Litvinov	Czech.	25	1	4	5	4	....	....	....	....	....
1991-92	Litvinov	Czech.	46	4	2	6	16	....	....	....	....	....
1992-93	Litvinov	Czech.	45	12	10	22	....	....	....	....	....	....
1993-94	Litvinov	Czech.	41	9	19	28	0	4	1	1	2	....
1994-95	Litvinov	Czech.	42	7	18	25	49	4	0	2	2	2
1995-96	**Los Angeles**	**NHL**	**11**	**1**	**4**	**5**	**4**	....	....	....	....	....
	Phoenix	IHL	47	0	9	9	34	4	0	2	2	4
1996-97	**Los Angeles**	**NHL**	**33**	**4**	**5**	**9**	**22**	....	....	....	....	....
	Phoenix	IHL	4	0	6	6	6	....	....	....	....	....
	NHL Totals		**44**	**5**	**9**	**14**	**26**	....	....	....	....	....

Rights traded to **Los Angeles** by **Hartford** for Los Angeles' fourth round choice (Ian MacNeil) in 1995 Entry Draft, May 31, 1995.

VOPAT, ROMAN (VOH-paht) L.A.

Center. Shoots left. 6'3", 216 lbs. Born, Litvinov, Czech., April 21, 1976.
(St. Louis' 4th choice, 172nd overall, in 1994 Entry Draft).

			Regular Season					Playoffs				
Season	Club	Lea	GP	G	A	TP	PIM	GP	G	A	TP	PIM
1993-94	Litvinov	Czech.	7	0	0	0	0	....	....	....	....	....
1994-95	Moose Jaw	WHL	72	23	20	43	141	10	4	1	5	28
	Peoria	IHL	....	....	....	....	....	6	0	2	2	2
1995-96	**St. Louis**	**NHL**	**25**	**2**	**3**	**5**	**48**	....	....	....	....	....
	Worcester	AHL	5	2	0	2	14	....	....	....	....	....
	Moose Jaw	WHL	7	0	4	4	34	....	....	....	....	....
	Prince Albert	WHL	22	15	5	20	81	18	9	8	17	57
1996-97	**Los Angeles**	**NHL**	**29**	**4**	**5**	**9**	**60**	....	....	....	....	....
	Phoenix	IHL	50	8	8	16	139	....	....	....	....	....
	NHL Totals		**54**	**6**	**8**	**14**	**108**	....	....	....	....	....

Traded to **Los Angeles** by **St. Louis** with Craig Johnson, Patrice Tardif, St. Louis fifth round choice (Peter Hogan) in 1996 Entry Draft and first round choice (Matt Zultek) in 1997 Entry Draft for Wayne Gretzky, February 27, 1996.

VOROBIEV, VLADIMIR (vah-roh-BEE-ehf) NYR

Left wing. Shoots right. 6', 185 lbs. Born, Cherepovets, USSR, October 2, 1972.
(NY Rangers' 10th choice, 240th overall, in 1992 Entry Draft).

			Regular Season					Playoffs				
Season	Club	Lea	GP	G	A	TP	PIM	GP	G	A	TP	PIM
1992-93	Cherepovets	CIS	42	18	5	23	18	....	....	....	....	....
1993-94	Moscow D'amo	CIS	11	3	1	4	2	....	....	....	....	....
1994-95	Moscow D'amo	CIS	48	9	20	29	28	14	1	7	8	2
1995-96	Moscow D'amo	CIS	42	19	9	28	49	9	2	8	10	2
1996-97	**NY Rangers**	**NHL**	**16**	**5**	**5**	**10**	**6**	....	....	....	....	....
	Binghamton	AHL	61	22	27	49	6	4	1	1	2	2
	NHL Totals		**16**	**5**	**5**	**10**	**6**	....	....	....	....	....

VORONOV, SERGEI (VOH-rohn-ahf) PIT.

Defense. Shoots left. 6'2", 200 lbs. Born, Moscow, USSR, February 5, 1971.
(Pittsburgh's 7th choice, 206th overall, in 1995 Entry Draft).

			Regular Season					Playoffs				
Season	Club	Lea	GP	G	A	TP	PIM	GP	G	A	TP	PIM
1992-93	Moscow D'amo	CIS	36	1	0	1	25	....	....	....	....	....
1993-94	Moscow D'amo	CIS	44	5	6	11	72	....	....	....	....	....
1994-95	Moscow D'amo	CIS	44	3	4	7	80	12	4	1	5	26
1995-96	Cleveland	IHL	2	0	0	0	4	....	....	....	....	....
	Hampton Rds.	ECHL	57	6	23	29	241	2	0	0	0	6
1996-97	Las Vegas	IHL	40	2	4	6	99	....	....	....	....	....

VUJTEK, VLADIMIR (VYOO-tehk) T.B.

Left wing. Shoots left. 6'1", 190 lbs. Born, Ostrava, Czech., February 17, 1972.
(Montreal's 4th choice, 73rd overall, in 1991 Entry Draft).

			Regular Season					Playoffs				
Season	Club	Lea	GP	G	A	TP	PIM	GP	G	A	TP	PIM
1988-89	Vitkovice	Czech.	3	0	1	1	0	....	....	....	....	....
1989-90	Vitkovice	Czech.	29	7	7	14	....	....	....	....	....	....
1990-91	Vitkovice	Czech.	26	7	4	11	....	....	....	....	....	....
	Tri-City	WHL	37	26	18	44	25	7	2	3	5	4
1991-92	**Montreal**	**NHL**	**2**	**0**	**0**	**0**	**0**	....	....	....	....	....
a	Tri-City	WHL	53	41	61	102	114	....	....	....	....	....
1992-93	**Edmonton**	**NHL**	**30**	**1**	**10**	**11**	**8**	....	....	....	....	....
	Cape Breton	AHL	20	10	9	19	14	1	0	0	0	0
1993-94	**Edmonton**	**NHL**	**40**	**4**	**15**	**19**	**14**	....	....	....	....	....
1994-95	Vitkovice	Czech.	18	5	7	12	51	....	....	....	....	....
	Cape Breton	AHL	30	10	11	21	30	....	....	....	....	....
	Las Vegas	IHL	1	0	0	0	0	....	....	....	....	....
1995-96	Vitkovice	Czech.	26	6	7	13	....	4	1	1	2	....
1996-97	Assat	Fin.	50	27	31	58	48	4	1	2	3	2
	NHL Totals		**72**	**5**	**25**	**30**	**22**	....	....	....	....	....

a WHL West First All-Star Team (1992)

Traded to **Edmonton** by **Montreal** with Shayne Corson and Brent Gilchrist for Vincent Damphousse and Edmonton's fourth round choice (Adam Wiesel) in 1993 Entry Draft, August 27, 1992. Traded to **Tampa Bay** by **Edmonton** with Edmonton's third round choice in 1998 Entry Draft for Brantt Myhres and a conditional draft choice, July 16, 1997.

VUKOTA, MICK (vuh-KOH-tuh) NYI

Right wing. Shoots right. 6'1", 225 lbs. Born, Saskatoon, Sask., September 14, 1966.

			Regular Season					Playoffs				
Season	Club	Lea	GP	G	A	TP	PIM	GP	G	A	TP	PIM
1983-84	Winnipeg	WHL	3	1	1	2	10	....	....	....	....	....
1984-85	Kelowna	WHL	66	10	6	16	247	....	....	....	....	....
1985-86	Spokane	WHL	64	19	14	33	369	9	6	4	10	68
1986-87	Spokane	WHL	61	25	28	53	*337	4	0	0	0	40
1987-88	**NY Islanders**	**NHL**	**17**	**1**	**0**	**1**	**82**	**2**	**0**	**0**	**0**	**23**
	Springfield	AHL	52	7	9	16	375	....	....	....	....	....
1988-89	**NY Islanders**	**NHL**	**48**	**2**	**2**	**4**	**237**	....	....	....	....	....
	Springfield	AHL	3	1	0	1	33	....	....	....	....	....
1989-90	**NY Islanders**	**NHL**	**76**	**4**	**8**	**12**	**290**	**1**	**0**	**0**	**0**	**17**
1990-91	**NY Islanders**	**NHL**	**60**	**2**	**4**	**6**	**238**	....	....	....	....	....
	Capital Dist.	AHL	2	0	0	0	9	....	....	....	....	....
1991-92	**NY Islanders**	**NHL**	**74**	**0**	**6**	**6**	**293**	....	....	....	....	....
1992-93	**NY Islanders**	**NHL**	**74**	**2**	**5**	**7**	**216**	**15**	**0**	**0**	**0**	**16**
1993-94	**NY Islanders**	**NHL**	**72**	**3**	**1**	**4**	**237**	**4**	**0**	**0**	**0**	**17**
1994-95	**NY Islanders**	**NHL**	**40**	**0**	**2**	**2**	**109**	....	....	....	....	....
1995-96	**NY Islanders**	**NHL**	**32**	**1**	**1**	**2**	**106**	....	....	....	....	....
1996-97	**NY Islanders**	**NHL**	**17**	**1**	**0**	**1**	**71**	....	....	....	....	....
	Utah	IHL	43	11	11	22	185	7	1	2	3	20
	NHL Totals		**510**	**16**	**29**	**45**	**1879**	**22**	**0**	**0**	**0**	**73**

Signed as a free agent by **NY Islanders**, March 2, 1987.

VUORIVIRTA, JUHA (voh-RIH-vihr-tah, YOO-hah) L.A.

Center. Shoots left. 6'3", 189 lbs. Born, Oulu, Finland, May 3, 1976.
(Los Angeles' 8th choice, 163rd overall, in 1995 Entry Draft).

			Regular Season					Playoffs				
Season	Club	Lea	GP	G	A	TP	PIM	GP	G	A	TP	PIM
1994-95	Tappara	Fin.	39	2	3	5	12	....	....	....	....	....
1995-96	Tappara	Fin. Jr.	4	2	5	7	0	....	....	....	....	....
	Tappara	Fin.	47	6	3	9	20	4	0	0	0	0
1996-97	Tappara	Fin.	49	5	3	8	20	3	0	0	0	0

VYSHEDKEVICH, SERGEI (vee-shehd-KAY-vihch) N.J.

Defense. Shoots left. 6', 185 lbs. Born, Dedovsk, USSR, January 3, 1975.
(New Jersey's 3rd choice, 70th overall, in 1995 Entry Draft).

			Regular Season					Playoffs				
Season	Club	Lea	GP	G	A	TP	PIM	GP	G	A	TP	PIM
1994-95	Moscow D'amo	CIS	49	6	7	13	67	14	2	0	2	12
1995-96	Moscow D'amo	CIS	49	5	4	9	12	13	1	1	2	6
1996-97	Albany	AHL	65	8	27	35	16	12	0	6	6	0

WALKER, SCOTT VAN.

Center. Shoots right. 5'10", 189 lbs. Born, Montreal, Que., July 19, 1973.
(Vancouver's 4th choice, 124th overall, in 1993 Entry Draft).

			Regular Season					Playoffs				
Season	Club	Lea	GP	G	A	TP	PIM	GP	G	A	TP	PIM
1991-92	Owen Sound	OHL	53	7	31	38	128	5	0	7	7	8
1992-93a	Owen Sound	OHL	57	23	68	91	110	8	1	5	6	16
	Cdn. National	....	2	3	0	3	0	....	....	....	....	....
1993-94	Hamilton	AHL	77	10	29	39	272	4	0	1	1	25
1994-95	Syracuse	AHL	74	14	38	52	334	....	....	....	....	....
	Vancouver	**NHL**	**11**	**0**	**1**	**1**	**33**	....	....	....	....	....
1995-96	**Vancouver**	**NHL**	**63**	**4**	**8**	**12**	**137**	....	....	....	....	....
	Syracuse	AHL	15	3	12	15	52	16	9	8	17	39
1996-97	**Vancouver**	**NHL**	**64**	**3**	**15**	**18**	**132**	....	....	....	....	....
	NHL Totals		**138**	**7**	**24**	**31**	**302**	....	....	....	....	....

a OHL Second All-Star Team (1993)

WALLIN, JESSE (WAHL-ihn) DET.

Defense. Shoots left. 6'2", 190 lbs. Born, Saskatoon, Sask., March 10, 1978.
(Detroit's 1st choice, 26th overall, in 1996 Entry Draft).

			Regular Season					Playoffs				
Season	Club	Lea	GP	G	A	TP	PIM	GP	G	A	TP	PIM
1994-95	Prince Albert	WHL	72	4	20	24	72	....	....	....	....	....
1995-96	Red Deer	WHL	70	5	19	24	61	9	0	3	3	4
1996-97	Red Deer	WHL	59	6	33	39	70	16	1	4	5	10

WALSH, KURT BUF.

Right wing. Shoots right. 6'2", 205 lbs. Born, St. John's, Nfld., September 26, 1977.
(Buffalo's 5th choice, 87th overall, in 1996 Entry Draft).

			Regular Season					Playoffs				
Season	Club	Lea	GP	G	A	TP	PIM	GP	G	A	TP	PIM
1993-94	Newmarket	OHL	35	1	2	3	23	....	....	....	....	....
1994-95	Sarnia	OHL	17	0	4	4	18	....	....	....	....	....
	Oshawa	OHL	42	6	10	16	31	....	....	....	....	....
1995-96	Oshawa	OHL	41	19	18	37	63	....	....	....	....	....
	Owen Sound	OHL	26	8	9	17	20	6	0	2	2	4
1996-97	Owen Sound	OHL	63	17	16	33	73	4	0	0	0	11

WALZ, WES (WAHLS)

Center. Shoots right. 5'10", 185 lbs. Born, Calgary, Alta., May 15, 1970.
(Boston's 3rd choice, 57th overall, in 1989 Entry Draft).

			Regular Season					Playoffs				
Season	Club	Lea	GP	G	A	TP	PIM	GP	G	A	TP	PIM
1988-89	Lethbridge	WHL	63	29	75	104	32	8	1	5	6	6
1989-90	**Boston**	**NHL**	**2**	**1**	**1**	**2**	**0**	....	....	....	....	....
a	Lethbridge	WHL	56	54	86	140	69	19	13	*24	*37	33
1990-91	**Boston**	**NHL**	**56**	**8**	**8**	**16**	**32**	**2**	**0**	**0**	**0**	**0**
	Maine	AHL	20	8	12	20	19	2	0	0	0	21
1991-92	**Boston**	**NHL**	**15**	**0**	**3**	**3**	**12**	....	....	....	....	....
	Maine	AHL	21	13	11	24	38	....	....	....	....	....
	Philadelphia	**NHL**	**2**	**1**	**0**	**1**	**0**	....	....	....	....	....
	Hershey	AHL	41	13	28	41	37	6	1	2	3	0
1992-93	Hershey	AHL	78	35	45	80	106	....	....	....	....	....
1993-94	**Calgary**	**NHL**	**53**	**11**	**27**	**38**	**16**	**6**	**3**	**0**	**3**	**2**
	Saint John	AHL	15	6	6	12	14	....	....	....	....	....
1994-95	**Calgary**	**NHL**	**39**	**6**	**12**	**18**	**11**	**1**	**0**	**0**	**0**	**0**
1995-96	**Detroit**	**NHL**	**2**	**0**	**0**	**0**	**0**	....	....	....	....	....
	Adirondack	AHL	38	20	35	55	58	....	....	....	....	....
1996-97	Zug	Switz.	41	24	22	46	67	9	5	1	6	39
	NHL Totals		**169**	**27**	**51**	**78**	**71**	**9**	**3**	**0**	**3**	**2**

a WHL East First All-Star Team (1990)

Traded to **Philadelphia** by **Boston** with Garry Galley and Boston's third round choice (Milos Holan) in 1993 Entry Draft for Gord Murphy, Brian Dobbin, Philadelphia's third round choice (Sergei Zholtok) in 1992 Entry Draft and Philadelphia's fourth round choice (Charles Paquette) in 1993 Entry Draft, January 2, 1992. Signed as a free agent by **Calgary**, August 26, 1993. Signed as a free agent by **Detroit**, September 6, 1995.

WARD, AARON DET.

Defense. Shoots right. 6'2", 200 lbs. Born, Windsor, Ont., January 17, 1973.
(Winnipeg's 1st choice, 5th overall, in 1991 Entry Draft).

			Regular Season					Playoffs				
Season	Club	Lea	GP	G	A	TP	PIM	GP	G	A	TP	PIM
1990-91	U. of Michigan	CCHA	46	8	11	19	126	....	....	....	....	....
1991-92	U. of Michigan	CCHA	42	7	12	19	64	....	....	....	....	....
1992-93	U. of Michigan	CCHA	30	5	8	13	73	....	....	....	....	....
	Cdn. National	....	4	0	0	0	8	....	....	....	....	....
1993-94	**Detroit**	**NHL**	**5**	**1**	**0**	**1**	**4**	....	....	....	....	....
	Adirondack	AHL	58	4	12	16	87	9	2	6	8	6
1994-95	Adirondack	AHL	76	11	24	35	87	4	0	1	1	0
	Detroit	**NHL**	**1**	**0**	**1**	**1**	**2**	....	....	....	....	....
1995-96	Adirondack	AHL	74	5	10	15	133	3	0	0	0	6
1996-97	**Detroit**	**NHL**	**49**	**2**	**5**	**7**	**52**	**19**	**0**	**0**	**0**	**17** ♦
	NHL Totals		**55**	**3**	**6**	**9**	**58**	**19**	**0**	**0**	**0**	**17**

Traded to **Detroit** by **Winnipeg** with Toronto's fourth round choice (previously acquired by Winnipeg — later traded to Detroit — Detroit selected John Jakopin) in 1993 Entry Draft for Paul Ysebaert and future considerations (Alan Kerr, June 18, 1993), June 11, 1993.

WARD, DIXON BUF.

Right wing. Shoots right. 6', 200 lbs. Born, Leduc, Alta., September 23, 1968.
(Vancouver's 6th choice, 128th overall, in 1988 Entry Draft).

			Regular Season					Playoffs				
Season	Club	Lea	GP	G	A	TP	PIM	GP	G	A	TP	PIM
1988-89	North Dakota	WCHA	37	8	9	17	26	....	....	....	....	....
1989-90	North Dakota	WCHA	45	35	34	69	44	....	....	....	....	....
1990-91a	North Dakota	WCHA	43	34	35	69	84	....	....	....	....	....
1991-92a	North Dakota	WCHA	38	33	31	64	90	....	....	....	....	....
1992-93	**Vancouver**	**NHL**	**70**	**22**	**30**	**52**	**82**	**9**	**2**	**3**	**5**	**0**
1993-94	**Vancouver**	**NHL**	**33**	**6**	**1**	**7**	**37**	....	....	....	....	....
	Los Angeles	**NHL**	**34**	**6**	**2**	**8**	**45**	....	....	....	....	....
1994-95	**Toronto**	**NHL**	**22**	**0**	**3**	**3**	**31**	....	....	....	....	....
	St. John's	AHL	6	3	3	6	19	....	....	....	....	....
	Detroit	IHL	7	3	6	9	7	5	3	0	3	7
1995-96	**Buffalo**	**NHL**	**8**	**2**	**2**	**4**	**6**	....	....	....	....	....
b	Rochester	AHL	71	38	56	94	74	19	11	*24	*35	8
1996-97	**Buffalo**	**NHL**	**79**	**13**	**32**	**45**	**36**	**12**	**2**	**3**	**5**	**6**
	NHL Totals		**246**	**49**	**70**	**119**	**237**	**21**	**4**	**6**	**10**	**6**

a WCHA Second All-Star Team (1991, 1992)
b Won Jack A. Butterfield Trophy (Playoff MVP - AHL) (1996)

Traded to **Los Angeles** by **Vancouver** for Jimmy Carson, January 8, 1994. Traded to **Toronto** by **Los Angeles** with Guy Leveque, Kelly Fairchild and Shayne Toporowski for Eric Lacroix, Chris Snell and Toronto's fourth round choice (Eric Belanger) in 1996 Entry draft, October 3, 1994. Signed as a free agent by **Buffalo**, September 20, 1995.

WARD, ED CGY.

Right wing. Shoots right. 6'3", 205 lbs. Born, Edmonton, Alta., November 10, 1969.
(Quebec's 7th choice, 108th overall, in 1988 Entry Draft).

			Regular Season					Playoffs				
Season	Club	Lea	GP	G	A	TP	PIM	GP	G	A	TP	PIM
1987-88	N. Michigan	WCHA	25	0	2	2	40	....	....	....	....	....
1988-89	N. Michigan	WCHA	42	5	15	20	36	....	....	....	....	....
1989-90	N. Michigan	WCHA	39	5	11	16	77	....	....	....	....	....
1990-91	N. Michigan	WCHA	46	13	18	31	109	....	....	....	....	....
1991-92	Greensboro	ECHL	12	4	8	12	21	....	....	....	....	....
	Halifax	AHL	51	7	11	18	65	....	....	....	....	....
1992-93	Halifax	AHL	70	13	19	32	56	....	....	....	....	....
1993-94	**Quebec**	**NHL**	**7**	**1**	**0**	**1**	**5**	....	....	....	....	....
	Cornwall	AHL	60	12	30	42	65	12	1	3	4	14
1994-95	Cornwall	AHL	56	10	14	24	118	....	....	....	....	....
	Calgary	**NHL**	**2**	**1**	**1**	**2**	**2**	....	....	....	....	....
	Saint John	AHL	11	4	5	9	20	5	1	0	1	10
1995-96	**Calgary**	**NHL**	**41**	**3**	**5**	**8**	**44**	....	....	....	....	....
	Saint John	AHL	12	1	2	3	45	16	4	4	8	27
1996-97	**Calgary**	**NHL**	**40**	**5**	**8**	**13**	**49**	....	....	....	....	....
	Saint John	AHL	1	0	0	0	0	....	....	....	....	....
	Detroit	IHL	31	7	6	13	45	....	....	....	....	....
	NHL Totals		**90**	**10**	**14**	**24**	**100**	....	....	....	....	....

Traded to **Calgary** by **Quebec** for Francois Groleau, March 23, 1995.

WARD, JASON MTL.

Right wing/center. Shoots right. 6'2", 184 lbs. Born, Chapleau, Ont., January 16, 1979.
(Montreal's 1st choice, 11th overall, in 1997 Entry Draft).

			Regular Season					Playoffs				
Season	Club	Lea	GP	G	A	TP	PIM	GP	G	A	TP	PIM
1995-96	Niagara Falls	OHL	64	15	35	50	139	10	6	4	10	23
1996-97	Erie	OHL	58	25	39	64	137	5	1	2	3	2

WARD, LANCE — N.J.

Defense. Shoots left. 6'3", 195 lbs. Born, Lloydminster, Alta., June 2, 1978.
(New Jersey's 1st choice, 10th overall, in 1996 Entry Draft).

			Regular Season					Playoffs				
Season	Club	Lea	GP	G	A	TP	PIM	GP	G	A	TP	PIM
1994-95	Red Deer	WHL	28	0	0	0	57	....	....	....	....	....
1995-96	Red Deer	WHL	72	4	13	17	127	10	0	4	4	10
1996-97	Red Deer	WHL	70	5	34	39	229	16	0	3	3	36

WARE, JEFF — (WAIR) TOR.

Defense. Shoots left. 6'4", 220 lbs. Born, Toronto, Ont., May 19, 1977.
(Toronto's 1st choice, 15th overall, in 1995 Entry Draft).

			Regular Season					Playoffs				
Season	Club	Lea	GP	G	A	TP	PIM	GP	G	A	TP	PIM
1994-95	Oshawa	OHL	55	2	11	13	86	7	1	1	2	6
1995-96	Oshawa	OHL	62	4	19	23	128	5	0	1	1	8
	St. John's	AHL	4	0	0	0	4	4	0	0	0	2
1996-97	**Toronto**	**NHL**	**13**	**0**	**0**	**0**	**6**	....	....	....	....	....
	Oshawa	OHL	24	1	10	11	38	13	0	3	3	34
	NHL Totals		**13**	**0**	**0**	**0**	**6**	....	....	....	....	....

WARRENER, RHETT — (WAHR-ihn-uhr, REHT) FLA.

Defense. Shoots left. 6'1", 209 lbs. Born, Shaunavon, Sask., January 27, 1976.
(Florida's 2nd choice, 27th overall, in 1994 Entry Draft).

			Regular Season					Playoffs				
Season	Club	Lea	GP	G	A	TP	PIM	GP	G	A	TP	PIM
1991-92	Saskatoon	WHL	2	0	0	0	0	....	....	....	....	....
1992-93	Saskatoon	WHL	68	2	17	19	100	9	0	0	0	14
1993-94	Saskatoon	WHL	61	7	19	26	131	16	0	5	5	33
1994-95	Saskatoon	WHL	66	13	26	39	137	10	0	3	3	6
1995-96	**Florida**	**NHL**	**28**	**0**	**3**	**3**	**46**	**21**	**0**	**1**	**1**	**0**
	Carolina	AHL	9	0	0	0	4	....	....	....	....	....
1996-97	**Florida**	**NHL**	**62**	**4**	**9**	**13**	**88**	**5**	**0**	**0**	**0**	**0**
	NHL Totals		**90**	**4**	**12**	**16**	**134**	**26**	**0**	**1**	**1**	**0**

WARRINER, TODD — (WAHR-ihn-uhr) TOR.

Left wing. Shoots left. 6'1", 188 lbs. Born, Blenheim, Ont., January 3, 1974.
(Quebec's 1st choice, 4th overall, in 1992 Entry Draft).

			Regular Season					Playoffs				
Season	Club	Lea	GP	G	A	TP	PIM	GP	G	A	TP	PIM
1990-91	Windsor	OHL	57	36	28	64	26	11	5	6	11	12
1991-92a	Windsor	OHL	50	41	41	82	64	7	5	4	9	6
1992-93	Windsor	OHL	23	13	21	34	29	....	....	....	....	....
	Kitchener	OHL	32	19	24	43	35	7	5	14	19	14
1993-94	Cdn. National	....	50	11	20	31	33	....	....	....	....	....
	Cdn. Olympic	....	4	1	1	2	0	....	....	....	....	....
	Kitchener	OHL	....	....	....	....	....	1	0	1	1	0
	Cornwall	AHL	....	....	....	....	....	10	1	4	5	4
1994-95	St. John's	AHL	46	8	10	18	22	4	1	0	1	2
	Toronto	**NHL**	**5**	**0**	**0**	**0**	**0**	....	....	....	....	....
1995-96	**Toronto**	**NHL**	**57**	**7**	**8**	**15**	**26**	**6**	**1**	**1**	**2**	**2**
	St. John's	AHL	11	5	6	11	16	....	....	....	....	....
1996-97	**Toronto**	**NHL**	**75**	**12**	**21**	**33**	**41**	....	....	....	....	....
	NHL Totals		**137**	**19**	**29**	**48**	**67**	**6**	**1**	**1**	**2**	**2**

a OHL First All-Star Team (1992)

Traded to **Toronto** by **Quebec** with Mats Sundin, Garth Butcher and Philadelphia's first round choice (previously acquired by Quebec — later traded to Washington — Washington selected Nolan Baumgartner) in 1994 Entry Draft for Wendel Clark, Sylvain Lefebvre, Landon Wilson and Toronto's first round choice (Jeffrey Kealty) in 1994 Entry Draft, June 28, 1994.

WASHBURN, STEVE — FLA.

Center. Shoots left. 6'2", 191 lbs. Born, Ottawa, Ont., April 10, 1975.
(Florida's 5th choice, 78th overall, in 1993 Entry Draft).

			Regular Season					Playoffs				
Season	Club	Lea	GP	G	A	TP	PIM	GP	G	A	TP	PIM
1991-92	Ottawa	OHL	59	5	17	22	10	11	2	3	5	4
1992-93	Ottawa	OHL	66	20	38	58	54	....	....	....	....	....
1993-94	Ottawa	OHL	65	30	50	80	88	17	7	16	23	10
1994-95	Ottawa	OHL	63	43	63	106	72	....	....	....	....	....
	Cincinnati	IHL	6	3	1	4	0	9	1	3	4	4
1995-96	**Florida**	**NHL**	**1**	**0**	**1**	**1**	**0**	**1**	**0**	**1**	**1**	**0**
	Carolina	AHL	78	29	54	83	45	....	....	....	....	....
1996-97	**Florida**	**NHL**	**18**	**3**	**6**	**9**	**4**	....	....	....	....	....
	Carolina	AHL	60	23	40	63	66	....	....	....	....	....
	NHL Totals		**19**	**3**	**7**	**10**	**4**	**1**	**0**	**1**	**1**	**0**

WASYLKO, STEVE — (WAH-sill-ko) CAR.

Center. Shoots left. 6'1", 173 lbs. Born, Ottawa, Ont., July 11, 1978.
(Hartford's 4th choice, 104th overall, in 1996 Entry Draft).

			Regular Season					Playoffs				
Season	Club	Lea	GP	G	A	TP	PIM	GP	G	A	TP	PIM
1995-96	Detroit	OHL	65	18	30	48	33	9	0	1	1	6
1996-97	Detroit	OHL	62	25	25	50	48	5	1	2	3	4

WASYLUK, TREVOR — (WAHZ-ah-luhk) CAR.

Left wing. Shoots left. 6'1", 187 lbs. Born, Saskatoon, Sask., May 4, 1978.
(Hartford's 1st choice, 34th overall, in 1996 Entry Draft).

			Regular Season					Playoffs				
Season	Club	Lea	GP	G	A	TP	PIM	GP	G	A	TP	PIM
1994-95	Medicine Hat	WHL	67	6	4	10	75	5	0	2	2	4
1995-96	Medicine Hat	WHL	69	25	21	46	59	5	0	2	2	15
1996-97	Medicine Hat	WHL	72	32	32	64	71	4	1	0	1	8
	Springfield	AHL	1	0	0	0	0	....	....	....	....	....

WATT, MIKE — EDM.

Left wing. Shoots left. 6'2", 212 lbs. Born, Seaforth, Ont., March 31, 1976.
(Edmonton's 3rd choice, 32nd overall, in 1994 Entry Draft).

			Regular Season					Playoffs				
Season	Club	Lea	GP	G	A	TP	PIM	GP	G	A	TP	PIM
1994-95	Michigan State	CCHA	39	12	6	18	64	....	....	....	....	....
1995-96	Michigan State	CCHA	37	17	22	39	60	....	....	....	....	....
1996-97	Michigan State	CCHA	39	24	17	41	109	....	....	....	....	....

WEBB, STEVE — NYI

Right wing. Shoots right. 6', 195 lbs. Born, Peterborough, Ont., April 20, 1975.
(Buffalo's 8th choice, 176th overall, in 1994 Entry Draft).

			Regular Season					Playoffs				
Season	Club	Lea	GP	G	A	TP	PIM	GP	G	A	TP	PIM
1992-93	Windsor	OHL	60	14	25	39	190	....	....	....	....	....
1993-94	Peterborough	OHL	35	6	16	22	126	6	1	1	2	10
1994-95	Peterborough	OHL	42	8	16	24	109	11	3	3	6	22
1995-96	Muskegon	ColHL	58	18	24	42	263	5	1	2	3	22
	Detroit	IHL	4	0	0	0	24	....	....	....	....	....
1996-97	**NY Islanders**	**NHL**	**41**	**1**	**4**	**5**	**144**	....	....	....	....	....
	Kentucky	AHL	25	6	6	12	103	2	0	0	0	19
	NHL Totals		**41**	**1**	**4**	**5**	**144**	....	....	....	....	....

Signed as a free agent by **NY Islanders**, October 10, 1996.

WEIGHT, DOUG — (WAYT) EDM.

Center. Shoots left. 5'11", 200 lbs. Born, Warren, MI, January 21, 1971.
(NY Rangers' 2nd choice, 34th overall, in 1990 Entry Draft).

			Regular Season					Playoffs				
Season	Club	Lea	GP	G	A	TP	PIM	GP	G	A	TP	PIM
1989-90	Lake Superior	CCHA	46	21	48	69	44	....	....	....	....	....
1990-91ab	Lake Superior	CCHA	42	29	46	75	86	....	....	....	....	....
	NY Rangers	**NHL**	....	....	....	....	....	**1**	**0**	**0**	**0**	**0**
1991-92	**NY Rangers**	**NHL**	**53**	**8**	**22**	**30**	**23**	**7**	**2**	**2**	**4**	**0**
	Binghamton	AHL	9	3	14	17	2	4	1	4	5	6
1992-93	**NY Rangers**	**NHL**	**65**	**15**	**25**	**40**	**55**	....	....	....	....	....
	Edmonton	**NHL**	**13**	**2**	**6**	**8**	**10**	....	....	....	....	....
1993-94	**Edmonton**	**NHL**	**84**	**24**	**50**	**74**	**47**	....	....	....	....	....
1994-95	Rosenheim	Ger.	8	2	3	5	18	....	....	....	....	....
	Edmonton	**NHL**	**48**	**7**	**33**	**40**	**69**	....	....	....	....	....
1995-96	**Edmonton**	**NHL**	**82**	**25**	**79**	**104**	**95**	....	....	....	....	....
1996-97	**Edmonton**	**NHL**	**80**	**21**	**61**	**82**	**80**	**12**	**3**	**8**	**11**	**8**
	NHL Totals		**425**	**102**	**276**	**378**	**379**	**20**	**5**	**10**	**15**	**8**

a CCHA First All-Star Team (1991)
b NCAA West Second All-American Team (1991)

Played in NHL All-Star Game (1996)

Traded to **Edmonton** by **NY Rangers** for Esa Tikkanen, March 17, 1993.

WEINRICH, ERIC — (WIGHN-rihc) CHI.

Defense. Shoots left. 6'1", 210 lbs. Born, Roanoke, VA, December 19, 1966.
(New Jersey's 3rd choice, 32nd overall, in 1985 Entry Draft).

			Regular Season					Playoffs				
Season	Club	Lea	GP	G	A	TP	PIM	GP	G	A	TP	PIM
1985-86	U. of Maine	H.E.	34	0	14	14	26	....	....	....	....	....
1986-87ab	U. of Maine	H.E.	41	12	32	44	59	....	....	....	....	....
1987-88	U. of Maine	H.E.	8	4	7	11	22	....	....	....	....	....
	U.S. National	....	38	3	9	12	24	....	....	....	....	....
	U.S. Olympic	....	3	0	0	0	0	....	....	....	....	....
1988-89	**New Jersey**	**NHL**	**2**	**0**	**0**	**0**	**0**	....	....	....	....	....
	Utica	AHL	80	17	27	44	70	5	0	1	1	4
1989-90	**New Jersey**	**NHL**	**19**	**2**	**7**	**9**	**11**	**6**	**1**	**3**	**4**	**17**
cd	Utica	AHL	57	12	48	60	38	....	....	....	....	....
1990-91e	**New Jersey**	**NHL**	**76**	**4**	**34**	**38**	**48**	**7**	**1**	**2**	**3**	**6**
1991-92	**New Jersey**	**NHL**	**76**	**7**	**25**	**32**	**55**	**7**	**0**	**2**	**2**	**4**
1992-93	**Hartford**	**NHL**	**79**	**7**	**29**	**36**	**76**	....	....	....	....	....
1993-94	**Hartford**	**NHL**	**8**	**1**	**1**	**2**	**2**	....	....	....	....	....
	Chicago	**NHL**	**54**	**3**	**23**	**26**	**31**	**6**	**0**	**2**	**2**	**6**
1994-95	**Chicago**	**NHL**	**48**	**3**	**10**	**13**	**33**	**16**	**1**	**5**	**6**	**4**
1995-96	**Chicago**	**NHL**	**77**	**5**	**10**	**15**	**65**	**10**	**1**	**4**	**5**	**10**
1996-97	**Chicago**	**NHL**	**81**	**7**	**25**	**32**	**62**	**6**	**0**	**1**	**1**	**4**
	NHL Totals		**520**	**39**	**164**	**203**	**383**	**58**	**4**	**19**	**23**	**51**

a Hockey East First All-Star Team (1987)
b NCAA East Second All-American Team (1987)
c AHL First All-Star Team (1990)
d Won Eddie Shore Plaque (Outstanding Defenseman - AHL) (1990)
e NHL/Upper Deck All-Rookie Team (1991)

Traded to **Hartford** by **New Jersey** with Sean Burke for Bobby Holik, Hartford's second round choice (Jay Pandolfo) in 1993 Entry Draft and future considerations, August 28, 1992. Traded to **Chicago** by **Hartford** with Patrick Poulin for Steve Larmer and Bryan Marchment, November 2, 1993.

WELLS, CHRIS — FLA.

Center. Shoots left. 6'6", 223 lbs. Born, Calgary, Alta., November 12, 1975.
(Pittsburgh's 1st choice, 24th overall, in 1994 Entry Draft).

			Regular Season					Playoffs				
Season	Club	Lea	GP	G	A	TP	PIM	GP	G	A	TP	PIM
1991-92	Seattle	WHL	64	13	8	21	80	11	0	0	0	15
1992-93	Seattle	WHL	63	18	37	55	111	5	2	3	5	4
1993-94	Seattle	WHL	69	30	44	74	150	9	6	5	11	23
1994-95a	Seattle	WHL	69	45	63	108	148	3	0	1	1	4
	Cleveland	IHL	3	0	1	1	2	....	....	....	....	....
1995-96	**Pittsburgh**	**NHL**	**54**	**2**	**2**	**4**	**59**	....	....	....	....	....
1996-97	Cleveland	IHL	15	4	6	10	9	....	....	....	....	....
	Florida	**NHL**	**47**	**2**	**6**	**8**	**42**	**3**	**0**	**0**	**0**	**0**
	NHL Totals		**101**	**4**	**8**	**12**	**101**	**3**	**0**	**0**	**0**	**0**

a WHL West First All-Star Team (1995)

Traded to **Florida** by **Pittsburgh** for Stu Barnes and Jason Woolley, November 19, 1996.

WELLS, JAY

Defense. Shoots left. 6'1", 210 lbs. Born, Paris, Ont., May 18, 1959.
(Los Angeles' 1st choice, 16th overall, in 1979 Entry Draft).

			Regular Season					Playoffs				
Season	**Club**	**Lea**	**GP**	**G**	**A**	**TP**	**PIM**	**GP**	**G**	**A**	**TP**	**PIM**
1977-78	Kingston	OHA	68	9	13	22	195	5	1	2	3	6
1978-79a	Kingston	OHA	48	6	21	27	100	11	2	7	9	29
1979-80	**Los Angeles**	**NHL**	**43**	**0**	**0**	**0**	**113**	**4**	**0**	**0**	**0**	**11**
	Binghamton	AHL	28	0	6	6	48	....	....	....	....	....
1980-81	**Los Angeles**	**NHL**	**72**	**5**	**13**	**18**	**155**	**4**	**0**	**0**	**0**	**27**
1981-82	**Los Angeles**	**NHL**	**60**	**1**	**8**	**9**	**145**	**10**	**1**	**3**	**4**	**41**
1982-83	**Los Angeles**	**NHL**	**69**	**3**	**12**	**15**	**167**	....	....	....	....	....
1983-84	**Los Angeles**	**NHL**	**69**	**3**	**18**	**21**	**141**	....	....	....	....	....
1984-85	**Los Angeles**	**NHL**	**77**	**2**	**9**	**11**	**185**	**3**	**0**	**1**	**1**	**0**
1985-86	**Los Angeles**	**NHL**	**79**	**11**	**31**	**42**	**226**	....	....	....	....	....
1986-87	**Los Angeles**	**NHL**	**77**	**7**	**29**	**36**	**155**	**5**	**1**	**2**	**3**	**10**
1987-88	**Los Angeles**	**NHL**	**58**	**2**	**23**	**25**	**159**	**5**	**1**	**2**	**3**	**21**
1988-89	**Philadelphia**	**NHL**	**67**	**2**	**19**	**21**	**184**	**18**	**0**	**2**	**2**	**51**
1989-90	**Philadelphia**	**NHL**	**59**	**3**	**16**	**19**	**129**	....	....	....	....	....
	Buffalo	**NHL**	**1**	**0**	**1**	**1**	**0**	**6**	**0**	**0**	**0**	**12**
1990-91	**Buffalo**	**NHL**	**43**	**1**	**2**	**3**	**86**	**1**	**0**	**1**	**1**	**0**
1991-92	**Buffalo**	**NHL**	**41**	**2**	**9**	**11**	**157**	....	....	....	....	....
	NY Rangers	**NHL**	**11**	**0**	**0**	**0**	**24**	**13**	**0**	**2**	**2**	**10**
1992-93	**NY Rangers**	**NHL**	**53**	**1**	**9**	**10**	**107**	....	....	....	....	....
1993-94	**NY Rangers**	**NHL**	**79**	**2**	**7**	**9**	**110**	**23**	**0**	**0**	**0**	**20** ♦
1994-95	**NY Rangers**	**NHL**	**43**	**2**	**7**	**9**	**36**	**10**	**0**	**0**	**0**	**8**
1995-96	**St. Louis**	**NHL**	**76**	**0**	**3**	**3**	**67**	**12**	**0**	**1**	**1**	**2**
1996-97	**Tampa Bay**	**NHL**	**21**	**0**	**0**	**0**	**13**	....	....	....	....	....
	NHL Totals		**1098**	**47**	**216**	**263**	**2359**	**114**	**3**	**14**	**17**	**213**

a OHA First All-Star Team (1979)

Traded to **Philadelphia** by **Los Angeles** for Doug Crossman, September 29, 1988. Traded to **Buffalo** by **Philadelphia** with Philadelphia's fourth round choice (Peter Ambroziak) in 1991 Entry Draft for Kevin Maguire and Buffalo's second round choice (Mikael Renberg) in 1990 Entry Draft, March 5, 1990. Traded to **NY Rangers** by **Buffalo** for Randy Moller, March 9, 1992. Traded to **St. Louis** by **NY Rangers** for Doug Lidster, July 31, 1995. Signed as a free agent by **Tampa Bay**, August 3, 1996.

WELSING, MARK (ROCKY) — ANA.

Defense. Shoots left. 6'3", 196 lbs. Born, Beloit, WI, February 8, 1976.
(Anaheim's 7th choice, 158th overall, in 1994 Entry Draft).

			Regular Season					Playoffs				
Season	**Club**	**Lea**	**GP**	**G**	**A**	**TP**	**PIM**	**GP**	**G**	**A**	**TP**	**PIM**
1994-95	N. Michigan	WCHA	38	0	8	8	129	....	....	....	....	....
1995-96	N. Michigan	WCHA	38	0	6	6	84	....	....	....	....	....
1996-97	N. Michigan	WCHA	33	2	1	3	77	....	....	....	....	....

WERENKA, BRAD (wuh-REHN-kuh) — PIT.

Defense. Shoots left. 6'2", 210 lbs. Born, Two Hills, Alta., February 12, 1969.
(Edmonton's 2nd choice, 42nd overall, in 1987 Entry Draft).

			Regular Season					Playoffs				
Season	**Club**	**Lea**	**GP**	**G**	**A**	**TP**	**PIM**	**GP**	**G**	**A**	**TP**	**PIM**
1986-87	N. Michigan	WCHA	30	4	4	8	35	....	....	....	....	....
1987-88	N. Michigan	WCHA	34	7	23	30	26	....	....	....	....	....
1988-89	N. Michigan	WCHA	28	7	13	20	16	....	....	....	....	....
1989-90	N. Michigan	WCHA	8	2	5	7	8	....	....	....	....	....
1990-91abc	N. Michigan	WCHA	47	20	43	63	36	....	....	....	....	....
1991-92	Cape Breton	AHL	66	6	21	27	95	5	0	3	3	6
1992-93	**Edmonton**	**NHL**	**27**	**5**	**4**	**9**	**24**	....	....	....	....	....
	Cdn. National	....	18	3	7	10	10	....	....	....	....	....
	Cape Breton	AHL	4	1	1	2	4	16	4	17	21	12
1993-94	**Edmonton**	**NHL**	**15**	**0**	**4**	**4**	**14**	....	....	....	....	....
	Cape Breton	AHL	25	6	17	23	19	....	....	....	....	....
	Cdn. Olympic	....	8	2	2	4	8	....	....	....	....	....
	Quebec	**NHL**	**11**	**0**	**7**	**7**	**8**	....	....	....	....	....
	Cornwall	AHL	....	....	....	....	....	12	2	10	12	22
1994-95	Milwaukee	IHL	80	8	45	53	161	15	3	10	13	36
1995-96	**Chicago**	**NHL**	**9**	**0**	**0**	**0**	**8**	....	....	....	....	....
	Indianapolis	IHL	73	15	42	57	85	5	1	3	4	8
1996-97de	Indianapolis	IHL	82	20	56	76	83	4	1	4	5	6
	NHL Totals		**62**	**5**	**15**	**20**	**54**	....	....	....	....	....

a WCHA First All-Star Team (1991)
b NCAA West First All-American Team (1991)
c NCAA Final Four All-Tournament Team (1991)
d IHL First All-Star Team (1997)
e Won Governors' Trophy (Top Defenseman - IHL) (1997)

Traded to **Quebec** by **Edmonton** for Steve Passmore, March 21, 1994. Signed as a free agent by **Chicago**, July 20, 1995. Signed as a free agent by **Pittsburgh**, July 31, 1997.

WERNBLOM, MAGNUS (VEHRN-blawm) — L.A.

Right wing. Shoots left. 6', 195 lbs. Born, Kramfors, Sweden, February 3, 1973.
(Los Angeles' 6th choice, 207th overall, in 1992 Entry Draft).

			Regular Season					Playoffs				
Season	**Club**	**Lea**	**GP**	**G**	**A**	**TP**	**PIM**	**GP**	**G**	**A**	**TP**	**PIM**
1990-91	MoDo	Swe.	16	4	2	6	8	....	....	....	....	....
1991-92	MoDo	Swe.	35	7	6	13	50	....	....	....	....	....
1992-93	MoDo	Swe.	37	8	3	11	36	3	0	0	0	0
1993-94	MoDo	Swe.	39	14	9	23	46	11	2	3	5	12
1994-95	MoDo	Swe.	38	12	10	22	50	....	....	....	....	....
1995-96	MoDo	Swe.	28	16	8	24	50	8	3	0	3	14
1996-97	MoDo	Swe.	50	26	9	35	78	....	....	....	....	....

WESENBERG, BRIAN (WEE-sehn-buhrg) — PHI.

Right wing. Shoots right. 6'3", 187 lbs. Born, Peterborough, Ont., May 9, 1977.
(Anaheim's 2nd choice, 29th overall, in 1995 Entry Draft).

			Regular Season					Playoffs				
Season	**Club**	**Lea**	**GP**	**G**	**A**	**TP**	**PIM**	**GP**	**G**	**A**	**TP**	**PIM**
1994-95	Guelph	OHL	66	17	27	44	81	14	2	3	5	18
1995-96	Guelph	OHL	66	25	33	58	161	16	4	11	15	34
1996-97	Guelph	OHL	64	37	43	80	186	18	4	9	13	59
	Philadelphia	AHL	....	....	....	....	....	3	0	0	0	7

Traded to **Philadelphia** by **Anaheim** for Anatoli Semenov and Mike Crowley, March 19, 1996.

WESLEY, GLEN — CAR.

Defense. Shoots left. 6'1", 197 lbs. Born, Red Deer, Alta., October 2, 1968.
(Boston's 1st choice, 3rd overall, in 1987 Entry Draft).

			Regular Season					Playoffs				
Season	**Club**	**Lea**	**GP**	**G**	**A**	**TP**	**PIM**	**GP**	**G**	**A**	**TP**	**PIM**
1983-84	Portland	WHL	3	1	2	3	0	....	....	....	....	....
1984-85	Portland	WHL	67	16	52	68	76	6	1	6	7	8
1985-86a	Portland	WHL	69	16	75	91	96	15	3	11	14	29
1986-87a	Portland	WHL	63	16	46	62	72	20	8	18	26	27
1987-88b	**Boston**	**NHL**	**79**	**7**	**30**	**37**	**69**	**23**	**6**	**8**	**14**	**22**
1988-89	**Boston**	**NHL**	**77**	**19**	**35**	**54**	**61**	**10**	**0**	**2**	**2**	**4**
1989-90	**Boston**	**NHL**	**78**	**9**	**27**	**36**	**48**	**21**	**2**	**6**	**8**	**36**
1990-91	**Boston**	**NHL**	**80**	**11**	**32**	**43**	**78**	**19**	**2**	**9**	**11**	**19**
1991-92	**Boston**	**NHL**	**78**	**9**	**37**	**46**	**54**	**15**	**2**	**4**	**6**	**16**
1992-93	**Boston**	**NHL**	**64**	**8**	**25**	**33**	**47**	**4**	**0**	**0**	**0**	**0**
1993-94	**Boston**	**NHL**	**81**	**14**	**44**	**58**	**64**	**13**	**3**	**3**	**6**	**12**
1994-95	**Hartford**	**NHL**	**48**	**2**	**14**	**16**	**50**	....	....	....	....	....
1995-96	**Hartford**	**NHL**	**68**	**8**	**16**	**24**	**88**	....	....	....	....	....
1996-97	**Hartford**	**NHL**	**68**	**6**	**26**	**32**	**40**	....	....	....	....	....
	NHL Totals		**721**	**93**	**286**	**379**	**599**	**105**	**15**	**32**	**47**	**109**

a WHL West All-Star Team (1986, 1987)
b NHL All-Rookie Team (1988)

Played in NHL All-Star Game (1989)

Traded to **Hartford** by **Boston** for Hartford's first round choices in 1995 (Kyle McLaren), 1996 (Jonathan Aitken) and 1997 (Sergei Samsonov) Entry Draft, August 26, 1994.

WHITE, BRIAN — T.B.

Defense. Shoots right. 6'1", 180 lbs. Born, Winchester, MA, February 7, 1976.
(Tampa Bay's 11th choice, 268th overall, in 1994 Entry Draft).

			Regular Season					Playoffs				
Season	**Club**	**Lea**	**GP**	**G**	**A**	**TP**	**PIM**	**GP**	**G**	**A**	**TP**	**PIM**
1994-95	U. of Maine	H.E.	28	1	1	2	16	....	....	....	....	....
1995-96	U. of Maine	H.E.	39	0	4	4	18	....	....	....	....	....
1996-97	U. of Maine	H.E.	35	4	12	16	36	....	....	....	....	....

WHITE, PETER — PHI.

Center. Shoots left. 5'11", 200 lbs. Born, Montreal, Que., March 15, 1969.
(Edmonton's 4th choice, 92nd overall, in 1989 Entry Draft).

			Regular Season					Playoffs				
Season	**Club**	**Lea**	**GP**	**G**	**A**	**TP**	**PIM**	**GP**	**G**	**A**	**TP**	**PIM**
1988-89	Michigan State	CCHA	46	20	33	53	17	....	....	....	....	....
1989-90	Michigan State	CCHA	45	22	40	62	6	....	....	....	....	....
1990-91	Michigan State	CCHA	37	7	31	38	28	....	....	....	....	....
1991-92	Michigan State	CCHA	41	26	49	75	32	....	....	....	....	....
1992-93	Cape Breton	AHL	64	12	28	40	10	16	3	3	6	12
1993-94	**Edmonton**	**NHL**	**26**	**3**	**5**	**8**	**2**	....	....	....	....	....
	Cape Breton	AHL	45	21	49	70	12	5	2	3	5	2
1994-95ab	Cape Breton	AHL	65	36	*69	*105	30	....	....	....	....	....
	Edmonton	**NHL**	**9**	**2**	**4**	**6**	**0**	....	....	....	....	....
1995-96	**Edmonton**	**NHL**	**26**	**5**	**3**	**8**	**0**	....	....	....	....	....
	Toronto	**NHL**	**1**	**0**	**0**	**0**	**0**	....	....	....	....	....
	St. John's	AHL	17	6	7	13	6	....	....	....	....	....
	Atlanta	IHL	36	21	20	41	4	3	0	3	3	2
1996-97ab	Philadelphia	AHL	80	*44	61	*105	28	10	6	8	14	6
	NHL Totals		**62**	**10**	**12**	**22**	**2**	....	....	....	....	....

a AHL Second All-Star Team (1995, 1997)
b Won John B. Sollenberger Trophy (Top Scorer - AHL) (1995, 1997)

Traded to **Toronto** by **Edmonton** with Edmonton's fourth round choice (Jason Sessa) in 1996 Entry Draft for Kent Manderville, December 4, 1995. Signed as a free agent by **Philadelphia**, August 19, 1996.

WHITE, TODD — CHI.

Center. Shoots left. 5'10", 180 lbs. Born, Kanata, Ont., May 21, 1975.

			Regular Season					Playoffs				
Season	**Club**	**Lea**	**GP**	**G**	**A**	**TP**	**PIM**	**GP**	**G**	**A**	**TP**	**PIM**
1993-94	Clarkson	ECAC	33	10	12	22	28	....	....	....	....	....
1994-95	Clarkson	ECAC	34	13	16	29	44	....	....	....	....	....
1995-96ab	Clarkson	ECAC	38	29	43	72	36	....	....	....	....	....
1996-97cd	Clarkson	ECAC	37	*38	*36	*74	22	....	....	....	....	....

a ECAC Second All-Star Team (1996)
b NCAA East Second All-American Team (1996)
c ECAC First All-Star Team (1997)
d NCAA East First All-American Team (1997)

Signed as a free agent by **Chicago**, August 6, 1997.

WHITE, TOM — CHI.

Center. Shoots left. 6'1", 185 lbs. Born, Chicago, IL, August 25, 1975.
(Chicago's 8th choice, 180th overall, in 1993 Entry Draft).

			Regular Season					Playoffs				
Season	**Club**	**Lea**	**GP**	**G**	**A**	**TP**	**PIM**	**GP**	**G**	**A**	**TP**	**PIM**
1993-94	Miami-Ohio	CCHA	31	1	6	7	26	....	....	....	....	....
1994-95	Miami-Ohio	CCHA	35	2	5	7	24	....	....	....	....	....
1995-96	Miami-Ohio	CCHA	36	7	4	11	56	....	....	....	....	....
1996-97	Miami-Ohio	CCHA	40	7	8	15	42	....	....	....	....	....

WHITFIELD, TRENT — BOS.

Center. Shoots left. 5'11", 176 lbs. Born, Estevan, Sask., June 17, 1977.
(Boston's 5th choice, 100th overall, in 1996 Entry Draft).

			Regular Season					Playoffs				
Season	**Club**	**Lea**	**GP**	**G**	**A**	**TP**	**PIM**	**GP**	**G**	**A**	**TP**	**PIM**
1993-94	Spokane	WHL	5	1	1	2	0	....	....	....	....	....
1994-95	Spokane	WHL	48	8	17	25	26	11	7	6	13	5
1995-96	Spokane	WHL	72	33	51	84	75	18	8	10	18	10
1996-97a	Spokane	WHL	58	34	42	76	74	9	5	7	12	10

a WHL West First All-Star Team (1997)

WHITNEY, RAY

Center. Shoots right. 5'9", 160 lbs.   Born, Fort Saskatchewan, Alta., May 8, 1972.
(San Jose's 2nd choice, 23rd overall, in 1991 Entry Draft).

			Regular Season					Playoffs				
Season	Club	Lea	GP	G	A	TP	PIM	GP	G	A	TP	PIM
1988-89	Spokane	WHL	71	17	33	50	16	....	....	....	....	....
1989-90	Spokane	WHL	71	57	56	113	50	6	3	4	7	6
1990-91abc	Spokane	WHL	72	67	118	*185	36	15	13	18	*31	12
1991-92	Koln	Ger.	10	3	6	9	4	....	....	....	....	....
	Cdn. National	....	5	1	0	1	6	....	....	....	....	....
	San Diego	IHL	63	36	54	90	12	4	0	0	0	0
	San Jose	**NHL**	2	0	3	3	0	....	....	....	....	....
1992-93	San Jose	NHL	26	4	6	10	4	....	....	....	....	....
	Kansas City	IHL	46	20	33	53	14	12	5	7	12	2
1993-94	San Jose	NHL	61	14	26	40	14	14	0	4	4	8
1994-95	San Jose	NHL	39	13	12	25	14	11	4	4	8	2
1995-96	San Jose	NHL	60	17	24	41	16	....	....	....	....	....
1996-97	San Jose	NHL	12	0	2	2	4	....	....	....	....	....
	Kentucky	AHL	9	1	7	8	2	....	....	....	....	....
	Utah	IHL	43	13	35	48	34	7	3	1	4	6
	NHL Totals		**200**	**48**	**73**	**121**	**52**	**25**	**4**	**8**	**12**	**10**

a   WHL West First All-Star Team (1991)
b   Memorial Cup All-Star Team (1991)
c   Won George Parsons Trophy (Memorial Cup Tournament Most Sportsmanlike Player) (1991)

WIDMER, JASON   S.J.

Defense. Shoots left. 6', 200 lbs.   Born, Calgary, Alta., August 1, 1973.
(NY Islanders' 8th choice, 176th overall, in 1992 Entry Draft).

			Regular Season					Playoffs				
Season	Club	Lea	GP	G	A	TP	PIM	GP	G	A	TP	PIM
1990-91	Lethbridge	WHL	58	2	12	14	55	16	0	1	1	12
1991-92	Lethbridge	WHL	40	2	19	21	181	5	0	4	4	9
1992-93	Lethbridge	WHL	55	3	15	18	140	4	0	3	3	2
	Capital Dist.	AHL	4	0	0	0	2	....	....	....	....	....
1993-94	Lethbridge	WHL	64	11	31	42	191	9	3	5	8	34
1994-95	Worcester	AHL	73	8	26	34	136	....	....	....	....	....
	Cdn. National	....	6	1	4	5	4	....	....	....	....	....
	NY Islanders	**NHL**	1	0	0	0	0	....	....	....	....	....
1995-96	**NY Islanders**	**NHL**	4	0	0	0	7	....	....	....	....	....
	Worcester	AHL	76	6	21	27	129	4	2	0	2	9
1996-97	**San Jose**	**NHL**	2	0	1	1	0	....	....	....	....	....
	Kentucky	AHL	76	4	24	28	105	4	0	0	0	8
	NHL Totals		**7**	**0**	**1**	**1**	**7**	....	....	....	....	....

Signed as a free agent by **San Jose**, September 11, 1996.

WIEMER, JASON   (WEE-muhr)   T.B.

Center. Shoots left. 6'1", 215 lbs.   Born, Kimberley, B.C., April 14, 1976.
(Tampa Bay's 1st choice, 8th overall, in 1994 Entry Draft).

			Regular Season					Playoffs				
Season	Club	Lea	GP	G	A	TP	PIM	GP	G	A	TP	PIM
1991-92	Portland	WHL	2	0	1	1	0	....	....	....	....	....
1992-93	Portland	WHL	68	18	34	52	159	16	7	3	10	27
1993-94	Portland	WHL	72	45	51	96	236	10	4	4	8	32
1994-95	Portland	WHL	16	10	14	24	63	....	....	....	....	....
	Tampa Bay	**NHL**	36	1	4	5	44	....	....	....	....	....
1995-96	**Tampa Bay**	**NHL**	66	9	9	18	81	6	1	0	1	28
1996-97	**Tampa Bay**	**NHL**	63	9	5	14	134	....	....	....	....	....
	Adirondack	AHL	4	1	0	1	7	....	....	....	....	....
	NHL Totals		**165**	**19**	**18**	**37**	**259**	**6**	**1**	**0**	**1**	**28**

WIKSTROM, JOHN   DET.

Defense. Shoots left. 6'3", 200 lbs.   Born, Lulea, Sweden, January 30, 1979.
(Detroit's 4th choice, 129th overall, in 1997 Entry Draft).

			Regular Season					Playoffs				
Season	Club	Lea	GP	G	A	TP	PIM	GP	G	A	TP	PIM
1995-96	Lulea	Swe.	9	0	0	0	2	....	....	....	....	....
1996-97	Lulea	Swe.	9	0	0	0	0	3	0	0	0	0

WILFORD, MARTY   CHI.

Defense. Shoots left. 6', 216 lbs.   Born, Cobourg, Ont., April 17, 1977.
(Chicago's 7th choice, 149th overall, in 1995 Entry Draft).

			Regular Season					Playoffs				
Season	Club	Lea	GP	G	A	TP	PIM	GP	G	A	TP	PIM
1994-95	Oshawa	OHL	63	1	6	7	95	7	1	1	2	4
1995-96	Oshawa	OHL	65	3	24	27	107	5	0	1	1	4
1996-97a	Oshawa	OHL	62	19	43	62	126	16	2	18	20	28

a   OHL Second All-Star Team (1997)

WILKIE, DAVID   MTL.

Defense. Shoots right. 6'2", 210 lbs.   Born, Ellensburgh, WA, May 30, 1974.
(Montreal's 1st choice, 20th overall, in 1992 Entry Draft).

			Regular Season					Playoffs				
Season	Club	Lea	GP	G	A	TP	PIM	GP	G	A	TP	PIM
1990-91	Seattle	WHL	25	1	1	2	22	....	....	....	....	....
1991-92	Kamloops	WHL	71	12	28	40	153	16	6	5	11	19
1992-93	Kamloops	WHL	53	11	26	37	109	6	4	2	6	2
1993-94	Kamloops	WHL	27	11	18	29	18	....	....	....	....	....
	Regina	WHL	29	27	21	48	16	4	1	4	5	4
1994-95	Fredericton	AHL	70	10	43	53	34	1	0	0	0	0
	Montreal	**NHL**	1	0	0	0	0	....	....	....	....	....
1995-96	**Montreal**	**NHL**	24	1	5	6	10	6	1	2	3	12
	Fredericton	AHL	23	5	12	17	20	....	....	....	....	....
1996-97	**Montreal**	**NHL**	61	6	9	15	63	2	0	0	0	2
	NHL Totals		**86**	**7**	**14**	**21**	**73**	**8**	**1**	**2**	**3**	**14**

WILKINSON, NEIL   PIT.

Defense. Shoots right. 6'3", 200 lbs.   Born, Selkirk, Man., August 15, 1967.
(Minnesota's 2nd choice, 30th overall, in 1986 Entry Draft).

			Regular Season					Playoffs				
Season	Club	Lea	GP	G	A	TP	PIM	GP	G	A	TP	PIM
1986-87	Michigan State	CCHA	19	3	4	7	18	....	....	....	....	....
1987-88	Medicine Hat	WHL	55	11	21	32	157	5	1	0	1	2
1988-89	Kalamazoo	IHL	39	5	15	20	96	....	....	....	....	....
1989-90	**Minnesota**	**NHL**	36	0	5	5	100	7	0	2	2	11
	Kalamazoo	IHL	20	6	7	.13	62	....	....	....	....	....
1990-91	**Minnesota**	**NHL**	50	2	9	11	117	22	3	3	6	12
	Kalamazoo	IHL	10	0	3	3	38	....	....	....	....	....
1991-92	**San Jose**	**NHL**	60	4	15	19	107	....	....	....	....	....
1992-93	**San Jose**	**NHL**	59	1	7	8	96	....	....	....	....	....
1993-94	**Chicago**	**NHL**	72	3	9	12	116	4	0	0	0	0
1994-95	**Winnipeg**	**NHL**	40	1	4	5	75	....	....	....	....	....
1995-96	**Winnipeg**	**NHL**	21	1	4	5	33	....	....	....	....	....
	Pittsburgh	**NHL**	41	2	10	12	87	15	0	1	1	14
1996-97	**Pittsburgh**	**NHL**	23	0	0	0	36	5	0	0	0	4
	Cleveland	IHL	2	0	1	1	0	....	....	....	....	....
	NHL Totals		**402**	**14**	**63**	**77**	**767**	**53**	**3**	**6**	**9**	**41**

Claimed by **San Jose** from **Minnesota** in Dispersal Draft, May 30, 1991. Traded to **Chicago** by **San Jose** as future considerations to complete June 18, 1993 trade for Jimmy Waite, July 9, 1993. Traded to **Winnipeg** by **Chicago** for Chicago's third round choice (previously acquired by Winnipeg — Chicago selected Kevin McKay) in 1995 Entry Draft, June 3, 1994. Traded to **Pittsburgh** by **Winnipeg** for Norm Maciver, December 28, 1995.

WILLIAMS, JEFF   N.J.

Center. Shoots left. 6', 175 lbs.   Born, Pointe-Claire, Que., February 11, 1976.
(New Jersey's 8th choice, 181st overall, in 1994 Entry Draft).

			Regular Season					Playoffs				
Season	Club	Lea	GP	G	A	TP	PIM	GP	G	A	TP	PIM
1993-94	Guelph	OHL	62	14	12	26	19	9	2	1	3	4
1994-95	Guelph	OHL	52	15	32	47	21	14	5	5	10	0
1995-96a	Guelph	OHL	63	15	49	64	42	16	13	15	28	10
1996-97	Raleigh	ECHL	20	4	8	12	8	....	....	....	....	....
	Albany	AHL	46	13	20	33	12	15	1	2	3	15

a   Canadian Major Junior Most Sportsmanlike Player of the Year (1996)

WILLIS, SHANE   CAR.

Right wing. Shoots right. 6', 176 lbs.   Born, Edmonton, Alta., June 13, 1977.
(Tampa Bay's 3rd choice, 56th overall, in 1995 Entry Draft).

			Regular Season					Playoffs				
Season	Club	Lea	GP	G	A	TP	PIM	GP	G	A	TP	PIM
1994-95	Prince Albert	WHL	65	24	19	43	38	13	3	4	7	6
1995-96	Prince Albert	WHL	69	41	40	81	47	18	11	10	21	18
1996-97a	Prince Albert	WHL	41	34	22	56	63	....	....	....	....	....
	Lethbridge	WHL	26	22	17	39	24	19	13	11	24	20

a   WHL East First All-Star Team (1997)

Re-entered NHL Entry Draft, **Carolina's** 4th choice, 88th overall, in 1997 Entry Draft.

WILLSIE, BRIAN   COL.

Right wing. Shoots right. 6', 179 lbs.   Born, London, Ont., March 16, 1978.
(Colorado's 7th choice, 146th overall, in 1996 Entry Draft).

			Regular Season					Playoffs				
Season	Club	Lea	GP	G	A	TP	PIM	GP	G	A	TP	PIM
1995-96	Guelph	OHL	65	13	21	34	18	16	4	2	6	6
1996-97	Guelph	OHL	64	37	31	68	37	18	15	4	19	10

WILM, CLARKE   (WIHLM)   CGY.

Center. Shoots left. 6', 202 lbs.   Born, Central Butte, Sask., October 24, 1976.
(Calgary's 5th choice, 150th overall, in 1995 Entry Draft).

			Regular Season					Playoffs				
Season	Club	Lea	GP	G	A	TP	PIM	GP	G	A	TP	PIM
1992-93	Saskatoon	WHL	69	14	19	33	71	9	4	2	6	13
1993-94	Saskatoon	WHL	70	18	32	50	181	16	0	9	9	19
1994-95	Saskatoon	WHL	71	20	39	59	179	10	6	1	7	21
1995-96	Saskatoon	WHL	72	49	61	110	83	4	1	1	2	4
1996-97	Saint John	AHL	62	9	19	28	107	5	2	0	2	15

WILSON, LANDON   BOS.

Right wing. Shoots right. 6'2", 216 lbs.   Born, St. Louis, MO, March 13, 1975.
(Toronto's 2nd choice, 19th overall, in 1993 Entry Draft).

			Regular Season					Playoffs				
Season	Club	Lea	GP	G	A	TP	PIM	GP	G	A	TP	PIM
1993-94	North Dakota	WCHA	35	18	15	33	*147	....	....	....	....	....
1994-95	North Dakota	WCHA	31	7	16	23	141	....	....	....	....	....
	Cornwall	AHL	8	4	4	8	25	13	3	4	7	68
1995-96	**Colorado**	**NHL**	7	1	0	1	6	....	....	....	....	....
	Cornwall	AHL	53	21	13	34	154	8	1	3	4	22
1996-97	**Colorado**	**NHL**	9	1	2	3	23	....	....	....	....	....
	Boston	**NHL**	40	7	10	17	49	....	....	....	....	....
	Providence	AHL	2	2	1	3	2	10	3	4	7	16
	NHL Totals		**56**	**9**	**12**	**21**	**78**	....	....	....	....	....

Traded to **Quebec** by **Toronto** with Wendel Clark, Sylvain Lefebvre and Toronto's first round choice (Jeffrey Kealty) in 1994 Entry Draft for Mats Sundin, Garth Butcher, Todd Warriner and Philadelphia's first round choice (previously acquired by Quebec — later traded to Washington — Washington selected Nolan Baumgartner) in 1994 Entry Draft, June 28, 1994. Traded to **Boston** by **Colorado** with Anders Myrvold for Boston's first round choice in 1998 Entry Draft, November 22, 1996.

WILSON, MIKE   BUF.

Defense. Shoots left. 6'6", 212 lbs.   Born, Brampton, Ont., February 26, 1975.
(Vancouver's 1st choice, 20th overall, in 1993 Entry Draft).

			Regular Season					Playoffs				
Season	Club	Lea	GP	G	A	TP	PIM	GP	G	A	TP	PIM
1992-93	Sudbury	OHL	53	6	7	13	58	14	1	1	2	2
1993-94	Sudbury	OHL	60	4	22	26	62	9	1	3	4	8
1994-95	Sudbury	OHL	64	13	34	47	46	18	1	8	9	10
1995-96	**Buffalo**	**NHL**	58	4	8	12	41	....	....	....	....	....
	Rochester	AHL	15	0	5	5	38	....	....	....	....	....
1996-97	**Buffalo**	**NHL**	77	2	9	11	51	10	0	1	1	2
	NHL Totals		**135**	**6**	**17**	**23**	**92**	**10**	**0**	**1**	**1**	**2**

Traded to **Buffalo** by **Vancouver** with Mike Peca and Vancouver's first round choice (Jay McKee) in 1995 Entry Draft for Alexander Mogilny and Buffalo's fifth round choice (Todd Norman) in 1995 Entry Draft, July 8, 1995.

WINDSOR, NICHOLAS — COL.

Defense. Shoots left. 6'1", 165 lbs. Born, Granby, Que., January 19, 1976.
(Quebec's 8th choice, 139th overall, in 1994 Entry Draft).

			Regular Season					Playoffs				
Season	Club	Lea	GP	G	A	TP	PIM	GP	G	A	TP	PIM
1994-95	Clarkson	ECAC	26	1	10	11	20	....	....	....	....	....
1995-96	Clarkson	ECAC	38	4	16	20	60	....	....	....	....	....
1996-97	Clarkson	ECAC	37	1	12	13	54	....	....	....	....	....

WISEMAN, BRIAN — TOR.

Center. Shoots left. 5'8", 175 lbs. Born, Chatham, Ont., July 13, 1971.

			Regular Season					Playoffs				
Season	Club	Lea	GP	G	A	TP	PIM	GP	G	A	TP	PIM
1990-91	U. of Michigan	CCHA	47	25	33	58	58	....	....	....	....	....
1991-92	U. of Michigan	CCHA	44	27	44	71	38	....	....	....	....	....
1992-93	U. of Michigan	CCHA	35	13	37	50	40	....	....	....	....	....
1993-94	U. of Michigan	CCHA	40	19	50	69	44	....	....	....	....	....
1994-95	Chicago	IHL	75	17	55	72	52	3	1	1	2	4
1995-96	Chicago	IHL	73	33	55	88	117	....	....	....	....	....
1996-97	**Toronto**	**NHL**	**3**	**0**	**0**	**0**	**0**	....	....	....	....	....
	St. John's	AHL	71	33	62	95	83	7	5	4	9	8
	NHL Totals		**3**	**0**	**0**	**0**	**0**	....	....	....	....	....

Signed as a free agent by **Toronto**, August 14, 1996.

WITT, BRENDAN — WSH.

Defense. Shoots left. 6'1", 205 lbs. Born, Humbolt, Sask., February 20, 1975.
(Washington's 1st choice, 11th overall, in 1993 Entry Draft).

			Regular Season					Playoffs				
Season	Club	Lea	GP	G	A	TP	PIM	GP	G	A	TP	PIM
1991-92	Seattle	WHL	67	3	9	12	212	15	1	1	2	84
1992-93a	Seattle	WHL	70	2	26	28	239	5	1	2	3	30
1993-94ab	Seattle	WHL	56	8	31	39	235	9	3	8	11	23
1994-95					DID NOT PLAY							
1995-96	**Washington**	**NHL**	**48**	**2**	**3**	**5**	**85**	....	....	....	....	....
1996-97	**Washington**	**NHL**	**44**	**3**	**2**	**5**	**88**	....	....	....	....	....
	Portland	AHL	30	2	4	6	56	5	1	0	1	30
	NHL Totals		**92**	**5**	**5**	**10**	**173**	....	....	....	....	....

a WHL West First All-Star Team (1993, 1994)
b Canadian Major Junior First All-Star Team (1994)

WOLANIN, CRAIG (wuh-LAN-ihn) — TOR.

Defense. Shoots left. 6'4", 215 lbs. Born, Grosse Pointe, MI, July 27, 1967.
(New Jersey's 1st choice, 3rd overall, in 1985 Entry Draft).

			Regular Season					Playoffs				
Season	Club	Lea	GP	G	A	TP	PIM	GP	G	A	TP	PIM
1984-85	Kitchener	OHL	60	5	16	21	95	4	1	1	2	2
1985-86	**New Jersey**	**NHL**	**44**	**2**	**16**	**18**	**74**	....	....	....	....	....
1986-87	**New Jersey**	**NHL**	**68**	**4**	**6**	**10**	**109**	....	....	....	....	....
1987-88	**New Jersey**	**NHL**	**78**	**6**	**25**	**31**	**170**	**18**	**2**	**5**	**7**	**51**
1988-89	**New Jersey**	**NHL**	**56**	**3**	**8**	**11**	**69**	....	....	....	....	....
1989-90	**New Jersey**	**NHL**	**37**	**1**	**7**	**8**	**47**	....	....	....	....	....
	Utica	AHL	6	2	4	6	2	....	....	....	....	....
	Quebec	**NHL**	**13**	**0**	**3**	**3**	**10**	....	....	....	....	....
1990-91	**Quebec**	**NHL**	**80**	**5**	**13**	**18**	**89**	....	....	....	....	....
1991-92	**Quebec**	**NHL**	**69**	**2**	**11**	**13**	**80**	....	....	....	....	....
1992-93	**Quebec**	**NHL**	**24**	**1**	**4**	**5**	**49**	**4**	**0**	**0**	**0**	**4**
1993-94	**Quebec**	**NHL**	**63**	**6**	**10**	**16**	**80**	....	....	....	....	....
1994-95	**Quebec**	**NHL**	**40**	**3**	**6**	**9**	**40**	**6**	**1**	**1**	**2**	**4**
1995-96	**Colorado**	**NHL**	**75**	**7**	**20**	**27**	**50**	**7**	**1**	**0**	**1**	**8** ♦
1996-97	**Tampa Bay**	**NHL**	**15**	**0**	**0**	**0**	**8**	....	....	....	....	....
	Toronto	**NHL**	**23**	**0**	**4**	**4**	**13**	....	....	....	....	....
	NHL Totals		**685**	**40**	**133**	**173**	**888**	**35**	**4**	**6**	**10**	**67**

Traded to **Quebec** by **New Jersey** with future considerations (Randy Velischek, August 13, 1990) for Peter Stastny, March 6, 1990. Traded to **Tampa Bay** by **Colorado** for Tampa Bay's second round choice in 1998 Entry Draft, July 29, 1996. Traded to **Toronto** by **Tampa Bay** for Toronto's third round choice in 1998 Entry Draft, January 31, 1997.

WOOD, DODY — S.J.

Center. Shoots left. 6', 200 lbs. Born, Chetwynd, B.C., March 18, 1972.
(San Jose's 4th choice, 45th overall, in 1991 Entry Draft).

			Regular Season					Playoffs				
Season	Club	Lea	GP	G	A	TP	PIM	GP	G	A	TP	PIM
1989-90	Ft. St. John	Jr. A	44	51	73	124	270	....	....	....	....	....
	Seattle	WHL	....	....	....	....	....	5	0	0	0	2
1990-91	Seattle	WHL	69	28	37	65	272	6	0	1	1	2
1991-92	Seattle	WHL	37	13	19	32	232	....	....	....	....	....
	Swift Current	WHL	3	0	2	2	14	7	2	1	3	37
1992-93	**San Jose**	**NHL**	**13**	**1**	**1**	**2**	**71**	....	....	....	....	....
	Kansas City	IHL	36	3	2	5	216	6	0	1	1	15
1993-94	Kansas City	IHL	48	5	15	20	320	....	....	....	....	....
1994-95	Kansas City	IHL	44	5	13	18	255	21	7	10	17	87
	San Jose	**NHL**	**9**	**1**	**1**	**2**	**29**	....	....	....	....	....
1995-96	**San Jose**	**NHL**	**32**	**3**	**6**	**9**	**138**	....	....	....	....	....
1996-97	**San Jose**	**NHL**	**44**	**3**	**2**	**5**	**193**	....	....	....	....	....
	Kansas City	IHL	6	3	6	9	35	....	....	....	....	....
	NHL Totals		**98**	**8**	**10**	**18**	**431**	....	....	....	....	....

WOOD, RANDY

Left wing/Center. Shoots left. 6', 195 lbs. Born, Princeton, NJ, October 12, 1963.

			Regular Season					Playoffs				
Season	Club	Lea	GP	G	A	TP	PIM	GP	G	A	TP	PIM
1982-83	Yale	ECAC	26	5	14	19	10	....	....	....	....	....
1983-84	Yale	ECAC	18	7	7	14	10	....	....	....	....	....
1984-85a	Yale	ECAC	32	25	28	53	23	....	....	....	....	....
1985-86bc	Yale	ECAC	31	25	30	55	26	....	....	....	....	....
1986-87	**NY Islanders**	**NHL**	**6**	**1**	**0**	**1**	**4**	**13**	**1**	**3**	**4**	**14**
	Springfield	AHL	75	23	24	47	57	....	....	....	....	....
1987-88	**NY Islanders**	**NHL**	**75**	**22**	**16**	**38**	**80**	**5**	**1**	**0**	**1**	**6**
	Springfield	AHL	1	0	1	1	0	....	....	....	....	....
1988-89	**NY Islanders**	**NHL**	**77**	**15**	**13**	**28**	**44**	....	....	....	....	....
	Springfield	AHL	1	1	1	2	0	....	....	....	....	....
1989-90	**NY Islanders**	**NHL**	**74**	**24**	**24**	**48**	**39**	**5**	**1**	**1**	**2**	**4**
1990-91	**NY Islanders**	**NHL**	**76**	**24**	**18**	**42**	**45**	....	....	....	....	....
1991-92	**NY Islanders**	**NHL**	**8**	**2**	**2**	**4**	**21**	....	....	....	....	....
	Buffalo	**NHL**	**70**	**20**	**16**	**36**	**65**	**7**	**2**	**1**	**3**	**6**
1992-93	**Buffalo**	**NHL**	**82**	**18**	**25**	**43**	**77**	**8**	**1**	**4**	**5**	**4**
1993-94	**Buffalo**	**NHL**	**84**	**22**	**16**	**38**	**71**	**6**	**0**	**0**	**0**	**0**
1994-95	**Toronto**	**NHL**	**48**	**13**	**11**	**24**	**34**	**7**	**2**	**0**	**2**	**6**
1995-96	**Toronto**	**NHL**	**46**	**7**	**9**	**16**	**36**	....	....	....	....	....
	Dallas	**NHL**	**30**	**1**	**4**	**5**	**26**	....	....	....	....	....
1996-97	**NY Islanders**	**NHL**	**65**	**6**	**5**	**11**	**61**	....	....	....	....	....
	NHL Totals		**741**	**175**	**159**	**334**	**603**	**51**	**8**	**9**	**17**	**40**

a ECAC Second All-Star Team (1985)
b ECAC First All-Star Team (1986)
c NCAA East Second All-Star Team (1986)

Signed as a free agent by **NY Islanders**, September 17, 1986. Traded to **Buffalo** by **NY Islanders** with Pat Lafontaine, Randy Hillier and NY Islanders' fourth round choice (Dean Melanson) in 1992 Entry Draft for Pierre Turgeon, Uwe Krupp, Benoit Hogue and Dave McLlwain, October 25, 1991. Claimed by **Toronto** from **Buffalo** in NHL Waiver Draft, January 18, 1995. Traded to **Dallas** by **Toronto** with Benoit Hogue for Dave Gagner and Dallas' sixth round choice (Dmitriy Yakushin) in 1996 Entry Draft, January 29, 1996. Signed as a free agent by **NY Islanders**, October 2, 1996.

WOOLLEY, JASON (WOO-lee) — PIT.

Defense. Shoots left. 6', 188 lbs. Born, Toronto, Ont., July 27, 1969.
(Washington's 4th choice, 61st overall, in 1989 Entry Draft).

			Regular Season					Playoffs				
Season	Club	Lea	GP	G	A	TP	PIM	GP	G	A	TP	PIM
1988-89	Michigan State	CCHA	47	12	25	37	26	....	....	....	....	....
1989-90	Michigan State	CCHA	45	10	38	48	26	....	....	....	....	....
1990-91ab	Michigan State	CCHA	40	15	44	59	24	....	....	....	....	....
1991-92	Cdn. National	....	60	14	30	44	36	....	....	....	....	....
	Cdn. Olympic	....	8	0	5	5	4	....	....	....	....	....
	Washington	**NHL**	**1**	**0**	**0**	**0**	**0**	....	....	....	....	....
	Baltimore	AHL	15	1	10	11	6	....	....	....	....	....
1992-93	**Washington**	**NHL**	**26**	**0**	**2**	**2**	**10**	....	....	....	....	....
	Baltimore	AHL	29	14	27	41	22	1	0	2	2	0
1993-94	**Washington**	**NHL**	**10**	**1**	**2**	**3**	**4**	**4**	**1**	**0**	**1**	**4**
	Portland	AHL	41	12	29	41	14	9	2	2	4	4
1994-95	Detroit	IHL	48	8	28	36	38	....	....	....	....	....
	Florida	**NHL**	**34**	**4**	**9**	**13**	**18**	....	....	....	....	....
1995-96	**Florida**	**NHL**	**52**	**6**	**28**	**34**	**32**	**13**	**2**	**6**	**8**	**14**
1996-97	**Florida**	**NHL**	**3**	**0**	**0**	**0**	**2**	....	....	....	....	....
	Pittsburgh	**NHL**	**57**	**6**	**30**	**36**	**28**	**5**	**0**	**3**	**3**	**0**
	NHL Totals		**183**	**17**	**71**	**88**	**94**	**22**	**3**	**9**	**12**	**18**

a CCHA First All-Star Team (1991)
b NCAA West First All-American Team (1991)

Signed as a free agent by **Florida**, February 15, 1995. Traded to **Pittsburgh** by **Florida** with Stu Barnes for Chris Wells, November 19, 1996.

WORRELL, PETER — FLA.

Left wing. Shoots left. 6'6", 249 lbs. Born, Pierre Fonds, Que., August 18, 1977.
(Florida's 7th choice, 166th overall, in 1995 Entry Draft).

			Regular Season					Playoffs				
Season	Club	Lea	GP	G	A	TP	PIM	GP	G	A	TP	PIM
1994-95	Hull	QMJHL	56	1	8	9	243	21	0	1	1	91
1995-96	Hull	QMJHL	63	23	36	59	464	18	11	8	19	81
1996-97	Hull	QMJHL	62	17	46	63	437	14	3	13	16	83

WOTTON, MARK (WAH-tuhn) — VAN.

Defense. Shoots left. 5'11", 187 lbs. Born, Foxwarren, Man., November 16, 1973.
(Vancouver's 11th choice, 237th overall, in 1992 Entry Draft).

			Regular Season					Playoffs				
Season	Club	Lea	GP	G	A	TP	PIM	GP	G	A	TP	PIM
1990-91	Saskatoon	WHL	45	4	11	15	37	....	....	....	....	....
1991-92	Saskatoon	WHL	64	11	25	36	92	....	....	....	....	....
1992-93	Saskatoon	WHL	71	15	51	66	90	9	6	5	11	18
1993-94a	Saskatoon	WHL	65	12	34	46	108	16	3	12	15	32
1994-95	Syracuse	AHL	75	12	29	41	50	....	....	....	....	....
	Vancouver	**NHL**	**1**	**0**	**0**	**0**	**0**	**5**	**0**	**0**	**0**	**4**
1995-96	Syracuse	AHL	80	10	35	45	96	15	1	12	13	20
1996-97	**Vancouver**	**NHL**	**36**	**3**	**6**	**9**	**19**	....	....	....	....	....
	Syracuse	AHL	27	2	8	10	25	2	0	0	0	4
	NHL Totals		**37**	**3**	**6**	**9**	**19**	**5**	**0**	**0**	**0**	**4**

a WHL East Second All-Star Team (1994)

WREN, BOB (REHN) — ANA.

Left wing. Shoots left. 5'10", 185 lbs. Born, Preston, Ont., September 16, 1974.
(Los Angeles' 3rd choice, 94th overall, in 1993 Entry Draft).

			Regular Season					Playoffs				
Season	Club	Lea	GP	G	A	TP	PIM	GP	G	A	TP	PIM
1991-92	Detroit	OHL	62	13	36	49	58	7	3	4	7	19
1992-93a	Detroit	OHL	63	57	88	145	91	15	4	11	15	20
1993-94a	Detroit	OHL	57	45	64	109	81	17	12	18	30	20
1994-95	Springfield	AHL	61	16	15	31	118	....	....	....	....	....
	Richmond	ECHL	2	0	1	1	0	....	....	....	....	....
1995-96	Knoxville	ECHL	50	21	35	56	257	8	4	11	15	32
	Detroit	IHL	1	0	0	0	0	....	....	....	....	....
1996-97	Baltimore	AHL	72	23	36	59	97	3	1	1	2	0

a OHL Second All-Star Team (1993, 1994)

Signed as a free agent by **Hartford**, September 6, 1994. Signed as a free agent by **Anaheim**, August 1, 1997.

WRIGHT, JAMIE — DAL.

Left wing. Shoots left. 6', 172 lbs. Born, Kitchener, Ont., May 13, 1976.
(Dallas' 3rd choice, 98th overall, in 1994 Entry Draft).

			Regular Season					Playoffs				
Season	Club	Lea	GP	G	A	TP	PIM	GP	G	A	TP	PIM
1993-94	Guelph	OHL	65	17	15	32	34	8	2	1	3	10
1994-95	Guelph	OHL	65	43	39	82	36	14	6	8	14	6
1995-96	Guelph	OHL	55	30	36	66	45	16	10	12	22	35
1996-97	Michigan	IHL	60	6	8	14	34	1	0	0	0	0

WRIGHT, SHAYNE — BUF.

Defense. Shoots left. 6', 189 lbs. Born, Welland, Ont., June 30, 1975.
(Buffalo's 12th choice, 277th overall, in 1994 Entry Draft).

			Regular Season					Playoffs				
Season	Club	Lea	GP	G	A	TP	PIM	GP	G	A	TP	PIM
1992-93	Owen Sound	OHL	62	9	21	30	101	8	2	0	2	5
1993-94	Owen Sound	OHL	64	11	24	35	95	9	1	10	11	4
1994-95	Owen Sound	OHL	63	11	50	61	114	10	1	9	10	34
	Rochester	AHL	2	0	0	0	0	4	0	1	1	0
1995-96	Rochester	AHL	48	0	7	7	99	5	0	1	1	8
1996-97	Rochester	AHL	80	7	30	37	124	10	2	3	5	6

WRIGHT, TYLER — PIT.

Center. Shoots right. 5'11", 185 lbs. Born, Canora, Sask., April 6, 1973.
(Edmonton's 1st choice, 12th overall, in 1991 Entry Draft).

			Regular Season					Playoffs				
Season	Club	Lea	GP	G	A	TP	PIM	GP	G	A	TP	PIM
1989-90	Swift Current	WHL	67	14	18	32	139	4	0	0	0	12
1990-91	Swift Current	WHL	66	41	51	92	157	3	0	0	0	6
1991-92	Swift Current	WHL	63	36	46	82	295	8	2	5	7	16
1992-93	**Edmonton**	**NHL**	**7**	**1**	**1**	**2**	**19**	....	....	....	....	....
	Swift Current	WHL	37	24	41	65	76	17	9	17	26	*49
1993-94	**Edmonton**	**NHL**	**5**	**0**	**0**	**0**	**4**	....	....	....	....	....
	Cape Breton	AHL	65	14	27	41	160	5	2	0	2	11
1994-95	Cape Breton	AHL	70	16	15	31	184	....	....	....	....	....
	Edmonton	**NHL**	**6**	**1**	**0**	**1**	**14**	....	....	....	....	....
1995-96	**Edmonton**	**NHL**	**23**	**1**	**0**	**1**	**33**	....	....	....	....	....
	Cape Breton	AHL	31	6	12	18	158	....	....	....	....	....
1996-97	**Pittsburgh**	**NHL**	**45**	**2**	**2**	**4**	**70**	....	....	....	....	....
	Cleveland	IHL	10	4	3	7	34	14	4	2	6	44
	NHL Totals		**86**	**5**	**3**	**8**	**140**	....	....	....	....	....

Traded to **Pittsburgh** by **Edmonton** for Pittsburgh's seventh round choice (Brandon Lafrance) in 1996 Entry Draft, June 22, 1996.

YACHMENEV, VITALI (yach-meh-NEHV) — L.A.

Right wing. Shoots left. 5'9", 180 lbs. Born, Chelyabinsk, USSR, January 8, 1975.
(Los Angeles' 3rd choice, 59th overall, in 1994 Entry Draft).

			Regular Season					Playoffs				
Season	Club	Lea	GP	G	A	TP	PIM	GP	G	A	TP	PIM
1992-93	Chelyabinsk	CIS 2	51	23	20	43	12	....	....	....	....	....
1993-94a	North Bay	OHL	66	*61	52	113	18	18	13	19	32	12
1994-95	North Bay	OHL	59	53	52	105	8	6	1	8	9	2
	Phoenix	IHL	....	....	....	....	....	4	1	0	1	0
1995-96	**Los Angeles**	**NHL**	**80**	**19**	**34**	**53**	**16**	....	....	....	....	....
1996-97	**Los Angeles**	**NHL**	**65**	**10**	**22**	**32**	**10**	....	....	....	....	....
	NHL Totals		**145**	**29**	**56**	**85**	**26**	....	....	....	....	....

a Canadian Major Junior Rookie of the Year (1994)

YAKE, TERRY (YAYK) — ST.L.

Right wing. Shoots right. 5'11", 190 lbs. Born, New Westminster, B.C., October 22, 1968.
(Hartford's 3rd choice, 81st overall, in 1987 Entry Draft).

			Regular Season					Playoffs				
Season	Club	Lea	GP	G	A	TP	PIM	GP	G	A	TP	PIM
1984-85	Brandon	WHL	11	1	1	2	0	....	....	....	....	....
1985-86	Brandon	WHL	72	26	26	52	49	....	....	....	....	....
1986-87	Brandon	WHL	71	44	58	102	64	....	....	....	....	....
1987-88	Brandon	WHL	72	55	85	140	59	3	4	2	6	7
1988-89	**Hartford**	**NHL**	**2**	**0**	**0**	**0**	**0**	....	....	....	....	....
	Binghamton	AHL	75	39	56	95	57	....	....	....	....	....
1989-90	**Hartford**	**NHL**	**2**	**0**	**1**	**1**	**0**	....	....	....	....	....
	Binghamton	AHL	77	13	42	55	37	....	....	....	....	....
1990-91	**Hartford**	**NHL**	**19**	**1**	**4**	**5**	**10**	**6**	**1**	**1**	**2**	**16**
	Springfield	AHL	60	35	42	77	56	15	9	9	18	10
1991-92	**Hartford**	**NHL**	**15**	**1**	**1**	**2**	**4**	....	....	....	....	....
	Springfield	AHL	53	21	34	55	63	8	3	4	7	2
1992-93	**Hartford**	**NHL**	**66**	**22**	**31**	**53**	**46**	....	....	....	....	....
	Springfield	AHL	16	8	14	22	27	....	....	....	....	....
1993-94	**Anaheim**	**NHL**	**82**	**21**	**31**	**52**	**44**	....	....	....	....	....
1994-95	**Toronto**	**NHL**	**19**	**3**	**2**	**5**	**2**	....	....	....	....	....
	Denver	IHL	2	0	3	3	2	17	4	11	15	16
1995-96	Milwaukee	IHL	70	32	56	88	70	5	3	6	9	4
1996-97	Rochester	AHL	78	34	*67	101	77	10	8	8	16	2
	NHL Totals		**205**	**48**	**70**	**118**	**106**	**6**	**1**	**1**	**2**	**16**

Claimed by **Anaheim** from **Hartford** in Expansion Draft, June 24, 1993. Traded to **Toronto** by **Anaheim** for David Sacco, September 28, 1994. Signed as a free agent by **Buffalo**, September 17, 1996. Signed as a free agent by **St. Louis**, August 12, 1997.

YAKHANOV, ANDREI (yah-KHAHN-ahf) — BOS.

Defense. Shoots right. 5'11", 190 lbs. Born, Ufa, USSR, July 23, 1973.
(Boston's 9th choice, 281st overall, in 1994 Entry Draft).

			Regular Season					Playoffs				
Season	Club	Lea	GP	G	A	TP	PIM	GP	G	A	TP	PIM
1992-93	Ufa Salavat	CIS	41	1	3	4	16	2	0	0	0	2
1993-94	Ufa Salavat	CIS	44	1	3	4	44	5	0	0	0	2
1994-95	Ufa Salavat	CIS	52	3	7	10	50	7	1	0	1	10
1995-96	Ufa Salavat	CIS	51	7	7	14	82	4	1	1	2	0
1996-97	Ufa Salavat	Rus.	44	3	10	13	52	10	0	1	1	22

YAKUSHIN, DMITRI (yah-KOO-shihn) — TOR.

Defense. Shoots left. 6', 198 lbs. Born, Kharkov, USSR, January 21, 1978.
(Toronto's 9th choice, 140th overall, in 1996 Entry Draft).

			Regular Season					Playoffs				
Season	Club	Lea	GP	G	A	TP	PIM	GP	G	A	TP	PIM
1995-96	Pembroke	Jr. A	31	8	5	13	62	....	....	....	....	....
1996-97	Edmonton	WHL	63	3	14	17	103	....	....	....	....	....

YASHIN, ALEXEI (YAH-shin) — OTT.

Center. Shoots right. 6'3", 215 lbs. Born, Sverdlovsk, USSR, November 5, 1973.
(Ottawa's 1st choice, 2nd overall, in 1992 Entry Draft).

			Regular Season					Playoffs				
Season	Club	Lea	GP	G	A	TP	PIM	GP	G	A	TP	PIM
1990-91	Sverdlovsk	USSR	26	2	1	3	10	....	....	....	....	....
1991-92	Moscow D'amo	CIS	35	7	5	12	19	....	....	....	....	....
1992-93	Moscow D'amo	CIS	27	10	12	22	18	10	7	3	10	18
1993-94	**Ottawa**	**NHL**	**83**	**30**	**49**	**79**	**22**	....	....	....	....	....
1994-95	Las Vegas	IHL	24	15	20	35	32	....	....	....	....	....
	Ottawa	**NHL**	**47**	**21**	**23**	**44**	**20**	....	....	....	....	....
1995-96	CSKA	CIS	4	2	2	4	4	....	....	....	....	....
	Ottawa	**NHL**	**46**	**15**	**24**	**39**	**28**	....	....	....	....	....
1996-97	**Ottawa**	**NHL**	**82**	**35**	**40**	**75**	**44**	**7**	**1**	**5**	**6**	**2**
	NHL Totals		**258**	**101**	**136**	**237**	**114**	**7**	**1**	**5**	**6**	**2**

Played in NHL All-Star Game (1994)

YAWNEY, TRENT (YAW-nee)

Defense. Shoots left. 6'3", 195 lbs. Born, Hudson Bay, Sask., September 29, 1965.
(Chicago's 2nd choice, 45th overall, in 1984 Entry Draft).

			Regular Season					Playoffs				
Season	Club	Lea	GP	G	A	TP	PIM	GP	G	A	TP	PIM
1982-83	Saskatoon	WHL	59	6	31	37	44	6	0	2	2	0
1983-84	Saskatoon	WHL	73	13	46	59	81	....	....	....	....	....
1984-85	Saskatoon	WHL	72	16	51	67	158	3	1	6	7	7
1985-86	Cdn. National	....	73	6	15	21	60	....	....	....	....	....
1986-87	Cdn. National	....	51	4	15	19	37	....	....	....	....	....
1987-88	Cdn. National	....	60	4	12	16	81	....	....	....	....	....
	Cdn. Olympic	....	8	1	1	2	6	....	....	....	....	....
	Chicago	**NHL**	**15**	**2**	**8**	**10**	**15**	**5**	**0**	**4**	**4**	**8**
1988-89	**Chicago**	**NHL**	**69**	**5**	**19**	**24**	**116**	**15**	**3**	**6**	**9**	**20**
1989-90	**Chicago**	**NHL**	**70**	**5**	**15**	**20**	**82**	**20**	**3**	**5**	**8**	**27**
1990-91	**Chicago**	**NHL**	**61**	**3**	**13**	**16**	**77**	**1**	**0**	**0**	**0**	**0**
1991-92	**Calgary**	**NHL**	**47**	**4**	**9**	**13**	**45**	....	....	....	....	....
	Indianapolis	IHL	9	2	3	5	12	....	....	....	....	....
1992-93	**Calgary**	**NHL**	**63**	**1**	**16**	**17**	**67**	**6**	**3**	**2**	**5**	**6**
1993-94	**Calgary**	**NHL**	**58**	**6**	**15**	**21**	**60**	**7**	**0**	**0**	**0**	**16**
1994-95	**Calgary**	**NHL**	**37**	**0**	**2**	**2**	**108**	**2**	**0**	**0**	**0**	**2**
1995-96	**Calgary**	**NHL**	**69**	**0**	**3**	**3**	**88**	**4**	**0**	**0**	**0**	**2**
1996-97	**St. Louis**	**NHL**	**39**	**0**	**2**	**2**	**17**	....	....	....	....	....
	NHL Totals		**528**	**26**	**102**	**128**	**675**	**60**	**9**	**17**	**26**	**81**

Traded to **Calgary** by **Chicago** for Stephane Matteau, December 16, 1991. Signed as a free agent by **St. Louis**, July 31, 1996.

YEGOROV, ALEXEI (yeh-GOH-rohv) — S.J.

Center. Shoots left. 5'11", 195 lbs. Born, St. Petersburg, USSR, May 21, 1975.
(San Jose's 3rd choice, 66th overall, in 1994 Entry Draft).

			Regular Season					Playoffs				
Season	Club	Lea	GP	G	A	TP	PIM	GP	G	A	TP	PIM
1992-93	St. Peterburg	CIS	17	1	2	3	10	6	3	1	4	6
1993-94	St. Peterburg	CIS	23	5	3	8	18	6	0	0	0	4
1994-95	St. Peterburg	CIS	10	2	1	3	10	....	....	....	....	....
	Fort Worth	CHL	18	4	10	14	15	....	....	....	....	....
1995-96	**San Jose**	**NHL**	**9**	**3**	**2**	**5**	**2**	....	....	....	....	....
	Kansas City	IHL	65	31	25	56	84	5	2	0	2	8
1996-97	**San Jose**	**NHL**	**2**	**0**	**1**	**1**	**0**	....	....	....	....	....
	Kentucky	AHL	75	26	32	58	59	4	0	1	1	2
	NHL Totals		**11**	**3**	**3**	**6**	**2**	....	....	....	....	....

YELLE, STEPHANE (YEHL-ee) — COL.

Center. Shoots left. 6'1", 162 lbs. Born, Ottawa, Ont., May 9, 1974.
(New Jersey's 8th choice, 186th overall, in 1992 Entry Draft).

			Regular Season					Playoffs				
Season	Club	Lea	GP	G	A	TP	PIM	GP	G	A	TP	PIM
1991-92	Oshawa	OHL	55	12	14	26	20	7	2	0	2	1
1992-93	Oshawa	OHL	66	24	50	74	20	10	2	4	6	4
1993-94	Oshawa	OHL	66	35	69	104	22	5	1	7	8	2
1994-95	Cornwall	AHL	40	18	15	33	22	13	7	7	14	8
1995-96	**Colorado**	**NHL**	**71**	**13**	**14**	**27**	**30**	**22**	**1**	**4**	**5**	**8** ♦
1996-97	**Colorado**	**NHL**	**79**	**9**	**17**	**26**	**38**	**12**	**1**	**6**	**7**	**2**
	NHL Totals		**150**	**22**	**31**	**53**	**68**	**34**	**2**	**10**	**12**	**10**

Traded to **Quebec** by **New Jersey** with New Jersey's eleventh round choice (Steven Low) in 1994 Entry Draft for Quebec's eleventh round choice (Mike Hansen) in 1994 Entry Draft, June 1, 1994.

YEPANCHINTSEV, VADIM (yeh-pahn-CHIHN-tsehv) — T.B.

Center. Shoots left. 5'9", 165 lbs. Born, Orsk, USSR, March 16, 1976.
(Tampa Bay's 3rd choice, 55th overall, in 1994 Entry Draft).

			Regular Season					Playoffs				
Season	Club	Lea	GP	G	A	TP	PIM	GP	G	A	TP	PIM
1993-94	Spartak	CIS	46	6	5	11	16	3	0	1	1	0
1994-95	Spartak	CIS	43	4	8	12	24	....	....	....	....	....
1995-96	Spartak	CIS	51	20	12	32	28	4	0	2	2	4
1996-97	Spartak	Rus.	38	10	8	18	74	....	....	....	....	....

YERKOVICH, SERGEI (yehr-KOH-vihch) — EDM.

Defense. Shoots left. 6'3", 210 lbs. Born, Minsk, USSR, September 3, 1974.
(Edmonton's 3rd choice, 68th overall, in 1997 Entry Draft).

			Regular Season					Playoffs				
Season	Club	Lea	GP	G	A	TP	PIM	GP	G	A	TP	PIM
1993-94	Tivali Minsk	CIS	39	2	1	3	34	....	....	....	....	....
1994-95	Tivali Minsk	CIS	45	3	1	4	52	....	....	....	....	....
1995-96	Tivali Minsk	CIS	41	5	3	8	30	....	....	....	....	....
1996-97	Las Vegas	IHL	76	6	19	25	167	....	....	....	....	....

YLONEN, JUHA (YOO-lih-nehn, YOO-hah) — PHO.

Center. Shoots left. 6', 180 lbs. Born, Helsinki, Finland, February 13, 1972.
(Winnipeg's 5th choice, 91st overall, in 1991 Entry Draft).

			Regular Season					Playoffs				
Season	Club	Lea	GP	G	A	TP	PIM	GP	G	A	TP	PIM
1990-91	Espoo	Fin. 2	40	12	21	33	4	....	....	....	....	....
1991-92	HPK	Fin.	43	7	11	18	8	....	....	....	....	....
1992-93	HPK	Fin.	48	8	18	26	22	12	3	5	8	2
1993-94	Jokerit	Fin.	37	5	11	16	2	12	1	3	4	8
1994-95	Jokerit	Fin.	50	13	15	28	10	11	3	2	5	0
1995-96	Jokerit	Fin.	24	3	13	16	20	11	4	5	9	4
1996-97	**Phoenix**	**NHL**	**2**	**0**	**0**	**0**	**0**	....	....	....	....	....
	Springfield	AHL	70	20	41	61	6	17	5	*16	21	4
	NHL Totals		**2**	**0**	**0**	**0**	**0**	....	....	....	....	....

YORK, HARRY — ST.L.

Center. Shoots left. 6'2", 215 lbs. Born, Panoka, Alta., April 16, 1974.

			Regular Season					Playoffs				
Season	Club	Lea	GP	G	A	TP	PIM	GP	G	A	TP	PIM
1994-95	Ft. McMurray	Jr. A	54	35	73	108	....	....	....	....	....	....
1995-96	Nashville	ECHL	64	33	50	83	122	....	....	....	....	....
	Atlanta	IHL	2	0	0	0	15	....	....	....	....	....
	Worcester	AHL	13	8	5	13	2	4	0	4	4	4
1996-97	**St. Louis**	**NHL**	**74**	**14**	**18**	**32**	**24**	**5**	**0**	**0**	**0**	**2**
	NHL Totals		**74**	**14**	**18**	**32**	**24**	**5**	**0**	**0**	**0**	**2**

Signed as a free agent by **St. Louis**, May 1, 1996.

YORK, JASON — OTT.

Defense. Shoots right. 6'2", 198 lbs. Born, Nepean, Ont., May 20, 1970.
(Detroit's 6th choice, 129th overall, in 1990 Entry Draft).

			Regular Season					Playoffs				
Season	Club	Lea	GP	G	A	TP	PIM	GP	G	A	TP	PIM
1989-90	Windsor	OHL	39	9	30	39	38	....	....	....	....	....
	Kitchener	OHL	25	11	25	36	17	17	3	19	22	10
1990-91	Windsor	OHL	66	13	80	93	40	11	3	10	13	12
1991-92	Adirondack	AHL	49	4	20	24	32	5	0	1	1	0
1992-93	**Detroit**	**NHL**	**2**	**0**	**0**	**0**	**0**	....	....	....	....	....
	Adirondack	AHL	77	15	40	55	86	11	0	3	3	18
1993-94	**Detroit**	**NHL**	**7**	**1**	**2**	**3**	**2**	....	....	....	....	....
a	Adirondack	AHL	74	10	56	66	98	12	3	11	14	22
1994-95	**Detroit**	**NHL**	**10**	**1**	**2**	**3**	**2**	....	....	....	....	....
	Adirondack	AHL	5	1	3	4	4	....	....	....	....	....
	Anaheim	**NHL**	**15**	**0**	**8**	**8**	**12**	....	....	....	....	....
1995-96	**Anaheim**	**NHL**	**79**	**3**	**21**	**24**	**88**	....	....	....	....	....
1996-97	**Ottawa**	**NHL**	**75**	**4**	**17**	**21**	**67**	**7**	**0**	**0**	**0**	**4**
	NHL Totals		**188**	**9**	**50**	**59**	**171**	**7**	**0**	**0**	**0**	**4**

a AHL First All-Star Team (1994)

Traded to **Anaheim** by **Detroit** with Mike Sillinger for Stu Grimson, Mark Ferner and Anaheim's sixth round choice (Magnus Nilsson) in 1996 Entry Draft, April 4, 1995. Traded to **Ottawa** by **Anaheim** with Shaun Van Allen for Ted Drury and the rights to Marc Moro, October 1, 1996.

YORK, MICHAEL — NYR

Center. Shoots right. 5'9", 179 lbs. Born, Pontiac, MI, January 3, 1978.
(NY Rangers' 7th choice, 136th overall, in 1997 Entry Draft).

			Regular Season					Playoffs				
Season	Club	Lea	GP	G	A	TP	PIM	GP	G	A	TP	PIM
1995-96	Michigan State	CCHA	39	12	27	39	20	....	....	....	....	....
1996-97	Michigan State	CCHA	37	18	29	47	42	....	....	....	....	....

YOUNG, B.J. — DET.

Right wing. Shoots right. 5'10", 178 lbs. Born, Anchorage, AK, July 23, 1977.
(Detroit's 5th choice, 157th overall, in 1997 Entry Draft).

			Regular Season					Playoffs				
Season	Club	Lea	GP	G	A	TP	PIM	GP	G	A	TP	PIM
1994-95	Tri-City	WHL	30	6	3	9	39	....	....	....	....	....
	Red Deer	WHL	21	5	9	14	33	....	....	....	....	....
1995-96	Red Deer	WHL	67	49	45	94	144	8	4	9	13	12
1996-97a	Red Deer	WHL	63	58	56	114	97	16	8	14	22	26

a WHL East First All-Star Team (1997)

YOUNG, SCOTT — COL.

Right wing. Shoots right. 6', 190 lbs. Born, Clinton, MA, October 1, 1967.
(Hartford's 1st choice, 11th overall, in 1986 Entry Draft).

			Regular Season					Playoffs				
Season	Club	Lea	GP	G	A	TP	PIM	GP	G	A	TP	PIM
1985-86	Boston U.	H.E.	38	16	13	29	31	....	....	....	....	....
1986-87	Boston U.	H.E.	33	15	21	36	24	....	....	....	....	....
1987-88	U.S. National	....	56	11	47	58	31	....	....	....	....	....
	U.S. Olympic	....	6	2	6	8	4	....	....	....	....	....
	Hartford	**NHL**	**7**	**0**	**0**	**0**	**2**	**4**	**1**	**0**	**1**	**0**
1988-89	**Hartford**	**NHL**	**76**	**19**	**40**	**59**	**27**	**4**	**2**	**0**	**2**	**4**
1989-90	**Hartford**	**NHL**	**80**	**24**	**40**	**64**	**47**	**7**	**2**	**0**	**2**	**2**
1990-91	**Hartford**	**NHL**	**34**	**6**	**9**	**15**	**8**	....	....	....	....	....
	Pittsburgh	**NHL**	**43**	**11**	**16**	**27**	**33**	**17**	**1**	**6**	**7**	**2** ♦
1991-92	Bolzano	Italy	18	22	17	39	6	5	4	3	7	7
	U.S. National	....	10	2	4	6	21	....	....	....	....	....
	U.S. Olympic	....	8	2	1	3	2	....	....	....	....	....
1992-93	**Quebec**	**NHL**	**82**	**30**	**30**	**60**	**20**	**6**	**4**	**1**	**5**	**0**
1993-94	**Quebec**	**NHL**	**76**	**26**	**25**	**51**	**14**	....	....	....	....	....
1994-95	Landshut	Ger.	4	6	1	7	6	....	....	....	....	....
	Frankfurt	Ger.	1	1	0	1	0	....	....	....	....	....
	Quebec	**NHL**	**48**	**18**	**21**	**39**	**14**	**6**	**3**	**3**	**6**	**2**
1995-96	**Colorado**	**NHL**	**81**	**21**	**39**	**60**	**50**	**22**	**3**	**12**	**15**	**10** ♦
1996-97	**Colorado**	**NHL**	**72**	**18**	**19**	**37**	**14**	**17**	**4**	**2**	**6**	**14**
	NHL Totals		**599**	**173**	**239**	**412**	**229**	**83**	**20**	**24**	**44**	**34**

Traded to **Pittsburgh** by **Hartford** for Rob Brown, December 21, 1990. Traded to **Quebec** by **Pittsburgh** for Bryan Fogarty, March 10, 1992.

YSEBAERT, PAUL (IGHS-bahrt) — T.B.

Center. Shoots left. 6'1", 190 lbs. Born, Sarnia, Ont., May 15, 1966.
(New Jersey's 4th choice, 74th overall, in 1984 Entry Draft).

			Regular Season					Playoffs				
Season	Club	Lea	GP	G	A	TP	PIM	GP	G	A	TP	PIM
1984-85	Bowling Green	CCHA	42	23	32	55	54	....	....	....	....	....
1985-86a	Bowling Green	CCHA	42	23	45	68	50	....	....	....	....	....
1986-87a	Bowling Green	CCHA	45	27	58	85	44	....	....	....	....	....
	Cdn. National	....	5	1	0	1	4	....	....	....	....	....
1987-88	Utica	AHL	78	30	49	79	60	....	....	....	....	....
1988-89	**New Jersey**	**NHL**	**5**	**0**	**4**	**4**	**0**	....	....	....	....	....
	Utica	AHL	56	36	44	80	22	5	0	1	1	4
1989-90	**New Jersey**	**NHL**	**5**	**1**	**2**	**3**	**0**	....	....	....	....	....
bcd	Utica	AHL	74	53	52	*105	61	5	2	4	6	0
1990-91	**New Jersey**	**NHL**	**11**	**4**	**3**	**7**	**6**	....	....	....	....	....
	Detroit	**NHL**	**51**	**15**	**18**	**33**	**16**	**2**	**0**	**2**	**2**	**0**
1991-92e	**Detroit**	**NHL**	**79**	**35**	**40**	**75**	**55**	**10**	**1**	**0**	**1**	**10**
1992-93	**Detroit**	**NHL**	**80**	**34**	**28**	**62**	**42**	**7**	**3**	**1**	**4**	**2**
1993-94	**Winnipeg**	**NHL**	**60**	**9**	**18**	**27**	**18**	....	....	....	....	....
	Chicago	**NHL**	**11**	**5**	**3**	**8**	**8**	**6**	**0**	**0**	**0**	**8**
1994-95	**Chicago**	**NHL**	**15**	**4**	**5**	**9**	**6**	....	....	....	....	....
	Tampa Bay	**NHL**	**29**	**8**	**11**	**19**	**12**	....	....	....	....	....
1995-96	**Tampa Bay**	**NHL**	**55**	**16**	**15**	**31**	**16**	**5**	**0**	**0**	**0**	**0**
1996-97	**Tampa Bay**	**NHL**	**39**	**5**	**12**	**17**	**4**	....	....	....	....	....
	NHL Totals		**440**	**136**	**159**	**295**	**183**	**30**	**4**	**3**	**7**	**20**

a CCHA Second All-Star Team (1986, 1987)
b AHL First All-Star Team (1990)
c Won John B. Sollenberger Trophy (Top Scorer - AHL) (1990)
d Won Les Cunningham Plaque (MVP - AHL) (1990)
e Won Alka-Seltzer Plus Award (1992)

Traded to **Detroit** by **New Jersey** for Lee Norwood and Detroit's fourth round choice (Scott McCabe) in 1992 Entry Draft, November 27, 1990. Traded to **Winnipeg** by **Detroit** with future considerations (Alan Kerr, June 18, 1993) for Aaron Ward and Toronto's fourth round choice (previously acquired by Winnipeg — later traded to Detroit — Detroit selected John Jakopin) in 1993 Entry Draft, June 11, 1993. Traded to **Chicago** by **Winnipeg** for Chicago's third round choice (later traded back to Chicago — Chicago selected Kevin McKay) in 1995 Entry Draft, March 21, 1994. Traded to **Tampa Bay** by **Chicago** with Rich Sutter for Jim Cummins, Tom Tilley and Jeff Buchanan, February 22, 1995.

YUSHKEVICH, DIMITRI (yoosh-KAY-vihch) — TOR.

Defense. Shoots right. 5'11", 208 lbs. Born, Yaroslavl, USSR, November 19, 1971.
(Philadelphia's 6th choice, 122nd overall, in 1991 Entry Draft).

			Regular Season					Playoffs				
Season	Club	Lea	GP	G	A	TP	PIM	GP	G	A	TP	PIM
1988-89	Yaroslavl	USSR	23	2	1	3	8	....	....	....	....	....
1989-90	Yaroslavl	USSR	41	2	3	5	39	....	....	....	....	....
1990-91	Yaroslavl	USSR	41	10	4	14	22	....	....	....	....	....
1991-92	Moscow D'amo	CIS	35	5	7	12	14	....	....	....	....	....
1992-93	**Philadelphia**	**NHL**	**82**	**5**	**27**	**32**	**71**	....	....	....	....	....
1993-94	**Philadelphia**	**NHL**	**75**	**5**	**25**	**30**	**86**	....	....	....	....	....
1994-95	Yaroslavl	CIS	10	3	4	7	8	....	....	....	....	....
	Philadelphia	**NHL**	**40**	**5**	**9**	**14**	**47**	**15**	**1**	**5**	**6**	**12**
1995-96	**Toronto**	**NHL**	**69**	**1**	**10**	**11**	**54**	**4**	**0**	**0**	**0**	**0**
1996-97	**Toronto**	**NHL**	**74**	**4**	**10**	**14**	**56**	....	....	....	....	....
	NHL Totals		**340**	**20**	**81**	**101**	**314**	**19**	**1**	**5**	**6**	**12**

Traded to **Toronto** by **Philadelphia** with Philadelphia's second round choice (Francis Larivee) in 1996 Entry Draft for Toronto's first round choice (Dainius Zubrus) in 1996 Entry Draft, second round choice (Jean-Marc Pelletier) in 1997 Entry Draft and Los Angeles' fourth round choice (previously acquired by Toronto — later traded to Los Angeles — Los Angeles selected Mikael Simons) in 1996 Entry Draft, August 30, 1995.

YZERMAN, STEVE (IGH-zuhr-muhn) — DET.

Center. Shoots right. 5'11", 185 lbs. Born, Cranbrook, B.C., May 9, 1965.
(Detroit's 1st choice, 4th overall, in 1983 Entry Draft).

			Regular Season					Playoffs				
Season	Club	Lea	GP	G	A	TP	PIM	GP	G	A	TP	PIM
1981-82	Peterborough	OHL	58	21	43	64	65	6	0	1	1	16
1982-83	Peterborough	OHL	56	42	49	91	33	4	1	4	5	0
1983-84a	**Detroit**	**NHL**	**80**	**39**	**48**	**87**	**33**	**4**	**3**	**3**	**6**	**0**
1984-85	**Detroit**	**NHL**	**80**	**30**	**59**	**89**	**58**	**3**	**2**	**1**	**3**	**2**
1985-86	**Detroit**	**NHL**	**51**	**14**	**28**	**42**	**16**	....	....	....	....	....
1986-87	**Detroit**	**NHL**	**80**	**31**	**59**	**90**	**43**	**16**	**5**	**13**	**18**	**8**
1987-88	**Detroit**	**NHL**	**64**	**50**	**52**	**102**	**44**	**3**	**1**	**3**	**4**	**6**
1988-89b	**Detroit**	**NHL**	**80**	**65**	**90**	**155**	**61**	**6**	**5**	**5**	**10**	**2**
1989-90	**Detroit**	**NHL**	**79**	**62**	**65**	**127**	**79**	....	....	....	....	....
1990-91	**Detroit**	**NHL**	**80**	**51**	**57**	**108**	**34**	**7**	**3**	**3**	**6**	**4**
1991-92	**Detroit**	**NHL**	**79**	**45**	**58**	**103**	**64**	**11**	**3**	**5**	**8**	**12**
1992-93	**Detroit**	**NHL**	**84**	**58**	**79**	**137**	**44**	**7**	**4**	**3**	**7**	**4**
1993-94	**Detroit**	**NHL**	**58**	**24**	**58**	**82**	**36**	**3**	**1**	**3**	**4**	**0**
1994-95	**Detroit**	**NHL**	**47**	**12**	**26**	**38**	**40**	**15**	**4**	**8**	**12**	**0**
1995-96	**Detroit**	**NHL**	**80**	**36**	**59**	**95**	**64**	**18**	**8**	**12**	**20**	**4**
1996-97	**Detroit**	**NHL**	**81**	**22**	**63**	**85**	**78**	**20**	**7**	**6**	**13**	**4** ♦
	NHL Totals		**1023**	**539**	**801**	**1340**	**694**	**113**	**46**	**65**	**111**	**46**

a NHL All-Rookie Team (1984)
b Won Lester B. Pearson Award (1989)

Played in NHL All-Star Game (1984, 1988-93, 1997)

ZABRANSKY, LIBOR (zah-BRAN-skee) — ST.L.

Defense. Shoots left. 6'3", 196 lbs. Born, Brno, Czech., November 25, 1973.
(St. Louis' 7th choice, 209th overall, in 1995 Entry Draft).

			Regular Season					Playoffs				
Season	Club	Lea	GP	G	A	TP	PIM	GP	G	A	TP	PIM
1994-95	Budejovice	Czech.	44	2	6	8	54	9	0	4	4	6
1995-96	Budejovice	Czech.	40	4	7	11	....	10	0	1	1	....
1996-97	**St. Louis**	**NHL**	**34**	**1**	**5**	**6**	**44**	....	....	....	....	....
	Worcester	AHL	23	3	6	9	24	5	2	5	7	6
	NHL Totals		**34**	**1**	**5**	**6**	**44**	....	....	....	....	....

ZALAPSKI, ZARLEY (zah-LAP-skee, ZAHR-lee) CGY.

Defense. Shoots left. 6'1", 215 lbs. Born, Edmonton, Alta., April 22, 1968.
(Pittsburgh's 1st choice, 4th overall, in 1986 Entry Draft).

			Regular Season					Playoffs				
Season	Club	Lea	GP	G	A	TP	PIM	GP	G	A	TP	PIM
1985-86	Cdn. National	....	32	2	4	6	10	....	....	....	....	....
1986-87	Cdn. National	....	74	11	29	40	28	....	....	....	....	....
1987-88	Cdn. National	....	47	3	13	16	32	....	....	....	....	....
	Cdn. Olympic	....	8	1	3	4	2	....	....	....	....	....
	Pittsburgh	**NHL**	**15**	**3**	**8**	**11**	**7**	....	....	....	....	....
1988-89a	**Pittsburgh**	**NHL**	**58**	**12**	**33**	**45**	**57**	**11**	**1**	**8**	**9**	**13**
1989-90	**Pittsburgh**	**NHL**	**51**	**6**	**25**	**31**	**37**	....	....	....	....	....
1990-91	**Pittsburgh**	**NHL**	**66**	**12**	**36**	**48**	**59**	....	....	....	....	....
	Hartford	**NHL**	**11**	**3**	**3**	**6**	**6**	**6**	**1**	**3**	**4**	**8**
1991-92	**Hartford**	**NHL**	**79**	**20**	**37**	**57**	**120**	**7**	**2**	**3**	**5**	**6**
1992-93	**Hartford**	**NHL**	**83**	**14**	**51**	**65**	**94**	....	....	....	....	....
1993-94	**Hartford**	**NHL**	**56**	**7**	**30**	**37**	**56**	....	....	....	....	....
	Calgary	**NHL**	**13**	**3**	**7**	**10**	**18**	**7**	**0**	**3**	**3**	**2**
1994-95	**Calgary**	**NHL**	**48**	**4**	**24**	**28**	**46**	**7**	**0**	**4**	**4**	**4**
1995-96	**Calgary**	**NHL**	**80**	**12**	**17**	**29**	**115**	**4**	**0**	**1**	**1**	**10**
1996-97	**Calgary**	**NHL**	**2**	**0**	**0**	**0**	**0**	....	....	....	....	....
	NHL Totals		**562**	**96**	**271**	**367**	**615**	**42**	**4**	**22**	**26**	**43**

a NHL All-Rookie Team (1989)
Played in NHL All-Star Game (1993)
Traded to **Hartford** by **Pittsburgh** with John Cullen and Jeff Parker for Ron Francis, Grant Jennings and Ulf Samuelsson, March 4, 1991. Traded to **Calgary** by **Hartford** with James Patrick and Michael Nylander for Gary Suter, Paul Ranheim and Ted Drury, March 10, 1994.

ZAMUNER, ROB (ZAM-nuhr) T.B.

Left wing. Shoots left. 6'2", 202 lbs. Born, Oakville, Ont., September 17, 1969.
(NY Rangers' 3rd choice, 45th overall, in 1989 Entry Draft).

			Regular Season					Playoffs				
Season	Club	Lea	GP	G	A	TP	PIM	GP	G	A	TP	PIM
1986-87	Guelph	OHL	62	6	15	21	8	....	....	....	....	....
1987-88	Guelph	OHL	58	20	41	61	18	....	....	....	....	....
1988-89	Guelph	OHL	66	46	65	111	38	7	5	5	10	9
1989-90	Flint	IHL	77	44	35	79	32	4	1	0	1	6
1990-91	Binghamton	AHL	80	25	58	83	50	9	7	6	13	35
1991-92	**NY Rangers**	**NHL**	**9**	**1**	**2**	**3**	**2**	....	....	....	....	....
	Binghamton	AHL	61	19	53	72	42	11	8	9	17	8
1992-93	**Tampa Bay**	**NHL**	**84**	**15**	**28**	**43**	**74**	....	....	....	....	....
1993-94	**Tampa Bay**	**NHL**	**59**	**6**	**6**	**12**	**42**	....	....	....	....	....
1994-95	**Tampa Bay**	**NHL**	**43**	**9**	**6**	**15**	**24**	....	....	....	....	....
1995-96	**Tampa Bay**	**NHL**	**72**	**15**	**20**	**35**	**62**	**6**	**2**	**3**	**5**	**10**
1996-97	**Tampa Bay**	**NHL**	**82**	**17**	**33**	**50**	**56**	....	....	....	....	....
	NHL Totals		**349**	**63**	**95**	**158**	**260**	**6**	**2**	**3**	**5**	**10**

Signed as a free agent by **Tampa Bay**, July 13, 1992.

ZANUTTO, MIKE BUF.

Center. Shoots left. 6', 190 lbs. Born, Burlington, Ont., January 1, 1977.
(Buffalo's 10th choice, 198th overall, in 1995 Entry Draft).

			Regular Season					Playoffs				
Season	Club	Lea	GP	G	A	TP	PIM	GP	G	A	TP	PIM
1994-95	North Bay	OHL	13	1	1	2	2	....	....	....	....	....
	Oshawa	OHL	42	13	17	30	2	7	4	1	5	0
1995-96	Oshawa	OHL	66	32	38	70	6	5	0	2	2	0
1996-97	Oshawa	OHL	62	23	33	56	18	18	6	6	12	12

ZEDNIK, RICHARD (ZEHD-nihk, REE-khahrd) WSH.

Left wing. Shoots left. 5'11", 172 lbs. Born, Bystrica, Czech., January 6, 1976.
(Washington's 10th choice, 249th overall, in 1994 Entry Draft).

			Regular Season					Playoffs				
Season	Club	Lea	GP	G	A	TP	PIM	GP	G	A	TP	PIM
1993-94	B. Bystrica	Slov. 2	25	3	6	9	....	....	....	....	....	....
1994-95	Portland	WHL	65	35	51	86	89	9	5	5	10	20
1995-96	**Washington**	**NHL**	**1**	**0**	**0**	**0**	**0**	....	....	....	....	....
a	Portland	WHL	61	44	37	81	154	7	8	4	12	23
	Portland	AHL	1	1	1	2	0	21	4	5	9	26
1996-97	**Washington**	**NHL**	**11**	**2**	**1**	**3**	**4**	....	....	....	....	....
	Portland	AHL	56	15	20	35	70	5	1	0	1	6
	NHL Totals		**12**	**2**	**1**	**3**	**4**	....	....	....	....	....

a WHL West Second All-Star Team (1996)

ZEHR, JEFF (ZAIR) NYI

Left wing/center. Shoots left. 6'3", 195 lbs. Born, Woodstock, Ont., December 10, 1978.
(NY Islanders' 3rd choice, 31st overall, in 1997 Entry Draft).

			Regular Season					Playoffs				
Season	Club	Lea	GP	G	A	TP	PIM	GP	G	A	TP	PIM
1995-96	Windsor	OHL	56	4	21	25	103	7	0	1	1	2
1996-97	Windsor	OHL	57	27	32	59	196	5	2	1	3	4

ZELENKO, BORIS (zeh-LEHN-koh) PIT.

Left wing. Shoots right. 6'1", 172 lbs. Born, Moscow, USSR, September 12, 1975.
(Pittsburgh's 11th choice, 206th overall, in 1994 Entry Draft).

			Regular Season					Playoffs				
Season	Club	Lea	GP	G	A	TP	PIM	GP	G	A	TP	PIM
1993-94	CSKA	CIS	34	5	1	6	10	1	0	0	0	0
1994-95	CSKA	CIS	35	5	1	6	12	1	0	0	0	0
1995-96	CSKA	CIS	26	4	2	6	8	3	1	0	1	0
1996-97	CSKA	Rus.	23	2	5	7	8	2	0	0	0	0

ZELEPUKIN, VALERI (zeh-leh-POO-kin) N.J.

Left wing. Shoots left. 6', 200 lbs. Born, Voskresensk, USSR, September 17, 1968.
(New Jersey's 13th choice, 221st overall, in 1990 Entry Draft).

			Regular Season					Playoffs				
Season	Club	Lea	GP	G	A	TP	PIM	GP	G	A	TP	PIM
1984-85	Khimik	USSR	5	0	0	0	2	....	....	....	....	....
1985-86	Khimik	USSR	33	2	2	4	10	....	....	....	....	....
1986-87	Khimik	USSR	19	1	0	1	4	....	....	....	....	....
1987-88	SKA MVO	USSR 2	18	18	6	24	....	....	....	....	....	....
	CSKA	USSR	19	3	1	4	8	....	....	....	....	....
1988-89	CSKA	USSR	17	2	3	5	2	....	....	....	....	....
1989-90	Khimik	USSR	46	17	14	31	26	....	....	....	....	....
1990-91	Khimik	USSR	34	11	6	17	38	....	....	....	....	....
1991-92	**New Jersey**	**NHL**	**44**	**13**	**18**	**31**	**28**	**4**	**1**	**1**	**2**	**2**
	Utica	AHL	22	20	9	29	8	....	....	....	....	....
1992-93	**New Jersey**	**NHL**	**78**	**23**	**41**	**64**	**70**	**5**	**0**	**2**	**2**	**0**
1993-94	**New Jersey**	**NHL**	**82**	**26**	**31**	**57**	**70**	**20**	**5**	**2**	**7**	**14**
1994-95	**New Jersey**	**NHL**	**4**	**1**	**2**	**3**	**6**	**18**	**1**	**2**	**3**	**12** ♦
1995-96	**New Jersey**	**NHL**	**61**	**6**	**9**	**15**	**107**	....	....	....	....	....
1996-97	**New Jersey**	**NHL**	**71**	**14**	**24**	**38**	**36**	**8**	**3**	**2**	**5**	**2**
	NHL Totals		**340**	**83**	**125**	**208**	**317**	**55**	**10**	**9**	**19**	**30**

ZENT, JASON OTT.

Left wing. Shoots left. 5'11", 204 lbs. Born, Buffalo, NY, April 15, 1971.
(NY Islanders' 3rd choice, 44th overall, in 1989 Entry Draft).

			Regular Season					Playoffs				
Season	Club	Lea	GP	G	A	TP	PIM	GP	G	A	TP	PIM
1990-91	U. Wisconsin	WCHA	39	19	18	37	51	....	....	....	....	....
1991-92a	U. Wisconsin	WCHA	39	22	17	39	128	....	....	....	....	....
1992-93	U. Wisconsin	WCHA	40	26	12	38	92	....	....	....	....	....
1993-94	U. Wisconsin	WCHA	42	20	21	41	120	....	....	....	....	....
1994-95	P.E.I.	AHL	55	15	11	26	46	9	6	1	7	6
1995-96	P.E.I.	AHL	68	14	5	19	61	5	2	1	3	4
1996-97	**Ottawa**	**NHL**	**22**	**3**	**3**	**6**	**9**	....	....	....	....	....
	Worcester	AHL	45	14	10	24	45	5	3	3	6	4
	NHL Totals		**22**	**3**	**3**	**6**	**9**	....	....	....	....	....

a NCAA All-Tournament Team (1992)
Traded to **Ottawa** by **NY Islanders** for Ottawa's fifth round choice (Andy Berenzweig) in 1996 Entry Draft, October 15, 1994.

ZETTLER, ROB TOR.

Defense. Shoots left. 6'3", 200 lbs. Born, Sept Iles, Que., March 8, 1968.
(Minnesota's 5th choice, 55th overall, in 1986 Entry Draft).

			Regular Season					Playoffs				
Season	Club	Lea	GP	G	A	TP	PIM	GP	G	A	TP	PIM
1985-86	S.S. Marie	OHL	57	5	23	28	92	....	....	....	....	....
1986-87	S.S. Marie	OHL	64	13	22	35	89	4	0	0	0	0
1987-88	Kalamazoo	IHL	2	0	1	1	0	7	0	2	2	2
	S.S. Marie	OHL	64	7	41	48	77	6	2	2	4	9
1988-89	**Minnesota**	**NHL**	**2**	**0**	**0**	**0**	**0**	....	....	....	....	....
	Kalamazoo	IHL	80	5	21	26	79	6	0	1	1	26
1989-90	**Minnesota**	**NHL**	**31**	**0**	**8**	**8**	**45**	....	....	....	....	....
	Kalamazoo	IHL	41	6	10	16	64	7	0	0	0	6
1990-91	**Minnesota**	**NHL**	**47**	**1**	**4**	**5**	**119**	....	....	....	....	....
	Kalamazoo	IHL	1	0	0	0	2	....	....	....	....	....
1991-92	**San Jose**	**NHL**	**74**	**1**	**8**	**9**	**99**	....	....	....	....	....
1992-93	**San Jose**	**NHL**	**80**	**0**	**7**	**7**	**150**	....	....	....	....	....
1993-94	**San Jose**	**NHL**	**42**	**0**	**3**	**3**	**65**	....	....	....	....	....
	Philadelphia	**NHL**	**33**	**0**	**4**	**4**	**69**	....	....	....	....	....
1994-95	**Philadelphia**	**NHL**	**32**	**0**	**1**	**1**	**34**	**1**	**0**	**0**	**0**	**2**
1995-96	**Toronto**	**NHL**	**29**	**0**	**1**	**1**	**48**	**2**	**0**	**0**	**0**	**0**
1996-97	**Toronto**	**NHL**	**48**	**2**	**12**	**14**	**51**	....	....	....	....	....
	Utah	IHL	30	0	10	10	60	....	....	....	....	....
	NHL Totals		**418**	**4**	**48**	**52**	**680**	**3**	**0**	**0**	**0**	**2**

Claimed by **San Jose** from **Minnesota** in Dispersal Draft, May 30, 1991. Traded to **Philadelphia** by **San Jose** for Viacheslav Butsayev, February 1, 1994. Traded to **Toronto** by **Philadelphia** for Toronto's fifth round choice (Per-Ragna Bergqvist) in 1996 Entry Draft, July 8, 1995.

ZEZEL, PETER (ZEH-zehl) N.J.

Center. Shoots left. 5'11", 200 lbs. Born, Toronto, Ont., April 22, 1965.
(Philadelphia's 1st choice, 41st overall, in 1983 Entry Draft).

			Regular Season					Playoffs				
Season	Club	Lea	GP	G	A	TP	PIM	GP	G	A	TP	PIM
1982-83	Toronto	OHL	66	35	39	74	28	4	2	4	6	0
1983-84	Toronto	OHL	68	47	86	133	31	9	7	5	12	4
1984-85	**Philadelphia**	**NHL**	**65**	**15**	**46**	**61**	**26**	**19**	**1**	**8**	**9**	**28**
1985-86	**Philadelphia**	**NHL**	**79**	**17**	**37**	**54**	**76**	**5**	**3**	**1**	**4**	**4**
1986-87	**Philadelphia**	**NHL**	**71**	**33**	**39**	**72**	**71**	**25**	**3**	**10**	**13**	**10**
1987-88	**Philadelphia**	**NHL**	**69**	**22**	**35**	**57**	**42**	**7**	**3**	**2**	**5**	**7**
1988-89	**Philadelphia**	**NHL**	**26**	**4**	**13**	**17**	**15**	....	....	....	....	....
	St. Louis	**NHL**	**52**	**17**	**36**	**53**	**27**	**10**	**6**	**6**	**12**	**4**
1989-90	**St. Louis**	**NHL**	**73**	**25**	**47**	**72**	**30**	**12**	**1**	**7**	**8**	**4**
1990-91	**Washington**	**NHL**	**20**	**7**	**5**	**12**	**10**	....	....	....	....	....
	Toronto	**NHL**	**32**	**14**	**14**	**28**	**4**	....	....	....	....	....
1991-92	**Toronto**	**NHL**	**64**	**16**	**33**	**49**	**26**	....	....	....	....	....
1992-93	**Toronto**	**NHL**	**70**	**12**	**23**	**35**	**24**	**20**	**2**	**1**	**3**	**6**
1993-94	**Toronto**	**NHL**	**41**	**8**	**8**	**16**	**19**	**18**	**2**	**4**	**6**	**8**
1994-95	**Dallas**	**NHL**	**30**	**6**	**5**	**11**	**19**	**3**	**1**	**0**	**1**	**0**
	Kalamazoo	IHL	2	0	0	0	0	....	....	....	....	....
1995-96	**St. Louis**	**NHL**	**57**	**8**	**13**	**21**	**12**	**10**	**3**	**0**	**3**	**2**
1996-97	**St. Louis**	**NHL**	**35**	**4**	**9**	**13**	**12**	....	....	....	....	....
	New Jersey	**NHL**	**18**	**0**	**3**	**3**	**4**	**2**	**0**	**0**	**0**	**10**
	NHL Totals		**802**	**208**	**366**	**574**	**417**	**131**	**25**	**39**	**64**	**83**

Traded to **St. Louis** by **Philadelphia** for Mike Bullard, November 29, 1988. Traded to **Washington** by **St. Louis** with Mike Lalor for Geoff Courtnall, July 13, 1990. Traded to **Toronto** by **Washington** with Bob Rouse for Al Iafrate, January 16, 1991. Acquired by **Dallas** from **Toronto** with Grant Marshall as compensation for Toronto's signing of free agent Mike Craig, August 10, 1994. Signed as a free agent by **St. Louis**, October 19, 1995. Traded to **New Jersey** by **St. Louis** for Chris McAlpine and New Jersey's ninth round choice in 1999 Entry Draft, February 11, 1997.

ZHAMNOV, ALEXEI (ZHAHM-nahf) CHI.

Center. Shoots left. 6'1", 195 lbs. Born, Moscow, USSR, October 1, 1970.
(Winnipeg's 5th choice, 77th overall, in 1990 Entry Draft).

			Regular Season					Playoffs				
Season	Club	Lea	GP	G	A	TP	PIM	GP	G	A	TP	PIM
1988-89	Moscow D'amo	USSR	4	0	0	0	0	....	....	....	....	....
1989-90	Moscow D'amo	USSR	43	11	6	17	21	....	....	....	....	....
1990-91	Moscow D'amo	USSR	46	16	12	28	24	....	....	....	....	....
1991-92	Moscow D'amo	CIS	39	15	21	36	28	....	....	....	....	....
1992-93	**Winnipeg**	**NHL**	**68**	**25**	**47**	**72**	**58**	**6**	**0**	**2**	**2**	**2**
1993-94	**Winnipeg**	**NHL**	**61**	**26**	**45**	**71**	**62**	....	....	....	....	....
1994-95a	**Winnipeg**	**NHL**	**48**	**30**	**35**	**65**	**20**	....	....	....	....	....
1995-96	**Winnipeg**	**NHL**	**58**	**22**	**37**	**59**	**65**	**6**	**2**	**1**	**3**	**8**
1996-97	**Chicago**	**NHL**	**74**	**20**	**42**	**62**	**56**	....	....	....	....	....
	NHL Totals		**309**	**123**	**206**	**329**	**261**	**12**	**2**	**3**	**5**	**10**

a NHL Second All-Star Team (1995)

Traded to **Chicago** by **Phoenix** with Craig Mills and Phoenix's first round choice (Ty Jones) in 1997 Entry Draft for Jeremy Roenick, August 16, 1996.

ZHITNIK, ALEXEI (ZHIHT-nihk) BUF.

Defense. Shoots left. 5'11", 204 lbs. Born, Kiev, USSR, October 10, 1972.
(Los Angeles' 3rd choice, 81st overall, in 1991 Entry Draft).

			Regular Season					Playoffs				
Season	Club	Lea	GP	G	A	TP	PIM	GP	G	A	TP	PIM
1989-90	Sokol Kiev	USSR	31	3	4	7	16	....	....	....	....	....
1990-91	Sokol Kiev	USSR	46	1	4	5	46	....	....	....	....	....
1991-92	CSKA	CIS	44	2	7	9	52	....	....	....	....	....
1992-93	**Los Angeles**	**NHL**	**78**	**12**	**36**	**48**	**80**	**24**	**3**	**9**	**12**	**26**
1993-94	**Los Angeles**	**NHL**	**81**	**12**	**40**	**52**	**101**	....	....	....	....	....
1994-95	**Los Angeles**	**NHL**	**11**	**2**	**5**	**7**	**27**	....	....	....	....	....
	Buffalo	**NHL**	**21**	**2**	**5**	**7**	**34**	**5**	**0**	**1**	**1**	**14**
1995-96	**Buffalo**	**NHL**	**80**	**6**	**30**	**36**	**58**	....	....	....	....	....
1996-97	**Buffalo**	**NHL**	**80**	**7**	**28**	**35**	**95**	**12**	**1**	**0**	**1**	**16**
	NHL Totals		**351**	**41**	**144**	**185**	**395**	**41**	**4**	**10**	**14**	**56**

Traded to **Buffalo** by **Los Angeles** with Robb Stauber, Charlie Huddy and Los Angeles' fifth round choice (Marian Menhart) in 1995 Entry Draft for Philippe Boucher, Denis Tsygurov and Grant Fuhr, February 14, 1995.

ZHOLTOK, SERGEI (ZHOL-tok) OTT.

Center. Shoots right. 6', 190 lbs. Born, Riga, Latvia, December 2, 1972.
(Boston's 2nd choice, 55th overall, in 1992 Entry Draft).

			Regular Season					Playoffs				
Season	Club	Lea	GP	G	A	TP	PIM	GP	G	A	TP	PIM
1990-91	Dynamo Riga	USSR	39	4	0	4	16	....	....	....	....	....
1991-92	Riga	CIS	27	6	3	9	6	....	....	....	....	....
1992-93	**Boston**	**NHL**	**1**	**0**	**1**	**1**	**0**	....	....	....	....	....
	Providence	AHL	64	31	35	66	57	6	3	5	8	4
1993-94	**Boston**	**NHL**	**24**	**2**	**1**	**3**	**2**	....	....	....	....	....
	Providence	AHL	54	29	33	62	16	....	....	....	....	....
1994-95	Providence	AHL	78	23	35	58	42	13	8	5	13	6
1995-96	Las Vegas	IHL	82	51	50	101	30	15	7	13	20	6
1996-97	**Ottawa**	**NHL**	**57**	**12**	**16**	**28**	**19**	**7**	**1**	**1**	**2**	**0**
	Las Vegas	IHL	19	13	14	27	20	....	....	....	....	....
	NHL Totals		**82**	**14**	**18**	**32**	**21**	**7**	**1**	**1**	**2**	**0**

Signed as a free agent by **Ottawa**, July 10, 1996.

ZHURIK, ALEXANDER (ZHUH-rihk) EDM.

Defense. Shoots left. 6'3", 195 lbs. Born, Minsk, USSR, May 29, 1975.
(Edmonton's 7th choice, 163rd overall, in 1993 Entry Draft).

			Regular Season					Playoffs				
Season	Club	Lea	GP	G	A	TP	PIM	GP	G	A	TP	PIM
1993-94	Kingston	OHL	59	7	23	30	92	6	0	0	0	4
1994-95	Kingston	OHL	54	3	21	24	51	6	0	0	0	0
1995-96	Cape Breton	AHL	80	5	36	41	85	....	....	....	....	....
1996-97	Hamilton	AHL	72	5	16	21	49	22	2	11	13	14

ZIB, LUKAS (ZIHB, LOO-kahsh) EDM.

Defense. Shoots right. 6'1", 200 lbs. Born, Ceske Budejovice, Czech., February 24, 1977.
(Edmonton's 3rd choice, 57th overall, in 1995 Entry Draft).

			Regular Season					Playoffs				
Season	Club	Lea	GP	G	A	TP	PIM	GP	G	A	TP	PIM
1994-95	Budejovice	Czech.	13	2	0	2	16	9	1	0	1	6
1995-96	Budejovice	Czech. Jr.	11	5	1	6	....	....	....	....	....	....
	Budejovice	Czech.	7	1	0	1	....	2	0	0	0	....
1996-97	Budejovice	Czech.	13	0	0	0	4	2	0	0	0	0

ZIMAKOV, SERGEI (zih-MAH-kahv) WSH.

Defense. Shoots left. 6'1", 194 lbs. Born, Moscow, USSR, January 15, 1978.
(Washington's 4th choice, 58th overall, in 1996 Entry Draft).

			Regular Season					Playoffs				
Season	Club	Lea	GP	G	A	TP	PIM	GP	G	A	TP	PIM
1995-96	Soviet Wings	CIS	49	2	7	9	36	....	....	....	....	....
1996-97	Soviet Wings	Rus.	39	4	3	7	57	2	0	0	0	0

ZMOLEK, DOUG (zuh-MOH-lehk) L.A.

Defense. Shoots left. 6'2", 220 lbs. Born, Rochester, MN, November 3, 1970.
(Minnesota's 1st choice, 7th overall, in 1989 Entry Draft).

			Regular Season					Playoffs				
Season	Club	Lea	GP	G	A	TP	PIM	GP	G	A	TP	PIM
1989-90	U. Minnesota	WCHA	40	1	10	11	52	....	....	....	....	....
1990-91	U. Minnesota	WCHA	34	11	6	17	38	....	....	....	....	....
1991-92ab	U. Minnesota	WCHA	41	6	20	26	84	....	....	....	....	....
1992-93	**San Jose**	**NHL**	**84**	**5**	**10**	**15**	**229**	....	....	....	....	....
1993-94	**San Jose**	**NHL**	**68**	**0**	**4**	**4**	**122**	....	....	....	....	....
	Dallas	**NHL**	**7**	**1**	**0**	**1**	**11**	**7**	**0**	**1**	**1**	**4**
1994-95	**Dallas**	**NHL**	**42**	**0**	**5**	**5**	**67**	**5**	**0**	**0**	**0**	**10**
1995-96	**Dallas**	**NHL**	**42**	**1**	**5**	**6**	**65**	....	....	....	....	....
	Los Angeles	**NHL**	**16**	**1**	**0**	**1**	**22**	....	....	....	....	....
1996-97	**Los Angeles**	**NHL**	**57**	**1**	**0**	**1**	**116**	....	....	....	....	....
	NHL Totals		**316**	**9**	**24**	**33**	**632**	**12**	**0**	**1**	**1**	**14**

a WCHA Second All-Star Team (1992)
b NCAA West Second All-American Team (1992)

Claimed by **San Jose** from **Minnesota** in Dispersal Draft, May 30, 1991. Traded to **Dallas** by **San Jose** with Mike Lalor and cash for Ulf Dahlen and Dallas' seventh round choice (Brad Mehalko) in 1995 Entry Draft, March 19, 1994. Traded to **Los Angeles** by **Dallas** with Shane Churla for Darryl Sydor and Los Angeles' fifth round choice (Ryan Christie) in 1996 Entry Draft, February 17, 1996.

ZOLOTOV, ROMAN (ZOH-loh-tov) PHI.

Defense. Shoots left. 6'1", 191 lbs. Born, Moscow, USSR, February 13, 1974.
(Philadelphia's 5th choice, 127th overall, in 1992 Entry Draft).

			Regular Season					Playoffs				
Season	Club	Lea	GP	G	A	TP	PIM	GP	G	A	TP	PIM
1991-92	Moscow D'amo	CIS	1	0	0	0	0	....	....	....	....	....
1992-93	Moscow D'amo	CIS Jr.			UNAVAILABLE							
1993-94	Moscow D'amo	CIS	33	0	2	2	20	5	0	1	1	6
1994-95	Moscow D'amo	CIS	25	0	2	2	24	8	1	2	3	6
1995-96	Moscow D'amo	CIS	41	0	2	2	94	9	0	1	1	6
1996-97	Moscow D'amo	Rus.	34	3	2	5	34	3	0	0	0	4

ZOMBO, RICK

Defense. Shoots right. 6'1", 202 lbs. Born, Des Plaines, IL, May 8, 1963.
(Detroit's 6th choice, 149th overall, in 1981 Entry Draft).

			Regular Season					Playoffs				
Season	Club	Lea	GP	G	A	TP	PIM	GP	G	A	TP	PIM
1981-82	North Dakota	WCHA	45	1	15	16	31	....	....	....	....	....
1982-83	North Dakota	WCHA	35	5	11	16	41	....	....	....	....	....
1983-84	North Dakota	WCHA	34	7	24	31	40	....	....	....	....	....
1984-85	**Detroit**	**NHL**	**1**	**0**	**0**	**0**	**0**	....	....	....	....	....
	Adirondack	AHL	56	3	32	35	70	....	....	....	....	....
1985-86	**Detroit**	**NHL**	**14**	**0**	**1**	**1**	**16**	....	....	....	....	....
	Adirondack	AHL	69	7	34	41	94	17	0	4	4	40
1986-87	**Detroit**	**NHL**	**44**	**1**	**4**	**5**	**59**	**7**	**0**	**1**	**1**	**9**
	Adirondack	AHL	25	0	6	6	22	....	....	....	....	....
1987-88	**Detroit**	**NHL**	**62**	**3**	**14**	**17**	**96**	**16**	**0**	**6**	**6**	**55**
1988-89	**Detroit**	**NHL**	**75**	**1**	**20**	**21**	**106**	**6**	**0**	**1**	**1**	**16**
1989-90	**Detroit**	**NHL**	**77**	**5**	**20**	**25**	**95**	....	....	....	....	....
1990-91	**Detroit**	**NHL**	**77**	**4**	**19**	**23**	**55**	**7**	**1**	**0**	**1**	**10**
1991-92	**Detroit**	**NHL**	**3**	**0**	**0**	**0**	**15**	....	....	....	....	....
	St. Louis	**NHL**	**64**	**3**	**15**	**18**	**46**	**6**	**0**	**2**	**2**	**12**
1992-93	**St. Louis**	**NHL**	**71**	**0**	**15**	**15**	**78**	**11**	**0**	**1**	**1**	**12**
1993-94	**St. Louis**	**NHL**	**74**	**2**	**8**	**10**	**85**	**4**	**0**	**0**	**0**	**11**
1994-95	**St. Louis**	**NHL**	**23**	**1**	**4**	**5**	**24**	**3**	**0**	**0**	**0**	**2**
1995-96	**Boston**	**NHL**	**67**	**4**	**10**	**14**	**53**	....	....	....	....	....
1996-97	Phoenix	IHL	23	0	6	6	22	....	....	....	....	....
	NHL Totals		**652**	**24**	**130**	**154**	**728**	**60**	**1**	**11**	**12**	**127**

Traded to **St. Louis** by **Detroit** for Vincent Riendeau, October 18, 1991. Traded to **Boston** by **St. Louis** for Fred Knipscheer, October 2, 1995. Signed as a free agent by **Los Angeles**, December 13, 1996.

ZUBOV, SERGEI (ZOO-bahf) DAL.

Defense. Shoots right. 6'1", 200 lbs. Born, Moscow, USSR, July 22, 1970.
(NY Rangers' 6th choice, 85th overall, in 1990 Entry Draft).

			Regular Season					Playoffs				
Season	Club	Lea	GP	G	A	TP	PIM	GP	G	A	TP	PIM
1988-89	CSKA	USSR	29	1	4	5	10	....	....	....	....	....
1989-90	CSKA	USSR	48	6	2	8	16	....	....	....	....	....
1990-91	CSKA	USSR	41	6	5	11	12	....	....	....	....	....
1991-92	CSKA	CIS	44	4	7	11	8	....	....	....	....	....
1992-93	CSKA	CIS	1	0	1	1	0	....	....	....	....	....
	NY Rangers	**NHL**	**49**	**8**	**23**	**31**	**4**	....	....	....	....	....
	Binghamton	AHL	30	7	29	36	14	11	5	5	10	2
1993-94	**NY Rangers**	**NHL**	**78**	**12**	**77**	**89**	**39**	**22**	**5**	**14**	**19**	**0** ♦
	Binghamton	AHL	2	1	2	3	0	....	....	....	....	....
1994-95	**NY Rangers**	**NHL**	**38**	**10**	**26**	**36**	**18**	**10**	**3**	**8**	**11**	**2**
1995-96	**Pittsburgh**	**NHL**	**64**	**11**	**55**	**66**	**22**	**18**	**1**	**14**	**15**	**26**
1996-97	**Dallas**	**NHL**	**78**	**13**	**30**	**43**	**24**	**7**	**0**	**3**	**3**	**2**
	NHL Totals		**307**	**54**	**211**	**265**	**107**	**57**	**9**	**39**	**48**	**30**

Traded to **Pittsburgh** by **NY Rangers** with Petr Nedved for Luc Robitaille and Ulf Samuelsson, August 31, 1995. Traded to **Dallas** by **Pittsburgh** for Kevin Hatcher, June 22, 1996.

ZUBRUS, DAINIUS (ZOO-bruhs) PHI.

Right wing. Shoots left. 6'3", 215 lbs. Born, Elektrenai, USSR, June 16, 1978.
(Philadelphia's 1st choice, 15th overall, in 1996 Entry Draft).

			Regular Season					Playoffs				
Season	Club	Lea	GP	G	A	TP	PIM	GP	G	A	TP	PIM
1995-96	Pembroke	Jr. A	28	19	13	32	73	....	....	....	....	....
	Caledon	Jr. A	7	3	7	10	2	17	11	12	23	4
1996-97	**Philadelphia**	**NHL**	**68**	**8**	**13**	**21**	**22**	**19**	**5**	**4**	**9**	**12**
	NHL Totals		**68**	**8**	**13**	**21**	**22**	**19**	**5**	**4**	**9**	**12**

ZUKIWSKY, JONATHAN (ZUH-kew-skee) ST.L.

Center. Shoots left. 6'2", 185 lbs. Born, St. Paul, Alta., October 7, 1977.
(St. Louis' 3rd choice, 95th overall, in 1996 Entry Draft).

			Regular Season					Playoffs				
Season	Club	Lea	GP	G	A	TP	PIM	GP	G	A	TP	PIM
1993-94	Red Deer	WHL	59	12	15	27	38	4	0	2	2	0
1994-95	Red Deer	WHL	71	19	24	43	45	....	....	....	....	....
1995-96	Red Deer	WHL	72	20	28	48	38	10	5	2	7	6
1996-97	Red Deer	WHL	66	27	26	53	41	16	6	5	11	10

ZULTEK, MATT (ZUHL-tehk) L.A.

Left wing. Shoots left. 6'4", 218 lbs. Born, Windsor, Ont., March 12, 1979.
(Los Angeles' 2nd choice, 15th overall, in 1997 Entry Draft).

			Regular Season					Playoffs				
Season	Club	Lea	GP	G	A	TP	PIM	GP	G	A	TP	PIM
1995-96	Caledon	Jr. A	50	19	26	45	82	....	....	....	....	....
1996-97	Ottawa	OHL	63	27	13	40	76	21	7	6	13	27

ZYUZIN, ANDREI (ZYOO-zin) S.J.

Defense. Shoots left. 6'1", 187 lbs. Born, Ufa, USSR, January 21, 1978.
(San Jose's 1st choice, 2nd overall, in 1996 Entry Draft).

			Regular Season					Playoffs				
Season	Club	Lea	GP	G	A	TP	PIM	GP	G	A	TP	PIM
1994-95	Ufa Salavat	CIS	30	3	0	3	16	....	....	....	....	....
1995-96	Ufa Salavat	CIS	41	6	3	9	24	....	....	....	....	....
1996-97	Ufa Salavat	Rus.	32	7	10	17	28	7	1	1	2	4

Retired NHL Player Index

Abbreviations: Teams/Cities: — **Ana.** – Anaheim; **Atl.** – Atlanta; **Bos.** – Boston, **Bro.** – Brooklyn; **Buf.** – Buffalo; **Cal.** – California; **Cgy.** – Calgary; **Cle.** – Cleveland; **Col.** – Colorado; **Dal.** – Dallas; **Det.** – Detroit; **Edm.** – Edmonton; **Fla.** – Florida; **Ham.** – Hamilton; **Hfd.** – Hartford; **K.C.** – Kansas City; **L.A.** – Los Angeles; **Min.** — Minnesota; **Mtl.** – Montreal; **Mtl. M.** – Montreal Maroons; **Mtl. W.** – Montreal Wanderers; **N.J.** – New Jersey; **NYA** – NY Americans; **NYI** – New York Islanders; **NYR** – New York Rangers; **Oak.** – Oakland; **Ott.** – Ottawa; **Phi.** – Philadelphia; **Pit.** – Pittsburgh; **Que.** – Quebec; **St. L.** – St. Louis; **S.J.** – San Jose; **T.B.** – Tampa Bay; **Tor.** – Toronto; **Van.** – Vancouver; **Wpg.** – Winnipeg; **Wsh.** – Washington.

Total seasons are rounded off to the nearest full season. **A** – assists; **G** – goals; **GP** – games played; **PIM** – penalties in minutes; **TP** – total points. ● – deceased. Assists not recorded during 1917-18 season.

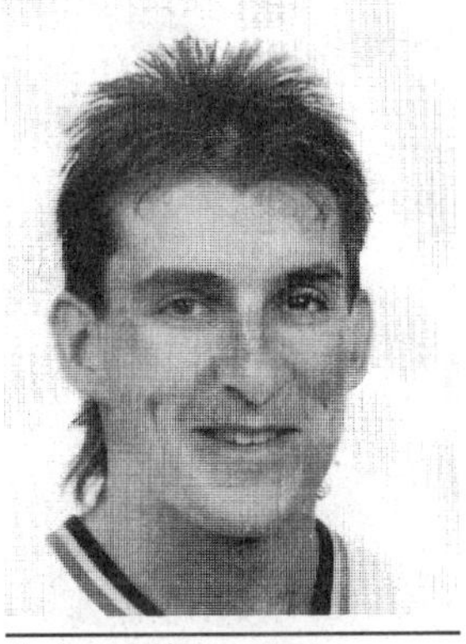

Jim Agnew

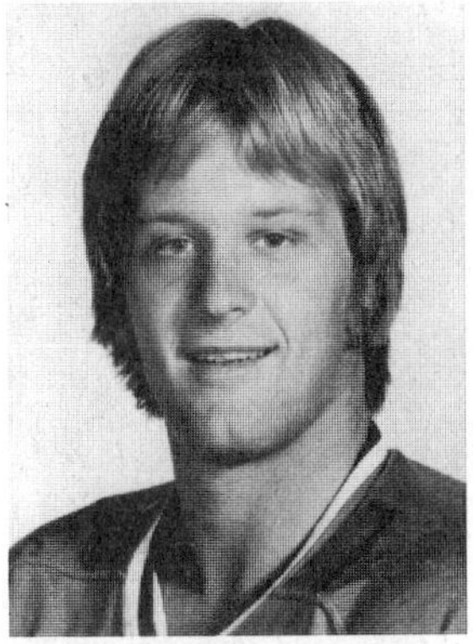

Russ Anderson

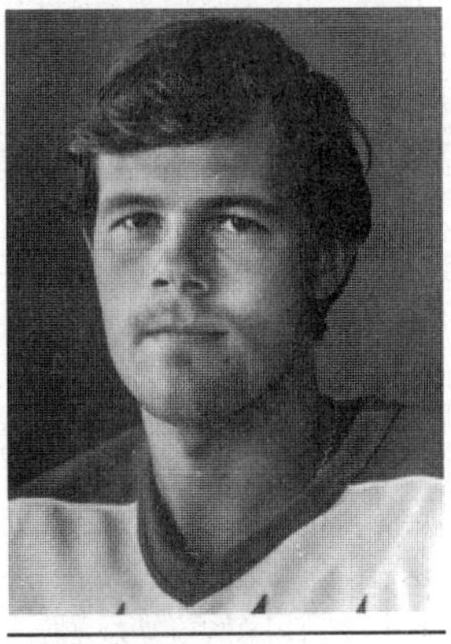

Peter Andersson

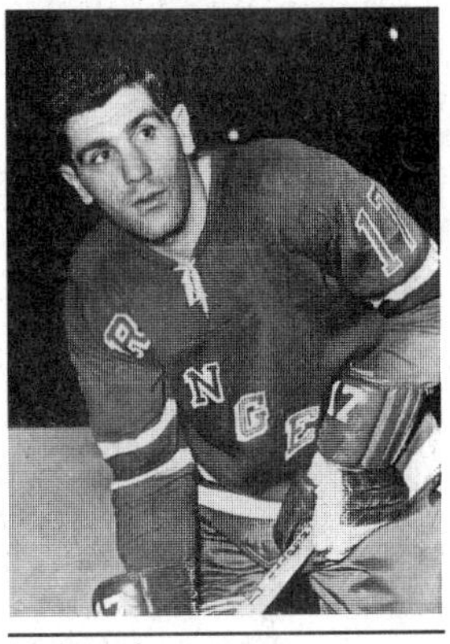

Lou Angotti

			Regular Schedule					Playoffs					NHL	First	Last
Name	NHL Teams	NHL Seasons	GP	G	A	TP	PIM	GP	G	A	TP	PIM	Cup Wins	NHL Season	NHL Season
A															
Abbott, Reg	Mtl.	1	3	0	0	0	0	....	....	....	....	....		1952-53	1952-53
● Abel, Clarence	NYR, Chi.	8	333	18	18	36	359	38	1	1	2	58	2	1926-27	1933-34
Abel, Gerry	Det.	1	1	0	0	0	0	....	....	....	....	....		1966-67	1966-67
Abel, Sid	Det., Chi.	14	612	189	283	472	376	97	28	30	58	79	3	1938-39	1953-54
Abgrall, Dennis	L.A.	1	13	0	2	2	4	....	....	....	....	....		1975-76	1975-76
Abrahamsson, Thommy	Hfd.	1	32	6	11	17	16	....	....	....	....	....		1980-81	1980-81
Achtymichuk, Gene	Mtl., Det.	4	32	3	5	8	2	....	....	....	....	....		1951-52	1958-59
Acomb, Doug	Tor.	1	2	0	1	1	0	....	....	....	....	....		1969-70	1969-70
Acton, Keith	Mtl., Min., Edm., Phi., Wsh., NYI	15	1023	226	358	584	1172	66	12	21	33	88	1	1979-80	1993-94
Adam, Douglas	NYR	1	4	0	1	1	0	....	....	....	....	....		1949-50	1949-50
Adam, Russ	Tor.	1	8	1	2	3	11	....	....	....	....	....		1982-83	1982-83
Adams, Greg C.	Phi., Hfd., Wsh., Edm., Van., Que., Det.	10	545	84	143	227	1173	43	2	11	13	153		1980-81	1989-90
Adams, Jack	Mtl.	1	42	6	12	18	11	3	0	0	0	0		1940-41	1940-41
● Adams, Jack J.	Tor., Ott.	7	173	82	29	111	307	10	3	0	3	12	2	1917-18	1926-27
● Adams, Stewart	Chi., Tor.	4	106	9	26	35	60	11	3	3	6	14		1929-30	1932-33
Adduono, Rick	Bos., Atl.	2	4	0	0	0	2	....	....	....	....	....		1975-76	1979-80
Affleck, Bruce	St.L., Van., NYI	7	280	14	66	80	86	8	0	0	0	0		1974-75	1983-84
Agnew, Jim	Van., Hfd.	6	81	0	1	1	257	4	0	0	0	6		1986-87	1992-93
Ahern, Fred	Cal., Cle., Col.	4	146	31	30	61	130	2	0	1	1	2		1974-75	1977-78
Ahlin, Tony	Chi.	1	1	0	0	0	0	....	....	....	....	....		1937-38	1937-38
Ahola, Peter	L.A., Pit., S.J., Cgy.	3	123	10	17	27	137	6	0	0	0	2		1991-92	1993-94
Ahrens, Chris	Min.	6	52	0	3	3	84	1	0	0	0	0		1973-74	1977-78
Ailsby, Lloyd	NYR	1	3	0	0	0	2	....	....	....	....	....		1951-52	1951-52
Aitken, Brad	Pit., Edm.	2	14	1	3	4	25	....	....	....	....	....		1987-88	1990-91
Albright, Clint	NYR	1	59	14	5	19	19	....	....	....	....	....		1948-49	1948-49
Aldcorn, Gary	Tor., Det., Bos.	5	226	41	56	97	78	6	1	2	3	4		1956-57	1960-61
Alexander, Claire	Tor., Van.	4	155	18	47	65	36	16	2	4	6	4		1974-75	1977-78
● Alexandre, Art	Mtl.	2	11	0	2	2	8	4	0	0	0	0		1931-32	1932-33
Allan, Jeff	Cle.	1	4	0	0	0	2	....	....	....	....	....		1977-78	1977-78
Allen, George	NYR, Chi., Mtl.	8	339	82	115	197	179	41	9	10	19	32		1938-39	1946-47
Allen, Keith	Det.	2	28	0	4	4	8	5	0	0	0	0	1	1953-54	1954-55
Allen, Viv	NYA	1	6	0	1	1	0	....	....	....	....	....		1940-41	1940-41
Alley, Steve	Hfd.	2	15	3	3	6	11	3	0	1	1	0		1979-80	1980-81
Allison, Dave	Mtl.	1	3	0	0	0	12	....	....	....	....	....		1983-84	1983-84
Allison, Mike	NYR, Tor., L.A.	10	499	102	166	268	630	82	9	17	26	135		1980-81	1989-90
Allison, Ray	Hfd., Phi.	7	238	64	93	157	223	12	2	3	5	20		1979-80	1986-87
● Allum, Bill	Chi, NYR	2	2	0	1	1	0	....	....	....	....	....		1939-40	1940-41
● Amadio, Dave	Det., L.A.	3	125	5	11	16	163	16	1	2	3	18		1957-58	1968-69
Ambroziak, Peter	Buf.	1	12	0	1	1	0	....	....	....	....	....		1994-95	1994-95
Amodeo, Mike	Wpg.	1	19	0	0	0	2	....	....	....	....	....		1979-80	1979-80
Anderson, Bill	Bos.	1	....	....	....	....	....	1	0	0	0	0		1942-43	1942-43
Anderson, Dale	Det.	1	13	0	0	0	6	2	0	0	0	0		1956-57	1956-57
Anderson, Doug	Mtl.	1	....	....	....	....	....	2	0	0	0	0	1	1952-53	1952-53
Anderson, Earl	Det., Bos.	3	109	19	19	38	22	5	0	1	1	0		1974-75	1976-77
Anderson, Jim	L.A.	1	7	1	2	3	2	....	....	....	....	....		1967-68	1967-68
Anderson, John	Tor., Que., Hfd.	12	814	282	349	631	263	37	9	18	27	2		1977-78	1988-89
Anderson, Murray	Wsh.	1	40	0	1	1	68	....	....	....	....	....		1974-75	1974-75
Anderson, Perry	St.L., N.J., S.J.	10	400	50	59	109	1051	36	2	1	3	161		1981-82	1991-92
Anderson, Ron C.	Det., L.A., St.L., Buf.	5	251	28	30	58	146	5	0	0	0	4		1967-68	1971-72
Anderson, Ron H.	Wsh.	1	28	9	7	16	8	....	....	....	....	....		1974-75	1974-75
Anderson, Russ	Pit., Hfd., L.A.	9	519	22	99	121	1086	10	0	3	3	28		1976-77	1984-85
● Anderson, Tom	Det., NYA, Bro.	8	319	62	127	189	190	16	2	7	9	8		1934-35	1941-42
Andersson, Kent-Erik	Min., NYR	7	456	72	103	175	78	50	4	11	15	4		1977-78	1983-84
Andersson, Peter	Wsh., Que.	3	172	10	41	51	81	7	0	2	2	2		1983-84	1985-86
Andersson, Peter	NYR, Fla.	2	47	6	13	19	20	....	....	....	....	....		1992-93	1993-94
Andrascik, Steve	NYR	1	....	....	....	....	....	1	0	0	0	0		1971-72	1971-72
Andrea, Paul	NYR, Pit., Cal., Buf.	4	150	31	49	80	10	....	....	....	....	....		1965-66	1970-71
Andrews, Lloyd	Tor.	4	53	8	5	13	10	7	2	0	2	5		1921-22	1924-25
Andrijevski, Alexander	Chi.	1	1	0	0	0	0	....	....	....	....	....		1992-93	1992-93
Andruff, Ron	Mtl., Col.,	5	153	19	36	55	54	2	0	0	0	0		1974-75	1978-79
Angotti, Lou	NYR, Chi., Phi., Pit., St.L.	10	653	103	186	289	228	65	8	8	16	17		1964-65	1973-74
Anholt, Darrel	Chi.	1	1	0	0	0	0	....	....	....	....	....		1983-84	1983-84
Anslow, Bert	NYR	1	2	0	0	0	0	....	....	....	....	....		1947-48	1947-48
Antonovich, Mike	Min., Hfd., N.J.	5	87	10	15	25	37	....	....	....	....	....		1975-76	1983-84
Apps, Syl (Jr.)	NYR, Pit., L.A.	10	727	183	423	606	311	23	5	5	10	23		1970-71	1979-80
Apps, Syl (Sr.)	Tor.	10	423	201	231	432	56	69	25	29	54	8	3	1936-37	1947-48
Arbour, Al	Det., Chi., Tor., St.L.	16	626	12	58	70	617	86	1	8	9	92	3	1953-54	1970-71
● Arbour, Amos	Mtl., Ham., Tor.	6	109	51	13	64	66	....	....	....	....	....		1918-19	1923-24
Arbour, Jack	Det., Tor.	2	47	5	1	6	56	....	....	....	....	....		1926-27	1928-29
Arbour, John	Bos., Pit., Van., St.L.	5	106	1	9	10	149	5	0	0	0	0		1965-66	1971-72
Arbour, Ty	Pit., Chi.	5	207	28	28	56	112	11	2	0	2	6		1926-27	1930-31
Archambault, Michel	Chi.	1	3	0	0	0	0	....	....	....	....	....		1976-77	1976-77
Archibald, Jim	Min.	3	16	1	2	3	45	....	....	....	....	....		1984-85	1986-87
Areshenkoff, Ronald	Edm.	1	4	0	0	0	0	....	....	....	....	....		1979-80	1979-80
Armstrong, Bill H.	Phi.	1	1	0	1	1	0	....	....	....	....	....		1990-91	1990-91
● Armstrong, Bob	Bos.	12	542	13	86	99	671	42	1	7	8	28		1950-51	1961-62
Armstrong, George	Tor.	21	1187	296	417	713	721	110	26	34	60	52	4	1949-50	1970-71
Armstrong, Murray	Tor., NYA, Bro., Det.	8	270	67	121	188	72	30	4	6	10	2		1937-38	1945-46
● Armstrong, Red	Tor.	1	7	1	1	2	2	....	....	....	....	....		1962-63	1962-63
Armstrong, Tim	Tor.	1	11	1	0	1	6	....	....	....	....	....		1988-89	1988-89
Arnason, Chuck	Mtl., Atl., Pit., K.C., Col., Cle., Min., Wsh.	8	401	109	90	199	122	9	2	4	6	4		1971-72	1978-79
Arniel, Scott	Wpg., Buf., Bos.	11	730	149	189	338	599	34	3	3	6	39		1981-82	1991-92
Arthur, Fred	Hfd., Phi.	3	80	1	8	9	49	4	0	0	0	2		1980-81	1982-83
Arundel, John	Tor.	1	3	0	0	0	9	....	....	....	....	....		1949-50	1949-50
● Ashbee, Barry	Bos., Phi.	5	284	15	70	85	291	17	0	4	4	22	1	1965-66	1973-74
● Ashby, Don	Tor., Col., Edm.	6	188	40	56	96	40	12	1	0	1	4		1975-76	1980-81
Ashton, Brent	Van., Col., N.J., Min., Que., Det., Wpg., Bos., Cgy.	14	998	284	345	629	635	85	24	25	49	70		1979-80	1992-93
Ashworth, Frank	Chi.	1	18	5	4	9	2	....	....	....	....	....		1946-47	1946-47
Asmundson, Oscar	NYR, Det., St.L., NYA, Mtl.	5	111	11	23	34	30	9	0	2	2	4	1	1932-33	1937-38
Atanas, Walt	NYR	1	49	13	8	21	40	....	....	....	....	....		1944-45	1944-45
Atkinson, Steve	Bos., Buf., Wsh.	6	302	60	51	111	104	1	0	0	0	0		1968-69	1974-75
Attwell, Bob	Col.	2	22	1	5	6	0	....	....	....	....	....		1979-80	1980-81
Attwell, Ron	St.L., NYR	1	22	1	7	8	8	....	....	....	....	....		1967-68	1967-68
Aubin, Norm	Tor.	2	69	18	13	31	30	1	0	0	0	0		1981-82	1982-83
Aubry, Pierre	Que., Det.	5	202	24	26	50	133	20	1	1	2	32		1980-81	1984-85
Aubuchon, Ossie	Bos., NYR	2	50	19	12	31	4	6	1	0	1	0		1942-43	1943-44
Auge, Les	Col.	1	6	0	3	3	4	....	....	....	....	....		1980-81	1980-81
● Aurie, Larry	Det.	12	489	147	129	276	279	24	6	9	15	10	2	1927-28	1938-39
Awrey, Don	Bos., St.L., Mtl., Pit., NYR, Col.	16	979	31	158	189	1065	71	0	18	18	150	2	1963-64	1978-79
● Ayres, Vern	NYA, Mtl.M., St.L., NYR	6	211	6	14	20	350	....	....	....	....	....		1930-31	1935-36

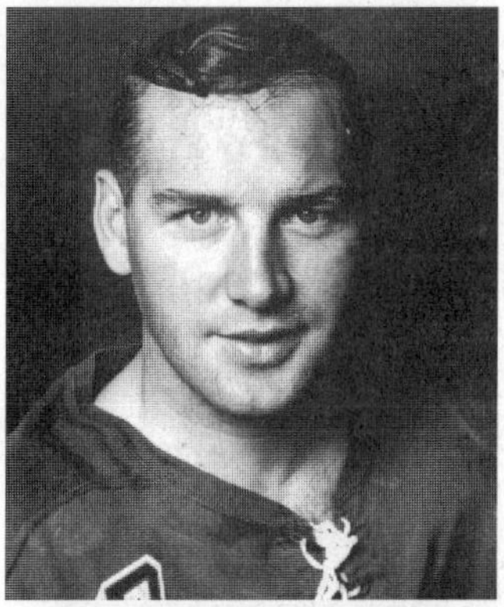

Dave Balon

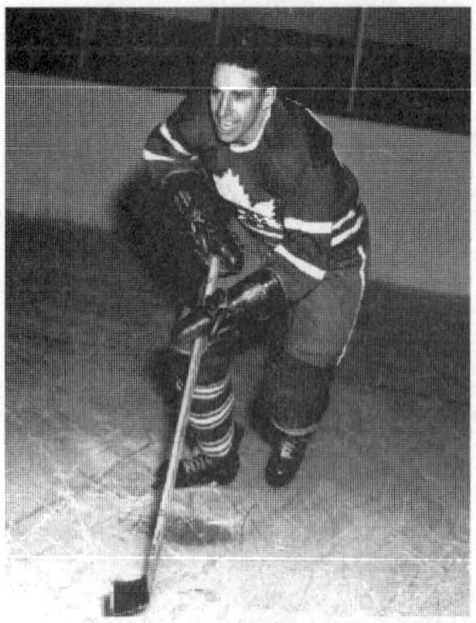

Max Bentley

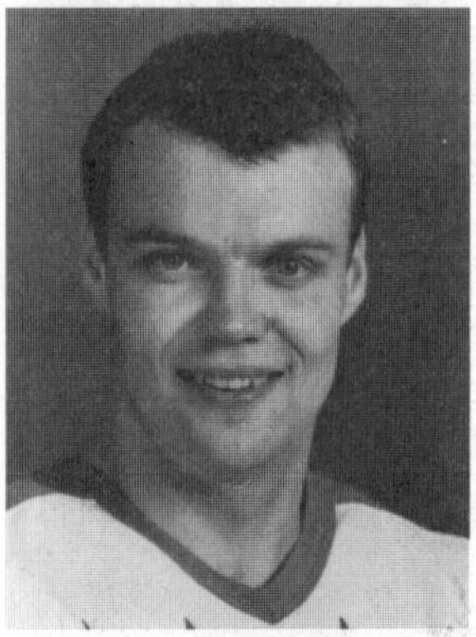

Timo Blomqvist

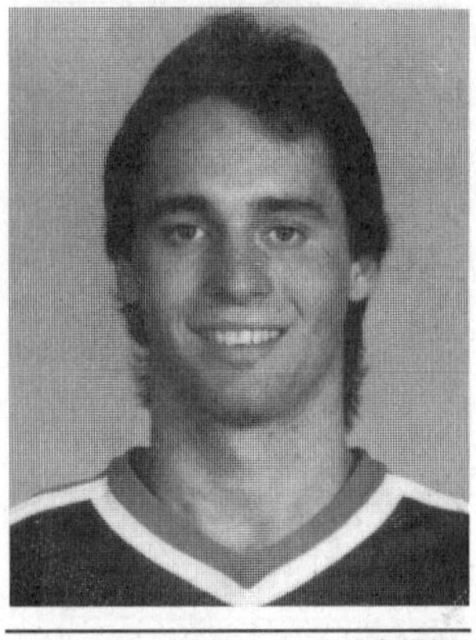

John Blum

Name	NHL Teams	NHL Seasons	Regular Schedule GP	G	A	TP	PIM	Playoffs GP	G	A	TP	PIM	NHL Cup Wins	First NHL Season	Last NHL Season
B															
Babando, Pete	Bos., Det., Chi., NYR	6	351	86	73	159	194	17	3	3	6	6	1	1947-48	1952-53
Babcock, Bobby	Wsh.	2	2	0	0	0	2	....	....	....	....	....		1990-91	1992-93
Babe, Warren	Min.	3	21	2	5	7	23	2	0	0	0	0		1987-88	1990-91
Babin, Mitch	St.L.	1	8	0	0	0	0	....	....	....	....	....		1975-76	1975-76
Baby, John	Cle., Min.	2	26	2	8	10	26	....	....	....	....	....		1977-78	1978-79
Babych, Wayne	St.L., Pit., Que., Hfd.	9	519	192	246	438	498	41	7	9	16	24		1978-79	1986-87
Baca, Jergus	Hfd.	2	10	0	2	2	14	....	....	....	....	....		1990-91	1991-92
Backman, Mike	NYR	3	18	1	6	7	18	10	2	2	4	2		1981-82	1983-84
Backor, Peter	Tor.	1	36	4	5	9	6	....	....	....	....	....	1	1944-45	1944-45
Backstrom, Ralph	Mtl., L.A., Chi.	17	1032	278	361	639	386	116	27	32	59	68	6	1956-57	1972-73
Bailey, Ace (G.)	Bos., Det., St.L., Wsh.	10	568	107	171	278	633	15	2	4	6	28	1	1968-69	1977-78
• Bailey, Ace (I.)	Tor.	8	313	111	82	193	472	21	3	4	7	12	1	1926-27	1933-34
Bailey, Bob	Tor., Det., Chi.	5	150	15	21	36	207	15	0	4	4	22		1953-54	1957-58
Bailey, Reid	Phi., Tor., Hfd.	4	40	1	3	4	105	16	0	2	2	25		1980-81	1983-84
Baillargeon, Joel	Wpg., Que.	3	20	0	2	2	31	....	....	....	....	....		1986-87	1988-89
Baird, Ken	Cal.	1	10	0	2	2	15	....	....	....	....	....		1971-72	1971-72
Baker, Bill	Mtl., Col., St.L., NYR	3	143	7	25	32	175	6	0	0	0	0		1980-81	1982-83
Bakovic, Peter	Van.	1	10	2	0	2	48	....	....	....	....	....		1987-88	1987-88
Balderis, Helmut	Min.	1	26	3	6	9	2	....	....	....	....	....		1989-90	1989-90
Baldwin, Doug	Tor., Det., Chi.	3	24	0	1	1	8	....	....	....	....	....		1945-46	1947-48
Balfour, Earl	Tor., Chi.,	7	288	30	22	52	78	26	0	3	3	4	1	1951-52	1960-61
• Balfour, Murray	Mtl., Chi., Bos.	8	306	67	90	157	393	40	9	10	19	45	1	1956-57	1964-65
Ball, Terry	Phi., Buf.	4	74	7	19	26	26	....	....	....	....	....		1967-68	1971-72
Balon, Dave	NYR, Mtl., Min., Van.	14	776	192	222	414	607	78	14	21	35	109	2	1959-60	1972-73
Baltimore, Byron	Edm.	1	2	0	0	0	4	....	....	....	....	....		1979-80	1979-80
Baluik, Stanley	Bos.	1	7	0	0	0	2	....	....	....	....	....		1959-60	1959-60
Bandura, Jeff	NYR	1	2	0	1	1	0	....	....	....	....	....		1980-81	1980-81
Banks, Darren	Bos.	2	20	2	2	4	73	....	....	....	....	....		1992-93	1993-94
Barahona, Ralph	Bos.	2	6	2	2	4	0	....	....	....	....	....		1990-91	1991-92
Barbe, Andy	Tor.	1	1	0	0	0	2	....	....	....	....	....		1950-51	1950-51
Barber, Bill	Phi.	12	903	420	463	883	623	129	53	55	108	109	2	1972-73	1984-85
Barber, Don	Min., Wpg., Que., S.J.	4	115	25	32	57	64	11	4	4	8	10		1988-89	1991-92
• Barilko, Bill	Tor.	5	252	26	36	62	456	47	5	7	12	104	4	1946-47	1950-51
Barkley, Doug	Chi., Det.	6	253	24	80	104	382	30	0	9	9	63		1957-58	1965-66
Barlow, Bob	Min.	2	77	16	17	33	10	6	2	2	4	6		1969-70	1970-71
Barnes, Blair	L.A.	1	1	0	0	0	0	....	....	....	....	....		1982-83	1982-83
Barnes, Norm	Phi., Hfd.	5	156	6	38	44	178	12	0	0	0	8		1976-77	1981-82
Baron, Normand	Mtl., St.L.	2	27	2	0	2	51	3	0	0	0	22		1983-84	1985-86
Barrault, Doug	Min., Fla.	2	4	0	0	0	2	....	....	....	....	....		1992-93	1993-94
Barrett, Fred	Min., L.A.	13	745	25	123	148	671	44	0	2	2	60		1970-71	1983-84
Barrett, John	Det., Wsh., Min.	8	488	20	77	97	604	16	2	2	4	50		1980-81	1987-88
Barrie, Doug	Pit., Buf., L.A.	3	158	10	42	52	268	....	....	....	....	....		1968-69	1971-72
Barry, Ed	Bos.	1	19	1	3	4	2	....	....	....	....	....		1946-47	1946-47
• Barry, Marty	NYA, Bos., Det., Mtl.	12	509	195	192	387	231	43	15	18	33	34	2	1927-28	1939-40
Barry, Ray	Bos.	1	18	1	2	3	6	....	....	....	....	....		1951-52	1951-52
Bartel, Robin	Cgy., Van.	2	41	0	1	1	14	6	0	0	0	16		1985-86	1986-87
Bartlett, Jim	Mtl., NYR, Bos.	5	191	34	23	57	273	2	0	0	0	0		1954-55	1960-61
• Barton, Cliff	Pit., Phi., NYR	3	85	10	9	19	22	....	....	....	....	....		1929-30	1939-40
Bathe, Frank	Det., Phi.,	9	224	3	28	31	542	27	1	3	4	42		1974-75	1983-84
Bathgate, Andy	NYR, Tor., Det., Pit.	17	1069	349	624	973	624	54	21	14	35	76	1	1952-53	1970-71
Bathgate, Frank	NYR	1	2	0	0	0	2	....	....	....	....	....		1952-53	1952-53
• Batters, Jeff	St.L.	2	16	0	0	0	28	....	....	....	....	....		1993-94	1994-95
• Bauer, Bobby	Bos.	9	327	123	137	260	36	48	11	8	19	6	2	1935-36	1951-52
Baumgartner, Mike	K.C.	1	17	0	0	0	0	....	....	....	....	....		1974-75	1974-75
Baun, Bob	Tor., Oak., Det.	17	964	37	187	224	1493	96	3	12	15	171	4	1956-57	1972-73
Bautin, Sergei	Wpg., Det., S.J.	3	132	5	25	30	176	6	0	0	0	2		1992-93	1995-96
Baxter, Paul	Que., Pit., Cgy.	8	472	48	121	169	1564	40	0	5	5	162		1979-80	1986-87
Beadle, Sandy	Wpg.	1	6	1	0	1	2	....	....	....	....	....		1980-81	1980-81
Beaton, Frank	NYR	2	25	1	1	2	43	....	....	....	....	....		1978-79	1979-80
Beattie, Red	Bos., Det., NYA	9	334	62	85	147	137	24	4	2	6	8		1930-31	1938-39
Beaudin, Norm	St.L., Min.	2	25	1	2	3	4	....	....	....	....	....		1967-68	1970-71
Beaudoin, Serge	Atl.	1	3	0	0	0	0	....	....	....	....	....		1979-80	1979-80
Beaudoin, Yves	Wsh.	3	11	0	0	0	5	....	....	....	....	....		1985-86	1987-88
Beck, Barry	Col., NYR, L.A.	10	615	104	251	355	1016	51	10	23	33	77		1977-78	1989-90
Beckett, Bob	Bos.	4	68	7	6	13	18	....	....	....	....	....		1956-57	1963-64
Bedard, James	Chi.	2	22	1	1	2	8	....	....	....	....	....		1949-50	1950-51
Bednarski, John	NYR, Edm.	4	100	2	18	20	114	1	0	0	0	17		1974-75	1979-80
Beers, Eddy	Cgy., St.L.	5	250	94	116	210	256	41	7	10	17	47		1981-82	1985-86
Behling, Dick	Det.	2	5	1	0	1	2	....	....	....	....	....		1940-41	1942-43
Beisler, Frank	NYA	2	2	0	0	0	0	....	....	....	....	....		1936-37	1939-40
Belanger, Alain	Tor.	1	9	0	1	1	6	....	....	....	....	....		1977-78	1977-78
Belanger, Roger	Pit.	1	44	3	5	8	32	....	....	....	....	....		1984-85	1984-85
Belisle, Danny	NYR	1	4	2	0	2	0	....	....	....	....	....		1960-61	1960-61
Beliveau, Jean	Mtl.	20	1125	507	712	1219	1029	162	79	97	176	211	10	1950-51	1970-71
• Bell, Billy	Mtl.W, Mtl., Ott.	6	61	3	1	4	7	9	0	0	0	0	1	1917-18	1923-24
Bell, Bruce	Que., St.L., NYR, Edm.	5	209	12	64	76	113	34	3	5	8	41		1984-85	1989-90
Bell, Harry	NYR	1	1	0	1	1	0	....	....	....	....	....		1946-47	1946-47
Bell, Joe	NYR	2	62	8	9	17	18	....	....	....	....	....		1942-43	1946-47
Belland, Neil	Van., Pit.	6	109	13	32	45	54	21	2	9	11	23		1981-82	1986-87
• Bellefeuille, Pete	Tor., Det.	4	92	26	4	30	58	....	....	....	....	....		1925-26	1929-30
• Bellemer, Andy	Mtl.M.	1	15	0	0	0	0	....	....	....	....	....		1932-33	1932-33
• Bend, Lin	NYR	1	8	3	1	4	2	....	....	....	....	....		1942-43	1942-43
Bennett, Adam	Chi., Edm.	3	69	3	8	11	69	....	....	....	....	....		1991-92	1993-94
Bennett, Bill	Bos., Hfd.	2	31	4	7	11	65	....	....	....	....	....		1978-79	1979-80
Bennett, Curt	St.L., NYR, Atl.	10	580	152	182	334	347	21	1	1	2	57		1970-71	1979-80
Bennett, Frank	Det.	1	7	0	1	1	2	....	....	....	....	....		1943-44	1943-44
Bennett, Harvey	Pit., Wsh., Phi., Min., St.L.	5	268	44	46	90	347	4	0	0	0	2		1974-75	1978-79
• Bennett, Max	Mtl.	1	1	0	0	0	0	....	....	....	....	....		1935-36	1935-36
Bennett, Rick	NYR	3	15	1	1	2	13	....	....	....	....	....		1989-90	1991-92
Benning, Brian	St.L., L.A., Phi., Edm., Fla.	11	568	63	233	296	963	48	3	20	23	74		1984-85	1994-95
Benning, Jim	Tor., Van.	9	605	52	191	243	461	7	1	1	2	2		1981-82	1989-90
• Benoit, Joe	Mtl.	5	185	75	69	144	94	11	6	3	9	11	1	1940-41	1946-47
Benson, Bill	NYA, Bro.	2	67	11	25	36	35	....	....	....	....	....		1940-41	1941-42
• Benson, Bobby	Bos.	1	8	0	1	1	4	....	....	....	....	....		1924-25	1924-25
• Bentley, Doug	Chi., NYR	13	566	219	324	543	217	23	9	8	17	8		1939-40	1953-54
• Bentley, Max	Chi., Tor., NYR	12	646	245	299	544	179	51	18	27	45	14	3	1940-41	1953-54
Bentley, Reggie	Chi.	1	11	1	2	3	2	....	....	....	....	....		1942-43	1942-43
Beraldo, Paul	Bos.	2	10	0	0	0	4	....	....	....	....	....		1987-88	1988-89
Berenson, Red	Mtl., NYR, St.L., Det.	17	987	261	397	658	305	85	23	14	37	49	2	1961-62	1977-78
Berezan, Perry	Cgy., Min., S.J.	9	378	61	75	136	279	31	4	7	11	34		1984-85	1992-93
Bergdinon, Fred	Bos.	1	2	0	0	0	0	....	....	....	....	....		1925-26	1925-26
Bergen, Todd	Phi.	1	14	11	5	16	4	17	4	9	13	8		1984-85	1984-85
Berger, Mike	Min.	2	30	3	1	4	67	....	....	....	....	....		1987-88	1988-89
Bergeron, Michel	Det., NYI, Wsh.	5	229	80	58	138	165	....	....	....	....	....		1974-75	1978-79
Bergeron, Yves	Pit.	2	3	0	0	0	0	....	....	....	....	....		1974-75	1976-77
Bergland, Tim	Wsh., T.B.	5	182	17	26	43	75	26	2	2	4	22		1989-90	1993-94
Bergloff, Bob	Min.	1	2	0	0	0	5	....	....	....	....	....		1982-83	1982-83
Berglund, Bo	Que., Min., Phi.	3	130	28	39	67	40	9	2	0	2	6		1983-84	1985-86
Bergman, Gary	Det., Min., K.C.	12	838	68	299	367	1249	21	0	5	5	20		1964-65	1975-76
Bergman, Thommie	Det.	6	246	21	44	65	243	7	0	2	2	2		1972-73	1979-80
Bergqvist, Jonas	Cgy.	1	22	2	5	7	10	....	....	....	....	....		1989-90	1989-90
• Berlinquette, Louis	Mtl., Mtl.M., Pit.	8	193	44	29	73	120	16	1	1	2	9		1917-18	1925-26
Bernier, Serge	Phi., L.A., Que.	7	302	78	119	197	234	5	1	1	2	0		1968-69	1980-81
Berry, Bob	Mtl., L.A.	8	541	159	191	350	344	26	2	6	8	6		1968-69	1976-77
Berry, Doug	Col.	2	121	10	33	43	25	....	....	....	....	....		1979-80	1980-81
Berry, Fred	Det.	1	3	0	0	0	0	....	....	....	....	....		1976-77	1976-77
Berry, Ken	Edm., Van.	4	55	8	10	18	30	....	....	....	....	....		1981-82	1988-89
Besler, Phil	Bos., Chi., Det.	2	30	1	4	5	18	....	....	....	....	....		1935-36	1938-39
• Bessone, Pete	Det.	1	6	0	1	1	6	....	....	....	....	....		1937-38	1937-38
Bethel, John	Wpg.	1	17	0	2	2	4	....	....	....	....	....		1979-80	1979-80
Bets, Maxim	Ana.	1	3	0	0	0	0	....	....	....	....	....		1993-94	1993-94

Name	NHL Teams	NHL Seasons	Regular Schedule GP	G	A	TP	PIM	Playoffs GP	G	A	TP	PIM	NHL Cup Wins	First NHL Season	Last NHL Season
Bettio, Sam	Bos.	1	44	9	12	21	32	....	....	....	....	....		1949-50	1949-50
Beverley, Nick	Bos., Pit., NYR, Min., L.A., Col.	11	502	18	94	112	156	7	0	1	1	0		1966-67	1979-80
Bialowas, Dwight	Atl., Min.	4	164	11	46	57	46	....	....	....	....	....		1973-74	1976-77
Bianchin, Wayne	Pit., Edm.	7	276	68	41	109	137	3	0	1	1	6		1973-74	1979-80
Bidner, Todd	Wsh.	1	12	2	1	3	7	....	....	....	....	....		1981-82	1981-82
Biggs, Don	Min.	2	12	2	0	2	8	....	....	....	....	....		1984-85	1984-85
Bignell, Larry	Pit.	2	20	0	3	3	2	3	0	0	0	2		1973-74	1974-75
Bilodeau, Gilles	Que.	1	9	0	1	1	25	....	....	....	....	....		1979-80	1979-80
Bionda, Jack	Tor., Bos.	4	93	3	9	12	113	11	0	1	1	14		1955-56	1958-59
Bissett, Tom	Det.	1	5	0	0	0	0	....	....	....	....	....		1990-91	1990-91
Bjugstad, Scott	Min., Pit., L.A.	9	317	76	68	144	144	9	0	1	1	2		1983-84	1991-92
Black, Stephen	Det., Chi.	2	113	11	20	31	77	13	0	0	0	13	1	1949-50	1950-51
Blackburn, Bob	NYR., Pit.	3	135	8	12	20	105	6	0	0	0	4		1968-69	1970-71
Blackburn, Don	Bos., Phi., NYR, NYI, Min.	6	185	23	44	67	87	12	3	0	3	10		1962-63	1972-73
Blade, Hank	Chi.	2	24	2	3	5	2	....	....	....	....	....		1946-47	1947-48
Bladon, Tom	Phi., Pit., Edm., Wpg., Det.	9	610	73	197	270	392	86	8	29	37	70	2	1972-73	1980-81
Blaine, Gary	Mtl.	1	1	0	0	0	0	....	....	....	....	....		1954-55	1954-55
● Blair, Andy	Tor., Chi.	9	402	74	86	160	323	38	6	6	12	32	1	1928-29	1936-37
Blair, Chuck	Tor.	2	3	0	0	0	0	....	....	....	....	....		1948-49	1950-51
Blair, George	Tor.	1	2	0	0	0	0	....	....	....	....	....		1950-51	1950-51
Blaisdell, Mike	Det., NYR, Pit., Tor.	9	343	70	84	154	166	6	1	2	3	10		1980-81	1988-89
Blake, Mickey	St.L., Bos., Tor.	2	16	1	1	2	6	....	....	....	....	....		1934-35	1935-36
● Blake, Toe	Mtl.M., Mtl.	15	578	235	292	527	272	58	25	37	62	23	3	1932-33	1947-48
Blight, Rick	Van., L.A.	7	326	96	125	221	170	5	0	5	5	2		1975-76	1982-83
● Blinco, Russ	Mtl.M, Chi.	6	268	59	66	125	24	19	3	3	6	4	1	1933-34	1938-39
Block, Ken	Van.	1	1	0	0	0	0	....	....	....	....	....		1970-71	1970-71
Blomqvist, Timo	Wsh., N.J.	5	243	4	53	57	293	13	0	0	0	24		1981-82	1986-87
Blomsten, Arto	Wpg., L.A.	3	25	0	4	4	8	....	....	....	....	....		1993-94	1995-96
Bloom, Mike	Wsh., Det.	3	201	30	47	77	215	....	....	....	....	....		1974-75	1976-77
Blum, John	Edm., Bos., Wsh., Det.	8	250	7	34	41	610	20	0	2	2	27		1982-83	1989-90
Bodak, Bob	Cgy., Hfd.	2	4	0	0	0	29	....	....	....	....	....		1987-88	1989-90
Boddy, Gregg	Van.	5	273	23	44	67	263	3	0	0	0	0		1971-72	1975-76
Bodnar, Gus	Tor., Chi., Bos.	12	667	142	254	396	207	32	4	3	7	10	2	1943-44	1954-55
Boehm, Ron	Oak.	1	16	2	1	3	10	....	....	....	....	....		1967-68	1967-68
Boesch, Garth	Tor.	4	197	9	28	37	205	34	2	5	7	18	3	1946-47	1949-50
Boh, Rick	Min.	1	8	2	1	3	4	....	....	....	....	....		1987-88	1987-88
Boileau, Marc	Det.	1	54	5	6	11	8	....	....	....	....	....		1961-62	1961-62
Boileau, Rene	NYA	1	7	0	0	0	0	....	....	....	....	....		1925-26	1925-26
Boimistruck, Fred	Tor.	2	83	4	14	18	45	....	....	....	....	....		1981-82	1982-83
Boisvert, Serge	Tor., Mtl.	5	46	5	7	12	8	23	3	7	10	4	1	1982-83	1987-88
Boivin, Claude	Phi., Ott.	4	132	12	19	31	364	....	....	....	....	....		1991-92	1994-95
Boivin, Leo	Tor., Bos., Det., Pit., Min.	19	1150	72	250	322	1192	54	3	10	13	59		1951-52	1969-70
Boland, Mike A.	Phi.	1	2	0	0	0	0	....	....	....	....	....		1974-75	1974-75
Boland, Mike J.	K.C., Buf.	2	23	1	2	3	29	3	1	0	1	2		1974-75	1978-79
Boldirev, Ivan	Bos., Cal., Chi., Atl., Van., Det.	15	1052	361	505	866	507	48	13	20	33	14		1970-71	1984-85
Bolduc, Danny	Det., Cgy.	3	102	22	19	41	33	1	0	0	0	0		1978-79	1983-84
Bolduc, Michel	Que.	2	10	0	0	0	6	....	....	....	....	....		1981-82	1982-83
Boll, Buzz	Tor., NYA, Bro., Bos.	12	437	133	130	263	148	31	7	3	10	13		1933-34	1943-44
Bolonchuk, Larry	Van., Wsh.	4	74	3	9	12	97	....	....	....	....	....		1972-73	1977-78
Bolton, Hughie	Tor.	8	235	10	51	61	221	17	0	5	5	14		1949-50	1956-57
Bonar, Dan	L.A.	3	170	25	39	64	208	14	3	4	7	22		1980-81	1982-83
Bonin, Marcel	Det., Bos., Mtl.	9	454	97	175	272	336	50	11	14	25	51	4	1952-53	1961-62
Boo, Jim	Min.	1	6	0	0	0	22	....	....	....	....	....		1977-78	1977-78
Boone, Buddy	Bos.	2	34	5	3	8	28	22	2	1	3	25		1956-57	1957-58
Boothman, George	Tor.	2	58	17	19	36	18	5	2	1	3	2		1942-43	1943-44
Bordeleau, Chris	Mtl., St.L., Chi.,	4	205	38	65	103	82	19	4	7	11	17	1	1968-69	1971-72
Bordeleau, J.P.	Chi.	10	519	97	126	223	143	48	3	6	9	12		1969-70	1979-80
Bordeleau, Paulin	Van.	3	183	33	56	89	47	5	2	1	3	0		1973-74	1975-76
Borotsik, Jack	St.L.	1	1	0	0	0	0	....	....	....	....	....		1974-75	1974-75
Boschman, Laurie	Tor., Edm., Wpg., N.J., Ott.	14	1009	229	348	577	2265	57	8	13	21	140		1979-80	1992-93
Bossy, Mike	NYI	10	752	573	553	1126	210	129	85	75	160	38	4	1977-78	1986-87
Bostrom, Helge	Chi.	4	96	3	3	6	58	13	0	0	0	16		1929-30	1932-33
Botell, Mark	Phi.	1	32	4	10	14	31	....	....	....	....	....		1981-82	1981-82
Bothwell, Tim	NYR, St.L., Hfd.	11	502	28	93	121	382	49	0	3	3	56		1978-79	1988-89
Botting, Cam	Atl.	1	2	0	1	1	0	....	....	....	....	....		1975-76	1975-76
Boucha, Henry	Det., Min., K.C., Col.	6	247	53	49	102	157	....	....	....	....	....		1971-72	1976-77
Bouchard, Dick	NYR	1	1	0	0	0	0	....	....	....	....	....		1954-55	1954-55
Bouchard, Edmond	Mtl., Ham., NYA, Pit.	8	220	19	20	39	105	....	....	....	....	....		1921-22	1928-29
Bouchard, Emile "Butch"	Mtl.	15	785	49	144	193	863	113	11	21	32	121	4	1941-42	1955-56
Bouchard, Pierre	Mtl., Wsh.	12	595	24	82	106	433	76	3	10	13	56	5	1970-71	1981-82
● Boucher, Billy	Mtl., Bos., NYA	7	213	93	35	128	391	21	9	3	12	35	1	1921-22	1927-28
● Boucher, Frank	Ott., NYR	14	557	161	262	423	119	56	16	18	34	12	2	1921-22	1943-44
● Boucher, George	Ott., Mtl.M, Chi.	15	449	122	62	184	739	44	11	3	14	105	4	1917-18	1931-32
● Boucher, Robert	Mtl.	1	12	0	0	0	0	....	....	....	....	....	1	1923-24	1923-24
Boudreau, Bruce	Tor., Chi.	8	141	28	42	70	46	9	2	0	2	0		1976-77	1985-86
Boudrias, Andre	Mtl., Min., Chi., St.L., Van.	12	662	151	340	491	218	34	6	10	16	12		1963-64	1975-76
Boughner, Barry	Oak., Cal.	2	20	0	0	0	11	....	....	....	....	....		1969-70	1970-71
Bourbonnais, Dan	Hfd.	2	59	3	25	28	11	....	....	....	....	....		1981-82	1983-84
Bourbonnais, Rick	St.L.	3	71	9	15	24	29	4	0	1	1	0		1975-76	1977-78
Bourcier, Conrad	Mtl.	1	6	0	0	0	0	....	....	....	....	....		1935-36	1935-36
Bourcier, Jean	Mtl.	1	9	0	1	1	0	....	....	....	....	....		1935-36	1935-36
● Bourgeault, Leo	Tor. NYR, Ott., Mtl.	8	307	24	20	44	269	24	1	1	2	18	1	1926-27	1934-35
Bourgeois, Charlie	Cgy., St.L., Hfd.	7	290	16	54	70	788	40	2	3	5	194		1981-82	1987-88
Bourne, Bob	NYI, L.A.	14	964	258	324	582	605	139	40	56	96	108	4	1974-75	1987-88
Boutette, Pat	Tor., Hfd., Pit.	10	756	171	282	453	1354	46	10	14	24	109		1975-76	1984-85
Boutilier, Paul	NYI, Bos., Min., NYR, Wpg.	8	288	27	83	110	358	41	1	9	10	45	1	1981-82	1988-89
Bowcher, Clarence	NYA	2	47	2	2	4	133	....	....	....	....	....		1926-27	1927-28
Bowman, Kirk	Chi.	3	88	11	17	28	19	7	1	0	1	0		1976-77	1978-79
● Bowman, Ralph	Ott., St.L., Det.	7	274	8	17	25	260	22	2	2	4	6	2	1933-34	1939-40
Bownass, Jack	Mtl., NYR	4	80	3	8	11	58	....	....	....	....	....		1957-58	1961-62
Bowness, Rick	Atl., Det., St. L, Wpg.	7	173	18	37	55	191	5	0	0	0	2		1975-76	1981-82
● Boyd, Bill	NYR, NYA	4	138	15	7	22	72	9	0	0	0	2	1	1926-27	1929-30
Boyd, Irwin	Bos., Det.	4	97	18	19	37	51	15	0	1	1	4		1931-32	1943-44
Boyd, Randy	Pit., Chi., NYI, Van.	8	257	20	67	87	328	13	0	2	2	26		1981-82	1988-89
Boyer, Wally	Tor., Chi., Oak. Pit.	7	365	54	105	159	163	15	1	3	4	0		1965-66	1971-72
Boyko, Darren	Wpg.	1	1	0	0	0	0	....	....	....	....	....		1988-89	1988-89
Bozek, Steve	L.A., Cgy., St.L., Van., S.J.	11	641	164	167	331	309	58	12	11	23	69		1981-82	1991-92
Bozon, Philippe	St.L.	4	144	16	25	41	101	19	2	0	2	31		1991-92	1994-95
● Brackenborough, John	Bos.	1	7	0	0	0	0	....	....	....	....	....		1925-26	1925-26
Brackenbury, Curt	Que., Edm., St.L.	4	141	9	17	26	226	2	0	0	0	0		1979-80	1982-83
Bradley, Barton	Bos.	1	1	0	0	0	0	....	....	....	....	....		1949-50	1949-50
Bradley, Lyle	Cal. Cle.	2	6	1	0	1	2	....	....	....	....	....		1973-74	1976-77
Bragnalo, Rick	Wsh.	4	145	15	35	50	46	....	....	....	....	....		1975-76	1978-79
● Brannigan, Andy	NYA, Bro.	2	27	1	2	3	31	....	....	....	....	....		1940-41	1941-42
Brasar, Per-Olov	Min., Van.	5	348	64	142	206	33	13	1	2	3	0		1977-78	1981-82
Brayshaw, Russ	Chi.	1	43	5	9	14	24	....	....	....	....	....		1944-45	1944-45
Breault, Francois	L.A.	3	27	2	4	6	42	....	....	....	....	....		1990-91	1992-93
Breitenbach, Ken	Buf.	3	68	1	13	14	49	8	0	1	1	4		1975-76	1978-79
Brennan, Dan	L.A.	2	8	0	1	1	9	....	....	....	....	....		1983-84	1985-86
Brennan, Doug	NYR	3	123	9	7	16	152	16	1	0	1	21	1	1931-32	1933-34
Brennan, Tom	Bos.	2	22	2	2	4	2	....	....	....	....	....		1943-44	1944-45
Brenneman, John	Chi., NYR, Tor., Det., Oak.	5	152	21	19	40	46	....	....	....	....	....		1964-65	1968-69
Bretto, Joe	Chi.	1	3	0	0	0	4	....	....	....	....	....		1944-45	1944-45
Brewer, Carl	Tor., Det., St.L.	12	604	25	198	223	1037	72	3	17	20	146	3	1957-58	1979-80
Brickley, Andy	Phi., Pit., N.J., Bos., Wpg.	11	385	82	140	222	81	17	1	4	5	4		1982-83	1993-94
Briden, Archie	Det., Pit.	2	72	9	5	14	56	....	....	....	....	....		1926-27	1929-30
Bridgman, Mel	Phi., Cgy., N.J., Det., Van.	14	977	252	449	701	1625	125	28	39	67	298		1975-76	1988-89
● Briere, Michel	Pit.	1	76	12	32	44	20	10	5	3	8	17		1969-70	1969-70
Brindley, Doug	Tor.	1	3	0	0	0	0	....	....	....	....	....		1970-71	1970-71
Brink, Milt	Chi.	1	5	0	0	0	0	....	....	....	....	....		1936-37	1936-37
Brisson, Gerry	Mtl.	1	4	0	2	2	4	....	....	....	....	....		1962-63	1962-63
Britz, Greg	Tor., Hfd.	3	8	0	0	0	4	....	....	....	....	....		1983-84	1986-87
● Broadbent, Harry	Ott. Mt.M, NYA	11	302	122	45	167	553	42	12	1	13	81	4	1918-19	1928-29
Brochu, Stephane	NYR	1	1	0	0	0	0	....	....	....	....	....		1988-89	1988-89

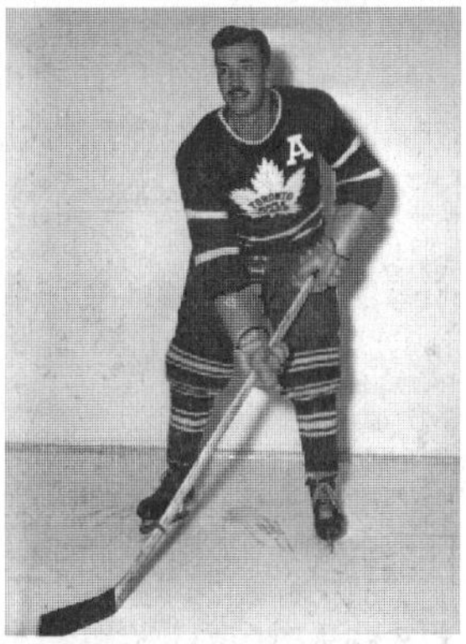

Garth Boesch

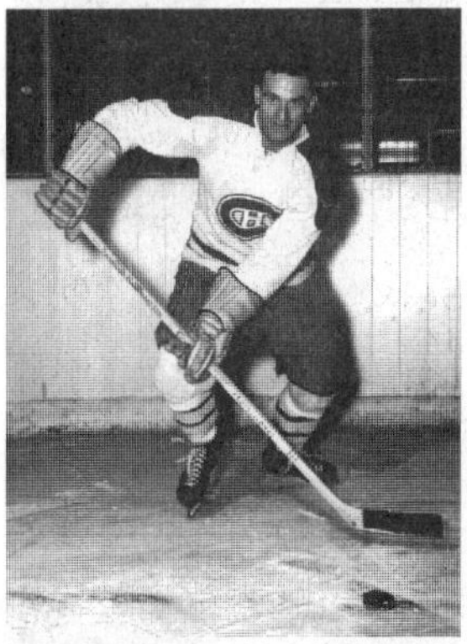

Marcel Bonin

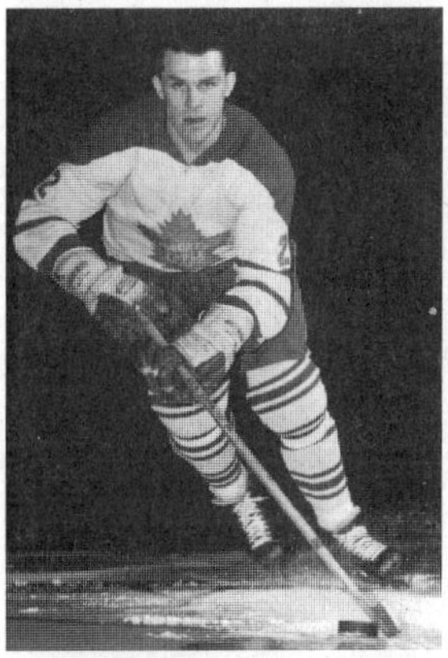

Carl Brewer

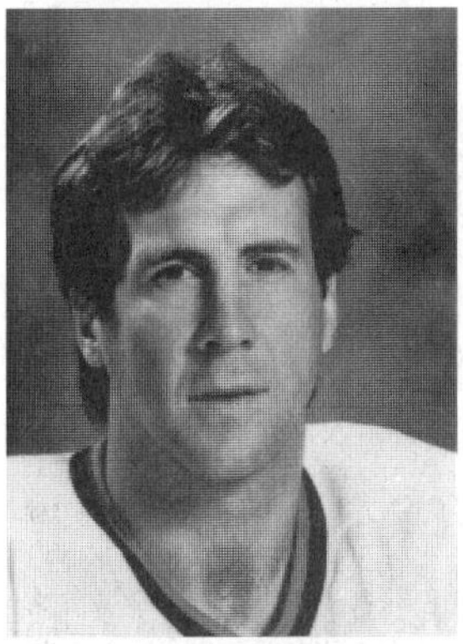

David Brown

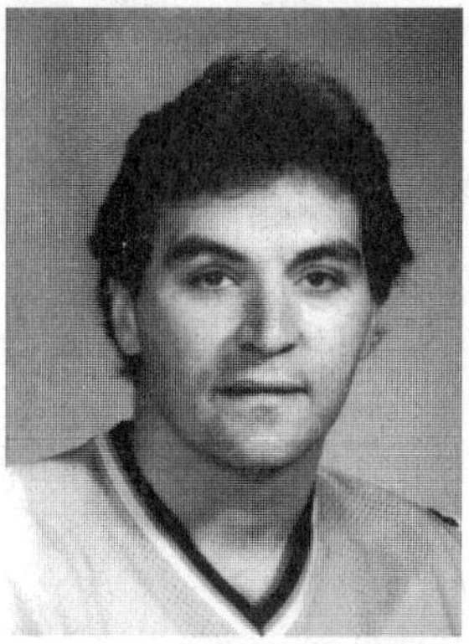

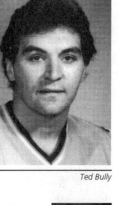

Ted Bully

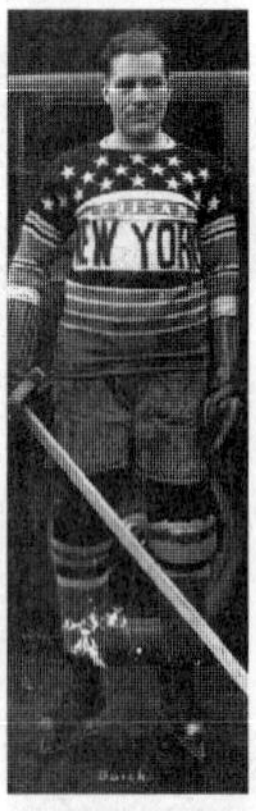

Billy Burch

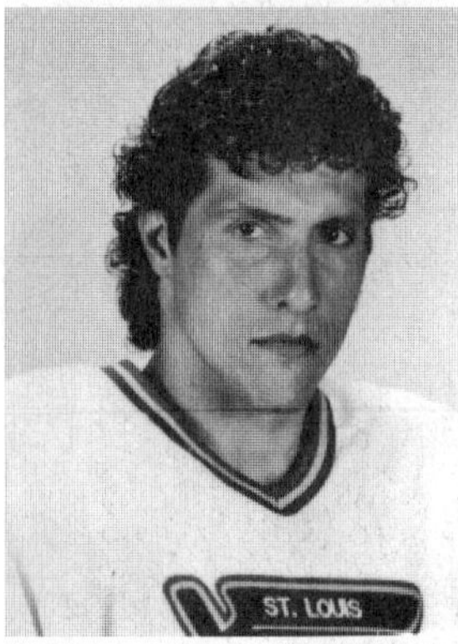

Gino Cavallini

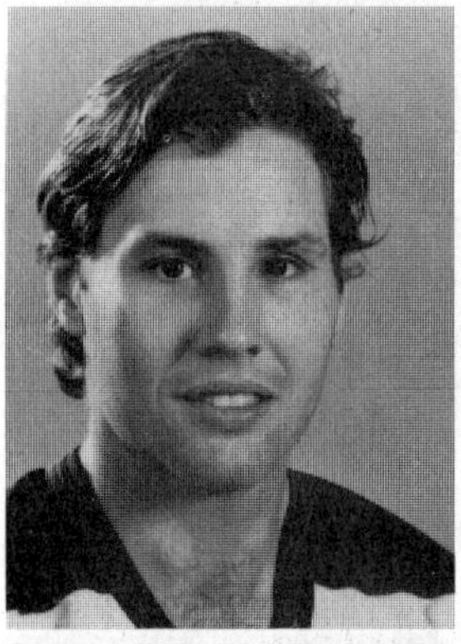

Paul Cavallini

			Regular Schedule					Playoffs							
Name	NHL Teams	NHL Seasons	GP	G	A	TP	PIM	GP	G	A	TP	PIM	NHL Cup Wins	First NHL Season	Last NHL Season
Broden, Connie	Mtl.	3	6	2	1	3	2	7	0	1	1	0	2	1955-56	1957-58
Brooke, Bob	NYR, Min., N.J.	7	447	69	97	166	520	34	9	9	18	59		1983-84	1989-90
Brooks, Gord	St.L., Wsh.	3	70	7	18	25	37	....	....	....	....	....		1971-72	1974-75
• Brophy, Bernie	Mtl.M, Det.	3	62	4	4	8	25	2	0	0	0	2		1925-26	1929-30
Brossart, Willie	Phi., Tor., Wsh.	6	129	1	14	15	88	1	0	0	0	0		1970-71	1975-76
Broten, Aaron	Col., N.J., Min., Que., Tor., Wpg.	12	748	186	329	515	441	34	7	18	25	40		1980-81	1991-92
• Brown, Adam	Det. Chi. Bos.	10	391	104	113	217	378	26	2	4	6	14	1	1941-42	1951-52
Brown, Arnie	Tor. NYR, Det., NYI, Atl.	12	681	44	141	185	738	22	0	6	6	23		1961-62	1973-74
Brown, Cam	Van.	1	1	0	0	0	7	....	....	....	....	....		1990-91	1990-91
Brown, Connie	Det.	5	91	15	24	39	12	14	2	3	5	0		1938-39	1942-43
Brown, David	Phi., Edm., S.J.	14	729	45	52	97	1789	80	2	3	5	209	1	1982-83	1995-96
Brown, Fred	Mtl.M	1	19	1	0	1	0	9	0	0	0	0		1927-28	1927-28
Brown, George	Mtl.	3	79	6	22	28	34	7	0	0	0	2		1936-37	1938-39
Brown, Gerry	Det.	2	23	4	5	9	2	12	2	1	3	4		1941-42	1945-46
Brown, Greg	Bos., Buf., Pit., Wpg.	4	94	4	14	18	86	6	0	1	1	4		1990-91	1994-95
Brown, Harold	NYR	1	13	2	1	3	2	....	....	....	....	....		1945-46	1945-46
Brown, Jim	L.A.	1	3	0	1	1	5	....	....	....	....	....		1982-83	1982-83
Brown, Keith	Chi., Fla.	16	876	68	274	342	916	103	4	32	36	184		1979-80	1994-95
Brown, Larry	NYR, Det., Phi., L.A.	9	455	7	53	60	180	35	0	4	4	10		1969-70	1977-78
• Brown, Stan	NYR, Det.	2	48	8	2	10	18	2	0	0	0	0		1926-27	1927-28
Brown, Wayne	Bos.	1	....	....	....	....	....	4	0	0	0	2		1953-54	1953-54
• Browne, Cecil	Chi.	1	13	2	0	2	4	....	....	....	....	....		1927-28	1927-28
Brownschidle, Jack	St.L., Hfd.	9	494	39	162	201	151	26	0	5	5	18		1977-78	1985-86
Brownschidle, Jeff	Hfd.	2	7	0	1	1	2	....	....	....	....	....		1981-82	1982-83
Brubaker, Jeff	Hfd., Mtl., Cgy., Tor., Edm., NYR, Det.	8	178	16	9	25	512	2	0	0	0	27		1979-80	1988-89
Bruce, Gordie	Bos.	3	28	4	9	13	13	7	2	3	5	4		1940-41	1945-46
Bruce, Morley	Ott.	4	72	8	1	9	27	12	0	0	0	2	2	1917-18	1921-22
Brumwell, Murray	Min., N.J.,	7	128	12	31	43	70	2	0	0	0	2		1980-81	1987-88
• Bruneteau, "Mud"	Det.	11	411	139	138	277	80	77	23	14	37	22	3	1935-36	1945-46
Bruneteau, Eddie	Det.	7	180	40	42	82	35	31	7	6	13	0		1940-41	1948-49
• Brydge, Bill	Tor., Det., NYA	9	368	26	52	78	506	2	0	0	0	4		1926-27	1935-36
Brydges, Paul	Buf.	1	15	2	2	4	6	....	....	....	....	....		1986-87	1986-87
• Brydson, Glenn	Mtl.M, St.L., NYR, Chi.	8	299	56	79	135	203	11	0	0	0	8		1930-31	1937-38
Brydson, Gord	Tor.	1	8	2	0	2	8	....	....	....	....	....		1929-30	1929-30
Bubla, Jiri	Van.	5	256	17	101	118	202	6	0	0	0	7		1981-82	1985-86
Buchanan, Al	Tor.	2	4	0	1	1	2	....	....	....	....	....		1948-49	1949-50
Buchanan, Bucky	NYR	1	2	0	0	0	0	....	....	....	....	....		1948-49	1948-49
Buchanan, Mike	Chi.	1	1	0	0	0	0	....	....	....	....	....		1951-52	1951-52
Buchanan, Ron	Bos., St.L.	2	5	0	0	0	0	....	....	....	....	....		1966-67	1969-70
Bucyk, John	Det., Bos.,	23	1540	556	813	1369	497	124	41	62	103	42	2	1955-56	1977-78
Bucyk, Randy	Mtl., Cgy.	2	19	4	2	6	8	2	0	0	0	0		1985-86	1987-88
Buhr, Doug	K.C.	1	6	0	2	2	4	....	....	....	....	....		1974-75	1974-75
Bukovich, Tony	Det.	2	17	7	3	10	6	6	0	1	1	0		1943-44	1944-45
Bullard, Mike	Pit., Cgy., St.L., Phi., Tor.	11	727	329	345	674	703	40	11	18	29	44		1980-81	1991-92
• Buller, Hy	Det., NYR	5	188	22	58	80	215	....	....	....	....	....		1943-44	1953-54
Bulley, Ted	Chi., Wsh., Pit.	8	414	101	113	214	704	29	5	5	10	24		1976-77	1983-84
Burakovsky, Robert	Ott.	1	23	2	3	5	6	....	....	....	....	....		1993-94	1993-94
• Burch, Billy	Ham., NYA, Bos., Chi.	11	390	137	53	190	251	2	0	0	0	0		1922-23	1932-33
Burchell, Fred	Mtl.	2	4	0	0	0	2	....	....	....	....	....		1950-51	1953-54
Burdon, Glen	K.C.	1	11	0	2	2	0	....	....	....	....	....		1974-75	1974-75
Burega, Bill	Tor.	1	4	0	1	1	4	....	....	....	....	....		1955-56	1955-56
Burke, Eddie	Bos., NYA	4	106	29	20	49	55	....	....	....	....	....		1931-32	1934-35
• Burke, Marty	Mtl., Pit., Ott., Chi.	11	494	19	47	66	560	31	2	4	6	44	2	1927-28	1937-38
Burmeister, Roy	NYA	3	67	4	3	7	2	....	....	....	....	....		1929-30	1931-32
Burnett, Kelly	NYR	1	3	1	0	1	0	....	....	....	....	....		1952-53	1952-53
Burns, Bobby	Chi.	3	20	1	0	1	8	....	....	....	....	....		1927-28	1929-30
Burns, Charlie	Det., Bos., Oak., Pit., Min.	11	749	106	198	304	252	31	5	4	9	6		1958-59	1972-73
Burns, Gary	NYR	2	11	2	2	4	18	5	0	0	0	2		1980-81	1981-82
• Burns, Norm	NYR	1	11	0	4	4	2	....	....	....	....	....		1941-42	1941-42
Burns, Robin	Pit., K.C.	5	190	31	38	69	139	....	....	....	....	....		1970-71	1975-76
Burrows, Dave	Pit., Tor.	10	724	29	135	164	373	29	1	5	6	25		1971-72	1980-81
Burry, Bert	Ott.	1	4	0	0	0	0	....	....	....	....	....		1932-33	1932-33
Burton, Cummy	Det.	3	43	0	2	2	21	3	0	0	0	0		1955-56	1958-59
Burton, Nelson	Wsh.	2	8	1	0	1	21	....	....	....	....	....		1977-78	1978-79
• Bush, Eddie	Det.	2	26	4	6	10	40	12	1	6	7	23		1938-39	1941-42
Buskas, Rod	Pit., Van., L.A., Chi.	11	556	19	63	82	1294	18	0	3	3	45		1982-83	1992-93
Busniuk, Mike	Phi.	2	143	3	23	26	297	25	2	5	7	34		1979-80	1980-81
Busniuk, Ron	Buf.	2	6	0	3	3	13	....	....	....	....	....		1972-73	1973-74
• Buswell, Walt	Det., Mtl.	8	368	10	40	50	164	24	2	1	3	10		1932-33	1939-40
Butcher, Garth	Van., St.L., Que., Tor.	14	897	48	158	206	2302	50	6	5	11	122		1981-82	1994-95
Butler, Dick	Chi.	1	7	2	0	2	0	....	....	....	....	....		1947-48	1947-48
Butler, Jerry	NYR, St.L., Tor., Van., Wpg.	11	641	99	120	219	515	48	3	3	6	79		1972-73	1982-83
Butters, Bill	Min.	2	72	1	4	5	77	....	....	....	....	....		1977-78	1978-79
Buttrey, Gord	Chi.	1	10	0	0	0	0	....	....	....	....	....		1943-44	1943-44
Buynak, Gordon	St. L	1	4	0	0	0	2	....	....	....	....	....		1974-75	1974-75
Byakin, Ilya	Edm., S.J.	2	57	8	25	33	44	....	....	....	....	....		1993-94	1994-95
Byce, John	Bos.	3	21	2	3	5	6	8	2	0	2	2		1989-90	1991-92
Byers, Gord	Bos.	1	1	0	1	1	0	....	....	....	....	....		1949-50	1949-50
Byers, Jerry	Min., Atl, NYR	4	43	3	4	7	15	....	....	....	....	....		1972-73	1977-78
Byers, Lyndon	Bos., S.J.	10	279	28	43	71	1081	37	2	2	4	96		1983-84	1992-93
Byers, Mike	Tor., Phi., Buf., L.A.	4	166	42	34	76	39	4	0	1	1	0		1967-68	1971-72
Byram, Shawn	NYI, Chi.	2	5	0	0	0	14	....	....	....	....	....		1990-91	1991-92

C

			Regular Schedule					Playoffs							
Name	NHL Teams	NHL Seasons	GP	G	A	TP	PIM	GP	G	A	TP	PIM	NHL Cup Wins	First NHL Season	Last NHL Season
• Caffery, Jack	Tor., Bos.	3	57	3	2	5	22	10	1	0	1	4		1954-55	1957-58
Caffery, Terry	Chi., Min.	2	14	0	0	0	0	1	0	0	0	0		1969-70	1970-71
• Cahan, Larry	Tor., NYR, Oak., L.A.	13	666	38	92	130	700	29	1	1	2	38		1954-55	1970-71
Cahill, Chuck	Bos.	2	32	0	1	1	4	....	....	....	....	....		1925-26	1926-27
• Cain, Herb	Mtl.M, Mtl., Bos.	13	570	206	194	400	178	67	16	13	29	13	2	1933-34	1945-46
• Cain, Jim	Mtl.M, Tor.	2	61	4	0	4	35	....	....	....	....	....	1	1924-25	1925-26
Cairns, Don	K.C., Col.	2	9	0	1	1	2	....	....	....	....	....		1975-76	1976-77
Calder, Eric	Wsh.	2	2	0	0	0	0	....	....	....	....	....		1981-82	1982-83
Calladine, Norm	Bos.	3	63	19	29	48	8	....	....	....	....	....		1942-43	1944-45
Callander, Drew	Phi., Van.	4	39	6	2	8	7	....	....	....	....	....		1976-77	1979-80
Callander, John "Jock"	Pit., T.B.	5	109	22	29	51	116	22	3	8	11	12	1	1987-88	1992-93
Callighen, Brett	Edm.	3	160	56	89	145	132	14	4	6	10	8		1979-80	1981-82
Callighen, Patsy	NYR	1	36	0	0	0	32	9	0	0	0	0	1	1927-28	1927-28
Camazzola, James	Chi.	2	3	0	0	0	0	....	....	....	....	....		1983-84	1986-87
Camazzola, Tony	Wsh.	1	3	0	0	0	4	....	....	....	....	....		1981-82	1981-82
Cameron, Al	Det., Wpg.	6	282	11	44	55	356	7	0	1	1	2		1975-76	1980-81
Cameron, Billy	Mtl., NYA	2	39	0	0	0	2	6	0	0	0	0	1	1923-24	1925-26
Cameron, Craig	Det., St.L., Min., NYI	9	552	87	65	152	196	27	3	1	4	17		1966-67	1975-76
Cameron, Dave	Col., N.J.	3	168	25	28	53	238	....	....	....	....	....		1981-82	1983-84
• Cameron, Harry	Tor., Ott., Mtl.	6	127	85	32	117	137	21	7	0	7	36	2	1917-18	1922-23
Cameron, Scotty	NYR	1	35	8	11	19	0	....	....	....	....	....		1942-43	1942-43
Campbell, Bryan	L.A., Chi.	5	260	35	71	106	74	22	3	4	7	2		1967-68	1971-72
Campbell, Colin	Pit., Col., Edm., Van., Det.	11	636	25	103	128	1292	45	4	10	14	181		1974-75	1984-85
• Campbell, Dave	Mtl.	1	3	0	0	0	0	....	....	....	....	....		1920-21	1920-21
Campbell, Don	Chi.	1	17	1	3	4	8	....	....	....	....	....		1943-44	1943-44
Campbell, Earl "Spiff"	Ott., NYA	3	77	5	1	6	12	2	0	0	0	0		1923-24	1925-26
Campbell, Scott	Wpg., St.L.	3	80	4	21	25	243	....	....	....	....	....		1979-80	1981-82
Campbell, Wade	Wpg., Bos.	6	213	9	27	36	305	10	0	0	0	20		1982-83	1987-88
Campeau, Tod	Mtl.	3	42	5	9	14	16	1	0	0	0	0		1943-44	1948-49
Campedelli, Dom	Mtl.	1	2	0	0	0	0	....	....	....	....	....		1985-86	1985-86
Capuano, Dave	Pit., Van., T.B., S.J.	4	104	17	38	55	56	6	1	1	2	5		1989-90	1993-94
Capuano, Jack	Tor., Van., Bos.	3	6	0	0	0	0	....	....	....	....	....		1989-90	1991-92
Carbol, Leo	Chi.	1	6	0	1	1	4	....	....	....	....	....		1942-43	1942-43
Cardin, Claude	St.L.	1	1	0	0	0	0	....	....	....	....	....		1967-68	1967-68
Cardwell, Steve	Pit.	3	53	9	11	20	35	4	0	0	0	2		1970-71	1972-73
• Carey, George	Que, Ham., Tor.	5	72	22	8	30	14	....	....	....	....	....		1919-20	1923-24
Carleton, Wayne	Tor., Bos., Cal.	7	278	55	73	128	172	18	2	4	6	14	1	1965-66	1971-72
Carlin, Brian	L.A.	1	5	1	0	1	0	....	....	....	....	....		1971-72	1971-72

			Regular Schedule					Playoffs							
Name	NHL Teams	NHL Seasons	GP	G	A	TP	PIM	GP	G	A	TP	PIM	NHL Cup Wins	First NHL Season	Last NHL Season
Carlson, Jack	Min., St.L.	6	236	30	15	45	417	25	1	2	3	72		1978-79	1986-87
Carlson, Kent	Mtl., St.L., Wsh.	5	113	7	11	18	148	8	0	0	0	13		1983-84	1988-89
Carlson, Steve	L.A.	1	52	9	12	21	23	4	1	1	2	7		1979-80	1979-80
Carlsson, Anders	N.J.	3	104	7	26	33	34	3	1	0	1	2		1986-87	1988-89
Carlyle, Randy	Tor., Pit., Wpg.	17	1055	148	499	647	1400	69	9	24	33	120		1976-77	1992-93
Carnback, Patrik	Mtl., Ana.	4	154	24	38	62	122	....	....	....	....	....		1992-93	1995-96
• Caron, Alain	Oak., Mtl.	2	60	9	13	22	18	....	....	....	....	....		1967-68	1968-69
• Carpenter, Eddie	Que, Ham.	2	44	10	4	14	23	....	....	....	....	....		1919-20	1920-21
Carr,	Que.	1	1	0	0	0	0	....	....	....	....	....		1919-20	1919-20
Carr, Al "Red"	Tor.	1	5	0	1	1	2	....	....	....	....	....		1943-44	1943-44
Carr, Gene	St.L., NYR, L.A., Pit., Atl.	8	465	79	136	215	365	35	5	8	13	66		1971-72	1978-79
Carr, Lorne	NYR, NYA, Tor.	13	594	204	222	426	132	53	10	9	19	13	2	1933-34	1945-46
Carriere, Larry	Buf. Atl, Van., L.A., Tor.	7	367	16	74	90	462	27	0	3	3	42		1972-73	1979-80
• Carrigan, Gene	NYR, StL, Det.	3	37	2	1	3	13	4	0	0	0	0		1930-31	1934-35
Carroll, Billy	NYI, Edm., Det.	7	322	30	54	84	113	71	6	12	18	18	4	1980-81	1986-87
Carroll, George	Mtl.M, Bos.	1	15	0	0	0	9	....	....	....	....	....		1924-25	1924-25
Carroll, Greg	Wsh., Det., Hfd.	2	131	20	34	54	44	....	....	....	....	....		1978-79	1979-80
Carruthers, Dwight	Det. Phi.	2	2	0	0	0	0	....	....	....	....	....		1965-66	1967-68
Carse, Bill	NYR, Chi.	4	124	28	43	71	38	16	3	2	5	0		1938-39	1941-42
Carse, Bob	Chi., Mtl.	5	167	32	55	87	52	10	0	2	2	2		1939-40	1947-48
• Carson, Bill	Tor., Bos.	4	159	54	24	78	156	11	3	0	3	14	1	1926-27	1929-30
• Carson, Frank	Mtl.M., NYA, Det.	7	248	42	48	90	166	31	0	2	2	9	1	1925-26	1933-34
• Carson, Gerry	Mtl., NYR, Mtl.M.	6	261	12	11	23	205	22	0	0	0	12	1	1928-29	1936-37
Carson, Lindsay	Phi., Hfd.	7	373	66	80	146	524	49	4	10	14	56		1981-82	1987-88
Carter, Billy	Mtl., Bos.	3	16	0	0	0	6	....	....	....	....	....		1957-58	1961-62
Carter, John	Bos., S.J.	8	244	40	50	90	201	31	7	5	12	51		1985-86	1992-93
Carter, Ron	Edm.	1	2	0	0	0	0	....	....	....	....	....		1979-80	1979-80
• Carveth, Joe	Det., Bos., Mtl.	11	504	150	189	339	81	69	21	16	37	28	2	1940-41	1950-51
Cashman, Wayne	Bos.	17	1027	277	516	793	1041	145	31	57	88	250	2	1964-65	1982-83
Cassidy, Bruce	Chi.	6	36	4	13	17	10	1	0	0	0	0		1983-84	1989-90
Cassidy, Tom	Pit.	1	26	3	4	7	15	....	....	....	....	....		1977-78	1977-78
Cassolato, Tony	Wsh.	3	23	1	6	7	4	....	....	....	....	....		1979-80	1981-82
Caufield, Jay	NYR, Min., Pit.	7	208	5	8	13	759	17	0	0	0	42	2	1986-87	1992-93
Cavallini, Gino	Cgy., St.L., Que.	9	593	114	159	273	507	74	14	19	33	66		1984-85	1992-93
Cavallini, Paul	Wsh., St.L., Dal.	10	564	56	177	233	750	69	8	27	35	114		1986-87	1995-96
Ceresino, Ray	Tor.	1	12	1	1	2	2	....	....	....	....	....		1948-49	1948-49
Cernik, Frantisek	Det.	1	49	5	4	9	13	....	....	....	....	....		1984-85	1984-85
Chabot, John	Mtl., Pit., Det.	8	508	84	228	312	85	33	6	20	26	2		1983-84	1990-91
Chad, John	Chi.	3	80	15	22	37	29	10	0	1	1	2		1939-40	1945-46
Chalmers, Bill "Chick"	NYR	1	1	0	0	0	0	....	....	....	....	....		1953-54	1953-54
Chalupa, Milan	Det.	1	14	0	5	5	6	....	....	....	....	....		1984-85	1984-85
• Chamberlain, Murph	Tor., Mtl., Bro., Bos.	12	510	100	175	275	769	66	14	17	31	96	2	1937-38	1948-49
Champagne, Andre	Tor.	1	2	0	0	0	0	....	....	....	....	....		1962-63	1962-63
Chapdelaine, Rene	L.A.	3	32	0	2	2	32	....	....	....	....	....		1990-91	1992-93
• Chapman, Art	Bos., NYA	10	438	62	176	238	140	26	1	5	6	9		1930-31	1939-40
Chapman, Blair	Pit., St.L.	7	402	106	125	231	158	25	4	6	10	15		1976-77	1982-83
Chapman, Brian	Hfd.	1	3	0	0	0	29	....	....	....	....	....		1990-91	1990-91
Charbonneau, Jose	Mtl., Van.	4	71	9	13	22	67	11	1	0	1	8		1987-88	1994-95
Charbonneau, Stephane	Que.	1	2	0	0	0	0	....	....	....	....	....		1991-92	1991-92
Charlebois, Bob	Min.	1	7	1	0	1	0	....	....	....	....	....		1967-68	1967-68
Charlesworth, Todd	Pit., NYR	6	93	3	9	12	47	....	....	....	....	....		1983-84	1989-90
Charron, Guy	Mtl., Det., K.C., Wsh.	12	734	221	309	530	146	....	....	....	....	....		1969-70	1980-81
Chartier, Dave	Wpg.	1	1	0	0	0	0	....	....	....	....	....		1980-81	1980-81
Chartraw, Rick	Mtl., L.A., NYR, Edm.	10	420	28	64	92	399	75	7	9	16	80	4	1974-75	1983-84
Check, Lude	Det., Chi.	2	27	6	2	8	4	....	....	....	....	....		1943-44	1944-45
Chernoff, Mike	Min.	1	1	0	0	0	0	....	....	....	....	....		1968-69	1968-69
Chernomaz, Rich	Col., N.J., Cgy.	7	51	9	7	16	18	....	....	....	....	....		1981-82	1991-92
Cherry, Dick	Bos., Phi.	3	145	12	10	22	45	4	1	0	1	4		1956-57	1969-70
Cherry, Don	Bos.	1	....	....	....	....	....	1	0	0	0	0		1954-55	1954-55
• Chevrefils, Real	Bos., Det.	8	387	104	97	201	185	30	5	4	9	20		1951-52	1958-59
Chibirev, Igor	Hfd.	2	45	7	12	19	2	....	....	....	....	....		1993-94	1994-95
Chicoine, Dan	Cle. Min.	3	31	1	2	3	12	1	0	0	0	0		1977-78	1979-80
Chinnick, Rick	Min.	2	4	0	2	2	0	....	....	....	....	....		1973-74	1974-75
Chipperfield, Ron	Edm., Que.,	2	83	22	24	46	34	....	....	....	....	....		1979-80	1980-81
Chisholm, Art	Bos.	1	3	0	0	0	0	....	....	....	....	....		1960-61	1960-61
Chisholm, Colin	Min.	1	1	0	0	0	0	....	....	....	....	....		1986-87	1986-87
• Chisholm, Lex	Tor.	2	54	10	8	18	19	3	1	0	1	0		1939-40	1940-41
Chorney, Marc	Pit. L.A.	4	210	8	27	35	209	7	0	1	1	2		1980-81	1983-84
• Chouinard, Gene	Ott.	1	8	0	0	0	0	....	....	....	....	....		1927-28	1927-28
Chouinard, Guy	Atl, Cgy., St.L.	10	578	205	370	575	120	46	9	28	37	12		1974-75	1983-84
Christian, Dave	Wpg., Wsh., Bos., St.L., Chi.	15	1009	340	433	773	284	102	32	25	57	27		1979-80	1993-94
Christie, Mike	Cal., Cle., Col., Van.	7	412	15	101	116	550	2	0	0	0	0		1974-75	1980-81
Christoff, Steve	Min. Cgy., L.A.	5	248	77	64	141	108	35	16	12	28	25		1979-80	1983-84
Chrystal, Bob	NYR	2	132	11	14	25	112	....	....	....	....	....		1953-54	1954-55
• Church, Jack	Tor., Bro., Bos.	5	130	4	19	23	154	25	1	1	2	18		1938-39	1945-46
Chychrun, Jeff	Phi., L.A., Pit., Edm.	8	262	3	22	25	744	19	0	2	2	65	1	1986-87	1993-94
Cichocki, Chris	Det., N.J.	4	68	11	12	23	27	....	....	....	....	....		1985-86	1988-89
• Ciesla, Hank	Chi., NYR	4	269	26	51	77	87	6	0	2	2	0		1955-56	1958-59
Cimellaro, Tony	Ott.	1	2	0	0	0	0	....	....	....	....	....		1992-93	1992-93
Cimetta, Robert	Bos., Tor.	4	103	16	16	32	66	1	0	0	0	15		1988-89	1991-92
Cirella, Joe	Col., N.J., Que., NYR, Fla., Ott.	15	828	64	211	275	1446	38	0	13	13	98		1981-82	1995-96
Cirone, Jason	Wpg.	1	3	0	0	0	2	....	....	....	....	....		1991-92	1991-92
Clackson, Kim	Pit., Que.	2	106	0	8	8	370	8	0	0	0	70		1979-80	1980-81
• Clancy, Francis "King"	Ott., Tor.	16	592	137	143	280	904	61	9	8	17	92	3	1921-22	1936-37
Clancy, Terry	Oak., Tor.	4	93	6	6	12	39	....	....	....	....	....		1967-68	1972-73
• Clapper, Dit	Bos.	20	833	228	246	474	462	82	13	17	30	50	3	1927-28	1946-47
Clark, Andy	Bos.	1	5	0	0	0	0	....	....	....	....	....		1927-28	1927-28
Clark, Dan	NYR	1	4	0	1	1	6	....	....	....	....	....		1978-79	1978-79
Clark, Dean	Edm.	1	1	0	0	0	0	....	....	....	....	....		1983-84	1983-84
Clark, Gordie	Bos.	2	8	0	1	1	0	1	0	0	0	0		1974-75	1975-76
Clarke, Bobby	Phi.	15	1144	358	852	1210	1453	136	42	77	119	152	2	1969-70	1983-84
• Cleghorn, Odie	Mtl., Pit.	10	180	95	29	124	147	24	9	3	12	13	1	1918-19	1927-28
• Cleghorn, Sprague	Ott. Tor. Mtl., Bos.	10	262	84	39	123	489	39	7	8	15	48	3	1918-19	1927-28
Clement, Bill	Phi., Wsh., Atl., Cgy.	11	719	148	208	356	383	50	5	3	8	26	2	1971-72	1981-82
Cline, Bruce	NYR	1	30	2	3	5	10	....	....	....	....	....		1956-57	1956-57
Clippingdale, Steve	L.A., Wsh.	2	19	1	2	3	9	1	0	0	0	0		1976-77	1979-80
Cloutier, Real	Que. Buf.	6	317	146	198	344	119	25	7	5	12	20		1979-80	1984-85
Cloutier, Rejean	Det.	2	5	0	2	2	2	....	....	....	....	....		1979-80	1981-82
Cloutier, Roland	Det., Que.	3	34	8	9	17	2	....	....	....	....	....		1977-78	1979-80
Clune, Wally	Mtl.	1	5	0	0	0	6	....	....	....	....	....		1955-56	1955-56
Coalter, Gary	Cal., K.C.	2	34	2	4	6	2	....	....	....	....	....		1973-74	1974-75
Coates, Steve	Det.	1	5	1	0	1	24	....	....	....	....	....		1976-77	1976-77
Cochrane, Glen	Phi., Van., Chi., Edm.	10	411	17	72	89	1556	18	1	1	2	31		1978-79	1988-89
Coflin, Hughie	Chi.	1	31	0	3	3	33	....	....	....	....	....		1950-51	1950-51
Colley, Tom	Min.	1	1	0	0	0	2	....	....	....	....	....		1974-75	1974-75
Collings, Norm	Mtl.	1	1	0	1	1	0	....	....	....	....	....		1934-35	1934-35
Collins, Bill	Min., Mtl., Det., St. L, NYR, Phi., Wsh.	11	768	157	154	311	415	18	3	5	8	12		1967-68	1977-78
Collins, Gary	Tor.	1	....	....	....	....	....	2	0	0	0	0		1958-59	1958-59
Collyard, Bob	St.L.	1	10	1	3	4	4	....	....	....	....	....		1973-74	1973-74
• Colman, Michael	S.J.	1	15	0	1	1	32	....	....	....	....	....		1991-92	1991-92
Colville, Mac	NYR	9	353	71	104	175	130	40	9	10	19	14	1	1935-36	1946-47
• Colville, Neil	NYR	12	464	99	166	265	213	46	7	19	26	32	1	1935-36	1948-49
Colwill, Les	NYR	1	69	7	6	13	16	....	....	....	....	....		1958-59	1958-59
Comeau, Rey	Mtl., Atl, Col.	9	564	98	141	239	175	9	2	1	3	8		1971-72	1979-80
Conacher, Brian	Tor., Det.	5	155	28	28	56	84	12	3	2	5	21	1	1961-62	1971-72
• Conacher, Charlie	Tor., Det., NYA	12	459	225	173	398	523	49	17	18	35	49	1	1929-30	1940-41
Conacher, Jim	Det., Chi., NYR	8	328	85	117	202	91	19	5	2	7	4		1945-46	1952-53
• Conacher, Lionel	Pit., NYA, Mtl.M., Chi.	12	498	80	105	185	882	35	2	2	4	34	2	1925-26	1936-37
Conacher, Pat	NYR, Edm., N.J., L.A., Cgy., NYI	13	521	63	76	139	235	66	11	10	21	40	1	1979-80	1995-96
Conacher, Pete	Chi., NYR, Tor.	6	229	47	39	86	57	7	0	0	0	0		1951-52	1957-58
• Conacher, Roy	Bos., Det., Chi.	11	490	226	200	426	90	42	15	15	30	14	2	1938-39	1951-52
Conn, Hugh "Red"	NYA	2	96	9	28	37	22	....	....	....	....	....		1933-34	1934-35
Connelly, Wayne	Mtl., Bos., Min., Det., St. L, Van.	10	543	133	174	307	156	24	11	7	18	4		1960-61	1971-72

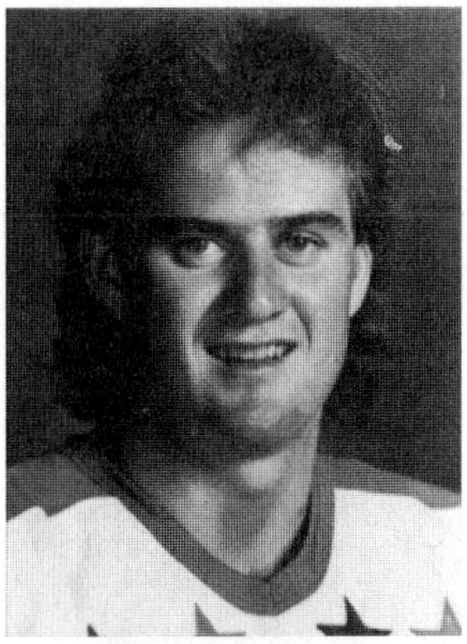
Dave Christian

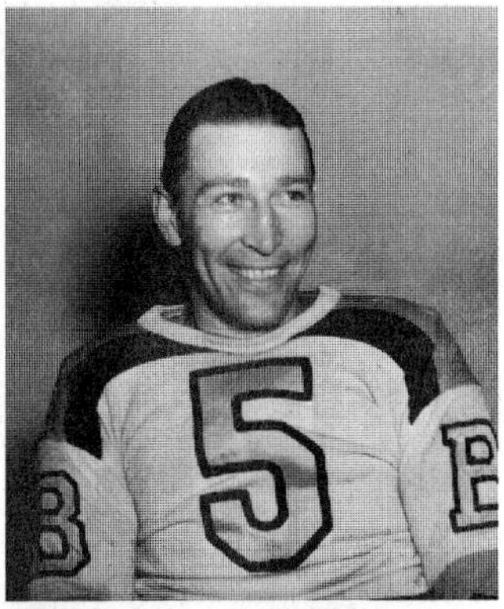
Dit Clapper

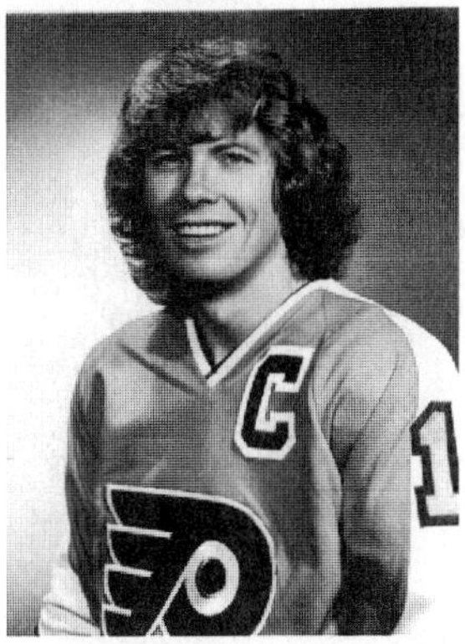
Bobby Clarke

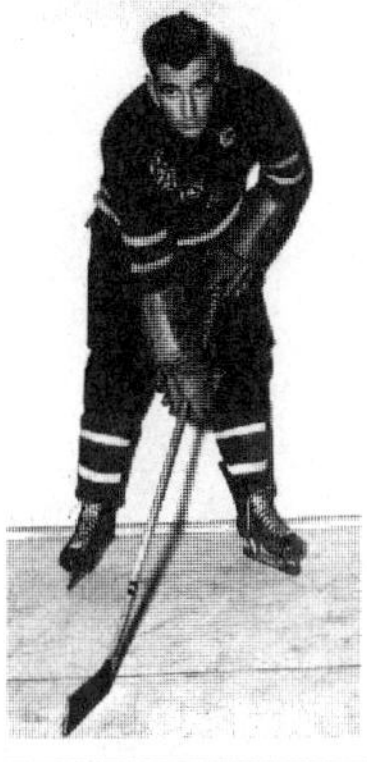
Neil Colville

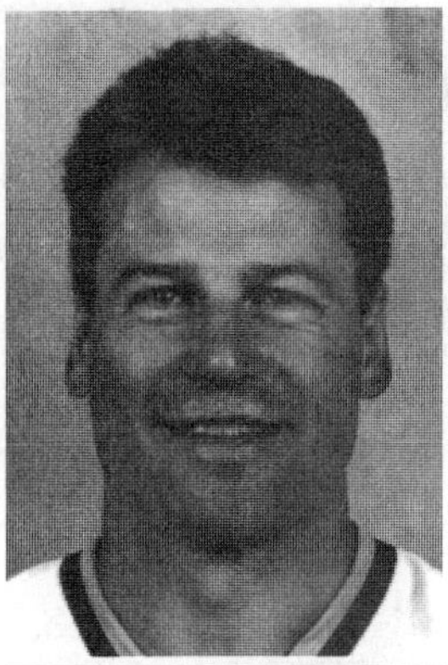

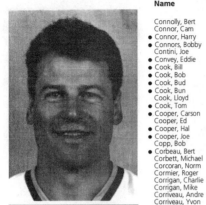

Pat Conacher

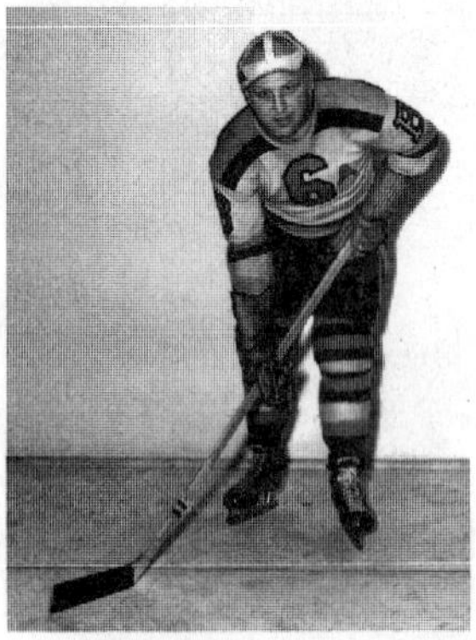

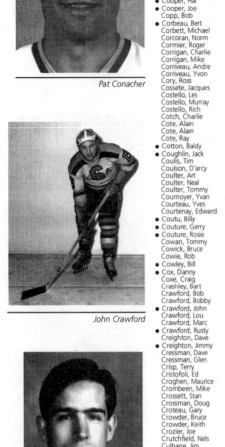

John Crawford

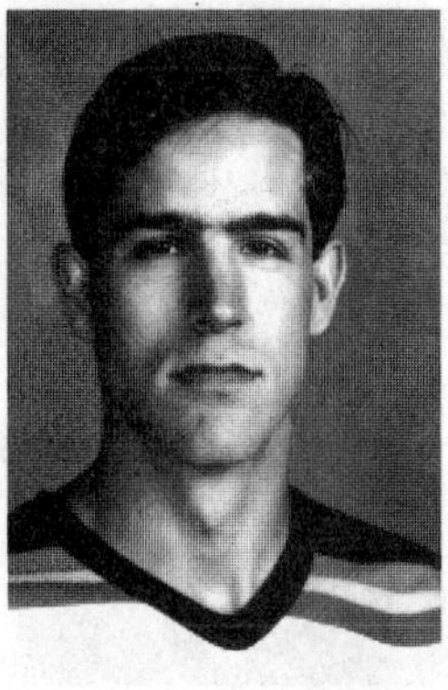

Brad Dalgarno

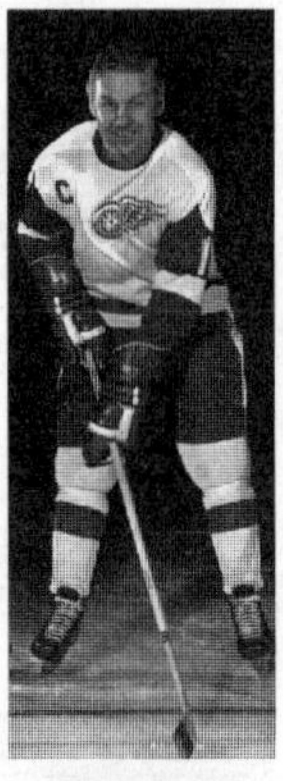

Alex Delvecchio

			Regular Schedule					Playoffs					NHL	First	Last
Name	NHL Teams	NHL Seasons	GP	G	A	TP	PIM	GP	G	A	TP	PIM	Cup Wins	NHL Season	NHL Season
Connolly, Bert	NYR, Chi.	3	87	13	15	28	37	14	1	0	1	0	1	1934-35	1937-38
Connor, Cam	Mtl., Edm., NYR	5	89	9	22	31	256	20	5	0	5	6	1	1978-79	1982-83
• Connor, Harry	Bos., NYA, Ott.	4	134	16	5	21	149	10	0	0	0	2		1927-28	1930-31
• Connors, Bobby	NYA, Det.	3	78	17	10	27	110	2	0	0	0	10		1926-27	1929-30
Contini, Joe	Col., Min.	3	68	17	21	38	34	2	0	0	0	0		1977-78	1980-81
• Convey, Eddie	NYR	3	36	1	1	2	33	....	....	....	....	....		1930-31	1932-33
• Cook, Bill	NYR	11	474	229	138	367	386	46	13	11	24	72	2	1926-27	1936-37
• Cook, Bob	Van., Det., NYI, Min.	4	72	13	9	22	22	....	....	....	....	....		1970-71	1974-75
• Cook, Bud	Bos., Ott., St.L.	3	51	5	4	9	22	....	....	....	....	....		1931-32	1934-35
• Cook, Bun	NYR, Bos.	11	473	158	144	302	444	46	15	3	18	50	2	1926-27	1936-37
Cook, Lloyd	Bos.	1	4	1	0	1	0	....	....	....	....	....		1924-25	1924-25
• Cook, Tom	Chi., Mtl.M.	9	349	77	98	175	184	24	2	4	6	19	1	1929-30	1937-38
• Cooper, Carson	Bos., Mtl., Det.	8	294	110	57	167	111	7	0	0	0	2		1924-25	1931-32
Cooper, Ed	Col.	2	49	8	7	15	46	....	....	....	....	....		1980-81	1981-82
• Cooper, Hal	NYR	1	8	0	0	0	2	....	....	....	....	....		1944-45	1944-45
• Cooper, Joe	NYR, Chi.	11	420	30	66	96	442	35	3	5	8	58		1935-36	1946-47
Copp, Bob	Tor.	2	40	3	9	12	26	....	....	....	....	....		1942-43	1950-51
• Corbeau, Bert	Mtl., Ham., Tor.,	10	257	65	33	98	611	14	2	0	2	10		1917-18	1926-27
Corbett, Michael	L.A.	1	....	....	....	....	....	2	0	1	1	2		1967-68	1967-68
Corcoran, Norm	Bos., Det., Chi.	4	29	1	3	4	21	4	0	0	0	6		1949-50	1955-56
Cormier, Roger	Mtl.	1	1	0	0	0	0	....	....	....	....	....		1925-26	1925-26
Corrigan, Charlie	Tor., NYA	2	19	2	2	4	2	....	....	....	....	....		1937-38	1940-41
Corrigan, Mike	L.A., Van., Pit.	10	594	152	195	347	698	17	2	3	5	20		1967-68	1977-78
Corriveau, Andre	Mtl.	1	3	0	1	1	0	....	....	....	....	....		1953-54	1953-54
Corriveau, Yvon	Wsh., Hfd., S.J.	9	280	48	40	88	310	29	5	7	12	50		1985-86	1993-94
Cory, Ross	Wpg.	2	51	2	10	12	41	....	....	....	....	....		1979-80	1980-81
Cossete, Jacques	Pit.	3	64	8	6	14	29	3	0	1	1	4		1975-76	1978-79
Costello, Les	Tor.	3	15	2	3	5	11	6	2	2	4	2	1	1947-48	1949-50
Costello, Murray	Chi., Bos., Det.	4	162	13	19	32	54	5	0	0	0	2		1953-54	1956-57
Costello, Rich	Tor.	2	12	2	2	4	2	....	....	....	....	....		1983-84	1985-86
Cotch, Charlie	Ham., Tor.	1	11	1	0	1	0	....	....	....	....	....		1924-25	1924-25
Cote, Alain	Bos., Wsh., Mtl., T.B., Que.	9	119	2	18	20	124	11	0	2	2	26		1985-86	1993-94
Cote, Alain	Que.	10	696	103	190	293	383	67	9	15	24	44		1979-80	1988-89
Cote, Ray	Edm.	3	15	0	0	0	4	14	3	2	5	0		1982-83	1984-85
• Cotton, Baldy	Pit., Tor., NYA	12	503	101	103	204	419	43	4	9	13	46	1	1925-26	1936-37
• Coughlin, Jack	Tor., Que, Mtl., Ham.	3	19	2	0	2	0	....	....	....	....	....		1917-18	1920-21
Coulis, Tim	Wsh., Min.	4	47	4	5	9	138	3	1	0	1	2		1979-80	1985-86
Coulson, D'arcy	Phi.	1	28	0	0	0	103	....	....	....	....	....		1930-31	1930-31
Coulter, Art	Chi., NYR	11	465	30	82	112	543	49	4	5	9	61	2	1931-32	1941-42
Coulter, Neal	NYI	3	26	5	5	10	11	....	....	....	....	....		1985-86	1987-88
Coulter, Tommy	Chi.	1	2	0	0	0	0	....	....	....	....	....		1933-34	1933-34
Cournoyer, Yvan	Mtl.	16	968	428	435	863	255	147	64	63	127	47	10	1963-64	1978-79
Courteau, Yves	Cgy., Hfd.	3	22	2	5	7	4	1	0	0	0	0		1984-85	1986-87
Courtenay, Edward	S.J.	2	44	7	13	20	10	....	....	....	....	....		1991-92	1992-93
• Coutu, Billy	Mtl., Ham., Bos.	10	239	33	18	51	350	32	2	0	2	42	1	1917-18	1926-27
• Couture, Gerry	Det., Mtl., Chi.,	10	385	86	70	156	89	45	9	7	16	4	1	1944-45	1953-54
• Couture, Rosie	Chi., Mtl.	8	309	48	56	104	184	23	1	5	6	15		1928-29	1935-36
Cowan, Tommy	Phi.	1	1	0	0	0	0	....	....	....	....	....		1930-31	1930-31
Cowick, Bruce	Phi., Wsh., St.L.	3	70	5	6	11	43	8	0	0	0	9	1	1973-74	1975-76
Cowie, Rob	L.A.	2	78	7	12	19	52	....	....	....	....	....		1994-95	1995-96
• Cowley, Bill	St.L., Bos.	13	549	195	353	548	143	64	12	34	46	22	2	1934-35	1946-47
• Cox, Danny	Tor., Ott., Det., NYR, St.L.	8	319	47	49	96	128	10	0	1	1	6		1926-27	1934-35
Coxe, Craig	Van., Cgy., St.L., S.J.	8	235	14	31	45	713	5	1	0	1	18		1984-85	1991-92
Crashley, Bart	Det., K.C., L.A.	6	140	7	36	43	50	....	....	....	....	....		1965-66	1975-76
Crawford, Bob	St.L., Hfd., NYR, Wsh.	7	246	71	71	142	72	11	0	1	1	8		1979-80	1986-87
Crawford, Bobby	Col., Det.	2	16	1	3	4	6	....	....	....	....	....		1980-81	1982-83
• Crawford, John	Bos.	13	548	38	140	178	202	66	4	13	17	36	2	1937-38	1949-50
Crawford, Lou	Bos.	2	26	2	1	3	29	....	....	....	....	....		1989-90	1991-92
Crawford, Marc	Van.	6	176	19	31	50	229	20	1	2	3	44		1981-82	1986-87
• Crawford, Rusty	Ott., Tor.,	2	38	10	3	13	84	2	2	1	3	0	1	1917-18	1918-19
Creighton, Dave	Bos., Chi., Tor., NYR	12	616	140	174	314	223	51	11	13	24	20		1948-49	1959-60
• Creighton, Jimmy	Det.,	1	11	1	0	1	2	....	....	....	....	....		1930-31	1930-31
Cressman, Dave	Min.	2	85	6	8	14	37	....	....	....	....	....		1974-75	1975-76
Cressman, Glen	Mtl.	1	4	0	0	0	2	....	....	....	....	....		1956-57	1956-57
Crisp, Terry	Bos., St.L., Phi., NYI	11	536	67	134	201	135	110	15	28	43	40	2	1965-66	1976-77
Cristofoli, Ed	Mtl.	1	9	0	1	1	4	....	....	....	....	....		1989-90	1989-90
Croghen, Maurice	Mtl.M.	1	16	0	0	0	4	....	....	....	....	....		1937-38	1937-38
Crombeen, Mike	Cle., St.L., Hfd.	8	475	55	68	123	218	27	6	2	8	32		1977-78	1984-85
Crossett, Stan	Phi.,	1	21	0	0	0	10	....	....	....	....	....		1930-31	1930-31
Crossman, Doug	Chi., Phi., NYI, Hfd., Det., T.B., St.L.	14	914	105	359	464	534	97	12	39	51	105		1980-81	1993-94
Croteau, Gary	L.A., Det., Cal., K.C., Col.	12	684	144	175	319	143	11	3	2	5	8		1968-69	1979-80
Crowder, Bruce	Bos., Pit.	4	243	47	51	98	156	31	8	4	12	41		1981-82	1984-85
Crowder, Keith	Bos., L.A.	10	662	223	271	494	1344	85	14	22	36	218		1980-81	1989-90
Crozier, Joe	Tor.,	1	5	0	3	3	2	....	....	....	....	....		1959-60	1959-60
Crutchfield, Nels	Mtl.	1	41	5	5	10	20	2	0	1	1	22		1934-35	1934-35
Culhane, Jim	Hfd.	1	6	0	1	1	4	....	....	....	....	....		1989-90	1989-90
Cullen, Barry	Tor., Det.	5	219	32	52	84	111	6	0	0	0	2		1955-56	1959-60
Cullen, Brian	Tor., NYR	7	326	56	100	156	92	19	3	0	3	2		1954-55	1960-61
Cullen, Ray	NYR, Det., Min., Van.	6	313	92	123	215	120	20	3	10	13	2		1965-66	1970-71
Cummins, Barry	Cal.	1	36	1	2	3	39	....	....	....	....	....		1973-74	1973-74
Cunningham, Bob	NYR	2	4	0	1	1	0	....	....	....	....	....		1960-61	1961-62
Cunningham, Jim	Phi.	1	1	0	0	0	4	....	....	....	....	....		1977-78	1977-78
Cunningham, Les	NYA, Chi.	2	60	7	19	26	21	1	0	0	0	2		1936-37	1939-40
Cupolo, Bill	Bos.	1	47	11	13	24	10	7	1	2	3	0		1944-45	1944-45
Curran, Brian	Bos., NYI, Tor., Buf., Wsh.	10	381	7	33	40	1461	24	0	1	1	122		1983-84	1993-94
Currie, Glen	Wsh., L.A.	8	326	39	79	118	100	12	1	3	4	4		1979-80	1987-88
Currie, Hugh	Mtl.	1	1	0	0	0	0	....	....	....	....	....		1950-51	1950-51
Currie, Tony	St.L., Hfd., Van.	8	290	92	119	211	83	16	4	12	16	14		1977-78	1984-85
Curry, Floyd	Mtl.	11	601	105	99	204	147	91	23	17	40	38	4	1947-48	1957-58
Curtale, Tony	Cgy.	1	2	0	0	0	0	....	....	....	....	....		1980-81	1980-81
Curtis, Paul	Mtl., L.A., St.L.	4	185	3	34	37	161	5	0	0	0	2		1969-70	1972-73
Cushenan, Ian	Chi., Mtl., NYR, Det.	5	129	3	11	14	134	....	....	....	....	....		1956-57	1963-64
Cusson, Jean	Oak.	1	2	0	0	0	0	....	....	....	....	....		1967-68	1967-68
Cyr, Denis	Cgy., Chi., St.L.	6	193	41	43	84	36	4	0	0	0	0		1980-81	1985-86
Cyr, Paul	Buf., NYR, Hfd.	9	470	101	140	241	623	24	4	6	10	31		1982-83	1991-92

D

Dahlin, Kjell	Mtl.	3	166	57	59	116	10	35	6	11	17	6	1	1985-86	1987-88
Dahlstrom, Cully	Chi.	8	342	88	118	206	58	29	6	8	14	4	1	1937-38	1944-45
Daigle, Alain	Chi.	6	389	56	50	106	122	17	0	1	1	0		1974-75	1979-80
Dailey, Bob	Van., Phi.	9	561	94	231	325	814	63	12	34	46	105		1973-74	1981-82
Daley, Frank	Det.	1	5	0	0	0	0	2	0	0	0	0		1928-29	1928-29
Daley, Pat	Wpg.	2	12	1	0	1	13	....	....	....	....	....		1979-80	1980-81
Dalgarno, Brad	NYI	10	321	49	71	120	332	27	2	4	6	37		1985-86	1995-96
Dallman, Marty	Tor.	2	6	0	1	1	0	....	....	....	....	....		1987-88	1988-89
Dallman, Rod	NYI, Phi.	4	6	1	0	1	26	1	0	1	1	0		1987-88	1991-92
Dame, Bunny	Mtl.	1	34	2	5	7	4	....	....	....	....	....		1941-42	1941-42
Damore, Hank	NYR	1	4	1	0	1	2	....	....	....	....	....		1943-44	1943-44
Daniels, Kimbi	Phi.	2	27	1	2	3	4	....	....	....	....	....		1990-91	1991-92
Daoust, Dan	Mtl., Tor.	8	522	87	167	254	544	32	7	5	12	83		1982-83	1989-90
Dark, Michael	St.L.	2	43	5	6	11	14	....	....	....	....	....		1986-87	1987-88
• Darragh, Harry	Pit., Phi., Bos., Tor.	8	308	68	49	117	50	16	1	3	4	4	1	1925-26	1932-33
• Darragh, Jack	Ott.	6	120	68	21	89	87	21	14	2	16	13	3	1917-18	1923-24
David, Richard	Que.	3	31	4	4	8	10	1	0	0	0	0		1979-80	1982-83
• Davidson, Bob	Tor.	12	491	94	160	254	398	82	5	17	22	79	2	1934-35	1945-46
Davidson, Gord	NYR	2	51	3	6	9	8	....	....	....	....	....		1942-43	1943-44
• Davie, Bob	Bos.	3	41	0	1	1	25	....	....	....	....	....		1933-34	1935-36
Davies, Ken	NYR	1	....	....	....	....	....	1	0	0	0	0		1947-48	1947-48
Davis, Bob	Det.	1	3	0	0	0	0	....	....	....	....	....		1932-33	1932-33
Davis, Kim	Pit., Tor.	4	36	5	7	12	51	4	0	0	0	0		1977-78	1980-81
Davis, Lorne	Mtl., Chi., Det., Bos.	6	95	8	12	20	20	18	3	1	4	10	1	1951-52	1959-60
Davis, Mal	Det., Buf.	6	100	31	22	53	34	7	1	0	1	0		1980-81	1985-86

Name	NHL Teams	NHL Seasons	Regular Schedule					Playoffs					NHL Cup Wins	First NHL Season	Last NHL Season
			GP	G	A	TP	PIM	GP	G	A	TP	PIM			
Davison, Murray	Bos.	1	1	0	0	0	0	....	....	....	....	....		1965-66	1965-66
Davydov, Evgeny	Wpg., Fla., Ott.	4	155	40	39	79	120	11	2	2	4	2		1991-92	1994-95
Dawes, Robert	Tor., Mtl.	4	32	2	7	9	6	10	0	0	0	2	1	1946-47	1950-51
• Day, Hap	Tor., NYA	14	581	86	116	202	601	53	4	7	11	56	1	1924-25	1937-38
Day, Joe	Hfd., NYI	3	72	1	10	11	87	....	....	....	....	....		1991-92	1993-94
Dea, Billy	Chi., NYR, Det., Pit.	8	397	67	54	121	44	11	2	1	3	6		1953-54	1970-71
Deacon, Don	Det.	3	30	6	4	10	6	2	2	1	3	0		1936-37	1939-40
Deadmarsh, Butch	Buf., ATL, K.C.	5	137	12	5	17	155	4	0	0	0	17		1970-71	1974-75
Dean, Barry	Col., Phi.	3	165	25	56	81	146	....	....	....	....	....		1976-77	1978-79
Debenedet, Nelson	Det., Pit.	2	46	10	4	14	13	....	....	....	....	....		1973-74	1974-75
DeBlois, Lucien	NYR, Col., Wpg., Mtl., Que., Tor.	15	993	249	276	525	814	52	7	6	13	38		1977-78	1991-92
Debol, David	Hfd.	2	92	26	26	52	4	3	0	0	0	0		1979-80	1980-81
Defazio, Dean	Pit.	1	22	0	2	2	28	....	....	....	....	....		1983-84	1983-84
DeGray, Dale	Cgy., Tor. L.A., Buf.	5	153	18	47	65	195	13	1	3	4	28		1985-86	1989-90
Delmonte, Armand	Bos.	1	1	0	0	0	0	....	....	....	....	....		1945-46	1945-46
Delorme, Gilbert	Mtl., St.L., Que., Det., Pit.	9	541	31	92	123	520	56	1	9	10	56		1981-82	1989-90
Delorme, Ron	Col., Van.	9	524	83	83	166	667	25	1	2	3	59		1976-77	1984-85
Delory, Valentine	NYR	1	1	0	0	0	0	....	....	....	....	....		1948-49	1948-49
Delparte, Guy	Col.	1	48	1	8	9	18	....	....	....	....	....		1976-77	1976-77
Delvecchio, Alex	Det.	24	1549	456	825	1281	383	121	35	69	104	29	3	1950-51	1973-74
• DeMarco, Ab	Chi., Tor., Bos., NYR	7	209	72	93	165	53	11	3	0	3	2		1938-39	1946-47
DeMarco, Albert	NYR, St.L., Pit., Van., L.A., Bos.	9	344	44	80	124	75	25	1	2	3	17		1969-70	1978-79
Demers, Tony	Mtl., NYR	6	83	20	22	42	23	3	0	0	0	0		1937-38	1943-44
Denis, Johnny	NYR	2	10	0	2	2	2	....	....	....	....	....		1946-47	1949-50
Denis, Lulu	Mtl.	2	3	0	1	1	0	....	....	....	....	....		1949-50	1950-51
• Denneny, Corbett	Tor., Ham., Chi.	9	175	99	29	128	138	15	7	4	11	9	2	1917-18	1927-28
• Denneny, Cy	Ott., Bos.	12	326	246	69	315	210	41	18	3	21	31	5	1917-18	1928-29
Dennis, Norm	St.L.	4	12	3	0	3	11	5	0	0	0	2		1968-69	1971-72
Denoird, Gerry	Tor.	1	15	0	0	0	0	....	....	....	....	....		1922-23	1922-23
DePalma, Larry	Min., S.J., Pit.	7	148	21	20	41	408	3	0	0	0	6		1985-86	1993-94
Derlago, Bill	Van., Bos., Wpg., Que., Tor.	9	555	189	227	416	247	13	5	0	5	8		1978-79	1986-87
• Desaulniers, Gerard	Mtl.	3	8	0	2	2	4	....	....	....	....	....		1950-51	1953-54
• Desilets, Joffre	Mtl., Chi.	5	192	37	45	82	57	7	1	0	1	7		1935-36	1939-40
Desjardins, Martin	Mtl.	1	8	0	2	2	2	....	....	....	....	....		1989-90	1989-90
• Desjardins, Vic	Chi., NYR	2	87	6	15	21	27	16	0	0	0	0		1930-31	1931-32
Deslauriers, Jacques	Mtl.	1	2	0	0	0	0	....	....	....	....	....		1955-56	1955-56
Devine, Kevin	NYI	1	2	0	1	1	8	....	....	....	....	....		1982-83	1982-83
• Dewar, Tom	NYR	1	9	0	2	2	4	....	....	....	....	....		1943-44	1943-44
Dewsbury, Al	Det., Chi.	9	347	30	78	108	365	14	1	5	6	16	1	1946-47	1955-56
Deziel, Michel	Buf.	1	....	....	....	....	....	1	0	0	0	0		1974-75	1974-75
Dheere, Marcel	Mtl.	1	11	1	2	3	2	5	0	0	0	6		1942-43	1942-43
Diachuk, Edward	Det.	1	12	0	0	0	19	....	....	....	....	....		1960-61	1960-61
Dick, Harry	Chi.	1	12	0	1	1	12	....	....	....	....	....		1946-47	1946-47
Dickens, Ernie	Tor., Chi.	6	278	12	44	56	98	13	0	0	0	4	1	1941-42	1950-51
Dickenson, Herb	NYR	2	48	18	17	35	10	....	....	....	....	....		1951-52	1952-53
Dietrich, Don	Chi., N.J.	2	28	0	7	7	10	....	....	....	....	....		1983-84	1985-86
• Dill, Bob	NYR	2	76	15	15	30	135	....	....	....	....	....		1943-44	1944-45
Dillabough, Bob	Det., Bos., Pit., Oak.	9	283	32	54	86	76	17	3	0	3	0		1961-62	1969-70
• Dillon, Cecil	NYR, Det.	10	453	167	131	298	105	43	14	9	23	14	1	1930-31	1939-40
Dillon, Gary	Col.	1	13	1	1	2	29	....	....	....	....	....		1980-81	1980-81
Dillon, Wayne	NYR, Wpg.	4	229	43	66	109	60	3	0	1	1	0		1975-76	1979-80
Dineen, Bill	Det., Chi.	5	323	51	44	95	122	37	1	1	2	18	2	1953-54	1957-58
Dineen, Gary	Min.	1	4	0	1	1	0	....	....	....	....	....		1968-69	1968-69
Dineen, Peter	L.A., Det.	2	13	0	2	2	13	....	....	....	....	....		1986-87	1989-90
Dinsmore, Chuck	Mtl.M	4	102	6	2	8	50	12	1	0	1	6	1	1924-25	1929-30
Dionne, Marcel	Det., L.A., NYR	18	1348	731	1040	1771	600	49	21	24	45	17		1971-72	1988-89
Djoos, Per	Det., NYR	3	82	2	31	33	58	....	....	....	....	....		1990-91	1992-93
Doak, Gary	Det., Bos., Van., NYR	16	789	23	107	130	908	78	2	4	6	121	1	1965-66	1980-81
Dobbin, Brian	Phi., Bos.	5	63	7	8	15	61	2	0	0	0	17		1986-87	1991-92
Dobson, Jim	Min., Col., Que.	4	12	0	0	0	6	....	....	....	....	....		1979-80	1983-84
• Doherty, Fred	Mtl.	1	3	0	0	0	0	....	....	....	....	....		1918-19	1918-19
Donaldson, Gary	Chi.	1	1	0	0	0	0	....	....	....	....	....		1973-74	1973-74
Donatelli, Clark	Min., Bos.	2	35	3	4	7	39	2	0	0	0	0		1989-90	1991-92
Donnelly, Babe	Mtl.M.	1	34	0	1	1	14	2	0	0	0	0		1926-27	1926-27
Donnelly, Dave	Bos., Chi., Edm.	5	137	15	24	39	150	5	0	0	0	0		1983-84	1987-88
• Doran, Red (J.)	NYA., Det., Mtl.	5	98	5	10	15	110	3	0	0	0	0		1933-34	1939-40
Doran, Red (L.)	Det.	1	24	3	2	5	10	....	....	....	....	....		1946-47	1946-47
• Doraty, Ken	Chi., Tor., Det.	5	103	15	26	41	24	15	7	2	9	2		1926-27	1937-38
Dore, Andre	NYR, St.L., Que.	7	257	14	81	95	261	23	1	2	3	32		1978-79	1984-85
Dore, Daniel	Que.	2	17	2	3	5	59	....	....	....	....	....		1989-90	1990-91
Dorey, Jim	Tor., NYR	4	232	25	74	99	553	11	0	2	2	40		1968-69	1971-72
Dorion, Dan	N.J.	2	4	1	1	2	2	....	....	....	....	....		1985-86	1987-88
Dornhoefer, Gary	Bos., Phi.	14	787	214	328	542	1291	80	17	19	36	203	2	1963-64	1977-78
Dorohoy, Eddie	Mtl.	1	16	0	0	0	6	....	....	....	....	....		1948-49	1948-49
Douglas, Jordy	Hfd., Min., Wpg.	6	268	76	62	138	160	6	0	0	0	4		1979-80	1984-85
Douglas, Kent	Tor., Oak., Det.	7	428	33	115	148	631	19	1	3	4	33	1	1962-63	1968-69
Douglas, Les	Det.	4	52	6	12	18	8	10	3	2	5	2	1	1940-41	1946-47
Downie, Dave	Tor.	1	11	0	1	1	2	....	....	....	....	....		1932-33	1932-33
Doyon, Mario	Chi., Que.	3	28	3	4	7	16	....	....	....	....	....		1988-89	1990-91
• Draper, Bruce	Tor.	1	1	0	0	0	0	....	....	....	....	....		1962-63	1962-63
• Drillon, Gordie	Tor., Mtl.	7	311	155	139	294	56	50	26	15	41	10	1	1936-37	1942-43
Driscoll, Pete	Edm.	2	60	3	8	11	97	3	0	0	0	0		1979-80	1980-81
Drolet, Rene	Phi., Det.	2	2	0	0	0	0	....	....	....	....	....		1971-72	1974-75
• Drouillard, Clarence	Det.	1	10	0	1	1	0	....	....	....	....	....		1937-38	1937-38
Drouin, Jude	Mtl., Min., NYI, Wpg.	12	666	151	305	456	346	72	27	41	68	33		1968-69	1980-81
• Drouin, Polly	Mtl.	6	156	23	50	73	80	5	0	1	1	5		1935-36	1940-41
Drulia, Stan	T.B.	1	24	2	1	3	10	....	....	....	....	....		1992-93	1992-93
Drummond, John	NYR	1	2	0	0	0	0	....	....	....	....	....		1944-45	1944-45
Drury, Herb	Pit., Phi.	6	213	24	13	37	203	4	1	1	2	0		1925-26	1930-31
Dube, Gilles	Mtl., Det.	2	12	1	2	3	2	2	0	0	0	0	1	1949-50	1953-54
Dube, Norm	K.C.	2	57	8	10	18	54	....	....	....	....	....		1974-75	1975-76
Duberman, Justin	Pit.	1	4	0	0	0	0	....	....	....	....	....		1993-94	1993-94
Duchesne, Gaetan	Wsh., Que., Min., S.J., Fla.	14	1028	179	254	433	617	84	14	13	27	97		1981-82	1994-95
Dudley, Rick	Buf., Wpg.	6	309	75	99	174	292	25	7	2	9	69		1972-73	1980-81
Duff, Dick	Tor., NYR, Mtl., L.A., Buf.	18	1030	283	289	572	743	114	30	49	79	78	6	1954-55	1971-72
Dufour, Luc	Bos., Que., St.L.	3	167	23	21	44	199	18	1	0	1	32		1982-83	1984-85
Dufour, Marc	NYR, L.A.	3	14	1	0	1	2	....	....	....	....	....		1963-64	1968-69
Duggan, Jack	Ott.	1	27	0	0	0	0	2	0	0	0	0		1925-26	1925-26
Duggan, Ken	Min.	1	1	0	0	0	0	....	....	....	....	....		1987-88	1987-88
Duguay, Ron	NYR, Det., Pit., L.A.	12	864	274	346	620	582	89	31	22	53	118		1977-78	1988-89
• Duguid, Lorne	Mtl.M, Det., Bos.	6	135	9	15	24	57	2	0	0	0	4		1931-32	1936-37
Dumart, Woody	Bos.	16	772	211	218	429	99	88	12	15	27	23	2	1935-36	1953-54
Dunbar, Dale	Van., Bos.	2	2	0	0	0	2	....	....	....	....	....		1985-86	1988-89
• Duncan, Art	Det., Tor.	5	156	18	16	34	225	5	0	0	0	4		1926-27	1930-31
Duncan, Iain	Wpg.	4	127	34	55	89	149	11	0	3	3	6		1986-87	1990-91
Dundas, Rocky	Tor.	1	5	0	0	0	14	....	....	....	....	....		1989-90	1989-90
Dunlap, Frank	Tor.	1	15	0	1	1	2	....	....	....	....	....		1943-44	1943-44
Dunlop, Blake	Min., Phi., St.L., Det.	11	550	130	274	404	172	40	4	10	14	18		1973-74	1983-84
Dunn, Dave	Van., Tor.	3	184	14	41	55	313	10	1	1	2	41		1973-74	1975-76
Dunn, Richie	Buf., Cgy., Hfd.	12	483	36	140	176	314	36	3	15	18	24		1977-78	1988-89
Dupere, Denis	Tor., Wsh., St.L., K.C., Col.	8	421	80	99	179	66	16	1	0	1	0		1970-71	1977-78
Dupont, Andre	NYR, St.L., Phi., Que.	13	800	59	185	244	1986	140	14	18	32	352	2	1970-71	1982-83
Dupont, Jerome	Chi., Tor.	6	214	7	29	36	468	20	0	2	2	56		1981-82	1986-87
Dupont, Norm	Mtl., Wpg., Hfd.	5	256	55	85	140	52	13	4	2	6	0		1979-80	1983-84
• Dupre, Yanick	Phi.	3	35	2	0	2	16	....	....	....	....	....		1991-92	1995-96
Durbano, Steve	St.L., Pit., K.C., Col.	6	220	13	60	73	1127	5	0	2	2	8		1972-73	1978-79
Duris, Vitezslav	Tor.	2	89	3	20	23	62	3	0	1	1	2		1980-81	1982-83
Dussault, Norm	Mtl.	4	206	31	62	93	47	7	3	1	4	0		1947-48	1950-51
• Dutkowski, Duke	Chi., NYA, NYR	5	200	16	30	46	172	6	0	0	0	6		1926-27	1933-34
• Dutton, Red	Mtl.M, NYA	10	449	29	67	96	871	18	1	0	1	33		1926-27	1935-36
Dvorak, Miroslav	Phi.	3	193	11	74	85	51	18	0	2	2	6		1982-83	1984-85
Dwyer, Mike	Col., Cgy.	4	31	2	6	8	25	1	1	0	1	0		1978-79	1981-82
Dyck, Henry	NYR	1	1	0	0	0	0	....	....	....	....	....		1943-44	1943-44

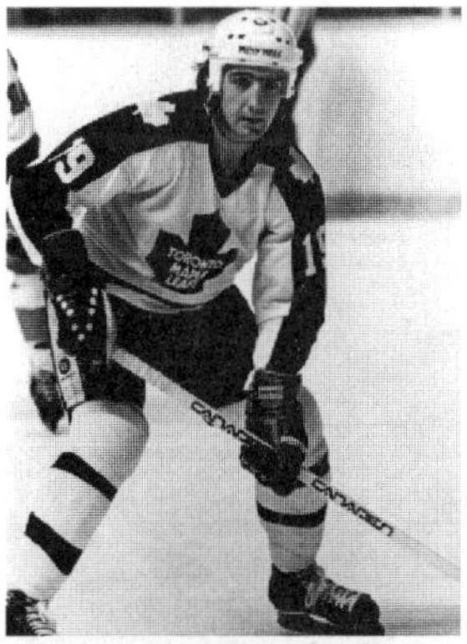
Bill Derlago

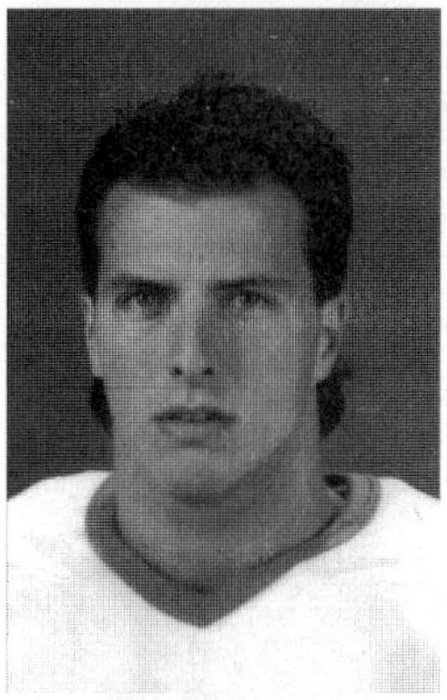
Daniel Dore

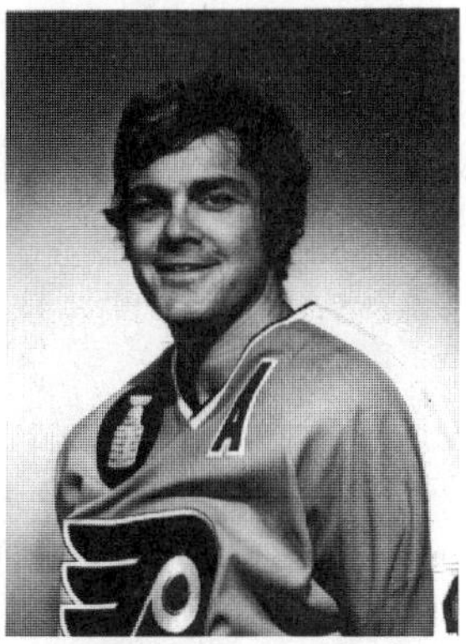
Gary Dornhoefer

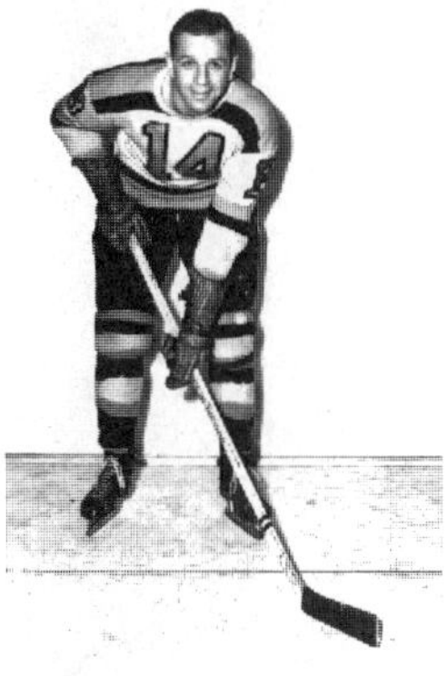
Woody Dumart

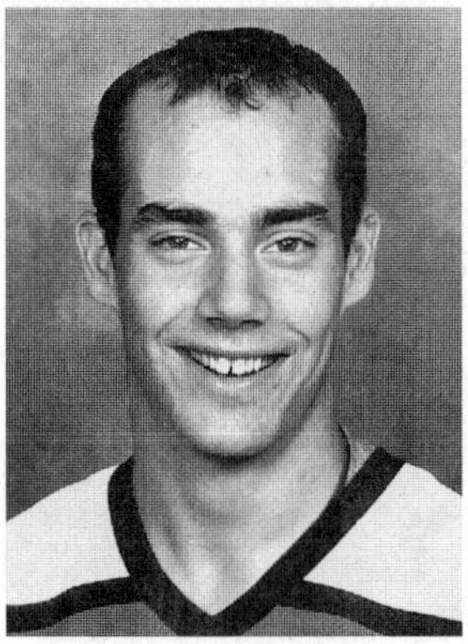

Yanick Dupre

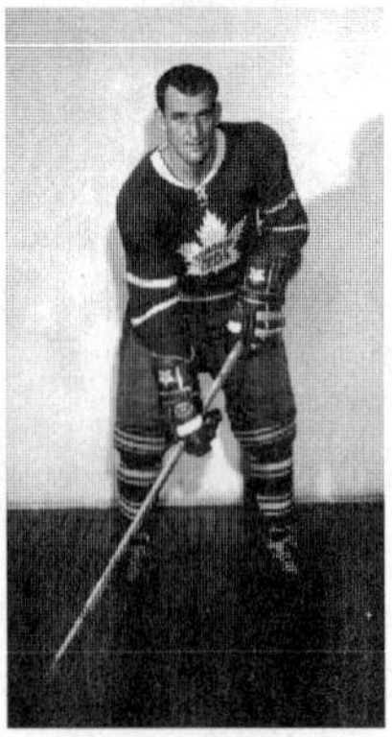

Gerry Ehman

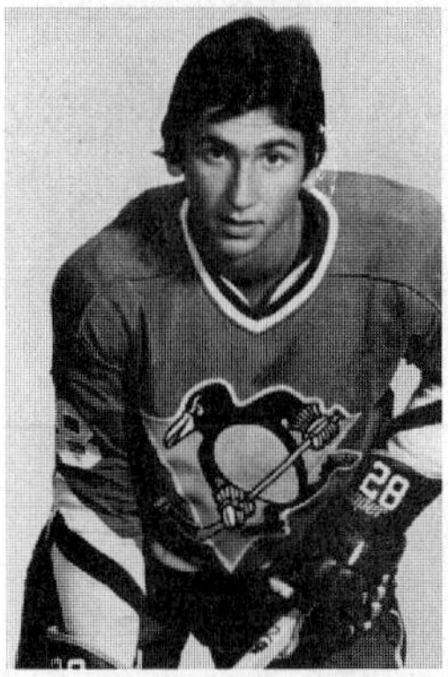

Mario Faubert

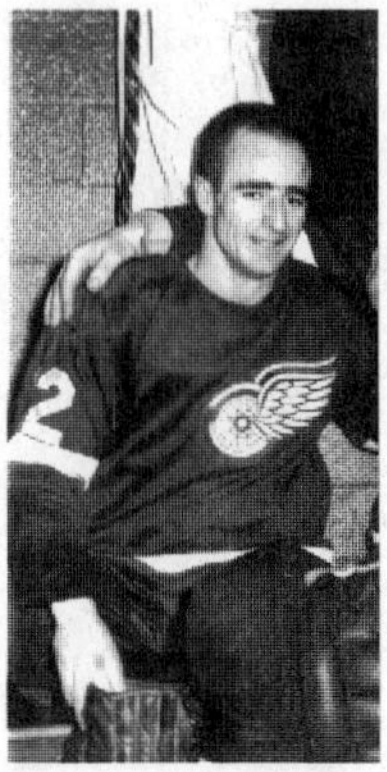

Val Fonteyne

			Regular Schedule					Playoffs					NHL	First	Last
Name	NHL Teams	NHL Seasons	GP	G	A	TP	PIM	GP	G	A	TP	PIM	Cup Wins	NHL Season	NHL Season
● Dye, Babe	Tor., Ham., Chi., NYA	11	269	202	41	243	200	15	11	2	13	18	1	1919-20	1930-31
Dykstra, Steven	Buf., Edm., Pit., Hfd.	5	217	8	32	40	545	1	0	0	0	2		1985-86	1989-90
Dyte, John	Chi.	1	27	1	0	1	31	....	....	....	....	....		1943-44	1943-44

E

Name	NHL Teams	NHL Seasons	GP	G	A	TP	PIM	GP	G	A	TP	PIM	NHL Cup Wins	First NHL Season	Last NHL Season
Eakin, Bruce	Cgy., Det.	4	13	2	2	4	4	....	....	....	....	....		1981-82	1985-86
Eatough, Jeff	Buf.	1	1	0	0	0	0	....	....	....	....	....		1981-82	1981-82
Eaves, Mike	Min., Cgy.	8	324	83	143	226	80	43	7	10	17	14		1978-79	1985-86
Eaves, Murray	Wpg., Det.	8	57	4	13	17	9	4	0	1	1	2		1980-81	1989-90
Ecclestone, Tim	St.L., Det., Tor., Atl.	11	692	126	233	359	344	48	6	11	17	76		1967-68	1977-78
Edberg, Rolf	Wsh.	3	184	45	58	103	24	....	....	....	....	....		1978-79	1980-81
● Eddolls, Frank	Mtl., NYR	8	317	23	43	66	114	31	0	2	2	10	1	1944-45	1951-52
Edestrand, Darryl	St.L., Phi., Pit., Bos., L.A.	10	455	34	90	124	404	42	3	9	12	57		1967-68	1978-79
Edmundson, Garry	Mtl., Tor.	3	43	4	6	10	49	11	0	1	1	8		1951-52	1960-61
Edur, Tom	Col., Pit	2	158	17	70	87	67	....	....	....	....	....		1976-77	1977-78
Egan, Pat	NYA, Bro., Det., Bos., NYR	11	554	77	153	230	776	44	9	4	13	44		1939-40	1950-51
Egers, Jack	NYR, St.L., Wsh.	7	284	64	69	133	154	32	5	6	11	32		1969-70	1975-76
Ehman, Gerry	Bos., Det., Tor., Oak, Cal.	9	429	96	118	214	100	41	10	10	20	12	1	1957-58	1970-71
Eklund, Pelle	Phi., Dal.	9	594	120	335	455	109	66	10	36	46	8		1985-86	1993-94
Eldebrink, Anders	Van., Que.	2	55	3	11	14	29	14	0	0	0	10		1981-82	1982-83
Elik, Boris	Det.	1	3	0	0	0	0	....	....	....	....	....		1962-63	1962-63
Elliot, Fred	Ott.	1	43	2	0	2	6	....	....	....	....	....		1928-29	1928-29
Ellis, Ron	Tor.	16	1034	332	308	640	207	70	18	8	26	20	1	1963-64	1980-81
Eloranta, Kari	Cgy., St.L.	5	267	13	103	116	155	26	1	7	8	19		1981-82	1986-87
Emberg, Eddie	Mtl.	1	....	....	....	....	....	2	1	0	1	0		1944-45	1944-45
Emmons, Gary	S.J.	1	3	1	0	1	0	....	....	....	....	....		1993-94	1993-94
● Emms, Hap	Mtl.M, NYA, Det., Bos.	10	320	36	53	89	311	14	0	0	0	12		1926-27	1937-38
Endean, Craig	Wpg.	1	2	0	1	1	0	....	....	....	....	....		1986-87	1986-87
Engblom, Brian	Mtl., Wsh., L.A., Buf., Cgy.	11	659	29	177	206	599	48	3	9	12	43	3	1976-77	1986-87
Engele, Jerry	Min.	3	100	2	13	15	162	2	0	1	1	0		1975-76	1977-78
English, John	L.A.	1	3	1	3	4	4	1	0	0	0	0		1987-88	1987-88
Ennis, Jim	Edm.	1	5	1	0	1	10	....	....	....	....	....		1987-88	1987-88
Erickson, Aut	Bos., Chi., Oak., Tor.	7	226	7	24	31	182	7	0	0	0	2	1	1959-60	1969-70
Erickson, Bryan	Wsh., L.A., Pit., Wpg.	9	351	80	125	205	141	14	3	4	7	7		1983-84	1993-94
Erickson, Grant	Bos., Min.	2	6	1	0	1	0	....	....	....	....	....		1968-69	1969-70
Eriksson, Peter	Edm.	1	20	3	3	6	24	....	....	....	....	....		1989-90	1989-90
Eriksson, Rolie	Min., Van.	3	193	48	95	143	26	2	1	0	1	0		1976-77	1978-79
Eriksson, Thomas	Phi.	5	208	22	76	98	107	19	0	3	3	12		1980-81	1985-86
Erixon, Jan	NYR	10	556	57	159	216	167	58	7	7	14	16		1983-84	1992-93
Esposito, Phil	Chi., Bos., NYR	18	1282	717	873	1590	910	130	61	76	137	138	2	1963-64	1980-81
Evans, Chris	Tor., Buf., St.L., Det., K.C.	5	241	19	42	61	143	12	1	1	2	8		1969-70	1974-75
Evans, Daryl	L.A., Wsh., Tor.	6	113	22	30	52	25	11	5	8	13	12		1981-82	1986-87
Evans, Doug	St.L., Wpg., Phi.	8	355	48	87	135	502	22	3	4	7	38		1985-86	1992-93
● Evans, Jack	NYR, Chi.	14	752	19	80	99	989	56	2	2	4	97	1	1948-49	1962-63
Evans, John	Phi.	3	103	14	25	39	34	1	0	0	0	0		1978-79	1982-83
Evans, Kevin	Min., S.J.	2	9	0	1	1	44	....	....	....	....	....		1990-91	1991-92
Evans, Paul	Tor.	2	11	1	1	2	21	2	0	0	0	0		1976-77	1977-78
Evans, Shawn	St. L., NYI	2	9	1	0	1	2	....	....	....	....	....		1985-86	1989-90
● Evans, Stewart	Det., Mtl.M., Mtl.	8	367	28	49	77	425	26	0	0	0	20	1	1930-31	1938-39
Ezinicki, Bill	Tor., Bos., NYR	9	368	79	105	184	713	40	5	8	13	87	3	1944-45	1954-55

F

Name	NHL Teams	NHL Seasons	GP	G	A	TP	PIM	GP	G	A	TP	PIM	NHL Cup Wins	First NHL Season	Last NHL Season
Fahey, Trevor	NYR	1	1	0	0	0	0	....	....	....	....	....		1964-65	1964-65
Fairbairn, Bill	NYR, Min. St.L.	11	658	162	261	423	173	54	13	22	35	42		1968-69	1978-79
Falkenberg, Bob	Det.	5	54	1	5	6	26	....	....	....	....	....		1966-67	1971-72
Farrant, Walt	Chi.	1	1	0	0	0	0	....	....	....	....	....		1943-44	1943-44
Farrish, Dave	NYR, Que, Tor.	7	430	17	110	127	440	14	0	2	2	24		1976-77	1983-84
Fashoway, Gordie	Chi.	1	13	3	2	5	14	....	....	....	....	....		1950-51	1950-51
Faubert, Mario	Pit.	7	231	21	90	111	292	10	2	2	4	6		1974-75	1981-82
Faulkner, Alex	Tor., Det.	3	101	15	17	32	15	12	5	0	5	2		1961-62	1963-64
Fauss, Ted	Tor.	2	28	0	2	2	15	....	....	....	....	....		1986-87	1987-88
Feamster, Dave	Chi.	4	169	13	24	37	154	33	3	5	8	61		1981-82	1984-85
Featherstone, Tony	Oak., Cal., Min.	3	130	17	21	38	65	2	0	0	0	0		1969-70	1973-74
Federko, Bernie	St.L., Det.	14	1000	369	761	1130	487	91	35	66	101	83		1976-77	1989-90
Fedotov, Anatoli	Wpg., Ana.	2	4	0	2	2	0	....	....	....	....	....		1992-93	1993-94
Felix, Chris	Wsh.	4	35	1	12	13	10	2	0	1	1	0		1987-88	1990-91
Felsner, Denny	St.L.	4	18	1	4	5	6	10	2	3	5	2		1991-92	1994-95
Feltrin, Tony	Pit., NYR	4	48	3	3	6	65	....	....	....	....	....		1980-81	1985-86
Fenton, Paul	Hfd., NYR, L.A., Wpg., Tor., Cgy., S.J.	8	411	100	83	183	198	17	4	1	5	27		1984-85	1991-92
Fenyves, David	Buf., Phi.	9	206	3	32	35	119	11	0	0	0	9		1982-83	1990-91
Fergus, Tom	Bos., Tor., Van.	12	726	235	346	581	499	65	21	17	38	48		1981-82	1992-93
Ferguson, George	Tor., Pit, Min	12	797	160	238	398	431	86	14	23	37	44		1972-73	1983-84
Ferguson, John	Mtl.	8	500	145	158	303	1214	85	20	18	38	260	5	1963-64	1970-71
Ferguson, Lorne	Bos., Det., Chi.	8	422	82	80	162	193	31	6	3	9	24		1949-50	1958-59
Ferguson, Norm	Oak., Cal.	4	279	73	66	139	72	10	1	4	5	7		1968-69	1971-72
Ferner, Mark	Buf., Wsh., Ana., Det.	6	91	3	10	13	51	....	....	....	....	....		1986-87	1994-95
Fidler, Mike	Cle., Min, Hfd., Chi.	7	271	84	97	181	124	....	....	....	....	....		1976-77	1982-83
● Field, Wilf	Bro., Mtl., Chi., NYA	6	219	17	25	42	151	5	0	0	0	2		1936-37	1944-45
Fielder, Guyle	Det., Chi., Bos.	4	9	0	0	0	2	6	0	0	0	2		1950-51	1957-58
Filimonov, Dmitri	Ott.	1	30	1	4	5	18	....	....	....	....	....		1993-94	1993-94
Fillion, Bob	Mtl.	7	327	42	61	103	84	33	7	4	11	10	2	1943-44	1949-50
Fillion, Marcel	Bos.	1	1	0	0	0	0	....	....	....	....	....		1944-45	1944-45
● Filmore, Tommy	Det., NYA, Bos.	4	117	15	12	27	33	....	....	....	....	....		1930-31	1933-34
Finkbeiner, Lloyd	NYA	1	1	0	0	0	0	....	....	....	....	....		1940-41	1940-41
Finney, Sid	Chi.	3	59	10	7	17	4	7	0	2	2	0		1951-52	1953-54
Finnigan, Ed	Bos.	2	15	1	1	2	2	....	....	....	....	....		1935-36	1935-36
● Finnigan, Frank	Ott., Tor., St.L.	14	553	115	88	203	405	39	6	9	15	22	2	1923-24	1936-37
Fischer, Ron	Buf.	2	18	0	7	7	6	....	....	....	....	....		1981-82	1982-83
Fisher, Alvin	Tor.	1	9	1	0	1	4	....	....	....	....	....		1924-25	1924-25
Fisher, Dunc	NYR, Bos., Det.	7	275	45	70	115	104	21	4	4	8	14	1	1947-48	1958-59
Fisher, Joe	Det.	4	66	8	12	20	13	15	2	1	3	6		1939-40	1942-43
Fitchner, Bob	Que	2	78	12	20	32	59	3	0	0	0	10		1979-80	1980-81
Fitzpatrick, Ross	Phi.	4	20	5	2	7	0	....	....	....	....	....		1982-83	1985-86
Fitzpatrick, Sandy	NYR, Min.	2	22	3	6	9	8	12	0	0	0	0		1964-65	1967-68
Flaman, Fern	Bos., Tor.	17	910	34	174	208	1370	63	4	8	12	93	1	1944-45	1960-61
Fleming, Gerry	Mtl.	2	11	0	0	0	42	....	....	....	....	....		1993-94	1994-95
Fleming, Reggie	Mtl., Chi., Bos., NYR, Phi., Buf.	12	749	108	132	240	1468	50	3	6	9	106	1	1959-60	1970-71
Flesch,	Ham.	1	1	0	0	0	0	....	....	....	....	....		1920-21	1920-21
Flesch, John	Min, Pit, Col.	4	124	18	23	41	117	....	....	....	....	....		1974-75	1979-80
Fletcher, Steven	Mtl., Wpg.	2	3	0	0	0	5	1	0	0	0	5		1987-88	1988-89
Flett, Bill	L.A., Phi., Tor., Atl, Edm.	11	689	202	215	417	501	52	7	16	23	42	1	1967-68	1979-80
Flichel, Todd	Wpg.	3	6	0	1	1	4	....	....	....	....	....		1987-88	1989-90
Flockhart, Rob	Van., Min	5	55	2	5	7	14	1	1	0	1	2		1976-77	1980-81
Flockhart, Ron	Phi., Pit., Mtl., St.L., Bos.	9	453	145	183	328	208	19	4	6	10	14		1980-81	1988-89
Floyd, Larry	N.J.	2	12	2	3	5	9	....	....	....	....	....		1982-83	1983-84
Fogarty, Bryan	Que., Pit., Mtl.	6	156	22	52	74	119	....	....	....	....	....		1989-90	1994-95
Fogolin, Lee	Buf., Edm.	13	924	44	195	239	1318	108	5	19	24	173	2	1974-75	1986-87
Fogolin, Lidio (Lee)	Det., Chi.	9	427	10	48	58	575	28	0	2	2	30	1	1947-48	1955-56
Folco, Peter	Van.	1	2	0	0	0	0	....	....	....	....	....		1973-74	1973-74
Foley, Gerry	Tor., NYR, L.A.	4	142	9	14	23	99	9	0	1	1	2		1954-55	1968-69
Foley, Rick	Chi., Phi., Det.	3	67	11	26	37	180	4	0	1	1	4		1970-71	1973-74
Foligno, Mike	Det., Buf., Tor., Fla.	15	1018	355	372	727	2049	57	15	17	32	185		1979-80	1993-94
Folk, Bill	Det.	2	12	0	0	0	4	....	....	....	....	....		1951-52	1952-53
Fontaine, Len	Det.	2	46	8	11	19	10	....	....	....	....	....		1972-73	1973-74
Fontas, Jon	Min.	2	2	0	0	0	0	....	....	....	....	....		1979-80	1980-81
Fonteyne, Val	Det., NYR, Pit.	13	820	75	154	229	26	59	3	10	13	8		1959-60	1971-72
Fontinato, Lou	NYR, Mtl.	9	535	26	78	104	1247	21	0	2	2	42		1954-55	1962-63
Forbes, Dave	Bos., Wsh.	6	363	64	64	128	341	45	1	4	5	13		1973-74	1978-79
Forbes, Mike	Bos., Edm.	3	50	1	11	12	41	....	....	....	....	....		1977-78	1981-82
Forey, Connie	St.L.	1	4	0	0	0	2	....	....	....	....	....		1973-74	1973-74
Forsey, Jack	Tor.	1	19	7	9	16	10	3	0	1	1	0		1942-43	1942-43
Forslund, Gus	Ott.	1	48	4	9	13	2	....	....	....	....	....		1932-33	1932-33

Name	NHL Teams	NHL Seasons	Regular Schedule GP	G	A	TP	PIM	Playoffs GP	G	A	TP	PIM	NHL Cup Wins	First NHL Season	Last NHL Season
Forslund, Tomas	Cgy.	2	44	5	11	16	12	....	....	....	....	....		1991-92	1992-93
Forsyth, Alex	Wsh.	1	1	0	0	0	0	....	....	....	....	....		1976-77	1976-77
Fortier, Charles	Mtl.	1	1	0	0	0	0	....	....	....	....	....		1923-24	1923-24
Fortier, Dave	Tor., NYI, Van.	4	205	8	21	29	335	20	0	2	2	33		1972-73	1976-77
Fortier, Marc	Que., Ott., L.A.	6	212	42	60	102	135	....	....	....	....	....		1987-88	1992-93
Fortin, Ray	St.L.	3	92	2	6	8	33	6	0	0	0	8		1967-68	1969-70
Foster, Dwight	Bos., Col., N.J., Det.	10	541	111	163	274	420	35	5	12	17	4		1977-78	1986-87
• Foster, Harry	NYR, Bos., Det.	4	83	3	2	5	32	....	....	....	....	....		1929-30	1934-35
Foster, Herb	NYR	2	5	1	0	1	5	....	....	....	....	....		1940-41	1947-48
Fotiu, Nick	NYR, Hfd., Cgy., Phi., Edm.	13	646	60	77	137	1362	38	0	4	4	67		1976-77	1988-89
• Fowler, Jimmy	Tor.	3	135	18	29	47	39	18	0	3	3	2		1936-37	1938-39
Fowler, Tom	Chi.	1	24	0	1	1	18	....	....	....	....	....		1946-47	1946-47
Fox, Greg	Atl, Chi., Pit.	8	494	14	92	106	637	44	1	9	10	67		1977-78	1984-85
Fox, Jim	L.A.	9	578	186	293	479	143	22	4	8	12	0		1980-81	1989-90
• Foyston, Frank	Det.	2	64	17	7	24	32	....	....	....	....	....		1926-27	1927-28
Frampton, Bob	Mtl.	1	2	0	0	0	0	3	0	0	0	0		1949-50	1949-50
Franceschetti, Lou	Wsh., Tor., Buf.	10	459	59	81	140	747	44	3	2	5	111		1981-82	1991-92
Francis, Bobby	Det.	1	14	2	0	2	0	....	....	....	....	....		1982-83	1982-83
• Fraser, Archie	NYR	1	3	0	1	1	0	....	....	....	....	....		1943-44	1943-44
Fraser, Curt	Van., Chi., Min.	12	704	193	240	433	1306	65	15	18	33	198		1978-79	1989-90
Fraser, Gord	Chi., Det., Mtl., Pit., Phi.	5	144	24	12	36	224	2	1	0	1	6		1926-27	1930-31
Fraser, Harry	Chi.	1	21	5	4	9	0	....	....	....	....	....		1944-45	1944-45
Fraser, Jack	Ham.	1	1	0	0	0	0	....	....	....	....	....		1923-24	1923-24
Frawley, Dan	Chi., Pit.	6	273	37	40	77	674	1	0	0	0	0		1983-84	1988-89
• Frederickson, Frank	Det., Bos., Pit.	5	165	37	36	73	206	10	2	5	7	26	1	1926-27	1930-31
Frew, Irv	Mtl.M, St.L., Mtl.	3	95	2	5	7	146	4	0	0	0	6		1933-34	1935-36
Friday, Tim	Det.	1	23	0	3	3	6	....	....	....	....	....		1985-86	1985-86
Fridgen, Dan	Hfd.	2	13	2	3	5	2	....	....	....	....	....		1981-82	1982-83
Friest, Ron	Min.	3	64	7	7	14	191	6	1	0	1	7		1980-81	1982-83
Frig, Len	Chi., Cal., Cle., St.L.	7	311	13	51	64	479	14	2	1	3	0		1972-73	1979-80
Frost, Harry	Bos.	1	3	0	0	0	0	1	0	0	0	0		1938-39	1938-39
Frycer, Miroslav	Que., Tor., Det., Edm.	8	415	147	183	330	486	17	3	8	11	16		1981-82	1988-89
Fryday, Bob	Mtl.	2	5	1	0	1	0	....	....	....	....	....		1949-50	1951-52
Ftorek, Robbie	Det., Que, NYR	8	334	77	150	227	262	19	9	6	15	28		1972-73	1984-85
Fullan, Larry	Wsh.	1	4	1	0	1	0	....	....	....	....	....		1974-75	1974-75
Fusco, Mark	Hfd.	2	80	3	12	15	42	....	....	....	....	....		1983-84	1984-85

G

Name	NHL Teams	NHL Seasons	Regular Schedule GP	G	A	TP	PIM	Playoffs GP	G	A	TP	PIM	NHL Cup Wins	First NHL Season	Last NHL Season
Gadsby, Bill	Chi., NYR, Det.	20	1248	130	438	568	1539	67	4	23	27	92		1946-47	1965-66
Gaetz, Link	Min., S.J.	3	65	6	8	14	412	....	....	....	....	....		1988-89	1991-92
Gage, Jody	Det., Buf.	6	68	14	15	29	26	....	....	....	....	....		1980-81	1991-92
Gagne, Art	Mtl., Bos., Ott., Det.	6	228	67	33	100	257	11	2	1	3	20		1926-27	1931-32
Gagne, Paul	Col., N.J., Tor., NYI	8	390	110	101	211	127	....	....	....	....	....		1980-81	1989-90
Gagne, Pierre	Bos.	1	2	0	0	0	0	....	....	....	....	....		1959-60	1959-60
Gagnon, Germaine	Mtl., NYI, Chi., K.C.	5	259	40	101	141	72	19	2	3	5	2		1971-72	1975-76
• Gagnon, Johnny	Mtl., Bos., NYA	10	454	120	141	261	295	32	12	12	24	37	1	1930-31	1939-40
Gainey, Bob	Mtl.	16	1160	239	262	501	585	182	25	48	73	151	5	1973-74	1988-89
• Gainor, Dutch	Bos., NYR, Ott., Mtl.M	7	246	51	56	107	129	25	2	1	3	14	2	1927-28	1934-35
Galarneau, Michel	Hfd.	3	78	7	10	17	34	....	....	....	....	....		1980-81	1982-83
• Galbraith, Percy	Bos., Ott.	8	347	29	31	60	224	31	4	7	11	24		1926-27	1933-34
• Gallagher, John	Mtl.M, Det., NYA	7	204	14	19	33	153	22	2	3	5	27	1	1930-31	1938-39
Gallant, Gerard	Det., T.B.	11	615	211	269	480	1674	58	18	21	39	178		1984-85	1994-95
Gallimore, Jamie	Min.	1	2	0	0	0	0	....	....	....	....	....		1977-78	1977-78
• Gallinger, Don	Bos.	5	222	65	88	153	89	23	5	5	10	19		1942-43	1947-48
Gamble, Dick	Mtl., Chi., Tor.	8	195	41	41	82	66	14	1	2	3	4	2	1950-51	1966-67
Gambucci, Gary	Min.	2	51	2	7	9	9	....	....	....	....	....		1971-72	1973-74
Ganchar, Perry	St. L., Mtl., Pit.	4	42	3	7	10	36	7	3	1	4	0		1983-84	1988-89
Gans, Dave	L.A.	2	6	0	0	0	2	....	....	....	....	....		1982-83	1985-86
• Gardiner, Herb	Mtl., Chi.	3	101	10	9	19	52	7	0	1	1	14		1926-27	1928-29
Gardner, Bill	Chi., Hfd.	9	380	73	115	188	68	45	3	8	11	17		1980-81	1988-89
Gardner, Cal	NYR, Tor., Chi., Bos.	12	696	154	238	392	517	61	7	10	17	20	2	1945-46	1956-57
Gardner, Dave	Mtl., St.L., Cal., Cle., Phi.	7	350	75	115	190	41	....	....	....	....	....		1972-73	1979-80
Gardner, Paul	Col., Tor., Pit., Wsh., Buf.	10	447	201	201	402	207	16	2	6	8	14		1976-77	1985-86
Gare, Danny	Buf., Det., Edm.	13	827	354	331	685	1285	64	25	21	46	195		1974-75	1986-87
Gariepy, Ray	Bos., Tor.	2	36	1	6	7	43	....	....	....	....	....		1953-54	1955-56
• Garland, Scott	Tor., L.A.	3	91	13	24	37	115	7	1	2	3	35		1975-76	1978-79
Garner, Bob	Pit.	1	1	0	0	0	0	....	....	....	....	....		1982-83	1982-83
• Garrett, Red	NYR	1	23	1	1	2	18	....	....	....	....	....		1942-43	1942-43
• Gassoff, Bob	St.L.	4	245	11	47	58	866	9	0	1	1	16		1973-74	1976-77
Gassoff, Brad	Van.	4	122	19	17	36	163	3	0	0	0	0		1975-76	1978-79
Gatzos, Steve	Pit.	4	89	15	20	35	83	1	0	0	0	0		1981-82	1984-85
Gaudreault, Armand	Bos.	1	44	15	9	24	27	7	0	2	2	8		1944-45	1944-45
• Gaudreault, Leo	Mtl.	3	67	8	4	12	30	....	....	....	....	....		1927-28	1932-33
Gaulin, Jean-Marc	Que.	4	26	4	3	7	8	1	0	0	0	0		1982-83	1985-86
Gaume, Dallas	Hfd.	1	4	1	1	2	0	....	....	....	....	....		1988-89	1988-89
Gauthier, Art	Mtl.	1	13	0	0	0	0	1	0	0	0	0		1926-27	1926-27
Gauthier, Daniel	Chi.	1	5	0	0	0	0	....	....	....	....	....		1994-95	1994-95
• Gauthier, Fern	NYR, Mtl., Det.	6	229	46	50	96	35	22	5	1	6	7		1943-44	1948-49
Gauthier, Jean	Mtl., Phi., Bos.	10	166	6	29	35	150	14	1	3	4	22	1	1960-61	1969-70
Gauthier, Luc	Mtl.	1	3	0	0	0	2	....	....	....	....	....		1990-91	1990-91
Gauvreau, Jocelyn	Mtl.	1	2	0	0	0	0	....	....	....	....	....		1983-84	1983-84
Gavin, Stewart	Tor., Hfd., Min.	13	768	130	155	285	584	66	14	20	34	75		1980-81	1992-93
Geale, Bob	Pit.	1	1	0	0	0	2	....	....	....	....	....		1984-85	1984-85
• Gee, George	Chi., Det.	9	551	135	183	318	345	41	6	13	19	32	1	1945-46	1953-54
Geldart, Gary	Min.	1	4	0	0	0	5	....	....	....	....	....		1970-71	1970-71
Gendron, Jean-Guy	NYR, Mtl., Bos., Phi.	14	863	182	201	383	701	42	7	4	11	47		1955-56	1971-72
Geoffrion, Bernie	Mtl., NYR	16	883	393	429	822	689	132	58	60	118	88	6	1950-51	1967-68
Geoffrion, Danny	Mtl., Wpg.	3	111	20	32	52	99	2	0	0	0	7		1979-80	1981-82
• Geran, Gerry "Duke"	Mtl.W., Bos.	2	37	5	1	6	6	....	....	....	....	....		1917-18	1925-26
• Gerard, Eddie	Ott., Tor.	6	128	50	30	80	106	27	7	3	10	23	4	1917-18	1922-23
Germain, Eric	L.A.	1	4	0	1	1	13	1	0	0	0	4		1987-88	1987-88
Getliffe, Ray	Bos., Mtl.	10	393	136	137	273	250	45	9	10	19	30	2	1935-36	1944-45
Giallonardo, Mario	Col.	2	23	0	3	3	6	....	....	....	....	....		1979-80	1980-81
Gibbs, Barry	Bos., Min., Atl., St.L., L.A.	13	797	58	224	282	945	36	4	2	6	67		1967-68	1979-80
Gibson, Don	Van.	1	14	0	3	3	20	....	....	....	....	....		1990-91	1990-91
Gibson, Doug	Bos., Wsh.	3	63	9	19	28	0	1	0	0	0	0		1973-74	1977-78
Gibson, John	L.A., Tor., Wpg.	3	48	0	2	2	120	....	....	....	....	....		1980-81	1983-84
Giesebrecht, Gus	Det.	4	135	27	51	78	13	17	2	3	5	0		1938-39	1941-42
Giffin, Lee	Pit.	2	27	1	3	4	9	....	....	....	....	....		1986-87	1987-88
Gilbert, Ed	K.C., Pit.	3	166	21	31	52	22	....	....	....	....	....		1974-75	1976-77
Gilbert, Greg	NYI, Chi., NYR, St.L.	15	837	150	228	378	576	133	17	33	50	162	3	1981-82	1995-96
Gilbert, Jeannot	Bos.	2	9	0	1	1	4	....	....	....	....	....		1962-63	1964-65
Gilbert, Rod	NYR	18	1065	406	615	1021	508	79	34	33	67	43		1960-61	1977-78
Gilbertson, Stan	Cal., St.L., Wsh., Pit.	6	428	85	89	174	148	3	1	1	2	2		1971-72	1976-77
Giles, Curt	Min., NYR, St.L.	14	895	43	199	242	733	103	6	16	22	118		1979-80	1992-93
Gillen, Don	Phi., Hfd.	2	35	2	4	6	22	....	....	....	....	....		1979-80	1981-82
Gillie, Ferrand	Det.	1	1	0	0	0	0	....	....	....	....	....		1928-29	1928-29
Gillies, Clark	NYI, Buf.	14	958	319	378	697	1023	164	47	47	94	287	4	1974-75	1987-88
Gillis, Jere	Que., Buf., Phi., Van., NYR	9	386	78	95	173	230	19	4	7	11	9		1977-78	1986-87
Gillis, Mike	Col., Bos.	6	246	33	43	76	186	27	2	5	7	10		1978-79	1983-84
Gillis, Paul	Que., Chi., Hfd.	11	624	88	154	242	1498	42	3	14	17	156		1982-83	1992-93
Gingras, Gaston	Mtl., Tor., St.L.	10	476	61	174	235	161	52	6	18	24	20	1	1979-80	1988-89
Girard, Bob	Cal., Cle., Wsh.	5	305	45	69	114	140	....	....	....	....	....		1975-76	1979-80
Girard, Kenny	Tor.	3	7	0	1	1	2	....	....	....	....	....		1956-57	1959-60
Giroux, Art	Mtl., Bos., Det.	3	54	6	4	10	14	2	0	0	0	0		1932-33	1935-36
Giroux, Larry	St.L., K.C., Det., Hfd.	7	274	15	74	89	333	5	0	0	0	4		1973-74	1979-80
Giroux, Pierre	L.A.	1	6	1	0	1	17	....	....	....	....	....		1982-83	1982-83
Gladney, Bob	L.A., Pit.	2	14	1	5	6	4	....	....	....	....	....		1982-83	1983-84
Gladu, Jean	Bos.	1	40	6	14	20	2	7	2	2	4	0		1944-45	1944-45
Glennie, Brian	Tor., L.A.	10	572	14	100	114	621	32	0	1	1	66		1969-70	1978-79
Glennon, Matt	Bos.	1	3	0	0	0	2	....	....	....	....	....		1991-92	1991-92
Gloeckner, Lorry	Det.	1	13	0	2	2	6	....	....	....	....	....		1978-79	1978-79

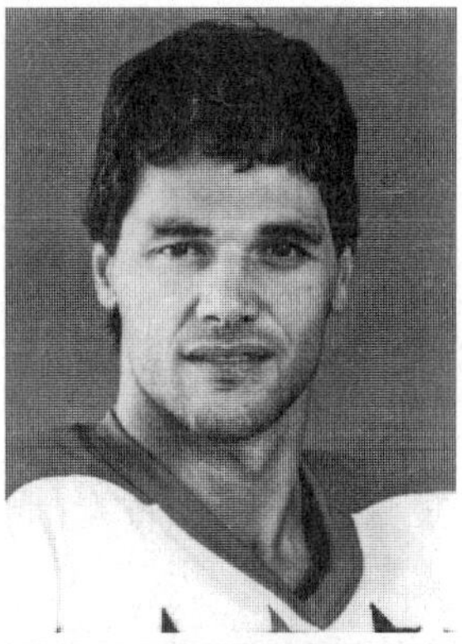
Lou Franceschetti

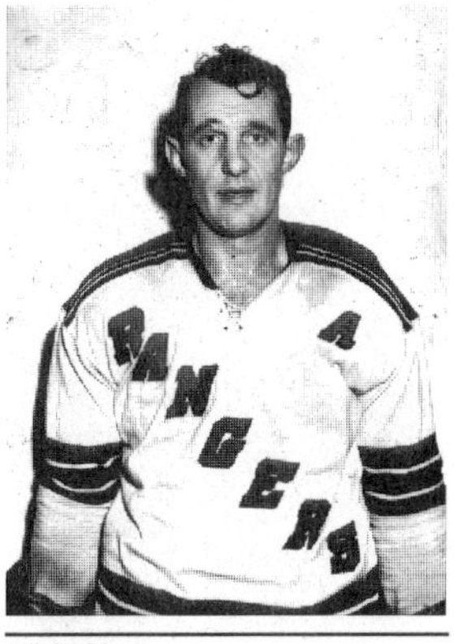

Bill Gadsby

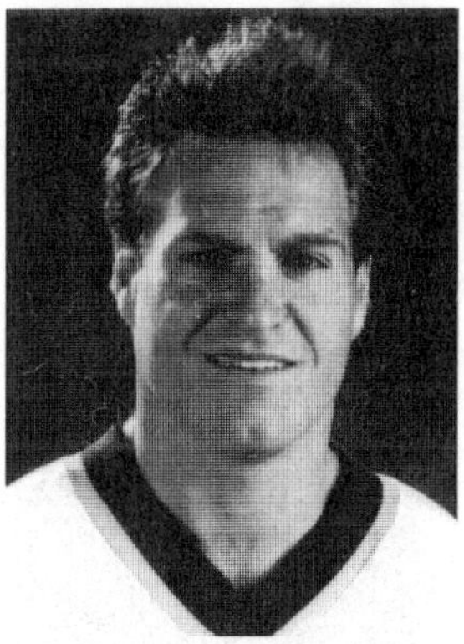
Greg Gilbert

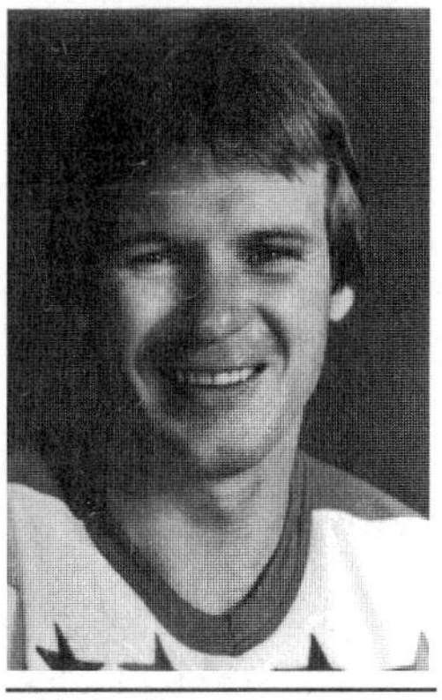
Bobby Gould

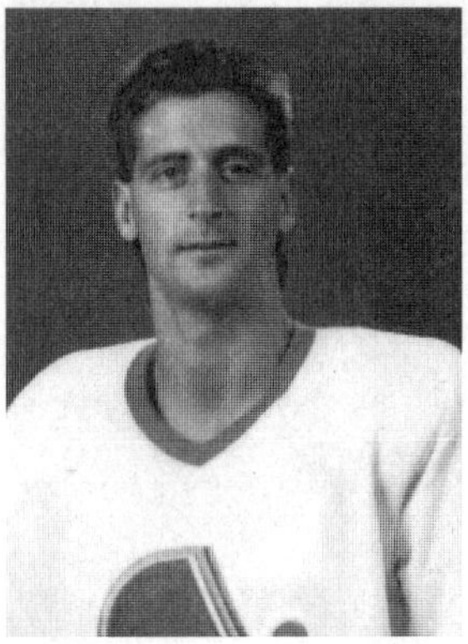

Stephane Guerard

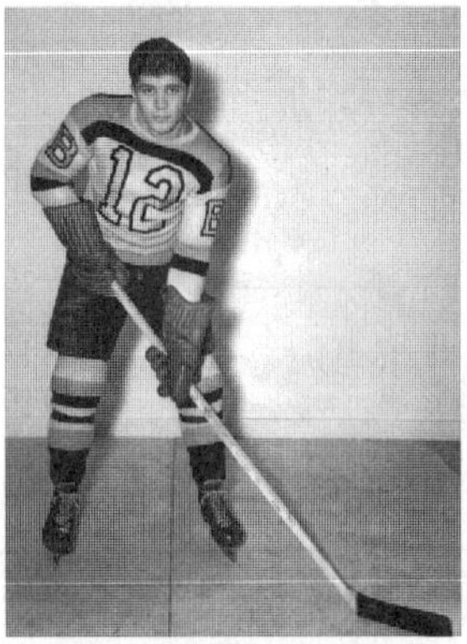

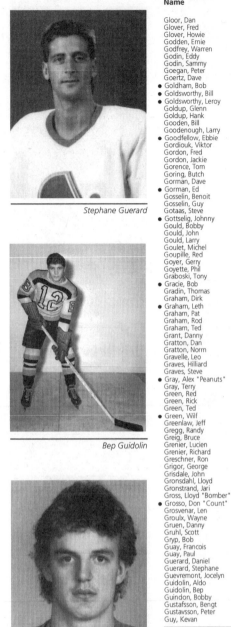

Bep Guidolin

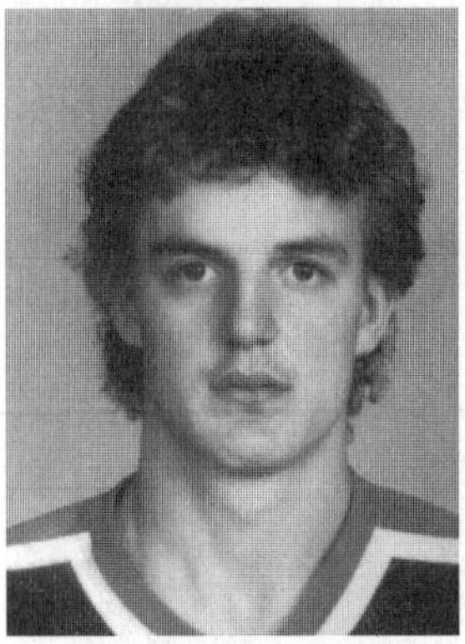

Marc Habscheid

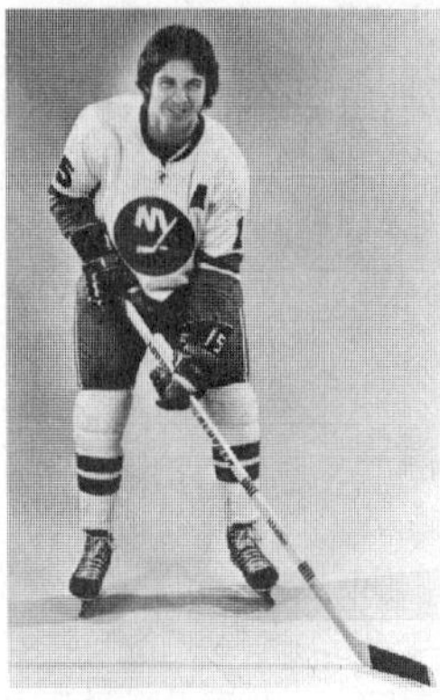

Billy Harris

Name	NHL Teams	NHL Seasons	Regular Schedule GP	G	A	TP	PIM	Playoffs GP	G	A	TP	PIM	NHL Cup Wins	First NHL Season	Last NHL Season
Gloor, Dan	Van.	1	2	0	0	0	0	....	....	....	....	....		1973-74	1973-74
Glover, Fred	Det., Chi.	5	92	13	11	24	62	8	0	0	0	0	1	1948-49	1952-53
Glover, Howie	Chi., Det., NYR, Mtl.	5	144	29	17	46	101	11	1	2	3	2		1958-59	1968-69
Godden, Ernie	Tor.	1	5	1	1	2	6	....	....	....	....	....		1981-82	1981-82
Godfrey, Warren	Bos., Det.	16	786	32	125	157	752	52	1	4	5	42		1952-53	1967-68
Godin, Eddy	Wsh.	2	27	3	6	9	12	....	....	....	....	....		1977-78	1978-79
Godin, Sammy	Ott., Mtl.	3	83	4	3	7	36	....	....	....	....	....		1927-28	1933-34
Goegan, Peter	Det., NYR, Min.	11	383	19	67	86	365	33	1	3	4	61		1957-58	1967-68
Goertz, Dave	Pit.	1	2	0	0	0	2	....	....	....	....	....		1987-88	1987-88
• Goldham, Bob	Tor., Chi., Det.	12	650	28	143	171	400	66	3	14	17	53	5	1941-42	1955-56
• Goldsworthy, Bill	Bos., Min., NYR	14	771	283	258	541	793	40	18	19	37	30		1964-65	1977-78
• Goldsworthy, Leroy	NYR, Det., Chi., Mtl., Bos., NYA	10	337	66	57	123	79	24	1	0	1	4	1	1929-30	1938-39
Goldup, Glenn	Mtl., L.A.	9	291	52	67	119	303	16	4	3	7	22		1973-74	1981-82
Goldup, Hank	Tor., NYR	6	202	63	80	143	97	26	5	1	6	6	1	1939-40	1945-46
Gooden, Bill	NYR	2	53	9	11	20	15	....	....	....	....	....		1942-43	1943-44
Goodenough, Larry	Phi., Van.	6	242	22	77	99	179	22	3	15	18	10	1	1974-75	1979-80
• Goodfellow, Ebbie	Det.	14	557	134	190	324	511	45	8	8	16	65	3	1929-30	1942-43
Gordiouk, Viktor	Buf.	2	26	3	8	11	0	....	....	....	....	....		1992-93	1994-95
Gordon, Fred	Det., Bos.	2	81	8	7	15	68	2	0	0	0	0		1926-27	1927-28
Gordon, Jackie	NYR	3	36	3	10	13	0	9	1	1	2	7		1948-49	1950-51
Gorence, Tom	Phi., Edm.	6	303	58	53	111	89	37	9	6	15	47		1978-79	1983-84
Goring, Butch	L.A., NYI, Bos.	16	1107	375	513	888	102	134	38	50	88	32	4	1969-70	1984-85
Gorman, Dave	Atl.	1	3	0	0	0	0	....	....	....	....	....		1979-80	1979-80
• Gorman, Ed	Ott., Tor.	4	113	14	5	19	108	8	0	0	0	2	1	1924-25	1927-28
Gosselin, Benoit	NYR	1	7	0	0	0	33	....	....	....	....	....		1977-78	1977-78
Gosselin, Guy	Wpg.	1	5	0	0	0	6	....	....	....	....	....		1987-88	1987-88
Gotaas, Steve	Pit., Min.	3	49	6	9	15	53	3	0	1	1	5		1987-88	1990-91
• Gottselig, Johnny	Chi.	16	589	176	195	371	203	43	13	13	26	18	2	1928-29	1944-45
Gould, Bobby	Atl., Cgy., Wsh., Bos.	11	697	145	159	304	572	78	15	13	28	58		1979-80	1989-90
Gould, John	Buf., Van., Atl.	9	504	131	138	269	113	14	3	2	5	4		1971-72	1979-80
Gould, Larry	Van.	1	2	0	0	0	0	....	....	....	....	....		1973-74	1973-74
Goulet, Michel	Que., Chi.	15	1089	548	604	1152	825	92	39	39	78	110		1979-80	1993-94
Goupille, Red	Mtl.	8	222	12	28	40	256	8	2	0	2	6		1935-36	1942-43
Goyer, Gerry	Chi.	1	40	1	2	3	4	3	0	0	0	2		1967-68	1967-68
Goyette, Phil	Mtl., NYR, St.L., Buf.	16	941	207	467	674	131	94	17	29	46	26	4	1956-57	1971-72
Graboski, Tony	Mtl.	3	66	6	10	16	24	3	0	0	0	6		1940-41	1942-43
• Gracie, Bob	Tor., Bos., NYA, Mtl.M., Mtl., Chi.	9	379	82	109	191	205	33	4	7	11	4	2	1930-31	1938-39
Gradin, Thomas	Van., Bos.	9	677	209	384	593	298	42	17	25	42	20		1978-79	1986-87
Graham, Dirk	Min., Chi.	12	772	219	270	489	917	90	17	27	44	92		1983-84	1994-95
• Graham, Leth	Ott., Ham.	6	26	3	0	3	0	1	0	0	0	0	1	1920-21	1925-26
Graham, Pat	Pit., Tor.	3	103	11	17	28	136	4	0	0	0	2		1981-82	1983-84
Graham, Rod	Bos.	1	14	2	1	3	7	....	....	....	....	....		1974-75	1974-75
Graham, Ted	Chi., Mtl.M., Det., St.L., Bos., NYA	9	343	14	25	39	300	23	3	1	4	34		1927-28	1936-37
Grant, Danny	Mtl., Min., Det., L.A.	13	736	263	273	536	239	43	10	14	24	19	1	1965-66	1978-79
Gratton, Dan	L.A.	1	7	1	0	1	5	....	....	....	....	....		1987-88	1987-88
Gratton, Norm	NYR, Atl., Buf., Min.	5	201	39	44	83	64	6	0	1	1	2		1971-72	1975-76
Gravelle, Leo	Mtl., Det.	5	223	44	34	78	42	17	4	1	5	2		1946-47	1950-51
Graves, Hilliard	Cal., Atl., Van., Wpg.	9	556	118	163	281	209	2	0	0	0	0		1970-71	1979-80
Graves, Steve	Edm.	3	35	5	4	9	10	....	....	....	....	....		1983-84	1987-88
• Gray, Alex "Peanuts"	NYR, Tor.	2	50	7	0	7	32	13	1	0	1	0	1	1927-28	1928-29
Gray, Terry	Bos., Mtl., L.A., St.L.	6	147	26	28	54	64	35	5	5	10	22		1961-62	1970-71
Green, Red	Ham., NYA, Bos., Det.	6	195	59	13	72	261	1	0	0	0	0	1	1923-24	1928-29
Green, Rick	Wsh., Mtl., Det., NYI	15	845	43	220	263	588	100	3	16	19	73	1	1976-77	1991-92
Green, Ted	Bos.	11	620	48	206	254	1029	31	4	8	12	54	1	1960-61	1971-72
• Green, Wilf	Ham., NYA	4	103	33	8	41	151	....	....	....	....	....		1923-24	1926-27
Greenlaw, Jeff	Wsh., Fla.	6	57	3	6	9	108	2	0	0	0	21		1986-87	1993-94
Gregg, Randy	Edm., Van.	10	474	41	152	193	333	137	13	38	51	127	5	1981-82	1991-92
Greig, Bruce	Cal.	2	9	0	1	1	46	....	....	....	....	....		1973-74	1974-75
Grenier, Lucien	Mtl., L.A.	4	151	14	14	28	18	2	0	0	0	0	1	1968-69	1971-72
Grenier, Richard	NYI	1	10	1	1	2	2	....	....	....	....	....		1972-73	1972-73
Greschner, Ron	NYR	16	982	179	431	610	1226	84	17	32	49	106		1974-75	1989-90
Grigor, George	Chi.	1	2	1	0	1	0	1	0	0	0	0		1943-44	1943-44
Grisdale, John	Tor., Van.	6	250	4	39	43	346	10	0	1	1	15		1972-73	1978-79
Gronsdahl, Lloyd	Bos.	1	10	1	2	3	0	....	....	....	....	....		1941-42	1941-42
Gronstrand, Jari	Min., NYR, Que., NYI	5	185	8	26	34	135	3	0	0	0	4		1986-87	1990-91
Gross, Lloyd "Bomber"	Tor., NYA, Bos., Det.	3	62	11	5	16	20	1	0	0	0	0		1926-27	1934-35
• Grosso, Don "Count"	Det., Chi., Bos.	9	336	87	117	204	90	49	15	14	29	63	1	1938-39	1946-47
Grosvenar, Len	Ott., NYA, Mtl.	6	147	9	11	20	78	4	0	0	0	2		1927-28	1932-33
Groulx, Wayne	Que.	1	1	0	0	0	0	....	....	....	....	....		1984-85	1984-85
Gruen, Danny	Det., Col.	3	49	9	13	22	19	....	....	....	....	....		1972-73	1976-77
Gruhl, Scott	L.A., Pit.	3	20	3	3	6	6	....	....	....	....	....		1981-82	1987-88
Gryp, Bob	Bos., Wsh.	3	74	11	13	24	33	....	....	....	....	....		1973-74	1975-76
Guay, Francois	Buf.	1	1	0	0	0	0	....	....	....	....	....		1989-90	1989-90
Guay, Paul	Phi., L.A., Bos., NYI	7	117	11	23	34	92	9	0	1	1	12		1983-84	1990-91
Guerard, Daniel	Ott.	1	2	0	0	0	0	....	....	....	....	....		1994-95	1994-95
Guerard, Stephane	Que.	2	34	0	0	0	40	....	....	....	....	....		1987-88	1989-90
Guevremont, Jocelyn	Van., Buf., NYR	9	571	84	223	307	319	40	4	17	21	18		1971-72	1979-80
Guidolin, Aldo	NYR	4	182	9	15	24	117	....	....	....	....	....		1952-53	1955-56
Guidolin, Bep	Bos., Det., Chi.	9	519	107	171	278	606	24	5	7	12	35		1942-43	1951-52
Guindon, Bobby	Wpg.	1	6	0	1	1	0	....	....	....	....	....		1979-80	1979-80
Gustafsson, Bengt	Wsh.	9	629	196	359	555	196	32	9	19	28	16		1979-80	1988-89
Gustavsson, Peter	Col.	1	2	0	0	0	0	....	....	....	....	....		1981-82	1981-82
Guy, Kevan	Cgy., Van.	6	156	5	20	25	138	5	0	1	1	23		1986-87	1991-92

H

Name	NHL Teams	NHL Seasons	Regular Schedule GP	G	A	TP	PIM	Playoffs GP	G	A	TP	PIM	NHL Cup Wins	First NHL Season	Last NHL Season
Haanpaa, Ari	NYI	3	60	6	11	17	37	6	0	0	0	10		1985-86	1987-88
Haas, David	Edm., Cgy.	2	7	2	1	3	7	....	....	....	....	....		1990-91	1993-94
Habscheid, Marc	Edm., Min., Det., Cgy.	11	345	72	91	163	171	12	1	3	4	13		1981-82	1991-92
Hachborn, Len	Phi., L.A.	3	102	20	39	59	29	7	0	3	3	7		1983-84	1985-86
Haddon, Lloyd	Det.	1	8	0	0	0	2	1	0	0	0	0		1959-60	1959-60
Hadfield, Vic	NYR, Pit.	16	1002	323	389	712	1154	73	27	21	48	117		1961-62	1976-77
Haggarty, Jim	Mtl.	1	5	1	1	2	0	3	2	1	3	0		1941-42	1941-42
• Hagglund, Roger	Que.	1	3	0	0	0	0	....	....	....	....	....		1984-85	1984-85
Hagman, Matti	Bos., Edm.	4	237	56	89	145	36	20	5	2	7	6		1976-77	1981-82
Haidy, Gord	Det.	1	....	....	....	....	....	1	0	0	0	0	1	1949-50	1949-50
Hajdu, Richard	Buf.	2	5	0	0	0	4	....	....	....	....	....		1985-86	1986-87
Hajt, Bill	Buf.	14	854	42	202	244	433	80	2	16	18	70		1973-74	1986-87
Hakansson, Anders	Min., Pit., L.A.	5	330	52	46	98	141	6	0	0	0	2		1981-82	1985-86
• Halderson, Slim	Det., Tor.	1	44	3	2	5	65	....	....	....	....	....		1926-27	1926-27
Hale, Larry	Phi.	4	196	5	37	42	90	8	0	0	0	12		1968-69	1971-72
Haley, Len	Det.	2	30	2	2	4	14	6	1	3	4	6		1959-60	1960-61
Hall, Bob	NYA	1	8	0	0	0	0	....	....	....	....	....		1925-26	1925-26
Hall, Del	Cal.	3	9	2	0	2	2	....	....	....	....	....		1971-72	1973-74
• Hall, Joe	Mtl.	2	37	15	1	16	145	12	0	2	2	31		1917-18	1918-19
Hall, Murray	Chi., Det., Min., Van.	9	164	35	48	83	46	6	0	0	0	0		1961-62	1971-72
Hall, Taylor	Van., Bos.	5	41	7	9	16	29	....	....	....	....	....		1983-84	1987-88
Hall, Wayne	NYR	1	4	0	0	0	0	....	....	....	....	....		1960-61	1960-61
• Halliday, Milt	Ott.	3	67	1	0	1	4	6	0	0	0	0	1	1926-27	1928-29
Hallin, Mats	NYI, Min.	5	152	17	14	31	193	15	1	0	1	13	1	1982-83	1986-87
Halward, Doug	Bos., L.A., Van., Det., Edm.	14	653	69	224	293	774	47	7	10	17	113		1975-76	1988-89
Hamel, Gilles	Buf., Wpg., L.A.	9	519	127	147	274	276	27	4	5	9	10		1980-81	1988-89
Hamel, Herb	Tor.	1	4	0	0	0	14	....	....	....	....	....		1930-31	1930-31
Hamel, Jean	St.L., Det., Que., Mtl.	12	699	26	95	121	766	33	0	2	2	44		1972-73	1983-84
• Hamill, Red	Bos., Chi.	12	419	128	94	222	160	24	1	2	3	20	2	1937-38	1950-51
Hamilton, Al	NYR, Buf., Edm.	7	257	10	78	88	258	7	0	0	0	2		1965-66	1979-80
Hamilton, Chuck	Mtl., St.L.	2	4	0	2	2	2	....	....	....	....	....		1961-62	1972-73
• Hamilton, Jack	Tor.	3	138	31	48	79	76	11	2	1	3	0		1942-43	1945-46
Hamilton, Jim	Pit.	8	95	14	18	32	28	6	3	0	3	0		1977-78	1984-85
• Hamilton, Reg	Tor., Chi.	12	424	21	87	108	412	57	3	8	11	46	2	1935-36	1946-47
Hammarstrom, Inge	Tor., St.L.	6	427	116	123	239	86	13	2	3	5	4		1973-74	1978-79
Hammond, Ken	L.A., Edm., NYR, Tor., Bos., S.J., Van., Ott.	8	193	18	29	47	290	15	0	0	0	24		1984-85	1992-93

Name	NHL Teams	NHL Seasons	Regular Schedule GP	G	A	TP	PIM	Playoffs GP	G	A	TP	PIM	NHL Cup Wins	First NHL Season	Last NHL Season
Hampson, Gord	Cgy.	1	4	0	0	0	5	....	....	....	....	....		1982-83	1982-83
Hampson, Ted	Tor., NYR, Det., Oak., Cal., Min.	12	676	108	245	353	94	35	7	10	17	2		1959-60	1971-72
Hampton, Rick	Cal., Cle., L.A.	6	337	59	113	172	147	2	0	0	0	0		1974-75	1979-80
Hamr, Radek	Ott.	2	11	0	0	0	0	....	....	....	....	....		1992-93	1993-94
Hamway, Mark	NYI	3	53	5	13	18	9	1	0	0	0	0		1984-85	1986-87
Handy, Ron	NYI, St.L.	2	14	0	3	3	0	....	....	....	....	....		1984-85	1987-88
Hangsleben, Al	Hfd., Wsh., L.A.	3	185	21	48	69	396	....	....	....	....	....		1979-80	1981-82
Hanna, John	NYR, Mtl., Phi.	5	198	6	26	32	206	....	....	....	....	....		1958-59	1967-68
• Hannigan, Gord	Tor.	4	161	29	31	60	117	9	2	0	2	8		1952-53	1955-56
Hannigan, Pat	Tor., NYR, Phi.	5	182	30	39	69	116	11	1	2	3	11		1959-60	1968-69
Hannigan, Ray	Tor.	1	3	0	0	0	2	....	....	....	....	....		1948-49	1948-49
Hansen, Ritchie	NYI, St.L.	4	20	2	8	10	4	....	....	....	....	....		1976-77	1981-82
Hanson, Dave	Det., Min.	2	33	1	1	2	65	....	....	....	....	....		1978-79	1979-80
Hanson, Emil	Det.	1	7	0	0	0	6	....	....	....	....	....		1932-33	1932-33
Hanson, Keith	Cgy.	1	25	0	2	2	77	....	....	....	....	....		1983-84	1983-84
Hanson, Ossie	Chi.	1	7	0	0	0	0	....	....	....	....	....		1937-38	1937-38
Harbaruk, Nick	Pit., St.L.	5	364	45	75	120	273	14	3	1	4	20		1969-70	1973-74
Harding, Jeff	Phi.	2	15	0	0	0	47	....	....	....	....	....		1988-89	1989-90
Hardy, Joe	Oak., Cal.	2	63	9	14	23	51	4	0	0	0	0		1969-70	1970-71
Hardy, Mark	L.A., NYR, Min.	15	915	62	306	368	1293	67	5	16	21	158		1979-80	1993-94
Hargreaves, Jim	Van.	2	66	1	7	8	105	....	....	....	....	....		1970-71	1972-73
Harlow, Scott	St.L.	1	1	0	1	1	0	....	....	....	....	....		1987-88	1987-88
Harmon, Glen	Mtl.	9	452	50	96	146	334	53	5	10	15	37	2	1942-43	1950-51
Harms, John	Chi.	2	44	5	5	10	21	3	3	0	3	2		1943-44	1944-45
Harnott, Happy	Bos.	1	6	0	0	0	6	....	....	....	....	....		1933-34	1933-34
Harper, Terry	Mtl., L.A., Det., St.L., Col.	19	1066	35	221	256	1362	112	4	13	17	140	5	1962-63	1980-81
Harrer, Tim	Cgy.	1	3	0	0	0	2	....	....	....	....	....		1982-83	1982-83
• Harrington, Hago	Bos., Mtl.	3	72	9	3	12	15	4	1	0	1	2		1925-26	1932-33
Harris, Billy	Tor., Det., Oak., Cal., Pit.	13	769	126	219	345	205	62	8	10	18	30	3	1955-56	1968-69
Harris, Billy	NYI, L.A., Tor.	12	897	231	327	558	394	71	19	19	38	48		1972-73	1983-84
Harris, Duke	Min., Tor.	1	26	1	4	5	4	....	....	....	....	....		1967-68	1967-68
Harris, Hugh	Buf.	1	60	12	26	38	17	3	0	0	0	0		1972-73	1972-73
Harris, Ron	Det., Oak., Atl., NYR	11	476	20	91	111	474	28	4	3	7	33		1962-63	1975-76
Harris, Smokey	Bos.	2	40	5	5	10	28	2	0	0	0	0		1924-25	1930-31
Harris, Ted	Mtl., Min., Det., St.L., Phi.	12	788	30	168	198	1000	100	1	22	23	230	5	1963-64	1974-75
Harrison, Ed	Bos., NYR	4	194	27	24	51	53	9	1	0	1	2		1947-48	1950-51
Harrison, Jim	Bos., Tor., Chi., Edm.	8	324	67	86	153	435	13	1	1	2	43		1968-69	1979-80
Hart, Gerry	Det., NYI, Que., St.L.	15	730	29	150	179	1240	78	3	12	15	175		1968-69	1982-83
• Hart, Gizzy	Det., Mtl.	3	96	6	8	14	12	8	0	1	1	0		1926-27	1932-33
Hartsburg, Craig	Min.	10	570	98	315	413	818	61	15	27	42	70		1979-80	1988-89
• Harvey, Doug	Mtl., NYR, Det., St.L.	20	1113	88	452	540	1216	137	8	64	72	152	6	1947-48	1968-69
Harvey, Fred	Min., Atl., K.C., Det.	7	407	90	118	208	131	14	0	2	2	8		1970-71	1976-77
Harvey, Hugh	K.C.	2	18	1	1	2	4	....	....	....	....	....		1974-75	1975-76
Hassard, Bob	Tor., Chi.	5	126	9	28	37	22	....	....	....	....	....		1949-50	1954-55
Hatoum, Ed	Det., Van.	3	47	3	6	9	25	....	....	....	....	....		1968-69	1970-71
Haworth, Alan	Buf., Wsh., Que.	8	524	189	211	400	425	42	12	16	28	28		1980-81	1987-88
Haworth, Gord	NYR	1	2	0	1	1	0	....	....	....	....	....		1952-53	1952-53
Hawryliw, Neil	NYI	1	1	0	0	0	0	....	....	....	....	....		1981-82	1981-82
Hay, Bill	Chi.	8	506	113	273	386	244	67	15	21	36	62		1959-60	1966-67
• Hay, George	Chi., Det.	7	242	74	60	134	84	8	2	3	5	2		1926-27	1933-34
Hay, Jim	Det.	3	75	1	5	6	22	9	1	0	1	2	1	1952-53	1954-55
Hayek, Peter	Min.	1	1	0	0	0	0	....	....	....	....	....		1981-82	1981-82
Hayes, Chris	Bos.	1	....	....	....	....	....	1	0	0	0	0	1	1971-72	1971-72
Haynes, Paul	Mtl.M., Bos., Mtl.	11	391	61	134	195	164	23	2	8	10	13		1930-31	1940-41
Hayward, Rick	L.A.	1	4	0	0	0	5	....	....	....	....	....		1990-91	1990-91
Hazlett, Steve	Van.	1	1	0	0	0	0	....	....	....	....	....		1979-80	1979-80
Head, Galen	Det.	1	1	0	0	0	0	....	....	....	....	....		1967-68	1967-68
Headley, Fern	Bos., Mtl.	1	27	1	1	2	6	5	0	0	0	0		1924-25	1924-25
Healey, Dick	Det.	1	1	0	0	0	2	....	....	....	....	....		1960-61	1960-61
Heaphy, Shawn	Cgy.	1	1	0	0	0	0	....	....	....	....	....		1992-93	1992-93
Heaslip, Mark	NYR, L.A.	3	117	10	19	29	110	5	0	0	0	2		1976-77	1978-79
Heath, Randy	NYR	2	13	2	4	6	15	....	....	....	....	....		1984-85	1985-86
Hebenton, Andy	NYR, Bos.	9	630	189	202	391	83	22	6	5	11	8		1955-56	1963-64
Hedberg, Anders	NYR	7	465	172	225	397	144	58	22	24	46	31		1978-79	1984-85
• Heffernan, Frank	Tor.	1	17	0	0	0	4	....	....	....	....	....		1919-20	1919-20
Heffernan, Gerry	Mtl.	3	83	33	35	68	27	11	3	3	6	8	1	1941-42	1943-44
Heidt, Mike	L.A.	1	6	0	1	1	7	....	....	....	....	....		1983-84	1983-84
• Heindl, Bill	Min., NYR	3	18	2	1	3	0	....	....	....	....	....		1970-71	1972-73
Heinrich, Lionel	Bos.	1	35	1	1	2	33	....	....	....	....	....		1955-56	1955-56
Heiskala, Earl	Phi.	3	127	13	11	24	294	....	....	....	....	....		1968-69	1970-71
Helander, Peter	L.A.	1	7	0	1	1	0	....	....	....	....	....		1982-83	1982-83
• Heller, Ott	NYR	15	647	55	176	231	465	61	6	8	14	61	2	1931-32	1945-46
Helman, Harry	Ott.	4	43	1	0	1	7	5	0	0	0	0	1	1922-23	1924-25
Helminen, Raimo	NYR, Min., NYI	3	117	13	46	59	16	2	0	0	0	0		1985-86	1988-89
Hemmerling, Tony	NYA	2	24	3	3	6	4	....	....	....	....	....		1935-36	1936-37
Henderson, Archie	Wsh., Min., Hfd.	3	23	3	1	4	92	....	....	....	....	....		1980-81	1982-83
Henderson, Murray	Bos.	8	405	24	62	86	305	41	2	3	5	23		1944-45	1951-52
Henderson, Paul	Det., Tor., Atl.	13	707	236	241	477	304	56	11	14	25	28		1962-63	1979-80
Hendrickson, John	Det.	3	5	0	0	0	4	....	....	....	....	....		1957-58	1961-62
Henning, Lorne	NYI	9	544	73	111	184	102	81	7	7	14	8	2	1972-73	1980-81
Henry, Camille	NYR, Chi., St.L.	14	727	279	249	528	88	47	6	12	18	7		1953-54	1969-70
Henry, Dale	NYI	6	132	13	26	39	263	14	1	0	1	19		1984-85	1989-90
Hepple, Alan	N.J.	3	3	0	0	0	7	....	....	....	....	....		1983-84	1985-86
• Herberts, Jimmy	Bos., Tor., Det.	6	216	83	26	109	263	9	3	0	3	10		1924-25	1929-30
Herchenratter, Art	Det.	1	10	1	2	3	2	....	....	....	....	....		1940-41	1940-41
Hergerts, Fred	NYA	2	20	2	4	6	2	....	....	....	....	....		1934-35	1935-36
Hergesheimer, Philip	Chi., Bos.	4	125	21	41	62	19	7	0	0	0	2		1939-40	1942-43
Hergesheimer, Wally	NYR, Chi.	7	351	114	85	199	106	5	1	0	1	0		1951-52	1958-59
Heron, Red	Tor., Bro., Mtl.	4	106	21	19	40	38	21	2	2	4	6		1938-39	1941-42
Heroux, Yves	Que.	1	1	0	0	0	0	....	....	....	....	....		1986-87	1986-87
Hervey, Matt	Wpg., Bos., T.B.	3	35	0	5	5	97	5	0	0	0	6		1988-89	1992-93
Hess, Bob	St.L., Buf., Hfd.	8	329	27	95	122	178	4	1	1	2	2		1974-75	1983-84
Heximer, Orville	NYR, Bos., NYA	3	85	13	7	20	28	5	0	0	0	2		1929-30	1934-35
Hextall, Bryan Jr.	NYR, Pit., Atl., Det., Min.	8	549	99	161	260	738	18	0	4	4	59		1962-63	1975-76
• Hextall, Bryan Sr.	NYR	11	449	187	175	362	227	37	8	9	17	19	1	1936-37	1947-48
Hextall, Dennis	NYR, L.A., Cal., Min., Det., Wsh.	13	681	153	350	503	1398	22	3	3	6	45		1968-69	1979-80
Heyliger, Vic	Chi.	2	34	2	3	5	2	....	....	....	....	....		1937-38	1943-44
Hicke, Bill	Mtl., NYR, Oak., Cal., Pit.	14	729	168	234	402	395	42	3	10	13	41	2	1958-59	1971-72
Hicke, Ernie	Cal., Atl., NYI, Min., L.A.	8	520	132	140	272	407	2	1	0	1	0		1970-71	1977-78
Hickey, Greg	NYR	1	1	0	0	0	0	....	....	....	....	....		1977-78	1977-78
Hickey, Pat	NYR, Col., Tor., Que., St.L.	10	646	192	212	404	351	55	5	11	16	37		1975-76	1984-85
Hicks, Doug	Min., Chi., Edm., Wsh.	9	561	37	131	168	442	18	2	1	3	15		1974-75	1982-83
Hicks, Glenn	Det.	2	108	6	12	18	127	....	....	....	....	....		1979-80	1980-81
• Hicks, Hal	Mtl.M., Det.	3	110	7	2	9	72	....	....	....	....	....		1928-29	1930-31
Hicks, Wayne	Chi., Bos., Mtl., Phi., Pit.	5	115	13	23	36	22	2	0	1	1	2	1	1959-60	1967-68
Hidi, Andre	Wsh.	2	7	2	1	3	9	2	0	0	0	0		1983-84	1984-85
Hiemer, Uli	N.J.	3	143	19	54	73	176	....	....	....	....	....		1984-85	1986-87
Higgins, Paul	Tor.	2	25	0	0	0	152	1	0	0	0	0		1981-82	1982-83
Higgins, Tim	Chi., N.J., Det.	11	706	154	198	352	719	65	5	8	13	77		1978-79	1988-89
Hildebrand, Ike	NYR, Chi.	2	41	7	11	18	16	....	....	....	....	....		1953-54	1954-55
Hill, Al	Phi.	8	221	40	55	95	227	51	8	11	19	43		1976-77	1987-88
Hill, Brian	Hfd.	1	19	1	1	2	4	....	....	....	....	....		1979-80	1979-80
• Hill, Mel	Bos., Bro., Tor.	9	324	89	109	198	128	43	12	7	19	18	3	1937-38	1945-46
Hiller, Dutch	NYR, Det., Bos., Mtl.	9	383	91	113	204	163	48	9	8	17	21	2	1937-38	1945-46
Hiller, Jim	L.A., Det., NYR	2	63	8	12	20	116	2	0	0	0	4		1992-93	1993-94
Hillier, Randy	Bos., Pit., NYI, Buf.	11	543	16	110	126	906	28	0	2	2	93	1	1981-82	1991-92
Hillman, Floyd	Bos.	1	6	0	0	0	10	....	....	....	....	....		1956-57	1956-57
Hillman, Larry	Det., Bos., Tor., Min., Mtl., Phi., L.A., Buf.	19	790	36	196	232	579	74	2	9	11	30	6	1954-55	1972-73
• Hillman, Wayne	Chi., NYR, Min., Phi.	13	691	18	86	104	534	28	0	3	3	19	1	1960-61	1972-73
Hilworth, John	Det.	3	57	1	1	2	89	....	....	....	....	....		1977-78	1979-80
Himes, Normie	NYA	9	402	106	113	219	127	2	0	0	0	0		1926-27	1934-35
Hindmarch, Dave	Cgy.	4	99	21	17	38	25	10	0	0	0	6		1980-81	1983-84
Hinse, Andre	Tor.	1	4	0	0	0	0	....	....	....	....	....		1967-68	1967-68

Doug Harvey

Wally Hergesheimer

Bryan Hextall, Sr.

Andre Hidi

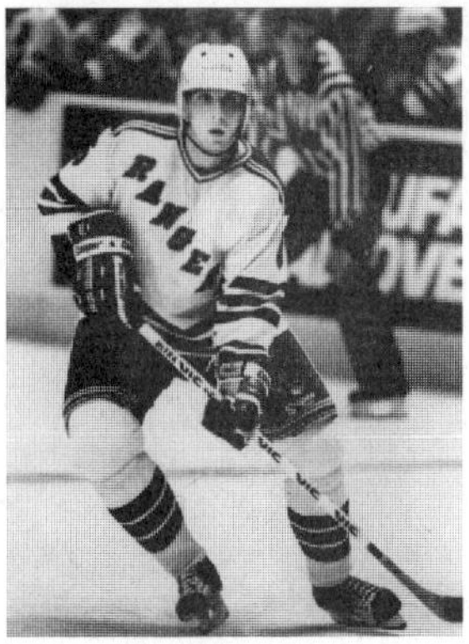

Miloslav Horava

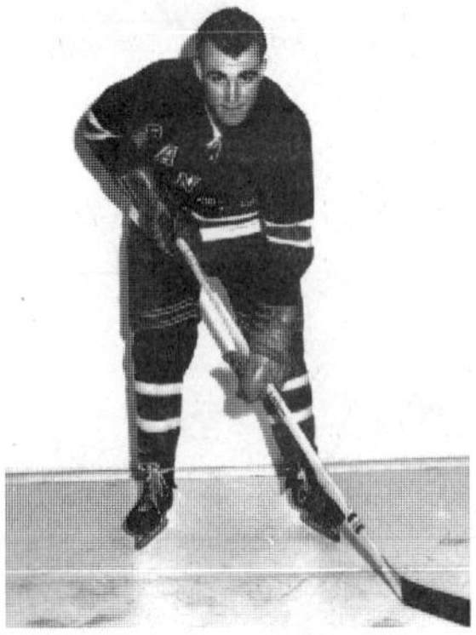

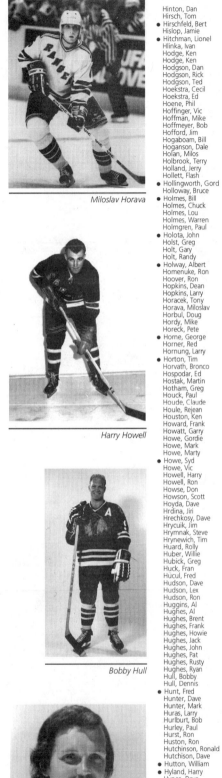

Harry Howell

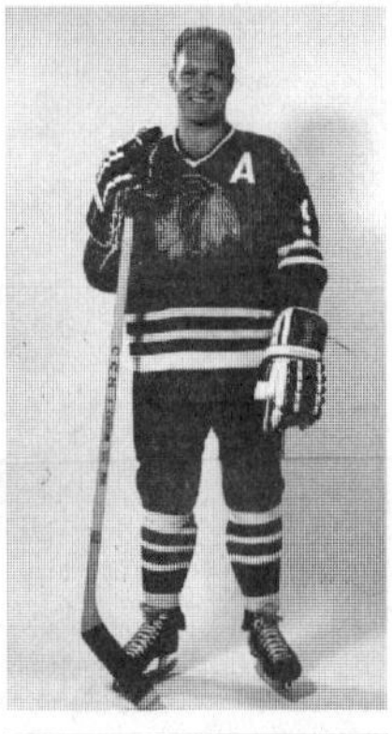

Bobby Hull

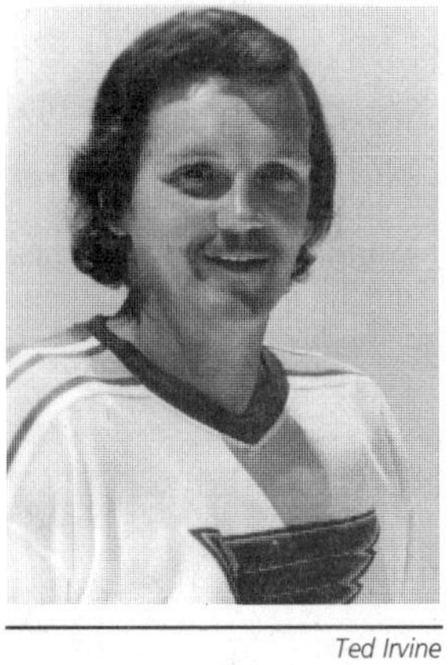

Ted Irvine

			Regular Schedule					Playoffs					NHL	First	Last
Name	NHL Teams	NHL Seasons	GP	G	A	TP	PIM	GP	G	A	TP	PIM	Cup Wins	NHL Season	NHL Season
Hinton, Dan	Chi.	1	14	0	0	0	16	....	....	....	....	....		1976-77	1976-77
Hirsch, Tom	Min.	3	31	1	7	8	30	12	0	0	0	6		1983-84	1987-88
• Hirschfeld, Bert	Mtl.	2	33	1	4	5	2	5	1	0	1	0		1949-50	1950-51
Hislop, Jamie	Que., Cgy.	5	345	75	103	178	86	28	3	2	5	11		1979-80	1983-84
• Hitchman, Lionel	Ott., Bos.	12	416	28	33	61	523	40	4	1	5	77	2	1922-23	1933-34
Hlinka, Ivan	Van.	2	137	42	81	123	28	16	3	10	13	8		1981-82	1982-83
Hodge, Ken	Min., Bos., T.B.	4	142	39	48	87	32	15	4	6	10	6		1988-89	1992-93
Hodge, Ken	Chi., Bos., NYR	14	881	328	472	800	779	97	34	47	81	120	2	1965-66	1977-78
Hodgson, Dan	Tor., Van.	4	114	29	45	74	64	....	....	....	....	....		1985-86	1988-89
Hodgson, Rick	Hfd.	1	6	0	0	0	6	1	0	0	0	0		1979-80	1979-80
Hodgson, Ted	Bos.	1	4	0	0	0	0	....	....	....	....	....		1966-67	1966-67
Hoekstra, Cecil	Mtl.	1	4	0	0	0	0	....	....	....	....	....		1959-60	1959-60
Hoekstra, Ed	Phi.	1	70	15	21	36	6	7	0	1	1	0		1967-68	1967-68
Hoene, Phil	L.A.	3	37	2	4	6	22	....	....	....	....	....		1972-73	1974-75
Hoffinger, Vic	Chi.	2	28	0	1	1	30	....	....	....	....	....		1927-28	1928-29
Hoffman, Mike	Hfd.	3	9	1	3	4	2	....	....	....	....	....		1982-83	1985-86
Hoffmeyer, Bob	Chi., Phi., N.J.	6	198	14	52	66	325	3	0	1	1	25		1977-78	1984-85
Hofford, Jim	Buf., L.A.	3	18	0	0	0	47	....	....	....	....	....		1985-86	1988-89
Hogaboam, Bill	Atl., Det., Min.	8	332	80	109	189	100	2	0	0	0	0		1972-73	1979-80
Hoganson, Dale	L.A., Mtl., Que.	7	343	13	77	90	186	11	0	3	3	12		1969-70	1981-82
Holan, Milos	Phi., Ana.	3	49	5	11	16	42	....	....	....	....	....		1993-94	1995-96
Holbrook, Terry	Min.	2	43	3	6	9	4	6	0	0	0	0		1972-73	1973-74
Holland, Jerry	NYR	2	37	8	4	12	6	....	....	....	....	....		1974-75	1975-76
Hollett, Flash	Tor., Ott., Bos., Det.	13	562	132	181	313	358	79	8	26	34	38	2	1933-34	1945-46
• Hollingworth, Gord	Chi., Det.	4	163	4	14	18	201	3	0	0	0	2		1954-55	1957-58
Holloway, Bruce	Van.	1	2	0	0	0	0	....	....	....	....	....		1984-85	1984-85
• Holmes, Bill	Mtl., NYA.	3	52	6	4	10	35	....	....	....	....	....		1925-26	1929-30
Holmes, Chuck	Det.	2	23	1	3	4	10	....	....	....	....	....		1958-59	1961-62
Holmes, Lou	Chi.	2	59	1	4	5	6	2	0	0	0	2		1931-32	1932-33
Holmes, Warren	L.A.	3	45	8	18	26	7	....	....	....	....	....		1981-82	1983-84
Holmgren, Paul	Phi., Min.	10	527	144	179	323	1684	82	19	32	51	195		1975-76	1984-85
• Holota, John	Det.	2	15	2	0	2	0	....	....	....	....	....		1942-43	1945-46
Holst, Greg	NYR	3	11	0	0	0	0	....	....	....	....	....		1975-76	1977-78
Holt, Gary	Cal., Clev., St.L.	5	101	13	11	24	133	....	....	....	....	....		1973-74	1977-78
Holt, Randy	Chi., Clev., Van., L.A., Cgy., Wsh., Phi.	10	395	4	37	41	1438	21	2	3	5	83		1974-75	1983-84
• Holway, Albert	Tor., Mtl.M., Pit.	5	113	7	2	9	48	8	0	0	0	2	1	1923-24	1928-29
Homenuke, Ron	Van.	1	1	0	0	0	0	....	....	....	....	....		1972-73	1972-73
Hoover, Ron	Bos., St.L.	3	18	4	0	4	31	8	0	0	0	18		1989-90	1991-92
Hopkins, Dean	L.A., Edm., Que.	6	223	23	51	74	306	18	1	5	6	29		1979-80	1988-89
Hopkins, Larry	Tor., Wpg.	4	60	13	16	29	26	6	0	0	0	2		1977-78	1982-83
Horacek, Tony	Phi., Chi.	5	154	10	19	29	316	2	1	0	1	2		1989-90	1994-95
Horava, Miloslav	NYR	3	80	5	17	22	38	2	0	1	1	0		1988-89	1990-91
Horbul, Doug	K.C.	1	4	1	0	1	2	....	....	....	....	....		1974-75	1974-75
Hordy, Mike	NYI	2	11	0	0	0	7	....	....	....	....	....		1978-79	1979-80
Horeck, Pete	Chi., Det., Bos.	8	426	106	118	224	340	34	6	8	14	43		1944-45	1951-52
• Horne, George	Mtl.M, Tor.	3	54	9	3	12	34	4	0	0	0	4		1925-26	1928-29
Horner, Red	Tor.	12	490	42	110	152	1254	71	7	10	17	170	1	1928-29	1939-40
Hornung, Larry	St.L.	2	48	2	9	11	10	11	0	2	2	2		1970-71	1971-72
• Horton, Tim	Tor., NYR, Buf., Pit.	24	1446	115	403	518	1611	126	11	39	50	183	4	1949-50	1973-74
Horvath, Bronco	NYR, Mtl., Bos., Chi., Tor., Min.	9	434	141	185	326	319	36	12	9	21	18		1955-56	1967-68
Hospodar, Ed	NYR, Hfd., Phi., Min., Buf.	9	450	17	51	68	1314	44	4	1	5	208		1979-80	1987-88
Hostak, Martin	Phi.	2	55	3	11	14	24	....	....	....	....	....		1990-91	1991-92
Hotham, Greg	Tor., Pit.	6	230	15	74	89	139	5	0	3	3	6		1979-80	1984-85
Houck, Paul	Min.	3	16	1	2	3	2	....	....	....	....	....		1985-86	1987-88
Houde, Claude	K.C.	2	59	3	6	9	40	....	....	....	....	....		1974-75	1975-76
Houle, Rejean	Mtl.	11	635	161	247	408	395	90	14	34	48	66	5	1969-70	1982-83
Houston, Ken	Atl., Cgy., Wsh., L.A.	9	570	161	167	328	624	35	10	9	19	66		1975-76	1983-84
Howard, Frank	Tor.	1	2	0	0	0	0	....	....	....	....	....		1936-37	1936-37
Howatt, Garry	NYI, Hfd., N.J.	12	720	112	156	268	1836	87	12	14	26	289	2	1972-73	1983-84
Howe, Gordie	Det., Hfd.	26	1767	801	1049	1850	1685	157	68	92	160	220	4	1946-47	1979-80
Howe, Mark	Hfd., Phi., Det.	16	929	197	545	742	455	101	10	51	61	34		1979-80	1994-95
Howe, Marty	Hfd., Bos.	6	197	2	29	31	99	15	1	2	3	9		1979-80	1984-85
• Howe, Syd	Ott., Phi., Tor., St.L., Det.	17	698	237	291	528	212	70	17	27	44	10	3	1929-30	1945-46
Howe, Vic	NYR	3	33	3	4	7	10	....	....	....	....	....		1950-51	1954-55
Howell, Harry	NYR, Oak., L.A.	21	1411	94	324	418	1298	38	3	3	6	32		1952-53	1972-73
Howell, Ron	NYR	2	4	0	0	0	0	....	....	....	....	....		1954-55	1955-56
Howse, Don	L.A.	1	33	2	5	7	6	2	0	0	0	0		1979-80	1979-80
Howson, Scott	NYI	2	18	5	3	8	4	....	....	....	....	....		1984-85	1985-86
Hoyda, Dave	Phi., Wpg.	4	132	6	17	23	299	12	0	0	0	17		1977-78	1980-81
Hrdina, Jiri	Cgy., Pit.	5	250	45	85	130	92	46	2	5	7	24	3	1987-88	1991-92
Hrechkosy, Dave	Cal., St.L.	4	140	42	24	66	41	3	1	0	1	2		1973-74	1976-77
Hrycuik, Jim	Wsh.	1	21	5	5	10	12	....	....	....	....	....		1974-75	1974-75
Hrymnak, Steve	Chi., Det.	2	18	2	1	3	4	2	0	0	0	0		1951-52	1952-53
Hrynewich, Tim	Pit.	2	55	6	8	14	82	....	....	....	....	....		1982-83	1983-84
Huard, Rolly	Tor.	1	1	1	0	1	0	....	....	....	....	....		1930-31	1930-31
Huber, Willie	Det., NYR, Van., Phi.	10	655	104	217	321	950	33	5	5	10	35		1978-79	1987-88
Hubick, Greg	Tor., Van.	2	77	6	9	15	10	....	....	....	....	....		1975-76	1979-80
Huck, Fran	Mtl., St.L.	3	94	24	30	54	38	11	3	4	7	2		1969-70	1972-73
Hucul, Fred	Chi., St.L.	5	164	11	30	41	113	6	1	0	1	10		1950-51	1967-68
Hudson, Dave	NYI, K.C., Col.	6	409	59	124	183	89	2	1	1	2	0		1972-73	1977-78
Hudson, Lex	Pit.	1	2	0	0	0	0	2	0	0	0	0		1978-79	1978-79
Hudson, Ron	Det.	2	33	5	2	7	2	....	....	....	....	....		1937-38	1939-40
Huggins, Al	Mtl.M	1	20	1	1	2	2	....	....	....	....	....		1930-31	1930-31
Hughes, Al	NYA	2	60	6	8	14	22	....	....	....	....	....		1930-31	1931-32
Hughes, Brent	L.A., Phi., St.L., Det., K.C.	8	435	15	117	132	440	22	1	3	4	53		1967-68	1974-75
Hughes, Frank	Cal.	1	5	0	0	0	0	....	....	....	....	....		1971-72	1971-72
Hughes, Howie	L.A.	3	168	25	32	57	30	14	2	0	2	2		1967-68	1969-70
Hughes, Jack	Col.	2	46	2	5	7	104	....	....	....	....	....		1980-81	1981-82
Hughes, John	Van., Edm., NYR	2	70	2	14	16	211	7	0	1	1	16		1979-80	1980-81
Hughes, Pat	Mtl., Pit., Edm., Buf., St.L., Hfd.	10	573	130	128	258	646	71	8	20	28	65	3	1977-78	1986-87
Hughes, Rusty	Det.	1	40	0	1	1	48	....	....	....	....	....		1929-30	1929-30
Hughes, Ryan	Bos.	1	3	0	0	0	0	....	....	....	....	....		1995-96	1995-96
Hull, Bobby	Chi., Wpg., Hfd.	16	1063	610	560	1170	640	119	62	67	129	102	1	1957-58	1979-80
Hull, Dennis	Chi., Det.	14	959	303	351	654	261	104	33	34	67	30		1964-65	1977-78
• Hunt, Fred	NYA, NYR	2	59	15	14	29	6	....	....	....	....	....		1940-41	1944-45
Hunter, Dave	Edm., Pit., Wpg.	10	746	133	190	323	918	105	16	24	40	211	3	1979-80	1988-89
Hunter, Mark	Mtl., St.L., Cgy., Hfd., Wsh.	12	628	213	171	384	1426	79	18	20	38	230	1	1981-82	1992-93
Huras, Larry	NYR	1	2	0	0	0	0	....	....	....	....	....		1976-77	1976-77
Hurlburt, Bob	Van.	1	1	0	0	0	2	....	....	....	....	....		1974-75	1974-75
Hurley, Paul	Bos.	1	1	0	1	1	0	....	....	....	....	....		1968-69	1968-69
Hurst, Ron	Tor.	2	64	9	7	16	70	3	0	2	2	4		1955-56	1956-57
Huston, Ron	Cal.	2	79	15	31	46	8	....	....	....	....	....		1973-74	1974-75
Hutchinson, Ronald	NYR	1	9	0	0	0	0	....	....	....	....	....		1960-61	1960-61
Hutchison, Dave	L.A., Tor., Chi., N.J.	10	584	19	97	116	1550	48	2	12	14	149		1974-75	1983-84
• Hutton, William	Bos., Ott., Phi.	2	64	3	2	5	8	2	0	0	0	0		1929-30	1930-31
• Hyland, Harry	Mtl.W, Ott.	1	16	14	0	14	9	....	....	....	....	....		1917-18	1917-18
Hynes, Dave	Bos.	2	22	4	0	4	2	....	....	....	....	....		1973-74	1974-75
Hynes, Gord	Bos., Phi.	2	52	3	9	12	22	12	1	2	3	6		1991-92	1992-93

I

Ihnacak, Miroslav	Tor., Det.	3	56	8	9	17	39	1	0	0	0	0		1985-86	1988-89
Ihnacak, Peter	Tor.	8	417	102	165	267	175	28	4	10	14	25		1982-83	1989-90
Imlach, Brent	Tor.	2	3	0	0	0	0	....	....	....	....	....		1965-66	1966-67
Ingarfield, Earl	NYR, Pit., Oak., Cal.	13	746	179	226	405	239	21	9	8	17	10		1958-59	1970-71
Ingarfield, Earl Jr.	Atl., Cgy., Det.	2	39	4	4	8	22	2	0	1	1	0		1979-80	1980-81
Inglis, Bill	L.A., Buf.	3	36	1	3	4	4	11	1	2	3	4		1967-68	1970-71
• Ingoldsby, Johnny	Tor.	2	29	5	1	6	15	....	....	....	....	....		1942-43	1943-44
Ingram, Frank	Bos., Chi.	4	102	24	16	40	69	11	0	1	1	2		1924-25	1931-32
Ingram, Ron	Chi., Det., NYR	4	114	5	15	20	81	2	0	0	0	0		1956-57	1964-65
• Irvin, Dick	Chi.	3	94	29	23	52	78	2	2	0	2	4		1926-27	1928-29
Irvine, Ted	Bos., L.A., NYR, St.L.	11	724	154	177	331	657	83	16	24	40	115		1963-64	1976-77
Irwin, Ivan	Mtl., NYR	5	155	2	27	29	214	5	0	0	0	8		1952-53	1957-58
Isaksson, Ulf	L.A.	1	50	7	15	22	10	....	....	....	....	....		1982-83	1982-83

Name	NHL Teams	NHL Seasons	Regular Schedule GP	G	A	TP	PIM	Playoffs GP	G	A	TP	PIM	NHL Cup Wins	First NHL Season	Last NHL Season
Issel, Kim	Edm.	1	4	0	0	0	0	....	....	....	....	....		1988-89	1988-89

J

Name	NHL Teams	NHL Seasons	GP	G	A	TP	PIM	GP	G	A	TP	PIM	NHL Cup Wins	First NHL Season	Last NHL Season
● Jackson, Art	Bos., Tor.	11	468	123	178	301	144	52	8	12	20	29	2	1934-35	1944-45
Jackson, Don	Min., Edm., NYR	10	311	16	52	68	640	53	4	5	9	147	2	1977-78	1986-87
● Jackson, Hal	Chi., Det.	8	219	17	34	51	208	31	1	2	3	33	2	1936-37	1946-47
● Jackson, Harvey "Busher"	Tor., Bos., NYA	15	633	241	234	475	437	71	18	12	30	53	1	1929-30	1943-44
Jackson, Jeff	Tor., NYR, Que., Chi.	8	263	38	48	86	313	6	1	1	2	16		1984-85	1991-92
Jackson, Jim	Cgy., Buf.	4	112	17	30	47	20	14	3	2	5	6		1982-83	1987-88
Jackson, John	Chi.	1	48	2	5	7	38	....	....	....	....	....		1946-47	1946-47
Jackson, Lloyd	NYA	1	14	1	1	2	0	....	....	....	....	....		1936-37	1936-37
Jackson, Stan	Tor., Bos., Ott.	5	85	9	4	13	74	....	....	....	....	....	1	1921-22	1926-27
Jackson, Walt "Red"	NYA, Bos.	4	84	16	11	27	18	....	....	....	....	....		1932-33	1934-35
● Jacobs, Paul	Tor.	1	1	0	0	0	0	....	....	....	....	....		1918-19	1918-19
Jacobs, Tim	Cal.	1	46	0	10	10	35	....	....	....	....	....		1975-76	1975-76
Jalo, Risto	Edm.	1	3	0	3	3	0	....	....	....	....	....		1985-86	1985-86
Jalonen, Kari	Cgy., Edm.	2	37	9	6	15	4	5	1	0	1	0		1982-83	1983-84
James, Gerry	Tor.	5	149	14	26	40	257	15	1	0	1	8		1954-55	1959-60
James, Val	Buf., Tor.	2	11	0	0	0	30	....	....	....	....	....		1981-82	1986-87
Jamieson, Jim	NYR	1	1	0	1	1	0	....	....	....	....	....		1943-44	1943-44
Jankowski, Lou	Det., Chi.	4	127	19	18	37	15	1	0	0	0	0		1950-51	1954-55
Jarrett, Doug	Chi., NYR	13	775	38	182	220	631	99	7	16	23	82		1964-65	1976-77
Jarrett, Gary	Tor., Det., Oak., Cal.	7	341	72	92	164	131	11	3	1	4	9		1960-61	1971-72
Jarry, Pierre	NYR, Tor., Det., Min.	7	344	88	117	205	142	5	0	1	1	0		1971-72	1977-78
Jarvenpaa, Hannu	Wpg.	3	114	11	26	37	83	....	....	....	....	....		1986-87	1988-89
Jarvi, Iiro	Que.	2	116	18	43	61	58	....	....	....	....	....		1988-89	1989-90
Jarvis, Doug	Mtl., Wsh., Hfd.	13	964	139	264	403	263	105	14	27	41	42	4	1975-76	1987-88
Jarvis, Jim "Bud"	Pit., Phi., Tor.	3	112	17	15	32	62	....	....	....	....	....		1929-30	1936-37
Jarvis, Wes	Wsh., Min., L.A., Tor.	9	237	31	55	86	98	2	0	0	0	2		1979-80	1987-88
Javanainen, Arto	Pit.	1	14	4	1	5	2	....	....	....	....	....		1984-85	1984-85
Jay, Bob	L.A.	1	3	0	1	1	0	....	....	....	....	....		1993-94	1993-94
Jeffrey, Larry	Det., Tor., NYR	8	368	39	62	101	293	38	4	10	14	42	1	1961-62	1968-69
Jelinek, Tomas	Ott.	1	49	7	6	13	52	....	....	....	....	....		1992-93	1992-93
Jenkins, Dean	L.A.	1	5	0	0	0	2	....	....	....	....	....		1983-84	1983-84
Jenkins, Roger	Tor., Chi., Mtl., Bos., Mtl.M., NYA	8	325	15	39	54	253	25	1	7	8	12	2	1930-31	1938-39
Jennings, Bill	Det., Bos.	5	108	32	33	65	45	20	4	4	8	6		1940-41	1944-45
Jensen, Chris	NYR, Phi.	6	74	9	12	21	27	....	....	....	....	....		1985-86	1991-92
Jensen, David A.	Hfd., Wsh.	4	69	9	13	22	22	11	0	0	0	2		1983-84	1987-88
Jensen, David H.	Min.	3	18	0	2	2	11	....	....	....	....	....		1983-84	1985-86
Jensen, Steve	Min., L.A.	7	438	113	107	220	318	12	0	3	3	9		1975-76	1981-82
● Jeremiah, Ed	NYA, Bos.	1	15	0	1	1	0	....	....	....	....	....		1931-32	1931-32
Jerrard, Paul	Min.	1	5	0	0	0	4	....	....	....	....	....		1988-89	1988-89
Jerwa, Frank	Bos.	4	81	11	16	27	53	....	....	....	....	....		1931-32	1931-32
● Jerwa, Joe	NYR, Bos., St.L., NYA	7	234	29	58	87	309	17	2	3	5	16		1930-31	1938-39
Jirik, Jaroslav	St.L.	1	3	0	0	0	0	....	....	....	....	....		1969-70	1969-70
Joanette, Rosario	Mtl.	1	2	0	1	1	4	....	....	....	....	....		1944-45	1944-45
Jodzio, Rick	Col., Clev.	1	70	2	8	10	71	....	....	....	....	....		1977-78	1977-78
Johannesen, Glenn	NYI	1	2	0	0	0	0	....	....	....	....	....		1985-86	1985-86
Johannson, John	N.J.	1	5	0	0	0	0	....	....	....	....	....		1983-84	1983-84
Johansen, Trevor	Tor., Col., L.A.	5	286	11	46	57	282	13	0	3	3	21		1977-78	1981-82
Johansson, Bjorn	Clev.	2	15	1	1	2	10	....	....	....	....	....		1976-77	1977-78
Johansson, Roger	Cgy., Chi.	4	161	9	34	43	163	5	0	1	1	2		1989-90	1994-95
Johns, Don	NYR, Mtl., Min.	6	153	2	21	23	76	....	....	....	....	....		1960-61	1967-68
Johnson, Al	Mtl., Det.	4	105	21	28	49	30	11	2	2	4	6		1956-57	1962-63
Johnson, Brian	Det.	1	3	0	0	0	5	....	....	....	....	....		1983-84	1983-84
● Johnson, Danny	Tor., Van., Det.	3	121	18	19	37	24	....	....	....	....	....		1969-70	1971-72
Johnson, Earl	Det.	1	1	0	0	0	0	....	....	....	....	....		1953-54	1953-54
● Johnson, Ivan	NYR, NYA	12	436	38	48	86	808	61	5	2	7	161	2	1926-27	1937-38
Johnson, Jim	NYR, Phi., L.A.	8	302	75	111	186	73	7	0	2	2	2		1964-65	1971-72
Johnson, Mark	Pit., Min., Hfd., St.L., N.J.	11	669	203	305	508	260	37	16	12	28	10		1979-80	1989-90
Johnson, Norman B.	Bos., Chi.	3	61	5	20	25	41	14	4	0	4	6		1957-58	1959-60
Johnson, Terry	Que., St.L., Cgy., Tor.	9	285	3	24	27	580	38	0	4	4	118		1979-80	1987-88
Johnson, Tom	Mtl., Bos.	17	978	51	213	264	960	111	8	15	23	109	6	1947-48	1964-65
● Johnson, Virgil	Chi.	3	75	2	9	11	27	19	0	3	3	4	1	1937-38	1944-45
Johnson, William	Tor.	1	1	0	0	0	0	....	....	....	....	....		1949-50	1949-50
Johnston, Bernie	Hfd.	2	57	12	24	36	16	3	0	1	1	0		1979-80	1980-81
Johnston, George	Chi.	4	58	20	12	32	2	....	....	....	....	....		1941-42	1946-47
Johnston, Greg	Bos., Tor.	9	187	26	29	55	124	22	2	1	3	12		1983-84	1991-92
Johnston, Jay	Wsh.	2	8	0	0	0	13	....	....	....	....	....		1980-81	1981-82
Johnston, Joey	Min., Cal., Chi.	6	331	85	106	191	320	....	....	....	....	....		1968-69	1975-76
Johnston, Larry	L.A., Det., K.C., Col.	7	320	9	64	73	580	....	....	....	....	....		1967-68	1976-77
Johnston, Marshall	Min., Cal.	7	251	14	52	66	58	6	0	0	0	2		1967-68	1973-74
Johnston, Randy	NYI	1	4	0	0	0	4	....	....	....	....	....		1979-80	1979-80
Johnstone, Eddie	NYR, Det.	10	426	122	136	258	375	55	13	10	23	83		1975-76	1986-87
Johnstone, Ross	Tor.	2	42	5	4	9	14	3	0	0	0	0	1	1943-44	1944-45
● Joliat, Aurel	Mtl.	16	654	270	190	460	757	54	14	19	33	89	3	1922-23	1937-38
Joliat, Bobby	Mtl.	1	1	0	0	0	0	....	....	....	....	....		1924-25	1924-25
Joly, Greg	Wsh., Det.	9	365	21	76	97	250	5	0	0	0	8		1974-75	1982-83
Joly, Yvan	Mtl.	3	2	0	0	0	0	1	0	0	0	0		1979-80	1982-83
Jonathon, Stan	Bos., Pit.	8	411	91	110	201	751	63	8	4	12	137		1975-76	1982-83
Jones, Bob	NYR	1	2	0	0	0	0	....	....	....	....	....		1968-69	1968-69
Jones, Brad	Wpg., L.A., Phi.	6	148	25	31	56	122	9	1	1	2	2		1986-87	1991-92
Jones, Buck	Det., Tor.	4	50	2	2	4	36	12	0	1	1	18		1938-39	1942-43
Jones, Jim	Cal.	1	2	0	0	0	0	....	....	....	....	....		1971-72	1971-72
Jones, Jimmy	Tor.	3	148	13	18	31	68	19	1	5	6	11		1977-78	1979-80
Jones, Ron	Bos., Pit., Wsh.	5	54	1	4	5	31	....	....	....	....	....		1971-72	1975-76
Jonsson, Tomas	NYI, Edm.	8	552	85	259	344	482	80	11	26	37	97	2	1981-82	1988-89
Joseph, Anthony	Wpg.	1	2	1	0	1	0	....	....	....	....	....		1988-89	1988-89
Joyal, Eddie	Det., Tor., L.A., Phi.	9	466	128	134	262	103	50	11	8	19	18		1962-63	1971-72
Joyce, Bob	Bos., Wsh., Wpg.	6	158	34	49	83	90	46	15	9	24	29		1987-88	1992-93
Joyce, Duane	Dal.	1	3	0	0	0	0	....	....	....	....	....		1993-94	1993-94
Juckes, Bing	NYR	2	16	2	1	3	6	....	....	....	....	....		1947-48	1949-50
Julien, Claude	Que.	2	14	0	1	1	25	....	....	....	....	....		1984-85	1985-86
Junker, Steve	NYI	2	5	0	0	0	0	3	0	1	1	0		1992-93	1993-94
Jutila, Timo	Buf.	1	10	1	5	6	13	....	....	....	....	....		1984-85	1984-85
Juzda, Bill	NYR, Tor.	9	398	14	54	68	398	42	0	3	3	46	2	1940-41	1951-52

K

Name	NHL Teams	NHL Seasons	GP	G	A	TP	PIM	GP	G	A	TP	PIM	NHL Cup Wins	First NHL Season	Last NHL Season
Kabel, Bob	NYR	2	48	5	13	18	34	....	....	....	....	....		1959-60	1960-61
Kachowski, Mark	Pit.	3	64	6	5	11	209	....	....	....	....	....		1987-88	1989-90
Kachur, Ed	Chi.	2	96	10	14	24	35	....	....	....	....	....		1956-57	1957-58
Kaese, Trent	Buf.	1	1	0	0	0	0	....	....	....	....	....		1988-89	1988-89
Kaiser, Vern	Mtl.	1	50	7	5	12	33	2	0	0	0	0		1950-51	1950-51
Kalbfleish, Walter	Ott., St.L., NYA, Bos.	4	36	0	4	4	32	5	0	0	0	2		1933-34	1936-37
● Kaleta, Alex	Chi., NYR	7	387	92	121	213	190	17	1	6	7	2		1941-42	1950-51
Kallur, Anders	NYI	6	383	101	110	211	149	78	12	23	35	32	4	1979-80	1984-85
● Kaminsky, Max	Ott., St.L., Bos., Mtl.M.	4	130	22	34	56	38	4	0	0	0	0		1933-34	1936-37
● Kampman, Bingo	Tor.	5	189	14	30	44	287	47	1	4	5	38	1	1937-38	1941-42
Kane, Frank	Det.	1	2	0	0	0	0	....	....	....	....	....		1943-44	1943-44
Kannegiesser, Gord	St.L.	2	23	0	1	1	15	....	....	....	....	....		1967-68	1971-72
Kannegiesser, Sheldon	Pit., NYR, L.A., Van.	8	366	14	67	81	292	18	0	2	2	10		1970-71	1977-78
Karabin, Ladislav	Pit.	1	9	0	0	0	2	....	....	....	....	....		1993-94	1993-94
Karamnov, Vitali	St.L.	3	92	12	20	32	65	2	0	0	0	2		1992-93	1994-95
Karjalainen, Kyosti	L.A.	1	28	1	8	9	12	3	0	1	1	2		1991-92	1991-92
Karlander, Al	Det.	4	212	36	56	92	70	4	0	1	1	0		1969-70	1972-73
Kasatonov, Alexei	N.J., Ana., St.L., Bos.	7	383	38	122	160	326	33	4	7	11	40		1989-90	1995-96
Kasper, Steve	Bos., L.A., Phi., T.B.	13	821	177	291	468	554	94	20	28	48	82		1980-81	1992-93
Kastelic, Ed	Wsh., Hfd.	7	220	11	10	21	719	8	1	0	1	32		1985-86	1991-92
Kaszycki, Mike	NYI, Wsh., Tor.	5	226	42	80	122	108	19	2	6	8	10		1977-78	1982-83
Kea, Ed	Atl., St.L.	10	583	30	145	175	508	32	2	4	6	39		1973-74	1982-83
Kearns, Dennis	Van.	10	677	31	290	321	386	11	1	2	3	8		1971-72	1980-81

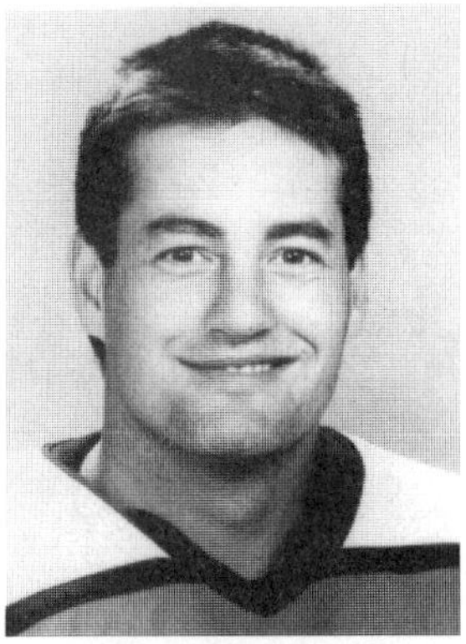
Chris Jensen

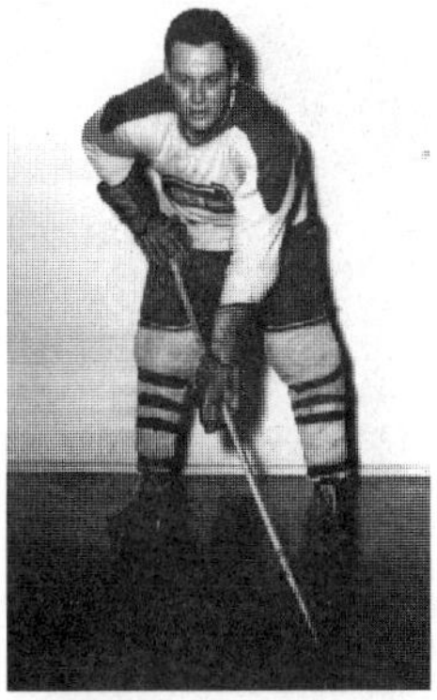
Tom Johnson

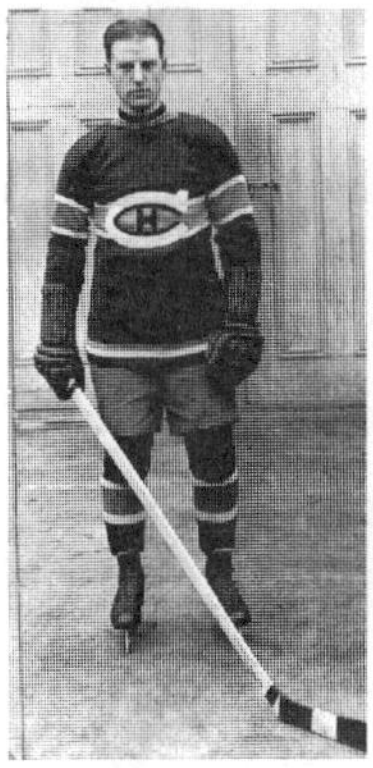
Aurel Joliat

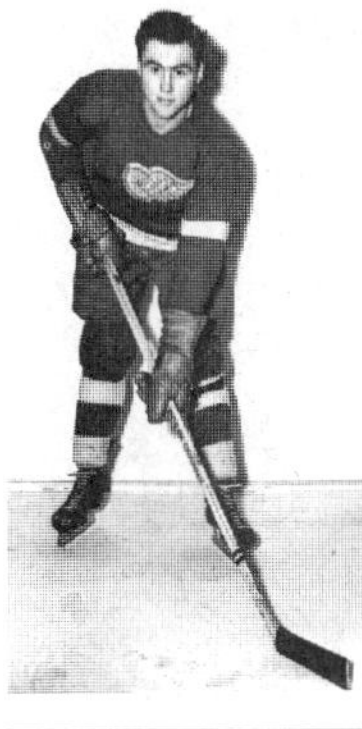
Red Kelly

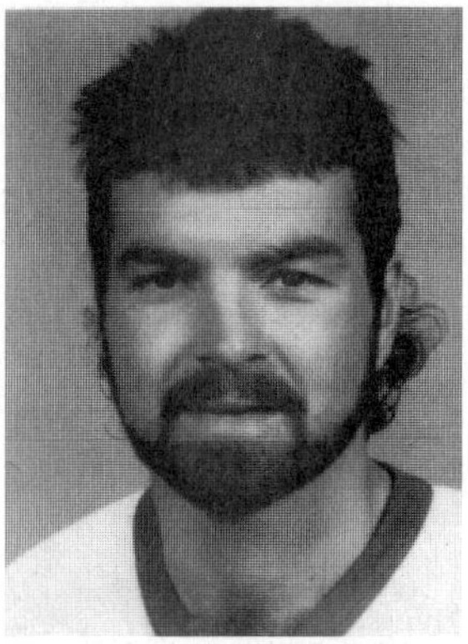

Chris Kotsopoulos

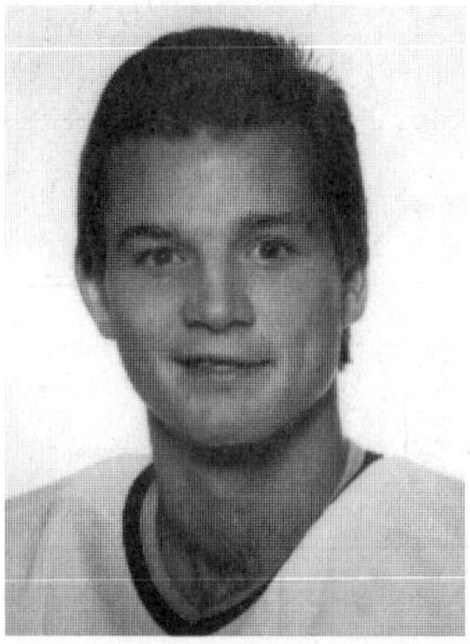

Mike Krushelnyski

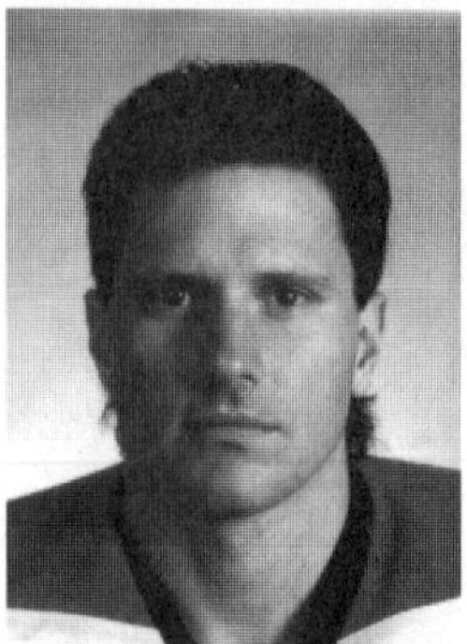

Bob Kudelski

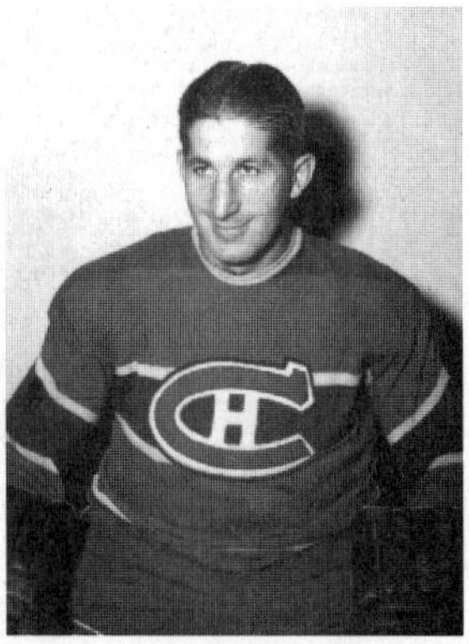

Elmer Lach

Name	NHL Teams	NHL Seasons	Regular Schedule GP	G	A	TP	PIM	Playoffs GP	G	A	TP	PIM	NHL Cup Wins	First NHL Season	Last NHL Season
• Keating, Jack	NYA	2	35	5	5	10	17	....	....	....	....	....		1931-32	1932-33
Keating, John	Det.	2	11	2	1	3	4	....	....	....	....	....		1938-39	1939-40
Keating, Mike	NYR	1	1	0	0	0	0	....	....	....	....	....		1977-78	1977-78
• Keats, Duke	Det., Chi.	3	82	30	19	49	113	....	....	....	....	....		1926-27	1928-29
• Keeling, Butch	Tor., NYR	12	525	157	63	220	331	47	11	11	22	34	1	1926-27	1937-38
Keenan, Larry	Tor., St.L., Buf., Phi.	6	233	38	64	102	28	46	15	16	31	12		1961-62	1971-72
Kehoe, Rick	Tor., Pit.	14	906	371	396	767	120	39	4	17	21	4		1971-72	1984-85
Kekalainen, Jarmo	Bos., Ott.	3	55	5	8	13	28	....	....	....	....	....		1989-90	1993-94
Keller, Ralph	NYR	1	3	1	0	1	6	....	....	....	....	....		1962-63	1962-63
Kellgren, Christer	Col.	1	5	0	0	0	0	....	....	....	....	....		1981-82	1981-82
Kelly, Bob	St.L., Pit., Chi.	6	425	87	109	196	687	23	6	3	9	40		1973-74	1978-79
Kelly, Bob	Phi., Wsh.	12	837	154	208	362	1454	101	9	14	23	172	2	1970-71	1981-82
Kelly, Dave	Det.	1	16	2	0	2	4	....	....	....	....	....		1976-77	1976-77
Kelly, John Paul	L.A.	7	400	54	70	124	366	18	1	1	2	41		1979-80	1985-86
Kelly, Pete	St.L., Det., NYA, Bro.	7	177	21	38	59	68	19	3	1	4	2	2	1934-35	1941-42
Kelly, Red	Det., Tor.	20	1316	281	542	823	327	164	33	59	92	51	8	1947-48	1966-67
• Kelly, Reg (Pep)	Tor., Chi., Bro.	8	288	74	53	127	105	38	7	6	13	10		1934-35	1941-42
Kemp, Kevin	Hfd.	1	3	0	0	0	4	....	....	....	....	....		1980-81	1980-81
Kemp, Stan	Tor.	1	1	0	0	0	2	....	....	....	....	....		1948-49	1948-49
Kendall, William	Chi., Tor.	5	131	16	10	26	28	6	0	0	0	0	1	1933-34	1937-38
Kennedy, Dean	L.A., NYR, Buf., Wpg., Edm.	12	717	26	110	136	1118	36	1	7	8	59		1982-83	1994-95
Kennedy, Forbes	Chi., Det., Bos., Phi., Tor.	11	603	70	108	178	988	12	2	4	6	64		1956-57	1968-69
Kennedy, Ted	Tor.	14	696	231	329	560	432	78	29	31	60	32	5	1942-43	1956-57
• Kenny, Eddie	NYR, Chi.	2	10	0	0	0	18	....	....	....	....	....		1930-31	1934-35
Keon, Dave	Tor., Hfd.	18	1296	396	590	986	117	92	32	36	68	6	4	1960-61	1981-82
Kerch, Alexander	Edm.	1	5	0	0	0	2	....	....	....	....	....		1993-94	1993-94
Kerr, Alan	NYI, Det., Wpg.	9	391	72	94	166	826	38	5	4	9	70		1984-85	1992-93
Kerr, Reg	Cle., Chi., Edm.	6	263	66	94	160	169	7	1	0	1	7		1977-78	1983-84
Kerr, Tim	Phi., NYR, Hfd.	13	655	370	304	674	596	81	40	31	71	58		1980-81	1992-93
Kessell, Rick	Pit., Cal.	5	135	4	24	28	6	....	....	....	....	....		1969-70	1973-74
Ketola, Veli-Pekka	Col.	1	44	9	5	14	4	....	....	....	....	....		1981-82	1981-82
Ketter, Kerry	Atl.	1	41	0	2	2	58	....	....	....	....	....		1972-73	1972-73
Kharin, Sergei	Wpg.	1	7	2	3	5	2	....	....	....	....	....		1990-91	1990-91
Kidd, Ian	Van.	2	20	4	7	11	25	....	....	....	....	....		1987-88	1988-89
Kiessling, Udo	Min.	1	1	0	0	0	2	....	....	....	....	....		1981-82	1981-82
Kilrea, Brian	Det., L.A.	2	26	3	5	8	12	....	....	....	....	....		1957-58	1967-68
• Kilrea, Hec	Ott., Det., Tor.	15	633	167	129	296	438	48	8	7	15	18	3	1925-26	1939-40
• Kilrea, Ken	Det.	5	91	16	23	39	8	15	2	2	4	4		1938-39	1943-44
Kilrea, Wally	Ott., Phi., NYA, Mtl.M., Det.	9	329	35	58	93	87	25	2	4	6	6	2	1929-30	1937-38
Kindrachuk, Orest	Phi., Pit., Wsh.	10	508	118	261	379	648	76	20	20	40	53	2	1972-73	1981-82
King, Frank	Mtl.	1	10	1	0	1	2	....	....	....	....	....		1950-51	1950-51
King, Wayne	Cal.	3	73	5	18	23	34	....	....	....	....	....		1973-74	1975-76
Kinsella, Brian	Wsh.	2	10	0	1	1	0	....	....	....	....	....		1975-76	1976-77
Kinsella, Ray	Ott.	1	14	0	0	0	0	....	....	....	....	....		1930-31	1930-31
• Kirk, Bobby	NYR	1	39	4	8	12	14	....	....	....	....	....		1937-38	1937-38
Kirkpatrick, Bob	NYR	1	49	12	12	24	6	....	....	....	....	....		1942-43	1942-43
Kirton, Mark	Tor., Det., Van.	6	266	57	56	113	121	4	1	2	3	7		1979-80	1984-85
Kisio, Kelly	Det., NYR, S.J., Cgy.	13	761	229	429	658	768	39	6	15	21	52		1982-83	1994-95
Kitchen, Bill	Mtl., Tor.	4	41	1	4	5	40	3	0	1	1	0		1981-82	1984-85
• Kitchen, Hobie	Mtl.M., Det.	2	48	5	4	9	58	....	....	....	....	....		1925-26	1926-27
Kitchen, Mike	Col., N.J.	8	474	12	62	74	370	2	0	0	0	2		1976-77	1983-84
Kjellberg, Patrik	Mtl.	1	7	0	0	0	2	....	....	....	....	....		1992-93	1992-93
Klassen, Ralph	Cal., Clev., Col., St.L.	9	497	52	93	145	120	26	4	2	6	12		1975-76	1983-84
Klein, Jim	Bos., NYA	8	164	30	24	54	68	5	0	0	0	2		1928-29	1937-38
Kleinendorst, Scot	NYR, Hfd., Wsh.	8	281	12	46	58	452	26	2	7	9	40		1982-83	1989-90
Klingbeil, Ike	Chi.	1	5	1	2	3	2	....	....	....	....	....		1936-37	1936-37
Klukay, Joe	Tor., Bos.	11	566	109	127	236	189	71	13	10	23	23	4	1942-43	1955-56
Kluzak, Gord	Bos.	7	299	25	98	123	543	46	6	13	19	129		1982-83	1990-91
Knibbs, Bill	Bos.	1	53	7	10	17	4	....	....	....	....	....		1964-65	1964-65
• Knott, Nick	Bro.	1	14	3	1	4	9	....	....	....	....	....		1941-42	1941-42
Knox, Paul	Tor.	1	1	0	0	0	0	....	....	....	....	....		1954-55	1954-55
Kolstad, Dean	Min., S.J.	3	40	1	7	8	69	....	....	....	....	....		1988-89	1992-93
Komadoski, Neil	L.A., St.L.	8	502	16	76	92	632	23	0	2	2	47		1972-73	1979-80
Konik, George	Pit.	1	52	7	8	15	26	....	....	....	....	....		1967-68	1967-68
Konroyd, Steve	Cgy., NYI, Chi., Hfd., Det., Ott.	15	895	41	195	236	863	97	10	15	25	99		1980-81	1994-95
Kopak, Russ	Bos.	1	24	7	9	16	0	....	....	....	....	....		1943-44	1943-44
Korab, Jerry	Chi., Van., Buf., L.A.	15	975	114	341	455	1629	93	8	18	26	201		1970-71	1984-85
• Kordic, John	Mtl., Tor., Wsh., Que.	7	244	17	18	35	997	41	4	3	7	131	1	1985-86	1991-92
Korn, Jim	Det., Tor., Buf., N.J., Cgy.	10	597	66	122	188	1801	16	1	2	3	109		1979-80	1989-90
Korney, Mike	Det., NYR	4	77	9	10	19	59	....	....	....	....	....		1973-74	1978-79
Koroll, Cliff	Chi.	11	814	208	254	462	376	85	19	29	48	67		1969-70	1979-80
Kortko, Roger	NYI	2	79	7	17	24	28	10	0	3	3	17		1984-85	1985-86
Kostynski, Doug	Bos.	2	15	3	1	4	4	....	....	....	....	....		1983-84	1984-85
Kotanen, Dick	NYR	1	1	0	0	0	0	....	....	....	....	....		1950-51	1950-51
Kotsopoulos, Chris	NYR, Hfd.,Tor., Det.	9	479	44	109	153	827	31	1	3	4	91		1980-81	1989-90
Kowal, Joe	Buf.	2	22	0	5	5	13	2	0	0	0	0		1976-77	1977-78
Kozak, Don	L.A., Van.	7	437	96	86	182	480	29	7	2	9	69		1972-73	1978-79
Kozak, Les	Tor.	1	12	1	0	1	2	....	....	....	....	....		1961-62	1961-62
• Kraftcheck, Stephen	Bos., NYR, Tor.	4	157	11	18	29	83	6	0	0	0	7		1950-51	1958-59
Krake, Skip	Bos., L.A., Buf.	7	249	23	40	63	182	10	1	0	1	17		1963-64	1970-71
Kravets, Mikhail	S.J.	2	2	0	0	0	0	....	....	....	....	....		1991-92	1992-93
Krentz, Dale	Det.	3	30	5	3	8	9	2	0	0	0	0		1986-87	1988-89
Krol, Joe	NYR, Bro.	3	26	10	4	14	8	....	....	....	....	....		1936-37	1941-42
Kromm, Rich	Cgy., NYI	9	372	70	103	173	138	36	2	6	8	22		1983-84	1992-93
Krook, Kevin	Col.	1	3	0	0	0	2	....	....	....	....	....		1978-79	1978-79
Krulicki, Jim	NYR, Det.	1	41	0	3	3	6	....	....	....	....	....		1970-71	1970-71
Kruppke, Gord	Det.	3	23	0	0	0	32	....	....	....	....	....		1990-91	1993-94
Krushelnyski, Mike	Bos., Edm., L.A., Tor., Det.	14	897	241	328	569	699	139	29	43	72	106	3	1981-82	1994-95
Krutov, Vladimir	Van.	1	61	11	23	34	20	....	....	....	....	....		1989-90	1989-90
Kryskow, Dave	Chi., Wsh., Det., Atl.	4	231	33	56	89	174	12	2	0	2	4		1972-73	1975-76
Kryznowski, Edward	Bos., Chi.	5	237	15	22	37	65	18	0	1	1	4		1948-49	1952-53
Kudelski, Bob	L.A., Ott., Fla.	9	442	139	102	241	218	22	4	4	8	4		1987-88	1995-96
Kuhn, Gord	NYA	1	12	1	1	2	4	....	....	....	....	....		1932-33	1932-33
Kukulowicz, Adolph	NYR	2	4	1	0	1	0	....	....	....	....	....		1952-53	1953-54
Kulak, Stu	Van., Edm., NYR, Que., Wpg.	4	90	8	4	12	130	3	0	0	0	2		1982-83	1988-89
Kullman, Arnie	Bos.	2	13	0	1	1	11	....	....	....	....	....		1947-48	1949-50
Kullman, Eddie	NYR	6	343	56	70	126	298	6	1	0	1	2		1947-48	1953-54
Kumpel, Mark	Que., Det., Wpg.	6	288	38	46	84	113	39	6	4	10	14		1984-85	1990-91
Kuntz, Alan	NYR	2	45	10	12	22	12	6	1	0	1	2		1941-42	1945-46
Kuntz, Murray	St.L.	1	7	1	2	3	0	....	....	....	....	....		1974-75	1974-75
Kurtenbach, Orland	NYR, Bos., Tor., Van.	13	639	119	213	332	628	19	2	4	6	70		1960-61	1973-74
Kurvers, Tom	Mtl., Buf., N.J., Tor., Van., NYI, Ana.	11	659	93	328	421	350	57	8	22	30	68	1	1984-85	1994-95
Kuryluk, Mervin	Chi.	1	....	....	....	....	....	2	0	0	0	0		1961-62	1961-62
Kushner, Dale	NYI, Phi.	3	84	10	13	23	215	....	....	....	....	....		1989-90	1991-92
Kuzyk, Ken	Clev.	2	41	5	9	14	8	....	....	....	....	....		1976-77	1977-78
Kvartalnov, Dmitri	Bos.	2	112	42	49	91	26	4	0	0	0	0		1992-93	1993-94
Kwong, Larry	NYR	1	1	0	0	0	0	....	....	....	....	....		1947-48	1947-48
• Kyle, Bill	NYR	2	3	0	3	3	0	....	....	....	....	....		1949-50	1950-51
• Kyle, Gus	NYR, Bos.	3	203	6	20	26	362	14	1	2	3	34		1949-50	1951-52
Kyllonen, Marku	Wpg.	1	9	0	2	2	2	....	....	....	....	....		1988-89	1988-89

L

Name	NHL Teams	NHL Seasons	GP	G	A	TP	PIM	GP	G	A	TP	PIM	NHL Cup Wins	First NHL Season	Last NHL Season
Labadie, Mike	NYR	1	3	0	0	0	0	....	....	....	....	....		1952-53	1952-53
Labatte, Neil	St.L.	2	26	0	2	2	19	....	....	....	....	....		1978-79	1981-82
L'Abbe, Moe	Chi.	1	5	0	1	1	0	....	....	....	....	....		1972-73	1972-73
Labine, Leo	Bos., Det.	11	643	128	193	321	730	60	11	12	23	82		1951-52	1961-62
Labossierre, Gord	NYR, L.A., Min.	6	215	44	62	106	75	10	2	3	5	28		1963-64	1971-72
Labovitch, Max	NYR	1	5	0	0	0	4	....	....	....	....	....		1943-44	1943-44
Labraaten, Dan	Det., Cgy.	4	268	71	73	144	47	8	1	0	1	4		1978-79	1981-82
Labre, Yvon	Pit., Wsh.	9	371	14	87	101	788	....	....	....	....	....		1970-71	1980-81
Labrie, Guy	Bos., NYR	2	42	4	9	13	16	....	....	....	....	....		1943-44	1944-45
Lach, Elmer	Mtl.	14	664	215	408	623	478	76	19	45	64	36	3	1940-41	1953-54
Lachance, Earl	Mtl.	1	1	0	0	0	0	....	....	....	....	....		1926-27	1926-27

Name	NHL Teams	NHL Seasons	Regular Schedule GP	G	A	TP	PIM	Playoffs GP	G	A	TP	PIM	NHL Cup Wins	First NHL Season	Last NHL Season
Lachance, Michel	Col.	1	21	0	4	4	22	....	....	....	....	....		1978-79	1978-79
Lacombe, Francois	Oak., Buf., Que.	4	78	2	17	19	54	3	1	0	1	0		1968-69	1979-80
Lacombe, Normand	Buf., Edm., Phi	7	319	53	62	115	196	26	5	1	6	49	1	1984-85	1990-91
Lacroix, Andre	Phi., Chi., Hfd.	6	325	79	119	198	44	16	2	5	7	0		1967-68	1979-80
Lacroix, Pierre	Que., Hfd.	4	274	24	108	132	197	8	0	2	2	10		1979-80	1982-83
Ladouceur, Randy	Det., Hfd., Ana.	14	930	30	126	156	1322	40	5	8	13	59		1982-83	1995-96
Lafleur, Guy	Mtl., NYR, Que.	17	1126	560	793	1353	399	128	58	76	134	67	5	1971-72	1990-91
Lafleur, Rene	Mtl.	1	1	0	0	0	0	....	....	....	....	....		1924-25	1924-25
Laforce, Ernie	Mtl.	1	1	0	0	0	0	....	....	....	....	....		1942-43	1942-43
LaForest, Bob	L.A.	1	5	1	0	1	2	....	....	....	....	....		1983-84	1983-84
Laforge, Claude	Mtl., Det., Phi.	8	193	24	33	57	82	5	1	2	3	15		1957-58	1968-69
LaForge, Marc	Hfd., Edm.	2	14	0	0	0	64	....	....	....	....	....		1989-90	1993-94
Laframboise, Pete	Cal., Wsh., Pit.	4	227	33	55	88	70	9	1	0	1	0		1971-72	1974-75
Lafrance, Adie	Mtl.	1	3	0	0	0	2	2	0	0	0	0		1933-34	1933-34
Lafrance, Leo	Mtl., Chi.	2	33	2	0	2	6	....	....	....	....	....		1926-27	1927-28
Lafreniere, Jason	Que., NYR, T.B.	5	146	34	53	87	22	15	1	5	6	19		1986-87	1993-94
Lafreniere, Roger	Det., St.L.	2	13	0	0	0	4	....	....	....	....	....		1962-63	1972-73
Lagace, Jean-Guy	Pit., Buf., K.C.	6	197	9	39	48	251	....	....	....	....	....		1968-69	1975-76
Laidlaw, Tom	NYR, L.A.	10	705	25	139	164	717	69	4	17	21	78		1980-81	1989-90
Laird, Robbie	Min.	1	1	0	0	0	0	....	....	....	....	....		1979-80	1979-80
Lajeunesse, Serge	Det., Phi.	5	103	1	4	5	103	....	....	....	....	....		1970-71	1974-75
Lalande, Hec	Chi., Det.	4	151	21	39	60	120	....	....	....	....	....		1953-54	1957-58
Lalonde, Bobby	Van., Atl., Bos., Cgy.	11	641	124	210	334	298	16	4	2	6	6		1971-72	1981-82
• Lalonde, Newsy	Mtl., NYA	6	99	124	27	151	122	12	22	1	23	19		1917-18	1926-27
Lalonde, Ron	Pit., Wsh.	7	397	45	78	123	106	....	....	....	....	....		1972-73	1978-79
• Lamb, Joe	Mtl.M., Ott., NYA, Bos., Mtl., St.L., Det.	11	443	108	101	209	601	18	1	1	2	51		1927-28	1937-38
Lambert, Lane	Det., NYR, Que.	6	283	58	66	124	521	17	2	4	6	40		1983-84	1988-89
Lambert, Yvon	Mtl., Buf.	10	683	206	273	479	340	90	27	22	49	67	4	1972-73	1981-82
Lamby, Dick	St.L.	3	22	0	5	5	22	....	....	....	....	....		1978-79	1980-81
• Lamirande, Jean-Paul	NYR, Mtl.	4	49	5	5	10	26	8	0	0	0	4		1946-47	1954-55
Lammens, Hank	Ott.	1	27	1	2	3	22	....	....	....	....	....		1993-94	1993-94
• Lamoureux, Leo	Mtl.	6	235	19	79	98	175	28	1	6	7	16	2	1941-42	1946-47
Lamoureux, Mitch	Pit., Phi.	3	73	11	9	20	59	....	....	....	....	....		1983-84	1987-88
Lampman, Mike	St.L., Van., Wsh.	4	96	17	20	37	34	....	....	....	....	....		1972-73	1976-77
Lancien, Jack	NYR	4	63	1	5	6	35	6	0	1	1	2		1946-47	1950-51
Landon, Larry	Mtl., Tor.	2	9	0	0	0	2	....	....	....	....	....		1983-84	1984-85
Lane, Gord	Wsh., NYI	10	539	19	94	113	1228	75	3	14	17	214	4	1975-76	1984-85
• Lane, Myles	NYR, Bos.	3	71	4	1	5	41	11	0	0	0	0	1	1928-29	1933-34
Langdon, Steve	Bos.	3	7	0	1	1	2	4	0	0	0	0		1974-75	1977-78
Langelle, Pete	Tor.	4	136	22	51	73	11	39	5	9	14	4	1	1938-39	1941-42
Langevin, Chris	Buf.	2	22	3	1	4	22	....	....	....	....	....		1983-84	1985-86
Langevin, Dave	NYI, Min., L.A.	8	513	12	107	119	530	87	2	17	19	106	4	1979-80	1986-87
Langlais, Alain	Min.	2	25	4	4	8	10	....	....	....	....	....		1973-74	1974-75
Langlois, Al	Mtl., NYR, Det., Bos.	9	497	21	91	112	488	53	1	5	6	50	3	1957-58	1965-66
Langlois, Charlie	Ham., NYA., Pit., Mtl.	4	151	22	3	25	201	2	0	0	0	0		1924-25	1927-28
Langway, Rod	Mtl., Wsh.	15	994	51	278	329	849	104	5	22	27	97	1	1978-79	1992-93
Lanthier, Jean-Marc	Van.	4	105	16	16	32	29	....	....	....	....	....		1983-84	1987-88
Lanyon, Ted	Pit.	1	5	0	0	0	4	....	....	....	....	....		1967-68	1967-68
Lanz, Rick	Van., Tor., Chi.	10	569	65	221	286	448	28	3	8	11	35		1980-81	1991-92
Laperriere, Jacques	Mtl.	12	691	40	242	282	674	88	9	22	31	101	6	1962-63	1973-74
Lapointe, Guy	Mtl., St.L., Bos.	16	884	171	451	622	893	123	26	44	70	138	6	1968-69	1983-84
Lapointe, Rick	Det., Phi., St.L., Que., L.A.	11	664	44	176	220	831	46	2	7	9	64		1975-76	1985-86
Lappin, Peter	Min., S.J.	2	7	0	0	0	2	....	....	....	....	....		1989-90	1991-92
Laprade, Edgar	NYR	10	501	108	172	280	42	18	4	9	13	4		1945-46	1954-55
LaPrairie, Ben	Chi.	1	7	0	0	0	0	....	....	....	....	....		1936-37	1936-37
Lariviere, Garry	Que., Edm.	4	219	6	57	63	167	14	0	5	5	8		1979-80	1982-83
Larmer, Jeff	Col., N.J., Chi.	5	158	37	51	88	57	5	1	0	1	2		1981-82	1985-86
Larmer, Steve	Chi., NYR	15	1006	441	571	1012	532	140	56	75	131	89	1	1980-81	1994-95
• Larochelle, Wildor	Mtl., Chi.	12	474	92	74	166	211	34	6	4	10	24	2	1925-26	1936-37
Larocque, Denis	L.A.	1	8	0	1	1	18	....	....	....	....	....		1987-88	1987-88
Larose, Bonner	Bos.	1	6	0	0	0	0	....	....	....	....	....		1925-26	1925-26
Larose, Claude	NYR	2	25	4	7	11	2	2	0	0	0	0		1979-80	1981-82
Larose, Claude	Mtl., Min., St.L.	16	943	226	257	483	887	97	14	18	32	143	5	1962-63	1977-78
Larouche, Pierre	Pit., Mtl., Hfd., NYR	14	812	395	427	822	237	64	20	34	54	16	2	1974-75	1987-88
Larson, Norman	NYA., Bro., NYR	3	89	25	18	43	12	....	....	....	....	....		1940-41	1946-47
Larson, Reed	Det., Bos., Edm., NYI, Min., Buf.	14	904	222	463	685	1391	32	4	7	11	63		1976-77	1989-90
Larter, Tyler	Wsh.	1	1	0	0	0	0	....	....	....	....	....		1989-90	1989-90
Latal, Jiri	Phi.	3	92	12	36	48	24	....	....	....	....	....		1989-90	1990-91
Latos, James	NYR	1	1	0	0	0	0	....	....	....	....	....		1988-89	1988-89
Latreille, Phil	NYR	1	4	0	0	0	2	....	....	....	....	....		1960-61	1960-61
Latta, David	Que.	4	36	4	8	12	4	....	....	....	....	....		1985-86	1990-91
Lauder, Marty	Bos.	1	3	0	0	0	2	....	....	....	....	....		1927-28	1927-28
Lauen, Mike	Wpg.	1	4	0	1	1	0	....	....	....	....	....		1983-84	1983-84
Laughlin, Craig	Mtl., Wsh., L.A., Tor.	8	549	136	205	341	364	33	6	6	12	20		1981-82	1988-89
Laughton, Mike	Oak., Cal.	4	189	39	48	87	101	11	2	4	6	0		1967-68	1970-71
Laurence, Red	Atl., St.L.	2	79	15	22	37	14	....	....	....	....	....		1978-79	1979-80
LaVallee, Kevin	Cgy., L.A., St.L., Pit.	7	366	110	125	235	85	32	5	8	13	21		1980-81	1986-87
Lavarre, Mark	Chi.	3	78	9	16	25	58	1	0	0	0	2		1985-86	1987-88
Lavender, Brian	St.L., NYI, Det., Cal.	4	184	16	26	42	174	3	0	0	0	2		1971-72	1974-75
Lavigne, Eric	L.A.	1	1	0	0	0	0	....	....	....	....	....		1994-95	1994-95
• Laviolette, Jack	Mtl.	1	18	2	0	2	6	2	0	0	0	0		1917-18	1917-18
Laviolette, Peter	NYR	1	12	0	0	0	6	....	....	....	....	....		1988-89	1988-89
Lavoie, Dominic	St.L., Ott., Bos., L.A.	6	38	5	8	13	32	....	....	....	....	....		1988-89	1993-94
Lawless, Paul	Hfd., Phi., Van., Tor.	7	239	49	77	126	54	3	0	2	2	2		1982-83	1989-90
Lawson, Danny	Det., Min., Buf.	5	219	28	29	57	61	16	0	1	1	2		1967-68	1971-72
Lawton, Brian	Min., NYR, Hfd., Que., Bos., S.J.	9	483	112	154	266	401	11	1	1	2	12		1983-84	1992-93
Laxdal, Derek	Tor., NYI	6	67	12	7	19	90	1	0	2	2	2		1984-85	1990-91
Laycoe, Hal	NYR, Mtl., Bos.	11	531	25	77	102	292	40	2	5	7	39		1945-46	1955-56
Lazaro, Jeff	Bos., Ott.	3	102	14	23	37	114	28	3	3	6	32		1990-91	1992-93
Leach, Jamie	Pit., Hfd., Fla.	5	81	11	9	20	12	....	....	....	....	....		1989-90	1993-94
Leach, Larry	Bos.	3	126	13	29	42	91	7	1	1	2	8		1958-59	1961-62
Leach, Reggie	Bos., Cal., Phi., Det.	13	934	381	285	666	387	94	47	22	69	22	1	1970-71	1982-83
Leavins, Jim	Det., NYR	2	41	2	12	14	30	....	....	....	....	....		1985-86	1986-87
Lebeau, Patrick	Mtl., Cgy., Fla.	3	7	2	2	4	4	....	....	....	....	....		1990-91	1993-94
LeBlanc, Fern	Det.	3	34	5	6	11	0	....	....	....	....	....		1976-77	1978-79
LeBlanc, J.P.	Chi., Det.	5	153	14	30	44	87	2	0	0	0	0		1968-69	1978-79
LeBrun, Al	NYR	2	6	0	2	2	4	....	....	....	....	....		1960-61	1965-66
Lecaine, Bill	Pit.	1	4	0	0	0	0	....	....	....	....	....		1968-69	1968-69
Leclair, Jackie	Mtl.	3	160	20	40	60	56	20	6	1	7	6	1	1954-55	1956-57
Leclerc, Rene	Det.	2	87	10	11	21	105	....	....	....	....	....		1968-69	1970-71
Lecuyer, Doug	Chi., Wpg., Pit.	4	126	11	31	42	178	7	4	0	4	15		1978-79	1982-83
Ledingham, Walt	Chi., NYI	3	15	0	2	2	4	....	....	....	....	....		1972-73	1976-77
• LeDuc, Albert	Mtl., Ott., NYR	10	383	57	35	92	614	28	5	6	11	32	2	1925-26	1934-35
LeDuc, Rich	Bos., Que.	4	130	28	38	66	69	5	0	0	0	9		1972-73	1980-81
• Lee, Bobby	Mtl.	1	1	0	0	0	0	....	....	....	....	....		1942-43	1942-43
Lee, Edward	Que.	1	2	0	0	0	5	....	....	....	....	....		1984-85	1984-85
Lee, Peter	Pit.	6	431	114	131	245	257	19	0	8	8	4		1977-78	1982-83
Lefley, Bryan	N.Y.I., K.C., Col.	5	228	7	29	36	101	2	0.	0	0	0		1972-73	1977-78
Lefley, Chuck	Mtl., St.L.	9	407	128	164	292	137	29	5	8	13	10	2	1970-71	1980-81
• Leger, Roger	NYR, Mtl.	5	187	18	53	71	71	20	0	7	7	14		1943-44	1949-50
Legge, Barry	Que., Wpg.	3	107	1	11	12	144	....	....	....	....	....		1979-80	1981-82
Legge, Randy	NYR	1	12	0	2	2	2	....	....	....	....	....		1972-73	1972-73
Lehmann, Tommy	Bos., Edm.	3	36	5	5	10	16	....	....	....	....	....		1987-88	1989-90
Lehto, Petteri	Pit.	1	6	0	0	0	4	....	....	....	....	....		1984-85	1984-85
Lehtonen, Antero	Wsh.	1	65	9	12	21	14	....	....	....	....	....		1979-80	1979-80
Lehvonen, Henri	K.C.	1	4	0	0	0	0	....	....	....	....	....		1974-75	1974-75
Leier, Edward	Chi.	2	16	2	1	3	2	....	....	....	....	....		1949-50	1950-51
Leinonen, Mikko	NYR, Wsh.	4	162	31	78	109	71	20	2	11	13	28		1981-82	1984-85
Leiter, Bobby	Bos., Pit., Atl.	10	447	98	126	224	144	8	3	0	3	2		1962-63	1975-76
Leiter, Ken	NYI, Min.	5	143	14	36	50	62	15	0	6	6	8		1984-85	1989-90
Lemaire, Jacques	Mtl.	12	853	366	469	835	217	145	61	78	139	63	8	1967-68	1978-79
Lemay, Moe	Van., Edm., Bos., Wpg.	8	317	72	94	166	442	28	6	3	9	55	1	1981-82	1988-89
Lemelin, Roger	K.C., Col.	4	36	1	2	3	27	....	....	....	....	....		1974-75	1977-78
Lemieux, Alain	St.L., Que., Pit.	6	119	28	44	72	38	19	4	6	10	0		1981-82	1986-87
Lemieux, Bob	Oak.	1	19	0	1	1	12	....	....	....	....	....		1967-68	1967-68

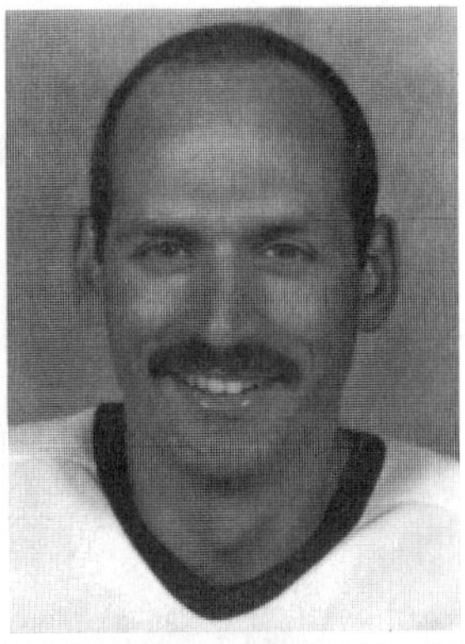
Randy Ladouceur

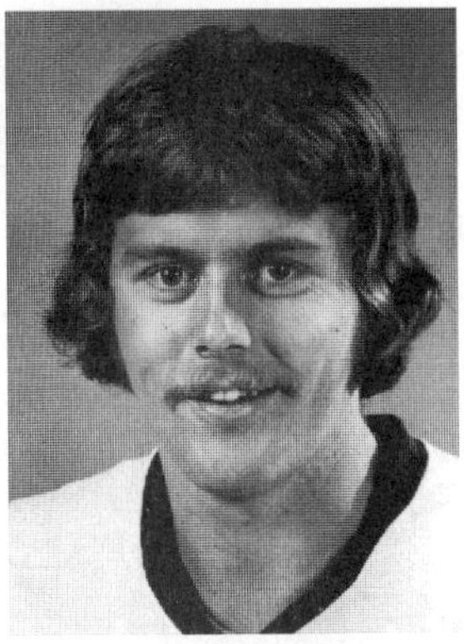
Walt Ledingham

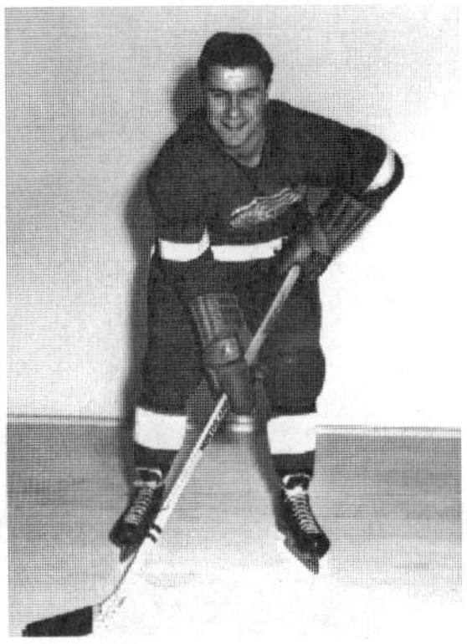
Tony Leswick

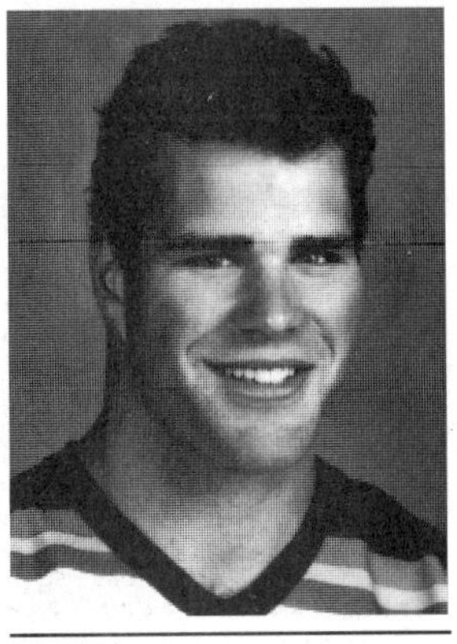
Brett Lindros

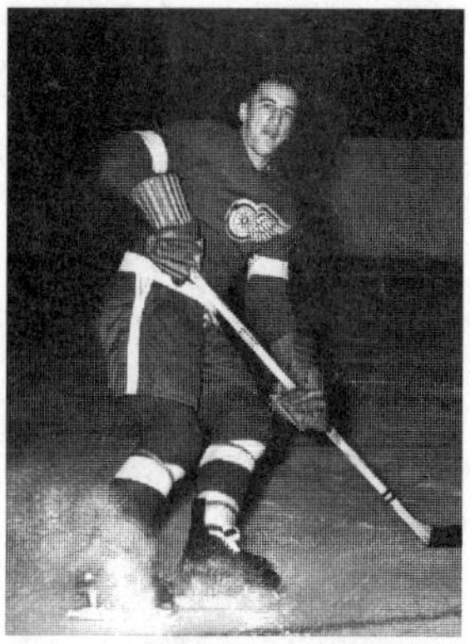

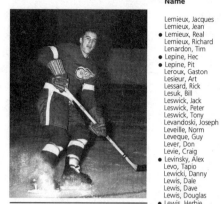

Ted Lindsay

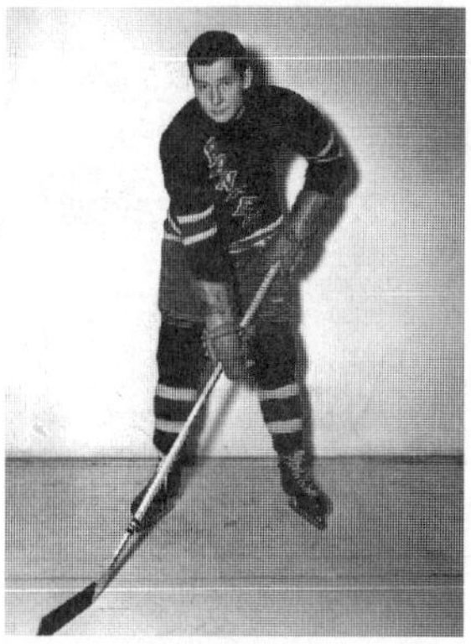

Pentti Lund

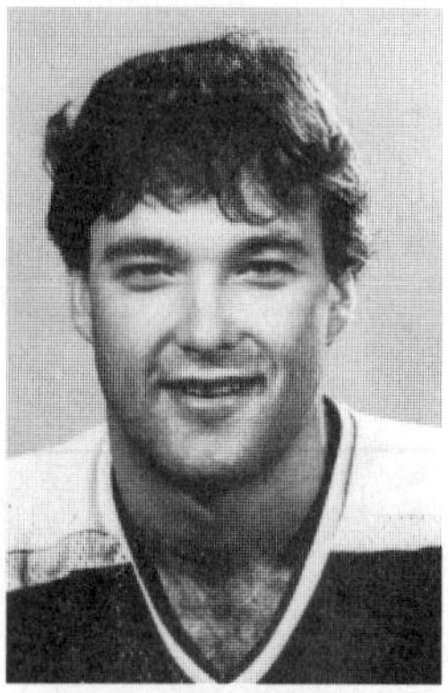

Dan Mandich

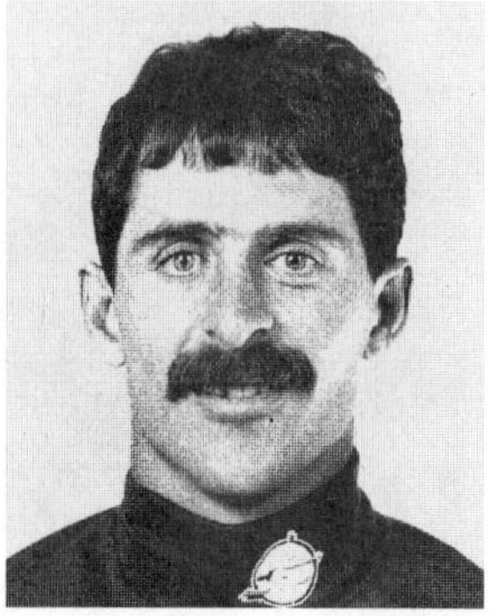

Moe Mantha

			Regular Schedule					Playoffs							
Name	NHL Teams	NHL Seasons	GP	G	A	TP	PIM	GP	G	A	TP	PIM	NHL Cup Wins	First NHL Season	Last NHL Season
Lemieux, Jacques	L.A.	3	19	0	4	4	8	1	0	0	0	0		1967-68	1969-70
Lemieux, Jean	L.A., Atl., Wsh.	5	204	23	63	86	39	3	1	1	2	0		1969-70	1977-78
• Lemieux, Real	Det., L.A., NYR, Buf.	8	456	51	104	155	262	18	2	4	6	10		1966-67	1973-74
Lemieux, Richard	Van., K.C., Atl.	5	274	39	82	121	132	2	0	0	0	0		1971-72	1975-76
Lenardon, Tim	N.J., Van.	2	15	2	1	3	4	....	....	....	....	....		1986-87	1989-90
• Lepine, Hec	Mtl.	1	33	5	2	7	2	....	....	....	....	....		1925-26	1925-26
• Lepine, Pit	Mtl.	13	526	143	98	241	392	41	7	5	12	26	2	1925-26	1937-38
Leroux, Gaston	Mtl.	1	2	0	0	0	0	....	....	....	....	....		1935-36	1935-36
Lesieur, Art	Mtl., Chi.	5	100	4	2	6	50	14	0	0	0	4	1	1928-29	1935-36
Lessard, Rick	Cgy., S.J.	3	15	0	4	4	18	....	....	....	....	....		1988-89	1991-92
Lesuk, Bill	Bos., Phi., L.A., Wsh., Wpg.	8	388	44	63	107	368	9	1	0	1	12	1	1968-69	1979-80
Leswick, Jack	Chi.	1	47	1	7	8	16	....	....	....	....	....	1	1933-34	1933-34
Leswick, Peter	NYA, Bos.	2	3	1	0	1	0	....	....	....	....	....		1936-37	1944-45
Leswick, Tony	NYR, Det., Chi.	12	740	165	159	324	900	59	13	10	23	91	3	1945-46	1957-58
Levandoski, Joseph	NYR	1	8	1	1	2	0	....	....	....	....	....		1946-47	1946-47
Leveille, Norm	Bos.	2	75	17	25	42	49	....	....	....	....	....		1981-82	1982-83
Leveque, Guy	L.A.	2	17	2	2	4	21	....	....	....	....	....		1992-93	1993-94
Lever, Don	Van., Atl., Cgy., Col., N.J., Buf.	15	1020	313	367	680	593	30	7	10	17	26		1972-73	1986-87
Levie, Craig	Wpg., Min., Van., St.L.	6	183	22	53	75	177	16	2	3	5	32		1981-82	1986-87
• Levinsky, Alex	Tor., Chi., NYR	9	368	19	49	68	307	37	2	1	3	26	2	1930-31	1938-39
Levo, Tapio	Col., N.J.	2	107	16	53	69	36	....	....	....	....	....		1981-82	1982-83
Lewicki, Danny	Tor., NYR, Chi.	9	461	105	135	240	177	28	0	4	4	8	1	1950-51	1958-59
Lewis, Dale	NYR	1	8	0	0	0	0	....	....	....	....	....		1975-76	1975-76
Lewis, Dave	NYI, L.A., N.J., Det.	15	1008	36	187	223	953	91	1	20	21	143		1973-74	1987-88
Lewis, Douglas	Mtl.	1	3	0	0	0	0	....	....	....	....	....		1946-47	1946-47
• Lewis, Herbie	Det.	11	483	148	161	309	248	38	13	10	23	6	2	1928-29	1938-39
Ley, Rick	Tor., Hfd.	6	310	12	72	84	528	14	0	2	2	20		1968-69	1980-81
Liba, Igor	NYR, L.A.	1	37	7	18	25	36	2	0	0	0	2		1988-89	1988-89
Libett, Nick	Det., Pit.	14	982	237	268	505	472	16	6	2	8	2		1967-68	1980-81
Licari, Anthony	Det.	1	9	0	1	1	0	....	....	....	....	....		1946-47	1946-47
Liddington, Bob	Tor.	1	11	0	1	1	2	....	....	....	....	....		1970-71	1970-71
Lindberg, Chris	Cgy., Que.	3	116	17	25	42	47	2	0	1	1	2		1991-92	1993-94
Lindgren, Lars	Van., Min.	6	394	25	113	138	325	40	5	6	11	20		1978-79	1983-84
Lindholm, Mikael	L.A.	1	18	2	2	4	2	....	....	....	....	....		1989-90	1989-90
Lindros, Brett	NYI	2	51	2	5	7	147	....	....	....	....	....		1994-95	1995-96
Lindsay, Ted	Det., Chi.	17	1068	379	472	851	1808	133	47	49	96	194	4	1944-45	1964-65
Lindstrom, Willy	Wpg., Edm., Pit.	8	582	161	162	323	200	57	14	18	32	24	2	1979-80	1986-87
Linseman, Ken	Phi., Edm., Bos., Tor.	14	860	256	551	807	1727	113	43	77	120	325	1	1978-79	1991-92
Liscombe, Carl	Det.	9	373	137	140	277	117	57	22	20	42	20	1	1937-38	1945-46
Litzenberger, Ed	Mtl., Chi., Det., Tor.	12	618	178	238	416	283	40	5	13	18	34	4	1952-53	1963-64
• Locas, Jacques	Mtl.	2	59	7	8	15	66	....	....	....	....	....		1947-48	1948-49
Lochead, Bill	NYR, Det., Col.	6	330	69	62	131	180	7	3	0	3	6		1974-75	1979-80
• Locking, Norm	Chi.	2	48	2	6	8	26	....	....	....	....	....		1934-35	1935-36
Lofthouse, Mark	Wsh., Det.	6	181	42	38	80	73	....	....	....	....	....		1977-78	1982-83
Logan, Dave	Chi., Van.	6	218	5	29	34	470	12	0	0	0	10		1975-76	1980-81
Logan, Robert	Buf., L.A.	3	42	10	5	15	0	....	....	....	....	....		1986-87	1988-89
Loiselle, Claude	Det., N.J., Que., Tor., NYI	13	616	92	117	209	1149	41	4	11	15	60		1981-82	1993-94
Lomakin, Andrei	Phi., Fla.	4	215	42	62	104	92	....	....	....	....	....		1991-92	1994-95
Loney, Troy	Pit., Ana., NYI, NYR	12	624	87	110	197	1091	67	8	14	22	97	2	1983-84	1994-95
Long, Barry	L.A., Det., Wpg.	5	280	11	68	79	250	5	0	1	1	18		1972-73	1981-82
• Long, Stanley	Mtl.	1	....	....	....	....	....	3	0	0	0	0		1951-52	1951-52
Lonsberry, Ross	Phi., Pit., Bos., L.A.	15	968	256	310	566	806	100	21	25	46	87	2	1966-67	1980-81
Loob, Hakan	Cgy.	6	450	193	236	429	189	73	26	28	54	16	1	1983-84	1988-89
Loob, Peter	Que.	1	8	1	2	3	0	....	....	....	....	....		1984-85	1984-85
Lorentz, Jim	NYR, Buf., Bos., St.L.	10	659	161	238	399	208	54	12	10	22	30	1	1968-69	1977-78
Lorimer, Bob	NYI, Col., N.J.	10	529	22	90	112	431	49	3	10	13	83	2	1976-77	1985-86
• Lorrain, Rod	Mtl.	6	179	28	39	67	30	11	0	3	3	0		1935-36	1941-42
• Loughlin, Clem	Det., Chi.	3	101	8	6	14	77	....	....	....	....	....		1926-27	1928-29
Loughlin, Wilf	Tor.	1	14	0	0	0	2	....	....	....	....	....		1923-24	1923-24
Lovsin, Ken	Wsh.	1	1	0	0	0	0	....	....	....	....	....		1990-91	1990-91
Lowdermilk, Dwayne	Wsh.	1	2	0	1	1	2	....	....	....	....	....		1980-81	1980-81
Lowe, Darren	Pit.	1	8	1	2	3	0	....	....	....	....	....		1983-84	1983-84
Lowe, Norm	NYR	1	4	1	1	2	0	....	....	....	....	....		1948-49	1949-50
• Lowe, Ross	Bos., Mtl.	3	77	6	8	14	82	2	0	0	0	0		1949-50	1951-52
• Lowery, Fred	Mtl.M., Pit.	2	54	1	0	1	10	2	0	0	0	6		1924-25	1925-26
• Lowrey, Eddie	Ott., Ham.	3	24	2	0	2	3	....	....	....	....	....		1917-18	1920-21
• Lowrey, Gerry	Tor., Pit., Phi., Chi., Ott.	7	226	48	48	96	170	4	1	0	1	8		1927-28	1932-33
Lucas, Danny	Phi.	1	6	1	0	1	0	....	....	....	....	....		1978-79	1978-79
Lucas, Dave	Det.	1	1	0	0	0	0	....	....	....	....	....		1962-63	1962-63
Luce, Don	NYR, Det., Buf., L.A., Tor.	13	894	225	329	554	364	71	17	22	39	52		1969-70	1981-82
Ludvig, Jan	N.J., Buf.	7	314	54	87	141	418	....	....	....	....	....		1982-83	1988-89
Ludzik, Steve	Chi., Buf.	9	424	46	93	139	333	44	4	8	12	70		1981-82	1989-90
Lukowich, Bernie	Pit., St.L.	2	79	13	15	28	34	2	0	0	0	0		1973-74	1974-75
Lukowich, Morris	Wpg., Bos., L.A.	8	582	199	219	418	584	11	0	2	2	24		1979-80	1986-87
Luksa, Charlie	Hfd.	1	8	0	1	1	4	....	....	....	....	....		1979-80	1979-80
Lumley, Dave	Mtl., Edm., Hfd.	9	437	98	160	258	680	61	6	8	14	131	2	1978-79	1986-87
Lund, Pentti	NYR, Bos.	7	259	44	55	99	40	19	7	5	12	0		1946-47	1952-53
Lundberg, Brian	Pit.	1	1	0	0	0	2	....	....	....	....	....		1982-83	1982-83
Lunde, Len	Min., Van., Det., Chi.	8	321	39	83	122	75	20	3	2	5	2		1958-59	1970-71
Lundholm, Bengt	Wpg.	5	275	48	95	143	72	14	3	4	7	14		1981-82	1985-86
Lundrigan, Joe	Tor., Wsh.	2	52	2	8	10	22	....	....	....	....	....		1972-73	1974-75
Lundstrom, Tord	Det.	1	11	1	1	2	0	....	....	....	....	....		1973-74	1973-74
Lundy, Pat	Det. Chi.	5	150	37	32	69	31	16	2	2	4	2		1945-46	1950-51
Lupien, Gilles	Mtl., Pit., Hfd.	5	226	5	25	30	416	25	0	0	0	21	2	1977-78	1981-82
Lupul, Gary	Van.	7	293	70	75	145	243	25	4	7	11	11		1979-80	1985-86
Lyle, George	Det., Hfd.	4	99	24	38	62	51	....	....	....	....	....		1979-80	1982-83
Lynch, Jack	Pit., Det., Wsh.	7	382	24	106	130	336	....	....	....	....	....		1972-73	1978-79
Lynn, Vic	Det., Mtl., Tor., Bos., Chi.	10	326	49	76	125	274	47	7	10	17	46	3	1943-44	1953-54
Lyon, Steve	Pit.	1	3	0	0	0	2	....	....	....	....	....		1976-77	1976-77
Lyons, Ron	Bos., Phi.	1	36	2	4	6	29	5	0	0	0	0		1930-31	1930-31
Lysiak, Tom	Atl., Chi.	13	919	292	551	843	567	76	25	38	63	49		1973-74	1985-86

M

MacAdam, Al	Phi., Cal., Cle., Min., Van.	12	864	240	351	591	509	64	20	24	44	21		1973-74	1984-85
MacDermid, Paul	Hfd., Wpg., Wsh., Que.	14	690	116	142	258	1303	43	5	11	16	116		1981-82	1994-95
MacDonald, Blair	Edm., Van.	4	219	91	100	191	65	11	0	6	6	2		1979-80	1982-83
MacDonald, Brett	Van.	1	1	0	0	0	0	....	....	....	....	....		1987-88	1987-88
MacDonald, Kevin	Ott.	1	1	0	0	0	2	....	....	....	....	....		1993-94	1993-94
• MacDonald, Kilby	NYR	4	151	36	34	70	47	15	1	2	3	4	1	1939-40	1944-45
MacDonald, Lowell	Det., L.A., Pit.	13	506	180	210	390	92	30	11	11	22	12		1961-62	1977-78
MacDonald, Parker	Tor., NYR, Det., Bos., Min.	14	676	144	179	323	253	75	14	14	28	20		1952-53	1968-69
MacDougall, Kim	Min.	1	1	0	0	0	0	....	....	....	....	....		1974-75	1974-75
MacEachern, Shane	St.L.	1	1	0	0	0	0	....	....	....	....	....		1987-88	1987-88
Macey, Hubert	NYR, Mtl.	3	30	6	9	15	0	8	0	0	0	0		1941-42	1946-47
MacGregor, Bruce	Det., NYR	14	893	213	257	470	217	107	19	28	47	44		1960-61	1973-74
MacGregor, Randy	Hfd.	1	2	1	1	2	2	....	....	....	....	....		1981-82	1981-82
MacGuigan, Garth	NYI	2	5	0	1	1	2	....	....	....	....	....		1979-80	1979-80
MacIntosh, Ian	NYR	1	4	0	0	0	4	....	....	....	....	....		1952-53	1952-53
MacIver, Don	Wpg.	1	6	0	0	0	2	....	....	....	....	....		1979-80	1979-80
MacKasey, Blair	Tor.	1	1	0	0	0	2	....	....	....	....	....		1976-77	1976-77
MacKay, Calum	Det., Mtl	8	237	50	55	105	214	38	5	13	18	20	1	1946-47	1954-55
Mackay, Dave	Chi.	1	29	3	0	3	26	5	0	1	1	2		1940-41	1940-41
• MacKay, Mickey	Chi., Pit., Bos.	4	147	44	19	63	79	11	0	0	0	6	1	1926-27	1929-30
MacKay, Murdo	Mtl.	4	19	0	3	3	0	15	1	2	3	0		1945-46	1947-48
Mackell, Fleming	Tor., Bos.	13	665	149	220	369	562	80	22	41	63	75	2	1947-48	1959-60
MacKenzie, Barry	Min.	1	6	0	1	1	6	....	....	....	....	....		1968-69	1968-69
• MacKenzie, Bill	Chi., Mtl.M., Mtl., NYR	7	264	15	14	29	145	21	1	1	2	11	1	1932-33	1939-40
Mackey, David	Chi., Min., St.L.	6	126	8	12	20	305	3	0	0	0	2		1987-88	1993-94
MacKey, Reggie	NYR	1	34	0	0	0	16	1	0	0	0	0		1926-27	1926-27
Mackie, Howie	Det.	2	20	1	0	1	4	8	0	0	0	0	1	1936-37	1937-38
MacKinnon, Paul	Wsh.	5	147	5	23	28	91	....	....	....	....	....		1979-80	1983-84
MacLean, Paul	St.L., Wpg., Det.	11	719	324	349	673	968	53	21	14	35	110		1980-81	1990-91

Name	NHL Teams	NHL Seasons	Regular Schedule GP	G	A	TP	PIM	Playoffs GP	G	A	TP	PIM	NHL Cup Wins	First NHL Season	Last NHL Season
MacLeish, Rick	Phi., Hfd., Pit., Det.	14	846	349	410	759	434	114	54	53	107	38	2	1970-71	1983-84
MacLellan, Brian	L.A., NYR, Min., Cgy., Det.	10	606	172	241	413	551	47	5	9	14	42		1982-83	1991-92
MacLeod, Pat	Min., S.J., Dal.	4	53	5	13	18	14	....	....	....	....	....		1990-91	1995-96
MacMillan, Billy	Tor., Atl., NYI	7	446	74	77	151	184	53	6	6	12	40		1970-71	1976-77
MacMillan, Bob	NYR, St.L., Atl., Cgy., Col., N.J., Chi.	11	753	228	349	577	260	31	8	11	19	16		1974-75	1984-85
MacMillan, John	Tor., Det.	5	104	5	10	15	32	12	0	1	1	2	2	1960-61	1964-65
MacNeil, Al	Tor., Mtl., Chi., NYR, Pit.	11	524	17	75	92	617	37	0	4	4	67		1955-56	1967-68
MacNeil, Bernie	St.L.	1	4	0	0	0	0	....	....	....	....	....		1973-74	1973-74
• MacPherson, Bud	Mtl.	7	259	5	33	38	233	29	0	3	3	21	1	1948-49	1956-57
• MacSweyn, Ralph	Phi.	5	47	0	5	5	10	8	0	0	0	6		1967-68	1971-72
MacWilliam, Mike	NYI	1	6	0	0	0	14	....	....	....	....	....		1995-96	1995-96
Madigan, Connie	St.L.	1	20	0	3	3	25	5	0	0	0	4		1972-73	1972-73
Madill, Jeff	N.J.	1	14	4	0	4	46	7	0	2	2	8		1990-91	1990-91
Magee, Dean	Min.	1	7	0	0	0	4	....	....	....	....	....		1977-78	1977-78
Maggs, Daryl	Chi., Cal., Tor.	3	135	14	19	33	54	4	0	0	0	0		1971-72	1979-80
Magnan, Marc	Tor.	1	4	0	1	1	5	....	....	....	....	....		1982-83	1982-83
Magnuson, Keith	Chi.	11	589	14	125	139	1442	68	3	9	12	164		1969-70	1979-80
Maguire, Kevin	Tor., Buf., Phi.	6	260	29	30	59	782	11	0	0	0	86		1986-87	1991-92
Mahaffy, John	Mtl., NYR	3	37	11	25	36	4	1	0	1	1	0		1942-43	1944-45
Mahovlich, Frank	Tor., Det., Mtl.	18	1181	533	570	1103	1056	137	51	67	118	163	6	1956-57	1973-74
Mahovlich, Pete	Det., Mtl., Pit.	16	884	288	485	773	916	88	30	42	72	134	4	1965-66	1980-81
Mailhot, Jacques	Que.	1	5	0	0	0	33	....	....	....	....	....		1988-89	1988-89
Mailley, Frank	Mtl.	1	1	0	0	0	0	....	....	....	....	....		1942-43	1942-43
Mair, Jim	Phi., NYI, Van.	5	76	4	15	19	49	3	1	2	3	4		1970-71	1974-75
• Majeau, Fern	Mtl.	2	56	22	24	46	43	1	0	0	0	0	1	1943-44	1944-45
Major, Bruce	Que.	1	4	0	0	0	0	....	....	....	....	....		1990-91	1990-91
Makela, Mikko	NYI, L.A., Buf., Bos.	7	423	118	147	265	139	18	3	8	11	14		1985-86	1994-95
Maki, Chico	Chi.	15	841	143	292	435	345	113	17	36	53	43	1	1960-61	1975-76
• Maki, Wayne	Chi., St.L., Van.	6	246	57	79	136	184	2	1	0	1	2		1967-68	1972-73
Makkonen, Karl	Edm.	1	9	2	2	4	0	....	....	....	....	....		1979-80	1979-80
Maley, David	Mtl., N.J., Edm., S.J., NYI	9	466	43	81	124	1043	46	5	5	10	111	1	1985-86	1993-94
Malinowski, Merlin	Col., N.J., Hfd.	5	282	54	111	165	121	....	....	....	....	....		1978-79	1982-83
Malone, Cliff	Mtl.	1	3	0	0	0	0	....	....	....	....	....		1951-52	1951-52
Malone, Greg	Pit., Hfd., Que.	11	704	191	310	501	661	20	3	5	8	32		1976-77	1986-87
• Malone, Joe	Mtl., Que., Ham.	7	125	146	21	167	35	9	5	0	5	0		1917-18	1923-24
Maloney, Dan	Chi., L.A., Det., Tor.	11	737	192	259	451	1489	40	4	7	11	35		1970-71	1981-82
Maloney, Dave	NYR, Buf.	11	657	71	246	317	1154	49	7	17	24	91		1974-75	1984-85
Maloney, Don	NYR, Hfd., NYI	13	765	214	350	564	815	94	22	35	57	101		1978-79	1990-91
Maloney, Phil	Bos., Tor., Chi.	5	158	28	43	71	16	6	0	0	0	0		1949-50	1959-60
Maluta, Ray	Bos.	2	25	2	3	5	6	2	0	0	0	0		1975-76	1976-77
Manastersky, Tom	Mtl.	1	6	0	0	0	11	....	....	....	....	....		1950-51	1950-51
Mancuso, Gus	Mtl., NYR	4	42	7	9	16	17	....	....	....	....	....		1937-38	1942-43
Mandich, Dan	Min.	4	111	5	11	16	303	7	0	0	0	2		1982-83	1985-86
Manery, Kris	Van., Wpg., Clev., Min.	4	250	63	64	127	91	....	....	....	....	....		1977-78	1980-81
Manery, Randy	L.A., Det., Atl.	10	582	50	206	256	415	13	0	2	2	12		1970-71	1979-80
Mann, Jack	NYR	2	9	3	4	7	0	....	....	....	....	....		1943-44	1944-45
Mann, Jimmy	Wpg., Que., Pit.	8	293	10	20	30	895	22	0	0	0	89		1979-80	1987-88
Mann, Ken	Det.	1	1	0	0	0	0	....	....	....	....	....		1975-76	1975-76
Mann, Norm	Tor.	3	31	0	3	3	4	2	0	0	0	0		1935-36	1940-41
Manners, Rennison	Pit., Phi.	2	37	3	2	5	14	....	....	....	....	....		1929-30	1930-31
Manno, Bob	Van., Tor., Det.	8	371	41	131	172	274	17	2	4	6	12		1976-77	1984-85
Manson, Ray	Bos., NYR	2	2	0	1	1	0	....	....	....	....	....		1947-48	1948-49
• Mantha, Georges	Mtl.	13	488	89	102	191	148	36	6	2	8	24	2	1928-29	1940-41
Mantha, Moe	Wpg., Pit., Edm., Min., Phi.	12	656	81	289	370	501	17	5	10	15	18		1980-81	1991-92
• Mantha, Sylvio	Mtl., Bos.	14	542	63	72	135	667	46	5	4	9	66	3	1923-24	1936-37
Maracle, Buddy	NYR	1	11	1	3	4	4	4	0	0	0	0		1930-31	1930-31
Marcetta, Milan	Tor., Min.	3	54	7	15	22	10	17	7	7	14	4	1	1966-67	1968-69
March, Mush	Chi.	17	759	153	230	383	540	45	12	15	27	41	2	1928-29	1944-45
Marchinko, Brian	Tor., NYI	4	47	2	6	8	0	....	....	....	....	....		1970-71	1973-74
Marcinyshyn, David	N.J., Que., NYR	3	16	0	1	1	49	....	....	....	....	....		1990-91	1992-93
Marcon, Lou	Det.	3	60	0	4	4	42	....	....	....	....	....		1958-59	1962-63
Marcotte, Don	Bos.	15	868	230	254	484	317	132	34	27	61	81	2	1965-66	1981-82
Marini, Hector	NYI, N.J.	5	154	27	46	73	246	10	3	6	9	14	2	1978-79	1983-84
• Mario, Frank	Bos.	2	53	9	19	28	24	....	....	....	....	....		1941-42	1944-45
• Mariucci, John	Chi.	5	223	11	34	45	308	12	0	3	3	26		1940-41	1947-48
Mark, Gordon	N.J., Edm.	4	85	3	10	13	187	....	....	....	....	....		1986-87	1994-95
Markell, John	Wpg., St. L., Min.	4	55	11	10	21	36	....	....	....	....	....		1979-80	1984-85
Marker, Gus	Det., Mtl.M., Tor., Bro.	10	322	64	69	133	133	46	5	7	12	36	1	1932-33	1941-42
Markham, Ray	NYR	1	14	1	1	2	21	7	1	0	1	24		1979-80	1979-80
Markle, Jack	Tor.	1	8	0	1	1	0	....	....	....	....	....		1935-36	1935-36
• Marks, Jack	Mtl.W, Tor., Que.	2	7	0	0	0	4	....	....	....	....	....		1917-18	1919-20
Marks, John	Chi.	10	657	112	163	275	330	57	5	9	14	60		1972-73	1981-82
Markwart, Nevin	Bos., Cgy.	8	309	41	68	109	794	19	1	0	1	33		1983-84	1991-92
Marois, Daniel	Tor., NYI, Bos., Dal.	8	350	117	93	210	419	19	3	3	6	28		1987-88	1995-96
Marois, Mario	NYR, Van., Que., Wpg., St.L.	15	955	76	357	433	1746	100	4	34	38	182		1977-78	1991-92
Marotte, Gilles	Bos., Chi., L.A., NYR, St.L.	12	808	56	265	321	872	29	3	3	6	26		1965-66	1976-77
Marquess, Mark	Bos.	1	27	5	4	9	6	4	0	0	0	0		1946-47	1946-47
Marsh, Brad	Atl., Cgy., Phi., Tor., Det., Ott.	15	1086	23	175	198	1241	97	6	18	24	124		1978-79	1992-93
Marsh, Gary	Det., Tor.	2	7	1	3	4	4	....	....	....	....	....		1967-68	1968-69
Marsh, Peter	Wpg., Chi.	5	278	48	71	119	224	26	1	5	6	33		1979-80	1983-84
Marshall, Bert	Det., Oak., Cal., NYR, NYI	14	868	17	181	198	926	72	4	22	26	99		1965-66	1978-79
Marshall, Don	Mtl., NYR, Buf., Tor.	19	1176	265	324	589	127	94	8	15	23	14	5	1951-52	1971-72
Marshall, Paul	Pit., Tor., Hfd.	4	95	15	18	33	17	1	0	0	0	0		1979-80	1982-83
Marshall, Willie	Tor.	4	33	1	5	6	2	....	....	....	....	....		1952-53	1958-59
Marson, Mike	Wsh., L.A.	6	196	24	24	48	233	....	....	....	....	....		1974-75	1979-80
• Martin, Clare	Bos., Det., Chi., NYR	6	237	12	28	40	78	27	0	2	2	6	1	1941-42	1951-52
Martin, Frank	Bos., Chi.	6	282	11	46	57	122	10	0	2	2	2		1952-53	1957-58
Martin, Grant	Van., Wsh.	4	44	0	4	4	55	1	1	0	1	2		1983-84	1986-87
Martin, Jack	Tor.	1	1	0	0	0	0	....	....	....	....	....		1960-61	1960-61
Martin, Pit	Det., Bos., Chi., Van.	17	1101	324	485	809	609	100	27	31	58	56		1961-62	1978-79
Martin, Rick	Buf., L.A.	11	685	384	317	701	477	63	24	29	53	74		1971-72	1981-82
Martin, Ron	NYA	2	94	13	16	29	36	....	....	....	....	....		1932-33	1933-34
Martin, Terry	Buf., Que., Tor., Edm., Min.	10	479	104	101	205	202	21	4	2	6	26		1975-76	1984-85
Martin, Tom	Wpg., Hfd., Min.	6	92	12	11	23	249	4	0	0	0	6		1984-85	1989-90
Martin, Tom	Tor.	1	3	1	0	1	0	....	....	....	....	....		1967-68	1967-68
Martineau, Don	Atl., Min., Det.	4	90	6	10	16	63	....	....	....	....	....		1973-74	1976-77
Martini, Darcy	Edm.	1	2	0	0	0	0	....	....	....	....	....		1993-94	1993-94
Martinson, Steven	Det., Mtl., Min.	4	49	2	1	3	244	1	0	0	0	10		1987-88	1991-92
Maruk, Dennis	Cal., Clev., Min., Wsh.	14	888	356	522	878	761	34	14	22	36	26		1975-76	1988-89
Masnick, Paul	Mtl., Chi., Tor.	6	232	18	41	59	139	33	4	5	9	27	1	1950-51	1957-58
• Mason, Charley	NYR, NYA, Det., Chi.	4	95	7	18	25	44	4	0	1	1	0		1934-35	1938-39
Massecar, George	NYA	3	100	12	11	23	46	....	....	....	....	....		1929-30	1931-32
Masters, Jamie	St.L.	3	33	1	13	14	2	2	0	0	0	0		1975-76	1978-79
• Masterton, Bill	Min.	1	38	4	8	12	4	....	....	....	....	....		1967-68	1967-68
Mathers, Frank	Tor.	3	23	1	3	4	4	....	....	....	....	....		1948-49	1951-52
Mathiasen, Dwight	Pit.	3	33	1	7	8	18	....	....	....	....	....		1985-86	1987-88
Mathieson, Jim	Wsh.	1	2	0	0	0	4	....	....	....	....	....		1989-90	1989-90
• Matte, Joe	Tor., Ham., Bos., Mtl.	4	64	18	14	32	43	....	....	....	....	....		1919-20	1925-26
Matte, Roland	Chi., Det.	2	24	0	3	3	8	....	....	....	....	....		1929-30	1942-43
Mattiussi, Dick	Pit., Oak., Cal.	4	200	8	31	39	124	8	0	1	1	6		1967-68	1970-71
Matz, Johnny	Mtl.	1	30	3	2	5	0	5	0	0	0	2		1924-25	1924-25
Maxner, Wayne	Bos.	2	62	8	9	17	48	....	....	....	....	....		1964-65	1965-66
Maxwell, Brad	Min., Que., Tor., Van., NYR	10	612	98	270	368	1292	79	12	49	61	178		1977-78	1986-87
Maxwell, Bryan	Min., St.L., Wpg., Pit.	8	331	18	77	95	745	15	1	1	2	86		1977-78	1984-85
Maxwell, Kevin	Min., Col., N.J.	3	66	6	15	21	61	16	3	4	7	24		1980-81	1983-84
Maxwell, Wally	Tor.	1	2	0	0	0	0	....	....	....	....	....		1952-53	1952-53
Mayer, Derek	Ott.	1	17	2	2	4	8	....	....	....	....	....		1993-94	1993-94
Mayer, Jim	NYR	1	4	0	0	0	0	....	....	....	....	....		1979-80	1979-80
Mayer, Pat	Pit.	1	1	0	0	0	4	....	....	....	....	....		1987-88	1987-88
Mayer, Shep	Tor.	1	12	1	2	3	4	....	....	....	....	....		1942-43	1942-43
• Mazur, Eddie	Mtl., Chi.	6	107	8	20	28	120	25	4	5	9	22	1	1950-51	1956-57
Mazur, Jay	Van.	4	47	11	7	18	20	6	0	1	1	8		1988-89	1991-92
McAdam, Gary	Buf., Pit., Det., Cgy., Wsh., N.J., Tor.	11	534	96	132	228	243	30	6	5	11	16		1975-76	1985-86
McAdam, Sam	NYR	1	5	0	0	0	0	....	....	....	....	....		1930-31	1930-31

Gilles Marotte

Dennis Maruk

Tom McCarthy

John McIntyre

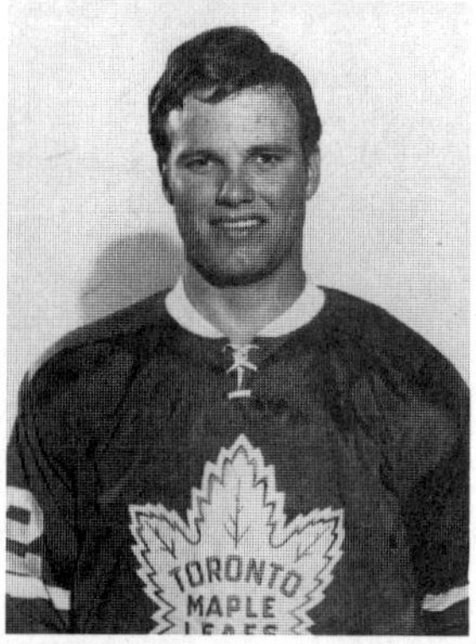

Jim McKenny

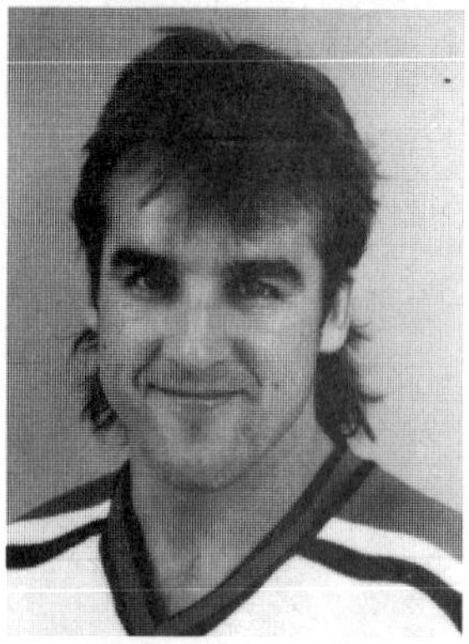

George McPhee

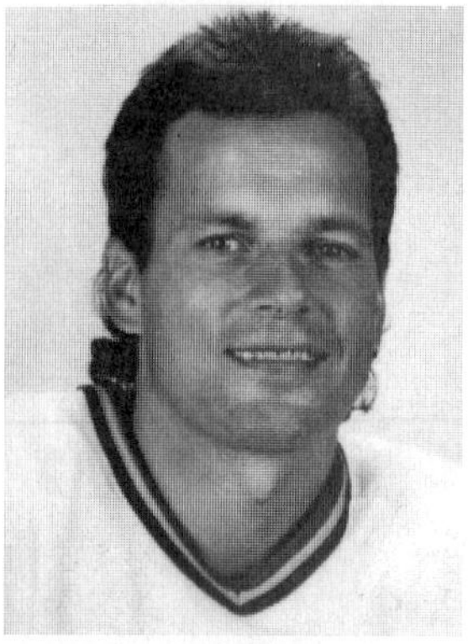

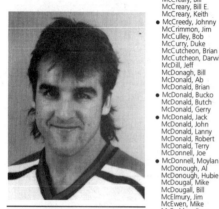

Rick Meagher

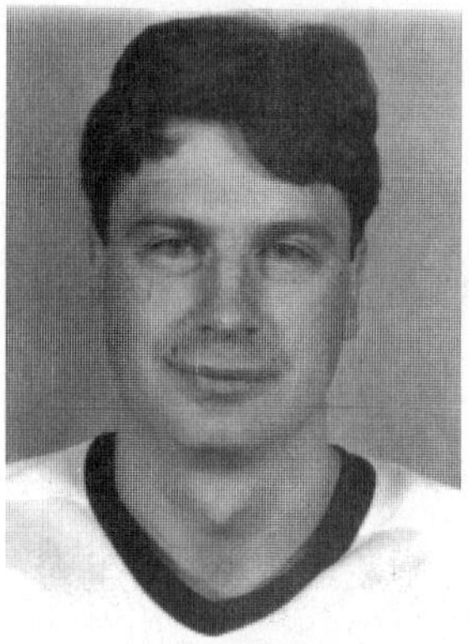

Oleg Mikulchik

Name	NHL Teams	NHL Seasons	Regular Schedule GP	G	A	TP	PIM	Playoffs GP	G	A	TP	PIM	NHL Cup Wins	First NHL Season	Last NHL Season
• McAndrew, Hazen	Bro.	1	7	0	1	1	6	....	....	....	....	....		1941-42	1941-42
McAneeley, Ted	Cal.	3	158	8	35	43	141	....	....	....	....	....		1972-73	1974-75
McAtee, Jud	Det.	3	46	15	13	28	6	14	2	1	3	0		1942-43	1944-45
McAtee, Norm	Bos.	1	13	0	1	1	0	....	....	....	....	....		1946-47	1946-47
McAvoy, George	Mtl.	1	....	....	....	....	....	4	0	0	0	0		1954-55	1954-55
McBain, Andrew	Wpg., Pit., Van., Ott.	11	608	129	172	301	633	24	5	7	12	39		1983-84	1993-94
McBean, Wayne	L.A., NYI, Wpg.	6	211	10	39	49	168	2	1	1	2	0		1987-88	1993-94
McBride, Cliff	Mtl.M., Tor.	2	2	0	0	0	0	....	....	....	....	....		1928-29	1929-30
McBurney, Jim	Chi.	1	1	0	1	1	0	....	....	....	....	....		1952-53	1952-53
• McCabe, Stan	Det., Mtl.M.	4	78	9	4	13	49	....	....	....	....	....		1929-30	1933-34
• McCaffrey, Bert	Tor., Pit., Mtl.	7	260	42	30	72	202	8	2	1	3	12	2	1924-25	1930-31
McCahill, John	Col.	1	1	0	0	0	0	....	....	....	....	....		1977-78	1977-78
McCaig, Douglas	Det., Chi.	7	263	8	21	29	255	7	0	1	1	10		1941-42	1950-51
• McCallum, Dunc	NYR, Pit.	5	187	14	35	49	230	10	1	2	3	12		1965-66	1970-71
McCalmon, Eddie	Chi., Phi.	2	39	5	0	5	14	....	....	....	....	....		1927-28	1930-31
McCann, Rick	Det.	6	43	1	4	5	6	....	....	....	....	....		1967-68	1974-75
McCarthy, Dan	NYR	1	5	4	0	4	4	....	....	....	....	....		1980-81	1980-81
McCarthy, Kevin	Phi., Van., Pit.	10	537	67	191	258	527	21	2	3	5	20		1977-78	1986-87
• McCarthy, Tom	Que., Ham.	2	34	19	3	22	10	....	....	....	....	....		1919-20	1920-21
McCarthy, Tom	Det., Bos.	4	60	8	9	17	8	....	....	....	....	....		1956-57	1960-61
McCarthy, Tom	Min., Bos.	9	460	178	221	399	330	68	12	26	38	67		1979-80	1987-88
McCartney, Walt	Mtl.	1	2	0	0	0	0	....	....	....	....	....		1932-33	1932-33
McCaskill, Ted	Min.	1	4	0	2	2	0	....	....	....	....	....		1967-68	1967-68
McClanahan, Rob	Buf., Hfd., NYR	5	224	38	63	101	126	34	4	12	16	31		1979-80	1983-84
McClelland, Kevin	Pit., Edm., Det., Tor., Wpg.	12	588	68	112	180	1672	98	11	18	29	281	4	1981-82	1993-94
McCord, Bob	Bos., Det., Min., St.L.	7	316	10	58	68	262	14	2	5	7	10		1963-64	1972-73
McCord, Dennis	Van.	1	3	0	0	0	6	....	....	....	....	....		1973-74	1973-74
McCormack, John	Tor., Mtl., Chi.	8	311	25	49	74	35	22	1	1	2	0	2	1947-48	1954-55
McCourt, Dale	Det., Buf., Tor.	7	532	194	284	478	124	21	9	7	16	6		1977-78	1983-84
McCreary, Bill	Tor.	1	12	1	0	1	4	....	....	....	....	....		1980-81	1980-81
McCreary, Bill E.	NYR, Det., Mtl., St.L.	8	309	53	62	115	108	48	6	16	22	14		1953-54	1970-71
McCreary, Keith	Mtl., Pit., Atl.	10	532	131	112	243	294	16	0	4	4	6		1961-62	1974-75
• McCreedy, Johnny	Tor.	2	64	17	12	29	25	21	4	3	7	16	2	1941-42	1944-45
McCrimmon, Jim	St.L.	1	2	0	0	0	0	....	....	....	....	....		1974-75	1974-75
McCulley, Bob	Mtl.	1	1	0	0	0	0	....	....	....	....	....		1934-35	1934-35
McCurry, Duke	Pit.	4	148	21	11	32	119	4	0	2	2	4		1925-26	1928-29
McCutcheon, Brian	Det.	3	37	3	1	4	7	....	....	....	....	....		1974-75	1976-77
McCutcheon, Darwin	Tor.	1	1	0	0	0	2	....	....	....	....	....		1981-82	1981-82
McDill, Jeff	Chi.	1	1	0	0	0	0	....	....	....	....	....		1976-77	1976-77
McDonagh, Bill	NYR	1	4	0	0	0	2	....	....	....	....	....		1949-50	1949-50
McDonald, Ab	Mtl., Chi., Bos., Det., Pit., St.L.	15	762	182	248	430	200	84	21	29	50	42	4	1957-58	1971-72
McDonald, Brian	Chi., Buf.	2	12	0	0	0	29	8	0	0	0	2		1967-68	1970-71
• McDonald, Bucko	Det., Tor., NYR	11	446	35	88	123	206	50	6	1	7	24	3	1934-35	1944-45
McDonald, Butch	Det., Chi.	2	66	8	20	28	2	5	0	2	2	10		1939-40	1944-45
McDonald, Gerry	Hfd.	2	8	0	0	0	4	....	....	....	....	....		1981-82	1981-82
• McDonald, Jack	Mtl.W, Mtl., Que., Tor.	5	73	27	11	38	22	12	2	0	2	5		1917-18	1921-22
McDonald, John	NYR	1	43	10	9	19	6	....	....	....	....	....		1943-44	1943-44
McDonald, Lanny	Tor., Col., Cgy.	16	1111	500	506	1006	899	117	44	40	84	120	1	1973-74	1988-89
McDonald, Robert	NYR	1	1	0	0	0	0	....	....	....	....	....		1943-44	1943-44
McDonald, Terry	K.C.	1	8	0	1	1	6	....	....	....	....	....		1975-76	1975-76
McDonnell, Joe	Van., Pit.	3	50	2	10	12	34	....	....	....	....	....		1981-82	1985-86
• McDonnell, Moylan	Ham.	1	20	1	1	2	0	....	....	....	....	....		1920-21	1920-21
McDonough, Al	L.A., Pit., Atl., Det.	5	237	73	88	161	73	8	0	1	1	2		1970-71	1977-78
McDonough, Hubie	L.A., NYI, S.J.	5	195	40	26	66	67	5	1	0	1	4		1988-89	1992-93
McDougal, Mike	NYR, Hfd.	4	61	8	10	18	43	....	....	....	....	....		1978-79	1982-83
McDougall, Bill	Det., Edm., T.B.	3	28	5	5	10	12	1	0	0	0	0		1990-91	1993-94
McElmury, Jim	Min., K.C., Col.	5	180	14	47	61	49	....	....	....	....	....		1972-73	1977-78
McEwen, Mike	NYR, Col., NYI, L.A., Wsh., Det., Hfd.	12	716	108	296	404	460	78	12	36	48	48	3	1976-77	1987-88
McFadden, Jim	Det., Chi.	8	412	100	126	226	89	49	10	9	19	30	1	1947-48	1953-54
McFadyen, Don	Chi.	4	179	12	33	45	77	11	2	2	4	5	1	1932-33	1935-36
McFall, Dan	Wpg.	2	9	0	1	1	0	....	....	....	....	....		1984-85	1985-86
McFarland, George	Chi.	1	2	0	0	0	0	....	....	....	....	....		1926-27	1926-27
McGeough, Jim	Wsh., Pit.	4	57	7	10	17	32	....	....	....	....	....		1981-82	1986-87
McGibbon, John	Mtl.	1	1	0	0	0	2	....	....	....	....	....		1942-43	1942-43
McGill, Bob	Tor., Chi., S.J., Det., NYI, Hfd.	13	705	17	55	72	1766	49	0	0	0	88		1981-82	1993-94
McGill, Jack	Mtl.	3	134	27	10	37	71	3	2	0	2	0		1934-35	1936-37
McGill, Jack G.	Bos.	4	97	23	36	59	42	27	7	4	11	17		1941-42	1946-47
McGill, Ryan	Chi., Phi., Edm.	4	151	4	15	19	391	....	....	....	....	....		1991-92	1994-95
McGregor, Sandy	NYR	1	2	0	0	0	2	....	....	....	....	....		1963-64	1963-64
McGuire, Mickey	Pit.	2	36	3	0	3	6	....	....	....	....	....		1926-27	1927-28
McHugh, Mike	Min., S.J.	4	20	1	0	1	16	....	....	....	....	....		1988-89	1991-92
McIlhargey, Jack	Phi., Van., Hfd.	8	393	11	36	47	1102	27	0	3	3	68		1974-75	1981-82
• McInenly, Bert	Det., NYA, Ott., Bos.	6	166	19	15	34	144	4	0	0	0	2		1930-31	1935-36
McIntosh, Bruce	Min.	1	2	0	0	0	0	....	....	....	....	....		1972-73	1972-73
McIntosh, Paul	Buf.	2	48	0	2	2	66	2	0	0	0	7		1974-75	1975-76
McIntyre, Jack	Bos., Chi., Det.	11	499	109	102	211	173	29	7	6	13	4		1949-50	1959-60
McIntyre, John	Tor., L.A., NYR, Van.	6	351	24	54	78	516	44	0	6	6	54		1989-90	1994-95
McIntyre, Larry	Tor.	2	41	0	3	3	26	....	....	....	....	....		1969-70	1972-73
McKay, Doug	Det.	1	....	....	....	....	....	1	0	0	0	0	1	1949-50	1949-50
McKay, Ray	Chi., Buf., Cal.	6	140	2	16	18	102	....	....	....	....	....		1968-69	1973-74
McKay, Scott	Ana.	1	1	0	0	0	0	....	....	....	....	....		1993-94	1993-94
McKechnie, Walt	Min., Cal., Bos., Det., Wsh., Clev., Tor., Col.	16	955	214	392	606	469	15	7	5	12	7		1967-68	1982-83
McKee, Mike	Que.	1	48	3	12	15	41	....	....	....	....	....		1993-94	1993-94
McKegney, Ian	Chi.	1	3	0	0	0	2	....	....	....	....	....		1976-77	1976-77
McKegney, Tony	Buf., Que., Min., NYR, St.L., Det., Chi.	13	912	320	319	639	517	79	24	23	47	56		1978-79	1990-91
• McKell, Jack	Ott.	2	42	4	1	5	42	12	0	0	0	0	1	1919-20	1920-21
McKendry, Alex	NYI, Cgy.	4	46	3	6	9	21	6	2	2	4	0	1	1977-78	1980-81
McKenna, Sean	Buf., L.A., Tor.	9	414	82	80	162	181	15	1	2	3	2		1981-82	1989-90
McKenney, Don	Bos., NYR, Tor., Det., St.L.	13	798	237	345	582	211	58	18	29	47	10	1	1954-55	1967-68
McKenny, Jim	Tor., Min.	14	604	82	247	329	294	37	7	9	16	10		1965-66	1978-79
McKenzie, Brian	Pit.	1	6	1	1	2	4	....	....	....	....	....		1971-72	1971-72
McKenzie, John	Chi., Det., NYR, Bos.	12	691	206	268	474	917	69	15	32	47	133	2	1958-59	1971-72
McKim, Andrew	Bos., Det.	3	38	1	4	5	6	....	....	....	....	....		1992-93	1994-95
McKinnon, Alex	Ham., NYA, Chi.	5	194	19	10	29	235	....	....	....	....	....		1924-25	1928-29
McKinnon, Bob	Chi.	1	2	0	0	0	0	....	....	....	....	....		1928-29	1928-29
• McKinnon, John	Mtl., Pit., Phi.	6	208	28	11	39	224	2	0	0	0	4		1925-26	1930-31
McLean, Don	Wsh.	1	9	0	0	0	6	....	....	....	....	....		1975-76	1975-76
• McLean, Fred	Que., Ham.	2	9	0	0	0	2	....	....	....	....	....		1919-20	1920-21
McLean, Jack	Tor.	3	67	14	24	38	76	13	2	2	4	8	1	1942-43	1944-45
McLean, Jeff	S.J.	1	6	1	0	1	0	....	....	....	....	....		1993-94	1993-94
• McLellan, John	Tor.	1	2	0	0	0	0	....	....	....	....	....		1951-52	1951-52
McLellan, Scott	Bos.	1	2	0	0	0	0	....	....	....	....	....		1982-83	1982-83
McLellan, Todd	NYI	1	5	1	1	2	0	....	....	....	....	....		1987-88	1987-88
• McLenahan, Roly	Det.	1	9	2	1	3	10	2	0	0	0	0		1945-46	1945-46
McLeod, Al	Det.	1	26	2	2	4	24	....	....	....	....	....		1973-74	1973-74
McLeod, Jackie	NYR	5	106	14	23	37	12	7	0	0	0	0		1949-50	1954-55
• McMahon, Mike C.	Mtl., Bos.	3	57	7	18	25	102	13	1	2	3	30	1	1942-43	1945-46
McMahon, Mike W.	NYR, Min., Chi., Det., Pit., Buf.	8	224	15	68	83	171	14	3	7	10	4		1963-64	1971-72
McManama, Bob	Pit.	3	99	11	25	36	28	8	0	1	1	6		1973-74	1975-76
McManus, Sammy	Mtl.M., Bos.	2	26	0	1	1	8	1	0	0	0	0	1	1934-35	1936-37
McMurchy, Tom	Chi., Edm.	4	55	8	4	12	65	....	....	....	....	....		1983-84	1987-88
McNab, Max	Det.	4	128	16	19	35	24	25	1	0	1	4	1	1947-48	1950-51
McNab, Peter	Buf., Bos., Van., N.J.	14	954	363	450	813	179	107	40	42	82	20		1973-74	1986-87
McNabney, Sid	Mtl.	1	....	....	....	....	....	5	0	1	1	2		1950-51	1950-51
• McNamara, Howard	Mtl.	1	11	1	0	1	2	....	....	....	....	....		1919-20	1919-20
• McNaughton, George	Que.B.	1	1	0	0	0	0	....	....	....	....	....		1919-20	1919-20
McNeill, Billy	Det.	6	257	21	46	67	142	4	1	1	2	4		1956-57	1963-64
McNeill, Michael	Chi., Que.	2	63	5	11	16	18	....	....	....	....	....		1990-91	1991-92
McNeill, Stu	Det.	3	10	1	1	2	2	....	....	....	....	....		1957-58	1959-60
McPhee, George	NYR, N.J.	7	115	24	25	49	257	29	5	3	8	69		1982-83	1988-89
McPhee, Mike	Mtl., Min., Dal.	11	744	200	199	399	661	134	28	27	55	193	1	1983-84	1993-94
McRae, Chris	Tor., Det.	3	21	1	0	1	122	....	....	....	....	....		1987-88	1989-90
McRae, Ken	Que., Tor.	7	137	14	21	35	364	6	0	0	0	4		1987-88	1993-94

Name	NHL Teams	NHL Seasons	Regular Schedule GP	G	A	TP	PIM	Playoffs GP	G	A	TP	PIM	NHL Cup Wins	First NHL Season	Last NHL Season
McReavy, Pat	Bos., Det.	4	55	5	10	15	4	22	3	3	6	9	1	1938-39	1941-42
McReynolds, Brian	Wpg., NYR, L.A.	3	30	1	5	6	8	....	....	....	....	....		1989-90	1993-94
McSheffrey, Bryan	Van., Buf.	3	90	13	7	20	44	....	....	....	....	....		1972-73	1974-75
McSween, Don	Buf., Ana.	5	47	3	10	13	55	....	....	....	....	....		1987-88	1995-96
McTaggart, Jim	Wsh.	2	71	3	10	13	205	....	....	....	....	....		1980-81	1981-82
McTavish, Gordon	St.L., Wpg.	2	11	1	3	4	2	....	....	....	....	....		1978-79	1979-80
• McVeigh, Charley	Chi., NYA	9	397	84	88	172	138	4	0	0	0	2		1926-27	1934-35
McVicar, Jack	Mtl.M.	2	88	2	4	6	63	6	0	0	0	2		1930-31	1931-32
Meagher, Rick	Mtl., Hfd., N.J., St.L.	12	691	144	165	309	383	62	8	7	15	41		1979-80	1990-91
Meehan, Gerry	Tor., Phi., Buf., Van., Atl., Wsh.	10	670	180	243	423	111	10	0	1	1	0		1968-69	1978-79
Meeke, Brent	Cal., Clev.	5	75	9	22	31	8	....	....	....	....	....		1972-73	1976-77
Meeker, Howie	Tor.	8	346	83	102	185	329	42	6	9	15	50	4	1946-47	1953-54
Meeker, Mike	Pit.	1	4	0	0	0	5	....	....	....	....	....		1978-79	1978-79
• Meeking, Harry	Tor., Det., Bos.	3	63	18	3	21	57	14	4	2	6	24	1	1917-18	1926-27
Meger, Paul	Mtl.	6	212	39	52	91	118	35	3	8	11	16	1	1949-50	1954-55
Meighan, Ron	Min., Pit.	2	48	3	7	10	18	....	....	....	....	....		1981-82	1982-83
Meissner, Barrie	Min.	2	6	0	1	1	4	....	....	....	....	....		1967-68	1968-69
Meissner, Dick	Bos., NYR	5	171	11	15	26	37	....	....	....	....	....		1959-60	1964-65
Melametsa, Anssi	Wpg.	1	27	0	3	3	2	....	....	....	....	....		1985-86	1985-86
Melin, Roger	Min.	2	3	0	0	0	0	....	....	....	....	....		1980-81	1981-82
Mellor, Tom	Det.	2	26	2	4	6	25	....	....	....	....	....		1973-74	1974-75
Melnyk, Gerry	Det., Chi., St.L.	6	269	39	77	116	34	53	6	6	12	6		1955-56	1967-68
Melnyk, Larry	Bos., Edm., NYR, Van.	10	432	11	63	74	686	66	2	9	11	127	1	1980-81	1989-90
Melrose, Barry	Wpg., Tor., Det.	6	300	10	23	33	728	7	0	2	2	38		1979-80	1985-86
Menard, Hillary	Chi.	1	1	0	0	0	0	....	....	....	....	....		1953-54	1953-54
Menard, Howie	Det., L.A., Chi., Oak.	4	151	23	42	65	87	19	3	7	10	36		1963-64	1969-70
Mercredi, Vic	Atl.	1	2	0	0	0	0	....	....	....	....	....		1974-75	1974-75
Meredith, Greg	Cgy.	2	38	6	4	10	8	5	3	1	4	4		1980-81	1982-83
Merkosky, Glenn	Hfd., N.J., Det.	5	66	5	12	17	22	....	....	....	....	....		1981-82	1989-90
Meronek, Bill	Mtl.	2	19	5	8	13	0	1	0	0	0	0		1939-40	1942-43
Merrick, Wayne	St.L., Cal., Clev., NYI	12	774	191	265	456	303	102	19	30	49	30	4	1972-73	1983-84
• Merrill, Horace	Ott.	2	11	0	0	0	0	....	....	....	....	....	1	1917-18	1919-20
Messier, Mitch	Min.	4	20	0	2	2	11	....	....	....	....	....		1987-88	1990-91
Messier, Paul	Col.	1	9	0	0	0	4	....	....	....	....	....		1978-79	1978-79
Metcalfe, Scott	Edm., Buf.	3	19	1	2	3	18	....	....	....	....	....		1987-88	1989-90
Metz, Don	Tor.	9	172	20	35	55	42	42	7	8	15	12	5	1939-40	1948-49
• Metz, Nick	Tor.	12	518	131	119	250	149	76	19	20	39	31	4	1934-35	1947-48
Michaluk, Art	Chi.	1	5	0	0	0	0	....	....	....	....	....		1947-48	1947-48
Michaluk, John	Chi.	1	1	0	0	0	0	....	....	....	....	....		1950-51	1950-51
Michayluk, Dave	Phi., Pit.	3	14	2	6	8	8	7	1	1	2	0	1	1981-82	1991-92
Micheletti, Joe	St.L., Col.	3	158	11	60	71	114	11	1	11	12	10		1979-80	1981-82
Micheletti, Pat	Min.	1	12	2	0	2	8	....	....	....	....	....		1987-88	1987-88
• Mickey, Larry	Chi., NYR., Tor., Mtl., L.A., Phi., Buf.	11	292	39	53	92	160	9	1	0	1	10		1964-65	1974-75
Mickoski, Nick	NYR, Chi., Det., Bos.	13	703	158	185	343	319	18	1	6	7.	6		1947-48	1959-60
Middendorf, Max	Que., Edm.	4	13	2	4	6	6	....	....	....	....	....		1986-87	1990-91
Middleton, Rick	NYR, Bos.	14	1005	448	540	988	157	114	45	55	100	19		1974-75	1987-88
Miehm, Kevin	St.L.	2	22	1	4	5	8	2	0	1	1	0		1992-93	1993-94
Migay, Rudy	Tor.	10	418	59	92	151	293	15	1	0	1	20		1949-50	1959-60
Mikita, Stan	Chi.	22	1394	541	926	1467	1270	155	59	91	150	169	1	1958-59	1979-80
Mikkelson, Bill	L.A., N.Y.I., Wsh.	4	147	4	18	22	105	....	....	....	....	....		1971-72	1976-77
Mikol, Jim	Tor., NYR	2	34	1	4	5	8	....	....	....	....	....		1962-63	1964-65
Mikulchik, Oleg	Wpg., Ana.	3	37	0	3	3	33	....	....	....	....	....		1993-94	1995-96
Milbury, Mike	Bos.	12	754	49	189	238	1552	86	4	24	28	219		1975-76	1986-87
• Milks, Hib	Pit., Phi., NYR, Ott.	8	317	87	41	128	179	9	0	0	0	2		1925-26	1932-33
Millar, Hugh	Det.	1	4	0	0	0	0	1	0	0	0	0		1946-47	1946-47
Millar, Mike	Hfd., Wsh., Bos., Tor.	5	78	18	18	36	12	....	....	....	....	....		1986-87	1990-91
Miller, Bill	Mtl.M., Mtl.	3	95	7	3	10	16	12	0	0	0	0	1	1934-35	1936-37
Miller, Bob	Bos., Col., L.A.	6	404	75	119	194	220	36	4	7	11	27		1977-78	1984-85
Miller, Brad	Buf., Ott., Cgy.	6	82	1	5	6	321	....	....	....	....	....		1988-89	1993-94
• Miller, Earl	Chi., Tor.	5	109	19	14	33	124	10	1	0	1	6	1	1927-28	1931-32
Miller, Jack	Chi.	2	17	0	0	0	4	....	....	....	....	....		1949-50	1950-51
Miller, Jason	N.J.	3	6	0	0	0	0	....	....	....	....	....		1990-91	1992-93
Miller, Jay	Bos., L.A.	7	446	40	44	84	1723	48	2	3	5	243		1985-86	1991-92
Miller, Paul	Col.	1	3	0	3	3	0	....	....	....	....	....		1981-82	1981-82
Miller, Perry	Det.	4	217	10	51	61	387	....	....	....	....	....		1977-78	1980-81
Miller, Tom	Det., NYI	4	118	16	25	41	34	....	....	....	....	....		1970-71	1974-75
Miller, Warren	NYR, Hfd.	4	262	40	50	90	137	6	1	0	1	0		1979-80	1982-83
Miner, John	Edm.	1	14	2	3	5	16	....	....	....	....	....		1987-88	1987-88
Minor, Gerry	Van.	5	140	11	21	32	173	12	1	3	4	25		1979-80	1983-84
Miszuk, John	Det., Chi., Phi., Min.	6	237	7	39	46	232	19	0	3	3	19		1963-64	1969-70
Mitchell, Bill	Det.	1	1	0	0	0	0	....	....	....	....	....		1963-64	1963-64
Mitchell, Herb	Bos.	2	53	6	0	6	38	....	....	....	....	....		1924-25	1925-26
Mitchell, Red	Chi.	3	83	4	5	9	67	....	....	....	....	....		1941-42	1944-45
Mitchell, Roy	Min.	1	3	0	0	0	0	....	....	....	....	....		1992-93	1992-93
Moe, Billy	NYR	5	261	11	42	53	163	1	0	0	0	0		1944-45	1948-49
Moffat, Lyle	Tor., Wpg.	3	97	12	16	28	51	....	....	....	....	....		1972-73	1979-80
• Moffat, Ron	Det.	3	37	1	1	2	8	7	0	0	0	0		1932-33	1934-35
Moher, Mike	N.J.	1	9	0	1	1	28	....	....	....	....	....		1982-83	1982-83
Mohns, Doug	Bos., Chi., Min., Atl., Wsh.	22	1390	248	462	710	1250	94	14	36	50	122		1953-54	1974-75
Mohns, Lloyd	NYR	1	1	0	0	0	0	....	....	....	....	....		1943-44	1943-44
Mokosak, Carl	Cgy., L.A., Phi., Pit., Bos.	6	83	11	15	26	170	1	0	0	0	0		1981-82	1988-89
Mokosak, John	Det.	2	41	0	2	2	96	....	....	....	....	....		1988-89	1989-90
Molin, Lars	Van.	3	172	33	65	98	37	19	2	9	11	7		1981-82	1983-84
Moller, Mike	Buf., Edm.	7	134	15	28	43	41	3	0	1	1	0		1980-81	1986-87
Moller, Randy	Que., NYR, Buf., Fla.	14	815	45	180	225	1692	78	6	16	22	197		1981-82	1994-95
Molloy, Mitch	Buf.	1	2	0	0	0	10	....	....	....	....	....		1989-90	1989-90
Molyneaux, Larry	NYR	2	45	0	1	1	20	10	0	0	0	8		1937-38	1938-39
Monahan, Garry	Mtl., Det., L.A., Tor., Van.	12	748	116	169	285	484	22	3	1	4	13		1967-68	1978-79
Monahan, Hartland	Cal., NYR, Wsh., Pit., L.A., St.L.	7	334	61	80	141	163	6	0	0	0	4		1973-74	1980-81
• Mondou, Armand	Mtl.	11	386	47	71	118	99	32	3	5	8	12	2	1928-29	1939-40
Mondou, Pierre	Mtl.	9	548	194	262	456	179	69	17	28	45	26	3	1976-77	1984-85
Mongeau, Michel	St.L., T.B.	4	54	6	19	25	10	2	0	1	1	0		1989-90	1992-93
Mongrain, Bob	Buf., L.A.	6	81	13	14	27	14	11	1	2	3	2		1979-80	1985-86
Monteith, Hank	Det.	3	77	5	12	17	6	4	0	0	0	0		1968-69	1970-71
Moore, Dickie	Mtl., Tor., St.L.	14	719	261	347	608	652	135	46	64	110	122	6	1951-52	1967-68
• Moran, Amby	Mtl., Chi.	2	35	1	1	2	24	....	....	....	....	....		1926-27	1927-28
• Morenz, Howie	Mtl., Chi., NYR	14	550	270	197	467	563	47	21	11	32	68	3	1923-24	1936-37
Moretto, Angelo	Clev.	1	5	1	2	3	2	....	....	....	....	....		1976-77	1976-77
Morin, Pete	Mtl.	1	31	10	12	22	7	1	0	0	0	0		1941-42	1941-42
Morin, Stephane	Que., Van.	5	90	16	39	55	52	....	....	....	....	....		1989-90	1993-94
Morris, Bernie	Bos.	1	6	2	0	2	0	....	....	....	....	....		1924-25	1924-25
Morris, Elwyn	Tor., NYR	4	135	13	29	42	58	18	4	2	6	16	1	1943-44	1948-49
Morris, Jon	N.J., S.J., Bos.	6	103	16	33	49	47	11	1	7	8	25		1988-89	1993-94
Morrison, Dave	L.A., Van.	4	39	3	3	6	4	....	....	....	....	....		1980-81	1984-85
Morrison, Don	Det., Chi.	3	112	18	28	46	12	3	0	1	1	0		1947-48	1950-51
Morrison, Doug	Bos.	4	23	7	3	10	15	....	....	....	....	....		1979-80	1984-85
Morrison, Gary	Phi.	3	43	1	15	16	70	5	0	1	1	2		1979-80	1981-82
Morrison, George	St.L.	2	115	17	21	38	13	3	0	0	0	0		1970-71	1971-72
Morrison, Jim	Bos., Tor., Det., NYR, Pit.	12	704	40	160	200	542	36	0	12	12	38		1951-52	1970-71
Morrison, John	NYA	1	18	0	0	0	0	....	....	....	....	....		1925-26	1925-26
Morrison, Kevin	Col.	1	41	4	11	15	23	....	....	....	....	....		1979-80	1979-80
Morrison, Lew	Phi., Atl., Wsh., Pit.	9	564	39	52	91	107	17	0	0	0	2		1969-70	1977-78
Morrison, Mark	NYR	2	10	1	1	2	0	....	....	....	....	....		1981-82	1983-84
Morrison, Roderick	Det.	1	34	8	7	15	4	3	0	0	0	0		1947-48	1947-48
Morrow, Ken	NYI	10	550	17	88	105	309	127	11	22	33	97	4	1979-80	1988-89
Morrow, Scott	Cgy.	1	4	0	0	0	0	....	....	....	....	....		1994-95	1994-95
Morton, Dean	Det.	1	1	1	0	1	2	....	....	....	....	....		1989-90	1989-90
Mortson, Gus	Tor., Chi., Det.	13	797	46	152	198	1380	54	5	8	13	68	4	1946-47	1958-59
Mosdell, Kenny	Bro., Mtl., Chi.	16	693	141	168	309	475	80	16	13	29	48	4	1941-42	1958-59
• Mosienko, Bill	Chi.	14	711	258	282	540	121	22	10	4	14	15		1941-42	1954-55
Mott, Morris	Cal.	3	199	18	32	50	49	....	....	....	....	....		1972-73	1974-75
• Motter, Alex	Bos., Det.	8	256	39	64	103	135	41	3	9	12	41	1	1934-35	1942-43
Moxey, Jim	Cal., Clev., L.A.	3	127	22	27	49	59	....	....	....	....	....		1974-75	1976-77
Mulhern, Richard	Atl., L.A., Tor., Wpg.	6	303	27	93	120	217	7	0	3	3	5		1975-76	1980-81

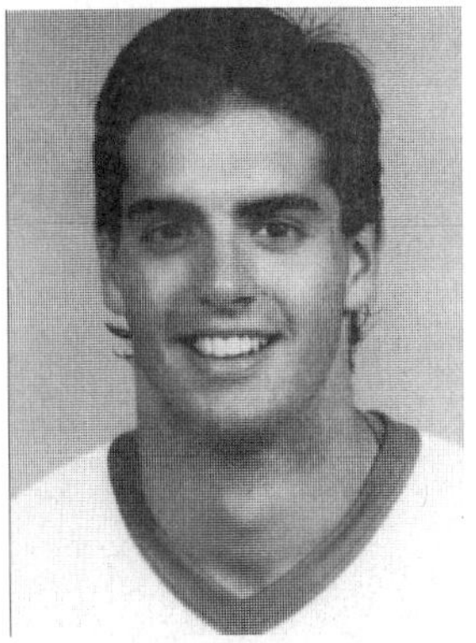

Dean Morton

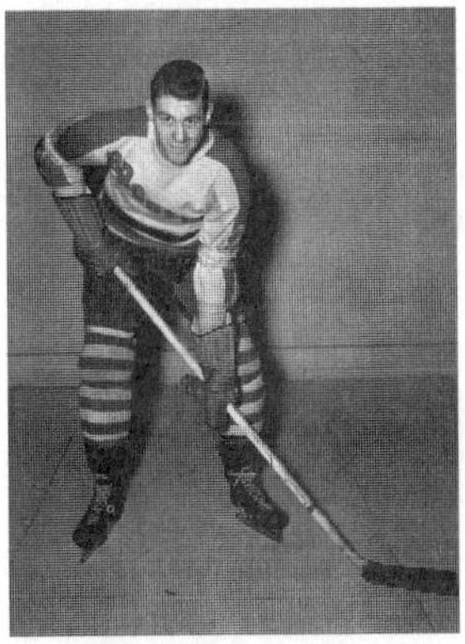

Ken Mosdell

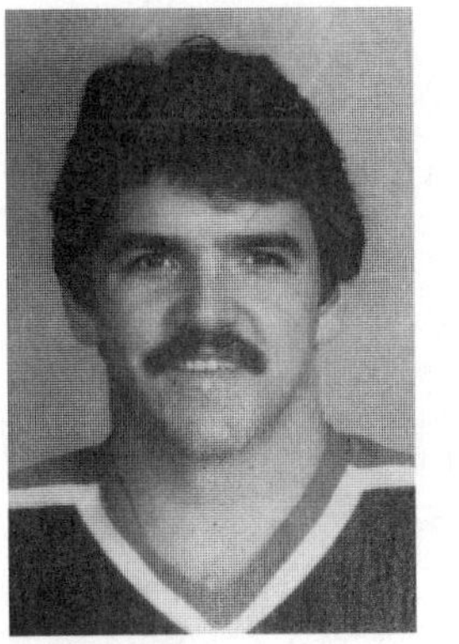

Paul Mulvey

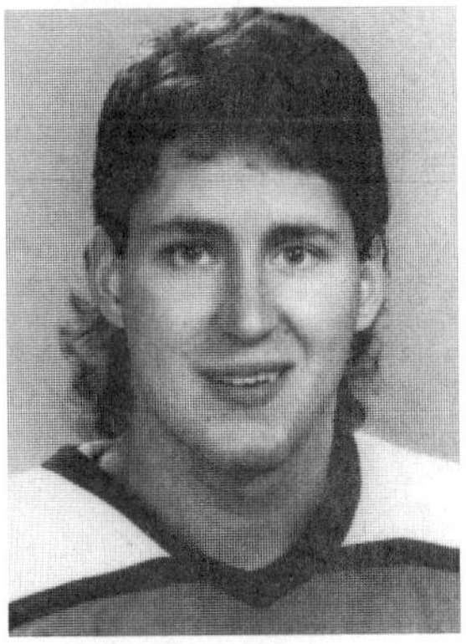

Pat Murray

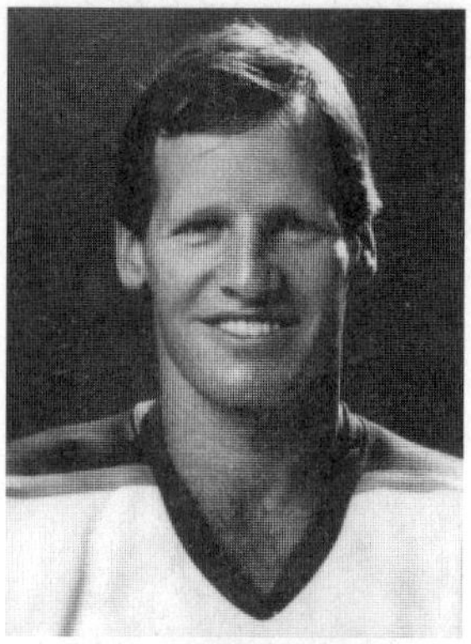

Mark Napier

Name	NHL Teams	NHL Seasons	Regular Schedule GP	G	A	TP	PIM	Playoffs GP	G	A	TP	PIM	NHL Cup Wins	First NHL Season	Last NHL Season
Mullen, Brian	Wpg., NYR, S.J., NYI	11	832	260	362	622	414	62	12	18	30	30		1982-83	1992-93
Muloin, Wayne	Det., Oak., Cal., Min.	3	147	3	21	24	93	11	0	0	0	2		1963-64	1970-71
Mulvenna, Glenn	Pit., Phi.	2	2	0	0	0	4	....	....	....	....	....		1991-92	1992-93
Mulvey, Grant	Chi., N.J.	10	586	149	135	284	816	42	10	5	15	70		1974-75	1983-84
Mulvey, Paul	Wsh., Pit., L.A.	4	225	30	51	81	613	....	....	....	....	....		1978-79	1981-82
• Mummery, Harry	Tor., Que., Mtl., Ham.	6	106	33	13	46	185	7	1	4	5	0	1	1917-18	1922-23
• Munro, Dunc	Mtl. M.	8	239	28	18	46	170	25	3	2	5	24	1	1924-25	1931-32
Munro, Gerry	Mtl. M., Tor.	2	33	1	0	1	22	....	....	....	....	....		1924-25	1925-26
Murdoch, Bob J.	Mtl., L.A., Atl., Cgy.	12	757	60	218	278	764	69	4	18	22	92	2	1970-71	1981-82
Murdoch, Bob L.	Cal., Clev., St.L.	4	260	72	85	157	127	....	....	....	....	....		1975-76	1978-79
Murdoch, Don	NYR, Edm., Det.	6	320	121	117	238	155	24	10	8	18	16		1976-77	1981-82
Murdoch, Murray	NYR	11	507	84	108	192	197	55	9	12	21	28	2	1926-27	1936-37
Murphy, Brian	Det.	1	1	0	0	0	0	....	....	....	....	....		1974-75	1974-75
Murphy, Mike	St.L. NYR, L.A.	12	831	238	318	556	514	66	13	23	36	54		1971-72	1982-83
Murphy, Rob	Van., Ott., L.A.	7	125	9	12	21	152	4	0	0	0	2		1987-88	1993-94
Murphy, Ron	NYR, Chi., Det., Bos.	18	889	205	274	479	460	53	7	8	15	26	1	1952-53	1969-70
Murray, Allan	NYA	7	271	5	9	14	163	....	....	....	....	....		1933-34	1939-40
Murray, Bob F.	Chi.	15	1008	132	382	514	873	112	19	37	56	106		1975-76	1989-90
Murray, Bob J.	Atl., Van.	4	194	6	16	22	98	10	1	1	2	15		1973-74	1976-77
Murray, Jim	L.A.	1	30	0	2	2	14	....	....	....	....	....		1967-68	1967-68
Murray, Ken	Tor., N.Y.I., Det., K.C.	5	106	1	10	11	135	....	....	....	....	....		1969-70	1975-76
Murray, Leo	Mtl.	1	6	0	0	0	2	....	....	....	....	....		1932-33	1932-33
Murray, Mike	Phi.	1	1	0	0	0	0	....	....	....	....	....		1987-88	1987-88
Murray, Pat	Phi.	2	25	3	1	4	15	....	....	....	....	....		1990-91	1991-92
Murray, Randy	Tor.	1	3	0	0	0	2	....	....	....	....	....		1969-70	1969-70
Murray, Terry	Cal., Phi., Det., Wsh.	8	302	4	76	80	199	18	2	2	4	10		1972-73	1981-82
Myers, Hap	Buf.	1	13	0	0	0	6	....	....	....	....	....		1970-71	1970-71
Myles, Vic	NYR	1	45	6	9	15	57	....	....	....	....	....		1942-43	1942-43

N

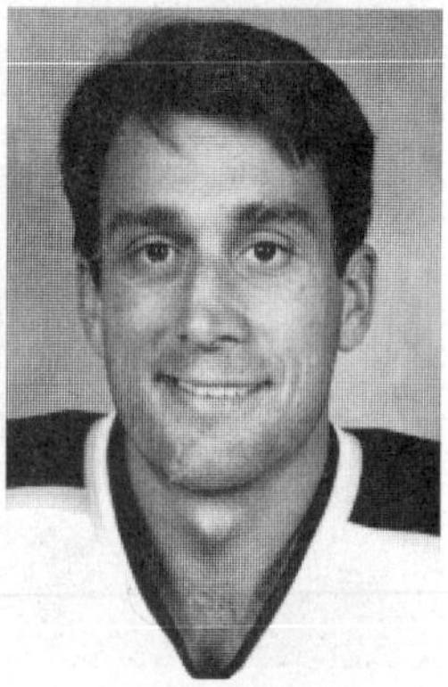

Cam Neely

Name	NHL Teams	NHL Seasons	Regular Schedule GP	G	A	TP	PIM	Playoffs GP	G	A	TP	PIM	NHL Cup Wins	First NHL Season	Last NHL Season
Nachbaur, Don	Hfd., Edm., Phi.	8	223	23	46	69	465	11	1	1	2	24		1980-81	1989-90
Nahrgang, Jim	Det.	3	57	5	12	17	34	....	....	....	....	....		1974-75	1976-77
Nanne, Lou	Min.	11	635	68	157	225	356	32	4	10	14	8		1967-68	1977-78
Nantais, Richard	Min.	3	63	5	4	9	79	....	....	....	....	....		1974-75	1976-77
Napier, Mark	Mtl., Min., Edm., Buf.	11	767	235	306	541	157	82	18	24	42	11	2	1978-79	1988-89
Naslund, Mats	Mtl., Bos.	9	651	251	383	634	111	102	35	57	92	33	1	1982-83	1994-95
Nattrass, Ralph	Chi.	4	223	18	38	56	308	....	....	....	....	....		1946-47	1949-50
Nattress, Ric	Mtl., St.L., Cgy., Tor., Phi.	11	536	29	135	164	377	67	5	10	15	60	1	1982-83	1992-93
Natyshak, Mike	Que.	1	4	0	0	0	0	....	....	....	....	....		1987-88	1987-88
Neaton, Pat	Pit.	1	9	1	1	2	12	....	....	....	....	....		1993-94	1993-94
Nechaev, Victor	L.A.	1	3	1	0	1	0	....	....	....	....	....		1982-83	1982-83
Nedomansky, Vaclav	Det., NYR, St.L.	6	421	122	156	278	88	7	3	5	8	0		1977-78	1982-83
Needham, Mike	Pit., Dal.	3	86	9	5	14	16	14	2	0	2	4	1	1991-92	1993-94
Neely, Bob	Tor., Col.	5	283	39	59	98	266	26	5	7	12	15		1973-74	1977-78
Neely, Cam	Van., Bos.	13	726	395	299	694	1241	93	57	32	89	168		1983-84	1995-96
Neilson, Jim	NYR, Cal., Clev.	16	1023	69	299	368	904	65	1	17	18	61		1962-63	1977-78
Nelson, Gordie	Tor.	1	3	0	0	0	11	....	....	....	....	....		1969-70	1969-70
Nelson, Todd	Wsh.	2	3	1	0	1	2	4	0	0	0	0		1994-95	1995-96
Nemeth, Steve	NYR	1	12	2	0	2	2	....	....	....	....	....		1987-88	1987-88
Nesterenko, Eric	Tor., Chi.	21	1219	250	324	574	1273	124	13	24	37	127	1	1951-52	1971-72
Nethery, Lance	NYR, Edm.	2	41	11	14	25	14	14	5	3	8	9		1980-81	1981-82
Neufeld, Ray	Hfd., Win., Bos.	11	595	157	200	357	816	28	8	6	14	55		1979-80	1989-90
• Neville, Mike	Tor., NYA	4	65	6	3	9	15	2	0	0	0	0	1	1917-18	1930-31
Nevin, Bob	Tor., NYR, Min., L.A.	18	1128	307	419	726	211	84	16	18	34	24	2	1957-58	1975-76
Newberry, John	Mtl., Hfd.	4	22	0	4	4	6	2	0	0	0	0		1982-83	1985-86
Newell, Rick	Det.	2	6	0	0	0	0	....	....	....	....	....		1972-73	1973-74
Newman, Dan	NYR, Mtl., Edm.	4	126	17	24	41	63	3	0	0	0	4		1976-77	1979-80
Newman, John	Det.	1	8	1	1	2	0	....	....	....	....	....		1930-31	1930-31
Nicholson, Al	Bos.	2	19	0	1	1	4	....	....	....	....	....		1955-56	1956-57
Nicholson, Edward	Det.	1	1	0	0	0	0	....	....	....	....	....		1947-48	1947-48
Nicholson, Graeme	Bos., Col., NYR	3	52	2	7	9	60	....	....	....	....	....		1978-79	1982-83
Nicholson, John	Chi.	1	2	1	0	1	0	....	....	....	....	....		1937-38	1937-38
Nicholson, Neil	Oak., N.Y.I.	4	39	3	1	4	23	2	0	0	0	0		1969-70	1977-78
Nicholson, Paul	Wsh.	3	62	4	8	12	18	....	....	....	....	....		1974-75	1976-77
Niekamp, Jim	Det.	2	29	0	2	2	37	....	....	....	....	....		1970-71	1971-72
Nienhuis, Kraig	Bos.	3	87	20	16	36	39	2	0	0	0	14		1985-86	1987-88
• Nighbor, Frank	Ott., Tor.	13	348	136	60	196	244	36	11	11	22	25	4	1917-18	1929-30
Nigro, Frank	Tor.	2	68	8	18	26	39	3	0	0	0	2		1982-83	1983-84
Nilan, Chris	Mtl., NYR, Bos.	13	688	110	115	225	3043	111	8	9	17	541	1	1979-80	1991-92
Nill, Jim	St.L., Van., Bos., Wpg., Det.	9	524	58	87	145	854	59	10	5	15	203		1981-82	1989-90
Nilsson, Kent	Atl., Cgy., Min., Edm.	9	553	264	422	686	116	59	11	41	52	14	1	1979-80	1994-95
Nilsson, Ulf	NYR	4	170	57	112	169	85	25	8	14	22	27		1978-79	1982-83
Nistico, Lou	Col.	1	3	0	0	0	0	....	....	....	....	....		1977-78	1977-78
• Noble, Reg	Tor., Mtl.M., Det.	16	509	167	79	246	830	32	4	5	9	33	3	1917-18	1932-33
Noel, Claude	Wsh.	1	7	0	0	0	0	....	....	....	....	....		1979-80	1979-80
Nolan, Pat	Tor.	1	2	0	0	0	0	....	....	....	....	....	1	1921-22	1921-22
Nolan, Ted	Det., Pit.	3	78	6	16	22	105	....	....	....	....	....		1981-82	1985-86
Nolet, Simon	Phi., K.C., Pit., Col.	10	562	150	182	332	187	34	6	3	9	8	1	1967-68	1976-77
Nordmark, Robert	St. L., Van.	4	236	13	70	83	254	7	3	2	5	8		1987-88	1990-91
Noris, Joe	Pit., St.L., Buf.	3	55	2	5	7	22	....	....	....	....	....		1971-72	1973-74
Norrish, Rod	Min.	2	21	3	3	6	2	....	....	....	....	....		1973-74	1974-75
• Northcott, Baldy	Mtl.M., Chi.	11	446	133	112	245	273	31	8	5	13	14	1	1928-29	1938-39
Norwich, Craig	Wpg., St.L., Col.	2	104	17	58	75	60	....	....	....	....	....		1979-80	1980-81
Norwood, Lee	Que., Wsh., St.L., Det., N.J., Hfd., Cgy.	12	503	58	153	211	1099	65	6	22	28	171		1980-81	1993-94
Novy, Milan	Wsh.	1	73	18	30	48	16	2	0	0	0	0		1982-83	1982-83
Nowak, Hank	Pit., Det., Bos.	4	180	26	29	55	161	13	1	0	1	8		1973-74	1976-77
Nykoluk, Mike	Tor.	1	32	3	1	4	20	....	....	....	....	....		1956-57	1956-57
Nylund, Gary	Tor., Chi., NYI	11	608	32	139	171	1235	24	0	6	6	63		1982-83	1992-93
• Nyrop, Bill	Mtl., Min.	4	207	12	51	63	101	35	1	7	8	22	3	1975-76	1981-82
Nystrom, Bob	NYI	14	900	235	278	513	1248	157	39	44	83	236	4	1972-73	1985-86

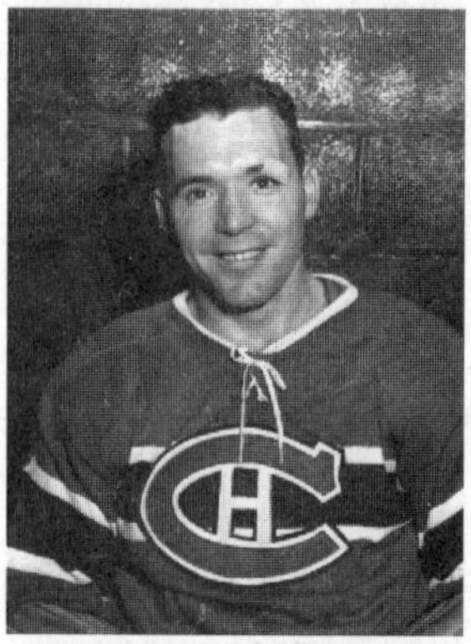

Buddy O'Connor

O

Name	NHL Teams	NHL Seasons	Regular Schedule GP	G	A	TP	PIM	Playoffs GP	G	A	TP	PIM	NHL Cup Wins	First NHL Season	Last NHL Season
• Oatman, Russell	Det., Mtl.M., NYR	3	120	20	9	29	100	15	1	0	1	18		1926-27	1928-29
O'Brien, Dennis	Min., Col., Clev., Bos.	10	592	31	91	122	1017	34	1	2	3	101		1970-71	1979-80
O'Brien, Obie	Bos.	1	2	0	0	0	0	....	....	....	....	....		1955-56	1955-56
O'Callahan, Jack	Chi., N.J.	7	389	27	104	131	541	32	4	11	15	41		1982-83	1988-89
O'Connell, Mike	Chi., Bos., Det.	13	860	105	334	439	605	82	8	24	32	64		1977-78	1989-90
• O'Connor, Buddy	Mtl., NYR	10	509	140	257	397	34	53	15	21	36	6	2	1941-42	1950-51
O'Connor, Myles	N.J., Ana.	4	43	3	4	7	69	....	....	....	....	....		1990-91	1993-94
Oddleifson, Chris	Bos., Van.	9	524	95	191	286	464	14	1	6	7	8		1972-73	1980-81
Odelein, Selmar	Edm.	3	18	0	2	2	35	....	....	....	....	....		1985-86	1988-89
O'Donnell, Fred	Bos.	2	115	15	11	26	98	5	0	1	1	5		1972-73	1973-74
O'Donoghue, Don	Oak., Cal.	3	125	18	17	35	35	3	0	0	0	0		1969-70	1971-72
Odrowski, Gerry	Det., Oak., St.L.	6	309	12	19	31	111	30	0	1	1	16		1960-61	1971-72
O'Dwyer, Bill	L.A., Bos.	5	120	9	13	22	113	10	0	0	0	2		1983-84	1989-90
O'Flaherty, Gerry	Tor., Van., Atl.	8	438	99	95	194	168	7	2	2	4	6		1971-72	1978-79
O'Flaherty, John	NYA, Bro.	2	21	5	1	6	0	....	....	....	....	....		1940-41	1941-42
Ogilvie, Brian	Chi., St.L.	6	90	15	21	36	29	....	....	....	....	....		1972-73	1978-79
O'Grady, George	Mtl.M.	1	4	0	0	0	0	....	....	....	....	....		1917-18	1917-18
Ogrodnick, John	Det., Que., NYR	14	928	402	425	827	260	41	18	8	26	6		1979-80	1992-93
Ojanen, Janne	N.J.	4	98	21	23	44	28	3	0	2	2	0		1988-89	1992-93
Okerlund, Todd	NYI	1	4	0	0	0	2	....	....	....	....	....		1987-88	1987-88
• Oliver, Harry	Bos., NYA	11	463	127	85	212	147	35	10	6	16	24	1	1926-27	1936-37
Oliver, Murray	Det., Bos., Tor., Min.	17	1127	274	454	728	320	35	9	16	25	10		1957-58	1974-75
Olmstead, Bert	Chi., Mtl., Tor.	14	848	181	421	602	884	115	16	43	59	101	5	1948-49	1961-62
Olsen, Darryl	Cgy.	1	1	0	0	0	0	....	....	....	....	....		1991-92	1991-92
Olson, Dennis	Det.	1	4	0	0	0	0	....	....	....	....	....		1957-58	1957-58
O'Neil, Paul	Van., Bos.	2	6	0	0	0	0	....	....	....	....	....		1973-74	1975-76
O'Neill, Jim	Bos., Mtl.	6	156	6	30	36	109	9	1	1	2	13		1933-34	1941-42
• O'Neill, Tom	Tor.	2	66	10	12	22	53	4	0	0	0	6	1	1943-44	1944-45
Orban, Bill	Chi., Min.	3	114	8	15	23	67	3	0	0	0	0		1967-68	1969-70

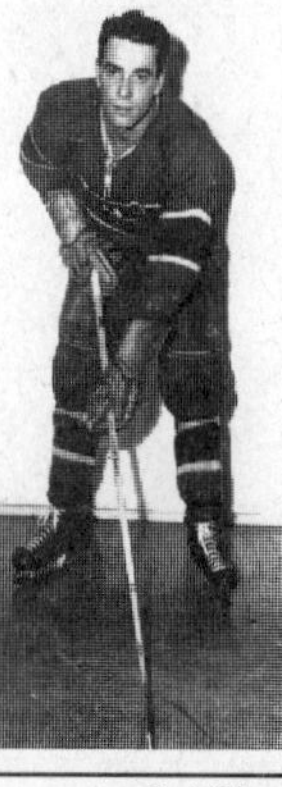

Bert Olmstead

Name	NHL Teams	NHL Seasons	Regular Schedule					Playoffs					NHL Cup Wins	First NHL Season	Last NHL Season
			GP	G	A	TP	PIM	GP	G	A	TP	PIM			
O'Ree, Willie	Bos.	2	45	4	10	14	26	....	....	....	....	....		1957-58	1960-61
O'Regan, Tom	Pit.	3	61	5	12	17	10	....	....	....	....	....		1983-84	1985-86
O'Reilly, Terry	Bos.	14	891	204	402	606	2095	108	25	42	67	335		1971-72	1984-85
Orlando, Gaetano	Buf.	3	98	18	26	44	51	5	0	4	4	14		1984-85	1986-87
Orlando, Jimmy	Det.	6	199	6	25	31	375	36	0	9	9	105	1	1936-37	1942-43
Orleski, Dave	Mtl.	2	2	0	0	0	0	....	....	....	....	....		1980-81	1981-82
Orr, Bobby	Bos., Chi.	12	657	270	645	915	953	74	26	66	92	107	2	1966-67	1978-79
Osborne, Keith	St.L., T.B.	2	16	1	3	4	16	....	....	....	....	....		1989-90	1992-93
Osborne, Mark	Det., NYR, Tor., Wpg.	14	919	212	319	531	1152	87	12	16	28	141		1981-82	1994-95
Osburn, Randy	Tor., Phi.	2	27	0	2	2	0	....	....	....	....	....		1972-73	1974-75
O'Shea, Danny	Min., Chi., St.L.	5	369	64	115	179	265	39	3	7	10	61		1968-69	1972-73
O'Shea, Kevin	Buf., St.L.	3	134	13	18	31	85	12	2	1	3	10		1970-71	1972-73
Osiecki, Mark	Cgy., Ott., Wpg., Min.	2	93	3	11	14	43	....	....	....	....	....		1991-92	1992-93
Otevrel, Jaroslav	S.J.	2	16	3	4	7	2	....	....	....	....	....		1992-93	1993-94
Ouelette, Eddie	Chi.	1	43	3	2	5	11	1	0	0	0	0		1935-36	1935-36
Ouelette, Gerry	Bos.	1	34	5	4	9	0	....	....	....	....	....		1960-61	1960-61
Owchar, Dennis	Pit., Col.	6	288	30	85	115	200	10	1	1	2	8		1974-75	1979-80
• Owen, George	Bos.	5	183	44	33	77	151	21	2	5	7	25	1	1928-29	1932-33

P

Name	NHL Teams	NHL Seasons	GP	G	A	TP	PIM	GP	G	A	TP	PIM	NHL Cup Wins	First NHL Season	Last NHL Season
Pachal, Clayton	Bos., Col.	3	35	2	3	5	95	....	....	....	....	....		1976-77	1978-79
Paddock, John	Wsh., Phi., Que.	5	87	8	14	22	86	5	2	0	2	0		1975-76	1982-83
Paiement, Rosaire	Phi., Van.	5	190	48	52	100	343	3	3	0	3	0		1967-68	1971-72
Paiement, Wilf	K.C. Col., Tor., Que., NYR, Buf., Pit.	14	946	356	458	814	1757	69	18	17	35	185		1974-75	1987-88
Palangio, Peter	Mtl., Det., Chi.	4	71	13	10	23	28	7	0	0	0	0	1	1926-27	1937-38
Palazzari, Aldo	Bos., NYR	1	35	8	3	11	4	....	....	....	....	....		1943-44	1943-44
Palazzari, Doug	St.L.	4	108	18	20	38	23	2	0	0	0	0		1974-75	1978-79
Palmer, Brad	Min., Bos.	3	168	32	38	70	58	29	9	5	14	16		1980-81	1982-83
Palmer, Rob H.	Chi.	3	16	0	3	3	2	....	....	....	....	....		1973-74	1975-76
Palmer, Rob R.	L.A., N.J.	7	320	9	101	110	115	8	1	2	3	6		1977-78	1983-84
• Panagabko, Ed	Bos.	2	29	0	3	3	38	....	....	....	....	....		1955-56	1956-57
Pankewicz, Greg	Ott.	1	3	0	0	0	2	....	....	....	....	....		1993-94	1993-94
Panteleev, Grigori	Bos., NYI	4	54	8	6	14	12	....	....	....	....	....		1992-93	1995-96
• Papike, Joe	Chi.	3	20	3	3	6	4	5	0	2	2	0		1940-41	1944-45
Pappin, Jim	Tor., Chi., Cal., Clev.	14	767	278	295	573	667	92	33	34	67	101	2	1963-64	1976-77
Paradise, Bob	Min., Atl., Pit., Wsh.	8	368	8	54	62	393	12	0	1	1	19		1971-72	1978-79
Pargeter, George	Mtl.	1	4	0	0	0	0	....	....	....	....	....		1946-47	1946-47
Parise, J.P.	Bos., Tor., Min., NYI, Clev.	14	890	238	356	594	706	86	27	31	58	87		1965-66	1978-79
Parizeau, Michel	St.L., Phi.	1	58	3	14	17	18	....	....	....	....	....		1971-72	1971-72
Park, Brad	NYR, Bos., Det.	17	1113	213	683	896	1429	161	35	90	125	217		1968-69	1984-85
Parker, Jeff	Buf., Hfd.	5	141	16	19	35	163	5	0	0	0	26		1986-87	1990-91
Parkes, Ernie	Mtl.M.	1	17	0	0	0	2	....	....	....	....	....		1924-25	1924-25
Parks, Greg	NYI	3	23	1	2	3	6	2	0	0	0	0		1990-91	1992-93
Parsons, George	Tor.	3	78	12	13	25	20	7	3	2	5	11		1936-37	1938-39
Pasek, Dusan	Min.	1	48	4	10	14	30	2	1	0	1	0		1988-89	1988-89
Pasin, Dave	Bos., L.A.	2	76	18	19	37	50	3	0	1	1	0		1985-86	1988-89
Paslawski, Greg	Mtl., St.L., Wpg., Buf., Que., Phi., Cgy.	11	650	187	185	372	169	60	19	13	32	25		1983-84	1993-94
Paterson, Joe	Det., Phi., L.A., NYR	9	291	19	37	56	829	22	3	4	7	77		1980-81	1988-89
Paterson, Mark	Hfd.	4	29	3	3	6	33	....	....	....	....	....		1982-83	1985-86
Paterson, Rick	Chi.	9	430	50	43	93	136	61	7	10	17	51		1978-79	1986-87
Patey, Doug	Wsh.	3	45	4	2	6	8	....	....	....	....	....		1976-77	1978-79
Patey, Larry	Cal., St.L., NYR	12	717	153	163	316	631	40	8	10	18	57		1973-74	1984-85
Patrick, Craig	Cal., St.L., K.C., Wsh.	8	401	72	91	163	61	2	0	1	1	0		1971-72	1978-79
Patrick, Glenn	St.L., Cal., Clev.	3	38	2	3	5	72	....	....	....	....	....		1973-74	1976-77
• Patrick, Lester	NYR	1	1	0	0	0	2	....	....	....	....	....		1926-27	1926-27
• Patrick, Lynn	NYR	10	455	145	190	335	240	44	10	6	16	22	1	1934-35	1945-46
Patrick, Muzz	NYR	5	166	5	26	31	133	25	4	0	4	34	1	1937-38	1945-46
Patrick, Steve	Buf., NYR, Que.	6	250	40	68	108	242	12	0	1	1	12		1980-81	1985-86
Patterson, Colin	Cgy., Buf.	10	504	96	109	205	239	85	12	17	29	57	1	1983-84	1992-93
Patterson, Dennis	K.C., Phi.	3	138	6	22	28	67	....	....	....	....	....		1974-75	1979-80
• Patterson, George	Bos., Det., St.L., Tor., Mtl., NYA	9	284	51	27	78	218	3	0	0	0	2		1926-27	1934-35
• Paul, Butch	Det.	1	3	0	0	0	0	....	....	....	....	....		1964-65	1964-65
• Paulhus, Rollie	Mtl.	1	33	0	0	0	0	....	....	....	....	....		1925-26	1925-26
Pavelich, Mark	NYR, Min., S.J.	7	355	137	192	329	340	23	7	17	24	14		1981-82	1991-92
Pavelich, Marty	Det.	10	634	93	159	252	454	91	13	15	28	74	4	1947-48	1956-57
Pavese, Jim	St.L., NYR, Det., Hfd.	8	328	13	44	57	689	34	0	6	6	81		1981-82	1988-89
• Payer, Evariste	Mtl.	1	1	0	0	0	0	....	....	....	....	....		1917-18	1917-18
Payne, Steve	Min.	10	613	228	238	466	435	71	35	35	70	60		1978-79	1987-88
Paynter, Kent	Chi., Wsh., Wpg., Ott.	7	37	1	3	4	69	4	0	0	0	10		1987-88	1993-94
Pearson, Mel	NYR, Pit.	5	38	2	6	8	25	....	....	....	....	....		1949-50	1967-68
Pedersen, Allen	Bos., Min., Hfd.	8	428	5	36	41	487	64	0	0	0	91		1986-87	1993-94
Pederson, Barry	Bos., Van., Pit., Hfd.	12	701	238	416	654	472	34	22	30	52	25		1980-81	1991-92
Pederson, Mark	Mtl., Phi., S.J., Det.	5	169	35	50	85	77	2	0	0	0	0		1989-90	1993-94
Peer, Bert	Det.	1	1	0	0	0	0	....	....	....	....	....		1939-40	1939-40
Peirson, Johnny	Bos.	11	545	153	173	326	315	49	9	17	26	26		1946-47	1957-58
Pelensky, Perry	Chi.	1	4	0	0	0	5	....	....	....	....	....		1983-84	1983-84
Pelletier, Roger	Phi.	1	1	0	0	0	0	....	....	....	....	....		1967-68	1967-68
Peloffy, Andre	Wsh.	1	9	0	0	0	0	....	....	....	....	....		1974-75	1974-75
Pelyk, Mike	Tor.	9	441	26	88	114	566	40	0	3	3	41		1967-68	1977-78
Penney, Chad	Ott.	1	3	0	0	0	2	....	....	....	....	....		1993-94	1993-94
Pennington, Cliff	Mtl., Bos.	3	101	17	42	59	6	....	....	....	....	....		1960-61	1962-63
Peplinski, Jim	Cgy.	11	711	161	263	424	1467	99	15	31	46	382	1	1980-81	1994-95
Perlini, Fred	Tor.	2	8	2	3	5	0	....	....	....	....	....		1981-82	1983-84
Perreault, Fern	NYR	2	3	0	0	0	0	....	....	....	....	....		1947-48	1949-50
Perreault, Gilbert	Buf.	17	1191	512	814	1326	500	90	33	70	103	44		1970-71	1986-87
Perry, Brian	Oak., Buf.	3	96	16	29	45	24	8	1	1	2	4		1968-69	1970-71
Persson, Stefan	NYI	9	622	52	317	369	574	102	7	50	57	69	4	1977-78	1985-86
Pesut, George	Cal.	2	92	3	22	25	130	....	....	....	....	....		1974-75	1975-76
• Peters, Frank	NYR	1	43	0	0	0	59	4	0	0	0	2		1930-31	1930-31
Peters, Garry	Mtl., NYR, Phi., Bos.	8	311	34	34	68	261	9	2	2	4	31	1	1964-65	1971-72
Peters, Jim	Det., Chi., Mtl., Bos.	9	574	125	150	275	186	60	5	9	14	22	3	1945-46	1953-54
Peters, Jimmy	Det., L.A.	9	309	37	36	73	48	11	0	2	2	2		1964-65	1974-75
Peters, Steve	Col.	1	2	0	1	1	0	....	....	....	....	....		1979-80	1979-80
Peterson, Brent	Det., Buf., Van., Hfd.	11	620	72	141	213	484	31	4	4	8	65		1979-80	1988-89
Petrenko, Sergei	Buf.	1	14	0	4	4	0	....	....	....	....	....		1993-94	1993-94
Petrov, Oleg	Mtl.	4	112	20	26	46	39	8	0	1	1	0	1	1992-93	1995-96
Pettersson, Jorgen	St.L., Hfd., Wsh.	6	435	174	192	366	117	44	15	12	27	4		1980-81	1985-86
• Pettinger, Eric	Ott., Bos., Tor.	3	98	7	12	19	83	4	1	0	1	8		1928-29	1930-31
Pettinger, Gord	Det., NYR, Bos.	8	292	42	74	116	77	47	4	5	9	11	4	1932-33	1939-40
Phair, Lyle	L.A.	3	48	6	7	13	12	1	0	0	0	0		1985-86	1987-88
Phillipoff, Harold	Atl., Chi.,	3	141	26	57	83	267	6	0	2	2	9		1977-78	1979-80
Phillips, Bat	Mtl.M.	1	27	1	1	2	6	4	0	0	0	2		1929-30	1929-30
• Phillips, Bill	Mtl.M., NYA.	8	302	52	31	83	232	28	6	2	8	19	1	1925-26	1932-33
Phillips, Charlie	Mtl.	1	17	0	0	0	6	....	....	....	....	....		1942-43	1942-43
Picard, Noel	Atl., Mtl., St.L.	7	335	12	63	75	616	50	2	11	13	167	1	1964-65	1972-73
Picard, Robert	Wsh. Tor., Mtl., Wpg., Que., Det.	13	899	104	319	423	1025	36	5	15	20	39		1977-78	1989-90
Picard, Roger	St.L.	1	15	2	2	4	21	....	....	....	....	....		1967-68	1967-68
Pichette, Dave	Que., St.L., N.J., NYR	7	322	41	140	181	348	28	3	7	10	54		1980-81	1987-88
Picketts, Hal	NYA.	1	48	3	1	4	32	....	....	....	....	....		1933-34	1933-34
Pidhirny, Harry	Bos.	1	2	0	0	0	0	....	....	....	....	....		1957-58	1957-58
Pierce, Randy	Col., N.J., Hfd.	8	277	62	76	138	223	2	0	0	0	0		1977-78	1984-85
Pike, Alf	NYR	6	234	42	77	119	145	21	4	2	6	12	1	1939-40	1946-47
Pilote, Pierre	Chi., Tor.	14	890	80	418	498	1251	86	8	53	61	102	1	1955-56	1968-69
Pinder, Gerry	Chi., Cal.	3	223	55	69	124	135	17	0	4	4	6		1969-70	1971-72
Pirus, Alex	Min., Det.	4	159	30	28	58	94	2	0	1	1	2		1976-77	1979-80
• Pitre, Didier	Mtl.	6	127	64	17	81	59	14	2	2	4	13		1917-18	1922-23
• Plager, Barclay	St.L.	10	614	44	187	231	1115	68	3	20	23	182		1967-68	1976-77
Plager, Bill	Min., St.L., Atl.	9	263	4	34	38	294	31	0	2	2	26		1967-68	1975-76
Plager, Bob	NYR, St.L.	14	644	20	126	146	802	74	2	17	19	195		1964-65	1977-78
Plamondon, Gerry	Mtl.	5	74	7	13	20	10	11	5	2	7	2	1	1945-46	1950-51
Plante, Cam	Tor.	1	2	0	0	0	0	....	....	....	....	....		1984-85	1984-85
Plante, Pierre	NYR, Que., Phi., St.L., Chi.	9	599	125	172	297	599	33	2	6	8	51		1971-72	1979-80
Plantery, Mark	Wpg.	1	25	1	5	6	14	....	....	....	....	....		1980-81	1980-81

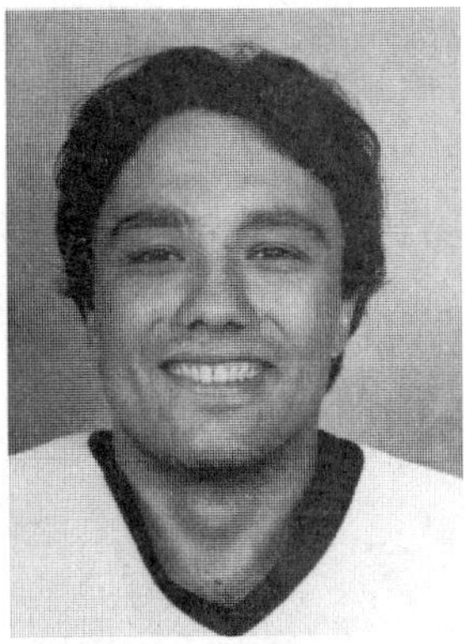
Grigori Panteleev

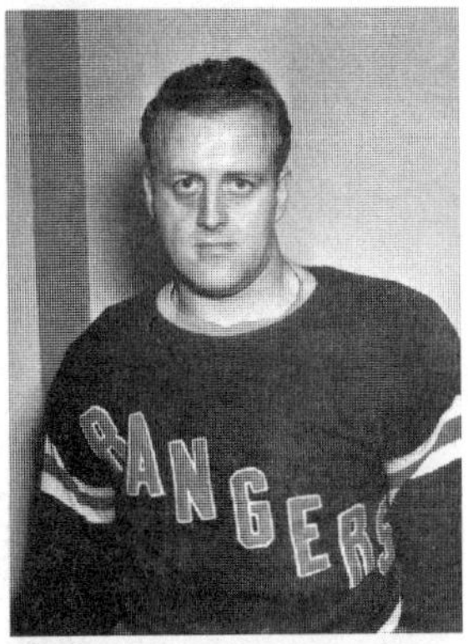

Lynn Patrick

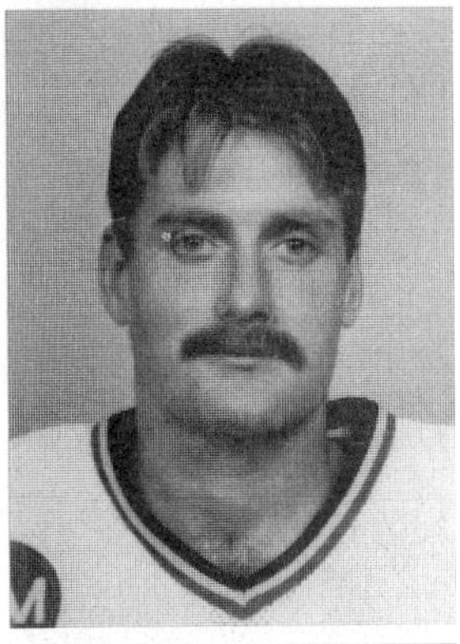
Pat Price

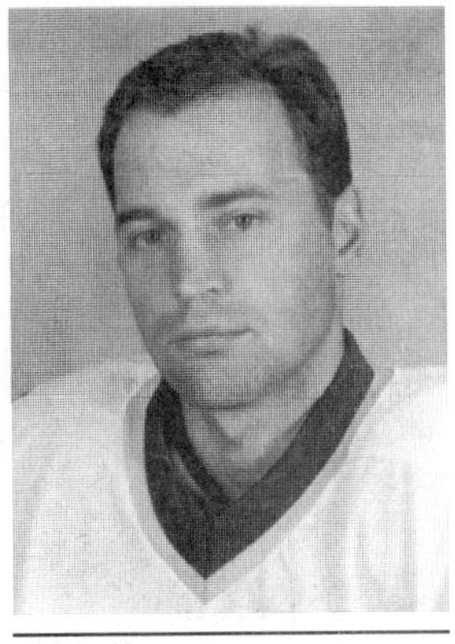
Vitali Prokhorov

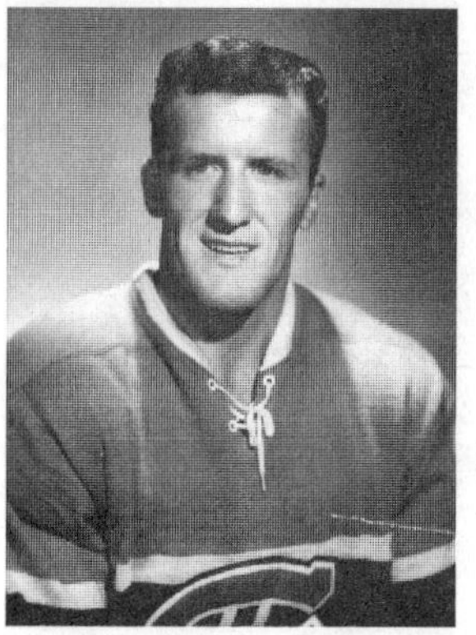

Claude Provost

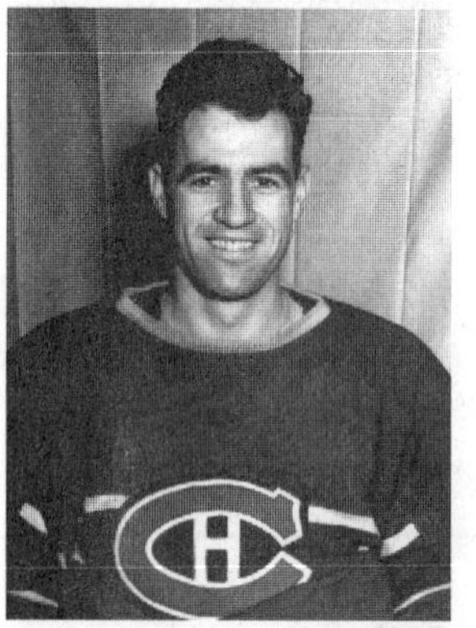

John Quilty

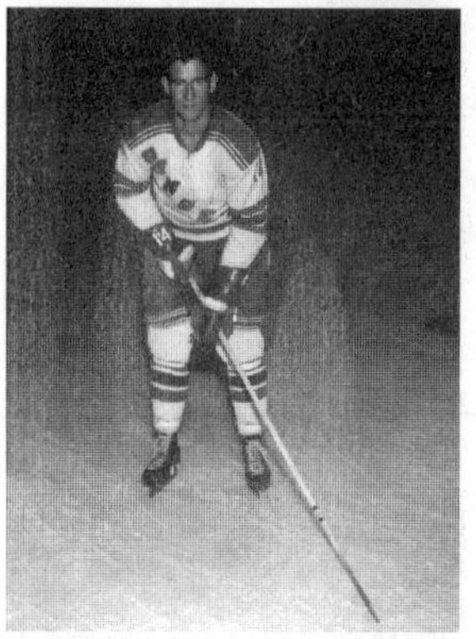

Jean Ratelle

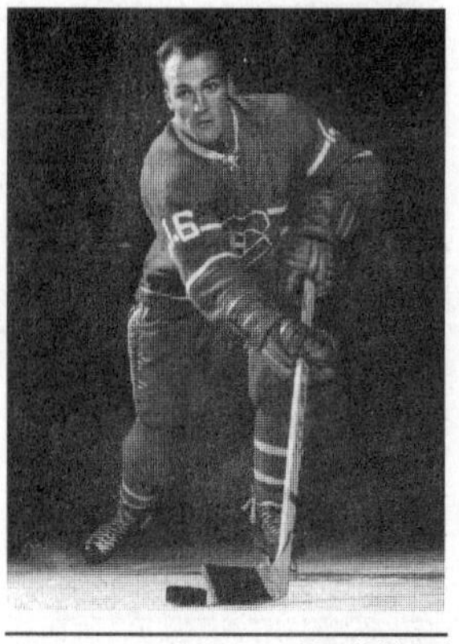

Henri Richard

			Regular Schedule					Playoffs					NHL	First	Last
Name	NHL Teams	NHL Seasons	GP	G	A	TP	PIM	GP	G	A	TP	PIM	Cup Wins	NHL Season	NHL Season
Plaxton, Hugh	Mtl.M.	1	15	1	2	3	4	....	....	....	....	....		1932-33	1932-33
Playfair, Jim	Edm., Chi.	3	21	2	4	6	51	....	....	....	....	....		1983-84	1988-89
Playfair, Larry	Buf., L.A.	12	688	26	94	120	1812	43	0	6	6	111		1978-79	1989-90
Pleau, Larry	Mtl.	3	94	9	15	24	27	4	0	0	0	0		1969-70	1971-72
Plett, Willi	Atl., Cgy., Min., Bos.	13	834	222	215	437	2572	83	24	22	46	466		1975-76	1987-88
Plumb, Rob	Det.	2	14	3	2	5	2	....	....	....	....	....		1977-78	1977-78
Plumb, Ron	Hfd.	1	26	3	4	7	14	....	....	....	....	....		1979-80	1979-80
Pocza, Harvie	Wsh.	2	3	0	0	0	2	....	....	....	....	....		1979-80	1981-82
Poddubny, Walt	Edm., Tor., NYR, Que., N.J.	11	468	184	238	422	454	19	7	2	9	12		1981-82	1991-92
Podloski, Ray	Bos.	1	8	0	1	1	22	....	....	....	....	....		1988-89	1988-89
Podolsky, Nels	Det.	1	1	0	0	0	0	7	0	0	0	4		1948-49	1948-49
Poeta, Anthony	Chi.	1	1	0	0	0	0	....	....	....	....	....		1951-52	1951-52
Poile, Bud	NYR, Bos., Det., Tor., Chi.,	7	311	107	122	229	91	23	4	5	9	8	1	1942-43	1949-50
Poile, Don	Det.	2	66	7	9	16	12	4	0	0	0	0		1954-55	1957-58
Poirer, Gordie	Mtl.	1	10	0	0	0	0	....	....	....	....	....		1939-40	1939-40
Polanic, Tom	Min.	2	19	0	2	2	53	5	1	1	2	4		1969-70	1970-71
Polich, John	NYR	2	3	0	1	1	0	....	....	....	....	....		1939-40	1940-41
Polich, Mike	Mtl., Min.	5	226	24	29	53	57	23	2	1	3	2	1	1976-77	1980-81
Polis, Greg	Pit., St.L., NYR, Wsh.	10	615	174	169	343	391	7	0	2	2	6		1970-71	1979-80
Poliziani, Daniel	Bos.	1	1	0	0	0	0	3	0	0	0	0		1958-59	1958-59
Polonich, Dennis	Det.	8	390	59	82	141	1242	7	1	0	1	19		1974-75	1982-83
Pooley, Paul	Wpg.	2	15	0	3	3	0	....	....	....	....	....		1984-85	1985-86
Popein, Larry	NYR, Oak.	8	449	80	141	221	162	16	1	4	5	6		1954-55	1967-68
Popiel, Paul	Bos., L.A., Det., Van., Edm.	7	224	13	41	54	210	4	1	0	1	4		1965-66	1979-80
• Portland, Jack	Mtl., Bos., Chi.	10	381	15	56	71	323	33	1	3	4	25	1	1933-34	1942-43
Porvari, Jukka	Col., N.J.	2	39	3	9	12	4	....	....	....	....	....		1981-82	1982-83
Posa, Victor	Chi.	1	2	0	0	0	2	....	....	....	....	....		1985-86	1985-86
Posavad, Mike	St.L.	2	8	0	0	0	0	....	....	....	....	....		1985-86	1986-87
Potvin, Denis	NYI	15	1060	310	742	1052	1354	185	56	108	164	253	4	1973-74	1987-88
Potvin, Jean	L.A., Min., Phi., NYI, Cle.	11	613	63	224	287	478	39	2	9	11	17	1	1970-71	1980-81
Poudrier, Daniel	Que.	3	25	1	5	6	10	....	....	....	....	....		1985-86	1987-88
Poulin, Dan	Min.	1	3	1	1	2	2	....	....	....	....	....		1981-82	1981-82
Poulin, Dave	Phi., Bos., Wsh.	13	724	205	325	530	482	129	31	42	73	132		1982-83	1994-95
Pouzar, Jaroslav	Edm.	4	186	34	48	82	135	29	6	4	10	16	3	1982-83	1986-87
Powell, Ray	Chi.	1	31	7	15	22	2	....	....	....	....	....		1950-51	1950-51
Powis, Geoff	Chi.	1	2	0	0	0	0	....	....	....	....	....		1967-68	1967-68
Powis, Lynn	Chi., K.C.	2	130	19	33	52	25	1	0	0	0	0		1973-74	1974-75
Prajsler, Petr	L.A., Bos.	4	46	3	10	13	51	4	0	0	0	0		1987-88	1991-92
• Pratt, Babe	Bos., NYR, Tor.	12	517	83	209	292	463	63	12	17	29	90	2	1935-36	1946-47
Pratt, Jack	Bos.	2	37	2	0	2	42	4	0	0	0	0		1930-31	1931-32
Pratt, Kelly	Pit.	1	22	0	6	6	15	....	....	....	....	....		1974-75	1974-75
Pratt, Tracy	Van., Col., Buf., Pit. Tor., Oak.	10	580	17	97	114	1026	25	0	1	1	62		1967-68	1976-77
Prentice, Dean	Pit., Min., Det., NYR, Bos.	22	1378	391	469	860	484	54	13	17	30	38		1952-53	1973-74
Prentice, Eric	Tor.	1	5	0	0	0	4	....	....	....	....	....		1943-44	1943-44
Preston, Rich	Chi., N.J.	8	580	127	164	291	348	47	4	18	22	56		1979-80	1986-87
Preston, Yves	Phi.	2	28	7	3	10	4	....	....	....	....	....		1978-79	1980-81
Priakin, Sergei	Cgy.	3	46	3	8	11	2	1	0	0	0	0		1988-89	1990-91
• Price, Bob	Ott.	1	1	0	0	0	0	....	....	....	....	....		1919-20	1919-20
Price, Jack	Chi.	3	57	4	6	10	24	4	0	0	0	0		1951-52	1953-54
Price, Noel	Pit., L.A., Det., Tor., NYR, Mtl., Atl.	14	499	14	114	128	333	12	0	1	1	8	1	1957-58	1975-76
Price, Pat	NYI, Edm., Pit., Que., NYR, Min.	13	726	43	218	261	1456	74	2	10	12	195		1975-76	1987-88
Price, Tom	Cal., Clev., Pit.	5	29	0	2	2	12	....	....	....	....	....		1974-75	1978-79
Priestlay, Ken	Buf., Pit.	6	168	27	34	61	63	14	0	0	0	21	1	1986-87	1991-92
• Primeau, Joe	Tor.	9	310	66	177	243	105	38	5	18	23	12	1	1927-28	1935-36
Primeau, Kevin	Van.	1	2	0	0	0	4	....	....	....	....	....		1980-81	1980-81
Pringle, Ellie	NYA	1	6	0	0	0	0	....	....	....	....	....		1930-31	1930-31
• Prodgers, Goldie	Tor., Ham.	6	110	63	22	85	33	....	....	....	....	....		1919-20	1924-25
Prokhorov, Vitali	St.L.	3	83	19	11	30	35	4	0	0	0	0		1992-93	1994-95
Pronovost, Andre	Mtl., Bos., Det., Min.	10	556	94	104	198	408	70	11	11	22	58	4	1956-57	1967-68
Pronovost, Jean	Wsh., Pit., Atl.	14	998	391	383	774	413	35	11	9	20	14		1968-69	1981-82
Pronovost, Marcel	Det., Tor.	21	1206	88	257	345	851	134	8	23	31	104	5	1950-51	1969-70
Propp, Brian	Phi., Bos., Min., Hfd.	15	1016	425	579	1004	830	160	64	84	148	151		1979-80	1993-94
Proulx, Christian	Mtl.	1	7	1	2	3	20	....	....	....	....	....		1993-94	1993-94
• Provost, Claude	Mtl.	15	1005	254	335	589	469	126	25	38	63	86	9	1955-56	1969-70
Pryor, Chris	Min., NYI	6	82	1	4	5	122	....	....	....	....	....		1984-85	1989-90
Prystai, Metro	Chi., Det.	11	674	151	179	330	231	43	12	14	26	8	2	1947-48	1957-58
• Pudas, Al	Tor.	1	4	0	0	0	0	....	....	....	....	....		1926-27	1926-27
Pulford, Bob	Tor., L.A.	16	1079	281	362	643	792	89	25	26	51	126	4	1956-57	1971-72
Pulkkinen, Dave	NYI	1	2	0	0	0	0	....	....	....	....	....		1972-73	1972-73
Purpur, Cliff (Fido)	Det., Chi., St.L.	5	144	25	35	60	46	16	1	2	3	4		1934-35	1944-45
Purves, John	Wsh.	1	7	1	0	1	0	....	....	....	....	....		1990-91	1990-91
• Pusie, Jean	Mtl., NYR, Bos.	5	61	1	4	5	28	7	0	0	0	0	1	1930-31	1935-36
Pyatt, Nelson	Det., Wsh., Col.	7	296	71	63	134	69	....	....	....	....	....		1973-74	1979-80

Q

Quackenbush, Bill	Det., Bos.	14	774	62	222	284	95	80	2	19	21	8		1942-43	1955-56
Quackenbush, Max	Bos., Chi.,	2	61	4	7	11	30	6	0	0	0	4		1950-51	1951-52
Quenneville, Joel	Tor., Col., N.J., Hfd., Wsh.	13	803	54	136	190	705	32	0	8	8	22		1978-79	1990-91
• Quenneville, Leo	NYR	1	25	0	3	3	10	3	0	0	0	0		1929-30	1929-30
• Quilty, John	Mtl., Bos.	4	125	36	34	70	81	13	3	5	8	9		1940-41	1947-48
Quinn, Pat	Tor., Van., Atl.	9	606	18	113	131	950	11	0	1	1	21		1968-69	1976-77
Quinney, Ken	Que.	3	59	7	13	20	23	....	....	....	....	....		1986-87	1990-91
Quintin, Jean-Francois	S.J.	2	22	5	5	10	4	....	....	....	....	....		1991-92	1992-93

R

Radley, Yip	NYA, Mtl.M.	2	18	0	1	1	13	....	....	....	....	....		1930-31	1936-37
Raglan, Clare	Det., Chi.	3	100	4	9	13	52	3	0	0	0	0		1950-51	1952-53
Raglan, Herb	St.L., Que., T.B., Ott.	9	343	33	56	89	775	32	3	6	9	50		1985-86	1993-94
Raleigh, Don	NYR	10	535	101	219	320	96	18	6	5	11	6		1943-44	1955-56
Ramage, Rob	Col., St.L., Cgy., Tor., Min., T.B., Mtl., Phi.	15	1044	139	425	564	2226	84	8	42	50	218	2	1979-80	1993-94
• Ramsay, Beattie	Tor.,	1	43	0	2	2	10	....	....	....	....	....		1927-28	1927-28
Ramsay, Craig	Buf.	14	1070	252	420	672	201	89	17	31	48	27		1971-72	1984-85
Ramsey, Les	Chi.	1	11	2	2	4	2	....	....	....	....	....		1944-45	1944-45
Ramsey, Wayne	Buf.	1	2	0	0	0	0	....	....	....	....	....		1977-78	1977-78
• Randall, Ken	Tor., Ham., NYA	10	215	67	28	95	415	14	3	1	4	43	2	1917-18	1926-27
Ranieri, George	Bos.	1	2	0	0	0	0	....	....	....	....	....		1956-57	1956-57
Ratelle, Jean	NYR, Bos.	21	1281	491	776	1267	276	123	32	66	98	24		1960-61	1980-81
Rathwell, John	Bos.	1	1	0	0	0	0	....	....	....	....	....		1974-75	1974-75
Ratushny, Dan	Van.	1	1	0	1	1	2	....	....	....	....	....		1992-93	1992-93
Rausse, Errol	Wsh.	3	31	7	3	10	0	....	....	....	....	....		1979-80	1981-82
Rautakallio, Pekka	Atl., Cgy.	3	235	33	121	154	122	23	2	5	7	8		1979-80	1981-82
Ravlich, Matt	Bos., Chi., Det., L.A.	10	410	12	78	90	364	24	1	5	6	16		1962-63	1972-73
Raymond, Armand	Mtl.	2	22	0	2	2	10	....	....	....	....	....		1937-38	1939-40
Raymond, Paul	Mtl.	4	76	2	3	5	6	5	0	0	0	2		1932-33	1937-38
Read, Mel	NYR	1	1	0	0	0	0	....	....	....	....	....		1946-47	1946-47
Reardon, Ken	Mtl.	7	341	26	96	122	604	31	2	5	7	62	1	1940-41	1949-50
• Reardon, Terry	Bos., Mtl.	7	193	47	53	100	73	30	8	10	18	12	1	1938-39	1946-47
Reaume, Marc	Tor., Det., Mtl., Van.	9	344	8	43	51	273	21	0	2	2	8		1954-55	1970-71
Reay, Billy	Det., Mtl.	10	479	105	162	267	202	63	13	16	29	43	2	1943-44	1952-53
Redahl, Gord	Bos.	1	18	0	1	1	2	....	....	....	....	....		1958-59	1958-59
Redding, George	Bos.	2	35	3	2	5	10	....	....	....	....	....		1924-25	1925-26
Redmond, Craig	L.A., Edm.	5	191	16	68	84	134	3	1	0	1	2		1984-85	1988-89
Redmond, Dick	Min., Cal., Chi., St.L., Atl., Bos.	13	771	133	312	445	504	66	9	22	31	27		1969-70	1981-82
Redmond, Keith	L.A.	1	12	1	0	1	20	....	....	....	....	....		1993-94	1993-94
Redmond, Mickey	Mtl., Det.	9	538	233	195	428	219	16	2	3	5	2	2	1967-68	1975-76
Reeds, Mark	St.L., Hfd.	8	365	45	114	159	135	53	8	9	17	23		1981-82	1988-89
• Regan, Bill	NYR, NYA	3	67	3	2	5	67	8	0	0	0	2		1929-30	1932-33
Regan, Larry	Bos., Tor.,	5	280	41	95	136	71	42	7	14	21	18		1956-57	1960-61
Regier, Darcy	Clev., NYI	3	26	0	2	2	35	....	....	....	....	....		1977-78	1983-84
Reibel, Earl	Det., Chi., Bos.	6	409	84	161	245	75	39	6	14	20	4	2	1953-54	1958-59

Name	NHL Teams	NHL Seasons	Regular Schedule					Playoffs					NHL Cup Wins	First NHL Season	Last NHL Season
			GP	G	A	TP	PIM	GP	G	A	TP	PIM			
Reid, Dave	Tor.	3	7	0	0	0	0	....	....	....	....	....		1952-53	1955-56
Reid, Gerry	Det.	1	....	....	....	....	....	2	0	0	0	2		1948-49	1948-49
Reid, Gordie	NYA	1	1	0	0	0	2	....	....	....	....	....		1936-37	1936-37
Reid, Reg	Tor.	2	40	2	0	2	4	2	0	0	0	0		1924-25	1925-26
Reid, Tom	Chi., Min.	11	701	17	113	130	654	42	1	13	14	49		1967-68	1977-78
Reierson, Dave	Cgy.	1	2	0	0	0	2	....	....	....	....	....		1988-89	1988-89
Reigle, Ed	Bos.	1	17	0	2	2	25	....	....	....	....	....		1950-51	1950-51
Reinhart, Paul	Atl., Cgy., Van.	11	648	133	426	559	277	83	23	54	77	42		1979-80	1989-90
Reinikka, Ollie	NYR	1	16	0	0	0	0	....	....	....	....	....		1926-27	1926-27
Reise, Leo Jr.	Chi., Det., NYR	9	494	28	81	109	399	52	8	5	13	68	2	1945-46	1953-54
• Reise, Leo Sr.	Ham., NYA, NYR	8	223	36	29	65	177	6	0	0	0	16		1920-21	1929-30
Renaud, Mark	Hfd., Buf.	5	152	6	50	56	86	....	....	....	....	....		1979-80	1983-84
Reynolds, Bobby	Tor.	1	7	1	1	2	0	....	....	....	....	....		1989-90	1989-90
Ribble, Pat	Atl., Chi., Tor., Wsh., Cgy.	8	349	19	60	79	365	8	0	1	1	12		1975-76	1982-83
Richard, Henri	Mtl.	20	1256	358	688	1046	928	180	49	80	129	181	11	1955-56	1974-75
Richard, Jacques	Alt., Buf., Que.	10	556	160	187	347	307	35	5	5	10	34		1972-73	1982-83
Richard, Jean-Marc	Que.	2	5	2	1	3	2	....	....	....	....	....		1987-88	1989-90
Richard, Maurice	Mtl.	18	978	544	421	965	1285	133	82	44	126	188	8	1942-43	1959-60
Richard, Mike	Wsh.	2	7	0	2	2	0	....	....	....	....	....		1987-88	1989-90
Richards, Todd	Hfd.	2	8	0	4	4	4	11	0	3	3	6		1990-91	1991-92
Richards, Travis	Dal.	2	3	0	0	0	2	....	....	....	....	....		1994-95	1995-96
Richardson, Dave	NYR, Chi., Det.	4	45	3	2	5	27	....	....	....	....	....		1963-64	1967-68
Richardson, Glen	Van.	1	24	3	6	9	19	....	....	....	....	....		1975-76	1975-76
Richardson, Ken	St.L.	3	49	8	13	21	16	....	....	....	....	....		1974-75	1978-79
Richer, Bob	Buf.	1	3	0	0	0	0	....	....	....	....	....		1972-73	1972-73
Richer, Stephane J. G.	T.B., Bos., Fla.	3	27	1	5	6	20	3	0	0	0	0		1992-93	1994-95
Richmond, Steve	NYR, Det., N.J., L.A.	5	159	4	23	27	514	4	0	0	0	12		1983-84	1988-89
Richter, Dave	Min., Phi., Van., St.L.	9	365	9	40	49	1030	22	1	0	1	80		1981-82	1989-90
Riley, Bill	Wsh., Wpg.	5	139	31	30	61	320	....	....	....	....	....		1974-75	1979-80
Riley, Jack	Det., Mtl., Bos.,	4	104	10	22	32	8	4	0	3	3	0		1932-33	1935-36
• Riley, Jim	Det., Chi.	1	17	0	2	2	14	....	....	....	....	....		1926-27	1926-27
Riopellie, Howard	Mtl.	3	169	27	16	43	73	8	1	1	2	2		1947-48	1949-50
Rioux, Gerry	Wpg.	1	8	0	0	0	6	....	....	....	....	....		1979-80	1979-80
Rioux, Pierre	Cgy.	1	14	1	2	3	4	....	....	....	....	....		1982-83	1982-83
• Ripley, Vic	Chi., Bos., NYR, St.L.	7	278	51	49	100	173	20	4	1	5	10		1928-29	1934-35
Risebrough, Doug	Mtl., Cgy.	13	740	185	286	471	1542	124	21	37	58	238	4	1974-75	1986-87
Rissling, Gary	Wsh., Pit.	7	221	23	30	53	1008	5	0	1	1	4		1978-79	1984-85
Ritchie, Bob	Phi., Det.	2	29	8	4	12	10	....	....	....	....	....		1976-77	1977-78
• Ritchie, Dave	Mtl.W, Ott., Tor., Que., Mtl.	6	54	15	3	18	39	1	0	0	0	0		1917-18	1925-26
Ritson, Alex	NYR	1	1	0	0	0	0	....	....	....	....	....		1944-45	1944-45
Rittinger, Alan	Bos.	1	19	3	7	10	0	....	....	....	....	....		1943-44	1943-44
Rivard, Bob	Pit.	1	27	5	12	17	4	....	....	....	....	....		1967-68	1967-68
• Rivers, Gus	Mtl.	3	88	4	5	9	12	16	2	0	2	2	2	1929-30	1931-32
Rivers, Shawn	T.B.	1	4	0	2	2	2	....	....	....	....	....		1992-93	1992-93
Rivers, Wayne	Det., Bos., St.L., NYR	7	108	15	30	45	94	....	....	....	....	....		1961-62	1968-69
Rizzuto, Garth	Van.	1	37	3	4	7	16	....	....	....	....	....		1970-71	1970-71
• Roach, Mickey	Tor., Ham., NYA	8	209	75	27	102	41	....	....	....	....	....		1919-20	1926-27
Roberge, Mario	Mtl.	5	112	7	7	14	314	15	0	0	0	24	1	1990-91	1994-95
Roberge, Serge	Que.	1	9	0	0	0	24	....	....	....	....	....		1990-91	1990-91
Robert, Claude	Mtl.	1	23	1	0	1	9	....	....	....	....	....		1950-51	1950-51
Robert, Rene	Tor., Pit., Buf., Col.	12	744	284	418	702	597	50	22	19	41	73		1970-71	1981-82
• Robert, Sammy	Ott.	1	1	0	0	0	0	....	....	....	....	....		1917-18	1917-18
Roberto, Phil	Mtl., St.L., Det., K.C., Col., Clev.	8	385	75	106	181	464	31	9	8	17	69	1	1969-70	1976-77
Roberts, Doug	Det., Oak., Cal., Bos.	10	419	43	104	147	342	16	2	3	5	46		1965-66	1974-75
Roberts, Gordie	Hfd., Min., Phi., St.L., Pit., Bos.	15	1097	61	359	420	1582	153	10	47	57	273	2	1979-80	1993-94
Roberts, Jim	Mtl., St.L.	15	1006	126	194	320	621	153	20	16	36	160	5	1963-64	1977-78
Roberts, Jimmy	Min.	3	106	17	23	40	33	2	0	0	0	0		1976-77	1978-79
Robertson, Fred	Tor., Det.,	2	34	1	0	1	35	7	0	0	0	0	1	1931-32	1933-34
Robertson, George	Mtl.	2	31	2	5	7	6	....	....	....	....	....		1947-48	1948-49
Robertson, Gordie	Buf.	1	5	1	2	3	7	....	....	....	....	....		1982-83	1982-83
Robertson, Torrie	Wsh., Hfd., Det.	10	442	49	99	148	1751	22	2	1	3	90		1980-81	1989-90
Robidoux, Florent	Chi.	3	52	7	4	11	75	....	....	....	....	....		1980-81	1983-84
Robinson, Doug	Chi., NYR, L.A.	7	239	44	67	111	34	11	4	3	7	0		1963-64	1970-71
Robinson, Earl	Mtl.M., Chi., Mtl.	11	417	83	98	181	133	25	5	4	9	0	1	1928-29	1939-40
Robinson, Larry	Mtl., L.A.	20	1384	208	750	958	793	227	28	116	144	211	6	1972-73	1991-92
Robinson, Moe	Mtl	1	1	0	0	0	0	....	....	....	....	....		1979-80	1979-80
Robinson, Rob	St.L.	1	22	0	1	1	8	....	....	....	....	....		1991-92	1991-92
Robinson, Scott	Min.	1	1	0	0	0	2	....	....	....	....	....		1989-90	1989-90
Robitaille, Mike	NYR, Det., Buf., Van.	8	382	23	105	128	280	13	0	1	1	4		1969-70	1976-77
• Roche, Earl	Mtl.M., Bos., Ott., St.L., Det.	4	147	25	27	52	48	2	0	0	0	0		1930-31	1934-35
Roche, Ernest	Mtl.	1	4	0	0	0	2	....	....	....	....	....		1950-51	1950-51
Roche, Michel	Mtl.M., Ott., St.L., Mtl., Det.	4	113	20	18	38	44	....	....	....	....	....		1930-31	1934-35
Rochefort, Dave	Det	1	1	0	0	0	0	....	....	....	....	....		1966-67	1966-67
Rochefort, Leon	NYR, Mtl., Phi., L.A., Det., Atl., Van.	15	617	121	147	268	93	39	4	4	8	16	2	1960-61	1975-76
Rochefort, Normand	Que., NYR, T.B.	13	598	39	119	158	570	69	7	5	12	82		1980-81	1993-94
Rockburn, Harvey	Det., Ott.	3	94	4	2	6	254	....	....	....	....	....		1929-30	1932-33
• Rodden, Eddie	Chi., Tor., Bos., NYR	4	98	6	14	20	152	2	0	1	1	0	1	1926-27	1930-31
Rogers, Alfred (John)	Min.	2	14	2	4	6	0	....	....	....	....	....		1973-74	1974-75
Rogers, Mike	Hfd., NYR, Edm.	7	484	202	317	519	184	17	1	13	14	6		1979-80	1985-86
Rohlicek, Jeff	Van.	2	9	0	0	0	8	....	....	....	....	....		1987-88	1988-89
Rolfe, Dale	Bos., L.A., Det., NYR	9	509	25	125	150	556	71	5	24	29	89		1959-60	1974-75
Romanchych, Larry	Chi., Atl	6	298	68	97	165	102	7	2	2	4	4		1970-71	1976-77
Rombough, Doug	Buf., NYI, Min.	4	150	24	27	51	80	....	....	....	....	....		1972-73	1975-76
• Romnes, Doc	Chi., Tor., NYA	10	360	68	136	204	42	43	7	18	25	4	2	1930-31	1939-40
• Ronan, Skene	Ott.	1	11	0	0	0	0	....	....	....	....	....		1918-19	1918-19
Ronson, Len	NYR, Oak.	2	18	2	1	3	10	....	....	....	....	....		1960-61	1968-69
Ronty, Paul	Bos., NYR, Mtl.	8	488	101	211	312	103	21	1	7	8	6		1947-48	1954-55
Rooney, Steve	Mtl., Wpg., N.J.	5	154	15	13	28	496	25	3	2	5	86	1	1984-85	1988-89
Root, Bill	Mtl., Tor., St.L., Phi.	6	247	11	23	34	180	22	1	2	3	25		1982-83	1987-88
• Ross, Art	Mtl.W	1	3	1	0	1	0	....	....	....	....	....		1917-18	1917-18
Ross, Jim	NYR	2	62	2	11	13	29	....	....	....	....	....		1951-52	1952-53
Rossignol, Roland	Det., Mtl.	3	14	3	5	8	6	1	0	0	0	2		1943-44	1945-46
Rota, Darcy	Chi., Atl., Van.	11	794	256	239	495	973	60	14	7	21	147		1973-74	1983-84
Rota, Randy	Mtl., L.A., K.C., Col.	5	212	38	39	77	60	5	0	1	1	0		1972-73	1976-77
• Rothschild, Sam	Mtl.M., NYA	4	92	8	6	14	24	10	0	0	0	0	1	1924-25	1927-28
• Roulston, Rolly	Det.	3	24	0	6	6	10	....	....	....	....	....		1935-36	1937-38
Roulston, Tom	Edm., Pit.	5	195	47	49	96	74	21	2	2	4	2		1980-81	1985-86
Roupe, Magnus	Phi.	2	40	3	5	8	42	....	....	....	....	....		1987-88	1988-89
Rousseau, Bobby	Mtl., Min., NYR	15	942	245	458	703	359	128	27	57	84	69	4	1960-61	1974-75
Rousseau, Guy	Mtl.	2	4	0	1	1	0	....	....	....	....	....		1954-55	1956-57
Rousseau, Roland	Mtl.	1	2	0	0	0	0	....	....	....	....	....		1952-53	1952-53
Routhier, Jean-Marc	Que.	1	8	0	0	0	9	....	....	....	....	....		1989-90	1989-90
Rowe, Bobby	Bos.	1	4	1	0	1	0	....	....	....	....	....		1924-25	1924-25
Rowe, Mike	Pit.	3	11	0	0	0	11	....	....	....	....	....		1984-85	1986-87
Rowe, Ron	NYR	1	5	1	0	1	0	....	....	....	....	....		1947-48	1947-48
Rowe, Tom	Wsh., Hfd., Det.	7	357	85	100	185	615	3	2	0	2	0		1976-77	1982-83
Roy, Stephane	Min.	1	12	1	0	1	0	....	....	....	....	....		1987-88	1987-88
Rozzini, Gino	Bos.	1	31	5	10	15	20	6	1	2	3	6		1944-45	1944-45
Rucinski, Mike	Chi.	2	1	0	0	0	0	2	0	0	0	0		1987-88	1988-89
Ruelle, Bernard	Det.	1	2	1	0	1	0	....	....	....	....	....		1943-44	1943-44
Ruff, Lindy	Buf., NYR	12	691	105	195	300	1264	52	11	13	24	193		1979-80	1990-91
Ruhnke, Kent	Bos.	1	2	0	1	1	0	....	....	....	....	....		1975-76	1975-76
Rundqvist, Thomas	Mtl.	1	2	0	1	1	0	....	....	....	....	....		1984-85	1984-85
• Runge, Paul	Bos., Mtl.M., Mtl.	7	140	18	22	40	57	7	0	0	0	6		1930-31	1937-38
Ruotsalainen, Reijo	NYR, Edm., N.J.	7	446	107	237	344	180	86	15	32	47	44	2	1981-82	1989-90
Rupp, Duane	NYR, Tor., Min., Pit.	10	374	24	93	117	220	10	2	2	4	8		1962-63	1972-73
Ruskowski, Terry	Chi., L.A., Pit., Min.	10	630	113	313	426	1354	21	1	6	7	86		1979-80	1988-89
Russell, Churchill	NYR	3	90	20	16	36	12	....	....	....	....	....		1945-46	1947-48
Russell, Phil	Chi., Atl., Cgy., N.J., Buf.	15	1016	99	325	424	2038	73	4	22	26	202		1972-73	1986-87
Ruuttu, Christian	Buf., Chi., Van.	9	621	134	298	432	714	42	4	9	13	49		1986-87	1994-95
Ruzicka, Vladimir	Edm., Bos., Ott.	5	233	82	85	167	129	30	4	14	18	2		1989-90	1993-94
Rymsha, Andy	Que.	1	6	0	0	0	23	....	....	....	....	....		1991-92	1991-92

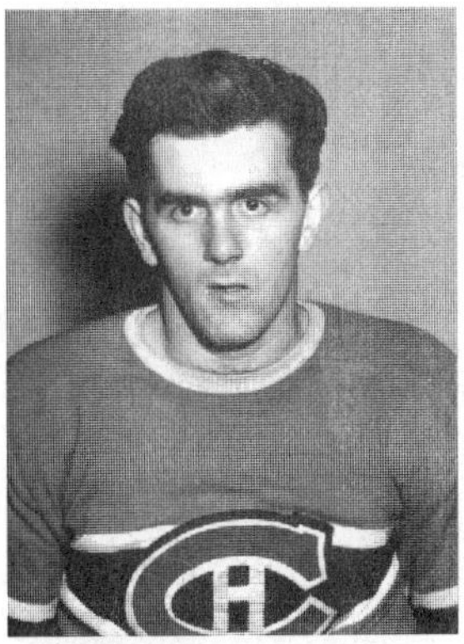
Maurice Richard

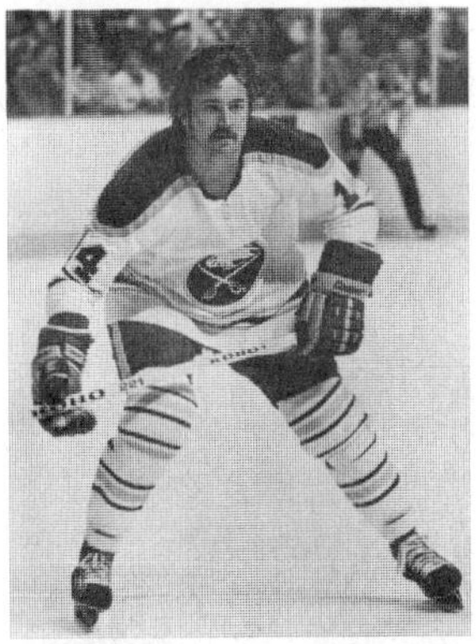
Rene Robert

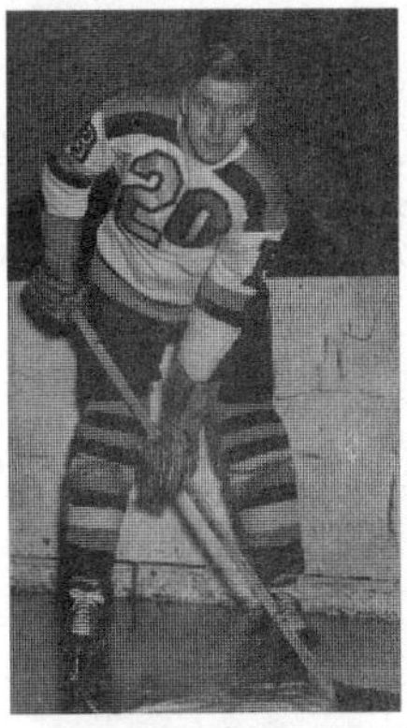
Paul Ronty

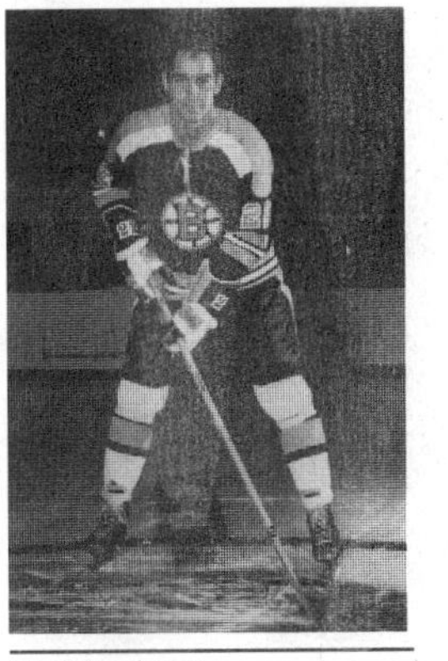
Derek Sanderson

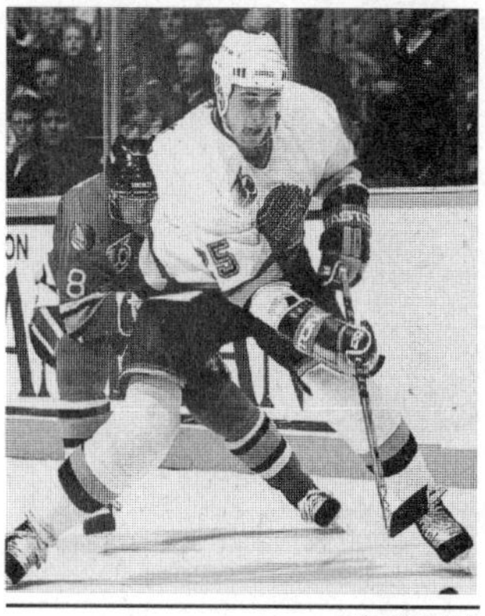

Jim Sandlak

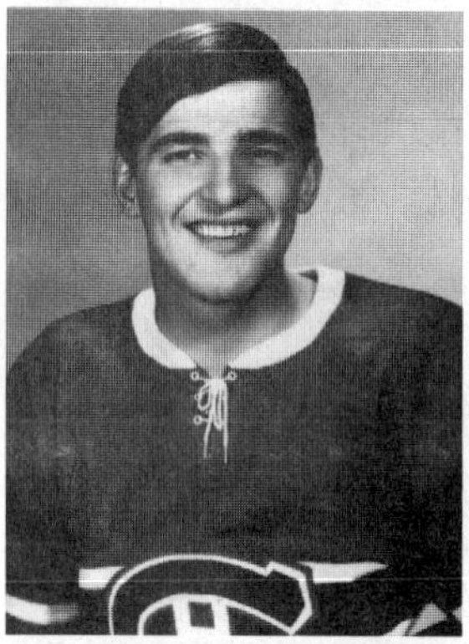

Serge Savard

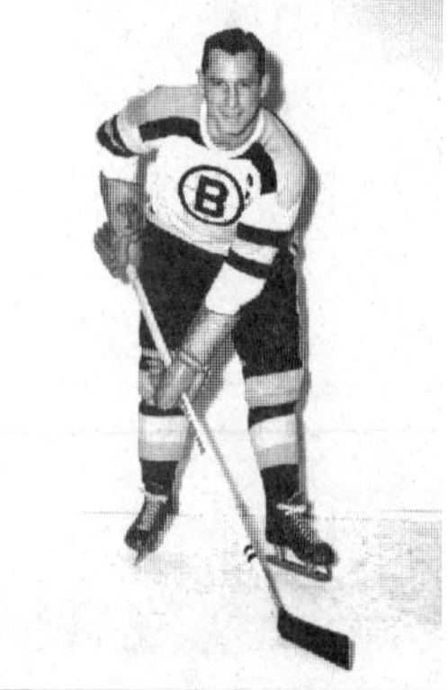

Milt Schmidt

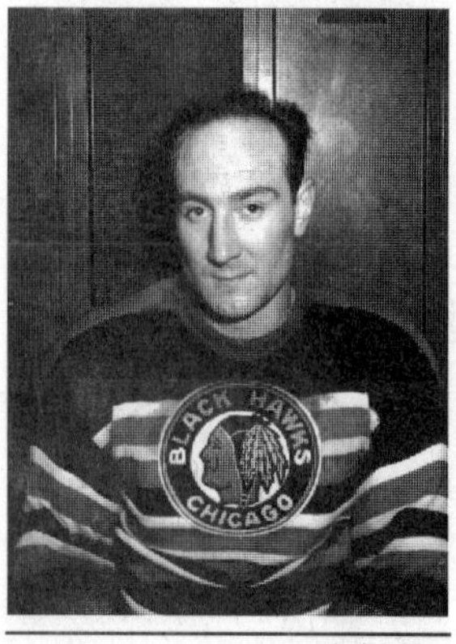

Earl Seibert

Name	NHL Teams	NHL Seasons	Regular Schedule GP	G	A	TP	PIM	Playoffs GP	G	A	TP	PIM	NHL Cup Wins	First NHL Season	Last NHL Season
S															
Saarinen, Simo	NYR	1	8	0	0	0	0	....	....	....	....	....		1984-85	1984-85
Sabol, Shaun	Phi.	1	2	0	0	0	0	....	....	....	....	....		1989-90	1989-90
Sabourin, Bob	Tor.	1	1	0	0	0	2	....	....	....	....	....		1951-52	1951-52
Sabourin, Gary	St.L., Tor., Cal., Clev.	10	627	169	188	357	397	62	19	11	30	58		1967-68	1976-77
Sabourin, Ken	Cgy., Wsh.	4	74	2	8	10	201	12	0	0	0	34	1	1988-89	1991-92
Sacharuk, Larry	NYR, St.L.	5	151	29	33	62	42	2	1	1	2	2		1972-73	1976-77
Saganiuk, Rocky	Tor., Pit.	6	259	57	65	122	201	6	1	0	1	15		1978-79	1983-84
St. Amour, Martin	Ott.	1	1	0	0	0	2	....	....	....	....	....		1992-93	1992-93
St. Laurent, Andre	NYI, Det., L.A., Pit.	11	644	129	187	316	749	59	8	12	20	48		1973-74	1983-84
St. Laurent, Dollard	Mtl., Chi.	12	652	29	133	162	496	92	2	22	24	87	5	1950-51	1961-62
St. Marseille, Frank	St.L., L.A.	10	707	140	285	425	242	88	20	25	45	18		1967-68	1976-77
St. Sauveur, Claude	Atl.	1	79	24	24	48	23	2	0	0	0	0		1975-76	1975-76
Saleski, Don	Phi., Col.	9	543	128	125	253	629	82	13	17	30	131	2	1971-72	1979-80
Salming, Borje	Tor., Det.	17	1148	150	637	787	1344	81	12	37	49	91		1973-74	1989-90
Salovaara, John Barry	Det.	2	90	2	13	15	70	....	....	....	....	....		1974-75	1975-76
Salvian, Dave	NYI	1	....	....	....	....	....	1	0	1	1	2		1976-77	1976-77
Samis, Phil	Tor.	2	2	0	0	0	0	5	0	1	1	2	1	1947-48	1949-50
Sampson, Gary	Wsh.	4	105	13	22	35	25	12	1	0	1	0		1983-84	1986-87
Sandelin, Scott	Mtl., Phi., Min.	4	25	0	4	4	2	....	....	....	....	....		1986-87	1991-92
Sanderson, Derek	Bos., NYR, St.L., Van., Pit.	13	598	202	250	452	911	56	18	12	30	187	2	1965-66	1977-78
Sandford, Ed	Bos., Det., Chi.	9	502	106	145	251	355	42	13	11	24	27		1947-48	1955-56
Sandlak, Jim	Van., Hfd.	11	549	110	119	229	821	33	7	10	17	30		1985-86	1995-96
● Sands, Charlie	Tor., Bos., Mtl., NYR	12	427	99	109	208	58	33	6	6	12	4	1	1932-33	1943-44
Sanipass, Everett	Chi., Que.	5	164	25	34	59	358	5	2	0	2	4		1986-87	1990-91
Sargent, Gary	L.A., Min.	8	402	61	161	222	273	20	5	7	12	8		1975-76	1982-83
Sarner, Craig	Bos.	1	7	0	0	0	0	....	....	....	....	....		1974-75	1974-75
Sarrazin, Dick	Phi.	3	100	20	35	55	22	4	0	0	0	0		1968-69	1971-72
Saskamoose, Fred	Chi.	1	11	0	0	0	6	....	....	....	....	....		1953-54	1953-54
Sasser, Grant	Pit.	1	3	0	0	0	0	....	....	....	....	....		1983-84	1983-84
Sather, Glen	Bos., Pit., NYR, St.L., Mtl., Min.	10	658	80	113	193	724	72	1	5	6	86		1966-67	1975-76
Saunders, Bernie	Que.	2	10	0	1	1	8	....	....	....	....	....		1979-80	1980-81
Saunders, Bud	Ott.	1	18	1	3	4	4	....	....	....	....	....		1933-34	1933-34
Saunders, David	Van.	1	56	7	13	20	10	....	....	....	....	....		1987-88	1987-88
Sauve, Jean-Francois	Buf., Que.	7	290	65	138	203	117	36	9	12	21	10		1980-81	1986-87
Savage, Joel	Buf.	1	3	0	1	1	0	....	....	....	....	....		1990-91	1990-91
Savage, Reggie	Wsh., Que.	3	34	5	7	12	28	....	....	....	....	....		1990-91	1993-94
● Savage, Tony	Bos., Mtl.	1	49	1	5	6	6	2	0	0	0	0		1934-35	1934-35
Savard, Andre	Bos., Buf., Que.	12	790	211	271	482	411	85	13	18	31	77		1973-74	1984-85
Savard, Jean	Chi, Hfd.	3	43	7	12	19	29	....	....	....	....	....		1977-78	1979-80
Savard, Serge	Mtl., Wpg.	17	1040	106	333	439	592	130	19	49	68	88	7	1966-67	1982-83
Scamurra, Peter	Wsh.	4	132	8	25	33	59	....	....	....	....	....		1975-76	1979-80
Sceviour, Darin	Chi.	1	1	0	0	0	0	....	....	....	....	....		1986-87	1986-87
Schaeffer, Butch	Chi.,	1	5	0	0	0	6	....	....	....	....	....		1936-37	1936-37
Schamehorn, Kevin	Det., L.A.	3	10	0	0	0	17	....	....	....	....	....		1976-77	1980-81
Schella, John	Van.	2	115	2	18	20	224	....	....	....	....	....		1970-71	1971-72
Scherza, Chuck	Bos., NYR	2	56	6	6	12	35	....	....	....	....	....		1943-44	1944-45
Schinkel, Ken	NYR, Pit.	12	636	127	198	325	163	19	7	2	9	4		1959-60	1972-73
Schlegel, Brad	Wsh., Cgy.	3	48	1	8	9	10	7	0	1	1	2		1991-92	1993-94
Schliebener, Andy	Van.	3	84	2	11	13	74	6	0	0	0	0		1981-82	1984-85
Schmautz, Bobby	Chi., Bos., Edm., Col., Van.	13	764	271	286	557	988	84	28	33	61	92		1967-68	1980-81
Schmautz, Cliff	Buf., Phi.	1	56	13	19	32	33	....	....	....	....	....		1970-71	1970-71
Schmidt, Clarence	Bos.,	1	7	1	0	1	2	....	....	....	....	....		1943-44	1943-44
Schmidt, Jackie	Bos.	1	45	6	7	13	6	5	0	0	0	0		1942-43	1942-43
Schmidt, Joseph	Bos.	1	2	0	0	0	0	....	....	....	....	....		1943-44	1943-44
Schmidt, Milt	Bos.	16	776	229	346	575	466	86	24	25	49	60	2	1936-37	1954-55
Schmidt, Norm	Pit.	4	125	23	33	56	73	....	....	....	....	....		1983-84	1987-88
● Schnarr, Werner	Bos.	2	25	0	0	0	0	....	....	....	....	....		1924-25	1925-26
Schock, Danny	Bos., Phi.	2	20	1	2	3	0	1	0	0	0	0	1	1969-70	1970-71
Schock, Ron	Bos., St.L., Pit., Buf.	15	909	166	351	517	260	55	4	16	20	29		1963-64	1977-78
Schoenfeld, Jim	Buf., Det., Bos.	13	719	51	204	255	1132	75	3	13	16	151		1972-73	1984-85
Schofield, Dwight	Det., Mtl., St.L., Wsh., Pit., Wpg.	7	211	8	22	30	631	9	0	0	0	55		1976-77	1987-88
Schreiber, Wally	Min.	2	41	8	10	18	12	....	....	....	....	....		1987-88	1988-89
● Schriner, Sweeney	NYA, Tor.	11	484	201	204	405	148	59	18	11	29	54	2	1934-35	1945-46
Schultz, Dave	Phi., L.A., Pit., Buf.	9	535	79	121	200	2294	73	8	12	20	412	2	1971-72	1979-80
Schurman, Maynard	Hfd.	1	7	0	0	0	0	....	....	....	....	....		1979-80	1979-80
Schutt, Rod	Mtl., Pit., Tor.	8	286	77	92	169	177	22	8	6	14	26		1977-78	1985-86
Scissons, Scott	NYI	3	2	0	0	0	0	1	0	0	0	0		1990-91	1993-94
Sclisizzi, Enio	Det., Chi.	6	81	12	11	23	26	13	0	0	0	6		1946-47	1952-53
Scott, Ganton	Tor., Ham., Mtl.M.	3	53	1	1	2	0	....	....	....	....	....		1922-23	1924-25
● Scott, Laurie	NYA, NYR	2	62	6	3	9	28	....	....	....	....	....	1	1926-27	1927-28
Scremin, Claudio	S.J.	2	17	0	1	1	29	....	....	....	....	....		1991-92	1992-93
Scruton, Howard	L.A.	1	4	0	4	4	9	....	....	....	....	....		1982-83	1982-83
Seabrooke, Glen	Phi.	3	19	1	6	7	4	....	....	....	....	....		1986-87	1988-89
Secord, Al	Bos., Chi., Tor, Phi.	12	766	273	222	495	2093	102	21	34	55	382		1978-79	1989-90
Sedlbauer, Ron	Van., Chi., Tor.	7	430	143	86	229	210	19	1	3	4	27		1974-75	1980-81
Seftel, Steve	Wsh.	1	4	0	0	0	2	....	....	....	....	....		1990-91	1990-91
Seguin, Dan	Min., Van.	2	37	2	6	8	50	....	....	....	....	....		1970-71	1973-74
Seguin, Steve	L.A.	1	5	0	0	0	9	....	....	....	....	....		1984-85	1984-85
● Seibert, Earl	NYR, Chi., Det.	15	645	89	187	276	746	66	11	8	19	76	2	1931-32	1945-46
Seiling, Ric	Buf., Det.	10	738	179	208	387	573	62	14	14	28	36		1977-78	1986-87
Seiling, Rod	Tor., NYR, Wsh., St.L., Atl.	17	979	62	269	331	601	77	4	8	12	55		1962-63	1978-79
Sejba, Jiri	Buf.	1	11	0	2	2	8	....	....	....	....	....		1990-91	1990-91
Selby, Brit	Tor., Phi., St.L.	8	350	55	62	117	163	16	1	1	2	8		1964-65	1971-72
Self, Steve	Wsh.	1	3	0	0	0	0	....	....	....	....	....		1976-77	1976-77
Selwood, Brad	Tor., L.A.	3	163	7	40	47	153	6	0	0	0	4		1970-71	1979-80
Semchuk, Brandy	L.A.	1	1	0	0	0	2	....	....	....	....	....		1992-93	1992-93
Semenko, Dave	Edm., Hfd., Tor.	9	575	65	88	153	1175	73	6	6	12	208	2	1979-80	1987-88
Senick, George	NYR	1	13	2	3	5	8	....	....	....	....	....		1952-53	1952-53
Seppa, Jyrki	Wpg.	1	13	0	2	2	6	....	....	....	....	....		1983-84	1983-84
Serafini, Ron	Cal.	1	2	0	0	0	2	....	....	....	....	....		1973-74	1973-74
Serowik, Jeff	Tor., Bos.	2	2	0	0	0	0	....	....	....	....	....		1990-91	1994-95
Servinis, George	Min.	1	5	0	0	0	0	....	....	....	....	....		1987-88	1987-88
Sevcik, Jaroslav	Que.	1	13	0	2	2	2	....	....	....	....	....		1989-90	1989-90
Shack, Eddie	NYR, Tor., Bos., L.A., Buf., Pit.	17	1047	239	226	465	1437	74	6	7	13	151	4	1958-59	1974-75
● Shack, Joe	NYR	2	70	23	13	36	20	....	....	....	....	....		1942-43	1944-45
Shakes, Paul	Cal.	1	21	0	4	4	12	....	....	....	....	....		1973-74	1973-74
Shanahan, Sean	Mtl., Col., Bos.	3	40	1	3	4	47	....	....	....	....	....		1975-76	1977-78
Shand, Dave	Atl., Tor., Wsh.	8	421	19	84	103	544	26	1	2	3	83		1976-77	1984-85
Shank, Daniel	Det., Hfd.	3	77	13	14	27	175	5	0	0	0	22		1989-90	1991-92
Shannon, Charles	NYA	1	4	0	0	0	2	....	....	....	....	....		1939-40	1939-40
● Shannon, Gerry	Ott., St.L., Bos., Mtl.M.	5	180	23	29	52	80	9	0	1	1	2		1933-34	1937-38
Sharples, Jeff	Det.	3	105	14	35	49	70	7	0	3	3	6		1986-87	1988-89
Sharpley, Glen	Min., Chi.	6	389	117	161	278	199	27	7	11	18	24		1976-77	1981-82
Shaunessy, Scott	Que.	2	7	0	0	0	23	....	....	....	....	....		1986-87	1988-89
Shaw, Brad	Hfd., Ott.	10	361	22	137	159	200	19	4	8	12	6		1985-86	1994-95
Shay, Norman	Bos., Tor.	2	53	5	2	7	34	....	....	....	....	....		1924-25	1925-26
Shea, Pat	Chi.	1	14	0	1	1	0	....	....	....	....	....		1931-32	1931-32
Shedden, Doug	Pit., Det., Que., Tor.	8	416	139	186	325	176	....	....	....	....	....		1981-82	1990-91
Sheehan, Bobby	Mtl., Cal., Chi., Det., NYR, Col., L.A.	9	310	48	63	111	50	25	4	3	7	8	1	1969-70	1981-82
Sheehy, Neil	Cgy., Hfd., Wsh.	9	379	18	47	65	1311	54	0	3	3	241		1983-84	1991-92
Sheehy, Tim	Det., Hfd.	2	27	2	1	3	0	....	....	....	....	....		1977-78	1979-80
Shelton, Doug	Chi.	1	5	0	1	1	2	....	....	....	....	....		1967-68	1967-68
Sheppard, Frank	Det.	1	8	1	1	2	0	....	....	....	....	....		1927-28	1927-28
Sheppard, Gregg	Bos., Pit.	10	657	205	293	498	243	82	32	40	72	31		1972-73	1981-82
Sheppard, Johnny	Det., NYA, Bos., Chi.	8	311	68	58	126	224	10	0	0	0	0	1	1926-27	1933-34
● Sherf, John	Det.	5	19	0	0	0	8	8	0	1	1	2	1	1935-36	1943-44
● Shero, Fred	NYR	3	145	6	14	20	137	13	0	2	2	8		1947-48	1949-50
Sherritt, Gordon	Det.	1	8	0	0	0	12	....	....	....	....	....		1943-44	1943-44
Sherven, Gord	Edm., Min., Hfd.	5	97	13	22	35	33	3	0	0	0	0		1983-84	1987-88
● Shewchuck, Jack	Bos.	6	187	9	19	28	160	20	0	1	1	19	1	1938-39	1944-45
Shibicky, Alex	NYR	8	322	110	91	201	161	39	12	12	24	12	1	1935-36	1945-46

Name	NHL Teams	NHL Seasons	Regular Schedule GP	G	A	TP	PIM	Playoffs GP	G	A	TP	PIM	NHL Cup Wins	First NHL Season	Last NHL Season
• Shields, Al	Ott., Phi., NYA, Mtl.M., Bos.	11	460	42	46	88	637	15	0	1	1	14	1	1927-28	1937-38
Shill, Bill	Bos.	3	79	21	13	34	18	7	1	2	3	2		1942-43	1946-47
• Shill, Jack	Tor., Bos., NYA, Chi.	6	163	15	20	35	70	27	1	6	7	13	1	1933-34	1938-39
Shinske, Rick	Clev., St.L.	3	63	5	16	21	10	....	....	....	....	....		1976-77	1978-79
Shires, Jim	Det., St.L., Pit.	3	56	3	6	9	32	....	....	....	....	....		1970-71	1972-73
Shmyr, Paul	Chi., Cal., Min., Hfd.	7	343	13	72	85	528	34	3	3	6	44		1968-69	1981-82
Shoebottom, Bruce	Bos.	4	35	1	4	5	53	14	1	2	3	77		1987-88	1990-91
• Shore, Eddie	Bos., NYA	14	553	105	179	284	1047	55	6	13	19	179	2	1926-27	1939-40
• Shore, Hamby	Ott.	1	18	3	0	3	17	....	....	....	....	....		1917-18	1917-18
Shores, Aubrey	Phi.	1	1	0	0	0	0	....	....	....	....	....		1930-31	1930-31
Short, Steve	L.A., Det.	2	6	0	0	0	2	....	....	....	....	....		1977-78	1978-79
Shudra, Ron	Edm.	1	10	0	5	5	6	....	....	....	....	....		1987-88	1987-88
Shutt, Steve	Mtl., L.A.	13	930	424	393	817	410	99	50	48	98	65	5	1972-73	1984-85
• Siebert, Babe	Mtl.M., NYR, Bos., Mtl.	14	596	140	156	296	982	53	8	7	15	64	2	1925-26	1938-39
Silk, Dave	NYR, Bos., Wpg., Det.	7	249	54	59	113	271	13	2	4	6	13		1979-80	1985-86
Siltala, Mike	Wsh., NYR	3	7	1	0	1	2	....	....	....	....	....		1981-82	1987-88
Siltanen, Risto	Edm., Hfd., Que.	8	562	90	265	355	266	32	6	12	18	30		1979-80	1986-87
Sim, Trevor	Edm.	1	3	0	1	1	2	....	....	....	....	....		1989-90	1989-90
Simard, Martin	Cgy., T.B.	3	44	1	5	6	183	....	....	....	....	....		1990-91	1992-93
Simmer, Charlie	Cal., Cle., L.A., Bos., Pit.	14	712	342	369	711	544	24	9	9	18	32		1974-75	1987-88
Simmons, Al	Cal., Bos.	3	11	0	1	1	21	1	0	0	0	0		1971-72	1975-76
Simon, Cully	Det., Chi.	3	130	4	11	15	121	14	0	1	1	6	1	1942-43	1944-45
Simon, Thain	Det.	1	3	0	0	0	0	....	....	....	....	....		1946-47	1946-47
Simon, Todd	Buf.	1	15	0	1	1	0	5	1	0	1	0		1993-94	1993-94
Simonetti, Frank	Bos.	4	115	5	8	13	76	12	0	1	1	8		1984-85	1987-88
Simpson, Bobby	Atl., St.L., Pit.	5	175	35	29	64	98	6	0	1	1	2		1976-77	1982-83
• Simpson, Cliff	Det.	2	6	0	1	1	0	2	0	0	0	2		1946-47	1947-48
Simpson, Craig	Pit., Edm., Buf.	10	634	247	250	497	659	67	36	32	68	56	2	1985-86	1994-95
• Simpson, Joe	NYA	6	228	21	19	40	156	2	0	0	0	0		1925-26	1930-31
Sims, Al	Bos., Hfd., L.A.	10	475	49	116	165	286	41	0	2	2	14		1973-74	1982-83
Sinclair, Reg	NYR, Det.	3	208	49	43	92	139	3	1	0	1	0		1950-51	1952-53
Singbush, Alex	Mtl.	1	32	0	5	5	15	3	0	0	0	4		1940-41	1940-41
Sinisalo, Ilkka	Phi., Min., L.A.	11	582	204	222	426	208	68	21	11	32	6		1981-82	1991-92
Siren, Ville	Pit., Min.	5	290	14	68	82	276	7	0	0	0	6		1985-86	1989-90
Sirois, Bob	Phi., Wsh.	6	286	92	120	212	42	....	....	....	....	....		1974-75	1979-80
Sittler, Darryl	Tor., Phi., Det.	15	1096	484	637	1121	948	76	29	45	74	137		1970-71	1984-85
• Sjoberg, Lars-Erik	Wpg.	1	79	7	27	34	48	....	....	....	....	....		1979-80	1979-80
Sjodin, Tommy	Min., Dal., Que.	2	106	8	40	48	52	....	....	....	....	....		1992-93	1993-94
• Skaare, Bjorne	Det.	1	1	0	0	0	0	....	....	....	....	....		1978-79	1978-79
Skarda, Randy	St.L.	2	26	0	5	5	11	....	....	....	....	....		1989-90	1991-92
• Skilton, Raymie	Mtl.W	1	1	1	0	1	0	....	....	....	....	....		1917-18	1917-18
• Skinner, Alf	Tor., Bos., Mtl.M., Pit.	4	70	26	4	30	76	7	8	1	9	0	1	1917-18	1925-26
Skinner, Larry	Col.	4	47	10	12	22	8	2	0	0	0	0		1976-77	1979-80
Skov, Glen	Det., Chi., Mtl.	12	650	106	136	242	413	53	7	7	14	48	3	1949-50	1960-61
Skriko, Petri	Van., Bos., Wpg., S.J.	9	541	183	222	405	246	28	5	9	14	4		1984-85	1992-93
Sleaver, John	Chi.	2	13	1	0	1	6	....	....	....	....	....		1953-54	1956-57
Sleigher, Louis	Que., Bos.	6	194	46	53	99	146	17	1	1	2	64		1979-80	1985-86
Sloan, Tod	Tor., Chi.	13	745	220	262	482	831	47	9	12	21	47	2	1947-48	1960-61
• Slobodzian, Peter	NYA	1	41	3	2	5	54	....	....	....	....	....		1940-41	1940-41
Slowinski, Eddie	NYR	6	291	58	74	132	63	16	2	6	8	6		1947-48	1952-53
Sly, Darryl	Tor., Min., Van.	4	79	1	2	3	20	....	....	....	....	....		1965-66	1970-71
Smail, Doug	Wpg., Min., Que., Ott.	13	845	210	249	459	602	42	9	2	11	49		1980-81	1992-93
Smart, Alex	Mtl.	1	8	5	2	7	0	....	....	....	....	....		1942-43	1942-43
Smedsmo, Dale	Tor.	1	4	0	0	0	0	....	....	....	....	....		1972-73	1972-73
Smillie, Don	Bos.	1	12	2	2	4	4	....	....	....	....	....		1933-34	1933-34
• Smith, Alex	Ott., Det., Bos., NYA	11	443	41	50	91	643	19	0	2	2	40	1	1924-25	1934-35
• Smith, Arthur	Tor., Ott.	4	144	15	10	25	249	4	1	1	2	8		1927-28	1930-31
Smith, Barry	Bos., Col.	3	114	7	7	14	10	....	....	....	....	....		1975-76	1980-81
Smith, Bobby	Min., Mtl.	15	1077	357	679	1036	917	184	64	96	160	245	1	1978-79	1992-93
Smith, Brad	Van., Atl., Cgy., Det., Tor.	9	222	28	34	62	591	20	3	3	6	49		1978-79	1986-87
• Smith, Brian D.	L.A., Min.	2	67	10	10	20	33	7	0	0	0	0		1967-68	1968-69
Smith, Brian S.	Det.	3	61	2	8	10	12	5	0	0	0	0		1957-58	1960-61
Smith, Carl	Det.	1	7	1	1	2	2	....	....	....	....	....		1943-44	1943-44
Smith, Clint	NYR, Chi.	11	483	161	236	397	24	42	10	14	24	2	1	1936-37	1946-47
Smith, Dallas	Bos., NYR	16	890	55	252	307	959	86	3	29	32	128	2	1959-60	1977-78
Smith, Dalton	NYA, Det.	1	10	1	2	3	0	....	....	....	....	....		1936-37	1943-44
Smith, Dennis	Wsh., L.A.	2	8	0	0	0	4	....	....	....	....	....		1989-90	1990-91
Smith, Derek	Buf., Det.	8	335	78	116	194	60	30	9	14	23	13		1975-76	1982-83
Smith, Derrick	Phi., Min., Dal.	10	537	82	92	174	373	82	14	11	25	79		1984-85	1993-94
Smith, Des	Mtl.M., Mtl., Chi., Bos.	5	196	22	25	47	236	25	1	4	5	18	1	1937-38	1941-42
• Smith, Don	Mtl.	1	10	1	0	1	4	....	....	....	....	....		1919-20	1919-20
Smith, Don A.	NYR	1	11	1	1	2	0	1	0	0	0	0		1949-50	1949-50
Smith, Doug	L.A., Buf., Edm., Van., Pit.	9	535	115	138	253	624	18	4	2	6	21		1981-82	1989-90
Smith, Floyd	Bos., NYR, Det., Tor., Buf.	13	616	129	178	307	207	48	12	11	23	16		1954-55	1971-72
Smith, George	Tor.	1	9	0	0	0	0	....	....	....	....	....		1921-22	1921-22
Smith, Glen	Chi.	1	2	0	0	0	0	....	....	....	....	....		1950-51	1950-51
Smith, Glenn	Tor.	1	9	0	0	0	0	....	....	....	....	....		1922-23	1922-23
Smith, Gord	Wsh., Wpg.	6	299	9	30	39	284	....	....	....	....	....		1974-75	1979-80
Smith, Greg	Cal., Clev., Min., Det., Wsh.	13	829	56	232	288	1110	63	4	7	11	106		1975-76	1987-88
• Smith, Hooley	Ott., Mtl.M., Bos., NYA	17	715	200	215	415	1013	54	11	8	19	109	2	1924-25	1940-41
Smith, Kenny	Bos.	7	331	78	93	171	49	30	8	13	21	6		1944-45	1950-51
Smith, Randy	Min.	2	3	0	0	0	0	....	....	....	....	....		1985-86	1986-87
Smith, Rick	Bos., Cal., St.L., Det., Wsh.	11	687	52	167	219	560	78	3	23	26	73	1	1968-69	1980-81
• Smith, Roger	Pit., Phi.	6	210	20	4	24	172	4	3	0	3	0		1925-26	1930-31
Smith, Ron	NYI	1	11	1	1	2	14	....	....	....	....	....		1972-73	1972-73
Smith, Sid	Tor.	12	601	186	183	369	94	44	17	10	27	2	3	1946-47	1957-58
Smith, Stan	NYR	2	9	2	1	3	0	....	....	....	....	....		1939-40	1940-41
Smith, Steve	Phi., Buf.	6	18	0	1	1	15	....	....	....	....	....		1981-82	1988-89
Smith, Stu E.	Mtl.	2	4	2	2	4	2	1	0	0	0	0		1940-41	1941-42
Smith, Stu G.	Hfd.	4	77	2	10	12	95	....	....	....	....	....		1979-80	1982-83
• Smith, Tommy	Que.B.	1	10	0	0	0	9	....	....	....	....	....		1919-20	1919-20
Smith, Vern	NYI	1	1	0	0	0	0	....	....	....	....	....		1984-85	1984-85
Smith, Wayne	Chi.	1	2	1	1	2	2	1	0	0	0	0		1966-67	1966-67
Smrke, John	St.L., Que.	3	103	11	17	28	33	....	....	....	....	....		1977-78	1979-80
• Smrke, Stan	Mtl.	2	9	0	3	3	0	....	....	....	....	....		1956-57	1957-58
Smyl, Stan	Van.	13	896	262	411	673	1556	41	16	17	33	64		1978-79	1990-91
• Smylie, Rod	Tor., Ott.	6	76	3	1	4	10	9	1	2	3	2	1	1920-21	1925-26
Snell, Ron	Pit.	2	7	3	2	5	6	....	....	....	....	....		1968-69	1969-70
Snell, Ted	Pit., K.C., Det.	2	104	7	18	25	32	....	....	....	....	....		1973-74	1974-75
Snepsts, Harold	Van., Min., Det., St.L.	17	1033	38	195	233	2009	93	1	14	15	231		1974-75	1990-91
Snow, Sandy	Det.	1	3	0	0	0	2	....	....	....	....	....		1968-69	1968-69
Snuggerud, Dave	Buf., S.J., Phi.	4	265	30	54	84	127	12	1	3	4	6		1989-90	1992-93
Sobchuk, Dennis	Det., Que.	2	35	5	6	11	2	....	....	....	....	....		1979-80	1982-83
Sobchuk, Gene	Van.	1	1	0	0	0	0	....	....	....	....	....		1973-74	1973-74
Solheim, Ken	Chi., Min., Det., Edm.	5	135	19	20	39	34	3	1	1	2	2		1980-81	1985-86
Solinger, Bob	Tor., Det.	5	99	10	11	21	19	....	....	....	....	....		1951-52	1959-60
• Somers, Art	Chi., NYR	6	222	33	56	89	189	30	1	5	6	20	1	1929-30	1934-35
Sommer, Roy	Edm.	1	3	1	0	1	7	....	....	....	....	....		1980-81	1980-81
Songin, Tom	Bos.	3	43	5	5	10	22	....	....	....	....	....		1978-79	1980-81
Sonmor, Glen	NYR	2	28	2	0	2	21	....	....	....	....	....		1953-54	1954-55
• Sorrell, John	Det., NYA	11	490	127	119	246	100	42	12	15	27	10	2	1930-31	1940-41
• Sparrow, Emory	Bos.	1	6	0	0	0	4	....	....	....	....	....		1924-25	1924-25
Speck, Fred	Det., Van.	3	28	1	2	3	2	....	....	....	....	....		1968-69	1971-72
• Speer, Bill	Pit., Bos.	4	130	5	20	25	79	8	1	0	1	4	1	1967-68	1970-71
Speers, Ted	Det.	1	4	1	1	2	0	....	....	....	....	....		1985-86	1985-86
• Spencer, Brian	Tor., NYI, Buf., Pit.	10	553	80	143	223	634	37	1	5	6	29		1969-70	1978-79
Spencer, Irv	NYR, Bos., Det.	8	230	12	38	50	127	16	0	0	0	8		1959-60	1967-68
Speyer, Chris	Tor., NYA	3	14	0	0	0	0	....	....	....	....	....		1923-24	1933-34
Spring, Don	Wpg.	4	259	1	54	55	80	6	0	0	0	10		1980-81	1983-84
Spring, Frank	Bos., St.L., Cal., Clev.	5	61	14	20	34	12	....	....	....	....	....		1969-70	1976-77
• Spring, Jesse	Ham., Pit., Tor., NYA	6	162	11	2	13	62	2	0	2	2	2		1923-24	1929-30
Spruce, Andy	Van., Col.	3	172	31	42	73	111	2	0	2	2	0		1976-77	1978-79
Srsen, Tomas	Edm.	1	2	0	0	0	0	....	....	....	....	....		1990-91	1990-91

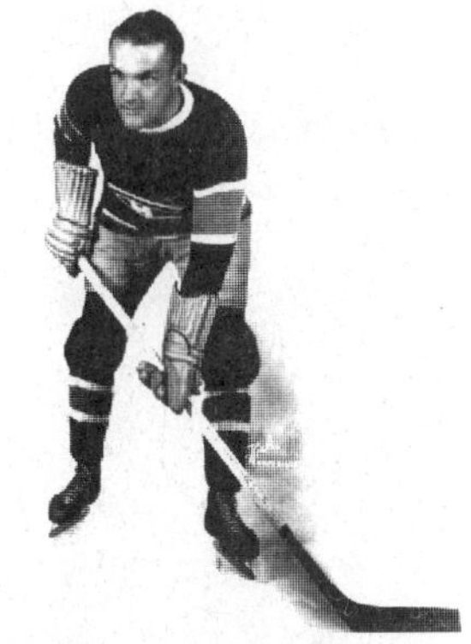
Babe Siebert

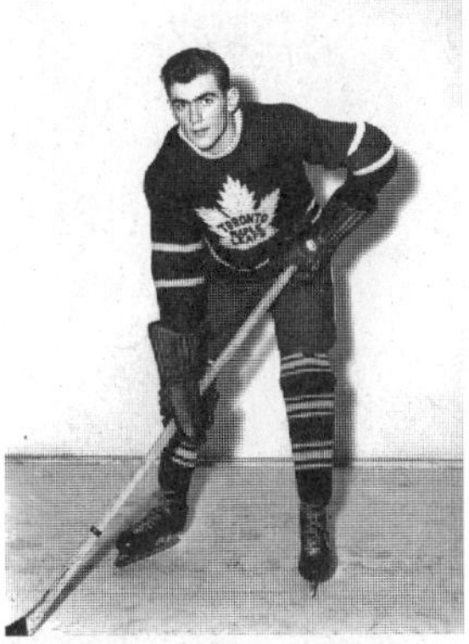
Tod Sloan

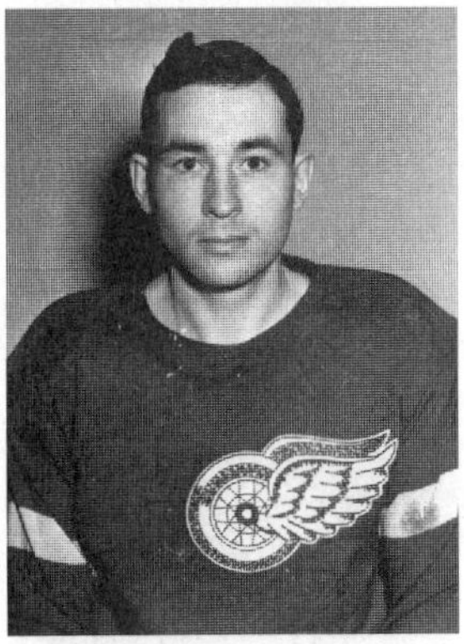
Jack Stewart

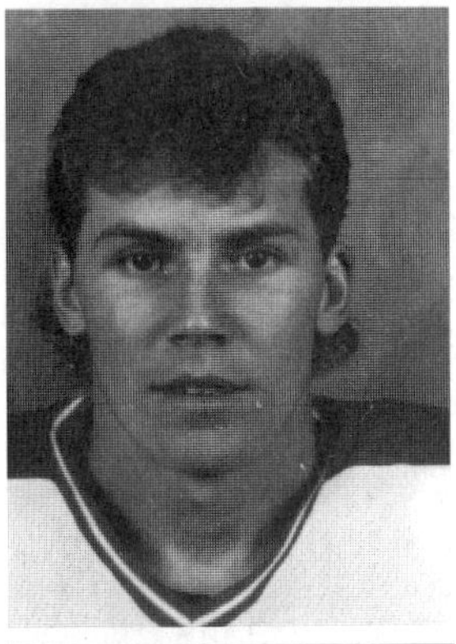
David Struch

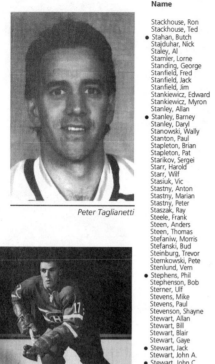

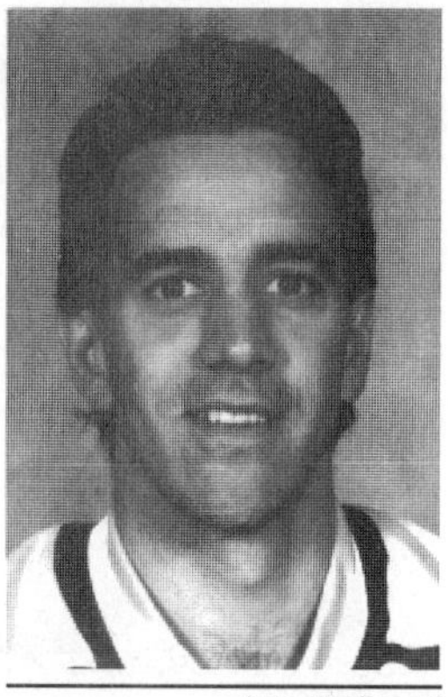
Peter Taglianetti

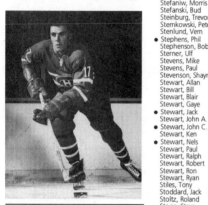

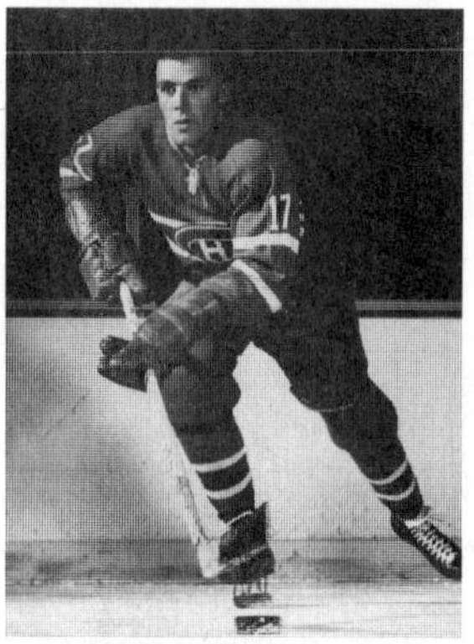
Jean-Guy Talbot

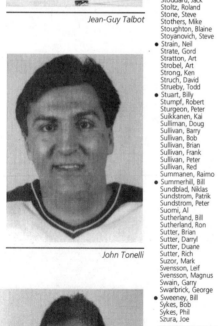

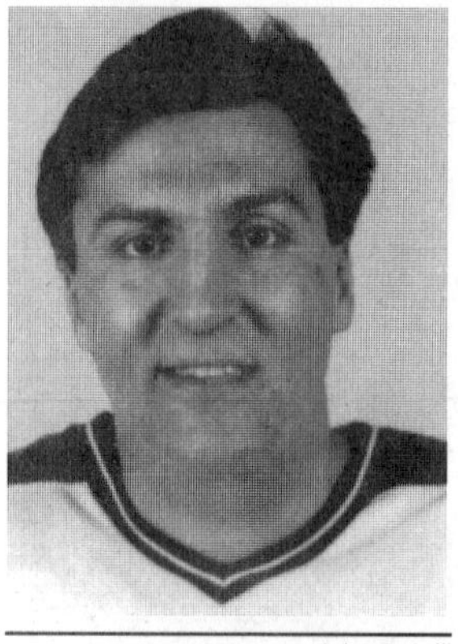
John Tonelli

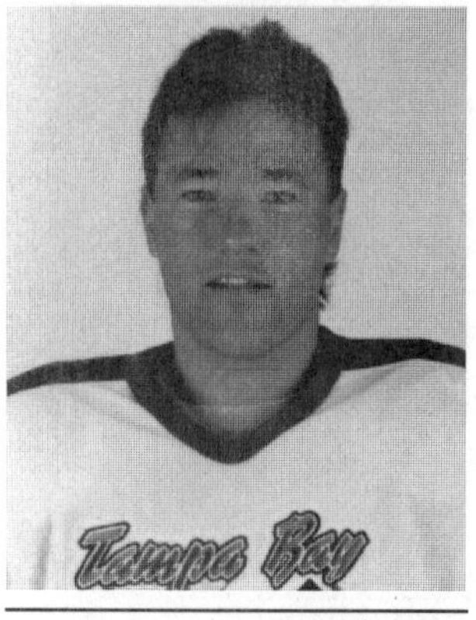

John Tucker

Name	NHL Teams	NHL Seasons	Regular Schedule					Playoffs					NHL Cup Wins	First NHL Season	Last NHL Season
			GP	G	A	TP	PIM	GP	G	A	TP	PIM			
Stackhouse, Ron	Cal., Det., Pit.	12	889	87	372	459	824	32	5	8	13	38		1970-71	1981-82
Stackhouse, Ted	Tor.	1	12	0	0	0	2	5	0	0	0	0	1	1921-22	1921-22
• Stahan, Butch	Mtl.	1	....	....	....	....	....	3	0	1	1	2		1944-45	1944-45
Stajduhar, Nick	Edm.	1	2	0	0	0	4	....	....	....	....	....		1995-96	1995-96
Staley, Al	NYR	1	1	0	1	1	0	....	....	....	....	....		1948-49	1948-49
Stamler, Lorne	L.A., Tor., Wpg.	4	116	14	11	25	16	....	....	....	....	....		1976-77	1979-80
Standing, George	Min.	1	2	0	0	0	0	....	....	....	....	....		1967-68	1967-68
Stanfield, Fred	Chi., Bos., Min., Buf.	14	914	211	405	616	134	106	21	35	56	10	2	1964-65	1977-78
Stanfield, Jack	Chi.	1	....	....	....	....	....	1	0	0	0	0		1965-66	1965-66
Stanfield, Jim	L.A.	3	7	0	1	1	0	....	....	....	....	....		1969-70	1971-72
Stankiewicz, Edward	Det.	2	6	0	0	0	2	....	....	....	....	....		1953-54	1955-56
Stankiewicz, Myron	St.L., Phi.	1	35	0	7	7	36	1	0	0	0	0		1968-69	1968-69
Stanley, Allan	NYR, Chi., Bos., Tor., Phi.	21	1244	100	333	433	792	109	7	36	43	80	4	1948-49	1968-69
• Stanley, Barney	Chi.	1	1	0	0	0	0	....	....	....	....	....		1927-28	1927-28
Stanley, Daryl	Phi., Van.	6	189	8	17	25	408	17	0	0	0	30		1983-84	1989-90
Stanowski, Wally	Tor., NYR	10	428	23	88	111	160	60	3	14	17	13	4	1939-40	1950-51
Stanton, Paul	Pit., Bos., NYI	5	295	14	49	63	262	44	2	10	12	66	2	1990-91	1994-95
Stapleton, Brian	Wsh.	1	1	0	0	0	0	....	....	....	....	....		1975-76	1975-76
Stapleton, Pat	Bos., Chi.	10	635	43	294	337	353	65	10	39	49	38		1961-62	1972-73
Starikov, Sergei	N.J.	1	16	0	1	1	8	....	....	....	....	....		1989-90	1989-90
Starr, Harold	Ott., Mtl.M., Mtl., NYR	7	205	6	5	11	186	15	1	0	1	4		1929-30	1935-36
Starr, Wilf	NYA, Det.	4	87	8	6	14	25	7	0	2	2	2	1	1932-33	1935-36
Stasiuk, Vic	Chi., Det., Bos.	14	745	183	254	437	669	69	16	18	34	40	2	1949-50	1962-63
Stastny, Anton	Que.	9	650	252	384	636	150	66	20	32	52	31		1980-81	1988-89
Stastny, Marian	Que., Tor.	5	322	121	173	294	110	32	5	17	22	7		1981-82	1985-86
Stastny, Peter	Que., N.J., St.L.	15	977	450	789	1239	824	93	33	72	105	123		1980-81	1994-95
Staszak, Ray	Det.	1	4	0	1	1	7	....	....	....	....	....		1985-86	1985-86
Steele, Frank	Det.	1	1	0	0	0	0	....	....	....	....	....		1930-31	1930-31
Steen, Anders	Wpg.	1	42	5	11	16	22	....	....	....	....	....		1980-81	1980-81
Steen, Thomas	Wpg.	14	950	264	553	817	753	56	12	32	44	62		1981-82	1994-95
Stefaniw, Morris	Atl.	1	13	1	1	2	2	....	....	....	....	....		1972-73	1972-73
Stefanski, Bud	NYR	1	1	0	0	0	0	....	....	....	....	....		1977-78	1977-78
Steinburg, Trevor	Que.	4	71	8	4	12	161	1	0	0	0	0		1985-86	1988-89
Stemkowski, Pete	Tor., Det., NYR, L.A.	15	967	206	349	555	866	83	25	29	54	136	1	1963-64	1977-78
Stenlund, Vern	Clev.	1	4	0	0	0	0	....	....	....	....	....		1976-77	1976-77
• Stephens, Phil	Mtl.W, Mtl.	2	8	1	0	1	0	....	....	....	....	....		1917-18	1921-22
Stephenson, Bob	Hfd., Tor.	1	18	2	3	5	4	....	....	....	....	....		1979-80	1979-80
Sterner, Ulf	NYR	1	4	0	0	0	0	....	....	....	....	....		1964-65	1964-65
Stevens, Mike	Van., NYI, Tor.	4	23	1	4	5	29	....	....	....	....	....		1984-85	1989-90
Stevens, Paul	Bos.	1	17	0	0	0	0	....	....	....	....	....		1925-26	1925-26
Stevenson, Shayne	Bos., T.B.	3	27	0	2	2	35	....	....	....	....	....		1990-91	1992-93
Stewart, Allan	N.J., Bos.	6	64	6	4	10	243	....	....	....	....	....		1985-86	1991-92
Stewart, Bill	Buf., St.L., Tor., Min.	8	261	7	64	71	424	13	1	3	4	11		1977-78	1985-86
Stewart, Blair	Det., Wsh., Que.	7	229	34	44	78	326	....	....	....	....	....		1973-74	1979-80
Stewart, Gaye	Tor., Chi., Det., NYR, Mtl.	11	502	185	159	344	274	25	2	9	11	16	2	1941-42	1953-54
• Stewart, Jack	Det., Chi.	12	565	31	84	115	765	80	5	14	19	143	2	1938-39	1951-52
Stewart, John A.	Pit., Atl., Cal.	5	258	58	60	118	158	4	0	0	0	10		1970-71	1974-75
• Stewart, John C.	Que.	1	2	0	0	0	0	....	....	....	....	....		1979-80	1979-80
Stewart, Ken	Chi.	1	6	1	1	2	2	....	....	....	....	....		1941-42	1941-42
• Stewart, Nels	Mtl.M., Bos., NYA	15	650	324	191	515	953	54	15	13	28	61	1	1925-26	1939-40
Stewart, Paul	Que.	1	21	2	0	2	74	....	....	....	....	....		1979-80	1979-80
Stewart, Ralph	Van., NYI	7	252	57	73	130	28	19	4	4	8	2		1970-71	1977-78
Stewart, Robert	Bos., Cal., Clev., St.L., Pit.	9	575	27	101	128	809	5	1	1	2	2		1971-72	1979-80
Stewart, Ron	Tor., Bos., St.L., NYR, Van., NYI	21	1353	276	253	529	560	119	14	21	35	60	3	1952-53	1972-73
Stewart, Ryan	Wpg.	1	3	1	0	1	0	....	....	....	....	....		1985-86	1985-86
Stiles, Tony	Cgy.	1	30	2	7	9	20	....	....	....	....	....		1983-84	1983-84
Stoddard, Jack	NYR	2	80	16	15	31	31	....	....	....	....	....		1951-52	1952-53
Stoltz, Roland	Wsh.	1	14	2	2	4	14	....	....	....	....	....		1981-82	1981-82
Stone, Steve	Van.	1	2	0	0	0	0	....	....	....	....	....		1973-74	1973-74
Stothers, Mike	Phi., Tor.	4	30	0	2	2	65	5	0	0	0	11		1984-85	1987-88
Stoughton, Blaine	Pit., Tor., Hfd., NYR	8	526	258	191	449	204	8	4	2	6	2		1973-74	1983-84
Stoyanovich, Steve	Hfd.	1	23	3	5	8	11	....	....	....	....	....		1983-84	1983-84
• Strain, Neil	NYR	1	52	11	13	24	12	....	....	....	....	....		1952-53	1952-53
Strate, Gord	Det.	3	61	0	0	0	34	....	....	....	....	....		1956-57	1958-59
Stratton, Art	NYR, Det., Chi., Pit., Phi.	4	95	18	33	51	24	5	0	0	0	0		1959-60	1967-68
Strobel, Art	NYR	1	7	0	0	0	0	....	....	....	....	....		1943-44	1943-44
Strong, Ken	Tor.	3	15	2	2	4	6	....	....	....	....	....		1982-83	1984-85
Struch, David	Cgy.	1	4	0	0	0	4	....	....	....	....	....		1993-94	1993-94
Strueby, Todd	Edm.	3	5	0	1	1	2	....	....	....	....	....		1981-82	1983-84
• Stuart, Billy	Tor., Bos.	7	194	30	17	47	145	17	1	0	0	12	1	1920-21	1926-27
Stumpf, Robert	St.L., Pit.	1	10	1	1	2	20	....	....	....	....	....		1974-75	1974-75
Sturgeon, Peter	Col.	2	6	0	1	1	2	....	....	....	....	....		1979-80	1980-81
Suikkanen, Kai	Buf.	2	2	0	0	0	0	....	....	....	....	....		1981-82	1982-83
Sulliman, Doug	NYR, Hfd., N.J., Phi.	11	631	160	168	328	175	16	1	3	4	2		1979-80	1989-90
Sullivan, Barry	Det.	1	1	0	0	0	0	....	....	....	....	....		1947-48	1947-48
Sullivan, Bob	Hfd.	1	62	18	19	37	18	....	....	....	....	....		1982-83	1982-83
Sullivan, Brian	N.J.	1	2	0	1	1	0	....	....	....	....	....		1992-93	1992-93
Sullivan, Frank	Tor., Chi.	4	8	0	0	0	2	....	....	....	....	....		1949-50	1955-56
Sullivan, Peter	Wpg.	2	126	28	54	82	40	....	....	....	....	....		1979-80	1980-81
Sullivan, Red	Bos., Chi., NYR	11	557	107	239	346	441	18	1	2	3	6		1949-50	1960-61
Summanen, Raimo	Edm., Van.	5	151	36	40	76	35	10	2	5	7	0		1983-84	1987-88
• Summerhill, Bill	Mtl., Bro.	4	72	14	17	31	70	3	0	0	0	2		1938-39	1941-42
Sundblad, Niklas	Cgy.	1	2	0	0	0	0	....	....	....	....	....		1995-96	1995-96
Sundstrom, Patrik	Van., N.J.	10	679	219	369	588	349	37	9	17	26	25		1982-83	1991-92
Sundstrom, Peter	NYR, Wsh., N.J.	6	338	61	83	144	120	23	3	3	6	8		1983-84	1989-90
Suomi, Al	Chi.	1	5	0	0	0	0	....	....	....	....	....		1936-37	1936-37
Sutherland, Bill	Mtl., Phi., Tor., St.L., Det.	6	250	70	58	128	99	14	2	4	6	0		1962-63	1971-72
Sutherland, Ron	Bos.	1	2	0	0	0	0	....	....	....	....	....		1931-32	1931-32
Sutter, Brian	St.L.	12	779	303	333	636	1786	65	21	21	42	249		1976-77	1987-88
Sutter, Darryl	Chi.	8	406	161	118	279	288	51	24	19	43	26		1979-80	1986-87
Sutter, Duane	NYI, Chi.	11	731	139	203	342	1333	161	26	32	58	405	4	1979-80	1989-90
Sutter, Rich	Pit., Phi., Van., St. L., Chi., T.B., Tor.	13	874	149	166	315	1411	78	13	5	18	133		1982-83	1994-95
Suzor, Mark	Phi., Col.	2	64	4	16	20	60	....	....	....	....	....		1976-77	1977-78
Svensson, Leif	Wsh.	2	121	6	40	46	49	....	....	....	....	....		1978-79	1979-80
Svensson, Magnus	Fla.	2	46	4	14	18	31	....	....	....	....	....		1994-95	1995-96
Swain, Garry	Pit.	1	9	1	1	2	0	....	....	....	....	....		1968-69	1968-69
Swarbrick, George	Oak., Pit., Phi.	4	132	17	25	42	173	....	....	....	....	....		1967-68	1970-71
• Sweeney, Bill	NYR	1	4	1	0	1	0	....	....	....	....	....		1959-60	1959-60
Sykes, Bob	Tor.	1	2	0	0	0	0	....	....	....	....	....		1974-75	1974-75
Sykes, Phil	L.A., Wpg.	10	456	79	85	164	519	26	0	3	3	29		1982-83	1991-92
Szura, Joe	Oak.	2	90	10	15	25	30	7	2	3	5	2		1967-68	1968-69

T

Name	NHL Teams	NHL Seasons	GP	G	A	TP	PIM	GP	G	A	TP	PIM	NHL Cup Wins	First NHL Season	Last NHL Season
Taft, John	Det.	1	15	0	2	2	4	....	....	....	....	....		1978-79	1978-79
Taglianetti, Peter	Wpg., Min., Pit., T.B.	11	451	18	74	92	1106	53	2	8	10	103	2	1984-85	1994-95
Talafous, Dean	Atl., Min., NYR	8	497	104	154	258	163	21	4	7	11	11		1974-75	1981-82
Talakoski, Ron	NYR	2	9	0	1	1	33	....	....	....	....	....		1986-87	1987-88
Talbot, Jean-Guy	Mtl., Min., Det., St.L., Buf.	17	1056	43	242	285	1006	150	4	26	30	142	7	1954-55	1970-71
Tallon, Dale	Van., Chi., Pit.	10	642	98	238	336	568	33	2	10	12	45		1970-71	1979-80
Tambellini, Steve	NYI, Col., N.J., Cgy., Van.	10	553	160	150	310	105	2	0	1	1	0	1	1978-79	1987-88
Tanguay, Chris	Que.	1	2	0	0	0	0	....	....	....	....	....		1981-82	1981-82
Tannahill, Don	Van.	2	111	30	33	63	25	....	....	....	....	....		1972-73	1973-74
Tanti, Tony	Chi., Van., Pit., Buf.	11	697	287	273	560	661	30	3	12	15	27		1981-82	1991-92
Tardif, Marc	Mtl., Que.	8	517	194	207	401	443	62	13	15	28	75	2	1969-70	1982-83
Tatarinov, Mikhail	Wsh., Que., Bos.	4	161	21	48	69	184	....	....	....	....	....		1990-91	1993-94
• Taylor, Billy	Tor., Det., Bos., NYR	7	323	87	180	267	120	33	6	18	24	13	1	1939-40	1947-48
• Taylor, Billy	NYR	1	2	0	0	0	0	....	....	....	....	....		1964-65	1964-65
• Taylor, Bob	Bos.	1	8	0	0	0	6	....	....	....	....	....		1929-30	1929-30
Taylor, Dave	L.A.	17	1111	431	638	1069	1589	92	26	33	59	145		1977-78	1993-94
Taylor, Harry	Tor., Chi.	3	66	5	10	15	30	1	0	0	0	0	1	1946-47	1951-52
Taylor, Mark	Phi., Pit., Wsh.	5	209	42	68	110	73	6	0	0	0	0		1981-82	1985-86
• Taylor, Ralph	Chi., NYR	3	99	4	1	5	169	4	0	0	0	10		1927-28	1929-30
Taylor, Ted	NYR, Det., Min., Van.	6	166	23	35	58	181	....	....	....	....	....		1964-65	1971-72

Name	NHL Teams	NHL Seasons	Regular Schedule GP	G	A	TP	PIM	Playoffs GP	G	A	TP	PIM	NHL Cup Wins	First NHL Season	Last NHL Season
Teal, Jeff	Mtl.	1	6	0	1	1	0	....	....	....	....	....		1984-85	1984-85
Teal, Skip	Bos.	1	1	0	0	0	0	....	....	....	....	....		1954-55	1954-55
Teal, Victor	NYI	1	1	0	0	0	0	....	....	....	....	....		1973-74	1973-74
Tebbutt, Greg	Que., Pit.	2	26	0	3	3	35	....	....	....	....	....		1979-80	1983-84
Tepper, Stephen	Chi.	1	1	0	0	0	0	....	....	....	....	....		1992-93	1992-93
Terbenche, Paul	Chi., Buf.	5	189	5	26	31	28	12	0	0	0	0		1967-68	1973-74
Terrion, Greg	L.A., Tor.	8	561	93	150	243	339	35	2	9	11	41		1980-81	1987-88
Terry, Bill	Min.	1	5	0	0	0	0	....	....	....	....	....		1987-88	1987-88
Tessier, Orval	Mtl., Bos.	3	59	5	7	12	6	....	....	....	....	....		1954-55	1960-61
Thatchell, Spence	NYR	1	1	0	0	0	0	....	....	....	....	....		1942-43	1942-43
Theberge, Greg	Wsh.	5	153	15	63	78	73	4	0	1	1	0		1979-80	1983-84
Thelin, Mats	Bos.	3	163	8	19	27	107	5	0	0	0	6		1984-85	1986-87
Thelven, Michael	Bos.	5	207	20	80	100	217	34	4	10	14	34		1985-86	1989-90
Therrien, Gaston	Que.	3	22	0	8	8	12	9	0	1	1	4		1980-81	1982-83
Thibaudeau, Gilles	Mtl., NYI, Tor.	5	119	25	37	62	40	8	3	3	6	2		1986-87	1990-91
Thibeault, Laurence	Det., Mtl.	2	5	0	2	2	2	....	....	....	....	....		1944-45	1945-46
Thiffault, Leo	Min.	1	....	....	....	....	....	5	0	0	0	0		1967-68	1967-68
Thomas, Cy	Chi., Tor.	1	14	2	2	4	12	....	....	....	....	....		1947-48	1947-48
Thomas, Reg	Que.	1	39	9	7	16	6	....	....	....	....	....		1979-80	1979-80
Thomas, Scott	Buf.	2	39	3	3	6	23	....	....	....	....	....		1992-93	1993-94
Thomlinson, Dave	St.L., Bos., L.A.	5	42	1	3	4	50	9	3	1	4	4		1989-90	1994-95
Thompson, Cliff	Bos.	2	13	0	1	1	2	....	....	....	....	....		1941-42	1948-49
Thompson, Errol	Tor., Det., Pit.	10	599	208	185	393	184	34	7	5	12	11		1970-71	1980-81
• Thompson, Kenneth	Mtl.W	1	1	0	0	0	0	....	....	....	....	....		1917-18	1917-18
• Thompson, Paul	NYR, Chi.	13	582	153	179	332	336	48	11	11	22	54	3	1926-27	1938-39
• Thoms, Bill	Tor., Chi., Bos.	13	548	135	206	341	153	44	6	10	16	6		1932-33	1944-45
Thomson, Bill	Det., Chi.	2	10	2	2	4	0	2	0	0	0	0		1938-39	1943-44
Thomson, Floyd	St.L.	8	411	56	97	153	341	10	0	2	2	6		1971-72	1979-80
Thomson, Jack	NYA	3	15	1	1	2	0	2	0	0	0	0		1938-39	1940-41
Thomson, Jim	Wsh., Hfd., N.J., L.A., Ott., Ana.	7	115	4	3	7	416	1	0	0	0	0		1986-87	1993-94
• Thomson, Jimmy	Tor., Chi.	13	787	19	215	234	920	63	2	13	15	135	4	1945-46	1957-58
• Thomson, Rhys	Mtl., Tor.	2	25	0	2	2	38	....	....	....	....	....		1939-40	1942-43
Thornbury, Tom	Pit.	1	14	1	8	9	16	....	....	....	....	....		1983-84	1983-84
• Thorsteinson, Joe	NYA	1	4	0	0	0	0	....	....	....	....	....		1932-33	1932-33
Thurier, Fred	NYA, Bro., NYR	3	80	25	27	52	18	....	....	....	....	....		1940-41	1944-45
Thurlby, Tom	Oak.	1	20	1	1	2	4	....	....	....	....	....		1967-68	1967-68
Thyer, Mario	Min.	1	5	0	0	0	0	1	0	0	0	2		1989-90	1989-90
Tichy, Milan	Chi., NYI	3	23	0	5	5	40	....	....	....	....	....		1992-93	1995-96
Tidey, Alex	Buf., Edm.	3	9	0	0	0	8	2	0	0	0	0		1976-77	1979-80
Tilley, Tom	St.L.	4	174	4	38	42	89	14	1	3	4	19		1988-89	1993-94
Timgren, Ray	Tor., Chi.	6	251	14	44	58	70	30	3	9	12	6	2	1948-49	1954-55
Tippett, Dave	Hfd., Wsh., Pit., Phi.	11	721	93	169	262	317	62	6	16	22	34		1983-84	1993-94
Titanic, Morris	Buf.	2	19	0	0	0	0	....	....	....	....	....		1974-75	1975-76
Tkaczuk, Walt	NYR	14	945	227	451	678	556	93	19	32	51	119		1967-68	1980-81
Toal, Mike	Edm.	1	3	0	0	0	0	....	....	....	....	....		1979-80	1979-80
Tomalty, Glenn	Wpg.	1	1	0	0	0	0	....	....	....	....	....		1979-80	1979-80
Tomlak, Mike	Hfd.	4	141	15	22	37	103	10	0	1	1	4		1989-90	1993-94
Tomlinson, Kirk	Min.	1	1	0	0	0	0	....	....	....	....	....		1987-88	1987-88
Tonelli, John	NYI, Cgy., L.A., Chi., Que.	14	1028	325	511	836	911	172	40	75	115	200	4	1978-79	1991-92
Tookey, Tim	Wsh., Que., Pit., Phi., L.A.	7	106	22	36	58	71	10	1	3	4	2		1980-81	1988-89
Toomey, Sean	Min.	1	1	0	0	0	0	....	....	....	....	....		1986-87	1986-87
Toppazzini, Jerry	Bos., Chi., Det.	12	783	163	244	407	436	40	13	9	22	13		1952-53	1963-64
Toppazzini, Zellio	Bos., NYR, Chi.	5	123	21	22	43	49	2	0	0	0	0		1948-49	1956-57
Torgayev, Pavel	Cgy.	1	41	6	10	16	14	1	0	0	0	0		1995-96	1995-96
Torkki, Jari	Chi.	1	4	1	0	1	0	....	....	....	....	....		1988-89	1988-89
Touhey, Bill	Mtl.M., Ott., Bos.	7	280	65	40	105	107	2	1	0	1	0		1927-28	1933-34
• Toupin, Jacques	Chi.	1	8	1	2	3	0	4	0	0	0	0		1943-44	1943-44
• Townsend, Art	Chi.	1	5	0	0	0	0	....	....	....	....	....		1926-27	1926-27
Townshend, Graeme	Bos., NYI, Ott.	5	45	3	7	10	28	....	....	....	....	....		1989-90	1993-94
Trader, Larry	Det., St.L., Mtl.	4	91	5	13	18	74	3	0	0	0	0		1982-83	1987-88
Trainor, Wes	NYR	1	17	1	2	3	6	....	....	....	....	....		1948-49	1948-49
• Trapp, Bobby	Chi.	2	82	4	4	8	129	2	0	0	0	4		1926-27	1927-28
Trapp, Doug	Buf.	1	2	0	0	0	0	....	....	....	....	....		1986-87	1986-87
Traub, Percy	Chi., Det.	3	130	3	3	6	217	4	0	0	0	6		1926-27	1928-29
Tredway, Brock	L.A.	1	....	....	....	....	....	1	0	0	0	0		1981-82	1981-82
Tremblay, Brent	Wsh.	2	10	1	0	1	6	....	....	....	....	....		1978-79	1979-80
Tremblay, Gilles	Mtl.	9	509	168	162	330	161	48	9	14	23	4	2	1960-61	1968-69
• Tremblay, J.C.	Mtl.	13	794	57	306	363	204	108	14	51	65	58	5	1959-60	1971-72
Tremblay, Marcel	Mtl.	1	10	0	2	2	0	....	....	....	....	....		1938-39	1938-39
Tremblay, Mario	Mtl.	12	852	258	326	584	1043	101	20	29	49	187	5	1974-75	1985-86
• Tremblay, Nels	Mtl.	2	3	0	1	1	0	2	0	0	0	0		1944-45	1945-46
Trimper, Tim	Chi., Wpg., Min.	6	190	30	36	66	153	2	0	0	0	2		1979-80	1984-85
Trottier, Bryan	NYI, Pit.	18	1279	524	901	1425	912	221	71	113	184	277	6	1975-76	1993-94
• Trottier, Dave	Mtl.M., Det.	11	446	121	113	234	517	31	4	3	7	39	1	1928-29	1938-39
Trottier, Guy	NYR, Tor.	3	115	28	17	45	37	9	1	0	1	16		1968-69	1971-72
Trottier, Rocky	N.J.	2	38	6	4	10	2	....	....	....	....	....		1983-84	1984-85
• Trudel, Louis	Chi., Mtl.	8	306	49	69	118	122	24	1	3	4	4	2	1933-34	1940-41
Trudell, Rene	NYR	3	129	24	28	52	72	5	0	0	0	2		1945-46	1947-48
Tsygurov, Denis	Buf., L.A.	3	51	1	5	6	45	....	....	....	....	....		1993-94	1995-96
Tucker, John	Buf., Wsh., NYI, T.B.	12	656	177	259	436	285	31	10	18	28	24		1983-84	1995-96
• Tudin, Connie	Mtl.	1	4	0	1	1	4	....	....	....	....	....		1941-42	1941-42
Tudor, Rob	Van., St.L.	3	28	4	4	8	19	3	0	0	0	0		1978-79	1982-83
Tuer, Allan	L.A., Min., Hfd.	4	57	1	1	2	208	....	....	....	....	....		1985-86	1989-90
Turcotte, Alfie	Mtl., Wpg., Wsh.	7	112	17	29	46	49	5	0	0	0	0		1983-84	1990-91
Turlick, Gord	Bos.	1	2	0	0	0	2	....	....	....	....	....		1959-60	1959-60
Turnbull, Ian	Tor., L.A., Pit.	10	628	123	317	440	736	55	13	32	45	94		1973-74	1982-83
Turnbull, Perry	St.L., Mtl., Wpg.	9	608	188	163	351	1245	34	6	7	13	86		1979-80	1987-88
Turnbull, Randy	Cgy.	1	1	0	0	0	2	....	....	....	....	....		1981-82	1981-82
Turner, Bob	Mtl., Chi.	8	478	19	51	70	307	68	1	4	5	44	5	1955-56	1962-63
Turner, Brad	NYI	1	3	0	0	0	0	....	....	....	....	....		1991-92	1991-92
Turner, Dean	NYR, Col., L.A.	4	35	1	0	1	59	....	....	....	....	....		1978-79	1982-83
Tustin, Norman	NYR	1	18	2	4	6	0	....	....	....	....	....		1941-42	1941-42
Tuten, Audley	Chi.	2	39	4	8	12	48	....	....	....	....	....		1941-42	1942-43
Tutt, Brian	Wsh.	1	7	1	0	1	2	....	....	....	....	....		1989-90	1989-90
Tuttle, Steve	St.L.	3	144	28	28	56	12	17	1	6	7	2		1988-89	1990-91

U V

Ubriaco, Gene	Pit., Oak., Chi.	3	177	39	35	74	50	11	2	0	2	4		1967-68	1969-70
Ullman, Norm	Det., Tor.	20	1410	490	739	1229	712	106	30	53	83	67		1955-56	1974-75
Unger, Garry	Tor., Det., St.L., Atl., L.A., Edm.	16	1105	413	391	804	1075	52	12	18	30	105		1967-68	1982-83
Vadnais, Carol	Mtl., Oak., Cal., Bos., NYR, N.J.	17	1087	169	418	587	1813	106	10	40	50	185	2	1966-67	1982-83
Vail, Eric	Atl, Cgy., Det.	9	591	216	260	476	281	20	5	6	11	6		1973-74	1981-82
• Vail, Melville	NYR	2	50	4	1	5	18	10	0	0	0	2		1928-29	1929-30
Vaive, Rick	Van., Tor., Chi., Buf.	13	876	441	347	788	1445	54	27	16	43	111		1979-80	1991-92
Valentine, Chris	Wsh.	3	105	43	52	95	127	2	0	0	0	4		1981-82	1983-84
Valiquette, Jack	Tor., Col.	7	350	84	134	218	79	23	3	6	9	4		1974-75	1980-81
Vallis, Lindsay	Mtl.	1	1	0	0	0	0	....	....	....	....	....		1993-94	1993-94
Van Boxmeer, John	Mtl., Col., Buf., Que.	11	588	84	274	358	465	38	5	15	20	37		1973-74	1983-84
Van Dorp, Wayne	Edm., Pit., Chi., Que.	6	125	12	12	24	565	27	0	1	1	42		1986-87	1991-92
Van Impe, Ed	Chi., Phi., Pit.	11	700	27	126	153	1025	66	1	12	13	131	2	1966-67	1976-77
Varvio, Jarkko	Dal.	2	13	3	4	7	4	....	....	....	....	....		1993-94	1994-95
Vasko, Elmer	Chi., Min.	13	786	34	166	200	719	78	2	7	9	73	1	1956-57	1969-70
Vasko, Rick	Det.	3	31	3	7	10	29	....	....	....	....	....		1977-78	1980-81
Vautour, Yvon	NYI, Col., N.J., Que.	6	204	26	33	59	401	....	....	....	....	....		1979-80	1984-85
Vaydik, Greg	Chi.	1	5	0	0	0	0	....	....	....	....	....		1976-77	1976-77
Veitch, Darren	Wsh., Det., Tor.	10	511	48	209	257	296	33	4	11	15	33		1980-81	1990-91
Velischek, Randy	Min., N.J., Que.	10	509	21	76	97	401	44	2	5	7	32		1982-83	1991-92
Vellucci, Mike	Hfd.	1	2	0	0	0	11	....	....	....	....	....		1987-88	1987-88
Venasky, Vic	L.A.	7	430	61	101	162	66	21	1	5	6	12		1972-73	1978-79
Veneruzzo, Gary	St.L.	2	7	1	1	2	0	9	0	2	2	2		1967-68	1971-72
Vermette, Mark	Que.	4	67	5	13	18	33	....	....	....	....	....		1988-89	1991-92
Verret, Claude	Buf.	2	14	2	5	7	2	....	....	....	....	....		1983-84	1984-85
Verstraete, Leigh	Tor.	3	8	0	1	1	14	....	....	....	....	....		1982-83	1987-88

Steve Vickers

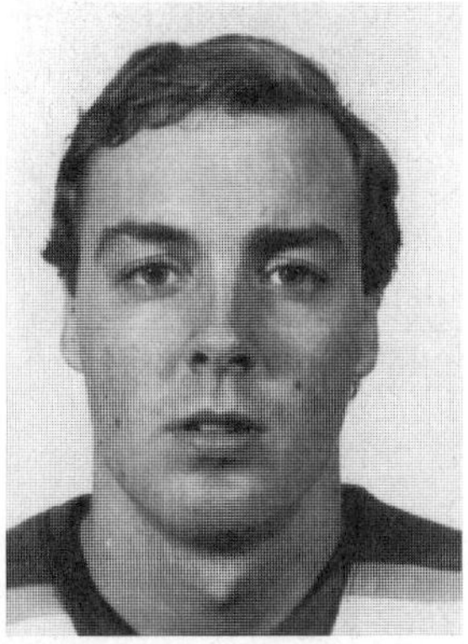
Hannu Virta

Mike Walton

Harry Watson

Bob Wilkie

Carey Wilson

Doug Wilson

Ron Wilson

Name	NHL Teams	NHL Seasons	Regular Schedule GP	G	A	TP	PIM	Playoffs GP	G	A	TP	PIM	NHL Cup Wins	First NHL Season	Last NHL Season
Ververgaert, Dennis	Van., Phi., Wsh.	8	583	176	216	392	247	8	1	2	3	6		1973-74	1980-81
Vesey, Jim	St.L., Bos.	3	15	1	2	3	7	....	....	....	....	....		1988-89	1991-92
Veysey, Sid	Van.	1	1	0	0	0	0	....	....	....	....	....		1977-78	1977-78
Vickers, Steve	NYR	10	698	246	340	586	330	68	24	25	49	58		1972-73	1981-82
Vigneault, Alain	St.L.	2	42	2	5	7	82	4	0	1	1	26		1981-82	1982-83
Vilgrain, Claude	Van., N.J., Phi.	5	89	21	32	53	78	11	1	1	2	17		1987-88	1993-94
Vincelette, Daniel	Chi., Que.	6	193	20	22	42	351	12	0	0	0	4		1986-87	1991-92
Vipond, Pete	Cal.	1	3	0	0	0	0	....	....	....	....	....		1972-73	1972-73
Virta, Hannu	Buf.	5	245	25	101	126	66	17	1	3	4	6		1981-82	1985-86
Vitolinsh, Harijs	Wpg.	1	8	0	0	0	4	....	....	....	....	....		1993-94	1993-94
Viveiros, Emanuel	Min.	3	29	1	11	12	6	....	....	....	....	....		1985-86	1987-88
Vokes, Ed	Chi.	1	5	0	0	0	0	....	....	....	....	....		1930-31	1930-31
Volcan, Mickey	Hfd., Cgy.	4	162	8	33	41	146	....	....	....	....	....		1980-81	1983-84
Volek, David	NYI	6	396	95	154	249	201	15	5	5	10	2		1988-89	1993-94
Volmar, Doug	Det., L.A.	4	62	13	8	21	26	2	1	0	1	0		1969-70	1972-73
• Voss, Carl	Tor., NYR, Det., Ott., St.L., Mtl.M., NYA, Chi.	8	261	34	70	104	50	24	5	3	8	0	1	1926-27	1937-38
Vyazmikin, Igor	Edm.	1	4	1	0	1	0	....	....	....	....	....		1990-91	1990-91

W

Name	NHL Teams	NHL Seasons	Regular Schedule GP	G	A	TP	PIM	Playoffs GP	G	A	TP	PIM	NHL Cup Wins	First NHL Season	Last NHL Season
Waddell, Don	L.A.	1	1	0	0	0	0	....	....	....	....	....		1980-81	1980-81
• Waite, Frank	NYR	1	17	1	3	4	4	....	....	....	....	....		1930-31	1930-31
Walker, Gord	NYR, L.A.	4	31	3	4	7	23	....	....	....	....	....		1986-87	1989-90
Walker, Howard	Wsh., Cgy.	3	83	2	13	15	133	....	....	....	....	....		1980-81	1982-83
• Walker, Jack	Det.	2	80	5	8	13	18	....	....	....	....	....		1926-27	1927-28
Walker, Kurt	Tor.	3	71	4	5	9	142	16	0	0	0	34		1975-76	1977-78
Walker, Russ	L.A.	2	17	1	0	1	41	....	....	....	....	....		1976-77	1977-78
Wall, Bob	Det., L.A., St.L.	8	322	30	55	85	155	22	0	3	3	2		1964-65	1971-72
Wallin, Peter	NYR	2	52	3	14	17	14	14	2	6	8	6		1980-81	1981-82
Walsh, Jim	Buf.	1	4	0	1	1	4	....	....	....	....	....		1981-82	1981-82
Walsh, Mike	NYI	2	14	2	0	2	4	....	....	....	....	....		1987-88	1988-89
Walter, Ryan	Wsh., Mtl., Van.	15	1003	264	382	646	946	113	16	35	51	62	1	1978-79	1992-93
Walton, Bobby	Mtl.	1	4	0	0	0	0	....	....	....	....	....		1943-44	1943-44
Walton, Mike	Tor., Bos., Van., Chi., St.L.	12	588	201	247	448	357	47	14	10	24	45	2	1965-66	1978-79
Wappel, Gord	Atl., Cgy.	3	20	1	1	2	10	2	0	0	0	4		1979-80	1981-82
Ward, Don	Chi., Bos.	2	34	0	1	1	16	....	....	....	....	....		1957-58	1959-60
• Ward, Jimmy	Mtl.M., Mtl.	12	527	147	127	274	455	36	4	4	8	26	1	1927-28	1938-39
Ward, Joe	Col.	1	4	0	0	0	2	....	....	....	....	....		1980-81	1980-81
Ward, Ron	Tor., Van.,	2	89	2	5	7	6	....	....	....	....	....		1969-70	1971-72
Ware, Michael	Edm.	2	5	0	1	1	15	....	....	....	....	....		1988-89	1989-90
Wares, Eddie	NYR, Det., Chi.	9	321	60	102	162	161	45	5	7	12	34	1	1936-37	1946-47
Warner, Bob	Tor.	2	10	1	1	2	4	4	0	0	0	0		1975-76	1976-77
Warner, Jim	Hfd.	1	32	0	3	3	10	....	....	....	....	....		1979-80	1979-80
Warwick, Bill	NYR	2	14	3	3	6	16	....	....	....	....	....		1942-43	1943-44
Warwick, Grant	NYR, Bos., Mtl.	9	395	147	142	289	220	16	2	4	6	6		1941-42	1949-50
• Wasnie, Nick	Chi., Mtl., NYA, Ott., St.L.	7	248	57	34	91	176	14	6	3	9	20	2	1927-28	1934-35
Watson, Bill	Chi.	4	115	23	36	59	12	6	0	2	2	0		1985-86	1988-89
Watson, Bryan	Mtl., Oak., Pit., Det., St.L., Wsh.	16	878	17	135	152	2212	32	2	0	2	70		1963-64	1978-79
Watson, Dave	Col.	2	18	0	1	1	10	....	....	....	....	....		1979-80	1980-81
Watson, Harry	Bro., Det., Tor., Chi.	14	809	236	207	443	150	62	16	9	25	27	5	1941-42	1956-57
Watson, Jim	Det., Buf.	8	221	4	19	23	345	....	....	....	....	....		1963-64	1971-72
Watson, Jimmy	Phi.	10	613	38	148	186	492	101	5	34	39	89	2	1972-73	1981-82
Watson, Joe	Bos., Phi., Col.	14	835	38	178	216	447	84	3	12	15	82	2	1964-65	1978-79
• Watson, Phil	NYR, Mtl.	13	590	144	265	409	532	45	10	25	35	67	2	1935-36	1947-48
Watters, Tim	Wpg., L.A.	14	741	26	151	177	1289	82	1	5	6	115		1981-82	1994-95
Watts, Brian	Det.	1	4	0	0	0	0	....	....	....	....	....		1975-76	1975-76
Webster, Aubrey	Phi., Mtl.M.	2	5	0	0	0	0	....	....	....	....	....		1930-31	1934-35
• Webster, Don	Tor.	1	27	7	6	13	28	5	0	0	0	12		1943-44	1943-44
Webster, John	NYR	1	14	0	0	0	4	....	....	....	....	....		1949-50	1949-50
Webster, Tom	Bos., Det., Cal.	5	102	33	42	75	61	1	0	0	0	0		1968-69	1979-80
• Weiland, Cooney	Bos., Ott., Det.	11	509	173	160	333	147	45	12	10	22	12	2	1928-29	1938-39
Weir, Stan	Cal., Tor., Edm., Col., Det.	10	642	139	207	346	183	37	6	5	11	4		1972-73	1982-83
Weir, Wally	Que., Hfd., Pit.	6	320	21	45	66	625	23	0	1	1	96		1979-80	1984-85
• Wellington, Duke	Que.	1	1	0	0	0	0	....	....	....	....	....		1919-20	1919-20
Wensink, John	Bos., Que., Col., N.J., St.L.	8	403	70	68	138	840	43	2	6	8	86		1973-74	1982-83
• Wentworth, Cy	Chi., Mtl.M., Mtl.	13	575	39	68	107	355	35	5	6	11	20	1	1927-28	1939-40
Wesley, Blake	Phi., Hfd., Que., Tor.	7	298	18	46	64	486	19	2	2	4	30		1979-80	1985-86
Westfall, Ed	Bos., NYI	18	1220	231	394	625	544	95	22	37	59	41	2	1961-62	1978-79
Wharram, Kenny	Chi.	14	766	252	281	533	222	80	16	27	43	38	1	1951-52	1968-69
Wharton, Len	NYR	1	1	0	0	0	0	....	....	....	....	....		1944-45	1944-45
Wheeldon, Simon	NYR, Wpg.	3	15	0	2	2	10	....	....	....	....	....		1987-88	1990-91
• Wheldon, Donald	St.L.	1	2	0	0	0	0	....	....	....	....	....		1974-75	1974-75
Whelton, Bill	Wpg.	1	2	0	0	0	0	....	....	....	....	....		1980-81	1980-81
Whistle, Rob	NYR, St.L.	2	51	7	5	12	16	4	0	0	0	2		1985-86	1987-88
White, Bill	L.A., Chi.	9	604	50	215	265	495	91	7	32	39	76		1967-68	1975-76
White, Moe	Mtl.	1	4	0	1	1	2	....	....	....	....	....		1945-46	1945-46
• White, Sherman	NYR	2	4	0	2	2	0	....	....	....	....	....		1946-47	1949-50
• White, Tex	Pit., NYA, Phi.	6	203	33	12	45	141	4	0	0	0	4		1925-26	1930-31
White, Tony	Wsh., Min.	5	164	37	28	65	104	....	....	....	....	....		1974-75	1979-80
Whitelaw, Bob	Det.	2	32	0	2	2	2	8	0	0	0	0		1940-41	1941-42
Whitlock, Bob	Min.	1	1	0	0	0	0	....	....	....	....	....		1969-70	1969-70
Whyte, Sean	L.A.	2	21	0	2	2	12	....	....	....	....	....		1991-92	1992-93
Wickenheiser, Doug	Mtl., St.L., Van., NYR, Wsh.	10	556	111	165	276	286	41	4	7	11	18		1980-81	1989-90
• Widing, Juha	NYR, L.A., Clev.	8	575	144	226	370	208	8	1	2	3	2		1969-70	1976-77
• Wiebe, Art	Chi.	11	414	14	27	41	201	31	1	3	4	10	1	1932-33	1943-44
Wiemer, Jim	Buf., NYR, Edm., L.A., Bos.	11	325	29	72	101	378	62	5	8	13	63	1	1982-83	1993-94
• Wilcox, Archie	Mtl.M., Bos., St.L.	6	208	8	14	22	158	12	1	0	1	8		1929-30	1934-35
Wilcox, Barry	Van.	2	33	3	2	5	15	....	....	....	....	....		1972-73	1974-75
Wilder, Arch	Det.	1	18	0	2	2	2	....	....	....	....	....		1940-41	1940-41
Wiley, Jim	Pit., Van.	5	63	4	10	14	8	....	....	....	....	....		1972-73	1976-77
Wilkie, Bob	Det., Phi.	2	18	2	5	7	10	....	....	....	....	....		1990-91	1993-94
Wilkins, Barry	Bos., Van., Pit.	9	418	27	125	152	663	6	0	1	1	4		1966-67	1975-76
Wilkinson, John	Bos.	1	9	0	0	0	6	....	....	....	....	....		1943-44	1943-44
Wilks, Brian	L.A.	4	48	4	8	12	27	....	....	....	....	....		1984-85	1988-89
Willard, Rod	Tor.	1	1	0	0	0	0	....	....	....	....	....		1982-83	1982-83
Williams, Burr	Det., St.L., Bos.	3	19	0	1	1	28	2	0	0	0	8		1933-34	1936-37
Williams, Darryl	L.A.	1	2	0	0	0	10	....	....	....	....	....		1992-93	1992-93
Williams, Dave	Tor., Van., Det., L.A., Hfd.	14	962	241	272	513	3966	83	12	23	35	455		1974-75	1987-88
Williams, David	S.J., Ana.	4	173	11	53	64	157	....	....	....	....	....		1991-92	1994-95
Williams, Fred	Det.	1	44	2	5	7	10	....	....	....	....	....		1976-77	1976-77
Williams, Gord	Phi.	2	2	0	0	0	2	....	....	....	....	....		1981-82	1982-83
Williams, Sean	Chi.	1	2	0	0	0	4	....	....	....	....	....		1991-92	1991-92
• Williams, Tom	Bos., Min., Cal., Wsh.	13	663	161	269	430	177	10	2	5	7	2		1961-62	1975-76
Williams, Tommy	NYR, L.A.	8	397	115	138	253	73	29	8	7	15	4		1971-72	1978-79
Williams, Warren	St.L., Cal.	3	108	14	35	49	131	....	....	....	....	....		1973-74	1975-76
Willson, Don	Mtl.	2	22	2	7	9	0	3	0	0	0	0		1937-38	1938-39
Wilson, Behn	Phi., Chi.	9	601	98	260	358	1480	67	12	29	41	190		1978-79	1987-88
• Wilson, Bert	NYR, L.A., St.L., Cgy.	8	478	37	44	81	646	21	0	2	2	42		1973-74	1980-81
Wilson, Bob	Chi.	1	1	0	0	0	0	....	....	....	....	....		1953-54	1953-54
Wilson, Carey	Cgy., Hfd., NYR	10	552	169	258	427	314	52	11	13	24	14		1983-84	1992-93
Wilson, Cully	Tor., Mtl., Ham., Chi.	5	125	60	23	83	232	2	1	0	1	6		1919-20	1926-27
Wilson, Doug	Chi., S.J.	16	1024	237	590	827	830	95	19	61	80	88		1977-78	1992-93
Wilson, Gord	Bos.	1	....	....	....	....	....	2	0	0	0	0		1954-55	1954-55
Wilson, Hub	NYA	1	2	0	0	0	0	....	....	....	....	....		1931-32	1931-32
Wilson, Jerry	Mtl.	1	3	0	0	0	2	....	....	....	....	....		1956-57	1956-57
Wilson, Johnny	Det., Chi., Tor., NYR	13	688	161	171	332	190	66	14	13	27	11	4	1949-50	1961-62
• Wilson, Larry	Det., Chi.	6	152	21	48	69	75	4	0	0	0	0	1	1949-50	1955-56
Wilson, Mitch	N.J., Pit.	2	26	2	3	5	104	....	....	....	....	....		1984-85	1986-87
Wilson, Murray	Mtl., L.A.	7	386	94	95	189	162	53	5	14	19	32	4	1972-73	1978-79
Wilson, Rick	Mtl., St.L., Det.	4	239	6	26	32	165	3	0	0	0	0		1973-74	1976-77
Wilson, Rik	St.L., Cgy., Chi.	6	251	25	65	90	220	22	0	4	4	23		1981-82	1987-88
Wilson, Roger	Chi.	1	7	0	2	2	6	....	....	....	....	....		1974-75	1974-75

Name	NHL Teams	NHL Seasons	Regular Schedule GP	G	A	TP	PIM	Playoffs GP	G	A	TP	PIM	NHL Cup Wins	First NHL Season	Last NHL Season
Wilson, Ron	Wpg., St.L., Mtl.	14	832	110	216	326	415	63	10	12	22	64		1979-80	1993-94
Wilson, Ron	Tor., Min.	7	177	26	67	93	68	20	4	13	17	8		1977-78	1987-88
Wilson, Wally	Bos.	1	53	11	8	19	18	1	0	0	0	0		1947-48	1947-48
Wing, Murray	Det.	1	1	0	1	1	0	....	....	....	....	....		1973-74	1973-74
Winnes, Chris	Bos., Phi.	4	33	1	6	7	6	1	0	0	0	0		1990-91	1993-94
• Wiseman, Eddie	Det., NYA, Bos.	10	456	115	165	280	136	43	10	10	20	16	1	1932-33	1941-42
Wiste, Jim	Chi., Van.	3	52	1	10	11	8	....	....	....	....	....		1968-69	1970-71
Witherspoon, Jim	L.A.	1	2	0	0	0	2	....	....	....	....	....		1975-76	1975-76
Witiuk, Steve	Chi.	1	33	3	8	11	14	....	....	....	....	....		1951-52	1951-52
Woit, Benny	Det., Chi.	7	334	7	26	33	170	41	2	6	8	18	3	1950-51	1956-57
Wojciechowski, Steven	Det.	2	54	19	20	39	17	6	0	1	1	0		1944-45	1946-47
Wolf, Bennett	Pit.	3	30	0	1	1	133	....	....	....	....	....		1980-81	1982-83
Wong, Mike	Det.	1	22	1	1	2	12	....	....	....	....	....		1975-76	1975-76
Wood, Robert	NYR	1	1	0	0	0	0	....	....	....	....	....		1950-51	1950-51
Woodley, Dan	Van.	1	5	2	0	2	17	....	....	....	....	....		1987-88	1987-88
Woods, Paul	Det.	7	501	72	124	196	276	7	0	5	5	4		1977-78	1983-84
Wortman, Kevin	Cgy.	1	5	0	0	0	2	....	....	....	....	....		1993-94	1993-94
• Woytowich, Bob	Bos., Min., Pit., L.A.	8	503	32	126	158	352	24	1	3	4	20		1964-65	1971-72
Wright, John	Van., St.L., K.C.	3	127	16	36	52	67	....	....	....	....	....		1972-73	1974-75
Wright, Keith	Phi.	1	1	0	0	0	0	....	....	....	....	....		1967-68	1967-68
Wright, Larry	Phi., Cal., Det.	5	106	4	8	12	19	....	....	....	....	....		1971-72	1977-78
Wycherley, Ralph	NYA, Bro.	2	28	4	7	11	6	....	....	....	....	....		1940-41	1941-42
Wylie, Duane	Chi.	2	14	3	3	6	2	....	....	....	....	....		1974-75	1976-77
• Wylie, William	NYR	1	1	0	0	0	0	....	....	....	....	....		1950-51	1950-51
Wyrozub, Randy	Buf.	4	100	8	10	18	10	....	....	....	....	....		1970-71	1973-74

Y Z

Name	NHL Teams	NHL Seasons	Regular Schedule GP	G	A	TP	PIM	Playoffs GP	G	A	TP	PIM	NHL Cup Wins	First NHL Season	Last NHL Season
• Yackel, Ken	Bos.	1	6	0	0	0	2	2	0	0	0	2		1958-59	1958-59
Yaremchuk, Gary	Tor.	4	34	1	4	5	28	....	....	....	....	....		1981-82	1984-85
Yaremchuk, Ken	Chi., Tor.	6	235	36	56	92	106	31	6	8	14	49		1983-84	1988-89
Yates, Ross	Hfd.	1	7	1	1	2	4	....	....	....	....	....		1983-84	1983-84
Young, Brian	Chi.	1	8	0	2	2	6	....	....	....	....	....		1980-81	1980-81
Young, C.J.	Cgy., Bos.	1	43	7	7	14	32	....	....	....	....	....		1992-93	1992-93
• Young, Doug	Mtl., Det.	10	388	35	45	80	303	28	1	5	6	16	2	1931-32	1940-41
Young, Howie	Det., Chi., Van.	8	336	12	62	74	851	19	2	4	6	46		1960-61	1970-71
Young, Tim	Min., Wpg., Phi.	10	628	195	341	536	438	36	7	24	31	27		1975-76	1984-85
Young, Warren	Min., Pit., Det.	7	236	72	77	149	472	....	....	....	....	....		1981-82	1987-88
Younghans, Tom	Min., NYR	6	429	44	41	85	373	24	2	1	3	21		1976-77	1981-82
Zabroski, Marty	Chi.	1	1	0	0	0	2	....	....	....	....	....		1944-45	1944-45
Zaharko, Miles	Atl., Chi.	4	129	5	32	37	84	3	0	0	0	0		1977-78	1981-82
Zaine, Rod	Pit., Buf.	2	61	10	6	16	25	....	....	....	....	....		1970-71	1971-72
Zanussi, Joe	NYR, Bos., St.L.	3	87	1	13	14	46	4	0	1	1	2		1974-75	1976-77
Zanussi, Ron	Min., Tor.	5	299	52	83	135	373	17	0	4	4	17		1977-78	1981-82
Zavisha, Brad	Edm.	1	2	0	0	0	0	....	....	....	....	....		1993-94	1993-94
Zeidel, Larry	Det., Chi., Phi.	5	158	3	16	19	198	12	0	1	1	12	1	1951-52	1968-69
Zemlak, Richard	Que., Min., Pit., Cgy.	5	132	2	12	14	587	1	0	0	0	10		1986-87	1991-92
Zeniuk, Ed	Det.	1	2	0	0	0	0	....	....	....	....	....		1954-55	1954-55
Zetterstrom, Lars	Van.	1	14	0	1	1	2	....	....	....	....	....		1978-79	1978-79
Zuke, Mike	St.L., Hfd.	8	455	86	196	282	220	26	6	6	12	12		1978-79	1985-86
Zunich, Ruby	Det.	1	2	0	0	0	2	....	....	....	....	....		1943-44	1943-44

Howie Young

Miles Zaharko

NOTE: Some players added to the Retired Player Index remain active in other leagues in North America and Europe. Players with NHL experience playing outside the NHL are placed in the Retired Player Index when they have completed one or more seasons of play after having been removed from an NHL club's reserve list. A player's age and his performance outside the NHL are considered in determining when he is moved from the active Player Register to the Retired Player Index.

Retired Players and Goaltenders Research Project

Throughout the Retired Players and Retired Goaltenders sections of this book, you will notice many players with a bullet (•) by their names. These players, according to our records, are deceased. The editors recognize that our information on the death dates of NHLers is incomplete. If you have documented information on the passing of any player not marked with a bullet (•) in this edition, we would like to hear from you. Please send this information to:

Retired Player Research Project
c/o NHL Publishing
194 Dovercourt Road
Toronto, Ontario
M6J 3C8 Canada
Fax: 416/531-3939

Many thanks to the following contributors in 1996-97:

Kevin Bixby, Corey Bryant, Paul R. Carroll, Jr., Bob Duff, Peter Fillman, Ernie Fitzsimmons, Scott Miller, Gary J. Pearce, Bill Schmidt, Ed Sweeney, Reginald Varin, Tim Zander.

Notes

1997-98 Goaltender Register

Note: The 1997-98 Goaltender Register lists every goaltender who appeared in an NHL game in the 1996-97 season, every goaltender drafted in the first six rounds of the 1997 Entry Draft, goaltenders on NHL Reserve Lists and other goaltenders.

Trades and roster changes are current as of August 22, 1997

To calculate a goaltender's goals-against-per-game average **(AVG)**, divide goals against **(GA)** by minutes played **(Mins)** and multiply this result by **60**.

Abbreviations: A list of league names can be found at the beginning of the Player Register. **Avg.** – goals against per game average; **GA** – goals against; **GP** – games played; **L** – losses; **Lea** – league; **SO** – shutouts; **T** – ties; **W** – wins; ♦ – member of Stanley Cup-winning team.

Player Register begins on page 257.

AEBISCHER, DAVID (IGH-bih-shuhr) COL.

Goaltender. Catches left. 6'1", 185 lbs. Born, Fribourg, Switz., February 7, 1978.
(Colorado's 7th choice, 161st overall, in 1997 Entry Draft).

			Regular Season								Playoffs						
Season	Club	Lea	GP	W	L	T	Mins	GA	SO	Avg	GP	W	L	Mins	GA	SO	Avg
1996-97	Fribourg	Switz.	10	....	....	....	577	34	....	3.53	3	....	....	184	13	....	4.24

ARSENAULT, DAVID (AR-seh-noh) DET.

Goaltender. Catches left. 6'2", 165 lbs. Born, Frankfurt, Germany, March 21, 1977.
(Detroit's 6th choice, 126th overall, in 1995 Entry Draft).

			Regular Season								Playoffs						
Season	Club	Lea	GP	W	L	T	Mins	GA	SO	Avg	GP	W	L	Mins	GA	SO	Avg
1994-95	St-Hyacinthe	QMJHL	19	3	10	0	862	75	0	5.22	....	....	....	....	....	....	....
	Drummondville	QMJHL	12	2	5	0	478	40	0	5.02	2	0	2	122	8	0	3.93
1995-96	Drummondville	QMJHL	21	8	10	1	1177	89	0	4.54	....	....	....	....	....	....	....
	Chicoutimi	QMJHL	6	1	1	1	207	14	0	4.06	5	0	1	....	....	....	5.61
1996-97	Chicoutimi	QMJHL	4	2	2	0	220	12	0	3.27	....	....	....	....	....	....	....
	Oshawa	OHL	41	24	9	5	2316	106	2	2.75	17	*11	6	1027	46	*1	*2.69

ASKEY, TOM ANA.

Goaltender. Catches left. 6'2", 185 lbs. Born, Kenmore, NY, October 4, 1974.
(Anaheim's 8th choice, 186th overall, in 1993 Entry Draft).

			Regular Season								Playoffs						
Season	Club	Lea	GP	W	L	T	Mins	GA	SO	Avg	GP	W	L	Mins	GA	SO	Avg
1992-93	Ohio State	NCAA	25	2	19	0	1235	125	....	6.07	....	....	....	....	....	....	....
1993-94	Ohio State	CCHA	27	3	19	4	1488	103	....	4.15	....	....	....	....	....	....	....
1994-95	Ohio State	CCHA	26	4	19	2	1387	121	0	5.23	....	....	....	....	....	....	....
1995-96a	Ohio State	CCHA	26	8	11	4	1340	68	....	3.05	....	....	....	....	....	....	....
1996-97	Baltimore	AHL	40	17	18	2	2238	140	1	3.75	3	0	3	137	11	0	4.79

a CCHA Second All-Star Team (1996)

AUBIN, JEAN-SEBASTIEN (OH-behn) PIT.

Goaltender. Catches right. 5'11", 179 lbs. Born, Montreal, Que., July 19, 1977.
(Pittsburgh's 2nd choice, 76th overall, in 1995 Entry Draft).

			Regular Season								Playoffs						
Season	Club	Lea	GP	W	L	T	Mins	GA	SO	Avg	GP	W	L	Mins	GA	SO	Avg
1994-95	Sherbrooke	QMJHL	27	13	10	1	1287	73	1	3.40	3	1	2	185	11	0	3.57
1995-96	Sherbrooke	QMJHL	40	18	14	2	2140	127	0	3.57	4	1	3	238	23	....	5.55
1996-97	Laval	QMJHL	11	2	6	1	532	41	0	4.62	....	....	....	....	....	....	....
	Moncton	QMJHL	22	9	12	0	1252	67	1	3.21	....	....	....	....	....	....	....
	Sherbrooke	QMJHL	4	3	1	0	249	8	0	1.93	1	0	1	60	4	0	4.00

BACH, RYAN (BAWK) DET.

Goaltender. Catches left. 6'1", 180 lbs. Born, Sherwood Park, Alta., October 21, 1973.
(Detroit's 11th choice, 262nd overall, in 1992 Entry Draft).

			Regular Season								Playoffs						
Season	Club	Lea	GP	W	L	T	Mins	GA	SO	Avg	GP	W	L	Mins	GA	SO	Avg
1992-93	Colorado	WCHA	4	1	3	0	239	11	0	2.76	....	....	....	....	....	....	....
1993-94	Colorado	WCHA	30	17	7	5	1733	105	0	3.64	....	....	....	....	....	....	....
1994-95ab	Colorado	WCHA	27	18	5	1	1522	83	0	3.27	....	....	....	....	....	....	....
1995-96ac	Colorado	WCHA	23	*17	4	2	1390	62	2	2.68	....	....	....	....	....	....	....
1996-97	Utica	ColHL	2	0	1	1	119	8	0	4.03	....	....	....	....	....	....	....
	Adirondack	AHL	13	2	3	1	450	29	0	3.86	1	0	0	45	3	0	3.92
	Toledo	ECHL	20	5	11	3	1168	74	0	3.80	....	....	....	....	....	....	....

a WCHA First All-Star Team (1995, 1996)
b NCAA West Second All-American Team (1995)
c NCAA West First All-American (1996)

BAILEY, SCOTT

Goaltender. Catches left. 6', 195 lbs. Born, Calgary, Alta., May 2, 1972.
(Boston's 3rd choice, 112th overall, in 1992 Entry Draft).

			Regular Season								Playoffs						
Season	Club	Lea	GP	W	L	T	Mins	GA	SO	Avg	GP	W	L	Mins	GA	SO	Avg
1990-91a	Spokane	WHL	46	33	11	0	2537	157	*4	3.71	....	....	....	....	....	....	....
1991-92a	Spokane	WHL	65	34	23	5	3798	206	1	3.30	10	5	5	605	43	0	4.26
1992-93	Johnstown	ECHL	36	13	15	3	1750	112	1	3.84	....	....	....	....	....	....	....
1993-94	Providence	AHL	7	2	2	2	377	24	0	3.82	....	....	....	....	....	....	....
	Charlotte	ECHL	36	22	11	3	2180	130	1	3.58	3	1	2	187	12	0	3.83
1994-95	Providence	AHL	52	25	16	9	2936	147	2	3.00	9	4	4	504	31	*2	3.69
1995-96	**Boston**	**NHL**	**11**	**5**	**1**	**2**	**571**	**31**	**0**	**3.26**	....	....	....	....	....	....	....
1996-97	**Boston**	**NHL**	**8**	**1**	**5**	**0**	**394**	**24**	**0**	**3.65**	....	....	....	....	....	....	....
	Providence	AHL	37	15	19	3	2210	120	1	3.26	2	1	1	119	6	0	3.03
	Providence	AHL	31	11	17	2	1735	112	0	3.87	7	3	4	452	23	0	3.05
	NHL Totals		**19**	**6**	**6**	**2**	**965**	**55**	**0**	**3.42**	....	....	....	....	....	....	....

a WHL West Second All-Star Team (1991, 1992)

BAKER, AARON CAR.

Goaltender. Catches right. 6'1", 174 lbs. Born, Eckville, Alta., February 17, 1978.
(Hartford's 6th choice, 143rd overall, in 1996 Entry Draft).

			Regular Season								Playoffs						
Season	Club	Lea	GP	W	L	T	Mins	GA	SO	Avg	GP	W	L	Mins	GA	SO	Avg
1995-96	Tri-City	WHL	20	11	6	0	1082	61	2	3.38	1	0	0	20	1	....	3.00
1996-97	Tri-City	WHL	34	11	19	1	1898	131	1	4.14	....	....	....	....	....	....	....

BALES, MICHAEL BUF.

Goaltender. Catches left. 6'1", 180 lbs. Born, Prince Albert, Sask., August 6, 1971.
(Boston's 4th choice, 105th overall, in 1990 Entry Draft).

			Regular Season								Playoffs						
Season	Club	Lea	GP	W	L	T	Mins	GA	SO	Avg	GP	W	L	Mins	GA	SO	Avg
1989-90	Ohio State	CCHA	21	6	13	2	1117	95	0	5.11	....	....	....	....	....	....	....
1990-91	Ohio State	CCHA	*39	11	24	3	*2180	184	0	5.06	....	....	....	....	....	....	....
1991-92	Ohio State	CCHA	36	11	20	5	2060	180	0	5.24	....	....	....	....	....	....	....
1992-93	**Boston**	**NHL**	**1**	**0**	**0**	**0**	**25**	**1**	**0**	**2.40**	....	....	....	....	....	....	....
	Providence	AHL	44	22	17	0	2363	166	1	4.21	2	0	2	118	8	0	4.07
1993-94	Providence	AHL	33	9	15	4	1757	130	0	4.44	....	....	....	....	....	....	....
1994-95	P.E.I.	AHL	45	25	16	3	2649	160	2	3.62	9	6	3	530	24	*2	2.72
	Ottawa	**NHL**	**1**	**0**	**0**	**0**	**3**	**0**	**0**	**0.00**	....	....	....	....	....	....	....
1995-96	**Ottawa**	**NHL**	**20**	**2**	**14**	**1**	**1040**	**72**	**0**	**4.15**	....	....	....	....	....	....	....
	P.E.I.	AHL	2	0	2	0	118	11	0	5.58	....	....	....	....	....	....	....
1996-97	**Ottawa**	**NHL**	**1**	**0**	**1**	**0**	**52**	**4**	**0**	**4.62**	....	....	....	....	....	....	....
	Baltimore	AHL	46	13	21	8	2543	130	3	3.07	....	....	....	....	....	....	....
	NHL Totals		**23**	**2**	**15**	**1**	**1120**	**77**	**0**	**4.12**	....	....	....	....	....	....	....

Signed as a free agent by **Ottawa**, July 4, 1994. Signed as a free agent by **Buffalo**, August 14, 1997.

BARRASSO, TOM (buh-RAH-soh) PIT.

Goaltender. Catches right. 6'3", 211 lbs. Born, Boston, MA, March 31, 1965.
(Buffalo's 1st choice, 5th overall, in 1983 Entry Draft).

			Regular Season								Playoffs						
Season	Club	Lea	GP	W	L	T	Mins	GA	SO	Avg	GP	W	L	Mins	GA	SO	Avg
1982-83	Acton-Boxboro	HS	23	....	....	....	1035	17	10	0.73	....	....	....	....	....	....	....
1983-84abcd	**Buffalo**	**NHL**	**42**	**26**	**12**	**3**	**2475**	**117**	**2**	**2.84**	**3**	**0**	**2**	**139**	**8**	**0**	**3.45**
1984-85ef	**Buffalo**	**NHL**	**54**	**25**	**18**	**10**	**3248**	**144**	***5**	***2.66**	**5**	**2**	**3**	**300**	**22**	**0**	**4.40**
	Rochester	AHL	5	3	1	1	267	6	1	1.35	....	....	....	....	....	....	....
1985-86	**Buffalo**	**NHL**	**60**	**29**	**24**	**5**	**3561**	**214**	**2**	**3.61**	....	....	....	....	....	....	....
1986-87	**Buffalo**	**NHL**	**46**	**17**	**23**	**2**	**2501**	**152**	**2**	**3.65**	....	....	....	....	....	....	....
1987-88	**Buffalo**	**NHL**	**54**	**25**	**18**	**8**	**3133**	**173**	**2**	**3.31**	**4**	**1**	**3**	**224**	**16**	**0**	**4.29**
1988-89	**Buffalo**	**NHL**	**10**	**2**	**7**	**0**	**545**	**45**	**0**	**4.95**	....	....	....	....	....	....	....
	Pittsburgh	**NHL**	**44**	**18**	**15**	**7**	**2406**	**162**	**0**	**4.04**	**11**	**7**	**4**	**631**	**40**	**0**	**3.80**
1989-90	**Pittsburgh**	**NHL**	**24**	**7**	**12**	**3**	**1294**	**101**	**0**	**4.68**	....	....	....	....	....	....	....
1990-91	**Pittsburgh**	**NHL**	**48**	**27**	**16**	**3**	**2754**	**165**	**1**	**3.59**	**20**	**12**	**7**	**1175**	**51**	***1**	***2.60** ♦
1991-92	**Pittsburgh**	**NHL**	**57**	**25**	**22**	**9**	**3329**	**196**	**1**	**3.53**	***21**	***16**	**5**	***1233**	**58**	**1**	**2.82** ♦
1992-93e	**Pittsburgh**	**NHL**	**63**	***43**	**14**	**5**	**3702**	**186**	**4**	**3.01**	**12**	**7**	**5**	**722**	**35**	***2**	**2.91**
1993-94	**Pittsburgh**	**NHL**	**44**	**22**	**15**	**5**	**2482**	**139**	**2**	**3.36**	**6**	**2**	**4**	**356**	**17**	**0**	**2.87**
1994-95	**Pittsburgh**	**NHL**	**2**	**0**	**1**	**1**	**125**	**8**	**0**	**3.84**	**2**	**0**	**1**	**80**	**8**	**0**	**6.00**
1995-96	**Pittsburgh**	**NHL**	**49**	**29**	**16**	**2**	**2799**	**160**	**2**	**3.43**	**10**	**4**	**5**	**558**	**26**	**1**	**2.80**
1996-97	**Pittsburgh**	**NHL**	**5**	**0**	**5**	**0**	**270**	**26**	**0**	**5.78**	....	....	....	....	....	....	....
	NHL Totals		**602**	**295**	**218**	**63**	**34624**	**1988**	**23**	**3.45**	**94**	**51**	**39**	**5418**	**281**	**5**	**3.11**

a NHL First All-Star Team (1984)
b Won Vezina Trophy (1984)
c Won Calder Memorial Trophy (1984)
d NHL All-Rookie Team (1984)
e NHL Second All-Star Team (1985, 1993)
f Shared William Jennings Trophy with Bob Sauve (1985)

Played in NHL All-Star Game (1985)

Traded to **Pittsburgh** by **Buffalo** with Buffalo's third round choice (Joe Dziedzic) in 1990 Entry Draft for Doug Bodger and Darrin Shannon, November 12, 1988.

BEAUBIEN, FREDERICK (boh-BEE-yehn) L.A.

Goaltender. Catches left. 6'1", 204 lbs. Born, Lauzon, Que., April 1, 1975.
(Los Angeles' 4th choice, 105th overall, in 1993 Entry Draft).

			Regular Season								Playoffs						
Season	Club	Lea	GP	W	L	T	Mins	GA	SO	Avg	GP	W	L	Mins	GA	SO	Avg
1992-93	St-Hyacinthe	QMJHL	33	8	16	3	1702	133	0	4.69	....	....	....	....	....	....	....
1993-94	St-Hyacinthe	QMJHL	47	19	19	5	2663	168	1	3.79	7	3	4	411	33	0	4.82
1994-95	St-Hyacinthe	QMJHL	51	19	24	4	2697	178	1	3.96	3	1	2	176	9	0	3.07
1995-96	Phoenix	IHL	36	13	9	7	1832	100	1	3.28	2	0	2	119	9	0	4.52
1996-97	Mississippi	ECHL	40	13	19	4	2217	130	2	3.52	3	0	3	188	14	0	4.45

BEAUPRE, DON (boh-PRAY)

Goaltender. Catches left. 5'10", 172 lbs. Born, Waterloo, Ont., September 19, 1961.
(Minnesota's 2nd choice, 37th overall, in 1980 Entry Draft).

			Regular Season								Playoffs						
Season	Club	Lea	GP	W	L	T	Mins	GA	SO	Avg	GP	W	L	Mins	GA	SO	Avg
1978-79	Sudbury	OHA	54	....	....	....	3248	260	2	4.78	10	....	....	600	44	0	4.20
1979-80a	Sudbury	OHA	59	28	29	2	3447	248	0	4.32	9	5	4	552	38	0	4.13
1980-81	**Minnesota**	**NHL**	**44**	**18**	**14**	**11**	**2585**	**138**	**0**	**3.20**	**6**	**4**	**2**	**360**	**26**	**0**	**4.33**
1981-82	**Minnesota**	**NHL**	**29**	**11**	**8**	**9**	**1634**	**101**	**0**	**3.71**	**2**	**0**	**1**	**60**	**4**	**0**	**4.00**
	Nashville	CHL	5	2	3	0	299	25	0	5.02	....	....	....	....	....	....	....
1982-83	**Minnesota**	**NHL**	**36**	**19**	**10**	**5**	**2011**	**120**	**0**	**3.58**	**4**	**2**	**2**	**245**	**20**	**0**	**4.90**
	Birmingham	CHL	10	8	2	0	599	31	0	3.11	....	....	....	....	....	....	....
1983-84	**Minnesota**	**NHL**	**33**	**16**	**13**	**2**	**1791**	**123**	**0**	**4.12**	**13**	**6**	**7**	**782**	**40**	**1**	**3.07**
	Salt Lake	CHL	7	2	5	0	419	30	0	4.30	....	....	....	....	....	....	....
1984-85	**Minnesota**	**NHL**	**31**	**10**	**17**	**3**	**1770**	**109**	**1**	**3.69**	**4**	**1**	**1**	**184**	**12**	**0**	**3.91**
1985-86	**Minnesota**	**NHL**	**52**	**25**	**20**	**6**	**3073**	**182**	**1**	**3.55**	**5**	**2**	**3**	**300**	**17**	**0**	**3.40**
1986-87	**Minnesota**	**NHL**	**47**	**17**	**20**	**6**	**2622**	**174**	**1**	**3.98**	....	....	....	....	....	....	....
1987-88	**Minnesota**	**NHL**	**43**	**10**	**22**	**3**	**2288**	**161**	**0**	**4.22**	....	....	....	....	....	....	....
1988-89	**Minnesota**	**NHL**	**1**	**0**	**1**	**0**	**59**	**3**	**0**	**3.05**	....	....	....	....	....	....	....
	Kalamazoo	IHL	3	1	2	0	179	9	1	3.02	....	....	....	....	....	....	....
	Washington	**NHL**	**11**	**5**	**4**	**0**	**578**	**28**	**1**	**2.91**	....	....	....	....	....	....	....
	Baltimore	AHL	30	14	12	2	1715	102	0	3.57	....	....	....	....	....	....	....
1989-90	**Washington**	**NHL**	**48**	**23**	**18**	**5**	**2793**	**150**	**2**	**3.22**	**8**	**4**	**3**	**401**	**18**	**0**	**2.69**
1990-91	**Washington**	**NHL**	**45**	**20**	**18**	**3**	**2572**	**113**	***5**	**2.64**	**11**	**5**	**5**	**624**	**29**	***1**	**2.79**
	Baltimore	AHL	2	2	0	0	120	3	0	1.50	....	....	....	....	....	....	....
1991-92	**Washington**	**NHL**	**54**	**29**	**17**	**6**	**3108**	**166**	**1**	**3.20**	**7**	**3**	**4**	**419**	**22**	**0**	**3.15**
	Baltimore	AHL	3	1	1	1	184	10	0	3.26	....	....	....	....	....	....	....
1992-93	**Washington**	**NHL**	**58**	**27**	**23**	**5**	**3282**	**181**	**1**	**3.31**	**2**	**1**	**1**	**119**	**9**	**0**	**4.54**
1993-94	**Washington**	**NHL**	**53**	**24**	**16**	**8**	**2853**	**135**	**2**	**2.84**	**8**	**5**	**2**	**429**	**21**	**1**	**2.94**
1994-95	**Ottawa**	**NHL**	**38**	**8**	**25**	**3**	**2161**	**121**	**1**	**3.36**	....	....	....	....	....	....	....
1995-96	**Ottawa**	**NHL**	**33**	**6**	**23**	**0**	**1770**	**110**	**1**	**3.73**	....	....	....	....	....	....	....
	Toronto	**NHL**	**8**	**0**	**5**	**0**	**336**	**26**	**0**	**4.64**	**2**	**0**	**0**	**20**	**2**	**0**	**6.00**
1996-97	**Toronto**	**NHL**	**3**	**0**	**3**	**0**	**110**	**10**	**0**	**5.45**	....	....	....	....	....	....	....
	St. John's	AHL	47	24	16	4	2622	128	3	2.93	....	....	....	....	....	....	....
	Utah	IHL	4	2	2	0	238	13	0	3.27	7	3	4	438	17	1	2.32
	NHL Totals		**667**	**268**	**277**	**75**	**37396**	**2151**	**17**	**3.45**	**72**	**33**	**31**	**3943**	**220**	**3**	**3.35**

a OHA First All-Star Team (1980)

Played in NHL All-Star Game (1981, 1992)

Traded to **Washington** by **Minnesota** for rights to Claudio Scremin, November 1, 1988. Traded to **Ottawa** by **Washington** for Ottawa's fifth round choice (Benoit Gratton) in 1995 Entry Draft, January 18, 1995. Traded to **NY Islanders** by **Ottawa** with Martin Straka and Bryan Berard for Damian Rhodes and Wade Redden, January 23, 1996. Traded to **Toronto** by **NY Islanders** with Kirk Muller for future considerations, January 23, 1996.

BEAUREGARD, STEPHANE (BOH-reh-gahrd)

Goaltender. Catches right. 5'11", 190 lbs. Born, Cowansville, Que., January 10, 1968.
(Winnipeg's 3rd choice, 52nd overall, in 1988 Entry Draft).

			Regular Season								Playoffs						
Season	Club	Lea	GP	W	L	T	Mins	GA	SO	Avg	GP	W	L	Mins	GA	SO	Avg
1986-87	St-Jean	QMJHL	13	6	7	0	785	58	0	4.43	5	1	3	260	26	0	6.00
1987-88ab	St-Jean	QMJHL	66	38	20	3	3766	229	2	3.65	7	3	4	423	34	0	4.82
1988-89	Moncton	AHL	15	4	8	2	824	62	0	4.51	....	....	....	....	....	....	....
	Fort Wayne	IHL	16	9	5	0	830	43	0	3.10	9	4	4	484	21	*1	*2.60
1989-90	**Winnipeg**	**NHL**	**19**	**7**	**8**	**3**	**1079**	**59**	**0**	**3.28**	**4**	**1**	**3**	**238**	**12**	**0**	**3.03**
	Fort Wayne	IHL	33	20	8	3	1949	115	0	3.54	....	....	....	....	....	....	....
1990-91	**Winnipeg**	**NHL**	**16**	**3**	**10**	**1**	**836**	**55**	**0**	**3.95**	....	....	....	....	....	....	....
	Moncton	AHL	9	3	4	1	504	20	1	2.38	1	1	0	60	1	0	1.00
	Fort Wayne	IHL	32	14	13	2	1761	109	0	3.71	*19	*10	9	*1158	57	0	2.95
1991-92	**Winnipeg**	**NHL**	**26**	**6**	**8**	**6**	**1267**	**61**	**2**	**2.89**	....	....	....	....	....	....	....
1992-93	**Philadelphia**	**NHL**	**16**	**3**	**9**	**0**	**802**	**59**	**0**	**4.41**	....	....	....	....	....	....	....
	Hershey	AHL	13	5	5	3	794	48	0	3.63	....	....	....	....	....	....	....
1993-94	**Winnipeg**	**NHL**	**13**	**0**	**4**	**1**	**418**	**34**	**0**	**4.88**	....	....	....	....	....	....	....
	Moncton	AHL	37	18	11	6	2082	121	1	3.49	*21	*12	9	*1305	57	*2	2.62
1994-95	Springfield	AHL	24	10	11	3	1381	73	2	3.17	....	....	....	....	....	....	....
1995-96cd	San Francisco	IHL	*69	*36	24	8	*4022	207	1	3.09	4	1	3	241	10	0	2.49
1996-97	Quebec	IHL	67	35	20	11	3945	174	4	2.65	9	5	3	498	19	0	2.29
	NHL Totals		**90**	**19**	**39**	**11**	**4402**	**268**	**2**	**3.65**	**4**	**1**	**3**	**238**	**12**	**0**	**3.03**

a QMJHL First All-Star Team (1988)
b Canadian Major Junior Goaltender of the year (1988)
c IHL First All-Star Team (1996)
d Won James Gatschene Memorial Trophy (MVP - IHL) (1996)

Traded to **Buffalo** by **Winnipeg** for Christian Ruuttu and future considerations, June 15, 1992. Traded to **Chicago** by **Buffalo** with Buffalo's fourth round choice (Eric Dazel) in 1993 Entry Draft for Dominik Hasek, August 7, 1992. Traded to **Winnipeg** by **Chicago** for Christian Ruuttu, August 10, 1992. Traded to **Philadelphia** by **Winnipeg** for future considerations, October 1, 1992. Traded to **Winnipeg** by **Philadelphia** for future considerations, June 11, 1993.

BELFOUR, ED (BEHL-fohr) DAL.

Goaltender. Catches left. 5'11", 182 lbs. Born, Carman, Man., April 21, 1965.

			Regular Season								Playoffs						
Season	Club	Lea	GP	W	L	T	Mins	GA	SO	Avg	GP	W	L	Mins	GA	SO	Avg
1986-87a	North Dakota	WCHA	34	29	4	0	2049	81	3	2.43	....	....	....	....	....	....	....
1987-88bc	Saginaw	IHL	61	32	25	0	*3446	183	3	3.19	9	4	5	561	33	0	3.53
1988-89	**Chicago**	**NHL**	**23**	**4**	**12**	**3**	**1148**	**74**	**0**	**3.87**	....	....	....	....	....	....	....
	Saginaw	IHL	29	12	10	0	1760	92	0	3.10	5	2	3	298	14	0	2.82
1989-90	Cdn. National	....	33	13	12	6	1808	93	0	3.08	....	....	....	....	....	....	....
	Chicago	**NHL**	....	....	....	....	....	....	....	....	**9**	**4**	**2**	**409**	**17**	**0**	**2.49**
1990-91 defghi	**Chicago**	**NHL**	***74**	***43**	**19**	**7**	***4127**	**170**	**4**	***2.47**	**6**	**2**	**4**	**295**	**20**	**0**	**4.07**
1991-92	**Chicago**	**NHL**	**52**	**21**	**18**	**10**	**2928**	**132**	***5**	**2.70**	**18**	**12**	**4**	**949**	**39**	**1**	***2.47**
1992-93deg	**Chicago**	**NHL**	***71**	**41**	**18**	**11**	***4106**	**177**	***7**	**2.59**	**4**	**0**	**4**	**249**	**13**	**0**	**3.13**
1993-94	**Chicago**	**NHL**	**70**	**37**	**24**	**6**	**3998**	**178**	***7**	**2.67**	**6**	**2**	**4**	**360**	**15**	**0**	**2.50**
1994-95gj	**Chicago**	**NHL**	**42**	**22**	**15**	**3**	**2450**	**93**	***5**	**2.28**	**16**	**9**	**7**	**1014**	**37**	**1**	**2.19**
1995-96	**Chicago**	**NHL**	**50**	**22**	**17**	**10**	**2956**	**135**	**1**	**2.74**	**9**	**6**	**3**	**666**	**23**	**1**	**2.07**
1996-97	**Chicago**	**NHL**	**33**	**11**	**15**	**6**	**1966**	**88**	**1**	**2.69**	....	....	....	....	....	....	....
	San Jose	**NHL**	**13**	**3**	**9**	**0**	**757**	**43**	**1**	**3.41**	....	....	....	....	....	....	....
	NHL Totals		**428**	**204**	**147**	**56**	**24436**	**1090**	**31**	**2.68**	**68**	**35**	**28**	**3942**	**164**	**3**	**2.50**

a WCHA First All-Star Team (1987)
b IHL First All-Star Team (1988)
c Shared Garry F. Longman Memorial Trophy (Top Rookie - IHL) (1988)
d NHL First All-Star Team (1991, 1993)
e Won Vezina Trophy (1991, 1993)
f Won Calder Memorial Trophy (1991)
g Won William M. Jennings Trophy (1991, 1993, 1995)
h Won Trico Goaltender Award (1991)
i NHL/Upper Deck All-Rookie Team (1991)
j NHL Second All-Star Team (1995)

Played in NHL All-Star Game (1992, 1993, 1996)

Signed as a free agent by **Chicago**, September 25, 1987. Traded to **San Jose** by **Chicago** for Chris Terreri, Ulf Dahlen, Michal Sykora and a conditional choice in 1998 Entry Draft, January 25, 1997. Signed as a free agent by **Dallas**, July 2, 1997.

BERGERON, JEAN-CLAUDE (BAIR-zhuhr-uhn)

Goaltender. Catches left. 6'2", 192 lbs. Born, Hauterive, Que., October 14, 1968.
(Montreal's 5th choice, 104th overall, in 1988 Entry Draft).

			Regular Season								Playoffs						
Season	Club	Lea	GP	W	L	T	Mins	GA	SO	Avg	GP	W	L	Mins	GA	SO	Avg
1987-88	Verdun	QMJHL	49	13	31	3	2715	265	0	5.86	....	....	....	....	....	....	....
1988-89	Verdun	QMJHL	44	8	34	1	2417	199	0	4.94	....	....	....	....	....	....	....
	Sherbrooke	AHL	5	4	1	0	302	18	0	3.58	....	....	....	....	....	....	....
1989-90abc	Sherbrooke	AHL	40	21	8	7	2254	103	2	*2.74	9	6	2	497	28	0	3.38
1990-91	**Montreal**	**NHL**	**18**	**7**	**6**	**2**	**941**	**59**	**0**	**3.76**	....	....	....	....	....	....	....
	Fredericton	AHL	18	12	6	0	1083	59	1	3.27	10	5	5	546	32	0	3.52
1991-92	Fredericton	AHL	13	5	7	1	791	57	0	4.32	....	....	....	....	....	....	....
	Peoria	IHL	27	14	9	3	1632	96	1	3.53	6	3	3	352	24	0	4.09
1992-93	**Tampa Bay**	**NHL**	**21**	**8**	**10**	**1**	**1163**	**71**	**0**	**3.66**	....	....	....	....	....	....	....
	Atlanta	IHL	31	21	7	1	1722	92	1	3.21	6	3	3	368	19	0	3.10
1993-94	**Tampa Bay**	**NHL**	**3**	**1**	**1**	**1**	**134**	**7**	**0**	**3.13**	....	....	....	....	....	....	....
d	Atlanta	IHL	48	27	11	7	2755	141	0	3.07	2	1	1	153	6	0	2.34
1994-95	Atlanta	IHL	6	3	3	0	324	24	0	4.44	....	....	....	....	....	....	....
	Tampa Bay	**NHL**	**17**	**3**	**9**	**1**	**883**	**49**	**1**	**3.33**	....	....	....	....	....	....	....
1995-96	**Tampa Bay**	**NHL**	**12**	**2**	**6**	**2**	**595**	**42**	**0**	**4.24**	....	....	....	....	....	....	....
	Atlanta	IHL	25	9	10	3	1326	92	0	4.16	....	....	....	....	....	....	....
1996-97	**Los Angeles**	**NHL**	**1**	**0**	**1**	**0**	**56**	**4**	**0**	**4.29**	....	....	....	....	....	....	....
	Phoenix	IHL	42	11	19	7	2296	127	0	3.32	....	....	....	....	....	....	....
	NHL Totals		**72**	**21**	**33**	**7**	**3772**	**232**	**1**	**3.69**	....	....	....	....	....	....	....

a AHL First All-Star Team (1990)
b Shared Harry "Hap" Holmes Trophy (fewest goals-against - AHL) with Andre Racicot (1990)
c Won Baz Bastien Memorial Trophy (Top Goaltender - AHL) (1990)
d Shared James Norris Memorial Trophy (fewest goals-against - IHL) with Mike Greenlay (1994)

Traded to **Tampa Bay** by **Montreal** for Frederic Chabot, June 19, 1992. Signed as a free agent by **Los Angeles**, August 28, 1996.

BERGQVIST, PER-RAGNAR (BUHRG-kvihst) PHI.

Goaltender. Catches left. 5'11", 183 lbs. Born, Leksand, Sweden, April 11, 1976.
(Philadelphia's 3rd choice, 124th overall, in 1996 Entry Draft).

			Regular Season								Playoffs						
Season	Club	Lea	GP	W	L	T	Mins	GA	SO	Avg	GP	W	L	Mins	GA	SO	Avg
1995-96	Leksand	Swe. Jr.	3	....	....	....	180	17	0	5.67	....	....	....	....	....	....	....
	Leksand	Swe.	6	....	....	....	327	17	0	3.12	1	....	....	60	1	0	1.00
1996-97	Leksard	Swe.	11	....	....	....	660	32	1	2.91	1	....	....	86	5	0	3.49

BESTER, ALLAN

Goaltender. Catches left. 5'7", 155 lbs. Born, Hamilton, Ont., March 26, 1964.
(Toronto's 3rd choice, 48th overall, in 1983 Entry Draft).

			Regular Season								Playoffs						
Season	Club	Lea	GP	W	L	T	Mins	GA	SO	Avg	GP	W	L	Mins	GA	SO	Avg
1981-82	Brantford	OHL	19	4	11	0	970	68	0	4.21	....	....	....	....	....	....	....
1982-83a	Brantford	OHL	56	29	21	3	3210	188	0	3.51	8	3	3	480	20	*1	*2.50
1983-84	**Toronto**	**NHL**	**32**	**11**	**16**	**4**	**1848**	**134**	**0**	**4.35**	....	....	....	....	....	....	....
	Brantford	OHL	23	12	9	1	1271	71	1	3.35	1	0	1	60	5	0	5.00
1984-85	**Toronto**	**NHL**	**15**	**3**	**9**	**1**	**767**	**54**	**1**	**4.22**	....	....	....	....	....	....	....
	St. Catharines	AHL	30	9	18	1	1669	133	0	4.78	....	....	....	....	....	....	....
1985-86	**Toronto**	**NHL**	**1**	**0**	**0**	**0**	**20**	**2**	**0**	**6.00**	....	....	....	....	....	....	....
	St. Catharines	AHL	50	23	23	3	2855	173	1	3.64	11	7	3	637	27	0	2.54
1986-87	**Toronto**	**NHL**	**36**	**10**	**14**	**3**	**1808**	**110**	**2**	**3.65**	**1**	**0**	**0**	**39**	**1**	**0**	**1.54**
	Newmarket	AHL	3	1	0	0	190	6	0	1.89	....	....	....	....	....	....	....
1987-88	**Toronto**	**NHL**	**30**	**8**	**12**	**5**	**1607**	**102**	**2**	**3.81**	**5**	**2**	**3**	**253**	**21**	**0**	**4.98**
1988-89	**Toronto**	**NHL**	**43**	**17**	**20**	**3**	**2460**	**156**	**2**	**3.80**	....	....	....	....	....	....	....
1989-90	**Toronto**	**NHL**	**42**	**20**	**16**	**0**	**2206**	**165**	**0**	**4.49**	**4**	**0**	**3**	**196**	**14**	**0**	**4.29**
	Newmarket	AHL	5	2	1	1	264	18	0	4.09	....	....	....	....	....	....	....
1990-91	**Toronto**	**NHL**	**6**	**0**	**4**	**0**	**247**	**18**	**0**	**4.37**	....	....	....	....	....	....	....
	Newmarket	AHL	19	7	8	4	1157	58	1	3.01	....	....	....	....	....	....	....
	Detroit	**NHL**	**3**	**0**	**3**	**0**	**178**	**13**	**0**	**4.38**	**1**	**0**	**0**	**20**	**1**	**0**	**3.00**
1991-92	**Detroit**	**NHL**	**1**	**0**	**0**	**0**	**31**	**2**	**0**	**3.87**	....	....	....	....	....	....	....
b	Adirondack	AHL	22	13	8	0	1268	78	0	3.69	*19	*14	5	1174	50	*1	*2.56
1992-93	Adirondack	AHL	41	16	15	5	2268	133	1	3.52	10	7	3	633	26	*1	2.46
1993-94	San Diego	IHL	46	22	14	6	2543	150	1	3.54	8	4	4	419	28	0	4.00
1994-95	San Diego	IHL	58	28	23	5	3250	183	1	3.38	4	2	2	272	13	0	2.86
1995-96	Orlando	IHL	51	32	16	2	2947	176	1	3.58	*23	11	12	*1343	65	2	2.90
	Dallas	**NHL**	**10**	**4**	**5**	**1**	**601**	**30**	**0**	**3.00**	....	....	....	....	....	....	....
1996-97	Orlando	IHL	61	37	13	3	3115	132	2	2.54	10	4	4	512	27	0	3.16
	NHL Totals		**219**	**73**	**99**	**17**	**11773**	**786**	**7**	**4.01**	**11**	**2**	**6**	**508**	**37**	**0**	**4.37**

a OHL First All-Star Team (1983)
b Won Jack Butterfield Trophy (Playoff MVP - AHL) (1992)

Traded to **Detroit** by **Toronto** for Detroit's sixth round choice (Alexander Kuzminsky) in 1991 Entry Draft, March 5, 1991. Signed as a free agent by **Anaheim**, September 9, 1993. Signed as a free agent by **Dallas**, January 21, 1996.

BIERK, ZAC (BUHRK, ZAK) T.B.

Goaltender. Catches left. 6'4", 186 lbs. Born, Peterborough, Ont., September 17, 1976.
(Tampa Bay's 8th choice, 212th overall, in 1995 Entry Draft).

			Regular Season								Playoffs						
Season	Club	Lea	GP	W	L	T	Mins	GA	SO	Avg	GP	W	L	Mins	GA	SO	Avg
1993-94	Peterborough	OHL	9	0	4	2	423	37	0	5.22	1	0	0	33	7	0	12.70
1994-95	Peterborough	OHL	35	11	15	5	1779	117	0	3.95	6	2	3	301	24	0	4.78
1995-96	Peterborough	OHL	58	31	16	6	3292	174	2	3.17	*22	*14	7	*1383	83	0	3.60
1996-97a	Peterborough	OHL	49	*28	16	0	2744	151	2	3.30	11	6	5	666	35	0	3.15

a OHL First All-Star Team (1997)

BILLINGTON, CRAIG — COL.

Goaltender. Catches left. 5'10", 170 lbs. Born, London, Ont., September 11, 1966.
(New Jersey's 2nd choice, 23rd overall, in 1984 Entry Draft).

			Regular Season								Playoffs						
Season	Club	Lea	GP	W	L	T	Mins	GA	SO	Avg	GP	W	L	Mins	GA	SO	Avg
1983-84	Belleville	OHL	44	20	19	0	2335	162	1	4.16	1	0	0	30	3	0	6.00
1984-85a	Belleville	OHL	47	26	19	0	2544	180	1	4.25	14	7	5	761	47	1	3.71
1985-86	New Jersey	NHL	18	4	9	1	901	77	0	5.13	....	....	....	....	....	....	....
	Belleville	OHL	3	2	1	0	180	11	0	3.67	20	9	6	1133	68	0	3.60
1986-87	New Jersey	NHL	22	4	13	2	1114	89	0	4.79	....	....	....	....	....	....	....
	Maine	AHL	20	9	8	2	1151	70	0	3.65	....	....	....	....	....	....	....
1987-88	Utica	AHL	*59	22	27	8	*3404	208	1	3.67	....	....	....	....	....	....	....
1988-89	New Jersey	NHL	3	1	1	0	140	11	0	4.71	....	....	....	....	....	....	....
	Utica	AHL	41	17	18	6	2432	150	2	3.70	4	1	3	220	18	0	4.91
1989-90	Utica	AHL	38	20	13	1	2087	138	0	3.97	....	....	....	....	....	....	....
1990-91	Cdn. National	....	34	17	14	2	1879	110	2	3.51	....	....	....	....	....	....	....
1991-92	New Jersey	NHL	26	13	7	1	1363	69	2	3.04	....	....	....	....	....	....	....
1992-93	New Jersey	NHL	42	21	16	4	2389	146	2	3.67	2	0	1	78	5	0	3.85
1993-94	Ottawa	NHL	63	11	41	4	3319	254	0	4.59	....	....	....	....	....	....	....
1994-95	Ottawa	NHL	9	0	6	2	472	32	0	4.07	....	....	....	....	....	....	....
	Boston	NHL	8	5	1	0	373	19	0	3.06	1	0	0	25	1	0	2.40
1995-96	Boston	NHL	27	10	13	3	1380	79	1	3.43	1	0	1	60	6	0	6.00
1996-97	Colorado	NHL	23	11	8	2	1200	53	1	2.65	1	0	0	20	1	0	3.00
	NHL Totals		241	80	115	19	12651	829	6	3.93	5	0	2	183	13	0	4.26

a OHL First All-Star Team (1985)

Played in NHL All-Star Game (1993)

Traded to **Ottawa** by **New Jersey** with Troy Mallette and New Jersey's fourth round choice (Cosmo Dupaul) in 1993 Entry Draft for Peter Sidorkiewicz and future considerations (Mike Peluso, June 26, 1993), June 20, 1993. Traded to **Boston** by **Ottawa** for NY Islanders' eighth round choice (previously acquired by Boston — Ottawa selected Ray Schultz) in 1995 Entry Draft, April 7, 1995. Signed as a free agent by **Florida**, September 5, 1996. Claimed by **Colorado** from **Florida** in NHL Waiver Draft, September 30, 1996.

BIRON, MARTIN (BIH-rohn) — BUF.

Goaltender. Catches left. 6'1", 154 lbs. Born, Lac St. Charles, Que., August 15, 1977.
(Buffalo's 2nd choice, 16th overall, in 1995 Entry Draft).

			Regular Season								Playoffs						
Season	Club	Lea	GP	W	L	T	Mins	GA	SO	Avg	GP	W	L	Mins	GA	SO	Avg
1994-95ab	Beauport	QMJHL	56	29	16	9	3193	132	3	*2.48	16	8	7	900	37	*4	2.47
1995-96	Buffalo	NHL	3	0	2	0	119	10	0	5.04	....	....	....	....	....	....	....
	Beauport	QMJHL	55	29	17	7	3201	152	1	2.85	*19	*12	7	1134	64	0	3.39
1996-97	Beauport	QMJHL	18	6	9	1	928	61	1	3.94	....	....	....	....	....	....	....
	Hull	QMJHL	16	11	4	1	974	43	2	2.65	6	3	1	325	19	0	3.51
	NHL Totals		3	0	2	0	119	10	0	5.04	....	....	....	....	....	....	....

a Canadian Major Junior First All-Star Team (1995)
b Canadian Major Junior Goaltender of the Year (1995)

BONNER, DOUG — TOR.

Goaltender. Catches left. 5'10", 175 lbs. Born, Tacoma, WA, October 15, 1976.
(Toronto's 3rd choice, 139th overall, in 1995 Entry Draft).

			Regular Season								Playoffs						
Season	Club	Lea	GP	W	L	T	Mins	GA	SO	Avg	GP	W	L	Mins	GA	SO	Avg
1992-93	Seattle	WHL	30	7	15	0	1212	93	1	4.60	....	....	....	....	....	....	....
1993-94	Seattle	WHL	29	9	15	0	1481	111	1	4.50	....	....	....	....	....	....	....
1994-95	Seattle	WHL	59	33	23	1	3386	205	1	3.63	3	0	3	193	10	0	3.11
1995-96	Seattle	WHL	58	20	27	7	3219	190	2	3.54	5	1	4	317	19	0	3.60
1996-97	St. John's	AHL	11	0	4	1	365	26	0	4.27	....	....	....	....	....	....	....
	Peoria	ECHL	23	13	8	1	1315	63	1	2.87	10	6	3	541	28	0	3.10

BOUCHER, BRIAN (BOO-shay) — PHI.

Goaltender. Catches left. 6'1", 190 lbs. Born, Woonsocket, RI, January 2, 1977.
(Philadelphia's 1st choice, 22nd overall, in 1995 Entry Draft).

			Regular Season								Playoffs						
Season	Club	Lea	GP	W	L	T	Mins	GA	SO	Avg	GP	W	L	Mins	GA	SO	Avg
1994-95	Tri-City	WHL	35	17	11	2	1969	108	1	3.29	13	6	5	795	50	0	3.77
1995-96	Tri-City	WHL	55	33	19	2	3183	181	1	3.41	11	6	5	653	37	*2	3.40
1996-97a	Tri-City	WHL	41	10	24	6	2458	149	1	3.64	....	....	....	....	....	....	....

a WHL West First All-Star Team (1997)

BRATHWAITE, FRED (BRAYTH-wayt)

Goaltender. Catches left. 5'7", 170 lbs. Born, Ottawa, Ont., November 24, 1972.

			Regular Season								Playoffs						
Season	Club	Lea	GP	W	L	T	Mins	GA	SO	Avg	GP	W	L	Mins	GA	SO	Avg
1989-90	Oshawa	OHL	20	11	2	1	886	43	1	2.91	10	4	2	451	22	0	*2.93
1990-91	Oshawa	OHL	39	25	6	3	1986	112	1	3.38	13	*9	2	677	43	0	3.81
1991-92	Oshawa	OHL	24	12	7	2	1248	81	0	3.89	....	....	....	....	....	....	....
	London	OHL	23	15	6	2	1325	61	*4	2.76	10	5	5	615	36	0	3.51
1992-93	Detroit	OHL	37	23	10	4	2192	134	0	3.67	15	9	6	858	48	1	3.36
1993-94	Edmonton	NHL	19	3	10	3	982	58	0	3.54	....	....	....	....	....	....	....
	Cape Breton	AHL	2	1	1	0	119	6	0	3.04	....	....	....	....	....	....	....
1994-95	Edmonton	NHL	14	2	5	1	601	40	0	3.99	....	....	....	....	....	....	....
1995-96	Edmonton	NHL	7	0	2	0	293	12	0	2.46	....	....	....	....	....	....	....
	Cape Breton	AHL	31	12	16	0	1699	110	1	3.88	....	....	....	....	....	....	....
1996-97	Manitoba	IHL	58	22	22	5	2945	167	1	3.40	....	....	....	....	....	....	....
	NHL Totals		40	5	17	4	1876	110	0	3.52	....	....	....	....	....	....	....

Signed as a free agent by **Edmonton**, October 6, 1993.

BROCHU, MARTIN (broh-SHOO) — WSH.

Goaltender. Catches left. 5'10", 200 lbs. Born, Anjou, Que., March 10, 1973.

			Regular Season								Playoffs						
Season	Club	Lea	GP	W	L	T	Mins	GA	SO	Avg	GP	W	L	Mins	GA	SO	Avg
1990-91	Granby	QMJHL	16	6	5	0	622	39	....	3.76	....	....	....	....	....	....	....
1991-92	Granby	QMJHL	52	15	29	2	2772	278	0	4.72	....	....	....	....	....	....	....
1992-93	Hull	QMJHL	29	9	15	1	1453	137	0	5.66	2	0	1	69	7	0	6.07
1993-94	Fredericton	AHL	32	10	11	3	1505	76	2	3.03	....	....	....	....	....	....	....
1994-95	Fredericton	AHL	44	18	18	4	2475	145	0	3.51	....	....	....	....	....	....	....
1995-96	Fredericton	AHL	17	6	8	2	986	70	0	4.26	....	....	....	....	....	....	....
	Wheeling	ECHL	19	10	6	2	1060	51	1	2.89	....	....	....	....	....	....	....
	Portland	AHL	5	2	2	1	287	15	0	3.14	12	7	4	700	28	*2	*2.40
1996-97	Portland	AHL	55	23	17	7	2962	150	2	3.04	5	2	3	323	13	0	2.41

Signed as a free agent by **Montreal**, September 22, 1992. Traded to **Washington** by **Montreal** for future considerations, March 15, 1996.

BRODEUR, MARTIN (broh-DOOR, MAHR-tihn) — N.J.

Goaltender. Catches left. 6'1", 205 lbs. Born, Montreal, Que., May 6, 1972.
(New Jersey's 1st choice, 20th overall, in 1990 Entry Draft).

			Regular Season								Playoffs						
Season	Club	Lea	GP	W	L	T	Mins	GA	SO	Avg	GP	W	L	Mins	GA	SO	Avg
1989-90	St-Hyacinthe	QMJHL	42	23	13	2	2333	156	0	4.01	12	5	7	678	46	0	4.07
1990-91	St-Hyacinthe	QMJHL	52	22	24	4	2946	162	2	3.30	4	0	4	232	16	0	4.14
1991-92	New Jersey	NHL	4	2	1	0	179	10	0	3.35	1	0	1	32	3	0	5.63
a	St-Hyacinthe	QMJHL	48	27	16	4	2846	161	2	3.39	5	2	3	317	14	0	2.65
1992-93	Utica	AHL	32	14	13	5	1952	131	0	4.03	4	1	3	258	18	0	4.19
1993-94bc	New Jersey	NHL	47	27	11	8	2625	105	3	2.40	17	8	9	1171	38	1	1.95
1994-95	New Jersey	NHL	40	19	11	6	2184	89	3	2.45	*20	*16	4	*1222	34	*3	*1.67 ♦
1995-96	New Jersey	NHL	77	34	30	12	*4433	173	6	2.34	....	....	....	....	....	....	....
1996-97de	New Jersey	NHL	67	37	14	13	3838	120	*10	*1.88	10	5	5	659	19	2	*1.73
	NHL Totals		235	119	67	39	13259	497	22	2.25	48	29	19	3084	94	6	1.83

a QMJHL Second All-Star Team (1992)
b NHL/Upper Deck All-Rookie Team (1994)
c Won Calder Memorial Trophy (1994)
d NHL Second All-Star Team (1997)
e Scored a goal in playoffs vs. Montreal, April 17, 1997.

Played in NHL All-Star Game (1996, 1997)

BUHLER, SCOTT (BEW-luhr) — BUF.

Goaltender. Catches left. 5'11", 169 lbs. Born, Osler, Sask., January 14, 1978.
(Buffalo's 10th choice, 222nd overall, in 1996 Entry Draft).

			Regular Season								Playoffs						
Season	Club	Lea	GP	W	L	T	Mins	GA	SO	Avg	GP	W	L	Mins	GA	SO	Avg
1994-95	Medicine Hat	WHL	1	0	1	0	60	5	0	5.00	....	....	....	....	....	....	....
1995-96	Medicine Hat	WHL	27	6	7	2	1130	80	1	4.25	2	0	0	48	6	0	7.50
1996-97	Medicine Hat	WHL	51	26	20	1	2845	173	2	3.65	1	0	1	12	4	0	20.00

BURKE, SEAN — CAR.

Goaltender. Catches left. 6'4", 208 lbs. Born, Windsor, Ont., January 29, 1967.
(New Jersey's 2nd choice, 24th overall, in 1985 Entry Draft).

			Regular Season								Playoffs						
Season	Club	Lea	GP	W	L	T	Mins	GA	SO	Avg	GP	W	L	Mins	GA	SO	Avg
1984-85	Toronto	OHL	49	25	21	3	2987	211	0	4.24	5	1	3	266	25	0	5.64
1985-86	Toronto	OHL	47	16	27	3	2840	233	0	4.92	4	0	4	238	24	0	6.05
1986-87	Cdn. National	....	42	27	13	2	2550	130	0	3.05	....	....	....	....	....	....	....
1987-88	Cdn. National	....	37	19	9	2	1962	92	1	2.81	....	....	....	....	....	....	....
	Cdn. Olympic	....	4	1	2	1	238	12	0	3.02	....	....	....	....	....	....	....
	New Jersey	NHL	13	10	1	0	689	35	1	3.05	17	9	8	1001	57	*1	3.42
1988-89	New Jersey	NHL	62	22	31	9	3590	230	3	3.84	....	....	....	....	....	....	....
1989-90	New Jersey	NHL	52	22	22	6	2914	175	0	3.60	2	0	2	125	8	0	3.84
1990-91	New Jersey	NHL	35	8	12	8	1870	112	0	3.59	....	....	....	....	....	....	....
1991-92	Cdn. National	....	31	18	6	4	1721	75	1	2.61	....	....	....	....	....	....	....
	Cdn. Olympic	....	7	5	2	0	429	17	0	2.37	....	....	....	....	....	....	....
	San Diego	IHL	7	4	2	1	424	17	0	2.41	3	0	3	160	13	0	4.88
1992-93	Hartford	NHL	50	16	27	3	2656	184	0	4.16	....	....	....	....	....	....	....
1993-94	Hartford	NHL	47	17	24	5	2750	137	2	2.99	....	....	....	....	....	....	....
1994-95	Hartford	NHL	42	17	19	4	2418	108	0	2.68	....	....	....	....	....	....	....
1995-96	Hartford	NHL	66	28	28	6	3669	190	4	3.11	....	....	....	....	....	....	....
1996-97	Hartford	NHL	51	22	22	6	2985	134	4	2.69	....	....	....	....	....	....	....
	NHL Totals		418	162	186	47	23541	1305	14	3.33	19	9	10	1126	65	1	3.46

Played in NHL All-Star Game (1989)

Traded to **Hartford** by **New Jersey** with Eric Weinrich for Bobby Holik, Hartford's second round choice (Jay Pandolfo) in 1993 Entry Draft and future considerations, August 28, 1992.

CARAVAGGIO, LUCIANO (car-ah-VAHJ-ee-oh) — N.J.

Goaltender. Catches left. 5'11", 175 lbs. Born, Etobicoke, Ont., October 3, 1975.
(New Jersey's 7th choice, 155th overall, in 1994 Entry Draft).

			Regular Season								Playoffs						
Season	Club	Lea	GP	W	L	T	Mins	GA	SO	Avg	GP	W	L	Mins	GA	SO	Avg
1993-94	Michigan Tech	WCHA	13	1	7	0	538	37	*1	4.13	....	....	....	....	....	....	....
1994-95	Michigan Tech	WCHA	31	12	5	3	1776	119	*1	4.02	....	....	....	....	....	....	....
1995-96	Michigan Tech	WCHA	25	7	11	4	1280	85	0	3.98	....	....	....	....	....	....	....
1996-97	Michigan Tech.	WCHA	28	7	14	4	1504	92	0	3.67	....	....	....	....	....	....	....

CAREY, JIM (CAIR-ee) — BOS.

Goaltender. Catches left. 6'2", 205 lbs. Born, Dorchester, MA, May 31, 1974.
(Washington's 2nd choice, 32nd overall, in 1992 Entry Draft).

			Regular Season								Playoffs						
Season	Club	Lea	GP	W	L	T	Mins	GA	SO	Avg	GP	W	L	Mins	GA	SO	Avg
1992-93a	U. Wisconsin	WCHA	26	15	8	1	1525	78	1	3.07	....	....	....	....	....	....	....
1993-94	U. Wisconsin	WCHA	*40	*24	13	1	*2247	114	*1	*3.04	....	....	....	....	....	....	....
1994-95bcd	Portland	AHL	55	30	14	11	3281	151	*6	2.76	....	....	....	....	....	....	....
e	Washington	NHL	28	18	6	3	1604	57	4	2.13	7	2	4	358	25	0	4.19
1995-96fg	Washington	NHL	71	35	24	9	4069	153	*9	2.26	3	0	1	97	10	0	6.19
1996-97	Washington	NHL	40	17	18	3	2293	105	1	2.75	....	....	....	....	....	....	....
	Boston	NHL	19	5	13	0	1004	64	0	3.82	....	....	....	....	....	....	....
	NHL Totals		158	75	61	15	8970	379	14	2.54	10	2	5	455	35	0	4.62

a WCHA Second All-Star Team (1993)
b AHL First All-Star Team (1995)
c Won Baz Bastien Memorial Trophy (Top Goaltender - AHL) (1995)
d Won Dudley "Red" Garrett Memorial Trophy (Top Rookie - AHL) (1995)
e NHL/Upper Deck All-Rookie Team (1995)
f NHL First All-Star Team (1996)
g Won Vezina Trophy (1996)

Traded to **Boston** by **Washington** with Anson Carter, Jason Allison, Washington's third round choice (Lee Goren) in 1997 Entry Draft and a conditional choice in 1998 Entry Draft for Bill Ranford, Adam Oates and Rick Tocchet, March 1, 1997.

CASEY, JON (CAY-see)

Goaltender. Catches left. 5'10", 155 lbs. Born, Grand Rapids, MN, March 29, 1962.

			Regular Season								Playoffs						
Season	Club	Lea	GP	W	L	T	Mins	GA	SO	Avg	GP	W	L	Mins	GA	SO	Avg
1980-81	North Dakota	WCHA	5	3	1	0	300	19	0	3.80							
1981-82	North Dakota	WCHA	18	15	3	0	1038	48	1	2.77							
1982-83	North Dakota	WCHA	17	9	6	2	1020	42	0	2.51							
1983-84	North Dakota	WCHA	37	25	10	2	2180	115	2	3.13							
	Minnesota	**NHL**	**2**	**1**	**0**	**0**	**84**	**6**	**0**	**4.29**							
1984-85abc	Baltimore	AHL	46	30	11	4	2646	116	*4	*2.63	*13	8	3	689	38	0	3.31
1985-86	**Minnesota**	**NHL**	**26**	**11**	**11**	**1**	**1402**	**91**	**0**	**3.89**							
	Springfield	AHL	9	4	3	1	464	30	0	3.88							
1986-87	Springfield	AHL	13	1	8	0	770	56	0	4.36							
	Indianapolis	IHL	31	14	15	0	1794	133	0	4.45							
1987-88	**Minnesota**	**NHL**	**14**	**1**	**7**	**4**	**663**	**41**	**0**	**3.71**							
	Kalamazoo	IHL	42	24	13	5	2541	154	2	3.64	7	3	3	382	26	0	4.08
1988-89	**Minnesota**	**NHL**	**55**	**18**	**17**	**12**	**2961**	**151**	**1**	**3.06**	**4**	**1**	**3**	**211**	**16**	**0**	**4.55**
1989-90	**Minnesota**	**NHL**	**61**	***31**	**22**	**4**	**3407**	**183**	**3**	**3.22**	**7**	**3**	**4**	**415**	**21**	**1**	**3.04**
1990-91	**Minnesota**	**NHL**	**55**	**21**	**20**	**11**	**3185**	**158**	**3**	**2.98**	***23**	***14**	**7**	***1205**	**61**	***1**	**3.04**
1991-92	**Minnesota**	**NHL**	**52**	**19**	**23**	**5**	**2911**	**165**	**2**	**3.40**	**7**	**3**	**4**	**437**	**22**	**0**	**3.02**
	Kalamazoo	IHL	4	2	1	1	250	11	0	2.64							
1992-93	**Minnesota**	**NHL**	**60**	**26**	**26**	**5**	**3476**	**193**	**3**	**3.33**							
1993-94	**Boston**	**NHL**	**57**	**30**	**15**	**9**	**3192**	**153**	**4**	**2.88**	**11**	**5**	**6**	**698**	**34**	**0**	**2.92**
1994-95	**St. Louis**	**NHL**	**19**	**7**	**5**	**4**	**872**	**40**	**0**	**2.75**	**2**	**0**	**1**	**30**	**2**	**0**	**4.00**
1995-96	**St. Louis**	**NHL**	**9**	**2**	**3**	**0**	**395**	**25**	**0**	**3.80**	**12**	**6**	**6**	**747**	**36**	**1**	**2.89**
	Peoria	IHL	43	21	19	2	2514	128	3	3.05							
1996-97	**St. Louis**	**NHL**	**15**	**3**	**8**	**0**	**707**	**40**	**0**	**3.39**							
	Worcester	AHL	4	2	1	1	244	10	0	2.45							
	NHL Totals		**425**	**170**	**157**	**55**	**23255**	**1246**	**16**	**3.21**	**66**	**32**	**31**	**3743**	**192**	**3**	**3.08**

a Won Baz Bastien Memorial Trophy (Top Goaltender - AHL) (1985)
b Won Harry "Hap" Holmes Memorial Trophy (fewest goals against - AHL) (1985)
c AHL First All-Star Team (1985)

Played in NHL All-Star Game (1993)

Signed as a free agent by **Minnesota**, April 1, 1984. Traded to **Boston** by **Dallas** for Andy Moog to complete June 20, 1993 trade which sent Gord Murphy to Dallas for future considerations, June 25, 1993. Signed as a free agent by **St. Louis**, June 29, 1994.

CASSIVI, FREDERIC (KASS-ih-vee) OTT.

Goaltender. Catches left. 6'4", 205 lbs. Born, Sorel, Que., June 12, 1975.
(Ottawa's 7th choice, 210th overall, in 1994 Entry Draft).

			Regular Season								Playoffs						
Season	Club	Lea	GP	W	L	T	Mins	GA	SO	Avg	GP	W	L	Mins	GA	SO	Avg
1993-94	St-Hyacinthe	QMJHL	35	15	13	3	1751	127	1	4.35							
1994-95	Halifax	QMJHL	24	9	12	1	1362	105	0	4.63							
	St-Jean	QMJHL	19	12	6	0	1021	55	1	3.23	5	2	3	258	18	0	4.19
1995-96	Thunder Bay	ColHL	12	6	4	2	715	51	0	4.28							
	P.E.I.	AHL	41	20	14	3	2347	128	1	3.27	5	2	3	317	24	0	4.54
1996-97	Syracuse	AHL	55	23	22	8	3069	164	2	3.21	1	0	1	59	3	0	3.01

CAVICCHI, TRENT (cah-VIH-kee) MTL.

Goaltender. Catches left. 6'3", 187 lbs. Born, Halifax, N.S., August 11, 1974.
(Montreal's 12th choice, 236th overall, in 1992 Entry Draft).

			Regular Season								Playoffs						
Season	Club	Lea	GP	W	L	T	Mins	GA	SO	Avg	GP	W	L	Mins	GA	SO	Avg
1992-93	N. Hampshire	H.E.	9	3	2	1	391	32	0	4.91							
1993-94	N. Hampshire	H.E.	25	14	7	1	1324	65	1	2.95							
1994-95	N. Hampshire	H.E.	23	14	6	1	1276	71	0	3.34							
1995-96	N. Hampshire	H.E.	24	9	12	3	1340	95	0	4.25							
1996-97	Knoxville	ECHL	11	2	7	1	616	56	0	5.45							
	Raleigh	ECHL	8	3	3	1	448	22	0	2.95							

CHABOT, FREDERIC (shah-BOH)

Goaltender. Catches left. 5'11", 175 lbs. Born, Hebertville-Station, Que., February 12, 1968.
(New Jersey's 10th choice, 192nd overall, in 1986 Entry Draft).

			Regular Season								Playoffs						
Season	Club	Lea	GP	W	L	T	Mins	GA	SO	Avg	GP	W	L	Mins	GA	SO	Avg
1986-87	Drummondville	QMJHL	62	31	29	0	3508	293	1	5.01	8	2	6	481	40	0	4.99
1987-88	Drummondville	QMJHL	58	27	24	4	3276	237	1	4.34	16	10	6	1019	56	*1	*3.30
1988-89a	Prince Albert	WHL	54	21	29	0	2957	202	2	4.10	4	1	1	199	16	0	4.82
1989-90	Sherbrooke	AHL	2	1	1	0	119	8	0	4.03							
	Fort Wayne	IHL	23	6	13	3	1208	87	1	4.32							
1990-91	**Montreal**	**NHL**	**3**	**0**	**0**	**1**	**108**	**6**	**0**	**3.33**							
	Fredericton	AHL	35	9	15	5	1800	122	0	4.07							
1991-92	Fredericton	AHL	30	17	9	4	1761	79	2	*2.69	7	3	4	457	20	0	2.63
	Winston-Salem	ECHL	24	15	7	2	1449	71	0	*2.94							
1992-93	**Montreal**	**NHL**	**1**	**0**	**0**	**0**	**40**	**1**	**0**	**1.50**							
	Fredericton	AHL	45	22	17	4	2544	141	0	3.33	4	1	3	261	16	0	3.68
1993-94	**Montreal**	**NHL**	**1**	**0**	**1**	**0**	**60**	**5**	**0**	**5.00**							
	Fredericton	AHL	3	0	1	1	143	12	0	5.03							
	Las Vegas	IHL	2	1	1	0	110	5	0	2.72							
	Philadelphia	**NHL**	**4**	**0**	**1**	**1**	**70**	**5**	**0**	**4.29**							
b	Hershey	AHL	28	13	5	6	1464	63	2	*2.58	11	7	4	665	32	0	2.89
1994-95	Cincinnati	IHL	48	25	12	7	2622	128	1	2.93	5	3	2	326	16	0	2.94
1995-96c	Cincinnati	IHL	38	23	9	4	2147	88	3	*2.46	14	9	5	854	37	1	2.60
1996-97de	Houston	IHL	*72	*39	26	7	*4265	180	*7	2.53	13	8	5	777	34	*2	2.63
	NHL Totals		**9**	**0**	**2**	**2**	**278**	**17**	**0**	**3.67**							

a WHL East All-Star Team (1989)
b Won Baz Bastien Award (Top Goaltender - AHL) (1994)
c IHL Second All-Star Team (1996)
d IHL First All-Star Team (1997)
e Won James Gatschene Memorial Trophy (MVP - IHL) (1997)

Signed as a free agent by **Montreal**, January 16, 1990. Claimed by **Tampa Bay** from **Montreal** in Expansion Draft, June 18, 1992. Traded to **Montreal** by **Tampa Bay** for J.C. Bergeron, June 19, 1992. Traded to **Philadelphia** by **Montreal** for cash, February 21, 1994. Signed as a free agent by **Florida**, August 11, 1994.

CHARPENTIER, SEBASTIEN (shahr-PUHNT-yay) WSH.

Goaltender. Catches left. 5'9", 161 lbs. Born, Drummondville, Que., April 18, 1977.
(Washington's 4th choice, 93rd overall, in 1995 Entry Draft).

			Regular Season								Playoffs						
Season	Club	Lea	GP	W	L	T	Mins	GA	SO	Avg	GP	W	L	Mins	GA	SO	Avg
1994-95	Laval	QMJHL	41	25	12	1	2152	99	2	2.76	16	9	4	886	45	0	3.05
1995-96	Laval	QMJHL	18	4	10	0	938	97	0	6.20							
	Val d'Or	QMJHL	33	21	9	1	1906	87	1	2.74	13	7	5	740	45	0	3.64
1996-97	Shawinigan	QMJHL	*62	*37	17	4	*3480	177	1	3.05	4	2	1	196	13	0	3.98

CHEVELDAE, TIM (SHEH-vehl-day)

Goaltender. Catches left. 5'10", 195 lbs. Born, Melville, Sask., February 15, 1968.
(Detroit's 4th choice, 64th overall, in 1986 Entry Draft).

			Regular Season								Playoffs						
Season	Club	Lea	GP	W	L	T	Mins	GA	SO	Avg	GP	W	L	Mins	GA	SO	Avg
1985-86	Saskatoon	WHL	36	21	10	3	2030	165	0	4.88	8	6	2	480	29	0	3.63
1986-87	Saskatoon	WHL	33	20	11	0	1909	133	2	4.18	5	4	1	308	20	0	3.90
1987-88a	Saskatoon	WHL	66	44	19	3	3798	235	1	3.71	6	4	2	364	27	0	4.45
1988-89	**Detroit**	**NHL**	**2**	**0**	**2**	**0**	**122**	**9**	**0**	**4.43**							
	Adirondack	AHL	30	20	8	0	1694	98	1	3.47	2	1	0	99	9	0	5.45
1989-90	**Detroit**	**NHL**	**28**	**10**	**9**	**8**	**1600**	**101**	**0**	**3.79**							
	Adirondack	AHL	31	17	8	6	1848	116	0	3.77							
1990-91	**Detroit**	**NHL**	**65**	**30**	**26**	**5**	**3615**	**214**	**2**	**3.55**	**7**	**3**	**4**	**398**	**22**	**0**	**3.32**
1991-92	**Detroit**	**NHL**	***72**	***38**	**23**	**9**	***4236**	**226**	**2**	**3.20**	**11**	**3**	**7**	**597**	**25**	***2**	**2.51**
1992-93	**Detroit**	**NHL**	**67**	**34**	**24**	**7**	**3880**	**210**	**4**	**3.25**	**7**	**3**	**4**	**423**	**24**	**0**	**3.40**
1993-94	**Detroit**	**NHL**	**30**	**16**	**9**	**1**	**1572**	**91**	**1**	**3.47**							
	Adirondack	AHL	2	1	0	1	125	7	0	3.36							
	Winnipeg	**NHL**	**14**	**5**	**8**	**1**	**788**	**52**	**1**	**3.96**							
1994-95	**Winnipeg**	**NHL**	**30**	**8**	**16**	**3**	**1571**	**97**	**0**	**3.70**							
1995-96	**Winnipeg**	**NHL**	**30**	**8**	**18**	**3**	**1695**	**111**	**0**	**3.93**							
	Hershey	AHL	8	4	3	0	457	31	0	4.07	4	2	2	250	14	0	3.36
1996-97	**Boston**	**NHL**	**2**	**0**	**1**	**0**	**93**	**5**	**0**	**3.23**							
	Fort Wayne	IHL	21	6	9	4	1137	75	0	3.96							
	NHL Totals		**340**	**149**	**136**	**37**	**19172**	**1116**	**10**	**3.49**	**25**	**9**	**15**	**1418**	**71**	**2**	**3.00**

a WHL East All-Star Team (1988)

Played in NHL All-Star Game (1992)

Traded to **Winnipeg** by **Detroit** with Dallas Drake for Bob Essensa and Sergei Bautin, March 8, 1994. Traded to **Philadelphia** by **Winnipeg** with Winnipeg's third round choice (Chester Gallant) in 1996 Entry Draft for Dominic Roussel, February 27, 1996. Signed as a free agent by **Boston**, August 27, 1996.

CLOUTIER, DAN (KLOO-tyay) NYR

Goaltender. Catches left. 6'1", 182 lbs. Born, Mont-Laurier, Que., April 22, 1976.
(NY Rangers' 1st choice, 26th overall, in 1994 Entry Draft).

			Regular Season								Playoffs						
Season	Club	Lea	GP	W	L	T	Mins	GA	SO	Avg	GP	W	L	Mins	GA	SO	Avg
1992-93	S.S. Marie	OHL	12	4	6	0	572	44	0	4.62	4	1	2	231	12	0	3.12
1993-94	S.S. Marie	OHL	55	28	14	6	2934	174	*2	3.56	14	*10	4	833	52	0	3.75
1994-95	S.S. Marie	OHL	45	15	26	2	2518	185	1	4.41							
1995-96	S.S. Marie	OHL	13	9	3	0	641	43	0	4.02							
a	Guelph	OHL	17	12	2	2	1004	35	2	2.09	16	11	5	993	52	*2	3.14
1996-97	Binghamton	AHL	60	23	28	8	3366	199	3	3.55	4	1	3	235	13	0	3.31

a OHL Second All-Star Team (1996)

COCKELL, MATT VAN.

Goaltender. Catches left. 5'11", 192 lbs. Born, Calgary, Alta., May 4, 1979.
(Vancouver's 7th choice, 117th overall, in 1997 Entry Draft).

			Regular Season								Playoffs						
Season	Club	Lea	GP	W	L	T	Mins	GA	SO	Avg	GP	W	L	Mins	GA	SO	Avg
1996-97	Saskatoon	WHL	47	14	26	4	2609	175	0	4.02							

COUSINEAU, MARCEL (koo-ZEE-noh) TOR.

Goaltender. Catches left. 5'9", 180 lbs. Born, Delson, Que., April 30, 1973.
(Boston's 3rd choice, 62nd overall, in 1991 Entry Draft).

			Regular Season								Playoffs						
Season	Club	Lea	GP	W	L	T	Mins	GA	SO	Avg	GP	W	L	Mins	GA	SO	Avg
1990-91	Beauport	QMJHL	49	13	29	3	2739	196	1	4.29							
1991-92	Beauport	QMJHL	*67	26	32	5	*3673	241	0	3.94							
1992-93	Drummondville	QMJHL	60	20	32	2	3298	225	0	4.09	9	3	6	498	37	*1	4.45
1993-94	St. John's	AHL	37	13	11	9	2015	118	0	3.51							
1994-95	St. John's	AHL	58	22	27	6	3342	171	4	3.07	3	0	3	179	9	0	3.01
1995-96	St. John's	AHL	62	21	26	13	3629	192	1	3.17	4	1	3	258	11	0	2.56
1996-97	**Toronto**	**NHL**	**13**	**3**	**5**	**1**	**566**	**31**	**1**	**3.29**							
	St. John's	AHL	19	7	8	3	1053	58	0	3.30	11	6	5	657	28	0	2.55
	NHL Totals		**13**	**3**	**5**	**1**	**566**	**31**	**1**	**3.29**							

Signed as a free agent by **Toronto**, November 13, 1993.

CRUICKSHANK, CURTIS (KRUHK-shank) WSH.

Goaltender. Catches left. 6'2", 209 lbs. Born, Ottawa, Ont., March 21, 1979.
(Washington's 3rd choice, 89th overall, in 1997 Entry Draft).

			Regular Season								Playoffs						
Season	Club	Lea	GP	W	L	T	Mins	GA	SO	Avg	GP	W	L	Mins	GA	SO	Avg
1996-97	Kingston	OHL	35	13	16	1	1792	118	2	3.95	1	0	1	26	4	0	9.23

CUGNET, JASON VAN.

Goaltender. Catches left. 6'1", 205 lbs. Born, North Battleford, Sask., July 31, 1976.
(Vancouver's 9th choice, 222nd overall, in 1995 Entry Draft).

			Regular Season								Playoffs						
Season	Club	Lea	GP	W	L	T	Mins	GA	SO	Avg	GP	W	L	Mins	GA	SO	Avg
1995-96	Kelowna	BCJHL	1	1	0	0	60	5	0	5.00							
1996-97	Colorado	WCHA	15	6	3	3	750	36	1	2.88							

DAFOE, BYRON (day-FOH) L.A.

Goaltender. Catches left. 5'11", 175 lbs. Born, Sussex, England, February 25, 1971.
(Washington's 2nd choice, 35th overall, in 1989 Entry Draft).

			Regular Season								Playoffs						
Season	Club	Lea	GP	W	L	T	Mins	GA	SO	Avg	GP	W	L	Mins	GA	SO	Avg
1988-89	Portland	WHL	59	29	24	3	3279	291	1	5.32	*18	10	8	*1091	81	*1	4.45
1989-90	Portland	WHL	40	14	21	3	2265	193	0	5.11							
1990-91	Portland	WHL	8	1	5	1	414	41	0	5.94							
	Prince Albert	WHL	32	13	12	4	1839	124	0	4.05							
1991-92	New Haven	AHL	7	3	2	1	364	22	0	3.63							
	Baltimore	AHL	33	12	16	4	1847	119	0	3.87							
	Hampton Rds.	ECHL	10	6	4	0	562	26	0	2.78							
1992-93	**Washington**	**NHL**	**1**	**0**	**0**	**0**	**1**	**0**	**0**	**0.00**							
	Baltimore	AHL	48	16	20	7	2617	191	1	4.38	5	2	3	241	22	0	5.48
1993-94	**Washington**	**NHL**	**5**	**2**	**2**	**0**	**230**	**13**	**0**	**3.39**	**2**	**0**	**2**	**118**	**5**	**0**	**2.54**
ab	Portland	AHL	47	24	16	4	2661	148	1	3.34	1	0	0	9	1	0	6.79
1994-95	Phoenix	IHL	49	25	16	6	2743	169	2	3.70							
	Washington	**NHL**	**4**	**1**	**1**	**1**	**187**	**11**	**0**	**3.53**	**1**	**0**	**0**	**20**	**1**	**0**	**3.00**
	Portland	AHL	6	5	0	0	330	16	0	2.91	7	3	4	416	29	0	4.18
1995-96	**Los Angeles**	**NHL**	**47**	**14**	**24**	**8**	**2666**	**172**	**1**	**3.87**							
1996-97	**Los Angeles**	**NHL**	**40**	**13**	**17**	**5**	**2162**	**112**	**0**	**3.11**							
	NHL Totals		**97**	**30**	**44**	**14**	**5246**	**308**	**1**	**3.52**	**3**	**0**	**2**	**138**	**6**	**0**	**2.61**

a AHL First All-Star Team (1994)
b Share Harry "Hap" Holmes Trophy (fewest goals-against - AHL) with Olaf Kolzig (1994)

Traded to **Los Angeles** by **Washington** with Dimitri Khristich for Los Angeles' first round choice (Alexander Volchkov) and Dallas' fourth round choice (previously acquired by Los Angeles — Washington selected Justin Davis) in 1996 Entry Draft, July 8, 1995.

DAIGLE, SYLVAIN (DAYG) PHO.

Goaltender. Catches right. 5'8", 185 lbs. Born, St-Hyacinthe, Que., October 20, 1976.
(Winnipeg's 7th choice, 136th overall, in 1995 Entry Draft).

							Regular Season							Playoffs			
Season	**Club**	**Lea**	**GP**	**W**	**L**	**T**	**Mins**	**GA**	**SO**	**Avg**	**GP**	**W**	**L**	**Mins**	**GA**	**SO**	**Avg**
1993-94	Shawinigan	QMJHL	31	14	11	3	1645	113	0	4.12	....	....	....	....	....	....	....
1994-95	Shawinigan	QMJHL	48	27	17	3	2831	159	3	3.37	14	7	6	824	57	0	4.15
1995-96	Shawinigan	QMJHL	49	23	14	5	2708	159	*3	3.52	6	2	4	389	22	0	3.39
1996-97	Springfield	AHL	13	8	3	0	691	23	1	2.00	6	1	4	311	18	0	3.47
	Mississippi	ECHL	34	20	8	5	1951	100	2	3.08	....	....	....	....	....	....	....
	Las Vegas	IHL	1	0	0	0	41	5	0	7.17	....	....	....	....	....	....	....

DAMPHOUSSE, JEAN-FRANCOIS (DAHM-fooz) N.J.

Goaltender. Catches left. 6', 165 lbs. Born, St-Alexis-des-Monts, Que., July 21, 1979.
(New Jersey's 1st choice, 24th overall, in 1997 Entry Draft).

							Regular Season							Playoffs			
Season	**Club**	**Lea**	**GP**	**W**	**L**	**T**	**Mins**	**GA**	**SO**	**Avg**	**GP**	**W**	**L**	**Mins**	**GA**	**SO**	**Avg**
1995-96	Ste-Foy	Midget	28	....	....	....	1165	85	2	3.06	....	....	....	....	....	....	....
1996-97	Moncton	QMJHL	39	6	25	2	2063	190	0	5.53	....	....	....	....	....	....	....

DAUBENSPECK, KIRK (DAW-behn-spehk) OTT.

Goaltender. Catches left. 6', 190 lbs. Born, Madison, WI, July 16, 1974.
(Philadelphia's 7th choice, 151st overall, in 1992 Entry Draft).

							Regular Season							Playoffs			
Season	**Club**	**Lea**	**GP**	**W**	**L**	**T**	**Mins**	**GA**	**SO**	**Avg**	**GP**	**W**	**L**	**Mins**	**GA**	**SO**	**Avg**
1993-94	U. Wisconsin	WCHA	7	2	2	0	280	19	0	4.07	....	....	....	....	....	....	....
1994-95	U. Wisconsin	WCHA	42	*23	15	4	*2503	146	0	3.51	....	....	....	....	....	....	....
1995-96	U. Wisconsin	WCHA	*39	*17	20	2	*2357	151	0	3.84	....	....	....	....	....	....	....
1996-97ab	U. Wisconsin	WCHA	33	13	18	2	1925	124	1	3.86	....	....	....	....	....	....	....

a WCHA Second All-Star Team (1997)
b NCAA West Second All-American Team (1997)

Traded to **Ottawa** by **Philadelphia** with Claude Boivin for Mark Lamb, March 5, 1994.

DEGAGNE, SHAWN (duh-GAH-nyay) NYR

Goaltender. Catches left. 5'11", 164 lbs. Born, North Bay, Ont., December 18, 1978.
(NY Rangers' 8th choice, 154th overall, in 1997 Entry Draft).

							Regular Season							Playoffs			
Season	**Club**	**Lea**	**GP**	**W**	**L**	**T**	**Mins**	**GA**	**SO**	**Avg**	**GP**	**W**	**L**	**Mins**	**GA**	**SO**	**Avg**
1995-96	Kitchener	OHL	3	0	1	0	53	5	0	5.66	....	....	....	....	....	....	....
1996-97	Kitchener	OHL	25	12	5	1	1111	61	0	3.29	6	0	1	168	8	0	2.86

DENIS, MARC (deh-NEE) COL.

Goaltender. Catches left. 6', 188 lbs. Born, Montreal, Que., August 1, 1977.
(Colorado's 1st choice, 25th overall, in 1995 Entry Draft).

							Regular Season							Playoffs			
Season	**Club**	**Lea**	**GP**	**W**	**L**	**T**	**Mins**	**GA**	**SO**	**Avg**	**GP**	**W**	**L**	**Mins**	**GA**	**SO**	**Avg**
1994-95	Chicoutimi	QMJHL	32	17	9	1	1688	98	0	3.48	6	4	2	372	19	1	3.06
1995-96	Chicoutimi	QMJHL	51	23	21	4	2951	157	2	3.19	16	8	8	957	69	0	4.33
1996-97	**Colorado**	**NHL**	**1**	**0**	**1**	**0**	**60**	**3**	**0**	**3.00**	....	....	....	....	....	....	....
abc	Chicoutimi	QMJHL	41	22	15	2	2323	104	4	*2.69	*21	*11	10	*1229	70	*1	3.42
	Hershey	AHL	....	....	....	....	....	....	....	....	4	1	0	55	1	0	1.08
	NHL Totals		**1**	**0**	**1**	**0**	**60**	**3**	**0**	**3.00**	....	....	....	....	....	....	....

a QMJHL First All-Star Team (1997)
b Canadian Major Junior First All-Star Team (1997)
c Canadian Major Junior Goaltender of the Year (1997)

DeROUVILLE, PHILIPPE (deh-ROO-vihl)

Goaltender. Catches left. 6'1", 185 lbs. Born, Victoriaville, Que., August 7, 1974.
(Pittsburgh's 5th choice, 115th overall, in 1992 Entry Draft).

							Regular Season							Playoffs			
Season	**Club**	**Lea**	**GP**	**W**	**L**	**T**	**Mins**	**GA**	**SO**	**Avg**	**GP**	**W**	**L**	**Mins**	**GA**	**SO**	**Avg**
1990-91	Longueuil	QMJHL	20	13	6	0	1030	50	0	2.91	....	....	....	....	....	....	....
1991-92	Verdun	QMJHL	34	20	6	3	1854	99	2	3.20	11	7	3	593	28	1	2.83
1992-93a	Verdun	QMJHL	61	30	27	2	3491	210	1	3.61	4	0	4	256	18	0	3.61
1993-94a	Verdun	QMJHL	51	28	22	0	2845	145	1	*3.06	4	0	4	210	14	0	4.00
1994-95	Cleveland	IHL	41	24	10	5	2369	131	1	3.32	4	1	3	263	18	0	4.09
	Pittsburgh	**NHL**	**1**	**1**	**0**	**0**	**60**	**3**	**0**	**3.00**	....	....	....	....	....	....	....
1995-96	Cleveland	IHL	38	19	11	3	2008	129	1	3.86	....	....	....	....	....	....	....
1996-97	**Pittsburgh**	**NHL**	**2**	**0**	**2**	**0**	**111**	**6**	**0**	**3.24**	....	....	....	....	....	....	....
	Kansas City	IHL	26	11	11	4	1470	69	2	2.82	2	0	1	32	4	0	7.35
	NHL Totals		**3**	**1**	**2**	**0**	**171**	**9**	**0**	**3.16**	....	....	....	....	....	....	....

a QMJHL Second All-Star Team (1993, 1994)

DESCHENES, FREDERIC (des-SHAYN)

Goaltender. Catches left. 5'9", 164 lbs. Born, Quebec, Que., January 12, 1976.
(Detroit's 4th choice, 114th overall, in 1994 Entry Draft).

							Regular Season							Playoffs			
Season	**Club**	**Lea**	**GP**	**W**	**L**	**T**	**Mins**	**GA**	**SO**	**Avg**	**GP**	**W**	**L**	**Mins**	**GA**	**SO**	**Avg**
1993-94	Granby	QMJHL	35	14	15	1	1861	132	0	4.26	7	3	4	372	27	0	4.35
1994-95	Granby	QMJHL	45	16	23	1	2375	160	0	4.04	11	3	7	553	35	1	3.80
1995-96 abcde	Granby	QMJHL	47	*34	7	0	2505	110	2	*2.63	14	8	2	....	....	....	2.98
1996-97	Rochester	AHL	38	15	13	3	1898	90	2	2.85	10	6	4	627	28	0	2.68
	Flint	ColHL	3	3	0	0	180	5	0	1.67	....	....	....	....	....	....	....

a QMJHL First All-Star Team (1996)
b Canadian Major Junior First All-Star Team (1996)
c Canadian Major Junior Goaltender of the Year (1996)
d Memorial Cup All-Star Team (1996)
e Won Hap Emms Memorial Trophy (Memorial Cup Tournament Top Goaltender) (1996)

DOVIGI, PATRICK EDM.

Goaltender. Catches left. 6', 180 lbs. Born, Sault Ste. Marie, Ont., July 2, 1979.
(Edmonton's 2nd choice, 41st overall, in 1997 Entry Draft).

							Regular Season							Playoffs			
Season	**Club**	**Lea**	**GP**	**W**	**L**	**T**	**Mins**	**GA**	**SO**	**Avg**	**GP**	**W**	**L**	**Mins**	**GA**	**SO**	**Avg**
1995-96	Elmira	Jr. B	33	10	12	1	....	....	4	4.53	....	....	....	....	....	....	....
1996-97	Erie	OHL	36	11	14	4	1764	114	3	3.88	5	1	4	303	18	0	3.56

DRAPER, TOM

Goaltender. Catches left. 5'11", 185 lbs. Born, Outremont, Que., November 20, 1966.
(Winnipeg's 8th choice, 165th overall, in 1985 Entry Draft).

							Regular Season							Playoffs			
Season	**Club**	**Lea**	**GP**	**W**	**L**	**T**	**Mins**	**GA**	**SO**	**Avg**	**GP**	**W**	**L**	**Mins**	**GA**	**SO**	**Avg**
1983-84	U. of Vermont	ECAC	20	8	12	0	1205	82	0	4.08	....	....	....	....	....	....	....
1984-85	U. of Vermont	ECAC	24	5	17	0	1316	90	0	4.11	....	....	....	....	....	....	....
1985-86	U. of Vermont	ECAC	29	15	12	1	1697	87	1	3.08	....	....	....	....	....	....	....
1986-87a	U. of Vermont	ECAC	29	16	13	0	1662	96	2	3.47	....	....	....	....	....	....	....
1987-88	Tappara	Fin.	28	16	3	9	1619	87	0	3.22	....	....	....	....	....	....	....
1988-89	**Winnipeg**	**NHL**	**2**	**1**	**1**	**0**	**120**	**12**	**0**	**6.00**	....	....	....	....	....	....	....
b	Moncton	AHL	*54	27	17	5	*2962	171	2	3.46	7	5	2	419	24	0	3.44
1989-90	**Winnipeg**	**NHL**	**6**	**2**	**4**	**0**	**359**	**26**	**0**	**4.35**	....	....	....	....	....	....	....
	Moncton	AHL	51	20	24	3	2844	167	1	3.52	....	....	....	....	....	....	....
1990-91	Moncton	AHL	30	15	13	2	1779	95	1	3.20	....	....	....	....	....	....	....
	Fort Wayne	IHL	10	5	3	1	564	32	0	3.40	....	....	....	....	....	....	....
	Peoria	IHL	10	6	3	1	584	36	0	3.70	4	2	1	214	10	0	2.80
1991-92	**Buffalo**	**NHL**	**26**	**10**	**9**	**5**	**1403**	**75**	**1**	**3.21**	**7**	**3**	**4**	**433**	**19**	**1**	**2.63**
	Rochester	AHL	9	4	3	2	531	28	0	3.16	....	....	....	....	....	....	....
1992-93	**Buffalo**	**NHL**	**11**	**5**	**6**	**0**	**664**	**41**	**0**	**3.70**	....	....	....	....	....	....	....
	Rochester	AHL	5	3	2	0	303	22	0	4.36	....	....	....	....	....	....	....
1993-94	**NY Islanders**	**NHL**	**7**	**1**	**3**	**0**	**227**	**16**	**0**	**4.23**	....	....	....	....	....	....	....
	Salt Lake	IHL	35	7	23	3	1933	140	0	4.34	....	....	....	....	....	....	....
1994-95	Minnesota	IHL	59	25	20	6	3063	187	1	3.66	2	0	2	118	10	0	5.07
1995-96	**Winnipeg**	**NHL**	**1**	**0**	**0**	**0**	**34**	**3**	**0**	**5.29**	....	....	....	....	....	....	....
	Milwaukee	IHL	31	14	12	3	1793	101	1	3.38	....	....	....	....	....	....	....
1996-97	Long Beach	IHL	39	28	7	3	2267	87	2	2.30	*18	*13	5	*1096	41	*2	2.24
	NHL Totals		**53**	**19**	**23**	**5**	**2807**	**173**	**1**	**3.70**	**7**	**3**	**4**	**433**	**19**	**1**	**2.63**

a ECAC First All-Star Team (1987)
b AHL Second All-Star Team (1989)

Traded to **St. Louis** by **Winnipeg** for future considerations (Jim Vesey, May 24, 1991), February 28, 1991. Traded to **Winnipeg** by **St. Louis** for future considerations, May 24, 1991. Traded to **Buffalo** by **Winnipeg** for Buffalo's seventh round choice (Artur Oktyabrev) in 1992 Entry Draft, June 22, 1991. Traded to **NY Islanders** by **Buffalo** for NY Islanders' seventh round choice (Stev Plouffe) in 1994 Entry Draft, September 30, 1993. Signed as a free agent by **Winnipeg**, December 14, 1995.

DUFFUS, PARRIS (DOO-fihz, PAIR-ihz)

Goaltender. Catches left. 6'2", 192 lbs. Born, Denver, CO, January 27, 1970.
(St. Louis' 6th choice, 180th overall, in 1990 Entry Draft).

							Regular Season							Playoffs			
Season	**Club**	**Lea**	**GP**	**W**	**L**	**T**	**Mins**	**GA**	**SO**	**Avg**	**GP**	**W**	**L**	**Mins**	**GA**	**SO**	**Avg**
1990-91	Cornell	ECAC	4	0	0	0	37	3	0	4.86	....	....	....	....	....	....	....
1991-92ab	Cornell	ECAC	28	14	11	3	1677	74	1	2.65	....	....	....	....	....	....	....
1992-93	Hampton Rds.	ECHL	4	3	1	0	245	13	0	3.18	....	....	....	....	....	....	....
	Peoria	IHL	37	16	15	4	2149	142	0	3.96	1	0	1	59	5	0	5.08
1993-94	Peoria	IHL	36	19	10	3	1845	141	0	4.58	2	0	1	92	6	0	3.88
1994-95	Peoria	IHL	29	17	7	3	1581	71	*3	2.69	7	4	2	409	17	0	2.49
1995-96	Minnesota	IHL	35	10	17	2	1812	100	1	3.31	....	....	....	....	....	....	....
1996-97	**Phoenix**	**NHL**	**1**	**0**	**0**	**0**	**29**	**1**	**0**	**2.07**	....	....	....	....	....	....	....
	Las Vegas	IHL	58	28	19	6	3266	176	3	3.23	3	0	3	175	8	0	2.73
	NHL Totals		**1**	**0**	**0**	**0**	**29**	**1**	**0**	**2.07**	....	....	....	....	....	....	....

a NCAA East First All-American Team (1992)
b ECAC Second All-Star Team (1992)

Signed as a free agent by **Winnipeg**, August 4, 1995.

DUNHAM, MICHAEL (DUHN-uhm) N.J.

Goaltender. Catches left. 6'3", 200 lbs. Born, Johnson City, NY, June 1, 1972.
(New Jersey's 4th choice, 53rd overall, in 1990 Entry Draft).

							Regular Season							Playoffs			
Season	**Club**	**Lea**	**GP**	**W**	**L**	**T**	**Mins**	**GA**	**SO**	**Avg**	**GP**	**W**	**L**	**Mins**	**GA**	**SO**	**Avg**
1990-91	U. of Maine	H.E.	23	14	5	2	1275	63	0	*2.96	....	....	....	....	....	....	....
1991-92	U. of Maine	H.E.	7	6	0	0	382	14	1	2.20	....	....	....	....	....	....	....
	U.S. National	....	3	0	1	1	157	10	0	3.82	....	....	....	....	....	....	....
1992-93ab	U. of Maine	H.E.	25	*21	1	1	1429	63	0	2.65	....	....	....	....	....	....	....
1993-94	U.S. National	....	33	22	9	2	1983	125	2	3.78	....	....	....	....	....	....	....
	U.S. Olympic	....	3	0	2	1	180	15	0	5.02	....	....	....	....	....	....	....
	Albany	AHL	5	2	2	1	304	26	0	5.12	....	....	....	....	....	....	....
1994-95cd	Albany	AHL	35	20	7	8	2120	99	1	2.80	7	6	1	419	20	1	2.86
1995-96e	Albany	AHL	44	30	10	2	2592	109	1	2.52	3	1	2	182	5	1	1.65
1996-97	**New Jersey**	**NHL**	**26**	**8**	**7**	**1**	**1013**	**43**	**2**	**2.55**	....	....	....	....	....	....	....
	Albany	AHL	3	1	1	1	184	12	0	3.91	....	....	....	....	....	....	....
	NHL Totals		**26**	**8**	**7**	**1**	**1013**	**43**	**2**	**2.55**	....	....	....	....	....	....	....

a Hockey East First All-Star Team (1993)
b NCAA East First All-American Team (1993)
c Shared Harry "Hap" Holmes Memorial Trophy (fewest goals against - AHL) with Corey Schwab (1995)
d Shared Jack A. Butterfield Trophy (Playoff MVP - AHL) with Corey Schwab (1995)
e AHL Second All-Star Team (1996)

ELLIOT, JASON DET.

Goaltender. Catches left. 6'2", 183 lbs. Born, Inuvik, N.W.T., November 10, 1975.
(Detroit's 7th choice, 205th overall, in 1994 Entry Draft).

							Regular Season							Playoffs			
Season	**Club**	**Lea**	**GP**	**W**	**L**	**T**	**Mins**	**GA**	**SO**	**Avg**	**GP**	**W**	**L**	**Mins**	**GA**	**SO**	**Avg**
1994-95	Cornell	ECAC	16	3	11	1	877	62	0	4.24	....	....	....	....	....	....	....
1995-96	Cornell	ECAC	19	12	2	1	971	38	2	2.35	....	....	....	....	....	....	....
1996-97	Cornell	ECAC	27	16	7	2	1475	67	0	2.73	....	....	....	....	....	....	....

ESCHE, ROBERT (EHSH) PHO.

Goaltender. Catches left. 6', 188 lbs. Born, Utica, NY, January 22, 1978.
(Phoenix's 5th choice, 139th overall, in 1996 Entry Draft).

							Regular Season							Playoffs			
Season	**Club**	**Lea**	**GP**	**W**	**L**	**T**	**Mins**	**GA**	**SO**	**Avg**	**GP**	**W**	**L**	**Mins**	**GA**	**SO**	**Avg**
1995-96	Detroit	OHL	23	13	6	0	1219	76	1	3.74	3	0	2	105	4	0	2.29
1996-97	Detroit	OHL	58	24	28	2	3241	206	2	3.81	5	1	4	317	19	0	3.60

ESSENSA, BOB (EH-sehn-suh)

Goaltender. Catches left. 6', 185 lbs. Born, Toronto, Ont., January 14, 1965.
(Winnipeg's 5th choice, 69th overall, in 1983 Entry Draft).

			Regular Season								Playoffs						
Season	Club	Lea	GP	W	L	T	Mins	GA	SO	Avg	GP	W	L	Mins	GA	SO	Avg
1983-84	Michigan State	CCHA	17	11	4	0	946	44	2	2.79	....	....	....	....	....	....	....
1984-85	Michigan State	CCHA	18	15	2	0	1059	29	2	1.64	....	....	....	....	....	....	....
1985-86a	Michigan State	CCHA	23	17	4	1	1333	74	1	3.33	....	....	....	....	....	....	....
1986-87	Michigan State	CCHA	25	19	3	1	1383	64	2	2.78	....	....	....	....	....	....	....
1987-88	Moncton	AHL	27	7	11	1	1287	100	1	4.66	....	....	....	....	....	....	....
1988-89	**Winnipeg**	**NHL**	**20**	**6**	**8**	**3**	**1102**	**68**	**1**	**3.70**	....	....	....	....	....	....	....
	Fort Wayne	IHL	22	14	7	0	1287	70	0	3.26	....	....	....	....	....	....	....
1989-90b	**Winnipeg**	**NHL**	**36**	**18**	**9**	**5**	**2035**	**107**	**1**	**3.15**	**4**	**2**	**1**	**206**	**12**	**0**	**3.50**
	Moncton	AHL	6	3	3	0	358	15	0	2.51	....	....	....	....	....	....	....
1990-91	**Winnipeg**	**NHL**	**55**	**19**	**24**	**6**	**2916**	**153**	**4**	**3.15**	....	....	....	....	....	....	....
	Moncton	AHL	2	1	0	1	125	6	0	2.88	....	....	....	....	....	....	....
1991-92	**Winnipeg**	**NHL**	**47**	**21**	**17**	**6**	**2627**	**126**	***5**	**2.88**	**1**	**0**	**0**	**33**	**3**	**0**	**5.45**
1992-93	**Winnipeg**	**NHL**	**67**	**33**	**26**	**6**	**3855**	**227**	**2**	**3.53**	**6**	**2**	**4**	**367**	**20**	**0**	**3.27**
1993-94	**Winnipeg**	**NHL**	**56**	**19**	**30**	**6**	**3136**	**201**	**1**	**3.85**	....	....	....	....	....	....	....
	Detroit	**NHL**	**13**	**4**	**7**	**2**	**778**	**34**	**1**	**2.62**	**2**	**0**	**2**	**109**	**9**	**0**	**4.95**
1994-95	San Diego	IHL	16	6	8	1	919	52	0	3.39	1	0	1	59	3	0	3.05
1995-96	Adirondack	AHL	3	1	2	0	179	11	0	3.69	....	....	....	....	....	....	....
	Fort Wayne	IHL	45	24	14	5	2529	122	1	2.89	5	2	3	299	12	0	2.41
1996-97	**Edmonton**	**NHL**	**19**	**4**	**8**	**0**	**868**	**41**	**1**	**2.83**	....	....	....	....	....	....	....
	NHL Totals		**313**	**124**	**129**	**34**	**17317**	**957**	**16**	**3.32**	**13**	**4**	**7**	**715**	**44**	**0**	**3.69**

a CCHA Second All-Star Team (1986)
b NHL All-Rookie Team (1990)

Traded to **Detroit** by **Winnipeg** with Sergei Bautin for Tim Cheveldae and Dallas Drake, March 8, 1994. Traded to **Edmonton** by **Detroit** for future considerations, June 14, 1996.

FANKHOUSER, SCOTT — ST.L.

Goaltender. Catches left. 6'2", 195 lbs. Born, Bismark, ND, July 1, 1975.
(St. Louis' 8th choice, 276th overall, in 1994 Entry Draft).

			Regular Season								Playoffs						
Season	Club	Lea	GP	W	L	T	Mins	GA	SO	Avg	GP	W	L	Mins	GA	SO	Avg
1994-95	Lowell	H.E.	11	4	4	1	499	37	0	4.44	....	....	....	....	....	....	....
1995-96	Melfort	Jr. A	45	....	....	....	2544	109	....	2.57	....	....	....	....	....	....	....
1996-97	Lowell	H.E.	11	2	4	1	517	38	0	4.41	....	....	....	....	....	....	....

FERNANDEZ, EMMANUEL — DAL.

Goaltender. Catches left. 6', 185 lbs. Born, Etobicoke, Ont., August 27, 1974.
(Quebec's 4th choice, 52nd overall, in 1992 Entry Draft).

			Regular Season								Playoffs						
Season	Club	Lea	GP	W	L	T	Mins	GA	SO	Avg	GP	W	L	Mins	GA	SO	Avg
1991-92	Laval	QMJHL	31	14	13	2	1593	99	1	3.73	9	3	5	468	39	0	5.00
1992-93	Laval	QMJHL	43	26	14	2	2347	141	1	3.60	13	*12	1	818	42	0	3.08
1993-94a	Laval	QMJHL	51	29	14	1	2776	143	*5	3.09	19	14	5	1116	49	*1	*2.63
1994-95b	Kalamazoo	IHL	46	21	10	9	2470	115	2	2.79	14	10	2	753	34	1	2.71
	Dallas	**NHL**	**1**	**0**	**1**	**0**	**59**	**3**	**0**	**3.05**	....	....	....	....	....	....	....
1995-96	**Dallas**	**NHL**	**5**	**0**	**1**	**1**	**249**	**19**	**0**	**4.58**	....	....	....	....	....	....	....
	Michigan	IHL	47	22	15	9	2664	133	*4	3.00	6	5	1	372	14	0	*2.26
1996-97	Michigan	IHL	48	20	24	2	2720	142	2	3.13	4	1	3	277	15	0	3.25
	NHL Totals		**6**	**0**	**2**	**1**	**308**	**22**	**0**	**4.29**	....	....	....	....	....	....	....

a QMJHL First All-Star Team (1994)
b IHL Second All-Star Team (1995)

Rights traded to **Dallas** by **Quebec** for Tommy Sjodin and Dallas' third round draft choice (Chris Drury) in 1994 Entry Draft, February 13, 1994.

FICHAUD, ERIC (FEE-shoh) — NYI

Goaltender. Catches left. 5'11", 171 lbs. Born, Anjou, Que., November 4, 1975.
(Toronto's 1st choice, 16th overall, in 1994 Entry Draft).

			Regular Season								Playoffs						
Season	Club	Lea	GP	W	L	T	Mins	GA	SO	Avg	GP	W	L	Mins	GA	SO	Avg
1992-93	Chicoutimi	QMJHL	43	18	13	1	2039	149	0	4.38	....	....	....	....	....	....	....
1993-94abc	Chicoutimi	QMJHL	*63	*37	21	3	*3493	192	4	3.30	*26	*16	10	*1560	86	*1	3.31
1994-95d	Chicoutimi	QMJHL	46	21	19	4	2637	151	4	3.44	7	2	5	428	20	0	2.80
1995-96	**NY Islanders**	**NHL**	**24**	**7**	**12**	**2**	**1234**	**68**	**1**	**3.31**	....	....	....	....	....	....	....
	Worcester	AHL	34	13	15	6	1989	97	1	2.93	2	1	1	127	7	0	3.30
1996-97	**NY Islanders**	**NHL**	**34**	**9**	**14**	**4**	**1759**	**91**	**0**	**3.10**	....	....	....	....	....	....	....
	NHL Totals		**58**	**16**	**26**	**6**	**2993**	**159**	**1**	**3.19**	....	....	....	....	....	....	....

a Canadian Major Junior Second All-Star Team (1994)
b Memorial Cup All-Star Team (1994)
c Won Hap Emms Memorial Trophy (Memorial Cup Tournament Top Goaltender) (1994)
d QMJHL First All-Star Team (1995)

Traded to **NY Islanders** by **Toronto** for Benoit Hogue, NY Islanders' third round choice (Ryan Pepperall) in 1995 Entry Draft and fifth round choice (Brandon Sugden) in 1996 Entry Draft, April 6, 1995.

FISCHER, KAI (FIH-shuhr, KIGH) — COL.

Goaltender. Catches left. 5'11", 176 lbs. Born, Forst, Germany, March 25, 1977.
(Colorado's 8th choice, 160th overall, in 1996 Entry Draft).

			Regular Season								Playoffs						
Season	Club	Lea	GP	W	L	T	Mins	GA	SO	Avg	GP	W	L	Mins	GA	SO	Avg
1995-96	Dusseldorf	Ger. Jr.								UNAVAILABLE							
1996-97	Dusseldorf	Ger.	2	....	....	....	125	7	0	3.36	....	....	....	....	....	....	....

FISET, STEPHANE (fih-SEHT) — L.A.

Goaltender. Catches left. 6'1", 195 lbs. Born, Montreal, Que., June 17, 1970.
(Quebec's 3rd choice, 24th overall, in 1988 Entry Draft).

			Regular Season								Playoffs						
Season	Club	Lea	GP	W	L	T	Mins	GA	SO	Avg	GP	W	L	Mins	GA	SO	Avg
1987-88	Victoriaville	QMJHL	40	15	17	4	2221	146	1	3.94	2	0	2	163	10	0	3.68
1988-89ab	Victoriaville	QMJHL	43	25	14	0	2401	138	1	*3.45	12	*9	2	711	33	0	*2.78
1989-90	**Quebec**	**NHL**	**6**	**0**	**5**	**1**	**342**	**34**	**0**	**5.96**	....	....	....	....	....	....	....
	Victoriaville	QMJHL	24	14	6	3	1383	63	1	*2.73	*14	7	6	*790	49	0	3.72
1990-91	**Quebec**	**NHL**	**3**	**0**	**2**	**1**	**186**	**12**	**0**	**3.87**	....	....	....	....	....	....	....
	Halifax	AHL	36	10	15	8	1902	131	0	4.13	....	....	....	....	....	....	....
1991-92	**Quebec**	**NHL**	**23**	**7**	**10**	**2**	**1133**	**71**	**1**	**3.76**	....	....	....	....	....	....	....
	Halifax	AHL	29	8	14	6	1675	110	*3	3.94	....	....	....	....	....	....	....
1992-93	**Quebec**	**NHL**	**37**	**18**	**9**	**4**	**1939**	**110**	**0**	**3.40**	**1**	**0**	**0**	**21**	**1**	**0**	**2.86**
	Halifax	AHL	3	2	1	0	180	11	0	3.67	....	....	....	....	....	....	....
1993-94	**Quebec**	**NHL**	**50**	**20**	**25**	**4**	**2798**	**158**	**2**	**3.39**	....	....	....	....	....	....	....
	Cornwall	AHL	1	0	1	0	60	4	0	4.00	....	....	....	....	....	....	....
1994-95	**Quebec**	**NHL**	**32**	**17**	**10**	**3**	**1879**	**87**	**2**	**2.78**	**4**	**1**	**2**	**209**	**16**	**0**	**4.59**
1995-96	**Colorado**	**NHL**	**37**	**22**	**6**	**7**	**2107**	**103**	**1**	**2.93**	**1**	**0**	**0**	**1**	**0**	**0**	**0.00** ♦
1996-97	**Los Angeles**	**NHL**	**44**	**13**	**24**	**5**	**2482**	**132**	**4**	**3.19**	....	....	....	....	....	....	....
	NHL Totals		**232**	**97**	**91**	**27**	**12866**	**707**	**10**	**3.30**	**6**	**1**	**2**	**231**	**17**	**0**	**4.42**

a QMJHL First All-Star Team (1989)
b Canadian Major Junior Goaltender of the Year (1989)

Traded to **Los Angeles** by **Colorado** with Colorado's first round choice in 1998 Entry Draft for Eric Lacroix and Los Angeles' first round choice in 1998 Entry Draft, June 20, 1996.

FITZPATRICK, MARK — FLA.

Goaltender. Catches left. 6'2", 198 lbs. Born, Toronto, Ont., November 13, 1968.
(Los Angeles' 2nd choice, 27th overall, in 1987 Entry Draft).

			Regular Season								Playoffs						
Season	Club	Lea	GP	W	L	T	Mins	GA	SO	Avg	GP	W	L	Mins	GA	SO	Avg
1985-86	Medicine Hat	WHL	41	26	6	1	2074	99	1	2.86	19	12	5	986	58	0	3.53
1986-87a	Medicine Hat	WHL	50	31	11	4	2844	159	4	3.35	20	12	8	1224	71	1	3.48
1987-88a	Medicine Hat	WHL	63	36	15	6	3600	194	2	3.23	16	12	4	959	52	*1	*3.25
1988-89	**Los Angeles**	**NHL**	**17**	**6**	**7**	**3**	**957**	**64**	**0**	**4.01**	....	....	....	....	....	....	....
	New Haven	AHL	18	10	5	1	980	54	1	3.31	....	....	....	....	....	....	....
	NY Islanders	**NHL**	**11**	**3**	**5**	**2**	**627**	**41**	**0**	**3.92**	....	....	....	....	....	....	....
1989-90	**NY Islanders**	**NHL**	**47**	**19**	**19**	**5**	**2653**	**150**	**3**	**3.39**	**4**	**0**	**2**	**152**	**13**	**0**	**5.13**
1990-91	**NY Islanders**	**NHL**	**2**	**1**	**1**	**0**	**120**	**6**	**0**	**3.00**	....	....	....	....	....	....	....
	Capital Dist.	AHL	12	3	7	2	734	47	0	3.84	....	....	....	....	....	....	....
1991-92b	**NY Islanders**	**NHL**	**30**	**11**	**13**	**5**	**1743**	**93**	**0**	**3.20**	....	....	....	....	....	....	....
	Capital Dist.	AHL	14	6	5	1	782	39	0	2.99	....	....	....	....	....	....	....
1992-93	**NY Islanders**	**NHL**	**39**	**17**	**15**	**5**	**2253**	**130**	**0**	**3.46**	**3**	**0**	**1**	**77**	**4**	**0**	**3.12**
	Capital Dist.	AHL	5	1	3	1	284	18	0	3.80	....	....	....	....	....	....	....
1993-94	**Florida**	**NHL**	**28**	**12**	**8**	**6**	**1603**	**73**	**1**	**2.73**	....	....	....	....	....	....	....
1994-95	**Florida**	**NHL**	**15**	**6**	**7**	**2**	**819**	**36**	**2**	**2.64**	....	....	....	....	....	....	....
1995-96	**Florida**	**NHL**	**34**	**15**	**11**	**3**	**1786**	**88**	**0**	**2.96**	**2**	**0**	**0**	**60**	**6**	**0**	**6.00**
1996-97	**Florida**	**NHL**	**30**	**8**	**9**	**9**	**1680**	**66**	**0**	**2.36**	....	....	....	....	....	....	....
	NHL Totals		**253**	**98**	**95**	**40**	**14241**	**747**	**6**	**3.15**	**9**	**0**	**3**	**289**	**23**	**0**	**4.78**

a Won Hap Emms Memorial Trophy (Memorial Cup Tournament Top Goaltender) (1987, 1988)
b Won Bill Masterton Memorial Trophy (1992)

Traded to **NY Islanders** by **Los Angeles** with Wayne McBean and future considerations (Doug Crossman, May 23, 1989) for Kelly Hrudey, February 22, 1989. Traded to **Quebec** by **NY Islanders** with NY Islanders' first round choice (Adam Deadmarsh) in 1993 Entry Draft for Ron Hextall and Quebec's first round choice (Todd Bertuzzi) in 1993 Entry Draft, June 20, 1993. Claimed by **Florida** from **Quebec** in Expansion Draft, June 24, 1993.

FLAHERTY, WADE (FLAY-uhr-tee) — NYI

Goaltender. Catches left. 6', 170 lbs. Born, Terrace, B.C., January 11, 1968.
(Buffalo's 10th choice, 181st overall, in 1988 Entry Draft).

			Regular Season								Playoffs						
Season	Club	Lea	GP	W	L	T	Mins	GA	SO	Avg	GP	W	L	Mins	GA	SO	Avg
1984-85	Kelowna	WHL	1	0	0	0	55	5	0	5.45	....	....	....	....	....	....	....
1985-86	Seattle	WHL	9	1	3	0	271	36	0	7.97	....	....	....	....	....	....	....
	Spokane	WHL	5	0	3	0	161	21	0	7.83	....	....	....	....	....	....	....
1986-87	Victoria	WHL	3	0	2	0	127	16	0	7.56	....	....	....	....	....	....	....
1987-88	Victoria	WHL	36	....	....	....	2052	135	0	3.95	5	....	....	300	18	0	3.60
1988-89	Victoria	WHL	42	21	19	0	2408	180	4	4.49	....	....	....	....	....	....	....
1989-90	Greensboro	ECHL	27	12	10	0	1308	96	0	4.40	....	....	....	....	....	....	....
1990-91	Kansas City	IHL	*56	16	31	4	2990	224	0	4.49	....	....	....	....	....	....	....
1991-92	**San Jose**	**NHL**	**3**	**0**	**3**	**0**	**178**	**13**	**0**	**4.38**	....	....	....	....	....	....	....
	Kansas City	IHL	43	26	14	3	2603	140	1	3.23	1	0	0	1	0	0	0.00
1992-93	**San Jose**	**NHL**	**1**	**0**	**1**	**0**	**60**	**5**	**0**	**5.00**	....	....	....	....	....	....	....
a	Kansas City	IHL	*61	*34	19	7	*3642	195	2	3.21	*12	6	6	733	34	*1	2.78
1993-94ab	Kansas City	IHL	*60	32	19	9	*3564	202	0	3.40	....	....	....	....	....	....	....
1994-95	**San Jose**	**NHL**	**18**	**5**	**6**	**1**	**852**	**44**	**1**	**3.10**	**7**	**2**	**3**	**377**	**31**	**0**	**4.93**
1995-96	**San Jose**	**NHL**	**24**	**3**	**12**	**1**	**1137**	**92**	**0**	**4.85**	....	....	....	....	....	....	....
1996-97	**San Jose**	**NHL**	**7**	**2**	**4**	**0**	**359**	**31**	**0**	**5.18**	....	....	....	....	....	....	....
	Kentucky	AHL	19	8	6	2	1032	54	1	3.14	3	1	2	199	11	0	3.30
	NHL Totals		**53**	**10**	**26**	**2**	**2586**	**185**	**1**	**4.29**	**7**	**2**	**3**	**377**	**31**	**0**	**4.93**

a Shared James Norris Memorial Trophy (fewest goals against - IHL) with Arturs Irbe (1992)
b IHL Second All-Star Team (1993, 1994)

Signed as a free agent by **San Jose**, September 3, 1991. Signed as a free agent by **NY Islanders**, July 22, 1997.

FOUNTAIN, MIKE — CAR.

Goaltender. Catches left. 6'1", 176 lbs. Born, North York, Ont., January 26, 1972.
(Vancouver's 4th choice, 69th overall, in 1992 Entry Draft).

			Regular Season								Playoffs						
Season	Club	Lea	GP	W	L	T	Mins	GA	SO	Avg	GP	W	L	Mins	GA	SO	Avg
1990-91	S.S. Marie	OHL	7	5	2	0	380	19	....	3.00	....	....	....	....	....	....	....
	Oshawa	OHL	30	17	5	1	1483	84	....	3.40	8	1	4	292	26	0	5.34
1991-92a	Oshawa	OHL	40	18	13	6	2260	149	1	3.96	7	3	4	429	26	0	3.64
1992-93	Cdn. National	....	13	7	5	1	745	37	1	2.98	....	....	....	....	....	....	....
	Hamilton	AHL	12	2	8	0	618	46	0	4.47	....	....	....	....	....	....	....
1993-94b	Hamilton	AHL	*70	*34	28	6	*4005	241	*4	3.61	3	0	2	146	12	0	4.92
1994-95	Syracuse	AHL	61	25	29	7	3618	225	2	3.73	....	....	....	....	....	....	....
1995-96	Syracuse	AHL	54	21	27	3	3060	184	1	3.61	15	8	7	915	57	*2	3.74
1996-97	**Vancouver**	**NHL**	**6**	**2**	**2**	**0**	**245**	**14**	**1**	**3.43**	....	....	....	....	....	....	....
	Syracuse	AHL	25	8	14	2	1462	78	1	3.20	2	0	2	119	12	0	6.02
	NHL Totals		**6**	**2**	**2**	**0**	**245**	**14**	**1**	**3.43**	....	....	....	....	....	....	....

a OHL First All-Star Team (1992)
b AHL Second All-Star Team (1994)

Signed as a free agent by **Carolina**, August 14, 1997.

FRANEK, PETR (FRAH-nehk) — COL.

Goaltender. Catches left. 5'11", 187 lbs. Born, Most, Czech., April 6, 1975.
(Quebec's 10th choice, 205th overall, in 1993 Entry Draft).

			Regular Season								Playoffs						
Season	Club	Lea	GP	W	L	T	Mins	GA	SO	Avg	GP	W	L	Mins	GA	SO	Avg
1992-93	Litvinov	Czech.	5	....	....	....	273	15	....	3.29	....	....	....	....	....	....	....
1993-94	Litvinov	Czech.	11	....	....	....	535	34	....	3.81	2	....	....	61	10	....	9.83
1994-95	Litvinov	Czech.	12	....	....	....	657	47	....	4.29	1	0	0	16	0	0	0.00
1995-96	Litvinov	Czech.	36	....	....	....	2096	85	3	2.43	16	....	....	948	47	....	2.97
1996-97	Hershey	AHL	15	4	1	0	457	23	3	3.02	....	....	....	....	....	....	....
	Brantford	ColHL	6	4	1	0	321	14	0	2.61	....	....	....	....	....	....	....
	Quebec	IHL	6	3	3	0	357	18	0	3.02	1	0	1	40	4	0	6.00

FRIESEN, TERRY — S.J.

Goaltender. Catches left. 5'11", 185 lbs. Born, Winkler, Man., October 29, 1977.
(San Jose's 3rd choice, 55th overall, in 1996 Entry Draft).

			Regular Season								Playoffs						
Season	Club	Lea	GP	W	L	T	Mins	GA	SO	Avg	GP	W	L	Mins	GA	SO	Avg
1995-96a	Swift Current	WHL	42	19	17	3	2504	155	2	3.71	6	2	4	338	21	0	3.73
1996-97	Swift Current	WHL	53	28	19	3	3090	170	1	3.30	10	6	4	592	27	0	2.74

a WHL East Second All-Star Team (1996)

FUHR, GRANT (FYOOR) ST.L.

Goaltender. Catches right. 5'9", 190 lbs. Born, Spruce Grove, Alta., September 28, 1962.
(Edmonton's 1st choice, 8th overall, in 1981 Entry Draft).

			Regular Season								Playoffs						
Season	Club	Lea	GP	W	L	T	Mins	GA	SO	Avg	GP	W	L	Mins	GA	SO	Avg
1979-80a	Victoria	WHL	43	30	12	0	2488	130	2	3.14	8	5	3	465	22	0	2.84
1980-81a	Victoria	WHL	59	48	9	1	3448	160	*4	*2.78	15	12	3	899	45	*1	*3.00
1981-82b	Edmonton	NHL	48	28	5	14	2847	157	0	3.31	5	2	3	309	26	0	5.05
1982-83	Edmonton	NHL	32	13	12	5	1803	129	0	4.29	1	0	0	11	0	0	0.00
	Moncton	AHL	10	4	5	1	604	40	0	3.98	....	....	....	....	....	....	....
1983-84	Edmonton	NHL	45	30	10	4	2625	171	1	3.91	16	11	4	883	44	1	2.99 ◆
1984-85	Edmonton	NHL	46	26	8	7	2559	165	1	3.87	*18	*15	3	1064	55	0	3.10 ◆
1985-86	Edmonton	NHL	40	29	8	0	2184	143	0	3.93	9	5	4	541	28	0	3.11
1986-87	Edmonton	NHL	44	22	13	3	2388	137	0	3.44	19	14	5	1148	47	0	2.46 ◆
1987-88cd	Edmonton	NHL	*75	*40	24	9	*4304	246	*4	3.43	*19	*16	2	*1136	55	0	2.90 ◆
1988-89	Edmonton	NHL	59	23	26	6	3341	213	1	3.83	7	3	4	417	24	1	3.45
1989-90	Edmonton	NHL	21	9	7	3	1081	70	1	3.89	....	....	....	....	....	....	....
	Cape Breton	AHL	2	2	0	0	120	6	0	3.01	....	....	....	....	....	....	....
1990-91	Edmonton	NHL	13	6	4	3	778	39	1	3.01	17	8	7	1019	51	0	3.00
	Cape Breton	AHL	4	2	2	0	240	17	0	4.25	....	....	....	....	....	....	....
1991-92	Toronto	NHL	66	25	33	5	3774	230	2	3.66	....	....	....	....	....	....	....
1992-93	Toronto	NHL	29	13	9	4	1665	87	1	3.14	....	....	....	....	....	....	....
	Buffalo	NHL	29	11	15	2	1694	98	0	3.47	8	3	4	474	27	1	3.42
1993-94e	Buffalo	NHL	32	13	12	3	1726	106	2	3.68	....	....	....	....	....	....	....
	Rochester	AHL	5	3	0	2	310	10	0	1.94	....	....	....	....	....	....	....
1994-95	Buffalo	NHL	3	1	2	0	180	12	0	4.00	....	....	....	....	....	....	....
	Los Angeles	NHL	14	1	7	3	698	47	0	4.04	....	....	....	....	....	....	....
1995-96	St. Louis	NHL	*79	30	28	16	4365	209	3	2.87	2	1	0	69	1	0	0.87
1996-97	St. Louis	NHL	73	33	27	11	4261	193	3	2.72	6	2	4	357	13	2	2.18
	NHL Totals		748	353	250	98	42273	2452	20	3.48	127	80	40	7428	371	5	3.00

a WHL First All-Star Team (1980, 1981)
b NHL Second All-Star Team (1982)
c NHL First All-Star Team (1988)
d Won Vezina Trophy (1988)
e Shared William M. Jennings Trophy with Dominik Hasek (1994)

Played in NHL All-Star Game (1982, 1984-86, 1988-89)

Traded to **Toronto** by **Edmonton** with Glenn Anderson and Craig Berube for Vincent Damphousse, Peter Ing, Scott Thornton, Luke Richardson, future considerations and cash, September 19, 1991. Traded to **Buffalo** by **Toronto** with Toronto's fifth round choice (Kevin Popp) in 1995 Entry Draft for Dave Andreychuk, Daren Puppa and Buffalo's first round choice (Kenny Jonsson) in 1993 Entry Draft, February 2, 1993. Traded to **Los Angeles** by **Buffalo** with Philippe Boucher and Denis Tsygurov for Alexei Zhitnik, Robb Stauber, Charlie Huddy and Los Angeles' fifth round choice (Marian Menhart) in 1995 Entry Draft, February 14, 1995. Signed as a free agent by **St. Louis**, July 14, 1995.

GAGE, JOAQUIN (GAYJ, YOH-ah-keen)

Goaltender. Catches left. 6', 200 lbs. Born, Vancouver, B.C., October 19, 1973.
(Edmonton's 6th choice, 109th overall, in 1992 Entry Draft).

			Regular Season								Playoffs						
Season	Club	Lea	GP	W	L	T	Mins	GA	SO	Avg	GP	W	L	Mins	GA	SO	Avg
1990-91	Portland	WHL	3	0	3	0	180	17	0	5.70	....	....	....	....	....	....	....
1991-92	Portland	WHL	63	27	30	4	3635	269	2	4.44	6	2	4	366	28	0	4.59
1992-93	Portland	WHL	38	21	16	1	2302	153	2	3.99	8	5	2	427	30	0	4.22
1993-94	Prince Albert	WHL	53	24	25	3	3041	212	1	4.18	....	....	....	....	....	....	....
1994-95	Cape Breton	AHL	54	17	28	5	3010	207	0	4.13	....	....	....	....	....	....	....
	Edmonton	NHL	2	0	2	0	99	7	0	4.24	....	....	....	....	....	....	....
1995-96	Edmonton	NHL	16	2	8	1	717	45	0	3.77	....	....	....	....	....	....	....
	Cape Breton	AHL	21	8	11	0	1162	80	0	4.13	....	....	....	....	....	....	....
1996-97	Hamilton	AHL	29	7	14	4	1558	91	0	3.50	....	....	....	....	....	....	....
	Wheeling	ECHL	3	1	0	0	120	8	0	4.00	....	....	....	....	....	....	....
	NHL Totals		18	2	10	1	816	52	0	3.82	....	....	....	....	....	....	....

GARNER, TYRONE CGY.

Goaltender. Catches left. 6'1", 164 lbs. Born, Stoney Creek, Ont., July 27, 1978.
(NY Islanders' 4th choice, 83rd overall, in 1996 Entry Draft).

			Regular Season								Playoffs						
Season	Club	Lea	GP	W	L	T	Mins	GA	SO	Avg	GP	W	L	Mins	GA	SO	Avg
1995-96	Oshawa	OHL	32	11	15	4	1697	112	0	3.96	....	....	....	....	....	....	....
1996-97	Oshawa	OHL	9	6	1	0	434	20	0	2.76	3	1	0	88	6	0	4.09

Traded to **Calgary** by **NY Islanders** with Marty McInnis and Calgary's sixth round choice (previously acquired by NY Islanders — Calgary selected Ilja Demidov) in 1997 Entry Draft for Robert Reichel, March 18, 1997.

GARON, MATHIEU (gah-ROHN) MTL.

Goaltender. Catches right. 6'1", 178 lbs. Born, Chandler, Que., January 9, 1978.
(Montreal's 2nd choice, 44th overall, in 1996 Entry Draft).

			Regular Season								Playoffs						
Season	Club	Lea	GP	W	L	T	Mins	GA	SO	Avg	GP	W	L	Mins	GA	SO	Avg
1995-96	Victoriaville	QMJHL	51	18	27	0	2709	189	1	4.19	12	7	4	676	38	1	3.39
1996-97	Victoriaville	QMJHL	53	29	18	3	3032	150	*6	2.97	6	2	4	330	23	0	4.18

GIGUERE, JEAN-SEBASTIEN (ZHEE-gair) CAR.

Goaltender. Catches left. 6', 175 lbs. Born, Montreal, Que., May 16, 1977.
(Hartford's 1st choice, 13th overall, in 1995 Entry Draft).

			Regular Season								Playoffs						
Season	Club	Lea	GP	W	L	T	Mins	GA	SO	Avg	GP	W	L	Mins	GA	SO	Avg
1993-94	Verdun	QMJHL	25	13	5	2	1234	66	1	3.21	....	....	....	....	....	....	....
1994-95	Halifax	QMJHL	47	14	27	5	2755	181	2	3.94	7	3	4	417	17	1	*2.45
1995-96	Halifax	QMJHL	55	26	23	2	3230	185	1	3.44	6	1	5	354	24	0	4.07
1996-97	Hartford	NHL	8	1	4	0	394	24	0	3.65	....	....	....	....	....	....	....
a	Halifax	QMJHL	50	28	19	3	3014	170	2	3.38	16	9	7	954	58	0	3.65
	NHL Totals		8	1	4	0	394	24	0	3.65	....	....	....	....	....	....	....

a QMJHL Second All-Star Team (1997)

GORDON, IAN CGY.

Goaltender. Catches left. 5'10", 160 lbs. Born, Yorkton, Sask., May 15, 1975.

			Regular Season								Playoffs						
Season	Club	Lea	GP	W	L	T	Mins	GA	SO	Avg	GP	W	L	Mins	GA	SO	Avg
1992-93	Swift Current	WHL	10	1	6	0	365	31	0	5.10	2	0	0	53	3	0	3.40
1993-94	Swift Current	WHL	65	29	27	4	3657	204	6	3.35	7	3	4	420	21	1	3.00
1994-95	Swift Current	WHL	17	6	9	1	994	62	1	3.74	....	....	....	....	....	....	....
	Saskatoon	WHL	41	24	9	7	2476	129	1	3.13	10	4	6	633	29	1	2.75
1995-96	Saint John	AHL	19	2	12	0	768	56	0	4.37	....	....	....	....	....	....	....
1996-97	Saint John	AHL	21	5	9	1	988	50	0	3.03	....	....	....	....	....	....	....
	Grand Rapids	IHL	5	2	2	0	257	15	0	3.50	1	0	0	0	0	0	0.00

Signed as a free agent by **Calgary**, October 6, 1995.

GOVERDE, DAVID (goh-VEHR-deh)

Goaltender. Catches right. 6', 210 lbs. Born, Toronto, Ont., April 9, 1970.
(Los Angeles' 4th choice, 91st overall, in 1990 Entry Draft).

			Regular Season								Playoffs						
Season	Club	Lea	GP	W	L	T	Mins	GA	SO	Avg	GP	W	L	Mins	GA	SO	Avg
1989-90	Sudbury	OHL	52	28	12	7	2941	182	0	3.71	7	3	3	394	25	0	3.81
1990-91	Phoenix	IHL	40	11	19	5	2007	137	0	4.10	....	....	....	....	....	....	....
1991-92	Los Angeles	NHL	2	1	1	0	120	9	0	4.50	....	....	....	....	....	....	....
	Phoenix	IHL	35	11	19	3	1951	129	1	3.97	....	....	....	....	....	....	....
	New Haven	AHL	5	1	3	0	248	17	0	4.11	....	....	....	....	....	....	....
1992-93	Los Angeles	NHL	2	0	2	0	98	13	0	7.96	....	....	....	....	....	....	....
	Phoenix	IHL	45	18	21	3	2569	173	1	4.04	....	....	....	....	....	....	....
1993-94	Los Angeles	NHL	1	0	1	0	60	7	0	7.00	....	....	....	....	....	....	....
	Phoenix	IHL	30	15	13	1	1716	93	0	3.25	....	....	....	....	....	....	....
	Portland	AHL	1	0	1	0	59	4	0	4.01	....	....	....	....	....	....	....
	Peoria	IHL	5	4	1	0	299	13	0	2.61	1	0	1	59	7	0	7.05
1994-95	Detroit	ColHL	4	4	0	0	240	10	0	2.50	....	....	....	....	....	....	....
	Phoenix	IHL	2	0	2	0	76	5	0	3.95	....	....	....	....	....	....	....
	Detroit	IHL	15	8	5	0	814	49	0	3.61	....	....	....	....	....	....	....
1995-96	Saint John	AHL	1	0	0	0	47	9	0	11.40	....	....	....	....	....	....	....
	Louisville	ECHL	12	5	5	1	697	46	*1	3.96	....	....	....	....	....	....	....
	Toledo	ECHL	31	23	3	4	1817	79	*1	2.61	11	8	3	666	32	0	2.88
1996-97	Toledo	ECHL	44	23	14	6	2554	126	*5	2.96	5	2	3	346	15	0	*2.59
	Fort Wayne	IHL	1	0	1	0	60	7	0	7.00	....	....	....	....	....	....	....
	NHL Totals		5	1	4	0	278	29	0	6.26	....	....	....	....	....	....	....

GRAHAME, JOHN BOS.

Goaltender. Catches left. 6'2", 210 lbs. Born, Denver, CO, August 31, 1975.
(Boston's 7th choice, 229th overall, in 1994 Entry Draft).

			Regular Season								Playoffs						
Season	Club	Lea	GP	W	L	T	Mins	GA	SO	Avg	GP	W	L	Mins	GA	SO	Avg
1994-95	Lake Superior	CCHA	28	16	7	3	1616	75	2	2.79	....	....	....	....	....	....	....
1995-96	Lake Superior	CCHA	29	21	4	2	1558	66	2	2.54	....	....	....	....	....	....	....
1996-97	Lake Superior	CCHA	37	19	13	4	2197	134	3	3.66	....	....	....	....	....	....	....

GUZDA, BRAD (GOOZ-dah) L.A.

Goaltender. Catches left. 6'3", 180 lbs. Born, Banff, Alta., April 28, 1973.

			Regular Season								Playoffs						
Season	Club	Lea	GP	W	L	T	Mins	GA	SO	Avg	GP	W	L	Mins	GA	SO	Avg
1995-96	Knoxville	ECHL	19	16	1	0	1083	69	0	3.82	7	3	4	433	24	0	3.33
	Muskegon	ColHL	2	0	0	0	12	5	0	24.50	....	....	....	....	....	....	....
1996-97	Knoxville	ECHL	35	12	18	2	1853	166	1	5.38	....	....	....	....	....	....	....
	Phoenix	IHL	5	0	1	2	165	12	0	4.37	....	....	....	....	....	....	....

Signed as a free agent by **Los Angeles**, May 28, 1996.

HACKETT, JEFF CHI.

Goaltender. Catches left. 6'1", 195 lbs. Born, London, Ont., June 1, 1968.
(NY Islanders' 2nd choice, 34th overall, in 1987 Entry Draft).

			Regular Season								Playoffs						
Season	Club	Lea	GP	W	L	T	Mins	GA	SO	Avg	GP	W	L	Mins	GA	SO	Avg
1986-87	Oshawa	OHL	31	18	9	2	1672	85	2	3.05	15	8	7	895	40	0	2.68
1987-88	Oshawa	OHL	53	30	21	2	3165	205	0	3.89	7	3	4	438	31	0	4.25
1988-89	NY Islanders	NHL	13	4	7	0	662	39	0	3.53	....	....	....	....	....	....	....
	Springfield	AHL	29	12	14	2	1677	116	0	4.15	....	....	....	....	....	....	....
1989-90a	Springfield	AHL	54	24	25	3	3045	187	1	3.68	*17	*10	5	934	60	0	3.85
1990-91	NY Islanders	NHL	30	5	18	1	1508	91	0	3.62	....	....	....	....	....	....	....
1991-92	San Jose	NHL	42	11	27	1	2314	148	0	3.84	....	....	....	....	....	....	....
1992-93	San Jose	NHL	36	2	30	1	2000	176	0	5.28	....	....	....	....	....	....	....
1993-94	Chicago	NHL	22	2	12	3	1084	62	0	3.43	....	....	....	....	....	....	....
1994-95	Chicago	NHL	7	1	3	2	328	13	0	2.38	2	0	0	26	1	0	2.31
1995-96	Chicago	NHL	35	18	11	4	2000	80	4	2.40	1	0	1	60	5	0	5.00
1996-97	Chicago	NHL	41	19	18	4	2473	89	2	2.16	6	2	4	345	25	0	4.35
	NHL Totals		226	62	126	16	12369	698	6	3.39	9	2	5	431	31	0	4.32

a Won Jack A. Butterfield Trophy (Playoff MVP - AHL) (1990)

Claimed by **San Jose** from **NY Islanders** in Expansion Draft, May 30, 1991. Traded to **Chicago** by **San Jose** for Chicago's third round choice (Alexei Yegorov) in 1994 Entry Draft, July 13, 1993.

HASEK, DOMINIK (HAH-shihk) BUF.

Goaltender. Catches left. 5'11", 168 lbs. Born, Pardubice, Czech., January 29, 1965.
(Chicago's 11th choice, 199th overall, in 1983 Entry Draft).

			Regular Season								Playoffs						
Season	Club	Lea	GP	W	L	T	Mins	GA	SO	Avg	GP	W	L	Mins	GA	SO	Avg
1981-82	Pardubice	Czech.	12	....	....	....	661	34	....	3.09	....	....	....	....	....	....	....
1982-83	Pardubice	Czech.	42	....	....	....	2358	105	....	2.67	....	....	....	....	....	....	....
1983-84	Pardubice	Czech.	40	....	....	....	2304	108	....	2.81	....	....	....	....	....	....	....
1984-85	Pardubice	Czech.	42	....	....	....	2419	131	....	3.25	....	....	....	....	....	....	....
1985-86a	Pardubice	Czech.	45	....	....	....	2689	138	....	3.08	....	....	....	....	....	....	....
1986-87ab	Pardubice	Czech.	43	....	....	....	2515	103	....	2.46	....	....	....	....	....	....	....
1987-88ac	Pardubice	Czech.	31	....	....	....	1862	93	....	3.00	....	....	....	....	....	....	....
1988-89abc	Pardubice	Czech.	42	....	....	....	2507	114	....	2.73	....	....	....	....	....	....	....
1989-90abc	Dukla Jihlava	Czech.	40	....	....	....	2251	80	....	2.13	....	....	....	....	....	....	....
1990-91	Chicago	NHL	5	3	0	1	195	8	0	2.46	3	0	0	69	3	0	2.61
d	Indianapolis	IHL	33	20	11	1	1903	80	*5	*2.52	1	1	0	60	3	0	3.00
1991-92e	Chicago	NHL	20	10	4	1	1014	44	1	2.60	3	0	2	158	8	0	3.04
	Indianapolis	IHL	20	7	10	3	1162	69	1	3.56	....	....	....	....	....	....	....
1992-93	Buffalo	NHL	28	11	10	4	1429	75	0	3.15	1	1	0	45	1	0	1.33
1993-94fgh	Buffalo	NHL	58	30	20	6	3358	109	*7	*1.95	7	3	4	484	13	2	*1.61
1994-95	Pardubice	Czech.	2	....	....	....	124	6	0	2.90	....	....	....	....	....	....	....
fg	Buffalo	NHL	41	19	14	7	2416	85	*5	*2.11	5	1	4	309	18	0	3.50
1995-96	Buffalo	NHL	59	22	30	6	3417	161	2	2.83	....	....	....	....	....	....	....
1996-97fgij	Buffalo	NHL	67	37	20	10	4037	153	5	2.27	3	1	1	153	5	0	1.96
	NHL Totals		278	132	98	35	15866	635	20	2.40	22	6	11	1218	48	2	2.36

a Czechoslovakian Goaltender-of-the-Year (1986, 1987, 1988, 1989, 1990)
b Czechoslovakian Player-of-the-Year (1987, 1989, 1990)
c Czechoslovakian First-Team All-Star (1988, 1989, 1990)
d IHL First All-Star Team (1991)
e NHL/Upper Deck All-Rookie Team (1992)
f NHL First All-Star Team (1994, 1995, 1997)
g Won Vezina Trophy (1994, 1995, 1997)
h Shared William M. Jennings Trophy with Grant Fuhr (1994)
i Won Lester B. Pearson Award (1997)
j Won Hart Trophy (1997)

Played in NHL All-Star Game (1996, 1997)

Traded to **Buffalo** by **Chicago** for Stephane Beauregard and Buffalo's fourth round choice (Eric Daze) in 1993 Entry Draft, August 7, 1992.

HEALY, GLENN — TOR.

Goaltender. Catches left. 5'10", 185 lbs. Born, Pickering, Ont., August 23, 1962.

			Regular Season								Playoffs						
Season	Club	Lea	GP	W	L	T	Mins	GA	SO	Avg	GP	W	L	Mins	GA	SO	Avg
1981-82	W. Michigan	CCHA	27	7	19	1	1569	116	0	4.44	....	....	....	....	....	....	....
1982-83	W. Michigan	CCHA	30	8	19	2	1732	116	0	4.01	....	....	....	....	....	....	....
1983-84	W. Michigan	CCHA	38	19	16	3	2241	146	0	3.90	....	....	....	....	....	....	....
1984-85	W. Michigan	CCHA	37	21	14	2	2171	118	0	3.26	....	....	....	....	....	....	....
1985-86	**Los Angeles**	**NHL**	**1**	**0**	**0**	**0**	**51**	**6**	**0**	**7.06**	....	....	....	....	....	....	....
	New Haven	AHL	43	21	15	4	2410	160	0	3.98	2	0	2	49	11	0	5.55
1986-87	New Haven	AHL	47	21	15	0	2828	173	1	3.67	7	3	4	427	19	0	2.67
1987-88	**Los Angeles**	**NHL**	**34**	**12**	**18**	**1**	**1869**	**135**	**1**	**4.33**	**4**	**1**	**3**	**240**	**20**	**0**	**5.00**
1988-89	**Los Angeles**	**NHL**	**48**	**25**	**19**	**2**	**2699**	**192**	**0**	**4.27**	**3**	**0**	**1**	**97**	**6**	**0**	**3.71**
1989-90	**NY Islanders**	**NHL**	**39**	**12**	**19**	**6**	**2197**	**128**	**2**	**3.50**	**4**	**1**	**2**	**166**	**9**	**0**	**3.25**
1990-91	**NY Islanders**	**NHL**	**53**	**18**	**24**	**9**	**2999**	**166**	**0**	**3.32**	....	....	....	....	....	....	....
1991-92	**NY Islanders**	**NHL**	**37**	**14**	**16**	**4**	**1960**	**124**	**1**	**3.80**	....	....	....	....	....	....	....
1992-93	**NY Islanders**	**NHL**	**47**	**22**	**20**	**2**	**2655**	**146**	**1**	**3.30**	**18**	**9**	**8**	**1109**	**59**	**0**	**3.19**
1993-94	**NY Rangers**	**NHL**	**29**	**10**	**12**	**2**	**1368**	**69**	**2**	**3.03**	**2**	**0**	**0**	**68**	**1**	**0**	**0.88** ♦
1994-95	**NY Rangers**	**NHL**	**17**	**8**	**6**	**1**	**888**	**35**	**1**	**2.36**	**5**	**2**	**1**	**230**	**13**	**0**	**3.39**
1995-96	**NY Rangers**	**NHL**	**44**	**17**	**14**	**11**	**2564**	**124**	**2**	**2.90**	....	....	....	....	....	....	....
1996-97	**NY Rangers**	**NHL**	**23**	**5**	**12**	**4**	**1357**	**59**	**1**	**2.61**	....	....	....	....	....	....	....
	NHL Totals		**372**	**143**	**160**	**42**	**20607**	**1184**	**11**	**3.45**	**36**	**13**	**15**	**1910**	**108**	**0**	**3.39**

Signed as a free agent by **Los Angeles**, June 13, 1985. Signed as a free agent by **NY Islanders**, August 16, 1989. Claimed by **Anaheim** from **NY Islanders** in Expansion Draft, June 24, 1993. Claimed by **Tampa Bay** from **Anaheim** in Phase II of Expansion Draft, June 25, 1993. Traded to **NY Rangers** by **Tampa Bay** for Tampa Bay's third round choice (previously acquired by NY Rangers — Tampa Bay selected Allan Egeland) in 1993 Entry Draft, June 25, 1993. Signed as a free agent by **Toronto**, August 8, 1997.

HEBERT, GUY (ay-BAIR, GEE) — ANA.

Goaltender. Catches left. 5'11", 185 lbs. Born, Troy, NY, January 7, 1967.
(St. Louis' 8th choice, 159th overall, in 1987 Entry Draft).

			Regular Season								Playoffs						
Season	Club	Lea	GP	W	L	T	Mins	GA	SO	Avg	GP	W	L	Mins	GA	SO	Avg
1985-86	Hamilton Coll.	NCAA	18	4	12	2	1011	69	2	4.09	....	....	....	....	....	....	....
1986-87	Hamilton Coll.	NCAA	18	12	5	0	1070	40	3	2.19	2	1	1	134	6	0	2.69
1987-88	Hamilton Coll.	NCAA	9	5	3	0	510	22	1	2.58	1	0	1	60	3	0	3.00
1988-89	Hamilton Coll.	NCAA	25	18	7	0	1454	62	2	2.56	2	1	1	126	4	0	1.90
1989-90	Peoria	IHL	30	7	13	7	1706	124	1	4.36	2	0	1	76	5	0	3.95
1990-91ab	Peoria	IHL	36	24	10	1	2093	100	2	2.87	8	3	4	458	32	0	4.19
1991-92	**St. Louis**	**NHL**	**13**	**5**	**5**	**1**	**738**	**36**	**0**	**2.93**	....	....	....	....	....	....	....
	Peoria	IHL	29	20	9	0	1731	98	0	3.40	4	3	1	239	9	0	2.26
1992-93	**St. Louis**	**NHL**	**24**	**8**	**8**	**2**	**1210**	**74**	**1**	**3.67**	**1**	**0**	**0**	**2**	**0**	**0**	**0.00**
1993-94	**Anaheim**	**NHL**	**52**	**20**	**27**	**3**	**2991**	**141**	**2**	**2.83**	....	....	....	....	....	....	....
1994-95	**Anaheim**	**NHL**	**39**	**12**	**20**	**4**	**2092**	**109**	**2**	**3.13**	....	....	....	....	....	....	....
1995-96	**Anaheim**	**NHL**	**59**	**28**	**23**	**5**	**3326**	**157**	**4**	**2.83**	....	....	....	....	....	....	....
1996-97	**Anaheim**	**NHL**	**67**	**29**	**25**	**12**	**3863**	**172**	**4**	**2.67**	**9**	**4**	**4**	**534**	**18**	**1**	**2.02**
	NHL Totals		**254**	**102**	**108**	**27**	**14220**	**689**	**13**	**2.91**	**10**	**4**	**4**	**536**	**18**	**1**	**2.01**

a Shared James Norris Memorial Trophy (fewest goals against - IHL) with Pat Jablonski (1991)
b IHL Second All-Star Team (1991)

Played in NHL All-Star Game (1997)

Claimed by **Anaheim** from **St. Louis** in Expansion Draft, June 24, 1993.

HEDBERG, JOHAN (HEHD-buhrg) — PHI.

Goaltender. Catches left. 5'11", 180 lbs. Born, Leksand, Sweden, May 5, 1973.
(Philadelphia's 8th choice, 218th overall, in 1994 Entry Draft).

			Regular Season								Playoffs						
Season	Club	Lea	GP	W	L	T	Mins	GA	SO	Avg	GP	W	L	Mins	GA	SO	Avg
1992-93	Leksand	Swe.	10	....	....	....	600	24	....	2.40	....	....	....	....	....	....	....
1993-94	Leksand	Swe.	17	....	....	....	1020	48	....	2.81	....	....	....	....	....	....	....
1994-95	Leksand	Swe.	17	....	....	....	986	58	....	3.53	....	....	....	....	....	....	....
1995-96	Leksand	Swe.	34	....	....	....	2013	95	....	2.83	4	....	....	240	13	....	3.25
1996-97	Leksand	Swe.	38	....	....	....	2260	95	3	2.52	8	....	....	581	18	1	1.86

HEIL, JEFF — NYR

Goaltender. Catches left. 6'1", 190 lbs. Born, Bloomington, MN, September 17, 1975.
(NY Rangers' 7th choice, 169th overall, in 1995 Entry Draft).

			Regular Season								Playoffs						
Season	Club	Lea	GP	W	L	T	Mins	GA	SO	Avg	GP	W	L	Mins	GA	SO	Avg
1994-95	Wisc.-River Falls	NCHA	25	13	7	3	1399	64	2	2.74	....	....	....	....	....	....	....
1995-96	Wisc.-River Falls	NCHA	16	13	2	0	943	28	2	1.78	....	....	....	....	....	....	....
1996-97	Wisc.-River Falls	NCHA	23	15	8	0	1335	52	4	2.34	....	....	....	....	....	....	....

HENRY, FREDERIC — N.J.

Goaltender. Catches left. 5'11", 155 lbs. Born, Cap-Rouge, Que., August 9, 1977.
(New Jersey's 10th choice, 200th overall, in 1995 Entry Draft).

			Regular Season								Playoffs						
Season	Club	Lea	GP	W	L	T	Mins	GA	SO	Avg	GP	W	L	Mins	GA	SO	Avg
1994-95	Granby	QMJHL	15	8	5	0	866	47	0	3.26	6	1	2	232	21	0	5.43
1995-96	Granby	QMJHL	28	19	5	2	1530	69	*3	2.71	12	9	2	610	21	2	*2.08
1996-97	Granby	QMJHL	57	33	16	6	3330	162	4	2.92	5	1	4	251	17	0	4.06
	Albany	AHL	1	1	0	0	60	3	0	3.00	....	....	....	....	....	....	....

HEXTALL, RON — PHI.

Goaltender. Catches left. 6'3", 192 lbs. Born, Brandon, Man., May 3, 1964.
(Philadelphia's 6th choice, 119th overall, in 1982 Entry Draft).

			Regular Season								Playoffs						
Season	Club	Lea	GP	W	L	T	Mins	GA	SO	Avg	GP	W	L	Mins	GA	SO	Avg
1981-82	Brandon	WHL	30	12	11	0	1398	133	0	5.71	3	0	2	103	16	0	9.32
1982-83	Brandon	WHL	44	13	30	0	2589	249	0	5.77	....	....	....	....	....	....	....
1983-84	Brandon	WHL	46	29	13	2	2670	190	0	4.27	10	5	5	592	37	0	3.75
1984-85	Hershey	AHL	11	4	6	0	555	34	0	3.68	....	....	....	....	....	....	....
	Kalamazoo	IHL	19	6	11	1	1103	80	0	4.35	....	....	....	....	....	....	....
1985-86ab	Hershey	AHL	*53	30	19	2	*3061	174	*5	3.41	13	5	7	780	42	*1	3.23
1986-87cdef	**Philadelphia**	**NHL**	***66**	**37**	**21**	**6**	***3799**	**190**	**1**	**3.00**	***26**	**15**	**11**	***1540**	**71**	***2**	**2.77**
1987-88g	**Philadelphia**	**NHL**	**62**	**30**	**22**	**7**	**3561**	**208**	**0**	**3.50**	**7**	**2**	**4**	**379**	**30**	**0**	**4.75**
1988-89h	**Philadelphia**	**NHL**	***64**	**30**	**28**	**6**	***3756**	**202**	**0**	**3.23**	**15**	**8**	**7**	**886**	**49**	**0**	**3.32**
1989-90	**Philadelphia**	**NHL**	**8**	**4**	**2**	**1**	**419**	**29**	**0**	**4.15**	....	....	....	....	....	....	....
	Hershey	AHL	1	1	0	0	49	3	0	3.67	....	....	....	....	....	....	....
1990-91	**Philadelphia**	**NHL**	**36**	**13**	**16**	**5**	**2035**	**106**	**0**	**3.13**	....	....	....	....	....	....	....
1991-92	**Philadelphia**	**NHL**	**45**	**16**	**21**	**6**	**2668**	**151**	**3**	**3.40**	....	....	....	....	....	....	....
1992-93	**Quebec**	**NHL**	**54**	**29**	**16**	**5**	**2988**	**172**	**0**	**3.45**	**6**	**2**	**4**	**372**	**18**	**0**	**2.90**
1993-94	**NY Islanders**	**NHL**	**65**	**27**	**26**	**6**	**3581**	**184**	**5**	**3.08**	**3**	**0**	**3**	**158**	**16**	**0**	**6.08**
1994-95	**Philadelphia**	**NHL**	**31**	**17**	**9**	**4**	**1824**	**88**	**1**	**2.89**	**15**	**10**	**5**	**897**	**42**	**0**	**2.81**
1995-96	**Philadelphia**	**NHL**	**53**	**31**	**13**	**7**	**3102**	**112**	**4**	***2.17**	**12**	**6**	**6**	**760**	**27**	**0**	**2.13**
1996-97	**Philadelphia**	**NHL**	**55**	**31**	**16**	**5**	**3094**	**132**	**5**	**2.56**	**8**	**4**	**3**	**444**	**22**	**0**	**2.97**
	NHL Totals		**539**	**265**	**190**	**58**	**30827**	**1574**	**19**	**3.06**	**92**	**47**	**43**	**5436**	**275**	**2**	**3.04**

a AHL First All-Star Team (1986)
b Won Dudley "Red" Garrett Memorial Trophy (Top Rookie - AHL) (1986)
c NHL First All-Star Team (1987)
d Won Vezina Trophy (1987)
e Won Conn Smythe Trophy (1987)
f NHL All-Rookie Team (1987)
g Scored a goal vs. Boston, December 8, 1987
h Scored a goal in playoffs vs. Washington, April 11, 1989

Played in NHL All-Star Game (1988)

Traded to **Quebec** by **Philadelphia** with Peter Forsberg, Steve Duchesne, Kerry Huffman, Mike Ricci, Chris Simon, Philadelphia's first round choice in the 1993 (Jocelyn Thibault) and 1994 (later traded to Toronto — later traded to Washington — Washington selected Nolan Baumgartner) Entry Drafts and cash for Eric Lindros, June 30, 1992. Traded to **NY Islanders** by **Quebec** with Quebec's first round choice (Todd Bertuzzi) in 1993 Entry Draft for Mark Fitzpatrick and NY Islanders' first round choice (Adam Deadmarsh) in 1993 Entry Draft, June 20, 1993. Traded to **Philadelphia** by **NY Islanders** with NY Islanders' sixth round choice (Dimitri Tertyshny) in 1995 Entry Draft for Tommy Soderstrom, September 22, 1994.

HILLIER, CRAIG — PIT.

Goaltender. Catches left. 6'1", 174 lbs. Born, Cole Harbour, N.S., February 28, 1978.
(Pittsburgh's 1st choice, 23rd overall, in 1996 Entry Draft).

			Regular Season								Playoffs						
Season	Club	Lea	GP	W	L	T	Mins	GA	SO	Avg	GP	W	L	Mins	GA	SO	Avg
1994-95	Ottawa	OHL	24	6	7	2	1078	69	1	3.84	....	....	....	....	....	....	....
1995-96a	Ottawa	OHL	44	24	14	3	2439	117	2	2.88	3	0	2	130	12	0	5.54
1996-97	Ottawa	OHL	36	23	6	4	2007	89	2	2.66	10	4	5	540	33	0	3.67

a OHL First All-Star Team (1996)

HIRSCH, COREY (HUHRSH) — VAN.

Goaltender. Catches left. 5'10", 160 lbs. Born, Medicine Hat, Alta., July 1, 1972.
(NY Rangers' 8th choice, 169th overall, in 1991 Entry Draft).

			Regular Season								Playoffs						
Season	Club	Lea	GP	W	L	T	Mins	GA	SO	Avg	GP	W	L	Mins	GA	SO	Avg
1988-89	Kamloops	WHL	32	11	12	2	1516	106	2	4.20	5	3	2	245	19	0	4.65
1989-90	Kamloops	WHL	*63	*48	13	0	3608	230	*3	3.82	*17	*14	3	*1043	60	0	*3.45
1990-91a	Kamloops	WHL	38	26	7	1	1970	100	3	*3.05	11	5	6	623	42	0	4.04
1991-92abcd	Kamloops	WHL	48	35	10	2	2732	124	*5	*2.72	*16	*11	5	954	35	*2	*2.20
1992-93	**NY Rangers**	**NHL**	**4**	**1**	**2**	**1**	**224**	**14**	**0**	**3.75**	....	....	....	....	....	....	....
efg	Binghamton	AHL	46	*35	4	5	2692	125	1	*2.79	14	7	7	831	46	0	3.32
1993-94	Cdn. National	....	45	24	17	3	2653	124	0	2.80	....	....	....	....	....	....	....
	Cdn. Olympic	....	8	5	2	1	495	17	0	2.06	....	....	....	....	....	....	....
	Binghamton	AHL	10	5	4	1	610	38	0	3.73	....	....	....	....	....	....	....
1994-95	Binghamton	AHL	57	31	20	5	3371	175	0	3.11	....	....	....	....	....	....	....
1995-96h	**Vancouver**	**NHL**	**41**	**17**	**14**	**6**	**2338**	**114**	**1**	**2.93**	**6**	**2**	**3**	**338**	**21**	**0**	**3.73**
1996-97	**Vancouver**	**NHL**	**39**	**12**	**20**	**4**	**2127**	**116**	**2**	**3.27**	....	....	....	....	....	....	....
	NHL Totals		**84**	**30**	**36**	**11**	**4689**	**244**	**3**	**3.12**	**6**	**2**	**3**	**338**	**21**	**0**	**3.73**

a WHL West First All-Star Team (1991, 1992)
b Canadian Major Junior Goaltender of the Year (1992)
c Memorial Cup All-Star Team (1992)
d Memorial Cup Tournament Top Goaltender (1992)
e Won Dudley "Red" Garrett Memorial Trophy (AHL Rookie of the Year) (1993)
f Shared Harry "Hap" Holmes Memorial Trophy (fewest goals-against - AHL) with Boris Rousson (1993)
g AHL First All-Star Team (1993)
h NHL All-Rookie Team (1996)

Traded to **Vancouver** by **NY Rangers** for Nathan Lafayette, April 7, 1995.

HITCHEN, ALLAN — VAN.

Goaltender. Catches left. 6'1", 195 lbs. Born, North York, Ont., March 6, 1978.

			Regular Season								Playoffs						
Season	Club	Lea	GP	W	L	T	Mins	GA	SO	Avg	GP	W	L	Mins	GA	SO	Avg
1995-96	Peterborough	OHL	17	4	6	3	727	60	0	4.95	3	2	1	126	9	0	4.29
1996-97	Peterborough	OHL	5	2	2	0	186	16	0	5.16	....	....	....	....	....	....	....
	London	OHL	25	5	15	0	1335	113	1	5.08	....	....	....	....	....	....	....

Signed as a free agent by **Vancouver**, October 3, 1996.

HODSON, KEVIN — DET.

Goaltender. Catches left. 6', 182 lbs. Born, Winnipeg, Man., March 27, 1972.

			Regular Season								Playoffs						
Season	Club	Lea	GP	W	L	T	Mins	GA	SO	Avg	GP	W	L	Mins	GA	SO	Avg
1990-91	S.S. Marie	OHL	30	18	11	0	1638	88	0	*3.22	10	*9	1	581	28	0	*2.89
1991-92	S.S. Marie	OHL	50	28	12	4	2722	151	0	3.33	18	12	6	1116	54	1	2.90
1992-93ab	S.S. Marie	OHL	26	18	5	2	1470	76	1	*3.10	14	11	2	755	34	0	2.70
	Indianapolis	IHL	14	5	9	0	777	53	0	4.09	....	....	....	....	....	....	....
1993-94	Adirondack	AHL	37	20	10	5	2082	102	2	2.94	3	0	2	89	10	0	6.77
1994-95	Adirondack	AHL	51	19	22	8	2731	161	1	3.54	4	0	4	237	14	0	3.53
1995-96	**Detroit**	**NHL**	**4**	**2**	**0**	**0**	**163**	**3**	**1**	**1.10**	....	....	....	....	....	....	....
	Adirondack	AHL	32	13	13	2	1654	87	0	3.16	3	0	2	150	8	0	3.21
1996-97	**Detroit**	**NHL**	**6**	**2**	**2**	**1**	**294**	**8**	**1**	**1.63**	....	....	....	....	....	....	....
	Quebec	IHL	2	1	1	0	118	7	0	3.54	....	....	....	....	....	....	....
	NHL Totals		**10**	**4**	**2**	**1**	**457**	**11**	**2**	**1.44**	....	....	....	....	....	....	....

a Memorial Cup All-Star Team (1993)
b Won Hap Emms Memorial Trophy (Memorial Cup Tournament Top Goaltender) (1993)

Signed as a free agent by **Chicago**, August 17, 1992. Signed as a free agent by **Detroit**, June 16, 1993.

HRUDEY, KELLY (ROO-dee) S.J.

Goaltender. Catches left. 5'10", 189 lbs. Born, Edmonton, Alta., January 13, 1961.
(NY Islanders' 2nd choice, 38th overall, in 1980 Entry Draft).

			Regular Season								Playoffs						
Season	Club	Lea	GP	W	L	T	Mins	GA	SO	Avg	GP	W	L	Mins	GA	SO	Avg
1978-79	Medicine Hat	WHL	57	12	34	7	3093	318	0	6.17	....	....	....	....	....	....	....
1979-80	Medicine Hat	WHL	57	25	23	4	3049	212	1	4.17	13	6	6	638	48	0	4.51
1980-81a	Medicine Hat	WHL	55	32	19	1	3023	200	4	3.97	4	1	3	244	17	0	4.18
	Indianapolis	CHL	....	....	....	....	....	....	....	....	2	....	....	135	8	0	3.56
1981-82bc	Indianapolis	CHL	51	27	19	4	3033	149	1	*2.95	13	11	2	842	34	*1	*2.42
1982-83bcd	Indianapolis	CHL	47	*26	17	1	2744	139	2	3.04	10	*7	3	*637	28	0	*2.64
1983-84	**NY Islanders**	**NHL**	**12**	**7**	**2**	**0**	**535**	**28**	**0**	**3.14**	....	....	....	....	....	....	....
	Indianapolis	CHL	6	3	2	1	370	21	0	3.40	....	....	....	....	....	....	....
1984-85	**NY Islanders**	**NHL**	**41**	**19**	**17**	**3**	**2335**	**141**	**2**	**3.62**	**5**	**1**	**3**	**281**	**8**	**0**	**1.71**
1985-86	**NY Islanders**	**NHL**	**45**	**19**	**15**	**8**	**2563**	**137**	**1**	**3.21**	**2**	**0**	**2**	**120**	**6**	**0**	**3.00**
1986-87	**NY Islanders**	**NHL**	**46**	**21**	**15**	**7**	**2634**	**145**	**0**	**3.30**	**14**	**7**	**7**	**842**	**38**	**0**	**2.71**
1987-88	**NY Islanders**	**NHL**	**47**	**22**	**17**	**5**	**2751**	**153**	**3**	**3.34**	**6**	**2**	**4**	**381**	**23**	**0**	**3.62**
1988-89	**NY Islanders**	**NHL**	**50**	**18**	**24**	**3**	**2800**	**183**	**0**	**3.92**	....	....	....	....	....	....	....
	Los Angeles	**NHL**	**16**	**10**	**4**	**2**	**974**	**47**	**1**	**2.90**	**10**	**4**	**6**	**566**	**35**	**0**	**3.71**
1989-90	**Los Angeles**	**NHL**	**52**	**22**	**21**	**6**	**2860**	**194**	**2**	**4.07**	**9**	**4**	**4**	**539**	**39**	**0**	**4.34**
1990-91	**Los Angeles**	**NHL**	**47**	**26**	**13**	**6**	**2730**	**132**	**3**	**2.90**	**12**	**6**	**6**	**798**	**37**	**0**	**2.78**
1991-92	**Los Angeles**	**NHL**	**60**	**26**	**17**	**13**	**3509**	**197**	**1**	**3.37**	**6**	**2**	**4**	**355**	**22**	**0**	**3.72**
1992-93	**Los Angeles**	**NHL**	**50**	**18**	**21**	**6**	**2718**	**175**	**2**	**3.86**	**20**	**10**	**10**	**1261**	**74**	**0**	**3.52**
1993-94	**Los Angeles**	**NHL**	**64**	**22**	**31**	**7**	**3713**	**228**	**1**	**3.68**	....	....	....	....	....	....	....
1994-95	**Los Angeles**	**NHL**	**35**	**14**	**13**	**5**	**1894**	**99**	**0**	**3.14**	....	....	....	....	....	....	....
1995-96	**Los Angeles**	**NHL**	**36**	**7**	**15**	**10**	**2077**	**113**	**0**	**3.26**	....	....	....	....	....	....	....
	Phoenix	IHL	1	0	1	0	50	5	0	5.95	....	....	....	....	....	....	....
1996-97	**San Jose**	**NHL**	**48**	**16**	**24**	**5**	**2631**	**140**	**0**	**3.19**	....	....	....	....	....	....	....
	NHL Totals		**649**	**267**	**249**	**86**	**36724**	**2112**	**16**	**3.45**	**84**	**36**	**46**	**5143**	**282**	**0**	**3.29**

a WHL Second All-Star Team (1981)
b CHL First All-Star Team (1982, 1983)
c Shared Terry Sawchuk Trophy (CHL's Leading Goaltender) with Rob Holland (1982, 1983)
d Won Tommy Ivan Trophy (CHL's Most Valuable Player) (1983)

Traded to **Los Angeles** by **NY Islanders** for Mark Fitzpatrick, Wayne McBean and future considerations (Doug Crossman, May 23, 1989) February 22, 1989. Signed as a free agent by **San Jose**, August 18, 1996.

HULTBERG, JOHN (HUHLT-buhrg) EDM.

Goaltender. Catches left. 5'11", 211 lbs. Born, Skokie, IL, April 25, 1977.
(Edmonton's 10th choice, 221st overall, in 1996 Entry Draft).

			Regular Season								Playoffs						
Season	Club	Lea	GP	W	L	T	Mins	GA	SO	Avg	GP	W	L	Mins	GA	SO	Avg
1995-96	Kingston	OHL	40	13	15	4	2036	125	1	3.68	3	1	2	206	17	0	4.95
1996-97	Kingston	OHL	8	1	5	1	398	33	0	4.97	....	....	....	....	....	....	....
	Barrie	OHL	27	14	4	3	1354	74	0	3.28	2	1	1	120	8	0	4.00

HURME, JANI (HOOR-meh) OTT.

Goaltender. Catches left. 6', 187 lbs. Born, Turku, Finland, January 7, 1975.
(Ottawa's 2nd choice, 58th overall, in 1997 Entry Draft).

			Regular Season								Playoffs						
Season	Club	Lea	GP	W	L	T	Mins	GA	SO	Avg	GP	W	L	Mins	GA	SO	Avg
1995-96	TPS	Fin.	16	....	....	....	946	34	2	2.16	10	....	....	545	22	2	2.42
	Kiekko-67	Fin. 2	16	....	....	....	968	39	1	2.42	....	....	....	....	....	....	....
	TPS	Fin. Jr.	13	....	....	....	777	34	1	2.63	....	....	....	....	....	....	....
1996-97	TPS	Fin.	48	31	11	6	2917	101	6	2.08	12	6	6	722	39	0	3.24

IRBE, ARTURS (UHR-bay, AHR-tuhrs) VAN.

Goaltender. Catches left. 5'8", 175 lbs. Born, Riga, Latvia, February 2, 1967.
(Minnesota's 11th choice, 196th overall, in 1989 Entry Draft).

			Regular Season								Playoffs						
Season	Club	Lea	GP	W	L	T	Mins	GA	SO	Avg	GP	W	L	Mins	GA	SO	Avg
1986-87	Dynamo Riga	USSR	2	....	....	....	27	1	0	2.22	....	....	....	....	....	....	....
1987-88a	Dynamo Riga	USSR	34	....	....	....	1870	86	4	2.69	....	....	....	....	....	....	....
1988-89	Dynamo Riga	USSR	40	....	....	....	2460	116	4	2.85	....	....	....	....	....	....	....
1989-90	Dynamo Riga	USSR	48	....	....	....	2880	115	2	2.42	....	....	....	....	....	....	....
1990-91	Dynamo Riga	USSR	46	....	....	....	2713	133	5	2.94	....	....	....	....	....	....	....
1991-92	**San Jose**	**NHL**	**13**	**2**	**6**	**3**	**645**	**48**	**0**	**4.47**	....	....	....	....	....	....	....
bc	Kansas City	IHL	32	24	7	1	1955	80	0	*2.46	*15	*12	3	914	44	0	*2.89
1992-93	**San Jose**	**NHL**	**36**	**7**	**26**	**0**	**2074**	**142**	**1**	**4.11**	....	....	....	....	....	....	....
	Kansas City	IHL	6	3	3	0	364	20	0	3.30	....	....	....	....	....	....	....
1993-94	**San Jose**	**NHL**	***74**	**30**	**28**	**16**	***4412**	**209**	**3**	**2.84**	**14**	**7**	**7**	**806**	**50**	**0**	**3.72**
1994-95	**San Jose**	**NHL**	**38**	**14**	**19**	**3**	**2043**	**111**	**4**	**3.26**	**6**	**2**	**4**	**316**	**27**	**0**	**5.13**
1995-96	**San Jose**	**NHL**	**22**	**4**	**12**	**4**	**1112**	**85**	**0**	**4.59**	....	....	....	....	....	....	....
	Kansas City	IHL	4	1	2	1	226	16	0	4.24	....	....	....	....	....	....	....
1996-97	**Dallas**	**NHL**	**35**	**17**	**12**	**3**	**1965**	**88**	**3**	**2.69**	**1**	**0**	**0**	**13**	**0**	**0**	**0.00**
	NHL Totals		**218**	**74**	**103**	**29**	**12251**	**683**	**11**	**3.35**	**21**	**9**	**11**	**1135**	**77**	**0**	**4.07**

a Soviet National League Rookie-of-the-Year (1988)
b IHL First All-Star Team (1992)
c Shared James Norris Memorial Trophy (fewest goals against - IHL) with Wade Flaherty (1992)

Played in NHL All-Star Game (1994)

Claimed by **San Jose** from **Minnesota** in Dispersal Draft, May 30, 1991. Signed as a free agent by **Dallas**, August 19, 1996.Signed as a free agent by **Vancouver**, August 5, 1997.

JABLONSKI, PAT CAR.

Goaltender. Catches right. 6', 180 lbs. Born, Toledo, OH, June 20, 1967.
(St. Louis' 6th choice, 138th overall, in 1985 Entry Draft).

			Regular Season								Playoffs						
Season	Club	Lea	GP	W	L	T	Mins	GA	SO	Avg	GP	W	L	Mins	GA	SO	Avg
1985-86	Windsor	OHL	29	6	16	4	1600	119	1	4.46	6	0	3	263	20	0	4.56
1986-87	Windsor	OHL	41	22	14	2	2328	128	*3	3.30	12	8	4	710	38	0	3.21
1987-88	Peoria	IHL	5	2	2	1	285	17	0	3.58	....	....	....	....	....	....	....
	Windsor	OHL	18	14	3	0	994	48	2	*2.90	9	*8	0	537	28	0	3.13
1988-89	Peoria	IHL	35	11	20	0	2051	163	1	4.77	3	0	2	130	13	0	6.00
1989-90	**St. Louis**	**NHL**	**4**	**0**	**3**	**0**	**208**	**17**	**0**	**4.90**	....	....	....	....	....	....	....
	Peoria	IHL	36	14	17	4	2023	165	0	4.89	4	1	3	223	19	0	5.11
1990-91	**St. Louis**	**NHL**	**8**	**2**	**3**	**3**	**492**	**25**	**0**	**3.05**	**3**	**0**	**0**	**90**	**5**	**0**	**3.33**
a	Peoria	IHL	29	23	3	2	1738	87	0	3.00	10	7	2	532	23	0	2.59
1991-92	**St. Louis**	**NHL**	**10**	**3**	**6**	**0**	**468**	**38**	**0**	**4.87**	....	....	....	....	....	....	....
	Peoria	IHL	8	6	1	1	493	29	1	3.53	....	....	....	....	....	....	....
1992-93	**Tampa Bay**	**NHL**	**43**	**8**	**24**	**4**	**2268**	**150**	**1**	**3.97**	....	....	....	....	....	....	....
1993-94	**Tampa Bay**	**NHL**	**15**	**5**	**6**	**3**	**834**	**54**	**0**	**3.88**	....	....	....	....	....	....	....
	St. John's	AHL	16	12	3	1	962	49	1	3.05	11	6	5	676	36	0	3.19
1994-95	Chicago	IHL	4	0	4	0	216	17	0	4.71	....	....	....	....	....	....	....
	Houston	IHL	3	1	1	1	179	9	0	3.01	....	....	....	....	....	....	....
1995-96	**St. Louis**	**NHL**	**1**	**0**	**0**	**0**	**8**	**1**	**0**	**7.50**	....	....	....	....	....	....	....
	Montreal	**NHL**	**23**	**5**	**9**	**6**	**1264**	**62**	**0**	**2.94**	**1**	**0**	**0**	**49**	**1**	**0**	**1.22**
1996-97	**Montreal**	**NHL**	**17**	**4**	**6**	**2**	**754**	**50**	**0**	**3.98**	....	....	....	....	....	....	....
	Phoenix	**NHL**	**2**	**0**	**1**	**0**	**59**	**2**	**0**	**2.03**	....	....	....	....	....	....	....
	NHL Totals		**123**	**27**	**58**	**18**	**6355**	**399**	**1**	**3.77**	**4**	**0**	**0**	**139**	**6**	**0**	**2.59**

a Shared James Norris Memorial Trophy (fewest goals against - IHL) with Guy Hebert (1991)

Traded to **Tampa Bay** by **St. Louis** with Steve Tuttle and Darin Kimble for future considerations, June 19, 1992. Traded to **Toronto** by **Tampa Bay** for cash, February 21, 1994. Claimed by **St. Louis** from **Toronto** in NHL Waiver Draft, October 2, 1995. Traded to **Montreal** by **St. Louis** for J.J. Daigneault, November 7, 1995. Traded to **Phoenix** by **Montreal** for Steve Cheredaryk, March 18, 1997. Signed as a free agent by **Carolina**, August 12, 1997.

JOHNSON, BRENT ST.L.

Goaltender. Catches left. 6'1", 175 lbs. Born, Farmington, MI, March 12, 1977.
(Colorado's 5th choice, 129th overall, in 1995 Entry Draft).

			Regular Season								Playoffs						
Season	Club	Lea	GP	W	L	T	Mins	GA	SO	Avg	GP	W	L	Mins	GA	SO	Avg
1994-95	Owen Sound	OHL	18	3	9	1	904	75	0	4.98	....	....	....	....	....	....	....
1995-96	Owen Sound	OHL	58	24	28	1	3211	243	1	4.54	6	2	4	371	29	0	4.69
1996-97	Owen Sound	OHL	50	20	28	1	2798	201	1	4.31	4	0	4	253	24	0	5.69

Traded to **St. Louis** by **Colorado** for San Jose's third round choice (previously acquired by St. Louis — Colorado selected Rick Berry) in 1997 Entry Draft and a conditional choice in 2000 Entry Draft, May 30, 1997.

JOSEPH, CURTIS EDM.

Goaltender. Catches left. 5'10", 185 lbs. Born, Keswick, Ont., April 29, 1967.

			Regular Season								Playoffs						
Season	Club	Lea	GP	W	L	T	Mins	GA	SO	Avg	GP	W	L	Mins	GA	SO	Avg
1988-89a	U. Wisconsin	WCHA	38	21	11	5	2267	94	1	2.49	....	....	....	....	....	....	....
1989-90	**St. Louis**	**NHL**	**15**	**9**	**5**	**1**	**852**	**48**	**0**	**3.38**	**6**	**4**	**1**	**327**	**18**	**0**	**3.30**
	Peoria	IHL	23	10	8	2	1241	80	0	3.87	....	....	....	....	....	....	....
1990-91	**St. Louis**	**NHL**	**30**	**16**	**10**	**2**	**1710**	**89**	**0**	**3.12**	....	....	....	....	....	....	....
1991-92	**St. Louis**	**NHL**	**60**	**27**	**20**	**10**	**3494**	**175**	**2**	**3.01**	**6**	**2**	**4**	**379**	**23**	**0**	**3.64**
1992-93	**St. Louis**	**NHL**	**68**	**29**	**28**	**9**	**3890**	**196**	**1**	**3.02**	**11**	**7**	**4**	**715**	**27**	***2**	**2.27**
1993-94	**St. Louis**	**NHL**	**71**	**36**	**23**	**11**	**4127**	**213**	**1**	**3.10**	**4**	**0**	**4**	**246**	**15**	**0**	**3.66**
1994-95	**St. Louis**	**NHL**	**36**	**20**	**10**	**1**	**1914**	**89**	**1**	**2.79**	**7**	**3**	**3**	**392**	**24**	**0**	**3.67**
1995-96	Las Vegas	IHL	15	12	2	1	874	29	1	1.99	....	....	....	....	....	....	....
	Edmonton	**NHL**	**34**	**15**	**16**	**2**	**1936**	**111**	**0**	**3.44**	....	....	....	....	....	....	....
1996-97	**Edmonton**	**NHL**	**72**	**32**	**29**	**9**	**4100**	**200**	**6**	**2.93**	**12**	**5**	**7**	**767**	**36**	**2**	**2.82**
	NHL Totals		**386**	**184**	**141**	**45**	**22023**	**1121**	**11**	**3.05**	**46**	**21**	**23**	**2826**	**143**	**4**	**3.04**

a WCHA First All-Star Team (1989)

Played in NHL All-Star Game (1994)

Signed as a free agent by **St. Louis**, June 16, 1989. Traded to **Edmonton** by **St. Louis** with the rights to Michael Grier for St. Louis' first round choices (previously acquired by Edmonton) in 1996 (Marty Reasoner) and 1997 (later traded to Los Angeles — Los Angeles selected Matt Zultek) Entry Drafts, August 4, 1995.

KEYES, TIM VAN.

Goaltender. Catches left. 5'11", 170 lbs. Born, Ganonoque, Ont., May 28, 1976.

			Regular Season								Playoffs						
Season	Club	Lea	GP	W	L	T	Mins	GA	SO	Avg	GP	W	L	Mins	GA	SO	Avg
1993-94	Kingston	OHL	6	0	2	0	171	16	0	5.61	....	....	....	....	....	....	....
1994-95	Kingston	OHL	16	7	2	2	750	56	0	4.48	1	0	0	27	5	0	11.11
1995-96	Ottawa	OHL	27	15	7	2	1497	73	1	2.93	3	0	2	110	12	0	6.55
1996-97	Ottawa	OHL	37	26	5	2	1990	87	2	2.62	17	10	5	929	50	0	3.23

Signed as a free agent by **Vancouver**, August 14, 1997.

KHABIBULIN, NIKOLAI (khah-bee-BOO-lihn) PHO.

Goaltender. Catches left. 6'1", 176 lbs. Born, Sverdlovsk, USSR, January 13, 1973.
(Winnipeg's 8th choice, 204th overall, in 1992 Entry Draft).

			Regular Season								Playoffs						
Season	Club	Lea	GP	W	L	T	Mins	GA	SO	Avg	GP	W	L	Mins	GA	SO	Avg
1988-89	Sverdlovsk	USSR	1	....	....	....	3	0	0	0.00	....	....	....	....	....	....	....
1989-90	Sverdlovsk Jrs.	USSR								UNAVAILABLE							
1990-91	Sputnik	USSR 3								UNAVAILABLE							
1991-92	CSKA	CIS	2	....	....	....	34	2	....	3.52	....	....	....	....	....	....	....
1992-93	CSKA	CIS	13	....	....	....	491	27	....	3.29	....	....	....	....	....	....	....
1993-94	CSKA	CIS	46	....	....	....	2625	116	....	2.65	3	....	....	193	11	....	3.42
	Russian Pen's	IHL	12	2	7	2	639	47	0	4.41	....	....	....	....	....	....	....
1994-95	Springfield	AHL	23	9	9	3	1240	80	0	3.87	....	....	....	....	....	....	....
	Winnipeg	**NHL**	**26**	**8**	**9**	**4**	**1339**	**76**	**0**	**3.41**	....	....	....	....	....	....	....
1995-96	**Winnipeg**	**NHL**	**53**	**26**	**20**	**3**	**2914**	**152**	**2**	**3.13**	**6**	**2**	**4**	**359**	**19**	**0**	**3.18**
1996-97	**Phoenix**	**NHL**	**72**	**30**	**33**	**6**	**4091**	**193**	**7**	**2.83**	**7**	**3**	**4**	**426**	**15**	**1**	**2.11**
	NHL Totals		**151**	**64**	**62**	**13**	**8344**	**421**	**9**	**3.03**	**13**	**5**	**8**	**785**	**34**	**1**	**2.60**

KHLOPTONOV, DENIS (khloh-POHT-nahv) FLA.

Goaltender. Catches left. 6'4", 198 lbs. Born, Moscow, USSR, January 27, 1978.
(Florida's 8th choice, 209th overall, in 1996 Entry Draft).

			Regular Season								Playoffs						
Season	Club	Lea	GP	W	L	T	Mins	GA	SO	Avg	GP	W	L	Mins	GA	SO	Avg
1995-96	CSKA	CIS Jr.								UNAVAILABLE							
1996-97	CSKA	Rus. 2	21	....	....	....	1260	42	0	2.00	....	....	....	....	....	....	....

KIDD, TREVOR — CGY.

Goaltender. Catches left. 6'2", 190 lbs. Born, Dugald, Man., March 29, 1972.
(Calgary's 1st choice, 11th overall, in 1990 Entry Draft).

			Regular Season								Playoffs						
Season	Club	Lea	GP	W	L	T	Mins	GA	SO	Avg	GP	W	L	Mins	GA	SO	Avg
1988-89	Brandon	WHL	32	11	13	1	1509	102	0	4.06	....	....	....	....	....	....	....
1989-90ab	Brandon	WHL	*63	24	32	2	*3676	254	2	4.15	....	....	....	....	....	....	....
1990-91	Brandon	WHL	30	10	19	1	1730	117	0	4.06	....	....	....	....	....	....	....
	Spokane	WHL	14	8	3	0	749	44	0	3.52	15	*14	1	926	32	2	*2.07
1991-92	Cdn. National	....	28	18	4	4	1349	79	2	3.51	....	....	....	....	....	....	....
	Cdn. Olympic	....	1	1	0	0	60	0	1	0.00	....	....	....	....	....	....	....
	Calgary	**NHL**	**2**	**1**	**1**	**0**	**120**	**8**	**0**	**4.00**	....	....	....	....	....	....	....
1992-93	Salt Lake	IHL	29	10	16	1	1696	111	1	3.93	....	....	....	....	....	....	....
1993-94	**Calgary**	**NHL**	**31**	**13**	**7**	**6**	**1614**	**85**	**0**	**3.16**	....	....	....	....	....	....	....
1994-95	**Calgary**	**NHL**	***43**	**22**	**14**	**6**	***2463**	**107**	**3**	**2.61**	**7**	**3**	**4**	**434**	**26**	**1**	**3.59**
1995-96	**Calgary**	**NHL**	**47**	**15**	**21**	**8**	**2570**	**119**	**3**	**2.78**	**2**	**0**	**1**	**83**	**9**	**0**	**6.51**
1996-97	**Calgary**	**NHL**	**55**	**21**	**23**	**6**	**2979**	**141**	**4**	**2.84**	....	....	....	....	....	....	....
	NHL Totals		**178**	**72**	**66**	**26**	**9746**	**460**	**10**	**2.83**	**9**	**3**	**5**	**517**	**35**	**1**	**4.06**

a WHL East First All-Star Team (1990)
b Canadian Major Junior Goaltender of the Year (1990)

KIPRUSOFF, MIIKKA (KIHP-ruh-sohf, MEE-kah) — S.J.

Goaltender. Catches left. 6', 176 lbs. Born, Turku, Finland, October 26, 1976.
(San Jose's 5th choice, 116th overall, in 1995 Entry Draft).

			Regular Season								Playoffs						
Season	Club	Lea	GP	W	L	T	Mins	GA	SO	Avg	GP	W	L	Mins	GA	SO	Avg
1994-95	TPS	Fin. Jr.	31	....	....	....	1896	92	....	2.91	....	....	....	....	....	....	....
	TPS	Fin.	4	....	....	....	240	12	0	3.00	2	....	....	120	7	....	3.50
1995-96	TPS	Fin. Jr.	3	....	....	....	180	9	....	3.00	....	....	....	....	....	....	....
	Kiekko-67	Fin. 2	5	....	....	....	300	7	....	1.40	....	....	....	....	....	....	....
	TPS	Fin.	12	....	....	....	550	38	0	4.14	3	....	....	114	4	....	2.11
1996-97	AIK	Swe.	42	....	....	....	2466	104	3	2.53	7	....	....	420	23	0	3.28

KNICKLE, RICK (kuh-NIHK-uhl)

Goaltender. Catches left. 5'10", 175 lbs. Born, Chatham, N.B., February 26, 1960.
(Buffalo's 7th choice, 116th overall, in 1979 Entry Draft).

			Regular Season								Playoffs						
Season	Club	Lea	GP	W	L	T	Mins	GA	SO	Avg	GP	W	L	Mins	GA	SO	Avg
1977-78	Brandon	WHL	49	34	5	7	2806	182	0	3.89	8	....	....	450	36	0	4.82
1978-79a	Brandon	WHL	38	26	3	8	2240	118	1	*3.16	16	12	3	886	41	*1	*2.78
1979-80	Brandon	WHL	33	11	14	1	1604	125	0	4.68	....	....	....	....	....	....	....
	Muskegon	IHL	16	....	....	....	829	52	0	3.76	3	....	....	156	17	0	6.54
1980-81b	Erie	EHL	43	....	....	....	2347	125	1	*3.20	8	....	....	446	14	0	*1.88
1981-82	Rochester	AHL	31	10	12	5	1753	108	1	3.70	3	0	2	125	7	0	3.37
1982-83	Flint	IHL	27	....	....	....	1638	92	2	3.37	3	....	....	193	10	0	3.11
	Rochester	AHL	4	0	3	0	143	11	0	4.64	....	....	....	....	....	....	....
1983-84c	Flint	IHL	60	32	21	5	3518	203	3	3.46	8	8	0	480	24	0	3.00
1984-85	Sherbrooke	AHL	14	7	6	0	780	53	0	4.08	....	....	....	....	....	....	....
	Flint	IHL	36	18	11	3	2018	115	2	3.42	7	3	4	401	27	0	4.04
1985-86	Saginaw	IHL	39	16	15	0	2235	135	2	3.62	3	2	1	193	12	0	3.73
1986-87	Saginaw	IHL	26	9	13	0	1413	113	0	4.80	5	1	4	329	21	0	3.83
1987-88	Flint	IHL	1	0	1	0	60	4	0	4.00	....	....	....	....	....	....	....
	Peoria	IHL	13	2	8	1	705	58	0	4.94	6	3	3	294	20	....	4.08
1988-89de	Fort Wayne	IHL	47	22	16	0	2716	141	1	*3.11	4	1	2	173	15	0	5.20
1989-90	Flint	IHL	55	25	24	1	2998	210	1	4.20	2	0	2	101	13	0	7.72
1990-91	Albany	IHL	14	4	6	2	679	52	0	4.59	....	....	....	....	....	....	....
	Springfield	AHL	9	6	0	2	509	28	0	3.30	....	....	....	....	....	....	....
1991-92c	San Diego	IHL	46	*28	13	4	2686	155	0	3.46	2	0	1	78	3	0	2.31
1992-93df	San Diego	IHL	41	33	4	4	2437	88	*4	*2.17	....	....	....	....	....	....	....
	Los Angeles	**NHL**	**10**	**6**	**4**	**0**	**532**	**35**	**0**	**3.95**	....	....	....	....	....	....	....
1993-94	**Los Angeles**	**NHL**	**4**	**1**	**2**	**0**	**174**	**9**	**0**	**3.10**	....	....	....	....	....	....	....
	Phoenix	IHL	25	8	9	3	1292	89	1	4.13	....	....	....	....	....	....	....
1994-95	Detroit	IHL	49	24	15	5	2725	134	*3	2.95	....	....	....	....	....	....	....
1995-96	Detroit	IHL	18	9	5	1	872	50	0	3.44	....	....	....	....	....	....	....
	Las Vegas	IHL	7	6	1	0	420	27	0	3.86	4	1	0	126	7	0	3.33
1996-97	Milwaukee	IHL	19	5	9	1	940	60	0	3.83	....	....	....	....	....	....	....
	NHL Totals		**14**	**7**	**6**	**0**	**706**	**44**	**0**	**3.74**	....	....	....	....	....	....	....

a WHL First All-Star Team (1979)
b EHL First All-Star Team (1981)
c IHL Second All-Star Team (1984, 1992)
d IHL First All-Star Team (1989, 1993)
e Won James Norris Memorial Trophy (fewest goals against - IHL) (1989)
f Shared James Norris Memorial Trophy (fewest goals against - IHL) with Clint Malarchuk (1993)

Signed as a free agent by **Montreal**, February 8, 1985. Signed as a free agent by **Los Angeles**, February 16, 1993.

KOLZIG, OLAF (KOHLT-zihg, OH-lahf) — WSH.

Goaltender. Catches left. 6'3", 225 lbs. Born, Johannesburg, South Africa, April 9, 1970.
(Washington's 1st choice, 19th overall, in 1989 Entry Draft).

			Regular Season								Playoffs						
Season	Club	Lea	GP	W	L	T	Mins	GA	SO	Avg	GP	W	L	Mins	GA	SO	Avg
1987-88	N. Westminster	WHL	15	6	5	0	650	48	1	4.43	3	0	3	149	11	0	4.43
1988-89	Tri-Cities	WHL	30	16	10	2	1671	97	1	*3.48	....	....	....	....	....	....	....
1989-90	**Washington**	**NHL**	**2**	**0**	**2**	**0**	**120**	**12**	**0**	**6.00**	....	....	....	....	....	....	....
	Tri-Cities	WHL	48	27	27	3	2504	250	1	4.38	6	4	0	318	27	0	5.09
1990-91	Baltimore	AHL	26	10	12	1	1367	72	0	3.16	....	....	....	....	....	....	....
	Hampton Rds.	ECHL	21	11	9	1	1248	71	2	3.41	3	1	2	180	14	0	4.66
1991-92	Baltimore	AHL	28	5	17	2	1503	105	1	4.19	....	....	....	....	....	....	....
	Hampton Rds.	ECHL	14	11	3	0	847	41	0	2.90	....	....	....	....	....	....	....
1992-93	**Washington**	**NHL**	**1**	**0**	**0**	**0**	**20**	**2**	**0**	**6.00**	....	....	....	....	....	....	....
	Rochester	AHL	49	25	16	4	2737	168	0	3.68	*17	9	8	*1040	61	0	3.52
1993-94	**Washington**	**NHL**	**7**	**0**	**3**	**0**	**224**	**20**	**0**	**5.36**	....	....	....	....	....	....	....
ab	Portland	AHL	29	16	8	5	1725	88	3	3.06	17	*12	5	1035	44	0	*2.55
1994-95	**Washington**	**NHL**	**14**	**2**	**8**	**2**	**724**	**30**	**0**	**2.49**	**2**	**1**	**0**	**44**	**1**	**0**	**1.36**
	Portland	AHL	2	1	0	1	125	3	0	1.44	....	....	....	....	....	....	....
1995-96	**Washington**	**NHL**	**18**	**4**	**8**	**2**	**897**	**46**	**0**	**3.08**	**5**	**2**	**3**	**341**	**11**	**0**	***1.94**
	Portland	AHL	5	5	0	0	300	7	1	1.40	....	....	....	....	....	....	....
1996-97	**Washington**	**NHL**	**29**	**8**	**15**	**4**	**1645**	**71**	**2**	**2.59**	....	....	....	....	....	....	....
	NHL Totals		**71**	**14**	**36**	**8**	**3630**	**181**	**2**	**2.99**	**7**	**3**	**3**	**385**	**12**	**0**	**1.87**

a Shared Harry "Hap" Holmes Trophy (fewest goals-against - AHL) with Byron Dafoe (1994)
b Won Jack Butterfield Trophy (Playoff MVP - IHL) (1994)

LABBE, JEAN-FRANCOIS (lah-BAY) — EDM.

Goaltender. Catches left. 5'9", 170 lbs. Born, Sherbrooke, Que., June 15, 1972.

			Regular Season								Playoffs						
Season	Club	Lea	GP	W	L	T	Mins	GA	SO	Avg	GP	W	L	Mins	GA	SO	Avg
1989-90	Trois-Rivieres	QMJHL	28	13	10	0	1499	106	1	4.24	3	1	1	132	8	0	3.64
1990-91	Trois-Rivieres	QMJHL	54	*35	14	0	2870	158	5	3.30	5	1	4	230	19	0	4.96
1991-92a	Trois-Rivieres	QMJHL	48	*31	13	3	2749	142	1	3.10	*15	*10	3	791	33	*1	*2.50
1992-93	Hull	QMJHL	46	26	18	2	2701	156	2	3.46	10	6	3	518	24	*1	*2.78
1993-94bcd	Thunder Bay	ColHL	52	*35	11	4	*2900	150	*2	*3.10	8	7	1	493	18	*2	*2.19
	P.E.I.	AHL	7	4	3	0	389	22	0	3.39	....	....	....	....	....	....	....
1994-95	P.E.I.	AHL	32	13	14	3	1817	94	2	3.10	....	....	....	....	....	....	....
1995-96	Cornwall	AHL	55	25	21	5	2972	144	3	2.91	8	3	5	471	21	1	2.68
1996-97efgh	Hershey	AHL	66	*34	22	9	3810	160	*6	*2.52	*23	*14	8	*1363	59	1	2.60

a QMJHL First All-Star Team (1992)
b ColHL First All-Star Team (1994)
c Named ColHL's Rookie of the Year (1994)
d Named ColHL's Outstanding Goaltender (1994)
e AHL First All-Star Team (1997)
f Won Harry "Hap" Holmes Memorial Trophy (fewest goals against - AHL) (1997)
g Won Baz Bastien Memorial Trophy (Top Goaltender - AHL) (1997)
h Won Les Cunningham Plaque (MVP - AHL) (1997)

Signed as a free agent by **Ottawa**, May 12, 1994. Traded to **Colorado** by **Ottawa** for a conditional draft choice, September 20, 1995. Signed as a free agent by **Edmonton**, August 8, 1997.

LABRECQUE, PATRICK (lah-BREHK)

Goaltender. Catches left. 6', 190 lbs. Born, Laval, Que., March 6, 1971.
(Quebec's 5th choice, 90th overall, in 1991 Entry Draft).

			Regular Season								Playoffs						
Season	Club	Lea	GP	W	L	T	Mins	GA	SO	Avg	GP	W	L	Mins	GA	SO	Avg
1990-91	St-Jean	QMJHL	59	17	34	6	3375	216	1	3.84	....	....	....	....	....	....	....
1991-92	Halifax	AHL	29	5	12	8	1570	114	0	4.36	....	....	....	....	....	....	....
1992-93	Greensboro	ECHL	11	6	3	2	650	31	0	2.86	1	0	1	59	5	0	5.08
	Halifax	AHL	20	3	12	2	914	76	0	4.99	....	....	....	....	....	....	....
1993-94	Cornwall	AHL	4	1	2	0	198	8	1	2.42	....	....	....	....	....	....	....
	Greensboro	ECHL	29	17	8	2	1609	89	0	3.32	1	0	0	22	4	0	10.80
1994-95	Fredericton	AHL	35	15	17	1	1913	104	1	3.26	*16	*10	6	*967	40	1	2.48
	Wheeling	ECHL	5	2	3	0	281	22	0	4.69	....	....	....	....	....	....	....
1995-96	**Montreal**	**NHL**	**2**	**0**	**1**	**0**	**98**	**7**	**0**	**4.29**	....	....	....	....	....	....	....
	Fredericton	AHL	48	23	18	6	2686	153	3	3.42	7	3	3	405	31	0	4.59
1996-97	Fredericton	AHL	12	1	7	1	601	31	0	3.09	....	....	....	....	....	....	....
	Quebec	IHL	9	2	6	0	482	29	0	3.61	....	....	....	....	....	....	....
	NHL Totals		**2**	**0**	**1**	**0**	**98**	**7**	**0**	**4.29**	....	....	....	....	....	....	....

Signed as a free agent by **Montreal**, June 21, 1994.

LACHER, BLAINE (LAW-kuhr)

Goaltender. Catches left. 6'1", 205 lbs. Born, Medicine Hat, Alta., September 5, 1970.

			Regular Season								Playoffs						
Season	Club	Lea	GP	W	L	T	Mins	GA	SO	Avg	GP	W	L	Mins	GA	SO	Avg
1991-92	Lake Superior	CCHA	9	5	3	0	410	22	0	3.22	....	....	....	....	....	....	....
1992-93	Lake Superior	CCHA	34	24	5	3	1915	86	2	2.70	....	....	....	....	....	....	....
1993-94	Lake Superior	CCHA	30	20	5	4	1785	59	6	*1.98	....	....	....	....	....	....	....
1994-95	**Boston**	**NHL**	**35**	**19**	**11**	**2**	**1965**	**79**	**4**	**2.41**	**5**	**1**	**4**	**283**	**12**	**0**	**2.54**
	Providence	AHL	1	0	1	0	59	3	0	3.03	....	....	....	....	....	....	....
1995-96	**Boston**	**NHL**	**12**	**3**	**5**	**2**	**671**	**44**	**0**	**3.93**	....	....	....	....	....	....	....
	Providence	AHL	9	3	5	0	462	30	0	3.90	....	....	....	....	....	....	....
	Cleveland	IHL	8	3	4	1	478	28	0	3.51	3	0	3	191	10	0	3.14
1996-97	Grand Rapids	IHL	11	1	8	1	510	32	0	3.76	....	....	....	....	....	....	....
	NHL Totals		**47**	**22**	**16**	**4**	**2636**	**123**	**4**	**2.80**	**5**	**1**	**4**	**283**	**12**	**0**	**2.54**

Signed as a free agent by **Boston**, June 2, 1994.

LaFOREST, MARK

Goaltender. Catches left. 5'11", 190 lbs. Born, Welland, Ont., July 10, 1962.

			Regular Season								Playoffs						
Season	Club	Lea	GP	W	L	T	Mins	GA	SO	Avg	GP	W	L	Mins	GA	SO	Avg
1981-82	Niagara Falls	OHL	24	10	13	1	1365	105	1	4.62	5	1	2	300	19	0	3.80
1982-83	North Bay	OHL	54	34	17	1	3140	195	0	3.73	8	4	4	474	31	0	3.92
1983-84	Adirondack	AHL	7	3	3	1	351	29	0	4.96	....	....	....	....	....	....	....
	Kalamazoo	IHL	13	4	5	2	718	48	1	4.01	....	....	....	....	....	....	....
1984-85	Adirondack	AHL	11	2	3	1	430	35	0	4.88	....	....	....	....	....	....	....
1985-86	**Detroit**	**NHL**	**28**	**4**	**21**	**0**	**1383**	**114**	**1**	**4.95**	....	....	....	....	....	....	....
	Adirondack	AHL	19	13	5	1	1142	57	0	2.99	*17	*12	5	*1075	58	0	3.24
1986-87	**Detroit**	**NHL**	**5**	**2**	**1**	**0**	**219**	**12**	**0**	**3.29**	....	....	....	....	....	....	....
a	Adirondack	AHL	37	23	8	0	2229	105	*3	2.83	....	....	....	....	....	....	....
1987-88	**Philadelphia**	**NHL**	**21**	**5**	**9**	**2**	**972**	**60**	**1**	**3.70**	**2**	**1**	**0**	**48**	**1**	**0**	**1.25**
	Hershey	AHL	5	2	1	2	309	13	0	2.52	....	....	....	....	....	....	....
1988-89	**Philadelphia**	**NHL**	**17**	**5**	**7**	**2**	**933**	**64**	**0**	**4.12**	....	....	....	....	....	....	....
	Hershey	AHL	3	2	0	0	185	9	0	2.92	12	7	5	744	27	1	2.18
1989-90	**Toronto**	**NHL**	**27**	**9**	**14**	**0**	**1343**	**87**	**0**	**3.89**	....	....	....	....	....	....	....
	Newmarket	AHL	10	6	4	0	604	33	1	3.28	....	....	....	....	....	....	....
1990-91ab	Binghamton	AHL	45	25	14	2	2452	129	0	3.16	9	3	4	442	28	1	3.80
1991-92	Binghamton	AHL	43	25	15	3	2559	146	1	3.42	11	7	4	662	34	0	3.08
1992-93	New Haven	AHL	30	10	18	1	1688	121	1	4.30	....	....	....	....	....	....	....
	Brantford	Col.	10	5	3	1	565	35	1	3.72	....	....	....	....	....	....	....
1993-94	**Ottawa**	**NHL**	**5**	**0**	**2**	**0**	**182**	**17**	**0**	**5.60**	....	....	....	....	....	....	....
	P.E.I.	AHL	43	9	25	5	2359	161	0	4.09	....	....	....	....	....	....	....
1994-95	Milwaukee	IHL	42	19	13	7	2325	123	2	3.17	15	8	7	937	40	*2	2.56
1995-96	Milwaukee	IHL	53	26	20	7	3079	191	0	3.72	5	2	3	315	18	0	3.42
1996-97	Binghamton	AHL	9	0	4	1	393	26	0	3.97	....	....	....	....	....	....	....
	Utica	ColHL	6	1	2	2	312	31	0	5.95	....	....	....	....	....	....	....
	NHL Totals		**103**	**25**	**54**	**4**	**5032**	**354**	**2**	**4.22**	**2**	**1**	**0**	**48**	**1**	**0**	**1.25**

a Won Baz Bastien Memorial Trophy (Top Goaltender - AHL) (1987, 1991)
b AHL Second All-Star Team (1991)

Signed as a free agent by **Detroit**, April 29, 1983. Traded to **Philadelphia** by **Detroit** for Philadelphia's second round choice (Bob Wilkie) in 1987 Entry Draft, June 13, 1987. Traded to **Toronto** by **Philadelphia** for Toronto's sixth round choice in 1991 Entry Draft and seventh round choice in 1991 Entry Draft, September 8, 1989. Traded to **NY Rangers** by **Toronto** with Tie Domi for Greg Johnston, June 28, 1990. Claimed by **Ottawa** from **NY Rangers** in Expansion Draft, June 18, 1992.

LAGRAND, SCOTT

Goaltender. Catches left. 6', 165 lbs. Born, Potsdam, NY, February 11, 1970.
(Philadelphia's 5th choice, 77th overall, in 1988 Entry Draft).

			Regular Season								Playoffs						
Season	Club	Lea	GP	W	L	T	Mins	GA	SO	Avg	GP	W	L	Mins	GA	SO	Avg
1989-90	Boston College	H.E.	24	17	4	0	1268	57	0	2.70	....	....	....	....	....	....	....
1990-91a	Boston College	H.E.	23	12	8	0	1153	63	2	3.28	....	....	....	....	....	....	....
1991-92b	Boston College	H.E.	30	11	16	2	1750	108	1	3.70	....	....	....	....	....	....	....
1992-93	Hershey	AHL	32	8	17	4	1854	145	0	4.69	....	....	....	....	....	....	....
1993-94	Hershey	AHL	40	16	13	3	2032	117	2	3.45	....	....	....	....	....	....	....
1994-95	Hershey	AHL	21	7	9	3	1104	71	1	3.86	....	....	....	....	....	....	....
	Atlanta	IHL	21	7	7	3	993	67	0	4.04	3	0	2	101	10	0	5.91
1995-96	Orlando	IHL	33	17	7	3	1618	103	1	3.82	3	0	0	51	1	0	1.17
1996-97	Orlando	IHL	35	16	10	2	1746	85	2	2.92	4	0	2	153	5	0	1.96

a Hockey East First All-Star Team (1991)
b NCAA East Second All-American Team (1992)

Traded to **Tampa Bay** by **Philadelphia** for Mike Greenlay, February 2, 1995.

LALIME, PATRICK (lah-LEEM) PIT.

Goaltender. Catches left. 6'2", 170 lbs. Born, St. Bonaventure, Que., July 7, 1974.
(Pittsburgh's 6th choice, 156th overall, in 1993 Entry Draft).

			Regular Season								Playoffs						
Season	Club	Lea	GP	W	L	T	Mins	GA	SO	Avg	GP	W	L	Mins	GA	SO	Avg
1992-93	Shawinigan	QMJHL	44	10	24	4	2467	192	0	4.67	....	....	....	....	....	....	....
1993-94	Shawinigan	QMJHL	48	22	20	0	2733	192	1	4.22	5	1	3	223	25	0	6.73
1994-95	Hampton Rds.	ECHL	26	15	7	3	1470	82	2	3.35	....	....	....	....	....	....	....
	Cleveland	IHL	23	7	10	4	1230	91	0	4.44	....	....	....	....	....	....	....
1995-96	Cleveland	IHL	41	20	12	7	2314	149	0	3.86	....	....	....	....	....	....	....
1996-97a	**Pittsburgh**	**NHL**	**39**	**21**	**12**	**2**	**2058**	**101**	**3**	**2.94**	....	....	....	....	....	....	....
	Cleveland	IHL	14	6	6	2	834	45	1	3.24	....	....	....	....	....	....	....
	NHL Totals		**39**	**21**	**12**	**2**	**2058**	**101**	**3**	**2.94**	....	....	....	....	....	....	....

a NHL All-Rookie Team (1997)

LAMBERT, JUDD N.J.

Goaltender. Catches left. 6'1", 175 lbs. Born, Richmond, B.C., June 3, 1974.
(New Jersey's 9th choice, 221st overall, in 1993 Entry Draft).

			Regular Season								Playoffs						
Season	Club	Lea	GP	W	L	T	Mins	GA	SO	Avg	GP	W	L	Mins	GA	SO	Avg
1993-94	Colorado	WCHA	11	6	4	0	620	33	0	3.19	....	....	....	....	....	....	....
1994-95	Colorado	WCHA	21	12	7	0	1060	57	*1	3.23	....	....	....	....	....	....	....
1995-96	Colorado	WCHA	19	16	1	2	1179	43	1	*2.19	....	....	....	....	....	....	....
1996-97	Colorado	WCHA	34	19	12	1	1993	101	3	3.04	....	....	....	....	....	....	....

LAMOTHE, MARC (luh-MAWTH) CHI.

Goaltender. Catches left. 6'1", 204 lbs. Born, New Liskeard, Ont., February 27, 1974.
(Montreal's 6th choice, 92nd overall, in 1992 Entry Draft).

			Regular Season								Playoffs						
Season	Club	Lea	GP	W	L	T	Mins	GA	SO	Avg	GP	W	L	Mins	GA	SO	Avg
1991-92	Kingston	OHL	42	10	25	2	2378	189	1	4.77	....	....	....	....	....	....	....
1992-93	Kingston	OHL	45	23	12	6	2489	162	1	3.91	15	8	5	753	48	1	3.82
1993-94	Kingston	OHL	48	23	20	5	2828	177	*2	3.76	6	2	2	224	12	0	3.21
1994-95	Fredericton	AHL	9	2	5	0	428	32	0	4.48	....	....	....	....	....	....	....
	Wheeling	ECHL	13	9	2	1	736	38	0	3.10	....	....	....	....	....	....	....
1995-96	Fredericton	AHL	23	5	9	3	1166	73	1	3.76	3	1	2	161	9	0	3.36
1996-97	Indianapolis	IHL	38	20	14	4	2271	100	1	2.64	1	0	0	20	1	0	3.00

Signed as a free agent by **Chicago**, September 26, 1996.

LANGKOW, SCOTT (LAING-kow) PHO.

Goaltender. Catches left. 5'11", 190 lbs. Born, Sherwood Park, Alta., April 21, 1975.
(Winnipeg's 2nd choice, 31st overall, in 1993 Entry Draft).

			Regular Season								Playoffs						
Season	Club	Lea	GP	W	L	T	Mins	GA	SO	Avg	GP	W	L	Mins	GA	SO	Avg
1991-92	Portland	WHL	1	0	0	0	33	2	0	3.46	....	....	....	....	....	....	....
1992-93	Portland	WHL	34	24	8	2	2064	119	2	3.46	9	6	3	535	31	0	3.48
1993-94a	Portland	WHL	39	27	9	1	2302	121	2	3.15	10	6	4	600	34	0	3.40
1994-95a	Portland	WHL	63	20	36	5	*3638	240	1	3.96	8	3	5	510	30	0	3.53
1995-96	**Winnipeg**	**NHL**	**1**	**0**	**0**	**0**	**6**	**0**	**0**	**0.00**	....	....	....	....	....	....	....
b	Springfield	AHL	39	18	15	6	2329	116	3	2.99	7	4	2	393	23	0	3.51
1996-97	Springfield	AHL	33	15	9	7	1928	85	0	2.64	....	....	....	....	....	....	....
	NHL Totals		**1**	**0**	**0**	**0**	**6**	**0**	**0**	**0.00**	....	....	....	....	....	....	....

a WHL West Second All-Star Team (1994, 1995)
b Shared Harry "Hap" Holmes Memorial Trophy (fewest goals against - AHL) with Manny Legace (1996)

LARIVEE, FRANCIS (la-RIHV-ay) TOR.

Goaltender. Catches left. 6'2", 198 lbs. Born, Montreal, Que., November 8, 1977.
(Toronto's 2nd choice, 50th overall, in 1996 Entry Draft).

			Regular Season								Playoffs						
Season	Club	Lea	GP	W	L	T	Mins	GA	SO	Avg	GP	W	L	Mins	GA	SO	Avg
1993-94	Val d'Or	QMJHL	36	....	....	....	1706	162	0	5.71	....	....	....	....	....	....	....
1994-95	Val d'Or	QMJHL	38	9	21	1	1795	132	0	4.41	....	....	....	....	....	....	....
1995-96	Val d'Or	QMJHL	*22	12	4	2	1162	73	0	3.77	....	....	....	....	....	....	....
	Laval	QMJHL	*39	9	24	1	2085	178	0	5.12	....	....	....	....	....	....	....
1996-97	Granby	QMJHL	1	1	0	0	60	1	0	1.00	1	0	0	50	4	0	4.80
	Laval	QMJHL	21	6	11	1	1068	77	1	4.33	....	....	....	....	....	....	....
	St. John's	AHL	4	3	1	0	244	9	0	2.21	2	0	0	1	0	0	0.00

LAROCQUE, MICHEL (lah-RAWK) S.J.

Goaltender. Catches left. 5'11", 198 lbs. Born, Lahr, West Germany, October 3, 1976.
(San Jose's 5th choice, 137th overall, in 1996 Entry Draft).

			Regular Season								Playoffs						
Season	Club	Lea	GP	W	L	T	Mins	GA	SO	Avg	GP	W	L	Mins	GA	SO	Avg
1995-96	Boston U.	H.E.	14	10	1	1	735	42	0	3.43	....	....	....	....	....	....	....
1996-97	Boston U.	H.E.	24	16	4	4	1466	58	0	*2.37	....	....	....	....	....	....	....

LEBLANC, RAYMOND (luh-BLAHNK)

Goaltender. Catches right. 5'10", 170 lbs. Born, Fitchburg, MA, October 24, 1964.

			Regular Season								Playoffs						
Season	Club	Lea	GP	W	L	T	Mins	GA	SO	Avg	GP	W	L	Mins	GA	SO	Avg
1983-84	Kitchener	OHL	54	....	....	....	2965	185	1	3.74	....	....	....	....	....	....	....
1984-85	Pinebridge	ACHL	40	....	....	....	2178	150	0	4.13	....	....	....	....	....	....	....
1985-86	Carolina	ACHL	42	....	....	....	2505	133	3	3.19	....	....	....	....	....	....	....
1986-87	Flint	IHL	64	33	23	1	3417	222	0	3.90	4	1	3	233	17	0	4.38
1987-88	Flint	IHL	62	27	19	8	3269	239	1	4.39	16	10	6	925	55	1	3.57
1988-89	Flint	IHL	15	5	9	0	852	67	0	4.72	....	....	....	....	....	....	....
	New Haven	AHL	1	0	0	0	20	3	0	9.00	....	....	....	....	....	....	....
	Saginaw	IHL	29	19	7	2	1655	99	0	3.59	1	0	1	5	9	0	3.05
1989-90	Indianapolis	IHL	23	15	6	2	1334	71	2	3.19	....	....	....	....	....	....	....
	Fort Wayne	IHL	15	3	3	3	680	44	0	3.88	3	0	2	139	11	0	4.75
1990-91	Fort Wayne	IHL	21	10	8	0	1072	69	0	3.86	....	....	....	....	....	....	....
	Indianapolis	IHL	3	2	0	0	145	7	0	2.90	1	0	0	19	1	0	3.20
1991-92	U.S. National	....	17	5	10	1	891	54	0	3.63	....	....	....	....	....	....	....
	U.S. Olympic	....	8	5	2	1	463	17	2	2.20	....	....	....	....	....	....	....
	Chicago	**NHL**	**1**	**1**	**0**	**0**	**60**	**1**	**0**	**1.00**	....	....	....	....	....	....	....
	Indianapolis	IHL	25	14	9	2	1468	84	2	3.43	....	....	....	....	....	....	....
1992-93	Indianapolis	IHL	56	23	22	7	3201	206	0	3.86	5	1	4	276	23	0	5.00
1993-94	Indianapolis	IHL	2	0	1	0	112	8	0	4.25	....	....	....	....	....	....	....
	Cincinnati	IHL	34	17	9	3	1779	104	1	3.51	5	0	3	159	9	0	3.39
1994-95	Chicago	IHL	44	19	14	6	2375	129	1	3.26	3	0	3	177	14	0	4.73
1995-96	Chicago	IHL	31	10	14	2	1614	97	0	3.61	....	....	....	....	....	....	....
1996-97	Chicago	IHL	38	15	14	2	1911	103	2	3.23	....	....	....	....	....	....	....
	NHL Totals		**1**	**1**	**0**	**0**	**60**	**1**	**0**	**1.00**	....	....	....	....	....	....	....

Signed as a free agent by **Chicago**, July 5, 1989.

LEGACE, MANNY (LEH-gah-see) CAR.

Goaltender. Catches left. 5'9", 162 lbs. Born, Toronto, Ont., February 4, 1973.
(Hartford's 5th choice, 188th overall, in 1993 Entry Draft).

			Regular Season								Playoffs						
Season	Club	Lea	GP	W	L	T	Mins	GA	SO	Avg	GP	W	L	Mins	GA	SO	Avg
1990-91	Niagara Falls	OHL	30	13	11	2	1515	107	0	4.24	4	1	1	119	10	0	5.04
1991-92	Niagara Falls	OHL	43	21	16	3	2384	143	0	3.60	14	8	5	791	56	0	4.25
1992-93a	Niagara Falls	OHL	48	22	19	3	2630	171	0	3.90	4	0	4	240	18	0	4.50
1993-94	Cdn. National	....	16	8	6	0	859	36	2	2.51	....	....	....	....	....	....	....
1994-95	Springfield	AHL	39	12	17	6	2169	128	2	3.54	....	....	....	....	....	....	....
1995-96bcd	Springfield	AHL	37	20	12	4	2196	83	*5	*2.27	4	1	3	220	18	0	4.91
1996-97	Springfield	AHL	36	17	14	5	2118	107	1	3.03	12	9	3	745	25	*2	2.01
	Richmond	ECHL	3	2	1	0	157	8	0	3.05	....	....	....	....	....	....	....

a OHL First All-Star Team (1993)
b AHL First All-Star Team (1996)
c Shared Harry "Hap" Holmes Memorial Trophy (fewest goals against - AHL) with Scott Langkow (1996)
d Won Baz Bastien Memorial Trophy (Top Goaltender - AHL) (1996)

LEITZA, BRIAN PIT.

Goaltender. Catches left. 6'2", 185 lbs. Born, Waukegin, IL, March 16, 1974.
(Pittsburgh's 14th choice, 284th overall, in 1994 Entry Draft).

			Regular Season								Playoffs						
Season	Club	Lea	GP	W	L	T	Mins	GA	SO	Avg	GP	W	L	Mins	GA	SO	Avg
1994-95	St. Cloud	WCHA	30	13	15	0	1626	93	0	3.43	....	....	....	....	....	....	....
1995-96	St. Cloud	WCHA	35	12	19	4	2068	129	2	3.74	....	....	....	....	....	....	....
1996-97	St. Cloud	WCHA	30	19	8	1	1738	93	0	3.21	....	....	....	....	....	....	....

LEMANOWICZ, DAVID FLA.

Goaltender. Catches left. 6'2", 190 lbs. Born, Edmonton, Alta., March 8, 1976.
(Florida's 9th choice, 218th overall, in 1995 Entry Draft).

			Regular Season								Playoffs						
Season	Club	Lea	GP	W	L	T	Mins	GA	SO	Avg	GP	W	L	Mins	GA	SO	Avg
1992-93	Spokane	WHL	16	3	11	0	738	61	1	4.96	....	....	....	....	....	....	....
1993-94	Spokane	WHL	6	1	2	0	256	21	0	4.92	....	....	....	....	....	....	....
1994-95	Spokane	WHL	16	5	5	1	761	41	2	3.23	....	....	....	....	....	....	....
1995-96a	Spokane	WHL	*62	*42	10	2	3362	162	*4	*2.89	18	9	6	1036	59	*2	3.42
1996-97	Carolina	AHL	33	11	18	0	1795	117	2	3.91	....	....	....	....	....	....	....
	Port Huron	ColHL	3	1	2	0	167	11	0	3.94	....	....	....	....	....	....	....

a WHL West First All-Star Team (1996)

LENARDUZZI, MIKE (leh-nahr-DOO-zee)

Goaltender. Catches left. 6'1", 165 lbs. Born, London, Ont., September 14, 1972.
(Hartford's 3rd choice, 57th overall, in 1990 Entry Draft).

			Regular Season								Playoffs						
Season	Club	Lea	GP	W	L	T	Mins	GA	SO	Avg	GP	W	L	Mins	GA	SO	Avg
1989-90	Oshawa	OHL	12	6	3	1	444	32	0	4.32	....	....	....	....	....	....	....
	S.S. Marie	OHL	20	....	....	....	1117	66	0	3.55	....	....	....	....	....	....	....
1990-91	S.S. Marie	OHL	35	19	8	3	1966	107	0	3.27	5	3	1	268	13	*1	2.91
1991-92	S.S. Marie	OHL	9	5	3	0	486	33	0	4.07	....	....	....	....	....	....	....
	Ottawa	OHL	18	5	12	1	986	60	1	3.65	....	....	....	....	....	....	....
	Sudbury	OHL	22	11	5	4	1201	84	2	4.20	11	4	7	651	38	0	3.50
	Springfield	AHL	....	....	....	....	....	....	....	....	1	0	0	39	2	0	3.08
1992-93	**Hartford**	**NHL**	**3**	**1**	**1**	**1**	**168**	**9**	**0**	**3.21**	....	....	....	....	....	....	....
	Springfield	AHL	36	10	17	5	1945	142	0	4.38	2	1	0	100	5	0	3.00
1993-94	**Hartford**	**NHL**	**1**	**0**	**0**	**0**	**21**	**1**	**0**	**2.86**	....	....	....	....	....	....	....
	Springfield	AHL	22	5	7	2	984	73	0	4.45	....	....	....	....	....	....	....
	Salt Lake	IHL	4	0	4	0	211	22	0	6.25	....	....	....	....	....	....	....
1994-95	London	ColHL	43	19	16	0	2198	172	0	4.69	5	1	2	274	20	0	4.37
1995-96	Saginaw	ColHL	43	14	15	3	2153	155	0	4.32	5	1	4	299	19	0	3.82
1996-97	Hershey	AHL	2	0	0	0	13	0	0	0.00	....	....	....	....	....	....	....
	Mobile	ECHL	37	15	10	8	1932	118	1	3.66	1	0	1	60	4	0	4.00
	NHL Totals		**4**	**1**	**1**	**1**	**189**	**10**	**0**	**3.17**	....	....	....	....	....	....	....

LINDSAY, EVAN CGY.

Goaltender. Catches left. 6'1", 180 lbs. Born, Calgary, Alta., May 15, 1979.
(Calgary's 2nd choice, 32nd overall, in 1997 Entry Draft).

			Regular Season								Playoffs						
Season	Club	Lea	GP	W	L	T	Mins	GA	SO	Avg	GP	W	L	Mins	GA	SO	Avg
1995-96	Olds	Jr. A	11	4	5	0	....	....	0	3.64	....	....	....	....	....	....	....
1996-97	Prince Albert	WHL	44	20	17	6	2651	153	1	3.46	4	0	4	240	16	0	4.00

LITTLE, NEIL — PHI.

Goaltender. Catches left. 6'1", 193 lbs. Born, Medicine Hat, Alta., December 18, 1971.
(Philadelphia's 10th choice, 226th overall, in 1991 Entry Draft).

			Regular Season								Playoffs						
Season	Club	Lea	GP	W	L	T	Mins	GA	SO	Avg	GP	W	L	Mins	GA	SO	Avg
1990-91	RPI	ECAC	18	9	8	0	1032	71	0	4.13							
1991-92	RPI	ECAC	28	11	11	3	1532	96	0	3.76							
1992-93ab	RPI	ECAC	*31	*19	9	3	*1801	88	0	2.93							
1993-94	RPI	ECAC	27	16	7	4	1570	88	0	3.36							
	Hershey	AHL	1	0	0	0	18	1	0	3.33							
1994-95	Hershey	AHL	19	5	7	3	919	60	0	3.91							
	Johnstown	ECHL	16	7	6	1	897	55	0	3.68	3	0	2	144	11	0	4.55
1995-96	Hershey	AHL	48	21	18	6	2680	149	0	3.34	1	0	1	60	4	0	4.02
1996-97	Philadelphia	AHL	54	31	12	7	3007	145	0	2.89	10	6	4	620	20	1	*1.94

a ECAC First All-Star Team (1993)
b NCAA East Second All-American Team (1993)

LITTMAN, DAVID

Goaltender. Catches left. 6', 183 lbs. Born, Cranston, RI, June 13, 1967.
(Buffalo's 12th choice, 211th overall, in 1987 Entry Draft).

			Regular Season								Playoffs						
Season	Club	Lea	GP	W	L	T	Mins	GA	SO	Avg	GP	W	L	Mins	GA	SO	Avg
1985-86	Boston College	H.E.	7	4	0	1	312	18	0	3.46							
1986-87	Boston College	H.E.	21	15	5	0	1182	68	0	3.45							
1987-88a	Boston College	H.E.	30	11	16	2	1726	116	0	4.03							
1988-89bc	Boston College	H.E.	*32	19	9	4	*1945	107	0	3.30							
1989-90	Rochester	AHL	14	5	6	1	681	37	0	3.26							
	Phoenix	IHL	18	8	7	2	1047	64	0	3.67							
1990-91	**Buffalo**	**NHL**	**1**	**0**	**0**	**0**	**36**	**3**	**0**	**5.00**							
de	Rochester	AHL	*56	*33	13	5	*3155	160	3	3.04	8	4	2	378	16	0	2.54
1991-92	**Buffalo**	**NHL**	**1**	**0**	**1**	**0**	**60**	**4**	**0**	**4.00**							
fg	Rochester	AHL	*61	*29	20	9	*3558	174	*3	2.93	15	8	7	879	43	*1	2.94
1992-93	**Tampa Bay**	**NHL**	**1**	**0**	**1**	**0**	**45**	**7**	**0**	**9.33**							
	Atlanta	IHL	44	23	12	4	2390	134	0	3.36	3	1	2	178	8	0	2.70
1993-94	Fredericton	AHL	16	8	7	0	872	63	0	4.33							
	Providence	AHL	25	10	11	3	1385	83	0	3.60							
1994-95	Richmond	ECHL	8	4	2	0	346	13	1	2.25	*17	*12	4	*952	37	*3	*2.33
1995-96	Los Angeles	IHL	43	17	16	5	2245	145	1	3.88							
1996-97	San Antonio	IHL	45	20	16	5	2437	138	2	3.40	4	1	3	230	11	0	2.87
	NHL Totals		**3**	**0**	**2**	**0**	**141**	**14**	**0**	**5.96**							

a Hockey East Second All-Star Team (1988)
b Hockey East First All-Star Team (1989)
c NCAA East Second All-American Team (1989)
d Shared Harry "Hap" Holmes Memorial Trophy (fewest goals against - AHL) with Darcy Wakaluk (1991)
e AHL First All-Star Team (1991)
f Won Harry "Hap" Holmes Memorial Trophy (fewest goals against - AHL) (1992)
g AHL Second All-Star Team (1992)

Signed as a free agent by **Tampa Bay**, August 27, 1992. Signed as a free agent by **Boston**, August 6, 1993.

LORENZ, DANNY

Goaltender. Catches left. 5'10", 187 lbs. Born, Murrayville, B.C., December 12, 1969.
(NY Islanders' 4th choice, 58th overall, in 1988 Entry Draft).

			Regular Season								Playoffs						
Season	Club	Lea	GP	W	L	T	Mins	GA	SO	Avg	GP	W	L	Mins	GA	SO	Avg
1986-87	Seattle	WHL	38	12	21	2	2103	199	0	5.68							
1987-88	Seattle	WHL	62	20	37	2	3302	314	0	5.71							
1988-89	Springfield	AHL	4	2	1	0	210	12	0	3.43							
a	Seattle	WHL	*68	31	33	4	*4003	240	*3	3.60							
1989-90a	Seattle	WHL	56	37	15	2	3226	221	0	4.11	13	6	7	751	40	0	3.21
1990-91	**NY Islanders**	**NHL**	**2**	**0**	**1**	**0**	**80**	**5**	**0**	**3.75**							
	Capital Dist.	AHL	17	5	9	2	940	70	0	4.47							
	Richmond	ECHL	20	6	9	2	1020	75	0	4.41							
1991-92	**NY Islanders**	**NHL**	**2**	**0**	**2**	**0**	**120**	**10**	**0**	**5.00**							
	Capital Dist.	AHL	53	22	22	7	3050	181	2	3.56	7	3	4	442	25	0	3.39
1992-93	**NY Islanders**	**NHL**	**4**	**1**	**2**	**0**	**157**	**10**	**0**	**3.82**							
	Capital Dist.	AHL	44	16	17	5	2412	146	1	3.63	4	0	3	219	12	0	3.29
1993-94	Salt Lake	IHL	20	4	12	0	982	91	0	5.56							
	Springfield	AHL	14	5	7	1	801	59	0	4.42	2	0	0	35	0	0	0.00
1994-95	Cincinnati	IHL	41	24	10	3	2222	126	0	3.40	5	2	3	308	16	0	3.12
1995-96	Cincinnati	IHL	46	28	12	5	2694	139	1	3.10	5	1	2	199	11	0	3.31
1996-97	Milwaukee	IHL	67	33	27	6	3903	221	0	3.40	3	0	3	187	11	0	3.53
	NHL Totals		**8**	**1**	**5**	**0**	**357**	**25**	**0**	**4.20**							

a WHL West First All-Star Team (1989, 1990)

Signed as a free agent by **Florida**, June 14, 1994.

LUONGO, ROBERTO — (loo-WAHN-goh) NYI

Goaltender. Catches left. 6'3", 181 lbs. Born, St-Leonard, Que., April 4, 1979.
(NY Islanders' 1st choice, 4th overall, in 1997 Entry Draft).

			Regular Season								Playoffs						
Season	Club	Lea	GP	W	L	T	Mins	GA	SO	Avg	GP	W	L	Mins	GA	SO	Avg
1995-96	Val d'Or	QMJHL	23	6	11	4	....	....	....	3.72	3	0	1	1195	74	0	4.48
1996-97	Val d'Or	QMJHL	60	32	22	2	3311	172	2	3.12	13	8	5	776	44	0	3.40

MacDONALD, AARON — FLA.

Goaltender. Catches left. 6'1", 193 lbs. Born, Grand Prairie, Alta., August 29, 1977.
(Florida's 2nd choice, 36th overall, in 1995 Entry Draft).

			Regular Season								Playoffs						
Season	Club	Lea	GP	W	L	T	Mins	GA	SO	Avg	GP	W	L	Mins	GA	SO	Avg
1993-94	Swift Current	WHL	18	6	6	0	710	48	0	4.06							
1994-95	Swift Current	WHL	53	24	20	6	2957	177	4	3.59	6	2	4	393	18	0	2.75
1995-96	Swift Current	WHL	29	14	12	2	1657	98	0	3.55							
	Calgary	WHL	19	2	14	1	1025	84	0	4.92							
1996-97	Calgary	WHL	30	6	19	3	1679	112	0	4.00	6	2	4	360	24	0	4.00
	Kelowna	WHL	23	17	6	0	1364	76	0	3.34							

MacDONALD, TODD — FLA.

Goaltender. Catches left. 6', 167 lbs. Born, Charlottetown, P.E.I., July 5, 1975.
(Florida's 7th choice, 109th overall, in 1993 Entry Draft).

			Regular Season								Playoffs						
Season	Club	Lea	GP	W	L	T	Mins	GA	SO	Avg	GP	W	L	Mins	GA	SO	Avg
1992-93	Tacoma	WHL	19	6	6	0	823	59	0	4.30							
1993-94	Tacoma	WHL	29	13	10	2	1606	109	1	4.07							
1994-95a	Tacoma	WHL	60	*35	21	2	3433	179	3	3.13	4	1	3	255	13	0	3.06
1995-96	Carolina	AHL	18	3	12	2	980	78	0	4.78							
	Detroit	ColHL	2	1	1	0	120	8	0	4.01	2	1	1	133	3	0	1.36
1996-97	Carolina	AHL	1	0	1	0	58	4	0	4.14							
	Cincinnati	IHL	31	11	9	5	1616	73	2	2.71	1	0	0	20	1	0	3.00

a WHL West First All-Star Team (1995)

MADELEY, DARRIN — (MAY-duh-lee)

Goaltender. Catches left. 5'11", 170 lbs. Born, Holland Landing, Ont., February 25, 1968.

			Regular Season								Playoffs						
Season	Club	Lea	GP	W	L	T	Mins	GA	SO	Avg	GP	W	L	Mins	GA	SO	Avg
1989-90	Lake Superior	CCHA	30	21	7	1	1683	68	1	2.42							
1990-91a	Lake Superior	CCHA	36	*29	3	3	2137	93	1	*2.61							
1991-92abc	Lake Superior	CCHA	36	23	6	4	2144	69	2	*2.05							
1992-93	**Ottawa**	**NHL**	**2**	**0**	**2**	**0**	**90**	**10**	**0**	**6.67**							
	New Haven	AHL	41	10	16	9	2295	127	0	3.32							
1993-94	**Ottawa**	**NHL**	**32**	**3**	**18**	**5**	**1583**	**115**	**0**	**4.36**							
	P.E.I.	AHL	6	0	4	0	270	26	0	5.77							
1994-95	**Ottawa**	**NHL**	**5**	**1**	**3**	**0**	**255**	**15**	**0**	**3.53**							
	P.E.I.	AHL	3	1	1	1	185	8	0	2.59							
	Detroit	IHL	9	7	2	0	498	20	1	2.41							
1995-96	P.E.I.	AHL	1	1	0	0	60	4	0	4.00							
	Detroit	IHL	40	16	14	4	2047	108	0	3.17	7	3	3	355	23	0	3.89
1996-97	Detroit	IHL	4	2	0	0	177	11	0	3.72							
	Saint John	AHL	46	11	18	11	2315	124	0	3.21	2	0	0	57	0	0	0.00
	NHL Totals		**39**	**4**	**23**	**5**	**1928**	**140**	**0**	**4.36**							

a NCAA West First All-American Team (1991, 1992)
b NCAA Final Four All-Tournament Team (1992)
c CCHA First All-Star Team (1992)
d AHL Second All-Star Team (1993)

Signed as a free agent by **Ottawa**, June 20, 1992. Signed as a free agent by **San Jose**, October 22, 1996.

MARACLE, NORM — (MAHR-ah-cuhl) DET.

Goaltender. Catches left. 5'9", 175 lbs. Born, Belleville, Ont., October 2, 1974.
(Detroit's 6th choice, 126th overall, in 1993 Entry Draft).

			Regular Season								Playoffs						
Season	Club	Lea	GP	W	L	T	Mins	GA	SO	Avg	GP	W	L	Mins	GA	SO	Avg
1991-92	Saskatoon	WHL	29	13	6	3	1529	87	1	3.41	15	9	5	860	37	0	3.38
1992-93a	Saskatoon	WHL	53	27	18	3	1939	160	1	3.27	9	4	5	569	33	0	3.48
1993-94bcd	Saskatoon	WHL	56	*41	13	1	3219	148	2	2.76	16	*11	5	940	48	*1	3.06
1994-95	Adirondack	AHL	39	12	15	2	1997	119	0	3.57							
1995-96	Adirondack	AHL	54	24	18	6	2949	135	2	2.75	1	0	1	30	4	0	8.11
1996-97e	Adirondack	AHL	*68	*34	22	9	*3843	173	5	2.70	4	1	3	191	10	1	3.13

a WHL East Second All-Star Team (1993)
b WHL East First All-Star Team (1994)
c Canadian Major Junior First All-Star Team (1994)
d Canadian Major Junior Goaltender of the Year (1994)
e AHL Second All-Star Team (1997)

MASON, CHRIS — ANA.

Goaltender. Catches left. 6', 200 lbs. Born, Red Deer, Alta., April 20, 1976.
(New Jersey's 7th choice, 122nd overall, in 1995 Entry Draft).

			Regular Season								Playoffs						
Season	Club	Lea	GP	W	L	T	Mins	GA	SO	Avg	GP	W	L	Mins	GA	SO	Avg
1993-94	Victoria	WHL	3	0	3	0	129	16	0	7.44							
1994-95	Prince George	WHL	44	8	30	1	2288	192	1	5.03							
1995-96	Prince George	WHL	59	16	37	1	3289	236	1	4.31							
1996-97	Prince George	WHL	50	19	24	4	2851	172	2	3.62	15	9	6	938	44	*1	2.81

Signed as a free agent by **Anaheim**, June 27, 1997.

McARTHUR, MARK — NYI

Goaltender. Catches left. 5'10", 175 lbs. Born, East York, Ont., November 16, 1975.
(NY Islanders' 5th choice, 112th overall, in 1994 Entry Draft).

			Regular Season								Playoffs						
Season	Club	Lea	GP	W	L	T	Mins	GA	SO	Avg	GP	W	L	Mins	GA	SO	Avg
1992-93	Guelph	OHL	35	14	14	3	1853	180	0	5.83							
1993-94	Guelph	OHL	51	25	18	5	2936	201	0	4.11	9	4	5	561	38	0	4.06
1994-95a	Guelph	OHL	48	*34	8	4	2776	130	1	*2.81	13	9	4	797	44	0	3.31
1995-96b	Utah	IHL	26	12	12	0	1482	77	0	3.12							
1996-97	Utah	IHL	56	28	20	6	3111	155	3	2.99							

a OHL Second All-Star Team (1995)
b Shared James Norris Memorial Trophy (fewest goals against - IHL) with Tommy Salo (1996)

McINERNEY, EOIN — (MAK-ih-NEHR-nee, OH-ehn) DAL.

Goaltender. Catches left. 5'10", 179 lbs. Born, Chatham, Ont., May 27, 1977.
(Dallas' 6th choice, 166th overall, in 1996 Entry Draft).

			Regular Season								Playoffs						
Season	Club	Lea	GP	W	L	T	Mins	GA	SO	Avg	GP	W	L	Mins	GA	SO	Avg
1994-95	London	OHL	28	2	15	1	1171	100	0	5.12	2	0	1	75	8	0	6.40
1995-96	London	OHL	50	3	34	3	2718	262	0	5.78							
1996-97	London	OHL	11	1	8	1	587	47	0	4.80							
	Sarnia	OHL	23	11	6	2	1109	73	0	3.95	5	1	0	143	4	1	1.68

McLEAN, JASON — NYR

Goaltender. Catches left. 6', 200 lbs. Born, Regina, Sask., September 3, 1979.
(NY Rangers' 5th choice, 126th overall, in 1997 Entry Draft).

			Regular Season								Playoffs						
Season	Club	Lea	GP	W	L	T	Mins	GA	SO	Avg	GP	W	L	Mins	GA	SO	Avg
1995-96	Moose Jaw	WHL	11	1	7	1	544	38	0	4.19							
1996-97	Moose Jaw	WHL	19	7	7	2	1014	60	0	3.55							

McLEAN, KIRK — VAN.

Goaltender. Catches left. 6', 195 lbs. Born, Willowdale, Ont., June 26, 1966.
(New Jersey's 6th choice, 107th overall, in 1984 Entry Draft).

			Regular Season								Playoffs						
Season	Club	Lea	GP	W	L	T	Mins	GA	SO	Avg	GP	W	L	Mins	GA	SO	Avg
1983-84	Oshawa	OHL	17	5	9	0	940	67	0	4.28							
1984-85	Oshawa	OHL	47	23	17	2	2581	143	1	*3.32	5	1	3	271	21	0	4.65
1985-86	**New Jersey**	**NHL**	**2**	**1**	**1**	**0**	**111**	**11**	**0**	**5.95**							
	Oshawa	OHL	51	24	21	2	2830	169	1	3.58	4	1	2	201	18	0	5.37
1986-87	**New Jersey**	**NHL**	**4**	**1**	**1**	**0**	**160**	**10**	**0**	**3.75**							
	Maine	AHL	45	15	23	4	2606	140	1	3.22							
1987-88	**Vancouver**	**NHL**	**41**	**11**	**27**	**3**	**2380**	**147**	**1**	**3.71**							
1988-89	**Vancouver**	**NHL**	**42**	**20**	**17**	**3**	**2477**	**127**	**4**	**3.08**	**5**	**2**	**3**	**302**	**18**	**0**	**3.58**
1989-90	**Vancouver**	**NHL**	***63**	**21**	**30**	**10**	***3739**	**216**	**0**	**3.47**							
1990-91	**Vancouver**	**NHL**	**41**	**10**	**22**	**3**	**1969**	**131**	**0**	**3.99**	**2**	**1**	**1**	**123**	**7**	**0**	**3.41**
1991-92a	**Vancouver**	**NHL**	**65**	***38**	**17**	**9**	**3852**	**176**	***5**	**2.74**	**13**	**6**	**7**	**785**	**33**	***2**	**2.52**
1992-93	**Vancouver**	**NHL**	**54**	**28**	**21**	**5**	**3261**	**184**	**3**	**3.39**	**12**	**6**	**6**	**754**	**42**	**0**	**3.34**
1993-94	**Vancouver**	**NHL**	**52**	**23**	**26**	**3**	**3128**	**156**	**3**	**2.99**	***24**	**15**	**9**	***1544**	**59**	***4**	**2.29**
1994-95	**Vancouver**	**NHL**	**40**	**18**	**12**	**10**	**2374**	**109**	**1**	**2.75**	**11**	**4**	**7**	**660**	**36**	**0**	**3.27**
1995-96	**Vancouver**	**NHL**	**45**	**15**	**21**	**9**	**2645**	**156**	**2**	**3.54**	**1**	**0**	**1**	**21**	**3**	**0**	**8.57**
1996-97	**Vancouver**	**NHL**	**44**	**21**	**18**	**3**	**2581**	**138**	**0**	**3.21**							
	NHL Totals		**493**	**207**	**213**	**58**	**28677**	**1561**	**19**	**3.27**	**68**	**34**	**34**	**4189**	**198**	**6**	**2.84**

a NHL Second All-Star Team (1992)

Played in NHL All-Star Game (1990, 1992)

Traded to **Vancouver** by **New Jersey** with Greg Adams for Patrik Sundstrom and Vancouver's fourth round choice (Matt Ruchty) in 1988 Entry Draft, September 15, 1987.

McLENNAN, JAMIE — ST.L.

Goaltender. Catches left. 6', 190 lbs. Born, Edmonton, Alta., June 30, 1971.
(NY Islanders' 3rd choice, 48th overall, in 1991 Entry Draft).

			Regular Season								Playoffs						
Season	Club	Lea	GP	W	L	T	Mins	GA	SO	Avg	GP	W	L	Mins	GA	SO	Avg
1989-90	Lethbridge	WHL	34	20	4	2	1690	110	1	3.91	13	6	5	677	44	0	3.90
1990-91a	Lethbridge	WHL	56	32	18	4	3230	205	0	3.81	*16	8	8	*970	56	0	3.46
1991-92	Capital Dist.	AHL	18	4	10	2	952	60	1	3.78	....	....	....	....	....	....	....
	Richmond	ECHL	32	16	12	2	1837	114	0	3.72	....	....	....	....	....	....	....
1992-93	Capital Dist.	AHL	38	17	14	6	2171	117	1	3.23	1	0	1	20	5	0	15.00
1993-94	**NY Islanders**	**NHL**	**22**	**8**	**7**	**6**	**1287**	**61**	**0**	**2.84**	**2**	**0**	**1**	**82**	**6**	**0**	**4.39**
	Salt Lake	IHL	24	8	12	2	1320	80	0	3.64	....	....	....	....	....	....	....
1994-95	**NY Islanders**	**NHL**	**21**	**6**	**11**	**2**	**1185**	**67**	**0**	**3.39**	....	....	....	....	....	....	....
	Denver	IHL	4	3	0	1	239	12	0	3.00	11	8	2	640	23	1	*2.15
1995-96	**NY Islanders**	**NHL**	**13**	**3**	**9**	**1**	**636**	**39**	**0**	**3.68**	....	....	....	....	....	....	....
	Utah	IHL	14	9	2	2	728	29	0	2.39	....	....	....	....	....	....	....
	Worcester	AHL	22	14	7	1	1216	57	0	2.81	2	0	2	119	8	0	4.04
1996-97	Worcester	AHL	39	18	13	4	2151	100	2	2.79	4	2	2	261	16	0	3.67
	NHL Totals		**56**	**17**	**27**	**9**	**3108**	**167**	**0**	**3.22**	**2**	**0**	**1**	**82**	**6**	**0**	**4.39**

a WHL East First All-Star Team (1991)

Signed as a free agent by **St. Louis**, July 15, 1996.

MIKLENDA, JAROSLAV (mih-KLEHN-da) — OTT.

Goaltender. Catches left. 6'1", 176 lbs. Born, Uherske Hradiste, Czech., March 7, 1974.
(Ottawa's 7th choice, 146th overall, in 1992 Entry Draft).

			Regular Season								Playoffs						
Season	Club	Lea	GP	W	L	T	Mins	GA	SO	Avg	GP	W	L	Mins	GA	SO	Avg
1991-92	Olomouc	Czech.	1	....	....	....	36	6	0	9.99	....	....	....	....	....	....	....
1992-93	Olomouc	Czech.	5	....	....	....	285	22	....	4.63	....	....	....	....	....	....	....
1993-94	TJ Vitkovice	Czech.	10	....	....	....	555	25	0	2.71	....	....	....	....	....	....	....
1994-95	Presov	Czech. 2	8	....	....	....	428	20	....	2.80	....	....	....	....	....	....	....
1995-96	Olomouc	Czech.	1	....	....	....	60	6	0	6.00	....	....	....	....	....	....	....
	Sumperk	Czech. 2	20	....	....	....	1200	54	....	2.70	....	....	....	....	....	....	....
1996-97	Sumperk	Czech. 2	21	....	....	....	1260	43	....	2.05	....	....	....	....	....	....	....

MILLER, AREN — DET.

Goaltender. Catches left. 6'2", 208 lbs. Born, Oxbow, Sask., January 13, 1978.
(Detroit's 2nd choice, 52nd overall, in 1996 Entry Draft).

			Regular Season								Playoffs						
Season	Club	Lea	GP	W	L	T	Mins	GA	SO	Avg	GP	W	L	Mins	GA	SO	Avg
1995-96	Spokane	WHL	23	8	7	2	965	50	1	3.11	3	0	3	81	8	0	5.93
1996-97	Spokane	WHL	52	22	20	3	2834	151	3	3.20	9	4	5	555	28	*1	3.03

MINARD, MIKE — EDM.

Goaltender. Catches left. 6'3", 205 lbs. Born, Owen Sound, Ont., November 1, 1976.
(Edmonton's 4th choice, 83rd overall, in 1995 Entry Draft).

			Regular Season								Playoffs						
Season	Club	Lea	GP	W	L	T	Mins	GA	SO	Avg	GP	W	L	Mins	GA	SO	Avg
1994-95	Chilliwack	Jr. A	40	....	....	....	2330	136	0	3.50	....	....	....	....	....	....	....
1995-96	Barrie	OHL	1	0	1	0	52	8	0	9.23	....	....	....	....	....	....	....
	Detroit	OHL	42	25	10	4	2314	128	2	3.32	17	9	6	922	55	1	3.58
1996-97	Hamilton	AHL	3	1	1	0	100	7	0	4.20	....	....	....	....	....	....	....
	Wheeling	ECHL	23	3	7	1	899	69	0	4.60	3	0	2	148	16	0	6.47

MOOG, ANDY (MOHG) — MTL.

Goaltender. Catches left. 5'8", 175 lbs. Born, Penticton, B.C., February 18, 1960.
(Edmonton's 6th choice, 132nd overall, in 1980 Entry Draft).

			Regular Season								Playoffs						
Season	Club	Lea	GP	W	L	T	Mins	GA	SO	Avg	GP	W	L	Mins	GA	SO	Avg
1978-79	Billings	WHL	26	13	5	4	1306	90	4	4.13	5	1	3	229	21	0	5.50
1979-80a	Billings	WHL	46	23	14	1	2435	149	1	3.67	3	2	1	190	10	0	3.16
1980-81	**Edmonton**	**NHL**	**7**	**3**	**3**	**0**	**313**	**20**	**0**	**3.83**	**9**	**5**	**4**	**526**	**32**	**0**	**3.65**
	Wichita	CHL	29	14	13	1	1602	89	0	3.33	5	3	2	300	16	0	3.20
1981-82	**Edmonton**	**NHL**	**8**	**3**	**5**	**0**	**399**	**32**	**0**	**4.81**	....	....	....	....	....	....	....
b	Wichita	CHL	40	23	13	3	2391	119	1	2.99	7	3	4	434	23	0	3.18
1982-83	**Edmonton**	**NHL**	**50**	**33**	**8**	**7**	**2833**	**167**	**1**	**3.54**	**16**	**11**	**5**	**949**	**48**	**0**	**3.03**
1983-84	**Edmonton**	**NHL**	**38**	**27**	**8**	**1**	**2212**	**139**	**1**	**3.77**	**7**	**4**	**0**	**263**	**12**	**0**	**2.74** ♦
1984-85	**Edmonton**	**NHL**	**39**	**22**	**9**	**3**	**2019**	**111**	**1**	**3.30**	**2**	**0**	**0**	**20**	**0**	**0**	**0.00** ♦
1985-86	**Edmonton**	**NHL**	**47**	**27**	**9**	**7**	**2664**	**164**	**1**	**3.69**	**1**	**1**	**0**	**60**	**1**	**0**	**1.00**
1986-87	**Edmonton**	**NHL**	**46**	**28**	**11**	**3**	**2461**	**144**	**0**	**3.51**	**2**	**2**	**0**	**120**	**8**	**0**	**4.00** ♦
1987-88	Cdn. National	....	27	10	7	5	1438	86	0	3.58	....	....	....	....	....	....	....
	Cdn. Olympic	....	4	4	0	0	240	9	1	2.25	....	....	....	....	....	....	....
	Boston	**NHL**	**6**	**4**	**2**	**0**	**360**	**17**	**1**	**2.83**	**7**	**1**	**4**	**354**	**25**	**0**	**4.24**
1988-89	**Boston**	**NHL**	**41**	**18**	**14**	**8**	**2482**	**133**	**1**	**3.22**	**6**	**4**	**2**	**359**	**14**	**0**	**2.34**
1989-90c	**Boston**	**NHL**	**46**	**24**	**10**	**7**	**2536**	**122**	**3**	**2.89**	**20**	**13**	**7**	**1195**	**44**	***2**	***2.21**
1990-91	**Boston**	**NHL**	**51**	**25**	**13**	**9**	**2844**	**136**	**4**	**2.87**	**19**	**10**	**9**	**1133**	**60**	**0**	**3.18**
1991-92	**Boston**	**NHL**	**62**	**28**	**22**	**9**	**3640**	**196**	**1**	**3.23**	**15**	**8**	**7**	**866**	**46**	**1**	**3.19**
1992-93	**Boston**	**NHL**	**55**	**37**	**14**	**3**	**3194**	**168**	**3**	**3.16**	**3**	**0**	**3**	**161**	**14**	**0**	**5.22**
1993-94	**Dallas**	**NHL**	**55**	**24**	**20**	**7**	**3121**	**170**	**2**	**3.27**	**4**	**1**	**3**	**246**	**12**	**0**	**2.93**
1994-95	**Dallas**	**NHL**	**31**	**10**	**12**	**7**	**1770**	**72**	**2**	**2.44**	**5**	**1**	**4**	**277**	**16**	**0**	**3.47**
1995-96	**Dallas**	**NHL**	**41**	**13**	**19**	**7**	**2228**	**111**	**1**	**2.99**	....	....	....	....	....	....	....
1996-97	**Dallas**	**NHL**	**48**	**28**	**13**	**5**	**2738**	**98**	**3**	**2.15**	**7**	**3**	**4**	**449**	**21**	**0**	**2.81**
	NHL Totals		**671**	**354**	**192**	**83**	**37814**	**2000**	**25**	**3.17**	**123**	**64**	**52**	**6978**	**353**	**3**	**3.04**

a WHL Second All-Star Team (1980)
b CHL Second All-Star Team (1982)
c Shared William Jennings Trophy with Rejean Lemelin (1990)

Played in NHL All-Star Game (1985, 1986, 1991, 1997)

Traded to **Boston** by **Edmonton** for Geoff Courtnall, Bill Ranford and Boston's second choice (Petro Koivunen) in 1988 Entry Draft, March 8, 1988. Traded to **Dallas** by **Boston** for Jon Casey to complete June 20, 1993 trade which sent Gord Murphy to Dallas for future considerations, June 25, 1993. Signed as a free agent by **Montreal**, July 17, 1997.

MOSS, TYLER — CGY.

Goaltender. Catches right. 6', 184 lbs. Born, Ottawa, Ont., June 29, 1975.
(Tampa Bay's 2nd choice, 29th overall, in 1993 Entry Draft).

			Regular Season								Playoffs						
Season	Club	Lea	GP	W	L	T	Mins	GA	SO	Avg	GP	W	L	Mins	GA	SO	Avg
1992-93	Kingston	OHL	31	13	7	5	1537	97	0	3.79	6	1	2	228	19	0	5.00
1993-94	Kingston	OHL	13	6	4	3	795	42	1	3.17	3	0	2	136	8	0	3.53
1994-95a	Kingston	OHL	*57	33	17	5	*3249	164	1	3.03	6	2	4	333	27	0	4.86
1995-96	Atlanta	IHL	40	11	19	4	2030	138	1	4.08	3	0	3	213	11	0	3.10
1996-97	Adirondack	AHL	11	1	5	2	507	42	1	4.97	....	....	....	....	....	....	....
	Grand Rapids	IHL	15	5	6	1	715	35	0	2.94	....	....	....	....	....	....	....
	Muskegon	ColHL	2	1	1	0	119	5	0	2.51	....	....	....	....	....	....	....
	Saint John	AHL	9	6	1	1	533	17	0	1.91	5	2	3	241	15	0	3.72

a OHL First All-Star Team (1995)

Traded to **Calgary** by **Tampa Bay** for Jamie Huscroft, March 18, 1997.

MUZZATTI, JASON (moo-ZAH-tee) — NYR

Goaltender. Catches left. 6'2", 210 lbs. Born, Toronto, Ont., February 3, 1970.
(Calgary's 1st choice, 21st overall, in 1988 Entry Draft).

			Regular Season								Playoffs						
Season	Club	Lea	GP	W	L	T	Mins	GA	SO	Avg	GP	W	L	Mins	GA	SO	Avg
1987-88a	Michigan State	CCHA	33	19	9	3	1915	109	0	3.41	....	....	....	....	....	....	....
1988-89	Michigan State	CCHA	42	32	9	1	2515	127	3	*3.03	....	....	....	....	....	....	....
1989-90bc	Michigan State	CCHA	33	*24	6	0	1976	99	0	3.01	....	....	....	....	....	....	....
1990-91	Michigan State	CCHA	22	8	10	2	1204	75	1	3.74	....	....	....	....	....	....	....
1991-92	Salt Lake	IHL	52	24	22	5	3033	167	2	3.30	4	1	3	247	18	0	4.37
1992-93	Cdn. National	....	16	6	9	0	880	53	0	3.84	....	....	....	....	....	....	....
	Indianapolis	IHL	12	5	6	1	707	48	0	4.07	....	....	....	....	....	....	....
	Salt Lake	IHL	13	5	6	1	747	52	0	4.18	....	....	....	....	....	....	....
1993-94	**Calgary**	**NHL**	**1**	**0**	**1**	**0**	**60**	**8**	**0**	**8.00**	....	....	....	....	....	....	....
	Saint John	AHL	51	26	21	3	2939	183	2	3.74	7	3	4	415	19	0	2.75
1994-95	Saint John	AHL	31	10	14	4	1741	101	2	3.48	....	....	....	....	....	....	....
	Calgary	**NHL**	**1**	**0**	**0**	**0**	**10**	**0**	**0**	**0.00**	....	....	....	....	....	....	....
1995-96	**Hartford**	**NHL**	**22**	**4**	**8**	**3**	**1013**	**49**	**1**	**2.90**	....	....	....	....	....	....	....
	Springfield	AHL	5	4	0	1	300	12	1	2.40	....	....	....	....	....	....	....
1996-97	**Hartford**	**NHL**	**31**	**9**	**13**	**5**	**1591**	**91**	**0**	**3.43**	....	....	....	....	....	....	....
	NHL Totals		**55**	**13**	**22**	**8**	**2674**	**148**	**1**	**3.32**	....	....	....	....	....	....	....

a CCHA Second All-Star Team (1988)
b CCHA First All-Star Team (1990)
c NCAA West Second All-American Team (1990)

Claimed on waivers by **Hartford** from **Calgary**, October 6, 1995. Traded to **NY Rangers** by **Carolina** for NY Rangers' fourth round choice in 1998 Entry Draft, August 8, 1997.

NABOKOV, YEVGENI (nuh-BAW-kahv, yehv-GEH-nee) — S.J.

Goaltender. Catches left. 6', 180 lbs. Born, Ust-Kamenogorsk, USSR, July 25, 1975.
(San Jose's 9th choice, 219th overall, in 1994 Entry Draft).

			Regular Season								Playoffs						
Season	Club	Lea	GP	W	L	T	Mins	GA	SO	Avg	GP	W	L	Mins	GA	SO	Avg
1992-93	Kamenogorsk	CIS	4	....	....	....	109	5	0	2.75	....	....	....	....	....	....	....
1993-94	Kamenogorsk	CIS	11	....	....	....	539	29	0	3.22	....	....	....	....	....	....	....
1994-95	Moscow D'amo	CIS	24	....	....	....	1265	40	....	1.89	....	....	....	....	....	....	....
1995-96	Moscow D'amo	CIS	39	....	....	....	2008	67	5	2.00	6	....	....	298	7	....	1.41
1996-97	Moscow D'amo	Rus.	27	....	....	....	1588	56	2	2.11	4	....	....	255	12	0	2.82

NOBLE, TOM — CHI.

Goaltender. Catches left. 5'10", 165 lbs. Born, Quincy, MA, March 21, 1975.
(Chicago's 12th choice, 284th overall, in 1993 Entry Draft).

			Regular Season								Playoffs						
Season	Club	Lea	GP	W	L	T	Mins	GA	SO	Avg	GP	W	L	Mins	GA	SO	Avg
1994-95	Boston U.	H.E.	18	15	2	0	1003	46	0	2.75	....	....	....	....	....	....	....
1995-96	Boston U.	H.E.	28	19	5	2	1536	77	....	3.01	....	....	....	....	....	....	....
1996-97a	Boston U.	H.E.	17	10	5	2	1017	53	0	3.13	....	....	....	....	....	....	....

a Hockey East All-Star Team (1997)

NORONEN, MIKA (NOH-rah-nehn, MEE-kah) — BUF.

Goaltender. Catches left. 6'1", 191 lbs. Born, Tampere, Finland, June 17, 1979.
(Buffalo's 1st choice, 21st overall, in 1997 Entry Draft).

			Regular Season								Playoffs						
Season	Club	Lea	GP	W	L	T	Mins	GA	SO	Avg	GP	W	L	Mins	GA	SO	Avg
1996-97	Tappara	Fin.	5	1	3	0	215	17	0	4.73	....	....	....	....	....	....	....

O'NEILL, MIKE

Goaltender. Catches left. 5'7", 160 lbs. Born, LaSalle, Que., November 3, 1967.
(Winnipeg's 1st choice, 15th overall, in 1988 Supplemental Draft).

			Regular Season								Playoffs						
Season	Club	Lea	GP	W	L	T	Mins	GA	SO	Avg	GP	W	L	Mins	GA	SO	Avg
1985-86	Yale	ECAC	6	3	1	0	389	17	0	3.53	....	....	....	....	....	....	....
1986-87a	Yale	ECAC	16	9	6	1	964	55	2	3.42	....	....	....	....	....	....	....
1987-88	Yale	ECAC	24	6	17	0	1385	101	0	4.37	....	....	....	....	....	....	....
1988-89ab	Yale	ECAC	25	10	14	1	1490	93	0	3.74	....	....	....	....	....	....	....
1989-90	Tappara	Fin.	41	23	13	5	2369	127	2	3.22	....	....	....	....	....	....	....
1990-91	Fort Wayne	IHL	8	5	2	1	490	31	0	3.80	....	....	....	....	....	....	....
	Moncton	AHL	30	13	7	6	1613	84	0	3.12	8	3	4	435	29	0	4.00
1991-92	**Winnipeg**	**NHL**	**1**	**0**	**0**	**0**	**13**	**1**	**0**	**4.62**	....	....	....	....	....	....	....
	Moncton	AHL	32	14	16	2	1902	108	1	3.41	11	4	7	670	43	*1	3.85
	Fort Wayne	IHL	33	22	6	3	1858	97	*4	3.13	....	....	....	....	....	....	....
1992-93	**Winnipeg**	**NHL**	**2**	**0**	**0**	**1**	**73**	**6**	**0**	**4.93**	....	....	....	....	....	....	....
	Moncton	AHL	30	13	10	4	1649	88	1	3.20	....	....	....	....	....	....	....
1993-94	**Winnipeg**	**NHL**	**17**	**0**	**9**	**1**	**738**	**51**	**0**	**4.15**	....	....	....	....	....	....	....
	Moncton	AHL	12	8	4	0	716	33	1	2.76	....	....	....	....	....	....	....
	Ft. Wayne	IHL	11	4	4	3	642	38	0	3.55	....	....	....	....	....	....	....
1994-95	Ft. Wayne	IHL	28	11	12	4	1603	109	0	4.08	....	....	....	....	....	....	....
	Phoenix	IHL	21	13	4	4	1256	64	1	3.06	9	4	5	535	33	0	3.70
1995-96	Baltimore	AHL	*74	31	31	7	*4250	250	2	3.53	12	6	6	689	43	0	3.75
1996-97	**Anaheim**	**NHL**	**1**	**0**	**0**	**0**	**31**	**3**	**0**	**5.81**	....	....	....	....	....	....	....
	Long Beach	IHL	45	26	12	6	2644	145	1	3.29	1	0	0	7	0	0	0.00
	NHL Totals		**21**	**0**	**9**	**2**	**855**	**61**	**0**	**4.28**	....	....	....	....	....	....	....

a ECAC First All-Star Team (1987, 1989)
b NCAA East First All-American Team (1989)

Signed as a free agent by **Anaheim**, July 14, 1995.

OSGOOD, CHRIS (AWS-gud) — DET.

Goaltender. Catches left. 5'10", 160 lbs. Born, Peace River, Alta., November 26, 1972.
(Detroit's 3rd choice, 54th overall, in 1991 Entry Draft).

			Regular Season								Playoffs						
Season	Club	Lea	GP	W	L	T	Mins	GA	SO	Avg	GP	W	L	Mins	GA	SO	Avg
1989-90	Medicine Hat	WHL	57	24	28	2	3094	228	0	4.42	3	0	3	173	17	0	5.91
1990-91a	Medicine Hat	WHL	46	23	18	3	2630	173	2	3.95	12	7	5	712	42	0	3.54
1991-92	Medicine Hat	WHL	15	10	3	0	819	44	0	3.22	....	....	....	....	....	....	....
	Brandon	WHL	16	3	10	1	890	60	1	4.04	....	....	....	....	....	....	....
	Seattle	WHL	21	12	7	1	1217	65	1	3.20	15	9	6	904	51	0	3.38
1992-93	Adirondack	AHL	45	19	19	4	2438	159	0	3.91	1	0	1	59	2	0	2.03
1993-94	**Detroit**	**NHL**	**41**	**23**	**8**	**5**	**2206**	**105**	**2**	**2.86**	**6**	**3**	**2**	**307**	**12**	**1**	**2.35**
	Adirondack	AHL	4	3	1	0	239	13	0	3.26	....	....	....	....	....	....	....
1994-95	**Detroit**	**NHL**	**19**	**14**	**5**	**0**	**1087**	**41**	**1**	**2.26**	**2**	**0**	**0**	**68**	**2**	**0**	**1.76**
	Adirondack	AHL	2	1	1	0	120	6	0	3.00	....	....	....	....	....	....	....
1995-96bc	**Detroit**	**NHL**	**50**	***39**	**6**	**5**	**2933**	**106**	**5**	**2.17**	**15**	**8**	**7**	**936**	**33**	**2**	**2.12**
1996-97c	**Detroit**	**NHL**	**47**	**23**	**13**	**9**	**2769**	**106**	**6**	**2.30**	**2**	**0**	**0**	**47**	**2**	**0**	**2.55** ♦
	NHL Totals		**157**	**99**	**32**	**19**	**8995**	**358**	**14**	**2.39**	**25**	**11**	**9**	**1358**	**49**	**3**	**2.16**

a WHL East Second All-Star Team (1991)
b NHL Second All-Star Team (1996)
c Shared William M. Jennings Trophy with Mike Vernon (1996, 1997)

Played in NHL All-Star Game (1996, 1997)

PARENT, RICH
(PEH-ruhn) **ST.L.**

Goaltender. Catches left. 6'3", 195 lbs. Born, Montreal, Que., January 12, 1973.

						Regular Season							Playoffs			
Season	**Club**	**Lea**	**GP**	**W**	**L**	**T**	**Mins**	**GA**	**SO**	**Avg**	**GP**	**W**	**L**	**Mins**	**GA**	**SO**	**Avg**
1994-95	Muskegon	ColHL	35	17	11	3	1867	112	1	3.60	13	7	3	725	47	1	3.89
1995-96	Muskegon	ColHL	36	23	7	4	2087	85	2	2.44	....	....	....	....	....	....	....
	Detroit	IHL	19	16	0	1	1040	48	2	2.77	7	3	3	363	22	0	3.64
1996-97a	Detroit	IHL	53	31	13	4	2815	104	4	2.22	15	8	3	786	21	1	*1.60

a Shared James Norris Memorial Trophy (fewest goals against - IHL) with Jeff Reese (1997)

Signed as a free agent by **St. Louis**, July 31, 1997.

PASSMORE, STEVE
EDM.

Goaltender. Catches left. 5'9", 165 lbs. Born, Thunder Bay, Ont., January 29, 1973.
(Quebec's 9th choice, 196th overall, in 1992 Entry Draft).

						Regular Season							Playoffs			
Season	**Club**	**Lea**	**GP**	**W**	**L**	**T**	**Mins**	**GA**	**SO**	**Avg**	**GP**	**W**	**L**	**Mins**	**GA**	**SO**	**Avg**
1990-91	Victoria	WHL	35	3	25	1	1838	190	0	6.20	....	....	....	....	....	....	....
1991-92	Victoria	WHL	*71	15	50	5	*4228	347	0	4.92	....	....	....	....	....	....	....
1992-93a	Victoria	WHL	43	14	24	2	2402	150	1	3.75	....	....	....	....	....	....	....
	Kamloops	WHL	25	19	6	0	1479	69	1	2.80	7	4	2	401	22	1	3.29
1993-94a	Kamloops	WHL	36	22	9	2	1927	88	1	*2.74	*18	*11	7	*1099	60	0	3.28
1994-95	Cape Breton	AHL	25	8	13	3	1455	93	0	3.83	....	....	....	....	....	....	....
1995-96	Cape Breton	AHL	2	1	0	0	90	2	0	1.33	....	....	....	....	....	....	....
1996-97b	Hamilton	AHL	27	12	12	3	1568	70	1	2.68	22	12	10	1325	61	*2	2.76
	Raleigh	ECHL	2	1	1	0	118	13	0	6.56	....	....	....	....	....	....	....

a WHL West First All-Star Team (1993, 1994)
b Won Fred Hunt Memorial Trophy (Sportsmanship - AHL) (1997)

Traded to **Edmonton** by **Quebec** for Brad Werenka, March 21, 1994.

PELLETIER, JEAN-MARC
(PEHL-tyay) **PHI.**

Goaltender. Catches left. 6'3", 200 lbs. Born, Atlanta, GA, March 4, 1978.
(Philadelphia's 1st choice, 30th overall, in 1997 Entry Draft).

						Regular Season							Playoffs			
Season	**Club**	**Lea**	**GP**	**W**	**L**	**T**	**Mins**	**GA**	**SO**	**Avg**	**GP**	**W**	**L**	**Mins**	**GA**	**SO**	**Avg**
1995-96	Cornell	ECAC	5	1	2	0	179	15	0	5.03	....	....	....	....	....	....	....
1996-97	Cornell	ECAC	11	5	2	3	679	28	1	2.47	....	....	....	....	....	....	....

PERSSON, JOAKIM
(PEHR-suhn) **BOS.**

Goaltender. Catches left. 5'11", 176 lbs. Born, Ostervala, Sweden, May 4, 1970.
(Boston's 10th choice, 259th overall, in 1993 Entry Draft).

						Regular Season							Playoffs			
Season	**Club**	**Lea**	**GP**	**W**	**L**	**T**	**Mins**	**GA**	**SO**	**Avg**	**GP**	**W**	**L**	**Mins**	**GA**	**SO**	**Avg**
1992-93	Hammarby	Swe. 2	40	....	....	....	2395	108	....	2.71	....	....	....	....	....	....	....
1993-94	Hammarby	Swe. 2	23	....	....	....	1380	59	....	2.57	....	....	....	....	....	....	....
	Providence	AHL	1	0	0	0	24	0	0	0.00	....	....	....	....	....	....	....
1994-95	AIK	Swe.	30	....	....	....	1800	103	1	3.43	....	....	....	....	....	....	....
1995-96	AIK	Swe.	24	....	....	....	1344	64	....	2.86	....	....	....	....	....	....	....
1996-97	Ratingen	Ger.	35	....	....	....	2111	154	0	4.37	6	....	....	360	29	0	4.83

PETRUK, RANDY
COL.

Goaltender. Catches right. 5'9", 178 lbs. Born, Cranbrook, B.C., April 23, 1978.
(Colorado's 5th choice, 107th overall, in 1996 Entry Draft).

						Regular Season							Playoffs			
Season	**Club**	**Lea**	**GP**	**W**	**L**	**T**	**Mins**	**GA**	**SO**	**Avg**	**GP**	**W**	**L**	**Mins**	**GA**	**SO**	**Avg**
1994-95	Kamloops	WHL	27	16	3	4	1462	71	1	2.91	7	5	2	423	19	0	2.70
1995-96	Kamloops	WHL	52	34	15	1	3071	181	1	3.54	16	9	6	990	58	0	3.52
1996-97	Kamloops	WHL	*60	25	28	5	*3475	210	0	3.63	....	....	....	....	....	....	....

PODOLKA, MICHAL
(poh-DOHL-kah) **DET.**

Goaltender. Catches right. 5'11", 146 lbs. Born, Most, Czech., August 11, 1977.
(Detroit's 4th choice, 135th overall, in 1996 Entry Draft).

						Regular Season							Playoffs			
Season	**Club**	**Lea**	**GP**	**W**	**L**	**T**	**Mins**	**GA**	**SO**	**Avg**	**GP**	**W**	**L**	**Mins**	**GA**	**SO**	**Avg**
1995-96	S.S. Marie	OHL	44	20	15	4	2391	149	1	3.74	1	0	1	60	6	0	6.00
1996-97	S.S. Marie	OHL	47	26	14	4	2626	134	1	3.06	11	6	4	662	35	*1	3.17

POTVIN, FELIX
(PAHT-vihn) **TOR.**

Goaltender. Catches left. 6', 190 lbs. Born, Anjou, Que., June 23, 1971.
(Toronto's 2nd choice, 31st overall, in 1990 Entry Draft).

						Regular Season							Playoffs			
Season	**Club**	**Lea**	**GP**	**W**	**L**	**T**	**Mins**	**GA**	**SO**	**Avg**	**GP**	**W**	**L**	**Mins**	**GA**	**SO**	**Avg**
1988-89	Chicoutimi	QMJHL	*65	25	31	1	*3489	271	*2	4.66	....	....	....	....	....	....	....
1989-90a	Chicoutimi	QMJHL	*62	*31	26	2	*3478	231	*2	3.99	....	....	....	....	....	....	....
1990-91bcde	Chicoutimi	QMJHL	54	33	15	4	3216	145	*6	*2.70	*16	*11	5	*992	46	0	*2.78
1991-92	**Toronto**	**NHL**	**4**	**0**	**2**	**1**	**210**	**8**	**0**	**2.29**	....	....	....	....	....	....	....
fgh	St. John's	AHL	35	18	10	6	2070	101	2	2.93	11	7	4	642	41	0	3.83
1992-93i	**Toronto**	**NHL**	**48**	**25**	**15**	**7**	**2781**	**116**	**2**	***2.50**	***21**	**11**	**10**	***1308**	**62**	**1**	**2.84**
	St. John's	AHL	5	3	0	2	309	18	0	3.50	....	....	....	....	....	....	....
1993-94	**Toronto**	**NHL**	**66**	**34**	**22**	**9**	**3883**	**187**	**3**	**2.89**	**18**	**9**	**9**	**1124**	**46**	**3**	**2.46**
1994-95	**Toronto**	**NHL**	**36**	**15**	**13**	**7**	**2144**	**104**	**0**	**2.91**	**7**	**3**	**4**	**424**	**20**	**1**	**2.83**
1995-96	**Toronto**	**NHL**	**69**	**30**	**26**	**11**	**4009**	**192**	**2**	**2.87**	**6**	**2**	**4**	**350**	**19**	**0**	**3.26**
1996-97	**Toronto**	**NHL**	***74**	**27**	**36**	**7**	***4271**	**224**	**0**	**3.15**	....	....	....	....	....	....	....
	NHL Totals		**297**	**131**	**114**	**42**	**17298**	**831**	**7**	**2.88**	**52**	**25**	**27**	**3206**	**147**	**5**	**2.75**

a QMJHL Second All-Star Team (1990)
b QMJHL First All-Star Team (1991)
c Canadian Major Junior Goaltender of the Year (1991)
d Memorial Cup All-Star Team (1991)
e Won Hap Emms Memorial Trophy (Memorial Cup Top Goaltender) (1991)
f Won Baz Bastien Memorial Trophy (Top Goaltender - AHL) (1992)
g Won Dudley "Red" Garrett Memorial Trophy (Top Rookie - AHL) (1992)
h AHL First All-Star Team (1992)
i NHL/Upper Deck All-Rookie Team (1993)

Played in NHL All-Star Game (1994, 1996)

PRESTIFILIPPO, JOE
(PREHS-tee-fihl-ih-poh) **NYI**

Goaltender. Catches left. 5'10", 170 lbs. Born, Newark, NJ, March 23, 1977.
(NY Islanders' 8th choice, 165th overall, in 1996 Entry Draft).

						Regular Season							Playoffs			
Season	**Club**	**Lea**	**GP**	**W**	**L**	**T**	**Mins**	**GA**	**SO**	**Avg**	**GP**	**W**	**L**	**Mins**	**GA**	**SO**	**Avg**
1995-96	Hotchkiss	HS	24	....	....	....	1440	56	3	2.33	....	....	....	....	....	....	....
1996-97	Harvard	ECAC	31	10	18	3	1866	99	1	3.18	....	....	....	....	....	....	....

PUPPA, DAREN
(POO-puh) **T.B.**

Goaltender. Catches right. 6'3", 205 lbs. Born, Kirkland Lake, Ont., March 23, 1965.
(Buffalo's 6th choice, 74th overall, in 1983 Entry Draft).

						Regular Season							Playoffs			
Season	**Club**	**Lea**	**GP**	**W**	**L**	**T**	**Mins**	**GA**	**SO**	**Avg**	**GP**	**W**	**L**	**Mins**	**GA**	**SO**	**Avg**
1983-84	RPI	ECAC	32	24	6	0	1816	89	0	2.94	....	....	....	....	....	....	....
1984-85	RPI	ECAC	32	31	1	0	1830	78	0	2.56	....	....	....	....	....	....	....
1985-86	**Buffalo**	**NHL**	**7**	**3**	**4**	**0**	**401**	**21**	**1**	**3.14**	....	....	....	....	....	....	....
	Rochester	AHL	20	8	11	0	1092	79	0	4.34	....	....	....	....	....	....	....
1986-87	**Buffalo**	**NHL**	**3**	**0**	**2**	**1**	**185**	**13**	**0**	**4.22**	....	....	....	....	....	....	....
a	Rochester	AHL	57	*33	14	0	3129	146	1	2.80	*16	*10	6	*944	48	*1	3.05
1987-88	**Buffalo**	**NHL**	**17**	**8**	**6**	**1**	**874**	**61**	**0**	**4.19**	**3**	**1**	**1**	**142**	**11**	**0**	**4.65**
	Rochester	AHL	26	14	8	2	1415	65	2	2.76	2	0	1	108	5	0	2.78
1988-89	**Buffalo**	**NHL**	**37**	**17**	**10**	**6**	**1908**	**107**	**1**	**3.36**	....	....	....	....	....	....	....
1989-90b	**Buffalo**	**NHL**	**56**	***31**	**16**	**6**	**3241**	**156**	**1**	**2.89**	**6**	**2**	**4**	**370**	**15**	**0**	**2.43**
1990-91	**Buffalo**	**NHL**	**38**	**15**	**11**	**6**	**2092**	**118**	**2**	**3.38**	**2**	**0**	**1**	**81**	**10**	**0**	**7.41**
1991-92	**Buffalo**	**NHL**	**33**	**11**	**14**	**4**	**1757**	**114**	**0**	**3.89**	....	....	....	....	....	....	....
	Rochester	AHL	2	0	2	0	119	9	0	4.54	....	....	....	....	....	....	....
1992-93	**Buffalo**	**NHL**	**24**	**11**	**5**	**4**	**1306**	**78**	**0**	**3.58**	....	....	....	....	....	....	....
	Toronto	**NHL**	**8**	**6**	**2**	**0**	**479**	**18**	**2**	**2.25**	**1**	**0**	**0**	**20**	**1**	**0**	**3.00**
1993-94	**Tampa Bay**	**NHL**	**63**	**22**	**33**	**6**	**3653**	**165**	**4**	**2.71**	....	....	....	....	....	....	....
1994-95	**Tampa Bay**	**NHL**	**36**	**14**	**19**	**2**	**2013**	**90**	**1**	**2.68**	....	....	....	....	....	....	....
1995-96	**Tampa Bay**	**NHL**	**57**	**29**	**16**	**9**	**3189**	**131**	**5**	**2.46**	**4**	**1**	**3**	**173**	**14**	**0**	**4.86**
1996-97	**Tampa Bay**	**NHL**	**6**	**1**	**1**	**2**	**325**	**14**	**0**	**2.58**	....	....	....	....	....	....	....
	Adirondack	AHL	1	1	0	0	62	3	0	2.90	....	....	....	....	....	....	....
	NHL Totals		**385**	**168**	**139**	**47**	**21423**	**1086**	**17**	**3.04**	**16**	**4**	**9**	**786**	**51**	**0**	**3.89**

a AHL First All-Star Team (1987)
b NHL Second All-Star Team (1990)

Played in NHL All-Star Game (1990)

Traded to **Toronto** by **Buffalo** with Dave Andreychuk and Buffalo's first round choice (Kenny Jonsson) in 1993 Entry Draft for Grant Fuhr and Toronto's fifth round choice (Kevin Popp) in 1995 Entry Draft, February 2, 1993. Claimed by **Florida** from **Toronto** in Expansion Draft, June 24, 1993. Claimed by **Tampa Bay** from **Florida** in Phase II of Expansion Draft, June 25, 1993.

RACICOT, ANDRE
(RAH-sih-KOH)

Goaltender. Catches left. 5'11", 165 lbs. Born, Rouyn-Noranda, Que., June 9, 1969.
(Montreal's 5th choice, 83rd overall, in 1989 Entry Draft).

						Regular Season							Playoffs			
Season	**Club**	**Lea**	**GP**	**W**	**L**	**T**	**Mins**	**GA**	**SO**	**Avg**	**GP**	**W**	**L**	**Mins**	**GA**	**SO**	**Avg**
1986-87	Longueuil	QMJHL	3	1	2	0	180	19	0	6.33	....	....	....	....	....	....	....
1987-88	Granby	QMJHL	30	15	11	1	1547	105	1	4.07	5	1	4	298	23	0	4.63
1988-89a	Granby	QMJHL	54	22	24	3	2944	198	0	4.04	4	0	4	218	18	0	4.95
1989-90	**Montreal**	**NHL**	**1**	**0**	**0**	**0**	**13**	**3**	**0**	**13.85**	....	....	....	....	....	....	....
b	Sherbrooke	AHL	33	19	11	2	1948	97	1	2.99	5	0	4	227	18	0	4.76
1990-91	**Montreal**	**NHL**	**21**	**7**	**9**	**2**	**975**	**52**	**1**	**3.20**	**2**	**0**	**1**	**12**	**2**	**0**	**10.00**
	Fredericton	AHL	22	13	8	1	1252	60	1	2.88	....	....	....	....	....	....	....
1991-92	**Montreal**	**NHL**	**9**	**0**	**3**	**3**	**436**	**23**	**0**	**3.17**	**1**	**0**	**0**	**1**	**0**	**0**	**0.00**
	Fredericton	AHL	28	14	8	5	1666	86	0	3.10	....	....	....	....	....	....	....
1992-93	**Montreal**	**NHL**	**26**	**17**	**5**	**1**	**1433**	**81**	**1**	**3.39**	**1**	**0**	**0**	**18**	**2**	**0**	**6.67** ♦
1993-94	**Montreal**	**NHL**	**11**	**2**	**6**	**2**	**500**	**37**	**0**	**4.44**	....	....	....	....	....	....	....
	Fredericton	AHL	6	1	4	0	292	16	0	3.28	....	....	....	....	....	....	....
1994-95	Portland	AHL	19	10	7	0	1080	53	1	2.94	....	....	....	....	....	....	....
	Phoenix	IHL	3	1	0	0	132	8	0	3.62	2	0	0	20	0	0	0.00
1995-96	Albany	AHL	2	2	0	0	120	4	0	2.00	....	....	....	....	....	....	....
	Columbus	ECHL	1	1	0	0	60	2	0	2.00	....	....	....	....	....	....	....
	Indianapolis	IHL	11	3	6	0	547	43	0	4.71	....	....	....	....	....	....	....
	Peoria	IHL	4	2	1	1	240	14	0	3.50	11	6	5	654	34	1	3.12
1996-97	Indianapolis	IHL	2	1	0	1	120	3	1	1.50	....	....	....	....	....	....	....
	Kansas City	IHL	6	1	4	0	273	21	0	4.60	....	....	....	....	....	....	....
	Las Vegas	IHL	13	6	5	1	759	40	1	3.16	....	....	....	....	....	....	....
	NHL Totals		**68**	**26**	**23**	**8**	**3357**	**196**	**2**	**3.50**	**4**	**0**	**1**	**31**	**4**	**0**	**7.74**

a QMJHL Second All-Star Team (1989)
b Shared Harry "Hap" Holmes Trophy (fewest goals-against - AHL) with J.C. Bergeron (1990)

Signed as a free agent by **Los Angeles**, September 22, 1994. Signed as a free agent by **Chicago**, August 25, 1995.

RACINE, BRUCE

Goaltender. Catches left. 6', 170 lbs. Born, Cornwall, Ont., August 9, 1966.
(Pittsburgh's 3rd choice, 58th overall, in 1985 Entry Draft).

						Regular Season							Playoffs			
Season	**Club**	**Lea**	**GP**	**W**	**L**	**T**	**Mins**	**GA**	**SO**	**Avg**	**GP**	**W**	**L**	**Mins**	**GA**	**SO**	**Avg**
1984-85	Northeastern	H.E.	26	11	14	1	1615	103	1	3.83	....	....	....	....	....	....	....
1985-86	Northeastern	H.E.	32	17	14	1	1920	147	0	4.56	....	....	....	....	....	....	....
1986-87ab	Northeastern	H.E.	33	12	18	3	1966	133	0	4.06	....	....	....	....	....	....	....
1987-88b	Northeastern	H.E.	30	15	11	4	1808	108	1	3.58	....	....	....	....	....	....	....
1988-89	Muskegon	IHL	51	*37	11	0	*3039	184	*3	3.63	5	4	1	300	15	0	3.00
1989-90	Muskegon	IHL	49	29	15	4	2911	182	1	3.75	9	5	4	566	32	1	3.34
1990-91	Albany	IHL	29	7	18	1	1567	104	0	3.98	....	....	....	....	....	....	....
	Muskegon	IHL	9	4	4	1	516	40	0	4.65	....	....	....	....	....	....	....
1991-92	Muskegon	IHL	27	13	10	3	1559	91	1	3.50	1	0	1	60	6	0	6.00
1992-93	Cleveland	IHL	35	13	16	6	1949	140	1	4.31	2	0	0	37	2	0	3.24
1993-94	St. John's	AHL	37	20	9	2	1875	116	0	3.71	1	0	0	20	1	0	0.00
1994-95	St. John's	AHL	27	11	10	4	1492	85	1	3.42	2	1	1	119	3	0	1.51
1995-96	**St. Louis**	**NHL**	**11**	**0**	**3**	**0**	**230**	**12**	**0**	**3.13**	**1**	**0**	**0**	**1**	**0**	**0**	**0.00**
	Peoria	IHL	22	11	10	1	1228	69	1	3.37	1	0	1	59	3	0	3.05
1996-97	San Antonio	IHL	44	25	14	2	2426	122	6	3.02	6	3	2	325	17	0	3.13
	NHL Totals		**11**	**0**	**3**	**0**	**230**	**12**	**0**	**3.13**	**1**	**0**	**0**	**1**	**0**	**0**	**0.00**

a Hockey East First All-Star Team (1987)
b NCAA East First All-American Team (1987, 1988)

Signed as a free agent by **Toronto**, August 11, 1993. Signed as a free agent by **St. Louis**, August 10, 1995.

RAM, JAMIE
S.J.

Goaltender. Catches left. 5'11", 175 lbs. Born, Scarborough, Ont., January 18, 1971.
(NY Rangers' 10th choice, 213th overall, in 1991 Entry Draft).

						Regular Season							Playoffs			
Season	**Club**	**Lea**	**GP**	**W**	**L**	**T**	**Mins**	**GA**	**SO**	**Avg**	**GP**	**W**	**L**	**Mins**	**GA**	**SO**	**Avg**
1990-91	Michigan Tech	WCHA	14	5	9	0	826	57	0	4.14	....	....	....	....	....	....	....
1991-92	Michigan Tech	WCHA	23	9	9	1	1144	83	0	4.35	....	....	....	....	....	....	....
1992-93ab	Michigan Tech	WCHA	*36	16	14	5	*2078	115	0	3.32	....	....	....	....	....	....	....
1993-94ab	Michigan Tech	WCHA	39	12	20	5	2192	117	*1	3.20	....	....	....	....	....	....	....
1994-95	Binghamton	AHL	26	12	10	2	1472	81	1	3.30	11	6	5	663	29	1	2.62
1995-96	**NY Rangers**	**NHL**	**1**	**0**	**0**	**0**	**27**	**0**	**0**	**0.00**	....	....	....	....	....	....	....
	Binghamton	AHL	40	18	16	3	2262	151	1	4.01	1	0	0	34	1	0	1.75
1996-97	Kentucky	AHL	50	25	19	5	2937	161	4	3.29	1	0	1	60	3	0	3.00
	NHL Totals		**1**	**0**	**0**	**0**	**27**	**0**	**0**	**0.00**	....	....	....	....	....	....	....

a WCHA First All-Star Team (1993, 1994)
b NCAA West First All-American Team (1993, 1994)

Signed as a free agent by **San Jose**, August 13, 1997.

RANFORD, BILL — WSH.

Goaltender. Catches left. 5'11", 185 lbs. Born, Brandon, Man., December 14, 1966.
(Boston's 2nd choice, 52nd overall, in 1985 Entry Draft).

			Regular Season								Playoffs						
Season	Club	Lea	GP	W	L	T	Mins	GA	SO	Avg	GP	W	L	Mins	GA	SO	Avg
1983-84	N. Westminster	WHL	27	10	14	0	1450	130	0	5.38	1	0	0	27	2	0	4.44
1984-85	N. Westminster	WHL	38	19	17	0	2034	142	0	4.19	7	2	3	309	26	0	5.05
1985-86	**Boston**	**NHL**	**4**	**3**	**1**	**0**	**240**	**10**	**0**	**2.50**	**2**	**0**	**2**	**120**	**7**	**0**	**3.50**
	N. Westminster	WHL	53	17	29	1	2791	225	0	4.84	....	....	....	....	....	....	....
1986-87	**Boston**	**NHL**	**41**	**16**	**20**	**2**	**2234**	**124**	**3**	**3.33**	**2**	**0**	**2**	**123**	**8**	**0**	**3.90**
	Moncton	AHL	3	3	0	0	180	6	0	2.00	....	....	....	....	....	....	....
1987-88	Maine	AHL	51	27	16	6	2856	165	1	3.47	....	....	....	....	....	....	....
	Edmonton	**NHL**	**6**	**3**	**0**	**2**	**325**	**16**	**0**	**2.95**	....	....	....	....	....	....	....
1988-89	**Edmonton**	**NHL**	**29**	**15**	**8**	**2**	**1509**	**88**	**1**	**3.50**	....	....	....	....	....	....	....
1989-90a	**Edmonton**	**NHL**	**56**	**24**	**16**	**9**	**3107**	**165**	**1**	**3.19**	***22**	***16**	**6**	***1401**	**59**	**1**	**2.53 ♦**
1990-91	**Edmonton**	**NHL**	**60**	**27**	**27**	**3**	**3415**	**182**	**0**	**3.20**	**3**	**1**	**2**	**135**	**8**	**0**	**3.56**
1991-92	**Edmonton**	**NHL**	**67**	**27**	**26**	**10**	**3822**	**228**	**1**	**3.58**	**16**	**8**	**8**	**909**	**51**	***2**	**3.37**
1992-93	**Edmonton**	**NHL**	**67**	**17**	**38**	**6**	**3753**	**240**	**1**	**3.84**	....	....	....	....	....	....	....
1993-94	**Edmonton**	**NHL**	**71**	**22**	**34**	**11**	**4070**	**236**	**1**	**3.48**	....	....	....	....	....	....	....
1994-95	**Edmonton**	**NHL**	**40**	**15**	**20**	**3**	**2203**	**133**	**2**	**3.62**	....	....	....	....	....	....	....
1995-96	**Edmonton**	**NHL**	**37**	**13**	**18**	**5**	**2015**	**128**	**1**	**3.81**	....	....	....	....	....	....	....
	Boston	**NHL**	**40**	**21**	**12**	**4**	**2307**	**109**	**1**	**2.83**	**4**	**1**	**3**	**239**	**16**	**0**	**4.02**
1996-97	**Boston**	**NHL**	**37**	**12**	**16**	**8**	**2147**	**125**	**2**	**3.49**	....	....	....	....	....	....	....
	Washington	**NHL**	**18**	**8**	**7**	**2**	**1009**	**46**	**0**	**2.74**	....	....	....	....	....	....	....
	NHL Totals		**573**	**223**	**243**	**67**	**32156**	**1830**	**14**	**3.41**	**49**	**26**	**23**	**2927**	**149**	**3**	**3.05**

a Won Conn Smythe Trophy (1990)

Played in NHL All-Star Game (1991)

Traded to **Edmonton** by **Boston** with Geoff Courtnall and future considerations for Andy Moog, March 8, 1988. Traded to **Boston** by **Edmonton** for Mariusz Czerkawski, Sean Brown and Boston's first round choice (Matthieu Descoteaux) in 1996 Entry Draft, January 11, 1996. Traded to **Washington** by **Boston** with Adam Oates and Rick Tocchet for Jim Carey, Anson Carter, Jason Allison, Washington's third round choice (Lee Goren) in 1997 Entry Draft and a conditional choice in 1998 Entry Draft, March 1, 1997.

REDDICK, ELDON (POKEY)

Goaltender. Catches left. 5'8", 170 lbs. Born, Halifax, N.S., October 6, 1964.

			Regular Season								Playoffs						
Season	Club	Lea	GP	W	L	T	Mins	GA	SO	Avg	GP	W	L	Mins	GA	SO	Avg
1982-83	Nanaimo	WHL	66	19	38	1	3549	383	0	6.46	....	....	....	....	....	....	....
1983-84	N. Westminster	WHL	50	24	22	2	2930	215	0	4.40	9	4	5	542	53	0	5.87
1984-85	Brandon	WHL	47	14	30	1	2585	243	0	5.64	....	....	....	....	....	....	....
1985-86a	Ft. Wayne	IHL	29	15	11	0	1674	86	*3	3.00	....	....	....	....	....	....	....
1986-87	**Winnipeg**	**NHL**	**48**	**21**	**21**	**4**	**2762**	**149**	**0**	**3.24**	**3**	**0**	**2**	**166**	**10**	**0**	**3.61**
1987-88	**Winnipeg**	**NHL**	**28**	**9**	**13**	**3**	**1487**	**102**	**0**	**4.12**	....	....	....	....	....	....	....
	Moncton	AHL	9	2	6	1	545	26	0	2.86	....	....	....	....	....	....	....
1988-89	**Winnipeg**	**NHL**	**41**	**11**	**17**	**7**	**2109**	**144**	**0**	**4.10**	....	....	....	....	....	....	....
1989-90	**Edmonton**	**NHL**	**11**	**5**	**4**	**2**	**604**	**31**	**0**	**3.08**	**1**	**0**	**0**	**2**	**0**	**0**	**0.00 ♦**
	Cape Breton	AHL	15	9	4	1	821	54	0	3.95	....	....	....	....	....	....	....
	Phoenix	IHL	3	2	1	0	185	7	0	2.27	....	....	....	....	....	....	....
1990-91	**Edmonton**	**NHL**	**2**	**0**	**2**	**0**	**120**	**9**	**0**	**4.50**	....	....	....	....	....	....	....
	Cape Breton	AHL	31	19	10	0	1673	97	2	3.48	2	0	2	124	10	0	4.84
1991-92	Cape Breton	AHL	16	5	3	3	765	45	0	3.53	....	....	....	....	....	....	....
	Ft. Wayne	IHL	14	6	5	2	787	40	1	3.05	7	3	4	369	18	0	2.93
1992-93b	Ft. Wayne	IHL	54	33	16	4	3043	156	3	3.08	*12	*12	0	723	18	0	*1.49
1993-94	**Florida**	**NHL**	**2**	**0**	**1**	**0**	**80**	**8**	**0**	**6.00**	....	....	....	....	....	....	....
	Cincinnati	IHL	54	31	12	6	2894	147	*2	3.05	10	6	2	498	21	*1	2.53
1994-95	Las Vegas	IHL	40	23	13	1	2075	104	*3	3.01	10	4	6	592	31	0	3.14
1995-96	Las Vegas	IHL	47	27	12	4	2636	129	1	2.94	15	8	6	770	43	0	3.35
1996-97	Grand Rapids	IHL	61	30	14	10	3244	134	6	2.48	5	2	3	335	13	0	2.32
	NHL Totals		**132**	**46**	**58**	**16**	**7162**	**443**	**0**	**3.71**	**4**	**0**	**2**	**168**	**10**	**0**	**3.57**

a Shared James Norris Memorial Trophy (fewest goals against - IHL) with Rick St. Croix (1986)
b Won "Bud" Poile Trophy (Playoff MVP - IHL) (1993)

Signed as a free agent by **Winnipeg**, September 27, 1985. Traded to **Edmonton** by **Winnipeg** for future considerations, September 28, 1989. Signed as a free agent by **Florida**, July 12, 1993.

REESE, JEFF

Goaltender. Catches left. 5'9", 180 lbs. Born, Brantford, Ont., March 24, 1966.
(Toronto's 3rd choice, 67th overall, in 1984 Entry Draft).

			Regular Season								Playoffs						
Season	Club	Lea	GP	W	L	T	Mins	GA	SO	Avg	GP	W	L	Mins	GA	SO	Avg
1983-84	London	OHL	43	18	19	0	2308	173	0	4.50	6	3	3	327	27	0	4.95
1984-85	London	OHL	50	31	15	1	2878	186	1	3.88	8	5	2	440	20	1	2.73
1985-86	London	OHL	57	25	26	3	3281	215	0	3.93	5	0	4	299	25	0	5.02
1986-87	Newmarket	AHL	50	11	29	0	2822	193	1	4.10	....	....	....	....	....	....	....
1987-88	**Toronto**	**NHL**	**5**	**1**	**2**	**1**	**249**	**17**	**0**	**4.10**	....	....	....	....	....	....	....
	Newmarket	AHL	28	10	14	3	1587	103	0	3.89	....	....	....	....	....	....	....
1988-89	**Toronto**	**NHL**	**10**	**2**	**6**	**1**	**486**	**40**	**0**	**4.94**	....	....	....	....	....	....	....
	Newmarket	AHL	37	17	14	3	2072	132	0	3.82	....	....	....	....	....	....	....
1989-90	**Toronto**	**NHL**	**21**	**9**	**6**	**3**	**1101**	**81**	**0**	**4.41**	**2**	**1**	**1**	**108**	**6**	**0**	**3.33**
	Newmarket	AHL	7	3	2	2	431	29	0	4.04	....	....	....	....	....	....	....
1990-91	**Toronto**	**NHL**	**30**	**6**	**13**	**3**	**1430**	**92**	**1**	**3.86**	....	....	....	....	....	....	....
	Newmarket	AHL	3	2	1	0	180	7	0	2.33	....	....	....	....	....	....	....
1991-92	**Toronto**	**NHL**	**8**	**1**	**5**	**1**	**413**	**20**	**1**	**2.91**	....	....	....	....	....	....	....
	Calgary	**NHL**	**12**	**3**	**2**	**2**	**587**	**37**	**0**	**3.78**	....	....	....	....	....	....	....
1992-93	**Calgary**	**NHL**	**26**	**14**	**4**	**1**	**1311**	**70**	**1**	**3.20**	**4**	**1**	**3**	**209**	**17**	**0**	**4.88**
1993-94	**Calgary**	**NHL**	**1**	**0**	**0**	**0**	**13**	**1**	**0**	**4.62**	....	....	....	....	....	....	....
	Hartford	**NHL**	**19**	**5**	**9**	**3**	**1086**	**56**	**1**	**3.09**	....	....	....	....	....	....	....
1994-95	**Hartford**	**NHL**	**11**	**2**	**5**	**1**	**477**	**26**	**0**	**3.27**	....	....	....	....	....	....	....
1995-96	**Hartford**	**NHL**	**7**	**2**	**3**	**0**	**275**	**14**	**1**	**3.05**	....	....	....	....	....	....	....
	Tampa Bay	**NHL**	**19**	**7**	**7**	**1**	**994**	**54**	**0**	**3.26**	**5**	**1**	**1**	**198**	**12**	**0**	**3.64**
1996-97	**New Jersey**	**NHL**	**3**	**0**	**2**	**0**	**139**	**13**	**0**	**5.61**	....	....	....	....	....	....	....
ab	Detroit	IHL	32	23	4	3	1763	55	4	*1.87	11	7	3	518	22	0	2.55
	NHL Totals		**172**	**52**	**64**	**17**	**8561**	**521**	**5**	**3.65**	**11**	**3**	**5**	**515**	**35**	**0**	**4.08**

a IHL Second All-Star Team (1997)
b Shared James Norris Memorial Trophy (fewest goals against - IHL) with Rich Parent (1997)

Traded to **Calgary** with Craig Berube, Alexander Godynyuk, Gary Leeman and Michel Petit for Doug Gilmour, Jamie Macoun, Ric Nattress, Rick Wamsley and Kent Manderville, January 2, 1992. Traded to **Hartford** by **Calgary** for Dan Keczmer, November 19, 1993. Traded to **Tampa Bay** by **Hartford** for Tampa Bay's ninth round choice (Ashhat Rakhmatullin) in 1996 Entry Draft, December 1, 1995. Traded to **New Jersey** by **Tampa Bay** with Chicago's second round choice (previously acquired by Tampa Bay — New Jersey selected Pierre Dagenais) in 1996 Entry Draft and Tampa Bay's eighth round choice (Jason Bertsch) in 1996 Entry Draft for Corey Schwab, June 22, 1996.

RHODES, DAMIAN — (ROHDZ) OTT.

Goaltender. Catches left. 6', 180 lbs. Born, St. Paul, MN, May 28, 1969.
(Toronto's 6th choice, 112th overall, in 1987 Entry Draft).

			Regular Season								Playoffs						
Season	Club	Lea	GP	W	L	T	Mins	GA	SO	Avg	GP	W	L	Mins	GA	SO	Avg
1987-88	Michigan Tech	WCHA	29	16	10	1	1625	114	0	4.20	....	....	....	....	....	....	....
1988-89	Michigan Tech	WCHA	37	15	22	0	2216	163	0	4.41	....	....	....	....	....	....	....
1989-90	Michigan Tech	WCHA	25	6	17	0	1358	119	0	6.26	....	....	....	....	....	....	....
1990-91	**Toronto**	**NHL**	**1**	**1**	**0**	**0**	**60**	**1**	**0**	**1.00**	....	....	....	....	....	....	....
	Newmarket	AHL	38	8	24	3	2154	144	1	4.01	....	....	....	....	....	....	....
1991-92	St. John's	AHL	43	20	16	5	2454	148	0	3.62	6	4	1	331	16	0	2.90
1992-93	St. John's	AHL	*52	27	16	8	*3074	184	1	3.59	9	4	5	538	37	0	4.13
1993-94	**Toronto**	**NHL**	**22**	**9**	**7**	**3**	**1213**	**53**	**0**	**2.62**	**1**	**0**	**0**	**1**	**0**	**0**	**0.00**
1994-95	**Toronto**	**NHL**	**13**	**6**	**6**	**1**	**760**	**34**	**0**	**2.68**	....	....	....	....	....	....	....
1995-96	**Toronto**	**NHL**	**11**	**4**	**5**	**1**	**624**	**29**	**0**	**2.79**	....	....	....	....	....	....	....
	Ottawa	**NHL**	**36**	**10**	**22**	**4**	**2123**	**98**	**2**	**2.77**	....	....	....	....	....	....	....
1996-97	**Ottawa**	**NHL**	**50**	**14**	**20**	**14**	**2934**	**133**	**1**	**2.72**	....	....	....	....	....	....	....
	NHL Totals		**133**	**44**	**60**	**23**	**7714**	**348**	**3**	**2.71**	**1**	**0**	**0**	**1**	**0**	**0**	**0.00**

Note: Played 10 seconds in playoff game vs. San Jose, May 6, 1994. Traded to **NY Islanders** by **Toronto** with Ken Belanger for future considerations, January 23, 1996. Traded to **Ottawa** by **NY Islanders** with Wade Redden for Don Beaupre, Martin Straka and Bryan Berard, January 23, 1996.

RICHTER, MIKE — (RIHK-tuhr) NYR

Goaltender. Catches left. 5'11", 187 lbs. Born, Abington, PA, September 22, 1966.
(NY Rangers' 2nd choice, 28th overall, in 1985 Entry Draft).

			Regular Season								Playoffs						
Season	Club	Lea	GP	W	L	T	Mins	GA	SO	Avg	GP	W	L	Mins	GA	SO	Avg
1985-86	U. Wisconsin	WCHA	24	14	9	0	1394	92	1	3.96	....	....	....	....	....	....	....
1986-87a	U. Wisconsin	WCHA	36	19	16	1	2136	126	0	3.54	....	....	....	....	....	....	....
1987-88	Colorado	IHL	22	16	5	0	1298	68	1	3.14	10	5	3	536	35	0	3.92
	U.S. National	....	29	17	7	2	1559	86	0	3.31	....	....	....	....	....	....	....
	U.S. Olympic	....	4	2	2	0	230	15	0	3.91	....	....	....	....	....	....	....
1988-89	Denver	IHL	*57	23	26	0	3031	217	1	4.30	4	0	4	210	21	0	6.00
	NY Rangers	**NHL**	....	....	....	....	....	....	....	....	**1**	**0**	**1**	**58**	**4**	**0**	**4.14**
1989-90	**NY Rangers**	**NHL**	**23**	**12**	**5**	**5**	**1320**	**66**	**0**	**3.00**	**6**	**3**	**2**	**330**	**19**	**0**	**3.45**
	Flint	IHL	13	7	4	2	782	49	0	3.76	....	....	....	....	....	....	....
1990-91	**NY Rangers**	**NHL**	**45**	**21**	**13**	**7**	**2596**	**135**	**0**	**3.12**	**6**	**2**	**4**	**313**	**14**	***1**	**2.68**
1991-92	**NY Rangers**	**NHL**	**41**	**23**	**12**	**2**	**2298**	**119**	**3**	**3.11**	**7**	**4**	**2**	**412**	**24**	**1**	**3.50**
1992-93	**NY Rangers**	**NHL**	**38**	**13**	**19**	**3**	**2105**	**134**	**1**	**3.82**	....	....	....	....	....	....	....
	Binghamton	AHL	5	4	0	1	305	6	0	1.18	....	....	....	....	....	....	....
1993-94	**NY Rangers**	**NHL**	**68**	***42**	**12**	**6**	**3710**	**159**	**5**	**2.57**	**23**	***16**	**7**	**1417**	**49**	***4**	**2.07 ♦**
1994-95	**NY Rangers**	**NHL**	**35**	**14**	**17**	**2**	**1993**	**97**	**2**	**2.92**	**7**	**2**	**5**	**384**	**23**	**0**	**3.59**
1995-96	**NY Rangers**	**NHL**	**41**	**24**	**13**	**3**	**2396**	**107**	**3**	**2.68**	**11**	**5**	**6**	**661**	**36**	**0**	**3.27**
1996-97	**NY Rangers**	**NHL**	**61**	**33**	**22**	**6**	**3598**	**161**	**4**	**2.68**	**15**	**9**	**6**	**939**	**33**	***3**	**2.11**
	NHL Totals		**352**	**182**	**113**	**34**	**20016**	**978**	**18**	**2.93**	**76**	**41**	**33**	**4514**	**202**	**9**	**2.68**

a WCHA Second All-Star Team (1987)

Played in NHL All-Star Game (1992, 1994)

RIENDEAU, VINCENT — (ree-EHN-doh)

Goaltender. Catches left. 5'10", 185 lbs. Born, St. Hyacinthe, Que., April 20, 1966.

			Regular Season								Playoffs						
Season	Club	Lea	GP	W	L	T	Mins	GA	SO	Avg	GP	W	L	Mins	GA	SO	Avg
1985-86a	Drummondville	QMJHL	57	33	20	3	3336	215	2	3.87	23	10	13	1271	106	1	5.00
1986-87b	Sherbrooke	AHL	41	25	14	0	2363	114	2	2.89	13	8	5	742	47	0	3.80
1987-88	**Montreal**	**NHL**	**1**	**0**	**0**	**0**	**36**	**5**	**0**	**8.33**	....	....	....	....	....	....	....
cd	Sherbrooke	AHL	44	27	13	3	2521	112	*4	*2.67	2	0	2	127	7	0	3.31
1988-89	**St. Louis**	**NHL**	**32**	**11**	**15**	**5**	**1842**	**108**	**0**	**3.52**	....	....	....	....	....	....	....
1989-90	**St. Louis**	**NHL**	**43**	**17**	**19**	**5**	**2551**	**149**	**1**	**3.50**	**8**	**3**	**4**	**397**	**24**	**0**	**3.63**
1990-91	**St. Louis**	**NHL**	**44**	**29**	**9**	**6**	**2671**	**134**	**3**	**3.01**	**13**	**6**	**7**	**687**	**35**	***1**	**3.06**
1991-92	**St. Louis**	**NHL**	**3**	**1**	**2**	**0**	**157**	**11**	**0**	**4.20**	....	....	....	....	....	....	....
	Detroit	**NHL**	**2**	**2**	**0**	**0**	**87**	**2**	**0**	**1.38**	**2**	**1**	**0**	**73**	**4**	**0**	**3.29**
	Adirondack	AHL	3	2	1	0	179	8	0	2.68	....	....	....	....	....	....	....
1992-93	**Detroit**	**NHL**	**22**	**13**	**4**	**2**	**1193**	**64**	**0**	**3.22**	....	....	....	....	....	....	....
1993-94	**Detroit**	**NHL**	**8**	**2**	**4**	**0**	**345**	**23**	**0**	**4.00**	....	....	....	....	....	....	....
	Adirondack	AHL	10	6	3	0	582	30	0	3.09	....	....	....	....	....	....	....
	Boston	**NHL**	**18**	**7**	**6**	**1**	**976**	**50**	**1**	**3.07**	**2**	**1**	**1**	**120**	**8**	**0**	**4.00**
1994-95	**Boston**	**NHL**	**11**	**3**	**6**	**1**	**565**	**27**	**0**	**2.87**	....	....	....	....	....	....	....
	Providence	AHL	....	....	....	....	....	....	....	....	1	1	0	60	3	0	3.00
1995-96	Riessersee	Ger.	47	....	....	....	2776	184	....	4.00	3	....	....	189	20	0	6.35
1996-97	Manitoba	IHL	41	10	18	5	1941	113	0	3.49	....	....	....	....	....	....	....
	NHL Totals		**184**	**85**	**65**	**20**	**10423**	**573**	**5**	**3.30**	**25**	**11**	**12**	**1277**	**71**	**1**	**3.34**

a QMJHL Second All-Star Team (1986)
b Won Harry "Hap" Holmes Memorial Trophy (fewest goals-against - AHL) (1987)
c Shared Harry "Hap" Holmes Memorial Trophy (fewest goals-against - AHL) with Jocelyn Perreault (1988)
d AHL Second All-Star Team (1988)

Signed as a free agent by **Montreal**, October 9, 1985. Traded to **St. Louis** by **Montreal** with Sergio Momesso for Jocelyn Lemieux, Darrell May and St. Louis' second round choice (Patrice Brisebois) in 1989 Entry Draft, August 9, 1988. Traded to **Detroit** by **St. Louis** for Rick Zombo, October 18, 1991. Traded to **Boston** by **Detroit** for Boston's fifth round choice (Chad Wilchynski) in 1995 Entry Draft, January 17, 1994.

ROCHE, SCOTT — (ROHSH) ST.L.

Goaltender. Catches left. 6'4", 220 lbs. Born, Lindsay, Ont., March 19, 1977.
(St. Louis' 2nd choice, 75th overall, in 1995 Entry Draft).

			Regular Season								Playoffs						
Season	Club	Lea	GP	W	L	T	Mins	GA	SO	Avg	GP	W	L	Mins	GA	SO	Avg
1993-94	North Bay	OHL	32	15	5	4	1587	93	0	3.52	5	2	1	191	10	0	*3.14
1994-95	North Bay	OHL	47	24	17	2	2599	167	2	3.86	6	2	4	348	30	0	5.17
1995-96	North Bay	OHL	53	12	29	5	2859	232	1	4.87	....	....	....	....	....	....	....
1996-97	North Bay	OHL	3	0	3	0	122	21	0	10.30	....	....	....	....	....	....	....
	Windsor	OHL	44	20	16	4	2496	152	1	3.65	5	1	4	267	26	0	5.84

ROLOSON, DWAYNE — CGY.

Goaltender. Catches left. 6'1", 180 lbs. Born, Simcoe, Ont., October 12, 1969.

			Regular Season								Playoffs						
Season	Club	Lea	GP	W	L	T	Mins	GA	SO	Avg	GP	W	L	Mins	GA	SO	Avg
1990-91	Lowell	H.E.	15	5	9	0	823	63	0	4.59	....	....	....	....	....	....	....
1991-92	Lowell	H.E.	12	3	8	0	660	52	0	4.73	....	....	....	....	....	....	....
1992-93	Lowell	H.E.	*39	20	17	2	*2342	150	0	3.84	....	....	....	....	....	....	....
1993-94ab	Lowell	H.E.	*40	*23	10	7	*2305	106	0	2.76	....	....	....	....	....	....	....
1994-95	Saint John	AHL	46	16	21	8	2734	156	1	3.42	5	1	4	298	13	0	2.61
1995-96	Saint John	AHL	67	*33	22	11	4026	190	1	2.83	16	10	6	1027	49	1	2.86
1996-97	**Calgary**	**NHL**	**31**	**9**	**14**	**3**	**1618**	**78**	**1**	**2.89**	....	....	....	....	....	....	....
	Saint John	AHL	8	6	2	0	480	22	1	2.75	....	....	....	....	....	....	....
	NHL Totals		**31**	**9**	**14**	**3**	**1618**	**78**	**1**	**2.89**	....	....	....	....	....	....	....

a Hockey East First All-Star Team (1994)
b NCAA East First All-Ameircan Team (1994)

Signed as a free agent by **Calgary**, July 4, 1994.

ROUSSEL, DOMINIC (roo-SEHL) PHI.

Goaltender. Catches left. 6'1", 191 lbs. Born, Hull, Que., February 22, 1970.
(Philadelphia's 4th choice, 63rd overall, in 1988 Entry Draft).

			Regular Season								Playoffs						
Season	Club	Lea	GP	W	L	T	Mins	GA	SO	Avg	GP	W	L	Mins	GA	SO	Avg
1987-88	Trois-Rivières	QMJHL	51	18	25	4	2905	251	0	5.18							
1988-89	Shawinigan	QMJHL	46	24	15	2	2555	171	0	4.02	10	6	4	638	36	0	3.39
1989-90	Shawinigan	QMJHL	37	20	14	1	1985	133	0	4.02	2	1	1	120	12	0	6.00
1990-91	Hershey	AHL	45	20	14	7	2507	151	1	3.61	7	3	4	366	21	0	3.44
1991-92	Philadelphia	NHL	17	7	8	2	922	40	1	2.60							
	Hershey	AHL	35	15	11	6	2040	121	1	3.56							
1992-93	Philadelphia	NHL	34	13	11	5	1769	111	1	3.76							
	Hershey	AHL	6	0	3	3	372	23	0	3.71							
1993-94	Philadelphia	NHL	60	29	20	5	3285	183	1	3.34							
1994-95	Philadelphia	NHL	19	11	7	0	1075	42	1	2.34	1	0	0	23	0	0	0.00
	Hershey	AHL	1	0	1	0	59	5	0	5.07							
1995-96	Philadelphia	NHL	9	2	3	2	456	22	1	2.89							
	Hershey	AHL	12	4	4	3	690	32	0	2.78							
	Winnipeg	NHL	7	2	2	0	285	16	0	3.37							
1996-97	Philadelphia	AHL	36	18	9	3	1852	82	2	2.66	1	0	0	26	3	0	6.93
	NHL Totals		146	64	51	14	7792	414	5	3.19	1	0	0	23	0	0	0.00

Traded to **Winnipeg** by **Philadelphia** for Tim Cheveldae and Winnipeg's third round choice (Chester Gallant) in 1996 Entry Draft, February 27, 1996. Signed as a free agent by **Philadelphia**, July 3, 1996.

ROY, PATRICK (WAH) COL.

Goaltender. Catches left. 6', 192 lbs. Born, Quebec City, Que., October 5, 1965.
(Montreal's 4th choice, 51st overall, in 1984 Entry Draft).

			Regular Season								Playoffs						
Season	Club	Lea	GP	W	L	T	Mins	GA	SO	Avg	GP	W	L	Mins	GA	SO	Avg
1982-83	Granby	QMJHL	54	13	35	1	2808	293	0	6.26							
1983-84	Granby	QMJHL	61	29	29	1	3585	265	0	4.44	4	0	4	244	22	0	5.41
1984-85	Montreal	NHL	1	1	0	0	20	0	0	0.00							
	Granby	QMJHL	44	16	25	1	2463	228	0	5.55							
	Sherbrooke	AHL	1	1	0	0	60	4	0	4.00	13	10	3	*769	37	0	*2.89
1985-86ab	Montreal	NHL	47	23	18	3	2651	148	1	3.35	20	*15	5	1218	39	*1	1.92 ♦
1986-87c	Montreal	NHL	46	22	16	6	2686	131	1	2.93	6	4	2	330	22	0	4.00
1987-88cd	Montreal	NHL	45	23	12	9	2586	125	3	2.90	8	3	4	430	24	0	3.35
1988-89cefg	Montreal	NHL	48	33	5	6	2744	113	4	*2.47	19	13	6	1206	42	2	*2.09
1989-90efg	Montreal	NHL	54	*31	16	5	3173	134	3	2.53	11	5	6	641	26	1	2.43
1990-91d	Montreal	NHL	48	25	15	6	2835	128	1	2.71	13	7	5	785	40	0	3.06
1991-92efh	Montreal	NHL	67	36	22	8	3935	155	*5	*2.36	11	4	7	686	30	1	2.62
1992-93a	Montreal	NHL	62	31	25	5	3595	192	2	3.20	20	*16	4	1293	46	0	*2.13 ♦
1993-94	Montreal	NHL	68	35	17	11	3867	161	*7	2.50	6	3	3	375	16	0	2.56
1994-95	Montreal	NHL	43	17	20	6	2566	127	1	2.97							
1995-96	Montreal	NHL	22	12	9	1	1260	62	1	2.95							
	Colorado	NHL	39	22	15	1	2305	103	1	2.68	*22	*16	6	*1454	51	*3	2.10 ♦
1996-97	Colorado	NHL	62	*38	15	7	3698	143	7	2.32	17	10	7	1034	38	*3	2.21
	NHL Totals		652	349	205	74	37921	1722	37	2.72	153	96	55	9452	374	11	2.37

a Won Conn Smythe Trophy (1986, 1993)
b NHL All-Rookie Team (1986)
c Shared William Jennings Trophy with Brian Hayward (1987, 1988, 1989)
d NHL Second All-Star Team (1988, 1991)
e Won Vezina Trophy (1989, 1990, 1992)
f NHL First All-Star Team (1989, 1990, 1992)
g Won Trico Goaltending Award (1989, 1990)
h Won William M. Jennings Award (1992)

Played in NHL All-Star Game (1988, 1990-94, 1997)

Traded to **Colorado** by **Montreal** with Mike Keane for Andrei Kovalenko, Martin Rucinsky and Jocelyn Thibault, December 6, 1995.

RUSSELL, BLAINE ANA.

Goaltender. Catches left. 5'11", 180 lbs. Born, Wetaskawin, Sask., January 11, 1977.
(Anaheim's 4th choice, 149th overall, in 1996 Entry Draft).

			Regular Season								Playoffs						
Season	Club	Lea	GP	W	L	T	Mins	GA	SO	Avg	GP	W	L	Mins	GA	SO	Avg
1995-96	Prince Albert	WHL	34	25	5	2	1920	98	2	3.06	7	4	2	380	20	0	3.16
1996-97	Lethbridge	WHL	6	4	1	1	370	17	0	2.76	14	*13	1	817	29	0	*2.13
	Prince Albert	WHL	29	9	15	3	1690	99	2	3.51							

SALO, TOMMY (SAH-loh) NYI

Goaltender. Catches left. 5'11", 173 lbs. Born, Surahammar, Sweden, February 1, 1971.
(NY Islanders' 5th choice, 118th overall, in 1993 Entry Draft).

			Regular Season								Playoffs						
Season	Club	Lea	GP	W	L	T	Mins	GA	SO	Avg	GP	W	L	Mins	GA	SO	Avg
1990-91	Vasteras	Swe.	2				100	11	0	6.60							
1991-92	Vasteras	Swe.								UNAVAILABLE							
1992-93	Vasteras	Swe.	24				1431	59	2	2.47	2			120	6	0	3.00
1993-94	Vasteras	Swe.	32				1896	106	0	3.35							
1994-95abcd	Denver	IHL	*65	*45	14	4	*3810	165	*3	*2.60	8	7	0	390	20	0	3.07
	NY Islanders	NHL	6	1	5	0	358	18	0	3.02							
1995-96	NY Islanders	NHL	10	1	7	1	523	35	0	4.02							
e	Utah	IHL	45	28	15	2	2695	119	*4	2.65	22	*15	7	1342	51	*3	2.28
1996-97	NY Islanders	NHL	58	20	27	8	3208	151	5	2.82							
	NHL Totals		74	22	39	9	4089	204	5	2.99							

a IHL First All-Star Team (1995)
b Won James Norris Memorial Trophy (Fewest goals against - IHL) (1995)
c Won Garry F. Longman Memorial Trophy (Top Rookie - IHL) (1995)
d Won James Gatschene Memorial Trophy (MVP - IHL) (1995)
e Shared James Norris Memorial Trophy (fewest goals against - IHL) with Mark McArthur (1996)

SARJEANT, GEOFF (SAHR-jehnt)

Goaltender. Catches left. 5'9", 180 lbs. Born, Newmarket, Ont., November 30, 1969.
(St. Louis' 1st choice, 17th overall, in 1990 Supplemental Draft).

			Regular Season								Playoffs						
Season	Club	Lea	GP	W	L	T	Mins	GA	SO	Avg	GP	W	L	Mins	GA	SO	Avg
1988-89	Michigan Tech	WCHA	6	0	3	2	329	22	0	4.01							
1989-90	Michigan Tech	WCHA	19	4	13	0	1043	94	0	5.41							
1990-91	Michigan Tech	WCHA	23	5	15	3	1540	97	0	3.78							
1991-92	Michigan Tech	WCHA	23	7	13	0	1201	90	1	4.50							
1992-93	Peoria	IHL	41	22	14	3	2356	130	0	3.31	3	0	3	179	13	0	4.36
1993-94a	Peoria	IHL	41	25	9	2	2275	93	*2	*2.45	4	2	2	211	13	0	3.69
1994-95	Peoria	IHL	55	32	12	8	3146	158	0	3.01	4	0	3	206	20	0	5.81
	St. Louis	NHL	4	1	0	0	120	6	0	3.00							
1995-96	San Jose	NHL	4	0	2	1	171	14	0	4.91							
	Kansas City	IHL	41	18	18	1	2167	140	1	3.88	2	0	1	99	3	0	1.82
1996-97	Cincinnati	IHL	59	32	20	5	3287	157	1	2.87	3	0	3	158	12	0	4.55
	NHL Totals		8	1	2	1	291	20	0	4.12							

a IHL First All-Star Team (1994)

Signed as a free agent by **San Jose**, September 23, 1995.

SCHAFER, PAXTON BOS.

Goaltender. Catches left. 5'9", 164 lbs. Born, Medicine Hat, Alta., February 26, 1976.
(Boston's 3rd choice, 47th overall, in 1995 Entry Draft).

			Regular Season								Playoffs						
Season	Club	Lea	GP	W	L	T	Mins	GA	SO	Avg	GP	W	L	Mins	GA	SO	Avg
1993-94	Medicine Hat	WHL	19	6	9	1	909	67	0	4.42							
1994-95a	Medicine Hat	WHL	61	32	26	2	3519	185	0	3.15	5	1	4	339	18	0	3.19
1995-96	Medicine Hat	WHL	60	24	30	3	3256	200	1	3.69	5	1	4	251	25	0	5.98
1996-97	Boston	NHL	3	0	0	0	77	6	0	4.68							
	Providence	AHL	22	9	10	0	1206	75	1	3.73							
	Charlotte	ECHL	4	3	1	0	239	7	0	1.75							
	NHL Totals		3	0	0	0	77	6	0	4.68							

a WHL East First All-Star Team (1995)

SCHWAB, COREY (SHWAHB) T.B.

Goaltender. Catches left. 6', 180 lbs. Born, North Battleford, Sask., November 4, 1970.
(New Jersey's 12th choice, 200th overall, in 1990 Entry Draft).

			Regular Season								Playoffs						
Season	Club	Lea	GP	W	L	T	Mins	GA	SO	Avg	GP	W	L	Mins	GA	SO	Avg
1988-89	Seattle	WHL	10	2	2	0	386	31	0	4.82							
1989-90	Seattle	WHL	27	15	2	1	1150	69	1	3.60	3	0	0	49	2	0	2.45
1990-91	Seattle	WHL	*58	32	18	3	*3289	224	0	4.09	6	1	5	382	25	0	3.93
1991-92	Utica	AHL	24	9	12	1	1322	95	0	4.31							
	Cincinnati	ECHL	8	6	0	1	450	31	0	4.13	9	6	3	540	29	0	3.22
1992-93	Utica	AHL	40	18	16	5	2387	169	*2	4.25	1	0	1	59	6	0	6.10
	Cincinnati	IHL	3	1	2	0	185	17	0	5.51							
1993-94	Albany	AHL	51	27	21	3	3058	184	0	3.61	5	1	4	298	20	0	4.02
1994-95abc	Albany	AHL	45	25	10	9	2711	117	3	*2.59	7	6	1	425	19	0	2.68
1995-96	New Jersey	NHL	10	0	3	0	331	12	0	2.18							
	Albany	AHL	5	3	2	0	299	13	0	2.61							
1996-97	Tampa Bay	NHL	31	11	12	1	1462	74	2	3.04							
	NHL Totals		41	11	15	1	1793	86	2	2.88							

a AHL Second All-Star Team (1995)
b Shared Harry "Hap" Holmes Memorial Trophy (fewest goals against - AHL) with Mike Dunham (1995)
c Shared Jack A. Butterfield Trophy (Playoff MVP - AHL) with Mike Dunham (1995)

Traded to **Tampa Bay** by **New Jersey** for Jeff Reese, Chicago's second round choice (previously acquired by Tampa Bay — New Jersey selected Pierre Dagenais) in 1996 Entry Draft and Tampa Bay's eighth round choice (Jason Bertsch) in 1996 Entry Draft, June 22, 1996.

SCOTT, TRAVIS ST.L.

Goaltender. Catches left. 6'2", 185 lbs. Born, Kanata, Ont., September 14, 1975.

			Regular Season								Playoffs						
Season	Club	Lea	GP	W	L	T	Mins	GA	SO	Avg	GP	W	L	Mins	GA	SO	Avg
1993-94	Windsor	OHL	45	20	18	0	2312	158	1	4.10	4	0	4	240	16	0	4.00
1994-95	Windsor	OHL	48	26	14	3	2644	147	3	3.34	3	0	1	94	6	1	3.83
1995-96	Oshawa	OHL	31	15	9	4	1763	78	3	2.65	5	1	4	315	23	0	4.38
1996-97	Baton Rouge	ECHL	10	5	2	1	501	22	0	2.63							
	Worcester	AHL	29	14	10	1	1482	75	1	3.04							

Signed as a free agent by **St. Louis**, December 30, 1996.

SHIELDS, STEVE BUF.

Goaltender. Catches left. 6'3", 210 lbs. Born, Toronto, Ont., July 19, 1972.
(Buffalo's 5th choice, 101st overall, in 1991 Entry Draft).

			Regular Season								Playoffs						
Season	Club	Lea	GP	W	L	T	Mins	GA	SO	Avg	GP	W	L	Mins	GA	SO	Avg
1990-91	U. of Michigan	CCHA	37	26	6	3	1963	106	0	3.24							
1991-92	U. of Michigan	CCHA	*37	*27	7	2	*2090	99	1	2.84							
1992-93ab	U. of Michigan	CCHA	*39	*30	6	2	2027	75	2	*2.22							
1993-94ab	U. of Michigan	CCHA	36	*28	6	1	1961	87	0	2.66							
1994-95	Rochester	AHL	13	3	8	0	673	53	0	4.72	1	0	0	20	3	0	9.00
	S. Carolina	ECHL	21	11	5	2	1157	52	2	2.69	3	0	2	144	11	0	4.58
1995-96	Buffalo	NHL	2	1	0	0	75	4	0	3.20							
	Rochester	AHL	43	20	17	2	2357	140	1	3.56	*19	*15	3	*1127	47	1	2.50
1996-97	Buffalo	NHL	13	3	8	2	789	39	0	2.97	10	4	6	570	26	1	2.74
	Rochester	AHL	23	14	6	2	1331	60	1	2.70							
	NHL Totals		15	4	8	2	864	43	0	2.99	10	4	6	570	26	1	2.74

a CCHA First All-Star Team (1993, 1994)
b NCAA West Second All-American Team (1993, 1994)

SHTALENKOV, MIKHAIL (shtuh-LEHN-kahf, mihk-HAIL) ANA.

Goaltender. Catches left. 6'2", 185 lbs. Born, Moscow, USSR, October 20, 1965.
(Anaheim's 5th choice, 108th overall, in 1993 Entry Draft).

			Regular Season								Playoffs						
Season	Club	Lea	GP	W	L	T	Mins	GA	SO	Avg	GP	W	L	Mins	GA	SO	Avg
1986-87a	Moscow D'amo	USSR	17				893	36	1	2.41							
1987-88	Moscow D'amo	USSR	25				1302	72	1	3.31							
1988-89	Moscow D'amo	USSR	4				80	3	0	2.25							
1989-90	Moscow D'amo	USSR	6				20	1	0	3.00							
1990-91	Moscow D'amo	USSR	31				1568	56	2	2.14							
1991-92	Moscow D'amo	CIS	27				1268	45	1	2.12							
1992-93b	Milwaukee	IHL	47	26	14	5	2669	135	2	3.03	3	1	2	209	11	0	3.16
1993-94	Anaheim	NHL	10	3	4	1	543	24	0	2.65							
	San Diego	IHL	28	15	11	2	1616	93	0	3.45							
1994-95	Anaheim	NHL	18	4	7	1	810	49	0	3.63							
1995-96	Anaheim	NHL	30	7	16	3	1637	85	0	3.12							
1996-97	Anaheim	NHL	24	7	8	1	1079	52	2	2.89	4	0	3	211	10	0	2.84
	NHL Totals		82	21	35	6	4069	210	2	3.10	4	0	3	211	10	0	2.84

a Soviet Rookie of the Year (1987)
b Won Garry F. Longman Memorial Trophy (Top Rookie - IHL) (1993)

SHULMISTRA, RICHARD N.J.

Goaltender. Catches right. 6'2", 185 lbs. Born, Sudbury, Ont., April 1, 1971.
(Quebec's 1st choice, 4th overall, in 1992 Supplemental Draft).

			Regular Season								Playoffs						
Season	Club	Lea	GP	W	L	T	Mins	GA	SO	Avg	GP	W	L	Mins	GA	SO	Avg
1990-91	Miami-Ohio	CCHA	20	2	12	2	920	80	0	5.21							
1991-92	Miami-Ohio	CCHA	19	3	5	2	850	67	0	4.72							
1992-93a	Miami-Ohio	CCHA	33	22	6	4	1949	88	1	2.71							
1993-94	Miami-Ohio	CCHA	27	13	12	1	1521	74	0	2.92							
1994-95	Cornwall	AHL	20	4	9	2	937	58	0	3.71	8	4	3	446	22	0	2.95
1995-96	Cornwall	AHL	36	9	18	2	1844	100	0	3.25	1	0	0	9	1	0	6.76
1996-97	Albany	AHL	23	5	9	2	1062	43	2	2.43	2	1	0	76	2	0	1.56

a CCHA Second All-Star Team (1993)

Signed as a free agent by **New Jersey**, August, 1997.

SIDORKIEWICZ, PETER (sih-DOHR-kuh-vihch) N.J.

Goaltender. Catches left. 5'9", 180 lbs. Born, Dabrowa Bialostocka, Pol., June 29, 1963.
(Washington's 5th choice, 91st overall, in 1981 Entry Draft).

			Regular Season								Playoffs						
Season	Club	Lea	GP	W	L	T	Mins	GA	SO	Avg	GP	W	L	Mins	GA	SO	Avg
1980-81	Oshawa	OHA	7	3	3	0	308	24	0	4.68	5	2	2	266	20	0	4.52
1981-82	Oshawa	OHL	29	14	11	1	1553	123	*2	4.75	1	0	0	13	1	0	4.62
1982-83	Oshawa	OHL	60	36	20	3	3536	213	0	3.61	17	15	1	1020	60	0	3.53
1983-84	Oshawa	OHL	52	28	21	1	2966	250	1	4.15	7	3	4	420	27	*1	3.86
1984-85	Binghamton	AHL	45	31	9	5	2691	137	3	3.05	8	4	4	481	31	0	3.87
	Fort Wayne	IHL	10	4	4	2	590	43	0	4.37	....	....	....	....	....	....	....
1985-86	Binghamton	AHL	49	21	22	3	2819	150	2	*3.19	4	1	3	235	12	0	3.06
1986-87a	Binghamton	AHL	57	23	16	0	3304	161	4	2.92	13	6	7	794	36	0	*2.72
1987-88	**Hartford**	**NHL**	**1**	**0**	**1**	**0**	**60**	**6**	**0**	**6.00**	....	....	....	....	....	....	....
	Binghamton	AHL	42	19	17	3	2345	144	0	3.68	3	0	2	147	8	0	3.27
1988-89b	**Hartford**	**NHL**	**44**	**22**	**18**	**4**	**2635**	**133**	**4**	**3.03**	**2**	**0**	**2**	**124**	**8**	**0**	**3.87**
1989-90	**Hartford**	**NHL**	**46**	**19**	**19**	**7**	**2703**	**161**	**1**	**3.57**	**7**	**3**	**4**	**429**	**23**	**0**	**3.22**
1990-91	**Hartford**	**NHL**	**52**	**21**	**22**	**7**	**2953**	**164**	**1**	**3.33**	**6**	**2**	**4**	**359**	**24**	**0**	**4.01**
1991-92	**Hartford**	**NHL**	**35**	**9**	**19**	**6**	**1995**	**111**	**2**	**3.34**	....	....	....	....	....	....	....
1992-93	**Ottawa**	**NHL**	**64**	**8**	**46**	**3**	**3388**	**250**	**0**	**4.43**	....	....	....	....	....	....	....
1993-94	**New Jersey**	**NHL**	**3**	**0**	**3**	**0**	**130**	**6**	**0**	**2.77**	....	....	....	....	....	....	....
	Albany	AHL	15	6	7	2	907	60	0	3.97	....	....	....	....	....	....	....
	Fort Wayne	IHL	11	6	3	0	591	27	*2	2.74	*18	10	8	*1054	59	*1	3.36
1994-95	Fort Wayne	IHL	16	8	6	1	941	58	1	3.70	3	1	2	144	12	0	5.00
1995-96	Albany	AHL	32	19	7	5	1809	89	3	2.95	1	0	1	59	3	0	3.06
1996-97	Albany	AHL	62	31	23	6	3539	171	2	2.90	16	7	8	920	48	0	3.13
	NHL Totals		**245**	**79**	**128**	**27**	**13864**	**831**	**8**	**3.60**	**15**	**5**	**10**	**912**	**55**	**0**	**3.62**

a AHL Second All-Star Team (1987)
b NHL All-Rookie Team (1989)

Played in NHL All-Star Game (1993)

Traded to **Hartford** by **Washington** with Dean Evason for David Jensen, March 12, 1985. Claimed by **Ottawa** from **Hartford** in Expansion Draft, June 18, 1992. Traded to **New Jersey** by **Ottawa** with future considerations (Mike Peluso, June 26, 1993) for Craig Billington, Troy Mallette and New Jersey's fourth round choice (Cosmo Dupaul) in 1993 Entry Draft, June 20, 1993.

SMANGS, HENRIK (SMOHNGS) PHO.

Goaltender. Catches left. 5'11", 174 lbs. Born, Leksand, Sweden, January 19, 1976.
(Winnipeg's 9th choice, 212th overall, in 1994 Entry Draft).

			Regular Season								Playoffs						
Season	Club	Lea	GP	W	L	T	Mins	GA	SO	Avg	GP	W	L	Mins	GA	SO	Avg
1995-96	Leksand	Swe. Jr.							UNAVAILABLE								
1996-97	Mora	Swe. 2	5	....	....	....	260	12	....	2.70	....	....	....	....	....	....	....

SNOW, GARTH PHI.

Goaltender. Catches left. 6'3", 200 lbs. Born, Wrentham, MA, July 28, 1969.
(Quebec's 6th choice, 114th overall, in 1987 Entry Draft).

			Regular Season								Playoffs						
Season	Club	Lea	GP	W	L	T	Mins	GA	SO	Avg	GP	W	L	Mins	GA	SO	Avg
1988-89	U. of Maine	H.E.	5	2	2	0	241	14	1	3.49	....	....	....	....	....	....	....
1989-90									DID NOT PLAY								
1990-91	U. of Maine	H.E.	25	*18	4	0	1290	64	2	2.98	....	....	....	....	....	....	....
1991-92a	U. of Maine	H.E.	31	*25	4	2	1792	73	*2	*2.44	....	....	....	....	....	....	....
1992-93b	U. of Maine	H.E.	23	*21	0	1	1210	42	1	*2.08	....	....	....	....	....	....	....
1993-94	U.S. National	....	23	13	5	3	1324	71	1	3.22	....	....	....	....	....	....	....
	U.S. Olympic	....	5	....	....	....	299	17	0	3.41	....	....	....	....	....	....	....
	Quebec	**NHL**	**5**	**3**	**2**	**0**	**279**	**16**	**0**	**3.44**	....	....	....	....	....	....	....
	Cornwall	AHL	16	6	5	3	927	51	0	3.30	13	8	5	790	42	0	3.19
1994-95	Cornwall	AHL	*62	*32	20	7	*3558	162	3	2.73	8	4	3	402	14	*2	*2.09
	Quebec	**NHL**	**2**	**1**	**1**	**0**	**119**	**11**	**0**	**5.55**	**1**	**0**	**0**	**9**	**1**	**0**	**6.67**
1995-96	**Philadelphia**	**NHL**	**26**	**12**	**8**	**4**	**1437**	**69**	**0**	**2.88**	**1**	**0**	**0**	**1**	**0**	**0**	**0.00**
1996-97	**Philadelphia**	**NHL**	**35**	**14**	**8**	**8**	**1884**	**79**	**2**	**2.52**	**12**	**8**	**4**	**699**	**33**	**0**	**2.83**
	NHL Totals		**68**	**30**	**19**	**12**	**3719**	**175**	**2**	**2.82**	**14**	**8**	**4**	**709**	**34**	**0**	**2.88**

a Hockey East Second All-Star Team (1992)
b NCAA Final Four All-Tournament Team (1993)

Traded to **Philadelphia** by **Colorado** for Philadelphia's third (later traded to Washington — Washington selected Shawn McNeil) and sixth (Kai Fischer) round choices in 1996 Entry Draft, July 12, 1995.

SODERSTROM, TOMMY (SAH-duhr-struhm)

Goaltender. Catches left. 5'7", 157 lbs. Born, Stockholm, Sweden, July 17, 1969.
(Philadelphia's 14th choice, 214th overall, in 1990 Entry Draft).

			Regular Season								Playoffs						
Season	Club	Lea	GP	W	L	T	Mins	GA	SO	Avg	GP	W	L	Mins	GA	SO	Avg
1989-90	Djurgarden	Swe.	4	....	....	....	240	14	0	3.50	....	....	....	....	....	....	....
1990-91	Djurgarden	Swe.	39	....	....	....	2340	104	3	2.67	7	....	....	423	10	2	1.42
1991-92	Djurgarden	Swe.	39	15	8	11	2340	109	4	2.79	10	....	....	635	28	0	2.65
1992-93	**Philadelphia**	**NHL**	**44**	**20**	**17**	**6**	**2512**	**143**	**5**	**3.42**	....	....	....	....	....	....	....
	Hershey	AHL	7	4	1	0	373	15	0	2.41	....	....	....	....	....	....	....
1993-94	**Philadelphia**	**NHL**	**34**	**6**	**18**	**4**	**1736**	**116**	**2**	**4.01**	....	....	....	....	....	....	....
	Hershey	AHL	9	3	4	1	461	37	0	4.81	....	....	....	....	....	....	....
1994-95	**NY Islanders**	**NHL**	**26**	**8**	**12**	**3**	**1350**	**70**	**1**	**3.11**	....	....	....	....	....	....	....
1995-96	**NY Islanders**	**NHL**	**51**	**11**	**22**	**6**	**2590**	**167**	**2**	**3.87**	....	....	....	....	....	....	....
1996-97	**NY Islanders**	**NHL**	**1**	**0**	**0**	**0**	**0**	**0**	**0**	**0.00**	....	....	....	....	....	....	....
	Rochester	AHL	2	2	0	0	120	8	0	4.00	....	....	....	....	....	....	....
	Utah	IHL	26	12	11	0	1463	76	0	3.12	....	....	....	....	....	....	....
	NHL Totals		**156**	**45**	**69**	**19**	**8188**	**496**	**10**	**3.63**	....	....	....	....	....	....	....

Traded to **NY Islanders** by **Philadelphia** for Ron Hextall and NY Islanders' sixth round choice (Dmitry Tertyshny) in 1995 Entry Draft, September 22, 1994.

SOUCY, CHRISTIAN (SOO-see)

Goaltender. Catches left. 5'11", 160 lbs. Born, Gatineau, Que., September 14, 1970.

			Regular Season								Playoffs						
Season	Club	Lea	GP	W	L	T	Mins	GA	SO	Avg	GP	W	L	Mins	GA	SO	Avg
1991-92	Vermont	ECAC	*30	15	11	3	*1783	81	0	2.83	....	....	....	....	....	....	....
1992-93a	Vermont	ECAC	29	11	15	3	1708	90	1	3.16	....	....	....	....	....	....	....
1993-94	**Chicago**	**NHL**	**1**	**0**	**0**	**0**	**3**	**0**	**0**	**0.00**	....	....	....	....	....	....	....
	Indianapolis	IHL	46	14	25	1	2302	159	1	4.14	....	....	....	....	....	....	....
1994-95	Indianapolis	IHL	42	15	17	5	2216	148	0	4.01	....	....	....	....	....	....	....
1995-96	Fort Worth	CHL	5	3	2	0	300	19	0	3.80	....	....	....	....	....	....	....
	Jacksonville	ECHL	3	2	1	0	179	11	0	3.68	....	....	....	....	....	....	....
	Indianapolis	IHL	22	12	9	0	1198	62	0	3.11	....	....	....	....	....	....	....
1996-97	Kentucky	AHL	3	0	2	0	138	11	0	4.77	....	....	....	....	....	....	....
	Baton Rouge	ECHL	46	18	20	3	2421	128	3	3.17	....	....	....	....	....	....	....
	NHL Totals		**1**	**0**	**0**	**0**	**3**	**0**	**0**	**0.00**	....	....	....	....	....	....	....

a ECAC Second All-Star Team (1993)

Signed as a free agent by **Chicago**, June 21, 1993.

STAUBER, ROBB (STAW-buhr) NYR

Goaltender. Catches left. 5'11", 180 lbs. Born, Duluth, MN, November 25, 1967.
(Los Angeles' 5th choice, 107th overall, in 1986 Entry Draft).

			Regular Season								Playoffs						
Season	Club	Lea	GP	W	L	T	Mins	GA	SO	Avg	GP	W	L	Mins	GA	SO	Avg
1986-87	U. Minnesota	WCHA	20	13	5	0	1072	63	0	3.53	....	....	....	....	....	....	....
1987-88abc	U. Minnesota	WCHA	44	34	10	0	2621	119	5	2.72	....	....	....	....	....	....	....
1988-89d	U. Minnesota	WCHA	34	26	8	0	2024	82	0	2.43	....	....	....	....	....	....	....
1989-90	**Los Angeles**	**NHL**	**2**	**0**	**1**	**0**	**83**	**11**	**0**	**7.95**	....	....	....	....	....	....	....
	New Haven	AHL	14	6	6	2	851	43	0	3.03	5	2	3	302	24	0	4.77
1990-91	New Haven	AHL	33	13	16	4	1882	115	1	3.67	....	....	....	....	....	....	....
	Phoenix	IHL	4	1	2	0	160	11	0	4.13	....	....	....	....	....	....	....
1991-92	Phoenix	IHL	22	8	12	1	1242	80	0	3.86	....	....	....	....	....	....	....
1992-93	**Los Angeles**	**NHL**	**31**	**15**	**8**	**4**	**1735**	**111**	**0**	**3.84**	**4**	**3**	**1**	**240**	**16**	**0**	**4.00**
1993-94	**Los Angeles**	**NHL**	**22**	**4**	**11**	**5**	**1144**	**65**	**1**	**3.41**	....	....	....	....	....	....	....
	Phoenix	IHL	3	1	1	0	121	13	0	6.42	....	....	....	....	....	....	....
1994-95	**Los Angeles**	**NHL**	**1**	**0**	**0**	**0**	**16**	**2**	**0**	**7.50**	....	....	....	....	....	....	....
	Buffalo	**NHL**	**6**	**2**	**3**	**0**	**317**	**20**	**0**	**3.79**	....	....	....	....	....	....	....
1995-96	Rochester	AHL	16	6	7	1	833	49	0	3.53	....	....	....	....	....	....	....
1996-97	Portland	AHL	30	13	13	2	1605	82	0	3.06	....	....	....	....	....	....	....
	NHL Totals		**62**	**21**	**23**	**9**	**3295**	**209**	**1**	**3.81**	**4**	**3**	**1**	**240**	**16**	**0**	**4.00**

a Won Hobey Baker Memorial Award (Top U.S. Collegiate Player) (1988)
b NCAA West First All-American Team (1988)
c WCHA First All-Star Team (1988)
d WCHA Second All-Star Team (1989)

Traded to **Buffalo** by **Los Angeles** with Alexei Zhitnik, Charlie Huddy and Los Angeles' fifth round choice (Marian Menhart) in 1995 Entry Draft for Philippe Boucher, Denis Tsygurov and Grant Fuhr, February 14, 1995. Signed as a free agent by **Washington**, August 27, 1996. Signed as a free agent by **NY Rangers**, August, 1997.

STORR, JAMIE (STOHR) L.A.

Goaltender. Catches left. 6', 170 lbs. Born, Brampton, Ont., December 28, 1975.
(Los Angeles' 1st choice, 7th overall, in 1994 Entry Draft).

			Regular Season								Playoffs						
Season	Club	Lea	GP	W	L	T	Mins	GA	SO	Avg	GP	W	L	Mins	GA	SO	Avg
1991-92	Owen Sound	OHL	34	11	16	1	1732	128	0	4.43	5	1	4	299	28	0	5.62
1992-93	Owen Sound	OHL	41	20	17	3	2362	180	0	4.57	8	4	4	454	35	0	4.63
1993-94a	Owen Sound	OHL	35	21	11	1	2004	120	1	3.59	9	4	5	547	44	0	4.83
1994-95	Owen Sound	OHL	17	5	9	2	977	64	0	3.93	....	....	....	....	....	....	....
	Los Angeles	**NHL**	**5**	**1**	**3**	**1**	**263**	**17**	**0**	**3.88**	....	....	....	....	....	....	....
	Windsor	OHL	4	3	1	0	241	8	1	1.99	10	6	3	520	34	1	3.92
1995-96	**Los Angeles**	**NHL**	**5**	**3**	**1**	**0**	**262**	**12**	**0**	**2.75**	....	....	....	....	....	....	....
	Phoenix	IHL	48	22	20	4	2711	139	2	3.08	2	1	1	118	4	1	2.03
1996-97	**Los Angeles**	**NHL**	**5**	**2**	**1**	**1**	**265**	**11**	**0**	**2.49**	....	....	....	....	....	....	....
	Phoenix	IHL	44	16	22	4	2441	147	0	3.61	....	....	....	....	....	....	....
	NHL Totals		**15**	**6**	**5**	**2**	**790**	**40**	**0**	**3.04**	....	....	....	....	....	....	....

a OHL First All-Star Team (1994)

SWANJORD, SCOTT N.J.

Goaltender. Catches left. 6'4", 210 lbs. Born, Sioux Falls, SD, October 8, 1975.
(New Jersey's 11th choice, 259th overall, in 1994 Entry Draft).

			Regular Season								Playoffs						
Season	Club	Lea	GP	W	L	T	Mins	GA	SO	Avg	GP	W	L	Mins	GA	SO	Avg
1994-95	Sioux City	USHL	24	14	7	0	1206	70	0	3.48	10	4	4	491	27	0	3.30
1995-96	Providence	H.E.	2	1	1	0	85	8	0	5.63	....	....	....	....	....	....	....
1996-97	Providence	H.E.							DID NOT PLAY								

TABARACCI, RICK (tab-uh-RA-chee) CGY.

Goaltender. Catches left. 6'1", 180 lbs. Born, Toronto, Ont., January 2, 1969.
(Pittsburgh's 2nd choice, 26th overall, in 1987 Entry Draft).

			Regular Season								Playoffs						
Season	Club	Lea	GP	W	L	T	Mins	GA	SO	Avg	GP	W	L	Mins	GA	SO	Avg
1986-87	Cornwall	OHL	59	23	32	3	3347	290	1	5.20	5	1	4	303	26	0	3.17
1987-88a	Cornwall	OHL	58	*33	18	6	3448	200	*3	3.48	11	5	6	642	37	0	3.46
	Muskegon	IHL	....	....	....	....	....	....	....	....	1	0	0	13	1	0	4.62
1988-89	**Pittsburgh**	**NHL**	**1**	**0**	**0**	**0**	**33**	**4**	**0**	**7.27**	....	....	....	....	....	....	....
b	Cornwall	OHL	50	24	20	5	2974	210	1	4.24	18	10	8	1080	65	*1	3.61
1989-90	Moncton	AHL	27	10	15	2	1580	107	2	4.06	....	....	....	....	....	....	....
	Fort Wayne	IHL	22	8	9	1	1064	73	0	4.12	3	1	2	159	19	0	7.17
1990-91	**Winnipeg**	**NHL**	**24**	**4**	**9**	**4**	**1093**	**71**	**1**	**3.90**	....	....	....	....	....	....	....
	Moncton	AHL	11	4	5	2	645	41	0	3.81	....	....	....	....	....	....	....
1991-92	**Winnipeg**	**NHL**	**18**	**6**	**7**	**3**	**966**	**52**	**0**	**3.23**	**7**	**3**	**4**	**387**	**26**	**0**	**4.03**
	Moncton	AHL	23	10	11	1	1313	80	0	3.66	....	....	....	....	....	....	....
1992-93	**Winnipeg**	**NHL**	**19**	**5**	**10**	**0**	**959**	**70**	**0**	**4.38**	....	....	....	....	....	....	....
	Moncton	AHL	5	2	1	2	290	18	0	3.72	....	....	....	....	....	....	....
	Washington	**NHL**	**6**	**3**	**2**	**0**	**343**	**10**	**2**	**1.75**	**4**	**1**	**3**	**304**	**14**	**0**	**2.76**
1993-94	**Washington**	**NHL**	**32**	**13**	**14**	**2**	**1770**	**91**	**2**	**3.08**	**2**	**0**	**2**	**111**	**6**	**0**	**3.24**
	Portland	AHL	3	3	0	0	176	8	0	2.72	....	....	....	....	....	....	....
1994-95	**Washington**	**NHL**	**8**	**1**	**3**	**2**	**394**	**16**	**0**	**2.44**	....	....	....	....	....	....	....
	Chicago	IHL	2	1	1	0	119	9	0	4.51	....	....	....	....	....	....	....
	Calgary	**NHL**	**5**	**2**	**0**	**1**	**202**	**5**	**0**	**1.49**	**1**	**0**	**0**	**19**	**0**	**0**	**0.00**
1995-96	**Calgary**	**NHL**	**43**	**19**	**16**	**3**	**2391**	**117**	**3**	**2.94**	**3**	**0**	**3**	**204**	**7**	**0**	**2.06**
1996-97	**Calgary**	**NHL**	**7**	**2**	**4**	**0**	**361**	**14**	**1**	**2.33**	....	....	....	....	....	....	....
	Tampa Bay	**NHL**	**55**	**20**	**25**	**6**	**3012**	**138**	**4**	**2.75**	....	....	....	....	....	....	....
	NHL Totals		**218**	**75**	**90**	**21**	**11524**	**588**	**13**	**3.06**	**17**	**4**	**12**	**1025**	**53**	**0**	**3.10**

a OHL First All-Star Team (1988)
b OHL Second All-Star Team (1989)

Traded to **Winnipeg** by **Pittsburgh** with Randy Cunneyworth and Dave McLlwain for Jim Kyte, Andrew McBain and Randy Gilhen, June 17, 1989. Traded to **Washington** by **Winnipeg** for Jim Hrivnak and Washington's second round choice (Alexei Budayev) in 1993 Entry Draft, March 22, 1993. Traded to **Calgary** by **Washington** for a conditional fifth round draft choice, April 7, 1995. Traded to **Tampa Bay** by **Calgary** for Aaron Gavey, November 19, 1996. Traded to **Calgary** by **Tampa Bay** for Calgary's fourth round choice in 1998 Entry Draft, June 21, 1997.

TALLAS, ROBBIE (TAL-as) BOS.

Goaltender. Catches left. 6', 163 lbs. Born, Edmonton, Alta., March 20, 1973.

			Regular Season								Playoffs						
Season	Club	Lea	GP	W	L	T	Mins	GA	SO	Avg	GP	W	L	Mins	GA	SO	Avg
1991-92	Seattle	WHL	14	4	7	0	708	52	0	4.41	....	....	....	....	....	....	....
1992-93	Seattle	WHL	58	24	23	3	3151	194	2	3.69	5	1	4	333	18	0	3.24
1993-94	Seattle	WHL	51	23	21	3	2849	188	0	3.96	9	5	4	567	40	0	4.23
1994-95	Charlotte	ECHL	36	21	9	3	2011	114	0	3.40	....	....	....	....	....	....	....
	Providence	AHL	2	1	0	0	82	4	1	2.90	....	....	....	....	....	....	....
1995-96	**Boston**	**NHL**	**1**	**1**	**0**	**0**	**60**	**3**	**0**	**3.00**	....	....	....	....	....	....	....
	Providence	AHL	37	12	16	7	2136	117	1	3.29	2	0	2	135	9	0	4.01
1996-97	**Boston**	**NHL**	**28**	**8**	**12**	**1**	**1244**	**69**	**1**	**3.33**	....	....	....	....	....	....	....
	Providence	AHL	24	9	14	1	1423	83	0	3.50	....	....	....	....	....	....	....
	NHL Totals		**29**	**9**	**12**	**1**	**1304**	**72**	**1**	**3.31**	....	....	....	....	....	....	....

Signed as a free agent by **Boston**, September 13, 1995.

TERRERI, CHRIS (tuh-RAIR-ee) CHI.

Goaltender. Catches left. 5'8", 160 lbs. Born, Providence, RI, November 15, 1964.
(New Jersey's 3rd choice, 87th overall, in 1983 Entry Draft).

			Regular Season								Playoffs						
Season	Club	Lea	GP	W	L	T	Mins	GA	SO	Avg	GP	W	L	Mins	GA	SO	Avg
1982-83	Providence	ECAC	11	7	1	0	528	17	2	1.93	....	....	....	....	....	....	....
1983-84	Providence	ECAC	10	4	2	0	391	20	0	3.07	....	....	....	....	....	....	....
1984-85ab	Providence	H.E.	33	15	13	5	1956	116	1	3.35	....	....	....	....	....	....	....
1985-86	Providence	H.E.	22	6	16	0	1320	84	0	3.74	....	....	....	....	....	....	....
1986-87	**New Jersey**	**NHL**	**7**	**0**	**3**	**1**	**286**	**21**	**0**	**4.41**	....	....	....	....	....	....	....
	Maine	AHL	14	4	9	1	765	57	0	4.47	....	....	....	....	....	....	....
1987-88	Utica	AHL	7	5	1	0	399	18	0	2.71	....	....	....	....	....	....	....
	U.S. National	....	26	17	7	2	1430	81	0	3.40	....	....	....	....	....	....	....
	U.S. Olympic	....	3	1	1	0	128	14	0	6.56	....	....	....	....	....	....	....
1988-89	**New Jersey**	**NHL**	**8**	**0**	**4**	**2**	**402**	**18**	**0**	**2.69**	....	....	....	....	....	....	....
	Utica	AHL	39	20	15	3	2314	132	0	3.42	2	0	1	80	6	0	4.50
1989-90	**New Jersey**	**NHL**	**35**	**15**	**12**	**3**	**1931**	**110**	**0**	**3.42**	**4**	**2**	**2**	**238**	**13**	**0**	**3.28**
1990-91	**New Jersey**	**NHL**	**53**	**24**	**21**	**7**	**2970**	**144**	**1**	**2.91**	**7**	**3**	**4**	**428**	**21**	**0**	**2.94**
1991-92	**New Jersey**	**NHL**	**54**	**22**	**22**	**10**	**3186**	**169**	**1**	**3.18**	**7**	**3**	**3**	**386**	**23**	**0**	**3.58**
1992-93	**New Jersey**	**NHL**	**48**	**19**	**21**	**3**	**2672**	**151**	**2**	**3.39**	**4**	**1**	**3**	**219**	**17**	**0**	**4.66**
1993-94	**New Jersey**	**NHL**	**44**	**20**	**11**	**4**	**2340**	**106**	**2**	**2.72**	**4**	**3**	**0**	**200**	**9**	**0**	**2.70**
1994-95	**New Jersey**	**NHL**	**15**	**3**	**7**	**2**	**734**	**31**	**0**	**2.53**	**1**	**0**	**0**	**8**	**0**	**0**	**0.00** ♦
1995-96	**New Jersey**	**NHL**	**4**	**3**	**0**	**0**	**210**	**9**	**0**	**2.57**	....	....	....	....	....	....	....
	San Jose	**NHL**	**46**	**13**	**29**	**1**	**2516**	**155**	**0**	**3.70**	....	....	....	....	....	....	....
1996-97	**San Jose**	**NHL**	**22**	**6**	**10**	**3**	**1200**	**55**	**0**	**2.75**	....	....	....	....	....	....	....
	Chicago	**NHL**	**7**	**4**	**1**	**2**	**429**	**19**	**0**	**2.66**	**2**	**0**	**0**	**44**	**3**	**0**	**4.09**
	NHL Totals		**343**	**129**	**141**	**38**	**18876**	**988**	**6**	**3.14**	**29**	**12**	**12**	**1523**	**86**	**0**	**3.39**

a Hockey East All-Star Team (1985)
b NCAA All-American Team (1985)

Traded to **San Jose** by **New Jersey** for San Jose's second round choice (later traded to Pittsburgh — Pittsburgh selected Pavel Skrbek) in 1996 Entry Draft, November 15, 1995. Traded to **Chicago** by **San Jose** with Ulf Dahlen, Michal Sykora and a conditional choice in 1998 Entry Draft for Ed Belfour, January 25, 1997.

THEODORE, JOSE (THEE-uh-dohr, joh-SAY) MTL.

Goaltender. Catches right. 5'11", 181 lbs. Born, Laval, Que., September 13, 1976.
(Montreal's 2nd choice, 44th overall, in 1994 Entry Draft).

			Regular Season								Playoffs						
Season	Club	Lea	GP	W	L	T	Mins	GA	SO	Avg	GP	W	L	Mins	GA	SO	Avg
1992-93	St-Jean	QMJHL	34	12	16	2	1776	112	0	3.78	3	0	2	175	11	0	3.77
1993-94	St-Jean	QMJHL	57	20	29	6	3225	194	0	3.61	5	1	4	296	18	0	3.65
1994-95a	Hull	QMJHL	*58	*32	22	2	*3348	193	5	3.46	*21	*15	6	*1263	59	*1	2.80
	Fredericton	AHL	....	....	....	....	....	....	....	....	1	0	1	60	3	0	3.00
1995-96	**Montreal**	**NHL**	**1**	**0**	**0**	**0**	**9**	**1**	**0**	**6.67**	....	....	....	....	....	....	....
a	Hull	QMJHL	48	33	11	2	2807	158	0	3.38	5	2	3	299	20	0	4.01
1996-97	**Montreal**	**NHL**	**16**	**5**	**6**	**2**	**821**	**53**	**0**	**3.87**	**2**	**1**	**1**	**168**	**7**	**0**	**2.50**
	Fredericton	AHL	26	12	12	0	1468	87	0	3.55	....	....	....	....	....	....	....
	NHL Totals		**17**	**5**	**6**	**2**	**830**	**54**	**0**	**3.90**	**2**	**1**	**1**	**168**	**7**	**0**	**2.50**

a QMJHL Second All-Star Team (1995, 1996)

THIBAULT, JOCELYN (tee-BOW) MTL.

Goaltender. Catches left. 5'11", 170 lbs. Born, Montreal, Que., January 12, 1975.
(Quebec's 1st choice, 10th overall, in 1993 Entry Draft).

			Regular Season								Playoffs						
Season	Club	Lea	GP	W	L	T	Mins	GA	SO	Avg	GP	W	L	Mins	GA	SO	Avg
1991-92	Trois Rivieres	QMJHL	30	14	7	1	1496	77	0	3.09	3	1	1	110	4	0	2.19
1992-93abc	Sherbrooke	QMJHL	56	34	14	5	3190	159	3	2.99	15	9	6	882	57	0	3.87
1993-94	**Quebec**	**NHL**	**29**	**8**	**13**	**3**	**1504**	**83**	**0**	**3.31**	....	....	....	....	....	....	....
	Cornwall	AHL	4	4	0	0	240	9	1	2.25	....	....	....	....	....	....	....
1994-95	Sherbrooke	QMJHL	13	6	6	1	776	38	1	2.94	....	....	....	....	....	....	....
	Quebec	**NHL**	**18**	**12**	**2**	**2**	**898**	**35**	**1**	**2.34**	**3**	**1**	**2**	**148**	**8**	**0**	**3.24**
1995-96	**Colorado**	**NHL**	**10**	**3**	**4**	**2**	**558**	**28**	**0**	**3.01**	....	....	....	....	....	....	....
	Montreal	**NHL**	**40**	**23**	**13**	**3**	**2334**	**110**	**3**	**2.83**	**6**	**2**	**4**	**311**	**18**	**0**	**3.47**
1996-97	**Montreal**	**NHL**	**61**	**22**	**24**	**11**	**3397**	**164**	**1**	**2.90**	**3**	**0**	**3**	**179**	**13**	**0**	**4.36**
	NHL Totals		**158**	**68**	**56**	**21**	**8691**	**420**	**5**	**2.90**	**12**	**3**	**9**	**638**	**39**	**0**	**3.67**

a QMJHL First All-Star Team (1993)
b Canadian Major Junior First All-Star Team (1993)
c Canadian Major Junior Goaltender of the Year (1993)

Traded to **Montreal** by **Colorado** with Andrei Kovalenko and Martin Rucinsky for Patrick Roy and Mike Keane, December 6, 1995.

THOMAS, TIM COL.

Goaltender. Catches left. 5'11", 180 lbs. Born, Flint, MI, April 15, 1974.
(Quebec's 11th choice, 217th overall, in 1994 Entry Draft).

			Regular Season								Playoffs						
Season	Club	Lea	GP	W	L	T	Mins	GA	SO	Avg	GP	W	L	Mins	GA	SO	Avg
1993-94	U. of Vermont	ECAC	*33	15	12	6	1864	94	0	3.03	....	....	....	....	....	....	....
1994-95ab	U. of Vermont	ECAC	34	18	13	2	2010	90	*4	*2.69	....	....	....	....	....	....	....
1995-96ac	U. of Vermont	ECAC	37	*26	7	4	*2254	88	*3	*2.34	....	....	....	....	....	....	....
1996-97	U. of Vermont	ECAC	36	22	11	3	2158	101	2	2.81	....	....	....	....	....	....	....

a ECAC First All-Star Team (1995, 1996)
b NCAA East Second All-American Team (1995)
c NCAA East First All-American Team (1996)

TORCHIA, MIKE (TOR-chee-ah)

Goaltender. Catches left. 5'11", 215 lbs. Born, Toronto, Ont., February 23, 1972.
(Minnesota's 2nd choice, 74th overall, in 1991 Entry Draft).

			Regular Season								Playoffs						
Season	Club	Lea	GP	W	L	T	Mins	GA	SO	Avg	GP	W	L	Mins	GA	SO	Avg
1988-89	Kitchener	OHL	30	14	9	4	1472	102	0	4.02	2	0	2	126	8	0	3.81
1989-90ab	Kitchener	OHL	40	25	11	2	2280	136	1	3.58	*17	*11	6	*1023	60	0	3.52
1990-91	Kitchener	OHL	57	25	24	7	*3317	219	0	3.95	6	2	4	382	30	0	4.71
1991-92	Kitchener	OHL	*55	25	24	3	*3042	203	1	4.00	14	7	7	900	47	0	3.13
1992-93	Cdn. National	....	5	5	0	0	300	11	1	2.20	....	....	....	....	....	....	....
	Kalamazoo	IHL	48	19	17	9	2729	173	0	3.80	....	....	....	....	....	....	....
1993-94	Kalamazoo	IHL	43	23	12	2	2168	133	0	3.68	4	1	3	221	14	*1	3.80
1994-95	Kalamazoo	IHL	41	19	14	5	2140	106	*3	2.97	6	0	4	257	17	0	3.97
	Dallas	**NHL**	**6**	**3**	**2**	**1**	**327**	**18**	**0**	**3.30**	....	....	....	....	....	....	....
1995-96	Portland	AHL	12	2	6	2	577	46	0	4.79	....	....	....	....	....	....	....
	Hampton Rds.	ECHL	5	2	2	0	260	17	0	3.92	....	....	....	....	....	....	....
	Michigan	IHL	1	1	0	0	60	1	0	1.00	....	....	....	....	....	....	....
	Orlando	IHL	7	3	1	1	341	17	0	2.99	....	....	....	....	....	....	....
	Baltimore	AHL	5	2	1	1	256	18	0	4.21	1	0	0	40	0	0	0.00
1996-97	Fort Wayne	IHL	57	20	31	3	2970	172	1	3.47	....	....	....	....	....	....	....
	Baltimore	AHL	....	....	....	....	....	....	....	....	1	0	0	40	4	0	6.00
	NHL Totals		**6**	**3**	**2**	**1**	**327**	**18**	**0**	**3.30**	....	....	....	....	....	....	....

a Memorial Cup All-Star Team (1990)
b Won Hap Emms Memorial Memorial Trophy (Memorial Cup Tournament Top Goaltender) (1990)

Traded to **Washington** by **Dallas** for future considerations, July 14, 1995. Traded to **Anaheim** by **Washington** for Todd Krygier, March 8, 1996.

TOSKALA, VESA (TAWS-kah-lah) S.J.

Goaltender. Catches left. 5'9", 172 lbs. Born, Tampere, Finland, May 20, 1977.
(San Jose's 4th choice, 90th overall, in 1995 Entry Draft).

			Regular Season								Playoffs						
Season	Club	Lea	GP	W	L	T	Mins	GA	SO	Avg	GP	W	L	Mins	GA	SO	Avg
1994-95	Ilves	Fin. Jr.	17	....	....	....	956	36	....	2.26	....	....	....	....	....	....	....
1995-96	Ilves	Fin. Jr.	3	....	....	....	180	3	....	1.00	....	....	....	....	....	....	....
	Koo-Vee	Fin. 2	2	....	....	....	119	5	....	2.51	....	....	....	....	....	....	....
	Ilves	Fin.	37	....	....	....	2073	109	1	3.16	2	....	....	78	11	....	8.49
1996-97	Ilves	Fin.	40	22	12	5	2270	108	0	2.85	8	3	5	479	29	0	3.63

TREFILOV, ANDREI (TREH-fee-lahf) BUF.

Goaltender. Catches left. 6', 190 lbs. Born, Kirovo-Chepetsk, USSR, August 31, 1969.
(Calgary's 14th choice, 261st overall, in 1991 Entry Draft).

			Regular Season								Playoffs						
Season	Club	Lea	GP	W	L	T	Mins	GA	SO	Avg	GP	W	L	Mins	GA	SO	Avg
1990-91	Moscow D'amo	USSR	20	....	....	....	1070	36	0	2.01	....	....	....	....	....	....	....
1991-92	Moscow D'amo	CIS	28	....	....	....	1326	35	0	1.58	....	....	....	....	....	....	....
1992-93	**Calgary**	**NHL**	**1**	**0**	**0**	**1**	**65**	**5**	**0**	**4.62**	....	....	....	....	....	....	....
	Salt Lake	IHL	44	23	17	3	2536	135	0	3.19	....	....	....	....	....	....	....
1993-94	**Calgary**	**NHL**	**11**	**3**	**4**	**2**	**623**	**26**	**2**	**2.50**	....	....	....	....	....	....	....
	Saint John	AHL	28	10	10	7	1629	93	0	3.42	....	....	....	....	....	....	....
1994-95	**Calgary**	**NHL**	**6**	**0**	**3**	**0**	**236**	**16**	**0**	**4.07**	....	....	....	....	....	....	....
	Saint John	AHL	7	1	5	1	383	20	0	3.13	....	....	....	....	....	....	....
1995-96	**Buffalo**	**NHL**	**22**	**8**	**8**	**1**	**1094**	**64**	**0**	**3.51**	....	....	....	....	....	....	....
	Rochester	AHL	5	4	1	0	299	13	0	2.61	....	....	....	....	....	....	....
1996-97	**Buffalo**	**NHL**	**3**	**0**	**2**	**0**	**159**	**10**	**0**	**3.77**	**1**	**0**	**0**	**5**	**0**	**0**	**0.00**
	NHL Totals		**43**	**11**	**17**	**4**	**2177**	**121**	**2**	**3.33**	**1**	**0**	**0**	**5**	**0**	**0**	**0.00**

Signed as a free agent by **Buffalo**, July 11, 1995.

TUGNUTT, RON OTT.

Goaltender. Catches left. 5'11", 155 lbs. Born, Scarborough, Ont., October 22, 1967.
(Quebec's 4th choice, 81st overall, in 1986 Entry Draft).

			Regular Season								Playoffs						
Season	Club	Lea	GP	W	L	T	Mins	GA	SO	Avg	GP	W	L	Mins	GA	SO	Avg
1984-85	Peterborough	OHL	18	7	4	2	938	59	0	3.77	....	....	....	....	....	....	....
1985-86	Peterborough	OHL	26	18	7	0	1543	74	1	2.88	3	2	0	133	6	0	2.71
1986-87a	Peterborough	OHL	31	21	7	2	1891	88	2	*2.79	6	3	3	374	21	1	3.37
1987-88	**Quebec**	**NHL**	**6**	**2**	**3**	**0**	**284**	**16**	**0**	**3.38**	....	....	....	....	....	....	....
	Fredericton	AHL	34	20	9	4	1964	118	1	3.60	4	1	2	204	11	0	3.24
1988-89	**Quebec**	**NHL**	**26**	**10**	**10**	**3**	**1367**	**82**	**0**	**3.60**	....	....	....	....	....	....	....
	Halifax	AHL	24	14	7	2	1368	79	1	3.46	....	....	....	....	....	....	....
1989-90	**Quebec**	**NHL**	**35**	**5**	**24**	**3**	**1978**	**152**	**0**	**4.61**	....	....	....	....	....	....	....
	Halifax	AHL	6	1	5	0	366	23	0	3.77	....	....	....	....	....	....	....
1990-91	**Quebec**	**NHL**	**56**	**12**	**29**	**10**	**3144**	**212**	**0**	**4.05**	....	....	....	....	....	....	....
	Halifax	AHL	2	0	1	0	100	8	0	4.80	....	....	....	....	....	....	....
1991-92	**Quebec**	**NHL**	**30**	**6**	**17**	**3**	**1583**	**106**	**1**	**4.02**	....	....	....	....	....	....	....
	Halifax	AHL	8	3	3	1	447	30	0	4.03	....	....	....	....	....	....	....
	Edmonton	**NHL**	**3**	**1**	**1**	**0**	**124**	**10**	**0**	**4.84**	**2**	**0**	**0**	**60**	**3**	**0**	**3.00**
1992-93	**Edmonton**	**NHL**	**26**	**9**	**12**	**2**	**1338**	**93**	**0**	**4.17**	....	....	....	....	....	....	....
1993-94	**Anaheim**	**NHL**	**28**	**10**	**15**	**1**	**1520**	**76**	**1**	**3.00**	....	....	....	....	....	....	....
	Montreal	**NHL**	**8**	**2**	**3**	**1**	**378**	**24**	**0**	**3.81**	**1**	**0**	**1**	**59**	**5**	**0**	**5.08**
1994-95	**Montreal**	**NHL**	**7**	**1**	**3**	**1**	**346**	**18**	**0**	**3.12**	....	....	....	....	....	....	....
1995-96	Portland	AHL	58	21	23	6	3068	171	2	3.34	13	7	6	782	36	1	2.76
1996-97	**Ottawa**	**NHL**	**37**	**17**	**15**	**1**	**1991**	**93**	**3**	**2.80**	**7**	**3**	**4**	**425**	**14**	**1**	**1.98**
	NHL Totals		**262**	**75**	**132**	**25**	**14053**	**882**	**5**	**3.77**	**10**	**3**	**5**	**544**	**22**	**1**	**2.43**

a OHL First All-Star Team (1987)

Traded to **Edmonton** by **Quebec** with Brad Zavisha for Martin Rucinsky, March 10, 1992. Claimed by **Anaheim** from **Edmonton** in Expansion Draft, June 24, 1993. Traded to **Montreal** by **Anaheim** for Stephan Lebeau, February 20, 1994. Signed as a free agent by **Washington**, September 25, 1995. Signed as a free agent by **Ottawa**, August 14, 1996.

TURCO, MARTY DAL.

Goaltender. Catches left. 5'11", 175 lbs. Born, Sault Ste. Marie, Ont., August 13, 1975.
(Dallas' 4th choice, 124th overall, in 1994 Entry Draft).

			Regular Season								Playoffs						
Season	Club	Lea	GP	W	L	T	Mins	GA	SO	Avg	GP	W	L	Mins	GA	SO	Avg
1994-95	U. of Michigan	CCHA	37	*27	7	1	2063	95	1	2.76	....	....	....	....	....	....	....
1995-96	U. of Michigan	CCHA	*42	*34	7	1	*2335	84	*5	*2.16	....	....	....	....	....	....	....
1996-97ab	U. of Michigan	CCHA	*41	*33	4	4	*2296	87	*4	*2.27	....	....	....	....	....	....	....

a CCHA First All-Star Team (1997)
b NCAA West First All-American Team (1997)

TUREK, ROMAN (TOOR-ehk) DAL.

Goaltender. Catches right. 6'3", 190 lbs. Born, Pisek, Czech., May 21, 1970.
(Minnesota's 6th choice, 113th overall, in 1990 Entry Draft).

			Regular Season								Playoffs						
Season	Club	Lea	GP	W	L	T	Mins	GA	SO	Avg	GP	W	L	Mins	GA	SO	Avg
1990-91	Budejovice	Czech.	26	....	....	....	1244	98	0	4.70	....	....	....	....	....	....	....
1991-92	Budejovice	Czech.2							UNAVAILABLE								
1992-93	Budejovice	Czech.	43	....	....	....	2555	121	....	2.84	....	....	....	....	....	....	....
1993-94	Budejovice	Czech.	44	....	....	....	2584	111	....	2.51	3	....	....	180	12	0	4.00
1994-95	Budejovice	Czech.	44	....	....	....	2587	119	....	2.76	9	....	....	498	25	....	3.01
1995-96	Nurnberg	Ger.	48	....	....	....	2787	154	....	3.31	5	....	....	338	14	....	2.48
1996-97	**Dallas**	**NHL**	**6**	**3**	**1**	**0**	**263**	**9**	**0**	**2.05**	....	....	....	....	....	....	....
	Michigan	IHL	29	8	13	4	1555	77	0	2.97	....	....	....	....	....	....	....
	NHL Totals		**6**	**3**	**1**	**0**	**263**	**9**	**0**	**2.05**	....	....	....	....	....	....	....

VAILLANCOURT, LUC (VIGH-an-koor) ANA.

Goaltender. Catches left. 6'1", 190 lbs. Born, Ferme-Neuve, Que., June 13, 1978.
(Anaheim's 4th choice, 125th overall, in 1997 Entry Draft).

			Regular Season								Playoffs						
Season	Club	Lea	GP	W	L	T	Mins	GA	SO	Avg	GP	W	L	Mins	GA	SO	Avg
1995-96	Beauport	QMJHL	22	7	8	0	882	71	0	4.83	2	1	0	80	3	0	2.25
1996-97	Beauport	QMJHL	51	18	27	1	2684	163	0	3.64	4	1	3	240	20	0	5.00

VALIQUETTE, STEPHEN (val-ih-KEHT) L.A.

Goaltender. Catches left. 6'5", 205 lbs. Born, Etobicoke, Ont., August 20, 1977.
(Los Angeles' 8th choice, 190th overall, in 1996 Entry Draft).

			Regular Season								Playoffs						
Season	Club	Lea	GP	W	L	T	Mins	GA	SO	Avg	GP	W	L	Mins	GA	SO	Avg
1994-95	Sudbury	OHL	4	2	0	0	138	6	0	2.61	....	....	....	....	....	....	....
1995-96	Sudbury	OHL	39	13	16	2	1887	123	0	3.91	....	....	....	....	....	....	....
1996-97	Sudbury	OHL	61	21	29	7	3311	232	1	4.20	....	....	....	....	....	....	....

VANBIESBROUCK, JOHN (van-BEES-bruhk) FLA.

Goaltender. Catches left. 5'8", 176 lbs. Born, Detroit, MI, September 4, 1963.
(NY Rangers' 5th choice, 72nd overall, in 1981 Entry Draft).

			Regular Season								Playoffs						
Season	Club	Lea	GP	W	L	T	Mins	GA	SO	Avg	GP	W	L	Mins	GA	SO	Avg
1980-81	S.S. Marie	OHA	56	31	16	1	2941	203	0	4.14	11	3	3	457	24	1	3.15
1981-82	**NY Rangers**	**NHL**	**1**	**1**	**0**	**0**	**60**	**1**	**0**	**1.00**	....	....	....	....	....	....	....
	S.S. Marie	OHL	31	12	12	2	1686	102	0	3.62	7	1	4	276	20	0	4.35
1982-83a	S.S. Marie	OHL	62	39	21	1	3471	209	0	3.61	16	7	6	944	56	*1	3.56
1983-84	**NY Rangers**	**NHL**	**3**	**2**	**1**	**0**	**180**	**10**	**0**	**3.33**	**1**	**0**	**0**	**1**	**0**	**0**	**0.00**
bcd	Tulsa	CHL	37	20	13	2	2153	124	*3	3.46	4	4	0	240	10	0	*2.50
1984-85	**NY Rangers**	**NHL**	**42**	**12**	**24**	**3**	**2358**	**166**	**1**	**4.22**	**1**	**0**	**0**	**20**	**0**	**0**	**0.00**
1985-86ef	**NY Rangers**	**NHL**	**61**	***31**	**21**	**5**	**3326**	**184**	**3**	**3.32**	**16**	**8**	**8**	**899**	**49**	***1**	**3.27**
1986-87	**NY Rangers**	**NHL**	**50**	**18**	**20**	**5**	**2656**	**161**	**0**	**3.64**	**4**	**1**	**3**	**195**	**11**	**1**	**3.38**
1987-88	**NY Rangers**	**NHL**	**56**	**27**	**22**	**7**	**3319**	**187**	**2**	**3.38**	....	....	....	....	....	....	....
1988-89	**NY Rangers**	**NHL**	**56**	**28**	**21**	**4**	**3207**	**197**	**0**	**3.69**	**2**	**0**	**1**	**107**	**6**	**0**	**3.36**
1989-90	**NY Rangers**	**NHL**	**47**	**19**	**19**	**7**	**2734**	**154**	**1**	**3.38**	**6**	**2**	**3**	**298**	**15**	**0**	**3.02**
1990-91	**NY Rangers**	**NHL**	**40**	**15**	**18**	**6**	**2257**	**126**	**3**	**3.35**	**1**	**0**	**0**	**52**	**1**	**0**	**1.15**
1991-92	**NY Rangers**	**NHL**	**45**	**27**	**13**	**3**	**2526**	**120**	**2**	**2.85**	**7**	**2**	**5**	**368**	**23**	**0**	**3.75**
1992-93	**NY Rangers**	**NHL**	**48**	**20**	**18**	**7**	**2757**	**152**	**4**	**3.31**	....	....	....	....	....	....	....
1993-94g	**Florida**	**NHL**	**57**	**21**	**25**	**11**	**3440**	**145**	**1**	**2.53**	....	....	....	....	....	....	....
1994-95	**Florida**	**NHL**	**37**	**14**	**15**	**4**	**2087**	**86**	**4**	**2.47**	....	....	....	....	....	....	....
1995-96	**Florida**	**NHL**	**57**	**26**	**20**	**7**	**3178**	**142**	**2**	**2.68**	***22**	**12**	**10**	**1332**	**50**	**1**	**2.25**
1996-97	**Florida**	**NHL**	**57**	**27**	**19**	**10**	**3347**	**128**	**2**	**2.29**	**5**	**1**	**4**	**328**	**13**	**1**	**2.38**
	NHL Totals		**657**	**288**	**256**	**79**	**37432**	**1959**	**25**	**3.14**	**65**	**26**	**34**	**3600**	**168**	**4**	**2.80**

a OHL Second All-Star Team (1983)
b CHL First All-Star Team (1984)
c Shared Terry Sawchuk Trophy (CHL's Leading Goaltender) with Ron Scott (1984)
d Shared Tommy Ivan Trophy (CHL's Most Valuable Player) with Bruce Affleck of Indianapolis (1984)
e Won Vezina Trophy (1986)
f NHL First All-Star Team (1986)
g NHL Second All-Star Team (1994)

Played in NHL All-Star Game (1994, 1996, 1997)

Traded to **Vancouver** by **NY Rangers** for future considerations (Doug Lidster, June 25, 1993), June 20, 1993. Claimed by **Florida** from **Vancouver** in Expansion Draft, June 24, 1993.

VERNON, MIKE S.J.

Goaltender. Catches left. 5'9", 165 lbs. Born, Calgary, Alta., February 24, 1963.
(Calgary's 2nd choice, 56th overall, in 1981 Entry Draft).

			Regular Season								Playoffs						
Season	Club	Lea	GP	W	L	T	Mins	GA	SO	Avg	GP	W	L	Mins	GA	SO	Avg
1980-81	Calgary	WHL	59	33	17	1	3154	198	1	3.77	22	14	8	1271	82	1	3.87
1981-82a	Calgary	WHL	42	22	14	2	2329	143	3	3.68	9	5	4	527	30	0	3.42
	Oklahoma City	CHL	....	....	....	....	....	....	....	....	1	0	1	70	4	0	3.43
1982-83	**Calgary**	**NHL**	**2**	**0**	**2**	**0**	**100**	**11**	**0**	**6.59**	....	....	....	....	....	....	....
ab	Calgary	WHL	50	19	18	2	2856	155	3	3.26	16	9	7	925	60	0	3.89
1983-84	**Calgary**	**NHL**	**1**	**0**	**1**	**0**	**11**	**4**	**0**	**22.22**	....	....	....	....	....	....	....
c	Colorado	CHL	46	30	13	2	2648	148	1	*3.35	6	2	4	347	21	0	3.63
1984-85	Moncton	AHL	41	10	20	4	2050	134	0	3.92	....	....	....	....	....	....	....
1985-86	**Calgary**	**NHL**	**18**	**9**	**3**	**3**	**921**	**52**	**1**	**3.39**	***21**	**12**	***9**	***1229**	**60**	**0**	**2.93**
	Moncton	AHL	6	3	1	2	374	21	0	3.37	....	....	....	....	....	....	....
	Salt Lake	IHL	10	6	4	0	600	34	1	3.40	....	....	....	....	....	....	....
1986-87	**Calgary**	**NHL**	**54**	**30**	**21**	**1**	**2957**	**178**	**1**	**3.61**	**5**	**2**	**3**	**263**	**16**	**0**	**3.65**
1987-88	**Calgary**	**NHL**	**64**	**39**	**16**	**7**	**3565**	**210**	**1**	**3.53**	**9**	**4**	**4**	**515**	**34**	**0**	**3.96**
1988-89d	**Calgary**	**NHL**	**52**	***37**	**6**	**5**	**2938**	**130**	**0**	**2.65**	***22**	***16**	**5**	***1381**	**52**	***3**	**2.26** ♦
1989-90	**Calgary**	**NHL**	**47**	**23**	**14**	**9**	**2795**	**146**	**0**	**3.13**	**6**	**2**	**3**	**342**	**19**	**0**	**3.33**
1990-91	**Calgary**	**NHL**	**54**	**31**	**19**	**3**	**3121**	**172**	**1**	**3.31**	**7**	**3**	**4**	**427**	**21**	**0**	**2.95**
1991-92	**Calgary**	**NHL**	**63**	**24**	**30**	**9**	**3640**	**217**	**0**	**3.58**	....	....	....	....	....	....	....
1992-93	**Calgary**	**NHL**	**64**	**29**	**26**	**9**	**3732**	**203**	**2**	**3.26**	**4**	**1**	**1**	**150**	**15**	**0**	**6.00**
1993-94	**Calgary**	**NHL**	**48**	**26**	**17**	**5**	**2798**	**131**	**3**	**2.81**	**7**	**3**	**4**	**466**	**23**	**0**	**2.96**
1994-95	**Detroit**	**NHL**	**30**	**19**	**6**	**4**	**1807**	**76**	**1**	**2.52**	**18**	**12**	**6**	**1063**	**41**	**1**	**2.31**
1995-96e	**Detroit**	**NHL**	**32**	**21**	**7**	**2**	**1855**	**70**	**3**	**2.26**	**4**	**2**	**2**	**243**	**11**	**0**	**2.72**
1996-97ef	**Detroit**	**NHL**	**33**	**13**	**11**	**8**	**1952**	**79**	**0**	**2.43**	***20**	***16**	**4**	***1229**	**36**	**1**	**1.76** ♦
	NHL Totals		**562**	**301**	**179**	**65**	**32192**	**1679**	**13**	**3.13**	**123**	**73**	**45**	**7308**	**328**	**5**	**2.69**

a WHL First All-Star Team (1982, 1983)
b Won Hap Emms Memorial Trophy (Memorial Cup Tournament Top Goaltender) (1983)
c CHL Second All-Star Team (1984)
d NHL Second All-Star Team (1989)
e Shared William M. Jennings Trophy with Chris Osgood (1996, 1997)
f Won Conn Smythe Trophy (1997)

Played in NHL All-Star Game (1988-91, 1993)

Traded to **Detroit** by **Calgary** for Steve Chiasson, June 29, 1994. Traded to **San Jose** by **Detroit** for a conditional choice in 1998 Entry Draft and a conditional choice in 1999 Entry Draft, August 18, 1997.

VOKOUN, TOMAS (voh-KOHN) MTL.

Goaltender. Catches right. 5'11", 208 lbs. Born, Karlovy Vary, Czech., July 2, 1976.
(Montreal's 11th choice, 226th overall, in 1994 Entry Draft).

			Regular Season								Playoffs						
Season	Club	Lea	GP	W	L	T	Mins	GA	SO	Avg	GP	W	L	Mins	GA	SO	Avg
1993-94	Kladno	Czech.	1	0	0	0	20	2	0	6.01	....	....	....	....	....	....	....
1994-95	Kladno	Czech.	26	....	....	....	1368	70	....	3.07	5	....	....	240	19	....	4.75
1995-96	Wheeling	ECHL	35	20	10	2	1912	117	0	3.67	7	4	3	436	19	0	2.61
	Fredericton	AHL	....	....	....	....	....	....	....	....	1	0	1	59	4	0	4.09
1996-97	**Montreal**	**NHL**	**1**	**0**	**0**	**0**	**20**	**4**	**0**	**12.00**	....	....	....	....	....	....	....
	Fredericton	AHL	47	12	26	7	2644	154	2	3.49	....	....	....	....	....	....	....
	NHL Totals		**1**	**0**	**0**	**0**	**20**	**4**	**0**	**12.00**	....	....	....	....	....	....	....

WAGNER, STEPHEN ST.L.

Goaltender. Catches left. 6'2", 200 lbs. Born, Red Deer, Alta., January 17, 1977.
(St. Louis' 5th choice, 159th overall, in 1996 Entry Draft).

			Regular Season								Playoffs						
Season	Club	Lea	GP	W	L	T	Mins	GA	SO	Avg	GP	W	L	Mins	GA	SO	Avg
1995-96	Olds	Jr. A	47	....	....	....	2787	139	2	2.99	....	....	....	....	....	....	....
1996-97	U. of Denver	WCHA	22	13	6	0	1202	57	1	2.85	....	....	....	....	....	....	....

WAITE, JIMMY (WAYT) CHI.

Goaltender. Catches left. 6'1", 180 lbs. Born, Sherbrooke, Que., April 15, 1969.
(Chicago's 1st choice, 8th overall, in 1987 Entry Draft).

			Regular Season								Playoffs						
Season	Club	Lea	GP	W	L	T	Mins	GA	SO	Avg	GP	W	L	Mins	GA	SO	Avg
1986-87a	Chicoutimi	QMJHL	50	23	17	3	2569	209	2	4.48	11	4	6	576	54	1	5.63
1987-88	Chicoutimi	QMJHL	36	17	16	1	2000	150	0	4.50	4	1	2	222	17	0	4.59
1988-89	**Chicago**	**NHL**	**11**	**0**	**7**	**1**	**494**	**43**	**0**	**5.22**	....	....	....	....	....	....	....
	Saginaw	IHL	5	3	1	0	304	10	0	1.97	....	....	....	....	....	....	....
1989-90	**Chicago**	**NHL**	**4**	**2**	**0**	**0**	**183**	**14**	**0**	**4.59**	....	....	....	....	....	....	....
bc	Indianapolis	IHL	54	*34	14	5	*3207	135	*5	*2.53	*10	*9	1	*602	19	*1	*1.89
1990-91	**Chicago**	**NHL**	**1**	**1**	**0**	**0**	**60**	**2**	**0**	**2.00**	....	....	....	....	....	....	....
	Indianapolis	IHL	49	*26	18	4	2888	167	3	3.47	6	2	4	369	20	0	3.25
1991-92	**Chicago**	**NHL**	**17**	**4**	**7**	**4**	**877**	**54**	**0**	**3.69**	....	....	....	....	....	....	....
	Indianapolis	IHL	13	4	7	1	702	53	0	4.53	....	....	....	....	....	....	....
	Hershey	AHL	11	6	4	1	631	44	0	4.18	6	2	4	360	19	0	3.17
1992-93	**Chicago**	**NHL**	**20**	**6**	**7**	**1**	**996**	**49**	**2**	**2.95**	....	....	....	....	....	....	....
1993-94	**San Jose**	**NHL**	**15**	**3**	**7**	**0**	**697**	**50**	**0**	**4.30**	**2**	**0**	**0**	**40**	**3**	**0**	**4.50**
1994-95	**Chicago**	**NHL**	**2**	**1**	**1**	**0**	**119**	**5**	**0**	**2.52**	....	....	....	....	....	....	....
	Indianapolis	IHL	4	2	1	1	239	13	0	3.25	....	....	....	....	....	....	....
1995-96	**Chicago**	**NHL**	**1**	**0**	**0**	**0**	**31**	**0**	**0**	**0.00**	....	....	....	....	....	....	....
	Indianapolis	IHL	56	28	18	6	3157	179	0	3.40	5	2	3	298	15	1	3.02
1996-97	**Chicago**	**NHL**	**2**	**0**	**1**	**1**	**105**	**7**	**0**	**4.00**	....	....	....	....	....	....	....
	Indianapolis	IHL	41	22	15	4	2450	112	4	2.74	4	1	3	222	13	0	3.51
	NHL Totals		**73**	**17**	**30**	**7**	**3562**	**224**	**2**	**3.77**	**2**	**0**	**0**	**40**	**3**	**0**	**4.50**

a QMJHL Second All-Star Team (1987)
b IHL First All-Star Team (1990)
c Won James Norris Memorial Trophy (fewest goals against - IHL) (1990)

Traded to **San Jose** by **Chicago** for future considerations (Neil Wilkinson, July 9, 1993), June 19, 1993. Traded to **Chicago** by **San Jose** for a conditional choice in 1997 Entry Draft, February 5, 1995.

WAKALUK, DARCY (WAHK-uh-luhk) PHO.

Goaltender. Catches left. 5'11", 180 lbs. Born, Pincher Creek, Alta., March 14, 1966.
(Buffalo's 7th choice, 144th overall, in 1984 Entry Draft).

			Regular Season								Playoffs						
Season	Club	Lea	GP	W	L	T	Mins	GA	SO	Avg	GP	W	L	Mins	GA	SO	Avg
1983-84	Kelowna	WHL	31	2	22	0	1555	163	0	6.29	....	....	....	....	....	....	....
1984-85	Kelowna	WHL	54	19	30	4	3094	244	0	4.73	5	1	4	282	22	0	4.68
1985-86	Spokane	WHL	47	21	22	1	2562	224	1	5.25	7	3	4	419	37	0	5.30
1986-87	Rochester	AHL	11	2	2	0	545	26	0	2.86	5	2	0	141	11	0	4.68
1987-88	Rochester	AHL	55	27	16	3	2763	159	0	3.45	6	3	3	328	22	0	4.02
1988-89	**Buffalo**	**NHL**	**6**	**1**	**3**	**0**	**214**	**15**	**0**	**4.21**	....	....	....	....	....	....	....
	Rochester	AHL	33	11	14	0	1566	97	1	3.72	....	....	....	....	....	....	....
1989-90	Rochester	AHL	56	31	16	4	3095	173	2	3.35	*17	*10	6	*1001	50	0	*3.01
1990-91	**Buffalo**	**NHL**	**16**	**4**	**5**	**3**	**630**	**35**	**0**	**3.33**	**2**	**0**	**1**	**37**	**2**	**0**	**3.24**
a	Rochester	AHL	26	10	10	3	1363	68	4	*2.99	9	6	3	544	30	0	3.31
1991-92	**Minnesota**	**NHL**	**36**	**13**	**19**	**1**	**1905**	**104**	**1**	**3.28**	....	....	....	....	....	....	....
	Kalamazoo	IHL	1	1	0	0	60	7	0	7.00	....	....	....	....	....	....	....
1992-93	**Minnesota**	**NHL**	**29**	**10**	**12**	**5**	**1596**	**97**	**1**	**3.65**	....	....	....	....	....	....	....
1993-94	**Dallas**	**NHL**	**36**	**18**	**9**	**6**	**2000**	**88**	**3**	**2.64**	**5**	**4**	**1**	**307**	**15**	**0**	**2.93**
1994-95	**Dallas**	**NHL**	**15**	**4**	**8**	**0**	**754**	**40**	**2**	**3.18**	**1**	**0**	**0**	**20**	**1**	**0**	**3.00**
1995-96	**Dallas**	**NHL**	**37**	**9**	**16**	**5**	**1875**	**106**	**1**	**3.39**	....	....	....	....	....	....	....
1996-97	**Phoenix**	**NHL**	**16**	**8**	**3**	**1**	**782**	**39**	**1**	**2.99**	....	....	....	....	....	....	....
	NHL Totals		**191**	**67**	**75**	**21**	**9756**	**524**	**9**	**3.22**	**8**	**4**	**2**	**364**	**18**	**0**	**2.97**

a Shared Harry "Hap" Holmes Memorial Trophy (fewest goals against - AHL) with David Littman (1991)

Traded to **Minnesota** by **Buffalo** for Minnesota's eighth round choice (Jiri Kuntos) in 1991 Entry Draft and Minnesota's fifth round choice (later traded to Toronto — Toronto selected Chris Deruiter) in 1992 Entry Draft, May 26, 1991. Signed as a free agent by **Phoenix**, July 23, 1996.

WEEKES, KEVIN FLA.

Goaltender. Catches left. 6', 158 lbs. Born, Toronto, Ont., April 4, 1975.
(Florida's 2nd choice, 41st overall, in 1993 Entry Draft).

			Regular Season								Playoffs						
Season	Club	Lea	GP	W	L	T	Mins	GA	SO	Avg	GP	W	L	Mins	GA	SO	Avg
1992-93	Owen Sound	OHL	29	9	12	5	1645	143	0	5.22	1	0	0	26	5	0	11.50
1993-94	Owen Sound	OHL	34	13	19	1	1974	158	0	4.80	....	....	....	....	....	....	....
1994-95	Ottawa	OHL	41	13	23	4	2266	153	1	4.05	....	....	....	....	....	....	....
1995-96	Carolina	AHL	60	24	25	8	3404	229	2	4.04	....	....	....	....	....	....	....
1996-97	Carolina	AHL	51	17	28	4	2898	172	1	3.56	....	....	....	....	....	....	....

WEIBEL, LARS (VIGH-behl) CHI.

Goaltender. Catches left. 6', 178 lbs. Born, Rapperswil, Switz., May 20, 1974.
(Chicago's 10th choice, 248th overall, in 1994 Entry Draft).

			Regular Season								Playoffs						
Season	Club	Lea	GP	W	L	T	Mins	GA	SO	Avg	GP	W	L	Mins	GA	SO	Avg
1992-93	Biel-Bienne	Switz.	14	....	....	....	674	54	....	4.80	....	....	....	....	....	....	....
1993-94	Lugano	Switz.	25	....	....	....	....	....	....	....	9	....	....	560	23	....	2.46
1994-95	Lugano	Switz.	35	....	....	....	2076	95	....	2.74	....	....	....	....	....	....	....
1995-96	Lugano	Switz.	36	....	....	....	2122	107	....	3.02	4	....	....	240	9	....	2.25
1996-97	Lugano	Switz.	45	....	....	....	2667	144	....	3.24	8	....	....	513	24	....	2.80

WENINGER, DAVE WSH.

Goaltender. Catches left. 6'1", 160 lbs. Born, Calgary, Alta., February 8, 1976.
(Washington's 5th choice, 74th overall, in 1996 Entry Draft).

			Regular Season								Playoffs						
Season	Club	Lea	GP	W	L	T	Mins	GA	SO	Avg	GP	W	L	Mins	GA	SO	Avg
1995-96	Michigan Tech.	WCHA	25	11	7	2	1300	70	0	3.23	....	....	....	....	....	....	....
1996-97	Michigan Tech.	WCHA	18	1	13	0	855	59	1	4.14	....	....	....	....	....	....	....

WHITMORE, KAY

Goaltender. Catches left. 5'11", 175 lbs. Born, Sudbury, Ont., April 10, 1967.
(Hartford's 2nd choice, 26th overall, in 1985 Entry Draft).

			Regular Season								Playoffs						
Season	Club	Lea	GP	W	L	T	Mins	GA	SO	Avg	GP	W	L	Mins	GA	SO	Avg
1983-84	Peterborough	OHL	29	17	8	0	1471	110	0	4.49	....	....	....	....	....	....	....
1984-85	Peterborough	OHL	53	*35	16	2	3077	172	*2	3.35	17	10	4	1020	58	0	3.41
1985-86a	Peterborough	OHL	41	27	12	2	2467	114	*3	*2.77	14	8	5	837	40	0	2.87
1986-87	Peterborough	OHL	36	14	17	5	2159	118	1	3.28	7	3	3	366	17	1	2.79
1987-88	Binghamton	AHL	38	17	15	4	2137	121	*3	3.40	2	0	2	118	10	0	5.08
1988-89	**Hartford**	**NHL**	**3**	**2**	**1**	**0**	**180**	**10**	**0**	**3.33**	**2**	**0**	**2**	**135**	**10**	**0**	**4.44**
	Binghamton	AHL	*56	21	29	4	*3200	241	1	4.52	....	....	....	....	....	....	....
1989-90	**Hartford**	**NHL**	**9**	**4**	**2**	**1**	**442**	**26**	**0**	**3.53**	....	....	....	....	....	....	....
	Binghamton	AHL	24	3	19	2	1386	109	0	4.72	....	....	....	....	....	....	....
1990-91	**Hartford**	**NHL**	**18**	**3**	**9**	**3**	**850**	**52**	**0**	**3.67**	....	....	....	....	....	....	....
b	Springfield	AHL	33	22	9	1	1916	98	1	3.07	*15	*11	4	*926	37	0	*2.40
1991-92	**Hartford**	**NHL**	**45**	**14**	**21**	**6**	**2567**	**155**	**3**	**3.62**	**1**	**0**	**0**	**19**	**1**	**0**	**3.16**
1992-93	**Vancouver**	**NHL**	**31**	**18**	**8**	**4**	**1817**	**94**	**1**	**3.10**	....	....	....	....	....	....	....
1993-94	**Vancouver**	**NHL**	**32**	**18**	**14**	**0**	**1921**	**113**	**0**	**3.53**	....	....	....	....	....	....	....
1994-95	**Vancouver**	**NHL**	**11**	**0**	**6**	**2**	**558**	**37**	**0**	**3.98**	**1**	**0**	**0**	**20**	**2**	**0**	**6.00**
1995-96	Detroit	IHL	10	3	5	0	501	33	0	3.95	....	....	....	....	....	....	....
	Los Angeles	IHL	30	10	9	7	1563	99	1	3.80	....	....	....	....	....	....	....
	Binghamton	AHL	11	6	4	1	663	37	0	3.35	2	0	2	127	9	0	4.27
1996-97	Sodertalje	Swe.	25	....	....	....	1320	85	0	3.86	....	....	....	....	....	....	....
	NHL Totals		**149**	**59**	**61**	**16**	**8335**	**487**	**4**	**3.51**	**4**	**0**	**2**	**174**	**13**	**0**	**4.48**

a OHL First All-Star Team (1986)
b Won Jack A. Butterfield Trophy (Playoff MVP - AHL) (1991)

Traded to **Vancouver** by **Hartford** for Corrie D'Alessio and future considerations, October 1, 1992. Traded to **NY Rangers** by **Vancouver** for Joe Kocur, March 20, 1996.

WICKENHEISER, CHRIS (wih-KEHN-high-zehr) EDM.

Goaltender. Catches left. 6'1", 185 lbs. Born, Lethbridge, Alta., January 20, 1976.
(Edmonton's 12th choice, 179th overall, in 1994 Entry Draft).

			Regular Season								Playoffs						
Season	Club	Lea	GP	W	L	T	Mins	GA	SO	Avg	GP	W	L	Mins	GA	SO	Avg
1993-94	Red Deer	WHL	29	11	13	0	1356	114	0	5.04	....	....	....	....	....	....	....
1994-95	Red Deer	WHL	47	13	26	3	2429	181	1	4.47	....	....	....	....	....	....	....
1995-96	Red Deer	WHL	48	17	27	2	2666	183	1	4.12	10	3	6	550	34	1	3.71
1996-97	Red Deer	WHL	1	0	1	0	60	4	0	4.00	....	....	....	....	....	....	....
a	Portland	WHL	40	24	13	3	2367	106	3	2.69	4	2	2	226	10	0	2.65

a WHL West Second All-Star Team (1997)

WILKINSON, DEREK T.B.

Goaltender. Catches left. 6', 170 lbs. Born, Lasalle, Que., July 29, 1974.
(Tampa Bay's 7th choice, 145th overall, in 1992 Entry Draft).

			Regular Season								Playoffs						
Season	Club	Lea	GP	W	L	T	Mins	GA	SO	Avg	GP	W	L	Mins	GA	SO	Avg
1991-92	Detroit	OHL	38	16	17	1	1943	138	1	4.26	7	3	2	313	28	0	5.37
1992-93	Detroit	OHL	*4	1	2	1	*245	18	0	4.41	....	....	....	....	....	....	....
	Belleville	OHL	*59	21	24	11	*3370	237	0	4.22	7	3	4	434	29	0	4.01
1993-94	Belleville	OHL	*56	24	16	4	2860	179	*2	3.76	12	6	6	700	39	*1	3.34
1994-95	Atlanta	IHL	46	22	17	2	2414	121	1	3.01	4	2	1	197	8	0	2.43
1995-96	**Tampa Bay**	**NHL**	**4**	**0**	**3**	**0**	**200**	**15**	**0**	**4.50**	....	....	....	....	....	....	....
	Atlanta	IHL	28	11	11	2	1433	98	1	4.10	....	....	....	....	....	....	....
1996-97	**Tampa Bay**	**NHL**	**5**	**0**	**2**	**1**	**169**	**12**	**0**	**4.26**	....	....	....	....	....	....	....
	Cleveland	IHL	46	20	17	6	2595	138	1	3.19	14	8	6	893	44	0	2.95
	NHL Totals		**9**	**0**	**5**	**1**	**369**	**27**	**0**	**4.39**	....	....	....	....	....	....	....

WILLIS, JORDAN DAL.

Goaltender. Catches left. 5'9", 155 lbs. Born, Kincardine, Ont., February 28, 1975.
(Dallas' 8th choice, 243rd overall, in 1993 Entry Draft).

			Regular Season								Playoffs						
Season	Club	Lea	GP	W	L	T	Mins	GA	SO	Avg	GP	W	L	Mins	GA	SO	Avg
1992-93	London	OHL	26	13	6	3	1428	101	1	4.24	7	....	....	355	19	0	3.21
1993-94	London	OHL	44	20	19	2	2428	158	1	3.90	1	0	0	8	1	0	7.50
1994-95	London	OHL	53	16	29	3	2824	202	0	4.29	3	0	3	165	15	0	5.45
1995-96	**Dallas**	**NHL**	**1**	**0**	**1**	**0**	**19**	**1**	**0**	**3.16**	....	....	....	....	....	....	....
	Michigan	IHL	38	17	9	9	2184	118	1	3.24	4	1	3	238	17	0	4.29
1996-97	Cdn. National	....	15	7	4	2	804	42	....	3.13	....	....	....	....	....	....	....
	Dayton	ECHL	8	4	4	0	429	25	0	3.50	....	....	....	....	....	....	....
	Michigan	IHL	2	0	2	0	102	8	0	4.70	....	....	....	....	....	....	....
	NHL Totals		**1**	**0**	**1**	**0**	**19**	**1**	**0**	**3.16**	....	....	....	....	....	....	....

WREGGET, KEN (REHG-eht) PIT.

Goaltender. Catches left. 6'1", 201 lbs. Born, Brandon, Man., March 25, 1964.
(Toronto's 4th choice, 45th overall, in 1982 Entry Draft).

			Regular Season								Playoffs						
Season	Club	Lea	GP	W	L	T	Mins	GA	SO	Avg	GP	W	L	Mins	GA	SO	Avg
1981-82	Lethbridge	WHL	36	19	12	0	1713	118	0	4.13	3	2	0	84	3	0	2.14
1982-83	Lethbridge	WHL	48	26	17	1	2696	157	0	3.49	20	14	5	1154	58	1	3.02
1983-84	**Toronto**	**NHL**	**3**	**1**	**1**	**1**	**165**	**14**	**0**	**5.09**	....	....	....	....	....	....	....
a	Lethbridge	WHL	53	32	20	0	3053	161	0	*3.16	4	1	3	210	18	0	5.14
1984-85	**Toronto**	**NHL**	**23**	**2**	**15**	**3**	**1278**	**103**	**0**	**4.84**	....	....	....	....	....	....	....
	St. Catharines	AHL	12	2	8	1	688	48	0	4.19	....	....	....	....	....	....	....
1985-86	**Toronto**	**NHL**	**30**	**9**	**13**	**4**	**1566**	**113**	**0**	**4.33**	**10**	**6**	**4**	**607**	**32**	***1**	**3.16**
	St. Catharines	AHL	18	8	9	0	1058	78	1	4.42	....	....	....	....	....	....	....
1986-87	**Toronto**	**NHL**	**56**	**22**	**28**	**3**	**3026**	**200**	**0**	**3.97**	**13**	**7**	**6**	**761**	**29**	**1**	**2.29**
1987-88	**Toronto**	**NHL**	**56**	**12**	**35**	**4**	**3000**	**222**	**2**	**4.44**	**2**	**0**	**1**	**108**	**11**	**0**	**6.11**
1988-89	**Toronto**	**NHL**	**32**	**9**	**20**	**2**	**1888**	**139**	**0**	**4.42**	....	....	....	....	....	....	....
	Philadelphia	**NHL**	**3**	**1**	**1**	**0**	**130**	**13**	**0**	**6.00**	**5**	**2**	**2**	**268**	**10**	**0**	**2.24**
1989-90	**Philadelphia**	**NHL**	**51**	**22**	**24**	**3**	**2961**	**169**	**0**	**3.42**	....	....	....	....	....	....	....
1990-91	**Philadelphia**	**NHL**	**30**	**10**	**14**	**3**	**1484**	**88**	**0**	**3.56**	....	....	....	....	....	....	....
1991-92	**Philadelphia**	**NHL**	**23**	**9**	**8**	**3**	**1259**	**75**	**0**	**3.57**	....	....	....	....	....	....	....
	Pittsburgh	**NHL**	**9**	**5**	**3**	**0**	**448**	**31**	**0**	**4.15**	**1**	**0**	**0**	**40**	**4**	**0**	**6.00** ♦
1992-93	**Pittsburgh**	**NHL**	**25**	**13**	**7**	**2**	**1368**	**78**	**0**	**3.42**	....	....	....	....	....	....	....
1993-94	**Pittsburgh**	**NHL**	**42**	**21**	**12**	**7**	**2456**	**138**	**1**	**3.37**	....	....	....	....	....	....	....
1994-95	**Pittsburgh**	**NHL**	**38**	***25**	**9**	**2**	**2208**	**118**	**0**	**3.21**	**11**	**5**	**6**	**661**	**33**	**1**	**3.00**
1995-96	**Pittsburgh**	**NHL**	**37**	**20**	**13**	**2**	**2132**	**115**	**3**	**3.24**	**9**	**7**	**2**	**599**	**23**	**0**	**2.30**
1996-97	**Pittsburgh**	**NHL**	**46**	**17**	**17**	**6**	**2514**	**136**	**2**	**3.25**	**5**	**1**	**4**	**297**	**18**	**0**	**3.64**
	NHL Totals		**504**	**198**	**220**	**45**	**27883**	**1752**	**8**	**3.77**	**56**	**28**	**25**	**3341**	**160**	**3**	**2.87**

a WHL East First All-Star Team (1984)

Traded to **Philadelphia** by **Toronto** for Philadelphia's first round choice (Rob Pearson) and Calgary's first round choice (previously acquired by Philadelphia — Toronto selected Steve Bancroft) in 1989 Entry Draft, March 6, 1989. Traded to **Pittsburgh** by **Philadelphia** with Rick Tocchet, Kjell Samuelsson and Philadelphia's third round choice (Dave Roche) in 1993 Entry Draft for Mark Recchi, Brian Benning and Los Angeles' first round choice (previously acquired by Pittsburgh — Philadelphia selected Jason Bowen) in 1992 Entry Draft, February 19, 1992.

YEREMEYEV, VITALI (yehr-eh-MAY-ehv) NYR

Goaltender. Catches left. 5'10", 167 lbs. Born, Ust-Kamenogorsk, USSR, September 23, 1975.
(NY Rangers' 11th choice, 209th overall, in 1994 Entry Draft).

			Regular Season								Playoffs						
Season	Club	Lea	GP	W	L	T	Mins	GA	SO	Avg	GP	W	L	Mins	GA	SO	Avg
1993-94	Kamenogorsk	CIS	19	....	....	....	1015	38	....	2.24	....	....	....	....	....	....	....
1994-95	CSKA	CIS	49	....	....	....	2733	97	....	2.13	....	....	....	....	....	....	....
1995-96	CSKA	CIS	25	....	....	....	1339	37	5	1.66	3	....	....	179	7	....	2.34
1996-97	CSKA	Rus.	14	....	....	....	635	35	0	3.31	1	....	....	59	3	0	3.05

YOUNG, WENDELL

Goaltender. Catches left. 5'9", 181 lbs. Born, Halifax, N.S., August 1, 1963.
(Vancouver's 3rd choice, 73rd overall, in 1981 Entry Draft).

			Regular Season								Playoffs						
Season	Club	Lea	GP	W	L	T	Mins	GA	SO	Avg	GP	W	L	Mins	GA	SO	Avg
1980-81	Kitchener	OHA	42	19	15	0	2215	164	1	4.44	14	9	1	800	42	*1	3.15
1981-82	Kitchener	OHL	60	38	17	2	3470	195	1	3.37	15	12	1	900	35	*1	*2.33
1982-83	Kitchener	OHL	61	41	19	0	3611	231	1	3.84	12	6	5	720	43	0	3.58
1983-84	Fredericton	AHL	11	7	3	0	569	39	1	4.11	....	....	....	....	....	....	....
	Milwaukee	IHL	6	4	1	1	339	17	0	3.01	....	....	....	....	....	....	....
	Salt Lake	CHL	20	11	6	0	1094	80	0	4.39	4	0	2	122	11	0	5.42
1984-85	Fredericton	AHL	22	7	11	3	1242	83	0	4.01	....	....	....	....	....	....	....
1985-86	**Vancouver**	**NHL**	**22**	**4**	**9**	**3**	**1023**	**61**	**0**	**3.58**	**1**	**0**	**1**	**60**	**5**	**0**	**5.00**
	Fredericton	AHL	24	12	8	4	1457	78	0	3.21	....	....	....	....	....	....	....
1986-87	**Vancouver**	**NHL**	**8**	**1**	**6**	**1**	**420**	**35**	**0**	**5.00**	....	....	....	....	....	....	....
	Fredericton	AHL	30	11	16	0	1676	118	0	4.22	....	....	....	....	....	....	....
1987-88	**Philadelphia**	**NHL**	**6**	**3**	**2**	**0**	**320**	**20**	**0**	**3.75**	....	....	....	....	....	....	....
abc	Hershey	AHL	51	*33	15	1	2922	135	1	2.77	12	*12	0	*767	28	*1	*2.19
1988-89	**Pittsburgh**	**NHL**	**22**	**12**	**9**	**0**	**1150**	**92**	**0**	**4.80**	**1**	**0**	**0**	**39**	**1**	**0**	**1.54**
	Muskegon	IHL	2	1	0	1	125	7	0	3.36	....	....	....	....	....	....	....
1989-90	**Pittsburgh**	**NHL**	**43**	**16**	**20**	**3**	**2318**	**161**	**1**	**4.17**	....	....	....	....	....	....	....
1990-91	**Pittsburgh**	**NHL**	**18**	**4**	**6**	**2**	**773**	**52**	**0**	**4.04**	....	....	....	....	....	....	....
1991-92	**Pittsburgh**	**NHL**	**18**	**7**	**6**	**0**	**838**	**53**	**0**	**3.79**	....	....	....	....	....	....	....
1992-93	**Tampa Bay**	**NHL**	**31**	**7**	**19**	**2**	**1591**	**97**	**0**	**3.66**	....	....	....	....	....	....	....
	Atlanta	IHL	3	3	0	0	183	8	0	2.62	....	....	....	....	....	....	....
1993-94	**Tampa Bay**	**NHL**	**9**	**2**	**3**	**1**	**480**	**20**	**1**	**2.50**	....	....	....	....	....	....	....
	Atlanta	IHL	2	2	0	0	120	6	0	3.00	....	....	....	....	....	....	....
1994-95	Chicago	IHL	37	14	11	7	1882	112	0	3.57	....	....	....	....	....	....	....
	Pittsburgh	**NHL**	**10**	**3**	**6**	**0**	**497**	**27**	**0**	**3.26**	....	....	....	....	....	....	....
1995-96	Chicago	IHL	61	30	20	6	3285	199	1	3.63	9	4	5	540	30	0	3.33
1996-97	Chicago	IHL	52	25	21	4	2931	170	1	3.48	4	1	3	256	13	0	3.04
	NHL Totals		**187**	**59**	**86**	**12**	**9410**	**618**	**2**	**3.94**	**2**	**0**	**1**	**99**	**6**	**0**	**3.64**

a AHL First All-Star Team (1988)
b Won Baz Bastien Memorial Trophy (Top Goaltender - AHL) (1988)
c Won Jack Butterfield Trophy (Playoff MVP - AHL) (1988)

Traded to **Philadelphia** by **Vancouver** with Vancouver's third round choice (Kimbi Daniels) in 1990 Entry Draft for Darren Jensen and Daryl Stanley, August 28, 1987. Traded to **Pittsburgh** by **Philadelphia** with Philadelphia's seventh round choice (Mika Valila) in 1990 Entry Draft for Pittsburgh's third round choice (Chris Therien) in 1990 Entry Draft, September 1, 1988. Claimed by **Tampa Bay** from **Pittsburgh** in Expansion Draft, June 18, 1992. Traded to **Pittsburgh** by **Tampa Bay** for future considerations, February 16, 1995.

Notes

John Davidson

Peter Ing

Terry Sawchuk

Gerry Desjardins

Gary Inness

Don Simmons

Ken Dryden

Phil Myre

Gump Worsley

Bill Durnan

Bernie Parent

Roy Worters

Retired NHL Goaltender Index

Abbreviations: Teams/Cities: — **Ana.** – Anaheim; **Atl.** – Atlanta; **Bos.** – Boston, **Bro.** – Brooklyn; **Buf.** – Buffalo; **Cal.** – California; **Cgy.** – Calgary; **Cle.** – Cleveland; **Col.** – Colorado; **Dal.** – Dallas; **Det.** – Detroit; **Edm.** – Edmonton; **Fla.** – Florida; **Ham.** – Hamilton; **Hfd.** – Hartford; **K.C.** – Kansas City; **L.A.** – Los Angeles; **Min.** — Minnesota; **Mtl.** – Montreal; **Mtl. M.** – Montreal Maroons; **Mtl. W.** – Montreal Wanderers; **N.J.** – New Jersey; **NYA** – NY Americans; **NYI** – New York Islanders; **NYR** – New York Rangers; **Oak.** – Oakland; **Ott.** – Ottawa; **Phi.** – Philadelphia; **Pit.** – Pittsburgh; **Que.** – Quebec; **St. L.** – St. Louis; **S.J.** – San Jose; **T.B.** – Tampa Bay; **Tor.** – Toronto; **Van.** – Vancouver; **Wpg.** – Winnipeg; **Wsh.** – Washington.

Avg. – goals against per 60 minutes played; **GA** – goals against; **GP** – games played; **Mins** – minutes played; **SO** – shutouts.

• – deceased. § - Forward, defenseman or coach who appeared in goal. For complete career, see Retired Player Index.

			Regular Schedule								Playoffs										
Name	NHL Teams	NHL Seasons	GP	W	L	T	Mins	GA	SO	Avg	GP	W	L	T	Mins	GA	SO	Avg	NHL Cup Wins	First NHL Season	Last NHL Season
Abbott, George	Bos.	1	1	0	1	0	60	7	0	7.00	....	....	....	....	....	....	....	....		1943-44	1943-44
Adams, John	Bos., Wsh.	2	22	9	10	1	1180	85	1	4.32	....	....	....	....	....	....	....	....		1972-73	1974-75
Aiken, Don	Mtl.	1	1	0	1	0	34	6	0	10.59	....	....	....	....	....	....	....	....		1957-58	1957-58
Aikenhead, Andy	NYR	3	106	47	43	16	6570	257	11	2.35	10	6	2	1	608	15	3	1.48	1	1932-33	1934-35
Almas, Red	Det., Chi.	3	3	0	2	1	180	13	0	4.33	5	1	3	0	263	13	0	2.97		1946-47	1952-53
• Anderson, Lorne	NYR	1	3	1	2	0	180	18	0	6.00	....	....	....	....	....	....	....	....		1951-52	1951-52
Astrom, Hardy	NYR, Col.	3	83	17	44	12	4456	278	0	3.74	....	....	....	....	....	....	....	....		1977-78	1980-81
Baker, Steve	NYR	4	57	20	20	11	3081	190	3	3.70	14	7	7	0	826	55	0	4.00		1979-80	1982-83
Bannerman, Murray	Van., Chi.	8	289	116	125	33	16470	1051	8	3.83	40	20	18	0	2322	165	0	4.26		1977-78	1986-87
Baron, Marco	Bos., L.A., Edm.	6	86	34	39	9	4822	292	1	3.63	1	0	1	0	20	3	0	9.00		1979-80	1984-85
Bassen, Hank	Chi., Det., Pit.	9	157	47	65	31	8779	441	5	3.01	5	1	3	0	274	11	0	2.41		1954-55	1967-68
• Bastien, Baz	Tor.	1	5	0	4	1	300	20	0	4.00	....	....	....	....	....	....	....	....		1945-46	1945-46
Bauman, Gary	Mtl., Min.	3	35	6	18	6	1718	102	0	3.56	....	....	....	....	....	....	....	....		1966-67	1968-69
Bedard, Jim	Wsh.	2	73	17	40	13	4232	278	1	3.94	....	....	....	....	....	....	....	....		1977-78	1978-79
Behrend, Marc	Wpg.	3	39	12	19	3	1991	160	1	4.82	7	1	3	0	312	19	0	3.65		1983-84	1985-86
Belanger, Yves	St.L., Atl., Bos.	6	78	29	33	6	4134	259	2	3.76	....	....	....	....	....	....	....	....		1974-75	1979-80
Belhumeur, Michel	Phi., Wsh.	3	65	9	36	7	3306	254	0	4.61	1	0	0	0	10	1	0	6.00		1972-73	1975-76
• Bell, Gordie	Tor., NYR	2	8	3	5	0	480	31	0	3.88	2	1	1	0	120	9	0	4.50		1945-46	1955-56
• Benedict, Clint	Ott., Mtl.M.	13	362	191	142	28	22321	859	58	2.31	48	25	18	4	2907	87	15	1.80	4	1917-18	1929-30
Bennett, Harvey	Bos.	1	25	10	12	2	1470	103	0	4.20	....	....	....	....	....	....	....	....		1944-45	1944-45
Bernhardt, Tim	Cgy., Tor.	4	67	17	36	7	3748	267	0	4.27	....	....	....	....	....	....	....	....		1982-83	1986-87
Berthiaume, Daniel	Wpg., Min., L.A., Bos., Ott.	9	215	81	90	21	11662	714	5	3.67	14	5	9	0	807	50	0	3.72		1985-86	1993-94
• Beveridge, Bill	Det., Ott., St.L., Mtl.M., NYR	9	297	87	166	42	18375	879	17	2.87	5	2	3	0	300	11	0	2.20		1929-30	1942-43
• Bibeault, Paul	Mtl., Tor., Bos., Chi.	7	214	81	107	25	12890	785	10	3.65	20	6	14	0	1237	71	2	3.44		1940-41	1946-47
Binette, Andre	Mtl.	1	1	1	0	0	60	4	0	4.00	....	....	....	....	....	....	....	....		1954-55	1954-55
Binkley, Les	Pit.	5	196	58	94	34	11046	575	11	3.12	7	5	2	0	428	15	0	2.10		1967-68	1971-72
Bittner, Richard	Bos.	1	1	0	0	1	60	3	0	3.00	....	....	....	....	....	....	....	....		1949-50	1949-50
Blake, Mike	L.A.	3	40	13	15	5	2117	150	0	4.25	....	....	....	....	....	....	....	....		1981-82	1983-84
Blue, John	Bos., Buf.	3	46	16	18	7	2521	126	1	3.00	2	0	1	0	96	5	0	3.13		1992-93	1995-96
Boisvert, Gilles	Det.	1	3	0	3	0	180	9	0	3.00	....	....	....	....	....	....	....	....		1959-60	1959-60
Bouchard, Dan	Atl., Cgy., Que., Wpg.	14	655	286	232	113	37919	2061	27	3.26	43	13	30	0	2549	147	1	3.46		1972-73	1985-86
• Bourque, Claude	Mtl., Det.	2	62	16	38	8	3830	192	5	3.01	3	1	2	0	188	8	1	2.55		1938-39	1939-40
Boutin, Rollie	Wsh.	3	22	7	10	1	1137	75	0	3.96	....	....	....	....	....	....	....	....		1978-79	1980-81
Bouvrette, Lionel	NYR	1	1	0	1	0	60	6	0	6.00	....	....	....	....	....	....	....	....		1942-43	1942-43
Bower, Johnny	NYR, Tor.	15	552	251	196	90	32016	1347	37	2.52	74	35	34	0	4378	184	5	2.52	4	1953-54	1969-70
§ Brannigan, Andy	NYA	1	1	0	0	0	7	0	0	0.00	....	....	....	....	....	....	....	....		1940-41	1940-41
Brimsek, Frank	Bos., Chi.	10	514	252	182	80	31210	1404	40	2.70	68	32	36	0	4365	186	2	2.56	2	1938-39	1949-50
• Broda, Turk	Tor.	14	629	302	224	101	38168	1609	62	2.53	101	60	39	1	5897	211	13	2.15	5	1936-37	1951-52
Broderick, Ken	Min., Bos.	3	27	11	12	1	1464	74	1	3.03	....	....	....	....	....	....	....	....		1969-70	1974-75
Broderick, Len	Mtl.	1	1	1	0	0	60	2	0	2.00	....	....	....	....	....	....	....	....		1957-58	1957-58
Brodeur, Richard	NYI, Van., Hfd.	9	385	131	176	62	21968	1410	6	3.85	33	13	20	0	2009	111	1	3.32		1979-80	1987-88
Bromley, Gary	Buf., Van.	6	136	54	44	28	7427	425	7	3.43	7	2	5	0	360	25	0	4.17		1973-74	1980-81
• Brooks, Arthur	Tor.	1	4	2	1	0	220	23	0	6.27	....	....	....	....	....	....	....	....		1917-18	1917-18
Brooks, Ross	Bos.	3	54	37	7	6	3047	134	4	2.64	1	0	0	0	20	3	0	9.00		1972-73	1974-75
• Brophy, Frank	Que.	1	21	3	18	0	1247	148	0	7.12	....	....	....	....	....	....	....	....		1919-20	1919-20
Brown, Andy	Det., Pit.	3	62	22	26	9	3373	213	1	3.79	....	....	....	....	....	....	....	....		1971-72	1973-74
Brown, Ken	Chi.	1	1	0	0	0	18	1	0	3.33	....	....	....	....	....	....	....	....		1970-71	1970-71
Brunetta, Mario	Que.	3	40	12	17	1	1967	128	0	3.90	....	....	....	....	....	....	....	....		1987-88	1989-90
Bullock, Bruce	Van.	3	16	3	9	3	927	74	0	4.79	....	....	....	....	....	....	....	....		1972-73	1976-77
Buzinski, Steve	NYR	1	9	2	6	1	560	55	0	5.89	....	....	....	....	....	....	....	....		1942-43	1942-43
Caley, Don	St.L.	1	1	0	0	0	30	3	0	6.00	....	....	....	....	....	....	....	....		1967-68	1967-68
Caprice, Frank	Van.	6	102	31	40	11	5589	391	1	4.20	....	....	....	....	....	....	....	....		1982-83	1987-88
Caron, Jacques	L.A., St.L., Van.	5	72	24	29	11	3846	211	2	3.29	12	4	7	0	639	34	0	3.19		1967-68	1973-74
Carter, Lyle	Cal.	1	15	4	7	0	721	50	0	4.16	....	....	....	....	....	....	....	....		1971-72	1971-72
• Chabot, Lorne	NYR, Tor., Mtl., Chi., Mtl.M., NYA	11	411	206	140	65	25309	861	73	2.04	37	13	17	6	2498	64	5	1.54	2	1926-27	1936-37
Chadwick, Ed	Tor., Bos.	6	184	57	92	35	10980	551	14	3.01	....	....	....	....	....	....	....	....		1955-56	1961-62
Champoux, Bob	Det., Cal.	2	17	2	11	3	923	80	0	5.20	1	1	0	0	55	4	0	4.36		1963-64	1973-74
Cheevers, Gerry	Tor., Bos.	13	418	230	103	74	24394	1175	26	2.89	88	53	34	0	5396	242	8	2.69	2	1961-62	1979-80
Chevrier, Alain	N.J., Wpg., Chi., Pit., Det.	6	234	91	100	14	12202	845	2	4.16	16	9	7	0	1013	44	0	2.61		1985-86	1990-91
§ • Clancy, "King"	Tor.	1	1	0	0	0	1	1	0	60.00	....	....	....	....	....	....	....	....		1931-32	1931-32
§ Cleghorn, Odie	Pit.	1	1	1	0	0	60	2	0	2.00	....	....	....	....	....	....	....	....		1925-26	1925-26
Clifford, Chris	Chi.	2	2	0	0	0	24	0	0	0.00	....	....	....	....	....	....	....	....		1984-85	1988-89
Cloutier, Jacques	Buf., Chi., Que.	12	255	82	102	24	12826	778	3	3.64	8	1	5	0	413	18	1	2.62		1981-82	1993-94
Colvin, Les	Bos.	1	1	0	1	0	60	4	0	4.00	....	....	....	....	....	....	....	....		1948-49	1948-49
§ • Conacher, Charlie	Tor., Det.	3	3	0	0	0	9	0	0	0.00	....	....	....	....	....	....	....	....		1932-33	1938-39
• Connell, Alex	Ott., Det., NYA, Mtl.M.	12	417	199	155	59	26030	830	81	1.91	21	8	5	8	1309	26	4	1.19	2	1924-25	1936-37
Corsi, Jim	Edm.	1	26	8	14	3	1366	83	0	3.65	....	....	....	....	....	....	....	....		1979-80	1979-80
Courteau, Maurice	Bos.	1	6	2	4	0	360	33	0	5.50	....	....	....	....	....	....	....	....		1943-44	1943-44
Cowley, Wayne	Edmonton	1	1	0	1	0	57	3	0	3.16	....	....	....	....	....	....	....	....		1993-94	1993-94
Cox, Abbie	Mtl.M., Det., NYA, Mtl.	3	5	1	1	2	263	11	0	2.51	....	....	....	....	....	....	....	....		1929-30	1935-36
Craig, Jim	Atl., Bos., Min.	3	30	11	10	7	1588	100	0	3.78	....	....	....	....	....	....	....	....		1979-80	1983-84
Crha, Jiri	Tor.	2	69	28	27	11	3942	261	0	3.97	5	0	4	0	186	21	0	6.77		1979-80	1980-81
• Crozier, Roger	Det., Buf., Wsh.	14	518	206	198	70	28567	1446	30	3.04	32	14	16	0	1789	82	1	2.75		1963-64	1976-77
• Cude, Wilf	Phi., Bos., Chi., Det., Mtl.	10	282	100	129	49	17486	798	24	2.74	19	7	11	1	1257	51	1	2.43		1930-31	1940-41
Cutts, Don	Edm.	1	6	1	2	1	269	16	0	3.57	....	....	....	....	....	....	....	....		1979-80	1979-80
• Cyr, Claude	Mtl.	1	1	0	0	0	20	1	0	3.00	....	....	....	....	....	....	....	....		1958-59	1958-59
Dadswell, Doug	Cgy.	2	27	8	8	3	1346	99	0	4.41	....	....	....	....	....	....	....	....		1986-87	1987-88
D'Alessio, Corrie	Hfd.	1	1	0	0	0	11	0	0	0.00	....	....	....	....	....	....	....	....		1992-93	1992-93
Daley, Joe	Pit., Buf., Det.	4	105	34	44	19	5836	326	3	3.35	....	....	....	....	....	....	....	....		1968-69	1971-72
Damore, Nick	Bos.	1	1	0	1	0	60	3	0	3.00	....	....	....	....	....	....	....	....		1941-42	1941-42
D'Amour, Marc	Cgy., Phi.	2	16	2	4	2	579	32	0	3.32	....	....	....	....	....	....	....	....		1985-86	1988-89
Daskalakis, Cleon	Bos.	3	12	3	4	1	506	41	0	4.86	....	....	....	....	....	....	....	....		1984-85	1986-87
Davidson, John	St.L., NYR	10	301	123	124	39	17109	1004	7	3.52	31	16	14	0	1862	77	1	2.48		1973-74	1982-83
Decourcy, Robert	NYR	1	1	0	1	0	29	6	0	12.41	....	....	....	....	....	....	....	....		1947-48	1947-48
Defelice, Norman	Bos.	1	10	3	5	2	600	30	0	3.00	....	....	....	....	....	....	....	....		1956-57	1956-57
DeJordy, Denis	Chi., L.A., Mtl., Det.	11	316	124	127	51	17798	929	15	3.13	18	6	9	0	946	55	0	3.49		1962-63	1973-74
DelGuidice, Matt	Bos.	2	11	2	5	1	434	28	0	3.87	....	....	....	....	....	....	....	....		1990-91	1991-92
Desjardins, Gerry	L.A., Chi., NYI, Buf.	10	331	122	153	44	19014	1042	12	3.29	35	15	15	0	1874	108	0	3.46		1968-69	1977-78
Dickie, Bill	Chi.	1	1	1	0	0	60	3	0	3.00	....	....	....	....	....	....	....	....		1941-42	1941-42
Dion, Connie	Det.	2	38	23	11	4	2280	119	0	3.13	5	1	4	0	300	17	0	3.40		1943-44	1944-45
Dion, Michel	Que., Wpg., Pit.	6	227	60	118	32	12695	898	2	4.24	5	2	3	0	304	22	0	4.34		1979-80	1984-85
Dolson, "Dolly"	Det.	3	93	35	44	13	5820	192	16	1.98	2	0	2	0	120	7	0	3.50		1928-29	1930-31
Dopson, Robert	Pit.	1	2	0	0	0	45	3	0	4.00	....	....	....	....	....	....	....	....		1993-94	1993-94
Dowie, Bruce	Tor.	1	2	0	1	0	72	4	0	3.33	....	....	....	....	....	....	....	....		1983-84	1983-84
Dryden, Dave	NYR, Chi., Buf., Edm.	9	203	66	76	31	10424	555	9	3.19	3	0	2	0	133	9	0	4.06		1961-62	1979-80
Dryden, Ken	Mtl.	8	397	258	57	74	23352	870	46	2.24	112	80	32	0	6846	274	10	2.40	6	1970-71	1978-79
Dumas, Michel	Chi.	2	8	2	1	2	362	24	0	3.98	1	0	0	0	19	1	0	3.16		1974-75	1976-77
Dupuis, Bob	Edm.	1	1	0	1	0	60	4	0	4.00	....	....	....	....	....	....	....	....		1979-80	1979-80
• Durnan, Bill	Mtl.	7	383	208	112	62	22945	901	34	2.36	45	27	18	0	2871	99	2	2.07	2	1943-44	1949-50
Dyck, Ed	Van.	3	49	8	28	5	2453	178	1	4.35	....	....	....	....	....	....	....	....		1971-72	1973-74
Edwards, Don	Buf., Cgy., Tor.	10	459	208	155	74	26181	1449	16	3.32	42	16	21	0	2302	132	1	3.44		1976-77	1985-86

			Regular Schedule								Playoffs										
Name	NHL Teams	NHL Seasons	GP	W	L	T	Mins	GA	SO	Avg	GP	W	L	T	Mins	GA	SO	Avg	NHL Cup Wins	First NHL Season	Last NHL Season
Edwards, Gary	St.L., L.A., Clev., Min., Edm., Pit.	13	286	88	125	51	16002	973	11	3.65	11	5	4	0	537	34	0	3.80		1968-69	1981-82
Edwards, Marv	Pit., Tor., Cal.	4	61	15	34	7	3467	218	2	3.77	....	....	....		....	....	....	....		1968-69	1973-74
Edwards, Roy	Det., Pit.	7	236	92	88	38	13109	637	12	2.92	4	0	3	0	206	11	0	3.20		1967-68	1973-74
Eliot, Darren	L.A., Det., Buf.	5	89	25	41	12	4931	377	1	4.59	1	0	0	0	40	7	0	10.50		1984-85	1988-89
Ellacott, Ken	Van.	1	12	2	3	4	555	41	0	4.43	....	....	....		....	....	....	....		1982-83	1982-83
Erickson, Chad	N.J.	1	2	1	1	0	120	9	0	4.50	....	....	....		....	....	....	....		1991-92	1991-92
Esposito, Tony	Mtl., Chi.	16	886	423	306	152	52585	2563	76	2.92	99	45	53	0	6017	308	6	3.07	1	1968-69	1983-84
• Evans, Claude	Mtl., Bos.	2	5	2	2	1	280	16	0	3.43	....	....	....		....	....	....	....		1954-55	1957-58
Exelby, Randy	Mtl., Edm.	2	2	0	1	0	63	5	0	4.76	....	....	....		....	....	....	....		1988-89	1989-90
Farr, Rocky	Buf.	3	19	2	6	3	722	42	0	3.49	....	....	....		....	....	....	....		1972-73	1974-75
Favell, Doug	Phi., Tor., Col.	12	373	123	153	69	20771	1096	18	3.17	21	5	16	0	1270	66	1	3.12		1967-68	1978-79
• Forbes, Jake	Tor., Ham., NYA, Phi.	13	210	84	114	11	12922	594	19	2.76	2	0	2	0	120	7	0	3.50		1919-20	1932-33
Ford, Brian	Que., Pit.	2	11	3	7	0	580	61	0	6.31	....	....	....		....	....	....	....		1983-84	1984-85
Foster, Norm	Bos., Edm.	2	13	7	4	0	623	34	0	3.27	....	....	....		....	....	....	....		1990-91	1991-92
Fowler, Hec	Bos.	1	7	1	6	0	420	43	0	6.14	....	....	....		....	....	....	....		1924-25	1924-25
Francis, Emile	Chi., NYR	6	95	31	52	11	5660	355	1	3.76	....	....	....		....	....	....	....		1946-47	1951-52
• Franks, Jim	Det., NYR, Bos.	4	43	12	23	7	2580	185	1	4.30	1	0	1	0	30	2	0	4.00	1	1936-37	1943-44
Frederick, Ray	Chi.	1	5	0	4	1	300	22	0	4.40	....	....	....		....	....	....	....		1954-55	1954-55
Friesen, Karl	N.J.	1	4	0	2	1	130	16	0	7.38	....	....	....		....	....	....	....		1986-87	1986-87
Froese, Bob	Phi., NYR	8	242	128	72	20	13451	694	13	3.10	18	3	9	0	830	55	0	3.98		1982-83	1990-91
Gagnon, David	Det.	1	2	0	1	0	35	6	0	10.29	....	....	....		....	....	....	....		1990-91	1990-91
• Gamble, Bruce	NYR, Bos., Tor., Phi.	10	327	109	149	47	18442	992	22	3.23	5	0	4	0	206	25	0	7.28		1958-59	1971-72
Gamble, Troy	Van.	4	72	22	29	9	3804	229	1	3.61	4	1	3	0	249	16	0	3.86		1986-87	1991-92
Gardiner, Bert	NYR, Mtl., Chi., Bos.	6	144	49	68	27	8760	554	3	3.79	9	4	5	0	647	20	0	1.85		1935-36	1943-44
• Gardiner, Chuck	Chi.	7	316	112	152	52	19687	664	42	2.02	21	12	6	3	1472	35	5	1.43	1	1927-28	1933-34
Gardner, George	Det., Van.	5	66	16	30	6	3313	207	0	3.75	....	....	....		....	....	....	....		1965-66	1971-72
Garrett, John	Hfd., Que., Van.	6	207	68	91	37	11763	837	1	4.27	9	4	3	0	461	33	0	4.30		1979-80	1984-85
Gatherum, Dave	Det.	1	3	2	0	1	180	3	1	1.00	....	....	....		....	....	....	....		1953-54	1953-54
Gauthier, Paul	Mtl.	1	1	0	0	1	70	2	0	1.71	....	....	....		....	....	....	....		1937-38	1937-38
Gelineau, Jack	Bos., Chi.	4	143	46	64	33	8580	447	7	3.13	4	1	2	0	260	7	1	1.62		1948-49	1953-54
Giacomin, Ed	NYR, Det.	13	610	289	206	97	35693	1675	54	2.82	65	29	35	0	3834	180	1	2.82		1965-66	1977-78
Gilbert, Gilles	Min., Bos., Det.	14	416	192	143	60	23677	1290	18	3.27	32	17	15	0	1919	97	3	3.03		1969-70	1982-83
Gill, Andre	Bos.	1	5	3	2	0	270	13	1	2.89	....	....	....		....	....	....	....		1967-68	1967-68
• Goodman, Paul	Chi.	3	52	23	20	9	3240	117	6	2.17	3	0	3	0	187	10	0	3.21	1	1937-38	1940-41
Gordon, Scott	Que.	2	23	2	16	0	1082	101	0	5.60	....	....	....		....	....	....	....		1989-90	1990-91
Gosselin, Mario	Que., L.A., Hfd.	9	241	91	107	14	12857	801	6	3.74	32	16	15	0	1816	99	0	3.27		1983-84	1993-94
Grahame, Ron	Bos., L.A., Que.	4	114	50	43	15	6472	409	5	3.79	4	2	1	0	202	7	0	2.08		1977-78	1980-81
• Grant, Ben	Tor., NYA., Bos.	6	50	17	26	4	2990	188	4	3.77	....	....	....		....	....	....	....		1928-29	1943-44
Grant, Doug	Det., St.L.	7	77	27	34	8	4199	280	2	4.00	....	....	....		....	....	....	....		1973-74	1979-80
Gratton, Gilles	St.L., NYR	2	47	13	18	9	2299	154	0	4.02	....	....	....		....	....	....	....		1975-76	1976-77
Gray, Gerry	Det., NYI	2	8	1	5	1	440	35	0	4.77	....	....	....		....	....	....	....		1970-71	1972-73
Gray, Harrison	Det.	1	1	0	0	0	40	5	0	7.50	....	....	....		....	....	....	....		1963-64	1963-64
Greenlay, Mike	Edm.	1	2	0	0	0	20	4	0	12.00	....	....	....		....	....	....	....		1989-90	1989-90
Guenette, Steve	Pit., Cgy.	5	35	19	16	0	1958	122	1	3.74	....	....	....		....	....	....	....		1986-87	1990-91
• Hainsworth, George	Mtl., Tor.	11	465	246	145	74	29415	937	94	1.91	52	22	25	5	3486	112	8	1.93	2	1926-27	1936-37
Hall, Glenn	Det., Chi., St.L.	18	906	407	327	163	53484	2239	84	2.51	115	49	65	0	6899	321	6	2.79	1	1952-53	1970-71
Hamel, Pierre	Tor., Wpg.	4	69	13	41	7	3766	276	0	4.40	....	....	....		....	....	....	....		1974-75	1980-81
Hanlon, Glen	Van., St.L., NYR, Det.	14	477	167	202	61	26037	1561	13	3.60	35	11	15	0	1756	92	4	3.14		1977-78	1990-91
Harrison, Paul	Min., Tor., Pit., Buf.	7	109	28	59	9	5806	408	2	4.22	4	0	1	0	157	9	0	3.44		1975-76	1981-82
Hayward, Brian	Wpg., Mtl., Min., S.J.	11	357	143	156	37	20025	1242	8	3.72	37	11	18	0	1803	104	0	3.46		1982-83	1992-93
Head, Don	Bos.	1	38	9	26	3	2280	161	2	4.24	....	....	....		....	....	....	....	1	1961-62	1961-62
• Hebert, Sammy	Tor., Ott.	2	4	1	3	0	200	19	0	5.70	....	....	....		....	....	....	....		1917-18	1923-24
Heinz, Rick	St.L., Van.	5	49	14	19	5	2356	159	2	4.05	1	0	0	0	8	1	0	7.50		1980-81	1984-85
Henderson, John	Bos.	2	45	15	15	15	2688	113	5	2.52	2	0	2	0	120	8	0	4.00		1954-55	1955-56
• Henry, Gord	Bos.	4	3	1	2	0	180	5	1	1.67	5	0	4	0	283	21	0	4.45		1948-49	1952-53
Henry, Jim	NYR, Chi., Bos.	9	405	161	173	70	24315	1166	27	2.88	29	11	18	0	1741	81	2	2.79		1941-42	1954-55
Herron, Denis	Pit., K.C., Mtl.	14	462	146	203	76	25608	1579	10	3.70	15	5	10	0	901	50	0	3.33		1972-73	1985-86
Highton, Hec	Chi.	1	24	10	14	0	1440	108	0	4.50	....	....	....		....	....	....	....		1943-44	1943-44
§ Himes, Normie	NYA	2	2	0	0	1	79	3	0	2.28	....	....	....		....	....	....	....		1927-28	1928-29
Hodge, Charlie	Mtl., Oak., Van.	13	358	152	124	60	20593	927	24	2.70	16	7	7	0	803	32	2	2.39	4	1954-55	1970-71
Hoffort, Bruce	Phi.	2	9	4	0	3	368	22	0	3.59	....	....	....		....	....	....	....		1989-90	1990-91
Hoganson, Paul	Pit.	1	2	0	1	0	57	7	0	7.37	....	....	....		....	....	....	....		1970-71	1970-71
Hogosta, Goran	NYI, Que.	2	22	5	12	3	1208	83	1	4.12	....	....	....		....	....	....	....		1977-78	1979-80
Holden, Mark	Mtl., Wpg.	4	8	3	2	1	372	25	0	4.03	....	....	....		....	....	....	....		1981-82	1984-85
Holland, Ken	Hfd.	2	4	0	2	1	206	17	0	4.95	....	....	....		....	....	....	....		1980-81	1980-81
Holland, Robbie	Pit.	2	44	11	22	9	2513	171	1	4.08	....	....	....		....	....	....	....		1979-80	1980-81
• Holmes, Harry	Tor., Det.	4	103	40	53	10	6510	264	17	2.43	7	4	3	0	420	28	0	4.00		1917-18	1927-28
§ Horner, Red	Tor.	1	1	0	0	0	1	1	0	60.00	....	....	....		....	....	....	....		1932-33	1932-33
Hrivnak, Jim	Wsh., Wpg., St.L.	5	85	34	30	3	4217	262	0	3.73	....	....	....		....	....	....	....		1989-90	1993-94
Ing, Peter	Tor., Edm., Det.	4	74	20	37	9	3941	266	1	4.05	....	....	....		....	....	....	....		1989-90	1993-94
Inness, Gary	Pit., Phi., Wsh.	7	162	58	61	27	8710	494	2	3.40	9	5	4	0	540	24	0	2.67		1973-74	1980-81
Ireland, Randy	Buf.	1	2	0	0	0	30	3	0	6.00	....	....	....		....	....	....	....		1978-79	1978-79
Irons, Robbie	St.L.	1	1	0	0	0	3	0	0	0.00	....	....	....		....	....	....	....		1968-69	1968-69
• Ironstone, Joe	NYA, Tor.	2	2	0	1	1	110	3	1	1.64	....	....	....		....	....	....	....		1925-26	1927-28
Jackson, Doug	Chi.	1	6	2	3	1	360	42	0	7.00	....	....	....		....	....	....	....		1947-48	1947-48
Jackson, Percy	Bos., NYA, NYR	4	7	1	3	1	392	26	0	3.98	....	....	....		....	....	....	....		1931-32	1935-36
Jaks, Pauli	L.A.	1	1	0	0	0	40	2	0	3.00	....	....	....		....	....	....	....		1994-95	1994-95
Janaszak, Steve	Min., Col.	2	3	0	1	1	160	15	0	5.62	....	....	....		....	....	....	....		1979-80	1981-82
Janecyk, Bob	Chi., L.A.	6	110	43	47	13	6250	432	2	4.15	3	0	3	0	184	10	0	3.26		1983-84	1988-89
§ Jenkins, Roger	NYA	1	1	0	1	0	30	7	0	14.00	....	....	....		....	....	....	....		1938-39	1938-39
Jensen, Al	Det., Wsh., L.A.	7	179	95	53	18	9974	557	8	3.35	12	5	5	0	598	32	0	3.21		1980-81	1986-87
Jensen, Darren	Phi.	2	30	15	10	1	1496	95	2	3.81	....	....	....		....	....	....	....		1984-85	1985-86
Johnson, Bob	St.L., Pit.	2	24	9	9	1	1059	66	0	3.74	....	....	....		....	....	....	....		1972-73	1974-75
Johnston, Eddie	Bos., Tor., St.L., Chi.	16	592	236	256	81	34215	1855	32	3.25	18	7	10	0	1023	57	1	3.34	2	1962-63	1977-78
Junkin, Joe	Bos.	1	1	0	0	0	8	0	0	0.00	....	....	....		....	....	....	....		1968-69	1968-69
Kaarela, Jari	Col.	1	5	2	2	0	220	22	0	6.00	....	....	....		....	....	....	....		1980-81	1980-81
Kampurri, Hannu	N.J.	1	13	1	10	1	645	54	0	5.02	....	....	....		....	....	....	....		1984-85	1984-85
• Karakas, Mike	Chi., Mtl.	8	336	114	169	53	20616	1002	28	2.92	23	11	12	0	1434	72	3	3.01	1	1935-36	1945-46
Keans, Doug	L.A., Bos.	9	210	96	64	26	11388	666	4	3.51	9	2	6	0	432	34	0	4.72		1979-80	1987-88
Keenan, Don	Bos.	1	1	0	1	0	60	4	0	4.00	....	....	....		....	....	....	....		1958-59	1958-59
• Kerr, Dave	Mtl.M., NYA, NYR	11	426	203	148	75	26519	960	51	2.17	40	18	19	3	2616	76	8	1.74	1	1930-31	1940-41
King, Scott	Det.	2	2	0	0	0	61	3	0	2.95	....	....	....		....	....	....	....		1990-91	1991-92
Kleisinger, Terry	NYR	1	4	0	2	0	191	14	0	4.40	....	....	....		....	....	....	....		1985-86	1985-86
Klymkiw, Julian	NYR	1	1	0	0	0	19	2	0	6.32	....	....	....		....	....	....	....		1958-59	1958-59
Kuntar, Les	Mtl.	1	6	2	2	0	302	16	0	3.18	....	....	....		....	....	....	....		1993-94	1993-94
Kurt, Gary	Cal.	1	16	1	7	0	838	60	0	4.30	....	....	....		....	....	....	....		1971-72	1971-72
Lacroix, "Frenchy"	Mtl.	1	5	1	4	0	280	15	0	3.21	....	....	....		....	....	....	....		1925-26	1925-26
LaFerriere, Rick	Col.	1	1	0	0	0	20	1	0	3.00	....	....	....		....	....	....	....		1981-82	1981-82
• Larocque, Michel	Mtl., Tor., Phi., St.L.	11	312	160	89	45	17615	978	17	3.33	14	6	6	0	759	37	1	2.92	4	1973-74	1983-84
Laskowski, Gary	L.A.	2	59	19	27	5	2942	228	0	4.65	....	....	....		....	....	....	....		1982-83	1983-84
Laxton, Gord	Pit.	4	17	4	9	0	800	74	0	5.55	....	....	....		....	....	....	....		1975-76	1978-79
§ LeDuc, Albert	Mtl.	1	1	0	0	0	2	1	0	30.00	....	....	....		....	....	....	....		1931-32	1931-32
Legris, Claude	Det.	2	4	0	1	1	91	4	0	2.64	....	....	....		....	....	....	....		1980-81	1981-82
• Lehman, Hugh	Chi.	2	48	20	24	4	3047	136	6	2.68	2	0	1	1	120	10	0	5.00		1926-27	1927-28
Lemelin, Reggie	Atl., Cgy., Bos.	15	507	236	162	63	28006	1613	12	3.46	59	23	25	0	3119	186	2	3.58		1978-79	1992-93
Lessard, Mario	L.A.	6	240	92	97	39	13529	843	9	3.74	20	6	12	0	1136	83	0	4.38		1978-79	1983-84
Levasseur, Jean-Louis	Min.	1	1	0	1	0	60	7	0	7.00	....	....	....		....	....	....	....		1979-80	1979-80
§ • Levinsky, Alex	Tor.	1	1	0	0	0	1	1	0	60.00	....	....	....		....	....	....	....		1932-33	1932-33
• Lindbergh, Pelle	Phi.	5	157	87	49	15	9151	503	7	3.30	23	12	10	0	1214	63	3	3.11		1981-82	1985-86
• Lindsay, Bert	Mtl.W., Tor.	2	20	6	14	0	1200	118	0	5.90	....	....	....		....	....	....	....		1917-18	1918-19
Liut, Mike	St. L., Hfd., Wsh.	13	663	294	271	74	38155	2219	25	3.49	67	29	32	0	3814	215	2	3.38		1979-80	1991-92
Lockett, Ken	Van.	2	55	13	15	8	2348	131	2	3.35	1	0	1	0	60	6	0	6.00		1974-75	1975-76
• Lockhart, Howie	Tor., Que., Ham., Bos.	5	57	17	40	0	3371	286	1	5.09	....	....	....		....	....	....	....		1919-20	1924-25
LoPresti, Pete	Min., Edm.	6	175	43	102	20	9858	668	5	4.07	2	0	2	0	77	6	0	4.68		1974-75	1980-81

Name	NHL Teams	NHL Seasons	Regular Schedule GP	W	L	T	Mins	GA	SO	Avg	Playoffs GP	W	L	T	Mins	GA	SO	Avg	NHL Cup Wins	First NHL Season	Last NHL Season
● LoPresti, Sam	Chi.	2	74	30	38	6	4530	236	4	3.13	8	3	5	0	530	17	1	1.92		1940-41	1941-42
Loustel, Ron	Wpg.	1	1	0	1	0	60	10	0	10.00	....	....	....	....	....	....	....	....		1980-81	1980-81
Low, Ron	Tor., Wsh., Det., Que., Edm., NJ	11	382	102	203	38	20502	1463	4	4.28	7	1	6	0	452	29	0	3.85		1972-73	1984-85
Lozinski, Larry	Det.	1	30	6	11	7	1459	105	0	4.32	....	....	....	....	....	....	....	....		1980-81	1980-81
Lumley, Harry	Det., NYR, Chi., Tor., Bos.	16	804	333	326	143	48100	2210	71	2.76	76	29	47	0	4760	199	7	2.51	1	1943-44	1959-60
MacKenzie, Shawn	N.J.	1	4	0	1	0	130	15	0	6.92	....	....	....	....	....	....	....	....		1982-83	1982-83
Malarchuk, Clint	Que., Wsh., Buf.	10	338	141	130	45	19030	1100	12	3.47	15	2	9	0	781	56	0	4.30		1981-82	1991-92
Maneluk, George	NYI	1	4	1	1	0	140	15	0	6.43	....	....	....	....	....	....	....	....		1990-91	1990-91
Maniago, Cesare	Tor., Mtl., NYR, Min., Van.	15	568	189	261	96	32570	1774	30	3.27	36	15	21	0	2245	100	3	2.67		1960-61	1977-78
Marois, Jean	Tor., Chi.	2	3	1	2	0	180	15	0	5.00	....	....	....	....	....	....	....	....		1943-44	1953-54
Martin, Seth	St.L.	1	30	8	10	7	1552	67	1	2.59	2	0	0	0	73	5	0	4.11		1967-68	1967-68
Mason, Bob	Wsh., Chi., Que., Van.	8	145	55	65	16	7988	500	1	3.76	5	2	3	0	369	12	1	1.95		1983-84	1990-91
Mattsson, Markus	Wpg., Min., L.A.	4	92	21	46	14	5007	343	6	4.11	....	....	....	....	....	....	....	....		1979-80	1983-84
May, Darrell	St. L.	2	6	1	5	0	364	31	0	5.11	....	....	....	....	....	....	....	....		1985-86	1987-88
Mayer, Gilles	Tor.	4	9	1	7	1	540	25	0	2.78	....	....	....	....	....	....	....	....		1949-50	1955-56
● McAuley, Ken	NYR	2	96	17	64	15	5740	537	1	5.61	....	....	....	....	....	....	....	....		1943-44	1944-45
McCartan, Jack	NYR	2	12	3	7	2	680	43	1	3.79	....	....	....	....	....	....	....	....		1959-60	1960-61
● McCool, Frank	Tor.	2	72	34	31	7	4320	242	4	3.36	13	8	5	0	807	30	4	2.23	1	1944-45	1945-46
McDuffe, Pete	St.L., NYR, K.C., Det.	5	57	11	36	6	3207	218	0	4.08	1	0	1	0	60	7	0	7.00		1971-72	1975-76
McGrattan, Tom	Det.	1	1	0	0	0	8	0	0	0.00	....	....	....	....	....	....	....	....		1947-48	1947-48
McKay, Ross	Hfd.	1	1	0	0	0	35	3	0	5.14	....	....	....	....	....	....	....	....		1990-91	1990-91
McKenzie, Bill	Det., K.C., Col.	6	91	18	49	13	4776	326	2	4.10	....	....	....	....	....	....	....	....		1973-74	1979-80
McKichan, Steve	Van.	1	1	0	0	0	20	2	0	6.00	....	....	....	....	....	....	....	....		1990-91	1990-91
McLachlan, Murray	Tor.	1	2	0	1	0	25	4	0	9.60	....	....	....	....	....	....	....	....		1970-71	1970-71
McLelland, Dave	Van.	1	2	1	1	0	120	10	0	5.00	....	....	....	....	....	....	....	....		1972-73	1972-73
McLeod, Don	Det., Phi.	2	18	3	10	1	879	74	0	5.05	....	....	....	....	....	....	....	....		1970-71	1971-72
McLeod, Jim	St.L.	1	16	6	6	4	880	44	0	3.00	....	....	....	....	....	....	....	....		1971-72	1971-72
McNamara, Gerry	Tor.	2	7	2	2	1	323	15	0	2.79	....	....	....	....	....	....	....	....		1960-61	1969-70
McNeil, Gerry	Mtl.	7	276	119	105	52	16535	650	28	2.36	35	17	18	0	2284	72	5	1.89	3	1947-48	1956-57
McRae, Gord	Tor.	5	71	30	22	10	3799	221	1	3.49	8	2	5	0	454	22	0	2.91		1972-73	1977-78
Melanson, Rollie	NYI, Min., L.A., N.J., Mtl.	11	291	129	106	33	16452	995	6	3.63	23	4	9	0	801	59	0	4.42	3	1980-81	1991-92
Meloche, Gilles	Chi., Cal., Cle., Min., Pit.	18	788	270	351	131	45401	2756	20	3.64	45	21	19	0	2464	143	2	3.48		1970-71	1987-88
Micalef, Corrado	Det.	5	113	26	59	15	5794	409	2	4.24	3	0	0	0	49	8	0	9.80		1981-82	1985-86
Middlebrook, Lindsay	Wpg., Min., N.J., Edm.	4	37	3	25	4	1845	152	0	4.94	....	....	....	....	....	....	....	....		1979-80	1982-83
● Millar, Al	Bos.	1	6	1	3	2	360	25	0	4.17	....	....	....	....	....	....	....	....		1957-58	1957-58
Millen, Greg	Pit., Hfd., St. L., Que., Chi., Det.	14	604	215	284	89	35377	2281	17	3.87	59	27	29	0	3383	193	0	3.42		1978-79	1991-92
● Miller, Joe	NYA, NYR, Pit., Phi.	4	130	24	90	16	7981	386	16	2.90	3	2	1	0	180	3	1	1.00	1	1927-28	1930-31
Mio, Eddie	Edm., NYR, Det.	7	192	64	73	30	10428	705	4	4.06	17	9	7	0	986	63	0	3.83		1979-80	1985-86
● Mitchell, Ivan	Tor.	3	20	11	9	0	1232	96	0	4.68	....	....	....	....	....	....	....	....		1919-20	1921-22
Moffat, Mike	Bos.	3	19	7	7	2	979	70	0	4.29	11	6	5	0	663	38	0	3.44		1981-82	1983-84
Moore, Alfie	NYA, Det., Chi.	4	21	7	14	0	1290	81	1	3.77	3	1	2	0	180	7	0	2.33	1	1936-37	1939-40
Moore, Robbie	Phi., Wsh.	2	6	3	1	1	257	8	2	1.87	5	3	2	0	268	18	0	4.03		1978-79	1982-83
Morissette, Jean	Mtl.	1	1	0	1	0	36	4	0	6.67	....	....	....	....	....	....	....	....		1963-64	1963-64
● Mowers, Johnny	Det.	4	152	65	61	26	9350	399	15	2.56	32	19	13	0	2000	85	2	2.55	1	1940-41	1946-47
Mrazek, Jerry	Phi.	1	1	0	0	0	6	1	0	10.00	....	....	....	....	....	....	....	....		1975-76	1975-76
● Mummery, Harry	Que., Ham.	2	4	2	1	0	191	20	0	6.28	....	....	....	....	....	....	....	....		1919-20	1921-22
● Murphy, Hal	Mtl.	1	1	1	0	0	60	4	0	4.00	....	....	....	....	....	....	....	....		1952-53	1952-53
Murray, Mickey	Mtl.	1	1	0	1	0	60	4	0	4.00	....	....	....	....	....	....	....	....		1929-30	1929-30
Myllys, Jarmo	Min., S.J.	4	39	4	27	1	1846	161	0	5.23	....	....	....	....	....	....	....	....		1988-89	1991-92
Mylnikov, Sergei	Que.	1	10	1	7	2	568	47	0	4.96	....	....	....	....	....	....	....	....		1989-90	1989-90
Myre, Phil	Mtl., Atl., St.L., Phi., Col., Buf.	14	439	149	198	74	25220	1482	14	3.53	12	6	5	0	747	41	1	3.29		1969-70	1982-83
Newton, Cam	Pit.	2	16	4	7	1	814	51	0	3.76	....	....	....	....	....	....	....	....		1970-71	1972-73
Norris, Jack	Bos., Chi., L.A.	4	58	19	26	4	3119	202	2	3.89	....	....	....	....	....	....	....	....		1964-65	1970-71
Oleschuk, Bill	K.C., Col.	4	55	7	28	10	2835	188	1	3.98	....	....	....	....	....	....	....	....		1975-76	1979-80
● Olesevich, Dan	NYR	1	1	0	0	1	29	2	0	4.14	....	....	....	....	....	....	....	....		1961-62	1961-62
Ouimet, Ted	St.L.	1	1	0	1	0	60	2	0	2.00	....	....	....	....	....	....	....	....		1968-69	1968-69
Pageau, Paul	L.A.	1	1	0	1	0	60	8	0	8.00	....	....	....	....	....	....	....	....		1980-81	1980-81
Paille, Marcel	NYR	7	107	33	52	21	6342	362	2	3.42	....	....	....	....	....	....	....	....		1957-58	1964-65
Palmateer, Mike	Tor., Wsh.	8	356	149	138	52	20131	1183	17	3.53	29	12	17	0	1765	89	2	3.03		1976-77	1983-84
Pang, Darren	Chi.	3	81	27	35	7	4252	287	0	4.05	6	1	3	0	250	18	0	4.32		1984-85	1988-89
Parent, Bernie	Bos., Tor., Phi.	13	608	270	197	121	35136	1493	54	2.55	71	38	33	0	4302	174	6	2.43	2	1965-66	1978-79
Parent, Bob	Tor.	2	3	0	2	0	160	15	0	5.62	....	....	....	....	....	....	....	....		1981-82	1982-83
Parro, Dave	Wsh.	4	77	21	36	10	4015	274	2	4.09	....	....	....	....	....	....	....	....		1980-81	1983-84
● Patrick, Lester	NYR	1	....	....	....	....	....	....	....	....	1	1	0	0	46	1	0	1.30	1	1927-28	1927-28
Peeters, Pete	Phi., Bos., Wsh.	13	489	246	155	51	27699	1424	21	3.08	71	35	35	0	4200	232	2	3.31		1978-79	1990-91
Pelletier, Marcel	Chi., NYR	2	8	1	6	1	395	33	0	5.01	....	....	....	....	....	....	....	....		1950-51	1962-63
Penney, Steve	Mtl., Wpg.	5	91	35	38	12	5194	313	1	3.62	27	15	12	0	1604	72	4	2.69		1983-84	1987-88
● Perreault, "Miche"	Mtl., Det., Bos.	3	31	8	16	6	1827	106	3	3.48	....	....	....	....	....	....	....	....		1955-56	1962-63
Pettie, Jim	Bos.	3	21	9	7	2	1157	71	1	3.68	....	....	....	....	....	....	....	....		1976-77	1978-79
Pietrangelo, Frank	Pit., Hfd.	7	141	46	59	6	7141	490	1	4.12	12	7	5	0	713	34	1	2.86	1	1987-88	1993-94
● Plante, Jacques	Mtl., NYR, St.L., Tor., Bos.	18	837	434	246	147	49533	1965	82	2.38	112	71	37	0	6651	240	14	2.17	6	1952-53	1972-73
Plasse, Michel	St.L., Mtl., K.C., Pit., Col., Que.	12	299	92	136	54	16760	1058	2	3.79	4	1	2	0	195	9	1	2.77	1	1970-71	1981-82
Plaxton, Hugh	Mtl.M.	1	1	0	1	0	59	5	0	5.08	....	....	....	....	....	....	....	....		1932-33	1932-33
Pronovost, Claude	Bos., Mtl.	2	3	1	1	0	120	7	1	3.50	....	....	....	....	....	....	....	....		1955-56	1958-59
Pusey, Chris	Det.	1	1	0	0	0	40	3	0	4.50	....	....	....	....	....	....	....	....		1985-86	1985-86
Raymond, Alain	Wsh.	1	1	0	1	0	40	2	0	3.00	....	....	....	....	....	....	....	....		1987-88	1987-88
Rayner, Chuck	NYA, Bro., NYR	10	424	138	209	77	25491	1294	25	3.05	18	9	9	0	1135	46	1	2.43		1940-41	1952-53
Reaugh, Daryl	Edm., Hfd.	3	27	8	9	1	1246	72	1	3.47	....	....	....	....	....	....	....	....		1984-85	1990-91
Redquest, Greg	Pit.	1	1	0	0	0	13	3	0	13.85	....	....	....	....	....	....	....	....		1977-78	1977-78
Reece, Dave	Bos.	1	14	7	5	2	777	43	2	3.32	....	....	....	....	....	....	....	....		1975-76	1975-76
Resch, Glenn	NYI, Col., N.J., Phi.	14	571	231	224	82	32279	1761	26	3.27	41	17	17	0	2044	85	2	2.50	1	1973-74	1986-87
Rheaume, Herb	Mtl.	1	31	10	19	1	1889	92	0	2.92	....	....	....	....	....	....	....	....		1925-26	1925-26
Ricci, Nick	Pit.	4	19	7	12	0	1087	79	0	4.36	....	....	....	....	....	....	....	....		1979-80	1982-83
Richardson, Terry	Det., St.L.	5	20	3	11	0	906	85	0	5.63	....	....	....	....	....	....	....	....		1973-74	1978-79
Ridley, Curt	NYR, Van., Tor.	6	104	27	47	16	5498	355	1	3.87	2	0	2	0	120	8	0	4.00		1974-75	1980-81
Riggin, Dennis	Det.	2	18	5	10	2	985	54	1	3.29	....	....	....	....	....	....	....	....		1959-60	1962-63
Riggin, Pat	Atl., Cgy., Wsh., Bos., Pit.	9	350	153	120	52	19872	1135	11	3.43	25	8	13	0	1336	72	0	3.23		1979-80	1987-88
Ring, Bob	Bos.	1	1	0	0	0	34	4	0	7.06	....	....	....	....	....	....	....	....		1965-66	1965-66
Rivard, Fern	Min.	4	55	9	27	11	2865	190	2	3.98	....	....	....	....	....	....	....	....		1968-69	1974-75
● Roach, John	Tor., NYR, Det.	14	491	219	204	68	30423	1246	58	2.46	34	15	16	3	2206	69	8	1.88	1	1921-22	1934-35
● Roberts, Moe	Bos., NYA, Chi.	4	10	2	5	0	506	31	0	3.68	....	....	....	....	....	....	....	....		1925-26	1951-52
● Robertson, Earl	NYA, Bro., Det.	6	190	60	95	34	11820	575	16	2.92	15	7	7	0	995	29	2	1.75	1	1936-37	1941-42
● Rollins, Al	Tor., Chi., NYR	9	430	139	205	84	25723	1196	28	2.79	13	6	7	0	755	30	0	2.38	1	1949-50	1959-60
Romano, Roberto	Pit., Bos.	6	126	46	63	8	7111	471	4	3.97	....	....	....	....	....	....	....	....		1982-83	1993-94
Rupp, Pat	Det.	1	1	0	1	0	60	4	0	4.00	....	....	....	....	....	....	....	....		1963-64	1963-64
Rutherford, Jim	Det., Pit., Tor., L.A.	13	457	151	227	59	25895	1576	14	3.65	8	2	5	0	440	28	0	3.82		1970-71	1982-83
Rutledge, Wayne	L.A.	3	82	27	41	6	4325	241	2	3.34	8	2	4	0	378	20	0	3.17		1967-68	1969-70
St. Croix, Rick	Phi., Tor.	8	129	49	54	18	7275	450	2	3.71	11	4	6	0	562	29	1	3.10		1977-78	1984-85
St. Laurent, Sam	N.J., Det.	5	34	7	12	4	1572	92	1	3.51	1	0	0	0	10	1	0	6.00		1985-86	1989-90
Sands, Charlie	Mtl.	1	1	0	0	0	25	5	0	12.00	....	....	....	....	....	....	....	....		1939-40	1939-40
Sands, Mike	Min.	2	6	0	5	0	302	26	0	5.17	....	....	....	....	....	....	....	....		1984-85	1986-87
Sauve, Bob	Buf., Det., Chi., N.J.	13	420	182	154	54	23711	1377	8	3.48	34	15	16	0	1850	95	4	3.08		1976-77	1987-88
● Sawchuk, Terry	Det., Bos., Tor., L.A., NYR	21	971	447	330	173	57184	2401	103	2.52	106	54	48	0	6310	267	12	2.54	4	1949-50	1969-70
Schaefer, Joe	NYR	2	2	0	1	0	86	8	0	5.58	....	....	....	....	....	....	....	....		1959-60	1960-61
Scott, Ron	NYR, L.A.	5	28	8	13	4	1450	91	0	3.77	1	0	0	0	32	4	0	7.50	1	1983-84	1989-90
Sevigny, Richard	Mtl., Que.	8	176	80	44	20	9485	507	5	3.21	4	0	3	0	208	13	0	3.75		1979-80	1986-87
Sharples, Scott	Cgy.	1	1	0	0	1	65	4	0	3.69	....	....	....	....	....	....	....	....		1991-92	1991-92
Shields, Al	NYA	1	2	0	0	0	41	9	0	13.17	....	....	....	....	....	....	....	....		1931-32	1931-32
Simmons, Don	Bos., Tor., NYR	11	247	98	104	39	14436	705	20	2.93	24	13	11	0	1436	64	3	2.67	2	1956-57	1968-69
Simmons, Gary	Cal., Clev., L.A.	4	107	30	57	15	6162	366	5	3.56	1	0	0	0	20	1	0	3.00		1974-75	1977-78
Skidmore, Paul	St.L.	1	2	1	1	0	120	6	0	3.00	....	....	....	....	....	....	....	....		1981-82	1981-82
Skorodenski, Warren	Chi., Edm.	5	35	12	11	4	1732	100	2	3.46	2	0	0	0	33	6	0	10.91		1981-82	1987-88
Smith, Al	Tor., Pit., Det., Buf., Hfd., Col.	10	233	74	99	36	12752	735	10	3.46	6	1	4	0	317	21	0	3.97		1965-66	1980-81
Smith, Billy	L.A., NYI	18	680	305	233	105	38431	2031	22	3.17	132	88	36	0	7645	348	5	2.73	4	1971-72	1988-89

Name	NHL Teams	NHL Seasons	Regular Schedule								Playoffs								NHL Cup Wins	First NHL Season	Last NHL Season
			GP	W	L	T	Mins	GA	SO	Avg	GP	W	L	T	Mins	GA	SO	Avg			
Smith, Gary	Tor., Oak., Cal., Chi., Van., Min., Wsh., Wpg.	14	532	173	261	74	29619	1675	26	3.39	20	5	13	0	1153	62	1	3.23		1965-66	1979-80
• Smith, Norman	Mtl.M., Det.	8	199	81	83	35	12297	475	17	2.32	12	9	2	0	820	18	3	1.32	2	1931-32	1944-45
Sneddon, Bob	Cal.	1	5	0	2	0	225	21	0	5.60	....	....	....	....	....	....	....	....		1970-71	1970-71
Soetaert, Doug	NYR, Wpg., Mtl.	12	284	110	104	42	15583	1030	6	3.97	5	1	2	0	180	14	0	4.67	1	1975-76	1986-87
Spooner, "Red"	Pit.	1	1	0	1	0	60	6	0	6.00										1929-30	1929-30
§ Staniowski, Ed	St.L., Wpg., Hfd.	10	219	67	104	21	12075	818	2	4.06	8	1	6	0	428	28	0	3.93		1975-76	1984-85
Starr, Harold	Mtl.M.	1	1	0	0	0	3	0	0	0.00										1931-32	1931-32
Stefan, Greg	Det.	9	299	115	127	30	16333	1068	5	3.92	30	12	17	0	1681	99	1	3.53		1981-82	1989-90
Stein, Phil	Tor.	1	1	0	0	0	70	2	0	1.71										1939-40	1939-40
Stephenson, Wayne	St.L., Phi., Wsh.	10	328	146	103	49	18343	937	14	3.06	26	11	12	0	1522	79	2	3.11	1	1971-72	1980-81
Stevenson, Doug	NYR, Chi.	2	8	2	6	0	480	39	0	4.88	....	....	....	....	....	....	....	....		1944-45	1945-46
Stewart, Charles	Bos.	3	77	31	41	5	4737	194	10	2.46	....	....	....	....	....	....	....	....		1924-25	1926-27
Stewart, Jim	Bos.	1	1	0	1	0	20	5	0	15.00	....	....	....	....	....	....	....	....		1979-80	1979-80
Stuart, Herb	Det.	1	3	1	2	0	180	5	0	1.67	....	....	....	....	....	....	....	....		1926-27	1926-27
Sylvestri, Don	Bos.	1	3	0	0	2	102	6	0	3.53	....	....	....	....	....	....	....	....		1984-85	1984-85
Takko, Kari	Min., Edm.	6	142	37	71	14	7317	475	1	3.90	4	0	1	0	109	7	0	3.85		1985-86	1990-91
Tanner, John	Que.	3	21	2	11	5	1084	65	1	3.60	....	....	....	....	....	....	....	....		1989-90	1991-92
Tataryn, Dave	NYR	1	2	1	1	0	80	10	0	7.50	....	....	....	....	....	....	....	....		1976-77	1976-77
Taylor, Bobby	Phi., Pit.	5	46	15	17	6	2268	155	0	4.10	....	....	....	....	....	....	....	....	1	1971-72	1975-76
• Teno, Harvey	Det.	1	5	2	3	0	300	15	0	3.00	....	....	....	....	....	....	....	....		1938-39	1938-39
Thomas, Wayne	Mtl., Tor., NYR	8	243	103	93	34	13768	766	10	3.34	15	6	8	0	849	50	1	3.53		1972-73	1980-81
• Thompson, Tiny	Bos., Det.	12	553	284	194	75	34174	1183	81	2.08	44	20	24	0	2972	93	7	1.88	1	1928-29	1939-40
Tremblay, Vince	Tor., Pit.	5	58	12	26	8	2785	223	1	4.80	....	....	....	....	....	....	....	....		1979-80	1983-84
Tucker, Ted	Cal.	1	5	1	1	1	177	10	0	3.39	....	....	....	....	....	....	....	....		1973-74	1973-74
Turner, Joe	Det.	1	1	0	0	1	60	3	0	3.00	....	....	....	....	....	....	....	....		1941-42	1941-42
• Vachon, Rogatien	Mtl., L.A., Det., Bos.	16	795	355	291	127	46298	2310	51	2.99	48	23	23	0	2876	133	2	2.77	3	1966-67	1981-82
Veisor, Mike	Chi., Hfd., Wpg.	10	139	41	62	26	7806	532	5	4.09	4	0	2	0	180	15	0	5.00		1973-74	1983-84
• Vezina, Georges	Mtl.	9	191	104	81	5	11564	633	13	3.28	26	17	8	0	1596	74	4	2.78	2	1917-18	1925-26
Villemure, Gilles	NYR, Chi.	10	205	100	65	28	11581	542	13	2.81	14	5	5	0	656	32	0	2.93		1963-64	1971-72
Wakely, Ernie	Mtl., St.L.	5	113	41	42	17	6244	290	8	2.79	10	2	6	0	509	37	1	4.36		1962-63	1971-72
• Walsh, James	Mtl.M., NYA	7	108	48	43	16	6461	250	12	2.32	8	2	4	2	570	16	2	1.68		1926-27	1932-33
Wamsley, Rick	Mtl., St.L., Cgy., Tor.	13	407	204	131	46	23123	1287	12	3.34	27	7	18	0	1397	81	0	3.48	1	1980-81	1992-93
Watt, Jim	St.L.	1	1	0	0	0	20	2	0	6.00	....	....	....	....	....	....	....	....		1973-74	1973-74
Weeks, Steve	NYR, Hfd., Van., NYI, L.A., Ott.	13	290	111	119	33	15879	989	5	3.74	12	3	5	0	486	27	0	3.33		1980-81	1992-93
Wetzel, Carl	Det., Min.	2	7	1	3	1	302	22	0	4.37	....	....	....	....	....	....	....	....		1964-65	1967-68
Wilson, Dunc	Phi., Van., Tor., NYR, Pit.	10	287	80	150	33	15851	988	8	3.74	....	....	....	....	....	....	....	....		1969-70	1978-79
Wilson, "Lefty"	Det., Tor., Bos.	3	3	0	0	1	85	1	0	0.71	....	....	....	....	....	....	....	....		1953-54	1957-58
• Winkler, Hal	NYR, Bos.	2	75	35	26	14	4739	126	21	1.60	10	2	3	5	640	18	2	1.69		1926-27	1927-28
Wolfe, Bernie	Wsh.	4	120	20	61	21	6104	424	1	4.17	....	....	....	....	....	....	....	....		1975-76	1978-79
Woods, Alec	NYA	1	1	0	1	0	70	3	0	2.57	....	....	....	....	....	....	....	....		1936-37	1936-37
Worsley, Gump	NYR, Mtl., Min.	21	861	334	349	148	50191	2432	43	2.91	70	40	26	0	4081	192	5	2.82	4	1952-53	1973-74
• Worters, Roy	Pit., NYA, Mtl.	12	484	171	233	68	30175	1143	66	2.27	11	3	6	2	690	24	3	2.09		1925-26	1936-37
Worthy, Chris	Oak., Cal.	3	26	5	10	4	1326	98	0	4.43	....	....	....	....	....	....	....	....		1968-69	1970-71
§ Young, Doug	Det.	1	1	0	0	0	21	1	0	2.86	....	....	....	....	....	....	....	....		1933-34	1933-34
Zanier, Mike	Edm.	1	3	1	1	1	185	12	0	3.89	....	....	....	....	....	....	....	....		1984-85	1984-85

1996-97 Transactions

July, 1996

10 – D **Tuomas Gronman** traded from Colorado to Chicago for Chicago's 2nd round pick in the 1998 Entry Draft.

18 – D **Frank Bialowas** traded from Washington to Philadelphia for future considerations.

29 – D **Craig Wolanin** traded from Colorado to Tampa Bay for Tampa Bay's 2nd round pick in the 1998 Entry Draft.

August, 1996

15 – RW **Sergei Gorbachev** traded from San Jose to Dallas for Dallas' 5th round pick in the 1998 Entry Draft.

16 – C **Jeremy Roenick** traded from Chicago to Phoenix for C **Alexei Zhamnov**, RW **Craig Mills** and Phoenix's 1st round pick in the 1997 Entry Draft (Ty Jones).

20 – D **Marty McSorley** traded from NY Rangers to San Jose for D **Jayson More**, C **Brian Swanson** and a conditional pick in the 1998 Entry Draft.

22 – D **Lyle Odelein** traded from Montreal to New Jersey for RW **Stephane Richer**.

22 – RW **Petr Klima** traded from Tampa Bay to Los Angeles for a conditional pick in the 1997 Entry Draft (Jan Sulc).

27 – RW **Dino Ciccarelli** traded from Detroit to Tampa Bay for a conditional pick in the 1998 Entry Draft.

September, 1996

4 – D **Brent Severyn** traded from NY Islanders to Colorado for Colorado's 3rd round pick in the 1997 Entry Draft. (Later traded to Calgary and then traded again to Carolina. Carolina selected Francis Lessard).

6 – C **Scott Thornton** traded from Edmonton to Montreal for RW **Andrei Kovalenko**.

30 – RW **Rob DiMaio** traded from San Jose to Boston for Boston's 5th round pick in the 1997 Entry Draft (Adam Nittel).

October, 1996

1 – C **Ted Drury** and the rights to D **Marc Moro** traded from Ottawa to Anaheim for D **Jason York** and C **Shaun Van Allen**.

1 – RW **Kevin Brown** traded from Anaheim to Hartford for the rights to C **Espen Knutsen**.

9 – D **Brian Glynn** and LW **Brendan Shanahan** traded from Hartford to Detroit for C **Keith Primeau**, D **Paul Coffey** and Detroit's 1st round pick in the 1997 Entry Draft (Nikos Tselios).

10 – C **Darby Hendrickson** traded from NY Islanders to Toronto for a conditional pick in the 1998 Entry Draft.

24 – C **Scott Fraser** traded from Montreal to Calgary for RW **David Ling** and Calgary's 6th round pick in the 1998 Entry Draft.

25 – RW **Petr Klima** traded from Los Angeles to Pittsburgh for a conditional pick in the 1997 Entry Draft.

29 – C **Pierre Turgeon**, D **Rory Fitzpatrick** and C **Craig Conroy** traded from Montreal to St. Louis for D **Murray Baron**, LW **Shayne Corson** and St. Louis' 5th round pick in the 1997 Entry Draft (Genady Razin).

November, 1996

2 – D **Curtis Leschyshyn** and LW **Chris Simon** traded from Colorado to Washington for RW **Keith Jones**, Washington's 1st round pick in the 1998 Entry Draft and a 4th round pick in the 1998 Entry Draft.

8 – RW **Jason MacDonald** traded from Detroit to Montreal for cash.

9 – D **Curtis Leschyshyn** traded from Washington to Hartford for C **Andrei Nikolishin**.

13 – LW **Donald Brashear** traded from Montreal to Vancouver for D **Jassen Cullimore**.

13 – LW **Sergio Momesso** traded from NY Rangers to St. Louis for RW **Brian Noonan**.

17 – C **Bryan Smolinski** traded from Pittsburgh to NY Islanders for D **Darius Kasparaitis** and C **Andreas Johansson**.

19 – C **Aaron Gavey** traded from Tampa Bay to Calgary for G **Rick Tabaracci**.

19 – C **Nick Vachon** traded from Los Angeles to NY Islanders for C **Chris Marinucci**.

19 – LW **Shawn Antoski** and D **Dmitri Mironov** traded from Pittsburgh to Anaheim for C **Alex Hicks** and D **Fredrik Olausson**.

19 – C **Stu Barnes** and D **Jason Woolley** traded from Florida to Pittsburgh for C **Chris Wells**.

19 – LW **Brian Bellows** traded from Tampa Bay to Anaheim for Anaheim's 6th round pick in the 1997 Entry Draft (Andrei Skopintsev).

22 – C **Neal Broten** traded from New Jersey to Los Angeles for future consideratons.

22 – D **Anders Myrvold** and RW **Landon Wilson** traded from Colorado to Boston for Boston's 1st round pick in the 1998 Entry Draft.

26 – D **Ricard Persson** and LW **Mike Peluso** traded from New Jersey to St. Louis for D **Ken Sutton** and St. Louis' 2nd pick in the 1999 Entry Draft.

27 – D **Christer Olsson** traded from St. Louis to Ottawa for LW **Pavol Demitra**.

27 – LW **Paul Kruse** traded from Calgary to NY Islanders for Colorado's 3rd round pick in the 1997 Entry Draft. (Previously acquired and later traded to Carolina. Carolina selected Francis Lessard.)

28 – RW **Brad Smyth** traded from Florida to Los Angeles for Los Angeles' 3rd round pick in the 1997 Entry Draft (Vratislav Cech).

December, 1996

7 – C **Craig Fisher** traded from NY Islanders to Florida for cash.

15 – D **Paul Coffey** and Hartford's 3rd round pick in the 1997 Entry Draft (Kris Mallette) traded from Hartford to Philadelphia for D **Kevin Haller**, Philadelphia's 1st round pick in the 1997 Entry Draft (later traded to San Jose; San Jose selected Scott Hannan) and Hartford's 7th round picfk in the 1997 Entry Draft (previously acquired – Andrew Merrick).

17 – D **Yves Racine** traded from San Jose to Calgary for cash.

18 – D **Ivan Droppa** traded from Chicago to Florida for D **Alain Nasreddine** and a conditional pick in the 1999 Entry Draft.

January, 1997

25 – G **Ed Belfour** traded from Chicago to San Jose for G **Chris Terreri**, RW **Ulf Dahlen**, D **Michal Sykora** and a conditional pick in the 1998 Entry Draft.

27 – RW **Tomas Sandstrom** traded from Pittsburgh to Detroit for C **Greg Johnson**.

31 – D **Craig Wolanin** traded from Tampa Bay to Toronto for Toronto's 3rd round pick in the 1998 Entry Draft.

February, 1997

6 – C **Mike Eastwood** and D **Dallas Eakins** traded from Phoenix to NY Rangers for D **Jayson More**.

11 – C **Peter Zezel** traded from St. Louis to New Jersey for D **Chris McAlpine** and New Jersey's 9th round pick in the 1999 Entry Draft.

21 – D **Jean-Jacques Daigneault** traded from Pittsburgh to Anaheim for LW **Garry Valk**.

25 – C **Doug Gilmour**, D **Dave Ellett** and a conditional draft pick traded from Toronto to New Jersey for C **Steve Sullivan**, D **Jason Smith** and the rights to C **Alyn McCauley**. New Jersey receives the conditional pick it had sent Toronto in a previous transaction.

March, 1997

1 – C **Adam Oates**, G **Bill Ranford** and RW **Rick Tocchet** traded from Boston to Washington for G **Jim Carey**, C **Anson Carter**, C **Jason Allison**, Washington's 3rd round pick in the 1997 Entry Draft (Lee Goren) and a conditional pick in the 1998 Entry Draft.

5 – D **Steve Chiasson** and a conditional pick in the 1997 Entry Draft traded from Calgary to Hartford for C **Hnat Domenichelli**, D **Glen Featherstone**, New Jersey's 2nd pick in the 1997 Entry Draft (previously acquired – Dmitri Kokorev) and Vancouver's 3rd round pick in the 1998 Entry Draft (previously acquired).

8 – C **Sergei Nemchinov** and RW **Brian Noonan** traded from New York Rangers to Vancouver for LW **Esa Tikkanen** and RW **Russ Courtnall**.

18 – G **Pat Jablonski** traded from Montreal to Phoenix for D **Steve Cheredaryk**.

18 – RW **Roman Oksiuta** traded from Anaheim to Pittsburgh for C **Richard Park**.

18 – LW **Josef Beranek** traded from Vancouver to Pittsburgh for future considerations.

18 – D **Marc Hussey** traded from Calgary to Chicago for LW **Ravil Gusmanov**.

18 – C **Ed Olczyk** traded from Los Angeles to Pittsburgh for RW **Glen Murray**.

18 – LW **Jon Battaglia** and Anaheim's 4th round pick in the 1998 Entry Draft traded from Anaheim to Hartford for C **Mark Janssens**.

18 – RW **Mike Prokopec** traded from Chicago to Ottawa for RW **Denis Chasse**, D **Kevin Bolibruck** and Ottawa's 6th round pick in the 1998 Entry Draft.

18 – D **Larry Murphy** traded from Toronto to Detroit for future considerations.

18 – LW **Derek King** traded from NY Islanders to Hartford for Hartford's 5th round pick in the 1997 Entry Draft (Adam Edinger).

18 – D **Frantisek Kucera** traded from Vancouver to Philadelphia for future considerations.

18 – D **Jamie Huscroft** traded from Calgary to Tampa Bay for G **Tyler Moss**.

18 – RW **Kelly Chase** traded from Hartford to Toronto for Toronto's 8th round pick in the 1998 Entry Draft.

18 – D **Dave Manson** traded from Phoenix to Montreal for RW **Chris Murray** and D **Murray Baron**.

18 – RW **Chris Murray** traded from Phoenix to Hartford to D **Gerald Diduck**.

18 – C **Robert Reichel** traded from Calgary to NY Islanders for LW **Marty McInnis**, G **Tyrone Garner** and Calgary's 6th round pick in the 1997 Entry Draft (previously acquired by NY Islanders – Ilja Demidov).

18 – D **Jeff Norton** traded from Edmonton to Tampa Bay for D **Drew Bannister** and the earlier of Tampa Bay or Anaheim's 6th round draft pick in the 1997 Entry Draft (Anaheim pick previously acquired by Tampa Bay – Peter Arno).

18 – LW **Miroslav Satan** traded from Edmonton to Buffalo for LW **Barrie Moore** and D **Craig Millar**.

18 – C **Kirk Muller** traded from Toronto to Florida for RW **Jason Podollan**.

May, 1997

28 – C **Martin Cerven** traded from Edmonton to Philadelphia for a conditional pick in the 1997 Entry Draft (Chad Hinz).

30 – G **Brent Johnson** traded from Colorado to St. Louis for San Jose's 3rd round pick in the 1997 Entry Draft (San Jose pick previously acquired by St. Louis – Rick Berry) and a conditional pick in the 2000 Entry Draft.

June, 1997

12 – D **Per Gustafsson** traded from Florida to Toronto for D **Mike Lankshear**.

21 – LW **Mike Peluso** traded from St. Louis to NY Rangers for future considerations.

21 – G **Rick Tabaracci** traded from Tampa Bay to Calgary for Calgary's 4th round pick in the 1998 Entry Draft.

21 – LW **Shawn Burr** traded from Tampa Bay to San Jose for San Jose's 5th round pick in the 1997 Entry Draft (Mark Thompson).

21 – LW **Mike Sullivan** traded from Calgary to Boston for Boston's 7th round pick in the 1997 Entry Draft (Brad Defauw) and 3rd round pick in the 1998 Entry Draft.

21 – Carolina traded Philadelphia's 1st round pick in the 1997 Entry Draft (previously acquired by Carolina – Scott Hannan) to San Jose for San Jose's 2nd round pick in the 1997 Entry Draft (Brad Defauw) and 3rd round pick in the 1998 Entry Draft.

27 – D **Alexander Godynyuk** and Carolina's 6th round pick in the 1998 Entry Draft traded from Carolina to St. Louis for RW **Stephen Leach**.

July, 1997

15 – LW **Vladimir Vujtek** and Edmonton's 3rd round pick in the 1998 Entry Draft traded from Edmonton to Tampa Bay for **Brantt Myhres** and a future conditional draft pick.

24 – LW **Stephane Matteau** traded from St. Louis to San Jose for **Darren Turcotte**.

25 – LW **Petri Varis** and San Jose's 6th round pick in the 1998 Entry Draft traded from San Jose to Chicago for LW **Murray Craven**.

25 – D **Ryan Risidore** and Carolina's 5th round pick in the 1998 Entry Draft traded from Carolina to Chicago for D **Enrico Ciccone**.

August, 1997

8 – G **Jason Muzzatti** traded from Carolina to NY Rangers for NY Rangers' 4th round pick in the 1998 Entry Draft.

12 – D **Jiri Slegr** traded from Edmonton to Pittsburgh for Pittsburgh's 3rd round pick in the 1998 Entry Draft.

18 – G **Mike Vernon** traded from Detroit to San Jose for a conditional pick in the 1998 Entry Draft and a conditional pick in the 1999 Entry Draft.

20 – **Karl Dykhuis** and **Mikael Renberg** traded from Philadelphia to Tampa Bay for Philadelphia's 1st round picks in the 1998, 1999, 2000 and 2001 Entry Drafts (previously acquired by Tampa Bay), August 20, 1997.

22 – **Vlastimil Kroupa** traded from San Jose to New Jersey for New Jersey's 3rd round pick in the 1998 Entry Draft.

Trade and free agent signings that occurred after August 22, 1997 are listed on page 256.

THREE STAR SELECTION...